32nd Conference on Uncertainty in Artificial Intelligence 2016

AA004429

Jersey City, New Jersey, USA
25-29 June 2016

Editors:

Alexander Ihler **Dominik Janzing**

ISBN: 978-1-5108-2780-6

Printed from e-media with permission by:

Curran Associates, Inc.
57 Morehouse Lane
Red Hook, NY 12571

Some format issues inherent in the e-media version may also appear in this print version.

Copyright© (2016) by Association For Uncertainty in Artificial Intelligence (AUAI)
All rights reserved.

Printed by Curran Associates, Inc. (2016)

For permission requests, please contact Association For Uncertainty in Artificial Intelligence (AUAI) at the address below.

Association For Uncertainty in Artificial Intelligence (AUAI)
Department of Computer Science
University of British Columbia
Vancouver BC Canada V6T 1Z4

Phone: (703) 787-8044
Fax: (703) 478-0829

www.auai.org

Additional copies of this publication are available from:

Curran Associates, Inc.
57 Morehouse Lane
Red Hook, NY 12571 USA
Phone: 845-758-0400
Fax: 845-758-2633
Email: curran@proceedings.com
Web: www.proceedings.com

Uncertainty in Artificial Intelligence

Proceedings of the Thirty-Second Conference (2016)

June 25-29, 2016, Jersey City, New Jersey, USA

Edited by
Alexander Ihler, University of California Irvine, USA
Dominik Janzing, Max Planck Institute for Intelligent Systems, Germany

General Chairs
Marina Meila, University of Washington, USA
Tom Heskes, Radboud University, Netherlands

Sponsored by
Artificial Intelligence Journal, Microsoft Research, Baidu Research, Google Inc., Adobe Systems Inc.

AUAI Press Corvallis, Oregon

Contents

Preface

The Conference on Uncertainty in Artificial Intelligence (UAI) is the premier international conference on research related to representation, inference, learning and decision making in the presence of uncertainty within the field of Artificial Intelligence. This volume contains all papers that were accepted for the 32nd UAI Conference, held in Jersey City, New Jersey, USA, from June 25 to 29, 2016. Papers appearing in this volume were subjected to a rigorous review process. 275 papers were submitted to the conference and each was peer-reviewed by 3 or more reviewers with the supervision of one Senior Program Committee member. A total of 85 papers were accepted, 26 for oral presentation and 59 for poster presentation, for an acceptance rate of 31%. We are very grateful to the program committee and senior program committee members for their diligent efforts. We are confident that the proceedings, like past UAI conference proceedings, will become an important archival reference for the field.

We are pleased to announce that the Microsoft Best Paper Award is awarded to Leonard Schulman and Piyush Srivastava for their paper, "Stability of Causal Inference". The Adobe Best Student Paper Award is awarded to Jan Leike (co-authored with Tor Lattimore, Laurent Orseau, and Marcus Hutter) for their paper, "Thompson Sampling is Asymptotically Optimal in General Environments".

In addition to the presentation of technical papers, we are very pleased to have four distinguished invited speakers at UAI 2016: Steven Low (Caltech), Andrew McCallum (University of Massachusetts Amherst), Steffen L. Lauritzen (University of Copenhagen) and, as Banquet Speaker, Farhan Feroz (Cambridge University). The UAI 2016 tutorials program, chaired by Jan Lemeire, consists of four tutorials: "Discrete Sampling and Integration in High Dimensional Spaces" by Supratik Chakraborty, Kuldeep S. Meel, and Moshe Y. Vardi, "Parallel and High-performance Computing for Speeding up Machine Learning Algorithms" by Anshul Gupta, "Integrative Logic-Based Causal Discovery" by Sofia Triantafillou and Ioannis Tsamardinos, and "Reasoning Under Uncertainty with Subjective Logic" by Audun Jøsang.

UAI 2016 also hosts three workshops, coordinated by workshops chair Melanie Zeilinger: "Causation: Foundation to Application" (Frederick Eberhardt, Ricardo Silva, Joris Mooij, Marloes Maathuis, Elias Bareinboim), "Bayesian Modeling Applications Workshop" (Rommel Carvalho, Kathryn Laskey), and "Machine Learning for Health" (Ke Yuan, Olivier Elemento, Edoardo Airoldi, Florian Markowetz).

Alexander Ihler and Dominik Janzing (Program Co-Chairs)
Marina Meila and Tom Heskes (General Co-Chairs)

Organizing Committee

General Chairs

Marina Meila, University of Washington, USA
Tom Heskes, Radboud University, Netherlands

Program Chairs

Alexander Ihler, University of California Irvine, USA
Dominik Janzing, Max Planck Institute for Intelligent Systems, Germany

Tutorials Chair

Jan Lemeire, Vrije Universiteit, Brussels

Workshops Chair

Melanie Zeilinger, ETH Zurich, Switzerland

Local Arrangements Chair

Changhe Yuan, City University of New York, USA

Acknowledgments

The success of a conference such as UAI depends greatly on the efforts of many individuals who volunteer their time to provide expert and detailed reviews of submitted papers. In particular, the Program Committee and Senior Program Committee for UAI 2016 were responsible for generating reviews and recommendations for the 275 submissions to the conference. Each submitted paper was reviewed by at least 3 members of the Program Committee. The Senior Program Committee then assessed the individual reviews for each paper, moderated discussion among Program Committee members if needed, and generated meta-reviews and recommendations for the program chairs. We are extremely grateful for the efforts of all of the individuals listed below.

Senior Program Committee

Ryan Adams	Harvard
Ayesha Ali	University of Guelph
Michel Besserve	Max Planck Institute
Craig Boutilier	Google
Emma Brunskill	Carnegie Mellon University
Francois Caron	Oxford
Kamalika Chaudhuri	University of California
Max Chickering	Microsoft Research
Fabio Cuzzolin	Oxford Brookes University
Adnan Darwiche	UCLA
Denver Dash	Magic Leap
Cassio de Campos	Queen's University Belfast
Jennifer Dy	Northeastern University
Gal Elidan	The Hebrew University of Jerusalem
Vibhav Gogate	The University of Texas at Dallas
Tommi Jaakkola	MIT
Helge Langseth	The Norwegian University of Science and Technology
Kathryn Laskey	George Mason University
Tze-Yun Leong	Singapore Management University, SINGAPORE
Marloes Maathuis	ETH Zurich
Benjamin Marlin	UMass Amherst
Brian Milch	Google
Claire Monteleoni	George Washington University
Joris Mooij	University of Amsterdam
Petri Myllymaki	Helsinki Institute for Information Technology
Thomas Nielsen	Aalborg University
David Poole	University of British Columbia
Thomas Richardson	University of Washington
Prakash Shenoy	University of Kansas
Ricardo Silva	University College London
David Sontag	New York University
Peter Spirtes	Carnegie Mellon University
Oliver Stegle	EMBL-EBI
Zoltan Szabo	University College London
Claudia Tarantola	University of Pavia
Ilya Tolstikhin	Max Planck Institute
Raquel Urtasun	University of Toronto
Yi Wang	IHPC, A*STAR

Dit-Yan Yeung	Hong Kong University of Science and Technology
Nevin Zhang	Hong Kong University of Science and Technology
Kun Zhang	CMU Pittsburg
Jun Zhu	Tsinghua University

Program Committee

Sophie Achard	CNRS
Tameem Adel	Radboud University Nijmegen
John Mark Agosta	Toyota Information Technology Center
Russell Almond	Florida State University
Christopher Amato	MIT
Leila Amgoud	IRIT - Universite Paul Sabatier
Eyal Amir	University of Illinois at Urbana-Champaign
Farhad Anaraki	University of Colorado, Boulder
Alessandro Antonucci	IDSIA
Cedric Archambeau	Amazon Berlin
Nimar Arora	Oracle
Reza Babanezhad Harikandeh	UBC
David Balduzzi	Victoria University Wellington
Akshay Balsubramani	UC San Diego
Elias Bareinboim	Purdue
Jay Bartroff	USC
Kim Bauters	Queen's University of Belfast
Nahla Ben Amor	ISG Tunis
Alessio Benavoli	IDSIA
Carlo Berzuini	University of Manchester
Debarun Bhattacharjya	IBM Research
Bozhena Bidyuk	Google
Benjamin Bloem-Reddy	Columbia
Alexandre Bouchard-Cote	UBC
Wray Buntine	Monash University
Cory Butz	University of Regina
Erik Cambria	Nanyang Technological University
Robert Castelo	Universitat Pompeu Fabra
Paola Cerchiello	University of Pavia
Hong Chang	Institute of Computing Technology
Junxiang Chen	Northeastern University
Changyou Chen	Duke University
Shang-Tse Chen	Georgia Tech
Yutian Chen	Google
William Cheung	Hong Kong Baptist University
Arthur Choi	UCLA
Jaesik Choi	Ulsan National Institute of Science and Technology
Tianjiao Chu	University of Pittsburgh
Kacper Chwialkowski	UCL / Gatsby Unit
Tom Claassen	Radboud University Nijmegen
Giorgio Corani	IDSIA
James Cussens	University of York
Christoph Dann	CMU
Jasper DeBock	Universiteit Gent
Sebastien Destercke	CNRS
Vanessa Didilez	University of Bristol
Nicolas Drougard	ONERA - The French Aerospace Lab
Marek Druzdzel	University of Pittsburgh
Elad Eban	Google
Frederick Eberhardt	Caltech
Zied Elouedi	ISG Tunis
Stefano Ermon	Stanford University
Robin Evans	University of Oxford

Fei Fang	USC
M. Julia Flores	University of Castilla - La Mancha (UCLM)
James Foulds	UC San Diego
Andrew Frank	Google
Kenji Fukumizu	Institute of Statistical Mathematics
Aram Galstyan	Information Sciences Institute
Minos Garofalakis	Technical University of Crete
Philipp Geiger	Max Planck Institute for Intelligent Systems
Phan Giang	George Mason University
Tobias Glasmachers	Institut fr Neuroinformatik
Clark Glymour	CMU
Lluis Godo	Artificial Intelligence Research Institute
Vicen Gomez	Universitat Pompeu Fabra
Manuel Gomez-Olmedo	Universidad de Granada
Mingming Gong	University of Technology Sydney
Christophe Gonzales	LIP6-UPMC
Perry Groot	Radboud University Nijmegen
Aritanan Gruber	University of Sao Paulo
Quanquan Gu	University of Virginia
Syriya Gunasekar	UT Austin
Yuhong Guo	Temple University
Hannaneh Hajishirzi	University of Washington
Elad Hazan	Princeton
Philipp Hennig	Max Planck Institute for Intelligent Systems
Jesse Hoey	University of Waterloo
Arjen Hommersom	University of Nijmegen
Antti Honkela	University of Helsinki
Jesse Hostetler	Oregon State University
Bert Huang	Virginia Tech
Marcus Hutter	Australian National University
Rishabh Iyer	University of Washington
David Jensen	University of Massachusetts Amherst
Alfredo Kalaitzis	Microsoft
Kalev Kask	UC Irvine
Kristian Kersting	University of Dortmund
Arto Klami	University of Helsinki
Mikko Koivisto	University of Helsinki
Kevin Korb	Monash University
Brian Kulis	Ohio State University
Branislav Kveton	Adobe Research
Balaji Lakshminarayanan	Gatsby/University College London
Jerome Lang	LAMSADE
Jan Lemeire	Vrije Universiteit Brussel
Philippe Leray	University of Nantes
Wu-Jun Li	Nanjing University
Yujia Li	University of Toronto
Lihong Li	Microsoft Research
Yingyu Liang	Princeton University
Moshe Lichman	UC Irvine
Lina Lin	University of Washington
Hailin Liu	CMU
Qiang Liu	Dartmouth
Weiru Liu	Queen's University Belfast
Yan Liu	USC
Dan Lizotte	University of Western Ontario
Po-Ling Loh	University of California
Qi Lou	UC Irvine
Daniel Lowd	University of Oregon
Aurelie Lozano	IBM
Peter Lucas	Radboud University Nijmegen

Manuel Luque	UNED
Michael Lyu	Chinese University of Hong Kong
Anders Madsen	Hugin Expert
Malik Magdon-Ismail	Rensselear Polytechnic Institute
Brandon Malone	University of Helsinki
Radu Marinescu	IBM Research
Maria Vanina Martinez	University of Oxford
Denis Mau	University of Sao Paulo
Krikamol Maundet	Max Planck Institute for Intelligent Systems
Julian McAuley	UC San Diego
Ole Mengshoel	Carnegie Mellon University
Ofer Meshi	Toyota Technological Institute at Chicago
Taneli Mielikainen	Yahoo
Thomas Minka	Microsoft Research UK
Karthika Mohan	UCLA
Mahesh Mohan	George Washington University
Preetam Nandy	ETH Zurich
Sriraam Natarajan	Indiana University
Deanna Needell	Claremont McKenna College
Truong-Huy Nguyen	Texas A&M University-Commerce
William Noble	University of Washington
Nuria Oliver	Telefonica Research
Pedro Ortega	University of Pennsylvenia
John Paisley	Columbia University
Hector Palacios	Universitat Pompeu Fabra
Xinghao Pan	University of California
Jose Pea	Linkping University
Jian Peng	UIUC
David Pennock	Microsoft Research
Anastasia Pentina	IST Austria
Jonas Peters	ETH Zurich
Marek Petrik	IBM Research
Wei Ping	UC Irvine
Kim-Leng Poh	National University of Singapore
Leonard Poon	The Hong Kong Institute of Education
Pascal Poupart	University of Waterloo
David Pynadath	USC Institute for Creative Technologies
Piyush Rai	Duke University
Aaditya Ramdas	UC Berkeley
Roland Ramsahai	University of Cambridge
Narges Razavian	New York University
Silja Renooij	Utrecht University
Teemu Roos	Helsinki Institute for Information Technology
Rafael Rumi	Almeria University
Brian Ruttenberg	Charles River Analytics
Regis Sabbadin	INRA
Antonio Salmeron	Universidad de Almeria
Alexander Schwing	University of Toronto
Uri Shalit	New York University
Ilya Shpitser	Johns Hopkins Univeristy
Tomi Silander	Xerox Research Centre Europe
Gerardo Simari	Universidad Nacional del Sur in Bahia Blanca and CONICET
Mathieu Sinn	IBM Research - Ireland
Kevin Small	Amazon
Jasper Snoek	Harvard
Le Song	Georgia Tech
Suvrit Sra	MIT
Bharath Sriperumbudur	Pennsylvania State University
Fabio Stella	University of Milan
Heiko Strathmann	University College London

Hang Su	Tsinghua University
L. Enrique Sucar	INAOE
Joe Suzuki	Osaka University
Umar Syed	Princeton
Vincent Tan	NUS
Graham Taylor	University of Guelph
Eric Tchetgen	Harvard
Johannes Textor	Utrecht University
Yuandong Tian	Facebook
Dustin Tran	Columbia
Ioannis Tsamardinos	University of Crete
Marco Valtorta	University of South Carolina
Twan van Laarhoven	Radboud University Nijmegen
Jirka Vomlel	Institute of Information Theory and Automation
Chong Wang	Carnegie Mellon University
Linbo Wang	University of Washington
Paul Weng	SYSU-CMU JIE
Ami Wiesel	Hebrew University
David Wipf	Microsoft Research Asia
Lirong Xia	Rensselaer Polytechnic Institute
Yang Xiang	University of Guelph
Minjie Xu	Tsinghua University
Eunho Yang	KAIST
Nan Ye	National University of Singapore
Junming Yin	University of Arizona
Changhe Yuan	City University of New York
Xiaotong Yuan	Nanjing University of Information Science & Technology
Yifeng Zeng	Teesside University
Jiji Zhang	Lingnan University
Yu Zhang	Hong Kong Baptist University
Chicheng Zhang	UC San Diego
Yi Zhen	Georgia Institute of Technology
Martin Zinkevich	Google

Additional Reviewers

Carolyn Augusta	University of Guelph
Iat Chong Chan	Bloomberg LP
Bryant Chen	UCLA
Juan Correa	Purdue
Mayukh Das	Indiana Univeristy
Rafael de Lima	Ulsan National Institute of Science and Technology
Yinpeng Dong	Tsinghua University
Yawen Fan	Shanghai Jiaotong University
Codruta Girlea	University of Illinois
Praveen Gupta	Purdue
Giyoung Jeon	Ulsan National Institute of Science and Technology
Marcin Kozniewski	University of Pittsburgh
Dongeun Lee	Ulsan National Institute of Science and Technology
Max Libbrecht	University of Washington
Miao Liu	MIT
Jianbing Ma	Queen's University Belfast
Francesca Mangili	IDSIA
Katerina Marazopoulou	University of Massachusetts Amherst
Teppo Niinimäki	University of Helsinki
Wen Pu	LinkedIn
Aswin Raghavan	Oregon State
Pedram Rooshenas	University of Oregon

Tomas Singliar	Microsoft
Anh Tong	UNIST
Lingjie Weng	LinkedIn
Shuang Wu	Shanghai Jiaotong University
Min Xu	University of California Berkeley
Junzhe Zhang	Purdue
Qin Zhou	Shanghai Jiaotong University

Additional Acknowledgments

A number of other people have made significant contributions towards making UAI 2016 possible. We acknowledge and thank:

- Moshe Lichmann for serving as the conference webmaster.
- Kasper Brink for setting up the registration.
- Local volunteers Cong Chen, Xiuyan Ni, and Cuiyuan Wang.
- Joris Mooij for providing local arrangement tips.
- Daniel Lowd for helping with the proceedings process.
- Kilian Weinberger for help setting up the automatic paper formatting checker.
- Zoltan Szabo for helpful CMT advice.
- Max Welling, Zoubin Ghahramani, and Hong Ge for sharing their Bayesan scoring model.
- The following student scholarship volunteers:

David Arbour	UMass Amherst
Matej Balog	University of Cambridge
Diana Borsa	UCL
Muthukumaran Chandrasekaran	University of Georgia
Xiangli Chen	University of Illinois at Chicago
Junxiang Chen	Northeastern University
Tianfan Fu	Shanghai Jiao Tong University
Joseph Futoma	Duke University
Tianxiang Gao	University of North Carolina at Chapel Hill
Hugo Gilbert	LIP6 UPMC
Biwei Huang	CMU/MPI
Viet Huynh	Deakin University
Hans Kersting	Max Plack Institute for Intelligent Systems
Tomáš Kocák	Inria Lille - Nord Europe
Chao Lan	University of Kansas
Yoad Lewenberg	The Hebrew University of Jerusalem
Katerina Marazopoulou	UMass Amherst
Mitchell McIntire	Stanford University
Julie Nutini	The University of British Columbia
Tahrima Rahman	The University of Texas at Dallas
Nan Rong Cornell	University
Md Amran Siddiqui	Oregon State University
Wen Sun	Carnegie Mellon University
Antonio Sutera	University of Liège
Xi Tan	Purdue University
Alexander Vervuurt	University of Oxford
Pengtao Xie	Carnegie Mellon University
Scott Yang	Courant Institute of Mathematical Sciences
Scott Young	New York University
Kun Zhang	Carnegie Mellon University

This page intentionally left blank.

Sponsors

We gratefully acknowledge the generous support provided by our sponsors, including support for best paper awards and travel scholarships. Without our sponsors' support it would not be feasible to organize a conference such as UAI 2016 without charging much higher registration fees.

Artificial Intelligence
www.elsevier.com/locate/artint

Microsoft Research

Baidu Research

Google

Adobe

Best Paper Awards

Microsoft Best Paper Award
Stability of Causal Inference
Leonard Schulman, Piyush Srivastava

Adobe Best Student Paper Award
Thompson Sampling is Asymptotically Optimal in General Environments
Jan Leike, Tor Lattimore, Laurent Orseau, Marcus Hutter

Proceedings

Gradient Methods for Stackelberg Security Games

Kareem Amin
University of Michigan
amkareem@umich.edu

Satinder Singh
University of Michigan
baveja@umich.edu

Michael P. Wellman
University of Michigan
wellman@umich.edu

Abstract

Stackelberg games are two-stage games in which the first player (called the leader) commits to a strategy, after which the other player (the follower) selects a best-response. These types of games have seen numerous practical application in security settings, where the leader (in this case, a defender) must allocate resources to protect various targets. Real world applications include the scheduling of US federal air marshals to international flights, and resource allocation at LAX airport. However, the best known algorithm for solving *general* Stackelberg games requires solving Integer Programs, and fails to scale beyond a few (significantly smaller than 100) number of leader actions, or follower types. In this paper, we present a new gradient-based approach for solving large Stackelberg games in security settings. Large-scale control problems are often solved by restricting the controller to a rich parameterized class of policies; the optimal control can then be computed using Monte Carlo gradient methods. We demonstrate that the same approach can be taken in a *strategic* setting. We evaluate our approach empirically, demonstrating that it can have negligible regret against the leader's true equilibrium strategy, while scaling to large games.

1 INTRODUCTION

Stackelberg games have received significant attention in the context of security applications, where a defender (the leader in the Stackelberg game) must deploy a limited number of security resources to protect a set of vulnerable targets to guard against an attacker (the follower in the Stackelberg game). Algorithms for these games have been deployed in real-world settings, e.g., to generate checkpoints and patrols at the Los Angeles International Airport [Pita et al., 2009], as well as to schedule US Federal Air Marshals (FAMS) to flights [Jain et al., 2010b, Tsai et al., 2009].

The best known solver for general Bayesian Stackelberg games is the DOBBS algorithm [Paruchuri et al., 2008], which was the first to formulate a Stackelberg game (given in normal form) as a Mixed Integer Linear Program (MILP). Since then, a great deal of research has been devoted to algorithms that scale to games of the size encountered in real settings. This has led to the development of a general class of Stackelberg Security Games (SSGs) [Korzhyk et al., 2011], which captures many of the key features of these real settings, along with algorithms including ORIGAMI, ERASER, ERASER-C [Kiekintveld et al., 2009], and ASPEN [Jain et al., 2010a], which can handle a large number of defender actions. With the exception of ASPEN, these algorithms work by assuming additional structure on the SSG, specifically on the pure strategy set of the defender. Similarly, the HBGS algorithm [Jain et al., 2011] scales to multiple attacker types by assuming hierarchical structure on the attacker types. Hence, these algorithms are able to solve MILPs more compact than would be generated from a game expressed in normal form.[1]

Among approximate methods, Monte-Carlo approaches have been used to solve games with infinite types [Kiekintveld et al., 2011], but also makes assumptions on what defender pure strategies are feasible. The HUNTER algorithm [Yin and Tambe, 2012], in contrast, can solve Stackelberg games with limited additional assumptions, but searches a game tree whose depth scales with the number of attacker types, and whose branching factor is the number of available targets. Approximate methods have also been utilized in recent work [Yang et al., 2012, 2013] considering attackers with bounded rationality, including attackers which behave according to the Quantal Response (QR) model [McKelvey and Palfrey, 1995]. This modeling assumption is made with limited loss of generality, as the degree of attacker rationally is specified by a parame-

[1]ORIGAMI makes the most restrictive assumptions on the game, and does not need to solve an MILP at all.

ter of the model. As we will see shortly, the algorithms in the present work can be seen as a refinement of the BRQR algorithm of Yang et al. [2013].

We introduce a different approach for finding good defender strategies in Stackelberg security games, which avoids imposing structure on the defender's *pure strategies*, the attackers' types, or the players' utilities. Instead, we propose restricting the search for defender strategies within a rich, but parameterized, class of mixed strategies. In a standard Stackelberg equilibrium the defender (who is the leader), plays an (unrestricted) mixed strategy, knowing that the attacker will select a best-response. In contrast, we will consider games where the defender's choice of mixed strategy must come from some fixed class of distributions.

This type of assumption is analogous to successful methods in AI and reinforcement learning such as policy gradient methods [Baxter and Bartlett, 2001], which avoid making assumptions about the dynamics of the environment, but rather, constrain the search for a good policy to within a parameterized family of policies. In this work, we will demonstrate how a similar approach can be applied to a *strategic* setting. We then apply Monte-Carlo gradient methods, a procedure we call STACKGRAD, to find solutions to the defender's optimization problem. In contrast to an ordinary optimal control problem, a unique feature of our derivation is that this gradient computation must pass through the attacker's response function. In order to maintain differentiability, we consider a smoothed version of the attacker's response function. We therefore consider an attacker in the QR model. While our primary motivation for this assumption is analytic, we reap the additional capability of modeling boundedly rational attackers.

Figure 1 provides a schematic of our approach. We begin with a Stackelberg game, consisting of the defender's set of mixed strategies, Δ, the attacker's response function g, and the defender's utility for playing $\mathcal{D} \in \Delta$, denoted $U(\mathcal{D}, g(\mathcal{D}))$. We then formulate an approximate Stackelberg game by restricting $\mathcal{D} \in \Delta(\Theta) \subset \Delta$ and smoothing $g \Rightarrow \tilde{g}$, where Θ denotes the parameterization of the defender strategy space. Finally, we solve for the defender's best strategy in the restricted game via gradient ascent.

Yang et al. [2013] propose finding approximate Stackelberg equilibria against QR attackers by finding local minima of the defender's expected utility function (over the unrestricted class of defender mixed strategies $\mathcal{D}$). This algorithm, called BRQR, relies on a black-box call to a procedure for finding such local minima. We can view our approach as an instantiation of BRQR where the restriction to defender strategies $\Delta(\Theta)$ bears fruit in two ways. First, we can explicitly find these local minima using gradient descent. In contrast, previous work relies on using black-box non-convex function optimization toolboxes. Secondly, we can scale to games with large pure strategy spaces in a principled manner, by designing $\Delta(\Theta)$ to have a compact parameterization.

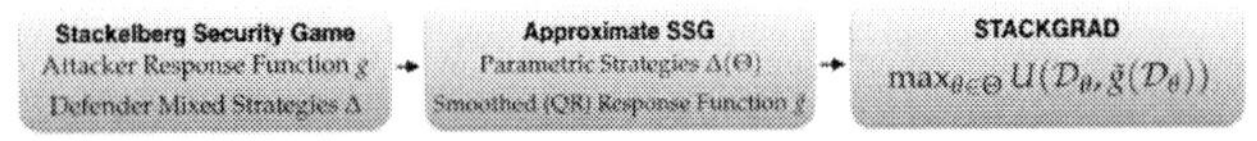

Figure 1: STACKGRAD optimizes the approximate game given considering a parametric class of leader (defender) strategies and by smoothing the follower's (attacker's) response function.

While any parameterized class of defender mixed strategies may be utilized, we propose two rich classes which yield heuristics with no computational dependence on the number of attacker types, and only mild dependencies on the size of the defender's pure strategy set. We then demonstrate empirically that STACKGRAD not only scales to large games, but also finds mixed strategies that are close to the defender's true Stackelberg optimal strategy.

Our primary contributions are in the derivation of a new algorithm for solving Stackelberg games approximately and in its empirical evaluation. Specifically, we define STACKGRAD, by deriving an approximate stochastic gradient of the defender's utility with respect to its strategy parameters through the (smoothed) best response function of the attacker. We argue analytically that STACKGRAD has no computational dependence on the number of attacker types in a Bayesian Stackelberg game, being able to handle any number (even infinite types). We then demonstrate empirically that, despite searching within a restricted class of mixed strategies, the solutions found by STACKGRAD have almost the same payoff to the defender as the true (unrestricted) Stackelberg optimum, computed directly using a solver for the unrestricted game. We also demonstrate the STACKGRAD has only a mild computational dependence on the number of pure strategies, by considering a game inspired by the Federal Air Marshal (FAMS) domain.

2 PRELIMINARIES

2.1 GENERAL SECURITY GAMES

We consider the *Stackelberg security game* introduced by Kiekintveld et al. [2009] (see Korzhyk et al. [2011] for a good overview).

An SSG is a two-player game between a defender and attacker. The attacker selects a target from a set $\mathcal{T} = \{t_1, \ldots, t_N\}$. The defender prevents attacks by guarding targets with various resources $\mathcal{R} = \{r_1, \ldots, r_K\}$. In the most general setting considered in previous work, resources may simultaneously cover a set of targets. For example, resources might be air marshals, and targets might be airline flights [Tsai et al., 2009]. An air marshal might protect a number of targets by flying a circuit which starts and ends at the marshal's home city; each flight along the circuit is considered covered. This is modeled by having the defender assign resources to *schedules*, where a schedule $S \subset \mathcal{T}$ is just a subset of the possible targets. Assigning a resource r_k to schedule S corresponds to covering each $t \in S$ with resource r_k. The set of schedules to which a resource r_k may be assigned is denoted by $\mathcal{S}_k$. $\mathcal{S}_k$ specifies the constraints induced by the domain. For example, in the air marshal SSG, $\mathcal{S}_k$ comprises sets of flights that can form a circuit that starts and ends in the marshal's home city.

A defender's pure strategy is an assignment of resources to schedules, which we denote by $\mathbf{s} \in \mathcal{S} \triangleq \mathcal{S}_1 \times \cdots \times \mathcal{S}_K$. Strategy component $\mathbf{s}_k$ is the schedule to which resource r_k is assigned. Strategy $\mathbf{s}$ induces a coverage vector $\mathbf{c} \in \{0,1\}^N$ (sometimes denoted $\mathbf{c}(\mathbf{s})$ when we wish to emphasize the dependence on $\mathbf{s}$) indicating which targets are covered: $\mathbf{c}_n = 1$ if $t_n \in \mathbf{s}_k$ for some k. An attacker's pure strategy is simply a target $t_n \in \mathcal{T}$.

Our methods also allow for non-binary coverage. That is, we can take $\mathbf{c}(\mathbf{s})$ to be an arbitrary function from $\mathcal{S}$ to $[0,1]^K$ representing the assignment of varying resource quantities to achieve degrees of target coverage. However, to simplify our expressions, and to stay consistent with previous work, we assume binary $\mathbf{c}_n$ unless otherwise noted.

If the defender plays a mixed strategy—a distribution $\mathcal{D}$ over pure strategies—we use $\bar{\mathbf{c}} \in [0,1]^d$ to denote the probability that each target is covered. In other words, $\bar{\mathbf{c}}(\mathcal{D}) = \mathbb{E}_{\mathbf{s} \sim \mathcal{D}}[\mathbf{c}(\mathbf{s})]$.

The players' utilities are functions of which target is attacked, and whether that target is covered (by any resource). Attacker and defender utilities are denoted $U_a : \{0,1\} \times \mathcal{T} \to \mathbb{R}$ and $U_d : \{0,1\} \times \mathcal{T} \to \mathbb{R}$ respectively. $U_a(0, t_n)$, for example, specifies the utility to the attacker if t_n is attacked and uncovered. The expected payoffs for playing defender mixed strategy $\mathcal{D}$ and attacker pure strategy t_n are given by:

$$\mathbf{U}_a(\mathcal{D}, t_n) = \bar{\mathbf{c}}(\mathcal{D}) U_a(1, t_n) + (1 - \bar{\mathbf{c}}(\mathcal{D})) U_a(0, t_n)$$
$$\mathbf{U}_d(\mathcal{D}, t_n) = \bar{\mathbf{c}}(\mathcal{D}) U_d(1, t_n) + (1 - \bar{\mathbf{c}}(\mathcal{D})) U_d(0, t_n)$$

In a security game, it is assumed that for all n, $M_{a,n} \triangleq U_a(0,t_n) - U_a(1,t_n) \geq 0$ and $M_{d,n} \triangleq U_d(1,t_n) - U_d(0,t_n) \geq 0$. The attacker never prefers that its target is covered. Similarly, the defender never prefers that the attacker's target is uncovered.

2.2 STACKELBERG EQUILIBRIA

The solution concept typically applied to security games is that of a *Stackelberg Equilibrium*, as opposed to the more conventional *Nash Equilibrium*. In a two-player Stackelberg game, one player—termed *leader*—first commits to a strategy. The other player—termed *follower*—observes this commitment, and plays a best response to the leader's chosen strategy. In security games, the defender is the leader and the attacker follows. This leader-follower interaction is argued to be better suited than simultaneous moves for modeling security domains, since after the defender deploys its resources, that deployment is subject to scrutiny by a malicious agent, who can use this information when deciding on its point of attack.

Due to the two-stage nature of the game, it is convenient to think of the follower as selecting a *response function* which maps each of the leader's mixed strategies to a pure strategy. With Δ the set of defender mixed strategies, we denote a response function by $g : \Delta \to \mathcal{T}$. Upon observing leader mixed strategy $\mathcal{D}$, the follower plays pure strategy $g(\mathcal{D})$.

We say that $(\mathcal{D}, g)$ forms a *Strong Stackelberg Equilibrium* (SSE) if, informally: (1) given response function g, the leader maximizes its payoff by playing $\mathcal{D}$, (2) g is not just a response function, but always returns a follower *best* response, and (3) if there are multiple follower best-response functions, g selects the one most beneficial to the leader.

Condition (3) is what distinguishes a *Strong* Stackelberg Equilibrium from an ordinary Stackelberg Equilibrium. It can be argued that this is a reasonable solution concept if one believes that the leader can always force the attacker to break ties in its favor. For our purposes, it will be necessary only to observe that the payoff to the leader in a SSE is the most that a leader can hope to guarantee against a rational follower. Below we state the definition of an SSE formally in the context of a security game.

Definition 1 (Follower Best-Response). *A follower response function $g : \Delta \to \mathcal{T}$ is a* best-response *function if for any other response function $g' : \Delta \to \mathcal{T}$ and leader strategy $\mathcal{D} \in \Delta$, $\mathbf{U}_a(\mathcal{D}, g(\mathcal{D})) \geq \mathbf{U}_a(\mathcal{D}, g'(\mathcal{D}))$.*

Definition 2 (Strong Stackelberg Equilibrium). *$(\mathcal{D}, g)$ where $\mathcal{D} \in \Delta$ and $g : \Delta \to \mathcal{T}$ is a* Strong Stackelberg Equilibrium *iff:*

1. *For all $\mathcal{D}' \in \Delta$, $\mathbf{U}_d(\mathcal{D}, g(\mathcal{D})) \geq \mathbf{U}_d(\mathcal{D}', g(\mathcal{D}'))$*
2. *g is a best-response function.*
3. *For any $\mathcal{D}' \in \Delta$ and best-response function g', $\mathbf{U}_d(\mathcal{D}', g(\mathcal{D}')) \geq \mathbf{U}_d(\mathcal{D}', g'(\mathcal{D}'))$*

The definition of a SSE ensures that, although there may be multiple such equilibria, they all give the same payoff to the defender. Given an instance of a security game $\mathcal{G}$, let $V_{\mathcal{G}}$ denote the payoff to the defender in equilibrium.

2.3 BAYESIAN STACKELBERG GAMES

An extension of the game described in the previous section allows the defender to model uncertainty over the potential attackers by a prior q over a set of attacker *types* Λ. Letting

g_λ denote the best response of attacker λ, the defender's utility in the Bayesian setting is given by:

$$\mathbf{U}_d(\mathcal{D}, \{g_\lambda\}) = \sum_{\lambda \in \Lambda} q(\lambda)\mathbf{U}_d(\mathcal{D}, g_\lambda(\mathcal{D})). \qquad (1)$$

As with a single attacker, if g_λ breaks ties in a consistent manner we can uniquely define $V_\mathcal{G}$ in the Bayesian setting. Given an arbitrary defender strategy $\mathcal{D}$, we define the competitive ratio of the defender's choice of strategy against the SSE solution. We assume that $\mathbf{U}_d(\mathcal{D}, \{g_\lambda\}) \geq 0$, and $V_\mathcal{G} > 0$.

Definition 3 (Competitive Ratio). *Given an instance of a Bayesian Stackelberg game $\mathcal{G}$, and defender strategy $\mathcal{D}$, define* $\mathrm{R}(\mathcal{D}) = \mathbf{U}_d(\mathcal{D}, \{g_\lambda\})/V_\mathcal{G}$.

The defender would like to maximize equation (1), or short of doing so, find a strategy $\mathcal{D}$ which attains a large competitive ratio. In this work, we propose using gradient methods to search for such strategies. However, in order to do so $\mathbf{U}_d$ will have to be differentiable with respect to its argument. In the next section, we describe the approximations needed to ensure this.

3 GAME APPROXIMATION

We now consider an approximation to general Bayesian Stackelberg games. We (1) assume a probabilistic model for the attacker, and (2) restrict the set of strategies available to the defender.

Recall that the *softmax* function $\sigma_\eta : \mathbb{R}^N \times \{1, \ldots, N\} \to [0, 1]$ provides a probabilistic approximation to the maximum element of the set. Given a vector $\mathbf{x} \in \mathbb{R}^N$, we let $\sigma_\eta(\mathbf{x}, i) = \frac{\exp(\eta \mathbf{x}_i)}{\sum_{i=1}^N \exp(\eta \mathbf{x}_i)}$. The categorical distribution over the set $\{1, \ldots, N\}$, which selects element i with probability $\sigma_\eta(\mathbf{x}, i)$ is called the *softmax distribution*. As the inverse temperature $\eta \to \infty$, softmax concentrates mass on the indices belonging to the maximum elements of $\mathbf{x}$.

The first step to approximating the security game of Section 2 is to have the attacker select its target according to the softmax distribution over its utilities, often times called a *quantal response* attacker [Yang et al., 2012]. Let $\mathbf{U}_\lambda$ denote the utility function corresponding to attacker type λ. Let us also define

$$\mathbf{u}_\lambda(\mathcal{D}) = [\mathbf{U}_\lambda(\mathcal{D}, t_1), \ldots, \mathbf{U}_\lambda(\mathcal{D}, t_N)],$$

the vector of expected payoffs to the attacker for each choice of target, assuming the defender plays mixed strategy $\mathcal{D}$. In the security game approximation, we assume that conditioned on the defender's choice of $\mathcal{D}$, and a fixed choice of η (a parameter of the approximation), the attacker selects target t_n with probability $\sigma_\eta(\mathbf{u}_\lambda(\mathcal{D}), n)$.

Second, we restrict the defender to select distributions from a parameterized class $\Delta_\Theta \subset \Delta$, where Θ denotes a set of parameters, and for each $\theta \in \Theta$, there is a corresponding distribution $\mathcal{D}_\theta \in \Delta_\Theta$. We denote the probability mass function (over $\mathcal{S}$) of $\mathcal{D}_\theta$ by $p(\cdot \mid \theta)$.

Putting these approximations together gives us a stochastic optimization problem from the perspective of the defender (summarized in the model below). First nature draws attacker type λ according to q. Given λ, η, and $\theta \in \Theta$, an attacker's (now random) response t_n is determined by a draw from the categorical distribution defined by $\sigma_\eta(\mathbf{u}_\lambda(\mathcal{D}_\theta), \cdot)$, rather than an exact best-response function g_λ. Upon independently drawing $\mathbf{s} \sim \mathcal{D}_\theta$, the defender receives $U_d(\mathbf{c}_n(\mathbf{s}), t_n)$.

Security Game Approximation

Defender selects $\theta \in \Theta$.
Nature draws $\lambda \sim q$
$n \sim \sigma_\eta(\mathbf{u}_\lambda(\mathcal{D}_\theta), \cdot)$, $\mathbf{s} \sim \mathcal{D}_\theta$
Defender receives payoff $U_d(\mathbf{c}_n(\mathbf{s}), t_n)$.

The goal of the defender in the security game approximation is to maximize its expected payoff, which is given by the following function:

$$\tilde{\mathbf{U}}_d(\theta) = \mathbf{E}\left[U_d(\mathbf{c}_n(\mathbf{s}), t_n)\right], \qquad (2)$$

The expectation here is taken according to the process just described.

If we take Δ_Θ identical to Δ and $\eta \to \infty$, then the logic of the model is that of a leader-follower game, and the defender strategy θ^* that maximizes $\tilde{\mathbf{U}}_d(\theta)$ is precisely its strategy in a Stackelberg equilibrium. However, maximizing $\tilde{\mathbf{U}}_d$ may not be tractable for larger games. If, on the other hand, Δ_Θ is restrictive ($\Delta_\Theta \neq \Delta$), the strategy $\mathcal{D}_{\theta^*}$ might suffer regret against an attacker best-response function g, but the parametric class may allow $\mathbf{U}_d$ to be efficiently maximized. Balancing these two effects is important. In the next section, we describe how given a fixed parametric class Θ, $\tilde{\mathbf{U}}_d$ can be maximized using gradient methods.

4 MONTE-CARLO GRADIENT ESTIMATE: STACKGRAD

If $\Theta \subset \mathbb{R}^d$ for some d, then gradient algorithms are natural candidates for maximizing Equation 2. However, to compute $\nabla\tilde{\mathbf{U}}_d(\theta)$ even at a single point θ, it might be necessary to sum over all of Λ, and the entire support of $\mathcal{D}_\theta$, which even for a parametric class of distributions might include all elements of $\mathcal{S}$. A more tractable approach is to take a Monte-Carlo estimate of $\nabla\tilde{\mathbf{U}}_d(\theta)$, which need not depend on the size of $\mathcal{S}$, and has *no* dependence on $|\Lambda|$.

The first step to producing such an estimate is to derive for any θ, an unbiased estimate $\tilde{\gamma}_\theta$ of $\nabla\tilde{\mathbf{U}}_d(\theta)$. Recall that given the defender's choice of parameter θ, the probability of schedule $\mathbf{s} \in \mathcal{S}$ is given by $p(\mathbf{s} \mid \theta)$. Let us denote the probability that the defender selects pure strategy $\mathbf{s}$, and an attacker of type λ selects target t_n by $p(\mathbf{s}, t_n \mid \theta, \lambda)$.

Thus, with probability $q(\lambda)p(\mathbf{s}, t_n \mid \theta, \lambda)$, the defender receives $U_d(\mathbf{s}, t_n)$, and so the gradient is

$$\nabla\tilde{\mathbf{U}}_d(\theta) = \sum_{\lambda\in\Lambda}\sum_{\mathbf{s}\in\mathcal{S},t_n\in\mathcal{T}} q(\lambda)U_d(\mathbf{c}_n(\mathbf{s}), t_n)\nabla p(\mathbf{s}, t_n \mid \theta, \lambda)$$

$$= \sum_{\lambda\in\Lambda}\sum_{\mathbf{s}\in\mathcal{S},t_n\in\mathcal{T}} \frac{p(\mathbf{s}, t_n \mid \theta, \lambda)}{p(\mathbf{s}, t_n \mid \theta, \lambda)} q(\lambda)U_d(\mathbf{c}_n(\mathbf{s}), t_n)\nabla p(\mathbf{s}, t_n \mid \theta, \lambda)$$

$$= \mathbb{E}\left[U_d(\mathbf{c}_n(\mathbf{s}), t_n)\frac{\nabla p(\mathbf{s}, t_n \mid \theta, \lambda)}{p(\mathbf{s}, t_n \mid \theta, \lambda)}\right]. \tag{3}$$

We can estimate $\nabla\tilde{\mathbf{U}}_d(\theta)$ by drawing m random samples according to the model. The gradient estimate for sample i is given by

$$\tilde{\gamma}_\theta^{(i)} = U_d(\mathbf{c}_n(\mathbf{s}^{(i)}), t_n^{(i)})\frac{\nabla p(\mathbf{s}^{(i)}, t_n^{(i)} \mid \theta, \lambda^{(i)})}{p(\mathbf{s}^{(i)}, t_n^{(i)} \mid \theta, \lambda^{(i)})},$$

and the overall gradient estimate by $\frac{1}{m}\sum_{i=1}^m \tilde{\gamma}_\theta^{(i)}$. This presumes that given realizations λ, $\mathbf{s}$ and t_n, the ratio $\frac{\nabla p(\mathbf{s},t_n|\theta,\lambda)}{p(\mathbf{s},t_n|\theta,\lambda)}$ can be efficiently computed. We examine classes Θ where this holds in the following sections.

For gradient methods to converge in expectation any unbiased estimate of $\nabla\tilde{\mathbf{U}}_d$ suffices (even taking $m = 1$), although lower variance estimates perform better in practice. Furthermore, $\frac{\nabla p(\mathbf{s},t_n|\theta,\lambda)}{p(\mathbf{s},t_n|\theta,\lambda)}$ depends on the realization $\lambda^{(i)}$, and not the entire set Λ. Thus, the computation required to estimate $\nabla\tilde{\mathbf{U}}_d$ is independent of $|\Lambda|$, and we expect such methods to scale to any number of attacker types (even infinitely many).

For completeness, we state the algorithm STACKGRAD, which is a projected stochastic gradient ascent, utilizing Monte-Carlo gradient estimates. Let $P_\Theta(x) = \min_{\theta\in\Theta}\|x - \theta\|_2$ denote the Euclidean projection of x onto Θ. We use the shorthand $\lambda, \mathbf{s}, t \sim M(\theta)$ to denote random variables sampled according to the stochastic approximation given defender parameter θ.

Algorithm STACKGRAD

Inputs: Class Θ, Horizon T, Sampling Parameter m
Initialize θ_0.
for $\tau = 1, \ldots, T$ **do**
  Sample $\lambda^{(i)}, \mathbf{s}^{(i)}, t_n^{(i)} \sim M(\theta_\tau)$ for $i = 1, \ldots, m$.
  Let $\tilde{\gamma}_\tau = \frac{1}{m}\sum_{i=1}^m U_d(\mathbf{c}_n(\mathbf{s}^{(i)}), t_n^{(i)})\frac{\nabla p(\mathbf{s}^{(i)},t_n^{(i)}|\theta_{\tau-1},\lambda^{(i)})}{p(\mathbf{s}^{(i)},t_n^{(i)}|\theta_{\tau-1},\lambda^{(i)})}$
  $\theta_\tau = P_\Theta(\theta_{\tau-1} + \frac{1}{\sqrt{T}}\tilde{\gamma}_\tau)$
end for
return θ_T

Standard results (e.g. Boyd et al. [2003]) tell us that after T iterations, the expected value of $\tilde{\mathbf{U}}_d(\theta_T)$ will be within $O(\frac{1}{\sqrt{T}})$ of a local maximum of the function $\tilde{\mathbf{U}}_d$. Therefore, if the quality of the defender strategy found by STACKGRAD, $R(\mathcal{D}_{\theta_T})$, is poor, it must either be because: (1) good mixed strategies for the *true* game exist only in $\Delta \setminus \Delta_\Theta$ (i.e. $\max_{\theta\in\Theta} V_\mathcal{G} - \tilde{\mathbf{U}}_d(\theta) \gg 0$), or (2) good defender strategies exist in Δ_Θ, but STACKGRAD converged to a suboptimal local maximum.

In what follows, we will see that in empirical validations, STACKGRAD exhibits good behavior on standard security games. This leads us to two questions, which we leave open for future theoretical research. (1) Are there classes of Stackelberg games, and parameterized strategies Θ, where the best strategy for the approximate game is guaranteed to be a good strategy for the true game? (2) Are there classes of Stackelberg games where STACKGRAD is guaranteed to exhibit good convergence properties?

5 INDEPENDENT RESOURCE ALLOCATION : CATEGORICAL DISTRIBUTIONS

In this section we demonstrate how to compute the ratio $\frac{\nabla p(\mathbf{s},t_n|\theta,\lambda)}{p(\mathbf{s},t_n|\theta,\lambda)}$ for a natural defender strategy class. We will then demonstrate how this parameterized class can be used to search for defender strategies in games with a large, even infinite number, of adversary types.

One simple, but rich class of defender strategies assumes that each defender resource is independently assigned to a schedule. For each resource k and schedule $s \in \mathcal{S}_k$, we assign resource k to s with some probability. This assignment is conducted independently across resources.

For each set of schedules $\mathcal{S}_k = \{s_{k,0}, \ldots, s_{k,d_k}\}$, we therefore introduce a parameter $\theta_{k,l}$ where for $l \geq 1$, $\theta_{k,l} \geq 0$ specifies the probability with which resource k is assigned to resource $s_{k,l}$. We require that $\sum_{l=1}^{d_k}\theta_{k,l} \leq 1$, and resource k is assigned to schedule $s_{k,0}$ with the remaining probability $\theta_{k,0} = 1 - \sum_{l=1}^{d_k}\theta_{k,l}$. Thus, this class of strategies is parameterized by $\Theta \subset \mathbb{R}^d$ where $d = \sum_{k=1}^K d_k$.

Notice that Δ_Θ is rich enough to describe any marginal distribution of an individual resource's assignment to schedules, including any pure strategy. However, Δ_Θ cannot capture mixed strategies which contain correlations between resource assignments.

In what follows, we derive $\frac{\nabla p(\mathbf{s},t_n|\theta,\lambda)}{p(\mathbf{s},t_n|\theta,\lambda)}$. We will need a helper lemma that characterizes the gradient of target coverage probabilities with respect to θ, the full proof of which is given in the supplemental material. In order to give the result, we will need some definitions. Given a joint assignment of resources to schedules $\mathbf{s}$, let $c_{-k,n}(\mathbf{s})$ indicate whether target n is covered by some resource other than resource k. In other words, $c_{-k,n}(\mathbf{s}) = \mathbf{1}[t_n \in \cup_{k'\neq k}\mathbf{s}_{k'}]$.

Also let $c_{k,l,n}$ indicate whether the lth schedule of resource k contains target t_n; $c_{k,l,n} = \mathbf{1}[t_n \in s_{k,l}]$.

Lemma 1. *For any target index n, resource index k, and schedule index $l \geq 1$,*

$$\frac{\partial}{\partial \theta_{k,l}} \bar{\mathbf{c}}_n(\mathcal{D}_\theta) = (c_{k,l,n} - c_{k,0,n}) \mathbb{P}_{\mathbf{s}\sim\mathcal{D}_\theta}(c_{-k,n}(\mathbf{s}) = 0)$$

The ratio $\frac{\nabla p(\mathbf{s},t_n|\theta,\lambda)}{p(\mathbf{s},t_n|\theta,\lambda)}$ can be written in terms of the derivative in Lemma 1. Let $\mathbf{s} = [s_{1,l_1}, \ldots, s_{K,l_K}]$, so that the indices of the selected schedules are given by $l_1, \ldots, l_K$. Define $z(\mathbf{s}, k, l) \in \{-1, 0, 1\}$ by letting $z(\mathbf{s}, k, l) = \mathbf{1}[l_k = k] - \mathbf{1}[l_k = 0]$. In other words $z(\mathbf{s}, k, l)$ provides a sign of 1 if resource k is assigned to schedule l, a sign of -1 if it is assigned to schedule 0 and a sign of 0 otherwise.

Theorem 1. *For any target t_n, schedule assignment $\mathbf{s}$, as well as resource index k and schedule index $l \geq 1$, we have that:*

$$\frac{\frac{\partial}{\theta_{k,l}} p(\mathbf{s}, t_n \mid \theta)}{p(\mathbf{s}, t_n \mid \theta)} = \frac{z(\mathbf{s}, k, l)}{\theta_{k,l_k}} - \eta M_{a,n} \frac{\partial}{\partial \theta_{k,l}} \bar{c}_n(\mathcal{D}_\theta) + \eta \sum_{n'=1}^{N} \sigma_\eta(\mathbf{u}(\mathcal{D}_\theta), n') M_{a,n'} \frac{\partial}{\partial \theta_{k,l}} \bar{c}_{n'}(\mathcal{D}_\theta)$$

Proof. Fix $\mathbf{s} = [s_{1,l_1}, \ldots, s_{K,l_K}]$. We have that $p(\mathbf{s} \mid \theta) = \prod_{k'=1}^{K} \theta_{k',l_{k'}}$. Now fix a resource index k and schedule index $l \geq 1$. We have that $\frac{\partial}{\partial \theta_{k,l}} p(\mathbf{s} \mid \theta) = \prod_{k' \neq k} \theta_{k',l_{k'}}$ if $l_k = l$; $\frac{\partial}{\partial \theta_{k,l}} p(\mathbf{s} \mid \theta) = -\prod_{k' \neq k} \theta_{k',l_{k'}}$ if $l_k = 0$; and $\frac{\partial}{\partial \theta_{k,l}} p(\mathbf{s} \mid \theta) = 0$ otherwise. From the definition of z:

$$\frac{\frac{\partial}{\partial \theta_{k,l}} p(\mathbf{s} \mid \theta)}{p(\mathbf{s} \mid \theta)} = \frac{z(\mathbf{s}, k, l)}{\theta_{k,l_k}} \tag{4}$$

Next fix a target index n, and note that $\frac{\partial}{\partial \theta_{k,l}} \exp(\eta \mathbf{u}_n(\mathcal{D}_\theta))) = \exp(\eta \mathbf{u}_n(\mathcal{D}_\theta)) \frac{\partial}{\partial \theta_{k,l}} \eta \mathbf{u}_n(\mathcal{D}_\theta) = -\eta \exp(\eta \mathbf{u}_n(\mathcal{D}_\theta)) M_{a,n} \frac{\partial}{\partial \theta_{k,l}} \bar{c}_n(\mathcal{D}_\theta)$

This lets us differentiate $\sigma_\eta(\mathbf{u}(\mathcal{D}_\theta), n)$:

$$\begin{aligned}
\frac{\partial}{\partial \theta_{k,l}} \sigma_\eta(\mathbf{u}(\mathcal{D}_\theta), n) &= \frac{\partial}{\partial \theta_{k,l}} \frac{\exp(\eta \mathbf{u}_n(\mathcal{D}_\theta)))}{\sum_{n'=1}^{N} \exp(\eta \mathbf{u}_{n'}(\mathcal{D}_\theta)))} \\
&= \frac{1}{\sum_{n'=1}^{N} \exp(\eta \mathbf{u}_{n'}(\mathcal{D}_\theta))} \frac{\partial}{\partial \theta_{k,l}} \exp(\eta \mathbf{u}_{n'}(\mathcal{D}_\theta)) \\
&+ \exp(\eta \mathbf{u}_n(\mathcal{D}_\theta)) \frac{\partial}{\partial \theta_{k,l}} \frac{1}{\sum_{n'=1}^{N} \exp(\eta \mathbf{u}_{n'}(\mathcal{D}_\theta))} \\
&= -\eta \sigma_\eta(\mathbf{u}(\mathcal{D}_\theta), n) M_{a,n} \frac{\partial}{\partial \theta_{k,l}} \bar{c}_n(\mathcal{D}_\theta) \\
&- \frac{\sigma_\eta(\mathbf{u}(\mathcal{D}_\theta), n)}{\sum_{n'=1}^{N} \exp(\eta \mathbf{u}_{n'}(\mathcal{D}_\theta))} \frac{\partial}{\partial \theta_{k,l}} \sum_{n'=1}^{N} \exp(\eta \mathbf{u}_{n'}(\mathcal{D}_\theta)) \\
&= -\eta \sigma_\eta(\mathbf{u}(\mathcal{D}_\theta), n) M_{a,n} \frac{\partial}{\partial \theta_{k,l}} \bar{c}_n(\mathcal{D}_\theta) \\
&+ \eta \sigma_\eta(\mathbf{u}(\mathcal{D}_\theta), n) \sum_{n'=1}^{N} \sigma_\eta(\mathbf{u}(\mathcal{D}_\theta), n') M_{a,n'} \frac{\partial}{\partial \theta_{k,l}} \bar{c}_{n'}(\mathcal{D}_\theta)
\end{aligned} \tag{5}$$

Using equations (4) and (5), we have:

$$\begin{aligned}
\frac{\frac{\partial}{\partial \theta_{k,l}} p(\mathbf{s}, t_n \mid \theta)}{p(\mathbf{s}, t_n \mid \theta)} &= \frac{\sigma_\eta(\mathbf{u}(\mathcal{D}_\theta), n) \frac{\partial}{\partial \theta_{k,l}} p(\mathbf{s} \mid \theta)}{p(\mathbf{s} \mid \theta) \sigma_\eta(\mathbf{u}(\mathcal{D}_\theta), n)} \\
&+ \frac{p(\mathbf{s} \mid \theta) \frac{\partial}{\partial \theta_{k,l}} \sigma_\eta(\mathbf{u}(\mathcal{D}_\theta), n)}{p(\mathbf{s} \mid \theta) \sigma_\eta(\mathbf{u}(\mathcal{D}_\theta), n)} \\
&= \frac{z(\mathbf{s}, k, l)}{\theta_{k,l_k}} - \eta M_{a,n} \frac{\partial}{\partial \theta_{k,l}} \bar{c}_n(\mathcal{D}_\theta) \\
&+ \eta \sum_{n'=1}^{N} \sigma_\eta(\mathbf{u}(\mathcal{D}_\theta), n') M_{a,n'} \frac{\partial}{\partial \theta_{k,l}} \bar{c}_{n'}(\mathcal{D}_\theta)
\end{aligned}$$

□

6 EXPERIMENTS SCALING WITH ATTACKER TYPES

The derivation from the previous section allows us to implement the STACKGRAD algorithm for a particular class of defender mixed strategies, specifically those that assign resources to schedules independently. We call the resulting algorithm STACKGRAD-I (where I follows from the independence assumption).

We now demonstrate that STACKGRAD-I scales very well on games with a large numbers of attacker types. Specifically, we will see that for a fixed choice of parameters T and m, both the run-time and quality of the solution θ_T found by STACKGRAD-I are *constant* in the number of attacker types.

Experiments were conducted on the patrolling domain introduced by Paruchuri et al. [2007], (see Paruchuri et al. [2008]). The goal is to assign a single security resource (such as a UAV or robot) to a sequence of targets $[t_{i_1}, \ldots, t_{i_d}]$, called its patrol. Thus, for patrol length d, the set of defender pure strategies $\mathcal{S}$ consists of all length d permutations of the target set.

In the original game, the coverage induced by strategy $\mathbf{s} = [t_{n_1}, \ldots, t_{n_d}]$ is not binary, and depends on the location of a target t_n in $\mathbf{s}$. That is, there are parameters $p_1, \ldots, p_d$ where $\mathbf{c}_n(\mathbf{s}) = p_j$ if $n = n_j$ and $\mathbf{c}_n(\mathbf{s}) = 0$ if $n \neq \{n_1, \ldots, n_d\}$. Target t_n is covered with probability p_j if it appears jth in the patrol, otherwise it is not covered at all. x

We use this formulation, but note that for this (non-binary) coverage function Lemma 1 must re-derived. Using the categorical distribution, there is a single parameter θ_l for each permutation in $\mathcal{S}$, and it is not difficult to show that $\frac{\partial}{\partial \theta_l} \bar{\mathbf{c}}_n(\mathcal{D}_\theta) = \mathbf{c}_n(\mathbf{s}_l) - \mathbf{c}_n(\mathbf{s}_0)$. The result of Theorem 1 is unchanged. Secondly, we note that for this particular game, the categorical distribution completely characterizes the set of mixed defender strategies ($\Delta = \Delta_\Theta$). Thus, for large enough inverse temperature in the softmax function ($\eta \to \infty$), maximizing $\tilde{U}_d(\theta)$ is equivalent to finding a Stackelberg equilibrium defender strategy.

Experiments where run on randomly generated instances of these games; $U_d(0, t_n)$, $M_{d,n}$, $U_\lambda(1, t_n)$ and $M_{\lambda,n}$ are chosen at random in $[0, 1]$. In all instances STACKGRAD-I is run with inverse temperature $\eta = 20$, and sampling parameter $m = 50$. Every data point is the average of 20 experiments. Experiments were run on a 2.5 GHz Intel Xeon E5-2680v3 processor, and Integer programs were solved using IBM CPLEX 12.4.

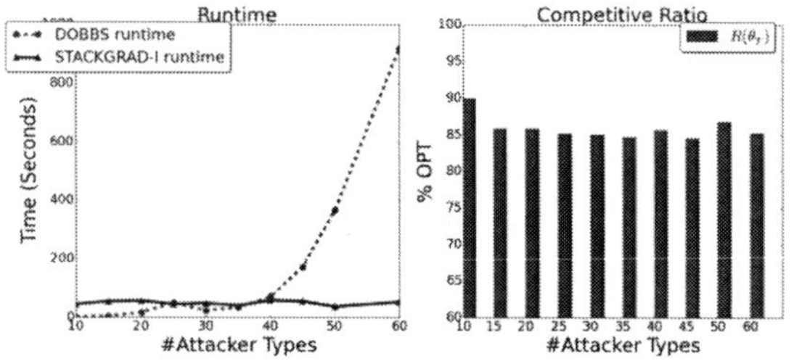

Figure 2: Patrol Game: STACKGRAD-I vs. DOBBS

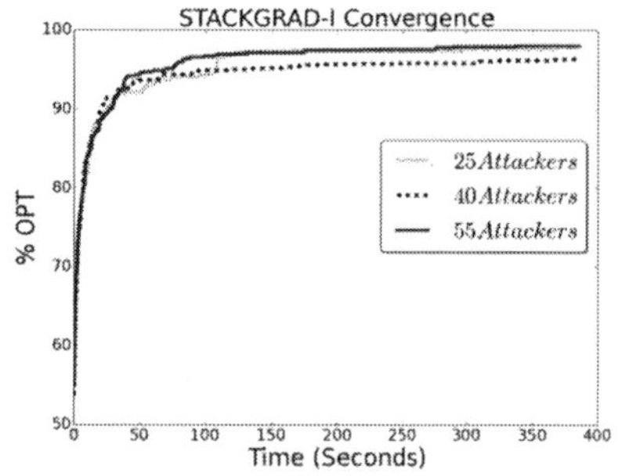

Figure 3: Competitive Ratio

In the left plot of Figure 2, we compare the running time of STACKGRAD-I and the DOBBS algorithm of Paruchuri et al. [2008], which is the fastest algorithm for general Stackelberg games, but must solve an integer program. Experiments were conducted on instances with 5 targets and patrol lengths of 2, for a total of 40 defender pure strategies. While the game is small enough to be tractable with a small number of defender pure strategies, as the number of attacker types is increased, the DOBBS algorithm begins to experience an exponential increase in its running time. In contrast, STACKGAD-I exhibits near constant average running time, with a range between 38 seconds and 59 seconds (against 55 attackers and 45 attackers respectively). Furthermore, as displayed on the right plot of Figure 2, scaling the game has no effect on the quality of the solution found by STACKGRAD-I. The competitive ratio of the solution θ^* found by STACKGRAD-I against the true optimum found by DOBBS ranges between 84.5% and 86.8%.

Of course both the running time and the quality of the solution found by STACKGRAD-I is a function of T, the number of iterations the gradient ascent is run. For the results in Figure 2, STACKGRAD-I was terminated after $T = 1000$ iterations.

In Figure 3, we show the results of running STACKGRAD-I for up to $T = 5000$ iterations, for $25, 40, 55$ attacker types. Here we see that the competitive ratio of the best solution found by STACKGRAD-I against the Stackelberg optimum quickly (displayed on the y axis) exceeds 90%. After 100 seconds (corresponding to about $T = 2500$), the average competitive ratio has reached above 94%.

STACKGRAD's constant running time, and performance, as the number of attackers is scaled up (but T is held constant), can be attributed to the fact that neither the parameterization nor the computation of the gradient depend on the size of Λ. Furthermore, the parameterization is complete, in the sense that all mixed strategies for the game are representable. The number of pure strategies, however, was kept small; with five targets and patrol of length two, there are a total of 20 defender pure strategies. In the next section, we demonstrate how STACKGRAD can be deployed to find solutions in games where the set of pure strategies is very large.

7 LARGE STRATEGY SETS

7.1 STRUCTURED PURE STRATEGIES

While the categorical distribution model of Section 5 demonstrates the power of gradient methods when the number of pure strategies are small, and the number of attacker types is large, most security games are concerned with settings in which there is a very large space of defender pure strategies. Recall that under the categorical model $\Theta \subset \mathbb{R}^d$, where $d = \sum_{k=1}^{K}(|\mathcal{S}_k| - 1)$. Thus, if $|\mathcal{S}_k|$ tends to be large, we would not expect STACKGRAD-I to perform very well. This is often the case in real security domains where the set of pure strategies exhibits a combinatorial explosion with the number of defender resources or potential targets.

In this Section, we introduce a new class of defender mixed strategies Θ which has a compact representation even as $|\mathcal{S}_k|$ grows large. We consider a setting in which schedules can be iteratively constructed. In the FAMS domain, for example, an air marshal r_k is assigned a schedule consisting of a sequence of flights $\mathbf{s}_k = [t_{n_1}, \ldots, t_{n_L}]$ (which we take to be ordered). The length of the schedule is bounded (there is some upper bound $L \leq B$), and must land the marshal back to its origin airport. Although the set of feasible schedules for a marshal r_k can be exponentially large in B, it has a natural combinatorial structure. In particular, given a subsequence of flights $\mathbf{s}_{k,1:l} = [t_{n_1}, \ldots, t_{n_l}]$, $l < L$, the set of feasible "next flights" can be efficiently computed.

Specifically, the subsequence of flights specified by $s_{k,1:l}$ lands the marshal at some airport A at some time τ. The viable choices for the $l+1$ flight are those flights leaving airport A after time τ, that can get the marshal back home in $B-l$ hops or fewer.[2]

More generally, we consider games where the schedules for some resource r_k is given by an ordered set of targets s_k. We will further assume that given some subseqence $s_{k,1:l}$, the set of feasible next targets $F(s_{k,1:l})$ can be efficiently computed. Formally, t_n belongs to $F(s_{k,1:l})$ if and only if there is some schedule $s_k \in \mathcal{S}_k$, where $s_k = [s_{k,1:l}, t_n, \ldots]$ (s_k begins with the prefix $s_{k,1:l}$).

7.2 PARAMETRIC MODEL

Following the recipe outlined in Section 4, we introduce a new parametric model Θ for games that exhibit the sequential structure just described.

We will consider a simple logistic model. For each resource k we introduce a vector $\mathbf{w}_k$ of dimension N, where N is the number of targets. We denote the nth element of $\mathbf{w}_k$ by $\mathbf{w}_{k,n}$. A resource r_k is assigned to schedule s_k according to a sequential stochastic process. Given a subsequence of targets of length l, $s_{k,1:l}$, the next target in resource r_k's schedule is selected with probability proportional to $\exp(\mathbf{w}_{k,n})$ when $t_n \in F(s_{k,1:l})$ and with probability 0 otherwise. For $t_n \in F(s_{k,1:l})$:

$$\mathbb{P}[s_k(l+1) = t_n \mid s_{k,1:l}] = \frac{\exp(\mathbf{w}_{k,n})}{\sum_{t_{n'} \in F(s_{k,1:l})} \exp(\mathbf{w}_{k,n'})} \tag{6}$$

Thus, $\mathbf{w}_{k,n}$ indicates the propensity for target t_n to be covered whenever that target is available in the feasible set of next targets. As was the case with the model of Section 5, each resource will be independently assigned to a schedule. Therefore $\theta = \{\mathbf{w}_1, \ldots, \mathbf{w}_K\}$, and $\Delta(\Theta)$ indicates the set of distributions over resource assignments where resources are independently assigned to schedules according to the aforementioned stochastic process. Notice that the dimension of θ is KN, where K is the number of resources and N is the number of targets. Therefore, the parameterization remains compact even if the size of $|\mathcal{S}|$ explodes.

We state $\frac{\nabla p(\mathbf{s}, t_n|\theta)}{p(\mathbf{s}, t_n|\theta)}$ for this new parametric class of strategies in the following Theorem. Due to space restrictions, the full proof is given in the supplemental material.

Theorem 2. *Let $t_{n_{k,l}}$ denote the lth target covered by the kth resource chosen by the defender. For any target t_{n^*} chosen by the attacker, schedule assignments* $\mathbf{s}$ *chosen by defender, and any parameter $\mathbf{w}_{k,n}$. $\frac{\partial}{\partial \mathbf{w}_{k,n}} p(\mathbf{s}, t_{n^*} \mid \theta)/p(\mathbf{s}, t_{n^*} \mid \theta)$ is given by the following equation:*

$$\sum_{l=1}^{L} \mathbf{1}[n = n_{k,l}] - \mathbb{P}[s_k(l) = t_n \mid s_{k,1:(l-1)}, \theta]$$
$$- \eta \sum_{n'=1}^{N} \sigma_\eta(\mathbf{u}_\lambda(\mathcal{D}_\theta), n') M_{a,n'} \frac{\partial}{\partial \mathbf{w}_{k,n}} \bar{\mathbf{c}}_{n'}(\mathcal{D}_\theta)$$
$$+ \eta M_{a,n^*} \frac{\partial}{\partial \mathbf{w}_{k,n}} \bar{\mathbf{c}}_{n^*}(\mathcal{D}_\theta)$$

[2]This computation is via a modification of Djikstra's algorithm.

Unlike the categorical model of Section 5, the partial derivative of $\bar{\mathbf{c}}_n(\mathcal{D}_\theta)$ cannot be easily computed in closed form. Changing the value of parameter $\mathbf{w}_{k,n}$, might effect the coverage of targets $t_{n'} \neq t_n$. In the federal air marshal (FAMS) domain, $\mathbf{w}_{k,n}$ corresponds to the likelihood that marshal r_k takes flight t_n. Increasing $\mathbf{w}_{k,n}$, however, also changes the coverage probabilities of other flights; flights departing from the destination airport of t_n also become more likely, as the marshal needs to return home.

Therefore, instead of computing the derivative in closed form, we use numerical differentiation. Given a set of parameters $\theta = \{\mathbf{w}_1, \ldots, \mathbf{w}_K\}$, let $\theta + \delta_{n,k}$ denote the set of parameters, where $\mathbf{w}_{k,n} = \mathbf{w}_{k,n} + \delta$, and all other parameters are unchanged. We estimate $\frac{\partial}{\partial \mathbf{w}_{k,n}} \bar{\mathbf{c}}_n(\theta)$ by sampling schedules $\mathbf{s}^{(i)}$ according to θ and schedules $\mathbf{s}_{n,k}^{(i)}$ according to $\theta + \delta_n^{(k)}$ for $i = 1, \ldots, m$. We then estimate $\frac{\partial}{\partial \mathbf{w}_{k,n}} \bar{c}_n(\theta)$ using $\frac{1}{m} \sum_{i=1}^{m} \frac{\mathbf{c}_n(\mathbf{s}^{(i)}) - \mathbf{c}_n(\mathbf{s}_{k,n}^{(i)})}{\delta}$.

8 EXPERIMENTS: SCALING WITH LARGE STRATEGY SETS

The derivation of the gradient for the model in the previous section gives us another instantiation of STACKGRAD, which we call STACKGRAD-L (where L follows from the logistic model). We now demonstrate the scalability of STACKGRAD-L in domains with a large number of defender pure strategies.

Recall that the STACKGRAD-L was derived to have no dependency on $|\mathcal{S}_k|$, the number of schedules available for any resource k. We compare against the state-of-the-art ASPEN algorithm [Jain et al., 2010a]. We note that the ASPEN algorithm was designed to eliminate the combinatorial explosion in *joint* schedules. If all $|\mathcal{S}_k| = X$, then there are X^K possible joint schedules if the Stackelberg game were to be expressed in normal form. Nevertheless, ASPEN still has a computational dependency the size of an individual set of schedules $\mathcal{S}_k$. In particular, ASPEN uses a column generation technique, where selecting each new column requires solving a network flow problem with at least $\sum_k^K |\mathcal{S}_k|$ edges.

We conduct experiments on games inspired by the FAMS domain. We begin with a fixed weighted network G^*, representing actual air travel between the 500 US airports with the most traffic [Colizza et al., 2007]. Nodes represent airports and the weights in G^* represent how many tickets were available between two airports in a given year. Given a parameter N, we generate a game instance as follows. We create a new network G, where G is generated by sampling 30 airports from G^* where at least 5 of these airports are chosen to be "hub" airports. We then create N edges in G corresponding to flights, where a flight between aiports v_1 and v_2 is present in G with probability proportional the weight on (v_1, v_2) in G^*. The edges in G are meant to be representative of actual flights between 30 US airports on a given day. Each edge represents a flight, and therefore a target. In this game, we have only a single attacker type. In all our experiments there are 3 marshals, who can take a tour of length $L \leq 5$ before returning to their home city. The home city is selected uniformly from one of the hubs for each of the marshals. We allow any such tour on G. [3]

We conduct experiments for various values of $N \in \{500, 1000, 1500, 2000, 2500, 5000, 10000\}$. $\mathcal{S}_k$ for a single marshal k consists of all tours from a start vertex of length at most 5 in a network consisting of up to 10000 directed edges. Even simply enumerating $\mathcal{S}_k$ for our larger instances is impossible. However, running ASPEN requires $\{\mathcal{S}_k\}$ to be given as input. Therefore, in order to allow ASPEN to complete in a reasonable amount of time, we generate subsets $\hat{\mathcal{S}}_k \subset \mathcal{S}_k$ by randomly sampling $Y = 10,000$ tours for each marshal. As a result, the performance of STACKGRAD-L is not reported as a competitive ratio to the true Stackelberg optimum, since ASPEN is also solving a restricted game.

Nevertheless, we can compare the performance of STACKGRAD-L to that of ASPEN as the size of the game is increased. In Figure 4 we compare the runtime of ASPEN with STACKGRAD-L for various values of N. Once Y is fixed, the size of the pure strategy set of ASPEN is constant. ASPEN is unaware of any of the pure strategies outside the set $\hat{\mathcal{S}}_1 \times \hat{\mathcal{S}}_2 \times \hat{\mathcal{S}}_3$. Nevertheless ASPEN must still solve a mixed integer linear program where the number of constraints scale with N. The average runtime of STACKGRAD-L increases as N grows as well, as the parameterization of STACKGRAD-L is in $\mathbb{R}^N$, but remains bounded by that of ASPEN for large N.

In Figure 4 we also display the average performance of each algorithm. Performance is measured as the direct payoff to the defender in the unrestricted game, in contrast to the results in Section 6, where we computed competitive ratios directly. We see that for smaller number of targets ASPEN finds a higher quality solution than STACKGRAD-L on average. However, as N is increased the solution found by STACKGRAD-L overtakes. We suspect this is due to the fact that fixing Y in ASPEN eliminates pure strategies that might be necessary for the defender, while any pure strategy can be represented by STACKGRAD-L. For large N, $\hat{\mathcal{S}}_k$ is a very small subset of all the possible tours of length 5.

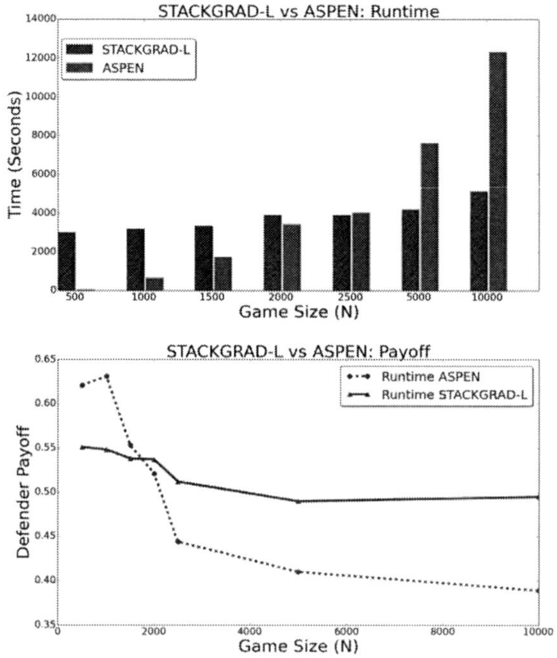

Figure 4: STACKGRAD-L vs ASPEN

9 CONCLUSIONS AND FUTURE WORK

We present a new algorithm, STACKGRAD, for solving Stackelberg security games, which works by performing a gradient ascent, rather than solving an integer program. We demonstrate a version of STACKGRAD with no computational dependence on the number of attacker types, and another version with a mild dependence on the number of defender pure strategies. Since the procedure restricts its search to within a parametric class of defender mixed strategies, and might find strategies bounded away from the true Stackelberg optimum, we also provide empirical evidence that the solutions found by STACKGRAD are of comparable quality to solutions in the unrestricted game. These empirical successes invite open questions for future research, chief among these being whether there are parametric classes of defender mixed strategies which are provably competitive with the true Stackelberg optimum.

[3] This permissiveness is somewhat artificial; in reality, a flight lands at its destination at a specified time, eliminating flights that leave sooner than that from consideration at the destination airport. This realism can be accounted for in the definition of F in the previous section. To keep the experiments simple, we allow any tour on G, and comment that this does not affect the scalability of STACKGRAD-L.

References

Jonathan Baxter and Peter L. Bartlett. Infinite-horizon policy-gradient estimation. *Journal of Artificial Intelligence Research*, 15:319–350, 2001.

Stephen Boyd, Lin Xiao, and Almir Mutapcic. Subgradient methods. Lecture notes of EE392o, Autumn Quarter, 2003.

Vittoria Colizza, Romualdo Pastor-Satorras, and Alessandro Vespignani. Reaction–diffusion processes and metapopulation models in heterogeneous networks. *Nature Physics*, 3(4):276–282, 2007.

Manish Jain, Erem Kardeş, and Fernando Ordóñez. Security games with arbitrary schedules: A branch and price approach. In *24th AAAI Conference on Artificial Intelligence*, pages 792–797, 2010a.

Manish Jain, Jason Tsai, James Pita, Christopher Kiekintveld, Shyamsunder Rathi, Milind Tambe, and Fernando Ordóñez. Software assistants for randomized patrol planning for the LAX airport police and the federal air marshal service. *Interfaces*, 40(4):267–290, 2010b.

Manish Jain, Christopher Kiekintveld, and Milind Tambe. Quality-bounded solutions for finite Bayesian Stackelberg games: Scaling up. In *10th International Conference on Autonomous Agents and Multi-Agent Systems*, pages 997–1004, 2011.

Christopher Kiekintveld, Manish Jain, Jason Tsai, James Pita, Fernando Ordóñez, and Milind Tambe. Computing optimal randomized resource allocations for massive security games. In *8th International Conference on Autonomous Agents and Multiagent Systems*, pages 689–696, 2009.

Christopher Kiekintveld, Janusz Marecki, and Milind Tambe. Approximation methods for infinite bayesian stackelberg games: Modeling distributional payoff uncertainty. In *10th International Conference on Autonomous Agents and Multiagent Systems*, pages 1005–1012, 2011.

Dmytro Korzhyk, Zhengyu Yin, Christopher Kiekintveld, Vincent Conitzer, and Milind Tambe. Stackelberg vs. Nash in security games: An extended investigation of interchangeability, equivalence, and uniqueness. *Journal of Artificial Intelligence Research*, 41:297–327, 2011.

Richard D McKelvey and Thomas R Palfrey. Quantal response equilibria for normal form games. *Games and economic behavior*, 10(1):6–38, 1995.

Praveen Paruchuri, Jonathan P. Pearce, Milind Tambe, Fernando Ordóñez, and Sarit Kraus. An efficient heuristic approach for security against multiple adversaries. In *6th International Joint Conference on Autonomous agents and Multiagent Systems*, pages 299–306, 2007.

Praveen Paruchuri, Jonathan P. Pearce, Janusz Marecki, Milind Tambe, Fernando Ordóñez, and Sarit Kraus. Playing games for security: An efficient exact algorithm for solving Bayesian Stackelberg games. In *7th International Joint Conference on Autonomous Agents and Multiagent Systems*, pages 895–902, 2008.

James Pita, Harish Bellamane, Manish Jain, Chris Kiekintveld, Jason Tsai, Fernando Ordóñez, and Milind Tambe. Security applications: Lessons of real-world deployment. *ACM SIGecom Exchanges*, 8(2):5, 2009.

Jason Tsai, Shyamsunder Rathi, Christopher Kiekintveld, Fernando Ordóñez, and Milind Tambe. IRIS: A tool for strategic security allocation in transportation networks. In *8th International Conference on Autonomous Agents and Multiagent Systems (Industrial Track)*, pages 37–44, 2009.

Rong Yang, Fernando Ordóñez, and Milind Tambe. Computing optimal strategy against quantal response in security games. In *11th International Conference on Autonomous Agents and Multiagent Systems*, pages 847–854, 2012.

Rong Yang, Christopher Kiekintveld, Fernando Ordóñez, Milind Tambe, and Richard John. Improving resource allocation strategies against human adversaries in security games: An extended study. *Artificial Intelligence*, 195:440–469, 2013.

Zhengyu Yin and Milind Tambe. A unified method for handling discrete and continuous uncertainty in Bayesian Stackelberg games. In *11th International Conference on Autonomous Agents and Multiagent Systems*, pages 855–862, 2012.

Inferring Causal Direction from Relational Data

David Arbour
darbour@cs.umass.edu

Katerina Marazopoulou
kmarazo@cs.umass.edu

David Jensen
jensen@cs.umass.edu

College of Information and Computer Sciences
University of Massachusetts Amherst
Amherst MA, 01003

Abstract

Inferring the direction of causal dependence from observational data is a fundamental problem in many scientific fields. Significant progress has been made in inferring causal direction from data that are independent and identically distributed (i.i.d.), but little is understood about this problem in the more general relational setting with multiple types of interacting entities. This work examines the task of inferring the *causal direction of peer dependence* in relational data. We show that, in contrast to the i.i.d. setting, the direction of peer dependence can be inferred using simple procedures, regardless of the form of the underlying distribution, and we provide a theoretical characterization on the identifiability of direction. We then examine the conditions under which the presence of confounding can be detected. Finally, we demonstrate the efficacy of the proposed methods with synthetic experiments, and we provide an application on real-world data.[1]

1 INTRODUCTION

Inferring the direction of causal dependence between two random variables from observational data is a fundamental problem in statistical reasoning. There have been many advances in this area for data sets that are independent and identically distributed (i.i.d.) [Janzing et al., 2012, Stegle et al., 2010, Lopez-Paz et al., 2015]. For relational data, recent work has studied the problem of inferring the effects of peers via *experimentation* [Muchnik et al., 2013, Bakshy et al., 2012, Toulis and Kao, 2013]. However, the problem of identifying causal direction from *observational* relational data has yet to receive the same focus. In this work, we study the problem of inferring the causal direction of peer dependence from observational relational data. We provide theoretical and experimental results to show that the causal direction of peer dependence can be robustly inferred from observational data by comparing the magnitude of two similarity measures (one for each candidate direction).

For example, consider a study on the causes of personal debt. Data consist of the net worth and the average monthly discretionary spending of a large set of individuals, along with the position of each individual within a social network. One reasonable question is whether a person's friends influence his or her spending habits. If a person's spending and wealth are correlated with the wealth and spending of their friends, what can be inferred about the *causal* dependence among these quantities? A person's spending could be caused by their friends' wealth or vice versa (direct dependence), or both quantities could be caused by an unobserved variable (confounding).

This paper examines when and how it is possible to differentiate among these scenarios. Specifically, we:

1. Identify a set of conditions under which the causal direction of relational dependence can be consistently inferred.
2. Investigate the effect of unobserved confounding on this approach to causal inference, and provide a simple test of relational confounding.
3. Provide an extension of our method to the case of nonlinear dependence via kernel embeddings.
4. Show that the proposed measures are robust to both the magnitude of the noise and the functional form of the true dependence, through a set of simulations under a variety of graph structures and functional forms.

The rest of the paper is structured as follows. Section 2 describes the problem setting. Section 3 presents a test of causal direction under deterministic linear dependence.

[1]A full version of this paper including supplementary material can be found at `http://kdl.cs.umass.edu/papers/arbour-et-al-uai2016.pdf`

Section 4 considers a relaxation of the assumptions by allowing for latent confounding and discusses the conditions under which latent confounding can be identified. Section 5 generalizes these results to the case where the similarity is measured by embedding the data in a reproducing kernel Hilbert space (RKHS). Section 6 presents experimental evaluation of these results using synthetic data and a variety of marginal and conditional distributions, as well as networks generated from the Erdős-Rényi, Watts-Strogatz, and Barabási-Albert models. Section 7 presents a demonstration of our method on Stack Overflow, a large online community where users ask and answer computer science related questions.

2 PROBLEM SETTING

Relational domains consist of multiple types of entities that interact with each other through multiple types of relationships. Consider, for example, the domain of academic publishing: authors write papers, papers cite other papers and so on. In this work, for clarity of exposition and without loss of generality, we focus on *networks*, a specific type of relational domains with a single type of entity (e.g., people) and a single type of relationship (e.g., friendship)[2].

An instantiation of a network consists of a set of people and a set of friendships among these people. This can be represented with an undirected graph $G = \langle V, E \rangle$ with n vertices. Nodes correspond to people and an edge denotes friendship between the nodes it connects. Every node of the graph $v_i \in V$ is associated with a pair of random variables, X_i and Y_i. These correspond to attributes of a person, for example wealth and spending habits. For every node, we can define a new random variable as a function of the random variables of its neighboring nodes. Specifically, in this section, we define a new random variable $X_i{}'$ as the sum of X_j over v_i's neighbors:

$$X_i{}' = \sum_{\{v_j | \langle v_i, v_j \rangle \in E\}} X_j$$

Similarly,

$$Y_i{}' = \sum_{\{v_j | \langle v_i, v_j \rangle \in E\}} Y_j.$$

For the remainder of the paper, we refer to functions of random variables of neighboring nodes, such as $X_i{}'$ and $Y_i{}'$, as *relational variables* and to random variables of the node, such as X_i and Y_i, as propositional variables. To avoid ambiguity, we refer to dependence between a relational variable and a propositional variable as *relational dependence.*

A very common assumption in relational domains is that of *templating*, i.e., random variables in different nodes follow the same distribution [Koller, 1999]. In our case, this would imply that the distribution of X_i is the same for all i (and the same for Y_i, $X_i{}'$, and $Y_i{}'$). This allows us to reason about four random variables on a model level: X, Y, X', and Y'. The task under consideration is determining the causal direction of relational dependence. Put in another way, we wish to determine whether $X' \to Y$ or $Y' \to X$ is the true generative process.

Since we are reasoning over random variables across all nodes of the network, it is convenient to represent them as vectors. Let $\mathbf{x} = \langle X_1, \ldots, X_n \rangle$ be a vector with the random variables X_i for every node and, similarly, $\mathbf{x}' = \langle X_1{}', \ldots, X_n{}' \rangle$. Let A denote the adjacency matrix of the graph defined as:

$$A_{ij} = \begin{cases} 1, & \text{if } (v_i, v_j) \in E. \\ 0, & \text{otherwise.} \end{cases}$$

We note that A is a symmetric matrix since G is an undirected graph. We can write the vector of the sum of the friends (i.e., the vector $\mathbf{x}'$) as $\mathbf{x}' = A\mathbf{x}$. Similarly, $\mathbf{y}' = A\mathbf{y}$.

We use D to denote the degree matrix of the graph:

$$D_{ij} = \begin{cases} d_i, & \text{if } i = j. \\ 0, & \text{otherwise.} \end{cases}$$

2.1 UNDERLYING ASSUMPTIONS

Throughout the paper, we make the following assumptions:

A1. *G is an undirected graph.*

A2. *Each node $v \in V$ has degree of at least 1.*

A3. *The distribution of X_i and Y_i is the same for all $v_i \in V$ (templating).*

A4. *There are no feedback cycles, i.e. $Y \to X \Rightarrow X \not\to Y$ for any two (relational or propositional) variables.*

Further, we initially assume (and later relax that assumption) that:

A5. *There are no confounding variables, i.e., unobserved variables that are common causes of the observed attributes.*

Section 4 is devoted to examining under which conditions this assumption can be loosened, while maintaining the ability to identify causal direction. Moreover, assumptions A4 and A5 mirror those found in the literature on determining causal direction between two propositional variables [Stegle et al., 2010, Janzing et al., 2012, Lopez-Paz et al., 2015].

[2]The extension to the more general multi-entity/multi-relationship case is straightforward. We provide the necessary details for this extension in the supplement.

3 DIRECTION UNDER LINEAR DEPENDENCE

In this section we show that, under the assumptions of linearity and a small amount of noise, peer dependence is asymmetric and the true causal direction can be consistently inferred. This is an inherent property of relational domains. The extension to non-linear dependencies is provided in Section 5.

To measure dependence between variables, we consider the square of Pearson's correlation, a common and widely employed measure of linear correlation between variables. Pearson's correlation between two variables X and Y can be computed from a sample $\mathbf{x}, \mathbf{y}$ as follows:

$$\rho(\mathbf{x}, \mathbf{y}) = \frac{\sum_{i=1}^{n}(x_i - \bar{x})(y_i - \bar{y})}{\sqrt{\sum_{i=1}^{n}(x_i - \bar{x})^2}\sqrt{\sum_{i=1}^{n}(y_i - \bar{y})^2}},$$

where $\bar{x}$ and $\bar{y}$ are the means of $\mathbf{x}$ and $\mathbf{y}$ respectively. We consider the square of the correlation to restrict the range of the metric to [0,1], rather than [-1,1].

Given a measure of dependence, a reasonable question is whether the measure is symmetric for relational data. Surprisingly, it is not. Given this, another reasonable question is what can be inferred by examining the dependence values in both directions. Surprisingly, the causal direction of dependence can be inferred from the resulting asymmetry.

We begin by handling a simplified case: Y is a deterministic function of the X values of related nodes. Specifically, we assume that Y_i is the scaled mean of the X_j variables of the related instances:

$$Y_i = \frac{\beta}{d_i}\sum_{i=1}^{d_i} X_j$$

Or, in matrix notation: $\mathbf{y} = \beta D^{-1}A\mathbf{x}$.

Under certain assumptions about the structure of the graph and the form of the dependence, the squared correlation in the causal direction will be greater that the squared correlation in the opposite direction.

Proposition 1. *Assume that G is a d-regular graph*[3]*, the true generative process is $\mathbf{y} = \beta D^{-1}A\mathbf{x}$ for some constant β, and assumptions A1-A5 hold. Then, $\rho^2(\mathbf{x}', \mathbf{y}) > \rho^2(\mathbf{y}', \mathbf{x})$.*

Proof. The left-hand-side of the inequality, given that by definition $\mathbf{x}' = A\mathbf{x}$, can be written as:

$$\rho^2(\mathbf{x}', \mathbf{y}) = \rho^2(A\mathbf{x}, \beta D^{-1}A\mathbf{x})$$
$$= \rho^2(A\mathbf{x}, \frac{\beta}{d}A\mathbf{x}) = 1$$

[3]A graph is d-regular if every vertex has degree d.

It remains to show that $1 > \rho^2(\mathbf{y}', \mathbf{x})$ which holds, unless $\rho^2(\mathbf{y}', \mathbf{x}) = 1$. Equality holds only when $\mathbf{y}' = \beta AD^{-1}A\mathbf{x}$ is a linear combination of $\mathbf{x}$, or in words, when the values of a node's friends of friends are a linear combination of that node's value. For random values of X, that happens for a degenerate network structure where every node has one friend of a friend and is the exact same starting node. This would happen, for example, in the case of a regular graph with degree 1 (pairs of nodes). □

In the case where Y is a noisy function of X, a similar inequality holds.

Proposition 2. *Assume that the true generative process is $\mathbf{y} = \beta D^{-1}A\mathbf{x} + \epsilon$ for some constant β, where ϵ is a vector with the noise terms. Moreover, assume that assumptions A1-A5 hold and X and Y are scaled to mean 0. Then the following holds:*

$$\rho^2(\mathbf{x}', \mathbf{y}) > \rho^2(\mathbf{y}', \mathbf{x}) \Leftrightarrow$$
$$\frac{Var(AD^{-1}A\mathbf{x}) + Var(A\epsilon)}{Var(D^{-1}A\mathbf{x}) + Var(\epsilon)} > \frac{Var(A\mathbf{x})}{Var(\mathbf{x})}.$$

A full derivation can be found in the supplement. The implication of proposition 2 is that the causal direction can be accurately inferred, as long as the relative influence of the noise distribution is small in comparison to the relationship between $AD^{-1}\mathbf{x}$ and $\mathbf{y}$. As we show during our experimental evaluation in Section 6, the method is quite robust to the effect of noise in practice.

4 REASONING ABOUT CONFOUNDING

Throughout Section 2 we assumed the absence of confounding influences (assumption A5). However, in many real-world settings, this proves to be an unrealistic assumption. Within the relational setting, there are two distinct ways in which the relationship between variables can be confounded:

1. $\mathbf{x}$ and $\mathbf{y}$ may share a common relational cause, $A\mathbf{z}$, i.e., $A\mathbf{z} \rightarrow \mathbf{x}$ and $A\mathbf{z} \rightarrow \mathbf{y}$.
2. There is a variable $\mathbf{z}$ that is a non-relational cause of $\mathbf{x}$ and a relational cause of $\mathbf{y}$, i.e., $\mathbf{z} \rightarrow \mathbf{x}$ and $A\mathbf{z} \rightarrow \mathbf{y}$.

In what follows, we show that the first scenario is identifiable from data, while the second one is not.

Proposition 3. *If $Cov(A\mathbf{x}, A\mathbf{y}) \geq Cov(A\mathbf{x}, \mathbf{y})$ and $Cov(A\mathbf{x}, A\mathbf{y}) \geq Cov(A\mathbf{x}, \mathbf{y})$, then there exists a relational variable which is a common cause of x and y.*

The proof is deferred to the supplement. Proposition 3 implies a very simple procedure for ruling out the presence of mutual relational confounding between two variables.

First, the relative dependence is measured between $A\mathbf{x}, \mathbf{y}$ and $A\mathbf{y}, \mathbf{x}$ respectively. Then, these two values are compared against the measured dependence between $A\mathbf{y}, A\mathbf{x}$. If neither are larger than the between-relational variable dependence no determination of direction is made, since observed dependence is likely due to confounding.

We now turn to scenario two, which yields the following negative result:

Corollary 1. *Under confounding scenario 2, in the absence of noise, a false conclusion of dependence $A\mathbf{x} \rightarrow \mathbf{y}$ will be made.*

Proof. Assume the generative structure is given by:

$$\mathbf{x} \sim \mathbf{z}$$
$$\mathbf{y} \sim D^{-1}A\mathbf{z}$$

It can be immediately seen that the form of this dependence is identical to the form of proposition 1, where we substituted $\mathbf{z}$ for the $\mathbf{x}$. It follows that, in the no-noise setting, an incorrect determination of direct causation will be made. □

Note that this also applies in the case of a small amount of noise, as implied by proposition 2. This result shows that without the assumption of no-confounding a determination of non-causation can be reliably implied, but the converse is not necessarily true.

5 AN EXTENSION TO NON-LINEAR DEPENDENCE

In the previous section, we showcased the applicability of our method for detecting linear dependence in relational data using correlation. An extension to more complex variables and non-linear dependence functions can be achieved by applying the kernel trick.

Some background on kernel embeddings is useful. Let $\mathcal{X}$ be a non-empty set, $(\mathcal{X}, \mathcal{A})$ be a measurable space where $\mathcal{A}$ is a σ-algebra on $\mathcal{X}$, and let $\mathscr{P}$ be the set of all probability measures, P, on $\mathcal{X}$. $\mathcal{H}$ is the RKHS of the functions $f : \mathcal{X} \rightarrow \mathbb{R}$ with the reproducing kernel $k : \mathcal{X} \times \mathcal{X} \rightarrow \mathbb{R}$. The *mean map* is a function $\mu : \mathscr{P} \rightarrow \mathcal{H}$ that defines a kernel embedding of a distribution into $\mathcal{H}$:

$$\mu_P = \mu(P) = \int_{\mathcal{X}} k(x, \cdot) dP(x)$$

If a characteristic kernel is used, then this mapping is unique, i.e., there is an injective function between a distribution and its kernel mean value. In this work, the purpose of kernel mean is twofold. For propositional variables, it is used to represent the underlying distribution and, as we shall see, can be used directly in a test for dependence. For relational variables, the mean embedding serves as an aggregation function for observations. The advantage of using the kernel mean embedding is that, under the assumption that the underlying distribution belongs to the exponential family, the underlying distributions are represented completely.

To reason over the distance between distributions, we define a second kernel, K, over the kernel means. Christmann and Steinwart [2010] showed that if the kernel inducing μ (k) is characteristic and K is the Gaussian kernel, then K is universal and thus, characteristic. This kernel is defined as:

$$K(\mu_x, \mu'_x) = e^{\frac{\|\mu_x - \mu'_x\|^2_{\mathcal{F}}}{2\theta}} \tag{1}$$

where $\sqrt{\theta}$ is the bandwidth of the kernel.

In addition to this measure of similarity between relational instances, we define a dependence measure. The centered *kernel target alignment* (KTA) is a normalized measure of dependence introduced by Cortes et al. [2012] within the context of multiple kernel learning. The measure is defined as:

$$\text{KTA}(\mathbf{x}, \mathbf{y}) = \frac{\langle K^c_{\mathbf{x}}, K^c_{\mathbf{y}} \rangle_{\mathcal{F}}}{\|K^c_{\mathbf{x}}\|_{\mathcal{F}} \|K^c_{\mathbf{y}}\|_{\mathcal{F}}} \tag{2}$$

Where $\|\cdot\|_{\mathcal{F}}$ is the Frobenius norm, $\langle K^c_{\mathbf{x}}, K^c_{\mathbf{y}} \rangle_{\mathcal{F}}$ is the Frobenius norm of the inner product between $K^c_{\mathbf{x}}$ and $K^c_{\mathbf{y}}$ which is calculated by taking the trace of the inner product. $K^c_{\mathbf{x}}$ is a centered kernel matrix, defined as:

$$K^c_{\mathbf{x}} = \left[\mathbf{I} - \frac{1}{m}\mathbf{1}\mathbf{1}^T\right] K_{\mathbf{x}} \left[\mathbf{I} - \frac{1}{m}\mathbf{1}\mathbf{1}^T\right]$$

where $\mathbf{I}$ is the identity matrix and $\mathbf{1}$ is a column vector of ones with length m. If a linear kernel is used, KTA reduces to squared Pearson's correlation, which has been our measure of focus thus far. Using this connection, the following corollary provides for consistent estimation of causal direction under the deterministic case with arbitrary functional dependence.

Corollary 2. *Under assumptions A1, A2, A3, A4, A5, and further assuming that the generative structure is given by $\mathbf{y} = D^{-1}A\phi(\mathbf{x})\beta$, then KTA$(A\mathbf{x}, \mathbf{y}) \geq$ KTA$(A\mathbf{y}, \mathbf{x})$.*

This follows as a straightforward extension of proposition 1. Because we are given by assumption that $KTA(A\mathbf{x}, \mathbf{y}) = 1$ and KTA is bounded from above by one, the inequality holds. Equality occurs only when the values of each node's friends of friends can be expressed as a sum of (feature-space embedded) values. For random values of X, this is reduced to the degenerate case of a graph of degree 1, as in proposition 1.

In practice, we note that the KTA based comparison relies on a number of hyper-parameters. The difficulty in choosing these parameters can result in poorer empirical performance. This problem has also been observed for other kernel-based approaches for causal inference [Zhang et al., 2011]. We leave the investigation of hyper-parameter selection as future work.

6 EXPERIMENTS

Our theoretical results focus on regular graphs, linear dependence, and absence of noise. In this section, we examine the effect that the network structure, the functional form of the dependence, and the presence of noise have on the efficacy of the linear and kernel based methods. [4]

6.1 REGULAR NETWORKS

We first considered regular graphs with linear dependence—a setting that matches our theoretical analysis—and we examined the effect of noise. We considered networks with the total number of nodes ranging from 100 to 500 and varied the degree between 2 and 22 by increments of 5. For every graph structure, we generated data as follows:

$$\begin{aligned}\mathbf{x} &\sim \mathcal{N}(0,1)\\ \epsilon &\sim \mathcal{N}(0,1)\\ \mathbf{y} &\sim D^{-1}A\mathbf{x} + \beta\epsilon\end{aligned}$$

where β is the coefficient of the noise and was varied between 0 and 2.

Figure 1 shows the relationship between $D^{-1}A\mathbf{x}$ and $\mathbf{y}$ for varying values of β. In the noiseless case (Figure 1a), $D^{-1}A\mathbf{x}$ and $\mathbf{y}$ are perfectly linearly correlated, as expected from the generating process. However, as the noise increases, the correlation between $D^{-1}A\mathbf{x}$ and $\mathbf{y}$ decays very quickly, approaching an adversarial case by the time the noise coefficient is $\beta = 1.0$.

We then measured dependence in each direction ($\mathbf{x}$ and $A\mathbf{y}$, $\mathbf{y}$ and $A\mathbf{x}$). The direction that produced the higher value for dependence was recorded as the inferred causal direction. To measure dependence, we used (i) the square of Pearson's correlation, and (ii) KTA using RBF kernels with a fixed bandwidth of 1.0 for all kernel calculations. Figure 2c shows the accuracy of both methods for a graph with 500 nodes and degree 7, while varying β. As expected from the our earlier theoretical results, both methods perform perfectly in the noise-less case, and continue to do so through $\beta = 0.5$. The linear method is significantly more robust to noise, remaining nearly perfect until $\beta = 1.0$.

We also examined the interplay between the graph structure (degree and number of nodes) and and the performance of each method. Figure 2a shows the performance for the case of a 500-node graph with noise coefficient of 1.0 with the degree varied between 2 and 22. Both methods become systematically worse as the degree (and thus the density of the network) increases. This is expected behaviour since an increase in the degree results in a lower *effective sample size* [Jensen and Neville, 2002], which will reduce the expected efficacy of both methods. The converse of this effect can be seen in Figure 2b, where the accuracy of the linear based approach improves significantly as the size of the network increases while the degree is kept constant (and thus the density of the network decreases).

6.2 NON-REGULAR NETWORKS

We next compared the performance of both methods to a departure from the assumption of network regularity. We considered the three most common generative models of graphs. The Erdős-Rényi model creates networks where two nodes are connected with a given probability. Throughout the experiments, we considered a fixed connection probability equal to 0.2. The Watts-Strogatz model generates "small-world networks". It begins with a lattice with a given neighborhood size and randomly rewires edges according to a fixed probability. For our experiments, we used neighborhood size 5 and rewiring probability equal to 0.2. The final generative model we considered was the Barabási-Albert model. This model generates graphs that display preferential attachment. For our experiments the power of preferential attachment was set to 1.0. For each network we considered sizes between 100 and 1000, by increments of 100, with 20 graphs being drawn for each size.

We then considered the following data generation scenarios for all graph types:

$$\begin{aligned}\mathbf{x} &\sim \mathcal{N}(0,1)\\ \epsilon &\sim \mathcal{N}(0,1)\\ \mathbf{y} &\sim f(D^{-1}A\mathbf{x}) + \beta\epsilon\end{aligned}$$

where $f(\cdot)$ is a function of $D^{-1}A\mathbf{x}$. We considered three functional forms:

- $f(\cdot)$ is a simple linear function (linear)
- $f(D^{-1}A\mathbf{x}) = \tan(D^{-1}A\mathbf{x})$ (nonlinear)
- $f(D^{-1}A\mathbf{x}) = \left(D^{-1}A\mathbf{x}\right)^4$ (quad)

For each setting, β was varied between 0 and 2 by increments of 0.25.

The performance of both the linear and KTA method for fixed network size of 1000 nodes with the magnitude of noise varied is shown in Figure 4. For the Barabási model under linear dependence, both the linear and kernel methods appear to be very robust up until a noise coefficient of

[4] Code is available at `https://github.com/darbour/RelationalCausalDirection.git`.

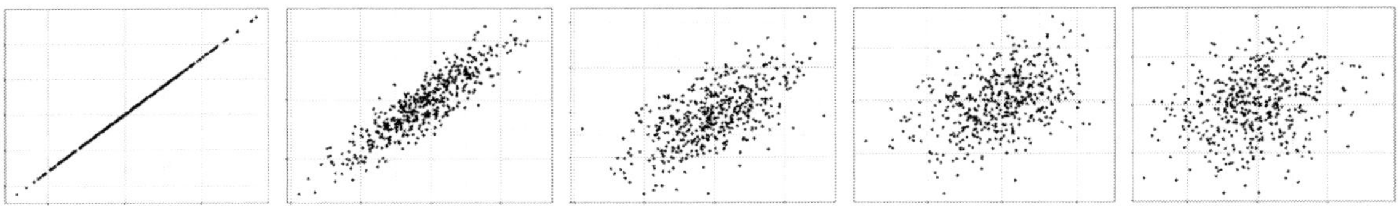

(a) $c_\epsilon = 0$ (b) $c_\epsilon = 0.25$ (c) $c_\epsilon = 0.5$ (d) $c_\epsilon = 1$ (e) $c_\epsilon = 2$

Figure 1: Scatterplots for the sum of X values of related nodes (x-axis) vs. the sum of X values of related nodes with additive Gaussian noise (y-axis). The noise coefficient (c_ϵ) varies from 0 to 2. The underlying network structure is a regular network of degree 10 with 500 nodes.

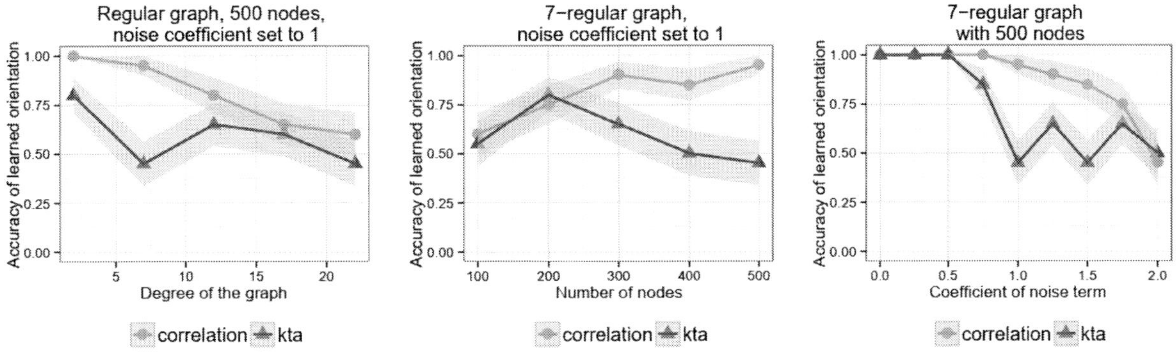

(a) (b) (c)

Figure 2: Orientation accuracy for regular graphs for varying degree (2a), size of network (2b), and noise coefficient (2c).

2.0. The KTA based method generally outperforms the linear dependence method for non-linear dependencies. This is to be expected, as Pearson's correlation is a measure of linear dependence.

The performance in the case where β is held to 0.5 and the size of the network is varied from 100 to 1000 can be seen in Figure 3. Here we can see that in both the Barabási-Albert and Watts-Strogatz graph models, Pearson's correlation and KTA achieve better performance under linear dependence as the size of the network increases. However, for in the case of the Erdős-Rényi models both methods perform poorly consistently as the size of the network increases. This is due to the nature of the graph-generation process. Both the Barabási-Albert and Watts-Strogatz models become increasingly sparse as the size of the network is increased. However, in the case of Erdős-Rényi, the probability connection is constant. As a result, the effective sample size remains low when the number of nodes increases. This likely accounts for the poor performance of the linear estimator. The opposite effect is seen in the case of the Barabási-Albert model. In nearly all cases the performance of the estimators is highest in the case of the Barabási-Albert networks.

6.3 A COMPARISON TO RELATIONAL BIVARIATE EDGE ORIENTATION

We also compared our results to the relational bivariate edge orientation (RBO) [Maier et al., 2013], the only other known method for testing causal direction in relational data. Maier et al. [2013] introduced the relational bivariate edge orientation (RBO) as an edge-orientation procedure within the context of learning causal models of relational domains. RBO is defined with respect to conditional independence properties of relational models. Specifically, rephrasing the definition of Maier et al. [2013] for single-entity/single-relationship networks, for a relational dependence between Y' and X, RBO checks if Y' is in the separating set of X and X'. If not, then Y' is effectively a "relational" collider and is oriented as such: $Y' \leftarrow X$. Otherwise, the only alternative model is $Y' \rightarrow X$, given that dependencies that induce feedback cycles (such as $X \rightarrow X'$) are excluded by assumption. The correctness of RBO is defined with respect to a conditional dependence oracle. In practice, Maier et al. [2013] follow the following procedure to infer causal direction between two relational variables:

1. Learn a linear model $\mathbf{x} \sim D^{-1}A\mathbf{x} + D^{-1}A\mathbf{y}$ to determine if $\mathbf{x} \perp\!\!\!\perp D^{-1}A\mathbf{x} \mid D^{-1}A\mathbf{y}$
2. If $\mathbf{x} \not\perp\!\!\!\perp D^{-1}A\mathbf{x} \mid D^{-1}A\mathbf{y}$, then return $D^{-1}A\mathbf{x} \rightarrow \mathbf{y}$,

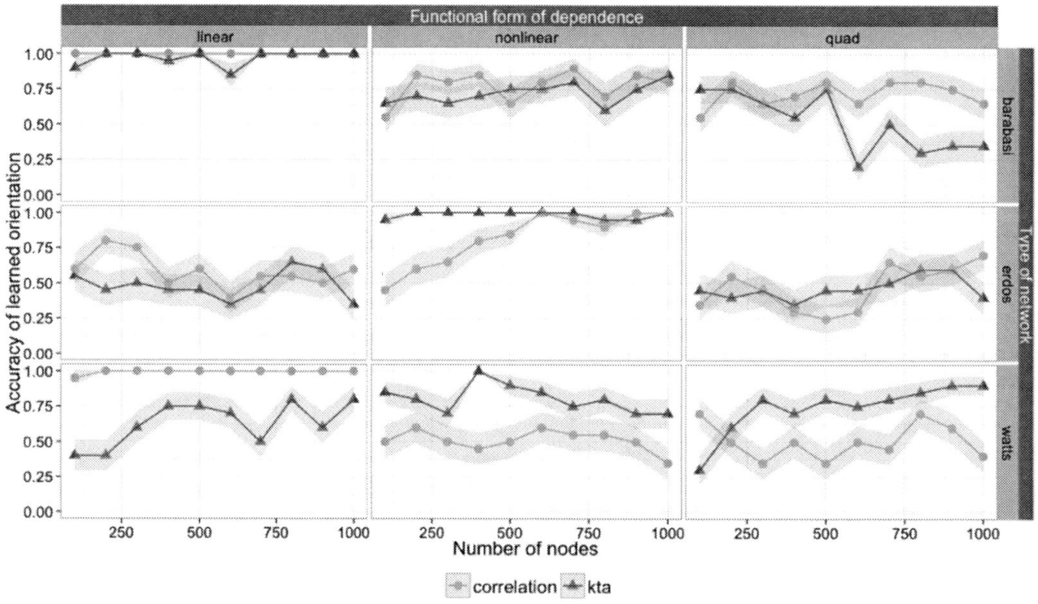

Figure 3: Orientation accuracy for various network types and functional forms, as the size of the graph increases. The noise coefficient is set to 0.5.

otherwise return $D^{-1}A\mathbf{y} \to \mathbf{x}$

We applied this procedure to the linear data-generating scenarios used in the previous two subsections, with one modification. Rather than testing a single perspective, we explicitly tested the conditional independence facts from the perspective of both $\mathbf{x}$ and $\mathbf{y}$. We found that between all scenarios, RBO failed to induce dependence in 80-90% of cases. This has important ramifications for the RCD algorithm of Maier et al. [2013]. As currently implemented, the RBO rule would have produced approximately %50 error rate, since it does not explicitly check both directions. Using our more conservative method, RBO would fire less frequently. In contrast, by incorporating the findings of the more direct marginal comparison presented here, vast numbers of edges would be accurately oriented. We plan on examining further integration of our findings into joint causal structure learning algorithms in future work.

7 REAL WORLD DEMONSTRATION

In contrast to the propositional setting, where there is a number of labeled ground-truth data-sets for testing novel methods of causal inference (e.g. [Lichman, 2013]), to our knowledge, there are no known publicly available datasets which contain ground-truth relational causal relationships. In the absence of the ability to verify the relative efficacy of our findings on real-world datasets, we provide a demonstration of our method on a real-world dataset. Specifically, we considered Stack Overflow, an online community where users pose and answer questions regarding software development. A user can post a question, which can be answered by anyone else within the community. Other users can then up/down vote questions and the given answers. These votes are tracked and the accrual of achieved points is displayed as the "reputation" of a user on the site. Moreover, users can comment on a question. Comments receive votes as well, but do not affect the reputation of a user. The dataset consists of all users, questions, answers, comments, and votes from the inception of the site to 2014.

We tested three questions about user behavior on Stack Overflow. For every question we consider 100 sub-samples of 1000 data points. We computed KTA and Pearson's correlation in each direction. Significance of dependence was determined by performing permutation tests with 1000 permutations. For all tests we set the significance threshold to be 0.01. When dependence was determined to be statistically significant, we also recorded how many times each direction was chosen by comparing test statistics in both directions.

The first question was: "Is there a relationship between the quality of a question and the quality of its subsequent answers?" To answer this, we used the scores of the questions and answers as proxies for their quality. All methods determined significance in both directions across all trials. However, the normalized statistics consistently determined the direction of dependence to be Question Quality $\to$ Answer Quality, while both of the un-normalized statistics consistently determined the direction of dependence to be

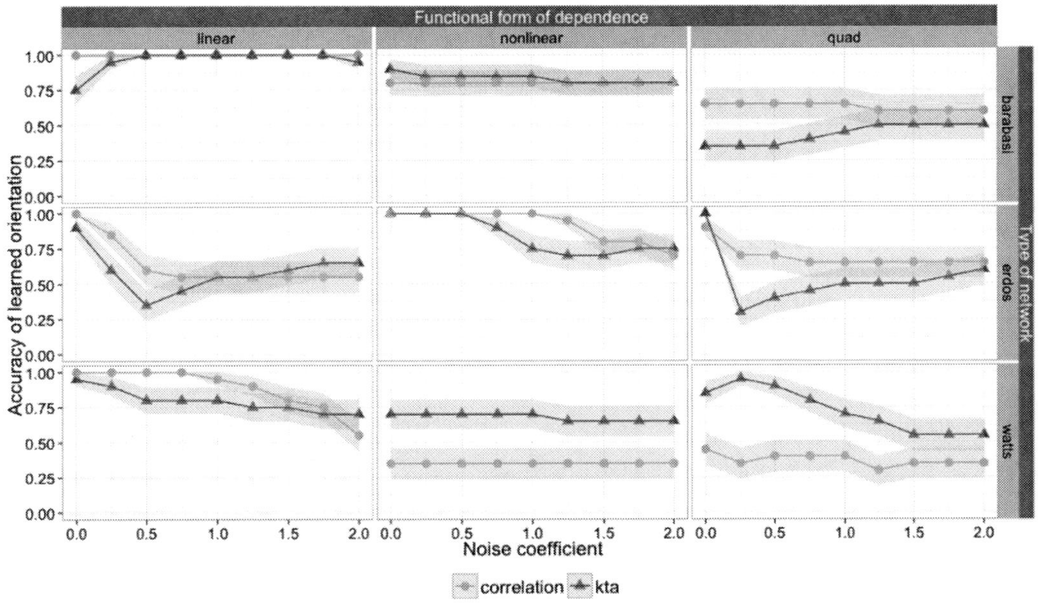

Figure 4: Orientation accuracy for various network types and functional forms, as the coefficient of the noise increases. The network size was kept constant at 1000 nodes.

Question Quality ← Answer Quality. Clearly, the former conclusion matches intuition and temporal ordering far better than the latter.

The second question we considered was whether users with high reputation receive higher quality answers. This was quantified by using the reputation of a user and the score of the answers as a proxy for quality. In this case, we found that KTA and Pearson both detected significance for both directions. For direction, we found that both KTA and Pearson determined direction to be Reputation → Answer Quality for over 90% of the cases. This indicates that there may be bias in the Stack Overflow community towards questions asked by high reputation users. We caution that this does not take into account the possible latent confounder of question quality, i.e., higher reputation users may simply ask higher quality questions.

Finally, we looked at the efficacy of comments as a quality improvement mechanism, i.e., whether allowing users to comment on a question causes the poster to improve or clarify her post. We constructed this test with the comments posted for a question and whether revisions were subsequently made to the question. In this case we found that all of the methods inferred that there was *not* a significant relationship between the score of the comments and subsequent revisions to posts. This negative result indicates that the commenting system provided by Stack Overflow is not an effective mechanism for improving the quality of questions on the site.

8 RELATED WORK

Relevant work to our investigation of methods for determining peer dependence in relational data falls into four basic categories. The most closely related work examines versions of this specific task with alternative methods. For example, Maier et al. [2013], Rattigan [2012], and Poole and Crowley [2013] provide scenarios in which an asymmetry may arise similar to that observed in our tests for direction. However, in contrast to prior work, we study the phenomenon of asymmetric dependence directly and provide a formal examination which provides guarantees to the circumstances under which this asymmetry can be reliably leveraged. Further, we provide extensive simulation experiments that further show conditions under which direction can be found by considering the difference in dependence in both directions.

A second category of related work focuses on measuring causal dependence in non-relational (i.i.d.) data. For example, Peters et al. [2014] examine the problem of determining the direction of dependence with i.i.d. data by either assuming non-Gaussian noise and linear dependence or non-linear dependence and Gaussian noise. The problem of identifying causal direction in the case of deterministic, i.e., non-noisy data, was studied by Daniusis et al. [2010]. The setting considered was propositional data, and the proposed solution leverages properties of information geometry in order to find asymmetries between the conditional distributions of the two variables. In contrast, the relational setting considered provides a much more direct mechanism for determining direction.

A third thread of related work aims to detect non-causal dependence in relational data. This task has attracted attention in both statistical relational learning (SRL) community and in multiple areas of the social sciences. In SRL, Jensen and Neville [2002] use a χ^2 test to detect auto-correlation in relational data and show its effect for feature selection. Angin and Neville [2008] introduce a shrinkage estimator for auto-correlation in the presence of varying dependence strength. However, both of these rely on empirical evaluation as evidence of correctness. Dhurandhar and Dobra [2012] and London et al. [2013] provide theoretical analysis for the inductive error of classification and regression in the relational setting.

In the social sciences, relational dependence has been examined under the monikers of peer influence, spillover, and interference. In the experimental setting, Eckles et al. [2014] characterize the threat to validity arising from the bias induced by relational dependence and provide experimental designs to reduce these effects. Manski [2013], VanderWeele [2008], and Aronow and Samii [2013] examine methods for removing the bias associated with relational dependence, assuming discrete or linearly dependent data. Toulis and Kao [2013] provide conditions for experimental design with binary treatments to identify peer influence. Ogburn and VanderWeele [2014] characterize relational dependence in terms of graphical models, but do not present an explicit testing procedure. Work studying homophily and contagion (e.g., Christakis and Fowler [2009], La Fond and Neville [2010]) is related but distinct in the task setup, as we do not assume the availability of temporal information.

Finally, our work is strongly connected and can serve as a complement to existing work on causal learning of relational domains. Maier et al. [2013] and Marazopoulou et al. [2015] present constraint-based algorithms to learn the structure of relational models from data. However, for their experiments they either rely on a d-separation oracle (without actual data), or use linear regression with mean-aggregation on synthetically generated data. As we showed in our synthetic experiments, these choices can lead to a large number of type II errors. This is especially troublesome for constraint-based structure learning algorithms where type II errors can lead to large deviations from the true causal model [Cornia and Mooij, 2014]. Such algorithms could leverage our test in order to improve results reported on data. Additionally, the directionality results presented in this paper have implications for future work in constraint-based structure learning algorithms, since they imply a smaller Markov-equivalence class than what is commonly assumed.

9 CONCLUSIONS AND FUTURE WORK

Inferring relational dependence is a task of general interest in a wide number of fields, from statistical relational learning to the social sciences. In this work, we have studied the problem of inferring causal direction in relational data. We have shown that, in contrast to the propositional setting, causal direction can be accurately inferred in relational data under the simplest functional forms such as linear deterministic dependence, without additional assumptions on the distribution of the underlying data. We then studied the problem of identifying confounding, showing the conditions when the presence of a relational confounding variable can be identified. Our experimental evaluation shows that these measures are robust, providing accurate inference under model and network mis-specification.

There are several promising avenues for future research. For causal learning, the ability to detect the direction of dependence in relational data implies that a different Markov equivalence class [Spirtes et al., 2000] holds for the relational setting than what is commonly assumed. Integration of the findings of this work into a causal learning algorithm could substantially improve the efficacy of existing methods such as RCD [Maier et al., 2013]. Further analysis of the interaction between the network structure and inference may further strengthen the robustness of the methods discussed here. Finally, the asymmetries shown to be inherent to relational data here may result in significant bias of conditional independence testing procedures. Incorporating this additional information is a first step in developing robust measures of conditional dependence in relational data to help determine causation, a problem which has broad application in both the statistical learning and social science communities.

Acknowledgements

Funding was provided by the U.S. Army Research Office (ARO) and Defense Advanced Research Projects Agency (DARPA) under Contract Number W911NF-11-C-0088. The content of the information in this document does not necessarily reflect the position or the policy of the Government, and no official endorsement should be inferred. The U.S. Government is authorized to reproduce and distribute reprints for Government purposes notwithstanding any copyright notation here on.

References

P. Angin and J. Neville. A shrinkage approach for modeling non-stationary relational autocorrelation. In *8th International Conference on Data Mining*, pages 707–712, 2008.

P. M. Aronow and C. Samii. Estimating average causal

effects under interference between units. *arXiv preprint arXiv:1305.6156*, 2013.

E. Bakshy, D. Eckles, R. Yan, and I. Rosenn. Social influence in social advertising: evidence from field experiments. In *Proceedings of the 13th ACM Conference on Electronic Commerce*, pages 146–161. ACM, 2012.

N. Christakis and J. Fowler. *Connected: The surprising power of our social networks and how they shape our lives*. Hachette Digital, Inc., 2009.

A. Christmann and I. Steinwart. Universal kernels on non-standard input spaces. In *Advances in Neural Information Processing Systems*, pages 406–414, 2010.

N. Cornia and J. M. Mooij. Type-II errors of independence tests can lead to arbitrarily large errors in estimated causal effects: An illustrative example. In *Proceedings of the UAI 2014 Workshop Causal Inference: Learning and Prediction*, pages 35–42, 2014.

C. Cortes, M. Mohri, and A. Rostamizadeh. Algorithms for learning kernels based on centered alignment. *The Journal of Machine Learning Research*, 13(1):795–828, 2012.

P. Daniusis, D. Janzing, J. Mooij, J. Zscheischler, B. Steudel, K. Zhang, B. Schölkopf, G. P. Spirtes, et al. Inferring deterministic causal relations. In *26th Conference on Uncertainty in Artificial Intelligence (UAI 2010)*, pages 143–150. AUAI Press, 2010.

A. Dhurandhar and A. Dobra. Distribution-free bounds for relational classification. *Knowledge and information systems*, 31(1):55–78, 2012.

D. Eckles, B. Karrer, and J. Ugander. Design and analysis of experiments in networks: Reducing bias from interference. *arXiv preprint arXiv:1404.7530*, 2014.

D. Janzing, J. Mooij, K. Zhang, J. Lemeire, J. Zscheischler, P. Daniušis, B. Steudel, and B. Schölkopf. Information-geometric approach to inferring causal directions. *Artificial Intelligence*, 182:1–31, 2012.

D. Jensen and J. Neville. Linkage and autocorrelation cause feature selection bias in relational learning. In *Proceedings of the 19th International Conference on Machine Learning*, pages 259–266, 2002.

D. Koller. Probabilistic relational models. In *Inductive logic programming*, pages 3–13. Springer, 1999.

T. La Fond and J. Neville. Randomization tests for distinguishing social influence and homophily effects. In *Proceedings of the 19th international conference on World wide web*, pages 601–610, 2010.

M. Lichman. UCI machine learning repository, 2013. URL `http://archive.ics.uci.edu/ml`.

B. London, B. Huang, B. Taskar, and L. Getoor. Collective stability in structured prediction: Generalization from one example. In *Proceedings of the 30th International Conference on Machine Learning (ICML-13)*, 2013.

D. Lopez-Paz, K. Muandet, and B. Recht. The randomized causation coefficient. *Journal of Machine Learning*, 2015.

M. Maier, K. Marazopoulou, D. Arbour, and D. Jensen. A sound and complete algorithm for learning causal models from relational data. In *Proceedings of the 29th Conference on Uncertainty in Artificial Intelligence*, pages 371–380, 2013.

C. F. Manski. Identification of treatment response with social interactions. *The Econometrics Journal*, 16(1):S1–S23, 2013.

K. Marazopoulou, M. Maier, and D. Jensen. Learning the structure of causal models with relational and temporal dependence. In *Proceedings of the 31st Conference on Uncertainty in Artificial Intelligence*, 2015.

L. Muchnik, S. Aral, and S. J. Taylor. Social influence bias: A randomized experiment. *Science*, 341(6146):647–651, 2013.

E. L. Ogburn and T. J. VanderWeele. Causal diagrams for interference. *Statistical Science*, 29(4):559–578, 2014.

J. Peters, J. M. Mooij, D. Janzing, and B. Schölkopf. Causal discovery with continuous additive noise models. *The Journal of Machine Learning Research*, 15(1): 2009–2053, 2014.

D. Poole and M. Crowley. Cyclic causal models with discrete variables: Markov chain equilibrium semantics and sample ordering. In *Proceedings of the 23rd international joint conference on Artificial Intelligence*, pages 1060–1068, 2013.

M. J. Rattigan. *Leveraging Relational Representations for Causal Discovery*. Ph.D. thesis, University of Massachusetts Amherst, 2012.

P. Spirtes, C. N. Glymour, and R. Scheines. *Causation, prediction, and search*. MIT press, 2000.

O. Stegle, D. Janzing, K. Zhang, J. M. Mooij, and B. Schölkopf. Probabilistic latent variable models for distinguishing between cause and effect. In *Advances in Neural Information Processing Systems*, pages 1687–1695, 2010.

P. Toulis and E. Kao. Estimation of causal peer influence effects. In *Proceedings of The 30th International Conference on Machine Learning*, pages 1489–1497, 2013.

T. J. VanderWeele. Ignorability and stability assumptions in neighborhood effects research. *Statistics in medicine*, 27(11):1934–1943, 2008.

K. Zhang, J. Peters, and D. Janzing. Kernel-based conditional independence test and application in causal discovery. In *In Uncertainty in Artificial Intelligence*. Citeseer, 2011.

Convex Relaxation Regression: Black-Box Optimization of Smooth Functions by Learning Their Convex Envelopes

Mohammad Gheshlaghi Azar
Rehabilitation Institute of Chicago
Northwestern University
Chicago, IL 60611

Eva L. Dyer
Rehabilitation Institute of Chicago
Northwestern University
Chicago, IL 60611

Konrad P. Körding
Rehabilitation Institute of Chicago
Northwestern University
Chicago, IL 60611

Abstract

Finding efficient and provable methods to solve non-convex optimization problems is an outstanding challenge in machine learning and optimization theory. A popular approach used to tackle non-convex problems is to use convex relaxation techniques to find a convex surrogate for the problem. Unfortunately, convex relaxations typically must be found on a problem-by-problem basis. Thus, providing a general-purpose strategy to estimate a convex relaxation would have a wide reaching impact. Here, we introduce *Convex Relaxation Regression* (CoRR), an approach for learning convex relaxations for a class of smooth functions. The idea behind our approach is to estimate the convex envelope of a function f by evaluating f at a set of T random points and then fitting a convex function to these function evaluations. We prove that with probability greater than $1-\delta$, the solution of our algorithm converges to the global optimizer of f with error $\mathcal{O}\big(\big(\frac{\log(1/\delta)}{T}\big)^{\alpha}\big)$ for some $\alpha > 0$. Our approach enables the use of convex optimization tools to solve non-convex optimization problems.

1 Introduction

Modern machine learning relies heavily on optimization techniques to extract information from large and noisy datasets (Friedman et al., 2001). Convex optimization methods are widely used in machine learning applications, due to fact that convex problems can be solved efficiently, often with a first order method such as gradient descent (Shalev-Shwartz and Ben-David, 2014; Sra et al., 2012; Boyd and Vandenberghe, 2004). A wide class of problems can be cast as convex optimization problems; however, many important learning problems, including binary classification with 0-1 loss, sparse and low-rank matrix recovery, and training multi-layer neural networks, are non-convex.

In many cases, non-convex optimization problems can be solved by first relaxing the problem: *convex relaxation* techniques find a convex function that approximates the original objective function (Tropp, 2006; Candès and Tao, 2010; Chandrasekaran et al., 2012). A convex relaxation is considered tight when it provides a tight lower bound to the original objective function. Examples of problems for which tight convex relaxations are known include binary classification (Cox, 1958), sparse and low-rank approximation (Tibshirani, 1996; Recht et al., 2010). The recent success of both sparse and low rank matrix recovery has demonstrated the power of convex relaxation for solving high-dimensional machine learning problems.

When a tight convex relaxation is known, then the underlying non-convex problem can often be solved by optimizing its convex surrogate in lieu of the non-convex problem. However, there are important classes of machine learning problems for which no such relaxation is known. These include a wide range of machine learning problems such as training deep neural nets, estimating latent variable models (mixture density models), optimal control, reinforcement learning, and hyper-parameter optimization. Thus, methods for finding convex relaxations of arbitrary non-convex functions would have wide reaching impacts throughout machine learning and the computational sciences.

Here we introduce a principled approach for black-box (zero-order) global optimization that is based on learning a convex relaxation to a non-convex function of interest (Sec. 3). To motivate our approach, consider the problem of estimating the convex envelope of the function f, i.e., the tightest convex lower bound of the function (Grotzinger, 1985; Falk, 1969; Kleibohm, 1967). In this case, we know that the envelope's minimum coincides with the minimum of the original non-convex function (Kleibohm, 1967). Unfortunately, finding the *exact* convex envelope of a non-convex function can be at least as hard as solving the original optimization problem. This is due to the fact that the problem of finding the convex envelope of a function is equivalent to the problem of computing its Legendre-Fenchel bi-conjugate (Rockafellar, 1997; Falk, 1969), which is in general as hard as optimizing f. Despite this result, we show that for a class of smooth (non-convex) functions, it is possible to accurately and efficiently *estimate* the convex envelope from a set of function evaluations.

The main idea behind our approach, *Convex Relaxation Regression* (CoRR), is to estimate the convex envelope of f and then optimize the resulting empirical convex envelope. We do this by solving a constrained ℓ_1 regression problem which estimates the convex envelope by a linear combination of a set of convex functions (basis vectors). As our approach only requires samples from the function, it can be used to solve optimization problems where gradient information is unknown. Whereas most methods for global optimization rely on local search strategies which find a new search direction to explore, CoRR takes a global perspective: it aims to form a global estimate of the function to "fill in the gaps" between samples. Thus CoRR provides an efficient strategy for global minimization through the use of convex optimization tools.

One of the main theoretical contributions of this work is the development of guarantees that CoRR can find accurate convex relaxations for a broad class of non-convex functions (Sec. 4). We prove in Thm. 1 that with probability greater than $1-\delta$, we can approximate the global minimizer with error of $\mathcal{O}\Big(\big(\frac{\log(1/\delta)}{T}\big)^{\alpha}\Big)$, where T is the number of function evaluations and $\alpha > 0$ depends upon the exponent of the Hölder-continuity bound on $f(x) - f^*$. This result assumes that the true convex envelope lies in the function class used to form a convex approximation. In Thm. 2, we extend this result for the case where the convex envelope is in the proximity of this set of functions. Our results may also translated to a bound with polynomial dependence on the dimension (Sec. 4.2.4).

The main contributions of this work are as follows. We introduce CoRR, a method for black-box optimization that learns a convex relaxation of a function from a set of random function evaluations (Sec. 3). Following this, we provide performance guarantees which show that as the number of function evaluations T grows, the error decreases polynomially in T (Sec. 4). In Thm. 1 we provide a general result for the case where the true convex envelope f_c lies in the function class $\mathcal{H}$ and extend this result to the approximate setting where $f_c \notin \mathcal{H}$ in Thm. 2. Finally, we study the performance of CoRR on several multi-modal test functions and compare it with a number of widely used approaches for global optimization (Sec. 5). These results suggest that CoRR can accurately find a tight convex lower bound for a wide class of non-convex functions.

2 Problem Setup

We now introduce relevant notation, setup our problem, and then provide background on global optimization of non-convex functions.

2.1 Preliminaries

Let n be a positive integer. For every $x \in \mathbb{R}^n$, its ℓ_2-norm is denoted by $\|x\|$, where $\|x\|^2 := \langle x, x\rangle$ and $\langle x, y\rangle$ denotes the inner product between two vectors $x \in \mathbb{R}^n$ and $y \in \mathbb{R}^n$. We denote the ℓ_2 metric by d_2 and the set of ℓ_2-normed bounded vectors in $\mathbb{R}^n$ by $\mathcal{B}(\mathbb{R}^n)$, where for every $x \in \mathcal{B}(\mathbb{R}^n)$ we assume that there exists some finite scalar C such that $\|x\| < C$. Let $(\mathcal{X}, d)$ be a metric space, where $\mathcal{X} \in \mathcal{B}(\mathbb{R}^n)$ is a convex set of bounded vectors and $d(., x)$ is convex w.r.t. its first argument for every $x \in \mathcal{B}(\mathbb{R}^n)$.[1] We denote the set of all bounded functions on $\mathcal{X}$ by $\mathcal{B}(\mathcal{X}, \mathbb{R})$, such that for every $f \in \mathcal{B}(\mathcal{X}, \mathbb{R})$ and $x \in \mathcal{X}$ there exists some finite scalar $C > 0$ such that $|f(x)| \leq C$. Finally, we denote the set of all convex bounded functions on $\mathcal{X}$ by $\mathcal{C}(\mathcal{X}, \mathbb{R}) \subset \mathcal{B}(\mathcal{X}, \mathbb{R})$. Also for every $\mathcal{Y} \subseteq \mathcal{B}(\mathbb{R}^n)$, we denote the convex hull of $\mathcal{Y}$ by $\mathrm{conv}(\mathcal{Y})$. Let $\mathcal{B}(x_0, r)$ denote an open ball of radius r centered at x_0. Let $\mathbf{1}$ denote a vector of ones.

The convex envelope of function $f : \mathcal{X} \to \mathbb{R}$ is denoted by $f_c : \mathcal{X} \to \mathbb{R}$. Let $\widetilde{\mathcal{H}}$ be the set of all convex functions defined over $\mathcal{X}$ such that $h(x) \leq f(x)$ for all $x \in \mathcal{X}$. The function f_c is the convex envelope of f if for every $x \in \mathcal{X}$ **(a)** $f_c(x) \leq f(x)$, **(b)** for every $h \in \widetilde{\mathcal{H}}$ the inequality $h(x) \leq f_c(x)$ holds. Convex envelopes are also related to the concepts of the convex hull and the epigraph of a function. For every function $f : \mathcal{X} \to \mathbb{R}$ the epigraph is defined as $\mathrm{epi} f = \{(\xi, x) : \xi \geq f(x), x \in \mathcal{X}\}$. One can then show that the convex envelope of f is obtained by $f_c(x) = \inf\{\xi : (\xi, x) \in \mathrm{conv}(\mathrm{epi} f)\}$, $\forall x \in \mathcal{X}$.

In the sequel, we will generate a set of function evaluations from f by evaluating the function over i.i.d. samples from ρ, where ρ denotes a probability distribution on $\mathcal{X}$ such that $\rho(x) > 0$ for all $x \in \mathcal{X}$. In addition, we approximate the convex envelope using a function class $\mathcal{H}$ that contains a set of convex functions $h(\cdot; \theta) \in \mathcal{H}$ parametrized by $\theta \in \Theta \subseteq \mathcal{B}(\mathbb{R}^p)$. We also assume that every $h \in \mathcal{H}$ can be expressed as a linear combination of a set of basis $\phi : \mathcal{X} \to \mathcal{B}(\mathbb{R}^p)$, that is, $h(x; \theta) = \langle \theta, \phi(x)\rangle$ for every $h(\cdot; \theta) \in \mathcal{H}$ and $x \in \mathcal{X}$.

2.2 Black-box Global Optimization Setting

We consider a *black-box* (zero-order) global optimization setting, where we assume that we do not have access to

[1] This also implies that $d(x, .)$ is convex w.r.t. its second argument argument for every $x \in \mathcal{B}(\mathbb{R}^n)$ due to the fact that the metric d by definition is symmetric.

information about the gradient of the function that we want to optimize. More formally, let $\mathcal{F} \subseteq \mathcal{B}(\mathcal{X}, \mathbb{R})$ be a class of bounded functions, where the image of every $f \in \mathcal{F}$ is bounded by R and $\mathcal{X}$ is a convex set. We consider the problem of finding the global minimum of the function f,

$$f^* := \min_{x \in \mathcal{X}} f(x). \tag{1}$$

We denote the set of minimizers of f by $\mathcal{X}_f^* \subseteq \mathcal{X}$.

In the black-box setting, the optimizer has only access to the inputs and outputs of the function f. In this case, we assume that our optimization algorithm is provided with a set of input points $\widehat{\mathcal{X}} = \{x_1, x_2, \ldots, x_T\}$ in $\mathcal{X}$ and a sequence of outputs $[f]_{\widehat{\mathcal{X}}} = \{f(x_1), f(x_2), \ldots, f(x_T)\}$. Based upon this information, the goal is to find an estimate $\widehat{x} \in \mathcal{X}$, such that the error $f(\widehat{x}) - f^*$ becomes as small as possible.

2.3 Methods for Black-box Optimization

Standard tools that are used in convex optimization, cannot be readily applied to solve non-convex problems as they only converge to local minimizers of the function. Thus, effective global optimization approaches must have a mechanism to avoid getting trapped in local minima. In low-dimensional settings, performing an exhaustive grid search or drawing random samples from the function can be sufficient (Bergstra and Bengio, 2012). However, as the dimension grows, smarter methods for searching for the global minimizer are required.

Non-adaptive search strategies. A wide range of global optimization methods are build upon the idea of iteratively creating a deterministic set (pattern) of points at each iteration, evaluating the function over all points in the set, and selecting the point with the minimum value as the next seed for the following iteration (Hooke and Jeeves, 1961; Lewis and Torczon, 1999). Deterministic pattern search strategies can be extended by introducing some randomness into the pattern generation step. For instance, simulated annealing (Kirkpatrick et al., 1983) (SA) and genetic algorithms (Bäck, 1996) both use randomized search directions to determine the next place that they will search. The idea behind introducing some noise into the pattern, is that the method can jump out of local minima that deterministic pattern search methods can get stuck in. While many of these search methods work well in low dimensions, as the dimension of problem grows, these algorithms often become extremely slow due to the curse of dimensionality.

Adaptive and model-based search. In higher dimensions, adaptive and model-based search strategies can be used to further steer the optimizer in good search directions (Mockus et al., 1978; Hutter, 2009). For instance, recent results in Sequential Model-Based Global Optimization (SMBO) have shown that Gaussian processes are useful priors for global optimization (Mockus et al., 1978; Bergstra et al., 2011). In these settings, each search direction is driven by a model (Gaussian process) and updated based upon the local structure of the function. These techniques, while useful in low-dimension problems, become inefficient in high-dimensional settings.

Hierarchical search methods take a different approach in exploiting the structure of the data to find the global minimizer (Munos, 2014; Bubeck et al., 2011; Azar et al., 2014; Munos, 2011). The idea behind hierarchical search methods is to identify regions of the space with small function evaluations to sample further (exploitation), as well as generate new samples in unexplored regions (exploration). One can show that it is possible to find the global optimum with a finite number of function evaluations using hierarchical search; however, the number of samples needed to achieve a small error increases exponentially with the dimension. For this reason, hierarchical search methods are often not efficient for high-dimensional problems.

Graduated optimization. Graduated optimization methods (Blake and Zisserman, 1987; Yuille, 1989), are another class of methods for non-convex optimization which have received much attention in recent years (Chapelle and Wu, 2010; Dvijotham et al., 2014; Hazan et al., 2015; Mobahi and III, 2015). These methods work by locally smoothing the problem, descending along this smoothed objective, and then gradually sharpening the resolution to hone in on the true global minimizer. Recently Hazan et al. (2015) introduced a graduated optimization approach that can be applied in the black-box optimization setting. In this case, they prove that for a class of functions referred to as σ-nice functions, their approach is guaranteed to converge to an ε-accurate estimate of the global minimizer at a rate of $\mathcal{O}(n^2/\varepsilon^4)$. To the best of our knowledge, this result represents the state-of-the-art in terms of theoretical results for global black-box optimization.

3 Algorithm

In this section, we introduce *Convex Relaxation Regression* (CoRR), a black-box optimization approach for global minimization of a bounded function f.

3.1 Overview

The main idea behind our approach is to estimate the convex envelope f_c of a function and minimize this surrogate in place of our original function. The following result guarantees that the minimizer of f coincides with the minimizer of f_c.

Proposition 1 (Kleibohm 1967). *Let f_c be the convex envelope of $f : \mathcal{X} \to \mathbb{R}$. Then (a) $\min_{x \in \mathcal{X}} f_c(x) = f^*$ and (b) $\mathcal{X}_f^* \subseteq \mathcal{X}_{f_c}^*$.*

This result suggests that one can find the minimizer of f by optimizing its convex envelope. Unfortunately, finding the exact convex envelope of a function is difficult in general. However, we will show that, for a certain class of functions, it is possible to estimate the convex envelope accurately from a set of function evaluations. Our aim is to estimate the convex envelope by fitting a convex function to these function evaluations.

The idea of fitting a convex approximation to samples from f is quite simple and intuitive. However, the best unconstrained convex fit to f does not necessarily coincide with f_c. Determining whether there exists a set of convex constraints under which the best convex fit to f coincides with f_c is an open problem. The following lemma, which is key to efficient optimization of f with CoRR, provides a solution. This lemma transforms our original non-convex optimization problem to a least-absolute-error regression problem with a convex constraint, which can be solved using convex optimization tools.

Lemma 1. *Let every $h \in \mathcal{H}$ and f be λ-Lipschitz for some $\lambda > 0$. Let $L(\theta) = \mathbb{E}[|h(x;\theta) - f(x)|]$ be the expected loss, where the expectation is taken with respect to the distribution ρ. Assume that there exists $\Theta_c \subseteq \Theta$ such that for every $\theta \in \Theta_c$, $h(x;\theta) = f_c(x)$ for all $x \in \mathcal{X}$. Consider the following optimization problem:*

$$\theta_\mu = \arg\min_{\theta \in \Theta} L(\theta) \quad s.t. \quad \mathbb{E}[h(x;\theta)] = \mu. \tag{2}$$

Then there exists a scalar $\mu \in [-R, R]$ for which $\theta_c \in \Theta_c$. In particular, $\theta_c \in \Theta_c$ when $\mu = \mathbb{E}(f_c(x))$.

The formal proof of this lemma is provided in the Supp. Materials. We prove this lemma by showing that for every $\theta \in \Theta$ where $\mathbb{E}[h(x;\theta)] = \mathbb{E}[f_c(x)]$, and for every $\theta_c \in \Theta_c$, the loss $L(\theta) \geq L(\theta_c)$. Equality is attained only when $\theta \in \Theta_c$. Thus, f_c is the only minimizer of $L(\theta)$ that satisfies the constraint $\mathbb{E}[h(x;\theta)] = \mathbb{E}[f_c(x)]$.

Optimizing μ. Lem. 1 implies that, for a certain choice of μ, Eqn. 2 provides us with the convex envelope f_c. However, finding the exact value of μ for which this result holds is difficult, as it requires knowledge of the envelope not available to the learner. Here we use an alternative approach to find μ which guarantees that the optimizer of $h(\cdot;\theta_\mu)$ lies in the set of true optimizers $\mathcal{X}_f^*$. Let x_μ denote the minimizer of $h(\cdot;\theta_\mu)$. We find a μ which minimizes $f(x_\mu)$:

$$\mu^* = \arg\min_{\mu \in [-R,R]} f(x_\mu). \tag{3}$$

Interestingly, one can show that x_{μ^*} lies in the set $\mathcal{X}_f^*$. To prove this, we use the fact that the minimizers of the convex envelope f_c and f coincide.This implies that $f(x_{\mu_c}) = f^*$, where $\mu_c := \mathbb{E}(f_c(x))$. It then follows that $f^* = f(x_{\mu_c}) \geq \min_{\mu \in [-R,R]} f(x_\mu) = f(x_{\mu^*})$. This combined with the fact that f^* is the minimizer of f implies that $f(x_{\mu^*}) = f^*$ and thus $x_{\mu^*} \in \mathcal{X}^*$.

3.2 Optimization Protocol

We now describe how we use the ideas presented in Sec. 3.1 to implement CoRR (see Alg. 1 for pseudocode). Our approach for black-box optimization requires two main ingredients: (1) samples from the function f and (2) a function class $\mathcal{H}$ from which we can form a convex approximation h. In practice, CoRR is initialized by first drawing two sets of T samples $\widehat{\mathcal{X}}_1$ and $\widehat{\mathcal{X}}_2$ from the domain $\mathcal{X} \subseteq \mathcal{B}(\mathbb{R}^n)$ and evaluating f over both of these sets. With these sets of function evaluations (samples) and a function class $\mathcal{H}$ in hand, our aim is to learn an approximation $h(x;\theta)$ to the convex envelope of f. Thus for a fixed value of μ, we solve the following constrained optimization problem (see the OPT procedure in Alg. 1):

$$\widehat{\theta}_c = \arg\min_{\theta \in \Theta} \widehat{\mathbb{E}}_1\left[|h(x;\theta) - f(x)|\right] \text{ s.t. } \widehat{\mathbb{E}}_2\left[h(x;\theta)\right] = \mu, \tag{4}$$

where the empirical expectation $\widehat{\mathbb{E}}_i[g(x)] := 1/T\sum_{x \in \widehat{\mathcal{X}}_i} g(x)$, for every $g \in \mathcal{B}(\mathcal{X}, \mathbb{R})$ and $i \in \{1, 2\}$. We provide pseudocode for optimizing Eqn. 4 in the OPT procedure of Alg. 1.

The optimization problem of Eqn. 4 is an empirical approximation of the optimization problem in Eqn. 2. However, unlike Eqn. 2, in which $L(\theta)$ is not easy to evaluate and optimize, the empirical loss can be optimized efficiently using standard convex optimization techniques. In addition, one can establish bounds on the error $|L(\widehat{\theta}_c) - L(\theta_c)|$ in terms of the sample size T using standard results from the literature on stochastic convex optimization (see, e.g., Thm. 1 in Shalev-Shwartz et al., 2009). Optimizing the empirical loss provides us with an accurate estimate of the convex envelope as the number of function evaluations increases.

The search for the best μ (Step 2 in Alg. 1) can be done by solving Eqn. 3. As μ is a scalar with known upper and lower bounds, we can employ a number of hyper-parameter search algorithms (Munos, 2011; Bergstra et al., 2011) to solve this 1D optimization problem. These algorithms guarantee fast convergence to the global minimizer in low dimensions and thus can be used to efficiently search for the solution to Eqn. 3. Let $\widehat{\mu}$ denote the final estimate of μ obtained in Step 2 of Alg. 1 and let $h(\cdot;\theta_{\widehat{\mu}})$ denote our final convex approximation to f_c. The final solution $\widehat{x}_{\widehat{\mu}}$ is then obtained by optimizing $h(\cdot;\theta_{\widehat{\mu}})$ (Step 2 of OPT).

To provide further insight into how CoRR works, we point the reader to Fig. 1. Here, we show examples of the convex surrogate obtained by OPT for different values of μ. We observe that as we vary μ, the minimum error is attained for $\mu \approx 0.47$. However, when we analytically compute the empirical expectation of convex envelope ($\widehat{E}_2[f_c(x)] = 0.33$) and use this value for μ, this produces a larger function evaluation. This may seem surprising, as we know that if we set $\mu = \mathbb{E}(f_c(x))$, then the solution of Eqn. 2 should provide us the exact convex envelope with the same opti-

Algorithm 1 Convex Relaxation Regression (CoRR)

Input: A black-box function f which returns a sample $f(x)$ when evaluated at a point x. The number of samples N to draw from f. A class $\mathcal{H} \subseteq \mathcal{B}(\mathcal{X}, \mathbb{R})$ of convex functions in $\mathcal{X}$ (parametrized by θ), a scalar R for which $\|f\|_\infty \leq R$, a sampling distribution ρ supported over $\mathcal{X}$.

1: **Random function evaluations.** Draw $2N$ i.i.d. samples according to the distribution ρ and partition them into two sets, $\widehat{\mathcal{X}} = \{\widehat{\mathcal{X}}_1, \widehat{\mathcal{X}}_2\}$. Generate samples $[f]_{\widehat{\mathcal{X}}_1}$ and $[f]_{\widehat{\mathcal{X}}_2}$, where $[f]_{\widehat{\mathcal{X}}_i} = \{f(x) : x \in \widehat{\mathcal{X}}_i\}$, $i = \{1,2\}\}$. Denote $[f]_{\widehat{\mathcal{X}}} = \{[f]_{\widehat{\mathcal{X}}_1}, [f]_{\widehat{\mathcal{X}}_2}\}$

2: **Optimize for μ.** Solve the 1D optimization problem

$$\widehat{\mu} = \underset{\mu \in [-R,R]}{\arg\min}\; f(\mathtt{OPT}(\mu, [f]_{\widehat{\mathcal{X}}})),$$

Output: $\widehat{x}_{\widehat{\mu}} = \mathtt{OPT}(\widehat{\mu}, [f]_{\widehat{\mathcal{X}}})$.

Procedure $\mathtt{OPT}(\mu, [f]_{\widehat{\mathcal{X}}})$

1: **Estimate the convex envelope.** Estimate $\widehat{f}_c = h(\cdot; \widehat{\theta}_\mu)$ by solving Eqn. 4.

2: **Optimize the empirical convex envelope.** Find an optimizer $\widehat{x}_\mu$ for $\widehat{f}_c$ by solving

$$\widehat{x}_\mu = \min_{x \in \mathcal{X}} \widehat{f}_c(x),$$

return $\widehat{x}_\mu$

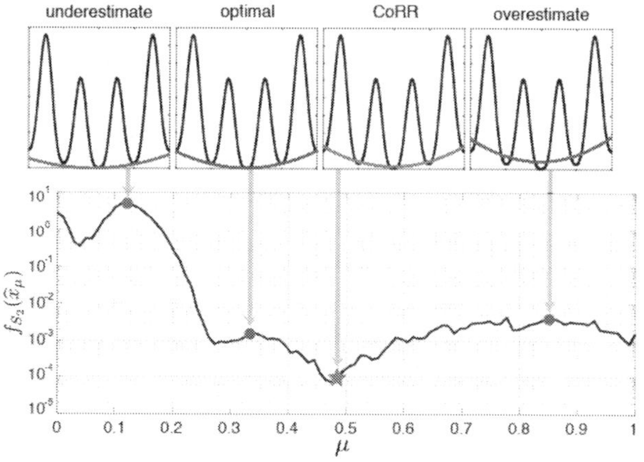

Figure 1: *Estimating the convex envelope of f with CoRR.* Here we demonstrate how CoRR learns a convex envelope by solving Eqn. 3. Along the top, we plot the test function f_{S_2} (see Sec. 5) and examples of the convex surrogates obtained for different values of μ. From left to right, we display the surrogate obtained for: an underestimate of μ, the empirical estimate of the convex envelope where $\mu \approx \widehat{\mathbb{E}}_2[f_c(x)]$, the result obtained by CoRR, and an overestimate of μ. Below, we display the value of the function f_{S_2} as we vary μ (solid blue).

mizer as f. This discrepancy can be explained by the approximation error introduced through solving the empirical version of Eqn. 2. This figure also highlights the stability of our approach for different values of μ. Our results suggest that our method is robust to the choice of μ, as a wide range of values of μ produce minimizers close to the true global minimum. Thus CoRR provides an accurate and robust approach for finding the global optimizer of f.

4 Theoretical Results

In this section, we provide our main theoretical results. We show that as the number of function evaluations T grows, the solution of CoRR converges to the global minimum of f with a polynomial rate. We also discuss the scalability of our result to high-dimensional settings.

4.1 Assumptions

We begin by introducing the assumptions required to state our results. The first assumption provides the necessary constraint on the candidate function class $\mathcal{H}$ and the set of all points in $\mathcal{X}$ that are minimizers for the function f.

Assumption 1 (Convexity). *Let $\mathcal{X}_f^*$ denote the set of minimizers of f. We assume that the following three convexity assumptions hold with regard to every $h(\cdot;\theta) \in \mathcal{H}$ and $\mathcal{X}_f^*$: (a) $h(x;\theta)$ is a convex function for all $x \in \mathcal{X}$, (b) h is a affine function of $\theta \in \Theta$ for all $x \in \mathcal{X}$, and (c) $\mathcal{X}_f^*$ is a convex set.*

Remark. Assumption 1c does not impose convexity on the function f. Rather, it requires that the set $\mathcal{X}_f^*$ is convex. This is needed to guarantee that both f_c and f have the same minimizers (see Prop. 1). Assumption 1c holds for a large class of non-convex functions. For instance, every continuous function with a unique minimizer satisfies this assumption (see, e.g., our example functions in Sect. 5).

Assumption 2 establishes the necessary smoothness assumption on the function f and the function class $\mathcal{H}$.

Assumption 2 (Lipschitz continuity). *We assume that f and h are Lipschitz continuous. That is for every $(x_1, x_2) \in \mathcal{X}^2$ we have that $|f(x_1) - f(x_2)| \leq d(x_1, x_2)$. Also for every $x \in \mathcal{X}$ and $(\theta_1, \theta_2) \in \Theta^2$ we have that $|h(x;\theta_1) - h(x;\theta_2)| \leq U d_2(\theta_1, \theta_2)$. We also assume that every $h \in \mathcal{H}$ is λ-Lipschitz on $\mathcal{X}$ w.r.t. the metric d for some $\lambda > 0$.*

We show that the optimization problem of Eqn. 1 provides us with the convex envelope f_c when the candidate class $\mathcal{H}$ contains f_c (see Lem. 1). The following assumption formalizes this condition.

Assumption 3 (Capacity of $\mathcal{H}$). *We assume that $f_c \in \mathcal{H}$, that is, there exist some $h \in \mathcal{H}$ and $\Theta \subseteq \Theta_c$ such that*

$h(x;\theta) = f_c(x)$ *for every* $x \in \mathcal{X}$ *and* $\theta \in \Theta_c$.

We also require that the following Hölder-type error bounds hold for the distances of our empirical estimates $\widehat{x}$ and $\widehat{\theta}$ from $\mathcal{X}_f^*$ and Θ_c, respectively.

Assumption 4 (Hölder-type error bounds). *Let* $\Theta^e := \{\theta|\theta \in \Theta, \mathbb{E}(h(x;\theta)) = f_c(x)\}$. *Also denote* $L^* := \min_{\theta\in\Theta^e} L(\theta)$. *We assume that there exists some finite positive scalars* γ_1, γ_2, β_1 *and* β_2 *such that for every* $x \in \mathcal{X}$ *and* $\theta \in \Theta^e$: *(a)* $f(x) - f^* \geq \gamma_1 d(x, \mathcal{X}_f^*)^{1/\beta_1}$. *(b)* $L(\theta) - L^* \geq \gamma_2 d_2(\theta, \Theta_c)^{1/\beta_2}$.

Assumption 4 implies that whenever the error terms $f(x) - f^*$ and $L(\theta) - L^*$ are small, the distances $d(x, \mathcal{X}_f^*)$ and $d_2(\theta, \Theta_c)$ are small as well. To see why Assumption 4 is required for the analysis of CoRR, we note that the combination of Assumption 4 with Assumption 2 leads to the following *local* bi-Hölder inequalities for every $x \in \mathcal{X}$ and $\theta \in \Theta^e$:

$$\begin{aligned} \gamma_1 d(x, \mathcal{X}_f^*)^{1/\beta_1} &\leq f(x) - f^* \leq d(x, \mathcal{X}_f^*) \\ \gamma_2 d_2(\theta, \Theta_c)^{1/\beta_2} &\leq L(\theta) - L^* \leq U d_2(\theta, \Theta_c) \end{aligned} \tag{5}$$

These inequalities determine the behavior of function f and L around their minimums as they establish upper and lower bounds on the errors $f(x) - f^*$ and $L(\theta) - L^*$. Essentially, Eqn. 5 implies that there is a direct relationship between $d(x, \mathcal{X}_f^*)$ ($d_2(\theta, \Theta_c)$) and $f(x) - f^*$ ($L(\theta) - L(\Theta_c)$). Thus, bounds on $d(x, \mathcal{X}_f^*)$ and $d_2(\theta, \Theta_c)$, respectively, imply bounds on $f(x) - f^*$ and $L(\theta) - L(\Theta_c)$ and vice versa. These bi-directional bounds are needed due to the fact that CoRR doest not directly optimize the function. Instead it optimizes the surrogate loss $L(\theta)$ to find the convex envelope and then it optimizes this empirical convex envelope to estimate the global minima. This implies that the standard result of optimization theory can only be applied to bound the error $L(\widehat{\theta}) - L^*$. The inequalities of Eqn. 5 are then required to convert the bound on $L(\widehat{\theta}) - L^*$ to a bound on $f(\widehat{x}_{\widehat{\mu}}) - f^*$, which ensures that the solution of CoRR converges to a global minimum as $L(\widehat{\theta}) - L^* \to 0$.

It is noteworthy that global error bounds such as those in Assumption 4 have been extensively analyzed in the literature of approximation theory and variational analysis (see, e.g., Azé, 2003; Corvellec and Motreanu, 2008; Azé and Corvellec, 2004; Fabian et al., 2010). Much of this body of work can be applied to study convex functions such as $L(\theta)$, where one can make use of the basic properties of convex functions to prove lower bounds on $L(\theta) - L^*$ in terms of the distance between θ and Θ_c (see, e.g., Thm. 1.16 in Azé, 2003). While these results are useful to further study the class of functions that satisfy Assumption 4, providing a direct link between these results and the error bounds of Assumption 4 is outside the scope of this paper.

Assumptions 3-4 can not be applied directly when $f_c \notin \mathcal{H}$. When $f_c \notin \mathcal{H}$, we make use of the following generalized version of these assumptions. We first consider a relaxed version of Assumption 3, which assumes that f_c can be approximated by some $h \in \mathcal{H}$.

Assumption 5 (υ-approachability of f_c by $\mathcal{H}$). *Let* υ *be a positive scalar. Define the distance between the function class* $\mathcal{H}$ *and* f_c *as* $\mathrm{dist}(f_c, \mathcal{H}) := \inf_{h\in\mathcal{H}} \mathbb{E}[|h(x;\theta) - f_c(x)|]$, *where the expectation is taken w.r.t. the distribution* ρ. *We then assume that the following inequality holds:* $\mathrm{dist}(f_c, \mathcal{H}) \leq \upsilon$.

The next assumption generalizes Assumption 4b to the case where $f_c \notin \mathcal{H}$:

Assumption 6. *Let* $\widetilde{p}$ *be a positive scalar. Assume that there exists a class of convex functions* $\widetilde{\mathcal{H}} \subseteq \mathcal{C}(\mathcal{X}, \mathbb{R})$ *parametrized by* $\theta \in \widetilde{\Theta} \subset \mathcal{B}(\mathbb{R}^{\widetilde{p}})$ *such that: (a)* $f_c \in \widetilde{\mathcal{H}}$, *(b) every* $h \in \widetilde{\mathcal{H}}$ *is linear in* θ *and (c)* $\mathcal{H} \subseteq \widetilde{\mathcal{H}}$. *Let* $\Theta_c \subseteq \widetilde{\Theta}$ *be the set of parameters for which* $h(x;\theta) = f_c(x)$ *for every* $x \in \mathcal{X}$ *and* $\theta \in \Theta_c$. *Also define* $\widetilde{\Theta}_e := \{\theta|\theta \in \widetilde{\Theta}, \mathbb{E}(h(x;\theta)) = f_c(x)\}$. *We assume that there exists some finite positive scalars* γ_2 *and* β_2 *such that for every* $x \in \mathcal{X}$ *and* $\theta \in \widetilde{\Theta}_e$

$$L(\theta) - L^* \geq \gamma_2 d_2(\theta, \widetilde{\Theta}_c)^{1/\beta_2}.$$

Intuitively speaking, Assumption 6 implies that the function class $\mathcal{H}$ is a subset of a larger unknown function class $\widetilde{\mathcal{H}}$ which satisfies the global error bound of Assumption 4b. Note that we do not require access to the class $\widetilde{\mathcal{H}}$, but we need that such a function class exists.

4.2 Performance Guarantees

We now present the two main theoretical results of our work and provide sketches of their proofs (the complete proofs of our results is provided in the Supp. Material).

4.2.1 Exact Setting

Our first result considers the case where the convex envelope $f_c \in \mathcal{H}$. In this case, we can guarantee that as the number of function evaluations grows, the solution of Alg. 1 converges to the optimal solution with a polynomial rate.

Theorem 1. *Let* δ *be a positive scalar. Let Assumptions 1, 2 ,3, and 4 hold. Then Alg. 1 returns* $\widehat{x}$ *such that with probability* $1 - \delta$

$$f(\widehat{x}) - f^* = \mathcal{O}\left[\xi_s \left(\frac{\log(1/\delta)}{T}\right)^{\beta_1\beta_2/2}\right],$$

where the smoothness coefficient $\xi_s := (\frac{1}{\gamma_1})^{\beta_2} (\frac{1}{\gamma_2})^{\beta_1\beta_2} U^{(1+\beta_2)\beta_1} (RB)^{\beta_2\beta_1}$.

Sketch of proof. To prove this result, we first prove bound on the error $L(\widehat{\theta}) - \min_{\theta\in\Theta_e} L(\theta)$ for which we rely on standard results from stochastic convex optimization. This combined with the result of Lem. 1 leads to a bound on $L(\widehat{\theta}) - L^*$. The bound on $L(\widehat{\theta}) - L^*$ combined with Assumption 4 translates to a bound on $d(\widehat{x}, \mathcal{X}_f^*)$. The result then follows by applying the Lipschitz continuity assumption (Assumption 2). □

Thm. 1 guarantees that as the number of function evaluations T grows, the solution of CoRR converges to f^* with a polynomial rate. The order of polynomial depends on the constants β_1 and β_2. The following corollary, which is an immediate result of Thm. 1, quantifies the number of function evaluations T needed to achieve an ε-optimal solution.

Corollary 1. *Let Assumptions 1, 2, 3, and 4 hold. Let ε and δ be some positive scalars. Then Alg. 1 needs $T = (\frac{\xi_s}{\varepsilon})^{2/(\beta_1\beta_2)}\log(1/\delta)$ function evaluations to return $\widehat{x}$ such that with probability $1-\delta$, $f(\widehat{x}) - f^* \leq \varepsilon$.*

This result implies that one can achieve an ε-accurate approximation of the global optimizer with CoRR with a polynomial number of function evaluations.

4.2.2 Approximate Setting

Thm. 1 relies on the assumption that the convex envelope f_c lies in the function class $\mathcal{H}$. However, in general, there is no guarantee that f_c belongs to $\mathcal{H}$. When the convex envelope $f_c \notin \mathcal{H}$, the result of Thm. 1 cannot be applied. However, one may expect that Alg. 1 still may find a close approximation of the global minimum as long as the distance between f_c and $\mathcal{H}$ is small. To prove that CoRR finds a near optimal solution in this case, we must show that $f(\widehat{x}) - f^*$ remains small when the distance between f_c and $\mathcal{H}$ is small. We now generalize Thm. 1 to the setting where the convex envelope f_c does not lie in $\mathcal{H}$ but is close to it.

Theorem 2. *Let Assumptions 1, 2, 5, and 6 hold. Then Alg. 1 returns $\widehat{x}$ such that for every $\zeta > 0$ with probability (w.p.) $1-\delta$*

$$f(\widehat{x}) - f^* = \mathcal{O}\left[\xi_s\left(\sqrt{\frac{\log(1/\delta)}{T}} + \zeta + \upsilon\right)^{\beta_1\beta_2}\right].$$

Sketch of proof. To prove this result, we rely on standard results from stochastic convex optimization to first prove a bound on the error $L(\widehat{\theta}) - \min_{\theta\in\Theta^c} L(\theta)$ when we set μ the empirical mean of the convex envelope. We then make use of Assumption 5 as well as Lem. 1 to transform this bound to a bound on $L(\widehat{\theta}) - L^*$. The bound on $f(\widehat{x}) - f^*$ then follows by combining this result with Assumptions 2 and 6. □

4.2.3 Approximation Error υ vs. Complexity of $\mathcal{H}$

From function approximation theory, it is known that for a sufficiently smooth function g, one can achieve an υ-accurate approximation of g by a linear combination of $p = \mathcal{O}(n/\upsilon)$ bases (Mhaskar, 1996; Girosi and Anzellotti, 1992). These results imply that one can make the error υ in Thm. 2 arbitrary small by increasing the complexity of function class $\mathcal{H}$ (i.e., increasing the number of convex bases p). Similar *shape preserving* results have been established for the case when the function and bases are both convex (see, e.g., Gal, 2010; Konovalový et al., 2010; Shvedov, 1981) under some mild assumptions on g. In particular, Konovalový et al. (2010) have proven that for a rather general class of $\mathcal{H}$, the approximation error between a convex function g and class $\mathcal{H}$, can be bounded in terms of the approximation error between g and $\mathcal{H}$ when no convexity constraint is imposed on $\mathcal{H}$. This implies that existing results in the approximation theory literature can be used to bound the approximation error υ in terms of the complexity of function class $\mathcal{H}$.

4.2.4 Dependence on Dimension

The results of Thm. 1 and Thm. 2 have no explicit dependence on the dimension n. However, the Lipschitz constant U can, in the worst-case scenario, be of $\mathcal{O}(\sqrt{p})$ (due to the Cauchy-Schwarz inequality). On the other hand to achieve an approximation error of υ the number of bases p needs be of $\mathcal{O}(n/\upsilon)$ (see Sect. 4.2.3). When we plug this result in the bound of Thm. 2, this leads to a dependency of $\mathcal{O}(n^{(1+\beta_2)\beta_1/2})$ on the dimension n due to the Lipschitz constant U. In the special case where $\beta_2 = \beta_1 = 1$, i.e., when the error bounds of Assumption 4 are linear, the dependency on n becomes linear. The linear dependency on n in this case matches the results of the black-box (zero-order) convex optimization (see, e.g., Duchi et al., 2015).

5 Numerical Results

In this section, we evaluate the performance of CoRR on several multi-dimensional test functions used for benchmarking non-convex optimization methods (Jamil and Yang, 2013).

Evaluation setup. Here we study CoRR's effectiveness in finding the global minimizer of the following test functions (Fig. 2a). We assume that all functions are supported over $\mathcal{X} = \mathcal{B}(0,2) \subseteq \mathbb{R}^n$, and otherwise rescale them to lie within this set. **(S1)** Salomon function: $f_S(x) = 1 - \cos(2\pi\|x\|) + 0.5\|x\|$. **(S2)** Squared Salomon: $f_{S_2}(x) = 0.1 f_S(x)^2$. **(SL)** Salomon and Langerman combination: $f_{SL}(x) = f_S(x) + f_L(x)\ \forall x \in \mathcal{B}(0,10) \cap \mathcal{B}(0,0.2)$ and $f_{SL}(x) = 0$, otherwise (before rescaling the domain). **(L)** Langerman function: $f_L(x) = -\exp(\|x-\alpha\|_2^2/\pi)\cos(\pi\|x-\alpha\|_2^2) + 1$, $\forall x \in \mathcal{B}(0,5)$ (before rescaling the domain). **(G)** The Griewank function: $f_G(x) = 0.1\left[1 + \frac{1}{4000}\sum_{i=1}^N x(i)^2 - \prod_{i=1}^N \frac{\cos(x)}{\sqrt{i}}\right]$, $\forall x \in \mathcal{B}(0,200)$ (before rescaling the domain). All of these functions have their minimum at the origin, except for the Langerman function which has its minimum at $x^* = c\mathbf{1}$ for $c = 0.5$.

All of the aforementioned functions exhibit some amount of global structure for which the convex envelope can be approximated by a quadratic basis (Fig. 2a). We thus use a quadratic basis to construct our function class $\mathcal{H}$. The basis functions $h(x;\theta) \in \mathcal{H}$ are parameterized by a vector of coefficients $\theta = [\theta_1, \theta_2, \theta_3]$, and can be written as $h(x;\theta) = \langle\theta_1, x^2\rangle + \langle\theta_2, x\rangle + \theta_3$. Thus, the number of parameters that we must estimate to find a convex approximation h equals $2n + 1$ (we drop the cross terms in our construction of the quadratic class). In practice, we impose a non-negativity constraint on all entries of the vector θ_1 to ensure that our approximation is convex.

Summary of results. To understand the difficulty of finding the minimizers for the test functions above, we compute the error $f(\widehat{x}) - f^*$ as we increase the number of function evaluations. Here, we show each of our five test functions (Fig. 2a) and their average scaling behavior in one dimension (Fig. 2b), where the error is averaged over 100 trials. We observe that CoRR quickly converges for all five test functions, with varying convergence rates. We observe the smallest initial error (for only 20 samples) for f_{SL} and the highest error for f_S. In addition, f_L achieves nearly perfect reconstruction of the global minimum after only 200 samples. The good scaling properties of f_L and f_{SL} is likely due the the fact that both of these functions have a wide basin around their global minimizer. This result provides nice insight into the scaling of CoRR in low dimensions.

Next, we study the approximation error as we vary the sample size and dimension for the Salomon function f_S (Fig. 2c-d). Just as our theory suggests, there is a clear dependence between the dimension and number of samples required to obtain small error. In Fig. 2c, we display the scaling behavior of CoRR as a function of both dimension and number of function evaluations T. In all of the tested dimensions, we obtain an error smaller than $1e^{-5}$ when we draw one million samples. In Fig. 2d, we compare the performance of CoRR (for fixed number of evaluations T) as we vary the dimension. In contrast, the quasi-Newton (QN) method and hybrid simulated annealing (SA) method (Hedar and Fukushima, 2004) recover the global minimizer for low dimensions but fail in dimensions greater than ten.[2] We posit that this is due to the fact the minimizer of the Salomon function lies at the center of its domain and as the dimension of the problem grows, drawing an initialization point (for QN) that is close to the global minimizer becomes extremely difficult.

[2]These methods are selected from a long list of candidates in MATLAB's global optimization toolbox. We report results for the methods that gave the best results for our test functions.

6 Discussion and Future Work

This paper introduced CoRR, an approach for learning a convex relaxation for a wide class of non-convex functions. The idea behind CoRR is to find an empirical estimate of the convex envelope of a function from a set of function evaluations. We demonstrate that CoRR is an efficient strategy for global optimization, both in theory and in practice. In particular, we provide theoretical results (Sec. 4) which show that CoRR is guaranteed to produce a convergent estimate of the convex envelope that exhibits polynomial dependence on the dimension. In numerical experiments (Sec. 5), we showed that CoRR provides accurate approximations to the global minimizer of multiple test functions and appears to scale well with dimension.

Our current instantiation of CoRR finds a convex surrogate for f based upon a set of samples that are drawn at random at the onset of the algorithm. In our evaluations, we draw i.i.d. samples from a uniform distribution over $\mathcal{X}$. However, the choice of the sampling distribution ρ has a significant impact on our estimation procedure. As such, selecting samples in an intelligent manner would significantly reduce the number of samples required to obtain an accurate estimate. A natural extension of CoRR is to the case where we can iteratively refine our distribution ρ based upon the output of the algorithm at previous steps.

An important factor in the success of our algorithm is the basis that we use to form our approximation. As discussed in Sec. 4.2.3, we know that a polynomial basis can be used to form a convex approximation to any convex function (Gal, 2010). However, finding a concise representation of the convex envelope using high-degree polynomials is not an easy task. Thus finding other well-suited bases for this approximation, such as the exponential basis, may improve the efficiency of CoRR by reducing the number of bases required. While outside the scope of this paper, exploring the use of constrained dictionary learning methods (Yaghoobi et al., 2009) for finding a good basis for our fitting procedure, is an interesting line for future work.

In our experiments, we observe that CoRR typically provides a good approximation to the global minimizer. However, in most cases, we do not obtain machine precision (like QN for low dimensions). Thus, we can combine CoRR with a local search method like QN by using the solution of CoRR as an initialization point for the local search. When using this hybrid approach, we obtain perfect reconstruction of the global minimum for the Salomon function for all of the dimensions we tested (Fig. 2d). This suggests that, as long the function does not fluctuate too rapidly around its global minimum (Asm. 2), CoRR can be coupled with other local search methods to quickly converge to the absolute global minimizer.

The key innovation behind CoRR is that one can efficiently

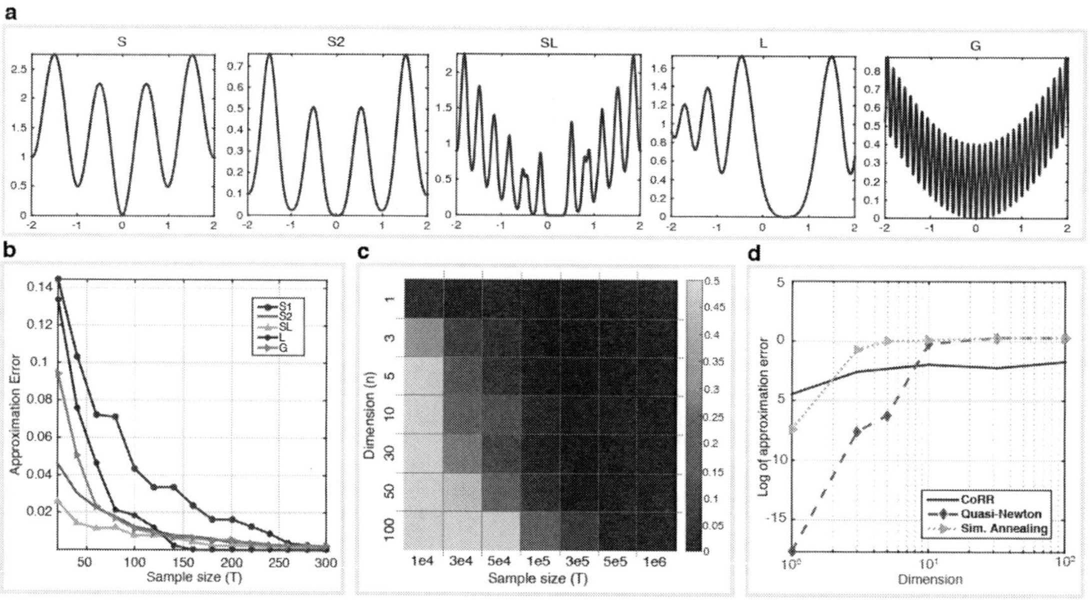

Figure 2: *Scaling behavior and performance of CoRR.* Along the top row in (a), we plot all five test functions studied in this paper. In (b), we display the mean approximation error between $f(\widehat{x}) - f^*$ as a function of the number of function evaluations T for all test functions in 1D. In (c), we display the mean approximation error as a function of the dimension and number of samples for the Salomon function. In (d), we compare CoRR's approximation error with other approaches for non-convex optimization, as we vary the dimension.

approximate the convex envelope of a non-convex function by solving a constrained regression problem which balances the approximation error with a constraint on the empirical expectation of the estimated convex surrogate. While our method could be improved by using a smart and adaptive sampling strategy, this paper provides a new way of thinking about how to relax non-convex problems. As such, our approach opens up the possibility of using the myriad of existing tools and solvers for convex optimization problems to efficiently solve non-convex problems.

References

Azar, M. G., Lazaric, A., and Brunskill, E. (2014). Stochastic optimization of a locally smooth function under correlated bandit feedback. In *ICML*.

Azé, D. (2003). A survey on error bounds for lower semicontinuous functions. In *ESAIM: ProcS*, volume 13, pages 1–17. EDP Sciences.

Azé, D. and Corvellec, J.-N. (2004). Characterizations of error bounds for lower semicontinuous functions on metric spaces. *ESAIM: Control, Optimisation and Calculus of Variations*, 10:409–425.

Bäck, T. (1996). *Evolutionary algorithms in theory and practice: evolution strategies, evolutionary programming, genetic algorithms*. Oxford University Press.

Bergstra, J. and Bengio, Y. (2012). Random search for hyper-parameter optimization. *J. Mach. Learn. Res.*, 13(1):281–305.

Bergstra, J. S., Bardenet, R., Bengio, Y., and Kégl, B. (2011). Algorithms for hyper-parameter optimization. In *NIPS*, pages 2546–2554.

Blake, A. and Zisserman, A. (1987). *Visual reconstruction*, volume 2. MIT Press Cambridge.

Boyd, S. and Vandenberghe, L. (2004). *Convex optimization*. Cambridge University Press.

Bubeck, S., Munos, R., Stoltz, G., and Szepesvari, C. (2011). X-armed bandits. *J. Mach. Learn. Res.*, 12:1655–1695.

Candès, E. J. and Tao, T. (2010). The power of convex relaxation: Near-optimal matrix completion. *IEEE Trans. Inf. Theory*, 56(5):2053–2080.

Chandrasekaran, V., Recht, B., Parrilo, P. A., and Willsky, A. S. (2012). The convex geometry of linear inverse problems. *Found Comput Math*, 12(6):805–849.

Chapelle, O. and Wu, M. (2010). Gradient descent optimization of smoothed information retrieval metrics. *Inform Retrieval*, 13(3):216–235.

Corvellec, J.-N. and Motreanu, V. V. (2008). Nonlinear error bounds for lower semicontinuous functions on metric spaces. *Math Program*, 114(2):291–319.

Cox, D. R. (1958). The regression analysis of binary sequences. *J R Stat Soc*, pages 215–242.

Duchi, J. C., Jordan, M. I., Wainwright, M. J., and Wibisono, A. (2015). Optimal rates for zero-order convex optimization: The power of two function evaluations. *IEEE Trans. Inf. Theory*, 61(5):2788–2806.

Dvijotham, K., Fazel, M., and Todorov, E. (2014). Universal convexification via risk-aversion. In *UAI*, pages 162–171.

Fabian, M. J., Henrion, R., Kruger, A. Y., and Outrata, J. V. (2010). Error bounds: Necessary and sufficient conditions. *Set-Valued and Variational Analysis*, 18(2):121–149.

Falk, J. E. (1969). Lagrange multipliers and nonconvex programs. *SIAM J Control Optim*, 7(4):534–545.

Friedman, J., Hastie, T., and Tibshirani, R. (2001). *The elements of statistical learning*, volume 1. Springer.

Gal, S. (2010). *Shape-preserving approximation by real and complex polynomials*. Springer.

Girosi, F. and Anzellotti, G. (1992). Convergence rates of approximation by translates. Technical report, Massachusetts Inst. of Tech. Cambridge Artificial Intelligence Lab.

Grotzinger, S. J. (1985). Supports and convex envelopes. *Math Program*, 31(3):339–347.

Hazan, E., Levy, K. Y., and Shalev-Swartz, S. (2015). On graduated optimization for stochastic non-convex problems. *arXiv:1503.03712 [cs.LG]*.

Hedar, A.-R. and Fukushima, M. (2004). Heuristic pattern search and its hybridization with simulated annealing for nonlinear global optimization. *Optim Method and Softw*, 19(3-4):291–308.

Hooke, R. and Jeeves, T. A. (1961). "Direct search" solution of numerical and statistical problems. *J ACM*, 8(2):212–229.

Hutter, F. (2009). Automated configuration of algorithms for solving hard computational problems. *University of British Columbia*.

Jamil, M. and Yang, X.-S. (2013). A literature survey of benchmark functions for global optimisation problems. *International Journal of Mathematical Modelling and Numerical Optimisation*, 4(2):150–194.

Kirkpatrick, S., Gelatt, C. D., Vecchi, M. P., et al. (1983). Optimization by simulated annealing. *Science*, 220(4598):671–680.

Kleibohm, K. (1967). Bemerkungen zum problem der nichtkonvexen programmierung. *Unternehmensforschung*, 11(1):49–60.

Konovalový, V., Kopotun, K., and Maiorov, V. (2010). Convex polynomial and ridge approximation of Lipschitz functions in $\mathbf{R}^d$. *Rocky Mountains Journal of Mathematics*, 40(3).

Lewis, R. M. and Torczon, V. (1999). Pattern search algorithms for bound constrained minimization. *SIAM J Optimiz*, 9(4):1082–1099.

Mhaskar, H. (1996). Neural networks for optimal approximation of smooth and analytic functions. *Neural Comput*, 8(1):164–177.

Mobahi, H. and III, J. W. F. (2015). A theoretical analysis of the optimization by gaussian continuation. In *AAAI*.

Mockus, J., Tiesis, V., and Zilinskas, A. (1978). The application of bayesian methods for seeking the extremum. *Towards global optimization*, 2(117-129):2.

Munos, R. (2011). Optimistic optimization of deterministic functions without the knowledge of its smoothness. In *NIPS*.

Munos, R. (2014). From bandits to monte-carlo tree search: The optimistic principle applied to optimization and planning. *Foundations and Trends in Machine Learning*, 7(1):1–129.

Recht, B., Fazel, M., and Parrilo, P. A. (2010). Guaranteed minimum-rank solutions of linear matrix equations via nuclear norm minimization. *SIAM Review*, 52(3):471–501.

Rockafellar, R. T. (1997). *Convex analysis*. Princeton University Press.

Shalev-Shwartz, S. and Ben-David, S. (2014). *Understanding machine learning: From theory to algorithms*. Cambridge University Press.

Shalev-Shwartz, S., Shamir, O., Srebro, N., and Sridharan, K. (2009). Stochastic convex optimization. In *COLT*.

Shvedov, A. S. (1981). Orders of coapproximation of functions by algebraic polynomials. *Mathematical Notes*, 29(1):63–70.

Sra, S., Nowozin, S., and Wright, S. J. (2012). *Optimization for machine learning*. MIT Press.

Tibshirani, R. (1996). Regression shrinkage and selection via the lasso. *J R Stat Soc*, pages 267–288.

Tropp, J. A. (2006). Algorithms for simultaneous sparse approximation. Part II: Convex relaxation. *Signal Process*, 86(3):589–602.

Yaghoobi, M., Blumensath, T., and Davies, M. E. (2009). Dictionary learning for sparse approximations with the majorization method. *IEEE Trans. Signal Process.*, 57(6):2178–2191.

Yuille, A. (1989). Energy functions for early vision and analog networks. *Biol Cybern*, 61(2):115–123.

The Mondrian Kernel

Matej Balog*
Department of Engineering
University of Cambridge

Balaji Lakshminarayanan
Gatsby Unit
University College London

Zoubin Ghahramani
Department of Engineering
University of Cambridge

Daniel M. Roy
Department of Statistical Sciences
University of Toronto

Yee Whye Teh
Department of Statistics
University of Oxford

Abstract

We introduce the Mondrian kernel, a fast *random feature* approximation to the Laplace kernel. It is suitable for both batch and online learning, and admits a fast kernel-width-selection procedure as the random features can be re-used efficiently for all kernel widths. The features are constructed by sampling trees via a Mondrian process [Roy and Teh, 2009], and we highlight the connection to Mondrian forests [Lakshminarayanan et al., 2014], where trees are also sampled via a Mondrian process, but fit independently. This link provides a new insight into the relationship between kernel methods and random forests.

1 INTRODUCTION

Kernel methods such as support vector machines and Gaussian processes are very popular in machine learning. While early work relied on dual optimization, recent large-scale kernel methods focus on the primal optimization problem where the input data are mapped to a finite-dimensional feature space and the weights are learned using fast linear optimization techniques, e.g., stochastic gradient descent. Rahimi and Recht [2007] proposed to approximate shift-invariant kernels by mapping the inputs to so-called *random features*, constructed so that the inner product of two mapped data points approximates the kernel evaluated at those two points (which is the inner product in the feature space corresponding to the kernel). Rahimi and Recht [2007] proposed two random feature construction schemes: *random Fourier features*, where data points are projected onto random vectors drawn from the Fourier transform of the kernel and then passed through suitable non-linearities; and *random binning*, where the input space is partitioned by a random regular grid into bins and data points are mapped to indicator vectors identifying which bins they end up in. Both of these approaches require specifying the kernel hyperparameters in advance, so that the appropriate distribution is used for sampling the random vectors or random grids, respectively. However, a suitable kernel width (length-scale) is often not known a priori and is found by cross-validation, or, where available, marginal likelihood optimization. In practice, this entails constructing a new feature space and training a linear learner from scratch for each kernel width, which is computationally expensive. Using a suitable kernel width is often more important than the choice of kernel type [Schölkopf and Smola, 2001], so a fast kernel width selection method is desirable.

We describe a connection between the Laplace kernel and the Mondrian process [Roy and Teh, 2009], and leverage it to develop a random feature approximation to the Laplace kernel that addresses the kernel width selection problem. This approximation, which we call the *Mondrian kernel*, involves random partitioning of data points using a Mondrian process, which can be efficiently reused for all kernel widths. The method preserves the nonparametric nature of kernel learning and is also suitable for online learning.

The Mondrian kernel reveals an interesting link between kernel methods and decision forests [Breiman, 2001, Criminisi et al., 2012], another popular class of nonparametric methods for black-box prediction tasks. The Mondrian kernel resembles *Mondrian forests*, a decision-forest variant introduced by Lakshminarayanan et al. [2014], where a Mondrian process is used as the randomization mechanism. The efficiently trainable Mondrian forests excel in the online setting, where their distribution is identical to the corresponding batch Mondrian forest, and have been successfully applied to both classification and regression [Lakshminarayanan et al., 2014, 2016]. Mondrian forests and the Mondrian kernel both lead to randomized, non-linear learning algorithms whose randomness stems from a Mondrian process. The former fits parameters corresponding to different Mondrian trees independently, while the latter fits them jointly. We compare these methods theoretically and thus establish a novel connection between the Laplace kernel and Mondrian forests via the Mondrian kernel.

*Also affiliated with Max-Planck Institute for Intelligent Systems, Tübingen, Germany.

The contributions of this paper are:

- a review of the Mondrian process using the simple notion of competing exponential clocks (Section 2);
- a novel connection between the Mondrian process and the Laplace kernel (Section 3), yielding a fast approximation to learning with the Laplace kernel;
- an efficient procedure for learning the kernel width from data (Section 4); and
- a comparison between Mondrian kernel and Mondrian forest that provides another connection between kernel learning and random forests (Section 6).

2 MONDRIAN PROCESS

For completeness, we review the Mondrian process [Roy and Teh, 2009, Roy, 2011, Chapter 5]. Although simple and perhaps well known to experts, our exposition through competing exponential clocks has not explicitly appeared in this form in the literature. Readers familiar with the Mondrian process may skip this section on first reading.

2.1 TERMINOLOGY

An *axis-aligned box* $\mathcal{X} = \mathcal{X}_1 \times \cdots \times \mathcal{X}_D \subseteq \mathbb{R}^D$ is a Cartesian product of D bounded intervals $\mathcal{X}_d \subseteq \mathbb{R}$. Their total length $|\mathcal{X}_1| + \cdots + |\mathcal{X}_D|$ is the *linear dimension of* $\mathcal{X}$. A *guillotine partition* of $\mathcal{X}$ is a hierarchical partitioning of $\mathcal{X}$ using axis-aligned cuts. Such a partition can be naturally represented using a strictly binary tree.

An *exponential clock with rate* r takes a random time $T \sim \text{Exp}(r)$ to ring after being started, where $\text{Exp}(r)$ is the exponential distribution with rate (inverse mean) r. The notion of *competing exponential clocks* refers to D independent exponential clocks with rates $r_1, \ldots, r_D$, started at the same time. It can be shown that (1) the time until some clock rings has $\text{Exp}(\sum r_d)$ distribution, (2) it is the d-th clock with probability proportional to r_d, and (3) once a clock rings, the remaining $D - 1$ clocks continue to run independently with their original distributions.

2.2 GENERATIVE PROCESS

The Mondrian process on an axis-aligned box $\mathcal{X} \subseteq \mathbb{R}^D$ is a time-indexed stochastic process taking values in guillotine-partitions of $\mathcal{X}$. It starts at time 0 with the trivial partition of $\mathcal{X}$ (no cuts) and as time progresses, new axis-aligned cuts randomly appear, hierarchically splitting $\mathcal{X}$ into more and more refined partitions. The process can be stopped at a lifetime $\lambda \in [0, \infty)$, which amounts to ignoring any cuts that would appear after time λ.

To describe the distribution of times and locations of new cuts as time progresses, we associate an independent exponential clock with rate $|\mathcal{X}_d|$ to each dimension d of $\mathcal{X}$. Let T be the first time when a clock rings and let d be the dimension of that clock. If $T > \lambda$ then this process terminates. Otherwise, a point a is chosen uniformly at random from $\mathcal{X}_d$ and $\mathcal{X}$ is split into $\mathcal{X}^< = \{\mathbf{x} \in \mathcal{X} \mid x_d < a\}$ and $\mathcal{X}^> = \{\mathbf{x} \in \mathcal{X} \mid x_d > a\}$ by a hyperplane in dimension d that is perpendicular to $\mathcal{X}_d$ at point a. After making this first cut, the remaining $D - 1$ clocks are discarded and the generative process restarts recursively and *independently* on $\mathcal{X}^<$ and $\mathcal{X}^>$. However, those processes start at time T rather than 0 and thus have less time left until the lifetime λ is reached.

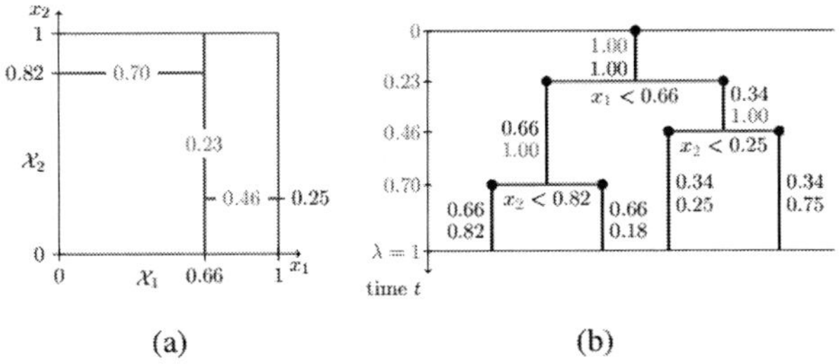

Figure 1: (a) Sample of a Mondrian process on the axis-aligned box $\mathcal{X} = [0, 1] \times [0, 1] \subseteq \mathbb{R}^2$ with lifetime $\lambda = 1.0$. Numbers on the cuts (shown in green) indicate the times when they appeared. The first cut appeared at time $T = 0.23$, in dimension $d = 1$, at location $a = 0.66 \in \mathcal{X}_1$. (b) Representing the Mondrian sample as a strictly binary tree, with new nodes (shown as circles) appearing as time (y-axis) progresses. The two numbers below each node show the rates of the two exponential clocks competing to split that node, with the winning clock's rate shown in green.

The specification of the generative process on $\mathcal{X}$ is now complete. Due to the properties of competing exponential clocks, the time until the first cut appears in $\mathcal{X}$ has exponential distribution with rate equal to the linear dimension of $\mathcal{X}$ and the dimension d in which the cut is made is chosen proportional to $|\mathcal{X}_d|$. This confirms equivalence of our generative process to the one proposed by Roy and Teh [2009]. Finally, we note that a.s. the Mondrian process does not explode, i.e., for every lifetime $\lambda \in [0, \infty)$, the process generates finitely many cuts with probability 1 [Roy, 2011].

2.3 PROJECTIVITY

If a Mondrian process runs on $\mathcal{X}$, what distribution of random partitions does it induce on an axis-aligned subbox $\mathcal{A} \subseteq \mathcal{X}$? (See Figure 2a for an illustration in $D = 2$ dimensions.) The Mondrian process was constructed so that the answer is the Mondrian process itself [Roy, 2011]. Here we explain this projectivity property using the notion of competing exponential clocks. To argue that the resulting process on $\mathcal{A}$ is indeed a Mondrian process, we show that the process running on $\mathcal{X}$ generates cuts in $\mathcal{A}$ in the same way as a Mondrian process running directly on $\mathcal{A}$ would.

Recall that each dimension d of $\mathcal{X}$ is associated with an exponential clock with rate $|\mathcal{X}_d|$ and if it rings first, the cut location is chosen uniformly at random from $\mathcal{X}_d$. This procedure can be equivalently represented using two competing clocks for each dimension (rather than just one):

- Clock $C^d_{\mathcal{A}}$ with rate $|\mathcal{A}_d|$. If this clock rings first, the cut location is chosen uniformly at random from $\mathcal{A}_d$.
- Clock $C^d_{\neg\mathcal{A}}$ with rate $|\mathcal{X}_d| - |\mathcal{A}_d|$. If it rings first, the cut location is sampled uniformly from $\mathcal{X}_d \setminus \mathcal{A}_d$.

(See Figure 2b.) Note that the clocks $C^1_{\mathcal{A}}, \ldots, C^D_{\mathcal{A}}$ represent the same cut distribution as a Mondrian process running on $\mathcal{A}$ would. If a clock $C^d_{\neg\mathcal{A}}$ rings first, a cut is made outside of $\mathcal{A}$ and all of $\mathcal{A}$ remains on one side of this cut. None of the clocks $C^d_{\mathcal{A}}$ have rung in that case and would usually be discarded and replaced with fresh clocks of identical rates, but by property (3) of competing exponential clocks, we can equivalently reuse these clocks (let them run) on the side of the cut containing $\mathcal{A}$. (Figure 2c shows a cut in dimension $d = 1$ that misses $\mathcal{A}$ and the reused clocks $C^d_{\mathcal{A}}$). Hence, cuts outside $\mathcal{A}$ do not affect the distribution of the first cut crossing $\mathcal{A}$, and this distribution is the same as if a Mondrian process were running just on $\mathcal{A}$. When a cut is made within $\mathcal{A}$ (see Figure 2d), the process continues on both sides recursively and our argument proceeds inductively, confirming that the Mondrian process on $\mathcal{X}$ generates cuts in $\mathcal{A}$ in the same way as a Mondrian process on $\mathcal{A}$ would.

2.4 MONDRIAN PROCESS ON $\mathbb{R}^D$

The Mondrian process on $\mathbb{R}^D$ is defined implicitly as a time-indexed stochastic process such that its restriction to any axis-aligned box $\mathcal{X} \subseteq \mathbb{R}^D$ is a Mondrian process as defined in section 2.2. Fortunately, this infinite-dimensional object can be compactly represented by instantiating the Mondrian process only in regions where we have observed data. As we observe new data points, the Mondrian sample can be extended using the *conditional Mondrian* algorithm [Roy and Teh, 2009], a simple and fast sampling procedure for extending a Mondrian sample in an axis-aligned box $\mathcal{A}$ to a larger axis-aligned box $\mathcal{X} \supseteq \mathcal{A}$. The conditional Mondrian is useful for online learning and prediction, as it can be used to extend Mondrian samples to (yet) unobserved parts of the input space [Lakshminarayanan et al., 2014].

3 MONDRIAN KERNEL

For concreteness, our running example will be regression: the problem of learning a function $f : \mathbb{R}^D \to \mathbb{R}$ from a set of N training examples $(\mathbf{x}_1, y_1), \ldots, (\mathbf{x}_N, y_N)$. However, the Mondrian kernel applies equally well to classification, or any other learning task.

Learning with kernels involves choosing a kernel function $k : \mathbb{R}^D \times \mathbb{R}^D \to \mathbb{R}$ to act as a similarity measure between input data points. Evaluating $k(\cdot, \cdot)$ on all pairs of N data

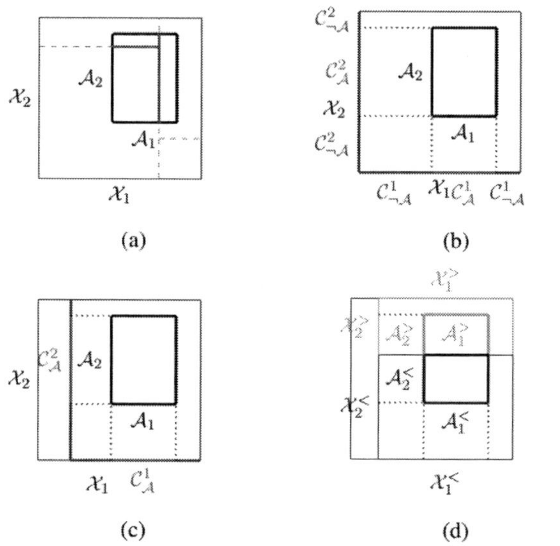

Figure 2: (a) A Mondrian process running on $\mathcal{X} = \mathcal{X}_1 \times \mathcal{X}_2$ generates cuts (dashed lines), some of which intersect $\mathcal{A} = \mathcal{A}_1 \times \mathcal{A}_2$ (green lines) and thus induces a random partition of $\mathcal{A}$. (b) Representing the first cut distribution using $2D = 4$ competing exponential clocks: in each dimension d, clock $C^d_{\mathcal{A}}$ corresponds to the region where making a cut splits $\mathcal{A}$ (shown in green) and clock $C^d_{\neg\mathcal{A}}$ to the (disconnected) region where making a cut misses $\mathcal{A}$ (shown in red). (c) Cut outside $\mathcal{A}$: reusing the clocks $C^1_{\mathcal{A}}$, $C^2_{\mathcal{A}}$ on the side of the cut containing $\mathcal{A}$. (d) Cut inside $\mathcal{A}$ (shown in black): the argument proceeds by induction on both sides.

points takes $\Omega(N^2)$ operations, with some models also requiring a $\Theta(N^3)$ operation on an $N \times N$ kernel matrix. This generally makes exact kernel methods unsuitable for large-scale learning. Rahimi and Recht [2007] proposed a fast approximation through a randomized construction of a low-dimensional feature map $\phi : \mathbb{R}^D \to \mathbb{R}^C$ such that

$$\forall \mathbf{x}, \mathbf{x}' \in \mathbb{R}^D \qquad k(\mathbf{x}, \mathbf{x}') \approx \phi(\mathbf{x})^T \phi(\mathbf{x}')$$

and then using a linear learning method in the feature space $\mathbb{R}^C$ implied by ϕ. For example, linear regression $\mathbf{y} \approx \mathbf{\Phi w}$, where $\mathbf{\Phi} \in \mathbb{R}^{N \times C}$ is the feature matrix with n-th row $\phi(\mathbf{x}_n)^T$, is solvable exactly in time linear in N. In general, the primal problem also lends itself naturally to stochastic gradient descent approaches for learning $\mathbf{w}$.

We use the Mondrian process to construct a randomized feature map for the (isotropic) *Laplace kernel*:

$$k(\mathbf{x}, \mathbf{x}') = \exp(-\lambda \|\mathbf{x} - \mathbf{x}'\|_1) = \exp(-\lambda \sum_{d=1}^{D} |x_d - x'_d|).$$

Here $\lambda \geq 0$ is the inverse kernel width (inverse length-scale), which we call the *lifetime* parameter of the kernel. We use a non-standard parametrization as this lifetime parameter will be linked to the Mondrian process lifetime.

3.1 MONDRIAN KERNEL

Consider the following randomized construction of a feature map $\phi : \mathbb{R}^D \to \mathbb{R}^C$:

1. Sample a partition of $\mathbb{R}^D$ via a Mondrian process on $\mathbb{R}^D$ with lifetime λ. Label the cells of the generated partition by $1, 2, \ldots$ in arbitrary order.
2. To encode a data point $\mathbf{x} \in \mathbb{R}^D$, look up the label c of the partion cell $\mathbf{x}$ falls into and set $\phi(\mathbf{x})$ to be the (column) indicator vector that has a single non-zero entry at position c, equal to 1.

The Mondrian process on $\mathbb{R}^D$ generates infinitely many partition cells and cannot be stored in memory, but projectivity comes to the rescue. As we only ever need to evaluate ϕ on finitely many data points, it suffices to run the Mondrian on the smallest axis-aligned box containing all these points. Also, we only label partition cells containing at least one data point, in effect removing features that would be 0 for all our data points. Then, the dimensionality C of ϕ equals the number of non-empty partiton cells and each data point has a single non-zero feature, equal to 1.

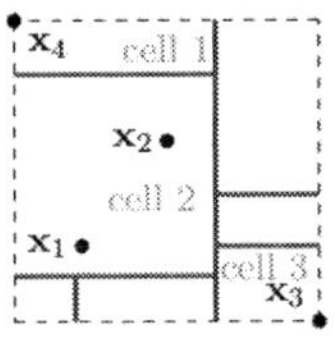

$\mathbf{x}$	$\phi(\mathbf{x})^T$
$\mathbf{x}_1$	[0 1 0]
$\mathbf{x}_2$	[0 1 0]
$\mathbf{x}_3$	[0 0 1]
$\mathbf{x}_4$	[1 0 0]

Figure 3: Feature expansions of 4 data points in $\mathbb{R}^2$.

However, note that the set of points on which the feature map ϕ is evaluated need not be known in advance and can even grow in an online fashion. Indeed, the conditional Mondrian algorithm discussed in section 2.4 allows us to extend Mondrian samples to larger boxes as necessary, and we can increase the dimensionality of ϕ whenever a data point is added to a previously empty partition cell.

This feature map ϕ induces a kernel

$$k_1(\mathbf{x}, \mathbf{x}') := \phi(\mathbf{x})^T \phi(\mathbf{x}') = \begin{cases} 1 & \text{if } \mathbf{x}, \mathbf{x}' \text{ in same partition cell} \\ 0 & \text{otherwise} \end{cases} \quad (1)$$

which we call a *Mondrian kernel* of order 1.

Instead of using a single Mondrian sample (partition), we can use M independent samples and construct a feature map ϕ by concatenating and normalizing the feature maps $\phi^{(1)}, \ldots, \phi^{(M)}$ obtained from each individual sample as above:

$$\phi(\mathbf{x}) := \frac{1}{\sqrt{M}} \left[\phi^{(1)}(\mathbf{x})^T \ \cdots \ \phi^{(M)}(\mathbf{x})^T \right]^T. \quad (2)$$

This feature expansion is *sparse*: every data point has exactly M non-zero features. The corresponding kernel, which we call a *Mondrian kernel of order M*, is

$$k_M(\mathbf{x}, \mathbf{x}') := \phi(\mathbf{x})^T \phi(\mathbf{x}') = \frac{1}{M} \sum_{m=1}^{M} \phi^{(m)}(\mathbf{x})^T \phi^{(m)}(\mathbf{x}').$$

This is the empirical frequency with which points $\mathbf{x}$ and $\mathbf{x}'$ end up in the same partition cell of a Mondrian sample.

Algorithm 1 Mondrian kernel

```
for m = 1 to M do
    construct feature map φ^(m)                ▷ section 3.1
join and rescale φ^(1), ..., φ^(M) into φ      ▷ equation (2)
map data X to feature representations Φ using φ
use linear learning method on Φ
```

3.2 MONDRIAN–LAPLACE LINK

By independence of the M Mondrian samples, a.s.

$$\lim_{M \to \infty} k_M(\mathbf{x}, \mathbf{x}') = \mathbb{E}\left[\phi^{(1)}(\mathbf{x})^T \phi^{(1)}(\mathbf{x}')\right] = \mathbb{E}\left[k_1(\mathbf{x}, \mathbf{x}')\right]$$

with convergence at the standard rate $\mathcal{O}_p(M^{-1/2})$. We thus define the *Mondrian kernel of order ∞* as

$$k_\infty(\mathbf{x}, \mathbf{x}') := \mathbb{E}[k_1(\mathbf{x}, \mathbf{x}')].$$

Proposition 1 (Mondrian-Laplace link). *The Mondrian kernel of order ∞ coincides with the Laplace kernel.*

Proof. As $k_1(\mathbf{x}, \mathbf{x}')$ (defined in (1)) is a binary random variable, $k_\infty(\mathbf{x}, \mathbf{x}')$ equals the probability that $\mathbf{x}$ and $\mathbf{x}'$ fall into the same partition cell of a Mondrian sample, which is equivalent to the sample having no cut in the minimal axis-aligned box spanned by $\mathbf{x}$ and $\mathbf{x}'$.

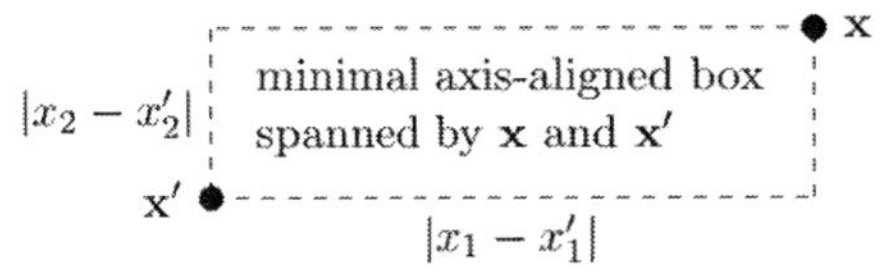

By projectivity, this probability is the same as the probability of not observing any cuts in a Mondrian process with lifetime λ running on just this minimal box. Noting that the linear dimension of this box is $\|\mathbf{x} - \mathbf{x}'\|_1$, we obtain

$$\begin{aligned} k_\infty(\mathbf{x}, \mathbf{x}') &= \mathbb{P}(\text{no cut between } \mathbf{x}, \mathbf{x}' \text{ until time } \lambda) \\ &= \mathbb{P}(T > \lambda) \text{ where } T \sim \text{Exp}(\|\mathbf{x} - \mathbf{x}'\|_1) \\ &= e^{-\lambda \|\mathbf{x} - \mathbf{x}'\|_1}. \end{aligned}$$ □

Note that the lifetime (inverse width) λ of the Laplace kernel corresponds to the lifetime of the Mondrian process used in the construction of the Mondrian kernel.

This link allows us to approximate the Laplace kernel with a Mondrian kernel k_M, which, unlike the Laplace kernel, admits a finite-dimensional feature expansion. The finite order M trades off kernel approximation error and computational costs (indirectly through the complexity of ϕ).

The following result confirms that the convergence of the Mondrian kernel approximation is exponentially fast in M *uniformly* on any fixed bounded input domain $\mathcal{X}$.

Proposition 2. *For any bounded input domain $\mathcal{X} \subseteq \mathbb{R}^D$ and $\delta > 0$, as $M \to \infty$,*

$$\mathbb{P}\left[\sup_{\mathbf{x},\mathbf{x}' \in \mathcal{X}} |k_M(\mathbf{x},\mathbf{x}') - k_\infty(\mathbf{x},\mathbf{x}')| > \delta\right] = \mathcal{O}\left(M^{2/3} e^{-M\delta^2/(12D+2)}\right).$$

Proof. Given in Supplement A. □

4 FAST KERNEL WIDTH LEARNING

This section discusses the main advantage of our Mondrian approximation to the Laplace kernel: the efficient learning of kernel width from data. In particular, the approximation allows for efficient evaluation of all kernel lifetimes (inverse widths) $\lambda \in [0, \Lambda]$, where the terminal lifetime $\Lambda > 0$ need not be fixed a priori.

4.1 FEATURE SPACE REUSAL

We make the following recollections from earlier sections:

- the Mondrian process runs through time, starting at time 0 and only refining the generated partition as time progresses (cuts are never removed)
- the Mondrian process with lifetime λ is obtained by ignoring any cuts that would occur after time λ
- the lifetime λ of the Mondrian process used in constructing an explicit feature map ϕ for a Mondrian kernel corresponds to the lifetime (inverse width) of the Laplace kernel that it approximates

Running the Mondrian process from time 0 to some terminal lifetime Λ thus sweeps through feature spaces approximating all Laplace kernels with lifetimes $\lambda \in [0, \Lambda]$. More concretely, we start with $\lambda = 0$ and ϕ the feature map corresponding to M trivial partitions, i.e., for any data point $\mathbf{x}$, the vector $\phi(\mathbf{x})$ has length M and all entries set to the normalizer $M^{-1/2}$. As we increase λ, at discrete time points new cuts appear in the M Mondrian samples used in constructing ϕ. Suppose that at some time λ, the partition cell corresponding to the c-th feature in ϕ is split into two by a new cut that first appeared at this time λ. We update the feature map ϕ by removing the c-th feature and appending two new features, one for each partition cell created by the split. See Figure 4 for an example with $M = 1$.

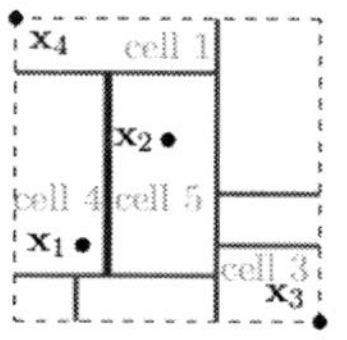

$\mathbf{x}$	$\phi(\mathbf{x})^T$
$\mathbf{x}_1$	[0 *1* 0 **1** **0**]
$\mathbf{x}_2$	[0 *1* 0 **0** **1**]
$\mathbf{x}_3$	[0 *0* 1 **0** **0**]
$\mathbf{x}_4$	[1 *0* 0 **0** **0**]

Figure 4: A new cut (shown in thick blue) appeared, splitting cell $c = 2$ (cf. Figure 3) into two new cells $c = 4$ and $c = 5$. The table shows the update to ϕ, with the removed feature in gray italics and the two new features in bold blue.

This procedure allows us to approximate all Laplace kernels with lifetimes $\lambda \in [0, \Lambda]$ without having to resample new feature spaces for each lifetime. The total computational cost is the same (up to a multiplicative constant) as of constructing a single feature space just for the terminal lifetime Λ. This is because a strictly binary tree with $C^{(m)}$ leaves (partition cells in the m-th Mondrian sample at time Λ) contains at most $C^{(m)} - 1$ internal nodes (features that had to be removed at some time point $\lambda < \Lambda$).

4.2 LINEAR LEARNER RETRAINING

Evaluating suitability of a lifetime (inverse kernel width) λ requires training and evaluating a linear model in the feature space implied by ϕ. This can also be done more efficiently than retraining a new model from scratch every time a new cut is added and ϕ updated. We discuss the example of ridge regression with exact solutions, and a general case of models trainable using gradient descent methods.

4.2.1 Ridge regression

The MAP weights of the primal ridge regression problem are $\hat{\mathbf{w}} = \mathbf{A}^{-1}\mathbf{\Phi}^T\mathbf{y}$, where $\mathbf{A} := (\mathbf{\Phi}^T\mathbf{\Phi} + \delta^2\mathbf{I}_C)$ is the regularized feature covariance matrix and δ^2 is the regularization hyperparameter. Instead of inverting $\mathbf{A}$, it is numerically more stable to work with its Cholesky factor $\text{chol}(\mathbf{A})$ [Seeger, 2003]. Phrasing the problem as Bayesian linear regression with, say, observation noise variance $\sigma_y^2 = \delta^2$ and prior weights variance $\sigma_w^2 = 1$, we can also obtain the log marginal likelihood $\mathcal{L}(\lambda)$ of the form

$$\mathcal{L}(\lambda) = -\frac{\|\mathbf{y} - \mathbf{\Phi}\hat{\mathbf{w}}\|_2^2}{2\delta^2} - \frac{\|\hat{\mathbf{w}}\|_2^2}{2} - \frac{1}{2}\ln\det\mathbf{A} + \text{const},$$

where the dependence on λ is implicit through ϕ.

When a new cut appears in one of the M Mondrian samples and ϕ is updated by deleting the c-th feature and appending two new ones, the corresponding update to the regularized feature covariance matrix $\mathbf{A}$ is to delete its c-th row and c-th column, and append two new rows and columns. Then both $\mathbf{A}^{-1}$ and $\text{chol}(\mathbf{A})$ can be appropriately updated in $\mathcal{O}(C^2)$ time, faster than $\mathcal{O}(C^3)$ recomputation from scratch. Updating the Cholesky factor when the c-th row and column are removed is slightly involved but can be achieved by first permuting the rows and columns so that the ones to be removed are the last ones [Seeger, 2004], after which the Cholesky factor is updated by deleting its last row and column. If C is the number of features at the terminal lifetime Λ, this $\mathcal{O}(C^2)$ update is performed $\mathcal{O}(C)$ times, for a total computational cost $\mathcal{O}(C^3)$. Note that performing the inversion or Cholesky factorization at just the terminal lifetime Λ would have the same time complexity.

After updating $\mathbf{A}^{-1}$ or $\text{chol}(\mathbf{A})$, the optimal weights $\hat{\mathbf{w}}$ can be updated in $\mathcal{O}(C^2 + N)$ time and the determinant of $\mathbf{A}$ required for the marginal likelihood $\mathcal{L}(\lambda)$ can be obtained from $\text{chol}(\mathbf{A})$ as the squared product of its diagonal elements in $\mathcal{O}(C)$ time. Exploiting sparsity of ϕ, evaluating the model on N_{test} data points takes $\mathcal{O}(N_{\text{test}}M)$ time.

Finally, we note that computing the marginal likelihood $\mathcal{L}(\lambda)$ for all $\lambda \in [0, \Lambda]$ and combining it with a prior $p(\lambda)$ supported on $[0, \Lambda]$ allows Bayesian inference over the kernel width λ^{-1}. We refer to Supplement B for more details.

4.2.2 Models trainable using gradient descent

Consider a linear model trained using a gradient descent method. If (an approximation to) the optimal weight vector $\mathbf{w}$ is available and then ϕ is updated by removing the c-th feature and appending two new features, a natural way of reinitializing the weights for subsequent gradient descent iterations is to remove the c-th entry of $\mathbf{w}$ and append two new entries, both set to the removed value (as points in the split cell are partitioned into the two new cells, this preserves all model predictions). Note that we have the freedom of choosing the number of gradient descent iterations after each cut is added, and we can opt to only evaluate the model (on a validation set, say) at several λ values on the first pass through $[0, \Lambda]$. One iteration of stochastic gradient descent takes $O(M)$ time thanks to sparsity of ϕ.

This efficient kernel width selection procedure can be especially useful with models where hyperparameters cannot be tweaked by marginal likelihood optimization (e.g., SVM).

5 ONLINE LEARNING

In this section, we describe how the Mondrian kernel can be used for online learning. When a new data point $\mathbf{x}_{N+1} \in \mathbb{R}^D$ arrives, incorporating it into M existing Mondrian samples (using the conditional Mondrian algorithm discussed in section 2.4) can create $0 \leq k \leq M$ new non-empty partition cells, increasing the dimensionality of the feature map ϕ. We set the new features to 0 for all previous data points $\mathbf{x}_1, \ldots, \mathbf{x}_N$.

In our running example of ridge regression, exact primal updates can again be carried out efficiently. The inverse $\mathbf{A}^{-1}$ or Cholesky factor $\text{chol}(\mathbf{A})$ of the regularized feature covariance matrix $\mathbf{A}$ can be updated in two steps:

1. extend $\mathbf{A}^{-1}$ or $\text{chol}(\mathbf{A})$ to incorporate the k new features (set to 0 for all existing data points) in $\mathcal{O}(C^2)$
2. incorporate the new data point $\mathbf{x}_{N+1}$, which is now a simple rank-1 update on $\mathbf{A}$, so $\mathbf{A}^{-1}$ or $\text{chol}(\mathbf{A})$ can again be updated efficiently in $\mathcal{O}(C^2)$ time

We refer to Supplement C for more details.

With gradient descent trainable models, we maintain (an approximation to) the optimal weights $\mathbf{w}$ directly. When a new data point arrives, we expand the dimensionality of ϕ as described above. The previously optimal weights can be padded with 0's in any newly added dimensions, and then passed to the gradient descent method as initialization.

6 LINK TO MONDRIAN FOREST

We contrast Mondrian kernel with Mondrian forest [Lakshminarayanan et al., 2014, 2016], another non-linear learning method based on the Mondrian process. They both start by sampling M independent Mondrians on $\mathbb{R}^D$ to provide M independent partitions of the data. However, these partitions are then used differently in the two models:

- In a Mondrian forest, parameters of predictive distributions in each tree are fitted independently of all other trees. The prediction of the forest is the average prediction among the M trees.
- With Mondrian kernel, the weights of all random features are fitted jointly by a linear learning method.

Let $C^{(m)}$ count the leaves (non-empty partition cells) in the m-th Mondrian sample and let $C = \sum_{m=1}^{M} C^{(m)}$ be the total number of leaves. Let $\phi_n^{(m)} := \phi^{(m)}(\mathbf{x}_n) \in \mathbb{R}^{C^{(m)}}$ be the indicator of the partition cell in the m-th sample into which the n-th data point falls (as in section 3.1). Also, as in equation (2), let $\phi_n := \phi(\mathbf{x}_n) \in \mathbb{R}^C$ be the normalized concatenated feature encoding of the n-th data point. Recall that each vector $\phi_n \in \mathbb{R}^C$ contains exactly M non-zero entries, all of which equal the normalizer $M^{-1/2}$.

For simplicity, we restrict our attention to ridge regression in this section and compare the learning objective functions of Mondrian kernel and Mondrian forest.

6.1 MONDRIAN KERNEL OBJECTIVE

The primal ridge regression problem in the feature space implied by ϕ is

$$\min_{\mathbf{w} \in \mathbb{R}^C} \sum_{n=1}^{N} (y_n - \mathbf{w}^T \phi_n)^2 + \delta^2 \|\mathbf{w}\|_2^2.$$

Decomposing $\mathbf{w} = M^{-1/2}[\mathbf{w}^{(1)T} \cdots \mathbf{w}^{(M)T}]^T$, so that each (rescaled) subvector $\mathbf{w}^{(m)}$ corresponds to features from the m-th Mondrian, denoting by $\hat{y}_n^{(m)} := \mathbf{w}^{(m)T} \phi_n^{(m)}$

the "contribution" of the m-th Mondrian to the prediction at the n-th data point, and writing $\text{loss}(y, \hat{y}) := (y - \hat{y})^2$, the Mondrian kernel objective function can be restated as

$$\min_{\mathbf{w} \in \mathbb{R}^C} \sum_{n=1}^{N} \text{loss}\left(y_n, \frac{1}{M} \sum_{m=1}^{M} \hat{y}_n^{(m)}\right) + \delta^2 \|\mathbf{w}\|_2^2. \quad (3)$$

6.2 MONDRIAN FOREST OBJECTIVE

Assuming a factorizing Gaussian prior over the leaves in each Mondrian tree (i.e., without the hierarchical smoothing used by Lakshminarayanan et al. [2016]), the predictive mean parameters $\mathbf{w}^{(m)}$ in the leaves of the m-th Mondrian tree are fitted by minimizing

$$\min_{\mathbf{w}^{(m)} \in \mathbb{R}^{C^{(m)}}} \sum_{n=1}^{N} (y_n - \mathbf{w}^{(m)T} \phi_n^{(m)})^2 + \gamma^2 \|\mathbf{w}^{(m)}\|_2^2$$

where γ^2 is the ratio of noise and prior variance in the predictive model. The parameters $\mathbf{w}^{(m)}$ are disjoint for different trees, so these M independent optimization problems are equivalent to minimizing the average of the M individual objectives. Writing $\hat{y}_n^{(m)} := \mathbf{w}^{(m)T} \phi_n^{(m)}$ for the m-th tree's prediction at the n-th data point and concatenating the parameters $\mathbf{w} := M^{-1/2} [\mathbf{w}^{(1)T} \cdots \mathbf{w}^{(M)T}]^T$, the Mondrian forest objective can be stated as

$$\min_{\mathbf{w} \in \mathbb{R}^C} \sum_{n=1}^{N} \frac{1}{M} \sum_{m=1}^{M} \text{loss}(y_n, \hat{y}_n^{(m)}) + \gamma^2 \|\mathbf{w}\|_2^2. \quad (4)$$

6.3 DISCUSSION

Comparing (3) and (4), we see that subject to regularization parameters (priors) chosen compatibly, the two objectives only differ in the contribution of an individual data point n to the total loss:

$$\text{Mondrian kernel:} \quad \text{loss}\left(y_n, \frac{1}{M} \sum_{m=1}^{M} \hat{y}_n^{(m)}\right)$$

$$\text{Mondrian forest:} \quad \frac{1}{M} \sum_{m=1}^{M} \text{loss}(y_n, \hat{y}_n^{(m)})$$

Specifically, the difference is in the order in which the averaging $\frac{1}{M} \sum_{m=1}^{M}$ over Mondrian samples/trees and the nonlinear loss function are applied. In both models predictions are given by $\hat{y} = \frac{1}{M} \sum_{m=1}^{M} \hat{y}^{(m)}$, so the Mondrian kernel objective is consistent with the aim of minimizing empirical loss on the training data, while the forest objective minimizes average loss across trees, not the loss of the actual prediction (when $M > 1$) [Ren et al., 2015].

Ren et al. [2015] address this inconsistency between learning and prediction by proposing to extend random forests with a *global refinement* step that optimizes all tree parameters jointly, minimizing the empirical training loss. Our approximation of the Laplace kernel via the Mondrian kernel can be interpreted as implementing this joint parameter fitting step on top of Mondrian forest, revealing a new connection between random forests and kernel methods.

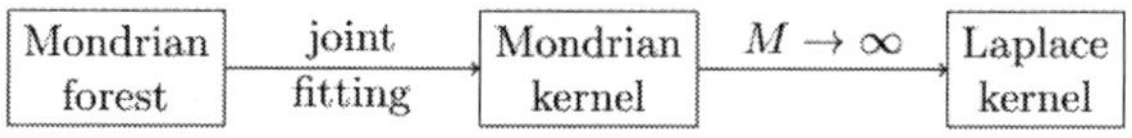

7 RELATED WORK

The idea of Rahimi and Recht [2007] to approximate shift-invariant kernels by constructing random features has been further developed by Le et al. [2013] and Yang et al. [2015], providing a faster method of constructing the random features when the input dimension D is high. The fast method of Dai et al. [2014] can adapt the number of random features, making it better-suited for streaming data. To the best of our knowledge, these methods require random features to be reconstructed from scratch for each new kernel width value; however, our solution allows us to efficiently learn this hyperparameter for the Laplace kernel.

Decision forests are popular for black-box classification and regression thanks to their competitive accuracy and computational efficiency. The most popular variants are Breiman's Random Forest [Breiman, 2001] and Extremely Randomized Trees [Geurts et al., 2006]. Breiman [2000] established a link between the Laplace kernel and random forests with an infinite number of trees, but unlike our work, made two additional strong assumptions, namely infinite data and a uniform distribution of features. From a computational perspective, Shen et al. [2006] approximated evaluation of an isotropic kernel using kd-trees, reducing computational complexity as well as memory requirements. Davies and Ghahramani [2014] constructed 'supervised' kernels using random forests and demonstrated that this can lead to linear-time inference. We refer to [Scornet, 2015] for a recent discussion on the connection between decision forests and kernel methods.

A key difference between decision forests and kernel methods is whether parameters are fit independently or jointly. In decision forests, the leaf node parameters for each tree are fit independently, whereas the weights of random features are fit jointly. Scornet [2015] shows that random forests can be interpreted as adaptive kernel estimates and discusses the theoretical properties of fitting parameters jointly. Ren et al. [2015] propose to extend random forests with a *global refinement* step, optimizing all tree parameters jointly to minimize empirical training loss.

The proposed Mondrian kernel establishes a link between Mondrian trees and Laplace kernel for finite data, without any assumptions on the distribution of the features. Unlike prior work, we exploit this connection to construct an adaptive random feature approximation and efficiently learn the kernel width.

8 EXPERIMENTS

We conducted three sets of experiments, with these goals:

1. verify that Mondrian kernel approximates the Laplace kernel, and compare to other random feature generation schemes (Section 8.1);
2. demonstrate usefulness of our efficient kernel width selection procedure, showing that it can quickly learn a suitable kernel width from data (Section 8.2); and
3. empirically compare the Mondrian kernel and Mondrian forests, supporting the insight into their relationship from Section 6 (Section 8.3).

With the exception of two experiments on synthetic data, we carried out our evaluation on the CPU dataset from [Rahimi and Recht, 2007], containing $N = 6554$ training and $N_{\text{test}} = 819$ test points with $D = 21$ attributes. Note that the CPU dataset is an adversarial choice here, as Rahimi and Recht [2007] report that random Fourier features perform better than binning schemes on this task. In all experiments, the ridge regularization constant was set to $\delta^2 = 10^{-4}$, the value used by Rahimi and Recht [2007], and the primal optimization problems were solved using stochastic gradient descent.

8.1 LAPLACE KERNEL APPROXIMATION

First we examined the absolute kernel approximation error $|k_\infty(\cdot,\cdot) - k_M(\cdot,\cdot)|$ directly. To this end, we sampled $N = 100$ data points uniformly at random in the unit square $[0,1]^2$ and computed the maximum absolute error over all N^2 pairs of points. The Laplace kernel k_∞ and Mondrian kernels k_M had a common lifetime (inverse width) $\lambda = 10$, so that several widths fit into the input domain $[0,1]^2$. We repeated the experiment 5 times for each value of M, showing the results in Figure 5. We plot the maximum error against the number M of non-zero features per data point, which is relevant for solvers such as Pegasos SVM [Shalev-Shwartz et al., 2007], whose running time scales with the number of non-zero features per data point. Under this metric, the Mondrian kernel and Random binning converged to the Laplace kernel faster than random Fourier features, showing that in some cases they can be a useful option. (The error of Random Fourier features would decrease faster when measured against the *total* number of features, as Mondrian kernel and Random binning generate sparse feature expansions.)

Second, we examined the approximation error indirectly via test set error on the CPU dataset. We repeated the experiment 5 times for each value of M and show the results in Figure 6. Even though Fourier features are better suited to this task, for a fast approximation with few ($M < 15$) non-zero features per data point, random binning and Mondrian kernel are still able to outperform the Fourier features.

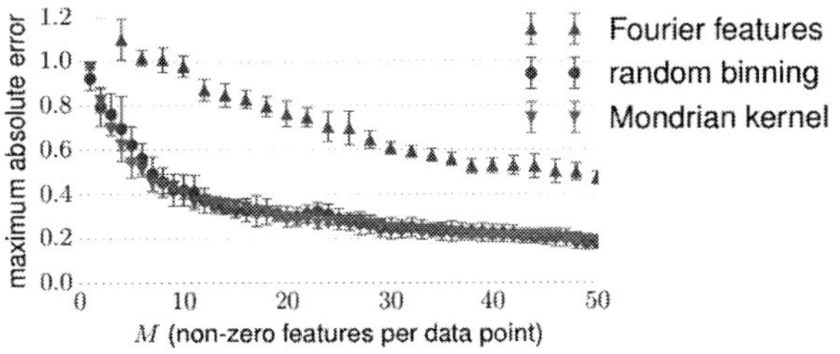

Figure 5: Maximum absolute kernel approximation error on all pairs of $N = 100$ data points in $[0,1]^2$.

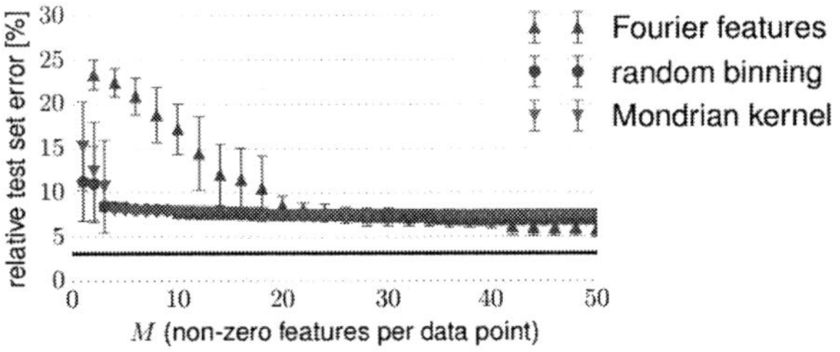

Figure 6: Test set error on the CPU dataset. The horizontal line at 3.1% indicates the error achieved with an exact, but expensive computation using the Laplace kernel.

8.2 FAST KERNEL WIDTH LEARNING

First, using a synthetic regression dataset generated from a Laplace kernel with known ground truth lifetime $\lambda_0 = 10$, we verified that the lifetime could be recovered using our kernel width selection procedure from Section 4. To this end, we let the procedure run until a terminal lifetime $\Lambda = 100$ and plotted the error on a held-out validation set as a function of the lifetime λ. The result in Figure 7 shows that the ground truth kernel lifetime $\lambda_0 = 10$ was recovered within an order of magnitude by selecting the lifetime $\hat{\lambda}$ minimizing validation set error. Moreover, this value of $\hat{\lambda}$ led to excellent performance on an independent test set.

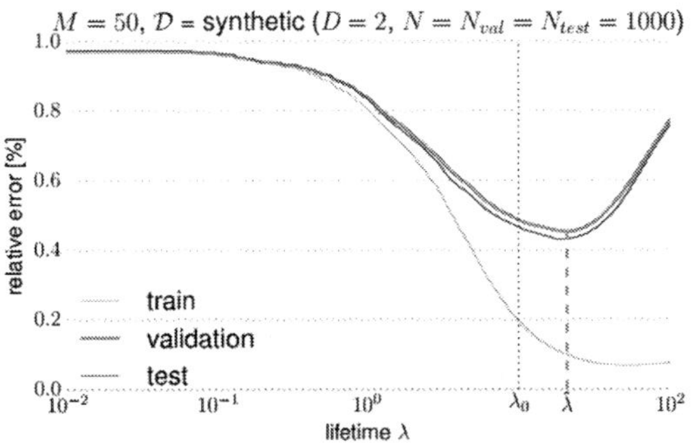

Figure 7: Recovering the ground truth lifetime $\lambda_0 = 10$ by selecting the value $\hat{\lambda} \approx 19$ minimizing validation set error.

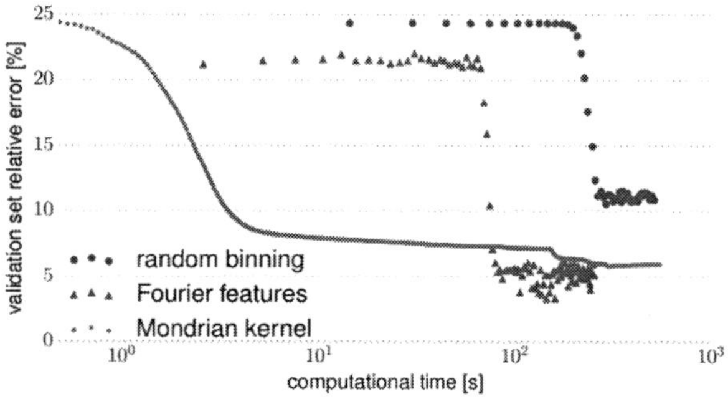

Figure 8: Validation set error as a function of computation time. Even though Fourier features are better suited to the CPU dataset [Rahimi and Recht, 2007] and eventually outperform the Mondrian kernel, the latter discovers suitable kernel widths at least an order of magnitude faster.

Second, we evaluated our kernel width selection procedure on the CPU dataset in order to demonstrate its practical usefulness. While the Mondrian kernel allows to efficiently sweep through lifetimes λ, Fourier features and random binning need to be reconstructed and retrained for each attempted lifetime value. We started the Fourier features and random binning at $\lambda = 1$, and in each step, we either doubled the maximum lifetime or halved the minimum lifetime considered so far, based on which direction seemed more promising. Once a good performing lifetime was found, we further optimized using a binary search procedure. All schemes were set to generate $M = 350$ non-zero features per datapoint. Figure 8 shows the performance of each scheme on a held-out validation set as a function of computation time. The result suggests that our kernel width learning procedure can be used to discover suitable lifetimes (inverse kernel widths) at least an order of magnitude faster than random Fourier features or random binning.

8.3 MONDRIAN KERNEL VS FOREST

We compared the performance of Mondrian kernel and "Mondrian forest" (quotes due to omission of hierarchical smoothing) based on the same $M = 50$ Mondrian samples, using the CPU dataset and varying the lifetime λ. Recall that higher values of λ lead to more refined Mondrian partitions, allowing more structure in the data to be modeled, but also increasing the risk of overfitting. Figure 9 shows that Mondrian kernel exploits the joint fitting of parameters corresponding to different trees and achieves a lower test error at lower lifetime values, thus producing a more compact solution based on simpler partitions. Figure 10 shows the parameter values learned by Mondrian kernel and Mondrian forest at the lifetime $\lambda = 2 \times 10^{-6}$. The distribution of weights learned by Mondrian kernel is more peaked around 0, as the joint fiting allows achieving more extreme predictions by adding together several smaller weights.

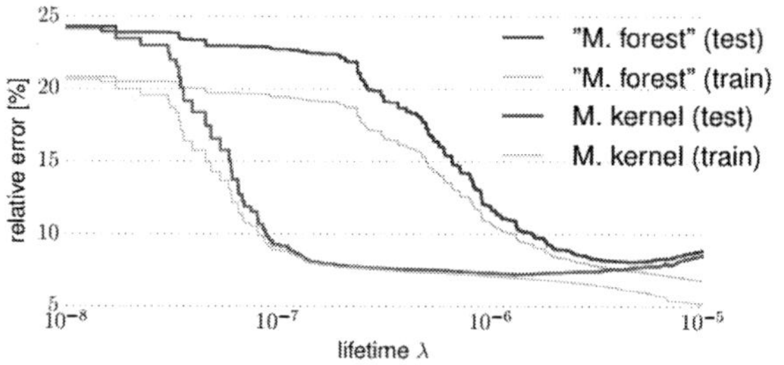

Figure 9: Comparison of Mondrian kernel and Mondrian forest models based on the same set of Mondrian samples.

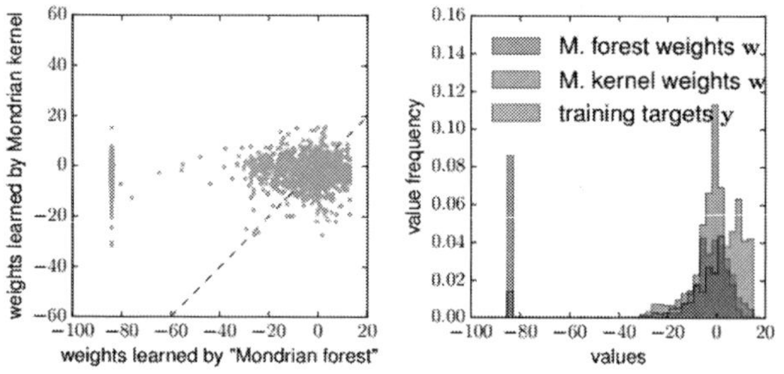

Figure 10: Weights learned by Mondrian forest and Mondrian kernel at the lifetime $\lambda = 2 \times 10^{-6}$ in Figure 9.

9 CONCLUSION

We presented the Mondrian kernel, a fast approximation to the Laplace kernel that admits efficient kernel width selection. When a different kernel or a different approximation is used, our procedure can provide a fast and simple way of initializing the kernel width for further optimization. While a Gaussian kernel is often considered a default choice, in many situations it imposes an inappropriately strong smoothness assumption on the modelled function and the Laplace kernel may in fact be a preferable option.

Our approach revealed a novel link between the Mondrian process and the Laplace kernel. We leave the discovery of similar links involving other kernels for future work.

Acknowledgements

We would like to thank Nilesh Tripuraneni for useful discussions. Part of this research was carried out while MB was at the University of Oxford. BL gratefully acknowledges generous funding from the Gatsby Charitable Foundation. ZG acknowledges funding from the Alan Turing Institute, Google, Microsoft Research and EPSRC Grant EP/N014162/1. DMR is supported by an NSERC Discovery Grant. YWT's research leading to these results has received funding from the European Research Council under the European Union's Seventh Framework Programme (FP7/2007-2013) ERC grant agreement no. 617071.

References

L. Breiman. Some infinity theory for predictor ensembles. Technical report, University of California at Berkeley, 2000.

L. Breiman. Random forests. *Mach. Learn.*, 45:5–32, 2001.

A. Criminisi, J. Shotton, and E. Konukoglu. Decision forests: A unified framework for classification, regression, density estimation, manifold learning and semi-supervised learning. *Found. Trends Comput. Graphics and Vision*, 2012.

B. Dai, B. Xie, N. He, Y. Liang, A. Raj, M.-F. F. Balcan, and L. Song. Scalable kernel methods via doubly stochastic gradients. In *Adv. Neural Information Proc. Systems (NIPS)*, 2014.

A. Davies and Z. Ghahramani. The random forest kernel and other kernels for big data from random partitions. *arXiv preprint arXiv:1402.4293v1*, 2014.

P. Geurts, D. Ernst, and L. Wehenkel. Extremely randomized trees. *Mach. Learn.*, 63(1):3–42, 2006.

B. Lakshminarayanan, D. M. Roy, and Y. W. Teh. Mondrian forests: Efficient online random forests. In *Adv. Neural Information Proc. Systems (NIPS)*, 2014.

B. Lakshminarayanan, D. M. Roy, and Y. W. Teh. Mondrian forests for large scale regression when uncertainty matters. In *Int. Conf. Artificial Intelligence Stat. (AISTATS)*, 2016.

Q. Le, T. Sarlós, and A. Smola. Fastfood-approximating kernel expansions in loglinear time. In *Proc. Int. Conf. Mach. Learn. (ICML)*, 2013.

A. Rahimi and B. Recht. Random features for large-scale kernel machines. In *Adv. Neural Information Proc. Systems (NIPS)*, 2007.

S. Ren, X. Cao, Y. Wei, and J. Sun. Global refinement of random forest. In *Proc. IEEE Conference on Computer Vision and Pattern Recognition*, pages 723–730, 2015.

D. M. Roy. *Computability, inference and modeling in probabilistic programming*. PhD thesis, Massachusetts Institute of Technology, 2011.

D. M. Roy and Y. W. Teh. The Mondrian process. In *Adv. Neural Information Proc. Systems (NIPS)*, 2009.

B. Schölkopf and A. J. Smola. *Learning with Kernels: Support Vector Machines, Regularization, Optimization, and Beyond*. MIT Press, Cambridge, MA, USA, 2001. ISBN 978-0-262-19475-4.

E. Scornet. Random forests and kernel methods. *arXiv preprint arXiv:1502.03836v2*, 2015.

M. Seeger. *Bayesian Gaussian Process Models: PAC-Bayesian Generalisation Error Bounds and Sparse Approximations*. PhD thesis, University of Edinburgh, 2003.

M. Seeger. Low rank updates for the Cholesky decomposition. Technical report, University of California at Berkeley, 2004.

S. Shalev-Shwartz, Y. Singer, and N. Srebro. Pegasos: Primal Estimated sub-GrAdient SOlver for SVM. In *Proc. Int. Conf. Mach. Learn. (ICML)*, 2007.

Y. Shen, A. Ng, and M. Seeger. Fast Gaussian process regression using KD-trees. In *Adv. Neural Information Proc. Systems (NIPS)*, 2006.

Z. Yang, A. J. Smola, L. Song, and A. G. Wilson. A la Carte - Learning Fast Kernels. In *Int. Conf. Artificial Intelligence Stat. (AISTATS)*, 2015.

Sequential Nonparametric Testing with the Law of the Iterated Logarithm

Akshay Balsubramani
University of California, San Diego

Aaditya Ramdas
University of California, Berkeley

Abstract

We propose a new algorithmic framework for sequential hypothesis testing with i.i.d. data, which includes A/B testing, nonparametric two-sample testing, and independence testing as special cases. It is novel in several ways: (a) it takes linear time and constant space to compute on the fly, (b) it has the same power guarantee (up to a small factor) as a non-sequential version of the test with the same computational constraints, and (c) it accesses only as many samples as are required – its stopping time adapts to the unknown difficulty of the problem. All our test statistics are constructed to be zero-mean martingales under the null hypothesis, and the rejection threshold is governed by a uniform non-asymptotic law of the iterated logarithm (LIL). For nonparametric two-sample mean testing, we also provide a finite-sample power analysis, and the first non-asymptotic stopping time analysis for this class of problems. We verify our predictions for type I and II errors and stopping times using simulations.

1 INTRODUCTION

Nonparametric statistical decision theory poses the problem of making a decision between a null (H_0) and alternate (H_1) hypothesis over a dataset with the aim of controlling both false positives and false negatives (in statistics terms, maximizing power while controlling type I error), all without making assumptions about the distribution of the data being analyzed. Such hypothesis testing is based on a "stochastic proof by contradiction" – the null hypothesis is thought of by default to be true, and is rejected only if the observed data are statistically very unlikely under the null.

There is increasing interest in solving such problems in a "big data" regime, in which the sample size N can be huge. We present a sequential testing framework for these problems that is particularly suitable for two related scenarios prevalent in many applications:

1) The dataset is extremely large and high-dimensional, so even a single pass through it is prohibitive.
2) The data is arriving as a stream, and decisions must be made with minimal storage.

Sequential tests have long been considered strong in such settings. Such a test accesses the data in an online/streaming fashion, assessing after every new datapoint whether it *then* has enough evidence to reject the null hypothesis. However, prior work tends to be univariate or parametric or asymptotic, while we are the first to provide non-asymptotic guarantees on multivariate nonparametric problems.

To elaborate on our motivations, suppose we have a gigantic amount of data from each of two unknown distributions, enough to detect even a minute difference in their means $\mu_1 - \mu_2$ if it exists. Further suppose that, unknown to us, deciding whether the means are equal is actually statistically easy ($|\mu_1 - \mu_2|$ is large), meaning that one can conclude $\mu_1 \neq \mu_2$ with high confidence by just considering a tiny fraction of the dataset. Can we take advantage of this, despite our ignorance of it?

A naive solution would be to discard most of the data and run a batch (offline) test on a small subset. However, we do not know how hard the problem is, and hence do not know how large a subset will suffice — sampling too little data might lead to incorrectly not rejecting the null, and sampling too much would unnecessarily waste computational resources. If we somehow knew $\mu_1 - \mu_2$, we would want to choose the fewest number of samples (say n^*) to reject the null while controlling type I error at some target level.

1.1 OVERVIEW OF OUR APPROACH

Our sequential test solves the problem by automatically stopping after seeing about n^* samples, while still controlling type I and II errors almost as well as the equivalent linear-time batch test. Without knowing the true problem difficulty, we are able to detect it with virtually no computational or statistical penalty. We devise and formally analyze a sequential algorithm for a variety of problems, starting with a basic test of the bias of a coin, and developing this to nonparametric two-sample mean testing, with further extensions to general nonparametric two-sample and independence testing.

Our proposed procedure only keeps track of a single scalar test statistic, which we construct to be a zero-mean random walk under the null hypothesis. It is used to test the null hypothesis each time a new data point is processed. A major statistical issue is dealing with the apparent multiple hypothesis testing problem – if our algorithm observes its first rejection of the null at time t, it might raise suspicions of being a false rejection, because $t-1$ hypothesis tests were already conducted and the t-th may have been rejected purely by chance. Applying some kind of multiple testing correction, like the Bonferroni or Benjamini-Hochberg procedure, is exceedingly conservative and produces very suboptimal results over a large number of tests. However, since the random walk moves only a relatively small amount every iteration, the tests are far from independent.

Formalizing this intuition requires adapting a classical probability result, the law of the iterated logarithm (LIL), with which we control for type I error (when H_0 is true). The LIL can be described as follows. Imagine tossing a fair coin, assigning $+1$ to heads and -1 to tails, and keeping track of the sum S_t of t coin flips. The LIL asserts that asymptotically, S_t always remains bounded between $\pm\sqrt{2t \ln \ln t}$ (and this "envelope" is tight).

When H_1 is true, we prove that the sequential algorithm does not need the whole dataset as a batch algorithm would, but automatically stops after processing just "enough" data points to detect H_1, depending on the unknown difficulty of the problem being solved. The near-optimal nature of this adaptive type II error control (when H_1 is true) is again due to the remarkable LIL.

As alluded to earlier, all of our test statistics can be thought of as random walks, which behave like S_t under H_0. The LIL then characterizes how such a random walk behaves under H_0 – our algorithm will keep observing new data since the random walk values will simply bounce around within the LIL envelope. Under H_1, the random walk is designed to have nonzero mean, and hence will eventually stray outside the LIL envelope, at which point the process stops and rejects the null hypothesis.

For practically applying this argument to finite samples and reasoning about type II error and stopping times, we cannot use the classical asymptotic form of the LIL typically stated in textbooks such as Feller (1950), instead adapting a finite-time extension of the LIL by Balsubramani (2015). As we will see, the technical contribution is necessary to investigate the stopping time, and control type I and II errors non-asymptotically *and* uniformly over all t.

In summary, our sequential testing framework has the following properties:

(A) Under H_0, it controls type I error, using a finite-time LIL computable in terms of empirical variance.

(B) Under H_1, and with type II error controlled at a target level, it automatically stops after seeing the same number of points as the corresponding computationally-constrained oracle batch algorithm.

(C) Each update takes $O(d)$ time and constant memory.

In later sections, we develop formal versions of these statements. The statistical observations, particularly the stopping time, follow from the finite-time LIL through simple concentration of measure arguments that extend to very general sequential testing settings, but have seemingly remained unobserved in the literature for decades because of the finite-time LIL necessary to make them.

We begin by describing a sequential test for the bias of a coin in Section 2. We then provide a sequential test for nonparametric two-sample *mean* testing in Section 3. We run extensive simulations in Section 4 to bear out predictions of our theory, followed by a comparison to the extensive existing literature on the subject. We also include extensions to general nonparametric two-sample and independence testing problems, in the appendices. All proofs (and code for experiments) are deferred to the full version (Balsubramani and Ramdas (2015)).

2 DETECTING THE BIAS OF A COIN

This section will illustrate how a simple sequential test can perform statistically as well as the best batch test in hindsight, while automatically stopping essentially as soon as possible. We will show that such early stopping can be viewed as quite a general consequence of concentration of measure. Just for this section, let K represent a constant that may take different values on each appearance, but is always absolute.

Consider observing i.i.d. binary flips $A_1, A_2, \dots \in \{-1, +1\}$ of a coin, which may be fair or biased towards

```
Fix N and compute p_N
if S_N > p_N then
    Reject H_0
else
    Fail to reject H_0
```

```
Fix N
for n = 1 to N do
    Compute q_n
    if S_n > q_n then
        Reject H_0 and return
Fail to reject H_0
```

Figure 1: Batch (left) and sequential (right) tests.

$+1$, with $P(A_i = +1) = \rho$. We want to test for fairness, detecting unfairness as soon as possible. Formulated as a hypothesis test, we wish to test, for $\delta \in (0, \frac{1}{2}]$:

$$H_0 : \rho = \frac{1}{2} \quad \text{vs.} \quad H_1(\delta) : \rho = \frac{1}{2} + \delta$$

For any sample size n, the natural test statistic for this problem is $S_n = \sum_{i=1}^{n} A_i$. S_n is a (scaled) simple mean-zero random walk under H_0. A standard hypothesis testing approach to our problem is a basic *batch* test involving S_N, which tests for deviations from the null for a fixed sample size N (Fig. 1, left). A basic Hoeffding bound shows that

$$S_N \leq \sqrt{\frac{N}{2} \ln \frac{1}{\alpha}} =: p_N$$

with probability $\geq 1 - \alpha$ under the null, so type I error is controlled at level α :

$$P_{H_0}(\text{reject } H_0) = P_{H_0}(S_N > p_N) \leq e^{-2p_N^2/N} = \alpha.$$

2.1 A SEQUENTIAL TEST

The main test we propose will be a sequential test as in Fig. 1. It sees examples as they arrive one at a time, up to a large time N, the maximum sample size we can afford. The sequential test is defined with a sequence of positive thresholds $\{q_n\}_{n \in [N]}$. We show how to set q_n to justify statements (A) and (B) in Section 1.1.

Type I Error. Just as the batch threshold p_N is determined by controlling the type I error with a concentration inequality, the sequential test also chooses $q_1, \ldots, q_N$ to control the type I error at α:

$$P_{H_0}(\text{reject } H_0) = P_{H_0}(\exists n \leq N : S_n > q_n) \leq \alpha \quad (1)$$

This inequality concerns the uniform concentration over infinite tails of S_n, but what $\{q_n\}_{n \in [N]}$ satisfies it? Asymptotically, the answer is governed by a foundational result, the LIL:

Theorem 1 (Law of the iterated logarithm (Khinchin (1924))). *With probability* 1, $\limsup_{n \to \infty} \frac{S_n}{\sqrt{n \ln \ln n}} = \sqrt{2}$.

The LIL says that q_n should have a $\sqrt{n \ln \ln n}$ asymptotic dependence on n, but does not specify its α dependence.

Our sequential testing insights rely on a stronger non-asymptotic LIL proved in (Balsubramani (2015), Theorem 2): with probability at least $1 - \alpha$, we have $|S_n| \leq \sqrt{Kn \ln\left(\frac{\ln n}{\alpha}\right)} =: q_n$ simultaneously for *all* $n \geq K \ln(\frac{4}{\alpha}) := n_0$. This choice of q_n satisfies (1) for $n_0 \leq n \leq N$, and specifies the sequential test as in Fig. 1. (Choosing q_n this way is unimprovable in all parameters up to absolute constants (Balsubramani (2015))).

Type II Error. For practical purposes, $\sqrt{\ln \ln n} \leq \sqrt{\ln \ln N}$ can be treated as a small constant (even when $N = 10^{20}, \sqrt{\ln \ln N} < 2$). Hence, $q_N \approx p_N$ (more discussion in the appendices), and the power is:

$$P_{H_1(\delta)}(\exists n \leq N : S_n > q_n) \geq P_{H_1(\delta)}(S_N > q_N) \quad (2)$$
$$\approx P_{H_1(\delta)}(S_N > p_N) \quad (3)$$

So the sequential test is essentially as powerful as a batch test with N samples (and similarly the nth round of the sequential test is like an n-sample batch test).

Early Stopping. The standard motivation for using sequential tests is that they often require few samples to reject statistically distant alternatives. To investigate this with our working example, suppose N is large and the coin is actually biased, with a fixed unknown $\delta > 0$. Then, if we somehow had full knowledge of δ when using the batch test and wanted to ensure a desired type II error $\beta < 1$, we would use just enough samples $n_\beta^*(\delta)$ (written as n^* in context):

$$n_\beta^*(\delta) = \min\left\{n : P_{H_1(\delta)}(S_n \leq p_n) \leq \beta\right\} \quad (4)$$

so that for all $n \geq n_\beta^*(\delta)$, since $p_n = o(n)$,

$$\beta \geq P_{H_1(\delta)}(S_n \leq p_n) = P_{H_1(\delta)}(S_n - n\delta \leq p_n - n\delta)$$
$$\geq P_{H_1(\delta)}(S_n - n\delta \leq -Kn\delta) \quad (5)$$

Examining (5), note that $S_n - n\delta$ is a mean-zero random walk. Therefore, standard lower bounds for the binomial tail tell us that $n_\beta^*(\delta) \geq \frac{K \ln(1/\beta)}{\delta^2}$ suffices, and no test can statistically use much less than $n^*_\beta(\delta)$ samples under $H_1(\delta)$ to control type II error at β.

How many samples does the sequential test use? The quantity of interest is the test's stopping time τ, which is $< N$ when it rejects H_0 and N otherwise. In fact, the expected stopping time is close to n^* under any alternate hypothesis:

Theorem 2. *For any δ and any $\beta > 0$, there exist absolute constants K_1, K_2 such that*

$$\mathbb{E}_{H_1}[\tau] \le \left(1 + \frac{K_1 \beta^{K_2}}{\ln \frac{1}{\beta}}\right) n^*_\beta(\delta)$$

Theorem 2 shows that the sequential test stops roughly as soon as we could hope for, under any alternative δ, despite our ignorance of δ! We will revisit these ideas when presenting our two-sample sequential test later in Section 3.1.

2.2 DISCUSSION

Before moving to the two-sample testing setting, we note the generality of these ideas. Theorem 2 is proved for biased coin flips, but it uses only basic concentration of measure ideas: upper and lower bounds on the tails of a statistic that is a cumulative sum incremented each timestep. Many natural test statistics follow this scheme, particularly those that can be efficiently updated on the fly. Our main sequential two-sample test in the next section does also.

Theorem 2 is notable for its uniformity over δ and β. Note that q_n (and therefore the sequential test) are independent of both of these – we need only to set a target type I error bound α. Under any alternative $\delta > 0$, the theorem holds for all β simultaneously. As β decreases, $n^*_\beta(\delta)$ of course increases, but the leading multiplicative factor $\left(1 + \frac{K_1 \beta^{K_2}}{\ln \frac{1}{\beta}}\right)$ decreases. In fact, with an increasingly stringent $\beta \to 0$, we see that $\frac{\mathbb{E}_{H_1}[\tau]}{n^*} \to 1$; so the sequential test in fact stops closer to n^*, and hence τ is almost *deterministically* best possible. Indeed, the proof of Theorem 2 also shows that $P_{H_1}(\tau \ge n) \le e^{-Kn\delta^2}$, so the probability of lasting n steps falls off exponentially in n, and is therefore quite sharply concentrated near the optimum $n^*_\beta(\delta)$.

We formalize this precise line of reasoning completely non-asymptotically in an even stronger high-dimensional setting, in the analysis of our main two-sample test in the next section.

3 TWO-SAMPLE MEAN TESTING

In this section, we present our main sequential two-sample test. Assume that we have samples $X_1, \dots, X_n, \dots \sim P$ and $Y_1, \dots, Y_n, \dots \sim Q$, with P, Q being unknown arbitrary continuous distributions on $\mathbb{R}^d$ with means $\mu_1 = \mathbb{E}_{X\sim P}[X], \mu_2 = \mathbb{E}_{Y\sim Q}[Y]$, and we need to test

$$H_0 : \mu_1 = \mu_2 \qquad \text{vs.} \qquad H_1 : \mu_1 \ne \mu_2 \tag{6}$$

Denote covariances of P, Q by Σ_1, Σ_2 and $\Sigma := \frac{1}{2}(\Sigma_1 + \Sigma_2)$. Define $\delta := \mu_1 - \mu_2$ so that $\delta = 0$ under H_0. Let $\Phi(\cdot)$ denote the standard Gaussian CDF, and $[\ln\ln]_+(x) := \ln\ln[\max(x, e^e)]$.

3.1 A LINEAR-TIME SEQUENTIAL TEST

Our sequential test follows the scheme in Fig. 1, so we only need to specify a sequence of rejection thresholds q_n. To do this, we denote

$$h_i = (X_{2i-1} - Y_{2i-1})^\top (X_{2i} - Y_{2i}).$$

and define our sequential test statistic as the following *stochastic process* evolving with n:

$$T_n = \sum_{i=1}^{n} h_i.$$

Under H_0, $\mathbb{E}[h_i] = 0$, and T_n is a zero-mean random walk.

Proposition 1. $\mathbb{E}[T_n] = \mathbb{E}[h] = n\|\delta\|^2$, *and*

$$\operatorname{var}(T_n) = n \operatorname{var}(h) = n(4\operatorname{tr}(\Sigma^2) + 4\delta^\top \Sigma \delta) =: nV_0.$$

We assume – for now – that our data are bounded, i.e.

$$\|X\|, \|Y\| \le 1/2,$$

so that by the Cauchy-Schwarz inequality, w.p. 1,

$$|T_n - T_{n-1}| = |(X_{2n-1} - Y_{2n-1})^\top (X_{2n} - Y_{2n})| \le 1$$

Since T_n has bounded differences, it exhibits Gaussian-like concentration under the null. We examine the cumulative variance process of T_n under H_0,

$$\sum_{i=1}^{n} \mathbb{E}\left[(T_i - T_{i-1})^2 \mid h_{1:(i-1)}\right] = \sum_{i=1}^{n} \operatorname{var}(h_i) = nV_0$$

Using this, we can control the behavior of T_n under H_0.

Theorem 3 (Balsubramani (2015)). *Take any $\xi > 0$. Then with probability $\ge 1 - \xi$, for all n simultaneously,*

$$|T_n| < C_0(\xi) + \sqrt{2C_1 nV_0 [\ln\ln]_+(nV_0) + C_1 nV_0 \ln\left(\frac{4}{\xi}\right)}$$

where $C_0(\xi) = 3(e-2)e^2 + 2\left(1+\sqrt{\frac{1}{3}}\right)\ln\left(\frac{8}{\xi}\right)$, *and* $C_1 = 6(e-2)$.

Unfortunately, we cannot use the theorem directly to get computable deviation bounds for type I error control, because the covariance matrix Σ is unknown a priori. nV_0 must instead be estimated on the fly as part of the sequential test, and its estimate must be concentrated tightly and *uniformly over time*, so as not to present a statistical bottleneck if the test runs for a long time. We prove such a result, necessary for sequential testing, relating nV_0 to the empirical variance process $\widehat{V}_n = \sum_i h_i^2$.

Lemma 4. *With probability* $\geq 1-\xi$, *for all* n *simultaneously, there is an absolute constant* C_3 *such that*

$$nV_0 \leq C_3(\widehat{V}_n + C_0(\xi))$$

Its proof uses a self-bounding argument and is in the Appendix. Now, we can combine these to prove a novel uniform *empirical* Bernstein inequality to (practically) establish concentration of T_n under H_0.

Theorem 5 (Uniform Empirical Bernstein Inequality for Random Walks). *Take any* $\xi > 0$. *Then with probability* $\geq 1-\xi$, *for all* n *simultaneously,*

$$|T_n| < C_0(\xi) + \sqrt{2\widehat{V}_n^* \left([\ln\ln]_+ \widehat{V}_n^* + \ln\left(\frac{4}{\xi}\right)\right)}$$

where $\widehat{V}_n^* := C_3(\widehat{V}_n + C_0(\xi))$, $C_0(\xi) = 3(e-2)e^2 + 2\left(1+\sqrt{\frac{1}{3}}\right)\ln\left(\frac{8}{\xi}\right)$ *and* C_3 *is an absolute constant.*

Its proof follows immediately from a union bound on Thm. 3 and Lem. 4. Thm. 5 depends on $\widehat{V}_n$, which is easily calculated by the algorithm on the fly in constant time per iteration. Ignoring constants for clarity, Thm. 5 effectively implies that our sequential test from Figure 1 controls type I error at α by setting

$$q_n \propto \ln\left(\frac{1}{\alpha}\right) + \sqrt{2\widehat{V}_n \ln\left(\frac{\ln \widehat{V}_n}{\alpha}\right)} \tag{7}$$

Practically, we suggest using the above threshold with a constant of 1.1 to guarantee type-I error approximately α (this is all one often wants anyway, since any particular choice of $\alpha = 0.05$ is anyway arbitrary). This is what we do in our experiments, with excellent success in simulations. For exact or conservative control, consider using a small constant multiple of the above threshold, such as 2.

The above sequential threshold is remarkable, because within the practically useful and simple expression lies a deep mathematical result – the uniform Bernstein LIL effectively involves a union bound for the error probability over an infinite sequence of times. Any other naive attempt to union bound the error probabilities for a possibly infinite sequential testing procedure will be too loose and hence too conservative. Furthermore, the classical LIL is known to be asymptotically tight including constants, and our non-asymptotic LIL is also tight up to small constant factors.

This type-I error control with an implicit infinite union bound surprisingly does not lead to a loss in power. Indeed, our statistic possesses essentially the same power as the corresponding linear-time batch two sample test, and also stops early for easy problems. We make this precise in the following two subsections.

3.2 A LINEAR-TIME BATCH TEST

Here we study a simple linear-time batch two-sample mean test, following the template in Fig. 1. Consider the linear-time statistic $T_N = \sum_{i=1}^{N} h_i$, where, as before, $h_i = (x_{2i-1} - y_{2i-1})^\top (x_{2i} - y_{2i})$. Note that the h_is are also i.i.d., and T_N relies on $2N$ data points from each distribution.

Let V_{N0}, V_{N1} be $\text{var}(T_N) = N\,\text{var}(h)$ under H_0, H_1 respectively. Recalling Proposition 1:

$$V_{N0} := NV_0 := 4N\,\text{tr}(\Sigma^2),$$
$$V_{N1} := NV_1 := N(4\,\text{tr}(\Sigma^2) + 4\delta^\top \Sigma\delta).$$

Then since T_N is a sum of i.i.d. variables, the central limit theorem (CLT) implies that (where $\xrightarrow{d}$ is convergence in distribution)

$$\frac{T_N}{\sqrt{V_{N0}}} \xrightarrow{d}_{H_0} \mathcal{N}(0,1) \tag{8a}$$

$$\frac{T_N - N\|\delta\|^2}{\sqrt{V_{N1}}} \xrightarrow{d}_{H_1} \mathcal{N}(0,1) \tag{8b}$$

Based on this information, our test rejects the null hypothesis whenever

$$T_N > \sqrt{V_{N0}}\, z_\alpha, \tag{9}$$

where z_α is the $1-\alpha$ quantile of the standard normal distribution. So Eq. (8a) ensures that

$$P_{H_0}\left(\frac{T_N}{\sqrt{V_{N0}}} > z_\alpha\right) \leq \alpha,$$

giving us type I error control under H_0.

In practice, we may not know V_{N0}, so we standardize the statistic using the empirical variance – since we assume N is large, these scalar variance estimates do not change the effective power analysis. For non-asymptotic type I error control, we can use an empirical Bernstein inequality (Maurer and Pontil, 2009, Thm. 11), based on an unbiased estimator of V_N. Specifically, the empirical variance of h_is ($\widehat{V}_N$) can be used to reject the null whenever

$$T_N > \sqrt{2\widehat{V}_N \ln(2/\alpha)} + \frac{7N\ln(2/\alpha)}{3(N-1)}. \quad (10)$$

Ignoring constants for clarity, the empirical Bernstein inequality effectively suggests that the batch test from Figure 1 will have type I error control of α on setting threshold

$$p_N \propto \ln\left(\frac{1}{\alpha}\right) + \sqrt{2\widehat{V}_N \ln\left(\frac{1}{\alpha}\right)} \quad (11)$$

For immediate comparison, we copy below the expression for q_n from Eq. (7):

$$q_n \propto \ln\left(\frac{1}{\alpha}\right) + \sqrt{2\widehat{V}_n\left(\ln\frac{\ln \widehat{V}_n}{\alpha}\right)}.$$

This similarity explains the optimal power and stopping time properties, detailed in the next subsection.

One might argue that if N is large, then $\widehat{V}_N \approx V_N$, and in this case we can simply derive the (asymptotic) power of the batch test given in Eq.(9) as

$$\begin{aligned} &P_{H_1}\left(\frac{T_N}{\sqrt{V_{N0}}} > z_\alpha\right) \quad (12)\\ &= P_{H_1}\left(\frac{T_N - N\|\delta\|^2}{\sqrt{V_{N1}}} > z_\alpha\sqrt{\frac{V_{N0}}{V_{N1}}} - \frac{N\|\delta\|^2}{\sqrt{V_{N1}}}\right)\\ &= \Phi\left(\frac{\sqrt{N}\|\delta\|^2}{\sqrt{8\,\mathrm{tr}(\Sigma^2) + 8\delta^\top\Sigma\delta}} - z_\alpha\sqrt{\frac{\mathrm{tr}(\Sigma^2)}{\mathrm{tr}(\Sigma^2) + \delta^\top\Sigma\delta}}\right) \end{aligned}$$

Note that the second term is a constant less than z_α. As a concrete example, when $\Sigma = \sigma^2 I$, and we denote the signal-to-noise ratio as $\Psi := \frac{\|\delta\|}{\sigma}$, then the power of the linear-time batch test is at least $\Phi\left(\frac{\sqrt{N}\Psi^2}{\sqrt{8d+8\Psi^2}} - z_\alpha\right)$.

3.3 POWER AND STOPPING TIME OF SEQUENTIAL TEST

The striking similarity of Eq. (11) and Eq. (7), mentioned in the previous subsection, is not coincidental. Indeed, both of these arise out of non-asymptotic versions of CLT-like control and LIL-like control, and we know that in the asymptotic regime for Bernoulli coin-flips, CLT thresholds and LIL threshold differ by just $\propto \sqrt{\ln\ln n}$ factors. Hence, it is not surprising to see the empirical Bernstein LIL match empirical Bernstein thresholds up to $\propto \sqrt{\ln\ln \widehat{V}_n}$ factors. Since the power of the sequential test is *at least* the probability of rejection at the very last step, and since $\sqrt{\ln\ln n} < 2$ even for $n = 10^{20}$, the power of the linear-time sequential and batch tests is essentially the same. However, a sequential test that rejects at the last step is of little practical interest, bringing us to the issue of early stopping.

Early Stopping. The argument is again identical to that Section 2, proving that $\mathbb{E}_{H_1}[\tau]$ is nearly optimal, and arbitrarily close to optimal as β tends to zero. Once more note that the "optimal" above refers to the performance of the oracle linear-time batch algorithm that was informed about the right number of points to subsample and use for the one-time batch test. Formally, let $n^*_\beta(\delta)$ denote this minimum sample size for the two-sample mean testing *batch* problem to achieve a power β, the * indicating that this is an oracle value, unknown to the user of the batch test. From Eq. (12), it is clear that for $N \geq \frac{8Tr(\Sigma^2)+8\delta^T\Sigma\delta}{\|\delta\|^4}(z_\beta + z_\alpha)^2$, the power becomes at least β. In other words,

$$n^*_\beta(\delta) \leq \frac{Tr(\Sigma^2) + \delta^T\Sigma\delta}{\|\delta\|^4} 8(z_\beta + z_\alpha)^2 \quad (13)$$

Theorem 6. *Under H_1, the sequential algorithm of Fig. 1 using q_n from Eq. (7) has expected stopping time $\propto n^*_\beta(\delta)$.*

For clarity, we simplify (7) and (11) by dropping the initial $\ln\left(\frac{1}{\alpha}\right)$ additive term since it is soon dominated by the second term and does not qualitatively affect the conclusion.

3.4 DISCUSSION

This section's arguments have given an illustration of the flexibility and great generality of the ideas we used to test the bias of the coin. In the two-sample setting, we simply design the statistic $T_N = \sum_{i=1}^n h_i$ to be a mean-zero random walk under the null. As in the coin's case, the LIL controls type I error, and the remaining arguments are identical because of the common concentration properties of all random walks.

Our test statistic T_N is chosen with several considerations in mind. First, the batch test is linear-time in the sample complexity, so we are comparing algorithms with the *same computational budget*, on a fair footing. There exist batch tests using U-statistics that have higher power than ours (Reddi et al. (2015)) for a given N, but they use more computational resources ($O(N^2)$ rather than $O(N)$).

Also, the batch statistic is a sum of random increments, a common way to write many hypothesis tests, and one that can be computed on the fly in the sequential setting. Note that T_N is a scalar, so our arguments do not change with d, and we inherit the favorable high-dimensional statistical performance of the statistic; Reddi et al. (2015) has more relevant discussion. The statistic also has been shown to have powerful generalizations in the recent statistics literature, which we discuss in the appendices.

Though we assume data scaled to have norm $\frac{1}{2}$ for convenience, this can be loosened. Any data with bounded norm $B > \frac{1}{2}$ can be rescaled by a factor $\frac{1}{B}$ just for the analysis, and then our results can be used. This results in an empirical Bernstein bound like Thm. 5, but of order $O\left(C_0(\xi) + \sqrt{\widehat{V}_n \ln\left(\frac{\ln(B\widehat{V}_n)}{\xi}\right)}\right)$. The dependence on B is very weak, and is negligible even when $B = \text{poly}(d)$.

In fact, we only require control of the higher moments (e.g. by Bernstein conditions, which generalize boundedness and sub-Gaussianity conditions) to prove the non-asymptotic Bernstein LIL in Balsubramani (2015), exactly as is the case for the usual Bernstein concentration inequalities for averages (Boucheron et al. (2013)). Therefore, our basic arguments hold for unbounded increments h_i as well. In fact, the LIL itself, as well as the non-asymptotic LIL bounds of Balsubramani (2015), apply to martingales – much more general versions of random walks capable of modeling dependence on the past history. Our ideas could conceivably be extended to this setting to devise more data-dependent tests, which would be interesting future work.

4 EMPIRICAL EVALUATION

In this section, we evaluate our proposed sequential test on synthetic data, to validate the predictions made by our theory concerning its type I/II errors and the stopping time.

We simulate data from two multivariate Gaussians ($d = 10$), motivated by our discussion at the end of Section 3.2: each Gaussian has covariance matrix $\Sigma = \sigma^2 I_d$, one has mean $\mu_1 = \mathbf{0}^d$ and the other has $\mu_2 = (\delta, 0, 0, \ldots, 0) \in \mathbb{R}^d$ for some $\delta \geq 0$. We keep $\sigma = 1$ here to keep the scale of the data roughly consistent with the biased-coin example, though we find the scaling of the data makes no practical difference, as we discussed.

4.1 RUNNING THE TEST AND TYPE I ERROR

Like typical hypothesis tests, ours is designed to control type I error. When implementing our algorithmic ideas, it suffices to set q_n as in (7), where the only unknown parameters are proportionality constants C, C_0: $q_n \propto C_0 + \sqrt{C\widehat{V}_n \left(\ln \frac{\ln \widehat{V}_n}{\alpha}\right)}$. The theory suggests that C, C_0 are absolute constants, and prescribes upper bounds for them, which can conceivably be loose because of the analytic techniques used (as Balsubramani (2015) discusses). On the other hand, in the asymptotic limit the bounds become tight; the empirical $\widehat{V}_n$ converges quickly to its mean V_n, and we know from second-moment versions of the LIL that $C = \sqrt{2}$ and $C_0 = 0$ are correct. However, as we consider smaller finite times, that bound must relax (at the extremely low $t = 1$ or 2 when flipping a fair coin, for instance).

Nevertheless, we find that in practice, for even moderate sample sizes like the ones we test here, the same reasonable constants suffice in all our experiments: $C = \sqrt{2}$ and $C_0 = \ln(\frac{1}{\alpha})$, with C_0 following Thm. 5 and similar fixed-sample Bennett bounds (Boucheron et al. (2013); Balsubramani (2015); also see the appendices). The situation is exactly analogous to how the Gaussian approximation is valid for even moderate sample sizes in batch testing, making possible a huge variety of common tests that are asymptotically and empirically correct with reasonable constants to boot.

To be more specific, consider the null hypothesis for the example of the coin bias testing given earlier; these fair coin flips are the most *anti*-concentrated possible bounded steps, and render our empirical Bernstein machinery ineffective, so they make a good test case. We choose C and C_0 as above, and plot the cumulative probability of type I violations $\Pr_{H_0}(\tau \leq n)$ up to time n for different α (where τ is the stopping time of the test), with the results in Fig. 2. To control type I error, the curves need to be asymptotically upper-bounded by the desired α levels (dotted lines). This does not appear true for our recommended settings of C, C_0, but the figure still indicates that type I error is controlled even for very high n with our settings. A slight further raise in C beyond $\sqrt{2}$ suffices to guarantee much stronger control.

Fig. 2 also seems to contain linear plots, which we cannot fully explain. We conjecture it is related to the standard proof of the classical LIL, which divides time into epochs of exponentially growing size (Feller (1950)). For more on provable correctness with low C, see the appendices.

4.2 TYPE II ERROR AND STOPPING TIME

Now we verify the results at the heart of the paper – uniformity over alternatives δ of the type II error and stopping time properties.

Fig. 3 plots the power of the sequential test $P_{H_1(\delta)}(\tau < N)$ against the maximum runtime N using the Gaussian

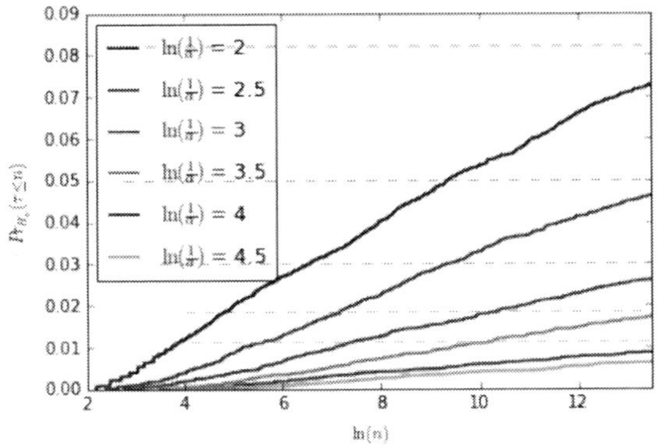

Figure 2: $\Pr_{H_0}(\tau \leq n)$ for different α, on biased coin. Dotted lines of corresponding colors are the target levels α.

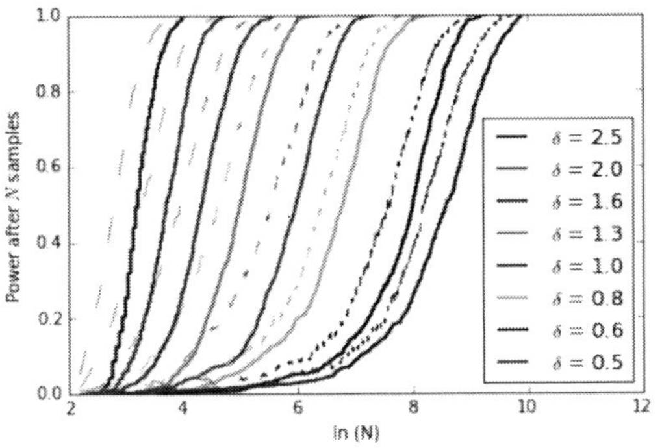

Figure 3: Power vs. $\ln(N)$ for different δ, on Gaussians. Dashed lines represent power of batch test with N samples.

data, at a range of different alternatives δ; the solid and dashed lines represent the power of the batch test (11) with N samples, and the sequential test with maximum runtime N. As we might expect, the batch test has somewhat higher power for a given sample size, but the sequential test consistently performs well compared to it. The role of N here is basically to set a desired tolerance for error; increasing N does not change the intermediate updates of the algorithm, but does increase the power by potentially running the test for longer. So each curve in Fig. 3 illustrates the statistical tradeoff inherent in hypothesis testing against a fixed simple alternative, but the great advantage of our sequential test is in achieving *all of them simultaneously with the same algorithm*.

To highlight this point, we examine the stopping time compared to the batch test for the Gaussian data, in Fig. 4. We see that the distributions of $\ln(\tau)$ are all quite concentrated, and that their medians (marked) fit well to a slope-4 line, showing the predicted $\frac{1}{\delta^4}$ dependence on δ. Some more experiments are in the appendices.

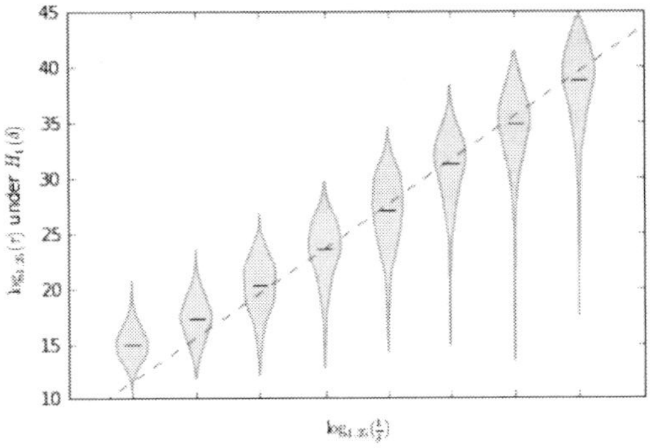

Figure 4: Distribution of $\log_{1.25}(\tau)$ for $\delta \in \{0.5(1.25)^c : c \in \{7, 6, \ldots, 0\}\}$, so that the abscissa values $\{\log_{1.25}(\frac{1}{\delta})\}$ are a unit length apart. Dashed line has slope 4.

5 RELATED WORK

Parametric or asymptotic methods. Our statements about the control of type I/II errors and stopping times are very general, following up on early sequential analysis work. Most sequential tests operate in the Wald's framework expounded in Wald (1945). In a seminal line of work, Robbins and colleagues delved into sequential hypothesis testing in an asymptotic sense Robbins (1985). Apart from being asymptotic, their tests were most often for simple hypotheses (point nulls and alternatives), were univariate, or parametric (assuming Gaussianity or known density). That said, two of their most relevant papers are Robbins (1970) and Darling and Robbins (1967), which discuss statistical methods related to the LIL. They give an asymptotic version of the argument of Section 2, using it to design sequential Kolmogorov-Smirnov tests with power one. Other classic works that mention using the LIL for testing various simple or univariate or parametric problems include Darling and Robbins (1968a,b); Lai (1977); Lerche (1986). These all operate in the asymptotic limit in which the classic LIL can be used to set q_N.

For testing a simple null against a simple alternative, the sequential probability ratio test (SPRT) was proved to be optimal by the seminal work of Wald and Wolfowitz (1948), but this applies when both the null and alternative have a known parametric form. The same authors also suggested a univariate nonparametric two-sample test in Wald and Wolfowitz (1940), but presumably found it unclear how to combine these two lines of work.

Bernstein-based methods. Finite-time uniform LIL-type concentration tools from Balsubramani (2015) are crucial to our analysis, and we adapt them in new ways; but novelty in this respect is not our primary focus here, because less recent concentration bounds can also be used to yield similar results. It is always possible to use a weighted union bound (allocating failure probability ξ over time as $\xi_n \propto \frac{\xi}{n^2}$) over fixed-$n$ Bernstein bounds, resulting in a deviation bound of $O\left(\sqrt{V_n \ln \frac{n}{\xi}}\right)$. A more advanced "peeling" argument, dividing time n into exponentially growing epochs, improves the bound to $O\left(\sqrt{V_n \ln \frac{\ln n}{\xi}}\right)$ (e.g. in Jamieson et al. (2014)). This suffices in many simple situations, but in general is still arbitrarily inferior to our bound of $O\left(\sqrt{V_n \ln\ln \frac{V_n}{\xi}}\right)$, precisely in the case $V_n \ll n$ in which we expect the second-moment Bernstein bounds to be most useful over Hoeffding bounds. A yet more intricate peeling argument, demarcating the epochs by exponential intervals in V_n rather than n, can be used to achieve our iterated-logarithm rate, in conjunction with the well-known second-order uniform martingale bound due to Freedman (1975). This serves as a sanity check on the non-asymptotic LIL bounds of Balsubramani (2015), where it is also shown that these bounds have the best possible dependence on all parameters. However, it can be verified that even a suboptimal uniform concentration rate like $O\left(\sqrt{V_n \ln \frac{V_n}{\xi}}\right)$ would suffice for the optimal stopping time properties of the sequential test to hold, with only a slight weakening of the power.

Bernstein inequalities that only depend on empirical variance have been used for stopping algorithms in Hoeffding races (Loh and Nowozin (2013)) and other even more general contexts (Mnih et al. (2008)). This line of work uses the empirical bounds very similarly to us, albeit in the nominally different context of direct estimation of a mean. As such, they too require uniform concentration over time, but achieve it with a crude union bound (failure probability $\xi_n \propto \frac{\xi}{n^2}$), resulting in a deviation bound of $O\left(\sqrt{\widehat{V}_n \ln \frac{n}{\xi}}\right)$. Applying the more advanced techniques above, it may be possible to get our optimal concentration rate, but to our knowledge ours is the first work to derive and use uniform LIL-type empirical Bernstein bounds.

Practical Usage. To our knowledge, implementing sequential testing in practice has previously invariably relied upon CLT-type results patched together with heuristic adjustments of the CLT threshold (e.g. the widely-used scheme for clinical trials of Peto et al. (1977) has an arbitrary conservative choice of $q_n = 0.001$ through the sequential process and $q_N = 0.05 = \alpha$ at the last datapoint). These perform as loose functional versions of our uniform finite-sample LIL upper bound, though without theoretical guarantees. In general, it is unsound to use an asymptotically normal distribution under the null at stopping time τ – the central limit theorem (CLT) applies to any *fixed* time t, but it may not apply to a *random* stopping time τ (see the random-sum CLT of Anscombe (1952), and Gut (2012) and references). This has caused myriad practical complications in implementing such tests (see Lai et al. (2008), Section 4). One of our contributions is to rigorously derive a directly usable finite-sample sequential test, in a way we believe can be extended to a large variety of testing problems.

We emphasize that there are several advantages to our proposed framework and analysis which, taken together, are unique in the literature. We tackle the multivariate nonparametric (possibly even high-dimensional) setting, with composite hypotheses. Moreover, we not only prove that the power is asymptotically one, but also derive finite-sample rates that illuminate dependence of other parameters on β, by considering non-asymptotic uniform concentration over finite times. The fact that it is not provable via purely asymptotic arguments is why our optimal stopping property has gone unobserved for a wide range of tests, even as basic as the biased coin. In our more refined analysis, it can be verified (Thm. 2) that the stopping time diverges to ∞ when the required type II error $\to 0$, i.e. power $\to 1$.

6 CONCLUSION

We have presented a sequential scheme for multivariate nonparametric hypothesis testing against composite alternatives, which comes with a full finite-sample analysis in terms of on-the-fly estimable quantities. Its desirable properties include type I error control by considering finite-time LIL concentration; near-optimal type II error compared to linear-time batch tests, due to the iterated-logarithm term in the LIL; and most importantly, essentially optimal early stopping, uniformly over a large class of alternatives. We presented some simple applications in learning and statistics, but our design and analysis techniques are general, and their extensions to other settings are of continuing future interest.

Acknowledgments

AB was supported in part by NSF grant IIS-1162581, and AR in part by ONR MURI grant N000140911052. The authors are grateful to the very helpful reviewers, and to the ITA workshop, at which this collaboration started.

References

Anscombe, F. J. (1952). Large-sample theory of sequential estimation. In *Mathematical Proceedings of the Cambridge Philosophical Society*, volume 48, pages 600–607. Cambridge Univ Press.

Balsubramani, A. (2015). Sharp uniform martingale concentration bounds. *arXiv preprint arXiv:1405.2639*.

Balsubramani, A. and Ramdas, A. (2015). Sequential nonparametric testing with the law of the iterated logarithm. *arXiv preprint arXiv:1506.03486*.

Boucheron, S., Lugosi, G., and Massart, P. (2013). *Concentration inequalities: A nonasymptotic theory of independence*. Oxford University Press.

Darling, D. and Robbins, H. (1967). Iterated logarithm inequalities. *Proceedings of the National Academy of Sciences of the United States of America*, pages 1188–1192.

Darling, D. and Robbins, H. (1968a). Some further remarks on inequalities for sample sums. *Proceedings of the National Academy of Sciences of the United States of America*, 60(4):1175.

Darling, D. and Robbins, H. (1968b). Some nonparametric sequential tests with power one. *Proceedings of the National Academy of Sciences of the United States of America*, 61(3):804.

Feller, V. (1950). *An Introduction to Probability Theory and Its Applications: Volume One*. John Wiley & Sons.

Freedman, D. A. (1975). On tail probabilities for martingales. *Ann. Probability*, 3:100–118.

Gut, A. (2012). Anscombe's theorem 60 years later. *Sequential Analysis*, 31(3):368–396.

Jamieson, K., Malloy, M., Nowak, R., and Bubeck, S. (2014). lil'ucb: An optimal exploration algorithm for multi-armed bandits. In *Conference on Learning Theory*.

Khinchin, A. Y. (1924). über einen satz der wahrscheinlichkeitsrechnung. *Fundamenta Mathematicae*, 6:9–20.

Lai, T. L. (1977). Power-one tests based on sample sums. *The Annals of Statistics*, pages 866–880.

Lai, T. L., Su, Z., et al. (2008). *Sequential nonparametrics and semiparametrics: Theory, implementation and applications to clinical trials*. Institute of Mathematical Statistics.

Lerche, H. R. (1986). Sequential analysis and the law of the iterated logarithm. *Lecture Notes-Monograph Series*, pages 40–53.

Loh, P.-L. and Nowozin, S. (2013). Faster hoeffding racing: Bernstein races via jackknife estimates. In *Algorithmic Learning Theory*, pages 203–217. Springer.

Maurer, A. and Pontil, M. (2009). Empirical bernstein bounds and sample variance penalization. *arXiv preprint arXiv:0907.3740*.

Mnih, V., Szepesvári, C., and Audibert, J.-Y. (2008). Empirical bernstein stopping. In *Proceedings of the 25th international conference on Machine learning*, pages 672–679. ACM.

Peto, R., Pike, M., Armitage, P., Breslow, N. E., Cox, D., Howard, S., Mantel, N., McPherson, K., Peto, J., and Smith, P. (1977). Design and analysis of randomized clinical trials requiring prolonged observation of each patient. ii. analysis and examples. *British journal of cancer*, 35(1):1.

Reddi, S. J., Ramdas, A., Póczos, B., Singh, A., and Wasserman, L. (2015). On the high dimensional power of a linear-time two sample test under mean-shift alternatives. In *Proceedings of the 18th International Conference on Artificial Intelligence and Statistics (AISTATS 2015)*.

Robbins, H. (1970). Statistical methods related to the law of the iterated logarithm. *The Annals of Mathematical Statistics*, pages 1397–1409.

Robbins, H. (1985). *Herbert Robbins Selected Papers*. Springer.

Wald, A. (1945). Sequential tests of statistical hypotheses. *The Annals of Mathematical Statistics*, 16(2):117–186.

Wald, A. and Wolfowitz, J. (1940). On a test whether two samples are from the same population. *The Annals of Mathematical Statistics*, 11(2):147–162.

Wald, A. and Wolfowitz, J. (1948). Optimum character of the sequential probability ratio test. *The Annals of Mathematical Statistics*, pages 326–339.

Budget Allocation using Weakly Coupled, Constrained Markov Decision Processes

Craig Boutilier
Google, Inc.
Mountain View, CA
cboutilier@google.com

Tyler Lu
Google, Inc.
Mountain View, CA
tylerlu@google.com

Abstract

We consider the problem of budget (or other resource) allocation in sequential decision problems involving a large number of concurrently running sub-processes, whose only interaction is through their consumption of budget. Our first contribution is the introduction of *budgeted MDPs (BMDPs)*, an MDP model in which policies/values are a *function of available budget*, (c.f. constrained MDPs which are solved given a *fixed* budget). BMDPs allow one to explicitly trade off allocated budget and expected value. We show that optimal value functions are concave, non-decreasing in budget, and piecewise-linear in the finite horizon case, and can be computed by dynamic programming (and support ready approximation). Our second contribution is a method that exploits BMDP solutions to allocate budget to a large number of independent BMDPs, coupled only by their common budget pool. The problem can be cast as a *multiple-choice knapsack problem*, which admits an efficient, optimal greedy algorithm. Empirical results in an online advertising domain confirm the efficacy of our methods.

1 INTRODUCTION

Markov decision processes (MDPs) [25, 7] are used widely throughout AI; but in many domains, actions consume limited resources and policies are subject to resource constraints, a problem often formulated using *constrained MDPs (CMDPs)* [2]. MDPs and CMDPs are even more complex when multiple independent MDPs, drawing from the same resources, must be controlled jointly, since the state and action spaces are formed by the cross-product of the individual subprocesses [23]. *Online advertising* is a domain with such properties: Archak et al. [4] propose a constrained MDP model for the optimal allocation of advertiser budget over an extended horizon that captures the sequential effect of multiple ads on a user's behavior.

Archak et al. [4] assume a fixed, predetermined budget for each user, and focus on optimally advertising to a user subject to this budget constraint. This formulation, however, does not determine a suitable budget, nor does it allow for making budget tradeoffs across different users, user types, or campaigns (e.g., different MDPs or different states of the same MDP). With this as motivation, we address these challenges by: (a) introducing *budgeted MDPs (BMDPs)*, which are solved as *a function of the (expected) budget available*; and (b) addressing budget tradeoffs across users using a *weakly coupled MDP* formulation [23] and optimally solving the allocation problem with a greedy algorithm that exploits local user BMDP solutions.

Our first contribution lies in the formulation and solution of BMDPs. The usual approach to resource constraints is CMDPs [2, 13]. While valuable models, CMDPs require *a priori* specification of fixed "budget" (e.g., a daily per-customer cap on ad spend). By contrast, BMDPs compute optimal policies and value functions (VFs) as a function of the budget made available. Effectively, we solve a CMDP *for all possible budget levels*, allowing one to explore the tradeoff between (optimal) expected value and allocated budget. Treating the budget b as a parameter, we show that, for any fixed state s of the BMDP, the optimal VF $V(s, b)$ is concave, non-decreasing in b; and for any finite horizon the VF is *piecewise-linear and concave (PWLC)*, defined by a finite set of *useful* resource levels. We derive a dynamic programming (DP) algorithm to compute this PWLC representation that supports approximation.

Our second contribution is a method for piecing together BMDP solutions to determine a joint policy over a set of BMDPs (e.g., for different users), subject to a global resource/budget constraint. Since the MDP is *weakly coupled* [23]—specifically, the individual customer BMDPs evolve independently, linked only through the consumption of shared budget—our aim is to determine an allocation of budget to each customer, which is turn dictates the optimal policy for that customer. We show that the budget allocation problem can be formulated as a *(multi-item variant of a) multiple-choice knapsack problem (MCKP)* [29], for which a straightforward greedy method can be used to construct the optimal budget allocation. We also discuss circumstances in which the dynamic, online *reallocation* of budget may be valuable, an approach rendered viable by the real-time nature of our method.

2 MDPS FOR BUDGET ALLOCATION

We describe an MDP model for engagement with users from a large, heterogeneous population. We use online advertising as our main motivation, though our techniques apply to the control of any large, distributed set of fully observable MDPs where actions consume limited resources. We abstract away a number of factors that arise in realistic ad domains to focus on budget allocation itself (e.g., partial observability and hidden state, control lag, incentives).

2.1 A WEAKLY COUPLED FORMULATION

We assume an advertiser has a fixed budget to spend on *advertising actions* for a target user population. Each action has a cost and is targeted to a specific user (e.g., a search, in-app or web page ad). Users respond stochastically in a way that may depend on their features (e.g., demographics), past actions (e.g., ad exposures) and past responses (e.g., click/purchase behavior).

Following Archak *et al.* [4], we model this as an MDP. We have a finite set of *users* $i \leq M$, who may be segmented into *types* reflecting static, observable characteristics that influence their responses. For ease of exposition, we assume all users have the same type; but the extension to multiple types is straightforward. We have a finite set S of *user states* $j \leq N$. At any time, user i is some state $s[i] \in S$. Let $\mathbf{S} = S^M$ be the *joint state space*, with the joint state denoted $\mathbf{s} = \langle s[1], \ldots, s[M] \rangle \in \mathbf{S}$. A user's state captures all relevant characteristics and history that influence her behavior. S may be small, or quite large in some contexts (e.g., the most recent search keyword on which the advertiser bid, or sufficient statistics summarizing historical interactions and user responses). A finite set A of *advertising actions* is available. At each stage, the advertiser selects an action $a[i]$ to apply to user i. Letting $\mathbf{A} = A^M$, a joint action is $\mathbf{a} = \langle a[1], \ldots, a[M] \rangle \in \mathbf{A}$.

Stochastic user response is captured by a *transition model* $P : S \times A \rightarrow \Delta(S)$, where $P(i, a, j) = p^a_{ij}$ is the probability that a user in state i moves to j when subjected to action a. *Reward* $R(i, a) = r^a_i$ reflects costs/payoffs when action a is applied to a user in state i. We decompose reward as $r^a_i = U(i) - C(i, a) = u_i - c^a_i$: *cost* C reflects action costs (e.g., cost of placing an ad, potential annoyance, etc.) and *utility function* U reflects benefits/payoffs (e.g., sales revenue, value of brand exposure, etc.).

The advertiser has a maximum *(global) budget* B that can be spent over the planning horizon. This global budget may be a hard limit in some settings; but we will require only that policies meet this constraint *in expectation.* We assume that the set of users is known, but our model easily handles new users who enter the system according to a known distribution over initial states. Different users will occupy many distinct states at any stage.

The optimal policy is defined w.r.t. the *joint constrained MDP*, with state space $\mathbf{S} = S^M$, action set $\mathbf{A} = A^M$, and a transition model, and cost, utility and reward functions defined as follows:

$$P(\mathbf{s}, \mathbf{a}, \mathbf{t}) = \prod_{i \leq M} P(s[i], a[i], t[i]); \quad U(\mathbf{s}) = \sum_{i \leq M} U(s[i]);$$

$$C(\mathbf{s}, \mathbf{a}) = \sum_{i \leq M} C(s[i], a[i]); \quad R(\mathbf{s}, \mathbf{a}) = U(\mathbf{s}) - C(\mathbf{s}, \mathbf{a}).$$

Joint transitions reflect the natural independence of user transitions. Costs and utilities are additive across users.

Our aim is to find a policy that maximizes expected discounted reward subject to the budget constraint: in expectation, the policy should spend no more than B. The optimal solution to this joint CMDP can be found by linear programming (LP) or DP. However, the exponential size of the state and action spaces (e.g., $O(N^M)$ states, or $\binom{M+N-1}{N-1}$ states if we use the "user count" for each state) makes this intractable. Fortunately, the MDP is *weakly coupled* [23]: users transitions are independent, with the local MDPs only coupled by their reliance on a single global budget. We take advantage of this below, solving the local MDPs such that their solutions can be effectively "pieced together" to form an approximate solution to the joint problem.

2.2 RELATED WORK

Budget Optimization. Allocation of advertising budgets is well-studied in marketing [19] with customer behavior and responses often modeled as a discrete or continuous Markov process [8, 24, 15]. Constrained budget optimization is of course critical to maximizing ROI in keyword auctions as well. [6, 16, 17, 12, 20].

Relatively little work has considered online budget optimization based on *sequential* user behavior. Markov models of web browsing and user response to online ads have been studied [10, 21]. Archak et al. [4] also assume Markovian user behavior in sponsored search—this is the behavioral model we adopt above. They propose a constrained MDP model and simple greedy algorithm that determines the optimal ad policy for a given user, assuming a fixed budget *for that user*. The same authors [5] demonstrate that user web search exhibits a "general to specific" behavior that is approximately Markovian. Other sequential work includes: budget optimization with advertiser response learning [3]; and reinforcement learning for optimal online ad strategies [27, 31] without budgets.

Constrained MDPs. We can extend the standard MDP model using *constrained MDPs (CMDPs)* [2, 13]: actions consume one or more resources (e.g., budget, energy) and policies must use no more than some set level of each resource in expectation. We outline a basic (one-dimensional) CMDP model.

Assume an underlying (local, not joint) MDP with states, actions, transitions, utilities and costs as above. Assuming a discounted infinite-horizon problem with discount factor

$0 \leq \gamma < 1$, our aim is to find an optimal (stationary, deterministic) policy that maximizes the expected sum of discounted rewards. The (unique) *optimal value function (VF)* $V^* : S \to \mathbb{R}$ satisfies the Bellman equation for all $i \in S$:

$$V^*(i) = \max_{a \in A} r_i^a + \gamma \sum_{j \in S} p_{ij}^a V^*(j),$$

while the optimal policy $\pi^*(i)$ selects the argmax of this expression. We will often use *Q-functions*, $Q(i, a) = r_i^a + \gamma \sum_{j \in S} p_{ij}^a V^*(j)$. The optimal VF and policy can be computed using DP algorithms (e.g., value/policy iteration) or LP methods [25, 7].

CMDPs extend this model by introducing constraints on the resources used by a policy [2]. We explicate the model using budgets (but it applies to any resource). A *budget constraint* B limits the cost of allowable policies, where the *expected discounted cost* of policy π at state i is:

$$C^\pi(i) = c_i^{\pi(i)} + \gamma \sum_{j \in S} p_{ij}^{\pi(i)} C^\pi(j).$$

An initial state (or distribution) is required for the constraint to be well-posed in general. The optimal solution (policy, VF) can be computed in poly-time using an LP [2]. There is always an optimal stationary policy for a CMDP, but unlike unconstrained MDPs, it may be stochastic.

Satisfying the budget constraint *in expectation* is suitable when a policy is executed many times, perhaps under different conditions, and budget is fungible over these instances, as in our ad domain. In other settings, the budget constraint may be *strict*—our model below easily accommodates strict budgets as well. We also allow costs in the budget constraint to be undiscounted (see below).

Weakly Coupled MDPs. The decomposition of MDPs into independent or semi-independent processes can often be used to mitigate the curse of dimensionality. Challenges lie in discovering a suitable decomposition structure and in determining how best to use the sub-process solutions to construct a (generally approximate) global solution. Many approaches have this flavor, in both standard MDPs and *decentralized (DEC)* MDPs and POMDPs [28, 1, 30, 22, 14]. The approach most related to ours is the decomposition method for *weakly-coupled MDPs* of [23]. There a joint MDP is comprised of a set of independent subprocesses, each itself a "local" MDP. Each local MDP reflects the task or objective of a specific agent, but the local policies require resources, both consumable and non-consumable. Their method: solves the local MDPs independently to produce local VFs parameterized by the resources available; uses the local VFs to assign resources to each local MDP; and reassigns unconsumed resources at each stage given the observed joint state. Our approach to budget decomposition is similar, but we use of the more standard *expected budget* constraint, and guarantee optimal composition. Our dynamic budget reallocation scheme is based on the reallocation mechanism of [23].

3 BUDGETED MDPS

We introduce *budgeted MDPs*, a variant of CMDPs in which budgets, or other resources, are (implicitly) treated as a part of the state, so that VFs/policies can vary with both the state *and available budget*. This allows budget-value tradeoffs to made quickly and easily.

3.1 THE BUDGETED MDP MODEL

A *(finite, one-dimensional) budgeted Markov decision process (BMDP)* $M = \langle S, A, P, U, C, B_{\max}, \gamma \rangle$ has the same components as a CMDP, but without a budget constraint. We allow an optional constant $B_{\max}$ that sets a plausible upper bound on useful or available budgets at any stage. We write $U(i) = u_i$ for the terminal utility at i if no action is taken (e.g., end of the planning horizon). We assume that, for each i, there is an a s.t. $c_i^a = 0$ (so a proper policy exists even with no budget).

We seek an optimal policy which maximizes expected reward over some horizon, but which consumes no more than some budget $b \leq B_{\max}$ in expectation. Unlike CMDPs, however, the policy should be a *function* of b.

3.2 DETERMINISTIC POLICIES

We begin by analyzing deterministic policies for finite-horizon problems, which develops useful intuitions. Define the *optimal deterministic t-stage-to-go VF* as follows. For all $i \in S, b \leq B_{\max}$, let $V_D^0(i, b) = u_i$, and define:

$$V_D^t(i, b) = \max_{\substack{a \in A \\ \mathbf{b} \in \mathbb{R}_+^n}} r_i^a + \gamma \sum_{j \leq n} p_{ij}^a V_D^{t-1}(j, b_j) \qquad (1)$$

$$\text{subj. to } c_i^a + \gamma \sum_{j \leq n} p_{ij}^a b_j \leq b \qquad (2)$$

The optimal policy $\pi_D^t(i, b)$ is obtained by taking the argmax. The VF reflects that doing a at i consumes c_i^a of the budget b, while optimal consumption at each reachable next state must be such that the *expected* budget used is no more than the remaining $b - c_i^a$. We discount the expected spend as is standard in CMDPs, but removing γ from Eq. 2 is also possible (we use undiscounted constraints below).

It is easy to see that $V_D^t(i, b)$ is monotone non-decreasing in b. While the optimal VF involves a continuous dimension b, it has a concise finite representation. For a fixed stage-to-go t and state i, define budget $0 \leq b \leq B_{\max}$ to be *(deterministically) useful* iff $V_D^t(i, b) > V_D^t(i, b - \varepsilon)$ for all $\varepsilon > 0$, and *useless* otherwise. We observe that:

Proposition 1. *For any finite t and state i, $V_D^t(i, \cdot)$ has a finite number of deterministically useful budget levels.*

We describe an algorithm to compute useful budgets (from which the proof of Prop. 1 follows).[1] Let $b_0^{i,t} = 0 < b_1^{i,t} < \ldots < b_M^{i,t}$ be the useful budget levels for (i, t). Prop. 1

[1] All proofs, and more detailed exposition, are available in a longer version of the paper, available at each author's web page.

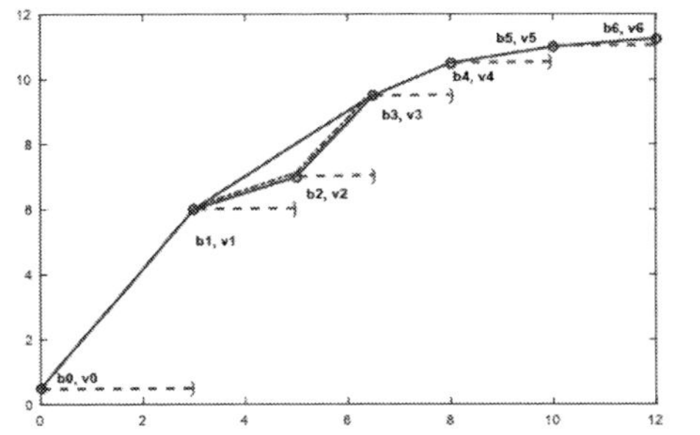

Fig. 1: An example VF $V_D(i, b)$. Useful budget levels are shown (the points (b, v)) along with: (a) the induced piecewise constant VF $V_D(i, b)$ (dashed line); and (b) the PWLC VF (solid line) for a randomized policy. Randomizing among b_0, b_1 for any expected spend $b \in (b_0, b_1)$ dominates deterministic spend b_0; and randomizing among b_1 and b_3 with expected spend b_2 dominates deterministic spend b_2 (dashed-dotted lines).

implies that $V_D^t(i, \cdot)$ is *piecewise constant* and monotone, with $V_D^t(i, b) = V_D^t(i, b_k^{i,t})$ for all $b \in [b_k^{i,t}, b_{k+1}^{i,t})$, for each $k < M$. We write $[\langle b_0^{i,t}, v_0^{i,t}\rangle, \ldots, \langle b_M^{i,t}, v_M^{i,t}\rangle]$ to denote this piecewise constant function (see Fig. 1).

Let the *reachable set* for state-action pair i, a be $S_i^a = \{j \in S | p_{ij}^a > 0\}$ and the *maximum out-degree* of an MDP be $d = \max_{i \in S, a \in A} |S_i^a|$. We compute the useful budgets for each state-stage pair—hence the optimal VF and policy—using a simple DP algorithm. Assume a piecewise constant representation of V_D^{t-1} (for V_D^0 this is trivial); and for ease of exposition, assume each i has $M + 1$ useful levels $b_0^{i,t-1}, \ldots, b_M^{i,t-1}$. We compute $V_D^t(i, b)$ as follows:

- Let $\sigma : S_i^a \to [M]$ be an assignment of each reachable state $j \in S_i^a$ to a useful budget level $b_{\sigma(j)}^{j,t-1}$, $\sigma(j) \leq M$, with $t - 1$ stages-to-go. Let Σ be the set of such mappings. We view $b_\sigma^{j,t-1}(j)$ as the budget to be consumed if we reach j after doing a; implicitly, σ dictates the $t - 1$-stage-to-go policy by selecting a budget level at each next state.
- Let the *potentially useful budget levels* for (i, t, a) be:

  $$\widetilde{B}_a^{i,t} = \{c_i^a + \sum_{j \in S_i^a} p_{ij}^a b_{\sigma(j)}^{j,t-1} \mid \sigma \in \Sigma\} \cap \{b \leq B_{\max}\}.$$

  Each $b_k^{i,t} \in \widetilde{B}_a^{i,t}$ is determined by some σ. The corresponding expected value is $v_k^{i,t} = r_i^a + \gamma \sum_j p_{ij}^a v_{\sigma(j)}^{j,t-1}$.
- Assume a reindexing of the entries in $\widetilde{B}_a^{i,t}$ so that the budget levels are ascending (ties broken arbitrarily). The *useful budget levels* for (i, t, a) are:

  $$B_a^{i,t} = \{b_k^{i,t} \in \widetilde{B}_a^{i,t} : \nexists k' < k \text{ s.t. } v_{k'}^{i,t} \geq v_k^{i,t}\}.$$

  That is, any potentially useful budget that is weakly dominated by a smaller budget is discarded. The useful budgets and corresponding values give us $Q^t(i, a, b)$.
- Let the *potentially useful budget levels* for (i, t) be $\widetilde{B}^{i,t} = \cup_{a \in A} B_a^{i,t}$, and let $B^{i,t}$ be the *useful budget levels*, obtained by pruning $\widetilde{B}^{i,t}$ as above. The useful budget levels and corresponding values give the VF $V^t(i, b)$.

While finite, the number of useful budget levels can grow exponentially in the horizon:

Proposition 2. *For any finite t and state i, $V_D^t(i, \cdot)$ has at most $O((|A|^d)^t)$ useful budget levels, where d is the maximum out-degree of the underlying MDP.*

This motivates approximating this set, as we discuss below in the context of stochastic policies.

3.3 STOCHASTIC POLICIES

Stochastic policies can offer greater value than deterministic policies due to their inherent flexibility, and thus have a rather different structure. Suppose at state-stage pair (i, t) the available budget b lies strictly between two deterministically useful levels, $b_k^{i,t} < b < b_{k+1}^{i,t}$. A stochastic policy that spends $b_{k+1}^{i,t}$ (and takes the corresponding action) with probability $p = \frac{b - b_k^{i,t}}{b_{k+1}^{i,t} - b_k^{i,t}}$, and $b_k^{i,t}$ with $1 - p$, provides greater expected value for (expected) spend b than the PW constant value offered by the optimal deterministic policy (see Fig. 1).

The optimal VF for such "single-stage randomized" policies is given by the *convex hull* of the useful budgets for (i, t) (see Fig. 1). Given useful budget set $B^{i,t} = \{0 = b_0^{i,t} < b_1^{i,t} < \ldots < b_M^{i,t}\}$, we say $b_k^{i,t}$ is *dominated* if there are two budgets $b_{k^-}^{i,t}, b_{k^+}^{i,t}$ $(k^- < k < k^+)$ s.t. $(1 - p)v_{k^-}^{i,t} + pv_{k^+}^{i,t} > v_k^{i,t}$. The convex hull is *piecewise linear and concave (PWLC)* and monotone, comprising the PWL function formed by the *non-dominated* points.

This PWLC structure is preserved by Bellman backups, and can be computed effectively in two stages: first, a simple *greedy algorithm* assigns budget incrementally to reachable next states, giving a PWLC representation of the Q-functions for each a; second, we compute the backed up VF by taking the convex hull of the union of these Q-functions.

Computing Q-functions. Assume $V^{t-1}(j, \cdot)$ is PWLC for all $j \in S$, with points $[\langle b_0^{j,t-1}, v_0^{j,t-1}\rangle, \ldots, \langle b_M^{j,t-1}, v_M^{j,t-1}\rangle]$, where each $b_k^{j,t-1}$ is non-dominated (for ease of exposition, assume each j has $M + 1$ non-dominated levels). Let $B(S_a^i) = \cup_{j \in S_a^i} B^{j,t-1}$, and re-index $B(S_a^i)$ in decreasing order of *bang-per-buck ratio (BpB)*:

$$BpB(b_k^{j,t-1}) = \frac{v_k^{j,t-1} - v_{k-1}^{j,t-1}}{b_k^{j,t-1} - b_{k-1}^{j,t-1}} = \frac{\Delta v_k^{j,t-1}}{\Delta b_k^{j,t-1}}.$$

(For $k = 0$, we leave BpB undefined, since $b_0^{j,t-1} = 0$ for all j.) This BpB expresses the (per-unit budget) increase in value when increasing budget at $(j, t - 1)$ from $b_{k-1}^{j,t-1}$ to $b_k^{j,t-1}$. Let $j(m), k(m), \Delta b(m), \Delta v(m)$ denote, resp., the state j, the useful budget index for j, the budget increment, and the value increment associated with the mth element of (sorted) $B(S_a^i)$. Let $M_i^* = |S_a^i| M$.

We define Q-functions as follows:

Definition 1. Let V^{t-1} be a VF such that, for all $j \in S$, $V^{t-1}(j, b)$ is bounded, monotone and PWLC in b with a finite number of budget points. Define:

- the 0th useful budget for a at i to be $b^{i,t}_{a,0} = c^a_i$, which gives value $v^{i,t}_{a,0} = r^a_i + \gamma \sum_{j \in S^a_i} p^a_{ij} v^{j,t-1}_0$;
- the mth useful budget, for $0 < m \leq M^*_i$, to be $b^{i,t}_{a,m} = \sum_{\ell \leq m} p^a_{i,j(\ell)} \Delta b(\ell)$ which gives value $v^{i,t}_{a,m} = r^a_i + \gamma \sum_{\ell \leq m} p^a_{i,j(\ell)} \Delta v(\ell)$.

For any $0 < m \leq M^*_i$, and b s.t. $b^{i,t}_{a,m-1} < b < b^{i,t}_{a,m}$, let $p^{i,t,a}_b = \frac{b - b^{i,t}_{a,m-1}}{b^{i,t}_{a,m} - b^{i,t}_{a,m-1}}$. Define *the Q-function for action a at stage t* as follows:

$$Q^t(i,a,b) = \begin{cases} \text{undefined} & \text{if } b < b^{i,t}_{a,0} \\ v^{i,t}_{a,m} & \text{if } b = b^{i,t}_{a,m} \\ p^{i,t,a}_b v^{i,t}_{a,m} + (1 - p^{i,t,a}_b) v^{i,t}_{a,m-1} & \text{if } b^{i,t}_{a,m-1} < b < b^{i,t}_{a,m} \\ v^{i,t}_{a,M^*_i} & \text{if } b > b^{i,t}_{a,M^*_i}. \end{cases}$$

This Q-function is optimal:

Theorem 3. *$Q^t(i,a,b)$ in Defn. 1 is the maximum expected value achievable when taking action a at state i with budget b with future value given by V^{t-1}.*

Q-functions can thus be computed with a simple greedy algorithm that allocates budget to "next states" in BpB-order (i.e., using a simple sorted merge of the linear segments of all reachable-state VFs, with each segment scaled by its transition probability; see Fig. 2 for an illustration). The intuitions are straightforward: once taking a at i, cost c^a_i is incurred, and the remaining budget $b' = b - c^a_i$ must be "allocated" to states in S^a_i. The first units of b' are most effectively used by state $j(1)$—i.e., the first in $B(S^i_a)$—since it has the greatest initial BpB. Budget up to $\Delta b(1) = b^{j(1),t-1}_{k(1)}$ to $j(1)$ gives an expected (future) value improvement of $\Delta v(1) = \Delta v^{j(1),t-1}_{k(1)}$ with probability $p^a_{i,j(1)}$, and has an expected spend of $p^a_{i,j(1)} \Delta b(1)$. This is the greatest expected (future) value attainable at i for any $b' \leq p^a_{ij} b^{j(1),t-1}_{k(1)}$. Similarly, the next $\Delta b(2)$ units of b' should be allocated to $j(2)$, giving a return of $BpB(b^{j(2),t-1}_{k(2)})$ per unit, with expected spend and return occurring with probability $p^a_{i,j(2)}$. This continues until all useful budgets from states in S^a_i have been allocated (reaching the max useful budget for (i,t)).

Computing Value Functions. Given the PWLC representation of the Q-functions, we can construct a similar PWLC representation of $V^t(i,b) = \max_a Q^t(i,a,b)$. We simply take the union of the points that determine each Q-function, and remove any dominated points (analogous to the move from deterministic to stochastic policies). More precisely, assuming a fixed state-stage (i,t), let Q_a be the set of budget-value points in a's Q-function, and let $Q_* = \cup_a Q_a$ be the union of of these points—we annotate each point with the action from which it was derived, so each has the form (b,v,a). We say (b,v,a) is *dominated* in Q_* if there are two (different) points $(b_1,v_1,a_1),(b_2,v_2,a_2) \in Q_*$ such that $b_1 \leq b \leq b_2$ and $(1-\alpha)v_1 + \alpha v_2 > v$, where $\alpha = \frac{b - b_1}{b_2 - b_1}$. Removing all dominated points from Q_* leaves the set of points that form the useful budget levels in the PWLC representation of $V^t(i,\cdot)$. In other words, we form the convex hull of Q_*. Clearly no dominated point (b,v,a) is useful in a stochastic policy, since a greater value can be attained, using the same expected budget, by α-mixing between actions a_1 and a_2 (and the corresponding budgets).

The construction above shows:

Theorem 4. *For any finite t and state i, $V^t(i,b)$ is piecewise linear, concave and monotone in b.*

The PWLC representation of $V^t(i,\cdot)$ can be constructed using any convex hull method. A basic *Graham scan* [18] is appropriate here, since Q-budget points are maintained in sorted order, and has complexity $O(|Q_*| \log |Q_*|)$.

Again, the number of useful levels grows exponentially, but is no greater than the number of deterministically useful levels, i.e., $V^t(i,\cdot)$ has size at most $O((|A|^d)^t)$. For infinite horizon problems, we may not have finitely many useful budgets, but the VF remains concave:

Theorem 5. *For any state i, the optimal infinite-horizon VF $V(i,b)$ is concave and monotone in b.*

Standard bounds apply when using the finite-horizon V^t to approximate the infinite-horizon VF: if Bellman error of V^t is ε, $||V^* - V^t|| \leq \frac{\varepsilon}{1-\gamma}$.

Approximation. The complexity of VF computation depends on the number of useful budget points. The VF can be approximated by removing non-dominated points that are "close" to lying strictly inside the convex hull. For instance, in Fig. 2(c), deletion of the second and third points results in a simpler Q-function, with a single segment from $(pb_0 + p'b'_0, pv_0 + p'v'_0)$ to $(pb_2 + p'b'_1, pv_2 + p'v'_1)$ replacing three true segments. It closely approximates the true Q-function since the slopes (BpBs) of all deleted segments are nearly identical.

Several simple pruning criteria can be added to the insertion step of the Graham scan (i.e., when transforming Q-functions to VFs). When inserting (b_{new}, v_{new}) with BpB β_{new}, we can delete the previously inserted point, (b_k, v_k) with BpB β_k, if $\beta_{new} \geq \beta_k - \varepsilon$, for some tolerance ε. This introduces a max-norm error of at most $\varepsilon(b_k - b_{k-1})$. Recursively applying this rule gives additive accumulation: s consecutive pruning steps gives error at most $s\varepsilon(b_k - b_{k-s})$. Since error also depends on the length of the segments being pruned, we can use both *slope* pruning and *length* pruning, or pruning dictated by their product, i.e., terminated when this product bound reaches some threshold τ. Standard MDP approximation bounds can be derived.

Policy Execution. Given the optimal VF V^*, we can readily determine the ideal level of (expected) spend b_0 given initial state i_0 (see our discussion of sweet spots below). While one could then solve the corresponding CMDP with budget b_0, the BMDP solution, in fact, embeds an optimal

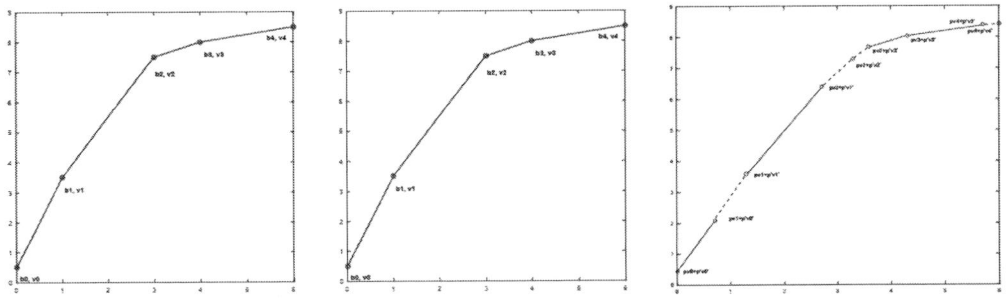

Fig. 2: (a) VF for state j; (b) VF for j'; (c) Q-function (future component) for a reaching j with prob. p and j' with $p' = 1 - p$.

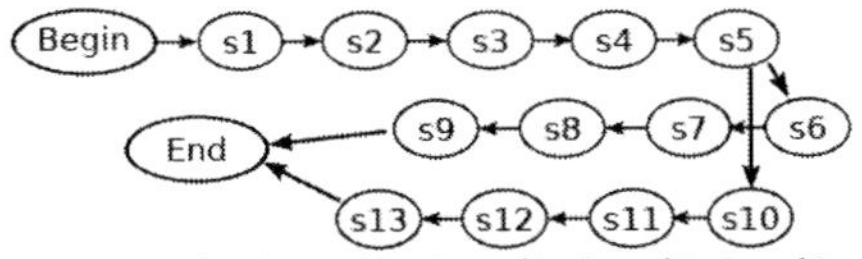

Search: s1: unint; s2: general int; s3: search1, s4: search2, s5:search3
Advertiser: s6: interest1; s7: interest2; s8: interest3, s9: conversion
Compt'r: s10: interest1; s11: interest2; s12: interest3, s13: conversion

Fig. 3: A synthetic ad MDP. "Begin" reflects the beginning of a customer search (transitions from it encode a prior over interest states). From an advertiser's perspective, the MDP for a specific customer can begin at any state of the process.

(non-stationary) CMDP solution for any budget level. The *execution* of the BMDP policy π^* is somewhat subtle, but straightforward. The optimization in Eqns. 1 and 2 generally assigns some future states a *greater* budget than what remains, $b_0 - c^a_{i_0}$, and some future states less—it is only *expected spend* that must not exceed the remaining budget. If state j's "assigned budget" b_j differs from $b_0 - c^a_{i_0}$, whether greater or less, then we must execute action $\pi^*(j, b_j)$ to ensure we achieve expected value $V^*(i_0, b_0)$. This requires that we record the optimal budget mapping σ at the final Bellman backup (assuming an infinite horizon problem) for each useful budget point at each state. When we reach any next state j, we "pass forward" its assigned budget $b_\sigma(j)$, at which point we take action $\pi^*(j, b_\sigma(j))$.

As in CMDPs, there can be substantial variance in actual spend when implementing the BMDP policy $\pi^*(i, b)$ (variance can be computed exactly during DP). We discuss strategies for mitigating the impact of variance below. A simple DP algorithm can be used to compute VFs with *strict* budgets [23], but allowing some variance in spend can improve expected value significantly.

3.4 EMPIRICAL EVALUATION

We evaluate the effectiveness of our DP method on several BMDPs, and measure the impact of approximation.

Synthetic Ad MDP. We begin with a small synthetic MDP that reflects the influence of ads on product search behavior. Its small size allows detailed examination of its optimal VF structure. The MDP (see Fig. 3) has 15 states reflecting various levels of customer interest in an advertiser's (or competitors') product, and five actions for different levels of ad intensity. Transitions for "nominal" (stochastic) progress through the search funnel are shown, with others omitted for clarity. More intense ad actions are more costly, but increase the odds of progressing in the funnel, and lower the odds of abandoning purchase intent.

We solve the BMDP ($\gamma = 0.975$, horizon 50) with four different degrees of approximation: exact (no pruning); mild pruning (slope/length pruning set to 0.01); aggressive pruning (both set to 0.05); and hybrid (mild pruning for 45 iterations, then exact computation for five). The following table shows the average (and min–max) number of segments in the PWLC VF over the 15 MDP states—the number of segments determines the complexity of the VFs—and computation time for each regime. For approximation schemes, we show the maximum absolute and relative errors (and the optimal value at which this error occurs).

	No prun.	Mild	Aggr.	Mild+No
Segments	3066 (0–5075)	18.3 (0–47)	10.4 (0–26)	480.8 (0–877)
Max Err	—	4.84 (26.61)	4.84 (26.61)	0.21 (58.77)
Max RelErr	—	40.9% (4.24)	48.7% (1.54)	2.3% (0.55)
CPU (s.)	1055.4	17.54	10.36	28.67

The optimal VF has a large number of segments per state but can be approximated quite well with very few segments. With mild/aggressive pruning, the VF is very compact, but has large maximum error (4.84, which is 18% rel. error at the point at which it occurs); the relative error is also significant, though it occurs at points with low value (hence gives small abs. error). The hybrid scheme works very well—by exploiting the contraction properties of the MDP, error associated with initial pruning is almost entirely overcome. It reduces the number of VF segments by an order of magnitude, and computation time by nearly two orders of magnitude, but gives very small max absolute (0.21, or 0.36%) and relative error (2.3%, or 0.0013).[2] Determining suitable pruning thresholds and schedules in general is an interesting open question.

Advertiser MDP. We next study two larger MDPs derived from the contact data of a large advertiser. The data consists of sequences of cross-channel touch points with users—each touch is labeled with a contact event (e.g., display ad, email, paid search ad, direct navigation to web site) or type of activity on the advertiser's web site (including transactions or "conversions"). There are 28 event types, and 3.6M trajectories comprising 10M events.

From this data, we learn (using MLE) several *variable-order Markov chain (VOMC) models* [9, 11] that predict

[2]CPU time using a simple Python prototype, on a 3.5GHz CPU with 32Gb of RAM.

transitions induced by the advertiser's policy. Predictions are based on a small sufficient history involving up to 10 preceding events. The histories comprising each VOMC form the state space of a Markov chain. From these we derive action-conditional transition models by substituting history end points with one of a small number of "controllable" events and using the VOMC model for these altered histories for transition predictions. We consider four actions (no-op, email, paid search, display ad), and two different models: the first is a VOMC model with a maximum state-order of 10 and an average state-order of five, giving an MDP with 451,582 states. The second is a two-component mixture of smaller VOMC models (maximum order of 3); we use the first component, with 1469 states.

We solve the BMDPs for both models (horizon 50, discount 0.975 as above). The table below shows pruning level, number of segments, and computation time for the 1469-state MDP using the same strategies as above.[3]

	No prun.	Mild	Aggr.	Mild+No
Segments	251.5 (74–359)	234.2 (77–342)	25.6 (5–39)	76.8 (18–321)
Max Err	—	5.13 (171.6)	28.9 (169.3)	3.9 (167.6)
Max RelErr	—	3.0% (171.6)	12.3% (169.3)	2.4% (167.6)
CPU (s.)	19918.9	10672.5	1451.8	2390.0

The 452K-state BMDP was solved only with aggressive pruning (slope 2.0, length 0.1), and averaged about 11.67 segments per state and 1168s. per DP iteration.

4 BUDGET ALLOCATED ACROSS MDPS

We now consider the problem facing an advertiser with a fixed maximum budget and a specific set of target customers, each of whom occupies the state of some underlying MDP. To solve the joint MDP above, we use the *weakly coupled* decomposition of [23], but merge the local solutions (and analyze this merge) in a different manner.

Offline Decomposition Our approach to decomposition is straightforward. We first solve each *single-user sub-MDP* as a BMDP with a some natural per-user maximum budget B_u. For ease of exposition, we assume just one user type, hence only one user MDP to solve (i.e., each user has the same dynamics). Users are distinguished only by their MDP state. The BMDP solution gives an optimal single-user policy π and VF V spanning all $s \in S, b \leq B_u$; indicating action choice and value *as a function of the budget available to be spent (in expectation) on that user alone.* We exploit this below. Indeed, this is why we do uses CMDPs, which do not indicate the value of allocating *varying* budgets to a user.

The Budget Allocation Problem Given initial (or current) joint state with M customers is $\mathbf{s} = \langle s[1], \cdots s[M] \rangle$, and budget B, a natural way to exploit the BMDP solution is to allocate some portion $b[i]$ of B to each customer $i \leq M$ s.t. we maximize the sum of expected values $v[i]$ assuming optimal engagement with i with budget $b[i]$. Specifically, the *budget allocation problem (BAP)* is :

$$\max_{b[i]:i \leq M} \sum_{i \leq M} V(s[i], b[i]) \text{ subj. to } \sum_{i \leq M} b[i] \leq B, \quad (3)$$

where V is the optimal VF for the underlying BMDP.

BAP determines an allocation $\mathbf{b}^* = \langle b^*[1], \ldots, b^*[M] \rangle$ that maximizes the expected value of *committing* a specific (expected) budget $b^*[i]$ to customer i. By simple linearity of expectation, we have:

Observation 6. *Let V be the optimal VF and π the optimal policy for the user MDP. Let $\mathbf{b}$ be the optimal solution to the budget allocation problem. Then the joint (non-stationary) policy $\overline{\pi}(\mathbf{s}) = \prod_i \pi(s[i], b[i])$ has expected value $\sum_i V(s[i], b[i])$ and expected spend $\sum_{i \leq M} b[i] \leq B$.*

We cannot guarantee this policy is truly optimal for the joint MDP, since this decomposed policy does not admit *recourse* in the execution of one user's MDP that depends on the realized outcome of some other user's MDP. However, we expect it to work well in practice (see below). For MDPs with large numbers of customers, or where the spend variance of the local BMDP policy is low, this form of suboptimality will be small. However, as we discuss below, *repeated online reallocation of budget* can sometimes overcome even this potential suboptimality in practice.

BAP (Eq. 3) can be viewed as a (multi-item variant of a) *multiple-choice knapsack problem (MCKP)* [29]. In the classic MCKP, we are given M classes of items, with each class i containing n_i items. To explain, we first begin with a restricted version of BAP, the *useful-budget assignment problem (UBAP)*. In UBAP, we require each user i be assigned a *useful* budget level from the discrete set $B^{s[i]}$. UBAP is exactly an MCKP: each user i is as an *item class* for whom exactly one budget must be chosen from the set of *items* $B^{s[i]}$ in that class. The *weight* of item $b \in B^{s[i]}$ is b (i.e., the amount of the budget it consumes); and the *profit* of assigning b to i is $V(s[i], b)$. The *capacity* is the global budget B, so total weight (budget assigned) cannot exceed B. We can view this as a *multi-item* variant of MCKP with multiple "copies" of the same class (namely, all users in a state j have the same items, weights and profits).

It is useful to consider an integer programming (IP) model of MCKP (where binary variable x_{ik} indicates that i is allocated the kth useful budget $\beta_{ik} = b_k^{s[i]}$):

$$\max_{x_{ik}} \quad \sum_{i \leq M} \sum_{k \in B^{s[i]}} V(s[i], \beta_{ik}) x_{ik} \quad (4)$$

$$\text{subject to} \quad \sum_{i \leq M} \sum_{k \in B^{s[i]}} \beta_{ik} x_{ik} \leq B \quad (5)$$

$$\sum_{k \in B^{s[i]}} x_{ik} = 1, \quad \forall i \leq M \quad (6)$$

$$x_{ik} \in \{0, 1\} \quad (7)$$

[3] The "no pruning" optimal benchmark uses slope/length pruning of 0.001/0.0001 for 20 iterations and 0.01/0.001 for 30. Aggressive is slope/length = 0.2/0.01; mild is 0.02/0.001.

We can collapse users in the same class using a counting (integer) variable as well.

Consider the LP relaxation of the IP Eq. 4—its optimal solution gives a (generally) fractional assignment of useful budget to any user i in state $s[i] = j$. Using a minor adaptation of the analysis of Sinha and Zoltners [29], we can show that the optimal allocation to any i is either integral (i.e., assigns a useful budget level to i), or is a mixture of two *consecutive* useful levels, in which case the expected budget $b^*[i]$ and induced expected value $v^*[i]$ in the LP corresponds to a point on the convex hull of the useful points. In other words, it lies on the PWLC VF $V(i,\cdot)$:

Proposition 7. *The optimal solution of the LP relaxation of UBAP IP Eq. 4 is such that, for each i: (a)* $x_{ik} = 1$ *for one value of k; or (b) there is some k such that only* $x_{ik}, x_{i,k+1} > 0$ *(i.e., only two budget levels are allocated, and they must be consecutive).*

We immediately obtain:

Corollary 8. *The optimal solution to the LP relaxation of UBAP is an optimal solution to BAP.*

The structure of the LP relaxation of MCKP is very valuable. Sinha and Zoltners [29] show that a simple greedy algorithm can be used to solve the relaxation. We adopt the same method, *greedy budget allocation (GBA)*, to solve BAP. For each state j, and each $1 \leq k \leq L$, define the *bang-for-buck ratio* as before:

$$BpB_{jk} = \frac{V(j, \beta_{jk}) - V(j, \beta_{jk-1})}{\beta_{jk} - \beta_{jk-1}}.$$

GBA assigns budget incrementally to each user in the order given by the BpB ratio. Initially each user i in state $s[i] = j$ is assigned a budget of $\beta_{j0} = 0$, and the unallocated budget is set to B (our budget constraint). At any stage of GBA, let b denote the unallocated budget, let β_{j,k_i} be i's current allocation and i's current ratio to be $BpB[i] = BpB_{jk_i+1}$. Let i be any *best user*, with maximum ratio $BpB[i]$. If sufficient budget remains, we increase i's allocation from β_{j,k_i} to β_{j,k_i+1}, then update i's ratio and the unallocated budget. We continue until the unallocated budget is less than $\beta_{j,k_i+1} - \beta_{j,k_i}$; then we allocate the remaining budget fractionally to the best i (β_{j,k_i} with probability p and β_{j,k_i+1} with $1-p$, for $p = \frac{(\beta_{j,k_i+1} - \beta_{j,k_i}) - b}{(\beta_{j,k_i+1} - \beta_{j,k_i})}$).

We can show that GBA finds the optimal solution to our BAP (see [29]). GBA can be modified to aggregate all users that lie in the same state, and to account for the stochastic arrival of customers of various types, or at various states.

Dynamic Budget Reallocation The variance in the spend of an optimal policy $\pi(i, b)$ means there is some risk over overspending the global budget. This risk is, of course, greater with small numbers of users than with large numbers. One way to alleviate this risk *dynamic budget reallocation (DBRA)*. Rather than committing to the optimal policy for each user given their initial allocation, we reallocate any remaining budget at each stage. More precisely, given the current joint state $\mathbf{s} = \langle s[1], \ldots, s[M] \rangle$ and remaining budget B, we: (a) use GBA to determine allocation $b[i], i \leq M$ given $(\mathbf{s}, B)$; (b) execute action $\pi(s[i], b[i])$ for each i, incurring the cost c_i^a; and (c) observe the next state $\mathbf{s}'$ and remaining B' and repeat. This approach (virtually) guarantees that the global budget B will not be overspent (if the BMDP policy randomizes, a small chance of a small violation may exist). It also offers a form of recourse; e.g., if the budget for some user is no longer useful (e.g., transition to an unprofitable state), it budget can be reallocated to a more profitable user.

Empirical Evaluation We test the effectiveness of GBA on the BMDPs described in Sec. 3.4. We study expected spend and value of the "implied" joint policies, as well as spend variance.

We consider several ways of implementing the joint policies induced by the GBA solution of BAP. The first is the *BMDP policy*, where once GBA allocates $b[i]$ to each user i, we implement the corresponding BMDP policy starting at state $s[i]$. This ensures that *expected spend* does not exceed $b[i]$, but doesn't guarantee budget satisfaction for any specific user. The second is the *static user budget policy (SUB)*: given the GBA allocation $b[i]$, we implement the first action $a = \pi(s[i], b[i])$ in the BMDP policy at $s[i]$ for each i; but when reaching next state, we take the action as if we only had that user's *remaining* budget $b[i] - c^a_{s[i]}$, ignoring the next state budget mapping from the BMDP policy. SUB thus recalibrates the actual spend to minimize the odds of overspending $b[i]$ on a per-user basis. We also use the reallocation scheme DBRA, which reduces the overspending risk collectively (not per-user).

Solving BMDPs and using GBA to allocate budget allows one to assess budget tradeoffs across different users in different states. Without a BMDP model or our budget-dependent VF, these tradeoffs must be made heuristically. In this case, we can use *uniform budget allocation (UBA)*, which apportions budget equally across all users, and then solves the induced CMDPs (one per occupied state).

Synthetic Ad MDP. In the synthetic MDP, our initial setup has 1000 customers starting in s_0. The following table shows the expected value obtained by 3 different policies for 4 different global budgets:

Total Bud.	BMDP Val.	DBRA Val.	SUB Val.
1000	8210	8579 (830.5)	4106 (707)
2000	10,905	11,019 (964)	4429 (825)
5000	15,692	15,658 (1239)	5270 (830.5)
10,000	18,110	17,942 (—)	6329 (1159)

BMDP value is the true expected value of the optimal BMDP policy. SUB and DBRA values are averaged over 100 trials, which execute the relevant policies for all 1000 users (sample std. dev. also shown). The optimal BMDP policy has a considerable advantage over a static policy that forbids the per-user budget to be exceeded, yielding 2-3 times the return.[4] BMDP values also show a clear pat-

[4]Values are discounted, net of budget spent.

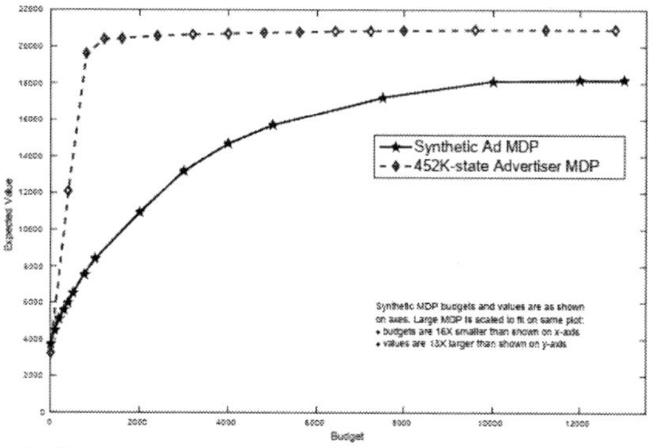

Fig. 4: Sweet spot curves: a plot of expected value vs. global budget for Synthetic and 452K-state MDPs (1000 users). The flat tails show that the maximal useful budget has been reached.

tern of diminishing return with increasing budget. Indeed, our MCKP-based GBA method allows one to *rapidly* assess the value of *optimally* using different global budgets to find the "sweet spot" in spend. Fig. 4 illustrates this *sweet spot curve*) for the joint MDP over 16 budget points.[5] The sweet spot curve is effectively the *Pareto frontier* expressing the tradeoff between two competing objectives, spend and expected return (for an in-depth survey of general multi-objective MDPs, please see [26]).

The optimal BMDP policy has considerable spend variance. In one run of 1000 customers (initial allocation 10 each), the sample average 10.012 is close to expected spend; but the sample std. dev. is 15.24. The empirical odds that a user exceeds the budget of 10 is 32.7%, and the odds of exceeding it by at least 50% is 28.7%. This alone explains the poor performance of the SUB allocation policy. Even with a large user base, overspending is possible: simulating the BMDP policy (1000 users) for 30 trials users, the global budget is exceeded in 13 of 30 trials, in 5 instances by over 3% (the largest overspend is by 11.7%). DBRA alleviates this risk—in all 100 trials the budget constraint is satisfied—while its average return matches or exceeds that of BMDP. With the very constrained budget (1000), DBRA also appears to offer the advantage of reallocating budget to more promising customers over time.

We also compare GBA to UBA on the same MDP, but with 1000 customers uniformly spread among the 12 nonterminal states (GBA and UBA are identical if all users start in the same state). The table below shows (exact) expected value of GBA and UBA for several global budgets.

Total Bud.	GBA Val.	UBA Val.
1000	39818.6	36997.2
2000	44559.5	40311.8
5000	53177.7	47142.4
10,000	58356.8	53773.8

The optimal BMDP solution allows GBA to make budget tradeoffs among customers in different states, giving greater value than a uniform scheme.

[5]The greedy algorithm averages 1.47ms. to compute the optimal allocation at each budget point.

Advertiser MDPs. We apply the same four methods to the advertiser-based MDPs. We first use GBA to derive "sweet spot" curves for the large MDP (results are similar for the 1469-state MDP). We assume 1000 customers, with 20 customers each entering the process in the 50 states with the largest "value spans" (i.e., difference in expected value given the minimal and maximal useful budget). Fig. 4 shows the budget-value tradeoff.

These MDPs model behavior that is quite random (i.e., not influenced very strongly by the actions). As a consequence, once the GBA algorithm is run, there is not a great difference between the BMDP and SUB policies. The table below shows results for the 452K-state BMDP for two fairly constrained budget levels (DBRA, SUB are averaged over 50 trials, BMDP and UBA values are exact).

Budg.	BMDP Val.	DBRA Val.	SUB Val.	UBA Val.
15	113358	99236 (3060)	112879 (1451)	106373
25	157228	142047 (3060)	157442 (2589)	149175

Neither BMDP nor SUB exhibit much variance in spend and both have similar expected values. SUB rarely overspends (e.g., maximum overspend for SUB with $B = 25$ is 0.16%). Variance tends to be greater when budgets are tighter. Among the 50 BMDP trials, 14 instances exceed the global budget, though only four instances exceed it by more than 4.0% (and one does so by 8.6%). DBRA eliminates the risk of overspending, but in this problem has a negative impact on expected value. GBA offers greater expected value than UBA (which is the only viable option if the BMDP has not been solved). GBA exceeds UBA by up to 6.5% over a range of constrained budgets.

5 CONCLUDING REMARKS

We have addressed the problem of budget (or other resource) allocation in MDPs so that budget-value tradeoffs can be addressed effectively. Our *budgeted MDP* model offers an alternative view of CMDPs that allows value to be derived as a function of available budget. We characterized the structure of optimal VFs and developed a DP algorithm that exploits the PWLC form of these VFs. Our second contribution was a method for exploiting BMDP solutions to allocate budget across independently operating BMDPs. We cast the problem as multi-item MCKP for which a simple greedy algorithm rapidly allocates budget optimally in a "committed" fashion. We also investigated dynamic reallocation of budget over time.

The extension of our methods to account for dynamic user populations is straightforward, but warrants empirical investigation. Future work includes the further study of and experimentation with our algorithms on richer models of user behavior. We are also interested in extending our models to partially observable settings (e.g., where user type estimation based on behavioral observations is needed).

References

[1] D. Adelman and A. Mersereau. Relaxations of weakly coupled stochastic dynamic programs. *Operations Research*, 56(3):712–727, 2008.

[2] E. Altman. *Constrained Markov Decision Processes*. Chapman and Hall, London, 1999.

[3] K. Amin, M. Kearns, P. Key, and A. Schwaighofer. Budget optimization for sponsored search: Censored learning in MDPs. In *UAI-12*, pp.543–553, 2012.

[4] N. Archak, V. Mirrokni, and S. Muthukrishnan. Budget optimization for online campaigns with positive carryover effects. In *WINE-12*, pp.86–99, 2012.

[5] N. Archak, V. Mirrokni, and S. Muthukrishnan. Mining advertiser-specific user behavior using adfactors. In *WWW 2010*, pp.31–40, 2010.

[6] C. Borgs, J. Chayes, O. Etesami, N. Immorlica, K. Jain, and M. Mahdian. Bid optimization in online advertisement auctions. In *Workshop on Sponsored Search Auctions*, 2006.

[7] C. Boutilier, T. Dean, and S. Hanks. Decision theoretic planning: Structural assumptions and computational leverage. *J. Artificial Intel. Res.*, 11:1–94, 1999.

[8] B. Bronnenberg. Advertising frequency decisions in a discrete Markov process under a budget constraint. *J. Marketing Res.*, 35(3):399–406, 1998.

[9] P. Bühlmann and A. Wyner. Variable-length Markov chains. *Annals of Stat.*, 27(2):480–513, 1999.

[10] M. Charikar, R. Kumar, P. Raghavan, S. Rajagopalan, and A. Tomkins. On targeting Markov segments. In *STOC-99*, pp.99–108, 1999.

[11] F. Chierichetti, R. Kumar, P. Raghavan, and T. Sarlos. Are web users really Markovian? In *WWW-12*, pp.609–618, 2012.

[12] B. DasGupta and S. Muthukrishnan. Stochastic budget optimization in internet advertising. *Algorithmica*, 65(3):634–661, 2013.

[13] D. Dolgov and E. Durfee. Stationary deterministic policies for constrained MDPs with multiple rewards, costs, and discount factors. In *IJCAI-05*, pp.1326–1331, 2005.

[14] D. Dolgov and E. Durfee. Optimal resource allocation and policy formulation in loosely-coupled Markov decision processes. In *ICAPS-04*, pp.315–324, 2004.

[15] G. Feichtinger, R. Hartl, and S. Sethi. Dynamic optimal control models in advertising: Recent developments. *Mgmt. Sci.*, 40(2):195–226, 1994.

[16] J. Feldmann, S. Muthukrishnan, M. Pál, and C. Stein. Budget optimization in search-based advertising auctions. In *ACM EC'07*, pp.40–49, 2007.

[17] A. Ghosh, P. McAfee, K. Papineni, and S. Vassilvitskii. Bidding for representative allocations for display advertising. In *WINE-09*, pp.208–219, 2009.

[18] R. Graham. An efficient algorithm for determining the convex hull of a finite planar set. *Inf. Proc. Letters*, 1(4):132–133, 1972.

[19] D. Holthausen, Jr. and G. Assmus. Advertising budget allocation under uncertainty. *Mgmt. Sci.*, 28(5):487–499, 1982.

[20] C. Karande, A. Mehta, and R. Srikant. Optimizing budget constrained spend in search advertising. In *WSDM-13*, pp.697–706, 2013.

[21] T. Li, N. Liu, J. Yan, G. Wang, F. Bai, and Z. Chen. A Markov chain model for integrating behavioral targeting into contextual advertising. In *ADKDD-09*, pp.1–9, 2009.

[22] F. Melo and M. Veloso. Decentralized MDPs with sparse interactions. *Artificial Intel.*, 175(11):1757–1789, 2011.

[23] N. Meuleau, M. Hauskrecht, K. Kim, L. Peshkin, L. P. Kaelbling, T. Dean, and C. Boutilier. Solving very large weakly coupled Markov decision processes. In *AAAI-98*, pp.165–172, 1998.

[24] P. Otter. On dynamic selection of households for direct marketing based on Markov chain models with memory. *Marketing Letters*, 18(1):73–84, 1981.

[25] M. Puterman. *Markov Decision Processes: Discrete Stochastic Dynamic Programming*. Wiley, 1994.

[26] D. Roijers, P. Vamplew, S. Whiteson, and R. Dazeley. A survey of multi-objective sequential decision-making. *J. Artificial Intel. Res.*, 48:67–113, 2013.

[27] D. Silver, L. Newnham, D. Barker, S. Weller, and J. McFall. Concurrent reinforcement learning from customer interactions. In *ICML-13*, pp.924–932, 2013.

[28] S. Singh and D. Cohn. How to dynamically merge Markov decision processes. In *NIPS 10*, pp.1057–1063, 1998.

[29] P. Sinha and A. Zoltners. The multiple-choice knapsack problem. *Op. Res.*, 27(3):503–515, 1979.

[30] M. Spaan and F. Melo. Interaction-driven Markov games for decentralized multiagent planning under uncertainty. In *AAMAS-08*, pp.525–532, 2008.

[31] G. Theocharous, P. Thomas, and M. Ghavamzadeh. Personalized ad recommendation systems for life-time value optimization with guarantees. In *IJCAI-15*, pp.1806–1812, 2015.

Analysis of Nyström Method with Sequential Ridge Leverage Score Sampling

Daniele Calandriello
SequeL team
INRIA Lille - Nord Europe

Alessandro Lazaric
SequeL team
INRIA Lille - Nord Europe

Michal Valko
SequeL team
INRIA Lille - Nord Europe

Abstract

Large-scale kernel ridge regression (KRR) is limited by the need to store a large kernel matrix $\mathbf{K}_t$. To avoid storing the entire matrix $\mathbf{K}_t$, Nyström methods subsample a subset of columns of the kernel matrix, and efficiently find an approximate KRR solution on the reconstructed $\widetilde{\mathbf{K}}_t$. The chosen subsampling distribution in turn affects the statistical and computational tradeoffs. For KRR problems, [16, 1] show that a sampling distribution proportional to the *ridge leverage scores* (RLSs) provides strong reconstruction guarantees for $\widetilde{\mathbf{K}}_t$. While exact RLSs are as difficult to compute as a KRR solution, we may be able to approximate them well enough. In this paper, we study KRR problems in a sequential setting and introduce the INK-ESTIMATE algorithm, that *incrementally* computes the RLSs estimates. INK-ESTIMATE maintains a small *sketch* of $\mathbf{K}_t$, that at each step is used to compute an intermediate estimate of the RLSs. First, our sketch update does not require access to previously seen columns, and therefore a *single pass* over the kernel matrix is sufficient. Second, the algorithm requires a fixed, small space budget to run dependent only on the *effective dimension* of the kernel matrix. Finally, our sketch provides strong approximation guarantees on the distance $\|\mathbf{K}_t - \widetilde{\mathbf{K}}_t\|_2$, and on the statistical risk of the approximate KRR solution at *any time*, because all our guarantees hold at any intermediate step.

1 INTRODUCTION

Kernel ridge regression [17, 18] (KRR) is a common nonparametric regression method with well studied theoretical advantages. Its main drawback is that, for n samples, storing and manipulating the kernel regression matrix $\mathbf{K}_n$ requires $\mathcal{O}(n^2)$ space, and can become quickly intractable when n grows. This includes batch large scale KRR, and online KRR, where the size of the dataset t grows over time as new samples are added to the problem. For this purpose, many different methods [23, 4, 10, 14, 11, 24] attempt to reduce the memory required to store the kernel matrix, while still producing an accurate solution.

For the batch case, the Nyström family of algorithms randomly selects a subset of m columns from the kernel matrix $\mathbf{K}_n$ that are used to construct a low rank approximation $\widetilde{\mathbf{K}}_t$ that requires only $\mathcal{O}(nm)$ space to store. The low-rank matrix is then used to find an approximate solution to the KRR problem. The quality of the approximate solution is strongly affected by the sampling distribution and the number of columns selected [16]. For example, uniform sampling is an approach with little computational overhead, but does not work well for datasets with high coherence [7], where the columns are weakly correlated. In particular, Bach [2] shows that the number of columns m necessary for a good approximation when sampling uniformly scales linearly with the maximum degree of freedoms of the kernel matrix. In linear regression, the notion of coherence is strongly related to the definition of leverage points or *leverage scores* of the dataset [6], where points with high (statistical) leverage score are more influential in the regression problem. For KRR, Alaoui and Mahoney [1] introduce a similar concept of *ridge* leverage scores (RLSs) of a square matrix, and shows that Nyström approximations sampled according to RLS have strong reconstruction guarantees of the form $\|\mathbf{K}_n - \widetilde{\mathbf{K}}_n\|_2$, that translate into good guarantees for the approximate KRR solution [1, 16]. Compared to the uniform distribution, a distribution based on RLSs better captures non-uniformities in the data, and can achieve good approximations using only a number of columns m, proportional to the average degrees of freedom of the matrix, called the *effective dimension* of the problem. The disadvantage of RLSs compared to uniform sampling is the high computational cost of exact RLSs, which is comparable to solving KRR itself. Alaoui and Mahoney [1] reduces this problem by showing that a distribution based on approximate RLSs can also provide the same strong guarantees, if the RLSs are approximated up to a constant error factor. They provide a fast method to compute these RLSs, but, unlike our approach, requires multiple passes over data. Another disadvantage of their approach, that we address, is the *inverse dependence on the minimal eigenvalue* of the kernel matrix in the error bound of Alaoui and Mahoney [1], which can be significant.

While Nyström methods are a typical choice in a batch setting, *online kernel sparsification* (OKS) [4, 5] examines each sample in the dataset sequentially. OKS maintains a small *dictionary* of relevant samples. Whenever a new sample arrive, if the dictionary is not able to accurately represent the new sample as a combination of the samples already stored, the dictionary is updated. This dictionary can be used to approximate KRR incrementally. OKS decides whether to include a sample using the correlation between samples in the dictionary and the new sample. This can measured using approximate linear dependency (ALD) [5], coherence [15], or the surprise criterion [12].

Generalization properties of online kernel sparsification were studied by Engel et al. [5], but depend on the empirical error and are not compared with an exact KRR solution on the whole dataset. Online kernel regression with the ALD rule was analyzed by Sun et al. [19], under the assumption that, asymptotically in n, the eigenvalues of the kernel matrix decay exponentially fast. Sun et al. [19] show that in this case the size of the dictionary grows sublinearly in t, or in other words that, asymptotically in n, the dictionary size converge to a fraction of n that will be small whenever the eigenvalues decay fast enough. This space guarantee is weaker than the fixed space requirements of Nyström methods, one of the reasons is that these methods (unlike ours) cannot remove a sample from the dictionary after inclusion. Furthermore, Van Vaerenbergh et al. [22] studies variants of online kernel regression with a forgetting factor for time-varying series, but these methods are not well studied in the normal KRR setting. Unlike in the batch setting, in the sequential setting we often require the guarantees not only at the end but also *in the intermediate steps* and this is our objective. Inspired by the advances in the analyses of the Nyström methods, in this paper, we focus on finding a space efficient algorithm capable of solving KRR problems in the sequential setting but that would be also equipped with generalization guarantees.

Main contributions We propose the INK-ESTIMATE algorithm that processes a dataset $\mathcal{D}$ of size n in *a single pass*. It requires only a small, fixed space budget, $\overline{q}$ proportional to the effective dimension of the problem and on the accuracy required. The algorithm maintains a Nyström approximation $\widetilde{\mathbf{K}}_t$, of the kernel matrix at time t, $\mathbf{K}_t$, based on RLSs estimates. At each step, it uses only the approximation and the newly received sample to incrementally update the RLSs estimate, and to compute $\widetilde{\mathbf{K}}_{t+1}$. Unlike in the batch Nyström setting, our challenge is to track RLSs and an effective dimension that *changes over time*. Sampling distributions based on RLSs can become obsolete and biased, but we show how to update them over time *without necessity of accessing previously seen samples* outside of the ones contained in $\widetilde{\mathbf{K}}_t$. Our space budget $\overline{q}$ scales with the average degree of freedom of the matrix, and not the larger maximum degree of freedom (as by Bach [2]), and does not imposes assumptions on the ridge regularization parameter, or on the smallest eigenvalue of the problem as the result of Alaoui and Mahoney [1]. However, we provide the same strong guarantees as batch RLSs based Nyström methods on $\|\mathbf{K}_n - \widetilde{\mathbf{K}}_n\|_2$ and on the risk of the approximate KRR solution. In addition to batch Nyström methods, all of these guarantees hold at any intermediate step t, and therefore the algorithm can output *accurate intermediate solutions*, or it can be interrupted at *any time* and return a solution with guarantees. Finally, it operates in a *sequential* setting, requiring only a single pass over the data.

If we compare INK-ESTIMATE to other online kernel regression methods (such as OKS), our algorithm provides generalization guarantees with respect to the exact KRR solution. Furthermore, it provides a new criteria for inclusion of a sample in the dictionary, in particular the ridge leverage scores. This criterion gives us a procedure that not only randomly includes samples in the dictionary, but that also randomly discards them to satisfy space constraints not only asymptotically, but at every step.

2 BACKGROUND

In this section we introduce the notation used through the paper and we introduce the kernel ridge regression problem [17] and Nyström approximation of the kernel matrix with ridge leverage scores.

Notation. We use curly capital letters $\mathcal{A}$ for collections. We use upper-case bold letters $\mathbf{A}$ for matrices, lower-case bold letters $\mathbf{a}$ for vectors, and lower-case letters a for scalars. We denote by $[\mathbf{A}]_{ij}$ and $[\mathbf{a}]_i$ the (i, j) element of a matrix and ith element of a vector respectively. We denote by $\mathbf{I}_n \in \mathbb{R}^{n\times n}$ the identity matrix of dimension n and by $\mathrm{Diag}(\mathbf{a}) \in \mathbb{R}^{n\times n}$ the diagonal matrix with the vector $\mathbf{a} \in \mathbb{R}^n$ on the diagonal. We use $\mathbf{e}_{i,n} \in \mathbb{R}^n$ to denote the indicator vector for element i of dimension n. When the dimensionality of $\mathbf{I}$ and $\mathbf{e}_i$ is clear from the context, we omit the n. We use $\mathbf{A} \succeq \mathbf{B}$ to indicate that $\mathbf{A} - \mathbf{B}$ is a PSD matrix. Finally, the set of integers between 1 and n is denoted by $[n] := \{1, \ldots, n\}$.

2.1 Exact Kernel Ridge Regression

Kernel regression. We consider a regression dataset $\mathcal{D} = \{(\mathbf{x}_t, y_t)\}_{t=1}^n$, with input $\mathbf{x}_t \in \mathcal{X} \subseteq \mathbb{R}^d$ and output $y_t \in \mathbb{R}$. We denote by $\mathcal{K} : \mathcal{X} \times \mathcal{X} \to \mathbb{R}$ a positive definite kernel function and by $\varphi : \mathcal{X} \to \mathbb{R}^D$ the corresponding feature map,[1] so that the kernel is obtained as $\mathcal{K}(\mathbf{x}, \mathbf{x}') = \varphi(\mathbf{x})^\mathsf{T}\varphi(\mathbf{x}')$. Given the dataset $\mathcal{D}$, we define the kernel matrix $\mathbf{K}_t \in \mathbb{R}^{t \times t}$ constructed on the first t samples as the application of the kernel function on all pairs of input values, i.e., $[\mathbf{K}_t]_{ij} = \mathcal{K}(\mathbf{x}_i, \mathbf{x}_j)$ for any $i, j \in [t]$ and we denote by $\mathbf{y}_t \in \mathbb{R}^t$ the vector with components y_i, $i \in [t]$. We also define the feature vectors $\phi_t = \varphi(\mathbf{x}_t) \in \mathbb{R}^D$ and after introducing the feature matrix

$$\mathbf{\Phi}_t = \left[\; \phi_1 \mid \phi_2 \mid \ldots \mid \phi_t \; \right] \in \mathbb{R}^{D \times t},$$

we can rewrite the kernel matrix as $\mathbf{K}_t = \mathbf{\Phi}_t^\mathsf{T}\mathbf{\Phi}_t$. Whenever a new point $\mathbf{x}_{t+1}$ arrives, the kernel matrix $\mathbf{K}_{t+1} \in \mathbb{R}^{t+1 \times t+1}$ is obtained by bordering $\mathbf{K}_t$ as

$$\mathbf{K}_{t+1} = \left[\begin{array}{c|c} \mathbf{K}_t & \overline{\mathbf{k}}_{t+1} \\ \hline \overline{\mathbf{k}}_{t+1}^\mathsf{T} & k_{t+1} \end{array} \right] \tag{1}$$

where $\overline{\mathbf{k}}_{t+1} \in \mathbb{R}^t$ is such that $[\overline{\mathbf{k}}_{t+1}]_i = \mathcal{K}(\mathbf{x}_{t+1}, \mathbf{x}_i)$ for any $i \in [t]$ and $k_{t+1} = \mathcal{K}(\mathbf{x}_{t+1}, \mathbf{x}_{t+1})$. According to the definition of the feature matrix $\mathbf{\Phi}_t$, we also have $\mathbf{k}_{t+1} = \mathbf{\Phi}_t^\mathsf{T}\phi_{t+1}$.

At any time t, the objective of *sequential* kernel regression is to find the vector $\widehat{\mathbf{w}}_t \in \mathbb{R}^t$ that minimizes the regularized quadratic loss

$$\widehat{\mathbf{w}}_t = \arg\min_{\mathbf{w}} \|\mathbf{y}_t - \mathbf{K}_t\mathbf{w}\|^2 + \mu\|\mathbf{w}\|^2, \tag{2}$$

where $\mu \in \mathbb{R}$ is a regularization parameter. This objective admits the closed form solution

$$\widehat{\mathbf{w}}_t = (\mathbf{K}_t + \mu\mathbf{I})^{-1}\mathbf{y}_t. \tag{3}$$

In the following, we use $\mathbf{K}_t^\mu$ as a short-hand for $(\mathbf{K}_t + \mu\mathbf{I})$. In batch regression, $\widehat{\mathbf{w}}_n$ is computed only once when all the samples of $\mathcal{D}$ are available, solving the linear system in Eq. 3 with $\mathbf{K}_n$. In the *fixed-design* kernel regression, the accuracy of resulting solution $\widehat{\mathbf{w}}_n$ is measured by the prediction error on the input set from $\mathcal{D}$. More precisely, the prediction of the estimator $\widehat{\mathbf{w}}_n$ in each point is obtained as $[\mathbf{K}_n\widehat{\mathbf{w}}_n]_i$, while the outputs y_i in the dataset are assumed to be a noisy observation of an unknown target function $f^* : \mathcal{X} \to \mathbb{R}$, evaluated in x_i i.e., for any $i \in [n]$,

$$y_i = f^*(x_i) + \eta_i,$$

where η_i is a zero-mean i.i.d. noise with bounded variance σ^2. Let $\mathbf{f}^* \in \mathbb{R}^n$ be the vector with components $f^*(x_i)$, then the risk of $\widehat{\mathbf{w}}_n$ is measured as

$$\mathcal{R}(\widehat{\mathbf{w}}_n) = \mathbb{E}_\eta\left[\|\mathbf{f}^* - \mathbf{K}_n\widehat{\mathbf{w}}_n\|_2^2\right]. \tag{4}$$

If the regularization parameter μ is properly tuned, it is possible to show that $\widehat{\mathbf{w}}_n$ has near-optimal risk guarantees (in a minmax sense). Nonetheless, the computation of $\widehat{\mathbf{w}}_n$ requires $\mathcal{O}(n^3)$ time and $\mathcal{O}(n^2)$ space, which becomes rapidly unfeasible for large datasets.

[1] where D can be very large or infinite (e.g. gaussian kernel)

2.2 Nyström Approximation with Ridge Leverage Scores

A common approach to reduce the complexity of kernel regression is to (randomly) select a subset of m samples out of $\mathcal{D}$, and compute the kernel between two points only when one of them is in the selected subset. This is equivalent to selecting a subset of columns of the $\mathbf{K}_n$ matrix. More formally, given the n samples in $\mathcal{D}$, a probability distribution $\mathbf{p}_n = [p_{1,n}, \ldots, p_{n,n}]$ is defined over all columns of $\mathbf{K}_n$ and $m \leq n$ columns are randomly sampled with replacement according to $\mathbf{p}_n$. We define by $\mathcal{I}_n$ the sequence of m indices $i \in [n]$ selected by the sampling procedure. From $\mathcal{I}_n$, we construct the corresponding selection matrix $\mathbf{S}_n \in \mathbb{R}^{n \times m}$, where each column $[\mathbf{S}_n]_{:,t} \in \mathbb{R}^n$ is all-zero except from the entry corresponding to the t-th element in $\mathcal{I}_n$ (i.e., $[\mathbf{S}]_{ij}$ is non-zero if at trial j the element i is selected). Whenever the non-zero entries of $\mathbf{S}_n$ are set to 1, sampling m columns from matrix $\mathbf{K}_n$ is equivalent to computing $\mathbf{K}_n\mathbf{S}_n \in \mathbb{R}^{n \times m}$. More generally, the non-zero entries of $\mathbf{S}_n$ could be set to some arbitrary weight $[\mathbf{S}]_{ij} = b_{ij}$. The resulting regularized Nyström approximation of the original kernel $\mathbf{K}_n$ is defined as

$$\widetilde{\mathbf{K}}_n = \mathbf{K}_n\mathbf{S}_n(\mathbf{S}_n^\mathsf{T}\mathbf{K}_n\mathbf{S}_n + \gamma\mathbf{I}_m)^{-1}\mathbf{S}_n^\mathsf{T}\mathbf{K}_n, \tag{5}$$

where γ is a regularization term (possibly different from μ). At this point, $\widetilde{\mathbf{K}}_n$ can be used to solve Eq. 3. Let $\mathbf{W} = (\mathbf{S}_n^\mathsf{T}\mathbf{K}_n\mathbf{S}_n + \gamma\mathbf{I}_m)^{-1} \in \mathbb{R}^{m \times m}$ and $\mathbf{C} = \mathbf{K}_n\mathbf{S}_n\mathbf{W}^{1/2} \in \mathbb{R}^{n \times m}$, applying the Woodbury inversion formula [8] we have

$$\begin{aligned}\widetilde{\mathbf{w}}_n =& (\widetilde{\mathbf{K}}_n + \mu\mathbf{I}_n)^{-1}\mathbf{y}_n = (\mathbf{C}\mathbf{I}_m\mathbf{C}^\mathsf{T} + \mu\mathbf{I}_n)^{-1}\mathbf{y}_n \\ =& \left(\frac{1}{\mu}\mathbf{I}_n - \frac{1}{\mu^2}\mathbf{I}_n\mathbf{C}\left(\mathbf{I}_m + \frac{1}{\mu}\mathbf{C}^\mathsf{T}\mathbf{C}\right)^{-1}\mathbf{C}^\mathsf{T}\mathbf{I}_n\right)\mathbf{y}_n \\ =& \frac{1}{\mu}\left(\mathbf{y}_n - \mathbf{C}\left(\mathbf{C}^\mathsf{T}\mathbf{C} + \mu\mathbf{I}_m\right)^{-1}\mathbf{C}^\mathsf{T}\mathbf{y}_n\right).\end{aligned} \tag{6}$$

Computing $\mathbf{W}^{1/2}$ and $\mathbf{C}$ takes $\mathcal{O}(m^3)$ and $\mathcal{O}(nm^2)$ time using a singular value decomposition, and so does solving the linear system. All the operations require to store at most an $n \times m$ matrix. Therefore the final complexity is reduced from $\mathcal{O}(n^3)$ to $\mathcal{O}(nm^2 + m^3)$ time, and from $\mathcal{O}(n^2)$ to $\mathcal{O}(nm)$ space. Rudi et al. [16] recently showed that in random design, the risk of the resulting solution $\widetilde{\mathbf{w}}_n$ strongly depends on the choice of m and the column sampling distribution $\mathbf{p}_n$. Early methods sampled columns uniformly, and Bach [2] shows that the using this distribution can provide a good approximation when the maximum diagonal entry of $\mathbf{K}_n(\mathbf{K}_n + \mu\mathbf{I})^{-1}$ is small. Following on this approach, Alaoui and Mahoney [1] propose a distribution proportional to these diagonal entries and calls them γ-Ridge Leverage Scores. We now restate their definition of RLS, corresponding sampling distribution, and the effective dimension.

Definition 1. *Given a kernel matrix* $\mathbf{K}_n \in \mathbb{R}^{n\times n}$, *the* γ-*ridge leverage score (RLS) of column* $i \in [n]$ *is*

$$\tau_{i,n}(\gamma) = \mathbf{k}_{i,n}^{\mathsf{T}}(\mathbf{K}_n + \gamma \mathbf{I}_m)^{-1}\mathbf{e}_{i,n}, \tag{7}$$

where $\mathbf{k}_{i,n} = \mathbf{K}_n \mathbf{e}_{i,n}$. *Furthermore, the effective dimension* $d_{\mathit{eff}}(\gamma)_n$ *of the kernel is defined as*

$$d_{\mathit{eff}}(\gamma)_n = \sum_{i=1}^{n} \tau_{i,n}(\gamma) = \mathrm{Tr}\left(\mathbf{K}_n(\mathbf{K}_n + \gamma \mathbf{I}_n)^{-1}\right). \tag{8}$$

The corresponding sampling distribution $\mathbf{p}_n$ *is defined as*

$$[\mathbf{p}_n]_i = p_{i,n} = \frac{\tau_{i,n}(\gamma)}{\sum_{j=1}^{n}\tau_{i,n}(\gamma)} = \frac{\tau_{i,n}}{d_{\mathit{eff}}(\gamma)_n}. \tag{9}$$

The RLSs are directly related to the structure of the kernel matrix and the regularized regression. If we perform an eigendecomposition of the kernel matrix as $\mathbf{K}_n = \mathbf{U}_n \mathbf{\Lambda}_n \mathbf{U}_n^{\mathsf{T}}$, then the RLS of a column $i \in [n]$ is

$$\tau_{i,n}(\gamma) = \sum_{j=1}^{n} \frac{\lambda_j}{\lambda_j + \gamma}[\mathbf{U}]_{i,j}^2, \tag{10}$$

which shows how the RLS is a weighted version of the standard leverage scores (i.e., $\sum_j [U]_{i,j}^2$), where the weights depend on both the spectrum of $\mathbf{K}_n$ and the regularization γ, which plays the role of a soft threshold on the rank of $\mathbf{K}_n$. Similar to the standard leverage scores [3], the RLSs measure the relevance of each point $\mathbf{x}_i$ for the overall kernel regression problem. Another interesting property of the RLSs is that their sum is the effective dimension $d_{\text{eff}}(\gamma)_n$, which measures the intrinsic capacity of the kernel $\mathbf{K}_n$ when its spectrum is soft-thresholded by a regularization γ.[2] We refer to the overall Nyström method using RLS and sampling according to to $\mathbf{p}_n$ in Eq. 9 as BATCH-EXACT, which is illustrated in Alg. 1. We single out the DIRECT-SAMPLE subroutine (which simply draws m independent samples from the multinomial distribution $\mathbf{p}_n$) to ease the introduction of our incremental algorithm in the next section.

With the following claim, Alaoui and Mahoney [1] prove that the regularized Nyström approximation $\widetilde{\mathbf{K}}_n$ obtained from Eq. 5 guarantees an accurate reconstruction of the original kernel matrix $\mathbf{K}_n$, and the risk of the associated solution $\widetilde{\mathbf{w}}_n$ is close to the risk of the exact solution $\widehat{\mathbf{w}}_n$.

Proposition 1 (Alaoui and Mahoney [1], App. A, Lem. 1). *Let* $\gamma \geq 1$, *let* $\mathbf{K}_n$ *be the full kernel matrix* ($t = n$), *and let* $\tau_{i,n}$, $d_{\mathit{eff}}(\gamma)_n$, $p_{i,n}$ *be defined according to Definition 1. For any* $0 \leq \varepsilon \leq 1$, *and* $0 \leq \delta \leq 1$, *if we run Alg. 1 using* DIRECT-SAMPLE *(Subroutine 1) with sampling budget* m,

$$m \geq \left(\frac{2d_{\mathit{eff}}(\gamma)}{\varepsilon^2}\right)\log\left(\frac{n}{\delta}\right),$$

to compute matrix $\mathbf{S}_n$, *then with probability* $1-\delta$ *the corresponding Nyström approximation* $\widetilde{\mathbf{K}}_n$ *in Eq. 5 satisfies the condition*

$$\mathbf{0} \preceq \mathbf{K}_n - \widetilde{\mathbf{K}}_n \preceq \frac{\gamma}{1-\varepsilon}\mathbf{K}_n(\mathbf{K}_n + \gamma \mathbf{I}_n)^{-1} \preceq \frac{\gamma}{1-\varepsilon}\mathbf{I}_n. \tag{11}$$

Furthermore, replacing $\mathbf{K}_n$ *by* $\widetilde{\mathbf{K}}_n$ *in Eq. 3 gives an approximation solution* $\widetilde{\mathbf{w}}_n$ *such that*

$$\mathcal{R}(\widetilde{\mathbf{w}}_n) \leq \left(1 + \frac{\gamma}{\mu}\frac{1}{1-\varepsilon}\right)^2 \mathcal{R}(\widehat{\mathbf{w}}_n).$$

Discussion This result directly relates the number of columns selected m with the accuracy of the approximation of the kernel matrix. In particular, the inequalities in Eq. 11 show that the distance $\|\mathbf{K}_n - \widetilde{\mathbf{K}}_n\|_2$ is smaller than $\gamma/(1-\varepsilon)$. This level of accuracy is then sufficient to guarantee that, when γ is properly tuned, the prediction error of $\widetilde{\mathbf{w}}_n$ is only a factor $(1+2\varepsilon)^2$ away from the error of the exact solution $\widehat{\mathbf{w}}$. As it was shown in [1], using $\widetilde{\mathbf{K}}_n$ in place of $\mathbf{K}_n$ introduces a bias in the solution $\widetilde{\mathbf{w}}_n$ of order γ. For appropriate choices of γ this bias is dominated by the ridge regularization bias controlled by μ. As a result, $\widetilde{\mathbf{w}}_n$ can indeed achieve almost the same risk as $\widehat{\mathbf{w}}_n$ and, at the same time, ignore all directions that are whitened by the regularization and only approximate those that are more relevant for ridge regression, thus reducing both time and space complexity. The RLSs quantify how important each column is to approximate these relevant directions but computing exact RLSs $\tau_{i,n}(\gamma)$ using Eq. 7 is as hard as solving the regression problem itself. Fortunately, in many cases it is computationally feasible to find an approximation of the RLSs. Alaoui and Mahoney [1] explore this possibility, showing that the accuracy and space guarantees are robust to perturbations in the distribution $\mathbf{p}_n$, and provide a two-pass method to compute such approximations. Unfortunately, the accuracy of their RLSs approximation is proportional to the smallest eigenvalue $\lambda_{\min}(\mathbf{K}_n)$, which in

---

Algorithm 1 BATCH-EXACT algorithm

Input: $\mathcal{D}$, regularization parameter γ, sampling budget m and probabilities $\mathbf{p}_n$ (Eq. 9)
Output: Nyström approximation $\widetilde{\mathbf{K}}_n$, matrix $\mathbf{S}_n$
1: Compute $\mathcal{I}_n$ using DIRECT-SAMPLE($\mathbf{p}_n, m$)
2: Compute $\mathbf{S}_n$ using $\mathcal{I}_n$ and weights $1/\sqrt{mp_{i,n}}$
3: Compute $\widetilde{\mathbf{K}}_n$ using $\mathbf{S}_n$ and Equation 5

Subroutine 1 DIRECT-SAMPLE($\mathbf{p}_n, m$) $\rightarrow \mathcal{I}_n$

Input: probabilities $\mathbf{p}_n$, sampling budget m
Output: subsampled column indices $\mathcal{I}_n$
1: **for** $j = \{1, \ldots, m\}$ **do**
2: Sample $i \sim \mathcal{M}(p_{1,n}, \ldots, p_{n,n})$
3: Add i to $\mathcal{I}_n$
4: **end for**

---

[2] Notice that indeed we have $d_{\text{eff}}(\gamma)_n \leq \mathrm{Rank}(\mathbf{K}_n)$.

Algorithm 2 The INK-ORACLE algorithm

Input: Dataset $\mathcal{D}$, regularization γ, sampling budget $\overline{q}$ and (α, β)-ORACLE
Output: $\widetilde{\mathbf{K}}_n$, $\mathbf{S}_n$

```
Initialize I_0 as empty, p̃_{1,0} = 1, b_{1,0} = 1, budget q̄
for t = 0, ..., n − 1 do
    Receive new column k̄_{t+1} and scalar k_{t+1}
    Receive α-leverage scores τ̃_{i,t+1} for any i ∈ I_t ∪ {t + 1} from (α, β)-ORACLE
    Receive β-approximate d̃_eff(γ)_{t+1} from (α, β)-ORACLE
    Set p̃_{i,t+1} = min{τ̃_{i,t+1}/d̃_eff(γ)_{t+1}, p̃_{i,t}}
    I_{t+1}, b_{t+1} = SHRINK-EXPAND(I_t, p̃_{t+1}, b_t, q̄)
    Compute S_{t+1} using I_{t+1} and weights √(b_{i,t+1})
    Compute K̃_{t+1} using S_{t+1} and Equation 5
end for
Return K̃_n and S_n
```

Subroutine 2 SHRINK-EXPAND$(\mathcal{I}_t, \widetilde{\mathbf{p}}_{t+1}, \mathbf{b}_t, \overline{q})$

Input: $\mathcal{I}_t$, app. pr. $\{(\widetilde{p}_{i,t+1}, b_{i,t}) : i \in \mathcal{I}_t\}$, $\widetilde{p}_{t+1,t+1}$, $\overline{q}$
Output: $\mathcal{I}_{t+1}$

```
for all j ∈ {1, ..., t} do                                  ▷SHRINK
    b_{i,t+1} = b_{i,t}
    while b_{i,t+1} p̃_{i,t+1} ≤ 1/q̄ and b_{i,t} ≠ 0 do
        Sample a random Bernoulli B( b_{i,t+1} / (b_{i,t+1}+1) )
        On success set b_{i,t+1} = b_{i,t+1} + 1
        On failure set b_{i,t+1} = 0
    end while
end for
b_{t+1,t+1} = 1                                             ▷EXPAND
while b_{t+1,t+1} p̃_{t+1,t+1} ≤ 1/q̄ and b_{t+1,t+1} ≠ 0 do
    Sample a random Bernoulli B( b_{t+1,t+1} / (b_{t+1,t+1}+1) )
    On success set b_{t+1,t+1} = b_{t+1,t+1} + 1
    On failure set b_{t+1,t+1} = 0
end while
Add to I_{t+1} all columns with b_{i,t+1} ≠ 0
```

some cases can be very small. In the rest of the paper, we propose an *incremental* approach that requires only a *single pass* over the data and, at the same time, does not depend on $\lambda_{\min}(\mathbf{K}_n)$ to be large as in [1], or on $\max_i \tau_{i,n}$ to be small as in [2].

3 INCREMENTAL ORACLE KERNEL APPROXIMATION WITH SEQUENTIAL SAMPLING

Our main goal is to extend the known ridge leverage score sampling to the *sequential setting*. This comes with several challenges that needs to be addressed *simultaneously:*

1. The RLSs change when a new sample arrives. We not only need to estimate them, but to *update* this estimate over iterations.
2. The effective dimension $\widetilde{d}_{\text{eff}}(\gamma)_t$, necessary to normalize the leverage scores for the sampling distribution $\mathbf{p}_n$, depends on the interactions of all columns, including the ones that we decided *not* to keep.
3. Due to changes in RLSs, our sampling distribution $\widetilde{\mathbf{p}}_t$ *changes over time.* We need to update to dictionary to reflect these changes, or it will quickly become *biased*, but once we completely drop a column, we cannot sample it again.

In this section, we address the third challenge of incremental updates of the columns with an algorithm for the approximation of the kernel matrix $\mathbf{K}_n$, assuming that the first and second issue are addressed by an *oracle* giving *both* good approximations of leverage scores and the effective dimension.

Definition 2. *At any step t, an (α, β)-oracle returns an α-approximate ridge leverage scores $\widetilde{\tau}_{i,t}$ which satisfy*

$$\frac{1}{\alpha}\tau_{i,t}(\gamma) \leq \widetilde{\tau}_{i,t} \leq \tau_{i,t}(\gamma),$$

for any $i \in [t]$ and and a β-approximate effective dimension $\widetilde{d}_{eff}(\gamma)_t$ which satisfy

$$d_{eff}(\gamma)_t \leq \widetilde{d}_{eff}(\gamma)_t \leq \beta d_{eff}(\gamma)_t.$$

We address the first and second challenge in Sect. 4 with an efficient implementation and (α, β)-oracle. In the following we give the *incremental* INK-ORACLE algorithm equipped with an (α, β)-oracle that after n steps it returns a kernel approximation with the same properties as if an (α, β)-oracle was used directly at time n.

3.1 The INK-ORACLE Algorithm

Apart from an (α, β)-ORACLE and the dataset $\mathcal{D}$, INK-ORACLE (Alg. 2) receives as input the regularization parameter γ used in constructing the final Nyström approximation and a sampling budget $\overline{q}$. It initializes the index dictionary $\mathcal{I}_0$ of stored columns as empty, and the estimated probabilities as $\widetilde{p}_{i,0} = 1$. Finally it initializes a set of integer weights $b_{i,0} = 1$. These weights will represent a discretized approximation of $1/\widetilde{p}_{i,t}$ (the inverse of the probabilities). At each time step t, it receives a new column $\overline{\mathbf{k}}_{t+1}$ and k_{t+1}. This can be implemented either by having a separate algorithm, constructing each column sequentially and stream it to INK-ORACLE, or by having INK-ORACLE store just the samples (for an additional $\mathcal{O}(td)$ space complexity) and independently compute the column once. The algorithm invokes the (α, β)-oracle to compute approximate probabilities $\widetilde{p}_{i,t+1} = \widetilde{\tau}_{i,t+1}/\widetilde{d}_{\text{eff}}(\gamma)_{t+1}$, and then takes the minimum $\min\{\widetilde{p}_{i,t+1}, \widetilde{p}_{i,t}\}$ for the sampling probability. As our analysis will reveal, this step is necessary to ensure that the SHRINK-EXPAND operation remains well defined, since the true probabilities $p_{i,t}$ decrease over time. It is important to notice that differently from the batch sampling setting, the approximate probabilities do not necessarily sum to one, but it is guaranteed that $\sum_{i=1}^{t} \widetilde{p}_{i,t} \leq 1$. The SHRINK-EXPAND procedure is composed of two steps. In the SHRINK step, we update the weights of the columns already in our dictionary. To decide whether a weight should be increased or not, the product of the weight at the preceding step $b_{i,t-1}$ and the new estimate $\widetilde{p}_{i,t}$ is compared to a threshold. If the product is above the threshold, it means the probability did not change much, and no action is necessary. If the product falls below the threshold, it means the decrease of $\widetilde{p}_{i,t}$ is significant, and the old weight is not representative anymore and should be increased. To increase the weight (e.g. from k to $k+1$), we draw a Bernoulli random variable $\mathcal{B}(\frac{k}{k+1})$, and if it succeeds we increase the weight to $k+1$, while if it fails we set the weight to 0. The more $\widetilde{p}_{i,t}$ decrease over time, the higher the chanches that $b_{i,t+1}$ is set to zero, and the index i (and the associated column $\mathbf{k}_{i,t+1}$) is completely dropped from the dictionary. Therefore, the SHRINK step randomly reduces the size of the dictionary to reflect the evolution of the probabilities. Conversely, the EXPAND step introduces the new column in the dictionary, and quickly updates its weight $b_{t,t}$ to reflect $\widetilde{p}_{t,t}$. Depending on the relevance (encoded by the RLS) of the new column, this means that it is possible that the new column is discarded at the same iteration as it is introduced. For a whole pass over the dataset, INK-ORACLE queries the oracle for each RLS at least once, but it *never* asks again for the RLS of a columns dropped from $\mathcal{I}_t$. As we will see in the next section, this greatly simplifies the construction of the oracle. Finally, after updating the dictionary, we use the updated weights $\sqrt{b_{i,t}}$ to update the approximation $\widetilde{\mathbf{K}}_t$, that can be used at any time and not only in the end.

3.2 Analysis of INK-ORACLE

The main result of this section is the lower bound on the number of columns required to be kept in order to guarantee a $\gamma/(1-\varepsilon)$ approximation of $\mathbf{K}_t$.

Theorem 1. *Let $\gamma > 1$. Given access to an (α, β)-oracle, for $0 \leq \varepsilon \leq 1$ and $0 \leq \delta \leq 1$, if we run Alg. 2 with parameter $\overline{q}$*

$$\overline{q} \geq \left(\frac{28\alpha\beta d_{\textit{eff}}(\gamma)_t}{\varepsilon^2}\right) \log\left(\frac{4t}{\delta}\right),$$

to compute a sequence of random matrices $\mathbf{S}_t$ with a random number of columns Q_t, then with probability $1-\delta$, for all t the corresponding Nyström approximation $\widetilde{\mathbf{K}}_t$ (Eq. 5) satisfies condition in Eq. 11,

$$\mathbf{0} \preceq \mathbf{K}_t - \widetilde{\mathbf{K}}_t \preceq \frac{\gamma}{1-\varepsilon}\mathbf{K}_t(\mathbf{K}_t + \gamma\mathbf{I})^{-1} \preceq \frac{\gamma}{1-\varepsilon}\mathbf{I}.$$

and the number of columns selected Q_t is such that

$$Q_t \leq 8\overline{q}.$$

Discussion Unlike in the batch setting, where the sampling procedure always returned m samples, the number of columns Q_t selected by INK-ORACLE is a random variable, but with high probability it will be not much larger than $\overline{q}$. Comparing INK-ORACLE to online kernel sparsification methods [19], we see that the number of columns, and therefore the space requirement, is guaranteed to be small not only asymptotically but at each step, and that no assumption on the spectrum of the matrix is required. Instead, the space complexity naturally scales with the effective dimension of the problem, and old samples that become superfluous are automatically discarded. Comparing Thm. 1 to Prop.1, INK-ORACLE achieves the same performance as its batch counterpart, as long as the space budget $\overline{q}$ is large enough. This budget depends on several quantities that are difficult to estimate, such as the effective dimension of the full kernel matrix. In practice, this quantity can be interpreted as the maximum amount of space that the user can afford for the algorithm to run. If the actual complexity of the problem exceeds this budget, the user can choose to run it again with another parameter γ or a worse accuracy ε. It is important to notice that, as we show in the proof, the distribution induced by the sampling procedure of INK-ORACLE is not the same as the distribution obtained by the multinomial sampling of BATCH-EXACT. Nonetheless, in our analysis we show that the bias introduced by the different distribution is small, and this allows INK-ORACLE to match the approximation guarantees given by Alaoui and Mahoney [1].

We give a detailed proof of Thm. 1 in App. B. In the rest of this section we sketch the proof and give the intuition for the most relevant parts.

The SHRINK step uses the thresholding condition to guarantee that the weight $b_{i,t}$ are good approximations of the $\widetilde{p}_{i,t}$. To make the condition effective, we require that the approximate probabilities $\widetilde{p}_{j,t}$ are decreasing. Because the approximate probabilities follow the true probabilities $p_{i,t}$, we first show that this decrease happens for the exact case.

Lemma 1. *For any kernel matrix $\mathbf{K}_t$ at time t, and its bordering $\mathbf{K}_{t+1}$ at time $t+1$ we have that the probabilities $p_{i,t}$ are monotonically decreasing over time t,*

$$\frac{\tau_{i,t+1}}{d_{\textit{eff}}(\gamma)_{t+1}} = p_{i,t+1} \leq p_{i,t} = \frac{\tau_{i,t+1}}{d_{\textit{eff}}(\gamma)_t}.$$

Since ridge leverage scores represent the importance of a column, when a new column arrives, there are two cases that can happen. If the column is orthogonal to the existing matrix, none of the previous leverage scores changes. If the new column can explain part of the previous columns, the previous columns should be picked less often, and we expect $\tau_{i,t}$ to decrease. Contrary to RLS, the effective dimension increases when the new sample is orthogonal to the existing matrix, while it stays the same when the new sample is a linear combination of the existing ones. In addition, the presence of γ regularizes both cases. When the vector is nearly orthogonal, the presence of $\gamma \mathbf{I}$ in the inverse will still penalize it, while the γ term at the denominator of Δ will reduce the influence of linearly correlated samples. Because $\tau_{i,t}$ decreases over time and $d_{\text{eff}}(\gamma)_{i,t}$ increases, the probabilities $p_{i,t}$ will overall decrease over time. This result itself is not sufficient to guarantee a well defined SHRINK step. Due to the (α, β)-approximation, it is possible that $p_{i,t+1} \leq p_{i,t}$ but $\widetilde{p}_{i,t+1} \not\leq \widetilde{p}_{i,t}$. To exclude this possibility, we adapt the following idea from Kelner and Levin [9].

Proposition 2 (Kelner and Levin [9]). *Given the approximate probabilities $\widetilde{\mathbf{p}}_t$ returned by an (α, β)-oracle at time t, and the approximate probabilities $\widetilde{\mathbf{p}}_{t+1}$ returned by an (α, β)-oracle at time $\{t+1\}$, then the approximate probabilities $\min^3\{\widetilde{\mathbf{p}}_t, \widetilde{\mathbf{p}}_{t+1}\}$ are also (α, β)-approximate for $\{t+1\}$. Therefore, without loss of generality, we can assume that $\widetilde{p}_{i,t+1} \leq \widetilde{p}_{i,t}$.*

Combining Lemma 1 and Proposition 2, we can guarantee that at each step the $\widetilde{p}_{i,t}$-s decrease. Unlike in the batch setting [1], we have to take additional care to consider correlations between iterations, the fact that the inclusion probabilities of Algorithm 2 are different from the multinomial ones of DIRECT-SAMPLE, and that the number of columns kept at each iteration is a *random* quantity Q_t. We adapt the approach of Pachocki [13] to the KRR setting to analyse this process. The key aspect is that the reweighting and rejection rule on line 3 of Algorithm 2 will only happen when the probabilities are truly changing. Finally, using a concentration inequality, we show that the number Q_t of columns selected is with high probability only a constant factor away from the budget $\overline{q}$ given to the algorithm.

4 LEVERAGE SCORES AND EFFECTIVE DIMENSION ESTIMATION

In the previous section we showed that our incremental sampling strategy based on (estimated) RLSs has strong space and approximation guarantees for $\widetilde{\mathbf{K}}_n$. While the analysis reported in the previous section relied on the existence of an (α, β)-oracle returning accurate leverage scores and effective dimension estimates, in this section we show that such an oracle *exists and can be implemented efficiently.* This is obtained by *two separate estimators* for the RLSs and effective dimension that are updated incrementally and combined together to determine the sampling probabilities.

4.1 Leverage Scores

We start by constructing an estimator that at each time t, takes as input an approximate kernel matrix $\widetilde{\mathbf{K}}_t$, and returns α-approximate RLS $\widetilde{\tau}_{i,t+1}$. The incremental nature of the estimator lies in the fact that it exploits access to the columns already in $\mathbf{S}_t$ and the new (exact) column $\overline{\mathbf{k}}_{t+1}$. We give the following approximation guarantees.

Lemma 2. *We assume that $\widetilde{\mathbf{K}}_t$ satisfies Eq. (11), and define $\overline{\mathbf{K}}_{t+1}$ as the matrix bordered with the new row and column*

$$\overline{\mathbf{K}}_{t+1} = \left[\begin{array}{c|c} \widetilde{\mathbf{K}}_t & \overline{\mathbf{k}}_{t+1} \\ \hline \overline{\mathbf{k}}_{t+1}^{\mathsf{T}} & k_{t+1} \end{array}\right].$$

Then

$$\mathbf{0} \preceq \mathbf{K}_{t+1} - \overline{\mathbf{K}}_{t+1} \preceq \frac{\gamma}{1-\varepsilon}\mathbf{I}.$$

Moreover let $\alpha = \frac{2-\varepsilon}{1-\varepsilon}$ and

$$\widetilde{\tau}_{i,t+1} = \frac{1}{\alpha\gamma}\left(k_{i,i} - \mathbf{k}_{i,t+1}\left(\overline{\mathbf{K}}_{t+1} + \alpha\gamma\mathbf{I}\right)^{-1}\mathbf{k}_{i,t+1}\right). \quad (12)$$

Then, for all i such that $\mathbf{k}_{i,t+1} \in \mathcal{I}_t \cup \{t+1\}$,

$$\frac{1}{\alpha}\tau_{i,t+1}(\gamma) \leq \widetilde{\tau}_{i,t+1} \leq \tau_{i,t+1}(\gamma).$$

Remark There are two important details that are used in proof of Lem. 2 (App. C). First, notice that using $\widetilde{\mathbf{K}}_t$ to approximate RLSs directly, would not be accurate enough. RLSs are defined as $\tau_{i,t}(\gamma) = \mathbf{e}_i^{\mathsf{T}}\mathbf{K}_t(\mathbf{K}_t + \gamma\mathbf{I})^{-1}\mathbf{e}_i$ and while the product $(\mathbf{K}_t + \gamma\mathbf{I})^{-1}\mathbf{e}_i$ can be accurately reconstructed using $(\widetilde{\mathbf{K}}_t + \gamma\mathbf{I})^{-1}\mathbf{e}_i$, the multiplication $\mathbf{K}_t\mathbf{e}_i$ cannot be approximated well using $\widetilde{\mathbf{K}}_t$. Since the nullspace of $\widetilde{\mathbf{K}}_t$ can be larger than the one of $\mathbf{K}_t$, it is possible that $\mathbf{e}_i$ partially falls into it, thus compromising the accuracy of the approximation of the RLS. In our approach, we deal with this problem by using the *actual columns* $\mathbf{k}_{i,t}$ of $\mathbf{K}_t$ to compute the RLS. This way, we preserve as much as exact information of the matrix as possible, while the expensive inversion operation is performed on the smaller approximation $\widetilde{\mathbf{K}}_t$. Since we require access to the stored columns $\mathbf{k}_{i,t}$, our approach can approximate the RLSs only for columns present in the dictionary but this is enough, since we are only interested in accurate probabilities for columns in the dictionary and for the new column $\overline{\mathbf{k}}_{t+1}$ (which is available at time $t+1$). As a comparison, the

[3] element-wise mininum

two-pass approach of Alaoui and Mahoney [1] uses the first pass just to compute an approximation $\widetilde{\mathbf{K}}_n$, and then approximates all leverage scores with $\widetilde{\mathbf{K}}_n(\widetilde{\mathbf{K}}_n + \gamma\mathbf{I})^{-1}$. This has an impact on their approximation factor α, that is proportional to $(\lambda_{\min}(\mathbf{K}_n) - \gamma\varepsilon)$. Therefore to have $\alpha \approx (\lambda_{\min}(\mathbf{K}_n) - \gamma\varepsilon) > 0$, it is necessary that $\gamma\varepsilon$ is of the order of $\lambda_{\min}(\mathbf{K}_n)$, which in some cases can be very small, and strongly increase the space requirements of the algorithm. Using the actual columns of the matrix in Eq. 12 allows us to compute an α-approximation independent of the smallest eigenvalue.

4.2 Effective Dimension

Using Eq. 12, we can estimate all the RLSs that we need to update $\mathbf{S}_t$. Nonetheless, to prove that the number of columns selected is not too large, the proof of Thm. 1 in the appendix requires that the sum of the probabilities $\widetilde{p}_{i,t}$ is smaller than 1. Therefore we not only need to compute the RLSs, but also a normalization constant. Indeed, a naïve definition of the probability $\widetilde{p}_{i,t}$ could be $p_{i,t} = \frac{\widetilde{\tau}_{i,t}}{\sum_{j=1}^{t}\widetilde{\tau}_{i,t}}$. A major challenge in our setting is that we cannot compute the sum of the approximate RLSs, because we do not have access to all the columns. Fortunately, we know that $\sum_{j=1}^{t}\widetilde{\tau}_{i,t} \leq \sum_{j=1}^{t}\tau_{i,t}(\gamma) = d_{\text{eff}}(\gamma)_t$. Therefore, one of our technical contribution is an estimator $\widetilde{d}_{\text{eff}}(\gamma)_t$ that does not use the approximate RLSs for the the columns that we no longer have. We now define this estimator and state its approximation accuracy.

Lemma 3. *Assume $\widetilde{\mathbf{K}}_t$ satisfies Eq. 11. Let $\alpha = \left(\frac{2-\varepsilon}{1-\varepsilon}\right)$ and $\beta = \left(\frac{2-\varepsilon}{1-\varepsilon}\right)^2(1+\rho)$ with $\rho = \frac{\lambda_{\max}(\mathbf{K}_n)}{\gamma}$. Define*

$$\widetilde{d}_{\text{eff}}(\gamma)_{t+1} = \widetilde{d}_{\text{eff}}(\gamma)_t + \alpha\widetilde{\Delta}_t \tag{13}$$

with

$$\begin{aligned}\widetilde{\Delta}_t = & \frac{1}{k_{t+1} + \gamma - \overline{\mathbf{k}}_{t+1}^{\mathsf{T}}\left(\widetilde{\mathbf{K}}_t + \alpha\gamma\mathbf{I}\right)^{-1}\overline{\mathbf{k}}_{t+1}} \\ & \times \left(k_{t+1} - \overline{\mathbf{k}}_{t+1}^{\mathsf{T}}\left(\widetilde{\mathbf{K}}_t + \alpha\gamma\mathbf{I}\right)^{-1}\overline{\mathbf{k}}_{t+1}\right. \\ & \left. - \frac{(1-\varepsilon)^2}{4}\gamma\overline{\mathbf{k}}_{t+1}^{\mathsf{T}}(\widetilde{\mathbf{K}}_t + \gamma\mathbf{I})^{-2}\overline{\mathbf{k}}_{t+1}\right).\end{aligned} \tag{14}$$

Then

$$d_{\textit{eff}}(\gamma)_{t+1} \leq \widetilde{d}_{\textit{eff}}(\gamma)_{t+1} \leq \beta d_{\textit{eff}}(\gamma)_{t+1}.$$

Discussion Since we cannot compute accurate RLSs for columns that are not present in the dictionary, we prefer to not estimate how each RLSs changes over time, but instead we directly estimate the increment of their sum. We do it by updating our estimate $\widetilde{d}_{\text{eff}}(\gamma)_{t+1}$ using our previous estimate $\widetilde{d}_{\text{eff}}(\gamma)_t$, and $\widetilde{\Delta}_t$. $\widetilde{\Delta}_t$ captures directly the interaction of the new sample with the *aggregate* of the previous samples, and allows us to estimate the increase in effective dimension using only the current matrix approximation $\widetilde{\mathbf{K}}_t$, the new column $\overline{\mathbf{k}}_{t+1}$ and the scalar k_{t+1}. Differently from the other terms we studied, the numerator of $\widetilde{\Delta}_t$ contains an additional $\gamma\overline{\mathbf{k}}_{t+1}^{\mathsf{T}}(\widetilde{\mathbf{K}}_t + \gamma\mathbf{I})^{-2}\overline{\mathbf{k}}_{t+1}$ second order term. The guarantees provided by Eq. 11 are not straightforward to extend because in general if $(\mathbf{K}_t + \gamma\mathbf{I})^{-1} \succeq (\widetilde{\mathbf{K}}_t + \alpha\gamma\mathbf{I})^{-1}$, it is not guaranteed that $(\mathbf{K}_t + \gamma\mathbf{I})^{-2} \succeq (\widetilde{\mathbf{K}}_t + \alpha\gamma\mathbf{I})^{-2}$. Nonetheless, we show that $\widetilde{\mathbf{K}}_t$ is still sufficient to estimate $\widetilde{\Delta}_t$, but, unlike α, the approximation error β is now dependent on the spectrum.

Algorithm 3 The INK-ESTIMATE algorithm

Input: Dataset $\mathcal{D}$, regularization γ, sampling budget $\overline{q}$
Output: $\widetilde{\mathbf{K}}_n$, $\mathbf{S}_n$

```
Initialize I_0 as empty, p̃_{1,0} = 1, b_{1,0} = 1, budget q̄
for t = 0, ..., n − 1 do
    Receive new column k̄_{t+1} and scalar k_{t+1}
    Compute α-leverage scores {τ̃_{i,t+1} : i ∈ I_t ∪ {t + 1}}, using K̃_{t+1}, k_i, k_{i,i}, and Eq. (12)
    Compute β-approximate d̃_eff(γ)_{t+1} using K̃_t, k̄_{t+1}, k_{t+1}, and Eq. (13)
    Set p̃_{i,t+1} = min{τ̃_{i,t+1}/d̃_eff(γ)_{t+1}, p̃_{i,t}}
    I_{t+1}, b_{t+1} = SHRINK-EXPAND(I_t, p̃_{t+1}, b_t, q̄)
    Compute S_{t+1} using I_{t+1} and weights √b_{i,t+1}
    Compute K̃_{t+1} using S_{t+1} and Equation 5
end for
Return K̃_n and S_n
```

4.3 Analysis of INK-ESTIMATE

With the separate estimates for leverage scores (Sect. 4.1) and effective dimension (Sect. 4.2), we have the necessary ingredients for the (α, β)-oracle and we are ready to present the final algorithm INK-ESTIMATE (Alg. 3).

Using the approximation guarantees of Lem. 2 and Lem. 3, we are ready to state the final result, instantiating the generic α and β terms of Thm. 2 with the values obtained in this section.

Theorem 2. *Let $\rho = \lambda_{\max}(\mathbf{K}_t)/\gamma$, $\alpha = \left(\frac{2-\varepsilon}{1-\varepsilon}\right)$, $\beta = \left(\frac{2-\varepsilon}{1-\varepsilon}\right)^2(1+\rho)$, and $\gamma > 1$. For any $0 \leq \varepsilon \leq 1$, and $0 \leq \delta \leq 1$, if we run Alg. 3 with parameter $\overline{q}$, where*

$$\overline{q} \geq \left(\frac{28\alpha\beta d_{\textit{eff}}(\gamma)_t}{\varepsilon^2}\right)\log\left(\frac{4t}{\delta}\right),$$

to compute a sequence of random matrices $\mathbf{S}_t$ with a random number of columns Q_t, then with probability $1-\delta$, for all t the corresponding Nyström approximation $\widetilde{\mathbf{K}}_t$ (Eq. 5) *satisfies condition 11*

$$\mathbf{0} \preceq \mathbf{K}_t - \widetilde{\mathbf{K}}_t \preceq \frac{\gamma}{1-\varepsilon}\mathbf{K}_t(\mathbf{K}_t + \gamma\mathbf{I})^{-1} \preceq \frac{\gamma}{1-\varepsilon}\mathbf{I}.$$

With the same prob., INK-ESTIMATE *requires at most*

$$\begin{aligned}&\mathcal{O}(n^2\overline{q}^2 + n\overline{q}^3)\\&\leq \mathcal{O}\left(\alpha^2\beta^2 n^2 d_{\mathit{eff}}(\gamma)_n^2 + \alpha^3\beta^3 n d_{\mathit{eff}}(\gamma)_n^3\right)\\&= \mathcal{O}\left(\alpha^4(1+\rho)^2 n^2 d_{\mathit{eff}}(\gamma)_n^2 + \alpha^6(1+\rho)^3 n d_{\mathit{eff}}(\gamma)_n^3\right)\end{aligned}$$

time and the space is bounded as

$$\mathcal{O}(n\overline{q}) \leq \mathcal{O}\left(\alpha\beta n d_{\mathit{eff}}(\gamma)_n\right) = \mathcal{O}\left(\alpha^2(1+\rho) n d_{\mathit{eff}}(\gamma)_n\right).$$

For the space complexity, from Theorem 1 we know we will not select more than $\mathcal{O}(\overline{q})$ columns in high probability. For the time complexity, at each iteration we need to solve linear systems involving $(\overline{\mathbf{K}}_{t+1} + \alpha\gamma\mathbf{I})^{-1}$ and $(\widetilde{\mathbf{K}}_t + \alpha\gamma\mathbf{I})^{-1}$. Approximating the inverse using transformations similar to Eq. (6) takes $\mathcal{O}(t\overline{q}^2 + \overline{q}^3)$ time, again using a singular value decomposition approach. To compute all leverage scores, we need to first compute an approximate inverse in $\mathcal{O}(t\overline{q}^2 + \overline{q}^3)$ time, and then solve Q_t systems, each using a multiplication costing $\mathcal{O}(tQ_t)$. With high probability, $Q_t \leq 8\overline{q}$, therefore computing all leverage scores costs $\mathcal{O}(t\overline{q}^2 + \overline{q}^3)$ for the first singular value decomposition, and $\mathcal{O}(t\overline{q})$ for each of the $\mathcal{O}(\overline{q})$ applications. To update the effective dimension estimate, we only have to compute another approximate inverse, and that costs $\mathcal{O}(t\overline{q}^2 + \overline{q}^3)$ as well. Finally, we have to sum the costs over n steps, and from $\sum_{t=1}^{n} t\overline{q}^2 \leq \overline{q}^2 n^2$, we obtain the final complexity. Even with a significantly different approach, INK-ESTIMATE achieves the same approximation guarantees as BATCH-EXACT. Consequently, it provides the same risk guarantees as the known batch version [1], stated in the following corollary.

Corollary 1. *For every $t \in \{1, \ldots, n\}$, let $\mathbf{K}_t$ be the kernel matrix at time t. Run Algorithm 3 with regularization parameter γ and space budget $\overline{q}$. Then, at any time t, the solution $\widetilde{\mathbf{w}}_t$ computed using the regularized Nyström approximation $\widetilde{\mathbf{K}}_t$ satisfies*

$$\begin{aligned}\mathcal{R}(\widetilde{\mathbf{w}}_t) &\leq \left(1 + \frac{\gamma}{\mu}\frac{1}{1-\varepsilon}\right)^2 \mathcal{R}(\widehat{\mathbf{w}}_t)\\&= \left(1 + \frac{\lambda_{\max}(\mathbf{K}_t)}{\rho\mu}\frac{1}{1-\varepsilon}\right)^2 \mathcal{R}(\widehat{\mathbf{w}}_t).\end{aligned}$$

Discussion Thm. 2 combines the generic result of Thm. 1 with the actual implementation of an oracle that we developed in this section. All the guarantees that hold for INK-ORACLE are inherited by INK-ESTIMATE, but now we can quantify the impact of the errors α and β on the algorithm. As we saw, the α error does not depends on the time, the spectrum of the kernel matrix or other quantities that increase over time. On the other hand, estimating the effective dimension without having access to all the leverage scores is a much harder task, and the β factor depends on the spectrum through the ρ coefficient. The influence that this coefficient exerts on the space and time complexity can vary significantly as the relative magnitude of $\lambda_{\max}(\mathbf{K}_n)$, γ and μ changes. If the largest eigenvalue grows too large without a corresponding increase in γ, the space and time requirements of INK-ESTIMATE can grow, but the risk bound, depending on γ/μ remains small. On the other hand, increasing γ without increasing μ reduces the computational complexity, but makes the guarantees on the risk of the solution $\widetilde{\mathbf{w}}_t$ much weaker. As an example, [1, Thm. 3] chooses, $\mu \geq \lambda_{\max}(\mathbf{K}_n)$ and $\gamma \approxeq \mu$. If we do the same, we recover their bound.

5 CONCLUSION

We presented a space-efficient algorithm for sequential Nyström approximation that requires only a single pass over the dataset to construct a low-rank matrix $\widetilde{\mathbf{K}}_n$ that accurately approximates the kernel matrix $\mathbf{K}_n$, and compute an approximate KRR solution $\widetilde{\mathbf{w}}_n$ whose risk is close to the exact solution $\widehat{\mathbf{w}}_n$. All of these guarantees do not hold only for the final matrix, but are valid for all intermediate matrices $\widetilde{\mathbf{K}}_t$ constructed by the sequential algorithm.

To address the challenges coming from the sequential setup, we introduced two separate estimators for RLSs and effective dimension that provide multiplicative error approximations of these two quantities across iterations. While the approximation of the RLSs is only a constant factor away from the exact RLSs, the error of the approximate effective dimension scales with the spectrum of the matrix through the coefficient ρ. A more careful analysis, or a different estimator might improve this dependence, and they can be easily plugged to the general analysis.

Our generalization results apply to the fixed design setting. An important extension of our work would be to consider a random design, such as in the work of Rudi et al. [16]. This extension would need even more careful tuning of the regularization parameter γ, needing to satisfy requirements of both generalization and the approximation of the (α, β)-oracle. Finally, the runtime analysis of the algorithm does not fully exploit the sequential nature of the updates. An implementation based on decompositions more amenable to updates (e.g., Cholesky decomposition), or on low-rank solvers that can exploit hot-start might further improve the time complexity.

Acknowledgements The research presented in this paper was supported by CPER Nord-Pas de Calais/FEDER DATA Advanced data science and technologies 2015-2020, French Ministry of Higher Education and Research, Nord-Pas-de-Calais Regional Council, French National Research Agency project ExTra-Learn (n.ANR-14-CE24-0010-01).

References

[1] Ahmed El Alaoui and Michael W. Mahoney. Fast randomized kernel methods with statistical guarantees. In *Neural Information Processing Systems*, 2015.

[2] Francis Bach. Sharp analysis of low-rank kernel matrix approximations. In *International Conference on Learning Theory*, 2013.

[3] Petros Drineas, Malik Magdon-Ismail, Michael W Mahoney, and David P. Woodruff. Fast approximation of matrix coherence and statistical leverage. *International Conference on Machine Learning*, 2012.

[4] Yaakov Engel, Shie Mannor, and Ron Meir. Sparse online greedy support vector regression. In *European Conference on Machine Learning*, 2002.

[5] Yaakov Engel, Shie Mannor, and Ron Meir. The kernel recursive least-squares algorithm. *IEEE Transactions on Signal Processing*, 52(8):2275–2285, 2004.

[6] B. S. Everitt. *The Cambridge dictionary of statistics*. Cambridge University Press, Cambridge, 2002.

[7] Alex Gittens and Michael Mahoney. Revisiting the Nyström method for improved large-scale machine learning. In *International Conference on Machine Learning*.

[8] Nicholas J Higham. *Accuracy and stability of numerical algorithms*. Society for Industrial and Applied Mathematics, 2002.

[9] Jonathan A. Kelner and Alex Levin. Spectral sparsification in the semi-streaming setting. *Theory of Computing Systems*, 53(2):243–262, 2012.

[10] Jyrki Kivinen, Alexander J. Smola, and Robert C. Williamson. Online learning with kernels. *IEEE Transactions on Signal Processing*, 52(8):2165–2176, 2004.

[11] Quoc Le, Tamás Sarlós, and Alex J Smola. Fastfood — Approximating kernel expansions in loglinear time. In *International Conference on Machine Learning*, 2013.

[12] Weifeng Liu, Il Park, and Jose C. Principe. An information theoretic approach of designing sparse kernel adaptive filters. *IEEE Transactions on Neural Networks*, 20(12):1950–1961.

[13] Jakub Pachocki. Analysis of resparsification. *arXiv preprint arXiv:1605.08194*, 2016.

[14] Ali Rahimi and Ben Recht. Random features for large-scale kernel machines. In *Neural Information Processing Systems*, 2007.

[15] Cédric Richard, José Carlos M. Bermudez, and Paul Honeine. Online prediction of time series data with kernels. *IEEE Transactions on Signal Processing*, 57 (3):1058–1067.

[16] Alessandro Rudi, Raffaello Camoriano, and Lorenzo Rosasco. Less is more: Nyström computational regularization. In *Neural Information Processing Systems*, 2015.

[17] Bernhard Schölkopf and Alexander J. Smola. *Learning with kernels: Support vector machines, regularization, optimization, and beyond*. MIT Press, 2001.

[18] John Shawe-Taylor and Nelo Cristianini. *Kernel methods for pattern analysis*. Cambridge University Press, 2004.

[19] Yi Sun, Jürgen Schmidhuber, and Faustino J. Gomez. On the size of the online kernel sparsification dictionary. In *International Conference on Machine Learning*, 2012.

[20] Joel A Tropp. Freedman's inequality for matrix martingales. *Electron. Commun. Probab*, 16:262–270, 2011.

[21] Joel A. Tropp. An introduction to matrix concentration inequalities. *Foundations and Trends in Machine Learning*, 8(1-2):1–230, 2015.

[22] Steven Van Vaerenbergh, Miguel Lázaro-Gredilla, and Ignacio Santamaría. Kernel recursive least-squares tracker for time-varying regression. *Neural Networks and Learning Systems, IEEE Transactions on*, 23(8):1313–1326, 2012.

[23] Christopher Williams and Matthias Seeger. Using the Nystrom method to speed up kernel machines. In *Neural Information Processing Systems*, 2001.

[24] Yuchen Zhang, John C. Duchi, and Martin J. Wainwright. Divide and conquer kernel ridge regression: A distributed algorithm with minimax optimal rates. *Journal Machine Learning Research*, 16:3299–3340, 2015.

Unsupervised Discovery of El Niño Using Causal Feature Learning on Microlevel Climate Data

Krzysztof Chalupka
Computation and
Neural Systems
Caltech

Tobias Bischoff
Environmental Science
and Engineering
Caltech

Pietro Perona
Electrical Engineering
Caltech

Frederick Eberhardt
Humanities and
Social Sciences
Caltech

Abstract

We show that the climate phenomena of El Niño and La Niña arise naturally as states of macro-variables when our recent causal feature learning framework (Chalupka et al., 2015, 2016) is applied to micro-level measures of zonal wind (ZW) and sea surface temperatures (SST) taken over the equatorial band of the Pacific Ocean. The method identifies these unusual climate states on the basis of the relation between ZW and SST patterns without any input about past occurrences of El Niño or La Niña. The simpler alternatives of (i) clustering the SST fields while disregarding their relationship with ZW patterns, or (ii) clustering the joint ZW-SST patterns, do not discover El Niño. We discuss the degree to which our method supports a causal interpretation and use a low-dimensional toy example to explain its success over other clustering approaches. Finally, we propose a new robust and scalable alternative to our original algorithm (Chalupka et al., 2016), which circumvents the need for high-dimensional density learning.

1 INTRODUCTION

The accurate characterization of macro-level climate phenomena is crucial to an understanding of climate dynamics, long term climate evolution and forecasting. Modern climate science models, despite their complexity, rely on an accurate and valid aggregation of micro-level measurements into macro-phenomena. While many aspects of the climate may indeed be subject fundamentally to chaotic dynamics, many large scale phenomena are deemed amenable to precise modeling. The El Niño–Southern Oscillation (ENSO) is arguably the most studied climate phenomenon at the inter-annual time scale, but much about its dynamics relating zonal winds (ZW) and sea surface temperatures (SST) remains poorly understood.

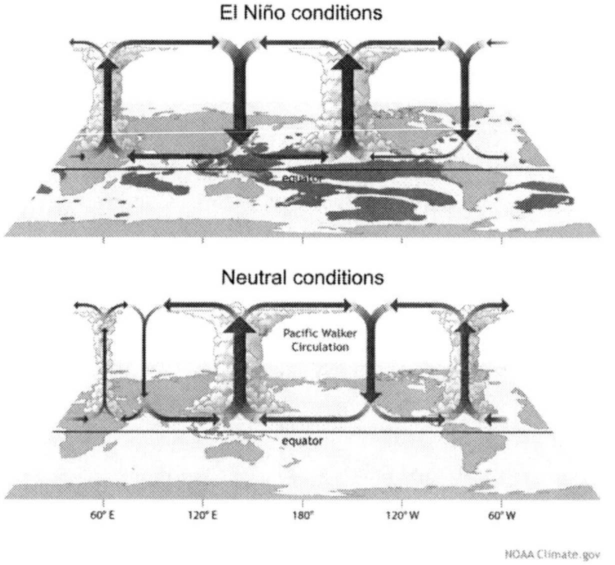

Figure 1: El Niño vs. neutral conditions from Di Liberto (2014). Top: An illustration of the state of the atmosphere and surface during typical El Niño conditions. Here, the colors indicate SST deviations from the neutral state with red being a positive and blue being a negative deviation. Bottom: Similar to the top panel but now showing neutral conditions of the Walker circulation (neither El Niño nor La Niña).

We apply our recent causal feature learning (CFL) framework (Chalupka et al., 2016) to learn causal macro-variables from the equatorial Pacific climate data. Our goal is threefold:

- apply CFL to real-world data, developing new practical algorithms as needed,
- test whether CFL can, without supervision, learn the ground truth that El Niño is an important macro-variable state in the ZW-SST system's dynamics,
- explore the theoretical and practical difference between CFL and clustering methods.

From the climate-science point of view, our research shows

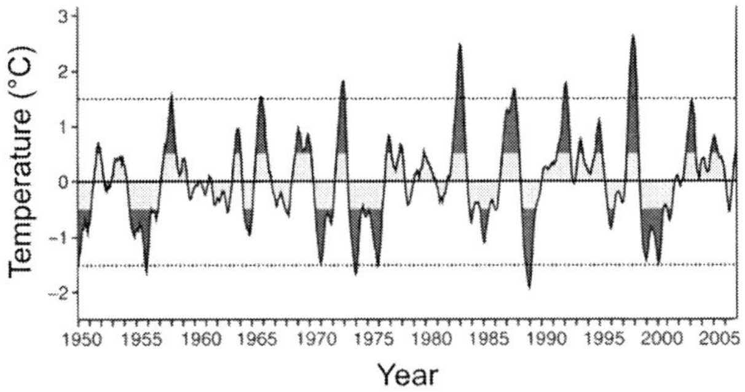

Figure 2: Niño 3.4 SST anomalies for the time period 1950–2005. The figure was adapted from McPhaden et al. (2006). Red shadings indicate El Niño years and blue shadings indicate La Niña years. The two dashed lines indicate the threshold for strong El Niño or La Niña events.

that CFL can be successfully used for an unbiased automated extraction of climate macro-variables, which would otherwise require tedious hand-crafting by domain experts. Moreover, the framework can directly suggest (computationally) expensive climate experiments (for example, through climate simulations) that could differentiate between true causes and mere correlations efficiently. Closer inspection of the output of CFL can also yield insights about new climate macro-phenomena (or important variants of existing ones) that inspire new physical models of the climate. Python code that reproduces our results and figures is available online at `http://vision.caltech.edu/~kchalupk/code.html`.

1.1 EL NIÑO–SOUTHERN OSCILLATION

El Niño is a weather pattern that is principally characterized by the state of eastern Pacific near-surface winds (ZW, zonal wind), sea surface temperature (SST) patterns, and the associated state of the atmospheric Walker circulation (see for example, Holton et al., 1989; Trenberth, 1997). The Walker circulation (see Fig. 1) is characterized by warm air rising over Indonesia and Papua New Guinea and cooler subsiding air over the eastern Pacific cold tongue region just west of equatorial South America (Lau and Yang, 2003). Near the surface, easterly winds (winds blowing from the east) drive water from east to west resulting in oceanic upwelling near the coast of equatorial South America (and downwelling east of Indonesia), that brings with it cold and nutrient rich waters from the deep oceans. During the ENSO warm phase, commonly referred to as El Niño (because it often occurs around and after Christmas), the Walker circulation weakens, ultimately resulting in weaker upwelling in the Eastern Pacific and thus in positive SST anomalies. Fig. 1 illustrates these phenomena.

ENSO-related weather in the tropics includes droughts, flooding, and may have direct impact on fisheries through reduced nutrient upwelling (e.g., Glantz, 2001). Atmospheric waves (ripples in wind, SST and rainfall patterns) generated by the change in circulation and SST anomalies in the tropics, make their way across the planet with dramatic impact (e.g, Ropelewski and Halpert, 1987; Changnon, 1999). Cashin et al. (2015) show that the economic impact of El Niño varies across regions. Economic activity may decline briefly in Australia, Chile, Indonesia, India, Japan, New Zealand, and South Africa after an El Niño event. Enhanced growth may be registered in other countries, such as the United States.

The ENSO cold phase, usually referred to as La Niña, is the opposing phase of El Niño with enhanced upwelling and colder SSTs in the eastern Pacific. Currently, predicting the strength of El Niño and La Niña events remains a difficult challenge for climate scientists as the period may vary between 3 and 7 years (see Fig. 2); as a consequence accurate forecasts are only possible less than a year in advance (e.g., Landsea and Knaff, 2000).

The National Oceanic and Atmospheric Administration (NOAA) defines El Niño as a positive three-month running mean SST anomaly of more than $0.5°$C from normal (for the 1971–2000 base period) in the Niño 3.4 region ($120°$W–$170°$W, $5°$N–$5°$S, see also Fig. 4). Similarly, La Niña conditions are defined as negative anomalies of more than $-0.5°$ C. Conditions in between $-0.5°$C and $0.5°$C are called neutral. This is illustrated using red and blue shadings in Fig. 2. Strong El Niño/La Niña events are defined as SST-anomalies greater than $1.5°$C. However, the definitions for El Niño and La Niña have evolved over time. For example, other regions than the Niño 3.4 region or other averaging conventions have been used in the specification of the SST anomalies.

1.2 CAUSAL FEATURES AND MACRO-VARIABLES

Climate experts view zonal winds as drivers of SST patterns. We take the view that if El Niño and La Niña are indeed genuine macro-level climate phenomena in their own right (and not just arbitrary quantities defined by convention) then they must consist of macro-level features of the relation between the high-dimensional micro-level ZT and SST patterns that can be detected by an unsupervised method. That is, it must be possible to identify El Niño and La Niña from a mass of air pressure and sea temperature readings, using a method that has no independent information about when such periods occurred.

In Chalupka et al. (2016) we developed a theoretically precise account of causal relations of macro-variables that supervene on micro-variables, and proposed an unsupervised method for their discovery, which we called Causal Feature Learning (CFL). We adopt the framework (summarized below) with a few interpretational adjustments for our climate setting. The method (originally inspired by the neuroscience setting, only tested on synthetic data) was designed to establish claims such as *"The presence of faces (in an image) causes specific neural processes in the brain."*, where a neural process identifies a class of spike trains across a large number of neurons recorded by electrodes. An ability to characterize such neural processes would provide the basis to explain, for example, what constitutes face recognition in the brain. There we considered as input visual stimuli (in the form of still images) and as output electrode recordings of the neural response of 1000 neurons (in the form of spike trains).

Formally, let an input (micro-)variable X take values in a high-dimensional domain $\mathcal{X}$ (in Chalupka et al. (2016), the pixel space of an image, in our case here ZW maps) and the output (micro-)variable Y take values in the high-dimensional domain $\mathcal{Y}$ (the space of neural spike trains then, the SST patterns here). The basic idea underlying our set-up is that the causal macro-variable relation is defined in terms of the *coarsest* aggregation of the micro-level spaces that preserves the probabilistic relations under intervention (hence, causal) between the micro-level spaces. Conceptually, macro-level causal variables group together micro-level states that make no causal difference. In Chalupka et al. (2016) we started by defining a micro-level manipulation (similar to Pearl's *do*()-operator (Pearl, 2000)):

Definition 1 (Micro-level Manipulation). *A* micro-level manipulation *is the operation $man(X = x)$ that changes the value of the micro-variable X to $x \in \mathcal{X}$, while not (directly) affecting any other variables. We write $man(x)$ if the manipulated variable X is clear from context.*

The micro-level manipulation is then used to define what we refer to as the *fundamental causal partition*:

Definition 2 (Fundamental Causal Partition, Causal Class). *Given the pair $(\mathcal{X}, \mathcal{Y})$, the* fundamental causal partition of *$\mathcal{X}$, denoted by $\Pi_c(\mathcal{X})$ is the partition induced by the equivalence relation $\overset{X}{\sim}$ such that*

$$x_1 \overset{X}{\sim} x_2 \quad \Leftrightarrow \quad \forall_y \; P(y \mid man(x_1)) = P(y \mid man(x_2)).$$

Similarly, the fundamental causal partition of $\mathcal{Y}$, *denoted by $\Pi_c(\mathcal{Y})$, is the partition induced by the equivalence relation $\overset{Y}{\sim}$ such that*

$$y_1 \overset{Y}{\sim} y_2 \quad \Leftrightarrow \quad \forall_x \; P(y_1 \mid man(x)) = P(y_2 \mid man(x)).$$

A cell of a causal partition is a causal class *of X or Y.*

The fundamental causal partitions then naturally give rise to the macro-level cause variable C and effect variable E that stand in a bijective relation to the cells of $\Pi_c(\mathcal{X})$ and $\Pi_c(\mathcal{Y})$, respectively. Thus, the macro-variable cause C ignores all the micro-level changes in X that do not have an effect on the probabilities over Y, and the macro-level effect E ignores all the micro-level detail in Y, which occur with the same probability given a manipulation to any $X = x$.

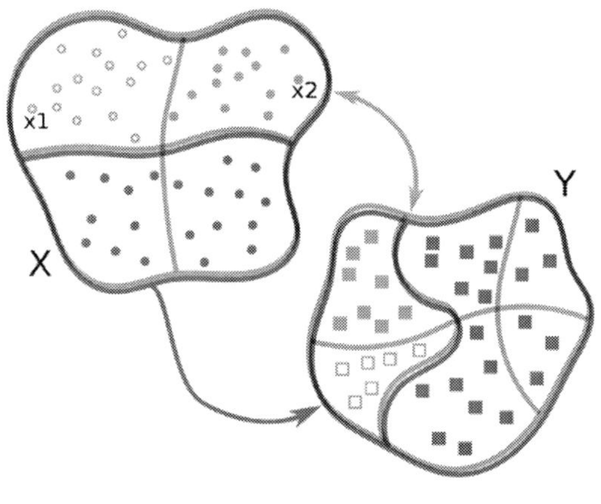

Figure 3: The Causal Coarsening Theorem, adapted from Chalupka et al. (2016). In this plot, the *observational* input macro-variable (top, gray) has four states, and has a well-defined joint with the observational output macro-variable (with six states). In each case, the *causal* macro-variable states are a coarsening of the observational states. For example, the input causal macro-variable merges the two top observational states. E.g. $P(Y \mid x_1) \neq P(Y \mid x_2)$, but $P(Y \mid man(x_1)) = P(Y \mid man(x_2))$.

With these definitions there is no reason *a priori* to think that macro-variables are common phenomena. In fact quite the opposite: The conditions that the probability distributions over X and Y must satisfy to give rise to non-trivial macro-variables C and E can easily be described as a measure-zero event when taken in their strict form. Consequently, our view is that to the extent that macro-variables are discussed in a scientific domain, there must be a presupposition that such strong conditions are satisfied at least approximately.

In the present context, our climate data consisting of ZW and SST measurements (we give a detailed description of the data in Section 1.3 below) is entirely observational. That is, the data is naturally sampled from $P(\text{SST}, \text{ZW})$ and not created by a (hypothetical) experimentalist from $P(\text{SST} \mid man(\text{ZW} = z))$ for different values of z. Nevertheless, we can identify the *observational* macro-variables that characterize the probabilistic relation between ZW and SST by replacing the probabilities in Definition 1.2 with observational probabilities $P(y \mid x)$:

Definition 3 (Fundamental Observational Partition, Observational Class). *Given the pair $(\mathcal{X}, \mathcal{Y})$, the* fundamental observational partition of $\mathcal{X}$, *denoted by $\Pi_o(\mathcal{X})$ is the partition induced by the equivalence relation $\overset{X}{\sim}$ such that*

$$x_1 \overset{X}{\sim} x_2 \quad \Leftrightarrow \quad \forall_y \; P(y \mid x_1) = P(y \mid x_2).$$

Similarly, the fundamental observational partition of $\mathcal{Y}$, *de-*

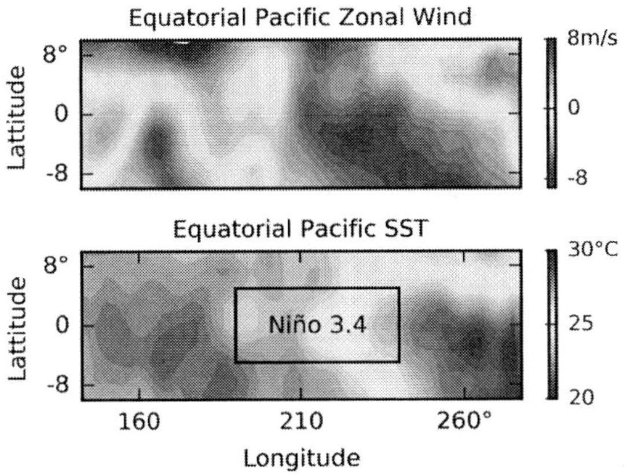

Figure 4: A micro-variable climate dataset. Top: A week's average ZW field. Bottom: A week's average SST field over the same region. In addition, the Niño 3.4 region is marked. Our dataset comprises 36 years' worth of overlapping weekly averages over the presented region.

noted by $\Pi_o(\mathcal{Y})$, is the partition induced by the equivalence relation $\overset{Y}{\sim}$ such that

$$y_1 \overset{Y}{\sim} y_2 \quad \Leftrightarrow \quad \forall_x\ P(y_1 \mid x) = P(y_2 \mid x).$$

A cell of an observational partition is an observational class *of X or Y.*

In Chalupka et al. (2016) we showed that the fundamental *causal* partition is almost always a *coarsening* of the corresponding fundamental *observational* partition, as illustrated in Fig. 3. We thus have some reason to expect that any macro-variables we do identify from our observational climate data will capture all the distinctions that are causal, but may in addition make some distinctions that do not support a causal inference. We return to this point in Section 6, where we discuss in more detail what causal insights can be drawn from this work. Our results should be seen as a step towards a characterization of macro-level causal variables for climate science, but we fully acknowledge that a complete causal characterization of the equatorial Pacific climate dynamics is beyond the scope of this paper.

1.3 DATASET

The data used for this study is based on the daily-averaged version of the NCEP-DOE Reanalysis 2 product for the time period 1979–2014 inclusive (Kanamitsu et al., 2002), a data product provided by the US National Centers for Environmental Protection (NCEP) and the Department of Energy (DOE). Reanalysis data sets are generated by fitting a complex climate model to all available data for a given period of time, thus generating estimates for times and locations that were not originally observed. In addition, we used the Geophysical Observational Analysis Tool (http://www.goat-geo.org) to interpolate the SST and zonal wind fields onto a 2.5° × 2.5° spatial grid for easier analysis. We chose to focus on the (140°, 280°)E×(-10°, +10°)N equatorial band of the Pacific Ocean. From the raw dataset, we extracted the zonal (west-to-east) wind component and SST data in this region (specifically, we extracted the fields at the 1000 hPa level near the surface). Finally, we smoothed the data by computing a running weekly average in each domain. The resulting dataset contains 13140 zonal wind and 13140 corresponding SST maps, each a 9×55 matrix. Fig. 4 shows sample data points.

2 PACIFIC MACRO-VARIABLES

To apply CFL in practice, we adapted our unsupervised causal feature learning algorithm (Chalupka et al., 2016) to more realistic scenarios. The new solution (Sec. 3) is more robust and applicable to high-dimensional real-world data. We start with a description of the results.

Throughout the article, we will refer to zonal wind *macro-variables* as W, and to temperature *macro-variables* as T. We first chose to search for four-state macro-variables (though we experiment with varying this number in Sec. 4.1) and considered a zero-time delay[1] between W and T. In the CFL framework, each macro-variable state corresponds to a cell of a partition of the respective micro-variable input space. Fig. 5 visualizes the W and T we learned by plotting the difference between each macro-variable cell's mean and the ZW (SST) mean across the whole dataset. The visualized states are easy to describe: For example, when W=WEqt there is a larger-than-average westerly wind component in the west-equatorial region, a feature often associated with the causes of El Niño (see Fig. 1). Indeed, Table 1 shows that the El Niño cell of T only arises in connection with W=WEqt. In addition, WEqt is often positively correlated with the T=Warm. Throughout the rest of the article, we will mostly focus on the T macro-variable. Our first goal is to quantitatively justify calling T=1 "El Niño" and calling T=2 "La Niña". Qualitatively, the warm and cold water tongues that reach westward across the Pacific and that are often used to describe the two phenomena, are evident in the image.

Following the standard definition of El Niño (see Section 1.1), we use the SST anomaly in the Niño 3.4 region to detect its presence (Trenberth, 1997). The anomaly is computed with respect to the climatological mean, that is the

[1]A zero time delay implies that CFL will attempt to relate the weekly moving ZW average to the weekly moving SST average. The question of different time delays turns out to be a very subtle issue in the study of El Niño as El Niño is not a periodic event, nor does it have a fixed duration (see Fig. 2). A careful discussion of other delays is not feasible in a short article and the zero-time delay was deemed a reasonable starting point by domain experts we consulted.

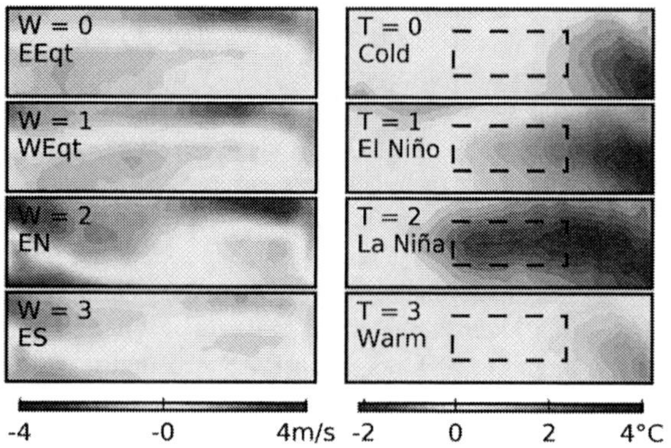

Figure 5: Macro-variables discovered by Alg. 1. For each state, the average difference from the dataset mean is shown. Left: Four states of W, the zonal wind macro-variable. We named the states "Easterly Equatorial" (EEqt),"Westerly Equatorial" (WEqt), "Easterly North of Equator" (EN) and "Easterly South of Equator" (ES). Right: Four states of T, the SST macro-variable. We named the states "Cold [American Coastal Waters]", "El Niño", "La Niña" and "Warm [American Coastal Waters]". The main text provides additional justification for calling T=1 and T=2 "El Niño" and "La Niña", respectively.

mean temperature *during the same week of the year* over all the weeks in our dataset. We will call a weekly average anomaly exceeding +.5°C a mild episode, and an anomaly exceeding +1.5°C a strong episode. The definition of La Niña is analogous, with negative thresholds. Fig. 6 shows that in the T=1 and T=2 cells, over 75% of all the points exceed the threshold for a mild (positive and negative, respectively) anomaly, and over 50% of the points exceed the strong threshold. The situation is different in the Warm and Cold cells, where almost no points exceed the strong threshold while the number of points falling in these non-anomalous cells is about 30% of the total. Since this macro-variable contains a state capturing a high proportion of El Niño-like patterns, we will say that this state has a "high precision" of detecting El Niño, while similarly, state T=2 has a high La Niña precision. Formally, we define the precision of a macro-variable state as follows:

Definition 4 (precision). *Let $T = \{T_1, \cdots, T_K\}$ be a partition of the set of all the SST maps used in our experiments. Let $n34 : SST \rightarrow \mathbb{R}$ be the function that computes the Niño 3.4 anomaly for a given map. Then, let*

$$c_\theta(T_k) = \begin{cases} \frac{1}{|T_k|} |\{t \in T_k \ s.t. \ n34(t) > \theta\}| & \text{if } \theta > 0 \\ \frac{1}{|T_k|} |\{t \in T_k \ s.t. \ n34(t) < \theta\}| & \text{if } \theta < 0 \end{cases}$$

be the function that computes for, a given cell T_k of the partition, the fraction of its members whose anomaly is greater than (if $\theta > 0$) or lesser than (if $\theta < 0$) a given threshold θ. Finally, call the four numbers $\max_k c_{.5}(T_k)$, $\max_k c_{1.5}(T_k)$, $\max_k c_{(-.5)}(T_k)$, $\max_k c_{(-1.5)}(T_k)$ *the mild/strong-El Niño and mild/strong-La Niña precision of the macro-variable T.*

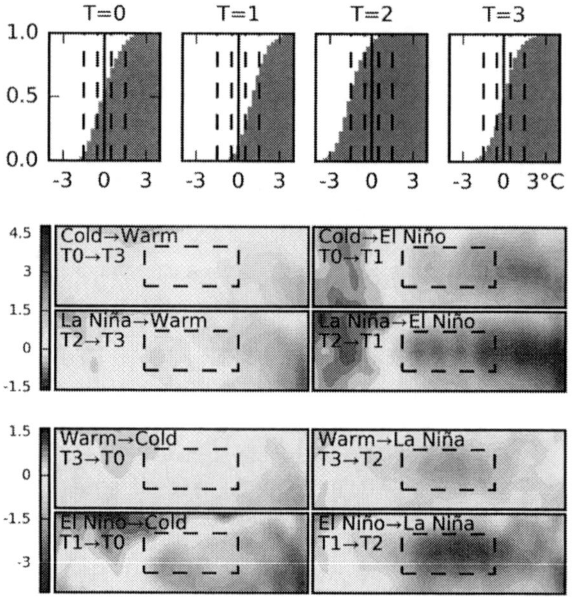

Figure 6: T=1 and T=2 are El Niño and La Niña. Top: Each plot shows the cumulative histogram of the Niño 3.4 anomalies, computed over all the weekly SST averages that belong to the given state of T. The dashed lines show the +/-0.5 and +/-1.5 "mild" and "strong" anomaly thresholds. Bottom: The minimal manipulations needed to transition from a given T-state into another (the exact procedure to obtain the plots is described in the text).

Together, the precisions indicate how well the partition T separates the mild and strong El Niño and La Niña anomalies from other structures in the data. In Fig. 6, for example, $c_{.5}(T) \approx .75$ and $c_{1.5}(T) \approx .25$ (both because of T=1), $c_{(-.5)}(T) \approx .85$ and $c_{(-1.5)}(T) \approx .5$ (both because of T=2). Thus, T has high mild-El Niño precision, and high mild-La Niña precision.

As further evidence that Alg. 1 recovered El Niño and La Niña, we show minimal state-to-state manipulations in Fig. 6. Take the La Niña→El Niño plot as an example. To compute it, we took all the SST maps for which T=La Niña, and for each found *the closest* (in the Euclidean space) map for which T=El Niño. We then averaged these differences. One of the insights the figure offers is that low SSTs in the Niño 3.4 region really are the distinguishing feature of T=La Niña. Similarly, an important difference between the T=Warm and T=El Niño is the characteristic tongue of warm water extending into the Niño 3.4 region. Adding this tongue is necessary to switch from T=Cold to T=El Niño, but not to switch from T=Cold or T=La Niña to T=Warm.

The CFL framework allows us to interpret W and T as stan-

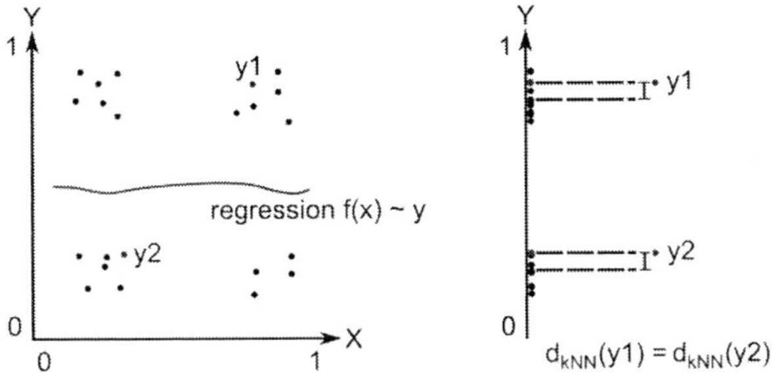

Figure 7: Alg. 1 vs. clustering. In this toy example, the data is sampled from the distribution $P(X) = U(\{1/5; 2/5)\} \cup \{3/5; 4/5\})$, $P(Y \mid X) = P(Y) = U(\{1/5; 2/5)\} \cup \{3/5; 4/5\})$. The clusters in the $\mathcal{X}$, $\mathcal{Y}$, and joint $\mathcal{X}, \mathcal{Y}$ space are evident. However, since X and Y are independent, we expect Alg. 1 to find only one macrolevel class of X. Indeed, (properly regularized) regression gives $f(x) = const\ \forall_x$, so $W(x) = 0\ \forall_x$. Incidentally, since the density of Y is similar in the neighborhood of each sample y (see data Y-projection on the right), $T(y) = 0\ \forall_y$.

dard probabilistic random variables with distribution we can estimate. Table 1 offers a probabilistic description of the system we learned. "When the equatorial zonal wind is unusually westerly, there is a 75% chance that the eastern Pacific is warm, and a 25% chance that El Niño arises." and "When the North-equatorial zonal wind is predominantly westerly, but the South-equatorial easterly, then the Eastern Pacific is most likely to be cold."—are example insights about the equatorial Pacific wind-SST system offered by CFL. We emphasize that both the macro-variables and the probabilities are learned from the data in an entirely unsupervised manner, without any a priori input about what constitutes ENSO events (except the fact that we restrict the SST and ZW fields to the equatorial Pacific region).

3 CFL: A ROBUST ALGORITHM

The practical bottleneck of the original CFL algorithm (Chalupka et al., 2016) is the need for joint density estimation of $p(X, Y)$. Density estimation is notoriously hard, especially in high dimensions. We modified the original algorithm to avoid explicit density estimation. An additional advantage of our approach (Alg. 1) is that it is very robust with respect to input space dimensionality: Input data is only used explicitly in regression, which can be implemented using any algorithm that easily handles high-dimensional inputs (we used neural nets).

Let $\mathcal{X}, \mathcal{Y}$ denote the micro-variable input and output space, respectively. Our algorithm is based on the insight that CFL only needs to detect the two equivalences

$$p(Y \mid x_1) = p(Y \mid x_2) \text{ for any } x_1, x_2 \in \mathcal{X} \text{ and} \quad (1)$$
$$p(y_1 \mid x) = p(y_2 \mid x) \text{ for any } y_1, y_2 \in \mathcal{Y}, x \in \mathcal{X}, \quad (2)$$

instead of actually computing the conditionals $p(Y \mid X)$.

Algorithm 1: Unsupervised Causal Feature Learning

input : $\mathcal{D} = \{(x_1, y_1), \cdots, (x_N, y_N)\}$
`Cluster` – a clustering algorithm
output: $W(x), T(y)$ – the causal class of each x, y.

1 Regress $f \leftarrow \mathrm{argmin}_f\, \Sigma_i (f(x_i) - y_i)^2$;
2 Let $W(x_i) \leftarrow$ `Cluster`$(f(x_1), \cdots, f(x_N))[x_i]$;
3 Let `Range`$(W) = \{0, \cdots, N\}$;
4 Let $\mathcal{Y}_w \leftarrow \{y \mid W(x) = w \text{ and } (x, y) \in \mathcal{D}\}$;
5 Let $g(y) \leftarrow [$`kNN`$(y, \mathcal{Y}_0), \cdots,$ `kNN`$(y, \mathcal{Y}_N)]$;
6 Let $T(y_i) \leftarrow$ `Cluster`$(g(y_1), \cdots, g(y_N))[y_i]$;

If Eq. (1) holds, we also have $\mathbb{E}[Y \mid x_1] = \mathbb{E}[Y \mid x_2]$. Computing conditional expectations is much easier than learning the full conditional: $f(X) = \mathbb{E}[Y \mid X]$ minimizes $\mathbb{E}[(Y - f(X))^2]$, so learning the conditional expectation amounts to regressing Y on X under the mean-squared error measure. Unfortunately, equal conditional expectations do not imply equal conditional distributions. However, arguably the practical risk of encountering differing conditionals with identical means is lower than the risk of failing at high-dimensional density learning. For this reason, we use $\mathbb{E}[Y \mid x_1] = \mathbb{E}[Y \mid x_2]$ as a heuristic indicator of the equivalence of the conditionals in Eq. (1) (see Line 2 in Alg. 1). For a more robust heuristic one could use more than just equal expectations to decide distribution equality. A promising direction would be to use a Mixture Density Network (Bishop, 1994) to approximate $P(Y \mid x)$ with a mixture of Gaussians for each x, and then cluster the mixtures.

Clustering the conditional expectations gives us the macro-variable class $W(x)$ of each input x. By construction (Chalupka et al., 2015), we have $p(Y \mid x) = P(Y \mid W(x))$ and by assumption the range of W is small. Instead of checking whether Eq. (2) holds for a given pair y_1, y_2 over all the $x \in \mathcal{X}$, it is thus enough to check whether $p(y_1 \mid W = w) = p(y_2 \mid W = w)$ for each value $w \in$ `Range`(W). For each given w we have a subset $\mathcal{Y}_w \subset \mathcal{Y}$ which consists of all the y's whose corresponding x's have causal class w. Consequently, Eq. (2) does not depend on the exact densities conditional on the micro-state, but only the densities conditional on the macro-level state. Thus, instead of trying to evaluate any given $p(y \mid w)$, Line 5 computes *the distance of y to the k-th nearest neighbor in $\mathcal{Y}_w$*. This idea is based on a principle that under-

	Cold	El Niño	La Niña	Warm
EEqt	2/3	0	1/3	0
WEqt	0	1/4	0	3/4
EN	~1/10	0	1/4	~2/3
ES	3/4	0	0	1/4

Table 1: Each row shows $P(T \mid W = w)$ for a given w.

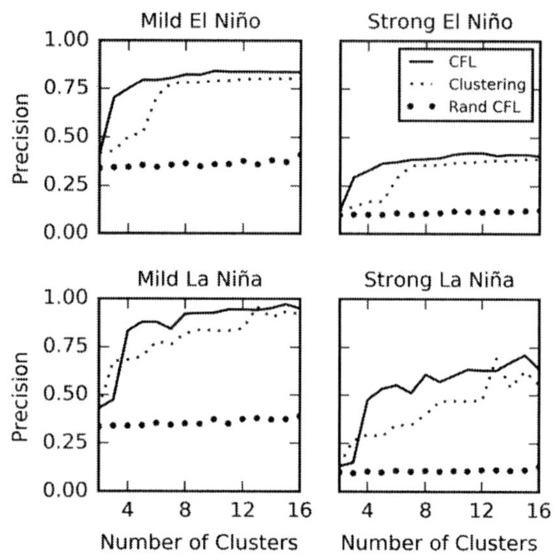

Figure 8: Changes in macro-variable precision as we vary the number of states in CFL, clustering, and CFL on reshuffled data ("Rand CFL"). With two states, it is impossible to differentiate El Niño and La Niña from other weather features, be it dynamic (CFL) or spatio-structural (clustering). Increasing the number of states reveals differences between the algorithms.

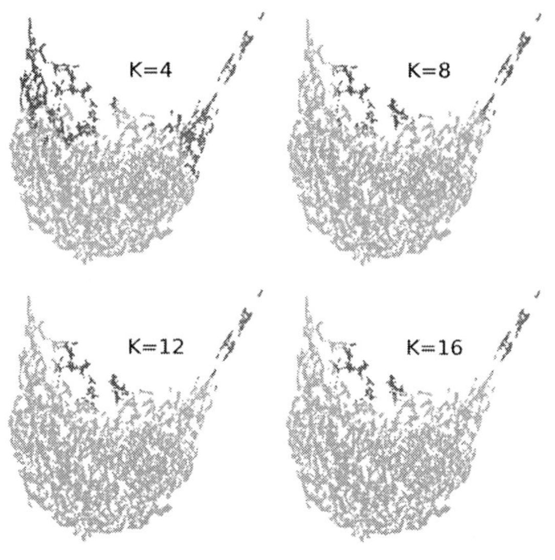

Figure 9: t-SNE (Van der Maaten and Hinton, 2008) embedding of the k-nn representation of SST data. The blue dots show, for varying K, the state of T with largest $c_{(-.5)}$ precision (see Def. 4). The red dots show the state with largest $c_{.5}$. Thus, the blue dots are "the" La Niña cluster for each K, and the red dots "the" El Niño cluster.

lies a whole class of nonparametric density estimation algorithms (Fukunaga and Hostetler, 1973; Mack and Rosenblatt, 1979): Where the density is high, samples from the distribution are closer to each other than where the density is low. This is illustrated in Fig 7. On the right, we plotted the projection of the data onto the y-space. In this projection, the distance of y_1 to its third-nearest neighbor is roughly the same as the distance of y_2 to its third-nearest neighbor. Indeed, this is the case for all the y's, because they are generated from a distribution that assigns equal density to all of them.

In Chalupka et al. (2016) we represented each y by an estimate of $[p(y \mid x_1), \cdots, p(y \mid x_N)]$, where N is the number of datapoints. The new approach represents each y sample by its 'k-nn representation', one scalar value for each $w \in \texttt{Range}(W)$ (Line 5). Clustering these representations gives us the causal state $T(y)$ for each y.

Algorithm 1 relies on a successful regression f that minimizes the mean squared error $\mathbb{E}[(f(x) - y)^2]$. In our experiments, we used the Theano (Bastien et al., 2012) and Lasagne packages to implement and train a three-hidden-layers, fully-connected neural network (Bishop, 1995) in Python. The data was sufficiently simple (compared to e.g. image datasets used to evaluate state-of-the-art neural nets in vision) that no regularization technique beyond simple weight decay and early stopping was necessary to minimize the validation error.

4 ROBUSTNESS OF THE RESULTS

In this section, we describe two additional studies we performed to ensure our algorithm behaves as expected, and that the results are robust with respect to changing the experimental parameters.

4.1 VARYING THE NUMBER OF STATES

Our choice of discovering four-state macro-variables was rather arbitrary. To check how varying the number of states changes the macro-variable precision (Def. 4), we repeated our experimental procedure, varying the number of states K from 2 to 16 (both in the ZW and SST space). Fig. 8 shows the precisions for each case. As expected, a low number of states (K=2, 3) doesn't allow the algorithm to precisely detect El Niño and La Niña. With K $>$ 4 however, a slowly growing trend persists at high precision values. El Niño and La Niña remain important features as K changes.

There are several possible behaviors of the algorithm given the slowly growing precision of the macro-variables with growing K: (1) The El Niño and La Niña states remain roughly constant, (2) CFL sub-divides the El Niño and La Niña states, (3) CFL finds better El Niño and La Niña regions, (3) A mix of the above. Fig. 9 suggests that (2) is true. As K grows, the clusters that most precisely detect the mild El Niño and mild La Niña phenomena form a chain of strict subsets.

	T1	T2	T3	T4
W1	.075	.40	.25	.27
W2	.083	.39	.25	.27
W3	.084	.39	.26	.27
W4	.080	.40	.24	.27

Table 2: Conditional probabilities $P(T \mid W)$ when Alg. 1 is applied to randomly (in time) reshuffled ZW and SST data.

4.2 RESHUFFLED DATA

As a sanity check, we ran Alg. 1 on randomly reshuffled (across the time dimension) ZW and SST data. We asked the algorithm to find K=4, ..., 16-state ZW and SST macro-variables. Table 2 shows $P(T \mid W)$, where W and T are the input and output macro-variables discovered in the randomized dataset with $K = 4$. Note that $P(T \mid W = W1)$, $P(T \mid W = W2)$, $P(T \mid W = W3)$ and $P(T \mid W = W4)$ are all equal. This is exactly as expected, since by reshuffling the data we removed any probabilistic dependence between the inputs and the outputs.

Applying Definition 2 to this data indicates that the algorithm implicitly only discovered one true input state, even though we explicitly asked it to look for a four-state macro-variable. The cardinality of the output macro-variable is three or four states, depending on whether .25 is close enough to .27 to apply Def. 2 to merge the last two columns. We performed the same reshuffled analysis for each K and computed as before the precision for the weak and strong El Niño and the weak and strong La Niña. Fig. 8, large dotted lines, shows that in each case none of the clusters contains a significant proportion of either El Niño or La Niña patterns. This experiment offers two insights:

- Alg. 1 passes the sanity check. When the inputs and outputs are independent, the input macro-variable is trivial, it has a single state.
- When SST patterns are clustered according to their probability of occurrence (e.g. as the W variable does in Table 2), El Niño and La Niña are not identified as macro-level climate states. We will return to this point in the Discussion.

5 WHY NOT NAIVE CLUSTERING?

It is instructive to compare our results with unsupervised clustering. Fig. 8 shows the precision coefficients for k-means clustering with k=4, ..., 16 (small dotted line), alongside our CFL results. Whereas CFL detects both El Niño and La Niña with high precision using only four states, k-means struggles to achieve a similar result even for larger K.

Barring particularities of the data (which we consider in the Discussion), there is in general no reason for CFL to give the same results as clustering. Consider the example in Fig. 7. Arguably, a reasonable clustering algorithm should find four linearly separable clusters in the joint $\mathcal{X}, \mathcal{Y}$ space, and two clusters in the $\mathcal{X}$ and $\mathcal{Y}$ space each. However, the variables are probabilistically independent. In contrast, CFL would only find a one-state input variable, since all values of X imply the same distribution over Y. Additionally, since $P(Y \mid X) = P(Y)$ is constant across all the samples, CFL would also only find a one-state output variable. The figure illustrates that Alg. 1 does precisely that (as should the original algorithm in Chalupka et al. (2016)).

6 DISCUSSION

The CFL framework we developed in Chalupka et al. (2015, 2016) aspires to solve an important problem in causal reasoning: how to automatically form macro-level variables from micro-level observations. In this work we have shown, for the first time, that these algorithms can be successfully applied to real-life data. We have recovered well-known, complex climate phenomena (El Niño, La Niña) as macro-variable states directly from climate data, in an entirely unsupervised manner. In order to do so, we developed a new, practical version of the original CFL algorithm.

We emphasize that our experiments use *observational* climate data, and we have to be cautious about causal conclusions. It is not even clear *a priori* whether the $ZW \rightarrow SST$ causal direction is a reasonable choice: it is known that wind patterns cause changes in SST and it in turn affects the wind by changing the atmospheric pressure. Feedback loops are commonplace in climate dynamics.

The Causal Coarsening Theorems in Chalupka et al. (2015, 2016) provide the basis for an efficient learning of causal relationships based on observational macro-variables – but some experiments are required. In addition, the theorems were only shown to hold for variables that are not subject to feedback. However, we are hopeful that an extension accounting for feedback can be proven. While real climate experiments are generally not feasible, such a theorem would provide the basis to perform large-scale climate experiments with detailed climate models, for example, to check whether *interventionally* shifting from the $W = 0$ zonal wind state to $W = 1$ in the climate model increases the likelihood of El Niño (i.e. of SST ending up in state T=1). Connecting the CFL framework with such experiments is an exciting future direction as it would also enable the possibility of using the macro-variables we have found to inform policy that aims to influence climate phenomena.

Our experiments that compare CFL with clustering showed that, as the number of clusters grows, k-means approaches never exceed CFL's precision in detecting El Niño and La Niña. One explanation for this finding is that while clustering looks for *spatial features* in the data, CFL looks for *relational probabilistic features*. Fig. 8 suggests that when the number of clusters is small there are strong spatial features in the data that supersede El Niño and La Niña in their distinctiveness. In contrast, CFL already detects El Niño with high precision with only four clusters. This indicates that either (1) There is something unique about $P(\text{El Niño} \mid \text{W})$ and $P(\text{La Niña} \mid \text{W})$, or (2) There is something unique about $P(\text{El Niño})$ and $P(\text{La Niña})$. Since we disproved the second hypothesis in Sec. 4.2, our results overall indicate that the El Niño and La Niña phenomena do not only constitute interesting spatial features of the SST map, but are also crucially characterized by the dynamic aspect of the interplay between zonal winds and sea surface temperatures.

Even when working with purely observational data, CFL offers an important causal insight not revealed by clustering methods. It guards against learning variables with ambiguous manipulation effects (Spirtes and Scheines, 2004). An illustrative example of an ambiguous macro-variable is total cholesterol. Low density lipids (LDL, commonly called "bad cholesterol") and high density lipids (HDL, "good cholesterol") can be aggregated together to count total cholesterol (TC), but TC has an ambiguous effect on heart disease because effects of LDL and HDL differ. The Causal Coarsening Theorem guarantees that each state of the observational macro-variable is causally unambiguous: no mixing of HDL and LDL can occur. In case of our El Niño setup, this means that two ZW states within the same cell are guaranteed to have the same effect on the SST macro-variable.

Finally, we note that there still is significant debate among climate scientists about what exactly constitutes El Niño and what its causes are. For example, recent research has shown that there may be multiple different types of El Niño states (Kao and Yu, 2009; Johnson, 2013) that all fall under NOAA's definition. Our results suggest that the current definition described in Section 1.1 coincides well with states of the probabilistic macro-variable discovered by CFL. In addition, Sec. 4.1 indicates that finer-grained structure does exist within the El Niño and La Niña clusters when they are analyzed from the relational-probabilistic standpoint. We leave this line of research as an important future direction.

Acknowledgements

KC's and PP's work was supported by the ONR MURI grant N00014-10-1-0933 and Gordon and Betty Moore Foundation. KC's, PP's and FE's work was supported by the NSF Award #1564330.

References

F. Bastien, P. Lamblin, R. Pascanu, J. Bergstra, I. J. Goodfellow, A. Bergeron, N. Bouchard, and Y. Bengio. Theano: new features and speed improvements. Deep Learning and Unsupervised Feature Learning NIPS 2012 Workshop, 2012.

C. M. Bishop. *Neural networks for pattern recognition*. Oxford university press, 1995.

Christopher M Bishop. Mixture density networks. 1994.

P. A. Cashin, K. Mohaddes, and M. Raissi. Fair weather or foul? The macroeconomic effects of El Niño. 2015.

K. Chalupka, P. Perona, and F. Eberhardt. Visual Causal Feature Learning. In *Thirty-First Conference on Uncertainty in Artificial Intelligence*, pages 181–190. AUAI Press, 2015.

K. Chalupka, P. Perona, and F. Eberhardt. Multi-Level Cause-Effect Systems. In *The 19th International Conference on Artificial Intelligence and Statistics*, 2016.

S. A. Changnon. Impacts of 1997-98 El Niño-generated weather in the United States. *Bulletin of the American Meteorological Society*, 80(9):1819, 1999.

T. Di Liberto. The Walker Circulation: ENSO's atmospheric buddy, 2014.

K. Fukunaga and L. D. Hostetler. Optimization of k nearest neighbor density estimates. *Information Theory, IEEE Transactions on*, 19(3):320–326, 1973.

M. H. Glantz. *Currents of change: impacts of El Niño and La Niña on climate and society*. Cambridge University Press, 2001.

J. R. Holton, R. Dmowska, and S. G. Philander. *El Niño, La Niña, and the southern oscillation*, volume 46. Academic press, 1989.

N. C. Johnson. How many ENSO flavors can we distinguish? *Journal of Climate*, 26(13):4816–4827, 2013.

M. Kanamitsu, W. Ebisuzaki, J. Woollen, S.-K. Yang, J. J. Hnilo, M. Fiorino, and G. L. Potter. NCEP-DOE AMIP-II reanalysis (r-2). *Bulletin of the American Meteorological Society*, 83(11):1631–1643, 2002.

H.-Y. Kao and J.-Y. Yu. Contrasting eastern-Pacific and central-Pacific types of ENSO. *Journal of Climate*, 22 (3):615–632, 2009.

C. W. Landsea and J. A. Knaff. How much skill was there in forecasting the very strong 1997-98 El Niño? *Bulletin of the American Meteorological Society*, 81(9):2107–2119, 2000.

K. M. Lau and S. Yang. Walker circulation. *Encyclopedia of atmospheric sciences*, pages 2505–2510, 2003.

Y. P. Mack and M. Rosenblatt. Multivariate k-nearest neighbor density estimates. *Journal of Multivariate Analysis*, 9(1):1–15, 1979.

M. J. McPhaden, S. E. Zebiak, and M. H. Glantz. Enso as an integrating concept in earth science. *Science*, 314 (5806):1740–1745, 2006.

J. Pearl. *Causality: Models, Reasoning and Inference*. Cambridge university press, 2000.

C. F. Ropelewski and M. S. Halpert. Global and regional scale precipitation patterns associated with the El Niño/Southern Oscillation. *Monthly Weather Review*, 115(8):1606–1626, 1987.

Peter Spirtes and Richard Scheines. Causal inference of ambiguous manipulations. *Philosophy of Science*, 71(5): 833–845, 2004.

K. E. Trenberth. The definition of El Niño. *Bulletin of the American Meteorological Society*, 78(12):2771–2777, 1997.

L. Van der Maaten and G. Hinton. Visualizing data using t-sne. *Journal of Machine Learning Research*, 9(2579-2605):85, 2008.

Individual Planning in Open and Typed Agent Systems

Muthukumaran Chandrasekaran
University of Georgia
Athens, GA 30602

Adam Eck
University of Nebraska
Lincoln, NE 68588

Prashant Doshi
University of Georgia
Athens, GA 30602

Leenkiat Soh
University of Nebraska
Lincoln, NE 68588

Abstract

Open agent systems are multiagent systems in which one or more agents may leave the system at any time possibly resuming after some interval and in which new agents may also join. Planning in such systems becomes challenging in the absence of inter-agent communication because agents must predict if others have left the system or new agents are now present to decide on possibly choosing a different line of action. In this paper, we prioritize open systems where agents of differing types may leave and possibly reenter but new agents do not join. With the help of a realistic domain – wildfire suppression – we motivate the need for individual planning in open environments and present a first approach for robust decision-theoretic planning in such multiagent systems. Evaluations in domain simulations clearly demonstrate the improved performance compared to previous methods that disregard the openness.

1 INTRODUCTION

The past year has been witness to one of the worst seasons of wildland fires, here onwards referred to as wildfires, on record in the United States. There were more than fifty thousand wildfires that burned more than nine million acres of wildland. Both ground and various types of aerial firefighting units are often deployed in suppressing these fires. Consider the decision-making task of a small ground unit of firefighters. As these fires are large, a unit needs to coordinate with others to focus their resources on the same area and make a difference. However, units may run out of suppressants (such as water and chemicals) or suffer from exhaustion causing them to temporarily leave. Consequently, wildfire fighting units form an *open* and *typed* multiagent system and a unit's decision making about its course of action becomes challenging if a leaving unit is unable to radio its intent to temporarily disengage.

Open agent systems such as the one described above are characterized by one or more interacting agents leaving the system at any time and possibly resuming after some interval, or new agents joining the system [1]. We refer to this characteristic as *agent openness*. A second form of openness is exhibited by a system when the types of agents alter at any time perhaps just briefly; we refer to this as *type openness*. The wildfire suppressing example presented above exhibits agent openness but not type openness.

In this paper, we prioritize systems exhibiting agent openness and further limit our attention to systems where agents may disengage at any time and possibly reenter the system but new agents do not enter the system. We are interested in how an individual agent, for example the ground firefighting unit, should plan its actions in such open and typed multiagent systems. A perspectivistic approach makes this investigation broadly applicable to cooperative, noncooperative and mixed settings all of which may exhibit agent openness.

Previous methods for individual decision-theoretic planning such as algorithms for the well-known interactive partially observable Markov decision process (I-POMDP) [2, 3] are well suited for typed systems but do not model agent openness so far. Similarly, algorithms for joint cooperative planning in frameworks such as the decentralized POMDP [4] are not easily amended for open agent systems. As such, there is a marked gap in the literature on principled planning for open systems. We present a first approach for modeling and planning in the context of agent openness when the physical state may not be perfectly observed. In keeping with our objective of individual planning and the presence of agents of various types, we generalize the I-POMDP-Lite framework [5] to allow for agent openness. This framework is more efficient than the general I-POMDP because it ascribes a nested MDP to model others rather than a belief hierarchy. We utilize a graph to model the interaction structure between various agents and extend the joint state to model the event that neighboring agents could have disengaged. In the absence of communication, we show how the agent's unexpected observations allow it to correct its model of the other agent *post hoc* after the agent has left or has reentered. Alternately, a *proactive* approach that seeks to predict when agent may disengage or reenter should exhibit improved benefit. However, the subject agent may not know how factors relevant to others' decisions to leave or reenter evolve.

The generalized I-POMDP-Lite is utilized to model the problem domain of wildfire suppression exhibiting open and typed agent systems. We continue with Hoang and Low's [5] use of interactive point-based value iteration to scalably plan and extend it appropriately to the generalized I-POMDP-Lite. Evaluations in simulations of the domain clearly demonstrate not only the improved performance of the individual agent but also the performance of the entire open system at a macro level in comparison to planning that disregards agent openness.

2 RELATED WORK

Agent openness is a challenging property of realistic multiagent systems that has been identified at various points in the literature. Shehory [1] noted that the openness of an agent system refers to the ability of introducing additional agents into the system in excess to the agents that comprise it initially. Calmet et al. [6] also studied openness in societies of agents where an open society is one that is open to new agents either with no definite goal or with goals not exceedingly relevant to the society. Both definitions focused on the system and software architecture to support openness.

Recently, additional properties for agent openness have been reported. Jamroga et al. [7] defined the degree of openness of multi-agency as the complexity of the minimal transformation that the system must undergo in order to add a new agent to the system or remove an existing one from the system. Jumadinova et al. [8] and Chen et al. [9] extended the notion of openness to include both agent openness and task openness to model the dynamic nature of the agents and tasks in the environment. They considered fluctuations in the availability of agents needed to perform tasks, as well as dynamic changes in the type of tasks that appear over time. In both papers, the degree of openness is defined as the rate at which agents/tasks join and leave the environment.

Relevant to modeling individual agents in open environments, Huynh et al. [10] studied the problem of developing trust and reputation models in open agent systems to enable agents (owned by a variety of stakeholders) to assess the quality of their peers' likely performance. Similarly, Pinyol and Sabater-Mir [11] studied, for open environments where agents' intentions are unknown, how to control the interactions among the agents in order to protect good agents from fraudulent entities, or to help agents find trustworthy or reputable agents.

In this paper, we adopt the notion of dynamic agent openness defined by Shehory, extended in Jumadinova et al. and Chen et al. Similar to Huynh et al. and Pinyol and Sabater-Mir, we are also interested in developing a solution to enable an agent to model its transient neighbors in open environments. However, our problem and approach differ in that we are interested in modeling *how neighbors will behave over time* (i.e., predicting what actions they might take, as well as their future presence in the environment which directly impacts when and how they might work together with or against an agent), instead of determining how reliable a neighbor might be. Similar to Jumadinova et al. and Chen et al., we also seek to design agents capable of strategic, self-interested reasoning, but we do so from the decision-theoretic perspective grounded in the tradition of Markov decision problems with an added focus on modeling peer behavior in order to plan and perform actions as a best response to the expected behavior of peers.

Finally, we note that ad hoc cooperation – coming together of multiple agents on the fly to meet a goal [12] – is just one characteristic of an open agent system. As this paper's focus is instead on agents dynamically departing the system and reentering, we do not discuss the emerging literature on online planning for ad hoc teamwork.

3 BACKGROUND

I-POMDP-Lite mitigates the complexity of I-POMDPs by predicting other agent's actions using a nested MDP; this assumes that the other perfectly observes the physical state. A nested MDP [5] is a scalable framework for individual planning in multiagent systems where the physical state and others' models are perfectly observable to each agent. It is defined as a tuple for agent i:

$$\mathcal{M}_{i,l} \triangleq \langle S, A, T_i, R_i, \{\pi_{j,d}, \pi_{k,d}, \ldots, \pi_{z,d}\}_{d=0}^{l-1}, OC_i \rangle$$

where:

- S is the set of physical states of the interacting agent system. The space may be factored as, $S = X_1 \times X_2 \times \ldots \times X_k$, where $X_1, \ldots, X_k$ are $k > 0$ factors;
- $A = A_i \times A_j \times \ldots \times A_z$ is the set of joint actions of all interacting agents in the system;
- Transition of a state due to the joint actions to another state may be stochastic and the transition function is defined as, $T_i : S \times A \times S \rightarrow [0, 1]$. The transition probabilities may be conditionally factored based on the factorization of the state space;
- R_i is the reward function of agent i that depends on the state and joint actions, $R_i : S \times A \rightarrow \mathbb{R}$;
- $\{\pi_{j,d}, \pi_{k,d}, \ldots, \pi_{z,d}\}_{d=0}^{l-1}$ is the set of other agents j, k, ..., z reasoning models at all levels from 0 to $l-1$. Each of these models is a policy which is a mapping from states

to distributions over actions and is obtained by solving a nested MDP for the agent at that level. However, a level-0 reasoning model is a uniform distribution over an agent's actions;

- OC_i is i's optimality criterion. In this paper, we utilize a finite horizon H with discount factor $\gamma \in (0, 1)$.

Analogous to MDPs, we may associate a horizon $0 < h \leq H$ value function with $\mathcal{M}_{i,l}$ that extends the standard Bellman equation. Let $A_{-i} = A_j \times A_k \times \ldots \times A_z$.

$$V^h_{i,l}(s) = \max_{a_i \in A_i} \sum_{\mathbf{a}_{-i} \in A_{-i}} \prod_{-i \in \{j,k,\ldots,z\}} \hat{\pi}_{-i,l-1}(s, a_{-i}) \times Q^h_{i,l}(s, a_i, \mathbf{a}_{-i}) \quad (1)$$

Here, $Q^h_{i,l}(s, a_i, \mathbf{a}_{-i})$ is defined recursively:

$$Q^h_{i,l}(s, a_i, \mathbf{a}_{-i}) = R_i(s, a_i, \mathbf{a}_{-i}) + \gamma \sum_{s' \in S} T_i(s, a_i, \mathbf{a}_{-i}, s') \times V^{h-1}_{i,l}(s') \quad (2)$$

Furthermore, $\hat{\pi}_{-i,l-1}$ in Eq. 1 is defined as a mixed strategy that has a distribution over reasoning models at all levels up to $l-1$. If $l - 1 = 0$ in Eq. 1 then $\hat{\pi}_{-i,l-1}$ is a uniform distribution over the other agent's actions.

$$\hat{\pi}_{j,l}(s, a_j) \triangleq \begin{cases} \sum_{d=0}^{l} Pr(d)\ \pi_{j,d}(s, a_j) & l \geq 1 \\ \frac{1}{|A_j|} & l = 0 \end{cases} \quad (3)$$

Policy $\pi_{j,d}(s, a_j)$ is obtained by solving the nested MDP of agent j at level d, which involves optimizing the corresponding value function similar to Eq. 1. Let Opt_j be the set of j's actions that optimizes it. Then, $\pi_{j,d}(s, a_j) = \frac{1}{|Opt_j|}$ if $a_j \in |Opt_j|$ otherwise $\pi_{j,d}(s, a_j)$ is 0. Distribution $Pr(d)$ on the nesting depth up to l is typically uniform but may also be learned from data as well.

With all agents modeling each other, solution of a nested MDP proceeds bottom up. Level-0 models of all agents default to uniform distributions. These are utilized in solving level-1 nested MDPs, $\mathcal{M}_{i,1}, \mathcal{M}_{j,1}, \ldots, \mathcal{M}_{z,1}$. Both level-0 and -1 solutions are utilized in solving nested MDPs at level 2; and so on up to level l. Consequently, in an N-agent system we solve $N-1$ models of others at any level and a total of $(N-1)l$ models. This is *linear* in both the number of nesting levels l and the number of agents, and scales well with both. If all N agents plan using nested MDPs then a total of $\mathcal{O}(N^2 l)$ such models are solved.

For individual planning in situations where the physical state is not perfectly observable to the subject agent i although the reasoning models of other agents are known and are supposed to possess the capability to observe the state perfectly, Hoang and Low [5] present the I-POMDP-Lite framework.

$$\text{I-POMDP}^{\mathcal{L}}_{i,l} \triangleq \langle S, A, \Omega_i, T_i, O_i, R_i, \{\mathcal{M}_{j,l-1}, \mathcal{M}_{k,l-1}, \ldots, \mathcal{M}_{z,l-1}\}, OC_i \rangle$$

Parameters S, A, T_i and R_i are as defined previously in the nested MDP framework. Ω_i is the set of agent i's observations and O_i is the observation function, which models the level of noise in the observations: $O_i : S \times A_i \times \Omega_i \rightarrow [0, 1]$. Notice that the observation distribution is conditionally independent of other agents' actions. $\{\mathcal{M}_{j,l-1}, \mathcal{M}_{k,l-1}, \ldots, \mathcal{M}_{z,l-1}\}$ are the nested MDPs of various interacting agents, and OC_i is the optimality criterion that may include a discount factor and an initial belief, b^0_i, over the state space.

Analogous to POMDPs, an agent maintains a belief over the states and the planning method associates a value function with the belief:

$$V^h_{i,l}(b_i) = \max_{a_i \in A_i} \left(\rho_i(b_i, a_i) + \gamma \sum_{s' \in S, o_i \in \Omega_i} \mathcal{T}^{a_i, o_i}_i(s', o_i | b_i, a_i) \times V^{h-1}_{i,l}(b'_i) \right) \quad (4)$$

where,

$$\rho_i(b_i, a_i) = \sum_{s \in S} \sum_{\mathbf{a}_{-i} \in A_{-i}} \prod_{-i \in \{j,k,\ldots,z\}} \pi_{-i,l-1}(s, a_{-i}) \times R_i(s, a_i, \mathbf{a}_{-i})\ b_i(s)$$

Policies $\pi_{-i,l-1}(s, a_{-i})$, $-i \in \{j, k, \ldots, z\}$ are solutions of the other agents' nested MDPs; and b'_i denotes the updated belief, $Pr(s'|o_i, a_i, \mathbf{a}_{-i}, b_i) \propto O_i(s', a_i, o_i) \times \sum_{s \in S} T_i(s, a_i, \mathbf{a}_{-i}, s')\ b_i(s)$.

Solution of I-POMDP$^{\mathcal{L}}_{i,l}$ requires solving the nested MDPs that are a part of its definition to obtain the policies. As we mentioned previously, this proceeds bottom up. At the top most level only, a POMDP is solved by decomposing the value function given in Eq. 4 into an inner product between a set of alpha vectors and the belief. While the total number of models that are solved remain linear in the nesting level and the number of agents, the computational complexity is higher because of the presence of a POMDP.

4 INDIVIDUAL PLANNING WITH AGENT OPENNESS

Planning that can assist fighting wildfires must deal with the event that units run out of suppressants – some types of units run out more quickly than others – due to which units temporarily leave the theater and thus the agent system. We seek to reason about the agent openness found in such environments as part of the individual planning in a principled way.

Systems of many agents in the real world often exhibit interaction structure. Specifically, not all agents interact with one another; rather, interactions often happen among small subgroups of agents.

Figure 1: (a) An example wildfire scenario with 5 firefighting units of three types situated in a 4×5 grid of forestland. (b) Firefighting units must often coordinate on suppressing fires. This coordination overlays an interaction graph.

A well-known data structure that explicates the interaction structure is an *interaction graph*, which is an undirected graph whose nodes represent agents and the absence of an edge between two agents indicates that the reward of each of the two agents is not dependent on any action of the other agent. Interaction structure may be exploited during planning for computational scalability [13, 14, 15]. We motivate the interaction structure using an example:

Example 1. *Figure 1(a) illustrates an example wildfire suppressing scenario that consists of ground and two types of aerial firefighting units. Units must coordinate on adjacent or diagonally located fires to gradually suppress them and prevent them from spreading. This coordination overlays an interaction graph that is shown in Fig. 1(b). Notice that the graph is not a clique and thus exhibits structure.*

Each vertex in the graph denotes an agent i in the set $\mathcal{N}$ of agents and an edge between a pair of agents whose individual payoffs depend on each other's actions. Let $\nu(i)$ be the set of nodes that are directly linked by an edge to node i. We refer to $\nu(i)$ as the set of i's neighboring agents.

4.1 Post Hoc Reasoning

Let $\dot{\mathbf{X}}$ be the set of distinguished state factor(s) in S whose value determines whether other agent $j \in \nu(i)$ temporarily leaves the network. For example, this variable could reflect j's suppressant level. If i determines that j has left the network, i replaces j's predicted actions – using j's policy obtained by solving its nested MDP $\mathcal{M}_{j,l-1}$ – with a no op action from then onward during which the agent does not act. [1] Consequently, A_j is replaced with $A_j \cup \{$no op$\}$. This is beneficial because we need not change the definitions of agent i's transition, observation and reward functions when an agent leaves the network if no op is already in A_j. Otherwise, these are modified to model the implications of j's no operation to allow for agent openness.

[1] A caveat of this approach is that the agent's absence is observationally equivalent with the agent intentionally not acting.

However, the problem of predicting when an agent has left the network remains challenging because the state is partially observable – the amount of j's suppressant cannot be directly observed as we preclude communication between the separated units. Similarly, the problem of predicting if and when an agent has resumed its activities is also challenging.

Define joint probability $\mathcal{T}_i^{a_i,o_i}(s', o_i|a_i, b_i)$ as,

$$\mathcal{T}_i^{a_i,o_i}(s', o_i|a_i, b_i) = \sum_{s \in S} b_i(s) \sum_{\mathbf{a}_{-i} \in A_{-i}} T_i(s, a_i, \mathbf{a}_{-i}, s')$$
$$O_i(s', a_i, \mathbf{a}_{-i}, o_i) \prod_{-i \in \{j,k,\ldots,z\}} \pi_{-i,l-1}(s, a_{-i})$$

We make the following key observation that facilitates progress in this challenging task:

Observation 1. Post hoc $\mathcal{T}_i^{a_i,o_i}(s', o_i|a_i, b_i)$ *immediately after a neighboring agent has left the system will be small but will generally increase with time until the agent reenters.*

While agent j may abruptly leave the system at time step t, the planning agent continues to predict j's actions as if it were part of the system until the observation at time $t+1$ reveals that the state did not transition as expected. In other words, joint $\mathcal{T}_i^{a_i,o_i}(s', o_i|a_i, b_i)$ will be small because next state s' that is obtained by predicting j's action incorrectly will have low likelihood given observation o_i.

Nevertheless, observation o_i when used in the belief update to obtain b'_i will cause the probability mass in b_i to shift to states that make o_i more likely. These are likely to be states at which $\pi_{j,l-1}(s', \text{no op})$ is high; i.e., j is not performing any significant action because j has left the system. With more such observations that support the fact that j has left the system, more probability mass in the updated beliefs settles on states at which j is predicted to not perform any significant action. Therefore, joint $\mathcal{T}_i^{a_i,o_i}(s', o_i|a_i, b_i)$ will start rising until another such event occurs. We illustrate this observation:

Example 2. *Let firefighting unit j exit a team that consists of units i and j who are coordinating on suppressing a high intensity wildfire. Unit i expects the intensity of the fire to continue reducing in the next time step but instead observes that the intensity remained the same as before. This low probability observation makes i subsequently believe that perhaps j is not fighting the fire anymore (because it may have left the system); a belief that gets strengthened further as the fire continues to burn at the same intensity despite i fighting it. When its predictions of j performing* no ops *are sufficiently certain, i may choose to coordinate on a different wildfire with another unit.*

Observation 1 continues to hold when $\nu(i)$ has two or more agents but i may not be able to pinpoint which agent has exited.

Moving forward, let agent j reenter the system and resume its actions. Again, agent i may experience a phenomenon similar to that described in Observation 1 where *post hoc* $T_i(s', o_i|a_i, b_i)$ drops because the observations do not support the next predicted state. This is because i is attributing no op to j despite j having reentered. However, persistent observations will shift the probability mass in i's belief to states at which j is predicted to be performing actions other than no op thereby modeling the fact that j is active again.

To illustrate, if unit i continued fighting the same wildfire as before, it may suddenly witness the intensity reducing significantly. This is indicative of the fact that unit j is active again and i's revised beliefs will emphasize those states at which j could also be suppressing the fire. On reentering, an agent can be expected to remain committed to fighting the fire if the intensity is steadily reducing, until the fire is suppressed or the agent's suppressant becomes low.

The observation below summarizes this subsection:

Observation 2. *Decision-theoretic planning that integrates modeling behaviors of other agents and a Bayesian belief update can reason about agent openness post hoc and plan accordingly with minimal extension.*

However, the limitation is that the adaptation of planning to the dynamic openness is delayed due to the *post hoc* reasoning.

4.2 Predicting Agent Openness

A better way to act in open agent systems would be to predict when a neighboring agent leaves or reenters the system. Presuming that the agent's departure is a policy-guided behavior and the agent's policy is known, we must predict changes in the distinguished state factors $\dot{\mathbf{X}}$ that may cause the other agent to leave the system. However, the main challenge is that the subject agent is usually uninformed about how these factors evolve over time.

For example, the rate at which the other firefighting unit consumes its suppressant is typically not known and may not be observed due to the separation between the two units. Nevertheless, observations related to the unit leaving the system over time provide information from which the rate could be gradually learned and utilized in the prediction.

Let $\dot{T}_i(\dot{\mathbf{x}}, a_i, \mathbf{a}_{-i}, \dot{\mathbf{x}}')$ be the transition distribution for $\dot{\mathbf{X}}$ given i's action a_i, neighbors' joint actions $\mathbf{a}_{-i}$, and previous value of the factor $\dot{\mathbf{x}} \in \dot{\mathbf{X}}$. For notational convenience, we assume that $\dot{T}_i$ may be factored out from function T_i. Subsequently, predicting when neighboring agents $j \in \nu(i)$ are likely to leave the system is dependent on knowing $\dot{T}_i(\dot{\mathbf{x}}, a_i, \mathbf{a}_{-i}, \dot{\mathbf{x}}')$ for all pairs of state factors and joint actions.

Our approach is Bayesian; it involves explicitly modeling the uncertainty over the distribution, updating it over time based on expected next states and utilizing it in the offline planning.

We may model the uncertainty over the distribution $\dot{T}_i(\dot{\mathbf{x}}, a_i, \mathbf{a}_{-i}, \cdot)$ as a Dirichlet process (DP), and the uncertainty over all such distributions as a system of Dirichlet processes. Formally, $\dot{T}_i(\dot{\mathbf{x}}, a_i, \mathbf{a}_{-i}, \cdot) \sim DP(n, C)$, where n is a positive integer and C is a distribution over $\dot{\mathbf{X}}$. Let factor(s) $\dot{\mathbf{X}}$ assume values $\{\dot{\mathbf{x}}_1, \dot{\mathbf{x}}_2, \ldots, \dot{\mathbf{x}}_{|\dot{\mathbf{X}}|}\}$, then

$$\Big(\dot{T}_i(\dot{\mathbf{x}}, a_i, \mathbf{a}_{-i}, \dot{\mathbf{x}}_1), \dot{T}_i(\dot{\mathbf{x}}, a_i, \mathbf{a}_{-i}, \dot{\mathbf{x}}_2), \ldots, \dot{T}_i(\dot{\mathbf{x}}, a_i, \mathbf{a}_{-i}, \dot{\mathbf{x}}_{|\dot{\mathbf{X}}|})\Big) \sim Dir(n \cdot \frac{c^{\dot{\mathbf{x}}\mathbf{a}\dot{\mathbf{x}}_1}}{n}, n \cdot \frac{c^{\dot{\mathbf{x}}\mathbf{a}\dot{\mathbf{x}}_2}}{n}, \ldots, n \cdot \frac{c^{\dot{\mathbf{x}}\mathbf{a}\dot{\mathbf{x}}_{|\dot{\mathbf{X}}|}}}{n}) \tag{5}$$

where $c^{\dot{\mathbf{x}}\mathbf{a}\dot{\mathbf{x}}_1}$ is the number of samples where transition $(\dot{\mathbf{x}}, a_i, \mathbf{a}_{-i}, \dot{\mathbf{x}}_1)$ occurs, and analogously for others; $n \triangleq \sum_{q=1}^{|\dot{\mathbf{X}}|} c^{\dot{\mathbf{x}}\mathbf{a}\dot{\mathbf{x}}_q}$ is the total number of samples. A Dirichlet process has the appealing property that the mean of its marginal, $E[\dot{T}_i(\dot{\mathbf{x}}, a_i, \mathbf{a}_{-i}, \dot{\mathbf{x}}_1)] = \frac{c^{\dot{\mathbf{x}}\mathbf{a}\dot{\mathbf{x}}_1}}{n}$ and the concentration parameter n inversely impacts the variance.

Let us obtain a sequence of n' next states $\{\dot{\mathbf{x}}'_1, \ldots, \dot{\mathbf{x}}'_{n'}\}$ given the current state $\dot{\mathbf{x}}$ and actions $a_i, \mathbf{a}_{-i}$ in independent draws. Then the posterior distributions become,

$$\Big(\dot{T}_i(\dot{\mathbf{x}}, a_i, \mathbf{a}_{-i}, \dot{\mathbf{x}}_1), \dot{T}_i(\dot{\mathbf{x}}, a_i, \mathbf{a}_{-i}, \dot{\mathbf{x}}_2), \ldots, \dot{T}_i(\dot{\mathbf{x}}, a_i, \mathbf{a}_{-i}, \dot{\mathbf{x}}_{|\dot{\mathbf{X}}|})\Big) |\dot{\mathbf{x}}'_1, \ldots, \dot{\mathbf{x}}'_{n'} \sim Dir\Big(n + n' \cdot \frac{c^{\dot{\mathbf{x}}\mathbf{a}\dot{\mathbf{x}}_1} + \sum_{q=1}^{n'} \delta_{\dot{\mathbf{x}}_1}(\dot{\mathbf{x}}_q)}{n+n'}, n + n' \cdot \frac{c^{\dot{\mathbf{x}}\mathbf{a}\dot{\mathbf{x}}_2} + \sum_{q=1}^{n'} \delta_{\dot{\mathbf{x}}_2}(\dot{\mathbf{x}}_q)}{n+n'}, \ldots, n + n' \cdot \frac{c^{\dot{\mathbf{x}}\mathbf{a}\dot{\mathbf{x}}_{|\dot{\mathbf{X}}|}} + \sum_{q=1}^{n'} \delta_{\dot{\mathbf{x}}_{|\dot{\mathbf{X}}|}}(\dot{\mathbf{x}}_q)}{n+n'}\Big) \tag{6}$$

where $\delta_{\dot{\mathbf{x}}'_1}(\dot{\mathbf{x}}_q)$ is a point mass located at $\dot{\mathbf{x}}_1$. As the posterior continues to be Dirichlet distributed, the posterior is also a Dirichlet process with concentration parameter that simply adds the count of new samples to the previous count and a base probability that is the proportion of the total number of samples in which say state $\dot{\mathbf{x}}_1$ occurs. As such, the Dirichlet process provides a conjugate family of priors over distributions.

By modeling the dynamic uncertainty over the transition function of distinguished state factors as a Dirichlet process, we may limit our attention to the counts of the different state samples. Let ϕ be the vector of counts of all transitions; its size is $|\dot{\mathbf{X}}|^2|A|$. Next, we show how to include the Dirichlet process in I-POMDP-Lite.

We augment the state space of I-POMDP$_{i,l}^{\mathcal{L}}$ to include this vector: $\mathcal{S} = S \times \Phi$ where Φ is the space of all such vectors and is of size $\mathbb{N}^{|\dot{\mathbf{X}}|^2|A|}$. Given the augmented state space, we redefine the transition, observation and reward functions of I-POMDP$^{\mathcal{L}}_{i,l}$ as follows:

$$\mathcal{T}_i(\langle s,\phi\rangle, a_i, \mathbf{a}_{-i}, \langle s',\phi'\rangle) = \begin{cases} T_i(s_{/\dot{\mathbf{x}}}, a_i, \mathbf{a}_{-i}, s'_{/\dot{\mathbf{x}}}) & \text{if } \phi' = \phi + \delta_{\dot{\mathbf{x}}\mathbf{a}\dot{\mathbf{x}}'} \\ \times E[\dot{T}_i(\dot{\mathbf{x}}, a_i, \mathbf{a}_{-i}, \dot{\mathbf{x}}')] & \\ 0 & \text{otherwise} \end{cases}$$

Here, $\delta_{\dot{\mathbf{x}}\mathbf{a}\dot{\mathbf{x}}'}$ is a vector of size $|\dot{\mathbf{X}}|^2|A|$ with all 0s except for a 1 at the location indexed by $(\dot{\mathbf{x}}, \mathbf{a}, \dot{\mathbf{x}}')$ where $\dot{\mathbf{x}}$ is the distinguished factor of state s and $\dot{\mathbf{x}}'$ is a factor of s'. *The expected transition probability is obtained from the posterior Dirichlet process.* The observation function is now defined as,

$$\mathcal{O}_i(\langle s,\phi\rangle, a_i, \mathbf{a}_{-i}, \langle s',\phi'\rangle, o_i) = \begin{cases} O_i(s', a_i, \mathbf{a}_{-i}, o_i) & \text{if } \phi' = \phi + \delta_{\dot{\mathbf{x}}\mathbf{a}\dot{\mathbf{x}}'} \\ 0 & \text{otherwise} \end{cases} \tag{7}$$

The reward function is straightforward: $\mathcal{R}_i(\langle s,\phi\rangle, a_i, \mathbf{a}_{-i}) = R_i(s, a_i, \mathbf{a}_{-i})$. The optimality criteria remains the same as before.

Consequently, the *augmented* I-POMDP$^{\mathcal{L}}_{i,l}$ is defined by the tuple $\langle \mathcal{S}, A, \mathcal{T}_i, \Omega_i, \mathcal{O}_i, \mathcal{R}_i, \{\mathcal{M}_{j,l-1}, \mathcal{M}_{k,l-1}, \ldots, \mathcal{M}_{z,l-1}\}, OC_i\rangle$, where the new parameters are defined as above. It shares commonality with the Bayes-adaptive I-POMDP framework [16] though we are uncertain over partial transition distributions only and our framework differs by limiting attention to nested MDPs as models of others. Acting optimally in response to observations in this augmented framework entails the standard balance between exploring to learn the transition distributions of the distinguished state factor(s) with greater confidence and exploiting the learned distributions for reward. However, compared to traditional online methods for reinforcement learning, this balance is achieved offline as an integral part of the planning.

The exact solution of the augmented I-POMDP$^{\mathcal{L}}_{i,l}$ is challenged by the infinite state space because the count vector ϕ grows unboundedly. If the count vector somehow reflects the true transition probabilities, then $\mathcal{T}_i$ effectively collapses into the true transition function and we may obtain the exact solution of the planning problem. However, by the law of large numbers we can only approach the true distributions asymptotically using counts. Nevertheless, the following observation provides guidance on how we can move forward:

Observation 3. *With increasing numbers of samples, means of the posterior Dirichlet processes $DP(n, C)$ come arbitrarily close to the true transition probabilities. Consequently, values of the policies using the estimated transition functions may also come arbitrarily close to the value of the exact policy.*

Indeed, Ross et al. [17] exploit the above observation in the context of POMDPs and identify an ϵ-dependent finite space of counts of both transitions and observations whose consideration leads to policies with values that are within ϵ of the exact (obtained using the infinite space). We extend these results to our context where the uncertainty is over the partial transition function only but involving multiple agents; this allows solving the augmented I-POMDP$^{\mathcal{L}}_{i,l}$ with finite state spaces as bounded approximation of the exact.

Let $\alpha^t(s, \phi; \pi_{i,l})$ be i's expected value of following policy $\pi_{i,l}$ from augmented state (s, ϕ) at some time step t. Let $\mathcal{N}^{\dot{\mathbf{x}}\mathbf{a}}_{\phi} = \sum_{q=1}^{|\dot{X}|} \phi_{\dot{\mathbf{x}}\mathbf{a}\dot{\mathbf{x}}_q}$ where $\phi_{\dot{\mathbf{x}}\mathbf{a}\dot{\mathbf{x}}_q}$ is the count for the transition $(\dot{\mathbf{x}}, \mathbf{a}, \dot{\mathbf{x}}_q)$ contained in the vector ϕ; and $\mathcal{N}^{\epsilon} = \max\left(\frac{|\dot{\mathbf{X}}|(1+\epsilon')}{\epsilon'}, \frac{1}{\epsilon''} - 1\right)$ where $\epsilon' = \frac{\epsilon(1-\gamma)^2}{8\gamma\mathcal{R}_{max}}$ and $\epsilon'' = \frac{\epsilon(1-\gamma)^2\, ln(\gamma^{-\epsilon})}{32\gamma\mathcal{R}_{max}}$. Here, $\mathcal{R}_{max}$ is the largest value in $\mathcal{R}$.

Proposition 1 shows that for transition counts that exceed $\mathcal{N}^{\epsilon}$, there exist counts less than or equal to $\mathcal{N}^{\epsilon}$ such that the negative impact of the reduced count on the expected value of following policy $\pi_{i,l}$ from the same state is bounded. More formally,

Proposition 1 (Bounded difference in value). *Given $\epsilon > 0$ and for any (s, ϕ) such that $\mathcal{N}^{\dot{\mathbf{x}}\mathbf{a}}_{\phi} > \mathcal{N}^{\epsilon}$ for all $\dot{\mathbf{x}}, \mathbf{a}$, there exist ϕ' such that $\mathcal{N}^{\dot{\mathbf{x}}\mathbf{a}}_{\phi'} \leq \mathcal{N}^{\epsilon}$ for all $\dot{\mathbf{x}}, \mathbf{a}$, and $|\alpha^h(s, \phi; \pi_{i,l}) - \alpha^h(s, \phi'; \pi_{i,l})| \leq \epsilon$.*

The proof of this proposition extends the proof of a similar proposition by Ross et al. [17] to the multiagent context of I-POMDP$^{\mathcal{L}}_{i,l}$ in a straightforward way. Let $\mathcal{S}^{\epsilon}$ be the set of augmented states of I-POMDP$^{\mathcal{L}}_{i,l}$ such that the count vectors are all limited to the following set, $\Phi^{\epsilon} = \{\phi \in \Phi : \mathcal{N}^{\dot{\mathbf{x}}\mathbf{a}}_{\phi} \leq \mathcal{N}^{\epsilon}\ \forall \dot{\mathbf{x}}, \mathbf{a}\}$; in other words, $\mathcal{S}^{\epsilon} = \mathcal{S} \times \Phi^{\epsilon}$. Then, define a new transition function over the augmented and bounded state space, $\mathcal{T}^{\epsilon}_i : \mathcal{S}^{\epsilon} \times A \times \mathcal{S}^{\epsilon} \rightarrow [0, 1]$ such that

$$\mathcal{T}^{\epsilon}_i(\langle s,\phi\rangle, a_i, \mathbf{a}_{-i}, \langle s',\phi'\rangle) = \begin{cases} T_i(s_{/\dot{\mathbf{x}}}, a_i, \mathbf{a}_{-i}, s'_{/\dot{\mathbf{x}}}) & \text{if } \phi' = \zeta(\phi + \delta_{\dot{\mathbf{x}}\mathbf{a}\dot{\mathbf{x}}'}) \\ \times E[\dot{T}_i(\dot{\mathbf{x}}, a_i, \mathbf{a}_{-i}, \dot{\mathbf{x}}')] & \\ 0 & \text{otherwise} \end{cases}$$

Here, ζ is a function that projects those counts which cause $\mathcal{N}^{\dot{\mathbf{x}}\mathbf{a}}_{\phi}$ to exceed $\mathcal{N}^{\epsilon}$ back to values so that the latter is not exceeded. If $\phi + \delta_{\dot{\mathbf{x}}\mathbf{a}\cdot}$ does not exceed $\mathcal{N}^{\epsilon}$, then ζ is an identity function. Observation function with the bounded state space also applies the projection ζ to Eq. 7 similarly to its use above. Finally, the reward function $\mathcal{R}^{\epsilon}_i(\langle s,\phi\rangle, a_i, \mathbf{a}_{-i}) = R_i(s, a_i, \mathbf{a}_{-i})$.

Subsequently, the definition of I-POMDP$^{\mathcal{L}}_{i,l}$ modifies to be the tuple $\langle \mathcal{S}^{\epsilon}, A, \mathcal{T}^{\epsilon}_i, \Omega_i, \mathcal{O}^{\epsilon}_i, \mathcal{R}_i, \{\mathcal{M}_{j,l-1}, \mathcal{M}_{k,l-1}, \ldots, \mathcal{M}_{z,l-1}\}, OC_i\rangle$. Let $\alpha^{h,\epsilon}(s, \phi; \pi_{i,l})$ be the expected value of following policy $\pi_{i,l}$ from state (s, ϕ) according to the modified framework with the bounded state space. Then, we may bound the negative impact on expected value due to using the new framework as follows:

Proposition 2 (Bounded difference in convergent value). *Given $\epsilon > 0$ and the augmented I-POMDP$_{i,l}^{\mathcal{L},\epsilon}$ with the bounded state space S^ϵ, the following holds:*

$$|\alpha^h(s, \phi; \pi_{i,l}) - \alpha^{h,\epsilon}(s, \phi'; \pi_{i,l})| \leq \frac{\epsilon}{1-\gamma}$$

for any $(s, \phi) \in S$ and some $(s, \phi') \in S^\epsilon$ where $\phi' = \zeta(\phi)$.

The proof of this proposition essentially generalizes Prop. 1 to the infinite horizon and is given in the Appendix. Consequently, Prop. 2 allows us to solve the augmented I-POMDP$_{i,l}^{\mathcal{L},\epsilon}$ while incurring a bounded loss.

In the context of open agent systems, the augmented framework provides a way to learn the transition probabilities of state factors that influence the other agents' decisions about whether they ought to leave the network, as a part of planning.

5 EXPERIMENTS

While the predictive method has the obvious advantage of potentially anticipating agent departures, it must first learn the transition probabilities accurately. Consequently, an empirical evaluation of the presented approaches on multiple configurations is needed.

5.1 Setup

We empirically evaluate our methods labeled **I-PBVI PostHoc** and **I-PBVI Predictive** using a realistic simulation of the complex wildfire domain (adapted from [18], similar to [19]). In the simulation, an agent obtains a reward of 1 each step and for each location that is not on fire, and a penalty of 100 for doing anything but a NOOP while recharging suppressant or trying to fight a nonexistent fire. Agents have three suppressant levels: empty and recharging, half full, and full with stochastic transitions between levels.

We measure the performance of agents employing both methods in two ways: (1) the average of discounted and cumulative rewards obtained by each agent; and (2) the average intensity of each fire over time (where intensity ranges from 0 for no fire to 4 for a burned-out location). The former evaluates the agent's planning method for maximizing rewards, whereas the latter evaluates the system-level performance of the team of agents in achieving their overall objective – suppressing the wildfire in the forest. Furthermore, we also include the performance of baselines that represent what would happen to the forest (1) if no agents were present (called **NOOP** as this situation is equivalent to all agents always taking NOOP actions), (2) if each agent randomly chooses between actions that put out fires or NOOP (labeled **Random**), representing a scenario where agents do not plan how or when to interact with their peers, and (3) if each agent carries out actions selected according to a heuristic-variant of Random (called **Heuristic**) – fight existing fires (chosen by random selection) only if the agent has available suppressant, else take a NOOP.

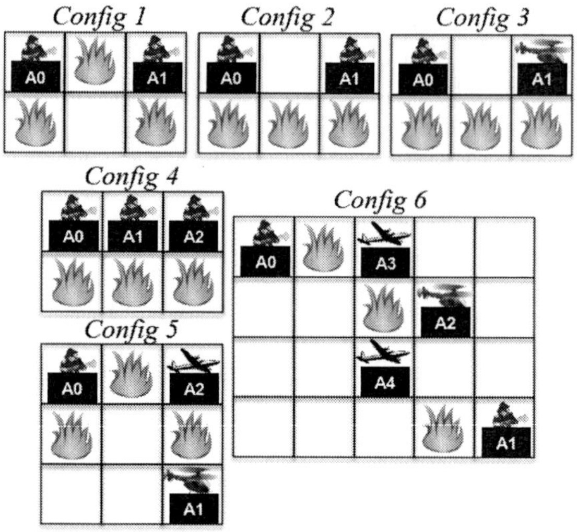

Figure 2: Illustration of experimental configurations.

To elicit different interactions between agents, we consider six configurations in our experiments, illustrated in Fig. 2: configurations C1, C2, and C3 where two agents are responsible for protecting the forest with three fires in each 2×3 grid, configuration C4 where three agents fight three fires in a 2×3 grid, configuration C5 where three agents fight three fires in a more spread out 3×3 grid, and configuration 6 where five agents fight 3 fires in a much larger 5×4 grid. In each of the six configurations, an agent can only put out a fire that is immediately adjacent – to its south, north, east, or west, or diagonal from the agent. In each configuration, I-PBVI PostHoc agents assume a uniform transition distribution for how peers' suppressant levels change, whereas I-PBVI Predictive agents perform random actions in simulation to learn the transition dynamics to better model openness and its impacts on joint behavior. After learning a transition model (i.e., after 100 steps and 30 trials), each agent in the predictive method will use this model for planning.

First configuration C1 contains two agents, each with an individual fire to fight (F0, F2, respectively) while also sharing a fire (F1). Each agent in C1 can lower the intensity of a fire by one. Configuration C2 represents an environment similar to C1, except all three fires are adjacent, and thus can spread to neighboring locations, increasing the pressure on agents to control the wildfires in the environment. Configuration C3, on the other hand, is the same as C2 except that agents are of differing types: A0 lowers the intensity of a fire by one, while A1 is more powerful and can accomplish twice as much reduction when it fights a fire. Together,

Table 1: Average team discounted rewards with 95% confidence intervals.

Configuration	I-PBVI Predictive	I-PBVI PostHoc	Heuristic	Random	NOOP
C1	16.635 ± 1.613	15.001 ± 0.479	5.709 ± 1.952	-380.114 ± 56.552	0.000 ± 0.000
C2	14.706 ± 0.573	14.681 ± 0.422	7.517 ± 2.369	-442.186 ± 58.427	0.000 ± 0.000
C3	27.459 ± 1.107	26.202 ± 1.267	11.455 ± 2.811	-488.988 ± 66.531	0.000 ± 0.000
C4	$\mathbf{49.607 \pm 3.211}$	44.340 ± 3.235	26.419 ± 3.606	-552.740 ± 74.620	0.000 ± 0.000
C5	$\mathbf{49.341 \pm 0.859}$	48.676 ± 1.773	25.365 ± 2.052	-844.951 ± 50.143	0.000 ± 0.000
C6	$\mathbf{103.735 \pm 2.859}$	87.532 ± 1.432	56.006 ± 14.481	-1272.801 ± 37.768	0.000 ± 0.000

Table 2: Average fire intensities with 95% confidence intervals.

Configuration	I-PBVI Predictive	I-PBVI PostHoc	Heuristic	Random	NOOP
C1	$\mathbf{2.597 \pm 0.038}$	2.686 ± 0.038	3.063 ± 0.032	3.379 ± 0.027	3.948 ± 0.005
C2	2.683 ± 0.038	2.695 ± 0.038	3.053 ± 0.033	3.630 ± 0.021	3.953 ± 0.004
C3	$\mathbf{1.537 \pm 0.039}$	1.670 ± 0.039	2.806 ± 0.035	3.250 ± 0.030	3.953 ± 0.004
C4	$\mathbf{0.834 \pm 0.031}$	1.024 ± 0.034	2.068 ± 0.039	2.841 ± 0.035	3.954 ± 0.004
C5	$\mathbf{1.361 \pm 0.038}$	1.374 ± 0.038	1.929 ± 0.040	2.222 ± 0.040	3.953 ± 0.004
C6	$\mathbf{1.025 \pm 0.018}$	1.222 ± 0.019	1.684 ± 0.015	1.999 ± 0.017	3.958 ± 0.002

these configurations enable us to evaluate (1) how agents are able to *balance between fighting a shared fire and their own individual fires* in C1; (2) how agents *behave under a more pressing situation* in C2; and (3) how *different types of agents interact* in C3.

In configuration C4, we extend C2 to add a third agent, which simultaneously *makes others' actions more difficult to predict* since each agent has an extra neighbor that it can work together with, while at the same time *provides more firefighting ability* to control wildfires in the forest. Note that agent A1 in C4 can fight all 3 fires. Configuration C5 adds to the complexity – it not only represents a larger, more spread out forest but it also involves *more intricate relationships among three agents*, each of different types. Namely, the three agents A0, A1, and A2 can each reduce the intensity of a fire by 1, 2, and 3 with each firefighting action, respectively. Thus, A2 (who shares fires with both A0 and A1) is quite powerful and is able to put out fires entirely by itself. As a result, its neighbors face interesting decisions of predicting what A2 will do in order to choose their optimal best response (either fighting a different fire, or conserving suppressant to fight future fires). Configuration C6 further adds to the complexity of C5 – it represents a much larger forest involving five agents. Agents A0-4 in C6 can reduce the fire intensity by 1, 1, 2, 3, and 3 respectively. Comparing all six of these configurations, we note that the complexity of agent reasoning increases as the configuration number increases, because more fire locations are shared between agents, more agents interact with one another, and more types of agents are introduced in the environment. For each configuration, we conducted 30 runs of 100 steps, and we average the results of our performance measures.

5.2 Results and Analysis

Tables 1 and 2 present the average discounted, cumulative rewards earned (summed across the team of agents) and the average intensity across all fires per time step, respectively. From these results, we first observe that agents using the I-PBVI Predictive and PostHoc solutions earned greater cumulative rewards, as well as achieved lower average fire intensities than the baseline approaches. This indicates that our approaches to planning about the presence of peer agents in open environments is indeed beneficial toward both agent performance as measured by cumulative rewards, as well as desired system behavior due to reduction in wildfires.

Comparing between our two approaches, we make several additional important observations. First, I-PBVI Predictive performed better than I-PBVI PostHoc in all configurations in terms of average fire intensity (with statistical significance at the $p = 0.05$ level in configurations C1, C3, C4, C5 and C6). Thus, learning how to predict when peer agents will be available and when they might be absent from the environment is indeed beneficial to helping agents achieve system-level goals (i.e., minimizing fires in our domain). In terms of discounted rewards, I-PBVI Predictive also outperformed I-PBVI PostHoc in larger configurations but with only a slight (non-statistically significant) advantage in smaller ones.

To better understand the differences in agent behavior produced by I-PBVI Predictive and PostHoc, we further investigated the different types of interactions between agents. These interactions are based on the types of actions chosen by agents, including putting out individual fires, collaborating with another agent in fighting a fire, fighting alone a fire that is shared by multiple agents, performing a NOOP due to recharging the agent's suppressant, performing a NOOP because there was no fire to fight, and performing a NOOP to conserve suppressant instead of fighting an available fire.

We discovered that I-PBVI Predictive consistently carried out a higher percentage of NOOP actions in order to conserve suppressant than did I-PBVI PostHoc–1.23 to 1.56 times more in configurations C1, C2, and C3, 2.18 times more in configuration C4, 20.36 times more in configuration

C5 and 28.21 times more in C6. Thus, I-PBVI Predictive caused an agent to conserve its valuable, limited suppressant so that it would be able to contribute when its potential partner agent becomes available to jointly fight the shared fire (as indicated by the combination of more NOOPs when fires were present and lower overall average fire intensity). Further, this provides evidence that learning to predict the presence of neighbors in open environments (using I-PBVI Predictive) does lead to agents that better consider the impacts of interactions between their joint actions, which in turn results in better global behavior toward system goals.

We also discovered that I-PBVI Predictive caused agents to be 2.85 and 1.13 times more likely to fight their own individual fires in C1 and C3, respectively, when there were fewest agents available to fight fires and more individual behavior was necessary. In the similar C2 environment where fires spread faster than C1 and agents had less overall firefighting ability than in C3 (where one agent could reduce fires faster), and thus it was more difficult to fight individual fires than in C1 and C3, both I-PBVI Predictive and PostHoc focused solely on fighting the joint fire that they could feasibly extinguish together. These results further indicate that learning to predict the presence of peers also helps agents better balance individual-centered behavior vs. collaborative behavior in open environments, depending on the needs of the environment.

6 CONCLUSION

As a first paper on modeling open agent systems from a decision-theoretic perspective, the focus of this effort was to study the impact of agents leaving and reentering from the perspective of an individual agent and to point out areas where existing frameworks can be generalized to tackle this problem in a principled manner. As an immediate next step, we are looking into Monte-Carlo based approaches for better scalability during planning. Furthermore, we are currently exploring how *anonymity* – the problem structure that it doesn't matter who fights the fire, but how many agents fight it – can be featured into frameworks like I-POMDP-Lite. Anonymity coupled with better planners may help scale to real-world problems involving 1000+ agents.

ACKNOWLEDGMENTS

This research is supported in part by grants from NSF IIS-0845036 and a grant from ONR N-00-0-141310870 (to PD). We thank James MacGlashan who authored the BURLAP codebase for invaluable assistance during implementation.

Appendix

Proposition 1 (Bounded difference in convergent value). *Given $\epsilon > 0$ and the augmented I-POMDP$^{\mathcal{C}}_{i,l}$ with the bounded state space S^ϵ, the following holds:*

$$|\alpha^{h,\epsilon}(s,\phi';\pi_{i,l}) - \alpha^h(s,\phi;\pi_{i,l})| \le \frac{\epsilon}{1-\gamma}$$

for any $(s,\phi) \in \mathcal{S}$ and some $(s,\phi') \in S^\epsilon$ where $\phi' = \zeta(\phi)$.

Proof. The proof of this proposition essentially generalizes Prop. 1 to the infinite horizon. Let $\mathcal{E}^h = \max_{\alpha^{h,\epsilon},\alpha^h,s,\phi} |\alpha^{h,\epsilon}(s,\phi';\pi_{i,l}) - \alpha^h(s,\phi;\pi_{i,l})|$. Omitting writing the max norm for brevity, we have,

$$\begin{aligned}
\mathcal{E} &= |\alpha^{h,\epsilon}(s,\phi';\pi_{i,l}) - \alpha^h(s,\phi';\pi_{i,l}) + \alpha^h(s,\phi';\pi_{i,l}) \\
&- \alpha^h(s,\phi;\pi_{i,l})| \\
&\le |\alpha^{h,\epsilon}(s,\phi';\pi_{i,l}) - \alpha^h(s,\phi';\pi_{i,l})| + |\alpha^h(s,\phi';\pi_{i,l}) \\
&- \alpha^h(s,\phi;\pi_{i,l})| \text{(from the law of triangle inequality)} \\
&\le |\alpha^{h,\epsilon}(s,\phi';\pi_{i,l}) - \alpha^h(s,\phi';\pi_{i,l})| + \epsilon \quad \text{(from Prop. 1)} \\
&= |\mathcal{R}^\epsilon_i(s,\phi',a_i,\mathbf{a}_{-i}) + \gamma \sum_{s'\in S,o_i\in\Omega_i} \mathcal{T}^\epsilon_i(\langle s,\phi'\rangle,a_i,\mathbf{a}_{-i}, \\
&\langle s',\phi''\rangle) \times \mathcal{O}^\epsilon_i(\langle s',\phi''\rangle,a_i,\mathbf{a}_{-i},o_i)\, \alpha^{h-1,\epsilon}_{o_i}(s',\phi'';\pi_{i,l}) \\
&- \mathcal{R}_i(s,\phi',a_i,\mathbf{a}_{-i}) + \gamma \sum_{s'\in S,o_i\in\Omega_i} \mathcal{T}_i(\langle s,\phi'\rangle,a_i,\mathbf{a}_{-i},\langle s',\phi''\rangle) \\
&\mathcal{O}_i(\langle s',\phi''\rangle,a_i,\mathbf{a}_{-i},o_i) \times \alpha^{h-1}_{o_i}(s',\phi'';\pi_{i,l}1)| + \epsilon \\
&= |R_i(s,\phi' a_i,\mathbf{a}_{-i}) + \gamma \sum_{s'\in S,o_i\in\Omega_i} T_i(s_{/\dot{\mathbf{x}}},a_i,\mathbf{a}_{-i},s'_{/\dot{\mathbf{x}}})) \\
&\quad E[\dot{T}_i(\dot{\mathbf{x}},a_i,\mathbf{a}_{-i},\dot{\mathbf{x}}')]\, O_i(s',a_i,\mathbf{a}_{-i},o_i)\, \alpha^{h-1,\epsilon}_{o_i}(s',\phi'';\pi_{i,l}) \\
&- R_i(s,\phi',a_i,\mathbf{a}_{-i}) + \gamma \sum_{s'\in S,o_i\in\Omega_i} T_i(s_{/\dot{\mathbf{x}}},a_i,\mathbf{a}_{-i},s'_{/\dot{\mathbf{x}}}) \\
&\quad E[\dot{T}_i(\dot{\mathbf{x}},a_i,\mathbf{a}_{-i},\dot{\mathbf{x}}')] \times O_i(s',a_i,\mathbf{a}_{-i},o_i) \\
&\alpha^{h-1}_{o_i}(s',\phi'';\pi_{i,l}1)| + \epsilon \\
&\le \gamma \sum_{s'\in S,o_i\in\Omega_i} T_i(s_{/\dot{\mathbf{x}}},a_i,\mathbf{a}_{-i},s'_{/\dot{\mathbf{x}}}))\, E[\dot{T}_i(\dot{\mathbf{x}},a_i,\mathbf{a}_{-i},\dot{\mathbf{x}}')] \\
&O_i(s',a_i,\mathbf{a}_{-i},o_i)|\alpha^{h-1,\epsilon}_{o_i}(s',\phi'';\pi_{i,l}) - \alpha^{h-1}_{o_i}(s',\phi'';\pi_{i,l})| + \epsilon \\
&\le \gamma \sum_{s'\in S,o_i\in\Omega_i} T_i(s_{/\dot{\mathbf{x}}},a_i,\mathbf{a}_{-i},s'_{/\dot{\mathbf{x}}}))\, E[\dot{T}_i(\dot{\mathbf{x}},a_i,\mathbf{a}_{-i},\dot{\mathbf{x}}')] \\
&O_i(s',a_i,\mathbf{a}_{-i},o_i) \max_{s',o_i,\phi''} |\alpha^{h+1,\epsilon}_{o_i}(s',\phi'';\pi_{i,l}) \\
&- \alpha^{h+1}_{o_i}(s',\phi'';\pi_{i,l})| + \epsilon \\
&= \gamma \max_{s',o_i,\phi''} |\alpha^{h-1,\epsilon}(s',\phi'';\pi_{i,l}) - \alpha^{h-1}(s',\phi'';\pi_{i,l})| + \epsilon \\
&= \gamma\, \mathcal{E}^{h-1} + \epsilon
\end{aligned}$$

Notice that $|\alpha^{1,\epsilon}(s',\phi'';\pi_{i,l}) - \alpha^1(s',\phi'';\pi_{i,l})| = |\mathcal{R}^\epsilon_i(s',\phi'',a_i,\mathbf{a}_{-i}) - \mathcal{R}_i(s',\phi'',a_i,\mathbf{a}_{-i})| = |R_i(s',a_i,\mathbf{a}_{-i}) - R_i(s',a_i,\mathbf{a}_{-i})| = 0$. The above recursion is a geometric series with a base case of 0. Therefore, $\mathcal{E}^h \le \frac{\epsilon}{1-\gamma}$. □

References

[1] O. Shehory. Software architecture attributes of multi-agent systems. In *1st International Workshop on Agent-Oriented Software Engineering, Revised papers*, pages 77–89. ACM, 2000.

[2] Piotr J. Gmytrasiewicz and Prashant Doshi. A framework for sequential planning in multiagent settings. *Journal of Artificial Intelligence Research*, 24:49–79, 2005.

[3] Prashant Doshi. Decision making in complex multiagent settings: A tale of two frameworks. *AI Magazine*, 33(4):82–95, 2012.

[4] Daniel S. Bernstein, Robert Givan, Neil Immerman, and Shlomo Zilberstein. The complexity of decentralized control of Markov decision processes. *Mathematics of Operations Research*, 27(4):819–840, 2002.

[5] Trong Nghia Hoang and Kian Hsiang Low. Interactive POMDP lite: Towards practical planning to predict and exploit intentions for interacting with self-interested agents. In *23rd International Joint Conference on AI (IJCAI)*, 2013.

[6] J. Calmet, A. Daemi, R. Endsuleit, and T. Mie. A liberal approach to openness in societies of agents. In *Engineering Societies in the Agents World IV, Lecture Notes in Computer Science*, volume 3071, pages 81–92, 2004.

[7] W. Jamroga, A. Meski, and M. Szreter. Modularity and openness in modeling multi-agent systems. In *Fourth International Symposium and Games, Automata, Logics and Formal Verification (GandALF)*, pages 224–239, 2013.

[8] J. Jumadinova, P. Dasgupta, , and L.-K. Soh. Strategic capability-learning for improved multi-agent collaboration in ad-hoc environments. *IEEE Transactions on Systems, Man, and Cybernetics-Part A*, 44(8):1003–1014, 2014.

[9] B. Chen, X. Chen, A. Timsina, and L.-K. Soh. Considering agent and task openness in ad hoc team formation (extended abstract). In *International Conference on Autonomous Agents and Multiagent Systems (AAMAS)*, pages 1861–1862, 2015.

[10] T. D. Huynh, N. R. Jennings an, and N. R. Shadbolt. An integrated trust and reputation model for open multi-agent systems. *Journal of Autonomous Agents and Multi-Agent Systems*, 13(2):119–154, 2006.

[11] I. Pinyol and J. Sabater-Mir. Computational trust and reputation models for open multi-agent systems: A review. *Artificial Intelligence Review*, 40:1–25, 2011.

[12] Peter Stone, Gal A. Kaminka, Sarit Kraus, and Jeffrey S. Rosenschein. Ad hoc autonomous agent teams: Collaboration without pre-coordination. In *Twenty-Fourth AAAI Conference on Artificial Intelligence*, 2010.

[13] Ranjit Nair, Pradeep Varakantham, Milind Tambe, and Makoto Yokoo. Networked distributed POMDPs: A synthesis of distributed constraint optimization and POMDPs. In *Twentieth AAAI Conference on Artificial Intelligence*, pages 133–139, 2005.

[14] Yoonheui Kim, Ranjit Nair, Pradeep Varakantham, Milind Tambe, and Makoto Yokoo. Exploiting locality of interaction in networked distributed POMDPs. In *AAAI Spring Symposium on Distributed Plan and Schedule Management*, 2006.

[15] Frans Oliehoek, Matthijs Spaan, Shimon Whiteson, and Nikos Vlassis. Exploiting locality of interaction in factored dec-POMDPs. In *Seventh International Joint Conference on Autonomous Agents and Multiagent Systems (AAMAS)*, pages 517–524, 2008.

[16] Brenda Ng, Kofi Boakye, Carol Meyers, and Andrew Wang. Bayes-adaptive interactive POMDPs. In *Twenty-Sixth AAAI Conference on Artificial Intelligence (AAAI)*, pages 1408 – 1414, 2012.

[17] Stephane Ross, Brahim Chaib-draa, and Joelle Pineau. Bayes-adaptive POMDPs. In *Neural Information Processing Systems (NIPS)*, 2007.

[18] D. Boychuk, W.J. Braun, R.J. Kulperger, Z.L. Krougly, and D.A. Stanford. A stochastic forest fire growth model. *Environmental and Ecological Statistics*, 16(2):133–151, 2009.

[19] N.K. Ure, S. Omidshafiei, B.T. Lopez, A.-A. Agha-Mohammadi, J.P. How, and J. Vian. Online heterogeneous multiagent learning under limited communication with applications to forest fire management. In *Intelligent Robotics and Systems (IROS)*, pages 5181–5188, 2015.

Modeling Transitivity in Complex Networks

Morteza Haghir Chehreghani*
Xerox Research Centre Europe - XRCE
6-8 Chemin de Maupertuis
38240 Meylan, France
morteza.chehreghani@xrce.xerox.com

Mostafa Haghir Chehreghani*
Department of Computer Science
KU Leuven
Leuven, 3001, Belgium
mostafa.chehreghani@gmail.com

Abstract

An important source of high clustering coefficient in real-world networks is *transitivity*. However, existing algorithms which model transitivity suffer from at least one of the following problems: *i*) they produce graphs of a specific class like bipartite graphs, *ii*) they do not give an analytical argument for the high clustering coefficient of the model, and *iii*) their clustering coefficient is still significantly lower than real-world networks. In this paper, we propose a new model for complex networks which is based on adding transitivity to scale-free models. We theoretically analyze the model and provide analytical arguments for its different properties. In particular, we calculate a lower bound on the clustering coefficient of the model which is independent of the network size, as seen in real-world networks. More than theoretical analysis, the main properties of the model are evaluated empirically and it is shown that the model can precisely simulate real-world networks from different domains with and different specifications.

1 Introduction

Most of real-world networks such as World Wide Web, social networks, Internet and biological networks exhibit structural properties which are not in either entirely regular or purely random graphs. For example, graphs produced by the model of Paul Erdős and Alfréd Rényi (the ER model) [10], do not have the two important properties observed in many real-world networks. The first property is related to the *degree distribution*. In a network, the *degree distribution* is defined as the probability distribution of the degrees of vertices over the whole network. In many real-world networks a *power-law distribution* is observed. More formally, the probability that the degree of a vertex is k is proportional to $k^{-\gamma}$. Networks with this property are called *scale-free* networks. However, the degree distribution of the graphs produced by the ER model converges to a *Poisson distribution*.

The second property is related to the *clustering coefficient*. Clustering coefficient is used to measure how well vertices in a network tend to be clustered together. In most of real-world networks, vertices tend to create tight groups characterized by dense ties [28]. However, in the ER model, every two vertices are connected with a constant and independent probability and therefore, the model generates graphs with a low clustering coefficient.

The β model (the Watts-Strogatz model), proposed by Watts and Strogatz [28], produces graphs with the *small-world* property and high *clustering coefficient*. In small-world networks, the distance between each pair of vertices is proportional to the logarithm of the number of vertices in the network. However, the β model produces an unrealistic degree distribution. The Barabási-Albert (BA) model, proposed by Albert-László Barabási and Réka Albert produces *scale-free* graphs [3]. The model is based on two important concepts: *growth* and *preferential attachment*. *Growth* means that the number of vertices in the network increases over time. *Preferential attachment* means that vertices with higher degree are more likely to receive new edges. The degree distribution of a graph resulting from the BA model is a power-law in the form of $\Pr[k] \sim k^{-3}$. However, the clustering coefficient of the graphs produced by the BA model is significantly lower than the clustering coefficient of real-world networks. Takemoto and Oosawa [25] propose a model for evolving networks by merging complete graphs (cliques) as building blocks. The model shows power-law degree distribution, power-law clustering spectra and high average clustering coefficients independent of the size of network. However, in most cases, real-world networks are evolved in a different way: they usually *grow* during the time by obtaining new vertices, rather than by merging complete graphs.

An important source of high clustering coefficient in net-

* The authors contributed equally.

works is *transitivity*. Transitivity means if u is connected to v and v is connected to w, the probability of having a connection between u and w is higher than any other pair of vertices in the network. Most of edges in real-world networks are *local* and they are drawn between vertices which have a common neighbor [18]. The model of [22] incorporates transitivity and generates graphs with high clustering coefficient. However, it produces bipartite networks which are limited to situations like company directors and movie actors. Clustering coefficient in the graphs produced by the model of [19] is still significantly lower than clustering coefficient of real-world networks. Leskovec et.al. [18] propose several mechanisms for modeling transitivity in complex networks. However, they do not provide any theoretical argument for the clustering coefficient of the mechanisms. The importance of such a theoretical analysis is that it guarantees that the model will reflect important properties of real-world networks, since a high clustering coefficient, independent of the network size, is seen in many real-world networks. On the other hand, for most of network models, it is not easy to theoretically analyze the clustering coefficient. For example, up to now, clustering coefficient of BA networks has only been determined by numerical simulations[1], and it is known to be very difficult to theoretically analyze it. Therefore, it is interesting to develop a model for transitivity in complex networks such that its clustering coefficient can be verified by theoretical arguments.

In this paper, we present the η model for modeling transitivity in complex networks. At every time interval t, the network obtains a new vertex and the new vertex is connected to some existing vertices. This step is similar to the BA model. Then, each vertex is selected with a probability proportional to its *degree* . If it is selected, then a pair of its neighbors are chosen randomly and an edge is drawn between them. The model has two adjustment parameter η and m. We theoretically analyze the model and prove that it produces networks with power-law degree distribution, high clustering coefficient and the small-world property. Compared to the clustering coefficient of random graphs or graphs produced by existing scale-free models, the clustering coefficient of the η model is significantly higher. In particular, by theoretical arguments, we prove that it is independent of the network size and depends solely on parameters like η and m. We also empirically evaluate the model and show that it can precisely simulate networks from different domains (biology, technology, social and information networks) with different characteristics.

The rest of this paper is organized as follows. In Second 2 we present the model and theoretically analyze its important properties. In Section 3 we empirically evaluate the model and show that it produces graphs very close to real-world networks. An overview of related work is given in Section 4, and finally the paper is concluded in Section 5.

[1]Numerical simulations show that clustering coefficient of a BA network with n vertices is $n^{-0.75}$.

Table 1: Symbols and their definitions.

Symbol	Definition
γ	The power-law exponent of the degree distribution in a scale-free network
η	A parameter of the proposed model ($\eta > 0$)
$\mathbf{G}$	A network produced by the η model
$V_{\mathbf{G}}$	The set of vertices of $\mathbf{G}$
$V_{\mathbf{G}}(t)$	The set of vertices of $\mathbf{G}$ at time t
$\mathbf{G}_0$	The initial graph
d_v	The degree of a vertex v
$d_v(t)$	The degree of a vertex v at time t
t_v	The time of adding v to the network
N_v	The set of neighbors of v
$N_v(t)$	The set of neighbors of v at time t
n	The number of vertices of the network
e	The number of edges of the network
$e(t)$	The number of edges of the network at time t
m	The number of edges drawn between a new vertex and the existing vertices of the network
$\langle CC \rangle$	The clustering coefficient
α	$\frac{2\eta+m}{2(\eta+m)}$
K	$\frac{2\eta}{2\eta+m}$

2 The η model

In this section, we first present the η model and then we theoretically analyze its important properties like power-law degree distribution, high clustering coefficient and the small-world property. Before that, in Table 1 we summarize symbols and notations that we will use in the paper.

Algorithm 1 describes the high level pseudo code of the η model proposed for modeling transitivity in complex networks. First a small graph $\mathbf{G}_0$ is produced. We refer to it as the *initial graph*. Then, at every time interval $t \in \{1, \ldots, \mathbf{T}\}$, the following steps are performed:
I. *growth*. A new vertex v is added to the network $\mathbf{G}$. We denote by t_v the time of adding v to $\mathbf{G}$.
II. *preferential attachment*. The vertex v is connected to m existing vertices. Existing vertices are chosen based on their degree. While every model which produces scale-free networks can be used, for the sake of simplicity, we here use the basic BA model. Therefore, for m times, a vertex w with probability

$$\frac{d_w(t)}{2e(t)} \tag{1}$$

is chosen and connected to v. We denote by $d_w(t)$ the degree of w at time interval t and by $e(t)$ the number of edges of the graph at time interval t.
III. *transitivity*. At this step each vertex w of the graph is

selected with probability

$$\frac{\eta d_w(t)}{2e(t)} \tag{2}$$

where η is a non-negative real number. Then, if w is selected, among the neighbors of w, two vertices are chosen *uniformly at random* and are connected to each other.

Algorithm 1 High level pseudo code of the η model.

GRAPHGENERATOR

Require: A non-negative real number η, a non-negative integer $\mathbf{T}$, a non-negative integer m.

Ensure: A graph $\mathbf{G}$ generated by the η model.

initialize $\mathbf{G}$ by a small graph
for $t = 1$ **to** $\mathbf{T}$ **do**
    {*growth*:}
    add a new vertex v to $\mathbf{G}$
    {*preferential attachment*:}
    connect v to m existing vertices {every existing vertex is selected proportional to its degree}
    {*transitivity*:}
    for every vertex $w \in V_{\mathbf{G}}$ **do**
        select w with probability $\frac{\eta d_w(t)}{2e(t)}$
        if w is selected **then**
            select two neighbors x and y of w uniformly at random
            draw an edge between x and y
        end if
    end for
end for
return $\mathbf{G}$

The authors of [18] investigated different cases of producing triangles in complex networks. In their scenario, a source vertex u decides to connect to some vertex w whose distance with u is two. u first selects a neighbor v and then v selects a neighbor $w \neq u$. u and v might use different policies to select v and w, e.g. uniform selection or selecting based on degree. Here we first select v proportional to its degree and then, u and w are selected uniformly at random. The main contribution of this work compared to [18] is that we precisely formulate the procedure, which gives us a possibility to analytically study the model. Particularly, we provide a lower bound on the clustering coefficient independent of the network size.

2.1 Expected number of edges

In this section, we calculate the expected number of edges of the network at every time interval t.

The number of edges at time interval t, i.e. $e(t)$, satisfies the following dynamical equation:

$$\frac{\partial e(t)}{\partial t} = \underbrace{m}_{\text{preferential attachment}} + \underbrace{\sum_{w \in V_{\mathbf{G}}(t)} \frac{\eta d_w(t)}{2e(t)}}_{\text{transitivity}} = m + \eta$$

where $V_{\mathbf{G}}(t)$ denotes vertices of $\mathbf{G}$ at time interval t. After solving this equation, we obtain

$$e(t) = (m + \eta)t + e(\mathbf{G}_0) \tag{3}$$

where $e(\mathbf{G}_0)$ denotes the number of edges in the initial graph. For large enough t, we sometimes discard $e(\mathbf{G}_0)$ and consider $e(t)$ as $(m + \eta)t$.

2.2 Power-law degree distribution

In this section, we show that in a graph produced by the η model, vertices (except those added at the very early time intervals) have a power-law degree distribution.

At every time interval $t \in \{1, \ldots, \mathbf{T}\}$, every vertex v in the network satisfies the following dynamical equation:

$$\begin{aligned}\frac{\partial d_v(t)}{\partial t} &\overset{(a)}{\approx} \underbrace{\sum_{u \in N_v(t)} \left(\frac{\eta d_u(t)}{2e(t)} \times \frac{2}{d_u(t)} \right)}_{\text{transitivity}} + \underbrace{\frac{m d_v(t)}{2e(t)}}_{\text{preferential attachment}} \\ &= \sum_{u \in N_v(t)} \left(\frac{\eta}{e(t)} \right) + \frac{m d_v(t)}{2e(t)} \\ &= \frac{\eta d_v(t)}{e(t)} + \frac{m d_v(t)}{2e(t)} \end{aligned} \tag{4}$$

where $N_v(t)$ refers to neighbors of vertex v at time interval t.

The approximation (a) is employed to make the computation of the dynamical equation $\frac{\partial d_v(t)}{\partial t}$ feasible, since, otherwise it would require taking the expectation of a function with a random variable at the denominator (i.e. the number of edges), which is computationally intractable. In principle, one could use the polynomial normal forms of such functions to eliminate the denominator. However, this transformation yields an exponential order in the number of conjunctions. Therefore, in mean-field theory, it is proposed to approximate the expectation via replacing the random denominator by its expectation, i.e. by $\mathbb{E}[f/g] \approx f/\mathbb{E}[g]$, where f is nonrandom [12, 13]. This approximation is exact in the thermodynamic limit, i.e. for large enough t, for example when $t > 20$. One can obtain higher order improvements of the approximation e.g. by a Taylor expansion around the expectation. The quality of such an approximation has been investigated in the context of mean-field theory by Markov Chain Monte Carlo (MCMC) simulations. Based on extensive experimental evidences, for example in [13, 23], the first-order approximation competes with more refined techniques such as the

TAP method [9]. Moreover, for large enough t, as mentioned earlier, the approximation becomes almost exact and the higher order approximation terms diminish. [2]

By replacing $e(t)$ with the value obtained in Equation 3, for large enough t, Equation 4 amounts to

$$\frac{\partial d_v(t)}{\partial t} = \frac{2\eta + m}{2(\eta + m)} \times \frac{d_v(t)}{t} = \frac{\alpha d_v(t)}{t} \tag{5}$$

where $\alpha = \frac{2\eta+m}{2(\eta+m)}$.

To solve Equation 5, we need to find the initial degree of vertex v, i.e. the number of edges v finds when it is added to the network at t_v. At time interval t_v, v finds m edges due to preferential attachment, and it expects to find $\frac{\eta m}{e(t_v)}$ edges due to transitivity. Therefore, its expected initial degree will be $m + \frac{\eta m}{(m+\eta)t_v}$.

Then, using the *continuum theory* [2], we obtain

$$d_v(t) = \left(m + \frac{\eta m}{(m+\eta)t_v}\right)\left(\frac{t}{t_v}\right)^{\alpha} \tag{6}$$

particularly

$$d_v(\mathbf{T}) = \left(m + \frac{\eta m}{(m+\eta)t_v}\right)\left(\frac{\mathbf{T}}{t_v}\right)^{\alpha} \tag{7}$$

If v is added to the network at a large enough time interval (i.e., t_v is larger than a lower bound L), Equations 6 and 7 can be written as

$$d_v(t) = m\left(\frac{t}{t_v}\right)^{\alpha} \tag{8}$$

and

$$d_v(\mathbf{T}) = m\left(\frac{\mathbf{T}}{t_v}\right)^{\alpha} \tag{9}$$

The probability that at time interval $\mathbf{T}$ a vertex v has a degree $d_v(\mathbf{T})$ smaller than k is

$$\Pr[d_v(\mathbf{T}) < k] = \Pr[m\left(\frac{\mathbf{T}}{t_v}\right)^{\alpha} < k] = \Pr[t_v > \frac{\mathbf{T} \times m^{\frac{1}{\alpha}}}{k^{\frac{1}{\alpha}}}] \tag{10}$$

and

$$\Pr[d_v(\mathbf{T}) < k] = 1 - \Pr[t_v \leq \frac{\mathbf{T} \times m^{\frac{1}{\alpha}}}{k^{\frac{1}{\alpha}}}] \tag{11}$$

We suppose that the vertices are added to the network at equal time intervals $\Pr[t_v] = \frac{1}{\mathbf{T}}$. Putting it into Equation 11, we get

$$\Pr[d_v(\mathbf{T}) < k] = 1 - \frac{\mathbf{T} \times m^{\frac{1}{\alpha}}}{\mathbf{T} \times k^{\frac{1}{\alpha}}} = 1 - \left(\frac{m}{k}\right)^{\frac{1}{\alpha}} \tag{12}$$

[2] In our MCMC simulations with $1,000$ runs, the approximation is unbiased, i.e. the difference between the mean of the empirical distribution and the approximated quantity is only 0.061 times the standard deviation.

Then, the degree distribution $\Pr[k]$ can be computed as

$$\Pr[k] = \frac{\partial \Pr[d_v(\mathbf{T}) < k]}{\partial k} = \frac{m^{\frac{1}{\alpha}}}{\alpha} \times k^{-(1+\frac{1}{\alpha})} \tag{13}$$

which means $\Pr[k] \sim k^{-(1+\frac{1}{\alpha})}$. Therefore, we have a power law degree distribution $\Pr[k] \sim k^{-\gamma}$, where

$$\gamma = 1 + \frac{1}{\alpha} = \frac{4\eta + 3m}{2\eta + m} = 2 + \frac{m}{2\eta + m} \tag{14}$$

2.3 The small world property

Reuven Cohen and Shlomo Havlin [8] showed that scale-free networks have a small diameter. In particular, they proved that the scale-free networks with $2 < \gamma < 3$ have a very small diameter which is proportional to $\ln\ln n$. They also showed that for $\gamma = 3$ the diameter is proportional to $\frac{\ln n}{\ln\ln n}$, and for $\gamma > 3$ it is proportional to $\ln n$. In all cases the scale-free network satisfies the small-world property. We note that here the diameter is the mean distance between vertices. As Equation 14 indicates, for the η model we have: $2 \leq \gamma \leq 3$. Particularly, for non-zero values of η and m, we have $2 < \gamma < 3$. This means that the η model satisfies the required conditions, i.e. it produces graphs with the small-world property where the diameter is proportional to $\ln n$.

2.4 Clustering coefficient

In this section, we provide a lower bound on the clustering coefficient of the networks produced by the η model, which is independent of the network size and depends only on the η and m parameters.

Watts and Strogatz [28] defined the clustering coefficient of a network as[3]

$$\langle CC \rangle = \frac{1}{n} \sum_{v \in V_G} \langle CC_v \rangle \tag{15}$$

where n is the number of vertices of the network and

$$\langle CC_v \rangle = \frac{C_v}{\binom{d_v}{2}} \tag{16}$$

where C_v is the number of edges among the neighbors of v. $\langle CC_v \rangle$ is called the local clustering coefficient of v.

For a network produced by the η model, C_v can be written as

$$C_v = \sum_{t=t_v}^{\mathbf{T}} (\langle C_v \rangle_T (t) + \langle C_v \rangle_P (t)) \tag{17}$$

where

[3] An alternative definition of the clustering coefficient which is also widely used, was introduced by Barrat and Weigt [4]: $\frac{3 \times \text{number of triangles in the network}}{\text{number of connected triples of vertices}}$.

- $\langle C_v \rangle_P(t)$ is the number of edges between neighbors of v which are added to $\mathbf{G}$ during the *preferential attachment* step at time interval t, and

- $\langle C_v \rangle_T$ is the number of edges between neighbors of v which are added to $\mathbf{G}$ during the *transitivity* step at time interval t.

Then, for a vertex v, at every time interval $t \geq t_v$, we define $\tau_v(t)$ as

$$\tau_v(t) = \sum_{t'=t_v}^{t} \langle C_v \rangle_T(t') \tag{18}$$

We have

$$C_v \geq \tau_v(\mathbf{T}) \tag{19}$$

Therefore

$$\langle CC_v \rangle \geq \frac{\tau_v(\mathbf{T})}{\binom{d_v(\mathbf{T})}{2}} \tag{20}$$

Suppose that v is added to the network at a time interval greater than a lower bound L (i.e. $t_v \geq L$) such that we can use Equation 8 to describe its degree. In the following, we compute $\tau_v(\mathbf{T})$.

For $t \geq t_v$, τ_v satisfies the dynamical equation

$$\frac{\partial \tau_v(t)}{\partial t} = \frac{\eta d_v(t)}{2e(t)} = \frac{\eta m t^{\alpha-1}}{2(\eta+m){t_v}^{\alpha}} \tag{21}$$

Then, at time interval $\mathbf{T}$, we will have:

$$\tau_v(\mathbf{T}) - \tau_v(t_v) = \int_{t_v}^{\mathbf{T}} \frac{\eta m}{2(m+\eta){t_v}^{\alpha}} \times t^{\alpha-1} \partial t \tag{22}$$

To solve this dynamical equation, we need to find $\tau_v(t_v)$. Since at time interval t_v vertex v finds $m + \frac{\eta m}{(m+\eta)t_v}$ edges, $\tau_v(t_v)$ will be:

$$\tau_v(t_v) = \frac{\eta \times \left(m + \frac{\eta+m}{(m+\eta)t_v}\right)}{2(m+\eta)t_v} \geq \frac{\eta m}{2(m+\eta)t_v} \tag{23}$$

Therefore after solving the integral of Equation 22, we will have

$$\tau_v(\mathbf{T}) \geq mK \times \left(\frac{\mathbf{T}^{\alpha}}{2{t_v}^{\alpha}} - \frac{1}{2}\right) + \frac{\eta m}{2(m+\eta)t_v} \tag{24}$$

$$\geq \frac{mK\mathbf{T}^{\alpha}}{2{t_v}^{\alpha}} - \frac{mK}{2} \tag{25}$$

where $K = \frac{\eta}{\alpha \times (m+\eta)} = \frac{2\eta}{2\eta+m}$.

Now, we use Equation 20 to find a lower bound for $\langle CC_v \rangle$:

$$\langle CC_v \rangle \geq \frac{\tau_v(\mathbf{T})}{\binom{d_v(\mathbf{T})}{2}} \geq \frac{2\tau_v(\mathbf{T})}{d_v(\mathbf{T})^2} \geq \frac{K{t_v}^{\alpha}}{m\mathbf{T}^{\alpha}} - \frac{K{t_v}^{2\alpha}}{m\mathbf{T}^{2\alpha}} \tag{26}$$

Let v be a vertex such that $L \leq t_v \leq \mathbf{T}$. Up to now, we have computed a lower bound for $\langle CC_v \rangle$. Now, we want to compute a lower bound for the clustering coefficient of the network induced by the vertices added to the network at time intervals $t_L, t_{L+1}, \ldots, t_{\mathbf{T}}$. We refer to this quantity as $\langle CC \rangle$ since it is almost the clustering coefficient of the whole network (compared to $\mathbf{T}$, L is very small and only for few vertices we cannot use Equation 8 to express the degree).

Using Equations 15 and 26, we obtain

$$\langle CC \rangle \geq \frac{1}{\mathbf{T}-L+1} \sum_{t_v=L}^{\mathbf{T}} \left(\frac{K{t_v}^{\alpha}}{m\mathbf{T}^{\alpha}} - \frac{K{t_v}^{2\alpha}}{m\mathbf{T}^{2\alpha}}\right) \tag{27}$$

A simple form of the Riemann sum [26] says

$$\sum_{x=a}^{b} x^r \geq \int_{a-1}^{b} x^r \partial x$$

where $r, a, b > 0$.

This inequality and Equation 27 yield

$$\langle CC \rangle \geq \frac{1}{\mathbf{T}-L+1} \int_{L-1}^{\mathbf{T}} \left(\frac{K{t_v}^{\alpha}}{m\mathbf{T}^{\alpha}} - \frac{K{t_v}^{2\alpha}}{m\mathbf{T}^{2\alpha}}\right) \partial t_v \tag{28}$$

After solving the integral, we obtain

$$\langle CC \rangle \geq \frac{K}{m(\alpha+1)} - \frac{K}{m(2\alpha+1)} \tag{29}$$

$$= \frac{2\eta(\eta+m)}{m(4\eta+3m)(3\eta+2m)} \tag{30}$$

Therefore, a lower bound is provided for the clustering coefficient of a η network, which is independent of the network size and depends on the η and m parameters. We refer to Equation 30 as B.

3 Simulating real-world networks

In this section, we consider several real-world networks, with different specifications and from different domains including biology, technology, social and information networks, and aim to simulate them using the η model. Table 2 summarizes the characteristics of different real-world networks and the networks simulating them. Note that we only describe one way of simulating the real-world networks by the η model which is not unique and the only existing way. In all simulated networks, the initial graph simply consists of two vertices connected by an edge.

Table 2: Real-world networks and the equivalent networks produced by the η model. $\mathcal{C}$ and $\mathcal{C}_\eta$ are clustering coefficient of the real-world networks and clustering coefficient of the networks produced by the η model, respectively. $\mathcal{C}_{BA}$ is the clustering coefficient of the simulated network if transitivity is not used.

Real-world networks				**Simulated networks**				
Network	# vertices	# edges	$\mathcal{C}$	m	η	# edges	$\mathcal{C}_\eta$	$\mathcal{C}_{BA}$
electronic circuits	24,097	53,248	0.03	2	0.23	53,121	0.034	0.009
email address books	16,881	57,029	0.13	3	0.5	58,041	0.11	0.0047
marine food web	135	598	0.23	4	0.54	599	0.24	0.148
neural network	307	2,359	0.28	5	2.8	2,341	0.29	0.098
Roget's thesaurus	1,022	5,103	0.15	4	1.4	5,389	0.14	0.038

The first real-world network studied here is the *electronic circuits* network. In this network vertices are electronic components e.g., logic gates in digital circuits and resistors, capacitors and diodes in analogic circuits, and edges are the wires [5]. It has $24,097$ vertices and $53,248$ edges and its clustering coefficient is 0.030. In order to simulate this network, we produce an η graph with these parameters: $m = 2$ and $\eta = 0.23$ and it has the same number of vertices as the electronic circuits network. The graph produced by the η model has $53,121$ edges, its clustering coefficient is 0.034 and its degree distribution is depicted in Figure 1(a).

The second real-world network is the network of *email address books* [21]. In this network, vertices represent computer users and an edge is drawn from user A to user B if B's email address appears in A's address book. This network has $16,881$ vertices and $57,029$ edges and its clustering coefficient is 0.13. We simulate this network by the η model using the following parameters: $m = 3$ and $\eta = 0.5$ and the number of vertices in the produced graph is $16,881$. The clustering coefficient of the simulated network is 0.11. However, if we remove transitivity from the network (and produce a BA network), its clustering coefficient will be only 0.0047. Figure 1(b) presents degree distribution of the simulated network.

The next two real-world networks are biological networks. In the *marine food web* network, vertices represent species in an ecosystem and an edge from vertex A to vertex B indicates that A preys on B [14] and [7]. This network has 135 vertices and 598 edges and its clustering coefficient is 0.23. The following parameters are used by the η model to simulate this network: $m = 4$, $\eta = 0.54$, and number of vertices is 135. The produced graph has 599 edges and its clustering coefficient is 0.24. Figure 1(c) presents degree distribution of the networks simulated by the η model.

The other important class of biological networks are *neural networks*. The neural network of the nematode C. Elegans reconstructed by White et al. [29] has 307 vertices and $2,359$ edges and its clustering coefficient is 0.28. We simulate it by a η network with $m = 5$ and $\eta = 2.8$. The clustering coefficient of the produced graph is 0.29. Degree distribution of the simulated network is shown in Figure 1(d).

The last real-world network investigated in this paper is the *Roget's thesaurus* network [17]. Each vertex of the graph corresponds to one of the $1,022$ categories in the $1,879$ edition of Peter Mark Roget's Thesaurus of English Words and Phrases. An edge is drawn between two categories if Roget gave a reference to the latter among the words and phrases of the former, or if the two categories were related to each other by their positions in Roget's book. This network has $5,103$ edges and its clustering coefficient is 0.15. We simulate it by a η network with $m = 4$ and $\eta = 1.4$. The produced graph has $5,389$ edges and its clustering coefficient is 0.14. Figure 1(e) presents degree distribution of the simulated network.

Note that when the graph is dense, since m is large, the preferential attachment step has a significant effect on the clustering coefficient. However, the bound B does not consider the clustering coefficient resulted by preferential attachment and as a result, for dense graphs (e.g., the *neural network* graph) it is not tight. In summary, the bound B is always tight for the clustering coefficient resulted by transitivity, and it is tight for the clustering coefficient of a network that is not very dense.

3.1 Empirical evaluation of the η model

In this section, we empirically evaluate the different properties of the η model. In order to investigate the impact of η, we fix m to 2 and n to $10,000$, and produce networks with different η: $0.4, 0.8, 1.2, 1.6, 2$. Figure 2 illustrates the degree distributions of the produced networks. If η is set to 0, a BA network is obtained. As we see in the figure, the degree distributions follow a power-law. Furthermore, by increasing η, the exponent γ slowly increases which is consistent with Equation 14. Figure 3(a) compares the clustering coefficient of the networks and the bound B obtained in Equation 30. In the produced networks, m is 2, n is $10,000$ and η varies between 0.4 and 2. It shows that by increasing the clustering coefficient, B increases as well. Table 3 summarizes the characteristics of the simulated networks. In the produced networks, by increasing η, the clustering coefficient, average degree increase and the diameter de-

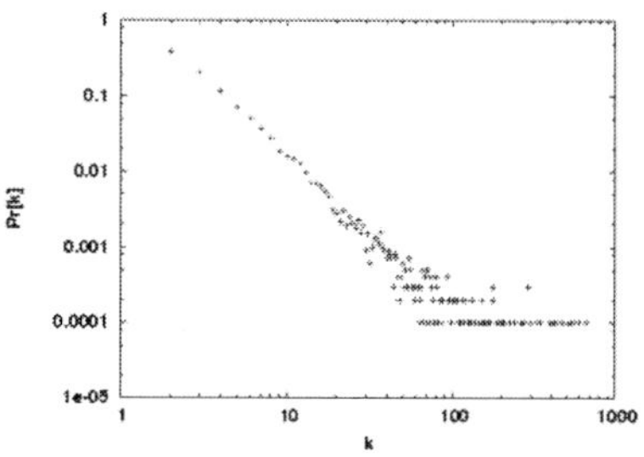

(a) Electronic circuits

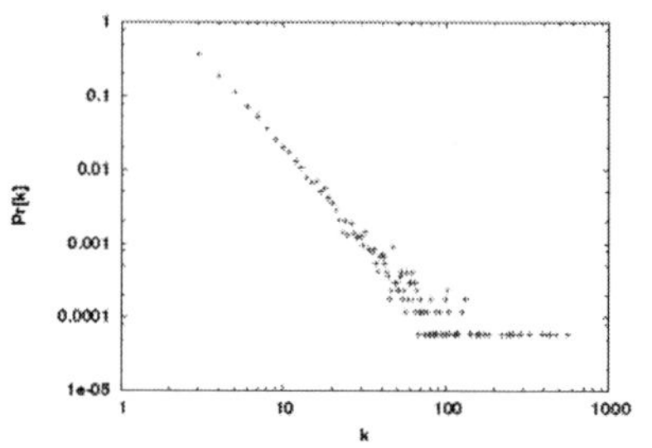

(b) Email address books

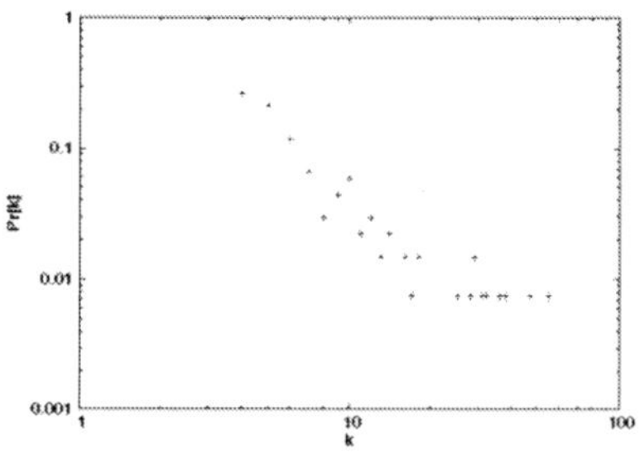

(c) marine food web

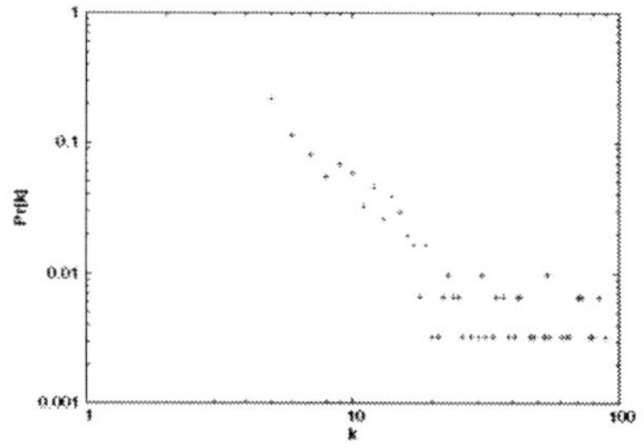

(d) nematode C. Elegans.

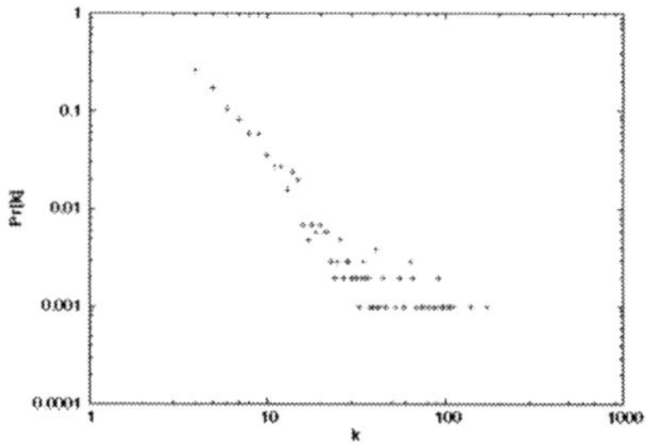

(e) Roget's thesaurus

Figure 1: Degree distributions of the η networks produced for the different real-world networks.

Table 3: Diameter, clustering coefficient, and average degree of networks produced by the η model for different values of η. n is set to $10,000$ and m is set to 2.

η	diameter	clustering coefficient	Avg. degree
0	5.28	0.0045	4
0.4	4.91	0.108	4.701
0.8	4.72	0.171	5.432
1.2	4.21	0.204	6.149
1.6	3.67	0.244	6.900
2	3.25	0.27	7.679

creases.

As depicted in Equations 6, 14 and 30, another parameter affecting the η networks is m. In order to evaluate the influence of m, we fix η to 1 and n to $10,000$, and produce networks with different values for m: 2, 3, 4 and 5. Figure 3 shows degree distributions of the produced networks. As depicted in the figure, the degree distributions follow a power-law. Similar to η, increasing m slightly increases the exponent γ, which is consistent with Equation 14. Figure 3(b) compares the clustering coefficient of the networks and the bound B obtained in Equation 30. In the produced networks, n is $10,000$ and η is 1 and m varies between 2 to 5. It shows that by decreasing B, the clustering coefficient decreases as well and as Equation 30 says, increasing m, reduces B. In Table 4, we describe the specifications of the networks. By increasing m, both the clustering coefficient and the diameter decrease but the average degree increases.

Table 4: Diameter, clustering coefficient, and average degree of networks produced by the η model for different values of m. n is set to 10000 and η is set to 1.

m	diameter	clustering coefficient	Avg. degree
2	4.34	0.19	5.826
3	3.88	0.09	7.804
4	3.32	0.0638	9.91
5	3.47	0.05	11.928

4 Related work

In [1], a power-law model $P(\alpha, \beta)$ is proposed as follows: let y be the number of vertices with degree x. $P(\alpha, \beta)$ assigns uniform probability to all graphs with $y = e^{\alpha}/x^{\beta}$. The authors study the giant component and the evolution of random graphs in this model. The authors of [27] present a model to explain social network searchability. Their model defines a class of searchable networks and a method for searching them.

Chung and Lu [6] consider a family of random graphs with a given expected degree sequence. In this model each edge is selected independently with probability proportional to the product of the expected degrees of its endpoints. Eubank et al. [11] show that many basic characteristics of the social network of the city of Portland, Oregon, USA, are well-modeled by the random graph model of Chung and Lu. They also present approximation algorithms for computing basic structural properties such as clustering coefficients and shortest paths distribution.

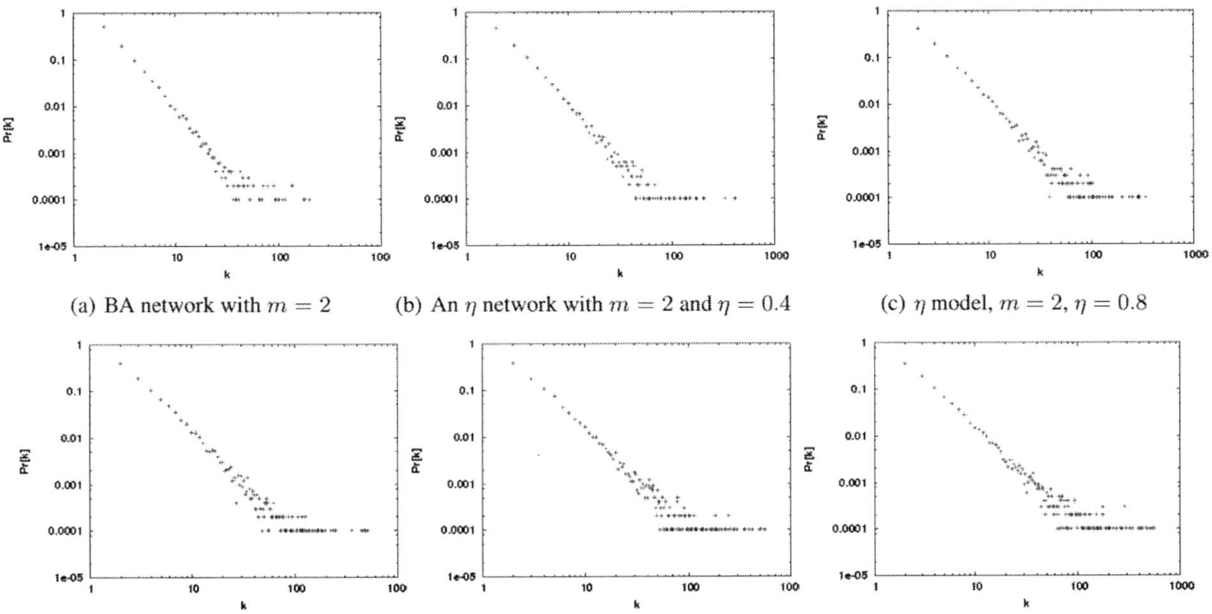

(a) BA network with $m = 2$ (b) An η network with $m = 2$ and $\eta = 0.4$ (c) η model, $m = 2$, $\eta = 0.8$

(d) An η network with $m = 2$ and $\eta = 1.2$ (e) η model, $m = 2$, $\eta = 1.6$ (f) η model, $m = 2$, $\eta = 2$

Figure 2: Comparison of degree distributions of a BA network and five η networks having different values of η.

In [20], the authors formulate models of the time evolution of the networks that obtain and lose vertices over time. They show that the model generates networks with power-law degree distributions. In their models new vertices obtain edges by preferential attachment, but the number of added vertices is equal to the number of deleted vertices. In [32] and [33], the authors study and analyze different properties such as degree distribution, clustering coefficient, average path length and phase transition of an evolving email network model.

Takemoto and Oosawa [25] propose a model for evolving networks by merging complete graphs (cliques) as building blocks. The model shows power-law degree distribution, power-law clustering spectra and high average clustering coefficients independent of the size of network. However, most real-world networks are formed in a different way: they *grow* over time by obtaining new vertices, rather than by merging cliques.

Serrano, Krioukov and Boguna [24] show that a class of hidden variable models with underlying metric spaces are able to reproduce specific properties (such as topology) in real-world networks. Li and Maini [19] propose an evolving network model that produces community structures. The model is based on two mechanisms: the inner-community preferential attachment and inter-community preferential attachment. However, while their theoretical and numerical simulations show that this network model has community structure, they do not provide a theoretical analysis for the clustering coefficient of the model. Furthermore, their numerical simulations show that the clustering coefficient of their model is still significantly lower than the clustering coefficient of real-world networks.

Yang and Leskovec [30] model the global influence of a vertex on the rate of diffusion through the network. The same authors in [31] investigate several large scale social, collaboration and information networks and find out that the community overlaps are more densely connected than the non-overlapping parts. Kin and Leskovec [16] propose the Multiplicative Attribute Graphs (MAG) model that employs interactions between the vertex attributes and the network structure. In this model, the probability of having an edge between two vertices is proportional to the attribute link formation affinities. The same authors in [15] present a parameter estimation method for the MAG model which is based on variational expectation maximization.

5 Conclusions

In this paper, we proposed a new model, called the η model, for describing transitivity relations in complex networks. We theoretically analyzed the model and calculated a lower bound on the clustering coefficient of the model which is independent of the network size and depends only on the model's parameters (η and m). We proved that the model satisfies important properties such as power-law degree distribution and the small-world property. We also evaluated the model empirically and showed that it can precisely simulate real-world networks from different domains with dif-

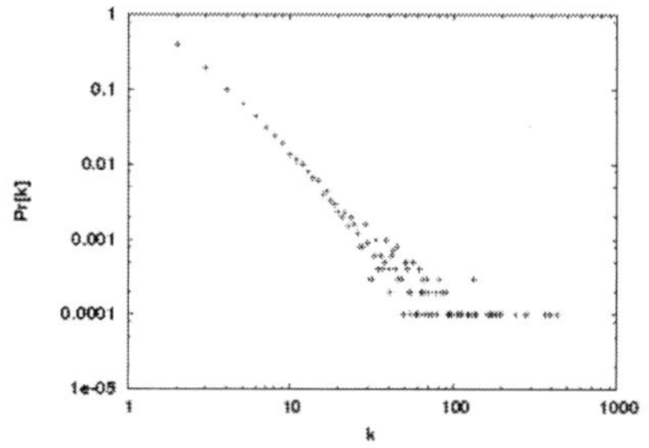

(a) $m = 2, \eta = 1$

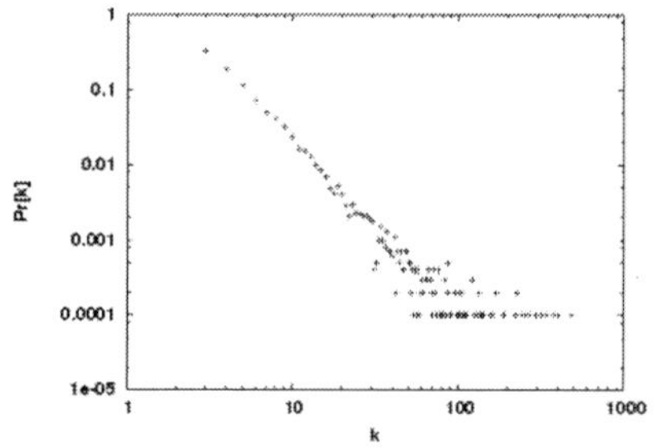

(b) $m = 3, \eta = 1$

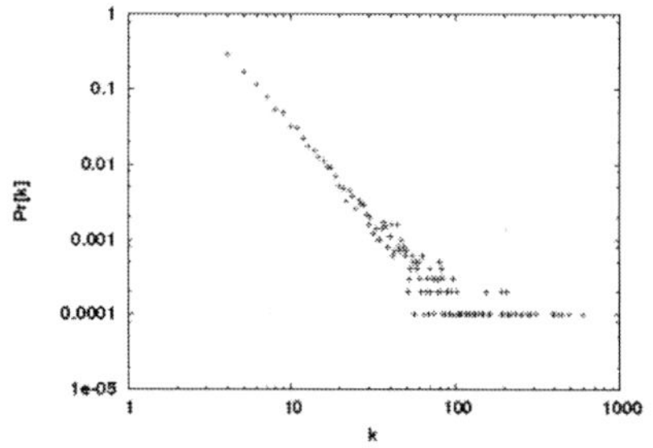

(c) $m = 4, \eta = 1$

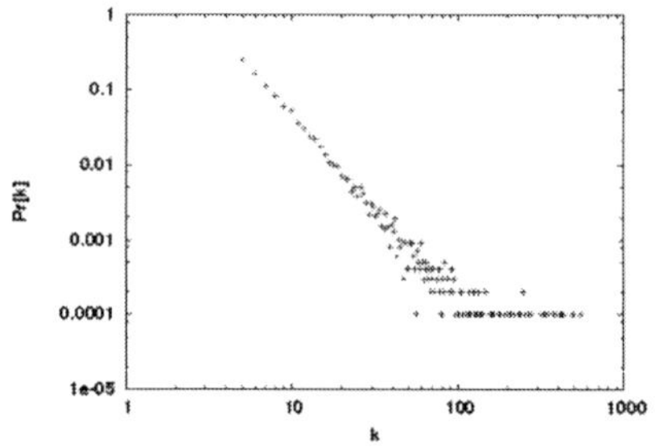

(d) $m = 5, \eta = 1$

Figure 4: Comparison of degree distributions of four η networks having different values of m.

ferent specifications.

References

[1] William Aiello, Fan Chung, and Linyuan Lu. A random graph model for massive graphs. In *Proceedings of the Thirty-second Annual ACM Symposium on Theory of Computing*, STOC, pages 171–180. ACM, 2000.

[2] Réka Albert and Albert-Lászlό Barabási. Statistical mechanics of complex networks. *Rev. Mod. Phys.*, 74(1):47–97, 2002.

[3] Albert-Laszlo Barabasi and Reka Albert. Emergence of scaling in random networks. *Science*, 286(5439):509–512, 1999.

[4] A. Barrat and M. Weigt. On the properties of small-world network models. *EUROP.PHYS.J.B*, 13:547, 2000.

[5] R. F. Cancho, C. Janssen, and R. V. Sole. Topology of technology graphs: Small world patterns in electronic circuits. *Phys. Rev. E*, 64, 2001.

[6] F. Chung and L. Lu. Connected components in random graphs with given expected degree sequences. *Annals of Combinatorics*, 6:125–145, 2002.

[7] Joel E. Cohen, Frederic Briand, and Charles M. Newman. *Community Food Webs: Data and Theory (Biomathematics)*, volume 20. Springer, 1990.

[8] R. Cohen and S. Havlin. Scale-Free Networks Are Ultrasmall. *Phys. Rev. Lett.*, 90:058701, 2003.

[9] P.W. Anderson D.J. Thouless and R.G. Palmer. A solution to a solvable model of a spin glass. *Philosophical Magazine*, page 35:593, 1977.

[10] P. Erdos and A Renyi. On the evolution of random graphs. pages 17–61, 1960.

[11] Stephen Eubank, V.S. Anil Kumar, Madhav V. Marathe, Aravind Srinivasan, and Nan Wang. Structural and algorithmic aspects of massive social networks. In *Proceedings of the Fifteenth Annual ACM-SIAM Symposium on Discrete Algorithms*, SODA '04, pages 718–727, 2004.

[12] Martin Grötschel, Sven O. Krumke, and Jörg Rambau, editors. *Online Optimization of Large Scale Systems*. Springer, 2001.

[13] Thomas Hofmann and Joachim M. Buhmann. Pairwise data clustering by deterministic annealing. *IEEE Trans. Pattern Anal. Mach. Intell.*, 19(1):1–14, 1997.

[14] M. Huxham, S. Beaney, and D. Raffaelli. Do parasites reduce the chances of triangulation in a real food web? *Oikos*, 76:284–300, 1996.

[15] Myunghwan Kim and Jure Leskovec. Modeling social networks with node attributes using the multiplicative attribute graph model. pages 400–409, 2011.

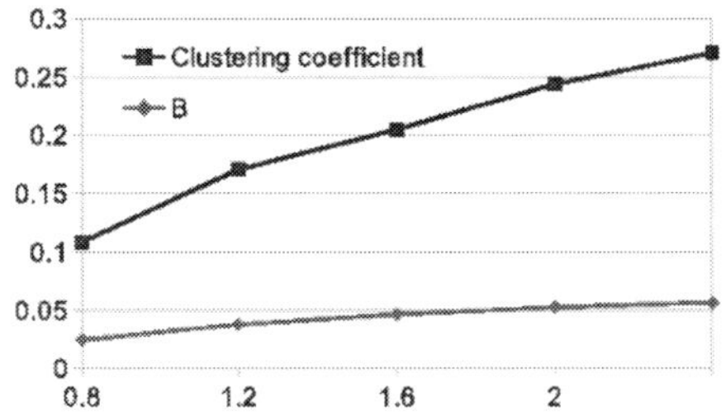

(a) The η parameter.

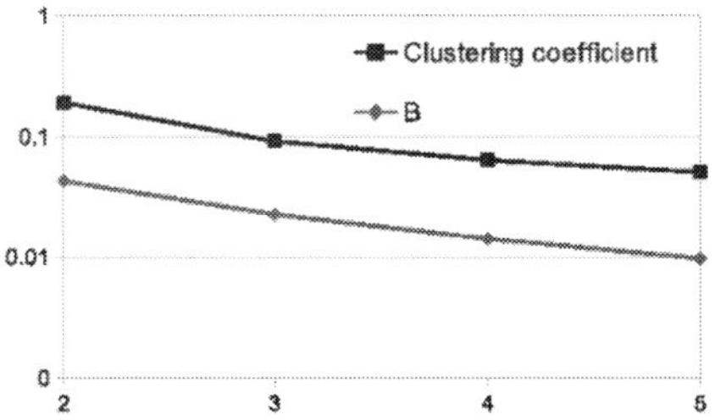

(b) The m parameter.

Figure 3: Effect of η and m on the clustering coefficient and the bound B.

[16] Myunghwan Kim and Jure Leskovec. Multiplicative attribute graph model of real-world networks. *Internet Mathematics*, 8(1-2):113–160, 2012.

[17] Donald E. Knuth. *The Stanford GraphBase - a platform for combinatorial computing*. ACM, 1993.

[18] Jure Leskovec, Lars Backstrom, Ravi Kumar, and Andrew Tomkins. Microscopic evolution of social networks. In *KDD '08: Proceeding of the 14th ACM SIGKDD international conference on Knowledge discovery and data mining*, pages 462–470, 2008.

[19] C. Li and P. K. Maini. An evolving network model with community structure. *Journal of Physics A: Mathematical and General*, 38:9741–9749, 2005.

[20] Cristopher Moore, Gourab Ghoshal, and M. E. J. Newman. Exact solutions for models of evolving networks with addition and deletion of nodes. 74(036121), 2006.

[21] M. E. J. Newman, Stephanie Forrest, and Justin Balthrop. Email networks and the spread of computer viruses. *Phys. Rev. E*, 66(3):035101, 2002.

[22] M. E. J. Newman, S. H. Strogatz, and D. J. Watts. Random graphs with arbitrary degree distributions and their applications. *Physical Review E*, 64(2):026118, 2001.

[23] Jan Puzicha, Thomas Hofmann, and Joachim M. Buhmann. A theory of proximity based clustering: structure detection by optimization. *Pattern Recognition*, 33(4):617–634, 2000.

[24] M Angeles Serrano, Dimitri Krioukov, and Marian Boguna. Self-similarity of complex networks and hidden metric spaces. *Phys. Rev. Lett.*, 100(078701), February 2008.

[25] Kazuhiro Takemoto and Chikoo Oosawa. Evolving networks by merging cliques. *Phys. Rev. E*, 742, 2005.

[26] G.B. Thomas and R.L. Finney. *Calculus and analytic geometry*. Calculus and Analytic Geometry. Addison-Wesley, 1996.

[27] D.J. Watts, P.S. Dodds, and M.E.J. Newman. Identity and search in social networks. *Science*, 296:1302, 2002.

[28] D.J. Watts and S.H. Strogatz. Collective dynamics of 'small-world' networks. *Nature*, (393):409–410, 1998.

[29] J.G. White, E. Southgate, J. N. Thomson, and S. Brenner. The structure of the nervous system of the nematode c. elegans. *Philosophical transactions Royal Society London*, 314:1–340, 1986.

[30] Jaewon Yang and Jure Leskovec. Modeling information diffusion in implicit networks. In *Proceedings of the 2010 IEEE International Conference on Data Mining*, ICDM '10, pages 599–608. IEEE Computer Society, 2010.

[31] Jaewon Yang and Jure Leskovec. Community-affiliation graph model for overlapping network community detection. In *Proceedings of the 2010 IEEE International Conference on Data Mining*, ICDM '12, pages 1170–1175. IEEE Computer Society, 2012.

[32] Chaopin Zhu and Anthony Kuh. On randomly evolving email networks. In *39th Annual Conference on Information Sciences and Systems*, 2006.

[33] Chaopin Zhu, Anthony Kuh, Juan Wang, and Philippe De Wilde. Analysis of an evolving email network. *Phys. Rev. E*, 74:046–109, 2006.

Adversarial Inverse Optimal Control for General Imitation Learning Losses and Embodiment Transfer

Xiangli Chen **Mathew Monfort** **Brian D. Ziebart**
University of Illinois at Chicago
Chicago, IL 60607
{xchen40,mmonfo2,bziebart}@uic.edu

Peter Carr
Disney Research
Pittsburgh, PA 15213
peter.carr@disneyresearch.com

Abstract

We develop a general framework for inverse optimal control that distinguishes between rationalizing demonstrated behavior and imitating inductively inferred behavior. This enables learning for more general imitative evaluation measures and differences between the capabilities of the demonstrator and those of the learner (i.e., differences in embodiment). Our formulation takes the form of a zero-sum game between a learner attempting to minimize an imitative loss measure, and an adversary attempting to maximize the loss by approximating the demonstrated examples in limited ways. We establish the consistency and generalization guarantees of this approach and illustrate its benefits on real and synthetic imitation learning tasks.

1 INTRODUCTION

Inverse optimal control (IOC) [Kalman, 1964, Rust, 1988, Boyd et al., 1994] and inverse reinforcement learning (IRL) [Ng and Russell, 2000, Abbeel and Ng, 2004] attempt to rationalize demonstrated sequential decision making by estimating a reward/cost function that makes observed decision sequences optimal. When the learned reward is defined over abstract properties of states and actions [Ng and Russell, 2000], it can generalize to new decision processes with states and actions that are similarly described. In contrast, methods that directly estimate a policy mapping from states to controls—also known as "behavioral cloning" [Pomerleau, 1989]—often generalize poorly when attempting to predict goal-directed sequential decisions when aspects of the decision process change.

Unfortunately, the basic IOC problem—selecting a reward function that makes demonstrated decision sequences optimal—is ill-posed, since degenerate solutions exist (e.g., setting all rewards to zero makes every decision sequence optimal) [Ng and Russell, 2000]. When demonstrated behavior is noisy, only degenerate solutions may remain as valid solutions to the basic IOC problem. Existing methods pose the problem in various ways to avoid degenerate solutions. Maximum margin planning (MMP) [Ratliff et al., 2006] seeks a reward function that makes demonstrated sequences have larger reward than all alternatives by a structured loss measure. Maximum (causal) entropy IRL [Ziebart et al., 2010], and its extensions [Boularias et al., 2011, Levine et al., 2011], seek an entropy-maximizing distribution over sequences/policies that matches the feature-based components of the reward function with demonstrated sequences. Each method is constructed around a specific loss function: MMP minimizes the the structured hinge loss, while MaxEnt IRL minimizes the (causal) log loss.

A typical assumption in IOC is that the demonstrator and the learner operate under identical decision processes. In other words, it is assumed that the demonstrator and imitator utilize the same action space, and have the same state transition dynamics. In such settings, imitation can be effectively accomplished by adequately predicting what a demonstrator would do in a new situation. We consider generalized imitation learning problems where the abilities of the demonstrator and the learner are different. This situation arises frequently in practice due to differences in embodiment between human demonstrators and robotic imitators [Nehaniv and Dautenhahn, 2002, Alissandrakis et al., 2002], and, more generally, when autonomously-controlled devices are more expensive and less capable than manually-controlled devices.

We propose a more general framework for inverse optimal control that is both consistent and computationally practical for a range of loss functions and situations where imitation learning across different embodiments is required. The key philosophy of our approach is that unknown properties of *how the demonstrator would behave in new situations* should be treated as pessimistically as possible, since any unwarranted assumptions could lead to substantial errors when behavior is evaluated under more general loss functions or transferred across embodiments. Our formulation produces a zero-sum game between: the learner seeking a control policy to minimize loss; and an adversary seeking a control policy that adequately characterizes the demonstrations, but maximizes the learner's loss. We establish consistency and generalization guarantees, develop algorithms for inference and learning under this formulation, and illustrate the benefits of this approach on synthetic and real imitation learning tasks.

2 BACKGROUND & NOTATION

In this paper, we denote single variables with assigned values in lowercase (e.g., a, s), multivariates with values in bold (e.g., $\mathbf{s}_{1:T}$), and random variables using uppercase (e.g., A_t or $\mathbf{S}_{1:T}$). **Decision processes** are defined by state and action sets ($\mathcal{S}$ and $\mathcal{A}$) and the state transition dynamics τ, which describe the distribution of next states $s_{t+1} \in \mathcal{S}$ given current state $s_t \in \mathcal{S}$ and action $a_t \in \mathcal{A}$: $\tau(s_{t+1}|s_t, a_t)$. We make use of **causally conditioned probability distributions** [Kramer, 1998],

$$P(\mathbf{y}_{1:T}||\mathbf{x}_{1:T}) \triangleq \prod_{t=1}^{T} P(y_t|\mathbf{y}_{1:t-1}, \mathbf{x}_{1:t}),$$

to compactly represent a decision process's **state transition dynamics**,

$$\tau(\mathbf{s}_{1:T}||\mathbf{a}_{1:T-1}) \triangleq \prod_{t=1}^{T} \tau(s_t|\mathbf{s}_{1:t-1}, \mathbf{a}_{1:t-1}),$$

and **stochastic control policy**,

$$\pi(\mathbf{a}_{1:T}||\mathbf{s}_{1:T}) \triangleq \prod_{t=1}^{T} \pi(a_t|\mathbf{a}_{1:t-1}, \mathbf{s}_{1:t}).$$

Multiplied together, these produce a joint probability distribution over the states and actions:

$$P(\mathbf{a}_{1:T}, \mathbf{s}_{1:T}) = \pi(\mathbf{a}_{1:T}||\mathbf{s}_{1:T})\tau(\mathbf{s}_{1:T}||\mathbf{a}_{1:T-1}).$$

We denote **deterministic control policies** (a special case of stochastic control policies) mapping from states or state histories to actions as $\delta(s_t)$ or $\delta(\mathbf{s}_{1:t})$. In addition to denoting the demonstrator's full control policy, π, under dynamics, τ, we also consider distributions of trajectories sampled from the demonstrator's distribution as $\tilde{\pi}$, $\tilde{\tau}$, and a learner's control policy, $\hat{\pi}$, under a (possibly different) set of dynamics $\hat{\tau}$, and estimates of the demonstrator's policy, $\check{\pi}$. We similarly denote states, actions, and deterministic policies corresponds to these different sources as $\tilde{s}, \hat{s}, \check{s}, \tilde{a}, \hat{a}, \hat{\delta}$, etc.

3 PROBLEM DEFINITION

We begin by formally defining the supervised learning task of imitation learning with general loss measures in Definition 1. The learner's performance is measured by a loss

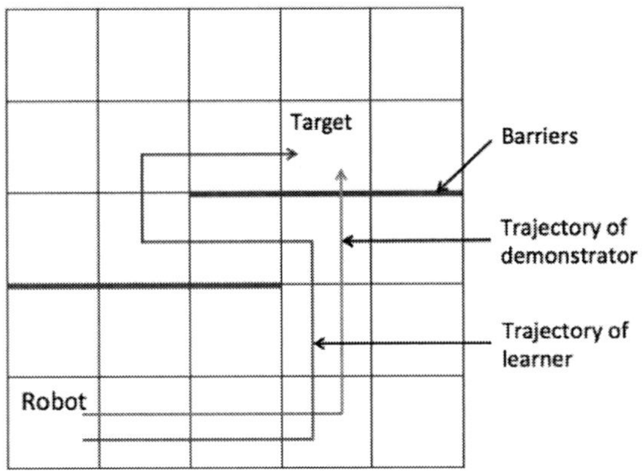

Figure 1: Learning to imitate a slower robot capable of walking over barriers.

function relating the expected state sequence of the learned control policy with the state sequence resulting from the demonstrator's control policy. The key inductive reasoning challenge is for the learner to produce a good control policy when demonstrations are unavailable by appropriately inferring the demonstrator's behaviors in such situations.

Definition 1. *In the task of* **imitation learning with general losses and embodiments**, *at training time: demonstrated traces of behavior are available from distribution $\tilde{P}(\mathbf{A}_{1:T}, \mathbf{S}_{1:T})$ under a dynamical system with known dynamics, $\tau(\mathbf{S}_{1:T}||\mathbf{A}_{1:T})$, and unknown control policy $\pi(\mathbf{A}_{1:T}||\mathbf{S}_{1:T})$. The learner attempts to choose a control policy $\hat{\pi}(\hat{\mathbf{A}}_{1:T}||\hat{\mathbf{S}}_{1:T})$ for potentially different dynamics, $\hat{\tau}(\hat{\mathbf{S}}_{1:T}||\hat{\mathbf{A}}_{1:T})$, that, at testing time, minimizes a given loss function relating (unknown) demonstration policies and learned policies: $\min_{\hat{\pi}} loss_{\tau,\hat{\tau}}(\pi, \hat{\pi})$.*

When the demonstrator and the learner operate under different state-action transition dynamics, $\tau \neq \hat{\tau}$, we refer to this setting as the **imitation learning across embodiments** problem. We assume that a loss function expressing the undesirability of the imitator's differences from the demonstrator is available. The key challenge is that the learner must still estimate the control policy of the demonstrator to be able to generalize to new situations, while also constructing its own control policy to overcome its differences in embodiment. We show a simple illustrative example of this in Figure 1.

The ability to minimize the desired imitative loss function when provided enough demonstration data and a sufficiently expressive characterization of decision policies is desired in an imitation learning algorithm. This is formally known as Fisher consistency (Def. 2).

Definition 2. *An imitation learning algorithm producing policy π_{imit} is* **Fisher consistent** *if, given the demonstrator's control policy for any demonstrator/imitator decision* *processes, $(\tau, \hat{\tau})$, and a sufficiently expressive feature representation for policies, the policy π_{imit} is a loss minimizer:*

$$\pi_{imit} \in \operatorname*{argmin}_{\hat{\pi}} \mathbb{E}\left[loss_{\tau,\hat{\tau}}(\pi, \hat{\pi})\right]. \quad (1)$$

We focus our attention in this work on loss functions that additively decompose over the state sequence[1]:

$$\mathbb{E}_{P(\mathbf{a}_{1:T},\mathbf{s}_{1:T},\hat{\mathbf{a}}_{1:T},\hat{\mathbf{s}}_{1:T})}\left[\sum_{t=1}^{T} \text{loss}(S_t, \hat{S}_t)\middle|\pi, \tau, \hat{\pi}, \hat{\tau}\right],$$

where the state-action distribution is obtained by combining a stochastic control policy with a state-transition dynamics distribution: $P(\mathbf{a}_{1:T}, \mathbf{s}_{1:T}, \hat{\mathbf{a}}_{1:T}, \hat{\mathbf{s}}_{1:T}) = \tau(\mathbf{s}_{1:T}||\mathbf{a}_{1:T-1})\ \pi(\mathbf{a}_{1:T}||\mathbf{s}_{1:T})\ \hat{\tau}(\hat{\mathbf{s}}_{1:T}||\hat{\mathbf{a}}_{1:T-1})\ \hat{\pi}(\hat{\mathbf{a}}_{1:T}||\hat{\mathbf{s}}_{1:T})$. Important to this problem definition is the independence between the demonstrator and the learner: there is no direct influence of one's actions on the other's state or actions, as shown in the factorization of the joint distribution.

4 ADVERSARIAL APPROACH

We develop an adversarial approach to the problem of imitation learning with general losses and embodiments (Definition 1) by combining the idea of rationalizing demonstrated behaviors from inverse optimal control [Abbeel and Ng, 2004] with a game-theoretic perspective [Topsøe, 1979, Grünwald and Dawid, 2004] that incorporates different imitative losses. Our approach assumes that except for certain properties of the limited samples of available demonstrated behavior, the demonstrator's policy is the worst-case possible for the learner. This avoids generalizing from available demonstrations in a optimistic manner that may be unrealistic and ultimately detrimental to the learner. Using tools from convex optimization (Theorem 3) and constraint generation (Algorithm 1), this formulation can be solved efficiently (Algorithm 2). Though the demonstrator's true policy is unlikely to be maximally detrimental to the learner, considering it as such leads to Fisher consistency (Theorem 1), provides strong generalization guarantees (Theorem 2), and avoids making any unwarranted assumptions.

4.1 ADVERSARIAL FORMULATION AND PROPERTIES

Our approach employs a game-theoretic formulation of the prediction task for additive state-based losses. We introduce an adversarially-estimated policy, $\check{\pi}$, which must be similar to demonstrated training data traces, but is the worst-case for the learner otherwise, as formalized in Definition 3.

[1]Loss functions for state-action pairs can also be incorporated by defining new states that (partially) "remember" previous state-action histories.

Definition 3. *The* **adversarial inverse optimal control** *learner for the joint demonstrator/learner transition dynamics, $(\tau, \hat{\tau})$ is defined as a zero-sum game in which each player chooses a stochastic control policy, $\hat{\pi}$ or $\check{\pi}$, optimizing:*

$$\min_{\hat{\pi}} \max_{\check{\pi}\in\tilde{\Xi}} \mathbb{E}\left[\sum_{t=1}^{T} loss(\hat{S}_t, \check{S}_t)\middle|\check{\pi}, \tau, \hat{\pi}, \hat{\tau}\right], \quad (2)$$

where $\tilde{\Xi}$ represents a convex set of constraints measured from characteristics of the demonstrated data (e.g., the moment-matching constraints: $\check{\pi} \in \tilde{\Xi} \iff \mathbb{E}[\sum_{t=1}^{T}\phi(\check{S}_t)|\check{\pi},\tau] = \tilde{\mathbf{c}} \triangleq \mathbb{E}[\sum_{t=1}^{T}\phi(S_t)|\tilde{\pi},\tilde{\tau}]$ of inverse reinforcement learning [Abbeel and Ng, 2004]) and the joint state-action distributions are realized by combining control policy and state-transition dynamics: e.g., $P(\hat{\mathbf{a}}_{1:T}, \hat{\mathbf{s}}_{1:T}) = \hat{\pi}(\hat{\mathbf{a}}_{1:T}||\hat{\mathbf{s}}_{1:T})\hat{\tau}(\hat{\mathbf{s}}_{1:T}||\hat{\mathbf{a}}_{1:T-1})$.

Though maximum margin methods, such as MMP [Ratliff et al., 2006] in the imitation learning setting, can similarly incorporate arbitrary structured loss functions, they are not Fisher consistent (Def. 2) even for the relatively simple Hamming loss (i.e., number of state mismatches between two sequences).[2] We establish the consistency of the adversarial inverse optimal control approach in Theorem 1.

Theorem 1. *Given a sufficiently rich feature representation defining the constraint set Ξ, the adversarial inverse optimal control learner is a Fisher consistent loss function minimizer for all additive, state-based losses.*

Proof. A sufficiently rich feature representation is equivalent to the constraint set Ξ containing only the true policy π. Then, under $\check{\pi} = \pi$, Eq. (2) then reduces to:

$$\min_{\hat{\pi}} \mathbb{E}\left[\sum_{t=1}^{T} \text{loss}(\hat{S}_t, \check{S}_t)\middle|\pi, \tau, \hat{\pi}, \hat{\tau}\right], \quad (3)$$

which is the loss function minimizer. □

An additional desirable property of this approach—even when the feature representation is not as expressive—is that if the set $\tilde{\Xi}$ can be defined to include the demonstrator's true policy, π, then generalization performance will be upper bounded by the expected adversarial training loss (Theorem 2).

Theorem 2. *The adversarial transfer IOC formulation (Definition 3) provides a useful generalization bound: if the true demonstrator policy π resides within the constraint set $\tilde{\Xi}$ with probability at least $1 - \alpha$, then the generalization*

[2]This follows directly from the Fisher inconsistency of multiclass classification [Liu, 2007, Tewari and Bartlett, 2007] using the Crammer-Singer multi-class generalization of the hinge loss [Crammer and Singer, 2002], which is a special case of the imitation learning setting with a single time step.

error will be worse than the training error (expected game value) with probability no more than α:

$$P(\pi \in \tilde{\Xi}) \geq 1 - \alpha \implies P\Bigg(\mathbb{E}\left[\sum_{t=1}^{T} loss(\hat{S}_t, S_t) | \pi, \tau, \hat{\pi}, \hat{\tau}\right] \geq \mathbb{E}\left[\sum_{t=1}^{T} loss(\hat{S}_t, \check{S}_t) | \check{\pi}, \tau, \hat{\pi}, \hat{\tau}\right]\Bigg) \leq \alpha. \quad (4)$$

Proof. If $\pi \in \tilde{\Xi}$, then

$$\mathbb{E}\left[\sum_{t=1}^{T} \text{loss}(\hat{S}_t, S_t) | \pi, \tau, \hat{\pi}, \hat{\tau}\right] \leq \mathbb{E}\left[\sum_{t=1}^{T} \text{loss}(\hat{S}_t, \check{S}_t) | \check{\pi}, \tau, \hat{\pi}, \hat{\tau}\right],$$

since replacing π with a worst case policy (maximizer of the set), $\check{\pi}$, only makes the expected loss worse. Thus, bounds on $P(\pi \in \tilde{\Xi})$ provide generalization guarantees with at least as much probability. □

4.2 LEARNING AND INFERENCE ALGORITHMS

Building on recently developed methods for tractably solving adversarial prediction problems for classification with cost-sensitive [Asif et al., 2015] and multivariate [Wang et al., 2015] performance measures, we employ the method of Lagrange multipliers to simplify from a game with one player's actions jointly constrained to a parameterized game with only probabilistic constraints on each player's policy (Theorem 3).

Theorem 3. *An equilibrium for the game of Definition 3 is obtained by solving an unconstrained zero-sum game parameterized by a vector of Lagrange multipliers:*

$$\min_{\mathbf{w}} \min_{\hat{\pi}} \max_{\check{\pi}} \mathbb{E}\left[\sum_{t=1}^{T} loss(\check{S}_t, \hat{S}_t) + \mathbf{w} \cdot \phi(\check{S}_t) \middle| \check{\pi}, \tau, \hat{\pi}, \hat{\tau}\right] - \mathbf{w} \cdot \tilde{\mathbf{c}}.$$

Proof. The proof follows from applying the method of Lagrangian multipliers (a) to the constrained optimization problem of Eq. (2), and then employing strong Lagrangian duality and minimax duality (b):

$$\min_{\hat{\pi}} \max_{\check{\pi} \in \tilde{\Xi}} \mathbb{E}\left[\sum_{t=1}^{T} \text{loss}(\hat{S}_t, \check{S}_t) \middle| \check{\pi}, \tau, \hat{\pi}, \hat{\tau}\right]$$
$$\stackrel{(a)}{=} \min_{\hat{\pi}} \max_{\check{\pi}} \min_{\mathbf{w}} \mathbb{E}\left[\sum_{t=1}^{T} \text{loss}(\hat{S}_t, \check{S}_t) + \mathbf{w} \cdot \left(\sum_{t=1}^{T} \phi(\check{S}_t) - \tilde{\mathbf{c}}\right) \middle| \check{\pi}, \tau, \hat{\pi}, \hat{\tau}\right]$$
$$\stackrel{(b)}{=} \min_{\mathbf{w}} \min_{\hat{\pi}} \max_{\check{\pi}} \mathbb{E}\left[\sum_{t=1}^{T} \text{loss}(\hat{S}_t, \check{S}_t) + \mathbf{w} \cdot \phi(\check{S}_t) \middle| \check{\pi}, \tau, \hat{\pi}, \hat{\tau}\right] - \mathbf{w} \cdot \tilde{\mathbf{c}}.$$

Note that we assume that the loss function is an expected loss over state predictions. The objective function of our optimization is therefore a bilinear function of the learner's strategy and the adversary's strategy, which provides the strong Lagrangian duality that we employ. No stronger assumption about the state-based loss function is needed so long as it takes this bilinear form. □

We form the stochastic policy of each player $\check{\pi}$, $\hat{\pi}$ as a mixture of deterministic policies: $\check{\delta}$ and $\hat{\delta}$. Conceptually, the payoff matrix of the zero-sum game can be constructed by specifying each combination of deterministic policies, $\check{\delta}$, $\hat{\delta}$, having payoff: $\mathbb{E}[\sum_{t=1}^{T} \text{loss}(\check{S}_t, \hat{S}_t) + \mathbf{w} \cdot \phi(\check{S}_t) | \check{\delta}, \tau, \hat{\delta}, \hat{\tau}]$. An example payoff matrix is shown in Table 1 with the adversary choosing a distribution over columns, and the learner choosing a distribution over rows.

Table 1: The payoff matrix for the adversarial IOC prediction game with $\ell(\check{\delta}, \hat{\delta}) = \mathbb{E}[\sum_{t=1}^{T} \text{loss}(\check{S}_t, \hat{S}_t) | \check{\delta}, \tau, \hat{\delta}, \hat{\tau}]$ and $\psi(\check{\delta}) = \mathbf{w} \cdot \mathbb{E}[\sum_{t=1}^{T} \phi(\check{S}_t) | \check{\delta}, \tau]$.

	$\check{\delta}_1$	$\check{\delta}_2$	...	$\check{\delta}_k$
$\hat{\delta}_1$	$\ell(\check{\delta}_1, \hat{\delta}_1) + \psi(\check{\delta}_1)$	$\ell(\check{\delta}_2, \hat{\delta}_1) + \psi(\check{\delta}_2)$	...	$\ell(\check{\delta}_k, \hat{\delta}_1) + \psi(\check{\delta}_k)$
$\hat{\delta}_2$	$\ell(\check{\delta}_1, \hat{\delta}_2) + \psi(\check{\delta}_1)$	$\ell(\check{\delta}_2, \hat{\delta}_2) + \psi(\check{\delta}_2)$	...	$\ell(\check{\delta}_k, \hat{\delta}_2) + \psi(\check{\delta}_k)$
⋮	⋮	⋮	⋱	⋮
$\hat{\delta}_j$	$\ell(\check{\delta}_1, \hat{\delta}_j) + \psi(\check{\delta}_1)$	$\ell(\check{\delta}_2, \hat{\delta}_j) + \psi(\check{\delta}_2)$	...	$\ell(\check{\delta}_k, \hat{\delta}_j) + \psi(\check{\delta}_k)$

Unfortunately, this leads to a payoff matrix with a size that is exponential in terms of the actions in the decision process. This cannot be explicitly constructed for practical problems of even modest size. We employ the double oracle method [McMahan et al., 2003] to construct a smaller sub-portion of the matrix that supports the Nash equilibrium strategy for the full game. The basic strategy, outlined in Algorithm 1, iteratively computes a Nash equilibrium for a payoff sub-matrix and augments the payoff matrix with an additional column and row that provide the most improvement for each player.

Finding the best response for each player:

$$\operatorname*{argmin}_{\hat{\delta}} \mathbb{E}\left[\sum_{t=1}^{T} \text{loss}(\check{S}_t, \hat{S}_t) \middle| \check{\pi}, \tau, \hat{\delta}, \hat{\tau}\right]; \text{ or} \quad (5)$$
$$\operatorname*{argmax}_{\check{\delta}} \mathbb{E}\left[\sum_{t=1}^{T} \text{loss}(\check{S}_t, \hat{S}_t) + \mathbf{w} \cdot \phi(\check{S}_t) \middle| \check{\delta}, \tau, \hat{\pi}, \hat{\tau}\right],$$

reduces to a time-varying optimal control problem. Consider finding the best demonstrator estimation policy $\check{\delta}^*$. The "expected loss" can be treated as a reward for state $s_t \in \mathcal{S}_D$ with a numerical value of:

$$\text{reward}(s_t) = \mathbb{E}[\text{loss}(s_t, \hat{S}_t) | \hat{\pi}] + \mathbf{w} \cdot \phi(s_t).$$

Algorithm 1 Double oracle method for adversarial IOC

Input: Demonstrator's state transition dynamics τ_D; learner's state transition dynamics, $\hat{\tau}$; loss function: $\text{loss}(s_t, \hat{s}_t)$; initial policy sets: $\check{\Pi}$ and $\hat{\Pi}$; feature function $\phi(s_t)$; and Lagrange multipliers $\mathbf{w}$.
Output: A Nash equilibrium $(\check{\pi}^*, \hat{\pi}^*)$.

repeat
  Compute Nash equilibrium $(\check{\pi}^*_D, \hat{\pi}^*)$ and its game value $\check{v}^*$ for sub-game $\check{\Pi}$, $\hat{\Pi}$, $\text{loss}(\cdot,\cdot)$, $\phi(\cdot)$, and $\mathbf{w}$
  Compute best response $\check{\delta}^*$ to $\hat{\pi}^*$ with value $\check{v}_{\check{\delta}^*}$
  if $\check{v}^* \neq v_{\check{\delta}^*}$ **then**
    Add action to set: $\check{\Pi} \leftarrow \check{\Pi} \cup \check{\delta}^*$
  end if
  Compute Nash equilibrium $(\check{\pi}^*, \hat{\pi}^*)$ and its game with value $\hat{v}^*$ for sub-game $\check{\Pi}$, $\hat{\Pi}$, $\text{loss}(\cdot,\cdot)$, $\phi(\cdot)$, and $\mathbf{w}$
  Compute best response $\hat{\delta}^*$ to $\check{\pi}$ value $\hat{v}_{\hat{\delta}^*}$
  if $\hat{v}^* \neq \hat{v}_{\hat{\delta}^*}$ **then**
    Add action to set: $\hat{\Pi} \leftarrow \hat{\Pi} \cup \hat{\delta}^*$
  end if
until $\check{v}_{\check{\delta}^*} = \hat{v}_{\hat{\delta}^*} = \check{v}^* = \hat{v}^*$
return $(\check{\pi}^*, \hat{\pi}^*)$

Once the reward function is constructed, this time-varying optimal control problem can be solved efficiently in $\mathcal{O}(|\mathcal{S}||\mathcal{A}|T)$ time using value iteration [Bellman, 1957]. We assume that the set of deterministic policies defining each player's stochastic policy is relatively small so that marginalizing to compute state rewards is dominated by the run time of solving the optimal control problem. Each player's best response can be constructed in this manner. Upon termination, neither player's (mixed) strategy can be improved with an additional game action (i.e., deterministic policy), and, thus, by definition $\check{\pi}^*$ and $\hat{\pi}^*$ must be an equilibrium pair [McMahan et al., 2003].

Algorithm 2 Learning algorithm for adversarial IOC

Input: Demonstration $\tilde{P}(\mathbf{A}_{1:T}, \mathbf{S}_{1:T})$ from given decision processes, $(\tau, \hat{\tau})$; loss function: $\text{loss}(\cdot,\cdot)$; and learning rate schedule λ_t
Output: Parameters $\mathbf{w}$ providing adversarial generalization

$\mathbf{w} \leftarrow \mathbf{0}$
while $\mathbf{w}$ not converged **do**
  Compute $\check{\pi}^*$ from parameters $\mathbf{w}$ using double oracle method (Alg. 1) given $\tau, \hat{\tau}$
  Gradient update of parameters: $\mathbf{w} \leftarrow \mathbf{w} - \lambda_t(\mathbb{E}_{P(\check{\mathbf{S}}_{1:T}, \check{\mathbf{A}}_{1:T})}[\sum_{t=1}^{T} \phi(\check{S}_t)|\check{\pi}^*, \tau] - \tilde{\mathbf{c}})$
end while

Model parameters $\mathbf{w}$ are estimated using a convex optimization routine described in Algorithm 2. We refer the reader to Asif et al. [Asif et al., 2015] for the proof of convexity for adversarial prediction learning problems of this form with payoff values that are constant with respect to the probability of each player's actions, but not the values themselves.

4.3 EXISTING METHOD RELATIONSHIPS

We conclude our development of the adversarial IOC method by highlighting its conceptual similarities to and differences from previous methods for imitating and predicting sequential decision making policies with the aid of Figure 2.

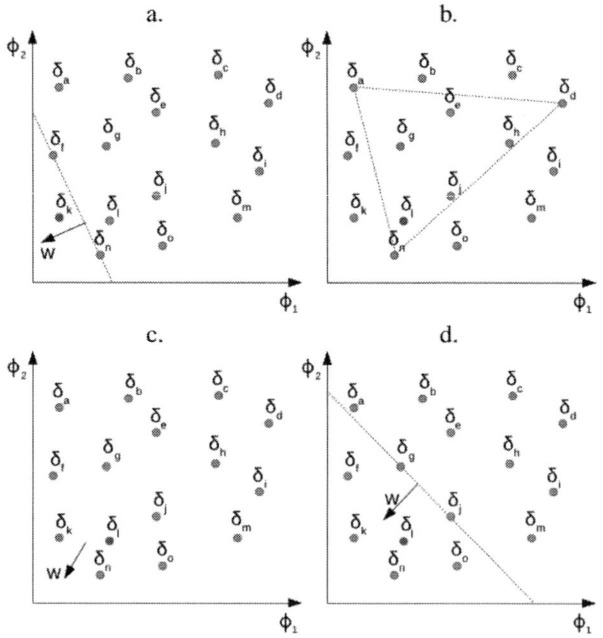

Figure 2: A set of deterministic policies, $\delta_a, \ldots, \delta_o$, represented as points in the two-dimensional feature space based on the expected sum of features under the policy, $\mathbb{E}[\sum_t \phi_k(S_t)|\delta]$. Maximum margin planning [Ratliff et al., 2006] chooses weight $\mathbf{w}$ to separate demonstration δ_k from δ_f and δ_n (top left); Abbeel & Ng's feature-matching algorithm [Abbeel and Ng, 2004] mixes between policies δ_a, δ_d, and δ_n (top right); maximum entropy IRL [Ziebart et al., 2010] chooses a weight direction and produces a probability distribution over all policies (bottom left); and our adversarial approach generates an equilibrium over deterministic policies, $\delta_f, \delta_g, \delta_j, \delta_k, \delta_l, \delta_n$, and δ_o, based on the learned weight $\mathbf{w}$ (bottom right).

When a single demonstrated trajectory resides on the convex hull of the expected feature space (e.g., δ_k in Figure 2a), Abbeel & Ng's feature-matching IRL algorithm [Abbeel and Ng, 2004], maximum margin planning [Ratliff et al., 2006], maximum causal entropy IRL [Ziebart et al., 2010] and our adversarial IOC approach will produce weight estimates $\mathbf{w}$ that make the demonstrated policy (uniquely) optimal. They differ in that Abbeel & Ng's algorithm will be satisfied with any weight $\mathbf{w}$ that makes δ_k uniquely optimal, since this would match feature counts with the distribution of demonstrated sequences: $\frac{1}{n}\sum_{i=1}^{n}\mathbb{E}[\sum_{t=1}^{T}\phi(S_t^{(i)})|\pi,\tau] = \frac{1}{n}\sum_{i=1}^{n}\sum_{t=1}^{T}\phi(s_t^{(i)})$, guaranteeing equivalent expected reward under the assumption that the reward function is linear in the feature vector, ϕ [Abbeel and Ng, 2004]. As a refinement to this idea, maximum margin planning [Ratliff et al., 2006] seeks parameter weights that make a demonstrated policy on the convex hull "more optimal" than other policies by a structured margin (using a structured loss to penalize being "almost as optimal" from a policy that is very different from the demonstration policy), as shown in Figure 2a. Maximum (causal) entropy inverse reinforcement learning [Ziebart et al., 2010], which employs a Boltzmann distribution over actions for each state, similarly converges to allocate all of its probability to the actions of the demonstrated policy. Adversarial IOC's behavior is equivalent to that of maximum margin planning (when a small amount of regularization is included) in this situation: it obtains a weight vector $\mathbf{w}$ so that the demonstrated policy is better than all alternatives by the structured loss.

When demonstrated trajectories are on the interior of the convex hull, as shown in Figure 2b-d, the behaviors of the methods differ substantially. Abbeel & Ng's feature-matching algorithm [Abbeel and Ng, 2004] produces a mixture of deterministic policies (e.g., a mixture of δ_a, δ_d, and δ_n with probabilities of 10%, 10%, and 80%, as shown in Figure 2b) that match demonstrated feature counts. Unfortunately, many such mixtures exist and switching between the extremes of the convex hull often proves to imitate poorly in practice. Maximum (causal) entropy inverse reinforcement learning [Ziebart et al., 2010] provides a distribution that places some probability on each deterministic policy, with higher probabilities specified by the learned weight vector $\mathbf{w}$, as shown in Figure 2c. This avoids mixing between extremely different deterministic policies [Abbeel and Ng, 2004], but requires a computationally expensive integration over all policies instead of using an optimal MDP policy solver as a sub-routine for learning.

An additional limitation of maximum (causal) entropy inverse reinforcement learning [Ziebart et al., 2010] is due to its global normalization over control policies. This normalization imposes burdensome implicit constraints on learned cost functions[3] due to cycle sensitivity [Monfort et al., 2015, Ziebart, 2010], as defined below and illustrated in Figure 3. These cost function constraints can increase the loss of resulting maximum entropy IRL predictions in practice even when demonstrated behavior trajectories do not include the states of the cycles. Conversely, removing a completely irrelevant cycle from a Markov decision process can drastically change the estimated reward/cost function.

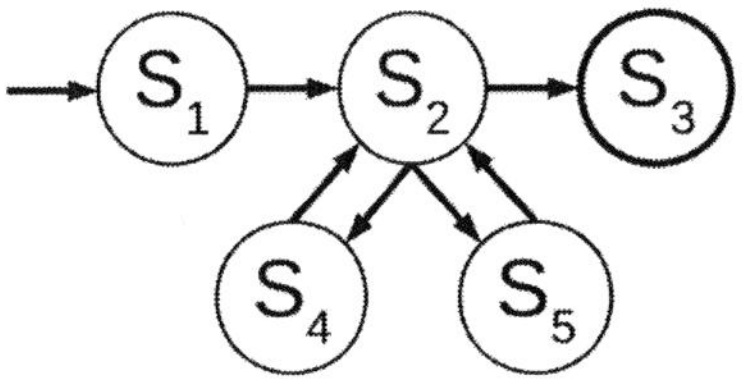

Figure 3: A deterministic Markov decision process with initial state s_1 and absorbing state s_3 in which we assume for simplicity that state two and four have identical features: $\phi(s_4) = \phi(s_5)$. Under maximum entropy inverse reinforcement learning [Ziebart et al., 2010], $P(s_{1:T}) \propto e^{-\mathbf{w}\cdot\sum_{t=1}^{T}\phi(s_t)}$ The number of paths terminating in the absorbing state of odd length $n \geq 3$ is $2^{\frac{n-3}{2}}$, each with cost of $C_0 + \frac{n-3}{2}C_1$, where $C_0 \triangleq \mathbf{w}\cdot(\phi(s_1)+\phi(s_2)+\phi(s_3))$ and $C_1 \triangleq \mathbf{w}\cdot(\phi(s_2)+\phi(s_4))$. The normalization constant under maximum entropy inverse optimal control is $\sum_{i=0}^{\infty}2^i e^{-C_0+iC_1} = e^{-C_0}\sum_{i=0}^{\infty}e^{i\ln 2-iC_1}$, and requires that $C_1 > \ln 2$ for it to be finite.

Definition 4. *An inverse optimal control method is characterized as being* **cycle sensitive** *when differences in a decision process's state representation and dynamics—independent from demonstrated trajectories through the decision process—can introduce arbitrary additional constraints on the estimated cost function.*

When provided with sub-optimal demonstration policies, our adversarial approach mixes together deterministic policies to match feature expectations with demonstrated policies. Unlike the extreme convex hull policies of the feature-matching algorithm [Abbeel and Ng, 2004], the deterministic policies mixed together by the adversarial IOC method are "competitive" with the demonstrated policy. They are specified by the learned weight vector $\mathbf{w}$, which determines thresholds for which deterministic policies need to be considered for mixing. For example, deterministic policies $\delta_k, \delta_n, \delta_o, \delta_l, \delta_j, \delta_g$ are included in the strategic game and appropriately mixed together when δ_l is demonstrated, as shown in Figure 2d. From this perspective, adversarial IOC can be viewed as combining the mixing behavior of Abbeel & Ng's feature-matching algorithm [Abbeel and Ng, 2004] with MMP's margin-like [Ratliff et al., 2006] selection of policies to mix, while avoiding the integration over all policies required by maximum (causal) entropy inverse reinforcement learning [Ziebart et al., 2010] and its sensitivity to irrelevant cycles in the MDP.

[3]These implicit cost function constraints are in contrast to explicit constraint, like cost function non-negativity to prevent negative cost cycles.

5 EXPERIMENTS

We demonstrate the benefits of our approach on synthetic and real imitation learning tasks with application-specific imitation losses and/or different embodiments.

5.1 NAVIGATION ACROSS A GRID

Our first experiment considers trajectories collected from simulated navigation across a discrete grid with various characteristics. For each task, a robot navigates through the environment to reach a target location. Each cell of the grid world is denoted by its horizontal and vertical positions, (x, y), where each is an integer value from 1 to N. The robot's goal is to reach the target location while minimizing the navigation cost within a fixed period of time. We define this fixed time horizon as the maximum number of steps needed to reach any cell of the grid world. The navigation task stops once the robot reaches the target, which is equivalent to representing that the robot stays in the cell where the target exists until the end of the final time step. We formulate the robot navigation problem to be an optimal sequential decision-making problem in a finite Markov decision process (MDP) in which the policy minimizes the expected cost of successful navigation.

Differing initial positions for the robot and the target location are sampled uniformly from the $N \times N$ cells. We generate the cost $C(s)$ for the demonstrator to traverse a particular grid cell (x, y position in the grid) in our simulations based on a linear function of feature vectors, $\phi(s)$, which characterize the state: $C(s) = \theta^T\phi(s) + \varepsilon(s)$, and a noise component, $\varepsilon(s)$. We employ a 7-element feature function vector, $\phi(s)$, in these grid experiments and choose each element of θ by sampling from the uniform distribution $U(0, 1)$. The noise component is similarly sampled from a uniform distribution, $U(0, \varepsilon)$, bounded by a scalar parameter ε that controls the amount of noise in the imitation learning task. We set $C(s) = 0$ when the robot reaches the cell where the target exists. Note that the cost is stationary; all values of $C(s)$ are sampled and fixed for each navigation task. The robot can attempt to move one step from its position in each of the cardinal directions (north, south, east and west), except it is unable to move beyond the boundaries of the grid. When the state transition dynamics are stochastic, the robot may accidentally move into another neighboring cell rather the intended one (e.g., north or south when attempting to move east). The state transition dynamics are formally then:

$$p(s_{t+1}|s_t, a_t) = \begin{cases} p_m & \text{matching the action} \\ \frac{1-p_m}{\text{number of neighbor cells}} & \text{neighbor cells} \end{cases}$$

where we call p_m the matching probability. The optimal policy from solving the finite MDP problem gives the robot's navigation strategy which then can generate a navigation trajectory for learning.

We establish a specific set of grid world navigation simulation characteristics as the base setting of our simulations:

- The size of the grid world is 9×9;
- The noise weight ε is 1; and
- The matching probability p_m is 0.7.

We repeat the simulation 200 times, yielding 200 navigation trajectories of which we use 100 as training data, and the remainder as testing data. We compare adversarial IOC to MMP [Ratliff et al., 2006] across various settings of the size of the grid, the amount of feature noise, the matching probability, and the number of training/testing datapoints. For our grid navigation experiments, we evaluate the loss as the Euclidean distance between the demonstrator's grid position (x, y) and the imitator's grid position $(\hat{x}, \hat{y})$, normalized by the maximum loss, m:

$$\frac{1}{N_{\text{test}}}\sum_{n=1}^{N_{\text{test}}} \mathbb{E}\left[\sum_{t=1}^{T} m^{-1}\sqrt{\left(X_t^{(n)} - \hat{X}_t^{(n)}\right)^2 + \left(Y_t^{(n)} - \hat{Y}_t^{(n)}\right)^2}\right],$$

where ($X_t^{(n)}$ and $Y_t^{(n)}$) are random variables under the demonstrator's control policy—the policy from solving the simulated finite MDP problem—and ($\hat{X}_t^{(n)}$ and $\hat{Y}_t^{(n)}$) are the ones with estimated policy. We employ this normalized Euclidean loss as the structured loss function for the margin in MMP and the game payoff in our adversarial method.

As shown in the first four plots of Figure 4, our adversarial IOC approach (Adv) provides significant improvements in reducing the imitation loss over the trajectory compared to maximum margin planning (MMP) under equivalent embodiment setting (i.e., standard imitation learning). Though the imitator's performance generally becomes worse as the imitation task becomes more difficult (less determinism in the state transition dynamics, increased amounts of noise influencing the demonstrator's optimal policy, and larger sizes of the grid), adversarial IOC consistently outperforms MMP across all of these settings. Very little dependence of the imitation performance on the number of training examples in the fourth plot reveals the general efficiency of training using IOC/IRL methods that estimate the motivating cost function.

We also compare the performance of our adversarial IOC imitation policy with the policy produced by MMP [Ratliff et al., 2006] when demonstrator and imitator have different embodiments. We assume that the demonstration robot's dynamics are noise free and more flexible. In our first experiment, the demonstrator has deterministic state transition dynamics with matching probability 1, and we evaluate the performance of the learner operating under stochastic dynamics with various matching probabilities from 0.9 to 0.5. In the second experiment, we set some obstacles in the grid world so that the imitating robot has to make a detour when it faces any of them, but the demonstrator does not. We evaluate the performance of learner on various number of obstacles from 20 to 60.

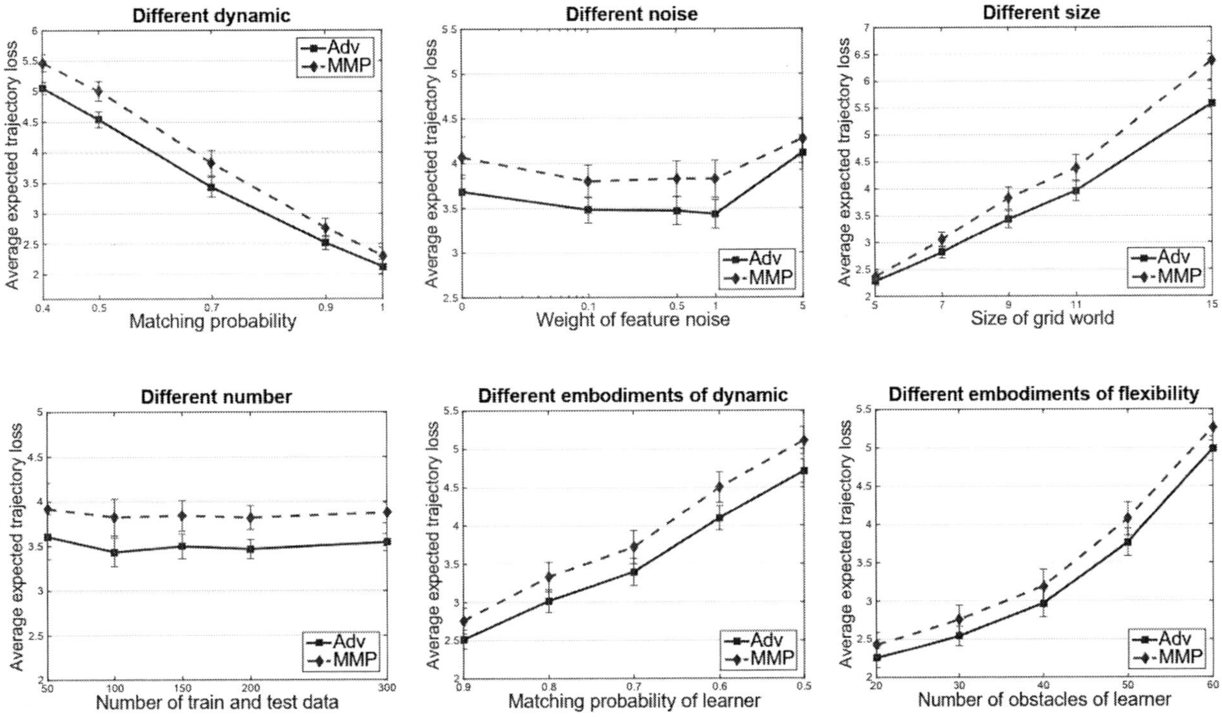

Figure 4: Experimental results with 95% confidence interval of various settings of the grid world's characteristics, including: the degree of stochasticity of the dynamics (top, left); varying amount of cost noise generating the demonstrator's trajectories (top, center); differences size of the grid world from 5x5 to 15x15 (top, right); different amount of training (test) data (bottom, left); the learner's dynamics differing from the demonstrator's (bottom, center); and the introduction of impassible obstacles for the learner (bottom, right).

The performance of the two methods under different embodiments is similarly evaluated according to the average expected trajectory loss of withheld test data, as shown in the final two plots of Figure 4. Our adversarial IOC method also outperforms MMP in these experimental settings.

5.2 LEARNING CAMERA CONTROL FROM DEMONSTRATION

We consider the task of learning to autonomously control a camera in a manner that appropriately captures the action of a basketball game based on human demonstrations of camera control [Chen and Carr, 2015]. The decision process characterizing camera control can be divided into a probabilistic model describing the state of the basketball game (the presence of players in different locations), and a dynamics model describing how camera movement controls effect the camera's state (quantized pan angle, θ, and quantize pan angle velocity, $\dot{\theta}$). As our focus is on the separation of rationalization and imitation evaluation measure, we assume that camera controls have no influence on the basketball game. Also based on this focus, we employ the empirical distribution of player locations rather than constructing a predictive model for those locations.

Our dataset is collected from high school basketball games. The camera recording the basketball game was operated by a human expert. The dataset consists of 46 sequences collected at 60Hz. The average number of frames for the sequences is 376. The output for each frame is the camera's horizontal pan angle, and the input is a 14 element vector that describes the state of the basketball game (the presence of players in different locations on the basketball court). The degree of the camera's pan angle in this dataset ranges from -30 degrees (left) to 30 degree (right), and we quantize the pan angle θ into discrete 61 levels. The pan angel velocity $\dot{\theta}$ of a particular frame is the difference between the current pan angle and the previous one, which is then mapped to 5 discrete levels $[-2, -1, 0, 1, 2]$ representing high speed of turning left to high speed of turning right. Overall, by combining the discrete pan angles and pan angle velocities, there are 305 total possible states for each frame. We use the first 23 sequences as our training dataset and the 23 remaining sequences as the testing dataset. We measure the performance of our adversarial IOC method and baseline methods using the average square

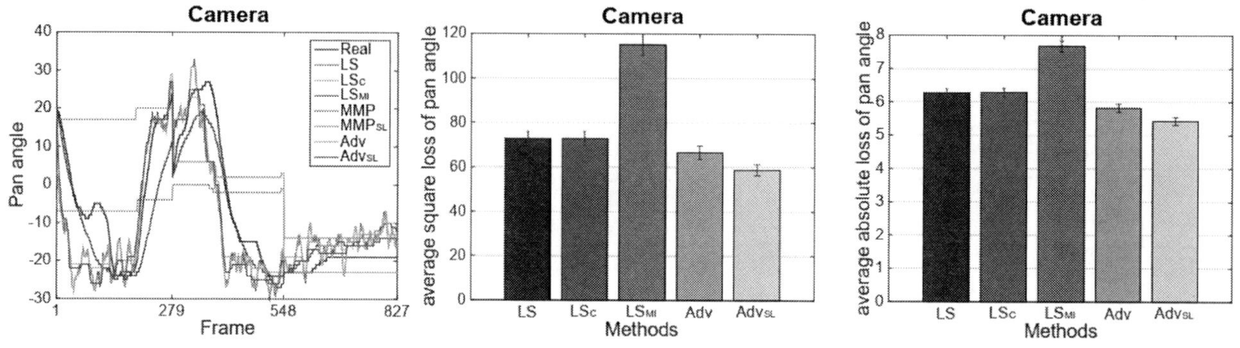

Figure 5: Imitating human camera operator's pan angle control (the Real trajectory on the left) using a regression approach, maximum margin planning, and our adversarial inverse optimal control method. Average squared loss and absolute loss of the imitator (with 95% mean confidence intervals estimates) are shown in the center and right plots, with maximum margin planning results suppressed due to being significantly worse and off of the presented scale.

loss per frame between pan angles:

$$\sum_{n=1}^{N}\sum_{t=1}^{T_n}(\theta_t^{(n)} - \hat{\theta}_t^{(n)})^2 / \sum_{n=1}^{N} T_n. \tag{6}$$

We compare our adversarial structured prediction method with a few forms of least squares linear regression models: one that is not constrained by the camera dynamics (**LS**); one that is constrained by the empirical dynamics of the camera (**LS$_{\mathbf{C}}$**); and one Markovian-based model that also conditions on the previous camera location (**LS$_{\mathbf{MI}}$**). Additionally, we consider two variants of maximum marginal planning methods: **MMP$_{\mathbf{SL}}$** is provided with the starting location of the human-operated camera, while **MMP** is not. Similarly, **Adv$_{\mathbf{SL}}$** is our adversarial IOC method provided with the starting location of the human-operated camera, while **Adv** is not. Let X_t denotes the 14 entry feature vector of the state of the basketball game at timestep t. The feature vector $\phi(S_t)$ of our adversarial method in Definition 3 is a 33 entry vector $[\theta, \theta^2, \dot{\theta}, \dot{\theta}^2, \theta X_t, \dot{\theta} X_t]$, which combines the basketball game state features and the camera angle and angle velocity state. For the regression models, the estimated sequence is a standard linear regression method $\hat{\theta}_t = \hat{a} X_t + \hat{b}$ where $\hat{a}$ and $\hat{b}$ are trained from the training dataset. For the constrained regression method, the predicted camera angle is projected to the closest angle for which transitioning is feasible.

The result of a test sequence of our experiment is shown in the left plot of Figure 5. The first two regression methods are generally very noisy as the predicted pan angle changes rapidly based on the rapid changes of the underlying inputs corresponding to the game state. The Markovian regression model performs well initially, but diverges from the demonstrated trajectory over time. Both of the MMP methods have much worse performance than the other methods presented. Our adversarial approaches tend to be similar to the regression model, but are much less noisy and provide a closer match to the demonstrated trajectory with significantly lower amounts of squared and absolute loss, as shown in the other plots of Figure 5.

6 CONCLUSION

In this paper, we introduced an adversarial framework for imitation learning using inverse optimal control. It takes the form of a game between an adversary seeking to maximize loss by approximating the training data, and a learner seeking to minimize the loss. Algorithmically, our approach possesses similarities with existing inverse optimal control methods, while resolving some of the deficiencies of those methods (e.g., lack of consistency, sensitivity to low cost cycles) in a principled manner. A key benefit of our approach is that it separates the rationalization of demonstrated decision sequences with the learner's optimization of an imitative loss function. We focused this added flexibility on the problem of learning to imitate under differences in embodiment. This is an underexplored, but important problem for imitation learning to be employed in practice. We established the consistency and useful generalization bounds for our adversarial inverse optimal control approach. We developed and presented efficient algorithms for inference and learning under this formulation. Finally, we demonstrated the benefits of adversarial inverse optimal control in a set of synthetic experiments and an autonomous camera control task where an autonomous camera is trained based on observations of human camera control. In the future, we plan to apply the developed framework to imitation learning settings for robotics applications for which we believe that generalizing across different embodiments will be especially useful.

Acknowledgments

The research in this paper was supported in part by NSF NRI Award No. 1227495 and NSF RI Award No. 1526379.

References

[Abbeel and Ng, 2004] Abbeel, P. and Ng, A. Y. (2004). Apprenticeship learning via inverse reinforcement learning. In *Proc. International Conference on Machine Learning*, pages 1–8.

[Alissandrakis et al., 2002] Alissandrakis, A., Nehaniv, C. L., and Dautenhahn, K. (2002). Imitation with alice: Learning to imitate corresponding actions across dissimilar embodiments. *Systems, Man and Cybernetics, Part A: Systems and Humans, IEEE Transactions on*, 32(4):482–496.

[Asif et al., 2015] Asif, K., Xing, W., Behpour, S., and Ziebart, B. D. (2015). Adversarial cost-sensitive classification. In *Proceedings of the Conference on Uncertainty in Artificial Intelligence*.

[Bellman, 1957] Bellman, R. (1957). A Markovian decision process. *Journal of Mathematics and Mechanics*, 6:679–684.

[Boularias et al., 2011] Boularias, A., Kober, J., and Peters, J. R. (2011). Relative entropy inverse reinforcement learning. In *International Conference on Artificial Intelligence and Statistics*, pages 182–189.

[Boyd et al., 1994] Boyd, S., El Ghaoui, L., Feron, E., and Balakrishnan, V. (1994). Linear matrix inequalities in system and control theory. *SIAM*, 15.

[Chen and Carr, 2015] Chen, J. and Carr, P. (2015). Mimicking human camera operators. In *IEEE Winter Conference on Applications of Computer Vision (WACV)*, pages 215–222. IEEE.

[Crammer and Singer, 2002] Crammer, K. and Singer, Y. (2002). On the algorithmic implementation of multiclass kernel-based vector machines. *The Journal of Machine Learning Research*, 2:265–292.

[Grünwald and Dawid, 2004] Grünwald, P. D. and Dawid, A. P. (2004). Game theory, maximum entropy, minimum discrepancy, and robust Bayesian decision theory. *Annals of Statistics*, 32:1367–1433.

[Kalman, 1964] Kalman, R. (1964). When is a linear control system optimal? *Trans. ASME, J. Basic Engrg.*, 86:51–60.

[Kramer, 1998] Kramer, G. (1998). *Directed Information for Channels with Feedback*. PhD thesis, Swiss Federal Institute of Technology (ETH) Zurich.

[Levine et al., 2011] Levine, S., Popovic, Z., and Koltun, V. (2011). Nonlinear inverse reinforcement learning with gaussian processes. In *Advances in Neural Information Processing Systems*, pages 19–27.

[Liu, 2007] Liu, Y. (2007). Fisher consistency of multicategory support vector machines. In *International Conference on Artificial Intelligence and Statistics*, pages 291–298.

[McMahan et al., 2003] McMahan, H. B., Gordon, G. J., and Blum, A. (2003). Planning in the presence of cost functions controlled by an adversary. In *International Conference on Machine Learning*, pages 536–543.

[Monfort et al., 2015] Monfort, M., Lake, B. M., Ziebart, B., Lucey, P., and Tenenbaum, J. (2015). Softstar: Heuristic-guided probabilistic inference. In *Advances in Neural Information Processing Systems*, pages 2746–2754.

[Nehaniv and Dautenhahn, 2002] Nehaniv, C. L. and Dautenhahn, K. (2002). The correspondence problem. *Imitation in animals and artifacts*, 41.

[Ng and Russell, 2000] Ng, A. Y. and Russell, S. (2000). Algorithms for inverse reinforcement learning. In *Proc. International Conference on Machine Learning*, pages 663–670.

[Pomerleau, 1989] Pomerleau, D. (1989). Alvinn: An autonomous land vehicle in a neural network. In *Advances in Neural Information Processing Systems 1*.

[Ratliff et al., 2006] Ratliff, N., Bagnell, J. A., and Zinkevich, M. (2006). Maximum margin planning. In *Proc. International Conference on Machine Learning*, pages 729–736.

[Rust, 1988] Rust, J. (1988). Maximum likelihood estimation of discrete control processes. *SIAM Journal on Control and Optimization*, 26:1006–1024.

[Tewari and Bartlett, 2007] Tewari, A. and Bartlett, P. L. (2007). On the consistency of multiclass classification methods. *The Journal of Machine Learning Research*, 8:1007–1025.

[Topsøe, 1979] Topsøe, F. (1979). Information theoretical optimization techniques. *Kybernetika*, 15(1):8–27.

[Wang et al., 2015] Wang, H., Xing, W., Asif, K., and Ziebart, B. D. (2015). Adversarial prediction games for multivariate losses. In *Advances in Neural Information Processing Systems (NIPS)*.

[Ziebart, 2010] Ziebart, B. D. (2010). *Modeling Purposeful Adaptive Behavior with the Principle of Maximum Causal Entropy*. PhD thesis, Carnegie Mellon University.

[Ziebart et al., 2010] Ziebart, B. D., Bagnell, J. A., and Dey, A. K. (2010). Modeling interaction via the principle of maximum causal entropy. In *Proc. International Conference on Machine Learning*, pages 1255–1262.

A Generative Block-Diagonal Model for Clustering

Junxiang Chen
Dept. of Electrical & Computer Engineering
Northeastern University
Boston, MA 02115
jchen@ece.neu.edu

Jennifer Dy
Dept. of Electrical & Computer Engineering
Northeastern University
Boston, MA 02115
jdy@ece.neu.edu

Abstract

Probabilistic mixture models are among the most important clustering methods. These models assume that the feature vectors of the samples can be described by a mixture of several components. Each of these components follows a distribution of a certain form. In recent years, there has been an increasing amount of interest and work in similarity-matrix-based methods. Rather than considering the feature vectors, these methods learn patterns by observing the similarity matrix that describes the pairwise relative similarity between each pair of samples. However, there are limited works in probabilistic mixture model for clustering with input data in the form of a similarity matrix. Observing this, we propose a generative model for clustering that finds the block-diagonal structure of the similarity matrix to ensure that the samples within the same cluster (diagonal block) are similar while the samples from different clusters (off-diagonal block) are less similar. In this model, we assume the elements in the similarity matrix follow one of beta distributions, depending on whether the element belongs to one of the diagonal blocks or to off-diagonal blocks. The assignment of the element to a block is determined by the cluster indicators that follow categorical distributions. Experiments on both synthetic and real data show that the performance of the proposed method is comparable to the state-of-the-art methods.

1 INTRODUCTION

In many applications, we want to divide the data into a few groups. Clustering is a task of finding the structure and interesting patterns in data, by grouping objects in such a way that objects in the same group are similar to each other, but objects in different groups are different. Recently, much research has been focused on developing clustering techniques and on applying these techniques to different fields such as image segmentation and text mining [26].

Probabilistic mixture models [3, 8] are among the most important clustering methods. These models assume that the feature vectors of data can be described by a mixture of several components. Each of these components follows a distribution of a certain form. Although different probabilistic mixture models differ in the detailed assumptions, most of them try to fit the feature vectors with a mixture of distributions.

In recent years, there has been an increasing amount of interest and work in similarity-matrix-based methods. Rather than observing the feature vectors of the data, as existing probabilistic mixture models do, similarity-matrix-based methods learn patterns by observing the similarity matrix that describes the pairwise relative similarity between each pair of data samples. One example of these methods is spectral clustering [14, 20]. Similarity-matrix-based methods have been very successful in different applications, because it could be applied to data of any form, as long as we can compare the similarity between samples. However, there are limited works in generative models for clustering where the input is a similarity matrix.

In clustering problems, we want to ensure that the samples within the same cluster are similar while the samples from different clusters are less similar. Therefore, given a similarity matrix, if we sort the indices of the similarity matrix according to the cluster indicators, the elements in diagonal blocks usually have larger values, because these elements measure the similarity between samples in the same cluster; while the elements in the off-diagonal blocks usually have smaller values, because these elements measure the similarity between samples from different clusters. The block structure in a similarity matrix is illustrated in Figure 1. Observing this, we propose to cluster by finding the block-diagonal structure in the

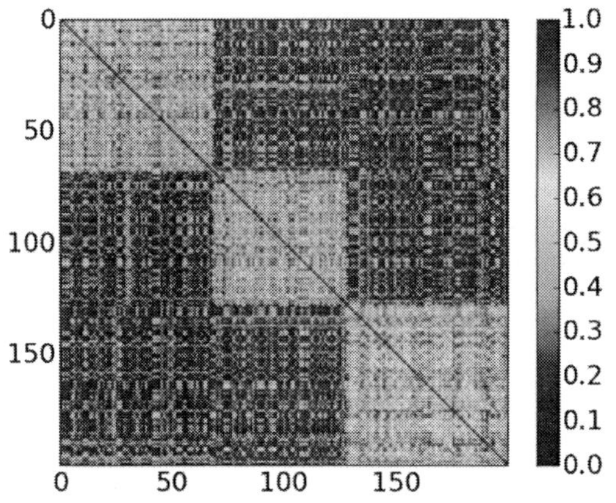

Figure 1: The block-diagonal structure in the similarity matrix. After we sort the indices of the similarity matrix according to the cluster indicators, elements in diagonal blocks have larger values, while elements in the off-diagonal blocks have smaller values.

similarity matrix.

Observing this, we propose a similarity-matrix-based probabilistic model for clustering, called *Block Mixture Model* (BMM). It is a generative model that discovers clusters by finding the block-diagonal structure in the similarity matrix. In BMM, we assume that the elements in the similarity matrix are drawn from a mixture of beta distributions, where the elements in the diagonal blocks are drawn from a beta distribution that is skewed towards one, and the elements in the off-diagonal blocks are drawn from a background beta distribution that is skewed towards zero. The assignment of each element to the blocks is determined by the cluster indicators for samples that follow categorical distributions. As a Bayesian method, BMM takes model uncertainty into consideration, allows us to provide an informative prior to the model, and safeguards against over-fitting [6].

Related Work Gaussian Mixture Model (GMM) [3] is the most well known generative model for clustering. GMM assumes data can be divided into several components and each component follows a Gaussian distribution. GMM usually has difficulty to cluster data with non-elliptical shape. To overcome this limitation, [8] proposes to warp a latent mixture of Gaussian distributions using Gaussian processes. This model can be applied when the clusters have more complex shapes. Although these generatives model methods differ in detailed assumptions, they all fit the real-valued feature vectors with a mixture of distributions. On the other hand, as a similarity-matrix-based method, BMM takes the similarity matrix as input. Therefore, it can be used to analyse any data types as long as the similarity between samples can be measured.

Spectral clustering [14, 20, 25, 21, 18] is a similarity-matrix-based clustering method. With this method, we first compute the eigenvectors of the Laplacian matrix that is derived from the similarity matrix. Then the clustering results are obtained by applying k-means [14, 20], or a probabilistic model [25, 21, 18] to analyse these eigenvectors. Unlike these methods, BMM is a generative model for the similarity matrix, which does not make use of the eigenvectors.

Stochastic blockmodels [24, 1, 10] are also generative models that find clusters. In these models, each sample belongs to a cluster and the connections between samples are determined by the corresponding pair of clusters. These methods are usually applied to an observed network, rather than similarity measures.

A generative clustering model for similarity matrices is proposed in [19]. It is assumed that the observed network is a noisy version of a latent network, where the latent network can be divided into several connected sub-networks. In contrast, BMM adopts a different strategy, where we try to find a block-diagonal structure in the similarity matrix. BMM tends to lead to better clustering results as demonstrated in the experiments (see Section 4).

The model proposed in [23] finds a block structure in Gaussian Graphical Models. Another related model is the orthogonal nonnegative matrix tri-factorization [4] that factorizes an observed matrix into 3 factors, which is equivalent to completing a non-negative matrix using a block structure. Both methods differ from BMM in that they are not probabilistic models and they are applied to the feature vectors directly but not on the similarity matrices.

Contributions of this work The contributions of this work can be summarized as follows:

1. We propose a new generative model for similarity-matrix-based clustering, we call *Block Mixture Model* (BMM), that searches for the diagonal-block structure in a similarity matrix.
2. We derive variational inference for BMM.
3. We test BMM on both synthetic and real data, and observe that the performance of BMM is comparable to the state-of-the-art methods.

2 MODEL FORMULATION

We propose a generative clustering model for the similarity matrix with a block-diagonal structure, we call *Block Mixture Model (BMM)*, to solve a clustering problem. To begin with, we construct a similarity matrix. Given a set of N data samples with C dimension $\{\boldsymbol{x}_1, \boldsymbol{x}_2, \ldots, \boldsymbol{x}_N\}$, where $\boldsymbol{x}_n \in \mathbb{R}^C$ for $n = 1, \ldots, N$. One possible way to construct a similarity matrix is to use the Gaussian kernel

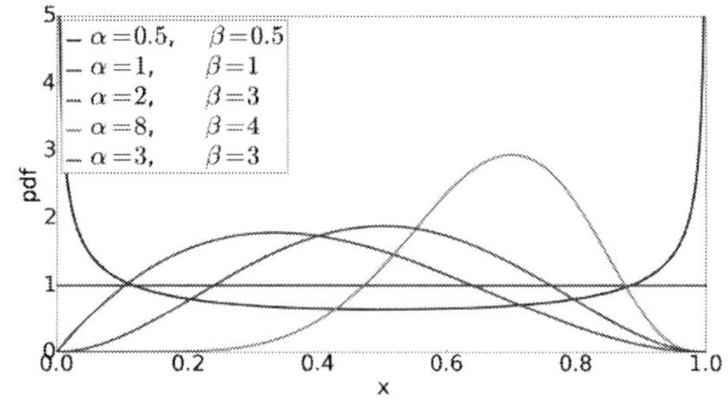

Figure 2: Beta distributions with different parameters

$\boldsymbol{W} \in \mathbb{R}^{N \times N}$ is defined as

$$\boldsymbol{W}_{ij} = \exp(-\frac{||\mathbf{x}_i - \mathbf{x}_j||^2}{2\sigma^2}), \ for\ i, j = 1, \ldots, N, \quad (1)$$

where σ is a positive real bandwidth parameter. In this paper, we focus our discussion on Gaussian kernel; but BMM can be applied to other similarity measures whose values range from 0 to 1 (e.g., cosine similarity).

In BMM, we assume that the data can be divided into K clusters, where K is a pre-defined integer. BMM can be easily extended to a nonparametric version, with Dirichlet process mixtures [7], such that the model can automatically find K. Since this is not the major focus of this paper, we introduce a simpler, more accessible version where K is pre-defined. We assign each sample $\boldsymbol{x}_n$ a K-element cluster indicator $\boldsymbol{z}_n = \{z_{nk}\}_{k=1}^K$ such that $z_{nk} = 1$ if and only if $\boldsymbol{x}_n$ belongs to the k-th cluster, and otherwise $z_{nk} = 0$. We let $\boldsymbol{z}_n$ follow a categorical distribution such that

$$\boldsymbol{z}_n \sim Categorical(\boldsymbol{\pi}), \quad (2)$$

where $\boldsymbol{\pi}$ is a K-element vector, representing the probability that each cluster is assigned. We let $\boldsymbol{\pi}$ be a sample from a symmetric Dirichlet distribution, with concentration parameter λ, i.e.

$$\boldsymbol{\pi} \sim Dirichlet(\lambda). \quad (3)$$

Note that in Gaussian kernel $\boldsymbol{W}$, all elements satisfying $0 < \boldsymbol{W}_{ij} \leq 1$, where a large $\boldsymbol{W}_{ij}$ indicates that the i-th and j-th samples are similar. Because of the range of $\boldsymbol{W}_{ij}$, we model it using beta distributions, which are distributions defined on the interval $(0, 1)$, parameterized by two positive shape parameters α and β. We choose beta distribution because it is a simple and flexible distribution that describes random variables between 0 and 1. We plot some probability density function (PDF) of beta distributions with different parameters in Figure 2.

If a random variable t follows a beta distribution such that $t \sim Beta(\alpha, \beta)$, then its expected value and variance are given by [9]

$$\mathbb{E}[x] = \frac{\alpha}{\alpha + \beta}, \quad (4)$$

$$\mathbf{Var}[x] = \frac{\alpha\beta}{(\alpha+\beta)^2(\alpha+\beta+1)} = \frac{\mathbb{E}[x](1-\mathbb{E}[x])}{\alpha+\beta+1}. \quad (5)$$

Now we assume that the similarity matrix $\mathbf{W}$ can be separated into K clusters. Then if we sort the indices of the similarity matrix according to the cluster indicators, we can observe a block-diagonal structure as shown in Figure 1. If $\boldsymbol{W}_{ij}$ is in one of the diagonal blocks, then it tends to have a large value. In this case, we let $\boldsymbol{W}_{ij}$ be a sample from a beta distribution that is parameterized by $\boldsymbol{\Theta}_k = (\alpha_k, \beta_k)$, such that it is skewed towards one. We assign a different parameter $\boldsymbol{\Theta}_k$ for each diagonal block, because in some clusters, the within cluster similarity might be larger than others. If $\boldsymbol{W}_{ij}$ is in off-diagonal blocks, then we let $\boldsymbol{\Theta}_0 = (\alpha_0, \beta_0)$ be the parameters for the beta distribution, such that it is close to zero. Since whether the i-th and j-th elements are in the diagonal or off-diagonal blocks can be derived by observing the cluster indicators $\boldsymbol{z}_i$ and $\boldsymbol{z}_j$ respectively, the probability density function of $\boldsymbol{W}_{ij}$ can be expressed as

$$p(\boldsymbol{W}_{ij}|\{\boldsymbol{\Theta_k}\}_{k=1}^K, \boldsymbol{\Theta}_0, \boldsymbol{Z}) = Beta(\boldsymbol{W}_{ij}|\alpha_0, \beta_0)^{1-\sum_k^K z_{ik}z_{jk}} \prod_{k=1}^K Beta(\boldsymbol{W}_{ij}|\alpha_k, \beta_k)^{z_{ik}z_{jk}}. \quad (6)$$

Note that if both samples $\mathbf{x}_i$ and $\mathbf{x}_j$ belong to the same cluster k, then $z_{ik}z_{jk} = 1$ and W_{ij} belongs to the k-th diagonal block. Therefore, in the equation, the term $z_{ik}z_{jk}$ is an indicator that $\boldsymbol{W}_{ij}$ is in the k-th diagonal block and the term $1 - \sum_k^K z_{ik}z_{jk}$ is an indicator that the $\boldsymbol{W}_{ij}$ is in the off-diagonal blocks. With the equation, we let elements in the diagonal blocks and off-diagonal blocks follow the corresponding beta distributions, respectively. Note that, we do not care about the diagonal elements in the similarity matrix $\{\boldsymbol{W}_{ii}\}_{i=1}^N$, because these elements do not contain clustering information. Because $\boldsymbol{W}$ is a symmetric matrix; in the generative process, we only need to generate the upper triangle of this matrix.

If the data contain clustering structure, the elements in the diagonal blocks should have larger values than the off-diagonal blocks. Therefore, we assign different prior distributions to the beta distribution parameters $\{\boldsymbol{\Theta_k}\}_{k=1}^K$ and $\boldsymbol{\Theta}_0$. We let

$$p(\boldsymbol{\Theta}_k|\boldsymbol{\zeta}) \propto Beta(\frac{\alpha_k}{\alpha_k + \beta_k}|\alpha_\zeta, \beta_\zeta) Lognormal(\alpha_k + \beta_k|\mu_\zeta, \sigma_\zeta^2), \quad (7)$$

$$p(\boldsymbol{\Theta}_0|\boldsymbol{\eta}) \propto Beta(\frac{\alpha_0}{\alpha_0 + \beta_0}|\alpha_\eta, \beta_\eta) Lognormal(\alpha_0 + \beta_0|\mu_\eta, \sigma_\eta^2), \quad (8)$$

where $\boldsymbol{\zeta} = \{\mu_\zeta, \sigma_\zeta^2, \alpha_\zeta, \beta_\zeta\}$ and $\boldsymbol{\eta} = \{\mu_\eta, \sigma_\eta^2, \alpha_\eta, \beta_\eta\}$ are the hyper-parameters for $\{\boldsymbol{\Theta_k}\}_{k=1}^K$ and $\boldsymbol{\Theta}_0$ respectively. The expected value of a beta distribution, as described in Equation (4), has a value between 0 and 1. Therefore, we use another beta distribution to model this expected value, which is represented by the first factor in Equations (7) and (8). As shown in Equation (5) that given its expected value, the variance of the beta distribution is inversely proportional to the value of $\alpha + \beta + 1$; therefore, we let $\alpha + \beta$ follow a log-normal distribution, which is

Algorithm 1 Generative Process

for $k \leftarrow 1$ to K **do**
  Generate $\boldsymbol{\Theta}_k$ according to Equation (7)
end for
Generate $\boldsymbol{\Theta}_0$ according to Equation (8)
Generate $\boldsymbol{\pi}$ according to Equation (3)
for $n \leftarrow 1$ to N **do**
  Generate $\boldsymbol{z}_n$ according to Equation (2)
end for
for $i \leftarrow 1$ to N **do**
  for $j \leftarrow 1$ to $i-1$ **do**
    Generate $\boldsymbol{W}_{ij}$ according to Equation (6)
    $\boldsymbol{W}_{ji} \leftarrow \boldsymbol{W}_{ij}$
  end for
end for

represented by the second factor in Equations (7) and (8). Since we multiply two distributions to form the prior distributions in Equations (7) and (8), we need to introduce a normalization constant to make sure the integral of the new pdf over the entire space is equal to one. With the prior distributions in Equations (7) and (8), we can control the expected value and the variance of a beta distribution by adjusting the hyper-parameters $\boldsymbol{\zeta}$ and $\boldsymbol{\eta}$.

We assign the hyper-parameters $\boldsymbol{\zeta}$ and $\boldsymbol{\eta}$ to make sure that the similarity matrix demonstrates a diagonal-block structure as shown in Figure 1. We want the diagonal blocks to be relatively dense and distributed with smaller variance. Therefore, we let the value μ_ζ to be relatively large, and α_ζ larger than β_ζ. In practice, we let $\mu_\zeta = 15$, $\sigma_\zeta^2 = 1$, $\alpha_\zeta = 80,000$ and $\beta_\zeta = 20,000$. We also want to make sure the off-diagonal blocks are relatively sparse and distributed with larger variance. Therefore, we let the value μ_η to be relatively small and α_η smaller than β_η. In practice, we let $\mu_\eta = 0$, $\sigma_\eta^2 = 1$, $\alpha_\eta = 1,000$ and $\beta_\eta = 9,000$. The prior seems relatively strong. However, note that the number of observations for each beta distribution is proportional to N^2. Therefore, the posterior distributions may still be very different from the prior distributions because of the large number of observations. We analyse the sensitivity of these hyper-parameters in Section 4.3

The model is described using a directed graphical model in Figure 3. The generative process of BMM is summarized in Algorithm 1. In the generative process, due to symmetry of the similarity matrix, we only generate the upper triangular elements, $\boldsymbol{W}_{ij}, i \in 1, \ldots, N$ and $j \in 1, \ldots, i-1$.

3 INFERENCE

In this section, we introduce how the latent variables in BMM model can be learned via variational inference. The joint probability of the model is given by

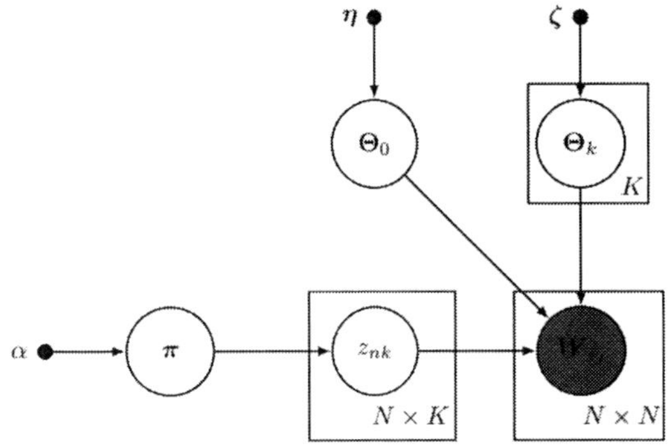

Figure 3: The graphical model. The dots represent the hyper-parameters. The regular circle represent latent random variables. The shaded circles represent observed random variables. The arrows represent the dependency between hyper-parameters and random variables. Each plate denotes that the structure inside the plate is repeated.

$$\begin{aligned}
&p(\boldsymbol{W}, \boldsymbol{\pi}, \boldsymbol{Z}, \{\boldsymbol{\Theta}_k\}_{k=1}^K, \boldsymbol{\Theta}_0 | \boldsymbol{\zeta}, \boldsymbol{\eta}, \lambda) \\
=&p(\boldsymbol{\Theta}_0|\boldsymbol{\eta}) \prod_{k=1}^{K} p(\boldsymbol{\Theta}_k|\boldsymbol{\zeta}) p(\boldsymbol{\pi}|\lambda) \prod_{n=1}^{N} p(\boldsymbol{z}_n|\boldsymbol{\pi}) \\
&\prod_{i=1}^{N}\prod_{j=1}^{i-1} p(\boldsymbol{W}_{ij}|\{\boldsymbol{\Theta}_k\}_{k=1}^K, \boldsymbol{\Theta}_0, \boldsymbol{Z})
\end{aligned} \tag{9}$$

We want to calculate the posterior distribution for the latent variables given the observed similarity matrix and the hyper-parameters, i.e. $p(\boldsymbol{\pi}, \boldsymbol{Z}, \{\boldsymbol{\Theta}_k\}_{k=1}^K, \boldsymbol{\Theta}_0 | \boldsymbol{W}, \boldsymbol{\zeta}, \boldsymbol{\eta}, \lambda)$. It is computationally intractable to directly calculate this posterior distribution. Therefore, we use a variational distribution $q(\boldsymbol{\pi}, \boldsymbol{Z}, \{\boldsymbol{\Theta}_k\}_{k=1}^K, \boldsymbol{\Theta}_0)$ to approximate the posterior distribution by minimizing the KL divergence $KL(q||p)$ [2]. As proven in [2], this is equivalent to maximizing a lower-bound $\mathcal{L}(q)$ that is defined as

$$\mathcal{L}(q) = \mathbb{E}_q[\log p(\boldsymbol{W}, \boldsymbol{\pi}, \boldsymbol{Z}, \{\boldsymbol{\Theta}_k\}_{k=1}^K, \boldsymbol{\Theta}_0) | \boldsymbol{\zeta}, \boldsymbol{\eta}, \lambda] + \mathcal{H}(q) \tag{10}$$

where $\mathbb{E}_q$ denotes that the expected value is taken with respect to the variational distribution q, and $\mathcal{H}(q)$ denotes the entropy of this variational distribution.

It is still impossible to directly calculate the variational distribution q. Therefore, we further assume that this distribution q can be factorized such that

$$q(\boldsymbol{\pi}, \boldsymbol{Z}, \{\boldsymbol{\Theta}_k\}_{k=1}^K, \boldsymbol{\Theta}_0) = q_{\boldsymbol{\pi}}(\boldsymbol{\pi}) \prod_{n=1}^{N} q_{\boldsymbol{z}_n}(\boldsymbol{z}_n) \prod_{k=1}^{K} q_{\boldsymbol{\Theta}_k}(\boldsymbol{\Theta}_k) q_{\boldsymbol{\Theta}_0}(\boldsymbol{\Theta}_0) \tag{11}$$

Because we do not use the conjugate prior distributions as the prior for the latent variables $\{\boldsymbol{\Theta}_k\}_{k=1}^K$ and $\boldsymbol{\Theta}_0$, we cannot estimate the distributions $q_{\boldsymbol{\Theta}_k}(\boldsymbol{\Theta}_k)$ and $q_{\boldsymbol{\Theta}_0}(\boldsymbol{\Theta}_0)$ in closed form. However, note that given the expected values $\mathbb{E}_{\boldsymbol{Z}}(\boldsymbol{Z})$, the distributions $q_{\boldsymbol{\Theta}_k}(\boldsymbol{\Theta}_k)$ and $q_{\boldsymbol{\Theta}_0}(\boldsymbol{\Theta}_0)$ are independent in the lower-bound $\mathcal{L}(q)$ described in

Equation (10). Therefore, we can find point estimators for $\{\widehat{\Theta}_k\}_{k=1}^K$ and $\widehat{\Theta}_0$ that maximizes $\mathcal{L}(q)$, such that

$$\widehat{\Theta}_k = \underset{(\alpha_k,\beta_k)}{\operatorname{argmax}} \mathcal{L}(q) \tag{12}$$

$$\widehat{\Theta}_0 = \underset{(\alpha_0,\beta_0)}{\operatorname{argmax}} \mathcal{L}(q) \tag{13}$$

We find these point estimators using the Broyden-Fletcher-Goldfarb-Shanno (BFGS) algorithm [17].

Given these point estimators, we calculate the optimal variational distributions $q_{\boldsymbol{\pi}}^*$ and $\{q_{\boldsymbol{z}_n}^*\}_{n=1}^N$. According to [2], with the factorization assumption introduced in Equation (11), the optimal factorized variational distribution $q_{\boldsymbol{Y}_j}^*(\boldsymbol{Y}_j)$ is given by

$$\log q_{\boldsymbol{Y}_j}^*(\boldsymbol{Y}_j) = \mathbb{E}_{i\neq j}[\log p(\boldsymbol{X}, \boldsymbol{Y})] + const \tag{14}$$

where $\boldsymbol{X}$ represents the observed data, $\boldsymbol{Y} = \{\boldsymbol{Y}_i\}_{i=1}^M$ represents all M factorized latent variables and $\mathbb{E}_{i\neq j}$ represents that the expected value is taken with respect to $\{q_{\boldsymbol{Y}_i}\}_{i\neq j}$.

By applying Equation (14), the optimal variational distribution $\{q_{\boldsymbol{z}_n}^*\}_{n=1}^N$ is given by

$$\begin{aligned}\log q_{\boldsymbol{z}_n}^*(\boldsymbol{z}_n) = &\sum_{k=1}^K z_{nk}\{\mathbb{E}_{\boldsymbol{\pi}}[\log \pi_k] \\ &+ \sum_{i\neq n} \mathbb{E}_{\boldsymbol{z}_i}[z_{ik}][\log \boldsymbol{B}(\hat{\alpha}_0, \hat{\beta}_0) - \log \boldsymbol{B}(\hat{\alpha}_k, \hat{\beta}_k) \\ &+ (\hat{\alpha}_k - \hat{\alpha}_0)\log W_{in} + (\hat{\beta}_k - \hat{\beta}_0)\log(1 - W_{in})]\} + const\end{aligned} \tag{15}$$

where $\boldsymbol{B}$ represents the beta function. By observing this equation, we conclude that

$$q_{\boldsymbol{z}_n}^*(\boldsymbol{z}_n) = Categorical(\boldsymbol{\omega}_n) \tag{16}$$

where $\boldsymbol{\omega}_n$ is a K-element vector such that

$$\begin{aligned}\omega_{nk} \propto exp(&\mathbb{E}_{\boldsymbol{\pi}}[\log \pi_k] + \sum_{i\neq n} \mathbb{E}_{\boldsymbol{z}_i}[z_{ik}]\{\log \boldsymbol{B}(\hat{\alpha}_0, \hat{\beta}_0) - \log \boldsymbol{B}(\hat{\alpha}_k, \hat{\beta}_k) \\ &+ (\hat{\alpha}_k - \hat{\alpha}_0)\log W_{in} + (\hat{\beta}_k - \hat{\beta}_0)\log(1 - W_{in})\})\end{aligned} \tag{17}$$

and $\boldsymbol{\omega}_n$ is normalized such that $\sum_{k=1}^K \omega_{nk} = 1$.

By applying Equation (14), the optimal variational distribution $q_{\boldsymbol{\pi}}^*$ is given by

$$\log q_{\boldsymbol{\pi}}^*(\boldsymbol{\pi}) = \sum_{k=1}^K \left(\lambda + \sum_{n=1}^N \mathbb{E}_{\boldsymbol{z}_n}[z_{nk}] - 1\right) \log \pi_k + const \tag{18}$$

By observing this equation, we note that

$$q_{\boldsymbol{\pi}}^*(\boldsymbol{\pi}) = Dirichlet(\boldsymbol{\phi}) \tag{19}$$

where $\boldsymbol{\phi}$ is a K-element vector, whose k-th element is given by

$$\phi_k = \lambda + \sum_{n=1}^N \mathbb{E}_{\boldsymbol{z}_n}[z_{nk}] \tag{20}$$

Algorithm 2 Variational Inference

> Initialize $\{q_{\boldsymbol{z}_n}^*\}_{n=1}^N$
> Initialize $q_{\boldsymbol{\pi}}^*$
> **repeat**
>   **for** $k \leftarrow 1$ to K **do**
>   Calculate $\widehat{\Theta}_k$ according to Equation (12)
>   **end for**
>   Calculate $\widehat{\Theta}_0$ according to Equation (13)
>   **for** $n \leftarrow 1$ to N **do**
>   Update $q_{\boldsymbol{z}_n}^*$ according to Equation (16)
>   **end for**
>   Update $q_{\boldsymbol{\pi}^*}$ according to Equation (19)
> **until** Convergence

We iteratively update $\{\widehat{\Theta}_k\}_{k=1}^K$, $\widehat{\Theta}_0$, $\{q_{\boldsymbol{z}_n}(\boldsymbol{z}_n)^*\}_{n=1}^N$ and $q_{\boldsymbol{\pi}}^*(\boldsymbol{\pi})$ until convergence. The expected values involved in the updates are obtained by

$$\mathbb{E}_{\boldsymbol{z}_n}[z_{nk}] = \boldsymbol{\omega}_{nk} \tag{21}$$

$$\mathbb{E}_{\boldsymbol{\pi}}[\log \pi_k] = \psi(\phi_k) - \psi\left(\sum_{i=1}^K \phi_i\right) \tag{22}$$

where ψ is the digamma function that is defined as the logarithmic derivative of the gamma function. The algorithm is summarized in Algorithm 2.

4 EXPERIMENTS

In this section, we test BMM using both synthetic and real data. We choose the bandwidth parameter of the Gaussian kernel σ in Equation (1) to be the median of the pairwise Euclidean distances. If not specified otherwise, the parameters for BMM are given as $\mu_\zeta = 15$, $\sigma_\zeta^2 = 1$, $\alpha_\zeta = 80,000$, $\beta_\zeta = 20,000$, $\mu_\eta = 0$, $\sigma_\eta^2 = 1$, $\alpha_\eta = 1,000$, $\beta_\eta = 9,000$ and $\lambda = 1$. We discuss the choice of the parameters in more details in Section 4.3. Because variational inference can only guarantee finding local minima, we run the algorithm with 10 different initial values, and select the solution with the maximum lower-bound value. We generate 5 of the initial values using random initialization, and generate the other 5 of the initial values using spectral clustering. Note that spectral clustering might give different results, because k-means is applied after embedding, and k-means only guarantees local optima.

4.1 SYNTHETIC 2D DATA

To demonstrate that BMM works when the clusters have complex shape , we test BMM using some 2-dimensional synthetic data. The clustering results of BMM , with each cluster shown in different color, are illustrated in Figure 4. We can observe that BMM is able to separate all of these

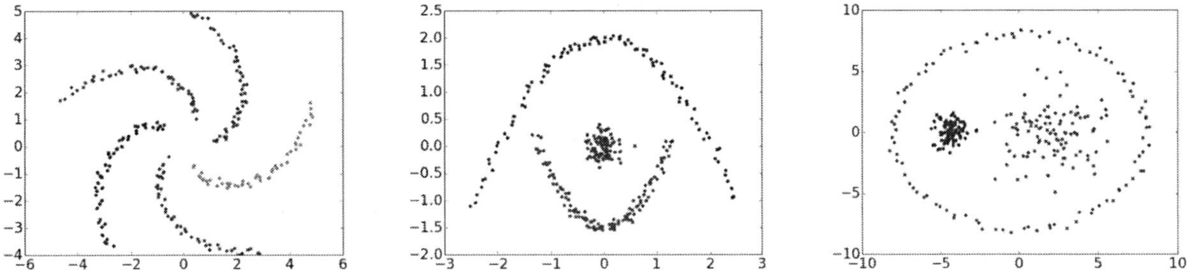

Figure 4: Clustering results for 2d synthetic data.

data perfectly. GMM fails to give similar results, because the cluster structure is complex shaped.

4.2 SYNTHETIC SIMILARITY MATRICES

In some applications, we are not directly given the feature vectors, but a similarity matrix. Similar to spectral clustering, BMM can also directly take a similarity matrix as an input. In this section, we test BMM using synthetic similarity matrices.

4.2.1 SIMILARITY MATRICES WITH A BLOCK-DIAGONAL STRUCTURE

To begin with, we test BMM using similarity matrices with different strength of block-diagonal structure. To generate a similarity matrix $\mathbf{W}$ with a block-diagonal structure, we let

$$\mathbf{W} = \mathbf{X}^T\mathbf{X}, \tag{23}$$

where $\boldsymbol{X}$ is a 100×3 matrix. Each row of $\boldsymbol{X}$ is a sample from a 3-element symmetric Dirichlet distribution with a positive concentration parameter α. We control the strength of the block-diagonal structure in the similarity matrix $\mathbf{W}$ by adjusting α. When α has a small value, the mass of the Dirichlet distribution tends to be concentrated in one of the three elements, and the similarly matrix has a strong block-diagonal structure, and vise versa. The ground-truth clustering label for each sample X_n is given by $L_n = \text{argmax}_{i=1,2,3} \boldsymbol{X}_{ni}$. To illustrate how α affects the block-diagonal structure, we plot $\boldsymbol{W}$ with different α in Figure 5, where indices of samples are sorted according to the ground-truth label $\mathbf{L} = \{L_n\}_{n=1}^{100}$. In the figure, we observe that when α is small (e.g., $\alpha = 0.25$), the block-diagonal structure is clear such that we can easily distinguish diagonal blocks from the off-diagonal blocks. However, when α is larger (e.g., $\alpha = 2$), the block structure is less clear.

We test BMM on $\mathbf{W}$ generated with different α between 0.06 to 4. For each α, we test BMM on 10 different random generated $\mathbf{W}$. We compare the clustering results of BMM against the results given by state-of-the-art methods that takes similarity matrices as input, including spectral

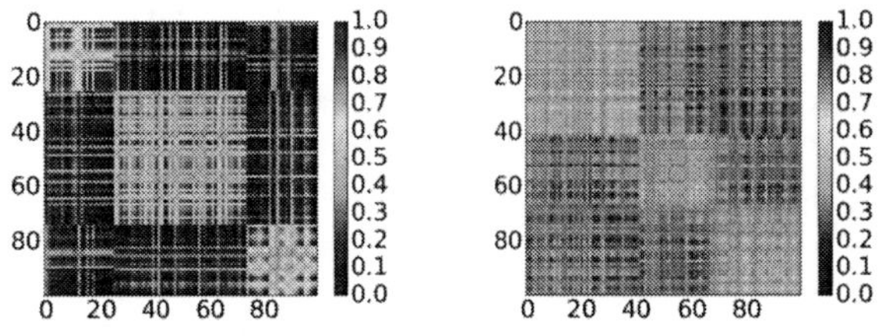

(a) $\alpha = 0.25$ (b) $\alpha = 2$

Figure 5: $\boldsymbol{W}$ with different α. The indices of samples are sorted according to the ground-truth labels L_n.

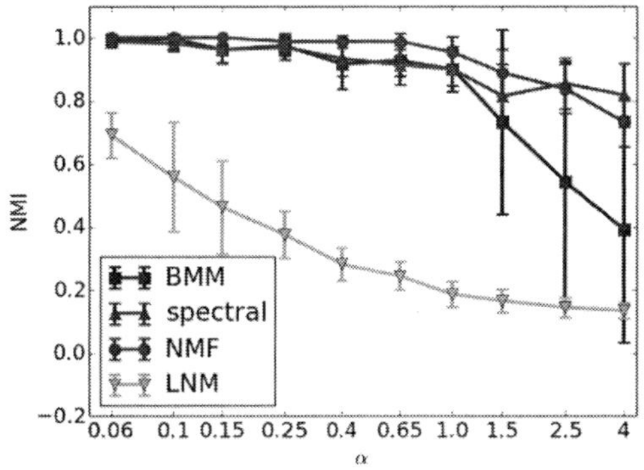

Figure 6: NMI on synthetic data $\mathbf{W}$ generated with different α. The line represents the mean value of the NMI, and the error bar demonstrates the standard deviation. The ticks on the horizontal axis are plotted with log scales.

clustering [14], Non-negative Matrix Factorization (NMF) [11] and Latent Network Model (LNM) [19]. We estimate the performance of the algorithms using Normalized Mutual Information (NMI) between the clustering results with respect to the labels $\mathbf{L}$. The NMI between two random variables X and Y is defined as [22]

$$\frac{\sum_{x \in X} \sum_{y \in Y} p(x,y)[\log p(x,y) - \log p(x)p(y)]}{\sqrt{\mathcal{H}(X)\mathcal{H}(Y)}} \tag{24}$$

where $\mathcal{H}(X)$ and $\mathcal{H}(Y)$ are the entropy for random variables X and Y respectively. The NMI ranges from 0 to 1, where a higher value indicates X and Y agree stronger with each other. We plot the mean values and standard deviations of NMI for the clustering results with respect to the ground-truth label $\mathbf{L}$ in Figure 6. In this figure the lines represent the mean values of NMI, and the error bars denote the standard deviations.

We can observe from the figure that NMF and spectral clustering outperform all other methods in this test. This is expected because $\mathbf{W}$ is generated based on non-negative matrix multiplication, which is consistent with the NMF assumption; and it is proved in [5] that there spectral clustering can be regarded as a relaxed version of NMF. We also observe from the figure that when $\alpha \leq 1$, the BMM results are comparable to the spectral clustering results. However, if $\alpha > 1$, the performance of BMM is worse. This is also expected since BMM gives clustering results based on the block-diagonal structure. When the similarity matrix contains a stronger block-diagonal structure, the performance of BMM is better. Note that in practice, we generate similarity matrices using Gaussian kernels that is described in Equation (1), with a bandwidth parameter σ set as the median value of the pairwise Euclidean distances. Therefore, the similarity matrix will be more similar to Figure 5(a) rather than Figure 5(b), because the pairwise similarity measures computed in this way usually differ significantly. LNM usually performs worse, because it only ensures samples in each cluster are well connected to their nearest neighbors respectively. LNM is more sensitive to the non-zero elements in the off-diagonal blocks.

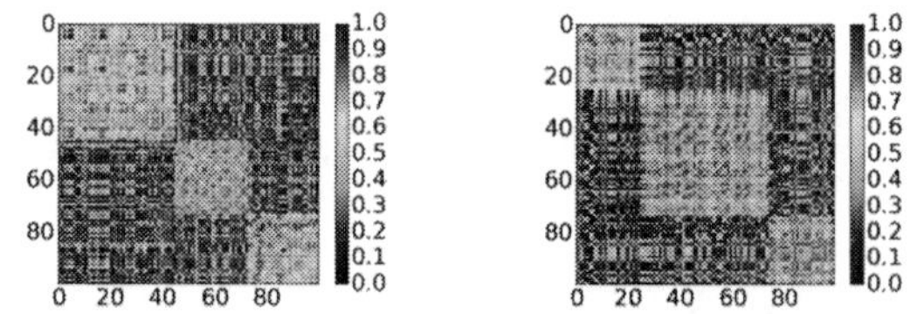

(a) Plot of $\boldsymbol{T}$, with indices sorted according to the labels $\mathbf{L}^{(1)}$.

(b) Plot of $\boldsymbol{T}$, with indices sorted according to the labels $\mathbf{L}^{(2)}$.

Figure 7: $\boldsymbol{T}$ is constructed such that $\boldsymbol{T} = \rho \boldsymbol{W}^{(1)} + (1-\rho)\boldsymbol{W}^{(2)}$, with $\rho = 0.45$. Both $\boldsymbol{W}^{(1)}$ and $\boldsymbol{W}^{(2)}$ contain a block-diagonal structure.

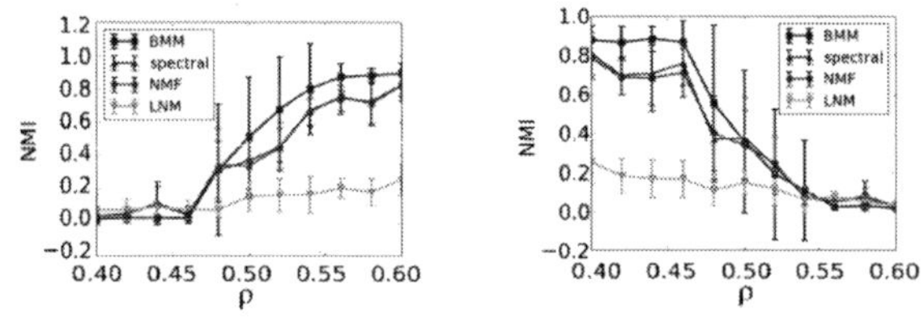

(a) NMI between the clustering results and the labels $\mathbf{L}^{(1)}$

(b) NMI between the clustering results and the labels $\mathbf{L}^{(2)}$

Figure 8: NMI on synthetic data. The line represents the mean value of the NMI, and the error bar demonstrates the standard deviation.

4.2.2 SIMILARITY MATRICES WITH STRUCTURED NOISE

Now we consider the case when the similarity matrices contain structured noise. We generate two similarity matrices $\boldsymbol{W}^{(1)}$ and $\boldsymbol{W}^{(2)}$ in the same way as described in Equation (23), with $\alpha = 0.25$ such that they contains clear block-diagonal structure. We denote the ground-truth labels samples represented by $\boldsymbol{W}^{(1)}$ and $\boldsymbol{W}^{(2)}$ using $\mathbf{L}^{(1)}$ and $\mathbf{L}^{(2)}$, respectively.

Then we generate a similarity matrix $\boldsymbol{T} = \rho\, \boldsymbol{W}^{(1)} + (1-\rho)\, \boldsymbol{W}^{(2)}$, where ρ is a real-value parameter between 0 and 1. By taking the weighted sum of matrices $\boldsymbol{W}^{(1)}$ and $\boldsymbol{W}^{(2)}$, we introduce structured noise to the similarity matrix. After summation, $\boldsymbol{T}$ simultaneously have two block-diagonal structures, this is illustrated in Figures 7(a) and 7(b). Note that both figures show the same matrix $\boldsymbol{T}$, but we sort it according to the block-diagonal structure of $\boldsymbol{W}^{(1)}$ and $\boldsymbol{W}^{(2)}$ respectively. Multiple possible block-diagonal structures indicate that there are more than one meaningful way to separate the data into clusters, which are common in real applications, because objects might be divided into groups by different criteria, or they can be interpreted in different ways [16, 15].

We vary the values of ρ between 0.4 to 0.6. For each ρ we generate 10 different matrices $\boldsymbol{W}$ and test BMM, spectral clustering, NMF and LNM using these matrices. The results are summarized in Figure 8.

In Figure 8, we observe that when $0.4 < \rho < 0.45$, the block-diagonal structure of $\boldsymbol{W}^{(2)}$ dominates the matrix $\boldsymbol{T}$, and we can consider $\mathbf{L}^{(2)}$ as the ground truth. As shown in Figure 8(b), BMM outperforms all other methods, since its results have a higher NMI with respect to $\mathbf{L}^{(2)}$. When $0.45 < \rho < 0.55$, the contribution of $\boldsymbol{W}^{(1)}$ or $\boldsymbol{W}^{(2)}$ becomes similar. We observed that BMM usually has a higher mean NMI value with respect to both $\mathbf{L}^{(1)}$ and $\mathbf{L}^{(2)}$ compared to other methods. In addition, BMM has a higher standard deviation. This indicates that BMM tends to reveal the block-diagonal structure of either $\boldsymbol{W}^{(1)}$ and $\boldsymbol{W}^{(2)}$, but other methods usually find neither of them. When $\rho > 0.55$, the block-diagonal structure of $\boldsymbol{W}^{(1)}$ dominates the matrix $\boldsymbol{W}$, and we can consider $\mathbf{L}^{(1)}$ as the ground truth. As shown in 8(a), BMM also outperforms spectral clustering, since its results have a higher mean NMI with respect to $\mathbf{L}^{(1)}$.

From the observation above, we conclude that BMM outperforms other methods if such structured noise is present. This is because spectral clustering finds the clusters by observing the eigenvectors of the Laplacian matrix that is derived from the similarity matrix. Spectral clustering can find the correct clusters for $W^{(1)}$ and $W^{(2)}$ individually according to these eigenvectors respectively. However, when we take the weighted sum of $W^{(1)}$ and $W^{(2)}$, the eigenvectors will change in general, and therefore, the clustering results given by spectral clustering are different from either $\mathbf{L}^{(1)}$ or $\mathbf{L}^{(2)}$. Due to the equivalence between NMF and spectral clustering [5], NMF performs similarly compared to spectral clustering. BMM avoids making use of the eigenvectors and looks for the strongest block-diagonal structure. It is more robust against the structured noise and is able to find the clusters similar to either $\mathbf{L}^{(1)}$ or $\mathbf{L}^{(2)}$.

In summary, in this section, we test BMM on synthetic similarity matrices. We observe that when the similarity matrix contains clear diagonal structure, BMM is comparable to spectral clustering. BMM is more robust to structured noise compared to spectral clustering and NMF.

4.3 HYPER-PARAMETER SENSITIVITY ANALYSIS

In this section, we discuss how the hyper-parameters $\mu_\zeta, \sigma_\zeta^2, \alpha_\zeta, \beta_\zeta, \mu_\eta, \sigma_\eta^2, \alpha_\eta$, and β_η affect the performance of BMM. We generate 10 synthetic random similarity matrices according to Equation (23) with $\alpha = 1$. We test BMM on each of the similarity matrices. In each test, we change one pair of the hyper-parameters at a time and keep all other hyper-parameters using the default values. We summarize the means of the NMI between the clustering results and the ground-truth label across the 10 similarity matrices, with each of the hyper-parameter settings, in Figure 9.

In Figures 9(a) and 9(b), we observe that the choices of $\mu_\zeta, \sigma_\zeta^2, \mu_\eta$ and σ_η^2 influence the clustering results less significantly. The mean NMI values are above 0.85, no matter what values are chosen. We set $\mu_\zeta = 15, \sigma_\zeta^2 = 1, \mu_\eta = 0$ and $\sigma_\eta^2 = 1$, since these values are consistent with the heuristic that the variance of the similarity measures in the diagonal blocks is smaller than that in the off-diagonal blocks. Note that they also provide high mean NMI.

From Figures 9(c) and 9(d), we can conclude that the values of $\alpha_\zeta, \beta_\zeta, \alpha_\eta$ and β_ζ have more effect on the clustering results. As mentioned in Section 2, we need to make sure the diagonal blocks are more dense than the off-diagonal blocks, i.e., $\alpha_\zeta/(\alpha_\zeta + \beta_\zeta) > \alpha_\eta/(\alpha_\eta + \beta_\eta)$. Therefore, we choose $\alpha_\zeta = 80,000$, $\beta_\zeta = 20,000$, $\alpha_\eta = 1,000$ and $\beta_\eta = 9,000$. We set hyper-parameters to these values in all other experiments in Section 4.

4.4 REAL DATA

In this section, we test BMM on several real dataset, and compare it with the state-of-the-art methods. Similar to spectral clustering, instead of just starting from the Gaussian kernel $\mathbf{W}$ defined in Equation (1), we also utilize the normalized similarly matrix that is defined as

$$\widetilde{W} = D^{-1/2} W D^{-1/2}, \tag{25}$$

where D is a diagonal matrix such that $D_{ii} = \sum_{j=1}^{N} W_{ij}$. In this , we present the results using both un-normalized W and normalized $\widetilde{W}$. In addition to the three similarity-matrix-based methods that are introduced in 4.2.1, we also compare BMM against k-means [13] and GMM [3].

First we introduce the experimental results on the Semeion handwritten digit dataset [12]. This dataset contains 1593 handwritten digits from 0 to 9 from 80 persons. The digits are stretched in a rectangular box 16x16 with $0/1$ values. We test the methods using different subsets of the dataset as different clustering tasks. In each task, we divide the dataset into 5 sets. We repeat the test 5 times, each time with one set taken out. The results are summarized in Table 1. The values in the table represent the means of the NMI. The values in the brackets represent the standard deviations. The values in bold is the largest mean NMI for each task.

We observe from Table 1 that BMM with the normalized similarity matrix $\widetilde{W}$ is one of the best methods. In some tasks, this method outperforms all other methods by a relatively large margin. For example in the task of distinguishing 6 from 8, this outperforms the second best method by more than 0.1 in terms of mean NMI.

We also observe that making use of the normalized similarity matrix $\widetilde{W}$ usually leads to better results, but in some tasks, such as the $\{0, 8\}$ and $\{4, 9\}$ tasks, utilizing the un-normalized similarity matrix W gives better results. However, in the $\{2, 3\}$ task, BMM with un-normalized similarity matrix W obtains a worse result compared to other methods. Although making the un-normalized similarity matrix might get better results in some of the tasks, we still recommend to use the normalized similarity matrix because its performance is better in general. In the $\{1, 7\}$ task, we observe that the performance of GMM is much better than all other methods. This might be due to that in the methods we compared, GMM is the only method that can scale the features. LNM usually performs worse, because it only ensures samples in each cluster are well connected to their nearest neighbors respectively, but do not guarantee that they are pairwise well connected. Note that BMM with normalized similarity matrix either performs comparably or outperforms spectral clustering and NMF in almost all tasks.

In addition to the Semeion data, we also compare BMM with the state-of-the-art methods using following UCI datasets [12]: iris dataset contains 150 samples from 3 classes of iris plants that are described using 4 features;

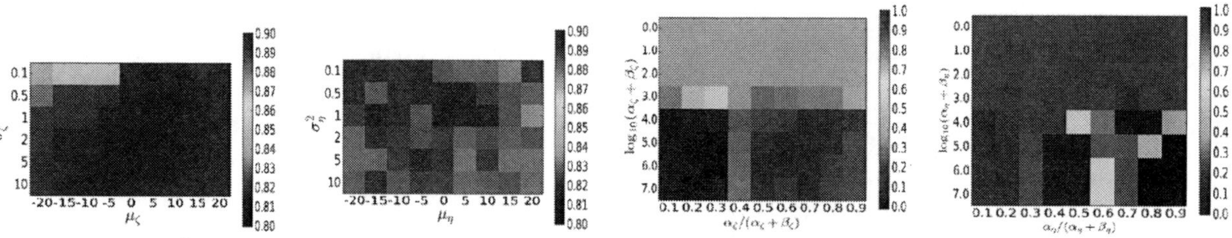

(a) μ_ζ vs. σ_ζ^2 (b) μ_η vs. σ_η^2 (c) α_ζ vs. β_ζ (d) α_η vs. β_η

Figure 9: Means NMI between the clustering results and the ground-truth label, with each hyper-parameter settings. We change a pair of hyper-parameters at a time.

Table 1: NMI on Semeion handwritten digit data

	BMM ($\boldsymbol{W}$)	BMM ($\boldsymbol{W}$)	Spectral	K-means	GMM	NMF	LNM
$\{0,8\}$	0.901(0.016)	**0.916(0.020)**	0.816 (0.017)	0.899(0.014)	0.820(0.028)	0.835(0.015)	0.191(0.025)
$\{1,7\}$	0.177(0.015)	0.258(0.038)	0.176(0.012)	0.210(0.049)	**0.588(0.073)**	0.183(0.041)	0.118(0.013)
$\{2,3\}$	**0.823(0.057)**	0.159(0.027)	0.531(0.033)	0.765(0.039)	0.708(0.042)	0.516(0.059)	0.095(0.031)
$\{4,9\}$	0.734(0.053)	**0.792(0.058)**	0.728(0.054)	0.774(0.054)	0.719(0.050)	0.740(0.058)	0.104(0.020)
$\{6,8\}$	**0.879(0.040)**	0.543(0.342)	0.617(0.019)	0.755(0.100)	0.688(0.033)	0.588(0.060)	0.155(0.018)
{0,1,2,3,4}	**0.740(0.005)**	0.610(0.009)	0.693(0.031)	0.690(0.018)	0.693(0.016)	0.606(0.047)	0.263(0.022)
{5,6,7,8,9}	**0.553(0.015)**	0.415(0.021)	0.542(0.018)	0.451(0.036)	0.419(0.022)	0.470(0.021)	0.195(0.047)
{0,1,2,3,4,5,6,7,8,9}	**0.522(0.037)**	0.501(0.032)	0.502(0.019)	0.497(0.051)	0.507(0.009)	0.512(0.046)	0.259(0.028)

Table 2: NMI on UCI data

	BMM ($\widetilde{\boldsymbol{W}}$)	BMM($\boldsymbol{W}$)	Spectral	K-means	GMM	NMF	LNM
Iris	0.631(0.035)	0.650(0.035)	0.624(0.020)	0.664(0.051)	**0.810(0.046)**	0.648(0.024)	0.350(0.025)
Synthetic Control	**0.781(0.012)**	0.739(0.013)	0.747(0.029)	0.696(0.012)	0.773(0.003)	0.686(0.030)	0.547(0.013)
Faults	**0.566(0.021)**	0.494(0.068)	0.493(0.070)	0.461(0.040)	0.494(0.081)	0.490(0.034)	0.336(0.035)
Wine	0.723(0.021)	**0.776(0.017)**	0.589(0.063)	0.707(0.032)	0.720(0.037)	0.690(0.043)	0.359(0.025)
CMU faces	0.834(0.083)	0.674(0.036)	**0.867(0.027)**	0.743(0.027)	0.852(0.019)	0.684(0.045)	0.462(0.077)

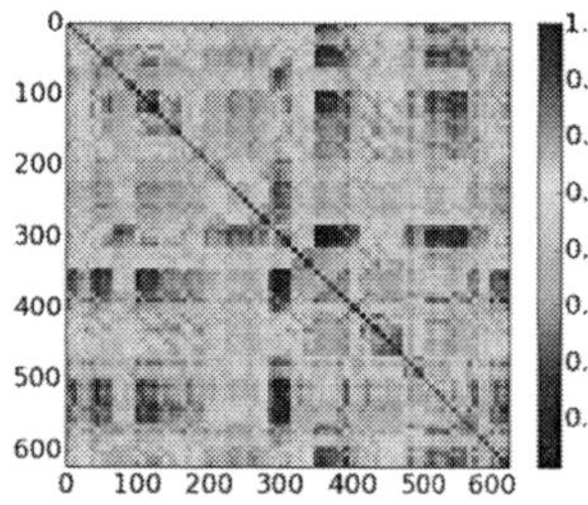

Figure 10: Similarity matrix for the CMU faces dataset.

synthetic control dataset contains 600 control charts that are synthetically generated from 6 classes; faults dataset contains 1,941 samples from 7 types of steel plates faults; wine dataset contains chemical analysis results of 178 samples of wines that are derived from 3 different cultivars; CMU faces dataset consists of 640 face images of 20 people taken at varying poses.

The results are summarized in Table 2. In this table, we observe GMM performs well in the iris dataset because the iris clusters are elliptically shaped. BMM with normalized similarity $\widetilde{\boldsymbol{W}}$ is one of the best methods in most of the tasks. It outperforms all other methods in the synthetic control and faults datasets, while it has a comparable performance with most of the methods in iris and wine datasets. However, we observe that in the CMU faces dataset, BMM performs slightly worse than spectral clustering. To illustrate why BMM perform worse, we plot the similarity matrix for this dataset, with indices sorted using the ground-truth identity labels in Figure 10. We observe the elements in the off-diagonal blocks differ significantly in values. Note that, BMM uses only one background beta distribution to model all elements in off-diagonal blocks. The CMU faces dataset violates this assumptions of BMM, making BMM perform worse.

5 CONCLUSION

In this paper, we propose Block Mixture Model (BMM), a generative model for the similarity matrix with block-diagonal structure, to solve the clustering problem. In this model, we assume the elements in the similarity matrix follow one of beta distributions, depending on whether the element belongs to either one of the diagonal blocks or to the off-diagonal blocks. We derive variational inference to learn the latent variables in BMM. Experiments on synthetic data demonstrate that BMM performs at least comparably to spectral clustering if the similarity matrix contains a clear block-diagonal structure, and it is more robust to structured noise. We test BMM on real data and observe that the performance of BMM is comparable to the state-of-the-art methods.

ACKNOWLEDGEMENTS

This work was partially supported by NIH/NHLBI grants R01HL089856 & R01HL089857 and by NSF IIS-1546428.

References

[1] E. M. Airoldi, D. M. Blei, S. E. Fienberg, and E. P. Xing. Mixed membership stochastic blockmodels. In *Advances in Neural Information Processing Systems*, pages 33–40, 2009.

[2] C. M. Bishop et al. *Pattern recognition and machine learning*, volume 1, chapter 10 Approximate Inference, pages 461 – 474. Springer, New York, 2006.

[3] A. P. Dempster, N. M. Laird, and D. B. Rubin. Maximum likelihood from incomplete data via the EM algorithm. *Journal of the royal statistical society. Series B (methodological)*, pages 1–38, 1977.

[4] C. Ding, T. Li, W. Peng, and H. Park. Orthogonal nonnegative matrix tri-factorizations for clustering. In *Proceedings of the 12th ACM SIGKDD international conference on Knowledge discovery and data mining*, pages 126–135. ACM, 2006.

[5] C. H. Ding, X. He, and H. D. Simon. On the equivalence of nonnegative matrix factorization and spectral clustering. In *SDM*, volume 5, pages 606–610. SIAM, 2005.

[6] R. O. Duda, P. E. Hart, and D. G. Stork. *Pattern classification*, chapter 3 Maximum Likelihood and Bayesian Parameter Estimation, pages 84 – 159. John Wiley & Sons, 2001.

[7] T. S. Ferguson. A Bayesian analysis of some nonparametric problems. *The annals of statistics*, pages 209–230, 1973.

[8] T. Iwata, D. Duvenaud, and Z. Ghahramani. Warped mixtures for nonparametric cluster shapes. In *Proceedings of the Conference on Uncertainty in Artificial Intelligence (UAI2013)*, 2013.

[9] N. L. Johnson, N. Balakrishnan, and S. I. Kotz. *Continuous Univariate Distributions*, volume 2. Wiley, 2nd edition, 1995.

[10] B. Karrer and M. E. Newman. Stochastic blockmodels and community structure in networks. *Physical Review E*, 83(1):016107, 2011.

[11] D. D. Lee and H. S. Seung. Algorithms for non-negative matrix factorization. In *Advances in Neural Information Processing Systems*, pages 556–562. MIT Press, 2001.

[12] M. Lichman. UCI machine learning repository. `http://archive.ics.uci.edu/ml`, 2013.

[13] J. MacQueen. Some methods for classification and analysis of multivariate observations. In *Proceedings of the fifth Berkeley symposium on mathematical statistics and probability*, volume 1, pages 281–297. Oakland, CA, USA., 1967.

[14] A. Y. Ng, M. I. Jordan, and Y. Weiss. On spectral clustering: Analysis and an algorithm. *Advances in Neural Information Processing Systems*, 2:849–856, 2002.

[15] D. Niu, J. G. Dy, M. Jordan, et al. Iterative discovery of multiple alternativeclustering views. *Pattern Analysis and Machine Intelligence, IEEE Transactions on*, 36(7):1340–1353, 2014.

[16] D. Niu, J. G. Dy, and M. I. Jordan. Multiple non-redundant spectral clustering views. In *Proceedings of the 27th International Conference on Machine Learning (ICML2010)*, pages 831–838, 2010.

[17] J. Nocedal and S. J. Wright. *Numerical Optimization*, chapter 6 Quasi-Newton Methods, pages 135 – 162. Springer, New York, 2nd edition, 2006.

[18] L. K. Poon, A. H. Liu, T. Liu, and N. L. Zhang. A model-based approach to rounding in spectral clustering. In *Proceedings of the 28th Conference on Uncertainty in Artificial Intelligence, 2012*, pages 685–694.

[19] R. Rosales and B. Frey. Learning generative models of similarity matrices. In *Proceedings of the Nineteenth conference on Uncertainty in Artificial Intelligence*, pages 485–492. Morgan Kaufmann Publishers Inc., 2002.

[20] J. Shi and J. Malik. Normalized cuts and image segmentation. In *IEEE Computer Society Conference on Computer Vision and Pattern Recognition*, pages 731–737. IEEE, 1997.

[21] R. Socher, A. L. Maas, and C. D. Manning. Spectral chinese restaurant processes: Nonparametric clustering based on similarities. In *AISTATS*, pages 698–706, 2011.

[22] A. Strehl and J. Ghosh. Cluster ensembles—a knowledge reuse framework for combining multiple partitions. *The Journal of Machine Learning Research*, 3:583–617, 2003.

[23] S. Sun, H. Wang, and J. Xu. Inferring block structure of graphical models in exponential families. In *Proceedings of the Eighteenth International Conference on Artificial Intelligence and Statistics*, pages 939–947, 2015.

[24] Y. J. Wang and G. Y. Wong. Stochastic blockmodels for directed graphs. *Journal of the American Statistical Association*, 82(397):8–19, 1987.

[25] T. Xiang and S. Gong. Spectral clustering with eigenvector selection. *Pattern Recognition*, 41(3):1012–1029, 2008.

[26] R. Xu and D. Wunsch. Survey of clustering algorithms. *Neural Networks, IEEE Transactions on*, 16(3):645–678, 2005.

Optimal Stochastic Strongly Convex Optimization with a Logarithmic Number of Projections

Jianhui Chen[1], Tianbao Yang[2], Qihang Lin[3], Lijun Zhang[4], and Yi Chang[1]

[1]Yahoo Research, Sunnyvale, CA 94089, USA
[2]Department of Computer Science, The University of Iowa, Iowa City, IA 52242, USA
[3]Department of Management Sciences, The University of Iowa, Iowa City, IA 52242, USA
[4]Key Laboratory for Novel Software Technology, Nanjing University, Nanjing 210023, China

Abstract

We consider stochastic strongly convex optimization with a complex inequality constraint. This complex inequality constraint may lead to computationally expensive projections in algorithmic iterations of the stochastic gradient descent (SGD) methods. To reduce the computation costs pertaining to the projections, we propose an Epoch-Projection Stochastic Gradient Descent (Epro-SGD) method. The proposed Epro-SGD method consists of a sequence of epochs; it applies SGD to an augmented objective function at each iteration within the epoch, and then performs a projection at the end of each epoch. Given a strongly convex optimization and for a total number of T iterations, Epro-SGD requires only $\log(T)$ projections, and meanwhile attains an optimal convergence rate of $O(1/T)$, both in expectation and with a high probability. To exploit the structure of the optimization problem, we propose a proximal variant of Epro-SGD, namely Epro-ORDA, based on the optimal regularized dual averaging method. We apply the proposed methods on real-world applications; the empirical results demonstrate the effectiveness of our methods.

1 INTRODUCTION

Recent years have witnessed an increased interest in adopting the stochastic (sub)gradient (SGD) methods [1, 3, 21] for solving large-scale machine learning problems. In each of the algorithmic iterations, SGD reduces the computation cost by sampling one (or a small number of) example for computing a stochastic (sub)gradient. Thus the computation cost in SGD is independent of the size of the data available for training; this property makes SGD appealing for large-scale optimization. However, when the optimization problems involve a complex domain (for example a positive definite constraint or a polyhedron one), the projection operation in each iteration of SGD, which is used to ensure the feasibility of the intermediate solutions, may become the computational bottleneck.

In this paper we consider to solve the following constrained optimization problem

$$\min_{\mathbf{x}\in\mathbb{R}^d} \quad f(\mathbf{x}) \qquad s.t. \quad c(\mathbf{x}) \le 0, \tag{1}$$

where $f(\mathbf{x})$ is β-strongly convex [23] and $c(\mathbf{x})$ is convex. We assume a stochastic access model for $f(\cdot)$, in which the only access to $f(\cdot)$ is via a stochastic gradient oracle; in other words, given arbitrary $\mathbf{x}$, this stochastic gradient oracle produces a random vector $\mathbf{g}(\mathbf{x})$, whose expectation is a subgradient of $f(\cdot)$ at the point $\mathbf{x}$, i.e., $\mathrm{E}[\mathbf{g}(\mathbf{x})] \in \partial f(\mathbf{x})$, where $\partial f(\mathbf{x})$ denotes the subdifferential set of $f(\cdot)$ at $\mathbf{x}$. On the other hand we have the full access to the (sub)gradient of $c(\cdot)$.

The standard SGD method [5] solves Eq. (1) by iterating the updates in Eq. (2) with an appropriate step size η_t, e.g., $\eta_t = 1/(\beta t)$), as below

$$\mathbf{x}_{t+1} = \mathcal{P}_{\{\mathbf{x}\in\mathbb{R}^d: c(\mathbf{x})\le 0\}}\left[\mathbf{x}_t - \eta_t \mathbf{g}(\mathbf{x}_t)\right], \tag{2}$$

and then returning $\widehat{\mathbf{x}}_T = \sum_{t=1}^T \mathbf{x}_t/T$ as the final solution for a total number of iterations T. Note that $\mathcal{P}_{\mathcal{D}}[\widehat{\mathbf{x}}]$ is a projection operator defined as

$$\mathcal{P}_{\mathcal{D}}[\widehat{\mathbf{x}}] = \arg\min_{\mathbf{x}\in\mathcal{D}} \|\mathbf{x} - \widehat{\mathbf{x}}\|_2^2. \tag{3}$$

If the involved constraint function $c(\mathbf{x})$ is complex (e.g., a polyhedral or a positive definite constraint), computing the associated projection may be computationally expensive; for example, a projection onto a positive definite cone over $\mathbb{R}^{d\times d}$ requires a full singular value decomposition (SVD) operation with time complexity of $O(d^3)$.

In this paper, we propose an epoch-based SGD method, called Epro-SGD, which requires only a logarithmic number of projections (onto the feasible set), and meanwhile achieves an optimal convergence rate for stochastic strongly convex optimization. Specifically, the proposed Epro-SGD method consists of a sequence of epochs; within each of the epochs, the standard SGD is applied to optimize a composite objective function augmented by the complex constraint function, hence avoiding the expensive projections steps; at the end of every epoch, a projection operation is performed to ensure the feasibility of the intermediate solution. Our analysis shows that given a strongly convex optimization and for a total number of T iterations, Epro-SGD requires only $\log(T)$ projections, and meanwhile achieves an optimal rate of convergence at $O(1/T)$, both in expectation and with a high probability.

To exploit the structure (for example the sparisty) of the optimization problem, we propose a proximal variant of the Epro-SGD method, namely Epro-ORDA, which utilizes an existing optimal dual averaging method to solve the involved proximal mapping. Our analysis shows that Epro-ORDA similarly requires only a logarithmic number of projections while enjoys an optimal rate of convergence.

For illustration we apply the proposed Epro-SGD methods on two real-world applications, i.e., the constrained Lasso formulation and the large margin nearest neighbor (LMNN) classification. Our experimental results demonstrate the efficiency of the proposed methods, in comparison to the existing methods.

2 RELATED WORK

The present work is inspired from the break-through work in [20], which proposed two novel one-projection-based stochastic gradient descent (OneProj) methods for stochastic convex optimizations. Specifically the first OneProj method was developed for general convex optimization; it introduces a regularized Lagrangian function as

$$L(\mathbf{x}, \lambda) = f(\mathbf{x}) + \lambda c(\mathbf{x}) - \frac{\gamma}{2}\lambda^2, \quad \lambda \geq 0,$$

then applies SGD to the convex-concave problem $\min_{\mathbf{x}\in\mathcal{B}} \max_{\lambda\geq 0} L(\mathbf{x}, \lambda)$, and finally performs only one projection at the end of all iterations, where $\mathcal{B}$ is a bounded ball subsuming $\mathcal{F} = \{\mathbf{x} \in \mathbb{R}^d : c(\mathbf{x}) \leq 0\}$ as a subset.

The second OneProj method was developed for strongly convex optimization. The proposed method introduced an augmented objective function

$$F(\mathbf{x}) = f(\mathbf{x}) + \gamma \ln\left(1 + \exp\left(\frac{\lambda c(\mathbf{x})}{\gamma}\right)\right), \quad (4)$$

where γ is a parameter dependent on the total number of iterations T, and λ is a problem specific parameter [20]. OneProj applies SGD to the augmented objective function, specifically using a stochastic subgradient of $f(\mathbf{x})$ and a subgradient of $c(\mathbf{x})$, and then performs a projection step after all iterations. For a total number T iterations, the OneProj method achieves a rate of convergence at $O(\log T/(\beta T))$, which is suboptimal for stochastic strongly convex optimization.

Several recent works [15, 26] propose optimal methods with optimal rates of convergence at $O(1/T)$ for stochastic strongly convex optimization. In particular, the Epoch-SGD method [15] consists of a sequence of epochs, each of which has a geometrically decreasing step size and a geometrically increasing iteration number. This method however needs to project the intermediate solutions onto a feasible set at every algorithmic iteration; when the involved constraint is complex, the involved projection is usually computationally expensive. This limitation restricts the practical applications on large scale data analysis. Therefore we are motivated to develop an optimal stochastic algorithm for strongly convex optimization but with a constant number of projections.

Another closely related work is the logT-SGD [33] for stochastic strongly convex and smooth optimization. LogT-SGD achieves an optimal rate of convergence, while require to perform $O(\kappa \log_2 T)$ projections, where κ is the ratio of the smoothness parameter to the strong convexity parameter. There are several key differences between our proposed Epro-SGD method and logT-SGD: (i) logT-SGD and its analysis rely on both the smoothness and the strong convexity of the objective function; in contrast, Epro-SGD only assumes that the objective function is strongly convex; (ii) the number of the required projections in logT-SGD is $O(\kappa \log_2 T)$, where the conditional number κ can be very large in real applications; in contrast, Epro-SGD requires at most $\log_2 T$ projections.

Besides reducing the number of projections in SGD, another line of research is based on the conditional gradient algorithms [7, 14, 17, 18, 32]; this type of algorithms mostly build upon the Frank-Wolfe technique [11], which eschews the projection in favor of a linear optimization step; however in general, they require the smoothness assumption in the objective function. On the other hand, [12, 16] extended Frank-Wolfe techniques to stochastic or online setting for general and strongly convex optimizations. Specifically [16] presents an online/stochastic Frank-Wolfe (OFW) algorithm with a convergence rate $O(1/T^{1/3})$ for general convex optimization problems, which is slower than the optimal rate $O(1/\sqrt{T})$. [12] presents an algorithm for online strongly convex optimization with an $O(\log T)$ regret bound, implying an $O(\log T/T)$ convergence rate for stochastic stronlgy convex optimization. This algorithm requires the problem domain to be a polytope, instead of a convex inequality constraint used in this paper; it also hinges on an efficient local linear optimization oracle that amounts to approximately solve a linear optimization problem over an intersection of a ball and and the feasible domain; furthermore the convergence result only holds in expectation and is sub-optimal.

3 EPOCH-PROJECTION SGD ALGORITHM

In this section, we present an epoch-projection SGD method, called Epro-SGD, for solving Eq. (1) and discuss its convergence result. Based on a stochastic dual averaging algorithm, we then present a proximal variant of the proposed Epro-SGD method.

3.1 SETUP AND BACKGROUND

Denote the optimal solution to Eq. (1) by $\mathbf{x}_*$ and its domain set by $\mathcal{D} = \{\mathbf{x} \in \mathbb{R}^d : c(\mathbf{x}) \leq 0\}$. Since $f(\mathbf{x})$ is β-strongly convex [23] and $c(\mathbf{x})$ is convex, the optimization problem in Eq. (1) is strongly convex. Note that the strong convexity in $f(\cdot)$ implies that $f(\mathbf{x}) \geq f(\mathbf{x}_*) + (\beta/2)\|\mathbf{x} - \mathbf{x}_*\|^2$ for any $\mathbf{x}$. Our analysis is based on the following assumptions:

A1. The stochastic subgradient $\mathbf{g}(\mathbf{x})$ is uniformly bounded by G_1, i.e., $\|\mathbf{g}(\mathbf{x})\|_2 \leq G_1$.

A2. The subgradient $\partial c(\mathbf{x})$ is uniformly bounded by G_2, i.e., $\|\partial c(\mathbf{x})\|_2 \leq G_2$ for any $\mathbf{x}$.

A3. There exists a positive value $\rho > 0$ such that

$$\left[\min_{c(\mathbf{x})=0,\, \mathbf{v} \in \partial c(\mathbf{x}),\, \mathbf{v} \neq 0} \|\mathbf{v}\|_2\right] \geq \rho. \tag{5}$$

Remarks Assumptions A1 and A2 respectively impose an upper bound on the stochastic subgradient of the objective function $f(\cdot)$ and the constraint function $c(\cdot)$. Assumption A3 ensures that the projection of a point onto a feasible domain does not deviate too much from this intermediate point. Note that Assumption A1 is previously used in [15]; a condition similar to Assumption A3 is used in [20], which however simply assumes that $\min_{c(\mathbf{x})=0} \|\nabla c(\mathbf{x})\|_2 \geq \rho$, without considering possible non-differentiability in $c(\cdot)$.

A key consequence of Assumption A3 is presented in the following lemma.

Lemma 1. *For any* $\widehat{\mathbf{x}}$, *let* $\widetilde{\mathbf{x}} = \arg\min_{c(\mathbf{x})\leq 0} \|\mathbf{x} - \widehat{\mathbf{x}}\|_2^2$. *If Assumption A3 holds, then*

$$\|\widehat{\mathbf{x}} - \widetilde{\mathbf{x}}\|_2 \leq \frac{1}{\rho}[c(\widehat{\mathbf{x}})]_+, \quad \rho > 0, \tag{6}$$

where $[s]_+$ *is a hinge operator defined as* $[s]_+ = s$ *if* $s \geq 0$, *and* $[s]_+ = 0$ *otherwise.*

Proof. If $c(\widehat{\mathbf{x}}_T) \leq 0$, we have $\widehat{\mathbf{x}} = \widetilde{\mathbf{x}}$; the inequality in Eq. (6) trivially holds. If $c(\widehat{\mathbf{x}}_T) > 0$, we can verify that $c(\widetilde{\mathbf{x}}_T) = 0$, and there exists $s \geq 0$ and $\mathbf{v} \in \partial c(\widetilde{\mathbf{x}}_T)$ such that $\widetilde{\mathbf{x}}_T - \widehat{\mathbf{x}}_T + s\mathbf{v} = 0$ (using duality theory). It follows that $\widehat{\mathbf{x}}_T - \widetilde{\mathbf{x}}_T = s\mathbf{v}$ ($\mathbf{v} \neq 0$), and thus $\widehat{\mathbf{x}}_T - \widetilde{\mathbf{x}}_T$ is the same direction as $\mathbf{v}$. It follows that

$$\begin{aligned} c(\widehat{\mathbf{x}}_T) &= c(\widehat{\mathbf{x}}_T) - c(\widetilde{\mathbf{x}}_T) \geq (\widehat{\mathbf{x}}_T - \widetilde{\mathbf{x}}_T)^\top \mathbf{v} \\ &= \|\mathbf{v}\|_2 \|\widehat{\mathbf{x}}_T - \widetilde{\mathbf{x}}_T\|_2 \geq \rho \|\widehat{\mathbf{x}}_T - \widetilde{\mathbf{x}}_T\|_2, \end{aligned}$$

where the last inequality uses Assumption A3. This completes the proof of this lemma. □

The result in Lemma 1 is closely related to *the polyhedral error bound condition* [13, 31]; this condition shows that the distance of a point to the optimal set of a convex optimization problem is bounded by the distance of the objective value at this point to the optimal objective value scaled by a constant. For illustration, we consider the optimization problem

$$\min_{\mathbf{x} \in \mathbb{R}^d} [c(\mathbf{x})]_+$$

with an optimal set as $\{\mathbf{x} \in \mathbb{R}^d : c(\mathbf{x}) = 0\}$. If $c(\widehat{\mathbf{x}}) > 0$, $\widetilde{\mathbf{x}} = \arg\min_{c(\mathbf{x})\leq 0} \|\mathbf{x} - \widehat{\mathbf{x}}\|_2^2 = \arg\min_{c(\mathbf{x})=0} \|\mathbf{x} - \widehat{\mathbf{x}}\|_2^2$ is the closest point in the optimal set to $\widehat{\mathbf{x}}$. Therefore, by *the polyhedral error bound condition* of a polyhedral convex optimization, if $c(\mathbf{x})$ is a polyhedral function, there exists a $\rho > 0$ such that

$$\|\widehat{\mathbf{x}} - \widetilde{\mathbf{x}}\|_2 \leq \frac{1}{\rho}\left([c(\widehat{\mathbf{x}})]_+ - \min_{\mathbf{x}}[c(\mathbf{x})]_+\right) = \frac{1}{\rho}[c(\widehat{\mathbf{x}})]_+.$$

Below we present three examples in which Assumption A3 or Lemma 1 is satisfied. Example 1: an affine function $c(\mathbf{x}) = \mathbf{c}^\top \mathbf{x} - b$ with $\rho = \|\mathbf{c}\|_2$. Example 2: the ℓ_1 norm constraint $\|\mathbf{x}\|_1 \leq B$ where $\rho = \min_{\mathbf{x}:\|\mathbf{x}\|_1 = B} \|\partial\|\mathbf{x}\|_1\|_2 \geq 1$. Example 3: the maximum of a finite number of affine functions $c(\mathbf{x}) = \max_{1\leq i\leq m} \mathbf{c}_i^\top \mathbf{x} - b_i$ satisfying Lemma 1 as well as the polyhedral error bound condition [31].

3.2 MAIN ALGORITHM

To solve Eq. (1) (using Epro-SGD), we introduce an augmented objective function by incorporating the constraint function as

$$F(\mathbf{x}) = f(\mathbf{x}) + \lambda[c(\mathbf{x})]_+. \tag{7}$$

It is worth noting that the augmented function in Eq. (7) does not have any iteration-dependent parameter, for example the parameter γ in Eq. (4). λ is a prescribed parameter satisfying $\lambda > G_1/\rho$, as illustrated in Lemma 2.

The details of our proposed Epro-SGD algorithm is presented in Algorithm 1. Similar to Epoch-SGD [15], Epro-SGD consists of a sequence of epochs, each of which has a geometrically decreasing step size and a geometrically increasing iteration number (Line 9 in Algorithm 1). The updates in every intra-epoch (Line 5 - 6) are standard SGD steps applied to the augmented objective function $F(\mathbf{x})$ with $\mathbf{x} = \mathbf{x}_t^k$. Epro-SGD is different from Epoch-SGD in that the former computes a projection only at the end of each epoch, while the latter computes a projection at each iteration. Consequently, when the projection step is computationally expensive (e.g., projecting onto a positive definite constraint), Epro-SGD may require much less computation time than Epoch-SGD.

Algorithm 1 Epoch-projection SGD (Epro-SGD)

```
Input: an initial step size η_1, total number of iterations T, and number of iterations in the first epoch T_1, a Lagrangian multiplier λ (λ > G_1/ρ)
Initialization: x_1^1 ∈ D and k = 1
while Σ_{i=1}^k T_i ≤ T do
  for t = 1, ..., T_k do
    Compute a stochastic gradient g(x_t^k)
    Compute x_{t+1}^k = x_t^k − η_k(g(x_t^k) + λ∂[c(x_t^k)]_+)
  end for
  Compute x̃_T^k = P_D[x̂_T^k], where x̂_T^k = Σ_{t=1}^{T_k} x_t^k / T_k
  Update x_1^{k+1} = x̃_T^k, T_{k+1} = 2T_k, η_{k+1} = η_k/2
  Set k = k + 1
end while
```

In Lemma 2, we present an important convergence analysis for the intra-epoch steps of Algorithm 1, which are key building blocks for deriving the main results in Theorem 1.

Lemma 2. *Under Assumptions A1∼A3, if we apply the update* $\mathbf{x}_{t+1} = \mathbf{x}_t - \eta(\widetilde{\nabla} f(\mathbf{x}_t;\varepsilon_t) + \lambda\nabla[c(\mathbf{x}_t)]_+)$ *for a number of T iterations, the following equality holds*

$$\mathrm{E}[f(\widetilde{\mathbf{x}}_T)] - f(\mathbf{x}_*) \leq \mu\left[\eta(G_1^2 + \lambda^2 G_2^2) + \frac{\mathrm{E}[\|\mathbf{x}_1 - \mathbf{x}_*\|_2^2]}{2\eta T}\right],$$

where $\mu = \rho/(\rho - G_1/\lambda)$.

Proof. Let $F(\mathbf{x}) = f(\mathbf{x}) + \lambda[c(\mathbf{x})]_+$ and denote by $\mathrm{E}_t[X]$ the expectation conditioned on the randomness until round $t-1$. It is easy to verify that $F(\mathbf{x}) \geq f(\mathbf{x})$, $F(\mathbf{x}) \geq f(\mathbf{x}) + \lambda c(\mathbf{x})$ and $F(\mathbf{x}_*) = f(\mathbf{x}_*)$. For any $\mathbf{x}$, we have

$$\begin{aligned}(\mathbf{x}_t - \mathbf{x})^\top \nabla F(\mathbf{x}_t) &\leq \frac{1}{2\eta}\left(\|\mathbf{x} - \mathbf{x}_t\|_2^2 - \|\mathbf{x} - \mathbf{x}_{t+1}\|_2^2\right) + \\ &\quad \frac{\eta}{2}\|\widetilde{\nabla} f(\mathbf{x}_t,\xi_t) + \lambda\nabla[c(\mathbf{x}_t)]_+\|_2^2 + \\ &\quad (\mathbf{x} - \mathbf{x}_t)^\top(\mathbf{g}(\mathbf{x}_t) - \nabla f(\mathbf{x}_t)) \\ &\leq \frac{1}{2\eta}\left(\|\mathbf{x} - \mathbf{x}_t\|_2^2 - \|\mathbf{x} - \mathbf{x}_{t+1}\|_2^2\right) + \\ &\quad \eta\left(G_1^2 + \lambda^2 G_2^2\right) + \zeta_t(\mathbf{x}),\end{aligned}$$

where $\zeta_t(\mathbf{x}) = (\mathbf{x} - \mathbf{x}_t)^\top(\mathbf{g}(\mathbf{x}_t) - \nabla f(\mathbf{x}_t))$. Furthermore by the convexity of $F(\mathbf{x})$, we have

$$\begin{aligned}F(\mathbf{x}_t) - F(\mathbf{x}) &\leq \frac{1}{2\eta}\left(\|\mathbf{x} - \mathbf{x}_t\|_2^2 - \|\mathbf{x} - \mathbf{x}_{t+1}\|_2^2\right) + \\ &\quad \eta(G_1^2 + \lambda^2 G_2^2) + \zeta_t(\mathbf{x}).\end{aligned}$$

Noting that $\mathrm{E}_t[\zeta_t(\mathbf{x})] = 0$, taking expectation over randomness and summation over $t = 1, \ldots, T$, we have

$$\begin{aligned}\frac{1}{T}\mathrm{E}\left[\sum_{t=1}^{T}(F(\mathbf{x}_t) - F(\mathbf{x}))\right] &= \mathrm{E}\left[F(\widehat{\mathbf{x}}_t) - F(\mathbf{x})\right] \\ &\leq \frac{\mathrm{E}[\|\mathbf{x}_1 - \mathbf{x}\|_2^2]}{2\eta T} + \eta(G_1^2 + \lambda^2 G_2^2).\end{aligned}$$

Let $B = \mathrm{E}[\|\mathbf{x}_1 - \mathbf{x}_*\|_2^2]/(2\eta T) + \eta(G_1^2 + \lambda^2 G_2^2)$. Since $\mathbf{x}_* \in \mathcal{D} \subseteq \mathcal{B}$, we have

$$\mathrm{E}\left[F(\widehat{\mathbf{x}}_t) - F(\mathbf{x}_*)\right] \leq B. \tag{8}$$

It follows that

$$\mathrm{E}[f(\widehat{\mathbf{x}}_T) + \lambda[c(\widehat{\mathbf{x}}_T)]_+] \leq f(\mathbf{x}_*) + B. \tag{9}$$

If $c(\widehat{\mathbf{x}}_T) \leq 0$, we have $\widetilde{\mathbf{x}}_T = \widehat{\mathbf{x}}_T$. Following from $F(\widetilde{\mathbf{x}}_T) \geq f(\widetilde{\mathbf{x}}_T)$ and $F(\mathbf{x}_*) = f(\mathbf{x}_*)$, we can verify that $\mathrm{E}[f(\widetilde{\mathbf{x}}_T)] - f(\mathbf{x}_*) \leq B$ and also $\mathrm{E}[f(\widetilde{\mathbf{x}}_T)] - f(\mathbf{x}_*) \leq \rho B/(\rho - G_1/\lambda)$ holds.

Next we show that $\mathrm{E}[f(\widetilde{\mathbf{x}}_T)] - f(\mathbf{x}_*) \leq \rho B/(\rho - G_1/\lambda)$ holds when $c(\widehat{\mathbf{x}}_T) > 0$. From Lemma 1, we have

$$c(\widehat{\mathbf{x}}_T) \geq \rho\|\widehat{\mathbf{x}}_T - \widetilde{\mathbf{x}}_T\|_2. \tag{10}$$

Moreover it follows from $\|\partial f(\mathbf{x})\|_2 \leq G_1$ and $f(\mathbf{x}_*) \leq f(\widetilde{\mathbf{x}}_T)$ that the following inequality holds

$$\begin{aligned}f(\mathbf{x}_*) - f(\widehat{\mathbf{x}}_T) &\leq f(\mathbf{x}_*) - f(\widetilde{\mathbf{x}}_T) + f(\widetilde{\mathbf{x}}_T) - f(\widehat{\mathbf{x}}_T) \\ &\leq G_1\|\widehat{\mathbf{x}}_T - \widetilde{\mathbf{x}}_T\|_2.\end{aligned} \tag{11}$$

Substituting Eqs. (10) and (11) into Eq. (9), we have

$$\begin{aligned}\lambda\rho\mathrm{E}[\|\widehat{\mathbf{x}}_T - \widetilde{\mathbf{x}}_T\|_2] &\leq \mathrm{E}[f(\mathbf{x}_*) - f(\widehat{\mathbf{x}}_T)] + B \\ &\leq G_1\mathrm{E}[\|\widehat{\mathbf{x}}_T - \widetilde{\mathbf{x}}_T\|_2] + B.\end{aligned}$$

By some rearrangement, we have $\mathrm{E}[\|\widehat{\mathbf{x}}_T - \widetilde{\mathbf{x}}_T\|_2] \leq B/(\lambda\rho - G_1)$. Furthermore we have

$$\begin{aligned}&\mathrm{E}[f(\widetilde{\mathbf{x}}_T)] - f(\mathbf{x}_*) \leq \mathrm{E}[f(\widetilde{\mathbf{x}}_T) - f(\widehat{\mathbf{x}}_T)] + \mathrm{E}[f(\widehat{\mathbf{x}}_T)] \\ &\quad - f(\mathbf{x}_*) \leq \mathrm{E}[G_1\|\widehat{\mathbf{x}}_T - \widetilde{\mathbf{x}}_T\|_2] + B \leq \frac{\lambda\rho}{\lambda\rho - G_1}B,\end{aligned}$$

where the second inequality follows from $\|\nabla f(\mathbf{x})\|_2 \leq \mathrm{E}\|\nabla f(\mathbf{x};\varepsilon)\| \leq G_1$, and $|f(\mathbf{x}) - f(\mathbf{y})| \leq G_1\|\mathbf{x} - \mathbf{y}\|_2$ for any $\mathbf{x}, \mathbf{y}$. This completes the proof of the lemma. □

We present a main convergence result of the Epro-SGD algorithm in the following theorem.

Theorem 1. *Under Assumptions A1∼A3 and given that $f(\mathbf{x})$ is β-strongly convex, if we let $\mu = \rho/(\rho - G_1/\lambda)$, $G^2 = G_1^2 + \lambda^2 G_2^2$, and set $T_1 = 8, \eta_1 = \mu/(2\beta)$, the total number of epochs $k^\dagger$ in Algorithm 1 is given by*

$$k^\dagger = \left\lceil \log_2\left(\frac{T}{8} + 1\right)\right\rceil \leq \log_2\left(\frac{T}{4}\right), \tag{12}$$

the solution $\mathbf{x}_1^{k^\dagger+1}$ enjoys a convergence rate of

$$\mathrm{E}[f(\mathbf{x}_1^{k^\dagger+1})] - f(\mathbf{x}_*) \leq \frac{32\mu^2 G^2}{\beta(T+8)}, \tag{13}$$

and $c(\mathbf{x}_1^{k^\dagger+1}) \leq 0$.

Proof. From the updating rule $T_{k+1} = 2T_k$, we can easily verify Eq. (12). Since $\mathbf{x}_1^{k^\dagger+1} = \widetilde{\mathbf{x}}_T^{k^\dagger} \in \mathcal{D}$, the inequality $c(\mathbf{x}_1^{k^\dagger+1}) \leq 0$ trivially holds.

Let $V_k = \mu^2 G^2 / (2^{k-2}\beta)$. It follows that $T_k = 2^{k+2} = 16\mu^2 G^2 / (V_k \beta)$ and $\eta_k = \mu / (2^k \beta) = V_k / (4\mu G^2)$. Next we show the inequality

$$\mathrm{E}[f(\mathbf{x}^k)] - f(\mathbf{x}_*) \leq V_k \tag{14}$$

holds by induction. Note that Eq. (14) implies $\mathrm{E}[f(\mathbf{x}_1^{k+1})] - f(\mathbf{x}_*) \leq 32\mu^2 G^2 / (\beta(T+8))$, due to $V_k < 32\mu^2 G^2 / (\beta(T+8))$. Let $\Delta_k = f(\mathbf{x}_1^k) - f(\mathbf{x}_*)$. It follows from Lemma 5 (detailed provided in Appendix), $\mu > 1$, and $G^2 > G_1^2$, the inequality in Eq. (14) holds when $k = 1$. Assuming that Eq. (14) holds for $k = k^\dagger$, we show that Eq. (14) holds for $k = {k^\dagger}_1 + 1$.

For a random variable X measurable with respect to the randomness up to epoch $k^\dagger + 1$. Let $\mathrm{E}_{k^\dagger}[X]$ denote the expectation conditioned on all the randomness up to epoch $k^\dagger$. Following Lemma 2, we have

$$\mathrm{E}_{k^\dagger}[\Delta_{k^\dagger+1}] \leq \mu \left[\eta_{k^\dagger} G^2 + \frac{\mathrm{E}[\|\mathbf{x}_1^{k^\dagger} - \mathbf{x}_*\|_2^2]}{2\eta_{k^\dagger} T_{k^\dagger}} \right].$$

Since $\Delta_{k^\dagger} = f(\mathbf{x}_1^{k^\dagger}) - f(\mathbf{x}_*) \geq \beta\|\mathbf{x}_1^{k^\dagger} - \mathbf{x}_*\|_2^2/2$ by the strong convexity in $f(\cdot)$, we have

$$\begin{aligned}
\mathrm{E}[\Delta_{k^\dagger+1}] &\leq \mu \left[\eta_{k^\dagger} G^2 + \frac{\mathrm{E}[\Delta_{k^\dagger}]}{\eta_{k^\dagger} T_{k^\dagger} \beta} \right] \\
&= \mu\eta_{k^\dagger} G^2 + \frac{V_{k^\dagger}\mu}{\eta_{k^\dagger} T_{k^\dagger} \beta} = \frac{V_{k^\dagger}}{4} + \frac{V_{k^\dagger}}{4} = V_{k^\dagger+1},
\end{aligned}$$

which completes the proof of this theorem. □

Remark We compare the obtained main results in Theorem 1 with several existing works. Firstly Eq. (13) implies that Epro-SGD achieves an optimal bound $O(1/T)$, matching the lower bound for a strongly convex problem [15]. Secondly in contrast to the OneProj method [20] with a convergence rate $O(\log T/T)$, Epro-SGD uses no more than $\log_2(T/4)$ projections to obtain an $O(1/T)$ convergence rate. Epro-SGD thus has better control over the solution for not deviating (too much) from the feasibility domain in the intermediate iterations. Thirdly compared to Epoch-SGD with its convergence rate bounded by $O(8G_1^2/(\beta T))$, the convergence rate bound of Epro-SGD is only worse by a factor of constant $4\mu^2 G^2/G_1^2$. Particularly consider a positive definite constraint with $\rho = 1$, $\mu = 2$, and $\lambda = 2G_1/\rho$, we have $G^2 = 5G_1^2$ and the bound of Epro-SGD is only worse by a factor of 80 than Epoch-SGD. Finally compared to the logT-SGD algorithm [33] which requires $O(\kappa \log_2 T)$ projections (κ is the conditional number), the number of projections in Epro-SGD is independent of the conditional number.

The main results in Lemma 2 and Theorem 1 are expected convergence bounds. In Theorem 2 (proof provided in Appendix) we show that Epro-SGD also enjoys a high probability bound under a boundedness assumption, i.e., $\|\mathbf{x}_* - \mathbf{x}_t\|_2 \leq D$ for all t. Note that the existing Epoch-SGD method [15] uses two different methods to derive its high probability bounds. Specifically the first method relies on an efficient function evaluator to select the best solutions among multiple trials of run; while the second one modifies the updating rule by projecting the solution onto the intersection of the domain and a center-shifted bounded ball with decaying radius. These two methods however may lead to additional computation steps, if being adopted for deriving high probability bounds for Epro-SGD.

Theorem 2. *Under Assumptions A1∼A3 and given* $\|\mathbf{x}_t - \mathbf{x}_*\|_2 \leq D$ *for all* t. *If we let* $\mu = \rho/(\rho - G_1/\lambda)$, $G^2 = G_1^2 + \lambda^2 G_2^2$, $C = (8G_1^2/\beta + 2G_1 D)\ln(m/\epsilon) + 2G_1 D$, *and set* $T_1 \geq \max(3C\beta/(\mu G^2), 9)$, $\eta_1 = \mu/(3\beta)$, *the total number of epochs* $k^\dagger$ *in Algorithm 1 is given by*

$$k^\dagger = \left\lfloor \log_2 \left(\frac{T}{T_1} + 1 \right) \right\rfloor \leq \log_2(T/4),$$

and the final solution $\mathbf{x}_1^{k^\dagger+1}$ *enjoys a convergence rate of*

$$f(\mathbf{x}_1^{k^\dagger+1}) - f(\mathbf{x}_*) \leq \frac{4T_1\mu^2 G^2}{\beta(T+T_1)}$$

with a probability at least $1 - \delta$, *where* $m = \lceil 2\log_2 T \rceil$.

Remark The assumption $\|\mathbf{x}_* - \mathbf{x}_t\|_2 \leq D$ can be satisfied practically, if we estimate the value of D such that $\|\mathbf{x}_*\|_2 \leq D/2$, and then project the intermediate solutions onto $\|\mathbf{x}\|_2 \leq D/2$ at every iteration. Note that Epoch-SGD [15] requires a total number of T projections, and its high probability bound of Epoch-SGD is denoted by $f(\mathbf{x}_1^{k^\dagger+1}) - f(\mathbf{x}_*) \leq 1200G_1^2 \log(1/\widetilde{\delta})/(\beta T)$ with a probability at lest $1 - \delta$, where $\widetilde{\delta} = \delta/(\lfloor \log_2(T/300+1) \rfloor)$.

3.3 A PROXIMAL VARIANT

We propose a proximal extension of Epro-SGD, by exploiting the structure of the objective function. Let the objective function in Eq. (1) be a sum of two components

$$\widehat{f}(\mathbf{x}) = f(\mathbf{x}) + g(\mathbf{x}),$$

where $g(\mathbf{x})$ is a relatively simple function, for example a squared ℓ_2-norm or ℓ_1-norm, such that the involved proximal mapping

$$\min_{\mathbf{x}\in\mathbb{R}^d} \quad g(\mathbf{x}) + \frac{1}{2}\|\mathbf{x} - \widehat{\mathbf{x}}\|_2^2$$

is easy to compute. The optimization problem in Eq. (1) can be rewritten as

$$\begin{aligned}
\min_{\mathbf{x}\in\mathbb{R}^d} &\quad f(\mathbf{x}) + g(\mathbf{x}) \\
s.t. &\quad c(\mathbf{x}) \leq 0.
\end{aligned} \tag{15}$$

Denote by $\mathbf{x}_*$ the optimal solution to Eq. (15). We similarly introduce an augmented objective function as

$$F(\mathbf{x}) = f(\mathbf{x}) + \lambda[c(\mathbf{x})]_+ + g(\mathbf{x}). \quad (16)$$

Subsequently the update of the proximal SGD method [9, 10, 22] is given by

$$\mathbf{x}_{t+1} = \arg\min_{\mathbf{x}\in\mathcal{D}} \frac{1}{2}\|\mathbf{x} - (\mathbf{x}_t - \eta\mathbf{g}(\mathbf{x}_t))\|_2^2 + \eta g(\mathbf{x}). \quad (17)$$

If $g(\mathbf{x})$ is a sparse regularizer, the proximal SGD can guarantee the sparsity in the intermediate solutions and usually yields better convergence than the standard SGD. However, given a complex constraint, solving the proximal mapping may be computational expensive. Therefore, we consider a proximal variant of Epro-SGD which involves only the proximal mapping of $g(\mathbf{x})$ without the constraint $\mathbf{x} \in \mathcal{D}$. An instinctive solution is to use the following update in place of step 6 in Algorithm 1:

$$\mathbf{x}_{t+1}^k = \arg\min_{\mathbf{x}\in\mathbb{R}^d} \frac{1}{2}\|\mathbf{x} - [\mathbf{x}_t^k - \eta_k(\mathbf{g}(\mathbf{x}_t^k) + \lambda\partial[c(\mathbf{x}_t^k)]_+)]\|_2^2 + \eta_k g(\mathbf{x}). \quad (18)$$

Based this update and using techniques in Lemma 2, we obtain similar convergence results (proof provided in Appendix), as presented in the following lemma [8].

Lemma 3. *Under Assumptions A1∼A3 and setting* $\mu = \rho/(\rho - G_1/\lambda)$, *by applying the update in Eq. (18) a number of* T *iterations, we have*

$$\mathrm{E}[\widehat{f}(\widetilde{\mathbf{x}}_T^k)] - \widehat{f}(\mathbf{x}_*) \leq \mu\mathrm{E}\left[\eta G^2 + \frac{\|\mathbf{x}_1^k - \mathbf{x}_*\|_2^2}{2\eta T} + \frac{g(\mathbf{x}_1^k) - g(\mathbf{x}_{T+1}^k)}{T}\right], \quad (19)$$

where $G^2 = (G_1^2 + \lambda^2 G_2^2)$, *and* $\widetilde{\mathbf{x}}_T^k$ *denotes the projected solution of the averaged solution* $\widehat{\mathbf{x}}_T^k = \sum_{t=1}^T \mathbf{x}_t^k / T$.

Different from the main result in Lemma 2, Eq. (19) has an additional term $(g(\mathbf{x}_1^k) - g(\mathbf{x}_{T+1}^k))/T_k$; it makes the convergence analysis in Epro-SGD difficult. To overcome this difficulty, we adopt the optimal regularized dual averaging (ORDA) algorithm [6] for solving Eq. (16). The details of ORDA are presented in Algorithm 2. The main convergence results of ORDA are summarized in the following lemma (proof provided in Appendix).

Lemma 4. *Under Assumptions A1∼A3 and setting* $\mu = \rho/(\rho - G_1/\lambda)$, *by running ORDA a number of* T *iterations for solving the augmented objective (16), we have*

$$\mathrm{E}[F(\widehat{\mathbf{x}}_T) - F(\mathbf{x}_*)] \leq \frac{4\|\mathbf{x}_1 - \mathbf{x}_*\|_2^2}{\eta\sqrt{T}} + \frac{2\eta(3G_1 + 2\lambda G_2)^2}{\sqrt{T}},$$

and

$$\mathrm{E}[\widehat{f}(\widetilde{\mathbf{x}}_T)] - \widehat{f}(\mathbf{x}_*) \leq \mu\mathrm{E}\left[\frac{4\|\mathbf{x}_1 - \mathbf{x}_*\|_2^2}{\eta\sqrt{T}} + \frac{2\eta(3G_1 + 2\lambda G_2)^2}{\sqrt{T}}\right],$$

Algorithm 2 Optimal Regularized Dual Averaging (ORDA)

Input: a step size η, the number iterations T, and the initial solution $\mathbf{x}_1$,
Set $\theta_t = \frac{2}{t+1}$, $\nu_t = \frac{2}{t}$, $\gamma_t = \frac{t^{3/2}}{\eta}$ and $\mathbf{z}_1 = \mathbf{x}_1$
for $t = 1, \ldots, T+1$ **do**
  compute $\mathbf{u}_t = (1 - \theta_t)\mathbf{x}_t + \theta_t \mathbf{z}_t$
  compute a stochastic subgradient $\mathbf{g}(\mathbf{x}_t)$ of $f(\mathbf{x})$ at $\mathbf{x}_t$ and a subgradient of $[c(\mathbf{x}_t)]_+$
  let $\bar{\mathbf{g}}_t = \theta_t\nu_t\left(\sum_{\tau=1}^t \frac{\mathbf{g}(\mathbf{x}_\tau) + \lambda\partial[c(\mathbf{x}_\tau)]_+}{\nu_\tau}\right)$
  compute $\mathbf{z}_{t+1} = \arg\min_{\mathbf{x}} \bar{\mathbf{g}}_t^\top \mathbf{x} + \frac{\theta_t\nu_t\gamma_{t+1}}{2}\|\mathbf{x} - \mathbf{x}_1\|_2^2 + g(\mathbf{x})$
  compute $\mathbf{x}_{t+1} = \arg\min_{\mathbf{x}} \mathbf{x}^\top(\mathbf{g}(\mathbf{x}_t) + \lambda\partial[c(\mathbf{x}_t)]_+) + \frac{\gamma_t}{2}\|\mathbf{x} - \mathbf{u}_t\|_2^2 + g(\mathbf{x})$
end for
Output: $\widehat{\mathbf{x}}_T = \mathbf{x}_{T+2}$

Algorithm 3 Epoch-projection ORDA (Epro-ORDA)

Input: an initial step size η_1, total number of iterations T, and number of iterations in the first epoch T_1, a Lagrangian multiplier $\lambda > G_1/\rho$
Initialization: $\mathbf{x}_1^1 \in \mathcal{D}$ and $k = 1$.
while $\sum_{i=1}^k T_i \leq T$ **do**
  Run ORDA to obtain $\widehat{\mathbf{x}}_T^k = \mathrm{ORDA}(\mathbf{x}_1^k, \eta_k, T_k)$
  Compute $\widetilde{\mathbf{x}}_T^k = \mathcal{P}_\mathcal{D}[\widehat{\mathbf{x}}_T^k]$
  Update $\mathbf{x}_1^{k+1} = \widetilde{\mathbf{x}}_T^k$, $T_{k+1} = 2T_k$, $\eta_{k+1} = \eta_k/\sqrt{2}$
  Set $k = k + 1$
end while

where $\widetilde{\mathbf{x}}_T$ *denotes the projected solution of the final solution* $\widehat{\mathbf{x}}_T$.

We present a proximal variant of Epro-SGD, namely Epro-ORDA, in Algorithm 3, and summarize its convergence results in Theorem 3. Note that Algorithm 2 and the convergence analysis in Lemma 4 are independent of the strong convexity in $\widehat{f}(\mathbf{x})$; the strong convexity is however used for analyzing the convergence of Epro-ORDA in Theorem 3 (proof provided in Appendix).

Theorem 3. *Under Assumptions A1∼A3 and given that* $\widehat{f}(\mathbf{x})$ *is* β*-strongly convex, if we let* $\mu = \rho/(\rho - G_1/\lambda)$ *and* $G = 3G_1 + 2\lambda G_2$, *and set* $T_1 = 16, \eta_1 = \mu/\beta$, *then the total number of epochs* $k^\dagger$ *in Algorithm 3 is given by*

$$k^\dagger = \left\lfloor \log_2\left(\frac{T}{17} + 1\right)\right\rfloor \leq \log_2(T/8),$$

and the final solution $\mathbf{x}_1^{k^\dagger+1}$ *enjoys a convergence rate of*

$$\mathrm{E}[\widehat{f}(\mathbf{x}_1^{k^\dagger+1})] - \widehat{f}(\mathbf{x}_*) \leq \frac{68\mu^2 G^2}{\beta(T+17)},$$

and $c(\mathbf{x}_1^{k^\dagger+1}) \leq 0$.

4 AN EXAMPLE OF SOLVING LMNN VIA EPRO-SGD

In this section, we discuss an application of applying the proposed Epro-SGD to solve a high dimensional distance metric learning (DML) with a large margin formulation, i.e., the large margin nearest neighbor (LMNN) classification method [30]. LMNN classification is one of the state-of-the-art methods for k-nearest neighbor classification. It learns a positive semi-definite distance metric, based on which the examples from the k-nearest neighbors always belong to the same class, while the examples from different classes are separated by a large margin.

To describe the LMNN method, we first present some notations. Let $(x_i, y_i), i = 1, 2, \cdots, \widehat{N}$, be a set of data points, where $x_i \in \mathbb{R}^d$ and $y \in \mathcal{Y}$ denote the feature representation and the class label, respectively. Let A be a positive definite matrix that defines a distance metric as $\text{dist}(x_1, x_2) = \|x_1 - x_2\|_A^2 = (x_1 - x_2)^\top A(x_1 - x_2)$. To learn a distance metric that separates the examples from different classes by a large margin, one needs to extract a set of similar examples (from the same class) and dissimilar examples (from a different class), denoted by $(x_1^j, x_2^j, x_3^j), j = 1, \ldots N$, where x_1^j shares the same class label to x_2^j and a different class from x_3^j. To this end, for each example $x_1^j = x_i$ one can form x_2^j by extracting the k nearest neighbors (defined by an Euclidean distance metric) that share the same class label to x_i, and form x_3^j by extracting a set of examples that have a different class label. Then an appropriate distance metric could be obtained from the following constrained optimization problem

$$\min_A \frac{c}{N}\sum_{j=1}^{N} \ell\left(A, x_1^j, x_2^j, x_3^j\right) + (1-c)tr(AL) + \frac{\mu_1}{2}\|A\|_F^2$$
$$s.t.\ A \succeq \epsilon I, \tag{20}$$

where $\ell(A, x_1^j, x_2^j, x_3^j) = \max(0, \|x_1^j - x_2^j\|_A^2 - \|x_1^j - x_3^j\|_A^2 + 1)$ is a hinge loss and $c \in (0, 1)$ is a trade-off parameter. In Eq. (20), $A \succeq \epsilon I$ is used as the constraint to ensure that Assumption A3 holds. Minimizing the first term is equivalent to maximizing the margin between $\|x_1^j - x_3^j\|_A^2$ and $\|x_1^j - x_2^j\|_A^2$. The matrix L encodes certain prior knowledge about the distance metric; for example, the original LMNN work [30] defines L as $L = \sum_{l=1}^{m} \|x_1^l - x_2^l\|_A^2/m$, where (x_1^l, x_2^l) are all k-nearest neighbor pairs from the same class. Other works [19] have used a weighted summation of distances between all data pairs $L = \sum_{i \neq j}^{n} w_{ij}\|x_i - x_j\|_A^2/n(n-1)$ or intra-class covariance matrix [25]. The last term $\|A\|_F^2/2$ is used as a regularization term and also makes the objective function strongly convex.

For data sets of very high dimensionality, i.e., $d \gg n$, LMNN in Eq. (20) usually produces a sub-optimal solution [25], as this formulation does not capture the sparsity structure of the features. Therefore we add a sparse regularizer and express the formulation below

$$\min_A \quad \frac{c}{N}\sum_{j=1}^{N} \ell\left(A, x_1^j, x_2^j, x_3^j\right) + (1-c)tr(AL)$$
$$+\frac{\mu_1}{2}\|A\|_F^2 + \mu_2\|A\|_1^{\text{off}}$$
$$s.t. \quad A \succeq \epsilon I, \tag{21}$$

where $\|A\|_1^{\text{off}} = \sum_{i \neq j} |A_{ij}|$ is an elmenent-wise ℓ_1-norm excluding the diagonal entries. Note that this sparse regularizer $\|A\|_1^{\text{off}}$ have been previously used in [25] for a different purpose.

Many standard optimization solvers or algorithms may not be efficient for solving Eq. (21). Firstly, the optimization problem in Eq. (21) can be formulated as a semi-definite program (SDP); however, general SDP solvers usually scale poorly with the number of triplets and is not suitable for large scale data analysis. Secondly, the gradient decent method presented in [30] requires to project intermediate solutions onto a positive definite cone; this operation invokes expensive singular value decomposition (SVD) for a large matrix and this limitation restricts the real-world applications of the gradient descent method. Thirdly, [25] employs a block coordinate descent (BCD) method to solve an L1-penalized log-det optimization problem; the BCD method is not suitable for solving Eq. (21), as the loss function is not linear in the variable A.

We employ the proposed Epro-SGD algorithm to solve the LMNN formulation in Eq. (21). Let $f(A) = \frac{c}{N}\sum_{j=1}^{N} \ell(A, x_1^j, x_2^j, x_3^j) + (1-c)tr(AL)$ and $g(A) = \frac{\mu_1}{2}\|A\|_F^2 + \mu_2\|A\|_1^{\text{off}}$. The positive definite constraint can be rewritten into an inequality constraint as $c(A) = \epsilon - \lambda_{\min}(A) \leq 0$, where $\lambda_{\min}(\cdot)$ denotes the minimum eigenvalue of the matrix A. We also make the correspondences $\mathbb{R}^d \to \mathbb{R}^{d \times d}$, $\mathbf{x} \to A$, $\|\mathbf{x}\|_2 \to \|A\|_F$, and provide necessary details below in a question-answer form

- How to compute the stochastic gradient of $f(A)$? First sample one triplet (x_1^j, x_2^j, x_3^j) (or a small number of triplets) and then compute $\widetilde{\nabla} f(A; \varepsilon) = c[(x_1^j - x_2^j)(x_1^j - x_2^j)^\top - (x_1^j - x_3^j)(x_1^j - x_3^j)^\top] + (1-c)L$ if $\ell(\|x_1^j - x_2^j\|_A^2 - \|x_1^j - x_3^j\|_A^2 + 1) > 0$, $\widetilde{\nabla} f(A; \varepsilon) = (1-c)L$ otherwise.

- How to compute the gradient of $[c(A)]_+ = [\epsilon - \lambda_{\min}(A)]_+$? By the theory of matrix analysis, the subgradient of $[c(A)]_+$ can be computed by $\partial c(A) = -\mathbf{u}\mathbf{u}^\top$ if $c(A) > 0$, and zero otherwise, where $\mathbf{u}$ denotes the eigevector of A associated with its minimum eigenvalue.

- What is the solution to the following proximal gradient step?

$$\min_A \frac{1}{2}\|A - \bar{A}_{t+1}\|_F^2 + \eta\left(\frac{\mu_1}{2}\|A\|_F^2 + \mu_2\|A\|_1^{\text{off}}\right).$$

The solution can be obtained via a soft-thresholding algorithm [2].

- What are the appropriate values for β, ρ, r, λ, that are necessary for running the algorithm? The value of $\beta = \mu_1$. The value of ρ is $\min_{c(A)=0} \|\nabla c(A)\|_F = 1$. The value of r can be set to $\sqrt{2c/\mu_1}$. The value of $G_2 = 1$. The value of G_1 can be estimated as $8cR^2 + (1-c)\|L\|_F + \mu_1 r + \mu_2 d$ if we assume $\|x_i\|_2 \leq R, i = 1, \ldots, n$. The value of $\lambda > G_1$ is usually tuned among a set of prespecified values.

Finally, we discuss the impact of employing Epro-SGD and Epro-ORDA method on accelerating the computation for solving LMNN. Note that at each iteration to compute the gradient of $c(A)$, we need to compute the minimum eigenvalue and its eigen-vector. For a dense matrix, it usually involves a time complexity of $O(d^2)$. However, by employing a proximal projection, we can guarantee that the intermediate solution A_t is a element-wise sparse solution, for which the computation of the last eigen-pair can be substantially reduced to be linear to the number of non-zeros elements in A_t.

To analyze the running time compared to the Epoch-SGD method, let us assume we are interested in a ϵ-accurate solution. In the following discussion, we take a particular choice of $\lambda = 2G_1$ and suppress the dependence on constants and only consider dependence on T, G_1 and d. The number of iterations required by Epro-SGD is $\Omega\left(G_1^2/\epsilon\mu_1\right)$, and that by Epro-ORDA is $\Omega\left(G_1^2/\epsilon\mu_1\right)$. Taking into account the running time per iteration, the total running time of Epoch-SGD is $\Omega\left(G_1^2 d^3/\left(\epsilon\mu_1\right)\right)$ and that of Epro-ORDA is $\Omega\left(G_1^2 d^2/\left(\epsilon\mu_1\right)\right)$. When d is very large, the speed-up can be orders of magnitude.

5 EXPERIMENTS

In this section, we empirically demonstrate the efficiency and effectiveness of the proposed Epro-SGD algorithm. We compare the following four algorithms:

- Stochastic sub-Gradient Descent method (SGD) [27]: we set the step size $\eta_t = 1/(\lambda t)$ and SGD achieves a rate of convergence $O(logT/T)$, requiring $O(T)$ projections for a constrained convex optimization problem.

- One-Projection SGD method (OneProj) [20]: we set the step size $\eta_t = 1/(\lambda t)$ and OneProj achieves a rate of convergence $O(logT/T)$, requiring only one projection for a constrained strongly convex optimization problem.

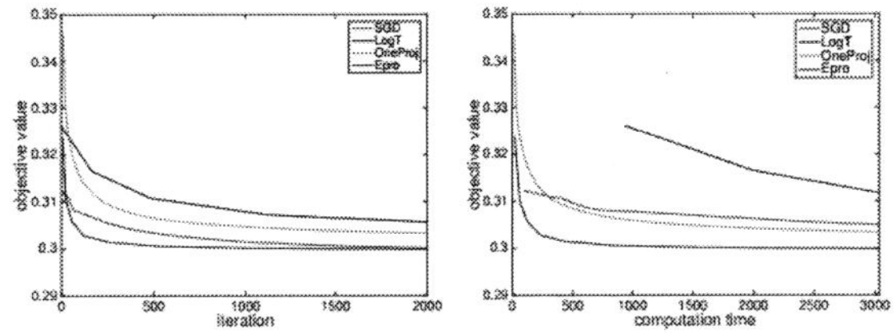

Figure 1: Empirical comparison of the four competing methods for solving Eq. (22). (1) Left plot: the change of the objective values with respect to the iteration number. (2) Right plot: the change of the objective values with respect to the computation time (in seconds).

- $O(logT)$-projections SGD method (logT) [33]: we set the step size $\eta_t = 1/(\sqrt{6}L)$ and logT achieves a rate of convergence $O(1/T)$, requiring $O(\log T)$ projections steps for a constrained strongly convex optimization problem.

- the proposed Epro-SGD with $O(logT)$ number of projections (Epro): we set the step size $\eta_t = 1/(\lambda t)$ and Epro archives a rate of convergence $O(1/T)$ with $O(\log T)$ projections steps for a constrained strongly convex optimization problem.

For illustration, we apply the competing algorithms for solving the constrained Lasso problem and the Large Margin Nearest Neighbor Classification (LMNN) in Eq. (21) respectively. We implement all algorithms using Matlab R2015a and conduct all simulations on an Intel(R) Xeon(R) CPU E5-2430 (15M Cache, 2.20 GHz).

5.1 EXPERIMENTS ON THE CONSTRAINED LASSO FORMULATION

We apply the proposed Epro-SGD algorithm and the other three competing algorithms to solve the L1-norm constrained least squares optimization problem

$$\begin{aligned} \min_w \quad & \frac{1}{2N}\sum_{i=1}^{N}\left(x_i^T w - y_i\right)^2 + \alpha\|w\|^2 \\ s.t. \quad & \|w\|_1 \leq \beta. \end{aligned} \tag{22}$$

Eq. (22) is an equivalent constrained counterpart of the well studied Lasso formation [29]. They aim at achieving entry-wise sparsity in the weight vector w while computing a linear predictor for regression.

We use the algebra data, a benchmark data from KDD Cup 2010 [28], for the following experiments. Specifically we use a preprocessed version of the algebra data[1] for our simulations. This preprocessed data set consists of $8,407,752$

[1] https://www.csie.ntu.edu.tw/ cjlin/libsvmtools/datasets/

samples from two classes, and each of the samples is represented as a feature feature of dimensionality $20,216,830$. In our experiments, we set $\alpha = 1$ and $\beta = 0.5$ for Eq. (22). We tune the initial step size respectively for each of the competing algorithms to get the (nearly) best performance; specifically in this experiments, we set $\eta_0 = 0.5$ for SGD, $\eta_0 = 0.3$ and $\lambda = 0.03$ for Epro, $\eta_0 = 0.1$ for OneProj, and $\eta_0 = 0.1$ for LogT.

In the experiments, we respectively run all competing algorithms for 2000 iterations; we then record the obtained objective values and the corresponding computation time. The experimental results are presented in Figure 1. The left plot shows how the objective value is changed with respect to the algorithm iteration. Note that for Eq. (22), the number of algorithm iterations is equal to the number of stochastic gradient computation (the access to the subgradient of the objective function). From this plot, we can observe that after running 2000 iterations, Epro and SGD attain smaller objective values, compared to OneProj and LogT; we can also observe that OneProj empirically converges slightly faster than logT. The right plot shows how the objective value is changed with respect to the computation time. For this experiment, we set the maximum computation time to 3035 seconds, which is the computation time required by running Epro for 2000 iterations. We can observe that Epro attain a smaller objective value, compared to the other three competing method; meanwhile, the standard SGD and OneProj attain similar objective values, given a fixed amount of computation time.

5.2 EXPERIMENTS ON THE LMNN FORMULATION

We apply the four competing algorithms to solve the LMNN formulation in Eq. (21). We use the Cora data [24] for the following experiments. Cora consists of 2708 scientific publications exclusively from 7 different categories. Each publication is represented by a normalized vector of length 1 and dimensionality 1433. From this data, we construct 5416 neighbor pairs (NP) by randomly selecting 2 publications of the same label; we then construct 16248 non-neighbor (NNT) by randomly selecting 3 non-neighbor publications (of a different label) for each of the NPs. Therefore, in each iteration of the SGD-type methods, we can use a NP and a NNT to construct a stochastic gradient for the optimization formulation. We set $c = 0.5$, $\mu_1 = 10^{-4}$, and $\mu_2 = 10^{-3}$ in Eq. (21). We terminate the algorithms when the iteration number is larger than $4,000$ or the relative change of the objective values in two iterations is smaller than 10^{-8}; we also record the obtained objective values, the required iteration number, and the computation time. Similarly we tune the initial step size respectively for the competing algorithms; specifically, we set $\eta_0 = 4 \times 10^{-8}$ for SGD, $\eta_0 = 10^{-5}$ and $\lambda = 0.1$ for Epro, $\eta_0 = 5 \times 10^{-7}$ for OneProj, and $\eta_0 = 10^{-6}$ for LogT.

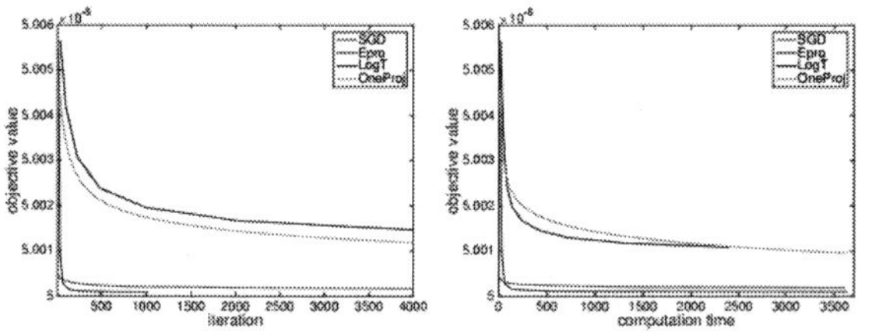

Figure 2: Empirical comparison of the four competing methods for solving Eq. (21). (1) Left plot: the change of the objective values with respect to the iteration number. (2) Right plot: the change of the objective value with respect to the computation time.

The experimental results are presented in Figure 2. Similarly in the left plot, we illustrate how the objective value changes with respect to the iteration number. For the LMNN formulation in Eq. (21), we can observe that Epro converges empirically much faster than all three competing algorithms; in particular, Epro converges after 1024 iterations, while the other 3 algorithms need more iterations. In the right plot, we illustrate how the objective value changes with respect to the computation time. We can observe that Epro converges using a smaller amount of computation time. specifically, in our experiment Epro converges with the computation time as 3622 seconds; while the other three competing algorithms need much more computation time.

6 CONCLUSIONS

We proposed an epoch-projection based SGD method, called Epro-SGD, for stochastic strongly convex optimization. The proposed Epro-SGD applies SGD on each iteration within its epochs and only performs a projection at the end of each epoch. Our analysis shows that Epro-SGD requires only a logarithmic number of projections, while achieves a guaranteed optimal rate of convergence both in expectation as well as with high probability. Additionally we proposed a variant of Epro-SGD based on an existing dual averaging method, called Epro-ORDA, which exploit structures of the optimization problems by incorporating an associated proximal mapping iteratively. For illustration, we applied the proposed Epro-SGD method for solving a large margin distance metric learning formulation and a constrained Lasso formulation respectively with a positive definite constraint. Our empirical results demonstrate the effectiveness of the proposed method.

References

[1] Bach, F., Moulines, E.: Non-asymptotic analysis of stochastic approximation algorithms for machine learning. In:

NIPS (2011)

[2] Beck, A., Teboulle, M.: A fast iterative shrinkage-thresholding algorithm for linear inverse problems. SIAM Journal on Imaging Sciences **2**(1), 183–202 (2009)

[3] Bottou, L.: Large-scale machine learning with stochastic gradient descent. In: COMPSTAT (2010)

[4] Boucheron, S., Lugosi, G., Bousquet, O.: Concentration inequalities. Advanced Lectures on Machine Learning pp. 208–240 (2004)

[5] Boyd, S., Vandenberghe, L.: Convex Optimization. Cambridge University Press (2004)

[6] Chen, X., Lin, Q., Pena, J.: Optimal regularized dual averaging methods for stochastic optimization. In: NIPS (2012)

[7] Clarkson, K.L.: Coresets, sparse greedy approximation, and the frank-wolfe algorithm. ACM Transactions on Algorithms **6**(4) (2010)

[8] Duchi, J., Singer, Y.: Efficient online and batch learning using forward backward splitting. Journal of Machine Learning Research **10**, 2899–2934 (2009)

[9] Duchi, J.C., Shalev-Shwartz, S., Singer, Y., Tewari, A.: Composite objective mirror descent. In: COLT (2010)

[10] Duchi, J.C., Singer, Y.: Efficient learning using forward-backward splitting. In: NIPS (2009)

[11] Frank, M., Wolfe, P.: An algorithm for quadratic programming. naval research logistics. Naval Research Logistics **3**(1-2), 95–110 (1956)

[12] Garber, D., Hazan, E.: A linearly convergent conditional gradient algorithm with applications to online and stochastic optimization. ArXiv:1301.4666 math.LG (2013)

[13] Gilpin, A., Peña, J., Sandholm, T.: First-order algorithm with log(1/epsilon) convergence for epsilon-equilibrium in two-person zero-sum games. Math. Program. **133**(1-2), 279–298 (2012)

[14] Hazan, E.: Sparse approximate solutions to semidefinite programs. In: LATIN, pp. 306–316 (2008)

[15] Hazan, E., Kale, S.: Beyond the regret minimization barrier: an optimal algorithm for stochastic strongly-convex optimization. Journal of Machine Learning Research - Proceedings Track **19**, 421–436 (2011)

[16] Hazan, E., Kale, S.: Projection-free online learning. In: ICML (2012)

[17] Jaggi, M.: Sparse convex optimization methods for machine learning. Ph.D. thesis, ETH Zurich (2011). DOI 10.3929/ethz-a-007050453

[18] Jaggi, M.: Revisiting frank-wolfe: Projection-free sparse convex optimization. In: ICML (2013)

[19] Liu, W., Tian, X., Tao, D., Liu, J.: Constrained metric learning via distance gap maximization. In: AAAI (2010)

[20] Mahdavi, M., Yang, T., Jin, R., Zhu, S., Yi, J.: Stochastic gradient descent with only one projection. In: NIPS (2012)

[21] Nemirovski, A., Juditsky, A., Lan, G., Shapiro, A.: Robust stochastic approximation approach to stochastic programming. SIAM Journal on Optimization **19**(4), 1574–1609 (2009)

[22] Nesterov, Y.: Gradient methods for minimizing composite objective function. Mathematical Programming **140**(1), 125–161 (2013)

[23] Nesterov, Y.: Introductory lectures on convex optimization: A basic course. Springer Science & Business Media (2013)

[24] Prithviraj, S., Galileo, N., Mustafa, B., Lise, G.: Collective classification in network data. AI Magazine **29**(3) (2008)

[25] Qi, G.J., Tang, J., Zha, Z.J., Chua, T.S., Zhang, H.J.: An efficient sparse metric learning in high-dimensional space via l1-penalized log-determinant regularization. In: ICML (2009)

[26] Rakhlin, A., Shamir, O., Sridharan, K.: Making gradient descent optimal for strongly convex stochastic optimization. In: ICML (2012)

[27] Shalev-Shwartz, S., Singer, Y., Srebro, N.: Pegasos: Primal estimated sub-gradient solver for svm. In: ICML (2007)

[28] Stamper, J., Niculescu-Mizil, A., Ritter, S., Gordon, G., Koedinger, K.: Algebra I 2008-2009. Challenge data set from KDD Cup 2010 Educational Data Mining Challenge. Find it at http://pslcdatashop.web.cmu.edu/KDDCup/downloads.jsp (2010)

[29] Tibshirani, R.: Regression shrinkage and selection via the lasso. Journal of the Royal Statistical Society: Series B **58**(1), 267–288 (1996)

[30] Weinberger, K.Q., Saul, L.K.: Distance metric learning for large margin nearest neighbor classification. Journal of Machine Learning Research **10**, 207–244 (2009)

[31] Yang, T., Lin, Q.: Stochastic subgradient methods with linear convergence for polyhedral convex optimization. arXiv:1510.01444 [cs.LG] (2015)

[32] Ying, Y., Li, P.: Distance metric learning with eigenvalue optimization. Journal of Machine Learning Research **13**(1), 1–26 (2012)

[33] Zhang, L., Yang, T., Jin, R., He, X.: O(logT) projections for stochastic optimization of smooth and strongly convex functions. In: ICML (2013)

Accelerated Stochastic Block Coordinate Gradient Descent for Sparsity Constrained Nonconvex Optimization

Jinghui Chen
Department of Systems and
Information Engineering
University of Virginia

Quanquan Gu
Department of Systems and
Information Engineering
University of Virginia

Abstract

We propose an accelerated stochastic block coordinate descent algorithm for nonconvex optimization under sparsity constraint in the high dimensional regime. The core of our algorithm is leveraging both stochastic partial gradient and full partial gradient restricted to each coordinate block to accelerate the convergence. We prove that the algorithm converges to the unknown true parameter at a linear rate, up to the statistical error of the underlying model. Experiments on both synthetic and real datasets backup our theory.

1 INTRODUCTION

High-dimensional statistics (Bühlmann and Van De Geer, 2011) deals with models in which the number of parameters d is comparable to or even larger than the sample size n. Since it is usually impossible to obtain a consistent estimator when both d and n increase, various types of statistical models with structural assumptions including sparse vectors, sparse matrices, low-rank matrices have been proposed and widely studied. In such a high dimensional regime, a general approach is solving a regularized optimization problem, which consists of a loss function measuring how well the model fits the data and some penalty function that encourages the assumed structures. For an overview of high dimensional statistics, please refer to Bühlmann and Van De Geer (2011); Negahban et al. (2009).

In this paper, instead of considering regularized estimator, we focus on the following sparsity constrained optimization problem:

$$\min_{\boldsymbol{\beta}} F(\boldsymbol{\beta}) \quad \text{subject to} \quad \|\boldsymbol{\beta}\|_0 \leq s, \qquad (1.1)$$

where $F(\boldsymbol{\beta}) = n^{-1}\sum_{i=1}^{n} f_i(\boldsymbol{\beta})$ is a sum of a finite number of convex and smooth functions, $\|\boldsymbol{\beta}\|_0$ is the number of nonzero elements in $\boldsymbol{\beta}$, and s is a tuning parameter that controls the sparsity of $\boldsymbol{\beta}$. The above problem is common in machine learning and statistics, such as the empirical risk minimization (ERM) and M-estimator, where $F(\boldsymbol{\beta})$ is the empirical loss function averaged over the training sample. For example, by choosing the squared loss $f_i(\boldsymbol{\beta}) = (\langle \boldsymbol{\beta}, \mathbf{x}_i \rangle - y_i)^2/2$, (1.1) becomes a sparsity constrained linear regression problem (Tropp and Gilbert, 2007).

Due to the nonconvexity of the sparsity constraint, the problem in (1.1) is in general NP hard. In order to obtain an approximate solution to (1.1), a variety of algorithms have been proposed. For example, when the objective function $F(\boldsymbol{\beta})$ is chosen to be the square loss function, it can be solved approximately by matching pursuit (Mallat and Zhang, 1993), orthogonal matching pursuit (Tropp and Gilbert, 2007), CoSaMP (Needell and Tropp, 2009), hard thresholding pursuit (Foucart, 2011), iterative hard thresholding (Blumensath and Davies, 2009) and forward backward feature selection algorithm (Zhang, 2011). For general loss functions, there also exists a set of algorithms such as forward feature selection (Shalev-Shwartz et al., 2010; Bahmani et al., 2013), forward backward feature selection algorithm (Jalali et al., 2011; Liu et al., 2013) and iterative gradient hard thresholding (Yuan et al., 2013; Jain et al., 2014). However, all the above algorithms are based on deterministic optimization such as gradient descent algorithm. In each iteration of gradient descent algorithm, it requires the evaluation of the full gradient over the n component functions, which is computationally very expensive, especially when n is large. In order to address this issue, Nguyen et al. (2014) proposed two stochastic iterative greedy algorithms. Yet neither of the algorithms attain linear rate of convergence for the objective function value. Li et al. (2016) proposed a stochastic variance reduced gradient hard thresholding algorithm. Nevertheless, it cannot leverage the coordinate block to accelerate the convergence.

In this paper, by leveraging the advantages of both stochastic gradient descent (Nemirovski et al., 2009; Lan, 2012) and randomized block coordinate descent (Shalev-Shwartz and Tewari, 2011; Nesterov, 2012; Beck and Tetruashvili, 2013; Richtárik and Takáč, 2014; Lu and Xiao, 2015), we propose a stochastic block coordinate gradient descent algorithm to solve the nonconvex sparsity constrained optimization problem in (1.1). The core of our algorithm is to exploit both stochastic partial gradient and full partial gradient restricted to each coordinate block. In detail, our algorithm consists of two layers of loops. For each iteration of the outer loop, the full gradient is computed once; while in the follow-up inner loop, partial stochastic gradient is computed to adjust the full gradient. We also incorporate mini-batch gradient computation into our algorithm, to further accelerate the convergence. Replacing full gradients with stochastic gradients restricted on coordinate blocks essentially trades the number of iterations with a low computational cost per iteration. We prove that the algorithm is guaranteed converge to the unknown true parameter $\boldsymbol{\beta}^*$ at a linear rate up to statistical error. The gradient complexity[1] of our algorithm is

$$\mathcal{O}\Big(\big(n + \kappa_{\tilde{s}}|\mathcal{B}|/k\big)\log(1/\epsilon)\Big),$$

where k is the number of coordinate blocks, $|\mathcal{B}|$ is the mini batch size, ϵ is the optimization error for the objective function value, and $\kappa_{\tilde{s}}$ is the condition number of the Hessian matrix $\nabla^2 F(\boldsymbol{\beta})$ restricted on any $\tilde{s} \times \tilde{s}$ principal submatrix. When $k = 1$ and $|\mathcal{B}| = 1$, our algorithm is reduced to accelerated gradient descent for the sparsity constrained nonconvex optimization problem. It improves the gradient complexity for gradient hard thresholding algorithms (Yuan et al., 2013; Jain et al., 2014) from $\mathcal{O}(n\kappa_{\tilde{s}}\log(1/\epsilon))$ to $\mathcal{O}[(n + \kappa_{\tilde{s}})\log(1/\epsilon)]$. Furthermore, for both sparse linear regression and sparse generalized linear model estimation, we show that the estimator from our algorithm attains the minimax optimal statistical rate. Experiments on both synthetic and real datasets backup our theory.

The remainder of this paper is organized as follows. In Section 2, we briefly review some related work. In Section 3, we review two examples of the optimization problems. We present the algorithm in Section 4, and analyze it in Section 5. In addition, we apply our theory to two specific examples and illustrate the corresponding theory for the two examples. We compare the proposed algorithm with existing algorithms in Section 6. Finally, we conclude this paper in Section 7.

Notation Let $\mathbf{A} = [A_{ij}] \in \mathbb{R}^{d\times d}$ be a matrix and $\mathbf{x} = [x_1, \ldots, x_d]^\top \in \mathbb{R}^d$ be vector. For $0 < q < \infty$, we define the ℓ_0, ℓ_q and ℓ_∞ vector norms as $\|\mathbf{x}\|_0 = \sum_{i=1}^d \mathbb{1}(x_i \neq 0)$, $\|\mathbf{x}\|_q = \Big(\sum_{i=1}^d |x_i|^q\Big)^{\frac{1}{q}}$ and $\|\mathbf{x}\|_\infty = \max_{1\leq i\leq d}|x_i|$, where $\mathbb{1}(\cdot)$ represents the indicator function. For a vector $\mathbf{x}$, we define $\mathrm{supp}(\mathbf{x})$ as the index set of nonzero entries of $\mathbf{x}$, and $\mathrm{supp}(\mathbf{x}, s)$ as the index set of the top s entries of $\mathbf{x}$ in terms of magnitude. In addition, we denote by $\mathbf{x}_S$ the restriction of $\mathbf{x}$ onto a index set S, such that $[\mathbf{x}_S]_i = x_i$ if $i \in S$, and $[\mathbf{x}_S]_i = 0$ if $i \notin S$. In addition, we denote by $\mathbf{x}_s$ the restriction of $\mathbf{x}$ onto the top s entries in terms of magnitude, i.e., $[\mathbf{x}_s]_i = x_i$ if $i \in \mathrm{supp}(\mathbf{x}, s)$, and $[\mathbf{x}_s]_i = 0$ if $i \notin \mathrm{supp}(\mathbf{x}, s)$. For a set $\mathcal{B}$, we denote its cardinality by $|\mathcal{B}|$. For a matrix $\mathbf{X}$, its i-th row is denoted by $\mathbf{X}_{i*}$ and its j-th column is denoted by $\mathbf{X}_{*j}$.

[1]Gradient complexity is defined to be the iteration complexity times the number of gradient evaluation on each component function

2 RELATED WORK

In this section, we briefly review additional lines of research beyond the sparsity constrained nonconvex optimization, that are relevant to our work.

Gradient descent is computationally expensive at each iteration, hence stochastic gradient descent is often used when the data set is large. At each iteration, only one or a mini-batch of the n component functions f_i is sampled (Nemirovski et al., 2009; Lan, 2012). Due to the variance in estimating the gradient by stochastic sampling, stochastic gradient descent has a sublinear rate of convergence even when $F(\boldsymbol{\beta})$ is strongly convex and smooth. To accelerate stochastic gradient descent, various types of accelerated stochastic gradient descent algorithms (Schmidt et al., 2013; Johnson and Zhang, 2013; Konečný and Richtárik, 2013; Defazio et al., 2014b; Mairal, 2014; Defazio et al., 2014a). The most relevant work to ours is stochastic variance reduced gradient (SVRG) (Johnson and Zhang, 2013) and its variants (Xiao and Zhang, 2014; Konečný et al., 2014a).

In contrast to gradient descent, block coordinate descent (BCD) (Shalev-Shwartz and Tewari, 2011; Nesterov, 2012; Beck and Tetruashvili, 2013; Richtárik and Takáč, 2014; Lu and Xiao, 2015) only computes the full gradient of $F(\boldsymbol{\beta})$ restricted on a randomly selected coordinate block at each iteration. Compared with gradient descent, the per-iteration time complexity of RBCD is much lower. However, such algorithms still compute the partial full gradient based on all the n component functions per iteration.

Stochastic block coordinate gradient descent was proposed recently (Dang and Lan, 2015; Xu and Yin, 2015; Reddi et al., 2014), which integrates the advantages of stochastic gradient descent and block coordinate descent. Such algorithms compute the stochastic partial gradient restricted to one coordinate block with respect to one component function, rather than the full partial derivative with respect to all the component functions. These algorithms essentially employ sampling of both coordinates and data instances at each iteration. However, they can only achieve a sublinear rate of convergence. Recently, randomized block coordinate descent using mini-batches (Zhao et al., 2014; Wang and Banerjee, 2014; Konečný et al., 2014b) are proposed independently to accelerate the convergence of stochastic block coordinate gradient descent.

Our work departs from the above studies by considering a sparsity constrained nonconvex optimization problem instead of convex optimization. Due to the nonconvex nature of (1.1), our algorithm is no longer guaranteed to converge to the global optimum. Nevertheless, by taking into account the underlying statistical models, we illustrate that proposed algorithm is guaranteed to converge to the unknown true model parameters up to the statistical error.

3 ILLUSTRATIVE EXAMPLES OF SPARSITY CONSTRAINED OPTIMIZATION

In this section, we give two examples of the statistical estimation problems, which fall in the sparsity constrained optimization problem in (1.1). We return to demonstrate the implication of our general algorithm and theory to these examples in Section 5.

Example 3.1 (Sparse Linear Regression). Consider the following linear regression model

$$\mathbf{y} = \mathbf{X}\boldsymbol{\beta}^* + \boldsymbol{\epsilon}, \tag{3.1}$$

where $\mathbf{y} \in \mathbb{R}^n$ denotes a vector of the responses, and $\mathbf{X} \in \mathbb{R}^{n\times d}$ is the design matrix, $\boldsymbol{\beta}^* \in \mathbb{R}^d$ is the unknown regression coefficient vector such that $\|\boldsymbol{\beta}^*\|_0 \le s^*$, and $\boldsymbol{\epsilon} \in \mathbb{R}^d$ is a noise vector. A commonly used estimator for the above sparse linear regression problem is the Lasso estimator (Tibshirani, 1996) with ℓ_1 norm penalty. An alternative estimator is the sparsity constrained estimator

$$\min_{\boldsymbol{\beta}\in\mathbb{R}^d} \frac{1}{2n}\|\mathbf{X}\boldsymbol{\beta} - \mathbf{y}\|_2^2 \quad \text{subject to} \quad \|\boldsymbol{\beta}\|_0 \le s, \tag{3.2}$$

where s is a tuning parameter, which controls the sparsity of $\boldsymbol{\beta}$. This is indeed an example of the nonconvex optimization problem in (1.1) where $F(\boldsymbol{\beta}) = 1/(2n)\|\mathbf{X}\boldsymbol{\beta} - \mathbf{y}\|_2^2$, $f_i(\boldsymbol{\beta}) = 1/2(\mathbf{x}_i^\top\boldsymbol{\beta} - y_i)^2$ and $\mathbf{x}_i \in \mathbb{R}^d$ is the i-th row of $\mathbf{X}$. Similar estimator has been studied by Tropp and Gilbert (2007); Zhang (2011); Jain et al. (2014), to mention a few.

Example 3.2 (Sparse Generalized Linear Models). We assume that the observations in each task are generated from generalized linear models

$$\mathbb{P}(y|\mathbf{x}, \boldsymbol{\beta}^*, \sigma) = \exp\left\{\frac{y\langle\boldsymbol{\beta}^*, \mathbf{x}\rangle - \Phi(\boldsymbol{\beta}^{*\top}\mathbf{x})}{c(\sigma)}\right\}, \tag{3.3}$$

where $\Phi(\cdot) : \mathbb{R} \to \mathbb{R}$ is a link function, $y \in \mathbb{R}$ is the response variable, $\mathbf{x} \in \mathbb{R}^d$ is the predictor vector, $\boldsymbol{\beta}^* \in \mathbb{R}^d$ is the parameter such that $\|\boldsymbol{\beta}^*\|_0 \le s^*$, and $c(\sigma) \in \mathbb{R}$ is fixed and known scale parameter. A special example of generalized linear model is the linear regression model where the noise follows from a Gaussian distribution, which corresponds to $c(\sigma) = \sigma^2$ and $\Phi(t) = t^2$. Logistic regression is another special case of the generalized linear model, where $\Phi(t) = \log(1 + \exp(t)), c(\sigma) = 1$ and $y \in \{0, 1\}$.

Given $\{\mathbf{x}_i, y_i\}_{i=1}^n$, a widely used estimator for $\boldsymbol{\beta}^*$ is the ℓ_1 regularized maximum likelihood estimator (Negahban et al., 2009; Loh and Wainwright, 2013). An alternative estimator is the sparsity constrained maximum likelihood estimator as follows

$$\min_{\boldsymbol{\beta}} -\frac{1}{n}\sum_{i=1}^n \frac{1}{c(\sigma)}\big[y_i\langle\boldsymbol{\beta}, \mathbf{x}_i\rangle - \Phi(\boldsymbol{\beta}^{*\top}\mathbf{x})\big],$$
$$\text{subject to} \quad \|\boldsymbol{\beta}\|_0 \le s. \tag{3.4}$$

The estimator in (3.4) has been investigated by Jalali et al. (2011); Yuan et al. (2013); Li et al. (2016).

For more examples, please refer to Yuan et al. (2013); Jain et al. (2014) and references therein.

4 THE PROPOSED ALGORITHM

In this section, we present an accelerated stochastic block coordinate descent algorithm based on nonconvex optimization for solving the proposed estimator in (1.1). The key motivation of the algorithm is using iterative hard thresholding to ensure cardinality constraint and mixed mini-batch partial gradient to reduce the variance of the stochastic gradient and accelerate the convergence. We display the algorithm in Algorithm 1.

Algorithm 1 Accelerated Stochastic Block Coordinate Gradient Descent with Hard Thresholding (ASBCDHT)

Initialization: $\widetilde{\boldsymbol{\beta}}^{(0)}$ **with** $\|\widetilde{\boldsymbol{\beta}}^{(0)}\|_0 \le s$
for $\ell = 1, 2, \ldots$ **do**
  $\widetilde{\boldsymbol{\beta}} = \widetilde{\boldsymbol{\beta}}^{(\ell-1)}$
  $\widetilde{\boldsymbol{\mu}} = \frac{1}{n}\sum_{i=1}^n \nabla f_i(\widetilde{\boldsymbol{\beta}})$
  $\boldsymbol{\beta}^{(0)} = \widetilde{\boldsymbol{\beta}}$
  Randomly sample z **uniformly from** $\{0, \ldots, m-1\}$
  for $t = 0, 1, \ldots, z-1$ **do**
    Randomly sample a mini-batch $\mathcal{B}$ **from** $\{1, \ldots, n\}$ **uniformly**
    Randomly sample j **from** $\{1, \ldots, k\}$ **uniformly**
    $[\mathbf{v}]_{\mathcal{G}_j} = \frac{1}{|\mathcal{B}|}\sum_{i\in\mathcal{B}} \nabla_{\mathcal{G}_j} f_i(\boldsymbol{\beta}^{(t)}) - \nabla_{\mathcal{G}_j} f_i(\widetilde{\boldsymbol{\beta}}) + \widetilde{\boldsymbol{\mu}}_{\mathcal{G}_j}$
    $\boldsymbol{\beta}^{(t+0.5)} = \boldsymbol{\beta}^{(t)} - \eta[\mathbf{v}]_{\mathcal{G}_j}$
    $\boldsymbol{\beta}^{(t+1)} = \mathrm{HT}(\boldsymbol{\beta}^{(t+0.5)}, s)$
  end for
  Set $\widetilde{\boldsymbol{\beta}}^{(\ell)} = \boldsymbol{\beta}^{(z)}$
end for

Note that in Algorithm 1, we have two layers of loops. In the outer loop, $\widetilde{\boldsymbol{\beta}}^{(r-1)}$ denotes the estimated parameter from previous stage, and $\widetilde{\boldsymbol{\mu}}$ denotes the full gradient computed based on $\widetilde{\boldsymbol{\beta}}^{(r-1)}$.

In the inner loop, Algorithm 1 integrates the advantages of randomized block coordinate descent and stochastic gradient descent together. Let $\{\mathcal{G}_1, \ldots, \mathcal{G}_k\}$ be a partition of all the d coordinates where $\mathcal{G}_j$ is a block of coordinates. In step 7, it uniformly samples a mini batch of component functions. And in step 8, it uniformly samples a coordinate block. The random sampling significantly reduces the computational cost. Based on the mini batch of component functions, and the coordinate block, it calculates the mixed partial gradient $[\mathbf{v}]_{\mathcal{G}_j}$ restricted on the selected coordinate block, which is the combination of the partial stochastic gradient and the partial full gradient (See step 9). Note that similar mixed gradient has been originally introduced in Johnson and Zhang (2013) and later adopted by Xiao and Zhang (2014); Konečný et al. (2014a); Zhao et al. (2014); Konečný et al. (2014b) to reduce the variance introduced by random sampling. More specifically, we can show that the variance of $[\mathbf{v}]_{\mathcal{G}_j}$ i.e., $\mathbb{E}[\|\mathbf{v}_{\widetilde{\mathcal{S}}} - \nabla_{\widetilde{\mathcal{S}}} F(\boldsymbol{\beta}^{(t)})\|_2^2]$ diminishes when $\boldsymbol{\beta}^{(t)}$ approaches the unknown true model parameter vector $\boldsymbol{\beta}^*$. $\boldsymbol{\beta}^{(t+0.5)}$ is the output of coordinate gradient descent step. Since $\boldsymbol{\beta}^{(t+0.5)}$ is not necessarily sparse after the coordinate descent update, in order to make it sparse, we apply a hard thresholding procedure (Yuan et al., 2013; Jain et al., 2014) right after coordinate descent step. The hard thresholding operator is defined as follows:

$$[\mathrm{HT}(\boldsymbol{\beta}, s)]_i = \begin{cases} \beta_i, & \text{if } i \in \mathrm{supp}(\boldsymbol{\beta}, s), \\ 0, & \text{otherwise.} \end{cases} \tag{4.1}$$

The hard thresholding step preserves the entries of $\boldsymbol{\beta}^{(t+0.5)}$ with the top s large magnitudes and sets the rest to zero. This gives rise to $\boldsymbol{\beta}^{(t+1)}$. Recall that s is a tuning parameter that controls the sparsity level.

5 MAIN THEORY AND IMPLICATIONS

In this section, we will present the main theory that characterizes the performance of Algorithm 1, followed which we show the consequences of our theory when it is applied to the two examples in Section 3.

5.1 MAIN THEORETICAL RESULTS

We first layout a set of definition and assumptions, that are essential for our main theory.

Definition 5.1 (Sparse Eigenvalues). Let $\widetilde{s}$ be a positive integer. The largest and smallest s-sparse eigenvalues of the Hessian matrix $\nabla^2 F(\boldsymbol{\beta})$ are

$$\rho_+(\widetilde{s}) = \sup_{\mathbf{v}} \left\{ \mathbf{v}^\top \nabla^2 F(\boldsymbol{\beta}) \mathbf{v} : \|\mathbf{v}\|_0 \le \widetilde{s}, \|\mathbf{v}\|_2 = 1, \boldsymbol{\beta} \in \mathbb{R}^d \right\},$$

$$\rho_-(\widetilde{s}) = \inf_{\mathbf{v}} \left\{ \mathbf{v}^\top \nabla^2 F(\boldsymbol{\beta}) \mathbf{v} : \|\mathbf{v}\|_0 \le \widetilde{s}, \|\mathbf{v}\|_2 = 1, \boldsymbol{\beta} \in \mathbb{R}^d \right\}.$$

Moreover, we define the restricted condition number $\kappa_{\widetilde{s}} = \rho_+(\widetilde{s})/\rho_-(\widetilde{s})$.

Based on the sparse eigenvalues, we make the following assumptions on $f_i(\boldsymbol{\beta})$ and $F(\boldsymbol{\beta})$ with respect to $\rho_+(\widetilde{s})$ and $\rho_-(\widetilde{s})$ mentioned above.

Assumption 5.2 (Restricted Strong Smoothness). $f_i(\boldsymbol{\beta})$ satisfies restricted strong smoothness condition at sparsity level $\widetilde{s}$ with a constant $\rho_+(\widetilde{s}) > 0$: for all $\boldsymbol{\beta}, \boldsymbol{\beta}'$ such that $\|\boldsymbol{\beta} - \boldsymbol{\beta}'\|_0 \le \widetilde{s}$, we have

$$f_i(\boldsymbol{\beta}) \le f_i(\boldsymbol{\beta}') + \nabla f_i(\boldsymbol{\beta}')^\top (\boldsymbol{\beta} - \boldsymbol{\beta}') + \frac{\rho_+(\widetilde{s})}{2} \|\boldsymbol{\beta} - \boldsymbol{\beta}'\|_2^2.$$

Assumption 5.3 (Restricted Strong Convexity). $F(\boldsymbol{\beta})$ satisfies restricted strong convexity condition at sparsity level $\widetilde{s}$ with a constant $\rho_-(\widetilde{s}) > 0$: for all $\boldsymbol{\beta}, \boldsymbol{\beta}'$ such that $\|\boldsymbol{\beta} - \boldsymbol{\beta}'\|_0 \le \widetilde{s}$, we have

$$F(\boldsymbol{\beta}) \ge F(\boldsymbol{\beta}') + \nabla F(\boldsymbol{\beta}')^\top (\boldsymbol{\beta} - \boldsymbol{\beta}') + \frac{\rho_-(\widetilde{s})}{2} \|\boldsymbol{\beta} - \boldsymbol{\beta}'\|_2^2.$$

Assumptions 5.2 and 5.3 indicate that function $f_i(\boldsymbol{\beta})$ is smooth and function $F(\boldsymbol{\beta})$ is strongly convex when restricted on to a sparse subspace. These restricted strong smoothness and strong convexity conditions ensure that the standard convex optimization results for strongly convex and smooth objective functions (Nesterov, 2004) can be applied to our problem settings as well. It is worth noting that we do not require each $f_i(\boldsymbol{\beta})$ to be restricted strongly convex, we only require their summation $F(\boldsymbol{\beta})$ is restricted strongly convex. $f_i(\boldsymbol{\beta})$ typically does not satisfy restricted strong convexity for $\widetilde{s} > 1$. Recall that, in Example 3.1, $f_i(\boldsymbol{\beta}) = 1/2(\mathbf{x}_i^\top \boldsymbol{\beta} - y_i)^2$, which is obviously not restricted strongly convex unless $\widetilde{s} = 1$.

Now we are ready to present our main theorem.

Theorem 5.4. Suppose Assumptions 5.2 and 5.3 hold with $\widetilde{s} = 2s + s^*$. In addition, assume that $0 < \eta \le 1/(18\rho_+(\widetilde{s}))$ and m, s are chosen such that,

$$\alpha = \frac{2k\tau^{m-1}(\tau - 1)}{\rho_-(\widetilde{s})\eta\gamma(\tau^m - 1)} + \frac{12\eta\rho_+(\widetilde{s})(n - |\mathcal{B}|)}{|\mathcal{B}|(n-1)\gamma} < 1,$$

where $\gamma = 1 - 12\eta\rho_+(\widetilde{s})(n - |\mathcal{B}|)/\big[|\mathcal{B}|(n-1)\big] - 6\eta\rho_+(\widetilde{s})$ and $\tau = 1 + 2\sqrt{s^*}/\sqrt{s - s^*}$. Then the estimator $\widetilde{\boldsymbol{\beta}}^{(\ell)}$ from Algorithm 1 satisfies

$$\mathbb{E}\big[F(\widetilde{\boldsymbol{\beta}}^{(\ell)}) - F(\boldsymbol{\beta}^*)\big] \le \alpha^\ell \mathbb{E}\big[F(\widetilde{\boldsymbol{\beta}}^{(0)}) - F(\boldsymbol{\beta}^*)\big] + \frac{3\eta}{2\gamma(1-\alpha)} \|\nabla_{\widetilde{\mathcal{S}}} F(\boldsymbol{\beta}^*)\|_2^2. \tag{5.1}$$

We have the following remarks regarding the above theorem results:

Remark 5.5. Theorem 5.4 implies that in order to achieve linear rate of convergence, the learning rate η need to be set sufficiently small, the sparsity constraint s and the number of inner loop iterations m should be set sufficiently large such that $\alpha \le 1$. Here we provide an example showing

Table 1: A comparison of gradient complexity for different algorithms.

Algorithms	Gradient Complexity
Nguyen et al. (2014)	$\mathcal{O}(1/\epsilon)$
Yuan et al. (2013)	$\mathcal{O}\big(n\kappa_{\widetilde{s}} \cdot \log(1/\epsilon)\big)$
Li et al. (2016)	$\mathcal{O}\big([n + \kappa_{\widetilde{s}}] \cdot \log(1/\epsilon)\big)$
Ours	$\mathcal{O}\big((n + \kappa_{\widetilde{s}}\lvert\mathcal{B}\rvert/k) \cdot \log(1/\epsilon)\big)$

this is absolutely achievable. Without loss of generality, we consider the simplified scenario where the batch size $|\mathcal{B}| = 1$ and coordinate block number $k = 1$. As stated in the theorem condition, suppose we choose $\eta = 1/(36\rho_+(\widetilde{s}))$, then we have $\gamma = 1/2$. This simplifies the expression of α to:

$$\alpha = 144\kappa_{\widetilde{s}} \cdot \frac{\tau^m}{\tau^m - 1}\Big(1 - \frac{1}{\tau}\Big) + \frac{2}{3},$$

Therefore, provided that s is chosen to be

$$s \geq \big(1 + 4(1728\kappa_{\widetilde{s}} - 1)^2\big)s^*, \ m \geq \log 2 \cdot (1728\kappa_{\widetilde{s}} - 1),$$

we have,

$$\frac{\tau^m}{\tau^m - 1} \leq 2, \ \Big(1 - \frac{1}{\tau}\Big) \leq \frac{1}{1728\kappa_{\widetilde{s}}},$$

which immediately verifies that $\alpha \leq \frac{5}{6} < 1$.

Remark 5.6. Theorem 5.4 illustrates the linear rate of convergence in objective function value gap. From (5.1), in order to ensure that the linear converging term satisfies $\alpha^\ell\big[F(\widetilde{\beta}^{(0)}) - F(\beta^*)\big] \leq \epsilon$, the number of stages should satisfy

$$\ell \geq \log_{\alpha^{-1}} \frac{F(\widetilde{\beta}^{(0)}) - F(\beta^*)}{\epsilon}.$$

Thus we need $\mathcal{O}(\log(1/\epsilon))$ outer iterations in Algorithm 1. Recall that from Remark 5.5, we have $m = \Omega(\kappa_{\widetilde{s}})$. Since in each outer iteration, we need to compute one full gradient and m mixed mini-batch gradient, the overall gradient complexity is $\mathcal{O}\big((n + \kappa_{\widetilde{s}} \cdot |\mathcal{B}|/k) \cdot \log(1/\epsilon)\big)$, where k is the number of coordinate blocks, $|\mathcal{B}|$ is the batch size, and $\kappa_{\widetilde{s}}$ is the restricted condition number of $\nabla^2 F(\beta^*)$. For the ease of comparison, we summarize the gradient complexity of our algorithm as well as the other state of the art algorithms in Table 1. As we can see, our proposed algorithm improves gradient complexity over previous work. In particular, with $k > 1$ and $|\mathcal{B}| = 1$, the gradient complexity of our algorithm outperforms that of Li et al. (2016). In the special case that $k = 1$ and $|\mathcal{B}| = 1$, our algorithm has the same gradient complexity as Li et al. (2016). In general, our algorithm provides more flexibility than Li et al. (2016) by incorporating mini-batch technique.

Theorem 5.4 immediately implies the following results.

Corollary 5.7. Under the same conditions of Theorem 5.4, the estimator $\widetilde{\beta}^{(\ell)}$ from Algorithm 1 satisfies

$$\mathbb{E}\|\widetilde{\beta}^{(\ell)} - \beta^*\|_2 \leq \underbrace{\alpha^{\ell/2}\sqrt{\frac{2\big[F(\widetilde{\beta}^{(0)}) - F(\beta^*)\big]}{\rho_-(\widetilde{s})}}}_{\text{Optimization Error}} + \underbrace{\left(\frac{2}{\rho_-(\widetilde{s})} + \sqrt{\frac{3\eta}{\gamma\rho_-(\widetilde{s})(1-\alpha)}}\right)\sqrt{\widetilde{s}}\|\nabla F(\beta^*)\|_\infty}_{\text{Statistical Error}}. \tag{5.2}$$

We have the following remark regarding the above result.

Remark 5.8. The right hand side of (5.2) consists of two terms. The first term is the optimization error, which goes to zero as ℓ increase, since $\alpha \in (0, 1)$. The second term corresponds to the statistical error, and is proportional to $\sqrt{\widetilde{s}}\|\nabla F(\beta^*)\|_\infty$. Since $\widetilde{s} = s + s^*$ and $s = O(s^*)$, the statistical is actually in the order of $\sqrt{s^*}\|\nabla F(\beta^*)\|_\infty$. Note that the statistical error of the regularized M estimators (Negahban et al., 2009; Loh and Wainwright, 2013) for sparse linear regression and generalized linear models, is also proportional to $\sqrt{s^*}\|\nabla F(\beta^*)\|_\infty$. Theorem 5.7 suggests that our algorithm attains a linear rate of convergence to the true parameter, up to the statistical error. In other words, our algorithm linearly converges to a local optima, which enjoys good statistical property.

5.2 IMPLICATION FOR SPECIFIC STATISTICAL ESTIMATION PROBLEMS

We now turn to the consequences of our algorithm and general theory for specific statistical estimation problems that arise in applications. In particular, we show the theoretical results by applying our theory to the two examples introduced in Section 3.

We begin with a corollary for the problem of sparse linear regression, as introduced in Example 3.1. We assume that the noise vector ϵ in (3.1) is zero-mean and has sub-Gaussian tails.

Assumption 5.9. ϵ is a zero mean random vector, and there exists a constant $\sigma > 0$ such that for any fixed $\|\mathbf{v}\|_2 = 1$, we have

$$\mathbb{P}\big(|\mathbf{v}^\top\epsilon| > \delta\big) \leq 2\exp\Big(-\frac{\delta^2}{2\sigma^2}\Big) \quad \text{for all} \quad \delta > 0.$$

In addition, without loss of generality, we make an additional assumption on the design matrices $\mathbf{X}$ in (3.1).

Assumption 5.10. For all columns in $\mathbf{X} \in \mathbb{R}^{n\times d}$, we have $\|\mathbf{X}_{*j}\|_2 \leq \sqrt{n}$, where $\mathbf{X}_{*j}$ is the j-th column of $\mathbf{X}$.

Note that Assumption 5.10 is often made in the analysis of Lasso estimator (Negahban et al., 2009; Zhang et al., 2009).

Corollary 5.11. Under the same conditions as Corollary 5.7, if Assumptions 5.9 and 5.10 hold, then with probability at least $1 - 1/d$, the estimator $\widetilde{\beta}^{(\ell)}$ from Algorithm 1 for sparse linear regression in (3.2) satisfies

$$\mathbb{E}\|\widetilde{\boldsymbol{\beta}}^{(\ell)} - \boldsymbol{\beta}^*\|_2 \le \underbrace{\alpha^{\ell/2}\sqrt{\frac{2\big[F(\widetilde{\boldsymbol{\beta}}^{(0)}) - F(\boldsymbol{\beta}^*)\big]}{\rho_-(\widetilde{s})}}}_{\text{Optimization Error}} + \underbrace{C\Bigg(\frac{2}{\rho_-(\widetilde{s})} + \sqrt{\frac{3\eta}{\gamma\rho_-(\widetilde{s})(1-\alpha)}}\Bigg)\sigma\sqrt{\frac{s^*\log d}{n}}}_{\text{Statistical Error}}, \quad (5.3)$$

where σ is the variance proxy of the sub-Gaussian random vector $\boldsymbol{\epsilon}$.

Corollary 5.11 suggests that when applying our algorithm to sparse linear regression, it achieves $O(\sqrt{s^* \log d/n})$ statistical error. It matches the minimax optimal rate for sparse linear regression (Raskutti et al., 2011).

We then provide a corollary for the problem of sparse generalized linear model estimation, as introduced in Example 3.2. For generalized linear model, we need the following assumption on its link function $\Phi(t)$, which is introduced in (3.3).

Assumption 5.12. There exists one $\alpha_u > 0$ such that the second derivative of the link function satisfies $\Phi''(t) \le \alpha_u$ for all $t \in \mathbb{R}$.

Similar assumption has been made in Loh and Wainwright (2013).

Corollary 5.13. Under the same conditions as Corollary 5.7, if Assumptions 5.10 and 5.12 hold, then with probability at least $1 - 1/d$, the estimator $\widetilde{\beta}^{(\ell)}$ from Algorithm 1 for sparse generalized linear models in (3.4) satisfies

$$\mathbb{E}\|\widetilde{\boldsymbol{\beta}}^{(\ell)} - \boldsymbol{\beta}^*\|_2 \le \underbrace{\alpha^{\ell/2}\sqrt{\frac{2\big[F(\widetilde{\boldsymbol{\beta}}^{(0)}) - F(\boldsymbol{\beta}^*)\big]}{\rho_-(\widetilde{s})}}}_{\text{Optimization Error}} + \underbrace{C\Bigg(\frac{2}{\rho_-(\widetilde{s})} + \sqrt{\frac{3\eta}{\gamma\rho_-(\widetilde{s})(1-\alpha)}}\Bigg)\alpha_u\sqrt{\frac{s^*\log d}{n}}}_{\text{Statistical Error}}, \quad (5.4)$$

where α_u is an upper bound on the second derivative of the link function $\Phi(t)$.

Corollary 5.13 demonstrates that when applying our algorithm to sparse generalized linear models, it achieves $O(\sqrt{s^* \log d/n})$ statistical error rate. It is also minimax rate-optimal.

6 EXPERIMENTS

In this section, we apply Algorithm 1 to the two examples discussed in Section 3, and present numerical results on both synthetic and large-scale real datasets to verify the performance of the proposed algorithm, and compare it with state-of-the-art sparsity cardinality constraint methods.

6.1 BASELINE METHODS

We compare our algorithm with several state-of-the-art baseline methods: (1) gradient descent with hard thresholding (GraHTP) by Yuan et al. (2013) ; (2) stochastic variance reduced gradient with hard thresholding by Li et al. (2016) (SVRGHT); (3) Our proposed accelerated stochastic block coordinate gradient descent with hard thresholding (ASBCDHT) with batch size $|\mathcal{B}| = 1$; and (4) Our proposed accelerated stochastic block coordinate descent with hard thresholding (ASBCDHT) with batch size $|\mathcal{B}| = 10$. Since our algorithm involves coordinate block, we set the block number as $k = 10$, where each block has (almost) the same number of coordinates. In addition, SVRGHT and ASBCDHT are based on mixed (partial) gradients, hence we need to specify the number of iterations for the inner loop. We simply choose $m = n$ since our theory demonstrates that m should be chosen as $\Omega(\kappa_{\widetilde{s}})$.

In order to fairly compare the above algorithms, we notice that at each iteration of GradHTP and SVRGHT, the gradient is updated with respect to all coordinates. When in our algorithm, at each iteration of Algorithm 1 the gradient is updated with respect to only a sampled coordinate block among all coordinates, so the computational cost is lower than that of gradient descent per iteration. Therefore, comparing algorithms that update the gradient with respect to different numbers of coordinates per iteration should be based on the same number of entire data passes (the least possible iterations for passing through the entire data set with respect to all coordinates).

6.2 SPARSE LINEAR REGRESSION

We first investigate the sparsity constrained linear regression problem in (3.2).

6.2.1 Synthetic Data

We generate an $n \times d$ design matrix $\mathbf{X}$ with rows drawn independently from a multivariate normal distribution $N(\mathbf{0}, \boldsymbol{\Sigma})$, where each element of $\boldsymbol{\Sigma}$ is defined by $\Sigma_{ij} = 0.6^{|i-j|}$. The true regression coefficient vector $\boldsymbol{\beta}^*$ has s^* nonzero entries that are drawn independently from the standard normal distribution. The response vector is generated by $\mathbf{y} = \mathbf{X}^\top\boldsymbol{\beta}^* + \boldsymbol{\epsilon}$, where each entry of $\boldsymbol{\epsilon}$ follows a normal distribution with zero mean and variance $\sigma^2 = 0.01$. In this part, we test our proposed algorithm

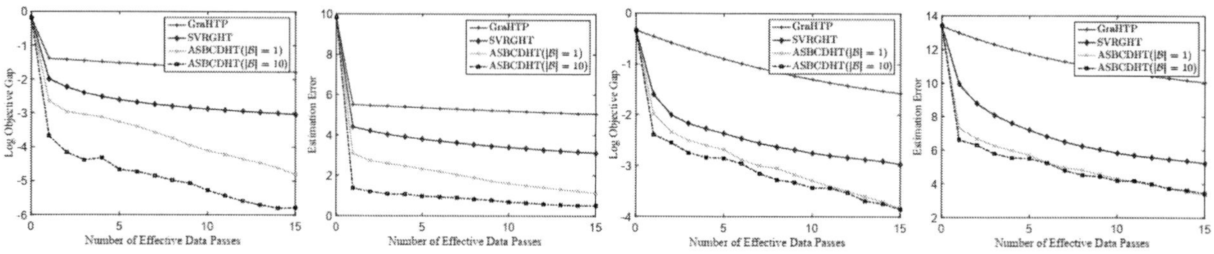

(a) (b) (c) (d)

Figure 1: Comparison of different algorithms for sparsity constrained sparse linear regression on the two synthetic datasets: (1) $n = 1000, d = 2000, s^* = 100$ (shown in (a) and (b)); (2) $n = 5000, d = 10000, s^* = 500$ (shown in (c) and (d)). (a) and (c) show the logarithm of the function value gap for the two datasets. (b) and (d) demonstrate the estimation error for the two datasets.

Table 2: Regression on E2006-TFIDF: MSE comparison of algorithms for the same entire effective data passes over 10 replications. The boldfaced results denote the lowest MSE among all the algorithms for the same entire effective data passes.

Method	#Data Passes=3	#Data Passes=6	#Data Passes=9	#Data Passes=12	#Data Passes=15
GraHTP	1.3388	1.1204	1.0522	1.0190	0.9970
SVRGHT	0.8809±0.0949	0.8150±0.0718	0.7819±0.0612	0.7574±0.0539	0.7385±0.0483
ASBCDHT($\|\mathcal{B}\|$ =1)	0.7039±0.1037	0.6835±0.0789	0.6709±0.0677	0.6607±0.0600	0.6518±0.0533
ASBCDHT($\|\mathcal{B}\|$ =10)	**0.7003**±0.1118	**0.6769**±0.0806	**0.6627**±0.0626	**0.6519**±0.0519	**0.6426**±0.0415

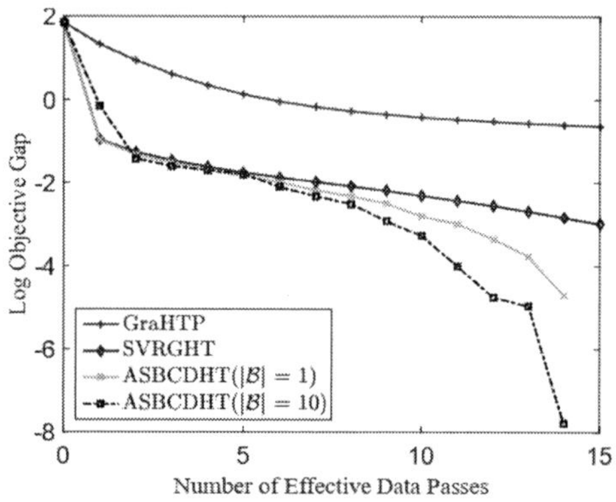

Figure 2: Comparison of different algorithms in terms of the logarithm of objective function value gap on E2006-TFIDF dataset.

along with with the state-of-the-art algorithms in two different settings: (1) $n = 1000, d = 2000, s^* = 100$; and (2) $n = 5000, d = 10000, s^* = 500$. Each experiment is repeated for 10 times. For each algorithm, we plot the logarithm of the objective function value gap and the estimation error $\|\boldsymbol{\beta}^{(t)} - \boldsymbol{\beta}^*\|_2$ for comparison. The sparsity parameter s is set to $s = 1.2s^*$ for all the algorithms according to the theory. The step size η of different algorithms is tuned by cross validation.

In Figure 1, we compare the logarithm of the function value gap and the estimation error in the above two datasets for all algorithms. Figure 1 (a) and (c) demonstrate that the optimization error decreases to zero at a linear rate while 1 (b) and (d) show that the estimation error of the estimator converges to certain level after some number of effective data passes. This is consistent with our theory in Corollary 5.11 that the estimation error of our algorithm consists of two terms: the optimization error that goes to zero, and the statistical error that depends on the problem parameters (d, n, s^* and so on). From Figure 1, it is obvious that our proposed algorithm outperforms other state-of-the-art algorithms in estimation error after the same number of effective data passes. Also note that when the data size is relatively small, our algorithm with batch size equals 10 performs better than the case when batch size equals 1, while this advantage decays as the data size grows. This is probably because the mini-batch sampling is more advantageous when the data are relatively small.

6.2.2 E2006-TFIDF Data

We use E2006-TFIDF dataset to test the sparsity constrained linear regression, which predicts risk from financial reports from thousands of publicly traded U.S. companies (Kogan et al., 2009). It contains 16,087 training instances, 3,308 testing instances and we randomly sample 50,000 features for this experiment. In this section, we choose $s = 2000$ and compare all algorithms using mean square error (MSE) for 15 entire effective data passes over 10 replications. The step size η is chosen by cross validation on the training data.

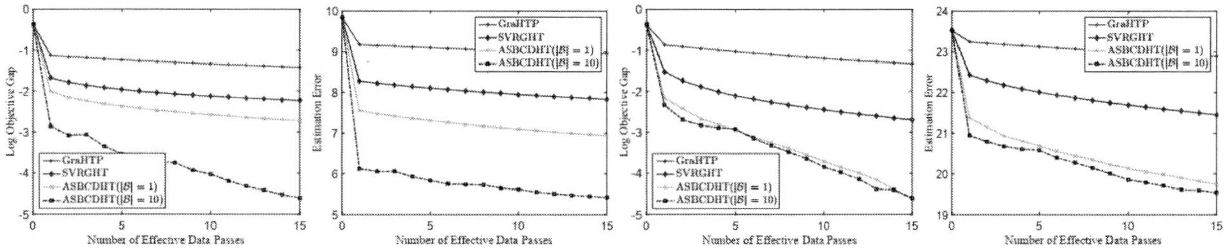

(a) (b) (c) (d)

Figure 3: Comparison of different algorithms for sparsity constrained sparse logistic regression on the two synthetic datasets: (1) $n = 1000, d = 2000, s^* = 100$ (shown in (a) and (b)); (2) $n = 5000, d = 10000, s^* = 500$ (shown in (c) and (d)). (a) and (c) show the logarithm of the function value gap for the two datasets. (b) and (d) are the estimation error for the two datasets.

Table 3: Classification on RCV1: classification error comparison of algorithms for the same entire effective data passes over 10 replications. The boldfaced results denote the lowest classification error among all the algorithms for the same entire effective data passes.

Method	#Data Passes=3	#Data Passes=6	#Data Passes=9	#Data Passes=12	#Data Passes=15
GraHTP	0.0758	0.0748	0.0739	0.0733	0.0727
SVRGHT	0.0848±0.0043	0.0763±0.0034	0.0708±0.0029	0.0677±0.0025	0.0671±0.0020
ASBCDHT($\|\mathcal{B}\|$ =1)	0.0662±0.0044	0.0648±0.0025	0.0644±0.0019	0.0642±0.0021	0.0639±0.0021
ASBCDHT($\|\mathcal{B}\|$ =10)	**0.0550**±0.0043	**0.0542**±0.0034	**0.0539**±0.0029	**0.0534**±0.0025	**0.0527**±0.0020

Figure 2 illustrates the logarithm of the objective function value gap for all the baseline algorithms and ours. We can see that our algorithm converges faster than the other baselines and our algorithm converges to much smaller objective function value than the other algorithms. In addition, Table 2 shows the mean value as well as the standard error of MSE for all the algorithms with respect to the number of effective data passes. Since there is no randomness in GraHTP, its standard error is zero. We can see that our algorithm attains much smaller mean square error than the other baseline algorithms for the same entire effective data passes. In particular, when the number of data passes equals 3, 6, 9 and 12, our ASBCDHT with batch size $\mathcal{B} = 10$ achieves the lowest MSE; and when the number of data passes equals 15, our ASBCDHT with batch size $\mathcal{B} = 1$ achieves the best performance.

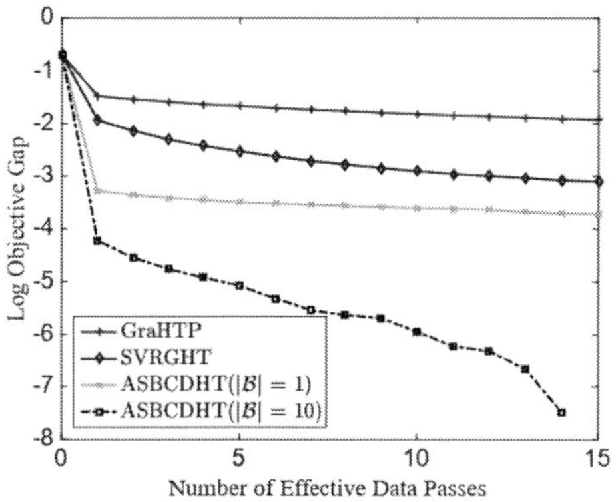

Figure 4: Comparison of different algorithms in terms of the logarithm of the objective function value gap on RCV1 dataset.

6.3 SPARSE LOGISTIC REGRESSION

We then evaluate the sparsity constrained generalized linear model, by considering a particular instance of sparse generalized linear model, i.e., sparse logistic regression. Its estimator is given by

$$\min_{\beta \in \mathbb{R}^d} \frac{1}{n} \sum_{i=1}^{n} \big[- y_i \cdot \mathbf{x}_i^\top \boldsymbol{\beta} + \log\big(1 + \exp(\mathbf{x}_i^\top \boldsymbol{\beta})\big)\big]$$
$$\text{subject to} \quad \|\boldsymbol{\beta}\|_0 \leq s,$$

where $y_i \in \{0, 1\}$. Similar estimator has been studied by Yuan et al. (2013).

6.3.1 Synthetic Data

We generate an $n \times d$ design matrix $\mathbf{X}$ with rows drawn independently from a multivariate normal distribution $N(\mathbf{0}, \mathbf{I})$, where $\mathbf{I}$ is a $d \times d$ identity matrix. The true regression coefficient vector $\boldsymbol{\beta}^*$ has s^* nonzero entries that are drawn independently from the standard normal distribution. Each response variable is generated from the logistic distribution

$$y_i = \begin{cases} 1, & \text{with probability } 1/(1 + \exp(\mathbf{x}_i^\top \boldsymbol{\beta}^*)), \\ 0, & \text{with probability } 1 - 1/(1 + \exp(\mathbf{x}_i^\top \boldsymbol{\beta}^*)). \end{cases}$$

In this part, we test our proposed algorithm along with the baseline algorithms in two different datasets: (1) $n = 1000, d = 2000, s^* = 100$; and (2) $n = 5000, d = 10000, s^* = 500$. Each experiment is repeated for 10 times and for all algorithms we plot the logarithm of the objective function value gap and the estimation error $\|\beta^{(t)} - \beta^*\|_2$ for comparison. The sparsity parameter s is again set to $s = 1.2s^*$. And the step size η is chosen by cross validation.

Figure 3 illustrates the logarithm of the function value gap and the estimation error $\|\beta^{(t)} - \beta^*\|_2$. The four sub-figures in Figure 3 demonstrate the similar trends as in Figure 1. Our proposed algorithm outperforms the other baseline algorithms by a large margin.

6.3.2 RCV1 Data

In order to evaluate the sparsity constrained logistic regression, we use RCV1 dataset, which is a Reuters Corpus Volume I data set for text categorization research (Lewis et al., 2004). Reuters Corpus Volume I (RCV1) is an archive of over 800,000 manually categorized newswire stories made available by Reuters, Ltd. for research purposes. This dataset contains $20,242$ training instances, $677,399$ testing instances and $47,236$ features. We use the whole training set and a subset of the test set, which contains $20,000$ testing instances for our experiment. In detail, we choose $s = 500$ and compare all algorithms in terms of their classification error on the test set for 15 entire effective data passes over 10 replications. The step size η is chosen by cross validation on the training set.

Table 3 demonstrates the classification results for the four algorithms including ours. It is obvious that our proposed algorithm achieves the lowest test error on RCV1 dataset on all periods of effective data passes and beats the other state-of-the-art baseline algorithms. Figure 4 further illustrates the logarithm of the objective function value gap for both the baseline algorithms and ours. This clearly demonstrates the superiority of our algorithm.

7 CONCLUSIONS

We proposed an accelerated stochastic block coordinate descent algorithm for sparsity constrained nonconvex optimization problems. We show that the algorithm enjoys a linear rate of convergence to the unknown true parameter up to the statistical error. Experiments on both synthetic and real datasets verify the effectiveness of our algorithm.

Acknowledgements

We would like to thank the anonymous reviewers for their helpful comments. Research was sponsored by Quanquan Gu's startup funding at Department of Systems and Information Engineering, University of Virginia.

References

BAHMANI, S., RAJ, B. and BOUFOUNOS, P. T. (2013). Greedy sparsity-constrained optimization. *The Journal of Machine Learning Research* **14** 807–841.

BECK, A. and TETRUASHVILI, L. (2013). On the convergence of block coordinate descent type methods. *SIAM Journal on Optimization* **23** 2037–2060.

BLUMENSATH, T. and DAVIES, M. E. (2009). Iterative hard thresholding for compressed sensing. *Applied and Computational Harmonic Analysis* **27** 265–274.

BÜHLMANN, P. and VAN DE GEER, S. (2011). *Statistics for high-dimensional data: methods, theory and applications.* Springer Science & Business Media.

DANG, C. D. and LAN, G. (2015). Stochastic block mirror descent methods for nonsmooth and stochastic optimization. *SIAM Journal on Optimization* **25** 856–881.

DEFAZIO, A., BACH, F. and LACOSTE-JULIEN, S. (2014a). Saga: A fast incremental gradient method with support for non-strongly convex composite objectives. In *Advances in Neural Information Processing Systems.*

DEFAZIO, A. J., CAETANO, T. S. and DOMKE, J. (2014b). Finito: A faster, permutable incremental gradient method for big data problems. In *Proceedings of the International Conference on Machine Learning.*

FOUCART, S. (2011). Hard thresholding pursuit: an algorithm for compressive sensing. *SIAM Journal on Numerical Analysis* **49** 2543–2563.

JAIN, P., TEWARI, A. and KAR, P. (2014). On iterative hard thresholding methods for high-dimensional m-estimation. In *Advances in Neural Information Processing Systems.*

JALALI, A., JOHNSON, C. C. and RAVIKUMAR, P. K. (2011). On learning discrete graphical models using greedy methods. In *Advances in Neural Information Processing Systems.*

JOHNSON, R. and ZHANG, T. (2013). Accelerating stochastic gradient descent using predictive variance reduction. In *Advances in Neural Information Processing Systems.*

KOGAN, S., LEVIN, D., ROUTLEDGE, B. R., SAGI, J. S. and SMITH, N. A. (2009). Predicting risk from financial reports with regression. In *Proceedings of Human Language Technologies: The 2009 Annual Conference of the North American Chapter of the Association for Computational Linguistics.* Association for Computational Linguistics.

KONEČNÝ, J., LIU, J., RICHTÁRIK, P. and TAKÁČ, M. (2014a). ms2gd: Mini-batch semi-stochastic gradient descent in the proximal setting. *arXiv:1410.4744* .

KONEČNÝ, J., QU, Z. and RICHTÁRIK, P. (2014b). Semi-stochastic coordinate descent. *arXiv:1412.6293* .

KONEČNÝ, J. and RICHTÁRIK, P. (2013). Semi-stochastic gradient descent methods. *arXiv:1312.1666* .

LAN, G. (2012). An optimal method for stochastic composite optimization. *Mathematical Programming* **133** 365–397.

LEWIS, D. D., YANG, Y., ROSE, T. G. and LI, F. (2004). Rcv1: A new benchmark collection for text categorization research. *The Journal of Machine Learning Research* **5** 361–397.

LI, X., ZHAO, T., ARORA, R., LIU, H. and HAUPT, J. (2016). Stochastic variance reduced optimization for nonconvex sparse learning. Tech. rep.

LIU, J., FUJIMAKI, R. and YE, J. (2013). Forward-backward greedy algorithms for general convex smooth functions over a cardinality constraint. *arXiv preprint arXiv:1401.0086* .

LOH, P.-L. and WAINWRIGHT, M. J. (2013). Regularized m-estimators with nonconvexity: Statistical and algorithmic theory for local optima. In *Advances in Neural Information Processing Systems*.

LU, Z. and XIAO, L. (2015). On the complexity analysis of randomized block-coordinate descent methods. *Mathematical Programming* **152** 615–642.

MAIRAL, J. (2014). Incremental majorization-minimization optimization with application to large-scale machine learning. *arXiv:1402.4419* .

MALLAT, S. G. and ZHANG, Z. (1993). Matching pursuits with time-frequency dictionaries. *Signal Processing, IEEE Transactions on* **41** 3397–3415.

NEEDELL, D. and TROPP, J. A. (2009). Cosamp: Iterative signal recovery from incomplete and inaccurate samples. *Applied and Computational Harmonic Analysis* **26** 301–321.

NEGAHBAN, S., YU, B., WAINWRIGHT, M. J. and RAVIKUMAR, P. K. (2009). A unified framework for high-dimensional analysis of m-estimators with decomposable regularizers. In *Advances in Neural Information Processing Systems*.

NEMIROVSKI, A., JUDITSKY, A., LAN, G. and SHAPIRO, A. (2009). Robust stochastic approximation approach to stochastic programming. *SIAM Journal on Optimization* **19** 1574–1609.

NESTEROV, Y. (2004). *Introductory lectures on convex optimization: A Basic Course*. Springer Science & Business Media.

NESTEROV, Y. (2012). Efficiency of coordinate descent methods on huge-scale optimization problems. *SIAM Journal on Optimization* **22** 341–362.

NGUYEN, N., NEEDELL, D. and WOOLF, T. (2014). Linear convergence of stochastic iterative greedy algorithms with sparse constraints. *arXiv preprint arXiv:1407.0088* .

RASKUTTI, G., WAINWRIGHT, M. J. and YU, B. (2011). Minimax rates of estimation for high-dimensional linear regression over-balls. *Information Theory, IEEE Transactions on* **57** 6976–6994.

REDDI, S., HEFNY, A., DOWNEY, C., DUBEY, A. and SRA, S. (2014). Large-scale randomized-coordinate descent methods with non-separable linear constraints. *arXiv preprint arXiv:1409.2617* .

RICHTÁRIK, P. and TAKÁČ, M. (2014). Iteration complexity of randomized block-coordinate descent methods for minimizing a composite function. *Mathematical Programming* **144** 1–38.

SCHMIDT, M., ROUX, N. L. and BACH, F. (2013). Minimizing finite sums with the stochastic average gradient. *arXiv:1309.2388* .

SHALEV-SHWARTZ, S., SREBRO, N. and ZHANG, T. (2010). Trading accuracy for sparsity in optimization problems with sparsity constraints. *SIAM Journal on Optimization* **20** 2807–2832.

SHALEV-SHWARTZ, S. and TEWARI, A. (2011). Stochastic methods for l 1-regularized loss minimization. *The Journal of Machine Learning Research* **12** 1865–1892.

TIBSHIRANI, R. (1996). Regression shrinkage and selection via the lasso. *Journal of the Royal Statistical Society. Series B (Methodological)* 267–288.

TROPP, J. A. and GILBERT, A. C. (2007). Signal recovery from random measurements via orthogonal matching pursuit. *Information Theory, IEEE Transactions on* **53** 4655–4666.

WANG, H. and BANERJEE, A. (2014). Randomized block coordinate descent for online and stochastic optimization. *arXiv preprint arXiv:1407.0107* .

XIAO, L. and ZHANG, T. (2014). A proximal stochastic gradient method with progressive variance reduction. *SIAM Journal on Optimization* **24** 2057–2075.

XU, Y. and YIN, W. (2015). Block stochastic gradient iteration for convex and nonconvex optimization. *SIAM Journal on Optimization* **25** 1686–1716.

YUAN, X.-T., LI, P. and ZHANG, T. (2013). Gradient hard thresholding pursuit for sparsity-constrained optimization. *arXiv preprint arXiv:1311.5750* .

ZHANG, T. (2011). Adaptive forward-backward greedy algorithm for learning sparse representations. *Information Theory, IEEE Transactions on* **57** 4689–4708.

ZHANG, T. ET AL. (2009). Some sharp performance bounds for least squares regression with l1 regularization. *The Annals of Statistics* **37** 2109–2144.

ZHAO, T., YU, M., WANG, Y., ARORA, R. and LIU, H. (2014). Accelerated mini-batch randomized block coordinate descent method. In *Advances in Neural Information Processing Systems*.

Online Bayesian Multiple Kernel Bipartite Ranking

Changying Du[1,2], Changde Du[3,4], Guoping Long[1], Qing He[2], Yucheng Li[1]
[1]Laboratory of Parallel Software and Computational Science, Institute of Software
Chinese Academy of Sciences (CAS), Beijing 100190, China
[2]Key Lab of Intelligent Information Processing of CAS, Institute of Computing Technology, CAS, Beijing 100190, China
[3]Key Laboratory of Optical Astronomy, National Astronomical Observatories, CAS, Beijing 100012, China
[4]University of Chinese Academy of Sciences, Beijing 100049, China
changying@iscas.ac.cn, cddu@nao.cas.cn, heq@ics.ict.ac.cn

Abstract

Bipartite ranking aims to maximize the area under the ROC curve (AUC) of a decision function. To tackle this problem when the data appears sequentially, existing online AUC maximization methods focus on seeking a point estimate of the decision function in a linear or predefined single kernel space, and cannot learn effective kernels automatically from the streaming data. In this paper, we first develop a Bayesian multiple kernel bipartite ranking model, which circumvents the kernel selection problem by estimating a posterior distribution over the model weights. To make our model applicable to streaming data, we then present a kernelized online Bayesian passive-aggressive learning framework by maintaining a variational approximation to the posterior based on data augmentation. Furthermore, to efficiently deal with large-scale data, we design a fixed budget strategy which can effectively control online model complexity. Extensive experimental studies confirm the superiority of our Bayesian multi-kernel approach.

1 INTRODUCTION

Aiming to learn a ranking decision function that is likely to place a positive instance before most negative ones, bipartite ranking [Agarwal and Roth, 2005; Clémençon *et al.*, 2008; Kotlowski *et al.*, 2011] is especially useful for imbalanced data sets, where the area under the ROC curve (AUC) [Hanley and McNeil, 1982; Bradley, 1997; Cortes and Mohri, 2004] is a commonly used evaluation metric. Recently, several online AUC maximization algorithms with pairwise loss functions were proposed to tackle this problem when the data appears sequentially [Zhao *et al.*, 2011a,b; Zhao and Hoi, 2012; Yang *et al.*, 2013; Gao *et al.*, 2013; Hu *et al.*, 2015; Ding *et al.*, 2015]. Furthermore, the generalization performance of online learning algorithms with pairwise loss functions have been investigated in [Wang *et al.*, 2012; Kar *et al.*, 2013].

Nevertheless, existing work only focus on seeking a point estimate of the decision function in a linear or predefined single kernel space, and cannot learn effective kernels automatically from the streaming data. As well known, choosing an appropriate kernel for real-world situations usually is not easy for users without enough domain knowledge. Multiple Kernel Learning (MKL) [Rakotomamonjy *et al.*, 2008; Gönen and Alpaydın, 2011] can circumvent such a problem by learning an optimal linear combination of a set of predefined kernels. However, conventional online MKL algorithms [Luo *et al.*, 2010; Hoi *et al.*, 2013; Sahoo *et al.*, 2014] are unsuitable for a direct use since AUC is a metric represented by the sum of pairwise losses between instances from different classes. More importantly, existing online MKL methods typically maintain a point estimate of their model weights, which can be affected seriously by online outliers and usually needs a tough tuning process for their penalty parameters.

Focusing on these problems, we first develop a Bayesian Bipartite Ranking model with Multiple Kernels (B^2RMK), which circumvents the kernel selection problem by estimating a posterior distribution over the model weights. Specifically, B^2RMK imposes global-local sparsity shrinkage priors on the weights of kernels and support vectors and adopts a margin-based ranking pseudo-likelihood function that mimics the pairwise hinge loss and can be expressed as a location-scale mixture of normals. Within the Bayesian formalism, the new model can automatically infer the weight penalty parameters and naturally alleviate overfitting to small training sets via model averaging over the posterior.

To make our model applicable to streaming data, we then present a kernelized online Bayesian Passive-Aggressive (PA) [Crammer *et al.*, 2006] learning framework. As far as we know, this is the first effort to perform online Bayesian learning with multiple kernels. The key of Bayesian PA is to maintain a posterior distribution at each time step. Unfortunately, exact posterior inference of B^{2}RMK is intractable, so we devise an efficient data augmentation [Tanner and Wong, 1987] based variational method to approximate the posterior with mean-field assumption.

Unlike most existing online MKL methods [Jin *et al.*, 2010; Luo *et al.*, 2010; Hoi *et al.*, 2013], which don't bound their model complexity and require more and more memory and computation when the data arrives sequentially, online B^{2}RMK only maintains two fixed-size buffers (one for positive instances, and another for negative ones) to store the learned support vectors, thus are much more efficient for large-scale data sets. When a buffer is full, we propose a principled strategy to update it, which can guarantee that the most important support vectors won't be discarded. As in [Hu *et al.*, 2015], smooth updating and compensation schemes are employed to further boost performance when updating the buffer. Extensive experimental studies confirm the superiority of our online Bayesian multi-kernel approach.

2 PRELIMINARIES

To better motivate our work, we first introduce some preliminaries, including bipartite ranking, AUC optimization and MKL. Let $\mathcal{X} = \{x \in \mathbb{R}^d\}$ be the instance space, $\mathcal{Y} = \{+1, -1\}$ be the label set, and $\mathbf{S} = \mathbf{S}_+ \cup \mathbf{S}_-$ be a set of training instances, where $\mathbf{S}_+$ and $\mathbf{S}_-$ include N_+ positive instances and N_- negative instances, respectively. The goal of bipartite ranking is to learn a ranking decision function that is likely to place a positive instance before most negative ones. AUC is a commonly used evaluation metric for bipartite ranking. For a ranking decision function $f : \mathcal{X} \to \mathbb{R}$, its AUC measure on $\mathbf{S}$ is defined as:

$$\mathrm{AUC}(f) = 1 - \frac{\sum_{i=1}^{N_+}\sum_{j=1}^{N_-}\mathbb{I}\big(f(x_i^+) \le f(x_j^-)\big)}{N_+N_-}$$

where $\mathbb{I}(\pi)$ is the indicator function that equals 1 when π is true and 0 otherwise. Since directly maximizing $\mathrm{AUC}(f)$ leads to a difficult combinatorial optimization problem, in practice, the indicator function is usually replaced by its convex surrogate, e.g., pairwise hinge loss [Hu *et al.*, 2015; Zhao *et al.*, 2011a] and squared loss [Gao *et al.*, 2013], which leads to minimizing the following regularized pairwise learning task [Christmann and Zhou, 2015]:

$$\mathcal{L}(f) = \frac{c}{2}\|f\|_{\mathcal{H}}^2 + \sum_{i=1}^{N_+}\sum_{j=1}^{N_-}\ell\left(f; x_i^+, x_j^-\right)$$

where $\|\cdot\|_{\mathcal{H}}$ denotes the norm in Reproducing Kernel Hilbert Space (RKHS), $\ell(\cdot)$ is the convex surrogate loss function and c is the regularization parameter balancing the model complexity and training errors.

A kernelized ranking decision function $f : \mathcal{X} \to \mathbb{R}$ that is used to predict the ranking score of a test instance x_i can be written as

$$f(x_i) = \boldsymbol{a}^\top \boldsymbol{k}_i + b$$

where $\boldsymbol{a} = [a_1, \ldots, a_N]^\top$ denotes the vector of weights assigned to each training instance ($N = N_+ + N_-$); b is the bias; and $\boldsymbol{k}_i = [\mathfrak{K}(x_1, x_i), \ldots, \mathfrak{K}(x_N, x_i)]^\top$, where $\mathfrak{K} : \mathcal{X} \times \mathcal{X} \to \mathbb{R}$ is a kernel function that measures the similarities between x_i and x_j, $j = 1, 2, \ldots, N$.

An important problem in single kernel learning is to prespecify the kernel parameters, which is often done in an empirical way. This problem can be circumvented by using the MKL framework [Rakotomamonjy *et al.*, 2008], which is a popular technique for learning an optimal linear combination of a set of predefined kernels. MKL algorithms basically use a weighted sum of P kernels $\{\mathfrak{K}_m : \mathcal{X} \times \mathcal{X} \to \mathbb{R}\}_{m=1}^P$ to get the following multi-kernel ranking decision function:

$$f(x_i) = \boldsymbol{a}^\top \left(\sum_{m=1}^{P} e_m \boldsymbol{k}_{m,i}\right) + b = \sum_{m=1}^{P} e_m \boldsymbol{a}^\top \boldsymbol{k}_{m,i} + b$$

where $\boldsymbol{k}_{m,i} = [\mathfrak{K}_m(x_1, x_i), \ldots, \mathfrak{K}_m(x_N, x_i)]^\top$, and e_m denotes the weight assigned to the m-th kernel.

In the sequel, the m-th $N \times N$ kernel matrix will be denoted by $\mathbf{K}_m$, and the vector of ranking scores of positive instances and negative instances will be denoted by $\mathbf{f}_+$ and $\mathbf{f}_-$, respectively, and $\mathbf{f} = \left[\mathbf{f}_+^\top \ \mathbf{f}_-^\top\right]^\top$.

3 BAYESIAN MULTIPLE KERNEL BIPARTITE RANKING

In this section, we formulate a probabilistic model for multi-kernel bipartite ranking. We impose a fairly general global-local shrinkage prior on the sample weights and kernel combination weights to keep the sparsity of them. Since pairwise hinge loss makes traditional Bayesian analysis hard, we then define a margin-based ranking pseudo-likelihood function to overcome this situation. After introducing a set of augmented variables and making the mean-field assumption, the intractable inference problem of our model can be transformed into a tractable one.

3.1 BAYESIAN SPARSITY SHRINKAGE PRIOR

Similar as in kernelized SVM, the sample weights $\boldsymbol{a}$ is often expected to be sparse for selecting support vectors actually needed in decision function. From the Bayesian perspective, a fairly general global-local shrinkage prior is the Three Parameter Beta Normal ($\mathcal{TPBN}$) [Armagan *et al.*, 2011], which favors strong shrinkage of small signals while having heavy tails to avoid over-shrinkage of the larger signals. Thus, concentrated at zero, $\mathcal{TPBN}$ can yield sparse model representations by suppressing unnecessary support vectors. In this paper, we select $\mathcal{TPBN}$ as the sparsity shrinkage prior due to its better mixing properties than priors such as spike-slab and Laplace. Besides, $\mathcal{TPBN}$ works well for high-dimensional settings since it can specify global and local properties independently. Assuming $\boldsymbol{a} \sim \prod_{i=1}^{N} \mathcal{TPBN}(a_i|\alpha_a, \beta_a, \phi)$, we have the following hierarchical prior:

$$\begin{aligned} a_i|\lambda_i &\sim \mathcal{N}(a_i|0, \lambda_i), \\ \lambda_i|\xi_i &\sim \Gamma(\lambda_i|\alpha_a, \xi_i), \qquad \xi_i|\phi \sim \Gamma(\xi_i|\beta_a, \phi), \\ \phi|\eta &\sim \Gamma(\phi|1/2, \eta), \qquad \eta \sim \Gamma(\eta|1/2, 1), \end{aligned}$$

where $\Gamma(\cdot)$ is the Gamma distribution (with shape-rate parameterization). Note that sample-level sparsity can be tuned by assigning suitable values to the hyper-parameters (α_a, β_a). Setting $\alpha_a = \beta_a = 0.5$, a special case of $\mathcal{TPBN}$ corresponds to the horseshoe prior.

Similarly, sparsity on kernel combination weights $\boldsymbol{e} = [e_1, \ldots, e_P]^\top$ is also desirable for better interpretability. So, we assume $\boldsymbol{e} \sim \prod_{m=1}^{P} \mathcal{TPBN}(e_m|\alpha_e, \beta_e, \rho)$, involving latent variables ω_m, φ_m and τ. Kernel-level sparsity can also be tuned by changing (α_e, β_e).

With the above priors on model weights, we assume the ranking scores of our B^{2}RMK model have the following distributions,

$$\begin{aligned} \mathbf{G}|\boldsymbol{a}, \{\mathbf{K}_m\}_{m=1}^{P}, \upsilon &\sim \prod_{m=1}^{P}\prod_{i=1}^{N} \mathcal{N}\left(g_{mi}|\boldsymbol{a}^\top \boldsymbol{k}_{m,i}, \upsilon^{-1}\right), \\ \mathbf{f}_+|\boldsymbol{e}, \mathbf{G}, b, c &\sim \prod_{i=1}^{N_+} \mathcal{N}\left(f_i|\boldsymbol{e}^\top \boldsymbol{g}_{\cdot i} + b, c^{-1}\right), \\ \mathbf{f}_-|\boldsymbol{e}, \mathbf{G}, b, c &\sim \prod_{j=1}^{N_-} \mathcal{N}\left(f_j|\boldsymbol{e}^\top \boldsymbol{g}_{\cdot j} + b, c^{-1}\right), \end{aligned}$$

where $\upsilon \sim \Gamma(\upsilon|\alpha_\upsilon, \beta_\upsilon)$, $b|\gamma \sim \mathcal{N}(b|0, \gamma^{-1})$, $\gamma \sim \Gamma(\gamma|\alpha_\gamma, \beta_\gamma)$, $c \sim \Gamma(c|\alpha_c, \beta_c)$. The intermediate variables g_{mi} ($m = 1, \ldots, P$, $i = 1, \ldots, N$) are introduced to make the inference procedures efficient. The $P \times N$ matrix of intermediate variables is denoted by $\mathbf{G}$, and the m-th row and i-th column of $\mathbf{G}$ by $\boldsymbol{g}_{m\cdot}$ and $\boldsymbol{g}_{\cdot i}$, respectively. In the sequel, all hyper-parameters will be denoted by $\Upsilon = \{\alpha_a, \beta_a, \alpha_e, \beta_e, \alpha_\upsilon, \beta_\upsilon, \alpha_\gamma, \beta_\gamma, \alpha_c, \beta_c\}$, while the priors by $\Psi = \{\boldsymbol{\lambda}, \boldsymbol{\xi}, \phi, \eta, \boldsymbol{\omega}, \boldsymbol{\varphi}, \rho, \tau, \upsilon, \gamma, c\}$ and the remaining variables by $\Omega = \{\boldsymbol{a}, b, \boldsymbol{e}, \mathbf{G}, \mathbf{f}_+, \mathbf{f}_-\}$.

3.2 MARGIN-BASED RANKING LIKELIHOOD

Several loss functions are available for bipartite ranking. Among them, pairwise hinge loss is the tightest convex upper bound on the rank loss, which is beneficial for better performance and faster convergence. Specifically, the pairwise hinge loss on data set $\mathbf{S}$ can be written as

$$\ell(f; \mathbf{S}) = \sum_{i=1}^{N_+}\sum_{j=1}^{N_-} \max\left(0, 1 - f(x_i^+) + f(x_j^-)\right),$$

which does not lend itself to a convenient description of a likelihood function. To overcome this situation, we propose to define a margin-based ranking pseudo-likelihood

$$L(\mathbf{y}|\mathbf{f}) = \prod_{i=1}^{N_+}\prod_{j=1}^{N_-} \exp\left(-2\max(0, 1 - f_i + f_j)\right),$$

where $\mathbf{y}$ is the label vector and has been divided out. With $\mathcal{TPBN}$ priors and the above margin-based ranking pseudo-likelihood, we can get the following pseudo posterior distribution using Bayes' rule

$$p(\Psi, \Omega|\mathbf{y}) = L(\mathbf{y}|\mathbf{f})p(\Omega|\Psi)p(\Psi)/p(\mathbf{y}|\Upsilon),$$

where $p(\mathbf{y}|\Upsilon)$ is the normalization constant. Note that it is hard to compute $p(\Psi, \Omega|\mathbf{y})$ analytically due to the max function in $L(\mathbf{y}|\mathbf{f})$. Fortunately, we can re-express $L(\mathbf{y}|\mathbf{f})$ as the product of $N_+ \cdot N_-$ location-scale mixtures of normals (see Supplement Section A) based on data augmentation idea [Tanner and Wong, 1987]

$$L(\mathbf{y}|\mathbf{f}) = \prod_{i=1}^{N_+}\prod_{j=1}^{N_-} \int_0^\infty \frac{\exp\left(\frac{(\theta_{ij}+1-f_i+f_j)^2}{-2\theta_{ij}}\right)}{\sqrt{2\pi\theta_{ij}}} d\theta_{ij}, \quad (1)$$

where θ_{ij} is the augmented variable. In the following, the matrix of augmented variables will be denoted by $\boldsymbol{\theta}$, and the i-th row and j-th column of $\boldsymbol{\theta}$ by $\boldsymbol{\theta}_{i\cdot}$ and $\boldsymbol{\theta}_{\cdot j}$, respectively. (1) indicates that the posterior distribution $p(\Psi, \Omega|\mathbf{y})$ can be expressed as the marginal of a higher-dimensional distribution that includes the augmented variables. Therefore, the augmented posterior distribution has the form

$$p(\Psi, \Omega, \boldsymbol{\theta}|\mathbf{y}) = \frac{L(\mathbf{y}, \boldsymbol{\theta}|\mathbf{f})p(\Omega|\Psi)p(\Psi)}{p(\mathbf{y}|\Upsilon)}, \quad (2)$$

where the unnormalized joint distribution of $\mathbf{y}$ and $\boldsymbol{\theta}$ conditioned on $\mathbf{f}$ is

$$L(\mathbf{y}, \boldsymbol{\theta}|\mathbf{f}) = \prod_{i=1}^{N_+}\prod_{j=1}^{N_-} \frac{1}{\sqrt{2\pi\theta_{ij}}} \exp\left(\frac{(\theta_{ij}+1-f_i+f_j)^2}{-2\theta_{ij}}\right).$$

3.3 VARIATIONAL APPROXIMATE INFERENCE

Directly solving for the augmented posterior is intractable due to the normalization constant $p(\mathbf{y}|\Upsilon)$, thus we appeal to the mean-field variational approximate Bayesian inference method, which is generally much more efficient than the Markov Chain Monte Calo (MCMC) based sampling methods. Specifically, we assume there are a family of factorable and free-form variational distributions

$$\begin{aligned} q(\Psi, \Omega, \boldsymbol{\theta}) = & q(\boldsymbol{\lambda})q(\boldsymbol{\xi})q(\phi)q(\eta)q(\boldsymbol{\omega})q(\boldsymbol{\varphi})q(\rho)q(\tau)q(\upsilon) \\ & \cdot q(\gamma)q(c)q(\boldsymbol{a})q(b, \boldsymbol{e})q(\mathbf{G})q(\mathbf{f}_+)q(\mathbf{f}_-)q(\boldsymbol{\theta}), \end{aligned}$$

and the objective is to get the optimal one which minimizes the Kullback-Leibler (KL) divergence between the approximating distribution and the target posterior, i.e.,

$$\min_{q(\Psi, \Omega, \boldsymbol{\theta}) \in \mathcal{P}} \mathrm{KL}\left(q(\Psi, \Omega, \boldsymbol{\theta}) \| p(\Psi, \Omega, \boldsymbol{\theta}|\mathbf{y})\right),$$

where $\mathcal{P}$ is the space of probability distributions. To this end, we first initialize the moments of all factor distributions of $q(\Psi, \Omega, \boldsymbol{\theta})$ appropriately and then iteratively optimize each of the factors in turn using the current estimates for all of the other factors. It can be shown that when keeping all other factors fixed the optimal distribution $q^*(\boldsymbol{a})$ satisfies

$$q^*(\boldsymbol{a}) \propto \exp\{\mathbb{E}_{-\boldsymbol{a}}[\log p(\Psi, \Omega, \boldsymbol{\theta}, \{\mathbf{K}_m\}_{m=1}^P, \mathbf{y})]\}, \quad (3)$$

where $\mathbb{E}_{-\boldsymbol{a}}$ denotes the expectation with respect to $p(\Psi, \Omega, \boldsymbol{\theta})$ over all variables except for $\boldsymbol{a}$, and $p(\Psi, \Omega, \boldsymbol{\theta}, \{\mathbf{K}_m\}_{m=1}^P, \mathbf{y})$ is the joint distribution of data and all variables, which has the following form

$$\begin{aligned} p(\Psi, \Omega, \boldsymbol{\theta}, \{\mathbf{K}_m\}_{m=1}^P, \mathbf{y}) = \\ L(\mathbf{y}, \boldsymbol{\theta}|\mathbf{f}) p(\mathbf{f}|\boldsymbol{e}, \mathbf{G}, b, c) p(\mathbf{G}|\boldsymbol{a}, \{\mathbf{K}_m\}_{m=1}^P, v) \\ \cdot p(\boldsymbol{a}|\boldsymbol{\lambda}) p(\boldsymbol{e}|\boldsymbol{\omega}) p(b|\gamma) p(\boldsymbol{\lambda}|\boldsymbol{\xi}) p(\boldsymbol{\xi}|\phi) p(\phi|\eta) p(\eta) \\ \cdot p(\boldsymbol{\omega}|\boldsymbol{\varphi}) p(\boldsymbol{\varphi}|\rho) p(\rho|\tau) p(\tau) p(v) p(\gamma) p(c). \end{aligned}$$

Expanding the right side of (3) and ignoring the terms unrelated to $\boldsymbol{a}$, we can further get[1]

$$\begin{aligned} q^*(\boldsymbol{a}) &\propto \exp\{\mathbb{E}_{-\boldsymbol{a}}[\log p(\mathbf{G}|\boldsymbol{a}, \{\mathbf{K}_m\}_{m=1}^P, v) + \log p(\boldsymbol{a}|\boldsymbol{\lambda})]\} \\ &= \mathcal{N}\left(\boldsymbol{\Sigma}_{\boldsymbol{a}}\left(\langle v\rangle \sum_{m=1}^P \mathbf{K}_m \langle \boldsymbol{g}_{m\cdot}^\top \rangle\right), \boldsymbol{\Sigma}_{\boldsymbol{a}}\right), \end{aligned}$$

where $\boldsymbol{\Sigma}_{\boldsymbol{a}} = \left(\langle v\rangle \sum_{m=1}^P \mathbf{K}_m \mathbf{K}_m^\top + \langle \Lambda_{\boldsymbol{\lambda}}^{-1}\rangle\right)^{-1}$ and $\Lambda_{\boldsymbol{\lambda}}^{-1} = \mathrm{diag}(\boldsymbol{\lambda})^{-1}$. Similarly, we can also get

$$q^*(b, \boldsymbol{e}) = \mathcal{N}\left(\Sigma_{(b,\boldsymbol{e})} \langle c\rangle \left[\mathbf{1}, \langle \mathbf{G}\rangle^\top\right]^\top \langle \mathbf{f}\rangle, \Sigma_{(b,\boldsymbol{e})}\right),$$

$$q^*(\mathbf{G}) = \prod_{i=1}^N \mathcal{N}\left(\mu_{\boldsymbol{g}\cdot i}, \left(\langle c\rangle \langle \boldsymbol{e}\boldsymbol{e}^\top\rangle + \langle v\rangle \mathbf{I}\right)^{-1}\right),$$

$$q^*(\mathbf{f}_+) = \mathcal{N}\Big(\mu_{\mathbf{f}_+}, \Big(\sum_{j=1}^{N_-} \langle \Lambda_{\boldsymbol{\theta}\cdot j}^{-1}\rangle + \langle c\rangle \mathbf{I}\Big)^{-1}\Big),$$

$$q^*(\mathbf{f}_-) = \mathcal{N}\Big(\mu_{\mathbf{f}_-}, \Big(\sum_{i=1}^{N_+} \langle \Lambda_{\boldsymbol{\theta}_{i\cdot}}^{-1}\rangle + \langle c\rangle \mathbf{I}\Big)^{-1}\Big),$$

$$q^*(\boldsymbol{\theta}) = \prod_{i=1}^{N_+} \prod_{j=1}^{N_-} \mathcal{GIG}\Big(\frac{1}{2}, 1, \langle (1 - f_i + f_j)^2\rangle\Big),$$

where

$$\Sigma_{(b,\boldsymbol{e})} = \begin{bmatrix} \langle c\rangle N + \langle \gamma\rangle, & \langle c\rangle \mathbf{1}^\top \langle \mathbf{G}^\top\rangle \\ \langle c\rangle \langle \mathbf{G}\rangle \mathbf{1}, & \langle c\rangle \langle \mathbf{G}\mathbf{G}^\top\rangle + \langle \Lambda_{\boldsymbol{\omega}}^{-1}\rangle \end{bmatrix}^{-1},$$

$$\mu_{\boldsymbol{g}\cdot i} = \Sigma_{\boldsymbol{g}\cdot i}(\langle c\rangle (\langle f_i\rangle \langle \boldsymbol{e}\rangle - \langle b\boldsymbol{e}\rangle) + \langle v\rangle \mathbf{K}_i^\top \langle \boldsymbol{a}\rangle),$$

$$\mu_{\mathbf{f}_+} = \Sigma_{\mathbf{f}_+}(N_- \mathbf{1} + \langle \boldsymbol{\theta}^{-1}\rangle (\langle \mathbf{f}_-\rangle + \mathbf{1}) + \langle c\rangle (\langle \mathbf{G}_+^\top\rangle \langle \boldsymbol{e}\rangle + \langle b\rangle \mathbf{1})),$$

$$\mu_{\mathbf{f}_-} = \Sigma_{\mathbf{f}_-}(\langle \boldsymbol{\theta}^{-1}\rangle^\top (\langle \mathbf{f}_+\rangle - \mathbf{1}) - N_+ \mathbf{1} + \langle c\rangle (\langle \mathbf{G}_-^\top\rangle \langle \boldsymbol{e}\rangle + \langle b\rangle \mathbf{1})).$$

[1] Here $\langle\cdot\rangle$ means the expectation operator, e.g., $\langle v\rangle$ means the expectation of v over its current optimal variational distribution.

Note that, $\boldsymbol{\theta}^{-1}$ is the element-wise inversion of $\boldsymbol{\theta}$, and $\mathbf{G}_+$ ($\mathbf{G}_-$) denotes the part of $\mathbf{G}$ corresponding to positive (negative) instances. The detailed derivations of the above equations together with the equations for all other variables can be found in the Supplement Section B.

4 ONLINE B^{2}RMK LEARNING

The above batch B^{2}RMK model still suffers from efficiency problems, e.g., huge memory consumption in dealing with large data sets and time-consuming re-training when the data appears sequentially. Online Passive-Aggressive (PA) [Crammer *et al.*, 2006] learning is a principled way to solve such problems. However, it is less explored under the Bayesian framework. Here, we present a fixed budget strategy to conduct online multiple kernel PA learning in Bayesian manner. Our method can be seen as an extension of the linear framework in [Shi and Zhu, 2014], which studied online max-margin topic models.

In the online setting, what we truly care about is how to update the current model, on the arrival of a new data. So, assume we already have an existing B^{2}RMK model at the t-th trial. In the updating of the kernel-based ranking decision function, the main problem is to compute the Gram matrix of pairwise kernel evaluations between the historical instances and new arriving instance, and we have to store all the received historical instances, making it impractical for large-scale online learning tasks. We address this challenge by maintaining only a small number of received historical instances. Specifically, we define two buffers B_t^+ and B_t^- of size $|B_t^+|$ and $|B_t^-|$, for storing the learned important positive and negative support vectors at the t-th trial, respectively. These support vectors in B_t^+ and B_t^- are essential for constructing the ranking decision function at the $(t+1)$-th trial, thus are expected to keep track of the global information of the decision boundary. To this end, existing online MKL methods [Luo *et al.*, 2010; Hoi *et al.*, 2013] typically assume an infinite buffer. However, their naive treatment of storing all received historical instances, requires more and more memory and computation when the data arrives sequentially. On the contrary, we control the computational complexity of our Online B^{2}RMK (OB^{2}RMK) model by fixing the buffer size to an appropriate value, assuming that the performance of OB^{2}RMK increases gradually with the increase of the buffer and it will be saturated when the buffer is large enough. As will be seen in the experimental section, such assumptions are well validated. Overall, the proposed OB^{2}RMK consists of two key modules, i.e., buffer update and model update.

4.1 UPDATE BUFFER

How to maintain the buffers with the most informative support vectors to get better generalization performance is a key challenge. Traditionally, First-In-First-Out (FIFO) and Reservoir Sampling (RS) are two typical stream oblivious policies to update the buffers and have demonstrated their effectiveness in online linear AUC maximization [Zhao *et al.*, 2011a]. However, FIFO and RS will cast off the important support vectors, thus will degrade the performance of the online learning algorithms. Compared with linear algorithms, this adverse impact will be more intense in the kernel-based algorithms which work with the Gram matrix of pairwise kernel evaluations [Yang *et al.*, 2013; Hu *et al.*, 2015]. In the following, we will propose a novel strategy to update the buffers for OB^{2}RMK, aiming to preserve the most important support vectors.

For the incoming new instance $(x_\star, y_\star)$, instead of counting its pairwise losses with all support vectors in the opposite buffer which is easily affected by outliers, we only count the pairwise losses with its k-nearest opposite support vectors X_k. This allows us to utilize the local information around $x_\star$ and improve the robustness of the ranking decision function [Hu *et al.*, 2015].

When the buffers B_t^+ and B_t^- are not full, the incoming new instance will be put into one of the buffers directly, thus the pairwise hinge loss at the $(t+1)$-th trial is

$$\ell(f; x_\star, X_k) = \begin{cases} \sum_{j=1}^k \max\left(0, 1 - f(x_\star) + f(x_j^-)\right), \; y_\star = 1, \\ \sum_{i=1}^k \max\left(0, 1 - f(x_i^+) + f(x_\star)\right), \; y_\star = -1. \end{cases}$$

When either buffer is full, one of the instances in this buffer should be discarded, to accommodate the incoming new instance. Recall that the $\mathcal{TPBN}$ prior concentrates at zero, thus a positive (negative) support vector x_i is likely to have a positive (negative) weight a_i to attain a discriminative decision function. Supposing B_t^+ (B_t^-) is full, we first search for a support vector x_r which has the smallest (largest) weight in the buffer. Instead of discarding x_r directly, we put x_r and $x_\star$ together to count the pairwise losses between them and X_k. This compensation scheme guarantees the useful information of x_r can be fully utilized before it is discarded. Hence, the pairwise hinge loss at the $(t+1)$-th trial is

$$\ell(f; x_\star, x_r, X_k) = \begin{cases} \sum_{j=1}^k \{\max(0, 1 - f(x_\star) + f(x_j^-)) \\ \quad + \max(0, 1 - f(x_r) + f(x_j^-))\}, \; y_\star = 1, \\ \sum_{i=1}^k \{\max(0, 1 - f(x_i^+) + f(x_\star)) \\ \quad + \max(0, 1 - f(x_i^+) + f(x_r))\}, \; y_\star = -1. \end{cases}$$

Concisely, the pairwise hinge loss at the $(t+1)$-th trial can be uniformly written as

$$\ell(f; x_\star, B_t) = \sum_{i=1}^{\tilde{N}_+} \sum_{j=1}^{\tilde{N}_-} \max\left(0, 1 - f(x_i^+) + f(x_j^-)\right),$$

where $B_t = B_t^+ \cup B_t^-$, and $\tilde{N}_+$ and $\tilde{N}_-$ are the number of positive and negative instances, respectively, in counting the pairwise hinge loss at the $(t+1)$-th trial. For example, we have $\tilde{N}_+ = 1, \tilde{N}_- = k$ when $y_\star = 1$ and B_t^+ was not full (i.e., without x_r), and $\tilde{N}_+ = 2, \tilde{N}_- = k$ when $y_\star = 1$ and B_t^+ was full (i.e., with x_r).

4.2 UPDATE MODEL

In online B^{2}RMK, the model parameters $\boldsymbol{a}$, b and $\boldsymbol{e}$ should vary with t, to update the ranking decision function. Note that the dimensionality of $\boldsymbol{a}$ will increase until the buffers are full, whereas b and $\boldsymbol{e}$ are always fixed-size.

4.2.1 Priors

Let $p_t(\boldsymbol{a}_t, b, \boldsymbol{e})$ denote the posterior distribution of $(\boldsymbol{a}, b, \boldsymbol{e})$ at the t-th trial, which will become a prior distribution at the $(t+1)$-th trial. Assuming $a_\star$ is the corresponding weight of $x_\star$ at the $(t+1)$-th trial. After imposing a $\mathcal{TPBN}$ prior on $a_\star$, i.e., $a_\star|\alpha_{a_\star}, \beta_{a_\star}, \phi_\star \sim \mathcal{TPBN}(a_\star|\alpha_{a_\star}, \beta_{a_\star}, \phi_\star)$, we have the hierarchical priors: $a_\star|\lambda_\star \sim \mathcal{N}(a_\star|0, \lambda_\star)$, $\lambda_\star|\xi_\star \sim \Gamma(\lambda_\star|\alpha_{a_\star}, \xi_\star)$, $\xi_\star|\phi_\star \sim \Gamma(\xi_\star|\beta_{a_\star}, \phi_\star)$, $\phi_\star|\eta_\star \sim \Gamma(\phi_\star|1/2, \eta_\star)$ and $\eta_\star \sim \Gamma(\eta_\star|1/2, 1)$.

The prior distributions of $\mathbf{G}$, $\mathbf{f}_+$, $\mathbf{f}_-$, v and c are omitted here as they are similar as in B^{2}RMK. Now let $\tilde{\Upsilon} = \{\alpha_{a_\star}, \beta_{a_\star}\}$, $\tilde{\Psi} = \{\lambda_\star, \xi_\star, \phi_\star, \eta_\star\}$ and $\tilde{\Omega} = \{\mathbf{f}_+, \mathbf{f}_-, \mathbf{G}, v, c\}$ for notational simplicity.

4.2.2 Posterior Updating

Since $\boldsymbol{a}, b, \boldsymbol{e}, \tilde{\Psi}$ and $\tilde{\Omega}$ actually are random variables, we have to average the loss $\ell(f; x_\star, B_t)$ over their joint distribution. Let $\mathbb{E}_{p(\boldsymbol{a},b,\boldsymbol{e},\tilde{\Psi},\tilde{\Omega})}$ denote the expectation over $p(\boldsymbol{a}, b, \boldsymbol{e}, \tilde{\Psi}, \tilde{\Omega})$, then we define the following expected pairwise hinge loss at the $(t+1)$-th trial:

$$\mathcal{R}(p(\boldsymbol{a}, b, \boldsymbol{e}, \tilde{\Psi}, \tilde{\Omega})) = \sum_{i=1}^{\tilde{N}_+} \sum_{j=1}^{\tilde{N}_-} \mathbb{E}_{p(\boldsymbol{a},b,\boldsymbol{e},\tilde{\Psi},\tilde{\Omega})}[\max(0, 1 - f_i + f_j)].$$

Note that, expected pairwise hinge loss is an upper bound of the pairwise hinge loss of the expected bipartite ranking model by Jensen's inequality, and is more convenient for our inference as shown below.

Now we can infer the new posterior distribution $p_{t+1}(\boldsymbol{a}, b, \boldsymbol{e})$ on the arrival of the new data $(x_\star, y_\star)$ by solving the following optimization problem:

$$\min_{p(\boldsymbol{a},b,\boldsymbol{e}) \in \mathcal{P}} \mathrm{KL}\left(p(\boldsymbol{a}, b, \boldsymbol{e}) \| p_t(\boldsymbol{a}_t, b, \boldsymbol{e}) p(a_\star)\right) + 2C \cdot \mathcal{R}(p(\boldsymbol{a}, b, \boldsymbol{e}, \tilde{\Psi}, \tilde{\Omega})), \quad (4)$$

where C is a positive regularization parameter, the constant 2 is just for convenience, and $\mathcal{R}(p(\boldsymbol{a}, b, \boldsymbol{e}, \tilde{\Psi}, \tilde{\Omega}))$ is the expected pairwise hinge loss at the $(t+1)$-th trial. Intuitively, we find a posterior distribution $p_{t+1}(\boldsymbol{a}, b, \boldsymbol{e})$ in the feasible zone that is not only close to $p_t(\boldsymbol{a}_t, b, \boldsymbol{e})p(a_\star)$, but also has small loss at the new trial. Note that $\boldsymbol{a} = \left[\boldsymbol{a}_t^\top \; a_\star\right]^\top$ at the $(t+1)$-th trial, but if B_t^+ (B_t^-) is already full and $y_\star = 1$ $(y_\star = -1)$, the weight vector $\boldsymbol{a}_t$ has been truncated one dimension before the optimization (4) to accommodate $a_\star$, which corresponds to an updating of the buffer.

Directly optimizing (4) with $\mathcal{R}$ is difficult and inefficient. Here we regard

$$L_{t+1}(\mathbf{y}|\boldsymbol{a}, b, \boldsymbol{e}) = \prod_{i=1}^{\tilde{N}_+}\prod_{j=1}^{\tilde{N}_-} \exp\left\{-2C \cdot \mathbb{E}_{p(\tilde{\Psi},\tilde{\Omega})}\left[\max(0, 1 - f_i + f_j)\right]\right\},$$

as the unnormalized pseudo-likelihood of label vector $\mathbf{y}$, then (4) can be rewritten as

$$\min_{p(\boldsymbol{a},b,\boldsymbol{e})\in\mathcal{P}} \mathrm{KL}\left(p(\boldsymbol{a}, b, \boldsymbol{e})\|p_t(\boldsymbol{a}_t, b, \boldsymbol{e})p(a_\star)\right) - \mathbb{E}_{p(\boldsymbol{a},b,\boldsymbol{e})}[\log(L_{t+1}(\mathbf{y}|\boldsymbol{a}, b, \boldsymbol{e}))].$$

It is straightforward to verify that the solution of this information theoretical optimization problem is

$$p(\boldsymbol{a}, b, \boldsymbol{e}) = \frac{p_t(\boldsymbol{a}_t, b, \boldsymbol{e})p(a_\star)L_{t+1}(\mathbf{y}|\boldsymbol{a}, b, \boldsymbol{e})}{p(\mathbf{y}|\tilde{\Upsilon})},$$

where $p(\mathbf{y}|\tilde{\Upsilon})$ is the normalization constant, and the posterior at the t-th trail $p_t(\boldsymbol{a}_t, b, \boldsymbol{e})$ becomes a prior. Since it is hard to compute the expectation with respect to $p(\tilde{\Psi}, \tilde{\Omega})$ in $L_{t+1}(\mathbf{y}|\boldsymbol{a}, b, e)$, we can regard the posterior distribution $p(\boldsymbol{a}, b, \boldsymbol{e})$ as the marginal of a higher-dimensional distribution that includes variables $\tilde{\Psi}$ and $\tilde{\Omega}$. Note that $\tilde{\Psi}$ and $\tilde{\Omega}$ will play only an auxiliary role in the inference procedure.

Therefore, the higher-dimensional distribution of $\boldsymbol{a}, b, \boldsymbol{e}, \tilde{\Psi}$ and $\tilde{\Omega}$ at the $(t+1)$-th trial satisfies the following form:

$$p_{t+1}(\boldsymbol{a}, b, \boldsymbol{e}, \tilde{\Psi}, \tilde{\Omega}) = \frac{p_t(\boldsymbol{a}_t, b, \boldsymbol{e})p(a_\star)p(\tilde{\Psi}, \tilde{\Omega})L_{t+1}(\mathbf{y}|\mathbf{f})}{p(\mathbf{y}|\tilde{\Upsilon})},$$

$$L_{t+1}(\mathbf{y}|\mathbf{f}) = \prod_{i=1}^{\tilde{N}_+}\prod_{j=1}^{\tilde{N}_-} \exp\left(-2C \cdot \max(0, 1 - f_i + f_j)\right),$$

which is intractable to compute analytically due to the max function in it. Similar as in B²RMK, where data augmentation presents an elegant way to deal with the challenging posterior inference problem, we transform $L_{t+1}(\mathbf{y}|\mathbf{f})$ into the product of $\tilde{N}_+ \cdot \tilde{N}_-$ location-scale mixtures of normals:

$$L_{t+1}(\mathbf{y}|\mathbf{f}) = \prod_{i=1}^{\tilde{N}_+}\prod_{j=1}^{\tilde{N}_-} \int_0^\infty \frac{\exp\left(\frac{(\theta_{ij}+C(1-f_i+f_j))^2}{-2\theta_{ij}}\right)}{\sqrt{2\pi\theta_{ij}}} d\theta_{ij}.$$

Now $L_{t+1}(\mathbf{y}|\mathbf{f})$ can also be seen as the marginal of the higher-dimensional distribution

$$L_{t+1}(\mathbf{y}, \boldsymbol{\theta}|\mathbf{f}) = \prod_{i=1}^{\tilde{N}_+}\prod_{j=1}^{\tilde{N}_-} \frac{\exp\left(\frac{(\theta_{ij}+C(1-f_i+f_j))^2}{-2\theta_{ij}}\right)}{\sqrt{2\pi\theta_{ij}}},$$

and the complete posterior distribution at the $(t+1)$-th trial can be expressed as

$$p_{t+1}(\boldsymbol{a}, b, \boldsymbol{e}, \tilde{\Psi}, \tilde{\Omega}, \boldsymbol{\theta}) = \frac{p_t(\boldsymbol{a}_t, b, \boldsymbol{e})p(a_\star)p(\tilde{\Psi}, \tilde{\Omega})L_{t+1}(\mathbf{y}, \boldsymbol{\theta}|\mathbf{f})}{p(\mathbf{y}|\tilde{\Upsilon})}.$$

4.2.3 Approximate Inference

We then make the variational approximate inference for $p_{t+1}(\boldsymbol{a}, b, \boldsymbol{e}, \tilde{\Psi}, \tilde{\Omega}, \boldsymbol{\theta})$. Specifically, assume there are a family of factorable and free-form variational distributions

$$q_{t+1}(\boldsymbol{a}, b, \boldsymbol{e}, \tilde{\Psi}, \tilde{\Omega}, \boldsymbol{\theta}) = q_{t+1}(\boldsymbol{a})q_{t+1}(b, \boldsymbol{e})q_{t+1}(\lambda_\star)q_{t+1}(\xi_\star)q_{t+1}(\phi_\star)q_{t+1}(\eta_\star) \cdot q_{t+1}(v)q_{t+1}(c)q_{t+1}(\mathbf{G})q_{t+1}(\mathbf{f}_+)q_{t+1}(\mathbf{f}_-)q_{t+1}(\boldsymbol{\theta}),$$

and the goal is to get the optimal one which minimizes $\mathrm{KL}(q_{t+1}(\boldsymbol{a}, b, \boldsymbol{e}, \tilde{\Psi}, \tilde{\Omega}, \boldsymbol{\theta})\|p_{t+1}(\boldsymbol{a}, b, \boldsymbol{e}, \tilde{\Psi}, \tilde{\Omega}, \boldsymbol{\theta}))$ between the approximating distribution and the target posterior. Following similar derivations as in B²RMK model, we can infer the optimal distributions for all involved variables at the $(t+1)$-th trial, and the detailed descriptions are shown in Supplement Section C.

5 CONVERGENCE, COMPLEXITY AND PREDICTION

In both B²RMK and OB²RMK, the inference mechanism sequentially updates the approximate posterior distributions of the model parameters and the augmented parameters until convergence, which is guaranteed because the KL divergence is convex with respect to each of the factors.

Rather than addressing the high-dimensionality problem directly, our kernel-based approach always transforms the original data into kernel matrices whose sizes only depend on the number of instances. Meanwhile, our online algorithm can naturally overcome the memory consumption challenge posed by large training sets.

For B²RMK, the computational complexity for transforming original data into kernel matrices $\{\mathbf{K}_m\}_{m=1}^P$ is $\mathrm{O}(N^2Pd)$, where d is the dimensionality of the original data. Note that $\sum_{m=1}^P \mathbf{K}_m\mathbf{K}_m^\top$ should be cached before starting inference to reduce the computation. The computational complexity for each iteration of the variational inference on training data is $\mathrm{O}(N^3 + P^3)$, where the matrix inversions for computing the covariances $\boldsymbol{\Sigma}_{\boldsymbol{a}}$ and $\boldsymbol{\Sigma}_{b,\boldsymbol{e}}$ consume $\mathrm{O}(N^3)$ and $\mathrm{O}(P^3)$ computation, respectively. Note that we can explore the symmetric positive semi-definite property to accelerate these matrix inversions.

For OB^2RMK, the computational complexity for the construction of P kernel matrices $\{\mathbf{K}_m\}_{m=1}^P$ at the t-th trial is $O(|B_t|\tilde{N}Pd)$, where $|B_t| = |B_t^+| + |B_t^-|$ and $\tilde{N} = \tilde{N}_+ + \tilde{N}_-$. The computational complexity for each iteration of the variational inference during training is $O(|B_t|^3 + P^3)$, which indicates that the computational complexity of OB^2RMK will be limited by the buffer size $|B_t|$ when P is given.

After obtaining the approximate posterior distributions $q^*(\boldsymbol{a})$ and $q^*(b, \boldsymbol{e})$, the ranking score for a new instance x_{new} can be calculated by:

$$f_{new} = \langle \boldsymbol{a} \rangle^\top \left(\sum_{m=1}^P \langle e_m \rangle \boldsymbol{k}_{m,new} \right) + \langle b \rangle.$$

6 EXPERIMENTS

In this section, we present extensive experimental results on real data sets to demonstrate the effectiveness of the proposed B^2RMK and OB^2RMK with fixed budgets. Specifically, we compare them with the following algorithms:

- Three batch learning algorithms, including SVM^{perf} for ordinal regression (SVM-OR) [Joachims, 2006], a bipartite ranking model with univariate logistic loss (Uni-Log) [Kotlowski *et al.*, 2011] and least square SVM (LS-SVM);
- Several state-of-the-art online AUC maximization algorithms, including one-pass AUC optimization (OPAUC) [Gao *et al.*, 2013], kernelized online imbalanced learning (KOIL) algorithm with fixed budgets [Hu *et al.*, 2015] and a bounded kernel-based online learning algorithm (Projectron++) [Orabona *et al.*, 2009];
- A latest online multiple kernel classification (OMKC) algorithm with infinite buffer size, which doesn't bound its model complexity, thus requires more and more computational resources when the data arrives sequentially [Hoi *et al.*, 2013].

6.1 EXPERIMENTAL TESTBED AND SETUP

We conduct experiments on a variety of data sets obtained from the UCI and the LIBSVM websites, as summarized in Table 1. To be consistent with previous studies [Gao *et al.*, 2013; Hu *et al.*, 2015], the features have been scaled to $[-1, 1]$ for all data sets, and multi-class data sets have been transformed into class-imbalanced binary ones. On each data set, we conduct four independent trials of 5-fold cross validation for all the algorithms, where four folds of the data are used for training while the rest for test in each trial. The averaged AUC value over these 20 runs is reported. For kernelized methods, we predefine a pool of 18 kernel functions on all features, including Gaussian kernels with 13 different widths $\{2^{-6}, 2^{-5}, \ldots, 2^6\}$ and polynomial kernels with 5 different degrees $\{1, 2, \ldots, 5\}$. Following [Gönen, 2012], all kernel matrices are normalized to have unit diagonal entries, i.e., spherical normalization, which can be done online. Note that our Bayesian multi-kernel approach infers model parameters automatically via posterior inference rather than time-consuming grid search. Though we still have to specify the hyper-parameters, they are fixed for all 15 data sets without re-adjustment on each data set.

Table 1: Details of the data sets used in our experiments.

Datasets	#instances	Datasets	#instances	Datasets	#instances
sonar	208	svmguide2	391	svmguide3	1243
glass	214	diabetes	768	segment	2310
heart	270	fourclass	862	satimage	4435
bupaliver	345	german	1000	spambase	4601
ionosphere	351	splice	1000	usps	9298

6.2 PERFORMANCE EVALUATION

6.2.1 Batch Learning

Though we mainly focus on online learning, we also briefly compare the proposed B^2RMK with three batch methods. We force sparsity at both sample-level and kernel-level by imposing sparsity-inducing priors ($\mathcal{TPBN}$) on the sample weights and kernel weights, respectively. Specifically, the hyper-parameters of the proposed B^2RMK are set to $(\alpha_a, \beta_a) = (\alpha_e, \beta_e) = (0.5, 0.5)$, $(\alpha_v, \beta_v) = (\alpha_c, \beta_c) = (10^{+2}, 10^{-2})$ and $(\alpha_\gamma, \beta_\gamma) = (10^{-2}, 10^{-2})$ for all data sets, while 5-fold cross validation is conducted on training sets to choose a better regularization parameter from $2^{[-10:10]}$ for other methods. The averaged AUC values of these batch algorithms are listed in Table 2, which show that B^2RMK performs significantly better than the competitors on 3 out of 5 data sets. Figure 1 illustrates the kernel weights and sample weights obtained by B^2RMK on 'fourclass' data set, which show that our model can effectively identify the key kernels and support vectors that are actually needed.

Table 2: Average AUC of batch learning methods.

Methods	diabetes	fourclass	german	splice	usps
SVM-OR	.832±.032	.831±.031	.793±.035	.924±.009	.963±.005
Uni-Log	**.833**±.032	.829±.031	**.799**±.034	.921±.011	.964±.004
LS-SVM	.832±.033	.831±.031	**.799**±.034	.925±.009	.963±.005
B^2RMK	.832±.028	**1.000**±.000	.795±.027	**.936**±.012	**.999**±.001

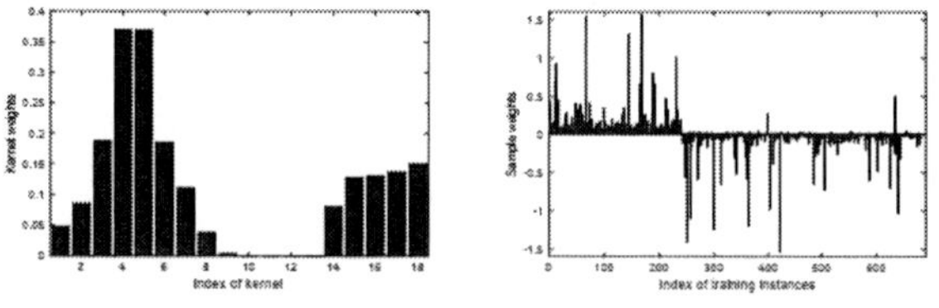

(a) (b)

Figure 1: (a) Kernel weights and (b) sample weights obtained by B^2RMK on 'fourclass' data set.

6.2.2 Online Learning

In real world online learning problems, there is usually very few training data at the beginning, and it is required to maintain a dynamic model with the sequentially arriving data. Since revisiting historical data is expensive for online algorithms, we cannot do cross validation on the entire training set. As such, we assume a half of one fold in the training data is available in a batch manner, and all algorithms tune their parameters on them.

For KOIL updated by RS++ or FIFO++, we set the learning rate $\eta = 0.01$ and select the penalty parameter C from $2^{[-10:10]}$ as suggested in their paper. For OPAUC, we select the learning rate parameter η and the regularization parameter λ from $2^{[-12:10]}$ and $2^{[-10:2]}$, respectively. For Projectron++, we select the parameter of projection difference η from $2^{[-10:10]}$. For OMKC, we adopt the deterministic updating and combination strategy, and the discount weight parameter β and smoothing parameter δ are fixed to 0.8 and 0.01, respectively. For OB^2RMK, we initially conduct B^2RMK on the half fold of training data to get the posterior distribution $p(\boldsymbol{a}, b, \boldsymbol{e})$. Then the hyper-parameters of OB^2RMK are set to $(\alpha_{a_*}, \beta_{a_*}) = (\alpha_v, \beta_v) = (\alpha_c, \beta_c) = (1, 1)$. The parameter k is fixed to 3, and the regularization parameter C is chosen from $\{0.1, 1, 3\}$. Furthermore, to provide KOIL and Projectron++ with multiple kernel information, we also run them with an unweighted combination of all the kernels as well as the best kernel among the pool of kernels. The symbols u and $*$ marked on the upper right corner are used for denoting them, respectively. All buffer sizes for KOIL and OB^2RMK are set to 100.

Table 3 summarizes the average AUC values of the compared online algorithms. We also list the performance of the proposed batch B^2RMK in the last column for reference. Several observations can be drawn as follows. First, by comparing the proposed OB^2RMK algorithm against the other online algorithms, we can find that the OB^2RMK performs considerably better on most data sets. In particular, the AUC values of OB^2RMK significantly surpass the baseline algorithms on some data sets. For example, on 'bupaliver', the AUC values for the baseline algorithms are lower than 71%, while OB^2RMK is able to achieve 75.8%. Secondly, online multiple kernel learning algorithms show better AUC performance than the single kernel and linear online learning algorithms on most data sets. This demonstrates the power of multiple kernel learning methods in classifying real-world data sets. Thirdly, OPAUC achieves fairly comparable or even better results than kernel-based algorithms on the data sets of 'svmguide2' and 'german'. We attribute this to the fact that a linear algorithm is enough to achieve good performance on some data sets, while the kernel-based algorithms may be easily affected by outliers. Finally, by examining the proposed OB^2RMK algorithm against the online multiple kernel learning algorithm $OMKC_{(D,D)}$ with infinite buffers, we can find that the OB^2RMK algorithm tends to outperform the $OMKC_{(D,D)}$ algorithm on most data sets. This encouraging result shows that the OB^2RMK algorithm with fixed buffer size is able to maintain an accurate sketch of historical training examples by exploring the compensation scheme.

6.3 SENSITIVITY ANALYSIS

The default values of parameter C, the buffer size and the number of iterations for each online updating are 1, 100 and 30 respectively. When we study one of them through varying its values, the other two are fixed to their default values. First, from Figure 2 we observe that the performance of OB^2RMK increases gradually with the increase of the buffer size and it is saturated when the size is relatively large, which is consistent with the observations in [Zhao *et al.*, 2011a; Hu *et al.*, 2015]. Then, we can conclude from Figure 3 (a) that the regularization parameter C should not be too large, whereas there is a relatively broad range between $[10^{-3}, 1]$ where OB^2RMK achieves good results. Finally, Figure 3 (b) shows that OB^2RMK converges rapidly, and typically stable results can be attained within 30 iterations.

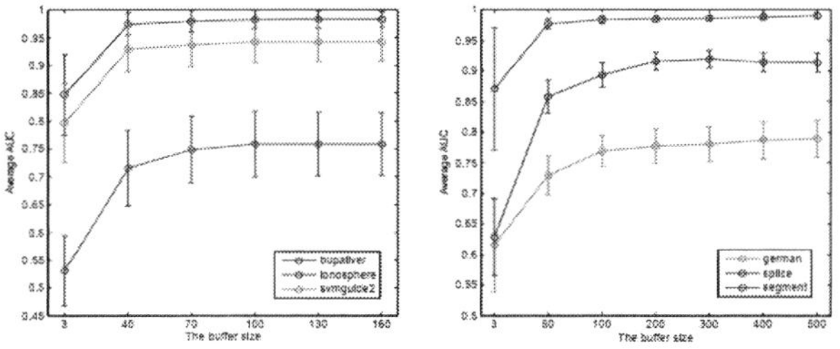

(a) Small data sets (b) Large data sets

Figure 2: Average AUC of OB^2RMK vs. buffer size.

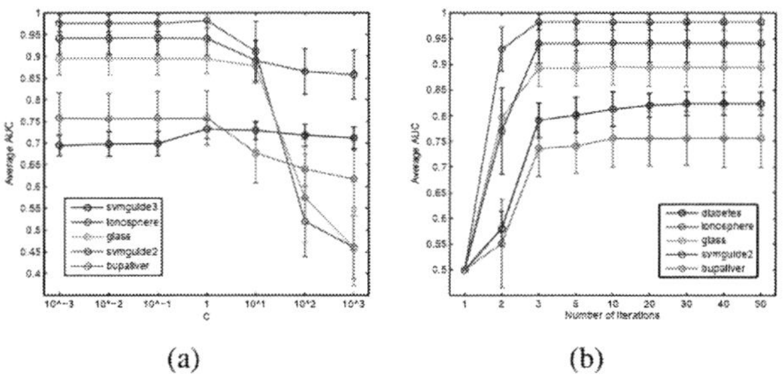

(a) (b)

Figure 3: Average AUC of OB^2RMK when different (a) parameter C and (b) number of iterations are used.

7 RELATED WORK

Online pairwise learning has gained increasing attention recently. In [Zhao *et al.*, 2011a], a buffer sampling based linear Online AUC maximization (OAM) model was proposed. In [Hu *et al.*, 2015], the Kernelized Online Imbal-

Table 3: Average AUC values (mean±std) on a variety of data sets. •/○ indicates that OB^2RMK is significantly better/worse than the corresponding method (pairwise t-tests at 95% significance level).

Datasets	OB^2RMK	$KOIL^u_{RS++}$	$KOIL^*_{RS++}$	$KOIL^u_{FIFO++}$	$KOIL^*_{FIFO++}$	$OMKC_{(D,D)}$	Projectron++^{u}	Projectron++*	OPAUC	B^2RMK
sonar	.915±.044	.865±.050•	.847±.051•	.865±.050•	.850±.049•	.916±.036	.713±.082•	.825±.071•	.813±.082•	**.942**±.034○
glass	.896±.035	.842±.050•	.784±.053•	.839±.052•	.785±.054•	.856±.071•	.582±.098•	.763±.066•	.822±.059•	**.898**±.034
heart	.895±.050	.893±.057	.895±.056	.894±.057	.895±.056	.854±.075•	.773±.056•	.806±.055•	.893±.051	**.905**±.053○
bupaliver	**.758**±.058	.703±.056•	.689±.062•	.707±.054•	.690±.059•	.654±.074•	.511±.020•	.587±.053•	.685±.068•	.755±.061
ionosphere	**.982**±.012	**.982**±.012	.971±.015•	**.982**±.012	.974±.018•	.969±.021•	.850±.041•	.898±.040•	.826±.075•	.980±.012
svmguide2	**.943**±.040	.939±.033	.924±.032•	.942±.032	.919±.038•	.921±.043•	.790±.065•	.836±.040•	.922±.035•	.942±.035
diabetes	.824±.028	.808±.039•	.789±.045•	.817±.036•	.798±.038•	.789±.022•	.574±.047•	.681±.041•	.742±.067•	**.832**±.028○
fourclass	**1.000**±.000	.987±.039•	.999±.001	.987±.039•	.999±.001	.999±.001	.815±.045•	.998±.002•	.830±.021•	**1.000**±.000
german	.768±.029	.760±.039•	.724±.046•	.761±.042•	.733±.041•	.723±.042•	.544±.030•	.625±.031•	.749±.043•	**.795**±.027○
splice	.894±.019	.886±.021•	.869±.018•	.887±.019•	.872±.024•	.906±.022○	.701±.030•	.797±.024•	.865±.020•	**.936**±.012○
svmguide3	.732±.023	.686±.039•	.620±.052•	.685±.051•	.625±.045•	.725±.034•	.503±.005•	.626±.031•	.715±.042•	**.807**±.026○
segment	.984±.005	.975±.006•	.959±.011•	.975±.006•	.957±.009•	.970±.006•	.789±.036•	.962±.010•	.895±.016•	**.998**±.001○
satimage	.978±.006	.958±.006•	.973±.007•	.956±.008•	.973±.007•	.974±.003	.903±.016•	.937±.006•	.848±.028•	**.991**±.002○
spambase	.944±.010	.938±.016•	.922±.017•	.938±.009•	.927±.015•	.958±.007○	.866±.021•	.893±.019•	.941±.009	**.983**±.004○
usps	.990±.003	.985±.004•	.988±.004	.984±.005•	.988±.003	.986±.002	.867±.030•	.976±.003•	.957±.003•	**.999**±.001○
win/tie/loss		12/3/0	12/3/0	12/3/0	12/3/0	9/4/2	15/0/0	15/0/0	13/2/0	0/5/10

anced Learning (KOIL) algorithm extended OAM to the nonlinear case with a predefined single kernel. Both of them provided regret bound based on pairwise hinge loss. [Ding *et al.*, 2015] extended OAM with adaptive gradient method which can exploit the knowledge of historical gradients. Besides, [Gao *et al.*, 2013] proposed a linear one-pass AUC optimization model which scans through the training data only once owing to the use of squared loss. A more recent squared loss based algorithm, named OPERA, was proposed in [Ying and Zhou, 2015], where a non-strongly convex objective was formulated in an unconstrained reproducing kernel Hilbert space. All the aforementioned methods seek point estimates of the decision function in a linear or single kernel space.

On the other hand, recent years witnessed the efforts on online extensions of multiple kernel learning due to its efficiency constrictions. Luo et al. [Luo *et al.*, 2010] first introduced an Online Multiclass Multi-kernel (OM2) classification algorithm with hinge loss. In [Hoi *et al.*, 2013], Hoi et al. proposed several Online Multiple Kernel Classification (OMKC) algorithms that aim to learn multiple kernelized classifiers and their linear combination simultaneously. In [Sahoo *et al.*, 2014], a family of Online Multiple Kernel Regression (OMKR) algorithms were proposed with sliding windows to address non-stationary times-series data. [Xia *et al.*, 2014] proposed an Online Multiple Kernel Similarity (OMKS) learning method, which learns a flexible nonlinear proximity function for visual search. These online MKL methods are effective for their specific applications, but generally involves several regularization parameters that are difficult to tune in real online scenario.

Bayesian learning is a principled way to infer the entire posterior distribution of various model parameters (e.g., kernel weights) from data automatically, providing the user a more simple way to accurately model data. In [Girolami and Rogers, 2005] and [Gönen, 2012], the authors studied Dirichlet and Gaussian priors for the kernel weights respectively. While both of them yield promising results, the former is difficult for inference. [Christoudias *et al.*, 2009] studied Bayesian localized MKL with Gaussian processes. So far, there is not only no online Bayesian MKL model but also no Bayesian multiple kernel AUC optimization model. Our margin-based model is the first combination of pairwise learning/AUC optimization with Bayesian MKL in the online setting.

8 CONCLUSION AND FUTURE WORK

We developed a Bayesian multi-kernel bipartite ranking model, which can circumvent the kernel selection problem by estimating a posterior distribution over the model weights. To make our model applicable to streaming data, we presented a kernelized online Bayesian PA learning framework by maintaining a variational approximation to the posterior. Furthermore, to efficiently deal with large-scale data, we maintained two fixed size buffers to control the number of support vectors while keeping track of the global information of the decision boundary. Extensive experimental studies confirmed the superiority of our Bayesian multi-kernel approach. In future, we plan to extend our model to deal with multi-source data with multi-task and transfer learning [Evgeniou *et al.*, 2005; Gönen and Margolin, 2014].

Acknowledgments

This work was supported by the National Natural Science Foundation of China (No. 61303059, 61573335, 91546122), Guangdong provincial science and technology plan projects (No. 2015B010109005), and the Science and Technology Funds of Guiyang (No. 201410012).

References

Shivani Agarwal and Dan Roth. Learnability of bipartite ranking functions. In *COLT*, pages 16–31, 2005.

Artin Armagan, Merlise Clyde, and David B Dunson. Generalized beta mixtures of gaussians. In *NIPS*, pages 523–531, 2011.

Andrew P Bradley. The use of the area under the roc curve in the evaluation of machine learning algorithms. *Pattern recognition*, 30(7):1145–1159, 1997.

Andreas Christmann and Ding-Xuan Zhou. On the robustness of regularized pairwise learning methods based on kernels. *arXiv preprint arXiv:1510.03267*, 2015.

Mario Christoudias, Raquel Urtasun, and Trevor Darrell. Bayesian localized multiple kernel learning. *Univ. California Berkeley, Berkeley, CA*, 2009.

Stéphan Clémençon, Gabor Lugosi, and Nicolas Vayatis. Ranking and empirical minimization of u-statistics. *The Annals of Statistics*, pages 844–874, 2008.

Corinna Cortes and Mehryar Mohri. Auc optimization vs. error rate minimization. In *NIPS*, 2004.

Koby Crammer, Ofer Dekel, Joseph Keshet, Shai Shalev-Shwartz, and Yoram Singer. Online passive-aggressive algorithms. *JMLR*, 7:551–585, 2006.

Yi Ding, Peilin Zhao, Steven CH Hoi, and Yew-Soon Ong. An adaptive gradient method for online auc maximization. In *AAAI*, 2015.

Theodoros Evgeniou, Charles A Micchelli, and Massimiliano Pontil. Learning multiple tasks with kernel methods. In *JMLR*, pages 615–637, 2005.

Wei Gao, Rong Jin, Shenghuo Zhu, and Zhi-Hua Zhou. One-pass AUC optimization. In *ICML*, 2013.

Mark Girolami and Simon Rogers. Hierarchic bayesian models for kernel learning. In *ICML*, 2005.

Mehmet Gönen and Ethem Alpaydın. Multiple kernel learning algorithms. *JMLR*, 12:2211–2268, 2011.

Mehmet Gönen and Adam A Margolin. Kernelized bayesian transfer learning. In *AAAI*, 2014.

Mehmet Gönen. Bayesian efficient multiple kernel learning. In *ICML*, pages 1–8, 2012.

James A Hanley and Barbara J McNeil. The meaning and use of the area under a receiver operating characteristic (roc) curve. *Radiology*, 143(1):29–36, 1982.

Steven C. H. Hoi, Rong Jin, Peilin Zhao, and Tianbao Yang. Online multiple kernel classification. *Machine Learning*, 90(2):289–316, 2013.

Junjie Hu, Haiqin Yang, Irwin King, Michael R. Lyu, and Anthony Man-Cho So. Kernelized online imbalanced learning with fixed budgets. In *AAAI*, 2015.

Rong Jin, Steven CH Hoi, and Tianbao Yang. Online multiple kernel learning: Algorithms and mistake bounds. In *Algorithmic Learning Theory*, pages 390–404, 2010.

Thorsten Joachims. Training linear svms in linear time. In *SIGKDD*, pages 217–226, 2006.

Purushottam Kar, Bharath K Sriperumbudur, Prateek Jain, and Harish C Karnick. On the generalization ability of online learning algorithms for pairwise loss functions. In *ICML*, 2013.

Wojciech Kotlowski, Krzysztof J Dembczynski, and Eyke Huellermeier. Bipartite ranking through minimization of univariate loss. In *ICML*, 2011.

Jie Luo, Francesco Orabona, Marco Fornoni, Barbara Caputo, and Nicolo Cesa-Bianchi. Om-2: An online multi-class multi-kernel learning algorithm. In *CVPR Workshop on Online Learning for Computer Vision*, 2010.

Francesco Orabona, Joseph Keshet, and Barbara Caputo. Bounded kernel-based online learning. *JMLR*, 10:2643–2666, 2009.

Alain Rakotomamonjy, Francis Bach, Stéphane Canu, and Yves Grandvalet. Simplemkl. *JMLR*, 9:2491–2521, 2008.

Doyen Sahoo, Steven CH Hoi, and Bin Li. Online multiple kernel regression. In *SIGKDD*, pages 293–302, 2014.

Tianlin Shi and Jun Zhu. Online bayesian passive-aggressive learning. In *ICML*, 2014.

Martin A Tanner and Wing Hung Wong. The calculation of posterior distributions by data augmentation. *Journal of the American Statistical Association*, 82(398):528–540, 1987.

Yuyang Wang, Roni Khardon, Dmitry Pechyony, and Rosie Jones. Generalization bounds for online learning algorithms with pairwise loss functions. In *COLT*, 2012.

Hao Xia, Steven CH Hoi, Rong Jin, and Peilin Zhao. Online multiple kernel similarity learning for visual search. *IEEE Transactions on PAMI*, 36(3):536–549, 2014.

Haiqin Yang, Junjie Hu, Michael R Lyu, and Irwin King. Online imbalanced learning with kernels. In *NIPS Workshop on Big Learning*, 2013.

Yiming Ying and Ding-Xuan Zhou. Online pairwise learning algorithms with kernels. *arXiv preprint arXiv:1502.07229*, 2015.

Peilin Zhao and Steven CH Hoi. Bduol: Double updating online learning on a fixed budget. In *Machine Learning and Knowledge Discovery in Databases*, pages 810–826. Springer, 2012.

Peilin Zhao, Steven C. H. Hoi, Rong Jin, and Tianbao Yang. Online AUC maximization. In *ICML*, pages 233–240, 2011.

Peilin Zhao, Steven CH Hoi, and Rong Jin. Double updating online learning. *JMLR*, 12:1587–1615, 2011.

Pruning Rules for Learning Parsimonious Context Trees

Ralf Eggeling **Mikko Koivisto**
University of Helsinki, Department of Computer Science,
Helsinki Institute for Information Techology HIIT, Finland
{eggeling,mkhkoivi}@cs.helsinki.fi

Abstract

We give a novel algorithm for finding a parsimonious context tree (PCT) that best fits a given data set. PCTs extend traditional context trees by allowing context-specific grouping of the states of a context variable, also enabling skipping the variable. However, they gain statistical efficiency at the cost of computational efficiency, as the search space of PCTs is of tremendous size. We propose pruning rules based on efficiently computable score upper bounds with the aim of reducing this search space significantly. While our concrete bounds exploit properties of the BIC score, the ideas apply also to other scoring functions. Empirical results show that our algorithm is typically an order-of-magnitude faster than a recently proposed memory-intensive algorithm, or alternatively, about equally fast but using dramatically less memory.

1 INTRODUCTION

The conditional distribution of a response variable y, given some explanatory variables $x_1, x_2, \ldots, x_d$, is a key ingredient in common probabilistic models. Often the modeler's interest is in distributions that admit a compact, structured representation, thereby facilitating statistically efficient learning and computationally efficient inference, as well as easy human interpretation.

Examples of general-purpose model classes include decision trees (Breiman et al., 1984; Friedman & Goldszmidt, 1996), decision graphs (Oliver, 1993; Chickering et al., 1997), multi-linear functions (Chavira & Darwiche, 2005), and conditional independence trees (Su & Zhang, 2005). These models allow for representing *context-specific independence* (Boutilier et al., 1996): given a *context*, i.e., an assignment for a *subset* of the explanatory variables x_i, the response y becomes independent of the rest.

When the explanatory variables are equipped with a natural linear ordering, more specialized models of context-specific independence are justified. In particular, *context trees* (CTs) of depth d over an alphabet Ω (Rissanen, 1983; Bühlmann & Wyner, 1999) model the distribution of the next symbol y after a sequence $x_d x_{d-1} \cdots x_1$ assuming each context is an assignment $a_\ell \cdots a_1$ for the $\ell \leq d$ immediate predecessors $x_\ell \cdots x_1$ of y, where the length ℓ may vary with the context. While context trees excel in computational efficiency, their statistical efficiency decays when there are long-range dependencies (requiring long contexts) and when the alphabet is non-binary.

To address the shortcoming of CTs, Bourguignon & Robelin (2004) proposed *parsimonious context trees* (PCTs), in which a context is a sequence $C_\ell \cdots C_1$ of *sets* of symbols $C_i \subseteq \Omega$. The idea is that the conditional distribution of y is the same of all assignments $a_d \cdots a_1$ that *match* the context, that is, $a_i \in C_i$ for $i = 1, \ldots, \ell$. In effect, PCTs allow for a compact representation and statistically efficient learning even in the presence of long-range dependencies. PCTs have found applications particularly within computational biology (Seifert et al., 2012; Eggeling et al., 2015b), where modeling sequential data over discrete alphabets constitutes a recurring challenge.

From a computational point of view, learning PCTs (i.e., maximizing a given scoring function) is, however, very challenging for larger depth d and alphabet size $|\Omega|$. The dynamic programming (DP) algorithm of Bourguignon & Robelin (2004) avoids explicit enumeration of all PCTs. Yet, it has to explore all possible contexts $C_\ell \cdots C_1$, with $\emptyset \subset C_i \subseteq \Omega$, each of which is a potential node of an optimal PCT and corresponds to a subproblem of optimizing the subtree rooted at it. Recently, Eggeling et al. (2015a) enhanced the DP algorithm by observing that two contexts of the same length are equivalent (i.e., have identical optimal subtrees) if they are matched by exactly the same set of data points; thus the respective subproblem needs to be solved only once. While this *memoization* variant is effective in reducing the time requirement of PCT optimization in practice, it has the disadvantage of increased memory consumption.

Here, we investigate a new idea to expedite PCT optimization in practice. We present pruning rules, which allow us to ignore subproblems that are guaranteed to not contribute to an optimal PCT. To obtain such guarantees, we derive upper bounds specifically for the BIC score, similar in spirit to the bounds on local scores by Tian (2000) and de Campos & Ji (2011) for structure learning in Bayesian networks. While for Bayesian networks also *global* bounds, useful in branch-and-bound search, can be derived by structural relaxations (de Campos & Ji, 2011; Yuan & Malone, 2013), with no assumptions on local scores, for PCTs a separate global view is absent and utilizing concrete properties of a particular score seems necessary.

As our subproblems form a so-called AND/OR search space (Dechter & Mateescu, 2007; Nilsson, 1980), we cannot prune a subproblem based solely on the associated bound, but we need to combine the bounds of a multitude of subproblems; in essence, we have to consider all alternative partitions of a subproblem into smaller subproblems, all of which need to be solved. To this end, we propose an efficient treatment, which resembles a simple pruning rule popular in structure learning in Bayesian networks (Teyssier & Koller, 2005); however, while the latter concerns the "is subset of" relation, our rule concerns the "refines" relation on set partitions. We note that our algorithm is an instantiation of so-called *General Branch and Bound* (Nau et al., 1984), but not of the more special A* algorithm for OR spaces.

Our pruning technique is orthogonal to the memoization technique of Eggeling et al. (2015a). In particular, our technique can be employed with or without memoization, resulting in high or low memory consumption, respectively. Because the effectiveness of our ideas is data-dependent, we evaluate the proposed algorithms empirically on a wide selection of real-world data sets.

2 PRELIMINARIES

In this section, we revisit the definition of PCTs, the basic structure learning algorithm, and a recently proposed memoization technique for improving it.

2.1 PARSIMONIOUS CONTEXT TREES

A *parsimonious context tree* (PCT) $\mathcal{T}$ of depth d over an alphabet Ω is a rooted, balanced, node-labeled tree of depth d with the following additional property: For each node of depth $\ell < d$ the labels of its children partition Ω, i.e., the labels of the children are pairwise disjoint nonempty subsets of Ω whose union is Ω.

We identify each node with the sequence of labels $V_\ell \cdots V_1$ of the nodes on the unique path from the node up to the root, denoted by $\mathbf{V}$ for short. We can also interpret the node $\mathbf{V}$ as the set of all sequences it represents. We say that a sequence $x_d \cdots x_1$ *matches* node $\mathbf{V}$, and denote it by $x_d \cdots x_1 \in \mathbf{V}$, if $x_i \in V_i$ for all positions $i = \ell, \ldots, 1$ (the remaining positions are ignored).

Given a PCT $\mathcal{T}$ and its node $\mathbf{V}$, we denote by $\mathcal{T}(\mathbf{V})$ the subtree of $\mathcal{T}$ rooted at $\mathbf{V}$. We say the subtree is *minimal* if it consists of a single chain of nodes down to a single leaf, thus all nodes labeled by Ω, and *maximal* if it consists only of nodes labeled with single symbols $a \in \Omega$, thus having $|\Omega|^{d-\ell(\mathbf{V})}$ leaves. Here, $\ell(\mathbf{V})$ denotes the depth of node $\mathbf{V}$.

To model the conditional distribution of the response variable y given a sequence $\mathbf{x}$, we equip each leaf $\mathbf{V}$ of a PCT with $|\Omega|$ parameters $\theta_{\mathbf{V}a}$, one parameter for each $a \in \Omega$. We interpret $\theta_{\mathbf{V}a}$ as the probability that y takes the value a given that $\mathbf{x}$ matches $\mathbf{V}$. In a data set $\mathbf{z} = (\mathbf{x}^t, y^t)_{t=1}^N$ we assume that, given $\mathbf{x}^t$, the response y^t is independent of the remainder of the data. Writing $\Theta_\mathcal{T}$ for the parameters of a PCT $\mathcal{T}$, we obtain the likelihood function

$$\mathcal{L}_\mathcal{T}(\Theta_\mathcal{T}) := \prod_{\text{leaf } \mathbf{V} \text{ of } \mathcal{T}} \prod_{a \in \Omega} \theta_{\mathbf{V}a}^{N_{\mathbf{V}a}}, \tag{1}$$

where $N_{\mathbf{V}a}$ denotes the count of the response a in data points where the explanatory variables match $\mathbf{V}$:

$$N_{\mathbf{V}a} := |\{t : \mathbf{x}^t \in \mathbf{V} \text{ and } y^t = a\}| . \tag{2}$$

We will further denote $N_\mathbf{V} := \sum_{a \in \Omega} N_{\mathbf{V}a}$.

2.2 BASIC STRUCTURE LEARNING

We consider a score-and-search approach to learn a PCT from a given data set. Suppose we are given a scoring function S that associates each PCT $\mathcal{T}$ with a real-valued score $S_\mathcal{T}$. The task is to find an optimal PCT,

$$\hat{\mathcal{T}} \in \operatorname*{argmax}_\mathcal{T} S_\mathcal{T} . \tag{3}$$

Aside from the fact that multiple PCTs may achieve the optimum, this task is practically equivalent to the task of finding the optimal score $S_{\hat{\mathcal{T}}}$. For convenience, we focus on the latter problem for the rest of the paper. An optimal tree $\hat{\mathcal{T}}$ can be constructed via, e.g., standard backtracking (see Section 2.3 for details).

Bourguignon & Robelin (2004) presented a dynamic programming algorithm for finding $S_{\hat{\mathcal{T}}}$. It relies on the mild assumption that the scoring function decomposes into a sum of leaf scores:

$$S_\mathcal{T} = \sum_{\text{leaf } \mathbf{V} \text{ of } \mathcal{T}} S(\mathbf{V}) . \tag{4}$$

This property is fulfilled by the log-likelihood function (Eq. 1) and thus also by scoring functions that can be written as penalized maximum log-likelihood with a decomposable penalty term, such as AIC (Akaike, 1974), BIC (Schwarz, 1978), and the Bayesian marginal likelihood with a decomposable prior.

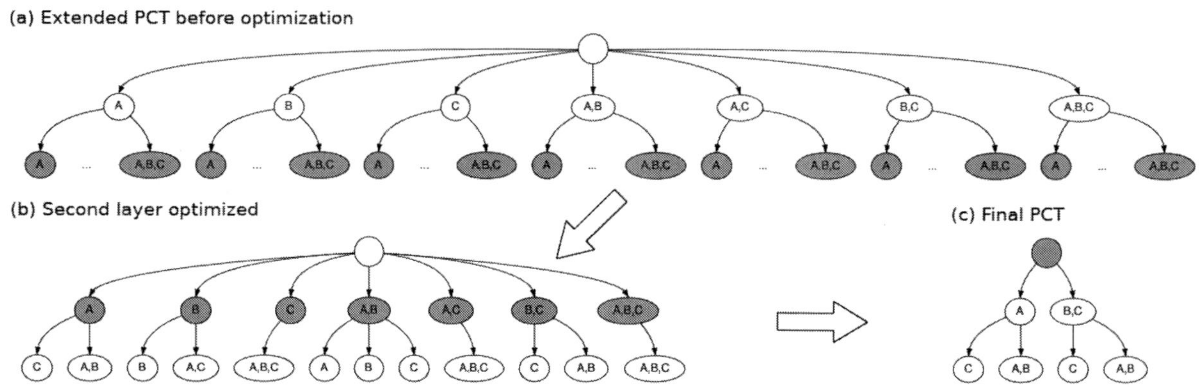

Figure 1: **Basic PCT optimization**. We show the bottom-up reduction of the extended PCT for a toy example of $d = 2$ and $\Omega = \{\mathsf{A}, \mathsf{B}, \mathsf{C}\}$. (a) Initially only the leaf scores of the extended PCT have an exact, optimal score assigned to them. (b) For each set of sibling leaves, the optimal valid selection of children is computed, the non-contributing siblings are discarded, and the winning score is propagated upwards to become the score of the parent. (c) The same principle is applied on the higher layer in order to select the optimal children of the root, obtaining a valid PCT with optimal score.

To describe the algorithm, we denote by $S_{\mathcal{T}(\mathbf{V})}(\mathbf{V})$ the sum of the leaf scores in the subtree $\mathcal{T}(\mathbf{V})$ rooted at an inner node $\mathbf{V}$ of $\mathcal{T}$; for a leaf $\mathbf{V}$, we put $S_{\mathcal{T}(\mathbf{V})}(\mathbf{V}) := S(\mathbf{V})$. We have the recurrence

$$S_{\mathcal{T}(\mathbf{V})}(\mathbf{V}) = \sum_{\text{child } \mathbf{C} \text{ of } \mathbf{V}} S_{\mathcal{T}(\mathbf{C})}(\mathbf{C}), \tag{5}$$

and, in particular, $S_{\mathcal{T}} = S_{\mathcal{T}}(\Lambda)$, where Λ is the root node of $\mathcal{T}$. Exploiting this recurrence, the algorithm of Bourguignon & Robelin (2004) optimizes the score over the subtrees rooted at $\mathbf{C}$, independently for each possible child node $\mathbf{C}$, and then selects a set of children that form an optimal partition of the parent node $\mathbf{V}$. For the base case of each leaf, the algorithm sets the optimal score $S_*(\mathbf{V}) := S(\mathbf{V})$, and for each inner node it computes the optimal score defined by

$$S_*(\mathbf{V}) := \max_{\substack{\{C_1,\ldots,C_r\} \\ \text{partition of } \Omega}} \{ S_*(C_1\mathbf{V}) + \cdots + S_*(C_r\mathbf{V}) \}. \tag{6}$$

It follows that the maximum score over all PCTs of depth d is obtained as

$$\max_{\mathcal{T}} S_{\mathcal{T}} = S_*(\Lambda). \tag{7}$$

The algorithm computes the leaf scores of $(2^{|\Omega|} - 1)^d$ possible leaves and, in addition, finds an optimal set of children in $O(3^{|\Omega|})$ time for each of slightly more than $(2^{|\Omega|} - 1)^{d-1}$ inner nodes. Since the complexity is a product of two terms which are both exponential in $|\Omega|$, PCTs are to date limited to applications of small to moderate alphabet size (Eggeling et al., 2015a).

2.3 INTERPRETATION AS REDUCTION OF EXTENDED PCT

The inner workings of the algorithm of Bourguignon & Robelin (2004) and the construction of the optimal PCT itself can be viewed as bottom-up reduction of a data structure called *extended PCT*, as illustrated in Figure 1. In contrast to a PCT, the sibling nodes in an extended PCT do not partition their parent node, but are labeled by all nonempty subsets of Ω. An extended PCT thus contains all possible PCTs as subtrees, as illustrated in Figure 1a. We denote the set of all nodes of an extended PCT by $\mathcal{V}$, and treat a PCT $\mathcal{T}$ as its proper subset, i.e., $\mathcal{T} \subset \mathcal{V}$.

Given an extended PCT, the base case of the algorithm requires the computation of leaf scores, and the task is now to reduce the extended PCT so that a PCT with maximal score remains. For each inner node it then (i) computes an optimal selection of children with the constraint that the node labels must form a partition of Ω, and (ii) removes all children and subtrees below that do not belong to this optimal partition.

Since an inner node can be optimized only if all of its children have already a score attached to them and are thus roots of valid PCT subtrees, the recursion leads essentially to a bottom-up reduction of the extended PCT beginning at the deepest *layer*, which comprises all nodes of the same depth, as displayed in Figure 1b. The optimization terminates once an optimal selection of children of the root node are computed; a possible final result is shown in Figure 1c.

2.4 MEMOIZATION

Eggeling et al. (2015a) proposed a *memoization* technique for speeding up PCT learning by exploiting regularities in the observed explanatory variables.

The core idea is to implement the algorithm of Bourguignon & Robelin (2004) in a top-down fashion and to store the result of subtree optimization for node $\mathbf{V}$ with the depth

$\ell(\mathbf{V})$ and the index set $I(\mathbf{V}) := \{t : \mathbf{x}^t \in \mathbf{V}\}$ as key, e.g., in a hash table. When the algorithm needs an optimal subtree (or its score) for another node $\mathbf{V}'$, the algorithm checks whether the key $(\ell(\mathbf{V}'), I(\mathbf{V}'))$ exists in the storage already and the associated result can be re-used. To work correctly, memoization requires that the score $S_*(\mathbf{V})$ depends on $\mathbf{V}$ only through $I(\mathbf{V})$ and $\ell(\mathbf{V})$. This property holds for many relevant scoring functions such as penalized maximum log-likelihood scores, but not for the Bayesian marginal likelihood with context-dependent pseudo-counts.

While memoization has shown to be rather effective particularly on highly structured data sets, it increases memory consumption. The original DP algorithm of Bourguignon & Robelin (2004) is relatively memory-efficient as only a small fraction of nodes of the extended PCT needs to be stored in memory at a given time, provided that the extended PCT is constructed, traversed, and reduced top-down in a depth-first manner. Memoization, in contrast, requires storing the scores and the associated data subset indices for all visited inner nodes of the extended PCT.

3 PRUNING RULES

We derive pruning rules, which utilize score upper bounds to decide at any given node whether we can avoid the explicit optimization over possible subtrees.

3.1 SCORING FUNCTION: BIC

In order to obtain effective upper bounds, we focus on the BIC score, derived from be Bayesian Information Criterion (Schwarz, 1978). It is an approximation of the Bayesian marginal likelihood and has been empirically shown to be suitable for PCT learning on real-world data due to its harsh penalty term, which favors sparse trees (Eggeling et al., 2014). The score can also be given a two-part-MDL interpretation (Rissanen, 1978). For a PCT $\mathcal{T}$, the BIC score is given by

$$S_{\mathcal{T}}^{\mathrm{BIC}} = \ln \mathcal{L}_{\mathcal{T}}(\hat{\Theta}_{\mathcal{T}}(\mathbf{z})) - \frac{k}{2} \ln N\,, \tag{8}$$

where $\hat{\Theta}_{\mathcal{T}}(\mathbf{z})$ denotes the maximum-likelihood parameter estimate on $\mathbf{z}$ and k denotes the number of free parameters. Since k is proportional to the number of leaves and since the likelihood (Eq. 1) is a product of leaf terms, the BIC score decomposes into a sum of

$$S^{\mathrm{BIC}}(\mathbf{V}) := \overbrace{\sum_a N_{\mathbf{V}a} \ln \frac{N_{\mathbf{V}a}}{N_{\mathbf{V}}}}^{L(\mathbf{V})} - \overbrace{\frac{1}{2}(|\Omega| - 1) \ln N}^{K}\,. \tag{9}$$

Here, $L(\mathbf{V})$ is the maximized log-likelihood of leaf $\mathbf{V}$ and K is the BIC penalty contribution of a single leaf, involving $|\Omega| - 1$ free parameters and a global sample size of N. We observe that the score of a leaf $\mathbf{V}$ does actually not depend on all data points in $\mathbf{z}$, but only on those that match $\mathbf{V}$.

3.2 UPPER BOUNDING THE BIC SCORE

Consider an inner node $\mathbf{V} \in \mathcal{V}$. To upper bound the BIC score over all possible subtrees rooted at $\mathbf{V}$, we upper bound the largest possible gain in the maximum-likelihood term on one hand, and lower bound the inevitable penalty due to increased model complexity on the other hand.

Consider first the likelihood term. We make use of the observation that every PCT is *nested* in the maximal PCT, which has $|\Omega|^d$ leaves, each representing a single realization of the explanatory variables. The same holds also locally for any PCT subtree below a particular node $\mathbf{V}$. Hence, the likelihood term is maximized by the maximal model, which partitions all realizations perfectly. We obtain the upper bound

$$\tilde{L}(\mathbf{V}) := \sum_{\mathbf{a} \in \Omega^{d-\ell(\mathbf{V})}} L(\mathbf{a}\mathbf{V})\,, \tag{10}$$

that is, we have $L(\mathbf{V}) \leq \tilde{L}(\mathbf{V})$. Here, $\mathbf{a}\mathbf{V}$ denotes the leaf node obtained by extending the context of node $\mathbf{V}$ with a single realization $\mathbf{a}$ of the remaining explanatory variables. Note that $\tilde{L}(\mathbf{V})$ can be computed fast by summing over the sequences $\mathbf{a}$ that occur in the data points that match $\mathbf{V}$. Now we distinguish:

Case 1 The minimal subtree is optimal. In this case, we can compute the exact score directly, without recursion.

Case 2 The minimal subtree is not optimal. Thus an optimal subtree makes at least one split, and therefore has at least two leaves. In this case, the likelihood term is upper bounded by $\tilde{L}(\mathbf{V})$ (Eq. 10), while the penalty term is at least $2K$.

Combining the two cases yields the following bound.

Proposition 1 (Score upper bound). *For an arbitrary inner node $\mathbf{V} \in \mathcal{V}$ it holds that*

$$S_*^{BIC}(\mathbf{V}) \leq S_0^{BIC}(\mathbf{V})\,,$$

with

$$S_0^{BIC}(\mathbf{V}) := \max\{L(\mathbf{V}) - K, \tilde{L}(\mathbf{V}) - 2K\}\,.$$

We will use this upper bound twice to device two pruning rules in the next two sections.

3.3 STOPPING RULE

First, we consider a simple rule for pruning, which is an immediate consequence of the aforementioned upper bound. The idea can be phrased as follows:

Stop optimizing the subtree below a node when context-specific independence can be declared already without even entering the recursion.

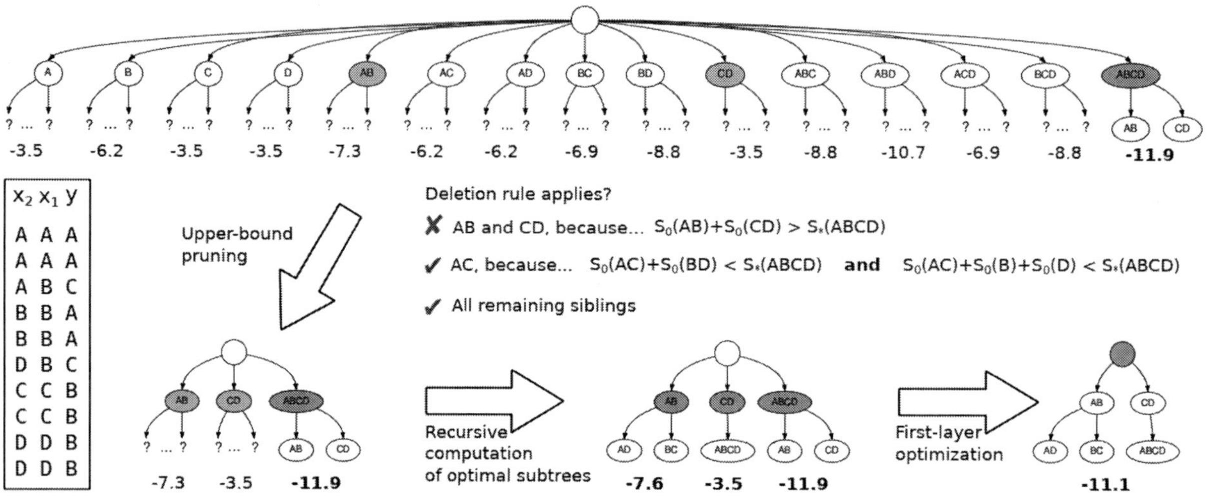

Figure 2: **Example of the deletion rule.** We consider a small data set of $N = 10$ for two explanatory variables over the alphabet $\Omega = \{\mathsf{A}, \mathsf{B}, \mathsf{C}, \mathsf{D}\}$ (bottom-left box). The root of each subtree for which exact BIC scores have been computed already is marked in green and corresponding score displayed in boldface below the subtree. The remaining other subtrees are associated with an upper bound on the BIC score. The root of a subtree which contributes to an upper-bounded partition score that is greater than the exact score of the maximal sibling node, and thus has to optimized explicitly, is displayed in orange.

Formally, we have the following.

Proposition 2 (Stopping rule)**.** *Let* $\mathbf{V} \in \mathcal{V}$ *with* $\ell(\mathbf{V}) < d$, *and let* $\mathcal{T}'$ *be the minimal subtree rooted at* $\mathbf{V}$. *If*

$$S_0^{BIC}(\mathbf{V}) = L(\mathbf{V}) - K\,,$$

then $S_*^{BIC}(\mathbf{V}) = S_{\mathcal{T}'}^{BIC}(\mathbf{V})$.

The correctness can be shown by contradiction. Assume $\mathcal{T}'$ does not yield the optimal score. Then $L(\mathbf{V}) - K < S_*^{\mathrm{BIC}}(\mathbf{V})$. But since $S_*^{\mathrm{BIC}}(\mathbf{V}) \leq S_0^{\mathrm{BIC}}(\mathbf{V})$, this violates the premise.

3.4 DELETION RULE

The idea of our second rule is to identify a node with so low a score that the node cannot appear in any optimal PCT. In an idealized form, the rule reads:

> *Delete a child node if the best set of children it belongs to is worse than some other set of children (to which the node does not belong).*

As we wish to delete as many potential child nodes as possible and not compute their optimal scores, we cannot assume the optimal scores of the sibling nodes are available. Thus, to make the rule concrete, we resort to upper bounds on the scores. Likewise, we need to lower bound the optimal score among the valid sets of children. While, in principle, various lower bounding schemes would be possible, we have chosen to use a particularly simple bound: the optimal score of the Ω-labeled child. We next describe the bounds and the rule more formally.

Consider a node $\mathbf{V}$. To efficiently check whether a child node $C\mathbf{V}$ can be deleted, we need an upper bound on the score obtained by a partition of $\mathbf{V}$ that includes $C\mathbf{V}$. To this end, we associate any set function $f : 2^\Omega \to \mathbb{R}$ with another function $f' : 2^\Omega \to \mathbb{R}$ defined by letting $f'(\emptyset) := 0$ and, for all $\emptyset \subset B \subseteq \Omega$,

$$f'(B) := \max_{\substack{\{C_1,\ldots,C_r\} \\ \text{partition of } B}} \{\, f(C_1) + \cdots + f(C_r)\,\}\,. \qquad (11)$$

A folklore dynamic programming algorithm computes f' for a given f in $O(3^{|\Omega|})$ time, based on the recurrence

$$f'(B) = \max_{\emptyset \subset C \subseteq B} \{f(C) + f'(B \setminus C)\}\,. \qquad (12)$$

Eggeling et al. (2015a) made use of this observation to compute the optimal score over all partitions of the alphabet, given by $f'(\Omega)$ with a suitable function f. Here, we apply it to score upper bounds, and we also use several of the values $f'(B)$ in order to stay within $O(3^{|\Omega|})$ for computing all upper bounds required:

Proposition 3 (Deletion rule)**.** *Let* $\mathbf{V} \in \mathcal{V}$ *with* $\ell(\mathbf{V}) < d$, *and let* $\emptyset \subset C \subset \Omega$. *Let* $f(C') := S_0(C'\mathbf{V})$ *for all* $\emptyset \subset C' \subseteq \Omega$. *If*

$$S_0(C\mathbf{V}) + f'(\Omega \setminus C) < S_*(\Omega\mathbf{V})\,,$$

then the node $C\mathbf{V}$ *does not belong to any optimal PCT.*

The correctness can be shown by contradiction. Suppose $C\mathbf{V}$ did belong to an optimal PCT even though the premise was fulfilled. Then $S_*(C\mathbf{V}) + f'(\Omega \setminus C) \geq S_*(\Omega\mathbf{V})$, leading to $S_0(C\mathbf{V}) < S_*(C\mathbf{V})$, which violates the property of S_0 being an an upper bound of S_*.

We illustrate the deletion rule by a small toy example in Figure 2. Here, we focus on the first layer, where only for the maximal node an optimal PCT subtree is computed and thus an exact score is available already, whereas for the other siblings only upper-bounded scores exist. Based on those scores, we compute the upper-bounded scores of every possible partition and observe and observe that only one partition, consisting of the two child nodes AB and CD, has an upper-bounded score that is greater than the exact score of the maximal sibling node ABCD. All other siblings can thus not contribute to an optimal partition of child nodes, as even the best partition they contribute to has an upper-bounded score smaller than what is already achieved. Hence, the corresponding subtrees do not need to be optimized explicitly and can be deleted.

The deletion rule does invest a certain amount of effort that the obtained savings need to compensate before the rule becomes effective: In the worst case, we need to compute the optimal partition of children twice for each inner node, once with the upper-bounded scores for excluding subtrees from further optimization, and once with the exact scores. As a positive side note, we observe that, while we focus on BIC upper bounds in this work, the deletion rule is in principle independent of the used scoring function, as long as an effective upper bound $S_0 \leq S_*$ can be specified.

3.5 LOOKAHEAD

The upper bound of Section 3.2 can be computed directly for a given node without entering the recursion. However, we can tighten the bound, if we do enter the recursion for one or more steps, in effect, performing a lookahead on the data. To this end, for all nodes $\mathbf{V}$ and number of steps $q = 1, \ldots, d - \ell(\mathbf{V})$, define

$$S_q(\mathbf{V}) := \max_{\substack{\{C_1,\ldots,C_r\} \\ \text{partition of } \Omega}} \sum_{i=1}^{r} S_{q-1}(C_i\mathbf{V}), \tag{13}$$

with $S_0(\mathbf{V})$ being the base case of a flat upper bound.

Proposition 4 (Lookahead bound). *For all $\mathbf{V} \in \mathcal{V}$ and $q = 1, \ldots, d - \ell(\mathbf{V})$, it holds that*

$$S_*(\mathbf{V}) \leq S_q(\mathbf{V}) \leq S_0(\mathbf{V}). \tag{14}$$

Using the lookahead bound with large q does constitute a substantial computational effort. If $q = d - \ell(\mathbf{V})$, the bound matched the optimal score and, in essence, is obtained by traversing through all possible PCT subtrees. Hence, the choice of q is critical in order to obtain a trade-off between gained savings and additional invested effort in relation to the flat bound.

One possibility to cope with that issue is to dynamically increase q, i.e., to first test whether pruning on flat upper bounds S_0 is possible. If this is not the case, q is increased by one, up to the maximal value of $d - \ell(\mathbf{V})$. However, in this work we refrain from exploring this procedure in full, as in our preliminary studies one-step lookahead ($q = 1$) turned out to perform the best in the vast majority of cases.

3.6 FINAL ALGORITHM

We combine the presented ideas using pseudo code. Consider first the task of computing, for all nonempty subsets $B \subseteq \Omega$, the maximum total score over all partitions of B, in other words, the set function f' for a given set function f, as defined in Eq. 11. The procedure MAX-PART given below completes this task based on the recurrence in Eq. 12.

```
MAX-PART(f)
g[∅] ← 0
for each ∅ ⊂ B ⊆ Ω in quasi-lexicographical order
    do g[B] ← −∞
       for each ∅ ⊂ C ⊆ B
           do g[B] ← max{g[B], f[C] + g[B \ C]}
return g
```

The main algorithm, given below as procedure MAX-PCT, calls MAX-PART(f) both with exact scores and with upper bounds, as specified by the argument f. The call MAX-PCT($\mathbf{V}$) returns the optimal score $S_*(\mathbf{V})$. We thus obtain the maximum score over all PCTs of depth d by calling MAX-PCT(Λ).

```
MAX-PCT(V)
score ← L(V) − K
if ℓ(V) < d and score < S_0^BIC(V)
   then s[Ω] ← MAX-PCT(ΩV)
        for each ∅ ⊂ B ⊆ Ω
            do u[C] ← S_q^BIC(CV)
        u' ← MAX-PART(u)
        for each ∅ ⊂ B ⊆ Ω
            do s[C] ← −∞
               if u[C] + u'[Ω \ C] > s[Ω]
                  then s[C] ← MAX-PCT(CV)
        s' ← MAX-PART(s)
        score ← s'[Ω]
return score
```

3.7 INCORPORATING MEMOIZATION

While we omitted it for the sake of simplicity in the pseudocode, incorporating the memoization technique of Eggeling et al. (2015a) into the proposed algorithm is straightforward.

We can add a test that checks whether the index set $I(\mathbf{V})$ has already occurred with some other node at the same depth directly when entering the function. If the test is positive, the score is re-used and the rest of the function is skipped. If the test is negative, the score is stored in a hash data structure at the end of the function with the current data subset (index set) and the depth of the node as key.

4 CASE STUDIES

In the empirical part of this work, we evaluate the effect of the proposed pruning techniques using a Java-implementetation based on the Jstacs library (Grau et al., 2012). We focus on the metric of *visited nodes* in the extended PCT, which includes all created nodes, included those used only for look-ahead computations. In addition, we also measure the elapsed *running time*. We consider the problem of modeling DNA binding sites of regulatory proteins such as transcription factors, which constitutes one established application of PCTs.

4.1 DATA AND PREDICTION STUDY

A data set of DNA binding sites consists of short sequences of the same length over the alphabet $\Omega = \{\mathsf{A}, \mathsf{C}, \mathsf{G}, \mathsf{T}\}$ that are considered to be recognized by the same DNA-binding protein. We use 25 data sets, which all show at least some degree of statistical dependence among sequence positions, from the publicly available data base JASPAR (Mathelier et al., 2013). The data sets differ in sequence length L from 10 to 21 symbols, in the sample size N from 156 to 3629 sequences, and in the strength of the signal.

To exhibit the general properties of this data, we perform a prediction experiment based on the model class and learning framework of Eggeling et al. (2014), which makes a position-specific use of PCTs. We perform a leave-one-out cross-validation for different PCT depths $d \in \{0, \ldots, 6\}$ and compute the mean log predictive probability over the test sequences from all iterations. We aggregate the resulting 7×25 mean log predictive probabilities in two different ways and visualize the results in Figure 3. First, we check for each data set, which d yields the highest predictive probability, and in case that several depths share rank one (which can happen if all subtrees below a certain depth are minimal), we note the smallest d. Second, we average the mean log predictive probabilities for each d over all 25 data sets.

We observe that all data sets contain indeed statistical dependencies to some degree, since $d = 0$ is never the best choice, and increasing d yields – on average – an increased predictive performance, though the magnitude of improvement decreases gradually. This indicates that (i) the used BIC score for PCT optimization works reasonably well in order to avoid overfitting, and (ii) the data sets have a non-trivial structure so that the optimization problem is hard.

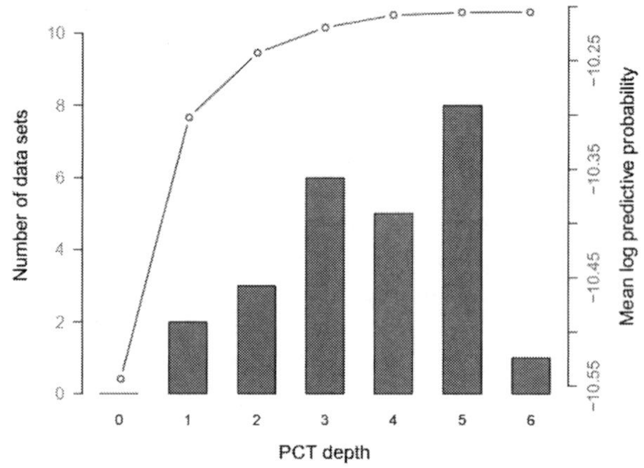

Figure 3: **Prediction study**. We show the results of a leave-one-out cross validation. Green bars indicate for how many data sets a certain PCT depth d is the smallest depth that yields an optimal prediction. The blue line shows the average predictive performance over all data sets as a function of d.

4.2 ONE DATA SET IN DETAIL

Next, we consider a single data set and investigate the effectiveness of the pruning rule in relation to the basic algorithm and to the memoization technique of Eggeling et al. (2015a). We focus on the DNA-binding protein CTCF (Kim et al., 2007), where the corresponding JASPAR data set consists of $N = 908$ sequences of length $L = 19$.

Figure 4a shows for this data set the *sequence logo* (Schneider & Stephens, 1990), which is a common visualization of the marginal distribution of the individual sequence positions. For each position, the four possible symbols are scaled relative to the marginal probability $\mathbf{p} = (p_{\mathsf{A}}, p_{\mathsf{C}}, p_{\mathsf{G}}, p_{\mathsf{T}})$ and the height of the symbol stack is scaled by $2 - \mathrm{H}(\mathbf{p})$ (which is often called *information content*), with H denoting the Shannon entropy in bits. Figure 4b shows the fraction of the visited nodes in the extended PCT of depth 5 for the pruning technique, the memoization technique, and the combination of both in relation to the basic algorithm.

We observe that pruning is effective in particular at positions where the marginal distribution of the response variable is far from uniform, with clear examples being position 10 and position 13. In fact, the correlation coefficient between the information content of the response variable and the common logarithm of fraction of visited nodes using the pruning rule in relation to the basic algorithm amounts -0.821. For memoization, a similar effect occurs, but here marginal distributions of the explanatory variables are the deciding factor: the largest saving occurs at position 14, where highly informative positions 10 and 13 are in the context.

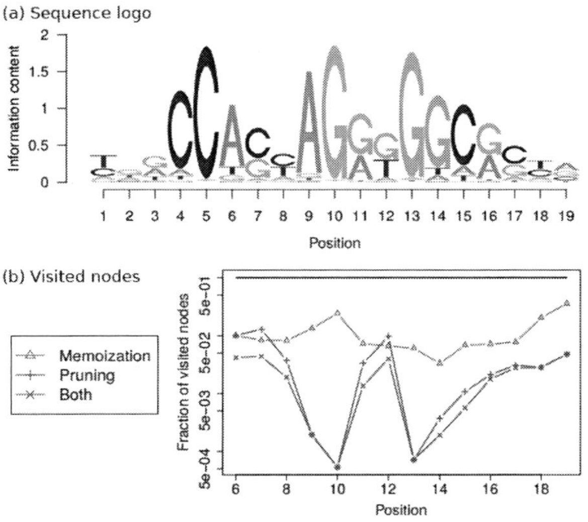

Figure 4: **Detailed result for CTCF data set.** Subfigure (a) shows the position-specific marginal nucleotide frequencies for each position in the sequence. Subfigure (b) shows the fraction of visited nodes required for PCT optimization ($d = 5$) for every sequence position $j = 6, \ldots, 19$, and for the three algorithmic variants in relation to the basic algorithm.

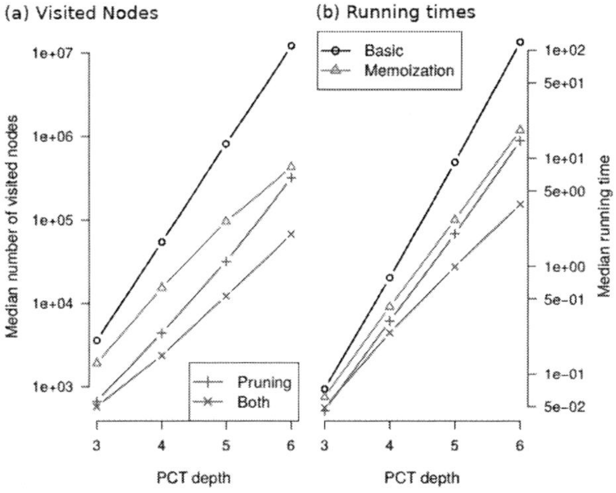

Figure 5: **Aggregated results for all four algorithmic variants.** For each data set, we average the visited nodes and running times over all sequence positions. We then plot (a) the median number of visited nodes and (b) median running times over all data sets.

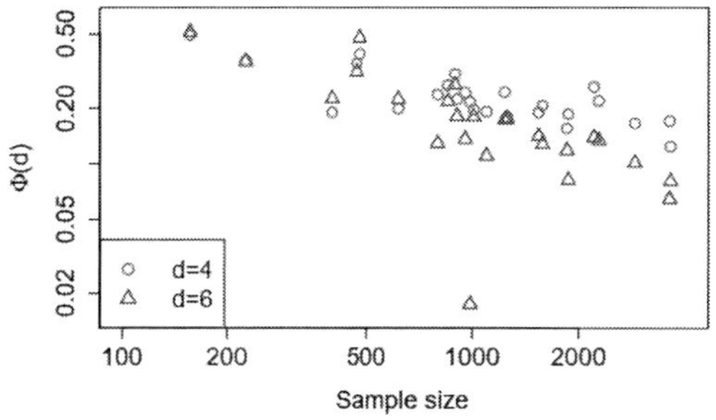

Figure 6: **Effect of sample size on savings ratio for pruning algorithm.** For all 25 data sets, for $d = \{4, 6\}$, we plot $\Phi(d)$ of Eq. 15 against the sample size N.

We summarize that the empirical performance does indeed satisfy the theoretical expectations: While memoization exploits regularities in the realizations of the explanatory variables, the pruning rules exploit regularity in the response variable, and the effect of the latter is often, though not always, greater. Combining both techniques generally resembles the sole application of pruning, albeit additional savings due to memoization do occur.

4.3 BROADER STUDY

We now take a broader view by considering all data sets. Given a PCT depth d, we (i) average the number of visited nodes and the absolute running times for each data set over all sequence positions, and (ii) take the median of average visited nodes and average running times over all data sets. The results are displayed for $d = 3, \ldots, 6$ in Figure 5, and confirm the observations made for a single data set in the previous section: Pruning outperforms memoization, yet the combination of both techniques yields the largest overall effect.

However, we observe a striking divergence between savings in terms of visited nodes in the extended PCT as displayed in Figure 5a and the improvements in terms of running times as displayed in Figure 5b. Whereas the savings in the first case are up to two orders of magnitude, the absolute running time yields a smaller improvement of roughly one order of magnitude for PCTs of $d = 5$.

In order to investigate this issue further, we measure how strong the runtime reduction deviates from the reduction in terms of visited nodes. Let $\mathrm{VN}(d)$ denote the number of visited nodes in the extended PCT for finding an optimal PCT of depth d using the pruning technique, and let $\mathrm{RT}(d)$ denote the corresponding running time. Let further $\mathrm{VN}_{\mathrm{basic}}(d)$ and $\mathrm{RT}_{\mathrm{basic}}(d)$ denote the same quantities for the basic algorithm. We define

$$\Phi(d) = \frac{\mathrm{VN}(d) \times \mathrm{RT}_{\mathrm{basic}}(d)}{\mathrm{VN}_{\mathrm{basic}}(d) \times \mathrm{RT}(d)}, \qquad (15)$$

which yields a value of 1, if the savings in visited nodes are translated one-to-one into savings in running times, and a value smaller than 1, if savings in terms of visited nodes are larger. Next, we plot $\Phi(4)$ and $\Phi(6)$ for each data set against the sample size (Figure 6).

We observe a correlation between Φ and sample size: for small data sets the discrepancy between running time and visited nodes is smaller than for larger data sets, which is beneficial since the statistical efficiency of PCTs is relevant in particular for small data settings. The one outlier in the plot at sample size close to 1000 where the $\Phi(6)$ is clearly off belongs to a highly-regular data set where pruning is so effective that reading the data and initializing all data structures becomes the dominating factor, albeit requiring only few milliseconds in absolute terms. Ignoring that outlier and extrapolating Φ in Figure 6 to a hypothetical sample size of zero, it appears that savings in running times and visited nodes could match.

To explain this behavior, we have to reconsider the theoretical expectations of the running time of the basic algorithm (Section 2.2). It assumes the work to be performed in each inner node to be dominated by the alphabet partitioning problem and thus constant for a fixed Ω. For small $|\Omega|$, however, data-management operations, such as determining $I(C\mathbf{V})$ given $I(\mathbf{V})$, become a significant factor. Unlike alphabet partitioning, data-management is not equally demanding within each node: Nodes close to the root match on average more data points than nodes close to the leaves. Moreover, assuming the siblings in the extended PCT are ordered quasi-lexicographically as in the example of Figure 1a, we observe that the right half of the extended PCT (or any subtree of it) matches on average more data points than the left half. However, the subtrees of the extended PCT not traversed explicitly due to the pruning or memoization technique are predominantly the subtrees that match comparably few data points, which explains why the savings in visited nodes do not directly translate into the same saving factors for running times.

5 CONCLUDING REMARKS

We have investigated a bound-and-prune approach to finding a maximum-score parsimonious context tree (PCT). Specifically, we derived local score upper bounds for the BIC score, with an option for a few-step lookahead, and we presented two pruning rules: a stopping rule and a deletion rule.

Empirical results on DNA binding site data showed that pruning alone, which essentially exploits regularities in the response variable, is slightly more effective than the memoization technique of Eggeling et al. (2015a), which exploits regularities in the explanatory variables. While the combination of pruning and memoization runs an about order-of-magnitude faster, it partially inherits the large memory requirements of memoization; however, pruning does reduce the memory requirement, too, as a smaller number of subproblems need to be solved explicitly. These finding suggest that pruning should always be included, and memoization can be added to gain further speedups provided that memory consumption is not an issue.

While we have restricted our attention to learning PCTs and to the BIC score, we believe many of the presented ideas are applicable more generally. First, the BIC score can, in principle, be replaced by any other scoring function for which good upper bounds similar to Proposition 1 can be established. Second, the techniques should easily extend to learning decision trees with many categorical explanatory variables. Third, the bound-and-prune approach might be effective also in expediting other algorithms that are based on recursive set partitioning, like the one by Kangas et al. (2014) for learning chordal Markov networks.

Acknowledgements

The authors thank the anonymous reviewers for valuable suggestions to improve the presentation. This work was supported by the Academy of Finland, Grant 276864 "Supple Exponential Algorithms".

References

Akaike, H. A new look at the statistical model identification. *IEEE Transactions on Automatic Control*, 19(6):716–723, 1974.

Bourguignon, P.-Y. and Robelin, D. Modèles de Markov parcimonieux: sélection de modele et estimation. In *Proceedings of the 5e édition des Journées Ouvertes en Biologie, Informatique et Mathématiques (JOBIM)*, 2004.

Boutilier, C., Friedman, N., Goldszmidt, M., and Koller, D. Context-specific independence in Bayesian networks. In *Proceedings of the 12th Conference on Uncertainty in Artificial Intelligence (UAI)*, 1996.

Breiman, L., Friedman, J.H., Olshen, R., and Stone, C.J. *Classification and Regression Trees*. Wadsworth, 1984.

Bühlmann, P. and Wyner, A.J. Variable length Markov chains. *Annals of Statistics*, 27:480–513, 1999.

Chavira, M. and Darwiche, A. Compiling Bayesian networks with local structure. In *Proceedings of the 19th International Joint Conference on Artificial Intelligence (IJCAI)*, 2005.

Chickering, D.M., Heckerman, D., and Meek, C. A Bayesian approach to learning Bayesian networks with local structure. In *Proceedings. of the 13th Conference on Uncertainty in Artificial Intelligence (UAI)*, 1997.

de Campos, C.P. and Ji, Q. Efficient structure learning of Bayesian networks using constraints. *Journal of Machine Learning Research*, 12:663–689, 2011.

Dechter, R. and Mateescu, R. AND/OR search spaces for graphical models. *Artificial Intelligence*, 171(2-3):73–106, 2007.

Eggeling, R., Roos, T., Myllymäki, P., and Grosse, I. Robust learning of inhomogeneous PMMs. In *Proceedings of the 17th International Conference on Artificial Intelligence and Statistics (AISTATS)*, 2014.

Eggeling, R., Koivisto, M., and Grosse, I. Dealing with small data: On the generalization of context trees. In *Proceedings of the 32nd International Conference on Machine Learning (ICML)*, 2015a.

Eggeling, R., Roos, T., Myllymäki, P., and Grosse, I. Inferring intra-motif dependencies of DNA binding sites from ChIP-seq data. *BMC Bioinformatics*, 16:375, 2015b.

Friedman, N. and Goldszmidt, M. Learning Bayesian networks with local structure. In *Proceedings of the 12th Conference on Uncertainty in Artificial Intelligence (UAI)*, 1996.

Grau, J., Keilwagen, J., Gohr, A., Haldemann, B., Posch, S., and Grosse, I. Jstacs: A Java framework for statistical analysis and classification of biological sequences. *Journal of Machine Learning Research*, 13:1967–1971, 2012.

Kangas, K., Koivisto, M., and Niinimäki, T. Learning chordal Markov networks by dynamic programming. In *Advances in Neural Information Processing Systems 27 (NIPS)*, 2014.

Kim, T.E., Abdullaev, Z.K., Smith, A.D., Ching, K.A., Loukinov, D.I., Green, R.D., Zhang, M.Q., Lobanenkov, V.V., and Ren, B. Analysis of the vertebrate insulator protein CTCF-binding sites in the human genome. *Cell*, 128:1231–1245, 2007.

Mathelier, A., Zhao, X., Zhang, A.W., Parcy, F., Worstley-Hunt, R., Arenillas, D.J., Buchman, S., Chen, C., Chou, A., Ienasescu, H., Lim, J., Shyr, C., Tan, G., Zhou, M., Lenhard, B., Sandelin, A., and Wasserman, W.W. JASPAR 2014: an extensively expanded and updated open-access database of transcription factor binding profiles. *Nucleic Acids Research*, 42(D1):D142–D147, 2013.

Nau, D.S., Kumar, V., and Kanal, L. General branch and bound, and its relation to A* and AO*. *Artificial Intelligence*, 23(1):29–58, 1984.

Nilsson, N.J. *Principles of Artificial Intelligence*. Tioga, Palo Alto, CA, 1980.

Oliver, J. Decision graphs – an extension of decision trees. In *Proceedings of the 4th International Workshop on Artificial Intelligence and Statistics (AISTATS)*, 1993.

Rissanen, J. Modeling by shortest data description. *Automatica*, 14:465–471, 1978.

Rissanen, J. A universal data compression system. *IEEE Transactions on Information Theory*, 29(5):656–664, 1983.

Schneider, T.D. and Stephens, R.M. Sequence logos: A new way to display consensus sequences. *Nucleic Acids Research*, 18(20):6097–6100, 1990.

Schwarz, G.E. Estimating the dimension of a model. *Annals of Statistics*, 2:461–464, 1978.

Seifert, M., Gohr, A., Strickert, M., and Grosse, I. Parsimonious higher-order hidden Markov models for improved array-CGH analysis with applications to Arabidopsis thaliana. *PLOS Computational Biology*, 8(1):e1002286, 2012.

Su, J. and Zhang, H. Representing conditional independence using decision trees. In *Proceedings of the 20th National Conference on Artificial Intelligence (AAAI)*, 2005.

Teyssier, M. and Koller, D. Ordering-based search: A simple and effective algorithm for learning Bayesian networks. In *Proceedings of the 21st Conference on Uncertainty in Artificial Intelligence (UAI)*, 2005.

Tian, J. A branch-and-bound algorithm for MDL learning in Bayesian networks. In *Proceedings of the 16th Conference on Uncertainty in Artificial Intelligence (UAI)*, 2000.

Yuan, C. and Malone, B. Learning optimal Bayesian networks: A shortest path perspective. *Journal of Artificial Intelligence Research*, 48:23–65, 2013.

Learning Network of Multivariate Hawkes Processes: A Time Series Approach

Jalal Etesami
Dep. of Industrial &
Enterprise Systems Eng.
Coordinated Science Lab.
UIUC, Urbana, IL 61801
etesami2@illinois.edu

Negar Kiyavash
Dep. of Industrial &
Enterprise Systems Eng.
Dep. of Electrical &
Computer Eng.
Coordinated Science Lab.
UIUC, Urbana, IL 61801
kiyavash@illinois.edu

Kun Zhang
Dep. of Philosophy
Carnegie Mellon University
Pittsburgh, PA 15213
kunz1@andrew.cmu.edu

Kushagra Singhal
Dep. of Electrical &
Computer Eng.
Coordinated Science Lab.
UIUC, Urbana, IL 61801
ksingha2@illinois.edu

Abstract

Learning the influence structure of multiple time series data is of great interest to many disciplines. This paper studies the problem of recovering the causal structure in network of multivariate linear Hawkes processes. In such processes, the occurrence of an event in one process affects the probability of occurrence of new events in some other processes. Thus, a natural notion of causality exists between such processes captured by the support of the excitation matrix. We show that the resulting causal influence network is equivalent to the Directed Information graph (DIG) of the processes, which encodes the causal factorization of the joint distribution of the processes. Furthermore, we present an algorithm for learning the support of excitation matrix of a class of multivariate Hawkes processes with exponential exciting functions (or equivalently the DIG). The performance of the algorithm is evaluated on synthesized multivariate Hawkes networks as well as a stock market and MemeTracker real-world dataset.

1 INTRODUCTION

In many disciplines, including biology, economics, social sciences, and computer science, it is important to learn the structure of interacting networks of stochastic processes. In particular, succinct representation of the causal interactions in the network is of interest.

A lot of studies in the causality fields focus on causal discovery from time series. To find causal relations from time series, one may fit vector autoregressive models on the time series, or more generally, evaluate the causal influences with transfer entropy [22] or directed information [19]. This paper considers learning causal structure for a specific type of time series, multivariate linear Hawkes process [8]. Hawkes processes were originally motivated by the quest for good statistical models for earthquake occurrences. Since then, they have been successfully applied to seismology [15], biology [21], criminology [13], computational finance [5, 12, 14], etc. It is desirable to develop specific causal discovery methods for such processes and study the properties of existing methods in this particular scenario.

In multivariate or mutually exciting point processes, occurrence of an event (arrival) in one process affects the conditional probability of new occurrences, i.e., the *intensity* function of other processes in the network. Such interdependencies between the intensity functions of a linear Hawkes process are modeled as follows: the intensity function of processes j is assumed to be a linear combination of different terms, such that each term captures only the effects of one other process (See Section 2.1). Therefore, a natural notion of functional dependence (causality) exists among the processes in the sense that in linear mutually exciting processes, if the coefficient pertaining to the effects of process i is non-zero in the intensity function of process j, we know that process i is influencing process j. This dependency is captured by the support of the excitation matrix of the network. As a result, estimation of the excitation (kernel) matrix of multivariate processes is crucial both for learning the structure of their causal network and for other inference tasks and has been the focus of research. For instance, maximum likelihood estimators were proposed for estimating the parameters of excitation matrices with exponential and Laguerre decay in [16, 25]. These estimators depend on existence of i.i.d. samples. However, often we do not have access to i.i.d. samples when analyzing time series. Second-order statistics of the multivariate Hawkes processes were used to estimate the kernel matrix of a subclass of multivariate Hawkes processes called symmetric Hawkes processes [1]. Utilizing the branching property of the Hawkes processes, an expectation maximization algorithm was proposed to estimate the excitation matrix in [10].

We aim to investigate efficient approaches to estimation of excitation matrix of Hawkes processes from time series that does not require i.i.d. samples and investigate how the concept of causality in such processes is related to other established approaches to analyze causal effects in time series.

1.1 SUMMARY OF RESULTS AND ORGANIZATION

Our contribution in this paper is two fold. First, we prove that for linear multivariate Hawkes processes, the causal relationships implied by the excitation matrix is equivalent to a specific factorization of the joint distribution of the system called *minimal generative model*. Minimal generative models encode causal dependencies based on a generalized notion of Granger causality, measured by causally conditioned directed information [20]. One significance of this result is that it provides a surrogate to directed information measure for capturing causal influences for Hawkes processes. Thus, instead of estimating the directed information, which often requires estimating a high dimensional joint distribution, it suffices to learn the support of the excitation matrix. Our second contribution is indeed providing an estimation method for learning the support of excitation matrices with exponential form using second-order statistics of the Hawkes processes.

Our proposed learning approach, in contrast with the previous work [1, 24], is not limited to symmetric Hawkes processes. In a symmetric Hawkes process, it is assumed that the Laplace transform of the excitation matrix can be factored into product of a diagonal matrix and a constant unitary matrix. Moreover, it is assumed that the expected values of all intensities are the same. A numerical method to approximate the excitation matrix from a set of coupled integral equations was recently proposed in [3]. Our approach is based on an exact analytical solution to find the excitation matrix. Interestingly, the exact approach turns out to be both more robust and less expensive in terms of complexity compared to the numerical method of [3].

The rest of this paper is organized as follows. Background material, some definitions, and the notation are presented in Section 2. Specifically, therein, we formally introduce multivariate Hawkes processes and directed information graphs. In Section 3, we establish the connection between the excitation matrix and the corresponding DIG. In Section 4, we propose an algorithm for learning the excitation matrix or equivalently the DIG of a class of stationary multivariate linear Hawkes processes. Section 5 illustrates the performance of the proposed algorithm in inferring the causal structure in a network of synthesized mutually exciting linear Hawkes processes and in stock market. Finally, we conclude our work in Section 6.

2 PRELIMINARY DEFINITIONS

In this Section we review some basic definitions and our notation. We denote random processes by capital letters and a collection of m random processes by $\underline{X}_{[m]} = \{X_1, ..., X_m\}$, where $[m] := \{1, ..., m\}$. We denote the ith random process at time t by $X_i(t)$, the random process X_i from time s up to time t by $X_{i,s}^t$, and a subset $\mathcal{K} \subseteq [m]$ of random process up to time t by $\underline{X}_{\mathcal{K}}^t$. The Laplace transform and Fourier Transform of X_i are denoted, respectively by

$$L[X_i](s) = \int_0^\infty X_i(t)e^{-st}dt, \tag{1}$$
$$\mathcal{F}[X_i](\omega) = \int_{-\infty}^{\infty} X_i(t)e^{-j\omega t}dt,$$

where $j = \sqrt{-1}$. The convolution between two functions f and g is defined as $f * g(t) := \int_{\mathbb{R}} f(x)g(t-x)dx$. The joint distribution of processes $\{X_1^n, ..., X_m^n\}$ is represented by $P_{\underline{X}}(n)$.

2.1 MULTIVARIATE HAWKES PROCESSES

Fix a complete probability space $(\Omega, \mathcal{F}, P)$. Let $N(t)$ denotes the counting process representing the cumulative number of events up to time t and let $\{\mathcal{F}^t\}_{t\geq 0}$ be a set of increasing σ-algebras such that $\mathcal{F}^t = \sigma\{N^t\}$. The non-negative, $\mathcal{F}^t$-measurable process $\lambda(t)$ is called the intensity of $N(t)$ if

$$P(N(t+dt) - N(t) = 1|\mathcal{F}^t) = \lambda(t)dt + o(dt).$$

A classical example of mutually exciting processes, a multivariate Hawkes process [8], is a multidimensional process $\underline{N}(t) = \{N_1, ..., N_m\}$ such that for each $i \in [m]$

$$P\left(dN_i(t) = 1|\underline{\mathcal{F}}^t\right) = \lambda_i(t)dt + o(dt), \tag{2}$$
$$P(dN_i(t) > 1|\underline{\mathcal{F}}^t) = o(dt),$$

where $\underline{\mathcal{F}}^t = \sigma\{\underline{N}^t\}$. The above equations imply that $\mathbb{E}[dN_i(t)/dt|\underline{\mathcal{F}}^t] = \lambda_i(t)$. Furthermore, the intensities are all positive and are given by

$$\lambda_i(t) = v_i + \sum_{k=1}^{m} \int_0^t \gamma_{i,k}(t-t')dN_k(t'). \tag{3}$$

The exciting functions $\gamma_{i,k}(\cdot)$s are in ℓ_1 such that $\lambda_i(t) \geq 0$ for all $t > 0$. Equivalently, in matrix representation:

$$\Lambda(t) = \mathbf{v} + \int_0^t \Gamma(t-t')d\underline{N}(t'), \tag{4}$$

where $\Gamma(\cdot)$ denotes an $m \times m$ matrix with entries $\gamma_{i,j}(\cdot)$; $d\underline{N}$, $\Lambda(\cdot)$, and $\mathbf{v}$ are $m \times 1$ arrays with entries dN_i, $\lambda_i(\cdot)$, and v_i, respectively. Matrix $\Gamma(\cdot)$ is called the excitation (kernel) matrix. Figure 1 illustrates the intensities of a multivariate Hawkes process comprised of two processes ($m = 2$) with the following parameters

$$\mathbf{v} = \begin{pmatrix} 0.5 \\ 0.4 \end{pmatrix}, \quad \Gamma(t) = \begin{pmatrix} 0.1e^{-t} & 0.3e^{-1.1t} \\ 0.5e^{-0.9t} & 0.3e^{-t} \end{pmatrix} u(t),$$

where $u(t)$ is the unit step function.

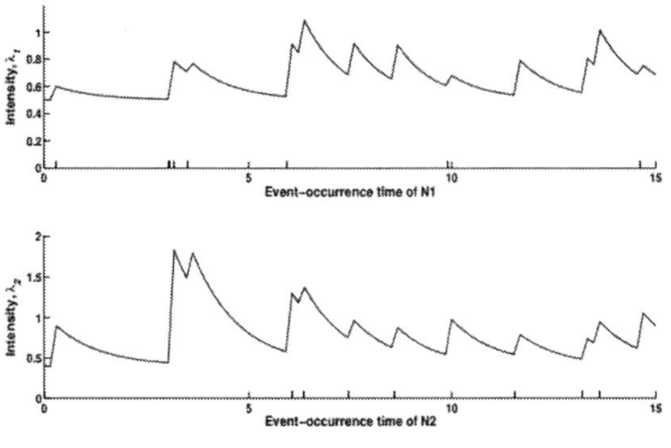

Figure 1: Intensities of the multivariate Hawkes process.

Assumption 1 *A joint distribution is called positive (non-degenerate), if there exists a reference measure ϕ such that $P_{\underline{X}} \ll \phi$ and $\frac{dP_{\underline{X}}}{d\phi} > 0$, where $P_{\underline{X}} \ll \phi$ denotes that $P_{\underline{X}}$ is absolutely continuous with respect to ϕ*[1].

Note that the Assumption 1 states that none of the processes is fully determined by the other processes.

2.2 CAUSAL STRUCTURE

A causal model allows the factorization of the joint distribution in some specific ways. *Generative model graphs* are a type of graphical model that similar to Bayesian networks [17] represent a causal factorization of the joint [19]. More precisely, it was shown in [19] that under Assumption 1, the joint distribution of a causal[2] discrete-time dynamical system with m processes can be factorized as follows,

$$P_{\underline{X}} = \prod_{i=1}^{m} P_{X_i||\underline{X}_{B_i}}, \tag{5}$$

where $B(i) \subseteq -\{i\}$ is the minimal[3] set of processes that causes process X_i, i.e., parent set of node i in the corresponding minimal generative model graph. Such factorization of the joint distribution is called minimal generative model. In Equation (5),

$$P_{X_i||\underline{X}_{B_i}} := \prod_{t=1}^{n} P_{X_i(t)|\underline{\mathcal{F}}^{t-1}_{B\cup\{i\}}},$$

and $\underline{\mathcal{F}}^{t-1}_{B\cup\{i\}} = \sigma\{\underline{X}^{t-1}_{B\cup\{i\}}\}$.

[1]A measure $P_{\underline{X}}$ on Borel subsets of the real line is absolutely continuous with respect to measure ϕ if for every measurable set B, $\phi(B) = 0$ implies $P_{\underline{X}}(B) = 0$.

[2]In causal systems, given the full past of the system, the present of the processes become independent.

[3]Minimal in terms of its cardinality.

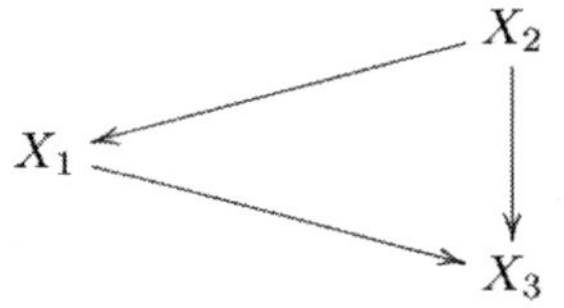

Figure 2: Minimal generative model graph of Example 1.

Extending the definition of generative model graphs to continuous-time systems requires some technicalities which are not necessary for the purpose of this paper. Hence we illustrate the general idea through an example.

The following example demonstrates the minimal generative model graph of a simple continuous-time system.

Example 1 *Consider a dynamical system in which the processes evolve over time horizon $[0, T]$ through the following coupled differential equations:*

$$dX_1 = f(X_1, X_2)dt + dW,$$
$$dX_2 = g(X_2)dt + dU,$$
$$dX_3 = h(X_1, X_2, X_3)dt + dV,$$

where W, U and V are independent exogenous noises. For small time dt, this becomes,

$$\begin{aligned} dX_1(t+dt) &\approx \Delta f(X_1(t), X_2(t)) + dW(t), \\ dX_2(t+dt) &\approx \Delta g(X_2(t)) + dU(t), \\ dX_3(t+dt) &\approx \Delta h(X_1(t), X_2(t), X_3(t)) + dV(t). \end{aligned} \tag{6}$$

In this example, since the system is causal, the corresponding joint distribution can be factorized as follows,

$$P_{\underline{X}} = \prod_{j=1}^{3}\prod_{k\geq 0} P_{X_j(T-kdt)|\underline{\mathcal{F}}^{T-(k+1)dt}}, \tag{7}$$

where $\underline{\mathcal{F}}^{T-(k+1)dt} = \sigma\{\underline{X}^{T-(k+1)dt}_{\{1,2,3\}}\}$. Due to (6), we can rewrite (7) as

$$P_{\underline{X}} = P_{X_1||X_2}P_{X_2}P_{X_3||X_1,X_2}. \tag{8}$$

Figure 2 demonstrates the corresponding generative model graph of the factorization in (8).

In general, the joint distribution of a causal dynamical system can be factorized as $P_{\underline{X}} = \prod_{i=1}^{m} P_{X_i||\underline{X}_{B_i}}$, where $B(i) \subseteq -\{i\}$ is the parent set of node i in the corresponding minimal generative model graph, and

$$P_{X_i||\underline{X}_{B_i}} = \prod_{k\geq 0} P_{X_i(T-kdt)|\underline{\mathcal{F}}^{T-(k+1)dt}_{B_i}}.$$

3 TWO EQUIVALENT NOTATIONS OF CAUSALITY FOR HAWKES PROCESSES

In linear multivariate Hawkes processes, a natural notion of causation exists in the following sense: if $\gamma_{i,j} \neq 0$, then occurrence of an event in jth process will affect the likelihood of the arrivals in ith process. Next, we establish the relationship between the excitation matrix of multivariate Hawkes processes and their generative model graph. To do so, first, we discuss the equivalence of directed information graphs and generative models graphs which was established in [20].

3.1 DIRECTED INFORMATION GRAPHS (DIGs)

An alternative graphical model to encode statistical interdependencies in stochastic causal dynamical systems are *directed information graphs* (DIGs) [19]. Such graphs are defined based on an information-theoretic quantity, *directed information* (DI) that generalizes the Granger causality and it was shown in [20] that under some mild assumptions, they are equivalent to the minimal generative model graphs. Hence, DIGs also represent a minimal factorization of the joint distribution.

In a DIG, to determine whether X_j causes X_i over a time horizon $[0, T]$ in a network of m random processes, two conditional probabilities are compared in KL-divergence sense: one is the conditional probability of $X_i(t+dt)$ given full past, i.e., $\underline{\mathcal{F}}^t := \sigma\{\underline{X}^t\}$ and the other one is the conditional probability of $X_i(t+dt)$ given full past except the past of X_j, i.e., $\underline{\mathcal{F}}^t_{-\{j\}} := \sigma\{\underline{X}^t_{-\{j\}}\}$. It is declared that there is no influence from X_j on X_i, if the two conditional probabilities are the same. More precisely, there is an influence from X_j on X_i if and only if the following directed information measure is positive [19],

$$I_T(X_j \to X_i||\underline{X}_{-\{i,j\}}) := \inf_{\mathbf{t}\in\mathcal{T}(0,T)} \tilde{I}_{\mathbf{t}}(X_j \to X_i||\underline{X}_{-\{i,j\}}), \tag{9}$$

where $-\{i,j\} := [m]\setminus\{i,j\}$, $\mathcal{T}$ denotes the set of all finite partitions of the time interval $[0, T]$ [23], and

$$\tilde{I}_{\mathbf{t}}(X_j \to X_i||\underline{X}_{-\{i,j\}}) := \sum_{k=0}^{n} I\left(X^{t_k}_{i,t_{k-1}}; X^{t_k}_{j,0}|\mathcal{F}^{t_{k-1}}_{-\{j\}}\right),$$

where $\mathbf{t} := (0 = t_0, t_1, ..., t_n = T)$. Finally, $I(X;Y|Z)$ represents the conditional mutual information between X and X given Z and it is given by

$$I(X;Y|Z) := \mathbb{E}_{P_{X,Y,Z}}\left[\log \frac{dP_{X|Y,Z}}{dP_{X|Z}}\right].$$

3.2 EQUIVALENCE BETWEEN GENERATIVE MODEL GRAPHS AND SUPPORT OF EXCITATION MATRIX

As mentioned earlier, the corresponding minimal generative model graph and the DIG of a causal dynamical system are equivalent. Thus, to characterize the corresponding minimal generative model graphs of a multivariate Hawkes system, we study the properties of its corresponding DIG.

Proposition 1 *Consider a set of mutually exciting processes $\underline{N}$ with excitation matrix $\Gamma(t)$. Under Assumption 1, $I_T(N_j \to N_i||\underline{N}_{-\{i,j\}}) = 0$ if and only if $\gamma_{i,j} \equiv 0$ over time interval $[0, T]$.*

Proof: See Section 7.1. □

Proposition 1 signifies that the support of the excitation matrix $\Gamma(\cdot)$ determines the adjacency matrix of the DIG and vice versa. Therefore, learning DIG of a mutually exciting Hawkes processes satisfying Assumption 1 is equivalent to learning the excitation matrix given samples from each of the processes. In other word, in the presence of side information that the processes are Hawkes, it is more efficient to learn the causal structure through learning the excitation matrix rather than the directed information needed for learning the DIG in general.

4 LEARNING THE EXCIATIONA MATRIX

In this section, we present an approach for learning the causal structure of a stationary Hawkes network with exponential exciting functions through learning the excitation matrix. This method is based on second order statistic of the Hawkes processes and it is suitable for the case when no i.i.d. samples are available. Note that when i.i.d. samples are available, non-parametric methods for learning the excitation matrix such as MMEL algorithm [25] exist. In this approach the exciting functions are expressed as linear combination of a set of base kernels and a penalized likelihood is used to estimate the parameters of the model. As mentioned earlier, we focus on learning the excitation matrix of multivariate Hawkes processes with exponential exciting functions. This class of Hawkes processes has been widely applied in many areas such as seismology, criminology, and finance [15, 21, 13, 5].

Definition 2 *The excitation matrix of a multivariate Hawkes processes with exponential exciting functions is defined as follows*

$$\mathcal{E}_{xp}(m) := \{\sum_{d=1}^{D} A_d e^{-\beta_d t}u(t) : A_d \in \mathbb{R}^{m\times m},$$
$$(\sum_{d=1}^{D} A_d e^{-\beta_d t})_{i,j} \geq 0, \rho(\sum_{d=1}^{D} \frac{A_d}{\beta_d}) < 1, D \in \mathbb{N}\}, \tag{10}$$

where $\{\beta_d\} > 0$ is called the set of exciting modes.

Example 2 *Consider a set of $m = 5$ mutually exciting processes with the following exponential excitation matrix*

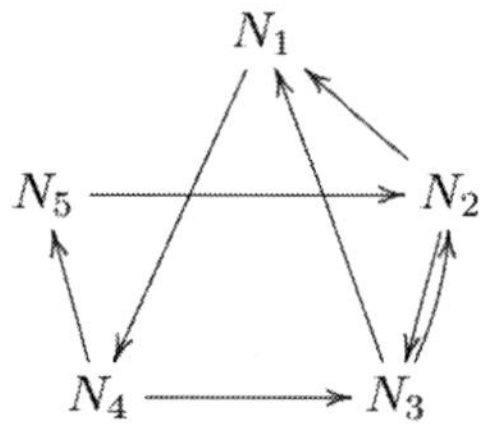

Figure 3: Corresponding DIG of the network in Example 2 with the excitation matrix given by (11)

$$\begin{pmatrix} 2 & 0 & 0 & 0 & 0 \\ 0 & 0 & .5 & 0 & 0 \\ 0 & 1.5 & 0 & 0 & 0 \\ 0 & 0 & 0 & 1.3 & 0 \\ 0 & 0 & 0 & 0 & 1 \end{pmatrix} \frac{e^{-t}}{20} + \begin{pmatrix} 0 & 0 & .5 & 0 & 0 \\ 0 & 0 & 0 & 0 & 2 \\ 0 & 1 & 0 & 2.5 & 0 \\ .1 & 0 & 0 & 0 & 0 \\ 0 & 0 & 0 & 1 & 0 \end{pmatrix} \frac{e^{-1.4t}}{20}$$
$$+ \begin{pmatrix} 1 & 1.5 & 1 & 0 & 0 \\ 0 & 0 & 0 & 0 & -1 \\ 0 & 0 & 2 & 0 & 0 \\ 2 & 0 & 0 & 0 & 0 \\ 0 & 0 & 0 & 0 & 0 \end{pmatrix} \frac{e^{-2t}}{20} \tag{11}$$

In this example $D = 3$ and the exciting modes are $\{1, 1.4, 2\}$. By Proposition 1, the adjacency matrix of the corresponding DIG of this network is given by the support of its excitation matrix. Figure 3 depicts the corresponding DIG.

Before describing our algorithm, we need to derive some useful properties of moments of the process. A multivariate Hawkes process with the excitation matrix Γ has stationary increments, i.e., the intensity processes is stationary, if and only if the following assumption holds [8, 6]:

Assumption 2 *The spectral radius (the supremum of the absolute values of the eigenvalues) of the matrix $\overline{\Gamma}$, where $[\overline{\Gamma}]_{i,j} = ||\gamma_{i,j}||_1$ is strictly less than one, i.e., $\rho(\overline{\Gamma}) < 1$.*

In this case, from (4) and Equation (2):

$$\Lambda = \mathbb{E}[\Lambda(t)] = \mathbf{v} + \int_0^t \Gamma(t-t')\mathbb{E}[d\underline{N}(t')]$$
$$= \mathbf{v} + \int_0^t \Gamma(t-t')\Lambda dt' = \mathbf{v} + \overline{\Gamma}\Lambda. \tag{12}$$

By Assumption 2, $\sum_{i\geq 0} \overline{\Gamma}^i$ converges to $(I - \overline{\Gamma})^{-1}$, thus $\Lambda = (I - \overline{\Gamma})^{-1}\mathbf{v}$. The normalized covariance matrix of a stationary multivariate Hawkes process with lag τ and window size $z > 0$ is defined by

$$\Sigma_z(\tau) := \frac{1}{z}\mathbb{E}\left[\int_t^{t+z} d\underline{N}(x) \int_{t+\tau}^{t+\tau+z} (d\underline{N}(y))^T\right] - \Lambda\Lambda^T z, \tag{13}$$

where $\int_t^{t+t'} d\underline{N}(x)$ denotes the number of events in time interval $(t, t+t']$.

Theorem 3 *[1] The Fourier transform of the normalized covariance matrix of a stationary multivariate Hawkes process with lag τ and window size $z > 0$ is given by*

$$\mathcal{F}[\Sigma_z](-\omega) \tag{14}$$
$$= 4\frac{\sin^2 z\omega/2}{\omega^2 z}\left(I - \mathcal{F}[\Gamma](\omega)\right)^{-1} diag(\Lambda) \left(I - \mathcal{F}[\Gamma](\omega)\right)^{-\dagger},$$

where $A^\dagger$ denotes the Hermitian conjugate of matrix A, and $diag(\Lambda)$ is a diagonal matrix with vector Λ as the main diagonal.

In order to learn the excitation matrix with exponential exciting functions, we need to learn the exciting modes $\{\beta_d\}$, the number of components D, and coefficient matrices $\{A_d\}$. Next results establishes the relationship between the exciting modes and the number of components D with the normalized covariance matrix of the process.

Corollary 4 *Consider a network of a stationary multivariate Hawkes processes with excitation matrix $\Gamma(t)$ belonging to $\mathcal{E}xp(m)$. Then the exciting modes of $\Gamma(t)$ are the absolute values of the zeros of $1/\operatorname{Tr}\mathcal{F}[\Sigma_z]^{-1}(\omega)$.*

Proof: See Section 7.2. □

Next, we need to find the coefficient matrices $\{A_d\}$. To do so, we use the covariance density of the processes. The covariance density of a stationary multivariate Hawkes process for $\tau > 0$ is defined as [8]

$$\Omega(\tau) := \mathbb{E}\left[(d\underline{N}(t+\tau)/dt - \Lambda)(d\underline{N}(t)/dt - \Lambda)^T\right]. \tag{15}$$

Since the processes have stationary increments, we have $\Omega(-\tau) = \Omega^T(\tau)$.

Lemma 5 *[8]*

$$\Omega(\tau) = \Gamma(\tau)diag(\Lambda) + \Gamma * \Omega(\tau), \tau > 0. \tag{16}$$

It has been shown in [3] that the above equation admit a unique solution for $\Gamma(\tau)$. Next proposition provides a system of linear equations that allows us to learn the coefficient matrices.

Proposition 6 *Consider a network of a stationary multivariate Hawkes processes with excitation matrix $\Gamma(t) \in \mathcal{E}xp(m)$, and exciting modes $\{\beta_1, ..., \beta_D\}$. Then $\{A_d\}$ are a solution of the linear system of equations: $\boldsymbol{S} = \boldsymbol{AH}$, where $\boldsymbol{H}_{m^2\times m^2}$ is a block matrix with (i,j)th block given by*

$$\boldsymbol{H}_{i,j} = \frac{diag(\Lambda) + \mathcal{L}[\Omega](\beta_j) + \mathcal{L}[\Omega]^T(\beta_i)}{\beta_j + \beta_i},$$

and $\boldsymbol{A} = [A_1, ..., A_D]$ and $\boldsymbol{S} = [\mathcal{L}[\Omega](\beta_1), ..., \mathcal{L}[\Omega](\beta_D)]$.

Proof: See Section 7.3.□

Combining the results of Corollary 4 and Proposition 6 allows us to learn the excitation matrix of exponential multivariate Hawkes processes from the second order moments. Consequently applying Proposition 1, the causal structure of the network can be learned by drawing an arrow from node i to j, when $\sum_{d=1}^{D} |(A_d)_{j,i}| > 0$.

4.1 ESTIMATION AND ALGORITHM

This section discusses estimators for the second order moments, namely the normalized covariance matrix and the covariance density of a stationary multivariate Hawkes processes from data. Once such estimators are available, the approach of previous section maybe used to learn the network. The most intuitive estimator for Λ defined by Equation (12) is $\underline{N}(T)/T$. It turns out that this estimator converges almost surely to Λ as T goes to infinity [2]. Furthermore, [2] proposes an empirical estimator for the normalized covariance matrix as follows

$$\widehat{\Sigma}_{z,T}(\tau) := \frac{1}{T}\sum_{i=1}^{\lfloor T/z \rfloor} (X_{iz} - X_{(i-1)z})(X_{iz+\tau} - X_{(i-1)z+\tau})^T, \tag{17}$$

where $X_t := \underline{N}(t) - \Lambda t$. In the same paper, it has been shown that under Assumption 2, the above estimator converges in ℓ_2 to the normalized covariance matrix (13), i.e., $\widehat{\Sigma}_{z,T}(\tau) \underset{T\to\infty}{\longrightarrow} \Sigma_z(\tau)$. Notice that the normalized covariance matrix and the covariance density are related by $\Sigma_{dt}(\tau)/dt = \Omega^T(\tau)$. Therefore, we can estimate the covariance density matrix using Equation (17) by choosing small enough window size $z = \Delta$. Namely, $\widehat{\Omega}_\Delta^T(\tau) = \widehat{\Sigma}_\Delta(\tau)/\Delta$.

Algorithm 1

1: $Input:\ \underline{N}^T$.
2: $Output:$ DIG.
3: $\widehat{\Lambda} \leftarrow \underline{N}(T)/T$
4: Choose $\sigma > 0$, $z > 0$, and small $\Delta > 0$.
5: Compute $\widehat{\Sigma}_{z,T}(\tau)$ and $\widehat{\Omega}_\Delta(\tau)$ using (17).
6: $\{\widehat{\beta}_d\}_{d=1}^{\widehat{D}} \leftarrow$ Zeros of $1/\operatorname{Tr}\mathcal{F}[\Sigma_z]^{-1}(\omega)$.
7: Compute $\mathcal{L}[\widehat{\Omega}_\Delta](\widehat{\beta}_d)$ for $d = 1, ..., \widehat{D}$.
8: Solve the set of equations arises from (20) for $\widehat{A}_d$.
9: Draw (j, i) if $\sum_{d=1}^{\widehat{D}} |(\widehat{A}_d)_{i,j}| \geq \sigma$.

Algorithm 1 summarizes the steps of our proposed approach for learning the excitation matrix and consequently the causal structure of an exponential multivariate Hawkes process.

5 EXPERIMENTAL RESULTS

In this section, we present our experimental results for both synthetic and real data.

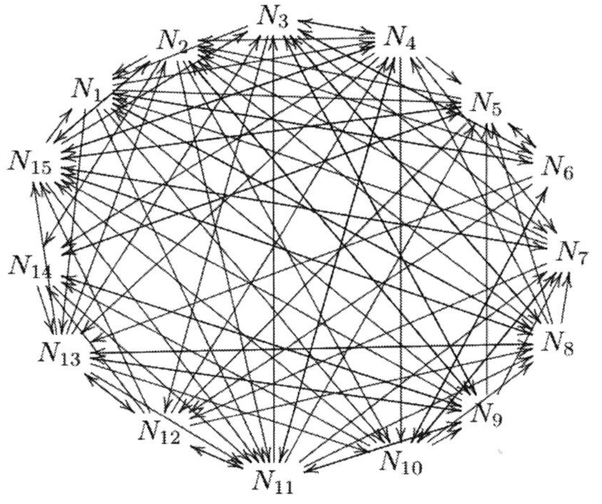

Figure 5: True causal structure of the synthesized example.

5.1 SYNTHETIC DATA

We apply the proposed algorithms to learn the causal structure of the multivariate Hawkes network of Example 2 with $\mathbf{v} = (0.5, 0.4, 0.5, 1, 0.3)^T$. This network satisfies Assumption 2, since $\rho(\overline{\Gamma}) \approx 0.16$. The exciting modes are $\{1, 1.4, 2\}$. We observed the arrivals of all processes during a time period T. Figure 4 depicts the outputs of algorithms 1 for $\Delta = 0.2$, $z = 2$, and observation lengths $T \in \{1000, 2100\}$. As illustrated in Figure 4, by increasing the length of observation T, the output graph converges the true DIG shown in Figure 3. As a comparison, we applied the MMEL algorithm proposed in [25] to learn the excitation matrix for this example and the numerical method based on Nystrom method proposed in [3] with $T = 2100$ and the number of quadrature $Q = 70$. Since MMEL requires i.i.d. samples, we generate 35 i.i.d. samples each of length 60 to obtain Figure 4(MMEL). Our proposed algorithm outperforms both MMEL and the numerical method of [3].

Furthermore, we conducted another experiment for a network of 15 processes with 102 edges illustrated in Figure 5. For a sample of length $T = 2500$, our algorithm was able to recover 70 edges correctly but identified 34 false arrows. MMEL could only recover 58 arrows correctly while detecting another 41 false arrows. The input for MMEL was 25 sequences each of length 100.

5.2 STOCK MARKET DATA

As an example of how our approach may discover causal structure in real-world data, we analyzed the causal relationship between stock prices of 12 technology companies of the New York Stock Exchange sourced from Google Finance. The prices were sampled every 2 minutes for twenty market days (03/03/2008 - 03/28/2008). Every time a stock price changed by $\pm 1\%$ of its current price an event was

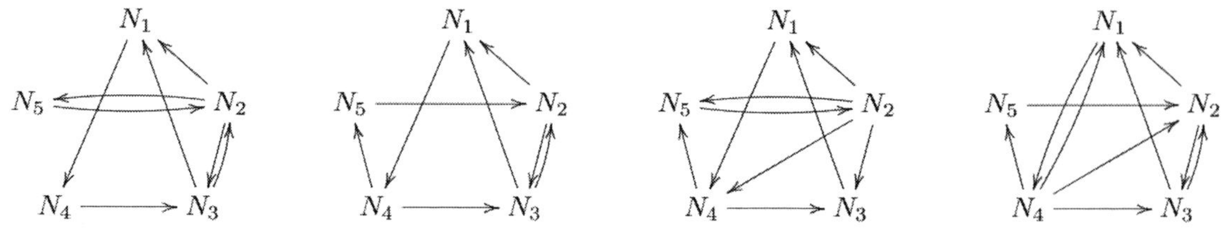

$(a)\ T = 1000$ $(b)\ T = 2100$ (c) Numerical method (d) MMEL

Figure 4: Recovered DIG of the network in Example 2 with the excitation matrix given by (11), (a), (b) Algorithm 1 with $\Delta = 0.2$, $z = 2$, and $T \in \{1000, 2100\}$, (c) the numerical method of [3] with $Q = 70$ and $T = 2100$, and (d) MMEL with 35 i.i.d. samples each of length 60. Our approach learns the graph with $T = 2100$, while other approaches fail at the same sample size.

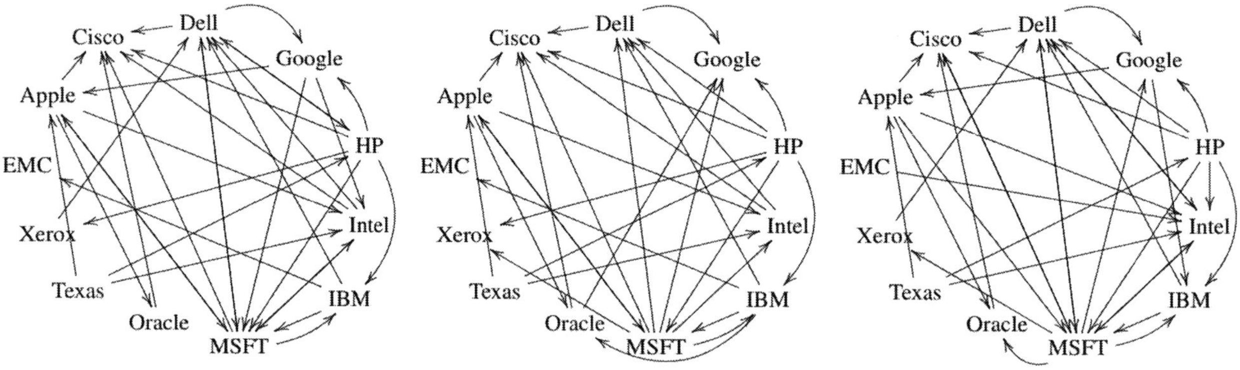

(a) Algorithm 1. (b) DIG. (c) MMEL.

Figure 6: Causal structures for the S&P (a) using Algorithm 1, (b) by estimating the directed information DIG, and (c) using MMEL algorithm.

logged on the stock's process. In order to prevent the substantial changes in stock's prices due to the opening and closing of the market, we ignored the samples at the beginning and at the end of each working day. For this part, we have assumed that the jumps occurring in stock's prices are correlated through a multivariate Hawkes process. This model class was advocated in [11, 2]. Figure 6(a) illustrate the causal graph resulting from Algorithm 1, with $z = 30$ and $\Delta = 2$ minutes.

To compare our learning approach with other approaches, we applied the MMEL algorithm to learn the corresponding causal graph. For this scenario, we assumed that the data collected from each day is generated i.i.d. Hence, a total of 20 i.i.d. samples were used. Figure 6(c) illustrates the resulting graph. As one can see, Figures 6(a) and 6(c) convey pretty much a similar causal interactions in the dataset. For instance both of these graphs suggest that one of the most influential companies in that period of time was Hewlett-Packard (HP). Looking into the global PC market share during 2008, we find that this was indeed the case.[4]

To use another modality, we derive the corresponding DIG of this network applying Equation (9). For this part, we used the market based on the Black-Scholes model [4] in which the stock's prices are modeled via a set of coupled stochastic PDEs. We assumed that the logarithm of the stock's prices are jointly Gaussian and therefore the corresponding DIs were estimated using Equation (24) in [7]. The resulting DIG is shown in Figure 6(b). Note that this DIG is derived from the logarithm of prices and not the jump processes we used earlier. Still it shares a lot of similarities with the two other graphs. For instance, it also identifies HP as one of the most influential companies and Microsoft as one the most influenced companies in that time period.

	Alg. 1	DIG	MMEL
Alg. 1	33	25	26
DIG	25	30	24
MMEL	26	24	34

This table shows the number of edges that each of the above approaches recovers and the number of edges that they jointly recover. This demonstrates the power of exponential kernels even when data does not come from such a model class.

[4]Gartner, `http://www.gartner.com/newsroom/id/856712`

5.3 MEMETRACKER DATA

We also studied causal influences in a blogosphere. The causal flow of information between media sites may be captured by studying hyperlinks provided in one media site to others. Specifically, the time of such linking can be modeled using a linear multivariate Hawkes processes with exponential exciting functions [25, 18]. This model is also intuitive in the sense that after emerging a new hot topic, in the first several days, the blogs or websites are more likely feature that topics and it is also more likely that the topic would trigger further discussions and create more hyperlinks. Thus, exponential exciting functions are well suited to capture such phenomenon as the exiting functions should have relatively large values at first and decay fast as time elapses.

For this experiment, we used the MemeTracker[5] dataset. The data contains time-stamped phrase and hyperlink information for news media articles and blog posts from over a million different websites. We extracted the times that hyperlinks to 10 well-known websites listed in Table 1 are created during August 2008 to April 2009. When a hyperlink to a website is created at a certain time, an arrival events is recorded at that time. More precisely, in this experiment, we picked 30 different phrases that appeared on different websites at different times. If a website that published one of the phrases at time t also contained a hyperlink to one of the 10 listed websites, an arrival event was recorded at time t for that website in our list.

Figure 7(a) illustrates the resulting causal structure learned by Algorithm 1 for $z = 12$ hours and $\Delta = 1$ hour. In this graph, an arrow from a node to another, say node Ye to Yo, means creating a hyperlink to `yelp.com` triggers creation of further hyperlinks to `youtube.com`.

We also applied the MMEL algorithm with one exponential kernel function to learn the excitation matrix. For this experiment, the data corresponding to each phrase was treated as an i.i.d. realization of the system. The resulting causal structure is depicted in Figure 7(b).

As Figure 7(a) illustrates, the nodes can be clustered into two main groups: $\{$Cr, Ye, Am, Yo$\}$ and $\{$Bb, Cn, Gu, Hu, Sp, Wi$\}$. The first group consists of mainly merchandise and reviewing websites and the second group contains the broadcasting websites. However, this is not as clear in Figure 7(b). This is because MMEL requires more i.i.d. samples (phrases) to be able to identify the correct arrows. Note that as we increase the number of phrases (110), Figure 7(c), both graphs become similar with two clearly visible main clusters.

[5] http://memetracker.org/data/links.html

Cr	craigslist.org
Ye	yelp.com
Am	amazon.com
Sp	spiegel.de
Wi	wikipedia.org
Yo	youtube.com
Cn	cnn.com
Gu	guardian.co.uk
Hu	humanevents.com
Bb	bbc.co.uk

Table 1: List of websites studied in MemeTracker experiment.

6 CONCLUSION

Learning the causal structure (DIG) of a stochastic network of processes requires estimation of conditional directed information (9). Estimating this quantity in general has high complexity and requires a large number of samples. However, the complexity of the learning task could be significantly reduced, if side information about the underlying structure of system dynamics is available. As proved in 1, for multivariate Hawkes processes, estimating the support of the excitation matrix suffices to learn the associated DIG. Therefore, all approaches for learning the excitation matrix of the multivariate Hawkes processes such as ML estimation [16, 25], EM algorithm [10], non-parametric estimation techniques proposed in [2], and the proposed method in this paper may be used to learn the causal interactions in such networks. The previous estimation approaches either require i.i.d. samples such as MMEL or are limited to the class of symmetric Hawkes processes. The proposed algorithm in this work allows us to learn the support of the excitation matrix in a larger class of matrices in the absence of i.i.d. samples.

Acknowledgements

This work was in part supported by NSF CCF 10- 54937 - CAREER, MURI grant ARMY W911NF-15-1-0479, and Army W911NF-15-1-0281 AB262.

7 TECHNICAL PROOFS

7.1 Proof of Proposition 1

Suppose $\gamma_{i,j} \equiv 0$. (3) implies that for every $t \le T$, $\lambda_i(t)$ is $\underline{\mathcal{F}}^t_{-\{j\}}(=\sigma\{\underline{N}^t_{-\{j\}}\})$-measurable and from (2), we have

$$P\left(dN_i(t)=1|\underline{\mathcal{F}}^t\right)=P(dN_i(t)=1|\underline{\mathcal{F}}^t_{-\{j\}}).$$

Equivalently, for every $0 \le t_{k-1} < t_k$,

$$I\left(N^{t_k}_{i,t_{k-1}};N^{t_k}_{j,0}|\mathcal{F}^{t_{k-1}}_{-\{j\}}\right)=0, \tag{18}$$

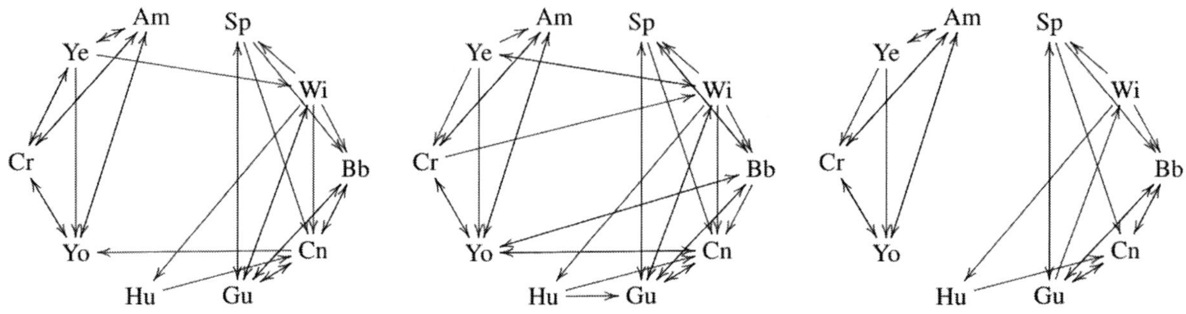

(a) Alg. 1 (30). (b) MMEL. (c) Both Alg. 1 & MMEL (110).

Figure 7: Recovered causal structure of the MemeTracker dataset using (a) Algorithm 1, (b) MMEL for 30 different phrases, and (c) both Algorithm 1 and MMEL for 110 different phrases.

and thus, $\tilde{I}_t(N_j \to N_i||\underline{N}_{-\{i,j\}}) = 0$, for any finite partition $\mathbf{t} \in \mathcal{T}(0,T)$.

For the converse we use proof by contradiction. Suppose $I_T(N_j \to N_i||\underline{N}_{-\{i,j\}}) = 0$ and $\gamma_{i,j} \neq 0$. Using the definition in (9), it is straightforward to observe that for any $t < T$,

$$I_t(N_j \to N_i||\underline{N}_{-\{i,j\}}) = 0.$$

Similarly, $I_{t+dt}(N_j \to N_i||\underline{N}_{-\{i,j\}}) = 0$. Consequently,

$$0 = I_{t+dt}(N_j \to N_i||\underline{N}_{-\{i,j\}}) - I_t(N_j \to N_i||\underline{N}_{-\{i,j\}})$$
$$= I\left(dN_i(t); N^t_{j,0}|\mathcal{F}^t_{-\{j\}}\right).$$

This implies $P(dN_i(t) = 1|\underline{\mathcal{F}}^t_{-\{j\}}) = \lambda_i(t)dt + o(dt)$, or $\lambda_i(t)$ is $\underline{\mathcal{F}}^t_{-\{j\}}$-measurable. Since, we have assumed $\gamma_{i,j} \neq 0$, we obtain $N_j(t)$ is $\underline{\mathcal{F}}^t_{-\{j\}}$-measurable, for all $t \leq T$. In words, jth process is determined by other processes which contradicts with the Assumption 1 that states there is no deterministic relationships between processes.

7.2 Proof of Corollary 4

If the excitation matrix belongs to $\mathcal{E}xp(m)$, from Equation (14) we have

$$\left(I - \sum_{d=1}^{D} \frac{A_d^T}{j\omega + \beta_d}\right) diag(\Lambda)^{-1} \left(I - \sum_{d=1}^{D} \frac{A_d}{-j\omega + \beta_d}\right)$$
$$= \frac{4\sin^2 z\omega/2}{\omega^2 z} \mathcal{F}[\Sigma_z]^{-1}(\omega).$$

By evaluating the trace of the above equation, we obtain

$$\sum_{i=1}^{m} \frac{|1-a_{i,i}|^2}{\lambda_i} + \sum_{i\neq j} \frac{|a_{i,j}|^2}{\lambda_i} = \frac{4\sin^2 z\omega/2}{\omega^2 z} \operatorname{Tr} \mathcal{F}[\Sigma_z]^{-1}(\omega), \tag{19}$$

where $a_{i,j} = \sum_{d=1}^{D} \frac{a_{i,j}^{(d)}}{-j\omega+\beta_d}$, and $A_d = [a_{i,j}^{(d)}]$. To learn the entire set $\{\pm j\beta_d\}$, we have to show that there are no pole zero cancellations in (19). That is, the nominator and denominator of (19) have no common roots. Let

$$g(\omega) := \left(\sum_{i=1}^{m} \frac{|1-a_{i,i}|^2}{\lambda_i} + \sum_{i\neq j} \frac{|a_{i,j}|^2}{\lambda_i}\right) \prod_{d=1}^{D} |-j\omega+\beta_d|^2,$$

which is the nominator of Equation (19). It is straightforward to check that for $\omega = -j\beta_k$, the above quantity is non-zero, due to the fact that β_ds are distinct and $A_k \neq \mathbf{0}$. Since $g(\omega)$ is a polynomial with real coefficients, from complex conjugate root theorem [9], we have $g(j\beta_k) \neq 0$. Therefore, the set $\{\pm j\beta_d\}$ contains all the poles of (19).

7.3 Proof of Proposition 6

From Lemma 5, the Laplace transform of the covariance density can be written as

$$\mathcal{L}[\Omega](s) = \mathcal{L}[\Gamma](s)\,(diag(\Lambda) + \mathcal{L}[\Omega](s))$$
$$+ \int_0^\infty \int_t^\infty \Gamma(t')\Omega^T(t) e^{-s(t'-t)} dt' dt.$$

When $\Gamma(t) \in \mathcal{E}xp(m)$, it can be shown that (1) becomes

$$\mathcal{L}[\Omega](s) = \sum_{d=1}^{D} \frac{A_d}{s+\beta_d}\left(diag(\Lambda) + \mathcal{L}[\Omega](s) + \mathcal{L}[\Omega]^T(\beta_d)\right). \tag{20}$$

If the set of exciting modes are given, we can insert $s = \beta_d$, for $d = 1, \ldots, D$ in the above equation and obtain the system of D equations.

References

[1] Emmanuel Bacry, Khalil Dayri, and Jean-Francois Muzy. Non-parametric kernel estimation for symmetric hawkes processes. application to high frequency financial data. *The European Physical Journal B*, 85(5):1–12, 2012.

[2] Emmanuel Bacry, Sylvain Delattre, Marc Hoffmann, and Jean-Francois Muzy. Some limit theorems for hawkes processes and application to financial statistics. *Stochastic Processes and their Applications*, 123(7):2475–2499, 2013.

[3] Emmanuel Bacry and Jean-Francois Muzy. Second order statistics characterization of hawkes processes and non-parametric estimation. *preprint arXiv:1401.0903*, 2014.

[4] Fischer Black and Myron Scholes. The pricing of options and corporate liabilities. *The journal of political economy*, pages 637–654, 1973.

[5] Clive G Bowsher. Modelling security market events in continuous time: Intensity based, multivariate point process models. *Journal of Econometrics*, 141(2):876–912, 2007.

[6] Pierre Brémaud and Laurent Massoulié. Stability of nonlinear hawkes processes. *The Annals of Probability*, pages 1563–1588, 1996.

[7] Jalal Etesami and Negar Kiyavash. Directed information graphs: A generalization of linear dynamical graphs. In *American Control Conference (ACC), 2014*, pages 2563–2568. IEEE.

[8] Alan G Hawkes. Spectra of some self-exciting and mutually exciting point processes. *Biometrika*, 58(1):83–90, 1971.

[9] Alan Jeffrey. *Complex analysis and applications*, volume 10. CRC Press, 2005.

[10] Erik Lewis and George Mohler. A nonparametric em algorithm for multiscale hawkes processes. *Preprint*, 2011.

[11] Scott W Linderman and Ryan P Adams. Discovering latent network structure in point process data. *preprint arXiv:1402.0914*, 2014.

[12] Thomas Josef Liniger. *Multivariate hawkes processes*. PhD thesis, Diss., Eidgenössische Technische Hochschule ETH Zürich, Nr. 18403, 2009, 2009.

[13] George O Mohler, Martin B Short, P Jeffrey Brantingham, Frederic Paik Schoenberg, and George E Tita. Self-exciting point process modeling of crime. *Journal of the American Statistical Association*, 106(493), 2011.

[14] Ioane Muni Toke and Fabrizio Pomponio. Modelling trades-through in a limited order book using hawkes processes. *Economics discussion paper*, (2011-32), 2011.

[15] Yosihiko Ogata. Seismicity analysis through point-process modeling: A review. *Pure and Applied Geophysics*, 155(2-4):471–507, 1999.

[16] T Ozaki. Maximum likelihood estimation of hawkes' self-exciting point processes. *Annals of the Institute of Statistical Mathematics*, 31(1):145–155, 1979.

[17] Judea Pearl. *Probabilistic reasoning in intelligent systems: networks of plausible inference*. Morgan Kaufmann, 1988.

[18] Julio Cesar Louzada Pinto, Tijani Chahed, and Eitan Altman. Trend detection in social networks using hawkes processes. In *Proceedings of the 2015 IEEE/ACM International Conference on Advances in Social Networks Analysis and Mining 2015*, pages 1441–1448. ACM, 2015.

[19] Christopher Quinn, Negar Kiyavash, and Todd P Coleman. Directed information graphs. *Transactions on Information Theory*, 61(12):6887–6909, 2015.

[20] Christopher J Quinn, Negar Kiyavash, and Todd P Coleman. Equivalence between minimal generative model graphs and directed information graphs. In *Information Theory Proceedings (ISIT), 2011 IEEE International Symposium on*, pages 293–297. IEEE, 2011.

[21] Patricia Reynaud-Bouret, Sophie Schbath, et al. Adaptive estimation for hawkes processes; application to genome analysis. *The Annals of Statistics*, 38(5):2781–2822, 2010.

[22] Thomas Schreiber. Measuring information transfer. *Physical review letters*, 85(2):461, 2000.

[23] Tsachy Weissman, Young-Han Kim, and Haim H Permuter. Directed information, causal estimation, and communication in continuous time. *Information Theory, IEEE Transactions on*, 59(3):1271–1287, 2013.

[24] Shuang-Hong Yang and Hongyuan Zha. Mixture of mutually exciting processes for viral diffusion. In *Proceedings of the 30th International Conference on Machine Learning (ICML-13)*, pages 1–9, 2013.

[25] Ke Zhou, Hongyuan Zha, and Le Song. Learning triggering kernels for multi-dimensional hawkes processes. In *Proceedings of the 30th International Conference on Machine Learning (ICML-13)*, pages 1301–1309, 2013.

Elliptical Slice Sampling with Expectation Propagation

Francois Fagan
Department of IEOR
Columbia University
New York, NY 10027
ff2316@columbia.edu

Jalaj Bhandari
Department of IEOR
Columbia University
New York, NY 10027
jb3618@columbia.edu

John P. Cunningham
Department of Statistics
Columbia University
New York, NY 10027
jpc2181@columbia.edu

Abstract

Markov Chain Monte Carlo techniques remain the gold standard for approximate Bayesian inference, but their practical issues — including onerous runtime and sensitivity to tuning parameters — often lead researchers to use faster but typically less accurate deterministic approximations. Here we couple the fast but biased deterministic approximation offered by expectation propagation with elliptical slice sampling, a state-of-the-art MCMC method. We extend our hybrid deterministic-MCMC method to include recycled samples and analytical slices, and we rigorously prove the validity of each enhancement. Taken together, we show that these advances provide an order of magnitude gain in efficiency beyond existing state-of-the-art sampling techniques in Bayesian classification and multivariate gaussian quadrature problems.

1 INTRODUCTION

Exact posterior inference in Bayesian models is rarely tractable, a fact which has prompted vast amounts of research into efficient approximate inference techniques. Deterministic methods such as the Laplace approximation, Variational Bayes, and Expectation Propagation offer fast and analytical posterior approximations, but introduce potentially significant bias due to their restricted form which can not capture important characteristics of the true posterior. Markov Chain Monte Carlo (MCMC) methods represent the target posterior with samples, which while asymptotically exact, can be slow, require substantial tuning, and perform poorly when variables are highly correlated.

Conceptually, these two techniques can be combined to great benefit: if a deterministic approximation can cover the true posterior mass accurately, then a subsequent MCMC sampler should be much faster and be less susceptible to inefficiency due to correlation (as the deterministic approximation would have captured this correlation). To do so, however, is practically quite difficult. First, both the Laplace and Variational Bayesian approximations fit local mass of a posterior (in Variational Bayes this is sometimes called the *exclusive* property of optimizing the Kullback-Liebler divergence from the approximation to the true posterior [Minka, 2005]). While excellent in many situations, this property is inappropriate for initializing an MCMC sampler, since it will be very difficult for that sampler to explore other areas of posterior mass (e.g., other modes). Expectation Propagation (EP, [Minka, 2001]), on the other hand, is typically derived as an inclusive approximation that, at least approximately, attempts to match the global sufficient statistics of the true posterior (most often the first and second moments, producing a Gaussian approximation). Such a choice is superior for an MCMC sampler.

Secondly, we require a sensible choice of MCMC sampler so as to leverage a deterministic approximation like EP. Given an unnormalized target distribution $p^*(\mathbf{x})$, we can write:

$$p^*(\mathbf{x}) \;=\; \hat{p}(\mathbf{x})\frac{p^*(\mathbf{x})}{\hat{p}(\mathbf{x})} \;\equiv\; \hat{p}(\mathbf{x})\hat{\mathcal{L}}(\mathbf{x}),$$

which allows us to treat the true posterior as the product of an effective prior $\hat{p}$ and likelihood $\hat{\mathcal{L}}$. We then have freedom to choose $\hat{p}$, which we will set to be the deterministic (Gaussian) posterior approximation from EP. Amongst all MCMC methods, Elliptical Slice Sampling (ESS, [Murray et al., 2010]) handles the above reformulations seamlessly. ESS has become an important and generic method for posterior inference with models that have a strong Gaussian prior. It inherits the attractive properties of slice sampling generally [Neal, 2003], and notably lacks tuning parameters that are often highly burdensome in other state-of-the-art methods like Hamiltonian Monte Carlo (HMC; Neal [2011]). The critical observation is that, if EP provides a quality posterior approximation $\hat{p} \approx p^*$, the likelihood term $\hat{\mathcal{L}}$ will typically be weak, which puts ESS in the regime where it is most efficient.

What results is a new MCMC sampler that combines EP and ESS, is faster than state-of-the-art samplers like HMC, and is able to explore the parameter space efficiently even in the presence of strong dependency among variables. Specifically, our contributions include:

1. In Section 2, we propose *Expectation Propagation based Elliptical Slice Sampling (EPESS)* where we justify the use of EP as the "prior" for ESS.

2. In Section 3, we investigate a method to improve the overall run time of ESS by sampling multiple points each iteration. It reduces the average number of shrinkage steps giving it a computational advantage. We call it *Recycled ESS* and integrate it with EPESS to further increase its efficiency.

3. We extend our method to *Analytic Elliptical Slice Sampling* in Section 4. As the name suggests, we can analytically find the region corresponding to a slice and sample uniformly from it. In addition to decorrelating samples, it offers the computational advantage of avoiding expensive shrinkage steps. It is applicable to only a few target distributions and we illustrate it, in the context of EPESS, for linear Truncated Multivariate Gaussian (TMG) quadrature.

4. We offer empirical evaluation of EPESS (Section 5), which show an order of magnitude improvement over the state-of-the art MCMC methods for TMG and probit models.

2 EXPECTATION PROPAGATION AND ELLIPTICAL SLICE SAMPLING

In this section we introduce our combined EP and ESS sampling method. We begin with background of the two building blocks of this method, to place them in context of current literature.

2.1 ELLIPTICAL SLICE SAMPLING

There are many problems where dependency between latent variables is induced through a Gaussian prior, for example in Gaussian Processes. Elliptical Slice Sampling (ESS, [Murray et al., 2010]) is specifically designed for efficiently sampling from such distributions and is considered state-of-the-art on these problems. ESS considers posteriors of the form

$$p^*(\mathbf{x}) = \frac{1}{Z}\mathcal{N}(\mathbf{x}; \mathbf{0}, \mathbf{\Sigma})\mathcal{L}(\mathbf{x}) \tag{1}$$

where $\mathcal{L}$ is a likelihood function, $\mathcal{N}(\mathbf{0}, \mathbf{\Sigma})$ is a multivariate Gaussian prior and Z is the normalizing constant.

ESS is a variant of slice sampling [Neal, 2003] that takes advantage of the Gaussian prior to improve mixing time and eliminate parameter tuning. At the beginning of each iteration of ESS two random variables are sampled. The first is the slice height y which is uniformly distributed over $[0, \mathcal{L}(\mathbf{x})]$, where $\mathbf{x}$ is the current sample. The second variable $\boldsymbol{\nu}$ is sampled from the prior $\mathcal{N}(\mathbf{x}; \mathbf{0}, \mathbf{\Sigma})$ and, together with the current sample $\mathbf{x}$, defines an ellipse:

$$\mathbf{x}'(\theta) = \mathbf{x}\cos(\theta) + \boldsymbol{\nu}\sin(\theta). \tag{2}$$

Next, a one-dimensional angle bracket $[\theta_{\min}, \theta_{\max}]$ of length 2π is proposed containing the point $\theta = 0$ (corresponding to the current point $\mathbf{x}$). The bracket is then shrunk toward $\theta = 0$ until a point is found within the bracket that satisfies $\mathcal{L}(\mathbf{x}'(\theta)) > y$. This point is accepted as the next point in the Markov chain.

ESS is known to work well when the prior aligns with the posterior and the likelihood is weak [Murray et al., 2010, Section 2.5]. However, when this is not the case then ESS can perform poorly, as we demonstrate below.

Figure 1 illustrates the problem when the prior and the posterior do not align: here we have a $\mathcal{N}(\mathbf{0}, \mathbf{I})$ prior with an observed Bernoulli likelihood $\mathcal{L}(\mathbf{x}) = \mathbb{1}(\mathbf{x} \in A)$ for some rectangle A. The posterior is a truncated Gaussian within A. In this example we have placed A away from the origin, with the result that that most of the posterior density lies vertically on the left boundary of the box. Accordingly, a good sampler should be able to make large vertical moves to effectively explore the posterior mass.

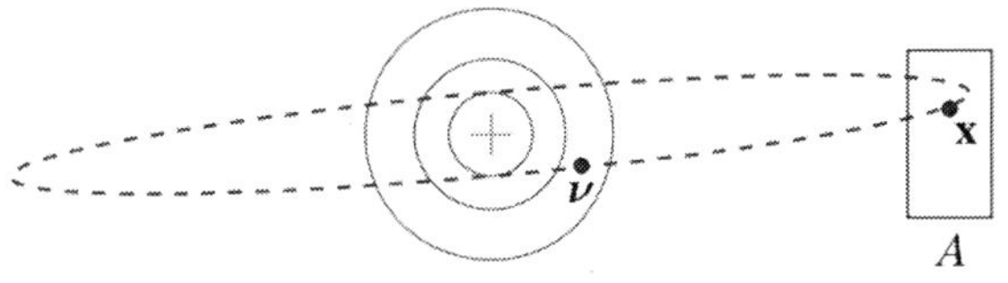

Figure 1: ESS ellipse shown in dashed red.

As the likelihood rectangle A moves further right, the posterior moves away from the prior. As a result most of the points proposed on the ellipse will not lie in A, so more shrinkage steps will be necessary until a point is accepted, leading to an inefficient algorithm. Moving A

further to the right also makes the ellipse more eccentric which prevents vertical movement, resulting in further inefficiency.

The other pathology afflicting ESS is that of strong likelihoods. This happens when $\mathcal{L}(\mathbf{x})$ is extremely large in regions of non-negligible posterior density. Once the sampler is in such a region, only with low probability will it be able to accept points proposed outside the region, hence it will get stuck. This will occur, for instance, when the prior underestimates the variance of the posterior and $\mathcal{L}(\mathbf{x})$ becomes large in the tails. We refer the reader to an extended explanation of this effect in [Nishihara et al., 2014]. Indeed, this motivates our choice of EP as a prior, since Variational Bayes and Laplace approximations are known to often underestimate posterior variance whereas EP does not [Minka, 2005].

We address both these problems by choosing an EP prior (Section 2.2) for ESS. How to incorporate EP into ESS is explained in Section 2.3.

2.2 EXPECTATION PROPAGATION

Expectation Propagation (EP) is a method for finding a Gaussian approximation q to a given distribution p^* by iteratively matching local moments and then updating the global approximation via a so-called 'tilted' distribution [Minka, 2001]. At termination the distribution q will optimize a global objective that approximates the Kullback-Liebler divergence $KL(p^*||q)$ [Wainwright and Jordan, 2008]. The resulting Gaussian approximation is an *inclusive* estimate of p^* that approximately matches its zeroth, first, and second moments.

Although EP has few theoretical guarantees [Dehaene and Barthelmé, 2015], it is known to be accurate for many models including truncated multivariate gaussian [Cunningham et al., 2011], probit and logistic regression [Nickisch and Rasmussen, 2008], log-Gaussian Cox processes [Ko and Seeger, 2015], and more [Minka, 2001]. It is also known to have superior performance compared to the Laplace approximation and Variational Bayes in terms of approximating marginal distributions accurately [Kuss and Rasmussen, 2005, Cseke and Heskes, 2011, Deisenroth and Mohamed, 2012].

2.3 ELLIPTICAL SLICE SAMPLING WITH EXPECTATION PROPAGATION

As outlined in Section 1, we incorporate a posterior approximation $\hat{p}$ as a proposal distribution for ESS. We do so by defining:

$$p^*(\mathbf{x}) = \hat{p}(\mathbf{x})\frac{p^*(\mathbf{x})}{\hat{p}(\mathbf{x})} = \hat{p}(\mathbf{x})\hat{\mathcal{L}}(\mathbf{x}) \quad (3)$$

where p^* is the posterior distribution of interest from Equation (1), $\hat{p}$ is our new prior and $\hat{\mathcal{L}}$ is our new likelihood. As explained in Section 2.1, for ESS to work well, $\hat{p}$ should have two desirable properties: *(i)* It should approximate the posterior p^*. The most obvious candidates for $\hat{p}$ includes Laplace, Variational Bayes and EP approximations, *(ii)* It should ensure that the new likelihood $\hat{\mathcal{L}} = p^*/\hat{p}$ is weak, in the sense as described in Section 2.1. Using either Laplace or Variational Bayes may result in large values of $\hat{\mathcal{L}}$ in the tails due to variance underestimation, which could cause the sampler to get stuck. The more inclusive nature of the EP estimate, on the other hand, makes it a sensible choice to obtain a Gaussian posterior approximation $\hat{p}$.

To demonstrate the power of this approach we return to the problematic example given in Figure 1. Using the EP approximation we can shift our prior to align with the posterior density on the left side of the likelihood rectange A. The ellipses become short and vertical, allowing ESS to mix efficiently. This is illustrated in Figure 2. To demonstrate the difference in the sampling behavior between EPESS and ESS, Figure 2.3 plots 400 samples from both EPESS and ESS. EPESS is clearly superior and manages to explore the entire distribution whereas ESS moves consistently less.

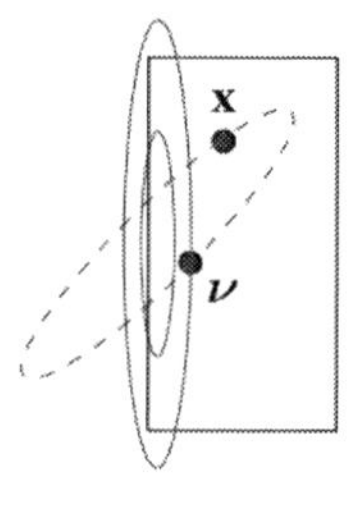

Figure 2: The EP approximation is in teal and an EPESS elliptical slice is in dashed red.

The idea of Equation (3) is not unique to this paper. Nishihara et al. [2014] use a similar construction where the Gaussian approximation is learned from samples. Although this has the advantage of not relying on EP to do moment matching, it requires parallelism and expensive moment calculations. EPESS will be simpler and more efficient when an accurate EP approximation is available. Braun and Bonfrer [2011] also have a similar method where they use the Laplace approximation, which as discussed, is a poor choice. We remark that using Power EP approximations is also a viable choice for a prior, a point that we will return to in Section 6.

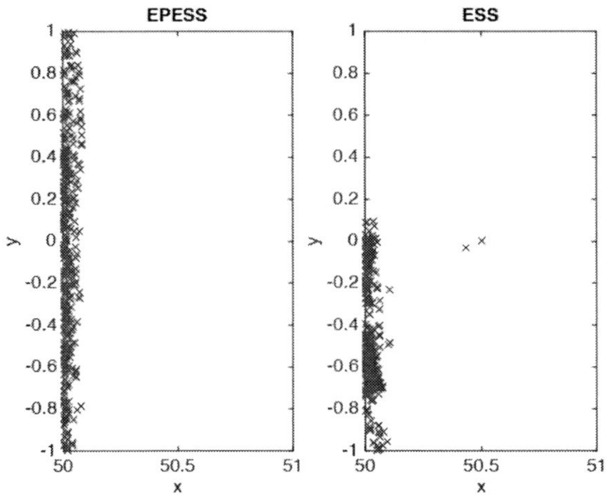

Figure 3: EPESS vs ESS: 400 samples of EPESS and ESS for a 2-d Gaussian $\mathcal{N}(\mathbf{0}, \mathbf{I})$ truncated in a rectangular box $\{50 \leq x \leq 51, -1 \leq y \leq 1\}$. EPESS explores the parameter space effectively whereas ESS does not.

Algorithm 1: `Recycled_ESS`

Input : Log-likelihood function $(\log \mathcal{L})$, initial point $\mathbf{x}_1^{(1)} \in \mathbb{R}^d$, prior $\mathcal{N}(\mathbf{0}, \mathbf{\Sigma})$, number of iterations N, number of recycled points J

Output: Samples from Markov Chain $((\mathbf{x}_1^{(1)}, ..., \mathbf{x}_J^{(1)}), ..., (\mathbf{x}_1^{(N)}, ..., \mathbf{x}_J^{(N)}))$

for $i = 1$ **to** N **do**
- $u \sim$ Uniform $[0, 1]$
- $\log y \leftarrow \log \mathcal{L}(\mathbf{x}_1^{(i-1)}) + \log u$
- $\boldsymbol{\nu} \sim \mathcal{N}(\mathbf{0}, \mathbf{\Sigma})$
- $\theta_{max} \sim$ Uniform $[0, 2\pi]$
- $\theta_{min} \leftarrow \theta_{max} - 2\pi$
- **for** $j = 1$ **to** J **do**
  - $(\hat{\mathbf{x}}_j^{(i)}, \theta_{min}, \theta_{max}) \leftarrow$ `ESS_inner_loop` $(\log \mathcal{L}, \log y, \boldsymbol{\nu}, \mathbf{x}_1^{(i-1)}, \theta_{min}, \theta_{max})$
- **end**
- $(\mathbf{x}_1^{(i)}, ..., \mathbf{x}_J^{(i)}) \leftarrow$ `rand_perm`$(\hat{\mathbf{x}}_1^{(i)}, ..., \hat{\mathbf{x}}_J^{(i)})$

end

return $((\mathbf{x}_1^{(1)}, ..., \mathbf{x}_J^{(1)}), ..., (\mathbf{x}_1^{(N)}, ..., \mathbf{x}_J^{(N)}))$

3 RECYCLED ELLIPTICAL SLICE SAMPLING

In this section we show how to sample $J > 1$ points at every ESS iteration without a significant increase in computational complexity. This idea is inspired by the work of Nishimura and Dunson [2015] on HMC. In that work an HMC algorithm is devised which "recycles" the intermediate points as valid samples from the target distribution. We borrow the phrase "recycling" from them and call our method *Recycled Elliptical Slice Sampling*.

Recall that in every ESS iteration, we propose points along an ellipse within an angle bracket, which is iteratively shrunk, until a point is accepted. In Recycled ESS, we don't stop after accepting the first point but continue to propose points starting from the last angle bracket used. This procedure is continued until J points are accepted. One of the J points is randomly selected to propagate the Markov chain.

As we shrink the angle bracket $[\theta_{\min}, \theta_{\max}]$ towards $\theta = 0$ (corresponding to the current point), the probability of the next proposal point being accepted tends to increase. Hence the number of shrinkage steps required to accept latter points is typically smaller than that for first accepted point. Since the number of likelihood function evaluations is proportional to the number of shrinkage steps, Recycled ESS is able to sample more points with only a small increase in computational complexity, leading to improved run times per sample. This approach is formalized in Algorithm 1, where `ESS_inner_loop` function is the regular ESS inner loop and can be found in Figure 2 of [Murray et al., 2010].

It is clear from Algorithm 1 that we treat each sample $\mathbf{x}_j^{(i)}$ as an element in a large Markov chain with state space $(\mathbf{x}_1^{(i)}, ..., \mathbf{x}_J^{(i)})$. We prove in Theorem 3.2 that each element $\mathbf{x}_j^{(i)}$ has its stationary marginal distribution as p^*. In order to do so, we first show in Lemma 3.1 that the transition operator of accepting the jth point is reversible.

Lemma 3.1. *Let T_j correspond to the transition operator from $\mathbf{x}_1^{(i-1)} \rightarrow \hat{\mathbf{x}}_j^{(i)}$. Then T_j is invariant to p^*.*

A detailed proof is given in the appendix. Theorem 3.2 easily follows:

Theorem 3.2. *Each element in the Recycled ESS Markov chain has marginal stationary distribution p^*.*

Proof. The sequence of points $\{\mathbf{x}_1^{(i)}\}$ follow a Markov Chain. At each step the transition operator is uniformly sampled from the set $\{T_j : j = 1, ..., J\}$, with each T_j being invariant to p^* (Lemma 3.1). Therefore we have that $\mathbf{x}_1^{(i)} \xrightarrow{dist.} \mathbf{x}^*$ where $\mathbf{x}^* \sim p^*$. Also, at any fixed iteration i, we have that all points in $\{\mathbf{x}_j^{(i)} : j = 1, ..., J\}$ are identically distributed. This follows from the random permutations:

$$p(\mathbf{x}_j^{(i)} | (\hat{\mathbf{x}}_1^{(i)}, ..., \hat{\mathbf{x}}_J^{(i)})) = \text{Uniform}(\hat{\mathbf{x}}_1^{(i)}, ..., \hat{\mathbf{x}}_J^{(i)}) = p(\mathbf{x}_k^{(i)} | (\hat{\mathbf{x}}_1^{(i)}, ..., \hat{\mathbf{x}}_J^{(i)})).$$

Integrating over $p(\hat{\mathbf{x}}_1^{(i)}, ..., \hat{\mathbf{x}}_J^{(i)})$ gives us that $p(\mathbf{x}_j^{(i)}) =$

$p(\mathbf{x}_1^{(i)})$ for any i, j. Since we have that $\mathbf{x}_1^{(i)} \xrightarrow{dist.} \mathbf{x}^*$, it follows that for all j: $\mathbf{x}_j^{(i)} \xrightarrow{dist.} \mathbf{x}^*$. $\square$

The downside of Recycled ESS is that the latter accepted points (corresponding to $j \approx J$) are sampled from a very small angle bracket and so are highly correlated. On the other hand these points only require a small number of function evaluations. Overall the effect of recycling is a small increase in the effective number of samples, with a small increase in computational complexity. Whether or not this is beneficial is investigated empirically in Section 5.

4 ANALYTIC ELLIPTICAL SLICE SAMPLING

Consider the ellipse

$$\mathcal{E} = \{\mathbf{x}' : \mathbf{x}'(\theta) = \mathbf{x}\cos(\theta) + \boldsymbol{\nu}\sin(\theta)\}$$

as in an ESS iteration as defined by Equation (2). Let $\mathcal{S}(y; \mathcal{E})$ be the slice corresponding to the acceptable points in $\mathcal{E}$ for a given slice height y:

$$\mathcal{S}(y; \mathcal{E}) = \{\mathbf{x}' \in \mathcal{E} : \mathcal{L}(\mathbf{x}') > y\}.$$

If we can analytically characterize $\mathcal{S}(y; \mathcal{E})$ then we only need to sample a point uniformly from the slice to propagate the Markov Chain [Neal, 2003]. This has three advantages: *(i)* We eliminate expensive slice shrinkage steps which reduces the computational cost of our sampler; *(ii)* In standard slice sampling algorithms, shrinkage steps bias the next sample to be close to the current sample thereby introducing correlations. Since we uniformly sample over $\mathcal{S}(y; \mathcal{E})$, the resulting samples are less correlated as we are not biased towards the current point; *(iii)* We can easily incorporate the recycling idea here resulting in an extremely efficient algorithm, which we refer to as *Analytic Elliptical Slice Sampling.*

As in Recycled ESS, in Analytic ESS we sample $J > 1$ points from each ellipse $\mathcal{E}$. We first sample J different y values, which are evenly spaced in a Quasi Monte-Carlo way. Corresponding to each y value, we analytically solve for $\mathcal{S}(y; \mathcal{E})$ (which has only a small amortized computational cost). One point is then uniformly sampled from each slice $\mathcal{S}(y; \mathcal{E})$. The pseudocode for Analytic ESS is given in Algorithm 2 and in Theorem 4.1 we prove its validity.

Theorem 4.1. *Each element in the Analytic ESS Markov chain has marginal stationary distribution p^*.*

Proof. The proof follows exactly the same argument as in Theorem 3.2. $\square$

Algorithm 2: `Analytic_Slice_Sampling`

Input : Likelihood $\hat{\mathcal{L}}$, prior $\hat{p}$, initial point $\mathbf{x}_1^{(0)}$, subroutine `Sample_Ellipse` to sample an ellipse, subroutine `Characterize_Slice` to analytically characterize $\mathcal{S}(\cdot; \mathcal{E})$, number of iterations N, number of slices per iteration J

Output: Samples from Markov Chain $((\mathbf{x}_1^{(1)}, ..., \mathbf{x}_J^{(1)}), ..., (\mathbf{x}_1^{(N)}, ..., \mathbf{x}_J^{(N)}))$

for $i = 1$ **to** N **do**
  $\mathcal{E} \leftarrow$ `Sample_Ellipse`$(\mathbf{x}_1^{(i-1)}, \hat{p})$
  $\mathcal{S}(\cdot; \mathcal{E}) \leftarrow$`Characterize_Slice`$(\mathcal{E})$
  $u \sim$ Uniform $[0, 1]$
  for $j = 1$ **to** J **do**
    $y \leftarrow (j - u)/J \cdot \hat{\mathcal{L}}(\mathbf{x}_1^{(i-1)})$
    $\mathbf{x}_j^{(i)} \leftarrow$ Uniform $\{\mathbf{x} : \mathbf{x} \in \mathcal{S}(y; \mathcal{E})\}$
  end
  $(\mathbf{x}_1^{(i)}, ..., \mathbf{x}_J^{(i)}) \leftarrow$ `rand_perm`$(\hat{\mathbf{x}}_1^{(i)}, ..., \hat{\mathbf{x}}_J^{(i)})$
end
return $((\mathbf{x}_1^{(1)}, ..., \mathbf{x}_J^{(1)}), ..., (\mathbf{x}_1^{(N)}, ..., \mathbf{x}_J^{(N)}))$

Unfortunately solving for $\mathcal{S}(y; \mathcal{E})$ in closed form is not possible in general, although it can be done for Truncated Multivariate Gaussian (TMG) quadrature as shown below.

4.1 ANALYTIC EPESS FOR TMG

The (linear) TMG distribution is defined as:

$$p^*(\mathbf{x}) = \frac{1}{Z}\mathcal{N}(\mathbf{x}; \mathbf{0}, \mathbf{I}) \prod_{j=1}^{M} \mathbb{1}(L_j^\top \mathbf{x} \geq 0).$$

Using the EP approximation $\mathcal{N}(\mathbf{x}; \boldsymbol{\mu}, \boldsymbol{\Sigma})$ and Equation (3), we can rewrite the density p^* as:

$$\begin{aligned}
p^*(\mathbf{x}) &\propto \mathcal{N}(\mathbf{x}; \mathbf{0}, \mathbf{I}) \prod_{j=1}^{m} \mathbb{1}(L_j^\top \mathbf{x} \geq 0) \\
&\propto \mathcal{N}(\mathbf{x}; \boldsymbol{\mu}, \boldsymbol{\Sigma}) \frac{\mathcal{N}(\mathbf{x}; \mathbf{0}, \mathbf{I})}{\mathcal{N}(\mathbf{x}; \boldsymbol{\mu}, \boldsymbol{\Sigma})} \prod_{j=1}^{m} \mathbb{1}(L_j^\top \mathbf{x} \geq 0) \\
&= \mathcal{N}(\mathbf{z}; \mathbf{0}, \boldsymbol{\Sigma}) \frac{\mathcal{N}(\mathbf{z}; -\boldsymbol{\mu}, \mathbf{I})}{\mathcal{N}(\mathbf{z}; \mathbf{0}, \boldsymbol{\Sigma})} \prod_{j=1}^{m} \mathbb{1}(L_j^\top (\mathbf{z} + \mu) \geq 0) \\
&\equiv \mathcal{N}(\mathbf{z}; \mathbf{0}, \boldsymbol{\Sigma}) \hat{\mathcal{L}}(\mathbf{z}) \\
&\equiv \tilde{p}(\mathbf{z})
\end{aligned}$$

where $\mathbf{x} = \mathbf{z} + \boldsymbol{\mu}$ is a transformation with identity Jacobian. We are able to apply Analytic ESS to $\tilde{p}(\mathbf{z})$ and can then recover samples for $\mathbf{x}$ by reversing the transformation. First we analytically characterize the slice:

$$\begin{aligned}\mathcal{S}(y;\mathcal{E}) &= \{\theta \in [0,2\pi) : \mathcal{L}(\mathbf{z}'(\theta)) > y\} \\ &= \cap_{j=1}^{m}\{\theta \in [0,2\pi) : L_j^{\top}\mathbf{z}'(\theta) + L_j^{\top}\mu \geq 0\} \\ &\quad \cap \{\theta \in [0,2\pi) : \frac{\mathcal{N}(\mathbf{z}'(\theta); -\boldsymbol{\mu}, \mathbf{I})}{\mathcal{N}(\mathbf{z}'(\theta); \mathbf{0}, \boldsymbol{\Sigma})} > y\} \\ &= \cap_{j=1}^{m}\Theta_j \cap \Theta_y,\end{aligned}$$

where $\mathbf{z}'(\theta) = \mathbf{z}\cos(\theta) + \boldsymbol{\nu}\sin(\theta)$. The region Θ_j is the part of the ellipse that lies in the halfspace defined by L_j. Since it is defined by a linear inequality of $\sin(\theta)$ and $\cos(\theta)$, it is easily characterized using basic trigonometry. The resulting region may be rewritten as $\Theta_j = [0, l_j] \cup [u_j, 2\pi]$ for some $l_j, u_j \in (0, 2\pi)$. Due to this nice structure, taking the intersection of all m regions can be computed in $\mathcal{O}(m)$. Region Θ_y can be simplified by taking logarithms on both sides of its inequality and reduces to the form:

$$a_0 + a_1\cos\theta + a_2\sin\theta + a_3\cos\theta\sin\theta + a_4\cos^2\theta > 0.$$

The roots of this inequality can be obtained by solving a quartic equation. This completes our analytic characterization of $\mathcal{S}(y;\mathcal{E})$.

The most expensive operations in Analytic ESS are generating $\mathcal{E}$ and characterizing $\mathcal{S}(y;\mathcal{E})$, as sampling from $\mathcal{S}(y;\mathcal{E})$ is relatively cheap. To see this, let d denote the dimension of $\mathbf{x}$ and m the number of linear truncations. To sample the ellipse $\mathcal{E}$ we must draw $\boldsymbol{\nu}$ from the Gaussian prior which costs $\mathcal{O}(d^2)$. Characterizing the slice $\mathcal{S}(y;\mathcal{E})$ involves m inner products of $\mathbf{x}$ and $\boldsymbol{\nu}$ with the linear truncations L_j and can be calculated in $\mathcal{O}(md)$. The total computational overhead is thus $\mathcal{O}(d^2 + md)$. Once this is done, sampling from $\mathcal{S}(y;\mathcal{E})$ is cheap. It involves sampling from an intersection of $\mathcal{O}(m)$ intervals which can be done in $\mathcal{O}(d + m)$ (here we have factored in the expense of storing each sample at a cost $\mathcal{O}(d)$).

Since the upfront cost of characterizing the slice $\mathcal{S}(y;\mathcal{E})$ is $\mathcal{O}(d^2 + md)$, we can sample $\mathcal{O}(d)$ points per ellipse $\mathcal{E}$ without significantly increasing the total computational complexity. This leads to a high effective sample size relative to the computational complexity.

The Exact-HMC algorithm for TMG [Pakman and Paninski, 2014] has an intimate relationship with Analytic ESS and inspired our analytic framework. We explain this connection in Section 5.2.

5 EXPERIMENTAL RESULTS

In this section we compare the empirical performance of the algorithms introduced in Sections 2.3–4 to other state-of-the-art MCMC methods. Comparisons are shown for the Probit regression and the TMG problem, both of which are often encountered in machine learning contexts, as well as the log-Gaussian Cox process. We quantify the mixing of MCMC samplers by comparing their effective number of samples. Effective sample size is estimated using the method as described in [Gelman et al., 2014] which is implemented in the MCMC Diagnostics Tool box for `Matlab` [Särkkä and Vehtari, 2014-02-34]. We compare the results in terms of effective sample size divided by the number of density function evaluations of p^*, which is the dominant computational expense of running the samplers.

5.1 PROBIT REGRESSION

Probit regression is one of the most common problems in machine learning and is often used as a benchmark for comparing Bayesian computation methods. A nice review of the state-of-the-art algorithms for probit can be found in [Chopin and Ridgway, 2015]. For our experiments, we choose 4 data sets of moderate size from UCI repository as listed in Table 1, with their dimension and number of datapoints. These are the Breast Cancer [Wolberg et al., 1995], Ionosphere [Sigillito, 1989], Sonar [Son] and Musk [AI Group at Arris Pharmaceutical Corporation, 1994] data sets. As is standard, each dataset is preprocessed to have zero mean and unit variance for each regressor, a unit intercept term has been included and the prior on each latent variable is $\mathcal{N}(0, 10)$.

Table 1: Datasets for probit: dimensions and number of data points.

DATASET	DIMENSION	DATA POINTS
Breast Cancer	31	569
Ionosphere	31	351
Sonar	61	97
Musk	165	419

We compare EPESS and Recycled EPESS (denoted by EPESS(J) where J is the number of recycled points per slice) against Metropolis-Hastings with an EP proposal (EPMH) and HMC using the No-U-Turn sampler as implemented in Stan [Carpenter et al., 2015]. EPMH is considered as state-of-the-art for Probit [Chopin and Ridgway, 2015] . The chains were initialized at the EP mean for all EPESS methods and the Stan implementation decides on its own initialization. We use the `R` package of Ridgway [2016] to find the EP approximation. Its CPU time is negligible compared to the time to run the samplers.

We run 100 chains with 20,000 samples per chain. For

EPMH we ran it until 20,000 unique samples (i.e., accepted proposed points) were collected to make it comparable with the other methods. The results are shown in the top three plots of Figure 4. EPESS outperforms HMC and EPMH by about a factor of 5 for effective sample size relative to number of function evaluations. As compared to EPMH, EPESS gives a slightly smaller effective number of samples but takes far fewer function evaluations. The number of function evaluations for Recycled EPESS is smaller than that of EPESS, however the effective number of samples are also proportionately small as the samples are highly correlated (this is expected: see Section 3). Overall Recycled EPESS does not improve the effective sample size relative to number of function evaluations above EPESS.

5.2 TRUNCATED MULTIVARIATE GAUSSIAN

The Truncated Multivariate Gaussian (TMG) is an important distribution which commonly arise in diverse models such as Probit/Tobit models, Neural models [Pillow et al., 2003], Bayesian bridge model in finance [Polson et al., 2014], True-skill model for competitions [Herbrich et al., 2006] and many others. There has been some recent work including [Lan and Shahbaba, 2015] focusing on sampling from TMG, but Exact-HMC algorithm [Pakman and Paninski, 2014] is considered to be state-of-the-art (see [Altmann et al., 2014] for a nice review). We treat it as the benchmark for comparisons in our experiments.

The equations of motion for Exact-HMC are the same as that of standard ESS,

$$\mathbf{x}'(t) = \mathbf{x}\cos(t) + \boldsymbol{\nu}\sin(t),$$

and so it suffers from the same problems as described in Section 2.1 and illustrated in Figure 1. The elliptical path enables *exact* calculation of where the HMC particle hits the truncations, hence the term *Exact*-HMC. These are the same calculations used to find the regions Θ_j in Analytic ESS, although being an HMC method, it does not have a slice height y with the corresponding region Θ_y. It also cannot incorporate an EP prior as this would destroy the elliptical path and render the calculations intractable. A tuning parameter T is required and for all our experiments we have fixed T to be $\pi/2$ as recommended by Pakman and Paninski [2014]. We only show comparative results for Analytic EPESS as it is faster than EPESS since it avoids slice shrinkages. We obtain an EP approximation for TMG using the method as described in [Cunningham et al., 2011] which is fast and scales well for high dimensions. It runs in negligible CPU time as compared to the running time of different sampling algorithms.

We run 100 chains with 20,000 samples per chain. The fourth plot in Figure 4 shows the results for a 2-d standard Gaussian where the truncated region is a rectangular box: $\{s \leq x \leq s+1, -1 \leq y \leq 1\}$. As we shift the box to the right, we see Analytic EPESS outperforming Exact-HMC by orders of magnitude. This trend carries over to higher dimensions as shown in the fifth plot in Figure 4. Results for $d = 500$ and $d = 1000$ have been omitted as Exact-HMC with $T = \pi/2$ takes prohibitively long to run.

5.3 LOG-GAUSSIAN COX PROCESS

We conducted experiments on a Log-Gaussian Cox Process (LGCP) applied to the coal mining disaster dataset as set up in the original ESS paper [Murray et al., 2010]. Although a convergent EP is available for the LGCP, it is not accurate with the EP mean substantially deviating from the true mean [Ko and Seeger, 2015]. Our experiments showed that EPESS fared no better than ESS on this problem, with the effective number of samples being about the same. This demonstrates the fact that EPESS will only perform well when EP is accurate.

6 DISCUSSION AND CONCLUSION

In this work we have shown how the ideas of ESS, EP and recycling can be combined to yield highly efficient MCMC methods. For both probit regression and Gaussian quadrature, performance exceeds state-of-the-art samplers by an order of magnitude. In the case of TMG, this can be multiple orders of magnitude.

We investigated two different types of recycling: sampling multiple points per slice (Recycled ESS), and sampling multiple points at different slice heights from the same ellipse (Analytic ESS). The benefit of Recycled ESS is questionable as it seems not to improve performance in probit, due to having highly correlated samples. It also introduces a tuning parameter which makes the algorithm more difficult to implement. Analytic EPESS for TMG does not have the above-mentioned issues of Recycled ESS. In this case recycling is of clear benefit as can be seen in the experimental results of Section 5.2. It is here where EPESS outperforms the state-of-the-art by the largest margin.

The example of the Log-Gaussian Cox process shows that EPESS will only offer an advantage over ESS when EP is accurate. This restricts the applicability of EPESS as a general method. Improving the accuracy of EP is a subject of active research and any developments made will be immediately be inherited by EPESS.

There are multiple directions of future work. Instead of

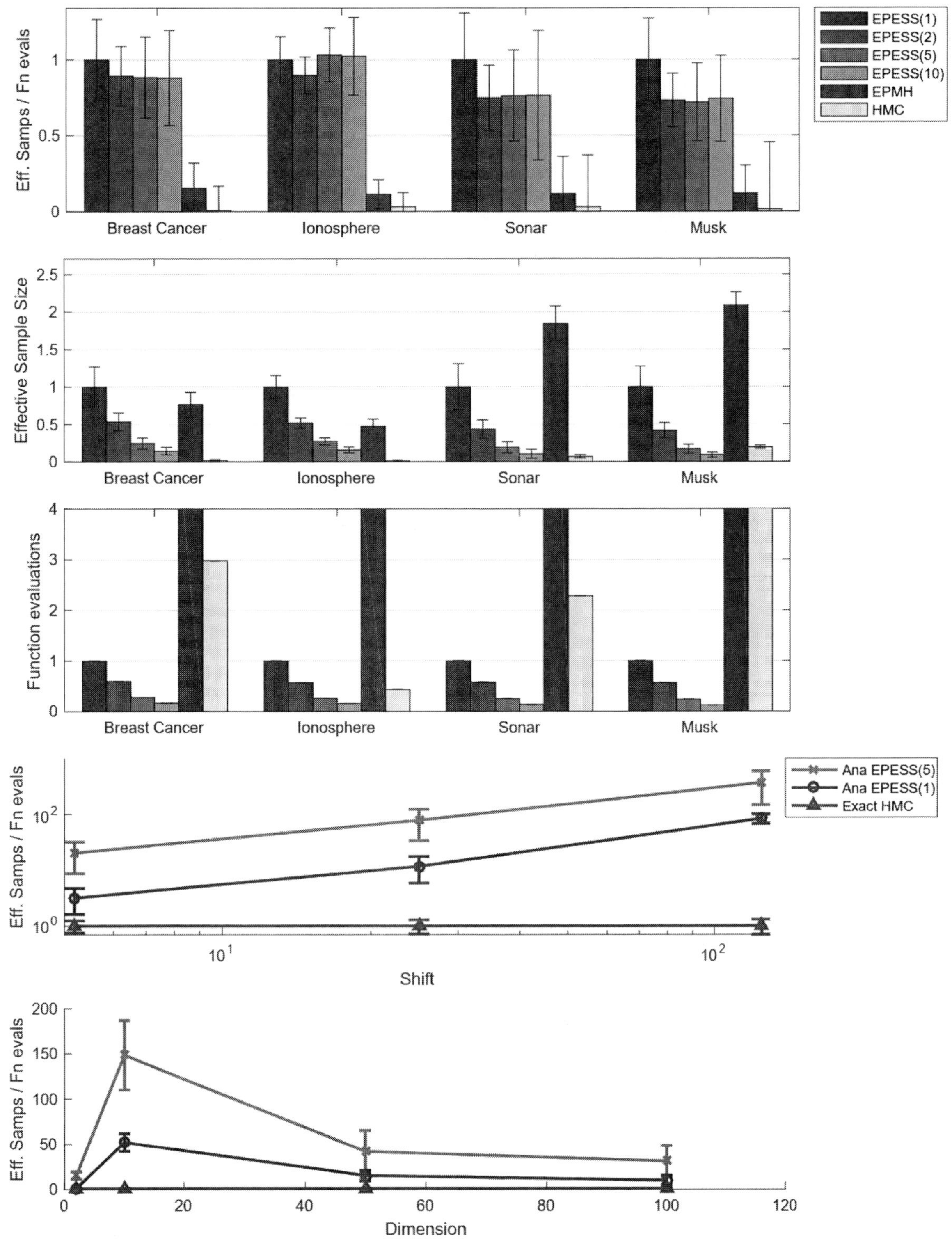

Figure 4: Plots of empirical results. In the top three plots all values are normalized so that EPESS(1) has value 1. In the bottom 2 plots all values are normalized so that Exact-HMC has value 1. The naming convention: EPESS(J) denotes Recycled EPESS with J points sampled per slice. EPESS(1) denotes EPESS without recycling. Ana EPESS(J) denotes Analytic EPESS with J threshold levels per iteration. Error bars in plot 3 for all algorithms are effectively zero.

choosing the prior that minimizes $\alpha = 1$ divergence, we could choose a prior corresponding to $\alpha > 1$ by replacing EP with Power-EP [Minka, 2004]. This might make the likelihood even weaker in EPESS and further improve performance.

Acknowledgements. We would like to thank Garud Iyengar for helpful discussions and Lichi Li for assisting in the code. FF is supported by a grant from Bloomberg. JPC is supported by Simons Foundation (SCGB#325171 and SCGB#325233), the Sloan Foundation, the McKnight Foundation, and the Grossman Center.

References

UCI machine learning repository. University of California, Irvine, School of Information and Computer Sciences.

AI Group at Arris Pharmaceutical Corporation. UCI Machine Learning Repository, 1994.

Yoann Altmann, Steve McLaughlin, and Nicolas Dobigeon. Sampling from a multivariate gaussian distribution truncated on a simplex: a review. In *Statistical Signal Processing (SSP), 2014 IEEE Workshop on*, pages 113–116. IEEE, 2014.

Michael Braun and Andre Bonfrer. Scalable inference of customer similarities from interactions data using dirichlet processes. *Marketing Science*, 30(3):513–531, 2011.

Bob Carpenter, Andrew Gelman, Matt Hoffman, Daniel Lee, Ben Goodrich, Michael Betancourt, Marcus A Brubaker, Jiqiang Guo, Peter Li, and Allen Riddell. Stan: a probabilistic programming language. *Journal of Statistical Software*, 2015.

Nicolas Chopin and James Ridgway. Leave pima indians alone: binary regression as a benchmark for bayesian computation. *arXiv preprint arXiv:1506.08640*, 2015.

Botond Cseke and Tom Heskes. Approximate marginals in latent gaussian models. *The Journal of Machine Learning Research*, 12:417–454, 2011.

John P Cunningham, Philipp Hennig, and Simon Lacoste-Julien. Gaussian probabilities and expectation propagation. *arXiv preprint arXiv:1111.6832*, 2011.

Guillaume P Dehaene and Simon Barthelmé. Bounding errors of expectation-propagation. In *Advances in Neural Information Processing Systems*, pages 244–252, 2015.

Marc Deisenroth and Shakir Mohamed. Expectation propagation in gaussian process dynamical systems. In *Advances in Neural Information Processing Systems*, pages 2609–2617, 2012.

Andrew Gelman, John B Carlin, Hal S Stern, and Donald B Rubin. *Bayesian data analysis*, volume 2. Taylor & Francis, 2014.

Ralf Herbrich, Tom Minka, and Thore Graepel. Trueskill: A bayesian skill rating system. In *Advances in Neural Information Processing Systems*, pages 569–576, 2006.

Young Jun Ko and Matthias Seeger. Expectation propagation for rectified linear poisson regression. In *Proceedings of the Seventh Asian Conference on Machine Learning*, number EPFL-CONF-214372, 2015.

Malte Kuss and Carl Edward Rasmussen. Assessing approximate inference for binary gaussian process classification. *The Journal of Machine Learning Research*, 6:1679–1704, 2005.

Shiwei Lan and Babak Shahbaba. Sampling constrained probability distributions using spherical augmentation. *arXiv preprint arXiv:1506.05936*, 2015.

Thomas Minka. Power EP. Technical report, Technical report, Microsoft Research, Cambridge, 2004.

Thomas Minka. Divergence measures and message passing. Technical report, 2005.

Thomas P Minka. Expectation propagation for approximate bayesian inference. In *Proceedings of the Seventeenth conference on Uncertainty in artificial intelligence*, pages 362–369. Morgan Kaufmann Publishers Inc., 2001.

Iain Murray, Ryan Prescott, Adams David, and J. C. Mackay. Elliptical slice sampling. In *Proceedings of the 13th International Conference on Artificial Intelligence and Statistics (AISTATS)*, 2010.

Radford Neal. Slice sampling. *Annals of Statistics*, 31: 705–741, 2003.

Radford M Neal. Mcmc using Hamiltonian dynamics. *Handbook of Markov Chain Monte Carlo*, 2, 2011.

Hannes Nickisch and Carl Edward Rasmussen. Approximations for binary gaussian process classification. *Journal of Machine Learning Research*, 9(10), 2008.

Robert Nishihara, Iain Murray, and Ryan P. Adams. Parallel mcmc with generalized elliptical slice sampling. *J. Mach. Learn. Res.*, 15(1):2087–2112, January 2014. ISSN 1532-4435.

Akihiko Nishimura and David Dunson. Recycling intermediate steps to improve Hamiltonian Monte Carlo. *arXiv preprint arXiv:1511.06925*, 2015.

Ari Pakman and Liam Paninski. Exact Hamiltonian Monte Carlo for truncated multivariate gaussians. *Journal of Computational and Graphical Statistics*, 23 (2):518–542, 2014.

Jonathan W Pillow, Liam Paninski, and Eero P Simoncelli. Maximum likelihood estimation of a stochastic integrate-and-fire neural model. In *NIPS*, pages 1311–1318. Citeseer, 2003.

Nicholas G Polson, James G Scott, and Jesse Windle. The bayesian bridge. *Journal of the Royal Statistical Society: Series B (Statistical Methodology)*, 76(4): 713–733, 2014.

James Ridgway. *EPGLM: Gaussian Approximation of Bayesian Binary Regression Models*, 2016. R package version 1.1.1.

S Särkkä and A Vehtari. Mcmc diagnostics for matlab. *Helsinki University of Technology*, 2014-02-34.

Vince Sigillito. UCI machine learning repository. University of California, Irvine, School of Information and Computer Sciences, 1989.

Martin J Wainwright and Michael I Jordan. Graphical models, exponential families, and variational inference. *Foundations and Trends® in Machine Learning*, 1(1-2):1–305, 2008.

William H. Wolberg, W. Nick Street, and Olvi L. Mangasarian. UCI machine learning repository. University of California, Irvine, School of Information and Computer Sciences, 1995.

Bayesian Learning of Kernel Embeddings

Seth Flaxman
flaxman@stats.ox.ac.uk
Department of Statistics
University of Oxford

Dino Sejdinovic
dino.sejdinovic@stats.ox.ac.uk
Department of Statistics
University of Oxford

John P. Cunningham
jpc2181@columbia.edu
Department of Statistics
Columbia University

Sarah Filippi
filippi@stats.ox.ac.uk
Department of Statistics
University of Oxford

Abstract

Kernel methods are one of the mainstays of machine learning, but the problem of kernel learning remains challenging, with only a few heuristics and very little theory. This is of particular importance in methods based on estimation of kernel mean embeddings of probability measures. For characteristic kernels, which include most commonly used ones, the kernel mean embedding uniquely determines its probability measure, so it can be used to design a powerful statistical testing framework, which includes nonparametric two-sample and independence tests. In practice, however, the performance of these tests can be very sensitive to the choice of kernel and its lengthscale parameters. To address this central issue, we propose a new probabilistic model for kernel mean embeddings, the Bayesian Kernel Embedding model, combining a Gaussian process prior over the Reproducing Kernel Hilbert Space containing the mean embedding with a conjugate likelihood function, thus yielding a closed form posterior over the mean embedding. The posterior mean of our model is closely related to recently proposed shrinkage estimators for kernel mean embeddings, while the posterior uncertainty is a new, interesting feature with various possible applications. Critically for the purposes of kernel learning, our model gives a simple, closed form marginal pseudolikelihood of the observed data given the kernel hyperparameters. This marginal pseudolikelihood can either be optimized to inform the hyperparameter choice or fully Bayesian inference can be used.

1 INTRODUCTION

A large class of popular and successful machine learning methods rely on kernels (positive semidefinite functions), including support vector machines, kernel ridge regression, kernel PCA (Schölkopf and Smola, 2002), Gaussian processes (Rasmussen and Williams, 2006), and kernel-based hypothesis testing (Gretton et al., 2005, 2008, 2012a). A key component for many of these methods is that of estimating kernel mean embeddings and covariance operators of probability measures based on data. The use of simple empirical estimators has been challenged recently (Muandet et al., 2016) and alternative, better-behaved frequentist shrinkage strategies have been proposed. In this article, we develop a Bayesian framework for estimation of kernel mean embeddings, recovering desirable shrinkage properties as well as allowing quantification of full posterior uncertainty. Moreover, the developed framework has an additional extremely useful feature. Namely, a persistent problem in kernel methods is that of kernel choice and hyperparameter selection, for which no general-purpose strategy exists. When a large dataset is available in a supervised setting, the standard approach is to use cross-validation. However, in unsupervised learning and kernel-based hypothesis testing, cross-validation is not straightforward to apply and yet the choice of kernel is critically important. Our framework gives a tractable closed-form marginal pseudolikelihood of the data allowing direct hyperparameter optimization as well as fully Bayesian posterior inference through integrating over the kernel hyperparameters. We emphasise that this approach is fully unsupervised: it is based solely on the modelling of kernel mean embeddings – going beyond marginal likelihood based approaches in, e.g., Gaussian process regression – and is thus broadly applicable in situations, such as kernel-based hypothesis testing, where the hyperparameter choice has thus far been mainly driven by heuristics.

In Section 2 we provide the necessary background on Reproducing Kernel Hilbert Spaces (RKHS) as well as describe some related works. In Section 3 we develop our Bayesian Kernel Embedding model, showing a rigorous Gaussian process prior formulation for an RKHS. In Section 4 we show how to perform kernel learning and posterior inference with our model. In Section 5 we empirically evaluate our model, arguing that our Bayesian Kernel Learning (BKL) objective should be considered as a "drop-in" replacement for heuristic methods of choosing kernel hyperparameters currently in use, especially in unsupervised settings such as kernel-based testing. We close in Section 6 with a discussion of various applications of our approach and future work.

2 BACKGROUND AND RELATED WORK

2.1 KERNEL EMBEDDINGS OF PROBABILITY MEASURES

For any positive definite kernel function $k : \mathcal{X} \times \mathcal{X} \to \mathbb{R}$, there exists a unique reproducing kernel Hilbert space (RKHS) $\mathcal{H}_k$. RKHS is an (often infinite-dimensional) space of functions $h : \mathcal{X} \to \mathbb{R}$ where evaluation can be written as an inner product, and in particular $h(x) = \langle h, k(\cdot, x)\rangle_{\mathcal{H}_k}$ for all $h \in \mathcal{H}_k, x \in \mathcal{X}$. Given a probability measure P on $\mathcal{X}$, its kernel embedding into $\mathcal{H}_k$ is defined as:

$$\mu_{\mathsf{P}} = \int k(\cdot, x)\, \mathsf{P}(dx). \tag{1}$$

Embedding μ_{P} is an element of $\mathcal{H}_k$ and serves as a representation of P akin to a characteristic function. It represents expectations of RKHS functions in the form of an inner product $\int h(x)\mathsf{P}(dx) = \langle h, \mu_{\mathsf{P}}\rangle_{\mathcal{H}_k}$. For a broad family of kernels termed *characteristic* (Sriperumbudur et al., 2011), every probability measure has a unique embedding – thus, such embeddings completely determine their probability measures and capture all of the moment information. This yields a framework for constructing nonparametric hypothesis tests for the two-sample problem and for independence, which are consistent against all alternatives (Gretton et al., 2008, 2012a) – we review this framework in the next section.

2.2 KERNEL MEAN EMBEDDING AND HYPOTHESIS TESTING

Given a kernel k and probability measures P and Q, the maximum mean discrepancy (MMD) between P and Q (Gretton et al., 2012a) is defined as the squared RKHS distance $\|\mu_{\mathsf{P}} - \mu_{\mathsf{Q}}\|^2_{\mathcal{H}_k}$ between their embeddings. A related quantity is the Hilbert Schmidt Independence Criterion (HSIC) (Gretton et al., 2005, 2008), a nonparametric dependence measure between random variables X and Y on domains $\mathcal{X}$ and $\mathcal{Y}$ respectively, defined as the squared RKHS distance $\|\mu_{\mathsf{P}_{XY}} - \mu_{\mathsf{P}_X\mathsf{P}_Y}\|^2_{\mathcal{H}_\kappa}$ between the embeddings of the joint distribution P_{XY} and of the product of the marginals $\mathsf{P}_X\mathsf{P}_Y$ with respect to a kernel $\kappa : (\mathcal{X} \times \mathcal{Y}) \times (\mathcal{X} \times \mathcal{Y}) \to \mathbb{R}$ on the product space. Typically, κ factorises, i.e. $\kappa((x, y), (x', y')) = k(x, x')l(y, y')$. The empirical versions of MMD and HSIC are used as test statistics for the two-sample ($\mathbf{H}_0 : \mathsf{P} = \mathsf{Q}$ vs. $\mathbf{H}_1 : \mathsf{P} \neq \mathsf{Q}$) and independence ($\mathbf{H}_0 : X \perp\!\!\!\perp Y$ vs. $\mathbf{H}_1 : X \not\perp\!\!\!\perp Y$) tests, respectively. With the help of the approximations to the asymptotic distribution under the null hypothesis, corresponding p-values can be computed (Gretton et al., 2012a). In addition, the so-called "witness function" which is proportional to $\mu_{\mathsf{P}} - \mu_{\mathsf{Q}}$ can be used to assess where the difference between the distributions arises.

2.3 KERNEL MEAN EMBEDDING ESTIMATORS

For a set of i.i.d. samples $x_1, \ldots, x_n$, the kernel mean embedding is typically estimated by its empirical version

$$\widehat{\mu_{\mathsf{P}}} = \mu_{\widehat{\mathsf{P}}} = \frac{1}{n}\sum_{i=1}^{n} k(\cdot, x_i), \tag{2}$$

from which various associated quantities, including the estimators of the squared RKHS distances between embeddings needed for kernel-based hypothesis tests, follow. As an empirical mean in an infinite-dimensional space, (2) is affected by Stein's phenomenon, as overviewed by Muandet et al. (2013) who also propose alternative shrinkage estimators similar to the well known James-Stein estimator. Improvements of test power using such shrinkage estimators are reported by Ramdas and Wehbe (2015). Connections between the James-Stein estimator and empirical Bayes procedures are classical (Efron and Morris, 1973), and thus a natural question to consider is whether a Bayesian formulation of the problem of kernel embedding estimation would yield similar shrinkage properties. In this paper, we will give a Bayesian perspective of the problem of kernel embedding estimation. In particular, we will construct a flexible model for underlying probability measures based on Gaussian measures in RKHSs which allows derivation of a full posterior distribution of μ_{P}, recovering similar shrinkage properties to Muandet et al. (2013), as discussed in Section 4.2. The model will give us a further advantage, however – as the marginal likelihood of the data given the kernel parameter can be derived leading to an informed choice of kernel parameters.

2.4 SELECTION OF KERNEL PARAMETERS

In supervised kernel methods like support vector machines, leave-one-out or k-fold crossvalidation is an effective and widely used method for kernel selection, and the myriad papers on multiple kernel learning (e.g. Bach et al. (2004); Sonnenburg et al. (2006); Gönen and Alpaydın (2011)) assume that some loss function is available and thus focus on effective ways of learning combinations of kernels. In the related but distinct world of smoothing kernels and kernel density estimation, there are a variety of long-standing approaches to bandwidth selection, again based on a loss function (in this case, mean integrated squared error is a popular choice (Bowman, 1985), and there is even a formula giving the optimal smoothing parameter asymptotically, see Rosenblatt (1956); Parzen (1962)) but we are not aware of work linking this literature to methods based on positive definite/RKHS kernels we study here. Separately,

Gaussian process learning can be undertaken by maximizing the marginal likelihood, which has a convenient closed form. This is noteworthy for its success and general applicability even for learning complicated combinations of kernels (Duvenaud et al., 2013) or rich kernel families (Wilson and Adams, 2013). Our approach has the same basic design as that of Gaussian process learning, yet it is applicable to learning kernel embeddings, which falls outside the realm of supervised learning.

As noted in Gretton et al. (2012b), the choice of the kernel k is critically important for the power of the tests presented in Section 2.2. However, no general, theoretically-grounded approaches for kernel selection in this context exist. The difficulty is that, unlike in supervised kernel methods, a simple cross-validation approach for the kernel parameter selection is not possible. What would be an ideal objective function – asymptotic test power – cannot be computed due to a complicated asymptotic null distribution. Moreover, even if we were able to estimate the power by performing tests on "training data" for each of the individual candidate kernels, in order to account for multiple comparisons, this training data would have to be disjoint from the one on which the hypothesis test is performed, which is clearly wasteful of power and appropriate only in the type of large-scale settings discussed in Gretton et al. (2012b). For these reasons, most users of kernel hypothesis tests in practice resort to using a parameterized kernel family such as squared exponential, and setting the length-scale parameter based on the "median heuristic."

The exact origins of the median heuristic are unclear (interestingly, it does not appear in the book that is most commonly cited as its source, Schölkopf and Smola (2002)) but it may have been derived from Takeuchi et al. (2006) and has precursors in classical work on bandwidth selection for kernel density estimation (Bowman, 1985). Note that there are two versions of the median heuristic in the literature: in both versions, given a set of observations $x_1, \ldots, x_n$ we calculate $\ell = \text{median}(\|x_i - x_j\|_2)$ and then one version (e.g. Mooij et al. (2015)) uses the Gaussian RBF / squared exponential kernel parameterized as $k(x, x') = \exp(-\frac{\|x-x'\|^2}{\ell^2})$ and the second version (e.g. Muandet et al. (2014)) uses the parameterization $k(x, x') = \exp(-\frac{\|x-x'\|^2}{2\ell^2})$. Some recent work has highlighted the situations in which the median heuristic can lead to poor performance (Gretton et al., 2012b). Cases in which the median heuristic performs quite well and also cases in which it performs quite poorly are discussed in (Reddi et al., 2015; Ramdas et al., 2015). We note that the median heuristic has also been used as a default value for supervised learning tasks (e.g. for the SVM implementation in R package `kernlab`) or when cross-validation is simply too expensive.

Outside of kernel methods, the same basic conundrum arises in spectral clustering in the choice of the parameters for the similarity graph (Von Luxburg, 2007, Section 8.1) and it is implicitly an issue in any unsupervised statistical method based on distances or dissimilarities, like the distance covariance (which is in fact equivalent to HSIC with a certain family of kernel functions (Sejdinovic et al., 2013)), or even the choice of the number of neighbors k in k-nearest neighbors algorithms.

3 OUR MODEL: BAYESIAN KERNEL EMBEDDING

Below, we will work with a parametric family of kernels $\{k_\theta(\cdot,\cdot)\}_{\theta\in\Theta}$. Given a dataset $\{x_i\}_{i=1}^n \sim \mathsf{P}$ of observations in $\mathbb{R}^D$ for an unknown probability distribution P, we wish to infer the kernel embedding $\mu_{\mathsf{P},\theta} = \int k_\theta(\cdot, x)\,\mathsf{P}(dx)$ for a given kernel k_θ in the parametric family. Moreover, we wish to construct a model that will allow inference of the kernel hyperparameter θ as well. Note that the two goals are related, since θ determines the space in which the embedding $\mu_{\mathsf{P},\theta}$ lies. When it is obvious from context, we suppress the dependence of the embeddings on the underlying measure P, writing μ_θ to emphasize the dependence on θ. Similarly, we will use $\widehat{\mu_\theta}$ to denote the simple empirical estimator from Eq. (2), which depends on a fixed sample $\{x_i\}_{i=1}^n$.

Our Bayesian Kernel Embedding (BKE) approach consists in specifying a prior on the kernel mean embedding μ_θ and a likelihood function linking it to the observations through the empirical estimator $\widehat{\mu_\theta}$. This will then allow us to infer the posterior distribution of the kernel mean embedding. The hyperparameter θ can itself have a prior, with the goal of learning a posterior distribution over the hyperparameter space.

3.1 PRIOR

A given hyperparameter θ (which can itself have a prior distribution), parameterizes a kernel k_θ and a corresponding RKHS $\mathcal{H}_{k_\theta}$. While it is tempting to define a $\mathcal{GP}(0, k_\theta(\cdot,\cdot))$ prior on μ_θ, this is problematic since draws from such prior would almost surely fall outside $\mathcal{H}_k$ (Wahba, 1990). Therefore, we define a GP prior over μ_θ as follows:

$$\mu_\theta \mid \theta \sim \mathcal{GP}(0, r_\theta(\cdot,\cdot)) \,, \tag{3}$$

$$r_\theta(x, y) := \int k_\theta(x, u) k_\theta(u, y) \nu(du) \,. \tag{4}$$

where ν is any finite measure on $\mathcal{X}$. This choice of r_θ ensures that $\mu_\theta \in \mathcal{H}_{k_\theta}$ with probability 1 by the *nuclear dominance* (Lukić and Beder, 2001; Pillai et al., 2007) of k_θ over r_θ for any stationary kernel k_θ and more broadly whenever $\int k_\theta(x, x)\nu(dx) < \infty$. For completeness, we provide details of this construction in the Appendix in Section A.2. Since Eq. (4) is the convolution of a kernel with itself with respect to ν, for typical kernels k_θ, the resulting kernel r_θ can be thought of as a smoother version of k_θ. A particularly convenient choice for $\mathcal{X} = \mathbb{R}^D$ is to take ν to be proportional to a Gaussian measure in which case r_θ can be computed analytically for a squared exponential kernel k_θ. The derivation is given in the Appendix in Section A.3, where we further show that if we set ν to be proportional to an isotropic Gaussian measure with a large variance parameter, r_θ becomes very similar to a squared exponential kernel with lengthscale $\theta\sqrt{2}$.

3.2 LIKELIHOOD

We need a likelihood linking the kernel mean embedding μ_θ to the observations $\{x_i\}_{i=1}^n$. We define the likelihood via the empirical mean embedding estimator of Eq. (2), $\widehat{\mu_\theta}$ which depends on $\{x_i\}_{i=1}^n$ and θ. Consider evaluating $\widehat{\mu_\theta}$ at some $x \in \mathbb{R}^D$ (which need not be one of our observations). The result is a real number giving an empirical estimate of $\mu_\theta(x)$ based on $\{x_i\}_{i=1}^n$ and θ. We link the empirical estimate, $\widehat{\mu_\theta}(x)$, to the corresponding modeled estimate, $\mu_\theta(x)$ using a Gaussian distribution with variance τ^2/n:

$$p(\widehat{\mu_\theta}(x)|\mu_\theta(x)) = \mathcal{N}(\widehat{\mu_\theta}(x); \mu_\theta(x), \tau^2/n), \quad x \in \mathcal{X}. \tag{5}$$

Our motivation for choosing this likelihood comes from the Central Limit Theorem. For a fixed location x, $\widehat{\mu_\theta}(x) = \frac{1}{n}\sum_{i=1}^n k_\theta(x_i, x)$ is an average of i.i.d. random variables so it satisfies:

$$\sqrt{n}(\widehat{\mu_\theta}(x) - \mu_\theta(x)) \xrightarrow{D} \mathcal{N}(0, \mathrm{Var}_{X\sim \mathsf{P}}[k_\theta(X,x)]). \tag{6}$$

We note that considering a heteroscedastic variance dependent on x in (5) would be a straightforward extension to our model, but we do not pursue this idea further here, i.e. while τ^2 can depend both on θ and x, we treat it as a single hyperparameter in the model.

3.3 JUSTIFICATION FOR THE MODEL

There are various ways to understand the construction of our hierarchical model. $\{x_i\}_{i=1}^n$ are drawn iid from P, which we do not have access to. We could estimate P directly (e.g. with a Gaussian mixture model) obtaining $\hat{\mathsf{P}}$, and then estimate $\mu_{\theta,\hat{\mathsf{P}}}$. But since density estimation is challenging in high dimensions, we posit a generative model for μ_θ directly.

Beginning at the top of the hierarchy, we have a fixed or random hyperparameter θ, which immediately defines k_θ and the corresponding RKHS $\mathcal{H}_{k_\theta}$. Then, we introduce a GP prior over μ_θ to ensure that $\mu_\theta \in \mathcal{H}_{k_\theta}$. A few realizations of μ_θ drawn from our prior are shown in Figure 1 (A), for an illustrative one-dimensional example where the prior is a Gaussian process with squared exponential kernel with lengthscale $\theta = 0.25$. Small values of θ yield rough functions and large values of θ yield smooth functions.

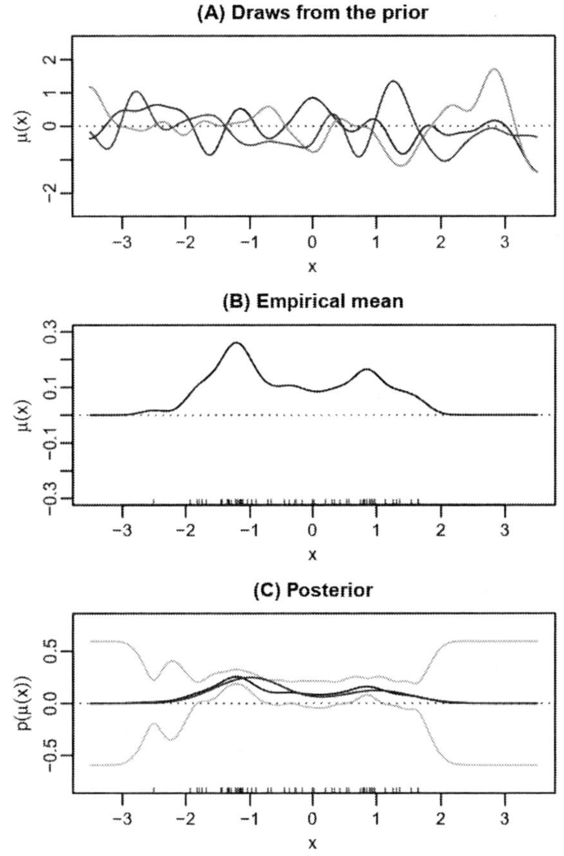

Figure 1: An illustration of the Bayesian Kernel Embedding model, where k_θ is a squared exponential kernel with lengthscale 0.1. Three draws of μ_θ from the prior are shown in (A). The empirical mean estimator $\widehat{\mu_\theta}$, which is the link function for the likelihood, is shown in (B) with the observations shown as a rug plot. In (C), the posterior mean embedding (black line) with uncertainty intervals (gray lines) is shown, as is the true mean embedding (blue line) based on the true data generating process (a mixture of Gaussians) and the same k_θ.

Next, we need to define the likelihood, which links these draws from the prior to the observations $\{x_i\}_{i=1}^n$. Since μ_θ is an infinite dimensional element in a Hilbert space and $\{x_i\}_{i=1}^n \in \mathcal{X}$ we need to transform the observations so that we can put a probability distribution over them. We use the empirical estimate of the mean embedding $\widehat{\mu_\theta}$ as our link function. Given a few observations, $\widehat{\mu_\theta}$ is shown in Figure 1 (B). Our likelihood links $\widehat{\mu_\theta}$ to μ_θ at the observation locations $\{x_i\}_{i=1}^n$ by assuming a squared loss function, i.e. Gaussian errors. As mentioned above, the motivation is the Central Limit Theorem, but also the convenient conjugate form that a Gaussian process with Gaussian likelihood yields. A plot of the posterior over the mean embedding is shown in Figure 1 (C). A few points are worth noting: since the empirical estimator is already quite smooth (notice its similarity to a kernel density estimate), the posterior mean embedding is only slightly smoother than the empirical mean embedding. Notice that unlike kernel density estimation, there is no requirement that the kernel mean embedding be non-negative, thus explaining the posterior uncertainty intervals which are below zero.

Our original motivation for considering a Bayesian model for kernel mean embeddings was to see whether there was a coherent Bayesian formulation that corresponded to the shrinkage estimators in Muandet et al. (2013), while also enabling us to learn the hyperparameters. The first difficulty we faced was how to define a valid prior over the RKHS and a reasonable likelihood function. Our choices are by no means definitive, and we hope to see further development in this area in the future. The second difficulty was that of developing a method for inferring hyperparameters, to which we turn in the next section.

4 BAYESIAN KERNEL LEARNING

In this section we show how to perform learning and inference in the Bayesian Kernel Embedding model introduced in the previous section. Our model inherits various attractive properties from the Gaussian process framework (Rasmussen and Williams, 2006). First, we derive the posterior and posterior predictive distributions for the kernel mean embedding in closed form due to the conjugacy of our model, and show the relationship with previously proposed shrinkage estimators. We then derive the tractable marginal likelihood of the observations given the hyperparameters allowing for efficient MAP estimation or posterior inference for hyperparameters.

4.1 POSTERIOR AND POSTERIOR PREDICTIVE DISTRIBUTIONS

Similarly to GP models, the posterior mean of μ_θ is available in closed form due to the conjugacy of Gaussians. Perhaps given our data we wish to infer μ_θ at a new location $x^* \in \mathbb{R}^D$. Given a value of the hyperparameter θ we can calculate the posterior distribution of μ_θ as well as the posterior predictive distribution $p(\mu_\theta(x^*)|\widehat{\mu_\theta}, \theta)$.

Standard GP results (Rasmussen and Williams, 2006) yield the posterior distribution as:

$$\begin{aligned}&[\mu_\theta(x_1), \ldots, \mu_\theta(x_n)]^\top \mid [\widehat{\mu_\theta}(x_1), \ldots, \widehat{\mu_\theta}(x_n)]^\top, \theta \\ &\quad \sim \mathcal{N}(R_\theta(R_\theta + (\tau^2/n)I_n)^{-1}[\widehat{\mu_\theta}(x_1), \ldots, \widehat{\mu_\theta}(x_n)]^\top, \\ &\qquad R_\theta - R_\theta(R_\theta + (\tau^2/n)I_n)^{-1}R_\theta),\end{aligned} \tag{7}$$

where R_θ is the $n \times n$ matrix such that its (i, j)-th element is $r_\theta(x_i, x_j)$. The posterior predictive distribution at a new location x^* is:

$$\begin{aligned}&\mu_\theta(x^*)^\top \mid [\widehat{\mu_\theta}(x_1), \ldots, \widehat{\mu_\theta}(x_n)]^\top, \theta \\ &\quad \sim \mathcal{N}(R_\theta^{*\top}(R_\theta + (\tau^2/n)I_n)^{-1}[\widehat{\mu_\theta}(x_1), \ldots, \widehat{\mu_\theta}(x_n)]^\top, \\ &\qquad r_\theta^{**} - R_\theta^{*\top}(R_\theta + (\tau^2/n)I_n)^{-1}R_\theta^*)\end{aligned} \tag{8}$$

where $R_\theta^* = [r_\theta(x^*, x_1), \ldots r_\theta(x^*, x_n)]^\top$ and $r_\theta^{**} = r_\theta(x^*, x^*)$.

As in standard GP inference, the time complexity is $\mathcal{O}(n^3)$ due to the matrix inverses and the storage is $\mathcal{O}(n^2)$ to store the $n \times n$ matrix R_θ.

4.2 RELATION TO THE SHRINKAGE ESTIMATOR

The spectral kernel mean shrinkage estimator (S-KMSE) of Muandet et al. (2013) for a fixed kernel k is defined as:

$$\check{\mu}_\lambda = \hat{\Sigma}_{XX}(\hat{\Sigma}_{XX} + \lambda I)^{-1}\hat{\mu}, \tag{9}$$

where $\hat{\mu} = \sum_{i=1}^n k(\cdot, x_i)$ is the empirical embedding, $\hat{\Sigma}_{XX} = \frac{1}{n}\sum_{i=1}^n k(\cdot, x_i) \otimes k(\cdot, x_i)$ is the empirical covariance operator on $\mathcal{H}_k$, and λ is a regularization parameter. (Muandet et al., 2013, Proposition 12) shows that $\check{\mu}_\lambda$ can be expressed as a weighted kernel mean $\check{\mu}_\lambda = \sum_{i=1}^n \beta_i k(\cdot, x_i)$, where

$$\begin{aligned}\beta &= \frac{1}{n}(K + n\lambda I)^{-1}K\mathbf{1} \\ &= (K + n\lambda I)^{-1}[\hat{\mu}(x_1), \ldots, \hat{\mu}(x_n)]^\top.\end{aligned}$$

Now, evaluating S-KMSE at any point x^* gives

$$\begin{aligned}\check{\mu}_\lambda(x^*) &= \sum_{i=1}^n \beta_i k(x^*, x_i) \\ &= K_*^\top(K + n\lambda I)^{-1}[\hat{\mu}(x_1), \ldots, \hat{\mu}(x_n)]^\top,\end{aligned}$$

where $K_* = [k(x^*, x_1), \ldots, k(x^*, x_n)]^\top$. Thus, the posterior mean in Eq. (7) recovers the S-KMSE estimator (Muandet et al., 2013), where the regularization parameter is related to the variance in the likelihood model (5), with a difference that in our case the kernel k_θ used to compute the empirical embedding is not the same as the kernel r_θ used to compute the kernel matrices. We note that our method has various advantages over the frequentist estimator $\check{\mu}_\lambda$: we have a closed-form uncertainty estimate, while we are not aware of a principled way of calculating the standard error of the frequentist estimators of embeddings. Our model also leads to a method for learning the hyperparameters, which we discuss next.

4.3 INFERENCE OF THE KERNEL PARAMETERS

In this section we focus on hyperparameter learning in our model. For the purposes of hyperparameter learning, we want to integrate out the kernel mean embedding μ_θ and consider the probability of our observations $\{x_i\}_{i=1}^n$ given the hyperparameters θ. In order to link our generative model directly to the observations, we use a pseudolikelihood approach as discussed in detail below.

We use the term pseudolikelihood because the model in this section will not correspond to the likelihood of the infinite dimensional empirical embedding; rather it will rely on the evaluations of the empirical embedding at a finite set of points. Let us fix a set of points $z_1, \ldots, z_m$ in $\mathcal{X} \subset \mathbb{R}^D$, with $m \geq D$. These points are not treated as random, and the inference method we develop does not require any specific choice of $\{z_j\}_{j=1}^m$. However, to ensure that there is a reasonable variability in the values of $k(x_i, z_j)$, these points should be placed in the high density regions of P. The simplest approach is to use a small held out portion of the data (with $m \ll n$ but $m \geq D$). Now, when we evaluate $\widehat{\mu_\theta}$ at these points, our modelling assumption from (5) on vector $\widehat{\mu_\theta}(\mathbf{z}) = [\widehat{\mu_\theta}(z_1), \ldots, \widehat{\mu_\theta}(z_m)]$ can be written as

$$\widehat{\mu_\theta}(\mathbf{z})|\mu_\theta \sim \mathcal{N}\left(\mu_\theta(\mathbf{z}), \frac{\tau^2}{n} I_m\right). \qquad (10)$$

However, as $\widehat{\mu_\theta}(z_j) = \frac{1}{n}\sum_{i=1}^n k_\theta(X_i, z_j)$ and all the terms $k_\theta(X_i, z_j)$ are independent given μ_θ, by Cramér's decomposition theorem, this modelling assumption is for the mapping $\phi_\mathbf{z} : \mathbb{R}^D \mapsto \mathbb{R}^m$, given by

$$\phi_\mathbf{z}(x) := [k_\theta(x, z_1), \ldots, k_\theta(x, z_m)] \in \mathbb{R}^m,$$

equivalent to:

$$\phi_\mathbf{z}(X_i)|\mu_\theta \sim \mathcal{N}\left(\mu_\theta(\mathbf{z}), \tau^2 I_m\right). \qquad (11)$$

Applying the change of variable $x \mapsto \phi_\mathbf{z}(x)$ and using the generalization of the change-of-variables formula to non-square Jacobian matrices as described in (Ben-Israel, 1999), we obtain a distribution for x conditionally on μ_θ and θ:

$$p(x|\mu_\theta, \theta) = p\left(\phi_\mathbf{z}(x)|\mu_\theta(\mathbf{z})\right) \operatorname{vol}\left[J_\theta(x)\right], \qquad (12)$$

where $J_\theta(x) = \left[\frac{\partial k_\theta(x, z_i)}{\partial x^{(j)}}\right]_{ij}$ is an $m \times D$ matrix, and

$$\begin{aligned}\operatorname{vol}\left[J_\theta(x)\right] &= \left(\det\left[J_\theta(x)^\top J_\theta(x)\right]\right)^{1/2} \\ &= \left(\det\left[\sum_{l=1}^m \frac{\partial k_\theta(x, z_l)}{\partial x^{(i)}} \frac{\partial k_\theta(x, z_l)}{\partial x^{(j)}}\right]_{ij}\right)^{1/2} \\ &=: \gamma_\theta(x). \end{aligned} \qquad (13)$$

The notation $\gamma_\theta(x)$ highlights the dependence on both θ and x. An explicit calculation of $\gamma_\theta(x)$ for squared exponential kernels is described in Section 4.4.

By the conditional independence of $\{\phi_\mathbf{z}(X_i)\}_{i=1}^n$ given μ_θ, we obtain the pseudolikelihood of all n observations:

$$\begin{aligned} p(x_1, \ldots, x_n|\mu_\theta, \theta) &= \prod_{i=1}^n \mathcal{N}\left(\phi_\mathbf{z}(x_i); \mu_\theta(\mathbf{z}), \tau^2 I_m\right) \gamma_\theta(x_i) \\ &= \mathcal{N}\left(\phi_\mathbf{z}(\mathbf{x}); \mathbf{m}_\theta(\mathbf{z}), \tau^2 I_{mn}\right) \prod_{i=1}^n \gamma_\theta(x_i), \end{aligned} \qquad (14)$$

where

$$\phi_\mathbf{z}(\mathbf{x}) = \left[\phi_\mathbf{z}(x_1)^\top \cdots \phi_\mathbf{z}(x_n)^\top\right]^\top = \operatorname{vec}\left\{K_{\theta,\mathbf{zx}}\right\} \in \mathbb{R}^{mn}$$

and in the mean vector $\mathbf{m}_\theta(\mathbf{z}) = \left[\mu_\theta(\mathbf{z})^\top \cdots \mu_\theta(\mathbf{z})^\top\right]^\top$, $\mu_\theta(\mathbf{z})$ repeats n times. Under the prior (3), this mean vector has mean $\mathbf{0}$ and covariance $\mathbf{1}_n\mathbf{1}_n^\top \otimes R_{\theta,\mathbf{zz}}$ where $R_{\theta,\mathbf{zz}}$ is the $m \times m$ matrix such that its (i,j)-th element is $r_\theta(z_i, z_j)$. Combining this prior and the pseudolikelihood in (14), we have the marginal pseudolikelihood:

$$\begin{aligned} p(x_1, \ldots, x_n|\theta) &= \int p(x_1, \ldots, x_n|\mu_\theta, \theta) p(\mu_\theta|\theta) d\mu_\theta \\ &= \int \mathcal{N}\left(\phi_\mathbf{z}(\mathbf{x}); \mathbf{m}_\theta(\mathbf{z}), \tau^2 I_{mn}\right) \left[\prod_{i=1}^n \gamma_\theta(x_i)\right] p(\mu_\theta|\theta) d\mu_\theta \\ &= \mathcal{N}\left(\phi_\mathbf{z}(\mathbf{x}); \mathbf{0}, \mathbf{1}_n\mathbf{1}_n^\top \otimes R_{\theta,\mathbf{zz}} + \tau^2 I_{mn}\right) \prod_{i=1}^n \gamma_\theta(x_i). \end{aligned} \qquad (15)$$

While the marginal pseudolikelihood in Eq. (15) involves a computation of the likelihood for an mn-dimensional normal distribution, the Kronecker structure of the covariance matrix allows efficient computation as described in Appendix A.4. The complexity for calculating this likelihood is $\mathcal{O}(m^3 + mn)$ (dominated by the inversion of $R_{\theta,\mathbf{zz}} + (\tau^2/n)I_m$). The Jacobian term depends on the parametric form of k_θ, but a typical cost as shown in Section 4.4 for the squared exponential kernel is $\mathcal{O}(nD^3 + nmD^2)$. In this case, the computation of matrices $R_{\theta,\mathbf{zz}}$ and $\phi_\mathbf{z}(\mathbf{x}) = \operatorname{vec}\{K_{\theta,\mathbf{zx}}\}$ is $\mathcal{O}(m^2 D)$ and $\mathcal{O}(mnD)$ respectively.

Just as in GP modeling, the marginal pseudolikelihood can be maximized directly for maximum likelihood II (also known as empirical Bayes) estimation, in which we look for a single best $\hat{\theta}$, or it can be used to construct an efficient MCMC sampler from the posterior of θ.

4.4 EXPLICIT CALCULATIONS FOR SQUARED EXPONENTIAL (RBF) KERNEL

Consider the isotropic squared exponential kernel with lengthscale matrix $\theta^2 I_D$ defined by

$$k_\theta(x, y) = \exp(-.5(x - y)^\top \theta^{-2} I_D (x - y)). \qquad (16)$$

In this case, we can analytically calculate $r_\theta(x, y)$, exact form is given in the Appendix in Section A.3.

The partial derivatives of $k_\theta(x, y)$ with respect to $x^{(i)}$ for $i = 1, \dots D$ can be easily derived as

$$\frac{\partial k_\theta(x, y)}{\partial x^{(i)}} = k_\theta(x, y)\frac{x^{(i)} - y^{(i)}}{\theta^2}$$

and therefore the Jacobian from Eq. (13) is equal to

$$\gamma_\theta(x) = \left(\det\left[\sum_{l=1}^{m} k_\theta(x, z_l)^2 \frac{(x^{(i)} - z_l^{(j)})^2}{\theta^4}\right]_{ij}\right)^{1/2}. \tag{17}$$

The computation of the matrix is $\mathcal{O}(mD^2)$ and the determinant is $\mathcal{O}(D^3)$. Since we must calculate $\gamma_\theta(x_i)$ for each x_i, the overall time complexity is $\mathcal{O}(nD^3 + nmD^2)$.

5 EXPERIMENTS

We demonstrate our approach on two synthetic datasets and one example on real data, focusing on two-sample testing with MMD and independence testing with HSIC. First, we use our Bayesian Kernel Embedding model and learn the kernel hyperparameters with maximum likelihood II, optimizing the marginal likelihood. Second, we take a fully Bayesian approach to inference and learning with our model. Finally, we apply the PC algorithm for causal structure discovery to a real dataset. The PC algorithm relies on a series of independence tests; we use HSIC with the lengthscales set with Bayesian Kernel Learning.

Choosing lengthscales with the median heuristic is often a very bad idea. In the case of two sample testing, Gretton et al. (2012b) showed that MMD with the median heuristic failed to reject the null hypothesis when comparing samples from a grid of isotropic Gaussians to samples from a grid of non-isotropic Gaussians. We repeated this experiment by considering a distribution P of a mixture of bivariate Gaussians centered on a grid with diagonal covariance and unit variance and a distribution Q of a mixture of bivariate Gaussians centered at the same locations but with rotated covariance matrices with a ratio ϵ of largest to smallest covariance eigenvalues.

As illustrated in Figures 2(A) and (B), for small values of ϵ both distributions are very similar whereas the distinction between P and Q becomes more apparent as ϵ increases. For different values of ϵ, we sample 100 observations from each mixture component, yielding 900 observations from P and 900 observations from Q and then perform a two-sample test ($\mathbf{H}_0 : \mathsf{P} = \mathsf{Q}$ vs. $\mathbf{H}_1 : \mathsf{P} \neq \mathsf{Q}$) using the MMD empirical estimate with an isotropic squared exponential kernel with one hyperparameter, the lengthscale. The type II error (i.e. probability that the test fails to reject the null hypothesis that $\mathsf{P} = \mathsf{Q}$ at $\alpha = 0.05$) is shown in Figure 2(C) for differently skewed covariances (ϵ from 0.5 to 15) when the median heuristic is chosen to select the kernel lengthscale or when using the Bayesian Kernel Learning. In this example, the median heuristic picks a kernel with a large lengthscale, since the median distance between points is large. With this large lengthscale MMD always fails to reject at $\alpha = 0.05$ even for simple cases where ϵ is large. When we use Bayesian Kernel Learning and optimize the marginal likelihood of Eq. (15) for $\tau^2 = 1$ (our results were not sensitive to the choice of this parameter, but in the fully Bayesian case below we show that we can learn it) we found the maximum marginal likelihood at a lengthscale of 0.85. With this choice of lengthscale, MMD correctly rejects the null hypothesis at $\alpha = 0.05$ even for very hard situations when $\epsilon = 2$. We observe that when ϵ is smaller than 2, the type II error of MMD is very high for both choices of lengthscale, because the two distributions P and Q are so similar that the test always retains the null hypothesis. In Figure 2(D) we illustrate the BKL marginal likelihood across a range of lengthscales. Interestingly, there are multiple local optima and the median heuristic lies between the two main modes. The plot indicates that multiple scales may be of interest for this dataset, which makes sense given that the true data generating process is a mixture model. This insight can be incorporated into the Bayesian Kernel Embedding framework by expanding our model, as discussed below. In Figure 2(E) we used the BKE posterior to estimate the witness function $\mu_{P,\theta} - \mu_{Q,\theta}$. This function is large in magnitude in the locations where the two distributions differ. For ease of visualization we do not try to include posterior uncertainty intervals, but these are readily available from our model, and we show them for a 1-dimensional case below.

Our model does not just provide a better way of choosing lengthscales. We can also use it in a fully Bayesian context, where we place priors over the hyperparameters θ and τ^2, and then integrate them out to learn a posterior distribution over the mean embedding. Switching to one dimension, we consider a distribution $\mathsf{P} = \mathcal{N}(0, 1)$ and a distribution $\mathsf{Q} = \text{Laplace}(0, \sqrt{.5})$. The densities are shown in Figure 3(A). Notice that the first two moments of these distributions are equal. To create a synthetic dataset we sampled n observations from each distribution, and then combined them together into a sample of size $2n$, following the strategy in the previous experiment to learn a single lengthscale and kernel mean embedding for the combined dataset. We ran a Hamiltonian Monte Carlo sampler (HMC) with NUTS (Stan source code is in the Appendix in Section B) for the Bayesian Kernel Embedding model with a squared exponential kernel, placing a $\text{Gamma}(1, 1)$ prior on the lengthscale θ of the kernel and a $\text{Gamma}(1, 1)$ prior on τ^2. We ran 4 chains for 400 iterations, discarding 200 iterations as warmup, with the chains starting at different random initial values. Standard convergence and mixing

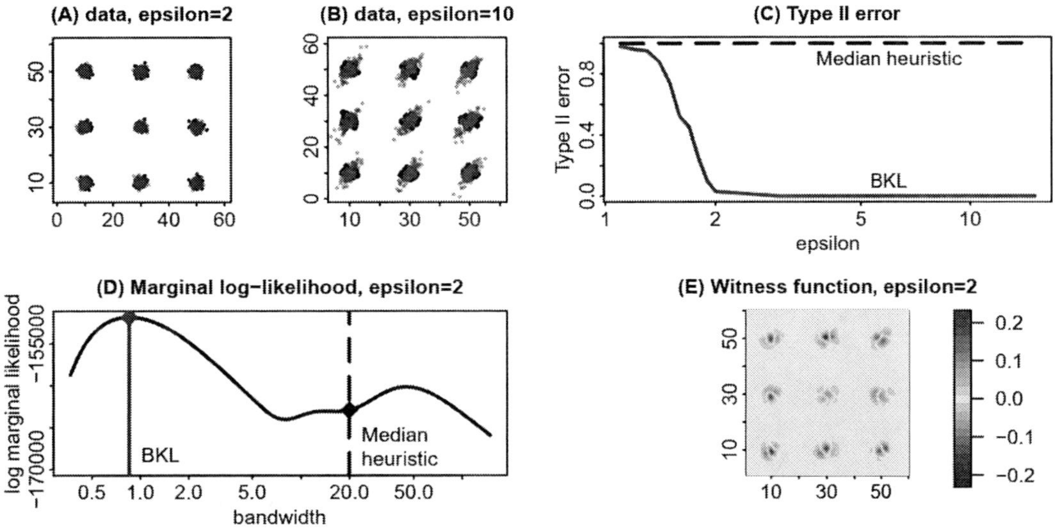

Figure 2: Two sample testing on a challenging simulated data set: comparing samples from a grid of isotropic Gaussians (black dots) to samples from a grid of non-isotropic Gaussians (red dots) with a ratio ϵ of largest to smallest covariance eigenvalues. Panels (A) and (B) illustrate such samples for two values of ϵ. (C) Type II error as a function of ϵ for significant level $\alpha = 0.05$ following the median heuristic or the BKL approach to choose the lengthscale. (D) BKL marginal log-likelihood across a range of lengthscales. It is maximised for a lengthscale of 0.85 whereas the median heuristic suggests a value of 20. (E) Witness function for the difficult case where $\epsilon = 2$ using the BKL lengthscale.

diagnostics were good ($\hat{R} \approx 1$), so we considered the result to be 800 draws from the posterior distribution. Recall that for fixed hyperparameters θ and τ^2 we can obtain a posterior distribution over $\mu_{P,\theta}$ and $\mu_{Q,\theta}$. For each of our 800 draws, we drew a sample from these two distributions and then calculated the witness function as the difference, thus obtaining a random function drawn from the posterior distribution over $\mu_{P,\theta} - \mu_{Q,\theta}$ (where in practice we evaluate this function at a fine grid for plotting purposes). We thus obtained the full posterior distribution over the witness function, integrating over the kernel hyperparameter. We followed this procedure twice to create a dataset with $n = 50$ and a dataset with $n = 400$. In Figure 3(B) we see that the witness function for the small dataset is not able to distinguish between the distributions as it rarely excludes 0. (Note that our model has the function 0 as its prior, which corresponds to the null hypothesis that the two distributions are equal. This could easily be changed to incorporate any relevant prior information.). As shown in Figure 3(C), with more data the witness function is able to distinguish between the two distributions, mostly excluding 0.

Finally, we consider the ozone dataset analyzed in Breiman and Friedman (1985), consisting of daily measurements of ozone concentration and eight related meteorological variables. Following the approach in Flaxman et al. (2015), we first pre-whiten the data to control for underlying temporal autocorrelation, then we use a combination of Gaussian process regression followed by HSIC to test for conditional independence. Each time we run HSIC, we set the kernel hyperparameters using Bayesian Kernel Learning. The graphical model that we learn is shown in Figure 4. The directed edge from the temperature variable to ozone is encouraging, as higher temperatures favor ozone formation through a variety of chemical processes which are not represented by variables in this dataset (Bloomer et al., 2009; Sillman, 1999). Note that this edge was not present in the graphical model in Flaxman et al. (2015) in which the median heuristic was used.

6 DISCUSSION

We developed a framework for Bayesian learning of kernel embeddings of probability measures. It is primarily designed for unsupervised settings, and in particular for kernel-based hypothesis testing. In these settings, one relies critically on a good choice of kernel and our framework yields a new method, termed Bayesian Kernel Learning, to inform this choice. We only explored learning the lengthscale of the squared exponential kernel, but our method extends to the case of richer kernels with more hyperparameters. We conceive of Bayesian Kernel Learning as a drop-in replacement for selecting the kernel hyperparameters in settings where cross-validation is unavailable. A sampling-based Bayesian approach is also demonstrated, enabling integration over kernel hyperparameters, and e.g., obtaining

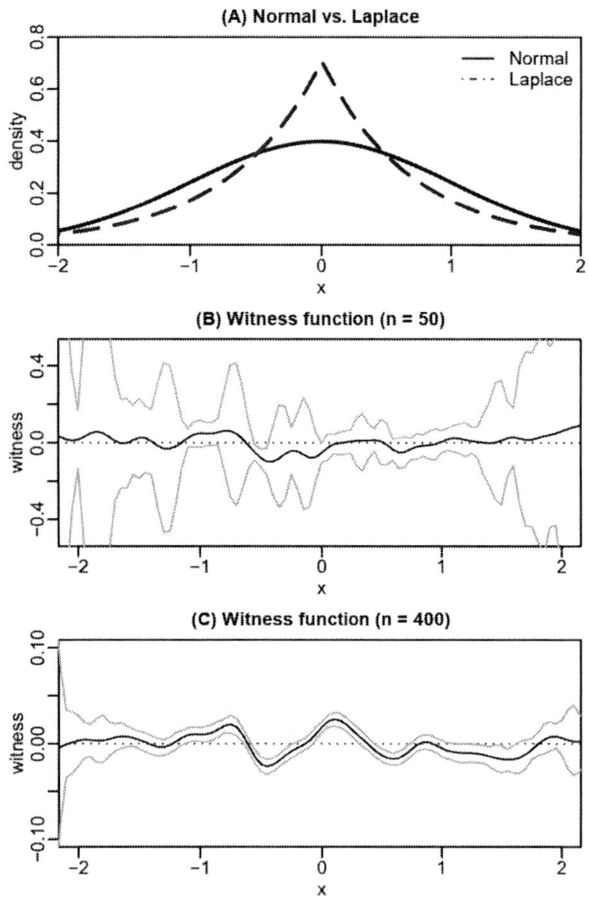

Figure 3: The true data generating process is shown in (A) where two samples of size n are drawn from distributions with equal means and variances. We then fit our Bayesian Kernel Embedding model, with priors over the hyperparameters θ and τ^2 to obtain a posterior over the witness function for two-sampling testing. The witness function indicates the model's posterior estimates of where the two distributions differ (when the witness function is zero, it indicates no difference between the distributions). Posterior means and 80% uncertainty intervals are shown. In (B) the small sample size means that the model does not effectively distinguish between samples from a normal and a Laplace distribution, while in (C) larger samples enable the model to find a clear difference, with much of the uncertainty envelope excluding 0.

the full posterior distribution over the witness function in two-sample testing.

While our method is designed for unsupervised settings, there are various reasons it might be helpful in supervised settings or in applied Bayesian modelling more generally. With the rise of large-scale kernel methods, it has become possible to apply, e.g. SVMs or GPs to very large datasets.

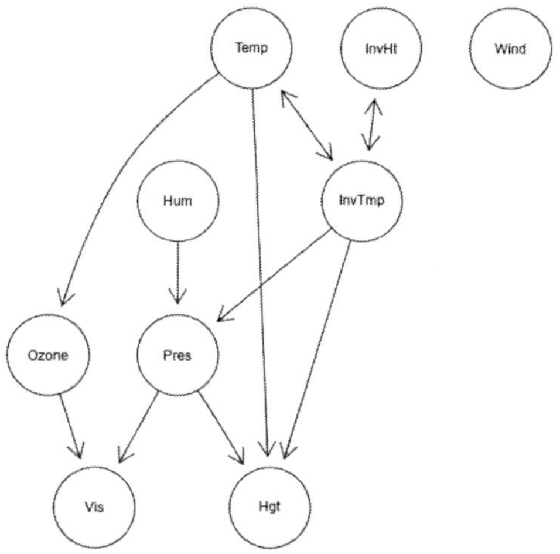

Figure 4: Graphical model representing an equivalence class of DAGs for the Ozone dataset from Breiman and Friedman (1985), learned using the PC algorithm following the approach in Flaxman et al. (2015) with HSIC to test for independence. We used BKL to set hyperparameters of HSIC. Singly directed edges represent causal links, while bidirected edges represent edges that the algorithm failed to orient. The causal edge from temperature to ozone accords with scientific understanding, and was not present in the graphical model learned in Flaxman et al. (2015) which employed the median heuristic.

But even with efficient methods, it can be very costly to run cross-validation over a large space of hyperparameters. In practice, when, e.g. large scale approximations based on random Fourier features (Rahimi and Recht, 2007) are used, we have not seen much attention paid to kernel learning – the features are often just one part of a complicated pipeline, so again the median heuristic is often employed. For these reasons, we think that the developed method for Bayesian Kernel Learning would be a judicious alternative. Moreover, it would be straightforward to develop scalable approximate versions of Bayesian Kernel Learning itself.

7 Acknowledgments

SRF was supported by the ERC (FP7/617071) and EPSRC (EP/K009362/1). Thanks to Wittawat Jitkrittum, Krikamol Muandet, Sayan Mukherjee, Jonas Peters, Aaditya Ramdas, Alex Smola, and Yee Whye Teh for helpful discussions.

References

Francis R Bach, Gert RG Lanckriet, and Michael I Jordan. Multiple kernel learning, conic duality, and the smo algorithm.

In *Proceedings of the twenty-first international conference on Machine learning*, page 6. ACM, 2004.

Adi Ben-Israel. The change-of-variables formula using matrix volume. *SIAM Journal on Matrix Analysis and Applications*, 21(1):300–312, 1999.

Bryan J. Bloomer, Jeffrey W. Stehr, Charles A. Piety, Ross J. Salawitch, and Russell R. Dickerson. Observed relationships of ozone air pollution with temperature and emissions. *Geophysical Research Letters*, 36(9), 2009. ISSN 1944-8007. L09803.

Adrian W Bowman. A comparative study of some kernel-based nonparametric density estimators. *Journal of Statistical Computation and Simulation*, 21(3-4):313–327, 1985.

Leo Breiman and Jerome H Friedman. Estimating optimal transformations for multiple regression and correlation. *Journal of the American Statistical Association*, 80(391):580–598, 1985.

David Duvenaud, James Lloyd, Roger Grosse, Joshua Tenenbaum, and Zoubin Ghahramani. Structure discovery in nonparametric regression through compositional kernel search. In *Proceedings of The 30th International Conference on Machine Learning*, pages 1166–1174, 2013.

Bradley Efron and Carl Morris. Stein's estimation rule and its competitors—an empirical bayes approach. *Journal of the American Statistical Association*, 68(341):117–130, 1973.

Seth R Flaxman, Daniel B Neill, and Alexander J Smola. Gaussian processes for independence tests with non-iid data in causal inference. *ACM Transactions on Intelligent Systems and Technology (TIST)*, 2015.

Mehmet Gönen and Ethem Alpaydın. Multiple kernel learning algorithms. *The Journal of Machine Learning Research*, 12: 2211–2268, 2011.

A. Gretton, K. Fukumizu, C.H. Teo, L. Song, B. Schoelkopf, and A. Smola. A kernel statistical test of independence. In J.C. Platt, D. Koller, Y. Singer, and S. Roweis, editors, *Advances in Neural Information Processing Systems 20*, Cambridge, MA, 2008. MIT Press.

Arthur Gretton, Olivier Bousquet, Alex Smola, and Bernhard Schölkopf. Measuring statistical dependence with hilbert-schmidt norms. In *Algorithmic learning theory*, pages 63–77. Springer, 2005.

Arthur Gretton, Karsten M Borgwardt, Malte J Rasch, Bernhard Schölkopf, and Alexander Smola. A kernel two-sample test. *The Journal of Machine Learning Research*, 13:723–773, 2012a.

Arthur Gretton, Dino Sejdinovic, Heiko Strathmann, Sivaraman Balakrishnan, Massimiliano Pontil, Kenji Fukumizu, and Bharath K Sriperumbudur. Optimal kernel choice for large-scale two-sample tests. In *Advances in neural information processing systems*, pages 1205–1213, 2012b.

Gopinath Kallianpur. Zero-one laws for Gaussian processes. *Transactions of the American Mathematical Society*, 149:199–211, 1970.

Milan N. Lukić and Jay H. Beder. Stochastic Processes with Sample Paths in Reproducing Kernel Hilbert Spaces. *Transactions of the American Mathematical Society*, 353(10):3945–3969, 2001.

Joris M Mooij, Jonas Peters, Dominik Janzing, Jakob Zscheischler, and Bernhard Schölkopf. Distinguishing cause from effect using observational data: methods and benchmarks. *The Journal of Machine Learning Research*, pages 1–96, 2015.

K. Muandet, B. Sriperumbudur, K. Fukumizu, A. Gretton, and B. Schölkopf. Kernel Mean Shrinkage Estimators. *Journal of Machine Learning Research (forthcoming)*, 2016.

Krikamol Muandet, Kenji Fukumizu, Bharath Sriperumbudur, Arthur Gretton, and Bernhard Schölkopf. Kernel mean estimation and Stein's effect. *arXiv preprint arXiv:1306.0842*, 2013.

Krikamol Muandet, Bharath Sriperumbudur, and Bernhard Schölkopf. Kernel mean estimation via spectral filtering. In *Advances in Neural Information Processing Systems*, pages 1–9, 2014.

Emanuel Parzen. On estimation of a probability density function and mode. *The Annals of Mathematical Statistics*, 33(3):1065–1076, 1962.

Natesh S Pillai, Qiang Wu, Feng Liang, Sayan Mukherjee, and Robert L Wolpert. Characterizing the function space for bayesian kernel models. *Journal of Machine Learning Research*, 8(8), 2007.

A. Rahimi and B. Recht. Random features for large-scale kernel machines. In *Advances in Neural Information Processing Systems (NIPS)*, pages 1177–1184, 2007.

Aaditya Ramdas and Leila Wehbe. Nonparametric independence testing for small sample sizes. *24th International Joint Conference on Artificial Intelligence (IJCAI)*, 2015.

Aaditya Ramdas, Sashank Jakkam Reddi, Barnabás Póczos, Aarti Singh, and Larry Wasserman. On the decreasing power of kernel and distance based nonparametric hypothesis tests in high dimensions. In *Twenty-Ninth AAAI Conference on Artificial Intelligence*, 2015.

Carl Edward Rasmussen and Christopher KI Williams. *Gaussian processes for machine learning*. MIT Press, Cambridge, MA, 2006.

Sashank J Reddi, Aaditya Ramdas, Barnabás Póczos, Aarti Singh, and Larry A Wasserman. On the high dimensional power of a linear-time two sample test under mean-shift alternatives. In *AISTATS*, 2015.

Murray Rosenblatt. Remarks on some nonparametric estimates of a density function. *The Annals of Mathematical Statistics*, 27 (3):832–837, 1956.

Bernhard Schölkopf and Alexander J Smola. *Learning with kernels: support vector machines, regularization, optimization and beyond*. the MIT Press, 2002.

Dino Sejdinovic, Bharath Sriperumbudur, Arthur Gretton, and Kenji Fukumizu. Equivalence of distance-based and rkhs-based statistics in hypothesis testing. *The Annals of Statistics*, 41(5):2263–2291, 2013.

Sanford Sillman. The relation between ozone, no x and hydrocarbons in urban and polluted rural environments. *Atmospheric Environment*, 33(12):1821–1845, 1999.

R. Silverman. Locally stationary random processes. *IRE Transactions on Information Theory*, 3(3):182–187, September 1957.

Sören Sonnenburg, Gunnar Rätsch, Christin Schäfer, and Bernhard Schölkopf. Large scale multiple kernel learning. *The Journal of Machine Learning Research*, 7:1531–1565, 2006.

B. Sriperumbudur, K. Fukumizu, and G. Lanckriet. Universality, characteristic kernels and RKHS embedding of measures. *Journal of Machine Learning Research*, 12:2389–2410, 2011.

Ingo Steinwart and Andreas Christmann. *Support Vector Machines*. Springer, 2008.

Ichiro Takeuchi, Quoc V Le, Timothy D Sears, and Alexander J Smola. Nonparametric quantile estimation. *The Journal of Machine Learning Research*, 7:1231–1264, 2006.

Ulrike Von Luxburg. A tutorial on spectral clustering. *Statistics and computing*, 17(4):395–416, 2007.

Grace Wahba. *Spline Models for Observational Data*. Society for Industrial and Applied Mathematics, 1990.

Andrew G Wilson and Ryan P Adams. Gaussian process kernels for pattern discovery and extrapolation. In *Proceedings of the 30th International Conference on Machine Learning (ICML-13)*, pages 1067–1075, 2013.

On the Theory and Practice of Privacy-Preserving Bayesian Data Analysis

James Foulds
Calit2 & CSE Department
UC San Diego
jfoulds@ucsd.edu

Joseph Geumlek
CSE Department
UC San Diego
jgeumlek@cs.ucsd.edu

Max Welling
Informatics Institute & QUVA Lab
University of Amsterdam
m.welling@uva.nl

Kamalika Chaudhuri
CSE Department
UC San Diego
kamalika@cs.ucsd.edu

Abstract

Bayesian inference has great promise for the privacy-preserving analysis of sensitive data, as posterior sampling automatically preserves differential privacy, an algorithmic notion of data privacy, under certain conditions (Dimitrakakis et al., 2014; Wang et al., 2015b). While this *one posterior sample* (OPS) approach elegantly provides privacy "for free," it is data inefficient in the sense of asymptotic relative efficiency (ARE). We show that a simple alternative based on the Laplace mechanism, the workhorse of differential privacy, is as asymptotically efficient as non-private posterior inference, under general assumptions. This technique also has practical advantages including efficient use of the privacy budget for MCMC. We demonstrate the practicality of our approach on a time-series analysis of sensitive military records from the Afghanistan and Iraq wars disclosed by the Wikileaks organization.

1 INTRODUCTION

Probabilistic models trained via Bayesian inference are widely and successfully used in application domains where privacy is invaluable, from text analysis (Blei et al., 2003; Goldwater and Griffiths, 2007), to personalization (Salakhutdinov and Mnih, 2008), to medical informatics (Husmeier et al., 2006), to MOOCs (Piech et al., 2013). In these applications, data scientists must carefully balance the benefits and potential insights from data analysis against the privacy concerns of the individuals whose data are being studied (Daries et al., 2014).

Dwork et al. (2006) placed the notion of privacy-preserving data analysis on a solid foundation by introducing *differential privacy* (Dwork and Roth, 2013), an algorithmic formulation of privacy which is a gold standard for privacy-preserving data-driven algorithms. Differential privacy measures the privacy "cost" of an algorithm. When designing privacy-preserving methods, the goal is to achieve a good trade-off between privacy and utility, which ideally improves with the amount of available data.

As observed by Dimitrakakis et al. (2014) and Wang et al. (2015b), Bayesian posterior sampling behaves synergistically with differential privacy because it automatically provides a degree of differential privacy under certain conditions. However, there are substantial gaps between this elegant theory and the practical reality of Bayesian data analysis. Privacy-preserving posterior sampling is hampered by data inefficiency, as measured by asymptotic relative efficiency (ARE). In practice, it generally requires artificially selected constraints on the spaces of parameters as well as data points. Its privacy properties are also not typically guaranteed for approximate inference.

This paper identifies these gaps between theory and practice, and begins to mend them via an extremely simple alternative technique based on the workhorse of differential privacy, the Laplace mechanism (Dwork et al., 2006). Our approach is equivalent to a generalization of Zhang et al. (2016)'s recently and independently proposed algorithm for beta-Bernoulli systems. We provide a theoretical analysis and empirical validation of the advantages of the proposed method. We extend both our method and Dimitrakakis et al. (2014); Wang et al. (2015b)'s *one posterior sample (OPS)* method to the case of approximate inference with privacy-preserving MCMC. Finally, we demonstrate the practical applicability of this technique by showing how to use a privacy-preserving HMM model to analyze sensitive military records from the Iraq and Afghanistan wars leaked by the Wikileaks organization. Our primary contributions are as follows:

- We analyze the privacy cost of posterior sampling for exponential family posteriors via OPS.
- We explore a simple Laplace mechanism alternative to OPS for exponential families.

- Under weak conditions we establish the consistency of the Laplace mechanism approach and its data efficiency advantages over OPS.
- We extend the OPS and Laplace mechanism methods to approximate inference via MCMC.
- We demonstrate the practical implications with a case study on sensitive military records.

2 BACKGROUND

We begin by discussing preliminaries on differential privacy and its application to Bayesian inference. Our novel contributions will begin in Section 3.1.

2.1 DIFFERENTIAL PRIVACY

Differential privacy is a formal notion of the privacy of data-driven algorithms. For an algorithm to be differentially private the probabilities of the outputs of the algorithms may not change much when one individual's data point is modified, thereby revealing little information about any one individual's data. More precisely, a randomized algorithm $\mathcal{M}(\mathbf{X})$ is said to be (ϵ, δ)-differentially private if

$$Pr(\mathcal{M}(\mathbf{X}) \in \mathcal{S}) \leq \exp(\epsilon) Pr(\mathcal{M}(\mathbf{X}') \in \mathcal{S}) + \delta \quad (1)$$

for all measurable subsets $\mathcal{S}$ of the range of $\mathcal{M}$ and for all datasets $\mathbf{X}$, $\mathbf{X}'$ differing by a single entry (Dwork and Roth, 2013). If $\delta = 0$, the algorithm is said to be ϵ-differentially private.

2.1.1 The Laplace Mechanism

One straightforward method for obtaining ϵ-differential privacy, known as the *Laplace mechanism* (Dwork et al., 2006), adds Laplace noise to the revealed information, where the amount of noise depends on ϵ, and a quantifiable notion of the sensitivity to changes in the database. Specifically, the $L1$ sensitivity $\triangle h$ for function h is defined as

$$\triangle h = \max_{\mathbf{X},\mathbf{X}'} \|h(\mathbf{X}) - h(\mathbf{X}')\|_1 \quad (2)$$

for all datasets $\mathbf{X}$, $\mathbf{X}'$ differing in at most one element. The Laplace mechanism adds noise via

$$\mathcal{M}_L(\mathbf{X}, h, \epsilon) = h(\mathbf{X}) + (Y_1, Y_2, \ldots, Y_d) \,, \quad (3)$$
$$Y_j \sim \text{Laplace}(\triangle h/\epsilon), \forall j \in \{1, 2, \ldots, d\} \,,$$

where d is the dimensionality of the range of h. The $\mathcal{M}_L(\mathbf{X}, h, \epsilon)$ mechanism is ϵ-differentially private.

2.1.2 The Exponential Mechanism

The exponential mechanism (McSherry and Talwar, 2007) aims to output responses of high utility while maintaining privacy. Given a utility function $u(\mathbf{X}, \mathbf{r})$ that maps database $\mathbf{X}$/output $\mathbf{r}$ pairs to a real-valued score, the exponential mechanism $\mathcal{M}_E(\mathbf{X}, u, \epsilon)$ produces random outputs via

$$Pr(\mathcal{M}_E(\mathbf{X}, u, \epsilon) = \mathbf{r}) \propto \exp\left(\frac{\epsilon u(\mathbf{X}, \mathbf{r})}{2\triangle u}\right) , \quad (4)$$

where the sensitivity of the utility function is

$$\triangle u \triangleq \max_{r, (\mathbf{X}^{(1)}, \mathbf{X}^{(2)})} \|u(\mathbf{X}^{(1)}, r) - u(\mathbf{X}^{(2)}, r)\|_1 \, , \quad (5)$$

in which $(\mathbf{X}^{(1)}, \mathbf{X}^{(2)})$ are pairs of databases that differ in only one element.

2.1.3 Composition Theorems

A key property of differential privacy is that it holds under composition, via an additive accumulation.

Theorem 1. *If $\mathcal{M}_1$ is (ϵ_1, δ_1)-differentially private, and $\mathcal{M}_2$ is (ϵ_2, δ_2)-differentially private, then $\mathcal{M}_{1,2}(\mathbf{X}) = (\mathcal{M}_1(\mathbf{X}), \mathcal{M}_2(\mathbf{X}))$ is $(\epsilon_1 + \epsilon_2, \delta_1 + \delta_2)$-differentially private.*

This allows us to view the total ϵ and δ of our procedure as a privacy "budget" that we spend across the operations of our analysis. There also exists an "advanced composition" theorem which provides privacy guarantees in an adversarial adaptive scenario called k-fold composition, and also allows an analyst to trade an increased δ for a smaller ϵ in this scenario (Dwork et al., 2010). Differential privacy is also immune to data-independent post-processing.

2.2 PRIVACY AND BAYESIAN INFERENCE

Suppose we would like a differentially private draw of parameters and latent variables of interest θ from the posterior $Pr(\theta|\mathbf{X})$, where $\mathbf{X} = \{\mathbf{x}_1, \ldots, \mathbf{x}_N\}$ is the private dataset. We can accomplish this by interpreting posterior sampling as an instance of the exponential mechanism with utility function $u(\mathbf{X}, \theta) = \log Pr(\theta, \mathbf{X})$, i.e. the log joint probability of the chosen θ assignment and the dataset $\mathbf{X}$ (Wang et al., 2015b). We then draw θ via

$$f(\theta; \mathbf{X}, \epsilon) \propto \exp\left(\frac{\epsilon \log Pr(\theta, \mathbf{X})}{2\triangle \log Pr(\theta, \mathbf{X})}\right) = Pr(\theta, \mathbf{X})^{\frac{\epsilon}{2\triangle \log Pr(\theta, \mathbf{X})}} \quad (6)$$

where the sensitivity is $\triangle \log Pr(\theta, \mathbf{X}) \triangleq$

$$\max_{\theta, (\mathbf{X}^{(1)}, \mathbf{X}^{(2)})} \| \log Pr(\theta, \mathbf{X}^{(1)}) - \log Pr(\theta, \mathbf{X}^{(2)})\|_1 \quad (7)$$

in which $\mathbf{X}^{(1)}$ and $\mathbf{X}^{(2)}$ differ in one element. If the data points are conditionally independent given θ,

$$\log Pr(\theta, \mathbf{X}) = \log Pr(\theta) + \sum_{i=1}^{N} \log Pr(\mathbf{x}_i|\theta) \, , \quad (8)$$

where $Pr(\theta)$ is the prior and $Pr(\mathbf{x}_i|\theta)$ is the likelihood term for data point $\mathbf{x}_i$. Since the prior does not depend on the data, and each data point is associated with a single log-likelihood term $\log Pr(\mathbf{x}_i|\theta)$ in $\log Pr(\theta, \mathbf{X})$, from the above two equations we have

$$\triangle \log Pr(\theta, \mathbf{X}) = \max_{\mathbf{x}, \mathbf{x}', \theta} |\log Pr(\mathbf{x}'|\theta) - \log Pr(\mathbf{x}|\theta)| . \quad (9)$$

This gives us the privacy cost of posterior sampling:

Theorem 2. *If* $\max_{\mathbf{x}, \mathbf{x}' \in \mathcal{X}, \theta \in \Theta} |\log Pr(\mathbf{x}'|\theta) - \log Pr(\mathbf{x}|\theta)| \leq C$*, releasing one sample from the posterior distribution* $Pr(\theta|\mathbf{X})$ *with any prior is* $2C$*-differentially private.*

Wang et al. (2015b) derived this form of the result from first principles, while noting that the exponential mechanism can be used, as we do here. Although they do not explicitly state the theorem, they implicitly use it to show two noteworthy special cases, referred to as the *One Posterior Sample (OPS)* procedure. We state the first of these cases:

Theorem 3. *If* $\max_{\mathbf{x} \in \mathcal{X}, \theta \in \Theta} |\log Pr(\mathbf{x}|\theta)| \leq B$*, releasing one sample from the posterior distribution* $Pr(\theta|\mathbf{X})$ *with any prior is* $4B$*-differentially private.*

This follows directly from Theorem 2, since if $|\log Pr(\mathbf{x}|\theta)| \leq B$, $C = \triangle \log Pr(\theta, \mathbf{X}) = 2B$.

Under the exponential mechanism, ϵ provides an adjustable knob trading between privacy and fidelity. When $\epsilon = 0$, the procedure samples from a uniform distribution, giving away no information about $\mathbf{X}$. When $\epsilon = 2\triangle \log Pr(\theta, \mathbf{X})$, the procedure reduces to sampling θ from the posterior $Pr(\theta|\mathbf{X}) \propto Pr(\theta, \mathbf{X})$. As ϵ approaches infinity the procedure becomes increasingly likely to sample the θ assignment with the highest posterior probability. Assuming that our goal is to sample rather than to find a mode, we would cap ϵ at $2\triangle \log Pr(\theta, \mathbf{X})$ in the above procedure in order to correctly sample from the true posterior. More generally, if our privacy budget is ϵ', and $\epsilon' \geq 2q\triangle \log Pr(\theta, \mathbf{X})$, for integer q, we can draw q posterior samples within our budget.

As observed by Huang and Kannan (2012), the exponential mechanism can be understood via statistical mechanics. We can write it as a Boltzmann distribution (a.k.a. a Gibbs measure)

$$f(\theta; \mathbf{x}, \epsilon) \propto \exp\left(\frac{-E(\theta)}{T}\right), T = \frac{2\triangle u(\mathbf{X}, \theta)}{\epsilon}, \quad (10)$$

where $E(\theta) = -u(\mathbf{X}, \theta) = -\log Pr(\theta, \mathbf{X})$ is the energy of state θ in a physical system, and T is the temperature of the system (in units such that Boltzmann's constant is one). Reducing ϵ corresponds to increasing the temperature, which can be understood as altering the distribution such that a Markov chain moves through the state space more rapidly.

3 PRIVACY FOR EXPONENTIAL FAMILIES: EXPONENTIAL VS LAPLACE

By analyzing the privacy cost of sampling from exponential family posteriors in the general case we can recover the privacy properties of many standard distributions. These results can be applied to full posterior sampling, when feasible, or to Gibbs sampling updates, as we discuss in Section 4. In this section we analyze the privacy cost of sampling from exponential family posterior distributions exactly (or at an appropriate temperature) via the exponential mechanism, following Dimitrakakis et al. (2014) and Wang et al. (2015b), and via a method based on the Laplace mechanism, which is a generalization of Zhang et al. (2016). The properties of the two methods are compared in Table 1.

3.1 THE EXPONENTIAL MECHANISM

Consider exponential family models with likelihood

$$Pr(\mathbf{x}|\theta) = h(\mathbf{x})g(\theta)\exp\left(\theta^\intercal S(\mathbf{x})\right),$$

where $S(\mathbf{x})$ is a vector of sufficient statistics for data point $\mathbf{x}$, and θ is a vector of natural parameters. For N i.i.d. data points, we have

$$Pr(\mathbf{X}|\theta) = \left(\prod_{i=1}^{N} h(\mathbf{x}^{(i)})\right)g(\theta)^N \exp\left(\theta^\intercal \sum_{i=1}^{N} S(\mathbf{x}^{(i)})\right).$$

Further suppose that we have a conjugate prior which is also an exponential family distribution,

$$Pr(\theta|\chi, \alpha) = f(\chi, \alpha)g(\theta)^\alpha \exp\left(\alpha\theta^\intercal \chi\right),$$

where α is a scalar, the number of prior "pseudo-counts," and χ is a parameter vector. The posterior is proportional to the prior times the likelihood,

$$Pr(\theta|\mathbf{X}, \chi, \alpha) \propto g(\theta)^{N+\alpha} \exp\left(\theta^\intercal \left(\sum_{i=1}^{N} S(\mathbf{x}^{(i)}) + \alpha\chi\right)\right). \quad (11)$$

To compute the sensitivity of the posterior, we have

$$|\log Pr(\mathbf{x}'|\theta) - \log Pr(\mathbf{x}|\theta)| \quad (12)$$
$$= |\theta^\intercal\left(S(\mathbf{x}') - S(\mathbf{x})\right) + \log h(\mathbf{x}') - \log h(\mathbf{x})| .$$

From Equation 9, we obtain $\triangle \log Pr(\theta, \mathbf{X}) =$

$$\sup_{\mathbf{x}, \mathbf{x}' \in \mathcal{X}, \theta \in \Theta} |\theta^\intercal\left(S(\mathbf{x}') - S(\mathbf{x})\right) + \log h(\mathbf{x}') - \log h(\mathbf{x})| . \quad (13)$$

A posterior sample at temperature T,

$$Pr_T(\theta|\mathbf{X}, \chi, \alpha) \propto g(\theta)^{\frac{N+\alpha}{T}} \exp\left(\theta^\intercal \frac{\sum_{i=1}^{N} S(\mathbf{x}^{(i)}) + \alpha\chi}{T}\right),$$
$$T = \frac{2\triangle \log p(\theta, X)}{\epsilon}, \quad (14)$$

Mechanism	Sensitivity	$S(\mathbf{X})$ is	Release	ARE	Pay Gibbs cost
Laplace	$\sup_{\mathbf{X},\mathbf{X}'} \Vert \sum_{i=1}^N S(\mathbf{x}'^{(i)}) - \sum_{i=1}^N S(\mathbf{x}^{(i)})\Vert_1$	Noised	Statistics	1	Once
Exponential (OPS)	$\sup_{\mathbf{x},\mathbf{x}'\in\mathcal{X},\theta\in\Theta} \vert\theta^\intercal\big(S(\mathbf{x}') - S(\mathbf{x})\big) + \log h(\mathbf{x}') - \log h(\mathbf{x})\vert$	Rescaled	One Sample	$1+T$	Per update (unless converged)

Table 1: Comparison of the properties of the two methods for private Bayesian inference.

has privacy cost ϵ, by the exponential mechanism. As an example, consider a beta-Bernoulli model,

$$
\begin{aligned}
Pr(p|\alpha,\beta) &= \frac{1}{B(\alpha,\beta)} p^{\alpha-1}(1-p)^{\beta-1} \\
&= \frac{1}{B(\alpha,\beta)} \exp((\alpha-1)\log p + (\beta-1)\log(1-p)) \\
Pr(x|p) &= p^x(1-p)^{1-x} = \exp(x\log p + (1-x)\log(1-p)
\end{aligned}
$$

where $B(\alpha,\beta)$ is the beta function. Given N binary-valued data points $\mathbf{X} = x^{(1)},\ldots,x^{(N)}$ from the Bernoulli distribution, the posterior is

$$
\begin{aligned}
&Pr(p|\mathbf{X},\alpha,\beta) \propto \\
&\quad \exp\Big(\big(n_+ + \alpha - 1\big)\log p + \big(n_- + \beta - 1\big)\log(1-p)\Big) \\
&\quad n_+ = \sum_{i=1}^N x^{(i)}, \quad n_- = \sum_{i=1}^N (1 - x^{(i)}) \,.
\end{aligned}
$$

The sufficient statistics for each data point are $S(x) = [x, 1-x]^\intercal$. The natural parameters for the posterior are $\theta = [\log p, \log(1-p)]^\intercal$, and $h(x) = 0$. The exponential mechanism sensitivity for a *truncated* version of this model, where $a_0 \leq p \leq 1 - a_0$, can be computed from Equation 13, $\triangle \log Pr(\theta, \mathbf{X}) =$

$$
\begin{aligned}
\sup_{x,x'\in\{0,1\},p\in[a_0,1-a_0]} &|x\log p + (1-x)\log(1-p) \\
&- \big(x'\log p + (1-x')\log(1-p)\big)| \\
&= -\log a_0 + \log(1-a_0)\,. \qquad (15)
\end{aligned}
$$

Note that if $a_0 = 0$, corresponding to a standard untruncated beta distribution, the sensitivity is unbounded. This makes intuitive sense because some datasets are impossible if $p = 0$ or $p = 1$, which violates differential privacy.

3.2 THE LAPLACE MECHANISM

One limitation of the exponential mechanism / OPS approach to private Bayesian inference is that the temperature T of the approximate posterior is fixed for any ϵ that we are willing to pay, regardless of the number of data points N (Equation 10). While the posterior becomes more accurate as N increases, and the OPS approximation becomes more accurate by proxy, the OPS approximation remains a factor of T flatter than the posterior at N data points. This is not simply a limitation of the analysis. An adversary

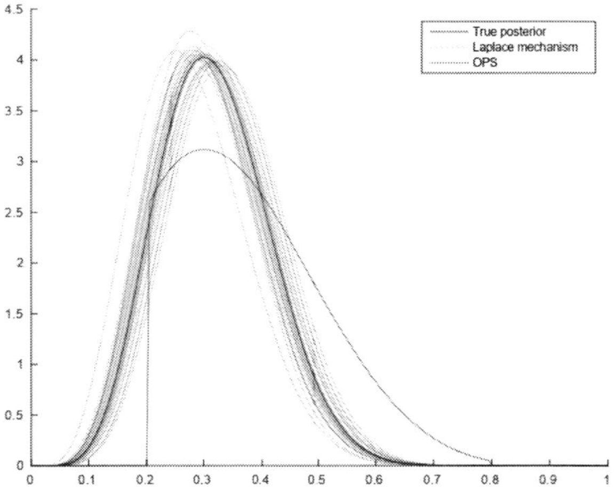

Figure 1: Privacy-preserving approximate posteriors for a beta-Bernoulli model ($\epsilon = 1$, the true parameter $p = 0.3$, OPS truncation point $a_0 = 0.2$, and number of observations $N = 20$). For the Laplace mechanism, 30 privatizing draws are rendered.

can choose data such that the dataset-specific privacy cost of posterior sampling approaches the worst case given by the exponential mechanism as N increases, by causing the posterior to concentrate on the worst-case θ (see the supplement for an example).

Here, we provide a simple Laplace mechanism alternative for exponential family posteriors, which becomes increasingly faithful to the true posterior with N data points, as N increases, for any fixed privacy cost ϵ, under general assumptions. The approach is based on the observation that for exponential family posteriors, as in Equation 11, the data interacts with the distribution only through the aggregate sufficient statistics, $S(\mathbf{X}) = \sum_{i=1}^N S(\mathbf{x}^{(i)})$. If we release privatized versions of these statistics we can use them to perform any further operations that we'd like, including drawing samples, computing moments and quantiles, and so on. This can straightforwardly be accomplished via the Laplace mechanism:

$$
\begin{aligned}
\hat{S}(\mathbf{X}) &= \mathrm{proj}(S(\mathbf{X}) + (Y_1, Y_2, \ldots, Y_d))\,, \qquad (16) \\
Y_j &\sim \mathrm{Laplace}(\triangle S(\mathbf{X})/\epsilon), \forall j \in \{1, 2, \ldots, d\}\,,
\end{aligned}
$$

where $\mathrm{proj}(\cdot)$ is a projection onto the space of sufficient statistics, if the Laplace noise takes it out of this region.

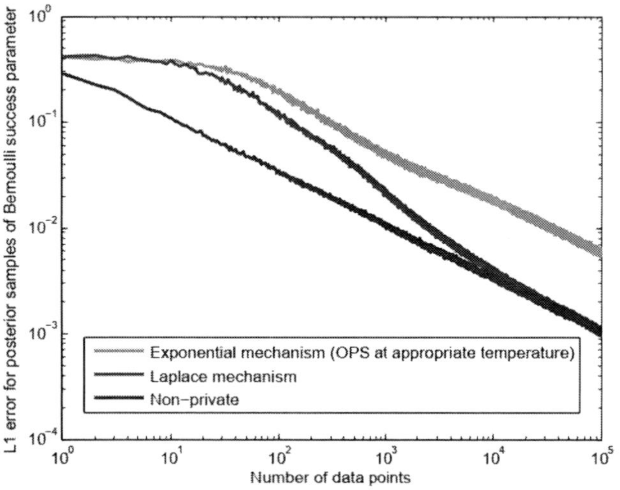

Figure 2: L1 error for private approximate samples from a beta posterior over a Bernoulli success parameter p, as a function of the number of Bernoulli(p) observations, averaged over 1000 repeats. The true parameter was $p = 0.1$, the exponential mechanism posterior was truncated at $a_0 = 0.05$, and $\epsilon = 0.1$.

For example, if the statistics are counts, the projection ensures that they are non-negative. The L_1 sensitivity of the aggregate statistics is

$$\triangle S(\mathbf{X}) = \sup_{\mathbf{X},\mathbf{X}'} \|\sum_{i=1}^{N} S(\mathbf{x}'^{(i)}) - \sum_{i=1}^{N} S(\mathbf{x}^{(i)})\|_1 \quad (17)$$
$$= \sup_{\mathbf{x},\mathbf{x}'} \|S(\mathbf{x}') - S(\mathbf{x})\|_1 \,,$$

where $\mathbf{X}$, $\mathbf{X}'$ differ in at most one element. Note that perturbing the sufficient statistics is equivalent to perturbing the parameters, which was recently and independently proposed by Zhang et al. (2016) for beta-Bernoulli models such as Bernoulli naive Bayes.

A comparison of Equations 17 and 13 reveals that the L1 sensitivity and exponential mechanism sensitivities are closely related. The L1 sensitivity is generally easier to control as it does not involve θ or $h(\mathbf{x})$ but otherwise involves similar terms to the exponential mechanism sensitivity. For example, in the beta posterior case, where $S(\mathbf{x}) = [x, 1 - x]$ is a binary indicator vector, the L1 sensitivity is 2. This should be contrasted to the exponential mechanism sensitivity of Equation 15, which depends heavily on the truncation point, and is unbounded for a standard untruncated beta distribution. The L1 sensitivity is fixed regardless of the number of data points N, and so the amount of Laplace noise to add becomes smaller relative to the total $S(\mathbf{X})$ as N increases.

Figure 1 illustrates the differences in behavior between the two privacy-preserving Bayesian inference algorithms for a beta distribution posterior with Bernoulli observations. The OPS estimator requires the distribution be truncated, here at $a_0 = 0.2$. This controls the exponential mechanism sensitivity, which determines the temperature T of the distribution, i.e. the extent to which the distribution is flattened, for a given ϵ. Here, $T = 2.7$. In contrast, the Laplace mechanism achieves privacy by adding noise to the sufficient statistics, which in this case are the pseudo-counts of successes and failures for the posterior distribution. In Figure 2 we illustrate the fidelity benefits of posterior sampling based on the Laplace mechanism instead of the exponential mechanism as the amount of data increases. In this case the exponential mechanism performs better than the Laplace mechanism only when the number of data points is very small (approximately $N = 10$), and is quickly overtaken by the Laplace mechanism sampling procedure. As N increases the accuracy of sampling from the Laplace mechanism's approximate posterior converges to the performance of samples from the true posterior at the current number of observations N, while the exponential mechanism behaves similarly to the posterior with fewer than N observations. We show this formally in the next subsection.

3.3 THEORETICAL RESULTS

First, we show that the Laplace mechanism approximation of exponential family posteriors approaches the true posterior distribution *evaluated at N data points.* Proofs are given in the supplementary.

Lemma 1. *For a minimal exponential family given a conjugate prior, where the posterior takes the form $Pr(\theta|\mathbf{X}, \chi, \alpha) \propto g(\theta)^{n+\alpha} \exp\Big(\theta^\intercal \big(\sum_{i=1}^{n} S(\mathbf{x}^{(i)}) + \alpha\chi\big)\Big)$, where $p(\theta|\eta)$ denotes this posterior with a natural parameter vector η, if there exists a $\delta > 0$ such that these assumptions are met:*

1. *The data $\mathbf{X}$ comes i.i.d. from a minimal exponential family distribution with natural parameter $\theta_0 \in \Theta$*
2. *θ_0 is in the interior of Θ*
3. *The function $A(\theta)$ has all derivatives for θ in the interior of Θ*
4. *$cov_{Pr(\mathbf{x}|\theta)}(S(\mathbf{x}))$ is finite for $\theta \in B(\theta_0, \delta)$*
5. *$\exists w > 0$ s.t. $\det(cov_{Pr(\mathbf{x}|\theta)}(S(\mathbf{x}))) > w$ for $\theta \in B(\theta_0, \delta)$*
6. *The prior $Pr(\theta|\chi, \alpha)$ is integrable and has support on a neighborhood of θ^**

then for any mechanism generating a perturbed posterior $\tilde{p}_N = p(\theta|\eta_N + \gamma)$ against a noiseless posterior $p_N = p(\theta|\eta_N)$ where γ comes from a distribution that does not *depend on the number of data observations N and has finite covariance, this limit holds:*

$\lim_{N\to\infty} E[KL(\tilde{p}_N \| p_N)] = 0$.

Corollary 2. *The Laplace mechanism on an exponential family satisfies the noise distribution requirements of Lemma 1 when the sensitivity of the sufficient statistics is finite and either the exponential family is minimal, or if the exponential family parameters θ are identifiable.*

These assumptions correspond to the data coming from a distribution where the Laplace regularity assumptions hold and the posterior satisfies the asymptotic normality given by the Bernstein-von Mises theorem. For example, in the beta-Bernoulli setting, these assumptions hold as long as the success parameter p is in the open interval $(0, 1)$. For $p = 0$ or 1, the relevant parameter is not in the interior of Θ, and the result does not apply. In the setting of learning a normal distribution's mean μ where the variance $\sigma^2 > 0$ is known, the assumptions of Lemma 1 always hold, as the natural parameter space is an open set. However, Corollary 2 does not apply in this setting because the sensitivity is infinite (unless bounds are placed on the data). Our efficiency result, in Theorem 4, follows from Lemma 1 and the Bernstein-von Mises theorem.

Theorem 4. *Under the assumptions of Lemma 1, the Laplace mechanism has an asymptotic posterior of $\mathcal{N}(\theta_0, 2\mathbb{I}^{-1}/N)$ from which drawing a single sample has an asymptotic relative efficiency of 2 in estimating θ_0, where $\mathbb{I}$ is the Fisher information at θ_0.*

Above, the asymptotic posterior refers to the normal distribution, whose variance depends on N, that the posterior distribution approaches as N increases. This ARE result should be contrasted to that of the exponential mechanism (Wang et al., 2015b).

Theorem 5. *The exponential mechanism applied to the exponential family with temperature parameter $T \geq 1$ has an asymptotic posterior of $\mathcal{N}(\theta^*, (1+T)\mathbb{I}^{-1}/N)$ and a single sample has an asymptotic relative efficiency of $(1 + T)$ in estimating θ^*, where $\mathbb{I}$ is the Fisher information at θ^*.*

Here, the ARE represents the ratio between the variance of the estimator and the optimal variance $\mathbb{I}^{-1}/N$ achieved by the posterior mean in the limit. Sampling from the posterior itself has an ARE of 2, due to the stochasticity of sampling, which the Laplace mechanism approach matches. These theoretical results provide an explanation for the difference in the behavior of these two methods as N increases seen in Figure 2. The Laplace mechanism will eventually approach the true posterior and the impact of privacy on accuracy will diminish when the data size increases. However, for the exponential mechanism with $T > 1$, the ratio of variances between the sampled posterior and the true posterior given N data points approaches $(1 + T)/2$, making the sampled posterior more spread out than the true posterior even as N grows large.

So far we have compared the ARE values for *sampling*, as an apples-to-apples comparison. In reality, the Laplace mechanism has a further advantage as it releases a full posterior with privatized parameters, while the exponential mechanism can only release a finite number of samples with a finite ϵ, which we discuss in Remark 1.

Remark 1. *Under the the assumptions of Lemma 1, by using the full privatized posterior instead of just a sample from it, the Laplace mechanism can release the privatized posterior's mean, which has an asymptotic relative efficiency of 1 in estimating θ^*.*

4 PRIVATE GIBBS SAMPLING

We now shift our discussion to the case of approximate Bayesian inference. While the analysis of Dimitrakakis et al. (2014) and Wang et al. (2015b) shows that posterior sampling is differentially private under certain conditions, exact sampling is not in general tractable. It does not directly follow that approximate sampling algorithms such as MCMC are also differentially private, or private at the same privacy level. Wang et al. (2015b) give two results towards understanding the privacy properties of approximate sampling algorithms. First, they show that if the approximate sampler is "close" to the true distribution in a certain sense, then the privacy cost will be close to that of a true posterior sample:

Proposition 3. *If procedure $\mathcal{A}$ which produces samples from distribution $P_{\mathbf{X}}$ is ϵ-differentially private, then any approximate sampling procedures $\mathcal{A}'$ that produces a sample from $P'_{\mathbf{X}}$ such that $\|P_{\mathbf{X}} - P'_{\mathbf{X}}\|_1 \leq \delta$ for any $\mathbf{X}$ is $(\epsilon, (1 + \exp(\epsilon)\delta)$-differentially private.*

Unfortunately, it is not in general feasible to verify the convergence of an MCMC algorithm, and so this criterion is not generally verifiable in practice. In their second result, Wang et al. study the privacy properties of stochastic gradient MCMC algorithms, including stochastic gradient Langevin dynamics (SGLD) (Welling and Teh, 2011) and its extensions. SGLD is a stochastic gradient method with noise injected in the gradient updates which converges in distribution to the target posterior.

In this section we study the privacy cost of MCMC, allowing us to quantify the privacy of many real-world MCMC-based Bayesian analyses. We focus on the case of Gibbs sampling, under exponential mechanism and Laplace mechanism approaches. By reinterpreting Gibbs sampling as an instance of the exponential mechanism, we obtain the "privacy for free" cost of Gibbs sampling. Metropolis-Hastings and annealed importance sampling also have privacy guarantees, which we show in the supplementary materials.

4.1 EXPONENTIAL MECHANISM

We consider the privacy cost of a Gibbs sampler, where data $\mathbf{X}$ are behind the privacy wall, current sampled values of parameters and latent variables $\theta = [\theta_1, \ldots, \theta_D]$ are publicly known, and a Gibbs update is a randomized algorithm which queries our private data in order to randomly select a new value θ'_l for the current variable θ_l. The transition kernel for a Gibbs update of θ_l is

$$T^{(Gibbs,l)}(\theta, \theta') = Pr(\theta'_l | \theta_{\neg l}, \mathbf{X}) \,, \quad (18)$$

where $\theta_{\neg l}$ refers to all entries of θ except l, which are held fixed, i.e. $\theta'_{\neg l} = \theta_{\neg l}$. This update can be understood via the exponential mechanism:

$$T^{(Gibbs,l,\epsilon)}(\theta, \theta') \propto Pr(\theta'_l, \theta_{\neg l}, \mathbf{X})^{\frac{\epsilon}{2\triangle \log Pr(\theta'_l, \theta_{\neg l}, \mathbf{X})}} \,, \quad (19)$$

with utility function $u(\mathbf{X}, \theta'_l; \theta_{\neg l}) = \log Pr(\theta'_l, \theta_{\neg l}, \mathbf{X})$, over the space of possible assignments to θ_l, holding $\theta_{\neg l}$ fixed. A Gibbs update is therefore ϵ-differentially private, with $\epsilon = 2\triangle \log Pr(\theta'_l, \theta_{\neg l}, \mathbf{X})$. This update corresponds to Equation 6 except that the set of responses for the exponential mechanism is restricted to those where $\theta'_{\neg l} = \theta_{\neg l}$. Note that

$$\triangle \log Pr(\theta'_l, \theta_{\neg l}, \mathbf{X}) \leq \triangle \log Pr(\theta, \mathbf{X}) \quad (20)$$

as the worst case is computed over a strictly smaller set of outcomes. In many cases each parameter and latent variable θ_l is associated with only the lth data point $\mathbf{x}_l$, in which case the privacy cost of a Gibbs scan can be improved over simple additive composition. In this case a random sequence scan Gibbs pass, which updates all N θ_l's exactly once, is $2\triangle \log Pr(\theta, \mathbf{X})$-differentially private by parallel composition (Song et al., 2013). Alternatively, a random scan Gibbs sampler, which updates a random Q out of N θ_l's, is $4\triangle \log Pr(\theta, \mathbf{X})\frac{Q}{N}$-differentially private from the *privacy amplification* benefit of subsampling data (Li et al., 2012).

4.2 LAPLACE MECHANISM

Suppose that the conditional posterior distribution for a Gibbs update is in the exponential family. Having privatized the sufficient statistics arising from the data for the likelihoods involved in each update, via Equation 16, and publicly released them with privacy cost ϵ, we may now perform the update by drawing a sample from the approximate conditional posterior, i.e. Equation 11 but with $S(\mathbf{X}) = \sum_{i=1}^{N}(\mathbf{x}^{(i)})$ replaced by $\hat{S}(\mathbf{X})$. Since the privatized statistics can be made public, we can also subsequently draw from an approximate posterior based on $\hat{S}(\mathbf{X})$ with any other prior (selected based on public information only), without paying any further privacy cost. This is especially valuable in a Gibbs sampling context, where the "prior" for a Gibbs update often consists of factors from

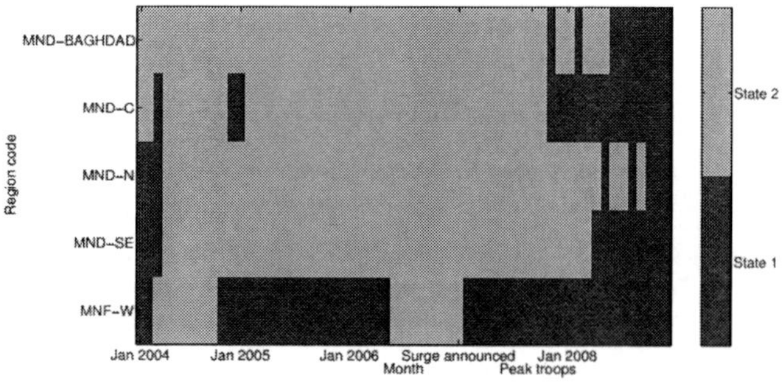

Figure 3: State assignments of privacy-preserving HMM on Iraq (Laplace mechanism, $\epsilon = 5$).

other variables and parameters to be sampled, which are updated during the course of the algorithm.

In particular, consider a Bayesian model where a Gibbs sampler interacts with data only via conditional posteriors and their corresponding likelihoods that are exponential family distributions. We can privatize the sufficient statistics of the likelihood just once at the beginning of the MCMC algorithm via the Laplace mechanism with privacy cost ϵ, and then approximately sample from the posterior by running the entire MCMC algorithm based on these privatized statistics without paying any further privacy cost. This is typically much cheaper in the privacy budget than exponential mechanism MCMC which pays a privacy cost for every Gibbs update, as we shall see in our case study in Section 5. The MCMC algorithm does not need to converge to obtain privacy guarantees, unlike the OPS method. This approach applies to a very broad class of models, including Bayesian parameter learning for fully-observed MRF and Bayesian network models. Of course, for this technique to be useful in practice, the aggregate sufficient statistics for each Gibbs update must be large relative to the Laplace noise. For latent variable models, this typically corresponds to a setting with many data points per latent variable, such as the HMM model with multiple emissions per timestep which we study in the next section.

5 CASE STUDY: WIKILEAKS IRAQ & AFGHANISTAN WAR LOGS

A primary goal of this work is to establish the practical feasibility of privacy-preserving Bayesian data analysis using complex models on real-world datasets. In this section we investigate the performance of the methods studied in this paper for the analysis of sensitive military data. In July and October 2010, the Wikileaks organization disclosed collections of internal U.S. military field reports from the wars in Afghanistan and Iraq, respectively. Both disclosures contained data from between January 2004 to December 2009, with ~75,000 entries from the war in Afghanistan, and ~390,000 entries from Iraq. Hillary Clinton, at that time

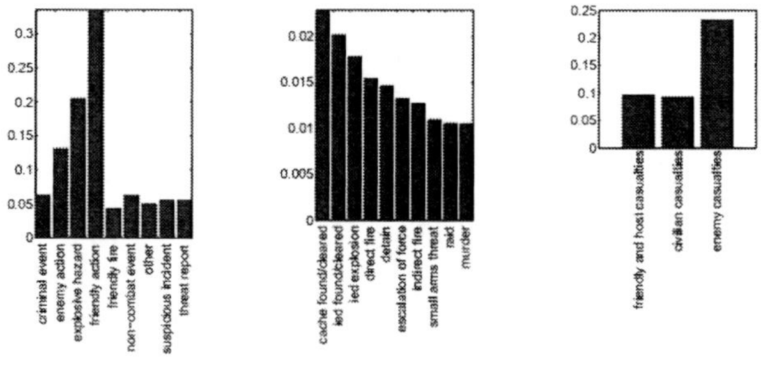

Figure 4: State 1 for Iraq (*type*, *category*, *casualties*).

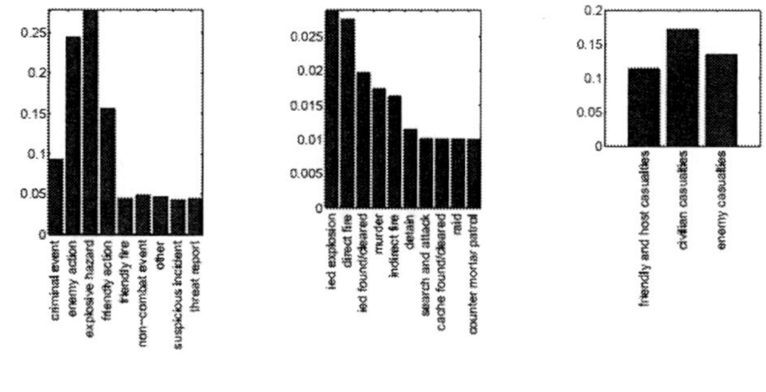

Figure 5: State 2 for Iraq (*type*, *category*, *casualties*).

the U.S. Secretary of State, criticized the disclosure, stating that it "puts the lives of United States and its partners' service members and civilians at risk."[1] These risks, and the motivations for the leak, could potentially have been mitigated by releasing a differentially private analysis of the data, which protects the contents of each individual log entry while revealing high-level trends. Note that since the data are publicly available, although our *models* were differentially private, other aspects of this manuscript such as the evaluation may reveal certain information, as in other works such as Wang et al. (2015a,b).

The disclosed war logs each correspond to an individual event, and contain textual reports, as well as fields such as coarse-grained *types* (*friendly action*, *explosive hazard*, ...), fine-grained *categories* (*mine found/cleared*, *show of force*, ...), and casualty counts (*wounded/killed/detained*) for the different factions (*Friendly*, *HostNation* (i.e. Iraqi and Afghani forces), *Civilian*, and *Enemy*, where the names are relative to the U.S. military's perspective). We use the techniques discussed in this paper to privately infer a hidden Markov model on the log entries. The HMM was fit to the non-textual fields listed above, with one timestep per month, and one HMM chain per region code. A naive Bayes conditional independence assumption was used in the emission probabilities for simplicity and parameter-count parsimony. Each field was modeled via a discrete distribution per latent state, with casualty counts binarized (0 versus > 0), and with *wounded/killed/detained* and *Friendly/HostNation* features combined, respectively, via disjunction of the binary values. This decreased the number of features to privatize, while slightly increasing the size of the counts per field to protect and simplifying the model for visualization purposes. After preprocessing to remove empty timesteps and near-empty region codes (see the supplementary), the median number of log entries per region/timestep pair was 972 for Iraq, and 58 for Afghanistan. The number of log entries per timestep was highly skewed for Afghanistan, due to an increase in density over time.

The models were trained via Gibbs sampling, with the transition probabilities collapsed out, following Goldwater and Griffiths (2007). We did not collapse out the naive Bayes parameters in order to keep the conditional likelihood in the exponential family. The details of the model and inference algorithm are given in the supplementary material. We trained the models for 200 Gibbs iterations, with the first 100 used for burn-in. Both privatization methods have the same overall computational complexity as the non-private sampler. The Laplace mechanism's computational overhead is paid once up-front, and did not greatly affect the runtime, while OPS roughly doubled the runtime. For visualization purposes we recovered parameter estimates via the posterior mean based on the latent variable assignments of the final iteration, and we reported the most frequent latent variable assignments over the non-burn-in iterations. We trained a 2-state model on the Iraq data, and a 3-state model for the Afghanistan data, using the Laplace approach with total $\epsilon = 5$ ($\epsilon = 1$ for each of 5 features).

Interestingly, when given 10 states, the privacy-preserving model only assigned substantial numbers of data points to these 2-3 states, while a non-private HMM happily fit a 10-state model to the data. The Laplace noise therefore appears to play the role of a regularizer, consistent with the noise being interpreted as a "random prior," and along the lines of noise-based regularization techniques such as (Srivastava et al., 2014; van der Maaten et al., 2013), although of course it may correspond to more regularization than we would typically like. This phenomenon potentially merits further study, beyond the scope of this paper.

We visualized the output of the Laplace HMM for Iraq in Figures 3–5. State 1 shows the U.S. military performing well, with the most frequent outcomes for each feature being *friendly action*, *cache found/cleared*, and *enemy casualties*, while the U.S. military performed poorly in State 2 (*explosive hazard*, *IED explosion*, *civilian casualties*). State 2 was prevalent in most regions until the situation improved to State 1 after the troop surge strategy of 2007. This transition typically occurred after troops peaked in Sept.–Nov. 2007. The results for Afghanistan, in the supplementary, provide a critical lens on the US military's performance, with enemy casualty rates (including

[1] Fallon, Amy (2010). "Iraq war logs: disclosure condemned by Hillary Clinton and Nato." The Guardian. Retrieved on 2/22/2016.

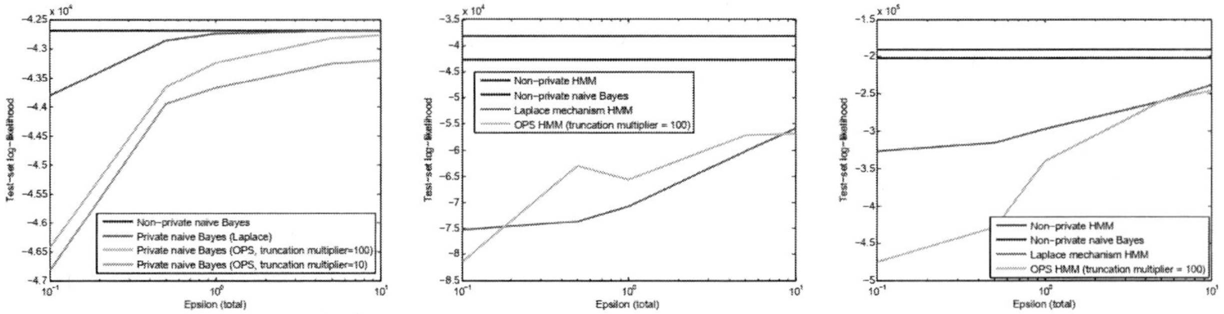

Figure 6: Log-likelihood results. **Left:** Naive Bayes (Afghanistan). **Middle**: Afghanistan. **Right**: Iraq. For OPS, Dirichlets were truncated at $a_0 = \frac{1}{MK_d}$, $M = 10$ or 100, where K_d = feature d's dimensionality.

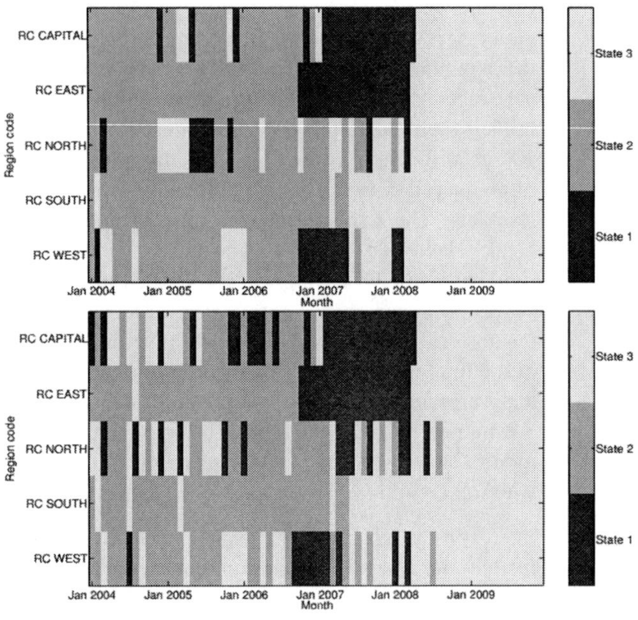

Figure 7: State assignments for OPS privacy-preserving HMM on Afghanistan. ($\epsilon = 5$, truncation point $a_0 = \frac{1}{100K_d}$). **Top**: Estimate from last 100 samples. **Bottom**: Estimate from last one sample.

detainments) lower than friendly/host casualties for all latent states, and lower than civilian casualties in 2 of 3 states.

We also evaluated the methods at prediction. A uniform random 10% of the timestep/region pairs were held out for 10 train/test splits, and we reported average test likelihoods over the splits. We estimated test log-likelihood for each split by averaging the test likelihood over the burned-in samples (Laplace mechanism), or using the final sample (OPS). All methods were given 10 latent states, and ϵ was varied between 0.1 and 10. We also considered a naive Bayes model, equivalent to a 1-state HMM. The Laplace mechanism was superior to OPS for the naive Bayes model, for which the statistics are corpus-wide counts, corresponding to a high-data regime in which our asymptotic analysis was applicable. OPS was competitive with the Laplace mechanism for the HMM on Afghanistan, where the amount of data was relatively low. For the Iraq dataset, where there was more data per timestep, the Laplace mechanism outperformed OPS, particularly in the high-privacy regime. For OPS, privacy at ϵ is only guaranteed if MCMC has converged. Otherwise, from Section 4.1, the worst case is an impractical $\epsilon^{(Gibbs)} \leq 400\epsilon$ (200 iterations of latent variable and parameter updates with worst-case cost ϵ). OPS only releases one sample, which harmed the coherency of the visualization for Afghanistan, as latent states of the final sample were noisy relative to an estimate based on all 100 post burn-in samples (Figure 7). Privatizing the Gibbs chain at a privacy cost of $\epsilon^{(Gibbs)}$ would avoid this.

6 CONCLUSION

This paper studied the practical limitations of using posterior sampling to obtain privacy "for free." We explored an alternative based on the Laplace mechanism, and analyzed it both theoretically and empirically. We illustrated the benefits of the Laplace mechanism for privacy-preserving Bayesian inference to analyze sensitive war records. The study of privacy-preserving Bayesian inference is only just beginning. We envision extensions of these techniques to other approximate inference algorithms, as well as their practical application to sensitive real-world data sets. Finally, we have argued that asymptotic efficiency is important in a privacy context, leading to an open question: how large is the class of private methods that are asymptotically efficient?

Acknowledgements

The work of K. Chaudhuri and J. Geumlek was supported in part by NSF under IIS 1253942, and the work of M. Welling was supported in part by Qualcomm, Google and Facebook. We also thank Mijung Park, Eric Nalisnick, and Babak Shahbaba for helpful discussions.

References

Blei, D. M., Ng, A. Y., and Jordan, M. I. (2003). Latent Dirichlet allocation. *Journal of Machine Learning Research*, 3:993–1022.

Daries, J. P., Reich, J., Waldo, J., Young, E. M., Whittinghill, J., Ho, A. D., Seaton, D. T., and Chuang, I. (2014). Privacy, anonymity, and big data in the social sciences. *Communications of the ACM*, 57(9):56–63.

Dimitrakakis, C., Nelson, B., Mitrokotsa, A., and Rubinstein, B. I. (2014). Robust and private Bayesian inference. In *Algorithmic Learning Theory (ALT)*, pages 291–305. Springer.

Dwork, C., McSherry, F., Nissim, K., and Smith, A. (2006). Calibrating noise to sensitivity in private data analysis. In *Theory of Cryptography*, pages 265–284. Springer.

Dwork, C. and Roth, A. (2013). The algorithmic foundations of differential privacy. *Theoretical Computer Science*, 9(3-4):211–407.

Dwork, C., Rothblum, G. N., and Vadhan, S. (2010). Boosting and differential privacy. In *The 51st Annual IEEE Symposium on Foundations of Computer Science (FOCS)*, pages 51–60.

Goldwater, S. and Griffiths, T. (2007). A fully Bayesian approach to unsupervised part-of-speech tagging. In *Proceedings of the 45th Annual Meeting of the Association of Computational Linguistics (ACL)*, pages 744–751.

Huang, Z. and Kannan, S. (2012). The exponential mechanism for social welfare: Private, truthful, and nearly optimal. In *Foundations of Computer Science (FOCS), 2012 IEEE 53rd Annual Symposium on*, pages 140–149. IEEE.

Husmeier, D., Dybowski, R., and Roberts, S. (2006). *Probabilistic modeling in bioinformatics and medical informatics*. Springer Science & Business Media.

Li, N., Qardaji, W., and Su, D. (2012). On sampling, anonymization, and differential privacy or, k-anonymization meets differential privacy. In *Proceedings of the 7th ACM Symposium on Information, Computer and Communications Security*, pages 32–33. ACM.

McSherry, F. and Talwar, K. (2007). Mechanism design via differential privacy. In *Foundations of Computer Science (FOCS), 2007 IEEE 48th Annual Symposium on*, pages 94–103. IEEE.

Piech, C., Huang, J., Chen, Z., Do, C., Ng, A., and Koller, D. (2013). Tuned models of peer assessment in MOOCs. In *Proceedings of the 6th International Conference on Educational Data Mining*, pages 153–160.

Salakhutdinov, R. and Mnih, A. (2008). Bayesian probabilistic matrix factorization using Markov chain Monte Carlo. In *Proceedings of the 25th International Conference on Machine Learning (ICML)*, pages 880–887.

Song, S., Chaudhuri, K., and Sarwate, A. D. (2013). Stochastic gradient descent with differentially private updates. In *Global Conference on Signal and Information Processing (GlobalSIP), 2013 IEEE*, pages 245–248. IEEE.

Srivastava, N., Hinton, G., Krizhevsky, A., Sutskever, I., and Salakhutdinov, R. (2014). Dropout: A simple way to prevent neural networks from overfitting. *The Journal of Machine Learning Research*, 15(1):1929–1958.

van der Maaten, L., Chen, M., Tyree, S., and Weinberger, K. Q. (2013). Learning with marginalized corrupted features. In *Proceedings of the 30th International Conference on Machine Learning (ICML)*, pages 410–418.

Wang, Y., Wang, Y.-X., and Singh, A. (2015a). Differentially private subspace clustering. In *Advances in Neural Information Processing Systems (NIPS)*, pages 1000–1008.

Wang, Y.-X., Fienberg, S. E., and Smola, A. (2015b). Privacy for free: Posterior sampling and stochastic gradient Monte Carlo. *Proceedings of The 32nd International Conference on Machine Learning (ICML)*, pages 2493–2502.

Welling, M. and Teh, Y. W. (2011). Bayesian learning via stochastic gradient Langevin dynamics. In *Proceedings of the 28th International Conference on Machine Learning (ICML)*, pages 681–688.

Zhang, Z., Rubinstein, B., and Dimitrakakis, C. (2016). On the differential privacy of Bayesian inference. In *Proceedings of the Thirtieth AAAI Conference on Artificial Intelligence (AAAI)*.

Taming the Noise in Reinforcement Learning via Soft Updates

Roy Fox*
Hebrew University

Ari Pakman*
Columbia University

Naftali Tishby
Hebrew University

Abstract

Model-free reinforcement learning algorithms, such as Q-learning, perform poorly in the early stages of learning in noisy environments, because much effort is spent unlearning biased estimates of the state-action value function. The bias results from selecting, among several noisy estimates, the apparent optimum, which may actually be suboptimal. We propose G-learning, a new off-policy learning algorithm that regularizes the value estimates by penalizing deterministic policies in the beginning of the learning process. We show that this method reduces the bias of the value-function estimation, leading to faster convergence to the optimal value and the optimal policy. Moreover, G-learning enables the natural incorporation of prior domain knowledge, when available. The stochastic nature of G-learning also makes it avoid some exploration costs, a property usually attributed only to on-policy algorithms. We illustrate these ideas in several examples, where G-learning results in significant improvements of the convergence rate and the cost of the learning process.

1 INTRODUCTION

The need to separate signals from noise stands at the center of any learning task in a noisy environment. While a rich set of tools to regularize learned parameters has been developed for supervised and unsupervised learning problems, in areas such as reinforcement learning there still exists a vital need for techniques that tame the noise and avoid overfitting and local minima.

One of the central algorithms in reinforcement learning is Q-learning [1], a model-free off-policy algorithm, which attempts to estimate the optimal value function Q, the cost-to-go of the optimal policy. To enable this estimation, a stochastic exploration policy is used by the learning agent to interact with its environment and explore the model. This approach is very successful and popular, and despite several alternative approaches developed in recent years [2, 3, 4], it is still being applied successfully in complex domains for which explicit models are lacking [5].

However, in noisy domains, in early stages of the learning process, the min (or max) operator in Q-learning brings about a bias in the estimates. This problem is akin to the "winner's curse" in auctions [6, 7, 8, 9]. With too little evidence, the biased estimates may lead to wrong decisions, which slow down the convergence of the learning process, and require subsequent unlearning of these suboptimal behaviors.

In this paper we present G-learning, a new off-policy information-theoretic approach to regularizing the state-action value function learned by an agent interacting with its environment in model-free settings.

This is achieved by adding to the cost-to-go a term that penalizes deterministic policies which diverge from a simple stochastic prior policy [10]. With only a small sample to go by, G-learning prefers a more randomized policy, and as samples accumulate, it gradually shifts to a more deterministic and exploiting policy. This transition is managed by appropriately scheduling the coefficient of the penalty term as learning proceeds.

In Section 4 we discuss the theoretical and practical aspects of scheduling this coefficient, and suggest that a simple linear schedule can perform well. We show that G-learning with this schedule reduces the value estimation bias by avoiding overfitting in its selection of the update policy. We further establish empirically the link between bias reduction and learning performance, that has been the underlying assumption in many approaches to reinforcement learning [11, 12, 13, 14]. The examples in Section 6 demonstrate the significant improvement thus obtained.

Furthermore, in domains where exploration incurs significantly higher costs than exploitation, such as the classic

*These authors contributed equally to this work.

cliff domain [2], G-learning with an ϵ-greedy exploration policy is exploration-aware, and chooses a less costly exploration policy, thus reducing the costs incurred during the learning process. Such awareness to the cost of exploration is usually attributed to on-policy algorithms, such as SARSA [2, 4] and Expected-SARSA [15, 16]. The remarkable finding that G-learning exhibits on-policy-like properties is illustrated in the example of Section 6.2.

In Section 2 we discuss the problem of learning in noisy environments. In Section 3 we introduce the penalty term, derive G-learning and prove its convergence. In Section 4 we determine a schedule for the coefficient of the information penalty term. In Section 5 we discuss related work. In Section 6 we illustrate the strengths of the algorithm through several examples.

2 LEARNING IN NOISY ENVIRONMENTS

2.1 NOTATION AND BACKGROUND

We consider the usual setting of a Markov Decision Process (MDP), in which an agent interacts with its environment by repeatedly observing its state $s \in S$, taking an action $a \in A$, with A and S finite, and incurring cost $c \in \mathbb{R}$. This induces a stochastic process $s_0, a_0, c_0, s_1, \ldots$, where s_0 is fixed, and where for $t \geq 0$ we have the Markov properties indicated by the conditional distributions $a_t \sim \pi_t(a_t|s_t)$, $c_t \sim \theta(c_t|s_t, a_t)$ and $s_{t+1} \sim p(s_{t+1}|s_t, a_t)$.

The objective of the agent is to find a time-invariant policy π that minimizes the total discounted expected cost

$$V^\pi(s) = \sum_{t \geq 0} \gamma^t \, \mathrm{E}[c_t|s_0 = s], \tag{1}$$

simultaneously for any $s \in S$, for a given discount factor $0 \leq \gamma < 1$. For each t, the expectation above is over all trajectories of length t starting at $s_0 = s$. A related quantity is the state-action value function

$$\begin{aligned} Q^\pi(s, a) &= \sum_{t \geq 0} \gamma^t \, \mathrm{E}[c_t|s_0 = s, a_0 = a] \\ &= \mathrm{E}_\theta[c|s, a] + \gamma \, \mathrm{E}_p[V^\pi(s')|s, a], \end{aligned} \tag{2}$$

which equals the total discounted expected cost that follows from choosing action a in state s, and then following the policy π.

If we know the distributions p and θ (or at least $\mathrm{E}_\theta[c|s, a]$), then it is easy to find the optimal state-action value function

$$Q^*(s, a) = \min_\pi Q^\pi(s, a) \tag{3}$$

using standard techniques, such as Value Iteration [17]. Our interest is in model-free learning, where the model parameters are unknown. Instead, the agent obtains samples from $p(s_{t+1}|s_t, a_t)$ and $\theta(c_t|s_t, a_t)$ through its interaction with the environment. In this setting, the Q-learning algorithm [1] provides a method for estimating Q^*. It starts with an arbitrary Q, and in step t upon observing s_t, a_t, c_t and s_{t+1}, performs the update

$$\begin{aligned} Q(s_t, a_t) \leftarrow\ & (1 - \alpha_t) Q(s_t, a_t) \\ & + \alpha_t \left(c_t + \gamma \sum_{a'} \pi(a'|s_{t+1}) Q(s_{t+1}, a') \right), \end{aligned} \tag{4}$$

with some learning rate $0 \leq \alpha_t \leq 1$, and the greedy policy for Q having

$$\pi(a|s) = \delta_{a, a^*(s)}; \qquad a^*(s) = \arg\min_a Q(s, a). \tag{5}$$

$Q(s, a)$ is unchanged for any $(s, a) \neq (s_t, a_t)$. If the learning rate satisfies

$$\sum_t \alpha_t = \infty; \qquad \sum_t \alpha_t^2 < \infty, \tag{6}$$

and the interaction itself uses an exploration policy that returns to each state-action pair infinitely many times, then Q is a consistent estimator, converging to Q^* with probability 1 [1, 17]. Similarly, if the update rule (4) uses a fixed update policy $\pi = \rho$, we call this algorithm Q^ρ-learning, because Q converges to Q^ρ with probability 1.

2.2 BIAS AND EARLY COMMITMENT

Despite the success of Q-learning in many situations, learning can proceed extremely slowly when there is noise in the distribution, given s_t and a_t, of either of the terms of (2), namely the cost c_t and the value of the next state s_{t+1}. The source of this problem is a negative bias introduced by the min operator in the estimator $\min_{a'} Q(s_{t+1}, a')$, when (5) is plugged into (4).

To illustrate this bias, assume that $Q(s, a)$ is an unbiased but noisy estimate of the optimal $Q^*(s, a)$. Then Jensen's inequality for the concave min operator implies that

$$\mathrm{E}[\min_a Q(s, a)] \leq \min_a Q^*(s, a), \tag{7}$$

with equality only when Q already reveals the optimal policy by having $\arg\min_a Q(s, a) = \arg\min_a Q^*(s, a)$ with probability 1, so that no further learning is needed. The expectation in (7) is with respect to the learning process, including any randomness in state transition, cost, exploration and internal update, given the domain.

This is an optimistic bias, causing the cost-to-go to appear lower than it is (or the reward-to-go higher). It is the well known "winner's curse" problem in economics and decision theory [6, 7, 8, 9], and in the context of Q-learning it was studied before in [3, 11, 12, 13]. A similar problem occurs when a function approximation scheme is used for Q instead of a table, even in the absence of transition or cost noise, because the approximation itself introduces noise [18].

As the sample size increases, the variance in $Q(s,a)$ decreases, which in turn reduces the bias in (7). This makes the update policy (5) more optimal, and the update increasingly similar to Value Iteration.

2.3 THE INTERPLAY OF VALUE BIAS AND POLICY SUBOPTIMALITY

It is insightful to consider the effect of the bias not only on the estimated value function, but also on the real value V^π of the greedy policy (5), since in many cases the latter is the actual output of the learning process. The central quantity of interest here is the gap $Q^*(s,a')-V^*(s)$, in a given state s, between the value of a non-optimal action a' and that of the optimal action.

Consider first the case in which the gap is large compared to the noise in the estimation of the $Q(s,a)$ values. In this case, a' indeed appears suboptimal with high probability, as desired. Interestingly, when the gap is very small relative to the noise, the learning agent should not worry, either. Confusing such a' for the optimal action has a limited effect on the value of the greedy policy, since choosing a' is near-optimal.

We conclude that the real value V^π of the greedy policy (5) is suboptimal only in the intermediate regime, when the gap is of the order of the noise, and neither is small. The effect of the noise can be made even worse by the propagation of bias between states, through updates. Such propagation can cause large-gap suboptimal actions to nevertheless appear optimal, if they lead to a region of state-space that is highly biased.

2.4 A DYNAMIC OPTIMISM-UNCERTAINTY LOOP

The above considerations were agnostic to the exploration policy, but the bias reduction can be accelerated by an exploration policy that is close to being greedy. In this case, high-variance estimation is self-correcting: an estimated state value with optimistic bias draws exploration towards that state, leading to a decrease in the variance, which in turn reduces the optimistic bias. This is a dynamic form of optimism under uncertainty. While in the usual case the optimism is externally imposed as an initial condition [19], here it is spontaneously generated by the noise and self-corrected through exploration.

The approach we propose below to reduce the variance is motivated by electing to represent the uncertainty explicitly, and not indirectly through an optimistic bias. We notice that although *in the end* of the learning process one obtains the deterministic greedy policy from $Q(a,s)$ as in (5), *during* the learning itself the bias in Q can be ameliorated by avoiding the hard min operator, and refraining from committing to a deterministic greedy policy. This can be achieved by adding to Q, at the early learning stage, a term that penalizes deterministic policies, which we consider next.

3 LEARNING WITH SOFT UPDATES

3.1 THE FREE-ENERGY FUNCTION G AND G-LEARNING

Let us adopt, before any interaction with the environment, a simple stochastic prior policy $\rho(a|s)$. For example, we can take the uniform distribution over the possible actions. The *information cost* of a learned policy $\pi(a|s)$ is defined as

$$g^\pi(s,a) = \log \tfrac{\pi(a|s)}{\rho(a|s)}, \tag{8}$$

and its expectation over the policy π is the Kullback-Leibler (KL) divergence of $\pi_s = \pi(\cdot|s)$ from $\rho_s = \rho(\cdot|s)$,

$$\mathrm{E}_\pi[g^\pi(s,a)|s] = \mathrm{D}_{\mathrm{KL}}[\pi_s \| \rho_s]. \tag{9}$$

The term (8) penalizes deviations from the prior policy and serves to regularize the optimal policy away from a deterministic action. In the context of the MDP dynamics $p(s_{t+1}|s_t,a_t)$, similarly to (1), we consider the total discounted expected information cost

$$I^\pi(s) = \sum_{t\geq 0} \gamma^t\, \mathrm{E}[g^\pi(s_t,a_t)|s_0=s]. \tag{10}$$

The discounting in (1) and (10) is justified by imagining a horizon $T \sim \mathrm{Geom}(1-\gamma)$, distributed geometrically with parameter $1-\gamma$. Then the cost-to-go V^π in (1) and the information-to-go I^π in (10) are the total (undiscounted) expected T-step costs.

Adding the penalty term (10) to the cost function (1) gives

$$\begin{aligned} F^\pi(s) &= V^\pi(s) + \tfrac{1}{\beta} I^\pi(s), \\ &= \sum_{t\geq 0} \gamma^t\, \mathrm{E}[\tfrac{1}{\beta} g^\pi(s_t,a_t) + c_t|s_0=s], \end{aligned} \tag{11}$$

called the *free-energy function* by analogy with a similar quantity in statistical mechanics [10].

Here β is a parameter that sets the relative weight between the two costs. For the moment, we assume that β is fixed. In following sections, we let β grow as the learning proceeds.

In analogy with the Q^π function (2), let us define the *state-action free-energy function* $G^\pi(s,a)$ as

$$\begin{aligned} G^\pi(s,a) &= \mathrm{E}_\theta[c|s,a] + \gamma\, \mathrm{E}_p[F^\pi(s')|s,a] \\ &= \sum_{t\geq 0} \gamma^t\, \mathrm{E}[c_t + \tfrac{\gamma}{\beta} g^\pi(s_{t+1},a_{t+1}))|s_0=s,a_0=a], \end{aligned} \tag{12}$$

and note that it does not involve the information term at time $t = 0$, since the action $a_0 = a$ is already known. From the definitions (11) and (12) it follows that

$$F^\pi(s) = \sum_a \pi(a|s) \left[\frac{1}{\beta} \log \frac{\pi(a|s)}{\rho(a|s)} + G^\pi(s,a) \right]. \quad (13)$$

It is easy to verify that, given the G function, the above expression for F^π has gradient 0 at

$$\pi(a|s) = \frac{\rho(a|s) e^{-\beta G(s,a)}}{\sum_{a'} \rho(a'|s) e^{-\beta G(s,a')}}, \quad (14)$$

which is therefore the optimal policy.

The policy (14) is the soft-min operator applied to G, with inverse-temperature β. When β is small, the information cost is dominant, and π approaches the prior ρ. When β is large, we are willing to diverge much from the prior to reduce the external cost, and π approaches the deterministic greedy policy for G.

Evaluated at the soft-greedy policy (14), the free energy (13) is

$$F^\pi(s) = -\frac{1}{\beta} \log \sum_a \rho(a|s) e^{-\beta G^\pi(s,a)}, \quad (15)$$

and plugging this expression into (12), we get that the optimal G^* is a fixed point of the equation

$$\begin{aligned} G^*(s,a) = {} & \mathrm{E}_\theta[c|s,a] && (16) \\ & - \frac{\gamma}{\beta} \mathrm{E}_p \left[\log \sum_{a'} \rho(a'|s') e^{-\beta G^*(s',a')} \right] \\ \equiv {} & \mathbf{B}^*[G^*]_{(s,a)}. && (17) \end{aligned}$$

Based on the above expression, we introduce G-learning as an off-policy TD-learning algorithm [2], that learns the optimal G^* from the interaction with the environment by applying the update rule

$$\begin{aligned} G(s_t,a_t) \leftarrow {} & (1-\alpha_t) G(s_t,a_t) && (18) \\ & + \alpha_t \left(c_t - \frac{\gamma}{\beta} \log \left(\sum_{a'} \rho(a'|s_{t+1}) e^{-\beta G(s_{t+1},a')} \right) \right). \end{aligned}$$

3.2 THE ROLE OF THE PRIOR

Clearly the choice of the prior policy ρ is significant in the performance of the algorithm. The prior policy can encode any prior knowledge that we have about the domain, and this can improve the convergence if done correctly. However an incorrect prior policy can hinder learning. We should therefore choose a prior policy that represents all of our prior knowledge, but nothing more. This prior policy has maximal entropy given the prior knowledge [20].

In our examples in Section 6, we use the uniform prior policy, representing no prior knowledge. Both in Q-learning and in G-learning, we could utilize the prior knowledge that moving into a wall is never a good action, by eliminating those actions. One advantage of G-learning is that it can utilize softer prior knowledge. For example, a prior policy that gives lower probability for moving into a wall represent the prior knowledge that such an action is usually (but not always) harmful, a type of knowledge that cannot be utilized in Q-learning.

We have presented G-learning in a fully parameterized formulation, where the function G is stored in a lookup table. Practical applications of Q-learning often resort to approximating the function Q through function approximations, such as linear expansions or neural networks [2, 3, 4, 21, 5]. Such an approximation generates inductive bias, which is another form of implicit prior knowledge. While G-learning is introduced here in its table form, preliminary results indicate that its benefits carry over to function approximations, despite the challenges posed by this extension.

3.3 CONVERGENCE

In this section we study the convergence of G under the update rule (18). Recall that the supremum norm is defined as $|x|_\infty = \max_i |x_i|$. We need the following Lemma, proved in the Supplementary Material.

Lemma 1. *The operator* $\mathbf{B}^*[G]_{(s,a)}$ *defined in* (17) *is a contraction in the supremum norm,*

$$\left|\mathbf{B}^*[G_1] - \mathbf{B}^*[G_2]\right|_\infty \le \gamma \left|G_1 - G_2\right|_\infty. \quad (19)$$

The update equation (18) of the algorithm can be written as a stochastic iteration equation

$$\begin{aligned} G_{t+1}(s_t,a_t) = {} & (1-\alpha_t) G_t(s_t,a_t) && (20) \\ & + \alpha_t (\mathbf{B}^*[G_t]_{(s_t,a_t)} + z_t(c_t,s_{t+1})) \end{aligned}$$

where the random variable z_t is

$$\begin{aligned} z_t(c_t,s_{t+1}) = {} & -\mathbf{B}^*[G_t]_{(s_t,a_t)} && (21) \\ & + c_t - \frac{\gamma}{\beta} \log \sum_{a'} \rho(a'|s_{t+1}) e^{-\beta G_t(s_{t+1},a')}. \end{aligned}$$

Note that z_t has expectation 0. Many results exist for iterative equations of the type (20). In particular, given conditions (6) for α_t, the contractive nature of $\mathbf{B}^*$, infinite visits to each pair (s_t, a_t) and assuming that $|z_t| < \infty$, G_t is guaranteed to converge to the optimal G^* with probability 1 [17, 22].

4 SCHEDULING β

In the previous section, we showed that running G-learning with a fixed β converges, with probability 1, to the optimal G^* for that β, given by the recursion in (12)–(14).

When $\beta = \infty$, the equations for G^* and F^* degenerate into the equations for Q^* and V^*, and G-learning becomes Q-learning. When $\beta = 0$, the update policy π in (14) is equal to the prior ρ. This case, denoted Q^ρ-learning, converges to Q^ρ.

In an early stage of learning, Q^ρ-learning has an advantage over Q-learning, because it avoids committing to a deterministic policy based on a noisy Q function. In a later stage of learning, when Q is a more precise estimate of Q^*, Q-learning gains the advantage by updating with a better policy than the prior. This is demonstrated in section 6.1.

We would therefore like to schedule β so that G-learning makes a smooth transition from Q^ρ-learning to Q-learning, just at the right pace to enjoy the early advantage of the former and the late advantage of the latter. As we argue below, such a β always exists.

4.1 ORACLE SCHEDULING

To consider the effect of the β scheduling on the correction of the bias (7), suppose that during learning we reach some G that is an unbiased estimate of G^*. $G(s_t, a_t)$ would remain unbiased if we update it towards

$$c_t + \gamma G(s_{t+1}, a^*) \tag{22}$$

with

$$a^* = \arg\min_{a'} G^*(s_{t+1}, a'), \tag{23}$$

but we do not have access to this optimal action. If we use the update rule (18) with $\beta = 0$, we update $G(s_t, a_t)$ towards

$$c_t + \gamma \sum_{a'} \rho(a'|s_{t+1}) G(s_{t+1}, a'), \tag{24}$$

which is always at least as large as (22), creating a positive bias. If we use $\beta = \infty$, we update $G(s_t, a_t)$ towards

$$c_t + \gamma \min_{a'} G(s_{t+1}, a'), \tag{25}$$

which creates a negative bias, as explained in Section 2.2. Since the right-hand side of (18) is continuous and monotonic in β, there must be some β for which this update rule is unbiased.

This is a non-constructive proof for the existence of a β schedule that keeps the value estimators unbiased (or at least does not accumulate additional bias). We can imagine a scheduling oracle, and a protocol for the agent by which to consult the oracle and obtain the β for its soft updates. At the very least, the oracle must be told the iteration index t, but it can also be useful to let β depend on any other aspect of the learning process, particularly the current world state s_t.

4.2 PRACTICAL SCHEDULING

A good schedule should increase β as learning proceeds, because as more samples are gathered the variance of G decreases, allowing more deterministic policies. In the examples of Section 6 we adopted the linear schedule

$$\beta_t = kt, \tag{26}$$

with some constant $k > 0$. Another possibility that we explored was to make β inversely proportional to a running average of the Bellman error, which decreases as learning progresses. The results were similar to the linear schedule.

The optimal parameter k can be obtained by performing initial runs with different values of k and picking the value whose learned policy gives empirically the lower cost-to-go. Although this exploration would seem costly compared to other algorithms for which no parameter tuning is needed, these initial runs do not need to be carried for many iterations. Moreover, in many situations the agent is confronted with a class of similar domains, and tuning k in a few initial domains leads to an improved learning for the whole class. This is the case in the domain-generator example in Section 6.1.

5 RELATED WORK

The connection between domain noise or function approximation, and the statistical bias in the Q function, was first discussed in [18, 3]. An interesting modification of Q-learning to address this problem is Double-Q-learning [11, 14], which uses two estimators for the Q function to alleviate the bias. Other modifications of Q-learning that attempt to reduce or correct the bias are suggested in [12, 13].

An early approach to Q-learning in continuous noisy domains was to learn, instead of the value function, the advantage function $A(s, a) = Q(s, a) - V(s)$ [23]. The algorithm represents A and V separately, and the optimal action is determined from $A(s, a)$ as $a^*(s) = \arg\min_a A(s, a)$. In noisy environments, learning A is shown in some examples to be faster than learning Q [23, 24].

More recently, it was shown that the advantage learning algorithm is a gap-increasing operator [25]. As discussed in Section 2.2, the action gap is a central factor in the generation of bias, and increasing the gap should also help reduce the bias. In Section 6.1 we compare our algorithm to the consistent Bellman operator $\mathcal{T}_C$, one of the gap-increasing algorithms introduced in [25].

For other works that study the effect of noise in Q-learning, although without identifying the bias (7), see [26, 27, 28].

Information considerations have received attention in recent years in various machine learning settings, with the free energy F^π and similar quantities used as a design principle for policies in known MDPs [10, 29, 30]. Other works have used related methods for reinforcement learning [31, 32, 33, 34, 35]. A KL penalty similar to ours is used in [35], in settings with known reward and transition functions, to encourage "curiosity".

Soft-greedy policies have been used before for exploration [2, 36], but to our knowledge G-learning is the first TD-learning algorithm to explicitly use soft-greedy policies in its updates.

Particularly relevant to our work is the approach studied in [32]. There the policy is iteratively improved by optimizing it in each iteration under the constraint that it only diverges slightly, in terms of KL-divergence, from the empirical distribution generated by the previous policy. In contrast, in G-learning we measure the KL-divergence from a fixed prior policy, and in each iteration allow the divergence to grow larger by increasing β. Thus the two methods follow different information-geodesics from the stochastic prior policy to more and more deterministic policies.

This distinction is best demonstrated by considering the Ψ-learning algorithm presented in [33, 34], based on the same approach as [32]. It employs the update rule

$$\begin{aligned}\Psi(s_t, a_t) \leftarrow\ & \Psi(s_t, a_t) \\ & + \alpha_t(c_t + \gamma\bar{\Psi}(s_{t+1}) - \bar{\Psi}(s_t)),\end{aligned} \quad (27)$$

with

$$\bar{\Psi}(s) = -\log \sum_a \rho(a|s) e^{-\Psi(s,a)}, \quad (28)$$

which is closely related to our update of G in (18).

Apart from lacking a β parameter, the most important difference is that the update of Ψ involves subtracting $\alpha_t\bar{\Psi}(s_t)$, whereas the update of G involves subtracting $\alpha_t G(s_t, a_t)$. This seemingly minor modification has a large impact on the behavior of the two algorithms. The update of G is designed to pull it towards the optimal state-action free energy G^*, for all state-action pairs. In contrast, subtracting the log-partition $\bar{\Psi}(s_t)$, in the long run pulls only $\Psi(s_t, a^*)$, with a^* the optimal action, towards its true value, while for the other actions the values grow to infinity. In this sense, the Ψ-learning update (27) is an information-theoretic gap-increasing Bellman operator [25].

The growth to infinity of suboptimal values separates them from the optimal value, and drives the algorithm to convergence. In G-learning, this parallels the increase in β with the accumulation of samples. However, there is a major benefit to keeping G reliable in all its parameters, and controlling it with a separate β parameter. In Ψ-learning, the Ψ function penalizes actions it deems suboptimal. If early noise causes an error in this penalty, the algorithm needs to unlearn it - a similar drawback to that of Q-learning. In Section 6, we demonstrate the improvement offered by G-learning.

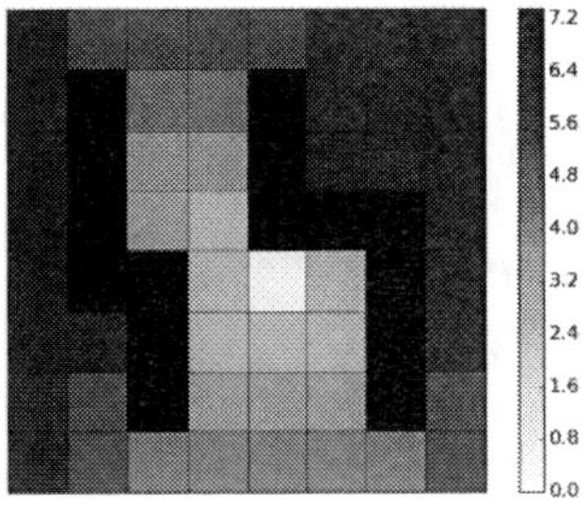

Figure 1: Gridworld domain. The agent can choose an adjacent square as the target to move to, and then may end up stochastically in a square adjacent to that target. The color scale indicates the optimal values V^* with a fixed cost of 1 per step.

6 EXAMPLES

This section illustrates how G-learning improves on existing model-free learning algorithms in several settings. The domains we use are clean and simple, to demonstrate that the advantages of G-learning are inherent to the algorithm itself.

We schedule the learning rate α_t as

$$\alpha_t = n_t(s_t, a_t)^{-\omega}, \quad (29)$$

where $n_t(s_t, a_t)$ is the number of times the pair (s_t, a_t) was visited. This scheme is widely used, and is consistent with (6) for $\omega \in (1/2, 1]$. We choose $\omega = 0.8$, which is within the range suggested in [37].

We schedule β linearly, as discussed in Section 4.2. In each case, we start with 5 preliminary runs of G-learning with various linear coefficients, and pick the coefficient with the lowest empirical cost. This coefficient is used in the subsequent test runs, whose results are plotted in Figure 2.

In all cases, we use a uniform prior policy ρ, a discount factor $\gamma = 0.95$, and 0 for the initial values ($Q_0 = 0$ in Q-learning, and similarly in the other algorithms). Except when mentioned otherwise, we employ random exploration, where s_t and a_t are chosen uniformly at the beginning of each time step, independently of any previous sample. This exploration technique is useful when comparing update rules, while controlling for the exploration process.

6.1 GRIDWORLD

Our first set of examples occurs in a gridworld of 8×8 squares, with some unavailable squares occupied by walls shown in black (Figure 1). The lightest square is the goal, and reaching it ends the episode.

At each time step, the agent can choose to move one square in any of the 8 directions (including diagonally), or stay in place. If the move is blocked by a wall or the edge of the board, it effectively attempts to stay in place. With some probability, the action performed by the agent is further followed by an additional random slide: with probability 0.15 to each vertically or horizontally adjacent available position, and with probability 0.05 to each diagonally adjacent available position.

The noise associated with these random transitions can be enhanced further by the possible variability in the costs incurred along the way. We consider three cases. In the first case, the cost in each step is fixed at 1. In the second case, the cost in each step is distributed normally i.i.d, with mean 1 and standard deviation 2. In the third case we define a distribution over domains, such that at the time of domain-generation the mean cost for each state-action is distributed uniformly i.i.d over $[1, 3]$. Once the domain has been generated and interaction begins, the cost itself in each step is again distributed normally i.i.d, with the generated mean and standard deviation 4.

We attempt to learn these domains using various algorithms. Figure 2 summarizes the results for Q-learning, G-learning, Double-Q-learning [11], Ψ-learning [33, 34] and the consistent Bellman operator $\mathcal{T}_C$ of [25]. We also include Q$^\rho$-learning, which performs updates as in (4) towards the prior policy ρ. Comparison with Speedy-Q-learning [12] is omitted, since it showed no improvement over vanilla Q-learning in these settings. In our experiments, these algorithms had comparable running times.

The β scheduling used in G-learning is linear, with the coefficient k equal to 10^{-3}, 10^{-4}, $5 \cdot 10^{-5}$ and 10^{-6}, respectively for the fixed-cost, noisy-cost, domain-generator and cliff domains (see Section 6.2).

For each case, Figure 2 shows the evolution over 250,000 algorithm iterations of the following three measures, averaged over $N = 100$ runs:

1. Empirical bias, defined as

$$\frac{1}{Nn}\sum_{i=1}^{N}\sum_{s=1}^{n}(V_{i,t}(s) - V_i^*(s)), \tag{30}$$

where i indexes the N runs and s the n states. Here $V_{i,t}$ is the greedy value based on the estimate obtained by each algorithm (Q, G, etc.), in iteration t of run i. The optimal value V_i^*, computed via Value Iteration, varies between runs in the domain-generator case.

2. Mean absolute error in V

$$\frac{1}{Nn}\sum_{i=1}^{N}\sum_{s=1}^{n}|V_{i,t}(s) - V_i^*(s)|. \tag{31}$$

A low bias could result from the cancellation of terms with high positive and negative biases. A convergence in the absolute error is more indicative of the actual convergence of the value estimates.

3. Increase in cost-to-go, relative to the optimal policy

$$\frac{1}{Nn}\sum_{i=1}^{N}\sum_{s=1}^{n}(V^{\pi_{i,t}}(s) - V_i^*(s)). \tag{32}$$

This measures the quality of the learned policy. Here $\pi_{i,t}$ is the greedy policy based on the state-action value estimates, and $V^{\pi_{i,t}}$ is its value in the model, computed via Value Iteration.

An algorithm is better when these measures reach zero faster. As is clear in Figure 2, in the domains with noisy cost (Rows 2 and 3), G-learning dominates over all the other competing algorithms by the three measures. The results are statistically significant, but plotting confidence intervals would clutter the figure.

An important and surprising point of Figure 2 is that Q$^\rho$-learning always outperforms Q-learning initially, before degrading. The reason is that the Q-learning updates initially rely on very few samples, so these harmful updates need to be undone by later updates. Q$^\rho$-learning, on the other hand, updates in the direction of a uniform prior. This gives an early advantage in mapping out the local topology of the problem, before long-range effects start pulling the learning towards the suboptimal Q^ρ.

The power of G-learning is that it enjoys the early advantage of Q$^\rho$-learning, and smoothly transitions to the convergence advantage of Q-learning. When β is small, the information cost g_t (8) outweighs the external costs c_t, and we update towards ρ. As samples keep coming in, and our estimates improve, β increases, and the updates gradually lean more towards a cost-optimizing policy. Unlike early stages in Q-learning, at this point G_t is already a good estimate, and we avoid overfitting. As mentioned above, Figure 2 shows that this effect is more manifest in noisier scenarios.

Finally, Figure 3 shows running averages of the Bellman error for the different algorithms considered. The Bellman error in G-learning is the coefficient multiplying α_t in (18),

$$\Delta G_t \equiv c_t - \tfrac{\gamma}{\beta}\log\left(\sum_{a'}\rho(a'|s_{t+1})e^{-\beta G_t(s_{t+1},a')}\right) - G_t(s_t, a). \tag{33}$$

When learning ends and $G = G^*$, the expectation of ΔG_t is zero (see (16)). Similar definitions hold for the other learning algorithms we compare with. As is clear from Figure 3, G-learning reaches zero average Bellman error faster than the competing methods, even while β is still increasing in order to make G^* converge to Q^*.

6.2 CLIFF WALKING

Cliff walking is a standard example in reinforcement learning [2], that demonstrates an advantage of on-policy algorithms such as SARSA [2, 4] and Expected-SARSA [15,

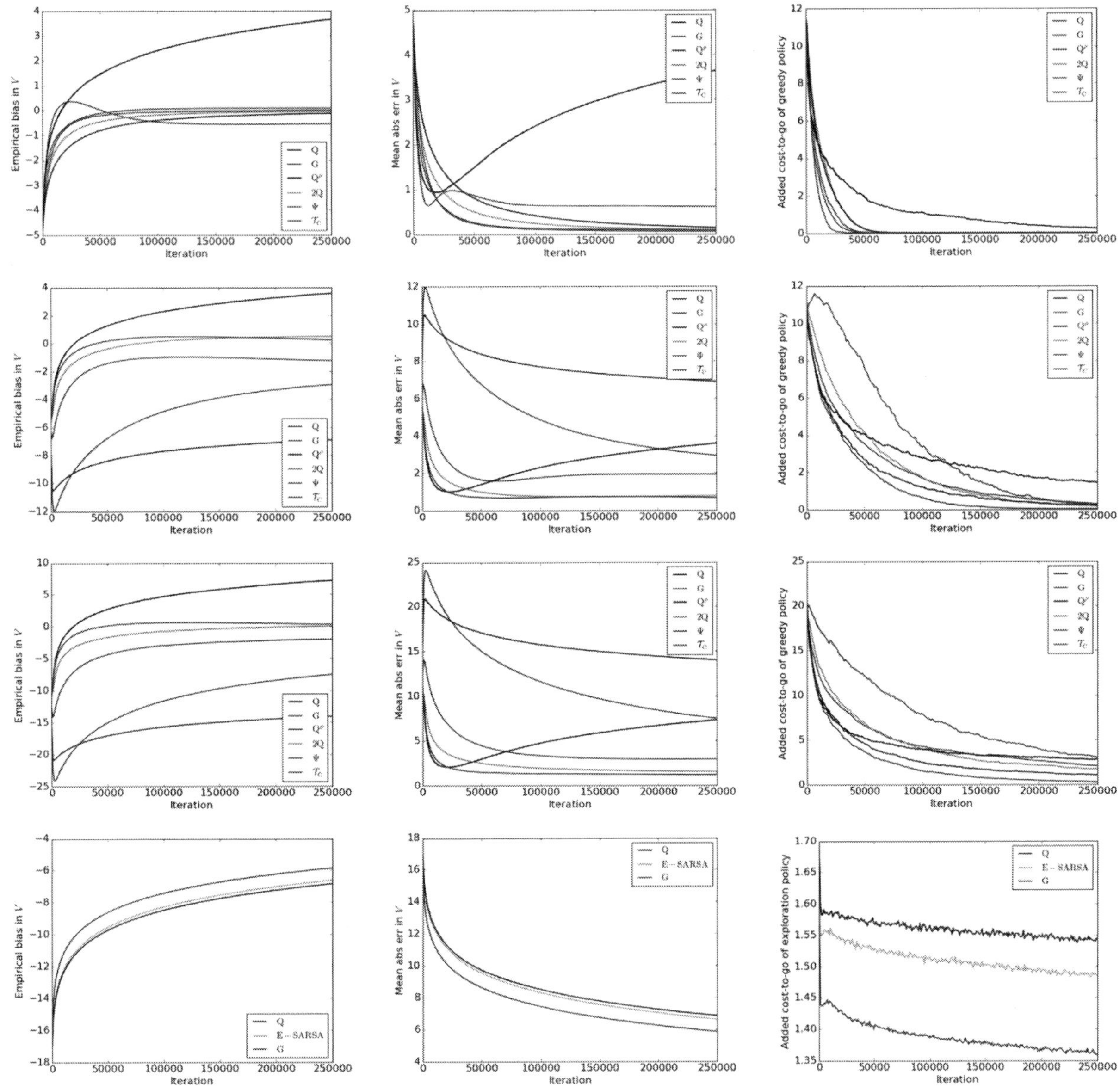

Figure 2: **Gridworld (Rows 1-3):** Comparison of Q-, G-, Q^{ρ}-, Double-Q-, Ψ- and $\mathcal{T}_C$-learning. **Row 1:** The cost in each step is fixed at 1. **Row 2:** The cost in each step is distributed as $\mathcal{N}(1, 2^2)$. **Row 3:** In each run, the domain is generated by drawing each $\mathrm{E}[c|s, a]$ uniformly over $[1, 3]$. The cost in each step is distributed as $\mathcal{N}(\mathrm{E}[c|s, a], 4^2)$. Note that in the noisy domains (Rows 2 and 3), G-learning dominates over all the other algorithms by the three measures. **Cliff (Row 4):** Comparison of Q- and G-learning, and Expected-SARSA. The cost in each step is 1, and falling off the cliff costs 5. **Left:** Empirical bias of V, relative to V^* (30). **Middle:** Mean absolute error between V and V^* (31). **Right:** Value of greedy policy, with the baseline V^* subtracted (32); except in Row 4, which shows the value of the exploration policy.

16] over off-policy learning approaches such as Q-learning. We use it to show another interesting strength of G-learning.

In this example, the agent can walk on the grid in Figure 4 horizontally or vertically, with deterministic transitions. Each step costs 1, except when the agent walks off the cliff (the bottom row), which costs 5, or reaches the goal (lower right corner), which costs 0. In either of these cases, the position resets to the lower left corner.

Exploration is now on-line, with s_t taken from the end of the previous step. The exploration policy in our simulations is ϵ-greedy with $\epsilon = 0.1$, i.e. with probability ϵ the agent

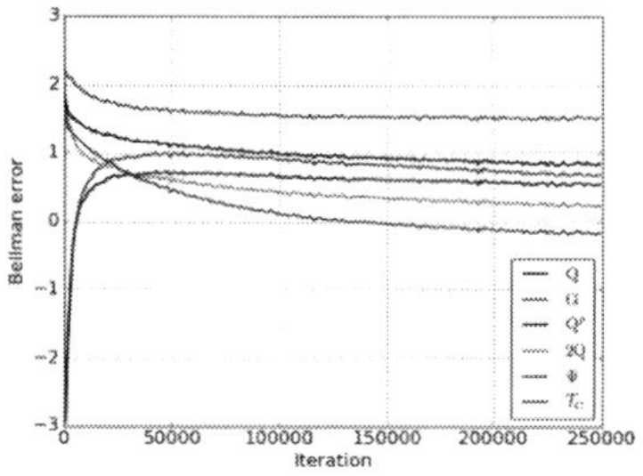

Figure 3: Running average of the Bellman error in the grid-world domain-generator example for Q-, G-, Q^{ρ}-, Double-Q-, Ψ- and $\mathcal{T}_C$-learning. The results for the other two grid-worlds of Figure 2 are similar.

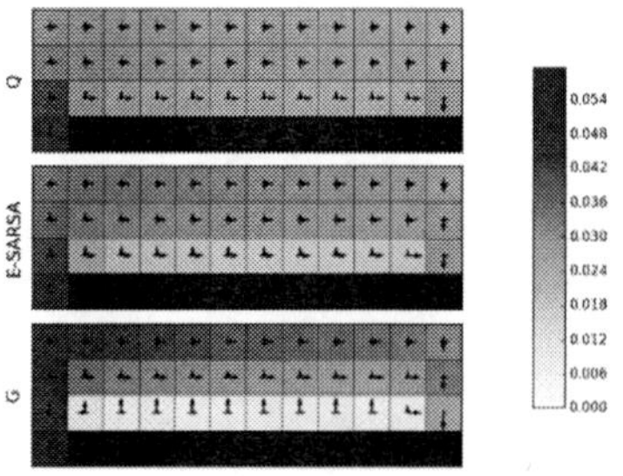

Figure 4: Cliff domain. The agent can choose a horizontally or vertically adjacent square, and moves there deterministically. The color scale and the arrow lengths indicate, respectively, the frequency of visiting each state and of making each transition, in the first 250,000 iterations of Q-learning, Expected-SARSA and G-learning. The near-greedy exploration policy of Q-learning has higher chance of taking the shortest path near the edge of the cliff at the bottom, than that of G-learning. As an off-policy algorithm, Q-learning fails to optimize for the exploration policy, whereas G-learning succeeds.

chooses a random action, and otherwise it takes deterministically the one that seems optimal. In practice, ϵ can be decreased after the learning phase, however it is also common to keep ϵ fixed for continued exploration [2].

In this setting, as shown in the bottom row of Figure 2, an off-policy algorithm like Q-learning performs poorly in terms of the value of its exploration policy, and the empirical cost it incurs. It learns a rough estimate of Q^* quickly, and then tends to use it and walk on the edge of the cliff. This leads to the agent occasionally exploring the possibility of falling off the cliff. In contrast, an on-policy algorithm like Expected-SARSA [15, 16] learns the value of its exploration policy, and quickly manages to avoid the cliff.

Figure 4 compares Q-learning, G-learning and Expected-SARSA in this domain, and shows that G-learning learns to avoid the cliff even better than an on-policy algorithm, although for a different reason. As an off-policy algorithm, G-learning does learn the value of the update policy, which prefers trajectories far from the cliff in the early stages of learning. This occurs because near the cliff, avoiding the cost of falling requires ruling out downward moves, which has a high information cost. On the other hand, trajectories far from the cliff, while paying a higher cost in overall distance to the goal, enjoy lower information cost because acting randomly is not costly for them.

As shown in the bottom row of Figure 2, by using a greedy policy for G as the basis of the ϵ-greedy exploration, we enjoy the benefits of being aware of the value of the exploration policy during the learning stage. At the same time, G-learning converges faster than either Q-learning or Expected-SARSA to the correct value function. In this case the "noise" that G-learning mitigates is related to the variability associated with the exploration.

7 CONCLUSIONS

The algorithm we have introduced successfully mitigates the slow learning problem of early stage Q-learning in noisy environments, that is caused by the bias generated by the hard optimization of the policy.

Although we have focused on Q-learning as a baseline, we believe that early-stage information penalties can also be applied to advantage in more sophisticated model-free settings, such as TD(λ), and combined with other incremental learning techniques, such as function approximation, experience replay and actor-critic methods.

G-learning takes a Frequentist approach to estimating the optimal Q function. This is in contrast to Bayesian Q-learning [38], which explicitly models the uncertainty about the Q function as a posterior distribution. It would be interesting to study the bias that hard optimization causes in the mean of this posterior, and to consider its reduction using methods similar to G-learning.

An important next step is to apply G-learning to more challenging domains, where an approximation of the G function is necessary. The simplicity of our linear β schedule (26) should facilitate such extensions, and allow G-learning to be combined with other schemes and algorithms. Further study should also address the optimal schedule for β. We leave these important questions for future work.

Acknowledgments

AP is supported by ONR grant N00014-14-1-0243 and IARPA via DoI/IBC contract number D16PC00003. RF and NT are supported by the DARPA MSEE Program, the Gatsby Charitable Foundation, the Israel Science Foundation and the Intel ICRI-CI Institute.

References

[1] Christopher JCH Watkins and Peter Dayan. Q-learning. *Machine learning*, 8(3-4):279–292, 1992.

[2] Richard S Sutton and Andrew G Barto. *Reinforcement learning: An introduction*. MIT press Cambridge, 1998.

[3] Warren B Powell. *Approximate Dynamic Programming: Solving the curses of dimensionality*, volume 703. John Wiley & Sons, 2007.

[4] Csaba Szepesvári. Algorithms for reinforcement learning. *Synthesis Lectures on Artificial Intelligence and Machine Learning*, 4(1):1–103, 2010.

[5] Volodymyr Mnih et al. Human-level control through deep reinforcement learning. *Nature*, 518(7540):529–533, 2015.

[6] Edward C Capen, Robert V Clapp, William M Campbell, et al. Competitive bidding in high-risk situations. *Journal of petroleum technology*, 23(06):641–653, 1971.

[7] Richard H Thaler. Anomalies: The winner's curse. *The Journal of Economic Perspectives*, pages 191–202, 1988.

[8] Eric Van den Steen. Rational overoptimism (and other biases). *American Economic Review*, pages 1141–1151, 2004.

[9] James E Smith and Robert L Winkler. The optimizer's curse: Skepticism and postdecision surprise in decision analysis. *Management Science*, 52(3):311–322, 2006.

[10] Jonathan Rubin, Ohad Shamir, and Naftali Tishby. Trading value and information in MDPs. In *Decision Making with Imperfect Decision Makers*, pages 57–74. Springer, 2012.

[11] Hado V Hasselt. Double Q-learning. In *NIPS*, 2010.

[12] Mohammad Ghavamzadeh, Hilbert J Kappen, Mohammad G Azar, and Rémi Munos. Speedy Q-learning. In *NIPS*, pages 2411–2419, 2011.

[13] Donghun Lee and Warren B Powell. An intelligent battery controller using bias-corrected Q-learning. In *AAAI*, 2012.

[14] Hado Van Hasselt, Arthur Guez, and David Silver. Deep reinforcement learning with Double Q-learning . In *AAAI*, 2016.

[15] Harm Van Seijen, Hado Van Hasselt, Shimon Whiteson, and Marco Wiering. A theoretical and empirical analysis of Expected Sarsa. In *ADPRL*, pages 177–184. IEEE, 2009.

[16] George H John. When the best move isn't optimal: Q-learning with exploration. In *AAAI*, page 1464, 1994.

[17] Dimitri P Bertsekas. *Dynamic programming and optimal control*, volume 1,2. Athena Scientific Belmont, MA, 1995.

[18] Sebastian Thrun and Anton Schwartz. Issues in using function approximation for reinforcement learning. In *Proceedings of the Fourth Connectionist Models Summer School*. Lawrence Erlbaum Publisher, Hillsdale, NJ, 1993.

[19] Ronen I Brafman and Moshe Tennenholtz. R-max-a general polynomial time algorithm for near-optimal reinforcement learning. *JMLR*, 3:213–231, 2003.

[20] Edwin T Jaynes. *Probability theory: The logic of science*. Cambridge University Press, 2003.

[21] Lucian Busoniu, Robert Babuska, Bart De Schutter, and Damien Ernst. *Reinforcement learning and dynamic programming using function approximators*, volume 39. CRC press, 2010.

[22] Vivek S Borkar. Stochastic approximation. *Cambridge Books*, 2008.

[23] Leemon C Baird III. Reinforcement learning in continuous time: Advantage updating. In *IEEE International Conference on Neural Networks*, volume 4, pages 2448–2453. IEEE, 1994.

[24] Mance E Harmon, Leemon C Baird III, and A Harry Klopf. Advantage updating applied to a differential game. *NIPS 7*, 7:353, 1995.

[25] Marc G Bellemare, Georg Ostrovski, Arthur Guez, Philip S Thomas, and Rémi Munos. Increasing the action gap: New operators for reinforcement learning. In *AAAI*, 2016.

[26] Mark D Pendrith and C Sammut. On reinforcement learning of control actions in noisy and non-Markovian domains. Technical report, 1994.

[27] Mark D Pendrith and Malcolm RK Ryan. Estimator variance in reinforcement learning: Theoretical problems and practical solutions. In *AAAI Workshop on On-Line Search*, 1997.

[28] Álvaro Moreno, José D Martín, Emilio Soria, Rafael Magdalena, and Marcelino Martínez. Noisy reinforcements in reinforcement learning: some case studies based on gridworlds. In *Proceedings of the 6th WSEAS international conference on applied computer science*, pages 296–300, 2006.

[29] Emanuel Todorov. Linearly-solvable Markov decision problems. In *NIPS*, pages 1369–1376, 2006.

[30] Hilbert J Kappen, Vicenç Gómez, and Manfred Opper. Optimal control as a graphical model inference problem. *Machine learning*, 87(2):159–182, 2012.

[31] Emanuel Todorov. Efficient computation of optimal actions. *Proceedings of the national academy of sciences*, 106(28):11478–11483, 2009.

[32] Jan Peters, Katharina Mülling, and Yasemin Altun. Relative entropy policy search. In *AAAI*, 2010.

[33] Konrad Rawlik, Marc Toussaint, and Sethu Vijayakumar. Approximate inference and stochastic optimal control. *arXiv preprint arXiv:1009.3958*, 2010.

[34] Mohammad Gheshlaghi Azar, Vicenç Gómez, and Hilbert J Kappen. Dynamic policy programming. *JMLR*, 13(1):3207–3245, 2012.

[35] Susanne Still and Doina Precup. An information-theoretic approach to curiosity-driven reinforcement learning. *Theory in Biosciences*, 131(3):139–148, 2012.

[36] Michel Tokic and Günther Palm. Value-difference based exploration: adaptive control between epsilon-greedy and softmax. In *KI 2011: Advances in Artificial Intelligence*, pages 335–346. Springer, 2011.

[37] Eyal Even-Dar and Yishay Mansour. Learning rates for Q-learning. *JMLR*, 5:1–25, 2004.

[38] Richard Dearden, Nir Friedman, and Stuart Russell. Bayesian Q-learning. In *AAAI/IAAI*, pages 761–768, 1998.

Quasi-Newton Hamiltonian Monte Carlo

Tianfan Fu
Computer Science Dept.
Shanghai Jiao Tong University
Shanghai 200240, China

Luo Luo
Computer Science Dept.
Shanghai Jiao Tong University
Shanghai 200240, China

Zhihua Zhang
Computer Science Dept.
Shanghai Jiao Tong University
Shanghai 200240, China

Abstract

The Hamiltonian Monte Carlo (HMC) method has become significantly popular in recent years. It is the state-of-the-art MCMC sampler due to its more efficient exploration to the parameter space than the standard random-walk based proposal. The key idea behind HMC is that it makes use of first-order gradient information about the target distribution. In this paper, we propose a novel dynamics using second-order geometric information about the desired distribution. The second-order information is estimated by using a quasi-Newton method (say, the BFGS method), so it does not bring heavy computational burden. Moreover, our theoretical analysis guarantees that this dynamics remains the target distribution invariant. As a result, the proposed quasi-Newton Hamiltonian Monte Carlo (QNHMC) algorithm traverses the parameter space more efficiently than the standard HMC and produces a less correlated series of samples. Finally, empirical evaluation on simulated data verifies the effectiveness and efficiency of our approach. We also conduct applications of QNHMC in Bayesian logistic regression and online Bayesian matrix factorization problems.

1 Introduction

Hamiltonian Monte Carlo (HMC) (Neal, 2011) is the state-of-the-art MCMC sampling algorithm. It defines a Hamiltonian function in terms of a potential energy—the negative logarithm of the target distribution and a kinetic energy parameterized by an auxiliary variable called momentum. By simulating from such a dynamical system, the proposal of distant states can be achieved. The attractive property of HMC is its rapid exploration to the state space. The main reason is that HMC makes use of the first-order gradient about the target distribution so that random-walk behaviors are suppressed to a great extent.

Along the idea of HMC, stochastic gradient MCMC algorithms have received great attention (Welling and Teh, 2011; Ahn, Korattikara, and Welling, 2012; Patterson and Teh, 2013; Chen, Fox, and Guestrin, 2014; Ding et al., 2014). Recently, Ma, Chen, and Fox (2015) proposed a general framework for this kind of stochastic gradient MCMC algorithms, which is built on a skew-symmetry structure. This structure represents determining traversing effect in HMC procedure and becomes one motivation of our new dynamics.

On the other hand, it is well established that the Newton or quasi-Newton methods using second-order information are more advanced than first-order gradient methods in the numerical optimization community (Nocedal and Wright, 2006). Since the Newton method is deemed to be computationally intensive, the quasi-Newton method is widely used in practice. In this paper, we explore the possibility of marrying the second-order gradient with HMC. Intuitively, a naive approach is to replace the first-order gradient in HMC with the second-order gradient about the negative logarithm of the target distribution using the quasi-Newton method. However, we will see that the resulting dynamics leads to an incorrect stationary distribution. Thus, it is challenging to incorporate second-order gradient into HMC.

Motivated by the work of Ma, Chen, and Fox (2015), we construct a skew-symmetry structure in our dynamics via adding the approximation of the inverse Hessian matrix to the standard Hamiltonian dynamics. We theoretically prove that this new dynamics keeps the target distribution invariant. Accordingly, we develop a quasi-Newton Hamiltonian Monte Carlo (QNHMC) algorithm. In QNHMC, both momentum and position variables are rescaled into a better condition using the geometric information estimated via a quasi-Newton method. Such an algorithm would produce a better proposal, take a large movement in the extended Hamiltonian dynamical system and enable a faster convergence rate to the desired distribution, which is verified by empirical results.

The remainder of the paper is organized as follows. Basic quasi-Newton and HMC methods are introduced in Section 2. We then describe our approach QNHMC in Section 3. Related studies are briefly reviewed in Section 4 while empirical results are shown in Section 5. Finally, we conclude our work in Section 6. All the proofs of theoretical results are given in Appendix.

2 Background

In this section we describe backgrounds on both quasi-Newton Approximation and Hamiltonian Monte Carlo.

2.1 Quasi-Newton Approximation

It is well-known that the Hessian matrix describes second-order curvature of the objective function $f: \mathbb{R}^d \to \mathbb{R}$. The time complexity and space complexity for exactly computing the Hessian matrix are both $O(d^2)$, which is computationally prohibitive for high-dimensional problems. Alternatively, quasi-Newton methods, including the BFGS method and its variant limited-memory BFGS(L-BFGS), are widely used (Nocedal and Wright, 2006).

In particular, let $\boldsymbol{\theta} \in \mathbb{R}^d$ be the parameter that needs to be estimated. Given the previous m estimates $\{\boldsymbol{\theta}_{k-m+1}, \boldsymbol{\theta}_{k-m+2}, \ldots, \boldsymbol{\theta}_k\}$ of $\boldsymbol{\theta}$ and the k-th estimate $\mathbf{B}_k$ of the inverse Hessian matrix, the BFGS updates $\mathbf{B}_{k+1}$ in the following way:

$$\mathbf{B}_{k+1} = (\mathbf{I} - \frac{\mathbf{s}_k \mathbf{y}_k^T}{\mathbf{y}_k^T \mathbf{s}_k})\mathbf{B}_k(\mathbf{I} - \frac{\mathbf{y}_k \mathbf{s}_k^T}{\mathbf{y}_k^T \mathbf{s}_k}) + \frac{\mathbf{s}_k \mathbf{s}_k^T}{\mathbf{s}_k^T \mathbf{y}_k}, \quad (1)$$

where $\mathbf{I}$ is the identity matrix, $\mathbf{s}_k = \boldsymbol{\theta}_{k+1} - \boldsymbol{\theta}_k$, and $\mathbf{y}_k = \nabla f(\boldsymbol{\theta}_{k+1}) - \nabla f(\boldsymbol{\theta}_k)$. It is implemented by storing the full $d \times d$ matrix $\mathbf{B}_k$. However, in the high-dimensional scenario (i.e., d is very large), the limited-memory BFGS is much more efficient. Specifically, in L-BFGS, $\mathbf{B}_{k-m+1}$ is set as $\gamma \mathbf{I}$ for some $\gamma > 0$, and $\{\mathbf{s}_{k-m+1}, \ldots, \mathbf{s}_{k-1}\}$ and $\{\mathbf{y}_{k-m+1}, \ldots, \mathbf{y}_{k-1}\}$ are stored. The involved matrix-vector product can be computed in linear time $O(md)$ by using a specially-designed recursive algorithm (Nocedal and Wright, 2006).

2.2 Hamiltonian Monte Carlo

We now briefly review the Hamiltonian Monte Carlo (Neal, 2011). HMC lies in Metropolis-Hastings (MH) framework. It can traverse long distances in the parameter space during a single transition. The proposals are generated from a Hamiltonian system by extending the state space via adding an auxiliary variable called momentum variable, and then simulating Hamiltonian dynamics to move long distances along the iso-probability contours in the extended parameter space.

Formally, suppose that $\boldsymbol{\theta} \in \mathbb{R}^d$ is the parameter of interest and $\pi(\boldsymbol{\theta})$ is the desired posterior distribution. Let $\mathbf{p}$ be the auxiliary variable which is independent of $\boldsymbol{\theta}$. For simplicity and generality, $\mathbf{p} \in \mathbb{R}^d$ is always assumed to be a zero-mean Gaussian with covariance $\mathbf{M}$.

Then a Hamiltonian is defined as the negative log-probability of the joint distribution $p(\boldsymbol{\theta}, \mathbf{p})$ as follows:

$$\begin{aligned} H(\boldsymbol{\theta}, \mathbf{p}) &= -\log p(\boldsymbol{\theta}, \mathbf{p}) \\ &= -\log \pi(\boldsymbol{\theta}) - \log p(\mathbf{p}) \\ &= U(\boldsymbol{\theta}) + \frac{1}{2}\mathbf{p}^T \mathbf{M}^{-1} \mathbf{p} + \text{const}, \end{aligned} \quad (2)$$

where $U(\boldsymbol{\theta}) = -\log \pi(\boldsymbol{\theta})$ is called the potential function. In the Hamiltonian system $\mathbf{M}$ is called a preconditioning mass matrix, $\boldsymbol{\theta}$ is regarded as a position variable, and $\mathbf{p}$ is called a momentum variable.

Given an initial state $(\boldsymbol{\theta}_0, \mathbf{p}_0)$, the state $(\boldsymbol{\theta}, \mathbf{p})$ is generated by deterministic simulation of Hamiltonian dynamics based on the following ordinary differential equation (ODE):

$$\begin{aligned} \dot{\boldsymbol{\theta}} &= \mathbf{M}^{-1}\mathbf{p}, \\ \dot{\mathbf{p}} &= -\nabla U(\boldsymbol{\theta}), \end{aligned} \quad (3)$$

where the dots denote the derivatives in time. In this paper we will also use $\mathbf{z} = (\boldsymbol{\theta}, \mathbf{p}) \in \mathbb{R}^{2d}$ to denote the joint variable of the position and momentum variables.

The trajectories of $\boldsymbol{\theta}$ and $\mathbf{p}$ produce proposals to the Metropolis-Hastings procedure. In particular, given the k-th estimate of the position variable $\boldsymbol{\theta}_k$, the standard HMC runs in the following steps: (i) draw $\mathbf{p}_k \sim \mathcal{N}(\mathbf{0}, \mathbf{M})$; (ii) compute the proposal$(\boldsymbol{\theta}^\star, \mathbf{p}^\star)$ by simulation from Eq. (3) using ϵ-discretization; (iii) compute the error caused by discretization $\nabla H = H(\boldsymbol{\theta}_k, \mathbf{p}_k) - H(\boldsymbol{\theta}^\star, \mathbf{p}^\star)$; (iv) accept new proposal $\boldsymbol{\theta}^\star$ with probability at $\min(\exp(\nabla H), 1)$.

It is worth mentioning that the error is only caused from the discretization and highly related to the step size ϵ. If the discretization error vanishes, that is to say, Eq. (3) is solved exactly, then Hamiltonian $H(\boldsymbol{\theta}, \mathbf{p})$ is conserved exactly and new proposal is always accepted. The details of HMC can be found in Neal (2011).

In practice, the mainstream integrator is the well-known leapfrog method in Algorithm 1, which is symplectic and time-reversible. The error is second-order in the step size ϵ, keeping acceptance rate a reasonable value. However, when the ODE described in Eq. (2) is stiff, the step size ϵ is required to be small to maintain a reasonable acceptance rate. This will cause the high-correlated series and reduce the effective sample size. A main reason is that only first-order gradient is not enough. That is, HMC fails to make sufficient use of the local geometric information, as shown by Girolami and Calderhead (2011); Zhang and Sut-

Algorithm 1 Standard Hamiltonian Monte Carlo(HMC)

Input: target posterior distribution $\pi(\boldsymbol{\theta})$ and potential function $U(\boldsymbol{\theta}) = -\log \pi(\boldsymbol{\theta})$, step size ϵ, number of leapfrog L, total number of sample N, burn-in samples K, start point $\boldsymbol{\theta}_0$, mass matrix $\mathbf{M}$

Output: $\{\boldsymbol{\theta}_{K+1}, \boldsymbol{\theta}_{K+2}, \ldots, \boldsymbol{\theta}_N\}$

Iteration counter $t = 1$.
while $t < N$ **do**
  Let $\mathbf{q} = \boldsymbol{\theta}_t$.
  Draw $\mathbf{p} \sim \mathcal{N}(\mathbf{0}, \mathbf{M})$.
  Compute the current energy E_0 using Eq. (2).
  First half step: $\mathbf{p} = \mathbf{p} - \epsilon \nabla U(\mathbf{q})/2$
  for $i = 1 : L$ **do**
    $\mathbf{q} = \mathbf{q} + \epsilon \mathbf{M}^{-1}\mathbf{p}$
    if $i \neq L$ **then**
      $\mathbf{p} = \mathbf{p} - \epsilon \nabla U(\mathbf{q})$
    end if
  end for
  Last half step: $\mathbf{p} = \mathbf{p} - \epsilon \nabla U(\mathbf{q})/2$
  Compute the proposed energy E_1 using Eq. (2).
  Draw $u \sim \text{Uniform}(0, 1)$
  if $u < \min\{1, \exp(E_1 - E_0)\}$ **then**
    Accept the proposal $\mathbf{q}$, i.e., $\boldsymbol{\theta}_{t+1} = \mathbf{q}$.
  else
    Reject, $\boldsymbol{\theta}_{t+1} = \boldsymbol{\theta}_t$.
  end if
  $t = t + 1$.
end while

ton (2011). We also demonstrate this problem empirically in Section 5.

3 Methodology

In this section, we first discuss the condition for variants of Hamiltonian dynamics to reach the correct stationary distribution and then propose a novel dynamics satisfying the condition. Accordingly, we develop a quasi-Newton Hamiltonian Monte Carlo (QNHMC) algorithm.

3.1 A Naive Replacement

Intuitively, the most straightforward approach to apply the quasi-Newton method on Hamiltonian Monte Carlo is simply to replace $\nabla U(\boldsymbol{\theta})$ in Algorithm 1 by $\mathbf{B}\nabla U(\boldsymbol{\theta})$, where $\mathbf{B}$ is the approximation to the inverse Hessian matrix. The resulting discrete time system can be viewed as an ϵ-discretization of the following continuous ODE:

$$\begin{aligned} \dot{\boldsymbol{\theta}} &= \mathbf{M}^{-1}\mathbf{p}, \\ \dot{\mathbf{p}} &= -\mathbf{B}(t)\nabla U(\boldsymbol{\theta}), \end{aligned} \tag{4}$$

where $\mathbf{B}(t) \in \mathbb{R}^{d \times d}$ is positive definite and varies with time t. For simplicity, we always ignore the time t and assume that $\mathbf{B}$ is not the identity matrix, i.e., $\mathbf{B} = \mathbf{B}(t) \neq \mathbf{I}$. Now we show that, as given by Corollary 1 below, $p(\boldsymbol{\theta}, \mathbf{p}) \propto \exp(-H(\boldsymbol{\theta}, \mathbf{p}))$ is no longer the stationary distribution of the dynamics described in Eq. (4). The following theorem shows a stronger result, a necessary condition for the invariance property, i.e., the dynamics governed by Eq. (4) can not conserve the entropy of p_t with time.

Theorem 1. *Let $p_t(\boldsymbol{\theta}, \mathbf{p})$ be the distribution of $(\boldsymbol{\theta}, \mathbf{p})$ at time t with dynamics described in Eq. (4). Define the entropy of $p_t(\boldsymbol{\theta}, \mathbf{p})$ as $h(p_t) = -\int_{\boldsymbol{\theta}, \mathbf{p}} f(p_t(\boldsymbol{\theta}, \mathbf{p})) d\boldsymbol{\theta} d\mathbf{p}$, where $f(x) = x \ln x$ is defined for measuring entropy. Assume p_t is a distribution with density and gradient vanishing at infinity and the gradient vanishes faster than $\frac{1}{\ln p_t}$. Then, the entropy of p_t varies over time.*

Intuitively, Theorem 1 is true because the standard Hamiltonian dynamics strictly preserve the entropy (Qian, 2012). The additional $\mathbf{B}$ can be seen as a noise, destroying the entropy preservation. This hints the fact that the distribution $p_t(z)$ tends toward far from the target distribution.

Based on Theorem 1, we conclude that the naive modification to Hamiltonian dynamics can not keep the target distribution invariant. That is,

Corollary 1. *The distribution of extended system $p(\boldsymbol{\theta}, \mathbf{p}) \propto exp(-H(\boldsymbol{\theta}, \mathbf{p}))$ is no longer invariant under the dynamics described by Eq. (4).*

This corollary claims the failure of dynamics governed by Eq. (4). In what follows, we will consider a general framework which builds the necessary and sufficient condition for variants of Hamiltonian dynamics to satisfy the invariance of the target distribution. Accordingly, this leads us to a new dynamics.

3.2 Motivation: A general recipe

In this section, we introduce a general framework for stochastic gradient MCMC algorithms proposed recently by Ma, Chen, and Fox (2015). It provides the sufficient and necessary condition for Hamiltonian systems to reach the invariant distribution.

Consider the following Stochastic Differential Equation (SDE) for continuous Markov processes for sampling:

$$d\mathbf{z} = f(\mathbf{z})dt + \sqrt{2D(\mathbf{z})}dW(t), \tag{5}$$

where $f(\cdot) : \mathbb{R}^{2d} \to \mathbb{R}^{2d}$ denotes the deterministic drift and is often related to the gradients of Hamiltonian $\nabla H(\mathbf{z})$, $W(t)$ is a $2d$-dimensional Wiener process, and $D(\mathbf{z}) \in \mathbb{R}^{2d \times 2d}$ is a positive semi-definite diffusion matrix. Obviously, not all choices of $f(\mathbf{z})$ and $D(\mathbf{z})$ can yield the stationary distribution $p(\boldsymbol{\theta}, \mathbf{q}) = p(\mathbf{z}) \propto \exp(-H(\mathbf{z}))$.

Ma, Chen, and Fox (2015) devised a recipe for constructing SDEs with the correct stationary distributions. They defined $f(\mathbf{z})$ directly in terms of the target distribution:

$$f(\mathbf{z}) = -[D(\mathbf{z}) + Q(\mathbf{z})]\nabla H(\mathbf{z}) + \Xi(\mathbf{z}),$$
$$\Xi_i(\mathbf{z}) = \sum_{j=1}^{d} \frac{\partial}{\partial \mathbf{z}_j}(D_{ij}(\mathbf{z}) + Q_{ij}(\mathbf{z})). \quad (6)$$

Here $\Xi_i(\cdot)$ is the i-th entry of the vector-valued function $\Xi(\cdot) : \mathbb{R}^{2d} \to \mathbb{R}^{2d}$, and $Q(\mathbf{z}) \in \mathbb{R}^{2d \times 2d}$ is a skew-symmetric curl matrix representing the determining traversing effects seen in the HMC procedure. It was proved that under certain conditions $p(\mathbf{z})$ is the unique stationary distribution of the dynamics governed by Eq. (5) (Ma, Chen, and Fox, 2015).

Theorem 2. *$p(\mathbf{z}) \propto \exp(-H(\mathbf{z}))$ is a stationary distribution of the dynamics described in Eq. (5) iff f is restricted to the form of Eq. (6), with $D(\mathbf{z})$ positive semidefinite and $Q(\mathbf{z})$ skew-symmetric.*

Since in this paper we restrict our attention to the deterministic dynamics, we can omit the term related to diffusion part $D(\mathbf{z})$. In this case, the SDE is reduced to an ODE. The skew-symmetry of $Q(\mathbf{z})$ inspires us to add $\mathbf{B}$ into update of the position variable $\boldsymbol{\theta}$ in the dynamics in Eq. (4).

In the next section we will consider skew-symmetric modification to the Hamiltonian dynamics that achieves the desired $p(\boldsymbol{\theta}, \mathbf{p})$ as the invariant distribution of the continuous Hamiltonian dynamical system.

3.3 Novel Dynamics in skew-symmetric structure

In this section, inspired by the skew-symmetric structure, we consider a variant on Hamiltonian dynamics as follows:

$$\dot{\boldsymbol{\theta}} = \mathbf{C}\mathbf{M}^{-1}\mathbf{p},$$
$$\dot{\mathbf{p}} = -\mathbf{C}\nabla U(\boldsymbol{\theta}), \quad (7)$$

where $\mathbf{C} \in \mathbb{R}^{d \times d}$ is a symmetric positive definite matrix, independent of $\boldsymbol{\theta}$ and $\mathbf{p}$.

Now we show that the new dynamics maintains the desired distribution as the invariant distribution.

Theorem 3. *$p(\boldsymbol{\theta}, \mathbf{p}) \propto exp(-H(\boldsymbol{\theta}, \mathbf{p}))$ is the unique stationary distribution of the dynamics governed by Eq. (7).*

Then it is easy to prove the entropy preservation of proposed dynamics directly using the intermediate results in Theorem 3.

Corollary 2. *Let $p_t(\boldsymbol{\theta}, \mathbf{p})$ be the distribution of $(\boldsymbol{\theta}, \mathbf{p})$ at time t with dynamics described in Eq. (7). Under almost the same condition with Theorem 1, i.e., the entropy of $p_t(\boldsymbol{\theta}, \mathbf{p})$ is defined as $h(p_t) = -\int_{\boldsymbol{\theta},\mathbf{p}} f(p_t(\boldsymbol{\theta}, \mathbf{p}))d\boldsymbol{\theta}d\mathbf{p}$, where $f(x) = x \ln x$. Assume p_t is an arbitrary distribution with density and gradient vanishing at infinity. Then, the entropy of p_t is strictly conserved with time.*

Algorithm 2 Quasi-Newton HMC (QNHMC)

Input: target distribution $\pi(\boldsymbol{\theta})$ and potential function $U(\boldsymbol{\theta}) = -\log \pi(\boldsymbol{\theta})$, step size ϵ, number of Leapfrog L, total number of sample N, burn-in samples K, start point $\boldsymbol{\theta}_0$, mass matrix $\mathbf{M}$, approximation of Hessian Matrix $\mathbf{B} = \mathbf{I}$.
Output: $\boldsymbol{\theta}_{K+1}, \boldsymbol{\theta}_{K+2}, \cdots, \boldsymbol{\theta}_N$.
1: Iteration counter $t = 1$.
2: **while** $t < N$ **do**
3:   Let $\mathbf{q} = \boldsymbol{\theta}_t$ and $\mathbf{C} = \mathbf{B}$.
4:   Draw $\mathbf{p} \sim \mathcal{N}(\mathbf{0}, \mathbf{M})$.
5:   Compute the current energy E_0 using Eq. (2).
6:   First half step: $\mathbf{p} = \mathbf{p} - \epsilon\mathbf{C}\nabla U(\mathbf{q})/2$.
7:   Update $\mathbf{B}$ using Eq. (1).
8:   **for** $i = 1 : L$ **do**
9:     $\mathbf{q} = \mathbf{q} + \epsilon\mathbf{C}\mathbf{M}^{-1}p$.
10:     **if** $i \neq L$ **then**
11:       $\mathbf{p} = \mathbf{p} - \epsilon\mathbf{C}\nabla U(\mathbf{q})$.
12:       Update $\mathbf{B}$ using Eq. (1).
13:     **end if**
14:   **end for**
15:   Last half step: $\mathbf{p} = \mathbf{p} - \epsilon\mathbf{C}\nabla U(\mathbf{q})/2$
16:   Update $\mathbf{B}$ using Eq. (1).
17:   Compute the proposed energy E_1 using Eq. (2).
18:   Draw $u \sim$ Uniform$(0, 1)$.
19:   **if** $u < \min\{1, \exp(E_1 - E_0)\}$ **then**
20:     Accept the proposal $\mathbf{q}$, i.e., $\boldsymbol{\theta}_{t+1} = \mathbf{q}$.
21:   **else**
22:     Reject, $\boldsymbol{\theta}_{t+1} = \boldsymbol{\theta}_t$. $\mathbf{B} = \mathbf{C}$.
23:   **end if**
24:   $t = t + 1$.
25: **end while**

In summary, we have shown that the dynamics given by Eq. (7) owns the invariance property. Furthermore, it is concise. When $\mathbf{C} = \mathbf{I}$, it reduces to Hamiltonian dynamics.

3.4 Quasi-Newton Hamiltonian Monte Carlo

In the previous section we mainly focus on the invariance property of the proposed dynamics given in Eq. (7), which in essence is a continuous ODE. However, in practice, we need a numerical solution to the continuous ODE in Eq. (7). Here, the discretization step employ leapfrog methods, inheriting from the standard HMC (Neal, 2011). In particular, the resulting Quasi-Newton Hamiltonian Monte Carlo **(QNHMC)** algorithm is shown in Algorithm 2.

It is worth noting that in Algorithm 2 the approximation $\mathbf{B}$ varies with iteration counter. In contrast, to keep the invariance property of the dynamics in Eq. (7), in each proposal (Step 3-15), $\mathbf{B}$ is kept as a constant $\mathbf{C}$. The update to $\mathbf{B}$ is only done when the proposal procedure ends and the proposal is accepted. The following theorem shows the correctness of Algorithm 2.

Theorem 4. *$\pi(\boldsymbol{\theta})$ is maintained as an invariant distribution for the whole chain produced by Algorithm 2.*

To gain some intuitions about the proposed QNHMC algorithm in physical interpretation, consider the well-known hockey puck instance widely used in the Hamiltonian dynamical system (Leimkuhler and Reich, 2004), where we can imagine the puck on an uneven surface. Here, $\mathbf{B}$ represents the approximation to the local geometric information. In HMC, when the local geometry is stiff, movements controlled by momentum $\mathbf{p}$ are always useless. By multiplying the matrix $\mathbf{B}$ ($\mathbf{C}$), the momentum variable and position variable are rescaled into the case where each dimension has a similar scale. This makes the movement in the extended Hamiltonian system more efficient. Empirically, it can traverse a large step in the state space. In the Bayesian scenario, this new dynamics produces a better proposal and less-autocorrelated series.

3.5 Computational Complexity

Two strategies (BFGS/L-BFGS) are used in estimating the matrix $\mathbf{B}$ according to the dimension of the parameter. When the dimension of the parameter d is high, the L-BFGS is adopted. In this case, $O(md)$ space complexity is needed. Moreover, since only matrix-vector product is required, the product $\mathbf{Bv}$ ($\mathbf{Cv}$) can be computed in linear time $O(md)$. It is worth noting that unlike in Algorithm 2, no need to update $\mathbf{B}$ in each leapfrog step when adopting L-BFGS. Instead, we choose to store $2m$ d-dimensional vectors as mentioned in Section 2. Only when the proposal is accepted, it is required to update $\mathbf{B}$.

On the other hand, when d is not high, BFGS is chosen. A $d \times d$ matrix needs to be stored so the complexity is $O(d^2)$. Each updating step requires $O(d)$ time without matrix-vector or matrix-matrix product.

In this paper, we mainly compare our QNHMC approach with the standard HMC (Neal, 2011). The gradient computation of the negative log-posterior $\nabla U(\boldsymbol{\theta})$ has already been done in the standard HMC in each leapfrog step. And, in practice, the gradient computation always contains expensive computations such as matrix-matrix/matrix-vector product. The size of matrix depends on both the dimension of the parameter and the number of the training instances. Our QNHMC algorithm can make use of the byproduct of leapfrog step, e.g., $\mathbf{s}_k$ and $\mathbf{y}_k$ in Eq. (1). Thus, the gradient computation is always dominant in computational time, which means that HMC and QNHMC cost the same order of magnitude running time in each proposal. Considering the larger step that QNHMC takes owing to more sufficient use of geometric information, QNHMC converges to the desired distribution faster than the standard HMC, which will be further validated by our empirical results.

4 Related Studies

In recent years, many approaches have been proposed to scale up Bayesian methods in machine learning community. As is well-known, gradient information of log-posterior distribution is widely used in Langevin/Hamiltonian dynamics. Among these methods, one large category is stochastic gradient Markov Chain Monte Carlo methods. The framework is to estimate the gradient from small mini-batches of observations instead of the whole dataset to cut the computational budget. The landmark of this kind of approaches is proposed by Welling and Teh (2011), which applied stochastic gradient on Langevin dynamics. Subsequently, a series of algorithms are developed to complete this framework (Ahn, Korattikara, and Welling, 2012; Patterson and Teh, 2013; Ahn, Shahbaba, and Welling, 2014; Chen, Fox, and Guestrin, 2014; Ding et al., 2014; Ma, Chen, and Fox, 2015). For instance, Chen, Fox, and Guestrin (2014) adapted stochastic gradient on Hamiltonian Monte Carlo (SGHMC) while Ding et al. (2014) devised a SGNHT algorithm by introducing a thermostat variable to make SGHMC more robust. Ma, Chen, and Fox (2015) developed a complete recipe for all stochastic gradient based MCMC approaches. There are some recent works (Bardenet, Doucet, and Holmes, 2014; Korattikara, Chen, and Welling, 2013; Maclaurin and Adams, 2015), attempting to perform Metropolis-Hastings rejection procedure using partial observations instead of whole dataset. These approaches mainly accelerate sampling procedure via a stochastic method applied on likelihood of data observations.

Another class of methods aim at sampler itself (Girolami and Calderhead, 2011; Zhang and Sutton, 2011; Calderhead and Sustik, 2012; Patterson and Teh, 2013; Wang, Mohamed, and Nando, 2013; Chao et al., 2015). Most of them are closely related to geometry. Concretely, they aim at finding the local geometric structure of posterior so that the random-walk behaviour in proposal can be significantly suppressed. Such algorithms allow a larger step size without loss of acceptance rate and make the sampling efficient. The representative work is Riemann Manifold Hamiltonian Monte Carlo proposed by Girolami and Calderhead (2011), which employed the high-order of geometric information about the local point. Chao et al. (2015) proposed an exponential integration to solve the high-oscillatory component of posterior more accurately than the integration used in the standard HMC method.

It is worth noting that Zhang and Sutton (2011) also proposed a quasi-Newton based Hamiltonian Monte Carlo method called HMC-BFGS. Different from our QNHMC, HMC-BFGS uses the geometric information in covariance of zero-mean proposal. In contrast, our QNHMC makes use of second-order information in scaling both momentum and position variables. Furthermore, HMC-BFGS devises an extended chain. The specially-designed structure may sacrifice the convergence rate and leads to a poor estimate of Hessian, validated by our empirical evaluations.

5 Empirical Evaluation

In this section, we empirically analyze the quasi-Newton HMC. We mainly compare our quasi-Newton HMC (QNHMC) with the standard HMC (Neal, 2011) and HMC-BFGS (Zhang and Sutton, 2011) in both efficiency and effectiveness. In all cases, QNHMC outperforms HMC and HMC-BFGS under the same settings of hyperparameters in both burn-in time and effective sample size.

5.1 Simulated data

First, we evaluate the scalability of our model on a high-dimensional zero-mean Gaussian distribution. The target distribution is high-dimensional Gaussian distribution $\mathcal{N}(\mathbf{0}, \mathbf{\Sigma})$. The covariance matrix is $\mathbf{\Sigma} = \mathbf{1}\mathbf{1}^T + 4\mathbf{I} \in \mathbb{R}^{d\times d}$, where $\mathbf{1}$ and $\mathbf{0}$ are the all-1 and all-0 vectors of d-dimension, respectively. This d-dimensional distribution is highly correlated in one direction. Hence, it is a challenging task for random-walk based sampler, such as MCMC.

The main evaluating metrics are as follows:

- Autocorrelation. Since the desired distribution is highly correlated, when computing the autocorrelation of samples, the samples are projected onto the direction of its largest eigenvalue ($\mathbf{x} = \mathbf{1}$). And the max number of lag m is set to 500. ρ_k is the autocorrelation at lag k.

- Effective sample size (ESS) is the common measurement, which summaries the amount of autocorrelation across different lags over all dimensions. ESS is formally defined as follows

$$\text{ESS} = \frac{n}{1 + 2\sum_{k=1}^{m} \rho_k},$$

  where n is the original sample size, m is the maximal number of lag and determined empirically. In this scenario, $m = 500$. Notice that ESS per second is also a metric to measure the efficiency of sampler.

- Convergence diagnostics. To compare the convergence rate fairly, we choose the starting position far away from the mode of the target distribution. Notice that the starting positions are same for all the samplers. Thus the chain should be run long enough to "forget" the starting position. This is the so-called burn-in period. Determining the length of burn-in period is critical. In this paper, we choose to monitor the probability of the samples, a mainstream method in convergence diagnostics (Gilks, Richardson, and Spiegelhalter, 1996). In particular, by observing the negative log-probability of samples $\mathbf{x}$ (i.e., $(\mathbf{x}-\mu)^T\mathbf{\Sigma}(\mathbf{x}-\mu)$, ignoring the normalizing constant), we can easily find that how long steps the chain takes to reach the highest posterior density (HPD) region and ends the burn-in period.

In this experiment, for fair comparison among these three methods, we adopt the same setting of the hyperparameters involved. In particular, we use the step size $\epsilon = 0.01$ and the number of leaps $L = 10$, the dimension of the problem $d = 100$. We draw 100K samples for each sampler. For HMC-BFGS, we need to choose an ensemble of K chains. If K is too large, there will be numerical unstability about the BFGS methods and the performance will degrade drastically. Here, K is chosen to be 5, following the setting of Zhang and Sutton (2011). The starting positions for these methods are the same, a randomly-generated point distant from the HPD region.

As illustrated in Figure 1, the chain of QNHMC only requires hundreds of samplings to end the burn-in period and reach the HPD region while the rest two algorithms need far more samplings. Hence, one advantage of QNHMC is that it can converge to the HDP region quicker than the other two algorithms.

Though QNHMC only requires hundreds of burn-in samples here, for fair comparison, when computing ESS and autocorrelation, we only use the last 50K samples for all the methods. The results are shown in Table 1. We observe that QNHMC can not only produce more "independent" series than the other methods, but also obtain the most effective sample size among the three methods under the same setting and draw samples from the desired distribution most efficiently.

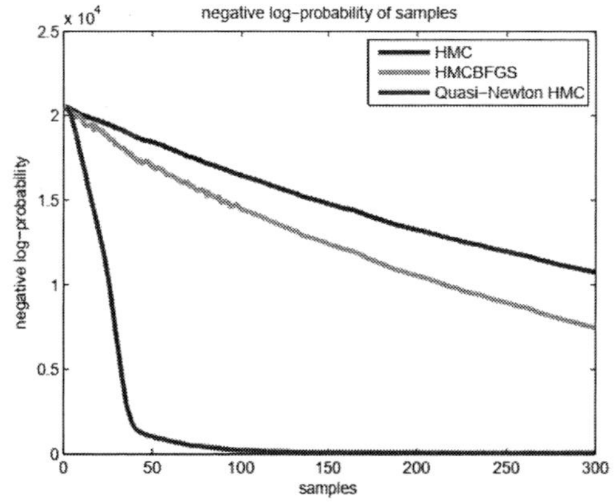

Figure 1: Performance of different samplers on simulated data: monitoring the convergence to HPD: negative log-probability of samples ($(\mathbf{x}-\mu)^T\mathbf{\Sigma}(\mathbf{x}-\mu)$) v.s. iteration

Table 1: Performance of different samplers on artificial data, as measured by sum of autocorrelation coefficient, burn-in time, Effective Sampler Size(ESS) and ESS per second. For the first two metric, lower is better while for the other two metric, higher is better.

Method	$\sum_{k=1}^{m} \|\rho_k\|$	burn-in time(second)	ESS	ESS per second
HMC	98.27	81	253	7.22
HMC-BFGS	49.74	47	497	9.65
QN-HMC	2.65	0.93	7936	93.36

Table 2: Performance of different methods on Bayesian Logistic Regression, as measured by sum of autocorrelation coefficient, burn-in time(in seconds) for sampling based methods, Effective Sampler Size(ESS) and ESS per second. GD is the abbreviation for gradient descent.

Method	burn-in time	ESS per second	Error
HMC	64	0.286	0.0493
HMC-BFGS	36	0.418	0.0501
QN-HMC	17	1.30	0.0496
GD	–	–	0.0578

5.2 Bayesian Logistic Regression

Next, we evaluate our method on a well-known handwritten digits classification task using the MNIST dataset[1]. In this task, we aim at discriminate digits "7" and "9". The number of training instances are 6265 and 5949 for "7" and "9", respectively while the number of test instances are 1028 and 1009 for "7" and "9", respectively.

We test four methods: gradient descent (GD), HMC, HMCBFGS and our QNHMC. For GD, we employ an ℓ_2 regularizer trial several time to choose the near-optimal hyperparameter. And in each iteration, we use all the training instances. For the sampling-based approaches, we take a fully Bayesian approach and place a weakly informative Gaussian prior on the weight, following Zhang and Sutton (2011); Girolami and Calderhead (2011).

The results for the sampling methods are shown in Table 2. The result with GD is provided as a baseline. We set the number of leapfrog L to 5 for all sampling based approaches. The step size ϵ is set to 0.1. Dimension $d = 784$ here, and L-BFGS method are used, where m is set to be 7. We can see that the Bayesian approaches are superior to the optimization based methods. Among the Bayesian approaches, QNHMC requires less burn-in time than the others and converges to a low test error faster. This shows its advantage over the other two HMC-related methods.

[1]http://yann.lecun.com/exdb/mnist/

5.3 Online Bayesian Matrix Factorization

Collaborative filtering is a popular theme. The target is to predict users' preference over a set of items, e.g., movies, music and produce recommendation. Owing to the sparsity in the ratings matrix (users versus items) in recommendation systems, over-fitting is a severe issue. Hence Bayesian approaches provide a natural solution. The most famous Bayesian algorithm for collaborative filtering is the online probabilistic matrix factorization proposed in Salakhutdinov and Mnih (2008).

In the experiment, the Root-Mean-Square Error (RMSE) is used to evaluate the performance of the three algorithms. It is defined as

$$\text{RMSE} = \|P_{\Omega_{\text{test}}}(\mathbf{X}) - P_{\Omega_{\text{test}}}(\mathbf{T})\|_F, \tag{8}$$

where Ω_{test} represents the index of all testing entries and $|\Omega_{test}|$ is the cardinality of Ω_{test}, and $\mathbf{X}$ is the solution from the algorithms and $P_{\Omega_{\text{test}}}(\mathbf{T})$ is corresponding partially observed labels, $\|\mathbf{X}\|_F$ represents the Frobenius norm of the matrix $\mathbf{X}$. $P_\Omega(\mathbf{X})$ represent the entry-wise projection of $\mathbf{X}$ onto Ω, defined by:

$$\{P_\Omega(\mathbf{X})\}_{ij} = \begin{cases} \mathbf{X}_{ij}, & (i,j) \in \Omega \\ 0, & \text{otherwise.} \end{cases}$$

We conduct the experiment in online Bayesian PMF on the Movielens-1M datasets[2]. The dataset contains about 1 million ratings of 3,952 movies by 6,040 users. The number of latent dimensions is set to 10. Other settings follow from the demo code given by Salakhutdinov and Mnih (2008). For HMC-related methods, step size ϵ is set to 0.01, length of leapfrog $L = 10$.

Performances of the different methods are shown in Table 3. The sampling-based methods (standard HMC, QNHMC and HMC-BFGS) provide better prediction results than the optimization-based methods (MAP), showing an advantage of Bayesian inference in this scenario, thus validating the need for scalable and efficient Bayesian algorithm such as QNHMC. In this experiment, prediction results for QNHMC, HMC and HMCBFGS are comparable. This experiment shows that QNHMC converges faster than the

[2]http://grouplens.org/datasets/movielens/

Table 3: Performance of different methods on Online Bayesian Matrix Factorization in terms of RMSE and running time. For RMSE, lower is better.

Method	RMSE	Running time(second)
MAP	0.8701	27.67
HMC	0.8607	202.5
QNHMC	0.8628	108.34
HMC-BFGS	0.8618	179.23

other two HMC-related approaches and can be seen as an effective choice for online Bayesian PMF.

6 Conclusion

In this paper we have proposed a novel quasi-Newton Hamiltonian Monte Carlo (QNHMC) algorithm to accelerate the Hamiltonian Monte Carlo sampler. Our theoretical analysis has guaranteed that the desired distribution is the unique stationary distribution under the proposed dynamics. The empirical results have verified the efficiency and effectiveness of our QNHMC on both simulated and practical datasets. A natural next step is to explore marrying stochastic gradient with QNHMC. More broadly, we believe that the unification of efficient optimization and sampling techniques, such as those described herein, will enable a significant scaling of Bayesian approaches.

Acknowledgements

This work has been supported by the National Natural Science Foundation of China (No. 61572017), Natural Science Foundation of Shanghai City (No. 15ZR1424200), and Microsoft Research Asia Collaborative Research Award.

Appendix

A: Proof of Theorem 1

Proof. Define

$$dz = d\begin{pmatrix} \theta \\ p \end{pmatrix} = \begin{pmatrix} M^{-1}p \\ -B\nabla U(\theta) \end{pmatrix} dt = G(z)dt \quad (9)$$

where $G(\cdot) : \mathbb{R}^{2d} \to \mathbb{R}^{2d}$ is a function and the i-th component of $G(\mathbf{z})$ is denoted by $G_i(\mathbf{z})$. According to the definition of FPE (Fokker-Planck Equation) (Kadanoff, 2000), the corresponding FPE is given by

$$\partial_t p_t(\boldsymbol{\theta}, \mathbf{p}) = \nabla^T[G(\mathbf{z})p_t(\boldsymbol{\theta}, \mathbf{p})] \quad (10)$$

The entropy at time t is defined by integrating out the joint variable $\mathbf{z}$, as follows:

$$h(p_t) = -\int_{\mathbf{z}} f(p_t(\mathbf{z}))d\mathbf{z} \quad (11)$$

The evolution of the entropy is governed by

$$\begin{aligned} \partial_t h(p_t(\mathbf{z})) &= -\partial_t \int_{\mathbf{z}} f(p_t(z))d\mathbf{z} \\ &= -\int_{\mathbf{z}} f'(p_t(\mathbf{z}))\partial_t p_t(\mathbf{z})d\mathbf{z} \\ &= -\int_{\mathbf{z}} f'(p_t(\mathbf{z}))\nabla^T[G(\mathbf{z})p_t(\mathbf{z})]d\mathbf{z} \\ &= -\int_{\mathbf{z}} f'(p_t(\mathbf{z}))\nabla^T[G(z)]p_t(\mathbf{z})d\mathbf{z} \\ &\quad -\int_{\mathbf{z}} f'(p_t(\mathbf{z}))(\nabla p_t(\mathbf{z}))^T[G(\mathbf{z})]d\mathbf{z} \end{aligned} \quad (12)$$

where the last equality uses the fact that

$$\begin{aligned} &\nabla^T[G(\mathbf{z})p_t(\boldsymbol{\theta}, \mathbf{p})] \\ &= p_t(\theta, \mathbf{p})\nabla^T[G(\mathbf{z})] + (\nabla p_t(\boldsymbol{\theta}, \mathbf{p}))^T[G(\mathbf{z})] \end{aligned} \quad (13)$$

The second term on the RHS of Equation 12 can be simplified into following form:

$$\begin{aligned} &-\int_{\mathbf{z}} f'(p_t(\mathbf{z}))(\nabla p_t(\mathbf{z}))^T[G(\mathbf{z})]d\mathbf{z} \\ &= -\int_{\mathbf{z}} (\nabla f(p_t(\mathbf{z})))^T[G(\mathbf{z})]d\mathbf{z} \\ &= \int_{\mathbf{z}} f(p_t(\mathbf{z}))\nabla^T[G(\mathbf{z})]d\mathbf{z} = 0 \end{aligned} \quad (14)$$

where the second equality is given by integrations by parts, using the fact that

$$\int_{\mathbf{z}} \nabla^T[f(p_t(\mathbf{z}))G(\mathbf{z})]d\mathbf{z} = 0 \quad (15)$$

which is based on the assumption that the probability density vanishes at infinity and $f(x) \to 0$ as $x \to 0$ such that $f(p_t(\mathbf{z}))[G(\mathbf{z})] \to 0$ as $\mathbf{z} \to \infty$.

Hence the entropy of p_t varies with rate of

$$\begin{aligned} \partial_t h(p_t(\mathbf{z})) &= -\int_{\mathbf{z}} f'(p_t(\mathbf{z}))\nabla^T[G(\mathbf{z})]p_t(\mathbf{z})d\mathbf{z} \\ &= -\int_{\mathbf{z}} f'(p_t(\mathbf{z}))(\mathbf{p}^T\mathbf{M}^{-T}(\mathbf{B}-\mathbf{I})\nabla U(\theta))p_t(\mathbf{z})d\mathbf{z} \end{aligned} \quad (16)$$

This is not equal to zero for $\mathbf{B}$ obviously. □

B: Proof of Theorem 3

Proof. Using FPE (Kadanoff, 2000), Eq. (7) can be written in the following decomposed form:

$$\begin{aligned} d\mathbf{z} &= d\begin{pmatrix} \boldsymbol{\theta} \\ \mathbf{p} \end{pmatrix} \\ &= \begin{pmatrix} \mathbf{0} & -\mathbf{C} \\ \mathbf{C} & \mathbf{0} \end{pmatrix}\begin{pmatrix} \nabla U(\boldsymbol{\theta}) \\ \mathbf{M}^{-1}\mathbf{p} \end{pmatrix} dt \\ &= \begin{pmatrix} -\mathbf{C}\mathbf{M}^{-1}\mathbf{p} \\ \mathbf{C}\nabla U(\boldsymbol{\theta}) \end{pmatrix} dt \\ &= \mathbf{F}(\mathbf{z})dt. \end{aligned} \quad (17)$$

The distribution evolution under this dynamical system is governed by a Fokker-Planck Equation as following:

$$\begin{aligned}
&\partial_t p_t(\mathbf{z}) \\
&= -\nabla^T[F(\mathbf{z})p_t(\mathbf{z})] \\
&= \sum_{i=1}^{2d} \partial_{\mathbf{z}_i}[\mathbf{F}_i(\mathbf{z})p_t(\mathbf{z})] \\
&= \sum_{i=1}^{d} \partial_{\theta_i}[\mathbf{f}_i(\mathbf{z})p(\mathbf{z})] + \sum_{j=1}^{d} \partial_{\mathbf{p}_j}[\mathbf{g}_j(\mathbf{z})p(\mathbf{z})] \\
&= \sum_{i=1}^{d}[\partial_{\theta_i}p(\mathbf{z})]\mathbf{f}_i(\mathbf{z}) + \sum_{j=1}^{d}[\partial_{\mathbf{p}_j}p(\mathbf{z})]\mathbf{g}_j(\mathbf{z}) \\
&= \sum_{i=1}^{d} p(\mathbf{z})[-\nabla U(\theta)]_i\mathbf{f}_i(\mathbf{z}) + \sum_{j=1}^{d} p(\mathbf{z})[\mathbf{M}^{-1}\mathbf{p}]_j\mathbf{g}_j(\mathbf{z}) \\
&= p(\mathbf{z})(\nabla U(\theta))^T(-\mathbf{CM}^{-1}\mathbf{p}) + p(\mathbf{z})(\mathbf{M}^{-1}\mathbf{p})^T(\mathbf{C}\nabla U(\theta)) \\
&= p(\mathbf{z})[(\nabla U(\theta))^T(-\mathbf{CM}^{-1}\mathbf{p}) + (\nabla U(\theta))^T\mathbf{C}^T(\mathbf{M}^{-1}\mathbf{p})] \\
&= 0
\end{aligned} \tag{18}$$

where $f(\cdot)$ and $g(\cdot)$ are functions defined as: $f(\cdot) : \mathbb{R}^{2d} \to \mathbb{R}^d$, $g(\cdot) : \mathbb{R}^{2d} \to \mathbb{R}^d$. $\mathbf{f}(\mathbf{z}) = \mathbf{f}(\mathbf{p}, \boldsymbol{\theta}) = -\mathbf{CM}^{-1}\mathbf{p}$ and $\mathbf{g}(\mathbf{z}) = \mathbf{g}(\mathbf{p}, \boldsymbol{\theta}) = C\nabla U(\boldsymbol{\theta})$. It satisfy that

$$F(\mathbf{z}) = \begin{pmatrix} -\mathbf{CM}^{-1}\mathbf{p} \\ \mathbf{C}\nabla U(\boldsymbol{\theta}) \end{pmatrix} = \begin{pmatrix} f(\mathbf{z}) \\ g(\mathbf{z}) \end{pmatrix} \tag{19}$$

$\mathbf{f}_i(\mathbf{z})$ and $\mathbf{g}_j(\mathbf{z})$ are the i-th entry and j-th entry of $\mathbf{f}(\mathbf{z})$ and $\mathbf{g}(\mathbf{z})$ respectively.

The fourth equality follows from the fact that function $f(\mathbf{z})$ only depend on $\mathbf{p}$ while function $g(\mathbf{z})$ only depend on $\boldsymbol{\theta}$. Hence, following happens.

$$\begin{aligned}
\partial_{\boldsymbol{\theta}_i} f_i &= 0 \\
\partial_{\mathbf{p}_i} g_i &= 0
\end{aligned} \tag{20}$$

Since $p(\mathbf{z}) = \pi(\boldsymbol{\theta}, \mathbf{p}) = \exp(-U(\boldsymbol{\theta}) - 1/2\mathbf{p}^T\mathbf{M}^{-1}\mathbf{p})$, we expand the partial derivation as following:

$$\begin{aligned}
\partial_{\boldsymbol{\theta}_i} p(\mathbf{z}) &= p(\mathbf{z})[-\nabla U(\boldsymbol{\theta})]_i \\
\partial_{\mathbf{p}_i} p(\mathbf{z}) &= p(\mathbf{z})[\mathbf{M}^{-1}\mathbf{p}]_i
\end{aligned} \tag{21}$$

Hence the fifth equality satisfies.

The last equality is given by the fact that $\mathbf{C}$ is symmetric, i.e., $\mathbf{C}^T = \mathbf{C}$. By calculating $\partial_t p_t(\mathbf{z}) = 0$, we show that the distribution p_t does not vary with time, i.e., $p(\mathbf{z}) = \pi(\boldsymbol{\theta}, \mathbf{p})$ is invariant under the dynamics described in Equation 7. □

C: Proof of Corollary 2

Proof. With the entropy defined in Eq. (11) and compact form of dynamics defined in Eq. (17), The evolution of the entropy is governed by

$$\begin{aligned}
\partial_t h(p_t(\mathbf{z})) &= \partial_t \int_{\mathbf{z}} f(p_t(\mathbf{z}))d\mathbf{z} \\
&= -\int_{\mathbf{z}} f'(p_t(\mathbf{z}))\partial_t p_t(\mathbf{z})d\mathbf{z} \\
&= -\int_{\mathbf{z}} f'(p_t(\mathbf{z}))\nabla^T[F(\mathbf{z})p_t(\mathbf{z})]d\mathbf{z} \\
&= 0,
\end{aligned} \tag{22}$$

where the first two equalities can be referred from part of Eq. (12) and the last equality follows from the conclusion in Eq. (18). □

D: Proof of Theorem 4

The idea behind the correctness of Algorithm 2 is that Theorem 3 guarantees the detailed balance condition for any neighboring samples (e.g., $\boldsymbol{\theta}_{i-1}$ and $\boldsymbol{\theta}_i$) while Theorem 4 strengthen this results on the whole chain.

Proof. Firstly, we define $\{\boldsymbol{\theta}_i\}_{i=1}^n$, the chain generated by Algorithm 2. At i-th iteration, $\mathbf{B}$ is denoted by $\mathbf{B}_i$. For every i, the approximation to inverse Hessian $\mathbf{B}_i$ is symmetric positive definite (Nocedal and Wright, 2006). As seen from Algorithm 2, in i-th proposal (Step 3-15), $\mathbf{B}_i$ is fixed. Moreover, according to Theorem 3 and ϵ-discretization, we obtain that the detailed balance condition hold for any neighboring samples $\boldsymbol{\theta}_{i-1}$ and $\boldsymbol{\theta}_i$, i.e.,

$$\pi(\boldsymbol{\theta}_{i-1})\mathcal{T}_i(\boldsymbol{\theta}_{i-1} \to \boldsymbol{\theta}_i) = \pi(\boldsymbol{\theta}_i)\mathcal{T}_i(\boldsymbol{\theta}_i \to \boldsymbol{\theta}_{i-1}) \tag{23}$$

where $\mathcal{T}_i(\cdot \to \cdot)$ is the transition kernel at i-th proposal.

Integrating out $\boldsymbol{\theta}_{i-1}$ on both sides, we obtain that

$$\begin{aligned}
\pi(\boldsymbol{\theta}_i) &= \int \pi(\boldsymbol{\theta}_i)\mathcal{T}_i(\boldsymbol{\theta}_i \to \boldsymbol{\theta}_{i-1})d\boldsymbol{\theta}_{i-1} \\
&= \int \pi(\boldsymbol{\theta}_{i-1})\mathcal{T}_i(\boldsymbol{\theta}_{i-1} \to \boldsymbol{\theta}_i)d\boldsymbol{\theta}_{i-1}
\end{aligned} \tag{24}$$

That is, distribution π is a stationary distribution with a single transition kernel $\mathcal{T}_i$, i.e.,

$$\mathcal{T}_i(\pi) = \pi \tag{25}$$

holds for every i.

Thus,

$$\mathcal{T}_n\mathcal{T}_{n-1}...\mathcal{T}_1(\pi) = \pi \tag{26}$$

Proved. □

References

Ahn, S.; Korattikara, A.; and Welling, M. 2012. Bayesian posterior sampling via stochastic gradient fisher scoring. *arXiv preprint arXiv:1206.6380.*

Ahn, S.; Shahbaba, B.; and Welling, M. 2014. Distributed stochastic gradient mcmc. In *Proceedings of the 31st International Conference on Machine Learning (ICML-14)*, 1044–1052.

Bardenet, R.; Doucet, A.; and Holmes, C. 2014. Towards scaling up markov chain monte carlo: an adaptive subsampling approach. In *Proceedings of the 31st International Conference on Machine Learning (ICML-14)*, 405–413.

Calderhead, B., and Sustik, M. A. 2012. Sparse approximate manifolds for differential geometric mcmc. In *Advances in Neural Information Processing Systems*, 2879–2887.

Chao, W.-L.; Solomon, J.; Michels, D. L.; and Sha, F. 2015. Exponential integration for hamiltonian monte carlo. In *Proceedings of the 32nd International Conference on Machine Learning (ICML-15)*, 1142–01151.

Chen, T.; Fox, E. B.; and Guestrin, C. 2014. Stochastic gradient hamiltonian monte carlo. *arXiv preprint arXiv:1402.4102*.

Ding, N.; Fang, Y.; Babbush, R.; Chen, C.; Skeel, R. D.; and Neven, H. 2014. Bayesian sampling using stochastic gradient thermostats. In *Advances in Neural Information Processing Systems*, 3203–3211.

Gilks, W. R.; Richardson, S.; and Spiegelhalter, D. J. 1996. Introducing markov chain monte carlo. *Markov chain Monte Carlo in practice* 1:19.

Girolami, M., and Calderhead, B. 2011. Riemann manifold langevin and hamiltonian monte carlo methods. *Journal of the Royal Statistical Society: Series B (Statistical Methodology)* 73(2):123–214.

Kadanoff, L. P. 2000. *Statistical physics: statics, dynamics and renormalization*. World Scientific.

Korattikara, A.; Chen, Y.; and Welling, M. 2013. Austerity in mcmc land: Cutting the metropolis-hastings budget. *arXiv preprint arXiv:1304.5299*.

Leimkuhler, B., and Reich, S. 2004. *Simulating hamiltonian dynamics*, volume 14. Cambridge University Press.

Ma, Y.-A.; Chen, T.; and Fox, E. 2015. A complete recipe for stochastic gradient mcmc. In *Advances in Neural Information Processing Systems*.

Maclaurin, D., and Adams, R. P. 2015. Firefly monte carlo: Exact mcmc with subsets of data. In *Proceedings of the 24th International Conference on Artificial Intelligence*, 4289–4295. AAAI Press.

Neal, R. M. 2011. Mcmc using hamiltonian dynamics. *Handbook of Markov Chain Monte Carlo* 2.

Nocedal, J., and Wright, S. 2006. *Numerical optimization*. Springer Science & Business Media.

Patterson, S., and Teh, Y. W. 2013. Stochastic gradient riemannian langevin dynamics on the probability simplex. In *Advances in Neural Information Processing Systems*, 3102–3110.

Qian, H. 2012. A hamiltonian-entropy production connection in the skew-symmetric part of a stochastic dynamics. *arXiv preprint arXiv:1205.6552*.

Salakhutdinov, R., and Mnih, A. 2008. Bayesian probabilistic matrix factorization using mcmc. *ICML08*.

Wang, Z.; Mohamed, S.; and Nando, D. 2013. Adaptive hamiltonian and riemann manifold monte carlo. In *Proceedings of the 30th International Conference on Machine Learning (ICML-13)*, 1462–1470.

Welling, M., and Teh, Y. W. 2011. Bayesian learning via stochastic gradient langevin dynamics. In *Proceedings of the 28th International Conference on Machine Learning (ICML-11)*, 681–688.

Zhang, Y., and Sutton, C. A. 2011. Quasi-newton methods for markov chain monte carlo. In *Advances in Neural Information Processing Systems*, 2393–2401.

Scalable Joint Modeling of Longitudinal and Point Process Data for Disease Trajectory Prediction and Improving Management of Chronic Kidney Disease

Joseph Futoma
Dept. of Statistical Science
Duke University
Durham, NC 27707

Mark Sendak
Institute for Health Innovation
School of Medicine
Duke University
Durham, NC 27707

C. Blake Cameron
Division of Nephrology
Duke University
Durham, NC 27707

Katherine Heller
Dept. of Statistical Science
Duke University
Durham, NC 27707

Abstract

A major goal in personalized medicine is the ability to provide individualized predictions about the future trajectory of a disease. Moreover, for many complex chronic diseases, patients simultaneously have additional comorbid conditions. Accurate determination of the risk of developing serious complications associated with a disease or its comorbidities may be more clinically useful than prediction of future disease trajectory in such cases. We propose a novel probabilistic generative model that can provide individualized predictions of future disease progression while jointly modeling the pattern of related recurrent adverse events. We fit our model using a scalable variational inference algorithm and apply our method to a large dataset of longitudinal electronic patient health records. Our model gives superior performance in terms of both prediction of future disease trajectories and of future serious events when compared to non-joint models. Our predictions are currently being utilized by our local accountable care organization during chart reviews of high risk patients.

1 INTRODUCTION

With the dawn of precision medicine and accountable care, it will become increasingly important for healthcare organizations to make accurate predictions about individual patients' future health risks to improve quality and contain costs. Accountable care organizations (ACOs) are organizations that bear financial responsibility for the quality and total cost of healthcare services provided to a defined population of patients. In order to deliver the right care at the right time in the right setting, ACOs need personalized prediction tools that identify individual patients in their populations at greatest risk of having poor clinical outcomes [Parikh et al., 2016, Bates et al., 2014]. Most ACOs currently lack these capabilities.[1] With the widespread adoption of electronic health records (EHRs), much of the data necessary to build such tools are already being collected during the course of routine medical care. In order to be clinically useful, such tools should be flexible enough (1) to accommodate the limitations inherent to operational EHR data [Hersh et al., 2014]; (2) to update predictions dynamically as new information becomes available; and (3) to scale to the massive size of modern health records.

We collaborated with Duke Connected Care, the ACO affiliated with the Duke University Health System, to develop predictive tools for chronic kidney disease (CKD). CKD is characterized by a gradual and generally symptomless loss of kidney function over time. CKD and its complications cause poor health, premature death, increased health service utilization, and excess economic costs. CKD is defined and staged by the degree to which a person's estimated glomerular filtration rate (eGFR) is impaired. eGFR is an approximation of overall kidney function and is calculated using a routinely obtained clinical laboratory test (serum creatinine) and demographic information (age, sex and race) [Levey et al., 2009; KDIGO, 2013]. Most clinical laboratories report eGFR automatically with every serum creatinine measurement.

Healthcare providers struggle at many levels to provide optimal care for patients with CKD. First, the majority of healthcare providers fail to recognize the presence of CKD, despite the fact that CKD can be readily identified using simple, eGFR-based laboratory criteria [Szcech et al., 2013; Tuot et al., 2011; Allen et al., 2011]. Second, among those patients with recognized CKD, both primary care providers and kidney specialists struggle to predict which patients will progress to kidney failure (requiring dialysis or kidney transplantation to survive) or suffer from other complications caused by CKD, such as early death from heart attack or stroke [Mendehlsson et al., 2011]. Third, providers often fail to prescribe appropriate preventive treatment to slow disease progression or address com-

[1] http://www.healthcare-informatics.com/article/survey-acos-still-cite-lack-interoperability-biggest-barrier

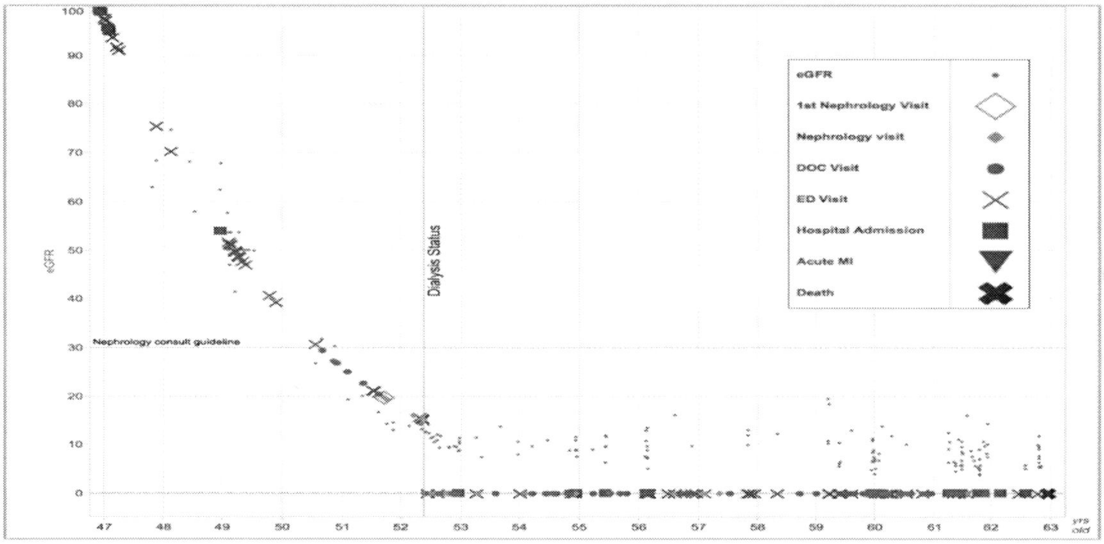

Figure 1: 15-year clinical course of an example patient who experienced both a rapid progression of CKD and a number of other serious health events. Y-axis indicates estimated glomerular filtration rate (eGFR), an estimate of overall kidney function (60-100 is normal, <60 indicates clinically significant kidney disease). X-axis indicates patient age in years. Markers indicate health service use and adverse events. Our model allows us to jointly model progression of CKD, as well as the association between the disease progression and risk for adverse events.

plications [Smart et al., 2014]. Medications such as RAAS drugs can slow progression of CKD if used early enough, while patient counseling and advanced planning can reduce the physical and psychological trauma when kidney failure is imminent.

From a population health management perspective, these characteristics make CKD an ideal condition to model and to develop high-impact care management programs. The challenges surrounding CKD care are best articulated with a representative clinical case, illustrated in Figure 1. A 47 year-old man makes first contact with our health system for emergency treatment of a stroke. His kidney function at this point is normal, although he possesses several risk factors for future CKD. Over the next 5 years, he receives sufficient medical care to detect that his kidney function is deteriorating rapidly (the normal annual rate of kidney function loss at his age is only about 1-2%). His kidney disease goes unnoticed by his healthcare providers, and he does not receive any treatment aimed at slowing progression to total kidney failure. At age 52, he is eventually referred to a kidney specialist, more than a year after his kidney function has fallen below the recommended threshold for such a referral. By this point, kidney failure is inevitable and there is too little time to make advanced preparations for kidney failure, such as pre-emptive kidney transplantation or at-home dialysis. Within 90 days of that first kidney specialist appointment, he develops symptoms of kidney failure and requires hospitalization for emergency dialysis initiation, which is both extremely traumatic and makes him among the most expensive type of patient to treat [Johnson et al., 2015]. He survives on dialysis for about a decade, suffering multiple cardiovascular complications from kidney failure, and ultimately dies at age 63. This patient's story is one of missed opportunities–opportunities that could have been acted upon with accurate predictions using machine learning methods and care management programs.

Our goal is to develop statistical methods that model both the risks of future loss of kidney function and the risks of future complications or adverse health events. The predictions from these models can then be used by healthcare organizations to connect high-risk patients to appropriately targeted interventions. Since the broad aim is to predict which patients will worsen in the near future, we need to model associations between CKD and the multitude of various health outcomes that could occur. CKD frequently coexists with and contributes to cardiovascular disease. In fact, most patients with advanced CKD pass away from cardiovascular complications before the onset of kidney failure. In this article, we choose to focus on two common types of adverse cardiovascular events: heart attacks (acute myocardial infarctions [AMIs]) and strokes (cerebrovascular accidents [CVAs]).

To this end, we develop a joint model that flexibly captures the eGFR trajectory of CKD progression, while simultaneously learning the association between disease trajectory and cardiovascular events. We formulate our approach as a hierarchical latent variable model. Each patient is represented by a set of latent variables characterizing both their disease trajectory and risk of having events. This approach captures dependencies between the disease trajectory and event risk.

Using our model, we study a large cohort of patients with CKD from the Duke University Health System and make predictions about the trajectory of their disease, as well as their risk of cardiovascular events. Our inference algorithm scales well to the large dataset, and makes accurate predictions that outperform several baselines.

2 PROPOSED JOINT MODEL FOR ELECTRONIC HEALTH RECORDS

In this section, we first describe the structure of electronic health records before introducing our proposed joint model for longitudinal and point process data.

Electronic Health Records

The Duke University Health System's electronic health record (Epic Systems, Madison, WI) stores nearly all available information captured about patients during their encounters within the health system. The EHR contains a large quantity of longitudinal patient data. The vast majority of the data are unstructured, contained within free-text notes and reports. Structured data include demographics, diagnosis and procedural codes, orders, laboratory results, and objective clinical observations (such as vital signs and various nursing assessments). Of particular interest to our work in modeling CKD patients are structured diagnosis codes and laboratory results.

The EHR stores granular information about medical diagnoses using structured, hierarchical codes conforming to ICD-9 (International Classification of Disease, 9th revision), a standardized taxonomy that is used principally for medical billing. For each medical encounter (such as a clinic or emergency department visit), a set of codes is assigned to document the primary problems or diseases that were addressed. In total, there are about 9,000 unique ICD-9 codes. Each clinical diagnosis may have multiple corresponding ICD-9 diagnosis codes. The Agency for Healthcare Research and Quality publishes the Clinical Classifications Software[2], a categorization tool that collapses the thousands of original codes into a few hundred clinically meaningful concepts. We use this mechanism to identify and aggregate codes for CVAs and AMIs, where we use the mean date among all relevant codes within monthly bins to account for multiple codes in a short time period that refer to the same clinical event.

In contrast to diagnosis codes, which capture clinicians' subjective diagnostic impressions, laboratory tests provide objective clinical data. A single medical encounter may include dozens, hundreds or (in the case of hospitalizations) thousands of discrete laboratory test results. Identifying and grouping relevant laboratory test results can be difficult due to lack of standardization and changing conventions over time. For example, serum creatinine, which is a lab test used to calculate eGFR, has more than 18 different names in our EHR that refer to the same value (e.g. "CREA", "Creatinine", "DUAP CREA"). Harmonizing and grouping these lab results required an exhaustive review of laboratory metadata by a subject matter expert.

There are numerous ongoing efforts to develop improved algorithms to identify chronic medical conditions and incident clinical events using a wide assortment of clinical data. Our model is agnostic to the particular algorithm used to identify clinical events. After cleaning and transforming the raw EHR data, we obtained a longitudinal set of eGFRs for each patient, and dates of CVA and AMI diagnoses.

[2]http://www.hcup-us.ahrq.gov/toolssoftware/ccs/ccs.jsp

Proposed Model

Our proposed hierarchical latent variable model jointly models longitudinal and point process data by creating different submodels for each type of data, with shared latent variables for each patient inducing dependencies between their two data types. Assume there are N patients, let $\vec{y_i} = \{y_{ij}\}_{j=1}^{N_i}$ denote the N_i observed readings of eGFR for patient i at times $\vec{t_i} = \{t_{ij}\}_{j=1}^{N_i}$, and let $\vec{u_i} = \{u_{ik}\}_{k=1}^{K_i}$ denote the K_i cardiac events patient i experiences (note that K_i may be 0). Let T_i^- be the time patient i is first seen in our sample of their health record, and T_i^+ the final time they are observed. Let z_i, b_i, f_i and v_i be a set of shared hierarchical latent variables for each patient i, to be defined subsequently. Conditioned on these latent variables, to be learned during inference, we make a common conditional independence assumption that the conditional likelihood for patient i factorizes:

$$p(\vec{y_i}, \vec{u_i}|z_i, b_i, f_i, v_i; x_i) = p(\vec{y_i}|z_i, b_i, f_i; x_i) \\ p(\vec{u_i}|z_i, b_i, f_i, v_i; x_i). \tag{1}$$

Longitudinal Submodel

We use a recently proposed model for disease trajectories for our longitudinal submodel [Schulam and Saria, 2015], that was shown to be extremely flexible and accurate at modeling continuous functions of disease progression. Given the set of latent variables for patient i, the longitudinal variables are conditionally independent, i.e. $p(\vec{y_i}|z_i, b_i, f_i) = \prod_{j=1}^{N_i} p(y_{ij}|z_i, b_i, f_i)$. The model assumes each observed longitudinal value is a normally distributed random variable containing a population component, a subpopulation component, an individual component, and a structured noise component:

$$y_i(t) = m_i(t) + \epsilon_i(t),\ \epsilon_i(t) \overset{iid}{\sim} N(0, \sigma_\epsilon^2) \tag{2}$$

$$m_i(t) = \Phi_p(t)^\top \Lambda x_{ip} + \Phi_z(t)^\top \beta_{z_i} + \Phi_l(t)^\top b_i + f_i(t). \tag{3}$$

The first term in (3) is the population component, where $\Phi_p(t) \in \mathbb{R}^{d_p}$ is a fixed basis expansion of time, $\Lambda \in \mathbb{R}^{d_p \times q_p}$ is a coefficient matrix, and $x_{ip} \in \mathbb{R}^{q_p}$ is a vector of baseline covariates.

The second term in (3) is the subpopulation component, where it is assumed person i belongs to latent subpopulation $z_i \in \{1, \ldots, G\}$. Each subpopulation is associated with a unique disease trajectory represented using B-splines, in particular, $\Phi_z(t) \in \mathbb{R}^{d_z}$ is a fixed B-spline basis expansion of time with $\beta_g \in \mathbb{R}^{d_z}$ the coefficient vector for group g. We assign z_i a multinomial logistic regression prior that depends on baseline covariates $x_{iz} \in \mathbb{R}^{q_z}$: $p(z_i = g) \propto \exp\{w_g^\top x_{iz}\}$, where $\{w_g\}_{g=1}^G$ are regression coefficients with $w_1 \equiv 0$ for identifiability.

The third term is the individual component, allowing for individual-specific long-term deviations in trajectory that are learned dynamically as more data is available. $\Phi_l(t) \in \mathbb{R}^{d_l}$ is a fixed basis expansion of time, and $b_i \in \mathbb{R}^{d_l}$ is a random effect for patient i, with prior $b_i \sim N(0, \Sigma_b)$.

Finally, $f_i(t)$ is the structured noise process that captures transient trends in disease trajectory. This is modeled using a zero-mean Gaussian process with Ornstein-Uhlenbeck covariance function $K_{OU}(t_1, t_2) = \sigma_f^2 \exp\{-\frac{|t_1 - t_2|}{l}\}$. This kernel is well-suited for this task, as it is mean-reverting and has no long-range dependence between deviations [Schulam and Saria, 2015].

Point Process Submodel

We choose to model the times $\vec{u_i} = \{u_{ik}\}_{k=1}^{K_i}$ that a person has an adverse event as a Poisson process. A common choice for the rate function from related literature in survival analysis corresponds to the hazard function from the Cox proportional hazards model. We make this choice in this work, for reasons both of simplicity and also computational efficiency as we discuss later. The conditional likelihood for the Poisson process for patient i on the interval $[T_i^-, T_i^+]$, with events at times $\{u_{ik}\}_{k=1}^{K_i}$, is given by:

$$p(\vec{u_i} | z_i, b_i, f_i, v_i) = \prod_{k=1}^{K_i} r_i(u_{ik}) \exp\{-\int_{T_i^-}^{T_i^+} r_i(t) dt\}, \tag{4}$$

where we specify the rate function for patient i as:

$$r_i(t) = r_0(t) \exp\{\gamma^\top x_{ir} + \alpha m_i(t) + \delta m_i'(t) + v_i\}. \tag{5}$$

We assume that $r_0(t)$ is a piecewise constant function with jumps at fixed quantiles of the event times, and heights $\{a_l\}_{l=1}^{N_r}$. The parameter $\gamma \in \mathbb{R}^{q_r}$ specifies the association between baseline covariates $x_{ir} \in \mathbb{R}^{q_r}$ and the risk for an event, while parameters α and δ specify the association between the risk for an event and the expected mean and expected slope of the longitudinal variable at that time, respectively.[3] Finally, the latent variable v_i, with prior $v_i \sim N(0, \sigma_v^2)$, represents an additional random effect (called a frailty term in survival analysis), multiplicatively adjusting an individual's overall risk for events. In order to compute the likelihood, we must compute the definite integral in (4) numerically. We find that the trapezoid rule works fine, although other options such as Gaussian quadrature are also possible.

3 RELATED WORK

There is a rich literature, mostly from biostatistics, on joint models typically for longitudinal data and time-to-event data with right censoring. See [Rizopoulos, 2012] for a thorough introduction to these types of joint models. A slightly different flavor of joint models is presented in [Proust-Lima et al., 2014]. These models differ in that instead of the longitudinal value directly influencing the event rate, they consider latent subpopulations of individuals within which it is assumed there is a different average profile of both the longitudinal value and risk of the event.

Most directly relevant to our work are several methods for modeling longitudinal data and recurrent event data [Liu and Huang, 2009; Kim et al., 2012; Han et al., 2007]. However, these methods share several notable weaknesses. First, the form for their longitudinal models are simplistic, all being mixed effects models. Such models are inflexible and will fail to capture the types of trajectories that our model can, through its mixture model and both long and short-term individual-specific deviations. In addition, these works as well as most of the literature on joint models rely on computationally expensive inference algorithms, thereby limiting their use to small datasets. Typically EM or gradient methods are employed for Maximum Likelihood Estimation, or MCMC in Bayesian settings. It is extremely uncommon to find a published joint model applied to a dataset of over 1000 individuals. However, our scalable variational inference algorithm, developed in the next section, is much more efficient, facilitating use in large-scale applications where there can be tens or even hundreds of thousands of patients.

Within the medical literature, there have been numerous studies on predicting adverse events such as kidney failure, death, or cardiac events in patients with CKD; for instance, [Tangri et al., 2011] is a common reference. In almost every case, the models developed are Cox proportional hazards models for time-to-event data, or logistic regression models for occurrence of an event in a specified time window. As such, these models are all static and use only a single snapshot of patient data to make predictions, which precludes the ability to generate dynamic predictions.

[3] Since $f_i(t)$ with an OU kernel is not differentiable, we let $m_i'(t)$ be the sum of the slopes of the first three terms in (3).

In recent years there has been much interest in machine learning in modeling electronic health records and other forms of healthcare data. For instance, [Lian et al., 2015] use hierarchical point processes to predict hospital admissions, and [Ranganath et al., 2015] develop a dynamic factor model to learn relationships between diseases and predict future diagnosis codes. Closest to our work in the application is [Perotte et al., 2015], who explore using time-series models to predict a time-to-event (progression from CKD stage 3 to stage 4) in CKD patients.

4 INFERENCE

As with most complex probabilistic generative models, the computational problem associated with fitting the model is estimation of the posterior distribution of latent variables and model parameters given the observed data. Exact computation of the posterior is intractable, and requires approximation to compute. To this end, we develop a mean field variational inference [Jordan et al., 1999] algorithm to approximate the posterior distribution of interest.

Variational methods transform the task of posterior inference into an optimization problem. The optimization problem posed by variational inference is to find a distribution q in some approximating family of distributions that is close in KL divergence to the true posterior. Equivalently, the problem can be viewed as maximizing what is known as the evidence lower bound (ELBO) [Bishop, 2006]:

$$\mathcal{L}(q) = E_q[\log p(y, u, z, b, f, v, \Theta) - \log q(z, b, f, v, \Theta)], \tag{6}$$

which forms a lower bound on the marginal likelihood $p(y, u)$ of our model.

Variational Approximation

Recall for our model that the model parameters are $\Theta = \{\Lambda, W, \beta, a, \gamma, \alpha, \delta\}$, and the local latent variables specific to each person are their subpopulation assignment z_i, random effects b_i and v_i, and structured noise function f_i. The joint distribution for our model can be expressed as:

$$p(y, u, z, b, f, v, \Theta) = p(\Theta) \prod_{i=1}^{N} \prod_{j=i}^{N_i} p(y_{ij} | z_i, b_i, f_i(t_{ij}), \Theta)$$
$$p(\vec{u_i} | z_i, b_i, f_i, v_i, \Theta) p(z_i) p(b_i) p(f_i) p(v_i) \tag{7}$$

We make the mean field assumption for the variational distribution, which assumes that in the approximate posterior q, all the latent variables are independent. This implies that $q(z, b, f, v, \Theta) = q(\Theta) \prod_{i=1}^{N} q_i(z_i, b_i, f_i, v_i)$, where:

$$q_i(z_i, b_i, f_i, v_i) = q_i(z_i | \nu_{z_i}) q_i(b_i | \mu_{b_i}, \Sigma_{b_i})$$
$$q_i(v_i | \mu_{v_i}, \sigma^2_{v_i}) q_i(f_i). \tag{8}$$

The assumed variational distributions for z_i, b_i, and v_i are the same family as their prior distribution, i.e. multinomial, multivariate normal, and univariate normal. For the variational form for f_i, we adapt ideas from the variational learning for sparse GPs literature [Lloyd et al., 2014; Titsias, 2009] to approximate the true posterior over f_i. In order to evaluate the ELBO in (6), we will need to evaluate $E_{q_i}[f_i]$ at times $\vec{t_i}$ for the longitudinal likelihood, as well as at $\vec{u_i}$ and at a grid of times t_i^{grid} for the point process likelihood (the grid is for the numerical integration). We choose to treat the observed observation times $\vec{t_i}$ as pseudo-inputs; this helps reduce overfitting and reduces the number of variational parameters to learn. In particular:

$$q_i(f_i(\vec{t_i}), f_i(\vec{u_i}), f_i(t_i^{\text{grid}})) = p(f_i(\vec{u_i}), f_i(t_i^{\text{grid}}) | f_i(\vec{t_i}))$$
$$q(f_i(\vec{t_i}) | \mu_{f_i}, \Sigma_{f_i}). \tag{9}$$

We allow a free-form multivariate Gaussian distribution for f_i at the longitudinal observation times, and use a so-called conditional Gaussian process for the distribution at $\vec{u_i}$, t_i^{grid}, i.e. the true conditional distribution of the joint multivariate normal, $f_i | f_i(\vec{t_i}) \sim \mathcal{GP}(\mu(t), \Sigma(t, t'))$:

$$\mu(t) = K_{t, \vec{t_i}} K^{-1}_{\vec{t_i}, \vec{t_i}} f_i(\vec{t_i}) \tag{10}$$

$$\Sigma(t, t') = K_{t,t'} - K_{t, \vec{t_i}} K^{-1}_{\vec{t_i}, \vec{t_i}} K_{\vec{t_i}, t'} \tag{11}$$

where $K_{t, \vec{t_i}}, K_{\vec{t_i}, \vec{t_i}}, K_{t,t'}$ are matrices evaluated at t, t', and $\vec{t_i}$ using the OU covariance kernel from Section 2.

Although priors on the model parameters Θ may be imposed, i.e. log-normal on a and normal on the rest, in our work we learn their maximum likelihood estimate (MLE) instead, and let $q(\Theta)$ be a delta function. Thus, the goal of our variational algorithm is to learn optimal variational parameters $\lambda_i = \{\nu_{z_i}, \mu_{b_i}, \Sigma_{b_i}, \mu_{v_i}, \sigma^2_{v_i}, \mu_{f_i}, \Sigma_{f_i}\}$ for each individual i, as well as a point estimate $\hat{\Theta}$ for the model parameters. In practice, we optimize the Cholesky decompositions L_{b_i}, L_{f_i} for the covariance matrices $\Sigma_{b_i}, \Sigma_{f_i}$.

Solving the Optimization Problem

In traditional settings for variational inference, the objective function is iteratively optimized by maximizing the variational parameters associated with each latent variable or parameter, holding the rest fixed. In models where the log complete conditional distributions (log of the conditional distribution of each latent variable given everything else) have analytic expectations with respect to the variational approximation, closed form EM-style updates are available for the variational parameters. This convenient property is typically observed in conditionally conjugate models, where each log complete conditional will be in the exponential family [Ghahramani and Beal, 2001].

Recently there has been much interest in applying variational methods to more complex models that do not exhibit conjugacy. In many cases, it is intractable to even evaluate the ELBO analytically, since one or both of the expectations in (6) have no closed form. In these cases, variational algorithms have been developed that rely on sampling from the variational approximation [Ranganath et al.,2014; Rezende et al., 2014]. However, because of the form we chose for r_i, it is possible to calculate a closed form approximation to the ELBO for our model (approximate due to the numerical integration; see Appendix for details). As such, we use the automatic differentiation package *autograd* [4] in Python to compute analytic gradients in order to optimize the bound. At each iteration of the algorithm, we optimize the local variational parameters in parallel using exact gradients. To optimize the global parameters, we turn to stochastic optimization.

Stochastic optimization has become a commonly used tool in variational inference. Rather than using every single observation to compute the gradient of the ELBO with respect to Θ, we can compute a noisy gradient based on a sampled batch of observations [Hoffman et al., 2013]. As long as the noisy gradient is unbiased and the learning rate ρ_t at each iteration satisfies the Robbins Monro conditions ($\sum_{t=1}^{\infty} \rho_t = \infty$, $\sum_{t=1}^{\infty} \rho_t^2 < \infty$), the stochastic optimization procedure will converge to a local maximum. To set the learning rate we use the AdaGrad algorithm, which adaptively allows for a different learning rate for each parameter. The learning rate for each parameter is scaled by the square root of a running sum of the squares of historical gradients [Duchi et al., 2011].

Algorithm

Algorithm 1 summarizes the procedure to learn an approximate posterior for the local latent variables and a point estimate for the model parameters.

Data: data y, u; hyperparameters.
Result: point estimate $\hat{\Theta}$, approximate posteriors q_i.
Initialize global parameters Θ.
repeat
  Randomly sample data for S patients, $\{y_s, u_s\}_{s=1}^{S}$.
  for *s = 1:S in parallel* **do**
    Optimize local variational parameters for q_s via gradient ascent.
  end
  Compute the noisy gradient for Θ.
  Update Θ using AdaGrad.
until *convergence of the ELBO*;

Algorithm 1: Stochastic Variational Inference algorithm for our Joint Model.

[4]https://github.com/HIPS/autograd

5 EMPIRICAL STUDY

In this section we describe our experimental setup and results on our real dataset.

Dataset

Our dataset comprises longitudinal and cardiac event data from 23,450 patients with stage 3 CKD or higher within our university health system. IRB approval (#Pro00066690) was obtained for this work. We first created an initial cohort of roughly 600,000 patients that had at least one encounter in the health system in the year prior to Feb. 1, 2015. This includes all types of encounters within the health system, including inpatient, outpatient, and emergency department visits. From this, we filtered to patients who had at least ten recorded values for serum creatinine, the laboratory value required to calculate eGFR. We next filtered to patients that had Stage 3 CKD or higher, indicative of moderate to severe kidney damage, defined as two eGFR measurements less than 60 mL/min separated by at least 90 days. Finally, since the recorded eGFR values are extremely noisy and eGFR is only a valid estimate of kidney function at steady state, we take the mean of eGFR readings in monthly time bins for each patient. Rapid fluctuations in acute illness are related to long term risk, but we have not yet explicitly incorporated this into our modeling.

After this preprocessing, on average each patient has 22.9 eGFR readings (std dev 13.6; median 19.0). In order to align the patients on a common time axis, for each patient we fix $t = 0$ to be their first recorded eGFR reading below 60 mL/min. The adverse events of interest in our experiments are AMIs and CVAs, and these were identified using ICD-9 codes as detailed in Section 2. 13.4% of patients had at least one code for AMI (among those with at least one: mean 4.1, std dev 7.1, median 2.0), and likewise 17.4% of patients had at least one code for CVA (mean 6.4, std dev 13.3, median 3.0). We use the same set of baseline covariates for x_{ip}, x_{iz}, x_{ir}: baseline age, race and gender, and indicator variables for hypertension and diabetes. Note that x_{ip}, x_{iz} include an intercept while x_{ir} does not.

For the experiments, we used ten fold cross validation with training sets of 21,105 patient records and test sets of 2,345 records. We fit separate joint models for CVA events and AMI events.

Evaluation Metrics

After learning a point estimate for the global model parameters during training, they are held fixed. Then, an approximate posterior is fit to each patient in the test set, where we allow the learning algorithm to see the first 60% of a patient's eGFR trajectory (and any events before then) and hold out the remaining 40% (and future events). Predictions about future disease trajectory and adverse events are made by drawing samples from the approximate posterior predictive distribution.

We evaluate our model on two tasks to asses predictive performance of each submodel. For the longitudinal submodel, we compute the mean squared error (MSE) and mean absolute error (MAE) for predictions about held-out eGFR values. For the point process submodel, we view the problem of predicting whether any event will occur in a given future time window (in our experiments, 1-5 years) as a binary classification problem. We report the area under the ROC curve (AUROC) and area under the precision-recall curve (AUPR) as evaluation metrics for each binary classification task. Calculating the probability of an event in a future time window $[T_i, T_i + c]$ for person i is easily computed as $1 - \exp\{-\int_{T_i}^{T_i+c} r_i(t)dt\}$.

Baselines

For the longitudinal submodel, we compare against the model in [Schulam and Saria, 2015], since we use their model as our longitudinal submodel. However, because our model was trained jointly with the point process submodel we do not in general learn the same model parameters, since the parameters for the learned trajectories are also influenced by the event data.

For the point process submodel, we compare against two standard baselines. The first is a simple Cox proportional hazards model from survival analysis, where we use the same set of time independent covariates x_{ir} as in our model. The likelihood is the same as (4), but now $r_i(t) = r_0(t)\exp\{\gamma^\top x_{ir}\}$. We also compare against a Cox model with time-dependent covariates, where $r_i(t) = r_0(t)\exp\{\gamma^\top x_{ir} + \alpha y_i(t)\}$, with $y_i(t)$ a step function denoting the most recent observed eGFR up until time t. Due to the lack of scalable inference algorithms for related works from the joint modeling literature, we were unable to compare against them on our large patient cohort.

Hyperparameters

We learn point estimates for hyperparameters $\sigma_\epsilon, \Sigma_b, \sigma_v, \sigma_f, l$ by maximizing the ELBO with respect to them. Additional hyperparameters include G, N_r, and the choice of basis expansions Φ_p, Φ_z, Φ_l in the longitudinal submodels. We let Φ_p and Φ_l be linear basis functions of time, thus allowing for population covariates and individual heterogeneity to shift the intercept and slope of eGFR trajectory. We let Φ_z be a B-spline expansion of time with degree two and twelve knots at equally spaced quantiles of eGFR observation times. We fix $G = 15$ and $N_r = 9$. Finally, we set the global scale parameter for AdaGrad to 0.1, and subsample 250 observations at a time. We experimented with other values for these fixed hyperparameters without major changes in performance.

Results

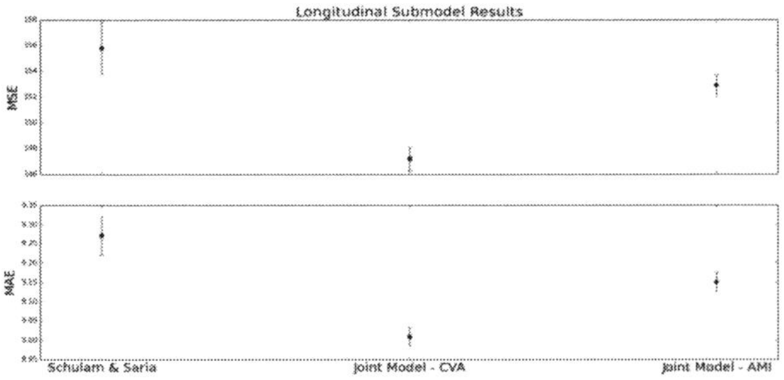

Figure 2: Mean MSE and MAE from longitudinal submodels. Error bars are one standard error.

Figure 2 highlights the results from the longitudinal submodel, where we present the mean MSEs and MAEs across the test sets. The longitudinal submodel from our joint model performs slightly better than the method of [Schulam and Saria, 2015] fit independently to the eGFR values. Figure 3 highlight the results from the point process submodel. Our proposed joint model performs substantially better than the two baselines at predicting future events, in terms of both AUROC and AUPR.

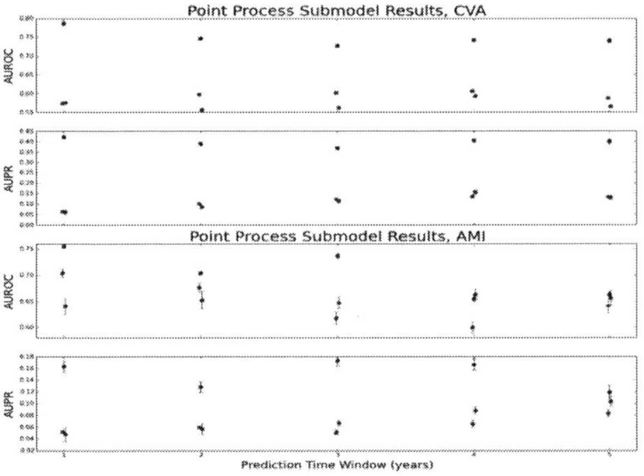

Figure 3: Mean AUROC and AUPR for CVA and AMI events. Blue is proposed Joint Model, red is Cox, green is time-varying Cox. Error bars are one standard error.

In addition, in this dataset it appears that prediction of CVA events is slightly easier than prediction of AMIs. For the CVA joint model, we estimate that $\alpha = -0.063$ and $\delta = -0.061$ while for the AMI joint model, $\alpha = -0.158$ and $\delta = -0.069$ (standard errors for all four estimates < 0.01, from the cross validation). The signs of these parameters agree with clinical intuition that patients with lower overall eGFR values and more rapid eGFR declines should be at higher risk for adverse events. It appears there is a slightly stronger association between eGFR trajectory and risk for AMIs compared to CVAs.

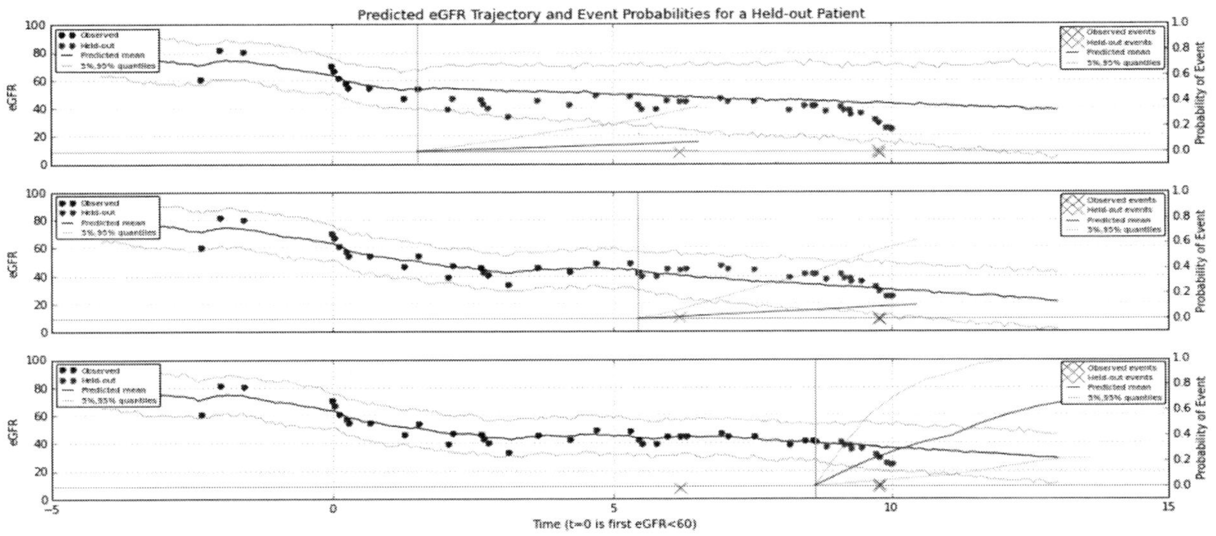

Figure 4: Dynamic predictions from our joint model. In each row, the parameters for this individual are refit as more data is made available (information to the left of the light blue lines is used to refit parameters). Blue circles and x's correspond to observed eGFR readings and CVA events, while green correspond to yet-unseen data.

Figure 4 shows an example of dynamic predictions over time for a test patient. In the three rows of the figure, we make predictions about the test patient after observing the first 25%, 50% and 75% of their disease trajectory and adverse events (in this example, CVAs). For each row we relearn the patient's parameters using information to the left of the vertical light blue line. As we observe more data, the longitudinal model updates its prediction about future disease trajectory and provides a reasonable forecast for the steady decline of this patient's eGFR. In the second row, as the model sees that the patient's trajectory is decreasing faster than in the first row, it correspondingly increases the probability of a future event. In the third row, after the model sees the patient's first CVA event, it further increases the probability of a future event.

6 DISCUSSION

In this paper, we have proposed a new joint model for longitudinal and point process data, and applied it to disease trajectory modeling and prediction of adverse events in patients with chronic kidney disease. We developed the first variational inference algorithm for this class of models, allowing us to fit our model to a large set of longitudinal patient data that is over an order of magnitude the size of datasets used by related methods. We find that our model yields good performance on the tasks of predicting future kidney function and predicting cardiovascular events.

Although our work is a promising first step for developing predictive models from EHR data and applying them to real clinical tasks, there are numerous inherent limitations to EHR data [Hersh et al., 2014]. Data quality is often poor, complicated by inaccurate, inconsistent or missing information. The EHR at a single organization may fail to capture the full patient story and all relevant outcomes of interest, as is the case when patients receive care from multiple, non-interoperable healthcare systems over time. Relevant patient reported outcomes, such as perceived quality of life, are rarely captured by EHRs. Events such as death may not be registered, particularly when patients die outside of the hospital. Data may be biased; certain laboratory tests may be performed only when a clinician suspects an abnormality. Furthermore, many clinical data are collected for billing purposes rather than patient care or research, distorting the relative importance of certain elements.

There are many directions in which we plan to extend this work. Future models will be multivariate in both longitudinal markers and in event processes. Inclusion of additional longitudinal variables such as blood pressure, albuminuria, and hemoglobin A1c will be important, since these are well known to be clinically important for monitoring cardiovascular and kidney health. Jointly modeling multiple event processes will allow us to learn correlations between different types of events. More flexible models, particularly for the event processes, should improve model performance, for instance using Gaussian Process modulated Poisson processes or Hawkes processes instead of employing the proportional hazards assumption as we do in this work. By further refining and deploying a flexible, scalable model such as ours, ACOs around the country can intervene on high-risk patients and realize the potential benefits of precision medicine.

Acknowledgements

Joseph Futoma is supported by an NDSEG fellowship. Dr. Cameron is supported by a Duke Training Grant in Nephrology (5T32DK007731). This project was funded by both the Duke Translational Research Institute and the Duke Institute for Health Innovation. Research reported in this publication was supported by the National Center for Advancing Translational Sciences of the NIH under Award Number UL1TR001117. The content is solely the responsibility of the authors and does not necessarily represent the official views of the NIH.

7 APPENDIX

We present the full derivation of the ELBO for our model. We can rewrite the expression for the ELBO in (6) as:

$$\mathcal{L}(q) = \sum_{i=1}^{N} \mathcal{L}(q_i), \tag{12}$$

$$\begin{aligned}\mathcal{L}(q_i) = {} & E_{q_i}[\log p(\vec{y_i}|z_i, b_i, f_i, \Theta) + \log p(\vec{u_i}|z_i, b_i, f_i, v_i, \Theta)] \\ & - KL(q_i(b_i)||p(b_i)) - KL(q_i(v_i)||p(v_i)) \\ & - KL(q_i(z_i)||p(z_i)) - KL(q_i(f_i(\vec{t_i}))||p(f_i(\vec{t_i}))).\end{aligned} \tag{13}$$

Computation of the KL divergence terms are standard. We focus our attention on the first two terms in (13).

The first term in (13) is the variational expectation of the log likelihood for the longitudinal submodel. To compute this, we need to calculate $E_{q_i}[(\vec{y_i} - m_i(\vec{t_i}))^\top(\vec{y_i} - m_i(\vec{t_i}))]$. It is straightforward to expand this product and calculate the expectation of each term. The relevant expectations are:

$$E_{q_i(z_i)}[\beta_{z_i}] = \sum_{g=1}^{G} \nu_{z_i,g}\beta_g \tag{14}$$

$$E_{q_i(b_i)}[b_i] = \mu_{b_i} \tag{15}$$

$$E_{q_i(f_i)}[f_i(\vec{t_i})] = \mu_{f_i} \tag{16}$$

$$E_{q_i(z_i)}[(\Phi_z(\vec{t_i})\beta_{z_i})^\top(\Phi_z(\vec{t_i})\beta_{z_i})] = \sum_{g=1}^{G} \nu_{z_i,g}(\Phi_z(\vec{t_i})\beta_g)^\top(\Phi_z(\vec{t_i})\beta_g) \tag{17}$$

$$E_{q_i(b_i)}[(\Phi_l(\vec{t_i})b_i)^\top(\Phi_l(\vec{t_i})b_i)] = \mathrm{Tr}(\Phi_l(\vec{t_i})\Sigma_{b_i}\Phi_l(\vec{t_i})^\top) + \mu_{b_i}^\top\Phi_l(\vec{t_i})^\top\Phi_l(\vec{t_i})\mu_{b_i} \tag{18}$$

$$E_{q_i(f_i(\vec{t_i}))}[f_i(\vec{t_i})^\top f_i(\vec{t_i})] = \mathrm{Tr}(\Sigma_{f_i}) + \mu_{f_i}^\top\mu_{f_i} \tag{19}$$

The second term in (13) is the variational expectation of the log likelihood for the point process submodel:

$$E_{q_i}[\log p(\vec{u_i}|z_i, b_i, f_i, v_i, \Theta)] = E_{q_i}[\sum_{k=1}^{K} \log r_i(u_{ik}) - \int_{T_i^-}^{T_i^+} r_i(t)dt]. \tag{20}$$

Each term in the summation in (20) is given by:

$$\begin{aligned}E_{q_i}[\log r_i(u_{ik})] = {} & \log r_0(u_{ik}) + \gamma^\top x_{ir} + \alpha E_{q_i}[m_i(u_{ik})] \\ & + \delta E_{q_i}[m_i'(u_{ik})] + E_{q_i}[v_i],\end{aligned} \tag{21}$$

where $E_{q_i}[v_i] = \mu_{v_i}$ and $E_{q_i}[m_i(u_{ik})], E_{q_i}[m_i'(u_{ik})]$ are simple to compute using (14) and (15), where we use the time derivatives of the bases $\Phi_p', \Phi_z', \Phi_l'$ in place of the actual bases for the latter. The only nontrivial term in $E_{q_i}[m_i(u_{ik})]$ is $E_{q_i}[f_i(u_{ik})]$. However, due to conjugacy, we have that for arbitrary t:

$$\begin{aligned}q_i(f_i(t)) &= \int p(f_i(t)|f_i(\vec{t_i}))q_i(f_i(\vec{t_i})) \\ &\equiv \mathcal{GP}(f_i; \mu(t), \Sigma(t, t'))\end{aligned} \tag{22}$$

$$\mu(t) = K_{t,\vec{t_i}}K_{\vec{t_i},\vec{t_i}}^{-1}\mu_{f_i} \tag{23}$$

$$\begin{aligned}\Sigma(t, t') = {} & K_{t,t'} - K_{t,\vec{t_i}}K_{\vec{t_i},\vec{t_i}}^{-1}K_{\vec{t_i},t'} \\ & + K_{t,\vec{t_i}}K_{\vec{t_i},\vec{t_i}}^{-1}\Sigma_{f_i}K_{\vec{t_i},\vec{t_i}}^{-1}K_{\vec{t_i},t'},\end{aligned} \tag{24}$$

so we can use (23) to compute $E_{q_i}[f_i(u_{ik})]$; the K matrices are the OU kernel evaluated at the relevant times.

The final term to compute is the integral in (20). Since we approximate it numerically, we need to evaluate $E_{q_i}[r_i(t)]$ for arbitrary times t:

$$E_{q_i}[r_i(t)] = r_0(t)e^{\gamma^\top x_{ir}}E_{q_i}[e^{\alpha m_i(t) + \delta m_i'(t) + v_i}]. \tag{25}$$

Using the mean field assumption, this expectation of products factorizes into products of expectations. There are no local latent variables corresponding to the population term in $m_i(t)$, so that term can be brought outside the expectation. Since $q_i(v_i) \sim N(\mu_{v_i}, \sigma_{v_i}^2)$ we have that e^{v_i} is log-normal, hence $E_{q_i}[e^{v_i}] = e^{\mu_{v_i} + \frac{\sigma_{v_i}^2}{2}}$. Expanding $m_i(t)$ and $m_i'(t)$ in (25) leads to three final expectations to compute. The first is:

$$E_{q_i(z_i)}[e^{(\alpha\Phi_z(t) + \delta\Phi_z'(t))^\top\beta_{z_i}}] = \sum_{g=1}^{G} \nu_{z_i,g}e^{(\alpha\Phi_z(t) + \delta\Phi_z'(t))^\top\beta_g} \tag{26}$$

The last two are $E_{q_i}[e^{(\alpha\Phi_l(t)^\top + \delta\Phi_l'(t)^\top)b_i}]$ and $E_{q_i}[e^{\alpha f_i(t)}]$. Since the variational distributions for b_i and $f_i(t)$ are multivariate normal (from (8) and (22)-(24)), the exponential of an affine transformation of them will be multivariate log-normal. We can use this with the fact that if $X \sim N(\mu, \Sigma)$ is multivariate normal, then $Y = e^X$ is multivariate log-normal with mean $E[Y]_i = e^{\mu_i + \frac{\Sigma_{ii}}{2}}$ to compute the desired variational expectations.

To compute noisy gradients of the ELBO with respect to Θ, we randomly sample S observations $\{y_s, u_s\}_{s=1}^S$ at each iteration, and compute the gradient of $\hat{\mathcal{L}}(q) \equiv \frac{N}{S}\sum_{s=1}^{S}\mathcal{L}(q_s)$, which equals $\mathcal{L}(q)$ in expectation.

References

A. Allen, J. Forman, et al. Primary Care Management of Chronic Kidney Disease. *Journal of General Internal Medicine*, 26(4):386-392, 2011.

D. W. Bates, S. Saria, L. Ohno-Machado, A. Shah, and G. Escobar. Big Data In Health Care: Using Analytics To Identify And Manage High-Risk And High-Cost Patients. *Health Affairs*, 33(7):1123-1131, 2014.

C. Bishop. *Pattern Recognition and Machine Learning*. Springer, New York., 2006.

J. Duchi, E. Hazan, and Y. Singer. Adaptive Subgradient Methods for Online Learning and Stochastic Optimization. *JMLR*, 12:2121-2158, 2011.

Z. Ghahramani and M. Beal. Propagation algorithms for variational Bayesian learning. *NIPS*, 2001.

J. Han, E. H. Slate, and E. A. Pena. Parametric latent class joint model for a longitudinal biomarker and recurrent events. *Stat Med* 26(29): 5285-5302, 2007.

W. Hersh, M. Weiner et al. Caveats for the Use of Operational Electronic Health Record Data in Comparative Effectiveness Research. *Medical Care* 51: S30-S37, 2013.

M. Hoffman, D. Blei, C. Wang, and J. Paisley. Stochastic variational inference. *JMLR*, 14:1303-1347, 2013.

T. Johnson, D. Rinehart, J. Durfee, et al. For Many Patients Who Use Large Amounts of Health Care Services, the Need Is Intense Yet Temporary. *Health Affairs*, 34(8): 1312-1319, 2015.

M. Jordan, Z. Ghahramani, T. Jaakkola, and L. Saul. Introduction to variational methods for graphical models. *Machine Learning*, 37:183-233, 1999.

KDIGO 2012. Clinical Practice Guideline for the Evaluation and Management of Chronic Kidney Disease. *Journal of the International Society of Nephrology*, (3)1, 2013.

S. Kim, D. Zeng, L. Chambless, and Y. Li. Joint Models of Longitudinal and Recurrent Events with Informative Terminal Event. *Stat Biosci* 4(2): 262-281, 2012.

A.S. Levey, L. A. Stevens, et al. A New Equation to Estimate Glomerular Filtration Rate. *Annals of internal medicine*,150(9):604-612, 2009.

W. Lian, R. Henao, V. Rao, J. Lucas, and L. Carin. A Multitask Point Process Predictive Model. *ICML*, 2015.

L. Liu and X. Huang. Joint Analysis of Correlated Repeated Measures and Recurrent Events Processes in the Presence of Death, With Application to a Study on Acquired Immune Deficiency Syndrome. *JRSS, C* 58(1):65-81, 2009.

C. Lloyd, T. Gunter, M. A. Osborne, and S. J. Roberts. Variational inference for Gaussian process modulated Poisson proceses. *ICML*, 2015.

D. Mendelssohn, B. Curtis, K. Yeates, et al. Suboptimal initiation of dialysis with and without early referral to a nephrologist. *Nephrology Dialysis Transplantation*, 26(9):2859-65, 2011.

R. B. Parikh, M. Kakad, and D. W. Bates. Integrating Predictive Analytics Into High-Value Care: The Dawn of Precision Delivery. *JAMA*, 315(7):651-652, 2016.

A. Perotte, R. Ranganath, J. S. Hirsch, D. Blei, and N. Elhadad. Risk prediction for chronic kidney disease progression using heterogeneous electronic health record data and time series analysis. *Journal of the American Medical Informatics Association*, 2015.

C. Proust-Lima, M. Sene, J. Taylor, H. Jacqmin-Gadda. Joint latent class models for longitudinal and time-to-event data: A review. *Statistical Methods in Medical Research* 23(1):74-90, 2014.

R. Ranganath, A. Perotte, N. Elhadad, and D. Blei. The Survival Filter: Joint Survival Analysis with a Latent Time Series. *UAI*, 2015.

R. Ranganath, S. Gerrish, and D. Blei. Black box variational inference. *AISTATS*, 2014.

D. Rezende, S. Mohamed, and D. Wierstra. Stochastic backpropagation and approximate inference in deep generative models. *ICML*, 2014.

D. Rizopoulos. *Joint Models for Longitudinal and Time-to-Event Data: With Applications in R*. Chapman and Hall / CRC Biostatistics Series, 2012.

P. Schulam and S. Saria. A Framework for Individualizing Predictions of Disease Trajectories by Exploiting Multi-Resolution Structure. *NIPS*, 2015.

N. Smart, G. Dieberg, M. Ladhanni, and T. Titus. Early referral to specialist nephrology services for preventing the progression to end-stage kidney disease. *Cochrane Database of Systematic Reviews*, 18(6), 2014.

L. Szczech, R. Stewart, H. Su, et al. Primary Care Detection of Chronic Kidney Disease in Adults with Type-2 Diabetes: The ADD-CKD Study. *PLoS ONE*, 9(11), 2014.

N. Tangri, L. A. Stevens, et al. A Predictive Model for Progression of Chronic Kidney Disease to Kidney Failure. *JAMA* 305(15):1553-1559, 2011.

M. Titsias. Variational learning of inducing variables in sparse Gaussian processes. *AISTATS*, 2009.

D. Tuot, L. Plantinga, C. Hsu, et al. Chronic Kidney Disease Awareness Among Individuals with Clinical Markers of Kidney Dysfunction. *Clinical Journal of the American Society of Nephrology*, 6(8):1838-1844, 2011.

Degrees of Freedom in Deep Neural Networks

Tianxiang Gao and **Vladimir Jojic**
Computer Science Department
University of North Carolina at Chapel Hill
Chapel Hill, NC, 27514, USA
{*tgao,vjojic*}*@cs.unc.edu*

Abstract

In this paper, we explore degrees of freedom in deep sigmoidal neural networks. We show that the degrees of freedom in these models are related to the expected *optimism*, which is the expected difference between test error and training error. We provide an efficient Monte-Carlo method to estimate the degrees of freedom for multi-class classification methods. We show that the degrees of freedom is less than the parameter count in a simple XOR network. We extend these results to neural nets trained on synthetic and real data and investigate the impact of network's architecture and different regularization choices. The degrees of freedom in deep networks is dramatically less than the number of parameters. In some real datasets, the number of parameters is several orders of magnitude larger than the degrees of freedom. Further, we observe that for fixed number of parameters, deeper networks have less degrees of freedom exhibiting a regularization-by-depth. Finally, we show that the degrees of freedom of deep neural networks can be used in a model selection criterion. This criterion has comparable performance to cross-validation with lower computational cost.

1 INTRODUCTION

Model selection is one of the key tasks in machine learning, as method's performance on training data is an optimistic estimate of its general performance. Efron [2004] provided an estimate of optimism, difference of error on test and training data, and related it to a measure of model's complexity deemed effective degrees of freedom. This result reflects Occam's razor since models with higher degrees of freedom tends to have higher optimism. Degrees of freedom, defined as parameter counts, have been frequently used in model selection. However, even in linear models, the number of parameters are not a good indicator of model's complexity. Straightforward examples of this behavior are models fit using sparsity penalties. In that context, degrees of freedom are related to the number of non-zero parameters instead of total parameter count.

Ye [1998] introduced the concept of Generalized Degrees of freedom (GDF) for complex modeling procedures with Gaussian distributed outputs. GDF is defined based on the sensitivity of the fitted values to the perturbations in observed values. Efron [2004] provided a framework for estimating degrees of freedom for modeling procedures with output in exponential family distribution. In order to estimate degrees of freedom in deep neural networks for classification problems, where the outputs can be regarded as a categorical distribution, we extend Efron's results to the context of multinomial logistic regression. Similar to Ye's GDF, the computation of the degrees of freedom involves assessing network's changes in output as a result of perturbation of the training data. The more sensitive the network's output to the perturbation, the more degrees of freedom it has.

We provide a straightforward algorithm for evaluating the degrees of freedom for any modeling procedure with outputs in categorical distribution form. This algorithm requires an additional run of the modeling procedure on the perturbed data. In the worst case, this amounts to doubling the running time of the procedure. Using this algorithm we first analyze the complexity of XOR network. This simple example highlights the fact that the degrees of freedom in a neural net is not simply equal to the total number of parameters in the network.

In our experiments, we aim to answer following questions:

1. How does the network's complexity (DoF) vary with its architecture? Specifically, how do the degrees of freedom grow with the depth of a neural network?

2. How does regularization affect network's complexity? Specifically, what is the impact of dropout, weight decay, adding noise on the degrees of freedom?

We answer these questions in the context of feed-forward sigmoidal networks employed on classification tasks on both synthetic and real datasets.

The prior work on the model complexity is rich, and we briefly review some key contributions. Bayesian Information Criterion (BIC) [Schwarz et al., 1978] and Akaike Information Criterions (AIC) [Akaike, 1974] are most commonly used techniques for model selection. Both aim to construct an estimate of the test log-likelihood by correcting the training set log likelihood with terms dependent on the number of parameters in the model in order to produce a score that is a less biased estimate of test log-likelihood. The weighting of the parameter count is different, BIC depends on the sample size, and AIC uses a constant. BIC applied to the family of models that contain the true model is consistent in the limit of the data. AIC, with some mild constraints, guarantees the selection of model with least square error, among models that do not include the true model. Crucial to the practical application of these methods is the correct count of parameters. Bayesian model selection elegantly avoids the need to specify the complexity of the network by evaluating evidence, a marginal probability of the data given the model. This approach marginalizes over all of the parameters, making models of different parameterizations comparable. The size of the parameter space directly impacts the evidence through this integration, as the prior on parameters gets spread thinly across high dimensional spaces. Unfortunately, the cost of computing such integrals is often prohibitive, but the models selected using these techniques have been shown to be very competitive. [MacKay, 2003, Neal, 1996, Guyon et al., 2004]. Kolmogorov-Chaitin complexity [Kolmogorov, 1965] describes dataset complexity in terms of a program that recapitulates the data. Generation of task-specific neural networks using algorithmically simple programs was explored by Schmidhuber [1997]. Networks whose parameters could not be captured by a simple program were avoided. A related method of Minimal Description Length reflects the desire for compact representation of the data. Its application [Hinton and Zemel, 1994] shows how the trade-off between the data and parameter compression can lead to an objective for training auto-encoders. Degrees of freedom of linear models fit with Lasso-type penalties have been analyzed, e.g. Lasso [Zou et al., 2007], Fused Lasso [Tibshirani et al., 2005] and Group Lasso [Vaiter et al., 2012]. The number of predictors and the number of degrees of freedom greatly differ due to the imposed sparsity and weight tying. Recent results on degrees of freedom for non-continuous procedures such as best subset regression and forward stagewise regression [Janson et al., 2015] highlight challenges in determining the complexity of these procedures as the estimators can be discontinuous. Research on Stein's Unbiased Risk Estimate has yielded model selection techniques [Stein, 1981] as well as algorithms for their estimation [Ye, 1998, Ramani et al., 2008]. Generalization of SURE to exponential families has been proposed by Eldar [2009]. However, its focus is on estimating parameter risk instead of prediction error. In linear models, the two neatly coincide. But this does not carry over to logistic regression and more broadly sigmoidal neural networks.

2 DEGREES OF FREEDOM FOR CATEGORICAL DISTRIBUTION

In this section, we derive the definition of degrees of freedom for categorical distribution from the optimism according to Efron [2004]. Then, we introduce an efficient Monte-Carlo sampling based method [Ramani et al., 2008] to estimate degrees of freedom.

2.1 DEFINITIONS

We focus on models aimed at multi-class classification task. The data is assumed to be composed of features $\mathbf{X} \in \mathbb{R}^{n \times p}$, and output labels $\mathbf{y}$ range over k categories. We will denote categorical distribution with $\mathcal{C}(\cdot)$. Categorical distribution over k categories can be parameterized using a vector of non-negative values with a sum of 1. We treat sample label y_i as realization of categorical random variables for a specific parameter vector $\boldsymbol{\mu}_i$. Hence $y_i \sim \mathcal{C}(\boldsymbol{\mu}_i)$, where $\boldsymbol{\mu}_i = [\mu_{i1}, \mu_{i2}, \dots, \mu_{ik}]$ is the **true probability** of sample y_i being in each class. $\mu_{ic} \in [0, 1]$ and $\sum_{c=1}^{k} \mu_{ic} = 1$. Members of exponential family follow form:

$$f(\mathbf{p}_i|\boldsymbol{\mu}_i) = r(\mathbf{p}_i) \exp\{\boldsymbol{\theta}(\boldsymbol{\mu}_i)^T \mathbf{p}_i - A(\boldsymbol{\mu}_i)\}$$

where $\mathbf{p}_i$ is the vector of sufficient statistics for sample i, $\boldsymbol{\theta}(\boldsymbol{\mu}_i)$ is the vector of natural parameters, $r(\mathbf{p}_i)$ is the base measure, $A(\boldsymbol{\mu}_i)$ is the log-partition function.

For categorical distribution with parameter $\boldsymbol{\mu}_i$, we have $\mathbf{p}_i = h(y_i) = [\delta(y_i - 1), \dots, \delta(y_i - k - 1)]^T$, where $\delta(\cdot)$ is the Kronecker delta function, $\delta(a) = 1$ if $a = 0$, $\delta(a) = 0$ if $a \neq 0$. In other words, $\mathbf{p}_i$ is a vector of the **observations** of sample i being in each class. Base measure is $r(\mathbf{p}_i) = 1$; natural parameters are $\theta_c(\boldsymbol{\mu}_i) = \ln \mu_{ic} - \ln(1 - \sum_{l=1}^{k-1} \mu_{il})$, and log partition function $A(\boldsymbol{\mu}_i) = \ln(1 + \sum_{c=1}^{k-1} e^{\theta_c(\boldsymbol{\mu}_i)})$. Note that both $\boldsymbol{\mu}_i$ and $\mathbf{p}_i$ are of dimension $k - 1$. Let $\mathbf{P} = [\mathbf{p}_1, \dots, \mathbf{p}_n]^T$ be the matrix of observations for all sample labels $y_1, \dots, y_n$.

2.2 OPTIMISM IN MODELS WITH CATEGORICAL DISTRIBUTION

Optimism is the difference between expected test log deviance error and training log deviance error for a model fitting procedure. It is related to the complexity of the model and degrees of freedom is derived from optimism. If the optimism for a modeling procedure can be estimated, we can use it for model selection. Efron [2004] provides the derivations of expected optimism for the single parameter exponential family. We follow Efron's approach to derive the definition of degrees of freedom for modeling procedure with output in categorical distribution form.

Given sample input $\mathbf{x}_i$, we assume that the output label $y_i \sim \mathcal{C}(\boldsymbol{\mu}_i)$. Let $\hat{\boldsymbol{\mu}}_i = \mathcal{L}(\mathbf{p}_i)$ be the **estimated probability** for sample i from observations $\mathbf{p}_i$. The log deviance error for $\hat{\boldsymbol{\mu}}_i$ and $\mathbf{p}_i$ is:

$$\begin{aligned} \text{err}_i &= -2\log f(\mathbf{p}_i|\hat{\boldsymbol{\mu}}_i^T) \\ &= -2[\boldsymbol{\theta}(\hat{\boldsymbol{\mu}}_i)^T\mathbf{p}_i - A(\hat{\boldsymbol{\mu}}_i)] \end{aligned}$$

Suppose we have another sample y_i^0 drawn from the same distribution as y_i, $y_i^0 \sim \mathcal{C}(\mu_i)$. Let $\mathbf{q}_i = h(y_i^0)$ be the vector of its observations. The expected log deviance error of $\mathbf{q}_i$ using $\hat{\boldsymbol{\mu}}_i$ is:

$$\begin{aligned} \text{Err}_i &= E_{y_i^0}\{-2\log f(\mathbf{q}_i|\hat{\boldsymbol{\mu}}_i)\} \\ &= -2[\boldsymbol{\theta}(\hat{\boldsymbol{\mu}}_i)^T\boldsymbol{\mu}_i + A(\hat{\boldsymbol{\mu}}_i)] \end{aligned}$$

The definition of optimism is:

$$\begin{aligned} O_i &= \text{Err}_i - \text{err}_i \\ &= 2\boldsymbol{\theta}(\hat{\boldsymbol{\mu}}_i)^T(\mathbf{p}_i - \boldsymbol{\mu}_i) \end{aligned}$$

Hence, optimism is the difference between log deviance error on the training set and expected log deviance error with respect to the true distribution.

The expected optimism over $y_i \sim \mathcal{C}(\boldsymbol{\mu}_i)$ for the estimated probability $\hat{\boldsymbol{\mu}}_i$ and true probability $\boldsymbol{\mu}_i$ is:

$$\Omega_i = 2E_{y_i}\{\boldsymbol{\theta}(\hat{\boldsymbol{\mu}}_i)^T(\mathbf{p}_i - \boldsymbol{\mu}_i).\}$$

As we do not know the true probability $\boldsymbol{\mu}_i$, we cannot compute the expected optimism. However, we can get an approximate measurement using Taylor series expansion. We can approximate $\boldsymbol{\theta}(\hat{\boldsymbol{\mu}}_i)$ by taking the Taylor series expansion at $\mathbf{p}_i = \boldsymbol{\mu}_i$ to obtain:

$$\boldsymbol{\theta}(\hat{\boldsymbol{\mu}}_i) \approx \boldsymbol{\theta}(\mathcal{L}(\boldsymbol{\mu}_i)) + \mathbf{D}^{(i)}(\mathbf{p}_i - \boldsymbol{\mu}_i).$$

$\mathbf{D}^{(i)}$ is the first derivative matrix where each entry $D_{jc}^{(i)} = \frac{\partial\theta_j(\mathcal{L}(\mathbf{v}))}{\partial v_c}|_{\mathbf{v}=\boldsymbol{\mu}_i}$.

Therefore, we can approximate expected optimism as:

$$\begin{aligned} \tilde{\Omega}_i &= 2E_{y_i}\{[\boldsymbol{\theta}(\mathcal{L}(\boldsymbol{\mu}_i)) + \mathbf{D}^{(i)}(\mathbf{p}_i - \boldsymbol{\mu}_i)]^T(\mathbf{p}_i - \boldsymbol{\mu}_i)\} \\ &= 2E_{y_i}\{\sum_{j=1}^{k-1}\sum_{l=1}^{k-1}(p_{ij} - \mu_{ij})(p_{il} - \mu_{il})D_{jl}^{(i)}\} \\ &= 2\sum_{j=1}^{k-1}\sum_{l=1}^{k-1}\text{cov}(p_{ij}, p_{il})\frac{\partial\theta_j(\mathcal{L}(\mathbf{v}))}{\partial v_l}|_{\mathbf{v}=\boldsymbol{\mu}_i} \end{aligned}$$

We can estimate the expected optimism by assuming $p_i \sim \mathcal{C}(\hat{\boldsymbol{\mu}}_i)$, so:

$$\hat{\Omega}_i = 2\sum_{j=1}^{k-1}\sum_{l=1}^{k-1}\text{cov}(p_{ij}, p_{il})\frac{\partial\theta_j(\mathcal{L}(\mathbf{v}))}{\partial v_l}|_{\mathbf{v}=\hat{\boldsymbol{\mu}}_i}. \quad (1)$$

In categorical distribution, $\text{cov}(p_{ij}, p_{il}) = -\hat{\mu}_{ij}\hat{\mu}_{il}$, if $i \neq j$. $\text{var}(p_{ij}) = \hat{\mu}_{ij}(1 - \hat{\mu}_{ij})$. Therefore, Equation (1) can be reduced to:

$$\hat{\Omega}_i = 2\sum_{j=1}^{k-1}\frac{\partial\mathcal{L}_j(\mathbf{v})}{\partial v_j}|_{\mathbf{v}=\hat{\boldsymbol{\mu}}_i}. \quad (2)$$

The proof is given in the supplementary material.

Equation (2) for $k = 2$ is exactly the result for Bernoulli distribution derived in [Efron, 2004]. Efron also showed that Eqn (2) gives the correct degrees of freedom for maximum likelihood estimation [Efron, 1975]. In a p-parameter curved exponential family, we have:

$$\sum_{i=1}^{n}\frac{\partial\mathcal{L}(\mathbf{v})}{\partial v_i}|_{\mathbf{v}=\hat{\boldsymbol{\mu}}_i} = p.$$

Here, we define the degrees of freedom for a classification model estimator $\hat{\boldsymbol{\mu}}_i = \mathcal{L}_i(\mathbf{P})$ on all the data samples $\mathbf{P}$ to be:

$$\text{df} = \sum_{i=1}^{n}\sum_{c=1}^{k-1}\frac{\partial\mathcal{L}_{ic}(\mathbf{P})}{\partial p_{ic}}. \quad (3)$$

This definition tells that the degrees of freedom is the sum of each sample's sensitivity of its estimated probability to the perturbations in its observation for all categories.

2.3 DEGREES OF FREEDOM FOR MODEL SELECTION

As degrees of freedom is related to the expected optimism, we can use degrees of freedom for model selection. According to Equation (2) and (3), the relationship between expected test and training log deviance errors is:

$$\sum_{i=1}^{n}E_{y_i}\{\text{Err}_i\} = \sum_{i=1}^{n}E_{y_i}\{\text{err}_i\} + 2\text{df}. \quad (4)$$

Euqation (4) is very similar to Akaike Information Criterions (AIC) Akaike [1974]:

$$\text{AIC} = \sum_{i=1}^{n}\text{err}_i + 2k, \quad (5)$$

where k is the number of parameters. We refer to 2df in Equation (4) and $2k$ in Equation (5) as "complexity correction" for training log deviance error. In simple linear regression models, df $= k$, and the complexity corrections are the same. However, in complex models such as deep neural networks, simply counting number of parameters can result in overestimate of the expected test log deviance error. Therefore, we introduce DoFAIC for model selection:

$$\text{DoFAIC} = \sum_{i=1}^{n} \text{err}_i + 2\text{df}. \quad (6)$$

DoFAIC uses degrees of freedom instead of the number of parameters for complexity correction. We assume that DoFAIC can produce a better criterion for model selection than Naïve AIC.

2.4 MONTE-CARLO ESTIMATE FOR DEGREES OF FREEDOM

For most practical estimators of the model's predictions with respect to the data derivatives, $\frac{\partial \mathcal{L}_{ic}(\mathbf{P})}{\partial p_{ic}}$ are not available in closed form. For example, fitting multinomial logistic regression using stochastic gradient descent with adaptive learning rates requires a fairly sophisticated derivation which accounts for changes in step-sizes as a result of data perturbation. For deep neural networks, this difficulty grows due to the use of back-propagation. In this paper, we used a sampling based method to efficiently estimate

Monte-Carlo estimation A theoretical result for a stochastic estimate of the degrees of freedom of nonlinear estimators has been proposed by Ramani et al. [2008]. We restate the key result from that paper here.

Theorem 1. *Let* $\mathbf{b}$ *be a zero mean i.i.d. random vector (that is independent of* $\mathbf{y}$*) with unit variance and bounded higher moments. Then*

$$\sum_i \frac{\partial f(\mathbf{y})}{\partial y_i} = \lim_{\epsilon \to 0} E_{\mathbf{b}} \left[\mathbf{b}^T \left(\frac{f(\mathbf{y} + \epsilon \mathbf{b}) - f(\mathbf{y})}{\epsilon} \right) \right]$$

provided that f *admits a well-defined second-order Taylor expansion.*

We sketch out a proof that the prediction in a neural net via forward pass is a smooth function of the observations of training labels. We will abbreviate "differentiable with respect to observations" as d.w.r.t.o. Sigmoid and soft-max are smooth functions of their inputs. The cross-entropy loss is a multivariate function that depends on data and weights, and all of its partial derivatives exist. For simplicity, we assume that the network is trained using gradient descent. Each update of the network's parameters is a linear combination of previous weights and a gradient of the loss. Assuming that the initial weights d.w.r.t.o. and loss is smooth then the update yields weights that are d.w.r.t.o. Random initialization and pre-training both yield initializations that are independent of observations, hence the partial derivatives of the initial weights with respect to observations are

Algorithm 1 Monte Carlo algorithm for computing degrees of freedom of a multi-class classifier

Input: training data $\mathbf{X} \in \mathbf{R}^{n \times p}$, $\mathbf{y} \in \{1, 2, .., k\}^n$
1: Compute observations matrix $\mathbf{P} = h(\mathbf{y})$
2: Train model on $\mathbf{X}$ and $\mathbf{P}$
3: Compute estimated probabilities for each sample $\mathcal{L}(\mathbf{P})$
4: Sample entries of $\mathbf{B}^{(t)} \in \mathbf{R}^{p \times k}$ from zero-mean, unit variance normal distribution
5: Train model on $\mathbf{X}$ and $\mathbf{P}^{(t)} = \mathbf{P} + \epsilon \mathbf{B}^{(t)}$
6: Using trained model compute estimated probabilities for each sample $\mathcal{L}(\mathbf{P}^{(t)})$;
7: Repeat 4-6 for T times;
8: Calculate *df* from Equation (7)

0. By induction, gradient descent, at any iteration, yields weights that are d.w.r.t.o. Forward pass through sigmoidal network yields estimated probabilities which are smooth with respect to observations. Thus, the Taylor expansion required by the above theorem exists.

Using this theorem, we can evaluate the derivative of a function $\frac{\partial f(x)}{\partial x}$ by perturbing the inputs. We applied a modified version of the method [Ramani et al., 2008] for categorical distribution. We applied random perturbation to the observations to estimate the degrees of freedom:

$$\text{df} = \sum_{i=1}^{n} \sum_{c=1}^{k-1} \frac{\partial \mathcal{L}_{ic}(\mathbf{P})}{\partial p_{ic}}$$
$$= \lim_{\epsilon \to 0} \left\{ E_{\mathbf{B}} \left[\sum_i \sum_c b_{ic} \left(\frac{\mathcal{L}_{ic}(\mathbf{P} + \epsilon \mathbf{B}) - \mathcal{L}_{ic}(\mathbf{P})}{\epsilon} \right) \right] \right\},$$

where $\mathbf{B}$ is a zero-mean i.i.d. random matrix with unit variance and bounded higher order moments. Therefore, we can approximate *df* with T independent samplings of $\mathbf{B}^{(t)}$:

$$df \approx \frac{1}{T} \sum_{t=1}^{T} \sum_{i=1}^{n} \sum_{c=1}^{k-1} b_{ic}^{(t)} \left(\frac{\mathcal{L}_{ic}(\mathbf{P} + \epsilon \mathbf{B}^{(t)}) - \mathcal{L}_{ic}(\mathbf{P})}{\epsilon} \right), \quad (7)$$

where ϵ is a small value. In our experiments, we choose $\epsilon = 10^{-5}$. To better estimate the sensitivity, we can use the average of multiple runs as the final estimation. The algorithm for estimating degrees of freedom is summarized in Algorithm 1.

Note that training on original and perturbed observations matrix can be performed in parallel. Finally, we also derived analytical derivatives for stochastic gradient descent learning which yields the same degrees of freedom as the algorithm presented above. However, this method requires maintenance of partial derivatives of each parameter with respect to each sample's observations. Such storage requirements make this method impractical for real world applications.

Variance reduction For deep neural networks, training takes a considerable amount of time. In order to estimate degrees of freedom in a reasonable computational time, we used a variance reduction technique – common random numbers – during Monte-Carlo sampling. When comparing the degrees of freedom on a specific data, fixed $\mathbf{P}$, for several different fitting procedures, we used the same perturbation matrix $\mathbf{B}$ for all the models. We used the same random seed for all models throughout the training. For example, in deep neural network training, we use the same random seed to initialize weights and bias; during pre-training with denoising-autoencoders, we use the same random seed for drop-out and input corruptions. For stochastic gradient descent methods, we use the same mini-batches splittings during training. In our experiment, we found that we can estimate degrees of freedom well enough using just one perturbed copy of the data when using these variance reduction techniques.

2.5 DEGREES OF FREEDOM IN MULTINOMIAL LOGISTIC REGRESSION

In order to validate the above algorithm in a setting with known degrees of freedom, we perform an empirical analysis of the degrees of freedom in different multinomial logistic regression models.

We generate an i.i.d. zero mean unit variance random design matrix $\mathbf{X}$ with $n = 100$ samples and $p = 20$ features. We represent each sample with $\mathbf{x}_i = [x_{i1}, x_{i2}, \ldots, x_{ip}]$. With $k = 4$ class, we generated a random weight matrix $\mathbf{W} \in \mathbb{R}^{p \times k}$, where each entry $w_{ic} \sim \mathcal{N}(0, 1)$. We generate each label from $y_i = \text{argmax}_j \, \mu_{ij}$, where $\boldsymbol{\mu}_i = e^{\mathbf{x}_i \mathbf{W}}$.

We fit 5 models using multinomial logistic regression. In ith model, we only use first $2i$ features in $\mathbf{X}$ to fit. Therefore, ith model only contains $2(i+1)(k-1)$ parameters and the degrees of freedom are equal to the number of parameters. We perform 5 Monte-Carlo degrees of freedom estimates for each model.

We plot degrees of freedom in Figure 1(a). We observed that degrees of freedom are very close to the number of parameters we used in the model. The standard error for Monte-Carlo estimate is small.

We also randomly generated 1000 samples for testing. Optimism is calculated by the difference between average testing log deviance error and training log deviance error. We plot the degrees of freedom and optimisms for all 5 models in Figure 1(b). It shows that the optimism has a linear relationship with degrees of freedom, as expected.

2.6 DEGREES OF FREEDOM OF A XOR NETWORK

We generated a small synthetic example using exclusive-or (XOR) operator, where $\text{XOR}(a, b) = 0$ if $a = b$, and $\text{XOR}(a, b) = 1$ if $a \neq b$. Given an input $x_1, x_2 \in \{0, 1\}$, the output $y = XOR(x_1, x_2)$, we hope to learn a model of

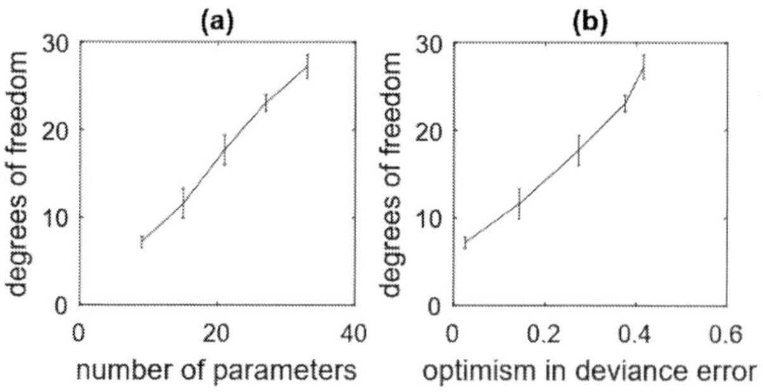

Figure 1: **(a)** Comparison between degrees of freedom estimates in multinomial logsitic regression and the true number of parameters used in the model. **(a)** Comparison between degrees of freedom estimates in multinomial logsitic regression and the optimism in log deviance error. In each plot, blue line is the mean of the five Monte-Carlo estimates. Error bar represents the standard error.

XOR operator. In general, we can build a neural network with two hidden nodes as shown in Figure 2 and weights in Table 1 to learn a perfect XOR classifier.

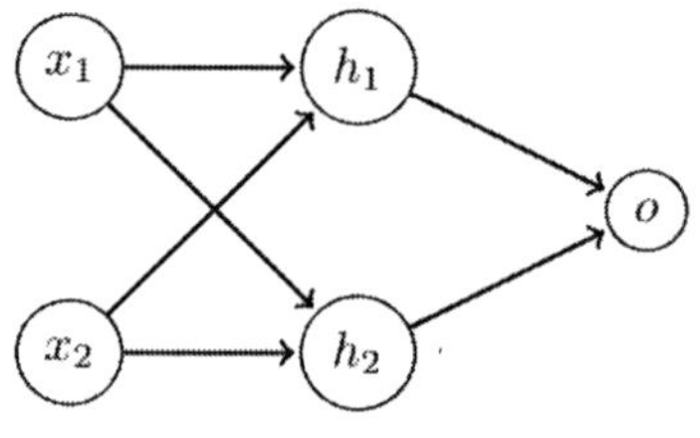

Figure 2: A Neural Network with 2 Hidden Nodes

Table 1: An XOR Network

x_1	0	1	0	1
x_2	0	0	1	1
$h_1 = \sigma(F(-0.5 + x_1 - x_2))$	0	1	0	0
$h_2 = \sigma(F(-0.5 - x_1 + x_2))$	0	0	1	0
$y = \sigma(K(-0.5 + h_1 + h_2))$	0	1	1	0

A network that trained properly should have weight matrix with form in Table 1. If x contains no noise, F, a multiplier, can be infinitely large to achieve perfect estimation. Therefore, we set y to be 0.9 instead of 1.

We train networks with different structures on XOR data using back-propagation and estimate their degrees of freedom using Monte-Carlo method. Even though there are 9 parameters in the network, we found that the degrees of freedom for all learned models is 4. We note that the symmetry in weights of the inputs to the two hidden nodes, eliminates degrees of freedom, as does implicit tying of the weights of inputs to the output node. To give an intuition why this tying occurs, we note that the predominantly correctly labeled data drives the network to keep the weights close to each other. Hence, a small perturbation in the labels can affect multiple weights simultaneously, but does not disturb their balance. This observation encourages us to investigate deeper models.

3 DEGREES OF FREEDOM IN DEEP NEURAL NETWORKS

In this section, we investigate degrees of freedom in deep neural network models. From the XOR example, we know that the degrees of freedom in a network is not equal the number of parameters in the model. The structure of the network and different regularization techniques will impact degrees of freedom.

3.1 TERMINOLOGIES AND SETTINGS

In the following experiments, we explore deep networks trained to solve larger classification problems. Each of the networks takes real value vector $\mathbf{x}_i \in \mathbb{R}^{p \times 1}$ as input and outputs the probability $\hat{\boldsymbol{\mu}}_i$ for this sample being in one of k categories. We use sigmoid activation function for all the hidden nodes and a soft-max in the last layer. The number of hidden layers is called "**depth**" of the network. We only consider networks with an equal number of units in each hidden layer, and we call this number "**width**" of the network. Next, we investigate degrees of freedom in networks with different width and depth.

Stacked-Auto-Encoder (SdA) pre-training We used SdA [Vincent et al., 2010] to pre-train the neural network with input dataset, as unsupervised pre-training helps the network to achieve a better generalization from the training data on supervised tasks [Erhan et al., 2010]. In denoising auto-encoder, **corruption** is used in layer-wised pre-training. The corruption is introduced by zeroing out input to the auto-encoder with a certain probability. The chosen probability of corruption is called **corruption rate**. **Dropout** [Srivastava et al., 2014] is also used during the pre-training of SdA, where output of hidden units are randomly zeroed with probability, which is called **dropout rate**. We assume that increasing in corruption rate or dropout rate will reduce degrees of freedom as they provide more regularization to the network.

Weight-decay We used a weight decay penalty on the sum of the squares of all the weights in the network during both pre-training and fine-tuning stage. Adding this penalty prevents the network from over-fitting. We refer to the multiplier associated with the sum of squares as **weight decay rate**. We expect to see that the degrees of freedom drops with increasing weight decay rate.

Implementation All our code are based on Theano [Bastien et al., 2012, Bergstra et al., 2010] and we ran experiments on a cluster of machines with NVIDIA Tesla compute cards.

3.2 DATA SETS

We prepared a synthetic dataset and two real datasets MNIST and CIFAR-10 to estimate degrees of freedom.

Synthetic We build a synthetic dataset from a randomly generated network with 30 input nodes, 2 hidden layers with 30 hidden nodes in each, and 4 output nodes. We generated $n = 5000$ random zero-mean unit variance inputs with 30 dimensions. Each layer was fully connected to the previous layer, and we generated weights $w \sim \mathcal{N}(0, 5)$. We used sigmoid activation function for each layer and a soft-max on top of the network. The output sample labels y are then sampled according to the probabilities from the soft-max layer. To get the optimism, we also generated another 5000 samples for test.

MNIST [1] [LeCun et al., 1998] is a benchmark dataset that contains handwritten digit images. Each sample is a 28×28 image from 10 classes. We used 50000 samples for training.

CIFAR-10 [2] [Krizhevsky and Hinton, 2009] is a dataset contains 32×32 tiny color images from 10 classes. Each sample has 3072 features. We used 50000 samples for training.

3.3 DEGREES OF FREEDOM AND THE STRUCTURE OF THE NETWORK

To investigate the degrees of freedom for networks with different structures, we estimated the degrees of freedom for networks with width $[10, 20, \ldots, 100]$ and depth with 1,2,3 and 4, where all the hidden layers have equal widths. We used SdA to pre-train with 0.1 dropout rate and 0.1 corruption rate. We use weight decay penalty $1e-5$ for both pre-training and fine-tuning. The estimated degrees of freedom is shown in Figure 3.

From the results, we found that networks with more width have more degrees of freedom. This is reasonable as increasing width leads to more independence between parameters. However, the degrees of freedom in deep networks is generally much less than the number of parameters it used. We see that the ratio of the parameters to degrees of freedom is on the order of 10^2. Loosely, one degree of freedom is acquired for 100 parameters. Among the models with the same number of parameters, deeper networks have

[1] `http://yann.lecun.com/expdb/mnist/`

[2] `https://www.cs.toronto.edu/~kriz/cifar.html`

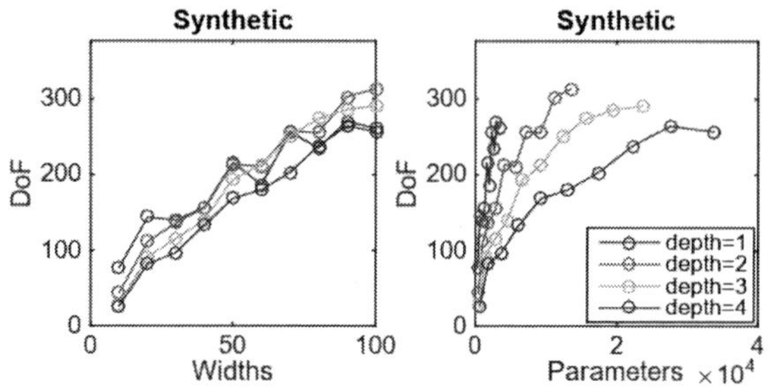

Figure 3: Degrees of freedom estimates for different models trained on synthetic data. Left: degrees of freedom vs network width. Right: degrees of freedom vs number of parameters in the network, which is linearly related to the network depth and quadratically related to the number of width. The line represent the degrees of freedom estimate from 1 Monte-Carlo run, and the color of each indicates the depth of the models.

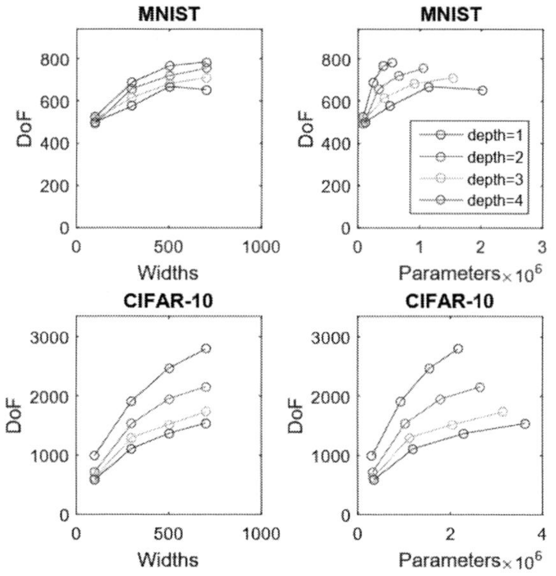

Figure 4: Degrees of freedom estimates for different models trained on MNIST and CIFAR-10. Left: degrees of freedom vs network width. Right: degrees of freedom vs the number of parameters in the network, which is linearly related to the network depth and quadratically related to the number of widths. The lines represent the degrees of freedom estimate from single Monte-Carlo sample and the color of each indicates the depth of that model.

less degrees of freedom. This observation indicates that the depth of the network has regularization on the complexity.

To further validate our assumption that deeper networks have less degrees of freedom, we also estimated degrees of freedom on MNIST and CIFAR-10 dataset. We tested networks with width $[100, 300, 500, 700]$, all other settings are the same as in the above synthetic experiment. The results are shown in Figure 4.

We observe that we can make the same conclusions hold for MNIST and CIFAR-10 as we did for synthetic data. The only difference is increasing depth results in more degrees of freedom than models trained with synthetic data. We attribute this to the differences of input data size and complexity between the real datasets, MNIST and CIFAR-10, and the much simpler synthetic datasets.

3.4 DEGREES OF FREEDOM AND REGULARIZATION TECHNIQUES

When training a deep neural network, many practical methods can be used for regularization. We investigate how the different techniques affect the degrees of freedom in the model.

We train networks using the same settings as in Section 3.3. In this experiment, we separately trained networks with different settings of penalty rates: corruption rate, dropout rate, and weight decay rate. We changed one rate at a time while keeping rest fixed.

tested the corruption rate, dropout rate, and weight decay penalty by keeping all others fixed and only changing one at a time.

For all three datasets, we trained network using corruption rate and dropout rate from $[0, 0.1, 0.2, \ldots, 0.9]$, and weight decay rate from 10^{-6} to 10^{-3}. For each setting of regularization parameters, we trained a 3 layer network $[30, 30, 30]$ for synthetic data and $[300, 300, 300]$ on MNIST and CIFAR-10 data. We used one Monte Carlo sample to estimate degrees of freedom in each model. The result is shown in Figure 5.

We found that neither corruption rate nor dropout rate affected degrees of freedom drastically for synthetic data. This is because the input of the synthetic data is generated randomly. Hence, pre-training cannot learn higher level features for synthetic data. For MNIST and CIFAR-10, we found that both corruption rate and dropout rate have an impact on degrees of freedom . In CIFAR-10, the regularization effect is much larger. These results suggest that the regularization strength from dropout and corruption can be data-specific.

Weight decay penalty has a very strong effect on the degrees of freedom for all three datasets. Further, the weight decay exhibited a highly non-linear impact on the degrees of freedom, in dramatic contrast to its effect in ridge regression.[3]

[3]Ridge regression degrees of freedom scale with $\frac{1}{1+\lambda}$ which is non-linear but much tamer multiplier than in neural networks

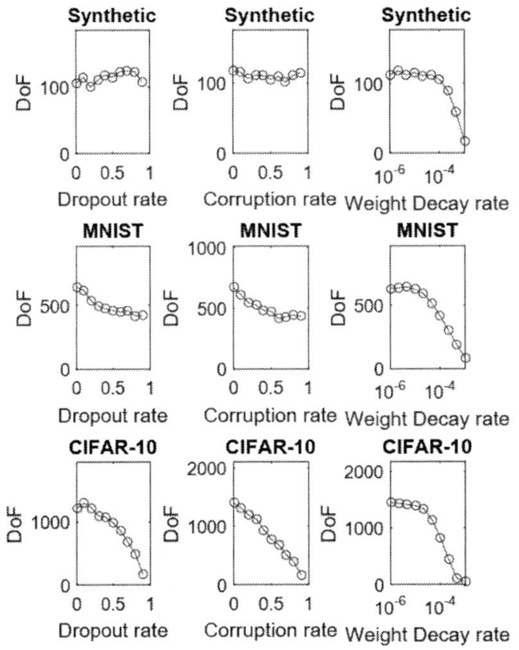

Figure 5: Degrees of freedom estimates for models trained on Synthetic data, MNIST and CIFAR-10 under different regularizations. The lines represent the degrees of freedom estimate.

3.5 MODEL SELECTION USING DEGREES OF FREEDOM

To validate that DoFAIC is a useful criterion for model selection, we compare it against model selection based on error estimates using cross validation. For brevity, we refer to the cross validation estimate of error as cross validation error. We performed a 5-fold cross-validation experiment for Synthetic, MNIST and CIFAR data on models with different network structures learned in Section 3.3. We calculated DoFAICs for all the models we trained using Equation (6) with the estimated degrees of freedom. We also calculated Naïve AIC using Equation (5) with the number of parameters in the network. We compared these estimates against cross-validation errors. The result is shown in Figure 6.

Further, we calculate the Spearman rank correlation between cross-validation log deviance errors and DoFAIC/Naïve AIC estimates for each dataset. The result is shown in Table 2.

We find that DoFAIC is very consistent with cross-validation error. Naïve AIC, on the other hand, exhibits negative correlation with cross validation error due to highly non-linear behavior. This is because Naïve AIC

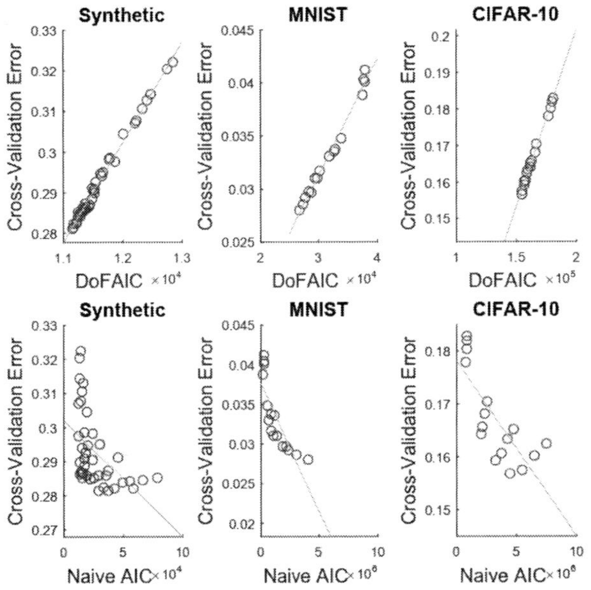

Figure 6: Comparison between DoFAIC (first row) / Naïve AIC (second row) and 5-fold cross validation. Each circle in the plot represents a model with a specific structure. The x-axis is the mean cross-validation log deviance error across 5 folds.

Table 2: Spearman Rank Correlation between Cross-validation error and DoFAIC/Naïve AIC

Dataset	DoFAIC ρ	Naïve AIC ρ
Synthetic	0.9865	-0.6711
MNIST	0.9853	-0.9471
CIFAR-10	0.9941	-0.7824

overestimates the complexity of the model by using the large number of parameters in the network. The actual complexity in deeper and larger networks are much less than the number of parameters.

For all three datasets, both DoFAIC and cross-validation chose the same model. This indicates that DoFAIC can be used for model selection. We note that k-fold cross-validation, which needs at most k rounds of training, while DoFAIC only requires at most 2 rounds of training. This makes DoFAIC an efficient model selection criterion.

4 DISCUSSION

In this paper, we investigated the degrees of freedom for classification models and presented an efficient method to estimate their degrees of freedom. We showed that for simple classification models, degrees of freedom is equal to the number of parameters in the model. In deep networks, the degrees of freedom is generally much less than the number of parameters in the model, and deeper networks tend to have less degrees of freedom. We also theoretically and empirically showed we can use DoFAIC as an efficient criterion for model selection, which has comparable performance to cross-validation.

Future work It would be interesting to investigate degrees of freedom in other deep architectures, such as Convolution Neural Network (CNN), Recurrent Neural Networks (RNN), denoising auto-encoders and contractive auto-encoders.

Acknowledgement

This work was supported by NSF INSPIRE award IOS-1343020 to VJ.

References

Hirotugu Akaike. A new look at the statistical model identification. *Automatic Control, IEEE Transactions on*, 19 (6):716–723, 1974.

Frédéric Bastien, Pascal Lamblin, Razvan Pascanu, James Bergstra, Ian J. Goodfellow, Arnaud Bergeron, Nicolas Bouchard, and Yoshua Bengio. Theano: new features and speed improvements. Deep Learning and Unsupervised Feature Learning NIPS 2012 Workshop, 2012.

James Bergstra, Olivier Breuleux, Frédéric Bastien, Pascal Lamblin, Razvan Pascanu, Guillaume Desjardins, Joseph Turian, David Warde-Farley, and Yoshua Bengio. Theano: a CPU and GPU math expression compiler. In *Proceedings of the Python for Scientific Computing Conference (SciPy)*, June 2010. Oral Presentation.

Bradley Efron. Defining the curvature of a statistical problem (with applications to second order efficiency). *The Annals of Statistics*, pages 1189–1242, 1975.

Bradley Efron. The estimation of prediction error. *Journal of the American Statistical Association*, 99(467), 2004.

Yonina C Eldar. Generalized SURE for exponential families: Applications to regularization. *Signal Processing, IEEE Transactions on*, 57(2):471–481, 2009.

Dumitru Erhan, Yoshua Bengio, Aaron Courville, Pierre-Antoine Manzagol, Pascal Vincent, and Samy Bengio. Why does unsupervised pre-training help deep learning? *The Journal of Machine Learning Research*, 11: 625–660, 2010.

Isabelle Guyon, Asa Ben Hur, Steve Gunn, and Gideon Dror. Result analysis of the nips 2003 feature selection challenge. In *Advances in Neural Information Processing Systems 17*, pages 545–552. MIT Press, 2004.

Geoffrey E. Hinton and Richard S. Zemel. Autoencoders, minimum description length and helmholtz free energy. In J. D. Cowan, G. Tesauro, and J. Alspector, editors, *Advances in Neural Information Processing Systems 6*, pages 3–10. Morgan-Kaufmann, 1994.

Lucas Janson, William Fithian, and Trevor J Hastie. Effective degrees of freedom: a flawed metaphor. *Biometrika*, page asv019, 2015.

Andrei N Kolmogorov. Three approaches to the quantitative definition of information. *Problems of information transmission*, 1(1):1–7, 1965.

Alex Krizhevsky and Geoffrey Hinton. Learning multiple layers of features from tiny images, 2009.

Yann LeCun, Corinna Cortes, and Christopher JC Burges. The MNIST database of handwritten digits, 1998.

David JC MacKay. *Information theory, inference and learning algorithms*. Cambridge university press, 2003.

Radford M. Neal. *Bayesian Learning for Neural Networks*. Springer-Verlag New York, Inc., Secaucus, NJ, USA, 1996. ISBN 0387947248.

Sathish Ramani, Thierry Blu, and Michael Unser. Monte-carlo sure: A black-box optimization of regularization parameters for general denoising algorithms. *Image Processing, IEEE Transactions on*, 17(9):1540–1554, 2008.

Jürgen Schmidhuber. Discovering neural nets with low kolmogorov complexity and high generalization capability. *Neural Networks*, 10(5):857–873, 1997.

Gideon Schwarz et al. Estimating the dimension of a model. *The annals of statistics*, 6(2):461–464, 1978.

Nitish Srivastava, Geoffrey Hinton, Alex Krizhevsky, Ilya Sutskever, and Ruslan Salakhutdinov. Dropout: A simple way to prevent neural networks from overfitting. *The Journal of Machine Learning Research*, 15(1):1929–1958, 2014.

Charles M Stein. Estimation of the mean of a multivariate normal distribution. *The annals of Statistics*, pages 1135–1151, 1981.

Robert Tibshirani, Michael Saunders, Saharon Rosset, Ji Zhu, and Keith Knight. Sparsity and smoothness via the fused lasso. *Journal of the Royal Statistical Society Series B*, 67(1):91–108, 2005. URL `https://ideas.repec.org/a/bla/jorssb/v67y2005i1p91-108.html`.

Samuel Vaiter, Charles Deledalle, Gabriel Peyré, Jalal M. Fadili, and Charles Dossal. The Degrees of Freedom of the Group Lasso. In *International Conference on Machine Learning Workshop (ICML)*, Edinburgh, United Kingdom, 2012. URL `https://hal.archives-ouvertes.fr/hal-00695292`.

Pascal Vincent, Hugo Larochelle, Isabelle Lajoie, Yoshua Bengio, and Pierre-Antoine Manzagol. Stacked denoising autoencoders: Learning useful representations in a deep network with a local denoising criterion. *The*

Journal of Machine Learning Research, 11:3371–3408, 2010.

Jianming Ye. On measuring and correcting the effects of data mining and model selection. *Journal of the American Statistical Association*, 93(441):120–131, 1998.

Hui Zou, Trevor Hastie, Robert Tibshirani, et al. On the "degrees of freedom" of the lasso. *The Annals of Statistics*, 35(5):2173–2192, 2007.

Training Deep Neural Nets to Aggregate Crowdsourced Responses

Alex Gaunt
Microsoft Research
Cambridge, UK

Diana Borsa
University College London,
London, UK

Yoram Bachrach
Microsoft Research
Cambridge, UK

Abstract

We propose a new method for aggregating crowdsourced responses, based on a deep neural network. Once trained, the aggregator network gets as input the responses of multiple participants to the same set of questions, and outputs its prediction for the correct response to each question. We empirically evaluate our approach on a dataset of responses to a standard IQ questionnaire, and show it outperforms existing state-of-the-art methods.

1 INTRODUCTION

Crowdsourcing platforms such as Amazon's Mechanical Turk are marketplaces which bring together participants who wish to take part in small micro-tasks in return for a fee and businesses or individuals who want to employ people for such tasks. A common use-case is data annotation and labelling, such as determining whether a caption correctly describes an image, or deciding whether the sentiment expressed in a text is positive, neutral or negative. Annotators may not always produce the correct responses to the questions posed to them. This might happen for several reasons: they may lack the sufficient knowledge to accurately answer every question or they might not be exerting the required effort to do well on a task. As annotators are not completely reliable in producing the correct responses to the posed questions, the resulting set of annotations would include errors, which results in an *inherent uncertainty* regarding which answers are correct. One instrument that can reduce the number of such errors is using *redundancy*: rather than asking a single participant to answer a question, the same question is posed to multiple participants; the multiple responses to the same question can then be *aggregated* into a single response to the question.

A commonly used aggregator is "majority vote", in which the chosen answer to each question is the one given most frequently by the participants. [1] This form of collective decision making has been heavily investigated. A result from the 18th century by the Marquis de Condorcet [5] states that the probability of majority vote to reach the correct conclusion to a question with two possible answers approaches 1 as the number of aggregated participants approaches infinity, assuming that participants are independent and each has a probability $p > \frac{1}{2}$ to provide the correct answer. [2]

Using crowdsourcing marketplaces it is possible to gather the responses of many participants to many questions in a very short time frame. Thus, such services make it easy to harness the collective intelligence of many participants. Given a set of responses of multiple participants to the same questions, one can use majority vote to get the aggregate responses to all the questions. However, this simple aggregator may be suboptimal, as some annotators produce higher quality results than others. For instance, if we know that the annotator Alice is more reliable than Bob, we might give her responses more weight when computing the aggregate solution. One way to determine the ability of annotators to provide correct responses is to evaluate each participant on a "gold-set" of questions, for which the correct answer is known. Given information about the ability of annotators evaluated on the gold-set, one can better aggregate the responses to a set of questions for which the correct answer is not known. However, what can be done to better aggregate responses in the absence of such a gold-set?

Earlier work has uncovered aggregation algorithms that outperform the majority vote aggregator, and that do not use external information such as a gold-set. Many such techniques are based on Bayesian models, that jointly infer information about the relative abilities and biases of participants, the difficulty levels of questions and the correct answer to each question [23, 2, 21]. As these techniques are Bayesian, they rely on a statistical model of the process through which the data was generated, reflecting model-

[1] The field of social choice refers to this aggregator as "plurality voting".

[2] The majority aggregator has also been shown to perform well in practice in multiple domains [22, 1, 10].

ing assumptions regarding the domain. Such assumptions are captured as random variables and the relation between them, consisting of the observed data and a set of assumed latent (unobserved) variables, along with a joint probability model tying the variables. While such techniques have been shown to be powerful tools for aggregating crowdsourced responses, their performance can be hindered when the modeling assumptions are incorrect or inaccurate – especially in the absence of large amounts of data.

Our contribution:

We propose a novel approach for aggregating crowdsourced responses. As opposed to existing Bayesian algorithms, at the heart of our approach lies a deep neural network, rather than a carefully engineered statistical model encoding an assumed relation between observed variables and possible latent factors. The network is trained by taking a small **seed dataset** of responses of participants to questions to which the correct answers are known. However, as opposed to the gold-set approach, we *only use the seed dataset to train the aggregator network*. Once the network is trained, we evaluate its ability to aggregate responses on a *completely separate* dataset, of both participants and questions the aggregator *has not encountered in the past*. Our training procedure involves using the small seed dataset to synthetically create a large training dataset, reflecting certain desiderata for aggregator functions.

We empirically evaluate our approach on a dataset of responses to a standard IQ questionnaire, and show it has a superior performance over existing methods. We examine the relation between the quantity of data available to our aggregator and its performance. Finally, we explore ways in which the network can infer not only the correct answers but also who the strong annotators are.

2 RELATED WORK

Earlier work in machine learning and artificial intelligence examined methods for merging the opinions of multiple people or agents, covering various aspects such as prediction markets [12] for predicting a future random event, aggregation of information in semantic web platforms [9], hybrid probabilistic relational frameworks [7] which combine logic based representations and probabilistic inference, and information aggregation in peer assessment systems [13].

A domain of particular interest is collective decision making and voting over candidate alternatives. Social choice theory focused on a set of rational agents, each of which has a preference order over the same set of candidates, and examined voting schemes which aggregate these preferences into a single aggregate decision [20] (such as who is the chosen candidate who wins the elections). Social choice theory shows how voting mechanisms allow reaching good group decisions [11], but has also uncovered ways in which voting rules are susceptible to manipulations by voters, who may lie about their true preferences so that the voting rule chooses an alternative their prefer [8]. We assume that the participants' responses reflect their true opinion and focus on the inference problem.

Our work focuses on aggregating crowdsourced opinions. A recent survey examines the implications of label noise in classification [6], and discusses label noise cleaning methods. One approach proposed for this problem is using EM [24], and another approach relies on modeling task difficulty [17]. Further, some algebraic bounds were provided for the binary rating case [4]. Other aggregation methods rely on probabilistic graphical models [23, 14, 18] including the state-of-the-art method of Bachrach et al. [2] (our empirical analysis shows we outperform this method).

3 PRELIMINARIES

We consider a set Q of $|Q| = q$ multiple choice questions, where each question has several possible answers. For simplicity, we denote the possible answers for each question as $[a] = \{1, 2, 3, \dots, a\}$. For each question $j \in Q$, there is exactly one correct answer $g_j \in [a]$ and we denote the set of correct answers to all the questions as the vector $g = (g_1, g_2, \dots, g_q) \in [a]^q$. The questions are posed to a set P of $|P| = p$ participants. Each participant $i \in P$ selects a response to each question j, reflecting which of the a possible answers they believe to be the correct one. We denote the response of participant $i \in P$ to question $j \in Q$ as $r_{i,j} \in [a]$. We collect the responses of all participants to all questions in a response matrix $M \in M_{p\times q}$ (where $M_{p\times q}$ denotes the set of all matrices with p rows and q columns) as follows: the element in the i'th row and j'th column in the matrix is the response of participant $i \in P$ to question $j \in Q$ (i.e. $M_{i,j} = r_{i,j} \in [a]$). Thus, each row in M represents a single participant's responses to each question and similarly, each column in M encodes the responses given by all the participants to a particular question.

Our goal is to use the response matrix M to uncover the correct answers g. This can be achieved if the responses of the participants to a question are correlated with the correct answer, though we do not make any specific model assumptions regarding the nature of this correlation. An aggregator is a function $f : M_{p\times q} \to [a]^q$ that takes a response matrix, produced by a set of participants for a set of questions, and outputs a proposed vector of correct answers – one for each of the considered questions. Given an input matrix $M \in M_{p\times q}$ and the vector of correct answers $g = (g_1, \dots, g_q) \in [a]^q$ for the considered q questions, we can measure the performance of the aggregator as the proportion of questions for which the inferred answers match the correct answers: $\frac{|Q_c|}{q}$ where Q_c denotes the set of questions for which the aggregator infers the correct responses $Q_c = \{j \in Q | f(M)_j = g_j\}$.

3.1 Desiderata for Aggreators

We now describe several properties of aggregator functions that intuitively characterize minimal requirements we expect fair aggregators to fulfill.

3.1.1 Participant ordering invariance

First, we have no a priori knowledge about the relative ability of the participants. In other words, the order of the participants whose opinions we aggregate is arbitrary, thus we expect a good aggregator to show no prejudice in favour or against a participant based on their position in the response matrix. We denote by $M^{r(x \leftrightarrow y)}$ the matrix M where the rows x and y are swapped,

$$M^{r(x \leftrightarrow y)}_{i,j} = \begin{cases} M_{y,j}, & i = x \\ M_{x,j}, & i = y \\ M_{i,j}, & otherwise \end{cases} \tag{1}$$

We say an aggregator $f : M_{p \times q} \to [a]^q$ is *participant location indifferent* if for any response matrix M and x, y we have $f(M^{r(x \leftrightarrow y)}) = f(M)$.

3.1.2 Question ordering invariance

Similarly, we may not attribute special meaning to the order in which the questions were posed to the participants. In other words, the choice of a specific column in the response matrix, where a certain question is placed reflects no knowledge we have regarding the question. We denote by $M^{c(x \leftrightarrow y)}_{i,j}$ the matrix M with columns x and y swapped:

$$M^{c(x \leftrightarrow y)}_{i,j} = \begin{cases} M_{i,y}, & j = x \\ M_{i,x}, & j = y \\ M_{i,j}, & otherwise \end{cases} \tag{2}$$

Given a vector $g \in [a]^q$ (representing either the true correct answers or a suggestion made by an aggregator regarding the correct answers), we denote by $g^{x \leftrightarrow y}$ the vector with the coordinates x and y swapped. We say an aggregator $f : M_{p \times q} \to [a]^q$ is *question location indifferent* if by swapping the order of two questions x, y, we obtain the same aggregated result, except the output differs in the order of answers, for the swapped questions, i.e. the required property is: $\forall M, x, y : f(M^{c(x \leftrightarrow y)}) = (f(M))^{x \leftrightarrow y}$.

3.1.3 Answer ordering invariance

Finally, we consider assigning meaning to the identities of the possible answers. The identities of answers are the set $[a] = 1, 2, \ldots, a$. In some cases, these identities reflect no knowledge we posses regarding the dataset. For instance, in an IQ questionnaire such as the one our empirical evaluation is based on. The unique correct answer has an equal probability of being placed in any location in the answer set. In contrast, in other datasets, the order in which the answers are shown is not arbitrary. For instance, consider the case of relevance judgement queries, where users are shown the current results of a search engine for a given query and are asked which is the most relevant. The search engine ranks results from best to worst, so if it is functioning well, the best match should be placed in the first place (or at least in one of the first few places). In this case, unless answers are deliberately shuffled, the correct response is far more likely to be one of the first responses than one of the last responses.

If we know the identities of answers are chosen arbitrarily, we may want to reflect this invariance. We denote by Π_a the set of all possible permutations over the set $[a]$ (i.e. any $\pi \in \Pi_a$ is a bijection $\pi : [a] \to [a]$). Consider a given $\pi_j \in \Pi_a$, and the column vector $r^T_{:,j} = (r_{1,j}, r_{2,j}, \ldots, r_{p,j})^T$ of given responses by p participants to a certain question j. We denote by $(r^{\pi}_{:,j})^T$ the column vector consisting of the answers by the p participants where the answer identities are shuffled through π, so $\pi(r_{:,j})^T = (\pi(r_{1,j}), \pi(r_{2,j}), \ldots, \pi(r_{p,j}))^T$. Given a response matrix $M \in M_{p \times q}$, we consider the case of permuting the answer identities for each question. Given a set of permutations $h = (\pi_1, \pi_2, \ldots, \pi_q)$ (where $\pi_j \in \Pi_a$), we consider shuffling the responses with these permutations for each of the questions. We denote by M^h the matrix where the responses of the participants where shuffled through the appropriate permutation, i.e. the j'th column of M^h is $\pi_j(r_{:,j})$. Similarly, given a vector $v \in [a]^q$ and a permutation sequence $h = (\pi_1, \pi_2, \ldots, \pi_q)$, we denote the vector where each element was shuffled by the respective permutation as $h(v) = (\pi_1(v_1), \pi_2(v_2), \ldots, \pi_q(v_q))$. We say an aggregator is *answer identity indifferent* if for any response matrix M and $h = (\pi_1, \pi_2, \ldots, \pi_p)$ we have $(f \circ h)(M) = (h \circ f)(M)$.

4 DeepAgg - TRAINING A NEURAL NETWORK AS AN AGGREGATOR

Our goal is to train a neural network as an aggregator $f_n : M_{p \times q} \to [a]^q$, following the desiderata of Section 3.1. We thus aim to generate an aggragtor that is participant location indifferent, question location indifferent and answer identity indifferent. This is a supervised learning problem, where the input is a response matrix $M \in M_{p \times q}$ and the desired output is the set of correct answers.

4.1 Constructing a Synthetic Training Set

The desired aggregator function is a complex mapping, so training a neural network requires a large training set. Given an infinite supply of participants and questions (along with their correct answers), we could repeatedly source q questions and p participants from the infinite supply source, pose the questions to the participants, collect the answers and thus obtain a large training set. However, in real-world settings we have a very limited supply of participants and questions.

Our solution relies on *synthetic data generation* through subsampling. We first take an original dataset, consisting of the responses of $p' > p$ participants to a set of $q' > q$ questions. We then select q questions at random from the q' available questions, and p participants of the p' available participants, and use only their responses. A single choice of q questions, $\mathcal{I}_q \in C(q', q)$ [3], and p participants, $\mathcal{I}_p \in C(p', p)$, results in a subsampled input matrix $M_{\mathcal{I}_p,\mathcal{I}_q} \in M_{p \times q}$. We repeat this process many times to generate a training dataset $D = \{(M_{\mathcal{I}_p,\mathcal{I}_q}, g_{\mathcal{I}_q})\}_{\mathcal{I}_q \in C(q',q), \mathcal{I}_p \in C(p',p)}$ where $g_{\mathcal{I}_q}$ denoted the correct responses for the subset of questions $\mathcal{I}_q$. In total we will have $\binom{q'}{q} \cdot \binom{p'}{p}$ choices of training instances. This augmented dataset enables us to transform a moderately small original dataset into one containing enough sub-sampled training examples to successfully train a neural net.

4.2 Adhering to Desiderata

Training a neural network involves optimizing the network's weight parameters based on the training set. The network could thus overfit the parameters to various properties of the training set that fail to generalize to the test set. For instance, if one answer is more common then others in the training set, a trained network might reflect this and select weights leading to this answer being chosen more often than others. When such trends are specific to the training data and do not occur on the test set, this overfitting is likely to lead to reduced performance. The Desiderata in Section 3.1 reflect assumptions regarding how the data was generated and the expected behavior of a good aggregator. Adhering to these properties avoids certain forms of overfitting. How should we design and train a neural network so it would achieve these properties and avoid overfitting?

One possibility is relying on the synthetic data generation process, and applying various *synthetic dataset perturbations*. Note that out of the three invariance properties identified in Section 3.1, the constructed dataset D encodes the first two. Thus in order to enforced the third invariance, we can permute the answer identities for each question in every subsampled data, by taking a set of random answer identity permutations $h = (\pi_1, \pi_2, \ldots, \pi_q)$ (where $\pi_j \in \Pi_a$), and shuffling the responses with these permutations for each of the questions. During the synthetic dataset construction, we generate a subsampled matrix $(M_{\mathcal{I}_p,\mathcal{I}_q}, g_{\mathcal{I}_q}) \in D$. Now we can expand this dataset by shuffling the answer identities via a random permutation h: $(h \circ (M_{\mathcal{I}_p,\mathcal{I}_q}, g_{\mathcal{I}_q})) = (h \circ (M_{\mathcal{I}_p,\mathcal{I}_q}), h \circ (g_{\mathcal{I}_q}))$. [4] As the answers identities are randomly shuffled, even if one answer identity is more frequently the correct answer in the original dataset, in the synthetic dataset any answer has an equal probability of being the correct answer. Hence, training on the synthetic dataset should result in an answer identity indifferent aggregator. Thus we get a large training dataset $\mathcal{D} = \{(h \circ (M_{\mathcal{I}_p,\mathcal{I}_q}, g_{\mathcal{I}_q})) | h \sim \Pi_a^q, (M_{\mathcal{I}_p,\mathcal{I}_q}, g_{\mathcal{I}_q}) \in D\}$.

An alternative approach to synthetic dataset perturbations is relying on the *chosen features* to achieve the desiderata: we simply create features that *abstract away* the irrelevant information. Under this approach we first construct the synthetic dataset D. We then take a training instance $(M_{\mathcal{I}_p,\mathcal{I}_q}, g_{\mathcal{I}_q}) \in D$, construct features representing this instance, denoted as $\phi(M_{\mathcal{I}_p,\mathcal{I}_q})$. Rather than training a neural network on the "raw" input $M \in D$, we train it on the feature representation, $\phi(M)$. Although any neural network must receive some *representation* of the training instance in some form, we will construct the feature representation in a way that eliminates information about participant locations, question locations or answer identities. More formally, we say a feature representation ϕ is participant location indifferent if changing the location of a participant in the matrix has no influence on the generated representation, so $\phi(M^{r(x \leftrightarrow y)}) = \phi(M)$ (for any $M \in D; x, y \in \mathcal{I}_p$). Similarly, we say a feature representation is question location indifferent if $\phi(M^{c(x \leftrightarrow y)}) = \phi(M), \forall M \in D; x, y \in \mathcal{I}_q$, and say that it is answer identity indifferent if $\phi(h \circ M) = \phi(M), \forall M \in D, h = (\pi_1, \pi_2, \ldots, \pi_p)$. [5]

4.3 An Overview of Our Approach

Our approach is indeed based on choosing a feature representation that adheres to our desiderata. Earlier work shows that while stronger aggregators do exist, majority vote is already powerful in aggregating crowdsourced responses [2]. Our architecture thus begins by using the majority vote rule to determine an initial answer sheet, and constructing features that describe participants and questions based on this initial chosen answer set; we then *gradually refine* this answer sheet, using two building blocks.

The first block is a neural network that predicts the probability that a participant would respond correctly to a specific question. We refer to these probabilities as "success probabilities". The input to the block is a proposed answer sheet, reflecting the "best guess" of the correct answer for each question. Given this answer sheet, the block constructs our feature representation of the participants and

[3] We denote by $C(n, k)$ the set of k-combinations that can be form using n elements

[4] See the definitions of these operators in Section 3.1.

[5] These properties of a *feature representation* are similar to those of an aggregator function, except in the case of a feature representation we refer to an *encoding* of the important bits of the input matrix that allow determining how to best aggregate the data, rather than to the end result consisting of the chosen answer for each question.

questions, and applies the neural network to compute the success probabilities.

The second building block focuses on a single question, and receives as input these success probabilities of the participants as well as the answer chosen by each participant, and outputs the chosen answer for the question. We propose two alternatives for constructing the second block, which both work by computing the total support for each possible answer, then outputting the answer with the strongest support. One alternative is using a neural network, and the other is a deterministic formula that weighs the success probabilities using a simplistic probabilistic model of the behavior of participants. [6]

Combining the two building blocks, we obtain a method for refining an answer sheet. The first block takes the current answer sheet and the responses of the participants, and computes the success probabilities; the second block uses these success probabilities to output an improved answer sheet. We call the application of the two building blocks a *refinement step*. We initialize the system with an answer sheet computed by majority vote, and perform multiple refinement steps to generate our final answer sheet. [7]

We now describe the features used to represent the participants and questions, then describe the building blocks and the overall network architecture in more detail.

4.4 Feature Representation of the Input

Consider an input matrix $M \in M_{p \times q}$ consisting of the responses of p participants to a set of q questions, and a proposed set of answers to these questions $g' \in [a]^n$. An element g'_i can be thought of as the current best guess for the answer to question i (our algorithms initialize g'_i as the majority vote to question i in the subsampled matrix). We refer to the vector g' of proposed responses as an answer sheet. A rough estimate for the success or ability of a participant i is the proportion of questions to which they responded correctly, assuming that the answer sheet g' is indeed correct: $a_i = \frac{|\{j \in [q] | M_{i,j} = g'_j\}|}{q}$. Similarly, a rough estimate for a difficulty of a question is the proportion of students who failed to provide the correct response to it: $d_j = 1 - \frac{|\{i \in [s] | M_{i,j} = g'_j\}|}{s}$. Clearly, the quality of the features a_i (for a participant i) and d_j (for a question j) depend on the answer sheet g': the higher the quality of g', the less noisy these features are.

The above features allow predicting whether a participant is likely to correctly answer a question, and can also be used to rank participants based on their ability or questions by their difficulty. Consider sorting the questions by their estimated difficulty, d_j, and partitioning this set into k parts, $D_1, \ldots, D_k$ by the estimated difficulty. For example, for $k = 2$ we partition the questions into two parts by estimated difficulty:the easiest half of the questions are D_1 (with the lower difficulty estimate d_j), and the hardest half of the questions are D_2 (with the highest difficulty estimate d_j). We can estimate the ability of a participant using only the questions in one part of the partition. For instance, for $k = 2$ the performance of participant i on the easiest questions D_1 is $a_i^1 = \frac{|\{j \in D_1 | M_{i,j} = g'_j\}|}{|D_1|}$, and their performance on the hardest questions is $a_i^2 = \frac{|\{j \in D_2 | M_{i,j} = g'_j\}|}{|D_2|}$. More generally, we choose a number of parts (the "width" k), and denote $a_i^t = \frac{|\{j \in D_t | M_{i,j} = g'_j\}|}{|D_t|}$ (where $t \in \{1, 2, \ldots, k\}$, and $|D_t| = \frac{q}{k}$, assuming that k divides q).

Consider partitioning the questions into two parts, the easy questions D_1 and hard questions D_2 (with difficulty estimated using the current answer sheet g'). We'd expect a student i to do better on the easy questions than on the hard questions, so a_i^1 is higher and a_i^2 is lower. If we have a student where a_i^1 is lower than a_i^2, we might infer that their success on the harder questions is due to luck rather than skill (and predict him to be less successful than a student v of identical average skill but where a_v^1 is higher than a_v^2). Thus $a_i^1, \ldots, a_i^k$ can serve as additional features providing further useful information, beyond just the average skill.

Similarly to partitioning the questions by their difficulty to build a more fine-grained representation of students, we can partition the students by ability to generate a better representation for questions. We sort the students by their estimated ability, a_i, and partition this set into k' parts, $E_1, \ldots, E'_k$. We estimate the difficulty of a question using only the students in one part of the partition (e.g. the difficulty of a question for the strong and weak students). We denote $d_j^t = 1 - \frac{|\{i \in E_t | M_{i,j} = g'_j\}|}{|E_t|}$ (where $t \in \{1, 2, \ldots, k'\}$, and $|E_t| = \frac{s}{k'}$, assuming that k' divides s).

The goal of our first building block is to take an input subsampled matrix M and a proposed answer sheet g' and determine the probability of a student i to correctly answer question j. We represent the students and questions using the above features: $\phi_{i,j}(M) = (a_i, a_i^1, \ldots, a_i^k, d_j, d_j^1, \ldots, d_j^{k'})$ (where the features are computed using g' as the answer sheet). We note that the representation ϕ is answer identity indifferent, participant location indifferent and question location indifferent.

4.5 Predicting Whether a Participant Will Answer a Question Correctly

We use a neural network which takes a representation of a single user and a single questions, and predicts the prob-

[6] In the empirical analysis in Section 5 we show both perform well on our dataset (with no significant performance difference between the two).

[7] If a refinement step does not change the answer sheet, we have reached a fixed point of the refinement function, and can terminate the process early.

ability that the user would correctly answer the question. The input to the network is $\phi_{i,j}(M)$ (where $i \in [p]$ and $j \in [q]$), as defined in Section 4.4. We have used the dimensions $k = k' = 3$, so both a user and a question are represented as 4 real numbers, meaning each input is a vector $\phi_{i,j}(M) \in \mathbb{R}^8$. Our network consists of three fully connected layers, each performing a linear transformation then a $\tanh$ operation. The first linear transformation maps the input to a hidden layer with a hidden state of size $h = 10$ neurons, and the following layers maintain this hidden state size. Following these layers, our network linearly maps the final layer into a single neuron.

Given a single subsampled matrix M and given the correct answer sheet g (consisting of the known correct answers to the subsampled questions), we use $y_{i,j}$ as an indicator variable denoting whether the participant i answered question j correctly, so $y_{i,j} = 1$ if $M_{i,j} = g_j$ and $y_{i,j} = 0$ otherwise. [8] Each subsampled matrix results in $p \cdot q$ representations for participant-question pairs, $\phi_{i,j}(M)$, and in $p \cdot q$ indicator variables $y_{i,j}$. Applying the network on all the representations of participant-question pairs, we obtain $p \cdot q$ activations of the final layer, denoted as $\hat{y}_{i,j}$. We use the cross entropy loss:

$$\mathcal{L} = \sum_{i=1}^{p}\sum_{j=1}^{q}[y_{i,j}\log\hat{y}_{i,j} + (1-\hat{y}_{i,j})\log(1-\hat{y}_{i,j})]$$

We train the network by randomly subsampling $n = 10,000$ matrices along with the correct responses to the questions. Once the network is trained, it can receive a representation $\phi_{i,j}$ of a participant i and a question j, and its output $\hat{y}_{i,j}$ can be interpreted as the probability that the participant would answer the question correctly. Figure 1 illustrates the structure of this neural network.

4.6 Computing Support for a Given Answer

The second building block in our approach considers a single question and the responses of p participants to that question. The goal of the block is to provide a score for each answer, such that the correct answer would receive the highest score. We refer to this as computing the aggregate support in favor of an answer. The output of the block is thus a vector of scores $s = (s_1, s_2, \ldots, s_a)$ where s_t is the score of answer t. We propose two alternatives for the construction of this building block.

The first alternative we propose is a neural network. Given the probability of a participant i to correctly answer the question, denoted b_i for brevity [9] and the responses of each participant to the question, denoted $m_i = r_{i,j}$ for the question j, we construct a $a \times p$ matrix U representing a probability distribution over the a possible answers.

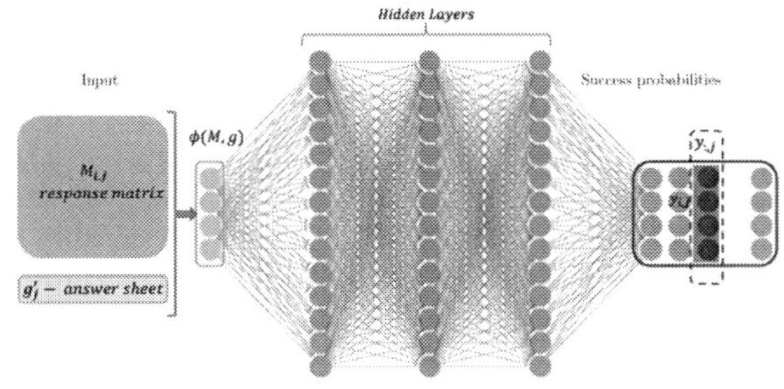

Figure 1: Visualization of the first building block: predicting success probabilities $y_{i,j}$, given a response matrix $M \in D$ and current answer sheet $g' = (g'_1, \cdots, g'_q)$

$$U_{i,k} = \begin{cases} b_i, & k = m_i \text{ (participant's chosen answer)} \\ \frac{1-b_i}{a-1}, & otherwise \end{cases} \quad (3)$$

This is an alternative to a "one-hot" encoding of $\{b_i\}_{i=1:p}$, reflecting the probability of a participant to choose each answer, assuming that the correct answer is indeed the one they chose, and that each incorrect answer is equally likely (the remaining mass $1 - b_i$ spread evenly across them).

The input to the network are the rows in matrix $U = (u_1^T, \cdots, u_a^T)$ – one for each possible answer. As the identity of each answer does not matter, we train a function f that takes a answer probability vector u and produces a score, s, for this answer vector. To learn the function we use a network of 3 fully connected layers, each consisting of a linear transformation followed by a $\tanh$ non-linearity, and a hidden size of $h = 15$, followed by another linear layer mapping the h neurons to a score s. We use the same mapping f to produce scores for all a possible answers, leading to $(s_1, \ldots, s_a) = (f(u_1), \ldots, f(u_a))$.

Each subsampled matrix used to train this network consists of q questions, where each question has an encoding, U, of size $p \cdot a$ representing the responses of the participants. Further, each subsampled matrix is considered along the vector of correct responses to each question $(g_1, \ldots, g_q)$. As we wish to optimize the network parameters so that the correct answer g_j to question j would receive the highest score s_j, the final layer of our network is a softmax operator: $\frac{\exp(s_i)}{\sum_{i=1}^{a}\exp(s_i)}$, and we use the cross-entropy loss. Figure 2 illustrates the structure of this neural network.

The second alternative we propose is a deterministic scor-

[8]Note that while training the network we use the ground truth correct answers. However, once the neural network is trained, it does not require this information, and can be used for any dataset. In our empirical analysis we train the network using one dataset, and use it on a completely separate dataset (both participants and questions that were not shown during training).

[9]Replacing the notation $\hat{y}_{i,j}$ as the question index is redundant

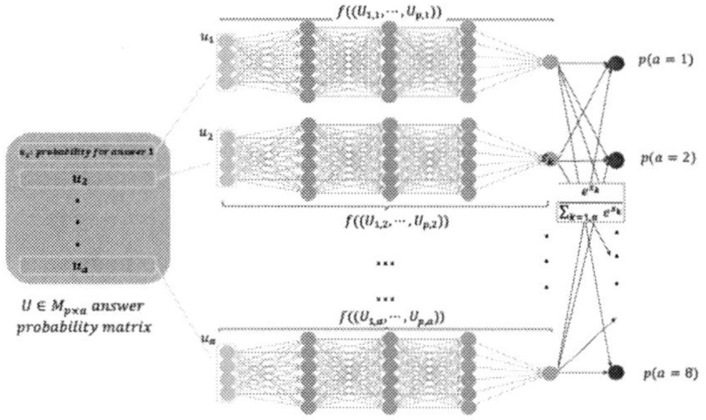

Figure 2: Visualization of the second building block: predicting the answer for a particular question j. Given the participants responses $M_{:,j}$ and the inferred probabilities of participants to be right or wrong $y_{:,j}$, we construct an answer probability matrix U as described in Eq. 3. Then for each possible answer k, we compute a score based on the participants' answer probabilities u_k: $s_k = f(u_k)$. These scores go through a `softmax` operator and finally we choose the answer with the highest probability.

ing function, based on a simple probabilistic model for the way in which the responses are chosen by the participant. Suppose that a priori each answer is equally likely to be the correct answer (reflecting answer identity invariance). Thus the correct answer is a random variable A, with a uniform distribution over the support $\{1, \ldots, a\}$. Assume that the probability of a participant i to choose the right answer to the question is b_i (given as the block's input), and that if i fails to choose the correct answer, they choose an answer uniformly at random from the remaining $a - 1$ answers. Finally, we assume that the participants are independent of one another. The responses of the participants are thus an observed random variable R over the support $[a]^p$.

Consider the case where the correct answer to the question as $r \in [a]$. Given the observed responses R, we can partition the participants into two sets: the participants who responded with the answer r as X_r (the correct participants), and those who responded with some other answer X_o (the incorrect participants). To obtain the observed responses R, each of the correct participants must have chosen the correct answer (with probability b_i), and each of the incorrect participant must have failed to chose the correct answer (with probability $1 - b_i$), and then choose exactly the incorrect answer they chose (there are $a - 1$ incorrect responses and each is equally probable). Thus, under our model, the probability of obtaining the observed responses R is:

$$P(R|A = r) = \prod_{f \in X_r} b_f \cdot \prod_{g \in X_o} \frac{1 - b_g}{a - 1} \quad (4)$$

The goal of the second building block is choosing the best response for a question given the input parameters $b1, \ldots, b_p$ and the observed responses R. By Bayes' theorem we have $P(A|R) = \frac{P(R|A) \cdot P(A)}{P(R)}$. Given the observed responses R and our assumed model, we seek the most probable answer $\arg\max_a P(A = a|R) = \frac{P(R|A=a) \cdot P(A=a)}{P(R)}$. As $P(R)$ is a normalizing constant and as we assumed that for any a we have $P(A = a) = \frac{1}{a}$, we have $\arg\max_a P(A = a|R) = \arg\max_a P(R|A = a)$. We can thus simply apply Equation 4 to compute the score $P(R|A = r)$ for each possible response $r \in [a]$, and return the answer with the maximal score.

4.7 Iterative Refinement

Section 4.4 discusses how we take a subsampled matrix M and a proposed answer sheet g'_0, and output a feature representation $\phi(M, g')$ for each user and question. Section 4.5 discusses how we take the feature representation and apply a neural network to predict $y_{i,j}$, the probability of each participant i to answer any question j. We call this step $cor(\phi(M, g'))$. Finally, section 4.6 discusses how we take the success probabilities $y = (y_{1,1}, y_{1,2}, \ldots, y_{1,q}, y_{2,1}, \ldots, y_{p,q})$ and the subsampled response matrix M and generate and refined answer sheet g' (either using a trained neural network, or through the formula on equation 4). We call this step $ref(y, M)$.

Our method, called DeepAgg, simply involves applying multiple such iterations (the number of iterations is the parameter $nIter$). Algorithm 1 describes this process.

Data: Reponse matrix $M \in M_{p \times q}$
Result: Aggregated responses $g' \in [a]^q$
$g' \leftarrow$ Maj(M) // Majority vote initialization ;
for $i \leftarrow 1$, ***nIter*** **do**
  $y \leftarrow cor(\phi(M, g'))$;
  $g' \leftarrow ref(y, M)$;
end
return g' ;

Algorithm 1: DeepAgg: Iterative Refinement

5 EMPIRICAL ANALYSIS

We empirically examine the DeepAgg method of Section 4, and evaluate its performance against both the majority vote aggregator and the DARE Bayesian aggregator of Bachrach et al. [2], using the same dataset described in that paper. This dataset consists of the responses of participants to the Raven's Standard Progressive Matrices (SPM) IQ test [15], an intelligence screening test. This test is a multiple choice questionnaire, consisting of $q' = 46$ questions, each with eight possible answers. [10] SPM is a popular intelligence

[10]The full test has 4 parts in increasing difficulty. We removed the easiest questions to focus on the more interesting cases where there is not a consensus between participants. Note that including all questions does not alter the qualitative conclusions of this paper.

test, that has been used for research purposes, clinical assessment and even military personnel screening [16]. The dataset contains the responses of $p' = 746$ participants, who took the test in the 2006, in the process of establishing the ability norms for the British market [15]. [11]

To conduct our experiments, we partitioned the dataset's questions into two parts, Q_a and Q_b, each with half (23) of the dataset's questions (where $Q_a \cup Q_b = \emptyset$). Similarly, we partitioned the participants into two parts, P_a and P_b, each with half (373) of the dataset's participants (with $Q_a \cup Q_b = \emptyset$). We trained DeepAgg using subsampled data from the responses of the participants in P_a to the questions in Q_a, and evaluated the performance using subsampled data from the responses of the participants in P_b to the questions in Q_b. This guarantees that the training and testing are done on separate datasets: not only are the training instances different from the test instances, effectively we are testing the aggregator on a completely unseen dataset.

5.1 Aggregation Quality

DeepAgg aggregates the responses of multiple participants and outputs the predicted correct answer for each question, similarly to majority vote or the DARE aggregator of Bachrach et al. [2]. We now compare the performance of these approaches. Our quality metric for an aggregator is simple. Given a response matrix $M^i \in M_{p \times q}$, an aggregator returns a vector $g'^i \in [a]^q$. Given the the set of actual correct responses $g^i \in [a]^q$, we denote the number of questions where the aggregator was correct as $c(g') = |\{j | g'^i_j = g^i_j\}|$. We denote the proportion of questions that were aggregated successfully as $s^i(g') = \frac{c^i(g'^i)}{q}$.

Figure 3 shows the quality of majority vote, DARE and our DeepAgg, as a function of the available date. When an aggregator has more available responses for each question, we expect it to achieve a better performance as it has more available data. The x-axis of Figure 3 shows the number of responses per question (the number of participants in the subsampled response matrix), and the y-axis shows the aggregation quality $\frac{1}{k}\sum_{i=1}^{k} s^i(g'^i)$, across $k = 10,000$ runs (each of which is a random subsampled response matrix).

Figure 3 shows that all methods achieve a better result as more data is available, but that the returns diminish as the number of participants increases (in agreement with the results reported in the work of Bachrach et al. [2]). For all data regimes, DeepAgg outperforms DARE.

The plot in Figure 3 was created with DeepAgg using equation 4 as the second building block. We have also run DeepAgg with the neural net implementation for the second block, with an almost identical performance, indicating that both are reasonable choices for that block.

[11]We thank the Psychometrics Centre of the University of Cambridge for making this dataset available for this research.

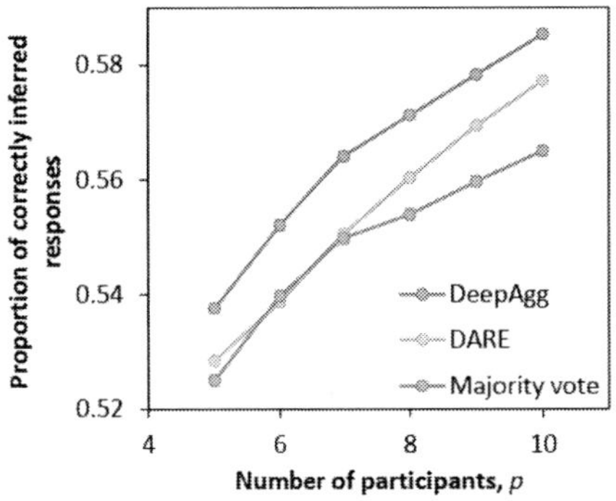

Figure 3: The performance of DeepAgg and alternative aggregators as a function of the size of the data

DeepAgg performs multiple iterations of improving the answer sheet, as described in Algorithm 1. Figure 4 shows the effect of the number of iterations on the quality of aggregation. The x-axis is the number of iterations ($nIter$ in Algorithm 1) and the y-axis is the average aggregation quality $\frac{1}{k}\sum_{i=1}^{k} s^i(g'^i)$ across $k = 10,000$ runs (with random subsampled response matrices). We find that performing multiple iterations improves the quality of aggregation, but that this improvement diminishes as the number of iterations increases. One possible cause for these diminishing returns is that if the answer sheet g' does not change following an iterations, we have reached a fixed point of this function, so there is no point in performing additional iterations.

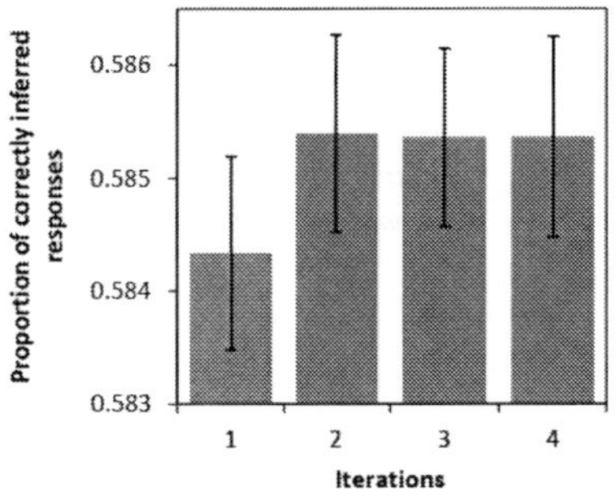

Figure 4: The effect of the number of DeepAgg iterations on aggregation quality

5.2 Evaluating the ability of participants

While the main stated goal of the DeepAgg aggregator is inferring the set of correct answers g, a common use-case in crowdsourcing settings is deciding which of the participants are good at the task and which are not.

One possible measure of the ability of a participant i given a response matrix M and a set of correct answers $g \in [a]^q$, is the proportion of questions which i answered correctly: $a_i = \frac{|\{j \in [q] | M_{i,j} = g_j\}|}{q}$. If we are not given the ground truth set of responses, g, we could use an approximate answer sheet g', and use $a'_i = \frac{|\{j \in [q] | M_{i,j} = g'_j\}|}{q}$ as an approximation. Clearly, the quality of this estimator depends on how well g' approximates g. As DeepAgg allows inferring an answer sheet g' given the response matrix M, one could thus use it as a tool for inferring the ability of participants.

Figure 5 investigates how well DeepAgg performs in inferring the ability of participants. This is a density plot which was generated by examining many data points, each describing a single random participant in a run of DeepAgg on a random subsampled matrix. The x-axis of each point represents the true ability of the participant, a_i, and the y-axis is the estimated ability of the participant, a'_i (using an answer sheet g' inferred using DeepAgg). The figure shows the density of the sampled points in each area on the chart.

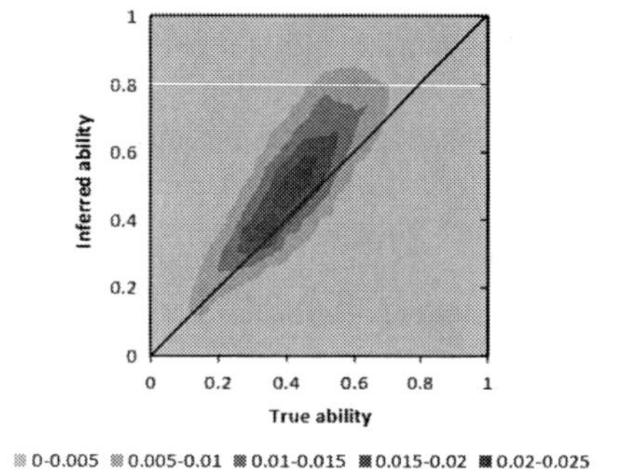

Figure 5: Using DeepAgg to infer the ability of participants

A perfect aggregator would result in a figure where points rest on the $y = x$ axis, and a Pearson correlation of 1. Figure 5 shows a very strong correlation between the inferred and true ability of each participant, even with few iterations. The Pearson correlation between the true ability of a participant and the inferred ability of that participant is $r = 0.79$, which is high considering the limited amount of data available to DeepAgg. This indicates that DeepAgg is a powerful tool not only in aggregating responses, but also for identifying skilled and less-skilled participants.

5.3 The Need for Computing Features

A major advantage of deep learning is its ability to learn feature representations without resorting to hand-crafted features [3, 19]. One might ask why we have used a method that relies on the features discussed in Section 4.4. A simpler architecture could use a deep neural net which simply operates on the input subsampled matrix M (for instance using a "one-hot" encoding for the chosen response of each participant on each question). We have indeed tested such an architecture, showing the performance it achieves to only match majority vote. A very deep network is theoretically capable of performing the overall computation we have done using DeepAgg. However, as this requires a very deep network, training the network using stochastic gradient descent (or similar variants) must search through an extremely large and complicated parameter space. The fact that a direct architecture does not achieve the high performance of DeepAgg indicates that the current optimization methods are incapable of finding this solution.

The computation in DeepAgg is quite deep: we apply a 3 layer deep network twice for each iteration (each building block is a network), so with even as few as 3 iterations this is a 18 layer deep architecture. Further, our computation relies on computing the desired features once in each iterations. Our ability to successfully train the network stems from the *constant supervision* we apply: a loss can be computed after every building block using the ground truth. In other words, once every basic building block, we apply a loss using the ground truth answer sheet g, allowing us to find excellent optimized parameters for each block.

6 LIMITATIONS AND CONCLUSIONS

We presented DeepAgg, an approach for aggregating crowdsourced responses, based on a deep neural network. Our empirical analysis shows that DeepAgg has a superior performance over the majority aggregator and a more sophisticated Bayesian approach. Our approach has some **inherent limitations**. Training the network requires taking an initial dataset and repeatedly sub-sampling parts of it to generate synthetic training examples. This training procedure is a computationally expensive calculation, which yields an aggregator taking the responses of p participants to q questions. Once the aggregator is trained, applying it to a new training instance is has a relatively low runtime complexity. However, if the input dimensions p or q are changed, the training process needs to be repeated to create a new aggregator. Further, we used a simple network architecture. A more elaborate structure could potentially improve performance. Finally, our method is desigend for the **complete data case**. It is difficult to adapting our method to the case of incomplete data, where some of the participants have only answered some of the questions. [12]

Several issues remain open for future research. How can our procedure be modified to handle the case of missing responses, where some participants may only provide responses to a subset of the questions? While it is easy to encode this in the input to the network, this may have a large impact of the quality of the aggregator. Second, is it possible to extend our approach to an active learning scenario, where we have control over the next question to ask a participant? Finally, could we take an aggregator training for certain input dimensions and convert it into an aggregator for other input sizes, without retraining a network?

[12] In contrast, Bayesian approaches are usually robust to missing data (for instance, in approaches based on graphical models, these can simply be treated as unobserved random variables).

References

[1] Y. Bachrach, T. Graepel, G. Kasneci, M. Kosinski, and J. Van Gael. Crowd IQ - aggregating opinions to boost performance. In *AAMAS*, 2012.

[2] Yoram Bachrach, Thore Graepel, Tom Minka, and John Guiver. How to grade a test without knowing the answers—a bayesian graphical model for adaptive crowdsourcing and aptitude testing. In *Proceedings of the 29th International Conference on Machine Learning (ICML-12)*, pages 1183–1190, 2012.

[3] Yoshua Bengio. Learning deep architectures for ai. *Foundations and trends® in Machine Learning*, 2(1):1–127, 2009.

[4] Nilesh Dalvi, Anirban Dasgupta, Ravi Kumar, and Vibhor Rastogi. Aggregating crowdsourced binary ratings. In *Proceedings of the 22nd international conference on World Wide Web*, pages 285–294. International World Wide Web Conferences Steering Committee, 2013.

[5] M.J.A.N. de Caritat et al. *Essai sur l'application de l'analyse à la probabilité des décisions rendues à la pluralité des voix*. L'imprimerie royale, 1785.

[6] Benoît Frénay and Michel Verleysen. Classification in the presence of label noise: a survey. *Neural Networks and Learning Systems, IEEE Transactions on*, 25(5):845–869, 2014.

[7] L. Getoor, N. Friedman, D. Koller, A. Pfeffer, and B. Taskar. 5 probabilistic relational models. *Statistical relational learning*, page 129, 2007.

[8] Allan Gibbard. Manipulation of voting schemes: a general result. *Econometrica: journal of the Econometric Society*, pages 587–601, 1973.

[9] G. Kasneci, J. Van Gael, R. Herbrich, and T. Graepel. Bayesian knowledge corroboration with logical rules and user feedback. In *ECML/PKDD*, 2010.

[10] M. Kosinski, Y. Bachrach, G. Kasneci, J. Van-Gael, and T. Graepel. Crowd IQ: Measuring the intelligence of crowdsourcing platforms. In *ACM Web Sciences*, 2012.

[11] A. McLennan. Consequences of the condorcet jury theorem for beneficial information aggregation by rational agents. *American Political Science Review*, pages 413–418, 1998.

[12] D.M. Pennock and R. Sami. Computational aspects of prediction markets, 2007.

[13] Chris Piech, Jonathan Huang, Zhenghao Chen, Chuong Do, Andrew Ng, and Daphne Koller. Tuned models of peer assessment in moocs. *arXiv preprint arXiv:1307.2579*, 2013.

[14] Guo-Jun Qi, Charu C Aggarwal, Jiawei Han, and Thomas Huang. Mining collective intelligence in diverse groups. In *Proceedings of the 22nd international conference on World Wide Web*, pages 1041–1052. International World Wide Web Conferences Steering Committee, 2013.

[15] J.C. Raven. Standard progressive matrices plus.

[16] J.C. Raven. The raven's progressive matrices: Change and stability over culture and time. *Cognitive Psychology*, 41(1):1–48, 2000.

[17] V.C. Raykar, S. Yu, L.H. Zhao, G.H. Valadez, C. Florin, L. Bogoni, and L. Moy. Learning from crowds. *JMLR*, 2010.

[18] Mahyar Salek, Yoram Bachrach, and Peter Key. Hotspotting-a probabilistic graphical model for image object localization through crowdsourcing. In *AAAI*, 2013.

[19] Jürgen Schmidhuber. Deep learning in neural networks: An overview. *Neural Networks*, 61:85–117, 2015.

[20] A. Sen. Social choice theory. *Handbook of mathematical economics*, 3:1073–1181, 1986.

[21] Bar Shalem, Yoram Bachrach, John Guiver, and Christopher M Bishop. Students, teachers, exams and moocs: Predicting and optimizing attainment in web-based education using a probabilistic graphical model. In *Machine Learning and Knowledge Discovery in Databases*, pages 82–97. Springer, 2014.

[22] James Surowiecki. *The wisdom of crowds*. Anchor, 2005.

[23] P. Welinder, S. Branson, S. Belongie, and P. Perona. The multidimensional wisdom of crowds. In *NIPS*, 2010.

[24] J. Whitehill, P. Ruvolo, T. Wu, J. Bergsma, and J. Movellan. Whose vote should count more: Optimal integration of labels from labelers of unknown expertise. *NIPS*, 22:2035–2043, 2009.

Model-Free Reinforcement Learning with Skew-Symmetric Bilinear Utilities

Hugo Gilbert[1], **Bruno Zanuttini**[4], **Paolo Viappiani**[1], **Paul Weng**[2,3], **Esther Nicart**[4,5]
[1]Sorbonne Universités, UPMC Univ Paris 06, CNRS, LIP6 UMR 7606, Paris, France
[2]SYSU-CMU Joint Institute of Engineering, Guangzhou, China
[3]SYSU-CMU Shunde International Joint Research Institute, Shunde, China
[4]Caen University, Normandy, France;
[5]Cordon Electronics DS2i, France;
{hugo.gilbert,paolo.viappiani}@lip6.fr, paweng@cmu.edu, {esther.nicart,bruno.zanuttini}@unicaen.fr

Abstract

In reinforcement learning, policies are typically evaluated according to the expectation of cumulated rewards. Researchers in decision theory have argued that more sophisticated decision criteria can better model the preferences of a decision maker. In particular, Skew-Symmetric Bilinear (SSB) utility functions generalize von Neumann and Morgenstern's expected utility (EU) theory to encompass rational decision behaviors that EU cannot accommodate. In this paper, we adopt an SSB utility function to compare policies in the reinforcement learning setting. We provide a model-free SSB reinforcement learning algorithm, *SSB Q-learning*, and prove its convergence towards a policy that is ϵ-optimal according to SSB. The proposed algorithm is an adaptation of fictitious play [Brown, 1951] combined with techniques from stochastic approximation [Borkar, 1997]. We also present some experimental results which evaluate our approach in a variety of settings.

1 INTRODUCTION

In problems of sequential decision-making under uncertainty (often represented as Markov Decision Problems—MDPs [Puterman, 1994]), an agent has to repeatedly choose according to her current state an action whose consequences are uncertain, in order to maximize a certain criterion in the long run. In most cases, the criterion chosen is the expectation of cumulated rewards, but it is not risk sensitive and fails to explain widely observed violations of axioms such as transitivity or von Neumann's independence axiom. One of the aims of decision theory is to provide criteria able to account for such behaviors.

Interestingly, the Skew-Symmetric Bilinear (SSB) utility theory [Fishburn, 1984] defines a family of decision criteria able to represent risk-averse and risk-seeking behaviors, intransitive choices and violations of the independence axiom. In particular it encompasses the expected utility (EU) model [von Neumann and Morgenstern, 1947], which is the most popular risk sensitive criterion in decision theory. In SSB theory a binary functional φ over probability distributions is given, where the sign of $\varphi(\mathbf{p}, \mathbf{q})$ gives the preference between two distributions $\mathbf{p}$ and $\mathbf{q}$. Furthermore, particular choices of φ allow decision criteria that only rely on ordinal pieces of information such as "this trajectory is preferred to this other trajectory" to be used. This property is of interest for MDPs as the optimal policy can be highly sensitive to the reward function, but specifying such a reward function is often difficult even for an expert user.

Such preference-based approaches have received much attention lately [Akrour *et al.*, 2012, Furnkranz *et al.*, 2012, Busa-fekete *et al.*, 2014, Wilson *et al.*, 2012, Wirth and Fürnkranz, 2013, Wirth and Neumann, 2015], and a special case of SSB utility function which optimizes the probability of yielding a preferred outcome has been investigated in various domains [Busa-fekete *et al.*, 2014, Dudík *et al.*, 2015, Rivest and Shen, 2010]. In reinforcement learning (RL), Busa-Fekete *et al.* [2014] provided a meta-heuristic algorithm using evolutionary strategies to compute a "good" policy. Designing a learning scheme for an RL problem using an SSB utility function would therefore enable RL problems to be solved for a large class of criteria including "preference-based" criteria.

The possibility of intransitive preferences in SSB utility theory could be seen as a significant barrier to its use in automated decision making. However, the seminal work of Gilbert *et al.* [2015a] shows that an SSB-optimal strategy always exists as a mixture of policies, and furthermore, that in a finite horizon MDP where the model is known, such an SSB-optimal strategy can be computed using a double oracle approach. Unfortunately, this approach suffers two drawbacks: its time and space requirements might become prohibitive if the optimal mixture of policies is composed of too many policies, and it does not generalize to the case where the model is unknown, and thus cannot be used to derive a model-free RL algorithm.

We remedy this by providing a new algorithm which behaves optimally in an MDP with an SSB utility function, from which we derive a model-free RL algorithm in order to learn an SSB-optimal policy when the model is unknown. While the approach is still based on game-theoretic arguments, the algorithm differs in spirit and resembles an adaptation of a fictitious play algorithm [Brown, 1951] combined with Q-learning [Watkins and Dayan, 1992] using stochastic approximation techniques with two timescales [Borkar, 2008]. Kalathil *et al.* [2014] recently exploited a similar two-timescale technique in MDPs, but in a different context; using the average expected reward criterion with vector rewards, their goal is to learn a policy whose vectorial value approaches a fixed set.

The paper is organized as follows. In Section 2, we give the background elements and introduce our notations. In Section 3, we give a game theoretic view of the resolution of an RL problem with an SSB utility function and present a fictitious play approach to solve it. Lastly, in Section 4, we present some experimental results.

2 SSB MARKOV DECISION PROCESSES

We study in this paper episodic MDPs with finite state and action spaces. An MDP $\mathcal{M}$ is formally defined by a tuple $(\mathcal{S}, \mathcal{F}, \mathcal{A}, \mathcal{P}, s_0)$ where: $\mathcal{S}$ is a finite collection of states; $\mathcal{F} = \{f_1, f_2, \ldots, f_{|\mathcal{F}|}\} \subset \mathcal{S}$ is a finite set of final states; $\mathcal{A} = \{\mathcal{A}_s | s \in \mathcal{S}\}$ is a collection of finite sets of possible actions, one for each state; $\mathcal{P}$ is the transition function where $\mathcal{P}(s'|s, a)$ is the probability that the state at time step $t+1$ is s', given that the state at time step t was s and that the agent performed action a; $s_0 \in \mathcal{S} \setminus \mathcal{F}$ is the initial state in which all episodes start.[1]

Whereas preferences over state-action pairs are typically modeled with numerical rewards, in our framework we assume that the final states summarize the preference information. More precisely, we assume that the decision maker has a preference relation $\succeq$ over possible final states, where $f \succeq f'$ means that ending in final state f is at least as good as ending in f'. Note that *we do not assume* $\succeq$ *to be total or even transitive*, thus accommodating a wide variety of preference behaviors, including those deviating from normative decision theory. A "standard" MDP (with rewards obtained at each time step) could still be represented in our setting with the notion of an *augmented MDP* [Gilbert *et al.*, 2015a] at the cost of introducing additional states.

We assume (as standard in RL) that $\mathcal{S}$, $\mathcal{A}$, s_0 and $\mathcal{F}$ are known, that $\mathcal{P}$ is unknown and that at each step the agent knows exactly which state she occupies.

We call *episode* a succession of state-action pairs $(s_0, a_0, s_1, \ldots, s_{t-1}, a_{t-1}, s_t)$, starting in s_0 and ending in a final state $s_t \in \mathcal{F}$. When the current episode ends, a new episode starts in state s_0. We further assume that the length of an episode is upper-bounded by a constant $T_{max} \in \mathbb{N}$.

[1] A probability distribution $\mathcal{P}_0$ over initial states can easily be accommodated by using a dummy state s_0 with one dummy action whose transitions to all the other states are governed by $\mathcal{P}_0$.

Table 1: Probabilities for Each Gardner Die

	1	2	3	4	5	6
$\mathbf{p}_A$	1/6	0	0	5/6	0	0
$\mathbf{p}_B$	0	0	5/6	0	0	1/6
$\mathbf{p}_C$	0	1/2	0	0	1/2	0

A *policy* π at horizon T indicates which action to perform in each nonfinal state for each time step $t < T$. A policy is *Markovian* if the action depends only on the current state and timestep (otherwise it may depend on all state-action pairs encoutered so far); *deterministic* if it prescribes exactly one action, or *randomized* if it prescribes a probability distribution over actions; *stationary* if the action prescribed does not depend on the timestep. We write Π_s for the set of Markovian stationary deterministic policies.

Importantly, given a set $\Pi = \{\pi^1, \pi^2, \ldots\}$ of policies, we define an enlarged set $\widetilde{\Pi}$ of policies, that denotes the set consisting of *mixtures* of policies, i.e., $\widetilde{\Pi} = \{\tilde{\pi} = (\pi^1|\alpha_1, \pi^2|\alpha_2, \ldots) : \sum_i \alpha_i = 1, \alpha_i \geq 0\}$, where $\tilde{\pi}$ is the *mixed policy*[2] that randomly selects policy π^i with probability α_i at the beginning of each episode.

Example 1. *As a running example, we consider a variant of the classical "Gardner dice" two-player game. Each player has three six-sided dice, written A, B, C and biased as shown in Table 1. Players simultaneously choose a die to throw, and whoever rolls the highest number wins.*

It is easy to see that die A rolls higher than B most of the time, so die A should be preferred to B, but B mostly beats C, and C mostly beats A, hence the relation "more likely to win" is cyclic. The optimal policy for this problem is to play dice A, B and C with probabilities $3/13$, $3/13$ and $7/13$, respectively [Gilbert et al.*, 2015a].*

For illustrative purposes, we consider a variant where each player makes sequential decisions: she must first choose whether to throw die A (action a_A) or not (a_{BC}). If she chooses a_{BC}, then she can choose to throw B (action a_B) or C (a_C). Clearly, this does not change the probabilities with which to throw each die in an optimal policy.

This problem can be represented as an MDP where T_{max} is 2, with an initial state s_0 where $\mathcal{A}_{s_0} = \{a_A, a_{BC}\}$; a state s_{BC} (reached by choosing action a_{BC} in s_0); and six final states $\{f_1, \ldots, f_6\}$ representing the numbers rolled. An example transition probability is $\mathcal{P}(f_3|s_{BC}, a_B) = 5/6$, and an example episode is $(s_0, a_{BC}, s_{BC}, a_C, f_5)$. An example (Markovian stationary deterministic) policy is $\pi_B(s_0) = a_{BC}, \pi_B(s_{BC}) = a_B$.

Using similar notation for A and C, the optimal policy is

[2] Not to be confused with the notion of randomized policies.

the mixed policy $\tilde{\pi}^* = (\pi_A|3/13, \pi_B|3/13, \pi_C|7/13)$, *which dictates that the player draws one of* π_A, π_B, π_C *at the start of an episode, following it for the whole episode.* [3]

Our aim is to find an optimal (defined in the next subsection) policy. Recall that the decision maker has a preference relation $\succeq$ over possible final states; we want to compare policies by considering this preference relation. In other words, we want to lift the preference relation $\succeq$ defined on final states to a preference relation defined on policies.

2.1 COMPARING POLICIES WITH AN SSB UTILITY FUNCTION

We assume throughout the paper that the agent's preferences between probability distributions are described by the SSB model as presented and axiomatized by Fishburn [1984]. In this model, an agent is endowed with a binary functional φ over ordered pairs $(f, f') \in \mathcal{F}^2$ of final states, indicating the intensity with which she prefers f to f', with $f \succeq f' \Leftrightarrow \varphi(f, f') \geq 0$. Functional φ is assumed to be skew-symmetric, i.e., $\varphi(f, f') = -\varphi(f', f)$ and is extended to the space of probability distributions over $\mathcal{F}$ by bilinearity (wrt the mixture operation on distributions). The SSB criterion for comparing $\mathbf{p}$ and $\mathbf{q}$ is then written:

$$\varphi(\mathbf{p}, \mathbf{q}) = \sum_{f, f' \in \mathcal{F}} p(f) q(f') \varphi(f, f') \qquad (1)$$

where $p(f)$ (resp. $q(f')$) denotes the probability of reaching the final state f (resp. f') in distribution $\mathbf{p}$ (resp. $\mathbf{q}$). We have $\mathbf{p} \succ \mathbf{q}$ if $\varphi(\mathbf{p}, \mathbf{q}) > 0$ (strict preference), and $\mathbf{p} \sim \mathbf{q}$ if $\varphi(\mathbf{p}, \mathbf{q}) = 0$ (indifference).

Any policy π in an MDP induces a probability distribution $\mathbf{p}^\pi$ over final states (reached after at most T_{max} time steps); $\mathbf{p}^\pi$ is referred to as the *final state distribution* of π. As comparing policies amounts to comparing their induced distributions, we write $\varphi(\pi, \pi')$ for $\varphi(\mathbf{p}^\pi, \mathbf{p}^{\pi'})$ to simplify notation and define the preference relation $\succsim$ over policies:

$$\pi \succsim \pi' \equiv \varphi(\pi, \pi') \geq 0 \qquad (2)$$

Example 2 (continued). *The goal of beating the opponent's roll can be expressed as* $\varphi(f_m, f_n) = 1$ *for* $m > n$, -1 *for* $m < n$, *and* 0 *for* $m = n$. *The deterministic policies* π_A, π_B, π_C *amount to rolling the corresponding die, inducing the final state distributions* $\mathbf{p}_A, \mathbf{p}_B, \mathbf{p}_C$ *of Table 1 over final states. We have (zero entries are irrelevant):*

$$\begin{aligned}
&\varphi(\mathbf{p}_A, \mathbf{p}_B) \\
&= \mathbf{p}_A(f_1)\mathbf{p}_B(f_3)\varphi(f_1, f_3) + \mathbf{p}_A(f_1)\mathbf{p}_B(f_6)\varphi(f_1, f_6) \\
&\quad + \mathbf{p}_A(f_4)\mathbf{p}_B(f_3)\varphi(f_4, f_3) + \mathbf{p}_A(f_4)\mathbf{p}_B(f_6)\varphi(f_4, f_6) \\
&= \frac{1}{6} \cdot \frac{5}{6} \cdot (-1) + \frac{1}{6} \cdot \frac{1}{6} \cdot (-1) + \frac{5}{6} \cdot \frac{5}{6} \cdot 1 + \frac{5}{6} \cdot \frac{1}{6} \cdot (-1) \\
&= 14/36 > 0,
\end{aligned}$$

showing that die A should be preferred to die B.

If we were to define φ *by* $\varphi(f_m, f_n) = m - n$, *the strength of a victory (or defeat) would be taken into account. The policies in this case would be compared wrt the expectation of the roll (as explained below).*

The SSB model is very general, as it can take into account choice intransitivity, which is widely observed in practice [Fishburn, 1991]. Moreover, the SSB model can represent different risk attitudes via an adequate choice of φ. For example, it represents risk-averse behavior (in the weak sense) if the certainty equivalent of a distribution $\mathbf{p}$ is less than or equal to its expected value, where the certainty equivalent of a distribution $\mathbf{p}$ is the element f such that $\varphi(\mathbf{p}, f) = 0$ (*i.e.*, $\mathbf{p} \sim f$). Nakamura [1989] shows how to design risk averse and risk seeking SSB utility functions.

The SSB model also encompasses many decision criteria, such as the expectation criterion $\varphi(f, f') = c(f) - c(f')$ (where c denotes a utility/cost function); the probability threshold criterion [Yu *et al.*, 1998] $\varphi(f, f') = 1_{c(f) \geq \tau} - 1_{c(f') \geq \tau}$, which states that $\mathbf{p} \succ \mathbf{q}$ if $\sum_{c(f) \geq \tau} p(f) > \sum_{c(f) \geq \tau} q(f)$ for a threshold $\tau \in \mathbb{R}$; and the dominance relation $\varphi(f, f') = 1$ (resp. $0, -1$) if $f \succ f'$ (resp. $f \sim f'$, $f \prec f'$), which states that $\mathbf{p} \succ \mathbf{q}$ if $\sum_{f \succ f'} p(f)q(f') > \sum_{f' \succ f} p(f)q(f')$ (as in Example 2). In other words $\mathbf{p}$ is preferred to $\mathbf{q}$ if a final state generated according to $\mathbf{p}$ is more likely to be preferred to a final state generated according to $\mathbf{q}$ than the converse. This is called *probabilistic dominance* in the following.

Probabilistic Dominance (PD) is interesting as it only relies on ordinal pieces of information. Its axiomatic characterization was given by Blavatskyy [2006] and it has been explored lately in various domains such as RL [Busa-fekete *et al.*, 2014], voting systems [Rivest and Shen, 2010] and dueling bandits [Dudík *et al.*, 2015]. In the latter work, the authors adopt the name of *von Neumann solution* for the PD optimal solution. Indeed, as will be discussed in the next section, finding an SSB-optimal policy (and in particular, finding an optimal policy according to PD) is equivalent to finding a Nash equilibrium in a finite zero-sum two-player game. Thus the existence of a von Neumann solution is implied by von Neumann's minimax theorem.

In standard MDPs, the optimal policy can be highly sensitive to the reward function used, and yet designing a numerical reward function is often cognitively difficult, even

[3] Note the difference with the *randomized* (stationary) policy π which draws a_A with probability $3/13$ in s_0, and, *independently of this*, draws a_B (resp. a_C) with probability $3/10$ (resp. $7/10$) in s_{BC}. The expectation of reaching each final state is nonetheless the same in π and $\tilde{\pi}^*$ (hence π is also optimal).

for an expert user. This issue is tackled in preference-based approaches [Akrour *et al.*, 2012, Weng and Zanuttini., 2013, Gilbert *et al.*, 2015b, Weng *et al.*, 2013, Busa-fekete *et al.*, 2014, Furnkranz *et al.*, 2012, Wilson *et al.*, 2012, Wirth and Fürnkranz, 2013, Wirth and Neumann, 2015] by only considering ordinal pieces of information, such as feedbacks of the type "this trajectory is preferable to that one". We can distinguish two types of approach. The first [Wirth and Fürnkranz, 2013, Wirth and Neumann, 2015, Weng *et al.*, 2013] aims to recover a numerical reward function that explains most of the expressed preferences of the user and can be used with classic criteria. The second [Busa-fekete *et al.*, 2014, Furnkranz *et al.*, 2012] deals with purely ordinal criteria, *e.g.*, Busa-Fekete *et al.* [2014] find a good policy (wrt to PD) using a meta-heuristic algorithm based on evolutionary strategies in finite horizon continuous MDPs.

Example 3. *Consider a car racing against the clock. The driver aims to complete the race in the shortest time possible, but must find the right compromise between speed and the risk of being eliminated; driving too fast can cause the car to run off the track and be eliminated from the competition; the relation between the car's speed and going off track is stochastic (the faster, the more likely). This is easily modeled as an MDP where policies induce a distribution over the race's possible outcomes. The preference $\succ$ over final states is determined by two conditions: (i) race completion is always strictly preferred to an elimination, and (ii) a trajectory completing the race in time t_1 is strictly preferred to completion in time $t_2 > t_1$.*

In this model, adopting SSB with probabilistic dominance finds the "best" policy for a driver who wants to maximize her chance of winning a race (against other drivers facing the same MDP). In contrast, traditional approaches would solve this problem by setting a (large) negative reward r_{elim} for an elimination and a small negative reward for each time step before completing the race, and then maximize expectation of rewards using, for example, Q-learning or any other classic algorithm. Different values of r_{elim} would result in very different policies, and while it might be possible to find a good compromise value allowing for a competitive behavior, manually tuning the reward function would be difficult in more complex scenarios.

Consequently, designing and implementing an algorithm for solving MDPs in an RL setting with an SSB utility function also gives us a tool to compute optimal policies for a large class of criteria, including "preference based" ones. A first step towards the design of this algorithm is to give a game-theoretic view of the problem.

2.2 A GAME ON POLICIES

When an MDP is fixed, Equations 1 and 2 induce a zero-sum two-player symmetric game where the set of strategies coincides with the set of possible policies. The players $i \in \{1, 2\}$ simultaneously choose a strategy $\tilde{\pi}_i$ (pure or mixed). The resulting payoff is then given by $\varphi(\tilde{\pi}_1, \tilde{\pi}_2)$. As emphasized by Gilbert *et al.* [2015a], an SSB optimal policy can be found by computing a Nash equilibrium of this game. Indeed, Nash equilibria $(\tilde{\pi}^*, \tilde{\pi}^*)$ are characterized by $\forall \tilde{\pi}, \varphi(\tilde{\pi}^*, \tilde{\pi}) \geq 0$.

Gilbert *et al.* [2015a] also showed that in this game, a best response to a strategy $\tilde{\pi}$ is given by a policy maximizing the expectation of cumulated rewards with reward function:

$$\mathcal{R}_{\mathbf{p}^{\tilde{\pi}}}(s) = \begin{cases} \mathbf{1}_i^\top \Phi \mathbf{p}^{\tilde{\pi}} & \text{if } s = f_i \in \mathcal{F} \\ 0 & \text{otherwise} \end{cases}$$

where $\mathbf{1}_i$ is the ith canonical vector, $^\top$ is the transpose operator and Φ is the SSB matrix (i.e., $\Phi_{i,j} = \varphi(f_i, f_j)$). Put another way, the reward obtained when arriving in the ith final state is given by the ith element of the vector $\Phi \mathbf{p}^{\pi}$ (the reward is 0 for nonfinal states). Since this defines a standard MDP, there is always a stationary, Markovian and deterministic optimal policy (i.e., the best response to $\tilde{\pi}$). Thus we can restrict ourselves to the finite game with Π_s as the set of pure strategies. To summarize, a Nash equilibrium of this game will give an SSB-optimal policy, in the form of a mixed policy $\tilde{\pi}^* \in \tilde{\Pi}_s$.

Example 4 (continued)**.** *The game induced by our running example has pure strategies π_A, π_B, π_C for both players, with payoff, e.g., $\varphi(\pi_A, \pi_B) = 14/36$ (Example 2). Consider the mixed policy $\tilde{\pi}_{AAB} = (\pi_A|2/3, \pi_B|1/3)$; Table 1 gives its final state distribution $\mathbf{p}^{\tilde{\pi}_{AAB}} = (2/18, 0, 5/18, 10/18, 0, 1/18)$. The value of response π_A to $\tilde{\pi}_{AAB}$ is given by*

$$\mathbf{p}^{\pi_A} \cdot \Phi \cdot \mathbf{p}^{\tilde{\pi}_{AAB}}$$
$$= (\frac{1}{6}, 0, 0, \frac{5}{6}, 0, 0)^\top (-\frac{16}{18}, -\frac{14}{18}, -\frac{9}{18}, \frac{6}{18}, \frac{16}{18}, \frac{17}{18}) = \frac{7}{54}$$

Similarly, the values of π_B, π_C are $-7/27$ and $1/18$ respectively, so a best response to $\tilde{\pi}_{AAB}$ is π_A. The second component of vector $\Phi \cdot \mathbf{p}^{\tilde{\pi}_{AAB}}$ can be computed as follows. We know that rolling 2 is worse than $16/18$ and better than $2/18$ of the outcomes of $\mathbf{p}^{\tilde{\pi}_{AAB}}$, and $\varphi(f_i, f_j)$ is always 1 for $i > j$. Therefore this component is $-1 \cdot 16/18 + 1 \cdot 2/18 = -14/18$.

In a finite zero-sum symmetric game, it is well-known that there exists a symmetric Nash Equilibrium (NE). We aim to compute this NE on policies characterized by payoff function φ (*solving the game*).

3 SOLVING THE GAME

Games in strategic forms can be solved by linear programming [Chvátal, 1983], unfortunately, here, the game is too large to be solved directly (we remind the reader that the number of pure strategies of the game is equal to the number of deterministic stationary policies of the MDP, which is exponential in the number of states).[4] If the model was known, one could rely on the double oracle algorithm of Gilbert *et al.* [2015a]. Unfortunately, that approach suffers some drawbacks. Firstly, if the optimal mixture of policies $\bar{\pi}^*$ is composed of too many policies, its time and space requirements might become prohibitive, as the double oracle algorithm would have to compute and store all polices that are in the support of $\bar{\pi}^*$. Secondly, this approach does not generalize to the case where the model is unknown. Thus it can not be used to derive a model-free RL algorithm. We therefore turn to a different approach, based on fictitious play and on a double timescale technique.

3.1 LEARNING SETTING

In RL, one typically expects convergence to playing an optimal policy at each step. Since in our case the optimal policy is mixed, this cannot be evaluated at each time step independently. Rather, after any number n of episodes, we consider the *final state distribution*, defined as $(f_1|\alpha_1, \ldots, f_{|\mathcal{F}|}|\alpha_{|\mathcal{F}|})$, where for all i, α_i is the fraction of episodes so far in which the final state was f_i.

We define the *loss* $L(\mathbf{p})$ of a distribution over final states to be the value of its best response against it:

$$L(\mathbf{p}) \stackrel{def}{=} \varphi(\mathbf{p}^{BR}, \mathbf{p})$$

where $\mathbf{p}^{BR}$ is the vector of final state frequencies of a policy which maximizes the expectation of cumulated rewards with respect to reward funtion $\mathcal{R}_{\mathbf{p}}$ (hence a best response to $\mathbf{p}$). Since $L(\mathbf{p}^{\bar{\pi}^*}) = 0$ characterizes SSB-optimal policies $\bar{\pi}^*$, it is natural to measure the quality of learning by the decrease in loss of the final state distribution so far $\mathbf{p}_n$, as n increases. Convergence to an SSB-optimal policy then amounts to $L(\mathbf{p}_n) \to 0$ with $n \to \infty$.

Rephrasing, we expect that, considering the final states reached from the beginning, in retrospect their frequencies are approximately equivalent to those we would have obtained had we played a mixed optimal policy from the start (and more and more exactly as n increases). This corresponds to the standard "on-line" setting of RL, in which success is measured from the start.

3.2 FICTITIOUS PLAY

Fictitious Play is an algorithm that only needs a best response procedure to solve a game. The algorithm maintains for each player her mixed policy so far $\bar{\pi}_n$, defined as $(\pi^1|\alpha_1, \ldots, \pi^k|\alpha_k)$, where for all i, α_i is the fraction of episodes so far in which the stationary, deterministic policy π^i has been played. At each time step, each player considers that $\bar{\pi}_n$ perfectly represents the mixed strategy that is used by the adversary and plays a best response to it. The algorithm converges to a Nash equilibrium of the game (in the sense that $L(\mathbf{p}_n)$ converges to 0) when the game is a finite zero-sum game. Fictitious play is represented in Algorithm 1 for a symmetric two-player zero-sum game. As the game is symmetric, we only need to consider the mixed policy so far, $\bar{\pi}_n$, of a player playing against herself.

Algorithm 1: Fictitious Play

Data: Game $\mathcal{G}$, arbitrary pure strategy π_0

1 **while** *True* **do**

2 Play π_n

3 # update current mixed policy

4 $\bar{\pi}_{n+1} = (\pi^1|\alpha_1, \ldots, \pi^k|\alpha_k)$ with

5 $\begin{cases} \alpha_i = n \cdot \alpha_i/(n+1) + 1/(n+1) & \text{for } \pi^i = \pi_n \\ \alpha_i = n \cdot \alpha_i/(n+1) & \text{for } \pi^i \neq \pi_n \end{cases}$

6 $\pi_{n+1} = \mathit{BestResponseTo}(\bar{\pi}_{n+1})$

Example 5 (continued). *Assume the agent chooses initial strategy $\pi_0 = \pi_B$, then after one episode/game we have $\bar{\pi}_1 = (\pi_B|1)$. Now π_A is a best response to $\bar{\pi}_1$ (Example 2), hence $\pi_1 = \pi_A$. So the agent plays π_A during the second episode, and we get $\bar{\pi}_2 = (\pi_A|1/2, \pi_B|1/2)$. Now it is easy to see that π_A is a best response to $\bar{\pi}_2$, so the agent again plays π_A and gets $\bar{\pi}_3 = (\pi_A|2/3, \pi_B|1/3)$. From Example 4 we get that π_A is a best response to $\bar{\pi}_3$, and that the loss of $\bar{\pi}_3$ is $L(\mathbf{p}^{\bar{\pi}_3}) = \varphi(\pi_A, \bar{\pi}_3) = 7/54$.*

3.3 SSB Q-LEARNING

This subsection makes a first step towards the adaptation of fictitious play to solve the game induced by an MDP and an SSB utility function. Recall from Section 2.2 that the best responses to the mixed strategy so far, $\bar{\pi}_n$, are exactly the optimal policies in the (standard) MDP with reward function $\mathcal{R}_{\mathbf{p}^{\bar{\pi}_n}}$. In other words, best responses can be computed as a function of $\mathbf{p}^{\bar{\pi}_n}$ only. Accordingly, instead of recording $\bar{\pi}_n$ as such, which involves an exponential number k of pure policies π^i in the worst case, as in Algorithm 1, it is enough to record the vector $\mathbf{p}_n = \mathbf{p}^{\bar{\pi}_n}$. Then we can rewrite Lines 4–6 of Algorithm 1 as:

$$\begin{aligned} \mathbf{p}_{n+1} &= n \cdot \mathbf{p}_n/(n+1) + \mathbf{p}^{\pi_n}/(n+1) \\ \pi_{n+1} &= \mathit{BestResponseTo}(\mathbf{p}_{n+1}) \end{aligned}$$

However, in practice, when policy π_n is played, one observes only one drawing from $\mathbf{p}^{\pi_n}$, and not the distribution itself. Hence our first adaptation of fictitious play is as given in Algorithm 2. Note that we do not know the model of the MDP, so we use *BestResponseTo* as an oracle. We find a better solution later in this section.

Example 6 (continued). *Let $\pi_0 = \pi_B$ again. Hence the agent plays π_B during one complete episode. If the die rolls 3, we get $\mathbf{p}_1 = (f_3|1)$. Then the best response is computed as one to a strategy which always yields f_3, and we get $\pi_1 = \pi_A$. The agent therefore plays π_A during one episode,*

[4] Our running example does not illustrate this combinatorial explosion, but it clearly arises, e.g., in the "intransitive grid" and the "race against the clock" (see Section 4).

Algorithm 2: Approximate Fictitious Play

Data: MDP $\mathcal{M}$, SSB function φ, arbitrary policy $\pi_0 \in \Pi_s$

while *True* **do**
- Play π_n for one episode
- f_i = final state reached
- $\mathbf{p}_{n+1} = n \cdot \mathbf{p}_n/(n+1) + \mathbf{1}_i/(n+1)$
- $\pi_{n+1} = \mathit{BestResponseTo}(\mathbf{p}_{n+1})$

and if the die rolls 4, we get $\mathbf{p}_2 = (f_3|1/2, f_4|1/2)$, to which a best response is $\pi_2 = \pi_A$. If the die then rolls 1, we get $\mathbf{p}_3 = (f_1|1/3, f_3|1/3, f_4|1/3)$. In this case the best response is π_A, just as in Example 4, but note that it has an estimated value $\mathbf{p}_A \cdot \Phi \cdot \mathbf{p}_3 = 5/6 \cdot 2/3 - 1/6 \cdot 2/3 = 4/9$, instead of $\varphi(\pi_A, \tilde{\pi}_{AAB}) = 7/54$ if $\mathbf{p}^{\tilde{\pi}_{AAB}}$ were directly observed.

The following theorem proves that observing only realizations of $\mathbf{p}^{\pi_n}$ does not prevent the convergence of $(\mathbf{p}_n)_{n\in\mathbb{N}}$ to the distribution of an SSB-optimal policy.

Theorem 1. *In Algorithm 2, $L(\mathbf{p}_n)$ tends to 0 as $n \to \infty$.*

Proof. Assume an optimal policy π_n with respect to $\mathcal{R}_{\mathbf{p}_n}$ is played during the $(n+1)$-th episode. At the end of the episode, a final state f_i is reached and $\mathbf{p}_{n+1}$ is defined by:

$$\mathbf{p}_{n+1} = \frac{n \cdot \mathbf{p}_n}{n+1} + \frac{\mathbf{1}_i}{n+1} = \mathbf{p}_n + \frac{1}{n+1}(\mathbf{1}_i - \mathbf{p}_n)$$

We rewrite this equation in the following way :

$$\mathbf{p}_{n+1} = \mathbf{p}_n + \frac{1}{n+1}(\mathbf{p}^{\pi_n} - \mathbf{p}_n + \boldsymbol{M}_{n+1}) \qquad (3)$$

where $\boldsymbol{M}_{n+1} = \mathbf{1}_i - \mathbf{p}^{\pi_n}$ is a square integrable martingale difference sequence. Equation 3 is a standard single timescale process with continuous differential inclusion:

$$\dot{\mathbf{p}}(t) \in \{\mathbf{p}^{\pi} - \mathbf{p}(t) : \pi \in \Pi(\mathbf{p}(t))\} \qquad (4)$$

where $\Pi(\mathbf{p})$ denotes the set of optimal policies with respect to reward $\mathcal{R}_{\mathbf{p}}$. A similar differential inclusion can be obtained for the standard fictitious play. However, here, as $\mathbf{p}_n$ is a distribution over final states (not over strategies) and as only a realization of $\mathbf{p}^{\pi}$ is observed, we need to invoke a stochastic approximation argument.

Indeed, the best response correspondence is upper-semicontinuous, with closed and convex values. Hence the existence of at least one solution $\mathbf{p}(t)$ through each initial value $\mathbf{p}(0)$, which is Lipschitz continuous and defined for all positive times, is guaranteed [Hofbauer, 1995]. Let $\mathbf{p}(t)$ be a solution of inclusion 4 and $\boldsymbol{\zeta}(t) = \mathbf{p}(t) + \dot{\mathbf{p}}(t) = \mathbf{p}^{\pi}$ for a best response $\pi \in \Pi(\mathbf{p}(t))$. By definition of L, we have $L(\mathbf{p}(t)) = \varphi(\boldsymbol{\zeta}(t), \mathbf{p}(t))$, and by the envelope theorem:

$$\frac{d}{dt}L(\mathbf{p}(t)) = \frac{\partial\varphi(\boldsymbol{\zeta}(t), \mathbf{p}(t))}{\partial\boldsymbol{\zeta}}\dot{\boldsymbol{\zeta}}(t) + \frac{\partial\varphi(\boldsymbol{\zeta}(t), \mathbf{p}(t))}{\partial\mathbf{p}}\dot{\mathbf{p}}(t)$$

As $\boldsymbol{\zeta}(t)$ maximizes $\varphi(., \mathbf{p}(t))$, the first term is null [Mas-Colell *et al.*, 1995, pp. 964–965], and by linearity:

$$\begin{aligned}\frac{d}{dt}L(\mathbf{p}(t)) &= \varphi(\boldsymbol{\zeta}(t), \dot{\mathbf{p}}(t)) \\ &= \varphi(\mathbf{p}(t), \dot{\mathbf{p}}(t)) + \underbrace{\varphi(\dot{\mathbf{p}}(t), \dot{\mathbf{p}}(t))}_{=0} \\ &= \varphi(\mathbf{p}(t), \dot{\mathbf{p}}(t)) + \underbrace{\varphi(\mathbf{p}(t), \mathbf{p}(t))}_{=0} \\ &= \varphi(\mathbf{p}(t), \boldsymbol{\zeta}(t)) = -\varphi(\boldsymbol{\zeta}(t), \mathbf{p}(t))\end{aligned}$$

as Φ is skew-symmetric (hence $\varphi(\mathbf{p}(t), \mathbf{p}(t)) = \varphi(\dot{\mathbf{p}}(t), \dot{\mathbf{p}}(t)) = 0$, and $\varphi(\mathbf{p}(t), \boldsymbol{\zeta}(t)) = -\varphi(\boldsymbol{\zeta}(t), \mathbf{p}(t))$). Thus, $\frac{d}{dt}L(\mathbf{p}(t)) = -L(\mathbf{p}(t))$, $L(\mathbf{p}(t)) = L(\mathbf{p}(0))e^{-t}$, and hence $L(\mathbf{p}(t))$ tends to 0 with $t \to \infty$. Thus, the set of final state distributions of the optimal strategies is globally attracting for the best response dynamic, which implies the convergence of the discrete stochastic approximation (3) [Benaïm *et al.*, 2006, Properties 1, 2]. □

If the model was known, one could use Algorithm 2. At each iteration of the **while** loop, the corresponding MDP would be solved using dynamic or linear programming to find the best response policy π_{n+1}. Unfortunately, as the model is unknown, this policy can not be computed directly and has to be learned. The "$\pi_{n+1} = \mathit{BestResponseTo}(\mathbf{p}_{n+1})$" line should therefore be replaced by, say, a Q-learning phase which converges asymptotically to the desired policy.

Recall that an agent using Q-learning (in a standard MDP) maintains an estimate of Q-values $Q(s, a)$ using:

$$\begin{aligned}&Q_{n+1}(s_n, a_n) = Q_n(s_n, a_n) \\ &+ \alpha_n(s_n, a_n)(r_{n+1} + \max_b\{Q_n(s_{n+1}, b)\} - Q_n(s_n, a_n))\end{aligned}$$

after taking action a_n in state s_n, ending up in state s_{n+1}, and observing the (numerical) reward r_{n+1}, and where $\alpha_n(s_n, a_n)$ is the value of the learning rate for (s_n, a_n) at timestep n. Note that from now on, for simplicity, we use n to denote the number of time steps (while previously it denoted the number of episodes). Exploitation is realized by choosing $a_n = \arg\max_a Q_n(s_n, a)$ at state s_n. Q-learning is known to converge to an optimal policy in the limit, provided the reward function is stationary [Watkins and Dayan, 1992].

Hence the idea is to adapt Algorithm 2 to run Q-learning while keeping its target reward function fixed to $\mathcal{R}_{\mathbf{p}_n}$ as when it started, and when it has converged (to an approximate best response to $\mathbf{p}_n$), to update $\mathbf{p}_n$ using what has been observed in this phase and start a new Q-learning phase. Unfortunately, the number of learning episodes required to learn an optimal or ϵ-optimal policy is unknown. Therefore, we want to avoid alternating the Q-learning phase and the reward update phase by using a technique from Borkar [1997] which interleaves both phases successfully using a two-timescale approach. In this approach, the following iterative equations are used concurrently:

$$\mathbf{p}_{n+1} = \mathbf{p}_n + \beta_n(\mathbf{1}_i - \mathbf{p}_n) \text{ when } f_i \in \mathcal{F} \text{ is reached} \quad (5)$$

$$Q_{n+1}(s_n, a_n) = Q_n(s_n, a_n) + \alpha_n(s_n, a_n)\Delta_{n+1} \quad (6)$$

$$\Delta_{n+1} = \mathcal{R}_{\mathbf{p}_n}(s_{n+1}) + \max_b\{Q_n(s_{n+1}, b)\} - Q_n(s_n, a_n)$$

$$\forall s, a, \left\{ \begin{array}{l} \sum_{n=0}^{\infty} \alpha_n(s,a) = \infty \text{ and } \sum_{n=0}^{\infty} \beta_n = \infty \\ \beta_n / \alpha_n(s,a) \to 0 \\ \sum_{n=0}^{\infty} \alpha_n(s,a)^2 + \beta_n^2 < \infty \end{array} \right\} \quad (7)$$

The intuition is that Q_n evolves more quickly than $\mathbf{p}_n$, giving time for Q_n, and hence the best response, to adapt to changes in the target reward $\mathcal{R}_{\mathbf{p}_n}$.

Write $\eta_{\mathbf{p}}$ (resp. $\eta_{s,a}$) for the number of times vector $\mathbf{p}_n$ (resp. state action-pair (s, a)) has been updated (resp. experienced). In our case, β_n is $1/(\eta_{\mathbf{p}} + 1)$ since Equation 5 tracks the final state distribution so far, so we can set α_n to $1/(\eta_{s,a} + 1)^{2/3}$ for instance. Note that this example works because $\mathbf{p}_n$ is updated after at most T_{max} steps, bounding the number of updates of α_n (for any (s, a)) between two consecutive updates of β_n. With these conditions, the two recursive equations on $\mathbf{p}_n$ and Q_n form a two-timescale stochastic approximation iteration, where $\mathbf{p}_n$ is on a slower timescale than Q_n. The following example gives the intuition behind the two time-scale technique; the convergence proof under Condition (7) is given in Theorem 2.

Example 7. *Suppose that at some point the Q-values of a_A and a_{BC} in s_0 are 0.1 and 0.2, respectively, and that those of a_B,a_C in s_{BC} are 0.3,−0.7. Assume moreover $\mathbf{p}_n$=$(1/5, 0, 1/5, 1/5, 1/5, 1/5)$, $n = 80$ (with 20 episodes of length 1 and 30 of length 2, hence $\eta_{\mathbf{p}} \simeq 0.02$) $\eta_{s_0,a_{BC}} = 30$ ($\alpha_n(s_0, a_{BC}) \simeq 0.1$) and $\eta_{s_{BC},a_B} = 20$ ($\alpha_n(s_{BC}, a_B) \simeq 0.13$).*

Hence the agent will choose a_{BC} in s_0, reach s_{BC} and update $Q(s_0, a_{BC})$ to $\simeq 0.2 + 0.1 \cdot (0 + 0.3 - 0.2) = 0.21$. In s_{BC} she will choose a_B and, if she rolls 3, update $Q(s_{BC}, a_B)$ to $\simeq 0.3 + 0.13 \cdot (\mathbf{1}_3 \cdot \Phi \cdot \mathbf{p}_n + 0 - 0.3) = 0.3 + 0.13 \cdot (-2/5 - 0.3) \simeq 0.2$, and $\mathbf{p}_n$ to $(10/51, 0, 11/51, 10/51, 10/51, 10/51)$.

Note that Q-values have evolved significantly more than $\mathbf{p}_n$ (and hence than the target numerical reward $\mathcal{R}_{\mathbf{p}_n}$).

3.4 HANDLING EXPLORATION

In order for Q-learning to converge, one needs to ensure that all state-action pairs are performed infinitely often. Usually, this exploration is guaranteed through some randomization, using an ϵ-greedy strategy, for instance. We present in this subsection an exploration strategy called *Episodic-ϵ-Greedy (EG for short)* that guarantees that we converge to an ϵ-optimal SSB strategy using the algorithm described by Equations 5 and 6. During learning, an episode will be generated using either the current best policy (defined by the Q-values), with probability $(1 - \epsilon)$, or the uniformly random policy, which we denote by π_U, with probability ϵ. If an episode is generated using π_U (i.e., the agent is exploring), then the update of Equation 5 is not performed at the end of the episode. This guarantees that the convergence of $\mathbf{p}_n$ is not biased by the exploration strategy. The final proposed algorithm is presented in Algorithm 3.

Algorithm 3: SSB Q-learning

Data: MDP $\mathcal{M}$, SSB function φ

while *True* **do**
- Choose a_n using the EG exploration strategy
- Play a_n, observe s_{n+1}, and let $r_{n+1} = \mathcal{R}_{\mathbf{p}_n}(s_{n+1})$
- $Q_{n+1}(s_n, a_n) = Q_n(s_n, a_n) + \alpha_n(s_n, a_n)(r_{n+1} + \max_b\{Q_n(s_{n+1}, b)\} - Q_n(s_n, a_n))$
- **if** $s_{n+1} = f_i \in \mathcal{F}$ *and exploration is off* **then**
  - $\mathbf{p}_{n+1} = \mathbf{p}_n + \frac{1}{\eta_{\mathbf{p}}+1}(\mathbf{1}_i - \mathbf{p}_n)$

We are now ready to prove the convergence of SSB Q-learning to an ϵ-optimal policy through two theorems.

Theorem 2. *Under Conditions (7) with $\beta_n = 1/(\eta_{\mathbf{p}} + 1)$, in Algorithm 3, $L(\mathbf{p}_n)$ tends to 0 almost surely as $n \to \infty$.*

Proof. The idea is that $\mathbf{p}_n$ can be viewed as quasi-static compared to Q_n. Indeed, let π_n be the greedy policy given by Q_n. We can rewrite the equations as:

$$\mathbf{p}_{n+1} = \mathbf{p}_n + \alpha_n(\epsilon_n + \mathbf{M}'_n) \quad (8)$$

$$Q_{n+1}(s_n, a_n) = Q_n(s_n, a_n) + \alpha_n(s_n, a_n)(T(Q_n)(s_n, a_n) - Q_n(s_n, a_n) + \mathbf{M}''_{n+1})$$

where $\epsilon_n = \frac{\beta_n}{\alpha_n}(\mathbf{p}^{\pi_n} - \mathbf{p}_n)$ and $\mathbf{M}'_n = \frac{\beta_n}{\alpha_n}(\mathbf{1}_i - \mathbf{p}^{\pi_n})$

$$T(Q_n)(s, a) = \sum_{s'} \mathcal{P}(s'|s, a)(\mathcal{R}_{\mathbf{p}_n}(s') + \max_b\{Q_n(s', b)\})$$

$$\mathbf{M}''_{n+1} = \mathcal{R}_{\mathbf{p}_n}(s_{n+1}) + \max_b\{Q_n(s_{n+1}, b)\} - T(Q_n)(s_n, a_n)$$

Clearly $\epsilon_n \to 0$ almost surely ($||\mathbf{p}^{\pi_n}||$ and $||\mathbf{p}_n||$ are bounded). Then $(\mathbf{p}_n, Q_n)$ will converge to the internally chain transitive invariant set of the ODE [Borkar, 2008]:

$$\dot{\mathbf{p}}(t) = 0 \qquad \dot{Q}(t) = T(Q(t)) - Q(t)$$

Let $Q^*(\mathbf{p}_n)$ denote the optimal Q-value function for reward function $\mathcal{R}_{\mathbf{p}_n}$. Therefore $Q_n - Q^*(\mathbf{p}_n) \to 0$ almost surely, which entails that $(\mathbf{p}_n, \pi_n)$ converges to the set $(\mathbf{p}, \pi^*(\mathbf{p}))$ with $\pi^*(\mathbf{p})$ a best response to $\mathbf{p}$. We then rewrite (5) to:

$$\mathbf{p}_{n+1} = \mathbf{p}_n + \beta_n(\mathbf{p}^{\pi^*(\mathbf{p}_n)} - \mathbf{p}_n + (\mathbf{p}^{\pi_n} - \mathbf{p}^{\pi^*(\mathbf{p}_n)}) + (\mathbf{1}_i - \mathbf{p}^{\pi_n}))$$

As $\mathbf{p}^{\pi_n} - \mathbf{p}^{\pi^*(\mathbf{p}_n)} \to 0$ almost surely, the asymptotic behavior is the same as in Theorem 1. Thus the loss of $\mathbf{p}_n$ converges to 0 with $n \to \infty$. □

The result of Theorem 2 uses the fact that with the EG exploration strategy, exploration has no impact on $\mathbf{p}_n$. The drawback of this strategy is that $\mathbf{p}_n$ does not truly represent the frequencies with which each final state has been obtained. If we let $\mathbf{p}_n^{real}$ represent the vector of true frequencies with which each final state has been obtained, then following theorem proves that $\mathbf{p}_n^{real}$ converges to the final state frequencies of an ϵ- optimal SSB-policy.

Theorem 3. *Under Conditions (7) with $\beta_n = 1/(\eta_{\mathbf{p}} + 1)$, when Algorithm 3 is run, $\mathbf{p}_n^{real}$ converges to the final state distribution of an ϵ-optimal SSB-policy almost surely.*

Proof. Let ϵ' denote the parameter of EG exploration and let $\mathbf{p}^{real} = \lim_{n \to \infty} \mathbf{p}_n^{real}$. Then asymptotically we have

$$\mathbf{p}^{real} = (1 - \epsilon')\mathbf{p}^* + \epsilon' \mathbf{p}^{\pi_U}$$

where $\mathbf{p}^*$ is the final state distribution of an optimal SSB-policy. Thus for any policy π:

$$\varphi(\mathbf{p}^{real}, \mathbf{p}^{\pi}) = (1 - \epsilon')\underbrace{\varphi(\mathbf{p}^*, \mathbf{p}^{\pi})}_{\geq 0} + \epsilon' \underbrace{\varphi(\mathbf{p}^{\pi_U}, \mathbf{p}^{\pi})}_{\geq -\varphi_{\max}}$$
$$\geq -\epsilon' \varphi_{\max}$$

with $\varphi_{\max} = \max_{f,f'} \varphi(f, f')$. Hence, with $\epsilon' = \epsilon/\varphi_{\max}$, Algorithm 3 converges to an ϵ-optimal SSB strategy. □

4 PROOF OF CONCEPT

Although SSB encompasses many different criteria, we focus here on the probabilistic dominance criterion as it is an important case for which no model-free algorithm that is provably correct has been proposed. We plot here the results of four experiments: "sequential Gardner dice", "who wants to be a millionaire", "intransitive grid" and "race against the clock" using the probabilistic dominance criterion (hence values are all in $[-1, 1]$). For all runs, $10,000,000$ steps were performed in the MDP, ϵ was set to 0.1, and α_n was set to $1/(\eta_{s,a} + 1)^{11/20}$.

Gardner Dice. We first present the results on Gardner's dice problem as formalized in Example 1. Figure 1(a) shows the evolution of the frequencies (f_A, f_B, f_C) with which each die has been played for a representative run. The optimal frequency vector $\mathbf{p}^* = (3/13, 3/13, 7/13)$ is shown as a green dot and the same vector biased by exploration $\mathbf{p}_\epsilon^* = (1 - \epsilon) * \mathbf{p}^* + \epsilon * \mathbf{p}^{\pi_U}$ by a red dot; the vector (f_A, f_B, f_C) tends towards $\mathbf{p}_\epsilon^*$, drawing triangles of decreasing surface around $\mathbf{p}_\epsilon^*$. Figure 1(b) presents the evolution of the Q-values of the three actions, a_A, a_B and a_C. One can see that the best die alternates between the three dice and that $\max\{Q_A, Q_B, Q_C\}$ tends towards 0. (The best response is always deterministic and so must be one of π_A, π_B, π_C. However at convergence its value has to be 0.)

Who wants to be a millionaire. In this popular television game show, a contestant answers 15 multiple-choice questions (with four possible answers) of increasing difficulty, for increasingly large sums, roughly doubling the pot each question. At each time step, the contestant may decide to walk away with the money currently won. If she answers incorrectly, then all winnings are lost except what has been earned at a "guarantee point" (questions 5 and 10). The player is allowed 3 lifelines (50:50, removing two of the choices, ask the audience and call a friend for suggestions); each can only be used once. We used the first model of the Spanish 2003 version of the game presented by Perea and Puerto [2007]. The probability of answering correctly is a function of the question's number and increased by the lifelines used (if any).

Intransitive grid. In this domain we study an episodic grid MDP containing 9 states. The agent always starts an episode in the bottom-right corner of the grid. Three terminal states, f_1, f_2 and f_3 can be attained at the three other corners of the grid. The agent can only go left and up. With a probability of 0.2, the agent makes a mistake and goes in the wrong direction. The preference relation between the final states is the following: $f_1 \succ f_2 \succ f_3 \succ f_1$.

Race against the clock. Lastly, we discuss the domain discussed in Example 3.[5] The racing circuit is represented by 6 physical positions $\{p_1, \ldots, p_6\}$ plus one, p_{el}, representing elimination. A state of the MDP is a triple (p, s, t) giving the current position $p \in \{p_1, \ldots, p_6, p_{el}\}$, the current speed of the car $s \in \{Slow, Medium, Fast\}$ and the current time $t \in \mathbf{N}$. In each state the agent can decide between 3 actions: accelerating, decelerating or keeping the same speed. At each time step t, the probability of running off the track is a function of s_t, p_t and a_t, taking into account both the speed of the car and the difficulty of the current part of the circuit. Finally, the time spent between two positions decreases stochastically with the current speed.

Results. Figure 1(c)-(f) shows the evolution of $L(\mathbf{p}_n^{real})$ and $L(\mathbf{p}_n)$ (i.e., the values of the optimal policies regarding reward functions defined by $\Phi\mathbf{p}_n^{real}$, $\Phi\mathbf{p}_n$) for each domain. The results are averaged over 20 runs. As expected the value of $L(\mathbf{p}_n)$ tends towards 0 as the number of learning steps increase. The value of $L(\mathbf{p}_n^{real})$ decreases and is much lower than ϵ $(= 0.1$ in the experiments) on all figures.

Finally, in Table 2, we compare the "race against the clock" results obtained by our SSB Q-learning algorithm to the results obtained by a standard Q-learning algorithm launched with three different reward functions $\mathbf{R}_1$, $\mathbf{R}_2$ and $\mathbf{R}_3$. For each reward function, a penalty of value $-t$ is received by the agent each time the circuit is completed in time t. For reward function $\mathbf{R}_i$, an elimination results in a penalty of value $r_{elem}^i \in \{-10, -25, -40\}$. For each algorithm we give the frequency of elimination f_{elem} and the average time T_{cc} of circuit completion. The final columns show the probabilities with which the SSB Q-learning agent would

[5] The complete description is given as supplementary material at hugogilbert.pythonanywhere.com.

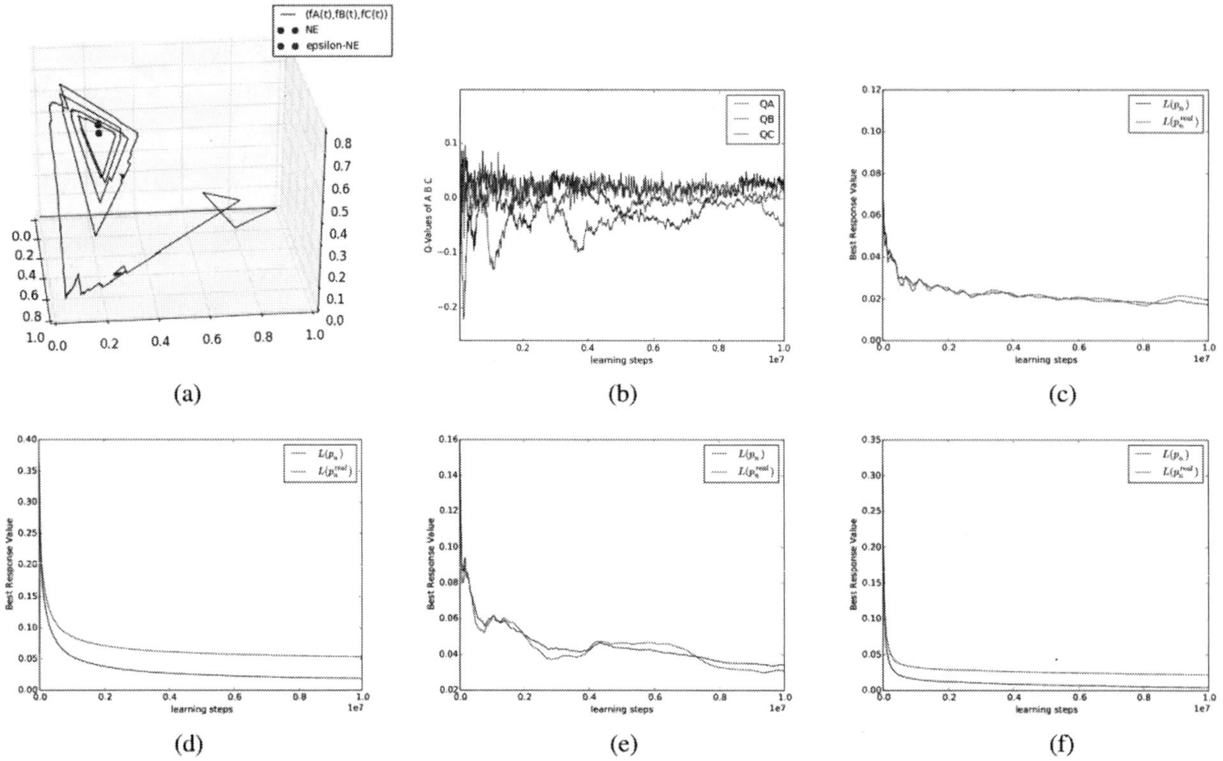

Figure 1: For the Gardner dice domain, **(a)** convergence of the policy in the space of die frequencies, **(b)** evolution of Q-values, **(c)** evolution of loss; For **(d)** Who wants to be a millionaire, **(e)** Intransitive grid and **(f)** Race against the clock, evolution of loss.

beat ($\mathbf{P}_{\succ}$) and at least tie with ($\mathbf{P}_{\succeq}$) each Q-learning agent. As expected, f_{elem} decreases and T_{cc} increases with the penalty value of an elimination. For a Q-learning agent, this penalty would have to be tuned to give the best compromise. The SSB Q-learning agent does not face this problem and the last two columns show that this agent is more likely to produce a preferred episode.

5 Conclusion

Skew-Symmetric Bilinear (SSB) utility is a useful general decision model that encompasses many decision criteria (e.g., EU, threshold probability, probabilistic dominance, etc.). We designed a model-free reinforcement learning algorithm to compute an epsilon SSB-optimal policy and provided experimental results.

Table 2: Comparisons of SSB Q-Learning with Three Q-Learning Algorithms (Results Averaged Over 20 Runs).

	f_{elem}	T_{cc}	$\mathbf{P}_{\succ}$	$\mathbf{P}_{\succeq}$
SSB Q-learning	0.41	5.29	–	–
Q-learning with $\mathbf{R}_1$	0.48	4.34	0.37	0.64
Q-learning with $\mathbf{R}_2$	0.31	7.14	0.48	0.66
Q-learning with $\mathbf{R}_3$	0.26	9.09	0.54	0.66

Our current work can be extended in several natural ways. For instance, it would be interesting to tackle non-episodic problems. Another direction is to use more elaborate RL algorithms than Q-learning for computing best responses.

Our work is currently being applied in an industrial context with good results. An automated information extraction (IE) treatment chain is modelled as an MDP, and improved using a reward function balancing extraction quality and treatment time. SSB utility theory is used to formalise qualitative preferences expressed by human operators on the output of the treatments.

Acknowledgement

Work supported by the French National Research Agency through the Idex Sorbonne Universités, ELICIT project under grant ANR-11-IDEX-0004-02.

References

[Akrour *et al.*, 2012] R. Akrour, M. Schoenauer, and M. Sebag. APRIL: active preference-learning based reinforcement learning. *CoRR*, abs/1208.0984, 2012.

[Benaïm *et al.*, 2006] M. Benaïm, J. Hofbauer, and S. Sorin. Stochastic Approximations and Differential

Inclusions, Part II: Applications. *Mathematics of Operations Research*, 31(4):673–695, November 2006.

[Blavatskyy, 2006] P. Blavatskyy. Axiomatization of a Preference for Most Probable Winner. *Theory and Decision*, 60(1):17–33, 02 2006.

[Borkar, 1997] V. S. Borkar. Stochastic approximation with two time scales. *Systems & Control Letters*, 29(5):291 – 294, 1997.

[Borkar, 2008] V. S. Borkar. *Stochastic approximation : a dynamical systems viewpoint.* Cambridge university press New Delhi, Cambridge, 2008.

[Brown, 1951] G. W. Brown. Iterative solution of games by fictitious play. *Activity Analysis of Production and Allocation*, 1951.

[Busa-fekete *et al.*, 2014] R. Busa-fekete, B. Szörényi, P. Weng, W. Cheng, and E. Hüllermeier. Preference-based evolutionary direct policy search, 2014.

[Chvátal, 1983] V. Chvátal. Matrix games. In *Linear programming*, chapter 15, pages 228–239. Freeman, 1983.

[Dudík *et al.*, 2015] M. Dudík, K. Hofmann, R. E. Schapire, A. Slivkins, and M. Zoghi. Contextual dueling bandits. *CoRR*, abs/1502.06362, 2015.

[Fishburn, 1984] P. Fishburn. SSB utility theory: an economic perspective. *Mathematical Social Sciences*, 8(1):63 – 94, 1984.

[Fishburn, 1991] P. Fishburn. Nontransitive preferences in decision theory. *Journal of Risk and Uncertainty*, 4(2):113–134, 1991.

[Furnkranz *et al.*, 2012] J. Furnkranz, E. Hullermeier, W. Cheng, and S. Park. Preference-based reinforcement learning: a formal framework and a policy iteration algorithm. *Machine Learning*, 89(1-2):123–156, 2012.

[Gilbert *et al.*, 2015a] H. Gilbert, O. Spanjaard, P. Viappiani, and P. Weng. Solving MDPs with Skew Symmetric Bilinear Utility Functions. In *IJCAI*, 2015.

[Gilbert *et al.*, 2015b] H. Gilbert, O. Spanjaard, P. Viappiani, and P. Weng. Reducing the number of queries in interactive value iteration. In *ADT*, pages 139–152, 2015.

[Hofbauer, 1995] J. Hofbauer. Stability for the best response dynamics. *Working Paper*, 1995.

[Kalathil *et al.*, 2014] D. M. Kalathil, V. S. Borkar, and R. Jain. A learning scheme for approachability in MDPs and Stackelberg stochastic games. *CoRR*, abs/1411.0728, 2014.

[Mas-Colell *et al.*, 1995] A. Mas-Colell, M. D. Whinston, and J. R. Green. *Microeconomic theory*. Oxford University press, New York, 1995.

[Nakamura, 1989] Y. Nakamura. Risk attitudes for nonlinear measurable utility. *Annals of Operations Research*, 19:pp. 311–333, 1989.

[Perea and Puerto, 2007] F. Perea and J. Puerto. Dynamic programming analysis of the TV game who wants to be a millionaire? *European Journal of Operational Research*, 183(2):805 – 811, 2007.

[Puterman, 1994] M. Puterman. *Markov Decision Processes: Discrete Stochastic Dynamic Programming*. John Wiley & Sons, Inc., New York, NY, USA, 1st edition, 1994.

[Rivest and Shen, 2010] R. Rivest and E. Shen. An optimal single-winner preferential voting system based on game theory. In V. Conitzer and J. Rothe, editors, *Proceedings Third International Workshop on Computational Social Choice*. Düsseldorf University Press, 2010.

[von Neumann and Morgenstern, 1947] J. von Neumann and O. Morgenstern. *Theory of games and economic behavior*. Princeton University Press, 1947.

[Watkins and Dayan, 1992] C. Watkins and P. Dayan. Q-learning. *Machine Learning*, 8:279–292, 1992.

[Weng and Zanuttini., 2013] P. Weng and B. Zanuttini. Interactive value iteration for Markov decision processes with unknown rewards. In *International Joint Conference in Artificial Intelligence*, 2013.

[Weng *et al.*, 2013] P. Weng, R. Busa-Fekete, and E. Hüllermeier. Interactive Q-Learning with Ordinal Rewards and Unreliable Tutor. In *ECML/PKDD Workshop Reinforcement Learning with Generalized Feedback*, 2013.

[Wilson *et al.*, 2012] A. Wilson, A. Fern, and P. Tadepalli. A Bayesian approach for policy learning from trajectory preference queries. In F. Pereira, C. Burges, L. Bottou, and K. Weinberger, editors, *Advances in Neural Information Processing Systems 25*, pages 1133–1141. Curran Associates, Inc., 2012.

[Wirth and Fürnkranz, 2013] C. Wirth and J. Fürnkranz. EPMC: every visit preference Monte Carlo for reinforcement learning. In *Asian Conference on Machine Learning, ACML 2013, Canberra, ACT, Australia, November 13-15, 2013*, pages 483–497, 2013.

[Wirth and Neumann, 2015] C. Wirth and G. Neumann. Model-free preference-based reinforcement learning. In *EWRL*, 2015.

[Yu *et al.*, 1998] S. Yu, Y. Lin, and P. Yan. Optimization models for the first arrival target distribution function in discrete time. *Journal of Mathematical Analysis and Applications*, 225(1):193–223, 1998.

Bridging Heterogeneous Domains With Parallel Transport For Vision and Multimedia Applications

Raghuraman Gopalan
Dept. of Video and Multimedia Technologies Research
AT&T Labs-Research
San Francisco, CA 94108

Abstract

Accounting for different feature types across datasets is a relatively under-studied problem in domain adaptation. We address this heterogeneous adaptation setting using principles from parallel transport and hierarchical sparse coding. By learning generative subspaces from each domain, we first perform label-independent cross-domain feature mapping using parallel transport, and obtain a collection of paths (bridges) that could compensate domain shifts. We encode the information contained in these bridges into an expanded prior, and then integrate the prior into a hierarchical sparse coding framework to learn a selective subset of codes representing holistic data properties that are robust to domain change and feature type variations. We then utilize label information on the sparse codes to perform classification, or in the absence of labels perform clustering, and obtain improved results on several previously studied heterogeneous adaptation datasets. We highlight the flexibility of our approach by accounting for multiple heterogeneous domains in training as well as in testing, and by considering the zero-shot domain transfer scenario where there are data categories in testing which are not seen during training. In that process we also empirically show how existing heterogeneous adaptation solutions can benefit from the findings of our study.

1 INTRODUCTION

Domain adaptation, which addresses the problem of change in data characteristics across training (source domain) and testing (target domain) datasets, has received substantial attention over the last few years [Daume III and Marcu, 2006, Gopalan et al., 2015]. Its utility for visual recognition problems has been adequately demonstrated by several efforts that have utilized principles from distance transforms [Saenko et al., 2010], max-margin methods [Duan et al., 2009], manifolds [Gong et al., 2012], dictionary learning [Qiu et al., 2012] among others. Many of these approaches have addressed settings where the source domain is labeled and the target domain is unlabeled (unsupervised adaptation), when the target domain also has partial labels (semi-supervised adaptation) and when there is more than one domain in the source and/or target (multiple domain adaptation). However they assume that data, across domains, is represented by same type of features with same dimensions. This is not always possible in practice, given the prevalence of multi-modal sensors, and there have been relatively few efforts in the literature addressing the heterogeneous domain adaptation (HDA) setting which allows different feature types across domains.

One of the earliest efforts is by [Dai et al., 2008] that proposed a translated learning framework using risk minimization principles to bridge data across different feature types. [Prettenhofer and Stein, 2010] utilized structural correspondence learning by identifying pivot features that share similarities across domains. While such models have restrictions on the type of applications where they can be deployed, [Shi et al., 2010] proposed a more generic heterogeneous spectral mapping framework that learns an embedding to obtain a common domain-invariant feature subspace that optimally represents data from each domain. Along similar lines, [Wang and Mahadevan, 2011] proposed a manifold alignment approach that bridges source and target domain manifolds through a latent space that in addition to preserving topology of each domain, maximizes the intra-class similarities and inter-class dis-similarities across domains. [Kulis et al., 2011] approached this problem by learning asymmetric kernel transformations that perform cross-domain data mapping using semantic similarity. More recently, [Li et al., 2014] proposed a feature augmentation strategy coupled with max-margin classifiers, whose formulation resembles multiple kernel learning that in turn guarantees global optimal solution, and [Yeh et al., 2014] studied the utility of canonical correlation subspaces to this problem. Most of these methods either address the HDA problem by learning projections for each domain onto a common latent space where certain properties are satisfied, or by learning feature mapping from one domain onto another directly.

We take a rather different approach which, instead of learning a *few complex transformations* to map domains, learns *several simpler transformations* that explain how data from different domains can be bridged. In learning such transformations we bring the domains to a common dimension using simpler generative information, instead of more complex objectives tied to the domain structure and data similarities. What we gain by doing so is a richer 'expanded' set of prior information which could be harnessed by hierarchical learning methodologies to perform inference. More specifically, given N domains, with each domain representing the data with different feature type (thus having different dimension), we group the data from each domain into k clusters based on their feature similarity and obtain generative subspaces corresponding to each cluster by doing principal component analysis (PCA). We fix all subspaces to have the same dimension p using a heuristic tied to the amount of energy preserved in doing the dimensionality reduction. We then perform parallel transport [Edelman et al., 1998] between subspaces in every domain pair and obtain several intermediate representations that describe how data across domains can be bridged. We subsequently project the data from each domain onto all these intermediate representations to obtain an expanded prior, and integrate it with hierarchical sparse coding [Jenatton et al., 2011] to obtain compact codes on which we use label information, if any, to perform cross-domain inference. More details are provided in Section 2. The construction of our approach has the following benefits.

Accommodating Unlabeled Data: In many practical situations, with the widespread availability of multi-modal data on the web, we have very few (or at times no) labeled data and lots of unlabeled data. Our approach can readily utilize such big unlabeled data as we rely on generative modeling in addressing the heterogeneous domain shift. By doing so, when the source and target domains contain the same categories/classes, our final inference can range from the classification scenario where we have labels for all categories in source domain and the target domain may or may not have partial labels, to the clustering scenario where both the source and target domains are unlabeled. The label information is utilized while training a discriminative classifier such as support vector machines (SVM) on the learnt sparse codes, and if no labels are available we perform clustering on the sparse codes using methods such as k-means.

Zero-Shot Domain Transfer: We can also address the zero-shot scenario in which there are categories in the target domain that are not present in the source domain. This is somewhat different from the scenarios discussed above where we at least had unlabeled data in source domain for all target categories to support inference models. We could handle such a zero-shot scenario as our model is generative and therefore the learned domain shift would have pertinent information for reasoning out new categories.

Multiple Heterogeneous Domains: Finally we can easily accommodate multiple heterogeneous domains in the source as well as in target since we obtain the expanded prior by doing parallel transport between each domain pair. This does not pose a computational bottleneck as we are eventually learning sparse codes in a hierarchical learning setting that could handle big data.

To the best of our knowledge, our proposed approach is the first to handle these varied aspects of the HDA problem, and while some existing methods could handle a subset of these in principle, we make explicit discussions on these practically relevant requirements. We tested our approach on existing heterogeneous adaptation datasets and obtained good performance improvement over previous results for diverse tasks such as object recognition, event classification, text categorization and sentiment analysis. Detailed experimental analysis is provided in Section 3, and concluding remarks are given in Section 4.

2 APPROACH

Problem Setting: We assume there are N heterogeneous domains $D = \{D_i\}_{i=1}^N$, where each domain $D_i = \{x_i^j, y_i^j\}_{j=1}^{n_i}$ contains n_i data samples with $x_i^j \in \mathbb{R}^{d_i}$ denoting the feature vector of dimension d_i and y_i^j denoting the corresponding label information (if any) belonging to one of M different categories. These domains could be partitioned into source and target domains depending on the problem situation. With this information, the goal of this work is to account for heterogeneous domain shift in inferring the labels of the unlabeled target domain data.

2.1 PRELIMINARIES

Before we proceed, we will first review relevant details about the tools we use in our approach.

Parallel Transport: We will be working on subspaces derived from the data, and we will generally have multiple subspaces extracted from each domain. In domain adaptation literature, the notion of geodesic on the Grassmann manifold has been used as a bridge to connect a pair of subspaces [Gopalan et al., 2011]. When we need to bridge two 'sets' of subspaces instead, parallel transport [Edelman et al., 1998] provides a way by learning multiple paths by which subspace sets can be bridged. More specifically, let $S_1 = \{S_1^i\}_i$ and $S_2 = \{S_2^i\}_i$ denote two sets of p-dimensional subspaces in $\mathbb{R}^d$ corresponding to domains D_1 and D_2 respectively, where each subspace say S_1^1 is a point on the Grassmannian $\mathcal{G}_{d,p}$. Let $g_A(t)$ denote the geodesic with the initial direction $A \in \mathbb{R}^{(d-p)\times p}$ connecting the means of S_1 and S_2, and $\bar{S}_1^1$ denote the tangent space representation of S_1^1 obtained using inverse exponential mapping computed at the mean of S_1. The parallel transport of $\bar{S}_1^1$ is then given as

$$\gamma \bar{S}_1^1(t) = Q_{S_1^1} \exp\left(t \begin{bmatrix} 0 & A^T \\ -A & 0 \end{bmatrix}\right) \begin{bmatrix} 0 \\ B \end{bmatrix} \quad (1)$$

where exp is the matrix exponential, $Q_{S_1^1} \in SO(d)$ is the orthogonal completion of S_1^1, and $B \in \mathbb{R}^{(d-p)\times p}$ is the initial direction to reach from S_1^1 to the exponential map of $\bar{S}_1^1$. Similar directions can be obtained for all subspaces in the sets S_1 and S_2 using the above tangent space approximation. Please refer to [Edelman et al., 1998] for more details. We will discuss how to utilize these directions (bridges) for HDA in Section 2.2.

Hierarchical Sparse Coding: In sparse coding [Yang et al., 2009] the goal is to represent each input vector $x \in \mathbb{R}^p$ as a sparse linear combination of basis vectors. Given a stacked input data matrix $X \in \mathbb{R}^{p\times n}$, where n is the number of data, it seeks to minimize:

$$\arg\min_{Z\in\mathcal{Z},C} ||X - ZC||_2^2 + \lambda\Omega(C) \quad (2)$$

where $Z \in \mathbb{R}^{p\times r}$ is the dictionary of basis vectors, $\mathcal{Z}$ is the set of matrices whose columns have small ℓ_2 norm and $C \in \mathbb{R}^{r\times n}$ is the code matrix, λ is a regularization hyperparameter, and Ω is the regularizer. In hierarchical sparse coding, such a scheme is extended in a layered fashion using a combination of coding and pooling steps and we pursue the schema presented in [Jenatton et al., 2011]. Our modification comes in the way in which the dictionary is initialized and we present the details in Section 2.2.

While there has been an attempt in using parallel transport for unsupervised homogeneous domain adaptation [Shrivastava et al., 2014], our construction vastly differs from that work as we handle multiple heterogeneous domains without using label information to bridge the domain shift. Moreover, ours is the first approach to integrate parallel transport information with hierarchical sparse coding for adaptation problems.

2.2 PROPOSED HETEROGENEOUS ADAPTATION ALGORITHM

Step 1: We first bring data from all N domains, $D = \{D_i\}_{i=1}^N$, onto a common dimension d by performing PCA on each D_i and choosing the resultant subspace dimension as the largest dimension required among all N subspaces such that 90% of the signal energy is preserved for that decomposition. Then we project data from each domain onto its corresponding subspace. We now have d-dimensional data across all domains, say $\bar{X} = \{\bar{x}_i^j\}_{i,j}$, where i ranges from 1 to N and j ranges from 1 to n_i.

Step 2: From each domain D_i, we then derive k generative subspaces by partitioning $\{\bar{x}_i^j\}_{j=1}^{n_i}$ into k clusters using the k-means algorithm based on the similarity of the d dimensional features, and performing PCA on each cluster. We ensure all the subspaces are of dimension p, by choosing p as the largest dimension required for a subspace, amongst all subspaces obtained by doing k-means in each of the N domains, such that 90% of the signal energy is preserved by that decomposition[1]. Thus from every domain D_i we have a set of p-dimensional subspaces in $\mathbb{R}^d$ denoted by $S_i = \{S_i^j\}_{j=1}^k$. Each subspace in this set is a point on the Grassmann manifold, $\mathcal{G}_{d,p}$. Let $X \in \mathbb{R}^{p\times n}, n = \sum_{i=1}^N n_i$ denote the matrix containing the projections of each data in $\bar{X}$ onto its appropriate subspace in $S = \{S_i\}_{i=1}^N$. This is our input data matrix for sparse coding.

Step 3: We then perform parallel transport between S_i's using the method described in Section 2.1, and obtain a collection of directions between each pair of (S_i, S_j), i=1,..N-1, $j = i$+1,..,N. We uniformly sample points along these directions using exponential mapping, which results in new subspaces that have information on how domain shift information flows between domains. We project each data in $\bar{X}$ onto these subspaces to get the expanded prior $\mathcal{P} \in \mathbb{R}^{p\times r}$, which we in turn use to initialize the dictionary Z.

Step 4: Finally we perform hierarchical sparse coding [Jenatton et al., 2011] with the input data matrix X from Step 2 and the initial dictionary Z obtained from Step 3. At the output of each layer of hierarchical sparse coding, we apply Steps 2 and 3 obtain another set of expanded prior which is then used to complement the dictionary of the following layer. Let the final output (from the last layer) of hierarchical sparse coding corresponding to the original data X be denoted by $\hat{X} = \{\hat{x}_i^j\}_{i,j}$, and their corresponding label information (if any) is denoted as before by $Y = \{y_i^j\}_{i,j}$. Note that we have not used any label information thus far.

2.3 INFERENCE

We now perform cross-domain inference using the information contained in $W = (\hat{X}, Y)$. Note that W contains data from both source and target domains, and depending on the dataset we may have one or more domains in the source and target.

Classification: For the classification scenarios widely studied in HDA, source domain contains labeled data for all M categories, and the target domain may or may not have partial labels, and both the source and target domains

[1] While this is a simple heuristic in addressing variations in feature dimensions, we show that it works well empirically. As stated in the introduction, our main proposal for HDA is by generating an expanded prior on how these domains interact, rather than addressing domain shift 'during' the process of bringing domains to a common dimension as done by most existing methods.

have the same M categories. So we consider labeled data present in W to train a multi-class SVM [Crammer and Singer, 2002] with default parameters for linear kernel, and then use the SVM similarity score to classify the unlabeled target domain data into one of M categories. Classification accuracy is computed as the percentage of unlabeled target data that were correctly assigned their category label (using ground truth). Note that while we could have used the label information in any of the previous stages, be it during parallel transport or in sparse coding, we did not because we would like the learned cross-domain representations $\hat{X}$ to be generic to support other inference scenarios discussed next. Nevertheless, we make some observations regarding this later in Section 3.6.

Clustering: We also address the clustering scenario where both source and target domain data are unlabeled, and they have the same M categories. In this case we cluster all the data in $\hat{X}$ into M groups using k-means, and compute the clustering accuracy using a standard method of labeling each of the resulting clusters with the majority class label according to the ground truth, and measuring the number of mis-classifications made by each cluster grouping.

Zero-shot Learning: We finally account for the zero-shot learning scenario where the target domain has some categories that are not a part of the M source domain categories. For this case, we use labels for M categories in the source domain and (if available) in the target domain to train the SVM as discussed for the classification scenario. We then threshold the SVM similiarity score for the unlabeled target data, with the hope that if such data comes outside of the M source categories, the similarity score will be less. We then cluster such data using k-means to obtain groupings, with the number of clusters set to the number of new target categories known apriori, and evaluate the accuracy as discussed above for the clustering scenario. If we do not even know the number of new target categories, then it becomes difficult to quantify clustering accuracy.

3 EXPERIMENTS

We first discuss the classification scenario and experiment with the setup used by [Li et al., 2014] for the problems of heterogeneous object recognition, text categorization and sentiment analysis. These experiments have only one domain each in the source and target. We then consider the event classification experiment designed by [Chen et al., 2013] which consists of multiple source domains and a single target domain. We then provide a detailed analysis of the findings from our study.

3.1 OBJECT RECOGNITION

We work with the Office dataset [Saenko et al., 2010] that contains a total of 4106 images from 31 categories collected from three sources: amazon (object images downloaded from Amazon), dslr (high-resolution images taken from a digital SLR camera) and webcam (low-resolution images taken from a web camera). SURF features are extracted for all the images. The images from amazon and webcam are clustered into 800 visual words by using k-means. After vector quantization, each image is represented as a 800 dimensional histogram feature. Similarly, we represent each image from dslr as a 600-dimensional histogram feature. In the experiments, dslr is used as the target domain, while amazon and webcam are considered as two individual source domains. For training the SVM, we randomly select 20 labeled images per category for the source domain amazon, and 8 labeled images per category for webcam as source domain. For the target domain dslr, 3 labeled images are randomly selected from each category. The remaining target domain data is used for testing. We present results of our HDA approach in Table 1 along with other methods studied in [Li et al., 2014].

Methods	Source Domain	
	amazon	webcam
[Shi et al., 2010]	42.8±2.4	42.2±2.6
[Wang and Mahadevan, 2011]	53.3±2.3	53.2±3.2
[Kulis et al., 2011]	53.1±2.4	53.0±3.2
[Li et al., 2014]	55.4±2.9	54.3±3.6
Ours	62.1±1.7	61.5±2.1

Table 1: Mean and std. deviation of classification accuracy (%) on Object Recognition Dataset with target domain dslr.

3.2 TEXT CATEGORIZATION

We use the Reuters multilingual dataset [Amini et al., 2009] which contains about 11K newswire articles from 6 categories in 5 languages namely, English, French, German, Italian and Spanish. All documents are represented by using the TF-IDF feature. We perform PCA based on the TF-IDF features from each domain with 60% energy preserved and thus the features for each language have the following dimensions respectively, 1131, 1230, 1417, 1041 and 807. We consider Spanish as the target domain in the experiments and use each of the other four languages as individual source domains. For each category, we randomly sample 100 labeled documents from the source domain and either 10 or 20 labeled documents from the target domain to train the SVM. The remaining documents in the target domain are used as the test data. We report classification results of our HDA approach in Table 2 along with the results of the other approaches discussed in [Li et al., 2014].

3.3 SENTIMENT ANALYSIS

We use the Cross-Lingual Sentiment (CLS) dataset [Prettenhofer and Stein, 2010], which is an extended version of the Multi-Domain Sentiment Dataset [Blitzer et al., 2007] widely used for domain adaptation. It is collected from

Methods	Source Domain							
	10 labels per target class				20 labels per target class			
	English	French	German	Italian	English	French	German	Italian
[Shi et al., 2010]	54.7±7.4	55.0±9.4	58.0±7.9	59.4±3.7	65.7±3.1	64.2±4.2	64.6±3.6	65.8±2.3
[Wang and Mahadevan, 2011]	65.0±2.9	66.9±2.1	67.5±2.1	68.5±2.8	72.4±2.4	72.8±2.0	72.9±2.3	73.3±2.1
[Kulis et al., 2011]	65.7±2.7	66.9±1.7	68.7±2.9	67.9±2.8	72.9±2.0	73.5±1.8	74.7±1.6	74.0±2.0
[Li et al., 2014]	68.6±2.3	69.5±1.9	69.8±2.7	69.8±2.5	75.3±1.7	75.7±1.6	76.1±1.5	75.8±1.8
Ours	73.2±1.6	73.8±1.9	74.1±2.3	74.0±1.7	83.5±2.4	84.1±1.9	83.8±2.1	84.2±1.5

Table 2: Mean and std. deviation of classification accuracy (%) on Reuters Multilingual Dataset with target domain Spanish

Methods	Target Domain		
	German	French	Japanese
[Shi et al., 2010]	50.4±0.6	49.8±0.6	51.3±1.0
[Wang and Mahadevan, 2011]	64.6±1.9	65.7±1.8	64.4±1.8
[Kulis et al., 2011]	58.3±3.0	59.4±4.3	57.5±1.9
[Li et al., 2014]	66.5±2.2	66.9±2.1	64.2±2.5
Ours	71.2±2.1	71.5±1.8	70.9±1.5

Table 3: Mean and std. deviation of classification accuracy (%) on Cross-lingual Sentiment Dataset with source domain English.

Methods	Target Domain	
	Kodak	CCV
[Bruzzone and Marconcini, 2010]	43.49	41.55
[Duan et al., 2012b]	44.21	38.56
[Duan et al., 2012a]	46.21	43.44
[Chen et al., 2013]	49.61	44.52
Ours	54.56	51.24

Table 4: Mean average precision (%) on the Event classification dataset with multiple heterogeneous source domains from Google image search, Bing image search and YouTube video search.

Amazon and contains about 800,000 reviews of three product categories: Books, DVDs and Music, and written in four languages: English, German, French, and Japanese. The English reviews were sampled from the Multi-Domain Sentiment Dataset and reviews in other languages are crawled from Amazon. For each category and each language, the dataset is partitioned into a training set, a test set consisting of 2,000 reviews each. We take English as the source domain and each of the other three languages as an individual target domain in the experiment. We randomly sample 500 reviews from the training set of the source domain and 100 reviews from the training set of the target domain as the labeled data to train the SVM. The test set is the official test set for each category and each language. As with text categorization experiment, we extracted the TF-IDF features and performed PCA with 60% energy preserved to result in dimensions 715, 929, 964 and 874 respectively for the four languages discussed above. Results on this dataset are presented in Table 3.

3.4 EVENT CLASSIFICATION

We then worked on the event classification dataset of [Chen et al., 2013] that accounts for multiple heterogeneous source domains and a single target domain. The events pertain to six classes namely, birthday, picnic, parade, show, sports and wedding. Three source domains correspond to Google and Bing image search, and Youtube video search corresponding to these events. Kodak and CCV dataset serve as the individual target domain. The Google and Bing domains are represented by a 4000 dimensional bag-of-words codebooks learnt on SIFT features, while YouTube, Kodak and CCV datasets are represented by 6000 dimensional spatio-temporal features corresponding to histogram of oriented gradient, histogram of optical flow and motion boundary histogram. By considering the source domains to be labeled and target domain completely unlabeled we trained the SVM on the source domain samples to perform separate inference on CCV and Kodak datasets as the target domain. The cross-domain event classification results are presented in Table 4.

3.5 DISCUSSION

Clustering and Zero-shot Learning: We see that our HDA approach outperforms existing methods on diverse heterogeneous classification tasks. We also performed these experiments for the clustering scenario by not considering any labeled data from the source and target domains using the approach discussed in Section 2.3. The performance decreased by around 15% on average from the classification results. While this is reasonable since label information always helps in performing class-specific inference, it also shows that our generative heterogeneous model outputs $\hat{X}$ contain information agnostic to domain and feature variations and thus is relevant in grouping data categories. We verified this by performing a baseline using k-means after Step 1 (i.e. without the adaptation procedure) and the results dropped further by around 18% on average.

We then considered the zero-shot learning scenario, by considering the classification experiments and holding out 10%, 20% and 30% of the categories as being exclusive to the target which the source domain has not seen. As per the discussion in Section 2.3, we first thresholded the SVM similarity scores for data from these new categories. With the similarity score ranging from 0 (low) to 1(high), we tried three thresholds namely 0.3, 0.2 and 0.1. Ideally these new categories should have lower similarities since they are not part of the trained model. On average we obtained a 95% filtering accuracy with these thresholds, across all datasets discussed before, and then we grouped the filtered data to get an accuracy of 85% on average. Note that these results are only for the new data categories, which are much less in number than those considered for classification scenario and hence can not be compared with those results. As a sanity check we tested the unlabeled data from the target categories that are present in the source, and observed that their SVM similarity scores were always greater than 0.3 for all datasets. These results convey that our model outputs are quite useful in reasoning out never seen before categories, which is very important in practice.

Parameter Tuning: For all the results discussed thus far, we used $k = 10$ clusters within each domain, and uniformly sampled 10 points on the parallel transport directions. We tried other values 8 and 12 for both clusters and sampling on directions, and PCA energy of 80% and 85% in learning the generative subspaces from the domains, and found the results decreased at the most by 2%. We used default parameters for other tools we have employed in the approach. This sheds light on the robustness of our approach. It takes about 5 to 10 seconds on a single 2GHz machine to perform inference over the range of scenarios discussed here.

Design Choice Analysis: We now analyze the rationale behind some choices we made in the approach. Firstly, we tested whether hierarchical sparse coding is necessary, or will a single layer sparse coding be sufficient. We also tested how many layers are necessary by experimenting up to five layers. The results reported in the paper are with three layers, and when we used four and five layers, the results reduced by 2.5% and 3% on average, using two layers saw average performance reduction of around 8% and using one layer saw a reduction of 17%. This suggests that hierarchical feature learning is useful, and the results reach a plateau around three layers for our experiments.

Then we inspect whether learning multiple bridges across domains using parallel transport is necessary, or just a single bridge using the geodesic will suffice. Results using only the geodesic was inferior by around 21% which highlights the utility of parallel transport to the HDA problem. We also test whether we need to do parallel transport to obtain expanded prior on the outputs of each layer of hierarchical sparse coding, by just initializing the first layer with the prior and doing hierarchical feature learning on it. That resulted in a performance drop of about 12% on average.

Multiple Source and Multiple Target Domains: Our experiments so far contained single source and single target domain, or multiple source domains and single target domain. We now pursue multiple source domains and multiple target domains on these datasets, where possible. Given N domains, we try all possible combinations across source and target domains. For example, if we have four domains, we consider 1 to 3 source domains that are accompanied by 3 to 1 target domains respectively. Our results for such a setting improves the results discussed in Sec 3.1 to 3.4 by at least 3% and up to 12%. This explains the utility of our method for HDA with increasing availability of domains.

3.6 EXTENSIONS

In this section we discuss some extensions of our approach, by relaxing certain assumptions that were made to facilitate its generalizability to different adaptation settings.

Using Label Information In Modeling Stage: Till now the labels were used only in the classification stage (Sec 2.3) and not in the modeling stage (Sec 2.2) as we wanted the model to handle classification, clustering and zero-shot learning. But in cases where say, the goal is just classification and there are labels available for training the model, it makes sense to use them in the model building stage itself. To support such a scenario, we modify our approach (in Step 4) by performing discriminative hierarchical sparse coding. We use the method of [Ji et al., 2011] and feed it with data labels contained in Y. Thus, we obtain the sparse codes output $\hat{X}$ which in addition to minimizing the reconstruction error of the data samples, also separates samples belonging to one class from other classes. Let us call this Case A. With this modification, the performance for classification experiments reported in Section 3.1 to 3.4 improved by at least 3% and up to 15% on average.

Another way to utilize label information is in forming the clusters within each domain (Step 2). Instead of using the similarity of the d dimensional features to group the data into k clusters, we group the data using their labels into M clusters and then perform the remaining steps as outlined in Section 2.2. So in this case the parallel transport information will have a notion of class discrimination in traversing the domain shift. Let us call this Case B. This resulted in an average performance improvement of at least 1.8% and up to 9% for the classification experiments reported in Section 3.1 to 3.4. We then used Case A and Case B together, and this improved the results by at least 5% and up to 20% on average.

Integrating With Other Heterogeneous Adaptation Strategies: As mentioned in the introduction, one of the goals of our study was to see how a large number of simple transformations would fare against few complex transformations to handle heterogeneous domain shift, which was the reason to map all domains to a common dimension using simpler generative information (Step 1). This strategy was shown to be successful through detailed experiments. Now we study how to get the best of both approaches. For this, instead of Step 1, we use outputs from existing heterogeneous adaptation techniques which map different dimensions onto a common one using more involved objectives related to domain structure. We tried two such techniques, one based on spectral mapping [Shi et al., 2010] and the

Domain		Classification accuracy (in %), mean±std. deviation					
Source	Target	No labeled target data			Few labeled target data		
		[Mahsa et al., 2014]	[Long et al., 2014]	Ours	[Ni et al., 2013]	[Mahsa et al., 2013]	Ours
Caltech	Amazon	52.3±1.1	46.76	56.3±1.1	49.5±2.6	61.8±2.5	65.3±1.2
Caltech	Dslr	53.0±2.3	44.59	55.2±1.8	76.7±3.9	65.8±3.5	79.8±1.2
Amazon	Caltech	44.4±1.4	39.45	49.2±1.3	27.4±2.4	47.8±1.5	51.1±0.3
Amazon	Webcam	48.5±2.6	42.03	51.6±2.1	72.0±4.8	72.5±3.1	75.5±1.1
Webcam	Caltech	39.3±0.5	30.19	42.8±1.8	29.7±1.9	43.6±1.2	45.5±2.8
Webcam	Amazon	44.3±0.9	29.96	45.2±2.5	49.4±2.1	53.4±1.9	55.5±1.7
Dslr	Amazon	39.4±1.1	32.78	44.3±1.2	48.9±3.8	56.9±1.6	57.5±1.5
Dslr	Webcam	88.8±1.0	85.42	91.2±1.7	72.6±2.1	89.1±1.6	92.3±2.6

Table 5: Comparison with homogeneous adaptation methods on the Office-Caltech dataset with 10 object categories.

other based on manifold alignment [Wang and Mahadevan, 2011]. The mapped output of these techniques, where the data from all domains $\{D_i\}_{i=1}^N$ will have the transformed to the same dimension d, signifies $\bar{X}$ which is then fed into Step 2, and the remaining steps from Sec 2.2 and 2.3 are followed. This resulted in a performance improvement of at least 5% and up to 18%, and at least 4.2% and up to 16.5% while using [Shi et al., 2010] and [Wang and Mahadevan, 2011] respectively, for classification, clustering, and zero-shot learning experiments reported in Section 3.1 to 3.5. These results hold promise on the utility of our approach to existing adaptation solutions.

Heterogeneous View Of Homogeneous Adaptation: Encouraged by these observations, we considered homogeneous adaptation problems that have been extensively studied in the literature [Saenko et al., 2010], which assumes the data is represented by same features (same dimensions) in both source and target domains. The goal of our study here is to represent such data with many different features, with each feature forming a separate domain, and empirically investigate whether multiple features can make adaptation problems easier to handle. We experiment with different combinations of heterogeneous features in the source and target and at the same time making sure that the same feature type is not used for both source and target. The results presented below are averaged over such combinations.

We first consider the Office-Caltech dataset [Gong et al., 2012] for adaptive object recognition that contains 10 objects with four domains namely, amazon, dslr, webcam, and Caltech. The data is represented by bag-of-words codebooks learnt from SURF features. We additionally extracted histogram of oriented gradients, local binary patterns, local phase quantization, and GIST descriptors. Thus we have five domains each in the source and target domain. We then followed the adaptation protocol of [Gong et al., 2012] that first considered labeled data from source domain and no labels from target domain, and then allows few labeled samples from target as well. Our results are provided in Table 5.

We then worked on adaptive face recognition and considered the following facial features, image intensities in RGB and HSV color spaces, edge magnitudes and gradient direction, multi-scale block LBP, self-quotient image and Gabor wavelets. We first followed the protocol of [Shekhar et al., 2013] that used the Multi-PIE dataset [Gross et al., 2010] with images of 129 subjects in frontal pose as the source domain, and five other off-frontal poses as the target domain. Images under five illumination conditions across source and target domains were used for training with which images from remaining 15 illumination conditions in the target domain were recognized. Face recognition accuracy for this experiment is given in Table 6. We also performed an experiment on the PIE dataset [Sim et al., 2002] using the protocol of [Ni et al., 2013], where the domain change is caused by illumination and blur. Frontal pose faces of 34 subjects under 11 different illumination conditions formed the source domain, while the unlabeled target domain consisted of frontal images of the same subjects under 10 other lighting conditions that were also blurred using four kernels, a Gaussian with standard deviation of 3 and 4 and motion blur with length 9, angle 135° and length 11, angle 45°. The results are provided in Table 7.

Method	Mean classification accuracy (%) Target domain pose				
	15°	30°	45°	60°	75°
[Sharma and Jacobs, 2011]	92.1	89.7	88.0	86.1	83.0
[Sharma et al., 2012]	99.7	99.2	98.6	94.9	95.4
[Yang et al., 2011]	96.8	90.6	94.4	91.4	90.5
[Shekhar et al., 2013]	98.4	98.2	98.9	99.1	98.8
Ours	99.5	99.3	99.1	99.4	98.9

Table 6: Comparison with homogeneous adaptation methods on CMU Multi-PIE dataset for face recognition across pose and lighting variations with few labeled target data.

Finally we performed adaptation experiments for action recognition on the IXMAS multi-view action dataset [Weinland et al., 2007] that contains eleven action categories including walk, kick and throw. Each action was performed three times by twelve actors taken from five different views, which include four side views and one top view. From each action video we extracted the following features, histograms of oriented gradients and optical flow (HOG/HOF), 3DHOG that is based on 3D gradi-

Method	Mean classification accuracy (%)			
	$\sigma = 3$	$\sigma = 4$	$len = 9$	$len = 11$
[Ahonen et al., 2008]	66.5	32.9	73.8	62.1
[Gopalan et al., 2011]	70.9	60.3	72.4	67.9
[Gong et al., 2012]	78.5	77.7	82.4	77.7
[Ni et al., 2013]	80.3	77.9	85.9	81.2
Ours	86.3	85.2	87.9	87.2

Table 7: Comparing homogeneous adaptation methods on CMU PIE dataset for face recognition across blur and lighting variations with no labeled target data. σ: std. deviation of the Gaussian blur, and len: length of linear motion blur.

ent orientations, and extended SURF descriptor for videos. The experiment was to recognize actions with the source and target domain pertaining to different views, thereby making 20 source-target combinations. The average cross-view recognition accuracy results for all these view combinations are given in Table 8. The correspondence mode contains matched instances across source and target domains, partial labels mode having fewer target labels and the non-discriminative virtual views (NDVV) comprising of partially-labeled and unlabeled target data, as studied in [Li and Zickler, 2012].

All these results show our method outperforming other homogeneous adaptation approaches, which suggests that such approaches could, in some form, benefit by expanding the type of features used to represent the data. The features we have used are only somewhat representative of the vast literature and more of them can be used with our approach.

4 CONCLUSION

We have approached the problem of bridging heterogeneous domains by learning a large set of intermediate representations, born out of simpler generative information, and integrated them with hierarchical feature learning mechanisms to perform inference pertaining to classification, clustering and zero-shot learning. We demonstrated superior empirical performance over existing methods on a wide range of problems involving different data modalities such as images, videos and natural language. We also discussed the utility of our design choices, and the robustness of the approach in dealing with multiple domains, feature types, unlabeled data and new unseen data categories. While our approach offers an alternative to many existing heterogeneous solutions that address domain shift through a latent space modeling, it also opens up opportunities for harnessing the benefits of the two strategies, which we highlighted through some initial studies. Such a mechanism could eventually pave way for establishing error bounds on the nature of heterogeneous shifts an approach can handle, within a reasonable set of domain shift assumptions reflecting practical data acquisition constraints.

References

Timo Ahonen, Esa Rahtu, Ville Ojansivu, and J Heikkila. Recognition of blurred faces using local phase quantization. In *ICPR*, 2008.

Massih Amini, Nicolas Usunier, and Cyril Goutte. Learning from multiple partially observed views-an application to multilingual text categorization. In *NIPS*, 2009.

John Blitzer, Mark Dredze, Fernando Pereira, et al. Biographies, bollywood, boom-boxes and blenders: Domain adaptation for sentiment classification. In *ACL*, 2007.

Lorenzo Bruzzone and Mattia Marconcini. Domain adaptation problems: A dasvm classification technique and a circular validation strategy. *IEEE TPAMI*, 32:770–787, 2010.

Chao-Yeh Chen and Kristen Grauman. Inferring unseen views of people. In *CVPR*, 2014.

Lin Chen, Lixin Duan, Dong Xu, and Dong Xu. Event recognition in videos by learning from heterogeneous web sources. In *CVPR*, 2013.

Koby Crammer and Yoram Singer. On the algorithmic implementation of multiclass kernel-based vector machines. *JMLR*, 2:265–292, 2002.

Wenyuan Dai, Yuqiang Chen, Gui-Rong Xue, Qiang Yang, and Yong Yu. Translated learning: Transfer learning across different feature spaces. In *NIPS*, 2008.

Hal Daume III and Daniel Marcu. Domain adaptation for statistical classifiers. *Journal of Artificial Intelligence Research*, pages 101–126, 2006.

Lixin Duan, Ivor W Tsang, Dong Xu, and Stephen J Maybank. Domain transfer svm for video concept detection. In *CVPR*, 2009.

Lixin Duan, Dong Xu, and Shih-Fu Chang. Exploiting web images for event recognition in consumer videos: A multiple source domain adaptation approach. In *CVPR*, 2012a.

Lixin Duan, Dong Xu, and Ivor W Tsang. Domain adaptation from multiple sources: A domain-dependent regularization approach. *IEEE Trans Neural Networks and Learning Systems*, 23:504–518, 2012b.

Alan Edelman, Tomás A Arias, and Steven T Smith. The geometry of algorithms with orthogonality constraints. *SIAM journal on Matrix Analysis and Applications*, 20: 303–353, 1998.

Boqing Gong, Yuan Shi, Fei Sha, and Kristen Grauman. Geodesic flow kernel for unsupervised domain adaptation. In *CVPR*, 2012.

Raghuraman Gopalan, Ruonan Li, and Rama Chellappa. Domain adaptation for object recognition: An unsupervised approach. In *ICCV*, 2011.

Method	Mean classification accuracy (%)		
	correspondence	partial labels	NDVV
[Liu et al., 2011]	75.3	-	-
[Chen and Grauman, 2014]	78.8	-	-
[Li and Zickler, 2012]	81.2	61.2	61.1, 26.0
[Zhang et al., 2013]	85.8	69.0	69.2, 35.3
Ours	89.5	74.3	75.3, 45.4

Table 8: Comparison with homogeneous adaptation methods on the IXMAS dataset for cross-view action recognition.

Raghuraman Gopalan, Ruonan Li, Vishal M Patel, and Rama Chellappa. Domain adaptation for visual recognition. *Foundations and Trends® in Computer Graphics and Vision*, 8(4):285–378, 2015.

Ralph Gross, Iain Matthews, Jeffrey Cohn, Takeo Kanade, and Simon Baker. Multi-pie. *Image and Vision Computing*, 28:807–813, 2010.

Rodolphe Jenatton, Julien Mairal, Guillaume Obozinski, and Francis Bach. Proximal methods for hierarchical sparse coding. *JMLR*, 12:2297–2334, 2011.

Zhengping Ji, Wentao Huang, Garrett Kenyon, and Luis Bettencourt. Hierarchical discriminative sparse coding via bidirectional connections. In *IJCNN*, 2011.

Brian Kulis, Kate Saenko, and Trevor Darrell. What you saw is not what you get: Domain adaptation using asymmetric kernel transforms. In *CVPR*, 2011.

Ruonan Li and Todd Zickler. Discriminative virtual views for cross-view action recognition. In *CVPR*, 2012.

Wen Li, Lixin Duan, Dong Xu, and Ivor W Tsang. Learning with augmented features for supervised and semi-supervised heterogeneous domain adaptation. *IEEE TPAMI*, 36:1134–1148, 2014.

Jingen Liu, Mubarak Shah, Benjamin Kuipers, and Silvio Savarese. Cross-view action recognition via view knowledge transfer. In *CVPR*, 2011.

Mingsheng Long, Jianmin Wang, Guiguang Ding, Jiaguang Sun, and Philip S Yu. Transfer joint matching for unsupervised domain adaptation. In *CVPR*, 2014.

Baktashmotlagh Mahsa, Mehrtash T Harandi, Brian C Lovell, and Mathieu Salzmann. Unsupervised domain adaptation by domain invariant projection. In *ICCV*, 2013.

Baktashmotlagh Mahsa, Mehrtash T Harandi, Brian C Lovell, and Mathieu Salzmann. Domain adaptation on the statistical manifold. In *CVPR*, 2014.

Jie Ni, Qiang Qiu, and Rama Chellappa. Subspace interpolation via dictionary learning for unsupervised domain adaptation. In *CVPR*, 2013.

Peter Prettenhofer and Benno Stein. Cross-language text classification using structural correspondence learning. In *ACL*, 2010.

Qiang Qiu, Vishal M Patel, Pavan Turaga, and Rama Chellappa. Domain adaptive dictionary learning. In *ECCV*. 2012.

Kate Saenko, Brian Kulis, Mario Fritz, and Trevor Darrell. Adapting visual category models to new domains. In *ECCV*. 2010.

Abhishek Sharma and David W Jacobs. Bypassing synthesis: Pls for face recognition with pose, low-resolution and sketch. In *CVPR*, 2011.

Abhishek Sharma, Abhishek Kumar, H Daume, and David W Jacobs. Generalized multiview analysis: A discriminative latent space. In *CVPR*, 2012.

Sumit Shekhar, Vishal M Patel, Hien V Nguyen, and Rama Chellappa. Generalized domain-adaptive dictionaries. In *CVPR*, 2013.

Xiaoxiao Shi, Qi Liu, Wei Fan, Philip S Yu, and Ruixin Zhu. Transfer learning on heterogenous feature spaces via spectral transformation. In *ICDM*, 2010.

Ashish Shrivastava, Sumit Shekhar, and Vishal M Patel. Unsupervised domain adaptation using parallel transport on grassmann manifold. In *WACV*, 2014.

Terence Sim, Simon Baker, and Maan Bsat. The cmu pose, illumination, and expression (pie) database. In *FG*, 2002.

Chang Wang and Sridhar Mahadevan. Heterogeneous domain adaptation using manifold alignment. In *IJCAI*, 2011.

Daniel Weinland, Edmond Boyer, and Remi Ronfard. Action recognition from arbitrary views using 3d exemplars. In *ICCV*, 2007.

Jianchao Yang, Kai Yu, Yihong Gong, and Thomas Huang. Linear spatial pyramid matching using sparse coding for image classification. In *CVPR*, 2009.

Meng Yang, David Zhang, and Xiangchu Feng. Fisher discrimination dictionary learning for sparse representation. In *ICCV*, 2011.

Yi-Ren Yeh, Chun-Hao Huang, and Yu-Chiang Frank Wang. Heterogeneous domain adaptation and classification by exploiting the correlation subspace. *IEEE Transactions on Image Processing*, 23, 2014.

Zhong Zhang, Chunheng Wang, Baihua Xiao, Wen Zhou, Shuang Liu, and Cunzhao Shi. Cross-view action recognition via a continuous virtual path. In *CVPR*, 2013.

Structured Prediction: From Gaussian Perturbations to Linear-Time Principled Algorithms

Jean Honorio
CS, Purdue
West Lafayette, IN 47907, USA
jhonorio@purdue.edu

Tommi Jaakkola
CSAIL, MIT
Cambridge, MA 02139, USA
tommi@csail.mit.edu

Abstract

Margin-based structured prediction commonly uses a maximum loss over all possible structured outputs (Altun & Hofmann, 2003; Collins, 2004; Taskar et al., 2003). In natural language processing, recent work (Zhang et al., 2014; Zhang et al., 2015) has proposed the use of the maximum loss over random structured outputs sampled independently from some proposal distribution. This method is linear-time in the number of random structured outputs and trivially parallelizable. We study this family of loss functions in the PAC-Bayes framework under Gaussian perturbations (McAllester, 2007). Under some technical conditions and up to statistical accuracy, we show that this family of loss functions produces a tighter upper bound of the Gibbs decoder distortion than commonly used methods. Thus, using the maximum loss over random structured outputs is a principled way of learning the parameter of structured prediction models. Besides explaining the experimental success of (Zhang et al., 2014; Zhang et al., 2015), our theoretical results show that more general techniques are possible.

1 INTRODUCTION

Structured prediction has been shown to be useful in many diverse domains. Application areas include natural language processing (e.g., named entity recognition, part-of-speech tagging, dependency parsing), computer vision (e.g., image segmentation, multiple object tracking), speech (e.g., text-to-speech mapping) and computational biology (e.g., protein structure prediction).

In dependency parsing, for instance, the observed input is a sentence and the desired structured output is a parse tree for the given sentence.

In general, structured prediction can be viewed as a kind of decoding. A *decoder* is a machine for predicting the structured output y given the observed input x. Such a decoder, depends on a parameter w. Given a fixed w, the task performed by the decoder is called *inference*. In this paper, we focus on the problem of learning the parameter w. Next, we introduce the problem and our main contributions.

We assume a distribution D on pairs (x, y) where $x \in \mathcal{X}$ is the observed input and $y \in \mathcal{Y}$ is the latent structured output, i.e., $(x, y) \sim D$. We also assume that we have a training set S of n i.i.d. samples drawn from the distribution D, i.e., $S \sim D^n$, and thus $|S| = n$.

We let $\mathcal{Y}(x) \neq \emptyset$ denote the countable set of feasible *decodings* of x. In general, $|\mathcal{Y}(x)|$ is exponential with respect to the input size.

We assume a fixed mapping ϕ from pairs to feature vectors, i.e., for any pair (x, y) we have the feature vector $\phi(x, y) \in \mathbb{R}^k \setminus \{0\}$. For a parameter $w \in \mathcal{W} \subseteq \mathbb{R}^k \setminus \{0\}$, we consider linear decoders of the form:

$$f_w(x) \equiv \arg\max_{y \in \mathcal{Y}(x)} \phi(x, y) \cdot w \tag{1}$$

In practice, very few cases of the above general *inference* problem are tractable, while most are NP-hard and also hard to approximate within a fixed factor. (We defer the details in theory of computation to Section 6.)

We also introduce the *distortion* function $d : \mathcal{Y} \times \mathcal{Y} \to [0, 1]$. The value $d(y, y')$ measures the amount of difference between two structured outputs y and y'. Disregarding the computational and statistical aspects, the ultimate goal is to set the parameter w in order to minimize the decoder distortion. That is:

$$\min_{w \in \mathcal{W}} \mathop{\mathbb{E}}_{(x,y) \sim D} [d(y, f_w(x))] \tag{2}$$

Computationally speaking, the above procedure is inefficient since $d(y, f_w(x))$ is a discontinuous function with respect to w and thus, it is in general an exponential-time optimization problem. Statistically speaking, the problem in eq.(2) requires access to the data distribution D and thus, in general it would require an infinite amount of data. In practice, we only have access to a small amount of training data.

Additionally, eq.(2) would potentially favor parameters w with low distortion, but that could be in a neighborhood of parameters with high distortion. In order to avoid this issue, we could optimize a more "robust" objective under Gaussian perturbations. More formally, let $\alpha > 0$ and let $Q(w)$ be a unit-variance Gaussian distribution centered at $w\alpha$ of parameters $w' \in \mathcal{W}$. The Gibbs decoder distortion of the perturbation distribution $Q(w)$ and data distribution D, is defined as:

$$L(Q(w), D) = \mathop{\mathbb{E}}_{(x,y)\sim D}\left[\mathop{\mathbb{E}}_{w'\sim Q(w)}[d(y, f_{w'}(x))]\right] \quad (3)$$

The minimization of the Gibbs decoder distortion can be expressed as:

$$\min_{w\in\mathcal{W}} L(Q(w), D)$$

The focus of our analysis will be to propose upper bounds of the Gibbs decoder distortion, with good computational and statistical properties. That is, we will propose upper bounds that can be computed in polynomial-time, and that require a small amount of training data.

For our analysis, we follow the same set of assumptions as in (McAllester, 2007). We define the margin $m(x, y, y', w)$ as the amount by which y is preferable to y' under the parameter w. More formally:

$$m(x, y, y', w) \equiv \phi(x, y) \cdot w - \phi(x, y') \cdot w$$

Let $c(p, x, y)$ be a nonnegative integer that gives the number of times that the part $p \in \mathcal{P}$ appears in the pair (x, y). For a part $p \in \mathcal{P}$, we define the feature p as follows:

$$\phi_p(x, y) \equiv c(p, x, y)$$

We let $\mathcal{P}(x) \neq \emptyset$ denote the set of $p \in \mathcal{P}$ such that there exists $y \in \mathcal{Y}(x)$ with $c(p, x, y) > 0$. We define the Hamming distance H as follows:

$$H(x, y, y') \equiv \sum_{p\in\mathcal{P}(x)} |c(p, x, y) - c(p, x, y')|$$

The commonly applied margin-based approach to learning w uses the maximum loss over all possible structured outputs (Altun & Hofmann, 2003; Collins, 2004; Taskar et al., 2003). That is:[1]

$$\min_{w\in\mathcal{W}} \frac{1}{n} \sum_{(x,y)\in S} \max_{\hat{y}\in\mathcal{Y}(x)} d(y, \hat{y})\, 1\begin{pmatrix} H(x, y, \hat{y}) \\ -m(x, y, \hat{y}, w) \geq 0 \end{pmatrix} + \lambda\|w\|_2^2 \quad (4)$$

[1]For computational convenience, the *convex* hinge loss $\max(0, 1 + z)$ is used in practice instead of the *discontinuous* 0/1 loss $1(z \geq 0)$.

In Section 2, we reproduce the results in (McAllester, 2007) and show that the above objective is related to an upper bound of the Gibbs decoder distortion in eq.(3). Note that evaluating the objective function in eq.(4) is as hard as the inference problem in eq.(1), since both perform maximization over the set $\mathcal{Y}(x)$.

Our main contributions are presented in Sections 3 and 4. Inspired by recent work in natural language processing (Zhang et al., 2014; Zhang et al., 2015), we show a tighter upper bound of the Gibbs decoder distortion in eq.(3), which is related to the following objective:[1]

$$\min_{w\in\mathcal{W}} \frac{1}{n} \sum_{(x,y)\in S} \max_{\hat{y}\in T(w,x)} d(y, \hat{y})\, 1\begin{pmatrix} H(x, y, \hat{y}) \\ -m(x, y, \hat{y}, w) \geq 0 \end{pmatrix} + \lambda\|w\|_2^2 \quad (5)$$

where $T(w, x)$ is a set of random structured outputs sampled i.i.d. from some proposal distribution with support on $\mathcal{Y}(x)$. Note that evaluating the objective function in eq.(5) is linear-time in the number of random structured outputs in $T(w, x)$.

2 FROM PAC-BAYES TO THE MAXIMUM LOSS OVER ALL POSSIBLE STRUCTURED OUTPUTS

In this section, we show the relationship between PAC-Bayes bounds and the commonly used maximum loss over all possible structured outputs.

As reported in (McAllester, 2007), by using the PAC-Bayes framework under Gaussian perturbations, we show that the commonly used maximum loss over all possible structured outputs is an upper bound of the Gibbs decoder distortion up to statistical accuracy ($\mathcal{O}(\sqrt{\log n/n})$ for n training samples).

Theorem 1 (McAllester, 2007). *Assume that there exists a finite integer value ℓ such that $|\cup_{(x,y)\in S}\mathcal{P}(x)| \leq \ell$. Fix $\delta \in (0, 1)$. With probability at least $1 - \delta/2$ over the choice of n training samples, simultaneously for all parameters $w \in \mathcal{W}$ and unit-variance Gaussian perturbation distributions $Q(w)$ centered at $w\sqrt{2\log(2n\ell/\|w\|_2^2)}$, we have:*

$$L(Q(w), D) \leq \frac{1}{n} \sum_{(x,y)\in S} \max_{\hat{y}\in\mathcal{Y}(x)} d(y, \hat{y})\, 1\begin{pmatrix} H(x, y, \hat{y}) \\ -m(x, y, \hat{y}, w) \geq 0 \end{pmatrix} + \frac{\|w\|_2^2}{n} + \sqrt{\frac{\|w\|_2^2 \log(2n\ell/\|w\|_2^2) + \log(2n/\delta)}{2(n-1)}}$$

(See Appendix A for detailed proofs.)

The proof of the above is based on the PAC-Bayes theorem and well-known Gaussian concentration inequalities.

As it is customary in generalization results, a *deterministic* expectation with respect to the data distribution D is upper-bounded by a *stochastic* quantity with respect to the training set S. This takes into account the statistical aspects of the problem.

Note that the upper bound uses maximization with respect to $\mathcal{Y}(x)$ and that in general, $|\mathcal{Y}(x)|$ is exponential with respect to the input size. Thus, the computational aspects of the problem have not been fully addressed yet. In the next section, we solve this issue by introducing randomness.

3 FROM PAC-BAYES TO THE MAXIMUM LOSS OVER RANDOM STRUCTURED OUTPUTS

In this section, we analyze the relationship between PAC-Bayes bounds and the maximum loss over random structured outputs sampled independently from some proposal distribution.

First, we will focus on the computational aspects. Instead of using maximization with respect to $\mathcal{Y}(x)$, we will perform maximization with respect to a set $T(w, x)$ of random structured outputs sampled i.i.d. from some proposal distribution $R(w, x)$ with support on $\mathcal{Y}(x)$. In order for this approach to be computationally appealing, $|T(w, x)|$ should be polynomial, even when $|\mathcal{Y}(x)|$ is exponential with respect to the input size.

Assumptions A and B will allow us to attain $|T(w,x)| = \mathcal{O}\left(\max\left(\frac{1}{\log(1/\beta)}, \|w\|_2^2\right)\right)$. The constant $\beta \in [0, 1)$ is properly introduced on Assumption A. It can be easily observed that β plays an important role in the number of random structured outputs that we need to draw from the proposal distribution $R(w, x)$. Next, we present our first assumption.

Assumption A (Maximal distortion). *The proposal distribution $R(w, x)$ fulfills the following condition. There exists a value $\beta \in [0, 1)$ such that for all $(x, y) \in S$ and $w \in \mathcal{W}$:*

$$\mathbb{P}_{y' \sim R(w,x)}[d(y, y') = 1] \geq 1 - \beta$$

In Section 4 we show examples that fulfill the above assumption, which include a *binary* distortion function for *any* type of structured output, as well as a distortion function that returns the number of different edges/elements for directed spanning trees, directed acyclic graphs and cardinality-constrained sets.

Next, we present our second assumption that allows obtaining $|T(w,x)| = \mathcal{O}\left(\max\left(\frac{1}{\log(1/\beta)}, \|w\|_2^2\right)\right)$. While Assumption A contributes with the term $\frac{1}{\log(1/\beta)}$ in $|T(w, x)|$, the following assumption contributes with the term $\|w\|_2^2$ in $|T(w, x)|$.

Assumption B (Low norm). *For any vector $z \in \mathbb{R}^k$, define:*

$$\mu(z) = \begin{cases} z/\|z\|_1 & \text{if } z \neq 0 \\ 0 & \text{if } z = 0 \end{cases}$$

The proposal distribution $R(w, x)$ fulfills the following condition for all $(x, y) \in S$ and $w \in \mathcal{W}$:[2]

$$\left\| \mathbb{E}_{y' \sim R(w,x)} [\mu(\phi(x, y) - \phi(x, y'))] \right\|_2 \leq \frac{1}{2\sqrt{n}} \leq \frac{1}{2\|w\|_2}$$

It is natural to ask whether there are instances that fulfill the above assumption. In Section 4 we provide two extreme cases: one example of a *sparse* mapping and a uniform proposal, and one example of a *dense* mapping and an *arbitrary* proposal distribution.

We will now focus on the statistical aspects. Note that randomness does not only stem from data, but also from sampling structured outputs. That is, in Theorem 1, randomness only stems from the training set S. We now need to produce generalization results that hold for all the sets $T(w, x)$ of random structured outputs. In addition, the uniform convergence of Theorem 1 holds for all parameters w. We now need to produce a generalization result that also holds for all possible proposal distributions $R(w, x)$. Therefore, we need a method for upper-bounding the number of possible proposal distributions $R(w, x)$. Assumption C will allow us to upper-bound this number.

Assumption C (Linearly inducible ordering). *The proposal distribution $R(w, x)$ depends solely on the linear ordering induced by the parameter $w \in \mathcal{W}$ and the mapping $\phi(x, \cdot)$. More formally, let $r(x) \equiv |\mathcal{Y}(x)|$ and thus $\mathcal{Y}(x) \equiv \{y_1 \dots y_{r(x)}\}$. Let $w, w' \in \mathcal{W}$ be any two arbitrary parameters. Let $\pi(x) = (\pi_1 \dots \pi_{r(x)})$ be a permutation of $\{1 \dots r(x)\}$ such that $\phi(x, y_{\pi_1}) \cdot w < \dots < \phi(x, y_{\pi_{r(x)}}) \cdot w$. Let $\pi'(x) = (\pi'_1 \dots \pi'_{r(x)})$ be a permutation of $\{1 \dots r(x)\}$ such that $\phi(x, y_{\pi'_1}) \cdot w' < \dots < \phi(x, y_{\pi'_{r(x)}}) \cdot w'$. For all $w, w' \in \mathcal{W}$ and $x \in \mathcal{X}$, if $\pi(x) = \pi'(x)$ then $KL(R(w, x)\|R(w', x)) = 0$. In this case, we say that the proposal distribution fulfills $R(\pi(x), x) \equiv R(w, x)$.*

Assumption C states that two proposal distributions $R(w, x)$ and $R(w', x)$ are the same provided that for the same permutation $\pi(x)$ we have $\phi(x, y_{\pi_1}) \cdot w < \dots < \phi(x, y_{\pi_{r(x)}}) \cdot w$ and $\phi(x, y_{\pi_1}) \cdot w' < \dots < \phi(x, y_{\pi_{r(x)}}) \cdot w'$. Geometrically speaking, for a fixed x we first project the feature vectors $\phi(x, y)$ of all the structured outputs $y \in \mathcal{Y}(x)$ onto

[2]The second inequality follows from an implicit assumption made in Theorem 1, i.e., $\|w\|_2^2/n \leq 1$. Note that if $\|w\|_2^2/n > 1$ then Theorem 1 provides an upper bound greater than 1, which is meaningless since the distortion function d is at most 1.

the lines w and w'. Let $\pi(x)$ and $\pi'(x)$ be the resulting ordering of the structured outputs after projecting them onto w and w' respectively. Two proposal distributions $R(w,x)$ and $R(w',x)$ are the same provided that $\pi(x) = \pi'(x)$. That is, the specific values of $\phi(x,y) \cdot w$ and $\phi(x,y) \cdot w'$ are irrelevant, and only their ordering matters.

In Section 4 we show examples that fulfill the above assumption, which include the algorithm proposed in (Zhang et al., 2014; Zhang et al., 2015) for directed spanning trees, and our proposed generalization to any type of data structure with computationally efficient local changes.

In what follows, by using the PAC-Bayes framework under Gaussian perturbations, we show that the maximum loss over random structured outputs sampled independently from some proposal distribution provides an upper bound of the Gibbs decoder distortion up to statistical accuracy ($\mathcal{O}(\log^{3/2} n/\sqrt{n})$ for n training samples).

Theorem 2. *Assume that there exist finite integer values ℓ and r such that $|\cup_{(x,y)\in S} \mathcal{P}(x)| \leq \ell$ and $|\mathcal{Y}(x)| \leq r$ for all $(x,y) \in S$. Assume that the proposal distribution $R(w,x)$ with support on $\mathcal{Y}(x)$ fulfills Assumption A with value β, as well as Assumptions B and C. Fix $\delta \in (0,1)$ and an integer $\mathfrak{s}$ such that $3 \leq \mathfrak{s} \leq \frac{9}{20}\sqrt{\ell+1}$. With probability at least $1-\delta$ over the choice of both n training samples and n sets of random structured outputs, simultaneously for all parameters $w \in \mathcal{W}$ with $\|w\|_0 \leq \mathfrak{s}$, unit-variance Gaussian perturbation distributions $Q(w)$ centered at $w\sqrt{2\log(2n\ell/\|w\|_2^2)}$, and for sets of random structured outputs $T(w,x)$ sampled i.i.d. from the proposal distribution $R(w,x)$ for each training sample $(x,y) \in S$, such that $|T(w,x)| = \left\lceil \frac{1}{2}\max\left(\frac{1}{\log(1/\beta)}, 32\|w\|_2^2\right)\log n \right\rceil$, we have:*

$$
\begin{aligned}
&L(Q(w), D) \\
&\leq \frac{1}{n}\sum_{(x,y)\in S} \max_{\hat{y}\in T(w,x)} d(y,\hat{y})\, 1\begin{pmatrix} H(x,y,\hat{y}) \\ -m(x,y,\hat{y},w) \geq 0 \end{pmatrix} \\
&+ \frac{\|w\|_2^2}{n} + \sqrt{\frac{\|w\|_2^2 \log(2n\ell/\|w\|_2^2) + \log(2n/\delta)}{2(n-1)}} + \sqrt{\frac{1}{n}} \\
&+ \max\left(\tfrac{1}{\log(1/\beta)}, 32\|w\|_2^2\right)\sqrt{\frac{\mathfrak{s}\log(\ell+1)\log^3(n+1)}{n}} \\
&+ 3\sqrt{\frac{\mathfrak{s}(\log\ell + 2\log(nr)) + \log(4/\delta)}{n}}
\end{aligned}
$$

(See Appendix A for detailed proofs.)

The proof of the above is based on Theorem 1 as a starting point. In order to account for the computational aspect of requiring sets $T(w,x)$ of polynomial size, we use Assumptions A and B for bounding a *deterministic* expectation. In order to account for the statistical aspects, we use Assumption C and Rademacher complexity arguments for bounding a *stochastic* quantity for all sets $T(w,x)$ of random structured outputs and all possible proposal distributions $R(w,x)$. The assumption of sparsity (i.e., $\|w\|_0 \leq \mathfrak{s}$) is pivotal for obtaining terms of order $\mathcal{O}(\sqrt{\mathfrak{s}\log \ell/n})$. Without sparsity, the terms would be of order $\mathcal{O}(\sqrt{\ell/n})$ which is not suited for high-dimensional settings.

3.1 Inference on Test Data

Note that the upper bound in Theorem 2 holds simultaneously for all parameters $w \in \mathcal{W}$. Therefore, our result implies that after learning the optimal parameter $\widehat{w} \in \mathcal{W}$ in eq.(5) from *training* data, we can bound the decoder distortion when performing *exact* inference on *test* data. More formally, Theorem 2 can be additionally invoked for a *test* set S', also with probability at least $1-\delta$. Thus, under the same setting as of Theorem 2, the Gibbs decoder distortion is upper-bounded with probability at least $1-2\delta$ over the choice of S and S'. In this paper, we focus on learning the parameter of structured prediction models. We leave the analysis of *approximate* inference on test data for future work.

4 EXAMPLES

In this section, we provide several examples that fulfill the three main assumptions of our theoretical result.

4.1 Examples for the Maximal Distortion Assumption

In what follows, we present some examples that fulfill our Assumption A. For a *binary* distortion function, we show that *any* type of structured output fulfills the above assumption. For a distortion function that returns the number of different edges/elements, we show that directed spanning trees, directed acyclic graphs and cardinality-constrained sets, fulfill the assumption as well.

For simplicity of analysis, most proofs in this part will assume a uniform proposal distribution $R(w,x) = R(x)$ with support on $\mathcal{Y}(x)$. In the following claim, we argue that we can perform a change of measure between different proposal distributions. Thus, allowing us to focus on uniform proposals afterwards.

Claim i (Change of measure). *Let $R(w,x)$ and $R'(w,x)$ two proposal distributions, both with support on $\mathcal{Y}(x)$. Assume that the proposal distribution $R(w,x)$ fulfills Assumption A with value β_1. Let $r_{w,x}(\cdot)$ and $r'_{w,x}(\cdot)$ be the probability mass functions of $R(w,x)$ and $R'(w,x)$ respectively. Assume that the total variation distance between $R(w,x)$ and $R'(w,x)$ is bounded as follows for all $(x,y) \in S$ and $w \in \mathcal{W}$:*

$$
\begin{aligned}
TV(R(w,x)\|R'(w,x)) &\equiv \frac{1}{2}\sum_{y\in\mathcal{Y}(x)} |r_{w,x}(y) - r'_{w,x}(y)| \\
&\leq \beta_2
\end{aligned}
$$

The proposal distribution $R'(w,x)$ fulfills Assumption A with $\beta = \beta_1 + \beta_2$ provided that $\beta_1 + \beta_2 \in [0,1)$.

Next, we provide a result for *any* type of structured output, but for a *binary* distortion function.

Claim ii (Any type of structured output). *Let $\mathcal{Y}(x)$ be an arbitrary countable set of feasible decodings of x, such that $|\mathcal{Y}(x)| \geq 2$ for all $(x,y) \in S$. Let $d(y,y') = 1(y \neq y')$. The uniform proposal distribution $R(w,x) = R(x)$ with support on $\mathcal{Y}(x)$ fulfills Assumption A with $\beta = 1/2$.*

The following claim pertains to directed spanning trees and for a distortion function that returns the number of different edges.

Claim iii (Directed spanning trees). *Let $\mathcal{Y}(x)$ be the set of directed spanning trees of v nodes. Let $A(y)$ be the adjacency matrix of $y \in \mathcal{Y}(x)$. Let $d(y,y') = \frac{1}{2(v-1)} \sum_{ij} |A(y)_{ij} - A(y')_{ij}|$. The uniform proposal distribution $R(w,x) = R(x)$ with support on $\mathcal{Y}(x)$ fulfills Assumption A with $\beta = \frac{v-2}{v-1}$.*

The next result is for directed acyclic graphs and for a distortion function that returns the number of different edges.

Claim iv (Directed acyclic graphs). *Let $\mathcal{Y}(x)$ be the set of directed acyclic graphs of v nodes and b parents per node, such that $2 \leq b \leq v-2$. Let $A(y)$ be the adjacency matrix of $y \in \mathcal{Y}(x)$. Let $d(y,y') = \frac{1}{b(2v-b-1)} \sum_{ij} |A(y)_{ij} - A(y')_{ij}|$. The uniform proposal distribution $R(w,x) = R(x)$ with support on $\mathcal{Y}(x)$ fulfills Assumption A with $\beta = \frac{b^2+2b+2}{b^2+3b+2}$.*

The final example is for cardinality-constrained sets and for a distortion function that returns the number of different elements.

Claim v (Cardinality-constrained sets). *Let $\mathcal{Y}(x)$ be the set of sets of b elements chosen from v possible elements, such that $b \leq v/2$. Let $d(y,y') = \frac{1}{2b}(|y - y'| + |y' - y|)$. The uniform proposal distribution $R(w,x) = R(x)$ with support on $\mathcal{Y}(x)$ fulfills Assumption A with $\beta = 1/2$.*

4.2 Examples for the Low Norm Assumption

Next, we present some examples that fulfill our Assumption B. We provide two extreme cases: one example for *sparse* mappings, and one example for *dense* mappings.

Next, we provide a result for a particular instance of a sparse mapping and a uniform proposal distribution.

Claim vi (Sparse mapping). *Let $b > 0$ be an arbitrary integer value. For all $(x,y) \in S$, let $\mathcal{Y}(x) = \cup_{p \in \mathcal{P}(x)} \mathcal{Y}_p(x)$, where the partition $\mathcal{Y}_p(x)$ is defined as follows:*

$$(\forall p \in \mathcal{P}(x))\ \mathcal{Y}_p(x) \equiv \{y' \mid |\phi_p(x,y) - \phi_p(x,y')| = b \wedge (\forall q \neq p)\ \phi_q(x,y) = \phi_q(x,y')\}$$

If $n \leq |\mathcal{P}(x)|/4$ for all $(x,y) \in S$, then the uniform proposal distribution $R(w,x) = R(x)$ with support on $\mathcal{Y}(x)$ fulfills Assumption B.

The following claim pertains to a particular instance of a dense mapping and an *arbitrary* proposal distribution.

Claim vii (Dense mapping). *Let $b > 0$ be an arbitrary integer value. Let $|\phi_p(x,y) - \phi_p(x,y')| = b$ for all $(x,y) \in S$, $y' \in \mathcal{Y}(x)$ and $p \in \mathcal{P}(x)$. If $n \leq |\mathcal{P}(x)|/4$ for all $(x,y) \in S$, then any arbitrary proposal distribution $R(w,x)$ fulfills Assumption B.*

4.3 Examples for the Linearly Inducible Ordering Assumption

In what follows, we present some examples that fulfill our Assumption C. We show that the algorithm proposed in (Zhang et al., 2014; Zhang et al., 2015) for directed spanning trees, fulfills the above assumption. We also generalize the algorithm in (Zhang et al., 2014; Zhang et al., 2015) to any type of data structure with computationally efficient local changes, and show that this generalization fulfills the assumption as well.

Next, we present the algorithm proposed in (Zhang et al., 2014; Zhang et al., 2015) for dependency parsing in natural language processing. Here, x is a sentence of v words and $\mathcal{Y}(x)$ is the set of directed spanning trees of v nodes.

Algorithm 1 Procedure for sampling a directed spanning tree $y' \in \mathcal{Y}(x)$ from a greedy local proposal distribution $R(w,x)$

```
Input: parameter w ∈ W, sentence x ∈ X
Draw uniformly at random a directed spanning tree ŷ ∈ Y(x)
repeat
  s ← post-order traversal of ŷ
  for each node t in the list s do
    for each node u before t in the list s do
      y ← change the parent of node t to u in ŷ
      if φ(x,y) · w > φ(x,ŷ) · w then
        ŷ ← y
      end if
    end for
  end for
until no refinement in last iteration
Output: directed spanning tree y' ← ŷ
```

The above algorithm has the following property:

Claim viii (Sampling for directed spanning trees). *Algorithm 1 fulfills Assumption C.*

Note that Algorithm 1 proposed in (Zhang et al., 2014; Zhang et al., 2015) uses the fact that we can perform local changes to a directed spanning tree in a computationally efficient manner. That is, changing parents of nodes in a post-order traversal will produce directed spanning trees. We can extend the above algorithm to any type of data structure where we can perform computationally efficient local changes. For instance, we can easily extend the method for directed acyclic graphs (traversed in post-order as well) and for sets with up to some prespecified number of elements.

Next, we generalize Algorithm 1 to any type of structured output.

Algorithm 2 Procedure for sampling a structured output $y' \in \mathcal{Y}(x)$ from a greedy local proposal distribution $R(w, x)$

Input: parameter $w \in \mathcal{W}$, observed input $x \in \mathcal{X}$
Draw uniformly at random a structured output $\hat{y} \in \mathcal{Y}(x)$
repeat
  Make a local change to $\hat{y}$ in order to increase $\phi(x, \hat{y}) \cdot w$
until no refinement in last iteration
Output: structured output $y' \leftarrow \hat{y}$

The above algorithm has the following property:

Claim ix (Sampling for any type of structured output). *Algorithm 2 fulfills Assumption C.*

5 EXPERIMENTAL RESULTS

In this section, we provide experimental evidence on synthetic data. Note that the work of (Zhang et al., 2014; Zhang et al., 2015) has provided extensive experimental evidence on real-world datasets, for part-of-speech tagging and dependency parsing in the context of natural language processing. Our experimental results are not only for directed spanning trees (Zhang et al., 2014; Zhang et al., 2015) but also for directed acyclic graphs and cardinality-constrained sets.

We performed 30 repetitions of the following procedure. We generated a ground truth parameter w^* with independent zero-mean and unit-variance Gaussian entries. Then, we generated a training set S of $n = 100$ samples. The fixed mapping ϕ from pairs (x, y) to feature vectors $\phi(x, y)$ is as follows. For every pair of possible edges/elements i and j, we define $\phi_{ij}(x, y) = 1\,(x_{ij} = 1 \wedge i \in y \wedge j \in y)$. For instance, for directed spanning trees of v nodes, we have $x \in \{0, 1\}^{\binom{v}{2}}$ and $\phi(x, y) \in \mathbb{R}^{\binom{v}{2}}$. In order to generate each training sample $(x, y) \in S$, we generated a random vector x with independent Bernoulli entries, each with equal probability of being 1 or 0. After generating x, we set $y = f_{w^*}(x)$. That is, we solved eq.(1) in order to produce the latent structured output y from the observed input x and the parameter w^*.

We compared two training methods: the maximum loss over all possible structured outputs as in eq.(4), and the maximum loss over random structured outputs as in eq.(5). For both minimization problems, we replaced the *discontinuous* 0/1 loss $1\,(z \geq 0)$ with the *convex* hinge loss $\max(0, 1 + z)$, as it is customary. For both problems, we used $\lambda = 1/n$ as suggested by Theorems 1 and 2, and we performed 20 iterations of the subgradient descent method with a decaying step size $1/\sqrt{t}$ for iteration t. For sampling random structured outputs in eq.(5), we implemented Algorithm 2 for directed spanning trees, directed acyclic graphs and cardinality-constrained sets. We considered directed spanning trees of 6 nodes, directed acyclic graphs of 5 nodes and 2 parents per node, and sets of 4 elements chosen from 15 possible elements. We used $\beta = 0.8$ for directed spanning trees, $\beta = 0.85$ for directed acyclic graphs, and $\beta = 0.5$ for cardinality-constrained sets, as prescribed by Claims iii, iv and v. After training, for inference on an independent test set, we used eq.(1) for the maximum loss over all possible structured outputs. For the maximum loss over random structured outputs, we use the following *approximate* inference approach:

$$\widetilde{f}_w(x) \equiv \underset{y \in T(w,x)}{\arg\max}\, \phi(x, y) \cdot w \qquad (6)$$

Table 1 shows the average over 30 repetitions, and the standard error at 95% confidence level of the following measurements. We report the runtime, the training distortion as well as the test distortion in an independently generated set of 100 samples. We also report the normalized distance of the learnt $\widehat{w}$ to the ground truth w^*, i.e., $\|\widehat{w} - w^*\|_2/\sqrt{\ell}$. Additionally, we report the angle of the learnt $\widehat{w}$ with respect to the ground truth w^*, i.e. $\arccos(\widehat{w} \cdot w^*/(\|\widehat{w}\|_2\|w^*\|_2))$. In the different study cases (directed spanning trees, directed acyclic graphs and cardinality-constrained sets), the maximum loss over random structured outputs outperforms the maximum loss over all possible structured outputs.

6 DISCUSSION

In this section, we provide more details regarding the computational complexity of the inference problem. We also present a brief review of the previous work and provide ideas for extending our theoretical result.

6.1 Computational Complexity of the Inference Problem

Very few cases of the general *inference* problem in eq.(1) are tractable. For instance, if $\mathcal{Y}(x)$ is the set of directed spanning trees, and w is a vector of edge weights (i.e., linear with respect to y), then eq.(1) is equivalent to the maximum directed spanning tree problem, which is polynomial-time. In general, the inference problem in eq.(1) is not

Table 1: Average over 30 repetitions, and standard error at 95% confidence level of several methods and measurements. For the maximum loss over all possible structured outputs (All) we used eq.(4) for training, and eq.(1) for inference on a test set. For the maximum loss over random structured outputs (Random and Random/All) we used eq.(5) for training. For inference, Random used eq.(6) while Random/All used eq.(1). Random outperforms All in the different study cases (directed spanning trees, directed acyclic graphs and cardinality-constrained sets). The difference between Random and Random/All is not statistically significant.

Problem	**Method**	**Training runtime**	**Training distortion**	**Test runtime**	**Test distortion**	**Distance to ground truth**	**Angle with ground truth**
Directed	All	1000	$52\% \pm 1.1\%$	12.4 ± 0.4	$61\% \pm 1.8\%$	0.56 ± 0.004	$74^\circ \pm 0.3^\circ$
spanning trees	Random	104 ± 3	$38\% \pm 2.1\%$	2.4 ± 0.1	$56\% \pm 1.9\%$	0.51 ± 0.005	$49^\circ \pm 0.6^\circ$
	Random/All			12.4 ± 0.3	$56\% \pm 1.9\%$		
Directed	All	1000	$41\% \pm 1.2\%$	10.8 ± 0.2	$45\% \pm 1.5\%$	0.60 ± 0.020	$61^\circ \pm 1.0^\circ$
acyclic graphs	Random	386 ± 21	$30\% \pm 1.3\%$	8.5 ± 0.2	$39\% \pm 1.6\%$	0.40 ± 0.008	$37^\circ \pm 1.0^\circ$
	Random/All			10.8 ± 0.2	$39\% \pm 1.6\%$		
Cardinality	All	1000	$42\% \pm 1.4\%$	11.1 ± 0.4	$45\% \pm 1.8\%$	0.58 ± 0.011	$65^\circ \pm 0.6^\circ$
constrained sets	Random	272 ± 9	$21\% \pm 1.2\%$	6.0 ± 0.2	$30\% \pm 1.9\%$	0.44 ± 0.008.	$30^\circ \pm 0.8^\circ$
	Random/All			10.9 ± 0.3	$29\% \pm 2.1\%$		

only NP-hard but also hard to approximate. For instance, if $\mathcal{Y}(x)$ is the set of directed acyclic graphs, and w is a vector of edge weights (i.e., linear with respect to y), then eq.(1) is equivalent to the maximum acyclic subgraph problem, which approximating within a factor better than $1/2$ is unique-games hard (Guruswami et al., 2008). As an additional example, consider the case where $\mathcal{Y}(x)$ is the set of sets with up to some prespecified number of elements (i.e., $\mathcal{Y}(x)$ is a cardinality constraint), and the objective $\phi(x, y) \cdot w$ is submodular with respect to y. In this case, eq.(1) cannot be approximated within a factor better than $1 - 1/e$ unless P=NP (Nemhauser et al., 1978).

These negative results made us to avoid interpreting the maximum loss over random structured outputs in eq.(5) as an approximate optimization algorithm for the maximum loss over all possible structured outputs in eq.(4).

6.2 Previous Work

Approximate inference was proposed in (Kulesza & Pereira, 2007), with an adaptation of the proof techniques in (McAllester, 2007). More specifically, (Kulesza & Pereira, 2007) performs maximization of the loss over a *superset* of feasible decodings of x, i.e., over $y \in \mathcal{Y}'(x) \supseteq \mathcal{Y}(x)$. Note that our upper bound of the Gibbs decoder distortion dominates the maximum loss over $y \in \mathcal{Y}(x)$, and the latter dominates the upper bound of (Kulesza & Pereira, 2007). One could potentially use a similar argument with respect to a *subset* of feasible decodings of x, i.e., with respect to $y \in \mathcal{Y}'(x) \subseteq \mathcal{Y}(x)$. Unfortunately, this approach does not obtain an upper bound of the Gibbs decoder distortion.

Tangential to our work, previous analyses have exclusively focused either on sample complexity or convergence. Sample complexity analyses include margin bounds (Taskar et al., 2003), Rademacher complexity (London et al., 2013) and PAC-Bayes bounds (McAllester, 2007; McAllester & Keshet, 2011). Convergence have been analyzed for specific algorithms for the separable (Collins & Roark, 2004) and nonseparable (Crammer et al., 2006) cases.

6.3 Concluding Remarks

The work of (Zhang et al., 2014; Zhang et al., 2015) has shown extensive experimental evidence for part-of-speech tagging and dependency parsing in the context of natural language processing. In this paper, we present a theoretical analysis that explains the experimental success of (Zhang et al., 2014; Zhang et al., 2015) for directed spanning trees. Our analysis was provided for a far more general setup, which allowed proposing algorithms for other types of structured outputs, such as directed acyclic graphs and cardinality-constrained sets. We hope that our theoretical work will motivate experimental validation on many other real-world structured prediction problems.

There are several ways of extending this research. While we focused on Gaussian perturbations, it would be interesting to analyze other distributions from the computational as well as statistical viewpoints. We analyzed a general class of proposal distributions that depend on the induced linear orderings. Algorithms that make greedy local changes, traverse the set of feasible decodings in a constrained fashion, by following allowed moves defined by some prespecified graph. The addition of these graph-theoretical constraints would enable obtaining tighter upper bounds. From a broader perspective, extensions of our work to latent models (Ping et al., 2014; Yu & Joachims, 2009) as well as maximum a-posteriori perturbation models (Gane et al., 2014; Papandreou & Yuille, 2011) would be of great interest. Finally, while we focused on learning the parameter of structured prediction models, it would be interesting to analyze *approximate* inference for prediction on an independent test set.

References

Altun, Y., & Hofmann, T. (2003). Large margin methods for label sequence learning. *European Conference on Speech Communication and Technology*, 145–152.

Bennett, J. (1956). Determination of the number of independent parameters of a score matrix from the examination of rank orders. *Psychometrika, 21*, 383–393.

Bennett, J., & Hays, W. (1960). Multidimensional unfolding: Determining the dimensionality of ranked preference data. *Psychometrika, 25*, 27–43.

Collins, M. (2004). Parameter estimation for statistical parsing models: Theory and practice of distribution-free methods. In *New developments in parsing technology*, vol. 23, 19–55. Kluwer Academic.

Collins, M., & Roark, B. (2004). Incremental parsing with the perceptron algorithm. *Annual Meeting of the Association for Computational Linguistics*, 111–118.

Cover, T. (1967). The number of linearly inducible orderings of points in d-space. *SIAM Journal on Applied Mathematics, 15*, 434–439.

Crammer, K., Dekel, O., Keshet, J., Shalev-Shwartz, S., & Singer, Y. (2006). Online passive-aggresive algorithms. *Journal of Machine Learning Research, 7*, 551–585.

Gane, A., Hazan, T., & Jaakkola, T. (2014). Learning with maximum a-posteriori perturbation models. *International Conference on Artificial Intelligence and Statistics, 33*, 247–256.

Guruswami, V., Manokaran, R., & Raghavendra, P. (2008). Beating the random ordering is hard: Inapproximability of maximum acyclic subgraph. *Foundations of Computer Science*, 573–582.

Kulesza, A., & Pereira, F. (2007). Structured learning with approximate inference. *Neural Information Processing Systems, 20*, 785–792.

London, B., Huang, B., Taskar, B., & Getoor, L. (2013). Collective stability in structured prediction: Generalization from one example. *International Conference on Machine Learning*, 828–836.

McAllester, D. (2007). Generalization bounds and consistency. In *Predicting structured data*, 247–261. MIT Press.

McAllester, D., & Keshet, J. (2011). Generalization bounds and consistency for latent structural probit and ramp loss. *Neural Information Processing Systems, 24*, 2205–2212.

Nemhauser, G., Wolsey, L., & Fisher, M. (1978). An analysis of approximations for maximizing submodular set functions—I. *Mathematical Programming, 14*, 265–294.

Neylon, T. (2006). *Sparse solutions for linear prediction problems*. Doctoral dissertation, New York University.

Papandreou, G., & Yuille, A. (2011). Perturb-and-MAP random fields: Using discrete optimization to learn and sample from energy models. *IEEE International Conference on Computer Vision*, 193–200.

Ping, W., Liu, Q., & Ihler, A. (2014). Marginal structured SVM with hidden variables. *International Conference on Machine Learning*, 190–198.

Taskar, B., Guestrin, C., & Koller, D. (2003). Max-margin Markov networks. *Neural Information Processing Systems, 16*, 25–32.

Yu, C., & Joachims, T. (2009). Learning structural SVMs with latent variables. *International Conference on Machine Learning*, 1169–1176.

Zhang, Y., Lei, T., Barzilay, R., & Jaakkola, T. (2014). Greed is good if randomized: New inference for dependency parsing. *Empirical Methods in Natural Language Processing*, 1013–1024.

Zhang, Y., Li, C., Barzilay, R., & Darwish, K. (2015). Randomized greedy inference for joint segmentation, POS tagging and dependency parsing. *North American Chapter of the Association for Computational Linguistics*, 42–52.

Efficient Feature Group Sequencing for Anytime Linear Prediction

Hanzhang Hu
hanzhang@cs.cmu.edu

Alexander Grubb
agrubb@cs.cmu.edu

J. Andrew Bagnell
dbagnell@ri.cmu.edu

Martial Hebert
hebert@ri.cmu.edu

Abstract

We consider *anytime* linear prediction in the common machine learning setting, where features are in groups that have costs. We achieve anytime (or interruptible) predictions by sequencing the computation of feature groups and reporting results using the computed features at interruption. We extend Orthogonal Matching Pursuit (OMP) and Forward Regression (FR) to learn the sequencing greedily under this group setting with costs. We theoretically guarantee that our algorithms achieve near-optimal linear predictions at each budget when a feature group is chosen. With a novel analysis of OMP, we improve its theoretical bound to the same strength as that of FR. In addition, we develop a novel algorithm that consumes cost $4B$ to approximate the optimal performance of *any* cost B, and prove that with cost less than $4B$, such an approximation is impossible. To our knowledge, these are the first anytime bounds at *all* budgets. We test our algorithms on two real-world data-sets and evaluate them in terms of anytime linear prediction performance against cost-weighted Group Lasso and alternative greedy algorithms.

1 INTRODUCTION AND BACKGROUND

First defined by Grass and Zilberstein [1996], anytime predictors output valid results even if they are interrupted at any point in time. The results improve with resources spent. In this work, we propose an anytime linear prediction algorithm under the common machine learning setting, where features are computed in groups with associated costs. We further assume that the cost of prediction is dominated by feature computation. Hence, we can achieve anytime predictions by computing feature groups in a specific order and outputting linear predictions using only computed features at interruption.

Formally, we are given n samples (x^i, y^i) from a feature matrix $X \in \mathbb{R}^{n \times D}$ and a response vector $Y \in \mathbb{R}^n$. We also have a partition of the D feature dimensions into J feature groups, $\mathcal{G}_1, \mathcal{G}_2, ..., \mathcal{G}_J$, and an associated cost of each group $c(\mathcal{G}_j)$. Our anytime prediction approach learns a sequencing of the feature groups, $G = g_1, g_2, ..., g_J$. For each budget limit B, the computed groups at cost B is a prefix of the sequencing, $G_{\langle B \rangle} = g_1, g_2, .., g_{J_{\langle B \rangle}}$, where $J_{\langle B \rangle} = \max\{j \leq J | \sum_{i \leq j} c(g_i) \leq B\}$ indexes the last group within the budget B. An ideal anytime algorithm seeks a sequencing G to minimize risk at all budgets B:

$$R(G_{\langle B \rangle}) := \min_w \frac{1}{2n} \|Y - X_{G_{\langle B \rangle}} w\|_2^2 + \frac{\lambda}{2} \|w\|_2^2, \quad (1)$$

where $X_{G_{\langle B \rangle}}$ contains features in $G_{\langle B \rangle}$, w is the associated linear predictor coefficient, and λ is a regularizing constant. Equivalently, if we assume that the y^i's have unit variance and zero mean by normalization, we can maximize the explained variance, $F(G_{\langle B \rangle}) := \frac{1}{2n} Y^T Y - R(G_{\langle B \rangle})$.

The above optimization problem is closest to the problem of subset selection for regression [Das and Kempe, 2011], which selects at most k features to optimize a linear regression. The problem is also similar to that of sparse model recovery [Tibshirani, 1994], which recovers coefficients of a true linear model. One common approach to these two problems is to select the features greedily via Forward Regression (FR) [Miller, 1984] or Orthogonal Matching Pursuit (OMP) [Pati et al., 1993]. Forward Regression greedily selects features that maximize the marginal increase in explained variance at each step. Orthogonal Matching Pursuit selects features as follows. The linear model coefficients of the unselected features are set to zero. At each step, the feature whose model coefficient has the largest gradient of the risk is selected. In this work, we extend FR and OMP to the setting where features are in groups that have costs. The extension to FR is intuitive: we only need to select feature groups using their marginal gain in objective per unit cost instead of using just the marginal gain. However, we have two notes about the extension to OMP. First, to incorporate feature costs, we need to evaluate a feature based on the squared norm of the associated weight vector gradient per unit cost instead of just the gradient norm. Second, when we compute the gradient norm for a feature group, ∇_g, we have to use the norm $\nabla_g^T(X_g^T X_g)^{-1}\nabla_g$, which is $\|\nabla_g\|_2^2$ if and only if each feature group g is whitened, which is an assumption in group OMP analysis by Lozano et al. [2009, 2011]. Our analysis sheds light on why this assumption is important in a group setting. Like previous analyses of greedy algorithms by Streeter and Golovin [2008], our analysis guarantees that our methods produce near-optimal linear predictions, measured by explained variance, at budgets where feature groups are selected. Thus, they exhibit the desired anytime behavior at those budgets. Finally, we extend our algorithm to account for *all* budgets and show a novel anytime result: for any budget B, if *OPT* is the optimal explained variance of cost B, then our proposed sequencing can approximate within a factor of *OPT* with cost at most $4B$. Furthermore, with a cost less than $4B$, a fixed sequence of predictors cannot approximate *OPT* in general. To our knowledge, these are the first anytime performance bounds at all budgets.

In previous works, both FR and OMP are theoretically analyzed for both the problem of subset selection and model recovery. Das and Kempe [2011] cast the subset selection problem as a submodular maximization that selects a set S with $|S| \leq k$ to maximize the explained variance and prove that FR and OMP achieve $(1 - e^{-\lambda^*})$ and $(1 - e^{-\lambda^{*2}})$ near-optimal explained variance, where λ^* is the minimum eigenvalue of the sample covariance, $\frac{1}{n}X^TX$. We can adopt these previous analyses to our extensions to FR and OMP under the group setting with costs and produce the same near-optimal results. We also present a novel analysis of OMP that leads to the same near-optimal factor $(1 - e^{-\lambda^*})$ as that of FR. Works on model recovery have also analyzed FR and OMP. Zhang [2009] proves that OMP discovers the true linear model coefficients, if they exist. This result was then extended by [Lozano et al., 2009, 2011] to the setting of feature groups using generalized linear models. However, we note that these theoretical analyses of model recovery assume that a true model exists. They focus on recovering model coefficients rather than directly analyzing prediction performance.

Besides greedy selection, another family of approaches to find the optimal subset S that minimizes $R(S)$ is to relax the NP-hard selection problem as a convex optimization. Lasso [Tibshirani, 1994], a well-known method, uses L_1 regularization to force sparsity in the linear model. To get an ordering of the features, compute the Lasso solution path by varying the L_1 regularization constant. Group Lasso [Yuan and Lin, 2006] extends Lasso to the group setting, replacing the L_1 norm with the sum of L_2 norms of feature groups. Group Lasso can also incorporate feature costs by scaling the L_2 norms of feature groups. Lasso-based methods are generally analyzed for model recovery, not prediction performance. We demonstrate experimentally that our greedy methods achieve better prediction performance than cost-weighted Group Lasso.

Various works have addressed anytime prediction previously. The most well-known family of approaches use *cascades* [Viola and Jones, 2001], which achieve anytime prediction by filtering out samples with a sequence of classifiers of increasing complexity and feature costs. At each stage, cascade methods [Sochman and Matas, 2005, Brubaker et al., 2008, Lefakis and Fleuret, 2010, Xu et al., 2014, Cai et al., 2015] typically achieve a target accuracy and assign a portion of samples with their final predictions. While this design frees up computation for the more difficult samples, it prevents recovery from early mistakes. Most cascade methods select features of each stage before being trained. Although the more recent works start to learn feature sequencing, the learned sequences are the same as those of cost-weighted Group Lasso [Chen et al., 2012] and greedy methods [Cai et al., 2015] when they are restricted to linear prediction. Hence our study of anytime linear prediction can help cascade methods choose features and learn cascades. Another branch of anytime prediction methods uses boosting. It outputs as results partial sums of the ensemble [Grubb and Bagnell, 2012] or averages of randomly sampled weak learners [Reyzin, 2011]. Our greedy methods can be viewed as a gradient boosting scheme by treating each feature as a weak learner. Some works approach anytime prediction with feature transformations [Xu et al., 2012, 2013] and learn cost-sensitive, non-linear transformation of features for linear classification. Similarly, Weinberger et al. [2009] hashes high dimensional features to low dimensional subspaces. These approaches operate on readily-computed features, which is orthogonal to our problem setting. Karayev et al. [2012] models the anytime prediction as a Markov Decision Process and learns a policy of applying intermediate learners and computing features through reinforcement learning.

Contributions

- We cast the problem of anytime linear prediction as a feature group sequencing problem and propose extensions to FR and OMP under the setting where features are in groups that have costs.
- We theoretically analyze our extensions to FR and OMP and show that they both achieve $(1 - e^{-\lambda^*})$ near-optimal explained variance with linear predictions at budgets when they choose feature groups.
- We develop the first anytime algorithm that provably approximates the optimal performance of *all* budgets B with cost of $4B$; we also prove it impossible to achieve a constant-factor approximation with cost less than $4B$.

2 COST-SENSITIVE GREEDY METHOD

This section formally introduces our extensions to FR and OMP to the group setting with costs. We assume that all feature dimensions and responses are normalized to have zero mean and unit variance. We define the regularized feature covariance matrix as $C := \frac{1}{n}X^TX + \lambda I_D$. Let C_{st} be the sub-matrix that selects rows from s and columns from t. Let C_S be short for C_{SS}. Given a non-empty union of selected feature groups S, the maximum explained variance $F(S)$ is achieved with the regularized optimal coefficient $w(S) = \frac{1}{n}(\frac{1}{n}X_S^TX_S + \lambda I)^{-1}(X_S^TY) = \frac{1}{n}C_S^{-1}X_S^TY$. When we take gradient of $F(S)$ with respect to the coefficient of a feature group g, if $g \subseteq S$ then the gradient is $\nabla_g F(S) = \frac{1}{n}X_g^T(Y - X_S w(S)) - \lambda w(S)_g$; if $g \cap S = \emptyset$ then we can extend $w(S)$ to dimensions of g, setting $w(S)_g = 0$, and then take the gradient to have $\nabla_g F(S) = \frac{1}{n}X_g^T(Y - X_S w(S))$. In both cases, we have $\nabla_g F(S) = \frac{1}{n}X_g^TY - C_{gS}w(S)$. We further shorten the notations by defining $b_g^S = \nabla_g F(S)$. If S is empty, we assume that coefficient $w(\emptyset)$ has zero for all features so that $F(\emptyset) = 0$. When $S = s_1, s_2, ...,$ is a sequence of feature groups, we define S_j to be the prefix sequence $s_1, s_2, ..., s_j$. We overload notations of a sequence S so that S also represents the union of its groups in notations such as $F(S)$, $w(S)$, C_S and b_S^S.

Algorithm 1: Cost Sensitive Group Orthogonal Matching Pursuit (CS-G-OMP)

---

input : The normalized feature matrix $X \in \mathbb{R}^{n \times D}$. The normalized response vector $Y \in \mathbb{R}^n$, which has a zero mean and unit variance. Feature groups $\mathcal{G}_1, ... \mathcal{G}_J$ that partition $\{1, .., D\}$, and group costs $c(\mathcal{G}_j)$. Regularization constant λ.

output: A sequence $G = g_1, g_2, ..., g_J$ of feature groups. For each $j \leq J$, a coefficient $w(G_j)$ for the prefix sequence $G_j = g_1, ..., g_j$.

1 $G_0 = \emptyset$;

2 **for** $j = 1, 2, ..., J$ **do**

   `// Learn linear model`

3   compute $w(G_{j-1}) = \frac{1}{n}C_{G_{j-1}}^{-1}X_{G_{j-1}}^TY$;

   `// Selection step (*)`

4   For each $g \notin G_{j-1}$, compute $b_g = \nabla_g F(G_{j-1}) = \frac{1}{n}X_g^T(Y - X_{G_{j-1}}w)$;

5   $g_j = \underset{g=\mathcal{G}_1,...,\mathcal{G}_J, g \notin G_{j-1}}{\text{argmax}} \frac{b_g^T(X_g^TX_g)^{-1}b_g}{c(g)}$;

6   $G_j = G_{j-1} \oplus g_j$;

7 compute $w(G_J)$;

In Algorithm 1, we present Cost-Sensitive Group Orthogonal Matching Pursuit (CS-G-OMP), which learns a near-optimal sequencing of the feature groups for anytime linear predictions. The feature groups are selected greedily. At the jth selection step $(*)$, we have chosen $j-1$ groups, $G_{j-1} = g_1, g_2, ..., g_{j-1}$, and have computed the best model using G_{j-1}, $w(G_{j-1})$. To evaluate a feature group g, we first compute the gradient $b_g = \nabla_g F(G_{j-1})$ of the explained variance F with respect to the coefficients of g. Then, we evaluate it with the whitened gradient L_2-norm square per unit cost, $\frac{b_g^T(X_g^TX_g)^{-1}b_g}{c(g)}$. We select the group g that maximizes this value as g_j, and continue until all groups are depleted. At test time, our proposed anytime prediction algorithm computes the feature groups in the order of $G = g_1, g_2, ..., g_J$. After each feature group g_j is available, we can compute and store prediction $\hat{y} = x^Tw(G_j)$ because we assumed that the costs of feature generation dominate the computations of linear predictions. At interruption, we can then report the latest prediction $\hat{y}$.

The learning procedure extending from Forward Regression is similar to Algorithm 1: we compute the linear models $w(G_{j-1} \oplus g)$ at line 4 instead of the gradients b_g and replace the selection criterion $\frac{b_g^T(X_g^TX_g)^{-1}b_g}{c(g)}$ at line 5 with the marginal gain in explained variance per unit cost, $\frac{F(G_{j-1} \oplus g) - F(G_{j-1})}{c(g)}$. We call this cost-sensitive FR extension as CS-G-FR.

Before we theoretically analyze our greedy methods in the next section, we provide an argument why **group whitening** at line 5 of Algorithm 1 is natural. OMP greedily selects features whose coefficients have the largest gradients of the objective function. In linear regression, the gradient for a feature g is the inner-product of X_g and the prediction residual $Y - \hat{Y}$. Hence OMP selects features that best reconstruct the residual. From this perspective, OMP under group setting should seek the feature group whose span contains the largest projection of the residual. Let the projection to feature group g be $P_g = X_g(X_g^TX_g)^{-1}X_g^T$ and recall projection matrices are idempotent. We observe that the criterion for CS-G-OMP selection step is $\frac{\|P_g(Y-\hat{Y})\|_2^2}{c(g)}$, i.e, a cost-weighted norm square of the projection of the residual onto a feature group. The name group whitening is chosen because the criterion is $\frac{\|b_g\|_2^2}{c(g)}$ if and only if feature groups are whitened. We assume *feature groups are whitened* in our formal analysis to make the criterion easier to analyze.

Besides the above greedy criterion, one may suggest other approaches to evaluate gradient vectors b_g for group g. For example, L_2 norm and L_∞ norm can be used to achieve greedy criteria $\frac{\|b_g\|_2^2}{c(g)}$ and $\frac{\|b_g\|_\infty^2}{c(g)}$, respectively. The former criterion forgoes group whitening, so we call it *no-whiten*. Thus, it overestimates a feature group that has correlated but effective features, an extreme example of which is a feature group of identical but effective features. The latter criterion evaluates only the best feature of each feature group, so we call it *single*. Thus, it underestimates a feature group that has a descriptive feature span but no top-performing individual feature dimensions. We will show in experiments that no-whiten and single are indeed inferior to our CS-G-OMP choice.

3 THEORETICAL ANALYSIS

This section proves that CS-G-FR and CS-G-OMP produce near-optimal explained variance F at budgets where features are selected. The main challenge of our analysis is to prove Lemma 3.1, which is a common stepping stone in submodular maximization analysis, e.g., Equation 8 in [Krause and Golovin, 2012]. The main Theorem 3.2 follows from the lemma by standard techniques, which we defer to the appendix.

Lemma 3.1 (main). *Let G_j be the first j feature groups selected by our greedy algorithm. There exists a constant $\gamma = \frac{\lambda^*+\lambda}{1+\lambda} > 0$ such that for any sequence S, total cost K, and indices $j = 1, 2, ..., J$, $F(S_{\langle K \rangle}) - F(G_{j-1}) \leq \frac{K}{\gamma}[\frac{F(G_j)-F(G_{j-1})}{c(g_j)}]$.*

Theorem 3.2. *Let $B = \sum_{i=1}^{L} c(g_i)$ for some L. There exists a constant $\gamma = \frac{\lambda^*+\lambda}{1+\lambda}$, such that for any sequence S and total cost K, $F(G_{\langle B \rangle}) > (1 - e^{-\gamma \frac{B}{K}})F(S_{\langle K \rangle})$.*

Before delving into the proof of Lemma 3.1, we first discuss some implications of Theorem 3.2, which argues that the explained variance of greedily selected features of cost B is within $(1 - e^{\gamma \frac{B}{K}})$-factor of that of any competing feature sequence of cost K. If we apply minimum regularization ($\lambda \to 0$), then the constant γ approaches λ^*. The resulting bound factor $(1 - e^{-\lambda^* \frac{B}{K}})$ is the bound for FR by Das and Kempe [2011]. However, we achieve the same bound for OMP, improving theoretical guarantees of OMP. We also note that less-correlated features lead to a higher λ^* and a stronger bound.

Lemma 3.1 for CS-G-FR is standard if we follow proofs in [Streeter and Golovin, 2008] and [Das and Kempe, 2011] because the objective F is γ-approximately submodular. However, we present a proof of Lemma 3.1 for CS-G-OMP without approximate submodularity to achieve the same constant γ. This proof in turn uses Lemma 3.3 and Lemma 3.4, whose proofs are based on the Taylor expansions of the regularized risk $\mathcal{R}[f_S] = R(S)$, a M-strongly smooth and m-strongly convex loss functional of predictors $f(x) = w^T x$. We defer these two proofs to the appendix and note that $M = m$ with our choice of R.

Lemma 3.3 (Using Smoothness). *Let S and G be some fixed sequences. Then $F(S) - F(G) \leq \frac{1}{2m}\langle b^G_{G\oplus S}, C^{-1}_{G\oplus S} b^G_{G\oplus S}\rangle$.*

Lemma 3.4 (Using Convexity). *For $j = 1, 2, ..., J$, $F(G_j) - F(G_{j-1}) \geq \frac{1}{2M}\langle b^{G_{j-1}}_{g_j}, C^{-1}_{g_j} b^{G_{j-1}}_{g_j}\rangle$.*

Note that in Lemma 3.4, since we assume feature groups are whitened, then $C_{g_j} = (1 + \lambda)I$. The bound of the lemma becomes $F(G_j) - F(G_{j-1}) \geq \frac{1}{2M(1+\lambda)}\langle b^{G_{j-1}}_{g_j}, b^{G_{j-1}}_{g_j}\rangle$. If feature groups are not whitened, the constant $(1+\lambda)$ can be scaled up to $(|\mathcal{G}_j|+\lambda)$, which detriments the strength of Theorem 3.2 especially when feature groups are large.

Proof. (of Lemma 3.1, using Lemma 3.3 and Lemma 3.4) Using Lemma 3.3, on $S_{\langle K \rangle}$ and G_{j-1}, we have:

$$F(S_{\langle K \rangle}) - F(G_{j-1}) \leq \frac{1}{2m}\langle b^{G_{j-1}}_{G_{j-1}\oplus S_{\langle K \rangle}}, C^G_{G_{j-1}\oplus S_{\langle K \rangle}} b^{G_{j-1}}_{G_{j-1}\oplus S_{\langle K \rangle}}\rangle \quad (2)$$

Note that the gradient $b^{G_{j-1}}_{G_{j-1}}$ equals 0, because $F(G_{j-1})$ is achieved by the linear model $w(G_{j-1})$. Then, using block matrix inverse formula, we have:

$$F(S_{\langle K \rangle}) - F(G_{j-1}) \leq \frac{1}{2m}\langle b^{G_{j-1}}_{S_{\langle K \rangle}}, C^G_{S_{\langle K \rangle}} b^{G_{j-1}}_{S_{\langle K \rangle}}\rangle \quad (3)$$

where $C^G_{S_{\langle K \rangle}} = C_{S_{\langle K \rangle}} - C_{S_{\langle K \rangle}G} C^{-1}_{S_{\langle K \rangle}} C_{GS_{\langle K \rangle}}$. Using spectral techniques in Lemmas 2.5 and 2.6 in [Das and Kempe, 2011] and noting that the minimum eigenvalue of C, $\lambda_{min}(C)$, is $\lambda^* + \lambda$, we have

$$\frac{1}{2m}\langle b^{G_{j-1}}_{S_{\langle K \rangle}}, C^G_{S_{\langle K \rangle}} b^{G_{j-1}}_{S_{\langle K \rangle}}\rangle \leq \frac{1}{2m(\lambda^*+\lambda)}\langle b^{G_{j-1}}_{S_{\langle K \rangle}}, b^{G_{j-1}}_{S_{\langle K \rangle}}\rangle. \quad (4)$$

Expanding $S_{\langle K \rangle}$ into individual groups s_i, we continue:

$$= \frac{1}{2m(\lambda^*+\lambda)} \sum_{s_i \in S_{\langle K \rangle}} \langle b^{G_{j-1}}_{s_i}, b^{G_{j-1}}_{s_i}\rangle \quad (5)$$

$$\leq \frac{1}{2m(\lambda^*+\lambda)} \sum_{s_i \in S_{\langle K \rangle}} c(s_i) \max_g \frac{\langle b^{G_{j-1}}_g, b^{G_{j-1}}_g\rangle}{c(g)} \quad (6)$$

$$= \frac{1}{2m(\lambda^*+\lambda)} \sum_{s_i \in S_{\langle K \rangle}} c(s_i) \frac{\langle b^{G_{j-1}}_{g_j}, b^{G_{j-1}}_{g_j}\rangle}{c(g_j)} \quad (7)$$

$$\leq \frac{M(1+\lambda)}{m(\lambda^*+\lambda)} \sum_{s_i \in S_{\langle K \rangle}} c(s_i) \frac{F(G_j) - F(G_{j-1})}{c(g_j)}. \quad (8)$$

The last equality follows from the greedy selection step of Algorithm 1 when feature groups are whitened. The last inequality is given by Lemma 3.4. The theorem then follows from $\gamma = (\frac{m}{M})\frac{\lambda^*+\lambda}{1+\lambda} = \frac{\lambda^*+\lambda}{1+\lambda}$. □

4 BI-CRITERIA APPROXIMATION AT ALL BUDGETS

Our analysis so far only bounds algorithm performance at budgets when new items are selected. However, an ideal analysis should apply to all budgets. As illustrated in Figure 1a, previous methods may choose expensive features early; until they are computed, we have no bounds. Figure 1b illustrates our proposed fix: each new item g_{j+1} cannot be more costly than the current sequence G_j.

This section proves two theorems of anytime prediction at *any* budget. Theorem 4.1 shows that to approximate the optimal explained variance of cost B within a constant factor, an anytime algorithm must cost at least $4B$. We then motivate and formalize our fix in Algorithm 2, which is shown in Theorem 4.3 to achieve this *bi-criteria approximation* bound for both budget and objective with the form: $F(G_{\langle B \rangle}) > (1 - e^{-\frac{\gamma^2}{1+\gamma}})F(S_{\langle \frac{B}{4} \rangle})$, where γ is the approximate submodular ratio, i.e., the maximum constant $\gamma \leq 1$ such that for all sets $A' \subseteq A$ and all element x,

$$\gamma(F(A \cup \{x\}) - F(A)) \leq F(A' \cup \{x\}) - F(A'). \quad (9)$$

We first illustrate the inherent difficulty in generating single sequences that are competitive at arbitrary budgets B by using the following budgeted maximization problem:

$$X = \{1, 2, \ldots\}, \ c(x) = x, \ F(S) = \sum_{x \in S} e^x. \quad (10)$$

The above problem originates from fitting the linear model $Y = \sum_{i=1}^{D} e^i X_i$, where X_i's are i.i.d. and X_i costs i.

Theorem 4.1. *Let $\mathcal{A}$ be any algorithm for selecting sequences $A = (a_1, \ldots)$. The best bi-criteria approximation that $\mathcal{A}$ can satisfy must be at least a 4-approximation in cost for the sequence described in Equation (10). That is, there does not exist a $C < 4$, and a $c_1 \in [0, 1)$, such that for any budget B and any sequence S,*

$$F(A_{\langle B \rangle}) > (1 - c_1) F(S_{\langle \frac{B}{C} \rangle}).$$

Proof. For any budget B, it is clear that the optimal selection contains a single item, B, whose value is e^B. For any budget B, let $m(B)$ denote the item of the maximum cost that is selected by the algorithm. If the bi-criteria bound holds, then $\sum_{k=1}^{m(B)} e^k \geq F(A_{\langle B \rangle}) > (1 - c_1) F(S_{\langle \frac{B}{C} \rangle})$. Taking the log of both sides and rearranging terms, we have $m(B) \geq \lfloor \frac{B}{C} \rfloor + \ln(1 - c_1) + \ln(e - 1) - 2$. Since $3 - \ln(1 - c_1) - \ln(e - 1) > 0$, we have for B large enough: $C \geq \frac{B}{m(B)}$. Hence, we need to minimize $\frac{B}{m(B)}$ for all B to minimize C. We can assume a_j to be increasing because otherwise we could remove the violating a_j from the sequence and decrease the ratio $\frac{B}{m(B)}$ for all subsequent j.

Let $b_j := c(A_j)$ and $\alpha_j := \frac{c(a_j)}{b_{j-1}}$. Then immediately before a_j is available, $\frac{B}{m(B)} \rightarrow \frac{c(A_j)}{c(a_{j-1})} \geq \frac{(1+\alpha_j)b_{j-1}}{b_{j-1}} = 1 + \alpha_j$. If we can bound $\frac{B}{m(B)} \leq C$ for all B, then there exists α_{max} such that $\alpha_j < \alpha_{max}$ for all j large enough. Immediately after a new a_j is selected, $\frac{B}{m(B)} = \frac{c(A_j)}{c(a_j)} = \frac{1+\alpha_j}{\alpha_j}$. For $\frac{B}{m(B)}$ to be bounded, there must exist some $\alpha_{min} > 0$ such that $\alpha_j > \alpha_{min}$ for large enough j. Now we consider the ratio $\frac{B}{m(B)}$ right before a_{j+1} is selected:

$$\frac{c(A_{j+1})}{c(a_j)} = \frac{b_j(1 + \alpha_{j+1})}{b_j \frac{\alpha_j}{1+\alpha_j}} = 1 + \frac{\alpha_{j+1}}{\alpha_j} + \alpha_{j+1} + \frac{1}{\alpha_j}. \quad (11)$$

Assume for seek of contradiction that $\frac{c(A_{j+1})}{c(a_j)}$ is bounded above by z for some $z \in (1, 4)$. Let $y := \frac{\alpha_{j+1}}{\alpha_j}$. Then we have: $z \geq 1 + y + y\alpha_j + \frac{1}{\alpha_j} \geq 1 + y + 2\sqrt{y} = (\sqrt{y} + 1)^2$. Hence $y \leq (\sqrt{z} - 1)^2 < 1$. So $a_{j+1} \leq (\sqrt{z} - 1)^2 a_j$, which implies that a_j converges to 0 and we have a contradiction. So $C \geq \frac{B}{m(B)} \rightarrow \frac{c(A_{j+1})}{c(a_j)} \geq 4$ for large j. □

(a) Before F is computed, we have no output or bounds.

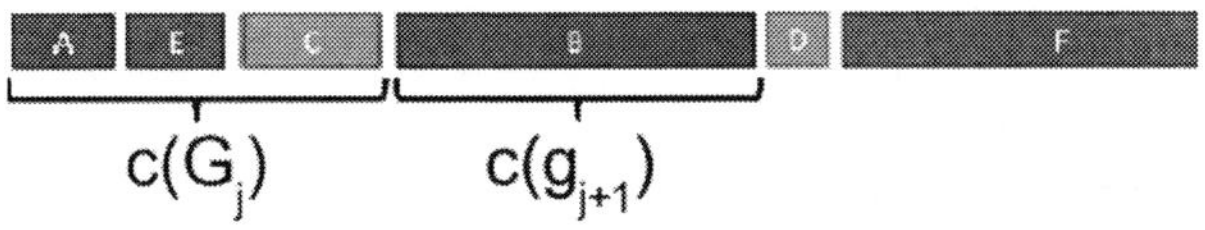

(b) Our constraint $c(g_{j+1}) \leq c(G_j)$ induces a smoother cost increase.

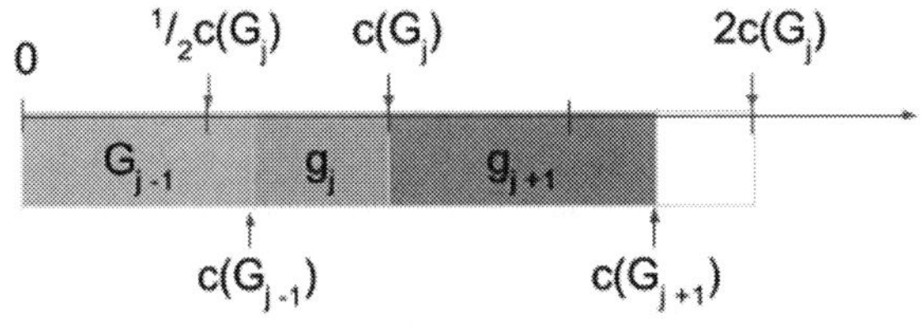

(c) Illustration of Doubling Algorithm Cost Constraint

Figure 1: Doubling Algorithm (b) has better anytime behaviors than greedy algorithm with no cost constraints (a).

The above proof lower bounds the cost approximation ratio C by Eq. 11, which is shown to be at least 4 for $C < \infty$. We note that *Eq.* 11 equals 4 if $\forall j, \alpha_j = 1$, which means the sequence total cost is doubled at each selection step. This observation leads to *Doubling Algorithm* (Alg. 2): we perform greedy selection in the same way as CS-G-FR, except that the total cost can be at most doubled at each step (illustrated in Figure 1c). The advantage of Doubling Algorithm over CS-G-FR is that the former prevents early computation of expensive features and induces a smoother increase of total cost; in most real-world data-sets, the two are identical after few steps because feature costs are often in a narrow range. We will analyze Doubling Algorithm with the following assumption, called *doubling capable*.

Definition 4.2. Let $G = (g_1, \ldots)$ be the sequence selected by the doubling algorithm. The set X and function F are *doubling capable* if, at every iteration j, the following set is non-empty: $\{x \mid x \in X \setminus G_{j-1}, \ c(x) \leq c(G_{j-1})\}$

Algorithm 2: Doubling Algorithm

input: objective function F, elements X, minimum cost $c_{\min}$

Let $g_1 = \underset{x \in X,\, c(x) \leq c_{\min}}{\operatorname{argmax}} \frac{F(\{x\})}{c(x)}$; Let $G_1 = g_1$;

for $j = 2, \ldots$ **do**

  Let $g_j = \underset{x \in X \setminus G_{j-1},\, c(x) \leq c(G_{j-1})}{\operatorname{argmax}} \frac{F(G_{j-1} \oplus \{x\}) - F(G_{j-1})}{c(x)}$;

  Let $G_j = G_{j-1} \oplus \{g_j\}$;

Theorem 4.3. *Let $G = (g_1, \ldots)$ be the sequence selected by the doubling algorithm (Algorithm 2). Fix some $B > c_{min}$. Let F be γ-approximately submodular as in Definition 9. For any sequence S,*

$$F(G_{\langle B \rangle}) > \left(1 - e^{-\frac{\gamma^2}{1+\gamma}}\right) F(S_{\langle \frac{B}{4} \rangle}).$$

Proof. Doubling capable easily leads to the observation that for all budgets B, there exists an index j such that $\frac{B}{2} \leq c(G_j) < B$. Choose K and k to be the largest integers such that $\frac{B}{2} \leq c(G_K) < B$ and $\frac{B}{8} \leq c(G_k) < \frac{B}{4}$. Since at each step we at most double the total cost and $4c(G_k) < B$, we observe $K \geq k + 2$. For each j, define $s_j = \frac{F(G_{j+1}) - F(G_j)}{c(g_{j+1})}$ as the best rate of improvement among the items Doubling Algorithm is allowed to consider after choosing G_j. Consider the item x in sequence $S_{\langle \frac{B}{4} \rangle}$ of the maximum cost.

(Case 1) If $c(x) \leq c(G_k)$, then every item in $S_{\langle \frac{B}{4} \rangle}$ was a candidate for g_j for all $j = k+1, ..., K$. So by approximate submodularity from Equation 9, we have

$$F(S_{\langle \frac{B}{4} \rangle}) \leq F(S_{\langle \frac{B}{4} \rangle} \cup G_j) \leq F(G_j) + \frac{B s_j}{4\gamma}. \quad (12)$$

Then using the standard submodular maximization proof technique, we define $\Delta_j = F(S_{\langle \frac{B}{4} \rangle}) - F(G_j)$. Applying $s_j = \frac{\Delta_j - \Delta_{j+1}}{c(g_{j+1})}$ in the above inequality, we have $\Delta_{k+j} \leq \Delta_k \prod_{j=k+1}^{k+j} (1 - \gamma \frac{4c(g_j)}{B})$. Maximizing the inequality by setting $c(g_j) = \frac{B}{K-k} \leq \frac{c(G_K) - c(G_k)}{4(K-k)}$, and using $(1 - z/l)^l < e^{-z}$, we have $F(G_K) > (1 - e^{-\gamma}) F(S_{\langle \frac{B}{4} \rangle})$.

From now on, we assume that $c(x) > c(G_k)$ and consider two cases by comparing $c(g_{k+2})$ and $c(G_k)$.

(Case 2.1) If $c(g_{k+2}) \geq c(G_k)$, then $c(G_K) - c(G_{k+1}) \geq c(g_{k+2}) \geq c(G_k)$. Since $c(G_{k+1}) \leq 2c(G_k)$ and $c(x) > c(G_k)$, we have $c(G_K) - c(G_{k+1}) \geq \frac{B}{2} - 2c(G_k)$. So $c(G_K) - c(G_{k+1}) \geq \max(c(G_k), \frac{B}{2} - 2c(G_k)) \geq \frac{B}{6}$. Thus, using the same proof techniques as in case 1, we can analyze the ratio between Δ_{k+1} and Δ_K, and have: $F(G_K) > (1 - e^{-\frac{2}{3}\gamma}) F(S_{\langle \frac{B}{4} \rangle})$.

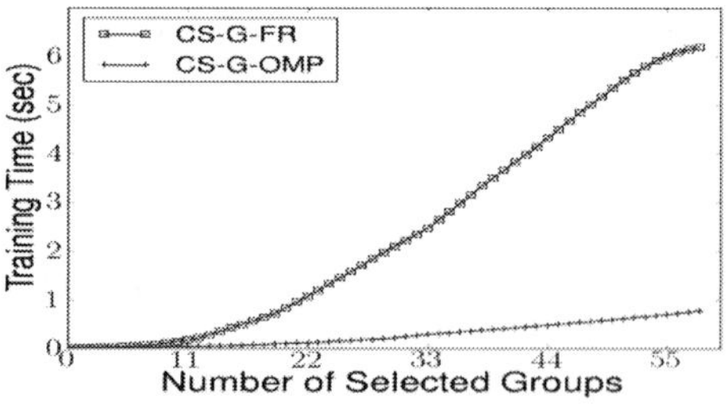

(a) Training Time OMP vs. FR (AGRICULTURAL)

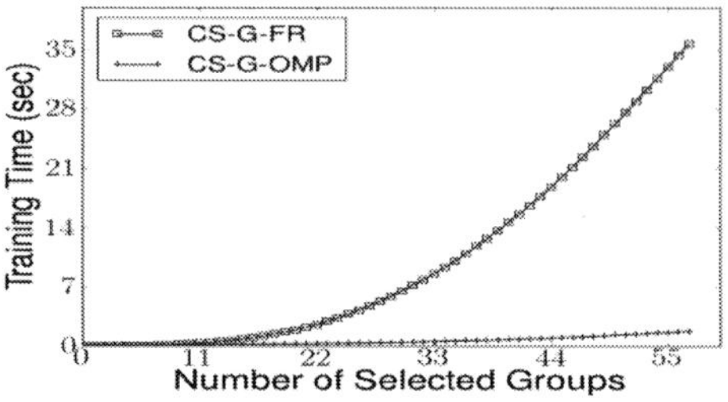

(b) Training Time OMP vs. FR (YAHOO! LTR)

Figure 2: The training time vs. the number of feature groups selected with two algorithms: CS-G-FR and CS-G-OMP. CS-G-OMP achieves a 8x and 20x overall training time speed-up on AGRICULTURAL and YAHOO! LTR.

(Case 2.2) Finally, if $c(g_{k+2}) < c(G_k) < c(x) < c(G_{k+1})$, g_{k+2} was a candidate for g_{k+1}, and x was a candidate for g_{k+2}. For an item y, let $r(y^j) = \frac{F(G_j \cup \{y\}) - F(G_j)}{c(y)}$ be the improvement rate of item y at G_j. Then we have $r(g_{k+1}^k) > r(g_{k+2}^k)$ and $r(g_{k+2}^{k+1}) > r(x^{k+1})$. Since the objective function is increasing, we have $r(x^k)c(x) \leq r(x^{k+1})c(x) + r(g_{k+1}^k)c(g_{k+1})$, so that $r(x^k) \leq r(x^{k+1}) + r(g_{k+1}^k)\frac{c(g_{k+1})}{c(x)}$. Then by the definition of γ in Equation 9, we have $\gamma r(g_{k+2}^{k+1}) \leq r(g_{k+2}^k)$. Hence we have $\gamma r(x^{k+1}) \leq r(g_{k+1}^k)$, which leads to $r(x^k) \leq r(g_{k+1}^k)(\frac{1}{\gamma} + \frac{c(g_{k+1})}{c(x)}) \leq r(g_{k+1}^k)(1 + \frac{1}{\gamma})$. Then inequality (12) holds with a coefficient adjustment and becomes $F(S_{\langle \frac{B}{4} \rangle}) \leq F(G_k) + \frac{B s_k (1+\gamma)}{4\gamma^2}$. Noting that the above inequality holds for all $j = k+1, ..., K$, we can replace the constant γ in the proof of case 1 with $\frac{\gamma^2}{1+\gamma}$ and have the following bound: $F(G_K) > (1 - e^{-\frac{\gamma^2}{1+\gamma}}) F(S_{\langle \frac{B}{4} \rangle})$. □

5 EXPERIMENTS

5.1 DATA-SETS AND SET-UP

We experiment our methods for anytime linear prediction on two real-world data-sets, each of which has a significant number of feature groups with associated costs.

Table 1: Test time 0.97-Timeliness measurement of different methods on AGRICULTURAL. We break the methods into OMP, FR and Oracle family: e.g., "Single" in the G-CS-OMP family means G-CS-OMP-Single, and "FR" in the Oracle family means the oracle curve derived from G-FR.

CS-G-OMP-Variants				CS-G-FR	Oracles		Sparse
CS-G-OMP	Single	No-Whiten	G-OMP		FR Oracle	OMP Oracle	
0.4406	0.4086	0.4340	0.4073	**0.4525**	**0.4551**	0.4508	0.3997

Table 2: Test time 0.99-Timeliness measurement of different methods on YAHOO! LTR.

Group	CS-G-OMP-Variants				CS-G-FR	Oracles		Sparse
Size	CS-G-OMP	Single	No-Whiten	G-OMP		FR	OMP	
5	**0.3188**	0.3039	0.3111	0.2985	**0.3222**	**0.3225**	0.3211	0.2934
10	**0.3142**	0.3117	0.3079	0.2909	**0.3205**	**0.3207**	0.3164	0.2858
15	**0.3165**	0.3159	0.3116	0.2892	**0.3213**	**0.3213**	0.3177	0.2952
20	**0.3161**	0.3124	0.3065	0.2875	**0.3180**	**0.3180**	0.3163	0.2895

- **Yahoo! Learning to Rank Challenge** [Chapelle and Chang, 2011] contains 883k web documents, each of which has a relevance score in $\{0, 1, 2, 3, 4\}$. Each of the 501 document features has an associated computational cost in $\{1, 5, 20, 50, 100, 150, 200\}$; the total feature cost is around 17K. The original data-set has no feature group structures, so we generated random group structures by grouping features of the same cost into groups of a given size s.[1]

- **Agriculture** is a proprietary data-set that contains 510k data samples, 328 features, and 57 feature groups. Each sample has a binary label in $\{1, 2\}$. Each feature group has an associated cost measured in its average computation time.[2]

5.2 EVALUATION METRIC, BASELINE AND ORACLE

Following the practice of Karayev et al. [2012], we use the area under the maximization objective F (explained variance) vs. cost curve normalized by the total area as the *timeliness* measurement of the anytime performance of an algorithm. In our data-sets, the performance of linear predictors plateaus much before all features are used, e.g., Figure 3a demonstrates this effect in YAHOO! LTR, where the last one percent of total improvement is bought by half of the total feature cost. Hence the majority of the timeliness measurement is from the plateau performance of linear predictors. The difference between timeliness of different anytime algorithms diminishes due to the plateau effect. Furthermore, the difference vanishes as we include additional redundant high cost features. To account for this effect, we stop the curve when it reaches the plateau. We define an α-*stopping cost* for parameter α in $[0, 1]$ as the cost at which our CS-G-OMP achieves α of the final objective value in training and ignore the objective vs. cost curve after the α-stopping cost. We call the timeliness measure on the shortened curve as α-*timeliness*; 1-timeliness equals the normalized area under the full curve and 0-timeliness is zero. If a curve does not pick a group at α-stopping cost, we linearly interpolate the objective value at the stopping cost to computr timeliness. We say an objective vs. cost curve has reached its final plateau if at least 95% of the total objective has been achieved and the next 1% requires more than 20% feature costs. (If the plateau does not exist, we use $\alpha = 1$.) Following this rule, we choose $\alpha = 0.97$ for AGRICULTURAL and $\alpha = 0.99$ for YAHOO! LTR.

Since an exhaustive search for the best feature sequencing is intractable, we approximate with the **Oracle** anytime performance following the approach of Karayev et al. [2012]. Given an objective vs. cost curve of a sequencing, we reorder the feature groups in descending order of their marginal benefit per unit cost, assuming that the marginal benefits stay the same after reordering. We specify which sequencing is used for creating **Oracle** in Section 5.5. For baseline performance, we use cost-weighted Group Lasso [Yuan and Lin, 2006], which scales the regularization constant of each group with the cost of the group. We note that the cascade design by Chen et al. [2012] can be reduced to this baseline if we enforce linear prediction. More specifically, the baseline solves the following minimization prob-

[1]We experiment on group sizes $s \in \{5, 10, 15, 20\}$. We choose regularizer $\lambda = 10^{-5}$ based on validation. We use $s = 10$ for qualitative results such as plots and illustrations, but we report quantitative results for all group size s. For our quantitative results, we report the average test performance. The initial risk is $R(\emptyset) = 0.85$.

[2] There are 6 groups of size 32; the other groups have sizes between 1 and 6. The cost of each group is its expected computation time in seconds, ranging between 0.0005 and 0.0088; the total feature cost is 0.111. We choose regularizer $\lambda = 10^{-7}$. The data-set is split into five 100k sets, and the remaining 10k are used for validation. We report the cross validation results on the five 100K sets as the test results. The initial risk is $R(\emptyset) = 0.091$.

[2]Karayev et al. [2012] define *timeliness* as the area under the average precision vs. time curve

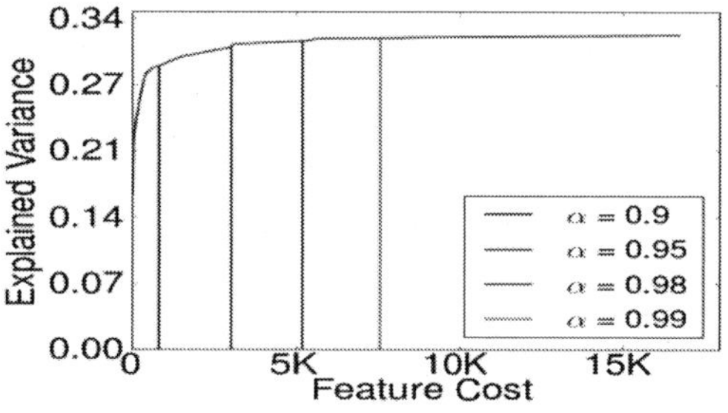

(a) Plateau Effect and α-Stopping Costs

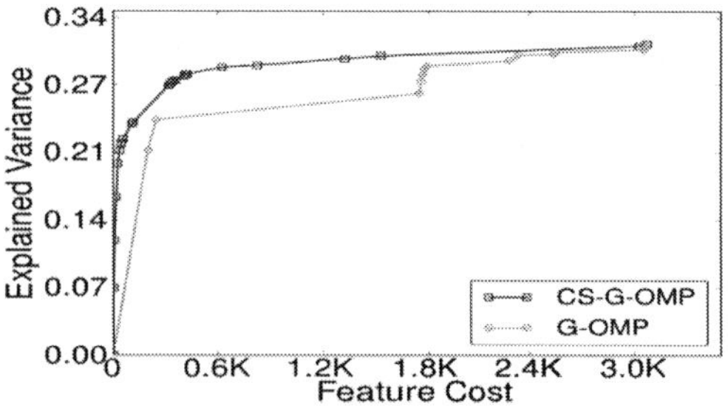

(b) Importance of Costs (CS-G-OMP vs. G-OMP)

Figure 3: (a) Explained Variance vs. Cost curve of CS-G-OMP in YAHOO! LTR. Vertical lines mark different α-stopping costs. (b) Explained Variance vs. Cost curve of CS-G-OMP and G-OMP on YAHOO! LTR set 1 with individual group size $s = 10$, stopped at 0.97-stop cost.

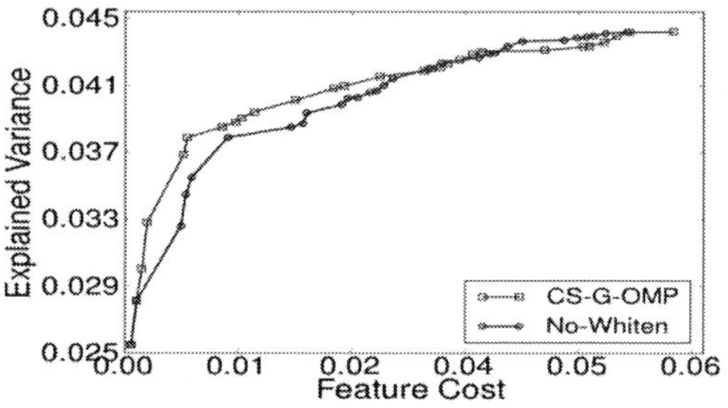

(a) Group Whiten vs. No-Whiten (AGRICULTURAL)

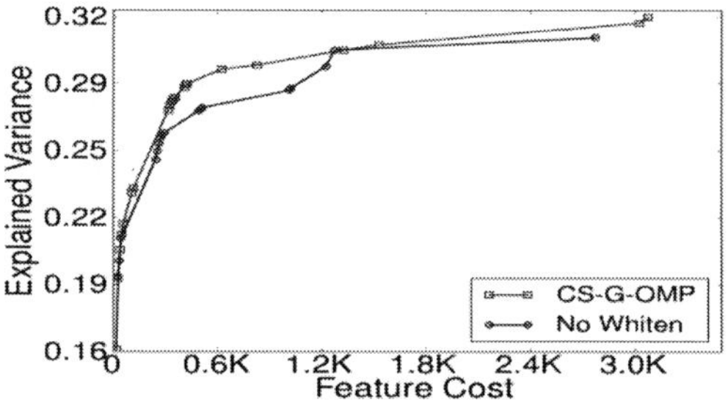

(b) Group Whiten vs. No-Whiten (YAHOO! LTR)

Figure 4: Explained Variance vs. Feature Cost curves on AGRICULTURAL (a) and YAHOO! LTR (b) comparing group whitening with no group whitening. The curves stop at 0.97-stopping cost.

lem: $\min_{w \in \mathbb{R}^D} \|Y - Xw\|_2^2 + \lambda \sum_{j=1}^{J} c(\mathcal{G}_j) \|w_{\mathcal{G}_j}\|_2$, and we vary value of regularization constant λ to obtain lasso paths. We call this baseline algorithm **Sparse**[3].

5.3 FEATURE COST

Our proposed CS-G-OMP differs from Group Orthogonal Matching Pursuit (G-OMP) [Lozano et al., 2009] in that G-OMP does not consider feature costs when evaluating features. We show that this difference is crucial for anytime linear prediction. In Figure 3b, we compare the objective vs. costs curves of CS-G-OMP and G-OMP that are stopped at 0.97-stopping cost on YAHOO! LTR. As expected, CS-G-OMP achieves a better overall prediction at every budget, qualitatively demonstrating the importance of incorporating feature costs. Table 1 and Table 2 quantify this effect, showing that CS-G-OMP achieves a better timeliness measure than regular G-OMP.

5.4 GROUP WHITENING

We provide experimental evidence that Group whitening, i.e., $X_g^T X_g = I_{D_g}$ for each group g, is a key assumption of both this work and previous feature group selection literature by Lozano et al. [2009, 2011]. In Figure 4, we compare anytime prediction performances using group whitened data against those using the common normalization scheme where each feature dimension is individually normalized to have zero mean and unit variance. The objective vs. cost curve qualitatively shows that group whitening consistently results in the better predictions. This behavior is expected from data-sets whose feature groups contain correlated features, e.g., group whitening effectively prevents selection step $(*)$ from overestimating the predictive power of feature groups of repeated good features. Table 1 and Table 2 demonstrate quantitatively the consistent better timeliness performance of CS-G-OMP over that of CS-G-OMP-no-whiten.

5.5 SELECTION CRITERION VARIANTS

This section compares CS-G-OMP and CS-G-FR, along with variants of these two methods and the baseline, Sparse. We formulated the variant of CS-G-OMP, *single*, in Section 2 and it intuitively chooses feature groups of the best single feature dimension per group cost. Our experiments show that this modification degrades prediction performance of CS-G-OMP. Since FR directly optimizes the objective at each step, we expect CS-G-FR to perform the best and use its curve to compute the **Oracle** curve as an approximate to the best achievable performance.

[3]We use an off-the-shelf software, SPAMS (SPArse Modeling Software [Jenatton et al., 2010]), to solve the optimization.

In Figure 5, we evaluate CS-G-FR, CS-G-OMP and CS-G-OMP-single based on the objective in Theorem 3.2, i.e., explained variance vs. feature cost curves. CS-G-FR, as expected, outperforms all other methods. CS-G-OMP outperforms the baseline method, Sparse, and the CS-G-OMP-Single variant. The performance advantage of CS-G-OMP over CS-G-OMP-Single is much clearer in the AGRICULTURAL data-set than in the YAHOO! LTR data-set. AGRICULTURAL has a natural group structure which may contain correlated features in each group. YAHOO! LTR has a randomly generated group structure whose features were filtered by feature selection before the data-set was published [Chapelle and Chang, 2011]. CS-G-FR and CS-G-OMP outperform the baseline algorithm, Sparse. We speculate that linearly scaling group regularization constants by group costs did not enforce Group-Lasso to choose the most cost-efficient features early. The test-time timeliness measures of each of the methods are recorded in Table 1 and Table 2, and quantitatively confirm the analysis above. Since AGRICULTURAL and YAHOO! LTR are originally a classification and a ranking data-set, respectively, we also report in Figure 5 the performance using classification accuracy and NDCG@5. This demonstrates the same qualitatively results as using explained variants.

As expected, when compared against CS-G-OMP, CS-G-FR consistently chooses more cost-efficient features at the cost of a longer training time. In the context of linear regression, let us assume that the group sizes are bounded by a constant when we are to select the number K feature group. We can then compute a new model of K groups in $O(K^2N)$ using Woodbury's matrix inversion lemma, evaluate it in $O(KN)$, and compute the gradients with respect to the weights of unselected groups in $O(N(J-K))$. Thus, CS-G-OMP requires $O(K^2N + JN)$ at step $K = 1, 2, 3, ..., J$ and CS-G-FR requires $O((J-K)K^2N)$, so the total training complexities for CS-G-OMP and CS-G-FR are $O(J^3N)$ and $O(J^4N)$, using $\sum_{K=1}^{J} K^2 = \frac{1}{6}J(J+1)(2J+1)$ and $\sum_{K=1}^{J} K^3 = \frac{1}{4}J^2(J+1)^2$. We also show this training complexity gap empirically in Figure 2, which plots the curves of training time vs. number of feature groups selected. When all feature groups are selected, CS-G-OMP achieves a 8x speed-up in AGRICULTURAL over CS-G-FR. In YAHOO! LTR, CS-G-OMP achieves a speed-up factor between 10 and 20; the smaller the sizes of the groups, the larger speed-up due to the increase in the number of groups. Both greedy methods are much faster than the Lasso path computation using SPAMS, however.

This work was conducted in part through collaborative participation in the Robotics Consortium sponsored by the U.S Army Research Laboratory under the Collaborative Technology Alliance Program, Cooperative Agreement W911NF-10-2-0016.

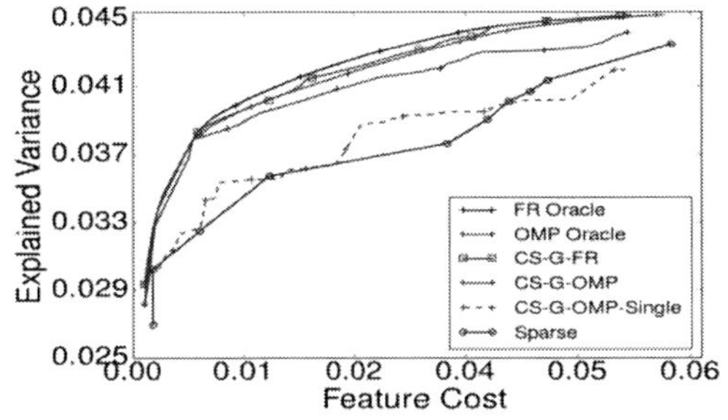

(a) FR vs. OMP vs. Sparse (AGRICULTURAL)

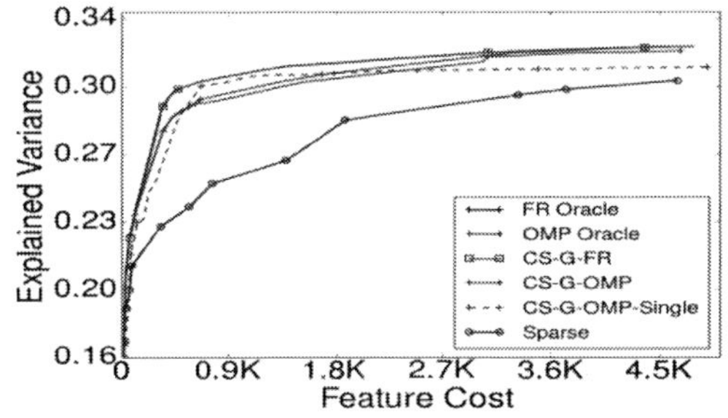

(b) FR vs. OMP vs. Sparse (YAHOO! LTR)

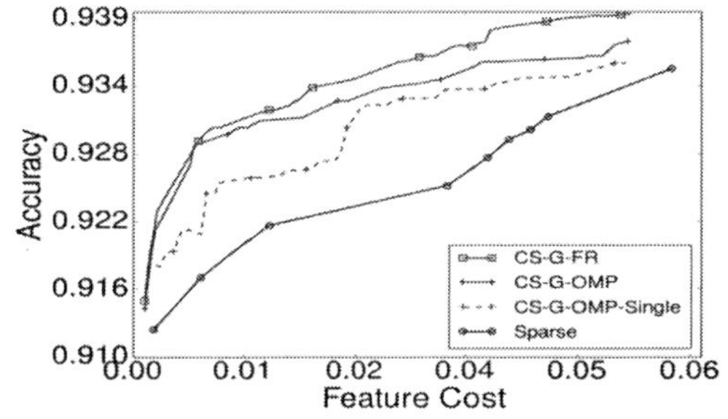

(c) FR vs. OMP vs. Sparse (AGRICULTURAL)

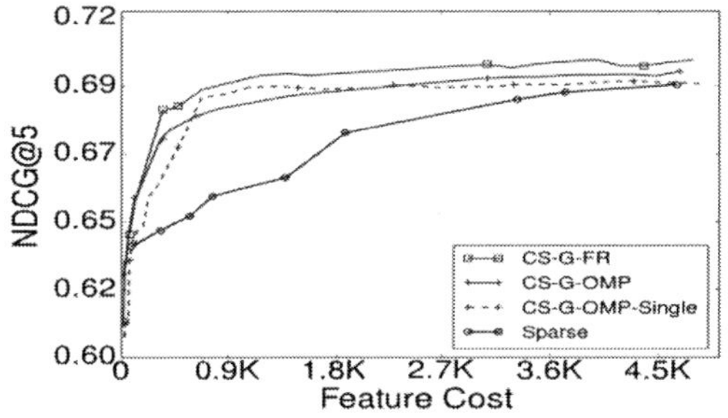

(d) FR vs. OMP vs. Sparse (YAHOO! LTR)

Figure 5: (a),(b): Explained Variance vs. Feature Cost curves on AGRICULTURAL and YAHOO! LTR(group-size=10), using CS-G-OMP, CS-G-FR and their Single variants. Curves stop at 0.97 and 0.98 stopping costs. (c),(d): Same curve with the natural objectives of the data-sets: accuracy and NDCG@5.

References

S. Brubaker, J. Wu, J. Sun, M. Mullin, and J. Rehg. On the Design of Cascades of Boosted Ensembles for Face Detection. *International Journal of Computer Vision*, pages 65–86, 2008.

Zhaowei Cai, Mohammad J. Saberian, and Nuno Vasconcelos. Learning Complexity-Aware Cascades for Deep Pedestrian Detection. In *International Conference on Computer Vision, ICCV*, 2015.

Olivier Chapelle and Yi Chang. Yahoo! Learning to Rank Challenge Overview. JMLR Workshop and Conference Proceedings, 2011.

Minmin Chen, Kilian Q. Weinberger, Olivier Chapelle, Dor Kedem, and Zhixiang Xu. Classifier Cascade for Minimizing Feature Evaluation Cost. In *Proceedings of the 15th International Conference on Artificial Intelligence and Statistics (AISTATS)*, 2012.

Abhimanyu Das and David Kempe. Submodular meets Spectral: Greedy Algorithms for Subset Selection, Sparse Approximation and Dictionary Selection . In *Proceedings of the 28th International Conference on Machine Learning (ICML)*, 2011.

Joshua Grass and Shlomo Zilberstein. Anytime Algorithm Development Tools. *SIGART Bulletin*, 1996.

Alexander Grubb and J. Andrew Bagnell. SpeedBoost: Anytime Prediction with Uniform Near-Optimality. In *the 15th International Conference on Artificial Intelligence and Statistics (AISTATS)*, 2012.

Rodolphe Jenatton, Julien Mairal, Guillaume Obozinski, and Francis R. Bach. Proximal Methods for Sparse Hierarchical Dictionary Learning. In *Proceedings of the 27th International Conference on Machine Learning (ICML)*, 2010.

Sergey Karayev, Tobias Baumgartner, Mario Fritz, and Trevor Darrell. Timely Object Recognition. In *Conference and Workshop on Neural Information Processing Systems (NIPS)*, 2012.

Andreas Krause and Daniel Golovin. Submodular Function Maximization. In *Tractability: Practical Approaches to Hard Problems*, 2012.

Leonidas Lefakis and Francois Fleuret. Joint Cascade Optimization Using a Product of Boosted Classifiers. In *Advances in Neural Information Processing Systems (NIPS)*. 2010.

Aurelie C. Lozano, Grzegorz Swirszcz, and Naoki Abe. Grouped Orthogonal Matching Pursuit for Variable Selection and Prediction. In *Neural Information Processing Systems (NIPS)*, 2009.

Aurelie C. Lozano, Grzegorz Swirszcz, and Naoki Abe. Group Orthogonal Matching Pursuit for Logistic Regression. In *Proceedings of the 14th International Conference on Artificial Intelligence and Statistics (AISTATS)*, volume 15, 2011.

Alan J. Miller. Subset Selection in Regression. In *Journal of the Royal Statistical Society. Series A (General), Vol. 147, No. 3, pp. 389-425*, 1984.

Y. Pati, R. Rezaiifar, and P. Krishnaprasad. Orthogonal Matching Pursuit : recursive function approximation with application to wavelet decomposition. In *Asilomar Conference on Signals, Systems and Computers*, 1993.

Lev Reyzin. Boosting on a budget: Sampling for feature-efficient prediction. In *the 28th International Conference on Machine Learning (ICML)*, 2011.

J. Sochman and J. Matas. WaldBoost: Learning for Time Constrained Sequential Detection. In *the 2005 IEEE Computer Society Conference on Computer Vision and Pattern Recognition (CVPR)*, 2005.

M. Streeter and D. Golovin. An Online Algorithm for Maximizing Submodular Functions. In *Proceedings of the 22nd Annual Conference on Neural Information Processing Systems (NIPS)*, 2008.

Robert Tibshirani. Regression Shrinkage and Selection Via the Lasso. *Journal of the Royal Statistical Society, Series B*, 58:267–288, 1994.

Paul A. Viola and Michael J. Jones. Rapid Object Detection using a Boosted Cascade of Simple Features. In *2001 IEEE Computer Society Conference on Computer Vision and Pattern Recognition (CVPR)*, 2001.

K.Q. Weinberger, A. Dasgupta, J. Langford, A. Smola, and J. Attenberg. Feature Hashing for Large Scale Multitask Learning. In *Proceedings of the 26th Annual International Conference on Machine Learning (ICML)*, 2009.

Z. Xu, K. Weinberger, and O. Chapelle. The Greedy Miser: Learning under Test-time Budgets. In *Proceedings of the 28th International Conference on Machine Learning (ICML)*, 2012.

Z. Xu, M. Kusner, G. Huang, and K. Q. Weinberger. Anytime Representation Learning. In *Proceedings of the 30th International Conference on Machine Learning (ICML)*, 2013.

Z. Xu, M. J. Kusner, K. Q. Weinberger, M. Chen, and O. Chapelle. Classifier cascades and trees for minimizing feature evaluation cost. *Journal of Machine Learning Research*, 15(1):2113–2144, 2014.

Ming Yuan and Yi Lin. Model Selection and Estimation in Regression with Grouped Variables. *Journal of the Royal Statistical Society*, 2006.

Tong Zhang. On the Consistency of Feature Selection using Greedy Least Squares Regression. *Journal of Machine Learning Research*, 10:555–568, 2009.

Scalable Nonparametric Bayesian Multilevel Clustering

Viet Huynh † **Dinh Phung** † **Svetha Venkatesh** †
† Center for Pattern Recognition and Data Analytics (PRaDA)
Deakin University, Australia

XuanLong Nguyen
Department of Statistics
University of Michigan, Ann Arbor, USA

Matt Hoffman
Adobe Research
Adobe Systems, Inc.

Hung Hai Bui
Adobe Research
Adobe Systems, Inc.

Abstract

Multilevel clustering problems where the content and contextual information are jointly clustered are ubiquitous in modern datasets. Existing works on this problem are limited to small datasets due to the use of the Gibbs sampler. We address the problem of scaling up multilevel clustering under a Bayesian nonparametric setting, extending the MC2 model proposed in (Nguyen *et al.*, 2014). We ground our approach in structured mean-field and stochastic variational inference (SVI) and develop a tree-structured SVI algorithm that exploits the interplay between content and context modeling. Our new algorithm avoids the need to repeatedly go through the corpus as in Gibbs sampler. More crucially, our method is immediately amendable to parallelization, facilitating a scalable distributed implementation on the Apache Spark platform. We conduct extensive experiments in a variety of domains including text, images, and real-world user application activities. Direct comparison with the Gibbs-sampler demonstrates that our method is an order-of-magnitude faster without loss of model quality. Our Spark-based implementation gains another order-of-magnitude speedup and can scale to large real-world datasets containing millions of documents and groups.

1 INTRODUCTION

A prominent feature in numerous modern datasets tackled in machine learning is how the data are naturally layered into groups in a hierarchical representation: text corpus as collection of documents, which are subdivided into words, user's activities are organized by users, whose sessions divided into actions, electronic medical records (EMR) organized as sets of ICD[1] codes diagnosed for the patient. Probabilistic modeling techniques for grouped data have become a standard tool in machine learning, including topic modeling (Blei *et al.*, 2003; Teh *et al.*, 2006) and multilevel data analysis (Hox, 2010; Diez-Roux, 2000). Another important feature in such datasets is the availability of rich sources of additional information known as contexts and group-specific meta-data (Phung *et al.*, 2012; Nguyen *et al.*, 2014). These include information about authorships, timestamps, various tags associated with texts and images, user's demographics, etc. For consistency, we shall refer to the content groups (e.g., text documents, images, user's activity session) broadly as *documents*, and its associated context as document-specific *context*.

The rich and interwoven nature of raw document contents and their contextual information provides an excellent opportunity for joint modeling and, in particular, clustering the content-units (e.g., forming topics from words) and the content-groups (e.g., forming cluster of documents) — a problem known as *multilevel clustering with context* (Nguyen *et al.*, 2014). There have been several attempts of multilevel clustering in the probabilistic topic modeling literature. A simple approach is to subdivide this task into two phases: first learn a topic model and then perform document clustering using the topic-induced representation of the documents (Lu *et al.*, 2011; Nguyen *et al.*, 2013; Phung *et al.*, 2014). An elegant approach is to unify these two steps into a single framework (Nguyen *et al.*, 2014; Xie & Xing, 2013; Rodriguez *et al.*, 2008; Wulsin *et al.*, 2012). Among these work, the Bayesian nonparametric approach to multilevel clustering with group-level contexts (MC2) (Nguyen *et al.*, 2014) offers a powerful method capable of jointly modeling both content and context in a flexible and nonparametric manner, generalizing on several previous modeling techniques. The key idea of the MC2 model is a special Dirichlet Process (DP) whose base-measure is a product between a context-generating measure and a content-generating DP. This construct enables both clustering of documents associating with their

[1]Stands for International Classification of Disease.

contexts and clustering of words into topics. Nguyen *et al.* (2014) have shown that their MC2 integrates the nested DP (Rodriguez *et al.*, 2008) and DP mixture (DPM) (Antoniak, 1974) into one single unified model wherein marginalizing out the documents' contents results in a DP mixture, and marginalizing out document-specific contexts results in a nested DP mixture.

The need for jointly accounting for both context and content data in a flexible Bayesian nonparametric fashion also underlies a formidable computational challenge for model fitting. In fact, the MC2 model of Nguyen *et al.* (2014) was originally equipped with a Gibbs sampler for inference; hence the usefulness of the model could only be demonstrated on relatively small datasets. This seriously hinders the usefulness and applicability of MC2 in tackling big real world datasets which can contain millions of documents or more, along with it the millions of useful pieces of contextual information.

Our goal in this work is to address the multilevel clustering with contexts problem at scale, by developing effective posterior inference algorithms for the MC2 using techniques from stochastic variational inference. A challenging aspect about inference for MC2 is the computational treatment in the clustering of discrete distributions of contents jointly with the context variables. Unlike either the Dirichlet process or HDP mixtures, the context-content linkage present in the MC2 model makes the model more expressive, while necessitating the inference of the joint context and content atoms. These are mathematically rich objects — while the context atoms take on usual contextual values, the content atoms represent probability distributions over words. To maintain an accurate approximation of the joint context and content atoms, we employ a *tree-structured mean-field* decomposition that explicitly links the model context and content atoms.

The result is a scalable stochastic variational inference (SVI) algorithm for MC2 (SVI-MC2) that, unlike Gibbs sampling, avoids the need to go through the corpus multiple times. Moreover, the SVI computation within each mini-batch can be easily parallelizable. To fully exploit this advantage of the SVI formulation, we further implement our proposed SVI for the MC2 algorithm on the Apache Spark platform. We demonstrate that even a sequential implementation of SVI-MC2 is several times faster than Nguyen *et al.* (2014)'s Gibbs sampler while yielding the same model perplexity. A parallel implementation can gain another order of magnitude improvement in speed; our Spark implementation can simultaneously find topics and clustering millions of documents and their context. Our contributions then can be summarized as: (a) a new theoretical development of stochastic variational inference for an important family of models to address the problem of multilevel clustering with contexts. We note this class of models (MC2) include nested DP, DPM, and HDP as the special cases; (b) a scalable implementation of the proposed SVI-MC2 on Apache Spark; and (c) the demonstration that our new algorithm can scale up to very large corpora.

2 RELATED WORK

Models for clustering documents

Two of the most well-known probabilistic models for learning from grouped data are Latent Dirichlet Allocation (LDA) (Blei *et al.*, 2003) and its nonparametric counterpart, Hierarchical Dirichlet process (HDP) (Teh *et al.*, 2006). These models allow us to exploit the group structure for word clustering but not to cluster the groups of data. To clustering documents, some authors employed a two-step process. In the first step, each document is represented by the feature of its topic proportion using topic models, e.g. LDA or HDP. Now each document is considered as an input data point for some clustering algorithm. Elango & Jayaraman (2005) used LDA combined with K-means to cluster images while Nguyen *et al.* (2013) exploited features by HDP and used Affinity Propagation for clustering human activities.

Incorporating topic modeling and clustering in one unique model is a more elegant approach. Nested DP (nDP) (Rodriguez *et al.*, 2008) is the first attempt to handle this challenge in the context of Bayesian nonparametric. The model by Rodriguez *et al.* (2008) has tried to group documents into clusters each of which shares the same distribution over the topics. However, in the original nDP, the documents do not share topics. An extension to nDP, the MLC-HDP model with 3-level clustering, has been done by Wulsin *et al.* (2012). This model can cluster words, documents and document-corpora with shared topic atoms throughout the group hierarchy with this model. Later, Multi-Grain Clustering Topic Model which allows mixing between global topics and document-cluster topics has been introduced by Xie & Xing (2013). The most recent work, the Bayesian nonparametric multilevel clustering with group-level contexts (MC2) (Nguyen *et al.*, 2014), offers a theoretically elegant joint model for both content and context. To our best of knowledge, this model is the current state-of-the-art for this problem.

However, authors in (Nguyen *et al.*, 2014) only provide a Gibbs sampling method for inference. This seriously hinder the usefulness and applicability of MC2 in tackling modern datasets which can contain millions of documents.

Stochastic Variational Inference

Between two main inference approaches for graphical model including MCMC and deterministic variational methods, variational inference is usually preferred due to its predictable convergence. In variational inference scheme, the problem of computing intractable posterior distribution is transformed into an optimization problem by introducing tractable variational distribution. One of the most popular approximation is mean-field which assumes that the variational distribution is fully factorized. The objective function called Evidence Lower BOund (ELBO) is defined as KL divergence between approximated distribution and the posterior distribution plus a constant. To solve this optimization problem, coordinate descent can be used. However, this optimization method is not suitable for modern datasets with millions of documents since all document are visited in each iteration. To circumvent this challenge, the earliest, but very recent, attempt can be traced back to (Hoffman *et al.*, 2010) where SVI framework for Bayesian nonparametric inference was proposed by combining mean-field approximation and stochastic optimization. SVI for the hierarchical Dirichlet process (HDP) was also presented in (Wang *et al.*, 2011).

Instead of using coordinate descent, stochastic variational inference (SVI) (Hoffman *et al.*, 2013) using stochastic gradient descent to optimize the ELBO. In order to keep optimization process converge faster, SVI uses the coordinate descent for the local update which is related to each data point and update global variables involving multiple data points with stochastic gradient. Moreover, as suggested by Amari (1998), learning with natural gradient may lead to faster convergence. In the SVI framework with exponential family distributions, the natural gradient updates are not only more likely to improve optimization speed but also produces simpler update equations.

We ground our methodology on (Hoffman *et al.*, 2013) and develop the SVI updates for MC2. However, we note at the outset that, unlike HDP, our model is not completely factorized, hence our solution does not simply follow a naive mean field, but rather a variant of structured mean field approximation of Bayesian nonparametric models.

3 MULTILEVEL CLUSTERING WITH CONTEXTS (MC2)

We first describe the MC2 model of (Nguyen *et al.*, 2014). The generative process for MC2 model (see Fig. 1a) is as follows

$$U \sim \text{DP}\left(\gamma\left(H \times \text{DP}\left(\upsilon Q_0\right)\right)\right) \text{ where } Q_0 \sim \text{DP}\left(\eta S\right),$$
$$\left(\theta_j, Q_j\right) \sim U \text{ for each group } j$$
$$x_j \sim F\left(\cdot \mid \theta_j\right), \quad \varphi_{ji} \sim Q_j, \quad w_{ji} \sim Y\left(\cdot \mid \varphi_{ji}\right).$$

In the above, U is a DP realization, hence a discrete measure with probability 1, and therefore enforces the clustering of documents. The sample pair $(\theta_j, Q_j) \sim U$ represents the context parameter and content-generating measures of the j-th document. Distinct measures Q_j are effectively drawn from DP(υQ_0) where $Q_0 \sim \text{DP}(\eta S)$, so the samples φ_{ji} share atoms just like in a hierarchical DP (HDP). $F(.|\theta_j)$ and $Y(.|\varphi_{ji})$ are the likelihoods for context and content with parameters θ_j and φ_{ji}. Their base-measures H and S are assumed to be conjugate with the respective likelihoods.

The stick-breaking representation for the MC2 model is given Fig. 1b. When integrated out the random stick length, the model has an intuitive Polya-Urn view known as the Chinese Restaurant Franchise Bus (CRF-Bus) (Nguyen *et al.*, 2014). Each word in a document is viewed as a customer in a bus. The buses deliver customers randomly to a set of restaurants following a Chinese Restaurant Process (CRP). After getting off the buses, the customers in the restaurants behave as in the HDP - Chinese Restaurant Franchise (CRF). The MC2 model thus inherits the metaphor of tables at restaurants and global dishes from the CRF. The detailed stick-breaking representations are

- Stick length for *content* generation $\epsilon = \{\epsilon_m\}_{m=1}^{\infty}$ and *content* shared atoms $\{\psi_m\}_{m=1}^{\infty}$

$$\epsilon \sim \text{GEM}\left(1, \gamma\right), \qquad \psi_m \sim S, \qquad Q_0 = \sum_{m=1}^{\infty} \epsilon_m \delta_{\psi_m}.$$

- Stick length for *context* generation $\beta = \{\beta_k\}_{k=1}^{\infty}$ and *context* shared atoms $\{\phi_k\}_{k=1}^{\infty}$

$$\beta \sim \text{GEM}\left(1, \eta\right), \qquad \phi_k \sim H, \qquad G = \sum_{t=1}^{\infty} \beta_k \delta_{\phi_k}.$$

- Choosing document group (restaurant) for document $j = 1, \ldots, J$ and generating *context observation*

$$z_j \sim \text{Cat}\left(\beta_{1:\infty}\right), \qquad x_j \sim F\left(\cdot \mid \phi_{z_i}\right).$$

- Stick length for each document group $k = 1, \ldots, \infty$, $\{\tau_{kt}\}_{t=1}^{\infty}$, choosing tables t, dishes c and generating *content word*, $j = 1, \ldots, J$ and $i = 1, \ldots, n_j$

$$\tau_k \sim \text{GEM}\left(1, \upsilon\right), \qquad t_{ji} \sim \text{Cat}\left(\tau_{z_j}\right),$$
$$c_{kt} \sim \text{Cat}\left(\epsilon\right), \qquad w_{ji} \sim Y\left(\cdot \mid \psi_{c_{z_j t_{ji}}}\right).$$

We consider general exponential family forms for the likelihoods[2] $Y(w \mid \psi) = \exp\left(\langle T(w), \psi\rangle - A(\psi)\right)$ and $F(x \mid \phi) = \exp\left(\langle T(x), \psi\rangle - A(\phi)\right)$. The prior $S(\psi \mid \cdot)$ and $H(\phi \mid \cdot)$ have the conjugate forms $p\left(\psi \mid \lambda_*^{\psi}\right) \propto \exp\left(\left\langle \lambda_*^{\psi}, [\psi; -A(\psi)]\right\rangle\right)$ and $p\left(\phi \mid \lambda_*^{\phi}\right) \propto \exp\left(\left\langle \lambda_*^{\phi}, [\phi; -A(\phi)]\right\rangle\right)$. The notation $[v; c]$ represents the stacking of two column vectors.

[2]Note that $T(w)$ and $T(x)$ may have different forms.

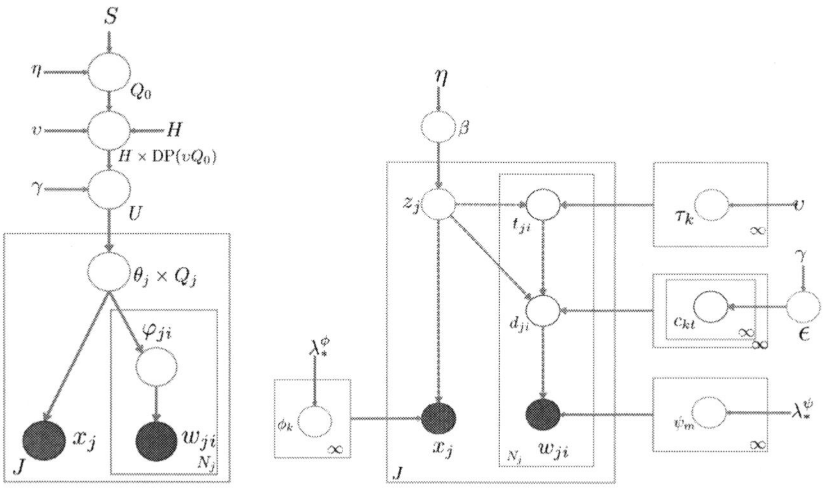

(a) Generative view.

(b) Stick-breaking view.

Figure 1: Graphical presentation for Multilevel clustering with contexts models.

4 SVI FOR MC2

4.1 TRUNCATED STICK-BREAKING REPRESENTATIONS

The approximation of DP by truncated stick-breaking representation has been introduced by (Ishwaran & James, 2001) and later used by (Blei & Jordan, 2006) for variational inference in DP mixtures model. In this work, we also use the truncated stick-breaking approximation for all three stick-breaking length variables of the model which are β, ϵ, and τ. As pointed by Ishwaran & James (2001), the truncated stick-breaking is equivalent to the generalized Dirichlet distribution (Connor & Mosiman, 1969; Wong, 1998) which is a distribution on $K-1$ simplex with $2(K-1)$-parameter $\lambda = \left(\lambda_{11}, \ldots \lambda_{(K-1)1,}, \lambda_{12}, \lambda_{(K-1)2}\right)$. Each pair of parameters $(\lambda_{k1}, \lambda_{k2})$ corresponds to the parameters for a Beta distribution in stick-breaking process. Generalized Dirichlet (GD) distribution is a member of the exponential family and is conjugate to Multinomial distributions (for more details, see the Appendix). For this reason, the mean-field update of a GD-distributed stick length also has a GD form. We used this conjugacy to compute the variational updates for stick-breaking variables.

4.2 MEAN-FIELD VARIATIONAL APPROXIMATION

The objective of inference problem with the model is to estimate the posterior distribution $p(\Theta \mid x, w)$ where Θ is the collection of parameter variable of the model, $\Theta \triangleq \{\beta, \epsilon, \tau, c, z, t, \psi, \phi\}$. In variational Bayes inference, this intractable posterior will be approximated with a tractable distribution called variational distribution, $q(\Theta)$. In order to ensure that $q(\Theta)$ is tractable, one usually uses mean-field assumption which assumes that all variational variables in Θ are independent. However, because of the nature of the MC2 model, two group of variables z_i (restaurant) and $t_{j1}, \ldots, t_{jn_j}$(tables) are highly correlated. We will maintain the joint distribution of these variables in as a collection of tree-structure graphical model. Thus, the variational distribution q is factorized as

$$q(\Theta) = q(\beta)\, q(\epsilon)\, q(\tau)\, q(c)\, q(z,t)\, q(\psi)\, q(\phi)\,.$$

All the factorized q's have exponential family form and for convenience we shall use either the natural or mean parameterization when appropriate. We use the following convention in naming the variational parameters: λ denotes a natural parameter, μ denotes a mean parameter, superscript denotes the collection of random variables of being parameterized and subscript denotes the index of variables. For instance, under this convention, λ_k^{ϕ} is the natural parameter for $q(\phi_k)$. The actual parameterization of q's are

- For the group of stick-breaking variables $q(\beta) = \text{GD}\left(\beta \mid \lambda^{\beta}\right)$, $q(\epsilon) = \text{GD}\left(\epsilon \mid \lambda^{\epsilon}\right)$, and $q(\tau) = \prod_{k=1}^{K} \text{GD}\left(\tau_k \mid \lambda_k^{\tau}\right)$ where λ^{β}, λ^{ϵ}, and λ_k^{τ} are $2K-2$, $2M-2$, and $2T-2$ dimension vector, respectively. K, M and T are the truncated levels for restaurants, dishes and tables in the CRF-Bus process respectively.
- For the group of content and context atoms $q(\psi) = \prod_{m=1}^{M} q\left(\psi_m \mid \lambda_m^{\psi}\right)$ and $q(\phi) = \prod_{k=1}^{K} q\left(\phi_k \mid \lambda_k^{\phi}\right)$.
- For the group of indicator variables $q(c) = \prod_{k=1}^{K} \prod_{t=1}^{T} \text{Mult}\left(c_{kt} \mid \mu_{kt}^{c}\right)$ and $q(z,t) = \prod_j \left[\text{Mult}\left(z_j \mid \mu_j^{z}\right) \prod_{i=1}^{n_j} \text{Mult}\left(t_{ji} \mid \mu_{jiz_j}^{t}\right)\right]$ where μ_j^{z}, μ_{kt}^{c}, and μ_{jik}^{t} are K, M, T-dimension vectors,

correspondingly. Note that two groups of variables z and t are not fully factorized but form a forest of trees, with each tree rooted at z_j.

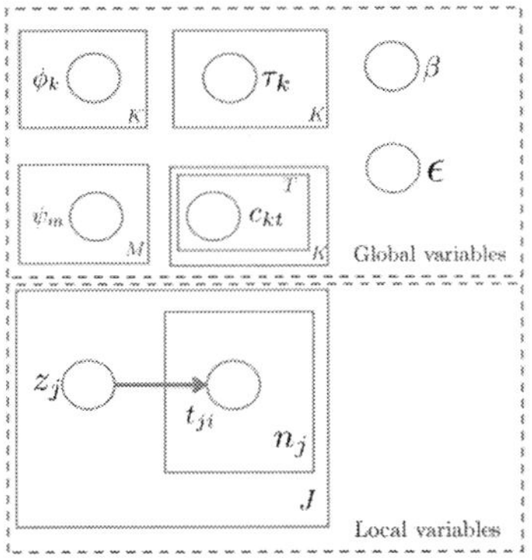

Figure 2: Variational factorization and global vs. local variables for SVI.

4.3 MEAN-FIELD UPDATES

All the individual q's in our model are in the exponential family and are locally conjugate. Thus, standard naive mean-field updates (Bishop *et al.*, 2006; Blei & Jordan, 2006), can be derived for all the variational parameters in a straight-forward manner. We provide more details on the update for the variational parameters of z and t since these are coupled and structured mean-field is needed (Wainwright & Jordan, 2008). At a high-level, for each tree rooted at z_j, exact inference needs to be done to convert from natural to mean parameters. The actual updates equation for these parameters are

$$\mu^t_{jikl} \propto \tilde{\mu}^t_{jikl}, \tag{1}$$

$$\mu^z_{jk} \propto \exp(\mathbb{E}\left[\ln \beta_k p(x_j \mid \phi_k)\right] + \sum_i \ln(\sum_{l=1}^{T} \tilde{\mu}^t_{jikl})),$$

where $\tilde{\mu}^t_{jikl}$ is the unnormalized value of μ^t_{jikl} and is $\exp\left(\sum_{m=1}^{M} \mu^c_{klm} \mathbb{E}\left[\ln p\left(w_{ji} \mid \psi_m\right)\right] + \mathbb{E}\left[\ln \tau_{kl}\right]\right)$.

The update for the rest of the parameters uses naive mean-field.

Two groups of variables, stick-breaking and atoms, contain similar variables. One variable in each group will be presented, the others have a similar forms and can be found in the appendix. The following equations includes updates for the content side of the stick-breaking and atom variables.

For the stick-breaking variational distribution $q(\epsilon)$

$$\lambda^\epsilon_{m1} = 1 + \sum_{k,t} \mu^c_{ktm} \qquad \lambda^\epsilon_{m2} = \gamma + \sum_{k,t} \sum_{l=m+1}^{M} \mu^c_{ktl}. \tag{2}$$

For the content-atom variational distribution $q(\psi)$

$$\lambda^\psi_m = \lambda^\psi_* + \sum_{j=1}^{J} \sum_{i=1}^{n_j} \left(\sum_{k=1}^{K} \mu^z_{jk} \sum_{l=1}^{T} \mu^c_{ktm} \mu^t_{jikl} \right) \left[T\left(w_{ji}\right); 1\right].$$

4.4 STOCHASTIC VARIATIONAL INFERENCE

We follow the SVI framework (Hoffman *et al.*, 2013) and divide the set of variables Θ in the posterior into the set of *local* variables $\{z, t\}$ with the rest as *global* variables (see Fig. 2). The variational Evidence Lower BOund (ELBO) function is

where $\Theta^g \triangleq \Theta \backslash \{z, t\}$ is the global parameters of the model.

We will reuse the coordinate descent updates for local variational parameters μ^z_j and μ^t_{jik} given in section 4.2. To derive the stochastic gradient descent update for the global parameters, instead of taking the gradient of $\mathcal{L}$ which would result in messages being passed from all the documents, we take the gradient of $\mathcal{L}_j$ which is sufficient to yield a stochastic gradient of $\mathcal{L}$. The gradients are multiplied with the inverse Fisher information matrix to obtain the natural gradients (denoted as $\frac{\partial^{(\text{ng})}}{\partial}$). The gradient with respect to the content atom and stick breaking variational parameters λ^ψ_m and $\lambda^\epsilon_{m1,2}$ are

$$\frac{\partial^{(\text{ng})} \mathcal{L}_j}{\partial \lambda^\psi_m} = \frac{-\lambda^\psi_m + \lambda^\psi_*}{J} + \sum_{i=1}^{n_j} (\sum_{k,l} \mu^z_{jk} \mu^c_{klm} \mu^t_{jikl}) \left[T\left(w_{ji}\right); 1\right]. \tag{3}$$

$$\frac{\partial^{(\text{ng})} \mathcal{L}_j}{\partial \lambda^\epsilon_{m1}} = \frac{-\lambda^\epsilon_{m1} + 1}{J} + \sum_{k,t} \mu^c_{ktm}, \tag{4}$$

$$\frac{\partial^{(\text{ng})} \mathcal{L}_j}{\partial \lambda^\epsilon_{m2}} = \frac{-\lambda^\epsilon_{m2} + \gamma}{J} + \sum_{k,t} \sum_{r=m+1}^{M} \mu^c_{ktr}$$

Computing the gradient w.r.t. $q(c_{kt})$ is easier using the minimal natural parameterization of the multinomial. Let λ^c_{kt} be the minimal natural parameter corresponding to the mean parameter μ^c_{kt}, the gradient w.r.t λ^c_{kt} is

$$\frac{\partial^{(\text{ng})} \mathcal{L}_j}{\partial \lambda^c_{ktm}} = \frac{-\lambda^c_{ktm} + \mathbb{E}\left[\ln \frac{\epsilon_m}{\epsilon_M}\right]}{J} + \left(a_{ktm} - a_{ktM}\right) \tag{5}$$

where $a_{ktm} = \mu^z_{jk} \sum_{i=1}^{n_j} \mu^t_{jikl} \mathbb{E}\left[\ln p\left(w_{ji} \mid \psi_m\right)\right]$ for $m = 1 \ldots M$. Conversion from natural to mean parameters for the multinomials are standard

$$\mu^c_{ktm} = \frac{\exp\left(\lambda^c_{ktm}\right)}{1 + \sum_{m=1}^{M-1} \exp\left(\lambda^c_{ktm}\right)}, m = 1, \ldots, M-1$$

and $\mu^c_{ktM} = 1 - \sum_{m=1}^{M-1} \mu_{ktm}$.

With above derivations, we can summarize the procedure of stochastic variational inference for MC2 model in Algorithm 1.

In the above, the stochastic gradient is obtained for each document. In practice, mini-batch of documents are used

Algorithm 1 Stochastic variational inference for MC2

Require: forgetting rate ι and delay ϱ
  Initialize $\lambda_m^{\psi(0)}, \lambda_k^{\phi(0)}$ and set $t = 1$;
  repeat
    Choose uniformly document j from data
    Compute μ_{jik}^{t} and μ_j^{z} with Eq. (1)
    Set $\varpi_t = (t + \varrho)^{-\iota}$
    Update stick-breaking variable hyperparameters $\lambda^{\beta}, \lambda^{\epsilon}, \lambda_k^{\tau}$ using corresponding gradient similar to Eq. (4) as follows
    $\lambda^{(t+1)} = \lambda^{(t)} + J\varpi_t \frac{\partial^{(\text{ng})}\mathcal{L}_j}{\partial\lambda}$
    Update content and context atom hyperparameters $\lambda^{\psi}, \lambda^{\phi}$ using corresponding gradient similar to Eq. (3) as follows
    $\lambda^{(t+1)} = \lambda^{(t)} + J\varpi_t \frac{\partial^{(\text{ng})}\mathcal{L}_j}{\partial\lambda}$
    Update "dish-table" indicator variable hyperparameters μ_{ktm}^{c} using gradient in Eq. (5).
  until convergence

in each update to reduce the variance (Hoffman *et al.*, 2010, 2013). In this case, the gradients with a single document in are replaced by the average gradients of all the documents in a mini-batch.

5 EXPERIMENTS

We evaluate our inference algorithm on real datasets with two different scale settings: small datasets with thousands of documents which can also be run using Gibbs sampler; large-scale data with millions of documents which can not be practically run with sampling methods. For small-scale settings, we illustrate competitive perplexity of our inference methods compare to Gibbs sampler but with much less computation time. We also report the running time and performance of our model for large-scale data sets.

5.1 DATASETS

As aforementioned, we use two groups of different scales of datasets. For the *small scale setting*, in order to compare with Gibbs sampler, we use the same datasets in (Nguyen *et al.*, 2014): a text dataset, NIPS, and image dataset, NUS-WIDE.

- NIPS[3] consists of 1740 document with the vocabulary size 13,649. To evaluate predictive performance, we randomly split into 90% training and 10% held-out for computing perplexity.
- NUS-WIDE (Chua *et al.*, 2009) contains a subset of 13 animal classes which totally include 3411 images. Held-out data includes 1357 images and the rest is used for training the model. For the image features, we use bag-of-word SIFT vector with dimension 500. For the context observations, we use the tags for each image which are 1000-dimension spare vectors.

[3]http://www.cs.nyu.edu/~roweis/data.html

For the *large-scale setting,* we use three different datasets including *Wikipedia*, *Pubmed*, and *Application Usage Activity (AUA)*.

- *Wikipedia* includes about 1.1 million documents downloaded from wikipedia.com. We pre-process data using a vocabulary list taken from the top 10,000 words in Project Gutenberg and remove all words less than three characters (Hoffman *et al.*, 2013). For the context features we use the (first) writer of the articles and the (top level) categories inferred from tagged categories in each article as described in (De Vries *et al.*, 2010).
- *PubMed* comprises 1.4 million abstracts acquired from pubmed.gov. These documents are filtered with the published year from 2000 onward. Similar to *Wikipedia,* we also extracted the vocabulary from the whole dataset and only kept words with more than 2 characters. A top list of 10.000 words is used as vocabulary list for computing bag-of-word. We further extract the Medical Subject Headings (MeSH) and consider as the context.
- *Application Usage Activity (AUA)*: This dataset contains the usage behavior from more than one million users of a popular software application. Each user is treated as a document in which a word refers to a specific functionality of the application and word frequency refers to the number of times the user interact with the corresponding functionality. The total number of functionalities (vocabulary size) is roughly 10,000. In addition to the current application, each user also uses a host of other related software products which can be used as the context of the user. Applying MC2 to this data effectively cluster the set of users into different segments. To measure the clustering quality, we simply use a ground-truth of two clusters of paid and free users. Note that this information is not present in the context or the word content.

5.2 EXPERIMENT SETUPS

Since our observed data are discrete, we assume that they are generated from either Categorical or Multinomial distributions endowed with Dirichlet priors. The learning rate for stochastic learning at iteration t is $\varpi_t = (t + \varrho)^{-\iota}$where $\varrho \geq 0$ is the delay parameter, and $\iota \in (.5, 1]$ is the forgetting rate which controls how quickly previous statistics is forgotten. In the experiment for computing perplexity, we fixed $\varrho = 1$ and $\iota = 0.8$. The hyperparameters for Dirichlet distributions are set to 0.01 and 0.1 for content and context, respectively.

Small-scale setting

The experiments for NIPS and NUSWIDE datasets are carried out on an Intel Xeon 2.6GHz machine with 16 cores, 16GB RAM using a C# implementation running on Windows 7. SVI method can be parallelized when computing local updates. We run the experiment using both datasets in serial and parallel modes. The parallel implementation is accomplished using the Task Parallel Library (TPL) in .NET framework.

Large-scale setting

In order to handle big datasets, we implement our algorithms on Apache Spark platform[4]. The experiments for *Wikipedia, Pubmed, AUA* are run in two main settings with no context observations, and with full context observations for each corresponding context. Since HDP implementation is not available on Spark, we use the LDA implementation provided by Spark machine learning library (MLLIB) to compare perplexity with our algorithm. We set the number of topics for LDA equal to the number of topic truncated in the MC2 model.

5.3 EVALUATION METRICS

Perplexity. We use perplexity as the evaluation metric to compare the modelling performance between inference algorithms (Gibbs vs. SVI) or between model (our model vs. LDA). The perplexity is defined as perplexity $(w^{\text{test}}) = \exp\left\{-\frac{\sum_j \ln p(w_{j.}|\mathcal{D})}{\sum_j n_j}\right\}$ where w^{test} is the content words in the test set and $\mathcal{D}$ is the training data. Since we wish to compare our SVI algorithm with Gibbs sampler, we implemented importance sampling (Wallach *et al.*, 2009) to computed $\ln p(w_{j.} \mid \mathcal{D})$ in both cases. In Spark MLLIB, there is no implementation for computing perplexity with importance sampling, we instead used the code given by Wallach *et al.* (2009).

Clustering performance. Since our model can carry out clustering for documents, we wish to compare clustering performance. However, documents usually do not have a "strong" ground truth and most of them are with multiple-cluster. For instance, with PubMed data, we use MeSH for each article as ground truth cluster but each article usually associates with several MeSH terms. Some popular clustering performance metrics including purity, Random Index(RI), Normalized Mutual Information (NMI), Fscore (Manning *et al.*, 2008, Chap16) are designed for single cluster ground truth. Whenever there is single cluster ground truth, for example, in the *AUA* dataset, we use the above four metrics. In other cases, we use the extended Normalized Mutual Information (eNMI) which is defined as follows. Let suppose that we have N objects each of which is belong to one of K clusters. A clustering algorithm will assign this object to one of T clusters. With N objects, we denote W as an $N \times K$ ground truth matrix where each row of this matrix represent a (transposed) one-hot vector encoding of the cluster it belongs. Similarly, we have $N \times T$ matrix as a result matrix. The joint probability when an object has the ground truth cluster k and is assigned to cluster t is $p(w,c) = W^{\top}C$. The mutual information between discovered clusters and ground truth cluster is $\text{MI}(W,C) = \sum_{k,t} p(w=k, c=t) \ln \frac{p(w=k,c=t)}{p(c=t)p(w=k)}$. The normalized mutual information is $\text{NMI}(W,C) = \frac{2\text{MI}(W,C)}{H(C)H(W)}$ where $H(\cdot)$ is the entropy of histogram of clusters. In the case of multiple clustering, we have the matrix W and C where each row is not one-hot vector but a vector with the sum as 1. We use some equations above for computing extended NMI (eNMI).

[4]http://spark.apache.org/

	Running time (s)	
	Sequential	Parallel
NIPS	11213	1431
NUSWIDE	8373	682

Table 1: Running time of two implementation version

5.4 EXPERIMENTAL RESULT

Results on small -scale setting

First, we demonstrate the performance of our proposed methods (SVI) compared with Gibbs sampler of (Nguyen *et al.*, 2014). For Gibbs samplers, we ran 1500 iterations and SVI with 50 documents in each mini-batch and compute perplexity. The Fig. 3 showed the predictive performance of them over running time. In both datasets, SVI can approach the performance of Gibbs sampler within one epoch[5]; after the first epoch, the perplexity only improved a little. To obtain the competitive performance with Gibbs sampler, our algorithm needs only one-fourth of the amount of running time. Furthermore, SVI algorithm is parallelizable. As shown in Table 1, running time with parallelized version on a single machine with 16 cores is further reduced significantly, 8 and 12 times for NIPS and NUS-WIDE, respectively. Note that our parallel SVI-MC2 only parallelize the local updates, hence, the per-core speedup also depends on the fraction of parallelizable local updates and the global update. In the case of NIPS data set, the dimension of the (global) content and context topic are 13,649 and 2037, respectively, while those of NUS-WIDE are 500 and 1000 which could explain why parallelization is more effective for NUS-WIDE.

[5]Each epoch is an iteration in which algorithm visited all data points.

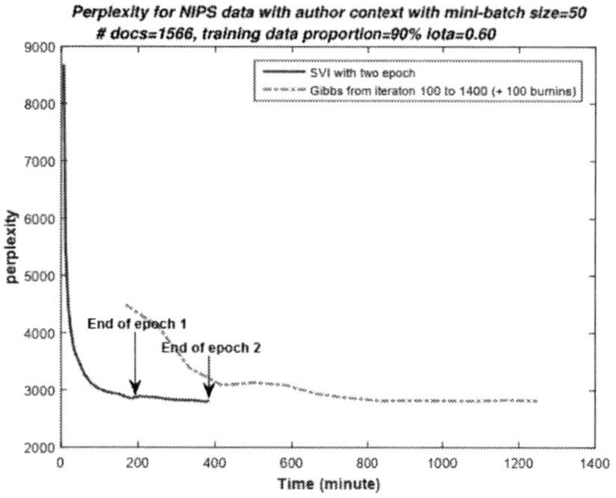

(a) NIPS - context: author

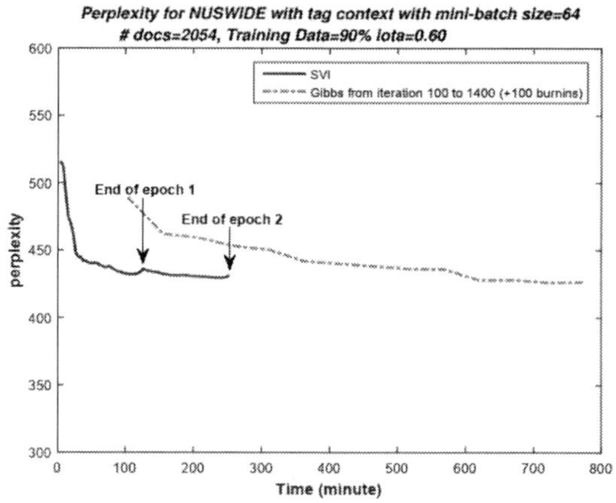

(b) NUS-WIDE - context: tag

Figure 3: Perplexity with respect to running time on two datasets: NIPS and NUS-WISE. The blue line denotes the change of perplexity over running time with two epochs of data for SVI learning algorithm while the green line depicts perplexity running with Gibbs samplers. The results for Gibbs sampler is shown for every 100 iteration from 100-th to 1400-th iteration (excluding 100 burn-in iteration).

	Context availability		LDA
	100%	0%	
Wikipedia - writer	**2,167**	2,280	2,635
Pubmed - MeSH	**2,294**	2.448	3,178
AUA - other products	**142.3**	149.7	209.3

Table 2: Log perplexity of Wikipedia and PubMed data

	Context availability	
	1%	0%
eNMI	**0.084**	0.065

Table 3: Extended Normalized mutual information (NMI) for Pubmed data

Results on large-scale setting

In this setting, we validate the robustness of our algorithm with large-scale datasets. We ran our inference algorithm with *Wikipedia, PubMed,* and *AUA* datasets together with the LDA baseline on an 8-node Spark cluster. We used writer, MeSH, and other products used as contexts for *Wikipedia*, *PubMed*, and *AUA*, respectively. For each dataset, we ran data with full observations of context and without context. Table 2 depict the perplexity for these datasets with and without context compared with LDA. The predictive performance of SVI-MC2 improved remarkably compared to LDA.

For *PubMed* dataset, we used MeSH as the ground truth for clustering evaluation. As each document contains several MeSH terms, we use extended NMI (eNMI) for computing clustering performance. For each mini-batch, we compute eNMI of this mini-batch with its ground truth. The table 3 depict the average eNMI for all mini-batches in an epoch. With a very little availability of the ground truth as context, our algorithm can considerably improve clustering performance.

For *AUA* dataset, three different levels of context availability are used including no context, 1%, and full context. Since the ground truth clusters do not overlap, we can use the conventional metrics for clustering evaluation such as NMI, RI, purity, and Fscore. We also compute the average of the above indices for all mini-batches in an epoch. The clustering results are are shown in table 4. All clustering metrics showed the advantage of context observation (very small percentage is needed) to improve the clustering performance.

It is not possible to run the Gibbs sampler for these large datasets; even the serial version of SVI took too much time, hence we only reported running time for Spark SVI-MC2. With the mini-batch size of 500, the best running times are achieved using an 8-node cluster: Wikipedia: 17 hours; Pubmed: 18.5 hours; AUA: 18 hours. However, using a single-node (with 16-core) could also suffice with running time roughly 1.5 times slower than on a full 8-node cluster. We note that the size of the mini-batch (500) in this case strongly affects the effectiveness of the distributed-cluster setting. For example, with a mini-batch size of 1000, the speed-up factor on an 8-node cluster (compared to single-node) increases from 1.5 to 1.8.

Context	Avail.	NMI	Purity	RI	Fscore
Other products used	0%	0.027	0.14	0.284	0.12
	1%	**0.035**	0.174	0.286	0.128
	100%	0.033	**0.179**	**0.287**	**0.131**

Table 4: Clustering performance for *AUA* data

6 CONCLUSION

We have presented a scalable method for Bayesian nonparametric multilevel clustering with contextual side information. We proposed a tree-structured SVI approximation for an efficient approximation of the model's posterior. The approach can be directly parallelizable, and we provide parallelized implementations that work both on a single machine and on a distributed Apache Spark cluster. The experimental results demonstrate that our method is several orders of magnitude faster than existing the Gibb-sampler while yield the same model quality. Most importantly, our work enables the applicability of multilevel clustering to modern real-world datasets which can contain millions of documents.

References

Amari, Shun-Ichi. 1998. Natural gradient works efficiently in learning. *Neural computation*, **10**(2), 251–276.

Antoniak, C.E. 1974. Mixtures of Dirichlet processes with applications to Bayesian nonparametric problems. *The Annals of Statistics*, **2**(6), 1152–1174.

Bishop, Christopher M, *et al.* 2006. *Pattern recognition and machine learning*. Vol. 1. springer New York.

Blei, D.M., & Jordan, M.I. 2006. Variational inference for Dirichlet process mixtures. *Bayesian Analysis*, **1**(1), 121–143.

Blei, D.M., Ng, A.Y., & Jordan, M.I. 2003. Latent Dirichlet Allocation. *Journal of Machine Learning Research*, **3**, 993–1022.

Chua, Tat-Seng, Tang, Jinhui, Hong, Richang, Li, Haojie, Luo, Zhiping, & Zheng, Yantao. 2009. NUS-WIDE: a real-world web image database from National University of Singapore. *Page 48 of: Proceedings of the ACM International Conference on Image and Video Retrieval*. ACM.

Connor, R. J., & Mosiman, J. E. 1969. Concepts of independence for proportions with a generalization of the Dirichlet distribution. *Journal of the American Statistical Association*, **64**, 194–206.

De Vries, Christopher M, Nayak, Richi, Kutty, Sangeetha, Geva, Shlomo, & Tagarelli, Andrea. 2010. Overview of the INEX 2010 XML mining track: Clustering and classification of XML documents. *Pages 363–376 of: Comparative evaluation of focused retrieval*. Springer Berlin Heidelberg.

Diez-Roux, Ana V. 2000. Multilevel analysis in public health research. *Annual review of public health*, **21**(1), 171–192.

Elango, Pradheep K, & Jayaraman, Karthik. 2005. Clustering Images Using the Latent Dirichlet Allocation Model. *University of Wisconsin*.

Hoffman, Matthew D, Blei, David M, Wang, Chong, & Paisley, John. 2013. Stochastic variational inference. *The Journal of Machine Learning Research*, **14**(1), 1303–1347.

Hoffman, M.D., Blei, D.M., & Bach, F. 2010. Online learning for latent dirichlet allocation. *Advances in Neural Information Processing Systems*, **23**, 856–864.

Hox, Joop. 2010. *Multilevel analysis: Techniques and applications*. Routledge.

Ishwaran, H., & James, L.F. 2001. Gibbs sampling methods for stick-breaking priors. *Journal of the American Statistical Association*, **96**(453), 161–173.

Lu, Yue, Mei, Qiaozhu, & Zhai, ChengXiang. 2011. Investigating task performance of probabilistic topic models: an empirical study of PLSA and LDA. *Information Retrieval*, **14**(2), 178–203.

Manning, C.D., Raghavan, P., & Schütze, H. 2008. *Introduction to Information Retrieval*. Vol. 1. Cambridge University Press Cambridge.

Nguyen, T. C., Phung, D., Gupta, S., & Venkatesh, S. 2013. Extraction of Latent Patterns and Contexts from Social Honest Signals Using Hierarchical Dirichlet Processes. *Pages 47–55 of: 2013 IEEE International Conference on Pervasive Computing and Communications (PerCom)*.

Nguyen, V., Phung, D., Venkatesh, S. Nguyen, X.L., & Bui, H. 2014. Bayesian Nonparametric Multilevel Clustering with Group-Level Contexts. *Pages 288–296 of: Proc. of International Conference on Machine Learning (ICML)*.

Phung, D., Nguyen, X., Bui, H., Nguyen, T.V., & Venkatesh, S. 2012. *Conditionally Dependent Dirichlet Processes for Modelling Naturally Correlated Data Sources*. Tech. rept. Pattern Recognition and Data Analytics, Deakin University.

Phung, D., Nguyen, T. C., Gupta, S., & Venkatesh, S. 2014. Learning Latent Activities from Social Signals with Hierarchical Dirichlet Process. *Pages 149–174 of:* et al.

Gita Sukthankar (ed), *Handbook on Plan, Activity, and Intent Recognition*. Elsevier.

Rodriguez, A., Dunson, D.B., & Gelfand, A.E. 2008. The nested Dirichlet process. *Journal of the American Statistical Association*, **103**(483), 1131–1154.

Teh, Y.W., Jordan, M.I., Beal, M.J., & Blei, D.M. 2006. Hierarchical Dirichlet Processes. *Journal of the American Statistical Association*, **101**(476), 1566–1581.

Wainwright, Martin J, & Jordan, Michael I. 2008. Graphical models, exponential families, and variational inference. *Foundations and Trends® in Machine Learning*, **1**(1-2), 1–305.

Wallach, H.M., Murray, I., Salakhutdinov, R., & Mimno, D. 2009. Evaluation methods for topic models. *Pages 1105–1112 of: Procs. of Int. Conference on Machine Learning (ICML)*. ACM.

Wang, C., Paisley, J., & Blei, D.M. 2011. Online variational inference for the hierarchical Dirichlet process. *In: Artificial Intelligence and Statistics*.

Wong, T.-T. 1998. Generalized Dirichlet distribution in Bayesian analysis. *Applied Mathematics and Computation*, **97**, 165–181.

Wulsin, D., Jensen, S., & Litt, B. 2012. A Hierarchical Dirichlet Process Model with Multiple Levels of Clustering for Human EEG Seizure Modeling. *In: Proc. of International Conference on Machine Learning (ICML)*.

Xie, Pengtao, & Xing, Eric P. 2013. Integrating Document Clustering and Topic Modeling. *Proceedings of the International Conference on Uncertainty in Artificial Intelligence*.

Hierarchical learning of grids of microtopics

Nebojsa Jojic
Microsoft Research,
Redmond, WA 98052

Alessandro Perina
Core Data Science, Microsoft
Redmond, WA 98053

Dongwoo Kim
Australia National University
Canberra, Australia

Abstract

The counting grid is a grid of *microtopics*, sparse word/feature distributions. The generative model associated with the grid does not use these microtopics individually, but in predefined groups which can only be (ad)mixed as such. Each allowed group corresponds to one of all possible overlapping rectangular windows into the grid. The capacity of the model is controlled by the ratio of the grid size and the window size. This paper builds upon the basic counting grid model and it shows that hierarchical reasoning helps avoid bad local minima, produces better classification accuracy and, most interestingly, allows for extraction of large numbers of coherent microtopics even from small datasets. We evaluate this in terms of consistency, diversity and clarity of the indexed content, as well as in a user study on word intrusion tasks. We demonstrate that these models work well as a technique for embedding raw images and discuss interesting parallels between hierarchical CG models and other deep architectures.

1 INTRODUCTION

Recently, a new breed of topic models, dubbed counting grids (CG) [1, 2], has been shown to have advantages in unsupervised learning over previous topic models, while at the same time providing a natural representation for visualization and user interface design [3]. CG models are *generative* models based on a grid of word distributions, which can best be thought of as the grounds for a massive Venn diagram of documents. The intersections among multiple documents (bags of words) create little intersection units with a very small number of words in them (or rather, a very sparse distribution of the words). The grid arrangement of these sparse distributions, which we will refer to here as *microtopics*, facilitates fast cumulative sum based inference and learning algorithms that chop up the documents into much smaller constitutive pieces than what traditional topic models typically do. For example, Fig. 1 shows a small part of such a grid with a few representative words with greatest probability from each microtopic. Each of the Science magazine abstracts used to train this grid is assumed to have been generated from a group of microtopics found in a single 4×4 window with equal weight given to all component microtopics. Thus, each microtopic can be 16 times sparser than the set of documents grouped into the window.

A document may share a window with another very similar document, but it is also mapped so that it only partially overlaps with a window that is the source for a set of slightly less related documents. The varying window overlap literally results in a varying overlap in document themes. This modeling assumption results in a trained grid where nearby microtopics tend to be related to each other as they are often used together to generate a document. Consider, e.g., the lower right 4×4 window in Fig. 1. The word distributions in these 16 cells are such that a variety of Science papers on evidence of ancient life on Earth could be generated by sampling words from there. (Note that each cell, though of very low entropy, contains a distribution over the entire vocabulary.) In the posterior distribution, this window is by far the most likely source for an article on a bizarre microorganism that produced nitrogen in cretaceous oceans. In the 4×4 window two cells to the left of this example we find mapped a variety of articles on even more ancient events on Earth, e.g. on how sulfur isotopes reveal a deep mantle storage of ancient crust. But there we also start to see words which increase the fit for articles that describe similar events on other planets. Further movement to the left gets us away from the Earth and into astronomy.

To demonstrate the refinement of the microtopics compared to topics from a typical topic model, the color labeling of the grid was created so as to reflect the Kullback-Leibler (KL) divergence of the individual microtopics to the topics trained on the same data through latent Dirichlet allocation (LDA). The LDA topics, hand-labeled after unsupervised training, correspond to fairly broad topics, while the CG represents the data as a group of slowly evolving microtopics. For example, all the yellow coded microtopics map to the "Physics" LDA topic, but they occupy a contiguous area in which from left to right the focus slowly shifts from electromagnetism and particle physics to material science. Furthermore, it is interesting to see the microtopics that occupy the boundaries between coarser topics that LDA model found, capturing the links among astronomy, physics and biology. It is immediately evident that the 2D CGs can have great use in data visualization, though the model can be trained for arbitrary dimensionality [1]. These models combine topic modeling and data embedding ideas in a way that facilitates intuitive regularization controls and allows creation of much larger sets of organized sparse topics. Furthermore, they lend them selves to elegant visualization and browsing strategies, and we encourage the reader to see the example `http://research.microsoft.com/en-us/um/people/jojic/CGbrowser.zip`.

However, the existing EM algorithm for CG learning is prone to local minima problems which occasionally lead to under performance [4, 5]. In addition, no direct testing of the microtopic coherence has been performed to date, which makes it unclear if they are meaningful outside their windowed grouping. After all, a variety of sophisticated topic models have been developed and tested by the research community, but LDA seems to still beat them often in practice. E.g., [16,17] raise doubts that various reported perplexity improvements over the basic LDA model are meaningful as they are sensitive to smoothing constants in the model, and also fail to translate to improvements in human judgement of topic quality. In fact, LDA usually outperforms more complex models on tasks that involve human judgement, which may be the main reason why practitioners of data science prefer this basic model to others [6]. Here we develop hierarchical versions of CG models, which in our experiments produced embeddings of considerably higher quality. We show that layering into deeper architectures primarily aids in avoiding bad local minima, rather than increasing representational capacity: The trained hierarchical model can be collapsed into an original counting grid form but with a much higher likelihood compared to the grids fit to the same data using EM with random restarts. The better data fit then translates into quantitatively better summaries of the data, as shown in numerical experiments as well as human evaluations of microtopics obtained through crowdsourcing.

2 HIERARCHICAL LEARNING OF GRIDS OF MICROTOPICS

The (C)CG grids [1, 2]: The basic counting grid $\pi_{\mathbf{k}}$ [1] is a set of distributions on the d-dimensional toroidal discrete grid $\mathbf{E}$ indexed by $\mathbf{k}$. The grids in this paper are bidimensional and typically from $(E_x = 32) \times (E_y = 32)$ to

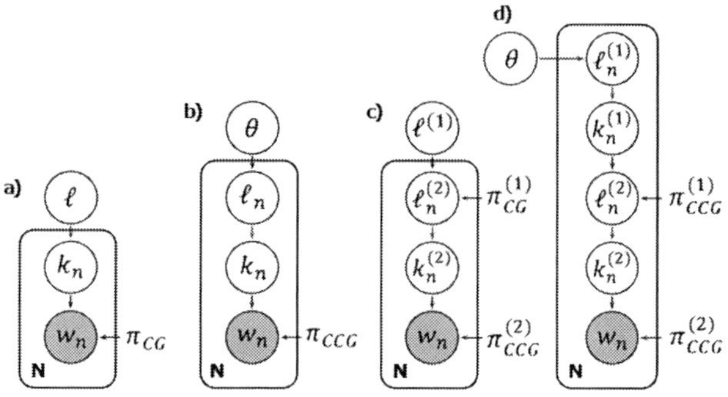

Figure 2: **a)** The basic counting grid, **b)** the componential counting grid, **c)** the hierarchical counting grid model (HCG) obtained by stacking a componential counting grid and a counting grid, and **d)** the hierarchical componential counting grid model (HCCG). Dotted circles represent the parameters of the models. Red links represents known conditional distributions $P(k_n|\ell_n) = U_\ell^W$ - Eq. 5. They are distributions over the grid locations, uniformly equal to $1/|\mathbf{W}|$ in the window of size $\mathbf{W}_\ell$ unequivocally identified by ℓ.

$(E_x = 64) \times (E_y = 64)$ in size. The index z indexes a particular word in the vocabulary $z = [1 \dots Z]$. Thus, $\pi_{\mathbf{i}}(z)$ is the probability of the word z at the d-dimensional discrete location $\mathbf{i}$, and $\sum_z \pi_{\mathbf{i}}(z) = 1$ at every location on the grid. The model generates bags of words, each represented by a list of words $\mathbf{w} = \{w_n\}_{n=1}^N$ with each word w_n taking an integer value between 1 and Z. The modeling assumption in the basic CG model is that each bag is generated from the distributions in a single window $\mathbf{W}$ of a preset size, e.g., $W_x = 5 \times W_y = 5$. A bag can be generated by first picking a window at a d-dimensional location ℓ, denoted as W_ℓ, then generating each of the N words by sampling a location $\mathbf{k}_n$ for a particular microtopic $\pi_{\mathbf{k}_n}$ uniformly within the window, and finally by sampling from that microtopic. Because the conditional distribution $p(\mathbf{k}_n|\ell)$ is a preset uniform distribution over the grid locations inside the window placed at location ℓ, the variable $\mathbf{k}_n$ can be summed out[1], and the generation can directly use the grouped histograms

$$h_\ell(z) = \frac{1}{|\mathbf{W}|} \sum_{\mathbf{j} \in W_\ell} \pi_{\mathbf{j}}(z), \tag{1}$$

where $|\mathbf{W}|$ is the area of the window, e.g. 25 when 5×5 windows are used. In other words, the position of the window ℓ in the grid is a latent variable given which we can write the probability of the bag as

$$P(\mathbf{w}|\ell) = \prod_{w_n \in \mathbf{w}} h_\ell(w_n) = \prod_{w_n \in \mathbf{w}} \Big(\frac{1}{|\mathbf{W}|} \cdot \sum_{\mathbf{j} \in W_\ell} \pi_{\mathbf{j}}(w_n)\Big) \tag{2}$$

As the grid is toroidal, a window can start at any position and there is as many h distributions as there are π distributions. The former will have a considerably higher entropy as they are averages of many π distributions. Although the basic CG model is essentially a simple mixture assuming the existence of a single source (one window) for all the features in one bag, it can have a very large number of (highly related) choices h to choose from. Topic models [7, 8], on the other hand, are admixtures that capture word

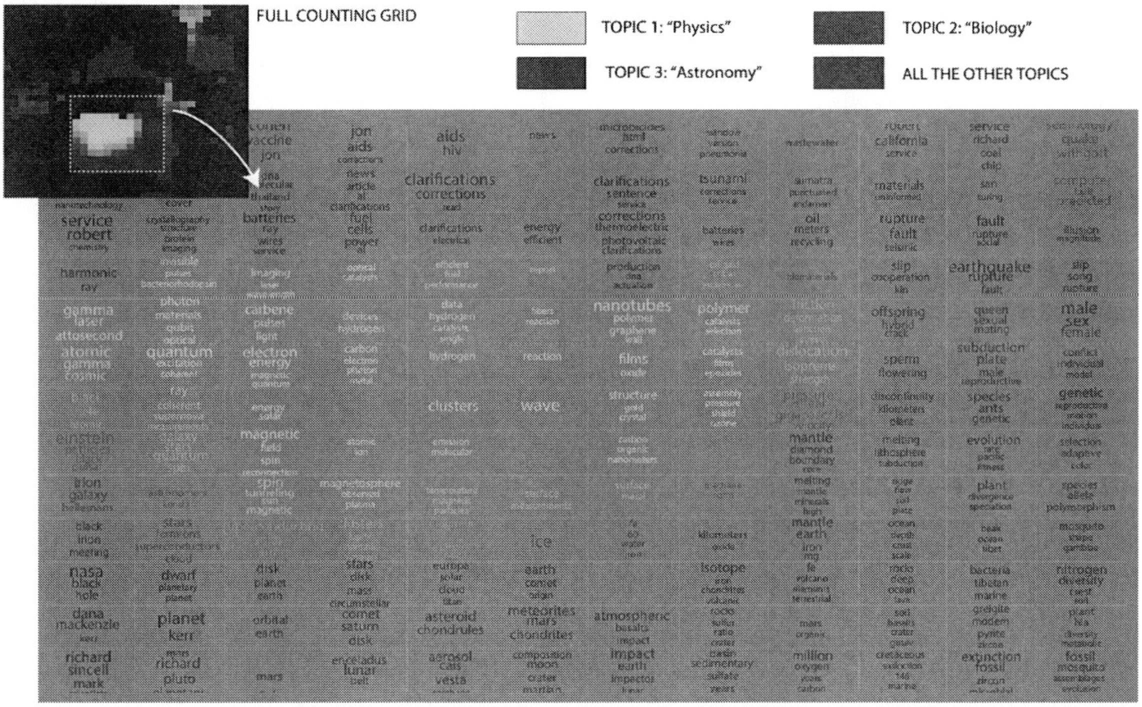

Figure 1: Clash of topics: LDA topics are mapped onto a counting grid. As shown in the top left panel, LDA's topics cluster in contiguous areas on the grid. In the enlarged part of the grid, for each microtopic we show the most likely words if they exceed a threshold.

co-occurrence statistics by using a much smaller number of topics that can be more freely combined to explain a single document. Componential Counting Grids (CCG) [2] combine these ideas, allowing multiple groups of broader topics h to be mixed to explain a single document. The entropic h distributions are still made of sparse microtopics π in the same way as in CG so that the CCG model can have a much larger number of topics than an LDA model without overtraining. More precisely, each word w_n can be generated from a different window, placed at location ℓ_n, but the choice of the window follows the same prior distributions θ_ℓ for all words. Within the window at location ℓ_n the word comes from a particular grid location k_n, and from that grid distribution the word is assumed to have been generated. The probability of a bag is now

$$P(\mathbf{w}|\pi) = \prod_{w_n \in \mathbf{w}} \sum_{\ell \in \mathbf{E}} \Big(\theta_\ell \cdot \big(\frac{1}{|\mathbf{W}|} \sum_{\mathbf{j} \in W_\ell} \cdot \pi_{\mathbf{j}}(w_n)\big)\Big) \quad (3)$$

In a well-fit CCG model, each data point has an inferred θ_ℓ distribution that usually hits multiple places in the grid, while in a CG, each data point tends to have a rather peaky posterior location distribution because the model is a mixture. Both models can be learned efficiently using the EM algorithm because the inference of the hidden variables, as well as updates of π and h can be performed using summed area tables [9], and are thus considerably faster than most of the sophisticated sampling procedures used to train other topic models. An intriguing property of these models is that even on a 32×32 grid with 1024 microtopics π and just as many grouped topics h, there is no room for too many independent groups. With a window size 8×8, for example, we can place only 16 windows without overlap, and the remaining windows are overlapping the pieces of these 16. The ratio between grid and window size is referred to as the *capacity* of the model, and the training set size necessary to avoid overtraining the model only needs to be 1-2 orders of magnitude above the capacity number. Thus a grid of 1024 microtopics may very well be trainable with thousands of data points, rather than 100s of thousands that traditional topic models usually require for that many topics.

Raw image embedding using (C)CGs: In previous applications of CG models to computer vision, images were represented as spatially disordered bags of features. We experimented with embedding raw images with full spatial information preserved, and we present this here as we feel that the image data helps in illuminating the benefits of hierarchical learning. An image described by a full intensity function $I(x, y)$ could be considered as a set of words, each word being an image location $z = (x, y)$. For a $N \times M$ image, we have a vocabulary of size $M \cdot N$. The number of repetitions of word (x, y) is then set to be proportional to the intensity I(x,y). (In case of color images, the number of features is simply tripled with each color channel treated in this way). In other words, an unwrapped image

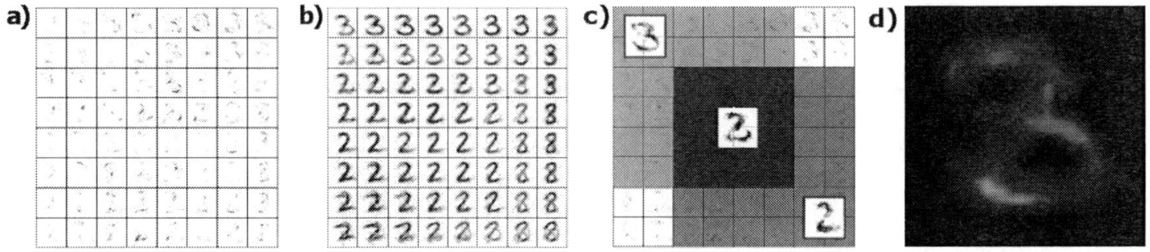

Figure 3: Intersecting digits on a grid of strokes. Each digit image is represented by counts (intensity) associated with image locations. **a)** π-distributions **b)** h-distributions **c-d)** Intersecting digits

is considered to be a word (location) histogram. π and h distributions can then also be seen as images, as they provide weights for different image locations. If we tile the image representations of these distributions we get additional insight into CGs as an embedding method. Fig. 3 shows a portion of a 48×48 grid trained on 2000 MNIST digits assuming a 6×6 window averaging. To illustrate the generative model, in c) we show the partial window sums for two overlapping windows over π. The green and blue areas form a window that generates a version of digit 3, which can be seen at the top left of this portion of the h grid (panel b)). The blue and red, on the other hand, combine into a window that represent a digit 2 at the position (3,3) in panel b). Partial sums for green, blue and red areas are shown in c) and these partial sums, color coded and overlapped are also illustrated in d). Careful observation of b) or the full grid in the appendix, demonstrates the slow deformation of digits from one to another in the h distributions. The appendix has additional examples of image dataset embedding, including rendered 3D head models and images of bold eagles retrieved by internet search. The CG π distributions shown here look like little strokes, while h distributions are full digits. The CCG model, on the other hand, combines multiple h distributions to represent a single image, and so h looks like a grid of strokes Fig. 4a, while π distributions are even sparser.

Hierarchical grids: By learning a model in which microtopics join forces with their neighbors to explain the data, (C-)CG models tend to exhibit high degrees of relatedness of nearby topics. As we slowly move away from one microtopic, the meaning of the topics we go over gradually shifts to related narrowly defined topics as illustrated by Fig. 1; this makes these grids attractive to HCI applications. But this also means that simple learning algorithms can be prone to local minima, as random initializations of the EM learning sometimes result in grouping certain related topics into large chunks, and sometime breaking these same chunks into multiple ones with more potential for suboptimal microtopics along boundaries. To illustrate this, in Fig. 4a we show a 48×48 grid of strokes h (Eq. 1) learned from 2000 MNIST digits using a CCG model assuming a 5×5 window averaging. Nearby features h are highly related to each other as they are the result of adding up features in overlapping windows over π (which is not shown). CCG is an admixture model, and so each digit indexed by t has a relatively rich posterior distribution θ^t over the locations in the grid that point to different strokes h. In Fig. 4, we show one of the main principal components of variation in θ as an image of the size of the grid. For three peaks there, we also show h-features at those locations. The combination of these three sparse features creates a longer contiguous stroke, which indicates that this longer stroke is often found in the data. Thus, the separation of these features across three distant parts of the map is likely a result of a local minimum in basic EM training. To transfer this reasoning to text models, consider the 5th cell in the first row in Fig. 1 with words HIV, AIDS, and the blue cell in the middle of the last column with words SELECTION, ADAPTIVE. The separation of these two things in faraway locations may very well be a result of a local minimum, which could be detected if location posteriors exhibit correlation. This illustration points to an idea on how to build better models. The distribution over locations ℓ that a data point t maps to (a posteriori) could be considered a new representation of the data point (digit in this case), with the mapped grid locations considered as features, and the posterior probabilities for these locations considered as feature counts. Thus another layer of a generative model can be added to generate the locations in the grid below, Fig. 2c-d. It is particularly useful to use another microtopic grid model as this added layer, because of the inherent relatedness of the nearby locations in the grid. The layer above can thus be either another admixture grid model (Componential Counting Grid - CCG), or a mixture (CG), and this layering can be continued to create a deep model. As CG is a mixture model, it terminates the layering: Its posterior distributions are peaky and thus uncorrelated. However, an arbitrary number of CCGs can be stacked on top of each other in this manner, terminating on top with a CG layer to form a hierarchical CG (HCG) model, or terminating in a CCG layer to form a hierarchical CCG (HCCG) model. In each layer, the pointers to features below are grouped, which should result in creating a contiguous longer stroke as discussed above in a grid cell that contains a combination of pointers to the lower layers.

For the sake of brevity, we only derive the HCG learning

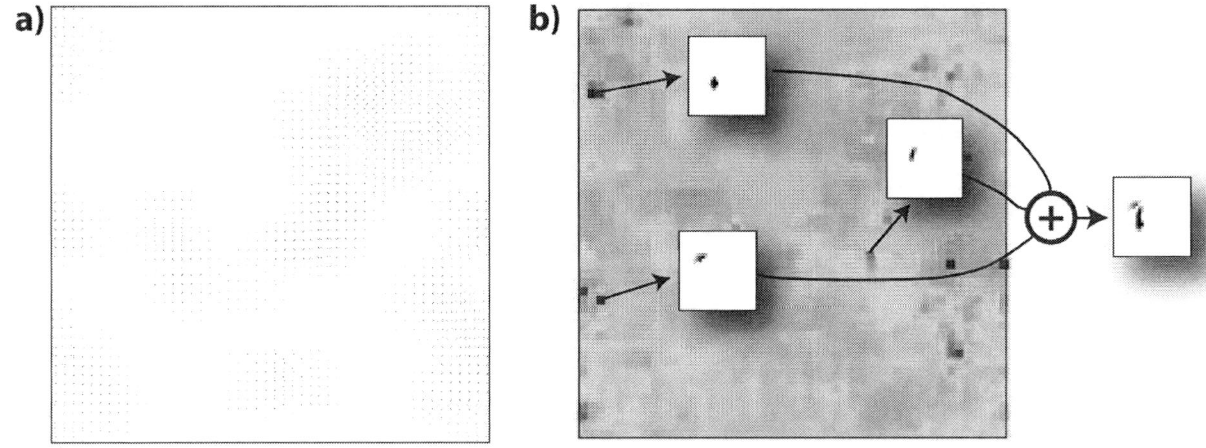

Figure 4: The benefits of hierarchical learning: **a)** h_{CCG} - a bigger higher resolution version in the appendix. **b)** Principal components of θ and three peaks put together.

algorithm with a single intermediate CCG layer. The extension to HCCG and higher order hierarchies is reported in the appendix. Variational inference and learning procedure for counting grid-based models utilizes cumulative sums and is only slower than training an individual (C)CG layer by a factor proportional to the number of layers. The graphical model for HCG is shown in Fig. 2c, where location variables pointing to grids in different layers have the same name, ℓ but carry a disambiguating superscript. *To avoid superscripts in the equations below, we renamed the CG's location variable from $\ell^{(1)}$ to m and dropped the superscript "$^{(2)}$" in the layer above.* The bottom CCG layer follows

$$P(w_n|k_n, \pi_{CCG}) = \pi_{CCG,k_n}(w_n) \tag{4}$$

$$P(k_n|\ell_n) = U^W_{\ell_n}(k_n) = \begin{cases} \frac{1}{|\mathbf{W}|} & \text{if } k_n \in \mathbf{W}_{\ell_n} \\ 0 & \text{Otherwise} \end{cases} \tag{5}$$

The latter is a pre-set distribution over the grid locations, uniform inside W_{ℓ_n}. Instead of the prior θ_ℓ the locations are generated from a top layer CG, indexed by m ($\ell^{(2)}$ in the figure),

$$P(\ell_n|m, \pi_{CG}) = \frac{1}{|\mathbf{W}|} \cdot \sum_{\mathbf{k} \in W_m} \pi_{CG,\mathbf{k}}(\ell_n) \tag{6}$$

This equation also shows that the lower-levels' grid locations act as observations in the higher level. We use the fully factorized variational posterior $q^t(\{k_n\}, \{\ell_n\}, m) = q^t(m) \cdot \prod_n \left(q^t(k_n) \cdot q^t(\ell_n)\right)$ to write the negative free energy $\mathcal{F}$ bounding the non-constant part of the loglikelihood of the data as

$$\begin{aligned} \mathcal{F} &= \sum_{t,n,k_n} q^t(k_n) \log \pi_{CCG,k_n}(w^t_n) \\ &+ \sum_{t,n,k_n,\ell_n} q^t(k_n) q^t(\ell_n) \log U^W_{\ell_n}(k_n) \\ &+ \sum_{t,m,\ell_n} q^t(m) q^t(\ell_n) \log \pi_{CG,m}(\ell_n) \\ &- \mathbb{H}(q(m, \{k_n\}, \{\ell_n\})) \end{aligned}$$

We maximize $\mathcal{F}$ with the EM algorithm which iterates E- and M-steps until convergence. E:

$$\begin{aligned} q^t(k_n = \mathbf{i}) &\propto \left(e^{\sum_{\ell_n} q^t(\ell_n) \log U^W_{\ell_n}(\mathbf{i})}\right) \cdot \pi_{CCG,\mathbf{i}}(w_n) \\ q^t(\ell_n = \mathbf{i}) &\propto \left(e^{\sum_{k_n} q^t(k_n) \log U^W_{\mathbf{i}}(k_n)}\right) \\ &\cdot \left(e^{\sum_m q^t(m) \log \pi_{CG,m}(\mathbf{i})}\right) \\ q^t(m = \mathbf{i}) &\propto e^{\sum_n \sum_{\ell_n} q^t(\ell_n) \cdot \log h_{CG,\mathbf{i}}(\ell_n)} \end{aligned}$$

The M step re-estimates the model parameters using these updatedposteriors:

$$\pi_{CCG,\mathbf{i}}(z) \propto \sum_t \sum_n q^t(k_n = \mathbf{i}) \cdot [w^t_n = z]$$

$$\pi_{CG,\mathbf{i}}(\mathbf{l}) \propto \hat{\pi}_{CG,\mathbf{i}}(\mathbf{l}) \cdot \sum_{t,n} q^t(\ell_n = \mathbf{l}) \cdot \sum_{\mathbf{k}|\mathbf{i} \in W_{\mathbf{k}}} \frac{q^t(k_n = \mathbf{i})}{\hat{h}_{CG,\mathbf{i}}(\mathbf{l})}$$

where the last (CG) update is performed analogous with [1]. Interestingly, training these hierarchical models stage by stage, reminiscent of deep models where such incremental learning was practically useful [10].
Although it has been shown that a deep neural network can be compressed into a shallow broader one through post training [11], the stacked (C-)CG models can be collapsed mathematically. In this sense we can view HCG and HCCG as *hierarchical learning algorithms* for CG and CCG, which are easier to visualize than deeper models. For example, for HCG in Fig. 2c-d, it is straightforward to see that the following grid defined over the original features $\{w_n\}$,

$$\pi_\ell(w_n) = \sum_{\mathbf{i}} \pi^{(1)}_{\cdot,\ell}(\mathbf{i}) \cdot h^{(2)}_{CCG,\mathbf{i}}(w_n) \tag{7}$$

can be used as a single layer grid that describes the same data distribution as the two-layer model[1]. However, the grids estimated from the hierarchical models should be more compact as the scattered groups of features are progressively merged in each new layer. *Learning in hierarchical models is thus more gradual and results in better*

[1] $h_{\mathbf{i}}$ are the grouped microtopics in the window $\mathbf{W}_{\mathbf{i}}$ - Eq. 1

local maxima, and we show below that the results are far superior to regular EM learning of the collapsed CG or CCG models.

3 EXPERIMENTS

In all the experiments we used models with two extra layers, although, in some experiments, we found that three levels worked slightly better. In general, the optimal number of layers will depend on the particular application.

Likelihood comparison: In the first experiment we compared the local maxima on models learned using the (full) MNIST data set. The two layer HCG model was first pretrained stage-wise as, e.g., [10], by training the higher level on the posterior distribution from the lower level as the input. Then, the model was refined by further variational EM training. The procedure is repeated 20 times with different random initializations to produce twenty hierarchical models. As discussed above, these models can be collapsed to a CG model by integrating out intermediate layers (7). These models were then compared with twenty models learned by directly learning CG models through previously published standard EM learning algorithm starting from twenty random initializations. Despite being collapsible to the same mathematical form, the HCG models consistently produced higher likelihood than the CG models directly learned using the standard method. *In fact, each CG model created by collapsing one of the learned HCG models had log likelihood at least two standard deviations above the highest log likelihood learned by basic EM (p-value $< 10^{-20}$).* Both learning approaches used the computation time equivalent to 1000 iterations of standard EM, which was more than enough for convergence.

Document classification: Next we ran test to see if the increased likelihood obtainable with a better learning algorithm translates into increased quality of representation when posterior distributions for individual text documents are considered as features in classification tasks. We considered the 20-newsgroup dataset[2] (20N) and the Mastercook dataset[3] (MC) composed by 4000 recipes divided in 15 classes. Previous work [12, 13] reduced 20-Newsgroup dataset into subsets with varying similarities and we considered the hardest subset composed by posts from the very similar newsgroups `comp.os.ms-windows`, `comp.windows.x` and `comp.graphics`. We considered the same complexities as in [2], using 10-fold cross validation and classified test document using maximum likelihood. Results for both datasets are shown in Tab. 1.

	CG	**HCG**	CCG	**HCCG**	linSVM
20N	82,3%	**83,5%**	83,4%	**85,0%**	77.5%
MC	38,7%	38,9%	76,2%	**78,9%**	71.3%

Table 1: Document classification. When bold, hierarchical grids outperformed the basic grids with statistical significance (HCG p-value =2.01e-4, HCCG p-values < 1e-3). "linSVM" stands for linear support vector machines which we reported as baseline.

Evaluation of microtopic quality using quantitative measures related to the use in visualization and indexing: We evaluated the coherence and the clarity of the microtopics comparing the collapsed (2 layers) hierarchical grids - HCG and HCCG with regular grids [1, 2], latent Dirichlet allocation (LDA) [7], the correlated topic model (CTM) [8] which allows to learn a large set of correlated topics and few non-parametric topic models [14, 15]. Generative models are often evaluated in terms of perplexity. However different models, even different learning algorithms applied to the same model, are very difficult to compare [16] and better perplexity does not always indicate better quality of topics as judged by human evaluators [17]. On the other hand, the subjective evaluation of topic quality is highly related to measures that have to do with data indexing, e.g. quality of word combinations when used for information retrieval. Thus we start with a novel evaluation procedure for topic models which is strongly related to information indexing and then show that we obtain similar evaluation results when we use human judgement. In the following experiments, we considered a corpus $\mathcal{D}$ composed of Science Magazine reports and scientific articles from the last 20 years. This is a very diverse corpus similar to the one used in [8]. As preprocessing step, we removed stop-words and applied the Porters' stemmer algorithm [18]. We considered grids of size $16 \times 16, 24 \times 24, 32 \times 32, 40 \times 40$ and 48×48 fixing the window size to 5×5. (Previous literature showed that counting grids are only sensitive to the ratio between grid and window area, as long as windows are sufficiently big.) We varied number of topics for LDA and CTM in $\{10, 15, \ldots, 100, 125, 150, \ldots, 1000\}$. For each complexity we trained 5 models starting with different random initializations and we averaged the results. In each repetition, we considered a random third of this corpus, for total of roughly $|\mathcal{D}| = 12K$ documents, $Z = 20K$ different words and more than $600K$ tokens.

To evaluate (micro)topics, we repetitively sampled k-tuples of words and checked for consistency, diversity and clarity of the indexed content. In the following, we describe the procedure used for evaluating grids. An equivalent procedure was used to evaluate other topic models for comparison.

To pick a tuple $\mathcal{T}$ of n words, we sampled a grid location $\hat{\ell}$. Then, we repetitively sampled the microtopic $\pi_{\hat{\ell}}$ to obtain the words in the tuple $\mathcal{T} = \{w_1, \ldots w_n\}$. We did not allow repetitions of words in the tuple. We considered 5000 dif-

[2] `http://www.cs.cmu.edu/afs/cs.cmu.edu/project/theo-20/www/data/news20.html`

[3] [2]

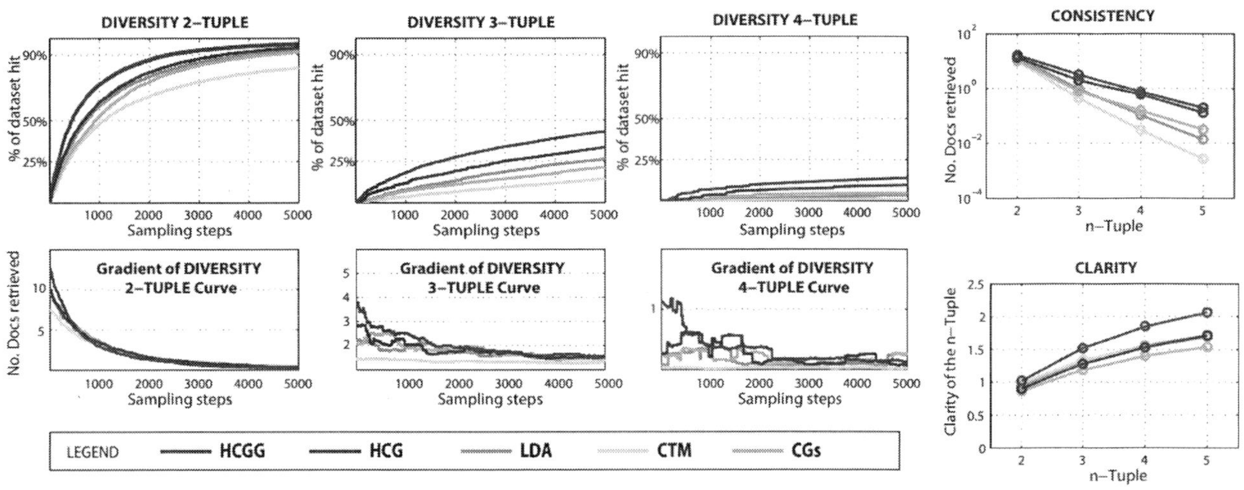

Figure 5: Microtopic evaluations. We compared 32×32 grids with the *best* result obtained by LDA and CTM. To avoid cluttering the graph, we did not report CCG results which were found inferior to the proposed hierarchical models. We also reported the gradient of the diversity curves to show that new samples steadily continue to contribute new tuples.

ferent $n = 2, 3, 4, 5$-tuples, not allowing repeated tuples. Then we checked for consistency, diversity and clarity of content indexed by each tuple. The **consistency** is quantified in terms of the average number of documents from the dataset that contained *all* words in $\mathcal{T}$. The **diversity** of indexed content is illustrated through the cumulative graph of acquired unique documents as more and more n-tuples are sampled and used to retrieve documents containing them. As this last curve depends on the sample order, we further repeated the process 5 times for a total of 25K different samples. Finally the **clarity** [19], measures the ambiguity of a query with respect to a collection of documents and it has been used to identify ineffective queries, on average, without relevance information.

Formally, the query clarity is measured as the entropy between the n-tuple and the language model $P(w)$ (unigram distributions) as $\sum_w P(w|T) \cdot \log_2 \frac{P(w|T)}{P(W)}$ where $P(w|T) = \sum_{d \in \mathcal{D}} P(w|\mathcal{D}) \cdot P(\mathcal{D}|T)$. We estimated the likelihood of an individual document model generating the tuple $P(T|\mathcal{D}) = \prod_{w_t \in T} P(w_t|\mathcal{D})$ and obtain $P(\mathcal{D}|T)$ using uniform prior probabilities for documents that contains a word in the tuple, and a zero prior for the rest. Finally, to estimate $P(w|T)$ we employed MonteCarlo sampling.

Results are illustrated in Fig.5 and should be appreciated by looking at all three measures together, as some can be over-optimized at the expense of others. The diversity curve that consistently grows as more tuples are sampled indicates that the sampled tuples belong to different subsets of the data, and are thus discriminative in segmenting the data into different clusters. The average tuple consistency, on the other hand, demonstrates that the sampled tuples do occur in large chunks of the data, demonstrating that the induced clusters are of significant size. The clarity measure shows that the clusters made of texts retrieved using different tuples have clear differentiation from the rest of the dataset in usage of all the words in the dictionary. We report results for the 32×32 grids and the best result of LDA and CTM which peaked respectively at 80 and 60 topics. Results for other grid sizes can be found in the additional material; they are stable across complexities with slightly better performances for larger grids.

All grid models show good consistency of words selected as they are optimized so that documents' words map into overlapping windows. Through positioning and intersection of many related documents the words end up being arranged in a fine-grained manner so as to reflect their higher-order co-occurrence statistics. Hierarchical learning greatly improved the results despite the fact that HCCG and HCG can be reduced to (C)CGs through marginalization (7).

Overall HCCG strongly outperformed all the methods, especially with a total gain of 0.5 bits on clarity, which is around third of the score for LDA/CTM. Despite allowing for correlated topics that enable CTM to learn larger topic models, CTM trails LDA in these graphs as topics were over expanded. We also considered non-parametric topic models such as "Dilan" [14] and the hierarchical Dirichlet process [15] but their best results were poor and we did not reported them in the figure. To get an idea, both models only indexed 25% of the content after 5000 2-Tuples samples and had a clarity lower of 0.7-1.2 bits than other topic models.

Human judgments of topic coherence: We next tested the quality of the inferred topics. Topic coherence is often measured based on co-occurrence of the top $k = 10$ words per topic. While good as a quick sanity check of a

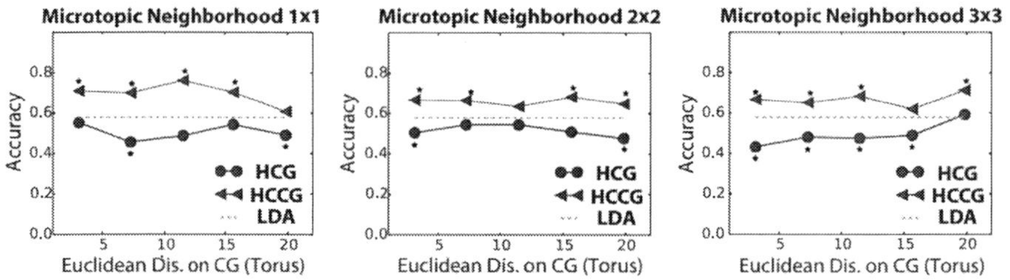

Figure 6: Result of word intrusion task. Statistical significance is denoted by *. *p-values and further details on the test are reported in the appendix*

single learned model, when this measure is used to compare models, it will favor models that lock onto top themes and distribute the rest of the words in the tails of the topic distributions. The LDA models usually have a large drop off in topic coherence when the number of topics is increased to force the model to address more correlations in the data. Indeed, using this measure, LDA topics outperform CG topics in case of small models. But as the number of topics grows, the microtopics trained by HCG significantly outperform both LDA and CG (see the appendix). A more interesting measure of topic quality, which not only depends on individual topic coherence but also on meaningful separation of different topics, requires human evaluation of *word intrusions*. In a word intrusion task [17], six randomly ordered words are presented to a human subject who then guesses which word is an outlier. In the original procedure a target topic is randomly selected and then the five words with *highest* probability are picked. Then, an intruder is added to this set. It is selected at random from the low probability words of the target topic that have high probability in some other topic. Finally the six words are shuffled and presented to the subject. If the target topic shows a lack of coherence or distinction from the intruding topic, the subject will often fail to correctly identify the intruder. This task is again geared towards only getting the top words right in a topic model and ignoring the rest of the distribution, which makes it unsuitable to comparison with microtopic models which attempt to extract much more correlation from the data. Thus instead of picking the top words from each topic, we sampled the words from the target topic to create the in-group. After sampling the location of a microtopic from the grid $\hat{\ell}$, we picked three randomly chosen words from $\pi_{\hat{\ell}}$ or from the small groups of microtopics in the window of size 2×2, and 3×3 around $\hat{\ell}$ (The latter is equivalent to computing the window distributions h using windows of smaller size than the ones used in training and should give us the indication if the granularity assumed in the window size was exaggerated: If it is then averaging of nearby topics should significantly reduce the noise due to forced topic splitting). For each of these groups we choose the intruder word using the standard procedure. If in this harder task humans can identify intruders better for microtopic models than for LDA models, this would indicate that the microtopics are not simply random subsamples of broader topics captured in h and similar in entropy to LDA topics. They would be a meaningful breakup of broad topics into finer ones. We compared LDA (known to performed better than CTM on intrusion tasks [17]), HCG, and HCCG, on randomly crawled 10K Wikipedia articles and used Amazon Mechanical Turk (24000 completed tasks from 345 different people). The trained grids were of size 32×32 and the windows 5×5. The optimal LDA size was chosen using likelihood cross-validation over the range of complexities as in the previous experiments (The peak performance there was at 80 topics). Results are shown in Fig.6 as a function of the Euclidean distance on the grid of the intruder word from the topic. HCCG outperformed LDA (p-values for the 3 tasks 1.20e-11, 1.88e-5, 2.97e-05) and HCG (p-values for the 3 tasks 3.97e-18, 1.01e-11, 3.14e-19) indicating that learning microtopics is possible with a good algorithm. Overall, *users were able to solve correctly 71% of HCCG problems and only 58% of LDA problems.* Interestingly, the performance of HCCG and HCG does not seem to depend on the distance of the intruder word: Even picking intruder word from a very close location rather than from a far away one lead to no additional confusion for the user. This shows that HCCG chops up the data into meaningful microtopics which are then combined into a large number of groups h that do not over broaden the scope. HCCG and HCG also outperformed respectively CG and CCG (see the appendix).

Learning to separate mixed digits. Finally, we show that an HCCG model can be used to perform a task that eludes most unsupervised *and* supervised models. We created a set of 10000 28×28 images, each containing two different MNIST digits overlapped, Fig. 7. We trained an HCCG model consisting of five 32×32 layers on this data stagewise by feeding $L^t(\ell) = \sum_n q^t(\ell_n = \ell)$ from one layer to the next. Windows of size 5×5 were used in all layers. From layer to layer, the new representations of the image consist of growing combinations of low level features h from the bottom layer (sparseness of which is similar to Fig. 4a). The hierarchical grouping is further encouraged by simply smoothing $L^t(\ell)$ with a 5×5 Gaussian kernel with deviation of 0.75, before feeding it to the next layer (This is motivated by the fact that nearby features in h are related and so if two distant locations should be grouped, so should those locations' neighbors). Once the model is

a)
b)

Figure 7: Unsupervised learning on mixed digits

collapsed to a single HCCG grid the components no longer look like short strokes but like whole digits, mostly free of overlap: The model has learned to approximately separate the images into constitutive digits. Reasoning on overlapping digits even eludes deep neural networks trained in a supervised manner, but here we did not use the information about which two digits are present in each of the training images.

4 CONCLUSIONS

We show that with new learning algorithms based on a hierarchy of CCG models, possibly terminated on the top with a CG, it is possible to learn large grids of sparse related microtopics from relatively small datasets. These microtopics correspond to intersections of multiple documents, and are considerably narrower than what traditional topic models can achieve without overtraining on the same data. Yet, these microtopics are well formed, as both the numerical measures of consistency, diversity and clarity and the user study on 345 mechanical turkers show. Another approach to capturing sparse intersections of broader topics is through product of expert models, e.g. RBMs [20], which consist of relatively broad topics but model the data through intersections rather than admixing. RBMs are also often stacked into deep structures. In future work it would be interesting to compare these models, though the tasks we used here would have to be somewhat changed to focus on the intersection modeling, rather than the topic coherence (as this is not what RBM topics are optimized for). HCCG and HCG models have a clear advantage in that it is easy to visualize how the data is represented, which is useful both to end users in HCI applications, and to machine learning experts during model development and debugging. Another parallel between the stacks of CCGs and other deep models is that the uniform connectivity of units is directly enforced through window constraints, rather than encouraged by dropout. Finally, in this specific context we illustrate a broader phenomenon that requires more methodical and broader treatment by the machine learning community. A more complex (deeper) model showed here large advantages in terms of training likelihood, but these advantages were *not* due to the expanded parameter space, because the resulting model is equivalent to a collapsed single layer model. Rather than being a reflection of increased representational abilities of the model, better likelihoods were thus the result of better fitting algorithm that consists of training a deep model (and then collapsing it into a simpler but equivalent parameterization). Similar phenomena are likely regularly encountered elsewhere in machine learning, but not always recognized as such, as in the absence of the full knowledge of the extrema of the fitting criterion, an increase in performance is often inappropriately ascribed to better modeling rather than better model fitting.

References

[1] Jojic, N., Perina, A.: Multidimensional counting grids: Inferring word order from disordered bags of words. In: Proceedings of conference on Uncertainty in artificial intelligence (UAI). (2011) 547–556

[2] Perina, A., Jojic, N., Bicego, M., Truski, A.: Documents as multiple overlapping windows into grids of counts. In Burges, C., Bottou, L., Welling, M., Ghahramani, Z., Weinberger, K., eds.: Advances in Neural Information Processing Systems 26. Curran Associates, Inc. (2013) 10–18

[3] Perina, A., Kim, D., Truski, A., Jojic, N.: Skim-reading thousands of documents in one minute: Data indexing and visualization for multifarious search. In: Workshop on Interactive Data Exploration and Analytics (IDEA'14) at KDD. (2014)

[4] Matt J. Kusner, Yu Sun, N.I.K.K.Q.W.: From word embeddings to document distances. In: Proceedings of the International Conference on Machine Learning. (2015)

[5] Hoffman, M., Blei, D.: Structured stochastic variational inference. CoRR **abs/1404.4114** (2014)

[6] Yi, X., Allan, J.: A comparative study of utilizing topic models for information retrieval. In: Proceedings of the 31th European Conference on IR Research on Advances in Information Retrieval. ECIR '09, Berlin, Heidelberg, Springer-Verlag (2009) 29–41

[7] Blei, D., Ng, A., Jordan, M.: Latent dirichlet allocation. Journal of machine Learning Research **3** (2003) 993–1022

[8] Blei, D.M., Lafferty, J.D.: Correlated topic models. In: NIPS. (2005)

[9] Crow, F.C.: Summed-area tables for texture mapping. In: Proceedings of the 11th Annual Conference on Computer Graphics and Interactive Techniques. SIGGRAPH '84, New York, NY, USA, ACM (1984) 207–212

[10] Hinton, G., Osinero, S.: A fast learning algorithm for deep belief nets. Neural Computation **18** (2006)

[11] Ba, L.J., Caurana, R.: Do deep nets really need to be deep? CoRR **abs/1312.6184** (2013)

[12] Banerjee, A., Basu, S.: Topic models over text streams: a study of batch and online unsupervised learning. In: In Proc. 7th SIAM Intl. Conf. on Data Mining. (2007)

[13] Reisinger, J., Waters, A., Silverthorn, B., Mooney, R.J.: Spherical topic models. In: ICML '10: Proceedings of the 27th international conference on Machine learning. (2010)

[14] Paisley, J., Wang, C., Blei, D.M.: The discrete infinite logistic normal distribution. Bayesian Analysis **7** (2012) 997–1034

[15] Teh, Y.W., Jordan, M.I., Beal, M.J., Blei, D.M.: Hierarchical dirichlet processes. Journal of the American Statistical Association **101** (2004)

[16] Asuncion, A., Welling, M., Smyth, P., Teh, Y.W.: On smoothing and inference for topic models. In: In Proceedings of Uncertainty in Artificial Intelligence. (2009)

[17] Chang, J., Boyd-Graber, J.L., Gerrish, S., Wang, C., Blei, D.M.: Reading tea leaves: How humans interpret topic models. In: NIPS. (2009)

[18] Porter, M.F.: Readings in information retrieval. Morgan Kaufmann Publishers Inc., San Francisco, CA, USA (1997) 313–316

[19] Cronen-Townsend, S., Croft, W.B.: Quantifying query ambiguity. In: Proceedings of the Second International Conference on Human Language Technology Research. HLT '02, San Francisco, CA, USA, Morgan Kaufmann Publishers Inc. (2002) 104–109

[20] Salakhutdinov, R., Hinton, G.: Replicated softmax: an undirected topic model. In: In Advances in Neural Information Processing Systems, NIPS. (2009)

Active Uncertainty Calibration in Bayesian ODE Solvers

Hans Kersting and Philipp Hennig
Max-Planck-Institute for Intelligent Systems
Spemannstraße, 72076 Tübingen, Germany
[hkersting|phennig]@tue.mpg.de

Abstract

There is resurging interest, in statistics and machine learning, in solvers for ordinary differential equations (ODEs) that return probability measures instead of point estimates. Recently, Conrad et al. introduced a sampling-based class of methods that are 'well-calibrated' in a specific sense. But the computational cost of these methods is significantly above that of classic methods. On the other hand, Schober et al. pointed out a precise connection between classic Runge-Kutta ODE solvers and Gaussian filters, which gives only a rough probabilistic calibration, but at negligible cost overhead. By formulating the solution of ODEs as approximate inference in linear Gaussian SDEs, we investigate a range of probabilistic ODE solvers, that bridge the trade-off between computational cost and probabilistic calibration, and identify the inaccurate gradient measurement as the crucial source of uncertainty. We propose the novel filtering-based method Bayesian Quadrature filtering (BQF) which uses Bayesian quadrature to actively learn the imprecision in the gradient measurement by collecting multiple gradient evaluations.

1 INTRODUCTION

The numerical solution of an initial value problem (IVP) based on an *ordinary differential equation* (ODE)

$$u^{(n)} = f(t, u(t), u'(t), \dots, u^{(n-1)}(t)),\ u(0) = u_0 \in \mathbb{R}^D \tag{1}$$

of order $n \in \mathbb{N}$, with $u : \mathbb{R} \to \mathbb{R}^D$, $f : [0,T] \times \mathbb{R}^{nD} \to \mathbb{R}^D$, $T > 0$, is an essential topic of numerical mathematics, because ODEs are the standard model for dynamical systems. Solving ODEs with initial values is an exceedingly well-studied problem (see Hairer et al., 1987, for a comprehensive presentation) and modern solvers are designed very efficiently. Usually, the original ODE (1) of order n is reduced to a system of n ODEs of first order

$$u'(t) = f(t, u(t)),\ u(0) = u_0 \in \mathbb{R}^D, \tag{2}$$

which are solved individually. The most popular solvers in practice are based on some form of Runge-Kutta (RK) method (as first introduced in Runge (1895) and Kutta (1901)) which employ a weighted sum of a fixed amount of gradients in order to iteratively extrapolate a discretized solution. That is, these methods iteratively collect 'observations' of approximate gradients of the solved ODE, by evaluating the dynamics f at an estimated solution, which is a linear combination of previously collected 'observations':

$$y_i = f\left(t_i, u_0 + \sum_{j<i} w_{ij} y_j\right). \tag{3}$$

The weights of s-stage RK methods of p-th order are carefully chosen so that the numerical approximation $\hat{u}$ and the Taylor series of the true solution u coincide up to the p-th term, thereby yielding a local truncation error of high order, $\|u(t_0 + h) - \hat{u}(t_0 + h)\| = \mathcal{O}(h^{p+1})$, for $h \to 0$. One can prove that $s \geq p$ in general, but for $p \leq 4$ there are RK methods with $p = s$. Hence, allowing for more function evaluations can drastically improve the speed of convergence to the true solution.

The polynomial convergence is impressive and helpful; but it does not actually quantify the true epistemic uncertainty about the accuracy of the approximate solution $\hat{u}$ for a concrete non-vanishing step-size h. One reason one may be concerned about this in machine learning is that ODEs are often one link of a chain of algorithms performing some statistical analysis. When employing classic ODE solvers and just plugging in the solution of the numerical methods in subsequent steps, the resulting uncertainty of the whole computation is ill-founded, resulting in overconfidence in a possibly wrong solution. It is thus desirable to model the epistemic uncertainty. Probability theory provides the framework to do so. Meaningful probability measures of the uncertainty about the result of deterministic computations (such as ODE solvers) can then be combined with probability measures modeling other sources of uncertainty, including 'real' aleatoric randomness (from e.g. sampling). Apart from quantifying our certainty over a computation, pinning down the main sources of uncertainty could furthermore improve the numerical solution and facilitate a more efficient allocation of the limited computational budget.

A closed framework to measure uncertainty over numerical computations was proposed by Skilling (1991) who pointed out that numerical methods can be recast as statistical inference of the latent true solution based on the observable results of tractable computations. Applying this idea to ordinary differential equations, Hennig & Hauberg (2014) phrased this notion more formally, as Gaussian process (GP) regression. Their algorithm class, however, could not guarantee the high polynomial convergence orders of Runge-Kutta methods. In parallel development, Chkrebtii et al. (2013) also introduced a probabilistic ODE solver of similar structure (i.e. based on a GP model), but using a Monte Carlo updating scheme. These authors showed a linear convergence rate of their solver, but again not the high-order convergence of classic solvers.
Recently, Schober et al. (2014) solved this problem by finding prior covariance functions which produce GP ODE solvers whose posterior means *exactly* match those of the optimal Runge-Kutta families of first, second and third order. While producing only a slight computational overhead compared to classic Runge-Kutta, this algorithm — as any GP-based algorithm — only returns Gaussian measures over the solution space.
In contrast, Conrad et al. (2015) recently provided a novel sampling-based class of ODE solvers which returns asymptotically non-parametric measures over the solution space, but creates significant computational overhead by running the whole classic ODE solvers multiple times over the whole time interval $[0, T]$ in order to obtain meaningful approximations for the desired non-parametric measure.
For practitioners, there is a trade-off between the desire for quantified uncertainty on the one hand, and low computational cost on the other. The currently available probabilistic solvers for ODEs either provide only a roughly calibrated uncertainty (Schober et al., 2014) at negligible overhead or a more fine-grained uncertainty supported by theoretical analysis (Conrad et al., 2015), at a computational cost increase so high that it rules out most practical applications. In an attempt to remedy this problem, we propose an algorithm enhancing the method of Schober et al. (2014) by improving the gradient measurement using modern probabilistic integration methods. By modeling the uncertainty where it arises, i.e. the imprecise prediction of where to evaluate f, we hope to gain better knowledge of the propagated uncertainty and arrive at well-calibrated posterior variances as uncertainty measures.

2 BACKGROUND

2.1 SAMPLING-BASED ODE SOLVERS

The probabilistic ODE solver by Conrad et al. (2015) modifies a classic deterministic one-step numerical integrator Ψ_h (e.g. Runge-Kutta or Taylor methods, cf. Hairer et al. (1987)) and models the discretization error of Ψ_h by adding suitably scaled i.i.d. Gaussian random variables $\{\xi_k\}_{k=0,\dots,K}$ after every step. Hence, it returns a discrete solution $\{U_k\}_{k=0,\dots,K}$ on a mesh $\{t_k = kh\}_{k=0,\dots,K}$ according to the rule

$$U_{k+1} = \Psi_h(U_k) + \xi_k. \quad (4)$$

This discrete solution can be extended into a continuous time approximation of the ODE, which is random by construction and can therefore be interpreted as a draw from a non-parametric probability measure Q_h on the solution space $C([0,T],\mathbb{R}^n)$, the Banach space of continuous functions. This probability measure can then be interpreted as a notion of epistemic uncertainty about the solution. This is correct in so far as, under suitable assumptions, including a bound on the variance of the Gaussian noise, the method converges to the true solution, in the sense that Q_h contracts to the Dirac measure on the true solution δ_u with the *same* convergence rate as the original numerical integrator Ψ_h, for $h \to 0$. This is a significant step towards a well-founded notion of uncertainty calibration for ODE solvers: It provides a probabilistic extension to classic method which does not break the convergence rate of these methods.

In practice, however, the precise shape of Q_h is *not* known and Q_h can only be interrogated by sampling, i.e. repeatedly running the entire probabilistic solver. After S samples, Q_h can be approximated by an empirical measure $Q_h(S)$. In particular, the estimated solution and uncertainty can only be expressed in terms of statistics of $Q_h(S)$, e.g. by the usual choices of the empirical mean and empirical variance respectively or alternatively by confidence intervals. For $S \to \infty$, $Q_h(S)$ converges in distribution to Q_h which again converges in distribution to δ_u for $h \to 0$:

$$Q_h(S) \overset{S\to\infty}{\to} Q_h \overset{h\to 0}{\to} \delta_u. \quad (5)$$

The theoretical analysis in Conrad et al. (2015) only concerns the convergence of the latent probability measures $\{Q_h\}_{h>0}$. Only the empirical measures $\{Q_h(S)\}_{S\in\mathbb{N}}$, however, can be observed. Consequently, it remains unclear whether the empirical mean of $Q_h(S)$ for a fixed stepsize $h > 0$ converges to the true solution as $S \to \infty$ and whether the empirical variance of $Q_h(S)$ is directly related, in an analytical sense, to the approximation error. In order to extend the given convergence results to the practically observable measures $\{Q_h(S)\}_{S\in\mathbb{N}}$ an analysis of the first convergence in (5) remains missing. The deterministic algorithm proposed below avoids this problem, by instead constructing a (locally parametric) measure from prior assumptions.

The computational cost of this method also seems to mainly depend on the rate of convergence of $Q_h(S) \to Q_h$ which determines how many (possibly expensive) runs of the numerical integrator Ψ_h over $[0, T]$ have to be computed and how many samples have to be stored for a sufficient approximation of Q_h. Furthermore, we expect that in practice the mean of Q_h, as approximated by $Q_h(S)$ might not be the best possible approximation, since in one step the random perturbation of the predicted solution by Gaussian noise ξ_k worsens our solution estimate with a probability of more than $1/2$, since - due to the full support of Gaussian distributions - the numerical sample solution is as likely to be perturbed away from as towards the true solution and - due to the tails of Gaussian distributions - it can also be perturbed way past the true solution with positive probability.

2.2 A FRAMEWORK FOR GAUSSIAN FILTERING FOR ODES

Describing the solution of ODEs as inference in a joint Gaussian model leverages state-space structure to achieve efficient inference. Therefore, we employ a Gauss-Markov prior on the state-space: *A priori* we model the solution function and $(q-1)$ derivatives $(u, \dot{u}, u^{(2)}, \dots, u^{(q-1)}) : [0, T] \to \mathbb{R}^{qD}$ as a draw from a q-times integrated Wiener process $X = (X_t)_{t\in[0,T]} = (X_t^{(1)}, \dots, X_t^{(q)})^T_{t\in[0,T]}$, i.e. the dynamics of X_t are given by the linear Itô stochastic differential equation (Karatzas & Shreve, 1991; Øksendal, 2003):

$$dX_t = F \cdot X_t dt + Q \cdot dW_t, \tag{6}$$

$$X_0 = \xi, \quad \xi \sim \mathcal{N}(m(0), P(0)), \tag{7}$$

with constant drift $F \in \mathbb{R}^{q\times q}$ and diffusion $Q \in \mathbb{R}^q$ given by

$$F = \begin{pmatrix} 0 & f_1 & 0 & \dots & 0 \\ 0 & 0 & f_2 & \dots & 0 \\ \vdots & & \ddots & \ddots & \vdots \\ 0 & & \dots & 0 & f_{q-1} \\ 0 & & \dots & 0 & 0 \end{pmatrix}, Q = \begin{pmatrix} 0 \\ 0 \\ \vdots \\ 0 \\ \sigma^2 \end{pmatrix} \tag{8}$$

for all $t \in [0, T]$ and some $f_1, \dots, f_{q-1} \in \mathbb{R}$, where W_t denotes a q-dimensional Wiener process ($q \geq n$). Hence, we are a priori expecting that $u^{(q)}$ behaves like a Brownian motion with variance σ^2 and that $u^{(i)}$ is modeled by $(q-1-i)$-times integrating this Brownian motion. The fact that the $(i+1)$-th component is the derivative of the i-th component in our state space is captured by a drift matrix with non-zero entries only on the first off-diagonal. The entries $f_1, \dots, f_{q-1}$ are damping factors. A standard choice is e.g. $f_i = i$. Without additional information, it seems natural to put white noise on the q-th derivative as the first derivative which is not captured in the state space. This gives rise to Brownian noise on the $(q-1)$-th derivative which is encoded in the diffusion matrix scaled by variance σ^2. Hence, we consider the integrated Wiener process a natural prior. For notational simplicity, only the case of scalar-valued functions, i.e. $D = 1$, is presented in the following. The framework can be extended to $D \geq 2$ in a straightforward way by modeling the output dimensions of f as independent stochastic processes.

Since X is the strong solution of a linear equation (6) with normally distributed initial value X_0, it follows from the theory of linear SDEs (Karatzas & Shreve, 1991) that X is a uniquely-determined Gauss-Markov process. This enables Bayesian inference in a highly efficient way by Gaussian filtering (Saatci, 2011)). For time invariant linear SDEs like (6), the fixed matrices for Gaussian filtering can be precomputed analytically (Särkkä, 2006).

In addition, Schober et al. (2014) showed that for $q \leq 3$ inference in this linear SDE yields Runge-Kutta steps.

Equipped with this advantageous prior we can perform Bayesian inference. The linearity and time-invariance of the underlying SDE permits to formulate the computation of the posterior as a Kalman filter (KF) (cf. (Särkkä, 2013) for a comprehensive introduction) with step size $h > 0$. The prediction step of the KF is given by

$$m^-_{t+h} = A(h)m_t, \tag{9}$$

$$P^-_{t+h} = A(h)P_t A(h)^T + Q(h), \tag{10}$$

with matrices $A(h), Q(h) \in \mathbb{R}^{q\times q}$ with entries

$$A(h)_{i,j} = \exp(h \cdot F)_{i,j} = \chi_{j\geq i} \frac{h^{j-i}}{(j-i)!} \left(\prod_{k=0}^{j-i-1} f_{i+k} \right), \tag{11}$$

$$Q(h)_{i,j} = \sigma^2 \cdot \left(\prod_{k_1=0}^{q-1+i} f_{i+k_1} \right) \cdot \left(\prod_{k_2=0}^{q-1+j} f_{j+k_2} \right) \cdot \tag{12}$$

$$\frac{h^{2q+1-i-j}}{(q-i)!(q-j)!(2q+1-i-j)}, \tag{13}$$

and followed by the update step

$$z = y - Hm^-_{t+h}, \tag{14}$$

$$S = HP^-_{t+h}H^T + R, \tag{15}$$

$$K = P^-_{t+h}H^T S^{-1}, \tag{16}$$

$$m_{t+h} = m^-_{t+h} + Kz, \tag{17}$$

$$P_{t+h} = P^-_{t+h} - KHP^-_{t+h}, \tag{18}$$

where $H = e_n^T \in \mathbb{R}^{1\times q}$ is the n-th unit vector.

Between the prediction and update step the n-th derivative of the true solution $\frac{\partial^n u}{\partial x^n}$ at time $t+h$ as a measurement for the n-th derivative and the noise of this measurement are estimated by the variable y and R. In order to derive precise values of y and R from the Gaussian prediction $\mathcal{N}(m_{t+h}, P_{t+h})$, we would have to compute the integrals

$$y = \int f(t+h, m_{t+h}^- + x) \cdot \mathcal{N}(x; 0, P_{t+h}^-)dx \qquad (19)$$

and

$$R = \int f(t+h, m_{t+h}^- + x) \cdot f(t+h, m_{t+h}^- + x)^T \cdot \mathcal{N}(x; 0, P_{t+h}^-)dx - yy^T, \qquad (20)$$

which are intractable for most choices of f. Below we investigate different ways to address the challenge of computing these integrals precisely while not creating too much computational overhead.

2.3 MEASUREMENT GENERATION OPTIONS FOR GAUSSIAN FILTERING

Schober et al. (2014) as, to the best of our knowledge, the first ones to point out the connection between Gaussian filtering and probabilistic ODE solvers, presents an algorithm which simply evaluates the gradient at the predicted mean, which is equivalent to setting y to be equal to its maximum likelihood estimator:

$$y = f(t+h, m_{t+h}^-),\ R = 0. \qquad (21)$$

While ensuring maximum speed, this is clearly not an ideal measurement. In our atomless predicted probability measure $\mathcal{N}(m_{t+h}^-, P_{t+h}^-)$ the mean predictor m_{t+h}^- is different from its true value $(u^{(0)}(t+h), \ldots, u^{(n)}(t+h))^T$ almost surely. Hence, for a non-constant f the estimate will be inaccurate most of the times. In particular this method deals poorly with 'skewed' gradient fields (a problem that leads to a phenomenon known as 'Lady Windermeres fan' (Hairer et al., 1987)). To get a better estimate of the true value of y, more evaluations of f seem necessary.

Therefore, we want to find numerical integration methods which capture y and R with sufficient precision, while using a minimal number of evaluations of f. Possible choices are:

(i) *Monte Carlo integration by sampling*:

$$y = \frac{1}{N}\sum_{i=1}^{N} f(t+h, x_i), \qquad (22)$$

$$R = \frac{1}{N}\sum_{i=1}^{N} f(t+h, x_i) \cdot f(t+h, x_i)^T - y \cdot y^T, \qquad (23)$$

$$x_i \sim \mathcal{N}(m_{t+h}^-, P_{t+h}^-), \qquad (24)$$

(which is *not* the same as the sampling over the whole time axis in (Conrad et al., 2015)).

(ii) *Approximation by a first-order Taylor series expansion:*

$$f(t+h, m_{t+h}^- + x) \simeq f(t+h, m_{t+h}^-) + \nabla f(t+h, m_{t+h}^- + x) \cdot x \qquad (25)$$

and thereby deriving moments of the linear transform of Gaussian distributions:

$$y = f(t+h, m_{t+h}^-), \qquad (26)$$

$$R = \nabla f(t+h, m_{t+h}^-) P_{t+h}^- \nabla f(t+h, m_{t+h}^-)^T. \qquad (27)$$

(iii) Integration by *Bayesian quadrature* with Gaussian weight function:

$$y = \alpha^T \cdot K^{-1} \cdot (f(x_1), \ldots, f(x_n))^T, \qquad (28)$$

$$R = \int\int k(x, x')w(x)w(x')dxdx' - \alpha^T K^{-1} \alpha. \qquad (29)$$

with $w(x) = \mathcal{N}(x; m_{t+h}^-, P_{t+h}^-)$, kernel matrix $K \in \mathbb{R}^{N\times N}$ with $K_{i,j} = k(x_i, x_j)$ and $\alpha = (\alpha(1), \ldots, \alpha(N))^T \in \mathbb{R}^N$ with $\alpha(i) = \int k(x, x_i)w(x)dx$ for a predefined covariance function k and evaluation points $(x_i)_{i=1,\ldots,N}$ (cf. section 2.4).

Our experiments, presented in Section 3, suggest that BQ is the most useful option.

Monte Carlo integration by sampling behaves poorly if the trajectory of the numerical solution passes through domain areas (as e.g. in the spikes of oscillators governed by non-stiff ODEs) where f takes highly volatile values since the random spread of samples from the domain are likely to return a skewed spread of values resulting in bad predictions of y with huge uncertainty R. Hence, the posterior variance explodes and the mean drifts back to its zero prior mean, i.e. $m_t \to 0$ and $\|P_t\| \to \infty$, for $t \to \infty$. Thus, we consider this method practically useless.

One may consider it a serious downside of Taylor-approximation based methods that the gradient only approximates the shape of f and thereby its mapping of the error on an 'infinitesimally small neighborhood' of m_{t+h}^-. Hence, it might ignore the true value of y completely, if the mean prediction is far off. However, for a highly regular f (e.g. Lipschitz-continuous in the space variable) this gradient approximation is very good.

Moreover, the approximation by a first-order Taylor series expansion needs an approximation of the gradient, which explicit ODE solvers usually do not receive as an input. However, in many numerical algorithms (e.g. optimization) the gradient is provided anyway. Therefore the gradient might already be known in real-world applications. While we find this method promising when the gradient is known or can be efficiently computed, we exclude it from our experiments because the necessity of a gradient estimate breaks the usual framework of ODE solvers.

In contrast, Bayesian quadrature avoids the risk of a skewed distortion of the samples for Monte Carlo integration by actively spreading a grid of deterministic sigma-points. It does not need the gradient of f and still can encode prior knowledge over f by the choice of the covariance function if more is known (Briol et al., 2015). The potential of using Bayesian quadrature as a part of a filter was further explored by Prüher & Simandl (2015), however in the less structured setting of nonlinear filtering where additional inaccuracy from the linear approximation in the prediction step arises. Moreover, Särkkä et al. (2015) recently pointed out that GPQ can be seen as sigma-point methods and gave covariance functions and evaluation points which reproduce numerical integration methods known for their favorable behavior (for example Gauss-Hermite quadrature, which is used for a Gaussian weight function).

Due to these advantages, we propose a new class of BQ-based probabilistic ODE filters named BQ Filtering.

2.4 BAYESIAN QUADRATURE FILTERING (BQF)

The crucial source of error for filtering-based ODE solvers is the calculation of the gradient measurement y and its variance R (c.f. Section 2.2). We propose the novel approach to use BQ to account for the uncertainty of the input and thereby estimate y and R. This gives rise a novel class of filtering-based solvers named *BQ Filter* (BQF). As a filtering-based method, one BQF-step consists of the KF prediction step (9) – (10), the calculation of y and R by BQ and the KF update step (14) – (18).

The KF prediction step outputs a Gaussian belief $\mathcal{N}(m^-_{t+h}, P^-_{t+h})$ over the true solution $u(t+h)$. This input value is propagated through f yielding a distribution over the gradient at time $t+h$. In other words, our belief over $\nabla f(t+h, u(t+h))$ is equal to the distribution of $Y := f(t, X)$, with uncertain input $X \sim \mathcal{N}(m^-_{t+h}, P^-_{t+h})$. For general f the distribution of Y will be neither Gaussian nor unimodal (as e.g. in Figure 1). But it is possible to compute the moments of this distribution under Gaussian assumptions on the input and the uncertainty over f (see for example Deisenroth (2009)). The equivalent formulation of prediction under uncertainty clarifies as numerical integration clarifies the connection to sigma-point methods, i.e. quadrature rules (Särkkä et al., 2015). Quadrature is as extensively studied and well-understood as the solution of ODEs. A basic overview can be found in Press et al. (2007). Marginalizing over X yields an integral with Gaussian weight function

$$\mathbb{E}[Y] = \int f(t+h, x) \cdot \underbrace{\mathcal{N}(x; m^-_{t+h}, P^-_{t+h})}_{=:w(x)}\, dx, \qquad (30)$$

which is classically solved by quadrature, i.e. evaluating f at a number of evaluation points $(x_i)_{i=1,\dots,N}$ and calculating a weighted sum of these evaluations. BQ can be interpreted as a probabilistic extension of these quadrature rules in the sense that their posterior mean estimate of the integral coincides with classic quadrature rules, while adding a posterior variance estimate at low cost (Särkkä et al., 2015).

By choosing a kernel k over the input space of f and evaluation points $(x_i)_{i=1,\dots,N}$, the function f is approximated by a GP regression (Rasmussen & Williams, 2006) with respect to the function evaluations $(f(x_i))_{i=1,\dots,N}$, yielding a GP posterior over f with mean m_f and covariance k_f denoted by $\mathcal{GP}(f)$. The integral is then approximated by integrating the GP approximation, yielding the predictive distribution for $\mathcal{I}[f]$:

$$\mathcal{I}[f] \sim \int \mathcal{GP}(f)(x) \cdot \mathcal{N}(x; m^-_{t+h}, P^-_{t+h}) dx. \qquad (31)$$

The uncertainty arising from the probability measure over the input is now split up in two parts: the uncertainty over the input value $x \sim \mathcal{N}(0, I)$ and the uncertainty over the precise value at this uncertain input, which can only be approximately inferred by its covariance with the evaluation points $(x_i)_{i=1,\dots,N}$, i.e. by $\mathcal{GP}(f)$. These two kinds of uncertainty are depicted in Figure 1. From the predictive distribution in (31), we can now compute a posterior mean and variance of $\mathcal{I}[f]$ which results in a weighted sum for the mean

$$y := \mathbb{E}[\mathcal{I}[f]]] = \alpha^T K^{-1} \left(f(x_1), \dots, f(x_n)\right)^T \qquad (32)$$

with

$$\alpha(i) = \int k(x, x_i) \mathcal{N}(x; 0, I) dx \qquad (33)$$

and variance

$$R := \mathrm{Var}[\mathcal{I}(f)] \qquad (34)$$

$$= \int\int k(x, x')w(x)w(x')dxdx' - \alpha^T K^{-1} \alpha, \qquad (35)$$

where $K \in \mathbb{R}^{N\times N}$ denotes the kernel matrix, i.e. $K_{i,j} = k(x_i, x_j)$.

The measurement generation in BQF is hence completely defined by the two free choices of BQ: the kernel k and the evaluation points $(x_i)_{i=1,\dots,n}$. By these choices, BQ and thereby the measurement generation in BQF is completely defined. For the squared exponential kernel (Rasmussen & Williams, 2006)

$$k(x, x') = \theta^2 \exp\left(-\frac{1}{2\lambda^2}\|x - x'\|^2\right), \qquad (36)$$

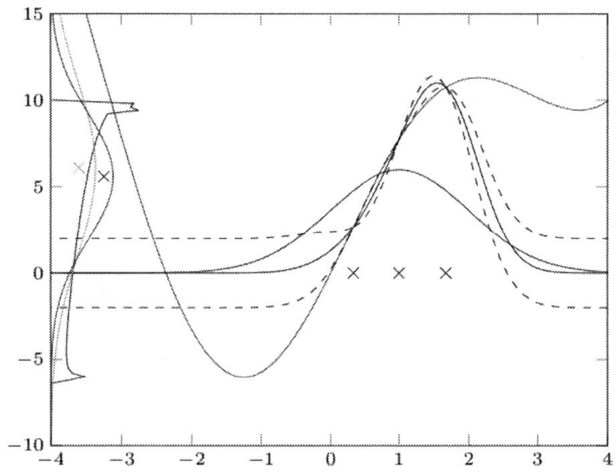

Figure 1: Prediction of function $f(x) = 8\sin(x) + x^2$ (red) under uncertain input $x \sim \mathcal{N}(x; 1, 1)$ (density in blue). $\mathcal{GP}(f)$ (black) derived from Gaussian grid evaluation points with $N = 3$ (blue crosses) as mean ± 2 standard deviation. True distribution of prediction in blue. Gaussian fit to true distribution in yellow and predicted distribution by BQ in green with crosses at means.

with lengthscale $\lambda > 0$ and output variance $\theta^2 > 0$, it turns out that y and R can be computed in closed form and that many classic quadrature methods which are known for their favorable properties can be computed in closed form (Särkkä et al., 2015), significantly speeding up computations. For the scalar case $nD = 1$, we obtain for (33) by straightforward computations:

$$\alpha(i) = \frac{\lambda\theta^2}{\sqrt{\lambda^2 + \sigma^2}} \exp\left(-\frac{(x_i - \mu)^2}{2(\lambda^2 + \sigma^2)}\right), \tag{37}$$

and

$$\int\int k(x, x')w(x)w(x')dxdx' = \frac{\theta^2}{\sqrt{1 + 2\sigma^2/\lambda^2}} \tag{38}$$

Hence, our BQ estimate for y is given by the sigma-point rule

$$y \approx \sum_{i=1}^{N} W_i f(t + h, x_i) \tag{39}$$

with easily computable weights

$$W_i = [\alpha \cdot K]_i. \tag{40}$$

Also the variance R takes a convenient shape

$$R = \frac{\theta^2}{\sqrt{1 + 2\sigma^2/\lambda^2}} - \alpha^T K^{-1} \alpha. \tag{41}$$

For $nD > 1$, we get slightly more complicated formulas which are given in Deisenroth (2009).

The other free choice in BQ, the evaluation points $(x_i)_{i=1,\dots,n}$, can also be chosen freely in every step of BQF. Usually, the nodes of BQ chosen are chosen so that the variance of the integral estimate is minimized (cf. Briol et al. (2015)). For this algorithm, the uncertainty has to be measured, not minimized though. Hence, we propose just to take a uniform grid scaled by $\mathcal{N}(m^-_{t+h}, P^-_{t+h})$ to measure the uncertainty in a comprehensive way.

Another promising choice is given by the roots of the physicists' version of the Hermite polynomials, since they yield Gauss-Hermite quadrature (GHQ), the standard numerical quadrature against Gaussian measures, as a posterior mean for a suitable covariance function (Särkkä et al., 2015). For GHQ, efficient algorithms to compute the roots and the weights are readily available (Press et al., 2007).

2.5 COMPUTATIONAL COST

All of the presented algorithms buy their probabilistic extension to classic ODE solvers by adding computational cost, sometimes more sometimes less. In most cases, evaluation of the dynamic function f forms the computational bottleneck, so we will focus on it here. Of course, the internal computations of the solver adds cost as well. Since all the models discussed here have linear inference cost, though, this additional overhead is manageable.
The ML-algorithm by Schober et al. (2014) is the fastest algorithm. By simply recasting a Runge-Kutta step as Gaussian filtering, rough probabilistic uncertainty is achieved with negligible computational overhead.
For the sampling method, the calculation of one individual sample of Q_h amounts to running the entire underlying ODE solver once, hence the overall cost is S times the original cost.
In contrast, the BQ-algorithm only has to run through $[0, T]$ once, but has to invert a $ND \times ND$ covariance matrix to perform Bayesian quadrature with N evaluation points. Usually, N will be small, since BQ performs well for a relatively small number of function evaluations (as e.g. illustrated by the experiments below). However, if the output dimension D is very large, Bayesian quadrature—like all quadrature methods—is not practical. BQ thus tends to be faster for small D, while MC tends to be faster for large D.

When considering these computational overheads, there is a nuanced point to be made about the value-to-cost trade-off of constructing a posterior uncertainty measure. If a classic numerical solver of order p is allotted a budget of M times its original one, it can use it to reduce its step-size by a factor of M, and thus reduce its approximation error by an order M^p. It may thus seem pointless to invest even such a linear cost increase into constructing an uncertainty measure around the classic estimate. But, in some practical settings, it may be more helpful to have a notion of uncertainty on a slightly less precise estimate than to produce a more precise estimate without a notion of error. In addition, classic solvers are by nature sequential algorithms, while the probabilistic extensions (both the sampling-based and Gaussian-filtering based ones) can be easily parallelized. Where parallel hardware is available, the effective time cost of probabilistic functionality may thus be quite limited (although we do not investigate this possibility in our present experiments).

With regards to memory requirements, the MC-method needs significantly more storage, since it requires saving all sample paths, in order to statistically approximate the entire non-parametric measure Q_h on $C([0,T],\mathbb{R})$. The BQ-algorithm only has to save the posterior GP, i.e. a mean and a covariance function, which is arguably the minimal amount to provide a notion of uncertainty. If MC reduces the approximation of Q_h to its mean and variance, it only requires this minimal storage as well.

3 EXPERIMENTS

This section explores applications of the probabilistic ODE solvers discussed in Section 2. The sampling-based algorithm by (Conrad et al., 2015) will be abbreviated as MC, the maximum-likelihood Gaussian filter ((Schober et al., 2014)) as ML and our novel BQ-based filter (BQF) as BQ. In particular, we assess how the performance of the purely deterministic class of Gaussian filtering based solvers compares to the inherently random class of sampling-based solvers.

We experiment on the Van der Pol oscillator (Hairer et al., 1987), a non-conservative oscillator with non-linear damping, which is a standard example for a non-stiff dynamical system. It is governed by the equation

$$\frac{\partial^2 u}{\partial t^2} = \mu(1-u^2)\frac{\partial u}{\partial t} - u, \qquad (42)$$

where the parameter $\mu \in \mathbb{R}$ indicates the non-linearity and the strength of the damping. We set $\mu = 5$ on a time axis $[10, 60]$, with initial values $(u(10), \dot{u}(10)) = (2, 10)$.

All compared methods use a model of order $q = 3$, and a step size $h = 0.01$. This induces a state-space model given by a twice-integrated Wiener process prior (cf. (6)) which yields a version of ML close to second-order Runge-Kutta (Schober et al., 2014). The same solver is used as the underlying numerical solver Ψ_h in MC. For the noise parameter, which scales the deviation of the evaluation point of f from the numerical extrapolation (i.e. the variance of the driving Wiener process for ML and BQ, and the variance of ξ_k for MC), we choose $\sigma^2 = 0.1$. The drift matrix F of the underlying integrated Wiener process is set to the default values $f_i = i$ for $i = 1, \dots, q-1$. The covariance function used in BQ is the widely popular squared exponential (36), with lengthscale $\lambda = 1$ and output variance $\theta^2 = 1$. (Since all methods use the same model, this tuning does not favor one algorithm over the other. In practice all these parameters should of course be set by statistical estimation.).

For a fair comparison in all experiments, we allow MC and BQ to make the same amount of function evaluations per time step. If MC draws N samples, BQ uses N evaluation points. The first experiment presents the solutions of the presented algorithms on the van der Pol oscillator (42) on the whole time axis in one plot, when we allow BQ and MC to make five function evaluations. Then, we examine more closely how the error of each methods changes as a function of the number of evaluations of f in Figure 3 and Figure 4.

3.1 SOLUTION MEASURES ON VAN DER POL OSCILLATOR

Figure 3 shows the solution estimates constructed by the three solvers across the time domain. In all cases, the mean estimates roughly follow the true solution (which e.g. Gaussian filtering with Monte Carlo integration by sampling (22) – (24) does not achieve). A fundamental difference between the filtering-based methods (ML and BQ) and the sampling-based MC algorithm is evident in both the mean and the uncertainty estimate.

While the filtering-based methods output a trajectory quite similar to the true solution with a small time lag, the MC algorithm produces a trajectory of a more varying shape. Characteristic points of the MC mean estimate (such as local extrema) are placed further away from the true value than for filtering-based methods.

The uncertainty estimation of MC appears more flexible as well. ML and BQ produce an uncertainty estimate which runs parallel to the mean estimate and appears to be strictly increasing. It appears to increase slightly in every step, resulting in an uncertainty estimate, which only changes very slowly. The solver accordingly appears overconfident in the spikes and underconfident in the valleys of the trajectory. The uncertainty of MC varies more, scaling up at the steep parts of the oscillator and decreasing again at the flat parts, which is a desirable feature.

Among the class of filtering-based solvers, the more refined BQ method outputs a better mean estimate with more confidence than ML.

3.2 QUALITY OF ESTIMATE AS A FUNCTION OF ALLOWED EVALUATIONS

Figure 3 and Figure 4 depict the value of the error of the mean approximation as a function of the allowed function evaluations N (i.e. N evaluation points for BQ and N samples for MC) at time points $t_1 = 18$ and $t_2 = 54$. Since the desired solution measure Q_h for MC can only be statistically approximated by the N samples, the mean estimate of MC is random. For comparison, the average of five MC-

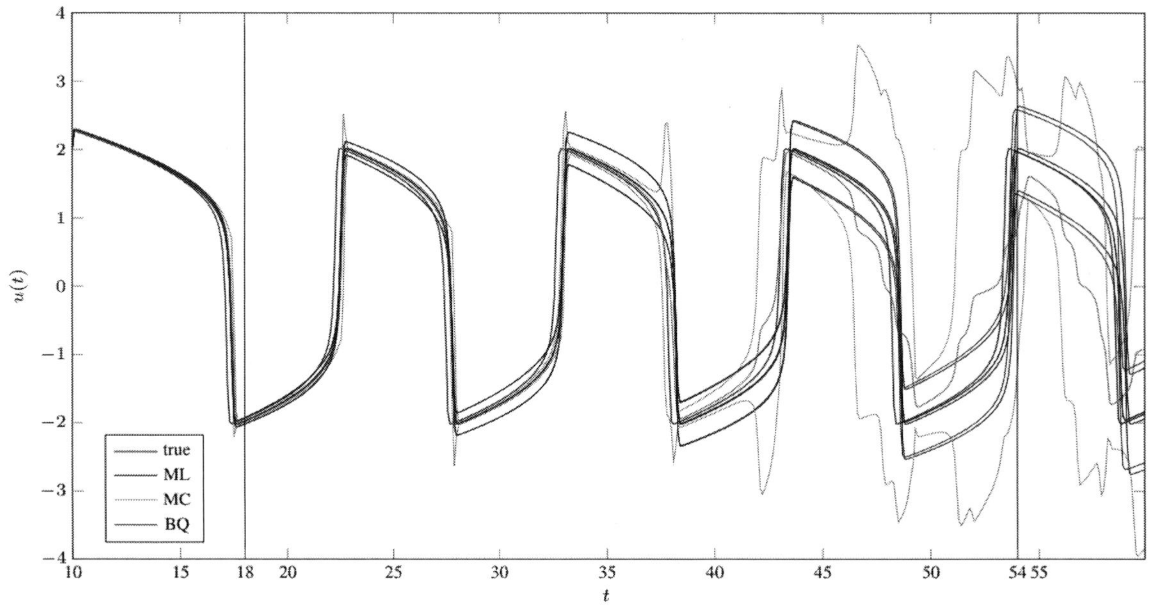

Figure 2: Solution estimates constructed on the Van der Pol oscillator (42). True solution in red. Mean estimates of ML, MC and BQ in black, green, blue, respectively. Uncertainty measures (drawn at two times standard deviation) as thin lines of the same color.

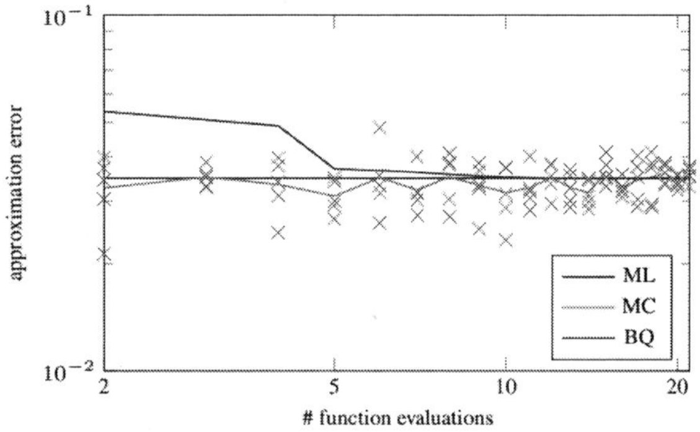

Figure 3: Plot of errors of the mean estimates at $t = 18$ of the methods MC (green) and BQ (blue) as a function of the allowed function evaluations. Maximum likelihood error in black. Single runs of the probabilistic MC solver as green crosses. Average over all runs as green line.

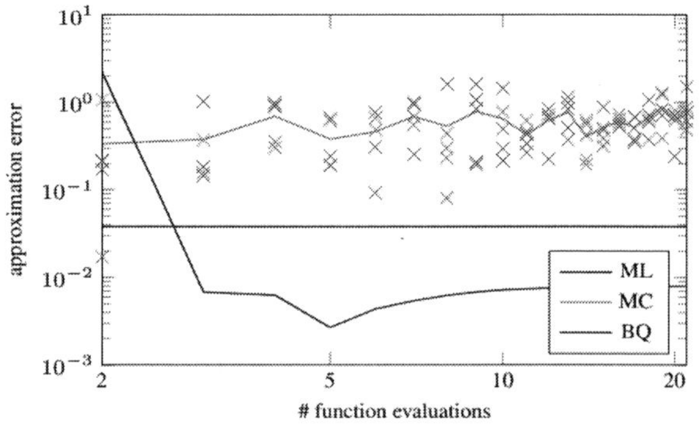

Figure 4: Plot of errors of the mean estimates at $t = 54$ of the methods MC (green) and BQ (blue) as a function of the allowed function evaluations. Maximum likelihood error in black. Single runs of the probabilistic MC solver as green crosses. Average over all runs as green line.

runs is computed.

At the early time point $t_1 = 18$, all trajectories are still close together and the methods perform roughly the same, as we allow more evaluations. There is a slight improvement for BQ with more evaluations, but the error remains above the one of ML error.

At the later time $t_2 = 54$, BQ improves drastically when at least five evaluations are allowed, dropping much below the ML error.

The average error by MC appears to be not affected by the number of samples. The ML error is constant, because it always evaluates only once.

4 DISCUSSION

The conducted experiments provide an interesting basis to discuss the differences between filtering-based methods (ML and BQ) and the sampling-based MC algorithm. We make the following observations:

(i) *Additional samples do not improve the random mean estimate of MC in expectation:*
Since the samples of MC are independent and identically distributed, the expectation of the random mean estimate of MC is the same, regardless of the amounts of samples. This property is reflected in Figure 3 and Figure 4, by the constant green line (up to random fluctuation). Additional samples are therefore only useful to improve the uncertainty calibration.

(ii) *The uncertainty calibration of MC appears more adaptive than of ML and BQ:*
Figure 3 suggests that MC captures the uncertainty more flexibly: It appropriately scales up in the steep parts of the oscillator, while expressing high confidence in the flat parts of the oscillator. The true trajectory is inside the interval between mean $\pm$ 2 standard deviations, which is not the case for BQ and ML. Moreover, MC produces a more versatile measure. The filtering-based methods appear to produce a strictly increasing uncertainty measure by adding to the posterior uncertainty in every step. MC avoids this problem by sampling multiple time over the whole time interval. We deem the resulting flexibility a highly desirable feature. BQ also outputs a meaningful uncertainty measure and we expect that adding Bayesian smoothing (Särkkä, 2013) would enable filtering-based methods to produce more adaptive measures as well.

(iii) *The expected error of MC-samples (and their mean) is higher than the error of ML:*
In the experiments, MC produced a higher error for the mean estimate, compared to both ML and BQ. We expect that this happens on all dynamical systems *by construction*: Given U_k, the next value U_{k+1} of a MC-sample is calculated by adding Gaussian noise ψ_k to the ML-extrapolation starting in U_k (cf. equation (4)). Due to the symmetry and full support of Gaussian distributions, the perturbed solution has a higher error than the unperturbed prediction, which coincides with the ML solution. Hence, every MC-sample accumulates with every step a positive expected error increment compared to the ML estimate. By the linearity of the average, the mean over all samples inherits the same higher error than the ML mean (and thereby also than the error of the more refined BQ mean).

Summing up, we argue that — at their current state — filtering-based methods appear to produce a 'better' mean estimate, while sampling-based methods produce in some sense a 'better' uncertainty estimate. Many applications might put emphasis on a good mean estimate, while needing a still well-calibrated uncertainty quantification. Our method BQF provides a way of combining a precise mean estimate with a meaningful uncertainty calibration. Sampling-based methods might not be able to provide this due to their less accurate mean estimate. For future work (which is beyond the scope of this paper), it could be possible to combine the advantages of both approaches in a unified method.

5 CONCLUSION

We have presented theory and methods for the probabilistic solution of ODEs which provide uncertainty measures over the solution of the ODE, contrasting the classes of (deterministic) filtering-based and (random) sampling-based solvers. We have provided a theoretical framework for Gaussian filtering as state space inference in linear Gaussian SDEs, highlighting the prediction of the gradient as the primary source of uncertainty. Of all investigated approximations of the gradient, Bayesian Quadrature (BQ) produces the best results, by actively learning the shape of the dynamic function f through deterministic evaluations. Hence, we propose a novel filtering-based method named *Bayesian Quadrature Filtering* (BQF), which employs BQ for the gradient measurement.

For the same amount of allowed gradient evaluations, the mean estimate of BQF appears to outperform the mean estimate of state-of-the-art sampling-based solvers on the Van der Pol oscillator, while outputting a better calibrated uncertainty than other filtering-based methods.

References

Briol, F-X., Oates, C. J., Girolami, M., Osborne, M. A., and Sejdinovic, D. Probabilistic integration: A role for statisticians in numerical analysis? *arXiv:1512.00933 [stat.ML]*, December 2015.

Chkrebtii, O., Campbell, D.A., Girolami, M.A., and Calderhead, B. Bayesian Uncertainty Quantification for Differential Equations. *arXiv prePrint 1306.2365*, 2013.

Conrad, P.R., Girolami, M., Särkkä, S., Stuart, A.M., and Zygalakis, K.C. Probability measures for numerical solution of differential equations. *arXiv:1506.04592 [stat.ME]*, June 2015.

Deisenroth, M.P. *Efficient Reinforcement Learning Using Gaussian Processes*. PhD thesis, Karlsruhe Institute of Technology, 2009.

Hairer, E., Nørsett, S.P., and Wanner, G. *Solving Ordinary Differential Equations I – Nonstiff Problems*. Springer, 1987.

Hennig, P. and Hauberg, S. Probabilistic Solutions to Differential Equations and their Application to Riemannian Statistics. In *Proc. of the 17th int. Conf. on Artificial Intelligence and Statistics (AISTATS)*, volume 33. JMLR, W&CP, 2014.

Karatzas, I. and Shreve, S.E. *Brownian Motion and Stochastic Calculus*. Springer, 1991.

Kutta, W. Beitrag zur näherungsweisen Integration totaler Differentialgleichungen. *Zeitschrift für Mathematik und Physik*, 46:435–453, 1901.

Øksendal, B. *Stochastic Differential Equations: An Introduction with Applications*. Springer, 6 edition, 2003.

Press, W.H., Teukolsky, S.A., Vetterling, W.T., and Flannery, B.P. *Numerical Recipes 3rd Edition: The Art of Scientific Computing*. Cambridge University Press, New York, NY, USA, 3 edition, 2007. ISBN 0521880688, 9780521880688.

Prüher, J. and Simandl, M. Bayesian quadrature in nonlinear filtering. In *Informatics in Control, Automation and Robotics (ICINCO), 2015 12th International Conference on*, volume 01, pp. 380–387, 2015.

Rasmussen, C.E. and Williams, C.K.I. *Gaussian Processes for Machine Learning*. MIT, 2006.

Runge, C. Über die numerische Auflösung von Differentialgleichungen. *Mathematische Annalen*, 46:167–178, 1895.

Saatci, Y. *Scalable Inference for Structured Gaussian Process Models*. PhD thesis, University of Cambridge, 2011.

Särkkä, S. *Recursive Bayesian Inference on Stochastic Differential Equations*. PhD thesis, Helsinki University of Technology, 2006.

Särkkä, S. *Bayesian filtering and smoothing*. Cambridge University Press, 2013.

Särkkä, S., Hartikainen, J., Svensson, L., and Sandblom, F. On the relation between gaussian process quadratures and sigma-point methods. *arXiv:1504.05994 [stat.ME]*, April 2015.

Schober, M., Duvenaud, D., and Hennig, P. Probabilistic ODE Solvers with Runge-Kutta Means. *Advances in Neural Information Processing Systems (NIPS)*, 2014.

Skilling, J. Bayesian solution of ordinary differential equations. *Maximum Entropy and Bayesian Methods, Seattle*, 1991.

Faster Stochastic Variational Inference using Proximal-Gradient Methods with General Divergence Functions

Mohammad Emtiyaz Khan
Ecole Polytechnique Fédérale de Lausanne
Lausanne Switzerland
emtiyaz@gmail.com

Reza Babanezhad
University of British Columbia
Vancouver, Canada
babanezhad@gmail.com

Wu Lin
University of Waterloo
Waterloo, Canada
wu.lin@uwaterloo.ca

Mark Schmidt
University of British Columbia
Vancouver, Canada
schmidtm@cs.ubc.ca

Masashi Sugiyama
University of Tokyo
Tokyo, Japan
sugi@k.u-tokyo.ac.jp

Abstract

Several recent works have explored stochastic gradient methods for variational inference that exploit the geometry of the variational-parameter space. However, the theoretical properties of these methods are not well-understood and these methods typically only apply to conditionally-conjugate models. We present a new stochastic method for variational inference which exploits the geometry of the variational-parameter space and also yields simple closed-form updates even for non-conjugate models. We also give a convergence-rate analysis of our method and many other previous methods which exploit the geometry of the space. Our analysis generalizes existing convergence results for stochastic mirror-descent on non-convex objectives by using a more general class of divergence functions. Beyond giving a theoretical justification for a variety of recent methods, our experiments show that new algorithms derived in this framework lead to state of the art results on a variety of problems. Further, due to its generality, we expect that our theoretical analysis could also apply to other applications.

1 INTRODUCTION

Variational inference methods are one of the most widely-used computational tools to deal with the intractability of Bayesian inference, while stochastic gradient (SG) methods are one of the most widely-used tools for solving optimization problems on huge datasets. The last three years have seen an explosion of work exploring SG methods for variational inference (Hoffman et al., 2013; Salimans et al., 2013; Ranganath et al., 2013; Titsias & Lázaro-Gredilla, 2014; Mnih & Gregor, 2014; Kucukelbir et al., 2014). In many settings, these methods can yield simple updates and scale to huge datasets.

A challenge that has been addressed in many of the recent works on this topic is that the "black-box" SG method ignores the geometry of the variational-parameter space. This has lead to methods like the stochastic variational inference (SVI) method of Hoffman et al. (2013), that uses *natural gradients* to exploit the geometry. This leads to better performance in practice, but this approach only applies to conditionally-conjugate models. In addition, it is not clear how using natural gradients for variational inference affects the theoretical convergence rate of SG methods.

In this work we consider a general framework that (i) can be stochastic to allow huge datasets, (ii) can exploit the geometry of the variational-parameter space to improve performance, and (iii) can yield a closed-form update even for non-conjugate models. The new framework can be viewed as a stochastic generalization of the proximal-gradient method of Khan et al. (2015), which splits the objective into conjugate and non-conjugate terms. By linearizing the non-conjugate terms, this previous method as well as our new method yield simple closed-form proximal-gradient updates even for non-conjugate models.

While proximal-gradient methods have been well-studied in the optimization community (Beck & Teboulle, 2009), like SVI there is nothing known about the convergence rate of the method of Khan et al. (2015) because it uses "divergence" functions which do not satisfy standard assumptions. Our second contribution is to *analyze the convergence rate* of the proposed method. In particular, we generalize an existing result on the convergence rate of stochastic mirror descent in non-convex settings (Ghadimi et al., 2014) to allow a general class of divergence functions that includes the cases above (in both deterministic and stochastic settings). While it has been observed empirically that including an appropriate divergence function enables larger steps than basic SG methods, this work gives the first theoretical result justifying the use of these more-general divergence functions. It in particular reveals how different factors affect the convergence rate such as the Lipschitz-continuity of the lower bound, the information geometry of the divergence functions, and the variance of the stochastic approximation. Our results also suggest conditions under which the proximal-gradient steps of Khan et al. (2015) can make more progress than (non-split) gradient steps, and sheds light on the choice of step-size for these methods. A notable aspect of our results is that, for the stochastic case and a fixed accuracy, there is always a sufficiently-small *fixed* step-size that leads to a solution with this accuracy or higher. Our experimental results indicate that the new method leads to improvements in performance on a variety of problems, and we note that the algorithm and theory might be useful beyond the variational inference scenarios we have considered in this work.

2 VARIATIONAL INFERENCE

Consider a general latent variable model where we have a data vector $\mathbf{y}$ of length N and a latent vector $\mathbf{z}$ of length D. In Bayesian inference, we are interested in computing the marginal likelihood $p(\mathbf{y})$, which can be written as the integral of the joint distribution $p(\mathbf{y}, \mathbf{z})$ over all values of $\mathbf{z}$. This integral is often intractable, and in variational inference we typically approximate it with the evidence lower-bound optimization (ELBO) approximation $\underline{\mathcal{L}}$. This approximation introduces a distribution $q(\mathbf{z}|\boldsymbol{\lambda})$ and chooses the variational parameters $\boldsymbol{\lambda}$ to maximize the following lower bound on the marginal likelihood:

$$\begin{aligned} \log p(\mathbf{y}) &= \log \int q(\mathbf{z}|\boldsymbol{\lambda}) \frac{p(\mathbf{y}, \mathbf{z})}{q(\mathbf{z}|\boldsymbol{\lambda})} d\mathbf{z}, \\ &\geq \max_{\boldsymbol{\lambda} \in \mathcal{S}} \underline{\mathcal{L}}(\boldsymbol{\lambda}) := \mathbb{E}_{q(\mathbf{z}|\boldsymbol{\lambda})} \left[\log \frac{p(\mathbf{y}, \mathbf{z})}{q(\mathbf{z}|\boldsymbol{\lambda})} \right]. \end{aligned} \tag{1}$$

The inequality follows from concavity of the logarithm function. The set $\mathcal{S}$ is the set of valid parameters $\boldsymbol{\lambda}$.

To optimize $\boldsymbol{\lambda}$, one of the seemingly-simplest approaches is gradient descent: $\boldsymbol{\lambda}_{k+1} = \boldsymbol{\lambda}_k + \beta_k \nabla \underline{\mathcal{L}}(\boldsymbol{\lambda}_k)$, which can be viewed as optimizing a quadratic approximation of $\underline{\mathcal{L}}$,

$$\boldsymbol{\lambda}_{k+1} = \underset{\boldsymbol{\lambda} \in \mathcal{S}}{\operatorname{argmin}} \left[-\boldsymbol{\lambda}^T \nabla \underline{\mathcal{L}}(\boldsymbol{\lambda}_k) + \frac{1}{2\beta_k} \|\boldsymbol{\lambda} - \boldsymbol{\lambda}_k\|_2^2 \right]. \tag{2}$$

While we can often choose the family q so that it has convenient computational properties, it might be impractical to apply gradient descent in this context when we have a very large dataset or when some terms in the lower bound are intractable. Recently, SG methods have been proposed to deal with these issues (Ranganath et al., 2013; Titsias & Lázaro-Gredilla, 2014): they allow large datasets by using random subsets (mini-batches) and can approximate intractable integrals using Monte Carlo methods that draw samples from $q(\mathbf{z}|\boldsymbol{\lambda})$.

A second drawback of applying gradient descent to variational inference is that it uses the Euclidean distance and thus ignores the *geometry of the variational-parameter space*, which often results in slow convergence. Intuitively, (2) implies that we should move in the direction of the gradient, but not move $\boldsymbol{\lambda}_{k+1}$ too far away from $\boldsymbol{\lambda}_k$ in terms of the Euclidean distance. However, the Euclidean distance is not appropriate for variational inference because $\boldsymbol{\lambda}$ is the parameter vector of a distribution; the Euclidean distance is often a poor measure of dissimilarity between distributions. The following example from Hoffman et al. (2013) illustrates this point: the two normal distributions $\mathcal{N}(0, 10000)$ and $\mathcal{N}(10, 10000)$ are almost indistinguishable, yet the Euclidean distance between their parameter vectors is 10, whereas the distributions $\mathcal{N}(0, 0.01)$ and $\mathcal{N}(0.1, 0.01)$ barely overlap, but their Euclidean distance between parameters is only 0.1.

Natural-Gradient Methods: The canonical way to address the problem above is by replacing the Euclidean distance in (2) with another divergence function. For example, the *natural gradient* method defines the iteration by using the symmetric Kullback-Leibler (KL) divergence (Hoffman et al., 2013; Pascanu & Bengio, 2013; Amari, 1998),

$$\begin{aligned} &\boldsymbol{\lambda}_{k+1} = \\ &\underset{\boldsymbol{\lambda} \in \mathcal{S}}{\operatorname{argmin}} \left[-\boldsymbol{\lambda}^T \nabla \underline{\mathcal{L}}(\boldsymbol{\lambda}_k) + \frac{1}{\beta_k} \mathbb{D}_{KL}^{sym}[q(\mathbf{z}|\boldsymbol{\lambda}) \,\|\, q(\mathbf{z}|\boldsymbol{\lambda}_k)] \right]. \end{aligned} \tag{3}$$

This leads to the update

$$\boldsymbol{\lambda}_{k+1} = \boldsymbol{\lambda}_k + \beta_k \left[\nabla^2 \mathbf{G}(\boldsymbol{\lambda}_k) \right]^{-1} \nabla \underline{\mathcal{L}}(\boldsymbol{\lambda}_k), \tag{4}$$

where $\mathbf{G}(\boldsymbol{\lambda})$ is the Fisher information-matrix,

$$\mathbf{G}(\boldsymbol{\lambda}) := \mathbb{E}_{q(\mathbf{z}|\boldsymbol{\lambda})} \left\{ [\nabla \log q(\mathbf{z}|\boldsymbol{\lambda})] [\nabla \log q(\mathbf{z}|\boldsymbol{\lambda})]^T \right\}.$$

Hoffman et al. (2013) show that the natural-gradient update can be computationally simpler than gradient descent for conditionally-conjugate exponential family models. In this family, we assume that the distribution of $\mathbf{z}$ factorizes as $\prod_i p(\mathbf{z}^i|\mathrm{pa}^i)$ where $\mathbf{z}^i$ are disjoint subsets of $\mathbf{z}$ and pa^i are the parents of the $\mathbf{z}^i$ in a directed acyclic graph. This family also assumes that each conditional distribution is in the exponential family,

$$p(\mathbf{z}^i|\mathrm{pa}^i) := h^i(\mathbf{z}^i) \exp\left[[\boldsymbol{\eta}^i(\mathrm{pa}^i)]^T \mathbf{T}^i(\mathbf{z}^i) - A^i(\boldsymbol{\eta}^i) \right],$$

where $\boldsymbol{\eta}^i$ are the natural parameters, $\mathbf{T}^i(\mathbf{z}^i)$ are the sufficient statistics, $A^i(\boldsymbol{\eta}^i)$ is the partition function, and $h^i(\mathbf{z}^i)$ is the base measure. Hoffman et al. (2013) consider a mean-field approximation $q(\mathbf{z}|\boldsymbol{\lambda}) = \prod_i q^i(\mathbf{z}^i|\boldsymbol{\lambda}^i)$ where each q^i belongs to the same exponential-family distribution as the joint distribution,

$$q^i(\mathbf{z}^i) := h^i(\mathbf{z}^i) \exp\left[(\boldsymbol{\lambda}^i)^T \mathbf{T}^i(\mathbf{z}^i) - A^i(\boldsymbol{\lambda}^i)\right].$$

The parameters of this distribution are denoted by $\boldsymbol{\lambda}^i$ to differentiate them from the joint-distribution parameters $\boldsymbol{\eta}^i$.

As shown by Hoffman et al. (2013), the Fisher matrix for this problem is equal to $\nabla^2 A^i(\boldsymbol{\lambda}^i)$ and the gradient of the lower bound with respect to $\boldsymbol{\lambda}^i$ is equal to $\nabla^2 A^i(\boldsymbol{\lambda}^i)(\boldsymbol{\lambda}^i - \boldsymbol{\lambda}^i_*)$ where $\boldsymbol{\lambda}^i_*$ are the mean-field parameters (see Paquet, 2014). Therefore, when computing the natural-gradient, the $\nabla^2 A^i(\boldsymbol{\lambda}^i)$ terms cancel out and the natural-gradient is simply $\boldsymbol{\lambda}^i - \boldsymbol{\lambda}^i_*$ which is much easier to compute than the actual gradient. Unfortunately, for non-conjugate models this cancellation does not happen and the simplicity of the update is lost. The Riemannian conjugate-gradient method of Honkela et al. (2011) has similar issues, in that computing $\nabla^2 A(\boldsymbol{\lambda})$ is typically very costly.

KL-Divergence Based Methods: Rather than using the symmetric-KL, Theis & Hoffman (2015) consider using the KL divergence $\mathbb{D}_{KL}[q(\mathbf{z}|\boldsymbol{\lambda}) \,\|\, q(\mathbf{z}|\boldsymbol{\lambda}_k)]$ within a stochastic proximal-point method:

$$\boldsymbol{\lambda}_{k+1} = \operatorname*{argmin}_{\boldsymbol{\lambda}\in\mathcal{S}} \left[-\underline{\mathcal{L}}(\boldsymbol{\lambda}) + \frac{1}{\beta_k}\mathbb{D}_{KL}[q(\mathbf{z}|\boldsymbol{\lambda}) \,\|\, q(\mathbf{z}|\boldsymbol{\lambda}_k)]\right]. \tag{5}$$

This method yields better convergence properties, but requires numerical optimization to implement the update even for conditionally-conjugate models. Khan et al. (2015) considers a deterministic proximal-gradient variant of this method by splitting the lower bound into $-\underline{\mathcal{L}} := f + h$, where f contains all the "easy" terms and h contains all the "difficult" terms. By linearizing the "difficult" terms, this leads to a closed-form update even for non-conjugate models. The update is given by:

$$\begin{aligned}\boldsymbol{\lambda}_{k+1} = \operatorname*{argmin}_{\boldsymbol{\lambda}\in\mathcal{S}} \Big[&\boldsymbol{\lambda}^T[\nabla f(\boldsymbol{\lambda}_k)] + h(\boldsymbol{\lambda}) \\ &+\frac{1}{\beta_k}\mathbb{D}_{KL}[q(\mathbf{z}|\boldsymbol{\lambda}) \,\|\, q(\mathbf{z}|\boldsymbol{\lambda}_k)]\Big].\end{aligned} \tag{6}$$

However, this method requires the exact gradients which is usually not feasible for large dataset and/or complex models.

Mirror Descent Methods: In the optimization literature, *mirror descent* (and stochastic mirror descent) algorithms are a generalization of (2) where the squared-Euclidean distance can be replaced by any Bregman divergence $\mathbb{D}_F(\boldsymbol{\lambda}\|\boldsymbol{\lambda}_k)$ generated from a strongly-convex function $F(\boldsymbol{\lambda})$ (Beck & Teboulle, 2003),

$$\boldsymbol{\lambda}_{k+1} = \operatorname*{argmin}_{\boldsymbol{\lambda}\in\mathcal{S}} \left\{-\boldsymbol{\lambda}^T \nabla\underline{\mathcal{L}}(\boldsymbol{\lambda}_k) + \frac{1}{\beta_k}\mathbb{D}_F(\boldsymbol{\lambda}\|\boldsymbol{\lambda}_k)\right\}. \tag{7}$$

The convergence rate of mirror descent algorithm has been analyzed in convex (Duchi et al., 2010) and more recently in non-convex (Ghadimi et al., 2014) settings. However, mirror descent does not cover the cases described above in (5) and (6) when a KL divergence between two exponential-family distributions is used with $\boldsymbol{\lambda}$ as the natural-parameter. For such cases, the Bregman divergence corresponds to a KL divergence with swapped parameters (see Nielsen & Garcia, 2009, Equation 29),

$$\begin{aligned}\mathbb{D}_A(\boldsymbol{\lambda}\|\boldsymbol{\lambda}_k) &:= A(\boldsymbol{\lambda}) - A(\boldsymbol{\lambda}_k) - [\nabla A(\boldsymbol{\lambda}_k)]^T(\boldsymbol{\lambda} - \boldsymbol{\lambda}_k) \\ &= \mathbb{D}_{KL}[q(\mathbf{z}|\boldsymbol{\lambda}_k) \,\|\, q(\mathbf{z}|\boldsymbol{\lambda})].\end{aligned} \tag{8}$$

where $A(\boldsymbol{\lambda})$ is the partition function of q. Because (5) and (6) both use a KL divergence where the second argument is fixed to $\boldsymbol{\lambda}_k$, instead of the first argument, they are not covered under the mirror-descent framework. In addition, even though mirror-descent has been used for variational inference (Ravikumar et al., 2010), Bregman divergences do not yield an efficient update in many scenarios.

3 PROXIMAL-GRADIENT SVI

Our proximal-gradient stochastic variational inference (PG-SVI) method extends (6) to allow stochastic gradients $\widehat{\nabla} f(\boldsymbol{\lambda}_k)$ and general divergence functions $\mathbb{D}(\boldsymbol{\lambda}\|\boldsymbol{\lambda}_k)$ by using the iteration

$$\boldsymbol{\lambda}_{k+1} = \operatorname*{argmin}_{\boldsymbol{\lambda}\in\mathcal{S}} \left\{\boldsymbol{\lambda}^T\left[\widehat{\nabla} f(\boldsymbol{\lambda}_k)\right] + h(\boldsymbol{\lambda}) + \frac{1}{\beta_k}\mathbb{D}(\boldsymbol{\lambda} \,\|\, \boldsymbol{\lambda}_k)\right\}. \tag{9}$$

This unifies a variety of existing approaches since it allows:

1. Splitting of $\underline{\mathcal{L}}$ into a difficult term f and a simple term h, similar to the method of Khan et al. (2015).
2. A stochastic approximation $\widehat{\nabla} f$ of the gradient of the difficult term, similar to SG methods.
3. Divergence functions $\mathbb{D}$ that incorporate the geometry of the parameter space, similar to methods discussed in Section 2 (see (3), (5), (6), and (7)).

Below, we describe each feature in detail, along with the precise assumptions used in our analysis.

3.1 SPLITTING

Following Khan et al. (2015), we split the lower bound into a sum of a "difficult" term f and an "easy" term h, enabling a closed-form solution for (9). Specifically, we split using $p(\mathbf{y}, \mathbf{z})/q(\mathbf{z}|\boldsymbol{\lambda}) = c\,\tilde{p}_d(\mathbf{z}|\boldsymbol{\lambda})\tilde{p}_e(\mathbf{z}|\boldsymbol{\lambda})$, where $\tilde{p}_d$ contains all factors that make the optimization difficult, and $\tilde{p}_e$ contains the rest (while c is a constant). By substituting in (1), we get the following split of the lower bound:

$$\underline{\mathcal{L}}(\boldsymbol{\lambda}) = \underbrace{\mathbb{E}_q[\log \tilde{p}_d(\mathbf{z}|\boldsymbol{\lambda})]}_{-f(\boldsymbol{\lambda})} + \underbrace{\mathbb{E}_q[\log \tilde{p}_e(\mathbf{z}|\boldsymbol{\lambda})]}_{-h(\boldsymbol{\lambda})} + \log c.$$

Note that $\tilde{p}_d$ and $\tilde{p}_e$ need not be probability distributions.

We make the following assumptions about f and h:

(A1) The function f is differentiable and its gradient is $L-$Lipschitz-continuous, i.e. $\forall \boldsymbol{\lambda}$ and $\boldsymbol{\lambda}' \in \mathcal{S}$ we have

$$\|\nabla f(\boldsymbol{\lambda}) - \nabla f(\boldsymbol{\lambda}')\| \leq L\|\boldsymbol{\lambda} - \boldsymbol{\lambda}'\|.$$

(A2) The function h can be a general convex function.

These assumptions are very weak. The function f can be non-convex and the Lipschitz-continuity assumption is typically satisfied in practice (and indeed the analysis can be generalized to only require this assumption on a smaller set containing the iterations). The assumption that h is convex seems strong, but note that we can always take $h = 0$ in the split if the function has no "nice" convex part. Below, we give several illustrative examples of such splits for variational-Gaussian inference with $q(\mathbf{z}|\boldsymbol{\lambda}) := \mathcal{N}(\mathbf{z}|\mathbf{m}, \mathbf{V})$, so that $\boldsymbol{\lambda} = \{\mathbf{m}, \mathbf{V}\}$ with $\mathbf{m}$ being the mean and $\mathbf{V}$ being the covariance matrix.

Gaussian Process (GP) Models: Consider GP models (Kuss & Rasmussen, 2005) for N input-output pairs $\{y_n, \mathbf{x}_n\}$ indexed by n. Let $z_n := f(\mathbf{x}_n)$ be the latent function drawn from a GP with mean 0 and covariance $\mathbf{K}$. We use a non-Gaussian likelihood $p(y_n|z_n)$ to model the output. We can then use the following split, where the non-Gaussian terms are in $\tilde{p}_d$ and the Gaussian terms are in $\tilde{p}_e$:

$$\frac{p(\mathbf{y}, \mathbf{z})}{q(\mathbf{z}|\boldsymbol{\lambda})} = \underbrace{\prod_{n=1}^{N} p(y_n|z_n)}_{\tilde{p}_d(\mathbf{z}|\boldsymbol{\lambda})} \underbrace{\frac{\mathcal{N}(\mathbf{z}|0, \mathbf{K})}{\mathcal{N}(\mathbf{z}|\mathbf{m}, \mathbf{V})}}_{\tilde{p}_e(\mathbf{z}|\boldsymbol{\lambda})}. \quad (10)$$

The detailed derivation is in the appendix. By substituting in (1), we obtain the lower bound $\underline{\mathcal{L}}(\boldsymbol{\lambda})$ shown below along with its split:

$$\underbrace{\sum_n \mathbb{E}_q[\log p(y_n|z_n)]}_{-f(\boldsymbol{\lambda})} - \underbrace{\mathbb{D}_{KL}[\mathcal{N}(\mathbf{z}|\mathbf{m}, \mathbf{V}) \,\|\, \mathcal{N}(\mathbf{z}|0, \mathbf{K})]}_{h(\boldsymbol{\lambda})}. \quad (11)$$

A1 is satisfied for common likelihoods, while it is easy to establish that h is convex. We show in Section 6 that this split leads to a closed-form update for iteration (9).

Generalized Linear Models (GLMs): A similar split can be obtained for GLMs (Nelder & Baker, 1972), where the non-conjugate terms are in $\tilde{p}_d$ and the rest are in $\tilde{p}_e$. Denoting the weights by $\mathbf{z}$ and assuming a standard Gaussian prior over it, we can use the following split:

$$\frac{p(\mathbf{y}, \mathbf{z})}{q(\mathbf{z}|\boldsymbol{\lambda})} = \underbrace{\prod_{n=1}^{N} p(y_n|\mathbf{x}_n^T\mathbf{z})}_{\tilde{p}_d(\mathbf{z}|\boldsymbol{\lambda})} \underbrace{\frac{\mathcal{N}(\mathbf{z}|0, \mathbf{I})}{\mathcal{N}(\mathbf{z}|\mathbf{m}, \mathbf{V})}}_{\tilde{p}_e(\mathbf{z}|\boldsymbol{\lambda})}.$$

We give further details about the bound for this case in the appendix.

Correlated Topic Model (CTM): Given a text document with a vocabulary of N words, denote its word-count vector by $\mathbf{y}$. Let K be the number of topics and $\mathbf{z}$ be the vector of topic-proportions. We can then use the following split:

$$\frac{p(\mathbf{y}, \mathbf{z})}{q(\mathbf{z}|\boldsymbol{\lambda})} = \underbrace{\prod_{n=1}^{N} \left[\sum_{k=1}^{K} \beta_{n,k} \frac{e^{z_k}}{\sum_j e^{z_j}}\right]^{y_n}}_{\tilde{p}_d(\mathbf{z}|\boldsymbol{\lambda})} \underbrace{\frac{\mathcal{N}(\mathbf{z}|\boldsymbol{\mu}, \boldsymbol{\Sigma})}{\mathcal{N}(\mathbf{z}|\mathbf{m}, \mathbf{V})}}_{\tilde{p}_e(\mathbf{z}|\boldsymbol{\lambda})},$$

where $\boldsymbol{\mu}, \boldsymbol{\Sigma}$ are parameters of the Gaussian prior and $\beta_{n,k}$ are parameters of K multinomials. We give further details about the bound in the appendix.

3.2 STOCHASTIC-APPROXIMATION

The approach of Khan et al. (2015) considers (9) in the special case of (6) where we use the exact gradient $\nabla f(\boldsymbol{\lambda}_k)$ in the first term. But in practice this gradient is often difficult to compute. In our framework, we allow a stochastic approximation of $\nabla f(\boldsymbol{\lambda})$ which we denote by $\widehat{\nabla} f(\boldsymbol{\lambda}_k)$.

As shown in the previous section, f might take a form $f(\boldsymbol{\lambda}) := \Sigma_{n=1}^{N} \mathbb{E}_q[\tilde{f}_n(\mathbf{z})]$ for a set of functions $\tilde{f}_n$ as in the GP model (11). In some situations, $\mathbb{E}_q[\tilde{f}_n(\mathbf{z})]$ is computationally expensive or intractable. For example, in GP models the expectation is equal to $\mathbb{E}_q[\log p(y_n|z_n)]$, which is intractable for most non-Gaussian likelihoods. In such cases, we can form a stochastic approximation by using a few samples $\mathbf{z}^{(s)}$ from $q(\mathbf{z}|\boldsymbol{\lambda})$, as shown below:

$$\nabla \mathbb{E}_q[\tilde{f}_n(\mathbf{z})] \approx \widehat{\mathbf{g}}(\boldsymbol{\lambda}, \boldsymbol{\xi}_n) := \frac{1}{S} \sum_{s=1}^{S} \tilde{f}_n(\mathbf{z}^{(s)}) \nabla[\log q(\mathbf{z}^{(s)}|\boldsymbol{\lambda})]$$

where $\boldsymbol{\xi}_n$ represents the noise in the stochastic approximation $\widehat{\mathbf{g}}$ and we use the identity $\nabla q(\mathbf{z}|\boldsymbol{\lambda}) = q(\mathbf{z}|\boldsymbol{\lambda})\nabla[\log q(\mathbf{z}|\boldsymbol{\lambda})]$ to derive the expression (Ranganath et al., 2013). We can then form a stochastic-gradient by randomly selecting a mini-batch of M functions $\tilde{f}_{n_i}(\mathbf{z})$ and employing the estimate

$$\widehat{\nabla} f(\boldsymbol{\lambda}) = \frac{N}{M} \sum_{i=1}^{M} \widehat{\mathbf{g}}(\boldsymbol{\lambda}, \boldsymbol{\xi}_{n_i}). \quad (12)$$

In our analysis we make the following two assumptions regarding the stochastic approximation of the gradient:

(A3) The estimate is unbiased: $\mathbb{E}[\widehat{\mathbf{g}}(\boldsymbol{\lambda}, \boldsymbol{\xi}_n)] = \nabla f(\boldsymbol{\lambda})$.

(A4) Its variance is upper bounded: $\text{Var}[\widehat{\mathbf{g}}(\boldsymbol{\lambda}, \boldsymbol{\xi}_n)] \leq \sigma^2$.

In both the assumptions, the expectation is taken with respect to the noise $\boldsymbol{\xi}_n$. The first assumption is true for the stochastic approximations of (12). The second assumption is stronger, but only needs to hold for all $\boldsymbol{\lambda}_k$ so is almost always satisfied in practice.

3.3 DIVERGENCE FUNCTIONS

To incorporate the geometry of q we incorporate a divergence function $\mathbb{D}$ between $\boldsymbol{\lambda}$ and $\boldsymbol{\lambda}_k$. The set of divergence functions need to satisfy two assumptions:

(A5) $\mathbb{D}(\boldsymbol{\lambda} \,\|\, \boldsymbol{\lambda}') > 0$, for all $\boldsymbol{\lambda} \neq \boldsymbol{\lambda}'$.

(A6) There exist an $\alpha > 0$ such that for all $\boldsymbol{\lambda}, \boldsymbol{\lambda}'$ generated by (9) we have:

$$(\boldsymbol{\lambda} - \boldsymbol{\lambda}')^T \nabla_{\boldsymbol{\lambda}} \mathbb{D}(\boldsymbol{\lambda} \,\|\, \boldsymbol{\lambda}') \geq \alpha \|\boldsymbol{\lambda} - \boldsymbol{\lambda}'\|^2. \qquad (13)$$

The first assumption is reasonable and is satisfied by typical divergence functions like the squared Euclidean distance and variants of the KL divergence. In the next section we show that, whenever the iteration (9) is defined and all $\boldsymbol{\lambda}_k$ stay within a compact set, the second assumption is satisfied for all divergence functions considered in Section 2.

4 SPECIAL CASES

Most methods discussed in Section 2 are special cases of the proposed iteration (9). We obtain gradient descent if $h = 0$, $f = -\underline{\mathcal{L}}$, $\widehat{\nabla} f = \nabla f$, and $\mathbb{D}(\boldsymbol{\lambda} \| \boldsymbol{\lambda}_k) = (1/2)\|\boldsymbol{\lambda} - \boldsymbol{\lambda}_k\|^2$ (in this case A6 is satisfied with $\alpha = 1$). From here, there are three standard generalizations in the optimization literature: SG methods do not require that $\widehat{\nabla} f = \nabla f$, proximal-gradient methods do not require that $h = 0$, and mirror descent allows $\mathbb{D}$ to be a different Bregman divergence generated by a strongly-convex function. Our analysis applies to all these variations on existing optimization algorithms because A1 to A5 are standard assumptions (Ghadimi et al., 2014) and, as we now show, A6 is satisfied for this class of Bregman divergences. In particular, consider the generic Bregman divergence shown in the left side of (8) for some strongly-convex function $A(\boldsymbol{\lambda})$. By taking the gradient with respect to $\boldsymbol{\lambda}$ and substituting in (13), we obtain that A6 is equivalent to

$$(\boldsymbol{\lambda} - \boldsymbol{\lambda}_k)^T [\triangledown A(\boldsymbol{\lambda}) - \triangledown A(\boldsymbol{\lambda}_k)] \geq \alpha \|\boldsymbol{\lambda} - \boldsymbol{\lambda}_k\|^2,$$

which is equivalent to strong-convexity of the function $A(\boldsymbol{\lambda})$ (Nesterov, 2004, Theorem 2.1.9).

The method of Theis & Hoffman (2015) corresponds to choosing $h = -\underline{\mathcal{L}}$, $f = 0$, and $\mathbb{D}(\boldsymbol{\lambda} \| \boldsymbol{\lambda}_k) := \mathbb{D}_{KL}[q(\mathbf{z}|\boldsymbol{\lambda}) \,\|\, q(\mathbf{z}|\boldsymbol{\lambda}_k)]$ where q is an exponential family distribution with natural parameters $\boldsymbol{\lambda}$. Since we assume h to be convex, only limited cases of their approach are covered under our framework. The method of Khan et al. (2015) also uses the KL divergence and focuses on the deterministic case where $\widehat{\nabla} f(\boldsymbol{\lambda}) = \nabla f(\boldsymbol{\lambda})$, but uses the split $-\underline{\mathcal{L}} = f + h$ to allow for non-conjugate models. In both of these models, A6 is satisfied when the Fisher matrix $\triangledown^2 A(\boldsymbol{\lambda})$ is positive-definite. This can be shown by using the definition of the KL divergence for exponential families (Nielsen & Garcia, 2009):

$$\begin{aligned} &\mathbb{D}_{KL}[q(\mathbf{z}|\boldsymbol{\lambda}) \,\|\, q(\mathbf{z}|\boldsymbol{\lambda}_k)] \\ &\quad := A(\boldsymbol{\lambda}_k) - A(\boldsymbol{\lambda}) - [\triangledown A(\boldsymbol{\lambda})]^T (\boldsymbol{\lambda}_k - \boldsymbol{\lambda}). \end{aligned} \qquad (14)$$

Taking the derivative with respect to $\boldsymbol{\lambda}$ and substituting in (13) with $\boldsymbol{\lambda}' = \boldsymbol{\lambda}_k$, we get the condition

$$(\boldsymbol{\lambda} - \boldsymbol{\lambda}_k)^T [\triangledown^2 A(\boldsymbol{\lambda})] (\boldsymbol{\lambda} - \boldsymbol{\lambda}_k) \geq \alpha \|\boldsymbol{\lambda} - \boldsymbol{\lambda}_k\|^2,$$

which is satisfied when $\triangledown^2 A(\boldsymbol{\lambda})$ is positive-definite over a compact set for α equal to its lowest eigenvalue on the set.

Methods based on natural-gradient using iteration (3) (like SVI) correspond to using $h = 0$, $f = -\underline{\mathcal{L}}$, and the symmetric KL divergence. Assumption A1 to A5 are usually assumed for these methods and, as we show next, A6 is also satisfied. In particular, when q is an exponential family distribution the symmetric KL divergence can be written as the sum of the Bregman divergence shown in (8) and the KL divergence shown in (14),

$$\begin{aligned} &\mathbb{D}_{KL}^{sym}[q(\mathbf{z}|\boldsymbol{\lambda}) \,\|\, q(\mathbf{z}|\boldsymbol{\lambda}_k)] \\ &:= \mathbb{D}_{KL}[q(\mathbf{z}|\boldsymbol{\lambda}_k) \,\|\, q(\mathbf{z}|\boldsymbol{\lambda})] + \mathbb{D}_{KL}[q(\mathbf{z}|\boldsymbol{\lambda}) \,\|\, q(\mathbf{z}|\boldsymbol{\lambda}_k)] \\ &= \mathbb{D}_A(\boldsymbol{\lambda} \| \boldsymbol{\lambda}_k) + \mathbb{D}_{KL}[q(\mathbf{z}|\boldsymbol{\lambda}) \,\|\, q(\mathbf{z}|\boldsymbol{\lambda}_k)] \end{aligned}$$

where the first equality follows from the definition of the symmetric KL divergence and the second one follows from (8). Since the two divergences in the sum satisfy A6, the symmetric KL divergence also satisfies the assumption.

5 CONVERGENCE OF PG-SVI

We first analyze the convergence rate of deterministic methods where the gradient is exact, $\widehat{\nabla} f(\boldsymbol{\lambda}) = \nabla f(\boldsymbol{\lambda})$. This yields a simplified result that applies to a wide variety of existing variational methods. Subsequently, we consider the more general case where a stochastic approximation of the gradient is used.

5.1 DETERMINISTIC METHODS

The following theorem establishes the convergence under a fixed step-size. We use $C_0 = \underline{\mathcal{L}}^* - \underline{\mathcal{L}}(\boldsymbol{\lambda}_0)$ as the initial (constant) sub-optimality, and express our result in terms of the quantity $\|\boldsymbol{\lambda}_{k+1} - \boldsymbol{\lambda}_k\|$.

Proposition 1. *Let A1, A2, A5, and A6 be satisfied. If we run t iterations of* (9) *with a fixed step-size* $\beta_k = \alpha/L$ *for all* k *and an exact gradient* $\nabla f(\boldsymbol{\lambda})$, *then we have*

$$\min_{k\in\{0,1,\ldots,t-1\}} \|\boldsymbol{\lambda}_{k+1} - \boldsymbol{\lambda}_k\|^2 \le \frac{2C_0}{\alpha t} \tag{15}$$

We give a proof in the appendix. Roughly, the theorem states that the minimum distance moved across all iterations must be in $O(1/t)$. If the objective is bounded below (C_0 is finite), then this result implies that the algorithm converges to a stationary point and also gives a rate of convergence.

Stating the result in terms of $\|\boldsymbol{\lambda}_{k+1} - \boldsymbol{\lambda}_k\|$ may appear to be unconventional, but this quantity is useful since it characterizes a fixed point of the algorithm. For example, consider the special case of gradient descent where $h = 0$ and $\mathbb{D}(\boldsymbol{\lambda}, \boldsymbol{\lambda}_k) = \frac{1}{2}\|\boldsymbol{\lambda} - \boldsymbol{\lambda}_k\|^2$. In this case, $\alpha = 1$ and $\beta_k = 1/L$, therefore we have $\|\boldsymbol{\lambda}_{k+1} - \boldsymbol{\lambda}_k\| = \|\nabla f(\boldsymbol{\lambda}_k)\|^2/L$ and Proposition 1 implies that $\min_k \|\nabla f(\boldsymbol{\lambda}_k)\|^2$ has a convergence rate of $O(1/t)$. This in turn shows that the method converges at a sublinear rate to an approximate stationary point, which would be a global minimum in the special case where f is convex.

If we use a divergence with $\alpha > 1$ then we can use a step-size larger than $1/L$ and the error will decrease faster than gradient-descent. To our knowledge, this is the first result that formally shows that natural-gradient methods can achieve faster convergence rates. The splitting of the objective into f and h functions is also likely to improve the step-size. Since L only depends on f, sometimes it might be possible to reduce the Lipschitz constant by choosing an appropriate split.

We next give a more general result that allows a per-iteration step size.

Proposition 2. *If we choose the step-sizes* β_k *to be such that* $0 < \beta_k \le 2\alpha/L$ *with* $\beta_k < 2\alpha/L$ *for at least one* k, *then,*

$$\min_{k\in\{0,1\ldots t-1\}} \frac{1}{\beta_k}\|\boldsymbol{\lambda}_{k+1} - \boldsymbol{\lambda}_k\|^2 \le \frac{C_0}{\sum_{k=0}^{t-1}(\alpha\beta_k - L\beta_k^2/2)} \tag{16}$$

We give a proof in the appendix. For gradient-descent, the above result implies that we can use any step-size less than $2/L$, which agrees with the classical step-size choices for gradient and proximal-gradient methods.

5.2 STOCHASTIC METHODS

We now give a bound for the more general case where we use a stochastic approximation of the gradient.

Proposition 3. *Let A1-A6 be satisfied. If we run t iterations of* (9) *for a fixed step-size* $\beta_k = \gamma\alpha_*/L$ *(where* $0 < \gamma < 2$ *is a scalar) and fixed batch-size* $M_k = M$ *for all* k *with a stochastic gradient* $\widehat{\nabla} f(\boldsymbol{\lambda})$, *then we have*

$$\mathbb{E}_{R,\boldsymbol{\xi}}(\|\boldsymbol{\lambda}_{R+1} - \boldsymbol{\lambda}_R\|^2) \le \frac{1}{2-\gamma}\left[\frac{2C_0}{\alpha_* t} + \frac{\gamma c \sigma^2}{ML}\right].$$

where c *is a constant such that* $c > 1/(2\alpha)$ *and* $\alpha_* := \alpha - 1/(2c)$. *The expectation is taken with respect to the noise* $\boldsymbol{\xi} := \{\boldsymbol{\xi}_0, \boldsymbol{\xi}_1, \ldots, \boldsymbol{\xi}_{t-1}\}$, *and a random variable* R *which follows the uniform distribution* $Prob(R = k) = 1/t, \forall k \in \{0, 1, 2, \ldots, t-1\}$.

Unlike the bound of Proposition 1, this bound depends on the noise variance σ^2 as well the mini-batch size M. In particular, as we would expect, the bound gets tighter as the variance gets smaller and as the size of our mini-batch grows. Notice that we can also make the second term smaller by decreasing the value of γ and the first term smaller by increasing the number of iterations. Therefore, this bound indicates that a small enough constant step-size γ (or a sufficiently-large batch-size M) can be used to reach any target level of accuracy. In the appendix, we give a more general result that allows a per-iteration step-size which can used to give an "anytime" algorithm that is able to converge to an arbitrary level of accuracy by using a decreasing sequence of step sizes (but we found that constant step-sizes work better empirically). Note that while stating the result in terms of a randomized iteration might seem strange, in practice we typically just take the last iteration as the minimizer.

6 CLOSED-FORM UPDATES FOR NON-CONJUGATE MODELS

We now give an example where iteration (9) attains a closed-form solution. We expect such closed-form solution to exist for a large class of problems, including models where q is an exponential-family distribution, but here we focus on the GP model discussed in Section 3.1.

For the GP model, we rewrite the lower bound (11) as

$$-\underline{\mathcal{L}}(\mathbf{m}, \mathbf{V}) := \underbrace{\sum_{n=1}^{N} f_n(m_n, v_n)}_{f(\boldsymbol{m},\boldsymbol{V})} + \underbrace{\mathbb{D}_{KL}[q \,\|\, p]}_{h(\boldsymbol{m},\boldsymbol{V})} \tag{17}$$

where we've used $q := \mathcal{N}(\mathbf{z}|\mathbf{m}, \mathbf{V})$, $p := \mathcal{N}(\mathbf{z}|0, \mathbf{K})$, and $f_n(m_n, v_n) := -\mathbb{E}_q[\log p(y_n|z_n)]$ with m_n being the entry n of $\mathbf{m}$ and v_n being the diagonal entry n of $\mathbf{V}$. We can compute a stochastic approximation of f using (12) by randomly selecting an example n_k (choosing $M = 1$) and using a Monte Carlo gradient approximation of f_{n_k}. Using this approximation, the linearized term in (9) can be simplified to the following:

$$\begin{aligned}\boldsymbol{\lambda}^T\left[\widehat{\nabla} f(\boldsymbol{\lambda}_k)\right] &= m_n \underbrace{N[\nabla_{m_n} f_{n_k}(m_{n_k,k}, v_{n_k,k})]}_{:=\alpha_{n_k,k}} \\ &+ v_n \underbrace{N[\nabla_{v_n} f_{n_k}(m_{n_k,k}, v_{n_k,k})]}_{:=2\,\gamma_{n_k,k}} \\ &= m_n \alpha_{n_k,k} + \tfrac{1}{2} v_n \gamma_{n_k,k} \end{aligned} \quad (18)$$

where $m_{n_k,k}$ and $v_{n_k,k}$ denote the value of m_n and v_n in the k'th iteration for $n = n_k$. By using the KL divergence as our divergence function in iteration (9), and by denoting $\mathcal{N}(\mathbf{z}|\mathbf{m}_k, \mathbf{V}_k)$ by q_k, we can express the two last two terms in (9) as a single KL divergence function as shown below:

$$\begin{aligned}&\boldsymbol{\lambda}^T\left[\widehat{\nabla} f(\boldsymbol{\lambda}_k)\right] + h(\boldsymbol{\lambda}) + \frac{1}{\beta_k}\mathbb{D}(\boldsymbol{\lambda}\|\boldsymbol{\lambda}_k), \\ &= (m_n\alpha_{n,k} + \tfrac{1}{2}v_n\gamma_{n,k}) + \mathbb{D}_{KL}[q \,\|\, p] + \frac{1}{\beta_k}\mathbb{D}_{KL}[q \,\|\, q_k], \\ &= (m_n\alpha_{n,k} + \tfrac{1}{2}v_n\gamma_{n,k}) + \frac{1}{1-r_k}\mathbb{D}_{KL}[q \,\|\, p^{1-r_k} q_k^{r_k}],\end{aligned}$$

where $r_k := 1/(1+\beta_k)$. Comparing this to (17), we see that this objective is similar to that of a GP model with a Gaussian prior[1] $p^{1-r_k} q_k^{r_k}$ and a linear Gaussian-like log-likelihood. Therefore, we can obtain closed-form updates for its minimization.

The updates are shown below and a detailed derivation is given in the appendix.

$$\begin{aligned}\widetilde{\gamma}_k &= r_k \widetilde{\gamma}_{k-1} + (1-r_k)\gamma_{n_k,k}\mathbf{1}_{n_k}, \\ \mathbf{m}_{k+1} &= \mathbf{m}_k - (1-r_k)(\mathbf{I} - \mathbf{K}\mathbf{A}_k^{-1})(\mathbf{m}_k + \alpha_{n_k,k}\boldsymbol{\kappa}_{n_k}), \\ v_{n_{k+1},k+1} &= \kappa_{n_{k+1},n_{k+1}} - \boldsymbol{\kappa}_{n_{k+1}}^T \mathbf{A}_k^{-1} \boldsymbol{\kappa}_{n_{k+1}}, \end{aligned} \quad (19)$$

where $\widetilde{\gamma}_0$ is initialized to a small positive constant to avoid numerical issues, $\mathbf{1}_{n_k}$ is a vector with all zero entries except n_k'th entry which is equal to 1, $\boldsymbol{\kappa}_k$ is n_k'th column of $\mathbf{K}$, and $\mathbf{A}_k := \mathbf{K} + [\text{diag}(\widetilde{\gamma}_k)]^{-1}$. For iteration $k+1$, we use $m_{n_{k+1},k+1}$ and $v_{n_{k+1},k+1}$ to compute the gradients $\alpha_{n_{k+1},k+1}$ and $\gamma_{n_{k+1},k+1}$, and run the above updates again. We continue until a convergence criteria is reached.

There are numerous advantages of these updates. First, We do not need to store the full covariance matrix $\mathbf{V}$. The updates avoid forming the matrix and only update $\mathbf{m}$. This works because we only need one diagonal element in each iteration to compute the stochastic gradient $\gamma_{n_k,k}$. For large N this is a clear advantage since the memory cost is $O(N)$ rather than $O(N^2)$. Second, computation of the mean vector $\mathbf{m}$ and a diagonal entry of $\mathbf{V}$ only require solving two linear equations, as shown in the second and third line of (19). In general, for a mini-batch of size M, we need a total of $2M$ linear equations, which is a lot cheaper than an explicit inversion. Finally, the linear equations at iteration $k+1$ are very similar to those at iteration k, since $\mathbf{A}_k$ differ only at one entry from $\mathbf{A}_{k+1}$. Therefore, we can reuse computations from the previous iteration to improve the computational efficiency of the updates.

[1]Since p and q are Gaussian, the product is a Gaussian.

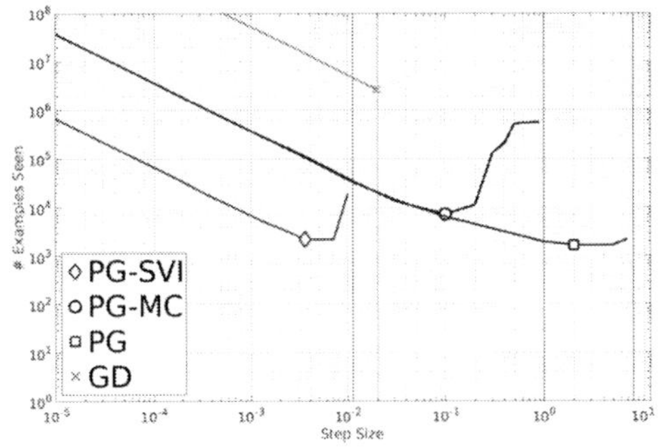

Figure 1: We show the number of examples required for convergence versus fixed step-sizes for binary GP classification. Methods based on proximal-gradient require fewer number of examples compared to gradient descent (GD). Step-size is upper bounded for all methods (upper bound shown with vertical lines). PG-SVI surprisingly converges at the same rate as PG.

7 EXPERIMENTAL RESULTS

In this section, we compare our method to many existing approaches such as SGD and four adaptive gradient-methods (ADAGRAD, ADADELTA, RMSprop, ADAM), as well as two variational inference methods for non-conjugate models (the Delta method and Laplace method). We show results on Gaussian process classification (Kuss & Rasmussen, 2005) and correlated topic models (Blei & Lafferty, 2007). The code to reproduce these experiments can be found at this link[2].

7.1 GAUSSIAN PROCESS CLASSIFICATION

We consider binary classification by using a GP model with Bernoulli-logit likelihood on three datasets: Sonar, Ionosphere, and USPS-3vs5. These datasets can be found at the UCI data repository[3] and their details are discussed in Kuss & Rasmussen (2005). For the GP prior, we use the zero mean-function, and a squared-exponential covariance function with hyperparameters σ and l as defined in Kuss & Rasmussen (2005) (see Eq. 33). We set the values of the hyperparameters using cross-validation. For the three datasets, the hyperparameters $(\log l, \log\sigma)$ are set to $(-1, 6)$, $(1, 2.5)$, and $(2.5, 5)$, respectively.

[2]https://github.com/emtiyaz/prox-grad-svi

[3]https://archive.ics.uci.edu/ml/datasets.html

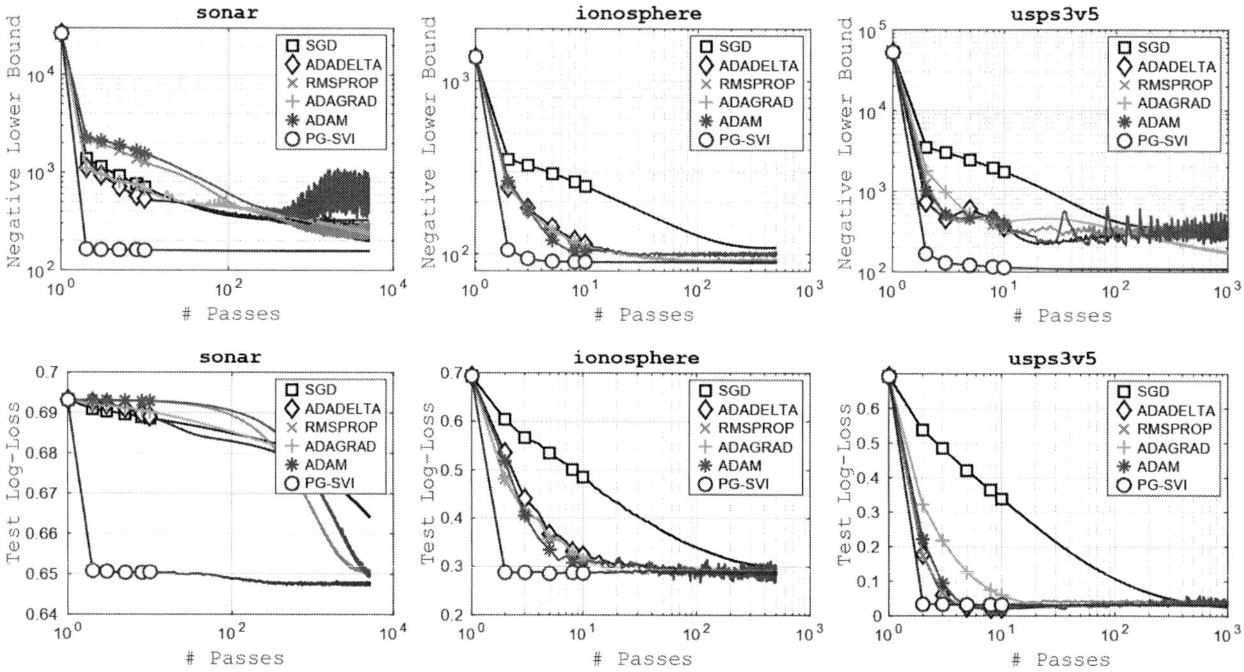

Figure 2: Comparison with adaptive gradient methods for binary classification using GP. We compare PG-SVI to SGD, ADADELTA, RMSprop, ADAGRAD, and ADAM on three datasets. Each column shows results for a dataset. Top row shows the negative of the lower bound, while the bottom row shows the test log-loss. In each plot, the X-axis shows the number of passes made through the data. Markers are shown at 0, 1, 2, 4, 7, and 9 passes through the data. Our method always converges within 10 passes through the data, while other methods more than 100 passes.

7.1.1 Performance Under a Fixed Step-Size

In our first experiment, we compare the performance under a fixed step-size. These results demonstrate that the step-size required for convergence is upper-bounded, as shown in our convergence analysis. The results also demonstrate the faster convergence of our method compared to gradient-descent methods. We compare the following four algorithms on the Ionosphere dataset: (1) batch gradient-descent (referred to as 'GD'), (2) batch proximal-gradient algorithm (referred to as 'PG'), (3) batch version of proximal-gradient algorithm with gradients approximated by using Monte-Carlo (referred to as 'PG-MC'), and (4) proposed proximal-gradient stochastic variational-inference (referred to as 'PG-SVI') where stochastic gradients are obtained using (12) with $M = 5$. For Monte Carlo approximation, we use $S = 500$ samples.

Figure 1 shows the number of examples required for convergence versus the step-size. A lower number implies faster convergence. The vertical lines show the step-size above which a method diverges. Convergence is assessed by monitoring the lower bound, and when the change in consecutive iterations do not exceed a certain threshold, we stop the algorithm.

We clearly see that GD requires many more passes through the data, and methods based on proximal-gradient method converge faster than GD. In addition, the upper bound on the step-size for PG is much larger than GD. This implies that PG can potentially take larger steps than the GD method. PG-SVI is surprisingly as fast as PG which shows the advantage of our approach over the approach of Khan et al. (2015).

7.1.2 Comparison with Adaptive Gradient Methods

We also compare PG-SVI to SGD and four adaptive methods, namely ADADELTA (Zeiler, 2012), RMSprop (Tieleman & Hinton, 2012), ADAGRAD (Duchi et al., 2011), and ADAM (Kingma & Ba, 2014). The implementation details of these algorithms are given in the appendix. We compare the value of the lower bound versus number of passes through the data. We also compare the average log-loss on the test data: $-\sum_n \log \hat{p}_n / N_*$ where $\hat{p}_n = p(y_n|\sigma, l, \mathcal{D}_t)$ is the predictive probabilities of the test point y_n given training data $\mathcal{D}_t$ and N_* is the total number of test-pairs. A lower value is better for the log-loss, and a value of 1 is equal to the performance of random coin-flipping.

Figure 2 summarizes the results. Each column shows results for a dataset. The top row shows the negative of the lower bound, while the bottom row shows the test log-loss.

Lower values are better for both. In all plots, the X-axis shows the number of passes made through the data. Markers are shown at 0, 1, 2, 4, 7, and 9 passes through the data (one pass means the number of randomly selected examples is equal to the total number of examples). Our method is much faster to converge than other methods, and it always converges within 10 passes through the data, while other methods requires more than 100 passes.

7.2 CORRELATED TOPIC MODEL

We now show results for correlated topic model on two collections of documents, namely NIPS dataset and Associated Press (AP) dataset. The NIPS[4] dataset contains 1500 documents from the NIPS conferences held between 1987 and 1999 (a vocabulary-size of 12,419 words and a total of around 1.9M words). The AP[5] collection contains 2,246 documents from the Associated Press (a vocabulary-size of 10,473 words and a total of 436K observed words). We use 50% of the documents for training and 50% for testing.

We compare to the Delta method and the Laplace method discussed in Wang & Blei (2013), and also to the original mean-field (MF) method of Blei & Lafferty (2007). For these methods, we use the implementation available at this link[6]. All of these methods approximate the lower bound by using approximations to the expectation of log-sum-exp functions (see Appendix for details). We compare these methods to the two versions of our algorithm which do not use such approximations, rather use a stochastic gradient as explain in Section 3.2. Specifically, we use the following two versions: one with full covariance (referred to as PG-SVI), and the other with diagonal covariance (referred to as PG-SVI-MF). For both of these algorithms, we use a fixed step-size of 0.001, and a mini-batch size of 2 documents.

Following Wang & Blei (2013), we compare the held-out log-likelihood, which is computed as follows: a new test document $\mathbf{y}$ is split into two halves $(\mathbf{y}^1, \mathbf{y}^2)$, then we compute the approximate posterior $q(\mathbf{z})$ to the posterior $p(\mathbf{z}|\mathbf{y}^1)$ using which we compute the held-out log-likelihood for each $y_n \in \mathbf{y}^2$ as follows:

$$\log p(y_n) \approx \log \int_z \left[\sum_{k=1}^{K} \beta_{n,k} \frac{e^{z_k}}{\sum_j e^{z_j}} \right]^{y_n} q(\mathbf{z}) d\mathbf{z} \quad (20)$$

We use Monte Carlo to approximate this quantity by using a large number of samples from q (unlike Wang & Blei (2013) who approximate it by using the Delta method). We report the average of this quantity over all words in $\mathbf{y}^2$.

Figure 3 shows the negative of the average held-out log-likelihood versus time for 10 topics. Lower values are better. Markers are shown at iterations after second and fifth passes through the data. We see that methods based on proximal-gradient algorithm converge a little bit faster than the existing methods. More importantly, they achieves better performance. This could be due to the fact that we do not approximate the expectation of the log-sum-exp function, unlike the Delta and Laplace method. We obtained similar results for different number of topics.

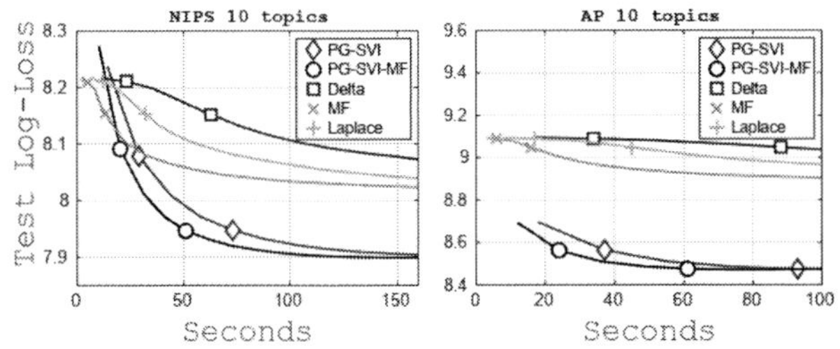

Figure 3: Results on NIPS (left) and AP (right) datasets using correlated topic model with 10 topics. We plot the negative of the average held-out log-likelihood versus time. Lower values are better. Methods based on proximal-gradient algorithm perform better.

8 DISCUSSION

This work has made two contributions. First, we proposed a new variational inference method that combines variable splitting, stochastic gradients, and general divergence functions. This method is well-suited for a huge variety of the variational inference problems that arise in practice, and we anticipate that it may improve over state of the art methods in a variety of settings. Our second contribution is a theoretical analysis of the convergence rate of this general method. Our analysis generalizes existing results for the mirror descent algorithm in optimization, and resolves the convergences of a variety of existing variational inference methods. Due to its generality we expect that this analysis could be useful to establish convergence of other algorithms that we have not thought of, perhaps beyond the variational inference settings we consider in this work.

One issue that we have not satisfactorily resolved is giving a theoretically-justified way to set the step-size in practice; our analysis only indicates that it must be sufficiently small. However, this problem is common in many methods in the literature and our analysis at least suggests the factors that should be taken into account. Another open issue is the applicability our method to many other latent variable models; in this paper we have shown applications to variational-Gaussian inference, but we expect that our method should result in simple updates for a larger class of latent variable models such as non-conjugate exponential family distribution models. Additional work on these issues will improve usability of our method.

[4]https://archive.ics.uci.edu/

[5]http://www.cs.columbia.edu/~blei/lda-c/index.html

[6]https://www.cs.princeton.edu/~chongw/resource.html

References

Amari, Shun-Ichi. Natural gradient works efficiently in learning. *Neural computation*, 10(2):251–276, 1998.

Beck, Amir and Teboulle, Marc. Mirror descent and nonlinear projected subgradient methods for convex optimization. *Operations Research Letters*, 31(3):167–175, 2003.

Beck, Amir and Teboulle, Marc. A fast iterative shrinkage-thresholding algorithm with application to wavelet-based image deblurring. In *IEEE International Conference on Acoustics, Speech and Signal Processing (ICASSP)*, pp. 693–696, 2009.

Blei, David M and Lafferty, John D. A correlated topic model of science. *The Annals of Applied Statistics*, pp. 17–35, 2007.

Duchi, John, Hazan, Elad, and Singer, Yoram. Adaptive subgradient methods for online learning and stochastic optimization. *The Journal of Machine Learning Research*, 12:2121–2159, 2011.

Duchi, John C, Shalev-Shwartz, Shai, Singer, Yoram, and Tewari, Ambuj. Composite objective mirror descent. *COLT*, 2010.

Ghadimi, Saeed, Lan, Guanghui, and Zhang, Hongchao. Mini-batch stochastic approximation methods for nonconvex stochastic composite optimization. *Mathematical Programming*, pp. 1–39, 2014.

Hoffman, Matthew D, Blei, David M, Wang, Chong, and Paisley, John. Stochastic variational inference. *The Journal of Machine Learning Research*, 14(1):1303–1347, 2013.

Honkela, A., Raiko, T., Kuusela, M., Tornio, M., and Karhunen, J. Approximate Riemannian conjugate gradient learning for fixed-form variational Bayes. *Journal of Machine Learning Research*, 11:3235–3268, 2011.

Khan, Mohammad Emtiyaz, Baque, Pierre, Flueret, Francois, and Fua, Pascal. Kullback-Leibler Proximal Variational Inference. In *Advances in Neural Information Processing Systems*, 2015.

Kingma, Diederik and Ba, Jimmy. Adam: A method for stochastic optimization. *arXiv preprint arXiv:1412.6980*, 2014.

Kucukelbir, Alp, Ranganath, Rajesh, Gelman, Andrew, and Blei, David. Fully automatic variational inference of differentiable probability models. In *NIPS Workshop on Probabilistic Programming*, 2014.

Kuss, M. and Rasmussen, C. Assessing approximate inference for binary Gaussian process classification. *Journal of Machine Learning Research*, 6:1679–1704, 2005.

Mnih, Andriy and Gregor, Karol. Neural variational inference and learning in belief networks. *arXiv preprint arXiv:1402.0030*, 2014.

Nelder, John A and Baker, R Jacob. Generalized linear models. *Encyclopedia of Statistical Sciences*, 1972.

Nesterov, Y. *Introductory Lectures on Convex Optimization: A Basic Course*. Kluwer Academic Publishers, Dordrecht, The Netherlands, 2004.

Nielsen, Frank and Garcia, Vincent. Statistical exponential families: A digest with flash cards. *arXiv preprint arXiv:0911.4863*, 2009.

Paquet, Ulrich. On the convergence of stochastic variational inference in Bayesian networks. *NIPS Workshop on variational inference*, 2014.

Pascanu, Razvan and Bengio, Yoshua. Revisiting natural gradient for deep networks. *arXiv preprint arXiv:1301.3584*, 2013.

Ranganath, Rajesh, Gerrish, Sean, and Blei, David M. Black box variational inference. *arXiv preprint arXiv:1401.0118*, 2013.

Ravikumar, Pradeep, Agarwal, Alekh, and Wainwright, Martin J. Message-passing for graph-structured linear programs: Proximal methods and rounding schemes. *The Journal of Machine Learning Research*, 11:1043–1080, 2010.

Salimans, Tim, Knowles, David A, et al. Fixed-form variational posterior approximation through stochastic linear regression. *Bayesian Analysis*, 8(4):837–882, 2013.

Theis, Lucas and Hoffman, Matthew D. A trust-region method for stochastic variational inference with applications to streaming data. *arXiv preprint arXiv:1505.07649*, 2015.

Tieleman, Tijmen and Hinton, Geoffrey. Lecture 6.5-RMSprop: Divide the gradient by a running average of its recent magnitude. *COURSERA: Neural Networks for Machine Learning 4*, 2012.

Titsias, Michalis and Lázaro-Gredilla, Miguel. Doubly stochastic variational Bayes for non-conjugate inference. In *International Conference on Machine Learning*, 2014.

Wang, Chong and Blei, David M. Variational inference in nonconjugate models. *Journal of Machine Learning Research*, 14(1):1005–1031, 2013.

Zeiler, Matthew D. ADADELTA: An adaptive learning rate method. *arXiv preprint arXiv:1212.5701*, 2012.

Probabilistic Size-constrained Microclustering

Arto Klami
Helsinki Institute for Information Technology HIIT
Department of Computer Science
University of Helsinki, Finland

Aditya Jitta
Helsinki Institute for Information Technology HIIT
Department of Computer Science
University of Helsinki, Finland

Abstract

Microclustering refers to clustering models that produce small clusters or, equivalently, to models where the size of the clusters grows sublinearly with the number of samples. We formulate probabilistic microclustering models by assigning a prior distribution on the size of the clusters, and in particular consider microclustering models with explicit bounds on the size of the clusters. The combinatorial constraints make full Bayesian inference complicated, but we manage to develop a Gibbs sampling algorithm that can efficiently sample from the joint cluster allocation of all data points. We empirically demonstrate the computational efficiency of the algorithm for problem instances of varying difficulty.

1 INTRODUCTION

Clustering is classically identified as the task of grouping similar objects into a number of clusters. Typical probabilistic formulations are based on mixture models [McLachlan and Peel, 2004], following the intuitive idea that each data point independently chooses a cluster by considering the product of some mixture weights and the likelihood of that cluster producing the data point. Because of these independent decisions, these models have very limited means for controlling the sizes of the clusters. Parametric mixture models are effectively agnostic of the cluster size; they can be tuned to a degree with the prior distribution of the weights, but in the end the likelihood overrides even the strongest priors for large sample sizes. Nonparametric mixture models such as Dirichlet process (DP) mixtures [Antoniak, 1974], Pitman-Yor mixtures [Dubey et al., 2014], and uniform process mixtures [Wallach et al., 2010] in turn induce some characteristic behavior for the size distribution. For example, DP mixtures assume that the number of clusters for a sample size of N grows proportionally to $\log(N)$ and the biggest clusters hold a large proportion of the data points due to the rich-get-richer property, which is not always consistent with reasonable clustering assumptions [Miller and Harrison, 2013]. The uniform process by Wallach et al. [2010] eliminates the rich-get-richer property, but in expectation produces clusters of all sizes with equal probability, resulting in total number of clusters proportional to $\sqrt{N}$.

Both being agnostic about the sizes of the clusters and explicitly assuming the rich-get-richer property are reasonable assumptions for a wide range of clustering tasks, as clearly demonstrated by the wide-spread usage of mixture models. For some clustering tasks, however, it would be useful to have finer control over the possible sizes of the clusters. For example, if the clustering model is used for creating teams of similar individuals [Kim et al., 2015] we would want to find clusters that are approximately of the same size, even as small as two to create working pairs. Another practical example is to use clustering to split a collection of items for further processing for distributed set of workers with limited capacity. We can expect the worker to perform the task more accurately and faster if the items are similar, and the clusters should contain at most a certain pre-given number of instances.

In this work, we consider probabilistic clustering models with explicit constraints on the sizes to address the illustrative scenarios above. Our model that assumes constant maximum size is a specific instance of the more general concept of *microclustering*, defined as clustering models for which the size of the clusters grows sublinearly with respect to the sample size [Miller et al., 2015] – here the size is explicitly forced to be constant, to guarantee small clusters even for extremely large data collections. Our microclustering model builds on standard parametric mixture models, but replaces the independent cluster assignments of individual data points with a joint assignment of all points that needs to satisfy the constraints.

Specifying the model for size-constrained microclustering is straightforward, requiring only a simple change in the prior distribution, and in fact similar models have earlier been discussed outside the probabilistic framework.

Banerjee [2006] considered distance-based clustering models that produce clusters of approximatively the same size, and Zhu et al. [2010] added explicit constraints to K-means to utilize prior knowledge on the cluster sizes. Their solutions correspond effectively to maximum likelihood estimation, which is easy given access to standard constrained optimization tools, whereas the core challenge in our case is in conducting full Bayesian inference over the model.

In this work we discuss the challenge of jointly sampling the cluster assignments of all data points in our microclustering model and present two alternative algorithms for that purpose, a dynamic programming algorithm based on depth-first branch-and-bound, and a simple rejection sampler. We empirically demonstrate that these two alternatives dominate in different conditions, the former being efficient for highly constrained cases and the latter being optimal for loose constraints. We then construct a final sampling algorithm that utilizes both parts to produce a Gibbs sampler that is a direct generalization of the corresponding algorithm for regular mixture models: In the absence of constraints it draws the samples independently with no computational overhead, whereas with increasingly tight constraints it starts using the dynamic programming algorithm for improved efficiency.

Besides introducing the size-constrained clustering model, the main message of this article is to highlight that full Bayesian inference is also feasible for models with combinatorial constraints, encouraging people to explore the opportunities outside independent samples. Even though probabilistic reasoning under combinatorial constraints is generally hard [Roth, 1996], many practical probabilistic models result in sufficiently small problem instances that can today be solved efficiently. Explicit constraints can hence be effective in constraining the model and often the computational overhead needed for finding the solution is small compared to the gain in overall performance. We are currently aware of only limited existing literature in this direction; Chen et al. [2005] and Dobra et al. [2006] presented MCMC algorithms for sampling contingency tables with constrained marginals, Klami [2012, 2013] considered posterior inference over permutations to solve cross-domain object matching problems, and Wang et al. [2015] presented an MCMC algorithm for combinatorial problems related to phylogenetic trees.

2 MICROCLUSTERING

Miller et al. [2015] define microclustering as any clustering model where the size of the clusters grow sublinearly with the total number of data points. Even though their formulation considers non-parametric models, the concept itself is useful also for parametric models where the number or size of the clusters is chosen via other means during the modeling process.

The core requirement for building probabilistic microclustering models is to have control over the sizes of the clusters. Regular mixture models have no control over the size distribution besides the prior weights (that can be dominated by the likelihood) because their independent data point assignment prior

$$p(\{z_n\}_{n=1}^N|\theta) = \prod_{n=1}^{N} p(z_n|\theta) \tag{1}$$

implies that the conditional posterior $p(z_n|\{z_n\}_{-n}, \theta) = p(z_n|\theta)$ is independent of the other assignments. Hence the sizes of the clusters cannot influence the decision of the individual sample. Marginalizing the parameters θ out introduces such a dependency, but its nature is completely determined by the prior used on θ and cannot be controlled easily. See Wallach et al. [2010] for both theoretical and empirical analysis of the resulting cluster size distributions for various non-parametric prior processes.

Explicit control over the cluster sizes is conceptually easy to obtain, by replacing the prior in (1) with one that factorizes over the clusters and not the samples:

$$p(\{z_n\}_{n=1}^N|\theta) = \prod_{k=1}^{K} p(s_k|\theta),$$

where s_k is the number of data points assigned to the kth cluster. It is linked to the assignments as $s_k = \sum_{n=1}^N \mathbb{I}(z_n = k)$ where $\mathbb{I}(\cdot)$ evaluates to one if its argument is true and otherwise to zero. In other words, we assume that all joint assignments that result in cluster sizes $\{s_k\}_{k=1}^K$ are equally probable, and their number does not directly influence the probability.

This general formulation leaves open the specific prior given for the sizes. Miller et al. [2015] introduced a non-parametric microclustering model that assumes the cluster sizes follow a negative binomial distribution, whereas we will be using constant priors over a set of legal cluster sizes. One might also imagine other practical choices, such as constant probability for some favoured cluster size with exponential decay for violations from that size. In general, this choice will be application-specific and hence the priors should be subjective, rather unconventionally for mixture modeling in general.

2.1 SIZE-CONSTRAINED MICROCLUSTERING

In this work, we consider microclustering models with explicit hard constraints on the cluster sizes, applicable for scenarios where the (typically maximum) size of a clusters is determined by external channel constraints. These clustering models clearly belong to the family of microclustering models, since the size of the clusters is constant with respect to the total number of data points and hence sublinear. The explicit constraints are easy to formulate but require constrained optimization techniques for inference.

Our model that restricts the sizes between L and U is

$$
\begin{aligned}
p(\{x_n\}|\phi,\{z_n\}) &= \prod_{n=1}^{N} p(x_n|\phi,z_n) = \prod_{n=1}^{N} g(x_n,\phi_{z_n}), \\
p(\{z_n\}) &= \prod_{k=1}^{K} p(s_k), \qquad (2) \\
p(s_k) &= \frac{1}{U-L+1}\delta(L \le s_k \le U),
\end{aligned}
$$

where $g(x_n, \phi_{z_n})$ is some likelihood function and the model is coupled with a suitable prior $p(\phi)$ on its parameters. In our experiments, we will use the Gaussian likelihood $\log g(x_n, \phi_k) = C - \frac{1}{2}(x_n - \mu_k)^T \tau (x_n - \mu_k)$ with diagonal precision τ and priors $\mu \sim N(\mu_0, \Sigma_0)$ and $\tau_d \sim \text{Gamma}(\alpha_0, \beta_0)$, but the core inference algorithms for $\{z\}$ works identically for any likelihood that factorizes over the samples. Here the constraints U and L are constant over the clusters, but all of the inference details apply also for cluster-specific constraints if such prior information is available.

3 INFERENCE

We now discuss the full Bayesian inference for the proposed model. The practical algorithmic details are given for a Gibbs sampler that samples the parameters ϕ of the clusters given the assignments and the assignments $\{z_n\}$ given the cluster parameters. The sampling equations for the cluster parameters are exactly as in any standard mixture model, and are not discussed here in any more detail.

The challenging part is sampling the assignments, which needs to be done jointly for all data points due to the prior distribution and constraints (2) defined for the whole collection instead of individual points. We will first briefly explain how the maximum likelihood solution is easy to find, and then proceed to present two alternatives algorithms for producing samples from the posterior distribution.

As a side remark, the microclustering model of Miller et al. [2015] sidesteps the issue of joint sampling by sampling the allocations of individual samples conditional on all others allocations, from $p(z_n|z_{-n})$. This is feasible in their model that does not have hard constraints, but results in long auto-correlation time due to aggressive conditioning. For our model such a sampler would be catastrophic if the constraints are tight; in the extreme case where the cluster sizes are forced to exact values it could never change the allocation since all clusters except the one where this data point was previously allocated at would be full.

3.1 THE MOST LIKELY ASSIGNMENT(S)

An important initial observation is that we can efficiently find the most likely assignment by solving the integer programming problem

$$
\begin{aligned}
&\max \sum_{n=1}^{N}\sum_{k=1}^{K} \log g(x_n, z_k)\pi_{k,n}, \qquad (3) \\
&s_k = \sum_n \pi_{k,n} \ge L \quad \forall k, \\
&s_k = \sum_n \pi_{k,n} \le U \quad \forall k, \\
&\sum_k \pi_{k,n} = 1 \quad \forall n,
\end{aligned}
$$

where π is a binary matrix whose element $\pi_{k,n}$ indicates whether the nth sample is assigned to the kth cluster. Any off-the-shelf linear programming solver will find the optimal solution in reasonable time for problems of practical size. By alternating between assignments obtained by solving (3) and maximum a posteriori choice for the cluster parameters ϕ_k, we would get a probabilistic variant of the size-constrained K-means model by Zhu et al. [2010].

Typical branch-and-bound algorithms used for solving (3) retain a list of solution candidates that are pruned away by comparing upper bounds for their value against a lower bound for the best candidate. They can be easily modified to retain a list of all possible solutions that are close enough to the optimal, to explicitly enumerate all solutions that are sufficiently likely. Given such a list of solutions $\{\pi^i\}$ and their associated log-probabilities $\{c^i\}$ we could easily sample a solution from $p(\pi = \pi^i) = \frac{\exp(c^i)}{\sum_i \exp(c^i)}$.

Unfortunately, explicitly enumerating all of the good solutions is infeasible for all but the smallest problems because their number becomes inordinately large. In the unconstrained case there are N^K possible allocations, all of which would need to be enumerated if the probabilities fall off of too slowly. We do not discuss this approach further since the cases for which it would be efficient are easy to solve by other means as well, but the optimization problem (3) is still important; we will use it for quickly creating an upper bound in our actual sampler, as well as for initializing the sampling chain.

3.2 CLUSTER SIZE ASSIGNMENT SAMPLER

3.2.1 Motivation

A more practical solution to the problem is a dynamic programming algorithm that operates in the space of possible cluster sizes, enumerating only the possible cluster size allocation vectors $r \in [L, U]^K$ instead of the sample allocation vectors $z \in [1, K]^N$. Even in the unconstrained case the maximum number of solutions to be enumerated in the end goes down from N^K to $\binom{N+K-1}{K-1}$, and for the constrained case with uniform maximum size U we have at most $\sum_{q=0}^{\min(K,\lfloor N/(U+1)\rfloor)}(-1)^q\binom{K}{q}\binom{N-q*(U+1)+K-1}{K-1}$ solutions. As a case in point, already for $N = 20$, $K = 8$ and

$U = 4$ these three numbers would be 2.6×10^{10}, 888.030 and 23.940. With minimum size $L = 2$ the number of possible solutions would further decrease to just 266. Enumerating 2.6×10^{10} solutions would be clearly infeasible, whereas the result set of at most 266 solutions would cause no trouble.

Operating in the space of cluster size allocations does come with a drawback as well, in the form of more difficult bounding of the solution candidates. Furthermore, the number of solution candidates in the intermediate stages is typically considerably higher than the size of the final set, but still orders of magnitude smaller than the number of individual solutions. We will next show how a reasonably efficient dynamic programming algorithm operating in the space of the cluster sizes can be designed.

3.2.2 Basic Concept

The algorithm operates on solution sets $A_a = (R_a, q_a)$, where each set contains a collection of solution candidates $R_a = \{r_a^i, p_a^i\}$ and the total probability of the set $q_a = \sum_i p_a^i$. Each solution i is characterized by a vector of cluster sizes $r_a^i \in \mathbb{N}^K$ and the associated probability p_a^i of that particular solution. Throughout the description of the algorithm, subscripts refer to the sets and superscripts to the individual solution candidates within the set, so that p_a^i means the probability of the ith solution candidate in set A_a.[1]

We build a forward-backward sampling algorithm based on dynamic programming reminiscent of the algorithm used for sampling the state sequence of Bayesian hidden Markov models [Scott, 2002]. Similar to that algorithm we make a forward pass to accumulate total probabilities of solutions and a backward pass to sample given the accumulated probabilities after each sample. For HMMs this algorithm can cover all possibilities since it only needs to keep track of K probabilities at each stage, but since we are keeping track of all possible cluster size allocations we also need to prune out solution candidates that will have negligible probability in the final set.

The overall algorithm is illustrated in Figure 1, which also demonstrates how the practical computations are performed.

3.2.3 Forward Pass

The forward pass starts by constructing N initial sets A_n, each storing the K possible cluster allocations for one sample. The probability of each solution is given by $p_n^k = g(x_n, z_k)$, and the total probability is $q_n = \sum_k p_n^k$.

[1] In practice we naturally store the values in the logarithmic domain for numerical stability, but the presentation below uses actual probabilities to avoid needing to write $\log \sum \exp(\cdot)$ for all cases where we sum up probabilities.

The first iteration of the forward pass picks two of these sets (denoted by i and j) and joins them to create a solution set $A_{i,j}$, containing all possible allocations of the two samples, stored still as the possible cluster size allocation vectors $r_{i,j}^i$ and their probabilities $p_{i,j}^i$. This join is performed by a collection of four basic operations described soon and illustrated in Figure 1.

After joining the two sets we proceed to join the resulting set with another of the initial N sets, denoted by l, this time producing the set $A_{i,j,l}$ that stores the joint allocations of all three samples. The process continues this way for $N - 1$ iterations, until all samples have been joined to the final set $A_{1:N}$. It stores the probabilities of all possible cluster size allocations that satisfy the constraints. Together with all of the intermediate sets it enables drawing a sample from the posterior using the backward pass described in Section 3.2.5.

3.2.4 Set operations

For manipulating the sets the algorithm requires four basic operations:

1. MERGE(A_a,A_b): Takes as input two sets and combines them, to produce a new set that contains all possible combinations of the solutions in the two sets: each solution in A_a is paired with each solution in A_b, so that the cluster size vectors are summed up and the probabilities are multiplied together. Note that this typically results in duplicate solution candidates, since the same sum $r_a^i + r_b^j$ can be reached in multiple ways.

2. COLLAPSE(A_a): Takes as input a solution set A_a with possible duplicates for the cluster size vectors r_a^i and returns the set so that each unique vector is represented only once. The probability of that set is obtained by summing over the probabilities associated with each duplicate: $p_a^i = \sum_j p_a^j \quad \forall r_a^j = r_a^i$.

3. CHECKCONSTRAINTS(A_a, U_a, L_a): Takes as input a solution set and returns a set that excludes all solutions that violate the constraints. That is, we keep only solutions for which $L_a \le r_a^i \le U_a$ holds for all K elements.

4. BOUND(A_a, b): Takes as input a solution set and returns a set that excludes all solutions for which the probability is below the bound, $p_a^i < b$.

A single iteration of the forward pass is simply a concatenation of all of the above operations: The initial sets are passed to MERGE, the result of that to COLLAPSE, and then to CHECKCONSTRAINTS and BOUND in either order. Without bounding or checking for the constraints the algorithm would simply proceed to enumerate all possible cluster size allocations, so the efficiency of the algorithm

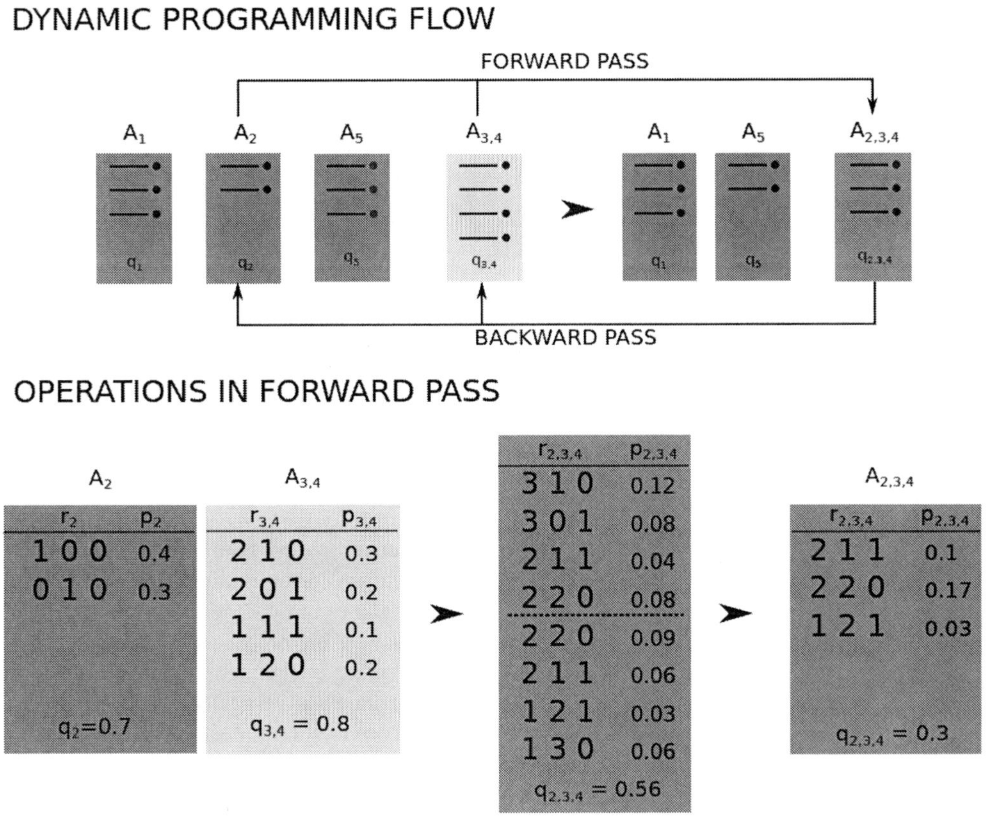

Figure 1: **Top:** Schematic overview of the dynamic programming algorithm. The forward pass computes the probabilities of possible cluster size allocation vectors by joining one sample at a time to the current overall solution set marked in yellow, producing the next overall solution set marked in orange. The backwards step then draws a sample by considering the probabilities in the intermediate sets created during the forward pass. **Bottom:** Example of an individual join. Each set stores all possible cluster size vectors r^i for the samples in that set with the associated probabilities p^i, as well as the total probability q that is their sum. The MERGE operation produces all possible combinations of the cluster size vectors of the two sets, here ordered so that the solutions above the dashed line correspond to r_2^1, and multiplies the probabilities. The COLLAPSE operation then sums up the probabilities for each unique solution, and CHECKCONSTRAINTS cuts out solutions that exceed the constraints; here solutions with cluster sizes above $U = 2$ were pruned out. Note that the total probability in the intermediate stage is simply the product of the probabilities for the incoming sets, but the probability of the final result is often considerably smaller. This allows pruning the other sets again since their upper bounds have decreased, here by $0.56 - 0.3 = 0.26$, resulting in A_5 now having only two valid solutions instead of three.

depends on how well we can cut out solution candidates based on the constraints and the bound on probabilities.

To efficiently bound the solutions in A_a we need to know an upper bound for the probability of still unprocessed samples, denoted by β_a^i, and a global lower bound for the probability of the most likely final solution, denoted by $G = \max_i p_{1:N}^i$. We can then prune out all solution candidates i in set A_a for which

$$p_a^i + \beta_a^i \leq G/\Delta,$$

where Δ is a threshold chosen sufficiently large; we use $\Delta = \exp(12)$ in our experiment, to indicate that we only prune out solutions that are guaranteed to be at least five orders of magnitude less likely than the optimal one. The bound β_a^i is obtained by inspecting the other sets A_m. Since we store with each set the total probability of all possible allocations as q_m, we obtain the bound $\beta_a^i = \sum_{m \neq a} q_m$ that is independent of the solution candidate itself. Note that the quantity G is in general unknown but we can use any lower bound for that instead and retain the validity (at the expense of longer computation time); we will return to the choice of G in Section 3.2.6.

The constraints used for CHECKCONSTRAINTS are not the original constraints, but instead we need to here look at what the remaining feasible solutions for this set are. For each set we can compute the minimum and maximum sizes of the clusters, denoted by $r_a^l = \min_i r_a^i$ and $r_a^u = \max_i r_a^i$, where the minimum and maximum are taken separately for each dimension. Then the constraints for the set A_a are given by

$$U_a = U - \sum_{m \neq a} r_m^l,$$

$$L_a = \max\left(L - \sum_{m \neq a} r_m^u, 0\right).$$

In other words, we can subtract from the global bound all the counts that we know for sure will be allocated in some future set, and we need to allocate in this set the counts that cannot be anymore allocated in the future sets.

3.2.5 Backward pass

The actual sample is produced by traversing the partial solution sets backwards, starting from the final set $A_{1:N}$. We normalize the probabilities of the possible solutions in that set and randomly sample one of those, denoting it by $r_{1:N}^l$. We then find all possible combinations of the last joined set m and its counterpart A_{-m}, that stores the solutions for all other samples, for which

$$r_m^i + r_{-m}^j = r_{1:N}^l.$$

That is, we find the possible solutions in each set that could have been paired up to create the final solution. For each of these we compute the probability $p_m^i \times p_{-m}^j$ and draw a categorical sample to indicate the cluster assignment for sample m. We then proceed backwards in the table repeating this same procedure, now using r_{-m}^j for the chosen allocation as the target vector, until at the very end we simply pick the only possible allocation for the first sample. This is guaranteed to produce a valid sample, the only error source coming from partial solution sets pruned away because of the upper bound being smaller than G/Δ.

3.2.6 Implementation Remarks

The efficiency of the algorithm depends on the order of the samples being merged into the final set. We use a simple heuristic that attempts to keep the size of the intermediate sets minimal, which proved efficient in our preliminary experiments: we keep track of the expected cluster size vector (obtained by summing simple matrix products for all remaining sets), and always join the sample that is expected to violate the maximum constraints most. If no such samples exist, we merge with the set having the smallest number of remaining solutions.

Another key element is keeping the total probabilities q_a associated with the unprocessed sets updated. Right after the initialization, we can typically exclude considerable number of solution candidates in the singleton sets because already that single assignment would make the full solution too unlikely. Since the bounding is based on the sum over all other sets, including the one that has already accumulated more samples, we should apply BOUND and CHECK-CONSTRAINTS again for all sets after each join.

Finally, we stated earlier that for bounding the candidates we need to know the probability G of the best final solution, so that we can prune out solutions for which the bounded probability is sufficiently smaller than that. Since we are operating in a depth-first manner we do not obtain such a bound with the algorithm itself. Instead, we find a lower bound for it by the following procedure: we first find the most likely individual solution by solving (3) and compute the cluster sizes $\hat{r}$ of that solution. We then solve the forward pass with constraints $L_k = U_k = \hat{r}_k$ and global bound G_0 corresponding to the total probability of all possible assignments without any constraints. This either produces a lower bound for the probability of the solution candidate corresponding to cluster sizes $\hat{r}$ or, if G_0 is too large, fails by producing an empty set. If the process failed we repeat the procedure using smaller G_0, until a valid lower bound is obtained. While this procedure is somewhat inefficient it generally still takes only a fraction of the total computation time, especially for hard instances. In our experiments, the resulting lower bound for G was also typically very close to the actual true maximum probability (seen after running the full forward pass).

Finally, for well-separated clusters it is typically not necessary to solve the whole problem in one go. Instead, we can partition the data set into disjoint subsets of data points that do not compete for the same clusters, using a simple greedy procedure. Then we can apply the algorithm for each subset separately, while still guaranteeing to produce an independent sample. In the empirical experiments we skip this step to keep the results as clear as possible (how often the problem splits into disjoint sets depends heavily on the data), but in practice it should be done since finding the disjoint sets is very light operation.

3.3 REJECTION SAMPLER

A considerably simpler algorithm for solving the same problem can be obtained by a rejection principle. Despite the simplicity, the rejection sampler presented next will still be a practical solution for some problem instances.

Given N samples to be allocated to K clusters, the rejection sampler simply allocates all samples independently, drawing the assignment for each from the normalized likelihoods $p(z_n = k) = \frac{g(x_n, z_k)}{Z}$, where Z sums over the probabilities for the different clusters k. Afterwards, the sampler checks whether the constraints on the cluster sizes are violated. If there are no violations we keep the sample. Otherwise we create another sample and check for the constraints again, continuing until a valid sample is produced.

This sampler is obviously inefficient for cases where the constraints rule out the most likely solutions, but for cases with loose constraints it is a practical tool. Often the very first sample will be accepted and the sampler is so fast that we can typically afford to re-sample quite many times.

4 EVALUATING THE ASSIGNMENT SAMPLERS

In the following we demonstrate the samplers on artificial problems. At this stage we do not consider the sampler as part of a full clustering model, but instead merely look at the process of sampling the cluster assignments given some log-probabilities for the individual assignments. In other words, we simply consider the constrained optimization task of finding all possible solutions to the maximization problem (3) that exceed a certain threshold and drawing a sample from that set.

4.1 PROBLEM INSTANCES

The difficulty of a problem instance can be described crudely along two axes: the optimality gap indicating how close the best individual solution is to the unconstrained optimal allocation, and how quickly the probabilities decay when forced to pick sub-optimal allocations. The former is tightly connected with the tightness of the constraints, whereas the latter related to the tightness and separation of the clusters.

Intuitively, the instances with small (or zero) optimality gap are good for the rejection sampler: Almost all samples produced are within the constraints and hence the sampler is almost as efficient as an unconstrained sampler would be. For the dynamic programming algorithm these instances are the worst possible ones, especially if the probabilities decay slowly; we need to enumerate an excessively large set of solutions. The other extreme of problems with tight constraints and large optimality gap is difficult for the rejection sampler, but easy for the dynamic programming variant as long as the probabilities decay quickly enough.

To study the behavior of the samplers under these characteristics we create random problem instances by sampling the log-probabilities from standard distributions and by controlling the tightness of the constraints. We do this instead of considering actual cluster assignment setups since it allows finer control over the characteristics; for real clustering instances the optimality gap and rate of decay are often correlated in a complicated manner. We return to actual clustering problems in Section 6.

4.2 RESULTS

We created random solution instances with $K \in [6, 15]$ and $N \in [36, 225]$, drawing the entries from normal distribution with zero mean and standard deviation $\sigma \in [4, 40]$. We then solved the problems with varying degree of constraints, so that each cluster size was allowed to differ from the mean by $[0, 3]$ samples. For each problem, we ran both of the above algorithms and stored the running time until a valid solution was found, terminating the samplers if it took more than 20 seconds.

We summarize the results in Figure 2, where we present the computation times as a function of the problem instance characteristics discussed above. The optimality gap is determined by simply comparing the solution of (3) to the unconstrained optimum, and for measuring the probability decay we use a simple proxy: we count for each sample the number of cluster assignments that have probability above $1/\Delta$ of the highest probability, excluding the top candidate itself, and sum them up. This approximates the number of free variables to be considered outside the best allocation, but need not correlate with the original problem size. For producing these plots we always grouped all problem instances satisfying specific conditions into one pool, reporting the quantiles of the computation time for that pool. For studying the effect of the optimality gap we only used instances for which the number of free variables is below 50, and for studying the effect of the free variables we considered cases with logarithmic optimality gap below 7.

The experiment confirms the intuitive expectations of the previous section: for small optimality gap the rejection sampler is optimal but it quickly becomes infeasible when the gap grows. The rejection sampler, meanwhile, is efficient for fast enough probability decay (or, equivalently, small enough effective problem size), but becomes extremely slow if the probabilities do not decay quickly enough. A notable observation is that the running time curves of both algorithms have a sharp curve with respect to one of the measures: The running time is reasonably constant and always manageable until some threshold in gap or probability decay, and after that the running time becomes quickly excessive. In other words, the instances with large optimality gap and small decay of probabilities are problematic for both samplers.

5 HYBRID SAMPLER

In light of the above experiments, we propose as the final sampling solution a hybrid algorithm that uses both the rejection sampler and the dynamic programming algorithm while avoiding the cases that are too slow for both of them.

For a given task of assigning N samples, we first try out with the rejection sampler for some number of tries; if we produce a valid sample we keep it and the process terminates. If we fail to produce a valid sample we proceed to evaluate the difficulty of the problem. If the problem is considered easy enough, we apply the dynamic programming algorithm to produce the sample.

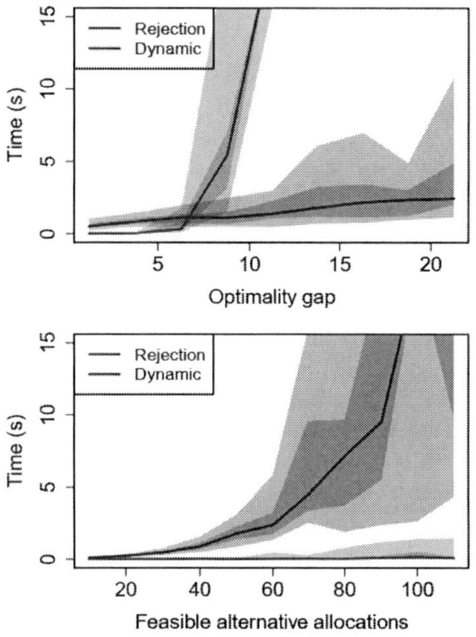

Figure 2: Comparison of running times of the two alternative sampling algorithms in producing a sample from posterior distributions $p(\{z_n\}|\{x_n\}, \phi)$ of varying difficulty. For both figures the dark shaded area indicates times between the 35% and 65% quantiles and the light shaded area between the 20% and 80% quantiles, and the times refer to single-core implementations. **Top:** The rejection sampler breaks down for logarithmic optimality gaps of roughly 7, meaning that the optimal allocation is roughly 1000 times more likely than the best feasible solution, but before that has effectively constant running time. The dynamic programming algorithm is largely insensitive to the optimality gap, but slightly slows down for the harder problems and occasionally takes longer time. **Bottom:** The dynamic programming sampler breaks down when the probabilities decay off too slowly. Here the horizontal axis denotes the count of non-optimal sample allocations with log-probabilities within 6 points of the most likely allocation for that sampler, and we see the algorithm becomes excessively slow around count 60.

If the problem is considered too challenging for the dynamic programming algorithm we split the problem into smaller chunks. We randomly divide the data point into two sets of $N/2$ instances each, and draw the assignments for each half conditional on the current assignments for the other half. For each half we again first try the rejection sampler and then consider the dynamic programming sampler or proceed to further subdivide the problem recursively. Assigning only a subset of the data points at a time naturally introduces auto-correlation in the overall sampling chain, but the time saved in not attempting to solve an overly difficult instance at once allows repeating the process enough times to produce an independent sample.

The exact criteria for when to split the problem into two halves should depend on the cost of sampling the cluster parameters ϕ given the assignments. For models where this stage is efficient, like our Gaussian likelihoods, the increased auto-correlation in sampling the assignments is not an issue and we can sample fairly small sets at once. In the other extreme, such as mixture models where approximative Bayesian computation [Csillery et al., 2010] is needed for sampling the cluster parameters, it pays off to solve the whole problem at once even if it takes a long time.

A full-blown analysis stage should inspect the rate of decline for the probabilities, the optimality gap, the number of solutions within the constraints, and possibly other statistics. In practice, however, we resort to a simpler heuristic to avoid the computation needed for the analysis (finding the optimality gap requires solving (3)); we simply use the same measure of effective problem size used in Section 4.2 and use the dynamic programming algorithm for cases where this number is small enough.

6 EVALUATING THE MICROCLUSTERING MODEL

Next we evaluate the final hybrid algorithm as part of a whole microclustering model to illustrate the balance between the two alternative solutions. As explained above, the algorithm has two parameters: The number of times the rejection sampler is tried before giving up, and the maximum complexity of the problem instance solved with the dynamic programming solver. Both parameters control how many samples can be jointly allocated; bigger values make it more likely that the sampler can allocate large number of data points at once, but at the same time increases the computational time per posterior sample. The relative ratio of these two parameters, in turn, controls how often each of the algorithms is in practice used; high number of tries and small complexity threshold imply that the rejection sampler allocates most samples, and vice versa.

Figure 3 illustrates the effect of the two parameters for an example clustering problem where the input data is uniformly distributed in a two-dimensional rectangle; the data has no natural cluster structure and hence the constraints are crucial in guaranteeing balanced cluster sizes. We show results for both 64 data points being clustered into $K = 8$ clusters and 256 data points being clustered into $K = 16$ clusters, constraining the clusters to be exactly identical in size. For both cases the results are similar: The rejection sampler takes care of the assignments of majority of the samples unless the maximum number of trials is very low, but using the dynamic sampler to solve harder problem instances helps assign more data points at a time. Both indi-

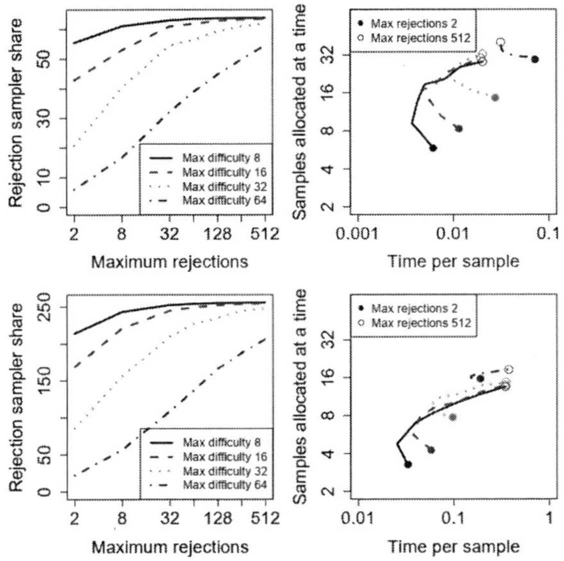

Figure 3: Illustration of the hybrid algorithm on two clustering problems. The top row corresponds to clustering $N = 64$ data points into $K = 8$ clusters and bottom row to clustering $N = 256$ samples into $K = 16$ clusters. For both cases the data points are uniformly distributed on a two-dimensional space, the clusters are forced to be of equal size, and the results are averaged over five randomly created data sets. **The left plots** show how many data points are on average assigned by the rejection sampler; the ratio naturally goes up if we try several times before giving up and down if we solve harder problems using the dynamic programming algorithm. The colored lines corresponding to different maximum difficulty scores, corresponding to the number of free variables in the problem instance as defined in Section 4.2. **The right plots** characterize the overall efficiency of the algorithm, plotting the average number of data points assigned jointly (by either algorithm) versus the computational time required for producing the whole posterior sample. Points closer to the top left corner are here the best, quickly allocating several data points at once, and we see that comparable results are obtained with several combinations for the two parameters as long as the extreme values are avoided. The color-codes in the right plot match the left one; for example, the red line shows how the behavior of the sampler evolves for maximum problem difficulty of 16 when the number of allowed rejections grows from 2 to 512.

vidual algorithms are hence useful for the overall solution. Importantly, a wide range of parameter values gives satisfactory results, suggesting that the overall algorithm is not very sensitive to the choice of the thresholds.

7 DISCUSSION

In this work we introduced a new microclustering model [Miller et al., 2015] for solving clustering tasks with predefined constraints on the sizes of the clusters, motivated by scenarios where the clusters are used, for example, in creating teams of fixed sizes [Kim et al., 2015] or for allocating items for further processing of (manual or automated) workers with limited capacity. To control the sizes we introduced a cluster assignment prior that does not factorize over the samples but instead over the clusters; this formulation is more general and can be used also for models without hard constraints. One straightforward extension would consider priors where the log-probability of the cluster decays linearly when moving away from some preferred size; for such a prior we can still find the most likely assignment easily and hence can generalize the whole sampler.

The model requires the cluster assignments to be drawn jointly for all data points, which increases the computational cost compared to standard mixture models. We discussed two alternative samplers and showed that each is efficient for a subclass of problems, and then proceeded to present a practical algorithm that can draw samples also for large data collections with the possible expense of increased auto-correlation for overly complex problem instances. The algorithm attempts to assign all samples jointly, but in case the problem instance is too difficult it recursively splits the problem into two parts and assigns the samples conditional on the assignments for the other part. Probabilistic treatment of clustering is most useful for fairly small cluster sizes that necessitate explicitly treating the full posterior, and we showed that for such setups we can draw posterior samples in a fraction of a second.

Finally, we want to encourage Bayesian practitioners to consider combinatorial constraints in their models. Even though the problem of finding all solutions that exceed a certain threshold is considerably harder than finding the best one, it is still feasible for problems of moderate size. Sampling-based probabilistic inference also comes with natural solution for splitting the problem into easier and smaller sub-problems, in form of conditioning based on a subset of the assignments. Consequently, we believe that several types of combinatorial constraints can be incorporated into typical latent-variable models and other probabilistic models with fairly low additional overhead. The auto-correlation of the sampling chain increases and the individual sampler steps typically take longer time, but one should not shy away from introducing the constraints if they are important for the model itself.

Acknowledgements

The work was supported by the Academy of Finland, via the Finnish Center of Excellence in Computational Inference Research (COIN) and grant 266969.

References

Charles E. Antoniak. Mixtures of Dirichlet processes with applications to Bayesian nonparametric problems. *Annals of Statistics*, 2(6):1152–1174, 1974.

Arindam Banerjee. Scalable clustering algorithms with balancing constraints. *Data mining and knowledge discovery*, 13(3):365–395, 2006.

Yuguo Chen, Persi Diaconis, Susan P. Holmes, and Jun S. Liu. Sequential Monte Carlo methods for statistical analysis of tables. *Journal of the American Statistical Association*, 100(469):109–120, 2005.

Katalin Csillery, Michael G.B. Blum, Oscar E. Gaggiotti, and Olivier Francois. Approximative Bayesian computation (ABC) in practice. *Trends in Ecology & Evolution*, 25(7):410–418, 2010.

Adrian Dobra, Claudia Tebaldi, and Mike West. Data augmentation in multi-way contingency tables with fixed marginal totals. *Journal of Statistical Planning and Inference*, 136(2):355–372, 2006.

Avinava Dubey, Sinead A. Williamson, and Eric P. Xing. Parallel Markov chain Monte Carlo for Pitman-Yor mixture models. In *Proceedings of Uncertainty in Artificial Intelligence*, 2014.

Byoung Wook Kim, Ja Mee Kim, Won Gyu Lee, and Jin Gon Shon. Parallel balanced team formation clustering based on MapReduce. In *Advances in Computer Science and Ubiquitous Computing*, volume 373 of *Lecture Notes in Electrical Engineering*, pages 671–675. Springer, 2015.

Arto Klami. Variational Bayesian matching. In *Proceedings of 4th Asian Conference on Machine Learning*, volume 25 of *JMLR: W&CP*, pages 205–220, 2012.

Arto Klami. Bayesian object matching. *Machine learning*, 92(2):225–250, 2013.

Geoff McLachlan and David Peel. *Finite mixture models*. Wiley, 2004.

Jeffrey Miller and Matthew Harrison. A simple example of Dirichlet process mixture inconsistency for the number of components. In *Advances in Neural Information Processing Systems 26*, pages 199–206, 2013.

Jeffrey Miller, Brenda Betancourt, Abbas Zaidi, Hanna Wallach, and Rebecca C. Steorts. Microclustering: When the cluster sizes grow sublinearly with the size of the data set. *arXiv:1512.00792*, 2015.

Dan Roth. On the hardness of approximative reasoning. *Artificial Intelligence*, 82(1–2):273–302, 1996.

Steven L. Scott. Bayesian methods for hidden Markov models. *Journal of the Americal Statistical Association*, 97(457):337–351, 2002.

Hanna M. Wallach, Shane T. Jensen, Lee Dicker, and Katherine A. Heller. An alternative prior process for nonparametric Bayesian clustering. In *Proceedings of the 13th International Conference on Artificial Intelligence and Statistics (AISTATS)*, volume 9 of *JMLR: W&CP*, 2010.

Liangliang Wang, Alexander Bouchard-Cote, and Arnaud Doucet. Bayesian phylogenetic inference using a combinatorial sequential Monte Carlo method. *Journal of the American Statistical Association*, 110(512):1362–1374, 2015.

Shunzhi Zhu, Dingding Wang, and Tao Li. Data clustering with size constraints. *Knowledge-Based Systems*, 23(8): 883–889, 2010.

Online learning with Erdős–Rényi side-observation graphs

Tomáš Kocák
SequeL team
INRIA Lille - Nord Europe

Gergely Neu
Universitat Pompeu Fabra
Barcelona, Spain

Michal Valko
SequeL team
INRIA Lille - Nord Europe

Abstract

We consider adversarial multi-armed bandit problems where the learner is allowed to observe losses of a number of arms beside the arm that it actually chose. We study the case where all non-chosen arms reveal their loss with an *unknown* probability r_t, independently of each other and the action of the learner. Moreover, we allow r_t to change in every round t, which rules out the possibility of estimating r_t by a well-concentrated sample average. We propose an algorithm which operates under the assumption that r_t is large enough to warrant at least one side observation with high probability. We show that after T rounds in a bandit problem with N arms, the expected regret of our algorithm is of order $\mathcal{O}\Big(\sqrt{\sum_{t=1}^{T}(1/r_t)\log N}\,\Big)$, given that $r_t \geq \log T/(2N-2)$ for all t. All our bounds are within logarithmic factors of the best achievable performance of any algorithm that is even allowed to know exact values of r_t.

1 INTRODUCTION

In sequential learning, a learner is repeatedly asked to choose an action for which it obtains a loss and receives a feedback from the environment (Cesa-Bianchi and Lugosi, 2006). We typically study two feedback settings: the learner either observes the losses for all the potential actions (full information) or it observes only the loss of the action it chose. This latter feedback scheme is known as the *bandit* setting (cf. Auer et al., 2002a). In this paper, instead of considering these two limit cases, we study a more refined feedback model, known as *bandit with side observations* (Mannor and Shamir, 2011; Alon et al., 2013; Kocák et al., 2014, 2016), that generalizes both of them. Typical examples for learning with full information and bandit feedback are sequential trading on a stock market (where all stock prices are fully observable after each trading period), and electronic advertising (where the learner can only observe the clicks on actually shown ads), respectively. However, advertising in a social network offers a more intricate user feedback than captured by the basic bandit model: when proposing an item to a user in a social network, the advertiser can often learn about the preferences of the user's connections as well. Naturally, the advertiser would want to improve its recommendation strategy by incorporating these side observations.

Besides advertising and recommender systems, side observations can also arise in sensor networks, where the action of the learner amounts to probing a particular sensor. In this setting, each sensor can reveal readings of some other sensors that are in its range. When our goal is to sequentially select a sensor maximizing a property of interest, a good learning strategy should be able to leverage these side readings.

In this paper, we follow the formalism of Mannor and Shamir (2011) who model side observations with a graph structure over the actions: two actions mutually reveal their losses if they are connected by an edge in the graph in question. In a realistic scenario this graph is *time dependent* and *unknown* to the learner (e.g., the advertiser or the algorithm scheduling sensor readings). All previous algorithms for the studied setting (Mannor and Shamir, 2011; Alon et al., 2013; Kocák et al., 2014, 2016) require the environment to reveal a substantial part of a graph, at least after the side observations have been revealed. Specifically, these algorithms require the knowledge of the *second neighborhood* (the set of neighbors of the neighbors) of the chosen action in order to update their internal loss estimates. On the other hand, they are able to handle arbitrary graph structures, potentially chosen by an adversary and prove performance guarantees using graph properties based on cliques or independence sets.

The main contribution of our work is a learning algorithm that, unlike previous solutions, does *not require the knowledge of the exact graph* underlying the observations, beyond knowing from which nodes the side observations came from. Relaxing this assumption, however, has to come with a price: As the very recent results of Cohen et al. (2016) show, achieving nontrivial advantages from side observations may be impossible without perfectly known side-observation graphs when an adversary is allowed to pick *both* the losses and the side-observation graphs. On the positive side, Cohen et al. offer efficient algorithms achieving strong improvements over the standard regret guarantees under the assumption that the losses are generated in an i.i.d. fashion and the graphs may be generated adversarially. Complementing these results, we consider the case of adversarial losses and make the assumption that the side-observation graph in round t is generated from an *Erdős–Rényi* model with an *unknown* and *time-dependent* parameter r_t. The main challenge for the learner is then the necessity to exploit the side observations despite not knowing the sequence (r_t). It is easy to see that this model can be equivalently understood as each non-chosen arm revealing its loss with probability r_t, independently of all other observations. That said, we still find it useful to think of the side observations as being generated from an Erdős–Rényi model, as it allows direct comparisons with the related literature. In particular, the case of learning with Erdős–Rényi side-observation graphs was considered before by Alon et al. (2013): Given *full access* to the underlying graph structure, their algorithm Exp3-SET can be shown to guarantee a regret bound of $\mathcal{O}\big(\sqrt{\sum_t (1/r_t)(1-(1-r_t)^N)\log N}\big)$. While the assumption of having full access to the graph be dropped relatively easily in this particular case, exact knowledge of r_t seems to be crucial for constructing reliable loss estimates and use them to guide the choice of action in each round.

It turns out that the problem of estimating r_t while striving to perform efficiently is in fact a major difficulty in our setting. Indeed, as we allow r_t to change arbitrarily between each round, we cannot rely on any past observations to construct well-concentrated estimates of these parameters. That is, the main challenge is estimating r_t from only a handful of samples. The core technical tool underlying our approach is a direct estimation procedure for the losses that does not estimate r_t explicitly.

Armed with this estimation procedure, we propose a learning algorithm called Exp3-Res that guarantees a regret of $\mathcal{O}(\sqrt{\sum_t (1/r_t)\log N})$, provided that $r_t \geq \log T/(2N-2)$ holds for all rounds t. This assumption essentially corresponds to requiring that, with high probability, at least 1 side observation is produced in every round, or, in other words, the side-observation graphs encountered are all *non-empty*. Notice that for the assumed range of r_t's, our regret bound improves upon the standard regret bound of Exp3, which is of $\mathcal{O}(\sqrt{NT\log N})$. It is easy to see that when r_t becomes smaller than $1/N$, side observations become unreliable and the bound of Exp3 cannot be improved. That is, if our assumption cannot be verified a priori, then ignoring all side observations and using the Exp3 algorithm of Auer et al. (2002a) instead can yield a better performance. On the other hand, given that our assumption holds, our bounds cannot be significantly improved as suggested by the lower-bound of $\Omega(\sqrt{T/r})$ proved for a static r by Alon et al. 2013.

Many other partial-information settings have been studied in previous work. One of the simplest of these settings is the label-efficient prediction game considered by Cesa-Bianchi et al. (2005), where the learner can observe either losses of all the actions or none of them, not even the loss of the chosen action. This observation can be queried by the learner at most an $\varepsilon < 1$ fraction of the total number of rounds, which means no losses are observed in the remaining rounds. An even more restricted information setting, label efficient bandit feedback was considered by Allenberg et al. (2006), where the learner can only query the loss of the chosen action, instead of all losses (see also Audibert and Bubeck, 2010). Algorithms for these two settings have regret of $\widetilde{\mathcal{O}}(\sqrt{T/\varepsilon})$ and $\widetilde{\mathcal{O}}(\sqrt{NT/\varepsilon})$, respectively. While these bounds may appear very similar to ours, notice that our setting offers a more intricate (and, for some problems, more realistic) feedback scheme, which also turns out to be much more challenging to exploit. In another related setting, Seldin et al. (2014) consider M side observations that the learner can proactively choose in each round without limitations. Seldin et al. deliver an algorithm with regret of $\widetilde{\mathcal{O}}(\sqrt{(N/M)T})$, also proving that choosing M observations uniformly at random is minimax optimal; given this sampling scheme, it is not even necessary to observe the loss of the chosen action. Their result is comparable to ours and the result by Alon et al. (2013) for Erdős–Rényi observation graphs with parameter $r = M/N$. However, Seldin et al. also assume that M is known, which obviates the need for estimating r. We provide a more technical discussion on the related work in Section 6.

In our paper, we assume that, just like the observation probabilities, the losses are *adversarial*, that is, they can change at each time step without restrictions. Learning with side observations and stochastic losses was studied by Caron et al. (2012) and Buccapatnam et al. (2014). While this is an easier setting that the adversarial one, the authors assumed, in both cases, that the graphs have to be known in advance. Recently, Carpentier and Valko (2016) studied another stochastic setting where the graph is also not known in advance, however their setting considers different feedback and loss structure (influence maximization) which differs from the side-observation setting.

Furthermore, Alon et al. (2015) considered a strictly more difficult setting than ours, where the loss of the chosen action may not be a part of the received feedback.

2 PROBLEM DEFINITION

We now formalize our learning problem. We consider a sequential interaction scheme between a learner and an environment, where the following steps are repeated in every round $t = 1, 2, \ldots, T$:

1. The environment chooses $r_t \in [0, 1]$ and a loss function over the arms, with $\ell_{t,i}$ being the loss associated with arm $i \in [N] \stackrel{\text{def}}{=} \{1, 2, \ldots, N\}$ at time t.
2. Based on its previous observations (and possibly some randomness), the learner draws an arm $I_t \in [N]$.
3. The learner suffers loss ℓ_{t,I_t}.
4. For all $i \neq I_t$, $O_{t,i}$ is independently drawn from a Bernoulli distribution with mean r_t. Furthermore, O_{t,I_t} is set as 1.
5. For all $i \in [N]$ such that $O_{t,i} = 1$, the learner observes the loss $\ell_{t,i}$.

The goal of the learner is to minimize its total expected losses, or, equivalently, to minimize the *total expected regret* (or, in short, regret) defined as

$$R_T = \max_{i \in [N]} \mathbb{E}\left[\sum_{t=1}^{T} (\ell_{t,I_t} - \ell_{t,i})\right].$$

We will denote the interaction history between the learner and the environment up to the beginning of round t by $\mathcal{F}_{t-1}$. We also define $p_{t,i} = \mathbb{P}[I_t = i | \mathcal{F}_{t-1}]$.

The main challenge in our setting is leveraging side observations *without knowing* r_t. Had we had access to the exact value of r_t, we would be able to define the following estimate of $\ell_{t,i}$:

$$\widehat{\ell}^{\star}_{t,i} = \frac{O_{t,i}\ell_{t,i}}{p_{t,i} + (1 - p_{t,i})r_t} \tag{1}$$

It is easy to see that the loss estimates defined this way are unbiased in the sense that $\mathbb{E}\left[\widehat{\ell}_{t,i}\middle| \mathcal{F}_{t-1}\right] = \ell_{t,i}$ for all t and i. It is also straightforward to show that an appropriately tuned instance of the Exp3 algorithm of Auer et al. (2002a) fed with these loss estimates is guaranteed to achieve a regret of $\mathcal{O}(\sqrt{\sum_t (1/r_t) \log N})$ (see also Seldin et al. 2014).

Then, one might consider a simple algorithm that devotes a number of observations to obtain an estimate $\widehat{r}_t$ of r_t and plug this estimate into (1). However, notice that since r_t is allowed to change arbitrarily over time, we can only work with a severely limited sample budget for estimating r_t: only $N - 1$ independent observations! Thus, we can obtain only very loose confidence intervals around r_t which translate to even more useless confidence intervals around $\widehat{\ell}^{\star}_{t,i}$.

Below, we describe a simple trick for obtaining loss estimates that have similar properties to the ones defined in (1) without requiring exact knowledge or even explicit estimation of r_t. Our procedure is based on the geometric resampling method of Neu and Bartók (2013). To get an intuition of the method, let us assume that we have access to the independent geometrically distributed random variable $G^{\star}_{t,i}$ with parameter $o_{t,i} = p_{t,i} + (1 - p_{t,i})r_t$. Then, replacing $1/o_{t,i}$ by $G^{\star}_{t,i}$ in the definition of $\widehat{\ell}^{\star}_t$ and ensuring that $G^{\star}_{t,i}$ is independent of $O_{t,i}$, we can obtain an unbiased loss estimate essentially equivalent to $\widehat{\ell}^{\star}_t$.

The challenge posed by this approach is that in our setting, we do not have exact sample access to the geometric random variable $G^{\star}_{t,i}$. In the next section, we describe our algorithm that is based on replacing $G^{\star}_{t,i}$ in the above definition by an appropriate surrogate.

3 ALGORITHM

Our algorithm is called Exp3-Res and displayed as Algorithm 1. It is based on the Exp3 algorithm of Auer et al. (2002a) and crucially relies on the construction of a surrogate $G_{t,i}$ of $G^{\star}_{t,i}$. Throughout this section, we will assume that $r_t \geq \frac{\log T}{2N-2}$, which implies that the probability of having no side observations in round t is of order $1/\sqrt{T}$.

The algorithm is initialized by setting $w_{1,i} = 1/N$ for all $i \in [N]$, and then performing the updates

$$w_{t+1,i} = \frac{1}{N} \exp\left(-\eta_{t+1}\widehat{L}_{t,i}\right) \tag{2}$$

after each round t, where $\eta_{t+1} > 0$ is a parameter of the algorithm called the *learning rate* in round t and $\widehat{L}_{t,i}$ is cumulative sum of the loss estimates $\widehat{\ell}_{s,i}$ up to (and including) time t. In round t, the learner draws its action I_t such that $I_t = i$ holds with probability $p_{t,i} \propto w_{t,i}$. To simplify some of the notation below, we introduce the shorthand notations $\mathbb{P}_t[\cdot] = \mathbb{P}[\cdot | \mathcal{F}_{t-1}]$ and $\mathbb{E}_t[\cdot] = \mathbb{E}[\cdot | \mathcal{F}_{t-1}]$.

For any fixed t, i, we now describe an efficiently computable surrogate $G_{t,i}$ for the geometrically distributed random variable $G^{\star}_{t,i}$ with parameter $o_{t,i}$ that will be used for constructing our loss estimates. In particular, our strategy will be to construct several independent copies $\{O'_{t,i}(k)\}$ of $O_{t,i}$ and choosing $G_{t,i}$ as the index k of the first copy with $O'_{t,i}(k) = 1$. It is easy to see that with infinitely many copies, we could exactly recover $G^{\star}_{t,i}$; our actual surrogate is going to be weaker thanks to the smaller sample size. For clarity of notation, we will omit most explicit references to t and i, with the understanding that all calculations need to be independently executed for all pairs t, i.

Let us now describe our mechanism for constructing the copies $\{O'(k)\}$. Since we need independence of $G_{t,i}$ and $O_{t,i}$ for our estimates, we use only side observations from actions $[N] \setminus \{I_t, i\}$. First, let's define σ as a uniform random permutation of $[N] \setminus \{I_t, i\}$. For all $k \in [N-2]$, we define $R(k) = O_{t,\sigma(k)}$. Note that due to the construction, $\{R(k)\}_{k=1}^{N-2}$ are pairwise independent Bernoulli random variables with parameter r_t, independent of $O_{t,i}$. Furthermore, knowing $p_{t,i}$ we can define $P(1), \ldots, P(N-2)$ as pairwise independent Bernoulli random variables with parameter $p_{t,i}$. Using $P(k)$ and $R(k)$ we define the random variable $O'(k)$ as

$$O'(k) = P(k) + (1 - P(k))R(k)$$

for all $k \in [N-2]$. Using independence of all previously defined random variables, it is easy to check that the variables $\{O'(k)\}_{k=1}^{N-2}$ are pairwise independent Bernoulli random variables with expectation $o_{t,i} = p_{t,i} + (1 - p_{t,i})r_t$. Now we are ready to define $G_{t,i}$ as

$$G_{t,i} = \min \{k \in [N-2] : O(k)' = 1\} \cup \{N-1\}. \quad (3)$$

The following lemma states some properties of $G_{t,i}$.

Lemma 1. *For any value of g we have*

$$\begin{aligned} \mathbb{E}[G_{t,i}] &= \frac{1}{o_{t,i}} - \frac{1}{o_{t,i}}(1 - o_{t,i})^{N-1} \\ \mathbb{E}\left[G_{t,i}^2\right] &= \frac{2 - o_{t,i}}{o_{t,i}^2} + \frac{1}{o_{t,i}^2}(1 - o_{t,i})^{N-2} \times \\ &\times \left(o_{t,i}^2 + o_{t,i} - 2 + 2o_{t,i}(N-2)(o_{t,i} - 1)\right) \end{aligned}$$

Proof. The proof follows directly from using the definition of $G_{t,i}$ and simplifying the sums

$$\begin{aligned} \mathbb{E}[G_{t,i}] &= \sum_{k=1}^{N-2} \left[k o_{t,i}(1 - o_{t,i})^{k-1}\right] + \\ &\quad + (N-1)(1 - o_{t,i})^{N-2}, \\ \mathbb{E}\left[G_{t,i}^2\right] &= \sum_{k=1}^{N-2} \left[k^2 o_{t,i}(1 - o_{t,i})^{k-1}\right] + \\ &\quad + (N-1)^2 (1 - o_{t,i})^{N-2}. \end{aligned}$$

□

Using Lemma 1, it is easy to see that $G_{t,i}$ follows a truncated geometric law in the sense that

$$\mathbb{P}[G_{t,i} = m] = \mathbb{P}\left[\min\left\{G_{t,i}^{\star}, N-1\right\} = m\right]$$

holds for all $m \in [N-1]$. Using all this notation, we construct an estimate of $\ell_{t,i}$ as

$$\widehat{\ell}_{t,i} = G_{t,i} O_{t,i} \ell_{t,i}. \quad (4)$$

The rationale underlying this definition of $G_{t,i}$ is rather delicate. First, note that $p_{t,i}$ is deterministic given the history $\mathcal{F}_{t-1}$ and therefore, does not depend on $O_{t,i}$. Second,

Algorithm 1 Exp3-Res

Input:
Set of actions $[N]$.
Initialization:
$\widehat{L}_{0,i} \leftarrow 0$ for $i \in [N]$.
Run:
for $t = 1$ **to** T **do**
  $\eta_t \leftarrow \sqrt{\log N \Big/ \left(N^2 + \sum_{s=1}^{t-1} \sum_{i=1}^{N} p_{s,i}(\widehat{\ell}_{s,i})^2\right)}$.
  $w_{t,i} \leftarrow (1/N)\exp(-\eta_t \widehat{L}_{t-1,i})$ for $i \in [N]$.
  $W_t \leftarrow \sum_{i=1}^{N} w_{t,i}$.
  $p_{t,i} \leftarrow w_{t,i}/W_t$.
  Choose $I_t \sim p_t = (p_{t,1}, \ldots, p_{t,N})$.
  Receive the observation set O_t.
  Receive the pairs $\{i, \ell_{t,i}\}$ for all i s.t. $O_{t,i} = 1$.
  Compute $G_{t,i}$ for all $i \in [N]$ using (3).
  $\widehat{\ell}_{t,i} \leftarrow \ell_{t,i} O_{t,i} G_{t,i}$ for all $i \in [N]$.
  $\widehat{L}_{t,i} = \widehat{L}_{t-1,i} + \widehat{\ell}_{t,i}$ for all $i \in [N]$.
end for

$O_{t,i}$ is also independent of $O_{t,j}$ for $j \notin \{i, I_t\}$. As a result, $G_{t,i}$ is independent of $O_{t,i}$, and we can use the identity $\mathbb{E}_t[G_{t,i} O_{t,i}] = \mathbb{E}_t[G_{t,i}]\,\mathbb{E}_t[O_{t,i}]$. The next lemma relates the loss estimates (4) to the true losses, relying on the observations above and the assumption $r_t \geq \frac{\log T}{2N-2}$.

Lemma 2. *Assume $r_t \geq \frac{\log T}{2N-2}$. Then, for all t and i,*

$$0 \leq \ell_{t,i} - \mathbb{E}_t\left[\widehat{\ell}_{t,i}\right] \leq \frac{1}{\sqrt{T}}.$$

Proof. Fix an arbitrary t and i. Using Lemma 1 along with $\mathbb{E}_t[O_{t,i}] = o_{t,i}$ and the independence of $G_{t,i}$ and $O_{t,i}$, we get

$$\mathbb{E}_t\left[\widehat{\ell}_{t,i}\right] = \mathbb{E}_t[G_{t,i} O_{t,i} \ell_{t,i}] = \ell_{t,i} - \ell_{t,i}(1 - o_{t,i})^{N-1},$$

which immediately implies the lower bound on $\ell_{t,i} - \mathbb{E}_t\left[\widehat{\ell}_{t,i}\right]$. For proving the upper bound, observe that

$$\ell_{t,i}(1 - o_{t,i})^{N-1} \leq (1 - r_t)^{N-1} \leq e^{-r_t(N-1)} \leq \frac{1}{\sqrt{T}}$$

holds by our assumption on r_t, where we used the elementary inequality $1 - x \leq e^x$ that holds for all $x \in \mathbb{R}$. □

The next theorem states our main result concerning Exp3-Res with an adaptive learning rate.

Theorem 1. *Assume that $r_t \geq \frac{\log T}{2N-2}$ holds for all t and set*

$$\eta_t = \sqrt{\frac{\log N}{N^2 + \sum_{s=1}^{t-1} \sum_{i=1}^{N} p_{s,i}(\widehat{\ell}_{s,i})^2}}.$$

Then, the expected regret of Exp3-Res *satisfies*

$$R_T \leq 2\sqrt{\left(N^2 + \sum_{t=1}^{T} \frac{1}{r_t}\right) \log N} + \sqrt{T}.$$

4 PROOF OF THEOREM 1

In this section, we present details of the proof of Theorem 1 but first, we state an auxiliary lemma.

Lemma 3 (Lemma 3.5 of Auer et al., 2002b). *Let b_1, b_2, ..., b_T be non-negative real numbers. Then*

$$\sum_{t=1}^{T} \frac{b_t}{\sqrt{\sum_{s=1}^{t} b_t}} \leq 2\sqrt{\sum_{t=1}^{T} b_t}.$$

Proof. The proof is based on the inequality $x/2 \leq 1 - \sqrt{1-x}$ for $x \leq 1$. Setting $x = b_t / \sum_{s=1}^{t} b_s$ and multiplying both sides of the inequality by $\sqrt{\sum_{s=1}^{t} b_s}$ we get

$$\frac{b_t}{\sqrt{\sum_{s=1}^{t} b_t}} \leq \sqrt{\sum_{s=1}^{t} b_s} - \sqrt{\sum_{s=1}^{t} b_s - b_t}.$$

The proof is concluded by summing over t. □

The first part of the analysis follows the proof of Lemma 1 by Györfi and Ottucsák (2007). Defining $W_t' = \frac{1}{N}\sum_{i=1}^{N} e^{-\eta_{t-1}\widehat{L}_{t-1,i}}$, we get

$$\begin{aligned}
\frac{1}{\eta_t} \log \frac{W_{t+1}'}{W_t} &= \frac{1}{\eta_t} \log \sum_{i=1}^{N} \frac{\frac{1}{N} e^{-\eta_t \widehat{L}_{t-1,i}} e^{-\eta_t \widehat{\ell}_{t,i}}}{W_t} \\
&= \frac{1}{\eta_t} \log \sum_{i=1}^{N} p_{t,i} e^{-\eta_t \widehat{\ell}_{t,i}} \\
&\leq \frac{1}{\eta_t} \log \sum_{i=1}^{N} p_{t,i} \left(1 - \eta_t \widehat{\ell}_{t,i} + (\eta_t \widehat{\ell}_{t,i})^2\right) \qquad (5) \\
&= \frac{1}{\eta_t} \log \left(1 - \eta_t \sum_{i=1}^{N} p_{t,i} \widehat{\ell}_{t,i} + \eta_t^2 \sum_{i=1}^{N} p_{t,i} (\widehat{\ell}_{t,i})^2\right),
\end{aligned}$$

where in (5), we used the inequality $\exp(-x) \leq 1 - x + x^2$ that holds for $x \geq -1$. Further, we used the inequality $\log(1-x) \leq -x$, which holds for all $x \leq 1$, to upper bound last term.

Using $\eta_{t+1} \leq \eta_t$ and Jensen's inequality, we get

$$\begin{aligned}
W_{t+1} &= \sum_{i=1}^{N} \frac{1}{N} e^{-\eta_{t+1} \widehat{L}_{t,i}} = \sum_{i=1}^{N} \frac{1}{N} \left(e^{-\eta_t \widehat{L}_{t,i}}\right)^{\frac{\eta_{t+1}}{\eta_t}} \\
&\leq \left(\sum_{i=1}^{N} \frac{1}{N} e^{-\eta_t \widehat{L}_{t,i}}\right)^{\frac{\eta_{t+1}}{\eta_t}} = (W_{t+1}')^{\frac{\eta_{t+1}}{\eta_t}},
\end{aligned}$$

which, together with the last inequality, gives us

$$\sum_{i=1}^{N} p_{t,i} \widehat{\ell}_{t,i} \leq \frac{\eta_t}{2} \sum_{i=1}^{N} p_{t,i} \left(\widehat{\ell}_{t,i}\right)^2 + \left[\frac{\log W_t}{\eta_t} - \frac{\log W_{t+1}}{\eta_{t+1}}\right]$$

for every $t \in [T]$. Taking expectations and summing over time, we get

$$\begin{aligned}
\mathbb{E}\left[\sum_{t=1}^{T}\sum_{i=1}^{N} p_{t,i}\widehat{\ell}_{t,i}\right] &\leq \mathbb{E}\left[\sum_{t=1}^{T} \frac{\eta_t}{2} \sum_{i=1}^{N} p_{t,i} \left(\widehat{\ell}_{t,i}\right)^2\right] \\
&\quad + \mathbb{E}\left[\sum_{t=1}^{T} \left(\frac{\log W_t}{\eta_t} - \frac{\log W_{t+1}}{\eta_{t+1}}\right)\right].
\end{aligned}$$

The goal of the second part of the analysis is to construct bounds for each of the three expectations in the previous inequality. For the term on the left-hand side, we use Lemma 2 to get the lower-bound

$$\mathbb{E}\left[\sum_{t=1}^{T}\sum_{i=1}^{N} p_{t,i}\widehat{\ell}_{t,i}\right] \geq \sum_{t=1}^{T}\sum_{i=1}^{N} p_{t,i}\ell_{t,i} + \sqrt{T}.$$

Note that is the only step in the analysis where the actual magnitude (and not just the sign) of the bias of the loss estimates shows up. Anything bigger than $\sqrt{T}$ would degrade our final regret bound.

We are left with bounding the two terms on the right-hand side. To simplify some notation below, let us define $b_t = \sum_{i=1}^{N} p_{t,i}(\widehat{\ell}_{t,i})^2$. By our definition of η_t and the help of Lemma 3, we can bound the first term on the right hand side as

$$\begin{aligned}
\mathbb{E}\left[\sum_{t=1}^{T} \frac{\eta_t b_t}{2}\right] &= \mathbb{E}\left[\sum_{t=1}^{T} \frac{b_t \sqrt{\log N}}{2\sqrt{N^2 + \sum_{s=1}^{t-1} b_s}}\right] \\
&\leq \mathbb{E}\left[\sqrt{\left(N^2 + \sum_{t=1}^{T} b_t\right) \log N}\right] \\
&\leq \sqrt{\left(N^2 + \sum_{t=1}^{T} \mathbb{E}\left[b_t\right]\right) \log N},
\end{aligned}$$

where we also used the fact that $N^2 \geq b_t$ and Jensen's inequality in the last line. We continue by bounding $\mathbb{E}\left[b_t\right]$:

$$\begin{aligned}
\mathbb{E}_t\left[\sum_{i=1}^{N} p_{t,i}(\widehat{\ell}_{t,i})^2\right] &= \sum_{i=1}^{N} p_{t,i}\ell_{t,i}^2 \mathbb{E}_t\left[O_{t,i}G_{t,i}^2\right] \\
&\leq \sum_{i=1}^{N} p_{t,i}o_{t,i} \frac{2 - o_{t,i}}{o_{t,i}^2} \leq \frac{2}{r_t},
\end{aligned} \qquad (6)$$

where we used $o_{t,i} \geq r_t$ together with the second part of Lemma 1 which gives us

$$\mathbb{E}_t\left[G_{t,i}^2\right] = \frac{2-o_{t,i}}{o_{t,i}^2} + \frac{1}{o_{t,i}^2}(1-o_{t,i})^{N-2}\times$$
$$\times\left(o_{t,i}^2 + o_{t,i} - 2 + 2o_{t,i}(N-2)(o-1)\right)$$
$$\leq \frac{2-o_{t,i}}{o_{t,i}^2},$$

since both $o_{t,i}^2 + o_{t,i} - 2$ and $2o_{t,i}(N-2)(o-1)$ are non-positive. Thus, we obtain

$$\mathbb{E}\left[\sum_{t=1}^{T}\frac{\eta_t b_t}{2}\right] \leq \sqrt{\left(\sum_{t=1}^{T}\frac{1}{r_t} + N^2\right)\log N}. \qquad (7)$$

Finally, using $W_1 = 1$, the sum in the last expectation telescopes to

$$\mathbb{E}\left[\sum_{t=1}^{T}\left(\frac{\log W_t}{\eta_t} - \frac{\log W_{t+1}}{\eta_{t+1}}\right)\right] = \mathbb{E}\left[-\frac{\log W_{T+1}}{\eta_{T+1}}\right].$$

Using the definition of W_t, we get that

$$\mathbb{E}\left[-\frac{\log W_{T+1}}{\eta_{T+1}}\right] \leq \mathbb{E}\left[-\frac{\log w_{T+1,j}}{\eta_{T+1}}\right]$$
$$\leq \mathbb{E}\left[\frac{\log N}{\eta_{T+1}}\right] + \mathbb{E}\left[\widehat{L}_{T,j}\right]$$

holds for any arm $j \in [N]$. Now note that the first term can be bounded by using the defintion of η_{T+1} with the help of (6) and Jensen's inequality. Using $\mathbb{E}_t\left[\widehat{\ell}_{t,i}\right] \leq \ell_{t,i}$ from Lemma 2 and combining everything together, we obtain the regret bound

$$R_T = \mathbb{E}\left[\sum_{t=1}^{T} p_{t,i}\ell_{t,i}\right] - \min_{j\in[N]}\mathbb{E}\left[\sum_{t\in T_k}\ell_{t,j}\right]$$
$$\leq 2\sqrt{\left(N^2 + \sum_{t=1}^{T}\frac{1}{r_t}\right)\log N} + \sqrt{T}.$$

5 EXPERIMENTS

In this section, we study the empirical performance of Exp3-Res compared to three other algorithms:

- Exp3 – a basic adversarial multi-armed bandit algorithm which uses only loss observations of chosen arms and discards all side observations.
- Oracle – full-information algorithm with access to losses of every action in every time step, regardless of the value of r_t. Our particular choice is Hedge (Littlestone and Warmuth, 1994; Freund and Schapire, 1997).
- Exp3-R – a variant of the Exp3-Res algorithm with access to the sequence $(r_t)_t^T$, using (1) to construct unbiased loss estimate instead of using geometric resampling.

The most interesting parameter of our experiment is the sequence (r_t), since it controls amount of side observation presented to the learner. In order to show that Exp3-Res can effectively make use of the additional information provided by the environment, we designed several sequences (r_t) with different amounts of side observation provided to the learner. In the case of small r_t-s, the problem is almost as difficult as the multi-armed bandit problem. On the other hand, in the case of large r_t-s, the problem is almost as easy as the full-information problem. Therefore, we expect that the performance of Exp3-Res will interpolate between the performance of the Exp3-R and Oracle algorithms depending on the values of the r_t-s. In the next section, we validate this claim empirically.

5.1 EXPERIMENT DETAILS

To ensure sufficient challenge for the algorithms, we have generated a sequence of losses as a random walk for each arm with independent increments uniformly distributed on $[-0.1, 0.1]$ while enforcing the random walks to stay within $[0, 1]$ by setting the value of a random walk to 0 or 1, respectively, if the random walk gets outside the boundaries. The loss sequence is fixed through all of the experiments to demonstrate the impact of the sequence $(r_t)_t^T$ on the regret of algorithms. We have observed qualitatively similar behavior for other loss sequences.

We fix the number of arms in all of the experiments as 50, and the time horizon as 500. Every curve represents an average of 100 runs.

5.2 RESULT OF THE EXPERIMENTS

We performed experiments on many different loss sequences and sequences of r_t-s. Since the results are essentially the same for all the different sequences, we included in the present paper just the results for one loss sequence with different sequences of r_t-s. In the case of $r_t \geq \log(T)/(2N-2)$, the case of high probability of having some side observation, the performance of the algorithm Exp3-Res proposed in the present paper is comparable to the performance of the idealistic Exp3-R which knows exact value of r_t in every time step. Moreover, if the average r_t is close to 1, the performance of the proposed algorithm is close to the performance of Oracle which observes all the losses. If the average r_t is close to zero, the performance of the algorithm is a little bit worse that the performance of basic Exp3. This is also supported by the theory, since our algorithm is not able to construct reliable estimates in the case of small r_t-s.

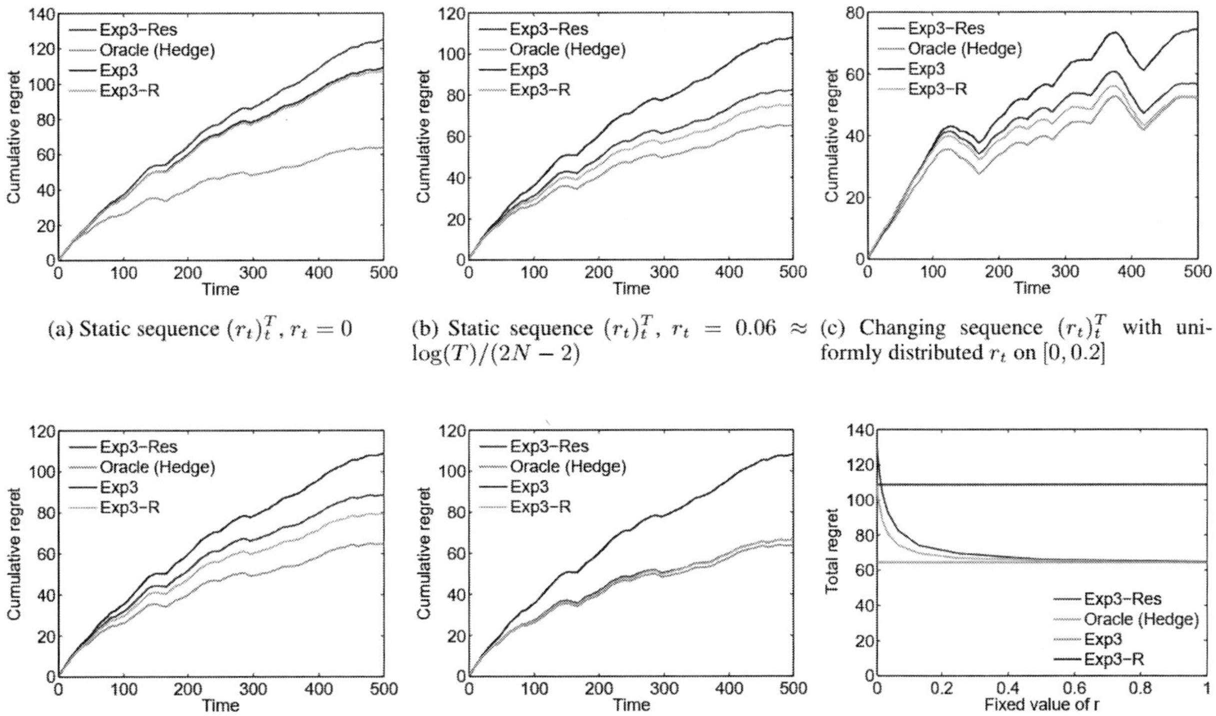

(a) Static sequence $(r_t)_t^T$, $r_t = 0$

(b) Static sequence $(r_t)_t^T$, $r_t = 0.06 \approx \log(T)/(2N-2)$

(c) Changing sequence $(r_t)_t^T$ with uniformly distributed r_t on $[0, 0.2]$

(d) Sequence $(r_t)_t^T$ generated as a random walk on $[0, 0.1]$

(e) Sequence $(r_t)_t^T$ generated as a random walk on $[0, 1]$

(f) Total regret for different values of static $(r_t)_t^T$

Figure 1: Comparison of algorithm for different amount of side information sequences (different sequences $(r_t)_t^T$)

6 CONCLUSION & FUTURE WORK

In this paper, we considered multi-armed bandit problems with stochastic side observations modeled by Erdős–Rényi graphs. Our contribution is a computationally efficient algorithm that operates under the assumption $r_t \geq \log T/(2N-2)$, which essentially guarantees that at least one piece of side observation is generated in every round, with high probability. In this case, our algorithm guarantees a regret bound of $\mathcal{O}\left(\sqrt{\log N \sum_{t=1}^{T} \frac{1}{r_t}}\right)$ (Theorem 1). In this section, we discuss several open questions regarding this result.

The most obvious question is whether it is possible to remove our assumptions on the values of r_t. We can only give a definite answer in the simple case when all r_t's are identical: In this case, one can think of simply computing the empirical frequency $\widehat{r}_t$ of all previous side observations in round t to estimate the constant r, plug the result into (1), and then use the resulting loss estimates in an exponential-weighting scheme. It is relatively straightforward (but also rather tedious) to show that the resulting algorithm satisfies a regret bound of $\widetilde{\mathcal{O}}\left(\sqrt{T/r}\right)$ for all possible values of r, thanks to the fact that $\hat{r}_t$ quickly concentrates around the true value of r. Notice however that this approach clearly breaks down if the r_t's change over time.

In the case of changing r_t's, the number of observations we can use to estimate r_t is severely limited, so much that we cannot expect any direct estimate of r_t to concentrate around the true value. Our algorithm proposed in Section 3 gets around this problem by directly estimating the importance weights $1/o_{t,i}$ instead of r_t, which enables us to construct reliable loss estimates, although only at the price of our assumption on the range of r_t. While we acknowledge that this assumption can be difficult to confirm a priori in practice, we remark that we find it quite surprising that *any algorithm whatsoever* can take advantage of such limited observations, even under such a restriction. We also point out that for values of r_t that are consistently below our bound, it is not possible to substantially improve the regret bounds of Exp3 which are of $\widetilde{\mathcal{O}}\left(\sqrt{TN}\right)$, as shown by the lower bounds of Alon et al. (2013). We expect that in several practical applications, one can verify whether the r_t's satisfy our assumption or not, and decide to use `Exp3-Res` or Exp3 accordingly. In fact, our experiments suggest that our algorithm performs well even if neither of these two assumptions are verified: we have seen that the empirical performance of `Exp3-Res` is only slightly worse than that of Exp3 even when the values of r_t are very small (Section 5). Still, finding out whether our restriction on r_t can be relaxed in general is a very important and interesting question left for future study.

An important corollary of our results is that, under some assumptions, it is possible to leverage side observations in a non-trivial way without having access to the second neighborhoods in the side-observation graphs as defined by Mannor and Shamir (2011). This complements the recent results of Cohen et al. (2016), who show that non-stochastic side-observations may provide non-trivial advantage over bandit feedback when the losses are stochastic even when the side-observation graphs are unobserved, but learning with unobserved feedback graphs can be as hard as learning with bandit feedback when both the losses and the graphs are generated by an adversary. A natural question that our work leads to is whether it is possible to efficiently leverage side-observations under significantly weaker assumptions on the observation model.

Acknowledgements The research presented in this paper was supported by CPER Nord-Pas de Calais/FEDER DATA Advanced data science and technologies 2015-2020, French Ministry of Higher Education and Research, Nord-Pas-de-Calais Regional Council, French National Research Agency project ExTra-Learn (n.ANR-14-CE24-0010-01), and by UPFellows Fellowship (Marie Curie COFUND program n° 600387).

References

Allenberg, C., Auer, P., Györfi, L., and Ottucsák, Gy. (2006). Hannan consistency in on-line learning in case of unbounded losses under partial monitoring. In *Algorithmic Learning Theory*, pages 229–243.

Alon, N., Cesa-Bianchi, N., Dekel, O., and Koren, T. (2015). Online learning with feedback graphs: Beyond bandits. In *Conference on Learning Theory*.

Alon, N., Cesa-Bianchi, N., Gentile, C., and Mansour, Y. (2013). From bandits to experts: A tale of domination and independence. In *Neural Information Processing Systems*.

Audibert, J.-Y. and Bubeck, S. (2010). Regret bounds and minimax policies under partial monitoring. *Journal of Machine Learning Research*, 11:2785–2836.

Auer, P., Cesa-Bianchi, N., Freund, Y., and Schapire, R. E. (2002a). The non-stochastic multi-armed bandit problem. *SIAM Journal on Computing*, 32(1):48–77.

Auer, P., Cesa-Bianchi, N., and Gentile, C. (2002b). Adaptive and self-confident on-line learning algorithms. *Journal of Computer and System Sciences*, 64:48–75.

Buccapatnam, S., Eryilmaz, A., and Shroff, N. B. (2014). Stochastic bandits with side observations on networks. In *International Conference on Measurement and Modeling of Computer Systems*.

Caron, S., Kveton, B., Lelarge, M., and Bhagat, S. (2012). Leveraging side observations in stochastic bandits. In *Uncertainty in Artificial Intelligence*.

Carpentier, A. and Valko, M. (2016). Revealing graph bandits for maximizing local influence. In *International Conference on Artificial Intelligence and Statistics*, pages 10–18.

Cesa-Bianchi, N. and Lugosi, G. (2006). *Prediction, learning, and games*. Cambridge University Press, New York, NY.

Cesa-Bianchi, N., Lugosi, G., and Stoltz, G. (2005). Minimizing regret with label efficient prediction. *IEEE Transactions on Information Theory*, 51(6):2152–2162.

Cohen, A., Hazan, T., and Koren, T. (2016). Online learning with feedback graphs without the graphs. In *International Conference on Machine Learning (to appear)*.

Freund, Y. and Schapire, R. E. (1997). A decision-theoretic generalization of on-line learning and an application to boosting. *Journal of Computer and System Sciences*, 55:119–139.

Györfi, L. and Ottucsák, Gy. (2007). Sequential prediction of unbounded stationary time series. *IEEE Transactions on Information Theory*, 53(5):1866–1872.

Kocák, T., Neu, G., and Valko, M. (2016). Online learning with noisy side observations. In *International Conference on Artificial Intelligence and Statistics*, pages 1186–1194.

Kocák, T., Neu, G., Valko, M., and Munos, R. (2014). Efficient learning by implicit exploration in bandit problems with side observations. In *Neural Information Processing Systems*, pages 613–621.

Littlestone, N. and Warmuth, M. (1994). The weighted majority algorithm. *Information and Computation*, 108(2):212–261.

Mannor, S. and Shamir, O. (2011). From bandits to experts: On the value of side-observations. In *Neural Information Processing Systems*.

Neu, G. and Bartók, G. (2013). An efficient algorithm for learning with semi-bandit feedback. In *Algorithmic Learning Theory*.

Seldin, Y., Bartlett, P., Crammer, K., and Abbasi-Yadkori, Y. (2014). Prediction with limited advice and multi-armed bandits with paid observations. In *International Conference on Machine Learning*.

Conjugate Conformal Prediction for Online Binary Classification

Mustafa A. Kocak
Tandon School of Engineering
New York University
Brooklyn, NY 11201
kocak@nyu.edu

Elza Erkip
Tandon School of Engineering
New York University
Brooklyn, NY 11201
elza@nyu.edu

Dennis E. Shasha
Courant Institute
New York University
New York, NY 10012
shasha@cs.nyu.edu

Abstract

Binary classification (rain or shine, disease or not, increase or decrease) is a fundamental problem in machine learning. We present an algorithm that can take any standard online binary classification algorithm and provably improve its performance under very weak assumptions, given the right to refuse to make predictions in certain cases. The extent of improvement will depend on the data size, stability of the algorithm, and room for improvement in the algorithms performance. Our experiments on standard machine learning data sets and standard algorithms (k-nearest neighbors and random forests) show the effectiveness of our approach, even beyond what is possible using previous work on conformal predictors upon which our approach is based. Though we focus on binary classification, our theory could be extended to multiway classification. Our code and data are available upon request.

1 INTRODUCTION

Reacting intelligently to incoming data lies at the heart of forecasting, trading, and many other applications. The simplest decision one has to make is binary (go/stop, buy/sell). However, in many cases one needs to assess the risk of a decision and refuse to make a decision at all if one is not confident enough. One of the well known methodologies for this task is using confidence predictors and declining to make a decision on ambiguous data points (Vovk, Gammerman, & Shafer, 2005). Intuitively, conformal predictors look at how previous predictions worked out for similar input data and let those results shape first whether to make a prediction at all and if so, which one to make. We extend existing conformal prediction approaches by permitting the use of multidimensional test statistics to provide more flexibility while keeping the theoretical guarantees of the original predictors. We apply this extended framework to the binary classification problem and show that our methods improve the performance of previous conformal predictors.

1.1 Related Work

Forecasting the upcoming data point in a data stream has been studied in econometrics, meteorology, finance, computer science, and many other disciplines (Box, Jenkins, Reinsel, & Ljung, 2015). In confidence predictors, the goal is to create a set of possible candidate outcomes such that the probability that the real outcome is not one of these candidates is less than a predetermined tolerance level. Some examples for the uses of confidence predictions include signal denoising (Ryabko & Ryabko, 2013), growth estimation for planning (Meade & Islam, 1995), among many similar forecast problems that requires bounds for the predicted values (Chatfield, 1993). Though most of the confidence prediction literature considers either parametric models or asymptotic results, Vovk, Gammerman and Shaffer (Vovk et al., 2005) introduced the conformal prediction framework, which provides exact finite-sample guarantees for exchangeable data sequences.

Binary classification problems where the classifier is allowed to decline making a decision has been studied both in online and offline settings. Optimal error-rejection tradeoffs are investigated under the names *selective classification* (El-Yaniv & Wiener, 2010, 2012), (Chaudhuri & Zhang, 2013) and *classification with reject option* (Denis & Hebiri, 2015), (Chow, 1970), (Herbei & Wegkamp, 2006).

Following this work, we focus on the conformal prediction approach to the online binary classification with reject option, and propose an extended framework to decrease the number of rejects while guaranteeing a small probability of error on the classified points.

1.2 Outline & Contributions

In Section 2, we describe our problem formally and provide some background information on online confidence prediction and conformal prediction. In Section 3, we extend the conformal prediction framework to multiple dimensions and then show how to preserve the theoretical error guarantees provided by the conformal framework, while rejecting less often.

The flexibility provided by this multidimensional framework is demonstrated in Section 4, where we introduce the notion of *conjugate conformal prediction*. Formally, a *conjugate conformal predictor* is a two dimensional conformal predictor derived from any given traditional conformal predictor. Intuitively, conjugate predictors not only compare the test point with the previous ones, but also compare the test point with its conjugate, i.e. the same point with its label flipped, to be able to make more aggressive predictions - not only when we have high confidence to accept the test point but also when we have high confidence to reject the conjugate point.

In Section 4.1, we define conjugate conformal predictors formally and prove their efficiency under mild stability assumptions on the set statistics used in the original predictor. Lastly, in Section 4.2. we present experimental results for classical conformal and conjugate conformal predictors on standard machine learning data sets from UCI ML Repository (Lichman, 2013) and standard machine learning algorithms (k nearest neighbors and random forests).

Finally, in Section 5 we conclude with a brief discussion of our results and planned future work.

2 PROBLEM SETUP & CONFORMAL PREDICTION

2.1 Data Model & Notation

In this work, we assume data points are revealed to the algorithm, one data point at a time. A data point generated at time t, consists of a feature vector x_t, which takes values from a feature space $\mathcal{X}$, and a label y_t, which takes values from a label space $\mathcal{Y}$. For the sake of brevity, we represent a data point with $z_t = (x_t, y_t) \in \mathcal{X} \times \mathcal{Y}$. We refer to the space $\mathcal{Z} = \mathcal{X} \times \mathcal{Y}$ as the data space.

The only statistical assumption about the data generating process is the *exchangeability* of the data points, that is: for any positive integer N, the probability of observing a data sequence $z_1, \ldots, z_N$ is invariant under any permutation of the data points, π, i.e.

$$Pr\left(z_1, \ldots, z_N\right) \quad = \quad Pr\left(z_{\pi(1)}, \ldots, z_{\pi(N)}\right).$$

Many processes (or variants of these processes) satisfy this assumption. For example, stock price histories are not exchangeable, but stock price returns (percentage up or down over a given time period) are. Echangeability can be considered as a generalization of the more common i.i.d assumption. We refer the reader to (Schervish, 2012) and (Kallenberg, 2006) for a thorough discussion of this assumption.

In addition, we also make use of a source of randomness: uniform random variables $\tau_1, \tau_2, \ldots$ on the unit interval, which are independent of the data. This will be used to randomize the prediction algorithms in such a way as to achieve validity guarantees.

Lastly, we use multi-sets throughout the paper. In other words, each set may contain the same element multiple times, in particular, we denote the (multi-)set of the first t data points as $\sigma_t = \{z_1, \ldots, z_t\}$ and we don't require the data points to be distinct. In addition, we use the following variations of σ_t for the sake of brevity of exposition:

- $\sigma_t^{(i)} = \{z_1, \ldots, z_{i-1}, z_{i+1}, \ldots, z_t\}$ stands for the set of first t data points except the ith one for any $i = 1, \ldots, t$.
- $\sigma_{t/y} = \{z_1, \ldots, z_{t-1}, (x_t, y)\}$ represents the set of first t data points assuming the tth label is equal to y, for any $y \in \mathcal{Y}$.
- $\sigma_{t/y}^{(i)}$ is the set of data points in $\sigma_{t/y}$ with the exception of the ith one, for $i = 1, \ldots, t$ and $y \in \mathcal{Y}$.

2.2 Online Prediction of Confidence

For the confidence prediction task, we assume the feature vector x_t is revealed at time t, but the corresponding label y_t is revealed only after the prediction is made and before the next feature vector x_{t+1} is revealed.

The task of the predictor is to predict a subset of the label space that contains the unseen label y_t with probability at least $1 - \epsilon$, for a given error tolerance level $\epsilon \in (0, 1)$. We denote the prediction set generated at time t as Γ_t^ϵ. Because Γ_t^ϵ is a set, we may be making a prediction of the form "the answer may be 1, 4, or 5". Formally:

Workflow for Online Confidence Prediction The fewer the errors, the more valid; the smaller the prediction set, the more efficient.

1: **for** $t = 1, 2, \ldots$ and given $\epsilon \in (0, 1)$ **do**
2: Nature reveals x_t.
3: Predictor calculates a prediction set $\Gamma_t^\epsilon \subseteq \mathcal{Y}$.
4: Nature reveals y_t and declares an error if $y_t \notin \Gamma_t^\epsilon$.

There are two main properties one expects from a good confidence predictor. The first is that the predictor should be *valid* (intuitively, the label value falls within the prediction set Γ_t^ϵ, fraction $1 - \epsilon$ of the time) and the other is that it is *efficient* (intuitively, $|\Gamma_t^\epsilon|$ is at least one but small).

The literature contains various ways of defining efficiency and validity measures, see (Vovk et al., 2014) for a detailed list. We use the following definitions:

- We call a confidence predictor *exactly valid* if the error events associated with its predictions occurs independently with probability ϵ. Additionally, we say a predictor is *conservatively valid* or simply *valid*, if it makes errors only on the data points on which some other exactly valid predictor makes errors. For further implications of this definition, see (Vovk et al., 2005).

- Since our results in Section 4 are focused on binary predictions, we use the cardinality of the predicted set, $|\Gamma_t^\epsilon|$, as a measure of efficiency. Particularly, we say the prediction at time t is *efficient* if $|\Gamma_t^\epsilon| = 1$. In binary classification setup, as in Section 4, an inefficient prediction at time t implies that the predictor chooses both possible values or none, effectively refusing to make a decision at t.

  Furthermore, we say a first predictor is more efficient than a second predictor at time t, if the first refuses to make a decision only if the second also refuses to make a decision at time t. Note that, such a comparison makes sense when both of the predictors are valid and have the same tolerance parameter, ϵ.

  For continuous label spaces, one can refer to the volume or size of the the prediction sets as a measure of efficiency (Lei, Robbins, & Wasserman, 2011).

2.3 Conformal Prediction

The main idea behind conformal predictors is to define a *nonconformity score* at time t between a candidate point $z = (x_t, y)$ for a candidate label $y \in \mathcal{Y}$ and the rest of the data $z_1, \ldots, z_{t-1}$, and to use it as a test statistic to decide whether a particular candidate label y will be included in the prediction set (candidate outcomes) or not. Intuitively, if data points similar to x_t have often mapped to y in the past, then y should belong to the prediction set for x_t.

The test statistic should take on smaller values the more probable the y is. One can create a non-conformity score based on a machine learning algorithm. Say that we employ the given algorithm, f, train it on the set σ_{t-1} and predict $\hat{y}_t = f_{\sigma_{t-1}}(x_t)$ as an estimate of y_t. Then we can derive a non-conformity score (also called the test statistic) to use at time t as $A_t(\sigma_{t-1}, z_t) = \phi\left(f_{\sigma_{t-1}}(x_t), y_t\right)$, where ϕ is any properly chosen loss function.

Because of the exchangeability assumption on the data, the conformity scores should be invariant to the order of data points in the training set σ_{t-1}. Therefore, the set of first t data points, σ_t, constitutes a complete sufficient statistic on the test statistic $A_t(\sigma_{t-1}, z_t)$. In our context, this means we can compute the exact probability distribution of the test statistic conditioned on σ_t. For a more detailed analysis of test statistics and how to compute their distribution under exchangeability, see Chapters 3.2 and 6.2 of (Cox & Hinkley, 1974).

Exploiting this idea leads to the following algorithm: calculate the non-conformity scores for each data point z_i that precedes t, based on the rest of the data preceding t plus the assumption that $y_t = y$ (the algorithm will do this one at a time for each label y for time t). We then calculate a confidence value, p_t^y, for the candidate label y as the fraction of the data points with greater non-conformity scores than the score of the last one (x_t, y). We will accept y into the confidence set provided this confidence value is greater than or equal to ϵ. Vovk (2005) has shown that, after some smoothing (using the additional source of randomness mentioned in section 2.1, the uniform random variable τ_t), this confidence value has a uniform distribution on $[0, 1]$ if the label y_t is really equal to y. The uniformity implies therefore that refusing to include y as a candidate point if its confidence value is less than ϵ would cause an error only with probability ϵ. The pseudocode is given in Algorithm 1, and further details are given in (Vovk et al., 2005).

Algorithm 1 (Smoothed) Conformal Prediction: The goal is to create a set of predicted values Γ_t^ϵ which covers the true label with probability $1 - \epsilon$, based on a confidence value p_t^y calculated from a given non-conformity measure A_t. In particular, p_t^y computes the fraction of data points with a larger non-conformity score than α_t^y, where τ_t is used to break the ties. The detailed definitions are in the text.

for $t = 1, 2, \ldots$ **do**
    $\Gamma_t^\epsilon \leftarrow \emptyset$
    for $y \in \mathcal{Y}$ **do**
        $y_t \leftarrow y$
        for $i = 1, \ldots, t$ **do**
            $\alpha_i^y \leftarrow A_t\left(\sigma_{t/y}^{(i)}, z_i\right)$
        $p_t^y = \left(|\{i : \alpha_i^y > \alpha_t^y,\}| + \tau_t|\{i : \alpha_i^y = \alpha_t^y\}|\right)/t$
        if $p_t^y \geq \epsilon$ **then**
            $\Gamma_t^\epsilon \leftarrow \Gamma_t^\epsilon \bigcup \{y\}$.

To appreciate the strength of the conformal predictors one can refer to the following results (Schafer & Vovk, 2008):

i. All (smoothed) conformal predictors are exactly valid (i.e. the error event at any time point is independent from others and occurs with probability ϵ) under the exchangeability assumption.

ii. If the data space is a Borel space, any given valid confidence predictor which is invariant to the order of the previous data points, there exists a conformal predictor that generates prediction sets not larger than the prediction sets generated by the given confidence predictor.

3 MULTIDIMENSIONAL CONFORMAL PREDICTION

In this section we will generalize the conformal prediction framework to multidimensional statistics and propose a principled extension to the algorithm presented above. This generalization is both simple and improves the efficiency of the formal prediction framework thus achieving practical improvements to standard algorithms.

The idea of the extension is to use non-conformity scores that take vector values instead of scalar ones, i.e. the range of A_t is $\mathbb{R}^d$ for some positive integer d. Such an approach may be helpful when we have several possible sets of data that may bear on a prediction. In such a scenario, one can use the non-conformity score of the candidate point to each of the several sets as components of a *non-conformity vector*.

The approach also helps in the application described in the next section, in which we focus on the case where the label space is binary, i.e. $\mathcal{Y} = \{0, 1\}$. In that setting, a one-dimensional non-conformity score $A_t(\sigma_{t-1}, (x_t, y))$ and its conjugate $A_t(\sigma_{t-1}, (x_t, 1-y))$ together provide a substantial improvement to the performance of the prediction compared to using just one score.

Just as in the one dimensional case, we assume that data points come from an exchangeable process and each component of the conformity vectors is invariant to the order of the points in the history, thus making the multi-dimensional conformity vectors exchangeable. Therefore, we can build a test statistic from them. However, in contrast to the scalar case, we don't have a linear order on these vectors, which complicates the decision of whether to include or exclude a label in the prediction set.

Instead of calculating a confidence value p^y for each $y \in \mathcal{Y}$ as before, we propose to select some subset of the d dimensional Euclidean space, which we call the *acceptance set* and denote it with S_t^y, for each y. We add the label y to the prediction set Γ_t^ϵ only if the corresponding nonconformity vector falls into the acceptance set, i.e. $y \in S_t^y$. Also, just as in the calculation of the one dimensional conformal prediction, we apply random smoothing on the boundary points of the acceptance set to guarantee exact validity. Specifically, we add y into the prediction set if the corresponding non-conformity vector is an interior point of the acceptance set, but if it is a boundary point of the set we include y iff τ_t is less than a specific value that is calibrated to the targeted error level. In Theorem 3.1 and the following Corollary 3.1.1, we provide some sufficient conditions on the acceptance sets to guarantee the validity of the associated predictor.

As an example, for the binary case, we propose to construct acceptance sets that include the points with smaller non-conformity scores than their conjugate scores in addition to some points with small non-conformity scores. This will satisfy the conditions given in Corollary 3.1.1 (See Figure 1). Such proposed acceptance sets will be investigated in detail in the next section.

The pseudocode for the described algorithm is given in Algorithm 2 below for generic acceptance sets. The following notation is used in the presentation of the algorithm to denote the acceptance sets:

- S_t^y: The acceptance set at time t for the prospective label y.
- $int\,(S_t^y)$: Interior points of the acceptance set.
- $\overline{int}\,(S_t^y)$: The set of points in the acceptance set, but not in the interior of it, i.e. $S_t^y / int\,(S_t^y)$.
- $\mathbf{v}_i^y$: The non-conformity vector for data point z_i, assuming $y_t = y$.
- Δ_t^y: Set of first t non-conformity vectors for $y_t = y$, i.e. $\{\mathbf{v}_1^y, \ldots, \mathbf{v}_t^y\}$.

Algorithm 2 Multidimensional Conformal Prediction: The goal is create a set of predicted outcomes Γ_t^ϵ based on d-dimensional statistics. See the definitions just above.

for $t = 1, 2, \ldots$ **do**
  $\Gamma_t^\epsilon \leftarrow \emptyset$
  for $y \in \mathcal{Y}$ **do**
    $y_t \leftarrow y$
    for $i = 1, \ldots, t$ **do**
      $\mathbf{v}_i^y \leftarrow A_t\left(\sigma_{t/y}^{(i)}, z_i\right)$
    Calculate $S_t^y \subseteq \mathbb{R}^d$ from $\sigma_{t/y}$
    if $\mathbf{v}_t^y \in int\,(S_t^y)$ **then**
      $\Gamma_t^\epsilon \leftarrow \Gamma_t^\epsilon \cup \{y\}$.
    if $\mathbf{v}_t^y \in \overline{int}\,(S_t^y)$ & $\tau_t \geq \frac{|S_t^y \cap \Delta_t^y| - (1-\epsilon)t}{|\overline{int}(S_t^y) \cap \Delta_t^y|}$ **then**
      $\Gamma_t^\epsilon \leftarrow \Gamma_t^\epsilon \cup \{y\}$.

The following theorem provides sufficient conditions for a sequence of acceptance sets using the above algorithm to guarantee that they lead to valid predictions. These conditions have the following intuitive interpretations: (i) S_t^y should not depend on the order of data points to preserve the exchangeability of the non-conformity vectors, and (ii) fraction $1-\epsilon$ of the non-conformity vectors should fall into the acceptance set, i.e $|S_t^y \cap \Delta_t^y| \simeq (1-\epsilon)\,t$, to make sure the probability of error is kept at ϵ. These requirements provide a guideline to design acceptance sets. In the next section, we will see that each conformal predictor can be represented in terms of acceptance sets satisfying this conditions. Also we will see an example of acceptance sets tailored for the binary classification problem.

Theorem 3.1 *For a given sequence of* d *dimensional conformity scores* A_t*, acceptance sets* S_t^y*, and smoothing parameters* τ_t*; if for all* $t = 1, 2, \ldots$ *and* $y \in \mathcal{Y}$*:*

i. S_t^y *is measurable conditioned on* $\sigma_{t/y}$,

ii. $|int(S_t^y) \cap \Delta_t^y| \le (1-\epsilon)t \le |S_t^y \cap \Delta_t^y|$,

then the multidimensional conformal predictor associated with these as described in Algorithm 2 is exactly valid.

The proof is based on the fact that any smoothed conformal predictor is exactly valid (Appendix of (Shafer & Vovk, 2008)). We simply construct a classical non-conformity score based on a given multidimensional predictor that satisfies the conditions of the theorem, and show that the associated predictors generate exactly the same prediction sets.

Proof: First, consider the acceptance set for label y and time t, S_t^y, and assume it satisfies both of the conditions given in the theorem statement. Then, define the non-conformity score

$$B_t\left(\sigma_{t/y}^{(i)}, z_i\right) = \begin{cases} 2 & \text{if } \mathbf{v}_i^y \notin S_t^y \\ 1 & \text{if } \mathbf{v}_i^y \in \overline{int}(S_t^y) \\ i/(t+1) & \text{if } \mathbf{v}_i^y \in int(S_t^y). \end{cases}$$

Next, we consider three exclusive and exhaustive scenarios to demonstrate the equivalence of the conformal predictor associated with B_t and the multidimensional one. Assuming, $z_t = (x_t, y)$, we calculate the p_t^y values for the conformal predictor associated with B_t in each scenario:

- If $\mathbf{v}_t^y \in int(S_t^y)$, then y is included in the prediction set for the multidimensional predictor. Also note that the first inequality of the second condition of the theorem implies:

$$p_t^y = \frac{\tau_t + t - |int(S_t^y) \cap \Delta_t^y|}{t} \ge \epsilon.$$

  Thus y is included for both of the predictors.

- If $\mathbf{v}_t^y \notin S_t^y$, the multidimensional predictor will reject y at time t, and also if we calculate the confidence value of y for the conformal predictor, by the second half of condition ii:

$$p_t^y = \frac{\tau_t(t - |S_t^y \cap \Delta_t^y|)}{t} < \frac{t - |S_t^y \cap \Delta_t^y|}{t} \le \epsilon.$$

- Lastly, if $\mathbf{v}_t^y \in boun(S_t^y)$, the corresponding confidence value becomes:

$$p_t^y = \frac{t - |S_t^y \cap \Delta_t^y| + \tau_t|\overline{int}(S_t^y) \cap \Delta_t^y|}{t},$$

  and this value is greater or equal to ϵ if and only if the second condition on the Line 10 of the Algorithm 2 holds.

Since both predictors behave exactly the same for all of these scenarios, we can declare they are equivalent and since the conformal predictor is valid, the multidimensional one also has to be valid. ■

In addition, we can omit the first half of the second assumed condition, i.e. $|int(S_t^y) \cap \Delta_t^y| \le (1-\epsilon)t$, at the cost of achieving conservative validity instead of exact validity.

This follows from the fact that the inequality $|int(S_t^y) \cap \Delta_t^y| \le (1-\epsilon)t$ is used only in the first scenario of the proof. In that scenario, the multi-dimensional predictor does not cause an error since the label y is included in the predicted set. However, the conformal predictor may cause an error if the inequality is violated. Thus the multidimensional predictor preserves its (conservative) validity. This argument is summarized in Corollary 3.1.1.

Corollary 3.1.1 *The multidimensional conformal predictor described in Algorithm 2 is valid, if* S_t^y *is* σ_t*-measurable and* $|S_t^y \cap \Delta_t^y| \ge (1-\epsilon)t$.

This section has extended the conformal prediction framework to multiple dimensional non-conformity scores and has provided some sufficient conditions to achieve the validity guarantees. However, we haven't touched the issue of "How one should choose acceptance sets to obtain efficient predictions?". The answer to this question depends on the choice of the non-conformity scores which will entail a specific design of acceptance sets. In the next section, we will present a simple choice of acceptance sets for 2-dimensional non-conformity vectors in the binary classification setup that achieves more efficient predictions than the traditional one dimensional conformal predictors under some stability assumptions.

4 CONJUGATE PREDICTION FOR BINARY CLASSIFICATION WITH REJECT OPTION

In this section, we focus on a special case of the confidence prediction problem, where the label space consists of only two elements $\mathcal{Y} = \{0, 1\}$. We propose a simple and effective way of choosing acceptance sets for two dimensional conformal predictors based on any given classical conformal predictor.

As mentioned in the introduction, this problem is equivalent to the scenario of *binary classification with reject option* (Denis & Hebiri, 2015), where at each time point t the predictor either makes a point prediction, i.e. 0 or 1, for y_t or refuses (rejects) to make one, i.e. $\Gamma_t^\epsilon = \{0, 1\}$.In this interpretation, validity implies the probability of error for each prediction is equal to or less than ϵ and efficiency implies the reject option is not used frequently. An asymptotic analysis of error and reject options for this scenario when the traditional conformal prediction is employed can be found at Chapter 3 of (Vovk et al., 2005).

The intuitive idea behind conformal prediction is that a prediction y should be taken if its non-conformity score (monotonic with the probability of error) takes on small values with respect to the non-conformity scores of the other data points. The proposed scheme, which we call *conjugate prediction*, says to make a prediction y if its non-conformity score takes a smaller value than the non-conformity score of the alternative prediction, namely $1-y$.

This approach in some sense tries to find a compromise between the maximum likelihood and conformal prediction. Specifically, it will usually choose the most conforming label, thus enhancing efficiency, while preserving validity by requiring the acceptance set to be large enough to cover at least $1-\epsilon$ fraction of the data points. In the next section, we define conjugate predictors rigorously and show their efficiency. In Section 4.2. we will present the comparison of conjugate and conformal predictors on standard machine learning data sets.

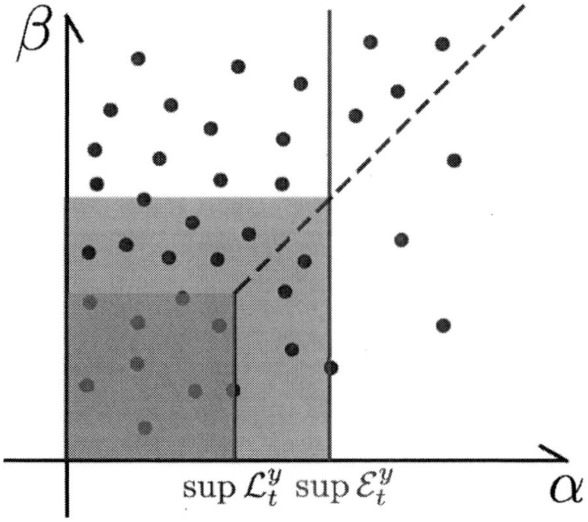

Figure 1: *(A Pictorial View of Conjugate Prediction)* In the figure α-β plane is sketched to illustrate the difference between the conformal and confidence prediction frameworks. For representative purposes, we choose $t = 40$ and $\epsilon = 0.2$. Each non-conformity vector is presented by a blue point assuming $y_t = y$, the acceptance set for conjugate prediction is on the right side of the red line, and the acceptance set for the conformal predictor is on the left of the green line. Assuming the green and red lines are approximately stable (i.e. they do not change based on an individual label value y), the conformal predictor declines to make a prediction if the test point, (x_t, y), falls into either green or red regions, however the conjugate predictor declines only on the red region.

4.1 Conjugate Conformal Prediction

Formally, a conjugate predictor associated with a given one dimensional non-conformity score A_t is a two-dimensional conformal predictor with the non-conformity vectors

$$\mathbf{v}_i^y = \begin{pmatrix} \alpha_i^y \\ \beta_i^y \end{pmatrix} = \begin{pmatrix} A_t\left(\sigma_{t/y}^{(i)}, (x_i, y_i)\right) \\ A_t\left(\sigma_{t/y}^{(i)}, (x_i, 1-y_i)\right) \end{pmatrix},$$

and the acceptance sets

$$S_t^y = \{(\alpha, \beta) : \alpha < \beta \text{ or } \alpha \leq \sup \mathcal{L}_t^y\},$$

where $\mathcal{L}_t^y = \{\gamma : |\{i : \alpha_i^y \leq \gamma \text{ or } \alpha_i < \beta_i^y\}| \leq (1-\epsilon)\,t\}$ and $\sup \emptyset = -\infty$.

For a more intuitive interpretation of the acceptance sets S_t^y, one can imagine to start with the set of points above the $\alpha = \beta$ line (see Figure 1) and combine it with the region $\alpha \leq \gamma$ where γ starts from $-\infty$ and increase the acceptance set until the total number of points in the set equals $(1-\epsilon)\,t$, i.e. $\alpha \leq \sup \mathcal{L}_t^y$, to make sure it satisfies the conditions given in Corollary 3.1.1.

Similarly, the traditional conformal predictor associated with A_t can also be represented as a two dimensional conformal predictor with the same non-conformity vectors $\mathbf{v}_i^y$ and acceptance sets:

$$\tilde{S}_t^y = \{\alpha : \alpha \leq \sup \mathcal{E}_t^y\}$$

where, $\mathcal{E}_t^y = \{\gamma : |\{i : \alpha_i^y \leq \gamma\}| \leq (1-\epsilon)\,t\}$.

As you can see in Figure 1, the traditional conformal predictor satisfies the same intuition as the conjugate predictor: start from $\gamma = -\infty$ and include points in the acceptance set until the number of non-conformity vectors that satisfy $\alpha \leq \gamma$ inequality become equal to $(1-\epsilon)\,t$. Note that this final γ value becomes equal to $\sup \mathcal{E}_t^y$.

In the following theorem, we argue that a conjugate conformal predictor is more efficient than the conformal predictor associated with the same non-conformity score, if the scoring functions are stable in the following sense. We say a scoring function A_t is stable if it changes little when any single label in the training set flips, i.e. $A_t\left(\sigma_{t/y}^{(i)}, z_i\right) \simeq A_t\left(\sigma_{t/1-y}^{(i)}, z_i\right)$ for any $i < t$. The notion of stability is studied thoroughly in statistical learning theory in the context of necessary conditions for learnability (Shalev-Shwartz, Shamir, Srebro, & Sridharan, 2010) (Bousquet & Elisseeff, 2002). In fact, many of the well-known learning algorithms, as well as the non-conformity scores derived from them, are stable to differing degrees, especially as the number of data points in the training sets increases, i.e. as t increases (Shave-Taylor & Cristianini, 2004), (Bousquet & Elisseeff, 2002), (Shalev-Shwartz & Ben-David, 2002).

In the following theorem, we first present a set of conditions in terms of the auxilary sets $\mathcal{L}_t^y$ and $\mathcal{E}_t^y$ for relative efficiency of the conjugate predictors and then intuitively discuss why the stability of the scoring functions imply these conditions.

Theorem 4.1 *Let scoring functions A_t and tolerance level $\epsilon \in [0,1]$ be given. Also assume the auxilary sets $\mathcal{L}_t^y$ and $\mathcal{E}_t^y$ are defined as:*

$$\begin{aligned} \mathcal{E}_t^y &= \{\gamma : |\{i : \alpha_i^y \leq \gamma\}| \leq (1-\epsilon)\,t\} \text{ and} \\ \mathcal{L}_t^y &= \{\gamma : |\{i : \alpha_i^y \leq \gamma \text{ or } \alpha_i^y < \beta_i^y\}| \leq (1-\epsilon)\,t\}. \end{aligned}$$

If $\sup \mathcal{L}_t^y \leq \sup \mathcal{E}_t^{1-y}$ for both $y \in \{0,1\}$, then the conjugate predictor associated with A_t is more efficient than the conformal predictor associated with the same non-conformity score at time t.

Proof: In the proof, we ignore the tie-breaking issues for the sake of brevity, but one can show, with a similar analysis, that the result holds as long as both the conjugate and conformal predictors use the same smoothing value, τ_t.

We start by assuming that the conjugate predictor declines to make a decision at time t, i.e. $|\Gamma_t^\epsilon| = 2$, which implies the non-conformity vector corresponding to the tth data point is included in the acceptance set regardless of the value of y, i.e. $\mathbf{v}_t^y \in S_t^y$ for both $y \in \{0,1\}$.

The definition of the non-conformity vector $\mathbf{v}_t^y = (\alpha_t^y, \beta_t^y)$, implies the equality $\alpha_t^y = \beta_t^{1-y}$ for all $y \in \{0,1\}$. Hence, the conditions for the rejection at time t can be written for any y as:

$$\begin{aligned} \mathbf{v}_t^y &\in \{(\alpha,\beta) : (\alpha < \beta \text{ or } \alpha \leq \sup \mathcal{L}_t^y) \\ &\qquad \text{and } (\alpha < \beta \text{ or } \alpha \leq \sup \mathcal{L}_t^{1-y})\} \\ &\subseteq \{(\alpha,\beta) : \max\{\alpha,\beta\} \leq \max_{y\in\{0,1\}} \sup \mathcal{L}_t^y\}. \end{aligned}$$

To simplify this last statement further, note $\sup \mathcal{L}_t^y \leq \sup \mathcal{E}_t^y$ from the definitions of the auxiliary sets $\mathcal{L}_t^y$ and $\mathcal{E}_t^y$. Combining this inequality with the hypothesis of the theorem, i.e. $\sup \mathcal{L}_t^y \leq \sup \mathcal{E}_t^{1-y}$, we obtain:

$$\max_{y\in\{0,1\}} \sup \mathcal{L}_t^y \leq \min_{y\in\{0,1\}} \sup \mathcal{E}_t^y.$$

Plugging this inequality in the previous statement:

$$\mathbf{v}_t^y \in \{(\alpha,\beta) : \max\{\alpha,\beta\} \leq \min_{y\in\{0,1\}} \sup \mathcal{E}_t^y\},$$

which implies $\mathbf{v}_t^y \in \tilde{S}_t^y$ and $\mathbf{v}_t^y \in \tilde{S}_t^{1-y}$. Therefore, the conformal predictor associated with A_t also declines to make a prediction.

Because the conformal predictor will decline to predict whenever the conjugate predictor will, the conjugate predictor is at least as efficient as the conformal predictor. Further, there are many cases where the conjugate predictor might predict even though the conformal predictor doesn't, for example if the test point fall into the green region in Figure 1. ■

Intuitively, the conditions given in the theorem hold for stable enough non-conformity scores, since stability implies $\sup \mathcal{E}_t^y \simeq \sup \mathcal{E}_t^{1-y}$, and as mentioned before $\sup \mathcal{L}_t^y \leq \sup \mathcal{E}_t^y$ follows directly from the definition of these sets.

The theorem says the conjugate predictor performs at least as efficiently as the original conformal predictor under these stability conditions. The validity of the conjugate predictors follows from Corollary 3.1.1.

In the next subsection, we investigate the relative performance of the conformal and conjugate predictors by comparing the error and rejection rates for different choices of non-conformity scores and datasets. Our main observation is that the conjugate predictors provide two type of gains. First, it reduces the rejection rate due to the extra information provided by the conjugate scores. Second, even if the conjugate score does not provide any extra information (i.e. the β_t^y can be calculated as a function of α_t^y), it reduces the error rate for a given rejection rate, by being more decisive about its choices on easy samples.

4.2 Empirical Results

In this section, we show the results of applying our algorithm and corresponding conformal predictor on some real data-sets from UCI Machine Learning Repository (Lichman, 2013). The details of the used non-conformity scores and the datasets are given in the following two subsections and the numerical results are given at the last subsection.

4.2.1 Experiments

Our experiments use two different non-conformity scores: one based on random forests and the other is based on nearest neighbor classifiers. The reason to choose these two example scores is to illustrate the effect of the conjugate predictor when the conjugate score providing new information about the data (as in the nearest neighbor case), or not (as in the random forests).

1. Out-of-bag Score in Random Forests: At each time t, we train a random forest consist of 100 randomized decision trees on $\sigma_{t/y}$. Randomization entails taking a bootstrap of the samples for training and restricting the optimization at the decision nodes to random subsets of the features as described in (Breiman, 2001). We used the Statistics and Machine Learning Toolbox's (MATLAB, 2013) under the default settings, which are the settings suggested by Breiman originally.

   The non-conformity score α_i^y of point z_i is calculated as the fraction of trees (using a training set that doesn't include z_i) that miss-classify the sample x_i, i.e. give the output $1 - y_i$. Note that this choice of non-conformity score implies $\beta_i^y = 1 - \alpha_i^y$, and thus the conjugate score does not provide any new information about the data. Nevertheless, conjugate prediction will still be useful for larger error tolerances.

2. *In-Class Distance in k-Nearest-Neighbor:* As the second scoring function, we built a non-conformity score based on the well-known k nearest neighbor algorithm. For each point z_i, we calculated the closest k data points with the same label y_i from the set $\sigma_{t/y}^{(i)}$ and used the arithmetic average of these k distances as the non-conformity score of α_i^y.

   In the implementation, we tried k values in the range 3 to 10, and we report the results for $k = 5$, which performed the best in all five data sets. Note that while larger values imply better stability, choosing k too large weakens the classifier's predictive power. We used Euclidean distance to measure the closeness of the data points after centering and scaling each feature to unit variance.

   Note that, in contrast to the non-conformity score used with random forests, this non-conformity score provides new information about the data, and as we see in Section 4.2.3, the advantage of using conjugate predictors is greater in this case.

4.2.2 Data Sets

We used the following data sets from UCI ML Repository (Lichman, 2013):

- Breast Cancer Wisconsin (Original) Data Set (Mangasarian & Wolberg, 1990): This data set consists of 699 data points, where each data point is collected from a patient that contains 10 integer valued features of a breast tumor and a binary label for its type (benign/malignant).
- Haberman's Survival Data Set: This data set contains 5 year survival information 306 patients after surgery for breast cancer. The data contain 3 integer features and 1 binary label (survived/died in 5 year.)
- Parkinson's Data Set (Little, McSharry, Hunter, & Ramig, 2008): This dataset contains data about 195 vocal recordings, where each record is represented by a 23 dimensional real vector and the goal is to predict if the subject has Parkinson's disease or not.
- Musk (v1) Data Set: This data set contains 476 data points on 92 types of molecules, each of which is represented by 166 features classifying them as musks and non-musks. The goal is to determine whether a new molecule will be a musk or not.
- Statlog (Australian Credit Approval) Data Set: This data set contains 690 data points on anonymized credit card applications described by 14 features, and classifying them as approved or rejected.

4.2.3 Results

In this part, we tested the above five data sets with both of the described non-conformity scores using error tolerance values of 0.03, 0.10, and 0.18. Because we assume exchangeability, we randomly permute the data before each experiment. Each experiment is repeated 10 times. The means are reported in Table 1,2,3, and 4.

In Tables 1 and 2, we report the cumulative error rate, i.e. fraction of mis-classified samples, for both conjugate and conformal predictors for each score, data, tolerance level combinations. Tables 3 and 4 give the cumulative rejection rates, i.e. the ratio of samples where the classifier declined to predict/classify.

Table 1: *Conjugate Conformal Predictors:* Mean Cumulative Error Rates. KNN means k nearest neighbor, and RF means random forest. B.C. means the breast cancer data set, Surv means survival, and Park. means Parkinson's.

	$\epsilon = 0.03$	$\epsilon = 0.10$	$\epsilon = 0.18$
KNN/B.C.	0.0284	0.0329	0.0335
KNN/Surv.	0.0363	0.1007	0.1699
KNN/Park.	0.0313	0.0836	0.1000
KNN/Musk	0.0336	0.1057	0.1473
KNN/Statlog	0.0358	0.1070	0.1574
RF/B.C.	0.0271	0.0334	0.0334
RF/Surv.	0.0366	0.1000	0.1788
RF/Park.	0.0313	00944.	0.1246
RF/Musk.	0.0372	0.1092	0.1571
RF/Statlog	0.0371	0.1035	0.1380

Table 2: *Classical Conformal Predictors:* Mean Cumulative Error Rates. Labels have the same meaning as in the previous table. Conjugate predictors (previous table) are more accurate or comparable in nearly all cases.

	$\epsilon = 0.03$	$\epsilon = 0.10$	$\epsilon = 0.18$
KNN/B.C.	0.0343	0.1048	0.1827
KNN/Surv.	0.0330	0.0971	0.1683
KNN/Park.	0.0354	0.0979	0.1692
KNN/Musk	0.0368	0.1038	0.1815
KNN/Statlog	0.0371	0.1133	0.1917
RF/B.C.	0.0307	0.1034	0.1892
RF/Surv.	0.0366	0.1000	0.1794
RF/Park.	0.0313	0.0985	0.1697
RF/Musk.	0.0372	0.1092	0.1824
RF/Statlog	0.0371	0.1045	0.1832

Additionally, in Table 5 the cumulative error rates for the native random forest and k nearest neighbor algorithms are presented. For the native implementation, at each time point t, the algorithm is trained on the first $t - 1$ data points and used to predict the tth one. In the for each combination, we report the error rates of the native algorithms over the

Table 3: *Conjugate Conformal Predictors:* Mean Cumulative Rejection Rates. Labels have the same meanings as in the previous tables.

	$\epsilon = 0.03$	$\epsilon = 0.10$	$\epsilon = 0.18$
KNN/B.C.	0.0570	0.0110	0.0098
KNN/Surv.	0.9255	0.7258	0.4507
KNN/Park.	0.4359	0.1410	0.0728
KNN/Musk	0.6149	0.2603	0.0981
KNN/Statlog	0.7581	0.2423	0.0174
RF/B.C.	0.0271	0.0146	0.0143
RF/Surv.	0.7461	0.5020	0.3010
RF/Park.	0.3503	0.1323	0.0805
RF/Musk.	0.4779	0.2088	0.1084
RF/Statlog	0.3964	0.0936	0.0293

Table 4: *Classical Conformal Predictors:* Mean Cumulative Rejection Rates. Labels have the same meanings as in the previous tables. Note that conjugate predictors (previous table) enjoy consistently lower rejection rates for k nearest neighbor algorithm and equivalent rejection rates to the conformal ones upto statistical fluctuations while keeping error rate at a lower level.

	$\epsilon = 0.03$	$\epsilon = 0.10$	$\epsilon = 0.18$
KNN/B.C.	0.6611	0.4246	0.2212
KNN/Surv.	0.9510	0.8013	0.6775
KNN/Park.	0.8195	0.6108	0.4615
KNN/Musk	0.8828	0.6903	0.5221
KNN/Statlog	0.9112	0.6878	0.4467
RF/B.C.	0.0255	0.0102	0.0095
RF/Surv.	0.7461	0.5020	0.3010
RF/Park.	0.3503	0.1297	0.0662
RF/Musk.	0.4779	0.2088	0.0962
RF/Statlog	0.3962	0.0929	0.0148

samples that corresponding conjugate predictors refused to make a prediction or not.

We observe that conjugate predictors always preserve validity (see Table 1), since they reach an error rate equal or less than the target tolerance level (up to statistical fluctuations). However, when the data is relatively easy to classify as in the breast cancer data (see Table 5), conjugate predictors are more decisive while also reducing the error rate by preserving the original validity guarantees.

Furthermore, the decisiveness of conjugate predictors reduces the rejection rates in our simulations (see Table 3 and 4). The gain is more pronounced when the data is relatively less noisy, i.e. easy to classify as in the breast cancer data, and the conjugate score of the base algorithm provides extra information about the data, as when using the k nearest neighbor algorithm.

Table 5: *Baseline:* Depending on the error tolerance ϵ, the conjugate algorithm refuses to predict on certain data points. For each box having format x/y, the table shows the error rate (x) of the underlying algorithm on the refused data points and the error rate (y) on the data points upon which the conjugate algorithm makes prediction. Note that, the error rate is significantly higher on the refused data points whenever the target error level ϵ is low, i.e. refusals are inevitable to preserve the validity.

	$\epsilon = 0.03$	$\epsilon = 0.10$	$\epsilon = 0.18$
KNN/B.C.	0.10/0.03	0.05/0.03	0.00/0.03
KNN/Surv.	0.26/0.54	0.24/0.37	0.23/0.31
KNN/Park.	0.19/0.05	0.21/0.10	0.14/0.11
KNN/Musk	0.23/0.09	0.27/0.14	0.29/0.16
KNN/Statlog	0.16/0.15	0.22/0.14	0.11/0.16
RF/B.C.	0.17/0.03	0.01/0.03	0.00/0.03
RF/Surv.	0.36/0.14	0.41/0.20	0.41/0.26
RF/Park.	0.29/0.05	0.22/0.12	0.06/0.14
RF/Musk.	0.33/0.08	0.37/0.15	0.30/0.19
RF/Statlog	0.26/0.06	0.33/0.12	0.08/0.14

5 DISCUSSION & CONCLUSION

Extending conformal predictors to multiple dimensions is both technically reasonable and practically beneficial. This paper has shown that the extension almost always increases the efficiency and always preserves the validity of machine learning algorithms compared with standard conformal predictors.

Other applications of this extension include scenarios where one may want to combine a set of conformal predictions to make better predictions even when there are breaks in exchangeability. For example, consider the problem of prediction under seasonal changes or other sources of concept drift.

Our conjugate prediction framework is an iterative method for finding hybrid non-conformity scores. As noted in the proof of Theorem 3.1, each multidimensional predictor can be equivalently represented as a conformal predictor. Thus, if one starts with a conformal predictor and can improve upon it by extending it to higher dimensions, as in the case of conjugate predictors, one will obtain a more effective conformal predictor.

The next steps in this work are to demonstrate the benefits of this extension to these other applications, to incorporate the resulting methods into standard machine learning software, and to explore further generalizations of conformal (and multi-dimensional/conjugate conformal) predictors.

References

Bousquet, O., & Elisseeff, A. (2002). Stability and generalization. *The Journal of Machine Learning Research*, 2, 499-526.

Box, G. E., Jenkins, G. M., Reinsel, G. C., & Ljung, G. M. (2015). *Time series analysis: forecasting and control.* John Wiley & Sons.

Chatfield, C. (1993). Calculating interval forecasts. *Journal of Business & Economic Statistics*, 11(2), 121-135.

Chaudhuri, K., & Zhang, C. (2013). Improved Algorithms for Confidence-Rated Prediction with Error Guarantees.

Chow, C. K. (1970). On optimum recognition error and reject tradeoff. *Information Theory, IEEE Transactions on*, 16(1), 41-46.

Cox, D. R., & Hinkley D.V. (1974). *Theoretical Statistics.* Chapman-Hall, London.

Denis, C., & Hebiri, M. (2015). Confidence Sets for Classification. *Statistical Learning and Data Sciences*, 301-312. Springer International Publishing.

El-Yaniv, R., & Wiener, Y. (2010). On the foundations of noise-free selective classification. *The Journal of Machine Learning Research*, 11, 1605-1641.

El-Yaniv, R., & Wiener, Y. (2012). Active learning via perfect selective classification. *The Journal of Machine Learning Research*, 13(1), 255-279.

Herbei, R., & Wegkamp, M. H. (2006). Classification with reject option. *Canadian Journal of Statistics*, 34(4), 709-721.

Kallenberg, O. (2006). *Probabilistic symmetries and invariance principles.* Springer Science & Business Media.

Lei, Jing. (2014). Classification with confidence. *Biometrika*, 101(4), 755-769, doi:10.1093/biomet/asu038.

Lei, J., Robins, J., & Wasserman, L. (2011). Efficient nonparametric conformal prediction regions. *arXiv preprint* arXiv:1111.1418.

Lichman, M. (2013). UCI Machine Learning Repository [http://archive.ics.uci.edu/ml]. Irvine, CA: University of California, School of Information and Computer Science.

Little, M. A., McSharry, P. E., Hunter, E. J., Spielman, J., & Ramig, L. O. (2009). Suitability of dysphonia measurements for telemonitoring of Parkinson's disease. *Biomedical Engineering, IEEE Transactions on*, 56(4), 1015-1022.

Mangasarian O.L., & Wolberg W.H. (1990). Cancer diagnosis via linear programming. *SIAM News*, 23(5), 1-18, September 1990.

MATLAB and Statistics and Machine Learning Toolbox Release 2013b, The MathWorks, Inc., Natick, Massachusetts, United States.

Meade, N., & Islam, T. (1995). Prediction intervals for growth curve forecasts. *Journal of Forecasting*, 14(5), 413-430.

Ryabko, B., & Ryabko, D. (2013). A confidence-set approach to signal denoising. *Statistical Methodology*, 15, 115-120.

Schervish, M. J. (2012). *Theory of statistics.* Springer Science & Business Media.

Shafer, G., & Vovk, V. (2008). A tutorial on conformal prediction. *The Journal of Machine Learning Research*, 9, 371-421.

Shalev-Shwartz, S., & Ben-David, S. (2014). *Understanding machine learning: From theory to algorithms.* Cambridge University Press.

Shalev-Shwartz, S., Shamir, O., Srebro, N., & Sridharan, K. (2010). Learnability, stability and uniform convergence. *The Journal of Machine Learning Research*, 11, 2635-2670.

Shawe-Taylor, J., & Cristianini, N. (2004). *Kernel methods for pattern analysis.* Cambridge university press.

Vovk, V., Fedorova, V., Nouretdinov, I., & Gammerman, A. (2014). Criteria of efficiency for conformal prediction. *Technical report, Royal Holloway University of London* (April 2014).

Vovk, V., Gammerman, A., & Shafer, G. (2005). *Algorithmic learning in a random world.* Springer Science & Business Media.

Online Forest Density Estimation

Frédéric Koriche
CRIL, CNRS UMR 8188
Université d'Artois, France
koriche@cril.fr

Abstract

Online density estimation is the problem of predicting a sequence of outcomes, revealed one at a time, almost as well as the best expert chosen from a reference class of probabilistic models. The performance of each expert is measured with the log-likelihood loss. The class of experts examined in this paper is the family of discrete, acyclic graphical models, also known as *Markov forests*. By coupling Bayesian mixtures with symmetric Dirichlet priors for parameter learning, and a variant of "Follow the Perturbed Leader" strategy for structure learning, we derive an online forest density estimation algorithm that achieves a regret of $\tilde{O}(\sqrt{T})$, with a per-round time complexity that is quasi-quadratic in the input dimension. Using simple and flexible update rules, this algorithm can be easily adapted to predict with Markov trees or mixtures of Markov forests. Empirical results indicate that our online algorithm is a practical alternative to the state-of-the-art batch algorithms for learning tree-structured graphical models.

1 INTRODUCTION

Graphical models have attracted considerable interest in AI, computational statistics, and machine learning (Wainwright and Jordan, 2008; Koller and Friedman, 2009). One of the key virtues of these models is to allow a separation between qualitative, structural aspects of uncertain knowledge, and quantitative, parametric aspects of uncertainty. As such, graphical models are able to represent, in a compact and intelligible way, high-dimensional probability distributions, using local interactions between variables. For *undirected* graphical models, also known as *Markov networks*, the structure is an undirected graph G, and the parameters are grouped into a set $\boldsymbol{\theta}$ of factors associated with the cliques of G. The probability $\mathbb{P}_M(\boldsymbol{x})$ assigned to an outcome $\boldsymbol{x}$ by a model $M = (G, \boldsymbol{\theta})$ is given by the product of factors in $\boldsymbol{\theta}$ which are activated by $\boldsymbol{x}$, divided by a normalization constant, known as the *partition function*.

A fundamental problem in graphical models is to extract from a series of observed outcomes, the structure and the parameters of a model that accurately predicts future, unseen, outcomes. This learning problem, which can be generalized to arbitrary probabilistic models, is often referred to as *density estimation* in the literature (Grünwald, 2007; Rissanen, 2012). In the *batch* density estimation setting, it is assumed that outcomes are sampled independently from a fixed (but unknown) target distribution. The data samples, available ahead of time, are separated into a training set for learning the model, and a test set for evaluating its performance. Contrastingly, in the *online* density estimation setting, there are no statistical assumptions about the series of outcomes (Merhav and Feder, 1998; Cesa-Bianchi and Lugosi, 2006). The learner receives inputs sequentially, and its performance is measured over all the observed sequence. The absence of statistical assumption makes online algorithms applicable in adaptive or "dynamic" environments, where the target distribution is allowed to arbitrarily change in response to various events, including the learner's decisions. Even in "static" environments, online algorithms can provide a practical alternative to batch algorithms, by processing only one outcome at a time. They are indeed particularly suited to handle streaming applications, where all the data is not available in advance, or large-scale domains with massive amounts of data.

Conceptually, online density estimation with graphical models can be viewed as a repeated game between the learner and its environment. The parameters of the game are an outcome space $\mathcal{X}$ and a class $\mathcal{M}$ of graphical models over $\mathcal{X}$, called *experts*. During each trial t of the game, the learner selects (possibly at random) a model $M^t \in \mathcal{M}$, the environment responds by an outcome $\boldsymbol{x}^t \in \mathcal{X}$, and the learner incurs the log-likelihood loss (or *log-loss*, for short) $\ell(M^t, \boldsymbol{x}^t) = -\ln \mathbb{P}_{M^t}(\boldsymbol{x}^t)$. The quality of an online learning algorithm is measured according to two standard metrics. The first, called *regret*, measures the difference in cumulative loss between the algorithm and the best expert in $\mathcal{M}$. Borrowing the terminology of game theory, an online learning algorithm is called *Hannan-consistent* if its regret over any possible sequence of T outcomes is only sublinear in T. The second metric is computational complexity, i.e. the amount of resources required to compute M^t at each round t, given the sequence of outcomes observed so far.

In this paper, we examine the problem of online density estimation for the class of *(discrete) Markov forests*, which represent discrete multivariate probability distributions where interdependencies are restricted to an acyclic graph. Markov forests are endowed with two remarkable properties, namely, (i) they can be factorized into a *closed form* which does not involve a partition function, and (ii) the space of all acyclic graphs upon which a Markov forest can be constructed is a *matroid*. As observed in (Pearl, 1988; Lauritzen, 1996), the closed-form expression of the probability distribution $\mathbb{P}_M$ associated with an n-dimensional Markov forest $M = (F, \boldsymbol{\theta})$ is given by

$$\mathbb{P}_M(\boldsymbol{x}) = \prod_{i=1}^{n} \theta_i(x_i) \prod_{(i,j)\in F} \frac{\theta_{ij}(x_i, x_j)}{\theta_i(x_i)\theta_j(x_j)} \qquad (1)$$

where $\theta_i(x_i)$ and $\theta_{ij}(x_i, x_j)$ are the marginal densities of the node i and the edge (i, j), respectively. Based on (1), probabilistic inference in Markov forests can be performed in linear time. Moreover, the matroid associated with the structure space of Markov forests allows linear optimization to be performed in low-polynomial time, using the greedy matroid algorithm.

Based on these properties, the "batch" forest density estimation problem can be solved in quasi-quadratic time (in the input dimension n), by finding a maximum weight spanning tree in the complete graph of order n, whose edges are weighted according to the empirical bivariate marginals measured on the training set. This simple and elegant strategy, due to Chow and Liu (1968), is the blueprint of more sophisticated algorithms for learning other tree-structured graphical models, such as constrained Markov forests (Liu et al., 2011; Tan et al., 2011), and mixtures of Markov trees (Meila and Jordan, 2000; Kumar and Koller, 2009). Beyond Markov forests and their variants, the problem of finding the structure and the parameters of a maximum likelihood graphical model is, in general, NP-hard (Chickering, 1995), even for the restricted classes of Bayesian polytrees (Dasgupta, 1999) and Markov networks of bounded treewidth (Srebro, 2003).

Our Results. The challenge of the "online" forest density estimation problem lies in the fact that outcomes are revealed only one at a time, thus forcing the learner to iteratively update both the structure and the parameters of a Markov forest, so as to minimize the cumulative log-loss over the sequence of outcomes observed so far. This difficulty naturally raises the question of whether there exist Hannan-consistent forest density estimation algorithms with a total runtime complexity comparable to that of batch learning algorithms. By exploiting the closed form of Markov forests and the matroid of their structure space, we answer this question in the affirmative using easily implementable update strategies.

The key point of our online learning algorithm and its regret analysis lies in the fact that the parameters and the structure of a forest can be updated in an *independent* way. Indeed, in light of the closed-form expression (1), the log-likelihood loss of a Markov forest can be additively decomposed to the nodes and the edges of a forest, in such a way that the contribution of the local components are independent of the forest structure. Thus, the regret of any algorithm producing the sequence $M^1, \cdots, M^T$ of Markov forests can be decomposed into a telescopic sum of two regret expressions, namely, a "parametric" part defined over the forest parameters $\boldsymbol{\theta}^1, \cdots, \boldsymbol{\theta}^T$, and a "structural" part defined over the forest structures $F^1, \cdots, F^T$.

By exploiting the additive decomposition of the log-loss, the parametric part can, in turn, be decomposed into a sum of "local" regrets defined over node and edge parameters. This observation naturally suggests the use of Bayesian mixtures under Dirichlet priors for estimating univariate marginals and bivariate marginals. Such mixtures, which have been extensively studied in the literature of density estimation (see e.g. Cesa-Bianchi and Lugosi (2006); Grünwald (2007)), can be implemented using very simple update rules. Namely, by selecting Jeffreys mixtures for univariate and bivariate marginal estimators, our strategy achieves a regret that is logarithmic in the number T of rounds, with a per-round time complexity that is quadratic in the input dimension n.

Concerning the structural part of the regret, the log-loss is an affine function of the forest structure. This, together with the matroid property of forest structures, opens up the possibility of using various online combinatorial optimization algorithms (see e.g. Koolen et al. (2010); Audibert et al. (2011)). Here, our structure-update strategy is based on the well-known *Follow the Perturbed Leader* (FPL) algorithm (Hannan, 1957; Kalai and Vempala, 2005), which essentially adds a random perturbation to the total loss observed so far, and selects the forest structure that minimizes the resulting cost function. In order to attenuate the possibly unstable effects of perturbations, our strategy uses a convex combination of forest structures, coupled with a swap-rounding method (Chekuri et al., 2010) for generating, at each iteration, a forest that is consistent with the current convex mixture. By ignoring logarithmic factors, this strategy achieves a regret of $\tilde{O}(\sqrt{T})$, with a quadratic per-round time complexity.

In a nutshell, our online forest density estimation algorithm achieves Hannan-consistency with a cumulative runtime complexity that is comparable to that of the Chow-Liu algorithm. Furthermore, our algorithm can be easily adapted to predict with Markov trees, and mixtures of Markov forests (with shared parameters). Experiments conducted on several real-world datasets support our theoretical approach. Notably, our online learning algorithm rapidly converges to the estimations of the state-of-the-art batch algorithms for Markov trees (Chow and Liu, 1968), and thresholded Markov forests (Tan et al., 2011).

Paper Structure. After introducing the necessary background in forest polytopes (Section 2) and Markov forests (Section 3), we present our online forest density estimation algorithm in Section 4. Its regret analysis is detailed in Section 5, and its experimental validation is presented in Section 6. Finally, Section 7 concludes with some related work in online learning, together with several perspectives of further research.

2 FOREST POLYTOPES

We start with some notations and definitions which will be used throughout the paper. Let $[n]$ denote the set $\{1, \cdots, n\}$, and $\binom{[n]}{2}$ denote the set $\{(i,j) \in [n] \times [n], i < j\}$. To simplify notation, we use the abbreviation $\boldsymbol{x}^{1:t}$ to designate any sequence of vectors $\boldsymbol{x}^1, \cdots, \boldsymbol{x}^t$. For $\boldsymbol{x}, \boldsymbol{y} \in \mathbb{R}^n$ and $p \in [1, \infty]$, we use $\|\boldsymbol{x}\|_p$ to denote the L_p norm of $\boldsymbol{x}$, and we use$\langle \boldsymbol{x}, \boldsymbol{y} \rangle$ to denote the scalar product of $\boldsymbol{x}$ and $\boldsymbol{y}$. For a subset $\boldsymbol{X} \subseteq \mathbb{R}^n$, we denote by $\operatorname{conv} \boldsymbol{X}$ the convex hull of $\boldsymbol{X}$.

In what follows, we shall adopt set and vector notations interchangeably for describing graphs over the node set $[n]$; in the set notation, G is a subset of $\binom{[n]}{2}$, and in the vector notation $\boldsymbol{g}$ is a vector in $\{0,1\}^{\binom{n}{2}}$, such that $g_{ij} = 1$ if and only if $(i,j) \in G$. As usual, a *forest* is an acyclic graph, and a *spanning tree* is an acyclic, connected graph that spans $[n]$. The spaces of all forests and all spanning trees of order n are denoted $\mathbf{F}_n$ and $\mathbf{T}_n$, respectively. It is well-known that the set of all forests of order n defines a *matroid* over the ground set $\binom{[n]}{2}$, where $\mathbf{F}_n$ is the collection of independent sets, and $\mathbf{T}_n$ is the collection of bases. The rank of this matroid is $n-1$, which corresponds to the size of any spanning tree over $[n]$.

The convex hull of $\mathbf{F}_n$, where elements are viewed in vector notation, is called the *forest polytope*. This polyhedron of dimension $n-1$ is characterized by the system of inequalities:

$$\operatorname{conv} \mathbf{F}_n = \left\{ \boldsymbol{p} \in \mathbb{R}_+^{\binom{n}{2}} : \langle \boldsymbol{p}, \boldsymbol{g} \rangle \leq n-1, \text{ for all } \boldsymbol{g} \in \{0,1\}^{\binom{n}{2}} \right\}$$

Such inequalities are often referred to as *acyclicity constraints* in the literature (Shrijver, 2003). The convex hull of $\mathbf{T}_n$, called the *spanning tree polytope*, is the subset of $\operatorname{conv} \mathbf{F}_n$ formed by the points $\boldsymbol{p}$ satisfying the equality $\langle \boldsymbol{p}, \mathbf{1} \rangle = n-1$, where $\mathbf{1}$ is the all-ones vector in $\mathbb{R}^n$. By Carathéodory's theorem, any point $\boldsymbol{p} \in \operatorname{conv} \mathbf{F}_n$ (resp. $\boldsymbol{p} \in \operatorname{conv} \mathbf{T}_n$) can be represented as a convex combination of $t \leq n-1$ forests (resp. spanning trees), i.e. $\boldsymbol{p} = \sum_{\tau=1}^{t} \alpha_\tau \boldsymbol{f}^\tau$, where $\boldsymbol{\alpha} \in \mathbb{R}_+^t$ and $\|\boldsymbol{\alpha}\|_1 = 1$.

Although the forest polytope and the spanning tree polytope are characterized by an exponential number N of acyclicity constraints, linear optimization under these combinatorial structures can be performed in low polynomial time. Indeed, by Edmond's theorem (1970), both $\operatorname{conv} \mathbf{F}_n$ and $\operatorname{conv} \mathbf{T}_n$ are totally dual-integral, and hence, any minimizer $\boldsymbol{p}^*$ of a linear objective $\langle \boldsymbol{w}, \boldsymbol{p} \rangle$ subject to $\boldsymbol{p} \in \operatorname{conv} \mathbf{F}_n$ (resp. $\boldsymbol{p} \in \operatorname{conv} \mathbf{T}_n$) is an extreme point in $\mathbf{F}_n$ (resp. $\mathbf{T}_n$). This point $\boldsymbol{p}^*$ can be found in $O(n^2 \log n)$ time, using the greedy matroid algorithm. Specifically, for the forest polytope, the greedy algorithm first sorts the $\binom{n}{2}$ edges in decreasing order according to the linear objective $\boldsymbol{w}$, next keeps the first m edges with non-positive weight, and then iteratively finds a minimum cost forest F over these m ordered edges. For the spanning tree polytope, the greedy algorithm coincides with Kruskal's method, which also sorts the edges according to $\boldsymbol{w}$, but uses (in the worst case) all the $\binom{n}{2}$ ordered edges for generating a minimum cost spanning tree.

Finally, in order to round fractional points in matroid polytopes, we shall focus on SWAP method proposed by Chekuri et al. (2010). This algorithm takes as input a fractional point $\boldsymbol{p} \in \operatorname{conv} \mathbf{F}_n$ (resp. $\boldsymbol{p} \in \operatorname{conv} \mathbf{T}_n$), given as a convex combination $\boldsymbol{p} = \sum_{\tau=1}^{t} \alpha_\tau \boldsymbol{f}^\tau$ of forests (resp. spanning trees), and iteratively generates the sequence of points $\boldsymbol{p}^1, \cdots, \boldsymbol{p}^t$, such that $\boldsymbol{p}^1 = \boldsymbol{p}$, $\boldsymbol{p}^t$ is an extreme point in $\mathbf{F}_n$ (resp. $\mathbf{T}_n$), and $\mathbb{E}[\boldsymbol{p}^\tau] = \boldsymbol{p}$ for all $\tau \in [t]$. Each point $\boldsymbol{p}^{\tau+1}$ is obtained from $\boldsymbol{p}^\tau$ by arbitrarily choosing two components $\alpha_i \boldsymbol{f}^i$ and $\alpha_j \boldsymbol{f}^j$ in $\boldsymbol{p}^\tau$, and by replacing them with a new component $(\alpha_i + \alpha_j)\boldsymbol{f}'$. Here, $\boldsymbol{f}'$ is generated in $O(n^2)$ time using random base exchanges. So, $\boldsymbol{p}$ can be rounded using $t-1$ quadratic-time operations. Importantly, SWAP can be interrupted at any iteration τ to give a convex combination $\boldsymbol{p}^\tau$ of $t+1-\tau$ graphical structures. In what follows, we use $\text{SWAP}_k(\boldsymbol{p})$ to denote the application of at most $\tau = t+1-k$ iterations of the SWAP algorithm, which returns a convex combination including at most k components.

3 MARKOV FORESTS

The graphical models examined in this paper are defined over a set $\{X_1, \cdots, X_n\}$ of multinomial random variables, each taking values over a finite alphabet $\{1, \cdots, m\}$, with $m \geq 2$.

A *probability table* for a random variable X_i, is a vector $\boldsymbol{\theta}_i$ in the m-dimensional probability simplex, where $\theta_i(u)$ denotes the probability that $X_i = u$. Similarly, a probability table for a pair of random variables (X_i, X_j) is a vector $\boldsymbol{\theta}_{ij}$ in the m^2-dimensional probability simplex, where $\theta_{ij}(u,v)$ indicates the probability that $X_i = u$ and $X_j = v$. By $\boldsymbol{\Theta}_{m,n}$, we denote the set of all mappings $\boldsymbol{\theta}$ that assign a probability table $\boldsymbol{\theta}_i$ to each $i \in [n]$, and a probability table $\boldsymbol{\theta}_{ij}$ to each $(i,j) \in \binom{[n]}{2}$, while satisfying the *marginalization constraints*:

$$\sum_{u=1}^{m} \theta_{ij}(u,v) = \theta_j(v) \text{ and } \sum_{v=1}^{m} \theta_{ij}(u,v) = \theta_i(u) \qquad (2)$$

Note that the dimension of $\boldsymbol{\theta}$ is $d = mn + m^2\binom{n}{2}$. The class of *m-ary n-dimensional Markov forests* is defined as $\mathcal{F}_{m,n} = \mathbf{F}_n \times \boldsymbol{\Theta}_{m,n}$, and the class of *$m$-ary n-dimensional Markov trees* is given by $\mathcal{T}_{m,n} = \mathbf{T}_n \times \boldsymbol{\Theta}_{m,n}$. For a class $\mathcal{M} \in \{\mathcal{F}_{m,n}, \mathcal{T}_{m,n}\}$, we denote by $\boldsymbol{P}(\mathcal{M})$ the matroid polytope associated with the structure space of $\mathcal{M}$, i.e. $\boldsymbol{P}(\mathcal{M}) = \operatorname{conv} \mathbf{F}_n$ if $\mathcal{M} = \mathcal{F}_{m,n}$, and $\boldsymbol{P}(\mathcal{M}) = \operatorname{conv} \mathbf{T}_n$ if $\mathcal{M} = \mathcal{T}_{m,n}$.

By taking into account the acyclicity constraints of $\mathbf{F}_n$ and the marginalization constraints of $\boldsymbol{\Theta}_{m,n}$, the probability distribution $\mathbb{P}_M$ over $\mathcal{X} = [m]^n$ represented by a Markov forest $M = (\boldsymbol{f}, \boldsymbol{\theta})$ is given by the closed-form expression (1). More generally, if $(\boldsymbol{p}, \boldsymbol{\theta})$ is a pair of vectors in $\boldsymbol{P}(\mathcal{M}) \times \boldsymbol{\Theta}_{m,n}$, then the corresponding distribution is given by

$$\mathbb{P}_{\boldsymbol{p},\boldsymbol{\theta}}(\boldsymbol{x}) = \prod_{i \in [n]} \theta_i(x_i) \prod_{(i,j) \in \binom{[n]}{2}} \left(\frac{\theta_{ij}(x_i, x_j)}{\theta_i(x_i)\theta_j(x_j)} \right)^{p_{ij}} \qquad (3)$$

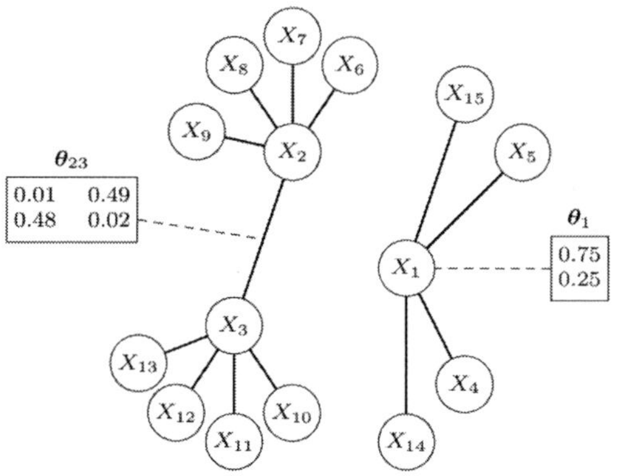

Figure 1: A binary Markov forest.

When $\boldsymbol{p}$ is described as a convex combination of forests (resp. trees), the pair $(\boldsymbol{p}, \boldsymbol{\theta})$ can be viewed as a *mixture* of Markov forests (resp. Markov trees) sharing the same parameters.

4 ONLINE MARKOV FORESTS

Recall that online learning can be viewed as a repeated game between a learning algorithm $\mathcal{A}$ and its environment. During each trial $t \in [T]$, the learner $\mathcal{A}$ starts by choosing (possibly at random) a model $M^t \in \mathcal{M}$, where $\mathcal{M}$ is a class of graphical models. Next, the environment responds by supplying an outcome $\boldsymbol{x}^t \in \mathcal{X}$, and then, $\mathcal{A}$ incurs the log-loss $\ell(M^t, \boldsymbol{x}^t) = -\ln \mathbb{P}_{M^t}(\boldsymbol{x}^t)$. The *(expected) regret* of the learning algorithm $\mathcal{A}$ with respect to the sequence of outcomes $\boldsymbol{x}^{1:T} = (\boldsymbol{x}^1, \cdots, \boldsymbol{x}^T)$ is given by

$$R_{\boldsymbol{x}^{1:T}}(\mathcal{A}) = \sum_{t=1}^{T} \mathbb{E}\left[\ell(M^t, \boldsymbol{x}^t)\right] - \min_{M \in \mathcal{M}} \sum_{t=1}^{T} \ell(M, \boldsymbol{x}^t) \quad (4)$$

where the expectation is taken with respect to the learner's internal randomization. By extension, the *minimax regret* of $\mathcal{A}$ at horizon T, denoted $R_T(\mathcal{A})$, is the maximum of $R_{\boldsymbol{x}^{1:T}}(\mathcal{A})$ over any sequence $\boldsymbol{x}^{1:T}$ in $\mathcal{X}^T$. $\mathcal{A}$ is called *Hannan-consistent* if its minimax regret is sublinear in T, or equivalently, if its average minimax regret $R_T(\mathcal{A})/T$ vanishes as $T \to \infty$.

The classes of experts investigated in this study are Markov forests and Markov trees, that is, $\mathcal{M} \in \{\mathcal{F}_{m,n}, \mathcal{T}_{m,n}\}$. The log-loss can be extended to $\boldsymbol{P}(\mathcal{M}) \times \boldsymbol{\Theta}_{m,n} \times \mathcal{X} \to \mathbb{R}$, using $\ell(\boldsymbol{p}, \boldsymbol{\theta}, \boldsymbol{x}) = -\ln \mathbb{P}_{\boldsymbol{p},\boldsymbol{\theta}}(\boldsymbol{x})$, where $\mathbb{P}_{\boldsymbol{p},\boldsymbol{\theta}}$ is defined according to the closed-form expression (3). Interestingly, we can observe that ℓ is an affine function of $\boldsymbol{p}$, given by

$$\ell(\boldsymbol{p}, \boldsymbol{\theta}, \boldsymbol{x}) = \psi(\boldsymbol{x}) + \langle \boldsymbol{p}, \boldsymbol{\phi}(\boldsymbol{x}) \rangle \quad (5)$$

where

$$\psi(\boldsymbol{x}) = \sum_{i \in [n]} \ln \frac{1}{\theta_i(x_i)} \text{ and } \phi_{ij}(x_i, x_j) = \ln \left(\frac{\theta_i(x_i)\theta_j(x_j)}{\theta_{ij}(x_i, x_j)} \right)$$

It is important to keep in mind that the sign of the components in the vector $\boldsymbol{\phi}(\boldsymbol{x}) \in \mathbb{R}^{\binom{n}{2}}$ can be positive or negative. A negative weight $\phi_{ij}(x_i, x_j)$ can be interpreted as a positive contribution (or gain) in favor of using the edge (i, j) in the graphical structure. Contrarily, a positive weight $\phi_{ij}(x_i, x_j)$ provides a negative contribution to the candidate edge (i, j).

With these notions in hand, we are now in position to examine the online forest density estimation (OFDE) algorithm. As specified in Algorithm 1, OFDE takes as input a class of experts $\mathcal{M} \in \{\mathcal{F}_{m,n}, \mathcal{T}_{m,n}\}$, and an upper bound k on the number of candidate structures maintained by its mixture. During each trial t, the learner maintains a pair $(\boldsymbol{p}^t, \boldsymbol{\theta}^t) \in \boldsymbol{P}(\mathcal{M}) \times \boldsymbol{\Theta}_{m,n}$, where $\boldsymbol{p}^t$ is a convex combination of at most k structures. The model $M^t = (\boldsymbol{f}^t, \boldsymbol{\theta}^t)$ used to predict the outcome $\boldsymbol{x}^t$ is obtained by generating $\boldsymbol{f}^t$ at random according to $\boldsymbol{p}^t$ (Line 4). After observing $\boldsymbol{x}^t$ (Line 5), the learner updates its parameters and its structure according to Lines 6-7 and Lines 8-12, respectively.

The vector of parameters $\boldsymbol{\theta}^t$ is updated by applying the Jeffreys (1946) rule to the probability table of each node $i \in [n]$ and each candidate edge $(i, j) \in \binom{[n]}{2}$. Here, t_u (resp. t_v) is the number of u's (resp. v's) in the sequence $x_i^1, \cdots, x_i^t$, and t_{uv} is the number of occurrences of (u, v) in $(x_i, x_j)^1, \cdots, (x_i, x_j)^t$.

The mixture $\boldsymbol{p}^t$ is updated using the following operations: first, apply the FPL strategy to produce an intermediate structure $\boldsymbol{f}^{t+\frac{1}{2}}$ (Lines 9-10); next, combine this structure with $\boldsymbol{p}^t$ to yield a new intermediate mixture $\boldsymbol{p}^{t+\frac{1}{2}}$ (Line 11), and then use SWAP$_k$ to build a new mixture with at most k components (Line 12). The values of the hyperparameters α_t and β_t, used to generate mixtures and perturbations, will be derived from regret analysis. Note that the same algorithmic scheme is used to learn with Markov forests and Markov trees. The key difference lies in the behavior of the greedy matroid algorithm; as mentioned above, the greedy algorithm uses only non-positive weights in $\phi^t(\boldsymbol{x}^t)$ to find an optimal point in conv $\mathbf{F}_n$ for the linear objective $\boldsymbol{w}^t$, while it uses all weights in $\phi^t(\boldsymbol{x}^t)$ to produce an optimal point in conv $\mathbf{T}_n$ for $\boldsymbol{w}^t$.

Theorem 1. The per-round time complexity of the OFDE algorithm is in $O(n^2m^2 + n^2 \log n + kn^2)$.

Proof. Based on the Jeffreys rule, the parameters $\boldsymbol{\theta}^{t+1}$ are computed in $O(d)$ time, where $d = mn + m^2\binom{n}{2}$. Furthermore, $\boldsymbol{f}^{t+\frac{1}{2}}$ is obtained in $O(n^2 \log n)$ time by applying the greedy matroid algorithm, and by exploiting the fact that the objective $\boldsymbol{w}^t$ can be maintained in $O(n^2)$ time per trial using $\boldsymbol{w}^0 = \boldsymbol{0}$ and $\boldsymbol{w}^t = \boldsymbol{w}^{t-1} + \phi^t(\boldsymbol{x}^t)$. Since $\boldsymbol{p}^{t+\frac{1}{2}}$ includes at most $k+1$ components, the updated mixture $\boldsymbol{p}^{t+1}$ and the updated forest $\boldsymbol{f}^{t+1}$ are obtained using SWAP in $O(n^2)$ time and $O(kn^2)$ time, respectively. □

Note that the time complexity of the Chow-Liu algorithm for a training set of size T is in $O(Tm^2n^2 + n^2 \log n)$. So, if k is constant or logarithmic in n, then the overall complexity of OFDE at horizon T is comparable to that of the Chow-Liu algorithm.

Algorithm 1: Online Forest Density Estimation (OFDE)

Input:
a class of experts $\mathcal{M} \in \{\mathcal{F}_{m,n}, \mathcal{T}_{m,n}\}$, and mixture size k

Initialization step

1 $\theta_i^1(u) \leftarrow \frac{1}{m}$ for all $i \in [n], u \in [m]$

2 $\theta_{ij}^1(u,v) \leftarrow \frac{1}{m^2}$ for all $(i,j) \in \binom{[n]}{2}, u, v \in [m]$

3 $\boldsymbol{p}^1 \leftarrow \mathbf{0}$

Trials

foreach $t \leftarrow 1, \ldots$ **do**

4 Play $M^t \leftarrow (\boldsymbol{f}^t, \boldsymbol{\theta}^t)$ where $\boldsymbol{f}^t = \textsc{Swap}_1(\boldsymbol{p}^t)$

5 Receive $\boldsymbol{x}^t$

Parameter update

6 $\theta_i^{t+1}(u) \leftarrow \dfrac{t_u + \frac{1}{2}}{t + \frac{m}{2}}$ for all $i \in [n], u \in [m]$

7 $\theta_{ij}^{t+1}(u,v) \leftarrow \dfrac{t_{uv} + \frac{1}{2}}{t + \frac{m^2}{2}}$ for all $(i,j) \in \binom{[n]}{2}, u, v \in [m]$

Structure update

8 Choose α_t and β_t in $(0,1)$

9 Draw $\boldsymbol{r}^t$ in $\left[0, \frac{1}{\beta_t}\right]^{\binom{n}{2}}$ uniformly at random

10 $\boldsymbol{f}^{t+\frac{1}{2}} \leftarrow \text{argmin}_{\boldsymbol{p} \in \boldsymbol{P}}(\boldsymbol{w}^t)$ where $\boldsymbol{w}^t \leftarrow \boldsymbol{r}^t + \sum_{\tau=1}^t \phi^\tau(\boldsymbol{x}^\tau)$

11 $\boldsymbol{p}^{t+\frac{1}{2}} \leftarrow \alpha_t \boldsymbol{p}^t + (1 - \alpha_t)\boldsymbol{f}^{t+\frac{1}{2}}$

12 $\boldsymbol{p}^{t+1} \leftarrow \textsc{Swap}_k(\boldsymbol{p}^{t+\frac{1}{2}})$

5 REGRET ANALYSIS

Based on the decomposable form of the log-loss (5), the regret of the OFDE algorithm can be expressed as a telescopic sum of two separate components, namely, a "parametric" regret with fixed structure and varying parameters, and a "structural" regret, with fixed parameters and varying structure. Formally, let $(\boldsymbol{p}, \boldsymbol{\theta})^{1:T} = ((\boldsymbol{p}^1, \boldsymbol{\theta}^1), \cdots, (\boldsymbol{p}^T, \boldsymbol{\theta}^T))$ be the sequence generated by the algorithm during T rounds. Then,

$$R_{\boldsymbol{x}^{1:T}}[(\boldsymbol{p}, \boldsymbol{\theta})^{1:T}] = R_{\boldsymbol{x}^{1:T}}(\boldsymbol{\theta}^{1:T}) + R_{\boldsymbol{x}^{1:T}}(\boldsymbol{p}^{1:T})$$

where

$$R_{\boldsymbol{x}^{1:T}}(\boldsymbol{p}^{1:T}) = \sum_{t=1}^T \ell(\boldsymbol{p}^t, \boldsymbol{\theta}^t, \boldsymbol{x}^t) - \ell(\boldsymbol{p}^*, \boldsymbol{\theta}^t, \boldsymbol{x}^t), \quad (6)$$

$$R_{\boldsymbol{x}^{1:T}}(\boldsymbol{\theta}^{1:T}) = \sum_{t=1}^T \ell(\boldsymbol{p}^*, \boldsymbol{\theta}^t, \boldsymbol{x}^t) - \ell(\boldsymbol{p}^*, \boldsymbol{\theta}^*, \boldsymbol{x}^t) \quad (7)$$

and where $(\boldsymbol{p}^*, \boldsymbol{\theta}^*)$ is any minimizer in $\boldsymbol{P}(\mathcal{M}) \times \boldsymbol{\Theta}_{m,n}$ of the cumulative log-loss $\sum_{t=1}^T \ell(\boldsymbol{p}, \boldsymbol{\theta}, \boldsymbol{x}^t)$. The rest of this section is devoted to the analysis of each separate part (7) and (6), and the unification of our results.

5.1 PARAMETRIC REGRET

For the analysis of the parametric regret $R_{\boldsymbol{x}^{1:T}}(\boldsymbol{\theta}^{1:T})$, we consider the problem of online density estimation problem with the class of experts $(\{\boldsymbol{p}\}, \boldsymbol{\Theta}_{m,n})$, where $\boldsymbol{p}$ is an arbitrary point in $\boldsymbol{P}$. As mentioned above, $\boldsymbol{p}$ can be viewed as a convex combination $\boldsymbol{p} = \mathbb{E}[\boldsymbol{f}]$ of graphical structures $\boldsymbol{f} \in \mathcal{M}$. Using the additive decomposition (5) and the linearity of expectations, we have

$$\begin{aligned} R_{\boldsymbol{x}^{1:T}}(\boldsymbol{\theta}^{1:T}) &= \mathbb{E}\left[\sum_{t=1}^T \ell(\boldsymbol{f}, \boldsymbol{\theta}^t, \boldsymbol{x}^t) - \ell(\boldsymbol{f}, \boldsymbol{\theta}^*, \boldsymbol{x}^t)\right] \\ &= \mathbb{E}\left[\ln \prod_{t=1}^T \frac{\mathbb{P}_{\boldsymbol{f},\boldsymbol{\theta}^*}(\boldsymbol{x}^t)}{\mathbb{P}_{\boldsymbol{f},\boldsymbol{\theta}^t}(\boldsymbol{x}^t)}\right] \end{aligned} \quad (8)$$

In light of the closed-form expression (1), the logarithmic term inside the expectation in (8) can be reformulated as

$$\ln \prod_{t=1}^T \frac{\mathbb{P}_{\boldsymbol{f},\boldsymbol{\theta}^*}(\boldsymbol{x}^t)}{\mathbb{P}_{\boldsymbol{f},\boldsymbol{\theta}_t}(\boldsymbol{x}^t)} = \sum_{i=1}^n \ln \frac{\theta_i^*(x_i^{1:T})}{\theta_i^{1:T}(x_i^{1:T})} + \sum_{(i,j) \in F} \ln \frac{\theta_{ij}^*(x_{ij}^{1:T})}{\theta_{ij}^{1:T}(x_{ij}^{1:T})} + \sum_{(i,j) \in F} \ln \frac{\theta_i^{1:T}(x_i^{1:T})}{\theta_i^*(x_i^{1:T})} \frac{\theta_j^{1:T}(x_j^{1:T})}{\theta_j^*(x_j^{1:T})} \quad (9)$$

where

$$\theta_i^*(x_i^{1:t}) = \prod_{\tau=1}^t \theta_i^*(x_i^\tau), \qquad \theta_i^{1:t}(x_i^{1:t}) = \prod_{\tau=1}^t \theta_i^\tau(x_i^\tau)$$

$$\theta_{ij}^*(x_{ij}^{1:t}) = \prod_{\tau=1}^t \theta_{ij}^*(x_i^\tau, x_j^\tau), \quad \theta_{ij}^{1:t}(x_{ij}^{1:t}) = \prod_{\tau=1}^t \theta_{ij}^\tau(x_i^\tau, x_j^\tau)$$

We may observe that (9) is essentially a composition of local regrets defined over univariate density estimators $\theta_i^{1:T}(x_i^{1:T})$ and bivariate density estimators $\theta_{ij}^{1:T}(x_{ij}^{1:T})$. Notably, for each edge $(i,j) \in F$, the regret of the bivariate estimator $\theta_{ij}^{1:T}(x_{ij}^{1:T})$ is compensated by the relative gains of the univariate estimators $\theta_i^{1:T}(x_i^{1:T})$ and $\theta_j^{1:T}(x_j^{1:T})$. Such a decomposition motivates the use of well-known Bayesian mixtures with Dirichlet priors for specifying the estimators. We focus here on *symmetric* Dirichlet priors, given by

$$p_\mu(\boldsymbol{\lambda}) = \frac{\Gamma(m\mu)}{\Gamma(\mu)^m} \prod_{v=1}^m (\lambda(v))^{\mu-1}$$

where $\boldsymbol{\lambda}$ is a vector in the m-dimensional probability simplex, $\Gamma(z) = \int_0^\infty t^{z-1}e^{-t}dt$ is the gamma function, and $\mu \in [0,1]$ is a hyperparameter. The corresponding Bayesian mixture $\lambda(x^{1:t})$ for the sequence $x^{1:t} = (x^1, \cdots, x^t)$ is given by

$$\int \prod_{\tau=1}^t \mathbb{P}_{\boldsymbol{\lambda}}(x^\tau) p_\mu(\boldsymbol{\lambda}) d\boldsymbol{\lambda} = \frac{\Gamma(m\mu)}{\Gamma(\mu)^m} \frac{\prod_{v=1}^m \Gamma(t_v + \mu)}{\Gamma(t + m\mu)} \quad (10)$$

where t_v is the number of v's in $x^{1:t}$. Thus, by applying (10) with $\mu = 1/2$ to the estimators $\theta_i^t(x_i^{1:t})$ and $\theta_{ij}^{1:t}(x_{ij}^{1:t})$, we derive the update rules specified by Lines 6-7 of the OFDE algorithm.

Before deriving a bound for the parametric regret (7), we present two useful double inequalities for log-gamma functions, summarized in the next lemma.

Lemma 1. Let m be a positive integer. Then for any $t > 0$,

$$-\ln\sqrt{2} \leq \ln\Gamma\left(t+\frac{1}{2}\right) - t\ln t + t - \ln\sqrt{2\pi} \leq 0 \quad (11)$$

$$0 \leq \ln\Gamma\left(t+\frac{m}{2}\right) - \ln\Gamma\left(t+\frac{1}{2}\right) - \frac{m-1}{2}\ln t \leq o(1) \quad (12)$$

Proof. (11) is a reformulation of Lemma 1 in (Watanabe and Roos, 2015), and the right-hand inequality of (12) follows from the classical asymptotic relation (see e.g. Qi and Luo (2013)):

$$\lim_{t\to\infty}\left[t^{b-a}\frac{\Gamma(t+a)}{\Gamma(t+b)}\right] = 1$$

using $a = {}^{m}/_{2}$ and $b = {}^{1}/_{2}$. For the left-hand inequality of (12), we can observe that

$$\ln\frac{\Gamma\left(t+\frac{m}{2}\right)}{\Gamma\left(t+\frac{1}{2}\right)} = \ln\frac{\Gamma\left(z+\frac{m-1}{2}\right)}{\Gamma\left(z+k\right)} + \ln\frac{\Gamma\left(z+k\right)}{\Gamma\left(z\right)} \quad (13)$$

where $z = t + {}^{1}/_{2}$ and $k = \lfloor\frac{m-1}{2}\rfloor$. Based on the identity $\ln\Gamma(z+k) = \ln\Gamma(z) + \sum_{i=0}^{k-1}\ln(z+i)$, the second term in the right-hand side of (13) is lower bounded by $k\ln z$. So, if m is odd, then $k = \frac{m-1}{2}$, and hence, (13) is lower bounded by $\frac{m-1}{2}\ln t$, as desired. Now, if m is even, then using $z' = t + k$, we can observe that the first term in the right-hand side of (13) can be rewritten as the log-ratio of $\Gamma(z'+1)$ to $\Gamma(z'+\frac{1}{2})$. Thus, by Wendel's inequality (1948), we have

$$\frac{1}{2}\ln z' \leq \ln\frac{\Gamma(z'+1)}{\Gamma(z'+\frac{1}{2})} \leq \frac{1}{2}\ln\left(z'+\frac{1}{2}\right)$$

By combining the lower bounds $k\ln z$ and $\frac{1}{2}\ln z'$, it follows that (13) is lower bounded by $(k+\frac{1}{2})\ln t = \frac{m-1}{2}\ln t$, which again yields the desired result. □

With these inequalities in hand, we can derive "sandwiching" bounds for the regret of the Jeffreys mixture. Specifically, using the Bayes mixture (10) with $\mu = {}^{1}/_{2}$, the regret expression $\ln\theta^*(x^{1:T}) - \ln\theta^{1:T}(x^{1:T})$ is equal to

$$\ln\left[\prod_{u=1}^{m}\left(\frac{t_u}{T}\right)^{t_u}\right] + \ln\frac{\Gamma\left(T+\frac{m}{2}\right)}{\prod_{u=1}^{m}\Gamma\left(t_u+\frac{1}{2}\right)} + C_m \quad (14)$$

where $C_m = m\ln\Gamma(\frac{1}{2}) - \ln\Gamma(\frac{m}{2})$. By coupling the double inequalities (11) and (12), we can deduce that

$$-\ln\sqrt{2} \leq \ln\Gamma\left(T+\frac{m}{2}\right) + T - T\ln T - \frac{m-1}{2}\ln T - \ln\sqrt{2\pi} \leq o(1)$$

Similarly, using the double inequality (11) and summing over m values, we can infer that

$$-m\ln\sqrt{2} \leq \ln\prod_{u=1}^{m}\Gamma\left(t_u+\frac{1}{2}\right) - \sum_{u=1}^{m}t_u\ln t_u + T - m\ln\sqrt{2\pi} \leq 0$$

Now, using the fact that the first term in (14) is equal to $\sum_{u=1}^{m}t_u\ln t_u - T\ln T$, we can combine the above two double inequalities to derive the sandwiching bounds:

$$-\ln\sqrt{2} \leq \ln\frac{\theta^*(x^{1:T})}{\theta^{1:T}(x^{1:T})} - \frac{m-1}{2}\ln\frac{T}{2\pi} - C_m \leq m\ln\sqrt{2} + o(1) \quad (15)$$

Unsurprisingly, the right-hand inequality of (15) coincides with the regret bound of the Jeffreys mixture established by Xie and Barron (2000). As shown below, the left-hand inequality of (15) will also prove useful for bounding the regret expression (9).

Lemma 2. The parametric regret $R_{\boldsymbol{x}^{1:T}}(\boldsymbol{\theta}^{1:T})$ of the OFDE algorithm is upper bounded by

$$\frac{n(m-1)+(n-1)(m-1)^2}{2}\ln\frac{T}{2\pi} + C_{m,n} + o(m^2 n)$$

where $C_{m,n} = nC_m + (n-1)(C_{m^2} - 2C_m)$.

Proof. As specified by Equality (8), any upper bound on the minimax regret of (9) is an upper bound on $R_{\boldsymbol{x}^{1:T}}(\boldsymbol{\theta}^{1:T})$. Based on this observation, consider the first term of (9), given by $\sum_{i=1}^{n}\ln[\theta_i^*(x_i^{1:T})/\theta_i^{1:T}(x_i^{1:T})]$. Using the right-hand inequality of (15) and summing over n nodes, this term is upper bounded by

$$\frac{n(m-1)}{2}\ln\frac{T}{2\pi} + nC_m + mn\ln\sqrt{2} + o(n)$$

Clearly, a similar strategy can be applied to the second term $\sum_{(i,j)\in F}\ln[\theta_{ij}^*(x_{ij}^{1:T})/\theta_{ij}^{1:T}(x_{ij}^{1:T})]$ of (9). Since $|F| \leq n-1$, this term is upper bounded by

$$\frac{(n-1)(m^2-1)}{2}\ln\frac{T}{2\pi} + (n-1)C_{m^2} + (n-1)m^2\ln\sqrt{2} + o(n)$$

Finally, the third term of (9) can be reformulated as a sum over each $(i,j) \in F$ of two components: $\ln[\theta_i^{1:T}(x_i^{1:T})/\theta_i^*(x_i^{1:T})]$ and $\ln[\theta_j^{1:T}(x_j^{1:T})/\theta_j^*(x_j^{1:T})]$. By applying the left-hand side inequality of (15) to each component, and summing over at most $n-1$ edges, this term is upper bounded by

$$-(n-1)(m-1)\ln\frac{T}{2\pi} - 2(n-1)C_m + 2(n-1)\ln\sqrt{2}$$

By combining the above three bounds, rearranging terms, and taking into account the fact that $[(n-1)(m^2+2)+mn]\ln\sqrt{2}$ is in $o(m^2 n)$ (for $m \geq 2$), we get the desired result. □

In the binomial case ($m = 2$), it is easy to check that $C_{2,n} = n \ln \pi$. By reporting this result into Lemma 2, we may derive for binary Markov forests a parametric regret bound of the form:

$$R_{\boldsymbol{x}^{1:T}}(\boldsymbol{\theta}^{1:T}) \leq \left(n - \frac{1}{2}\right) \ln T + o(n) \tag{16}$$

5.2 STRUCTURAL REGRET

Before deriving a bound for the structural part of the regret, we first examine some analytic properties of the loss function (5), specified as an affine function of the predicted structure.

Lemma 3. Given a class of models $\mathcal{M} \in \{\mathcal{F}_{m,n}, \mathcal{T}_{m,n}\}$, let $\boldsymbol{\theta}^{1:T}$ be the sequence of parameters in $\boldsymbol{\Theta}_{m,n}$ generated by the OFDE algorithm on the sequence of outcomes $\boldsymbol{x}^{1:T}$. Then, for any $t \in [T]$, any $\boldsymbol{p}, \boldsymbol{q} \in \boldsymbol{P}(\mathcal{M})$, and any $\boldsymbol{x} \in \mathcal{X}$,

$$\left\|\boldsymbol{\phi}^t(\boldsymbol{x})\right\|_\infty \leq \ln\left(\frac{T}{2} + \frac{m^2}{4}\right)$$
$$\|\boldsymbol{p} - \boldsymbol{q}\|_1 \leq 2(n-1)$$

Proof. For the first property, consider two values $u, v \in [m]$. We may observe that $\phi_{ij}^1(u,v) = 0 < \ln(T/2 + m^2/4)$, for $m \geq 2$. Furthermore, using the Jeffreys update rule, we have

$$\begin{aligned}\phi_{ij}^{t+1}(u,v) &= \ln\frac{(t_u + 1/2)(t_v + 1/2)}{(t + m/2)^2} + \ln\frac{t + m^2/2}{t_{uv} + 1/2}\\ &\leq \ln\frac{1}{4} + \ln\frac{t + m^2/2}{t_{uv} + 1/2} \leq \ln\left(\frac{T}{2} + \frac{m^2}{4}\right)\end{aligned}$$

where the first inequality follows from the fact that the maximizer of $(t_u + 1/2)(t_v + 1/2)$ subject to the constraint $t_u + t_v \leq t$ is given by $t_u = t_v = \frac{t}{2}$. Concerning the second property, recall that the dimension of $\boldsymbol{P}(\mathcal{M})$ is $n-1$, which implies that $\|\boldsymbol{p}\|_1 \leq n-1$ for all $\boldsymbol{p} \in \boldsymbol{P}(\mathcal{M})$. This, together with the fact that $\|\boldsymbol{p} - \boldsymbol{q}\|_1 \leq \|\boldsymbol{p}\|_1 + \|\boldsymbol{q}\|_1$, implies the result. □

Based on these properties, we derive a regret bound for the structural part of the OFDE algorithm by analyzing the update rules in Lines 10-12. Specifically, the expression (6) is decomposed into the telescopic sum:

$$\begin{aligned}R_{\boldsymbol{x}^{1:T}}(\boldsymbol{p}^{1:T}) \leq& \sum_{t=1}^{T} \langle \boldsymbol{p}^t, \boldsymbol{\ell}^t\rangle - \langle \boldsymbol{p}^{t+\frac{1}{2}}, \boldsymbol{\ell}^t\rangle &(17)\\ &+ \sum_{t=1}^{T} \langle \boldsymbol{p}^{t+\frac{1}{2}}, \boldsymbol{\ell}^t\rangle - \langle \boldsymbol{f}^{t+\frac{1}{2}}, \boldsymbol{\ell}^t\rangle &(18)\\ &+ \sum_{t=1}^{T} \langle \boldsymbol{f}^{t+\frac{1}{2}}, \boldsymbol{\ell}^t\rangle - \langle \boldsymbol{p}^*, \boldsymbol{\ell}^t\rangle &(19)\end{aligned}$$

where $\boldsymbol{\ell}^t$ is used here as a shorthand of $\boldsymbol{\phi}^t(\boldsymbol{x}^t)$. Recall that each point $\boldsymbol{p}^t$ in the sequence $\boldsymbol{p}^{1:T}$ includes at most k forests. So, the difference (17) captures the regret of the OFDE algorithm with respect to its *unbounded* version, where the swap rounding step at Line 12 is omitted.

Lemma 4. The OFDE algorithm has no regret with respect to its unbounded version: $\sum_{t=1}^{T} \langle \boldsymbol{p}^t, \boldsymbol{\ell}^t\rangle - \langle \boldsymbol{p}^{t+\frac{1}{2}}, \boldsymbol{\ell}^t\rangle = 0$.

Proof. Let $\tilde{\boldsymbol{p}}^{1:T}$ be the sequence of points given by the unbounded version of OFDE, that is, $\tilde{\boldsymbol{p}}^1 = \boldsymbol{p}^1$ and $\tilde{\boldsymbol{p}}^{t+1} = \alpha_t \tilde{\boldsymbol{p}}^t + (1-\alpha_t)\boldsymbol{f}^{t+\frac{1}{2}}$ for each $t \in [T]$. We prove that $\mathbb{E}[\boldsymbol{p}^t] = \boldsymbol{p}^{t+\frac{1}{2}}$ by induction on $t \in [T]$. The case $t = 1$ follows from $\boldsymbol{p}^1 = \tilde{\boldsymbol{p}}^1$. Suppose by induction hypothesis that $\mathbb{E}[\boldsymbol{p}^t] = \tilde{\boldsymbol{p}}^t$. Using the SWAP algorithm, $\mathbb{E}[\boldsymbol{p}^{t+1}] = \alpha_t \boldsymbol{p}^t + (1-\alpha_t)\boldsymbol{f}^{t+\frac{1}{2}}$. Furthermore, by induction hypothesis, we also know that $\mathbb{E}[\alpha_t \boldsymbol{p}^t + (1-\alpha_t)\boldsymbol{f}^{t+\frac{1}{2}}] = \alpha_t \mathbb{E}[\boldsymbol{p}^t] + (1-\alpha_t)\boldsymbol{f}^{t+\frac{1}{2}} = \tilde{\boldsymbol{p}}^{t+1}$. Since $\mathbb{E}[\mathbb{E}[\boldsymbol{p}^{t+1}]] = \mathbb{E}[\boldsymbol{p}^{t+1}]$, it follows that $\mathbb{E}[\boldsymbol{p}^{t+1}] = \tilde{\boldsymbol{p}}^{t+1}$, as desired. Based on this invariant, the result follows from the linearity of expectations: $\sum_{t=1}^{T} \langle \mathbb{E}[\boldsymbol{p}^t], \boldsymbol{\ell}^t\rangle - \langle \boldsymbol{p}^{t+\frac{1}{2}}, \boldsymbol{\ell}^t\rangle = \sum_{t=1}^{T} \mathbb{E}\langle \boldsymbol{p}^{t+\frac{1}{2}} - \boldsymbol{p}^{t+\frac{1}{2}}, \boldsymbol{\ell}^t\rangle = 0$. □

With this result in hand, the structural regret of the OFDE algorithm is reduced to the sum of (18) and (19). Using appropriate choices for the hyperparameters α_t and β_t we can derive sublinear regret bounds in both the horizon-dependent setting (where T is known) and the horizon-independent setting.

Lemma 5. Let $\gamma = \ln(T/2 + m^2/4)$. The structural regret $R_{\boldsymbol{x}^{1:T}}(\boldsymbol{p}^{1:T})$ of the OFDE algorithm is bounded by

- $n^2\gamma\sqrt{2T}$ in the horizon-dependent case, using $0 < \alpha_t \leq \frac{1}{2\sqrt{2t}}$ and $\beta_t = \frac{1}{\gamma n}\sqrt{2/t}$;
- $n^2(\gamma+1)^2\sqrt{2T}$ in the horizon-independent case, using $0 < \alpha_t \leq \frac{1}{4\sqrt{2t}}$ and $\beta_t = \frac{1}{n}\sqrt{2/t}$.

Proof. Consider the regret expression (18), and let $\alpha_t = \alpha'/\sqrt{t}$. Using the specification of $\boldsymbol{p}^{t+\frac{1}{2}}$ given at Line 11, we get

$$\begin{aligned}\sum_{t=1}^{T} \langle \boldsymbol{p}^{t+\frac{1}{2}} - \boldsymbol{f}^{t+\frac{1}{2}}, \boldsymbol{\ell}^t\rangle &= \sum_{t=1}^{T} \alpha_t \langle \boldsymbol{p}^t - \boldsymbol{f}^{t+\frac{1}{2}}, \boldsymbol{\ell}^t\rangle\\ &\leq 2(n-1)\gamma \sum_{t=1}^{T} \alpha_t \leq 4(n-1)\gamma\alpha'\sqrt{T}\end{aligned}$$

where the first inequality follows from Hölder's inequality $\langle \boldsymbol{p}^t - \boldsymbol{f}^{t+\frac{1}{2}}, \boldsymbol{\ell}^t\rangle \leq \|\boldsymbol{p}^t - \boldsymbol{f}^{t+\frac{1}{2}}\|_1 \|\boldsymbol{\ell}^t\|_\infty$, and the application of Lemma 3. The last inequality follows from $\sum_{t=1}^{T} 1/\sqrt{t} \leq 2\sqrt{T}$. Now, observe that (19) is the regret of the FPL strategy. Let $\beta_t = \beta'/\sqrt{t}$. By applying Theorem 3.3 in (Kalai and Vempala, 2005), we can derive that

$$\begin{aligned}\sum_{t=1}^{T} \langle \boldsymbol{f}^{t+\frac{1}{2}} - \boldsymbol{p}^*, \boldsymbol{\ell}^t\rangle &\leq 2\beta' RA\sqrt{T} + \tfrac{D}{\beta'}\sqrt{T}\\ &\leq (n-1)n^2\gamma^2\beta'\sqrt{T} + \tfrac{2(n-1)}{\beta'}\sqrt{T}\end{aligned}$$

using the facts that $R = \max_{t\in[T]} \langle \boldsymbol{f}^{t+\frac{1}{2}}, \boldsymbol{\ell}^t\rangle \leq 2(n-1)\gamma$ from Hölder inequality, $A = \max_{t\in[T]} \|\boldsymbol{\ell}^t\|_1 \leq \gamma n^2/2$, and

$D = \max_{t\in[T]} \|f^{t+\frac{1}{2}} - f^{t-\frac{1}{2}}\|_1 \leq 2(n-1)$. Combining the derived bounds for (18) and (19), and rearranging, yields

$$R_{x^{1:T}}(p^{1:T}) \leq (n-1)\sqrt{T}\left(4\gamma\alpha' + n^2\gamma^2\beta' + \frac{2}{\beta'}\right)$$

In the horizon-dependent case, we can take $\beta' = \sqrt{2}/\gamma n$ to derive that $R_{x^{1:T}}(p^{1:T}) \leq \gamma(n-1)(4\alpha' + n\sqrt{2})\sqrt{T}$, which is bounded by $n^2\gamma\sqrt{2T}$ for $\alpha' \leq 1/2\sqrt{2}$. In the horizon-independent case, γ is unknown. So, using $\beta' = \sqrt{2}/n$, we get that $R_{x^{1:T}}(p^{1:T}) \leq (n-1)[4\gamma\alpha' + (n/\sqrt{2})(\gamma^2+1)]\sqrt{T}$, which is bounded by $n^2(\gamma+1)^2\sqrt{2T}$ for $\alpha' \leq 1/4\sqrt{2}$. □

5.3 MAIN RESULTS

We have now all ingredients in hand to prove the Hannan-consistency of our online learning algorithm. The next theorem is obtained by coupling Lemma 2 with Lemma 5. The corollary is simply derived by replacing the bound in Lemma 2 with (16).

Theorem 2. For the classes of Markov forests $\mathcal{F}_{m,n}$ and Markov trees $\mathcal{T}_{m,n}$, there exists an online density estimation algorithm achieving a minimax regret in $O(m^2 n \ln T + n^2 \ln T\sqrt{T})$ in the horizon-dependent case, and $O(m^2 n \ln T + n^2 (\ln T)^2 \sqrt{T})$ in the horizon-independent case.

Corollary 1. For the classes of binary Markov forests $\mathcal{F}_{2,n}$ and Markov trees $\mathcal{T}_{2,n}$, there exists an online density estimation algorithm that attains (in the horizon-dependent case) a minimax regret of $n^2 \ln(\frac{T}{2}+1)\sqrt{2T} + (n - \frac{1}{2})\ln T + o(n)$.

To conclude the theoretical part of this study, recall that the competitor used in both parts (6) and (7) of the regret analysis is an expert in $(\boldsymbol{P}(\mathcal{M}), \Theta_{m,n})$. As mentioned above, such experts are tree-structured mixtures sharing the same parameters, which predict according to the probability distribution (3). As stated in Lemma 2, the parametric regret $R_{x^{1:T}}(\theta^{1:T})$ of the OFDE algorithm with respect to these experts is in $O(m^2 n \ln T)$. Since the regret bounds in Lemma 5 also hold for these competitors, it follows that OFDE is Hannan-consistent with respect to tree-structured mixtures.

6 EXPERIMENTS

In order to empirically evaluate our algorithm, we performed simulations on 4 publicly available datasets[1], listed in Table 1. Though all these datasets are binary-valued, they differ in the number of variables and the number of instances.

Our experimental objective was to compare the OFDE algorithm with respect to batch learning algorithms which have the benefit of hindsight for the train set. To this end, we used the Chow-Liu (CL) algorithm (Chow and Liu, 1968) that learns a Markov tree, and the Chow-Liu with Thresholding (CLT) algorithm (Tan et al., 2011), that learns a Markov forest by pruning the

[1] alchemy.cs.washington.edu/papers/davis10a/

Dataset	Train set	Tune set	Test set	Vars (n)
Abalone	3,134	417	626	31
Covertype	30,000	4,000	6,000	84
KDDCup 2000	180,092	19,907	34,955	64
MSNBC	291,326	38,843	58,265	17

Table 1: Dataset Characteristics.

Chow-Liu tree. The CL and OFDE algorithms were trained without using the tune set. As CLT relies on a user-supplied threshold parameter $\epsilon \in (0,1)$, we performed experiments using several values $\{1/4, 1/2, 3/4\}$ for this parameter and kept in our results the best choice of ϵ measured on the tune set. In our implementation of CLT, we used a slight refinement of the original pruning rule: any edge (i,j) for which the empirical mutual information is lower than $n^{-\epsilon}$ is removed from the tree. Our OFDE algorithm was trained with both reference classes $\mathcal{F}_{2,n}$ and $\mathcal{T}_{2,n}$. Here, we denote by OFDE$_F$ (resp. OFDE$_T$) the instantiation of OFDE with Markov forests (resp. Markov trees). Both instances of OFDE were trained under the horizon-independent setting, using $k = \ln n$, $\alpha_t = \frac{1}{4\sqrt{2t}}$, and $\beta_t = \frac{1}{n}\sqrt{2/t}$.

The batch algorithms CL and CLT were trained on the whole train set, and their generalization performance was measured using the average log-loss evaluated on the test set. For the online learners OFDE$_F$ and OFDE$_T$, the instances were revealed only one at a time and, at the end of each iteration, the performance was measured by evaluating the average log-loss on the test set. The sequence of observations was generated by simply listing the instances of the train set.

The results, averaged over 10 experiments per dataset, are reported in Figure 2. Unsurprisingly, the performance of OFDE$_T$ is generally better than OFDE$_F$, since the batch tree learner CL outperforms its forest variant CLT. Yet, it is apparent that OFDE$_T$ and OFDE$_F$ respectively converge to the estimations of CL and CLT. The convergence rates are particularly remarkable for the datasets Covertype, KDDCup 2000, and MSNBC, where a logarithmic scale is used for the number of iterations.

Concerning runtimes, the three algorithms were implemented in C++ and tested on a Quad-core Intel XEON X5550. For all datasets, the per-round runtime of OFDE (using forests or trees) is less than 3 ms. This indicates that OFDE can be used as practical alternative to CL(T) for handling streaming applications.

7 DISCUSSION

As a fundamental result in universal prediction, it is known that the optimal solution achieving minimax regret for any class $\mathcal{M}$ of discrete probabilistic models is obtained by the *normalized maximum likelihood* strategy (Shtarkov, 1987). Unfortunately, for this optimal strategy, the time horizon T must be known in advance, and the computation of the log-loss at each round $t \in [T]$ requires the evaluation of exponentially many marginalization terms. Thus, one of the key challenges in online density estimation is to devise horizon-independent strategies that pro-

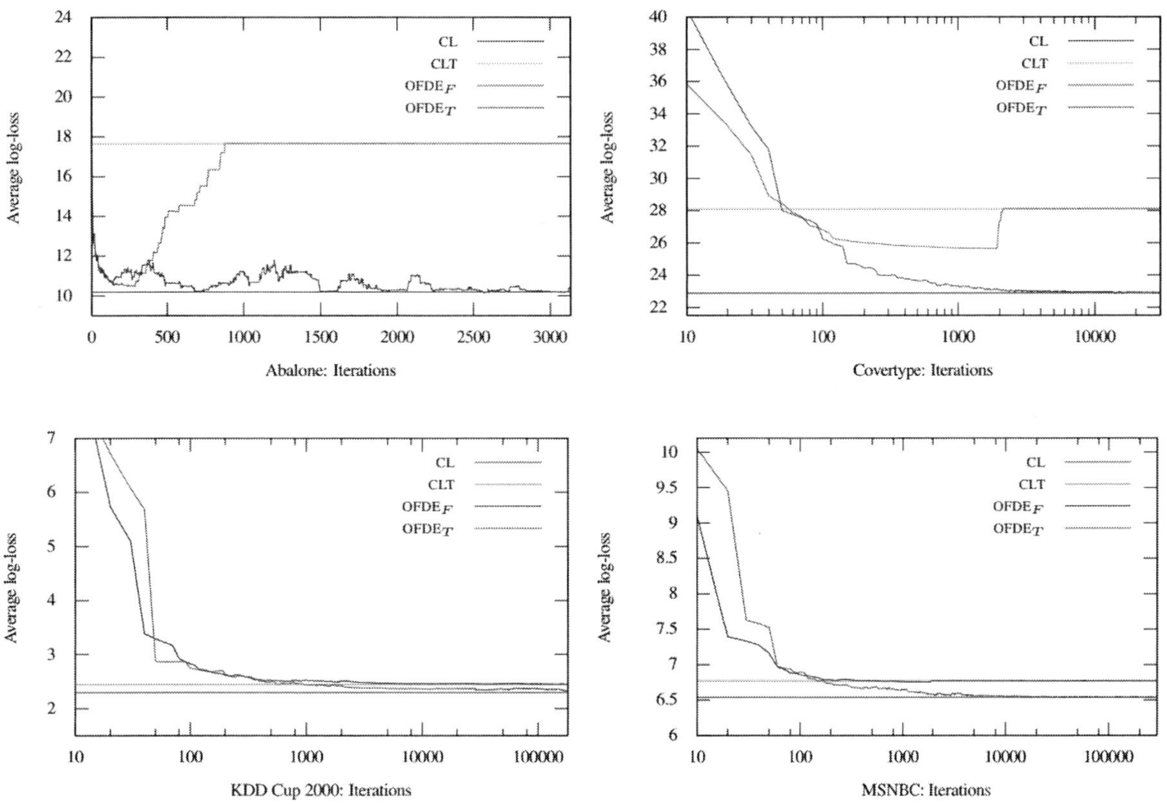

Figure 2: Comparison of $\text{OFDE}_\mathcal{T}$ and $\text{OFDE}_\mathcal{F}$ with CL and CLT on the four datasets.

vide a good compromise between minimax optimality and computational complexity. Several easily implementable nearly optimal strategies have been proposed for unidimensional probabilistic models, including binomial and multinomial families (Freund, 1996; Xie and Barron, 2000; Watanabe and Roos, 2015), and, more generally, univariate exponential families (Takimoto and Warmuth, 2000; Azoury and Warmuth, 2001; Kotłowski and Grünwald, 2011). Much less is known, however, about multidimensional families, especially the classes of graphical models characterized by multiple interdependencies between variables. A notable exception is the work by Bauer et al. (1997) for sequentially predicting the parameters of a Bayesian network. Yet, the target network structure is known in advance. To our knowledge, the present paper is one of the first studies that investigates both structural and parametric aspects of graphical models in online density estimation.

By considering classes of experts defined over varying structures, our study has intimate connections with *online combinatorial optimization*, a topic of online learning where the reference classes are combinatorial spaces. Several Hannan-consistent algorithms have been proposed in this setting, including the *Follow the Perturbed Leader* (FPL) strategy (Hannan, 1957; Kalai and Vempala, 2005), and the *Online Mirror Descent* (OMD) strategy (Koolen et al., 2010; Audibert et al., 2011; Rajkumar and Agarwal, 2014). Though OMD is known to achieve better regret bounds than FPL, it relies on a projection step performed at each iteration, in order to maintain the current estimate in the convex hull of the combinatorial space. The computational complexity of this projection step is typically much worse than the cost of linear optimization, especially when the combinatorial space is a matroid. The FPL strategy, advocated in this study, provides a reasonable compromise between optimality and computational complexity. Yet, alternative strategies can be devised in our setting such as, for example, online Franck-Wolfe optimization methods (Hazan and Kale, 2012).

A natural perspective of research that emerges from our study is to devise *lower bounds* for the minimax regret of forest density estimators. In a related setting, Kveton et al. (2014) have recently shown that such lower bounds are essentially logarithmic in T for the reference class of partition matroids. We conjecture that similar bounds holds for graphical matroids, and more generally for the classes $\mathcal{F}_{m,n}$ and $\mathcal{T}_{m,n}$. Finally, our work is also related to mixtures of trees (Meila and Jordan, 2000; Kumar and Koller, 2009). To this point, we have shown that OFDE is Hannan-consistent with mixtures of forests (or trees) sharing the *same* parameters. An interesting open question is to determine whether *arbitrary* mixtures of trees are learnable in the online density estimation setting.

References

J-Y. Audibert, S. Bubeck, and G. Lugosi. Minimax policies for combinatorial prediction games. In *Proc. of COLT*, pages 107–132, 2011.

K. Azoury and M. Warmuth. Relative loss bounds for online-learning density estimation with the exponential family of distributions. *Machine Learning*, 43:211–246, 2001.

E. Bauer, D. Koller, and Y. Singer. Update rules for parameter estimation in Bayesian networks. In *Proc. of UAI*, pages 3–13, 1997.

N. Cesa-Bianchi and G. Lugosi. *Prediction, Learning, and Games*. Cambridge University Press, 2006.

C. Chekuri, J. Vondrák, and R. Zenklusen. Dependent randomized rounding via exchange properties of combinatorial structures. In *Proc. of FOCS*, pages 575–584, 2010.

D. M. Chickering. Learning Bayesian networks is NP-complete. In *Proc. of AISTATS*, pages 121–130, 1995.

C. K. Chow and C. N. Liu. Approximating discrete probability distributions with dependence trees. *IEEE Transactions on Information Theory*, 14(3):462–467, 1968.

S. Dasgupta. Learning polytrees. In *Proc. of UAI*, pages 134–141, 1999.

J. Edmonds. Submodular functions, matroids, and certain polyhedra. In *Proc. Calgary International Conference on Combinatorial Structures and their Applications*, pages 69–87, 1970.

Y. Freund. Predicting a binary sequence almost as well as the optimal biased coin. In *Proc. of COLT*, pages 89–98, 1996.

P. Grünwald. *The Minimum Description Length Principle*. MIT Press, 2007.

J. Hannan. Approximation to Bayes risk in repeated plays. In *Contributions to the Theory of Games*, volume 3, pages 97–139. Princeton University Press, 1957.

E. Hazan and S. Kale. Projection-free online learning. In *Proc. of ICML*, 2012.

H. Jeffreys. An invariant form for the prior probability in estimation problems. In *Proc. of Royal Society London*, number 186 in A, pages 453–461, 1946.

A. Kalai and S. Vempala. Efficient algorithms for online decision problems. *Journal of Computer and System Sciences*, 71(3):291–307, 2005.

D. Koller and N. Friedman. *Probabilistic Graphical Models*. MIT Press, 2009.

W. Koolen, M. Warmuth, and J. Kivinen. Hedging structured concepts. In *Proc. of COLT*, pages 93–105, 2010.

W. Kotłowski and P. Grünwald. Maximum likelihood vs. sequential normalized maximum likelihood in on-line density estimation. In *Proc. of COLT*, pages 457–476, 2011.

M. P. Kumar and D. Koller. Learning a small mixture of trees. In *Proc. of NIPS*, pages 1051–1059, 2009.

B. Kveton, Z. Wen, A. Ashkan, H. Eydgahi, and B. Eriksson. Matroid bandits: Fast combinatorial optimization with learning. In *Proc. of UAI*, pages 420–429, 2014.

S. Lauritzen. *Graphical Models*. Clarendon Press, 1996.

H. Liu, M. Xu, H. Gu, A. Gupta, J. Lafferty, and L. Wasserman. Forest density estimation. *Journal of Machine Learning Research*, 12:907–951, 2011.

M. Meila and M. I. Jordan. Learning with mixtures of trees. *Journal of Machine Learning Research*, 1:1–48, 2000.

N. Merhav and M. Feder. Universal prediction. *IEEE Transactions on Information Theory*, 48:1947–1958, 1998.

J. Pearl. *Probabilistic Reasoning in Intelligent Systems: Networks of Plausible Inference*. Morgan Kaufmann, 1988.

F. Qi and Q-M. Luo. Bounds for the ratio of two Gamma functions: from Wendel's asymptotic relation to Elezović-Giordano-Pečarić's theorem. *Journal of Inequalities and Applications*, 2013(1):1–20, 2013.

A. Rajkumar and S. Agarwal. Online decision-making in general combinatorial spaces. In *Proc. of NIPS*, pages 3482–3490, 2014.

J. Rissanen. *Optimal Estimation of Parameters*. Cambridge, 2012.

A. Shrijver. *Combinatorial Optimization: Polyhedra and Efficiency*, volume B. Springer, 2003.

Y. Shtarkov. Universal sequential coding of single messages. *Problems of Information Transmission*, 23(3):175–186, 1987.

N. Srebro. Maximum likelihood bounded tree-width Markov networks. *Artificial Intelligence*, 143(1):123–138, 2003.

E. Takimoto and M. Warmuth. The last-step minimax algorithm. In *Proc. of ALT*, pages 279–290, 2000.

V. Tan, A. Anandkumar, and A. Willsky. Learning high-dimensional Markov forest distributions: Analysis of error rates. *Journal of Machine Learning Research*, 12: 1617–1653, 2011.

M. Wainwright and M. Jordan. Graphical models, exponential families, and variational inference. *Foundations and Trends in Machine Learning*, 1(1-2):1–305, 2008.

K. Watanabe and T. Roos. Achievability of asymptotic minimax regret by horizon-dependent and horizon-independent strategies. *Journal of Machine Learning Research*, 16:1–48, 2015.

J. Wendel. Note on the Gamma function. *The American Mathematical Monthly*, 55(9):563–564, 1948.

Q. Xie and A. Barron. Asymptotic minimax regret for data compression, gambling, and prediction. *IEEE Transactions on Information Theory*, 46(2):431–445, 2000.

Towards a Theoretical Understanding of Negative Transfer in Collective Matrix Factorization

Chao Lan
EECS Department
University of Kansas
Lawrence, KS 66045
clan@ittc.ku.edu

Jianxin Wang
School of Information Science and Engineering
Central South University
Changsha, China
jxwang@mail.csu.edu.cn

Jun Huan
EECS Department
University of Kansas
Lawrence, KS 66045
jhuan@ittc.ku.edu

Abstract

Collective matrix factorization (CMF) is a popular technique to improve the overall factorization quality of multiple matrices presuming they share the same latent factor. However, it suffers from performance degeneration when this assumption fails, an effect called *negative transfer (n.t.)*. Although the effect is widely admitted, its theoretical nature remains a mystery to date.

This paper presents a first theoretical understanding of $n.t.$ in theory. Under the statistical mini-max framework, we derive lower bounds for the CMF estimator and gain two insights. First, the $n.t.$ effect can be explained as the rise of a bias term in the standard lower bound, which depends only on the structure of factor space but neither the estimator nor samples. Second, the $n.t.$ effect can be explained as the rise of an d_{th}-root function on the learning rate, where d is the dimension of a Grassmannian containing the subspaces spanned by latent factors. These discoveries are also supported in simulation, and suggest $n.t.$ may be more effectively addressed via model construction other than model selection.

1 INTRODUCTION

Collective matrix factorization (CMF) is a popular technique to factorize multiple matrices in hope of improving their overall factorization quality (e.g. [7, 23, 17, 11, 16, 2, 12, 3, 21, 26]). The key assumption of CMF is that all matrices share the same low-rank factor, under which its estimator proves to be consistent [5]. However, when this assumption fails, CMF is known to suffer from performance degeneration – an effect called *negative transfer*. Several algorithmic solutions have been proposed, which alternatively assume different matrix factors are drawn from the same distribution [24, 1] or partially shared [10].

Although negative transfer has been long accused for causing the performance degeneration, the theoretical understanding on its nature appears surprisingly scarce, i.e. no study was done to justify its existence or how it may hurt CMF. *What can we say about negative transfer in theory?* This is the question we aim to address in the paper.

Our investigation is performed under the mini-max framework in statistical decision theory. We first cast CMF into this framework and design a collective hypothesis testing problem that captures the negative transfer effect. By reducing the CMF estimation problem to this testing problem, we manage to derive a lower bound of the CMF estimator, through which a new bias term is discovered that worsens the standard bound. In particular, the bias only depends on the structure of the factor space, but neither the choice of estimator nor training samples. This suggests negative transfer is an intrinsic difficulty of learning, which may only be resolved at the model construction phase but neither model selection nor data collection. This is also supported from another observation that negative transfer down-weights the contribution of estimation accuracy in the lower bound.

For better interpretability, we further refine the lower bound by capturing more problem characteristics. In particular, we derive a learning rate of $\Omega(1/|\omega|^{\frac{1}{d}})$, where $\vec{\omega}$ is the index set of all matrix observations and d is the dimension of a Grassmannian containing the subspaces spanned by latent factors. Pessimistically, this rate is d_{th}-root slower than the standard rate $\Omega(1/|\omega|)$ where negative transfer does not exist. This discovery is also supported in our simulation.

The rest of this paper is organized as follows: the notations are introduced in section two; our primary lower bound is presented in section three, and the refined bound is presented in section four; proofs and remarks are given in section five, followed by simulation in section six and conclusions in section seven.

2 PRELIMINARIES

In this section we introduce the major notations, concepts and assumptions used in analysis. For the ease of presentation, we focus on two matrix factorization, but all discussions are readily generalizable.

Matrix Notations. For a matrix M, let M_{ij} be its entry at row i and column j, let $[M]$ be its column space, $||M||$ be its Frobenius norm [1] and M^T be its transpose. Given two matrices M, M' of the same column size, let $\vec{M} = [M, M']$ be their column concatenation. Let I be an identify matrix properly sized by the context.

Sets. Let $\mathbb{M}_k^{n\cdot}$ be a set of rank-k matrices with row dimension n and arbitrary column dimension, and $\mathbb{M}_k^{n,p} \subseteq \mathbb{M}_k^{n\cdot}$ be its subset with column dimension p. Let $\mathbb{G}_k^n$ be the Grassmannian defined as the set of k-dimensional subspaces in $\mathbb{R}^n$ (a metric will be equipped later). Note each element in $\mathbb{G}_k^n$ is a subspace. Let $\mathbb{S}_k^n$ be the set of orthonormal matrices in $\mathbb{R}^{k\times n}$.

Metrics. Let d be the metric on $\mathbb{M}_k^{n,p}$ such that

$$d(M, M') = ||M - M'||, \tag{1}$$

for all $M, M' \in \mathbb{M}_k^{n,p}$. It will be used for any choice of p. Let ρ be the metric on $\mathbb{G}_k^n$ such that for any $\mathcal{G}, \mathcal{G}' \in \mathbb{G}_k^n$,

$$\rho(\mathcal{G}, \mathcal{G}') = ||\mathrm{P}_{\mathcal{G}} - \mathrm{P}_{\mathcal{G}'}||, \tag{2}$$

where $\mathrm{P}_{\mathcal{G}}$ is the orthogonal projection matrix onto $\mathcal{G}$. It is defined as $\mathrm{P}_{\mathcal{G}} = DD^T$ for any basis $D \in \mathbb{S}_k^n$ of $\mathcal{G}$. See [4, Section 2.5] for more explanations.

Factorization Model. We focus on full-rank matrix factorization, which is typically assumed in CMF (e.g. [17, 5]). The factorization model is generally denoted as $M = DA$, where D is called the *factor* and A is called the *loading*. For the ease of presentation, we assume $D \in \mathbb{S}_k^n$ but all discussions are generalizable. (See Remark 11 for a justification.) In general the loading will not be specified in analysis, as long as it is a properly sized full rank matrix. All matrices are assumed bounded.

The Shared-Factor Assumption of CMF. The CMF assumption can be stated as: *any input $M, M' \in \mathbb{M}_k^{n\cdot}$ admit factorization $M = DA$ and $M' = D'A'$ such that* $[D] = [D']$. Note although CMF assumes $D = D'$, in essence it only requires $[D] = [D']$. Also note $[D] \in \mathbb{G}_k^n$.

Probability Notations. We mainly use two styles of probability notations with different focuses: 1) notation $\Pr\{\cdot\}$ focuses on the uncertainty over random samples, e.g. in section 3 where we prove the mini-max bound randomized over samples; 2) notation $\mathbb{P}$ focuses on treating the probability as a subject of interest, e.g. in section 4 where we pick a finite set of probabilities for testing which one generates the random sample.

Sampling Model. In many applications M is not fully observed (e.g. matrix completion [17]). Let ω be the index set of observed entries and M_ω be the input matrix. Assume ω is randomly sampled. Given a concatenated matrix $\vec{M}$, we use $\vec{\omega}$ to denote its index set of observations (induced from the observations of each matrix).

Generative Model. The matrix generative model is needed for refining the mini-max bound, but not for modeling negative transfer. In our analysis, only one generative model needs to be defined on the concatenated matrix $\vec{M}$.

Suppose $\vec{M} \in \mathbb{M}_k^{n,\vec{p}}$. Let $\mathcal{P}$ be a set of probabilities defined on $\mathbb{M}_k^{n,\vec{p}}$ such that each $\mathbb{P} \in \mathcal{P}$ is a matrix-variate normal distribution (e.g. [6, Chapter 2]),

$$\mathbb{P}_{\bar{M}}(\vec{M}) = \mathcal{N}(\bar{M}, \sigma^2\mathrm{I}, \sigma^2\mathrm{I}'), \tag{3}$$

with mean matrix $\bar{M}$ and covariance matrices $\sigma^2\mathrm{I}$ (among rows) and $\sigma^2\mathrm{I}'$ (among columns). It follows

$$\mathbb{P}_{\bar{M}}(\vec{M}) = \prod\nolimits_{(i,j)} \tilde{\mathbb{P}}_{\bar{M}}(\vec{M}_{ij}), \tag{4}$$

where $\tilde{\mathbb{P}}_{\bar{M}}(\vec{M}_{ij}) = \tilde{\mathcal{N}}(\bar{M}_{ij}, \sigma^2)$ is a univariate normal distribution and the product is taken over all indices of $\vec{M}$. We note in passing $\mathbb{P}_{\bar{M}}$ is similar to the probabilistic matrix factorization model assumed in [15, Equation 1]. Define

$$\mathbb{P}_{\bar{M}}(\vec{M}_{\vec{\omega}}) = \prod\nolimits_{(i,j)\in\vec{\omega}} \tilde{\mathbb{P}}_{\bar{M}}(\vec{M}_{ij}). \tag{5}$$

Mapping. Since each M admits a unique $[D]$ in factorization $M{=}DA$ (Remark 12), we have a mapping $\theta : \mathbb{M}_k^{n\cdot} \to \mathbb{G}_k^n$ such that $\theta(M) = [D]$. This is the mapping from a rank-k matrix with n rows to its column space in $\mathbb{R}^n$. Note θ applies to any column dimension.

CMF Estimator. Recall $\vec{M}_{\vec{\omega}}$ is the random observation of two matrices. Define CMF estimator as $\hat{\theta} : \{\vec{M}_{\vec{\omega}}\} \to \mathbb{G}_k^n$. Note it realizes the shared-factor assumption by mapping two matrix observations into a single subspace. Write $\hat{\theta}_{\vec{\omega}}$ for $\hat{\theta}(\vec{M}_{\vec{\omega}})$. The quality of $\hat{\theta}$ is evaluated by

$$\ell_{\vec{\omega}}(\hat{\theta}|\vec{M}) = \frac{1}{2}\left[\rho(\hat{\theta}_{\vec{\omega}}, \theta(M)) + \rho(\hat{\theta}_{\vec{\omega}}, \theta(M'))\right]. \tag{6}$$

Define the maximum risk of any CMF estimator as

$$\mathfrak{M}(\hat{\theta}) = \sup\nolimits_{\vec{M}} \mathbb{E}_{\vec{\omega}} \ell_{\vec{\omega}}(\hat{\theta}|\vec{M}), \tag{7}$$

where expectation $\mathbb{E}_\omega$ is taken over the randomness of $\vec{M}_{\vec{\omega}}$.

It was noted when the shared-factor assumption is satisfied, CMF is equivalent to factorizing on a single matrix $\vec{M}$ [10].

Packing. This notion is used to define the following hypothesis testing problem and widely used in proof. For any

[1] This notation should not cause confusion since we only consider Frobenius norm in this paper.

set $\mathcal{X}$ equipped with a metric $\rho_{\mathcal{X}}$, let $\{x_v\}_{v\in\mathcal{V}}$ be an arbitrary subset of $\mathcal{X}$ indexed by a set $\mathcal{V}$. For any $\delta > 0$, we say this subset is a δ-packing of $\mathcal{X}$ with respect to $\rho_{\mathcal{X}}$ if $\rho_{\mathcal{X}}(x_v, x_{v'}) \geq \delta$ whenever $v \neq v'$.

Collective Hypothesis Testing. To lower bound $\mathfrak{M}(\hat{\theta})$, we employ the classic estimation-to-testing reduction method (e.g. [22]). To capture the negative transfer effect, we additionally design a *collective hypothesis testing* problem.

Let $\{\mathcal{G}_v\}_{v\in\mathcal{V}}$ be a 2δ-packing of $\mathbb{G}_k^n$ indexed by a finite set $\mathcal{V}$, and V, V' be two random variables taking values $v, v' \in \mathcal{V}$ respectively. Our testing problem is stated as follows:

Step 1: choose V, V' (with replacement) from $\mathcal{V}$ independently and uniformly at random.

Step 2: conditioned on $(V = v, V' = v')$, randomly choose $(D, D') \in \mathbb{S}_k^n \times \mathbb{S}_k^n$ satisfying $([D], [D']) = (\mathcal{G}_v, \mathcal{G}_{v'})$.

Step 3: generate $(M, M') = (DA, D'A')$ with some random A, A'; then generate observation $\vec{M}_{\vec{\omega}}$ from $\vec{M}$.

Step 4: apply a collective testing function $\hat{V} : \{\vec{M}_{\vec{\omega}}\} \to \mathcal{V}$ defined as [2]

$$\hat{V}(\vec{M}_{\vec{\omega}}) := \arg\min\nolimits_{v\in\mathcal{V}} \rho(\hat{\theta}(\vec{M}_{\vec{\omega}}), \mathcal{G}_v). \tag{8}$$

To our knowledge, the collective hypothesis testing problem, albeit simple, is the first attempt to theoretically model the negative transfer effect in CMF. It also allows incorporation of richer information such as prior distribution, and can be applied to other problems besides CMF, as will be exemplified in later discussions.

3 A PRIMARY LOWER BOUND

The following proposition presents a primary lower bound, which reveals our main idea and insights.

Proposition 1. *Suppose $\mathbb{G}_k^n$ admits a 2δ-packing indexed by a finite set $\mathcal{V}$, and V is a uniform random variable on $\mathcal{V}$. Then, any CMF estimator $\hat{\theta}$ satisfies*

$$\mathfrak{M}(\hat{\theta}) \geq \frac{\delta}{2} \cdot \left(C_\delta + \frac{1}{|\mathcal{V}|} \Pr\{\hat{V}(\vec{M}_{\vec{\omega}}) \neq V\} \right), \tag{9}$$

where $C_\delta = 1 - |\mathcal{V}|^{-1}$ and the probability is defined over the random choice of V and $\vec{M}_{\vec{\omega}}$ [3].

Our main idea of proving the proposition is to first reduce the estimation problem into the collective hypothesis testing problem. Then, if two matrices are generated from different subspaces (i.e. $\theta(M) \neq \theta(M')$), $\hat{V}$ is guaranteed to make mistake on at least one matrix by a geometrical argument in Figure 1. This inevitable mistake gives rise to bias C_δ in the lower bound, which does not depend on the choice of estimator nor observations. On the other hand, the testing error $\Pr\{\hat{V}(\vec{M}_{\vec{\omega}}) \neq V\}$ is obtained by standard arguments, conditioned on the case when two matrices are indeed generated from the same subspace.

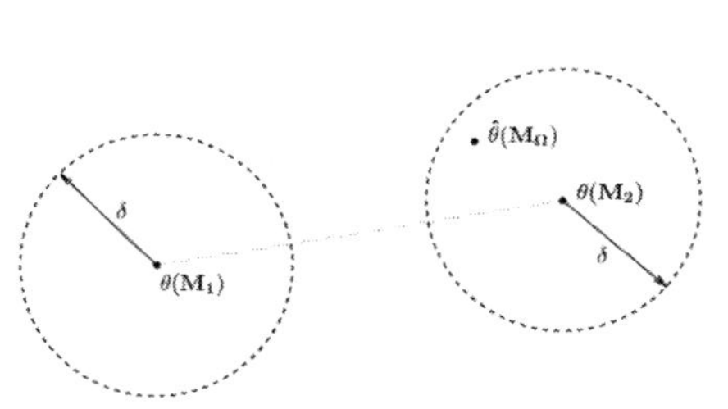

Figure 1: When two matrices are generated from different subspaces, no CMF estimator $\hat{\theta}$ can simultaneously fall into the two δ-balls centered at $\theta(M_2)$ and $\theta(M_2)$ respectively. As a result, the testing function $\hat{V}$ is guaranteed to make a mistake on at least one matrix.

Next, we discuss the implications of Proposition 1. For comparison, consider the case when negative transfer does not exist (i.e. $V = V'$). In this case, by Remark 13 we have

$$\mathfrak{M}(\hat{\theta}) \geq \delta \cdot \Pr\{\hat{V}(\vec{M}_{\vec{\omega}}) \neq V\}. \tag{10}$$

Comparing the lower bounds in (9) and (10), we see negative transfer has caused two changes: 1) introduce a bias term C_δ; 2) down-weight the testing error by $1/(2|\mathcal{V}|)$. In particular, the bias term depends merely on the structure of $\mathbb{G}_k^n$, pessimistically suggesting that CMF may never succeed in a mini-max sense, disregarding the choice of estimator $\hat{\theta}$ or observation $\vec{M}_{\vec{\omega}}$. Combining both aspects, it seems finding a good factor space may be more important than finding a good estimator or sample for mitigating the negative transfer effect.

When negative transfer does not exist, we may obtain another indirect implication by comparing CMF with independent matrix factorization (IMF) [4]. To elaborate the latter, let $\hat{\theta}_s : \{M_\omega\} \to \mathbb{G}_k^n$ be an IMF estimator and define its maximum risk as

$$\mathfrak{M}_s(\hat{\theta}_s) = \sup\nolimits_M \mathbb{E}\, \rho(\hat{\theta}_s(M_\omega), \theta(M)), \tag{11}$$

where the expectation is taken over the randomness of ω. Let $\hat{V}_s : \{M_\omega\} \to \mathcal{V}$ be any testing function on a single matrix, which possibly induces $\hat{V}$. By standard mini-max arguments it is easy to verify that

$$\mathfrak{M}_s(\hat{\theta}_s) \geq \delta \cdot \Pr\{\hat{V}_s(M_\omega) \neq V\}. \tag{12}$$

A comparison between the lower bounds in (10) and (12) suggests CMF estimator performs *no worse* than IMF estimator on at least one matrix. The reason is $\hat{V}(\vec{M}_{\vec{\omega}}) \neq V$ implies inclusively either $\hat{V}_s(M_\omega) \neq V$ or $\hat{V}_s(M'_{\omega'}) \neq V$.

[2] Note $\vec{M}_{\vec{\omega}}$ depends on v, v' in Steps 3 and 4.

[3] Both V and $\hat{V}(\vec{M}_{\vec{\omega}})$ are random variables on $\mathcal{V}$.

[4] This is the technique that separately factorizes each matrix based on its own observations.

(Otherwise, $\hat{V}$ would not make the mistake if, say, it is simply defined as the random choice of one $\hat{V}_s$.) Taking M_w for instance, we thus have

$$\Pr\{\hat{V}(\vec{M}_{\vec{\omega}}) \neq V\} \leq \Pr\{\hat{V}_s(M_\omega) \neq V\}. \quad (13)$$

Further detailing (13) is beyond the scope of this paper. Nevertheless, it is not difficult to conjecture the inequality holds typically when M has insufficient observation (thus CMF improves over IMF on at least one matrix) and the equality holds otherwise. It should be noted even without negative transfer, our lower bound does not suggest CMF always improves over IMF. We note this is neither concluded from the upper bound analysis of CMF assuming no negative transfer [5].

Next we present two extensions of the proposition.

3.1 A BOUND WITH PRIOR

In [16], authors assumed a prior distribution over the factor space. A natural question for us is how such intrinsic prior may affect the negative transfer effect. For simplicity assume all sets are measurable.

Let ν be a probability measure defined on the factor space $\mathbb{S}_k^n$, as assumed in [16]. It naturally induces a probability measure μ over $\mathbb{G}_k^n$ such that for any $\mathcal{G} \in \mathbb{G}_k^n$,

$$\mu(\mathcal{G}) := \int_{[D]=\mathcal{G}} 1 \, d\nu(D). \quad (14)$$

Define $\tilde{\mu} := \mu/N$ as a normalized probability measure with proper choice of N. We can replace *Step 1* in the collective hypothesis testing problem with

Step 1^**: choose both* V, V' *(with replacement) by* $\tilde{\mu}(\mathcal{G}_V)$.

By the same arguments for Proposition 1, and now

$$\Pr\{V = V'\} = \sum\nolimits_{v \in \mathcal{V}} \tilde{\mu}^2(\mathcal{G}_v), \quad (15)$$

it is easy to verify the following result.

Corollary 2. *Suppose* $\mathbb{G}_k^n$ *admits a* 2δ*-packing indexed by a finite set* $\mathcal{V}$. *Let* V *be a uniform random variable on* $\mathcal{V}$. *Replace Step* 1 *in collective hypothesis testing with Step* 1^*. *Then, any CMF estimator* $\hat{\theta}$ *satisfies*

$$\mathfrak{M}(\hat{\theta}) \geq \frac{\delta}{2} \cdot \left(\tilde{C}_\delta + \tilde{N}_\delta \Pr\{\hat{V}(\vec{M}_{\vec{\omega}}) \neq V\}\right), \quad (16)$$

where $\tilde{N}_\delta = \sum_{v \in \mathcal{V}} \tilde{\mu}^2(\mathcal{G}_v)$, $\tilde{C}_\delta = 1 - \tilde{N}_\delta$, *and the probability is defined over the random choice of* $\vec{M}_{\vec{\omega}}$ *and* V.

The implication of Corollary 2 is clear: since $\tilde{N}_\delta$ reaches its minimum when $\tilde{\mu}(\mathcal{G}_V)$ is the same for all choices of V (by Chebyshev's sum inequality), resulting in the maximum bias $\tilde{C}_\delta$, we see CMF suffers most negative transfer when nature chooses V uniformly.

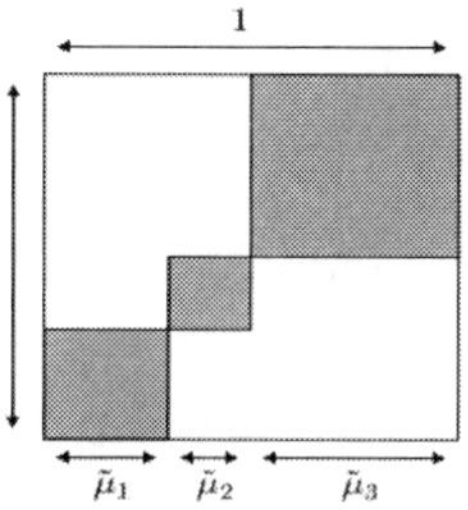

Figure 2: A packing of three points, each indexing a gray square in the figure with its prior $\mu_i := \mu(\mathcal{G}_i)$, $i = 1, 2, 3$. The total area of three squares equals to $\tilde{N}_\delta$. Clearly, this area reaches its maximum value 1 when $\mu_i = 1$ for any i. This corresponds to the most concentrated prior μ.

On the other hand, a simple geometric argument in Figure 2 shows the more concentrated $\tilde{\mu}$ nature uses, the less negative transfer CMF suffers.

3.2 A BOUND FOR MATRIX RECOVERY

A major use of CMF is for recovering the missing values of incomplete matrices (e.g. [17]). This section presents a technique to extend Proposition 1 for the recovery task under mild conditions. The main strategy is to convert the recovery error back to $\rho(\hat{\mathcal{G}}, \mathcal{G})$ using the following variant of [18, Theorem 2.3].

Lemma 3. *Let* $\mathcal{G}, \mathcal{G}'$ *respectively be the column spaces of any* $M, M' \in \mathbb{M}_k^{n,p}$. *Let* $s_k(M)$ *be the smallest non-zero singular value of* M. *Then*

$$\rho(\mathcal{G}, \mathcal{G}') \leq \sqrt{2}||M - M'||/s_k(M). \quad (17)$$

For simplicity, we focus on a set $\tilde{\mathbb{M}}_k^{n\cdot} \subseteq \mathbb{M}_k^{n\cdot}$ whose matrices have their smallest non-zero singular values bounded away from zero. A similar assumption was made for matrix recovery in [9, Theorem I.2.].

Let $\tilde{\mathbb{G}}_k^n \subseteq \mathbb{G}_k^n$ be the set induced from $\tilde{\mathbb{M}}_k^{n\cdot}$ such that for every $\mathcal{G} \in \tilde{\mathbb{G}}_k^n$ there is an $M \in \tilde{\mathbb{M}}_k^{n\cdot}$ satisfying $\theta(M) = \mathcal{G}$. For a matrix M and a factor $\hat{D}$ estimated from its observation M_ω, define the recovery error as

$$er_M(\hat{D}) = \min_A ||M - \hat{D}A||^2. \quad (18)$$

This is similar to the reconstructive error in [13, page 1]. Define the recovery loss as

$$\ell_{\mathfrak{r}|\vec{\omega}}(\hat{\theta}|\vec{M}) = \frac{1}{2}\left[er_M(\hat{\theta}(\vec{M}_{\vec{\omega}})) + er_{M'}(\hat{\theta}(\vec{M}_{\vec{\omega}}))\right], \quad (19)$$

and the maximum risk of any CMF estimator as

$$\mathfrak{M}_{\mathfrak{r}}(\hat{\theta}) = \sup\nolimits_{\vec{M} \in \tilde{\mathbb{M}}_k^{n\cdot} \times \tilde{\mathbb{M}}_k^{n\cdot}} \mathbb{E}_{\vec{\omega}} \ell_{\mathfrak{r}|\vec{\omega}}(\hat{\theta}|\vec{M}). \quad (20)$$

Our recovery bound is stated as follows.

Corollary 4. *Given a $\tilde{\mathbb{M}}_k^{n\cdot}$ and its induced $\tilde{\mathbb{G}}_k^n$ that admits a 2δ-packing indexed by a finite set $\mathcal{V}$. Let V be a uniform random variable on $\mathcal{V}$. Then, there is a $c > 0$ (depending on $\tilde{\mathbb{M}}_k^{n\cdot}$) bounded away from zero such that every CMF estimator $\hat{\theta}$ satisfies*

$$\tilde{\mathfrak{M}}_{\mathfrak{r}}(\hat{\theta}) \geq \frac{\delta \cdot c}{2\sqrt{2}} \left(C_\delta + \frac{1}{|\mathcal{V}|} \Pr\{\hat{V}(\vec{M}_{\vec{\omega}}) \neq V\} \right), \quad (21)$$

where $C_\delta = 1 - |\mathcal{V}|^{-1}$ and the probability is defined over the random choice of $\vec{M}_{\vec{\omega}}$ and V.

Corollary 4 shows a recovery error bound that maintains the same order as the estimation error bound.

4 A FINER LOWER BOUND

In this section, we first introduce a few more machinery used to refine the lower bound in Proposition 1, and then present the refined bound.

Generalized Fano Method for CMF. The first piece of information is related to the generalized Fano method in [22, Lemma 3], which will be the starting point of our proof.

Let $I(;)$ denote the mutual information between two variables. The following lemma is our extension of the generalized Fano method for the CMF problem.

Lemma 5. *Let $\{M_v \in \mathbb{M}_k^{n\cdot}\}_{v\in\mathcal{V}} \subseteq \mathcal{P}$ be a collection of matrices indexed by $\mathcal{V}$ such that for any $v \neq v'$,*

$$\rho(\theta(M_v), \theta(M_{v'})) \geq 2\delta. \quad (22)$$

Further, suppose

$$I(V; \vec{M}_{\vec{\omega}}) \leq \beta, \quad (23)$$

where V is a uniform random variable on $\mathcal{V}$. Then

$$\begin{aligned} \max_{v,v'\in\mathcal{V}} \mathbb{E}_\omega \frac{1}{2} \left(d(\hat{\theta}, \theta(M_v)) + d(\hat{\theta}, \theta(M_{v'})) \right) \\ \geq \frac{\delta}{2} \left(1 - \frac{\beta + \log 2}{|\mathcal{V}| \log |\mathcal{V}|} \right). \end{aligned} \quad (24)$$

Comparing (24) with the standard bound [22, Lemma 3] [5]

$$\frac{\delta}{2} \left(1 - \frac{\beta + \log 2}{\log |\mathcal{V}|} \right), \quad (25)$$

our generalization introduces an additional $|\mathcal{V}|$ in the denominator, which significantly speeds up the growth of the lower bound as $|\mathcal{V}|$ increases. This coincides with with our discovery in Proposition 1, and provides a finer implication of the negative transfer effect. In result we retain the mutual information (instead of relaxing it to KL divergence) to facilitate later application.

[5] While [22] focused on probability set, we focus on matrix set to facilitate later application. Nevertheless, our extension is also applicable on probability set and will give result similar to (24).

A few things should be clarified about the lemma. First, it does not require M_v's to have the same column dimension. Second, $I(V; \vec{M}_{\vec{\omega}})$ is derived from $\Pr\{\hat{v}(\vec{M}_{\vec{\omega}}) \neq V\}$ in Proposition 1 and thus inherits the condition that two matrices share the same latent factor.

Packing Number. The second piece of information is related to the packing number on Grassmannian $\mathbb{G}_k^n$, which will be used to bound $|\mathcal{V}|$ in Lemma 5.

Let $M(\mathbb{G}_k^n, \rho, \delta)$ be the packing number on $\mathbb{G}_k^n$ with respect to metric ρ and radius δ. It is the largest size of $\mathcal{V}$ that indexes an admitted δ-packing on $\mathbb{G}_k^n$. Let $\tau(\mathbb{G}_k^n)$ and d be the diameter and dimension of $\mathbb{G}_k^n$, respectively. The following result is a variant of [19, Proposition 8].

Lemma 6. *There exist universal constants $c_1, c_2 > 0$ such that for any $\delta \in (0, \tau(\mathbb{G}_k^n)]$,*

$$(c_1\tau(\mathbb{G}_k^n)/\delta)^d \leq M(\mathbb{G}_k^n, \rho, \delta) \leq (c_2\tau(\mathbb{G}_k^n)/\delta)^d. \quad (26)$$

Mutual Information. The third piece of information is related to the mutual information $I(V; \vec{M}_{\vec{\omega}})$ appeared in Lemma 5, which will be used for deriving its upper bound.

Let $D_{k\ell}$ denote KL divergence. Recall the probability notation $\mathbb{P}$ introduced in section 2. A classic approach (e.g. [22, page 428]) to bound $I(V; \vec{M}_{\vec{\omega}})$ is by

$$I(V; \vec{M}_{\vec{\omega}}) \leq \frac{1}{|\mathcal{V}|^2} \sum_{v,v'} D_{k\ell}(\mathbb{P}_v || \mathbb{P}_{v'}). \quad (27)$$

However, this does not directly apply to our setting since $\mathbb{P}_v$ is not easy to specify. The following technique is from [8, Equation 110], which addresses the problem.

Lemma 7. *Let $T(\vec{M}_{\vec{\omega}})$ be any side information. Then*

$$I(V; \vec{M}_{\vec{\omega}}) \leq I(V; \vec{M}_{\vec{\omega}} | T(\vec{M}_{\vec{\omega}})). \quad (28)$$

Write $\vec{T}$ for $T(\vec{M}_{\vec{\omega}})$. We notice

$$I(V; \vec{M}_{\vec{\omega}} | \vec{T}) \leq \frac{\sum_{v,v'} \mathbb{E} D_{k\ell}(\mathbb{P}_v(\cdot|\vec{T}) || \mathbb{P}_{v'}(\cdot|\vec{T}))}{|\mathcal{V}|^2}, \quad (29)$$

where expectation $\mathbb{E}$ is taken over the randomness of $\vec{T}$.

KL Divergence. The last piece of information is related to KL divergence, which is used to specify the bound in (29).

Recall the generative model introduced in section 2. For a matrix $\vec{M}$ and its observation index $\vec{\omega}$, let W_ω be a matrix of the same size as $\vec{M}$ such that $W_{ij|\vec{\omega}} = 1$ if $(i,j) \in \vec{\omega}$ and $W_{ij|\vec{\omega}} = 0$ otherwise. Let $\circ$ denote the Hadamard product between matrices. We remark the following result.

Lemma 8. *For any $\vec{M}, \vec{M}' \in \mathbb{M}_k^{n,\vec{p}}$ and $\vec{\omega}$,*

$$D_{k\ell}(\mathbb{P}_{\vec{M}|\vec{\omega}} || \mathbb{P}_{\vec{M}'|\vec{\omega}}) = \frac{1}{2\sigma^4} ||W_{\vec{\omega}} \circ (\vec{M} - \vec{M}')||^2. \quad (30)$$

4.1 THE FINER BOUND

Recall the factorization model $M = DA$ and A is randomly generated. Let $\Sigma_A = \mathbb{E}||A||^2$. Our finer bound is based on the setting of Proposition 1 and stated as follows.

Theorem 9. *Every CMF estimator $\hat{\theta}$ satisfies*

$$\mathfrak{M}(\hat{\theta}) \geq c \cdot \tau(\mathbb{G}_k^n)^{1-1/d}(|\vec{\omega}|\Sigma_A/\sigma^4)^{-1/d}, \qquad (31)$$

where $c > 0$ depends on the nature of $\mathbb{G}_k^n$ and absorbs lower order terms.

The new lower bound can be interpreted as follows.

- $|\vec{\omega}|$: larger observation number $|\vec{\omega}|$ leads to smaller lower bound. This makes sense, as more observations improve the accuracy of testing. However, we see its impact is significantly restricted by d, resulting in a learning rate $\Omega(|\vec{\omega}|^{-1/d})$. Based on (25) and our arguments for the theorem, one can easily derive a learning rate without negative transfer as $\Omega(|\vec{\omega}|^{-1})$. Thus we see negative transfer significantly slows down learning. This shall not be too surprising, however, since in Lemma 5 the lower bound has already become linearly dependent on $|\mathcal{V}|$ (instead of logarithmically) due to the negative transfer effect.

- d: for simplicity, assume $\tau(\mathbb{G}_k^n)|\vec{\omega}|\Sigma_A/\sigma^4 \geq 1$. Then, larger d leads to larger lower bound. In particular, a very large d significantly weakens the impact of other parameters (except $\tau(\mathbb{G}_k^n)$) on the lower bound. This coincides with our discovery in Proposition 1, where the impact of estimation quality (and now its related parameters) is down-weighted.

  We notice the dimension $d = k(n-k)$ is quadratic to matrix rank k and reaches its maximum at $k = n/2$ (and thus the worst bound). It is unclear how to explain such role of k, but we have another consistent observation based mainly on combinatoric arguments: Assume $\mathbb{M}_k^{n\cdot}$ is defined on a finite field of order q (which is common in problems such as recommendation system). Then the number of its column spaces (thus factor spaces) is the q-binomial coefficient $\binom{n}{k}_q$ based on [14]. Clearly, the more subspaces $\mathbb{M}_k^{n\cdot}$ induces, the more difficult estimation/testing will be. In particular, we notice $\binom{n}{k}_q$ is also a quadratic-style function of k and reaches its maximum at $k = n/2$.

- $\tau(\mathbb{G}_k^n)$: larger diameter of $\mathbb{G}_k^n$ leads to larger lower bound. This makes sense, since a larger hypothesis set admits a larger packing (see Lemma 6), resulting in a more challenging testing problem. In addition, we see the impact of diameter is slightly restricted by the dimension d of $\mathbb{G}_k^n$. Specifically, a large diameter hurts more when the dimension is high.

- Σ_A and σ: we are not particularly interested in these two terms, but note in passing that larger Σ_A or smaller σ leads to smaller lower bound.

- c : this coefficient arises from the universal constants in Lemma 6 that depend on the nature of $\mathbb{G}_k^n$. Then it absorbs lower order terms through derivation, but this shall not affect the order of interested parameters.

5 PROOFS AND REMARKS

Proof of Proposition 1.

Write $\hat{\theta}$ for $\hat{\theta}(\vec{M}_{\vec{\omega}})$, $\vec{V}$ for (V, V') and $\vec{v}$ for (v, v'). Let notation $\vee$ denote the logical disjunction. Following standard mini-max arguments, we first have

$$\begin{aligned}
&\sup_{\vec{M}}\mathbb{E}_{\vec{\omega}}\left[\rho(\hat{\theta},\theta(M)) + \rho(\hat{\theta},\theta(M'))\right] \\
&\geq \sup_{\vec{M}}\mathbb{E}\left[\delta\,\mathbf{1}\{\rho(\hat{\theta},\theta(M)) \geq \delta \vee \rho(\hat{\theta},\theta(M')) \geq \delta\}\right] \\
&= \delta \cdot \sup_{\vec{M}}\Pr\{\rho(\hat{\theta},\theta(M)) \geq \delta \vee \rho(\hat{\theta},\theta(M')) \geq \delta\},
\end{aligned} \qquad (32)$$

where the inequality is based on the fact that total distance is greater than δ if any one distance is greater than δ.

Reducing the above estimation problem into the collective hypothesis testing problem (with a 2δ-packing $\{\theta_v\}_{v\in\mathcal{V}}$), we have

$$\begin{aligned}
&\sup_{\vec{M}}\Pr\{\rho(\hat{\theta},\theta(M)) \geq \delta \vee \rho(\hat{\theta},\theta(M')) \geq \delta\} \\
&\geq \frac{1}{|\mathcal{V}|^2}\sum_{\vec{v}}\Pr\{\rho(\hat{\theta},\theta_v) \geq \delta \vee \rho(\hat{\theta},\theta_{v'}) \geq \delta \mid \vec{V} = \vec{v}\},
\end{aligned} \qquad (33)$$

where the coefficient is based on the uniform sampling assumption on $\mathcal{V}$ so that $\Pr\{\vec{V} = \vec{v}\} = 1/|\mathcal{V}|^2$.

Now we introduce the negative transfer effect. Consider two cases $v = v'$ and $v \neq v'$. Clearly the second one captures the violation of the shared-factor assumption. Then

$$\begin{aligned}
&\Pr\{\rho(\hat{\theta},\theta_v) \geq \delta \vee \rho(\hat{\theta},\theta_{v'}) \geq \delta \mid \vec{V} = \vec{v}\} \\
&= \Pr\{\rho(\hat{\theta},\theta_v) \geq \delta \vee \rho(\hat{\theta},\theta_{v'}) \geq \delta \mid v \neq v', \vec{V} = \vec{v}\} \\
&\quad \cdot \Pr\{v \neq v' \mid \vec{V} = \vec{v}\} \\
&\quad + \Pr\{\rho(\hat{\theta},\theta_v) \geq \delta \vee \rho(\hat{\theta},\theta_{v'}) \geq \delta \mid v = v', \vec{V} = \vec{v}\} \\
&\quad \cdot \Pr\{v = v' \mid \vec{V} = \vec{v}\} \\
&= 1 \cdot \Pr\{v \neq v' \mid \vec{V} = \vec{v}\} \\
&\quad + \Pr\{\rho(\hat{\theta},\theta_v) \geq \delta \vee \rho(\hat{\theta},\theta_{v'}) \geq \delta \mid v = v', \vec{V} = \vec{v}\} \\
&\quad \cdot \Pr\{v = v' \mid \vec{V} = \vec{v}\},
\end{aligned} \qquad (34)$$

where the second equality is based on the geometric argument illustrated in Figure 1, i.e. if $v \neq v'$, then no $\hat{\theta}$ can be simultaneously δ-close to both θ_v and $\theta_{v'}$, which implies $\Pr\{\rho(\hat{\theta}, \theta_v) \geq \delta \vee \rho(\hat{\theta}, \theta_{v'}) \geq \delta\} = 1$.

Putting all above arguments together and in addition: 1) $\rho(\hat{\theta}, \theta_{v_t}) \geq \delta$ as implied by $\hat{V}(\vec{M}_{\vec{\omega}}) \neq v_t$ (by the definition of $\hat{V}$); 2) average over all possible $\vec{v}$, we have

$$\begin{aligned} &\sup_{\vec{M}} \mathbb{E}\left[\rho(\hat{\theta}, \theta(M)) + \rho(\hat{\theta}, \theta(M'))\right] \\ &\geq \delta \left(\Pr\{V \neq V'\} + \frac{1}{|\mathcal{V}|}\Pr\{\hat{V}(\vec{M}_{\vec{\omega}}) \neq V | V = V'\}\right). \end{aligned} \tag{35}$$

It remains to simplify the above lower bound. First, by uniform sampling $\Pr\{V \neq V'\} = 1 - |\mathcal{V}|^{-1}$. Second, $\Pr\{\hat{V} \neq V | V = V'\} = \Pr\{\hat{v} \neq V\}$, where the left side probability is over the randomness of both V, V', while the right side probability is merely over the randomness of V. Putting all together proves the proposition.

Proof of Corollary 4.

Recall $s_k(M)$ is the smallest non-zero singular value of matrix M. By our assumption $c = \inf_{M \in \tilde{\mathbb{M}}_k^{n \cdot}} s_k(M)$ is positive and bounded away from zero. Combining with Lemma 3, this implies any $M, M' \in \tilde{\mathbb{M}}_k^{n \cdot}$ satisfy

$$\rho(\mathcal{G}, \mathcal{G}') \leq \sqrt{2}||M - M'||/c. \tag{36}$$

Writing $\hat{\theta} := \hat{\theta}(\vec{M}_\omega)$, this further implies

$$er_M(\hat{\theta}) \geq c \cdot \rho(\hat{\theta}, \theta(M))/\sqrt{2}. \tag{37}$$

Hence over all $\vec{M} \in \tilde{\mathbb{M}}_k^{n \cdot} \times \tilde{\mathbb{M}}_k^{n \cdot}$, we have

$$\begin{aligned} &\sup_{\vec{M}} \mathbb{E}_{\vec{\omega}}\left[er_M(\hat{\theta}) + er_{M'}(\hat{\theta})\right] \\ &\geq \frac{c}{\sqrt{2}} \sup_{\vec{M}} \mathbb{E}_{\vec{\omega}}\left[\rho(\hat{\theta}, \theta(M)) + \rho(\hat{\theta}, \theta(M'))\right]. \end{aligned} \tag{38}$$

Applying Proposition 1 yields the corollary.

Proof of Lemma 5.

The proof is similar to [22, Lemma 3], with the main difference that we study a joint estimation problem (instead of a single one) and apply our own reduction technique.

By assumption $\{\phi(\mathbb{P}_v)\}_{v \in \mathcal{V}}$ is a 2δ-packing on $\mathbb{G}_k^n$. Applying the arguments in Proposition 1 gives a lower bound

$$\frac{\delta}{2}\left(C_\alpha + \frac{1}{|\mathcal{V}|}\Pr\{\hat{V}(\vec{M}_{\vec{\omega}}) \neq V\}\right), \tag{39}$$

where $C_\alpha = 1 - |\mathcal{V}|^{-1}$.

Further, following the same arguments in the generalized Fano method [22, Lemma 3] (in particular, the Fano's inequality and data processing inequality), we have

$$\Pr\{\hat{V}(\vec{M}_{\vec{\omega}}) \neq V\} \geq 1 - \frac{I(V; \vec{M}_{\vec{\omega}}) + \log 2}{\log |\mathcal{V}|}. \tag{40}$$

Combining both with $I(V; \vec{M}_{\vec{\omega}}) \leq \beta$ proves the lemma.

Proof of Lemma 6.

Let $N(\mathbb{G}_k^n, \rho, \delta)$ be the covering number of $\mathbb{G}_k^n$ with respect to metric ρ and covering radius δ. It is defined as

$$\min\{|\mathcal{V}| : \mathbb{G}_k^n \text{ admits a } \delta\text{-cover indexed by } \mathcal{V}\}, \tag{41}$$

where a *δ-cover* is a set of points in $\mathbb{G}_k^n$ such that the union of their δ-balls contains $\mathbb{G}_k^n$. It is stated [19, Proposition 8] there are universal constants $s_1, s_2 > 0$ such that

$$(s_1 \cdot D_g/\delta)^d \leq N(\mathbb{G}_k^n, \rho, \delta) \leq (s_2 \cdot D_g/\delta)^d. \tag{42}$$

In addition, it is well-known that (e.g. [25, Equation 1.5]).

$$N(\mathbb{G}_k^n, \rho, \delta) \leq M(\mathbb{G}_k^n, \rho, \delta) \leq N(\mathbb{G}_k^n, \rho, \delta/2). \tag{43}$$

Putting two together we have

$$(s_1 \cdot D_g/\delta)^d \leq M(\mathbb{G}_k^n, \rho, \delta) \leq (2s_2 \cdot D_g/\delta)^d. \tag{44}$$

Setting $c_1 = s_1$ and $c_2 = 2s_2$ proves the lemma.

Proof of Lemma 8.

Recall the generative model in section 2, where $\mathcal{P} = \{\mathbb{P}\}$ is a set of probabilities defined on $\mathbb{M}_k^{n,\vec{p}}$. For clarity we first derive the case when $\vec{M}$ is complete, and its generalization for $\vec{M}_{\vec{\omega}}$ naturally follows. Remark the following result.

Remark 10. *For any $\bar{M}, \bar{M}' \in \mathbb{M}_k^{n,\vec{p}}$,*

$$D_{k\ell}(\mathbb{P}_{\bar{M}}(M)||\mathbb{P}_{\bar{M}'}(M)) = \frac{1}{2\sigma^4}||\bar{M} - \bar{M}'||^2. \tag{45}$$

Proof. By the definition of KL divergence,

$$D_{k\ell}(\mathbb{P}_{\bar{M}}||\mathbb{P}_{\bar{M}'}) = \mathbb{E}_{\mathbb{P}_{\bar{M}}} \log\left(\mathbb{P}_{\bar{M}}/\mathbb{P}_{\bar{M}'}\right), \tag{46}$$

where expectation $\mathbb{E}_{\mathbb{P}_{\bar{M}}}$ is taken over $\mathbb{P}_{\bar{M}}$. Further, by the definition of matrix-variate normal distribution (e.g. [6]),

$$\mathbb{P}_{\bar{M}}(\vec{M}) = \exp\left(-||(\vec{M} - \bar{M}||^2/2\sigma^4\right)/\sqrt{(2\pi)^{np}}. \tag{47}$$

This implies

$$\log\frac{\mathbb{P}_{\bar{M}}}{\mathbb{P}_{\bar{M}'}} = -\frac{1}{2\sigma^4}(||\vec{M} - \bar{M}||^2 - ||\vec{M} - \bar{M}'||^2). \tag{48}$$

In addition,

$$\begin{aligned} &\mathbb{E}_{\mathbb{P}_M} ||\vec{M} - \bar{M}||^2 - ||\vec{M} - \bar{M}'||^2 \\ &= \mathbb{E}\sum_{i,j}(\vec{M}_{ij} - \bar{M}_{ij})^2 - (\vec{M}_{ij} - \bar{M}'_{ij})^2 \\ &= \mathbb{E}\sum_{i,j} 2\vec{M}_{ij}(\bar{M}'_{ij} - \bar{M}_{ij}) + \bar{M}_{ij}^2 - (\bar{M}'_{ij})^2 \\ &= \sum_{i,j} 2\bar{M}_{ij}(\bar{M}'_{ij} - \bar{M}_{ij}) + \bar{M}_{ij}^2 - (\bar{M}'_{ij})^2 \\ &= \sum_{i,j}(\bar{M}'_{ij} - \bar{M}_{ij})^2 = ||\bar{M}' - \bar{M}||^2. \end{aligned} \tag{49}$$

Putting all together completes the proof. □

The arguments for Lemma 8 is almost the same as those for Remark 10, except now we have

$$\mathbb{P}_{\vec{M}|\vec{\omega}}(\vec{M}) = \prod_{(i,j)\in\vec{\omega}} \tilde{\mathbb{P}}_{\vec{M}}(\vec{M}_{ij}), \tag{50}$$

which admits a matrix form (can be easily verified)

$$\mathbb{P}_{\vec{M}|\vec{\omega}}(\vec{M}) = \frac{\exp\left(-\frac{1}{2\sigma^4}||W_{\vec{\omega}} \circ (\vec{M} - \bar{M})||^2\right)}{\sqrt{(2\pi)^{|\vec{\omega}|}}}. \tag{51}$$

Keeping $W_{\vec{\omega}}$ through the derivation proves the lemma.

Proof of Theorem 9.

The first step is to apply the extended generalized Fano method (Lemma 5) to derive a lower bound. To do so, we need to fulfill its two conditions (22) and (23) respectively.

Let $\{\vec{M}_v \in \mathbb{M}_k^{n,\vec{p}}\}_{v\in\mathcal{V}}$ be a set inducing a 2δ-packing on $\mathbb{G}_k^n$, i.e. $\rho(\theta(\vec{M}_v), \theta(\vec{M}_{v'})) \geq 2\delta$ for any $v \neq v'$. This set fulfills (22). Note we have chosen all matrices from $\mathbb{M}_k^{n,\vec{p}}$, which does not weaken the analysis since this set can induce the entire $\mathbb{G}_k^n$ through θ.

It takes more effort to fulfill (23). Recall $I(V; \vec{M}_{\vec{\omega}})$ is based on the condition that input matrices share the same factor. Then our problem is equivalent to testing V using a single matrix $\vec{M}$ randomly drawn from $\mathbb{M}_k^{n,\vec{p}}$. This allows us to apply the generative model on $\mathbb{M}_k^{n,\vec{p}}$ in section 2.

For any $\vec{M} \in \mathbb{M}_k^{n,\vec{p}}$, let $\vec{A} \in \mathbb{R}^{k\times\vec{p}}$ be a loading in its factorization and $\vec{W} \in \mathbb{R}^{n\times\vec{p}}$ be its mask such that $\vec{W}_{ij} = 1$ if $\vec{M}_{ij}$ is observed and $\vec{W}_{ij} = 0$ otherwise. We have

$$\begin{aligned}
&I(V; \vec{M}_{\vec{\omega}}) \\
&\leq I(V; \vec{M}_{\vec{\omega}}|\vec{A}) \\
&\leq \mathbb{E}_{\vec{A}} \frac{1}{|\mathcal{V}|^2} \sum_{v,v'\in\mathcal{V}} D_{k\ell}(\mathbb{P}_v(\vec{M}|\vec{A})||\mathbb{P}_{v'}(\vec{M}|\vec{A})) \\
&\leq \frac{1}{|\mathcal{V}|^2} \sum_{v,v'} \mathbb{E} D_{k\ell}(\mathbb{P}_v(\vec{M}|\vec{A})||\mathbb{P}_{v'}(\vec{M}|\vec{A})) \\
&= \frac{1}{|\mathcal{V}|^2} \sum_{v,v'} \mathbb{E} \frac{1}{2\sigma^4} ||\vec{W} \circ (D_{\mathcal{G}_v} - D_{\mathcal{G}_{v'}})\vec{A}||^2 \\
&\leq \frac{1}{|\mathcal{V}|^2} \sum_{v,v'} \frac{||\vec{W}||^2}{2\sigma^4} ||D_{\mathcal{G}_v} - D_{\mathcal{G}_{v'}}||^2 \cdot \mathbb{E}||\vec{A}||^2 \\
&\leq \frac{1}{|\mathcal{V}|^2} \sum_{v,v'} \frac{|\vec{\omega}|}{2\sigma^4} \cdot \rho(\mathcal{G}_v, \mathcal{G}_{v'}) \cdot \Sigma_{\vec{A}} \\
&\leq \frac{1}{2\sigma^4} |\vec{\omega}| \cdot \tau(\mathbb{G}_k^n) \cdot \Sigma_{\vec{A}},
\end{aligned} \tag{52}$$

where the first inequality is based on Lemma 7 where we condition both probabilities on a loading A; the second inequality is based on (29); the third inequality is due to the convexity of $\mathbb{E}_{\vec{A}}$; the first equality is based on Lemma 8; the fourth inequality is based on simple algebra argument (see Remark 14), and the fifth inequality is based on an extended argument of [20, Lemma A.1.2.] (see Remark 15); the last inequality is by the fact that $\rho(\mathcal{G}_v, \mathcal{G}_{v'}) \leq \tau(\mathbb{G}_k^n)$.

Till now we have fulfilled both conditions in the generalized Fano method described in Lemma 5. Together with Lemma 6 that bounds $|\mathcal{V}|$, this implies a lower bound

$$\frac{\delta}{2}\left(1 - \frac{|\vec{\omega}|\tau(\mathbb{G}_k^n)\Sigma_A/2\sigma^4 + \log 2}{d\,(\tau(\mathbb{G}_k^n)c/\delta)^d \log(\tau(\mathbb{G}_k^n)c/\delta)}\right). \tag{53}$$

As a standard strategy, it remains to choose a proper δ so that the 'big' fraction in (53) is upper bounded by $1/2$.

We are mainly interested in the order of parameters. First relax the lower order term $\log(\tau(\mathbb{G}_k^n)c/\delta) \geq \log(2c)$ since $\tau(\mathbb{G}_k^n) \geq 2\delta$ and the constant $\log 2 \geq \log 1 = 0$. Rearranging terms, we wish to choose a δ satisfying

$$\delta \geq \left(\frac{c^d \cdot d \cdot \log 2c \cdot \tau(\mathbb{G}_k^n)^d \cdot 2\sigma^4}{2|\vec{\omega}|\tau(\mathbb{G}_k^n)\Sigma_A}\right)^{1/d}. \tag{54}$$

Further, since $d = k(n-k)$ is a positive integer, it is easy to verify $d^{1/d} \leq 1.45$ and $(\log(2c))^{1/d} \leq \log(2c)$. Plugging both in the above lower bound and merging constants and terms depending on c into c', we have

$$\delta \geq c' \cdot \tau(\mathbb{G}_k^n)^{1-1/d} \cdot \left(|\vec{\omega}|\Sigma_A/\sigma^4\right)^{-1/d}. \tag{55}$$

Plugging this back to the lower bound (53) and merging constants again proves the theorem.

5.1 REMARKS

Remark 11. *Any $M, M' \in \mathbb{M}_k^{n\cdot}$ admit a joint full-rank factorization $M = QA$ and $M' = QA'$ for some $Q \in \mathbb{R}^{n\times k}$ if and only if they admit a joint factorization $M = DB$ and $M' = DB'$ for some $D \in \mathbb{S}_k^n$.*

Proof. A well known fact is that that every subspace of $\mathbb{R}^n$ admits an orthonormal basis (by Gram-Schmidt process). Thus for one direction, any Q induces a subspace $span(Q)$, which admits an orthonormal basis $D \in \mathbb{S}_k^n$. This means $Q = DL$ for some expressive coefficient matrix L and thus $M = QA = D(LA)$. The other direction is trivial. □

Remark 12. *Every $M \in \mathbb{M}_k^{n\cdot}$ admits exactly one $\mathcal{S} \in \mathbb{G}_k^n$ such that $\mathcal{S} = [D]$ for any $D \in \mathbb{S}_k^n$ satisfying $M = DA$.*

Proof. Given any two factorizations $M = DA = D'A'$ with $D, D' \in \mathbb{S}_k^n$, to justify the remark it suffices to show $span(D) \subseteq span(D')$ and $span(D) \supseteq span(D')$.

For the first direction, it suffices to find a $W \in \mathbb{R}^{k\times k}$ such that $D'W = D$. This is easy as $(D')^T D'$ is invertible since $D' \in \mathbb{S}_k^n$. (In fact, we only need D' to have full column rank.) Thus one can set $W = ((D')^T D')^{-1}(D')^T D$. Similar arguments apply for the other direction. □

Remark 13. *In Proposition 1, if one always has* $\theta(M) = \theta(M')$, *then* $\mathfrak{M}(\hat{\theta}) \geq \delta \cdot \Pr\{\hat{V}(\vec{M}_{\vec{\omega}}) \neq V\}$.

Proof. Condition $\theta(M) = \theta(M')$ implies we can fix $V = V'$ while designing the collective hypothesis testing problem. This means $\Pr\{V \neq V'\} = 0$ and $\Pr\{V = V'\} = 1$. Plugging both into the proof of Proposition 1 (last inequality) justifies the remark. □

Remark 14. *For any same sized matrices* A *and* B, *we have* $||A \circ B||^2 \leq ||A||^2 \cdot ||B||^2$.

Proof. For all sums taken over all matrix indices, it follows $||A \circ B||^2 = \sum(A_{ij}B_{ij})^2 = \sum(A_{ij})^2(B_{ij})^2 \leq \sum(A_{ij})^2 \sum(B_{i'j'})^2 = ||A||^2||B||^2$, where the inequality is by the fact that $(B_{ij})^2 \leq \sum(B_{i'j'})^2$ for any (i,j). □

Remark 15. *For any* $D, D' \in \mathbb{S}_k^n$,

$$||D - D'||^2 \leq ||DD^T - D'(D')^T||^2. \tag{56}$$

Proof. This remark is a matrix extension of [20, Lemma A.1.2]. Let $D_{:j}$ denote the column j of D. We have

$$\begin{aligned} &||DD^T - D'(D')^T||^2 \\ &= \sum_j ||D_{:j}D_{:j}^T - D'_{:j}(D'_{:j})^T||^2 \\ &\leq \sum_j ||D_{:j} - D'_{:j}||^2 = ||D - D'||^2, \end{aligned} \tag{57}$$

where the inequality is based on [20, Lemma A.1.2] and the fact that $||D_{:j} - D'_{:j}|| \leq \sqrt{2}$ since $D, D' \in \mathbb{S}_k^n$. □

6 SIMULATION

In this section we empirically evaluate the learning rate of CMF under two settings, one without negative transfer and the other with negative transfer (NT):

NT-Free: in this case, we randomly generate a factor $D \in \mathbb{S}_k^n$ and two loadings $A \in \mathbb{R}^{n \times p}$ and $A' \in \mathbb{R}^{n \times p'}$ to construct matrices $M = DA$ and $M' = D'A'$. By this means, M, M' are guaranteed to share the same factor and negative transfer does not exist.

NT-Likely: in this case, we randomly and independently generate two factors $D, D' \in \mathbb{S}_k^n$ and two loadings A, A' same sized as in the NT-Free case. The two matrices are constructed by $M = DA$ and $M' = D'A'$. By this means, it is likely $[D] \neq [D']$ and thus negative transfer exists.

In evaluation we simply set n, p, p' to 50 and set k to 10. To examine the learning rate, the ratio of observations, denoted by r, is varied from 0.1, 0.3, 0.5, 0.7 to 0.9. At each choice of r, we randomly select $r \cdot np$ number of entries in each matrix to form the observation $\vec{M}_{\vec{\omega}}$. The CMF algorithm in [17] is implemented with no use of prediction link

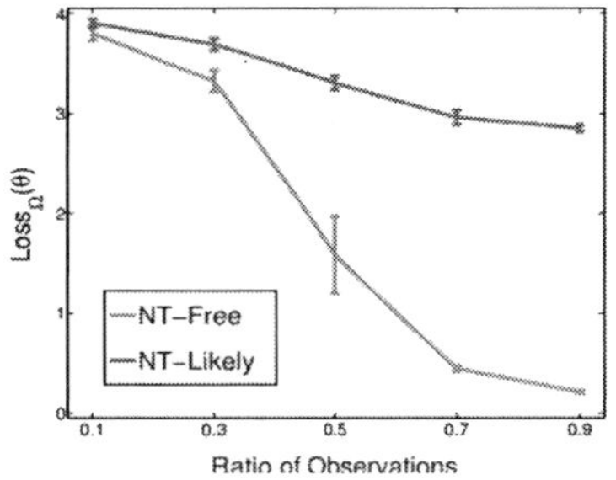

Figure 3: Performance simulation.

function. After performing CMF on $\vec{M}$, the loss function in the proposition is evaluated. Rewrite its notation as

$$Loss_{\omega}(\hat{\theta}) = \frac{1}{2}\left[\rho(\hat{\theta}, \theta(M)) + \rho(\hat{\theta}, \theta(M'))\right]. \tag{58}$$

In addition, fpr each r we repeat the random choice of $\vec{M}_{\vec{\omega}}$ for 10 times and report the averaged loss in Figure 3.

From Figure 3 it is clear that CMF converges much slower when negative transfer exists, as compared with the case when negative transfer does not exist. The bias is also quite obvious. These coincide with our theoretical discoveries.

7 CONCLUSION AND DISCUSSION

This paper presents a first theoretical explanation of negative transfer in collective matrix factorization. We present a min-max lower bound of the CMF estimator and show negative transfer gives rise to an additional bias term that depends only on the structure of the factor space. We further present a finer lower bound and show negative transfer slows the learning rate from $\Omega(|\vec{\omega}|^{-1})$ to $\Omega(|\vec{\omega}|^{-1/d})$, where d is the dimension of Grassmannian containing the subspaces spanned by matrix factors.

A limitation of this study is we assumed full-rank factorization. As suggested by the theory, increasing k may mitigate negative transfer, but clearly at the cost of increasing estimation variance. How these two aspects trade with each other remains unclear, even though our analysis may be naively extended for a larger k' (by simply basing everything on $\mathbb{G}_{k'}^n$). In addition, in reality two matrices may have different ranks and their induced subspaces may partly overlap [10]. This partial overlapping is merely implicitly captured in our analysis (thorough the choice of δ) and stronger results may be obtained by explicitly modeling it.

Acknowledgements

The authors would like to thank the anonymous reviewers for their valuable comments and suggestions to improve the quality of the paper. This work was supported in part by the National Natural Science Foundation of China under Grant No.61232001 and No.61420106009 for Jianxin Wang and NSF grant 1513324 to Jun Huan.

References

[1] Deepak Agarwal, Bee-Chung Chen, and Bo Long. Localized factor models for multi-context recommendation. In *SIGKDD*, 2011.

[2] Guillaume Bouchard, Dawei Yin, and Shengbo Guo. Convex collective matrix factorization. In *AISTATS*, 2013.

[3] Thomas Franz, Antje Schultz, Sergej Sizov, and Steffen Staab. Triplerank: Ranking semantic web data by tensor decomposition. In *International Semantic Web Conference (ISWC)*, 2009.

[4] Gene H Golub and Charles F Van Loan. *Matrix computations*, volume 3. JHU Press, 2012.

[5] Suriya Gunasekar, Makoto Yamada, Dawei Yin, and Yi Chang. Consistent collective matrix completion under joint low rank structure. In *AISTATS*, 2015.

[6] Arjun K Gupta and Daya K Nagar. *Matrix variate distributions*, volume 104. CRC Press, 1999.

[7] David Cohn Thomas Hofmann. The missing link-a probabilistic model of document content and hypertext connectivity. In *NIPS*, 2001.

[8] Alexander Jung, Yonina Eldar, and Norbert Gortz. On the minimax risk of dictionary learning. *Information Theory, IEEE Transactions on*, 62(3):1501–1515, 2016.

[9] Raghunandan H Keshavan, Sewoong Oh, and Andrea Montanari. Matrix completion from a few entries. In *Information Theory, 2009. ISIT 2009. IEEE International Symposium on*, pages 324–328. IEEE, 2009.

[10] Arto Klami, Guillaume Bouchard, Abhishek Tripathi, et al. Group-sparse embeddings in collective matrix factorization. In *Proceedings of International Conference on Learning Representations (ICLR) 2014*, 2014.

[11] Christoph Lippert, Stefan Hagen Weber, Yi Huang, Volker Tresp, Matthias Schubert, and Hans-Peter Kriegel. Relation prediction in multi-relational domains using matrix factorization. In *NIPS Workshop: Structured Input-Structured Output*, 2008.

[12] Bo Long, Zhongfei Mark Zhang, Xiaoyun Wu, and Philip S Yu. Spectral clustering for multi-type relational data. In *ICML*, 2006.

[13] Andreas Maurer and Massimiliano Pontil. K-dimensional coding schemes in hilbert spaces. *Information Theory, IEEE Transactions on*, 56(11):5839–5846, 2010.

[14] Amritanshu Prasad. Counting subspaces of a finite vector space. *Resonance*, 15(11):977–987, 2010.

[15] Ruslan Salakhutdinov and Andriy Mnih. Bayesian probabilistic matrix factorization using Markov chain Monte Carlo. In *Proceedings of the 25th international conference on Machine learning*, pages 880–887. ACM, 2008.

[16] Ajit Singh and Geoffrey Gordon. A Bayesian matrix factorization model for relational data. In *UAI*, 2010.

[17] Ajit P Singh and Geoffrey J Gordon. Relational learning via collective matrix factorization. In *SIGKDD*, 2008.

[18] Ji-Guang Sun. Perturbation of angles between linear subspaces. *Journal Of Computational Mathematics*, 5(1), 1987.

[19] Stanisław Szarek. Nets of Grassmann manifold and orthogonal group. In *Proceedings of Banach Space Workshop, University of Iowa Press*, pages 169–185, 1982.

[20] Vincent Q Vu and Jing Lei. Minimax rates of estimation for sparse PCA in high dimensions. In *International Conference on Artificial Intelligence and Statistics*, pages 1278–1286, 2012.

[21] Kenan Y Yılmaz, Ali T Cemgil, and Umut Simsekli. Generalised coupled tensor factorisation. In *NIPS*, 2011.

[22] Bin Yu. Assouad, Fano, and Le Cam. In *Festschrift for Lucien Le Cam*, pages 423–435. Springer, 1997.

[23] Kai Yu, Shipeng Yu, and Volker Tresp. Multi-label informed latent semantic indexing. In *SIGIR*, 2005.

[24] Yu Zhang, Bin Cao, and Dit-Yan Yeung. Multi-domain collaborative filtering. In *UAI*, 2010.

[25] Ding-Xuan Zhou. Capacity of reproducing kernel spaces in learning theory. *Information Theory, IEEE Transactions on*, 49(7):1743–1752, 2003.

[26] Jiayu Zhou, Fei Wang, Jianying Hu, and Jieping Ye. From micro to macro: Data driven phenotyping by densification of longitudinal electronic medical records. In *SIGKDD*, 2014.

Budgeted Semi-supervised Support Vector Machine

Trung Le*, **Phuong Duong, Mi Dinh**
Faculty of Information Technology
University of Pedagogy, Vietnam
{trunglm, phuongdth, midtt}@hcmup.edu.vn

Tu Dinh Nguyen, Vu Nguyen, Dinh Phung
Centre for Pattern Reccognition and Data Analytics
Deakin University, Australia
{tu.nguyen, v.nguyen, dinh.phung}@deakin.edu.au

Abstract

Due to the prevalence of unlabeled data, semi-supervised learning has drawn significant attention and has been found applicable in many real-world applications. In this paper, we present the so-called Budgeted Semi-supervised Support Vector Machine (BS3VM), a method that leverages the excellent generalization capacity of kernel-based method with the adjacent and distributive information carried in a spectral graph for semi-supervised learning purpose. The fact that the optimization problem of BS3VM can be solved directly in the primal form makes it fast and efficient in memory usage. We validate the proposed method on several benchmark datasets to demonstrate its accuracy and efficiency. The experimental results show that BS3VM can scale up efficiently to the large-scale datasets where it yields a comparable classification accuracy while simultaneously achieving a significant computational speed-up compared with the baselines.

1 Introduction

Supervised learning constitutes one of the most fundamental problems in machine learning. While in no doubt this theory has been applied successfully to many real-world applications, a key limitation of this theory lies in the requirement of annotated labels during training. However, manual labeling process for large-scale data is labor intensive and error-prone. Consequently, the collected datasets frequently consist of a collection of labeled data jointly with a larger collection of unlabeled data. Semi-supervised learning (SSL) involves utilizing the intrinsic information carried in unlabeled data to enhance the generalization capacity of the learning algorithms. During the past decade, SSL has attracted significant attention and has been found applicable in a variety of problems including text categorization [Joachims, 1999], and bioinformatics [Kasabov et al., 2005] to name a few.

A notable approach to semi-supervised learning paradigm is to employ a spectral graph for representing the adjacent and distributive information in data. Several existing works have leveraged on the expressiveness of spectral graphs for SSL, including mincut [Blum et al., 2004], graph random walk [Azran, 2007], manifold regularization [Belkin et al., 2006], and spectral graph [Duong et al., 2015].

Inspired from the seminal work of [Joachims, 1999], a large body of works has attempted to advance kernel methods such as Support Vector Machine (SVM) [Cortes and Vapnik, 1995] within the semi-supervised learning paradigm. The underlying idea is to *solve standard SVM problem while treating the unknown labels as optimization variables* [Chapelle et al., 2008]. This leads to a non-convex optimization problem with a combinatorial explosion of label assignments. A wide spectrum of techniques have been proposed to solve this optimization problem including local combination search [Joachims, 1999], gradient descent [Chapelle and Zien, 2005], convex-concave procedures [Collobert et al., 2006], and deterministic annealing [Sindhwani et al., 2006, Le et al., 2013, Nguyen et al., 2014]. Although these approaches can somehow deal with the combinatorial intractability, their requirement of repeated retraining the model renders them impractical for many real-world problems.

At the intersection between kernel method and the spectral graph theory, several existing works have attempted to incorporate information carried in a spectral graph to build a better kernel function [Smola and Kondor, 2003, Zhu et al., 2004]. These works basically employed the Laplacian matrix induced from the spectral graph to construct the kernel function which can capture the features of ambient space. Manifold regularization framework [Belkin et al., 2006] exploited the geometry property of the probability distribution that generates data and incorporated it as an additional regularization term. Two regularization terms

*This work was carried out when the first author was supported and visiting the Centre for Pattern Recognition and Data Analytics, Deakin University, Australia in 2015.

were introduced to control the complexity of the classifier in the ambient space and to control the complexity measured by the geometry property of the data distribution. However, the computational complexity for manifold regularization approach is cubical in the training size. Hence, other approaches have been proposed to scale it up [Tsang and Kwok, 2006, Melacci and Belkin, 2011]. In particular, the work of [Melacci and Belkin, 2011] (the Laplacian Support Vector Machine or LapSVM) made use of preconditioned conjugate gradient to solve the optimization problem of manifold regularization approach in the primal form. This allows the computational complexity to be scaled up to quadratic. However, this approach was to solve the corresponding optimization problem in the first dual layer instead of in the primal form, hence renders the solution infeasible for online setting. Furthermore, LapSVM requires storing a full Hessian matrix of the training size in the memory, resulting in a quadratic memory complexity.

Recently, stochastic gradient descent (SGD) method [Shalev-Shwartz and Singer, 2007, Kakade and Shalev-Shwartz, 2008, Lacoste-Julien et al., 2012, Rakhlin et al., 2012, Hazan and Kale, 2014] has emerged as a promising framework to scale up fast and online learning algorithms. SGD possesses three key advantages: i) very fast; ii) capacity to run in online mode; and iii) economic memory usage. However, SGD-based methods are vulnerable to the *curse of kernelization* [Wang et al., 2012], that is, the model size linearly grows up with the training size accumulated over time. To bound the model size, budget-based algorithms limit the model size to a predefined budget B. When the model size exceeds the budget, a budget maintenance procedure is invoked to decrease the model size by one. Three widely-used budget maintenance strategies are removal, projection, and merging. In the removal strategy, the most redundant support vector is simply discarded [Crammer et al., 2004, Cavallanti et al., 2007, Wang and Vucetic, 2010, Le et al., 2016]. In the projection strategy, the information of the most redundant support vector is partly preserved through its projection onto the linear span of the remaining support vectors [Wang and Vucetic, 2010, Wang et al., 2012, Le et al., 2016]. The merging strategy first selects two vectors, and then merges them into one before discarding them [Wang et al., 2012].

Leveraging on the advantages of kernel method, spectral graph theory and stochastic gradient descent, we propose in this paper a novel approach to semi-supervised learning, termed as *Budgeted Semi-supervised Support Vector Machine* (BS3VM). To devise BS3VM, we first conjoin the theory of kernel method with the framework of spectral-graph-based semi-supervised learning. This allows us to form a specific optimization problem which involves the core optimization problem of kernel method and simultaneously enables the label propagation. We then apply SGD method to solve the incurred optimization problem directly in the primal form. To avoid the curse of kernelization, we employ two budgets B_l and B_u for the labeled and unlabeled portions. When either the labeled or unlabeled portion in the model exceeds its budget, the corresponding budget maintenance strategy will be invoked accordingly. We also establish a rigorous convergence analysis for BS3VM. The theoretical result shows that there exists a gap between the proposed and optimal solutions. This gap can be explicitly quantified and crucially depends on the budget maintenance rates and the coefficients accompanied with the removed vectors. We further establish the extensive experiments on several real-world datasets. The experimental results show that our proposed BS3VM can offer a comparable predictive performance while simultaneously achieving a significant computational speed-up comparing with the state-of-the-art baselines.

2 Spectral-graph-based Semi-supervised Learning

2.1 Spectral Graph

Spectral graph is a useful tool to capture the geometrical and distributive information carried in data. It is usually an undirected graph whose vertices are data instances. In the context of semi-supervised learning, we are given a training set $X = X_l \cup X_u$ where $X_l = \{(x_i, y_i)\}_{i=1}^{l}$ specifies labeled data and $X_u = \{x_i\}_{i=l+1}^{l+u}$ identifies unlabeled data. We can start constructing the spectral graph $\mathcal{G} = (\mathcal{V}, \mathcal{E})$ with the vertex set $\mathcal{V}$ including all labeled and unlabeled instances (i.e., $\mathcal{V} = \{x_i\}_{i=1}^{l+u}$). An edge $e_{ij} = \overline{x_i x_j} \in \mathcal{E}$ between two vertices x_i, x_j represents the similarity of these two instances. Let μ_{ij} be the weight of this edge. The principle is that if μ_{ij} is sufficiently large then two labels y_i, y_j are expected to be the same. The set of edges $\mathcal{G}$ and its weighs can be established using the following ways:

- *Fully connected graph*: every pair of vertices x_i, x_j is connected by an edge. The edge weight decreases when the distance $\|x_i - x_j\|$ increases. The Gaussian kernel weight function widely used is given by

  $$\mu_{ij} = e^{-\|x_i - x_j\|^2/(2\sigma^2)}$$

  where σ is known as the bandwidth parameter and controls how quickly the weight decreases.

- *k-NN*: each vertex x_i defines its k nearest neighbors (k-NN) and makes an edge with one of its k-NN. The Gaussian kernel weight function can be used for the edge weight. Empirically, k-NN graphs with small k tend to perform well.

- *ε-NN*: we connect x_i and x_j if $\|x_i - x_j\| \leq \varepsilon$. Again the Gaussian kernel weight function can be used to weight the connected edges. In practice, ε-NN graphs are easier to construct than k-NN graphs.

It is noteworthy that when constructing the spectral graph, we avoid connecting the edge of two labeled instances since we do not need to propagate the label between them.

2.2 Label Propagation

After constructing the spectral graph, a semi-supervised learning problem is cast to assign labels to the unlabeled vertices. To this end, we need a mechanism to rationally propagate labels from the labeled vertices to the unlabeled ones. The key idea is that if μ_{ij} is large, then the two labels y_i, y_j are expected to be the same.

To assign labels to the unlabeled instances, it is desirable to learn a map $f : \mathscr{X} \longrightarrow \mathscr{Y}$ where $\mathscr{X}$ and $\mathscr{Y}$ are domains of data and label, respectively such that

- $f(x_i)$ is as closest to its label y_i as possible for all labeled instances x_i $(1 \leq i \leq l)$.
- f should be smooth on the whole graph $\mathscr{G}$, i.e., if x_i is very close to x_j (i.e., x_i, x_j are very similar or μ_{ij} is large), the discrepancy between f_i and f_j (i.e., $|f_i - f_j|$) is small.

Therefore, the following optimization problem is proposed to solve

$$\min_f \left(\infty . \sum_{i=1}^{l} (f_i - y_i)^2 + \sum_{(i,j)\in\mathscr{E}} \mu_{ij} |f_i - f_j| \right) \quad (1)$$

where by convention we define $\infty.0 = 0$ and $f_i = f(x_i)$.

The optimization problem in Eq. (1) peaks its minimum as the first term is exactly 0 and the second term is as smallest as possible. It is therefore rewritten as follows

$$\min_f \left(\sum_{(i,j)\in\mathscr{E}} \mu_{ij} |f_i - f_j| \right) \quad (2)$$
$$\text{s.t.} : \forall_{i=1}^{l} : f_i = y_i$$

To extend the representation ability of the prediction function f, we relax the discrete function f to be a real-valued. The drawback of the relaxation is that in the solution, $f(x)$ is now real-valued, hence does not directly correspond to a label. This can however be addressed by thresholding $f(x)$ at zero to produce discrete label predictions, i.e., if $f(x) \geq 0$, predict $y = 1$, and if $f(x) < 0$, predict $y = -1$.

3 Budgeted Semi-supervised Support Vector Machine

In this section, we present our proposed Budgeted Semi-supervised Support Vector Machine (BS3VM). We start this section with the introduction of the optimization problem of BS3VM. We then propose SGD-based solution for BS3VM with two budgets for the labeled and unlabeled portions, followed by the convergence analysis.

3.1 BS3VM Optimization Problem

Let $\Phi : \mathscr{X} \longrightarrow \mathscr{H}$ be a transformation from the input space $\mathscr{X}$ to a Reproducing Hilbert Kernel Space (RHKS) $\mathscr{H}$. We use the function $f(x) = \mathbf{w}^{\mathsf{T}}\Phi(x) - \rho = \sum_{i=1}^{l+u} \alpha_i K(x_i, x) - \rho$, where $\mathbf{w} = \sum_{i=1}^{l+u} \alpha_i \Phi(x_i)$ and $K(.,.)$ is kernel function, to predict label. Inspired from the optimization problem in Eq. (2), the following optimization problem is proposed

$$\min_{\mathbf{w}} \left(\frac{1}{2} \|\mathbf{w}\|^2 + \frac{C}{l} \sum_{i=1}^{l} \xi_i + \frac{C'}{|\mathscr{E}|} \sum_{(i,j)\in\mathscr{E}} \mu_{ij} |f_i - f_j| \right) \quad (3)$$
$$\text{s.t.} : \forall_{i=1}^{l} : y_i \left(\mathbf{w}^{\mathsf{T}}\Phi(x_i) - \rho \right) \geq 1 - \xi_i$$
$$\forall_{i=1}^{l} : \xi_i \geq 0$$

where $f_i = \mathbf{w}^{\mathsf{T}}\Phi(x_i) - \rho$.

In the optimization formulation of Eq. (3), we minimize $\frac{1}{2}\|\mathbf{w}\|^2$ to maximize the margin for motivating the generalization capacity. At the same time, we minimize $\sum_{(i,j)\in\mathscr{E}} \mu_{ij} |f_i - f_j|$ to make the prediction function smoother on the spectral graph.

We rewrite the optimization problem in Eq. (3) in the primal form as follows[1]

$$\min_{\mathbf{w}} \left(\frac{1}{2} \|\mathbf{w}\|^2 + \frac{C}{l} \sum_{i=1}^{l} l(\mathbf{w}; z_i) + \frac{C'}{|\mathscr{E}|} \sum_{(i,j)\in\mathscr{E}} \mu_{ij} l_1 \left(\mathbf{w}^{\mathsf{T}}\Phi_{ij} \right) \right) \quad (4)$$

where $z_i = (x_i, y_i)$, $l(\mathbf{w}; x, y) = \max\{0, 1 - y\mathbf{w}^{\mathsf{T}}\Phi(x)\}$, $\Phi_{ij} = \Phi(x_i) - \Phi(x_j)$, $l_p(t) = |t|^p$ with $t \in \mathbb{R}$, and $p \geq 1$.

3.2 Budgeted SGD-based Solution for BS3VM

We now present the SGD-based solution for the optimization problem in Eq. (4). To resolve the curse of kernelization, we employ two budgets for the labeled and unlabeled portions whose budget sizes are B_l and B_u, respectively. When either the size of labeled or unlabeled portion in the current model exceeds its budget, the corresponding budget maintenance strategy is executed to maintain the model.

Let us denote the objective function in Eq. (4) by $J(\mathbf{w})$. At the iteration t, we construct the instantaneous objective function $J_t(\mathbf{w})$ which is defined as

$$J_t(\mathbf{w}) = \frac{1}{2} \|\mathbf{w}\|^2 + Cl(\mathbf{w}; x_{i_t}, y_{i_t}) + C' \mu_{u_t v_t} l_1 \left(\mathbf{w}^{\mathsf{T}}\Phi_{u_t v_t} \right)$$

where i_t is uniformly sampled from $\{1, ..., l\} = [l]$ and the edge (u_t, v_t) connected x_{u_t} and x_{v_t} is uniformly sampled from the set of edges $\mathscr{E}$.

[1]We can eliminate the bias ρ by simply adjusting the kernel.

Inspired from the SGD method, we update $\mathbf{w}_t$ as

$$\mathbf{w}_{t+1} = \mathbf{w}_t - \eta_t g_t = \mathbf{w}_t - \frac{1}{t} J^{'}(\mathbf{w}_t) = \frac{t-1}{t}\mathbf{w}_t + \frac{C\alpha_t y_{i_t}\Phi(x_{i_t})}{t} + C^{'}\frac{\mu_{u_t v_t}\beta_t\left(\Phi(x_{u_t}) - \Phi(x_{v_t})\right)}{t} \quad (5)$$

where $\alpha_t = -l_o^{'}(\mathbf{w}_t; x_{i_t}, y_{i_t})$, $\beta_t = -\text{sign}\left(\mathbf{w}_t^{\mathsf{T}}\Phi_{u_t v_t}\right)$, the learning rate $\eta_t = \frac{1}{t}$, and $g_t = J^{'}(\mathbf{w}_t)$.

It is noteworthy that we denote $o = \mathbf{w}^{\mathsf{T}}\Phi(x)$ which implies $l(\mathbf{w}; x, y)$ is now a function of o, and $l_o^{'}(\mathbf{w}; x, y)$ is the derivative of the loss function w.r.t the variable o.

The update formula shown in Eq. (5) is vulnerable to the curse of kernelization, that is, the model size linearly grows with the data size accumulated over time. To address this issue, we propose to use two budgets for the labeled and unlabeled portions whose sizes are B_l and B_u, respectively.

Algorithm 1 Algorithm for training BS3VM.

Input: $B_l, B_u, K(.,.), C, C^{'}, \sigma$

1: $\mathbf{w}_1 = \mathbf{0}$
2: $b_l = 0$
3: $b_u = 0$
4: **for** $t = 1$ **to** T **do**
5: Uniformly sample i_t from $[l]$
6: Uniformly sample the edge (u_t, v_t) from $\mathcal{E}$
7: Update

$$\mathbf{w}_{t+1} = \frac{t-1}{t}\mathbf{w}_t + \frac{C}{t}\alpha_t y_{i_t}\Phi(x_{i_t}) + \frac{C'}{t}\mu_{u_t v_t}\beta_t\left(\Phi(x_{u_t}) - \Phi(x_{v_t})\right)$$

8: $b_l = b_l + 1 + \mathbb{I}_{u_t \le l} + \mathbb{I}_{v_t \le l}$
9: $b_u = b_u + \mathbb{I}_{u_t > l} + \mathbb{I}_{v_t > l}$
10: **if** $b_l > B_l$ **then**
11: $BM(\mathbf{w}_{t+1}, 'l')$ *// labeled portion*
12: $b_l = B_l$
13: **end if**
14: **if** $b_u > B_u$ **then**
15: $BM(\mathbf{w}_{t+1}, 'u')$ *// unlabeled portion*
16: $b_u = B_u$
17: **end if**
18: **end for**

Output: $\overline{\mathbf{w}}_T = \frac{1}{T}\sum_{t=1}^{T}\mathbf{w}_t$ or $\mathbf{w}_{T+1}$

Algorithm 1 presents the pseudocode of BS3VM. The model of BS3VM is represented through the labeled and unlabeled portions whose current sizes are b_l and b_u, respectively. When either b_l or b_u exceeds its budget, a budget maintenance procedure is triggered to maintain the model size (cf. lines 11 and 15 in Algorithm 1). We have two kinds of budget maintenance (BM) which involve the labeled and unlabeled portions, respectively. To differentiate these two kinds of BM, we employ the second argument in BM procedure wherein $'l'$ involves BM for the labeled portion and $'u'$ involves BM for the unlabeled portion. In addition, two options (i.e., $'l'$ or $'u'$) involve the same functional activity. The only difference is that they refer to either labeled or unlabeled portions. In addition, we utilize the fully connected spectral graph wherein the edge weights are computed on the fly as necessary.

3.3 Budget Maintenance Strategy

In this section, we present the BM strategies used in this paper which are removal and projection. The original projection strategy can partly preserve the information of the removed vectors and hence, usually offers better predictive performance than removal strategy. However, it requires a costly computation of the inverse of a matrix whose dimension is either B_l or B_u. To resolve this computational burden, we propose two special projection strategies which are nearest-neighbor projection (NNP) and random-neighbor projection (RNP). At the outset of this section, we define the index sets of the labeled and unlabeled portions at the iteration t as $I_t^l \subset [l]$[2] and $I_t^u \subset [l+1 : l+u]$[3], respectively. Hence, the current model $\mathbf{w}_t$ can be written as

$$\mathbf{w}_t = \sum_{i \in I_t^l} \delta_i \Phi(x_i) + \sum_{i \in I_t^u} \delta_i \Phi(x_i)$$

Both the removal and projection strategies involve the vectors whose coefficients have smallest absolute values in the labeled and unlabeled portions. We now define

$$l_t = \underset{i \in I_t^l}{\text{argmin}}\ |\delta_i| \text{ and } u_t = \underset{i \in I_t^u}{\text{argmin}}\ |\delta_i|$$

3.3.1 Removal

In the removal strategy, we simply remove $\Phi(x_{l_t})$ or $\Phi(x_{u_t})$. This strategy is efficient, but the information of the removed vectors are completely vanished.

3.3.2 Projection

To keep the information of the removed vector, the original projection strategy performs a projection of this vector onto the linear span of the remaining vectors. Although this full projection can efficiently preserve the information of the removed vector, it requires a costly computation of the inverse of B_l (or B_u) by B_l (or B_u) matrix which costs cubically over the budget sizes. Furthermore, decreasing the budget sizes to reduce the computational cost may significantly compromise the learning performance. To speed up the computation and omit the computational dependence of the projection on the budget sizes, we propose two variations of the projection which are nearest-neighbor projec-

[2] We denote $[l] = \{1, 2, \ldots, l\}$.
[3] We denote $[l+1 : l+u] = \{l+1, l+2, \ldots, l+u\}$.

tion (NNP) and random-neighbor projection (RNP) strategies. For brevity in presentation, we denote

$$x_{r_t} = \begin{cases} x_{l_t} & \text{for the option 'l' of BM} \\ x_{u_t} & \text{for the option 'u' of BM} \end{cases}$$

Nearest-Neighbor Projection (NNP). To efficiently preserve the information of x_{r_t}, before removing it, we find k-NN of x_{r_t} and do projection of x_{r_t} onto the linear span of this set. Our intuition is that if the vector x falls into the k-NN of x_{r_t} then x is close to x_{r_t}; consequently the induced dot product $K(x, x_{r_t}) = \Phi(x)^{\mathsf{T}} \Phi(x_{r_t})$ is high and hence, $\Phi(x)$ can largely keep the information of $\Phi(x_{r_t})$.

Random-Neighbor Projection (RNP). To further speed up the NNP strategy, we propose random-neighbor projection (NNP) wherein we first randomly choose k vectors from the support set and then project $\Phi(x_{r_t})$ onto the linear span of these vectors to preserve its information.

3.4 Convergence Analysis

In what follows we present the convergence analysis for BS3VM. Given an instance x, in a BM procedure, we replace this instance by its approximation $A(x)$ which incurs the difference vector $D(x) = \Phi(x) - A(x)$. In particular, with the removal strategy, $A(x) = 0, \forall x$, with the full projection strategy, $A(x) = \mathbb{P}_L(x), \forall x$ where $\mathbb{P}_L(x)$ specifies the linear span of the remaining vectors in the support set, and with NNP or RNP strategy, $A(x) = \mathbb{P}_L(x), \forall x$ where $\mathbb{P}_L(x)$ specifies the linear span of k corresponding vectors. We further define $\mathbf{w}^* = \underset{\mathbf{w}}{\operatorname{argmin}}\, J(\mathbf{w})$. For simplification, we assume that $\|\Phi(x)\| = K(x,x)^{1/2} = 1, \forall x$.

Let us denote two Bernoulli random variables which indicate whether the budget maintenances for the labeled portion (i.e., the option 'l') and for the unlabeled portion (i.e., the option 'u') are performed by Z_t^l, Z_t^u. The update rule is

$$\mathbf{w}_{t+1} = \mathbf{w}_t - \eta_t g_t - Z_t^l \delta_{l_t} D(x_{l_t}) - Z_t^u \delta_{u_t} D(x_{u_t}) \quad (6)$$

It is noteworthy that the update rule in Eq. (6) covers all BM strategies. In addition, our convergence analysis can be applied to all aforementioned BM strategies but for comprehensibility, we present the theoretical results for the removal strategy.

Lemma 1 establishes an upper bound on $\|\mathbf{w}_t\|$, followed by Lemma 2 which establishes an upper bound on $\|g_t\|$.

Lemma 1. *The following statement holds*

$$\|\mathbf{w}_t\| \le C + 2C', \forall t$$

Lemma 2. *The following statement holds*

$$\|g_t\| \le G = 2\left(C + 2C'\right), \forall t$$

In Algorithm 1, the labeled-vertex sampling (cf. line 5) updates the coefficient of one labeled support vector while the edge sampling (cf. line 6) updates two coefficients of two support vectors. To proceed the convergence analysis, we assume that before removed, the coefficient of the labeled vector $\Phi(x_{l_t})$ is updated at most m times via the labeled-vertex sampling and n times via the edge sampling and the coefficient of the unlabeled vector $\Phi(x_{u_t})$ is updated at most p times via the edge sampling. Particularly, in the context of online learning, the labeled vector $\Phi(x_{l_t})$ might be sampled from a continuous distribution and so might be the edge. It follows that $m = n = p = 1$ and the assumption is naturally valid.

Lemma 3. *Given two positive integer numbers m, n, assume that before removed, the coefficient of $\Phi(x_{l_t})$ is updated at most m times via the labeled-vertex sampling and n times via the edge sampling. We then have*

$$|\delta_{l_t}| \le \left(mC + nC'\right)/t, \forall t$$

Lemma 4. *Given a positive integer number p, assume that before removed, the coefficient of $\Phi(x_{u_t})$ is updated at most p times via the edge sampling. We then have*

$$|\delta_{u_t}| \le pC'/t, \forall t$$

Lemma 5 establishes an upper bound on $\|h_t\|$, followed by Lemma 6 establishing an upper bound on $\mathbb{E}\left[\|\mathbf{w}_t - \mathbf{w}^*\|^2\right]^{1/2}$.

Lemma 5. *We define $\rho_i = \frac{\delta_i}{\eta_t} = t\delta_i$ and $h_t = Z_t^l \rho_{l_t} D(x_{l_t}) + Z_t^u \rho_{u_t} D(x_{u_t})$. Then we have*

$$\|h_t\| \le H = mC + (n+p)C', \forall t$$

Lemma 6. *The following statement holds*

$$\mathbb{E}\left[\|\mathbf{w}_t - \mathbf{w}^*\|^2\right]^{1/2} \le W = H + \sqrt{H^2 + (G+H)^2}, \forall t$$

We can now state Theorem 7 which establishes an upper bound on the regret. This theorem also reveals that there exists a gap between the rendered and optimal solutions. This gap crucially depends on the budget maintenance rates for the labeled and unlabeled portions.

Theorem 7. *Let us consider the running of Algorithm 1. The following statement holds*

$$\begin{aligned}
\mathbb{E}[J(\overline{\mathbf{w}}_t)] - J(\mathbf{w}^*) &\le \frac{1}{T}\sum_{t=1}^{T} \mathbb{E}[J(\mathbf{w}_t)] - J(\mathbf{w}^*) \\
&\le \frac{(G+H)^2(\log T + 1)}{2T} \\
&\quad + \frac{W}{T}\sum_{t=1}^{T} \mathbb{P}\left(Z_t^l = 1\right)\mathbb{E}\left[\rho_{l_t}^2\right]^{1/2} \\
&\quad + \frac{W}{T}\sum_{t=1}^{T} \mathbb{P}(Z_t^u = 1)\,\mathbb{E}\left[\rho_{u_t}^2\right]^{1/2}
\end{aligned}$$

where $\rho_{l_t} = \delta_{l_t}/\eta_t$ *and* $\rho_{u_t} = \delta_{u_t}/\eta_t$.

Remark 8. The theoretical result gained in Theorem 7 also encompasses the standard analysis. In particular, if the BM procedures never happen (i.e., $\mathbb{P}\left(Z_t^l = 1\right) = \mathbb{P}\left(Z_t^u = 1\right) = 0, \forall t$), we achieve the logarithm regret bound $\frac{(G+H)^2(\log T+1)}{T}$. Furthermore, to minimize the gap, we should choose to remove the vectors with the smallest absolute coefficients (since $\rho_{l_t} = \frac{\delta_{l_t}}{\eta_t}$ and $\rho_{u_t} = \frac{\delta_{u_t}}{\eta_t}$).

4 Experiments

We establish quantitative experiments to investigate the influence of the budget sizes (i.e., B_l and B_u) to the accuracy and training time, and to prove the accuracy and efficiency of our proposed BS3VM on several benchmark datasets. The data statistics is given in Table 1. To simulate the semi-supervised learning context, we randomly remove 80% and 90% data labels in each dataset. We create three versions of our approach: BS3VM with the removal strategy (BS3VM-R), BS3VM with the nearest-neighbor projection strategy (BS3VM-NNP), and BS3VM with the random-neighbor projection strategy (BS3VM-RNP).

Baselines. In order to investigate the efficiency and accuracy of BS3VM, we compare with the following baselines:

- LapSVM [Melacci and Belkin, 2011]: Laplacian Support Vector Machine is a state-of-the-art method in semi-supervised classification based on manifold regularization framework. It can reduce the computational complexity from $O\left(n^3\right)$ to $O\left(n^2\right)$ where n is the training size using the preconditioned conjugate gradient and an early stopping strategy.
- CCCP-TSVM [Collobert et al., 2006]: A kernel-based semi-supervised method was proposed to solve the optimization problem using convex-concave procedures.

All codes of the baselines are achieved from the corresponding authors. All compared methods run on a Windows machine with the configuration of 24-vcore CPU Xeon 3.47 GHz and 96GB RAM.

Hyperparameter Setting. The standard RBF kernel, given by $K\left(x,x'\right) = e^{-\gamma\left\|x-x'\right\|^2}$, is used in the experiments. For LapSVM, we use the parameter settings proposed in [Melacci and Belkin, 2011], wherein the parameters γ_A and γ_I are searched in the range $\left\{10^{-6}, 10^{-4}, 10^{-2}, 10^{-1}, 1, 10, 100\right\}$. In all experiments with LapSVM, we utilize the preconditioned conjugate gradient version, which is more suitable for the LapSVM optimization problem [Melacci and Belkin, 2011]. For CCCP-TSVM, we use the setting CCCP-TSVM$|_{UC*=LC}^{s=0}$. The trade-off parameter C is tuned in the range $\left\{2^{-5}, 2^{-3}, \ldots, 2^3, 2^5\right\}$ and the width of kernel δ is varied in the range $\left\{2^{-5}, 2^{-3}, \ldots, 2^3, 2^5\right\}$. Regarding our proposed BS3VM, the bandwidth σ of Gaussian kernel weight function is set as to $\frac{1}{2\sigma^2} = \gamma$, and the second trade-off parameter C' is set to be equal the first trade-off parameter C. We employ the standard training-testing split with 90% of data for training and 10% of data for testing. We run 5-fold cross-validation, and then select the parameter set that yields the highest classification accuracy. We set the number of iterations T in BS3VM to $\lceil 0.01 \times (l+u) \rceil$ for the large-scale datasets such as MUSHROOMS, W5A, W8A, COD-RNA, and COVTYPE, and to $\lceil 0.1 \times (l+u) \rceil$ for the remaining datasets. Each experiment is carried out five times to compute the average of the reported measures.

Dataset	Dimension	Size
G50C	50	551
COIL20	1,014	145
USPST	256	601
AUSTRALIAN	14	690
A1A	123	1,605
MUSHROOM	112	8,124
SVMGUIDE3	21	1,243
SVMGUIDE2	20	391
W5A	300	9,888
W8A	300	49,749
COR-RNA	8	59,535
COVTYPE	54	100,945

Table 1: The statistics of the experimental datasets.

Experimental Results. The experimental results are reported in Tables 2 and 3. For readability, we emphasize in boldface the highest accuracy and in italics the shortest training time. Regarding the classification accuracy, our proposed BS3VMs are comparable with other baselines and CCCP-TSVM is slightly better than others. However, our BS3VMs scale impressively with the large-scale datasets whilst CCCP-TSVM scale unsatisfactorily. The version BS3VM-R wins the shortest training time over all experimental datasets, except for the dataset W5A under 80%-unlabeled setting. Besides, two other versions BS3VM-NNP and BS3VM-RNP also scale efficiently with the training size, and their training times only slightly exceed those of BS3VM-R on all datasets. This implies that the simplified projection strategies (i.e., NNP and RNP) do not incur a significant computational burden. Interestingly, BS3VM-R always offers comparable accuracies comparing with BS3VM-NNP and BS3VM-RNP, which indicates that the information loss occurring in the removal of vector in BS3VM-R is tolerant. It is noteworthy that although we only set small budgets for all datasets (i.e., 50 or 100), the classification accuracies attained by three versions on all datasets are still remarkable. This fact confirms the effectiveness of our proposed budget maintenance strategies in eliminating the redundant vectors and in keeping the core vectors which sufficiently characterize the training set.

Datasets [B]	BS3VM-R		BS3VM-NNP		BS3VM-RNP		LapSVM		CCCP	
	Acc	Time	Acc	Time	Acc	Time	Acc	Time	Acc	Time
G50C [50]	95.45	*0.131*	95.45	0.14	95.45	0.133	96.2	0.29	**98.18**	0.141
COIL20 [50]	**100**	*0.083*	**100**	0.094	**100**	0.088	**100**	0.39	98.1	1.078
USPST [50]	99.17	*0.091*	99.17	0.217	99.17	0.134	99.2	0.28	**99.58**	0.61
AUSTRALIAN [50]	**88.41**	0.041	87.68	0.098	86.96	0.085	85.9	0.94	81.88	*0.002*
A1A [50]	**80.1**	*0.146*	78.19	0.192	79.44	0.167	**80.1**	0.21	79.75	0.953
MUSHROOM [50]	96.12	*0.506*	96.86	0.874	97.05	0.566	98.8	5.25	**100**	28.078
SVMGUIDE3 [50]	78.23	*0.056*	77.02	0.289	78.23	0.116	75.8	0.33	**81.45**	1.421
SVMGUIDE2 [50]	76.12	*0.02*	79.1	0.03	86.57	0.024	85.1	0.41	**90.27**	0.078
W5A [50]	96.46	1.732	96.97	2.471	97.27	2.348	97	*1.18*	**98.33**	146.28
W8A [100]	97.02	*18*	97.02	18.15	96.8	18.1	**97.4**	26.15	97.1	1,380.16
COR-RNA [100]	85.53	*0.545*	85.95	0.937	86.53	0.836	85.7	13.14	**88.47**	3,900.43
COVTYPE [100]	**87.07**	*8.273*	84.56	8.931	84.12	8.51	81.8	19.75	85.91	5,958.07

Table 2: Cross-validation accuracies (in %) and training times (in second) on the experimental datasets when 80% of data labels are removed. We set the same value for B_l and B_u which is the notation [B] next to the dataset name.

Datasets [B]	BS3VM-R		BS3VM-NNP		BS3VM-RNP		LapSVM		CCCP	
	Acc	Time	Acc	Time	Acc	Time	Acc	Time	Acc	Time
G50C [50]	**95.45**	*0.129*	94.55	0.128	**95.45**	0.131	94.5	0.29	94.55	0.509
COIL20 [50]	92.86	*0.011*	96.43	0.025	**100**	0.015	**100**	0.16	**100**	0.366
USPST [50]	**100**	*0.012*	**100**	0.032	**100**	0.017	99.6	0.38	**100**	2.17
AUSTRALIAN [50]	86.23	*0.004*	85.51	0.013	85.51	0.009	86.2	0.32	**89.85**	0.031
A1A [50]	82.24	*0.018*	81.26	0.035	81.62	0.024	81.6	0.24	**82.37**	0.047
MUSHROOM [50]	91.38	*0.09*	91.02	0.141	94.29	0.105	97.5	0.334	**99.96**	8.82
SVMGUIDE3 [50]	77.82	*0.005*	77.42	0.017	77.02	0.005	77.9	0.28	**83.37**	0.054
SVMGUIDE2 [50]	82.09	*0.004*	79.1	0.007	79.1	0.005	80.6	0.38	**85.12**	0.02
W5A [50]	97.17	*0.329*	97.27	0.412	91.17	0.323	**97.5**	0.521	97.39	7.41
W8A [100]	97.03	*3.215*	96.93	3.982	97.01	3.79	**97.32**	9.15	97.18	379.06
COR-RNA [100]	83.33	*0.519*	82.73	0.82	**92.92**	0.682	86.1	11.42	89.74	326.72
COVTYPE [100]	80.98	*4.628*	86.89	5.142	**86.38**	4.897	80.2	34.02	85.75	1,275.22

Table 3: Cross-validation accuracies (in %) and training times (in second) on the experimental datasets when 90% of data labels are removed. We set the same value for B_l and B_u which is the notation [B] next to the dataset name.

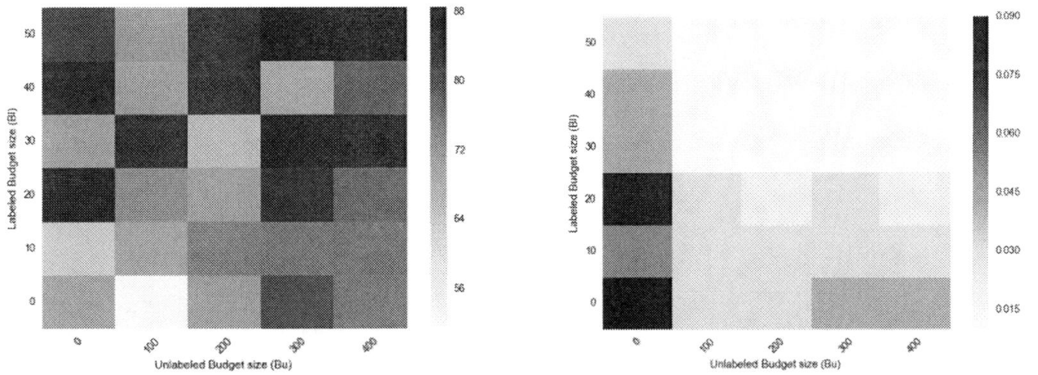

(a) The variation of the classification accuracy.

(b) The variation of the training time.

Figure 1: The variations of the classification accuracy and training time on the dataset AUSTRALIAN when two budget sizes B_l and B_u are varied.

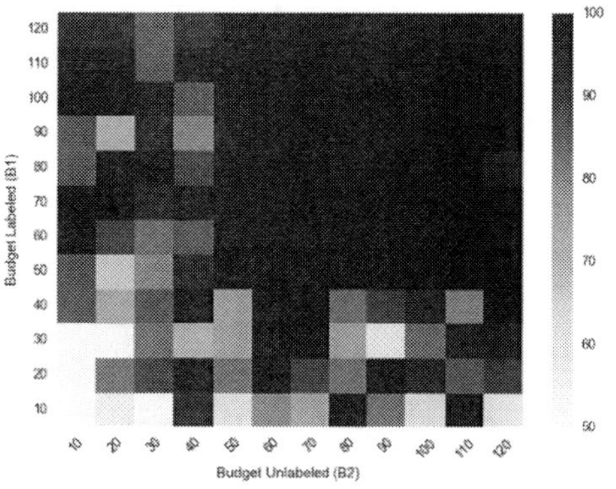

(a) The variation of the classification accuracy.

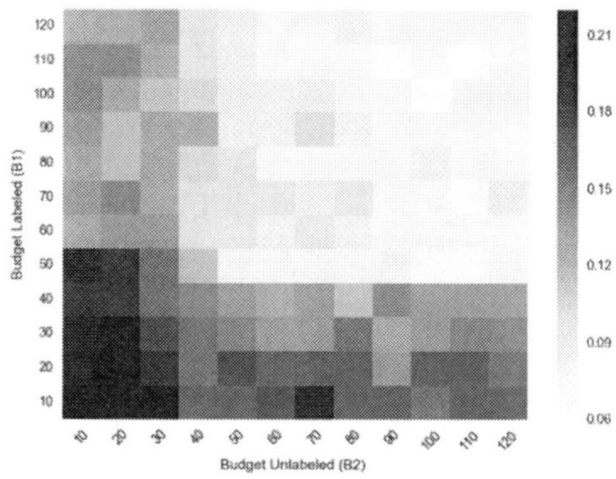

(b) The variation of the training time.

Figure 2: The variations of the classification accuracy and training time on the dataset COIL20 when two budget sizes B_l and B_u are varied.

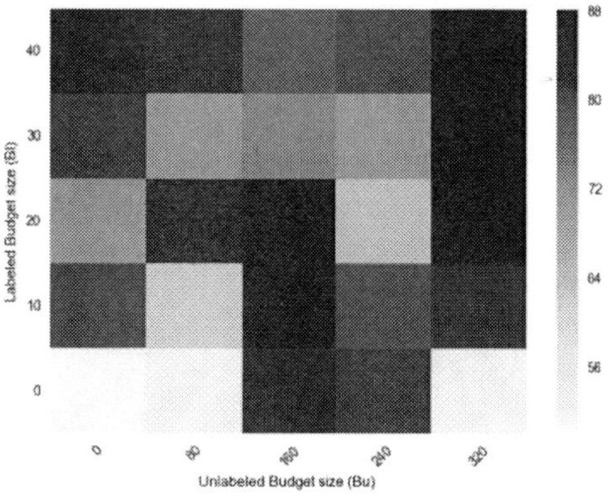

(a) The variation of the classification accuracy.

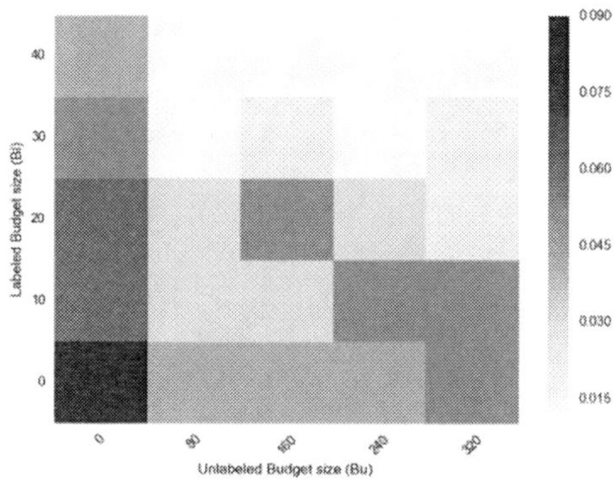

(b) The variation of the training time.

Figure 3: The variations of the classification accuracy and training time on the dataset G50C when two budget sizes B_l and B_u are varied.

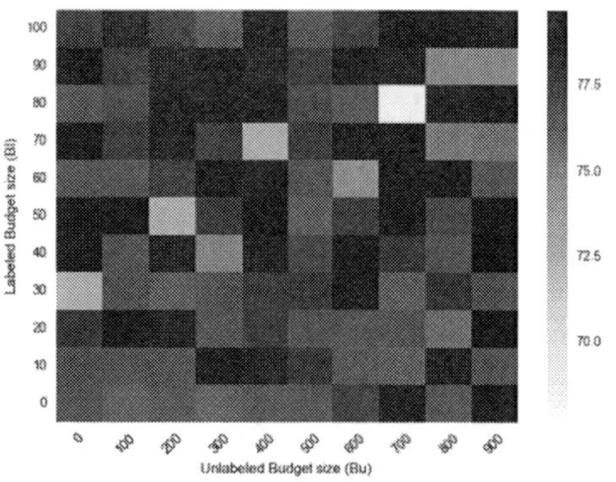

(a) The variation of the classification accuracy.

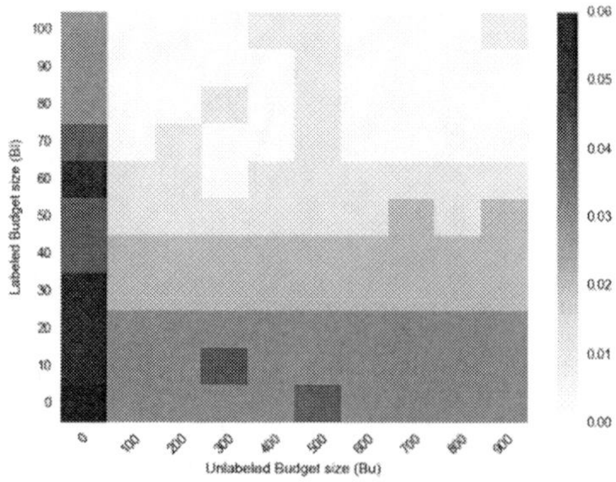

(b) The variation of the training time.

Figure 4: The variations of the classification accuracy and training time on the dataset SVMGUIDE3 when two budget sizes B_l and B_u are varied.

Influence of Budget Sizes to Learning Performance. We investigate the influence of the budget sizes (i.e., B_l and B_u) to the learning performance. We choose to conduct a simulation study on 4 datasets AUSTRALIAN, COIL20, G50C, and SVMGUIDE3. For each dataset, we simultaneously vary the labeled budget size B_l and the unlabeled budget size B_u to measure the classification accuracy and the training time. We visualize the classification accuracies and the training times using heat maps shown in Figures 1, 2, 3, and 4. It can be observed that when increasing the budget sizes (i.e., B_l and B_u), the classification accuracy tends to increase and the training time tends to decrease or fluctuate. The reason is that large budget sizes enrich the expressiveness of the model, and hence boost the accuracy. In the meanwhile, when increasing the budget sizes, there appears a trade-off between the computational cost in each iteration and the budget maintenance rate which fluctuates the training time depending on which factor dominates. In practice, using these heat maps, one can conveniently find the optimal pair (B_l, B_u) that balances the classification accuracy and the training time for example $(50, 300)$ for AUSTRALIAN, $(50, 50)$ for COIL20, $(40, 320)$ for G50C, and $(60, 300)$ for SVMGUIDE3. Another observation is that the increases of B_l and B_u fairly equally affect the classification accuracy while increasing B_u strongly affects to the training time than increasing B_l. Finally, the training time becomes worst if we set one budget size to a small value and gradually increase another.

5 Conclusion

In this paper, we have proposed Budgeted Semi-supervised Support Vector Machine (BS3VM) for semi-supervised learning purpose. We first leverage the theory of kernel method with the framework of spectral-graph-based semi-supervised learning to form a specific optimization problem, which involves the core optimization problem of kernel method for learning on labeled data and simultaneously allows the label propagation. We then apply the SGD method to directly solve such optimization problem in the primal form. To resolve the curse of kernelization, we employ two budgets for the labeled and unlabeled portions in the model. We further establish a rigorous convergence analysis for BS3VM. The theoretical results reveal that there exists a gap between the rendered and optimal solutions. This gap crucially depends on the budget maintenance rates and the coefficients accompanied with the removed vectors. Finally, we conduct extensive experiments on several benchmark datasets. The experimental results show that BS3VM yields a comparable classification accuracy while simultaneously achieving a significant computational speed-up comparing with the state-of-the-art baselines.

References

A. Azran. The rendezvous algorithm: Multiclass semi-supervised learning with markov random walks. In *Proceedings of the 24th International Conference on Machine Learning*, ICML 2007, pages 49–56, 2007.

M. Belkin, P. Niyogi, and V. Sindhwani. Manifold regularization: A geometric framework for learning from labeled and unlabeled examples. *J. Mach. Learn. Res.*, 7: 2399–2434, December 2006.

A. Blum, J. D. Lafferty, M. R. Rwebangira, and R. Reddy. Semi-supervised learning using randomized mincuts. In *ICML*, volume 69, 2004.

G. Cavallanti, N. Cesa-Bianchi, and C. Gentile. Tracking the best hyperplane with a simple budget perceptron. *Machine Learning*, 69(2-3):143–167, 2007.

O. Chapelle and A. Zien. Semi-supervised classification by low density separation, 2005.

O. Chapelle, V. Sindhwani, and S.S. Keerthi. Optimization techniques for semi-supervised support vector machines. *Journal of Machine Learning Research*, 9:203–233, June 2008.

R. Collobert, F. Sinz, J. Weston, L. Bottou, and T. Joachims. Large scale transductive svms. *Journal of Machine Learning Research*, 2006.

C. Cortes and V. Vapnik. Support-vector networks. In *Machine Learning*, pages 273–297, 1995.

K. Crammer, J. Kandola, and Y. Singer. Online classification on a budget. In *Advances in Neural Information Processing Systems 16*. MIT Press, 2004.

P. Duong, V. Nguyen, M. Dinh, T. Le, D. Tran, and W. Ma. Graph-based semi-supervised support vector data description for novelty detection. In *2015 International Joint Conference on Neural Networks (IJCNN)*, pages 1–6, July 2015.

E. Hazan and S. Kale. Beyond the regret minimization barrier: Optimal algorithms for stochastic strongly-convex optimization. *J. Mach. Learn. Res.*, 15(1):2489–2512, January 2014. ISSN 1532-4435.

T. Joachims. Transductive inference for text classification using support vector machines. In *International Conference on Machine Learning (ICML)*, pages 200–209, Bled, Slowenien, 1999.

S. Kakade and Shalev-Shwartz. Mind the duality gap: Logarithmic regret algorithms for online optimization. In *NIPS*, 2008.

N. Kasabov, D. Zhang, and P.S. Pang. Incremental learning in autonomous systems: evolving connectionist systems for on-line image and speech recognition. In *Advanced Robotics and its Social Impacts, 2005. IEEE Workshop on*, pages 120 – 125, june 2005.

S. Lacoste-Julien, M. W. Schmidt, and F. Bach. A simpler approach to obtaining an o(1/t) convergence rate for the projected stochastic subgradient method. *CoRR*, 2012.

T. Le, D. Tran, T. Tran, K. Nguyen, and W. Ma. Fuzzy entropy semi-supervised support vector data description. In *2013 International Joint Conference on Neural Networks (IJCNN)*, pages 1–5, Aug 2013.

T. Le, V. Nguyen, D. T. Nguyen, and D. Phung. Nonparametric budgeted stochastic gradient descent. In *Proceedings of the 19th International Conference on Artificial Intelligence and Statistics*, pages 654–662, 2016.

S. Melacci and M. Belkin. Laplacian support vector machines trained in the primal. *J. Mach. Learn. Res.*, 12: 1149–1184, jul 2011.

V. Nguyen, T. Le, T. Pham, M. Dinh, and T. H. Le. Kernel-based semi-supervised learning for novelty detection. In *2014 International Joint Conference on Neural Networks (IJCNN)*, pages 4129–4136, July 2014.

A. Rakhlin, O. Shamir, and K. Sridharan. Making gradient descent optimal for strongly convex stochastic optimization. In *ICML 2012*, pages 449–456, 2012.

S. Shalev-Shwartz and Y. Singer. Logarithmic regret algorithms for strongly convex repeated games. In *The Hebrew University*, 2007.

V. Sindhwani, S.S. Keerthi, and O. Chapelle. Deterministic annealing for semi-supervised kernel machines. In *Proceedings of the 23rd international conference on Machine learning*, ICML 2006, pages 841–848, 2006.

A. J. Smola and I. R. Kondor. Kernels and regularization on graphs. In *Proceedings of the Annual Conference on Computational Learning Theory*, 2003.

I. W. Tsang and J. T. Kwok. Large-scale sparsified manifold regularization. pages 1401–1408. MIT Press, 2006.

Z. Wang and S. Vucetic. Online passive-aggressive algorithms on a budget. In *AISTATS*, volume 9, pages 908–915, 2010.

Z. Wang, K. Crammer, and S. Vucetic. Breaking the curse of kernelization: Budgeted stochastic gradient descent for large-scale svm training. *Journal of Machine Learning Research*, 13(1):3103–3131, 2012.

X. Zhu, J. S. Kandola, Z. Ghahramani, and J. D. Lafferty. Nonparametric transforms of graph kernels for semi-supervised learning. In *NIPS 2004*, pages 1641–1648, 2004.

A Characterization of Markov Equivalence Classes of Relational Causal Models under Path Semantics

Sanghack Lee and **Vasant Honavar**
Artificial Intelligence Research Laboratory
College of Information Sciences and Technology
The Pennsylvania State University, University Park, PA 16802
{sxl439, vhonavar}@ist.psu.edu

Abstract

Relational Causal Models (RCM) generalize Causal Bayesian Networks so as to extend causal discovery to relational domains. We provide a novel and elegant characterization of the Markov equivalence of RCMs under *path semantics*. We introduce a novel representation of unshielded triples that allows us to efficiently determine whether an RCM is Markov equivalent to another. Under path semantics, we provide a sound and complete algorithm for recovering the structure of an RCM from conditional independence queries. Our analysis also suggests ways to improve the orientation recall of algorithms for learning the structure of RCM under *bridge burning semantics* as well.

1 INTRODUCTION

The discovery of causal relationships from observational and, when available, experimental data is a central problem in artificial intelligence. Of particular interest is causal discovery in real-world settings consist of inherently interrelated entities and the resulting data exhibit a rich *relational* (Chen, 1976) structure. The past three decades have seen major advances in causal discovery (Pearl, 2000; Spirtes et al., 2000). However, the vast majority of this work has focused on Causal Bayesian Networks (CBN), directed graphical models that model causal relationships between a set of random variables of interest. Such models lack the expressive power to model causal relationships in relational domains.

Maier et al. (2010) showed that the Directed Acyclic Probabilistic Entity-Relationship model (DAPER) (Heckerman et al., 2007) which generalizes both Probabilistic Relational Models (PRM) (Friedman et al., 1999) and plate models (Buntine, 1994) is sufficient to represent causality in relational domains. Maier et al. (2010) proposed Relational PC (RPC), a relational extension of the PC algorithm (Spirtes et al., 2000) for learning the structure of Relational Causal Model (RCM), which is a particular class of DAPER, under *bridge burning semantics* (BBS). However, RPC is not complete, and is prone to erroneous orientation of edges (Maier et al., 2013a). To overcome the limitations of RPC, Maier et al. (2013a) introduced the Relational Causal Discovery (RCD) algorithm which reduces learning the structure of an RCM to learning the structure of Abstract Ground Graph (AGG, Maier et al., 2013b), a directed acyclic graph that is intended to correctly abstract the *ground instances* of the RCM, and Lee and Honavar (2016) proposed RCD-Light, a more efficient alternative to RCD. However, all of existing algorithms for learning RCM are provably *not complete* (Lee and Honavar, 2016).

Against this background, we characterize the *Markov equivalence* of RCMs, an essential step in specifying a provably complete constraint-based algorithms for learning the structure of RCM under *path semantics*, a more elegant alternative to BBS. The key idea is to show that two RCMs are Markov equivalent *if and only if* their corresponding sets of ground instances are Markov equivalent. We introduce *canonical unshielded triples,* a novel graphical construct that can be used to test the Markov equivalence of two RCMs. We provide an efficient algorithm to enumerate a subset of canonical unshielded triples of an RCM that suffice for testing whether an RCM is Markov equivalent to another. Finally, we provide an algorithm to construct a *completed partially-directed RCM*, a unique compact representation of the Markov equivalence class of an RCM.

The main contributions of this paper are: (i) a novel characterization of Markov equivalence of RCMs, using a novel representation of the relational counterparts of unshielded triples and efficient identification thereof; (ii) revelation of problematic behaviors of BBS (Maier et al., 2013a,b; Lee and Honavar, 2015, 2016), and proposal of a viable alternative, namely, *path semantics*, which is more intuitive and retains the desirable properties of BBS while avoiding its drawbacks; and (iii) the first sound and complete algorithm for learning the structure of an RCM under path semantics.

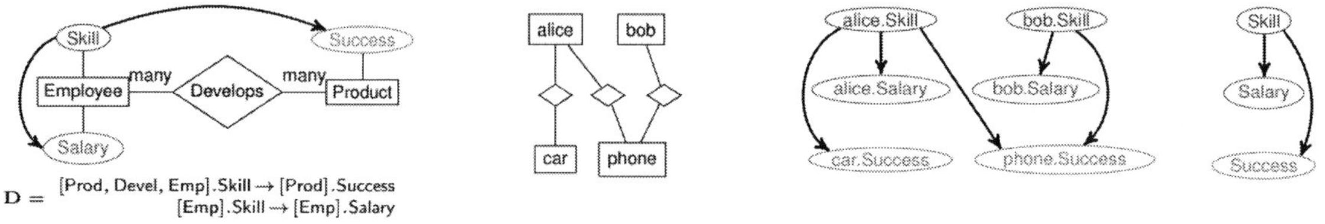

(a) RCM $\mathcal{M} = (\mathcal{S}, \mathbf{D})$ (b) relational skeleton $\sigma \in \Sigma_{\mathcal{S}}$ (c) ground graph $\mathcal{G}_{\sigma}^{\mathcal{M}}$ (d) CDG $\mathcal{G}_{\mathcal{A}}^{\mathcal{M}}$

Figure 1: An example of an RCM drawn over its underlying relational schema together with a relational skeleton, ground graph, and class dependency graph (both bridge burning and path semantics yield the same ground graph.)

2 PRELIMINARIES

We follow the notational conventions for Causal Bayesian Networks (Pearl, 2000; Spirtes et al., 2000) and the literature on RCM (Maier et al., 2013a; Lee and Honavar, 2015). A graph is specified by a set of vertices and the edges that connect them. An edge may be directed ($\rightarrow$) or undirected ($-$), but not both. A partially directed acyclic graph (PDAG) includes undirected as well as directed edges but no directed cycles. A directed acyclic graph (DAG) is a PDAG with no undirected edges. Let $\mathcal{G}$ be a PDAG and X be a vertex in $\mathcal{G}$, i.e., $X \in \mathbb{V}(\mathcal{G})$. Then, parents of X, $pa(\mathcal{G}, X)$, are vertices that have a direct edge towards X. Children (ch) are analogously defined. Neighbors (ne) of X are vertices connected to X via an undirected edge while adjacencies (adj) of X are those connected to X via an edge either directed or undirected. A *walk* on a graph is an ordered sequence of vertices where consecutive vertices in the sequence are adjacent to each other in the graph, and a *path* is a walk in which every vertex is distinct.

Relational Domain A relational domain comprises of entities that are interdependent through relationships. The specification of such relational domain is called a relational schema (schema for short). A schema, denoted by $\mathcal{S}$, is a tuple of entity classes, relationship classes, attribute classes, and cardinality constraints, denoted by $\mathcal{E}$, $\mathcal{R}$, $\mathcal{A}$, and $card$, respectively. For example, *Employee* and *Product* are entity classes in a business domain (Figure 1). *Develops* is a relationship class between them. *Employee* has *Salary* as an attribute class. Each employee may develop *multiple* products; and each product may be developed by *multiple* employees. We collectively call $\mathcal{E}$ and $\mathcal{R}$ item classes. Every item class is associated with a set of attribute classes. We denote $\mathcal{A}(I)$ a set of attribute classes associate with an item class I. A relationship class consists of participating entity classes. We denote $E \in R$ if E is a participating entity class of a relationship class R. For simplicity, we drop role indicators (as in other literature on RCM), which allow participation of an entity class in a relationship class in multiple ways. A cardinality constraint defines how many relationships an entity can participate in. Following RCM literature, $card$ is a partial function from $\mathcal{R} \times \mathcal{E}$ to $\{one, many\}$.

A relational skeleton (skeleton for short) is a particular realization of a schema, which is an undirected graph where vertices are items (i.e., instances of item classes). An edge is defined between a relationship and an entity if the entity participates in the relationship. We denote a skeleton by σ, a member of all possible skeletons $\Sigma_{\mathcal{S}}$. We denote by $\sigma(I)$ the set of items of item class I.

2.1 RELATIONAL CAUSAL MODEL

A relational causal model (RCM) (Maier et al., 2010, 2013a) consists of a set of cause-effect relationships and parameters where the cause and the effect are related in the given relational schema. For example, "the success of a product depends on the skills of employees who develop the product" is encoded as a *relational dependency*, "[Product, Develops, Employee].Skill→[Product].Success". We elaborate on each component of an RCM more precisely in what follows.

A *relational path* is an alternating sequence of entity and relationship classes. The relational path corresponds to a *walk* (with some restrictions) in the given schema where item classes are vertices and the participation of an entity class to a relationship class is an undirected edge between them. A relational path is similar to a slot chain in PRM (Friedman et al., 1999) and a first-order constraint in DAPER (Heckerman et al., 2007). The first and the last item class of a relational path is called *base* and *terminal* item class, respectively. The path explains the relation of the terminal item class from the *perspective* of the base item class. Hence the base item class is also called the *perspective*. A relational path is *canonical* if it is of unit length. A *relational variable* is a pair of a relational path and an attribute class, which belongs to the terminal item class of the path. For example, a relational variable $P.X$ consists of a path P and an attribute class X where X is an attribute class associated with the terminal item class of P. Then, an RCM $\mathcal{M} = (\mathcal{S}, \mathbf{D}, \mathbf{\Theta})$ is a set of relational dependencies $\mathbf{D}$ along with parameters $\mathbf{\Theta}$ given a schema $\mathcal{S}$. A relational dependency $P.Y \rightarrow Q.X$ consists of two relational variables as an effect and its cause where the effect relational variable is canonical, $Q = [I]$ where $X \in \mathcal{A}(I)$, and the base of P is I. To emphasize the use of canonical relational

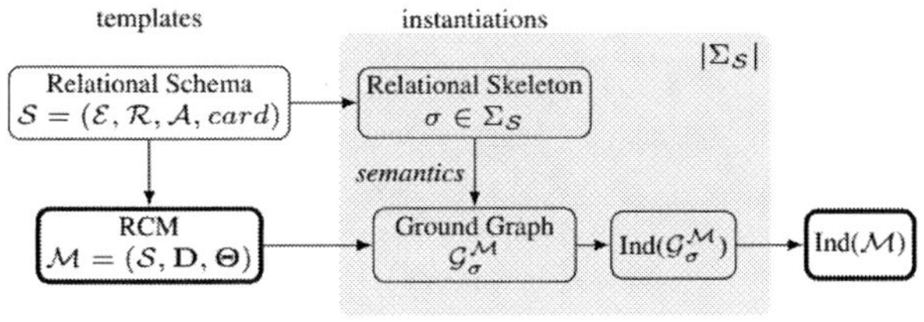

Figure 2: Schematic showing a relational schema, an RCM, and their respective instantiations, i.e., relational skeleton, and ground graphs and the independence relations of the RCM entailed from the independence relations admitted by the ground graphs.

variable, we denote a canonical relational variable with an attribute class X by $\mathcal{V}_X$.

An RCM is said to be acyclic if its *class dependency graph* $\mathcal{G}_\mathcal{A}^\mathcal{M} \triangleq (\mathcal{A}, \{Y \to X \mid P.Y \to \mathcal{V}_X \in \mathbf{D}\})$ is a DAG (see Figure 1(d)). Hence, $\mathcal{A}$ is a partially-ordered set where we denote $Z \prec_\mathcal{A} X$ if there exists a directed path from Z to X in $\mathcal{G}_\mathcal{A}^\mathcal{M}$. This implies that dependencies of the same pair of attribute classes must have the same orientation (i.e., it is impossible to have both $P.Y \to \mathcal{V}_X$ and $Q.X \to \mathcal{V}_Y$).

An RCM (or its partially directed variant) is *not* a traditional graphical model defined over relational variables: edges (i.e., relational dependencies) are only well-defined between a pair of relational variables where one of them is canonical. Hence, graphical relation (i.e., adj, ch, pa, and ne) is well-defined only if its argument is a canonical relational variable. For example, if $P.Y \to \mathcal{V}_X \in \mathcal{M}$, then $pa(\mathcal{M}, \mathcal{V}_X) = \{P.Y\}$ but $ch(\mathcal{M}, P.Y)$ is undefined if P is not canonical.

Relational d-separation An RCM defines a set of dependencies at the schema level. Given a skeleton σ, the RCM $\mathcal{M}$ is realized as a ground graph $\mathcal{G}_\sigma^\mathcal{M}$ (see Figure 1(c)), which is a DAG where vertices are attributes of items in the skeleton (e.g., $i.X$ for $X \in \mathcal{A}(I)$ of an item $i \in \sigma(I)$) and each directed edge is interpreted as a direct cause (e.g., $j.Y \to i.X$). If the RCM is an actual model of given relational data, then the ground graph will correspond to the underlying causal process that governs the attribute values of the items in the skeleton (i.e., relational data). An edge $j.Y \to i.X$ exists if there exists a dependency $P.Y \to \mathcal{V}_X \in \mathbf{D}$ such that j is *reachable* (which we will formally define in Section 3) from i along P in the skeleton. We denote by $P|_i^\sigma$ a *terminal set*, a set of reachable items from i along P in σ, which is determined according to the chosen semantics, e.g., BBS (Maier et al., 2013a; Maier, 2014). For simplicity, we drop σ if it is either unnecessary or can be inferred without ambiguity.

In RCM, we are especially interested in conditional independence between relational variables. We might ask, for example, is the success of a product independent of its developers' salaries given their skills? This conditional independence query can be represented as [Product].Success $\perp\!\!\!\perp$ [Product, Develops, Employee].Salary | [Product, Develops, Employee].Skill. If true, this implies that each product's success is independent of its developers' salary given their skills (in every company). Formally, an independence query is of the form $U \perp\!\!\!\perp V \mid \mathbf{W}$ where $\{U, V\} \cup \mathbf{W}$ is a set of relational variables of the same perspective, say $B \in \mathcal{E} \cup \mathcal{R}$. Then, the query is equivalent to checking

$$\forall_{\sigma \in \Sigma_S} \forall_{i \in \sigma(B)}\ U|_i^\sigma \perp\!\!\!\perp V|_i^\sigma \mid \mathbf{W}|_i^\sigma, \qquad (1)$$

in all of the instantiations of the RCM (Maier et al., 2013b) (see Figure 2). In other words, the existence of a relational skeleton $\sigma \in \Sigma_S$ and a base item $i \in \sigma(B)$ such that $U|_i^\sigma \not\perp\!\!\!\perp V|_i^\sigma \mid \mathbf{W}|_i^\sigma$ in a ground graph $\mathcal{G}_\sigma^\mathcal{M}$ is the necessary and sufficient condition for $U \not\perp\!\!\!\perp V \mid \mathbf{W}$.

3 RCM SEMANTICS

We proceed to describe two alternative semantics for interpreting relational paths, and hence translating relational dependencies of an RCM into causal relationships on attributes of items of a skeleton. Let P be a relational path of n item classes. We denote the length of P by $|P|$, the reverse of the path P by $\tilde{P}$, the ℓth item class of P by P^ℓ, and the subpath of P from ℓ to m (inclusive) by $P^{\ell:m}$. We might omit the beginning or ending index if the subpath is from the beginning (i.e., prefix) or to the end of the path (i.e., suffix). i.e., $P^{:m} = P^{1:m}$ and $P^{\ell:} = P^{\ell:n}$.

We first introduce *path semantics*, where the term path exactly means what path is defined in graph theory. Let $i \overset{P,\sigma}{\rightsquigarrow} j$ denote the fact that items i and j are connected by a path of items $\mathbf{p}$ from i to j in the given skeleton σ, where the item class of ℓth item of $\mathbf{p}$ is the ℓth item class of P for $1 \leq \ell \leq |P|$. Then, under path semantics, the terminal set $P|_i^\sigma$ is simply defined as,

$$P|_i^\sigma \triangleq \{j \mid i \overset{P,\sigma}{\rightsquigarrow} j\}.$$

Bridge burning semantics (BBS) (Maier et al., 2013b; Maier, 2014) computes $P|_i^\sigma$ as the set of leaves of the tree obtained by traversing the given skeleton σ along P in breadth-first order starting at i. Formally, BBS defines $P|_i^\sigma$ iteratively as $P^{:1}|_i^\sigma \triangleq \{i\}$ and

$$P^{:m}|_i^\sigma \triangleq \{k \in \sigma(P^m) \cap ne(\sigma, j) \mid j \in P^{:m-1}|_i^\sigma\} \setminus \bigcup_{\ell < m} P^{:\ell}|_i^\sigma$$

The choice of BBS has following implications, which are not fully considered in the existing RCM literature. First, given a more complex relational skeleton, BBS may yield, counterintuitively, a sparser ground graph because, as we can clearly see in the definition, if P' is a proper prefix of P and $j \in P'|_i$, then $j \notin P|_i$ even though there exists a path of items from i to j along P. Compare Figure 3(f) with 3(c). The addition of two edges e_1–r_1'–e_2'

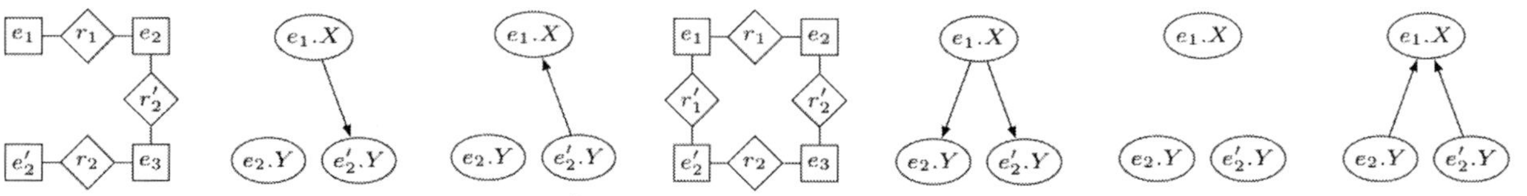

(a) skeleton σ (b) $\mathcal{G}_{\sigma}^{(\mathcal{S},\{D\})}$ (c) $\mathcal{G}_{\sigma}^{(\mathcal{S},\{\tilde{D}\})}$ (d) skeleton σ' (e) $\mathcal{G}_{\sigma'}^{(\mathcal{S},\{D\})}$ (f) $\mathcal{G}_{\sigma'}^{(\mathcal{S},\{\tilde{D}\})}$ BBS (g) $\mathcal{G}_{\sigma'}^{(\mathcal{S},\{\tilde{D}\})}$ PS

Figure 3: Comparison of ground graphs under bridge burning semantics and path semantics. Let $\mathcal{S}$ be a schema with $\mathcal{E} = \{E_1, E_2, E_3\}$, $X \in \mathcal{A}(E_1)$, $Y \in \mathcal{A}(E_2)$, and $\mathcal{R} = \{R_1, R_2\}$ where $E_1, E_2 \in R_1$ and $E_2, E_3 \in R_2$ with cardinality greater than 1. $D = [E_2, R_2, E_3, R_2, E_2, R_1, E_1].X \to [E_2].Y$. Both semantics yield the same ground graphs (b), (c), and (e) for the relational skeleton σ. However, the two semantics yield different ground graphs (f,), (g) for $\mathcal{M} = (\mathcal{S}, \{\tilde{D}\})$ for relational skeleton σ'.

in σ' compared to σ make $e_2' \in [E_1, R_1, E_2]|_{e_1}^{\sigma'}$ and, hence, $e_2' \notin [E_1, R_1, E_2, R_2, E_3, R_2, E_2]|_{e_1}^{\sigma'}$. Second, the two RCMs that differ only with respect to the directionality of their dependencies may have different (undirected) adjacencies in their ground graphs (compare Figure 3(f) with 3(e)). This is because $j \in P|_i$ does not entail $i \in \tilde{P}|_j$ under BBS since the fact that Q is a prefix of P does not necessarily imply that $\tilde{Q}$ is a prefix of $\tilde{P}$.

In this paper, we consider RCMs under path semantics, which is an elegant and more intuitive alternative to BBS. Further, path semantics shares the desirable properties of BBS (Maier, 2014): both semantics do not permit revisiting the base item. However, path semantics does not suffer from the counter-intuitive consequences of BBS and easier to analyze as we will see in the rest of paper.

4 MARKOV EQUIVALENCE OF RCMS UNDER PATH SEMANTICS

Recall that, in general, there can be Markov equivalent CBNs that represent a given set of independence relations (Pearl, 2000). Because RCMs are essentially relational counterparts of CBNs, it follows that there can be multiple RCMs that encode a given set of independence relations in relational domains.

Definition 1 (Markov Equivalence of RCMs). Two RCMs are *Markov equivalent* if they entail the same set of relational *d*-separation conditions.

The previous attempts to characterize the Markov equivalence of RCMs under BBS (Maier et al., 2013a; Marazopoulou et al., 2015) had relied on analyses of the Abstract Ground Graph (AGG) representation of an RCM. However, Lee and Honavar (2015) have shown that AGGs cannot faithfully represent the independence relations encoded by RCMs under BBS. Consequently, the RCD algorithm (Maier et al., 2013a), which relies on AGGs to learn the structure of an RCM under BBS is *not* complete Lee and Honavar (2016). Hence, we proceed to characterize the Markov equivalence of RCMs under path semantics.

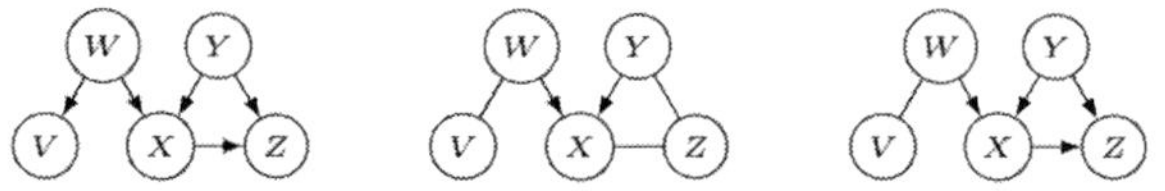

(a) (b) (c)

Figure 4: An example of a DAG, its pattern, and its CPDAG where (W, X, Y) is an unshielded collider and (V, W, X) and (W, X, Z) are unshielded non-colliders.

Recall that the relational d-separation $U \perp\!\!\!\perp V \mid \mathbf{W}$ in an RCM is equivalent to $U|_i \perp\!\!\!\perp V|_i \mid \mathbf{W}|_i$ for every base item i in *every* ground graph of the RCM. Hence, a sufficient condition for two RCMs to be Markov equivalent is that, for *every* relational skeleton, the corresponding sets of ground graphs of the two RCMs be Markov equivalent:

$$\forall_{\sigma \in \Sigma_{\mathcal{S}}} [\mathcal{G}_{\sigma}^{\mathcal{M}}] = [\mathcal{G}_{\sigma}^{\mathcal{M}'}] \Rightarrow [\mathcal{M}] = [\mathcal{M}'] \qquad (2)$$

where $[\mathcal{M}]$ and $[\mathcal{G}]$ denote the Markov equivalence class of an RCM and a DAG $\mathcal{G}$, respectively. In Section 4.1, we will demonstrate that the converse of Equation 2 holds as well, thereby establishing a necessary and sufficient condition for two RCMs to be Markov equivalent.

Markov equivalence of DAG First, we recall the characterization of Markov equivalence of DAG (see Figure 4, Verma and Pearl, 1990; Andersson et al., 1997). Let $\mathcal{G}$ be a DAG with random variables $\mathbf{V}$ as vertices. Let X, Y, and Z be in $\mathbf{V}$. A triple (X, Y, Z) is an *unshielded triple* if both X and Z are adjacent to Y but X and Z are not adjacent. It is an *unshielded collider* if they are oriented as $X \to Y \leftarrow Z$ in the given DAG. Let $\mathcal{G}'$ be a DAG that share the same vertices of $\mathcal{G}$. Then, $\mathcal{G}$ and $\mathcal{G}'$ are said to be *Markov equivalent* if they entail identical independence relations among $\mathbf{V}$. Two DAGs are Markov equivalent if and only if their *patterns* are the same (Verma and Pearl, 1990). The *pattern* of a DAG is a PDAG where all *unshielded colliders* are oriented and the only oriented edges are unshielded colliders. A Markov equivalence class is represented by a *completed PDAG* (CPDAG or *essential graph*), a PDAG in which a directed edge $X \to Y$ implies that every DAG in the class shares the edge $X \to Y$ (*compelled edge*) while an undi-

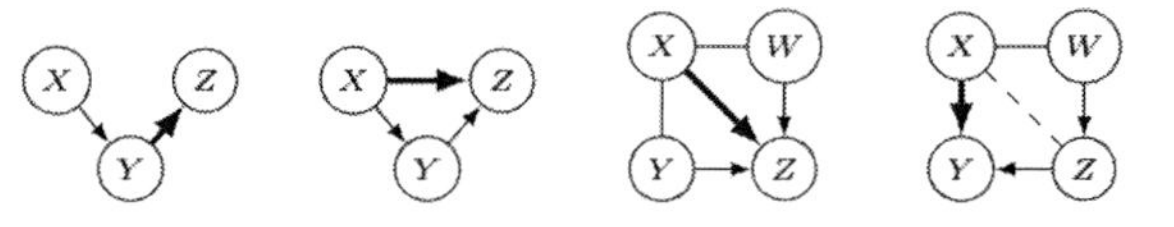

(a) R1 (b) R2 (c) R3 (d) R4

Figure 5: Orientation rules to construct a CPDAG from a pattern and background knowledge where the orientation of a thick edge is determined by the other given edges. The edge between X and Z in R4 might be undirected or directed in any direction.

rected edge $X - Y$ implies that there exist two DAGs in the class where one has $X \to Y$ and the other has $X \leftarrow Y$ (*reversible edge*).

There are at least two systematic methods to discover the CPDAG from a pattern: The first method uses orientation rules (Meek, 1995) (Figure 5). The three rules (R1–R3) are sufficient to discover CPDAG from a pattern, and an additional rule R4 can deal with background knowledge (i.e., known orientations other than those implied by the pattern), if available. The second method exploits an algorithm for *extensibility* of a PDAG (Dor and Tarsi, 1992), which examines whether there exists a DAG which is a *consistent extension* of the PDAG, that is, the DAG shares the same sets of adjacencies, unshielded colliders, and oriented edges (if any) of the PDAG. We proceed to characterize Markov equivalence of RCM by generalizing the notions of unshielded triples, pattern, and CPDAG from the setting of CBNs to the (relational) setting of RCMs.

4.1 THE PATTERN OF AN RCM

We consider unshielded triples in ground graphs of an RCM and relate them to the RCM under path semantics. Let $i.X$, $j.Y$, and $k.Z$ be three different vertices in the ground graph $\mathcal{G}_\sigma^{\mathcal{M}}$ of an RCM $\mathcal{M}$ for an arbitrary skeleton $\sigma \in \Sigma_\mathcal{S}$. Then, $(i.X, j.Y, k.Z)$ is an unshielded triple in $\mathcal{G}_\sigma^{\mathcal{M}}$ only if $P.Y \in adj\,(\mathcal{M}, \mathcal{V}_X)$ and $Q.Z \in adj\,(\mathcal{M}, \mathcal{V}_Y)$ where $j \in P|_i^\sigma$ and $k \in Q|_j^\sigma$ for $i.X$ and $k.Z$ to be connected to $j.Y$. Furthermore, $R.Z$ must not be in $adj\,(\mathcal{M}, \mathcal{V}_X)$ for every path R such that $k \in R|_i^\sigma$ for $i.X$ and $k.Z$ to be disconnected in $\mathcal{G}_\sigma^{\mathcal{M}}$. Then, we define a *canonical unshielded triple* as follows:

Definition 2 (Canonical Unshielded Triple). Let $\mathcal{M}$ be an RCM defined on a relational schema $\mathcal{S}$. Suppose $(i.X, j.Y, k.Z)$ is an unshielded triple (UT) in the ground graph $\mathcal{G}_\sigma^{\mathcal{M}}$ for some $\sigma \in \Sigma_\mathcal{S}$. There must be two (not necessarily distinct) dependencies $P.Y - \mathcal{V}_X$ and $Q.Z - \mathcal{V}_Y$ of $\mathcal{M}$ (ignoring directions) such that $j \in P|_i^\sigma$ and $k \in Q|_j^\sigma$. Then, we say that $(\mathcal{V}_X, \mathbf{P}.Y, R.Z)$ is a *canonical unshielded triple* (CUT) of $\mathcal{M}$ for every $R \in \{T \mid k \in T|_i^\sigma\}$ where $\mathbf{P} = \{T \mid j \in T|_i^\sigma\}$.

Since whenever $(i.X, j.Y, k.Z)$ is a UT in $\mathcal{G}_\sigma^{\mathcal{M}}$, so is $(k.Z, j.Y, i.X)$, it follows that whenever $(\mathcal{V}_X, \mathbf{P}.Y, R.Z)$ is a CUT of $\mathcal{M}$, there exists a CUT $(\mathcal{V}_Z, \mathbf{Q}.Y, \tilde{R}.X)$ for some relational paths $\mathbf{Q}$.

Theorem 3. *Two RCMs defined over the same relational schema are Markov equivalent if and only if their ground graphs are Markov equivalent for every relational skeleton of the relational schema:*

$$[\mathcal{M}] = [\mathcal{M}'] \Leftrightarrow \forall_{\sigma \in \Sigma_\mathcal{S}} [\mathcal{G}_\sigma^{\mathcal{M}}] = [\mathcal{G}_\sigma^{\mathcal{M}'}].$$

Proof. (If part) By the definition of relational d-separation. (Only if part) Let $[\mathcal{G}_\sigma^{\mathcal{M}}] \neq [\mathcal{G}_\sigma^{\mathcal{M}'}]$ for some $\sigma \in \Sigma_\mathcal{S}$. Then, the two ground graphs $\mathcal{G}_\sigma^{\mathcal{M}}$and $\mathcal{G}_\sigma^{\mathcal{M}'}$differ either in their (i) adjacencies or in their (ii) unshielded colliders.
Case (i): There must exist a relational dependency $P.Y \to \mathcal{V}_X$ in $\mathcal{M}$ while both $P.Y \to \mathcal{V}_X$ and $\tilde{P}.X \to \mathcal{V}_Y$ are not in $\mathcal{M}'$ (or vice versa). Then, either $P.Y \perp\!\!\!\perp \mathcal{V}_X \mid pa(\mathcal{M}', \mathcal{V}_X)$ or $\tilde{P}.X \perp\!\!\!\perp \mathcal{V}_Y \mid pa(\mathcal{M}', \mathcal{V}_Y)$ hold in $\mathcal{M}'$ by causal Markov condition. However, both tests will be false in $\mathcal{M}$ since there exists a relational skeleton σ yielding $i.X \to j.Y$ in $\mathcal{G}_\sigma^{\mathcal{M}}$ where $\{P\} = \{T \mid i \in T|_j^\sigma\}$ while $P.Y \notin pa(\mathcal{M}', \mathcal{V}_X)$ and $\tilde{P}.X \notin pa(\mathcal{M}', \mathcal{V}_Y)$.
Case (ii): There must exist a CUT $(\mathcal{V}_X, \mathbf{P}.Y, R.Z)$ corresponding to an unshielded triple $(i.X, j.Y, k.Z)$, which is an unshielded collider in $\mathcal{G}_\sigma^{\mathcal{M}}$ and unshielded non-collider in $\mathcal{G}_\sigma^{\mathcal{M}'}$ (or vice versa). Because $R.Z \notin adj\,(\mathcal{M}, \mathcal{V}_X)$ for every $R \in \{T \mid k \in T|_i^\sigma\}$, there must exist a separating set $\mathbf{S} \subseteq adj(\mathcal{M}, \mathcal{V}_X)$ such that $\mathcal{V}_X \perp\!\!\!\perp R.Z \mid \mathbf{S}$ in $\mathcal{M}$ assuming $X \not\to_\mathcal{A} Z$ without loss of generality.[1] By the definition of relational d-separation, $\mathbf{S}$ must be disjoint with $\mathbf{P}.Y$. However, in $\mathcal{M}'$, $\mathcal{V}_X \not\perp\!\!\!\perp R.Z \mid \mathbf{S}$ since $\mathbf{S}$ is disjoint from $\mathbf{P}.Y$, and $i.X$ and $k.Z$ are d-connected with $j.Y$ unblocked. □

We derive the definition of the *pattern* of an RCM taking into account the fact that acyclicity of an RCM is defined at an attribute class level.

Definition 4 (Pattern of RCM). Let $\mathcal{M} = (\mathcal{S}, \mathbf{D})$ be an RCM and $\mathfrak{C}^{\mathcal{M}}$ be all canonical unshielded colliders of $\mathcal{M}$. We define the set of *attribute class level colliders* as

$$\mathfrak{C}_\mathcal{A}^{\mathcal{M}} \triangleq \{(X, Y, Z) \mid (\mathcal{V}_X, \mathbf{P}.Y, R.Z) \in \mathfrak{C}^{\mathcal{M}}\}.$$

Then, the *pattern* of $\mathcal{M}$, $pattern(\mathcal{M})$, is a partially-directed RCM $(\mathcal{S}, \mathbf{D}' \cup \mathbf{D}'')$ where $\mathbf{D}' = \{Q.X \to \mathcal{V}_Y \in \mathbf{D} \mid (X, Y, Z) \in \mathfrak{C}_\mathcal{A}^{\mathcal{M}}\}$ and $\mathbf{D}'' = \{P.Y - \mathcal{V}_X \mid P.Y \to \mathcal{V}_X \in \mathbf{D} \setminus \mathbf{D}'\}$.

Lemma 5. $[\mathcal{M}] = [\mathcal{M}'] \Leftrightarrow pattern(\mathcal{M}) = pattern(\mathcal{M}')$.

Proof. The proof follows from Theorem 3. □

[1] Otherwise, the proof can be obtained using $(\mathcal{V}_Z, \tilde{\mathbf{Q}}.Y, \tilde{R}.X)$.

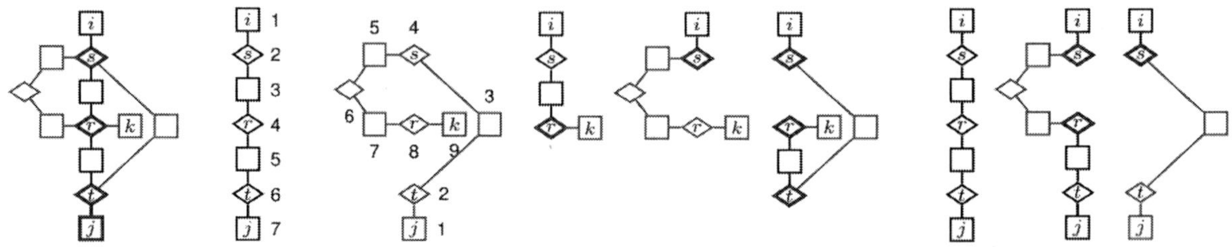

(a) σ (b) $\mathbf{p}$ (c) $\mathbf{q}$ (d) paths of items for R_r, R_s, and R_t (e) paths of items for $\mathbf{P}$

Figure 6: Illustration of key concepts used to characterize CUTs for a hypothetical RCM $\mathcal{M}$ with $P.Y \in adj(\mathcal{M}, \mathcal{V}_X)$ and $Q.Z \in adj(\mathcal{M}, \mathcal{V}_Y)$ yielding a UT $(i.X, j.Y, k.Z)$ in $\mathcal{G}_\sigma^{\mathcal{M}}$ where P and Q correspond to item classes of $\mathbf{p}$ and $\mathbf{q}$, respectively.

Unlike in the case of DAGs, it is not immediately obvious how to identify all CUTs of an RCM. Fortunately, to discover the pattern of an RCM, it suffices to identify only one CUT from the set of CUTs for each triple of attribute classes if exists.

4.1.1 Characterization of Canonical Unshielded Triples for Pattern of RCM

How can we identify a subset of CUTs of an RCM that is sufficient to identify the pattern of the RCM? One approach is to enumerate all relational skeletons, identify the UTs in the corresponding ground graphs, and the corresponding CUTs. Because such an approach is not computationally tractable, we consider the following alternative: enumerate the skeletons that are just large enough to include a UT in the corresponding ground graph, and the corresponding CUT. We first investigate conditions under which a relational skeleton includes a UT in the corresponding ground graph, and then provide a characterization of CUTs in terms of such UTs, which leads to an efficient CUT enumeration algorithm whose time complexity is polynomial in the number of dependencies, $|\mathbf{D}|$, and $\max\{|P| \mid P.X \to \mathcal{V}_Y \in \mathbf{D}\}$ (the maximum length of dependencies, which is typically bounded by a small constant).

Relational Skeleton of an Unshielded Triple Each shielded or unshielded triple of item-attributes associates with two dependencies non-exclusively. Consider a triple $(i.X, j.Y, k.Z)$ in some skeleton $\sigma \in \Sigma_S$. Let $P.Y \in adj(\mathcal{M}, \mathcal{V}_X)$ and $Q.Z \in adj(\mathcal{M}, \mathcal{V}_Y)$ (the two are the same if $Q.Z = \tilde{P}.X$) that admit the triple, that is, $j \in P|_i^\sigma$ and $k \in Q|_j^\sigma$. Let $\mathbf{p} = [i, \ldots, j]$ and $\mathbf{q} = [j, \ldots, k]$ be paths of items from i to j along P and j to k along Q, respectively. Since $\mathbf{p}$ and $\mathbf{q}$ must share at least one item j, there must be a non-empty set of items shared by $\mathbf{p}$ and $\mathbf{q}$. We define *anchors*, denoted by $\mathbf{J}_{\mathbf{p},\mathbf{q}}$, to be the set of pairs of indices of items shared by $\mathbf{p}$ and $\mathbf{q}$:

$$\mathbf{J}_{\mathbf{p},\mathbf{q}} \triangleq \{(a, b) \mid \mathbf{p}_a = \mathbf{q}_b\}.$$

For example, $\mathbf{J}_{\mathbf{p},\mathbf{q}} = \{(2,4), (4,8), (6,2), (7,1)\}$ in Figure 6. Anchors permit us to construct a small relational skeleton made of items for P and Q. Thus, we can enumerate the candidate anchors and verify if they are indeed anchors by constructing a relational skeleton that conforms to the equalities implied by $\mathbf{J}_{\mathbf{p},\mathbf{q}}$.

Characteristic Anchors We consider anchors that allow us to efficiently enumerate a subset of CUTs that suffice to identify the pattern of an RCM $\mathcal{M}$. We identify three special anchors (a_r, b_r), (a_s, b_s), and (a_t, b_t) among the anchors in $\mathbf{J}_{\mathbf{p},\mathbf{q}}$, and derive three relational paths R_r, R_s, and R_t from the special anchors.

Consider the item j that is the last shared item of $\mathbf{p}$ and the first shared item of $\mathbf{q}$such that $(|P|, 1) \in \mathbf{J}_{\mathbf{p},\mathbf{q}}$. Since $\mathbf{J}_{\mathbf{p},\mathbf{q}}$ is not empty, there must be a last shared item for $\mathbf{q}$ at the following anchor:

$$(a_r, b_r) \triangleq \arg\max_{(a,b) \in \mathbf{J}_{\mathbf{p},\mathbf{q}}} b.$$

No item in $\mathbf{p}_{:a_r}$ and $\mathbf{q}_{b_r:}$ is shared other than the item at the anchor (a_r, b_r) and, hence, there exists a path of items from i to k. We define $R_r \triangleq P^{:a_r} \bowtie Q^{b_r:}$ where the symbol "$\bowtie$" is a path concatenation operator (e.g., $[E_1, R_1, E_2] \bowtie [E_2, R_2] = [E_1, R_1, E_2, R_2]$). We can infer that $R_r.Z \notin adj(\mathcal{M}, \mathcal{V}_X)$ since $i.X$ and $k.Z$ are disconnected. Next, we define an anchor for the first shared item of $\mathbf{p}$:

$$(a_s, b_s) \triangleq \arg\min_{(a,b) \in \mathbf{J}_{\mathbf{p},\mathbf{q}}} a.$$

We characterize the given unshielded triple by considering following two cases where (a_s, b_s) is identical to (a_r, b_r) and where it is not.

Case $(a_r, b_r) = (a_s, b_s)$: A path of items corresponding to R_r is the *only* path from i to k that consists of items only in $\mathbf{p}$ and $\mathbf{q}$, and $\{R_r\} \subseteq \{T \mid k \in T|_i^\sigma\}$.

Case $(a_r, b_r) \neq (a_s, b_s)$: In a similar manner we define R_r with (a_r, b_r), we define $R_s \triangleq P^{:a_s} \bowtie Q^{b_s:}$, which satisfies $k \in R_s|_i^\sigma$. Note that $R_r = R_s$ if $P^{a_s:a_r} = Q^{b_s:b_r}$. Observing that $a_s < a_r \leq |P|$ and $1 \leq b_s < b_r$, we infer that $(|P|, 1)$ can be neither (a_r, b_r) nor (a_s, b_s).

Hence, there must exist at least three distinct anchors in $\mathbf{J}_{\mathbf{p},\mathbf{q}}$: $\{(|P|,1),(a_r,b_r),(a_s,b_s)\} \subseteq \mathbf{J}_{\mathbf{p},\mathbf{q}}$. The existence of characteristic anchors further implies that there must be an anchor (a,b) such that $a_r < a \leq |P|$ and $1 \leq b < b_s$. Among such anchors, if $\mathbf{p}_{a_r:a:-1}$ and $\mathbf{q}_{b:b_s:-1}$ do not share any items except the item at (a,b), then there exists a path of items from i to k, $\mathbf{p}_{:a_s} \bowtie \mathbf{q}_{b:b_s:-1} \bowtie \mathbf{p}_{a_r:a:-1} \bowtie \mathbf{q}_{b_r:}$, where the subpath with ": -1" represents the reverse of the subpath. There do exist such anchors:

$$(a_t,b_t) \triangleq \arg\max_{(a,b)\in\mathbf{J}_{\mathbf{p},\mathbf{q}},a_r<a,b<b_s} b,$$

and we likewise define $R_t \triangleq P^{:a_s} \bowtie Q^{b_t:b_s:-1} \bowtie P^{a_r:a_t:-1} \bowtie Q^{b_r:}$. We call such a set of anchors, *characteristic anchors*. Given the characteristic anchors $\{(a_r,b_r),(a_s,b_s),(a_t,b_t)\} \subseteq \mathbf{J}_{\mathbf{p},\mathbf{q}}$, we retrieve three relational paths, R_r, R_s, and R_t, such that $\{R_r,R_s,R_t\} \subseteq \{T \mid k \in T|_i^{\sigma}\}$. See Figure 6(d) for characteristic anchors $(a_s,b_s)=(2,4)$, $(a_r,b_r)=(4,8)$, and $(a_t,b_t)=(6,2)$, and for paths of items corresponding to R_r, R_s, and R_t.

Construction of CUTs with Characteristic Anchors The characteristic anchors permit the construction of a relational skeleton σ such that the corresponding ground graph $\mathcal{G}_\sigma^{\mathcal{M}}$ includes a UT. First, since all triples characterized by a given characteristic anchor share common relational path(s) from i to k, the existence of a dependency $R_r.Z - \mathcal{V}_X$ (ignoring its direction) makes the triple "shielded" if $(a_r,b_r)=(a_s,b_s)$. Similarly, we can test "shieldedness" in the case of $(a_r,b_r) \neq (a_s,b_s)$ by checking $adj(\mathcal{M},\mathcal{V}_X) \cap \{R_r,R_s,R_t\}.Z$ is non-empty. Second, we can devise an efficient and complete procedure that (virtually) constructs a relational skeleton σ that includes an unshielded triple in $\mathcal{G}_\sigma^{\mathcal{M}}$. Hence, characteristic anchors can be used to identify the CUTs of an RCM without enumerating the entire set of anchors $\mathbf{J}_{\mathbf{p},\mathbf{q}}$.

We proceed to outline an algorithm (see supplementary material for details) that, given a pair of dependencies of an RCM, constructs a CUT. The algorithm initialize candidate anchors $\mathbf{J}_{\mathbf{p},\mathbf{q}}$ by checking pairs of indices (a,b) where $P^a = Q^b$. Then, the algorithm picks an anchor as (a_r,b_r), checks whether (a_r,b_r) can be (a_s,b_s) and yields a UT. Then, it outputs a CUT $(\mathcal{V}_X, \{P.Y,(P^{:a_r} \bowtie Q^{:b_r:-1}).Y\}, R_r.Z)$ where the (virtually constructed) relational skeleton σ' satisfies $\{R_r\}=\{T \mid k \in T|_i^{\sigma'}\}$ and $\{P, P^{:a_r} \bowtie Q^{:b_r:-1}\} = \{T \mid j \in T|_i^{\sigma'}\}$. If (a_r,b_r) must differ from (a_s,b_s), then the algorithm explores valid candidates for (a_s,b_s) and (a_t,b_t). If all necessary conditions are passed, then it yields a CUT from among the following: $(\mathcal{V}_X,\mathbf{P}.Y,R_r.Z)$, $(\mathcal{V}_X,\mathbf{P}.Y,R_s.Z)$, and $(\mathcal{V}_X,\mathbf{P}.Y,R_t.Z)$ where σ' satisfies $\{R_r,R_s,R_t\}=\{T \mid k \in T|_i^{\sigma'}\}$ and $\mathbf{P}=\{T \mid j \in T|_i^{\sigma'}\}$, which consists of at most six relational paths[2]. For example, paths of items in Figure 6(e) correspond to three distinct relational paths of $\mathbf{P}$.

4.2 COMPLETED PARTIALLY-DIRECTED RCM

The pattern of an RCM is a partially-directed RCM (PRCM) wherein each directed dependency is covered by some CUT of the RCM. Completed PRCM (CPRCM) is a PRCM where a dependency is directed if and only if all valid RCMs with the same pattern have the dependency oriented in the same direction as in the CPRCM. Since acyclicity of RCM is defined at the attribute class level, we orient edges on a partially-directed class dependency graph $\mathcal{G}_\mathcal{A}$ (initialized with $\mathcal{G}_\mathcal{A}^{pattern(\mathcal{M})}$) with a set of attribute class level non-colliders, denoted by $\mathfrak{N}_\mathcal{A}^{\mathcal{M}}$ ($\mathfrak{N}$ for short), derived from canonical unshielded non-colliders obtained as a byproduct of discovering the pattern of an RCM. Then, orientations from *completed* partially-directed CDG are used to orient undirected dependencies in the pattern of RCM resulting the CPRCM.

Given a canonical unshielded non-collider $(\mathcal{V}_X,\mathbf{P}.Y,R.Z)$, corresponding attribute class level non-collider is (X,Y,Z). It is the case that $X=Z$, that is, $(X,Y,X)\in\mathfrak{N}$. Then, we can orient as $Y \to X$, which corresponds to Relational Bivariate Orientation (RBO, Maier et al., 2013a). For simplicity, we assume that all edges of $\mathcal{G}_\mathcal{A}$ that can be oriented using RBO have been oriented, and we exclude them (e.g., (X,Y,X)) from $\mathfrak{N}$. Otherwise if $X \neq Z$, then X and Z may be connected making (X,Y,Z) *shielded*. This is why the term "unshielded" is dropped in attribute class level non-colliders. To obtain the CPRCM given the pattern of an RCM, we provide a *sound* set of rules and a *sound* and *complete* extensibility-based method. The former can be used even when the set of non-colliders is not complete whereas the latter requires a complete set of non-colliders. Before we proceed, we characterize $\mathcal{G}_\mathcal{A}^{pattern(\mathcal{M})}$ and $\mathfrak{N}_\mathcal{A}^{\mathcal{M}}$:

Proposition 6. *Let (X,Y,Z) be an unshielded collider in $\mathcal{G}_\mathcal{A}^{\mathcal{M}}$, then $X \to Y \leftarrow Z$ in $\mathcal{G}_\mathcal{A}^{pattern(\mathcal{M})}$.*

Proof. This follows from Lemma 4.4.1 in (Maier, 2014) for the existence of a triple. Since there is no dependency between X and Z, the triple must be unshielded. □

Corollary 7. *For every unshielded non-collider $(X,Y,Z)\in\mathcal{G}_\mathcal{A}^{\mathcal{M}}$, $(X,Y,Z)\in\mathfrak{N}_\mathcal{A}^{\mathcal{M}}$.*

Hence, $\mathfrak{N}$ is simply a set of non-colliders that includes all unshielded non-colliders.

Sound Rules The four rules in Figure 5 can be used to correctly orient the edges in a partially-directed CDG $\mathcal{G}_\mathcal{A}$ (Corollary 7). We provide three additional rules that make use of $\mathfrak{N}$. First, if $(X,Y,Z)\in\mathfrak{N}$ and $X \to Y$, then $Y \to Z$. This can be viewed as a generalization of R1 that

[2] P, $P^{:a_w} \bowtie Q^{:b_w:-1}$, $P^{:a_s} \bowtie Q^{:b_s:-1}$, $P^{:a_s} \bowtie Q^{b_t:b_s:-1} \bowtie P^{a_t:}$, $P^{:a_s} \bowtie Q^{b_s:b_r} \bowtie P^{a_r:}$, and $P^{:a_s} \bowtie Q^{b_s:b_r} \bowtie P^{a_r:a_w} \bowtie Q^{:b_w:-1}$ with $a_w \triangleq a_t - \gamma + 1$ and $b_w \triangleq b_t - \gamma + 1$ where $\gamma = LLRSP(P^{a_r:a_t:-1}, Q^{:b_t:-1})$ (see Lee and Honavar, 2015).

Algorithm 1 Completing a PDAG given non-colliders.

procedure *completes*(PDAG $\mathcal{G}$, non-colliders $\mathfrak{N}$)
  $\mathbf{U} := \{X \rightarrow Y, Y \rightarrow X\}_{X-Y \in \mathcal{G}}$
  for $X \rightarrow Y$ in $\mathbf{U}$ **do**
    $\mathcal{G}' := (\mathcal{G} \setminus \{X - Y\}) \cup \{X \rightarrow Y\}$
    if $\forall_{V \in pa(\mathcal{G},Y)} (X, Y, V) \notin \mathfrak{N}$ **and** $ext(\mathcal{G}', \mathfrak{N})$ **then**
      remove edges of $\mathcal{G}'$ from $\mathbf{U}$
    else orient $Y \rightarrow X$ in $\mathcal{G}$, remove $Y \rightarrow X$ from $\mathbf{U}$

procedure $ext(\mathcal{G}, \mathfrak{N})$
  $\mathcal{H} := copy(\mathcal{G})$
  repeat
    for X in $\mathbb{V}(\mathcal{H})$ **such that** $ch(\mathcal{H}, X) = \emptyset$ **do**
      if $(V_1, X, V_2) \notin \mathfrak{N}$ for every $V_1, V_2 \in adj(\mathcal{H}, X)$
        orient $Y \rightarrow X$ in $\mathcal{G}$ for every $Y \in ne(\mathcal{H}, X)$
        $\mathcal{H} := \mathcal{H} \setminus \{X\}$
        break
    else return False
  until $\mathcal{H}$ is empty
  return True

avoids checking unshieldedness. Second, if $(X, Y, Z) \in \mathfrak{N}$ and $X \rightarrow Z$, then $Y \rightarrow Z$. This is similar to R4 in the sense that $Y \rightarrow Z$ is a common orientation among possible orientations of a non-collider that does not create a directed cycle. Finally, we can identify a shielded collider from the fact that there must be a sink in any undirected cycle. If there exists an undirected cycle of length $n \geq 3$ where every subsequent triple in the cycle except one is non-collider, then the triple that is not a *non-collider* must be a collider. The preceding rules are clearly sound. However, without further characterization of non-colliders $\mathfrak{N}$ in a partially-directed CDG, we cannot prove that they are complete for learning the structure of an RCM.

Extensibility with Shielded Non-Colliders We generalize the algorithm for determining whether a PDAG admits an oriented extension (PDAG extensibility) (Dor and Tarsi, 1992) to work with a set of non-colliders that may be, but not necessarily, shielded. The original PDAG extensibility algorithm finds a vertex without outgoing edges where all undirected edges on the vertex can be oriented towards the vertex (i.e., sinkable) without creating new unshielded colliders. If such a vertex is found, the undirected edges between it and its neighbors are oriented towards it. The preceding steps are repeated after removing the vertex from the PDAG. The algorithm returns failure if some edges remain undirected in the PDAG and no sinkable vertex can be found. The original algorithm exploits the observation that a sinkable vertex cannot be "the middle of unshielded non-colliders", which we generalize to "the middle of non-colliders $\mathfrak{N}$". Because the unshieldedness of non-colliders plays no role in the proof of correctness of the original algorithm, the proof holds for the modified algorithm (Algorithm 1).

Theorem 8. *Let $\mathcal{G}$ be a PDAG. Let $\mathfrak{N}$ be a set of non-colliders which includes all unshielded non-colliders in $\mathcal{G}$. Then, algorithm ext correctly decides whether there exists a DAG that is a consistent extension of $\mathcal{G}$ satisfying constraints imposed by $\mathfrak{N}$.*

Proof. Let $ce(\mathcal{G}, \mathfrak{N})$ be a set of DAGs that consistently extend $\mathcal{G}$ for a given set of attribute level non-colliders $\mathfrak{N}$. Let $\mathfrak{N}(\mathcal{G}) = \{(X, Y, Z) \in \mathfrak{N} \mid \{X, Y, Z\} \subseteq \mathbb{V}(\mathcal{G})\}$ be a set of *induced* non-colliders. Whenever there exists a DAG $\mathcal{G}' \in ce(\mathcal{G}, \mathfrak{N})$, there must exist X, a sink of $\mathcal{G}$, such that $ce(\mathcal{G} - X, \mathfrak{N}(\mathcal{G} - X))$ is non-empty since $\mathcal{G}' - X$ satisfies $\mathfrak{N}(\mathcal{G} - X)$. Thus the algorithm 1 will maximally orient the PDAG and return True.

Let $\mathcal{G}''$ be a DAG in $ce(\mathcal{G} - X, \mathfrak{N}(\mathcal{G} - X))$ and $\mathcal{G}'''$ be a *reconstructed* graph $\mathcal{G}'' \cup \{X\} \cup \{Y \rightarrow X \mid Y \in ne(\mathcal{G}, X)\}$. Then, $\mathcal{G}'''$ is in $ce(\mathcal{G}, \mathfrak{N})$: (i) $\mathcal{G}'''$ is a DAG since adding a vertex as a sink to a DAG results a DAG; and (ii) $\mathcal{G}'''$ satisfies $\mathfrak{N}(\mathcal{G}) \setminus \mathfrak{N}(\mathcal{G} - X)$ since, for every reconstructed (shielded or unshielded) collider $Y \rightarrow X \leftarrow Z$, $(Y, X, Z) \notin \mathfrak{N}$ (by the definition of sinkable vertex). Therefore, ext finds a DAG in $ce(\mathcal{G}, \mathfrak{N})$ and returns True whenever $\mathcal{G}$ is extensible; and returns False otherwise. □

5 CAUSAL DISCOVERY ALGORITHM

We proceed to present RpCD, a sound and complete causal discovery algorithm for RCM under path semantics under the usual assumptions namely, causal Markov condition, sufficiency, and faithfulness (Spirtes et al., 2000), that allow us to interpret every ground graph of RCM as a CBN. We also assume access to an independence oracle that correctly answers independence queries with respect to the RCM. We further assume, as in (Maier et al., 2013a), that the maximum hop length of dependencies is known *a priori* which ensures that only a finite number of candidate dependencies need to be considered.

RpCD (see Algorithm 2) extends the key ideas of the PC algorithm (Spirtes et al., 2000) to the relational domain. Phase I of RpCD identifies adjacencies (Lines 1–11) and phase II orients the dependencies (Lines 12–23). The phase I is nearly identical to that of RCD (Maier et al., 2013a). Given a maximum hop threshold h, all candidate dependencies are enumerated. Then, spurious dependencies are removed through conditional independence tests. In Lines 12–23, it orients undirected dependencies through conditional independence tests on CUTs. Redundant tests are avoided by skipping (i) already known non-colliders (Line 15), (ii) already oriented edges (Line 16), and (iii) inactive non-colliders (Line 17). At an attribute class level, edges are oriented if forming a collider (Line 19) or forming a non-collider having the same attribute classes on its flanking elements (Line 20, RBO). All orientations that can be inferred from the sound orientation rules (see Section 4.2) are enforced (Line 22). Finally, Line 23 maximally-orients partially-directed class dependency graph with a complete

Algorithm 2 RpCD

Input: $\mathcal{S}$ schema, $\mathcal{O}$ independence tester, h hop threshold

1: initialize $\mathbf{D}$ with candidate dependencies up to h hops.
2: initialize an undirected graph $\mathcal{G}$ with undirected $\mathbf{D}$.
3: $\ell := 0$
4: **repeat**
5:   **for** every ordered pair $(P.Y, \mathcal{V}_X)$ **s.t.** $P.Y - \mathcal{V}_X \in \mathcal{G}$ **do**
6:     **for** every $\mathbf{S} \subseteq ne(\mathcal{G}, \mathcal{V}_X) \setminus \{P.Y\}$ **s.t.** $|\mathbf{S}| = \ell$ **do**
7:       **if** $\mathcal{V}_X \perp\!\!\!\perp P.Y \mid \mathbf{S}$ **then**
8:         remove $\{P.Y - \mathcal{V}_X, \tilde{P}.X - \mathcal{V}_Y\}$ from $\mathcal{G}$.
9:         **break**
10:   $\ell := \ell + 1$
11: **until** $|ne(\mathcal{G}, \mathcal{V}_X)| - 1 < \ell$ for every $X \in \mathcal{A}$
12: initialize $\mathfrak{U}$ with canonical unshielded triples from $\mathcal{G}$.
13: $\mathfrak{N} := \emptyset$, $\mathcal{H} := \langle \mathcal{A}, \{X - Y \mid P.Y - \mathcal{V}_X \in \mathcal{G}\} \rangle$
14: **for** every $(\mathcal{V}_X, \mathbf{P}.Y, R.Z) \in \mathfrak{U}$ **do**
15:   **continue if** $(X, Y, Z) \in \mathfrak{N}$ **or**
16:           $\{X, Z\} \cap ne(\mathcal{H}, Y) = \emptyset$ **or**
17:           $\{X, Z\} \cap ch(\mathcal{H}, Y) \neq \emptyset$
18:   **if** exists $\mathbf{S} \subseteq adj(\mathcal{G}, \mathcal{V}_X)$ **s.t.** $R.Z \perp\!\!\!\perp \mathcal{V}_X \mid \mathbf{S}$ **then**
19:     **if** $\mathbf{S} \cap \mathbf{P}.Y = \emptyset$ **then** orient $X \rightarrow Y \leftarrow Z$ in $\mathcal{H}$
20:     **else if** $X = Z$ **then** orient $Y \rightarrow X$ in $\mathcal{H}$
21:     **else** add (X, Y, Z) to $\mathfrak{N}$
22:   orient edges in $\mathcal{H}$ with sound rules with $\mathfrak{N}$.
23: $completes(\mathcal{H}, \mathfrak{N})$
24: **return** $\bigcup_{P.Y - \mathcal{V}_X \in \mathcal{G}} \begin{cases} P.Y \rightarrow \mathcal{V}_X & Y \rightarrow X \in \mathcal{H} \\ P.Y - \mathcal{V}_X & Y - X \in \mathcal{H} \end{cases}$

set of attribute class level non-colliders $\mathfrak{N}$ (except the inactive ones that play no role in the orientation of the edges). RpCD outputs undirected and directed dependencies reflecting orientations recovered from Phase II (Line 24).

Theorem 9 (Soundness and Completeness). *Let $\mathcal{M}$ be an RCM whose maximum hop length of dependencies is less than or equal to h. Given access to an independence oracle and h, RpCD is sound and complete for learning the structure of the RCM under path semantics.*

Proof. The proof follows from (Maier et al., 2013a) for Phase I and, for Phase II, from the Markov equivalence of RCMs (Theorem 3) with the completeness of (i) CUTs for UTs, (ii) the CUT-enumerating algorithm for (non-)colliders ($\mathfrak{C}_{\mathcal{A}}^{\mathcal{M}}$ and $\mathfrak{N}_{\mathcal{A}}^{\mathcal{M}}$), and (iii) generalized extensibility (Theorem 8). □

Causal Discovery of RCM under BBS It is easy to see that a modification of RCD (Maier et al., 2013a) to take advantage of valid CUTs under BBS will improve the orientation recall of RCD. Given the implications of BBS (Section 3), one can check whether a CUT of an RCM under path semantics correspond to a UT in some ground graph of the RCM under BBS. The "valid" CUTs under BBS can then replace UTs of AGG (Maier et al., 2013b; Lee and Honavar, 2016) used by RCD for orientating the edges. Note that each UT of AGG is a special case of CUT where $(a_r, b_r) = (a_s, b_s)$ with $P^{a_r:} = Q^{:b_r:-1}$.

6 SUMMARY AND DISCUSSION

Relational causal models (RCM) offer an attractive approach to modeling causality in real world settings that are modeled by relational domains. Previous studies of RCM have assumed bridge burning semantics (BBS). A careful examination of RCM under BBS reveals its counter-intuitive behavior. We consider RCM under path semantics which offers a viable alternative to BBS while preserving its desirable properties while avoiding its counterintuitive consequences. We introduced canonical unshielded triples, a novel graphical construct that we use to characterize Markov equivalence of RCM under path semantics. We described RpCD, a sound and complete algorithm for recovering the structure of an RCM under path semantics from conditional independence queries. We also suggested ways to improve the orientation recall of algorithms for learning the structure of RCM under BBS.

We conclude by listing some promising directions for further research: (i) Our analysis is based on perfect independence tests. In practice, the reliability of independence tests depends on the accuracy of parametric assumption for the underlying distribution, and the quantity of available data. Many methods have been developed to make the structure learning algorithm for causal Bayesian networks (CBNs) robust to such errors including adjacency-conservative (Lemeire et al., 2012), orientation-conservative (Ramsey et al., 2006) and order-independent (Colombo and Maathuis, 2014) PC algorithms. It would be interesting to consider variants of RpCD that incorporate such approaches in the relational setting. (ii) There are variants of CBN that relax some of its restrictive assumptions (Richardson and Spirtes, 2002). Similar extensions of RCMs would be interesting to consider. (iii) It would be interesting to consider methods for estimating a spillover effect in the presence of interference (Tchetgen Tchetgen and VanderWeele, 2012) due to violation of stable unit treatment variable assumption. (iv) RCM currently does not allow class dependency graph level cycles even if such cycles are guaranteed to not introduce a cycle in any of the ground graphs of the model. For example, a person's traits are inherited from those of his/her biological parents. We can consider relaxing the acyclicity assumptions underlying RCM to permit such cycles.

Acknowledgments

The authors are grateful to UAI 2016 anonymous reviewers for their thorough reviews. This research was supported in part by the Edward Frymoyer Endowed Professorship held by Vasant Honavar and in part by the Center for Big Data Analytics and Discovery Informatics which is co-sponsored by the Institute for Cyberscience, the Huck Institutes of the Life Sciences, and the Social Science Research Institute at the Pennsylvania State University.

References

Andersson, S. A., Madigan, D., and Perlman, M. D. (1997). A characterization of Markov equivalence classes for acyclic digraphs. *The Annals of Statistics*, 25(2):505–541.

Buntine, W. L. (1994). Operations for learning with graphical models. *Journal of Artificial Intelligence Research*, 2:159–225.

Chen, P. P.-S. (1976). The entity-relationship model - toward a unified view of data. *ACM Transactions on Database Systems*, 1(1):9–36.

Colombo, D. and Maathuis, M. H. (2014). Order-independent constraint-based causal structure learning. *Journal of Machine Learning Research*, 15:3921–3962.

Dor, D. and Tarsi, M. (1992). A simple algorithm to construct a consistent extension of a partially oriented graph. Technical Report R-185, Cognitive Systems Laboratory, UCLA.

Friedman, N., Getoor, L., Koller, D., and Pfeffer, A. (1999). Learning probabilistic relational models. In *Proceedings of the Sixteenth International Joint Conference on Artificial Intelligence*, pages 1300–1309. Morgan Kaufmann.

Heckerman, D., Meek, C., and Koller, D. (2007). Probabilistic entity-relationship models, PRMs, and plate models. In Getoor, L. and Taskar, B., editors, *Introduction to Statistical Relational Learning*, pages 201–238. MIT Press.

Lee, S. and Honavar, V. (2015). Lifted representation of relational causal models revisited: Implications for reasoning and structure learning. In *Proceedings of the UAI 2015 Workshop on Advances in Causal Inference*, pages 56–65. CEUR-WS.

Lee, S. and Honavar, V. (2016). On learning causal models from relational data. In *Proceedings of the Thirtieth AAAI Conference on Artificial Intelligence*. AAAI Press.

Lemeire, J., Meganck, S., Cartella, F., and Liu, T. (2012). Conservative independence-based causal structure learning in absence of adjacency faithfulness. *International Journal of Approximate Reasoning*, 53(9):1305–1325.

Maier, M., Marazopoulou, K., Arbour, D., and Jensen, D. (2013a). A sound and complete algorithm for learning causal models from relational data. In *Proceedings of the Twenty-Ninth Conference on Uncertainty in Artificial Intelligence*, pages 371–380. AUAI Press.

Maier, M., Marazopoulou, K., and Jensen, D. (2013b). Reasoning about independence in probabilistic models of relational data. In *Approaches to Causal Structure Learning Workshop, UAI-13*.

Maier, M., Taylor, B., and Jensen, D. (2010). Learning causal models of relational domains. In *Proceedings of the Twenty-Fourth AAAI Conference on Artificial Intelligence*, pages 531–538. AAAI Press.

Maier, M. E. (2014). *Causal Discovery for Relational Domains: Representation, Reasoning, and Learning*. PhD thesis, University of Massachusetts Amherst.

Marazopoulou, K., Maier, M., and Jensen, D. (2015). Learning the structure of causal models with relational and temporal dependence. In *Proceedings of the Thirty-First Conference on Uncertainty in Artificial Intelligence*, pages 572–581.

Meek, C. (1995). Causal inference and causal explanation with background knowledge. In *Proceedings of the Eleventh Conference on Uncertainty in Artificial Intelligence*, pages 403–410. Morgan Kaufmann.

Pearl, J. (2000). *Causality: Models, Reasoning, and Inference*. Cambridge University Press.

Ramsey, J., Zhang, J., and Spirtes, P. L. (2006). Adjacency-faithfulness and conservative causal inference. In *Proceedings of the Twenty-Second Conference on Uncertainty in Artificial Intelligence*, pages 401–408. AUAI Press.

Richardson, T. and Spirtes, P. (2002). Ancestral graph Markov models. *The Annals of Statistics*, 30(4):962–1030.

Spirtes, P., Glymour, C. N., and Scheines, R. (2000). *Causation, Prediction, and Search*. MIT Press.

Tchetgen Tchetgen, E. J. and VanderWeele, T. J. (2012). On causal inference in the presence of interference. *Statistical Methods in Medical Research*, 21(1):55–75.

Verma, T. and Pearl, J. (1990). Equivalence and synthesis of causal models. In *Proceedings of the Sixth Conference on Uncertainty in Artificial Intelligence*, pages 220–227. AUAI Press.

Improving Imprecise Compressive Sensing Models

Dongeun Lee and **Rafael Lima** and **Jaesik Choi**
School of Electrical and Computer Engineering
Ulsan National Institute of Science and Technology
Ulsan, 44919, Korea
{eundong, rafael_glima, jaesik}@unist.ac.kr

Abstract

Random sampling in compressive sensing (CS) enables the compression of large amounts of input signals in an efficient manner, which is useful for many applications. CS reconstructs the compressed signals exactly with overwhelming probability when incoming data can be sparsely represented with a few components. However, the theory of CS framework including random sampling has been focused on exact recovery of signal; impreciseness in signal recovery has been neglected. This can be problematic when there is uncertainty in the number of sparse components such as signal sparsity in dynamic systems that can change over time. We present a new theoretical framework that handles uncertainty in signal recovery from the perspective of recovery success and quality. We show that the signal recovery success in our model is more accurate than the success probability analysis in the CS framework. Our model is then extended to the case where the success or failure of signal recovery can be relaxed. We represent the number of components included in signal recovery with a right-tailed distribution and focus on recovery quality. Experimental results confirm the accuracy of our model in dynamic systems.

1 INTRODUCTION

Continuous flows of big data are generated by many sources nowadays. Among these, resource limited devices occupy a significant portion. For these devices, sensing and transmitting massive data are important challenges, as they are concerned with saving resources.

Compressive sensing (CS) (Seeger & Nickisch, 2008; Hsu et al., 2009; Lopes, 2013; Malioutov & Varshney, 2013; Zhu & Gu, 2015) is a well suited choice for resource limited devices because it enables the sensing and compression of massive data without the complexity burden imposed by conventional schemes. Recent advances in CS reduce the complexity burden even further with *random sampling*, by which CS schemes have been successfully applied to broader application areas such as sampling of spatio-temporal data (Foucart & Rauhut, 2013; Lee & Choi, 2014).

CS reconstructs the exact signals from the compressed measurements with overwhelming probability when incoming data can be sparsely represented (i.e., small numbers of components). Therefore, most CS frameworks are built based on the assumption that incoming data with sparse representation can be *exactly* recovered when an enough number of measurements is given.

Unfortunately, this assumption does not hold in practice when there is no guarantee of enough measurements for varying signal sparsity. This *uncertainty* occurs especially with many dynamic systems where the numbers of components change over time. The assumption also implies that the reconstruction would fail when input signals have more components (denser) than a predefined threshold. This prevents deriving a tight probabilistic model which takes account of the numbers of components and measurements in signal recovery. In this regard, recently introduced dynamic CS frameworks (Malioutov et al., 2010; Sejdinovic et al., 2010; Shahrasbi et al., 2011; Vaswani & Lu, 2010; Ziniel & Schniter, 2013) provide the way of reducing the number of necessary measurements exploiting temporal correlation between measurements. Nevertheless, a recovery success/quality analysis with uncertainty in signal sparsity has not been provided by existing CS frameworks yet.

This paper presents a new theoretical framework for the random sampling in CS that handles *impreciseness* in signal recovery when the number of measurements lacks for varying signal sparsity. Our framework incorporates the beta distribution to present the signal recovery success more accurately than the success probability analysis in the CS framework. Furthermore, we relax the concept of signal recovery success and present the number of components included in the signal recovery as a varying quantity, for which we propose right-tailed distribution modeling. We believe our new framework will bridge the gap between success and failure of signal recovery in CS frameworks.

2 COMPRESSIVE SENSING AND RANDOM SAMPLING

Compressive sensing, or compressed sampling (CS), is an efficient signal processing framework which incorporates signal acquisition and compression simultaneously (Baraniuk, 2007; Candès & Wakin, 2008). CS enables a signal to be acquired with a number of samples that is far fewer than an original signal dimension and of the same order as the number of (significant) components.

2.1 COMPRESSING WHILE SENSING

In CS, a signal is projected onto random vectors whose cardinality is far below the dimension of the signal. Consider a signal $\mathbf{x} \in \mathbb{R}^N$ is compactly represented with a sparsifying basis $\mathbf{\Psi}$ having just a few components: $\mathbf{x} = \mathbf{\Psi}\mathbf{s}$, where $\mathbf{s} \in \mathbb{R}^N$ is the vector of transformed coefficients with a few significant coefficients. Here, $\mathbf{\Psi}$ could be a basis that makes $\mathbf{x}$ sparse in a transform domain such as the DCT, wavelet transform domains, or even the canonical basis, i.e., the identity matrix $\mathbf{I}$, if $\mathbf{x}$ is sparse itself without the help of a transform.

Definition (K-sparse Signal). *A signal* $\mathbf{x}$ *is called* K*-sparse if it is a linear combination of only* $K \ll N$ *basis vectors such that* $\sum_{i=1}^{K} s_{n_i} \boldsymbol{\psi}_{n_i}$*, where* $\{n_1, \ldots, n_K\} \subset \{1, \ldots, N\}$*;* s_{n_i} *is a coefficient in* $\mathbf{s}$*; and* $\boldsymbol{\psi}_{n_i}$ *is a column of* $\mathbf{\Psi}$*.*

In practice, some signals may not be exactly K-sparse. Rather, they can be closely approximated with K basis vectors by ignoring many small coefficients close to zero. This type of signal is called *compressible* (Baraniuk, 2007; Foucart & Rauhut, 2013).

CS projects $\mathbf{x}$ onto a random sensing basis $\mathbf{\Phi} \in \mathbb{R}^{M \times N}$ as follows ($M < N$):

$$\mathbf{y} = \mathbf{\Phi}\mathbf{x} = \mathbf{\Phi}\mathbf{\Psi}\mathbf{s}, \tag{1}$$

where $\mathbf{\Phi}$ should have the *restricted isometry property* (RIP).[1] A conventional approach for $\mathbf{\Phi}$ to satisfy RIP is sampling its independent identically distributed (i.i.d.) elements from the Gaussian distribution or other sub-Gaussian distributions (e.g., Rademacher/Bernoulli distribution).

The system shown in (1) is underdetermined, as the number of equations M is smaller than the number of variables N, i.e., there are infinitely many $\mathbf{x}$'s that satisfy $\mathbf{y} = \mathbf{\Phi}\mathbf{x}$. Nevertheless, this system can be solved with overwhelming probability exploiting the fact that $\mathbf{s}$ is K-sparse. Here $M = O(K \log(N/K))$ in the case of Gaussian and sub-Gaussian sensing matrices (Candès & Wakin, 2008).

2.2 RANDOM SAMPLING

Random sampling is a variant of CS which can further reduce the computational complexity to a constant time (Foucart & Rauhut, 2013; Lee & Choi, 2014). The random sampling scheme is based on the fact that it is possible to construct $\mathbf{\Phi}$ in (1) from a random selection of rows from the identity matrix $\mathbf{I}$, which is equivalent to the random sampling of coefficients in $\mathbf{x}$.

Note that the sparsifying basis $\mathbf{\Psi}$ should be *incoherent*[2] with $\mathbf{I}$, such as the DCT and wavelet transform bases, for the successful recovery of the original signal (Candès & Wakin, 2008; Foucart & Rauhut, 2013). Unless they are incoherent, the measurement vector $\mathbf{y} \in \mathbb{R}^M$ in (1) would contain zero entries. Here, the number of required measurements M is larger than in the cases of Gaussian and sub-Gaussian matrices, that is, $M = O(K \log N)$.

2.3 RECOVERY OF SIGNAL

A signal recovery algorithm takes measurements $\mathbf{y}$, a random sensing matrix $\mathbf{\Phi}$, and the sparsifying basis $\mathbf{\Psi}$. The sensing matrix $\mathbf{\Phi}$ and sparsifying basis $\mathbf{\Psi}$ are assumed to be known to a decoder. The signal recovery algorithm then recovers $\mathbf{s}$ knowing that $\mathbf{s}$ is sparse. Once we recover $\mathbf{s}$, the original signal $\mathbf{x}$ can be recovered through $\mathbf{x} = \mathbf{\Psi}\mathbf{s}$. The recovery algorithm reconstructs $\mathbf{s}$ by the following linear program:

$$\operatorname{argmin} \|\tilde{\mathbf{s}}\|_1 \quad \text{subject to} \quad \mathbf{\Phi}\mathbf{\Psi}\tilde{\mathbf{s}} = \mathbf{y}. \tag{2}$$

The optimization problem in (2) is solved by a ℓ_1-minimization method (basis pursuit) (Boyd & Vandenberghe, 2004), greedy methods such as orthogonal matching pursuit (Pati et al., 1993), or thresholding-based methods such as iterative hard thresholding (Blumensath & Davies, 2008). Choosing a specific algorithm depends on $\mathbf{\Phi}$, M, N, and K: recovery success rates and speed can only be determined by numerical tests (Foucart & Rauhut, 2013).[3] In this paper, we reconstruct signals by the *basis pursuit*.

Specifically in the case of random sampling, the solution $\mathbf{s}^\star$ to (2) obeys

$$\|\mathbf{s}^\star - \mathbf{s}\|_2 \le C_1 \cdot \|\mathbf{s} - \mathbf{s}_K\|_1 \tag{3}$$

[1] The random sensing basis $\mathbf{\Phi}$ have RIP if $(1-\delta)\|\mathbf{s}\|_2^2 \le \|\mathbf{\Phi}\mathbf{\Psi}\mathbf{s}\|_2^2 \le (1+\delta)\|\mathbf{s}\|_2^2$ for small $\delta \ge 0$, and this condition applies to all K-sparse $\mathbf{s}$.

[2] The two bases $\mathbf{\Phi}$ and $\mathbf{\Psi}$ are incoherent when the rows of $\mathbf{\Phi}$ cannot sparsely represent the columns of $\mathbf{\Psi}$ and vice versa.

[3] Note that greedy methods are not always fast.

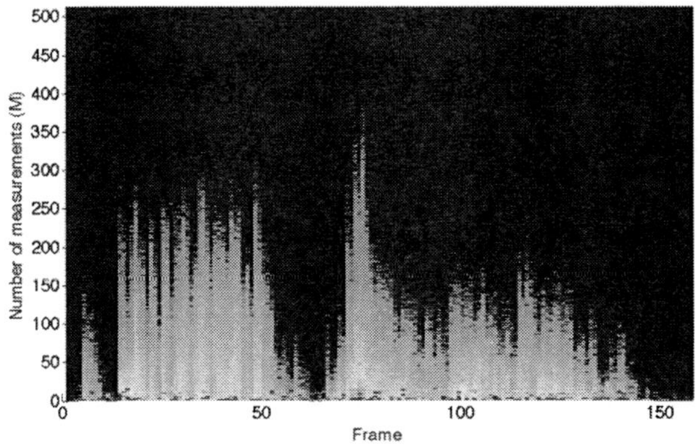

Figure 1: Recovery error of audio data for different numbers of measurements M over time. Each frame has a signal length $N = 512$. Colors close to blue represent smaller errors, whereas colors close to red represent larger errors.

for some constant $C_1 > 0$, where $\mathbf{s}_K$ is the vector $\mathbf{s}$ with all but the largest K components set to 0. When an original signal is exactly K-sparse, then $\mathbf{s} = \mathbf{s}_K$ with $M = O(K \log N)$ measurements, which implies that the recovery is exact, i.e., $\mathbf{s}^\star = \mathbf{s}$.

3 A NEW PERSPECTIVE ON RECOVERY SUCCESS

The success of signal reconstruction in compressive sensing (CS) is not deterministic. For instance, when we say an exact recovery of a K-sparse signal is achievable with overwhelming probability, it implies there is also the chance of recovery not being exact.

Most CS literature assumes a sufficient number of measurements M such that an exact recovery is almost always achievable (Candès & Wakin, 2008; Foucart & Rauhut, 2013), which is based on an assumption that sparsity K is already known or does not exceed a certain bound. However, the signal sparsity in dynamic systems may change over time and an excessive number of measurements may waste resources such as network bandwidth and storage space. For example, Figure 1 shows recovery error over time for audio data (a 7 second recording of a trumpet solo) (Ziniel et al., 2012), where varying signal sparsity incurs different recovery error with a fixed number of measurements over time. Here we cannot simply increase the number of measurements to eliminate error, as it is unreasonable in terms of compression. Therefore, we propose a new theoretical framework for the random sampling of CS and provide a new perspective on signal recovery.

3.1 COMPRESSIVE SENSING FRAMEWORK

In the random sampling of CS, the number of required measurements $M = O(K \log N)$ can be detailed as follows (Foucart & Rauhut, 2013):

$$M \geq C \cdot K \ln(N) \ln(\epsilon^{-1}) \tag{4}$$

for some constant $C > 0$, where $\epsilon \in (0,1)$ denotes the probability of an *inexact* recovery of the K-sparse signal. In particular, the signal recovery succeeds with a probability of at least $1 - \epsilon$ if (4) holds.[4]

We can then express (4) with regard to the probability of failure ϵ, which is given by

$$\mathbf{P}(\mathbf{s}^\star \neq \mathbf{s} \mid M, N, K) := \epsilon \leq \exp\left(-\frac{M}{C \cdot \ln(N) K}\right). \tag{5}$$

Thus, the probability of failure (inexact recovery) $\mathbf{P}(\mathbf{s}^\star \neq \mathbf{s} \mid M, N, K)$ is conditional upon M, N, and K. Since we are interested in the dynamic signal sparsity K, we model K as a *random variable* with M and N as *fixed quantities*.

If we denote an arbitrary probability density function (pdf) of K as $f_K(k)$, we can marginalize over k and find the upper bound of failure probability as follows:

$$\begin{aligned}\mathbf{P}(\mathbf{s}^\star \neq \mathbf{s} \mid M, N) &= \int_k \mathbf{P}(\mathbf{s}^\star \neq \mathbf{s} \mid M, N, K) \cdot f_K(k)\, \mathrm{d}k \\ &\leq \int_k \exp\left(-\frac{M}{C \cdot \ln(N) K}\right) f_K(k)\, \mathrm{d}k.\end{aligned} \tag{6}$$

Therefore, we can state that a signal recovery succeeds with a probability of at least $1 - \int_k \exp(-M/(C \cdot \ln(N)K)) f_K(k) \mathrm{d}k$, given the distribution of signal sparsity $f_K(k)$.

The upper bound in (6) may have an analytic solution when K follows certain distributions such as the *inverse Gaussian distribution* and the *gamma distribution*.[5]

Remark Assuming $f_K(k) = \mathrm{IG}(\mu, \lambda)$, the upper bound of (6) is

$$\frac{\sqrt{\lambda} \exp(\lambda/\mu - \sqrt{2\lambda/\mu^2}\sqrt{M/(C \cdot \ln(N)) + \lambda/2})}{\sqrt{2M/(C \cdot \ln(N)) + \lambda}}, \tag{7}$$

where μ and λ are the mean and the shape parameter of the inverse Gaussian distribution, respectively.

Remark Assuming $f_K(k) = \mathrm{Gamma}(\kappa, \theta)$, the upper bound of (6) is

$$\frac{2}{\Gamma(\kappa)} \left(\frac{M}{C \cdot \ln(N)\theta}\right)^{\kappa/2} K_{-\kappa}\left(2\sqrt{\frac{M}{C \cdot \ln(N)\theta}}\right), \tag{8}$$

[4]See Theorem 12.20 (Foucart & Rauhut, 2013).

[5]Since $K \geq 0$, probability distributions supported on semi-infinite intervals, i.e., $(0, \infty)$, are rational choices.

where κ and θ are the shape parameter and the scale parameter of the gamma distribution, respectively; $\Gamma(\cdot)$ is the gamma function; and $K_{-\kappa}(\cdot)$ is the modified Bessel function of the second kind.

3.2 MODELING SUCCESS AND FAILURE

Unfortunately, the probability of signal recovery failure ϵ given in (5) does not hold in practice because there is a discrepancy between the failure probabilities in the CS framework and actual random sampling, as will be further explained in Section 5.1. Thus we have to model the success or failure probability of signal recovery from a new perspective.

We can model the new pdf of *signal recovery success* using the mixture of the *Dirac delta function* and the *beta distribution*, which incorporates both stochastic and deterministic cases. We introduce $K_{\min}$ and $K_{\max}$ to denote the minimum and the maximum signal sparsities which yield stochastic probability, as opposed to a deterministic result where signal recovery always succeeds or always fails.

Definition (Recovery Success Model). *Let* $\mathbf{P}(\mathbf{s}^{\star}{=}\mathbf{s}|M,N) := \Pi$. *The pdf of* Π *given* K *is given by*[6]

$$f_{\Pi|K}(\pi \mid k) := \begin{cases} \delta(\pi - 1) & k < K_{\min} \\ \mathrm{Beta}(\alpha_K, \beta_K) & K_{\min} \le k \le K_{\max}. \\ \delta(\pi) & K_{\max} < k \end{cases} \quad (9)$$

Combining this definition with an arbitrary pdf $f_K(k)$ of the dynamic signal sparsity K, we can find the success probability distribution marginalized over k as follows:

$$\begin{aligned} f_\Pi(\pi) &= \int_k f_{\Pi|K}(\pi \mid k) f_K(k)\, dk \\ &= \int_0^{K_{\min}} \delta(\pi - 1) f_K(k)\, dk \\ &\quad + \int_{K_{\min}}^{K_{\max}} \mathrm{Beta}(\alpha_K, \beta_K) \cdot f_K(k)\, dk \\ &\quad + \int_{K_{\max}}^{\infty} \delta(\pi) f_K(k)\, dk \\ &= \delta(\pi - 1) F_K(K_{\min}) + \delta(\pi)(1 - F_K(K_{\max})) \\ &\quad + \int_{K_{\min}}^{K_{\max}} \mathrm{Beta}(\alpha_K, \beta_K) \cdot f_K(k)\, dk, \end{aligned} \quad (10)$$

where $F_K(\cdot)$ is the cumulative distribution function (CDF) of K.

The two Dirac delta function terms in (10) can be interpreted as probability masses. Since $\int_{K_{\min}}^{K_{\max}} \mathrm{Beta}(\alpha_K, \beta_K) \cdot f_K(k)\, dk$ does not have an analytic solution, we compute this value numerically.

[6] $\mathrm{Beta}(\alpha_K, \beta_K)$ here is used to denote the pdf of the beta distribution.

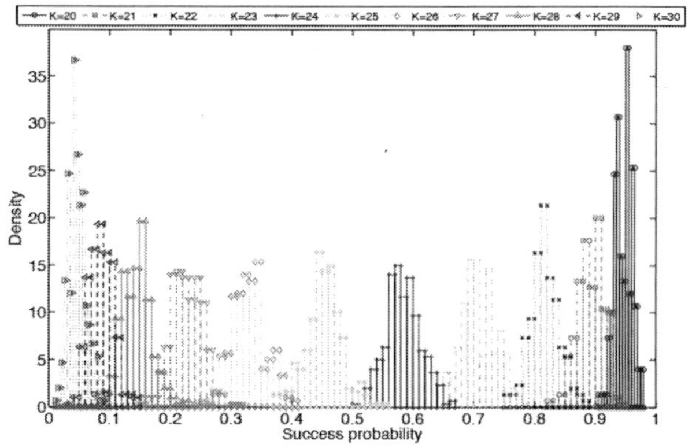

Figure 2: Histograms of success probability for various K's. Success probability distribution for each K was obtained with 300 different random signed spike vectors for $N = 512$ and $M = 100$. A single success probability for each signed spike vector was calculated with 300 experiments.

As an illustrative example, suppose that we examine the success probability by generating many different signed spike (± 1) vectors for each signal sparsity and then performing experiments for each signed spike vector.[7] Figure 2 shows histograms of success probability for various signal sparsities, where $K_{\min} = 20$ and $K_{\max} = 30$.

The success probability shown in Figure 2 naturally follows the beta distribution with its parameters α and β depending on signal sparsity, i.e., $\mathbf{P}(\mathbf{s}^{\star}{=}\mathbf{s} \mid M, N, K) \sim \mathrm{Beta}(\alpha_K, \beta_K)$.[8] The beta distribution is well known as the conjugate prior for the Bernoulli and the binomial distributions which are ideal for modeling success/failure.

3.3 MODELING ACCURACY

Here, we present the main theoretical contribution: the recovery success model defined in (9) is tighter than the lower bound of that in the existing CS framework explained in Section 3.1, when the number of measurements is not enough. We show the failure probability in the CS framework (5) is incapable of reflecting the actual failure probability of signal recovery. Not only can't the inequality $\mathbf{P}(\mathbf{s}^{\star} \neq \mathbf{s} \mid M, N, K) \le \exp(-M/(C \cdot \ln(N)K))$ provide tight probability of failure, but the inequality itself is inaccurate.

This inaccuracy results from the slowly decaying lower bound of success probability, that is, $1 - \exp(-M/(C \cdot \ln(N)K))$. In fact, we can show this lower bound decays slower than a power-law decay by the following lemma.

[7] Detailed settings are explained in Section 5.1.

[8] If more than 300 experiments had been performed, each success probability distribution would have been more sharply peaked due to a smaller variance.

Lemma 1 (Slackness of Recovery Success Probability). *There exists $K_0 > 0$ such that for all $K > K_0$, the lower bound of recovery success probability in the CS framework (Section 3.1) is greater than the value of a power-law-decay function.*

Proof. We need to show the following inequality

$$1 - \exp\left(-\frac{M}{C \cdot \ln(N)K}\right) > K^{-\alpha} \quad (11)$$

holds if $K > K_0$ for some $K_0 > 0$, where $\alpha > 0$. Adding, subtracting, and taking the power K on both sides yields

$$(1 - K^{-\alpha})^K > \exp\left(-\frac{M}{C \cdot \ln(N)}\right). \quad (12)$$

We now use the *binomial approximation* on the left-hand side: $(1 - K^{-\alpha})^K \geq 1 - K \cdot K^{-\alpha}$. Thus we instead prove the following inequality

$$1 - K^{1-\alpha} > \exp\left(-\frac{M}{C \cdot \ln(N)}\right) \quad (13)$$

holds if $K > K_0$ for some $K_0 > 0$.

If we assume $\alpha > 1$, then adding, subtracting, and taking the power $1/(1-\alpha)$ on both sides of (13) yields

$$\left(1 - \exp\left(-\frac{M}{C \cdot \ln(N)}\right)\right)^{1/(1-\alpha)} < K. \quad (14)$$

Setting $K_0 = (1 - \exp(-M/(C \cdot \ln(N))))^{1/(1-\alpha)}$, we can argue that for all $K > K_0$, the lower bound of recovery success probability is greater than the value of a power-law-decay function. □

Corollary 2. *In the CS framework (Section 3.1), there is always a chance of succeeding at signal recovery however large K is.*

Proof. The power-law-decay function $K^{-\alpha}$ in (11) *slowly* converges to zero as $K \to \infty$: its value is noticeably greater than zero even with a large K. As the lower bound of recovery success probability is greater than the value of the power-law-decay function for all $K > K_0$, there is always a chance of recovery success however large K is. □

The claim of the CS framework in Corollary 2 is in fact implausible because it says we can even set $K > M$ and there is still a chance of success. We cannot expect signal recovery with a number of measurements M less than K. We now show that our recovery success model provides more accurate success probability by the following theorem.

Theorem 3. *The recovery success model in (9) is tighter than the lower bound of recovery success probability given by the CS framework (Section 3.1) with a limited number of measurements.*

Proof. In contrast to Corollary 2, our recovery success model can yield $\mathbf{P}(\mathbf{s}^\star = \mathbf{s} \mid M, N, K) = 0$ with a bounded $K_{\max}$. In particular, we can let the mean of $\text{Beta}(\alpha_K, \beta_K)$, $\alpha_K/(\alpha_K + \beta_K)$, converge to zero with $\alpha_{K_{\max}} \to 0$.

Similarly, we show this mean converges to one ($\mathbf{P}(\mathbf{s}^\star = \mathbf{s} \mid M, N, K) = 1$) with $K_{\min}$ which is not so close to zero, whereas the lower bound of the recovery success probability given by the CS framework converges to one only if K is very close to zero.

We can let $\alpha_K/(\alpha_K + \beta_K)$ converge to one with $\beta_{K_{\min}} \to 0$. In contrast, $1 - \exp(-M/(C \cdot \ln(N)K)) \to 1$ if, and only if, $K \to 0$. Since $0 < K_{\min} < K_{\max} < \infty$, we can argue that our recovery success model can provide tighter recovery success probability. □

3.4 PARAMETER LEARNING IN DYNAMIC SYSTEMS

When the signal sparsity K changes in dynamic systems, it does not change in an abrupt manner; rather, it tends to smoothly change over time (Vaswani & Lu, 2010; Ziniel & Schniter, 2013). One simple way to model this correlation between K's is to utilize the *Markov model* (Ziniel & Schniter, 2013). In this setup, each K makes up a state and each state is associated with the recovery success probability. This can be best modeled by the hidden Markov model, where each state K generates success/failure according to the emission probability.

In our scenario, signal recovery success is observed in an environment where the signal sparsity varies over time. We want to estimate parameters of the hidden Markov model, especially the emission probabilities. Since our recovery success model employs the beta distribution as conjugate distributions (prior and posterior), we can learn its parameters α_K and β_K for each state K.

Specifically, the decoder can observe signal recovery success/failure and corresponding signal sparsity K at each decoding step. Then using these emission and state sequences, it can sequentially update the parameters α_K and β_K for each state K (Durbin et al., 1998), by simply incrementing the value of α_K by 1 for each success or the value of β_K by 1 for each failure.

In order to prevent over-fitting with insufficient observations, it is preferable to have hyperparameters of the prior beta distribution set according to K's. In Figure 2, we can clearly see the trend of α_K and β_K for different K's: α_K decreases, whereas β_K increases as K grows.[9] Therefore, these hyperparameters can act as the effective numbers of observations of recovery success/failure, reflecting our prior belief on signal recovery success for different K's.

[9]Also, see the proof of Theorem 3.

4 FURTHER ANALYSIS ON RECOVERY QUALITY

When a signal of interest is not exactly K-sparse but compressible, as discussed in Section 2.1, the signal recovery in Section 2.3 can be treated from a different perspective (Lee & Choi, 2015). In particular, the inequality (3) is considered differently.

If an original signal is compressible, then the quality of a recovered signal is proportional to that of the K most significant pieces of information. We get progressively better results as we compute more measurements M, since $M = O(K \log N)$ (Candès & Wakin, 2008). Therefore, $\mathbf{\Psi s}^\star \in \mathbb{R}^N$ also makes progress on its quality as M increases.[10]

From this viewpoint, the success or failure of signal recovery no longer exists. Rather, we can view the number of components included in the signal recovery as a *varying quantity*. Specifically, if a signal recovery is about to fail with a given K, then K can be lowered to make the recovery eventually succeed. Here the number of *included* components K varies for different recoveries and signals, as analogous to the success probability in Section 3.2 that can be calculated with different recoveries and varies for different signals.

In this regard, (3) can be utilized to infer varying K's over different recoveries and signals. Here our assumption is that the upper bound in (3) is *tight* such that we solve the following optimization problem:

$$\max K \qquad \text{subject to} \qquad \|\mathbf{s}^\star - \mathbf{s}\|_2 \leq C_1 \cdot \|\mathbf{s} - \mathbf{s}_K\|_1. \tag{15}$$

In (15), C_1 has to be determined, where the maximum signal sparsity $K_{\max}$ introduced in Section 3.2 plays a key role to set the upper limit on how large K can be, since $K > K_{\max}$ is not reasonable.

In particular, we can generate a compressible signal $\mathbf{s}_i \in S$ such that $\|\mathbf{s}_i\|_1 = C_{\ell_1}$ and $\|\mathbf{s}_i\|_2 = C_{\ell_2}$ for all i, where S is the set containing many different signals; $C_{\ell_1} > 0$ and $C_{\ell_2} > 0$ are constants. For each $\mathbf{s}_i$, we have a set $S_i^\star$ which contains many different recoveries $\mathbf{s}_{ij}^\star$. Then C_1 can be found as follows:

$$C_1 = \frac{\min \|\mathbf{s}_{ij}^\star - \mathbf{s}_i\|_2}{\|\mathbf{s}_i - \mathbf{s}_i^{K_{\max}}\|_1}, \tag{16}$$

where $\mathbf{s}_i^{K_{\max}}$ denotes the compressible signal $\mathbf{s}_i$ with all but the largest $K_{\max}$ components set to 0.

Varying K's obtained through (15) can be represented by a pdf, which has been empirically shown to follow the *gamma distribution* (Lee & Choi, 2015). We are interested in the shape of this pdf, which is shown by the following proposition.

Proposition 1. *The pdf of K, the number of components included in the signal recovery of a compressible signal, is skewed to the right, i.e., right tailed.*

Proof. Since $\|\mathbf{s}_i\|_1 = C_{\ell_1}$ and $\|\mathbf{s}_i\|_2 = C_{\ell_2}$ for all i, we can conceive the same sequence $\{s_n\}$ of elements (absolute values) in $\mathbf{s}_i$ for all i. Then we have

$$\|\mathbf{s}_i - \mathbf{s}_i^K\|_1 = \sum_{n=1}^{N-K} s_n. \tag{17}$$

Without loss of generality, we consider the partial sum $\sum_{n=1}^{N-K} s_n$ in (17) to be an *arithmetic series* which can be represented by a quadratic function in terms of K. We also assume the inequality constraint in (15) is the equality constraint such that $\|\mathbf{s}^\star - \mathbf{s}\|_2 = C_1 \cdot \|\mathbf{s} - \mathbf{s}_K\|_1$.

If we take the (partial) inverse function of the quadratic function, we have $K \sim K_{\max} - \sqrt{\|\mathbf{s}^\star - \mathbf{s}\|_2 - (\min \|\mathbf{s}_{ij}^\star - \mathbf{s}_i\|_2)}$. Assuming the distribution of $\|\mathbf{s}^\star - \mathbf{s}\|_2$ is *symmetric* (zero skewness), this asymptotic relation says $\|\mathbf{s}^\star - \mathbf{s}\|_2$ will be *compressed* as it becomes large, which in turn makes the pdf of K right tailed.

A similar claim can be made if we consider the partial sum $\sum_{n=1}^{N-K} s_n$ to be a *geometric series*, where $K \sim N - \log(\|\mathbf{s}^\star - \mathbf{s}\|_2)$. In this case, the pdf of K is skewed to the right as well. □

4.1 ERROR ANALYSIS IN DYNAMIC SYSTEMS

Since the success or failure of signal recovery does not exist in this framework, we instead investigate the amount of error occurring during the recovery procedure in an *expected value* sense. In particular, the best K-term approximation $\|\mathbf{s} - \mathbf{s}_K\|_1$ in (3) is known to be bounded as follows (Baraniuk et al., 2010):

$$\|\mathbf{s} - \mathbf{s}_K\|_1 \leq \frac{2G}{K}, \tag{18}$$

where the constant G can be learned by the power-law decay such that each magnitude of components in $\mathbf{s}$, sorted in decreasing order, is upper bounded by G/i^2. ($i = 1, \ldots, N$ is the sorted index.)

Then we can analyze the ℓ_2 error E of signal recovery assuming $f_K(k) = \mathrm{Gamma}(\kappa, \theta)$, which is given by

$$E = \int_k C_1 \cdot \frac{2G}{k} f_K(k)\,\mathrm{d}k = \frac{2C_1 G}{\theta} \mathrm{B}(\kappa - 1, 1), \tag{19}$$

where $\mathrm{B}(\cdot,\cdot)$ is the beta function (Lee & Choi, 2015). Here the pdf $f_K(k)$ is employed to represent varying K's.[11]

[10] The error bound follows (3) as well if $\mathbf{\Psi}$ is an orthogonal matrix, which is usually the case.

[11] Note that this pdf is different from the one introduced in Section 3.

In this framework, there is no longer such an indicator as the timely varying signal sparsity K in Section 3, because signals are compressible and their coefficients are already populated with small, but non-zero, coefficients. Thus, we may assume the same gamma distribution over time, whose parameters κ and θ can then be estimated.

In order to prevent over-fitting to insufficient observations, we introduce the conjugate prior for the gamma distribution. It is known that the conjugate prior of the gamma distribution has the following form (Miller, 1980; Fink, 1997).

$$\mathbf{P}(\kappa, \theta \mid p, q, r, s) = \frac{1}{Z} \cdot \frac{p^{\kappa-1} \exp(-q/\theta)}{\Gamma(\kappa)^r \theta^{s\kappa}}, \tag{20}$$

where $p, q, r, s > 0$ are hyperparameters that are sequentially updated with $p' = pk$, $q' = q + k$, $r' = r + 1$, and $s' = s + 1$;[12] and the normalizing constant Z is

$$Z = \int_0^\infty \frac{p^{\kappa-1}\Gamma(s\kappa + 1)}{\Gamma(\kappa)^r q^{s\kappa+1}} \,\mathrm{d}\kappa. \tag{21}$$

Using (19) and (20), we can marginalize over κ and θ to estimate error $\widehat{E}$ as follows:

$$\begin{aligned}\widehat{E} &= \int_\kappa \int_\theta E \cdot \mathbf{P}(\kappa, \theta \mid p, q, r, s) \,\mathrm{d}\theta \,\mathrm{d}\kappa \\ &= \frac{2C_1 G}{Z} \int_0^\infty \frac{p^{\kappa-1}}{(\kappa-1)\Gamma(\kappa)^r} \int_0^\infty \frac{\exp(-q/\theta)}{\theta^{s\kappa+1}} \,\mathrm{d}\theta \,\mathrm{d}\kappa \\ &= \frac{2C_1 G}{Z} \int_0^\infty \frac{p^{\kappa-1}\Gamma(s\kappa)}{(\kappa-1)\Gamma(\kappa)^r q^{s\kappa}} \,\mathrm{d}\kappa, \end{aligned} \tag{22}$$

which can be computed numerically.

5 EXPERIMENTAL RESULTS

5.1 RECOVERY SUCCESS

In Section 3, we discussed the discrepancy between the failure probabilities in the CS framework and actual random sampling. In order to show this discrepancy, we *artificially* generated signed spikes ± 1 at random locations in proportion to desired sparsities and *densified* these spikes using $\mathbf{\Psi}$[13] to perform the random sampling.

For each signal sparsity K, the actual failure probability can be calculated for different recovery experiments. To this end, we adopted a standard optimization method (*basis pursuit*) to solve the optimization problem in (2) (Chen et al., 1998). Specifically, the primal-dual algorithm based on the interior point method was employed to solve (2) (Boyd & Vandenberghe, 2004).

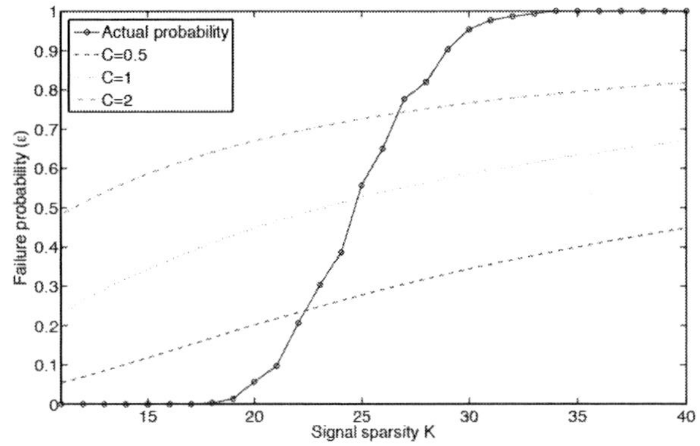

Figure 3: Comparison between actual failure probability and failure probabilities given in (5) with varying C's. Actual failure probability of each signal sparsity K was obtained with 300 experiments for $N = 512$ and $M = 100$.

Figure 3 shows that the actual failure probability of signal recovery with varying signal sparsity does not follow the failure probability given in the CS framework. The failure probability in (5) cannot model the actual failure probability of signal recovery, regardless of the value chosen for constant C. This result confirms Lemma 1 and Corollary 2.

Moreover, in Section 3.2 we modeled the new pdf of signal recovery success $f_{\Pi}(\pi)$ in (10). We compared this new pdf with the upper bound of failure in (6), given a dynamic signal sparsity K. Specifically, we employed the inverse Gaussian distribution such that $f_K(k) = \mathrm{IG}(30, 200)$. Figure 4 exhibits the efficacy of our recovery success model, where the lower bounds of success probability given in the CS framework fail to capture actual success probability in random sampling case. This result confirms Theorem 3.

Note that our recovery success model provides the baseline of recovery success for any CS frameworks that are specifically designed to handle varying signal sparsity. For instance, Figure 5 shows histograms of success probability for various signal sparsities using Modified-CS (Vaswani & Lu, 2010).[14] Compared with Figure 2, the success probability shown in Figure 5 also follows the beta distribution; but success probability is higher than that of basis pursuit for a given sparsity K ($K_{\min} = 21$ and $K_{\max} = 31$), thanks to the ability of Modified-CS to handle dynamic signal sparsity. The recovery success model in (9) is still effective here as a theoretical framework, or the recovery success model using the basis pursuit may promise a minimum guarantee for the recovery success of other CS frameworks.

We also employed real-world environmental data sets ob-

[12] Here, p', q', r', and s' are updated posterior hyperparameters; and k is a single observation.

[13] We used DCT as the sparsifying basis $\mathbf{\Psi}$ throughout experiments.

[14] Results were obtained with two frames where the second frame has one more spike than the first frame so that Modified-CS could exploit smoothly varying signal sparsity. Histograms in Figure 5 are the success probabilities of the second frame.

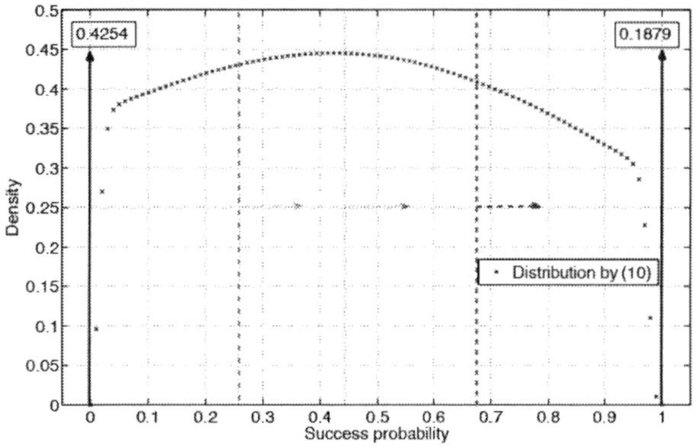

Figure 4: Comparison between our new success probability distribution in (10) and the lower bounds of success probability obtained by (6) with varying C's. The inverse Gaussian distribution was used for $f_K(k)$. Two probability masses are shown by vertical arrows, where solid boxes atop the arrows denote their probabilities. Three vertical dashed/dotted lines represent the lower bounds by (6): $C = 0.5$ at 0.6781; $C = 1$ at 0.4450; and $C = 2$ at 0.2596. Here, $K_{\min} = 20$ and $K_{\max} = 30$.

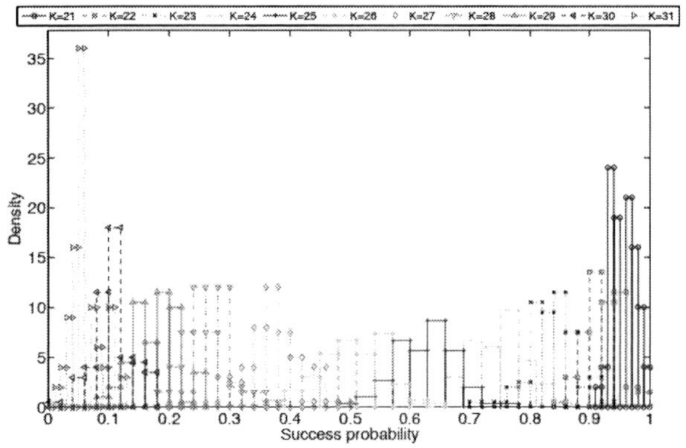

Figure 5: Histograms of success probability for various K's using Modified-CS (Vaswani & Lu, 2010). Success probability distribution for each K was obtained with 100 different random signed spike vectors for $N = 512$ and $M = 100$. A single success probability for each signed spike vector was calculated with 100 experiments. Compared with the results with basis pursuit in Figure 2, success probability is higher for a given sparsity K. Note also that 100 experiments resulted in a larger variance for each K.

tained from wireless sensor network deployments (Quer et al., 2012): humidity and temperature. In addition, audio data shown in Figure 1 was used for comparison as well. Random numbers representing the dynamic signal sparsity K were drawn from the inverse Gaussian distribution ($f_K(k) = \mathrm{IG}(30, 200)$) and we used this K to randomly choose components sorted in decreasing order; other components were set to zero. Figure 6 shows the success probability of signal recovery follows the shape of Figure 4.

5.2 RECOVERY QUALITY

When a signal is compressible and not exactly K-sparse, this signal is basically *dense*. In Section 4, we regarded the number of components included in the signal recovery as a varying quantity. We are interested in the general shape of this quantity in distribution. In order to verify Proposition 1, we performed experiments using real data sets as well as artificially generated random signed spikes.

We first provide results with real-world data sets to verify Proposition 1. Figure 7 displays the histograms of K, the number of components included in each signal recovery, which was obtained using the method explained in Section 4. We can identify that Proposition 1 actually holds here, as all distributions are skewed to the right. Furthermore, the distributions follow the gamma distribution, which is also natural since the gamma distribution has positive skewness, i.e., right tailed.

In addition, random signed spikes were artificially generated in different magnitudes at random locations and densified to perform random sampling. In particular, we considered an arithmetic sequence of length 50 $(2, 4, 6, \ldots, 98, 100)$, whose elements were placed at random locations in each vector. These signals are dense enough to be used for experiments because signal recovery always fails when $K > 30$ in our case, as shown in Figure 3. Figure 8 displays the histogram of K and the gamma distribution fitting, where we can again see that Proposition 1 holds.

Furthermore, we analyze the ℓ_2 error E of signal recovery assuming $f_K(k) = \mathrm{Gamma}(\kappa, \theta)$ using (19). In order to show its efficacy, we compared the solutions of (19) with real data sets. For humidity data, $E = 94.3533$ while the average ℓ_2 norm of data is 564.8585; for temperature data, $E = 75.5441$ while the average ℓ_2 norm of data is 627.8038; and for audio data, $E = 5.0979$ while the average ℓ_2 norm of data is 1.5866. Apart from the case of audio data, (19) provides useful estimators for the upper bound of amount of error during recovery. It should be noted that this bound is rather loose due to a large constant G in (18), which could be improved with a less conservative G.

6 CONCLUSION

We have presented a new theoretical CS framework in random sampling which handles uncertainty in signal recovery from a new perspective. The success probability of signal recovery in random sampling was investigated when signal sparsity can vary with an insufficient number of measurements. The success probability analysis in the existing CS framework was shown to be incapable of reflecting actual

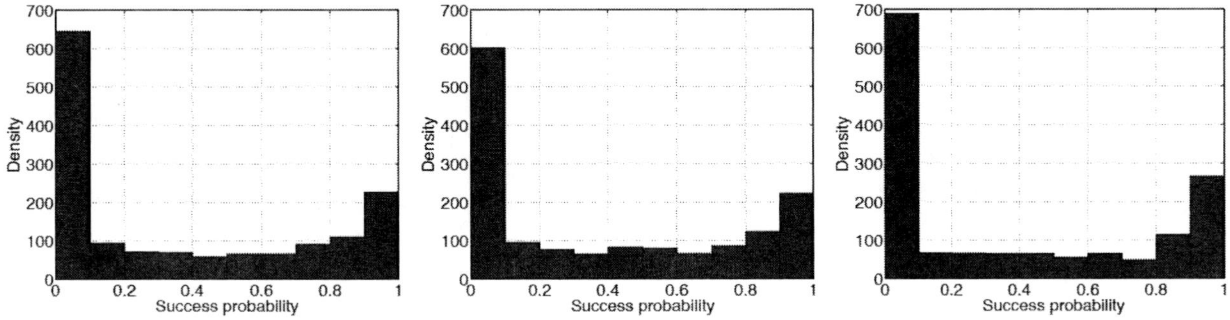

(a) humidity (b) temperature (c) audio

Figure 6: Histograms of success probability for (a) humidity data, (b) temperature data, and (c) audio data. Histogram was obtained with 1,500 random number generations (the inverse Gaussian distribution) to choose different signals and 100 different experiments for each signal with $N = 512$ and $M = 100$. All histograms closely follow the shape of Figure 4.

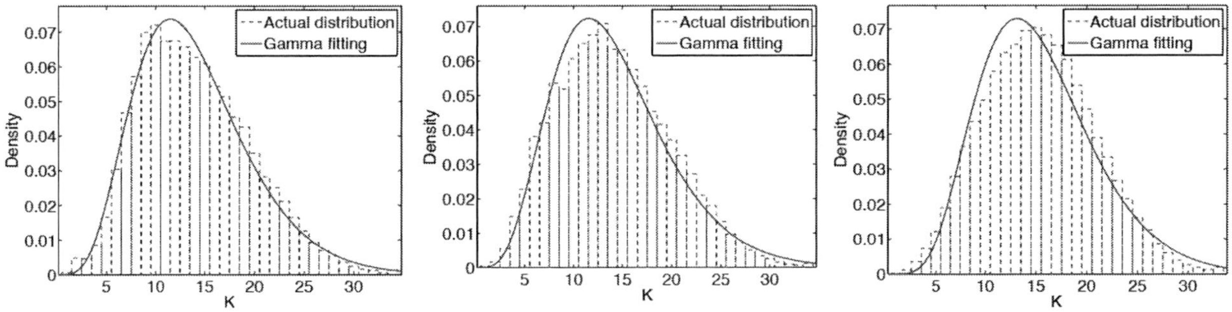

(a) humidity (b) temperature (c) audio

Figure 7: Distributions of K fitted with gamma distributions for (a) humidity data ($\mathrm{Gamma}(5.69, 2.45)$), (b) temperature data ($\mathrm{Gamma}(5.56, 2.54)$), and (c) audio data ($\mathrm{Gamma}(6.92, 2.21)$). Histograms were obtained with 34 different signals and 1,000 different experiments for each signal (a and b); with 153 different signals and 500 different experiments for each signal (c), with $N = 512$ and $M = 100$.

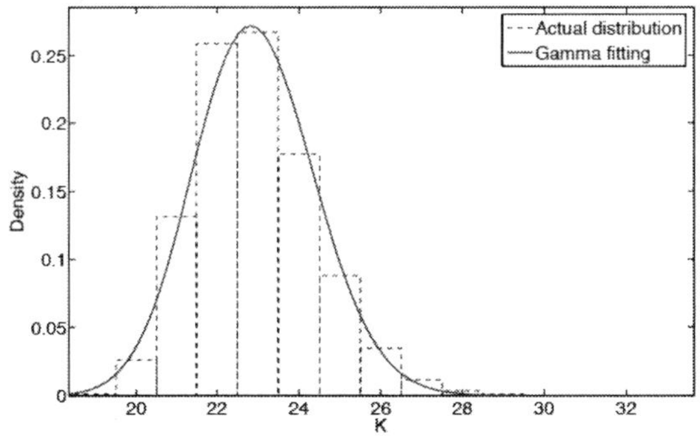

Figure 8: Distribution of K fitted with a gamma distribution $\mathrm{Gamma}(242.81, 0.09)$, using the maximum likelihood estimation. Histogram was obtained with 300 different signals and 300 different experiments for each signal, with $N = 512$ and $M = 100$.

success probability by both theoretical analysis and experiments. On the contrary, our recovery success model could closely reflect actual success probability.

We also considered signals which cannot be exactly represented with sparse representations, where we could alternatively view the number of components included in the signal recovery as a varying quantity. This quantity was shown by both theoretical analysis and experiments to follow a right-tailed distribution such as the gamma distribution. We provided error analysis for these signals.

Acknowledgements

This work was supported by Basic Science Research Program through the National Research Foundation of Korea (NRF) grant funded by the Ministry of Science, ICT & Future Planning (MSIP) (NRF-2014R1A1A1002662, NRF-2014M2A8A2074096). Jaesik Choi is the corresponding author.

References

Baraniuk, Richard G. Compressive sensing [lecture notes]. *IEEE Signal Process. Mag.*, 24(4):118–121, Jul. 2007.

Baraniuk, Richard G., Cevher, Volkan, Duarte, Marco F., and Hegde, Chinmay. Model-based compressive sensing. *IEEE Trans. Inf. Theory*, 56(4):1982–2001, Apr. 2010.

Blumensath, Thomas and Davies, Mike E. Iterative thresholding for sparse approximations. *J. Fourier Anal. Appl.*, 14(5-6):629–654, Dec. 2008.

Boyd, Stephen and Vandenberghe, Lieven. *Convex Optimization*. Cambridge University Press, 2004.

Candès, Emmanuel J. and Wakin, Michael B. An introduction to compressive sampling. *IEEE Signal Process. Mag.*, 25(2):21–30, Mar. 2008.

Chen, Scott S., Donoho, David L., and Saunders, Michael A. Atomic decomposition by basis pursuit. *SIAM J. Sci. Comput.*, 20(1):33–61, Jan. 1998.

Durbin, Richard, Eddy, Sean R, Krogh, Anders, and Mitchison, Graeme. *Biological Sequence Analysis: Probabilistic Models of Proteins and Nucleic Acids*. Cambridge University Press, 1998.

Fink, Daniel. A compendium of conjugate priors, 1997.

Foucart, Simon and Rauhut, Holger. *A Mathematical Introduction to Compressive Sensing*. Springer, 2013.

Hsu, Daniel, Kakade, Sham, Langford, John, and Zhang, Tong. Multi-label prediction via compressed sensing. In *Proc. NIPS*, pp. 772–780, 2009.

Lee, Dongeun and Choi, Jaesik. Low complexity sensing for big spatio-temporal data. In *Proc. IEEE BigData*, pp. 323–328, 2014.

Lee, Dongeun and Choi, Jaesik. Learning compressive sensing models for big spatio-temporal data. In *Proc. SDM*, pp. 667–675, 2015.

Lopes, Miles. Estimating unknown sparsity in compressed sensing. In *Proc. ICML*, pp. 217–225, 2013.

Malioutov, Dmitry and Varshney, Kush. Exact rule learning via boolean compressed sensing. In *Proc. ICML*, pp. 765–773, 2013.

Malioutov, Dmitry M., Sanghavi, Sujay R., and Willsky, Alan S. Sequential compressed sensing. *IEEE J. Sel. Top. Signal Process.*, 4(2):435–444, Apr. 2010.

Miller, Robert B. Bayesian analysis of the two-parameter gamma distribution. *Technometrics*, 22(1):65–69, Feb. 1980.

Pati, Yagyensh C., Rezaiifar, Ramin, and Krishnaprasad, P. S. Orthogonal matching pursuit: Recursive function approximation with applications to wavelet decomposition. In *Proc. ACSSC*, pp. 40–44, 1993.

Quer, Giorgio, Masiero, Riccardo, Pillonetto, Gianluigi, Rossi, Michele, and Zorzi, Michele. Sensing, compression, and recovery for WSNs: Sparse signal modeling and monitoring framework. *IEEE Trans. Wireless Commun.*, 11(10):3447–3461, Oct. 2012.

Seeger, Matthias W. and Nickisch, Hannes. Compressed sensing and bayesian experimental design. In *Proc. ICML*, pp. 912–919, 2008.

Sejdinovic, Dino, Andrieu, Christophe, and Piechocki, Robert. Bayesian sequential compressed sensing in sparse dynamical systems. In *Proc. Allerton*, pp. 1730–1736, 2010.

Shahrasbi, Behzad, Talari, Ali, and Rahnavard, Nazanin. TC-CSBP: Compressive sensing for time-correlated data based on belief propagation. In *Proc. CISS*, pp. 1–6, 2011.

Vaswani, Namrata and Lu, Wei. Modified-CS: Modifying compressive sensing for problems with partially known support. *IEEE Trans. Signal Process.*, 58(9):4595–4607, Sep. 2010.

Zhu, Rongda and Gu, Quanquan. Towards a lower sample complexity for robust one-bit compressed sensing. In *Proc. ICML*, pp. 739–747, 2015.

Ziniel, Justin and Schniter, Philip. Dynamic compressive sensing of time-varying signals via approximate message passing. *IEEE Trans. Signal Process.*, 61(21): 5270–5284, Nov. 2013.

Ziniel, Justin, Rangan, Sundeep, and Schniter, Philip. A generalized framework for learning and recovery of structured sparse signals. In *Proc. IEEE Statistical Signal Processing Workshop*, pp. 325–328, 2012.

Bounded Rational Decision-Making in Feedforward Neural Networks

Felix Leibfried[1,2,3] and **Daniel A. Braun**[1,2]
[1]Max Planck Institute for Intelligent Systems, Tübingen, Germany
[2]Max Planck Institute for Biological Cybernetics, Tübingen, Germany
[3]Graduate Training Center of Neuroscience, Tübingen, Germany

Abstract

Bounded rational decision-makers transform sensory input into motor output under limited computational resources. Mathematically, such decision-makers can be modeled as information-theoretic channels with limited transmission rate. Here, we apply this formalism for the first time to multilayer feedforward neural networks. We derive synaptic weight update rules for two scenarios, where either each neuron is considered as a bounded rational decision-maker or the network as a whole. In the update rules, bounded rationality translates into information-theoretically motivated types of regularization in weight space. In experiments on the MNIST benchmark classification task for handwritten digits, we show that such information-theoretic regularization successfully prevents overfitting across different architectures and attains results that are competitive with other recent techniques like dropout, dropconnect and Bayes by backprop, for both ordinary and convolutional neural networks.

1 INTRODUCTION

Intelligent systems in biology excel through their ability to flexibly adapt their behavior to changing environments so as to maximize their (expected) benefit. In order to understand such biological intelligence and to design artificial intelligent systems, a central goal is to analyze adaptive behavior from a theoretical point of view. A formal framework to achieve this goal is decision theory. An important idea, originating from the foundations of decision theory, is the principle of maximum expected utility [1]. According to the principle of maximum expected utility, an intelligent agent is formalized as a decision-maker that chooses optimal actions that maximize the expected benefit of an outcome, where the agent's benefit is quantified by a utility function.

A fundamental problem of the maximum expected utility principle is that it does not take into account computational resources that are necessary to identify optimal actions—it is for example computationally prohibitive to compute an optimal chess move because of the vast amount of potential board configurations. One way of taking computational resources into account is to study optimal decision-making under information-processing constraints [2, 3]. In this study, we use an information-theoretic model of bounded rational decision-making [4, 5, 6] that has precursors in the economic literature [7, 8, 9] and that is closely related to recent advances harnessing information theory for machine learning and perception-action systems [10, 11, 12, 13, 14, 15, 16, 17, 18, 19, 20].

Previously, this information-theoretic bounded rationality model was applied to derive a synaptic weight update rule for a single reward-maximizing spiking neuron [21]. It was shown that such a neuron tries to keep its firing rate close to its average firing rate, which ultimately leads to economizing of synaptic weights. Mathematically, such economizing is equivalent to a regularization that prevents synaptic weights from growing without bounds. The bounded rational weight update rule furthermore generalizes the synaptic weight update rule for an ordinary reward-maximizing spiking neuron as presented for example in [22]. In our current work, we extend the framework of information-theoretic bounded rationality to networks of neurons, but restrict ourselves for a start to deterministic settings. In particular, we investigate two scenarios, where either each single neuron is considered as a bounded rational decision-maker or the network as a whole.

The remainder of this manuscript is organized as follows. In Section 2, we explain the information-theoretic bounded rationality model that we use. In Section 3, we apply this model to derive bounded rational synaptic weight update rules for single neurons and networks of neurons. In Section 4, we demonstrate the regularizing effect of these bounded rational weight update rules on the MNIST benchmark classification task. In Section 5, we conclude.

2 BACKGROUND ON BOUNDED RATIONAL DECISION-MAKING

2.1 A FREE ENERGY PRINCIPLE FOR BOUNDED RATIONALITY

A decision-maker is faced with the task to choose an optimal action out of a set of actions. Each action y is associated with a given task-specific utility value $U(y)$. A fully rational decision-maker picks the action y^* that globally maximizes the utility function, where $y^* = \arg\max_y U(y)$, assuming for notational simplicity that the global maximum is unique. Under limited computational resources however, the decision-maker may not be able to identify the globally optimal action y^* which leads to the question of how limited computational resources should be quantified. In general, the decision-maker's behavior can be expressed as a probability distribution over actions $p(y)$. The basic idea of information-theoretic bounded rationality is that changes in such probability distributions are costly and necessitate computational resources. More precisely, computational resources are quantified as informational cost evoked by changing from a prior probabilistic strategy $p_0(y)$ to a posterior probabilistic strategy $p(y)$ during the deliberation process preceding the choice. Mathematically, this informational cost is given by the Kullback-Leibler divergence $D_{KL}(p(y)||p_0(y)) \leq B$ between prior and posterior strategy, where computational resources are modeled as an upper bound $B \geq 0$ [10, 5, 6, 13, 14, 15, 17, 18, 19, 20, 8, 9]. Accordingly, bounded rational decision-making can be formalized by the following free energy objective

$$\begin{aligned} p^*(y) &= \arg\max_{p(y)} \ (1-\beta) \langle U(y) \rangle_{p(y)} - \beta D_{KL}(p(y)||p_0(y)) \\ &= \arg\max_{p(y)} \left\langle (1-\beta)U(y) - \beta \ln \frac{p(y)}{p_0(y)} \right\rangle_{p(y)}, \end{aligned} \tag{1}$$

where $\beta \in (0;1)$ controls the trade-off between expected utility and informational cost. Note that the upper bound B imposed on the Kullback-Leibler divergence determines the value of β. Choosing the value of B is hence equivalent to choosing the value of β.

The free energy objective in Equation (1) is concave with respect to $p(y)$ and the optimal solution $p^*(y)$ can be expressed in closed analytic form:

$$p^*(y) = \frac{p_0(y) \exp(\frac{1-\beta}{\beta} U(y))}{\sum_{y'} p_0(y') \exp(\frac{1-\beta}{\beta} U(y'))}. \tag{2}$$

In the limit cases of none ($\beta \to 1$) and infinite ($\beta \to 0$) resources, the optimal strategy from Equation (2) becomes

$$\lim_{\beta \to 1} p^*(y) = p_0(y), \tag{3}$$

$$\lim_{\beta \to 0} p^*(y) = \delta_{yy^*}, \tag{4}$$

respectively, where $y^* = \arg\max_y U(y)$ represents an action that globally maximizes the utility function. A decision-maker without any computational resources ($\beta \to 1$) sticks to its prior strategy $p_0(y)$, whereas a decision-maker that can access an arbitrarily large amount of resources ($\beta \to 0$) always picks a globally optimal action and recovers thus the fully rational decision-maker.

2.2 A RATE DISTORTION PRINCIPLE FOR CONTEXT-DEPENDENT DECISION-MAKING

In the face of multiple contexts, fully rational decision-making requires to find an optimal action y for each environment x, where optimality is defined through a utility function $U(x,y)$. Bounded rational decision-making in multiple contexts means to compute multiple strategies, expressed as conditional probability distributions $p(y|x)$, under limited computational resources. Limited computational resources are modeled through an upper bound $B \geq 0$ on the expected Kullback-Leibler divergence $\langle D_{KL}(p(y|x)||p_0(y)) \rangle_{p(x)} \leq B$ between the strategies $p(y|x)$ and a common prior $p_0(y)$, averaged over all possible environments described by the distribution $p(x)$ [4, 15]. The resulting optimization problem may be formalized as

$$\begin{aligned} p^*(y|x) = \arg\max_{p(y|x)} \ & (1-\beta) \langle U(x,y) \rangle_{p(x,y)} \\ & - \beta \langle D_{KL}(p(y|x)||p_0(y)) \rangle_{p(x)}, \end{aligned} \tag{5}$$

where $\beta \in (0;1)$ governs the trade-off between expected utility and informational cost. It can be shown that the most economic prior $p_0(y)$ is given by the marginal distribution $p_0(y) = p(y) = \sum_x p(y|x)p(x)$, because the marginal distribution minimizes the expected Kullback-Leibler divergence for a given set of conditional distributions $p(y|x)$—see [23]. In this case, the expected Kullback-Leibler divergence becomes identical to the mutual information $I(x,y)$ between the environment x and the action y [4, 21, 11, 12, 7, 16]. Accordingly, bounded rational decision-making can be formalized through the following objective

$$\begin{aligned} p^*(y|x) &= \arg\max_{p(y|x)} \ (1-\beta) \langle U(x,y) \rangle_{p(x,y)} - \beta I(x,y) \\ &= \arg\max_{p(y|x)} \left\langle (1-\beta)U(x,y) - \beta \ln \frac{p(y|x)}{p(y)} \right\rangle_{p(x,y)}, \end{aligned} \tag{6}$$

which is mathematically equivalent to the rate distortion problem from information theory [24].

The rate distortion objective in Equation (6) is concave with respect to $p(y|x)$ but there is unfortunately no closed analytic form solution. It is however possible to express the optimal solution as a set of self-consistent equations:

$$p^*(y|x) = \frac{p(y)\exp(\frac{1-\beta}{\beta}U(x,y))}{\sum_{y'} p(y')\exp(\frac{1-\beta}{\beta}U(x,y'))}, \quad (7)$$

$$p(y) = \sum_x p^*(y|x)p(x). \quad (8)$$

These self-consistent equations are solved by replacing $p(y)$ with an initial arbitrary distribution $q(y)$ and iterating through Equations (7) and (8) in an alternating fashion. This procedure is known as Blahut-Arimoto algorithm [25, 26] and is guaranteed to converge to a global optimum [27] presupposed that $q(y)$ does not assign zero probability mass to any y.

In the limit cases of none ($\beta \to 1$) and infinite ($\beta \to 0$) resources, the optimal strategy from Equations (7) and (8) may be expressed in closed analytic form

$$\lim_{\beta\to 1} p^*(y|x) = p(y) = \delta_{yy^*}, \quad (9)$$

$$\lim_{\beta\to 0} p^*(y|x) = \delta_{yy^*_x}, \quad (10)$$

where $y^* = \arg\max_y \langle U(x,y)\rangle_{p(x)}$ refers to an action that globally maximizes the expected utility averaged over all possible environments, and y^*_x refers to an action that globally maximizes the utility for one particular environment x—assuming for notational simplicity that global maxima are unique in both cases. In the absence of any computational resources ($\beta \to 1$), the decision-maker chooses the same strategy no matter which environment is encountered in order to minimize the deviation between the conditional strategies $p(y|x)$ and the average strategy $p(y)$. The decision-maker chooses however a strategy that maximizes the average expected utility. In case of access to an arbitrarily large amount of computational resources ($\beta \to 0$), the decision-maker picks the best action for each environment and recovers thus the fully rational decision-maker.

3 THEORETICAL RESULTS: SYNAPTIC WEIGHT UPDATE RULES

3.1 PARAMETERIZED STRATEGIES AND ONLINE RULES

Computing the optimal solution to the rate distortion problem in Equation (6) with help of Equations (7) and (8) through the Blahut-Arimoto algorithm has two severe drawbacks. First, it requires to compute and store the conditional strategies $p(y|x)$ and the marginal strategy $p(y)$ explicitly, which is prohibitive for large environment and action spaces. And second, it requires that the decision-maker is able to evaluate the utility function for arbitrary environment-action pairs (x, y), which is a plausible assumption in planning, but not in reinforcement learning where samples from the utility function can only be obtained from interactions with the environment.

We therefore assume a parameterized form of the strategy $p_w(y|x)$, from which the decision-maker can draw samples y for a given sample of the environment x, and optimize the rate distortion objective from Equation (6) with help of gradient ascent [21]—also referred to as policy gradient in the reinforcement learning literature [22]. Gradient ascent requires to compute the derivative of the objective function $L(w)$ with respect to the strategy parameters w and to update the parameters according to the rule $w \leftarrow w + \alpha \cdot \frac{\partial}{\partial w}L(w)$ in each time step, where $\alpha > 0$ denotes the learning rate and $\frac{\partial}{\partial w}L(w)$ is defined as

$$\frac{\partial}{\partial w}L(w) = \left\langle \left(\frac{\partial}{\partial w}\ln p_w(y|x)\right)(1-\beta)U(x,y)\right\rangle_{p_w(x,y)} - \left\langle \left(\frac{\partial}{\partial w}\ln p_w(y|x)\right)\beta\ln\frac{p_w(y|x)}{p_w(y)}\right\rangle_{p_w(x,y)}. \quad (11)$$

Note that the update rule from Equation (11) requires the computation of an expected value over $p_w(x, y)$. This expected value can be approximated through environment-action samples (x, y) in either a batch or an online manner. For the rest of this paper, we assume an online update rule where the agent adapts its behavior instantaneously after each interaction with the environment in response to an immediate reward signal $U(x, y)$ as is typical for reinforcement learning.

Informally, the rate distortion model for bounded rational decision-making translates into a specific form of regularization that penalizes deviations of the decision-maker's instantaneous strategy $p_w(y|x)$, given the current environment x, from the decision-maker's mean strategy $p_w(y) = \sum_x p_w(y|x)p(x)$, averaged over all possible environments. Previously, Equation (11) was applied to a single spiking neuron that was stochastic [21]. Here, we generalize this approach to deterministic networks of neurons that have neural input (environmental context x), neural output (action y) and a reward signal (utility U). We derive parameter update rules in the style of Equation (11) that allow to adjust synaptic weights in an online fashion. In particular, we investigate two scenarios where either each single neuron is considered as a bounded rational decision-maker or the network as a whole.

3.2 A STOCHASTIC NEURON AS A BOUNDED RATIONAL DECISION-MAKER

A stochastic neuron may be considered as a bounded rational decision-maker [21]: the neuron's presynaptic input is interpreted as environmental context and the neuron's output is interpreted as action variable. The neuron's parameterized strategy corresponds to its firing behavior and is given by

$$p_{\mathbf{w}}(y|\mathbf{x}) = y \cdot \rho(\mathbf{w}^\top \mathbf{x}) + (1-y)\cdot(1-\rho(\mathbf{w}^\top \mathbf{x})), \quad (12)$$

where $y \in \{0, 1\}$ is a binary variable reflecting the neuron's current firing state, $\mathbf{x}$ is a binary column vector representing the neuron's current presynaptic input and $\mathbf{w}$ is a real-valued column vector representing the strength of presynaptic weights. $\rho \in (0; 1)$ is a monotonically increasing function denoting the neuron's current firing probability. In a similar way, the neuron's mean firing behavior can be expressed as:

$$p_{\mathbf{w}}(y) = y \cdot \bar{\rho}(\mathbf{w}) + (1-y)\cdot(1-\bar{\rho}(\mathbf{w})), \quad (13)$$

where $\bar{\rho}(\mathbf{w}) = \sum_{\mathbf{x}} \rho(\mathbf{w}^\top \mathbf{x})p(\mathbf{x})$ denotes the neuron's mean firing probability averaged over all possible inputs $\mathbf{x}$. The mean firing probability $\bar{\rho}(\mathbf{w})$ can be easily estimated with help of an exponential window in an online manner according to

$$\bar{\rho}(\mathbf{w}) \leftarrow (1-\frac{1}{\tau})\bar{\rho}(\mathbf{w}) + \frac{1}{\tau}\rho(\mathbf{w}^\top \mathbf{x}), \quad (14)$$

where τ is a constant defining the time horizon [21].

Assuming a task-specific utility function $U(\mathbf{x}, y)$ determining the neuron's instantaneous reward and assuming furthermore that the neuron's output y does not impact the presynaptic input $\mathbf{x}$ of the next time step, the bounded rational neuron may be thought of as optimizing a rate distortion objective according to Equation (6) with gradient ascent as outlined in Section 3.1 [21]. Equation (11) is then applicable by using the quantities

$$\frac{\partial}{\partial w_i} \ln p_{\mathbf{w}}(y|\mathbf{x}) = x_i \rho'(\mathbf{w}^\top \mathbf{x}) \left(\frac{y}{\rho(\mathbf{w}^\top \mathbf{x})} - \frac{1-y}{1-\rho(\mathbf{w}^\top \mathbf{x})} \right), \quad (15)$$

and

$$\ln \frac{p_{\mathbf{w}}(y|\mathbf{x})}{p_{\mathbf{w}}(y)} = y \ln \frac{\rho(\mathbf{w}^\top \mathbf{x})}{\bar{\rho}(\mathbf{w})} + (1-y)\ln \frac{1-\rho(\mathbf{w}^\top \mathbf{x})}{1-\bar{\rho}(\mathbf{w})}. \quad (16)$$

By averaging over the binary quantity y, a more concise weight update rule is derived [21]:

$$\frac{\partial}{\partial w_i} L(\mathbf{w}) = \left\langle x_i \rho'(\mathbf{w}^\top \mathbf{x})(1-\beta)\Delta U(\mathbf{x}) \right\rangle_{p(\mathbf{x})} - \left\langle x_i \rho'(\mathbf{w}^\top \mathbf{x})\beta \ln \frac{\rho(\mathbf{w}^\top \mathbf{x})(1-\bar{\rho}(\mathbf{w}))}{\bar{\rho}(\mathbf{w})(1-\rho(\mathbf{w}^\top \mathbf{x}))} \right\rangle_{p(\mathbf{x})}, \quad (17)$$

where $\Delta U(\mathbf{x}) = U(\mathbf{x}, y=1) - U(\mathbf{x}, y=0)$ denotes the difference in utility between firing ($y = 1$) and not firing ($y = 0$) for a given $\mathbf{x}$. If the conditional and marginal strategies are initialized to be roughly equal $p_{\mathbf{w}_0}(y) \approx p_{\mathbf{w}_0}(y|\mathbf{x})$, where $\mathbf{w}_0 \approx \mathbf{0}$ refers to the initial value of $\mathbf{w}$, the hyperparameter β determines how fast the decision-maker's strategy converges. A high value of β implies little computational resources and quick convergence due to the fact that conditional and marginal strategies are initially almost equal. On the opposite, a low value of β indicating vast computational resources allows the decision-maker to find an optimal strategy for each environment where conditional and marginal strategies may deviate substantially.

3.3 A DETERMINISTIC NEURON AS A BOUNDED RATIONAL DECISION-MAKER

In a deterministic setup, the neuron's parameterized firing behavior in a small time window Δt may be expressed through its firing rate $\phi(\mathbf{w}^\top \boldsymbol{\xi})$ as:

$$p_{\mathbf{w}}(y|\boldsymbol{\xi}) = y \cdot \phi(\mathbf{w}^\top \boldsymbol{\xi})\Delta t + (1-y)\cdot(1-\phi(\mathbf{w}^\top \boldsymbol{\xi})\Delta t), \quad (18)$$

where $\boldsymbol{\xi}$ is a real-valued column vector indicating the presynaptic firing rates and $\phi > 0$ is a monotonically increasing function. In a similar fashion, the neuron's mean firing behavior is given by

$$p_{\mathbf{w}}(y) = y \cdot \bar{\phi}(\mathbf{w})\Delta t + (1-y)\cdot(1-\bar{\phi}(\mathbf{w})\Delta t), \quad (19)$$

where $\bar{\phi}(\mathbf{w}) = \sum_{\boldsymbol{\xi}} \phi(\mathbf{w}^\top \boldsymbol{\xi})p(\boldsymbol{\xi})$ refers to the neuron's mean firing rate averaged over all possible presynaptic firing rates $\boldsymbol{\xi}$. In accordance with the previous section, the mean firing rate $\bar{\phi}(\mathbf{w})$ can be conveniently approximated in an online manner through an exponential window with a time constant τ as:

$$\bar{\phi}(\mathbf{w}) \leftarrow (1-\frac{1}{\tau})\bar{\phi}(\mathbf{w}) + \frac{1}{\tau}\phi(\mathbf{w}^\top \boldsymbol{\xi}). \quad (20)$$

Using the quantities introduced above, we can define a mutual information rate between the presynaptic firing rates $\boldsymbol{\xi}$ and the instantaneous firing state of the neuron $y \in \{0; 1\}$:

$$\lim_{\Delta t \to 0} \frac{1}{\Delta t} I(\boldsymbol{\xi}, y) = \lim_{\Delta t \to 0} \frac{1}{\Delta t} \left\langle \sum_y p_{\mathbf{w}}(y|\boldsymbol{\xi}) \ln \frac{p_{\mathbf{w}}(y|\boldsymbol{\xi})}{p_{\mathbf{w}}(y)} \right\rangle_{p(\boldsymbol{\xi})} = \left\langle \phi(\mathbf{w}^\top \boldsymbol{\xi}) \ln \frac{\phi(\mathbf{w}^\top \boldsymbol{\xi})}{\bar{\phi}(\mathbf{w})} \right\rangle_{p(\boldsymbol{\xi})}. \quad (21)$$

A derivation of Equation (21) can be found in Section A.1. Assuming a rate-dependent utility function $U(\boldsymbol{\xi}, \phi(\mathbf{w}^\top \boldsymbol{\xi}))$, a deterministic neuron can be interpreted as a bounded rational decision-maker similar to Equation (6) with the following rate distortion objective

$$\begin{aligned}\mathbf{w}^* &= \arg\max_{\mathbf{w}} \ (1-\beta)\left\langle U(\boldsymbol{\xi},\phi(\mathbf{w}^\top\boldsymbol{\xi}))\right\rangle_{p(\boldsymbol{\xi})} \\ &\quad - \beta \lim_{\Delta t\to 0}\frac{1}{\Delta t} I(\boldsymbol{\xi},y) \\ &= \arg\max_{\mathbf{w}} \ \left\langle (1-\beta)U(\boldsymbol{\xi},\phi(\mathbf{w}^\top\boldsymbol{\xi}))\right\rangle_{p(\boldsymbol{\xi})} \\ &\quad - \left\langle \beta\phi(\mathbf{w}^\top\boldsymbol{\xi})\ln\frac{\phi(\mathbf{w}^\top\boldsymbol{\xi})}{\bar{\phi}(\mathbf{w})}\right\rangle_{p(\boldsymbol{\xi})}.\end{aligned} \tag{22}$$

Optimizing the neuron's weights with gradient ascent, a similar weight update rule as in Equation (17) is derived for the deterministic case:

$$\begin{aligned}&\frac{\partial}{\partial w_i}L(\mathbf{w}) = \\ &\left\langle \xi_i\phi'(\mathbf{w}^\top\boldsymbol{\xi})(1-\beta)\frac{\partial}{\partial\phi}U(\boldsymbol{\xi},\phi(\mathbf{w}^\top\boldsymbol{\xi}))\right\rangle_{p(\boldsymbol{\xi})} \\ &- \left\langle \xi_i\phi'(\mathbf{w}^\top\boldsymbol{\xi})\beta\ln\frac{\phi(\mathbf{w}^\top\boldsymbol{\xi})}{\bar{\phi}(\mathbf{w})}\right\rangle_{p(\boldsymbol{\xi})},\end{aligned} \tag{23}$$

where $\frac{\partial}{\partial\phi}U(\boldsymbol{\xi},\phi(\mathbf{w}^\top\boldsymbol{\xi}))$ denotes the derivative of the utility function with respect to the neuron's firing rate. The solution in Equation (23) requires the derivative of two terms with respect to w_i. The derivative of the expected utility $\left\langle U(\boldsymbol{\xi},\phi(\mathbf{w}^\top\boldsymbol{\xi}))\right\rangle_{p(\boldsymbol{\xi})}$ is straightforward, whereas the derivative of the mutual information rate $\lim_{\Delta t\to 0}\frac{1}{\Delta t}I(\boldsymbol{\xi},y)$ is not so trivial and explained in more detail in Section A.2.

3.4 A NEURAL NETWORK OF BOUNDED RATIONAL DETERMINISTIC NEURONS

Here, we consider a feedforward multilayer perceptron that can be imagined to consist of individual bounded rational deterministic neurons as described in the previous section. Assuming that all neurons aim at maximizing a global utility function while at the same time minimizing their local mutual information rate, each neuron n may be interpreted as solving a deterministic rate distortion objective where the utility function is shared among all neurons but the mutual information cost is neuron-specific:

$$\begin{aligned}\mathbf{w}^{n*} &= \arg\max_{\mathbf{w}^n} \ (1-\beta)\left\langle U(\boldsymbol{\xi}^{\text{in}},\mathbf{f}(\mathcal{W},\boldsymbol{\xi}^{\text{in}}))\right\rangle_{p(\boldsymbol{\xi}^{\text{in}})} \\ &\quad - \beta\lim_{\Delta t\to 0}\frac{1}{\Delta t}I(\boldsymbol{\xi}^n,y^n),\end{aligned} \tag{24}$$

where $\mathbf{w}^n$, $\boldsymbol{\xi}^n$ and y^n refer to the presynaptic weight vector, the presynaptic firing rates and the current firing state of neuron n respectively and where $\mathcal{W}$ denotes the entirety of all weights in the whole neural network. The global utility $U(\boldsymbol{\xi}^{\text{in}},\mathbf{f}(\mathcal{W},\boldsymbol{\xi}^{\text{in}}))$ is expressed as a function of the network's input rates $\boldsymbol{\xi}^{\text{in}}$ and the network's output rates $\mathbf{f}(\mathcal{W},\boldsymbol{\xi}^{\text{in}})$.

The corresponding synaptic weight update rule for gradient ascent is similar to Equation (23) and given by

$$\begin{aligned}&\frac{\partial}{\partial w_i^n}L^n(\mathcal{W}) = \\ &\left\langle (1-\beta)\frac{\partial}{\partial w_i^n}U(\boldsymbol{\xi}^{\text{in}},\mathbf{f}(\mathcal{W},\boldsymbol{\xi}^{\text{in}}))\right\rangle_{p(\boldsymbol{\xi}^{\text{in}})} \\ &- \left\langle \beta\xi_i^n\phi'(\mathbf{w}^{n\top}\boldsymbol{\xi}^n)\ln\frac{\phi(\mathbf{w}^{n\top}\boldsymbol{\xi}^n)}{\bar{\phi}(\mathbf{w}^n)}\right\rangle_{p(\boldsymbol{\xi}^{\text{in}})},\end{aligned} \tag{25}$$

where $L^n(\mathcal{W})$ refers to the rate distortion objective of neuron n. The derivative of the utility function with respect to the weight $\frac{\partial}{\partial w_i^n}U(\boldsymbol{\xi}^{\text{in}},\mathbf{f}(\mathcal{W},\boldsymbol{\xi}^{\text{in}}))$ can be straightforwardly derived via ordinary backpropagation [28].

3.5 A DETERMINISTIC NEURAL NETWORK AS A BOUNDED RATIONAL DECISION-MAKER

While focusing on individual neurons as bounded rational decision-makers in the previous section, it is also possible to interpret an entire feedforward multilayer perceptron as one bounded rational decision-maker. To allow for this interpretation, we consider in the following the network's output rates $f_j(\mathcal{W},\boldsymbol{\xi}) \in (0;1)$ as the event probabilities of a categorical distribution (for example, by using a softmax activation function in the last layer). Importantly, the categorical distribution is considered as a bounded rational strategy

$$p_{\mathcal{W}}(\mathbf{y}|\boldsymbol{\xi}) = \sum_j y_j f_j(\mathcal{W},\boldsymbol{\xi}), \tag{26}$$

that generates a binary unit output vector $\mathbf{y}$ given the input rates $\boldsymbol{\xi}$ and the set of all weights in the entire network denoted by $\mathcal{W}$. The average bounded rational strategy is then given by

$$p_{\mathcal{W}}(\mathbf{y}) = \sum_j y_j \bar{f}_j(\mathcal{W}), \tag{27}$$

where $\bar{f}_j(\mathcal{W})$ is the mean rate of output unit j that can again be approximated in an online manner according to

$$\bar{f}_j(\mathcal{W}) \leftarrow (1-\frac{1}{\tau})\bar{f}_j(\mathcal{W}) + \frac{1}{\tau}f_j(\mathcal{W},\boldsymbol{\xi}), \tag{28}$$

by use of an exponential window with a time constant τ in line with previous sections.

Accordingly, the informational cost can be quantified by the mutual information between $\boldsymbol{\xi}$ and $\mathbf{y}$:

$$\begin{aligned}I(\boldsymbol{\xi},\mathbf{y}) &= \left\langle \sum_{\mathbf{y}} p_{\mathcal{W}}(\mathbf{y}|\boldsymbol{\xi})\ln\frac{p_{\mathcal{W}}(\mathbf{y}|\boldsymbol{\xi})}{p_{\mathcal{W}}(\mathbf{y})}\right\rangle_{p(\boldsymbol{\xi})} \\ &= \left\langle \sum_j f_j(\mathcal{W},\boldsymbol{\xi})\ln\frac{f_j(\mathcal{W},\boldsymbol{\xi})}{\bar{f}_j(\mathcal{W})}\right\rangle_{p(\boldsymbol{\xi})}.\end{aligned} \tag{29}$$

Presupposing again a rate dependent utility function $U(\boldsymbol{\xi}, \mathbf{f}(\mathcal{W}, \boldsymbol{\xi}))$, the entire deterministic network may be interpreted to solve the subsequent rate distortion objective

$$\begin{aligned}\mathcal{W}^* &= \arg\max_{\mathcal{W}} \ (1-\beta)\,\langle U(\boldsymbol{\xi}, \mathbf{f}(\mathcal{W}, \boldsymbol{\xi}))\rangle_{p(\boldsymbol{\xi})} \\ &\quad - \beta I(\boldsymbol{\xi}, \mathbf{y}) \\ &= \arg\max_{\mathcal{W}} \ \langle (1-\beta) U(\boldsymbol{\xi}, \mathbf{f}(\mathcal{W}, \boldsymbol{\xi}))\rangle_{p(\boldsymbol{\xi})} \\ &\quad - \left\langle \beta \sum_j f_j(\mathcal{W}, \boldsymbol{\xi}) \ln \frac{f_j(\mathcal{W}, \boldsymbol{\xi})}{\bar{f}_j(\mathcal{W})} \right\rangle_{p(\boldsymbol{\xi})},\end{aligned} \tag{30}$$

Assuming that synaptic weights are updated via gradient ascent, the following weight update rule can be derived

$$\begin{aligned}&\frac{\partial}{\partial w_i^n} L(\mathcal{W}) = \\ &\left\langle (1-\beta) \sum_j \left(\frac{\partial}{\partial w_i^n} f_j(\mathcal{W}, \boldsymbol{\xi})\right) \left(\frac{\partial}{\partial f_j} U(\boldsymbol{\xi}, \mathbf{f}(\mathcal{W}, \boldsymbol{\xi}))\right) \right\rangle_{p(\boldsymbol{\xi})} \\ &- \left\langle \beta \sum_j \left(\frac{\partial}{\partial w_i^n} f_j(\mathcal{W}, \boldsymbol{\xi})\right) \ln \frac{f_j(\mathcal{W}, \boldsymbol{\xi})}{\bar{f}_j(\mathcal{W})} \right\rangle_{p(\boldsymbol{\xi})},\end{aligned} \tag{31}$$

where $\frac{\partial}{\partial w_i^n}$ denotes the derivative with respect to the ith weight of neuron n, and $\frac{\partial}{\partial f_j} U(\boldsymbol{\xi}, \mathbf{f}(\mathcal{W}, \boldsymbol{\xi}))$ denotes the derivative of the utility function with respect to the firing rate of the jth output neuron. Equation (31) requires to differentiate two terms with respect to w_i^n. The derivative of the expected utility is straightforward while the derivative of the mutual information is explained in Section A.3.

Note that the derivative of the rate distortion objective $\frac{\partial}{\partial w_i^n} L(\mathcal{W})$ takes a convenient form which can be easily computed by extending ordinary backpropagation [28]. In ordinary backpropagation, the quantity $\frac{\partial}{\partial f_j} U(\boldsymbol{\xi}, \mathbf{f}(\mathcal{W}, \boldsymbol{\xi}))$ is propagated backwards through the network. The core algorithm of ordinary backpropagation can be employed for computing $\frac{\partial}{\partial w_i^n} L(\mathcal{W})$ by simply replacing the derivative of the utility function $\frac{\partial}{\partial f_j} U(\boldsymbol{\xi}, \mathbf{f}(\mathcal{W}, \boldsymbol{\xi}))$ with the more general quantity $(1-\beta)\frac{\partial}{\partial f_j} U(\boldsymbol{\xi}, \mathbf{f}(\mathcal{W}, \boldsymbol{\xi})) - \beta \ln \frac{f_j(\mathcal{W}, \boldsymbol{\xi})}{\bar{f}_j(\mathcal{W})}$.

4 EXPERIMENTAL RESULTS: MNIST CLASSIFICATION

In our simulations, we applied both types of rate distortion regularization (the local type from Section 3.4 and the global type from Section 3.5) on the MNIST benchmark classification task. In particular, we investigated in how far this information-theoretically motivated regularization subserves generalization. To this end, we trained classification on the MNIST training set, consisting of $60,000$ grayscale images of handwritten digits, and tested generalization on the MNIST test set, consisting of $10,000$ examples. For all our simulations, we used a network with two hidden layers of rectified linear units [29] and a top layer of 10 softmax units implemented in Lua with Torch [30]. We chose as optimization criterion the negative cross entropy between the class labels and the network output [31]

$$U(\boldsymbol{\xi}, \mathbf{f}(\mathcal{W}, \boldsymbol{\xi})) = \sum_j \delta_{jl(\boldsymbol{\xi})} \ln f_j(\mathcal{W}, \boldsymbol{\xi}), \tag{32}$$

where δ denotes the Kronecker delta and $\boldsymbol{\xi}$ the vectorized input image—note that pixels were normalized to lie in the range $[0; 1]$. The variable $j \in \{1, 10\}$ is an index over the network's output units and $l(\boldsymbol{\xi}) \in \{1, 10\}$ denotes the label of image $\boldsymbol{\xi}$.

In order to assess the robustness of our regularizers, we performed our experiments with networks of different architectures. In particular, we used network architectures with two hidden layers and varied the number of neurons $\#_{\text{neu}} \in \{529, 1024, 2025, 4096\}$ per hidden layer. We performed gradient ascent with a learning rate $\alpha = 0.01$ updating weights online after each training example. We trained the networks for 70 epochs where one epoch corresponded to one sweep through the entire training set. After each epoch, the learning rate decayed according to $\alpha \leftarrow \frac{\alpha}{1+t\cdot\eta}$ where t denotes the current epoch and $\eta = 0.002$ is a decay parameter. Weights were updated by use of a momentum $\gamma = 0.9$ according to $\Delta w_i^n \leftarrow \gamma \Delta w_i^n + (1-\gamma)\frac{\partial}{\partial w_i^n} L(\mathcal{W})$ and were randomly initialized in the range $(-(\#_{\text{in}}(n))^{-0.5}; (\#_{\text{in}}(n))^{-0.5})$ with help of a uniform distribution at the beginning of the simulation where $\#_{\text{in}}(n)$ denotes the number of inputs to neuron n. Each non-input neuron had an additional bias weight that was initialized in the same way as the presynaptic weights of that neuron. Rate distortion regularization required furthermore to compute the mean firing rate $\bar{\phi}(\mathbf{w}^n)$ of individual neurons n through an exponential window in an online fashion with a time constant $\tau = 1000$. In order to ensure numerical stability when using rate distortion regularization, terms of the form $\ln \frac{\phi(\mathbf{w}^{n\top}\boldsymbol{\xi}^n)}{\bar{\phi}(\mathbf{w}^n)}$ in the weight update rules were computed according to $\ln \max\{\phi(\mathbf{w}^{n\top}\boldsymbol{\xi}^n), \varepsilon\} - \ln \max\{\bar{\phi}(\mathbf{w}^n), \varepsilon\}$ with $\varepsilon = 2.22 \cdot 10^{-16}$.

To find optimal values for the rate distortion trade-off parameter β, we conducted pilot studies with small networks comprising 529 neurons per hidden layer that were trained for only 50 epochs on the MNIST training set according to the aforementioned training scheme and subsequently evaluated on the MNIST test set. While this might induce overfitting of β on the test set in the small networks, we used the same β-values as a heuristic for all larger architectures and did not tune the hyperparameter any further. In global rate distortion regularization (Grdi), the best test error was achieved around $\beta = 0.2$ although Grdi seems to behave rather robust in the range $\beta \in [0; 0.8]$—see middle left panel in Figure 1. In local rate distortion regularization (Lrdi), the best test error was achieved for $\beta = 0$ with ordinary utility maximization without regularization—see middle right panel. However, when measuring the performance in terms of expected utility on the test set, Lrdi achieved a significant performance increase compared to ordinary utility maximization in the range $\beta \in [10^{-5}, 5 \cdot 10^{-4}]$—see upper right panel. In our final studies, we could furthermore ascertain that Lrdi performs reasonably well on larger architectures as it achieved a test error of 1.26% compared to 1.43% in ordinary utility maximization when increasing the number of units per hidden layer to 4096.

Table 1: Classification Errors on the MNIST Test Set in the Permutation Invariant Setup

Method	$\#_{\text{neu}}$	Error [%]
Bayes by backprop [10]	1200	1.32
Dropout [32]	800	1.28
Dropconnect [32]	800	1.20
Dropout [33]	4096	**1.01**
Local rate distortion (Lrdi) $\beta = 10^{-5}$	529	1.36
	1024	1.34
	2025	1.28
	4096	**1.26**
Global rate distortion (Grdi) $\beta = 0.2$	529	1.23
	1024	1.17
	2025	1.14
	4096	**1.11**

The results of our final studies where we trained networks for 70 epochs are illustrated in Table 1 which compares rate distortion regularization to other techniques from the literature for different network architectures comprising two hidden layers. It can be seen that both local and global rate distortion regularization (Lrdi and Grdi respectively) attain results in the permutation invariant setting (Lrdi: 1,26%, Grdi: 1.11%) that are competitive with other recent techniques like dropout (1.01% [33] and 1.28% [32]), dropconnect (1.20% [32]) and Bayes by backprop (1.32% [10]). It is furthermore shown that both rate distortion regularizers lead to a decreasing generalization error when increasing the number of neurons in hidden layers which demonstrates successful prevention of overfitting. Successful prevention of overfitting is additionally demonstrated by applying global rate distortion regularization (Grid, $\beta = 0.2$) to a convolutional neural network with an architecture according to [32]—see Section B.2 in [32]—attaining an error of 0.61% without tuning any hyperparameters (see Table 2). This result is also competitive with other recent techniques in the permutation non-invariant setting—compare to dropout (0.59% [32]) and dropconnect (0.63% [32]). In line with [33], we preprocessed the input with ZCA whitening and added a max-norm regularizer to limit the size of presynaptic weight vectors to at most 3.5.

Table 2: Classification Errors on the MNIST Test Set in the Permutation Non-Invariant Setup

Method	Error [%]
Conv net + Dropconnect [32]	0.63
Conv net + Grdi ($\beta = 0.2$)	0.61
Conv net + Dropout [32]	**0.59**

The lower panels of Figure 1 show the development of the test set error over epochs for both rate distortion regularizers (red) compared to ordinary utility maximization without regularization (Umax, black) for the different network architectures that we used in the permutation invariant setting. It can be seen that the global variant of our regularizer (Grdi with $\beta = 0.2$, see lower left panel in Figure 1) leads to a significant increase in performance across different architectures as demonstrated by the two separate clusters of trajectories. In addition, Grdi also leads to faster learning as the red trajectories in the lower left panel of Figure 1 decrease significantly faster then the black trajectories during the first ten epochs of training. For the local variant of our regularizer (Lrdi with $\beta = 10^{-5}$, see lower right panel in Figure 1), the performance improvements are less prominent when compared to the global variant.

5 CONCLUSION

Previously, a synaptic weight update rule for a single reward-maximizing spiking neuron was devised, where the neuron was interpreted as a bounded rational decision-maker under limited computational resources with help of rate distortion theory [21]. It was shown that such a bounded rational weight update rule leads to an efficient regularization by preventing synaptic weights from growing without bounds. In our current work, we extend these results to deterministic neurons and neural networks. On the MNIST benchmark classification task, we have demonstrated the regularizing effect of our approach as networks were successfully prevented from overfitting. These results are robust as we conducted experiments with different network architectures achieving performance competitive with other recent techniques like dropout [33], dropconnect [32] and Bayes by backprop [10] for both ordinary and convolutional networks. The strength of rate distortion regularization is that it is a more principled approach than for example dropout and dropconnect as it may be applied to general artificial agents with parameterized policies and not only to neural networks. Parameterized policies that optimize the rate distortion objective have been previously applied to unsupervised density estimation tasks with autoencoder networks [12]. Our current work extends this kind of approach to the theory of reinforcement and supervised learning with feedforward neural networks, and also provides evidence that this approach scales well on large data sets.

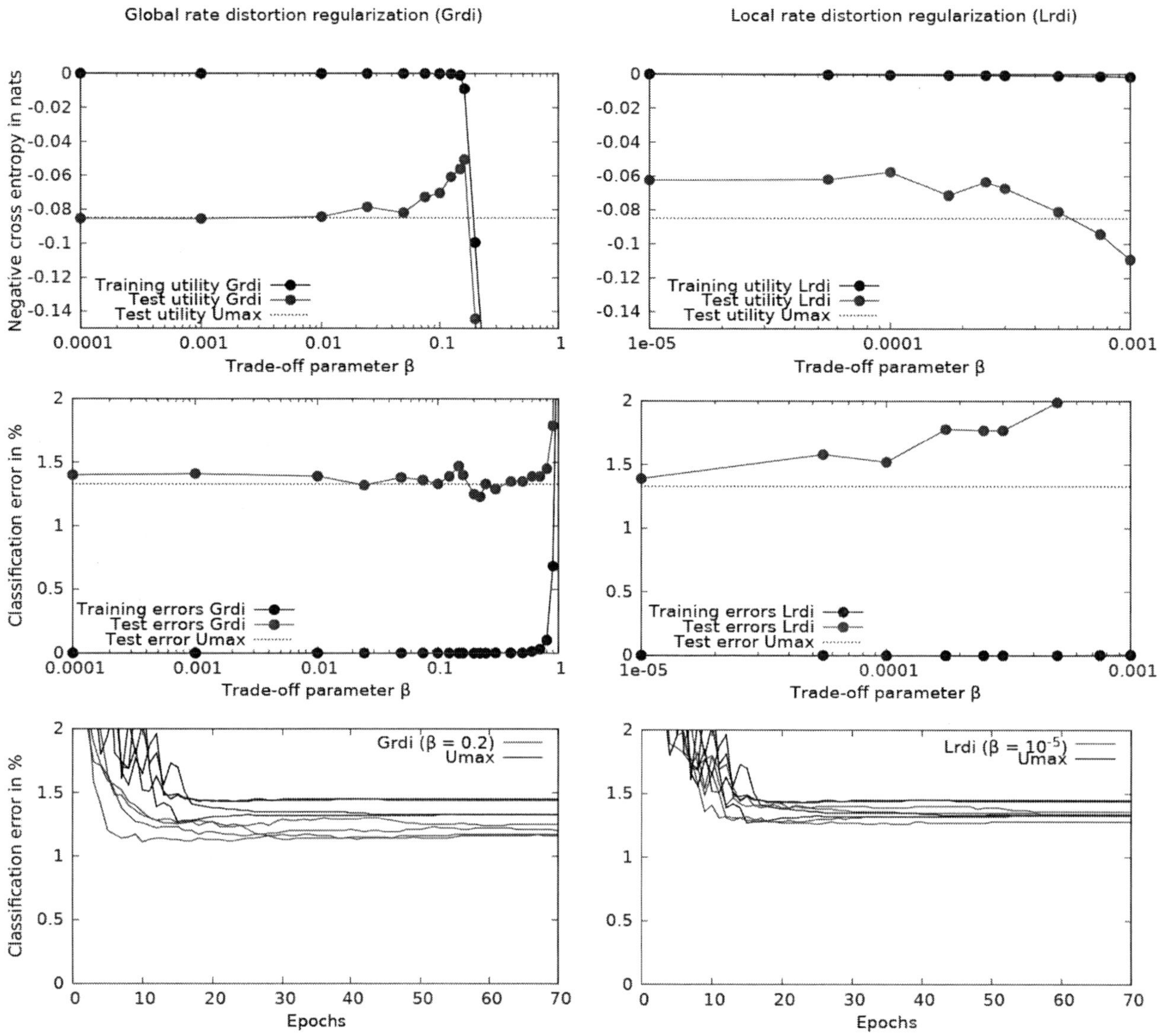

Figure 1: Performance on MNIST in the Permutation Invariant Setup. The left column refers to analyses with global rate distortion regularization (Grdi) and the right column to analyses with local rate distortion regularization (Lrdi). The *upper and middle panels* show the results of the pilot studies on the smallest network architecture. Trajectories in the upper panels illustrate the expected utility (the negative cross entropy) after 50 epochs of training for different values of β—black solid lines reflect the expected utility on the training set, red solid lines reflect the expected utility on the test set and red dashed horizontal lines reflect the expected utility on the test set in ordinary utility maximization (Umax, $\beta = 0$). The middle panels show classification errors instead of utility values. In the Grdi case, the negative cross entropy drops sharply for larger betas, because the regularization drives the output rates towards a flatter distribution, even though the mode of the distribution is maintained, which allows for robust performance in terms of classification error. The *lower panels* show the results of our final simulations with four different network architectures and fixed β-values. The plots compare the development of the test set error over epochs between ordinary utility maximization (black trajectories, Umax) and rate distortion regularization (red trajectories, Grdi with $\beta = 0.2$ and Lrdi with $\beta = 10^{-5}$ respectively). Each trajectory corresponds to one of the four different network architectures.

A APPENDIX

A.1 MUTUAL INFORMATION RATE OF A DETERMINISTIC NEURON

$$\begin{aligned}
&\lim_{\Delta t \to 0} \frac{1}{\Delta t} I(\boldsymbol{\xi}, y) \\
&= \lim_{\Delta t \to 0} \frac{1}{\Delta t} \left\langle \sum_y p_{\mathbf{w}}(y|\boldsymbol{\xi}) \ln \frac{p_{\mathbf{w}}(y|\boldsymbol{\xi})}{p_{\mathbf{w}}(y)} \right\rangle_{p(\boldsymbol{\xi})} \\
&= \lim_{\Delta t \to 0} \frac{1}{\Delta t} \left\langle \phi(\mathbf{w}^\top \boldsymbol{\xi}) \Delta t \ln \frac{\phi(\mathbf{w}^\top \boldsymbol{\xi})}{\bar{\phi}(\mathbf{w})} \right\rangle_{p(\boldsymbol{\xi})} \\
&+ \lim_{\Delta t \to 0} \frac{1}{\Delta t} \left\langle (1 - \phi(\mathbf{w}^\top \boldsymbol{\xi}) \Delta t) \underbrace{\ln \frac{1 - \phi(\mathbf{w}^\top \boldsymbol{\xi}) \Delta t}{1 - \bar{\phi}(\mathbf{w}) \Delta t}}_{\to 0} \right\rangle_{p(\boldsymbol{\xi})} \\
&= \left\langle \phi(\mathbf{w}^\top \boldsymbol{\xi}) \ln \frac{\phi(\mathbf{w}^\top \boldsymbol{\xi})}{\bar{\phi}(\mathbf{w})} \right\rangle_{p(\boldsymbol{\xi})} .
\end{aligned} \tag{33}$$

A.2 DERIVATIVE OF THE MUTUAL INFORMATION RATE

$$\begin{aligned}
&\frac{\partial}{\partial w_i} \lim_{\Delta t \to 0} \frac{1}{\Delta t} I(\boldsymbol{\xi}, y) \\
&= \lim_{\Delta t \to 0} \frac{1}{\Delta t} \frac{\partial}{\partial w_i} \left\langle \sum_y p_{\mathbf{w}}(y|\boldsymbol{\xi}) \ln \frac{p_{\mathbf{w}}(y|\boldsymbol{\xi})}{p_{\mathbf{w}}(y)} \right\rangle_{p(\boldsymbol{\xi})} \\
&= \lim_{\Delta t \to 0} \frac{1}{\Delta t} \left\langle \sum_y \left(\frac{\partial}{\partial w_i} p_{\mathbf{w}}(y|\boldsymbol{\xi}) \right) \ln \frac{p_{\mathbf{w}}(y|\boldsymbol{\xi})}{p_{\mathbf{w}}(y)} \right\rangle_{p(\boldsymbol{\xi})} \\
&+ \lim_{\Delta t \to 0} \frac{1}{\Delta t} \underbrace{\left\langle \sum_y p_{\mathbf{w}}(y|\boldsymbol{\xi}) \left(\frac{\partial}{\partial w_i} \ln p_{\mathbf{w}}(y|\boldsymbol{\xi}) \right) \right\rangle_{p(\boldsymbol{\xi})}}_{= \left\langle \sum_y \frac{\partial}{\partial w_i} p_{\mathbf{w}}(y|\boldsymbol{\xi}) \right\rangle_{p(\boldsymbol{\xi})} = \frac{\partial}{\partial w_i} 1 = 0} \\
&- \lim_{\Delta t \to 0} \frac{1}{\Delta t} \underbrace{\left\langle \sum_y p_{\mathbf{w}}(y|\boldsymbol{\xi}) \left(\frac{\partial}{\partial w_i} \ln p_{\mathbf{w}}(y) \right) \right\rangle_{p(\boldsymbol{\xi})}}_{= \sum_y \frac{\partial}{\partial w_i} p_{\mathbf{w}}(y) = \frac{\partial}{\partial w_i} 1 = 0} \\
&= \lim_{\Delta t \to 0} \frac{1}{\Delta t} \left\langle \xi_i \phi'(\mathbf{w}^\top \boldsymbol{\xi}) \Delta t \ln \frac{\phi(\mathbf{w}^\top \boldsymbol{\xi})}{\bar{\phi}(\mathbf{w})} \right\rangle_{p(\boldsymbol{\xi})} \\
&- \lim_{\Delta t \to 0} \frac{1}{\Delta t} \left\langle \xi_i \phi'(\mathbf{w}^\top \boldsymbol{\xi}) \Delta t \underbrace{\ln \frac{1 - \phi(\mathbf{w}^\top \boldsymbol{\xi}) \Delta t}{1 - \bar{\phi}(\mathbf{w}) \Delta t}}_{\to 0} \right\rangle_{p(\boldsymbol{\xi})} \\
&= \left\langle \xi_i \phi'(\mathbf{w}^\top \boldsymbol{\xi}) \ln \frac{\phi(\mathbf{w}^\top \boldsymbol{\xi})}{\bar{\phi}(\mathbf{w})} \right\rangle_{p(\boldsymbol{\xi})} .
\end{aligned} \tag{34}$$

A.3 DERIVATIVE OF THE GLOBAL MUTUAL INFORMATION

$$\begin{aligned}
&\frac{\partial}{\partial w_i^n} I(\boldsymbol{\xi}, \mathbf{y}) \\
&= \frac{\partial}{\partial w_i^n} \left\langle \sum_{\mathbf{y}} p_{\mathcal{W}}(\mathbf{y}|\boldsymbol{\xi}) \ln \frac{p_{\mathcal{W}}(\mathbf{y}|\boldsymbol{\xi})}{p_{\mathcal{W}}(\mathbf{y})} \right\rangle_{p(\boldsymbol{\xi})} \\
&= \left\langle \sum_{\mathbf{y}} \left(\frac{\partial}{\partial w_i^n} p_{\mathcal{W}}(\mathbf{y}|\boldsymbol{\xi}) \right) \ln \frac{p_{\mathcal{W}}(\mathbf{y}|\boldsymbol{\xi})}{p_{\mathcal{W}}(\mathbf{y})} \right\rangle_{p(\boldsymbol{\xi})} \\
&+ \underbrace{\left\langle \sum_{\mathbf{y}} p_{\mathcal{W}}(\mathbf{y}|\boldsymbol{\xi}) \left(\frac{\partial}{\partial w_i^n} \ln p_{\mathcal{W}}(\mathbf{y}|\boldsymbol{\xi}) \right) \right\rangle_{p(\boldsymbol{\xi})}}_{= \left\langle \sum_{\mathbf{y}} \frac{\partial}{\partial w_i^n} p_{\mathcal{W}}(\mathbf{y}|\boldsymbol{\xi}) \right\rangle_{p(\boldsymbol{\xi})} = \frac{\partial}{\partial w_i^n} 1 = 0} \\
&- \underbrace{\left\langle \sum_{\mathbf{y}} p_{\mathcal{W}}(\mathbf{y}|\boldsymbol{\xi}) \left(\frac{\partial}{\partial w_i^n} \ln p_{\mathcal{W}}(\mathbf{y}) \right) \right\rangle_{p(\boldsymbol{\xi})}}_{= \sum_{\mathbf{y}} \frac{\partial}{\partial w_i^n} p_{\mathcal{W}}(\mathbf{y}) = \frac{\partial}{\partial w_i^n} 1 = 0} \\
&= \left\langle \sum_j \left(\frac{\partial}{\partial w_i^n} f_j(\mathcal{W}, \boldsymbol{\xi}) \right) \ln \frac{f_j(\mathcal{W}, \boldsymbol{\xi})}{\bar{f}_j(\mathcal{W})} \right\rangle_{p(\boldsymbol{\xi})} .
\end{aligned} \tag{35}$$

Acknowledgements

This study was supported by the DFG, Emmy Noether grant BR4164/1-1.

References

[1] J von Neumann and O Morgenstern. *Theory of Games and Economic Behavior*. Princeton University Press, 1944.

[2] S J Gershman, E J Horvitz, and J B Tenenbaum. Computational rationality: a converging paradigm for intelligence in brains, minds, and machines. *Science*, 349(6245):273–278, 2015.

[3] H A Simon. Theories of bounded rationality. *Decision and Organization*, 1:161–176, 1972.

[4] T Genewein, F Leibfried, J Grau-Moya, and D A Braun. Bounded rationality, abstraction and hierarchical decision-making: an information-theoretic optimality principle. *Frontiers in Robotics and AI*, 2(27), 2015.

[5] P A Ortega, D A Braun, J Dyer, K-E Kim, and N Tishby. Information-theoretic bounded rationality. *arXiv preprint arXiv:1512.06789*, 2015.

[6] P A Ortega and D A Braun. Thermodynamics as a theory of decision-making with information-processing costs. *Proceedings of the Royal Society A*, 469(2153):1–26, 2013.

[7] C A Sims. Rational inattention and monetary economics. In *Handbook of Monetary Economics*, volume 3, chapter 4. Elsevier, 2011.

[8] D H Wolpert. Information theory - the bridge connecting bounded rational game theory and statistical physics. In *Complex Engineered Systems*, chapter 12. Springer, 2004.

[9] L G Mattsson and J W Weibull. Probabilistic choice and procedurally bounded rationality. *Games and Economic Behavior*, 41(1):61–78, 2002.

[10] C Blundell, J Cornebise, K Kavukcuoglu, and D Wierstra. Weight uncertainty in neural networks. In *Proceedings of the 32nd International Conference on Machine Learning*, 2015.

[11] S Still. Lossy is lazy. In *Workshop on Information Theoretic Methods in Science and Engineering*, pages 17–21, 2014.

[12] L G Sanchez Giraldo and J C Principe. Rate-distortion auto-encoders. *arXiv preprint arXiv:1312.7381*, 2013.

[13] H J Kappen, V Gómez, and M Opper. Optimal control as a graphical model inference problem. *Machine Learning*, 87(2):159–182, 2012.

[14] K Rawlik, M Toussaint, and S Vijayakumar. On stochastic optimal control and reinforcement learning by approximate inference. *Proceedings Robotics: Science and Systems*, 2012.

[15] J Rubin, O Shamir, and N Tishby. Trading value and information in MDPs. In *Decision Making with Imperfect Decision Makers*, chapter 3. Springer, 2012.

[16] N Tishby and D Polani. Information theory of decisions and actions. In *Perception-Action Cycle*, chapter 19. Springer, 2011.

[17] K Friston. The free-energy principle: a unified brain theory? *Nature Reviews Neuroscience*, 11(2):127–138, 2010.

[18] J Peters, K Muelling, and Y Altun. Relative entropy policy search. In *Proceedings of the National Conference on Artificial Intelligence*, 2010.

[19] S Still. Information-theoretic approach to interactive learning. *Europhysics Letters*, 85(2):28005, 2009.

[20] E Todorov. Efficient computation of optimal actions. *Proceedings of the National Academy of Sciences of the United States of America*, 106(28):11478–11483, 2009.

[21] F Leibfried and D A Braun. A reward-maximizing spiking neuron as a bounded rational decision maker. *Neural Computation*, 27(8):1686–720, 2015.

[22] X Xie and H S Seung. Learning in neural networks by reinforcement of irregular spiking. *Physical Review E*, 69(4 Pt 1):041909, 2004.

[23] N Tishby, F C Pereira, and W Bialek. The information bottleneck method. In *Proceedings of the 37th Annual Allerton Conference on Communication, Control and Computing*, pages 368–377, 1999.

[24] C E Shannon. Coding theorems for a discrete source with a fidelity criterion. *Institute of Radio Engineers, International Convention Record*, 7:142–163, 1959.

[25] S Arimoto. An algorithm for computing the capacity of arbitrary discrete memoryless channels. *IEEE Transactions on Information Theory*, 18(1):14–20, 1972.

[26] R Blahut. Computation of channel capacity and rate-distortion functions. *IEEE Transactions on Information Theory*, 18(4):460–473, 1972.

[27] I. Csiszar. On the computation of rate-distortion functions. *IEEE Transactions on Information Theory*, 20(1):122–124, 1974.

[28] Y LeCun, L Bottou, G B Orr, and K R Müller. Efficient backprop. In *Neural Networks: Tricks of the Trade*, volume 1524, chapter 2, pages 9–50. Springer Berlin Heidelberg, 1998.

[29] X Glorot, A Bordes, and Y Bengio. Deep sparse rectifier neural networks. In *Proceedings of the Fourteenth International Conference on Artificial Intelligence and Statistics*, pages 315–323, 2011.

[30] R Collobert, K Kavukcuoglu, and C Farabet. Torch7: a matlab-like environment for machine learning. In *BigLearn, NIPS Workshop. No. EPFL-CONF-192376*, 2011.

[31] P Y Simard, D Steinkraus, and J C Platt. Best practices for convolutional neural networks applied to visual document analysis. In *Proceedings of the Seventh International Conference on Document Analysis and Recognition*, 2003.

[32] L Wan, M Zeiler, S Zhang, Y LeCun, and R Fergus. Regularization of neural networks using dropconnect. In *Proceedings of the 30th International Conference on Machine Learning*, 2013.

[33] N Srivastava, G E Hinton, A Krizhevsky, I Sutskever, and R Salakhutdinov. Dropout : a simple way to prevent neural networks from overfitting. *Journal of Machine Learning Research*, 15:1929–1958, 2014.

Thompson Sampling is Asymptotically Optimal in General Environments

Jan Leike
Australian National University
jan.leike@anu.edu.au

Tor Lattimore
University of Alberta
tor.lattimore@gmail.com

Laurent Orseau
Google DeepMind
lorseau@google.com

Marcus Hutter
Australian National University
marcus.hutter@anu.edu.au

Abstract

We discuss a variant of Thompson sampling for nonparametric reinforcement learning in countable classes of general stochastic environments. These environments can be non-Markov, nonergodic, and partially observable. We show that Thompson sampling learns the environment class in the sense that (1) asymptotically its value converges to the optimal value in mean and (2) given a recoverability assumption regret is sublinear.

Keywords. General reinforcement learning, Thompson sampling, asymptotic optimality, regret, discounting, recoverability, AIXI.

1 INTRODUCTION

In reinforcement learning (RL) an agent interacts with an unknown environment with the goal of maximizing rewards. Recently reinforcement learning has received a surge of interest, triggered by its success in applications such as simple video games [MKS$^+$15]. However, theory is lagging behind application and most theoretical analyses has been done in the bandit framework and for Markov decision processes (MDPs). These restricted environment classes fall short of the full reinforcement learning problem and theoretical results usually assume ergocity and visiting every state infinitely often. Needless to say, these assumptions are not satisfied for any but the simplest applications.

Our goal is to lift these restrictions; we consider *general reinforcement learning*, a top-down approach to RL with the aim to understand the fundamental underlying problems in their generality. Our approach to general RL is *nonparametric*: we only assume that the true environment belongs to a given countable environment class.

We are interested in agents that maximize rewards *optimally*. Since the agent does not know the true environment in advance, it is not obvious what optimality should mean. We discuss two different notions of optimality: *asymptotic optimality* and *worst-case regret*.

Asymptotic optimality requires that asymptotically the agent learns to act optimally, i.e., that the discounted value of the agent's policy π converges to the optimal discounted value, $V^*_\mu - V^\pi_\mu \to 0$ for all environments μ from the environment class. This convergence is impossible for deterministic policies since the agent has to explore infinitely often and for long stretches of time, but there are policies that converge almost surely in Cesàro average [LH11]. Bayes-optimal agents are generally not asymptotically optimal [Ors13]. However, asymptotic optimality can be achieved through an exploration component on top of a Bayes-optimal agent [Lat13, Ch. 5] or through optimism [SH15].

Asymptotic optimality in mean is essentially a weaker variant of *probably approximately correct* (PAC) that comes without a concrete convergence rate: for all $\varepsilon > 0$ and $\delta > 0$ the probability that our policy is ε-suboptimal converges to zero (at an unknown rate). Eventually this probability will be less than δ. Since our environment class can be very large and non-compact, concrete PAC/convergence rates are likely impossible.

Regret is how many expected rewards the agent forfeits by not following the best informed policy. Different problem classes have different regret rates, depending on the structure and the difficulty of the problem class. Multi-armed bandits provide a (problem-independent) worst-case regret bound of $\Omega(\sqrt{KT})$ where K is the number of arms [BB12]. In Markov decision processes (MDPs) the lower bound is $\Omega(\sqrt{DSAT})$ where S is the number of states, A the number of actions, and D the diameter of the MDP [AJO10]. For a countable class of environments given by state representation functions that map histories to MDP states, a regret of $\tilde{O}(T^{2/3})$ is achievable assuming the resulting MDP is weakly communicating [NMRO13]. A problem class is considered *learnable* if there is an algorithm that has a sublinear regret guarantee.

This paper continues a narrative that started with definition of the Bayesian agent AIXI [Hut00] and the proof that it satisfies various optimality guarantees [Hut02]. Recently it was revealed that these optimality notions are trivial or subjective [LH15]: a Bayesian agent does not explore enough to lose the prior's bias, and a particularly bad prior can make the agent conform to any arbitrarily bad policy as long as this policy yields some rewards. These negative results put the Bayesian approach to (general) RL into question. In this paper we remedy the situation by showing that using Bayesian techniques an agent can indeed be optimal in an objective sense.

The agent we consider is known as *Thompson sampling*, *posterior sampling*, or the *Bayesian control rule* [Tho33]. It samples an environment ρ from the posterior, follows the ρ-optimal policy for one effective horizon (a lookahead long enough to encompass most of the discount function's mass), and then repeats. We show that this agent's policy is asymptotically optimal in mean (and, equivalently, in probability). Furthermore, using a recoverability assumption on the environment, and some (minor) assumptions on the discount function, we prove that the worst-case regret is sublinear. This is the first time convergence and regret bounds of Thompson sampling have been shown under such general conditions.

Thompson sampling was originally proposed by Thompson as a bandit algorithm [Tho33]. It is easy to implement and often achieves quite good results [CL11]. In multi-armed bandits it attains optimal regret [AG11, KKM12]. Thompson sampling has also been considered for MDPs: as model-free method relying on distributions over Q-functions with convergence guarantee [DFR98], and as a model-based algorithm without theoretical analysis [Str00]. Bayesian and frequentist regret bounds have also been established [ORvR13, OR14, GM15]. PAC guarantees have been established for an optimistic variant of Thompson sampling for MDPs [ALL+09].

For general RL Thompson sampling was first suggested in [OB10] with resampling at every time step. The authors prove that the action probabilities of Thompson sampling converge to the action probability of the optimal policy almost surely, but require a finite environment class and two (arguably quite strong) technical assumptions on the behavior of the posterior distribution (akin to ergodicity) and the similarity of environments in the class. Our convergence results do not require these assumptions, but we rely on an (unavoidable) recoverability assumption for our regret bound.

Appendix A contains a list of notation and Appendix B contains omitted proofs.

2 PRELIMINARIES

The set $\mathcal{X}^* := \bigcup_{n=0}^{\infty} \mathcal{X}^n$ is the set of all finite strings over the alphabet $\mathcal{X}$ and the set $\mathcal{X}^\infty$ is the set of all infinite strings over the alphabet $\mathcal{X}$. The empty string is denoted by ϵ, not to be confused with the small positive real number ε. Given a string $x \in \mathcal{X}^*$, we denote its length by $|x|$. For a (finite or infinite) string x of length $\geq k$, we denote with $x_{1:k}$ the first k characters of x, and with $x_{<k}$ the first $k-1$ characters of x.

The notation $\Delta\mathcal{Y}$ denotes the set of probability distributions over $\mathcal{Y}$.

In reinforcement learning, an agent interacts with an environment in cycles: at time step t the agent chooses an *action* $a_t \in \mathcal{A}$ and receives a *percept* $e_t = (o_t, r_t) \in \mathcal{E}$ consisting of an *observation* $o_t \in \mathcal{O}$ and a real-valued *reward* r_t; the cycle then repeats for $t+1$. We assume that rewards are bounded between 0 and 1 and that the set of actions $\mathcal{A}$ and the set of percepts $\mathcal{E}$ are finite.

We fix a *discount function* $\gamma : \mathbb{N} \to \mathbb{R}$ with $\gamma_t \geq 0$ and $\sum_{t=1}^{\infty} \gamma_t < \infty$. Our goal is to maximize discounted rewards $\sum_{t=1}^{\infty} \gamma_t r_t$. The *discount normalization factor* is defined as $\Gamma_t := \sum_{k=t}^{\infty} \gamma_k$. The *effective horizon* $H_t(\varepsilon)$ is a horizon that is long enough to encompass all but an ε of the discount function's mass:

$$H_t(\varepsilon) := \min\{k \mid \Gamma_{t+k}/\Gamma_t \leq \varepsilon\} \tag{1}$$

A *history* is an element of $(\mathcal{A} \times \mathcal{E})^*$. We use $æ \in \mathcal{A} \times \mathcal{E}$ to denote one interaction cycle, and $æ_{<t}$ to denote a history of length $t-1$. We treat action, percepts, and histories both as outcomes and as random variables. A *policy* is a function $\pi : (\mathcal{A} \times \mathcal{E})^* \to \Delta\mathcal{A}$ mapping a history $æ_{<t}$ to a distribution over the actions taken after seeing this history; the probability of action a is denoted $\pi(a \mid æ_{<t})$. An *environment* is a function $\nu : (\mathcal{A} \times \mathcal{E})^* \times \mathcal{A} \to \Delta\mathcal{E}$ mapping a history $æ_{<t}$ and an action a_t to a distribution over the percepts generated after this history; the probability of percept e is denoted $\nu(e \mid æ_{<t} a_t)$.

A policy π and an environment ν generate a probability measure ν^π over infinite histories $(\mathcal{A} \times \mathcal{E})^\infty$, defined by its values on the cylinder sets $\{h \in (\mathcal{A} \times \mathcal{E})^\infty \mid h_{<t} = æ_{<t}\}$:

$$\nu^\pi(æ_{<t}) := \prod_{k=1}^{t-1} \pi(a_k \mid æ_{<k}) \nu(e_k \mid æ_{<k} a_k)$$

When we take an expectation $\mathbb{E}_\nu^\pi$ of a random variable $X_t(æ_{<t})$ this is to be understood as the expectation of the history $æ_{<t}$ for a fixed time step t drawn from ν^π, i.e.,

$$\mathbb{E}_\nu^\pi[X_t(æ_{<t})] := \sum_{æ_{<t}} \nu^\pi(æ_{<t}) X_t(æ_{<t}).$$

We often do not explicitly add the subscript t to time-dependent random variables.

Definition 1 (Value Function). The *value* of a policy π in an environment ν given history $æ_{<t}$ is defined as

$$V_\nu^\pi(æ_{<t}) := \frac{1}{\Gamma_t}\mathbb{E}_\nu^\pi\left[\sum_{k=t}^{\infty}\gamma_k r_k \,\middle|\, æ_{<t}\right],$$

if $\Gamma_t > 0$ and $V_\nu^\pi(æ_{<t}) := 0$ if $\Gamma_t = 0$. The *optimal value* is defined as $V_\nu^*(h) := \sup_\pi V_\nu^\pi(h)$.

The normalization constant $1/\Gamma_t$ ensures that values are bounded between 0 and 1. We also use the *truncated value function*

$$V_\nu^{\pi,m}(æ_{<t}) := \frac{1}{\Gamma_t}\mathbb{E}_\nu^\pi\left[\sum_{k=t}^{m}\gamma_k r_k \,\middle|\, æ_{<t}\right].$$

For each environment μ there is an *optimal policy* π_μ^* that takes an *optimal action* for each history [LH14, Thm. 10]:

$$\pi_\mu^*(a_t \mid æ_{<t}) > 0 \implies a_t \in \arg\max_a V_\mu^*(æ_{<t}a)$$

Let $\mathcal{M}$ denote a countable class of environments. We assume that $\mathcal{M}$ is large enough to contain the true environment (e.g. the class of all computable environments). Let $w \in \Delta\mathcal{M}$ be a prior probability distribution on $\mathcal{M}$ and let

$$\xi := \sum_{\nu\in\mathcal{M}} w(\nu)\nu$$

denote the corresponding Bayesian mixture over the class $\mathcal{M}$. After observing the history $æ_{<t}$ the prior w is updated to the posterior

$$w(\nu \mid æ_{<t}) := w(\nu)\frac{\nu(æ_{<t})}{\xi(æ_{<t})}.$$

We also use the notation $w(\mathcal{M}' \mid æ_{<t}) := \sum_{\nu\in\mathcal{M}'} w(\nu \mid æ_{<t})$ for a set of environments $\mathcal{M}' \subseteq \mathcal{M}$. Likewise we define $\nu(A \mid æ_{<t}) := \sum_{h\in A}\nu(h \mid æ_{<t})$ for a prefix-free set of histories $A \subseteq (\mathcal{A}\times\mathcal{E})^*$.

Let $\nu, \rho \in \mathcal{M}$ be two environments, let π_1, π_2 be two policies, and let $m \in \mathbb{N}$ be a lookahead time step. The *total variation distance* is defined as

$$D_m(\nu^{\pi_1}, \rho^{\pi_2} \mid æ_{<t}) := \sup_{A\subseteq(\mathcal{A}\times\mathcal{E})^m}\left|\nu^{\pi_1}(A \mid æ_{<t}) - \rho^{\pi_2}(A \mid æ_{<t})\right|.$$

with $D_\infty(\nu^{\pi_1}, \rho^{\pi_2} \mid æ_{<t}) := \lim_{m\to\infty} D_m(\nu^{\pi_1}, \rho^{\pi_2} \mid æ_{<t})$.

Lemma 2 (Bounds on Value Difference). *For any policies π_1, π_2, any environments ρ and ν, and any horizon $t \leq m \leq \infty$,*

$$|V_\nu^{\pi_1,m}(æ_{<t}) - V_\rho^{\pi_2,m}(æ_{<t})| \leq D_m(\nu^{\pi_1}, \rho^{\pi_2} \mid æ_{<t})$$

Proof. See Appendix B. □

3 THOMPSON SAMPLING IS ASYMPTOTICALLY OPTIMAL

Strens proposes following the optimal policy for one episode or "related to the number of state transitions the agent is likely to need to plan ahead" [Str00]. We follow Strens' suggestion and resample at the effective horizon.

Let ε_t be a monotone decreasing sequence of positive reals such that $\varepsilon_t \to 0$ as $t \to \infty$. We define our Thompson-sampling policy π_T in Algorithm 1.

Algorithm 1 Thompson sampling policy π_T

```
1: while true do
2:     sample ρ ~ w( · | æ_{<t})
3:     follow π*_ρ for H_t(ε_t) steps
```

Note that π_T is a stochastic policy since we occasionally sample from a distribution. We assume that this sampling is independent of everything else.

Definition 3 (Asymptotic Optimality). A policy π is *asymptotically optimal in an environment class* $\mathcal{M}$ iff for all $\mu \in \mathcal{M}$

$$V_\mu^*(æ_{<t}) - V_\mu^\pi(æ_{<t}) \to 0 \text{ as } t \to \infty \tag{2}$$

on histories drawn from μ^π.

There are different types of asymptotic optimalities based on the type of stochastic convergence in (2). If this convergence occurs almost surely, it is called *strong asymptotic optimality* [LH11, Def. 7]; if this convergence occurs in mean, it is called *asymptotic optimality in mean*; if this convergence occurs in probability, it is called *asymptotic optimality in probability*; and if the Cesàro averages converge almost surely, it is called *weak asymptotic optimality* [LH11, Def. 7].

3.1 ASYMPTOTIC OPTIMALITY IN MEAN

This subsection is dedicated to proving the following theorem.

Theorem 4 (Thompson Sampling is Asymptotically Optimal in Mean). *For all environments $\mu \in \mathcal{M}$,*

$$\mathbb{E}_\mu^{\pi_T}\left[V_\mu^*(æ_{<t}) - V_\mu^{\pi_T}(æ_{<t})\right] \to 0 \text{ as } t \to \infty.$$

This theorem immediately implies that Thompson sampling is also asymptotically optimal in probability: The convergence in mean of the random variables $X_t := V_\mu^*(æ_{<t}) - V_\mu^{\pi_T}(æ_{<t})$ stated in Theorem 4 is equivalent to convergence in probability in the sense that $\mu^{\pi_T}[X_t > \varepsilon] \to 0$ as $t \to \infty$ for all $\varepsilon > 0$ because the random variables X_t are nonnegative and bounded. However, this does not imply almost sure convergence (see Section 3.3).

Define the *Bayes-expected total variation distance*

$$F_m^\pi(æ_{<t}) := \sum_{\rho\in\mathcal{M}} w(\rho \mid æ_{<t}) D_m(\rho^\pi, \xi^\pi \mid æ_{<t})$$

for $m \leq \infty$.

If we replace the distance measure D_m by cross-entropy, then the quantity $F_m^\pi(æ_{<t})$ becomes the Bayes-expected *information gain* [Lat13, Eq. 3.5].

For the proof of Theorem 4 we need the following lemma.

Lemma 5 (F Vanishes On-Policy). *For any policy π and any environment μ,*

$$\mathbb{E}_\mu^\pi[F_\infty^\pi(æ_{<t})] \to 0 \textit{ as } t \to \infty.$$

Proof. See Appendix B. □

Proof of Theorem 4. Let $\beta, \delta > 0$ and let $\varepsilon_t > 0$ denote the sequence used to define π_T in Algorithm 1. We assume that t is large enough such that $\varepsilon_k \leq \beta$ for all $k \geq t$ and that δ is small enough such that $w(\mu \mid æ_{<t}) > 4\delta$ for all t, which holds since $w(\mu \mid æ_{<t}) \not\to 0$ μ^π-almost surely for any policy π [Hut09, Lem. 3i].

The stochastic process $w(\nu \mid æ_{<t})$ is a ξ^{π_T}-martingale since

$$\begin{aligned}
&\mathbb{E}_\xi^{\pi_T}[w(\nu \mid æ_{1:t}) \mid æ_{<t}] \\
&= \sum_{a_t e_t} \xi^{\pi_T}(æ_t \mid æ_{<t}) w(\nu) \frac{\nu^{\pi_T}(æ_{1:t})}{\xi^{\pi_T}(æ_{1:t})} \\
&= \sum_{a_t e_t} \xi^{\pi_T}(æ_t \mid æ_{<t}) w(\nu \mid æ_{<t}) \frac{\nu^{\pi_T}(æ_t \mid æ_{<t})}{\xi^{\pi_T}(æ_t \mid æ_{<t})} \\
&= w(\nu \mid æ_{<t}) \sum_{a_t e_t} \nu^{\pi_T}(æ_t \mid æ_{<t}) \\
&= w(\nu \mid æ_{<t}).
\end{aligned}$$

By the martingale convergence theorem [Dur10, Thm. 5.2.8] $w(\nu \mid æ_{<t})$ converges ξ^{π_T}-almost surely and because $\xi^{\pi_T} \geq w(\mu)\mu^{\pi_T}$ it also converges μ^{π_T}-almost surely.

We argue that we can choose t_0 to be one of π_T's resampling time steps large enough such that for all $t \geq t_0$ the following three events hold simultaneously with μ^{π_T}-probability at least $1 - \delta$.

(i) There is a finite set $\mathcal{M}' \subset \mathcal{M}$ with $w(\mathcal{M}' \mid æ_{<t}) > 1 - \delta$ and $w(\nu \mid æ_{<k}) \not\to 0$ as $k \to \infty$ for all $\nu \in \mathcal{M}'$.

(ii) $|w(\mathcal{M}'' \mid æ_{<t}) - w(\mathcal{M}'' \mid æ_{<t_0})| \leq \delta$ for all $\mathcal{M}'' \subseteq \mathcal{M}'$.

(iii) $F_\infty^{\pi_T}(æ_{<t}) < \delta\beta w_{\min}^2$.

where $w_{\min} := \inf\{w(\nu \mid æ_{<k}) \mid k \in \mathbb{N}, \nu \in \mathcal{M}'\}$, which is positive by (i).

(i) and (ii) are satisfied eventually because the posterior $w(\,\cdot \mid æ_{<t})$ converges μ^{π_T}-almost surely. Note that the set $\mathcal{M}'$ is random: the limit of $w(\nu \mid æ_{<t})$ as $t \to \infty$ depends on the history $æ_{1:\infty}$. Without loss of generality, we assume the true environment μ is contained in $\mathcal{M}'$ since $w(\mu \mid æ_{<t}) \not\to 0$ μ^{π_T}-almost surely. (iii) follows from Lemma 5 since convergence in mean implies convergence in probability.

Moreover, we define the horizon $m := t + H_t(\varepsilon_t)$ as the time step of the effective horizon at time step t. Let $æ_{<t}$ be a fixed history for which (i-iii) is satisfied. Then we have

$$\begin{aligned}
\delta\beta w_{\min}^2 &> F_\infty^{\pi_T}(æ_{<t}) \\
&= \sum_{\nu\in\mathcal{M}} w(\nu \mid æ_{<t}) D_\infty(\nu^{\pi_T}, \xi^{\pi_T} \mid æ_{<t}) \\
&= \mathbb{E}_{\nu\sim w(\,\cdot\mid æ_{<t})}\left[D_\infty(\nu^{\pi_T}, \xi^{\pi_T} \mid æ_{<t})\right] \\
&\geq \mathbb{E}_{\nu\sim w(\,\cdot\mid æ_{<t})}\left[D_m(\nu^{\pi_T}, \xi^{\pi_T} \mid æ_{<t})\right] \\
&\geq \beta w_{\min}^2 w(\mathcal{M} \setminus \mathcal{M}'' \mid æ_{<t})
\end{aligned}$$

by Markov's inequality where

$$\mathcal{M}'' := \left\{\nu \in \mathcal{M} \mid D_m(\nu^{\pi_T}, \xi^{\pi_T} \mid æ_{<t}) < \beta w_{\min}^2\right\}.$$

For our fixed history $æ_{<t}$ we have

$$\begin{aligned}
1 - \delta &< w(\mathcal{M}'' \mid æ_{<t}) \\
&\overset{(i)}{\leq} w(\mathcal{M}'' \cap \mathcal{M}' \mid æ_{<t}) + \delta \\
&\overset{(ii)}{\leq} w(\mathcal{M}'' \cap \mathcal{M}' \mid æ_{<t_0}) + 2\delta \\
&\overset{(i)}{\leq} w(\mathcal{M}'' \mid æ_{<t_0}) + 3\delta
\end{aligned}$$

and thus we get

$$1 - 4\delta < w\left[D_m(\nu^{\pi_T}, \xi^{\pi_T} \mid æ_{<t}) < \beta w_{\min}^2 \;\middle|\; æ_{<t_0}\right]. \tag{3}$$

In particular, this bound holds for $\nu = \mu$ since $w(\mu \mid æ_{<t_0}) > 4\delta$ by assumption.

It remains to show that with high probability the value $V_\mu^{\pi_\rho^*}$ of the sample ρ's optimal policy π_ρ^* is sufficiently close to the μ-optimal value V_μ^*. The worst case is that we draw the worst sample from $\mathcal{M}' \cap \mathcal{M}''$ twice in a row. From now on, let ρ denote the sample environment we draw at time step t_0, and let t denote some time step between t_0 and $t_1 := t_0 + H_{t_0}(\varepsilon_{t_0})$ (before the next resampling). With probability $w(\nu' \mid æ_{<t_0}) w(\nu' \mid æ_{<t_1})$ we sample ν' both at t_0 and t_1 when following π_T. Therefore we have for all $æ_{t:m}$ and all $\nu \in \mathcal{M}$

$$\begin{aligned}
&\nu^{\pi_T}(æ_{1:m} \mid æ_{<t}) \\
&\geq w(\nu' \mid æ_{<t_0}) w(\nu' \mid æ_{<t_1}) \nu^{\pi_{\nu'}^*}(æ_{1:m} \mid æ_{<t}).
\end{aligned}$$

Thus we get for all $\nu \in \mathcal{M}'$ (in particular ρ and μ)

$$
\begin{aligned}
& D_m(\mu^{\pi_T}, \rho^{\pi_T} \mid æ_{<t}) \\
& \geq \sup_{\nu' \in \mathcal{M}} \sup_{A \subseteq (\mathcal{A} \times \mathcal{E})^m} \Big| w(\nu' \mid æ_{<t_0}) w(\nu' \mid æ_{<t_1}) \\
& \qquad (\mu^{\pi^*_{\nu'}}(A \mid æ_{<t}) - \rho^{\pi^*_{\nu'}}(A \mid æ_{<t})) \Big| \\
& \geq w(\nu \mid æ_{<t_0}) w(\nu \mid æ_{<t_1}) \\
& \qquad \sup_{A \subseteq (\mathcal{A} \times \mathcal{E})^m} \Big| \mu^{\pi^*_\nu}(A \mid æ_{<t}) - \rho^{\pi^*_\nu}(A \mid æ_{<t}) \Big| \\
& \geq w^2_{\min} D_m(\mu^{\pi^*_\nu}, \rho^{\pi^*_\nu} \mid æ_{<t}).
\end{aligned}
$$

For $\rho \in \mathcal{M}''$ we get

$$
\begin{aligned}
& D_m(\mu^{\pi_T}, \rho^{\pi_T} \mid æ_{<t}) \\
& \leq D_m(\mu^{\pi_T}, \xi^{\pi_T} \mid æ_{<t}) + D_m(\rho^{\pi_T}, \xi^{\pi_T} \mid æ_{<t}) \\
& \overset{(3)}{<} \beta w^2_{\min} + \beta w^2_{\min} = 2\beta w^2_{\min},
\end{aligned}
$$

which implies together with Lemma 2 and the fact that rewards in $[0, 1]$

$$
\begin{aligned}
& \Big| V^{\pi^*_\nu}_\mu(æ_{<t}) - V^{\pi^*_\nu}_\rho(æ_{<t}) \Big| \\
& \leq \frac{\Gamma_{t+H_t(\varepsilon_t)}}{\Gamma_t} + \Big| V^{\pi^*_\nu, m}_\mu(æ_{<t}) - V^{\pi^*_\nu, m}_\rho(æ_{<t}) \Big| \\
& \leq \varepsilon_t + D_m(\mu^{\pi^*_\nu}, \rho^{\pi^*_\nu} \mid æ_{<t}) \\
& \leq \varepsilon_t + \tfrac{1}{w^2_{\min}} D_m(\mu^{\pi_T}, \rho^{\pi_T} \mid æ_{<t}) \\
& < \beta + 2\beta = 3\beta.
\end{aligned}
$$

Hence we get (omitting history arguments $æ_{<t}$ for simplicity)

$$
\begin{aligned}
V^*_\mu &= V^{\pi^*_\mu}_\mu < V^{\pi^*_\mu}_\rho + 3\beta \leq V^*_\rho + 3\beta \\
&= V^{\pi^*_\rho}_\rho + 3\beta < V^{\pi^*_\rho}_\mu + 3\beta + 3\beta = V^{\pi^*_\rho}_\mu + 6\beta.
\end{aligned} \tag{4}
$$

With μ^{π_T}-probability at least $1-\delta$ (i), (ii), and (iii) are true, with μ^{π_T}-probability at least $1-\delta$ our sample ρ happens to be in $\mathcal{M}'$ by (i), and with $w(\cdot \mid æ_{<t_0})$-probability at least $1 - 4\delta$ the sample is in $\mathcal{M}''$ by (3). All of these events are true simultaneously with probability at least $1 - (\delta + \delta + 4\delta) = 1 - 6\delta$. Hence the bound (4) transfers for π_T such that with μ^{π_T}-probability $\geq 1 - 6\delta$ we have

$$
V^*_\mu(æ_{<t}) - V^{\pi_T}_\mu(æ_{<t}) < 6\beta.
$$

Therefore $\mu^{\pi_T}[V^*_\mu(æ_{<t}) - V^{\pi_T}_\mu(æ_{<t}) \geq 6\beta] < 6\delta$ and with $\delta \to 0$ we get that $V^*_\mu(æ_{<t}) - V^{\pi_T}_\mu(æ_{<t}) \to 0$ as $t \to \infty$ in probability. The value function is bounded, thus it also converges in mean by the dominated convergence theorem. □

3.2 WEAK ASYMPTOTIC OPTIMALITY

It might appear that convergence in mean is more natural than the convergence of Cesàro averages of weak asymptotic optimality. However, both notions are not so fundamentally different because they both allow an infinite number of bad mistakes (actions that lead to $V^*_\mu - V^\pi_\mu$ being large). Asymptotic optimality in mean allows bad mistakes as long as their probability converges to zero; weak asymptotic optimality allows bad mistakes as long as the total time spent on bad mistakes grows sublinearly.

Lattimore and Hutter show that weak asymptotic optimality is possible in a countable class of deterministic environments using an MDL-agent that explores through bursts of random walks [LH11, Def. 10]. For classes of stochastic environments, BayesExp is weakly asymptotically optimal [Lat13, Ch. 5]. However, this requires the additional condition that the effective horizon grows sublinearly, $H_t(\varepsilon_t) \in o(t)$, while Theorem 4 does not require this condition.

Generally, weak asymptotic optimality and asymptotic optimality in mean are incomparable because the notions of convergence are incomparable for (bounded) random variables. First, for deterministic sequences (i.e. deterministic policies in deterministic environments), convergence in mean is equivalent to (regular) convergence, which implies convergence in Cesàro average, but not vice versa. Second, convergence in probability (and hence convergence in mean for bounded random variables) does not imply almost sure convergence of Cesàro averages [Sto13, Sec. 14.18]. We leave open the question whether the policy π_T is weakly asymptotically optimal.

3.3 STRONG ASYMPTOTIC OPTIMALITY

Strong asymptotic optimality is known to be impossible for deterministic policies [LH11, Thm. 8.1], but whether it is possible for stochastic policies is an open question. However, we show that Thompson sampling is not strongly asymptotically optimal.

Example 6 (Thompson Sampling is not Strongly Asymptotically Optimal). Define $\mathcal{A} := \{\alpha, \beta\}$, $\mathcal{E} := \{0, 1/2, 1\}$, and assume geometric discounting, $\gamma_t := \gamma^t$ for $\gamma \in (0, 1)$. Consider the following class of environments $\mathcal{M} := \{\nu_\infty, \nu_1, \nu_2, \ldots\}$ (transitions are labeled with action, reward):

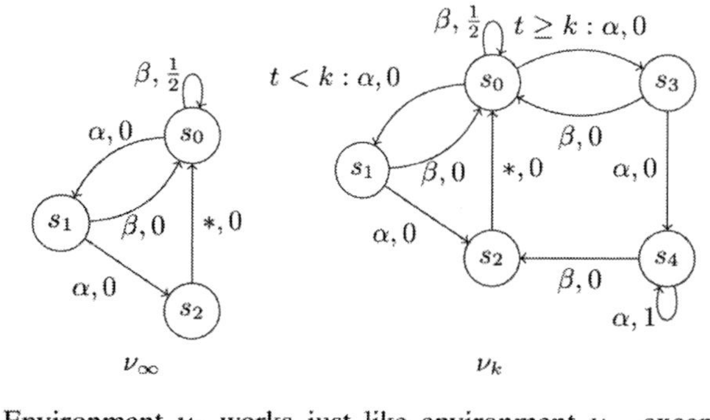

Environment ν_k works just like environment ν_∞ except that after time step k, the path to state s_3 gets unlocked and the optimal policy is to take action α twice from state s_0. The class $\mathcal{M}$ is a class of deterministic weakly communicating MDPs (but as an MDP ν_k has more than 5 states). The optimal policy in environment ν_∞ is to always take action β, the optimal policy for environment ν_k is to take action β for $t < k$ and then take action β in state s_1 and action α otherwise.

Suppose the policy π_T is acting in environment ν_∞. Since it is asymptotically optimal in the class $\mathcal{M}$, it has to take actions $\alpha\alpha$ from s_0 infinitely often: for $t < k$ environment ν_k is indistinguishable from ν_∞, so the posterior for ν_k is larger or equal to the prior. Hence there is always a constant chance of sampling ν_k until taking actions $\alpha\alpha$, at which point all environments ν_k for $k \leq t$ become falsified.

If the policy π_T decides to explore and take the first action α, it will be in state s_1. Let $æ_{<t}$ denote the current history. Then the ν_∞-optimal action is β and

$$V^*_{\nu_\infty}(æ_{<t}) = (1-\gamma)\left(0 + \gamma\frac{1}{2} + \gamma^2\frac{1}{2} + \ldots\right) = \frac{\gamma}{2}.$$

The next action taken by π_T is α since any optimal policy for any sampled environment that takes action α once, takes that action again (and we are following that policy for an ε_t-effective horizon). Hence

$$V^{\pi_T}_{\nu_\infty}(æ_{<t}) \leq (1-\gamma)\left(0 + 0 + \gamma^2\frac{1}{2} + \gamma^3\frac{1}{2} + \ldots\right) = \frac{\gamma^2}{2}.$$

Therefore $V^*_{\nu_\infty} - V^{\pi_T}_{\nu_\infty} \geq (\gamma - \gamma^2)/2 > 0$. This happens infinitely often with probability one and thus we cannot get almost sure convergence. ◊

We expect that strong asymptotic optimality can be achieved with Thompson sampling by resampling at every time step (with strong assumptions on the discount function).

4 REGRET

4.1 SETUP

In general environments classes worst-case regret is linear because the agent can get caught in a trap and be unable to recover [Hut05, Sec. 5.3.2]. To achieve sublinear regret we need to ensure that the agent can recover from mistakes. Formally, we make the following assumption.

Definition 7 (Recoverability). An environment ν satisfies the *recoverability assumption* iff

$$\sup_\pi \left| \mathbb{E}^{\pi^*_\nu}_\nu[V^*_\nu(æ_{<t})] - \mathbb{E}^\pi_\nu[V^*_\nu(æ_{<t})] \right| \to 0 \text{ as } t \to \infty.$$

Recoverability compares following the worst policy π for $t-1$ time steps and then switching to the optimal policy π^*_ν to having followed π^*_ν from the beginning. The recoverability assumption states that switching to the optimal policy at any time step enables the recovery of most of the value.

Note that Definition 7 demands that it becomes less costly to recover from mistakes as time progresses. This should be regarded as an effect of the discount function: if the (effective) horizon grows, recovery becomes easier because the optimal policy has more time to perform a recovery. Moreover, recoverability is on the optimal policy, in contrast to the notion of ergodicity in MDPs which demands returning to a starting state regardless of the policy.

Remark 8 (Weakly Communicating POMDPs are Recoverable). If the effective horizon is growing, $H_t(\varepsilon) \to \infty$ as $t \to \infty$, then any weakly communicating finite state partially observable MDP satisfies the recoverability assumption.

Definition 9 (Regret). The *regret* of a policy π in environment μ is

$$R_m(\pi, \mu) := \sup_{\pi'} \mathbb{E}^{\pi'}_\mu \left[\sum_{t=1}^m r_t\right] - \mathbb{E}^\pi_\mu \left[\sum_{t=1}^m r_t\right].$$

Note that regret is undiscounted and always nonnegative. Moreover, the supremum is always attained by some policy (not necessarily the (V_μ-)optimal policy π^*_μ because that policy uses discounting), since the space of possible different policies for the first m actions is finite since we assumed the set of actions $\mathcal{A}$ and the set of percepts $\mathcal{E}$ to be finite.

Assumption 10 (Discount Function). *Let the discount function γ be such that*

(a) $\gamma_t > 0$ for all t,

(b) γ_t is monotone decreasing in t, and

(c) $H_t(\varepsilon) \in o(t)$ for all $\varepsilon > 0$.

This assumption demands that the discount function is somewhat well-behaved: the function has no oscillations, does not become 0, and the horizon is not growing too fast.

Assumption 10 is satisfied by geometric discounting: $\gamma_t := \gamma^t > 0$ (a) for some fixed constant $\gamma \in (0, 1)$ is monotone decreasing (b), $\Gamma_t = \gamma^t/(1-\gamma)$, and $H_t(\varepsilon) = \lceil \log_\gamma \varepsilon \rceil \in o(t)$ (c).

The problem with geometric discounting is that it makes the recoverability assumption very strong: since the horizon is not growing, the environment has to enable *faster recovery* as time progresses; in this case weakly communicating partially observable MDPs are *not* recoverable.

A choice with $H_t(\varepsilon) \to \infty$ that satisfies Assumption 10 is $\gamma_t := e^{-\sqrt{t}}/\sqrt{t}$ [Lat13, Sec. 2.3.1]. For this discount function $\Gamma_t \approx 2e^{-\sqrt{t}}$, $H_t(\varepsilon) \approx -\sqrt{t}\log\varepsilon + (\log\varepsilon)^2 \in o(t)$, and thus $H_t(\varepsilon) \to \infty$ as $t \to \infty$.

4.2 SUBLINEAR REGRET

This subsection is dedicated to the following theorem.

Theorem 11 (Sublinear Regret). *If the discount function γ satisfies Assumption 10, the environment $\mu \in \mathcal{M}$ satisfies the recoverability assumption, and π is asymptotically optimal in mean, i.e.,*

$$\mathbb{E}_\mu^\pi\left[V_\mu^*(æ_{<t}) - V_\mu^\pi(æ_{<t})\right] \to 0 \text{ as } t \to \infty,$$

then $R_m(\pi, \mu) \in o(m)$.

If the items in Assumption 10 are violated, Theorem 11 can fail:

- If $\gamma_t = 0$ for some time steps t, our policy does not care about those time steps and might take actions that have large regret.
- Similarly if γ oscillates between high values and very low values: our policy might take high-regret actions in time steps with comparatively lower γ-weight.
- If the horizon grows linearly, infinitely often our policy might spend some constant fraction of the current effective horizon exploring, which incurs a cost that is a constant fraction of the total regret so far.

To prove Theorem 11, we apply the following technical lemma.

Lemma 12 (Value and Regret). *Let $\varepsilon > 0$ and assume the discount function γ satisfies Assumption 10. Let $(d_t)_{t\in\mathbb{N}}$ be a sequence of numbers with $|d_t| \leq 1$ for all t. If there is a time step t_0 with*

$$\frac{1}{\Gamma_t}\sum_{k=t}^{\infty}\gamma_k d_k < \varepsilon \quad \forall t \geq t_0 \tag{5}$$

then

$$\sum_{t=1}^{m} d_t \leq t_0 + \varepsilon(m - t_0 + 1) + \frac{1+\varepsilon}{1-\varepsilon}H_m(\varepsilon)$$

Proof. This proof essentially follows the proof of [Hut06, Thm. 17]; see Appendix B. □

Proof of Theorem 11. Let $(\pi_m)_{m\in\mathbb{N}}$ denote any sequence of policies, such as a sequence of policies that attain the supremum in the definition of regret. We want to show that

$$\mathbb{E}_\mu^{\pi_m}\left[\sum_{t=1}^{m} r_t\right] - \mathbb{E}_\mu^{\pi}\left[\sum_{t=1}^{m} r_t\right] \in o(m).$$

For

$$d_k^{(m)} := \mathbb{E}_\mu^{\pi_m}[r_k] - \mathbb{E}_\mu^{\pi}[r_k] \tag{6}$$

we have $-1 \leq d_k^{(m)} \leq 1$ since we assumed rewards to be bounded between 0 and 1. Because the environment μ satisfies the recoverability assumption we have

$$\left|\mathbb{E}_\mu^{\pi_\mu^*}[V_\mu^*(æ_{<t})] - \mathbb{E}_\mu^{\pi}[V_\mu^*(æ_{<t})]\right| \to 0 \text{ as } t \to \infty, \text{ and}$$

$$\sup_m \left|\mathbb{E}_\mu^{\pi_\mu^*}[V_\mu^*(æ_{<t})] - \mathbb{E}_\mu^{\pi_m}[V_\mu^*(æ_{<t})]\right| \to 0 \text{ as } t \to \infty,$$

so we conclude that

$$\sup_m \left|\mathbb{E}_\mu^{\pi}[V_\mu^*(æ_{<t})] - \mathbb{E}_\mu^{\pi_m}[V_\mu^*(æ_{<t})]\right| \to 0$$

by the triangle inequality and thus

$$\sup_m \mathbb{E}_\mu^{\pi_m}[V_\mu^*(æ_{<t})] - \mathbb{E}_\mu^{\pi}[V_\mu^*(æ_{<t})] \to 0 \text{ as } t \to \infty. \tag{7}$$

By assumption the policy π is asymptotically optimal in mean, so we have

$$\mathbb{E}_\mu^{\pi}[V_\mu^*(æ_{<t})] - \mathbb{E}_\mu^{\pi}[V_\mu^\pi(æ_{<t})] \to 0 \text{ as } t \to \infty,$$

and with (7) this combines to

$$\sup_m \mathbb{E}_\mu^{\pi_m}[V_\mu^*(æ_{<t})] - \mathbb{E}_\mu^{\pi}[V_\mu^\pi(æ_{<t})] \to 0 \text{ as } t \to \infty.$$

From $V_\mu^*(æ_{<t}) \geq V_\mu^{\pi_m}(æ_{<t})$ we get

$$\limsup_{t\to\infty}\left(\sup_m \mathbb{E}_\mu^{\pi_m}[V_\mu^{\pi_m}(æ_{<t})] - \mathbb{E}_\mu^{\pi}[V_\mu^\pi(æ_{<t})]\right) \leq 0. \tag{8}$$

For $\pi' \in \{\pi, \pi_1, \pi_2, \ldots\}$ we have

$$\begin{aligned}\mathbb{E}_\mu^{\pi'}[V_\mu^{\pi'}(æ_{<t})] &= \mathbb{E}_\mu^{\pi'}\left[\frac{1}{\Gamma_t}\mathbb{E}_\mu^{\pi'}\left[\sum_{k=t}^{\infty}\gamma_k r_k \,\middle|\, æ_{<t}\right]\right] \\ &= \mathbb{E}_\mu^{\pi'}\left[\frac{1}{\Gamma_t}\sum_{k=t}^{\infty}\gamma_k r_k\right] \\ &= \frac{1}{\Gamma_t}\sum_{k=t}^{\infty}\gamma_k \mathbb{E}_\mu^{\pi'}[r_k],\end{aligned}$$

so from (6) and (8) we get

$$\limsup_{t\to\infty}\sup_m \frac{1}{\Gamma_t}\sum_{k=t}^{\infty}\gamma_k d_k^{(m)} \leq 0.$$

Let $\varepsilon > 0$ and choose t_0 independent of m and large enough such that $\sup_m \sum_{k=t}^{\infty}\gamma_k d_k^{(m)}/\Gamma_t < \varepsilon$ for all $t \geq t_0$. Now we let $m \in \mathbb{N}$ be given and apply Lemma 12 to get

$$\begin{aligned}\frac{R_m(\pi,\mu)}{m} &= \frac{\sum_{k=1}^{m} d_k^{(m)}}{m} \\ &\leq \frac{t_0 + \varepsilon(m - t_0 + 1) + \frac{1+\varepsilon}{1-\varepsilon}H_m(\varepsilon)}{m}.\end{aligned}$$

Since $H_t(\varepsilon) \in o(t)$ according to Assumption 10c we get $\limsup_{m\to\infty} R_m(\pi,\mu)/m \leq 0$. □

Example 13 (Converse of Theorem 11 is False). Let μ be a two-armed Bernoulli bandit with means 0 and 1 and suppose we are using geometric discounting with discount factor $\gamma \in [0, 1)$. This environment is recoverable. If our policy π pulls the suboptimal arm exactly on time steps $1, 2, 4, 8, 16, \ldots$, regret will be logarithmic. However, on time steps $t = 2^n$ for $n \in \mathbb{N}$ the value difference $V^*_\mu - V^\pi_\mu$ is deterministically at least $1 - \gamma > 0$. ◊

4.3 IMPLICATIONS

We get the following immediate consequence.

Corollary 14 (Sublinear Regret for the Optimal Discounted Policy). *If the discount function γ satisfies Assumption 10 and the environment μ satisfies the recoverability assumption, then $R_m(\pi^*_\mu, \mu) \in o(m)$.*

Proof. From Theorem 11 since the policy π^*_μ is (trivially) asymptotically optimal in μ. □

If the environment does not satisfy the recoverability assumption, regret may be linear *even on the optimal policy*: the optimal policy maximizes discounted rewards and this short-sightedness might incur a tradeoff that leads to linear regret later on if the environment does not allow recovery.

Corollary 15 (Sublinear Regret for Thompson Sampling). *If the discount function γ satisfies Assumption 10 and the environment $\mu \in \mathcal{M}$ satisfies the recoverability assumption, then $R_m(\pi_T, \mu) \in o(m)$ for the Thompson sampling policy π_T.*

Proof. From Theorem 4 and Theorem 11. □

5 DISCUSSION

In this paper we introduced a reinforcement learning policy π_T based on Thompson sampling for general countable environment classes (Algorithm 1). We proved two asymptotic statements about this policy. Theorem 4 states that π_T is asymptotically optimal in mean: the value of π_T in the true environment converges to the optimal value. Corollary 15 states that the regret of π_T is sublinear: the difference of the expected average rewards between π_T and the best informed policy converges to 0. Both statements come without a concrete convergence rate because of the weak assumptions we made on the environment class.

Asymptotic optimality has to be taken with a grain of salt. It provides no incentive to the agent to avoid traps in the environment. Once the agent gets caught in a trap, all actions are equally bad and thus optimal: asymptotic optimality has been achieved. Even worse, an asymptotically optimal agent has to explore all the traps because they might contain hidden treasure. Overall, there is a dichotomy between the asymptotic nature of asymptotic optimality and the use of discounting to prioritize the present over the future. Ideally, we would want to give finite guarantees instead, but without additional assumptions this is likely impossible in this general setting. Our regret bound could be a step in the right direction, even though itself asymptotic in nature.

For Bayesians asymptotic optimality means that the posterior distribution $w(\cdot \mid æ_{<t})$ concentrates on environments that are indistinguishable from the true environment (but generally not on the true environment). This is why Thompson sampling works: any optimal policy of the environment we draw from the posterior will, with higher and higher probability, also be (almost) optimal in the true environment.

If the Bayesian mixture ξ is inside the class $\mathcal{M}$ (as it is the case for the class of lower semicomputable chronological semimeasures [Hut05]), then we can assign ξ a prior probability that is arbitrarily close to 1. Since the posterior of ξ is the same as the prior, Thompson sampling will act according to the Bayes-optimal policy most of the time. This means the Bayes-value of Thompson sampling can be very good; formally, $V^*_\xi(\epsilon) - V^{\pi_T}_\xi(\epsilon)$ can be made arbitrarily small, and thus Thompson sampling can have near-optimal Legg-Hutter intelligence [LH07].

In contrast, the Bayes-value of Thompson sampling can also be very bad: Suppose you have a class of $(n+1)$-armed bandits indexed $1, \ldots, n$ where bandit i gives reward $1 - \varepsilon$ on arm 1, reward 1 on arm $i + 1$, and reward 0 on all other arms. For geometric discounting and $\varepsilon < (1 - \gamma)/(2 - \gamma)$, it is Bayes-optimal to pull arm 1 while Thompson sampling will explore on average $n/2$ arms until it finds the optimal arm. The Bayes-value of Thompson sampling is $1/(n - \gamma_{n-1})$ in contract to $(1 - \varepsilon)$ achieved by Bayes. For a horizon of n, the Bayes-optimal policy suffers a regret of εn and Thompson sampling a regret of $n/2$, which is much larger for small ε.

The exploration performed by Thompson sampling is qualitatively different from the exploration by BayesExp [Lat13, Ch. 5]. BayesExp performs phases of exploration in which it maximizes the expected information gain. This explores the environment class completely, even achieving off-policy prediction [OLH13, Thm. 7]. In contrast, Thompson sampling only explores on the optimal policies, and in some environment classes this will not yield off-policy prediction. So in this sense the exploration mechanism of Thompson sampling is more reward-oriented than maximizing information gain.

Possible avenues of future research are providing concrete convergence rates for specific environment classes and results for uncountable (parameterized) environment classes. For the latter, we have to use different analysis techniques because the true environment μ is typically assigned a prior probability of 0 (only a positive density) but the proofs of Lemma 5 and Theorem 4 rely on dividing by or taking a minimum over prior probabilities. We also left open whether Thompson sampling is weakly asymptotically optimal.

Acknowledgements

Example 6 was developed jointly with Stuart Armstrong. We thank Tom Everitt and Djallel Bouneffouf for proofreading.

REFERENCES

[AG11] Shipra Agrawal and Navin Goyal. Analysis of Thompson sampling for the multi-armed bandit problem. In *Conference on Learning Theory*, 2011.

[AJO10] Peter Auer, Thomas Jaksch, and Ronald Ortner. Near-optimal regret bounds for reinforcement learning. *Journal of Machine Learning Research*, 11:1563–1600, 2010.

[ALL+09] John Asmuth, Lihong Li, Michael L Littman, Ali Nouri, and David Wingate. A Bayesian sampling approach to exploration in reinforcement learning. In *Uncertainty in Artificial Intelligence*, pages 19–26, 2009.

[BB12] Sébastien Bubeck and Cesa-Nicolò Bianchi. Regret analysis of stochastic and nonstochastic multi-armed bandit problems. *Foundations and Trends in Machine Learning*, 5(1):1–122, 2012.

[BD62] David Blackwell and Lester Dubins. Merging of opinions with increasing information. *The Annals of Mathematical Statistics*, pages 882–886, 1962.

[CL11] Olivier Chapelle and Lihong Li. An empirical evaluation of Thompson sampling. In *Neural Information Processing Systems*, pages 2249–2257, 2011.

[DFR98] Richard Dearden, Nir Friedman, and Stuart Russell. Bayesian Q-learning. In *AAAI*, pages 761–768, 1998.

[Dur10] Rick Durrett. *Probability: Theory and Examples*. Cambridge University Press, 4th edition, 2010.

[GM15] Aditya Gopalan and Shie Mannor. Thompson sampling for learning parameterized Markov decision processes. In *Conference on Learning Theory*, pages 861–898, 2015.

[Hut00] Marcus Hutter. A theory of universal artificial intelligence based on algorithmic complexity. Technical report, 2000. `http://arxiv.org/abs/cs.AI/0004001`.

[Hut02] Marcus Hutter. Self-optimizing and Pareto-optimal policies in general environments based on Bayes-mixtures. In *Computational Learning Theory*, pages 364–379. Springer, 2002.

[Hut05] Marcus Hutter. *Universal Artificial Intelligence: Sequential Decisions Based on Algorithmic Probability*. Springer, 2005.

[Hut06] Marcus Hutter. General discounting versus average reward. In *Algorithmic Learning Theory*, pages 244–258. Springer, 2006.

[Hut09] Marcus Hutter. Discrete MDL predicts in total variation. In *Neural Information Processing Systems*, pages 817–825, 2009.

[KKM12] Emilie Kaufmann, Nathaniel Korda, and Rémi Munos. Thompson sampling: An asymptotically optimal finite-time analysis. In *Algorithmic Learning Theory*, pages 199–213. Springer, 2012.

[Lat13] Tor Lattimore. *Theory of General Reinforcement Learning*. PhD thesis, Australian National University, 2013.

[LH07] Shane Legg and Marcus Hutter. Universal intelligence: A definition of machine intelligence. *Minds & Machines*, 17(4):391–444, 2007.

[LH11] Tor Lattimore and Marcus Hutter. Asymptotically optimal agents. In *Algorithmic Learning Theory*, pages 368–382. Springer, 2011.

[LH14] Tor Lattimore and Marcus Hutter. General time consistent discounting. *Theoretical Computer Science*, 519:140–154, 2014.

[LH15] Jan Leike and Marcus Hutter. Bad universal priors and notions of optimality. In *Conference on Learning Theory*, pages 1244–1259, 2015.

[MKS+15] Volodymyr Mnih, Koray Kavukcuoglu, David Silver, Andrei A Rusu, Joel Veness, Marc G Bellemare, Alex Graves, Martin Riedmiller, Andreas K Fidjeland, Georg Ostrovski, Stig Petersen, Charles Beattie, Amir Sadik, Ioannis Antonoglou, Helen King, Dharshan Kumaran, Daan Wierstra, Shane Legg, and Demis Hassabis. Human-level control through deep reinforcement learning. *Nature*, 518(7540):529–533, 2015.

[NMRO13] Phuong Nguyen, Odalric-Ambrym Maillard, Daniil Ryabko, and Ronald Ortner. Competing with an infinite set of models in reinforcement learning. In *Artificial Intelligence and Statistics*, pages 463–471, 2013.

[OB10] Pedro A Ortega and Daniel A Braun. A minimum relative entropy principle for learning and acting. *Journal of Artificial Intelligence Research*, pages 475–511, 2010.

[OLH13] Laurent Orseau, Tor Lattimore, and Marcus Hutter. Universal knowledge-seeking agents for stochastic environments. In *Algorithmic Learning Theory*, pages 158–172. Springer, 2013.

[OR14] Ian Osband and Benjamin Van Roy. Model-based reinforcement learning and the eluder dimension. In *Neural Information Processing Systems*, pages 1466–1474, 2014.

[Ors13] Laurent Orseau. Asymptotic non-learnability of universal agents with computable horizon functions. *Theoretical Computer Science*, 473:149–156, 2013.

[ORvR13] Ian Osband, Dan Russo, and Benjamin van Roy. (More) efficient reinforcement learning via posterior sampling. In *Neural Information Processing Systems*, pages 3003–3011, 2013.

[SH15] Peter Sunehag and Marcus Hutter. Rationality, optimism and guarantees in general reinforcement learning. *Journal of Machine Learning Research*, 16:1345–1390, 2015.

[Sto13] Jordan M Stoyanov. *Counterexamples in Probability*. Courier Corporation, 3rd edition, 2013.

[Str00] Malcolm Strens. A Bayesian framework for reinforcement learning. In *International Conference on Machine Learning*, pages 943–950, 2000.

[Tho33] William R Thompson. On the likelihood that one unknown probability exceeds another in view of the evidence of two samples. *Biometrika*, pages 285–294, 1933.

A Formal Solution to the Grain of Truth Problem

Jan Leike
Australian National University
jan.leike@anu.edu.au

Jessica Taylor
Machine Intelligence Research Inst.
jessica@intelligence.org

Benya Fallenstein
Machine Intelligence Research Inst.
benya@intelligence.org

Abstract

A Bayesian agent acting in a multi-agent environment learns to predict the other agents' policies if its prior assigns positive probability to them (in other words, its prior contains a *grain of truth*). Finding a reasonably large class of policies that contains the Bayes-optimal policies with respect to this class is known as the *grain of truth problem*. Only small classes are known to have a grain of truth and the literature contains several related impossibility results. In this paper we present a formal and general solution to the full grain of truth problem: we construct a class of policies that contains all computable policies as well as Bayes-optimal policies for every lower semicomputable prior over the class. When the environment is unknown, Bayes-optimal agents may fail to act optimally even asymptotically. However, agents based on Thompson sampling converge to play ε-Nash equilibria in arbitrary unknown computable multi-agent environments. While these results are purely theoretical, we show that they can be computationally approximated arbitrarily closely.

Keywords. General reinforcement learning, multi-agent systems, game theory, self-reflection, asymptotic optimality, Nash equilibrium, Thompson sampling, AIXI.

1 INTRODUCTION

Consider the general setup of multiple reinforcement learning agents interacting sequentially in a known environment with the goal to maximize discounted reward.[1] Each agent knows how the environment behaves, but does not know the other agents' behavior. The natural (Bayesian) approach would be to define a class of possible policies that the other agents could adopt and take a prior over this class. During the interaction, this prior gets updated to the posterior as our agent learns the others' behavior. Our agent then acts optimally with respect to this posterior belief.

[1]We mostly use the terminology of reinforcement learning. For readers from game theory we provide a dictionary in Table 1.

Reinforcement learning	Game theory
stochastic policy	mixed strategy
deterministic policy	pure strategy
agent	player
multi-agent environment	infinite extensive-form game
reward	payoff/utility
(finite) history	history
infinite history	path of play

Table 1: Terminology dictionary between reinforcement learning and game theory.

A famous result for infinitely repeated games states that as long as each agent assigns positive prior probability to the other agents' policies (a *grain of truth*) and each agent acts Bayes-optimal, then the agents converge to playing an ε-Nash equilibrium [KL93].

As an example, consider an infinitely repeated prisoners dilemma between two agents. In every time step the payoff matrix is as follows, where C means cooperate and D means defect.

	C	D
C	3/4, 3/4	0, 1
D	1, 0	1/4, 1/4

Define the set of policies $\Pi := \{\pi_\infty, \pi_0, \pi_1, \dots\}$ where policy π_t cooperates until time step t or the opponent defects (whatever happens first) and defects thereafter. The Bayes-optimal behavior is to cooperate until the posterior belief that the other agent defects in the time step after the next is greater than some constant (depending on the discount function) and then defect afterwards. Therefore Bayes-optimal behavior leads to a policy from the set Π

(regardless of the prior). If both agents are Bayes-optimal with respect to some prior, they both have a grain of truth and therefore they converge to a Nash equilibrium: either they both cooperate forever or after some finite time they both defect forever. Alternating strategies like TitForTat (cooperate first, then play the opponent's last action) are not part of the policy class Π, and adding them to the class breaks the grain of truth property: the Bayes-optimal behavior is no longer in the class. This is rather typical; a Bayesian agent usually needs to be more powerful than its environment [LH15b].

Until now, classes that admit a grain of truth were known only for small toy examples such as the iterated prisoner's dilemma above [SLB09, Ch. 7.3]. The quest to find a large class admitting a grain of truth is known as the *grain of truth problem* [Hut09, Q. 5j]. The literature contains several impossibility results on the grain of truth problem [FY01, Nac97, Nac05] that identify properties that cannot be simultaneously satisfied for classes that allow a grain of truth.

In this paper we present a formal solution to multi-agent reinforcement learning and the grain of truth problem in the general setting (Section 3). We assume that our multi-agent environment is computable, but it does not need to be stationary/Markov, ergodic, or finite-state [Hut05]. Our class of policies is large enough to contain all computable (stochastic) policies, as well as all relevant Bayes-optimal policies. At the same time, our class is small enough to be limit computable. This is important because it allows our result to be computationally approximated.

In Section 4 we consider the setting where the multi-agent environment is unknown to the agents and has to be learned in addition to the other agents' behavior. A Bayes-optimal agent may not learn to act optimally in unknown multi-agent environments *even though it has a grain of truth*. This effect occurs in non-recoverable environments where taking one wrong action can mean a permanent loss of future value. In this case, a Bayes-optimal agent avoids taking these dangerous actions and therefore will not explore enough to wash out the prior's bias [LH15a]. Therefore, Bayesian agents are not *asymptotically optimal*, i.e., they do not always learn to act optimally [Ors13].

However, asymptotic optimality is achieved by Thompson sampling because the inherent randomness of Thompson sampling leads to enough exploration to learn the entire environment class [LLOH16]. This leads to our main result: if all agents use Thompson sampling over our class of multi-agent environments, then for every $\varepsilon > 0$ they converge to an ε-Nash equilibrium asymptotically.

The central idea to our construction is based on *reflective oracles* [FST15, FTC15b]. Reflective oracles are probabilistic oracles similar to halting oracles that answer whether the probability that a given probabilistic Turing machine T outputs 1 is higher than a given rational number p. The oracles are reflective in the sense that the machine T may itself query the oracle, so the oracle has to answer queries about itself. This invites issues caused by self-referential liar paradoxes of the form "if the oracle says that I return 1 with probability $> 1/2$, then return 0, else return 1." Reflective oracles avoid these issues by being allowed to randomize if the machines do not halt or the rational number is *exactly* the probability to output 1. We introduce reflective oracles formally in Section 2 and prove that there is a limit computable reflective oracle.

2 REFLECTIVE ORACLES

2.1 PRELIMINARIES

Let $\mathcal{X}$ denote a finite set called *alphabet*. The set $\mathcal{X}^* := \bigcup_{n=0}^{\infty} \mathcal{X}^n$ is the set of all finite strings over the alphabet $\mathcal{X}$, the set $\mathcal{X}^\infty$ is the set of all infinite strings over the alphabet $\mathcal{X}$, and the set $\mathcal{X}^\sharp := \mathcal{X}^* \cup \mathcal{X}^\infty$ is their union. The empty string is denoted by ϵ, not to be confused with the small positive real number ε. Given a string $x \in \mathcal{X}^\sharp$, we denote its length by $|x|$. For a (finite or infinite) string x of length $\geq k$, we denote with $x_{1:k}$ the first k characters of x, and with $x_{<k}$ the first $k-1$ characters of x. The notation $x_{1:\infty}$ stresses that x is an infinite string.

A function $f : \mathcal{X}^* \to \mathbb{R}$ is *lower semicomputable* iff the set $\{(x, p) \in \mathcal{X}^* \times \mathbb{Q} \mid f(x) > p\}$ is recursively enumerable. The function f is *computable* iff both f and $-f$ are lower semicomputable. Finally, the function f is *limit computable* iff there is a computable function ϕ such that

$$\lim_{k \to \infty} \phi(x, k) = f(x).$$

The program ϕ that limit computes f can be thought of as an *anytime algorithm* for f: we can stop ϕ at any time k and get a preliminary answer. If the program ϕ ran long enough (which we do not know), this preliminary answer will be close to the correct one.

We use $\Delta\mathcal{Y}$ to denote the set of probability distributions over $\mathcal{Y}$. A list of notation can be found in Appendix A.

2.2 DEFINITION

A *semimeasure* over the alphabet $\mathcal{X}$ is a function $\nu : \mathcal{X}^* \to [0, 1]$ such that (i) $\nu(\epsilon) \leq 1$, and (ii) $\nu(x) \geq \sum_{a \in \mathcal{X}} \nu(xa)$ for all $x \in \mathcal{X}^*$. In the terminology of measure theory, semimeasures are probability measures on the probability space $\mathcal{X}^\sharp = \mathcal{X}^* \cup X^\infty$ whose σ-algebra is generated by the *cylinder sets* $\Gamma_x := \{xz \mid z \in \mathcal{X}^\sharp\}$ [LV08, Ch. 4.2]. We call a semimeasure (probability) a *measure* iff equalities hold in (i) and (ii) for all $x \in \mathcal{X}^*$.

Next, we connect semimeasures to Turing machines. The literature uses *monotone Turing machines*, which naturally correspond to lower semicomputable semimeasures [LV08, Sec. 4.5.2] that describe the distribution that arises when piping fair coin flips into the monotone machine. Here we take a different route.

A *probabilistic Turing machine* is a Turing machine that has access to an unlimited number of uniformly random coin flips. Let $\mathcal{T}$ denote the set of all probabilistic Turing machines that take some input in $\mathcal{X}^*$ and may query an oracle (formally defined below). We take a Turing machine $T \in \mathcal{T}$ to correspond to a semimeasure λ_T where $\lambda_T(a \mid x)$ is the probability that T outputs $a \in \mathcal{X}$ when given $x \in \mathcal{X}^*$ as input. The value of $\lambda_T(x)$ is then given by the chain rule

$$\lambda_T(x) := \prod_{k=1}^{|x|} \lambda_T(x_k \mid x_{<k}). \tag{1}$$

Thus $\mathcal{T}$ gives rise to the set of semimeasures $\mathcal{M}$ where the *conditionals* $\lambda(a \mid x)$ are lower semicomputable. In contrast, the literature typically considers semimeasures whose *joint* probability (1) is lower semicomputable. This set $\mathcal{M}$ contains all computable measures. However, $\mathcal{M}$ is a proper subset of the set of all lower semicomputable semimeasures because the product (1) is lower semicomputale, but there are some lower semicomputable semimeasures whose conditional is not lower semicomputable [LH15c, Thm. 6].

In the following we assume that our alphabet is binary, i.e., $\mathcal{X} := \{0, 1\}$.

Definition 1 (Oracle). An *oracle* is a function $O : \mathcal{T} \times \{0,1\}^* \times \mathbb{Q} \to \Delta\{0,1\}$.

Oracles are understood to be probabilistic: they randomly return 0 or 1. Let T^O denote the machine $T \in \mathcal{T}$ when run with the oracle O, and let λ_T^O denote the semimeasure induced by T^O. This means that drawing from λ_T^O involves two sources of randomness: one from the distribution induced by the probabilistic Turing machine T and one from the oracle's answers.

The intended semantics of an oracle are that it takes a *query* (T, x, p) and returns 1 if the machine T^O outputs 1 on input x with probability greater than p when run with the oracle O, i.e., when $\lambda_T^O(1 \mid x) > p$. Furthermore, the oracle returns 0 if the machine T^O outputs 1 on input x with probability less than p when run with the oracle O, i.e., when $\lambda_T^O(1 \mid x) < p$. To fulfill this, the oracle O has to make statements about itself, since the machine T from the query may again query O. Therefore we call oracles of this kind *reflective oracles*. This has to be defined very carefully to avoid the obvious diagonalization issues that are caused by programs that ask the oracle about themselves. We impose the following self-consistency constraint.

Definition 2 (Reflective Oracle). An oracle O is *reflective* iff for all queries $(T, x, p) \in \mathcal{T} \times \{0,1\}^* \times \mathbb{Q}$,

(i) $\lambda_T^O(1 \mid x) > p$ implies $O(T, x, p) = 1$, and

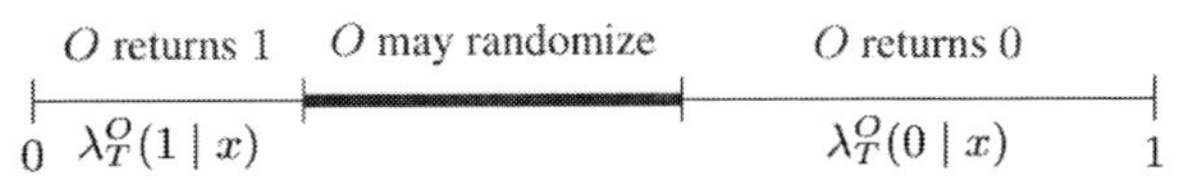

Figure 1: Answer options of a reflective oracle O for the query (T, x, p); the rational $p \in [0, 1]$ falls into one of the three regions above. The values of $\lambda_T^O(0 \mid x)$ and $\lambda_T^O(1 \mid x)$ are depicted as the length of the line segment under which they are written.

(ii) $\lambda_T^O(0 \mid x) > 1 - p$ implies $O(T, x, p) = 0$.

If p under- or overshoots the true probability of $\lambda_T^O(\cdot \mid x)$, then the oracle must reveal this information. However, in the critical case when $p = \lambda_T^O(1 \mid x)$, the oracle is allowed to return anything and may randomize its result. Furthermore, since T might not output any symbol, it is possible that $\lambda_T^O(0 \mid x) + \lambda_T^O(1 \mid x) < 1$. In this case the oracle can reassign the non-halting probability mass to 0, 1, or randomize; see Figure 1.

Example 3 (Reflective Oracles and Diagonalization). Let $T \in \mathcal{T}$ be a probabilistic Turing machine that outputs $1 - O(T, \epsilon, 1/2)$ (T can know its own source code by quining [Kle52, Thm. 27]). In other words, T queries the oracle about whether it is more likely to output 1 or 0, and then does whichever the oracle says is less likely. In this case we can use an oracle $O(T, \epsilon, 1/2) := 1/2$ (answer 0 or 1 with equal probability), which implies $\lambda_T^O(1 \mid \epsilon) = \lambda_T^O(0 \mid \epsilon) = 1/2$, so the conditions of Definition 2 are satisfied. In fact, for this machine T we must have $O(T, \epsilon, 1/2) = 1/2$ for all reflective oracles O. ◇

The following theorem establishes that reflective oracles exist.

Theorem 4 ([FTC15a, App. B]). *There is a reflective oracle.*

Definition 5 (Reflective-Oracle-Computable). A semimeasure is called *reflective-oracle-computable* iff it is computable on a probabilistic Turing machine with access to a reflective oracle.

For any probabilistic Turing machine $T \in \mathcal{T}$ we can complete the semimeasure $\lambda_T^O(\cdot \mid x)$ into a reflective-oracle-computable measure $\overline{\lambda}_T^O(\cdot \mid x)$: Using the oracle O and a binary search on the parameter p we search for the crossover point p where $O(T, x, p)$ goes from returning 1 to returning 0. The limit point $p^* \in \mathbb{R}$ of the binary search is random since the oracle's answers may be random. But the main point is that the expectation of p^* exists, so $\overline{\lambda}_T^O(1 \mid x) = \mathbb{E}[p^*] = 1 - \overline{\lambda}_T^O(0 \mid x)$ for all $x \in \mathcal{X}^*$. Hence $\overline{\lambda}_T^O$ is a measure. Moreover, if the oracle is reflective, then $\overline{\lambda}_T^O(x) \geq \lambda_T^O(x)$ for all $x \in \mathcal{X}^*$. In this sense the oracle O can be viewed as a way of 'completing' all semimeasures λ_T^O to measures by arbitrarily assigning the non-halting probability mass. If the oracle O is reflective this is consistent in the sense that Turing machines who run other Turing machines will be completed in the same way. This is especially important for a universal machine that runs all other Turing machines to induce a Solomonoff-style distribution.

2.3 A LIMIT COMPUTABLE REFLECTIVE ORACLE

The proof of Theorem 4 given in [FTC15a, App. B] is non-constructive and uses the axiom of choice. In Section 2.4 we give a constructive proof for the existence of reflective oracles and show that there is one that is limit computable.

Theorem 6 (A Limit Computable Reflective Oracle). *There is a reflective oracle that is limit computable.*

This theorem has the immediate consequence that reflective oracles cannot be used as halting oracles. At first, this result may seem surprising: according to the definition of reflective oracles, they make concrete statements about the output of probabilistic Turing machines. However, the fact that the oracles may randomize some of the time actually removes enough information such that halting can no longer be decided from the oracle output.

Corollary 7 (Reflective Oracles are not Halting Oracles). *There is no probabilistic Turing machine T such that for every prefix program p and every reflective oracle O, we have that $\lambda_T^O(1 \mid p) > 1/2$ if p halts and $\lambda_T^O(1 \mid p) < 1/2$ otherwise.*

Proof. Assume there was such a machine T and let O be the limit computable oracle from Theorem 6. Since O is reflective we can turn T into a deterministic halting oracle by calling $O(T, p, 1/2)$ which deterministically returns 1 if p halts and 0 otherwise. Since O is limit computable, we can finitely compute the output of O on any query to arbitrary finite precision using our deterministic halting oracle. We construct a probabilistic Turing machine T' that uses our halting oracle to compute (rather than query) the oracle O on $(T', \epsilon, 1/2)$ to a precision of $1/3$ in finite time. If $O(T', \epsilon, 1/2) \pm 1/3 > 1/2$, the machine T' outputs 0, otherwise T' outputs 1. Since our halting oracle is entirely deterministic, the output of T' is entirely deterministic as well (and T' always halts), so $\lambda_{T'}^O(0 \mid \epsilon) = 1$ or $\lambda_{T'}^O(1 \mid \epsilon) = 1$. Therefore $O(T', \epsilon, 1/2) = 1$ or $O(T', \epsilon, 1/2) = 0$ because O is reflective. A precision of $1/3$ is enough to tell them apart, hence T' returns 0 if $O(T', \epsilon, 1/2) = 1$ and T' returns 1 if $O(T', \epsilon, 1/2) = 0$. This is a contradiction. □

A similar argument can also be used to show that reflective oracles are not computable.

2.4 PROOF OF THEOREM 6

The idea for the proof of Theorem 6 is to construct an algorithm that outputs an infinite series of *partial oracles* converging to a reflective oracle in the limit.

The set of queries is countable, so we can assume that we have some computable enumeration of it:

$$\mathcal{T} \times \{0,1\}^* \times \mathbb{Q} =: \{q_1, q_2, \ldots\}$$

Definition 8 (k-Partial Oracle). A *k-partial oracle* $\tilde{O}$ is function from the first k queries to the multiples of 2^{-k} in $[0, 1]$:

$$\tilde{O} : \{q_1, q_2, \ldots, q_k\} \to \{n2^{-k} \mid 0 \leq n \leq 2^k\}$$

Definition 9 (Approximating an Oracle). A k-partial oracle $\tilde{O}$ *approximates* an oracle O iff $|O(q_i) - \tilde{O}(q_i)| \leq 2^{-k-1}$ for all $i \leq k$.

Let $k \in \mathbb{N}$, let $\tilde{O}$ be a k-partial oracle, and let $T \in \mathcal{T}$ be an oracle machine. The machine $T^{\tilde{O}}$ that we get when we run T with the k-partial oracle $\tilde{O}$ is defined as follows (this is with slight abuse of notation since k is taken to be understood implicitly).

1. Run T for at most k steps.
2. If T calls the oracle on q_i for $i \leq k$,
   (a) return 1 with probability $\tilde{O}(q_i) - 2^{-k-1}$,
   (b) return 0 with probability $1 - \tilde{O}(q_i) - 2^{-k-1}$, and
   (c) halt otherwise.
3. If T calls the oracle on q_j for $j > k$, halt.

Furthermore, we define $\lambda_T^{\tilde{O}}$ analogously to λ_T^O as the distribution generated by the machine $T^{\tilde{O}}$.

Lemma 10. *If a k-partial oracle $\tilde{O}$ approximates a reflective oracle O, then $\lambda_T^O(1 \mid x) \geq \lambda_T^{\tilde{O}}(1 \mid x)$ and $\lambda_T^O(0 \mid x) \geq \lambda_T^{\tilde{O}}(0 \mid x)$ for all $x \in \{0,1\}^*$ and all $T \in \mathcal{T}$.*

Proof. This follows from the definition of $T^{\tilde{O}}$: when running T with $\tilde{O}$ instead of O, we can only lose probability mass. If T makes calls whose index is $> k$ or runs for more than k steps, then the execution is aborted and no further output is generated. If T makes calls whose index $i \leq k$, then $\tilde{O}(q_i) - 2^{-k-1} \leq O(q_i)$ since $\tilde{O}$ approximates O. Therefore the return of the call q_i is underestimated as well. □

Definition 11 (k-Partially Reflective). A k-partial oracle $\tilde{O}$ is *k-partially reflective* iff for the first k queries (T, x, p)

- $\lambda_T^{\tilde{O}}(1 \mid x) > p$ implies $\tilde{O}(T, x, p) = 1$, and

- $\lambda_T^{\tilde{O}}(0 \mid x) > 1 - p$ implies $\tilde{O}(T, x, p) = 0$.

It is important to note that we can check whether a k-partial oracle is k-partially reflective in finite time by running all machines T from the first k queries for k steps and tallying up the probabilities to compute $\lambda_T^{\tilde{O}}$.

Lemma 12. *If O is a reflective oracle and $\tilde{O}$ is a k-partial oracle that approximates O, then $\tilde{O}$ is k-partially reflective.*

Lemma 12 only holds because we use semimeasures whose conditionals are lower semicomputable.

Proof. Assuming $\lambda_T^{\tilde{O}}(1 \mid x) > p$ we get from Lemma 10 that $\lambda_T^O(1 \mid x) \geq \lambda_T^{\tilde{O}}(1 \mid x) > p$. Thus $O(T, x, p) = 1$ because O is reflective. Since $\tilde{O}$ approximates O, we get $1 = O(T, x, p) \leq \tilde{O}(T, x, p) + 2^{-k-1}$, and since $\tilde{O}$ assigns values in a 2^{-k}-grid, it follows that $\tilde{O}(T, x, p) = 1$. The second implication is proved analogously. □

Definition 13 (Extending Partial Oracles). A $k+1$-partial oracle $\tilde{O}'$ *extends* a k-partial oracle $\tilde{O}$ iff $|\tilde{O}(q_i) - \tilde{O}'(q_i)| \leq 2^{-k-1}$ for all $i \leq k$.

Lemma 14. *There is an infinite sequence of partial oracles $(\tilde{O}_k)_{k \in \mathbb{N}}$ such that for each k, $\tilde{O}_k$ is a k-partially reflective k-partial oracle and $\tilde{O}_{k+1}$ extends $\tilde{O}_k$.*

Proof. By Theorem 4 there is a reflective oracle O. For every k, there is a canonical k-partial oracle $\tilde{O}_k$ that approximates O: restrict O to the first k queries and for any such query q pick the value in the 2^{-k}-grid which is closest to $O(q)$. By construction, $\tilde{O}_{k+1}$ extends $\tilde{O}_k$ and by Lemma 12, each $\tilde{O}_k$ is k-partially reflective. □

Lemma 15. *If the $k+1$-partial oracle $\tilde{O}_{k+1}$ extends the k-partial oracle $\tilde{O}_k$, then $\lambda_T^{\tilde{O}_{k+1}}(1 \mid x) \geq \lambda_T^{\tilde{O}_k}(1 \mid x)$ and $\lambda_T^{\tilde{O}_{k+1}}(0 \mid x) \geq \lambda_T^{\tilde{O}_k}(0 \mid x)$ for all $x \in \{0,1\}^*$ and all $T \in \mathcal{T}$.*

Proof. $T^{\tilde{O}_{k+1}}$ runs for one more step than $T^{\tilde{O}_k}$, can answer one more query and has increased oracle precision. Moreover, since $\tilde{O}_{k+1}$ extends $\tilde{O}_k$, we have $|\tilde{O}_{k+1}(q_i) - \tilde{O}_k(q_i)| \leq 2^{-k-1}$, and thus $\tilde{O}_{k+1}(q_i) - 2^{-k-1} \geq \tilde{O}_k(q_i) - 2^{-k}$. Therefore the success to answers to the oracle calls (case 2(a) and 2(b)) will not decrease in probability. □

Now everything is in place to state the algorithm that constructs a reflective oracle in the limit. It recursively traverses a tree of partial oracles. The tree's nodes are the partial oracles; level k of the tree contains all k-partial oracles. There is an edge in the tree from the k-partial oracle $\tilde{O}_k$ to the i-partial oracle $\tilde{O}_i$ if and only if $i = k+1$ and $\tilde{O}_i$ extends $\tilde{O}_k$.

For every k, there are only finitely many k-partial oracles, since they are functions from finite sets to finite sets. In particular, there are exactly two 1-partial oracles (so the search tree has two roots). Pick one of them to start with, and proceed recursively as follows. Given a k-partial oracle $\tilde{O}_k$, there are finitely many $(k+1)$-partial oracles that extend $\tilde{O}_k$ (finite branching of the tree). Pick one that is $(k+1)$-partially reflective (which can be checked in finite time). If there is no $(k+1)$-partially reflective extension, backtrack.

By Lemma 14 our search tree is infinitely deep and thus the tree search does not terminate. Moreover, it can backtrack to each level only a finite number of times because at each level there is only a finite number of possible extensions. Therefore the algorithm will produce an infinite sequence of partial oracles, each extending the previous. Because of finite backtracking, the output eventually stabilizes on a sequence of partial oracles $\tilde{O}_1, \tilde{O}_2, \ldots$. By the following lemma, this sequence converges to a reflective oracle, which concludes the proof of Theorem 6.

Lemma 16. *Let $\tilde{O}_1, \tilde{O}_2, \ldots$ be a sequence where $\tilde{O}_k$ is a k-partially reflective k-partial oracle and $\tilde{O}_{k+1}$ extends $\tilde{O}_k$ for all $k \in \mathbb{N}$. Let $O := \lim_{k \to \infty} \tilde{O}_k$ be the pointwise limit. Then*

(a) $\lambda_T^{\tilde{O}_k}(1 \mid x) \to \lambda_T^O(1 \mid x)$ and $\lambda_T^{\tilde{O}_k}(0 \mid x) \to \lambda_T^O(0 \mid x)$ as $k \to \infty$ for all $x \in \{0,1\}^*$ and all $T \in \mathcal{T}$, and

(b) O is a reflective oracle.

Proof. First note that the pointwise limit must exists because $|\tilde{O}_k(q_i) - \tilde{O}_{k+1}(q_i)| \leq 2^{-k-1}$ by Definition 13.

(a) Since $\tilde{O}_{k+1}$ extends $\tilde{O}_k$, each $\tilde{O}_k$ approximates O. Let $x \in \{0,1\}^*$ and $T \in \mathcal{T}$ and consider the sequence $a_k := \lambda_T^{\tilde{O}_k}(1 \mid x)$ for $k \in \mathbb{N}$. By Lemma 15, $a_k \leq a_{k+1}$, so the sequence is monotone increasing. By Lemma 10, $a_k \leq \lambda_T^O(1 \mid x)$, so the sequence is bounded. Therefore it must converge. But it cannot converge to anything strictly below $\lambda_T^O(1 \mid x)$ by the definition of T^O.

(b) By definition, O is an oracle; it remains to show that O is reflective. Let $q_i = (T, x, p)$ be some query. If $p < \lambda_T^O(1 \mid x)$, then by (a) there is a k large enough such that $p < \lambda_T^{\tilde{O}_t}(1 \mid x)$ for all $t \geq k$. For any $t \geq \max\{k, i\}$, we have $\tilde{O}_t(T, x, p) = 1$ since $\tilde{O}_t$ is t-partially reflective. Therefore $1 = \lim_{k \to \infty} \tilde{O}_k(T, x, p) = O(T, x, p)$. The case $1 - p < \lambda_T^O(0 \mid x)$ is analogous. □

3 A GRAIN OF TRUTH

3.1 NOTATION

In reinforcement learning, an agent interacts with an environment in cycles: at time step t the agent chooses an *action* $a_t \in \mathcal{A}$ and receives a *percept* $e_t = (o_t, r_t) \in \mathcal{E}$

consisting of an *observation* $o_t \in \mathcal{O}$ and a real-valued *reward* $r_t \in \mathbb{R}$; the cycle then repeats for $t+1$. A *history* is an element of $(\mathcal{A} \times \mathcal{E})^*$. In this section, we use $æ \in \mathcal{A} \times \mathcal{E}$ to denote one interaction cycle, and $æ_{<t}$ to denote a history of length $t-1$.

We fix a *discount function* $\gamma : \mathbb{N} \to \mathbb{R}$ with $\gamma_t \geq 0$ and $\sum_{t=1}^{\infty} \gamma_t < \infty$. The goal in reinforcement learning is to maximize discounted rewards $\sum_{t=1}^{\infty} \gamma_t r_t$. The *discount normalization factor* is defined as $\Gamma_t := \sum_{k=t}^{\infty} \gamma_k$. The *effective horizon* $H_t(\varepsilon)$ is a horizon that is long enough to encompass all but an ε of the discount function's mass:

$$H_t(\varepsilon) := \min\{k \mid \Gamma_{t+k}/\Gamma_t \leq \varepsilon\} \tag{2}$$

A *policy* is a function $\pi : (\mathcal{A} \times \mathcal{E})^* \to \Delta\mathcal{A}$ that maps a history $æ_{<t}$ to a distribution over actions taken after seeing this history. The probability of taking action a after history $æ_{<t}$ is denoted with $\pi(a \mid æ_{<t})$. An *environment* is a function $\nu : (\mathcal{A} \times \mathcal{E})^* \times \mathcal{A} \to \Delta\mathcal{E}$ where $\nu(e \mid æ_{<t}a_t)$ denotes the probability of receiving the percept e when taking the action a_t after the history $æ_{<t}$. Together, a policy π and an environment ν give rise to a distribution ν^π over histories. Throughout this paper, we make the following assumptions.

Assumption 17. *(a) Rewards are bounded between* 0 *and* 1.

(b) The set of actions $\mathcal{A}$ and the set of percepts $\mathcal{E}$ are both finite.

(c) The discount function γ and the discount normalization factor Γ are computable.

Definition 18 (Value Function). The *value* of a policy π in an environment ν given history $æ_{<t}$ is defined recursively as $V_\nu^\pi(æ_{<t}) := \sum_{a \in \mathcal{A}} \pi(a \mid æ_{<t}) V_\nu^\pi(æ_{<t}a)$ and

$$V_\nu^\pi(æ_{<t}a_t) := \frac{1}{\Gamma_t} \sum_{e_t \in \mathcal{E}} \nu(e_t \mid æ_{<t}a_t)\Big(\gamma_t r_t + \Gamma_{t+1} V_\nu^\pi(æ_{1:t})\Big)$$

if $\Gamma_t > 0$ and $V_\nu^\pi(æ_{<t}a_t) := 0$ if $\Gamma_t = 0$. The *optimal value* is defined as $V_\nu^*(æ_{<t}) := \sup_\pi V_\nu^\pi(æ_{<t})$.

Definition 19 (Optimal Policy). A policy π is *optimal in environment ν (ν-optimal)* iff for all histories $æ_{<t} \in (\mathcal{A} \times \mathcal{E})^*$ the policy π attains the optimal value: $V_\nu^\pi(æ_{<t}) = V_\nu^*(æ_{<t})$.

We assumed that the discount function is summable, rewards are bounded (Assumption 17a), and actions and percepts spaces are both finite (Assumption 17b). Therefore an optimal deterministic policy exists for every environment [LH14, Thm. 10].

3.2 REFLECTIVE BAYESIAN AGENTS

Fix O to be a reflective oracle. From now on, we assume that the action space $\mathcal{A} := \{\alpha, \beta\}$ is binary. We can treat computable measures over binary strings as environments: the environment ν corresponding to a probabilistic Turing machine $T \in \mathcal{T}$ is defined by

$$\nu(e_t \mid æ_{<t}a_t) := \overline{\lambda}_T^O(y \mid x) = \prod_{i=1}^{k} \overline{\lambda}_T^O(y_i \mid x y_1 \ldots y_{i-1})$$

where $y_{1:k}$ is a binary encoding of e_t and x is a binary encoding of $æ_{<t}a_t$. The actions $a_{1:\infty}$ are only *contextual*, and not part of the environment distribution. We define

$$\nu(e_{<t} \mid a_{<t}) := \prod_{k=1}^{t-1} \nu(e_k \mid æ_{<k}).$$

Let $T_1, T_2, \ldots$ be an enumeration of all probabilistic Turing machines in $\mathcal{T}$. We define the *class of reflective environments*

$$\mathcal{M}_{\text{refl}}^O := \left\{\overline{\lambda}_{T_1}^O, \overline{\lambda}_{T_2}^O, \ldots\right\}.$$

This is the class of all environments computable on a probabilistic Turing machine with reflective oracle O, that have been completed from semimeasures to measures using O.

Analogously to AIXI [Hut05], we define a Bayesian mixture over the class $\mathcal{M}_{\text{refl}}^O$. Let $w \in \Delta\mathcal{M}_{\text{refl}}^O$ be a lower semicomputable prior probability distribution on $\mathcal{M}_{\text{refl}}^O$. Possible choices for the prior include the *Solomonoff prior* $w(\overline{\lambda}_T^O) := 2^{-K(T)}$, where $K(T)$ denotes the length of the shortest input to some universal Turing machine that encodes T [Sol78].[2] We define the corresponding Bayesian mixture

$$\xi(e_t \mid æ_{<t}a_t) := \sum_{\nu \in \mathcal{M}_{\text{refl}}^O} w(\nu \mid æ_{<t}) \nu(e_t \mid æ_{<t}a_t) \tag{3}$$

where $w(\nu \mid æ_{<t})$ is the (renomalized) posterior,

$$w(\nu \mid æ_{<t}) := w(\nu) \frac{\nu(e_{<t} \mid a_{<t})}{\overline{\xi}(e_{<t} \mid a_{<t})}. \tag{4}$$

The mixture ξ is lower semicomputable on an oracle Turing machine because the posterior $w(\cdot \mid æ_{<t})$ is lower semicomputable. Hence there is an oracle machine T such that $\xi = \lambda_T^O$. We define its completion $\overline{\xi} := \overline{\lambda}_T^O$ as the completion of λ_T^O. This is the distribution that is used to compute the posterior. There are no cyclic dependencies since $\overline{\xi}$ is called on the shorter history $æ_{<t}$. We arrive at the following statement.

Proposition 20 (Bayes is in the Class). $\overline{\xi} \in \mathcal{M}_{\text{refl}}^O$.

Moreover, since O is reflective, we have that $\overline{\xi}$ dominates all environments $\nu \in \mathcal{M}_{\text{refl}}^O$:

$$\overline{\xi}(e_{1:t} \mid a_{1:t})$$

[2]Technically, the lower semicomputable prior $2^{-K(T)}$ is only a semidistribution because it does not sum to 1. This turns out to be unimportant.

$$= \overline{\xi}(e_t \mid æ_{<t}a_t)\overline{\xi}(e_{<t} \mid a_{<t})$$
$$\geq \xi(e_t \mid æ_{<t}a_t)\overline{\xi}(e_{<t} \mid a_{<t})$$
$$= \overline{\xi}(e_{<t} \mid a_{<t}) \sum_{\nu \in \mathcal{M}^O_{\text{refl}}} w(\nu \mid æ_{<t})\nu(e_t \mid æ_{<t}a_t)$$
$$= \overline{\xi}(e_{<t} \mid a_{<t}) \sum_{\nu \in \mathcal{M}^O_{\text{refl}}} w(\nu)\frac{\nu(e_{<t} \mid a_{<t})}{\overline{\xi}(e_{<t} \mid a_{<t})}\nu(e_t \mid æ_{<t}a_t)$$
$$= \sum_{\nu \in \mathcal{M}^O_{\text{refl}}} w(\nu)\nu(e_{1:t} \mid a_{1:t})$$
$$\geq w(\nu)\nu(e_{1:t} \mid a_{1:t})$$

This property is crucial for on-policy value convergence.

Lemma 21 (On-Policy Value Convergence [Hut05, Thm. 5.36]). *For any policy π and any environment $\mu \in \mathcal{M}^O_{refl}$ with $w(\mu) > 0$,*

$$V^\pi_\mu(æ_{<t}) - V^\pi_{\overline{\xi}}(æ_{<t}) \to 0 \ \mu^\pi\text{-almost surely as } t \to \infty.$$

3.3 REFLECTIVE-ORACLE-COMPUTABLE POLICIES

This subsection is dedicated to the following result that was previously stated but not proved in [FST15, Alg. 6]. It contrasts results on arbitrary semicomputable environments where optimal policies are not limit computable [LH15b, Sec. 4].

Theorem 22 (Optimal Policies are Oracle Computable). *For every $\nu \in \mathcal{M}^O_{refl}$, there is a ν-optimal (stochastic) policy π^*_ν that is reflective-oracle-computable.*

Note that even though deterministic optimal policies always exist, those policies are typically not reflective-oracle-computable.

To prove Theorem 22 we need the following lemma.

Lemma 23 (Reflective-Oracle-Computable Optimal Value Function). *For every environment $\nu \in \mathcal{M}^O_{refl}$ the optimal value function V^*_ν is reflective-oracle-computable.*

Proof. This proof follows the proof of [LH15b, Cor. 13]. We write the optimal value explicitly as

$$V^*_\nu(æ_{<t}) = \frac{1}{\Gamma_t} \lim_{m\to\infty} \underset{æ_{t:m}}{\text{max}\!\!\!\!\sum} \sum_{k=t}^{m} \gamma_k r_k \prod_{i=t}^{k} \nu(e_i \mid æ_{<i}), \tag{5}$$

where $\text{max}\!\!\!\!\sum$ denotes the expectimax operator:

$$\underset{æ_{t:m}}{\text{max}\!\!\!\!\sum} := \max_{a_t \in \mathcal{A}} \sum_{e_t \in \mathcal{E}} \ldots \max_{a_m \in \mathcal{A}} \sum_{e_m \in \mathcal{E}}$$

For a fixed m, all involved quantities are reflective-oracle-computable. Moreover, this quantity is monotone increasing in m and the tail sum from $m+1$ to ∞ is bounded by Γ_{m+1} which is computable according to Assumption 17c and converges to 0 as $m \to \infty$. Therefore we can enumerate all rationals above and below V^*_ν. □

Proof of Theorem 22. According to Lemma 23 the optimal value function V^*_ν is reflective-oracle-computable. Hence there is a probabilistic Turing machine T such that

$$\lambda^O_T(1 \mid æ_{<t}) = \big(V^*_\nu(æ_{<t}\alpha) - V^*_\nu(æ_{<t}\beta) + 1\big)/2.$$

We define a policy π that takes action α if $O(T, æ_{<t}, 1/2) = 1$ and action β if $O(T, æ_{<t}, 1/2) = 0$. (This policy is stochastic because the answer of the oracle O is stochastic.)

It remains to show that π is a ν-optimal policy. If $V^*_\nu(æ_{<t}\alpha) > V^*_\nu(æ_{<t}\beta)$, then $\lambda^O_T(1 \mid æ_{<t}) > 1/2$, thus $O(T, æ_{<t}, 1/2) = 1$ since O is reflective, and hence π takes action α. Conversely, if $V^*_\nu(æ_{<t}\alpha) < V^*_\nu(æ_{<t}\beta)$, then $\lambda^O_T(1 \mid æ_{<t}) < 1/2$, thus $O(T, æ_{<t}, 1/2) = 0$ since O is reflective, and hence π takes action β. Lastly, if $V^*_\nu(æ_{<t}\alpha) = V^*_\nu(æ_{<t}\beta)$, then both actions are optimal and thus it does not matter which action is returned by policy π. (This is the case where the oracle may randomize.) □

3.4 SOLUTION TO THE GRAIN OF TRUTH PROBLEM

Together, Proposition 20 and Theorem 22 provide the necessary ingredients to solve the grain of truth problem.

Corollary 24 (Solution to the Grain of Truth Problem). *For every lower semicomputable prior $w \in \Delta\mathcal{M}^O_{refl}$ the Bayes-optimal policy $\pi^*_{\overline{\xi}}$ is reflective-oracle-computable where ξ is the Bayes-mixture corresponding to w defined in* (3).

Proof. From Proposition 20 and Theorem 22. □

Hence the environment class $\mathcal{M}^O_{\text{refl}}$ contains any reflective-oracle-computable modification of the Bayes-optimal policy $\pi^*_{\overline{\xi}}$. In particular, this includes computable multi-agent environments that contain other Bayesian agents over the class $\mathcal{M}^O_{\text{refl}}$. So any Bayesian agent over the class $\mathcal{M}^O_{\text{refl}}$ has a grain of truth even though the environment may contain other Bayesian agents *of equal power*. We proceed to sketch the implications for multi-agent environments in the next section.

4 MULTI-AGENT ENVIRONMENTS

This section summarizes our results for multi-agent systems. The proofs can be found in [Lei16].

4.1 SETUP

In a *multi-agent environment* there are n agents each taking sequential actions from the finite action space $\mathcal{A}$. In each time step $t = 1, 2, \ldots$, the environment receives action a^i_t from agent i and outputs n percepts $e^1_t, \ldots, e^n_t \in \mathcal{E}$, one for

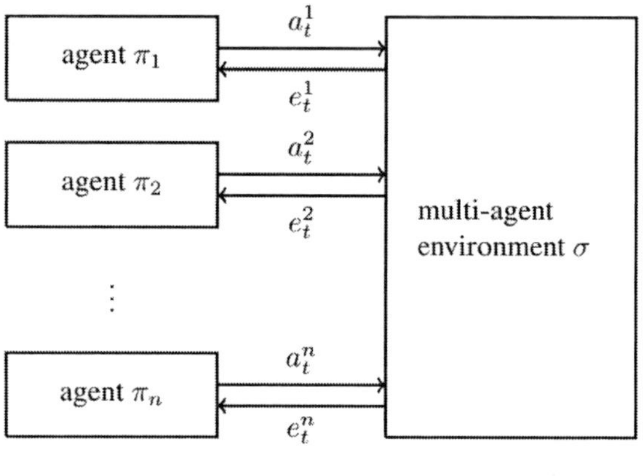

Figure 2: Agents $\pi_1, \ldots, \pi_n$ interacting in a multi-agent environment.

each agent. Each percept $e_t^i = (o_t^i, r_t^i)$ contains an observation o_t^i and a reward $r_t^i \in [0,1]$. Importantly, agent i only sees its own action a_t^i and its own percept e_t^i (see Figure 2). We use the shorthand notation $a_t := (a_t^1, \ldots, a_t^n)$ and $e_t := (e_t^1, \ldots, e_t^n)$ and denote $æ_{<t}^i = a_1^i e_1^i \ldots a_{t-1}^i e_{t-1}^i$ and $æ_{<t} = a_1 e_1 \ldots a_{t-1} e_{t-1}$.

We define a multi-agent environment as a function

$$\sigma : (\mathcal{A}^n \times \mathcal{E}^n)^* \times \mathcal{A}^n \to \Delta(\mathcal{E}^n).$$

The agents are given by n policies $\pi_1, \ldots, \pi_n$ where $\pi_i : (\mathcal{A} \times \mathcal{E})^* \to \Delta\mathcal{A}$. Together they specify the *history distribution*

$$\begin{aligned} \sigma^{\pi_{1:n}}(\epsilon) &:= 1 \\ \sigma^{\pi_{1:n}}(æ_{1:t}) &:= \sigma^{\pi_{1:n}}(æ_{<t} a_t) \sigma(e_t \mid æ_{<t} a_t) \\ \sigma^{\pi_{1:n}}(æ_{<t} a_t) &:= \sigma^{\pi_{1:n}}(æ_{<t}) \prod_{i=1}^n \pi_i(a_t^i \mid æ_{<t}^i). \end{aligned}$$

Each agent i acts in a *subjective environment* σ_i given by joining the multi-agent environment σ with the policies $\pi_1, \ldots, \pi_{i-1}, \pi_{i+1}, \ldots, \pi_n$ by marginalizing over the histories that π_i does not see. Together with policy π_i, the environment σ_i yields a distribution over the histories of agent i

$$\sigma_i^{\pi_i}(æ_{<t}^i) := \sum_{æ_{<t}^j, j \neq i} \sigma^{\pi_{1:n}}(æ_{<t}).$$

We get the definition of the subjective environment σ_i with the identity $\sigma_i(e_t^i \mid æ_{<t}^i a_t^i) := \sigma_i^{\pi_i}(e_t^i \mid æ_{<t}^i a_t^i)$. It is crucial to note that the subjective environment σ_i and the policy π_i are ordinary environments and policies, so we can use the formalism from Section 3.

Our definition of a multi-agent environment is very general and encompasses most of game theory. It allows for cooperative, competitive, and mixed games; infinitely repeated games or any (infinite-length) extensive form games with finitely many players.

The policy π_i is an *ε-best response* after history $æ_{<t}^i$ iff

$$V_{\sigma_i}^*(æ_{<t}^i) - V_{\sigma_i}^{\pi_i}(æ_{<t}^i) < \varepsilon.$$

If at some time step t, all agents' policies are ε-best responses, we have an *ε-Nash equilibrium*. The property of multi-agent systems that is analogous to asymptotic optimality is convergence to an ε-Nash equilibrium.

4.2 INFORMED REFLECTIVE AGENTS

Let σ be a multi-agent environment and let $\pi_{\sigma_1}^*, \ldots \pi_{\sigma_n}^*$ be such that for each i the policy $\pi_{\sigma_i}^*$ is an optimal policy in agent i's subjective environment σ_i. At first glance this seems ill-defined: The subjective environment σ_i depends on each other policy $\pi_{\sigma_j}^*$ for $j \neq i$, which depends on the subjective environment σ_j, which in turn depends on the policy $\pi_{\sigma_i}^*$. However, this circular definition actually has a well-defined solution.

Theorem 25 (Optimal Multi-Agent Policies). *For any reflective-oracle-computable multi-agent environment σ, the optimal policies $\pi_{\sigma_1}^*, \ldots, \pi_{\sigma_n}^*$ exist and are reflective-oracle-computable.*

Note the strength of Theorem 25: each of the policies $\pi_{\sigma_i}^*$ is acting optimally *given the knowledge of everyone else's policies*. Hence optimal policies play 0-best responses by definition, so if every agent is playing an optimal policy, we have a Nash equilibrium. Moreover, this Nash equilibrium is also a *subgame perfect* Nash equilibrium, because each agent also acts optimally on the counterfactual histories that do not end up being played. In other words, Theorem 25 states the existence and reflective-oracle-computability of a subgame perfect Nash equilibrium in any reflective-oracle-computable multi-agent environment. From Theorem 6 we then get that these subgame perfect Nash equilibria are limit computable.

Corollary 26 (Solution to Computable Multi-Agent Environments). *For any computable multi-agent environment σ, the optimal policies $\pi_{\sigma_1}^*, \ldots, \pi_{\sigma_n}^*$ exist and are limit computable.*

4.3 LEARNING REFLECTIVE AGENTS

Since our class $\mathcal{M}_{\text{refl}}^O$ solves the grain of truth problem, the result by Kalai and Lehrer [KL93] immediately implies that for any Bayesian agents $\pi_1, \ldots, \pi_n$ interacting in an infinitely repeated game and for all $\varepsilon > 0$ and all $i \in \{1, \ldots, n\}$ there is almost surely a $t_0 \in \mathbb{N}$ such that for all $t \geq t_0$ the policy π_i is an ε-best response. However, this hinges on the important fact that every agent has to know the game and also that all other agents are Bayesian agents. Otherwise the convergence to an ε-Nash equilibrium may fail, as illustrated by the following example.

At the core of the following construction is a *dogmatic prior* [LH15a, Sec. 3.2]. A dogmatic prior assigns very high probability to going to hell (reward 0 forever) if the agent deviates from a given computable policy π. For a Bayesian agent it is thus only worth deviating from the policy π if the agent thinks that the prospects of following π are very poor already. This implies that for general multi-agent environments and without additional assumptions on the prior, we cannot prove any meaningful convergence result about Bayesian agents acting in an unknown multi-agent environment.

Example 27 (Reflective Bayesians Playing Matching Pennies)**.** In the game of *matching pennies* there are two agents ($n = 2$), and two actions $\mathcal{A} = \{\alpha, \beta\}$ representing the two sides of a penny. In each time step agent 1 wins if the two actions are identical and agent 2 wins if the two actions are different. The payoff matrix is as follows.

	α	β
α	1,0	0,1
β	0,1	1,0

We use $\mathcal{E} = \{0, 1\}$ to be the set of rewards (observations are vacuous) and define the multi-agent environment σ to give reward 1 to agent 1 iff $a_t^1 = a_t^2$ (0 otherwise) and reward 1 to agent 2 iff $a_t^1 \neq a_t^2$ (0 otherwise). Note that neither agent knows a priori that they are playing matching pennies, nor that they are playing an infinite repeated game with one other player.

Let π_1 be the policy that takes the action sequence $(\alpha\alpha\beta)^\infty$ and let $\pi_2 := \pi_\alpha$ be the policy that always takes action α. The average reward of policy π_1 is $2/3$ and the average reward of policy π_2 is $1/3$. Let ξ be a universal mixture (3). By Lemma 21, $V_\xi^{\pi_1} \to c_1 \approx 2/3$ and $V_\xi^{\pi_2} \to c_2 \approx 1/3$ almost surely when following policies (π_1, π_2). Therefore there is an $\varepsilon > 0$ such that $V_\xi^{\pi_1} > \varepsilon$ and $V_\xi^{\pi_2} > \varepsilon$ for all time steps. Now we can apply [LH15a, Thm. 7] to conclude that there are (dogmatic) mixtures ξ_1' and ξ_2' such that $\pi^*_{\xi_1'}$ always follows policy π_1 and $\pi^*_{\xi_2'}$ always follows policy π_2. This does not converge to a (ε-)Nash equilibrium. $\diamondsuit$

A policy π is *asymptotically optimal in mean in an environment class* $\mathcal{M}$ iff for all $\mu \in \mathcal{M}$

$$\mathbb{E}_\mu^\pi\left[V_\mu^*(æ_{<t}) - V_\mu^\pi(æ_{<t})\right] \to 0 \text{ as } t \to \infty \qquad (6)$$

where $\mathbb{E}_\mu^\pi$ denotes the expectation with respect to the probability distribution μ^π over histories generated by policy π acting in environment μ.

Asymptotic optimality stands out because it is currently the only known nontrivial objective notion of optimality in general reinforcement learning [LH15a].

The following theorem is the main convergence result. It states that for asymptotically optimal agents we get convergence to ε-Nash equilibria in any reflective-oracle-computable multi-agent environment.

Theorem 28 (Convergence to Equilibrium)**.** *Let σ be an reflective-oracle-computable multi-agent environment and let $\pi_1, \dots, \pi_n$ be reflective-oracle-computable policies that are asymptotically optimal in mean in the class $\mathcal{M}^O_{refl}$. Then for all $\varepsilon > 0$ and all $i \in \{1, \dots, n\}$ the $\sigma^{\pi_{1:n}}$-probability that the policy π_i is an ε-best response converges to 1 as $t \to \infty$.*

In contrast to Theorem 25 which yields policies that play a subgame perfect equilibrium, this is not the case for Theorem 28: the agents typically do not learn to predict off-policy and thus will generally not play ε-best responses in the counterfactual histories that they never see. This weaker form of equilibrium is unavoidable if the agents do not know the environment because it is impossible to learn the parts that they do not interact with.

Together with Theorem 6 and the asymptotic optimality of the Thompson sampling policy [LLOH16, Thm. 4] that is reflective-oracle computable we get the following corollary.

Corollary 29 (Convergence to Equilibrium)**.** *There are limit computable policies $\pi_1, \dots, \pi_n$ such that for any computable multi-agent environment σ and for all $\varepsilon > 0$ and all $i \in \{1, \dots, n\}$ the $\sigma^{\pi_{1:n}}$-probability that the policy π_i is an ε-best response converges to 1 as $t \to \infty$.*

5 DISCUSSION

This paper introduced the class of all reflective-oracle-computable environments $\mathcal{M}^O_{\text{refl}}$. This class solves the grain of truth problem because it contains (any computable modification of) Bayesian agents defined over $\mathcal{M}^O_{\text{refl}}$: the optimal agents and Bayes-optimal agents over the class are all reflective-oracle-computable (Theorem 22 and Corollary 24).

If the environment is unknown, then a Bayesian agent may end up playing suboptimally (Example 27). However, if each agent uses a policy that is asymptotically optimal in mean (such as the Thompson sampling policy [LLOH16]) then for every $\varepsilon > 0$ the agents converge to an ε-Nash equilibrium (Theorem 28 and Corollary 29).

Our solution to the grain of truth problem is purely theoretical. However, Theorem 6 shows that our class $\mathcal{M}^O_{\text{refl}}$ allows for computable approximations. This suggests that practical approaches can be derived from this result, and reflective oracles have already seen applications in one-shot games [FTC15b].

Acknowledgements

We thank Marcus Hutter and Tom Everitt for valuable comments.

REFERENCES

[FST15] Benja Fallenstein, Nate Soares, and Jessica Taylor. Reflective variants of Solomonoff induction and AIXI. In *Artificial General Intelligence*. Springer, 2015.

[FTC15a] Benja Fallenstein, Jessica Taylor, and Paul F Christiano. Reflective oracles: A foundation for classical game theory. Technical report, Machine Intelligence Research Institute, 2015. `http://arxiv.org/abs/1508.04145`.

[FTC15b] Benja Fallenstein, Jessica Taylor, and Paul F Christiano. Reflective oracles: A foundation for game theory in artificial intelligence. In *Logic, Rationality, and Interaction*, pages 411–415. Springer, 2015.

[FY01] Dean P Foster and H Peyton Young. On the impossibility of predicting the behavior of rational agents. *Proceedings of the National Academy of Sciences*, 98(22):12848–12853, 2001.

[Hut05] Marcus Hutter. *Universal Artificial Intelligence*. Springer, 2005.

[Hut09] Marcus Hutter. Open problems in universal induction & intelligence. *Algorithms*, 3(2):879–906, 2009.

[KL93] Ehud Kalai and Ehud Lehrer. Rational learning leads to Nash equilibrium. *Econometrica*, pages 1019–1045, 1993.

[Kle52] Stephen Cole Kleene. *Introduction to Metamathematics*. Wolters-Noordhoff Publishing, 1952.

[Lei16] Jan Leike. *Nonparametric General Reinforcement Learning*. PhD thesis, Australian National University, 2016.

[LH14] Tor Lattimore and Marcus Hutter. General time consistent discounting. *Theoretical Computer Science*, 519:140–154, 2014.

[LH15a] Jan Leike and Marcus Hutter. Bad universal priors and notions of optimality. In *Conference on Learning Theory*, pages 1244–1259, 2015.

[LH15b] Jan Leike and Marcus Hutter. On the computability of AIXI. In *Uncertainty in Artificial Intelligence*, pages 464–473, 2015.

[LH15c] Jan Leike and Marcus Hutter. On the computability of Solomonoff induction and knowledge-seeking. In *Algorithmic Learning Theory*, pages 364–378, 2015.

[LLOH16] Jan Leike, Tor Lattimore, Laurent Orseau, and Marcus Hutter. Thompson sampling is asymptotically optimal in general environments. In *Uncertainty in Artificial Intelligence*, 2016.

[LV08] Ming Li and Paul M. B. Vitányi. *An Introduction to Kolmogorov Complexity and Its Applications*. Texts in Computer Science. Springer, 3rd edition, 2008.

[Nac97] John H Nachbar. Prediction, optimization, and learning in repeated games. *Econometrica*, 65(2):275–309, 1997.

[Nac05] John H Nachbar. Beliefs in repeated games. *Econometrica*, 73(2):459–480, 2005.

[Ors13] Laurent Orseau. Asymptotic non-learnability of universal agents with computable horizon functions. *Theoretical Computer Science*, 473:149–156, 2013.

[SLB09] Yoav Shoham and Kevin Leyton-Brown. *Multiagent Systems: Algorithmic, Game-Theoretic, and Logical Foundations*. Cambridge University Press, 2009.

[Sol78] Ray Solomonoff. Complexity-based induction systems: Comparisons and convergence theorems. *IEEE Transactions on Information Theory*, 24(4):422–432, 1978.

Bayesian Hyperparameter Optimization for Ensemble Learning

Julien-Charles Lévesque[*] **Christian Gagné**
Laboratoire de vision et systèmes numériques
Dép. de génie électrique et de génie informatique
Université Laval, Québec, Canada

Robert Sabourin
Laboratoire d'imagerie, de vision et d'IA
Dép. de génie de la production automatisée
École de technologie supérieure, Montréal, Canada

Abstract

In this paper, we bridge the gap between hyperparameter optimization and ensemble learning by performing Bayesian optimization of an ensemble with regards to its hyperparameters. Our method consists in building a fixed-size ensemble, optimizing the configuration of one classifier of the ensemble at each iteration of the hyperparameter optimization algorithm, taking into consideration the interaction with the other models when evaluating potential performances. We also consider the case where the ensemble is to be reconstructed at the end of the hyperparameter optimization phase, through a greedy selection over the pool of models generated during the optimization. We study the performance of our proposed method on three different hyperparameter spaces, showing that our approach is better than both the best single model and a greedy ensemble construction over the models produced by a standard Bayesian optimization.

1 INTRODUCTION

For a long time, the tuning of hyperparameters for learning algorithms was solved by simple exhaustive methods such as grid search guided by cross-validation error. Grid search does work in practice, but it suffers from serious drawbacks such as a search space complexity that grows exponentially with the number of hyperparameters tuned. Recently, other strategies such as sequential model-based parameter optimization (Hutter et al., 2011), random search (Bergstra and Bengio, 2012), and Bayesian optimization (Snoek et al., 2012) have been shown to be better alternatives to grid search for non-trivial search spaces.

While hyperparameter optimization focuses on the performance of a single model, it is generally accepted that ensembles can perform better than single classifiers, one of many striking examples being the winning entry of the Netflix challenge (Bell and Koren, 2007). More recent machine learning competitions such as Kaggle competitions are also often won by ensemble methods (Sun and Pfahringer, 2011). Given these previous results, it is logical to combine Bayesian hyperparameter optimization techniques with ensemble methods to further push generalization accuracy. Feurer et al. (2015a) performed post-hoc ensemble generation by reusing the product of a completed hyperparameter optimization, winning phase 1 of the ChaLearn AutoML challenge (Guyon et al., 2015). Lastly, Snoek et al. (2015) also constructed post-hoc ensembles of neural networks for image captioning.

These two lines of previous work make for a compelling argument to directly apply Bayesian optimization of hyperparameters for ensemble learning. Rather than trying to model the whole space of ensembles, which is likely hard and inefficient to optimize, we pose a performance model of the ensemble at hand when adding a new classifier with some given hyperparameters. This is achieved by reusing models previously assessed during the optimization, evaluating performance change induced by adding them one at a time to the ensemble. This allows us to compute observations of the true ensemble loss with regards to the hyperparameter values. These observations are used to condition a Bayesian optimization prior, creating mean and variance estimates over the hyperparameter space which will be used to optimize the configuration of a new classifier to add to the ensemble. Finally, we consider different possibilities to maintain and build the ensemble as the optimization progresses, and settle on a round-robin optimization of the classifiers in the ensemble. This ensemble optimization procedure comes at a very small additional cost compared with a regular Bayesian optimization of hyperparameter yet yields better generalization accuracy for the same number of trained models.

We evaluate our proposed approach on a benchmark of medium datasets for two different hyperparameter spaces, one consisting solely of SVM algorithms with different ker-

*julien-charles.levesque.1@ulaval.ca

nel types, and one larger space with various families of learning algorithms. In both search spaces, our approach is shown to outperform regular Bayesian optimization as well as post-hoc ensemble generation from pools of classifiers obtained by classical Bayesian optimization of hyperparameters. We also evaluate our approach on a search space of convolutional neural networks trained on the CIFAR-10 dataset. The proposed approach is also able to provide better performance in this case.

The paper is structured as follows: Section 2 presents the problem of Bayesian hyperparameter optimization and highlights some related work. Section 3 presents the main contributions of this paper, which can be summarized as a methodology for Bayesian optimization of ensembles through hyperparameter tuning. Finally, Section 4 presents the experiments and an analysis of the results.

2 HYPERPARAMETER OPTIMIZATION

The behavior of a learning algorithm A is often tunable with regards to a set of external parameters, called hyperparameters $\gamma = \{\gamma_1, \gamma_2, \ldots\} \in \Gamma$, which are not learned during training. The hyperparameter selection problem is one stage of a bi-level optimization problem, where the first objective is the tuning of the model's parameters θ and the second objective is the performance with regards to the hyperparameters γ.

The procedure requires two datasets, one for training and one for hyperparameter optimization (also called validation), namely $\mathcal{X}_T$ and $\mathcal{X}_V$, each assumed to be sampled *i.i.d.* from an underlying distribution $\mathcal{D}$. The objective function to minimize for hyperparameter optimization takes the form of the empirical generalization error on $\mathcal{X}_V$:

$$f(\gamma) = L(h_\gamma|\mathcal{X}_V) + \epsilon \tag{1}$$

$$L(h_\gamma|\mathcal{X}_V) = \frac{1}{|\mathcal{X}_V|}\sum_{i=1}^{|\mathcal{X}_V|} l_{0-1}(h_\gamma(x_i), y_i), \tag{2}$$

where ϵ is some noise on the observation of the generalization error, l_{0-1} is the zero-one loss function, and the model h_γ is obtained by running the training algorithm with hyperparameters γ, $h_\gamma = A(\mathcal{X}_T, \gamma)$. Other loss functions could be applied, but unless otherwise specified, the loss function will be the zero-one loss.

In order to solve this problem, Bayesian optimization consists in posing a probabilistic regression model of the generalization error of trained models with respect to their hyperparameters γ, and exploiting this model to select new hyperparameters to explore. At each iteration, a model of $f(\gamma)$ is conditioned on the set of previously observed hyperparameter values and associated losses $\{\gamma_i, L(h_{\gamma_i}|\mathcal{X}_V)\}_{i=1}^t$. Selection of the next hyperparameters to evaluate is performed by maximizing an *acquisition function* $a(\gamma|f(\gamma))$, a criterion balancing exploration and exploitation given mean and variance estimates obtained from the model of $f(\gamma)$. Among the model families for $f(\gamma)$, two interesting choices are Gaussian Processes (Rasmussen and Williams, 2006; Snoek et al., 2012) and Random Forests (Hutter et al., 2011), both providing information about the mean and variance of the fitted distribution over the whole search space.

A typical hyperparameter optimization is executed iteratively, subsequently generating a model of $f(\gamma)$ from observations, selecting hyperparameter tuples γ to evaluate, training a classifier h_γ with the given training data, evaluating it on the validation data, and looping until the maximum number of iterations or time budget is spent.

Recent advances in hyperparameter optimization have primarily focused on making optimization faster, more accurate and applicable to a wider set of applications. In order to speed up convergence, Feurer et al. (2015b) have shown that hyperparameter optimization can be warm started with meta features about datasets. Touching on both speed and optimality, the design of better acquisition functions has seen a lot of interest, and predictive entropy search was shown to be less greedy than expected improvement in locating the optima of objective functions (Hernández-Lobato et al., 2014). New applications have also emerged, one notable example being the optimization of hyperparameters for anytime algorithms with freeze-and-thaw Bayesian optimization (Swersky et al., 2014).

2.1 HYPERPARAMETER OPTIMIZATION AND ENSEMBLES

The idea of generating ensembles with hyperparameter optimization has already received some attention. Bergstra and Cox (2013) applied hyperparameter optimization in a multi-stage approach akin to boosting in order to generate better representations of images. Lacoste et al. (2014b) proposed the Sequential Model-based Ensemble Optimization (SMBEO) method to optimize ensembles based on bootstrapping the validation datasets to simulate multiple independent hyperparameter optimization processes and combined the results with the agnostic Bayesian combination method.

The process of hyperparameter optimization generates many trained models, and is usually concluded by selecting a model according to the hold-out (or cross-validation) generalization error $\gamma^* = \arg\min_\gamma L(h_\gamma|\mathcal{X}_V)$. This single model selection at the end of the optimization is the equivalent of a point estimate, and it can result in overfitting. One strategy to limit this overfitting in the selection of a final model is to select multiple models instead of one, reducing the risk of overfitting and thus increasing the generalization performance.

A simple strategy to build an ensemble from a hyperparameter optimization is to keep the trained models as they are generated for evaluation instead of discarding them (Feurer et al., 2015a). This effectively generates a *pool* of classifiers to combine at the end of the optimization, a process which is called **post-hoc ensemble generation**. Forward greedy selection has been shown to perform well in the context of pruning a pool of classifiers (Caruana et al., 2004). At each iteration, given a pool of trained classifiers H to select from, a new classifier is added to the ensemble, selected according to the minimum ensemble generalization error. At the first iteration, the classifier added is simply the single best classifier. At step t, given the ensemble $E = \{h_{e_1}, h_{e_2}, \ldots, h_{e_{t-1}}\}$, the next classifier is chosen to minimize the empirical error on the validation dataset when added to E:

$$h_t = \arg\min_{h \in H} L(E \cup \{h\} | \mathcal{X}_V) \tag{3}$$

$$L(E \cup \{h\} | \mathcal{X}_V) = \sum_{i=0}^{|\mathcal{X}_V|} l_{0-1}\left(g(x_i, E \cup \{h\}), y_i\right), \tag{4}$$

where $g(x_i, E)$ is a function combining the predictions of the classifiers in E on sample x_i. In this case, the combination rule is majority voting, as it is less prone to overfitting (Caruana et al., 2004; Feurer et al., 2015a). Other possible combination rules include weighted voting, stacking (Kuncheva, 2004) and agnostic Bayesian combination (Lacoste et al., 2014a), to name only a few. Such an approach can be shown to perform better than the single best classifier produced by the hyperparameter optimization, due in part to a reduction of the classifiers' variance through combination.

3 ENSEMBLE OPTIMIZATION

In this work, we aim at directly optimizing an ensemble of classifiers through Bayesian hyperparameter optimization. The strategies discussed in the previous section mostly aimed at reusing the product of a completed hyperparameter optimization after the fact. The goal is to make an online selection of hyperparameters that could be more interesting for an ensemble, but which do not necessarily maximize the objective function of Equation 1 on their own. Directly posing a model on the space of all possible ensembles of a given size $f(E) = f(\gamma_1, \ldots, \gamma_m)$ would result in a very hard and inefficient optimization problem, effectively duplicating the training of many models.

In order to palliate this, we propose a more focused approach. We define the objective function to be the performance of a given ensemble E when it is augmented with a new classifier trained with hyperparameters γ, or h_γ. In other words, the objective function is the empirical error provided by adding a model h_γ to the ensemble E:

$$f(\gamma | E) = L(E \cup A(\gamma, \mathcal{X}_T) | \mathcal{X}_V), \tag{5}$$

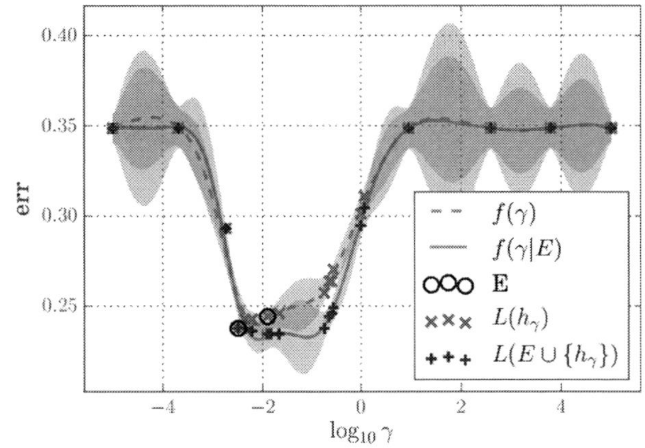

Figure 1: Example of an ensemble optimization. The red marks represent trained models and their standalone generalization error, and black circles represent two models selected for the current ensemble E. Blue marks represent the performance of an ensemble when we add the trained model with corresponding hyperparameters γ.

again using the empirical loss on a hold-out validation set $\mathcal{X}_V$. Contrarily to the post-hoc ensemble generation, a probabilistic model is fit on the performance that a model trained with given hyperparameters would provide to the ensemble. In order to do this, two things are required: 1) an already established ensemble, and 2) a pool of trained classifiers available to compute *observations* of Equation 5 to condition our model on. Given the history of trained models so far $H = \{h_1, \ldots, h_t\}$ and an ensemble defined by a selection of classifiers within the history $E = \{h_{e_1}, \ldots, h_{e_m}\}$, the observations used to model $f(\gamma)$ are obtained by reusing the trained classifiers in H, keeping E constant. Consequently, the objective function models the true ensemble error. Given a zero-one loss function and an empty ensemble $E = \varnothing$, Equation 5 falls back to a classical hyperparameter optimization problem, and the objective function will be minimized by the best hyperparameters for a single model γ^*.

The power of the suggested framework is illustrated with an example shown in Figure 1. This figure presents one iteration of ensemble optimization given 20 trained SVMs in a one-dimensional hyperparameter space, where the single hyperparameter is the width of the RBF kernel ($\sigma \in [10^{-5}, 10^5]$). The dataset used is the Pima Indian Diabetes dataset available from UCI (Frank and Asuncion, 2010), with separate training and validation splits. The current ensemble E consists of two models selected by forward greedy selection shown by black circles. Ensemble evaluation and member selection strategies will be discussed further; for now let us assume a fixed ensemble. The red Xs represent the generalization error of single models and the red curve represents a Gaussian Process prior conditioned on those observations, in other words, a model of

$f(\gamma)$. The blue crosses represent the generalization error of the ensemble E when the corresponding classifiers are added to it, and the blue curve is again a Gaussian Process prior conditioned on the ensemble observations, or, more generally speaking, a model of $f(\gamma|E)$. For both Gaussian Processes, the variance estimates are represented by shaded areas. The next step would be to apply an acquisition function with the ensemble mean and variance estimates to select the next hyperparameters to evaluate.

Figure 1 shows that the objective function of an ensemble and a single classifier can be different. It can also be observed in this case that the generalization error of the ensemble is lower than that of a single model, hence the interest in optimizing ensembles directly.

3.1 ALTERNATE FORMULATIONS

In order to be able to generalize over the space of hyperparameters, it is crucial to have an ensemble which does not contain all the classifiers in H, because if it did there would be no information added in the computation of Equation 5. A different problem formulation could be derived which compares classifiers with the whole pool of trained models, which would take the form $f(\gamma|H) = q(h_\gamma|H, \mathcal{X}_V)$, where $q(\cdot)$ is a metric of performance for a classifier with regards to the pool. For example, a diversity inducing metric such as pairwise disagreement (Kuncheva, 2004) could be used, but this would lead to degenerate pools of classifiers, as diversity is easily increased by trivial and degenerate classifiers (voting all for one class or the other).

Multi-objective optimization approaches have been considered for the maximization of both diversity and accuracy, a problem typically solved with genetic algorithms (Tsymbal et al., 2005). However, this problem formulation does not guarantee a better performing ensemble – only a more diverse pool of classifiers – with the hope that it will lead to better generalization performance. Directly optimizing diversity in classifier ensembles is questionable, and the evidence thus far is mixed (Didaci et al., 2013; Kuncheva, 2003).

Lastly, an inverse problem could be posed, measuring the difference in the generalization error by removing classifiers from the history one by one, and optimizing this difference. One problem with such a model is that it would be vulnerable to redundancy – very good hyperparameters present in multiple copies in the history would be falsely marked as having no impact on the generalization error.

For the reasons stated above, the best solution appears to be the use of a fixed ensemble which is maintained and updated as the optimization progresses. Thus it is possible to build an accurate Bayesian model of how well an ensemble would perform if we added a model trained with hyperparameters γ. This means that we need to store the trained

Algorithm 1 Ensemble Optimization Procedure

Input: $\mathcal{X}_T, \mathcal{X}_V, B, m, A, \Gamma, L$
Output: H, history of models; E, the final ensemble

$H, G, E \leftarrow \varnothing$
for $i \in 1, \ldots, B$ **do**
  $j \leftarrow i \mod m$
  $E \leftarrow E \setminus \{h_j\}$
  $\mathbf{L}_i \leftarrow \{L(E \cup h|\mathcal{X}_V)\}_{h \in H}$
  $f(\gamma|E) \leftarrow \mathrm{BO}(G, \mathbf{L}_i)$ // Fit model
  $\gamma_i \leftarrow \arg\max_{\gamma \in \Gamma} a(\gamma|f(\gamma|E))$ // Next hypers
  $h_i \leftarrow \mathrm{A}(\mathcal{X}_T, \gamma_i)$ // Train model
  $G \leftarrow G \cup \{\gamma_i\}$
  $H \leftarrow H \cup \{h_i\}$
  $h_j \leftarrow \arg\min_{h \in H} L(E \cup \{h\})$ // New model at j
  $E \leftarrow E \cup \{h_j\}$ // Update ensemble
end for

classifiers in a database (or store their predictions on the validation and testing splits) to permit ensemble construction and evaluation in the subsequent iterations.

3.2 ENSEMBLE UPDATE

The problem defined above is straightforward as long as the ensemble is given beforehand. In this section we will tackle the problem of building and updating the ensemble as the optimization progresses. To make things simpler, an ensemble size m will be fixed beforehand – this number can be fine-tuned at the end of the optimization. Each iteration of the optimization procedure will contain two steps: first the evaluation as described in Section 3, maintaining a fixed ensemble, and then an ensemble update step. Since members of the ensemble should be changed as the optimization moves forward and better models are found, a round-robin strategy will be used for the ensemble construction. The ensemble E will in fact consist of m fixed positions, and at every iteration i, the classifier at position $j = (i \mod m)$ will be removed from the ensemble before finding hyperparameters which minimize Equation 5 – effectively optimizing the classifier at this position for the given iteration. At the end of an iteration the ensemble is updated again greedily, selecting the new best classifier (it could be the same classifier or a better one). The whole procedure is described in Algorithm 1 and in Figure 2.

In addition, it is expected that some classifiers will specialize given the fixed state of a large part of the ensemble for each iteration. For instance, when replacing an individually strong classifier, another strong classifier will most likely be required. Figure 3 shows an example of optimization on a one-dimensional hyperparameter space run for 50 iterations, where an ensemble of five classifiers was optimized. The ensemble is represented by the five diamonds and its generalization error is shown by the dotted and dashed line at the bottom of the figure. Then, each of the five members

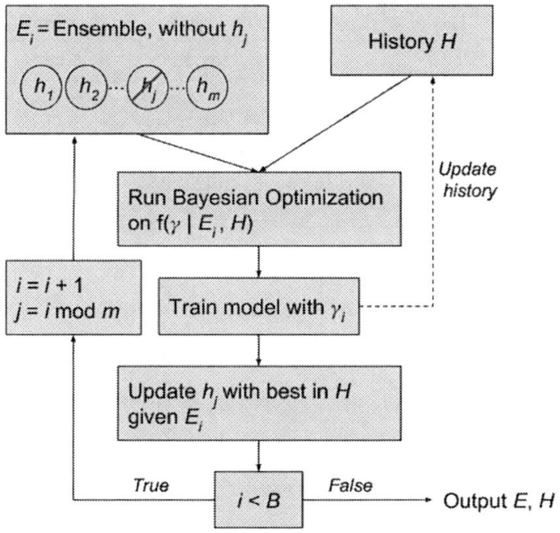

Figure 2: Schema of the Ensemble Optimization procedure.

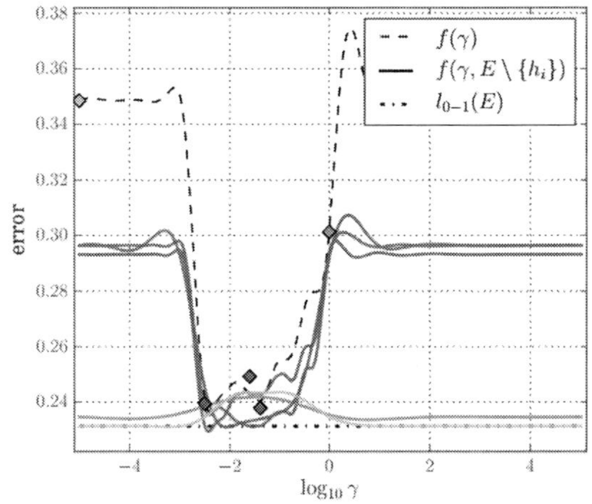

Figure 3: Example of objective function $f(\gamma | E \setminus \{h_i\})$ given a pool of 50 trained classifiers on a 1-D hyperparameter optimization problem. Each color represents the performance of an ensemble when removing its member h_i represented by a diamond of the same color in the plot.

i is independently removed and a Gaussian Process model is fit on the performance of an ensemble given the remaining models in the pool – this corresponds to the five colored lines of Figure 3. We can see from this figure that the hyperparameters which minimize the ensemble error are different for each *slot* in the ensemble, illustrating our concept.

3.3 COMPUTATIONAL COMPLEXITY

The *computational overhead* of the proposed method comes mainly from the evaluation of the empirical error of ensembles. It is very small with regards to the cost of running most learning algorithms (which is usually quadratic or worse in the number of samples), and also with the cost of conditioning the probabilistic model on the observations (which is cubic in the number of iterations). The computation of the empirical error of ensembles takes place in step 5 in Algorithm 1. Given an ensemble of size m, a validation dataset of size n, and a history of trained classifiers of size t, the complexity of this step is $O(t(mn + n)) = O(tmn)$ since it requires one pass over all models in the history, and for each of those the combination of the classifiers through majority voting (mn) and the computation of the empirical error n.

3.4 LOSS FUNCTION

The objective function defined in Equation 5 contains a loss function, which up until now referred to the empirical loss of the ensemble, or the zero-one loss. However, the zero-one loss contains a strong discontinuity and can result in optimization procedures failing due to the majority voting combination. For instance, if all classifiers of the ensemble are wrong on some instances, replacing one of those poor classifiers with a better one will not make the ensemble correctly classify those instances, resulting in the same performance with regards to the objective function, even though this classifier would be a good choice for the ensemble.

The performance of ensembles will be considered with regards to their classification *margin*, which will let us derive a more suitable loss function (Schapire and Freund, 2012). Given an ensemble of classifiers E outputting label predictions on a binary problem $\mathcal{Y} \in \{-1, 1\}$, the *normalized* margin for a sample $\{x, y\}$ is defined as follows:

$$M(E, x, y) = \frac{1}{|E|} \sum_{h \in E} yh(x). \tag{6}$$

The normalized margin $M \in [-1, 1]$ takes the value 1 when all classifiers of the ensemble correctly classify the sample x, -1 when all the classifiers are wrong, and somewhere in between otherwise. In the case of multi-class problems, predictions of classifiers can be brought back to a binary domain by attributing 1 for a correct classification and -1 for a misclassification. The margin becomes:

$$M_{mc}(E, x, y) = \frac{1}{|E|} \sum_{h \in E} [1 - 2l_{0-1}(h(x), y)]. \tag{7}$$

We will now derive some loss functions from the margin. The margin itself could be the objective, since it is desirable that the margin of the ensemble be high. It must be rescaled to really become a loss function, giving a margin-based loss function:

$$l_M(E, x, y) = \frac{1 - M(E, x, y)}{2}. \tag{8}$$

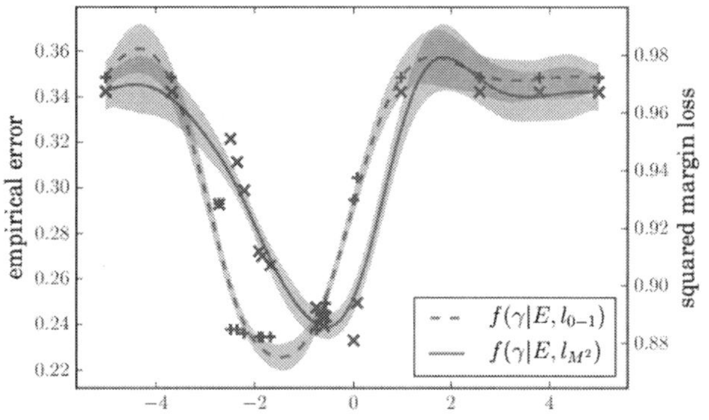

Figure 4: Examples of ensemble loss functions for a 1-D hyperparameter optimization. Blue curve legend is on the left, red curve legend is on the right.

This loss function should not be used to optimize an ensemble because it is directly maximized only by the accuracy of individual classifiers. In other words, given a validation dataset $\mathcal{X}_V$ and a set of classifiers H to evaluate, the classifier minimizing Equation 8 is always the classifier with the lowest empirical error on its own, without regards to the ensemble performance. Therefore, the loss function must not give the same weight to all classifiers without regards to ensemble performance, while also being smooth. A loss function which achieves this is the margin-based loss function taken to the power of two:

$$l_{M^2}(E, x, y) = \frac{(1 - M(E, x, y))^2}{4}. \tag{9}$$

This places a higher emphasis on samples misclassified by the ensemble, and decreases the importance of samples as the margin grows closer to 1. Since it meets the required properties, the squared margin loss function will be used as the ensemble loss function in this work.

Figure 4 shows an example of the two loss functions discussed in this section, the zero-one loss and the squared margin loss, applied on the same ensemble. Both losses have different scales, with the empirical error scale on the left and the squared margin scale on the right of the figure. We can see that these two loss functions lead to different optimal hyperparameters given the same ensemble. In other words, the hyperparameters minimizing the objective function according to the models of $f(\gamma|E)$ are different with the two loss functions.

Considering that a loss function other than the empirical error will be used during the optimization, it will probably be beneficial to rebuild an ensemble from scratch using the final pool of classifiers trained once the optimization is over. Hence, a post-hoc ensemble generation will be performed after the hyperparameter optimization.

Table 1: Benchmarking datasets and abbreviations

Dataset	Instances	Features	Classes
Adult (adlt)	48,842	14	2
Bank (bnk)	4,521	16	2
Car (car)	1,728	6	4
Chess-krvk (ches)	28,506	6	18
Letter (ltr)	20,000	16	26
Magic (mgic)	19,020	10	2
Musk-2 (msk)	6,598	166	2
Page-blocks (p-blk)	5,473	10	5
Pima (pim)	768	8	2
Semeion (sem)	1,593	256	10
Spambase (spam)	4,601	57	2
Stat-german-credit (s-gc)	1,000	24	2
Stat-image (s-im)	2,310	18	7
Stat-shuttle (s-sh)	58,000	9	7
Steel-plates (s-pl)	1,941	27	7
Titanic (tita)	2,201	3	2
Thyroid (thy)	7,200	21	6
Wine-quality-red (wine)	1,599	11	6

4 EXPERIMENTS

We showcase the performance of our ensemble optimization approach on three different problems. The first two problems consist of different algorithms and hyperparameter spaces evaluated on the same benchmark of medium datasets available from the UCI repository, presented in Table 1. For every repetition, a different hold-out testing partition was sampled with 33% of the total dataset size (unless the dataset had a pre-specified testing split, in which case it was used for all repetitions). The remaining instances of the dataset were used to complete a 5-fold cross-validation procedure. Final models are retrained on all the data available for training and validation.

In every case, the prior on the objective function is a Gaussian Process (GP) with Matérn-52 kernel using automatic relevance determination[1]. The noise, amplitude, and length-scale parameters are obtained through slice sampling (Snoek et al., 2012). The slice sampling of GP hyperparameters for ensemble optimization must be reinitialized at every iteration given that different ensembles E can change the properties of the optimized function drastically. The acquisition function is the Expected Improvement over the best solution found so far. The compared methods and their abbreviated names are the following:

- Classical Bayesian optimization (BO-best). It returns a single model selected with argmin on validation performance (Snoek et al., 2012).
- Post-hoc ensemble constructed from the pool of classifiers with Bayesian optimization (BO-post). The post-hoc ensemble is initiated by picking the three best classifiers from the pool before proceeding with forward

[1] Code from http://github.com/JasperSnoek/spearmint.

greedy selection – this form of warm starting is recommended in (Caruana et al., 2004) to reduce overfitting.
- The proposed ensemble optimization method using the squared margin loss function (EO).
- Post-hoc ensemble constructed from the pool of classifiers generated by ensemble optimization (EO-post). The same post-hoc procedure as with BO-post is executed.

The hyperparameter spaces can contain continuous, discrete, and categorical parameters (e.g., base classifier or kernel choice). In the case of categorical and discrete parameters, they are represented using a continuous parameter which is later discretized. This does not deal with the fact that hyperparameter spaces of different classifiers are disjoint and should not be modeled jointly, but since all the compared methods are using this same technique, the comparison is fair.

4.1 SVM SEARCH SPACE

The models used in this benchmark are SVM models, and the parameterization includes the choice of the kernel along with the various hyperparameters needed per kernel. The hyperparameter space Γ optimized can be described as follows:

- One hyperparameter for the kernel choice: linear, RBF, polynomial, or sigmoid;
- Configurable error cost $C \in [10^{-5}, 10^{5}]$ (for all kernels);
- RBF and sigmoid kernels both have a kernel width parameter $\gamma_{RBF} \in [10^{-5}, 10^{5}]$;
- Polynomial kernel has a degree parameter $d \in [1, 10]$;
- Sigmoid and polynomial kernels both have an intercept parameter, $c \in [10^{-2}, 10^{2}]$.

All compared approaches optimized the same search space. Each method is given a budget of $B = 200$ iterations, or 200 hyperparameter tuples tested, to optimize hyperparameters with a 5-fold cross-validation procedure. The ensemble selection stage exploits this cross-validation procedure, considering the next classifier which reduces the most the generalization error over all the cross-validation folds. Selected hyperparameters are retrained on the whole training and validation data, and combined directly on the testing split to generate the generalization error values presented in this section. The ensemble optimization method is run with an ensemble size $m = 12$. This ensemble size was selected empirically and may not be optimal. Future work could investigate strategies to dynamically size the ensemble as the optimization progresses, with no fixed limit.

The generalization error on the test split for the selected methods is presented in Table 2, averaged over 10 repetitions. The last column shows the ranks of each method averaged over all datasets, where the best rank is 1 and the worst rank is 4.

Table 3: Wilcoxon pairwise test p-values for the SVM hyperparameter space. Bold entries highlight significant differences ($p \leq 0.05$) and parentheses are added when method at row i is worse than the method at column j according to ranks.

	1	2	3	4
1 - BO-best	–	(0.33)	**(0.00)**	**(0.00)**
2 - BO-post	0.33	–	**(0.01)**	**(0.00)**
3 - EO	**0.00**	**0.01**	–	0.21
4 - EO-post	**0.00**	**0.00**	(0.21)	–

A Wilcoxon signed-rank test is used to measure the statistical significance of the results. The Wilcoxon signed-rank test is a strong statistical test for comparing methods across multiple datasets, which is an nonparametric version of the Student's t-test that does not assume normal distributions and is less sensitive to outliers (Demšar, 2006). The input for the Wilcoxon test is the generalization error of a method i on each dataset d, averaged across the R repetitions:

$$\mathbf{e}_i = \{\frac{1}{R}\sum_{r=1}^{R} e_{i,d,r}\}_d, \tag{10}$$

where $e_{i,d,r}$ is the generalization error produced by method i on dataset d at repetition r. The Wilcoxon test is then computed for all pairs of methods $(\mathbf{e}_i, \mathbf{e}_j)$. The results of this procedure are shown in Table 3.

From Table 2 we can see that it is beneficial to build an ensemble from the output of a classical hyperparameter optimization, as seen by the lower rank of BO-post with regards to BO-best. However, the performance improvement is not shown to be significant according to the Wilcoxon test. Both the ensemble optimization methods seem to outperform classical Bayesian optimization strategies in terms of rankings. The Wilcoxon test shows that EO and EO-post both performed significantly better than BO-best and BO-post. It should be noted that there is no significant difference between EO and EO-post, highlighting that there was not a significant gain from the post-hoc ensemble construction. Caruana et al., 2004 presented some strategies to reduce overfitting in the forward greedy procedure – such as bagging from the pool of models – which could be considered in order to achieve more with the same pool, although this is left for future work.

Another test which can be used to assess the performance of the evaluated methods is the Friedman test with post-hoc tests on classifier ranks averaged across datasets. A Friedman test with the four methods presented in this section finds a significant difference between them with a p-value of 5.5×10^{-4}. The Friedman test is then usually followed by a post-hoc test to measure whether the difference in ranks is above a critical difference level, such as the Nemenyi test (Demšar, 2006). Figure 5 shows the results of

Table 2: Generalization error on SVM hyperparameter space, averaged over 10 repetitions, 5-fold cross-validation. Last column shows the rank of methods averaged over all datasets.

	adlt	bnk	car	ches	ltr	mgic	msk	p-blk	pim	sem	spam	s-gc	s-im	s-sh	s-pl	thy	tita	wine	Ranks
BO-best	15.52	10.67	1.27	16.86	2.45	12.49	0.29	3.06	25.52	4.43	6.47	23.20	3.57	0.10	23.91	3.09	20.59	35.28	3.39
BO-post	15.38	10.71	1.56	16.72	2.50	12.21	0.28	3.01	25.65	4.37	6.47	23.45	2.94	0.08	22.58	3.17	20.59	35.09	2.81
EO	15.39	10.44	0.81	15.06	2.34	12.18	0.30	3.14	23.70	4.58	6.45	23.05	2.73	0.09	22.61	2.51	20.27	33.29	1.89
EO-post	15.27	10.60	0.95	15.08	2.36	12.21	0.28	2.97	24.03	4.40	6.36	23.40	2.55	0.09	22.63	2.69	20.57	33.70	1.92

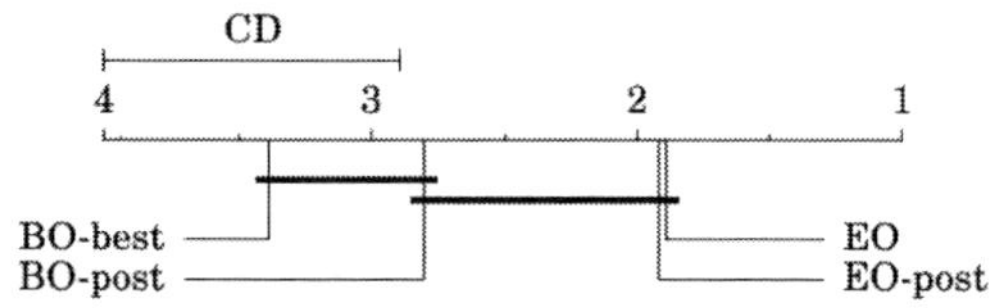

Figure 5: Methods by rank and significant differences according to a post-hoc Nemenyi test with significance level at $p = 0.05$ for the SVM hyperparameter space.

such a test, with methods linked by bold lines being found not significantly different by the test for a significance level of $p = 0.05$. The Nemenyi post-hoc test gives a more visual insight as to what is going on, but it is more sensitive to the pool of tested methods – the outcome of the test can change if new methods are inserted in the experiments. According to this test, EO and EO-post are both significantly different from BO-best, meaning that ensemble optimization is significantly better than the single best classifier returned by Bayesian optimization.

4.2 SCIKIT-LEARN MODELS SEARCH SPACE

The same methods as in the previous section were repeated for a different search space consisting of multiple base algorithms, all available from `scikit-learn`[2]. The models and their hyperparameters are *K nearest neighbors* with the number of neighbors `n_neighbors` in $[1, 30]$; *RBF SVM* with the penalty `C` logarithmically in $[10^{-5}, 10^5]$ and the width of the RBF kernel γ_{RBF} logarithmically in $[10^{-5}, 10^5]$; *linear SVM* with the penalty `C` logarithmically scaled in $[10^{-5}, 10^5]$; *decision tree* with the maximal depth `max_depth` in $[1, 10]$, the minimum number of examples in a node to split `min_samples_split` in $[2, 100]$, and the minimum number of training examples in a leaf `min_samples_leaf` in $[2, 100]$; *random forest* with the number of trees `n_estimators` in $[1, 30]$, the maximal depth `max_depth` in $[1, 10]$, the minimum number of examples in a node to split `min_samples_split` in $[2, 100]$, and the minimum number of training examples in a leaf `min_samples_leaf` in $[2, 100]$; *AdaBoost* with the number of weak learners `n_estimators` in $[1, 30]$; *Gaussian Naive Bayes (GNB)* and *Linear Discriminant Analysis (LDA)* both without any hyperparameters; and

[2]Available at `http://scikit-learn.org/`.

Table 5: Wilcoxon pairwise tests p-values for the scikit-learn hyperparameter space. Bold entries highlight significant differences ($p \leq 0.05$) and parentheses are added when method at row i is worse than the method at column j according to ranks.

	1	2	3	4
1 - BO-best	–	**(0.05)**	**(0.00)**	**(0.00)**
2 - BO-post	**0.05**	–	**(0.00)**	**(0.00)**
3 - EO	**0.00**	**0.00**	–	**0.03**
4 - EO-post	**0.00**	**0.00**	(0.03)	–

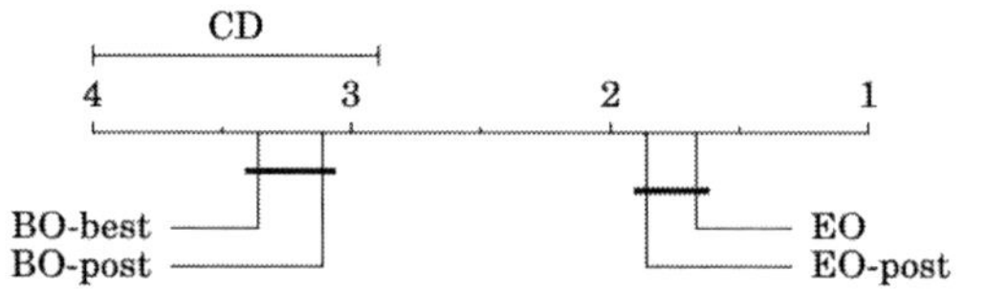

Figure 6: Methods by rank and significant differences according to a post-hoc Nemenyi test with significance level at $p = 0.05$ for the scikit-learn hyperparameter space.

Quadratic Discriminant Analysis (QDA) with the regularization `reg_param` logarithmically in $[10^{-3}, 10^3]$.

The set of hyperparameter optimization strategies is the same as in the previous section, and the maximum number of iterations B is set to 100. Tables 4 and 5 show the same metrics and Wilcoxon pairwise tests as introduced in Section 4.1.

Conclusions are similar for this hyperparameter space, whereas the generation of a post-hoc ensemble is again shown to be beneficial to the generalization accuracy for both BO and EO. In this case the post-hoc ensemble for BO is found significantly better than the single best classifier according to the Wilcoxon test. The overall best method is EO, which significantly outperforms all other methods, including EO-post, as seen in Table 5. For some datasets, the ensemble optimization procedure achieves a large drop in the generalization error, see for example datasets letter (ltr), musk-2 (msk) and semeion (sem) in Table 4.

A Friedman test on this suite of experiments is again run and found significant with a p-value of 1.5×10^{-5}. Figure 6 shows the results of the Nemenyi post-hoc test, with

Table 4: Generalization error on the scikit-learn hyperparameter space, averaged over 10 repetitions, 5-fold cross-validation. Last column shows the rank of methods averaged over all datasets.

	adlt	bnk	car	ches	ltr	mgic	msk	p-blk	pim	sem	spam	s-gc	s-im	s-sh	s-pl	thy	tita	wine	Ranks
BO-best	14.70	11.04	4.77	25.73	4.72	12.06	2.13	3.41	23.25	8.82	5.80	23.15	3.72	0.12	26.91	1.19	22.74	35.96	3.36
BO-post	14.62	10.53	4.80	25.73	4.72	11.99	2.18	3.26	23.38	8.82	5.53	23.15	3.64	0.11	26.16	1.20	22.74	35.71	3.11
EO	14.35	10.30	0.81	19.39	2.81	12.38	0.28	2.80	24.09	4.37	5.02	22.75	2.84	0.08	22.69	1.21	20.66	35.19	1.67
EO-post	14.32	10.39	1.01	20.47	2.76	12.48	0.28	2.94	23.38	4.37	5.24	22.90	2.99	0.07	23.50	1.10	21.20	35.47	1.86

methods linked by bold lines being found not significantly different by the test for a significance level of $p = 0.05$. According to this test, EO-post and EO are significantly different from both BO and BO-best, meaning that ensemble optimization approaches significantly outperform both Bayesian optimization baselines.

4.3 CONVOLUTIONAL NEURAL NETWORKS

Lastly, we evaluated the performance of our approach when fine-tuning the parameters of a convolutional neural network for the CIFAR-10 dataset. In order to have a reproducible baseline, the `cuda-convet` implementation was used with the reference model files given which achieves 18% generalization error on the testing dataset[3]. One batch of the training data was set aside for validation (batches 1-4 used for training, 5 for validation, and 6 for testing). Performance of the baseline configuration on the given training batches was around $22.4\% \pm 0.9$ for 250 epochs of training. The parameters optimized were the same as in (Snoek et al., 2012), namely the learning rates and weight decays for the convolution and softmax layers, and the parameters of the local response normalization layer (size, power and scale). The number of training epochs was kept fixed at 250.

We computed 10 repetitions of a standard Bayesian optimization and our proposed ensemble optimization with ensemble size $m = 7$, both with a budget of $B = 100$ hyperparameter tuples to evaluate. Figure 7 shows the performance of ensembles generated from both pools of classifiers with a post-hoc ensemble generation. In order to limit overfitting, the first three models of each ensemble were selected directly based on accuracy, as suggested in (Caruana et al., 2004). In both cases, the ensemble size benefits the generalization accuracy, although the classifiers generated by the ensemble optimization procedure do perform slightly better. The difference in generalization error between BO-post and EO-post at the last iteration is found significant by a Wilcoxon test with a p-value of 0.005. Further work should investigate strategies to use the remaining validation data once the models are chosen, to further improve generalization accuracy.

[3]Code available at `https://code.google.com/archive/p/cuda-convnet/` and network configuration file used is `layers-18pct.cfg`.

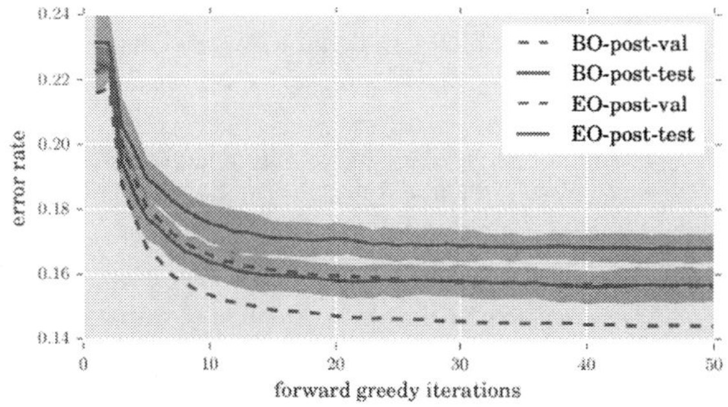

Figure 7: Generalization errors of a post-hoc ensemble with classical Bayesian optimization (BO-post) and a post-hoc ensemble generated from our ensemble optimization approach (EO-post) on the CIFAR-10 dataset with regards to the number of classifiers in the final ensemble. Results averaged over 10 repetitions.

5 CONCLUSION

In this work, we presented a methodology to achieve Bayesian optimization of ensembles through hyperparameter tuning. We tackle the various challenges posed by ensemble optimization in this context, and the result is an optimization strategy that is able to exploit trained models and generate better ensembles of classifiers at the computational cost of a regular hyperparameter optimization.

We showcase the performance of our approach on three different problem suites, and in all cases show a significant difference in generalization accuracy between our approach and post-hoc ensembles built on top of a classical hyperparameter optimization, according to Wilcoxon signed-rank tests. This is a strong validation of our method, especially considering that it involves little extra computation.

Acknowledgements

This research benefitted from the computing resources provided by Calcul Québec, Compute Canada and Nvidia. We would also like to thank Annette Schwerdtfeger for proofreading this paper.

References

Bell, Robert M. and Yehuda Koren (Dec. 2007). "Lessons from the Netflix prize challenge". In: *ACM SIGKDD Explorations Newsletter* 9.2, pp. 75–79.

Bergstra, James and Yoshua Bengio (2012). "Random Search for Hyper-Parameter Optimization". In: *Journal of Machine Learning Research* 13, pp. 281–305.

Bergstra, James and David D. Cox (2013). "Hyperparameter Optimization and Boosting for Classifying Facial Expressions: How good can a " Null " Model be?" In: *Proceedings of the ICML Workshop on Representation and Learning.*

Caruana, Rich, Alexandru Niculescu-Mizil, Geoff Crew, and Alex Ksikes (2004). "Ensemble Selection from Libraries of Models". In: *Proceedings of the 21st International Conference on Machine Learning*, p. 9.

Demšar, Janez (2006). "Statistical Comparisons of Classifiers over Multiple Data Sets". In: *The Journal of Machine Learning Research* 7, pp. 1–30.

Didaci, Luca, Giorgio Fumera, and Fabio Roli (2013). "Diversity in Classifier Ensembles : Fertile Concept or Dead End ?" In: *Multiple Classifier Systems*, pp. 37–48.

Feurer, Matthias, Aaron Klein, Katharina Eggensperger, Jost Tobias Springenberg, Manuel Blum, and Frank Hutter (2015a). "Efficient and Robust Automated Machine Learning". In: *Advances in Neural Information Processing Systems.*

Feurer, Matthias, Jost Tobias Springenberg, and Frank Hutter (2015b). "Initializing Bayesian Hyperparameter Optimization via Meta-Learning". In: *Proceedings of the Twenty-Ninth AAAI Conference on Artificial Intelligence.*

Frank, A. and A. Asuncion (2010). *UCI Machine Learning Repository*. URL: `https://archive.ics.uci.edu/ml/datasets.html`.

Guyon, Isabelle, Kristin Bennett, Gavin Cawley, Hugo Jair Escalante, Sergio Escalera, Tin Kam Ho, Núria Macià, Bisakha Ray, Mehreen Saeed, Alexander Statnikov, and Evelyne Viegas (2015). "Design of the 2015 ChaLearn AutoML Challenge". In: *2015 International Joint Conference on Neural Networks (IJCNN).* ChaLearn.

Hernández-Lobato, José Miguel, Matthew W. Hoffman, and Zoubin Ghahramani (2014). "Predictive Entropy Search for Efficient Global Optimization of Black-box Functions". In: *Advances in Neural Information Processing Systems.*

Hutter, Frank, Holger H. Hoos, and Kevin Leyton-Brown (2011). "Sequential Model-Based Optimization for General Algorithm Configuration". In: *Learning and Intelligent Optimization*, pp. 507–523.

Kuncheva, Ludmila I. (2003). "That Elusive Diversity in Classifier Ensembles". In: *Pattern Recognition and Image Analysis*, pp. 1126–1138.

Kuncheva, Ludmila I. (2004). *Combining Pattern Classifiers: Methods and Algorithms*. Wiler-Interscience.

Lacoste, Alexandre, Hugo Larochelle, Mario Marchand, and François Laviolette (2014a). "Agnostic Bayesian Learning of Ensembles". In: *Proceedings of the 31st International Conference on Machine Learning* 32.

Lacoste, Alexandre, Hugo Larochelle, Mario Marchand, and François Laviolette (2014b). "Sequential Model-Based Ensemble Optimization". In: *Uncertainty in Artificial Intelligence.*

Rasmussen, Carl Edward and Christopher K. I. Williams (2006). *Gaussian Processes for Machine Learning*. MIT Press.

Schapire, Robert E. and Yoav Freund (2012). *Boosting: Foundations and Algorithms*. MIT Press.

Snoek, Jasper, Hugo Larochelle, and Ryan P. Adams (2012). "Practical Bayesian Optimization of Machine Learning Algorithms". In: *Advances in Neural Information Processing Systems.*

Snoek, Jasper, Oren Rippel, Kevin Swersky, Ryan Kiros, Nadathur Satish, Narayanan Sundaram, Md. Mostofa Ali Patwary, Prabhat, and Ryan P. Adams (2015). "Scalable Bayesian Optimization Using Deep Neural Networks". In: *Proceedings of the 32nd International Conference on Machine Learning.*

Sun, Quan and Bernhard Pfahringer (2011). "Bagging Ensemble Selection". In: *AI 2011: Advances in Artificial Intelligence* 7106, pp. 251–260.

Swersky, Kevin, Jasper Snoek, and Ryan P. Adams (2014). "Freeze-Thaw Bayesian Optimization". In: *arXiv preprint*, pp. 1–12. arXiv: `arXiv:1406.3896v1`.

Tsymbal, Alexey, Mykola Pechenizkiy, and Pádraig Cunningham (2005). "Diversity in Search Strategies for Ensemble Feature Selection". In: *Information Fusion* 6.1, pp. 83–98.

Political Dimensionality Estimation Using a Probabilistic Graphical Model

Yoad Lewenberg
The Hebrew University
of Jerusalem, Israel
yoadlew@cs.huji.ac.il

Yoram Bachrach
Microsoft Research,
Cambridge, United Kingdom
yobach@microsoft.com

Lucas Bordeaux
Microsoft Research,
Cambridge, United Kingdom
lucasb@microsoft.com

Pushmeet Kohli
Microsoft Research,
Redmond, WA, USA
pkohli@microsoft.com

Abstract

This paper attempts to move beyond the left-right characterization of political ideologies. We propose a trait based probabilistic model for estimating the manifold of political opinion. We demonstrate the efficacy of our model on two novel and large scale datasets of public opinion. Our experiments show that although the political spectrum is richer than a simple left-right structure, peoples' opinions on seemingly unrelated political issues are very correlated, so fewer than 10 dimensions are enough to represent peoples' entire political opinion.

1 Introduction

The problem of best describing political variation has been a key issue in social sciences for over a century, and many models have been proposed over the years. The most prominent system for classifying political positions, ideologies and parties is the Left-Right classification. The notions of "Left" and "Right" in politics originate from the seating arrangements in the French legislative body during the French Revolution of 1789: the aristocracy sat on the right of the Speaker and the commoners sat on the left. The key ideological point of contention was the "old order", with the Right supporting aristocratic interests and the church, and with the Left supporting republicanism, secularism, and civil liberties.

However, is using the left-right terminology justified by *data* about political opinions? The terms left-wing and right-wing have evolved to capture a somewhat different meaning in modern day USA than their meaning in the years following the French Revolution. The left-wing generally refers to egalitarianism, social policies supporting the working class, and multiculturalism, typically including socialists and libertarians, identifying with the Democratic party; The right-wing refers to conservative Christian values, support for a free-market system, and traditional family values, and including conservatives and free-market supporters, identifying with the Republican party.

Opinions regarding a *single* issue can easily be expressed on a single axis. Parties or people can be placed on the axis depending on the degree of support to a stance relating to this issue; those whose strongly support a position can be placed on one side, followed by those with who slightly support it, and so on, ending with those strongly opposing the stance. For example, we can place parties who strongly support heavy regulation of businesses on the far left, those who want complete business freedom under any circumstances on the far right, and those who support light regulation of some businesses in the center.

However, most political parties take an ideological stand regarding *many* issues: immigration, free medical care, minimum wage, regulating banks, religious freedom, abortions, gay and lesbian rights, regulating drugs and alcohol, and many others. When the ideology of parties spans multiple issues, representing these ideologies requires a *political spectrum* — a system for classifying different political positions using *several* geometric axes, each representing an independent political dimension. For example, a spectrum with two axes may include one axis for sociocultural issues (relating for example to supporting or opposing a heavy investment in welfare) and one for economic issues (for example, supporting or opposing de-regulation of business).

One way to define a political spectrum is by using a dimension for each of the important issues the people and parties care about. Given a political spectrum of K dimensions we can express people's opinions and the political ideology of parties as K-dimensional vectors. However, a large dimensionality makes it cumbersome for people to explain their views, so clearly we would like to use the smallest possible dimensionality that can fully express the opinions of most people and parties. Political scientists have noted that the wide popularity of the left-right identification stems from the surprising fact that in many countries, it *is* possible to map parties into a single left-right axis [39, 17]. For example, Von Beyme [38] categorized European parties into nine "families" that described most parties, and was able to linearly order seven such families from left to right: communist, socialist, green, liberal, Christian democratic, conservative and right-wing extremist. Although a single left-right axis can describe many parties, in many countries parties may take any combination of several issues [24, 39]. Common examples are the issues of economic freedom (taxation, free trade, free enterprise) and personal freedom (drug legalization, abortion and conscription). Some populations require a large dimensionality to represent, as individuals or parties may take any combination of positions regarding many issues, whereas other populations can be represented using less dimensions, due to strong correlations between stances on many issues.

Currently, 98 out of the 100 members in the United States Senate are affiliated with either the Democratic party (left) or the Republican party (right). This low-dimensional political landscape contrasts to other countries. For instance, in the United Kingdom, the House of Commons is composed of 11 parties. This disparity in the number of parties suggests that the political spectrum in the USA has fewer dimensions than the political spectrum in the UK.

Political scientists have to infer the key dimensions in a political spectrum representation using *data mining* techniques. For example, Ferguson [10] has used a set of questions pertaining to many issues: birth control, capital punishment, censorship, communism, evolution, law, patriotism, theism, treatment of criminals, and war. He used People's responses to questions pertaining to these issues as the input to a *factor analysis process*, trying to describe the variability between the correlated responses on different issues, using a low number of latent factors. His analysis showed that three dimensions, which he called Religionism, Humanitarianism, and Nationalism, were sufficient to capture much of the variability in the data. In other words, most people in the dataset could be described using three numbers, so that their position regarding *all* issues could be predicted given these numbers with high accuracy.

Such factor analysis based techniques for building a political spectrum can be thought of in terms of *dimensionality reduction*. This process transforms the data in the high-dimensional space into a representation in a space of fewer dimensions. Many such techniques are based on algebraic methods, such as SVD (singular value decomposition) or PCA (principal component analysis). Given the data and a target number K of dimensions, they find a good representation of the original data in a Kdimensional space. In this sense, these techniques can be thought of as a lossy compression technique. They receive peoples' opinions on many questions, and attempt to characterize both people and questions using very concise descriptions (vectors in a low dimension space). The original responses of the people regarding the political stances can then be reconstructed approximately. However, the approximation quality depends on the compression ratio: with a high dimensionality it is possible to represent people on the spectrum so that the full opinion regarding any issue can be determined accurately, and with a low dimensionality individuals may be represented very concisely, but with a higher error.

Although factor analysis can be a useful tool in inferring possible dimensions on the political spectrum, it is still unclear what the dimensionality of the political spectrum should be. How can we use data mining and machine learning tools in order to determine the true dimensionality of the data? How accurately can we infer peoples' political opinions using their location in this political spectrum?

1.1 Our Contribution:

We analyze the optimal number of political dimensions to use. In contrast to earlier data driven approaches for analyzing data so as to construct a political spectrum, we do not use an algebraic dimensionality reduction technique. Rather, we use a *Bayesian* model selection approach.

We use a *probabilistic graphical model* for dimensionality reduction, representing both users and questions regarding political stances as feature vectors in a low dimensional space, where similarity is measured by the inner product. Thus, each coordinate in the low dimensional space relates to one political dimension. Any choice of the number of dimensions in the low dimensional space results in a slightly different model. We choose the most plausible number of dimensions given the data, by taking the model with the *maximal evidence*.

We apply the technique on two datasets, each containing People's responses regarding various questions about their political stances. The first dataset consists of the responses of 38,000 UK users who ranked political issues by their importance. The second dataset consists of the responses of 1,500 users from the USA, sourced from Amazon's Mechanical Turk, who rated the degree to which they agree to 56 sentences representing a political stance. In each of these we use our approach to determine the optimal dimensionality of the political spectrum.

On the one hand, our results indicate the political spectrum is richer than simple "left-right" structure represented using a single dimension. On the other hand, they indicate that peoples' opinions on seemingly unrelated political issues are very correlated, so fewer than 10 dimensions are enough to represent peoples' entire political opinion.

2 Methodology

The key issue we focus on is determining how many dimensions underly the political positions of people with respect to a broad range of questions. We use statistical tools akin to factor analysis. Factor analysis methods attempt to represent a set of observed correlated variables in terms of several 'common' factors. The common factors are not directly observed in the data and thus are sometime called latent variables. Existing approaches use factor analysis to identify the main factors in political values, but use an algebraic factor analysis, where the number of political dimensions is an *input* of the factor analysis algorithm [10, 9]. In contrast, we use a Bayesian approach, which chooses the optimal dimensionality to use.

We first describe our high level methodology. Our technique receives an input dataset which contains the responses of many participants, P, regarding a set of political questions, Q. Each such question represents a political stand, and the participant is asked to express the degree to which they agree or disagree with the stand, on a numerical scale. For example, such an item may be "Alcohol and cigarettes should be heavily taxed.", and a participant must rate the item on a seven-point scale between strongly disagreeing (1) and strongly agreeing (7) with the statement.[1] When the dataset relates to $|P|$ participants responding to $|Q|$ questions, the dataset is thus a matrix of $|P| \cdot |Q|$ numbers.

Given the dataset, we apply a dimensionality reduction procedure that models both participants and questions as low dimensional vectors. If the dimensionality used in our procedure is chosen to be K, each participant and question are represented by vectors in $\mathbb{R}^K$. Let $p' \in \mathbb{R}^K$ be the representation chosen for the participant, and let $q' \in \mathbb{R}^K$ be the representation chosen for the question. The procedure is devised so that the *predicted* rating the participant $p \in P$ would give to a question $q \in Q$ is the inner product of these two vectors $\langle p', q' \rangle$. The dimensionality reduction is based on a probabilistic graphical model. Any choice of a dimensionality K for the political spectrum results in a slightly different such model $\mathcal{H}_K$. We use the dimensionality for which the evidence under the model is maximized.

3 PMPS Model

The dimensionality reduction model we use is a Probabilistic Model for expressing the Political Spectrum, or PMPS for short. PMPS is a probabilistic graphical model which resembles other Bayesian models for matrix factorization [2, 28, 33, 6].

Graphical models were first introduced by Pearl [27]. We use the more general framework of factor graphs (see e.g., [19]) in order to describe the factored structure of the assumed joint probability distribution among the variables. Once the graphical model is defined and the values of the observed variables are set, inference algorithms (such as approximate message-passing methods) can be used in order to infer the marginal probability distribution of the unknown variables [19].

[1]For a ranking of political issues, we assign integer scores for these topics in consecutive order.

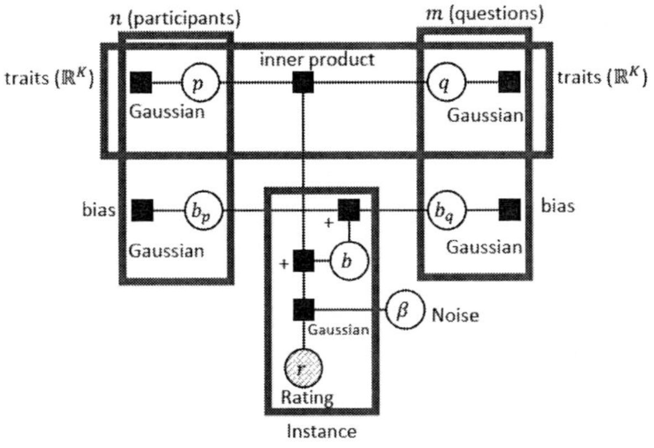

Figure 1: **Factor graph for the PMPS model.** The large plates indicate parts of the graph which are repeated with repetition indexed by the participant, question or trait.

The data fed to the model is a set of observations of the form (p, q, r) where $p \in P$ is the participant, $q \in Q$ is the political stance question, and $r \in \mathbb{N}$ is the rating given by the participant, expressing the degree to which they agree to the stance presented in the question.

The model assumes that the participants and questions can be characterized by K underlying "traits". These traits might be, for instance, the user's opinion on economy related issues. Note that the number of dimensions K of the model, i.e., the size of the participant and question vector has to be determined before the construction of the model. We model the process by which a participant $p \in P$ produces an answer r to a question $q \in Q$ as inner product between two K dimensional vectors of unobserved (latent) variables, one for the participant and one for the question. Thus we assume that: every participant has a latent trait vector and a latent bias; and Each question has a latent trait vector and a latent bias. The bias captures the fact that some participants give higher ratings than others, and that some questions receive higher ratings than others on average. Information such as the latent vector and bias of the participants and questions are modeled as unobserved variables, whereas the given response to a question by a user is modeled as an observed variable.

PMPS is a joint probabilistic model whose factor graph is given in Figure 1. Namely, the rating r that a participant with a latent vector $p \in \mathbb{R}^K$ gives to a question with a latent vector $q \in \mathbb{R}^K$ is modeled as

$$\Pr(r|t, s, b) = \mathcal{N}\left(r|p^T q + b_p + b_q, \beta^2\right), \qquad (1)$$

where β is the standard deviation of the observation noise, and $b_p + b_q$ are the participant and question bias, respectively.

In order to do inference on the model, we must first define prior distributions for the variable of interest. We assume factorizing Gaussian priors for the participant vector traits $p_i \sim \mathcal{N}(\mu_p, \sigma_p^2)$ and bias $b_p \sim \mathcal{N}(\mu_p, \sigma_p^2)$, and question vector traits $q_i \sim \mathcal{N}(\mu_q, \sigma_q^2)$ and bias $b_q \sim \mathcal{N}(\mu_q, \sigma_q^2)$. The Gaussian prior was chosen as it allows us to specify a range of plausible values using two parameters, and to admit a relative simple approximation inference. Also, it characterizes the assumption that a priory we expect that extreme ratings would be uncommon. In this work we set $\mu_p = \mu_q = 0$ and $\sigma_p = \sigma_q = \beta = 1$.

Inference in this model is done using message passing algorithms. We implemented the model using the Infer.NET [25] framework for probabilistic graphical models. Inference was done approximately, using the Expectation Propagation (EP) algorithm [26]. EP calculates marginal distributions on a given factor graph by iteratively computing messages along edges that propagate information across the factor graph. EP runs iteratively until convergence, so its runtime is linear in the model's size, which in the case of PMPS is of size $O(|P| \cdot |Q|)$. We note that while in our dataset all observations were present (i.e. we had the rating of every participant to every question), PMPS can also handle a partial set of observations (i.e. the case where we cannot observe the response of some participants to some of the questions).

3.1 Model Selection

For a specific K the model $\mathcal{H}_K$ was built, however different K values produce different models. The task of selecting the most plausible statistical model from a set of candidates $\mathcal{H}_1, \ldots, \mathcal{H}_N$ given the data is called *model selection.*

An important aspect of model selection is that we should not compare models solely based on how well it fits the data, but also based on their simplicity.[2] In other words, a good model selection technique should be balanced, achieving a good trade-off between *goodness of fit* and *simplicity* [40]. A key advantage of a Bayesian approach is the existence of a well-accepted methodology for achieving such a trade-off.

The posterior probability, $\Pr(\mathcal{H}_K|D)$ of the model $\mathcal{H}_K$ given the data D, is given by Bayes's theorem:

$$\Pr(\mathcal{H}_K|D) = \frac{\Pr(D|\mathcal{H}_K)\Pr(\mathcal{H}_K)}{\Pr(D)}. \tag{2}$$

[2]As an example, consider a dataset with five points in 2D space. One model that has a perfect fit is to use a fourth-degree polynomial; however if we look at the points and find that they are approximately on a straight line, we will favour a much simpler linear model that simply assumes some amount of noise.

This gives the following probability ratio between model $\mathcal{H}_i$ and model $\mathcal{H}_j$ [23]:

$$\frac{\Pr(\mathcal{H}_i|D)}{\Pr(\mathcal{H}_j|D)} = \frac{\Pr(D|\mathcal{H}_i)}{\Pr(D|\mathcal{H}_j)}\frac{\Pr(\mathcal{H}_i)}{\Pr(\mathcal{H}_j)}. \tag{3}$$

If we have a uniform prior over models, i.e. no a priori belief that either $\mathcal{H}_i$ or $\mathcal{H}_j$ is more probable, Equation 3 simplifies to $\Pr(D|\mathcal{H}_i)/\Pr(D|\mathcal{H}_j)$, this ratio is known as the *Bayes factor* [18]. We thus wish to find the model that maximizes $\Pr(D|\mathcal{H}_K)$. The density $\Pr(D|\mathcal{H}_K)$ is obtained by integrating over the unknown parameters values in that model:

$$\Pr(D|\mathcal{H}_K) = \int_{\theta_K} \Pr(D|\mathcal{H}_K, \theta_K)\Pr(\theta_K|\mathcal{H}_K)\,\mathrm{d}\theta_K, \tag{4}$$

where θ_K are the parameters under $\mathcal{H}_K$, $\Pr(\theta_K|\mathcal{H}_K)$ is the prior density and $\Pr(D|\mathcal{H}_K, \theta_K)$ is the probability of the data given the model $\mathcal{H}_K$ with parameters θ_K. The quantity in Equation 4 is called the *evidence* for model $\mathcal{H}_K$.

Simple models tend to make precise predictions and complex models, by their nature, are capable of making a greater variety of predictions. Therefore, in the case where the data are compatible with both models, the simpler model will turn out as more probable. The dimension K that results in the highest model evidence, suggests that the latent dimension of the data is that K.

4 Results

We now present our results, produced by applying PMPS learning and alternative methods on the UK and US datasets. We first describe the datasets, then discuss the empirical evaluation and the results.

4.1 Datasets

In both UK and USA datasets, users were directly asked to give their opinion regards several issues.[3]

4.1.1 UK Dataset

The website 38DEGREES[4] [1] has conducted a poll in which users from across the UK were asked to rank 18 issues according to their priorities. The issues were: The

[3]Asking users directly for their political opinions is one route for obtaining data. An alternative is mining social network data to infer political opinions [37, 35]. These could then be correlated with other inferred user psycho-demographic traits [21, 20, 4, 36] or socio-economic perceptions [22, 29, 11] (similarly to our analysis here). We used a direct survey as it offers less noisy observations than inferred traits (and although this limited the amount of data we collected, we believe the size of our dataset is sufficient for our analysis).

[4]http://www.38degrees.org.uk/

- Having an abortion is the choice of the mother. No one else has the right to decide this for her.
- Life begins at conception. Babies are people and deserve to be protected from abortion by law.
- It is morally a role of the state to provide basic medical care for everyone.
- Immigrants help grow our economy.
- Access to guns should be severely controlled.
- Owning a gun should be a fundamental right.
- My country has the duty to bring democracy to the world.
- Alcohol and cigarettes should be heavily taxed to discourage their use.
- Education including higher education should be free to all.
- The government should extend paid maternity leave to 3 months for every working mother.

Figure 2: An example of a few questions from the questionnaire

	Immigration	Poverty	Environment	Cost of living	The EU
Climate change	-0.3535	0.01949	0.58	-0.3272	-0.2592
Immigration		-0.3583	-0.2245	0.0636	0.4757
Poverty			-0.0804	0.0669	-0.3491
Environment				-0.2956	-0.1842
Cost of living					-0.0628

Table 1: The correlation between the issues

NHS[5], Banking, Privacy, Tax dodging, The economy, Animal welfare, Climate change, Poverty, Human rights, Education, Transport, Energy, Immigration, Environment, The EU, Housing, Cost of living and Privatisation of public services.

The results of this poll were generously shared with us. The dataset consists of 38,000 records of users, where every user is identified with his/her postcode.

4.1.2 USA Dataset

Using Amazon Mechanical Turk [34], We asked 1,500 users from different states in the USA to fill a questionnaire with 56 statements. For each statement, each user was asked give his/hers opinion and select one option from the seven-point scale from disagree strongly to agree strongly.

The statement were about different topics such as: religious, abortion, gay and lesbian rights, public health care and immigration. An example of a few questions can be found in Figure 2, the complete questionnaire is available online.[6]

[5]NHS is the British National Health Service

[6]http://tinyurl.com/h7t339v

4.1.3 Correlations Between Responses to Different Questions

Unsurprisingly, when examining the issue ratings in the UK dataset we note that some issues' rankings are correlated. Table 1 shows the correlations between the ratings of various issues. For example, as can be seen in Table 1, a user that ranked *Environment* at a high place is likely to do the same for *Climate change*, and a user who ranked *Immigration* at a high place is likely to rank *Climate change* at a low place.

Similar correlations between the responses to different political stance questions also occur in the USA dataset, indicating that many political issues are inter-correlated.

4.2 Predictive Performance

The high correlation between various items indicates that it should be possible to predict the responses of a participant to some of the questions based on the way their responded to other questions. Given a specific single question $q \in Q$, we can train a linear regression model to predict how a person $p \in P$ would respond to that question given their responses to some other subset of questions $S \subset Q$. If we are interested in predicting the responses to *multiple* questions,

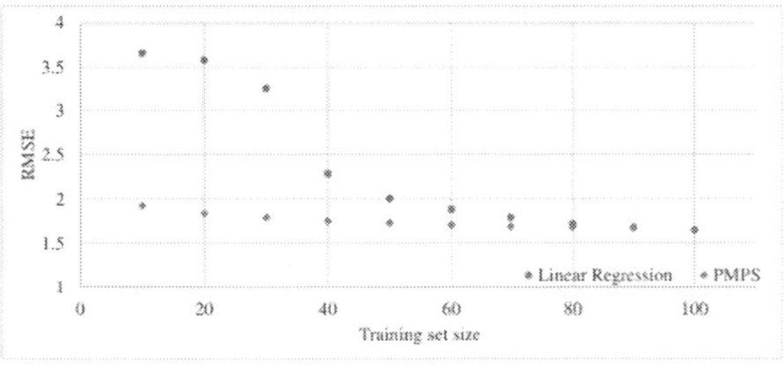

Figure 3: The prediction error (RMSE) of linear regression and PMPS.

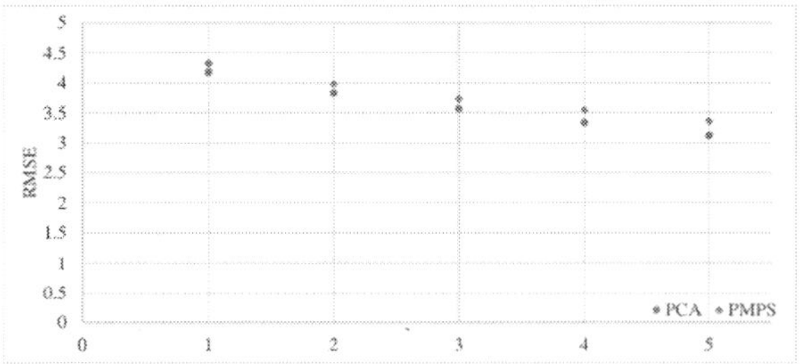

Figure 4: The error (RMSE) of PCA and PMPS against the number principal components on the UK data.

$T \subset Q$ based on the responses to some of the other questions, $S \subset Q$ (where $S \cap T = \emptyset$), we can train $|T|$ linear regression models, each taking as features the responses to the questions in S and predicting the responses to one of the questions $t_i \in T$.

An alternative approach is to use our PMPS model to generate the predictions. In this approach we learn to express questions as a posterior distribution over vectors in a low-dimensional space. Then, given a partial set of responses given by the person p to a subset S of the questions, we also obtain a representation of that person as a posterior distribution over vectors in the low dimensional space. Thus, PMPS would also produce a posterior distribution over the possible responses p would have to all the remaining questions, $Q \setminus S$ (including of course the questions in T). We can then take the mode of the posterior distribution over the responses to an unobserved question $t_i \in T$ and use them as a prediction for the response p would give to t_i.

We first designed an experiment to contrast the predictive performance of PMPS with that of linear regression models, using the USA dataset. The experiment goal was to predict the responses of users to questions in our USA dataset. In each trial we randomly select a subset $P^b \subset P$ of the participants to use for training. We let the model (either the linear regression model or PMPS) to observe the responses of these training participants to all the questions. We then select a subset of test participants $P^t \subset P$ (such that $P^b \cap P^t = \emptyset$). We also select a set $T \subset Q$ of target questions and a set of predictor questions $S \subset Q$ (where $S \cap T = \emptyset$). We first train the model using the training participants P^b, then let the model observe the responses of each test participants $p_j \in P^t$ to the target questions S (and *only* these questions). Next, we use the model to predict the responses of each test participant to each of the target questions, and examine the prediction error. In our experiments we used $|S| = 30$ predictor questions and $|T| = 26$ questions (so S and T form a partition of the question set). In our experiments we fixed $|P^t| = 20$ and we varied the number of training participants $|P^b|$ between 10 participants and 100 participants. We used 1,000 trials to measure the average prediction error of each model (linear regression or PMPS).

Our results regarding the predictive performance of PMPS and linear regression are given in Figure 3. The x-axis is the number of training participants, $|P^b|$, reflecting the amount of training data available to the model. The y-axis is the prediction root mean squared error (RMSE), averaged across the trials, with cross-validation. The figure shows that PMPS achieves a superior prediction quality over a linear regression method. The quality gap is especially big for treatments with less training data (fewer training participants). Figure 3 shows the results for PMPS model with $K = 6$, though other K values showed similar results and outperformed linear regression.

4.3 Latent Traits

The high correlation between the issues suggests that the response data can be compressed. For example, consider the UK dataset, where the full data for each user consists of an 18-dimensional vectors, representing that person's importance rating for each of the issues. Rather than representing the entries of the dataset as 18-dimensional vectors, with one number per issue / question, we can project them into a lower dimension using either PMPS or traditional linear techniques such as PCA. This results in "compressing" the opinions dataset, at the cost of introducing some noise to the the entries.

We note that as opposed to the predictive performance experiment in Section 4.2, the goal of using such a dimensionality reduction is a lossy compression of the data, rather then predicting some entries or responses of a user based on their responses to other questions. In particular, in order to find a person's representation as a low dimensional vector, we process *all* of their responses.

For both PMPS and PCA the projection into a low dimensional vector is revertible, i.e. we can easily interpret the low-dimensional representation back into the 18-dimensional space. For PMPS this is done by plugging the learned weights and low-dimensional vectors in the model

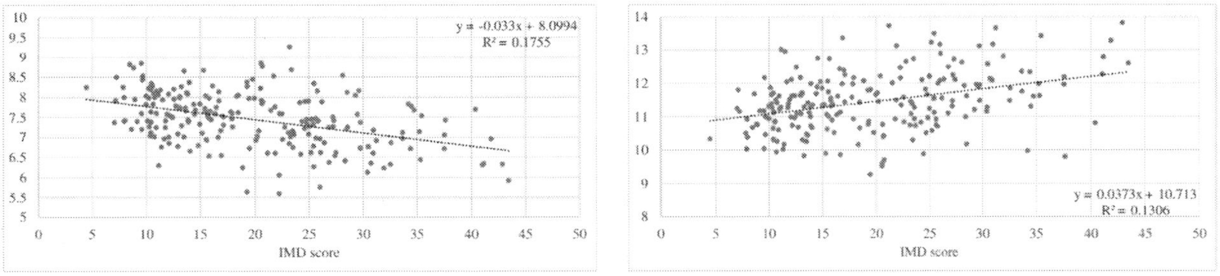

(a) The average rank of "Poverty" as a function of the IMD score. (b) The average rank of "The EU" as a function of the IMD score.

Figure 5: Correlation between the IMD score of LA and the average rank the issues in the LAs.

and inferring, rather than observing, the rating r of each question—this key operation is the inner product.

As the data is not perfectly reconstructed from this compression, a good measure of the noise resulting from the compression is the RMSE of the reconstructed 18-dimensional point compared to the original.

Figure 4 reports the compression RMSEs for both PCA and PMPS. Two conclusions can be drawn from the figure:

- Both PCA and PMPS can be used to characterize a *political spectrum*, which allows a tradeoff between the conciseness of peoples' description and the error in predicting their responses using this compressed description. The tradeoff between the compression and the error is very similar for these methods.
- Applying PCA on the data does not give a clear indication on the *true dimensionality* of the data: even for relatively high dimensions, the RMSE is not negligible.

As we discussed in section 3.1, one significant advantage of a Bayesian method such as PMPS over non-Bayesian methods is that they can trade-off some of the accuracy of compression for a greater simplicity of the representation, and that they allow for a rigorous method for choosing the "correct" dimensionality of the spectrum used.

4.3.1 Socio-Demographic Factors

The latent traits of a user, captured by their representation in the low dimensional space, may not correspond to an objective and observable measure of that individual. However, in the case of our political data, some correlations between ratings of different items can be explained as a result of socio-demographic influence.

Consider, for example, the participants in the UK dataset. It stands to reason that poor areas would be more concerned about issues such as poverty. To examine the correlations between rating and socio-demographic influence in the UK, we use the English Index of Multiple Deprivation (IMD) [12]. The IMD is a score that is given to every local authority (LA) in the UK. This score is based on employment, income, extent and concentration of the local authority. It ranges between 0 and 50: the higher the score, the more deprived the local authority.

There is a high correlation between the average rank of an issue in a specific LA and the IMD score of the LA. As, for example, it is shown in Figure 5, the average rank of "Poverty" (5a) is generally lower (more important) in LA's with high IMD, than in LA's with low IMD; and the average rank of "The EU" (5b) is generally higher in LA's with low IMD than in LA's with high IMD. Thus, LA's that ranked "Poverty" in a relatively high location are likely to rank "The EU" in a relatively low location and vice versa. Therefore, observing the IMD score of the user's LA could give us information about the ranks of the issues.

This analysis illustrates that it may be possible to capture a lot of the variability in People's responses to political questions by considering some of their objective traits, such as poverty.

4.4 Model Dimensionality

Our main goal is determining the true dimensionality of the political spectrum required to accurately represent peoples' stances regarding a wide range of political issues. To this end, we applied PMPS learning to our UK dataset and USA dataset. In both cases we examined the model evidence of every dimension so as to reveal the dimensionality of the datasets.

4.4.1 Dimensionality in the UK Dataset

When analyzing the UK dataset, we applied the PMPS model to the *entire UK data*, as well as the data from *specific UK local authorities*. As there is a high correlation between the IMD score of LA and the average rank of an issue, one of the latent dimension, in the PMPS model might be related to the IMD score, and the dimension of the data

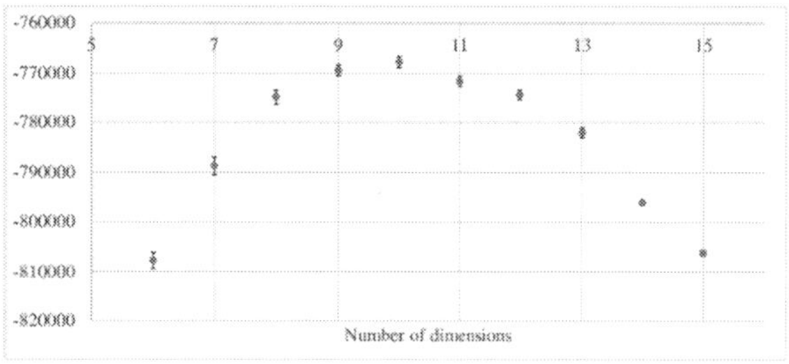

Figure 6: Log model evidence as a function of the dimension, on the data from UK.

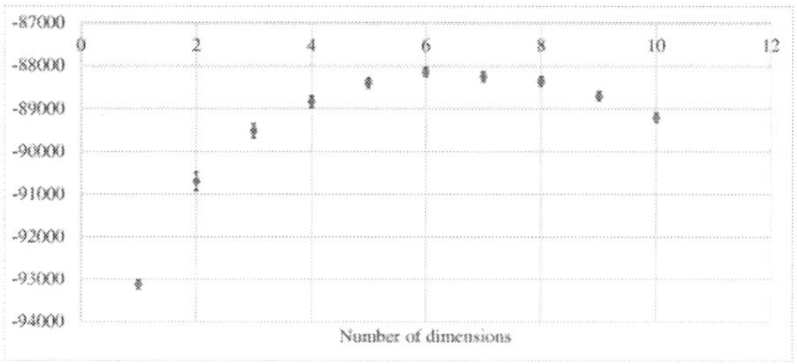

Figure 7: Log model evidence as a function of the dimension, on the data from USA.

is likely to be lower than 18.[7] The log of the model evidence as a function of the dimension can be found in Figure 6. The model in which the latent dimension was 10 resulted in the highest model evidence, and therefore the data suggests that the dimension is 10. We applied the same technique for every LA. In this experiment the dimension ranged from 7 (Metropolitan Borough of Wigan) to 11 (Rossendale District), with average of 9.717 and standard deviation of 0.678. Thus, the dimension of the data remains relatively homogeneous across local authorities.

4.4.2 Dimensionality in the USA Dataset

In the 114th United States Congress, out of 435 seats 431 are occupied by members of the Democrat and Republican parties. That is, the vast majority of the people in the US are represented by the two parties. For comparison, in the Parliament of the United Kingdom, there are 11 parties.

Historically, the Democratic party supports gun control laws, keeps elective abortions legal, and tends to favor equal rights for gay and lesbian couples. In contrast, the Republican Party opposes gun control laws, and the Republican party's agenda states that abortions should not be legal and marriage should be between a man and a woman. Hence, it appears that a single left-right axis could describe the two parties.

However, it is not clear why, for example, a person who supports abortion is likely to opposes state involvement with religious institutions. Therefore, we attempted to investigate whether the political dimension in the US is indeed lower than in the UK and, whether two parties can truly represent the American people. Alternatively, it could be the case that the election system in the USA results in a two party system, even though more parties are actually needed to truly represent the electors.

[7] Obviously, one needs to know the ranks of 17 issues in order to give an accurate prediction on the rank of the remaining issues. However, the PMPS model is not aware to the fact that for every user every rank appears only once.

In order to find the dimensionality of the data, we applied PMPS learning. The log of the model evidence as a function of the dimension can be found in Figure 7. The model in which the latent dimension was 6 resulted in the highest model evidence, and therefore data suggested that the dimension is 6, while the same technique suggested that the dimension within UK is 10. In addition, we applying PMPS learning on the data from different states. Unlike the data from UK, the results were less homogeneous across states, and range from 4 in Texas and California, to 6 in Michigan, New York and Florida.

5 Related Work

While the traditional political spectrum is a simple left-right axis, it has been doubted whether ordinary citizens actually use the specific ideology associated with this representation (see, e.g., [8]). Many Political scientists have suggested more complex, multidimensional representations of the political spectrum. One of the earliest work is by Ferguson [10], who suggested that peoples' positions with regard to 10 broad topics were influenced by 3 broad underlying dimensions: Religionism (with issues such as evolution, birth control and God), Humanitarianism (with issues such as war, capital punishment and treatment of criminals) and Nationalism (censorship, law patriotism and communisim).

Christie, and Meltzer [7] suggested a four dimensions diagram: fabianism to radicalism, fascism to anarchism, conservatism to social democracy and capitalist individualism to state communism. A similar research has been done by Eysenck [9] in the United Kingdom and in Germany. The research identified two independent principles: *Radicalism* (R) and *Tender-Mindedess* (T). In both countries, all but one attitude were found to have the same coordinates on the R-T Cartesian coordinate system. In Sweden, Husen showed a similar pattern [15].

Our method for determining the dimensionality of a political spectrum given a dataset is a Bayesian one, relying on a dimensionality reduction Probabilistic Graphical Model. Graphical models [27] have been widely studied in the context of AI. For example, Porteous et al. [28] use graphical model for Bayesian probabilistic matrix factorization. Schmidt et al. [30] dealt with learning the structure of undirected graphical using L1 regression. Bachrach et al. [5] presented a graphical model for inferring the correct answers, difficulty levels of questions and ability levels of participants in multiple problem domains. A line of work has considered Bayesian methods and matrix factorization techniques for collaborative filtering based recommender systems [14, 13, 16, 32], which also capture peoples' ratings of various items. Our model is similar to the Matchbox recommendation system [33], in which users and items are mapped into a low-dimensional 'trait space'.

We used a rigorous and theoretically justified method for dimensionality selection. Alternative model selection techniques such as AIC [3] and BIC [31] have been previously for other domains. These technique also trade-off bias and variance, using the likelihood function, number of parameters of the model and the number of sampled data.

6 Conclusions

We proposed an approach for choosing the optimal dimensionality of the political spectrum, based on a dataset of responses of participants regarding political stands. Our method uses a probabilistic graphical model for dimensionality reduction, allowing us to express the political spectrum dimensionality selection problem as a Bayesian model selection problem, which we solve by choosing the dimensionality of the model with maximal evidence.

We applied the model on two types of datasets. The UK dataset contains participants ranking regarding many political issues, whereas in the US dataset participants rate their degree of agreement with many sentences representing a political stand. Our model indicates that for both datasets, there are correlations in the data regarding seemingly unrelated political issues, allowing for a more concise representation of peoples' political stand than the naive encoding of their responses to all questions. Further, our analysis of the UK dataset indicates that socio-demographic factors correlate with political opinions. This allows predicting political stands based on such socio-demographic factors.

Despite these correlations between responses to different questions (or between socio-demographic factors and these responses), our model indicates that a "left-right" political spectrum, or even a two dimensional spectrum, are far too simplistic, and insufficient to represent peoples' political opinion. Our model's choice for the optimal dimensionality is 10 dimensions for the UK dataset, and 6 for US dataset. Interestingly, the optimal dimensionality for the political spectrum differs across states in the USA.

Many questions are left open for future research. First, the political dimensions found by our model are the result of the feature extraction during the dimensionality reduction. Could these dimensions be interpreted in a human understandable form? Second, would alternative Bayesian models for dimensionality reduction achieve a lower error, and perhaps result in a different choice of dimensionality for the political spectrum, or is this dimensionality an inherent property of the data? Finally, our results indicated correlations between socio-demographic features of participants and their political opinions. To what degree of accuracy is it possible to predict demographic traits of people based solely on their political stand?

References

[1] 38 Degrees. 38 degrees — people. power. change., 2014.

[2] D. Agarwal and B.-C. Chen. flda: matrix factorization through latent dirichlet allocation. In *Proceedings of the third ACM international conference on Web search and data mining*, pages 91–100. ACM, 2010.

[3] H. Akaike. Information theory and an extension of the maximum likelihood principle. In *Selected Papers of Hirotugu Akaike*, pages 199–213. Springer, 1998.

[4] Y. Bachrach. Human judgments in hiring decisions based on online social network profiles. In *DSAA*, pages 1–10. IEEE, 2015.

[5] Y. Bachrach, T. Graepel, T. Minka, and J. Guiver. How to grade a test without knowing the answers—a bayesian graphical model for adaptive crowdsourcing and aptitude testing. *ICML*, 2012.

[6] Y. Bachrach, O. Lev, Y. Lewenberg, and Y. Zick. Tracking performance and forming study groups for prep courses using probabilistic graphical models. In *AAMAS*, 2016.

[7] S. Christie and A. Meltzer. *The floodgates of anarchy*. PM Press, 1970.

[8] P. E. Converse. The nature of belief systems in mass publics (1964). *Critical Review*, 18(1-3):1–74, 1964.

[9] H. J. Eysenck. *Sense and nonsense in psychology*. Penguin Books, 1963.

[10] L. W. Ferguson. The stability of the primary social attitudes: I. religionism and humanitarianism. *The Journal of Psychology*, 12(2):283–288, 1941.

[11] M. I. Gorinova, Y. Lewenberg, Y. Bachrach, A. Kalaitzis, M. Fagan, D. Carignan, and N. Gautam. Predicting gaming related properties from twitter accounts. In *AAAI*, 2016.

[12] GOV.UK. English indices of deprivation 2010: local authority summaries, 2010.

[13] T. Hofmann. Latent semantic models for collaborative filtering. *ACM Trans. Inf. Syst.*, 22(1):89–115, Jan. 2004.

[14] T. Hofmann and J. Puzicha. Latent class models for collaborative filtering. In *IJCAI*, volume 99, pages 688–693, 1999.

[15] T. Husen. Matningar av intressen och attityder. *Personalen och Foretaget*, pages 80–87, 1951.

[16] R. Jin, L. Si, and C. Zhai. Preference-based graphic models for collaborative filtering. In *UAI*, pages 329–336, 2002.

[17] J. T. Jost, C. M. Federico, and J. L. Napier. Political ideology: Its structure, functions, and elective affinities. *Annual review of psychology*, 60:307–337, 2009.

[18] R. E. Kass and A. E. Raftery. Bayes factors. *Journal of the american statistical association*, 90(430):773–795, 1995.

[19] D. Koller and N. Friedman. *Probabilistic graphical models: principles and techniques*. MIT press, 2009.

[20] M. Kosinski, Y. Bachrach, P. Kohli, D. Stillwell, and T. Graepel. Manifestations of user personality in website choice and behaviour on online social networks. *Machine learning*, 95(3):357–380, 2014.

[21] M. Kosinski, D. Stillwell, and T. Graepel. Private traits and attributes are predictable from digital records of human behavior. *Proceedings of the National Academy of Sciences*, 110(15):5802–5805, 2013.

[22] Y. Lewenberg, Y. Bachrach, and S. Volkova. Using emotions to predict user interest areas in online social networks. In *DSAA*, pages 1–10. IEEE, 2015.

[23] D. J. MacKay. *Information theory, inference, and learning algorithms*, volume 7. Citeseer, 2003.

[24] W. S. Maddox and S. A. Lilie. *Beyond liberal and conservative: Reassessing the political spectrum*. Cato Institute, 1984.

[25] T. Minka, J. Winn, J. Guiver, S. Webster, Y. Zaykov, B. Yangel, A. Spengler, and J. Bronskill. Infer.NET 2.6, 2014.

[26] T. P. Minka. Expectation propagation for approximate bayesian inference. In *Proceedings of the Seventeenth conference on Uncertainty in artificial intelligence*, pages 362–369. Morgan Kaufmann Publishers Inc., 2001.

[27] J. Pearl. *Probabilistic reasoning in intelligent systems: networks of plausible inference*. Morgan Kaufmann, 1988.

[28] I. Porteous, A. U. Asuncion, and M. Welling. Bayesian matrix factorization with side information and dirichlet process mixtures. In *AAAI*, 2010.

[29] D. Preoţiuc-Pietro, S. Volkova, V. Lampos, Y. Bachrach, and N. Aletras. Studying user income through language, behaviour and affect in social media. *PloS one*, 10(9):e0138717, 2015.

[30] M. Schmidt, A. Niculescu-Mizil, K. Murphy, et al. Learning graphical model structure using l1-regularization paths. In *AAAI*, volume 7, pages 1278–1283, 2007.

[31] G. Schwarz et al. Estimating the dimension of a model. *The annals of statistics*, 6(2):461–464, 1978.

[32] L. Si and R. Jin. Flexible mixture model for collaborative filtering. In *ICML*, volume 3, pages 704–711, 2003.

[33] D. H. Stern, R. Herbrich, and T. Graepel. Matchbox: large scale online bayesian recommendations. In *WWW*, pages 111–120. ACM, 2009.

[34] A. M. Turk. Amazon mechanical turk, 2014.

[35] S. Volkova and Y. Bachrach. On predicting sociodemographic traits and emotions from communications in social networks and their implications to online self-disclosure. *Cyberpsychology, Behavior, and Social Networking*, 18(12):726–736, 2015.

[36] S. Volkova, Y. Bachrach, M. Armstrong, and V. Sharma. Inferring latent user properties from texts published in social media. In *AAAI*, pages 4296–4297, 2015.

[37] S. Volkova, G. Coppersmith, and B. Van Durme. Inferring user political preferences from streaming communications. In *ACL (1)*, pages 186–196, 2014.

[38] K. Von Beyme. *Political parties in Western democracies*. Gower Publishing Company, Limited, 1985.

[39] A. Ware. *Political parties and party systems*, volume 9. Oxford University Press Oxford, 1996.

[40] E. Wit, E. v. d. Heuvel, and J.-W. Romeijn. all models are wrong...: an introduction to model uncertainty. *Statistica Neerlandica*, 66(3):217–236, 2012.

Correlated Tag Learning in Topic Model

Shuangyin Li*, Rong Pan†, Yu Zhang* and Qiang Yang*
*Department of Computer Science and Engineering, Hong Kong University of Science and Technology, China
{shuangyinli, zhangyu, qyang}@cse.ust.hk
†School of Data and Computer Science, Sun Yat-sen University, Guang Zhou, China. panr@sysu.edu.cn

Abstract

It is natural to expect that the documents in a corpus will be correlated, and these correlations are reflected by not only the words but also the observed tags in each document. Most previous works model this type of corpus, which are called the semi-structured corpus, without considering the correlations among the tags. In this work, we develop a Correlated Tag Learning (CTL) model for semi-structured corpora based on the topic model to enable the construction of the correlation graph among tags via a logistic normal participation process. For the inference of the CTL model, we devise a variational inference algorithm to approximate the posterior. In experiments, we visualize the tag correlation graph generated by the CTL model on the DBLP corpus and for the tasks of document retrieval and classification, the correlation graph among tags is helpful to improve the generalization performance compared with the state-of-the-art baselines.

1 INTRODUCTION

Documents are usually composed of a group of words with different word frequencies, leading to the 'bag-of-words' representation. Besides, it is natural to expect that documents in a corpus are highly correlated with each other. This implicit relationship among documents may be embodied in the semantic meanings of the words in each document, where we can use topic models or other related methods to learn the correlations. However, most of the documents contain not only unstructured contexts (e.g., the plain text) but also metadata (e.g., tags). The metadata usually consists of several tags, such as authors in an article, keywords for a web page, and categories for a product. To model this type of documents which are called semi-structured documents, the metadata information would play an important role in organizing, understanding, and summarizing them in many applications.

Obviously, the tags in a corpus come from a compacted space, taking higher-level semantic as one type of semantic abstraction than words. Thus, the tags should be highly correlated with each other, which is consistent with documents' correlations. That is, the correlation between two documents can be reflected via their tags. Thus, modeling the correlations among tags can benefit the learning of the relations among documents and help obtain more meaningful representations for documents, which can be helpful for the consequent tasks such as document classification and retrieval. On the other hand, to model the documents, only considering the word information is obviously not enough if the tag information is available. Meanwhile, ignoring the correlations among tags is deficient, because the correlations can help understand the documents in a better way. Hence, how to model the correlations among tags together with the words is interesting and important for document modeling.

In fact, tags can be treated as high-level 'topics' in a corpus. While differently, the observed tags would be very complicated and high-dimensional, and belong to a different semantic space, compared with latent topics discovered by topic models. Thus, there should be a connection between the observed tags and the latent topics, such as a distribution over topics for each tag. In previous works such as the tag-weighted topic model [15], the author topic model [18], and the labeled-LDA [21], almost all of them define continuous distributions for the observed tags over the latent topics. Each tag is defined as a vector sampled from a certain probability distribution such as a Dirichlet distribution in [15], where the vector for a tag indicates the distribution over all the latent topics. In this way, the observed tags and the latent topics are combined together. However, under the Dirichlet distribution, the tags are modeled to be independent, which ignores the correlations among the tags.

On the other hand, we may model the correlations among the tags only using the co-occurrence of the tags. However, there are two main limitations in this approach. Firstly, it ignores the importance of different tags in a specific document, where some tags are more relevant to a document than others but in another document the situation can be totally different. Secondly, as described above, the tags are a set of semantic topic distributions, which are learned from plain text, and so the correlations should be modeled from the semantic level, while only considering the co-occurrences is not enough.

In this paper, we propose a novel CTL model based on the topic model to learn the correlations among the tags. In the CTL model, participation vectors of the observed tags, which take advantage of both the text information and the tags, for a semi-structured corpus are used to learn the correlations. For inference, an effective inference method is devised to learn the model parameters. The outputs of the CTL model are the tags' correlation matrix and the latent topics for documents, which are learned by utilizing the learned tag correlations. After learning the CTL, we can obtain a correlational graph which shows the relationships among the tags by ranking the correlational values. In experiments, we trained the proposed model on the DBLP corpus, where we treated authors as tags and we can visualize the correlational graph among the authors. Also, for one special author, there is a ranking list to show the relevant authors not only from the co-author information but also from whether they have similar research interests. We also apply the CTL model to the document retrieval and classification tasks on the Wikipedia corpus and the results show that the CTL model outperforms the state-of-the-art baselines.

2 RELATED WORKS

To date, many models are proposed for document modeling via different approaches such as undirected graphical models [24, 20, 13, 26, 25] or directed graphical models. As directed graphical models, topic models [11, 3, 1, 2, 4, 10] have been found to play an important role in analyzing unstructured texts. These models have been applied to many text mining areas, including information retrieval [28], document classification [6], and so on. However, most of these undirected and directed graphical models just consider the unstructured text with the bag-of-word assumption.

More and more text mining tasks are emerging in real-world applications to handle the semi-structured corpora, such as document classification described in [5, 16]. Based on the topic model, many methods have been proposed to deal with the semi-structured corpora, such as the author topic model [18], labeled-LDA [21], DMR [19], Tag-Weighted Topic Model (TWTM) [15], Tag-Weighted Dirichlet Allocation (TWDA) [14], partially LDA [22], TMBP [9], cFTM [8], statistical topic models [23], and so on. Most of the models take advantage of some given meta data (e.g., tags, labels, or contextual information) in a document with different assumptions. For example, the author topic model defines the distributions of the authors over the latent topics and the authors are assumed to be independent under a Dirichlet prior. In the labeled-LDA and partially LDA, the labels are defined as a set of distributions over the words from a vocabulary. For the TWTM and TWDA, a weight vector is used to generate the topic distribution of a document with the given tags. The DMR model is a Dirichlet-multinomial regression topic model which defines a log-linear prior on the document-topic distributions. In [23], Timothy et al. investigate a class of generative topic models for multi-label documents that associate individual word tokens with different labels, where the dependency-LDA is proposed to model the relations among the labels and words. Some of the aforementioned models can obtain the topic distribution of the tags, which can be used to measure the distance between the tags. However, they fail to directly model the correlations among tags.

3 THE CTL MODEL

In this section, we will mathematically define the Correlated Tag Learning (CTL) model, and discuss the learning and inference methods.

We use the following terminologies and notations to describe a corpus where each document is associated with a set of tags, which we call the semi-structured corpus.

Semi-Structured Corpus As a collection of M documents, we define the corpus $D = \{(\mathbf{w}^1, \mathbf{t}^1), \ldots, (\mathbf{w}^M, \mathbf{t}^M)\}$, where each 2-tuple $(\mathbf{w}^d, \mathbf{t}^d)$ denotes a document with its tag vector. Let $\mathbf{w}^d = (w_1^d, \ldots, w_N^d)$ denote the vector of N words associated with document d. Let $\mathbf{t}^d = (t_1^d, \ldots, t_L^d)$ represent the tag vector, each element of which is a binary indicator for a tag, with L as the number of all the tags in the corpus D.

Tag Matrix Here $\mathbf{t}^d$ is expanded to a $l^d \times L$ tag matrix T^d, where l^d is the number of tags in document d for the convenience of the inference. For each $i \in \{1, \ldots, l^d\}$, $T_{i\cdot}^d$ is a binary vector, where $T_{ij}^d = 1$ if

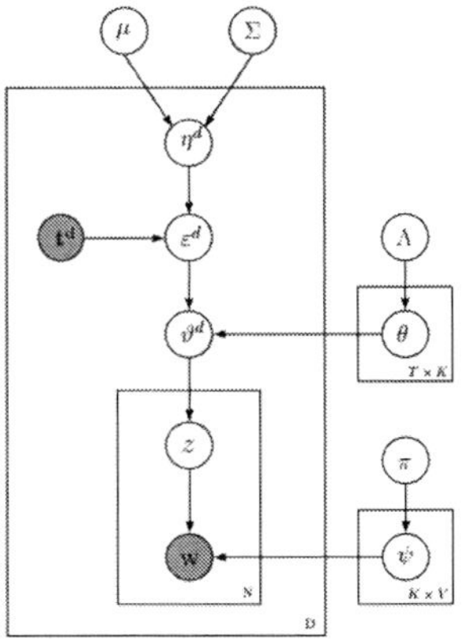

Figure 1: The graphical model of the CTL model, where each node denotes a random variable, a shaded node represents an observed variable, and edges indicate possible dependencies.

and only if the i-th tag in the document d is the j-th tag in the tag set of the corpus D.

Topic Proportions Each document is associated with a set of topic proportions ϑ. For a document d, ϑ^d is a multinomial distribution over topics and it reflects the probabilities of the words in document d drawing from latent topics.

3.1 The Model

The proposed CTL model is a hierarchical Bayesian model based on the topic model with assumptions that each document in a corpus is modeled by an underlying set of latent topics and that each topic defines a multinomial distribution over words. Besides, the CTL model assumes that the topic distribution of each document is determined by the given tags with a set of participation values. With the participation values in a participation vector, the CTL can model the topic proportions of each document as the product between the participation vector and the topic distributions of each tags in the document.

In this paper, we use ϑ_d to denote the topic distribution of the document d, as shown in Figure 1. Let θ represent a $T \times K$ matrix, where K is the number of the latent topics and each row in θ describes the distribution of one tag belonging to the latent topics. Let ψ represent a $K \times V$ distribution matrix, where each row is a distribution vector of one topic over words and V is the number of words in the dictionary of D.

3.1.1 Participation Vectors

ε^d, as shown in Figure 1, denotes the participation vector of the given tags in the document d. In the TWTM [15] and TWDA [14] models, it is called a weight vector which follows a Dirichlet distribution. As discussed above, under a Dirichlet distribution, the components of the participation vector are nearly independent, leading to a strong and unrealistic assumption that the presence of one observed tag is not correlated to the presence of another one. In order to overcome this assumption, we use a flexible logistic normal distribution to model the observed tags. As shown in Figure 1, Σ is the covariance matrix of the logistic normal distribution, μ is the expected value vector of the random variables, and η^d is a L-dimensional row vector that follows the normal distribution with Σ as the covariance and μ the mean. So the participation vector is defined as follows:

$$\varepsilon^d = \exp\{T^d \times (\eta^d)^{\mathrm{T}}\},$$

where $(\eta^d)^{\mathrm{T}}$ is the transpose of η^d, and ε^d is a $l^d \times 1$ column vector associated with the document d. Note that ε^d does not satisfy $\sum_i \varepsilon_i^d = 1$, hence we call it a participation vector instead of a weight vector.

With the participation vector, instead of a Dirichlet distribution, we use a logistic normal distribution to model the topic distribution of the document d:

$$\vartheta^d = \frac{(\varepsilon^d)^T \times T^d \times \theta}{\sum_i((\varepsilon^d)^T \times T^d \times \theta)_i},$$

where $(\cdot)_i$ denotes the i-th entry in a vector and ϑ^d, the multinomial topic proportions of the document d, satisfies $\sum_i \vartheta_i^d = 1$. With the multinomial topic proportions ϑ obtained by a participation vector and a set of the observed tags in a document, we can generate each word for the document in a similar way to the topic model.

Thus, the CTL model assumes that a corpus with M documents arises from the following generative process:

1. For each topic $k \in \{1, \ldots, K\}$, draw $\psi_k \sim \mathrm{Dir}(\pi)$, where $\mathrm{Dir}(\cdot)$ denotes a Dirichlet distribution and π is a V-dimensional vector of hyperparameters.

2. For each tag $t \in \{1, \ldots, L\}$, draw $\theta_t \sim \mathrm{Dir}(\Lambda)$, where Λ is a K dimensional prior vector of θ.

3. For each document d:

   (a) Draw $\eta^d \sim \mathcal{N}(\mu, \Sigma)$ where $\mathcal{N}(\cdot, \cdot)$ denotes a multivariate normal distribution.

   (b) Generate T^d by $\mathbf{t}^d$.

   (c) Generate $\varepsilon^d = \exp\{T^d \times (\eta^d)^{\mathrm{T}}\}$.

   (d) Generate $\vartheta^d = \frac{(\varepsilon^d)^T \times T^d \times \theta}{\sum_i((\varepsilon^d)^T \times T^d \times \theta)_i}$.

   (e) For each word w_{dn}:

i. Draw z_{dn} ~Mult(ϑ^d) where Mult(·) denotes a multinomial distribution.

ii. Draw w_{dn} ~Mult($\psi_{z_{dn}}$).

The CTL model is different from the TWTM model [15] where the weight vector in a document for the given tags is drawn from a Dirichlet distribution. The Dirichlet distribution is computationally convenient but it has a nearly independent assumption among the components of the weight vector. Differently, entries in the participation vector of the observed tags is highly correlated as we described above.

The covariance matrix Σ induces the dependencies between the components of the participation vector, and allows a general pattern of variability between the components. Using the covariance matrix of the logistic normal distribution, we can capture the correlated relationships between the given tags associated with each document.

3.2 Variational Inference

The logistic normal distribution used here brings not only the capacity to model the correlations among tags but also a challenge for the posterior inference procedure since it is not a conjugate prior for the multinomial distribution. We present a variational expectation-maximization (EM) algorithm [12, 27] for the inference. In the variational EM algorithm, the E-step approximates the posterior by minimizing the Kullback-Leibler (KL) divergence between the variational distribution and the true posterior distribution. This method casts the inference problem as an optimization problem to approximate the posterior distribution of this latent model and some study in [2] shows that minimizing the KL divergence is equivalent to maximizing the evidence lower bound (ELBO) denoted by $\mathcal{L}(\cdot)$.

For the CTL model, the ELBO can be derived by using Jensen's inequality:

$$\mathcal{L}(\cdot) = \sum_d^D E_q[\log p(\eta^d|\mu,\Sigma)] + \sum_d^D\sum_n^N E_q[\log p(z_n|\vartheta^d)] + \sum_d^D\sum_n^N E_q[\log p(w_n|\psi, z_n)] + \sum_i^L E_q[\log p(\theta_i|\Lambda)] + H(q), \quad (1)$$

where $q(\cdot)$ denotes a variational distribution of the latent variables, $E_q[\cdot]$ denotes the expectation with respect to q, and $H(q)$ is the entropy of the variational distribution whose definition is:

$$H(q) = -\sum_d^D E_q[\log q(\eta^d)] - \sum_d^D\sum_n^N E_q[\log q(z_n)] - \sum_i^L E_q[\log q(\theta_i)].$$

For the variational distribution $q(\cdot)$, we choose a fully factorized distribution where all the variables are assumed to be independent:

$$q(\eta, z, \theta|u, \sigma^2, \gamma, \lambda) = \prod_i^L \mathrm{Dir}(\theta_i|\lambda_i) \prod_d^D \left(\mathcal{N}(\eta^d|u,\sigma^2)\prod_n^N \mathrm{Mult}(z_n|\gamma_n)\right),$$

where λ in the Dirichlet distribution, γ in the multinomial distribution, and (u, σ^2) in the Gaussian distribution are the variational parameters.

Before discussing the optimization procedure, we describe how to compute the ELBO in Eq. (1). In the CTL model, the key inferential problem that we need to solve is to compute the second term in Eq. (1), which is the expected logorithm of a topic assignment subject to a normalized multinomial parameter and can be computed as

$$\begin{aligned} E_q[\log p(z_n|\vartheta^d)] &= E_q\left[\log p\left(z_n|\frac{(\varepsilon^d)^T \times T^d \times \theta}{\sum_i((\varepsilon^d)^T \times T^d \times \theta)_i}\right)\right] \\ &= \sum_k^K \gamma_{nk} E_q\left[\log\left(\frac{(\varepsilon^d)^T \times T^d \times \theta}{\sum_i((\varepsilon^d)^T \times T^d \times \theta)_i}\right)_k\right], \end{aligned}$$

where γ_{nk} denotes the probability of the k-th topic assigned to the n-th word. We see that computing the CTL's ELBO relies on the calculation of the expected normalized topic distribution of a document, which can be computed as

$$\begin{aligned} &E_q\left[\log\left(\frac{(\varepsilon^d)^T \times T^d \times \theta}{\sum_i((\varepsilon^d)^T \times T^d \times \theta)_i}\right)_k\right] \\ =&E_q\left[\log((\varepsilon^d)^T \times T^d \times \theta)_k\right] - E_q\left[\log(\sum_i((\varepsilon^d)^T \times T^d \times \theta)_i)\right] \\ =&E_q\left[\log\sum_i^{l^d} \varepsilon_i^d \theta_k^{(i)}\right] - E_q\left[\log\sum_i^{l^d}\varepsilon_i^d\right] \\ =&E_q\left[\log\sum_i^{l^d} \exp\{\eta_{(i)}^d\}\theta_k^{(i)}\right] - E_q\left[\log\sum_i^{l^d}\exp\{\eta_{(i)}^d\}\right], \end{aligned}$$

where $\theta^{(i)}$ denotes the vector of the topic distributions for the i-th tags in the document d corresponding to a row in θ and $\eta_{(i)}^d$ is the i-th entry of $T^d \times (\eta^d)^{\mathrm{T}}$.

By following the correlated topic model [1], the above two expectations can be computed approximately with Taylor expansions, respectively:

$$E_q[\log\sum_i^{l^d}\exp\{\eta_{(i)}^d\}\theta_k^{(i)}] \approx \log\alpha + \frac{1}{\alpha}\sum_i^{l^d} E_q[\exp\{\eta_{(i)}^d\}]E_q[\theta_k^{(i)}] - 1$$

and

$$E_q[\log \sum_i^{l^d} \exp\{\eta^d_{(i)}\}] \approx \log \beta + \frac{1}{\beta} \sum_i^{l^d} E_q[\exp\{\eta^d_{(i)}\}] - 1,$$

where we introduce two new variational parameter α and β. Note that $E_q[\exp\{\eta^d_{(i)}\}]$ is the mean of a log-normal distribution and equals $\exp\{u_{(i)}+\sigma^2_{(i)}/2\}$. The expectation of a Dirichlet random variable, $E_q[\theta^{(i)}_k]$, is equal to $[\lambda_k / \sum_j^K \lambda_j]_{(i)}$. Thus, for a document d, we have

$$\begin{aligned} &\sum_n^N E_q[\log p(z_n|\vartheta^d)] \\ &\approx \sum_n^N \sum_k^K \gamma_{nk}\Big(\log \alpha + \frac{1}{\alpha}\sum_i^{l^d} \exp\{u_{(i)} + \sigma^2_{(i)}/2\}\left[\frac{\lambda_k}{\sum_j^K \lambda_j}\right]_{(i)} \\ &\quad - \log \beta - \frac{1}{\beta}\sum_i^{l^d} \exp\{u_{(i)} + \sigma^2_{(i)}/2\}\Big). \end{aligned}$$

Thus, we can use the block coordinate-ascent variational inference to maximize Eq. (1) with respect to variational parameters including σ^2, u, γ, λ, α, and β.

We first maximize $\mathcal{L}(\cdot)$ with respect to σ^2 for the document d with the objective function formulated as

$$\begin{aligned} \mathcal{L}(\sigma^2) &= -\frac{1}{2}\mathrm{tr}(\mathrm{diag}(\sigma^2)\Sigma^{-1}) + \sum_i^L \frac{1}{2}\log \sigma^2_{(i)} \\ &+ \sum_n^N \sum_k^K \frac{\gamma_{nk}}{\alpha}\Big(\sum_i^{l^d} \exp\{u_{(i)} + \sigma^2_{(i)}/2\}\left[\frac{\lambda_k}{\sum_j^K \lambda_j}\right]_{(i)}\Big) \\ &- \frac{N}{\beta}\sum_i^{l^d} \exp\{u_{(i)} + \sigma^2_{(i)}/2\}, \end{aligned} \tag{2}$$

where $\mathrm{tr}(\cdot)$ denotes the trace of a square matrix and $\mathrm{diag}(\cdot)$ converts a vector to a diagonal matrix. Obviously the problem with respect to σ has no analytic solution and we solve it via the Newton's method with gradient computed as

$$\begin{aligned} \mathcal{L}'(\sigma^2_i) =& \frac{1}{2}\sum_n^N \sum_k^K \frac{\gamma_{nk}}{\alpha}\exp\{u_{(i)} + \sigma^2_{(i)}/2\}\left[\frac{\lambda_k}{\sum_j^K \lambda_j}\right]_{(i)} \\ &- \frac{N}{2\beta}\exp\{u_{(i)} + \sigma^2_{(i)}/2\} + \frac{1}{2\sigma^2_{(i)}} - \frac{1}{2}\Sigma^{-1}_{ii}, \end{aligned} \tag{3}$$

where the subscript $(i) \in (1, \cdots, l^d)$ indicates the i-th tag in a specific document d.

The objective function with respect to u is formulated as

$$\begin{aligned} \mathcal{L}(u) &= -\frac{1}{2}(u-\mu)^T\Sigma^{-1}(u-\mu) - \frac{N}{\beta}\sum_i^{l^d}\exp\{u_{(i)} + \frac{\sigma^2_{(i)}}{2}\} \\ &+ \sum_n^N \sum_k^K \frac{\gamma_{nk}}{\alpha}(\sum_i^{l^d}\exp\{u_{(i)} + \sigma^2_{(i)}/2\}\left[\frac{\lambda_k}{\sum_j^K \lambda_j}\right]_{(i)}). \end{aligned} \tag{4}$$

We use the conjugate gradient algorithm to solve this problem, where the derivative is computed as

$$\begin{aligned} \mathcal{L}'(u) =& \sum_n^N \sum_k^K \frac{\gamma_{nk}}{\alpha}\exp\{u_{(i)} + \sigma^2_{(i)}/2\}\left[\frac{\lambda_k}{\sum_j^K \lambda_j}\right]_{(i)} \\ &- \frac{N}{\beta}\exp\{u_{(i)} + \sigma^2_{(i)}/2\} - \Sigma^{-1}(u-\mu). \end{aligned} \tag{5}$$

We maximize Eq. (1) with respect to γ_{nk} to find the maximizer as

$$\begin{aligned} \gamma_{nk} \propto \psi_{k,v^{w_n}} \exp\Bigg\{&\frac{1}{\alpha}(\sum_i^{l^d}\exp\{u_{(i)} + \sigma^2_{(i)}/2\}\left[\frac{\lambda_k}{\sum_j^K \lambda_j}\right]_{(i)}) \\ &+ \log \alpha\Bigg\}, \end{aligned} \tag{6}$$

where v^{w_n} denotes the index of w_n in the dictionary.

For the variational parameter λ, the objective function is formulated as

$$\begin{aligned} \mathcal{L}(\lambda) =& \sum_k^K(\Lambda_k - 1)(\Psi(\lambda_k) - \Psi(\sum_j^K \lambda_j)) - \log\Gamma(\sum_j^K \lambda_j) \\ &+ \sum_n^N \sum_k^K \frac{\gamma_{nk}}{\alpha}\Big(\sum_i^{l^d}\exp\{u_{(i)} + \sigma^2_{(i)}/2\}\left[\frac{\lambda_k}{\sum_j^K \lambda_j}\right]_{(i)}\Big) \\ &+ \sum_k^K \log\Gamma(\lambda_k) + \sum_k^K(\lambda_k - 1)(\Psi(\lambda_k) - \Psi(\sum_j^K \lambda_j)). \end{aligned} \tag{7}$$

We use the gradient descent method to solve it, where the derivative with respect to λ_k is:

$$\begin{aligned} \mathcal{L}'(\lambda_k) =& \sum_n^N \frac{\gamma_{nk}(\sum_j^K \lambda_j - \lambda_k)}{\alpha(\sum_j^K \lambda_j)^2}\exp\{u_{(i)} + \sigma^2_{(i)}/2\} \\ &+ (\Lambda_k - \lambda_k)(\Psi'(\lambda_k) - \Psi'(\sum_j^K \lambda_j)). \end{aligned} \tag{8}$$

For α and β, the optimal solutions can easily be found as

$$\alpha \propto \frac{\sum_n^N \sum_k^K \gamma_{nk}\Big(\sum_i^{l^d}\exp\{u_{(i)} + \sigma^2_{(i)}/2\}\left[\frac{\lambda_k}{\sum_j^K \lambda_j}\right]_{(i)}\Big)}{\sum_n^N \sum_k^K \gamma_{nk}} \tag{9}$$

$$\beta \propto \sum_i^{l^d}\exp\{u_{(i)} + \sigma^2_{(i)}/2\}. \tag{10}$$

In the E-Step of the variational EM algorithm, we iteratively update the variational parameters including σ^2 , u, γ, λ, α and β.

3.3 Parameter Estimation

The parameters of the CTL model include Σ, μ, ψ and Λ. In the M-step, given the semi-structured corpus, we can estimate the parameters by maximizing a lower-bound of the log-likelihood based on the variational

E-step. The update rules for Σ, μ and ψ can easily be obtained:

$$\mu \propto \frac{1}{D}\sum_{d}^{D} u_d, \tag{11}$$

$$\Sigma \propto \frac{1}{D}\sum_{d}^{D}\Big(I\sigma_d^2 + (u_d-\mu)(u_d-\mu)^T\Big), \tag{12}$$

$$\psi_{kj} \propto \sum_{d}^{D}\sum_{n}^{N}\gamma_{nk}(w^d)_n^j, \tag{13}$$

where $(w^d)_n^j$ is the count for the n-th word in the document d. For the Dirichlet parameter Λ, its objective function is formulated as

$$\mathcal{L}(\Lambda) = \sum_{l}^{L}\Bigg(\log\Gamma(\sum_{j}^{K}\Lambda_j) - \sum_{i}^{K}\log\Gamma(\Lambda_i) + \sum_{i}^{K}(\Lambda_i - 1)\Big(\Psi(\lambda_i^l) - \Psi(\sum_{j}^{K}\lambda_j^l)\Big)\Bigg). \tag{14}$$

The derivative with respect to Λ_i is computed as

$$\mathcal{L}'(\Lambda_i) = L\Big(\Psi(\sum_{j}^{K}\Lambda_j) - \Psi(\lambda_i)\Big) + \sum_{l}^{L}\Big(\Psi(\lambda_i^l) - \Psi(\sum_{j}^{K}\lambda_j^l)\Big). \tag{15}$$

We can use the linear-time Newton-Raphson algorithm to estimate Λ.

4 DISCUSSION

The proposed CTL model can capture the correlations among the tags in a semi-structured corpus, not just only by considering the co-occurrences of the tags. The CTL model presents the participation vector for each document to estimate the correlations of the tags, and the participation vector is learned by the text information with the basic assumption on latent topics. In other words, the co-occurrence vector is binary, which means that one tag is present or absent, while the participation vector is non-binary and the values in participation vector denote the importance of the tags.

Actually, we can train the CTL model by only considering the co-occurrence information of tags in each document. In this case, different tags have equal importance in a document d and hence η^d is observed for each document, where η_j^d is set to 1 if and only if the document d has the j-th tag. So the CTL model will consist of two parts, as shown in Figure 2. The left figure in Figure 2 is the first part containing Σ, μ, η^d, ξ^d and $\mathbf{t}^d$, where η^d, ξ^d and $\mathbf{t}^d$ are the observed variables. We can use the traditional maximum likelihood estimation to learn the correlation matrix Σ with the D samples:

$$\mu = \frac{1}{D}\sum_{d}^{D}\mathbf{t}^d, \quad \Sigma = \frac{1}{D}\sum_{d}^{D}(\mathbf{t}^d-\mu)(\mathbf{t}^d-\mu)^{\mathrm{T}}.$$

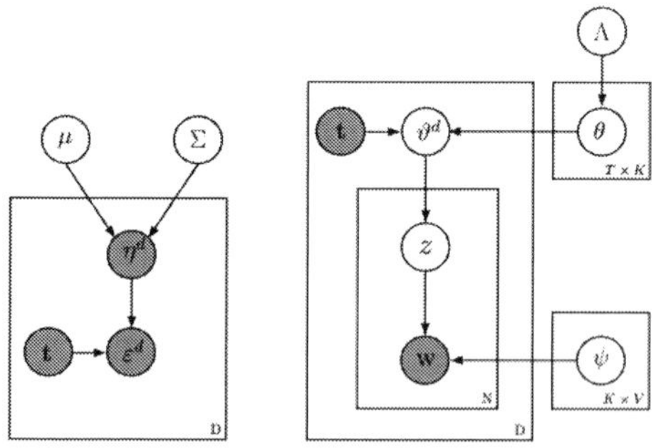

Figure 2: The two parts of the CTL model will be degenerated if η^d becomes equal to $\mathbf{t}^d$, which means that all the tags have the same effect on the document.

The second part shown in the right figure of Figure 2 means that all the tags have equal impacts on the topic distribution ϑ^d. We can see that the second part is a variant of the author topic model described in [18]. Thus, we can use the variational inference process to compute the new ELBO bound as:

$$\begin{aligned}\mathcal{L}_{new} =& \sum_{d}^{D}E_q[\log p(\mathbf{t}^d|\mu,\Sigma)] + \sum_{d}^{D}\sum_{n}^{N}E_q[\log p(z_n|\vartheta^d)] \\ &+ \sum_{d}^{D}\sum_{n}^{N}E_q[\log p(w_n|\psi,z_n)] + \sum_{i}^{L}E_q[\log p(\theta_i|\Lambda)] \\ &- \sum_{d}^{D}E_q[\log q(\mathbf{t}^d)] - \sum_{d}^{D}\sum_{n}^{N}E_q[\log q(z_n)] \\ &- \sum_{i}^{L}E_q[\log q(\theta_i)],\end{aligned}$$

where $\sum_d^D E_q[\log p(\mathbf{t}^d|\mu,\Sigma)]$ and $\sum_d^D E_q[\log q(\mathbf{t}^d)]$ are fixed, $\sum_d^D\sum_n^N E_q[\log p(z_n|\vartheta^d)]$ does not involve σ^2 and u since η^d and ξ^d are known. In this case, $\mathcal{L}_{new} < \mathcal{L}$, which means the new lower bound $\mathcal{L}_{new}$ is lower than the former one when convergence. Thus, treating the tags equally will not be a good choice.

Compared with the tag-weighted topic model [15], we would obtain document embeddings with better quality when the tags in the corpus are highly correlated. Thus, we will study the CTL model under this setting in our experiments.

5 EXPERIMENTS

In this section, we will present the performance of the proposed CTL model on document modeling, document classification, and document retrieval, respectively.

5.1 Experimental Settings

We used two semi-structured corpora to evaluate the CTL model. The first corpus is the Digital Bibliography and Library Project (DBLP),[1] which is a collection of bibliographic information of technical papers published in major computer science journals and conferences. We use the authors as the tags and removed the authors that occur in fewer than 5 papers. We use a subset of the DBLP that contains abstracts of $D = 40,108$ papers with $72,748$ words by removing stop words and $L = 6,348$ unique tags. The second corpus is from Wikipedia.[2] The Wikipedia corpus we used contains $43,217$ articles. The size of the vocabulary is $22,344$ by removing stop words. We use the category information, which is located at the bottom of each article and provided by the MediaWiki software, of articles as the tags, and in total there are $2,900$ tags. Moreover, each article belongs to different portals which can be viewed as the class label and all the articles used in the experiments belong to 20 classes, such as arts, sports, history, biography, education and so on.

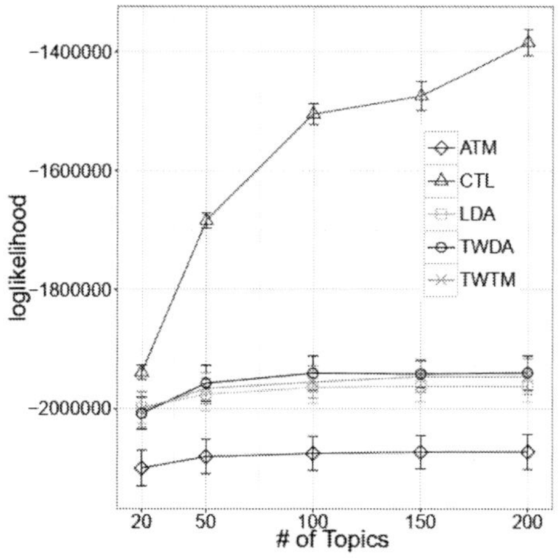

Figure 3: The 5-fold cross-validated held-out log-likelihood of different models on the Wikipedia corpus with different number of topics.

5.2 Experiments on Document Modeling

To demonstrate the performance of the different models on document modeling, we computed the log-likelihood of the held-out data given a model estimated from the remaining data by using five-fold cross validation, implying that 80% documents are for training and the remaining 20% for testing. We compared the CTL model with the Author Topic Model (ATM), TWTM, TWDA, and LDA by varying the number of latent topics. Since the LDA could not handle the tag information directly, we treated the given tags as the word features and added them into the document as the input for the LDA model.

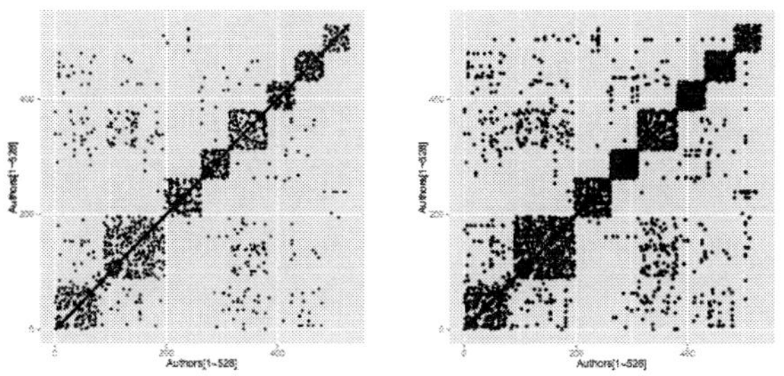

(a) penalty factor $p = 0.25$ (b) penalty factor $p = 0.5$

Figure 4: The scatter plots of the selected 528 authors on the DBLP corpus, where a point is drawn if the corresponding two authors are neighbors.

Figure 3 shows the average log-likelihood for each model on the held-out set. The results demonstrate that the CTL model has much better performance than other baselines. One possible reason is that the tags contained in Wikipedia corpus are highly correlated and with the help of the logistic normal distribution, the CTL model can obtain a more reasonable and effective participation vector to form the topic distribution for each document.

5.3 Analysis on Tag Graph

The covariance of the logistic normal distribution for the participation vector can be used to visualize the relations among tags. Thus, we use the covariance matrix to form a tag graph, where the nodes represent the tags appeared in the corpus and the edges denote the relations between tags. To construct the tag graph, we use the method introduced in [17] for neighborhood selection based on the Lasso. As described in [17], the neighborhood selection with the Lasso is used to estimate the conditional dependency separately for each node in the graph. In the CTL model, for a document d, η^d follows a normal distribution with mean u and covariance Σ. Thus, $\{\eta^d\}$ are treated as independent observations sampled from the normal distribution $\mathcal{N}(\mu, \Sigma)$, which are used to estimate the neighborhood based on [17].

We use the DBLP corpus for the experiment. For the convenience of display, we select 528 authors to illustrate the correlated connections among them by drawing an edge if the corresponding two authors are neighbors with different penalty factor $p = 0.25$ and

[1] `http://www.informatik.uni-trier.de/~ley/db/`
[2] http://www.wikipedia.org/

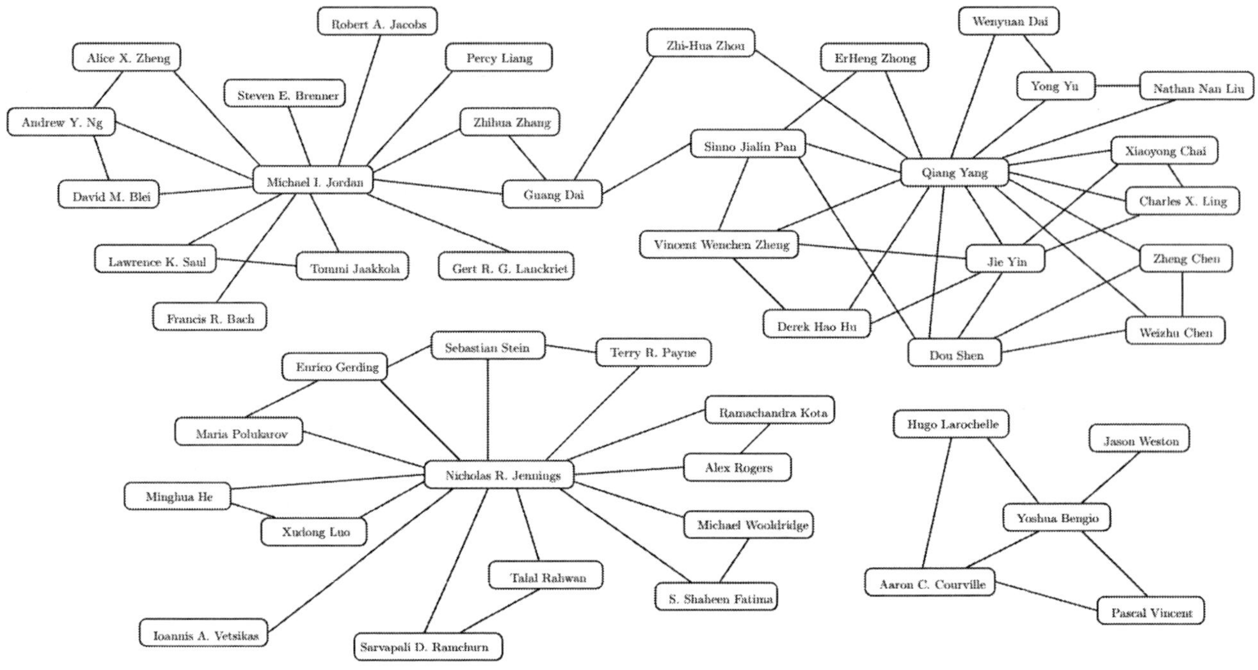

Figure 5: A subset of the author graph learned from 40,108 abstracts of the DBLP. The edges between authors are computed by the neighborhood selection method [17] based on the Lasso.

Table 1: The ranking list of top correlated authors with eight authors on the DBLP corpus.

Michael I. Jordan	Alice X. Zheng(0.157837), Francis R. Bach(0.116478), Gert R. G. Lanckriet(0.107671), David M. Blei(0.103741), Steven E. Brenner(0.092675), Zhihua Zhang(0.090492), Percy Liang(0.089226), Robert A. Jacobs(0.085318), Tommi Jaakkola (0.082044), Guang Dai(0.058045), Lawrence K. Saul(0.057545), Martin J. Wainwright(0.045444), Nebojsa Jojic(0.043731), David A. Patterson(0.041441), Tamar Flash(0.035152), Erik B. Sudderth(0.033563), Andrew Y. Ng(0.013234)
Yoshua Bengio	Pascal Vincent(0.410208), Hugo Larochelle(0.265349), Aaron C. Courville(0.132399), Jason Weston(0.049443)
Qiang Yang	Dou Shen(0.149414), Derek Hao Hu(0.144670), Sinno Jialin Pan(0.134137), Xiaoyong Chai(0.115358), Nathan Nan Liu (0.0.113420), ErHeng Zhong(0.107736), Weizhu Chen(0.104334), Yong Yu(0.091473), Charles X. Ling(0.081368), Jie Yin (0.077154), Wenyuan Dai(0.071907), Vincent Wenchen Zheng(0.062750), Zheng Chen(0.060292), Zhi-Hua Zhou(0.057265)
Nicholas R. Jennings	Alex Rogers(0.243331), Ramachandra Kota(0.142240), Maria Polukarov(0.137646), Talal Rahwan(0.134888), Ioannis A. Vetsikas(0.126621), S. Shaheen Fatima(0.121799), Sebastian Stein(0.117208), Enrico Gerding(0.027282), Minghua He(0.106050), Xudong Luo(0.086897), Sarvapali D. Ramchurn(0.071510), Terry R. Payne(0.068713), Michael Wooldridge(0.065824)
Micha Sharir	Pankaj K. Agarwal(0.273844), Emo Welzl(0.170932), Natan Rubin(0.139646), Jnos Pach(0.110192), Haim Kaplan (0.106137), Vladlen Koltun(0.104685), Boris Aronov(0.102123), Shakhar Smorodinsky(0.088530), Esther Ezra(0.083021), Dan Halperin(0.074751, Rom Pinchasi(0.056282), Bernard Chazelle(0.044011), Jir Matousek(0.027263)
Jiawei Han	Xiaoxin Yin(0.196956), Deng Cai(0.103920), Guozhu Dong(0.101735), V. S. Lakshmanan(0.100016), Xin Jin(0.098451), Charu C. Aggarwal(0.098256), Anthony K. H. Tung(0.092360), Jianyong Wang(0.087017), Hongjun Lu(0.072772), ChengXiang Zhai(0.048570), Jiong Yang(0.042489), Philip S. Yu(0.036918), Ke Wang(0.032003)
Jennifer Rexford	David Walker(0.247776), Mung Chiang(0.162803), Eric Keller(0.152502), Renata Teixeira(0.141469), Minlan Yu(0.123096), Nick Feamster(0.115787), Albert G. Greenberg(0.111072), Aman Shaikh(0.093805), Matthew Caesar(0.049353), Michael J. Freedman(0.039058), Kang G. Shin(0.031615)
Franco Zambonelli	Marco Mamei(0.372887), Letizia Leonardi(0.213969), Giacomo Cabri(0.195711), Gabriella Castelli(0.188215), Nicola Bicocchi(0.080601), Andrea Omicini(0.054696), Robert Tolksdorf(0.040949), Sara Montagna(0.020905), Matthias Baumgarten(0.012859), Alberto Rosi(0.012646)

0.5, respectively. After using the spectral clustering based on the conditional dependency obtained by the method in [17], as shown in Figure 4, we clearly see that the authors cluster together to different groups, where the authors in a group may have similar research interests.

We plot the author graph to show the correlations among the 518 authors and in Figure 5, a part of the graph is shown, where the nodes represent authors and the edges denote the correlations between the authors.

In this graph, we can find some interesting insight. For example, two authors 'Zhi-Hua Zhou' and 'Guang Dai', who did not coauthor any paper, have a connection between them since they have similar research interests, which shows an advantage of the CTL model over only using the coauthorship information that it can find meaningful relations at the semantic level.

The CTL model can give a ranking list based on how the authors are correlated. In Table 1, we pick several authors from the 528 authors, and for each selected author, we rank other authors according to their correlational values, which can be obtained by the process of neighborhood selection (see [17]). Based on the results, we can easily see how close the two authors are in the research and answer interesting questions including that whether researcher A has more similar interests to researcher B than to researcher C.

5.4 Document Classification and Retrieval

In this section, we conduct experiments on document classification and retrieval tasks.

We first test the classification performance by comparing the performance of the LDA, ATM, TWTM, TWDA, and the proposed CTL model with the number of topics as 50 and 100, respectively. The LIBSVM [7] with the Gaussian kernel and default parameters is used as the classifier. In experiments, we use a subset of the Wikipedia corpus which contains 14,400 documents belonging to 20 classes. We reported in Figure 6 the precision of different methods on the Wikipedia corpus by using the five-fold cross validation. According to Figure 6, the performance of the CTL model is significantly better than that of other baseline methods. One possible reason is that the CTL model can learn a better topic distribution for each document than others.

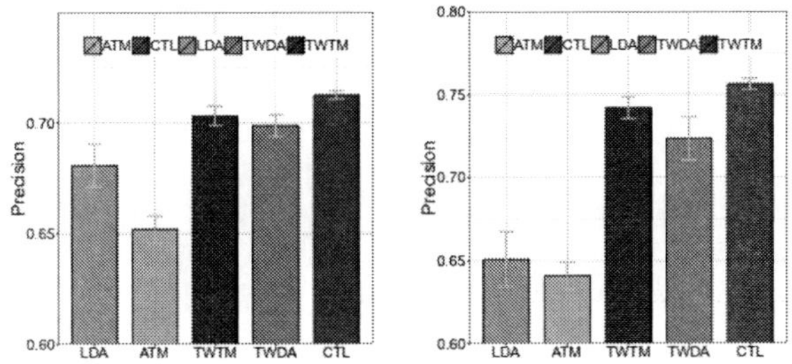

(a) $K = 50$ (b) $K = 100$

Figure 6: Classification results on the Wikipedia corpus for the LDA, ATM, TWTM, TWDA and CTL models with five-fold cross validation.

Moreover, we use the Wikipedia corpus to evaluate the performance on the document retrieval task. In this experiment, each document is represented by the vector of topic distribution generated by different models with the topic number as $K = 100$. The Wikipedia corpus used here is just the data set used in the above classification experiment. We randomly sample 12,400 documents for training and the rest for testing. For each query, documents in the database were ranked using the cosine distance as the similarity metric. For evaluation, we check whether a retrieved document has the same class label as the query document to decide whether the retrieved document is relevant to the query document. Figure 7 shows the F1 scores and the precision-recall curves of the LDA, ATM, TWTM, TWDA and CTL models. The experimental results demonstrate the superiority of the embedding learned by the CTL model for the document retrieval task.

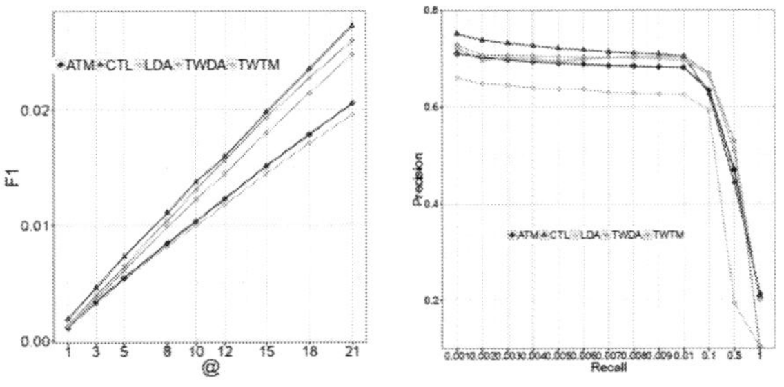

(a) F1-Score (b) Precision-Recall curves

Figure 7: F1-score and precision-recall curves for document retrieval on the Wikipedia corpus for the LDA, ATM, TWTM, TWDA, and CTL models with $K = 100$.

6 CONCLUSION

In this paper, we propose the CTL model, a statistical model of semi-structured corpora, based on the topic model to discover highly correlational relationships among the tags observed in the semi-structured corpus. Besides, the experimental results demonstrated that this method can model semi-structured corpora better than the state-of-the-art models when the tags are highly correlated.

In our future study, we will apply the CTL model to more text applications. Another possible direction is to devise parallel algorithms for the CTL model to further improve its efficiency.

ACKNOWLEDGEMENT

We thank the support of China National 973 project 2014CB340304 and Hong Kong CERG projects 16211214 and 16209715.

References

[1] David M. Blei and John D. Lafferty. Correlated topic models. In *NIPS*, 2005.

[2] David M. Blei and Jon D. McAuliffe. Supervised topic models. In *NIPS*, 2007.

[3] David M. Blei, Andrew Y. Ng, and Michael I. Jordan. Latent Dirichlet allocation. *Journal of Machine Learning Research*, 3:993–1022, 2003.

[4] Jordan L. Boyd-Graber and David M. Blei. Syntactic topic models. *CoRR*, abs/1002.4665, 2010.

[5] Andrej Bratko and Bogdan Filipic. Exploiting structural information for semi-structured document categorization. *Information Processing and Management*, 42(3):679 – 694, 2006.

[6] Deng Cai, Qiaozhu Mei, Jiawei Han, and Chengxiang Zhai. Modeling hidden topics on document manifold. In *CIKM*, pages 911–920, 2008.

[7] Chih-Chung Chang and Chih-Jen Lin. Libsvm: A library for support vector machines. *ACM Transactions on Intelligent Systems and Technology*, 2(3):27, 2011.

[8] Xu Chen, Mingyuan Zhou, and Lawrence Carin. The contextual focused topic model. In *KDD*, pages 96–104, 2012.

[9] Hongbo Deng, Jiawei Han, Bo Zhao, Yintao Yu, and Cindy Xide Lin. Probabilistic topic models with biased propagation on heterogeneous information networks. In *KDD*, pages 1271–1279, 2011.

[10] Matthew D. Hoffman, David M. Blei, and Francis R. Bach. Online learning for latent Dirichlet allocation. In *NIPS*, pages 856–864, 2010.

[11] Thomas Hofmann. Probabilistic latent semantic indexing. In *SIGIR*, pages 50–57, 1999.

[12] Michael I. Jordan, Zoubin Ghahramani, Tommi Jaakkola, and Lawrence K. Saul. An introduction to variational methods for graphical models. *Machine Learning*, 37(2):183–233, 1999.

[13] Hugo Larochelle and Stanislas Lauly. A neural autoregressive topic model. In *NIPS*, pages 2717–2725, 2012.

[14] Shuangyin Li, Guan Huang, Ruiyang Tan, and Rong Pan. Tag-weighted Dirichlet allocation. In *ICDM*, pages 438–447, 2013.

[15] Shuangyin Li, Jiefei Li, and Rong Pan. Tag-weighted topic model for mining semi-structured documents. In *IJCAI*, 2013.

[16] Pierre-Francois Marteau, Gildas Ménier, and Eugen Popovici. Weighted naive Bayes model for semi-structured document categorization. *CoRR*, abs/0901.0358, 2009.

[17] Nicolai Meinshausen and Peter Bühlmann. High-dimensional graphs and variable selection with the lasso. *The Annals of Statistics*, pages 1436–1462, 2006.

[18] Rosen-Zvi Michal, Chemudugunta Chaitanya, Griffiths Thomas, Smyth Padhraic, and Steyvers Mark. Learning author-topic models from text corpora. *ACM Transactions on Information Systems*, 28(1):1–38, 2010.

[19] David M. Mimno and Andrew McCallum. Topic models conditioned on arbitrary features with Dirichlet-multinomial regression. In *UAI*, pages 411–418, 2008.

[20] Srivastava Nitish, Ruslan Salakhutdinov, and Geoffrey E. Hinton. Modeling documents with a deep Boltzmann machine. In *UAI*, 2013.

[21] Daniel Ramage, David Hall, Ramesh Nallapati, and Christopher D. Manning. Labeled LDA: A supervised topic model for credit attribution in multi-labeled corpora. In *EMNLP*, pages 248–256, 2009.

[22] Daniel Ramage, Christopher D. Manning, and Susan Dumais. Partially labeled topic models for interpretable text mining. In *SIGKDD*, pages 457–465, 2011.

[23] Timothy N Rubin, America Chambers, Padhraic Smyth, and Mark Steyvers. Statistical topic models for multi-label document classification. *Machine learning*, 88(1-2):157–208, 2012.

[24] Ruslan Salakhutdinov and Geoffrey E. Hinton. Replicated softmax: an undirected topic model. In *NIPS*, pages 1607–1614, 2009.

[25] Nitish Srivastava and Ruslan Salakhutdinov. Learning representations for multimodal data with deep belief nets. In *ICML Workshop*, 2012.

[26] Nitish Srivastava and Ruslan Salakhutdinov. Multimodal learning with deep Boltzmann machines. In *NIPS*, pages 2222–2230, 2012.

[27] Martin J. Wainwright and Michael I. Jordan. Graphical models, exponential families, and variational inference. *Foundations and Trends in Machine Learning*, 1(1-2):1–305, 2008.

[28] Xing Wei and W. Bruce Croft. LDA-based document models for ad-hoc retrieval. In *SIGIR*, pages 178–185, 2006.

Utilize Old Coordinates: Faster Doubly Stochastic Gradients for Kernel Methods

Chun-Liang Li
Machine Learning Department
Carnegie Mellon University
Pittsburgh, PA 15213
chunlial@cs.cmu.edu

Barnabás Póczos
Machine Learning Department
Carnegie Mellon University
Pittsburgh, PA 15213
bapoczos@cs.cmu.edu

Abstract

To address the scalability issue of kernel methods, random features are commonly used for kernel approximation (Rahimi and Recht, 2007). They map the input data to a randomized low-dimensional feature space and apply fast linear learning algorithms on it. However, to achieve high precision results, one might still need a large number of random features, which is infeasible in large-scale applications. Dai et al. (2014) address this issue by recomputing the random features of small batches in each iteration instead of pre-generating for the whole dataset and keeping them in the memory. The algorithm increases the number of random features linearly with iterations, which can reduce the approximation error to arbitrarily small. A drawback of this approach is that the large number of random features slows down the prediction and gradient evaluation after several iterations. We propose two algorithms to remedy this situation by "utilizing" old random features instead of adding new features in certain iterations. By checking the expected descent amount, the proposed algorithm selects "important" old features to update. The resulting procedure is surprisingly simple without enhancing the complexity of the original algorithm but effective in practice. We conduct empirical studies on both medium and large-scale datasets, such as ImageNet, to demonstrate the power of the proposed algorithms.

1 INTRODUCTION

Kernel methods are powerful tools for learning non-linear hypotheses. Many algorithms can be combined with kernel methods, including SVM and logistic regression. However, kernel methods are usually considered as non-scalable due to the kernel matrix $K \in \mathbb{R}^{n \times n}$, where n is the number of examples. For large-scale datasets, such as MNIST-8M (8.1 million) and ImageNet (1.3 million), the memory usage makes kernels methods prohibitive for these applications.

One line of research is devoted to kernel approximation with limited memory usage (Williams and Seeger, 2000; Rahimi and Recht, 2007). Random Features (Rahimi and Recht, 2007), inspired by Bochner's theory, approximate the kernel mapping via a simple sampling procedure. After mapping the input data into the randomized feature space created by random features, we then apply existing fast linear learning algorithms. It has attracted machine learning community's interest because of its simplicity and effectiveness in practice. The extensions of random features include Rahimi and Recht (2008); Yang et al. (2012); Le et al. (2013); Yang et al. (2014); Chen et al. (2015); Bach (2015). However, both theoretical (Rahimi and Recht, 2007) and empirical studies show one might still need a large number of random features to achieve high precision results. If we pre-generate the random features and keep them in the memory, it is still infeasible in modern large-scale applications.

Dai et al. (2014) propose a remedy which generates random features on the fly by connecting functional gradients and random features, which is called *Doubly Stochastic Gradient Descent* (DSG). DSG re-computes the random features for a small batch of data in each iteration instead of keeping them in the memory. The re-computing manner allows DSG to increase the number of random features in every iteration. The algorithm can also be treated as a variant of random coordinate gradient (RCD) algorithm, because DSG updates the newly increased feature (coordinate) in every iteration. Therefore, by increasing the number of features, DSG can achieve arbitrarily small approximation error if one have sufficient budget of time. On the flip side, increasing features in every iteration causes the number of random features to grow linearly with number iterations. After several iterations, the large number of used random features makes prediction and computing gradients slow.

In this paper, we make the following contributions. First,

we solve the drawback of large number of random features by updating old coordinates instead of increasing features in certain iterations (Section 4) to reduce the number of the used random features. One simple extension is sampling from old coordinates uniformly and periodically as typical RCD over the finite dimensions, which is called *DSG with Uniform Sampling* (UDSG). We make the second contribution by analyzing the convergence rate of UDSG. Although UDSG usually works well in practice, our theoretical analysis suggests the descent amount of UDSG is not as much as Dai et al. (2014) in the worst case. We then make our third contribution by proposing the other non-trivial algorithm, *DSG with Checking* (CDSG), which chooses the old coordinate by checking the expected descent amount and derive a expected line search methodology to further boost the performance. Theoretically, CDSG enjoys the same convergence rate as DSG. Empirically, it outperforms other algorithms. Last, we conduct experiments on large-scale datasets, including ImageNet, and further study the comparison with deep neural nets in Section 5. We then conclude in Section 6 and make a guideline of choosing algorithms in practice.

2 PRELIMINARIES

The problem we are interested in this paper is as follows. Assume the data point $(\mathbf{x}, y) \in \mathcal{X} \times \mathcal{Y}$ is an *i.i.d.* sample from a distribution $\mathbb{P}(\mathbf{x}, y)$, where $\mathcal{X} \subseteq \mathbb{R}^d$, we want to estimate a function $f : \mathcal{X} \to \mathcal{Y}$ in Reproducing Hilbert Space (RKHS) $\mathcal{H}$ by optimizing

$$f_* = \underset{f \in \mathcal{H}}{\operatorname{argmin}} R(f) = \underset{f \in \mathcal{H}}{\operatorname{argmin}} \frac{\lambda}{2}\|f\|_{\mathcal{H}}^2 + \mathbb{E}_{(\mathbf{x},y)}[\ell(f(\mathbf{x}), y)], \tag{1}$$

where $\ell(z, y)$ is a convex loss function in z. Commonly used loss functions are hinge loss (SVM), logistic loss (logistic regression) and square loss (ridge regression). Note that if the data comes from a batch setting, we replace the above expectation with the empirical expectation (average).

2.1 RKHS AND KERNEL

The RKHS $\mathcal{H}$ on $\mathcal{X}$ is a Hilbert space of functions from $\mathcal{X}$ to $\mathbb{R}$. One typical way to define RKHS is via kernel functions $k(\mathbf{x}, \mathbf{x}') : \mathcal{X} \times \mathcal{X} \to \mathbb{R}$, which encodes the similarity between two data points. The kernel function k is symmetric and positive definite. $\mathcal{H}$ is RKHS if and only if there exists a kernel $k(\mathbf{x}, \mathbf{x}')$ such that $\forall \mathbf{x} \in \mathcal{X}, k(\mathbf{x}, \cdot) \in \mathcal{H}$ and $\langle k(\mathbf{x}, \cdot), k(\mathbf{x}', \cdot)\rangle_{\mathcal{H}} = k(\mathbf{x}, \mathbf{x}')$. Also, if $f \in \mathcal{H}$, $f(\mathbf{x}) = \langle f, k(\mathbf{x}, \cdot)\rangle_{\mathcal{H}}$. One commonly used kernel is Gaussian RBF kernel $k(\mathbf{x}, \mathbf{x}') = \exp\left(-\frac{\|\mathbf{x}-\mathbf{x}'\|^2}{2\sigma^2}\right)$. The training bottleneck of using kernels is to compute and store the kernel matrix $K \in \mathbb{R}^{n \times n}$ for n data points. It brings the computational concern in both time and space complexity and makes designing scalable algorithms for large-scale problems a challenging task. There are several approach to addressing this difficulty by making trade-off between and time as space. For example, LIBSVM (Chang and Lin, 2011) only caches some columns of kernel matrix to save the memory usage and re-compute the columns where there is a cache miss.

2.2 RANDOM FEATURE

The other way to define kernel is finding the explicit feature mapping $\phi(\mathbf{x})$ such that $k(\mathbf{x}, \mathbf{x}') = \phi(\mathbf{x})^\top \phi(\mathbf{x}')$. Bochner's theorem suggests a way to find this mapping for the stationary (shift-invariant) kernel, *i.e.*, $k(\mathbf{x}, \mathbf{x}') = k(\mathbf{x} - \mathbf{x}')$, and draws the community's attention in this decade (Rahimi and Recht, 2007).

Theorem 1. *(Bochner's Theorem) A continuous, real-valued, symmetric and shift-invariant function k on $\mathbb{R}^d$ is a positive definite kernel if and only if there is a positive finite measure $\mathbb{P}(\boldsymbol{\omega})$ such that*

$$\begin{aligned} k(\mathbf{x} - \mathbf{x}') &= \int_{\mathbb{R}^d} 2\left(\cos(\boldsymbol{\omega}^\top \mathbf{x}) \cos(\boldsymbol{\omega}^\top \mathbf{x}')\right. \\ &\quad \left. + \sin(\boldsymbol{\omega}^\top \mathbf{x}) \sin(\boldsymbol{\omega}^\top \mathbf{x}')\right) d\mathbb{P}(\omega), \end{aligned}$$

For Gaussian RBF kernel, the corresponding density $\mathbb{P}(\omega)$ is the Gaussian distribution.

Inspired from Bochner's Theorem, we can approximate the kernel evaluation by the Monte-Carlo approximation. Define $\phi_\omega(\mathbf{x}) = \sqrt{2}[\cos(\boldsymbol{\omega}^\top \mathbf{x}), \sin(\boldsymbol{\omega}^\top \mathbf{x})]$ and $z(\mathbf{x}) = \frac{1}{\sqrt{m}}[\phi_{\omega_1}(\mathbf{x}), \cdots, \phi_{\omega_m}(\mathbf{x})]$, where $\omega_1, \ldots, \omega_m$ are i.i.d. samples from $\mathbb{P}(\boldsymbol{\omega})$. We then have

$$k(\mathbf{x} - \mathbf{x}') = \mathbb{E}_\omega\left(\phi_\omega(\mathbf{x})\phi_\omega(\mathbf{x}')\right) \approx z(\mathbf{x})^\top z(\mathbf{x}')$$

and (1) can be transformed to

$$\mathbf{w}_* = \underset{\mathbf{w}}{\operatorname{argmin}} \frac{\lambda}{2}\|\mathbf{w}\|^2 + \mathbb{E}_{(\mathbf{x},y)}[l(\mathbf{w}^\top z(\mathbf{x}), y)], \tag{2}$$

which can be solved by fast linear learning algorithms to handle million-scale data easily (Fan et al., 2008).

3 DOUBLY STOCHASTIC KERNEL MACHINE

By using random features, we can represent the feature mapping with a finite-length vector $z(\mathbf{x})$ and approximate the kernel evaluation by the inner product $k(\mathbf{x}, \mathbf{x}') \approx z(\mathbf{x})^\top z(\mathbf{x}')$. We are then able to transform problem (1) into the linear learning problem (2). The approximation error $\mathbb{E}[(f_*(\mathbf{x}) - \mathbf{w}_*^\top(\mathbf{x}))^2] \leq \epsilon$ can be bounded by ϵ with $O(1/\epsilon)$ number of random features (Rahimi and Recht, 2007), which is the consequence of the bound of Monte-Carlo approximation. More discussions on the optimality can be referred to Sriperumbudur and Szabó (2015).

Suppose we use m random features for approximation, then the space complexity for storing the transformed data is $O(nm)$, where n is the number of data points. One line of research is to replace the simple Monte-Carlo with different sampling scheme to improve the learning with random features. Le et al. (2013) propose an efficient sampling procedure to save the feature generation time. Yang et al. (2014); Chen et al. (2015); Bach (2015) use different sampling strategies with faster convergence rate to reduce m.

In practice, to achieve accurate results, m usually has to be large, which cause the space cost for storing. For example, MNIST-8M data contains eight million training points. If we use 10^5 random features with `double` type, it takes more than 1T memory to store the transformed data, which is prohibitive to many machines. On the other hand, the kernel matrix K is approximated by $z(\mathbf{X})z(\mathbf{X})^\top$, where $z(\mathbf{X}) \in \mathbb{R}^{n\times m}$. However, K is not low rank and has long-tailed eigenvalue distributions for many commonly used kernels (Weyl, 1912; Wathen and Zhu, 2015), which implies there is no hope to accurately approximate K with small m.

Therefore, the other line of research is to save memory usage with large m. Yen et al. (2014) propose a algorithm by imposing a sparsity constraint in (2) to reduce the memory usage. However, the sparsity constraint makes the problem not an unbiased approximation of (1). Dai et al. (2014) propose to re-generate the random features repeatedly during the training to save the memory usage, which makes using a large number of random features possible.

3.1 DOUBLY STOCHASTIC GRADIENT

Dai et al. (2014) propose a novel algorithm by using "doubly functional gradient" to address the scalability issue of kernel methods. Given a data point $(\mathbf{x}, y)$, the stochastic functional gradient of (1) is $\nabla_f R(f) = \lambda f(\cdot) + \mathbb{E}_{(\mathbf{x},y)}[\xi(\cdot)]$, where $\xi(\cdot) = \ell'(f(\mathbf{x}), y)k(\mathbf{x}, \cdot)$. By Bocher's theorem, we could further approximate the functional gradient $\xi(\cdot)$ by the random feature $\phi_\omega(\mathbf{x})$. That is, given $\omega \sim \mathbb{P}(\omega)$ and a data point $(\mathbf{x}, y)$, the doubly stochastic gradient of $\ell(f(\mathbf{x}), y)$ with respect to $f \in \mathcal{H}$ is $\zeta(\cdot) = l'(f(\mathbf{x}), y)\phi_\omega(\mathbf{x})\phi_\omega(\cdot)$, where $\mathbb{E}_\omega(\zeta(\cdot)) = \xi(\cdot)$. The following formula connects the randomness from data $(\mathbf{x}, y)$ and random feature ω,

$$\begin{aligned}\nabla_f R(f) &= \lambda f(\cdot) + \mathbb{E}_{(\mathbf{x},y)}[\xi(\cdot)] \\ &= \lambda f(\cdot) + \mathbb{E}_{(\mathbf{x},y)}\mathbb{E}_\omega[\zeta(\cdot)].\end{aligned}$$

In each iteration t, the doubly stochastic gradient of $\ell(f(\mathbf{x}_t), y_t)$ is $\zeta_t(\cdot) = \ell'(f_t(\mathbf{x}_t), y_t)\phi_{\omega_t}(\mathbf{x}_t)\phi_{\omega_t}(\cdot)$ by sampling ω_t from $\mathbb{P}(\omega)$ and $(\mathbf{x}_t, y_t)$ from $\mathbb{P}(\mathbf{x}, y)$. The update rule for the algorithm is

$$f_{t+1}(\cdot) = f_t(\cdot) - \gamma_t\left(\lambda f_t(\cdot) + \zeta_t(\cdot)\right) = \sum_{i=1}^{t} a_t^i \zeta_i(\cdot),$$

where a_t^i are coefficients from λ and γ_t in each iteration. For each data point $\mathbf{x}$, we do not need to pre-generate the corresponding $z(\mathbf{x})$ until we want to evaluate the function as well as the doubly stochastic gradient on $\mathbf{x}$. The potential problem is how to regenerate the $z(\mathbf{x})$ every time. If we store $\omega_1, \ldots, \omega_t$, which takes $O(dt)$, when both d and t are large, it is still infeasible in practice. Thanks for the pseudo-randomness used in modern computers, we could use different random seeds for different iterations, then we are guaranteed to sample the same ω back. Then the space complexity is only $O(t)$ for storing $\alpha_t^i = a_t^i \ell'(f_i(\mathbf{x}_i), y_i)\phi_\omega(\mathbf{x}_i)$. We call the algorithm as DSG, which is shown in Algorithm 1. The convergence rate of DSG is proved in Dai et al. (2014) under the conditions of Assumption 2.

Algorithm 1 $\{\alpha_i\}_{i=1}^t$ = **DSG**($\mathbb{P}(\mathbf{x}, y)$)

```
for i = 1, ..., t do
    Sample (x_i, y_i) ~ P(x, y).
    Sample ω_i ~ P(ω) with seed i.
    f(x_i) = Predict(x_i, {α_j}_{j=1}^{i-1}).
    α_i = -γ_i l'(f(x_i), y_i) φ_{ω_i}(x_i).
    α_j = (1 - γ_i λ) α_j for j = 1, ..., i - 1.
end for
```

Algorithm 2 $f(\mathbf{x})$ = **Predict**($\mathbf{x}$, $\{\alpha_i\}_{i=1}^m$)

```
Set f(x) = 0.
for i = 1, ..., m do
    Sample ω_i ~ P(ω) with seed i.
    f(x) = f(x) + α_i φ_{ω_i}(x).
end for
```

Assumption 2.

1. *The optimal solution f_* to the problem* (1) *exists.*
2. *Loss function $\ell(u, y) : \mathbb{R} \times \mathbb{R} \to \mathbb{R}$ and its first-order derivative is L-Lipschitz continous in terms of the first argument.*
3. *There exists $M > 0$, such that $|\ell'(f_t(\mathbf{x}_t), y_t)| \leqslant M$. Note that in our situation $M < \infty$ exists since we assume bounded domain and the functions f_t we generate are always bounded as well.*
4. *There exists $\kappa > 0$ and $\phi > 0$, such that $k(\mathbf{x}, \mathbf{x}') \leqslant \kappa$, $|\phi_\omega(\mathbf{x})\phi_\omega(\mathbf{x}')| \leqslant \phi, \forall \mathbf{x}, \mathbf{x}' \in \mathcal{X}, \omega \in \Omega$. For Gaussian RBF kernel, we have $\kappa = 1$, $\phi = 2$.*

Theorem 3 (Convergence rate of DSG (Dai et al., 2014)). *When $\gamma_t = \frac{\theta}{t}$ with $\theta > 0$ such that $\theta\lambda \in (1, 2) \cup \mathbb{Z}_+$, for any $x \in \mathcal{X}$,*

$$\mathbb{E}_{\mathcal{D}^t, \omega^t}\left[|f_{t+1}(x) - f_*(x)|^2\right] \leqslant \frac{2C_0^2 + 2\kappa S_0^2}{t},$$

where

$$S_0 = \max\left\{\|f_*\|_{\mathcal{H}}, \frac{Q_0 + \sqrt{Q_0^2 + Z(1+\theta\lambda)^2\theta^2\kappa M^2}}{Z}\right\},$$

with $Z = 2\lambda\theta - 1$, $Q_0 = \sqrt{2}\kappa^{1/2}LC_0\theta$, *and* $C_0 = 2(\kappa + \phi)M\theta$.

4 FAST DOUBLY STOCHASTIC KERNEL MACHINES

The $O(1/t)$ convergence rate in Theorem 3 is already optimal as proved in Dai et al. (2014). However, we could still improve DSG. In in each iteration, DSG is required to evaluate $f(\mathbf{x})$ for calculating gradients in each iteration, which needs to go through $\omega_1, \dots, \omega_t$ to compute $\phi_{\omega_i}(\mathbf{x})$ in Algorithm 2. For continuous distributions, such as Gaussian distribution $\mathbb{P}(\omega)$ for Gaussian kernel, the collision probability of sampling is zero. After t iterations, we have t different $\omega_1, \dots, \omega_t$ for the feature generation. Then the complexity of the tth iteration is $O(td)$, and the total complexity from iteration 1 to iteration t is $O(t^2d)$, which makes DSG less efficient when t is large.

On the other hand, DSG could be treated as a random coordinate descent (RCD) with mini-batch. In each iteration t, sampling ω_t can be treated as choosing one coordinate to update. Since the collision probability is zero, it is equivalent to updating a new coordinate in every iteration. From the perspective of RCD, we could also choose an "old" coordinate to update instead of sampling new ω in certain iterations. Then we could reduce the number of used coordinates.

In what follows, we will present two algorithms, UDSG and CDSG, which "utilize" previous coordinates. UDSG is a nature extension from RCD. Studying its theoretical analysis gives us deeper insight to design the non-trivial algorithm CDSG, which enjoys the better bound of sample complexity than UDSG. In some following descriptions, we will abuse ω_i as the coordinate index for convenience.

4.1 UTILIZE WITH UNIFORM SAMPLING

A simple strategy is using empirical distribution to approximate $\mathbb{P}(\omega)$, which is a widely-used technique in statistics. Assume we already independently sample $\mathbf{\Omega}^m = \{\omega_1, \dots, \omega_m\}$ from $\mathbb{P}(\omega)$, then we could create an empirical distribution $\hat{\mathbb{P}}_m(\omega)$, which is a uniform distribution on $\omega_1, \dots, \omega_m$. Sampling from $\hat{\mathbb{P}}_m(\omega)$ is unbiased since $\mathbb{E}_{\mathbf{\Omega}^m}\mathbb{E}_{\omega\sim\hat{\mathbb{P}}_m}[\omega|\mathbf{\Omega}^m] = \mathbb{E}_{\omega\sim\mathbb{P}}(\omega)$. When m is large, we could expect the empirical distribution $\hat{\mathbb{P}}_m(\omega)$ to be a good approximation of $\mathbb{P}(\omega)$. Note that it is similar to typical RCD algorithm over a finite number of dimensions.

Here we study one simple algorithm for a concise presentation, which periodically samples from $\mathbb{P}(\omega)$ for G iterations and then sample from the empirical distribution $\hat{\mathbb{P}}(\omega)$ for U iterations. The number of random features m after t iterations is $O(Gt/G + U)$. The proposed algorithm, doubly stochastic gradients descent with uniform sampling, which is called UDSG and shown in Algorithm 3. Based on Assumption 2, the convergence rate of UDSG is shown in Theorem 4.

Algorithm 3 $\{\alpha_i\}_{i=1}^m$ = **UDSG**($\mathbb{P}(\mathbf{x}, y)$)

```
m = 0
for i = 1, ..., t do
  Sample (x_i, y_i) ~ P(x, y).
  f(x_i) = Predict(x_i, {α_j}_{j=1}^m).
  if mod(i, G + U) < G then
    Sample ω_{m+1} ~ P(ω) with seed m + 1.
    α_j = (1 − γ_i λ)α_j for j = 1, ..., m.
    α_{m+1} = −γ_i ℓ'(f(x_i), y_i) φ_{ω_{m+1}}(x_i).
    m = m + 1
  else
    Sample ω_k ~ P̂_m(ω), where 1 ≤ k ≤ m.
    α_j = (1 − γ_i λ)α_j for j = 1, ..., m.
    α_k = α_k − γ_i ℓ'(f(x_i), y_i) φ_{ω_k}(x_i).
  end if
end for
```

Theorem 4 (Convergence rate of UDSG). *When* $\gamma_t = \frac{\theta}{t}$ *with* $\theta > 0$ *such that* $\theta\lambda \in (1, 2) \cup \mathbb{Z}_+$, *for any* $\mathbf{x} \in \mathcal{X}$,

$$\mathbb{E}_{\mathcal{D}^t,\omega^t}\left[|f_{t+1}(\mathbf{x}) - f_*(\mathbf{x})|^2\right] \leqslant \frac{2C_1^2 + 2\kappa S_1^2}{t},$$

where

$$S_1 = \max\left\{\|f_*\|_{\mathcal{H}}, \frac{Q_1 + \sqrt{Q_1^2 + Z(1+\theta\lambda)^2\theta^2\kappa M^2}}{Z}\right\},$$

with $Z = 2\lambda\theta - 1$, $Q_1 = \sqrt{2}\kappa^{1/2}LC_1\theta$, *and* $C_1 = 2(\kappa + \phi)M\theta\sqrt{1 + \frac{2U}{G+U} + \frac{2U^2}{G(G+U)} + \frac{2U(U-1)}{Gt}}$

4.1.1 PROOF OF THEOREM 4

We provide a proof sketch here. Our analysis closely follows Dai et al. (2014) but we need to carefully deal with several cross-terms as shown in (3) later. Some technical lemmas are in Appendix.

We decompose the error into two terms,

$$|f_t(\mathbf{x}) - f^*(\mathbf{x})|^2 \leq 2|f_t(\mathbf{x}) - h_t(\mathbf{x})|^2 + 2\kappa\|h_t - f^*\|_{\mathcal{H}}^2,$$

where

$$h_t(\cdot) = \mathbb{E}_\omega[f_t(\cdot)] = \mathbb{E}_\omega[\sum_{i=1}^t a_t^i \zeta_{\omega_i}(\cdot)] = \sum_{i=1}^t a_t^i \xi_{\omega_i}(\cdot).$$

Since $\mathbb{E}_{\mathcal{D}^t,\omega^t}\left[\|h_{t+1} - f_*\|_{\mathcal{H}}^2\right] \leqslant \frac{S^2}{t}$, where S is a constant related to $\mathbb{E}_{\mathcal{D}^t,\omega^t}\left(|f_{t+1}(\mathbf{x}) - h_{t+1}(\mathbf{x})|^2\right)$ as shown in Dai et al. (2014), the remaining task is to bound $\mathbb{E}_{\mathcal{D}^t,\omega^t}\left(|f_{t+1}(\mathbf{x}) - h_{t+1}(\mathbf{x})|^2\right)$. We define the following terms to simplify the notations.

- $\mathcal{G} = \{x | (x-1) \bmod (G+U) < G \text{ and } 1 \le x \le t\}$.
- $\mathcal{G}_k = \{x | x \in \mathcal{G} \text{ and } \lceil x/(G+U) \rceil = k\}$.
- $\mathcal{U}_k = \{x | x \notin \mathcal{G}, \lceil x/(G+U) \rceil = k \text{ and } 1 \le x \le t\}$.
- $V_i(\mathbf{x}) = a_t^i (\zeta_t(\mathbf{x}) - \xi_t(\mathbf{x}))$.

By definition, we have $\mathbb{E}_{\mathcal{D}^t,\omega^t}(|f_{t+1}(\mathbf{x}) - h_{t+1}(\mathbf{x})|^2) = \mathbb{E}_{\mathcal{D}^t,\omega^t}\left[\left(\sum_{i=1}^t V_i(\mathbf{x})\right)^2\right]$, then

$$
\begin{aligned}
&\mathbb{E}_{\mathcal{D}^t,\omega^t}\left[\left(\sum_{i=1}^t V_i(\mathbf{x})\right)^2\right] \\
= \;& \mathbb{E}_{\mathcal{D}^t,\omega^t}\left[\left(\sum_{\mathcal{G}} V_i(\mathbf{x}) + \sum_{k=1}^{\lceil t/(G+U)\rceil} \sum_{i\in\mathcal{U}_k} V_i(\mathbf{x})\right)^2\right] \\
\le \;& \mathbb{E}_{\mathcal{D}^t,\omega^t}\left[\left(\sum_{\mathcal{G}} V_i(\mathbf{x})\right)^2 + \sum_{k=1}^{\lceil t/(G+U)\rceil} \left(\sum_{i\in\mathcal{U}_k} V_i(\mathbf{x})\right)^2\right. \\
&+2\sum_{k=1}^{\lceil t/(G+U)\rceil}\left(\sum_{i\in\mathcal{U}_k} V_i(\mathbf{x})\right)\left(\sum_{\mathcal{G}} V_i(\mathbf{x})\right) \\
&\left.\sum_{p=1}^{\lceil \frac{t}{G+U}\rceil -1}\sum_{q=p+1}^{\lceil \frac{t}{G+U}\rceil}\left(\sum_{i\in\mathcal{U}_p} V_i(\mathbf{x})\right)\left(\sum_{i\in\mathcal{U}_q} V_i(\mathbf{x})\right)\right].
\end{aligned} \tag{3}
$$

We complete the proof by bounding each term. For details please refer to the Appendix.

4.1.2 TOTAL COMPLEXITY

The sample complexity bound in Theorem 4 is clearly worse than the result in Theorem 3 for DSG. However, we should take the complexity of single iteration into account for comparison. After t iterations, the ratio of the number of used ω between UDSG and DSG is $O(G/G+U)$.

We suppose Q_1^2 in Theorem 4 dominates $Z(1+\theta\lambda)^2\theta^2\kappa M^2$. Also, we assume $S_0 > \|f_*\|_{\mathcal{H}}$ and $S_1 > \|f_*\|_{\mathcal{H}}$ in Theorem 3 and Theorem 4, respectively. The ratio between sample complexities of Theorem 3 and Theorem 4 is close to $O(1+\frac{2U}{G+U}+\frac{2U^2}{G(G+U)}+\frac{2U(U-1)}{Gt})$. Then the ratio r between the total complexity of DSG and UDSG is

$$
\begin{aligned}
r &\ge \left(1+\frac{2U}{G+U}+\frac{2U^2}{G(G+U)}\right)\times\frac{G}{G+U} \\
&= \left(1+\frac{2U}{G+U}\times\frac{G+U}{G}\right)\frac{G}{G+U} \\
&= \frac{G+2U}{G+U},
\end{aligned}
$$

This result suggests setting U to be zero to minimize the complexity, which implies DSG is theoretically no worse than UDSG under certain conditions. However, this pessimistic result inspires us to design a better algorithm in Section 4.2.

4.2 UTILIZE WITH CHECKING

In each iteration t, we could either pick up the coordinate we have used, or sample a new coordinate from $\mathbb{P}(\omega)$ to update. The uniform sampling strategy algorithm, UDSG, has a worse bound than DSG, which implies updating a new coordinate $\omega \sim \mathbb{P}(\omega)$ reduces the objective more than updating old coordinates in expectation. Therefore, before updating, we should "*check*" the old coordinate to ensure the chosen coordinate ω_k is as effective as the newly sampled coordinate $\omega \sim \mathbb{P}(\omega)$.

We start by investigating the reason that causes UDSG to be worse than DSG in expectation. We take the simple case that we sample $\omega_1, \ldots, \omega_{t-1}$ from $\mathbb{P}(\omega)$ as DSG and set $\omega_t = \omega_k$, where $1 \le k \le t-1$. Then $\mathbb{E}_{\mathcal{D}^t,\omega^t}(|f_{t+1}(\mathbf{x}) - h_{t+1}(\mathbf{x})|^2) = \mathbb{E}_{\mathcal{D}^t,\omega^t}\left[\left((\sum_{i=1,i\neq k}^{t-1} V_i(\mathbf{x})) + (V_k(\mathbf{x}) + V_t(\mathbf{x}))\right)^2\right]$. We abbreviate $\mathbb{E}_{\mathcal{D}^t,\omega^t}(\cdot)$ as $\mathbb{E}(\cdot)$ in the following context for a succinct representation.

Lemma 5. *(Dai et al., 2014)*

If ω_i and ω_j are i.i.d. samples from $\mathbb{P}(\omega)$, $\mathbb{E}\left[(V_i(\mathbf{x}) + V_j(\mathbf{x}))^2\right] = \mathbb{E}\left(V_i(\mathbf{x})^2\right) + \mathbb{E}\left(V_j(\mathbf{x})^2\right)$.

We then have the bound

$$
\begin{aligned}
&\mathbb{E}\left[\left(\sum_{i=1}^t V_i(\mathbf{x})\right)^2\right] \\
\le\; &\sum_{i=1,i\neq k}^{t-1} \mathbb{E}\left(V_i(\mathbf{x})^2\right) + \mathbb{E}\left[(|V_k(\mathbf{x})| + |V_t(\mathbf{x})|)^2\right].
\end{aligned} \tag{4}
$$

In contrast, the bound of DSG is

$$
\mathbb{E}_{\mathcal{D}^t,\omega^t}\left[\left(\sum_{i=1}^t V_i(\mathbf{x})\right)^2\right] \le \sum_{i=1}^t \mathbb{E}_{\mathcal{D}^t,\omega^t}\left(V_i(\mathbf{x})^2\right). \tag{5}
$$

The cross term $\mathbb{E}_{\mathcal{D}^t,\omega^t}(|V_k(\mathbf{x})||V_t(\mathbf{x})|)$ from expanding the quadratic term in (4) causes a worse bound than (5). The generalization of this simple example is Theorem 4 in Section 4.1. The cross terms cause a larger constant C_1 in Theorem 4 than C_0 in Theorem 3.

Without any further knowledge about $V_k(\mathbf{x})$ and $V_t(\mathbf{x})$, the upper bound in (4) is unavoidable. Therefore, in iteration t, we should choose $1 \le k \le t-1$ such that the upper bound U_t of $\mathbb{E}\left[(V_k(\mathbf{x}) + V_t(\mathbf{x}))^2\right]$ can be bounded by the bound of $\mathbb{E}\left(V_k(\mathbf{x})^2\right) + \mathbb{E}\left(V_t(\mathbf{x})^2\right)$. To be specific, we should select k such that

$$
U_t \le \mathbb{E}\left[\left(a_t^k \ell'(f_k(\mathbf{x}_k), y_k)\right)^2 + \left(a_t^t \ell'(f_t(\mathbf{x}_t), y_t)\right)^2\right](\kappa+\phi)^2. \tag{6}
$$

For convenience, we let $g_i = \ell'(f_i(\mathbf{x}_i), y_i)$ and $\Phi_{\mathbf{x}}(\omega_i, \mathbf{x}_k) = \phi_{\omega_i}(\mathbf{x}_k)\phi_{\omega_k}(\mathbf{x}) - k(\mathbf{x}_k, \mathbf{x})$. Expanding

$V_k(\mathbf{x})$ and $V_t(\mathbf{x})$ results the upper bound U_t as

$$\begin{aligned} & \mathbb{E}\left[(V_k(\mathbf{x}) + V_t(\mathbf{x}))^2\right] \\ = & \mathbb{E}\left[\left(a_t^k g_k \Phi_{\mathbf{x}}(\omega_k, \mathbf{x}_k) + a_t^t g_t \Phi_{\mathbf{x}}(\omega_t, \mathbf{x}_t) + \right.\right. \\ & \left.\left. a_t^t g_t \Phi_{\mathbf{x}}(\omega_k, \mathbf{x}_k) - a_t^t g_t \Phi_{\mathbf{x}}(\omega_k, \mathbf{x}_k)\right)^2\right] \\ \leq & 2\mathbb{E}\left[\left(a_t^k g_k + a_t^t g_t\right)^2\right](\kappa + \phi)^2 \\ & +2\left((a_t^t M)^2\right)\mathbb{E}\left[\left(\Phi_{\mathbf{x}}(\omega_k, \mathbf{x}_t) - \Phi_{\mathbf{x}}(\omega_k, \mathbf{x}_k)\right)^2\right]. \end{aligned} \tag{7}$$

Note that we suppose $\omega_t = \omega_k$.

If x_1 and x_2 are *i.i.d.* samples from $\mathbb{P}(x)$, then $\mathbb{E}\left((x_1 - x_2)^2\right) = 2\mathrm{Var}(x)$. Let $\sigma^2 = \mathbb{E}_{\omega_k}\left[\mathrm{Var}_y\left(\Phi_{\mathbf{x}}(\omega_k, y)\right)\right]$ and $\beta_t^k = a_t^k g_k$. Incorporating (7) into (6) with the above fact of variance results the selection criterion as choosing ω_k such that

$$\begin{aligned} & 2\mathbb{E}\left[(\beta_t^k + a_t^t g_t)^2\right](\kappa + \phi)^2 + 2\left(a_t^t M \sigma(\kappa + \phi)\right)^2 \\ \leq & \mathbb{E}\left[(\beta_t^k)^2 + (a_t^t g_t)^2\right](\kappa + \phi)^2. \end{aligned} \tag{8}$$

4.2.1 MINI-BATCH AND EXPECTED LINE SEARCH

In (8), smaller $a_t^t M \sigma(\kappa + \phi)$ makes it easier to find an ω_k which satisfies (8). Reducing $a_t^t M \sigma(\kappa + \phi)$ comes for free by using the mini-batch extension of stochastic gradient descent. If the batch size is B, the variance of $\frac{1}{B}\sum_{i=1}^{B} \Phi_{\mathbf{x}_i}(\omega_k, y)$ is $\frac{1}{B}\mathrm{Var}_y\left(\Phi_{\mathbf{x}}(\omega_k, y)\right)$.

Also, instead of setting $a_t^t = -\gamma_t$, we could further do line-search in expectation for a steeper descent with a larger step size. Assume the step size is η, and we want to keep the error upper bounded by DSG. Therefore, given $\omega_1, \ldots, \omega_{t-1}$, combining with the mini-batch extension, We find the largest step size $\eta < -\gamma_t$, such that

$$2(\beta_t^k + \eta g_t)^2 + \frac{2\left(\eta M \sigma\right)^2}{B^2} \leq (\beta_t^k)^2 + (a_t^t g_t)^2. \tag{9}$$

The optimization problem (9) is a quadratic inequality, which can be solved with the analytical solution. We then choose ω_k with the max step size $|\eta_k|$ to update. We call the algorithm as "doubly stochastic gradient descent with checking" (CDSG), which is shown in Algorithm 4. For simplicity, we show the case when $B = 1$ in Algorithm 4, but one can extend it to general $B > 1$ cases.

Convergence rate of CDSG. The convergence rate of CDSG is exactly the same as Theorem 3. We omit the proof in the Appendix.

5 EXPERIMENT

In this section, we first study medium-scale data, which allows us to do thorough comparisons to understand the trade-off between different algorithms. We then also show the results on the large-scale datasets. Last, we compare DSG-based algorithms with deep neural nets. The details of the datasets are shown in Table 1.

Algorithm 4 $\{\alpha_i\}_{i=1}^m = \mathbf{CDSG}(\mathbb{P}(\mathbf{x}, y))$

```
m = 0
for i = 1, ..., t do
  Sample (x_i, y_i) ~ P(x, y).
  f(x_i) = Predict(x_i, {α_j}_{j=1}^m).
  Compute step sizes η_1, ..., η_m via (9), and suppose
  |η_k| = argmax_j |η_j|.
  if |η_j| ≤ γ_t then
    α_j = (1 − γ_i λ)α_j for j = 1, ..., m.
    α_{m+1} = −γ_i ℓ'(f(x_i), y_i) φ_{ω_{m+1}}(x_i).
    β_j = (1 − γ_i λ)β_j for j = 1, ..., m.
    β_{m+1} = −γ_i ℓ'(f(x_i), y_i).
    m = m + 1
  else
    α_j = (1 − η_k λ)α_j for j = 1, ..., m.
    α_k = α_k − η_k ℓ'(f(x_i), y_i) φ_{ω_k}(x_i).
    β_j = (1 − η_k λ)α_j for j = 1, ..., m.
    β_k = α_k − η_k ℓ'(f(x_i), y_i).
  end if
end for
```

Dataset	# train	# test	# classes
CIFAR-10	60K	10K	10
Epsilon	0.4M	0.1M	2
Year	0.46M	51K	$\mathbb{R}$
MNIST-8M	8.1 M	10K	10
ImageNet 2012	1.3 M	0.1M	1000

Table 1: The dataset information for experiments, where the label of Year is real number.

General Setting In all experiments, we use Gaussian kernel. The kernel bandwidth is obtained by the median trick (Smola, 2004). For UDSG, we set $G = 1$ and $U = 1$. The other parameters will be specified later.

5.1 MEDIUM-SCALE DATA

We observed that the algorithms tend to overfit the medium-scale data without carefully tunning regularization terms. In this subsection, we only compare the training objectives, which is a natural criterion for optimization problems.

Setting for Medium-Scale Data For the CIFAR-10, we use raw pixels as input. Also, we conduct PCA to reduce the number of dimension of every datasets to be no more than 100. The parameters for DSG-based algorithms are shown in Table 2, where the feature block F means we sample F random features in each iteration. For non-DSG-

Dataset	Batch Size B	Feature Block F	λ
CIFAR10	$4,096$	256	10^{-5}
Epsilon	$10,000$	512	10^{-5}
Year	$10,000$	512	10^{-5}

Table 2: Parameters for DSG-based algorithms on medium-scale datasets.

based algorithms, which pre-generate random features for the data points, we set the number of random features as $4F$.

Compare with Other Approximation There are several competitors that can be considered, such as Kivinen et al. (2004), kernel SDCA (Shalev-Shwartz and Zhang, 2013), and several stochastic optimization algorithms with random feature or Nyström method (Shalev-Shwartz and Zhang, 2013; Johnson and Zhang, 2013; Nesterov, 2012). Here we only choose SVRG (Johnson and Zhang, 2013) with random features, which has been shown to be one of the best among the above algorithms.

We compare DSG, UDSG, CDSG and SVRG (Johnson and Zhang, 2013) with multi-class kernel logistic regression and kernel ridge regression. The results are shown in Figure 1.

We first look at Figure 1(a), Figure 1(b) and Figure 1(c). Since we only use $4F$ random features for SVRG, is not surprising that SVRG with limited random features converges to unsatisfactory results at the early stage. Without the enough number of the random features, the bottleneck of the learning is the approximation error instead of the optimization algorithms. Although we can use more features than $4F$ to achieve better performance for medium-scale data, it takes longer time and more memory for training. This issue becomes more critical in the large-scale applications. The memory usage can even make this approach prohibitive to large-scale problems. Note that we do not show SVRG in Figure 1(d), Figure 1(e) and Figure 1(f) since it converges out of the range.

Second, we compare DSG-based algorithms. In Figure 1(b), UDSG performs worse than DSG, which confirms the bound of Theorem 4 and the worst-case discussion of uniform sampling in Section 4.2. However, we observe that the worst case does not occur often in practice. Although the analysis in Section 4.1.2 is pessimistic, UDSG generally outperforms DSG in Figure 1. On the other hand, the proposed CDSG outperforms both DSG and UDSG in all datasets, which justifies the correctness of the validity of the proposed checking rule and expected line search in Section 4.2.

Compare with Exact Optimization We compare DSG-based algorithms with LIBSVM (Chang and Lin, 2011), which is the state-of-the-art solver for kernel learning by using kernel matrices. We consider kernel SVM in this comparison since there is no kernel logistic regression implementation in LIBSVM. We report the performance of each algorithm when LIBSVM converges. CIFAR-10 and Epsilon take LIBSVM 583 and 8457 seconds to converge, respectively. The results are shown in Table 3.

	LIBSVM	DSG	UDSG	CDSG
CIFAR-10	0.386	0.407	0.402	0.402
Epsilon	0.143	0.145	0.146	0.145

Table 3: The training error of each algorithm at the time when LIBSVM converges.

In these experiments, to achieve high-precision results, the exact optimization is always preferable in practice if we have enough memory. We observe that in both CIFAR-10 and Epsilon, DSG-based algorithms achieve the satisfactory performance quickly, but they take longer time to converge to the precise results. For example, all DSG-based algorithms can achieve 0.15 error of Epsilon within 150 seconds. Especially, CDSG can achieve 0.147. However, they take more than $10,000$ seconds to get the error lower than 0.144. We address this issue to the variance from doubly stochastic methodology, which requires the learning rate to be small and make the learning slow in the later iterations as the typical SGD algorithms (Johnson and Zhang, 2013; Shalev-Shwartz and Zhang, 2013).

5.2 LARGE-SCALE DATA

We study MNIST-8M digit recognition dataset, which contains 8.1 million training data and 10 classes. We reduce the raw pixel to 100 dimensions as feature and set $B = 20,000$, $F = 4096$ and $\lambda = 10^{-6}$. LIBSVM cannot run on this dataset due to the memory limitation, and we can only load 500 pre-generated random features into our memory, which results in unsatisfactory result (0.05 training and testing error) with any algorithms, such as SVRG. Therefore, we focus on the comparison on DSG-based algorithms. The result is shown in Figure 2[1].

As one can see from Figure 2, CDSG consistently outperforms the other two algorithms in both training objectives and testing error as well as under different loss functions. The results justify the correctness and usefulness of the proposed CDSG again. In contrast, UDSG does not perform as well as Figure 1, which confirms the worst case analysis in Theorem 4.

5.3 STUDY WITH DEEP NEURAL NET

We follow Dai et al. (2014) to compare DSG-based algorithms with deep neural nets on image classification

[1]Compared with multi-class logistic regression, the training objective of one-vs-one kernel SVM is less meaningful, so we do not compare it.

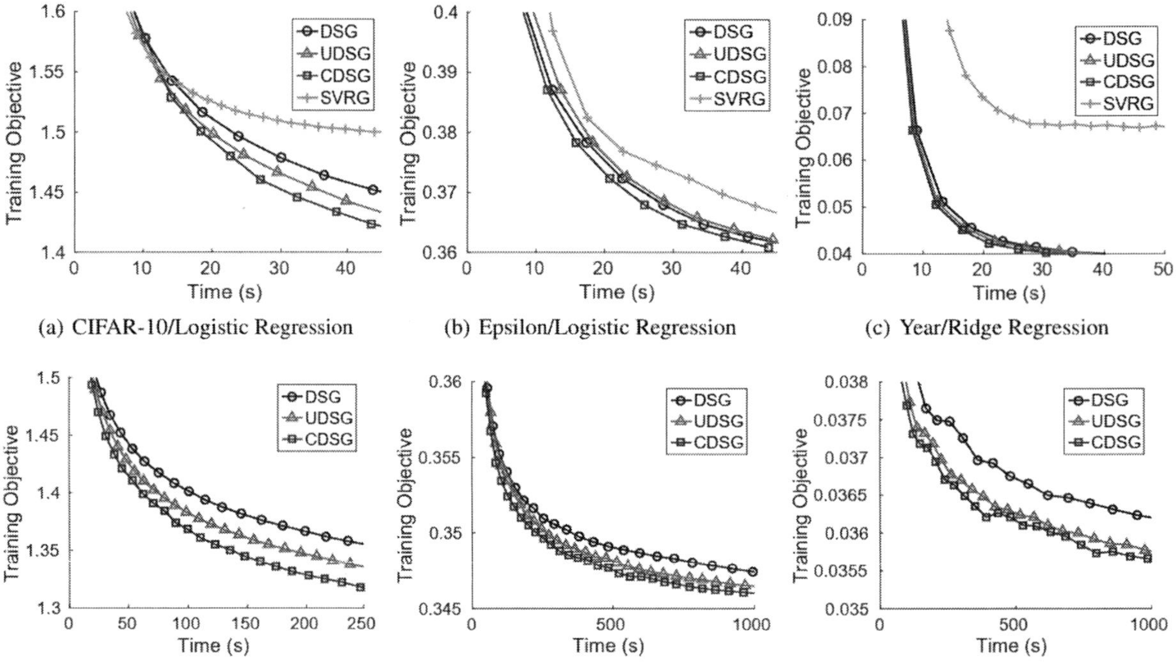

(a) CIFAR-10/Logistic Regression (b) Epsilon/Logistic Regression (c) Year/Ridge Regression

(d) CIFAR-10/Logistic Regression (e) Epsilon/Logistic Regression (f) Year/Ridge Regression

Figure 1: Training objective of different algorithms on each datasets.

Data	Batch Size b	Feature Block r	λ
CIFAR-10	32768	512	0.0005
MNIST-8M	16384	512	0.0005
ImageNet	16384	128	0.0005

Table 4: The parameters for DSG-based algorithms.

tasks. Besides CIFAR-10 and MNIST-8M, we also study ImageNet-2012, which is one of the most challenging image classification data currently. Since we do not aim to compare the representation learning ability, we use the pre-trained features provided by Dai et al. (2014). The detailed information of the used neural-net architectures (LeCun et al., 1998; Krizhevsky et al., 2012) can be found in the Appendix.

We study the following algorithms and the parameters are shown in Table 4.

- **Joint:** Put two fully connected layers at the top of the neural net for classification and train these two layers and the pre-trained layers "jointly".
- **Fixed:** Put two fully connected layers at the top of the neural net for classification and only train these two layers and without modifying pre-trained layers.
- **DSG-based:** Apply DSG algorithms on the pre-trained features.

	DSG	UDSG	CDSG	Fixed	Joint
CIFAR-10	16.0	15.9	**15.8**	18.0	19.1
MNIST-8M	6.1	5.9	**5.3**	7.1	8.5
ImageNet	45.1	44.9	**44.7**	48.2	58.6

Table 5: The testing error (%) of each dataset when CDSG converges.

	DSG	UDSG	CDSG	Fixed	Joint
CIFAR-10	15.8	15.9	**15.8**	15.8	15.9
MNIST-8M	5.3	5.4	**5.3**	7.1	6.2
ImageNet	44.9	44.8	44.7	46.2	**42.4**

Table 6: The converged results (%) of all algorithms for each dataset.

Since the joint-trained neural net takes much more time than other algorithms, we report the results when CDSG converges in Table 5. The result shows that DSG-based algorithms converge faster than deep neural nets, and CDSG is the best in this family. For example, CDSG converges to 44.7% testing error on ImageNet. At the same time, the joint-trained neural net only achieves 58.6% testing error.

The converged results of all algorithms are shown in Table 6. In both CIFAR-10 and MNIST-8M, the CDSG algorithm is better than neural nets, which suggests proposed CDSG is not only efficient but also effective in some tasks. However, in ImageNet, the joint-trained neural net is still

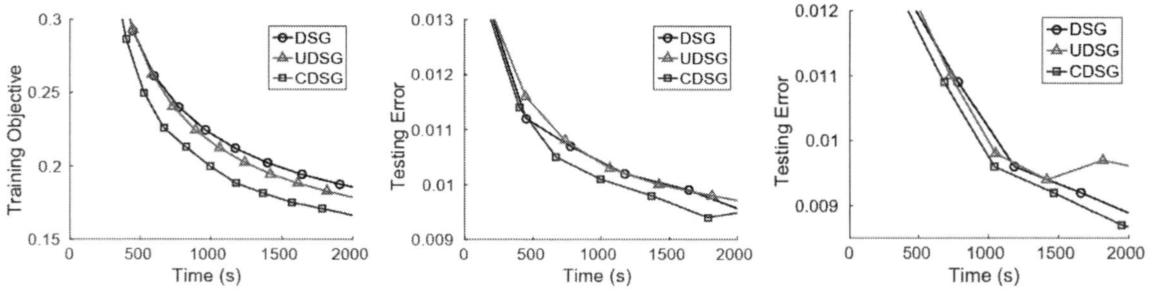

(a) Training objective of logistic regression (b) Testing error of logistic regression (c) Testing error of SVM

Figure 2: Training objective of logistic regression on MNIST-8M.

the state-of-art by using more than twice of the training time needed for CDSG. We address the performance gap to the unsatisfactory representativeness of the pre-trained features, because the time for learning pre-trained features provided by Dai et al. (2014) only takes less than 10% of the training time. We could expect better pre-trained features could result in better performance of CDSG, but it takes more time for getting pre-trained features. Also, if we only have limited training time budget, such as the fine-tunning step in training deep neural networks, CDSG enjoys the advantage of the fast training to achieve satisfactory results quickly as shown in Table 5.

6 CONCLUSION

In this paper, we extended the DSG algorithm (Dai et al., 2014) to be more efficient by utilizing previous coordinates. We studied two algorithms including UDSG and CDSG. UDSG samples old coordinates with uniform sampling, which results in a worse convergence bound than the original DSG, though it outperforms DSG usually in practice. We also propose the other variant, CDSG, which selects previous coordinates in a more conservative way by checking the upper bound of the expected error. In the theoretical side, CDSG enjoys the same bound as DSG; in the practical side, CDSG is demonstrated to have better performance than DSG and UDSG consistently in all datasets we studied.

From our empirical study, we make the following suggestions.

Medium-Scale Data: If the size of memory permits and we want to achieve high-precision result, the solver with exact optimization by computing kernel matrices is still preferable, such as LIBSVM. However, they take longer time than the time needed for CDSG to achieve satisfactory performance (less than 5 minutes in all datasets we studied). For some medium-scale data we studied, the exact optimization solver takes hours to converge.

Large-Scale Data: For large-scale problems, such as ImageNet, the proposed CDSG algorithm enjoys several advantages. First, it is memory efficient, so we are allowed to use a large number of random features for kernel approximation, Second, it is computationally efficient and much faster than the original DSG algorithm. Under the situation with limited time budget, CDSG can quickly achieve satisfactory performance. However, if we want to achieve the state-of-the-art performance as deep neural nets, the proposed kernel approximation needs better feature representation as input to achieve better performance. Otherwise, the jointly-trained neural net may be preferable. The other alternative is combining the recent development of unsupervised training of deep neural networks (Doersch et al., 2015) with CDSG, which could possibly give us competitive performance with jointly-trained neural nets.

References

Bach, F. R. (2015). On the equivalence between quadrature rules and random features. *CoRR*.

Chang, C.-C. and Lin, C.-J. (2011). LIBSVM: A library for support vector machines. *ACM Transactions on Intelligent Systems and Technology*.

Chen, X., Yang, H., King, I., and Lyu, M. R. (2015). Training-efficient feature map for shift-invariant kernels. In *Proceedings of the Twenty-Fourth International Joint Conference on Artificial Intelligence*.

Dai, B., Xie, B., He, N., Liang, Y., Raj, A., Balcan, M., and Song, L. (2014). Scalable kernel methods via doubly stochastic gradients. In *Advances in Neural Information Processing Systems*.

Doersch, C., Gupta, A., and Efros, A. A. (2015). Unsupervised visual representation learning by context prediction. In *International Conference on Computer Vision*.

Fan, R.-E., Chang, K.-W., Hsieh, C.-J., Wang, X.-R., and Lin, C.-J. (2008). LIBLINEAR: A library for large linear classification. *Journal of Machine Learning Research*.

Johnson, R. and Zhang, T. (2013). Accelerating stochastic

gradient descent using predictive variance reduction. In *Advances in Neural Information Processing Systems.*

Kivinen, J., Smola, A. J., and Williamson, R. C. (2004). Online Learning with Kernels. *IEEE Transactions on Signal Processing.*

Krizhevsky, A., Sutskever, I., and Hinton, G. E. (2012). Imagenet classification with deep convolutional neural networks. In *Advances in Neural Information Processing Systems.*

Le, Q. V., Sarlós, T., and Smola, A. J. (2013). Fastfood - computing hilbert space expansions in loglinear time. In *Proceedings of the International Conference on Machine Learning.*

LeCun, Y., Bottou, L., Bengio, Y., and Haffner, P. (1998). Gradient-based learning applied to document recognition. In *Proceedings of the IEEE.*

Nesterov, Y. (2012). Efficiency of coordinate descent methods on huge-scale optimization problems. *SIAM Journal on Optimization.*

Rahimi, A. and Recht, B. (2007). Random features for large-scale kernel machines. In *NIPS.*

Rahimi, A. and Recht, B. (2008). Weighted sums of random kitchen sinks: Replacing minimization with randomization in learning. In *Advances in Neural Information Processing Systems.*

Shalev-Shwartz, S. and Zhang, T. (2013). Stochastic dual coordinate ascent methods for regularized loss. *Journal of Machine Learning Research.*

Smola, A. J. (2004). An introduction to machine learning with kernels lecture 5.

Sriperumbudur, B. K. and Szabó, Z. (2015). Optimal rates for random fourier features.

Wathen, A. J. and Zhu, S. (2015). On spectral distribution of kernel matrices related to radial basis functions. *Numerical Algorithms.*

Weyl, H. (1912). Das asymptotische verteilungsgesetz der eigenwerte linearer partieller differentialgleichungen (mit einer anwendung auf die theorie der hohlraumstrahlung). *Mathematische Annalen.*

Williams, C. K. I. and Seeger, M. W. (2000). Using the nyström method to speed up kernel machines. In *Advances in Neural Information Processing Systems.*

Yang, J., Sindhwani, V., Avron, H., and Mahoney, M. W. (2014). Quasi-monte carlo feature maps for shift-invariant kernels. In *Proceedings of the International Conference on Machine Learning.*

Yang, T., Li, Y.-F., Mahdavi, M., Jin, R., and Zhou, Z.-H. (2012). "nystr"om method vs random fourier features: A theoretical and empirical comparison". In *Advances in Neural Information Processing Systems.*

Yen, I. E., Lin, T., Lin, S., Ravikumar, P. K., and Dhillon, I. S. (2014). Sparse random feature algorithm as coordinate descent in hilbert space. In *Advances in Neural Information Processing Systems.*

On Hyper-Parameter Estimation in Empirical Bayes: A Revisit of the MacKay Algorithm

Chune Li[1], **Yongyi Mao**[2], **Richong Zhang**[1] and **Jinpeng Huai**[1] *
[1]School of Computer Science and Engineering, Beihang University, Beijing, P. R. China 100191
[2]School of Electrical Engineering and Computer Science, University of Ottawa, Ottawa, ON K1N 6N5, Canada

Abstract

An iterative procedure introduced in MacKay's evidence framework is often used for estimating the hyper-parameter in empirical Bayes. Despite its effectiveness, the procedure has stayed primarily as a heuristic to date. This paper formally investigates the mathematical nature of this procedure and justifies it as a well-principled algorithm framework. This framework, which we call the MacKay algorithm, is shown to be closely related to the EM algorithm under certain Gaussian assumption.

1 INTRODUCTION

As a bridge between full Bayesian models and completely frequentist models, the empirical Bayesian method (also known as empirical Bayes in short, or type-II maximum likelihood) has been applied to many learning, inference or prediction applications (see. e.g. [Schäfer and Strimmer, 2005, Efron, 2012, Heskes, 2000, Yang et al., 2004, Frost and Savarino, 1986, DuMouchel and Pregibon, 2001]). The generic setup of empirical Bayes consists the observed data $\mathbf{D}$, the model parameter $\mathbf{z}$ that parametrizes the data likelihood function $p(\mathbf{D}|\mathbf{z})$, and the prior distribution $p(\mathbf{z})$ of the model parameter. In the parametric version of empirical Bayes (Figure 1), the prior distribution is parameterized by certain hyper-parameter α, namely, as $p(\mathbf{z}|\alpha)$, and the philosophy of empirical Bayes is to estimate the hyper-parameter α from the observed data $\mathbf{D}$.

As empirical Bayes treats the model parameter $\mathbf{z}$ as a latent random variable, the estimation of the hyper-parameter α naturally fits in the framework of the EM algorithm [Dempster et al., 1977, Carlin and Louis, 1997], and the EM-based solutions have been developed to solve this problem in various application domains (see, e.g., [Inoue and Tanaka, 2001, Clyde and George, 2000]). Among other approaches to this problem, a technique introduced by MacKay is also widely adopted in practice[Bishop, 1999, Tipping, 2001, Tipping et al., 2003, Wipf and Nagarajan, 2008, Tan and Févotte, 2009].

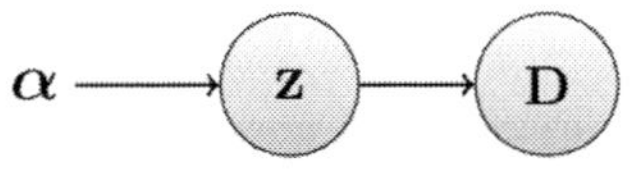

Figure 1: The generic model of empirical Bayesian method

In his "evidence framework" [MacKay, 1992b, MacKay and Neal, 1994, MacKay, 1995], MacKay considers a hierarchical Bayesian model similar to that in Figure 1 but with one distinction: an additional hyper-prior $p(\alpha|\mathcal{H})$, which depends on the choice $\mathcal{H}$ of model, is placed on the hyper-parameter α. In this setting, the evidence framework addresses three levels of inference problems: 1) given the hyper-parameter α, inferring $\mathbf{z}$, 2) given the model $\mathcal{H}$, inferring α, and 3) evaluating model $\mathcal{H}$. MacKay shows [MacKay, 1995] that the three levels of inference may be combined for prediction and for automatic shrinkage of parameter spaces (namely, Automatic Relevance Determination, or ARD) for neural network regression models. The second-level inference in the evidence framework is closely related to empirical Bayes. In particular, when a flat hyper-prior $p(\alpha|\mathcal{H})$ is placed on α, the objective of the second-level inference coincides with the objective of empirical Bayes. For the second-level inference, MacKay introduces a procedure that alternates between inferring $\mathbf{z}$ given α (first-level inference) and inferring α given $\mathbf{z}$. This procedure, although well appreciated in some classical papers (e.g., [Bishop, 1999]) and highly cited in ARD related literature (e.g., [Bishop, 1999, Tipping, 2001, Tan and Févotte, 2009]), is called the *MacKay algorithm* in this paper.

This work is supported partly by China 973 program (No. 2014CB340305), by the National Natural Science Foundation of China (No. 61300070, 61421003), and by the Beijing Advanced Innovation Center for Big Data and Brain Computing. Richong Zhang is the corresponding author of this work (email: zhangrc@act.buaa.edu.cn)

Since its birth, the MacKay algorithm has been applied to various empirical Bayes models and its performance is often compared with the EM algorithm. For example, the MacKay algorithm is applied to the Bayesian PCA model [Bishop, 1999] and a non-negative matrix factorization model [Tan and Févotte, 2009] for automated shrinkage of the latent-space dimensions. In [Tipping, 2001], the MacKay algorithm is applied to SVM regression models for promoting sparsity, and it is shown to converge faster than the EM algorithm.

Despite its effectiveness, the mathematical principle and optimization objective of the MacKay algorithm are however not well characterized in the literature to date. In MacKay's original exposition [MacKay and Neal, 1994, MacKay, 1995], the second-level inference task is clearly stated, but the justification of the iterative procedure (i.e., the MacKay algorithm) is mainly heuristic. In addition, since the MacKay's algorithm is often implemented with a particular update procedure, known as the fixed-point iteration [Solomon, 2015, Hyvärinen, 1999], or the "MacKay update", the boundary between the *framework* of the MacKay algorithm and MacKay's fixed-point *update rule* is often blurred in the literature. This makes the MacKay algorithm often understood in a narrow sense as this specific fixed-point update rule, rather than as an *algorithm framework*.

In this paper, under a generic formulation of the empirical Bayes model (Figure 1), we re-formulate the MacKay algorithm as a coordinate-ascent procedure for solving a well-defined optimization problem. This optimization problem shares some similarity with the optimization problem underlying the EM algorithm: its objective function is a lower bound of the true objective function defining the optimization objective of empirical Bayes. Also similar to the EM algorithm, this lower bound is not "far" from the true objective function and one of the two update steps in the coordinate-ascent procedure guarantees to make the lower bound meet the true objective function. This understanding justifies the MacKay algorithm (whether or not implemented with the MacKay update) as a well-principled algorithm framework, juxtaposed on equal footing with the EM framework.

Under a specific linear regression model, it has been observed that the MacKay update and the EM algorithm are closely reated [Murphy, 2012]. It is then curious to investigate the relationship between the two algorithms in a more general setting. To that end, we show that as long as the the posterior distribution $p(\mathbf{z}|\mathbf{D},\boldsymbol{\alpha})$ is a Gaussian distribution, the objective function for the MacKay algorithm is simply a restriction of the EM objective function where two of the three variables are restricted on a curve. Under this Gaussian condition, we show that the MacKay optimization problem is a relaxation of the original optimization problem in empirical Bayes, and that the EM optimization problem is a relaxation of the MacKay optimization problem. In addition, the three problems attain their optimum at the same configuration of the hyper-parameter $\boldsymbol{\alpha}$. These understandings then help to explain why the MacKay algorithm converge faster than the EM algorithm.

The objective of this paper is to rigorously formulate the MacKay algorithm and to investigate its connection to the EM algorithm. We have made an effort to be pedagogical in our presentation. In particular, we use a linear regression model and the Bayesian PCA model as running examples throughout the paper.

2 SETUP

The generic model for empirical Bayes is given in Figure 1, where $\mathbf{D}$ is the observed data, $\mathbf{z}$ is the model parameter, and $\boldsymbol{\alpha}$ is the hyper-parameter. We note that both $\mathbf{z}$ and $\boldsymbol{\alpha}$ can be a scalar, a vector, a matrix or of an arbitrary form. The model is specified by the likelihood function $p(\mathbf{D}|\mathbf{z})$ and the prior distribution $p(\mathbf{z}|\boldsymbol{\alpha})$. The objective of empirical Bayes is then to estimate the hyper-parameter $\boldsymbol{\alpha}$ from the data $\mathbf{D}$.

Let

$$l(\boldsymbol{\alpha}) := \log p(\mathbf{D}|\boldsymbol{\alpha}) = \log \int p(\mathbf{D}|\mathbf{z})p(\mathbf{z}|\boldsymbol{\alpha})d\mathbf{z} \quad (1)$$

be the log-marginal likelihood or the "log-evidence" [MacKay, 1992b] of the hyper-parameter $\boldsymbol{\alpha}$. Then the estimation of $\boldsymbol{\alpha}$ can be naturally formulated as solving the following optimization problem.

Opt-I

Find $\boldsymbol{\alpha}$ that maximizes $l(\boldsymbol{\alpha})$.

We now use the examples of linear regression and Bayesian PCA[Bishop, 1999] to illustrate this. Throughout the paper, we will use $\mathcal{N}(x;\mu,\Lambda)$ to denote the Gaussian density function with variable x, mean μ and covariance matrix Λ, and we will use I_d to denote the $d\times d$ identity matrix, $\mathrm{Tr}(\cdot)$ to denote the trace operator, $\mathrm{Det}(\cdot)$ to denote the determinant operator, $\|\cdot\|$ to denote L2 norm, and $\mathbb{E}_q[\cdot]$ to denote expectation under distribution q.

Linear Regression Example–1 *Let* $\mathbf{D} := \{(x_{(i)}, y_{(i)}) : i = 1,2,\ldots,n\}$ *be the observed data, where each* $x_{(i)}$ *is a vector in* $\mathbb{R}^d$*, and each* $y_{(i)}$ *is a scalar in* $\mathbb{R}$*. The dependency of* $y_{(i)}$ *on* $x_{(i)}$ *is modelled as*

$$y_{(i)} = \mathbf{z}^T x_{(i)} + \epsilon_{(i)}.$$

Here $\epsilon_{(i)}$ *is a zero-mean Gaussian noise with variance* σ^2*, and* $\mathbf{z}$ *is the model parameter, which is modelled as a d-dimensional spherical Gaussian variable with zero mean and variance* $1/\boldsymbol{\alpha}$*. For simplicity, we assume that the parameter* σ^2 *is known and the objective of empirical Bayes* *is to estimate the hyper-parameter $\boldsymbol{\alpha}$. Then the objective function in* Opt-I *is:*

$$l(\boldsymbol{\alpha})=\log\int\mathcal{N}(\mathbf{z};0,\frac{1}{\boldsymbol{\alpha}}I_d)\prod_{i=1}^{n}\mathcal{N}(y_{(i)};\mathbf{z}^T x_{(i)},\sigma^2)d\mathbf{z}$$

Bayesian PCA Example–1 *Following [Bishop, 1999], let $\mathbf{D} := \{t_{(i)} : i = 1, 2, \ldots, n\}$ be the observed data, where each $t_{(i)}$ is a vector in $\mathbb{R}^m$. Each observed vector $t_{(i)}$ depends on a latent variable $x_{(i)} \in \mathbb{R}^d$ via*

$$t_{(i)} = \mathbf{z}x_{(i)} + \epsilon_{(i)}.$$

Here $x_{(i)}$ is a zero-mean Gaussian variable with covariance I_d, $\epsilon_{(i)}$ is a spherical Gaussian noise with zero mean and known variance σ^2, and parameter $\mathbf{z} \in \mathbb{R}^{m\times d}$ ($d < m$) is modelled as a random matrix whose kth column $\mathbf{z}_k$ is drawn from a spherical Gaussian distribution with zero mean and variance $1/\boldsymbol{\alpha}_k$. Let $\boldsymbol{\alpha} := \{\boldsymbol{\alpha}_k : k = 1, 2, \ldots, d\}$. Then $\boldsymbol{\alpha}$ is the hyper-parameter on $\mathbf{z}$ and Opt-I *has the following objective function:*

$$l(\boldsymbol{\alpha}) = \log\left(\int\prod_{k=1}^{d}\mathcal{N}(\mathbf{z}_k;0,\frac{1}{\boldsymbol{\alpha}_k}I_m)\right.$$
$$\left.\prod_{i=1}^{n}\int\mathcal{N}(x_{(i)};0,I_d)\mathcal{N}(t_{(i)};\mathbf{z}x_{(i)},\sigma^2 I_m)dx_{(i)}\right)d\mathbf{z}$$

The optimization problem Opt-I can sometimes be solved easily, for instance, in the above linear regression setting. In practice, however, this problem is usually difficult and requires special algorithmic techniques. The above Bayesian PCA setting is one such example.

The EM approach to Opt-I is well-known. In the remainder of this paper, we develop the MacKay algorithm for this problem. To compare and relate to EM, we also present the EM algorithm in parallel. The above linear regression and Bayesian PCA settings will be carried along our development as illustrative examples.

3 THE TWO ALGORITHMS

In this section, we will show that both the EM algorithm and the MacKay algorithm can be formulated as optimizing a lower bound of the objective function $l(\boldsymbol{\alpha})$ via coordinate ascent. While this is well known for the EM algorithm, it has been quite obscure for the MacKay algorithm.

3.1 THE EM ALGORITHM

The Expectation-Maximization (EM) algorithm [Dempster et al., 1977] is a classical method for maximizing the log-likelihood function or log-posterior density function in which certain latent variables have been integrated over. When applied to the optimization problem Opt-I, the EM algorithm implicitly constructs a lower bound $\mathcal{F}_{\mathrm{EM}}$ of the objective function $l(\boldsymbol{\alpha})$.

$$\begin{aligned}\mathcal{F}_{\mathrm{EM}}(q,\boldsymbol{\alpha}) &:= \mathbb{E}_q\left[\log\frac{p(\mathbf{D}|\mathbf{z})p(\mathbf{z}|\boldsymbol{\alpha})}{q(\mathbf{z})}\right]\\ &= \int q(\mathbf{z})\log\frac{p(\mathbf{D}|\mathbf{z})p(\mathbf{z}|\boldsymbol{\alpha})}{q(\mathbf{z})}d\mathbf{z}\end{aligned} \tag{2}$$

where $q(\cdot)$ is an arbitrary probability distribution on the space of $\mathbf{z}$. By the Jensen's Inequality[Jensen, 1906], the follow result is well-known in the literature of the EM algorithm [Dempster et al., 1977].

Lemma 1. *$\mathcal{F}_{\mathrm{EM}}(q,\boldsymbol{\alpha}) \le l(\boldsymbol{\alpha})$, where the equality is achieved if and only if $q(\mathbf{z})$ is the posterior distribution $p(\mathbf{z}|\mathbf{D},\boldsymbol{\alpha})$.*

Instead of optimizing the original objective function $l(\boldsymbol{\alpha})$, we now define an alternative optimization problem.

> OptEM
>
> Find $\boldsymbol{\alpha}$ and a distribution q that maximize $\mathcal{F}_{\mathrm{EM}}(q,\boldsymbol{\alpha})$.

The EM algorithm is then the coordinate ascent solver for OptEM. More precisely, the update rule at the tth iteration of the coordinate ascent is given below.

EM Algorithm

E-Step:

$$\begin{aligned}q^{(t)} &:= \arg\max_q \mathcal{F}_{\mathrm{EM}}(q,\boldsymbol{\alpha}^{(t)})\\ &= p(\mathbf{z}|\mathbf{D},\boldsymbol{\alpha}^{(t)})\end{aligned}$$

M-Step:

$$\begin{aligned}\boldsymbol{\alpha}^{(t+1)} &:= \arg\max_{\boldsymbol{\alpha}} \mathcal{F}_{\mathrm{EM}}(q^{(t)},\boldsymbol{\alpha})\\ &= \arg\max_{\boldsymbol{\alpha}} \mathbb{E}_{q^{(t)}}\left[\log p(\mathbf{z}|\boldsymbol{\alpha})\right]\end{aligned}$$

We note that by Lemma 1, at the end of E-Step,

$$\mathcal{F}_{\mathrm{EM}}(q^{(t)},\boldsymbol{\alpha}^{(t)}) = l(\boldsymbol{\alpha}^{(t)}). \tag{3}$$

This gives rise to the following lemma [Dempster et al., 1977].

Lemma 2. *The iteration of the EM algorithm continuously increases the log-evidence function $l(\boldsymbol{\alpha})$ and therefore is guaranteed to converge.*

Linear Regression Example–2 *For the linear regression model, let $[x_{(1)}, x_{(2)}, \ldots, x_{(n)}]$ be denoted by a matrix $X \in \mathbb{R}^{d\times n}$ and $[y_{(1)}, y_{(2)}, \ldots, y_{(n)}]^T$ denoted by a vector*

$Y \in \mathbb{R}^n$. The objective function (2) is

$$\mathcal{F}_{\mathrm{EM}}(q, \boldsymbol{\alpha}) = \frac{1}{\sigma^2}\sum_{i=1}^{n} y_{(i)} x_{(i)}^T \mathbb{E}_q[\mathbf{z}]$$
$$- \frac{1}{2\sigma^2}\mathbb{E}_q\left[\mathbf{z}^T\left(\sum_{i=1}^{n} x_{(i)}x_{(i)}^T + \boldsymbol{\alpha}\sigma^2 I_d\right)\mathbf{z}\right]$$
$$- \mathbb{E}_q\left[\log q(\mathbf{z})\right] + \frac{n+d}{2}\log 2\pi + \frac{n}{2}\log\sigma^2$$
$$+ \frac{d}{2}\log\boldsymbol{\alpha} - \frac{1}{2\sigma^2}\sum_{i=1}^{n} y_{(i)}^2$$

It is easy to verify that the posterior distribution of $\mathbf{z}$ is also Gaussian and the E-Step update becomes

$$q^{(t)}(\mathbf{z}) = \mathcal{N}\left(\mathbf{z}; \mu_{\mathrm{LR}}(\boldsymbol{\alpha}^{(t)}), K_{\mathrm{LR}}(\boldsymbol{\alpha}^{(t)})\right) \qquad (4)$$

where

$$\mu_{\mathrm{LR}}(\boldsymbol{\alpha}) := \frac{1}{\sigma^2}\left(\frac{1}{\sigma^2}XX^T + \boldsymbol{\alpha}I_d\right)^{-1} XY, \qquad (5)$$

and

$$K_{\mathrm{LR}}(\boldsymbol{\alpha}) := \left(\frac{1}{\sigma^2}XX^T + \boldsymbol{\alpha}I_d\right)^{-1}. \qquad (6)$$

For the M-Step update, noting that

$$\mathcal{F}_{\mathrm{EM}}(q^{(t)}, \boldsymbol{\alpha}) = -\frac{\boldsymbol{\alpha}}{2}\left\|\mu_{\mathrm{LR}}(\boldsymbol{\alpha}^{(t)})\right\|^2$$
$$- \frac{\boldsymbol{\alpha}}{2}\mathrm{Tr}\left(K_{\mathrm{LR}}(\boldsymbol{\alpha}^{(t)})\right) + \frac{d}{2}\log\boldsymbol{\alpha} + const,$$

it is possible to express the maximizing $\boldsymbol{\alpha}$ for this function directly in terms of $\boldsymbol{\alpha}^{(t)}$ as:

$$\boldsymbol{\alpha}^{(t+1)} = \frac{d}{\left\|\mu_{\mathrm{LR}}(\boldsymbol{\alpha}^{(t)})\right\|^2 + \mathrm{Tr}\left(K_{\mathrm{LR}}(\boldsymbol{\alpha}^{(t)})\right)} \qquad (7)$$

That is, the updates in E-Step and M-Step can be combined into the single update equation (7).

Bayesian PCA Example–2 *For the BPCA model, the objective function (2) is*

$$\mathcal{F}_{\mathrm{EM}}(q, \boldsymbol{\alpha}) = -\frac{n}{2}\mathbb{E}_q\left[\log\mathrm{Det}(\mathbf{z}\mathbf{z}^T + \sigma^2 I_m)\right]$$
$$- \frac{1}{2}\sum_{i=1}^{n}\mathbb{E}_q\left[t_{(i)}^T(\mathbf{z}\mathbf{z}^T + \sigma^2 I_m)^{-1}t_{(i)}\right]$$
$$- \frac{1}{2}\sum_{k=1}^{d}\boldsymbol{\alpha}_k\mathbb{E}_q\left[\|\mathbf{z}_k\|^2\right] - \mathbb{E}_q\left[\log q(\mathbf{z})\right]$$
$$+ \sum_{k=1}^{d}\frac{m}{2}\log\boldsymbol{\alpha}_k - \frac{dn+dm}{2}\log 2\pi.$$

The M-Step update is then

$$\boldsymbol{\alpha}_k^{(t+1)} = \frac{m}{\mathbb{E}_{q^{(t)}}\left[\|\mathbf{z}_k\|^2\right]}. \qquad (8)$$

However, the E-Step update of $q^{(t)}$ can not be expressed in explicit forms and one usually relies on various approximation techniques. For example, a sampling approach [Neal, 1993] may be used for this purpose. Later in this paper, we will discuss the approach that approximates the posterior as a Gaussian.

3.2 MACKAY ALGORITHM

In [MacKay, 1992a, MacKay, 1992c, MacKay, 1992b, MacKay, 1995], MacKay presented the influential evidence framework that addresses inference as three levels. A heuristic iterative procedure is introduced for the second-level inference, namely, for inferring the hyperparameter. Here, we re-formulate the this procedure as a well-principled algorithm framework, and call it the *MacKay algorithm*.

To begin, note that the objective function $l(\boldsymbol{\alpha})$ can be expressed as

$$l(\boldsymbol{\alpha}) = \log p(\mathbf{D}, \mathbf{z}|\boldsymbol{\alpha}) - \log p(\mathbf{z}|\mathbf{D}, \boldsymbol{\alpha}),$$

for any $\mathbf{z}$ (with $p(\mathbf{z}|\mathbf{D}, \boldsymbol{\alpha})$ non-zero). Define

$$\mathcal{F}_{\mathrm{MacKay}}(\mathbf{z}, \boldsymbol{\alpha}) := \log p(\mathbf{D}, \mathbf{z}|\boldsymbol{\alpha}) - \max_{\mathbf{z}'}\log p(\mathbf{z}'|\mathbf{D}, \boldsymbol{\alpha}). \qquad (9)$$

The following lemma is easy to verify.

Lemma 3. *$\mathcal{F}_{\mathrm{MacKay}}(\mathbf{z}, \boldsymbol{\alpha}) \leq l(\boldsymbol{\alpha})$, where the equality is achieved if and only if $\mathbf{z} = \arg\max_{\mathbf{z}}\log p(\mathbf{D}, \mathbf{z}|\boldsymbol{\alpha})$.*

We now introduce another optimization problem.

> OptMacKay
>
> Find $\boldsymbol{\alpha}$ and $\mathbf{z}$ that maximize $\mathcal{F}_{\mathrm{MacKay}}(\mathbf{z}, \boldsymbol{\alpha})$.

The MacKay algorithm is then defined as the following coordinate ascent procedure for optimizing $\mathcal{F}_{\mathrm{MacKay}}$.

MacKay Algorithm

z-Step:

$$\mathbf{z}^{(t)} := \arg\max_{\mathbf{z}}\mathcal{F}_{\mathrm{MacKay}}(\mathbf{z}, \boldsymbol{\alpha}^{(t)}) = \arg\max_{\mathbf{z}}\log p(\mathbf{D}, \mathbf{z}|\boldsymbol{\alpha}^{(t)})$$

$\boldsymbol{\alpha}$-Step:

$$\boldsymbol{\alpha}^{(t+1)} := \arg\max_{\boldsymbol{\alpha}}\mathcal{F}_{\mathrm{MacKay}}(\mathbf{z}^{(t)}, \boldsymbol{\alpha}).$$

At the end of z-Step, by Lemma 3,

$$\mathcal{F}_{\mathrm{MacKay}}(\mathbf{z}^{(t)}, \boldsymbol{\alpha}^{(t)}) = l(\boldsymbol{\alpha}^{(t)}). \qquad (10)$$

This property clearly parallels Equation (3) of the EM algorithm. That is, although the MacKay algorithm maximizes the lower bound $\mathcal{F}_{\text{MacKay}}$ of the true objective function $l(\boldsymbol{\alpha})$, the lower bound $\mathcal{F}_{\text{MacKay}}$ is in fact "not far" below $l(\boldsymbol{\alpha})$ and at the end of each $\mathbf{z}$-Step update, the lower-bound meets $l(\boldsymbol{\alpha})$. Then by the coordinate-ascent nature of the MacKay algorithm, we have the following lemma, parallel to Lemma 2 of the EM algorithm.

Lemma 4. *The iteration of the MacKay algorithm continuously increases the log-evidence function $l(\boldsymbol{\alpha})$ and therefore is guaranteed to converge.*

In the MacKay algorithm, it is worth noting that the update in the $\boldsymbol{\alpha}$-Step is usually performed with a "fixed-point iteration" procedure [Solomon, 2015, MacKay, 1992a, Bishop, 1999, Murphy, 2012], which we describe next for self-containedness.

Fixed-Point Iteration Suppose that the equation

$$\partial \mathcal{F}_{\text{MacKay}}(\mathbf{z}, \boldsymbol{\alpha}) / \partial \boldsymbol{\alpha} = 0$$

can be reduced to the form $\boldsymbol{\alpha} = h(\boldsymbol{\alpha}, \mathbf{z})$. The fixed-point iteration approach for the α-Step update in the MacKay algorithm is the following update rule.

$$\boldsymbol{\alpha}^{(t+1)} = h(\boldsymbol{\alpha}^{(t)}, \mathbf{z}^{(t)}).$$

Linear Regression Example–3 *In the linear regression model, the lower bound $\mathcal{F}_{\text{MacKay}}$ is*

$$\begin{aligned}\mathcal{F}_{\text{MacKay}}(\mathbf{z}, \boldsymbol{\alpha}) = & \frac{1}{\sigma^2}\sum_{i=1}^{n} y_{(i)} x_{(i)}^T \mathbf{z} - \frac{1}{2\sigma^2}\sum_{i=1}^{n} y_{(i)}^2 \\ & - \frac{1}{2\sigma^2}\mathbf{z}^T \left(\sum_{i=1}^{n} x_{(i)} x_{(i)}^T + \boldsymbol{\alpha}\sigma^2 I_d\right)\mathbf{z} \\ & + \frac{n+d}{2}\log 2\pi + \frac{n}{2}\log\sigma^2 + \frac{d}{2}\log\boldsymbol{\alpha} \\ & + \frac{1}{2}\log\text{Det}\left(2\pi K_{\text{LR}}(\boldsymbol{\alpha})\right)\end{aligned} \tag{11}$$

The $\mathbf{z}$-Step turns out to be

$$\mathbf{z}^{(t)} = \mu_{\text{LR}}(\boldsymbol{\alpha}^{(t)}).$$

Note

$$\frac{\partial \mathcal{F}_{\text{MacKay}}(\mathbf{z}, \boldsymbol{\alpha})}{\partial \boldsymbol{\alpha}} = \frac{d}{2\boldsymbol{\alpha}} - \frac{1}{2}\|\mathbf{z}\|^2 - \frac{1}{2}\text{Tr}\left(K_{\text{LR}}(\boldsymbol{\alpha})\right).$$

When setting $\frac{\partial \mathcal{F}_{\text{MacKay}}(\mathbf{z}, \boldsymbol{\alpha})}{\partial \boldsymbol{\alpha}} = 0$, we obtain

$$\boldsymbol{\alpha} = \frac{d - \boldsymbol{\alpha}\text{Tr}\left(K_{\text{LR}}(\boldsymbol{\alpha})\right)}{\|\mathbf{z}\|^2}$$

This gives rise to the fixed-point iteration of the $\boldsymbol{\alpha}$-Step:

$$\boldsymbol{\alpha}^{(t+1)} = \frac{d - \boldsymbol{\alpha}^{(t)}\text{Tr}\left(K_{\text{LR}}(\boldsymbol{\alpha}^{(t)})\right)}{\|\mathbf{z}^{(t)}\|^2}.$$

Bayesian PCA Example–3 *For the BPCA model, the objective function $\mathcal{F}_{\text{MacKay}}$ is*

$$\begin{aligned}\mathcal{F}_{\text{MacKay}}(\mathbf{z}, \boldsymbol{\alpha}) = & -\frac{n}{2}\log\text{Det}\left(\mathbf{z}\mathbf{z}^T + \sigma^2 I_m\right) \\ & - \frac{1}{2}\sum_{i=1}^{n} t_{(i)}^T (\mathbf{z}\mathbf{z}^T + \sigma^2 I_m)^{-1} t_{(i)} \\ & - \frac{1}{2}\sum_{k=1}^{d} \alpha_k \|\mathbf{z}_k\|^2 - \max_{\mathbf{z}'} p(\mathbf{z}'|\mathbf{D}, \boldsymbol{\alpha}) \\ & + \sum_{k=1}^{d} \frac{m}{2}\log\boldsymbol{\alpha}_k - \frac{dn+dm}{2}\log 2\pi\end{aligned}$$

The $\mathbf{z}$-Step and $\boldsymbol{\alpha}$-Step updates then become

$$\begin{aligned}\mathbf{z}^{(t)} &= \arg\max_{\mathbf{z}} p(\mathbf{z}|\mathbf{D}, \boldsymbol{\alpha}^{(t)}) \\ \boldsymbol{\alpha}^{(t+1)} &= \arg\max_{\boldsymbol{\alpha}} \left[-\frac{1}{2}\sum_{k=1}^{d} \boldsymbol{\alpha}_k \left\|\mathbf{z}_k^{(t)}\right\|^2 \right. \\ & \left. - \max_{\mathbf{z}'} p(\mathbf{z}'|\mathbf{D}, \boldsymbol{\alpha}) + \sum_{k=1}^{d} \frac{m}{2}\log\boldsymbol{\alpha}_k\right]\end{aligned}$$

Since in general there does not exist closed-form solution for the $\mathbf{z}$-Step update, the two update equations can not be further expressed. In practice, a Gaussian approximation is applied to the posterior function $p(\mathbf{z}|\mathbf{D}, \boldsymbol{\alpha}^{(t)})$ in order to derive these update equations (see next section).

It is perhaps worth noting that the z-step update of the MacKay algorithm resembles the E-step update of an approximate version of the EM algorithm, known as "Hard EM" (or "Viterbi-EM" in the context of Hidden Markov Models)[Allahverdyan and Galstyan, 2011]. However, the M-step of Hard EM/Viterbi-EM is different from the $\boldsymbol{\alpha}$-step of the MacKay algorithm, due to the fact the OptEM and OptMacKay have different objective functions. It is not clear whether there is a more direct connection between Hard EM and the MacKay algorithm bypassing the generic EM algorithm, although we suspect that the answer is "no".

4 GAUSSIAN APPROXIMATION

As seen above, in both the EM algorithm and the MacKay algorithm, it is desirable to compute the posterior distribution of model parameter, namely, $p(\mathbf{z}|\mathbf{D}, \boldsymbol{\alpha})$. In the case of EM, this is for updating q in the E-Step and in the case of MacKay, this is for updating $\mathbf{z}$ in the $\mathbf{z}$-Step. For some models, such Bayesian PCA, it is difficult to carry out explicit computation of the posterior. A commonly used technique is to approximate the posterior as a Gaussian density function, namely,

$$p(\mathbf{z}|\mathbf{D}, \boldsymbol{\alpha}) \approx \mathcal{N}(\mathbf{z}; \mu, K), \text{ for some } \mu,\ K. \tag{12}$$

Clearly, the mean vector μ and the covariance matrix K of the Gaussian density depend on the hyper-parameter $\boldsymbol{\alpha}$ and will be denoted by $\mu(\boldsymbol{\alpha})$ and $K(\boldsymbol{\alpha})$ respectively.

When $p(\mathbf{z}|\mathbf{D},\boldsymbol{\alpha})$ is a continuous function of $\mathbf{z}$, a common technique for obtain such an approximation (12) is the following [MacKay, 1995].

Let $\widehat{\mathbf{z}}$ maximizes $p(\mathbf{z}|\mathbf{D},\boldsymbol{\alpha})$. By Taylor-expanding $\log p(\mathbf{z}|\mathbf{D},\boldsymbol{\alpha})$ at $\mathbf{z}=\widehat{\mathbf{z}}$, up to the second-order terms, it is easy to see that

$$\log p(\mathbf{z}|\mathbf{D},\boldsymbol{\alpha}) \approx \log p\left(\widehat{\mathbf{z}}|\mathbf{D},\boldsymbol{\alpha}\right)+\frac{1}{2}\left(\mathbf{z}-\widehat{\mathbf{z}}\right)^T H(\boldsymbol{\alpha})\left(\mathbf{z}-\widehat{\mathbf{z}}\right)$$

where $H(\boldsymbol{\alpha})$ denotes the Hessian matrix of function $\log p(\mathbf{z}|\mathbf{D},\boldsymbol{\alpha})$ at $\mathbf{z}=\widehat{\mathbf{z}}$. This gives the customary approximation of $p(\mathbf{z}|\mathbf{D},\boldsymbol{\alpha})$ as [MacKay, 1995]

$$p(\mathbf{z}|\mathbf{D},\boldsymbol{\alpha}) \approx \mathcal{N}\left(\mathbf{z};\widehat{\mathbf{z}},-H(\boldsymbol{\alpha})^{-1}\right)$$

Then $\mu(\boldsymbol{\alpha})$ and $K(\boldsymbol{\alpha})$ in the Gaussian approximation (12) can be taken as

$$\mu(\boldsymbol{\alpha})=\widehat{\mathbf{z}},\ K(\boldsymbol{\alpha})=-H(\boldsymbol{\alpha})^{-1}. \tag{13}$$

We note that in (12), the approximation is sometimes accurate, namely, that the strict equality is satisfied. In such cases, the Gaussian approximation as stated in (12) and (13) in fact holds precisely.

Linear Regression Example–4 *As seen in (4), (5) and (6), the posterior distribution $p(\mathbf{z}|\mathbf{D},\boldsymbol{\alpha})$ is indeed a Gaussian density function. That is, the Gaussian approximation (12) holds with equality, where $\mu(\boldsymbol{\alpha})=\mu_{\text{LR}}(\boldsymbol{\alpha})$ and $K(\boldsymbol{\alpha})=K_{\text{LR}}(\boldsymbol{\alpha})$ (defined in (5) and (6) respectively).*

Bayesian PCA Example–4 *Let $\mathbf{Z}$ be the vector representation of matrix $\mathbf{z}$, namely, $\mathbf{Z}$ is a length-md vector obtained by stacking columns of the matrix $\mathbf{z}$. That is, $\mathbf{Z}:=(\mathbf{z}_1^T,\mathbf{z}_2^T,\ldots,\mathbf{z}_d^T)^T$. Let $\widehat{\mathbf{Z}}$ denote the maximizing configuration for function $p(\mathbf{Z}|\mathbf{D},\boldsymbol{\alpha})$, and similarly let $H(\boldsymbol{\alpha})$ denote the Hessian of $\log p(\mathbf{Z}|\mathbf{D},\boldsymbol{\alpha})$ at $\mathbf{Z}=\widehat{\mathbf{Z}}$. The Gaussian approximation (12) then becomes*

$$p(\mathbf{Z}|\mathbf{D},\boldsymbol{\alpha}) \approx \mathcal{N}(\mathbf{Z};\mu_{\text{BPCA}}(\boldsymbol{\alpha}),K_{\text{BPCA}}(\boldsymbol{\alpha})) \tag{14}$$

where

$$\mu_{\text{BPCA}}(\boldsymbol{\alpha}):=\widehat{\mathbf{Z}},\ K_{\text{BPCA}}(\boldsymbol{\alpha}):=-H(\boldsymbol{\alpha})^{-1}.$$

We note that in this case, (12) is only an approximation. In addition, since $\widehat{\mathbf{Z}}$ and $H(\boldsymbol{\alpha})^{-1}$ are difficult to compute analytically, numerical solutions are usually sought.

In the remainder of this section, we assume that (12) holds with equality and further investigate the optimization problems in the EM and MacKay algorithms.

4.1 EM

Recall that with the EM algorithm, the objective function in the optimization problem is $\mathcal{F}_{\text{EM}}$ in (2). Since the optimizing distribution q for any given $\boldsymbol{\alpha}$ is the posterior $p(\mathbf{z}|D,\boldsymbol{\alpha})$, this, under the Gaussian assumption (12) of the posterior, allows us to restrict q to the form $\mathcal{N}(\mathbf{z};u,S)$ parametrized by mean vector u and covariance S. The the objective function $\mathcal{F}_{\text{EM}}(q,\boldsymbol{\alpha})$ can then be re-expressed as $\mathcal{F}_{\text{EM}}(u,S,\boldsymbol{\alpha})$. That is,

$$\begin{aligned}\mathcal{F}_{\text{EM}}(u,S,\boldsymbol{\alpha}) &= \mathbb{E}_{\mathcal{N}(\mathbf{z};u,S)}\left[\log\frac{p(\mathbf{D}|\mathbf{z})p(\mathbf{z}|\boldsymbol{\alpha})}{\mathcal{N}(\mathbf{z};u,S)}\right]\\ &= \mathbb{E}_{\mathcal{N}(\mathbf{z};u,S)}\left[\log p(\mathbf{D}|\mathbf{z})p(\mathbf{z}|\boldsymbol{\alpha})\right]\\ &\quad+\frac{J}{2}\log 2\pi+\frac{1}{2}\log\text{Det}(S)+\frac{J}{2}\end{aligned} \tag{15}$$

where J is the length of the vector $\mathbf{z}$. The following lemma is established by noting the following two-way factorization of $p(\mathbf{D},\mathbf{z}|\boldsymbol{\alpha})$.

$$p(\mathbf{D},\mathbf{z}|\boldsymbol{\alpha})=p(\mathbf{D}|\mathbf{z})p(\mathbf{z}|\boldsymbol{\alpha})=p(\mathbf{D}|\boldsymbol{\alpha})p(\mathbf{z}|\mathbf{D},\boldsymbol{\alpha}) \tag{16}$$

Lemma 5. *When the Gaussian approximation (12) holds with equality, the function $\mathcal{F}_{\text{EM}}$ can be re-expressed as*

$$\begin{aligned}\mathcal{F}_{\text{EM}}(u,S,\boldsymbol{\alpha}) &= \log\mathcal{N}(u;\mu(\boldsymbol{\alpha}),K(\boldsymbol{\alpha}))-\frac{1}{2}\text{Tr}(K^{-1}(\boldsymbol{\alpha})S)\\ &\quad+\log p(\mathbf{D}|\boldsymbol{\alpha})+\frac{J}{2}\log 2\pi+\frac{1}{2}\log\text{Det}(S)+\frac{J}{2}\end{aligned}$$

To derive the update rule for the EM algorithm under the Gaussian approximation (12), we prove the following results.

Lemma 6. *For any given S and $\boldsymbol{\alpha}$,*

$$\arg\max_u \mathcal{F}_{\text{EM}}(u,S,\boldsymbol{\alpha})=\mu(\boldsymbol{\alpha}).$$

Proof: Based on Lemma 5, we express $\mathcal{F}_{\text{EM}}(u,S,\boldsymbol{\alpha})$ further.

$$\begin{aligned}\mathcal{F}_{\text{EM}}(u,S,\boldsymbol{\alpha}) &= -\frac{J}{2}\log 2\pi-\frac{1}{2}\log\text{Det}(K(\boldsymbol{\alpha}))\\ &\quad-\frac{1}{2}\left(u-\mu(\boldsymbol{\alpha})\right)^T K^{-1}(\boldsymbol{\alpha})(u-\mu(\boldsymbol{\alpha}))\\ &\quad-\frac{1}{2}\text{Tr}\left(K^{-1}(\boldsymbol{\alpha})S\right)+\log p(\mathbf{D}|\boldsymbol{\alpha})\\ &\quad+\frac{J}{2}\log 2\pi+\frac{1}{2}\log\text{Det}(S)+\frac{J}{2}.\end{aligned}$$

$$\frac{\partial\mathcal{F}_{\text{EM}}}{\partial u}=-\frac{1}{2}\left(K^{-1}(\boldsymbol{\alpha})+(K^{-1}(\boldsymbol{\alpha}))^T\right)(u-\mu(\boldsymbol{\alpha}))$$

By setting $\frac{\partial\mathcal{F}_{\text{EM}}}{\partial u}$ to zero, we prove the result. □

Lemma 7. *For any u and $\boldsymbol{\alpha}$,*

$$\arg\max_S \mathcal{F}_{\text{EM}}(u,S,\boldsymbol{\alpha})=K(\boldsymbol{\alpha}).$$

Proof: By the expression of $\mathcal{F}_{\rm EM}(u,S,\boldsymbol{\alpha})$ in Lemma 5,

$$\frac{\partial \mathcal{F}_{\rm EM}}{\partial S} = -\frac{1}{2}\frac{\partial}{\partial S}{\rm Tr}(K^{-1}(\boldsymbol{\alpha})S) + \frac{1}{2}\frac{\partial}{\partial S}\log {\rm Det}(S).$$

By ${\rm Tr}(AB) = \sum_i\sum_j A_{ij}B_{ji}$, we have

$$\begin{aligned}{\rm Tr}(K^{-1}(\boldsymbol{\alpha})S) &= \sum_i\sum_j (K^{-1}(\boldsymbol{\alpha}))_{ij}S_{ji};\\ \frac{\partial}{\partial S_{ij}}{\rm Tr}(K^{-1}(\boldsymbol{\alpha})S) &= (K^{-1}(\boldsymbol{\alpha}))_{ji}\\ \frac{\partial}{\partial S}{\rm Tr}(K^{-1}(\boldsymbol{\alpha})S) &= (K^{-1}(\boldsymbol{\alpha}))^T.\end{aligned}$$

On the other hand, since $\frac{\partial {\rm Det}(S)}{\partial S_{ij}} = {\rm Det}(S)(S^{-1})_{ji}$, we have

$$\begin{aligned}\frac{\partial}{\partial S_{ij}}\log {\rm Det}(S) &= (S^{-1})_{ji}\\ \frac{\partial}{\partial S}\log {\rm Det}(S) &= (S^{-1})^T.\end{aligned}$$

Then

$$\frac{\partial \mathcal{F}_{\rm EM}}{\partial S} = -\frac{1}{2}(K^{-1}(\boldsymbol{\alpha}))^T + \frac{1}{2}(S^{-1})^T.$$

The lemma is then proved by setting this derivative to zero. □

As a corollary of Lemma 6, Lemma 7 and (15), the update rule of the EM algorithm can be established.

Lemma 8. *When the Gaussian approximation (12) holds with equality, the EM algorithm becomes the following EM-Gauss Procedure.*

EM-Gauss Procedure:

E-Step:

$$\begin{aligned}u^{(t)} &:= \mu(\boldsymbol{\alpha}^{(t)})\\ S^{(t)} &:= K(\boldsymbol{\alpha}^{(t)})\end{aligned}$$

M-Step:

$$\boldsymbol{\alpha}^{(t+1)} := \arg\max_{\boldsymbol{\alpha}} \mathbb{E}_{\mathcal{N}(\mathbf{z};u^{(t)},S^{(t)})}\left[\log p(\mathbf{z}|\boldsymbol{\alpha})\right]$$

Linear Regression Example–5 *In the linear regression model, the Gaussian assumption (12) holds true. The E-Step then reduces to (4), which can be integrated into the M-Step. The EM update can then be expressed as a single update equation (7), the same as that in Linear Regression Example-2.*

Bayesian PCA Example–5 *Note that $\mu_{\rm BPCA}(\boldsymbol{\alpha})$ is a vector of length md and $K_{\rm BPCA}(\boldsymbol{\alpha})$ is an $md\times md$ matrix. Let $\mu_{{\rm BPCA},k}(\boldsymbol{\alpha})$ denote the component of $\mu_{\rm BPCA}(\boldsymbol{\alpha})$ corresponding to $\mathbf{z}_k$ component of $\widehat{\mathbf{Z}}$, and $K_{{\rm BPCA},k}(\boldsymbol{\alpha})$ denote the sub-matrix of $K_{\rm BPCA}(\boldsymbol{\alpha})$ that serves as the covariance matrix of $\mathbf{z}_k$. With the Gassian approximation (14) holds with equality, the update (8) of $\boldsymbol{\alpha}$ becomes*

$$\boldsymbol{\alpha}_k^{(t+1)} = \frac{m}{\left\|\mu_{{\rm BPCA},k}(\boldsymbol{\alpha}^{(t)})\right\|^2 + {\rm Tr}\left(K_{{\rm BPCA},k}(\boldsymbol{\alpha}^{(t)})\right)}.$$

4.2 MACKAY

Lemma 9. *When the Gaussian approximation (12) holds with equality, the function $\mathcal{F}_{\rm MacKay}$ in (9) becomes*

$$\mathcal{F}_{\rm MacKay}(\mathbf{z},\boldsymbol{\alpha}) = \log p(\mathbf{D},\mathbf{z}|\boldsymbol{\alpha}) + \frac{1}{2}\log {\rm Det}(2\pi K(\boldsymbol{\alpha})).$$

Proof: This lemma follows from $\max_{\mathbf{z}'}\log p(\mathbf{z}'|\mathbf{D},\boldsymbol{\alpha}) = -\frac{1}{2}\log {\rm Det}(2\pi K(\boldsymbol{\alpha}))$. □

Lemma 10. *When the Gaussian approximation (12) holds with equality, for any $\boldsymbol{\alpha}$,*

$$\arg\max_{\mathbf{z}} \log p(\mathbf{D},\mathbf{z}|\boldsymbol{\alpha}) = \mu(\boldsymbol{\alpha}).$$

The proof of this lemma follows the same line as that of Lemma 6. The MacKay algorithm under the Gaussian approximation (12) can then be established from Lemma 10 and Lemma 9.

Lemma 11. *When the Gaussian approximation (12) holds with equality, the MacKay algorithm becomes the following MacKay-Gauss Procedure.*

MacKay-Gauss Procedure:

z-Step:

$$\mathbf{z}^{(t)} := \mu(\boldsymbol{\alpha}^{(t)})$$

$\boldsymbol{\alpha}$-Step:

$$\boldsymbol{\alpha}^{(t+1)} := \arg\max_{\boldsymbol{\alpha}}\left[\log p(\mathbf{z}^{(t)}|\boldsymbol{\alpha}) + \frac{1}{2}\log {\rm Det}(K(\boldsymbol{\alpha}))\right]$$

Linear Regression Example–6 *Since the Gaussian assumption (12) holds true in linear regression, the updates of the MacKay algorithm are those in Linear Regression Example–3.*

Bayesian PCA Example–6 *Assuming that the Gassian approximation (12) holds with equality, the $\mathbf{z}$-Step and $\boldsymbol{\alpha}$-Step updates become*

$$\begin{aligned}\mathbf{Z}^{(t)} &= \mu_{\rm BPCA}(\boldsymbol{\alpha}^{(t)})\\ \boldsymbol{\alpha}^{(t+1)} &= \arg\max_{\boldsymbol{\alpha}}\left[-\frac{1}{2}\sum_{k=1}^{d}\alpha_k\left\|\mathbf{z}_k^{(t)}\right\|^2\right.\\ &\quad\left. +\frac{1}{2}\log {\rm Det}\left(K_{\rm BPCA}(\boldsymbol{\alpha})\right) + \sum_{k=1}^{d}\frac{m}{2}\log \alpha_k\right]\end{aligned}$$

When setting $\frac{\partial \mathcal{F}_{\text{MacKay}}(\mathbf{z},\boldsymbol{\alpha})}{\partial \boldsymbol{\alpha}_k} = 0$, *we can obtain*

$$\boldsymbol{\alpha}_k = h(\boldsymbol{\alpha}_k, \mathbf{z}) = \frac{m - \boldsymbol{\alpha}_k \text{Tr}\left(K_{\text{BPCA},k}(\boldsymbol{\alpha})\right)}{\|\mathbf{z}_k\|^2}.$$

This gives rise to the fixed-point iteration of the $\boldsymbol{\alpha}$*-Step*

$$\boldsymbol{\alpha}_k^{(t+1)} = \frac{m - \boldsymbol{\alpha}_k^{(t)} \text{Tr}\left(K_{\text{BPCA},k}(\boldsymbol{\alpha}^{(t)})\right)}{\left\|\mathbf{z}_k^{(t)}\right\|^2}$$

4.3 THE RELATIONSHIP BETWEEN MAKCAY AND EM

As is shown earlier, the MacKay and EM algorithms correspond to solving two different optimization problems. However, we will show next that when the Gaussian approximation (12) holds exactly, the two algorithms are closely related.

First note that $\mathcal{F}_{\text{EM}}$ is a trivariate function whereas $\mathcal{F}_{\text{MacKay}}$ is a bivariate function. The theorem below suggests that if the Gaussian approximation of the posterior distribution $p(\mathbf{z}|\mathbf{D}, \boldsymbol{\alpha})$ is exact, then by setting its covariance variable S of $\mathcal{F}_{\text{EM}}$ to the covariance matrix of the posterior, the function $\mathcal{F}_{\text{EM}}$ reduces $\mathcal{F}_{\text{MacKay}}$.

Theorem 1. *When the Gaussian approximation (12) holds with equality,* $\mathcal{F}_{\text{EM}}(u, K(\boldsymbol{\alpha}), \boldsymbol{\alpha}) = \mathcal{F}_{\text{MacKay}}(u, \boldsymbol{\alpha})$, *where* $K(\boldsymbol{\alpha})$ *is defined in (13).*

Proof: Suppose that the Gaussian approximation (12) holds with equality. Invoking (16), we have

$$\begin{aligned}\mathcal{F}_{\text{MacKay}}(\mathbf{z}, \boldsymbol{\alpha}) &= \log p(\mathbf{D}, \mathbf{z}|\boldsymbol{\alpha}) + \frac{1}{2}\log \text{Det}(2\pi K(\boldsymbol{\alpha})) \\ &= \log \mathcal{N}(\mathbf{z}; \mu(\boldsymbol{\alpha}), K(\boldsymbol{\alpha})) + \log p(\mathbf{D}|\boldsymbol{\alpha}) \\ &\quad + \frac{1}{2}\log \text{Det}(2\pi K(\boldsymbol{\alpha}))\end{aligned}$$

But by Lemma 5, we have

$$\begin{aligned}\mathcal{F}_{\text{EM}}(\mathbf{z}, K(\boldsymbol{\alpha}), \boldsymbol{\alpha}) &= \log \mathcal{N}(\mathbf{z}; \mu(\boldsymbol{\alpha}), K(\boldsymbol{\alpha})) \\ &\quad - \frac{1}{2}\text{Tr}\left(K^{-1}(\boldsymbol{\alpha})K(\boldsymbol{\alpha})\right) + \log p(\mathbf{D}|\boldsymbol{\alpha}) \\ &\quad + \frac{J}{2}\log 2\pi + \frac{1}{2}\log \text{Det}(K(\boldsymbol{\alpha})) + \frac{J}{2} \\ &= \log \mathcal{N}(\mathbf{z}; \mu(\boldsymbol{\alpha}), K(\boldsymbol{\alpha})) + \log p(\mathbf{D}|\boldsymbol{\alpha}) \\ &\quad + \frac{1}{2}\log \text{Det}(2\pi K(\boldsymbol{\alpha})) \\ &= \mathcal{F}_{\text{MacKay}}(\mathbf{z}, \boldsymbol{\alpha})\end{aligned}$$

This proves the theorem. □

Theorem 1 suggests that the function $\mathcal{F}_{\text{MacKay}}$ is a restriction of function $\mathcal{F}_{\text{EM}}$. Denote by $\mathfrak{C}$ the set of all $(S, \boldsymbol{\alpha})$ configurations with $S = K(\boldsymbol{\alpha})$. That is, $\mathfrak{C}$ is the curve on the $(S, \boldsymbol{\alpha})$ plane specified by $S = K(\boldsymbol{\alpha})$. Under this notation, $\mathcal{F}_{\text{MacKay}}$ is the function $\mathcal{F}_{\text{EM}}$ with variables $(S, \boldsymbol{\alpha})$ restricted on the curve $\mathfrak{C}$.

Theorem 2. *When the Gaussian approximation (12) holds with equality,*

$$\mathcal{F}_{\text{MacKay}}(u, \boldsymbol{\alpha}) = \max_S \mathcal{F}_{\text{EM}}(u, S, \boldsymbol{\alpha}), \tag{17}$$

$$l(\boldsymbol{\alpha}) = \max_u \mathcal{F}_{\text{MacKay}}(u, \boldsymbol{\alpha}). \tag{18}$$

Proof: Denote $S^* := \arg\max_S \mathcal{F}_{\text{EM}}(u, S, \boldsymbol{\alpha}) = K(\boldsymbol{\alpha})$. Thus

$$\max_S \mathcal{F}_{\text{EM}}(u, S, \boldsymbol{\alpha}) = \mathcal{F}_{\text{EM}}(u, S^*, \boldsymbol{\alpha}) = \mathcal{F}_{\text{EM}}(u, K(\alpha), \boldsymbol{\alpha}).$$

Then the equation (17) holds by Theorem 1, On the other hand, by Lemma 3, $\mathcal{F}_{\text{MacKay}}(\mathbf{z}, \boldsymbol{\alpha}) \leq l(\boldsymbol{\alpha})$ and the equality can be achieved. We thus obtain the equation (18). □.

The following result follows immediately from Theorem 2.

Corollary 1. *The optimizing configurations for* Opt-l, OptEM *and* OptMacKay *are identical in* $\boldsymbol{\alpha}$.

Theorem 2 and Corollary 1 essentially suggest that OptMacKay is a relaxation of Opt-l, that OptEM is a relaxation of OptMacKay, and that such successive relaxations do not alter the solution of the original problem Opt-l.

Lemma 12. *The EM-Gauss Procedure is identical to the 3-way coordinate ascent on* $\mathcal{F}_{\text{EM}}$, *namely, iterating over the following three steps.*

$$\begin{aligned}u^{(t)} &:= \arg\max_u \mathcal{F}_{\text{EM}}(u, S^{(t-1)}, \boldsymbol{\alpha}^{(t)}) \\ S^{(t)} &:= \arg\max_S \mathcal{F}_{\text{EM}}(u^{(t)}, S, \boldsymbol{\alpha}^{(t)}) \\ \boldsymbol{\alpha}^{(t+1)} &:= \arg\max_{\boldsymbol{\alpha}} \mathcal{F}_{\text{EM}}(u^{(t)}, S^{(t)}, \boldsymbol{\alpha})\end{aligned}$$

Proof: This follows from the fact that in the EM-Gauss Procedure, the update of u is independent of S and the update of S is independent of u. □

Since OptEM is a relaxation of OptMacKay, it has higher degrees of freedom during optimization. This extra degree of freedom is fully explored in the three-way coordinate descent of EM-Gauss, making its convergence slower than that of MacKay-Gauss. This slower convergence of EM-Gauss can also be understood from another perspective, in which MacKay-Gauss and EM-Gauss are both considered as optimizing the function $\mathcal{F}_{\text{EM}}$.

Lemma 13. *The MacKay-Gauss Procedure is equivalent to the following two-way coordinate-ascent on* $\mathcal{F}_{\text{EM}}$.

$$\begin{aligned}u^{(t)} &:= \arg\max_u \mathcal{F}_{\text{EM}}(u, S^{(t-1)}, \boldsymbol{\alpha}^{(t-1)}) \\ \left(S^{(t)}, \boldsymbol{\alpha}^{(t)}\right) &:= \arg\max_{(S,\boldsymbol{\alpha})\in\mathfrak{C}} \mathcal{F}_{\text{EM}}(u^{(t)}, S, \boldsymbol{\alpha}).\end{aligned}$$

Following directly from the Lemma 11 and Theorem 1, this lemma suggests that MacKay-Gauss can be viewed as optimizing the same objective function $\mathcal{F}_{\text{EM}}$ as EM-Gauss, but taking a particular coordinate-ascent path, namely, alternating between maximization over u and maximization over (S, α) *along the curve* $\mathfrak{C}$. This allows MacKay-Gauss to take a "shorter-cut" than EM-Gauss.

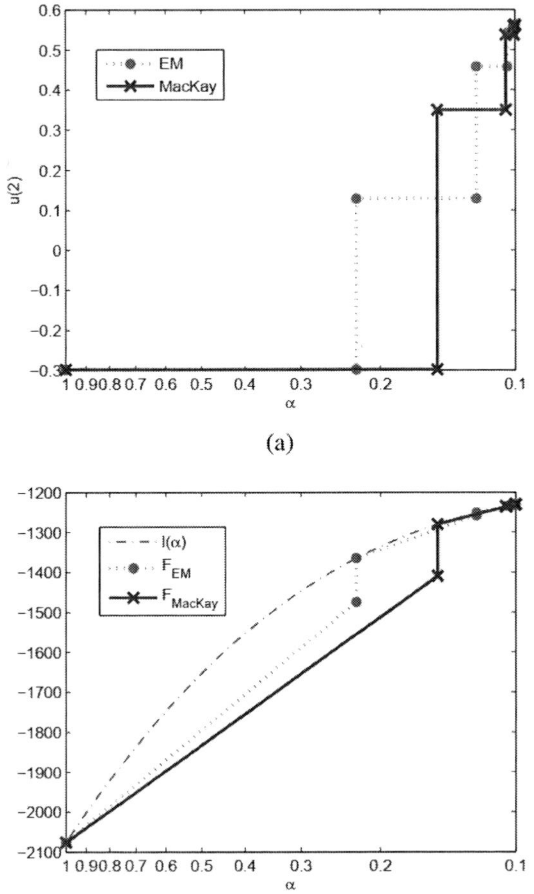

(b)

Figure 2: The convergence of both the EM algorithm and the MacKay algorithm from the initial configuration $\alpha = 1$ to the final configuration $\alpha \approx 0.1$. (a) The (α, u)-trajectories of the EM and MacKay algorithms, where an arbitrary component (in this case, the second component $u(2)$) of vector u is taken as a representative for u. (b) the function $\mathcal{F}_{\text{EM}}$ evaluated along the EM trajectory and the function $\mathcal{F}_{\text{MacKay}}$ evaluated along the MacKay trajectory, and the log-evidence function $l(\alpha)$ plotted using its closed-form expression.

4.4 Experiments

Experiments are performed to study the dynamics of the MacKay algorithm and the EM algorithm. We generate a simulated dataset $\mathbf{D}$ for a linear regression model according to the setup in Linear Regression Example–1 with $n = 300, d = 200, \sigma^2 = 10, \alpha = 0.1$ where each each $x_{(i)}$ is drawn uniformly at random from the open interval $(0, 1)$. Both the EM algorithm (in Linear Regression Example-2) and the MacKay algorithm (in Linear Regression Example-3) are used to estimate α from $\mathbf{D}$. For both algorithms, α is initialized to 1 and σ^2 is treated as known.

The optimization trajectories of the two algorithms in Figure 2 (a) show that the MacKay algorithm converges faster towards the fixed point (top right corner) than the EM algorithm. In Figure 2 (b), we see that both the MacKay algorithm and the EM algorithm increase their respective objective functions along their optimization paths, but MacKay achieves higher value of the log-evidence function $l(\alpha)$ than EM at every iteration step.

5 Concluding Remarks

In his influential evidence framework, MacKay presented practical Bayesian methods for inference at the parameter level, at the hyper-parameter level and at the model level. For inference at the hyper-parameter level, MacKay introduced a heuristic procedure that iterates between estimating the parameter for a given hyper-parameter setting and estimating the hyper-parameter for the previous parameter setting. Although this procedure is widely adopted in empirical Bayesian methods, its mathematical principle had not been carefully explored prior to this work. In this paper, we formulate this procedure as a well-principled algorithmic framework, and call it the MacKay algorithm.

We show that the MacKay algorithm, like the EM algorithm, can be understood as a coordinate-ascent solution to optimizing a lower bound of the objective function in empirical Bayes. Although this lower bound is different from the lower bound that is optimized by the EM algorithm, we show that as long as the posterior distribution of the parameter is a Gaussian density function, the two algorithms are closely related. In particular, the EM optimization problem, the MacKay optimization problem, and the original empirical Bayes optimization problem all have the same solution. In addition, the MacKay problem is a relaxation of the original problem, and the EM problem is a relaxation of the MacKay problem. This understanding provides and intuitive explanation as to why the MacKay algorithm converges faster than the EM algorithm.

We believe that the close relationship between the MacKay algorithm and the EM algorithm revealed in this paper strongly depends on the Gaussian condition. Although this paper does not show the necessity of this condition, we believe that, in case of non-Gaussian posterior or non-Gaussian models, this relationship will break down, and the MacKay algorithm will diverge from the EM algorithm towards its own optimization objective and along its own optimization path. This makes the MacKay algorithm a framework in its own right. We hope that this paper inspire more applications of the MacKay algorithm to more general models, a territory appearing completely unexplored.

References

[Allahverdyan and Galstyan, 2011] Allahverdyan, A. and Galstyan, A. (2011). Comparative analysis of viterbi training and maximum likelihood estimation for hmms. In *Advances in Neural Information Processing Systems*, pages 1674–1682.

[Bishop, 1999] Bishop, C. M. (1999). Bayesian PCA. *Advances in neural information processing systems*, pages 382–388.

[Carlin and Louis, 1997] Carlin, B. P. and Louis, T. A. (1997). Bayes and empirical Bayes methods for data analysis. *Statistics and Computing*, 7(2):153–154.

[Clyde and George, 2000] Clyde, M. and George, E. I. (2000). Flexible empirical Bayes estimation for wavelets. *Journal of the Royal Statistical Society: Series B (Statistical Methodology)*, 62(4):681–698.

[Dempster et al., 1977] Dempster, A. P., Laird, N. M., and Rubin, D. B. (1977). Maximum likelihood from incomplete data via the em algorithm. *Journal of the royal statistical society. Series B (methodological)*, pages 1–38.

[DuMouchel and Pregibon, 2001] DuMouchel, W. and Pregibon, D. (2001). Empirical Bayes screening for multi-item associations. In *Proceedings of the seventh ACM SIGKDD international conference on Knowledge discovery and data mining*, pages 67–76. ACM.

[Efron, 2012] Efron, B. (2012). *Large-scale inference: empirical Bayes methods for estimation, testing, and prediction*, volume 1. Cambridge University Press.

[Frost and Savarino, 1986] Frost, P. A. and Savarino, J. E. (1986). An empirical Bayes approach to efficient portfolio selection. *Journal of Financial and Quantitative Analysis*, 21(03):293–305.

[Heskes, 2000] Heskes, T. (2000). Empirical bayes for learning to learn. In *ICML*, pages 367–374.

[Hyvärinen, 1999] Hyvärinen, A. (1999). Fast and robust fixed-point algorithms for independent component analysis. *Neural Networks, IEEE Transactions on*, 10(3):626–634.

[Inoue and Tanaka, 2001] Inoue, J.-i. and Tanaka, K. (2001). Dynamics of the maximum marginal likelihood hyperparameter estimation in image restoration: Gradient descent versus expectation and maximization algorithm. *Phys. Rev. E*, 65:016125.

[Jensen, 1906] Jensen, J. L. W. V. (1906). Sur les fonctions convexes et les ingalits entre les valeurs moyennes. *Acta Mathematica*, 30(1):175–193.

[MacKay, 1992a] MacKay, D. J. (1992a). Bayesian interpolation. *Neural computation*, 4(3):415–447.

[MacKay, 1992b] MacKay, D. J. (1992b). The evidence framework applied to classification networks. *Neural computation*, 4(5):720–736.

[MacKay, 1992c] MacKay, D. J. (1992c). A practical Bayesian framework for backpropagation networks. *Neural computation*, 4(3):448–472.

[MacKay, 1995] MacKay, D. J. (1995). Probable networks and plausible predictions: a review of practical bayesian methods for supervised neural networks. *Network: Computation in Neural Systems*, 6(3):469–505.

[MacKay and Neal, 1994] MacKay, D. J. and Neal, R. M. (1994). Automatic relevance determination for neural networks. In *Technical Report in preparation*. Cambridge University.

[Murphy, 2012] Murphy, K. P. (2012). *Machine learning: a probabilistic perspective*. MIT press.

[Neal, 1993] Neal, R. (1993). Probabilistic inference using markov chain monte carlo methods. Technical Report CRG-TR -93-1, Dept. of Computer Science, University of Toronto.

[Schäfer and Strimmer, 2005] Schäfer, J. and Strimmer, K. (2005). An empirical Bayes approach to inferring large-scale gene association networks. *Bioinformatics*, 21(6):754–764.

[Solomon, 2015] Solomon, J. (2015). *Numerical Algorithms: Methods for Computer Vision, Machine Learning, and Graphics*. CRC Press.

[Tan and Févotte, 2009] Tan, V. Y. and Févotte, C. (2009). Automatic relevance determination in nonnegative matrix factorization. In *SPARS'09-Signal Processing with Adaptive Sparse Structured Representations*.

[Tipping, 2001] Tipping, M. E. (2001). Sparse Bayesian learning and the relevance vector machine. *The journal of machine learning research*, 1:211–244.

[Tipping et al., 2003] Tipping, M. E., Faul, A. C., et al. (2003). Fast marginal likelihood maximisation for sparse bayesian models. In *AISTATS*.

[Wipf and Nagarajan, 2008] Wipf, D. P. and Nagarajan, S. S. (2008). A new view of automatic relevance determination. In *Advances in neural information processing systems*, pages 1625–1632.

[Yang et al., 2004] Yang, D., Zakharkin, S. O., Page, G. P., Brand, J. P., Edwards, J. W., Bartolucci, A. A., and Allison, D. B. (2004). Applications of Bayesian statistical methods in microarray data analysis. *American Journal of Pharmacogenomics*, 4(1):53–62.

Dantzig Selector with an Approximately Optimal Denoising Matrix and its Application in Sparse Reinforcement Learning

Bo Liu
Auburn University
boliuauburn@gmail.com

Luwan Zhang
University of Wisconsin-Madison
luwanzhang@gmail.com

Ji Liu
University of Rochester
ji.liu.uwisc@gmail.com

Abstract

Dantzig Selector (DS) is widely used in compressed sensing and sparse learning for feature selection and sparse signal recovery. Since the DS formulation is essentially a linear programming optimization, many existing linear programming solvers can be simply applied for scaling up. The DS formulation can be explained as a basis pursuit denoising problem, wherein the data matrix (or measurement matrix) is employed as the denoising matrix to eliminate the observation noise. However, we notice that the data matrix may not be the optimal denoising matrix, as shown by a simple counter-example. This motivates us to pursue a better denoising matrix for defining a general DS formulation. We first define the optimal denoising matrix through a minimax optimization, which turns out to be an NP-hard problem. To make the problem computationally tractable, we propose a novel algorithm, termed as "Optimal" Denoising Dantzig Selector (ODDS), to approximately estimate the optimal denoising matrix. Empirical experiments validate the proposed method. Finally, a novel sparse reinforcement learning algorithm is formulated by extending the proposed ODDS algorithm to temporal difference learning, and empirical experimental results demonstrate to outperform the conventional "vanilla" DS-TD algorithm.

1 Introduction

We consider consider the classic problem in compressed sensing, sparse learning, and statistics [Donoho, 2006, Candes and Tao, 2007, Bickel et al., 2009]:

Given a data (measurement) matrix $X \in \mathbb{R}^{n\times m}$ ($m \gg n$) and a noisy observation vector $y \in \mathbb{R}^n$ satisfying $y = X\beta^* + \epsilon$ where ϵ is the noise vector following the Gaussian distribution $N(0, \sigma^2 I)$[1] and β^* is the truth model which is a sparse vector. How to recover the sparse vector β^* from this under-determined system?

Dantzig Selector (DS) [Candes and Tao, 2007] is a widely used approach to solving this problem. The standard DS is formulated as

$$\text{(DS)} \quad \hat{\beta}_{\text{DS}} = \arg\min_{\beta} \ \|\beta\|_1 \qquad \text{(1a)}$$

$$\text{s.t.} \ \|X^T(X\beta - y)\|_\infty \leq \lambda. \qquad \text{(1b)}$$

DS has a very similar performance to another famous formulation LASSO [Tibshirani, 1996] both empirically and theoretically [Bickel et al., 2009]. The DS formulation (1) can be formulated as a linear programming (LP) problem, thus many matured LP solvers can be directly applied to address this problem with large-scale problem settings. The DS formulation or its variation has been widely used in reinforcement learning [Geist et al., 2012, Liu et al., 2012, Mahadevan and Liu, 2012, Qin et al., 2014], computational bioinformatics [Liu, 2014], and computer vision [Cong et al., 2011].

The motivation of this paper is to explore the role of X^T (the transpose of X) in DS formulation (1). We note that the constraint in (1b) follows two principles: 1) the defined feasible region should contain the true solution β^* with high probability; and 2) to make $\hat{\beta}_{\text{DS}}$ close to β^* the feasible region defined by the constraint should be as small as possible, that is, λ is expected to a small value. Taking $\beta = \beta^*$ into the constraint leads to the smallest possible value for $\lambda = \|X^T(X\beta^* - y)\|_\infty = \|X^T\epsilon\|_\infty$. If columns of X are normalized to 1, we have $\lim_{n\to\infty} \|X^T\epsilon\|_\infty \to 0$ with high probability Candes and Tao [2007]. Therefore, the factor X^T in the constraint actually plays the role of *denoising*. This motivates us to ask two questions: 1) is X^T the optimal denoising matrix for the recovery of the sparse signal β^*?; and 2) if not, how to measure the the optimality of the denoising matrix and how to compute the optimal denoising matrix?

[1]The Gaussian distribution can be generalized to any sub-Gaussian distribution.

Unfortunately, X^T is *not* the optimal denoising matrix in general. We provide a counter-example in Section 3. The main contributions of this paper are summarized below:

- We propose a generalized denoising Dantzig selector formulation (GDDS) and define the optimal denoising matrix for sparse signal recovery via a minimax formulation;
- A two-stage approach is proposed to compute the approximately optimal denoising matrix;
- We apply the proposed ODDS algorithm to an important application in reinforcement learning: the temporal difference learning problem for sparse value function approximation.

This paper is organized as follows: Related work is introduced in Section 2. Section 3, which is the core part of this paper, proposes the general Dantzig Selector formulation with both intuitive motivations as well as the mathematical backgrounds. A generalized error bound is proposed, which leads to the definition of the optimal denoising matrix, which is NP-hard in general. To address this problem, a two-stage algorithm for approximately computing the optimal denoising matrix is given. Then in Section 4, the algorithm is applied to reinforcement learning to design a new algorithm for sparse value function approximation. The experimental results are presented in Section 5, which validate the effectiveness of the proposed algorithm.

2 Related Work

The problem considered in this paper has received substantial attentions in compressed sensing, sparse learning, and statistics. The study starts from the special case, i.e. the noiseless case $\epsilon = 0$. To recover the sparse vector β^*, there are two types of approaches: ℓ_1 norm minimization and greedy algorithms. The ℓ_1 norm minimization solves the following optimization problem to estimate β^* [Chen and Donoho, 1994, Candes and Tao, 2005]

$$\min_{\beta} \quad \|\beta\|_1 \quad \text{s.t.} \quad X\beta = y. \tag{2}$$

The theoretical study [Candes and Tao, 2005] suggests that under the restricted isometric property (RIP) condition, the ℓ_1 norm minimization formulation can recover the true solution β^* exactly. The greedy approaches include the forward greedy algorithm (or OMP) [Tropp, 2004] and the backward greedy algorithm. A similar theoretical guarantee of exact recovery is proven for the forward greedy algorithm in Zhang [2011b].

Now let us turn to the noisy case, i.e. $\epsilon \neq 0$. The noisy case is more challenging than the noiseless case. It also mainly includes two types of approaches: ℓ_1 norm minimization approaches and greedy algorithms. To deal with the noise, there are several popular formulations including DS [Candes and Tao, 2007], LASSO [Tibshirani, 1996], and basis pursuit denoising (BPDN) [Chen et al., 2001]. They essentially apply different manners to denoise. BPDN uses the ℓ_2 norm penalty to denoise:

$$\hat{\beta}_{\text{BPDN}} = \arg\min_{\beta} \|\beta\|_1 \quad \text{s.t.} \quad \|X\beta - y\|_2 \leq \varepsilon, \tag{3}$$

where the constraint basically restricts the noise ϵ by $\|\epsilon\| \leq \varepsilon$. DS uses the ℓ_∞ norm penalty to denoise $\|X^T\epsilon\|_\infty \leq \lambda$ as shown above. LASSO applies the same spirit as DS [Bickel et al., 2009] to denoise, but uses a different formulation

$$\hat{\beta}_{\text{LASSO}} = \arg\min_{\beta} \frac{1}{2}\|X\beta - y\|_2^2 + \lambda\|\beta\|_1. \tag{4}$$

The theoretical error bound for LASSO and DS is similar [Bickel et al., 2009] and better than BPDN in some sense. The key reason lies in that the noise constraint used in DS and LASSO $\|X^T\epsilon\|_\infty \leq \lambda$ is sharper than the noise constraint used in BPDN $\|\epsilon\| \leq \varepsilon$.[2] The greedy approaches mainly include the forward greedy algorithm [Zhang, 2009] and the forward-backward greedy algorithm [Zhang, 2011a, Liu et al., 2013].

While Dantzig Selector primarily focuses on ℓ_1 regularization for sparsity, the group-sparsity structures was explored [Liu et al., 2010a], and was recently extended to generalized norm [Chatterjee et al., 2014]. Other variants includes weighted Dantzig Selector [Candes et al., 2008] by re-weighting the sparse signal, multi-stage Dantzig Selector [Liu et al., 2010b] for iterative sparse signal recovery, etc. As for the computational achievements, besides the primal-dual interior point method [Candes and Tao, 2007], TFOCS [Becker et al., 2011] is also widely used. Later, inexact alternating direction method of multipliers (ADMM) formulations are proposed in [Lu et al., 2012, Wang and Yuan, 2012], which are computationally efficient.

3 Algorithm

We first show the generic error bound when "X^T" in (1b) is substituted by an arbitrary denoising matrix Q^T. Then a counter example is provided to show why X^T is not the optimal choice for Q^T. We prove an approximate method to pursue the optimal denoising matrix Q^T in the end of this section.

3.1 Generalized Denoising Dantzig Selector and its Error Bound

With the backgrounds of the denoising matrix introduced above, one intuitive question is that if X^T the optimal denoising matrix for sparse signal recovery of β^*? The answer is actually NO! To explain this, we first introduce the

[2] From the optimization perspective, BPDN seems consistent with LASSO, but the theoretical error bound is worse than LASSO and DS for some subtle reasons, which is beyond the scope of this paper.

generalized denoising Dantzig Selector formulation. Next, an error bound w.r.t the GDDS and regular DS is proposed, and it can be proven that for regular DS, the error bound is tighter than the existing error bound provided in [Candes and Tao, 2007] and [Bickel et al., 2009]. Then a simple counter-example is proposed to argue that X^T may not be the optimal denoising matrix. We here present some definitions and notations in Figure 1.

- h_T, h_{T^c}: T and T^c are two complementary subsets in $\{1, 2, \cdots, m\}$. We denote by $h_T \in \mathbb{R}^m$ the vector taking the same values as h on T and zeros in the rest; the same for $h_{T^c} \in \mathbb{R}^m$;
- $|T|$ returns the cardinality of the set T;
- $\|W\|_\infty$ is defined as the induced ∞ norm of matrix $W \in \mathbb{R}^{m\times m}$, i.e. $\|W\|_\infty = \max_x \frac{\|Wx\|_\infty}{\|x\|_\infty}$ where the vector infinity norm $\|Wx\|_\infty$ and $\|x\|_\infty$ are defined as usual;
- $\leq_{(P)}$: less than or equal to with high probability;

Figure 1: Notation used in this paper

First we define a generalized denoising Dantzig Selector (GDDS) formulation by using a general denoising matrix Q^T ($Q \in \mathbb{R}^{n\times m}$) to replace the X^T in the constraint:

$$\text{(GDDS)} \quad \min_\beta : \|\beta\|_1 \quad \text{s.t.} : \|Q^T(X\beta - y)\|_\infty \leq \lambda. \tag{5}$$

Next we will propose an error bound for the proposed GDDS in (5) and regular DS. Since the denoising matrix is not necessarily X^T anymore, the commonly used RIP condition or restricted eigenvalue (RE) condition [Van De Geer et al., 2009] are not eligible here. To extend to the general case, we define a new condition termed as *generalized restricted (GR) constant.*

Definition 1. *(GR constant) Given $X, Q \in \mathbb{R}^{n\times m}$ and $p \in [1, \infty]$, the general restricted constant $\rho(Q^T X, p, s)$ is defined as*

$$\rho(Q, X, p, s) := \min_{|T|\leq s, \|h_{T^c}\|_1 \leq \|h_T\|_1} \frac{\|Q^T Xh\|_\infty}{\|h\|_p}. \tag{6}$$

This definition essentially provides the lower bound of the ratio between $\|Q^T Xh\|_\infty$ and $\|h\|_p$ over h in a subset of $\mathbb{R}^p$, which characterizes the property of $Q^T X$. The GR constant leads to a weaker condition to exactly recover the sparse signal β^* for the noiseless case ($\epsilon = 0$) and a tighter error bound for the noisy case ($\epsilon \neq 0$) than the existing analysis, as shown by Theorem 1. Based on the definition for GR constant in Definition 1, we have the following error bound on $\|\hat{\beta}_{\text{GDDS}} - \beta^*\|_p$.

Theorem 1. *Assume that the GR condition is satisfied, i.e. the GR constant $\rho(Q, X, p, \|\beta^*\|_0) > 0$. Choose $\lambda = \|Q^T\epsilon\|_\infty$ in (5). We have*

$$\|\hat{\beta}_{GDDS} - \beta^*\|_p \leq \frac{2\|Q^T\epsilon\|_\infty}{\rho(Q, X, p, \|\beta^*\|_0)}, \tag{7}$$

where $\hat{\beta}_{GDDS}$ is the solution to (5) and p can be any value in the range $[1, \infty]$.

It should be noted that albeit with a more general error bound, Theorem 1 does not weaken the existing analysis based on the following two observations:

- In the noiseless case, i.e. $\epsilon = 0$, if the GR condition is satisfied, then $\hat{\beta}_{\text{GDDS}}$ is able to exactly recover β^*. Note that the GR condition is weaker than the RIP condition for $Q = X$ [Candes, 2008]. In other words, the RIP condition leads to GR condition when $Q = X$. The detailed interpretation is provided in Appendix.
- In the noisy case, i.e. $\epsilon \neq 0$, this bound (7) is a tighter bound than the bound $\|\hat{\beta}_{\text{DS}} - \beta^*\|_p$ for DS in [Candes and Tao, 2007, Bickel et al., 2009] for $Q = X$. Please also refer to Appendix for detailed comparisons.

The key reason why Theorem 1 does not loose the existing analysis lies in that the definition of the GR constant $\rho(Q, X, p, s)$ skips many relaxation steps by directly indicating the relationship between $\|Q^T\epsilon\|_\infty$ and $\|\hat{\beta}_{\text{GDDS}} - \beta^*\|^2$. Given p, s and X, $\rho(Q, X, p, s)$ reflects the ability for sparse signal recovery of β^* of the denoising matrix Q^T: *The larger $\rho(Q, X, p, s)$ is, the better Q is able to recover the sparse signal β^*.* Therefore, since the error bound provided in Theorem is tight enough, it is reasonable to use the bound in (7) as the evaluation criteria to see why X^T is not the optimal denoising matrix and define the optimal denoising matrix.

3.2 A Counter-Example

To see why X^T may not be the optimal denoising matrix, we show an example of Q which gives a lower value for the bound in (7). To construct such a matrix Q, we require the same conditions on Q as X, i.e. all columns of Q have been normalized with norm 1. We can verify that any Q with unit column norm, the value of $\|Q^T\epsilon\|_\infty$ is comparable to $\|X^T\epsilon\|_\infty$, according to the following standard results in Lemma 1.

Lemma 1. *For any $Q \in \mathbb{R}^{n\times m}$ satisfying $\|Q_{.i}\| = 1$ for $i = 1, \cdots, m$, we have*

$$\|Q^T\epsilon\|_\infty \leq \sigma\sqrt{\log m}$$

with high probability at least $1 - O(1/m)$.

The key reason why $\|Q^T\epsilon\|_\infty$ and $\|X^T\epsilon\|_\infty$ are comparable lies in that all entries in random vectors $Q^T\epsilon \in \mathbb{R}^p$

and $X^T\epsilon \in \mathbb{R}^p$ follow the same Gaussian distribution $\mathcal{N}(0, \sigma^2)$. Since $\|Q^T\epsilon\|_\infty$ and $\|X^T\epsilon\|_\infty$ are comparable, we only need to find an example for Q such that $\rho(Q, X, p, s) > \rho(X, X, p, s)$ for some X. Let $s = 1$ for simplicity and

$$X = \begin{pmatrix} \sqrt{3}/2 & 1/2 \\ 1/2 & \sqrt{3}/2 \end{pmatrix}, \; Q = \begin{pmatrix} 1 & 0 \\ 0 & 1 \end{pmatrix}. \tag{8}$$

We have

$$X^T X = \begin{pmatrix} 1 & \sqrt{3}/2 \\ \sqrt{3}/2 & 1 \end{pmatrix} \tag{9}$$

$$\begin{aligned} \rho(X, X, p, 1) = & \min_{\substack{|T| \le 1 \\ \|h_{T^c}\|_1 \le \|h_T\|_1}} \frac{\|X^T X h\|_\infty}{\|h_T\|_p} \\ = & 1 - \sqrt{3}/2 = 0.134, \\ \rho(Q, X, p, 1) = & \min_{\substack{|T| \le 1 \\ \|h_{T^c}\|_1 \le \|h_T\|_1}} \frac{\|Q^T X h\|_\infty}{\|h_T\|_p} \\ = & \sqrt{3}/2 - 1/2 = 0.366, \end{aligned}$$

where in both cases the optimal value of h is $h = [1, -1]^T$ regardless of the value of p. Thus, this example shows that X^T may not always be the optimal denoising matrix.

3.3 Optimal Denoising Matrix and its Approximation

From the counter-example in the previous section, we know that X is not the optimal option for Q to maximize $\rho(Q, X, p, s)$. Therefore, it raises an optimization problem to find the optimal Q:

$$Q^* = \operatorname*{argmax}_{\|Q_{.i}\| \le 1} \min_{\substack{|T| \le s \\ \|h_{T^c}\|_1 \le \|h_T\|_1}} \frac{\|Q^T X h\|_\infty}{\|h_T\|_p}. \tag{10}$$

However, this formulation is extremely difficult to solve. Although we can solve it easily for small n, m as in our example above, it is NP-hard in general. Therefore, it is unrealistic to solve this problem exactly. To find a reasonable approximation, we consider an alternative way to finding an optimal matrix $W \approx Q^T X$:

$$W^* = \operatorname*{argmax}_{\|W\|_\infty \le 1} \min_{\substack{|T| \le s \\ \|h_{T^c}\|_1 \le \|h_T\|_1}} \frac{\|W h\|_\infty}{\|h_T\|_p}. \tag{11}$$

One can easily verify that the optimal solution is $W^* = I$.[3] The second step is to find the optimal Q. We try to find the best Q from another perspective. Intuitively, we want $Q^T X$ to be close to the identity matrix. We estimate Q by the following:

$$\min_Q : \; \|Q^T X - I\|_p \quad \text{s.t.} : \quad \|Q_{.i}\| \le 1 \tag{12}$$

[3] Actually, it is not important which norm is used to restrict W. For most norms we verified, the optimal solution for W should be a diagonal matrix with equal values.

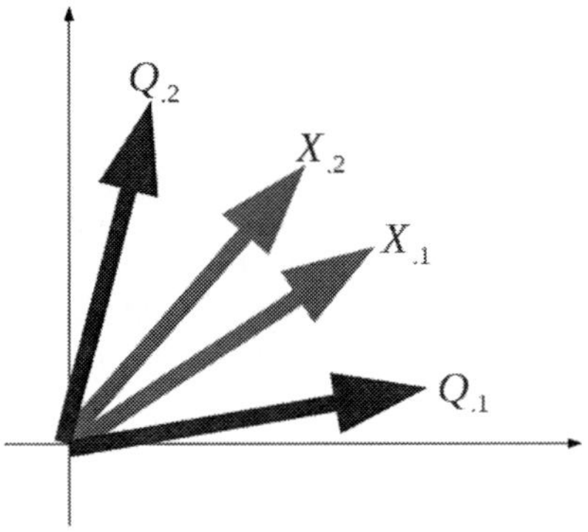

Figure 2: An example of X and Q.

where $p \in [1, \infty]$ and $\|X\|_p := (\sum_{i,j} |X_{ij}|^p)^{1/p}$. We have many options for choosing $p \in [1, \infty]$. Based on our empirical study, a reasonable empirical value for p is $p = 2$, and thus the problem can be recast as a strongly convex problem

$$\min_Q : \; \|Q^T X - I\|_2^2 \quad \text{s.t.} : \quad \|Q_{.i}\| \le 1 \tag{13}$$

There are many optimization algorithms to address this problem. We use Nesterov's accelerated gradient method [Nesterov, 2004]. Note that the empirical Q obtained from (12) or (13) is generally different from the optimal one defined in (10). And the optimal denoising Dantzig Selector algorithm is summarized as in Algorithm 1.

Algorithm 1 "Optimal" Denoising Dantzig Selector (ODDS)

Require: $X \in \mathbb{R}^{n \times m}, y \in \mathbb{R}^n$
Ensure: β
  Compute the denoising matrix Q^T via Eq. (13)
  Compute β via Eq. (5)

Figure 2 provides an example of Q and X in the two-dimensional case. Intuitively, Q is an approximation to X by slightly modifying all feature (column) vectors of X such that they are as different from each other as possible.

4 Reinforcement Learning

Dantzig selector has an important application in reinforcement learning. This section first briefly introduces reinforcement learning and then shows how to apply the proposed ODDS method to it.

A *Markov Decision Process* (MDP) is defined by the tuple $(S, A, P_{ss'}^a, R, \gamma)$, comprised of a set of states S, a set of actions A, a dynamical system model comprised of the transition kernel $P_{ss'}^a$ specifying the probability of transition from state $s \in S$ to state $s' \in S$ under action $a \in A$, a reward model $R(s, a) : S \times A \to \mathbb{R}$, and $0 \le \gamma < 1$ is a discount factor. A policy $\pi : S \to A$ is a deterministic mapping from states to actions. Associated with each policy π is a value function V^π, which is the fixed point of the Bellman equation:

$$V^\pi = T^\pi(V^\pi) = R^\pi + \gamma P^\pi V^\pi,$$

for a given state $s \in S$, $R^\pi(s) = R(s, \pi(s))$, and P^π is the state transition function under fixed policy π, and T^π is known as the *Bellman operator*. In what follows, we often drop the dependence of V^π, T^π, R^π on π, for notation simplicity. In linear value function approximation, a value function is assumed to lie in the linear span of a basis function matrix Φ of dimension $|S| \times d$, where d is the number of linear independent features. It is easy to show that the "best" approximation $\hat{v}_{\text{best}}$ of the true value function V satisfies the following equation,

$$\hat{v}_{\text{best}} = \Pi V = \Pi L^{-1} R, \tag{14}$$

where $\Pi = \Phi(\Phi^T \Xi \Phi)^{-1} \Phi^T \Xi$, Ξ is a diagonal matrix where the i-th diagonal entry ξ_i is the stationary state distribution w.r.t state s_i. and $L = I - \gamma P$. However, L^{-1} is also computationally prohibitive. To this end, a more practical way is to compute a Galerkin-Bubnov approximate solution [Yu and Bertsekas, 2010] is via solving a fixed-point equation

$$\hat{v} = \Pi_\Phi^X T \hat{v} \tag{15}$$

w.r.t an oblique projection Π_Φ^X onto span(Φ) orthogonal to X, i.e., $\Pi_\Phi^X = \Phi(X^T\Phi)^{-1}X^T$. The existence and uniqueness of the solution can be verified since T is a contraction mapping, Π_Φ^X is a non-expansive mapping, and thus $\Pi_\Phi^X T$ is a contraction mapping. As for the optimal solution $\hat{v}_{\text{best}}$, we have $X_{\text{best}} = (L^T)^{-1}\Xi\Phi$, which is also computational expensive. An often used X used in the fixed-point equation (15) is $X_{TD} = \Xi\Phi$, which is computationally affordable, and the corresponding solution to the fixed-point equation is $\hat{v}_{TD}$. The other often used X is $X_{BR} = \Xi L \Phi$ [Scherrer, 2010], which we will not explained in details here. However, it is obvious that none of X_{TD} or X_{BR} is the optimal solution. In fact, it has been shown that $||V - \hat{v}_{TD}||_\Xi \leq \frac{1}{1-\gamma}||V - \hat{v}_{\text{best}}||_\Xi$ [Tsitsiklis and Van Roy, 1997], which implies that approximation error $||V - \hat{v}_{TD}||_\Xi$ between the true value function V and $\hat{v}_{TD}$ can be arbitrarily bad when $\gamma \to 1$. Given a fixed-point equation (15), we have

$$\Pi_\Phi^X T\hat{v} - \hat{v} = \Pi_\Phi^X (T\hat{v} - \hat{v}) = \Phi(X^T\Phi)^{-1}X^T(T\hat{v} - \hat{v}) \tag{16}$$

Thus we can formulate the approximation error via constraining $||X^T(T\hat{v} - \hat{v})||_\infty \leq \lambda$.

Since the P, R, Ξ models are not accessible, the sample-based estimation is used. Given n training samples of the form $(s_i, a_i, r_i, s_i')_{i=1}^n$, $s_i \sim \Xi$, $r_i = r(s_i, a_i)$, $a_i \sim \pi_b(\cdot|s_i)$, $s_i' \sim P(\cdot|s_i, a_i)$, the empirical Bellman operator $\hat{T}$ is thus written as

$$\hat{T}(\hat{\Phi}\theta) = \hat{R} + \gamma\hat{\Phi}'\theta \tag{17}$$

We denote $\hat{\Phi}$ (resp. $\hat{\Phi}'$) the empirical feature matrices whose i-th row is the feature vector $\phi(s_i)^T$ (resp. $\phi(s_i')^T$), and $\hat{R} \in \mathbb{R}^n$ the empirical reward vector with corresponding r_i as the i-th row. And the error constraint can be formulated as $||Q^T(A\theta - b)||_\infty \leq \lambda$, where $A = \hat{\Phi} - \gamma\hat{\Phi}'$, $b = \hat{R}$, and $Q \in \mathbb{R}^{n \times d}$. So given Q and a pre-defined error λ, the Dantzig Selector temporal difference learning problem can be formulated as

$$\hat{\theta}_{\text{DS-TD}} = \underset{\theta}{\text{argmin}} \, ||\theta||_1 \quad \text{s.t.} \quad ||Q^T(A\theta - b)||_\infty \leq \lambda.$$

If $Q = \hat{\Phi}$, then the algorithm is the DS-TD algorithm [Geist et al., 2012]. Motivated by the GDDS algorithm to find the optimal denoising matrix Q^T, we design a new Dantzig Selector temporal difference learning algorithm to compute the optimal Q^T for sparse value function approximation as follows

$$\hat{\theta}_{\text{ODDS-TD}} = \underset{\theta}{\text{argmin}} \, ||\theta||_1 \quad \text{s.t.} \quad ||Q^T(A\theta - b)||_\infty \leq \lambda \tag{18}$$

where Q is computed from solving

$$\min_Q : \; ||Q^T A - I||_F^2 \quad \text{s.t.} : \quad ||Q_{.i}|| \leq 1 \tag{19}$$

Based on above, we propose the following ODDS-TD algorithm.

Algorithm 2 "Optimal" Denoising Dantzig Selector for Temporal Difference Learning with (ODDS-TD)

Require: A, b

Ensure: $\hat{\theta}_{\text{ODDS-TD}}$

Compute the denoising matrix Q^T via Eq. (19)

Compute $\hat{\theta}_{\text{ODDS-TD}}$ via Eq. (18)

5 Empirical Experiment

Experiments are first conducted on synthetic data with small-scale size and medium-scale respectively. Next, we apply the proposed method to a reinforcement learning problem on real data sets to show its advantage over existing algorithms.

5.1 Small-Scale Experiment

In this experiment, we conduct the comparison study between the regular Dantzig Selector (DS) and ODDS. We first compare the performance of different algorithms w.r.t different sparsity and noise levels. We set $n = 100, m = 150$, the true signal β^* is preset, with different numbers of non-zero elements (NNZ) among $10, 15, 20, 25$. We also change different noise level varying among $\sigma = 0.1, 0.2, 0.3$. Figure 3 shows the performance comparison of the two algorithms, wherein in each subfigure, the noise level is the same, and the x-axis denotes the NNZ level, and the result is measured by the difference of the learned sparse signal with β^*. From Figure 3, we can see that $||\hat{\beta}_{\text{ODDS}} - \beta^*||_2$ is much smaller than $||\hat{\beta}_{\text{DS}} - \beta^*||_2$.

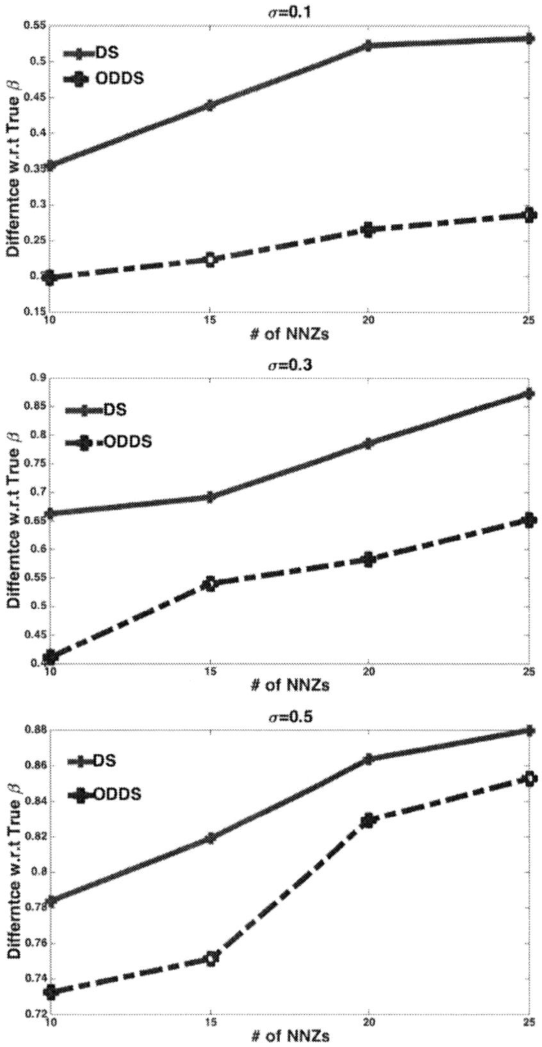

Figure 3: Small-scale Experiment w.r.t different sparsity levels.

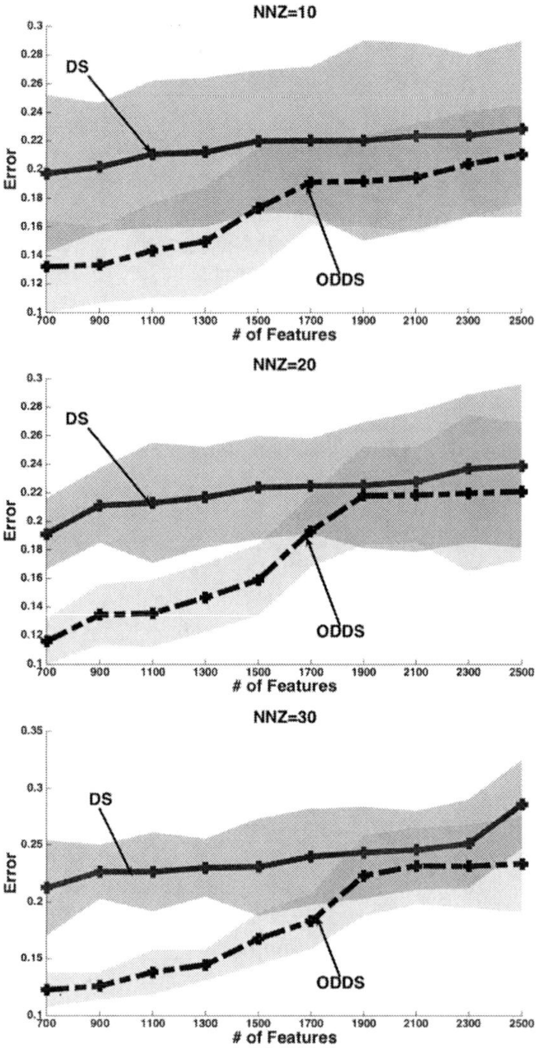

Figure 4: Comparison w.r.t different number of features.

5.2 Medium-Scale Experiment

In this experiment, we conduct the comparison study between the regular DS and ODDS. The experimental setting is that given $n = 500$, the number of features m goes among $700, 900, \cdots, 2500$, and $NNZ = 10$. The noise level $\sigma = 0.01$, and λ is chosen as $\lambda = \sigma\sqrt{2\log n}$ as suggested by [Candes and Tao, 2007] for a fair comparison between DS and ODDS, and the result is averaged by the mean-squares error (MSE), which is averaged over 50 runs. From Figure 4, we can see that the performance of ODDS is much better than that of regular DS, with both much lower MSE error and less variance.

5.3 ODDS-TD Experiment

In this experiment, we compare the performance of the DS-TD [Geist et al., 2012] and the proposed ODDS-TD algorithm. We test the performances of the two algorithms on the 20-state corrupted chain domain, wherein the two goal-states are $s \in [1, 20]$ with the reward signal $+1$, and the probability transition to the nearest goal-state is 0.9. The features are constructed as follows. 5 radial basis functions (RBF) are constructed, and one constant is used as an offset, and all other noisy features are randomly drawn from Gaussian distribution. So for each sample s_t, the feature vector $\phi(s) = [1, \mathrm{RBF}(1), \cdots, \mathrm{RBF}(5), s_1, \cdots, s_n]$. 200 off-policy samples are collected via randomly sampling the state space. Two comparison studies are carried out. In the first experiment, there are 300 noisy features, so altogether there are 306 features, and the value function approximation result is shown in the first subfigure of Figure 5, where v_{ODDS} and v_{DS} are the value function approximation results of ODDS and regular DS. From the figures, one can see that the v_{ODDS} is much more accurate than that of v_{DS}. The second experiment poses an even more challenging task, where the number of noisy features is set to be 600, so altogether there are 606 features, which makes the feature selection task much more difficult, and the result is shown in the second subfigure of Figure 5. We can see that

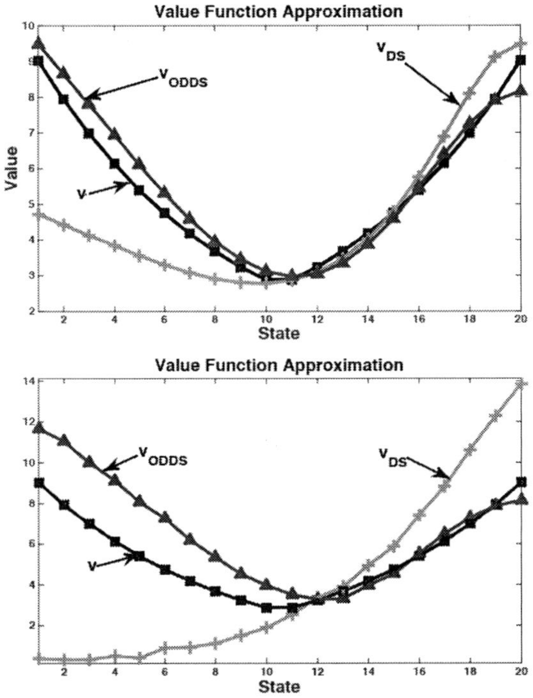

Figure 5: Comparison between ODDS-TD and DS-TD

v_{DS} has been severely distorted, whereas v_{ODDS} is still able to well preserve the topology of the value function, and is able to generate the right policy.

6 Conclusion

In this paper, motivated by achieving a better sparse signal recovery, we propose a generalized denoising matrix Dantzig selector formulation. A two-stage algorithm is proposed to find the optimal denoising matrix. The algorithm is then applied to sparse value function approximation problem in temporal difference learning field, and the empirical results validate the efficacy of the proposed algorithm. There are many interesting future directions along this research topic. For example, the ODDS framework can be extended to weighted Dantzig Selector (WDS) [Candes et al., 2008], multi-stage Dantzig Selector [Liu et al., 2010b], group Dantzig Selector [Liu et al., 2010a] and generalized Dantzig Selector [Chatterjee et al., 2014], which are parallel research directions of the Dantzig Selector algorithms family.

7 Acknowledgements

Bo Liu is partially funded by NSF Grant IIS-1216467, and the startup funding at Auburn University. Ji Liu is funded by NSF Grant CNS-1548078, the NEC fellowship, and the startup funding at the University of Rochester.

A Theoretical Analysis of ODDS

Proof to Theorem 1

Proof. Denote the difference between the solution to (5) $\hat{\beta}_{\text{GDDS}}$ and the true model β^* as $h = \hat{\beta}_{\text{GDDS}} - \beta^*$. Denote the support set of β^* by $T \subset \{1, 2, \cdots, m\}$. First we verify that the true model β^* is a feasible point to the problem (5) due to the following observation

$$\|Q^T(X\beta^* - y)\|_\infty = \|Q^T\epsilon\|_\infty \leq \lambda.$$

Since $\hat{\beta}_{\text{GDDS}}$ is the minimizer of problem (5), it follows that

$$\begin{aligned}
&\|\hat{\beta}_{\text{GDDS}}\|_1 \leq \|\beta^*\|_1 \\
\Rightarrow &\sum_{j\in T} |(\hat{\beta}_{\text{GDDS}})_j| + \sum_{j\in T^c} |(\hat{\beta}_{\text{GDDS}})_j| \leq \sum_{j\in T} |\beta_j^*| \\
\Rightarrow &\sum_{j\in T^c} |(\hat{\beta}_{\text{GDDS}})_j| \leq \sum_{j\in T} |\beta_j^* - (\hat{\beta}_{\text{GDDS}})_j| \\
\Rightarrow &\|h_{T^c}\|_1 \leq \|h_T\|_1.
\end{aligned}$$

From the definition of $\rho(Q, X, p, s)$ in (6), we have

$$\rho(Q, X, p, \|\beta^*\|_0)\|h\|_p \leq \|Q^T X h\|_\infty$$

which indicates

$$\|h\|_p \leq \frac{\|Q^T X h\|_\infty}{\rho(Q, X, p, \|\beta^*\|_0)}. \tag{20}$$

It follows that

$$\begin{aligned}
\|Q^T X h\|_\infty =&\|Q^T X(\hat{\beta}_{\text{GDDS}} - \beta^*)\|_\infty \\
=&\|Q^T(X\hat{\beta}_{\text{GDDS}} - y + \epsilon)\|_\infty \\
\leq&\|Q^T(X\hat{\beta}_{\text{GDDS}} - y)\|_\infty + \|Q^T\epsilon\|_\infty \\
\leq&2\|Q^T\epsilon\|_\infty.
\end{aligned}$$

Combining (20), we obtain the desired error bound

$$\|h\|_p \leq \frac{2\|Q^T\epsilon\|_\infty}{\rho(Q, X, p, \|\beta^*\|_0)}.$$

It completes the proof. □

Proof of Lemma 1

Proof. This proof follows the standard union bound proof. For completion, we provide the proof below. Since $\epsilon \sim \mathcal{N}(0, I_{n\times n}\sigma^2)$, for each linear combination of ϵ, we have $Q_{.i}^T\epsilon \sim \mathcal{N}(0, \sigma^2)$. Recall that for any $t > 0$, we have that

$$\int_t^\infty e^{-x^2/2}dx \leq e^{-t^2/2}/t. \tag{21}$$

Denote the event $A_i = \{|Q_{.i}^T\epsilon| \leq \lambda\}, i = 1, 2, \cdots, m$:

$$\begin{aligned}
\{\|Q^T\epsilon\|_\infty \leq \lambda\} &= \{\max_{1\leq i\leq m} |Q_{.i}^T\epsilon| \leq \lambda\} \\
&= \cap_{i=1}^m A_i.
\end{aligned}$$

We derive the probability as follows:

$$\begin{aligned}\Pr(\cap_{i=1}^m A_i) &= 1-\Pr(\cup_{i=1}^m A_i^c)\\ &\geq 1-\sum_{i=1}^m \Pr(A_i^c)\\ &= 1-m\Pr(|\xi|\geq \lambda/\sigma)\\ &\geq 1-2\frac{m\sigma}{\lambda}e^{-\lambda^2/2\sigma^2},\end{aligned}$$

where the second inequality holds by union bound and the last inequality follows (21) since $\xi \sim \mathcal{N}(0,1)$. Thus, we can take $\lambda = 2\sigma\sqrt{\log m}$ so that

$$\Pr(\|Q^T\epsilon)\|_\infty \leq \lambda) \geq 1-1/m\sqrt{\log m} = 1-O(1/m).$$

It completes the proof. □

RIP Condition Implies GR Condition

Recall that to exactly recover β^* the RIP condition requires that $\delta_{2s} > \sqrt{2}-1$ [Candes, 2008], where $s = \|\beta^*\|_0$ and δ_{2s} is defined as for matrix X^TX is defined as

$$1-\delta_{2s} \leq \frac{\|Xg\|^2}{\|g\|^2} \leq 1+\delta_{2s} \quad \forall \, \|g\|_0 \leq 2s.$$

Now we need to prove that $\delta_{2s} > \sqrt{2}-1$ leads to the GR condition $\rho(X, X, 2, \|\beta^*\|_0) > 0$.

Consider an arbitrary vector h and an arbitrary index set $T_0 \subset \{1, 2, \cdots, m\}$ with cardinality s satisfying $\|h_{T_0}\|_1 \geq \|h_{T_0^c}\|_1$. T_1 corresponds to the locations of the s largest coefficients of $h_{T_0^c}$; T_2 to the locations of the next s largest coefficients of $h_{T_0^c}$, and so on. We use T_{01} to denote $T_0 \cup T_1$ for short.

Note the fact that if $Xh \neq 0$, then $X^TXh \neq 0$. To obtain $\rho(X, X, 2, \|\beta^*\|_0) > 0$, it suffices to show that for any nonzero h satisfying $\|h_{T_0^c}\|_1 \leq \|h_{T_0}\|_1$, the following ratio is positive

$$\|Xh\|/\|h\| > 0. \tag{22}$$

We have

$$\begin{aligned}&|\langle Xh, Xh_{T_{01}}\rangle|\\ \geq&\|Xh_{T_{01}}\|^2 - \sum_{j\geq 2}|\langle Xh_{T_{01}}, Xh_{T_j}\rangle|\\ \geq&\|Xh_{T_{01}}\|^2 - \sum_{j\geq 2}|\langle Xh_{T_0}, Xh_{T_j}\rangle| - \sum_{j\geq 2}|\langle Xh_{T_1}, Xh_{T_j}\rangle|\\ \geq&\|Xh_{T_{01}}\|^2 - \delta_{2s}\sum_{j\geq 2}(\|h_{T_0}\|+\|h_{T_1}\|)\|h_{T_j}\|\\ \geq&\|Xh_{T_{01}}\|^2 - \sqrt{2}\|h_{T_{01}}\|\delta_{2s}\sum_{j\geq 2}\|h_{T_j}\|\\ \geq&\|Xh_{T_{01}}\|^2 - \sqrt{2}\|h_{T_{01}}\|\delta_{2s}\|h_{T_0^c}\|_1 s^{-1/2}\\ \geq&(1-\delta_{2s})\|h_{T_{01}}\|^2 - \sqrt{2}\delta_{2s}\|h_{T_{01}}\|^2\\ \geq&(1-(\sqrt{2}+1)\delta_{2s})\|h_{T_{01}}\|^2,\end{aligned}$$

where the third inequality uses the result $|\langle Xh_{T_i}, Xh_{T_j}\rangle| \leq \delta_{2s}\|h_{T_i}\|\|h_{T_j}\|$ if $i \neq j$, see Lemma 2.1 Candes [2008]). It follows from the fact $|\langle Xh, Xh_{T_{01}}\rangle| \leq \|Xh\|\|Xh_{T_{01}}\|$ that

$$\|Xh\| \geq (1-(\sqrt{2}+1)\delta_{2s})\|h_{T_{01}}\|. \tag{23}$$

From $\|h_{T_0^c}\|_1 \leq \|h_{T_0}\|_1$, we have $\|h\| \leq 2\|h_{T_{01}}\|$, see the last line of the proof for Theorem 1.2 in [Candes, 2008]. It also can be found from [Candes and Tao, 2007, Bickel et al., 2009]. Together with (23) and the RIP condition $\delta_{2s} < \sqrt{2}-1$, we obtain

$$\|Xh\| \geq (1-(\sqrt{2}+1)\delta_{2s})\|h_{T_{01}}\| \geq \frac{(1-(\sqrt{2}+1)\delta_{2s})}{2}\|h\|,$$

which verifies (22).

Comparison to Existing Error Bounds for DS

This section aims to show that the error bound provided in (7) is a tighter bound than two existing results in [Candes and Tao, 2007] and [Bickel et al., 2009]. For simpler notations, we denote the difference between the estimate $\hat{\beta}_{\text{DS}}$ by DS and the true model β^* as $h = \hat{\beta}_{\text{DS}} - \beta^*$, T denotes the support set of β^*, and s denotes the sparsity of β^*. The complete comparison requires extensive space to basically repeat the proofs in [Candes and Tao, 2007] and [Bickel et al., 2009]. Here, we just show their results, highlight the key point in their original proofs, and illustrate why our error bound does not loose theirs.

Existing results conducted in [Candes and Tao, 2007] and [Bickel et al., 2009] are only based on the following facts

- (FACT 1) $\|h_{T^c}\|_1 \leq \|h_T\|_1$ (Please refer to Eq. (3.2) in [Candes and Tao, 2007] and Eq. (B.12) in [Bickel et al., 2009]);
- (FACT 2) $\|X^TXh\|_\infty \leq 2\|X^T\epsilon\|_\infty \leq_{(\text{P})} 2\sigma\sqrt{\log m}$ (Please refer to Eq. (3.3) in [Candes and Tao, 2007] and Eq. (B.7) in [Bickel et al., 2009]).

which are also the foundations to provide our error bound in (7).

The error bound provided in Theorem 1.1 of [Candes and Tao, 2007] is derived from (see the end of Proof of Theorem 1.1 in [Candes and Tao, 2007])

$$\begin{aligned}\|h\| &\overset{\text{(FACT 1)}}{\leq} \frac{2\sqrt{s}}{1-\delta-\theta}\|X^TXh\|_\infty\\ &\overset{\text{(FACT 2)}}{\leq} \frac{2\sqrt{s}}{1-\delta-\theta}2\|X^T\epsilon\|_\infty.\end{aligned} \tag{24}$$

Please check the original paper for the definitions of δ and θ. The error bound (with $p = 2$, $m = s$) provided in [Bickel et al., 2009] is derived from

$$\begin{aligned}\|h\| &\overset{\text{(FACT 1)}}{\leq} \frac{32s}{\kappa(s,s,1)}\|X^TX\epsilon\|_\infty\\ &\overset{\text{(FACT 2)}}{\leq} \frac{32s}{\kappa(s,s,1)}2\|X^T\epsilon\|_\infty.\end{aligned} \tag{25}$$

Please refer to the original paper for the definition of $\kappa(s, s, 1)$.

From these two bounds in (24) and (25), they essentially uses FACT 1 to find an upper bound for $\|h\|/\|X^T Xh\|_\infty$. This observation motivates us to directly define the upper bound through the definition of $\rho(\cdot,\cdot,\cdot)$ in (6)

$$\rho(X, X, s, 2) \leq \frac{\|X^T Xh\|_\infty}{\|h\|} \quad \forall h \text{ under FACT 1.}$$

Then we simply apply FACT 2 as (24) and (25) to obtain the error bound in (7). Therefore, our analysis provides a tighter error bound than Candes and Tao [2007] and Bickel et al. [2009].

References

S. R. Becker, E. J. Candès, and M. C. Grant. Templates for convex cone problems with applications to sparse signal recovery. *Mathematical Programming Computation*, 3 (3):165–218, 2011.

P. J. Bickel, Y. Ritov, and A. B. Tsybakov. Simultaneous analysis of lasso and dantzig selector. *The Annals of Statistics*, pages 1705–1732, 2009.

E. Candes and T. Tao. The Dantzig selector: Statistical estimation when p is much larger than n. *The Annals of Statistics*, pages 2313–2351, 2007.

E. J. Candes. The restricted isometry property and its implications for compressed sensing. *Comptes Rendus Mathematique*, 346(9):589–592, 2008.

E. J. Candes and T. Tao. Decoding by linear programming. *IEEE Transactions on Information Theory*, 51 (12):4203–4215, 2005.

E. J. Candes, M. B. Wakin, and S. P. Boyd. Enhancing sparsity by reweighted l1 minimization. *Journal of Fourier analysis and applications*, 14(5-6):877–905, 2008.

S. Chatterjee, S. Chen, and A. Banerjee. Generalized dantzig selector: Application to the k-support norm. In *Advances in Neural Information Processing Systems*, pages 1934–1942, 2014.

S. Chen and D. Donoho. Basis pursuit. In *IEEE the Twenty-Eighth Asilomar Conference onSignals, Systems and Computers*, volume 1, pages 41–44, 1994.

S. S. Chen, D. L. Donoho, and M. A. Saunders. Atomic decomposition by basis pursuit. *SIAM review*, 43(1):129–159, 2001.

Y. Cong, J. Yuan, and J. Liu. Sparse reconstruction cost for abnormal event detection. In *Computer Vision and Pattern Recognition (CVPR), 2011 IEEE Conference on*, pages 3449–3456. IEEE, 2011.

D. L. Donoho. Compressed sensing. *IEEE Transactions on Information Theory*, 52(4):1289–1306, 2006.

M. Geist, B. Scherrer, A. Lazaric, and M. Ghavamzadeh. A Dantzig Selector Approach to Temporal Difference Learning. In *International Conference on Machine Learning*, 2012.

B. Liu, S. Mahadevan, and J. Liu. Regularized off-policy TD-learning. In *Advances in Neural Information Processing Systems*, pages 845–853, 2012.

H. Liu, J. Zhang, X. Jiang, and J. Liu. The group dantzig selector. In *International Conference on Artificial Intelligence and Statistics*, pages 461–468, 2010a.

J. Liu. *Statistical Methods for Genome-wide Association Studies and Personalized Medicine*. PhD thesis, University of Wisconsin-Madison, 2014.

J. Liu, P. Wonka, and J. Ye. Multi-stage dantzig selector. In *Advances in Neural Information Processing Systems*, pages 1450–1458, 2010b.

J. Liu, R. Fujimaki, and J. Ye. Forward-backward greedy algorithms for general convex smooth functions over a cardinality constraint. *ICML*, 2013.

Z. Lu, T. K. Pong, and Y. Zhang. An alternating direction method for finding dantzig selectors. *Computational Statistics & Data Analysis*, 56(12):4037–4046, 2012.

S. Mahadevan and B. Liu. Sparse q-learning with mirror descent. *arXiv preprint arXiv:1210.4893*, 2012.

Y. Nesterov. *Introductory lectures on convex optimization: A basic course*, volume 87. Springer, 2004.

Z. Qin, W. Li, and F. Janoos. Sparse reinforcement learning via convex optimization. In *Proceedings of the 31st International Conference on Machine Learning (ICML-14)*, pages 424–432, 2014.

B. Scherrer. Should one compute the temporal difference fix point or minimize the bellman residual? the unified oblique projection view. In *ICML*, pages 52–68, 2010.

R. Tibshirani. Regression shrinkage and selection via the lasso. *Journal of the Royal Statistical Society. Series B (Methodological)*, pages 267–288, 1996.

J. A. Tropp. Greed is good: Algorithmic results for sparse approximation. *IEEE Transactions on Information Theory*, 50(10):2231–2242, 2004.

J. Tsitsiklis and B. Van Roy. An analysis of temporal-difference learning with function approximation. *IEEE Transactions on Automatic Control*, 42:674–690, 1997.

S. A. Van De Geer, P. Bühlmann, et al. On the conditions used to prove oracle results for the lasso. *Electronic Journal of Statistics*, 3:1360–1392, 2009.

X. Wang and X. Yuan. The linearized alternating direction method of multipliers for dantzig selector. *SIAM Journal on Scientific Computing*, 34(5):A2792–A2811, 2012.

H. Yu and D. P. Bertsekas. Error bounds for approximations from projected linear equations. *Mathematics of Operations Research*, 35(2):306–329, 2010.

T. Zhang. On the consistency of feature selection using greedy least squares regression. In *Journal of Machine Learning Research*, pages 555–568, 2009.

T. Zhang. Adaptive forward-backward greedy algorithm for learning sparse representations. *IEEE Transactions on Information Theory*, 57(7):4689–4708, 2011a.

T. Zhang. Sparse recovery with orthogonal matching pursuit under rip. *IEEE Transactions on Information Theory*, 57(9):6215–6221, 2011b.

Importance Weighted Consensus Monte Carlo for Distributed Bayesian Inference

Qiang Liu
Computer Science
Dartmouth College
qiang.liu@dartmouth.edu

Abstract

The recent explosion in big data has created a significant challenge for efficient and scalable Bayesian inference. In this paper, we consider a divide-and-conquer setting in which the data is partitioned into different subsets with communication constraints, and a proper combination strategy is used to aggregate the Monte Carlo samples drawn from the local posteriors based on the dataset subsets. We propose a new importance weighted consensus Monte Carlo method for efficient Bayesian inference in this setting. Our method outperforms the previous one-shot combination strategies in terms of accuracy, and is more computation- and communication-efficient than the previous iterative combination methods that require iterative re-sampling and communication steps. We provide two practical versions of our approach, and illustrate their properties both theoretically and empirically.

1 INTRODUCTION

Bayesian inference provides a powerful paradigm for reasoning with uncertain data by reducing inference problems into computational problems that can be routinely solved using efficient methods like Monte Carlo (MC) or Markov chain Monte Carlo (MCMC) methods. However, the recent explosion in big data has created a significant challenge for efficient and scalable Bayesian inference due to the difficulty for evaluating the likelihood across all the data points; traditional methods like Gibbs sampling and Metropolis-Hastings are extremely slow when the size of datasets is large.

We consider a divide-and-conquer approach for Bayesian computation under big data, in which case we partition the data into multiple subsets, and draw posterior samples on each subset separately, and then combine the results properly. Typical combination methods mostly rely on first approximating the subset posteriors using certain density estimation method and then combine the corresponding estimated densities. For example, the *consensus Monte Carlo* by Scott et al. (2013) fits the subset samples using normal distributions in which case the density combination reduces to a simple weighted linear averaging on the samples; Neiswanger et al. (2013) instead approximates each subset posterior using kernel density estimator (KDE), and uses another MCMC to draw sample from the product of KDEs. These methods are "one-shot" in that they do not require any further communication beyond passing the posterior samples; however, these methods critically rely on the qualities of the density estimators and often do not perform well in practice. Other *iterative* methods (e.g., Wang & Dunson, 2013; Xu et al., 2014) propose to iteratively resample from the local posteriors with adjusted local priors to enforce a consistency between the subset posteriors. Although being able to improve the performance iteratively, these methods require to re-draw the samples repeatedly, resulting higher computation and communication costs.

We propose a new importance weighted consensus Monte Carlo method for efficient distributed Bayesian inference. The key ingredient of our method is an importance weighted consensus strategy that efficiently combines the subset samples by leveraging their likelihood information. Our method performs significantly better than the pervious one-shot methods based on density estimations that solely rely on the subset samples and ignore the likelihood information. In addition, we show that our method can perform as efficient as the iterative combination methods, but with much less communication and computational costs.

Related Work The divided-and-conquer approach for scalable Bayesian computation has been studied in a series of recent works (Huang & Gelman, 2005; Scott et al., 2013; Neiswanger et al., 2013; Wang & Dunson, 2013; Xu et al., 2014; Minsker et al., 2014; Rabinovich et al., 2015). Another major approach for scalable Bayesian inference is based on efficient subsampling; see e.g., Korattikara et al. (2014); Welling & Teh (2011); Maclaurin & Adams (2014);

Bardenet et al. (2014). Despite being a relatively new topic, there are already a rich set of comprehensive reviews (Bardenet et al., 2015; Green et al., 2015; Zhu et al., 2014; Baker et al., 2015; Angelino et al., 2015).

Outline The rest of this paper is organized as follows. Section 2 introduces backgrounds and review the existing methods. Section 3 introduces our main method, where we propose two practical versions of our method and study their properties. Section 4 presents empirical results on both simulated and real-world datasets. The conclusion is made in Section 5.

2 BACKGROUND AND EXISTING METHODS

Consider a probabilistic model $p(D|x)$ where x is a random parameter with prior $p(x)$ and D is the observed data. Bayesian computation involves inferring the posterior distribution $f(x) \propto p(D|x)p(x)$, often in terms of calculating posterior moments of form $\mathbb{E}_f[h(x)] = \int h(x)f(x)dx$, where $h(x)$ is a test function, including the mean, variance or credible intervals. Typical Monte Carlo methods work by drawing samples from the posterior $\{x_i\}_{i=1}^n \sim f(x)$, and approximating the posterior moments by $\sum_{i=1}^n h(x_i)/n$; this gives a consistent estimator with mean squared error $\mathrm{var}_f[h(x)]/n$ with i.i.d. samples. Unfortunately, directly sampling from $p(D|x)$ requires to repeatedly evaluate the posterior probability and can be prohibitively slow when the number of data instances in D is very large.

We consider a divided-and-conquer approach in which case the data D is partitioned into m independent, non-overlapping subsets $D^1, \ldots, D^m$, so that we have

$$f(x) \overset{def}{=} p(x|D) \propto p(x)\prod_{k=1}^m p(D^k|x).$$

This allows us to decompose the global posterior $f(x)$ into a product of "local posteriors" $f_k(x)$:

$$f(x) \propto \prod_k f_k(x), \qquad f_k(x) = p(D^k|x)p(x)^{1/m},$$

where each local posterior $f_k(x)$ receives $1/m$ of the original prior. Note that we do not assume D^m to have the same size nor follow a same probabilistic model.

Since each subset contains less data points, it is easier to sample from each of the local posteriors independently, which can be done in a parallel fashion. A critical problem, however, is how to inference about the global posterior $f(x)$, or estimate $\mathbb{E}_f[h(x)]$, using the samples from the local posteriors $\{x_i^k\}_{i=1}^n \sim f_k(x)$, $k = 1, \ldots, m$.

Existing Methods Useful perspectives can be obtained by considering the special case when $f_k(x)$ are assumed to be normal distributions, e.g., $f_k(x) = \mathcal{N}(x; \mu_k, \Sigma_k)$. This is justified by Bernstein-Von Mises Theorem, which says that the posterior $f_k(x)$ is close to normal when the number of data points in D^k is large. An important property of Gaussian distributions is that the product $f \propto \prod_k f_k$ of the densities f_k is equivalent to the density function of a weighted averaging $\bar{x} = \sum_k w_k x^k$, where $w_k = (\sum_k \Sigma_k^{-1})^{-1}\Sigma_k^{-1}$ and $x^k \sim f_k$. This motivates the consensus Monte Carlo (CMC) method (Scott et al., 2013) that combines the subset posterior samples by

$$\bar{x}_i = \sum_k \hat{w}_k x_i^k, \quad \hat{w}_k = (\sum_k \hat{\Sigma}_k^{-1})^{-1}\hat{\Sigma}_k^{-1},$$

where the exact covariance matrix Σ_k is replaced by the empirical covariance matrix $\hat{\Sigma}_k$ of $\{x_i^k\}_{i=1}^n$.

Unfortunately, CMC does not provide guarantees for non-Gaussian cases. Neiswanger et al. (2013) proposed a more general approach which approximates each subset posterior $f_k(x)$ with a Gaussian kernel density estimator (KDE), and then sample from the product of the KDEs using MCMC. This methods, however, does not scale well in high dimensions due to the use of non-parametric density estimation; in particular, the MSE of this method is $O(n^{-2/(2+d)})$, where d is the dimension of x; when $d > 2$, this is worse than the typical parametric rate $O(n^{-1/2})$ that we would get from the global posterior sampling.

In fact, we argue that inferring the global posterior $f \propto \prod_k f_k$ using only the subset samples $x_i^k \sim f_k(x)$ is fundamentally difficult, since it involves evaluating non-linear functionals of form $\int h(x)\prod_k f_k(x)dx$ for which certain non-parametric density estimates of f_k are unavoidable, and subjects to non-parametric minimax lower bounds that are generally worse than $O(n^{-1/2})$; see, for example, Birge & Massart (1995); Krishnamurthy et al. (2015, 2014) for discussions related to estimating the simpler form $\int f_1(x)f_2(x)dx$.

Therefore, acquiring further information is critical for improving the performance. Several authors (Wang & Dunson, 2013; Xu et al., 2014) have proposed to iteratively adjust and resample from the local posteriors to improve the results. Specifically, they set the local posteriors to be $f_k(x) \propto p(D^k|x)p_k(x)$, where $p_k(x)$ is a local "prior" that is adjusted iteratively. In particular, Xu et al. (2014) takes $p_k(x) = \prod_{k' \neq k} \hat{g}_{k'}(x)$ where $\hat{g}_k$ is an approximation of $p(D|x)/p(D^k|x)$ based on the current subset samples. In this way, we have $f_k \approx f$, and hence the subset samples can be treated as drawn from the global posterior f approximately.

In Wang & Dunson (2013), $p_k(x)$ are instead chosen to enforce the local samples $\{x_i^k\}_{i=1}^n$ to be consistent with each other; in particular, it is based on the observation that

$$\prod_k f_k(x) = \int \prod_k f_k(x^k) \exp\left[-\frac{(x^k - x)^2}{2h^2}\right] dx^k + O(h^2)$$

for small h, and evaluates the above integral using a Gibbs sampler that alternatively sample $\{x^k\}$ and x. This methods, however, critically depends on the value of h, since large h gives poor approximation (we need $h = O(n^{-1/4})$ to obtain an $O(n^{-1/2})$ approximation error), while small h makes Gibbs sampler difficult to converge. Wang & Dunson (2013) proposed to gradually decrease the value of h, making it essentially an annealed MCMC (Gibbs sampling) algorithm over the augmented distribution of $\{x^k\}$ and x; it is therefore difficult to formally guarantee the convergence of this algorithm. In addition, each iteration of the Gibbs sampling has a relatively expensive computation and communication cost in that it requires a fully convergent sampling from the local posteriors as well as communicating the subset posterior samples between the local subsets and the fusion center.

The above methods use only the information in the local posterior samples and do not make use of the values of their posterior probabilities which can carry important information. In this work, we propose a new combination method that avoids the density estimation using an important sampling strategy that assigns importance weights to the subset samples based on their likelihood values. We show that our method can significantly improve over the one-shot combination methods based on density estimations, while avoiding the expensive resampling steps in the iterative methods. We provide two versions of our method: our *Method I* is a valid importance sampling estimator and hence provides a consistent estimator with a typical parametric $O(n^{-1/2})$ estimator for generic non-Gaussian cases; our *Method II* provides a heuristic that works exceptionally well when f_k are nearly Gaussian, although without a formal consistency guarantee in generic cases.

3 IMPORTANCE WEIGHTED CONSENSUS MONTE CARLO

Assume we want to combine the local samples $\boldsymbol{x}_i = [x_i^1, \ldots, x_i^m]$ via a generic consensus function $\bar{x}_i = \phi(x_i^1, \ldots, x_i^m) = \phi(\boldsymbol{x})$; this includes, but does not limit to, the weighted averaging function $\bar{x} = \sum_{k=1}^m w_k x^k$. The key component of our approach is an auxiliary distribution over $[x^1, \ldots, x^m]$ under which the consensus $\bar{x} = \phi(\boldsymbol{x})$ is distributed according to the global posterior $f = \prod_k f_k$.

Proposition 3.1. *Let $g(x^1, \ldots, x^m)$ be an arbitrary density function, and $g(\bar{x})$ is the corresponding density function of $\bar{x} = \phi(\boldsymbol{x})$, that is,*

$$g(\bar{x}) = \int_{S_{\bar{x}}} g(x^1, \ldots, x^m) dS_{\bar{x}},$$

where the integral is over on the surface $S_{\bar{x}} = \{\boldsymbol{x} \colon \phi(\boldsymbol{x}) = \bar{x}\}$. We define an auxiliary distribution

$$\begin{aligned} p(x^1, \ldots, x^m) &= f(\bar{x}) g(x^1, \ldots, x^m \mid \bar{x}) \\ &= f(\bar{x}) g(x^1, \ldots, x^m) / g(\bar{x}), \end{aligned}$$

then the distribution $p(\bar{x})$ of $\bar{x}$ under $p(x^1, \ldots, x^m)$ equals $f(\cdot)$, that is, $p(\bar{x}) = f(\bar{x})$, and hence

$$\mathbb{E}_f[h(x)] = \mathbb{E}_p[h(\bar{x})].$$

for any function $h(x)$.

Proof. Simply note that

$$p(\bar{x}) = \int_{S_{\bar{x}}} f(\bar{x}) g(x^1, \ldots, x^m) / g(\bar{x}) dS_{\bar{x}} = f(\bar{x}). \quad \square$$

This result allows us to transform the estimation problem of $f(x)$ to that of a higher dimensional distribution $p(x^1, \ldots, x^m)$. Now given the local posterior samples $\{x_i^k\}_{i=1}^n \sim f_k$, we can treat $\boldsymbol{x}_i = [x_i^1, \ldots, x_i^m]$ as drawn from the product distribution $\prod_k f_k(x_k) \overset{def}{=} q(\boldsymbol{x})$. Using $q(\boldsymbol{x})$ as a proposal distribution allows us to construct a convenient importance sampling estimator:

$$\mathbb{E}_f[h(x)] = \mathbb{E}_p[h(\bar{x})] \approx \frac{\sum_{i=1}^n w(\boldsymbol{x}_i) h(\bar{x}_i)}{\sum_{i=1}^n w(\boldsymbol{x}_i)} \overset{def}{=} \hat{z}_h, \quad (1)$$

where $\bar{x}_i = \phi(\boldsymbol{x}_i)$ and the estimator $\hat{z}_h$ is a self normalized importance sampling estimator with importance weights

$$w(\boldsymbol{x}_i) = \frac{p(\boldsymbol{x}_i)}{q(\boldsymbol{x}_i)} = \frac{g(x_i^1, \ldots, x_i^m) \prod_k f_k(\bar{x}_i)}{g(\bar{x}_i) \prod_k f_k(x_i^k)}. \quad (2)$$

Note that we do not need to know the normalization constants in $f_k(x)$ to calculate $\hat{z}_h$; calculating the normalization constants is often a critically difficult task.

Since $\hat{z}_h$ is a standard importance sampling estimator, it forms a consistent estimator for $z_h = \mathbb{E}_f[h(x)]$ in that $\Pr(\lim_{n \to \infty} \hat{z}_h = z_h) = 1$ if $q(\boldsymbol{x}) > 0$ whenever $p(\boldsymbol{x}) > 0$ (see e.g., Theorem 9.2 in Owen (2013)). In addition, the asymptotic MSE $\mathbb{E}[(\hat{z}_h - z_h)^2]$ can be calculated using the Delta method:

$$\mathbb{E}[(\hat{z}_h - z_h)^2] \asymp \frac{1}{n} \mathbb{E}_q[(h(\bar{x}) - z_h)^2 w(\boldsymbol{x})^2]. \quad (3)$$

Therefore, $\hat{z}_h$ approximates z_h with a typical parametric $O(n^{-1/2})$ error rate.

The MSE (3) depends on the test function $h(\cdot)$; a more generic measure of efficiency that is independent of $h(x)$ is the variance of the importance weights,

$$\operatorname{var}_q(w(\boldsymbol{x})) = \int q(\boldsymbol{x}) \left[\frac{p(\boldsymbol{x})}{q(\boldsymbol{x})} - 1\right]^2 d\boldsymbol{x}, \quad (4)$$

or equivalently, the effective sample size (ESS) $n/(\text{var}_q(w(\boldsymbol{x})) + 1)$. We would like to have the importance weights $w(\boldsymbol{x})$ to be as uniform as possible, having a small variance or a large effective sample size [1] (ideally $w(\boldsymbol{x}) = 1$, $\forall \boldsymbol{x}$, in which case $q(\boldsymbol{x}) = p(\boldsymbol{x})$).

3.1 OPTIMAL CHOICE OF $\phi(\cdot)$ AND $g(\cdot)$

The estimator $\hat{z}_h$ depends on both the consensus function $\phi(\cdot)$ and the auxiliary distribution $g(\cdot)$. In this section, we discuss the optimal choice of $\phi(\cdot)$ and $g(\cdot)$ in terms of minimizing the variance $\text{var}_q(w(\boldsymbol{x}))$ of the importance weights.

Proposition 3.2. *(i). The optimal* $g(x^1, \ldots, x^m)$ *that minimizes the variance* $\text{var}_q(w(\boldsymbol{x}))$ *is*

$$g^*(x^1, \ldots, x^m) = \prod_{k=1}^{m} f_k(x^k),$$

in which case $g^*(\bar{x}) = \int_{S_{\bar{x}}} \prod_{k=1}^{m} f_k(x^k) dS_{\bar{x}}$ *with* $S_{\bar{x}} = \{\boldsymbol{x}\colon \bar{x} = \phi(\boldsymbol{x})\}$ *and* $w(\boldsymbol{x}) = \prod_{k=1}^{m} f_k(\bar{x})/g^*(\bar{x})$.

(ii). With $g = g^*$, *the optimal consensus function* $\bar{x} = \phi(\boldsymbol{x})$ *should be chosen such that* $g^*(\bar{x}) \propto \prod_k f_k(\bar{x})$. *In the special case when* $f_k(x)$ *are Gaussian, that is,* $f_k(x) = \mathcal{N}(x; \mu_k, \Sigma_k)$, *the optimal* $\phi(\cdot)$ *is the weighted averaging* $\phi(x) = \sum_{k=1}^{m} w_k x^k$ *with* $w_k = (\sum_k \Sigma_k^{-1})^{-1}\Sigma_k^{-1}$, *and in this case, we have* $w(x) = 1$, $\forall x$ *and* $\text{var}_q(w(x)) = 0$. *But there is no closed form for such an optimal* $\phi(\cdot)$ *in general cases.*

Proof. (i). Since $\mathbb{E}_q[w(\boldsymbol{x})] = 1$, minimizing the variance $\text{var}_q(w(\boldsymbol{x}))$ is equivalent to minimizing $\mathbb{E}_q[w(\boldsymbol{x})^2]$,

$$\mathbb{E}_q[w(\boldsymbol{x})^2] = \int \frac{p(\boldsymbol{x})^2}{q(\boldsymbol{x})} d\boldsymbol{x} = \int \frac{\prod_k f_k(\bar{x})^2}{g(\bar{x})^2} \Phi_g(\bar{x}) d\bar{x},$$

where $\Phi_g(\bar{x}) = \int_{S_{\bar{x}}} \frac{g(\boldsymbol{x})^2}{\prod_k f_k(x^k)} dS_{\bar{x}}$; one can show that g^* minimizes $\Phi_g(\bar{x})$ for any fixed $\bar{x}$, and hence minimizes $\mathbb{E}_q[w(\boldsymbol{x})^2]$.

(ii). With $g = g^*$, we have $\Phi_{g^*}(\bar{x}) = g^*(\bar{x})$ and hence $\mathbb{E}_q[w(\boldsymbol{x})^2] = \int \frac{\prod_k f_k(\bar{x})^2}{g^*(\bar{x})} d\bar{x}$, which is minimized when $g^*(\bar{x}) \propto \prod_k f_k(\bar{x})$. □

Remark With $g^*(\boldsymbol{x}) = \prod_k f_k(x^k)$, our estimator $\hat{z}_h$ can be treated as simply an importance sampler on $f(\bar{x})$ with proposal $g^*(\bar{x})$. The difficulty, however, is that $g^*(\bar{x})$ is usually intractable to calculate, making it essential to find suboptimal $g(\boldsymbol{x})$ that is more computationally tractable.

[1] A simple connection between (4) and (3) is that $(\text{var}_q(w(\boldsymbol{x})) + 1)/n$ can be treated as the expectation of the MSE $\mathbb{E}[(\hat{z}_h - z_h)^2]$ when the value of $h(x)$, $\forall x$ is drawn from standard normal distribution.

Algorithm 1 Importance Weighted Consensus Monte Carlo

Input: Samples from the local posteriors $\{x_i^k\}_{i=1}^n \sim f_k, \forall k = 1, \ldots, m$. Test function $h(x)$.

Output: Estimate $\mathbb{E}(h(x))$ under the global posterior $f(x) \propto \prod_k f_k(x)$.

Consensus: Let $\hat{\Sigma}_k$ be the empirical covariance matrix of subsample $\{x_i^k\}_{i=1}^n$. Calculate

$$\bar{x}_i = \sum_i w_k x_i^k, \quad \text{where } w_k = (\sum_k \hat{\Sigma}_k^{-1})^{-1}\hat{\Sigma}_k^{-1}.$$

Reweighting: Calculate the importance weights $w(\boldsymbol{x}_i)$ by *Method I* as defined in (5) or *Method II* in (6).

Estimating: $\mathbb{E}(h) \approx \sum_i w_i h(\bar{x}_i)/\sum_i w_i$

3.2 PRACTICAL IMPLEMENTATION

Although the optimal choices in Proposition 3.2 are intractable in general cases, we can leverage Bernstein-von Mises theorem to obtain near optimal choices. In particular, Proposition 3.2 justified the use of the weighted averaging $\phi(\boldsymbol{x}) = \sum_{k=1}^{m} w_k x^k$, with weights decided by the empirical variance $w_k = (\sum_k \hat{\Sigma}_k^{-1})^{-1}\hat{\Sigma}_k^{-1}$, which is the same as the consensus MC in Scott et al. (2013). Our method also requires to set a good auxiliary distribution $g(\boldsymbol{x})$; we explore two simple choices in this paper:

1. *Method I.* Motivated by Bernstein-von Mises theorem, we approximate each $f_k(x)$ by a Gaussian $\hat{f}_k(x) = \mathcal{N}(x;\ \hat{\mu}_k, \hat{\Sigma}_k)$, where $\hat{\mu}_k$ and $\hat{\Sigma}_k$ are the empirical mean and covariance matrices of the k-th local sample $\{x_i^k : i \in [n]\}$, respectively. We then construct the auxiliary distribution $g(\boldsymbol{x})$ to be $g(\boldsymbol{x}) = \prod_k \hat{f}_k(x_k)$, under which we have $g(\bar{x}) = \mathcal{N}(\bar{x};\ \bar{\mu}, \bar{\Sigma})$, with $\bar{\mu} = \sum_k w_k \hat{\mu}_k$, and $\bar{\Sigma}^{-1} = (\sum_k w_k \hat{\Sigma}_k^{-1})$. In this case, the importance weight in (2) reduces to

$$w(\boldsymbol{x}_i) = \frac{\prod_k f_k(\bar{x}_i)}{\mathcal{N}(\bar{x}_i; \bar{\mu}, \bar{\Sigma})} \cdot \frac{\prod_k \mathcal{N}(x_i^k; \hat{\mu}_k, \hat{\Sigma}_k)}{\prod_k f_k(x_i^k)}. \quad (5)$$

2. *Method II.* Instead of approximating each f_k, we explicitly set the auxiliary distribution $g(\boldsymbol{x})$ to be the optimal choice suggested in Proposition 3.2, that is, $g(\boldsymbol{x}) = \prod_k f_k(x^k)$, and then approximate the corresponding $g(\bar{x})$ with a Gaussian distribution, that is, we approximate $g(\bar{x})$ by $\hat{g}(\bar{x}) = \mathcal{N}(\bar{x}, \bar{\mu}, \bar{\Sigma})$, which gives an importance weight of form

$$w(\boldsymbol{x}_i) = \frac{\prod_k f_k(\bar{x}_i)}{\mathcal{N}(\bar{x}_i; \bar{\mu}, \bar{\Sigma})}. \quad (6)$$

This can be justified in two possible scenarios: a) when each f_k is close to Gaussian by Bernstein-von Mises theorem, the distribution $g(\bar{x})$ of their averaging $\bar{x} =$

$\sum_{k=1}^{m} w_k x_i^k$ should also be close to Gaussian; b) when the number m of subsets is large, the averaging $\bar{x} = \sum_{k=1}^{m} w_k x_i^k$ is approximately Gaussian by the central limit theorem.

Comparing with (5), the importance weight in (6) simply drops the terms that involve x_i^k, and hence should have smaller variance, but with the risk of introducing additional biases. We note that although *Method I* is a valid importance sampling (IS) estimator, and gives consistent estimates in general cases, *Method II* is no longer a valid IS estimator, and hence is not consistent for general non-Gaussian distributions. Nevertheless, we find that *Method II* often performs surprisingly well in practice, and has attractive theoretical properties when f_k are indeed Gaussian.

3.3 GAUSSIAN CASES

It is illustrative to study the properties of *Method I* and *Method II* under the simple case when f_k are Gaussian. In particular, we show that, despite being inconsistent for non-Gaussian cases, *Method II* is guaranteed to outperform *Method I* in Gaussian cases, that is, it exploits the Gaussianity more aggressively.

Assume $f_k(x) = \mathcal{N}(x; \mu_k, \Sigma_k)$ and denote by $\hat{f}_k(x) = \mathcal{N}(x; \hat{\mu}_k, \hat{\Sigma}_k)$, where $\hat{\mu}_k, \hat{\Sigma}_k$ are the empirical mean and covariance of the local sample $\{x_i^k\}_{i=1}^n$ on the k-th subset. Let $\theta = \{\mu_k, \Sigma_k^{-1} \colon \forall k\}$ be the set of true parameters and $\hat{\theta} = \{\hat{\mu}_k, \hat{\Sigma}_k^{-1} \colon \forall k\}$ the empirical estimates; correspondingly we denote $q(\boldsymbol{x}|\theta) = \prod_k f_k(x^k)$ and $q(\boldsymbol{x}|\hat{\theta}) = \prod_k \hat{f}_k(x^k)$. Then $\hat{\theta}$ is the maximum likelihood estimator of θ based on data $\{\boldsymbol{x}_i\}_{i=1}^n$.

Denote by $\hat{z}_h^I$ and $\hat{z}_h^{II}$ the estimates given by *Method I* and *Method II*, respectively. Let $t(\boldsymbol{x}) = h(\boldsymbol{x})\frac{p(\boldsymbol{x})}{q(\boldsymbol{x})}$, then

$$\hat{z}_h^I = \frac{1}{n}\sum_{i=1}^{n} t(\boldsymbol{x}_i), \qquad \hat{z}_h^{II} = \frac{\sum_{i=1}^{n} \omega(\boldsymbol{x}_i) t(\boldsymbol{x}_i)}{\sum_{i=1}^{n} \omega(\boldsymbol{x}_i)}.$$

where $\omega(\boldsymbol{x}_i) = \frac{q(\boldsymbol{x}_i|\theta)}{q(\boldsymbol{x}_i|\hat{\theta})}$. Note that here the weights $\omega(\boldsymbol{x}_i)$ should be very close to one when the sample size n is large since $\hat{\theta}$ is a maximum likelihood estimator of θ (assuming all f_k are Gaussian). However, as observed in Henmi et al. (2007); Henmi & Eguchi (2004), the $\omega(\boldsymbol{x}_i)$ in fact can act as a control variate to cancel part of the variance in $t(\boldsymbol{x}_i)$. As a result, $\hat{z}_h^{II}$ is guaranteed to have lower variance than $\hat{z}_h^I$ when all f_k are Gaussian.

Lemma 3.3 (Henmi et al. (2007)). *Assume each f_k is Gaussian, e.g., $f_k(x) = \mathcal{N}(x; \mu_k, \Sigma_k)$, $\forall k \in [m]$. Denote by $\hat{s} = \sum_{i=1}^{n} \nabla_\theta \log q(\boldsymbol{x}_i|\theta)/n$, then $\mathbb{E}\hat{s} = 0$ and*

$$\hat{z}_h^{II} = \hat{z}_h^I - \mathbb{E}[\hat{z}_h^I \hat{s}^\top][\mathrm{var}(\hat{s})]^{-1}\hat{s} + O_p(1/n).$$

Proof. See the proof of Theorem 1 and Equation (10) in Henmi et al. (2007). □

Therefore, $\hat{z}_h^{II}$ is asymptotically equivalent to a variance reduced version of $\hat{z}_h^I$ by using the score function $\hat{s}$ as a control variate; see e.g., Owen (2013) for background on control variate.

Theorem 3.4. *Assume $f_k(x) = \mathcal{N}(x; \mu_k, \Sigma_k)$, $\forall k \in [m]$. Denote by $\mathrm{MSE}(\hat{z}_h) = \lim_{n\to+\infty} n\mathbb{E}[(\hat{z}_h - z_h)^2]$ the asymptotic mean square error of $\hat{z}_h$, then we have*

$$\mathrm{MSE}(\hat{z}_h^I) = \mathrm{var}_f(h(x)) \geq \mathrm{MSE}(\hat{z}_h^{II}), \tag{7}$$

where $\mathrm{var}_f(h(x))$ is the variance of $h(x)$ under the global posterior $f(x) \propto \prod_k f_k(x)$.

Proof. The fact that $\mathrm{MSE}(\hat{z}_h^I) \geq \mathrm{MSE}(\hat{z}_h^{II})$ is a result of Lemma 3.3 by the property of control variate (also see Henmi et al. (2007, Theorem 1)). The proof of $\mathrm{MSE}(\hat{z}_h^I) = \mathrm{var}_f(h(x))$ is shown in the Appendix. □

Therefore, despite being inconsistent in general non-Gaussian cases, *Method II* is guaranteed to outperform *Method I* in Gaussian cases, that is, it relies on a stronger assumption, and works well if the assumption is indeed satisfied. In contrast, *Method I* is more robust in that it is a consistent estimator for generic non-Gaussian f_k (but may also have large variances in bad cases). In practical cases when the size of each local dataset D^k is large, each f_k is close to Gaussian by Bernstein-von-Mises theorem, and we observe that *Method II* often performs better than *Method I* empirically.

3.4 FURTHER DISCUSSIONS

Our algorithm is summarized in Algorithm 1. We further discuss some issues here.

Communication Cost. Our methods outperform the previous *one-shot* combination methods such as Scott et al. (2013) and Neiswanger et al. (2013) in that *Method I* gives a consistent estimator for general f_k with a parametric $O(n^{-1/2})$ rate, while *Method II* provides exceptionally good estimates when f_k are (nearly) Gaussian. This is not surprising given that our methods leverage more information: it depends on both the local posterior samples x_i^k and their (unnormalized) likelihoods $f_k(x_i^k)$, as well as the (unnormalized) likelihoods $f_k(\bar{x}_i)$ of the combined sample $\bar{x}_i$. Therefore, compared with the *one-shot* methods, our methods require two additional rounds of communication between the subsets and the fusion center to evaluate and communicate the likelihood of the combined sample $\{\bar{x}_i\}$. The overall communication cost of our method is $O(mn(2d+1))$, where m is the number of machines, n is the Monte Carlo sample size and d is the dimension of the parameter, while that of Neiswanger et al. (2013) is $O(mnd)$, and that of Scott et al. (2013) is $O(d^2)$ which only needs to communicate the first two moments of the subset samples.

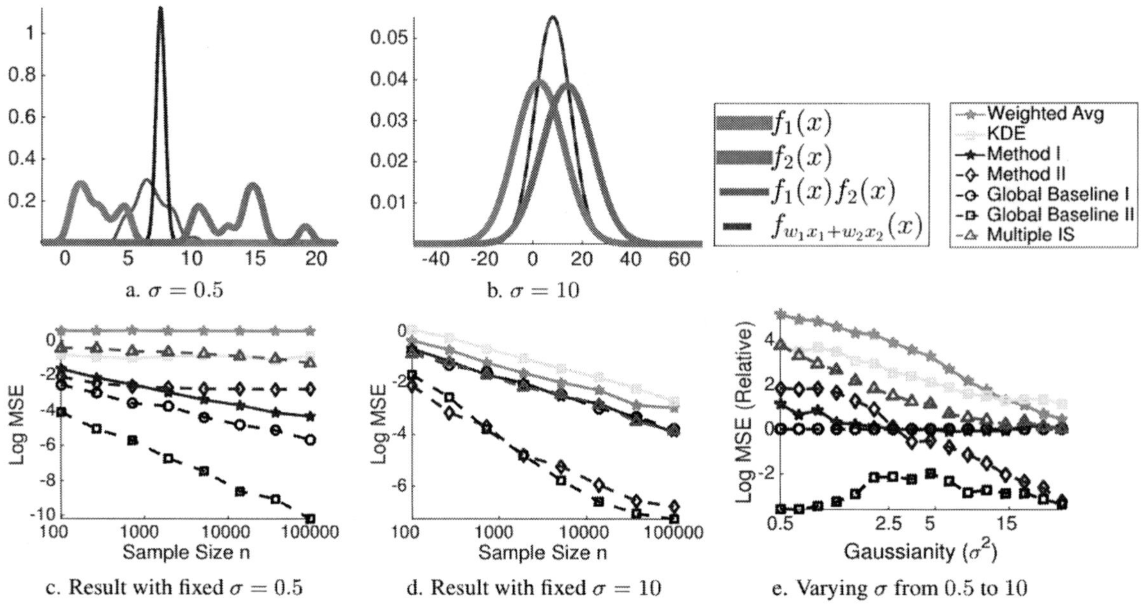

a. $\sigma = 0.5$ b. $\sigma = 10$

c. Result with fixed $\sigma = 0.5$ d. Result with fixed $\sigma = 10$ e. Varying σ from 0.5 to 10

Figure 1: Results on the toy Gaussian mixture model. (a)-(b) The simulated distributions $f_1(x)$ and $f_2(x)$ when $\sigma = 0.5$ (highly non-Gaussian) and $\sigma = 10$ (highly Gaussian), respectively. (c)-(d) The MSE for estimating the mean $\mathbb{E}_f[x]$ under the two cases shown in (a) and (b), respectively. (e) The relative MSE compared to *Global Baseline I* when we vary σ from 0.5 to 10, so that $f_1(x)$ and $f_2(x)$ change from being highly non-Gaussian to highly Gaussian.

Meanwhile, our method is still much more communication-efficient compared with the *iterative* combination methods that require more iterative rounds of communications, and resampling steps. The communication complexity of Wang & Dunson (2013) with T iterations is $O(mndT)$, and that of Xu et al. (2014) is $O(nd^2T)$ because it only passes the first two empirical moments instead of the samples. Our method has a significant advantage because the main practical bottleneck is often the number of communication rounds, regardless of the amount of information exchanged at each round. In our empirical results, we show that our methods work competitively with the iterative methods at their convergence.

Computational Cost. The total computational cost of our combination method is $O(nm(d^3 + L))$ where d^3 is due to the inverse of the covariance matrices and L denotes the cost for evaluating the local posterior probability $f_k(x)$; this is slightly worse than the linear averaging (Scott et al., 2013) which costs $O(nmd^3)$, but has advantage over Neiswanger et al. (2013) which requires a full MCMC procedure over the product of the KDEs for the combination. Further, the *iterative* combination methods have significantly higher computational cost, because they requires to re-draw subset samples iteratively, which is often much more expensive than the combination steps.

Random Permutation. The total size of all the local posterior samples is mn, while the size of the combined sample $\{\bar{x}_i\}$ is only n, that is, we lose a size of $(m-1)n$ when making the combination. To obtain more combined samples, we can randomly permute each subset sample $\{x_i^k : i \in [n]\}$ and combined the permuted subset samples, and repeat the process for multiple times. However, our empirical results do not suggest a significant improvement of performance by using multiple random permutations (e.g., we did not find significant improvement by averaging 10 random permutations).

4 EXPERIMENTS

We report empirical results for our method using a toy example of mixture of Gaussians as well as a Bayesian probit model with both simulated and real world datasets. We compare with the following algorithms:

1. Our *Method I* and *Method II* as shown in Algorithm 1.

2. *Global Baseline I* and *Global Baseline II*, which draw sample $\{x_i^*\}$ from the global posterior $f(x) \propto \prod_k f_k(x)$, and estimate $\mathbb{E}_f(h(x))$ by

$$\hat{z}_h^{*I} = \frac{1}{n}\sum_i h(x_i^*), \quad \hat{z}_h^{*II} = \frac{\sum_i \omega(x_i^*) h(x_i^*)}{\sum_i \omega(x_i^*)},$$

respectively, where $\omega(x_i^*) = f(x_i^*)/\hat{f}(x_i^*)$, and $\hat{f}(x) = \mathcal{N}(x;\ \hat{\mu}^*,\ \hat{\Sigma}^*)$ with $\hat{\mu}^*$ and $\hat{\Sigma}^*$ being the empirical mean and covariance matrix of $\{x_i^*\}$. Note that $\hat{z}_h^{*I}$ and $\hat{z}_h^{*II}$ can be treated as the global version of *Method I* and *Method II*, respectively; following Henmi et al. (2007), we can show

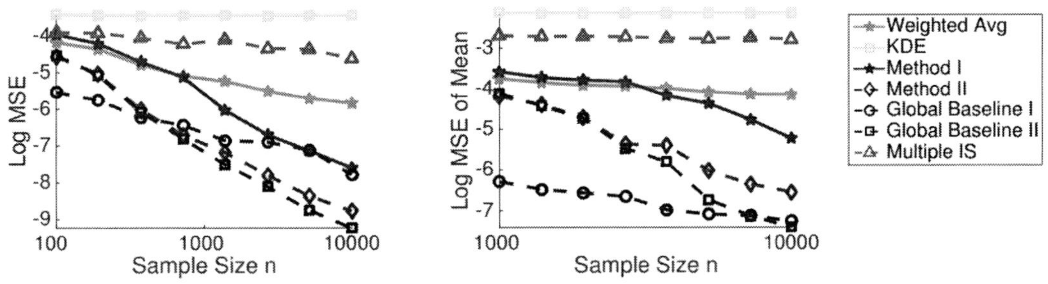

a. Estimating $\mathbb{E}_f[x]$ ($p = 10$, $m = 10$) c. Estimating $\mathbb{E}_f[x]$ ($p = 50$, $m = 10$)

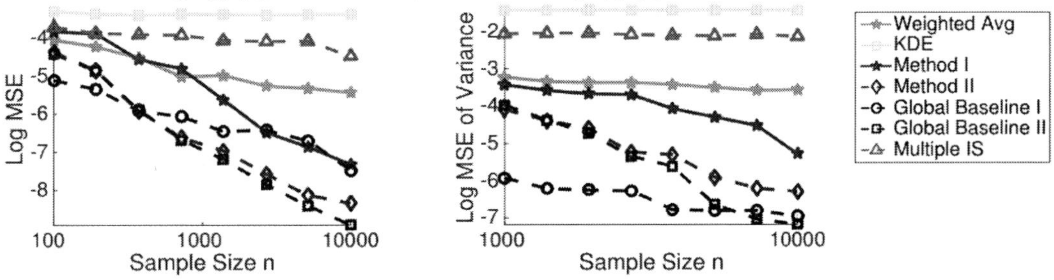

b. Estimating $\mathbb{E}_f[x^2]$ ($p = 10$, $m = 10$) d. Estimating $\mathbb{E}_f[x^2]$ ($p = 50$, $m = 10$)

Figure 2: Results on probit regression model with simulated data D of size $12,000$, partitioned into $m = 10$ subsets. (a)-(b) The MSE for estimating $\mathbb{E}_f[x]$ and $\mathbb{E}_f[x^2]$, respectively, when the dimension p of x is 10. (c)-(d) The results when the dimension p increases to 50. All the results are averaged over 500 random trials.

that $\hat{z}_h^{*II}$ always has smaller variance than $\hat{z}_h^{*I}$ when $f(x)$ is a Gaussian distribution.

3. *Weighted Avg*, which is the consensus Monte Carlo method by Scott et al. (2013).

4. The *KDE* method by Neiswanger et al. (2013).[2]

5. An naive *multiple importance weighted estimator (Multiple IS)* in which each subset sample $\{x_i^k\}_{i=1}^n \sim f_k$ is used to directly construct an importance sampling estimator for $\mathbb{E}_f(h(x))$:

$$\hat{z}_h^k = \frac{\sum_i h(x_i^k) w(x_i^k)}{\sum_i w(x_i^k)}, \quad \text{where} \quad w(x_i^k) = \frac{f(x_i^k)}{f_k(x_i^k)},$$

and the results from different subsets are combined by a weighted linear averaging:

$$\hat{z}_h^{MIS} = \frac{\sum_k v_k \hat{z}_h^k}{\sum_i v_k},$$

where v_k is chosen to be $v_k = 1/\hat{\text{var}}(\hat{z}_h^i)$.

6. The sampling via moment sharing (SMS) method by Xu et al. (2014),[3] which iteratively adjusts the local priors and draw local samples repeatedly.

[2]We used the code available at `https://www.cs.cmu.edu/~wdn/research/embParMCMC/index.html`.

[3]We used the code available at `https://github.com/BigBayes/SMS`

4.1 TOY EXAMPLE

We first consider two Gaussian mixtures with 10 components,

$$f_k(x) = \frac{1}{10}\sum_{j=1}^{10} \mathcal{N}(x; \mu_{jk}, \sigma^2), \quad k = 1, 2,$$

where μ_{jk} is randomly drawn from $\text{Uniform}([0, 10])$ for $f_1(x)$ and $\text{Uniform}([10, 20])$ for $f_2(x)$. The variance σ^2 is used to adjust the Gaussianity of $f_k(x)$. With a small σ (see Figure 1a), $f_1(x)$ and $f_2(x)$ are highly multi-modal, and are far away from each other; with a large σ (see Figure 1b), $f_1(x)$ and $f_2(x)$ become close to Gaussian and have a significant overlap with each other.

Figure 1(a) & (b) also shows the shapes of the corresponding product $f(x) \propto f_1(x)f_2(x)$ and the density function $f_{\bar{x}}(x)$ of the weighted averaging $\bar{x} = w_1x_1 + w_2x_2$ with $w_i \propto 1/\text{var}_{f_i}(x)$. We see that with a small σ, $f_{\bar{x}}(x)$ is very different from $f(x)$ but still covers a large part of $f(x)$, and hence can serve as a good importance sampling proposal (as approximately used in our methods). With a large σ, both $f(x)$ and $f_{\bar{x}}(x)$ are Gaussian like and are almost identical with each other.

Figure 1(c) & (e) shows the MSE of different algorithms when estimating the posterior mean $\mathbb{E}_f(h(x))$ with $h(x) = x$. Figure 1(c) shows the results of different algorithms when $\sigma = 0.5$ (the highly non-Gaussian case), in which we find that *Method I* works better than *Method II* and

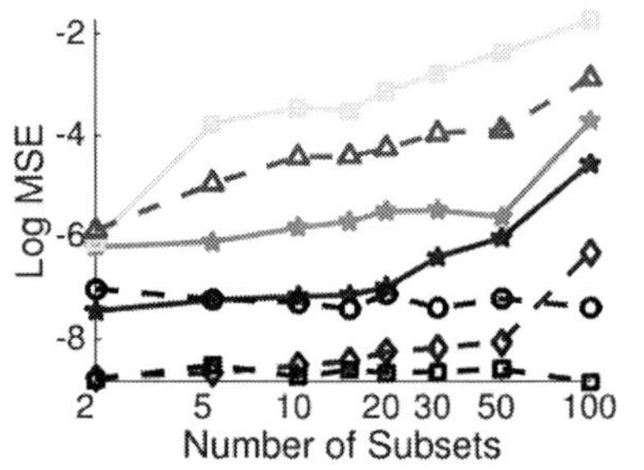

a. Estimating $\mathbb{E}_f[x]$ ($p = 10, n = 5 \times 10^3$)

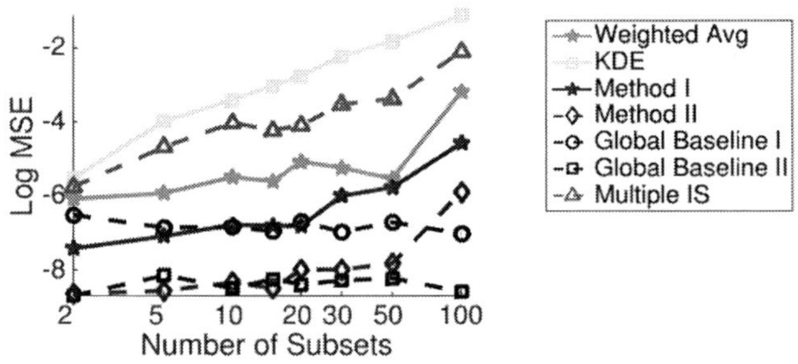

b. Estimating $\mathbb{E}_f[x^2]$ ($p = 10, n = 5 \times 10^3$)

Figure 3: Results on probit regression model with simulated data D of size 12,000, partitioned into m subsets, with m ranging from 2 to 100. (a)-(b) The MSE for estimating $\mathbb{E}_f[x]$ and $\mathbb{E}_f[x^2]$, respectively; the posterior sample size is fixed to be $n = 5 \times 10^3$ in both cases. All the results are averaged over 500 random trials.

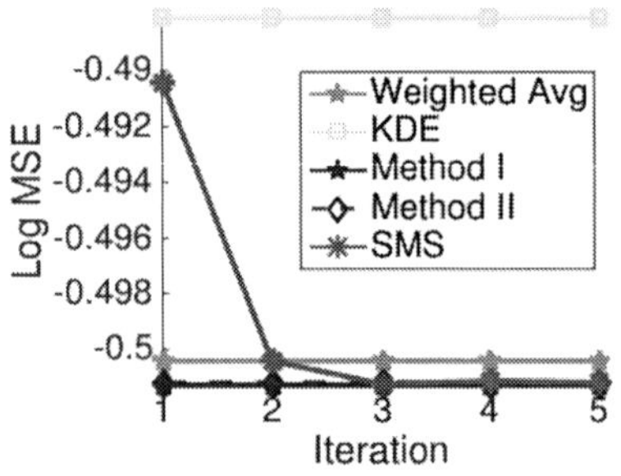

Figure 4: Comparing with SMS by Xu et al. (2014) on Bayesian probit regression. The setting is the same as that in Figure 3, except with fixed subset number $m = 10$.

Method II is clearly inconsistent in that its MSE stops decrease when the sample increases. Figure 1d shows the result of different algorithms when $\sigma = 10$ (the almost Gaussian case), in which we find that *Method II* works better than *Method I* as predicted by Theorem 3.4.

Figure 1(e) shows the results of different algorithms when we range σ from 0.5 to 10 (from highly non-Gaussian to highly Gaussian), and we can find that the performance of *Method I* converges to that of *Global baseline I* as predicted by Theorem 3.4, and that of *Method II* converges to *Global baseline II*. In all the cases, we find that both *Weighted Avg* and *KDE* perform much worse. *Multiple IS* tends to perform well when f_1 and f_2 are close to each other, but is worse when they are far apart from each other.

4.2 BAYESIAN PROBIT REGRESSION

We consider the Bayesian probit regression model for binary classification. Let $D = \{\chi_\ell, \zeta_\ell\}_{\ell=1}^N$ be a set of observed data with p-dimensional features $\chi_\ell \in \mathbb{R}^p$ and binary labels $\zeta_\ell \in \{0, 1\}$. The probit model is

$$p(D|x) = \prod_{\ell=1}^{N} \left[\zeta_\ell \Phi(x^\top \chi_\ell) + (1 - \zeta_\ell)(1 - \Phi(x^\top \chi_\ell))\right],$$

where $\Phi(\cdot)$ represents the cumulative distribution function of the standard normal distribution. We use an uninformative Gaussian prior $p(x) = \mathcal{N}(x; 0, 0.1)$ on x throughout our experiments.

We start with testing our methods on simulated datasets, where we first generate a true value of x with 50% zero elements and 50% elements drawn randomly from standard normal distribution, and then simulate a dataset $D = \{\chi_\ell, \zeta_\ell\}_{\ell=1}^N$ that is subsequently evenly partitioned into m subsets $\{D^k\}_{k=1}^m$, each of which includes N/m data points. We simulate $N = 12,000$ number of points throughout our experiments.

Figure 2(a) & (b) show the mean square error when estimating the posterior mean $\mathbb{E}_f[x]$ and the second order moment $\mathbb{E}_f[x^2]$, respectively, both when the dataset D is partitioned into $m = 10$ subsets (so that each subset D^k receives 1,200 data points). We can see that as the posterior sample size n of the subset samples $\{x_i^k\}_{i=1}^n \sim p(x|D^k)$ increases, our *Method I* and *Method II* match closely with the *Global Baseline I* and *Global Baseline II*, respectively; this may suggest that the local posteriors f_k are close to Gaussian in this case. The other methods, including *Weighted Avg*, *KDE* and *Multiple IS*, work significantly worse than both of our methods.

Figure 2(c) & (d) shows the results under the same setting as Figure 2(a) & (b), except when the dimension p increases to 50, where we observe that our *Method I* and *Method II* match less closely with the corresponding global baselines, but still tend to significantly outperform all the other distributed algorithms.

Figure 3(a) & (b) show the results when we fix the dimension $p = 10$ and a posterior sample size of $n = 5 \times 10^3$ and partition the dataset D into different number m of subsets (so that each subset D^k receives $12,000/m$ data points), with m range from 2 to 100. We observed that our *Method I* and *Method II* again match closely with the *Global Baseline I* and *Global Baseline II*, except when the partition number m is very high (e.g., $m \geq 30$ for *Method I*, and

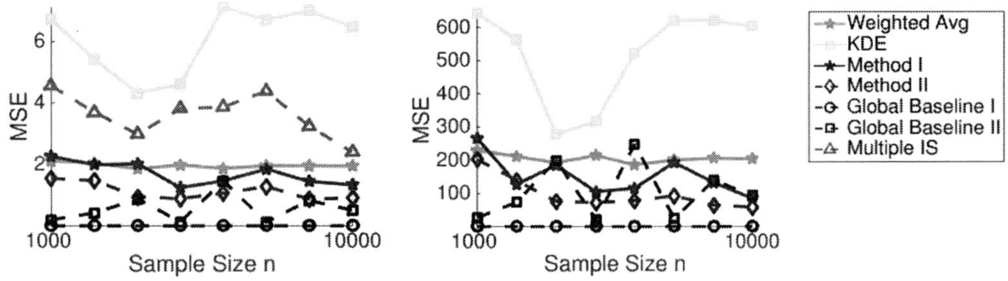

a. Estimating $\mathbb{E}_f[x]$ ($p = 54$, $m = 10$) b. Estimating $\mathbb{E}_f[x^2]$ ($p = 54$, $m = 10$)

Figure 5: Probit regression on the CoverType dataset. The dataset is partitioned evenly into 10 subsets. The result of *Multiple IS* in (b) is much worse than the other methods and is not shown in the figure.

$m \geq 100$ for *Method II*).

Figure 4 shows the result when we compare our methods with the iterative SMS method by Xu et al. (2014), where we find that our *Method I* and *Method II* tend to perform as well as SMS at its convergence, but has the advantage of requiring no iterative communication or re-sampling. We also tested the Weistrass sampler by Wang & Dunson (2013) (result does not report), but find it often performs worse (results similar to Figure 3 of Xu et al. (2014)).

In addition, we experimented with an iterative version of our method which introduces local priors $p_k(x)$ that satisfy $\prod_k p_k(x) = p(x)$ where $p(x)$ is the original global prior, and iteratively updates $p_k(x)$ to make the local posteriors $f_k(x) = p(D^k|x)p_k(x)$ match with each other. We observe that this iterative version does not improve the result significantly, likely because the non-iterative version of our method is already good enough.

Binary CoverType Dataset We then test our methods on the Forest Covertype dataset from the UCI machine learning repository (Bache & Lichman, 2013); it has 54 features, and is reprocessed to get binary labels following Collobert et al. (2002). For our experiment, we take the first 12,000 data points, and partition them into 10 subsets. The results of different algorithms are shown in Figure 5, in which we see that our *Method I* and *Method II* still perform significantly better than the other distributed algorithms.

5 CONCLUSION

We propose an importance weighted consensus Monte Carlo approach for distributed Bayesian inference. Two practical versions of our method are proposed, and their properties are studied both theoretically and empirically. Our methods have significant advantages over the previous one-shot methods based on density estimates in terms of accuracy, as well as the iterative methods in terms of computational and communication costs.

APPENDIX

Proof of Theorem 3.4. We only prove $\mathrm{MSE}(z_h^I) = \mathrm{var}_f(h(x))$ here; the fact that $\mathrm{MSE}(z_h^I) \geq \mathrm{MSE}(z_h^{II})$ can be found in Henmi et al. (2007, Theorem 1).

Let $\mathrm{MLE}_n(\hat{z}_h^I) = n\mathbb{E}[(\hat{z}_h^I - z_h)^2]$; using the Delta method we can show that $\mathrm{MLE}_n(z_h^I) \asymp \mathbb{E}_q[(h(\bar{x}) - z_h)^2 w_n(\boldsymbol{x})^2]$, with

$$w_n(\boldsymbol{x}) = \frac{p_n(\boldsymbol{x})}{q(\boldsymbol{x})} = \frac{\mathcal{N}(\bar{x}, \mu_0, \Sigma_0)}{\mathcal{N}(\bar{x}, \hat{\mu}_0, \hat{\Sigma}_0)} \prod_k \frac{\mathcal{N}(x^k, \mu_k, \Sigma_k)}{\mathcal{N}(x^k, \hat{\mu}_k, \hat{\Sigma}_k)},$$

where $q(\boldsymbol{x}) = \prod_k \mathcal{N}(x_k;\ \mu_k, \Sigma_k)$, and $p_n(\boldsymbol{x}) = \mathcal{N}(\bar{x};\ \mu_0, \Sigma_0) \prod_k \mathcal{N}(x_k;\ \hat{\mu}_k, \hat{\Sigma}_k) / \mathcal{N}(\bar{x};\ \hat{\mu}_0, \hat{\Sigma}_0)$; here $w_n(\boldsymbol{x})$ and $p_n(\boldsymbol{x})$ are indexed with sample size n since they dependent on the empirical means and variances. Since $\mathrm{var}_f(h(x)) = \mathbb{E}_{p_n}[(h(\bar{x}) - z_h)^2]$ by Proposition 3.1, we have

$$\begin{aligned}
&\mathrm{MSE}_n(z_h^I) - \mathrm{var}_f(h(x)) \\
&\asymp \mathbb{E}_q[(h(\bar{x}) - z_h)^2 w_n(\boldsymbol{x})^2] - \mathbb{E}_{p_n}[(h(\bar{x}) - z_h)^2] \\
&= \mathbb{E}_{p_n}[(h(\bar{x}) - z_h)^2 w_n(\boldsymbol{x})] - \mathbb{E}_{p_n}[(h(\bar{x}) - z_h)^2] \\
&= \mathbb{E}_{p_n}[(h(\bar{x}) - z_h)^2 (w_n(\boldsymbol{x}) - 1)]
\end{aligned}$$

Using Cauchy-Schwarz inequality, we have

$$\begin{aligned}
&\left(\mathrm{MSE}(z_h^I) - \mathrm{var}_f(h(x))\right)^2 \\
&\leq \mathbb{E}_{p_n}[(h(\bar{x}) - z_h)^4] \cdot \mathbb{E}_{p_n}[(w_n(\boldsymbol{x}) - 1)^2] \\
&= \mathbb{E}_f[(h(x) - z_h)^4] \cdot \mathbb{E}_q[w_n(\boldsymbol{x})(w_n(\boldsymbol{x}) - 1)^2].
\end{aligned}$$

Therefore, we just need to show that $\mathbb{E}_q[w_n(\boldsymbol{x})(w_n(\boldsymbol{x}) - 1)^2] \to 0$. This can be done using dominant convergence theorem: Let $\psi_n(\boldsymbol{x}) = q(\boldsymbol{x}) w_n(\boldsymbol{x})(w_n(\boldsymbol{x}) - 1)^2$, then we have $\psi_n(x) \to 0$, $\forall \boldsymbol{x}$ since $\hat{\mu}_k \to \mu_k$, $\hat{\Sigma}_k \to \Sigma_k$ and hence $w_n(\boldsymbol{x}) \to 1$ for $\forall \boldsymbol{x}$; in addition, we can show that $|\psi_n(\boldsymbol{x})| \leq q(\boldsymbol{x})^{1/2}$ for large enough n and $q(\boldsymbol{x})^{1/2}$ is an integrable function.

□

References

Angelino, E., Johnson, M. J., and Adams, R. P. Patterns of scalable Bayesian inference. *http://arxiv.org/abs/1602.05221*, 2015.

Bache, K. and Lichman, M. UCI machine learning repository, 2013. URL `http://archive.ics.uci.edu/ml`.

Baker, J., Fearnhead, P., and Fox, E. Computational statistics for big data. 2015.

Bardenet, R., Doucet, A., and Holmes, C. Towards scaling up Markov chain Monte Carlo: an adaptive subsampling approach. In *ICML*, pp. 405–413, 2014.

Bardenet, R., Doucet, A., and Holmes, C. On Markov chain Monte Carlo methods for tall data. *arXiv preprint arXiv:1505.02827*, 2015.

Birge, L. and Massart, P. Estimation of integral functionals of a density. *The Annals of Statistics*, pp. 11–29, 1995.

Collobert, R., Bengio, S., and Bengio, Y. A parallel mixture of SVMs for very large scale problems. *Neural computation*, 14(5):1105–1114, 2002.

Green, P. J., Łatuszyński, K., Pereyra, M., and Robert, C. P. Bayesian computation: a summary of the current state, and samples backwards and forwards. *Statistics and Computing*, 25(4):835–862, 2015.

Henmi, M. and Eguchi, S. A paradox concerning nuisance parameters and projected estimating functions. *Biometrika*, 91(4):929–941, 2004.

Henmi, M., Yoshida, R., and Eguchi, S. Importance sampling via the estimated sampler. *Biometrika*, 94(4):985–991, 2007.

Huang, Z. and Gelman, A. Sampling for Bayesian computation with large datasets. *Available at SSRN 1010107*, 2005.

Korattikara, A., Chen, Y., and Welling, M. Austerity in MCMC land: Cutting the Metropolis-Hastings budget. In *ICML*, 2014.

Krishnamurthy, A., Kandasamy, K., Poczos, B., and Wasserman, L. Nonparametric estimation of Renyi divergence and friends. In *ICML*, 2014.

Krishnamurthy, A., Kandasamy, K., Poczos, B., and Wasserman, L. On estimating L_2^2 divergence. In *AISTATS*, 2015.

Maclaurin, D. and Adams, R. P. Firefly Monte Carlo: Exact MCMC with subsets of data. In *UAI*, 2014.

Minsker, S., Srivastava, S., Lin, L., and Dunson, D. B. Robust and scalable Bayes via a median of subset posterior measures. *arXiv preprint arXiv:1403.2660*, 2014.

Neiswanger, W., Wang, C., and Xing, E. Asymptotically exact, embarrassingly parallel MCMC. *arXiv preprint arXiv:1311.4780*, 2013.

Owen, A. B. *Monte Carlo theory, methods and examples*. 2013.

Rabinovich, M., Angelino, E., and Jordan, M. I. Variational consensus Monte Carlo. *arXiv preprint arXiv:1506.03074*, 2015.

Scott, S. L., Blocker, A. W., Bonassi, F. V., Chipman, H., George, E., and McCulloch, R. Bayes and big data: The consensus Monte Carlo algorithm. In *EFaBBayes 250 conference*, volume 16, 2013.

Wang, X. and Dunson, D. B. Parallel MCMC via Weierstrass sampler. *arXiv preprint arXiv:1312.4605*, 2013.

Welling, M. and Teh, Y. W. Bayesian learning via stochastic gradient Langevin dynamics. In *ICML*, pp. 681–688, 2011.

Xu, M., Lakshminarayanan, B., Teh, Y. W., Zhu, J., and Zhang, B. Distributed Bayesian posterior sampling via moment sharing. In *NIPS*, pp. 3356–3364, 2014.

Zhu, J., Chen, J., and Hu, W. Big learning with Bayesian methods. *arXiv preprint arXiv:1411.6370*, 2014.

Large-scale Submodular Greedy Exemplar Selection with Structured Similarity Matrices

Dmitry Malioutov
IBM Research
Yorktown Heights, NY

Abhishek Kumar
IBM Research
Yorktown Heights, NY

Ian E.H. Yen
Computer Science Department
University of Texas at Austin

Abstract

Exemplar clustering attempts to find a subset of data-points that summarizes the entire data-set in the sense of minimizing the sum of distances from each point to its closest exemplar. It has many important applications in machine learning including document and video summarization, data compression, scalability of kernel methods and Gaussian processes, active learning and feature selection. A key challenge in the adoption of exemplar clustering to large-scale applications has been the availability of accurate and scalable algorithms. We propose an approach that combines structured similarity matrix representations with submodular greedy maximization that can dramatically increase the scalability of exemplar clustering and still enjoys good approximation guarantees. Exploiting structured similarity matrices within the context of submodular greedy algorithms is by no means trivial, as naive approaches still require computing all the entries of the matrix. We propose a randomized approach based on sampling sign-patterns of columns of the similarity matrix and establish accuracy guarantees. We demonstrate significant computational speed-ups while still achieving highly accurate solutions, and solve problems with up-to millions of data-points in around a minute or less on a single commodity computer.

1 Introduction

With the prevalence of large-scale datasets coming from social media, computational biology, finance and engineering it has been difficult to apply some of the more computationally intensive machine learning approaches such as probabilistic Graphical models, kernel methods and Gaussian processes. Simple tools like logistic regression trained via stochastic gradient descent are instead prevalent in web companies that need to deal with hundreds of millions and more samples [16]. Exemplar clustering suggests a path to extend some of the powerful ML methods to such domains by finding small representative subsets of data to summarize the large dataset, and apply the method on the summary. Other uses of exemplar clustering include summarizing data for humans (document and video summarization [14]), facility location in OR, and active learning [7] to prioritize the annotation in large unlabeled datasets where annotating the entire dataset is out of the question.

An integer programming formulation for exemplar clustering is itself intractable, being an NP-hard problem [21]. Hence, a variety of approximate schemes have been developed including LP relaxations [3, 27], message-passing algorithms [8, 13], and heuristic algorithms such as Partitioning around Medoids (PAM) [11]. The most successful methods balancing scalability and good accuracy guarantees[1] have been based on the theory of submodular maximization [12]. Exemplar clustering (with some mild assumptions) can be shown to be submodular, i.e. to satisfy diminishing marginal gains. Thus, invoking the celebrated result of [21], the greedy approach that adds exemplars in order of their marginal gains has an $1 - 1/e$ approximation guarantee. A lazy evaluation approach called "Lazy Greedy" further exploits the diminishing marginal gains property to accelerate the solution [18].

Nevertheless, for very large scale data-sets even greedy algorithms become computationally infeasible, as the exemplar clustering cost-function is non-local, and evaluating the marginal gains for each exemplar candidate requires evaluating the distance to each other point in the dataset. A number of directions have been considered to speed up basic greedy (and lazy greedy) methods. Simple surrogate functions (such as modular bounds) approximating the submodular function have been proposed in [26]. The paper also introduced a nearest neighbors pruning approach

[1]There is a rich theory on LP relaxations for exemplar clustering, but the methods are less scalable, having to solve linear programs with $O(n^2)$ variables, where n is the number of datapoints.

to reduce the set of candidates to consider. This idea has been further explored in [15]. A distributed algorithm that randomly splits the data among several machines, selects exemplars from each subset, and then combines them was proposed in [20]. This however requires further approximation by a factor of $1/min(k, m)$ where k is the number of exemplars, and m is the number of machines. A stochastic sub-sampling idea called "Lazier than lazy greedy" was proposed in [19] which takes a small random subset of potential exemplars into consideration at each stage. By taking the sample size proportional to $n/k \log(1/\epsilon)$ the running time of the algorithm executed for k iterations becomes independent of k, and is still able to achieve an $1 - 1/e - \epsilon$ approximation guarantee (in expectation). This result was also applied in the streaming setting [2].

We pursue a different approach where we assume that the similarity matrices are either exactly represented as certain structured matrices (such as low-rank, sparse plus low-rank, product of sparse matrices, Toeplitz, e.t.c), or can be approximated by such. For example, using the popular word2vec representation for words and sentences [17] along with cosine similarity gives rise to an explicit low-rank similarity matrix. Squared Euclidean distance matrices (and corresponding similarity matrices) are also exactly low-rank for low-dimensional feature spaces. While simply using the structured matrix for the greedy algorithm reduces its memory footprint, it still requires quadratic computation in number of samples n. We show that the bottleneck of the problem involves a low-rank positive column sum problem. We develop a randomized approximation technique based on sampling column sign-patterns and establish theoretical guarantees which can reduce the computation to linear in n. The proposed approach is guaranteed to generate a better solution than the stochastic sampling approach [19] at the cost of a very modest increase in computation. We consider numerical studies on a number of large-scale machine learning problems and demonstrate dramatic increase in speed compared to plain greedy and lazy-greedy methods with only a minor corresponding loss in objective values.

The outline of the paper is as follows. We first overview submodular maximization, and prior work on exact and approximate greedy algorithms in Section 2. We discuss structured approximation matrices and our approach for approximate greedy optimization in Section 3. We present theoretical guarantees in Section 4 and experimental results in Section 5.

2 Background: submodular optimization

In this paper we consider an approach for exemplar clustering based on *submodular maximization*. We start by reviewing the notions of submodularity, greedy algorithms and their guarantees, and the recent extensions.

Let $\mathcal{V}$ be a set of size n. A set function $f : 2^{\mathcal{V}} \to \mathbb{R}$ is called submodular if it satisfies a diminishing marginal gains property: if $A \subseteq B$, and $a \in \mathcal{V}$ then

$$f(A \cup a) - f(A) \geq f(B \cup a) - f(B)$$

Intuitively, there is more benefit (higher marginal gain) to add a new element a to the smaller set A than to its superset B. If for all $A \subseteq B$ it holds that $f(A) \leq f(B)$ then the function is called *monotone submodular*. If $f(\varnothing) = 0$ then the function is called homogeneous. A celebrated result by Neumhauser et. al establishes that a simple greedy algorithm achieves an $1 - \frac{1}{e}$ approximation to the optimal objective to non-negative cardinality constrained monotone submodular maximization [21]. The greedy algorithm starts with an empty set, and at each stage adds the element which has the maximum marginal gain $\Delta f(a|A) = f(A \cup a) - f(A)$ to the current selected set A.

The exemplar clustering problem that we consider in the paper has the following form. We have a collection $\mathcal{V}$ of data-points,[2] and a similarity function $s : \mathcal{V} \times \mathcal{V} \to \mathbb{R}^+$. We would like to faithfully summarize the entire data-set (maximize the pairwise similarity between each point and its exemplar) using at most k exemplars:

$$\max_{A \subset \mathcal{V}} \sum_{i \in \mathcal{V}} \max_{j \in A} s(i, j) \text{ where } |S| \leq k \qquad (1)$$

One can verify that the exemplar clustering problem above corresponds to nonnegative monotone submodular maximization with a cardinality constraint, and hence the greedy algorithm can be applied with the corresponding approximation guarantee. The greedy algorithm can be sped up further using the same diminishing returns property of marginal gains [18] by lazy evaluation, by keeping the elements in a priority queue sorted according to marginal gain.

Unfortunately, the evaluation of the marginal gain for a single candidate exemplar requires $O(n)$ computation, and we consider $O(n)$ candidates at each stage. Hence the greedy algorithm still does not scale to very large data-sets beyond a few hundred thousand data points. Improving the scalability of the greedy algorithm for exemplar clustering has been an active research area and a number of approximation strategies have been proposed at the cost of worse approximation guarantees. The existing proposals include stochastic greedy, distributed algorithms and nearest-neighbor graph approximations that we have described in the introduction. Next we describe how we can exploit structured similarity matrices and a randomized ap-

[2] All our results also extend to the non-symmetric version of the problem where the data-points come from set $\mathcal{V}_1$ and exemplars have to be selected from $\mathcal{V}_2$, for example the facility location problem in Operations Research. Also, allowing rewards $h_i \geq 0$ for making data-point i an exemplar, still keeps the problem monotone and submodular.

proach based on sampling sign-patterns of columns to propose an elegant scalable solution for exemplar clustering with good approximation guarantees.

3 Greedy exemplar selection with low-rank similarity matrices

We consider the greedy approach for exemplar clustering. As inputs we have the similarity matrix S and a budget k. At each stage t we have the current active set $\mathcal{A}^t$ of exemplars chosen at the previous iteration. We would like to evaluate the marginal gain of new elements $a \in \mathcal{V} \setminus \mathcal{A}^t$.

Suppose that at step t we have computed the optimal assignment $\hat{j}^t(i) = \arg\max_{j \in \mathcal{A}^t} s(i,j)$ for each datapoint i. We will refer to the attained objective as $z_i = s(i, \hat{j}^t(i))$. At iteration $t+1$, we compute the marginal gain for each $a \in \mathcal{V} \setminus \mathcal{A}^t$. The closest element to i in $\mathcal{A}^t \cup a$ either remains the same as in the previous step, or it becomes a. Hence the marginal gain $\Delta f(a|A)$ of adding a to $\mathcal{A}^t$ is

$$\sum_i \max\left(s(i,a),\ s(i,\hat{j}^t(i))\right) - s(i,\hat{j}^t(i)) \qquad (2)$$

Define $[X]_+ = \max(X, 0)$. Then the computational bottleneck is computing the vector of marginal gains, i.e. the maximum positive column sum of the matrix $R = S - \mathbf{z}\mathbf{1}^T$:

$$\max_j \sum_i [R_{ij}]_+ = \max_j \sum_i [S_{ij} - z_i]_+ \qquad (3)$$

Naive implementation requires computing all the elements of this matrix[3]. We show that if the matrix S has a structured representation and allows fast matrix action (mutliplication of the matrix by a vector) – then we can exploit a randomized algorithm with good guarantees.

We first analyze the case of low-rank matrices, $S = \tilde{U}\tilde{V}^T$, where $\tilde{U}$ and $\tilde{V}$ are $n \times d$. We show that we can use a number of other structured matrices in Section 3.4. Now, if S is low-rank with rank d then R is also low-rank with rank at most $d+1$. Let $U = [\tilde{U},\ -\mathbf{z}]$ and $V = [\tilde{V},\ \mathbf{1}]$. Then $R = UV^T = S - \mathbf{z}\mathbf{1}^T$. Note that computing the plain column sum for low-rank matrices is trivial: $\mathbf{1}^T R = (\mathbf{1}^T U)V^T$ thus reducing the computational complexity from $O(n^2)$ to $O(nd)$. However, the positive sign in $\mathbf{1}^T[R]_+$ makes it considerably more difficult to exploit the low-rank factorization. We study this problem next.

3.1 Maximum positive column sum problem

We would like to efficiently compute the maximum positive column sum for a low-rank matrix $R = UV^T$:

$$\max_j \sum_i [R_{ij}]_+ = \max_j \sum_i \left([UV^T]_+\right)_{ij} \qquad (4)$$

[3]Lazy greedy algorithms avoid computing some elements but still evaluate a large number of columns of this matrix.

Algorithm 1 Approximate max-positive column sum

1. Uniformly at random sample r columns from the matrix R and compute their sign patterns $\mathbf{q}_i$.
2. Aggregate sign-patterns into matrix $Q = [\mathbf{q}_1, \ldots \mathbf{q}_r]$.
3. Let $Y = (Q^T U)V$ and let $\mathbf{y} = \max_i Y_{ij}$.
4. Find $\hat{j} = \arg\max_j \mathbf{y}_j$.

Suppose we knew the binary ($\{0,1\}$) sign-pattern $\hat{\mathbf{q}}$ of the column achieving the maximum in (4), i.e. $q_i = 1_{\{R_{i\hat{j}} > 0\}}$ where $\hat{j}$ is the column achieving the arg max in (4). Then we could compute

$$\max_j \sum_i [R_{ij}]_+ = \max_j \sum_i \left([UV^T]_+\right)_{ij} = \max_j [(\hat{\mathbf{q}}^T U)V^T]_j \qquad (5)$$

Also note, that for an arbitrary sign-pattern $\mathbf{q}$, we have

$$\max_j [(\hat{\mathbf{q}}^T U)V^T]_j \geq \max_j [(\mathbf{q}^T U)V^T]_j \qquad (6)$$

We suggest to take a collection of r random sign-patterns $\{\mathbf{q}_1, \ldots, \mathbf{q}_r\}$ and evaluate the maximum value of the r.h.s. in (6) over all of them. We take the sign-patterns from a subset of columns of R sampled uniformly at random (another choice can be i.i.d. binary vectors). Surprisingly, such a simple scheme can be shown to satisfy good approximation guarantees, which we describe in Section 4, and also to give very accurate numerical results. In particular, it is guaranteed to produce better results than the stochastic greedy approach [19] with the same subset of columns.

The procedure is described in Algorithm 1. It produces a lower bound $\sum_i R_{i\hat{j}}$ on the maximum positive column sum of R:

$$\hat{j} := \arg\max_j \max_{\tilde{j} \in \{j(1), \ldots, j(r)\}} \mathbf{q}_{\tilde{j}}^T R_{:,j}. \qquad (7)$$

3.2 Scalable submodular greedy algorithm

Now, to use this algorithm for efficient greedy submodular optimization, we have to repeat it for k rounds of greedy to generate k exemplars. At each round we simply recompute the vector $\mathbf{z}$ and $R = [\tilde{U},\ -\mathbf{z}][\tilde{V},\ \mathbf{1}]^\top$ and invoke Algorithm 1. At the initial stage the vector $\mathbf{z}$ is zero, and the initial marginal gains are simply the column-sums of S. We summarize the steps in Algoritm 2.

The greedy algorithm is recovered if we find the exact column maximizing marginal gains: $\arg\max_j \sum_i ([R]_+)_{ij}$. This however would require $O(n^2)$ computation. By using the approach from Section 3.1 with r random signs, it can be reduced to $O(nr)$ by allowing approximate answers.

3.3 Further speed-ups

The approach proposed in the previous section can dramatically reduce the computation of the greedy method from

Algorithm 2 Low Rank GReedy (LRGR)

Input: $S = \tilde{U}\tilde{V}^T$
Initialize: $\hat{j}^1 = \arg\max_j \sum_i [\tilde{U}\tilde{V}^T]_{ij}$. Set $\mathcal{A}^1 = \{\hat{j}^1\}$. Evaluate $z_i = s(i, \hat{j}^1)$. Set $t = 1$.
for $i = 1 \dots r$ **do**
i. Advance $t \to t + 1$
ii. Let $R = \tilde{U}\tilde{V}^T - \mathbf{z}\mathbf{1}^T$.
iii. Use (7) to approximately find $\hat{j}^t \approx \arg\max_j \sum_i ([R]_+)_{ij}$.
iv. $\mathcal{A}^t = \mathcal{A}^{t-1} \cup \hat{j}^t$
v. Update $\mathbf{z}^t$: $z_i^{t+1} = \max_{j \in \mathcal{A}^t} s(i, j)$
end for

$O(n^2)$ to $O(nr)$ per each round of the greedy method. Yet, we can improve the running time and accuracy further.

In the previous section the matrix Q of sign-patterns was recomputed from scratch at each greedy iteration. Note that if we store this matrix from the previous iteration, then we only need to update $Q^T\mathbf{z}$, while $Q^T\tilde{U}$ remains the same. While reusing the same matrix Q on all iterations may significantly impact accuracy, we can keep generating new sign patterns but also keep re-using the computationally inexpensive pre-computed old-sign patterns.

We also note that we can compute the complement sign-patterns very inexpensively. Let $\bar{\mathbf{q}} = \mathbf{1} - \mathbf{q}$. Then $(\bar{\mathbf{q}}^T U)V^T = (\mathbf{1}^T U)V^T - (\mathbf{q}^T U)V^T$. Thus we can add another r complement sign-patterns at the cost of computing the column sum of $R = UV^T$.

Finally, the algorithm proposed in the previous section aims to speed up the computation of the plain greedy algorithm. In [19] an extension of stochastic greedy was proposed to also accelerate the lazy-greedy approach by caching previously computed marginal gains and storing them in a priority queue. The same ideas can be used with our randomized sign-pattern approach to develop its lazy-greedy variant.

3.4 Low-rank and other structured similarity matrices

In Sections 3.1 and 3.2 we assumed that the similarity matrix S is low-rank, which can happen if we use inner-product similarity measure in a low-dimensional vector space (e.g word2vec). Note that the matrix of pairwise squared Euclidean distances is also low-rank for low-dimensional feature spaces, and this also holds for matrices based on arbitrary Bregman divergences, and hence for the corresponding similarity matrices.

In addition to the low-rank assumption, we can also use a variety of other structured matrix factorizations in exactly the same way, as long as they allow fast-matrix action. Suppose $S = \tilde{U}\tilde{V}^T$, then to apply the approach in Section 3.1 we simply need to be able to quickly compute $Q\tilde{U}$ and $(Q\tilde{U})\tilde{V}^T$. For example if $\tilde{U}$ and $\tilde{V}$ have high-dimensional but very sparse rows (e.g. the sparse one-hot bag-of-words representation for text), then the matrix-vector products depend on the number of non-zero entries in $\tilde{U}$ and $\tilde{V}$.

Other factorizations allowing fast matrix action include sparse plus low-rank matrices, Fourier matrices, circulant and convolution matrices, and even more advanced matrix approximations including block-diagonal low-rank matrices [24] and matrices with low displacement operators [25].

4 Theoretical analysis

In this section we show that LRGR achieves an approximately optimal solution in expectation when sufficiently many sign patterns are sampled. In the first part we show approximation bounds that do not assume any structure on the similarity matrix S. Subsequently, we try to provide intuition behind how the low-rank structure on S can help in achieving better solution by analyzing the case of rank-2 similarity matrix. Finally, we analyze the case of data distributed across tight clusters.

4.1 Structure-oblivious approximation guarantees

The results in this section do not exploit the structure on the similarity matrix. The proof proceeds along similar lines as [19]. We prove the result for the symmetric case when the candidate exemplars belong to the set of points. Let $\mathcal{A}^*$ be the optimal solution of problem (1) with $|\mathcal{A}^*| = k$ (if the algorithm terminates with $|\mathcal{A}^*| < k$, it will return the optimal solution [21]), and $\mathcal{A}^t$ be the solution of LRGR at step t. Let $\mathcal{V}$ denote the full index set of all the points ($\mathcal{V} = \{1, 2, \dots, n\}$). Let $f(\mathcal{A}^t)$ be the objective value for set $\mathcal{A}^t$ and $\Delta(a|\mathcal{A}^t) := f(\mathcal{A}^t \cup a) - f(\mathcal{A}^t)$.

Using submodularity, we have

$$f(\mathcal{A}^*) - f(\mathcal{A}^t) \leq \sum_{a \in \mathcal{A}^* \setminus \mathcal{A}^t} \Delta(a|\mathcal{A}^t) \tag{8}$$

The following Lemma bounds the expected potential gain of LRGR after step t.

Lemma 4.1. *Given a current solution $\mathcal{A}^t$, the expected gain of LRGR in the next step is at least $\frac{1-e^{-kr/n}}{k} \sum_{a \in \mathcal{A}^* \setminus \mathcal{A}^t} \Delta(a|\mathcal{A}^t)$ when signs from r randomly picked columns are used.*

Proof. Let $\mathcal{R}$ be the set of randomly picked columns with $|\mathcal{R}| = r$. The probability that one of the columns from $\mathcal{A}^* \setminus \mathcal{A}^t$ is picked, is given by

$$P[\mathcal{R} \cap (\mathcal{A}^* \setminus \mathcal{A}^t) \neq \phi] = 1 - P[\mathcal{R} \cap (\mathcal{A}^* \setminus \mathcal{A}^t) = \phi]$$
$$= 1 - \left(1 - \frac{|\mathcal{A}^* \setminus \mathcal{A}^t|}{|\mathcal{V} \setminus \mathcal{A}^t|}\right)^r$$
$$\geq 1 - e^{-\frac{r|\mathcal{A}^* \setminus \mathcal{A}^t|}{|\mathcal{V} \setminus \mathcal{A}^t|}} \geq 1 - e^{-\frac{r|\mathcal{A}^* \setminus \mathcal{A}^t|}{n}}$$

Since $0 \leq |\mathcal{A}^* \setminus \mathcal{A}^t| \leq k$, using Jensen's inequality we have

$$1 - e^{-\frac{r|\mathcal{A}^* \setminus \mathcal{A}^t|}{n}} \geq \left(1 - e^{-\frac{rk}{n}}\right) \frac{|\mathcal{A}^* \setminus \mathcal{A}^t|}{k}$$

If LRGR picks one of the columns from $\mathcal{A}^* \setminus \mathcal{A}^t$, the score for that column will be evaluated exactly. Scores for the columns whose sign pattern matches that of the picked column will also be evaluated exactly. The scores for all other columns will be underestimated. As LRGR takes a maximum over all the scores, it will add a column to $\mathcal{A}^t$ which will give a gain equal to at least that of the picked column from $\mathcal{A}^* \setminus \mathcal{A}^t$. As any of the columns from $\mathcal{A}^* \setminus \mathcal{A}^t$ is equally likely to be picked, the exemplar a^{t+1} added by LRGR will yield

$$\mathbf{E}[\Delta(a^{t+1}|\mathcal{A}^t)] \geq P[\mathcal{R} \cap (\mathcal{A}^* \setminus \mathcal{A}^t) \neq \phi] \frac{\sum_{a \in \mathcal{A}^* \setminus \mathcal{A}^t} \Delta(a|\mathcal{A})}{|\mathcal{A}^* \setminus \mathcal{A}^t|}$$
$$\geq \frac{1 - e^{-kr/n}}{k} \sum_{a \in \mathcal{A}^* \setminus \mathcal{A}^t} \Delta(a|\mathcal{A}^t).$$

□

Combining Lemma 4.1 with Eq. 8 we get

$$f(\mathcal{A}^*) - f(\mathcal{A}^t) \leq \frac{k}{1 - e^{-kr/n}} \mathbf{E}[f(\mathcal{A}^{t+1}) - f(\mathcal{A}^t)] \quad (9)$$

Taking expectation over $\mathcal{A}^t$, we have

$$\mathbf{E}[f(\mathcal{A}^{t+1}) - f(\mathcal{A}^t)] \geq \frac{1 - e^{-kr/n}}{k} \mathbf{E}[f(\mathcal{A}^*) - f(\mathcal{A}^t)] \quad (10)$$

Unrolling the above by induction, we get

$$\mathbf{E}[f(\mathcal{A}^k)] \geq \left(1 - \left(1 - \frac{1 - e^{-kr/n}}{k}\right)^k\right) f(\mathcal{A}^*)$$
$$\geq \left(1 - e^{-(1 - e^{-kr/n})}\right) f(\mathcal{A}^*)$$
$$\geq \left(1 - e^{-1}(1 + e^{-kr/n})\right) f(\mathcal{A}^*)$$
$$= (1 - 1/e - e^{-kr/n}) f(\mathcal{A}^*).$$

Note that the above bound turns vacuous for $r \leq \frac{n}{k} \ln \frac{1}{1-1/e} \approx 0.459\frac{n}{k}$. When the similarity matrix is allowed to have negative entries, the submodular objective function may lose nonnegativity but it still remains monotonic. In this case, one can obtain a guarantee of the form:

$$f(\mathcal{A}^*) - \mathbf{E}[f(\mathcal{A}^k)] \leq (e^{\frac{1-k}{k}} + e^{\frac{-kr}{n}})(f(\mathcal{A}^*) - \mathbf{E}[f(\mathcal{A}^1)]).$$

4.2 Approximation guarantee under low-rank assumption

The analysis in the previous section did not use the low-rank assumption on the matrix R. We show that this assumption is helpful not only to improve the computational complexity of the proposed algorithm, but also to improve the approximation compared to the stochastic greedy approach. To build some intuition of why the low-rank assumption is helpful, consider the maximum possible number of distinct sign-patterns of columns of the matrix R. If the matrix is full-dimensional, then any sign-pattern is possible, and there are 2^n such sign patterns out of which n are chosen. However, if $R = UV^T$, and U and V are $n \times d$, then for a fixed U, the number of possible sign-patterns of columns of R is reduced. In particular, as we show below, for the 2-dimensional case, the number of possible sign-patterns is $2n$ (instead of 2^n): U has two columns, and the sign patterns of any linear combinations of these two columns generate only a small subset of possible sign patterns.

More generally, if U is d-dimensional, then using the results in [10] for number of regions created by n hyperplanes (in general position) in d dimensions, we have that the number of possible sign-patterns of R for a fixed U is given by:

$$2\sum_{i=1}^{d} \binom{n-1}{i-1} \quad (11)$$

For the 2-dimensional case, this number is $2n$. If we assumed that the column sign-patterns in our matrix R are sampled uniformly at random with replacement from the $2n$ possible choices, then the expected number of unique sign-patterns is $\sum_{i=0}^{n-1}(\frac{2n-1}{2n})^i = 2n(1-(1-1/(2n))^n) \approx 0.787n$. So we expect some number of columns with repeated sign-patterns in the low-dimensional case. This makes it easier for us to get a sign-pattern from our r sampled columns of R that matches the sign-pattern of one of the exemplars.

Let $\mathcal{A}^*$ be the index set of optimal k exemplars. For the 2-dimensional case, we consider the probability that at least one of the r randomly sampled columns, indexed by set $\mathcal{R}$, will completely agree in signs with at least one of the exemplars. The worst case for this probability is when all the exemplars have exactly the same sign pattern since we reduce our set of candidate signs that the sampled columns can match to. This worst case probability is given as:

$$P(\mathcal{R} \cap A^* \neq \phi) + P(\mathcal{R} \cap A^* = \phi)(1 - ((2n-1)/2n)^r)$$
$$= 1 - (1 - k/n)^r + (1 - k/n)^r(1 - ((2n-1)/2n)^r)$$
$$\geq 1 - e^{-kr/n}e^{-r/(2n)}.$$

The first term in the first line corresponds to the probability of selecting one of the r sampled columns to be one of the exemplars, and the second term corresponds to picking a column that misses the set of exemplars, but whose sign-pattern agrees with the sign pattern of one of the exemplars. This probability of at least one agreement in sign patterns is also a lower bound on the probability of Algorithm 1 recovering a column whose score is at least that of one of the exemplars. For the best case when all the exemplars differ with each other in at least one place in sign patterns, the lower bound on the recovery probability increases to $(1 - e^{-kr/n} e^{-kr/(2n)})$. If we ignore the structure on R, the lower bound loosens to $(1 - e^{-kr/n})$ which was used in Section 4.1.

We should also note that this bound, although better than stochastic greedy [19], is based on several worst-case scenarios and is still highly pessimistic for practical settings. The uniform sampling assumption of sign patterns implies that all regions created by the n hyperplanes [10] are equally likely to contribute to the sign patterns, whereas in practice the data is often non-uniformly distributed and even occurs in clusters.

Furthermore, the analysis does not consider inexact matches, where the sampled columns differ in sign patterns with the exemplars only at a few places. This disagreement in a small number of places will result in underestimating the positive sum of the exemplar column to some extent. However, if the score of the exemplar is mainly contributed by a few data points (i.e., a few rows) and the gap between exemplar score and the best non-exemplar score is sufficient, the algorithm may still have a good chance in picking the exemplar column in next iteration. If this gap is low, we do not lose much in terms of objective value by picking one of the runner-up columns. Indeed, we empirically observe a considerable performance gain (in terms of objective value) over stochastic greedy on several real datasets in Section 5.

4.3 Approximation guarantees under cluster assumption

Here we consider another simplified scenario for better understanding of the sampling approach (7). We assume data points form K disjoint clusters $\mathcal{C}_1, \mathcal{C}_2, ..., \mathcal{C}_K$ satisfying $0 < m \leq |\mathcal{C}_k| \leq M \leq n$ and

(a) $S_{ij} \geq \kappa, \forall i, j \in \mathcal{C}_k$ for some constant $\kappa > \frac{4}{4+m/M}$.

(b) $S_{ij} \in [c - \epsilon/2, c + \epsilon/2]$ for i, j not in the same cluster, where c, ϵ are constants satisfying $c < (\kappa - \epsilon)/2$ and $\epsilon < \frac{m}{4n}\kappa$.

The cluster assumption ensures that points in the same cluster $\mathcal{C}_k$ have similarity at least κ, while points of different clusters has similarity of bounded variance (in range $[c - \epsilon/2, c + \epsilon/2]$). Note the low-variance condition for points of different clusters is often satisfied in problem of higher dimension due to the *curse of dimensionality*, where uncorrelated points can have maximum distance indiscernible to the minimum distance [4]. For example, in document categorization, the semantically-unrelated documents have only *stop words* in common, which causes unrelated documents to have almost the same similarity to each others. Under the cluster assumptions (a)-(b), we show that the sampling estimator (7) has approximation error bounded by $2n\epsilon$ as follows. A related clustering assumption was used to analyze convex relaxations for exemplar clustering in [6].

Theorem 4.1. *Let j^* and $\hat{j}$ denote the greedy column selected by exact criteria (3) and sampling criteria (7) with r samples respectively. For data satisfying clustering assumption (a)-(b), we have*

$$\sum_{i=1}^{n} [R_{i\hat{j}}]_+ \geq \sum_{i=1}^{n} [R_{ij^*}]_+ - 2n\epsilon \tag{12}$$

holds for each iteration $t \leq K$ with probability at least $1 - \delta$ if

$$r \geq \frac{n}{|\mathcal{C}(j^*)|} \ln(\frac{1}{\delta}). \tag{13}$$

where $|\mathcal{C}(j^*)|$ is the size of the cluster that contains j^*.

Proof. For $t = 1$, (12) holds directly since $R = S$ and no sampling is used (so $\hat{j} = j^*$). For $t > 1$, $\mathcal{C}(j^*)$ must be a cluster that does not contain any exemplar chosen in previous iterations. Otherwise, suppose $\mathcal{C}(j^*)$ contains an exemplar j' selected in previous iterate. We have

$$\begin{aligned} \sum_{i=1}^{n} [R_{ij^*}]_+ &\leq \sum_{i \in \mathcal{C}(j^*)} [S_{ij^*} - S_{ij'}]_+ + \sum_{i \notin \mathcal{C}} [R_{ij^*}]_+ \\ &\leq |\mathcal{C}(j^*)|(1-\kappa) + n\epsilon \\ &< \frac{m\kappa}{4} + \frac{m\kappa}{4} = m\kappa/2. \end{aligned}$$

by assumption (a)-(b). However, picking any point j from a cluster $\mathcal{C}$ that does not contain exemplar from previous iterates gives

$$\begin{aligned} \sum_{i=1}^{n} [R_{ij}]_+ &\geq \sum_{i \in \mathcal{C}(j^*)} [S_{ij^*} - (c + \frac{\epsilon}{2})]_+ \\ &\geq \sum_{i \in \mathcal{C}(j^*)} [\kappa - \kappa/2]_+ \geq m\kappa/2, \end{aligned}$$

which leads to contradiction.

Given that $\mathcal{C}(j^*)$ is a cluster not containing exemplar selected from previous iterates, consider $\hat{j}$ selected by the sampling estimator (7). With number of samples r satisfying (13), we have at least $1 - \delta$ probability that one of the sign-pattern vectors $\mathbf{q}_{\hat{j}}$ is produced by a point $\hat{j} \in \mathcal{C}(j^*)$, which has

$$q_{i\hat{j}} := 1[S_{i\hat{j}} - z_i] = 1 \ , \ \forall i \in \mathcal{C}(j^*) \tag{14}$$

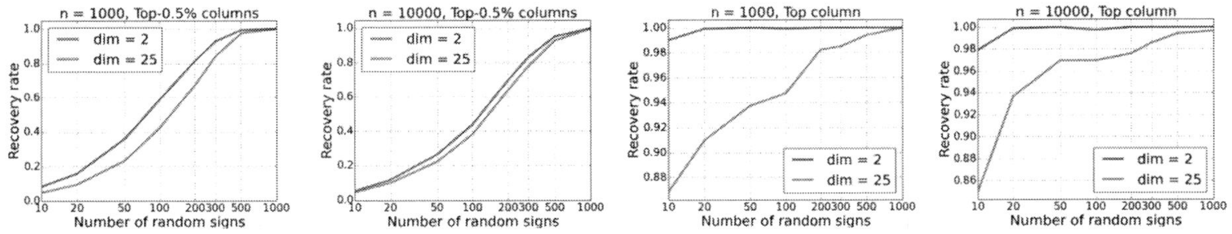

Figure 1: Average recovery rates vs. number of sampled columns (log-scale) for Algorithm 1 over 100 random trials. Data is generated from uniform distribution on the unit sphere (left two plots) and standard Cauchy distribution (right two plots).

since $z_i = S_{ij}$ for some $j \notin \mathcal{C}(j^*)$. Therefore, we have

$$\begin{aligned}\sum_{i=1}^{n}[R_{i\hat{j}}]_+ &\geq \max_{j\in\{j(1),..,j(r)\}} \sum_{i=1}^{n} q_{ij}R_{i\hat{j}} \\ &\geq \max_{j\in\{j(1),..,j(r)\}} \sum_{i=1}^{n} q_{ij}R_{ij^*} \geq \sum_{i=1}^{n} q_{i\bar{j}}R_{ij^*} \\ &\geq \sum_{i\in\mathcal{C}(j^*)} q_{i\bar{j}}R_{ij^*} + \sum_{i\notin\mathcal{C}(j^*)} q_{i\bar{j}}R_{ij^*} \\ &\geq \sum_{i\in\mathcal{C}(j^*)} [R_{ij^*}]_+ - n\epsilon,\end{aligned} \tag{15}$$

where the last inequality is due to (14), assumption (b) and $R_{ij^*} := S_{ij^*} - S_{ij} > 0$ for some $j \notin \mathcal{C}(j^*)$. On the other hand,

$$\begin{aligned}\sum_{i=1}^{n}[R_{ij^*}]_+ &= \sum_{i\in\mathcal{C}(j^*)} [R_{ij^*}]_+ + \sum_{i\notin\mathcal{C}(j^*)} [R_{ij^*}]_+ \\ &\leq \sum_{i\in\mathcal{C}(j^*)} [R_{ij^*}]_+ + n\epsilon.\end{aligned} \tag{16}$$

Combining (15) and (16) leads to the conclusion (12). □

5 Experimental results

We now study the performance of the proposed approach on numerical experiments. We first consider the low-rank maximum positive column sum problem from Section 3.1 corresponding to one stage of the greedy algorithm, and then the low-rank greedy algorithm from Section 3.2.

5.1 Synthetic experiments

In this section we perform numerical simulations to study the behavior of the proposed sign sampling approach in Section 3.1 in recovering the top scoring columns. In the first experiment, we independently sample rows of $U \in \mathbb{R}^{n\times d}$ and $V \in \mathbb{R}^{n\times d}$ from a uniform distribution on the unit sphere $\mathbb{S}^{d-1}$, and take the similarity matrix to be $S = UV^\top$. We conduct 100 random trials of generating pairs of U and V. For every sampled pair U and V, we randomly sample 100 different sets of sign patterns and use Algorithm 1 to estimate the highest scoring column using each set. We report the fraction of times the estimated column is among the top scoring 0.5% columns over all these random trials. Figure 1 shows the recovery rate versus the number of sign patterns for $n = 1K, 10K$ and $d = 2, 25$ which clearly increases with the number of sampled columns.

We repeat the same experiment with U and V generated according to the heavy-tailed Cauchy distribution, and we report the much more stringent recovery rate of the top scoring column this time. We observe that Algorithm 1 performs exceptionally well in recovering the top scoring column for both $d = 2$ and 25. Intuitively, this happens due to the heavy tailed nature of Cauchy distribution, where only a small subset of rows of S will contain the maximums and minimums for each column. Hence, getting the correct sign-pattern for these few rows will greatly increase the probability of recovering the top column by Algorithm 1. This example highlights the fact that the proposed LRGR is capable of taking advantage of the underlying distribution whereas stochastic greedy approach [19] remains oblivious to the distribution of entries of S since it computes the maximum only over the sampled subset of columns. In the Cauchy example, stochastic greedy will have a recovery probability of ~ 0.01 for $n = 10K, r = 100$ irrespective of d, whereas Algorithm 1 empirically shows a recovery rate of ~ 0.96 for $d = 25$.

5.2 Experiments on Machine learning datasets

We compare hte proposed randomized low-rank greedy approach (LRGR) to several other competing methods for approximate exemplar clustering, focusing on alternative approximate greedy methods. We have not considered integer programming and message passing based methods as they do not scale to the dataset sizes we consider in the experiments. We describe the contestants first[4]. We consider both data-sets with low-dimensional feature representations, and data-sets with high-dimensional but sparse feature representation. For simplicity we focus on the inner-product similarity measure here. The experiments are run on a sin-

[4]All the algorithms are written in python relying on *numpy* and *scipy* packages for dense and sparse linear algebra.

gle commodity computer with 16 Gb of RAM.

Plain and lazy greedy As a baseline we used the standard greedy and lazy greedy algorithms, which do use the low-rank structure to reduce the memory footprint, but which compute all the required entries of the similarity matrix. We also use the efficient update for the t-th step of the greedy method, where we do not recompute the optimal assignment of points to exemplars from scratch, but we re-use the previous assignment at the $t-1$-st step – and only compare its best assignment to the new added exemplar. Lazy greedy achieves the same objective value as plain greedy. In our experiments with small number of exemplars the running time of lazy-greedy was similar or slower than plain greedy, so the time is not reported. Lazy-greedy can become significantly faster than plain greedy when the number of exemplars is much higher, and it typically accelerates (benefits more from lazy evaluation) at later stages.

Random subset As a very simple baseline we obtain a random subset of points as exemplars, and compute the cost of optimal assignments of points to these exemplars.

K-means with cluster medoids (KmeansCTR). K-means algorithm produces cluster centers that are not data-points but their convex combinations. We use a heuristic that ignores k-means cluster centers, and instead computes the centroid (1-medoid) for each of the k-clusters independently. Initialization is done using k-means++ [1]. Note that for similarity matrices other than cosine similarity comparison with k-means will not be meaningful, as k-means assumes Euclidean distance between data-points.

Stochastic greedy (StochGr) The approach [19] selects at each step a small subset of columns of the similarity matrix, and only searches for exemplars among this set. We use the same subset-size 100 as for the proposed algorithm.

KNN-greedy (KnnGr) A K-nearest neighbor graph for the data is used to create a sparse approximation to the similarity matrix which is non-zero for the K nearest neighbors only [15, 26]. We use 100 nearest neighbors to give the same number of parameters as stochastic greedy and the proposed algorithm. We report two times for this algorithm: total time taken including the construction of the KNN-graph (pre-processing step needed to run the algorithm), and just the time for exemplar clustering starting with the sparse KNN graph already provided.

LR-greedy (LRGR) This is our proposed algorithm which uses sign-patterns of 100 random columns selected at each iteration from the similarity matrix.

Datasets. We use a collection of standard machine learning datasets from the UCI archive [5] of various sizes and numbers of features (both dense and sparse), and report the time and approximation quality in the table below. The data-sets with label (RF) use a Random-Feature Kernel Approximation method [23] to perform exemplar clustering with (RBF-Laplacian) Kernelized features, namely the Random Binning Features.

The final data-set is the World TSP data set which contains the latitude and longitude of 1,904,711 cities in the world[5]. We use geographical distance (computed via polar coordinate flat-Earth formula) between pairs of cities. To obtain a low-rank approximation to the distance matrix $\mathbb{D}$, we sampled $100n$ pairs of distances and use low-rank matrix completion[6] to find $UV^T \approx \mathbb{D}$. Using rank $d = 20$, we obtain a decomposition UV^T with testing RMSE $< 10^{-2}$. We use the corresponding similarity matrix $S = D_{\max} - UV^T$, where $D_{\max}$ is the maximum element of $\mathbb{D}$. Note that due to the non-Euclidean nature of the similarity matrix, comparison with Kmeans-CTR is not meaningful.

Results We report the objective values in table 1 and the timing numbers in table 2. The number of exemplars is kept small in these experiments as all the contesting methods scale linearly with the number of exemplars. To reduce this linear scaling one could either use the algorithms in a distributed setting proposed in [20] or combine with lazy-evaluation using a priority queue for marginal gains. For methods involving stochasticity (e.g. random subset selection in stochastic greedy, the proposed LRGR method, and k-means initialization) we report an average objective value and run-time over 10 trials.

We can see that the proposed low-rank greedy approach with random projections provides a very close approximation to the exact greedy objective values at an orders of magnitude faster time. We also see that among all the approximate algorithms the proposed method typically provides the best objective value (excluding the exact greedy method), and always within the top two results. The time is also competitive with other algorithms. K-means followed by finding cluster centroids is quite a good contender on small-dimensional data-sets, but its approximation quality can be poor on high-dimensional sparse data-sets. Furthermore, K-means assumes a Euclidean distance between data-points and does not apply to more general distance matrices.[7]. For KNN-greedy the time is dominated by the construction of the sparse nearest neighbors graph. Once the graph is constructed the algorithm is fast, and provides solutions which are quite reasonable although not as good as the proposed approach. The construction of the KNN graph can be accelerated using approximate

[5]Data is at http://www.math.uwaterloo.ca/tsp/world/.

[6]We use the low-rank matrix completion solver provided by the authors of [28].

[7]For example, k-means can not be used with spherical geodesic, transportation or string-edit distances, while there are no such constraints for exemplar clustering.

Table 1: Objective values achieved by greedy submodular algorithms with inner product similarity metric and 10 exemplars. Here d_{avg} is the average number of features per sample. Number of exemplars is 10. The best solution (after exact plain greedy which we aim to approximate) is marked with one star, and second-best with two stars. The proposed approach (LRGR) is typically most accurate, and is within the top 2 in all of our experiments.

Data	N (M)	d	d_{avg}	RND	KmeansCtr	StochGR	KnnGR	LRGR	Greedy
Satimage	4435	36	36	3587.77	**3997.6***	3969.38	3977.13	**3983.4****	3976.42
Sector	6412	55197	163	381.5	667.01	717.96	**777.23****	**779.24***	787.53
Pendigits	7494	16	16	6925.22	**7171.33***	7122.27	7024.70	**7146.24****	7147.87
Pendigit-RF	7494	12891	100	2194.15	2962.44	2901.8	**2994.0****	**3004.27***	3015.23
RCV1	20242	47236	74	1217.67	1946.44	2003.26	**2175.85****	**2193.92***	2239.40
CodRNA	59535	8	8	53256.81	**56442.23***	55845.54	55411.42	**56133.72****	56146.50
CodRNA-RF	59535	7611	50	22290.93	**26353.32****	25909.36	n/a (mem)	**26533.53***	26746.18
Covtype	581012	54	11.9	490120.3	521045.25	**521188****	n/a (mem)	**523629.12***	n/a
Covtype-RF	581012	54509	50	86973.72	**136830.64****	136357.15	n/a (mem)	**146731.86***	n/a
World-Scale	1904711	20	20	6974224.6	n/a	**7309125.1****	n/a (mem)	**7408043.0***	n/a

Table 2: Timing results of greedy submodular algorithms with inner product similarity metric. We allowed up-to 1 hour for all the competing approaches.

Data	N (M)	d	d_{avg}	KmeansCtr	StochGR	KnnGR	KnnGR-Ttl	LRGR	Greedy
Satimage	4435	36	36	0.085s	0.114s	0.178	1.36	0.15s	2.056s
Sector	6412	55197	163	2.613s	1.227s	0.366	7.49	4.82s	68.682s
Pendigits	7494	16	16	0.115s	0.232s	0.356	1.73	0.229s	5.430s
Pendigit-RF	7494	12891	100	2.240s	0.909s	0.313	6.46	3.24s	59.515s
RCV1	20242	47236	74	5.561s	2.106s	1.304	40.83	7.52s	375.067s
CodRNA	59535	8	8	0.637s	1.550s	3.974	19.77	1.82s	593.721s
CodRNA-RF	59535	7611	50	15.981s	5.818s	n/a	n/a	15.17s	2995.639s
Covtype	581012	54	11.94	9.107s	17.302s	n/a	n/a	24.17s	n/a
Covtype-RF	581012	54509	50	102.257s	37.214s	n/a	n/a	140.96s	n/a
World-Scale	1904711	20	20	n/a	53.4s	n/a	n/a	67.5s	n/a

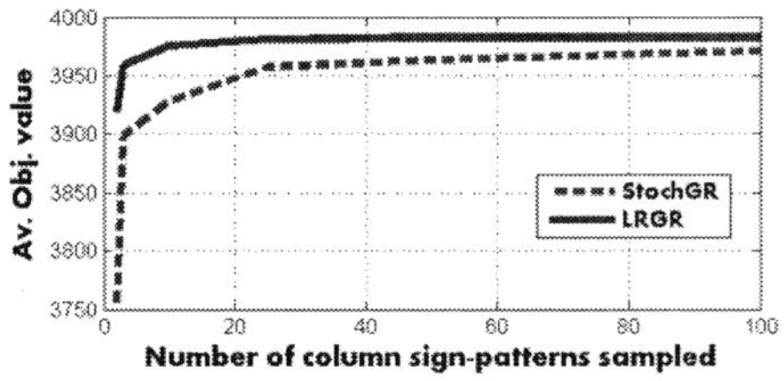

Figure 2: Av. objective values for LRGR and StochGR vs. num. sampled columns on Satimage data. 25 trials.

nearest neighbors (ANN) techniques, for example based on locality-sensitive-hashing (LSH) [9, 22], but that would also affect the quality of the results. Finally, it is quite clear that selecting random subsets is a rather poor (albeit very fast) data-summarization approach and any other method can provide a significant improvement.

The proposed low-rank greedy method achieved a slightly better objective than the exact greedy method that it tries to approximate in one experiment. This is not a contradiction as selecting a suboptimal exemplar in the current step may possibly improve the objective in further steps.

Dependence on the number of sampled columns. In Figure 2 we plot the average objective value achieved via Stochastic greedy and the proposed LRGR method vs. the number of sampled columns. The values are averages over 25 trials. We see that LRGR achieves better values by making better use of the samples, especially for smaller numbers of sampled columns.

6 Concluding Remarks

We developed a new approach for large-scale exemplar clustering based on submodular greedy maximization with structured similarity matrices. We propose a randomized sign-pattern sampling approach to approximate the bottleneck computation of finding the element with the maximal marginal gain. We establish accuracy guarantees, and evaluate the approach on large scale exemplar clustering problems on machine learning data-sets including up-to millions of data-points. Our current approach is serial and uses a single processor, but it can also be used as a sub-routine in previously proposed distributed approaches to extend exemplar clustering to problems of much larger scale.

We thank Baruch Schieber and Robert Hildebrand for helpful discussions.

References

[1] D. Arthur and S. Vassilvitskii. k-means++: The advantages of careful seeding. In *Proc. 18th ACM-SIAM symposium on Discrete algorithms*, 2007.

[2] A. Badanidiyuru, B. Mirzasoleiman, A. Karbasi, and A. Krause. Streaming submodular maximization: Massive data summarization on the fly. In *Proc. Int. conf. Knowledge discovery and data mining*, 2014.

[3] F. Barahona and F. Chudak. Near-optimal solutions to large-scale facility location problems. *Discrete Optimization*, 2(1):35–50, 2005.

[4] K. Beyer, J. Goldstein, R. Ramakrishnan, and U. Shaft. When is nearest neighbor meaningful? In *Database theory - ICDT99*. Springer, 1999.

[5] C. Blake and C. J. Merz. UCI repository of machine learning databases. 1998.

[6] E. Elhamifar, G. Sapiro, and R. Vidal. Finding exemplars from pairwise dissimilarities via simultaneous sparse recovery. In *Proc. NIPS*, 2012.

[7] E. Elhamifar, G. Sapiro, A. Yang, and S. S. Sasrty. A convex optimization framework for active learning. In *IEEE Int. Conf. on Computer Vision*, 2013.

[8] B. J. Frey and D. Dueck. Clustering by passing messages between data points. *Science*, 315(5814):972–976, 2007.

[9] A. Gionis, P. Indyk, and R. Motwani. Similarity search in high dimensions via hashing. In *VLDB*, volume 99, pages 518–529, 1999.

[10] C. Ho and S. Zimmerman. On the number of regions in an m-dimensional space cut by n hyperplanes. *Australian Math. Society Gazette*, 33(4), Sep. 2006.

[11] L. Kaufman and P. Rousseeuw. *Clustering by means of medoids*. North-Holland, 1987.

[12] A. Krause and D. Golovin. Submodular function maximization. *Tractability: Practical Approaches to Hard Problems*, 3:19, 2012.

[13] N. Lazic, B. J. Frey, and P. Aarabi. Solving the uncapacitated facility location problem using message passing algorithms. In *AISTATS*, 2010.

[14] H. Lin and J. Bilmes. A class of submodular functions for document summarization. In *Proc. ACL*, 2011.

[15] E. M. Lindgren, S. Wu, and A. G. Dimakis. Sparse and greedy: Sparsifying submodular facility location problems. In *NIPS Systems Workshop*, 2015.

[16] H. B. McMahan, G. Holt, D. Sculley, M. Young, Dietmar Ebner, Julian Grady, L. Nie, T. Phillips, E. Davydov, and D. Golovin. Ad click prediction: a view from the trenches. In *Proc. 19th ACM SIGKDD Int. Conf. on Knowledge discovery and Data mining*, 2013.

[17] T. Mikolov, I. Sutskever, K. Chen, G.S. Corrado, and J. Dean. Distributed representations of words and phrases and their compositionality. In *Advances in Neural Information Processing Systems*, 2013.

[18] Michel Minoux. Accelerated greedy algorithms for maximizing submodular set functions. In *Optimization Techniques*, pages 234–243. Springer, 1978.

[19] B. Mirzasoleiman, A. Badanidiyuru, A. Karbasi, J. Vondrak, and A. Krause. Lazier than lazy greedy. *arXiv preprint arXiv:1409.7938*, 2014.

[20] B. Mirzasoleiman, A. Karbasi, R. Sarkar, and A. Krause. Distributed submodular maximization: Identifying representative elements in massive data. In *Adv. Neural Information Proc. Systems*, 2013.

[21] G. L. Nemhauser, L. A. Wolsey, and M. L. Fisher. An analysis of approximations for maximizing submodular set functions i. *Mathematical Programming*, 14(1):265–294, 1978.

[22] B. Neyshabur and N. Srebro. On symmetric and asymmetric LSH for inner product search. In *International Conference on Machine learning*, 2015.

[23] A. Rahimi and B. Recht. Random features for large-scale kernel machines. In *Advances in neural information processing systems*, pages 1177–1184, 2007.

[24] S. Si, C.J Hsieh, and I. Dhillon. Memory efficient kernel approximation. In *Proc. of the 31st Int. Conf. on Machine Learning*, 2014.

[25] V. Sindhwani, T. Sainath, and S. Kumar. Structured transforms for small-footprint deep learning. In *Advances in Neural Information Processing Systems*, pages 3070–3078, 2015.

[26] K. Wei, R. Iyer, and J. Bilmes. Fast multi-stage submodular maximization. In *Proc. of Int. Conf. on Machine Learning (ICML)*, 2014.

[27] I. E.H. Yen, D. Malioutov, and A. Kumar. Scalable exemplar clustering and facility location via augmented block coordinate descent with column generation. In *Proc. AISTATS*, 2016.

[28] H.F. Yu, Hsieh C.J., S. Si, and I.S. Dhillon. Scalable coordinate descent approaches to parallel matrix factorization for recommender systems. In *IEEE International Conference of Data Mining*, 2012.

Sparse Gaussian Processes for Bayesian Optimization

Mitchell McIntire
Stanford University
Stanford, CA 94305
mcint286@stanford.edu

Daniel Ratner
SLAC National Accelerator Laboratory
Menlo Park, CA 94025
dratner@slac.stanford.edu

Stefano Ermon
Stanford University
Stanford, CA 94305
ermon@cs.stanford.edu

Abstract

Bayesian optimization schemes often rely on Gaussian processes (GP). GP models are very flexible, but are known to scale poorly with the number of training points. While several efficient sparse GP models are known, they have limitations when applied in optimization settings.

We propose a novel Bayesian optimization framework that uses sparse online Gaussian processes. We introduce a new updating scheme for the online GP that accounts for our preference during optimization for regions with better performance. We apply this method to optimize the performance of a free-electron laser, and demonstrate empirically that the weighted updating scheme leads to substantial improvements to performance in optimization.

1 Introduction

Bayesian nonparametric models have seen growing popularity due to their flexibility and modeling power. The core strength of nonparametrics lies in their ability to scale in complexity with the data, making them useful in cases where parametric model selection is challenging. These models have therefore been used successfully in a variety of applications (Kulis & Jordan (2012); Tank et al. (2015); Miller et al. (2015); Johnson & Willsky (2013)).

Gaussian processes (GPs) have emerged as an elegant nonparametric approach to regression. GPs provide a full probabilistic model of the data, and allow us to compute not only the model's prediction at input points but also to quantify the uncertainty in the predictions. While powerful and elegant, the application of GP regression is limited by the poor scaling of GPs (Rasmussen & Williams (2005)). This limitation has motivated the introduction of numerous efficient approaches for approximating the exact GP solution, e.g. Gal et al. (2014); Hensman et al. (2013); Ranganathan et al. (2011).

A common approach to this approximation is to use sparse GPs, which rely on lower-dimensional representations defined by a smaller set of "inducing points" to represent the full GP. Various types of sparse GPs have been introduced, e.g. Snelson & Ghahramani (2006); Lawrence et al. (2003); Titsias (2009); Csató & Opper (2002); Seeger et al. (2003). These varieties tend to differ most in how they perform the selection and management of inducing points; usually a greedy method of some form is used to select points from the data set that minimize an entropy or information loss criterion. A notable exception is the method of Snelson & Ghahramani (2006), who treat inducing point selection as a continuous optimization problem.

Our focus here is on optimization when it is extremely costly to evaluate the objective function. Bayesian optimization is a natural choice in this setting (Jones et al. (1998)). In Bayesian optimization, a probabilistic model of the objective function is used to select sampling points by maximizing an acquisition function based on e.g. the expected improvement in the target variable. Gaussian processes are naturally applicable to Bayesian optimization due to their full probabilistic formulation, which can effectively model the observations of the optimization process; see e.g. Osborne et al. (2009); Snoek et al. (2012) for recent applications of Bayesian optimization using GPs. Other approaches to Bayesian optimization include deep neural networks, as in Snoek et al. (2015).

To date, applications of GPs to Bayesian optimization have typically used full Gaussian process regression. In these settings, it is either assumed that computation time is relatively less important (as compared to e.g. function evaluations), or that convergence will occur quickly enough that the size of the full GP is not an issue. These assumptions might not hold in large parameter spaces, however, particularly in settings with noisy observations that can significantly slow the rate of convergence.

As a result, we consider the application of sparse GPs to Bayesian optimization, as in Nickson et al. (2014). Since sparse GPs have bounded size, the time taken to update during optimization will not increase regardless of how long the procedure takes to converge. Using sparse GPs for Bayesian optimization presents a different set of challenges than in a typical regression problem, however. In particular, existing sparse GP approaches seek to model the full GP as accurately as possible given the limited size of their representation. This goal is obviously desirable for regression, but has key shortcomings in optimization, namely that the limited resources of the sparse GP may be allocated to closely model regions of parameter space that perform poorly and are therefore less important for optimization.

We propose weighted-update online Gaussian processes (WOGP) as an alternative to typical sparse GP set selection that is better suited to optimization; rather than tailoring the sparse GP for predictive accuracy, WOGPs use an online update scheme that weights the feature space of the GP according to which regions are promising from the optimization perspective. During Bayesian optimization over a large parameter space, this ensures that the sparse model does not waste resources by attempting to accurately model regions that are clearly irrelevant to the optimization problem.

Our work is motivated by an application of Bayesian optimization to improve the performance of the Linac Coherent Light Source (LCLS) free-electron laser (FEL) at the SLAC National Accelerator Laboratory (Emma et al. (2010)). The operational costs of this machine are daunting, and current tuning procedures consume hundreds of hours of machine (and machine operator) time annually that could be better spent conducting the various scientific experiments that rely on LCLS. In this setting, we demonstrate empirically that WOGPs significantly outperform competing techniques.

2 Background

In this section we describe Gaussian process regression and the online sparse GP algorithm introduced in Csató (2002). This algorithm uses online updates and a sparse representation to reduce the GP training complexity. This online scheme is particularly useful for large scale and online regression tasks, since it reduces the time taken to update the GP in each iteration with efficient individual updates.

2.1 Review of Gaussian Process Regression

Formally, a Gaussian process is a collection of random variables $\mathcal{X}$ such that any finite subset $(X_1, \cdots, X_n) \subset \mathcal{X}$ have a joint Gaussian distribution. For example, if we have a GP over the interval $[0, 1]$, then the joint distribution of any finite set of points in $[0, 1]$ is multivariate normal; the mean and covariance of this distribution will be discussed shortly. This GP can be thought of as a distribution over functions $f : [0, 1] \to \mathbb{R}$, as every assignment of values to this interval (or any domain on which a GP is defined) has some probability associated with it via this joint distribution.

A Gaussian process prior is fully defined by its covariance function $K : \mathcal{X} \times \mathcal{X} \to \mathbb{R}$ and its prior mean $\mu_0 : \mathcal{X} \to \mathbb{R}$. To simplify the discussion, we will assume that the prior mean function is zero, though this need not be the case. The covariance function is required only to be a valid covariance function in that the Gram matrix $K_{i,j} = K(\boldsymbol{x}_i, \boldsymbol{x}_j)$ of values of any finite subset of $\mathcal{X}$ must be positive semidefinite.

In Gaussian process regression, a GP prior is conditioned on training data to obtain the posterior distribution over the function space. Following the notation of Rasmussen & Williams (2005), given training samples X with corresponding observations $\boldsymbol{f}$ and test inputs X_*, distribution of training observations and test outputs $\boldsymbol{f}_*$ is multivariate Gaussian; conditioning the latter on the former gives us

$$\boldsymbol{f}_*|X, X_*, \boldsymbol{f} \sim \mathcal{N}(K(X_*, X)K(X, X)^{-1}\boldsymbol{f}, \\ K(X_*, X_*) - K(X_*, X)K(X, X)^{-1}K(X, X_*)) . \quad (1)$$

The resulting posterior at the test locations is a multivariate Gaussian distribution whose mean and covariance are then used in regression. Incorporating the assumption of i.i.d. Gaussian noise into this model is straightforward, involving a simple change to the covariance function according to the standard deviation σ of the assumed noise. This yields the posterior distribution conditioned on noisy observations $\boldsymbol{y}$:

$$\boldsymbol{f}_*|X, X_*, \boldsymbol{y} \sim \mathcal{N}(K(X_*, X)[K(X, X) + \sigma^2 I]^{-1}\boldsymbol{y}, \\ K(X_*, X_*) - K(X_*, X)[K(X, X) + \sigma^2 I]^{-1}K(X, X_*)) . \quad (2)$$

See Rasmussen & Williams (2005) for a full treatment of GP regression and Gaussian processes in general.

For a predictive distribution conditioned on n training inputs, the time complexity of Gaussian process regression is $\mathcal{O}(n^3)$. This is prohibitively expensive for applications with more than a few thousand inputs (or fewer in settings where runtime is an important consideration). Several approaches have been introduced for approximating full GP regression with more efficient algorithms. The most common category for these approximations is the sparse GP, several varieties of which are listed in Section 1. See Quionero-Candela & Rasmussen (2005) for a thorough treatment of the variety and theory of sparse approximations to full Gaussian process regression.

The common thread among these methods is the attempt to represent the full Gaussian process using a set of $m < n$ inducing inputs, typically leading to a complexity of $\mathcal{O}(m^2 n)$ to train the sparse GP. These inducing inputs are often chosen as a subset of the input data, leading to a difficult combinatorial problem that is typically solved using some form

Algorithm 1 Online GP Update

Input: data point $\boldsymbol{x}$, output y
Persistent: Inducing variables $X_{\mathcal{I}}$, GP model parameters
Assess novelty γ of point $\boldsymbol{x}$.
if $\gamma < \epsilon_{tol}$ **then**
  Perform sparse update without expanding the model.
else
  Perform full update, adding $\boldsymbol{x}$ to $X_{\mathcal{I}}$ and extending GP model parameters.
end if
if Model size exceeds m **then**
  Score inducing inputs $X_{\mathcal{I}}$ on impact of removal.
  Remove the lowest-scoring element of $X_{\mathcal{I}}$; update the GP model to minimize the impact of removal.
end if

of greedy minimization of information loss. Snelson & Ghahramani (2006) provide one alternative, in which inducing variable selection is treated as a continuous optimization problem. Our approach is most closely related to the algorithm introduced in Csató (2002), which iteratively trains the approximating GP by processing each input individually. This method selects inducing points by continually comparing new data points to the existing set of inducing variables in the model and keeping whichever subset yields the best approximation. This method is described in more detail below.

2.2 Online Sparse GPs

The online sparse GP algorithm of Csató & Opper (2002); Csató (2002) handles the sparse selection problem by observing input data one point at a time. In each iteration, the new data point is added to the sparse model (assuming that the sample passes a geometric novelty threshold), which may increase its size to $m + 1$ inducing variables. A reduction step is then performed, which removes one of these inducing variables to restore the sparse GP to size m. Pseudocode for the online update is given in Algorithm 1.

Following Csató (2002), we represent a GP by its covariance function K and its posterior parameterization after t iterations in terms of the $(m \times 1)$ dimensional vector $\boldsymbol{\alpha}_t$ of inducing point coefficients and the $(m \times m)$ matrix C_t which specifies the posterior covariance. We denote by $X_{\mathcal{I}}$ the set of inducing variables, giving us the posterior predictive distribution at query points X^* as

$$\mathcal{N}(K(X^*, X_{\mathcal{I}})\boldsymbol{\alpha}_t, \\ K(X^*, X^*) + K(X^*, X_{\mathcal{I}})C_t K(X_{\mathcal{I}}, X^*)) \,. \quad (3)$$

The covariance function K corresponds to a (possibly infinite-dimensional) feature space $\mathcal{F}$. Specifically, if d is the dimension of the data, there exists a function $\phi : \mathbb{R}^d \to \mathcal{F}$ such that $K(x_i, x_j) = \langle \phi(x_i), \phi(x_j) \rangle_{\mathcal{F}}$ is the inner product of $x_i, x_j \in \mathbb{R}^d$ in $\mathcal{F}$. It is shown in Csató (2002) that the Gaussian process can be viewed as a Gaussian distribution in $\mathcal{F}$. Let Φ be the feature space representation of $X_{\mathcal{I}}$, so $K_{\mathcal{I}} \equiv K(X_{\mathcal{I}}, X_{\mathcal{I}}) = \Phi^{\top}\Phi$. Then in the feature space $\mathcal{F}$ we have

$$\mathrm{GP}_K(\boldsymbol{\alpha}, C) \sim \mathcal{N}(\Phi\boldsymbol{\alpha}, I_{\mathcal{F}} + \Phi C \Phi^{\top}) \,, \quad (4)$$

where $I_{\mathcal{F}}$ is the identity matrix in $\mathcal{F}$ and we use the notation $\mathrm{GP}_K(\boldsymbol{\alpha}, C)$ to denote the GP with the corresponding covariance function and parameters. Henceforth we will omit the K in this notation, as it will be clear from context.

This allows for a straightforward computation of the Kullback-Leibler (KL) divergence between two GPs that have the same kernel function. The KL divergence between distributions P and Q is defined as

$$D_{KL}(P\|Q) = \int_{\mathcal{F}} P(\boldsymbol{x}) \log \frac{P(\boldsymbol{x})}{Q(\boldsymbol{x})} d\boldsymbol{x} \,. \quad (5)$$

Note that we need never concern ourselves with the cases $P(\boldsymbol{x}) = 0$ or $Q(\boldsymbol{x}) = 0$ since we deal exclusively with normal distributions in this paper.

Suppose that in iteration $t + 1$ a new inducing variable is added to the model, increasing its size to $m + 1$. In the approach of Csató (2002), the optimal reduced parameters $\hat{\boldsymbol{\alpha}}$ and $\hat{C}$ are computed by minimizing the KL divergence between $GP \sim \mathrm{GP}(\alpha, C)$, the over-sized GP that we are reducing, and the approximation $\widehat{GP} \sim \mathrm{GP}(\hat{\boldsymbol{\alpha}}, \hat{C})$, subject to the constraint that $\hat{\boldsymbol{\alpha}}$ and $\hat{C}$ have entries of zero corresponding to some inducing variable (i.e. there exists an index i such that the ith element of $\hat{\boldsymbol{\alpha}}$ and the ith row and column of $\hat{C}$ are zero). We assume without loss of generality that it is the last inducing variable that is removed.

Csató (2002) minimizes $D_{KL}(\widehat{GP}\|GP)$ with respect to the parameters $\hat{\boldsymbol{\alpha}}$ and $\hat{C}$, resulting in the update equations (3.19) and (3.22). With $Q \equiv K_{\mathcal{I}}^{-1}$, these equations are

$$\hat{\boldsymbol{\alpha}} = \boldsymbol{\alpha}^{(r)} - \frac{\alpha^*}{c^* + q^*}(\boldsymbol{C}^* + \boldsymbol{Q}^*) \\ \hat{C} = C^{(r)} + \frac{1}{q^*}\boldsymbol{Q}^*\boldsymbol{Q}^{*\top} - \frac{1}{c^* + q^*}(\boldsymbol{C}^* + \boldsymbol{Q}^*)(\boldsymbol{C}^* + \boldsymbol{Q}^*)^{\top} \,, \quad (6)$$

where $\boldsymbol{\alpha}^{(r)}$ denotes the first m entries of $\boldsymbol{\alpha}$, $C^{(r)}$ is the $(m \times m)$ matrix obtained by omitting the last row and column of C, α^*, c^*, and q^* are the last elements of $\boldsymbol{\alpha}$, $\mathrm{diag}(C)$, and $\mathrm{diag}(Q)$ respectively, and the $(m \times 1)$ vectors $\boldsymbol{C}^*$ and $\boldsymbol{Q}^*$ are the last columns of C and Q respectively, excluding the last entry. Applying the block matrix inversion formula, we can also compute the reduced inverse

Algorithm 2 Bayesian optimization

while Not converged **do**
  Compute $\boldsymbol{x}_{t+1} = \arg\max_{\boldsymbol{x}}(EI(\boldsymbol{x}))$.
  Query objective function at $\boldsymbol{x}_{t+1}$ to get y_{t+1}.

  Augment the data: $\mathcal{D}_{t+1} = \{\mathcal{D}_t, (\boldsymbol{x}_{t+1}, y_{t+1})\}$
  Update the model: $\mathcal{M}_{t+1} = \mathcal{M}_t \leftarrow (\boldsymbol{x}_{t+1}, y_{t+1})$
  $t = t + 1$
end while

Gram matrix $\hat{Q}$:

$$K_{\mathcal{I}} = Q^{-1} \Rightarrow K_{\mathcal{I}}^{(r)} = (Q^{(r)} - \frac{1}{q^*}\boldsymbol{Q}^*\boldsymbol{Q}^{*\top})^{-1}$$
$$\Rightarrow \hat{Q} = Q^{(r)} - \frac{1}{q^*}\boldsymbol{Q}^*\boldsymbol{Q}^{*\top}. \quad (7)$$

Using the update equations (6), scores are computed for each of the $m+1$ inducing variables based on the minimum KL divergence that can be achieved when omitting them. The worst-scoring point is then removed, with updates (6) performed to the appropriate coordinate.

2.3 Bayesian Optimization

Bayesian optimization is a probabilistic approach to optimization that is generally used when queries to the function being optimized are expensive. This method lessens the number of evaluations needed, shifting the burden instead to computation over probabilities by utilizing information from all of the function evaluations to choose the next sampling location. We deal here with Bayesian optimization using Gaussian processes as probabilistic models.

Let $\mathcal{D}_t = \{(\boldsymbol{x}_i, y_i)_{i=1}^t\}$ be the observed data of the first t iterations of optimization, where y_i is the observation of the target variable at the location $\boldsymbol{x}_i$ in parameter space. Then we denote by $\mathcal{M}_t$ the model trained on $\mathcal{D}_t$ (where the ordering of $\mathcal{D}_t$ may matter, e.g. if the model is an online sparse GP). Let $\mathcal{M}_t(\boldsymbol{x}) = (\mu_t(\boldsymbol{x}), \sigma_t(\boldsymbol{x}))$, so that μ and σ give the posterior mean function and variance of the model.

The central idea behind Bayesian optimization is to explore according to an acquisition function which incorporates the current set of observations. In this paper we use the expected improvement as our acquisition function. If $\boldsymbol{x}^*$ is the observed location that maximizes μ_t, the improvement at a point $\boldsymbol{x}$ is defined[1] as

$$I_t(\boldsymbol{x}) = \max(0, \mu_t(\boldsymbol{x}) - \mu_t(\boldsymbol{x}^*)). \quad (8)$$

As seen in Jones et al. (1998) the expected improvement at a point $\boldsymbol{x}$ can be computed as

$$EI(\boldsymbol{x}) \equiv E[I_t(\boldsymbol{x})] =$$
$$\begin{cases} (\mu_t(\boldsymbol{x}) - \mu_t(\boldsymbol{x}^*))\Phi(Z) + \sigma_t(\boldsymbol{x})\phi(Z) & \sigma_t(\boldsymbol{x}) > 0 \\ 0 & \sigma_t(\boldsymbol{x}) = 0 \end{cases},$$
$$Z = \frac{\mu_t(\boldsymbol{x}) - \mu_t(\boldsymbol{x}^*)}{\sigma_t(\boldsymbol{x})}. \quad (9)$$

Here Φ and ϕ respectively represent the CDF and PDF of the standard normal distribution. Recently, Bull (2011) showed that optimization using the EI criterion gives provably efficient convergence in many settings.

With EI defined and the method of updating the GP model specified, Bayesian optimization is straightforward; pseudocode for this procedure is given in Algorithm 2. Note that to maximize expected improvement we use numerical optimization, since EI cannot be maximized analytically but is extremely cheap to evaluate as compared with the objective function. See Brochu et al. (2010) for a more thorough introduction to Bayesian optimization.

3 Online Sparse Gaussian Processes for Bayesian Optimization

In this section we apply online sparse GPs to Bayesian optimization. This is complicated by the limited size of the sparse GP, which can reduce exploitation by preventing the information gained in an iteration from being fully incorporated, as well as hinder exploration of promising areas by dedicating resources to model regions of poor performance. We therefore introduce the weighted-update online GP (WOGP), our modified online sparse GP scheme, and the resulting Bayesian optimization algorithm. Our approach to online sparse GPs is similar to that of Csató (2002); Csató & Opper (2002), but utilizes a weighted measure of divergence between the Gaussian processes' predictive distributions. This allows us to better allocate the limited modeling capacity of the sparse GP to further the goal of optimization (rather than predictive accuracy).

For example, imagine that we are attempting to maximize performance over a large parameter space. The online sparse GPs studied previously may devote multiple inducing points to modeling a complex region of low performance to minimize the divergence in this area. These points may serve our goal of maximization better by improving the model's resolution in promising regions of parameter space while maintaining only a vague notion of poor performance in other regions.

3.1 The Weighted KL Divergence

We now describe a weighted divergence measure between distributions and compute this divergence for two GPs.

[1]We use $\mu_t(\boldsymbol{x}^*)$ rather than the best observation itself to account for the assumed noise in the observations.

Definition 1. *For probability distributions P and Q and real-valued weighting function f, we define the weighted KL divergence as*

$$D^f_{KL}(P\|Q) = \int_{\mathcal{F}} P(\boldsymbol{x}) \log \left(\frac{P(\boldsymbol{x})}{Q(\boldsymbol{x})}\right)^{f(\boldsymbol{x})} d\boldsymbol{x}$$
$$= \int_{\mathcal{F}} f(\boldsymbol{x}) P(\boldsymbol{x}) \log \frac{P(\boldsymbol{x})}{Q(\boldsymbol{x})} d\boldsymbol{x}\,. \tag{10}$$

We note that f should be non-negative to prevent rewarding differences between the distributions; the goal of weighting is to regard divergence in low-weighted areas not as good, but as acceptable if accuracy in highly weighted regions can be obtained in its place.

Proposition 1. *For real-valued weighting function f, and constant $c \in \mathbb{R}$, the following hold:*

$$D^{cf}_{KL} = cD^f_{KL},\; D^{f+c}_{KL} = D^f_{KL} + cD_{KL}\,. \tag{11}$$

Proof. Easily computed from (5) and (10). □

We can also see from Proposition 1 that scaling f by a constant factor does not affect relative divergence.

We can write the prediction of GP at a point $\boldsymbol{x}$ in feature space as $\boldsymbol{x}^\top \Phi \boldsymbol{\alpha}$, since $\boldsymbol{x}^\top \Phi$ is the inner product in the feature space corresponding to the evaluation of the kernel function K (see Equation 3). Then we define f^* in terms of the proportional improvement expected at $\boldsymbol{x}$:

$$f^*(\boldsymbol{x}) = 1 + \frac{\boldsymbol{x}^\top \Phi \boldsymbol{\alpha} - y^*}{|y^*|} = \frac{\boldsymbol{x}^\top \Phi \boldsymbol{\alpha}}{|y^*|}\,, \tag{12}$$

where y^* is the best value observed thus far during optimization.

This weighting function f^* will cause promising regions of feature space to be weighted more heavily in the divergence computation. Of course, we immediately see that f^* is negative wherever the GP's posterior mean is negative. In our motivating application this is not much of a concern, as we deal with a non-negative target (laser pulse energy). In other settings and with other weighting functions, adjustments may be necessary to prevent f being negative.

These adjustments may simply take the form of shifting the observations to be positive; if the minimum observation is y_{min} and the minimum value attained by the GPs prior mean function is p_{min}, then we can define $y_0 = -\min(y_{min}, p_{min})$. Incrementing the prior mean and observations of the GP by y_0 simply shifts its posterior mean function above zero without changing the shape of the distribution. This can be seen from the linearity of the GP formulation, for example in Equation 2.

Alternatively, f can be shifted directly to prevent it being negative; from Proposition 1 we have $D^{f+c}_{KL} = D^f_{KL} + cD_{KL}$, so this has the effect of averaging the weighted and unweighted divergences in order to ensure that differences between the distributions P and Q where $f < 0$ are not rewarded (since the rewards given by D^f_{KL} in these regions will be offset by the cD_{KL} term).

Surprisingly, we can compute a closed form equation for $D^{f^*}_{KL}(GP\|\widehat{GP})$ in terms of m- and $(m+1)$-dimensional GP parameters $\hat{\boldsymbol{\alpha}}$, $\hat{C}$, $\boldsymbol{\alpha}$, and C, despite its formulation in the possible infinite dimensional feature space $\mathcal{F}$. The derivation of this equation can be found the full version of this paper, available online (McIntire et al. (2016b)).

Proposition 2. *Let $GP = \mathrm{GP}(\boldsymbol{\alpha}, C)$, $\widehat{GP} = \mathrm{GP}(\hat{\boldsymbol{\alpha}}, \hat{C})$ be GPs which share the same inducing inputs and covariance function K. Let $K_{\mathcal{I}} = K(X_{\mathcal{I}}, X_{\mathcal{I}}) \equiv Q^{-1}$ and define*

$$\Gamma = I + \frac{(I + K_{\mathcal{I}} C)^\top}{\boldsymbol{\alpha}^\top K_{\mathcal{I}} \boldsymbol{\alpha}},\; \hat{V} = (\hat{C} + Q)^{-1},$$
$$w = \mathrm{Tr}[(C+Q)\hat{V} - I] - \log|(C+Q)\hat{V}|\,. \tag{13}$$

Then the weighted KL divergence (10) between GP and $\widehat{GP}$ using weighting function f^* (12) is given by

$$D^{f^*}_{KL}(GP\|\widehat{GP}) \propto 2\boldsymbol{\alpha}^\top(\Gamma^\top - I)\hat{V}(\boldsymbol{\alpha} - \hat{\boldsymbol{\alpha}}) +$$
$$(\boldsymbol{\alpha} - \hat{\boldsymbol{\alpha}})^\top \hat{V} (\boldsymbol{\alpha} - \hat{\boldsymbol{\alpha}}) + w$$
$$= (2\Gamma\boldsymbol{\alpha} - (\boldsymbol{\alpha} + \hat{\boldsymbol{\alpha}}))^\top \hat{V}(\boldsymbol{\alpha} - \hat{\boldsymbol{\alpha}}) + w\,. \tag{14}$$

We can obtain some intuition for this formula by separately considering the cases $\hat{\boldsymbol{\alpha}} = \boldsymbol{\alpha}$ and $\hat{C} = C$. In the former case, the first term of (14) vanishes, while if $\hat{C} = C$ the second term vanishes; we can therefore infer roughly that the first term encodes the loss due to reducing α, while w measures loss from reducing C to $\hat{C}$. For a noise-free, full (non-sparse) GP, we have $C = -K_{\mathcal{I}}^{-1} \Rightarrow \Gamma = I$. In this case, (14) reduces to the unweighted KL divergence:

$$D_{KL}(GP\|\widehat{GP}) = (\boldsymbol{\alpha} - \hat{\boldsymbol{\alpha}})^\top \hat{V}(\boldsymbol{\alpha} - \hat{\boldsymbol{\alpha}}) + w\,. \tag{15}$$

Note that the full GP is used to weight the divergence rather than the reduced approximating GP. The reduced $\widehat{GP}$ that minimizes (14) is therefore a moment projection (or M-projection) of GP onto the space of reduced size-m GPs. As shown by Koller & Friedman (2009), this type of projection punishes $\widehat{GP}$ (viewed as a normal distribution) for failing to assign probability mass to regions which are assigned non-negligible probability by GP. The reverse direction $D^f_{KL}(\widehat{GP}\|GP)$ corresponds to the I-projection, which instead punishes $\widehat{GP}$ for assigning probability to regions that GP considers low-probability. Interpreting this in terms of the function space defined by the GPs, we use the M-projection, which ensures that all functions plausible under GP are assigned some probability by $\widehat{GP}$, a highly desirable property as contrasted with the I-projection.

3.2 WOGPs: Weighted Sparse GP Reduction

We now address the problem of reducing the full GP to $\widehat{GP}$, which uses only m of the inducing variables. The goal of this reduction is of course to minimize the impact of removing an inducing variable; in our case, we attempt to minimize $D^{f^*}_{KL}(GP\|\widehat{GP})$.

Note that the weighting function f^* uses the full GP prediction rather than the reduced GP. This is desirable for two reasons. First, we expect the full GP to predict more accurately than the reduced GP because it is fully utilizing the information from the size-m model of the previous iteration and the new point, while the reduced GP must approximate this information. Second, using the reduced GP's predictions to weight the feature space confounds the optimization problem, since the weighting of the feature space is then malleable; for example, if f is the prediction of $\widehat{GP}$, it may be optimal to simply let $\hat{\boldsymbol{\alpha}} = 0 \Rightarrow f = 0$, but this is not helpful in approximating the full GP.

Fix $GP = \mathrm{GP}(\boldsymbol{\alpha}, C)$ and $K_{\mathcal{I}}$. Let $d^*(\hat{\boldsymbol{\alpha}}, \hat{C}) = cD^{f^*}_{KL}(GP\|\widehat{GP})$ be the weighted KL divergence (times scaling constant c) between this GP and its approximation $\widehat{GP} = \mathrm{GP}(\hat{\boldsymbol{\alpha}}, \hat{C})$. Recall our definition of $\hat{Q}$, the update to the inverse Gram matrix, from Equation 7 (and note that $\hat{Q}$ is a function only of Q).

Formally we address the following problem:

$$\begin{aligned} \underset{\hat{\boldsymbol{\alpha}},\hat{C}}{\text{minimize}} \quad & d^*(\hat{\boldsymbol{\alpha}}, \hat{C}) \\ \text{subject to} \quad & \hat{\boldsymbol{\alpha}}^\top \boldsymbol{e}_{m+1} = 0 \\ & \hat{C}\boldsymbol{e}_{m+1} = \mathbf{0}_{m+1} \\ & \hat{C} = \hat{C}^\top \\ & (\hat{C} + \hat{Q}) \succeq 0 \\ & |\hat{C} + Q| > 0. \end{aligned} \tag{16}$$

Here $\boldsymbol{e}_{m+1}$ is the final standard basis vector and $\mathbf{0}_{m+1}$ is the zero vector in $\mathbb{R}^{m+1}$.

Proposition 3. *For fixed $\hat{C}$, the optimization problem (16) is convex with respect to $\hat{\boldsymbol{\alpha}}$.*

Proof. Differentiating (14) with respect to the nonzero entries of $\hat{\boldsymbol{\alpha}}$ yields

$$\begin{aligned} \frac{\partial\, d^*(\hat{\boldsymbol{\alpha}}, \hat{C})}{\partial \hat{\boldsymbol{\alpha}}} &= -2[I_m\mathbf{0}_m]\hat{V}(\Gamma - I)\boldsymbol{\alpha} \\ &\quad - 2[I_m\mathbf{0}_m]\hat{V}(\boldsymbol{\alpha} - [I_m\mathbf{0}_m]^\top\hat{\boldsymbol{\alpha}}) \\ &= -2[I_m\mathbf{0}_m]\hat{V}(\Gamma\boldsymbol{\alpha} - [I_m\mathbf{0}_m]^\top\hat{\boldsymbol{\alpha}}), \end{aligned} \tag{17}$$

where $\hat{\boldsymbol{\alpha}}$ is now assumed to be m-dimensional, I_m represents the m-dimensional identity matrix, $\mathbf{0}_m$ is a column vector of m zeros, and $[I_m\mathbf{0}_m]$ denotes the corresponding $(m \times (m+1))$-dimensional matrix.

Now let $\boldsymbol{v}_i$ denote the ith column of $\hat{V}$, excluding the last entry, and observe that

$$\frac{\partial^2\, d^*(\hat{\boldsymbol{\alpha}}, \hat{C})}{\partial \hat{\alpha}_i \hat{\alpha}_j} = 2\frac{\partial\,(\boldsymbol{v}_i^\top \hat{\boldsymbol{\alpha}})}{\partial \hat{\alpha}_j} = 2\hat{V}_{i,j}\,. \tag{18}$$

Thus we have that the Hessian matrix of $d^*(\hat{\boldsymbol{\alpha}}, \hat{C})$ with respect to $\hat{\boldsymbol{\alpha}}$ is just twice the leading $(m \times m)$ submatrix of $\hat{V}$, which we denote $\hat{V}^{(r)}$.

Note that we can compute $\hat{V}^{(r)}$ using block matrix inversion:

$$\hat{V}^{(r)} = (\hat{C} + Q^{(r)} - \frac{1}{q^*}Q^*Q^{*\top})^{-1} = (\hat{C} + \hat{Q})^{-1}\,. \tag{19}$$

Our result follows from the constraints $(\hat{C} + \hat{Q}) \succeq 0$ and $|\hat{C} + Q| > 0$, with the additional observation that the domain of (16) in $\hat{\boldsymbol{\alpha}}$ is a convex set. □

Having established convexity, we now use Equation 17 to compute an update rule for $\hat{\boldsymbol{\alpha}}$ that minimizes the resulting weighted KL divergence. Solving (17) for zero, we have

$$\begin{aligned} &[I_m\mathbf{0}_m]\hat{V}(\Gamma\boldsymbol{\alpha} - [I_m\mathbf{0}_m]^\top\hat{\boldsymbol{\alpha}}) = \mathbf{0}_m \Rightarrow \\ &\quad \hat{V}(\Gamma\boldsymbol{\alpha} - [I_m\mathbf{0}_m]^\top\hat{\boldsymbol{\alpha}}) = [\mathbf{0}_m^\top\ u]^\top \Rightarrow \\ &\Gamma\boldsymbol{\alpha} - [I_m\mathbf{0}_m]^\top\hat{\boldsymbol{\alpha}} = (\hat{C} + Q)[\mathbf{0}_m^\top\ u]^\top = u[\boldsymbol{Q}^{*\top} q^*]^\top, \end{aligned} \tag{20}$$

where in the last step we recall that the last column of $\hat{C}$ is zero. We let $\Gamma^{(r)}$ denote the first m rows of Γ and $\boldsymbol{\Gamma}^*$ the last row of Γ; observe then that

$$\boldsymbol{\Gamma}^*\boldsymbol{\alpha} = uq^* \Rightarrow u = \frac{\boldsymbol{\Gamma}^*\boldsymbol{\alpha}}{q^*}\,, \tag{21}$$

which leads us to the following solution.

Proposition 4. *The update rule for $\hat{\boldsymbol{\alpha}}$ which minimizes $D^{f^*}_{KL}(GP\|\widehat{GP})$ is given by*

$$\hat{\boldsymbol{\alpha}} = \Gamma^{(r)}\boldsymbol{\alpha} - \frac{\boldsymbol{\Gamma}^*\boldsymbol{\alpha}}{q^*}\boldsymbol{Q}^*\,. \tag{22}$$

Fixing $\hat{\boldsymbol{\alpha}}$ to be optimal in the above sense, we would then like to solve the optimization problem (16) with respect to $\hat{C}$. Unfortunately, this problem is not easily solved for local minima. Differentiating Equation 14 with respect to $\hat{C}$, we have

$$\begin{aligned} \frac{\partial d^*(\hat{\boldsymbol{\alpha}}, \hat{C})}{\partial \hat{C}} &= \frac{\partial w}{\partial \hat{C}} + \\ &- [I_m\mathbf{0}_m]\hat{V}(2\Gamma\boldsymbol{\alpha} - (\boldsymbol{\alpha} + \hat{\boldsymbol{\alpha}}))(\boldsymbol{\alpha} - \hat{\boldsymbol{\alpha}})^\top\hat{V}[I_m\mathbf{0}_m]^\top\,. \end{aligned} \tag{23}$$

Evaluating the derivative of w in the same way, we arrive at

$$\begin{aligned} \frac{\partial w}{\partial \hat{C}} &= [I_m\mathbf{0}_m]\hat{V}[I_m\mathbf{0}_m]^\top \\ &\quad - [I_m\mathbf{0}_m]\hat{V}(C + Q)\hat{V}[I_m\mathbf{0}_m]^\top \end{aligned} \tag{24}$$

However, we are not aware of a way to solve Equation 23 to minimize $D_{KL}^{f^*}(GP\|\widehat{GP})$ analytically with respect to $\hat{C}$.

Furthermore, we find that the objective $d^*(\hat{\alpha}, \hat{C})$ is not convex with respect to $\hat{C}$: since $\log|X|$ is known to be concave, the second term of w

$$-\log|(C+Q)\hat{V}| = \log|\hat{C}+Q| - \log|C+Q| \quad (25)$$

is concave. This prevents us from using convex optimization to solve for $\hat{C}$. However, we have the following:

Proposition 5. *For fixed $\hat{\alpha}$, the objective $d^*(\hat{\alpha}, \hat{C})$ can be written as $d^*(\hat{\alpha}, \hat{C}) = g_1(\hat{C}) - g_2(\hat{C})$, where g_1, g_2 are real-valued convex functions on the intersection of $\mathbb{R}^{(m+1)\times(m+1)}$ with the constraints on $\hat{C}$ in (16).*

Proof. Due to Theorem 1 of Yuille & Rangarajan (2003), we can show this by demonstrating that the Hessian of $d^*(\hat{\alpha}, \hat{C})$ for fixed $\hat{\alpha}$ is bounded. Since $\mathrm{Tr}[X^{-1}]$ is convex, we already have the desired result for w and will therefore compute only the Hessian of

$$d_0^*(\hat{C}) \equiv (2\Gamma\boldsymbol{\alpha} - (\boldsymbol{\alpha} + \hat{\boldsymbol{\alpha}}))^\top \hat{V} (\boldsymbol{\alpha} - \hat{\boldsymbol{\alpha}}) \, . \quad (26)$$

To do this, we first compute

$$\frac{\partial d_0^*}{\partial \hat{C}} = -[I_m \mathbf{0}_m] \hat{V} (2\Gamma\boldsymbol{\alpha} - (\boldsymbol{\alpha}+\hat{\boldsymbol{\alpha}}))(\boldsymbol{\alpha}-\hat{\boldsymbol{\alpha}})^\top \hat{V} [I_m \mathbf{0}_m]^\top \, , \quad (27)$$

where we use the matrices $[I_m \mathbf{0}_m]$ to confine the expression to the $(m \times m)$ derivative with respect to the nonzero entries of $\hat{C}$. Let $\boldsymbol{u}_1 = 2\Gamma\boldsymbol{\alpha} - (\boldsymbol{\alpha} + \hat{\boldsymbol{\alpha}})$ and $\boldsymbol{u}_2 = (\boldsymbol{\alpha} - \hat{\boldsymbol{\alpha}})$ for notational convenience. Confining this expression to a particular entry, we arrive at

$$\frac{\partial d_0^*}{\partial \hat{C}_{i,j}} = -\boldsymbol{v}_i^\top \boldsymbol{u}_1 \boldsymbol{u}_2^\top \boldsymbol{v}_j \, , \quad (28)$$

letting $\boldsymbol{v}_i$ denote the ith column of $\hat{V}$ (and recalling that $\hat{V}$ is symmetric).

Let $H_{k,l}^{i,j}$ represent an entry of the Hessian matrix of d_0^*, and compute

$$H_{k,l}^{i,j} = \frac{\partial^2 d_0^*}{\partial \hat{C}_{i,j} \partial \hat{C}_{k,l}} = -\frac{\partial}{\partial \hat{C}_{k,l}} \boldsymbol{v}_i^\top \boldsymbol{u}_1 \boldsymbol{u}_2^\top \boldsymbol{v}_j$$
$$= \boldsymbol{u}_1^\top (\hat{V}_{i,k} \boldsymbol{v}_l \boldsymbol{v}_j^\top + \hat{V}_{j,k} \boldsymbol{v}_i \boldsymbol{v}_l^\top) \boldsymbol{u}_2 \, . \quad (29)$$

Evidently $H_{k,l}^{i,j}$ is bounded for all i, j, k, l, and thus we have the desired result. □

The above result allows us to employ methods of concave-convex minimization, e.g. the CCCP procedure of Yuille & Rangarajan (2003). Specifically, to minimize $g_1 - g_2$ we employ an iterative method of updating $\hat{C}$ according to the rule

$$\frac{\partial g_1}{\partial \hat{C}}(\boldsymbol{x}^{t+1}) = \frac{\partial g_2}{\partial \hat{C}}(\boldsymbol{x}^t) \, . \quad (30)$$

It is not straightforward to explicitly decompose d^* into convex terms g_1 and g_2 due to the difficulty of solving Equation 23, so we instead use the iterative method for optimization given in Yuille & Rangarajan (2003) for such cases, which finds $\boldsymbol{x}^{t+1}$ in each step by minimizing a function of $\boldsymbol{x}^{t+1}$ and $\boldsymbol{x}^t$.

In Section 4, we demonstrate that CCCP optimization of $\hat{C}$ can significantly reduce the weighted KL divergence of the online GP update. Since we are minimizing with respect to the matrix $\hat{C}$, the size of the CCCP optimization problem is $\mathcal{O}(m^2)$. For larger sparse models, this approach may therefore not be feasible if computation time is a primary concern. As runtime is extremely costly for our application, we also propose as a heuristic the update rule for $\hat{C}$ of Csató (2002), given in Equation 6, which minimizes the unweighted divergence between the distributions as well as the w-term of the weighted divergence. The analytic form for this update can provide a significant speedup over CCCP if m is large; we justify this heuristic by comparing with CCCP updating for $\hat{C}$ in Section 4.

4 Experiments

We perform two types of experiments to demonstrate the efficacy of WOGPs in Bayesian optimization. First, we provide easily visualized examples of the comparative performance of WOGPs and standard online sparse GPs on synthetic optimization problems. Second, we use data from the LCLS free-electron laser to test the optimization algorithms in a real-world setting with noisy observations.

4.1 Example Problem

First, we consider the simple problem of optimizing over a function given by $y = 20 + x - (x-1)^2(x+1)^2$, shown in Figure 1a, which achieves a maximum slightly greater than 21 at $x \approx 1.1$ and has a local maximum at $x \approx -.84$. Each type of model is allowed at most five inducing variables. In each trial, we choose five training points in $[-3, 3]$ uniformly at random and train each model on them. The Bayesian optimization procedure described in Section 2.3 is then performed for 80 iterations. Figure 1b shows the results of this experiment averaged across 80 trials. On average, both models tend to quickly find a value near the global optimum; however, while the WOGP tends to converge near this optimum, the unweighted model does not. Instead, when the unweighted model explores other areas, it essentially loses focus on the optimal area by devoting some of its limited resources to modeling the new, lower-scoring region. This can be seen in the decline on average of the unweighted model's score to roughly $y = 19$, in which it converges within the near-plateau between $x = -1$ and $x = 0$.

In the bottom of Figure 1, examples are shown of the con-

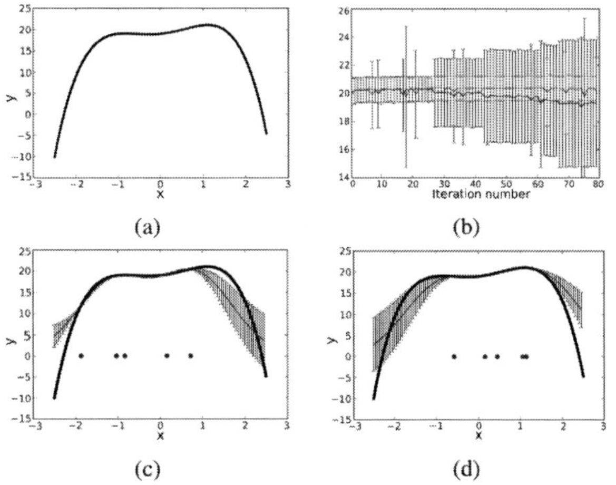

Figure 1: Simple 1-D optimization problem. (a) The objective function. (b) Average y-value explored in each iteration, for unweighted (blue) and weighted (red) models. Standard deviations are shown as error bars. (c,d) Sample unweighted and weighted (respectively) final GP models. The objective is shown in black, GP mean function with uncertainty in blue, and inducing points as red dots.

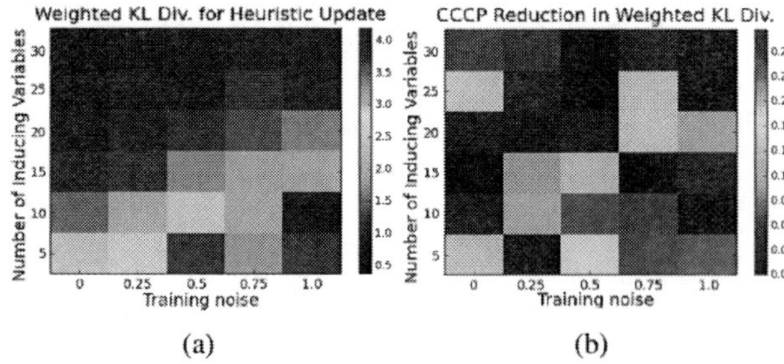

Figure 2: Results demonstrating the effectiveness of CCCP for optimization over $\hat{C}$, shown for a particular event. Each pixel shows the median value over 20 trials at the given configuration. (a) The weighted KL divergence d^* obtained using the heuristic (6) update rule for $\hat{C}$. (b) The proportional reduction in d^* from CCCP optimization over $\hat{C}$.

verged online GP models in this problem. In (1c), the unweighted model is plotted in blue with its predictive variance, while the underlying function $f(x)$ is plotted in black. The red dots underneath show the locations of the inducing variables for each model. The models were trained on the same points, and both initially explore in the region around $x = -1$. However, the unweighted model allocates one of its inducing variables to $x \approx -2$ in order to capture the curvature of $f(x)$ in the negative direction. The weighted model instead stabilizes its inducing variables around $x = -1$ and $x = 0$ during its exploration in $x < 0$ and then begins to explore in $x > 0$. This rightward exploration quickly converges around $x = 1$.

4.2 FEL Performance Optimization

Free-electron lasers operate by accelerating electrons to nearly the speed of light, and then passing this electron beam through a series of magnetic dipoles to separate the electrons into coherent microbunches (Huang & Kim (2007)). Through this coherence, an FEL can generate x-ray pulses 10 billion fold brighter than any other x-ray source. Here, we focus on the tuning of quadrupole magnets, which are placed upstream of the FEL to manipulate the shape of the electron beam.

Currently at LCLS, quadrupole magnets are tuned by hand to optimize the beam pulse energy. The existing tuning procedure is repeated frequently due to machine configuration changes and drift over time. This extensive tuning time is problematic due to the operational cost of the beam and the heavy over-subscription of LCLS users; the FEL is used by scientists in a variety of disciplines for field-leading research, and the demand for machine time outstrips its availability by a factor of 5. Reducing the time spent tuning the machine would directly increase its availability for scientific use.

Our experiments on the FEL data thus far have used isolated optimization 'events': we define such an event as a consecutive period of time using a fixed accelerator configuration, such that the measured x-ray pulse energy is a function only of the controlled variables, i.e. quadrupole magnet settings. Under this assumption, we then train two online GP models with the same number of inducing variables, one using a WOGP, and one using a standard online sparse GP, on a noisy subset of the event data. A much larger sparse GP (with e.g. 500 inducing variables) is trained on the event data without noise. This large 'truth' model is then used in the Bayesian optimization procedure, with its predictions used as feedback for the online GP optimizers. We introduce noise for the online GP models and not the truth model to simulate the use case of online tuning, which must be done each time the beam is used due to the tendency of the machine settings to drift over time.

We first use this data to test the WOGP update rules for $\hat{C}$. Using CCCP to minimize $D^{f^*}_{KL}(GP\|\widehat{GP})$ with respect to $\hat{C}$ can be used to minimize the weighted KL divergence of the approximating GP. Alternatively, we propose as a heuristic the update given by Csató (2002), shown in (6), which is optimal for the KL divergence (5) between $\widehat{GP}$ and GP, and optimal for the w term of $D^{f^*}_{KL}(GP\|\widehat{GP})$.

Figure 2 shows results of a comparison between these update rules for $\hat{C}$. For this testing, a single representative event was chosen, and 20 optimization trials were run for a short time with various levels of training noise and numbers of inducing variables. For each trial, the value of $D^{f^*}_{KL}$ is then computed for an additional size reduction step for both

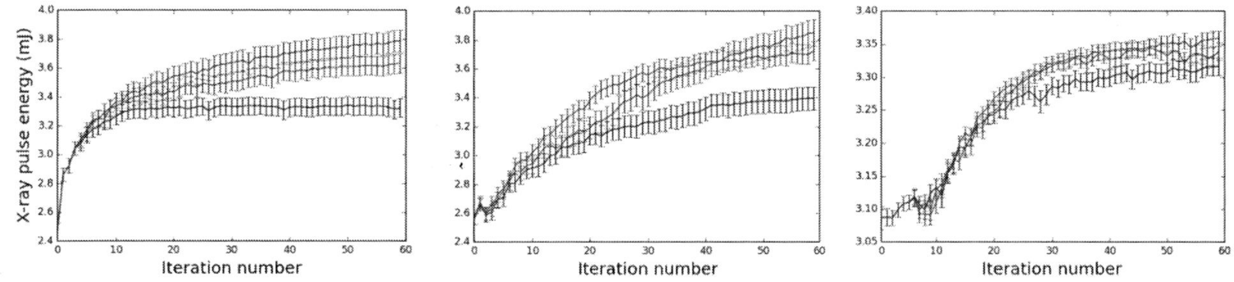

(a) (b) (c)

Figure 3: Results of optimization on FEL data, with events at different beam configurations and electron energies of 11.45, 13.2, and 14.5 GeV respectively. The plots show the average x-ray pulse energy in mJ of the region explored in each iteration by the weighted (red) and unweighted (blue) sparse optimizers, as well as by a full GP, shown in green. Error bars indicate the normalized standard deviation of the values in each iteration.

the heuristic and CCCP-computed values of $\hat{C}$. In Figure 2a, the median value of $D^{f^*}_{KL}$ obtained using the heuristic update for $\hat{C}$ across these trials is shown for each configuration. Note that as the modeling problem becomes more challenging (as noise increases and the number of inducing variables decrease), the typical divergence of the update increases. We do not show a similar plot for the CCCP updating because it is visually very similar.

In Figure 2b, the percentage decrease in $D^{f^*}_{KL}$ achieved by using CCCP updating is shown. We see that using CCCP to optimize the value of $\hat{C}$ typically leads to a 5-15% decrease in the weighted KL divergence of the update. This demonstrates that the heuristic update for $\hat{C}$ is justified in cases where the runtime of CCCP is prohibitive. These results also indicate that the CCCP updating scheme detailed here can provide nontrivial improvements to $D^{f^*}_{KL}$ over the heuristic update. Over the course of optimization the accumulated benefit from the CCCP updating may lead to substantial improvements in performance.

Next, we compare the performance of WOGPs and standard online sparse GPs in optimization over the FEL data events described above. Results from three such events, averaged over 200 trials (with different, randomly sampled initial training data), are shown in Figure 3. The results of optimization are compared in terms of final y-value and regret (which is an additive constant away from the negative sum of observations), which accounts for speed of improvement as well. We can see that in general WOGPs tend to yield better performance than the unweighted sparse GP: in the first two events (3a) and (3b), the difference in final y-values is statistically significant ($p < .001$, $p < .002$ respectively in the two-sided t-test), as is the difference in regret ($p < .05$, $p < .005$). In the final event (3c), we can see that the WOGP performs similarly to the full GP, though its improvement over the unweighted sparse GP is not statistically significant for this event.

5 Conclusions

Bayesian optimization is known to be effective for optimization in settings where the objective function is expensive to evaluate. A complex parameter space and noisy observations can slow the convergence of Bayesian optimization, however, and using a full Gaussian process model leads to poor scaling in these cases. In this paper, we introduce sparse online GPs for Bayesian optimization.

Our main contribution is a novel weighted updating scheme for sparse online GPs, which enables a trade-off during optimization between overall predictive accuracy and a specific focus on better-performing regions of parameter space. This addresses the core problem with using sparse GPs in Bayesian optimization: the limited size of the GP representation, which prevents the information from new data from being fully incorporated into the model. As a result, traditional sparse GPs perform poorly since the sparse set selection does not necessarily attempt to preserve resolution in promising areas of parameter space and may even 'blur' local optima to preserve accuracy elsewhere.

Our new weighted-update online GP, WOGP, outperforms the standard online sparse GP in optimization by preferentially updating the model to incorporate information that is more valuable to the optimization procedure. We are able to analytically evaluate the weighted KL divergence between Gaussian processes for a simple weighting function, and we demonstrate empirically that updating the sparse GP to minimize this weighted divergence significantly improves performance during Bayesian optimization. Live tests of this approach are currently underway at LCLS (McIntire et al. (2016a)).

Acknowledgements

Work is supported by Department of Energy Contract No. DE-AC02-76SF00515. SE is partially supported by NSF grant 1522054 through subcontract 72954-10597.

References

Brochu, Eric, Cora, Vlad M, and de Freitas, Nando. A tutorial on Bayesian optimization of expensive cost functions, with application to active user modeling and hierarchical reinforcement learning. eprint arXiv:1012.2599, arXiv.org, December 2010.

Bull, Adam D. Convergence rates of efficient global optimization algorithms. *Journal of Machine Learning Research*, 12:2879–2904, November 2011.

Csató, Lehel. *Gaussian Processes - Iterative Sparse Approximations*. PhD thesis, Aston University, 2002.

Csató, Lehel and Opper, Manfred. Sparse on-line Gaussian processes. *Neural Computation*, 14(3):641–668, 2002.

Emma, P. et al. First lasing and operation of an ngstrom-wavelength free-electron laser. *Nature Photonics*, 4:641 – 647, 2010.

Gal, Yarin, van der Wilk, Mark, and Rasmussen, Carl. Distributed variational inference in sparse Gaussian process regression and latent variable models. In *Advances in Neural Information Processing Systems 27*, pp. 3257–3265. Curran Associates, Inc., 2014.

Hensman, James, Fusi, Nicoló, and Lawrence, Neil D. Gaussian processes for big data. In *Proceedings of the Twenty-Ninth Conference on Uncertainty in Artificial Intelligence*, 2013.

Huang, Z. and Kim, K. J. Review of x-ray free-electron laser theory. *Phys. Rev. ST Accel. Beams*, 10, 2007.

Johnson, Matthew J. and Willsky, Alan S. Bayesian nonparametric hidden semi-markov models. *J. of Machine Learning Research*, 14(1):673–701, February 2013.

Jones, Donald R., Schonlau, Matthias, and Welch, William J. Efficient global optimization of expensive black-box functions. *J. of Global Optimization*, 13(4): 455–492, December 1998.

Koller, Daphne and Friedman, Nir. *Probabilistic Graphical Models: Principles and Techniques - Adaptive Computation and Machine Learning*. The MIT Press, 2009.

Kulis, Brian and Jordan, Michael I. Revisiting k-means: New algorithms via Bayesian nonparametrics. In *Proceedings of the 29th Int'l Conference on ML*, 2012.

Lawrence, Neil, Seeger, Matthias, and Herbrich, Ralf. Fast sparse Gaussian process methods: The informative vector machine. In *Advances in Neural Information Processing Systems 15*, pp. 625–632. MIT Press, 2003.

McIntire, Mitchell, Cope, Tyler, Ermon, Stefano, and Ratner, Daniel. Bayesian optimization of FEL performance at LCLS. In *Proceedings of the 7th International Particle Accelerator Conference*, 2016a.

McIntire, Mitchell, Ratner, Daniel, and Ermon, Stefano. Sparse Gaussian processes for Bayesian optimization: Technical report. Technical report, 2016b.

Miller, Andrew et al. A Gaussian process model of quasar spectral energy distributions. In *Advances in Neural Information Processing Systems 28*, 2015.

Nickson, Thomas, Osborne, Michael A., Reece, Steven, and Roberts, Stephen. Automated machine learning using stochastic algorithm tuning. In *NIPS Workshop on Bayesian Optimization*, 2014.

Osborne, Michael A., Garnett, Roman, and Roberts, Stephen J. Gaussian processes for global optimization. In *In Learning and Intelligent Optimization*, 2009.

Quionero-Candela, Joaquin and Rasmussen, Carl Edward. A unifying view of sparse approximate Gaussian process regression. *Journal of Machine Learning Research*, 6: 1939–1959, 2005.

Ranganathan, A., Yang, M. H., and Ho, J. Online sparse Gaussian process regression and its applications. *IEEE Transactions on Image Processing*, 20(2), Feb 2011.

Rasmussen, Carl Edward and Williams, Christopher K. I. *Gaussian Processes for Machine Learning (Adaptive Computation and ML)*. The MIT Press, 2005.

Seeger, Matthias, Williams, Christopher K. I., and Lawrence, Neil D. Fast forward selection to speed up sparse gaussian process regression. In *Workshop on AI and Statistics 9*, 2003.

Snelson, Edward and Ghahramani, Zoubin. Sparse Gaussian processes using pseudo-inputs. In *Advances in Neural Information Processing Systems*, pp. 1257–1264. MIT press, 2006.

Snoek, Jasper, Larochelle, Hugo, and Adams, Ryan P. Practical Bayesian optimization of machine learning algorithms. In *Advances in Neural Information Processing Systems 25*, pp. 2960–2968, 2012.

Snoek, Jasper et al. Scalable bayesian optimization using deep neural networks. In *Proceedings of the 32nd Int'l Conference on Machine Learning (ICML-15)*, 2015.

Tank, A., Foti, N., and Fox, E.B. Streaming variational inference for Bayesian nonparametric mixture models. In *Proc. Int'l Conference on AI and Statistics*, May 2015.

Titsias, Michalis K. Variational learning of inducing variables in sparse Gaussian processes. In *In Artificial Intelligence and Statistics 12*, pp. 567–574, 2009.

Yuille, A. L. and Rangarajan, Anand. The concave-convex procedure. *Neural Computation*, 15(4):915–936, 2003.

A General Statistical Framework for Designing Strategy-proof Assignment Mechanisms

Harikrishna Narasimhan
Harvard University
Cambridge, MA 02138, USA
hnarasimhan@seas.harvard.edu

David C. Parkes
Harvard University
Cambridge, MA 02138, USA
parkes@eecs.harvard.edu

Abstract

We develop a statistical framework for the design of a strategy-proof assignment mechanism that closely approximates a target outcome rule. The framework can handle settings with and without money, and allows the designer to employ techniques from machine learning to control the space of strategy-proof mechanisms searched over, by providing a rule class with appropriate capacity. We solve a sample-based optimization problem over a space of mechanisms that correspond to *agent-independent price functions* (virtual prices in the case of settings without money), subject to a feasibility constraint on the sample. A transformation is applied to the obtained mechanism to ensure feasibility on all type profiles, and strategy-proofness. We derive a sample complexity bound for our approach in terms of the capacity of the chosen rule class and provide applications for our results.

1 INTRODUCTION

Mechanism design studies situations where a set of self-interested agents each hold private information regarding their preferences over different outcomes. Originating from microeconomic theory, mechanism design has become important in the design of open, algorithmic systems that involve multiple stakeholders. A mechanism receives claims about agent types, selects an outcome, and may additionally charge payments. An important property of a mechanism is that of *strategy-proofness*, where it is in the best interest for each agent to make truthful reports.

The existing theory of mechanism design provides positive and negative results in regard to properties that can be achieved together with strategy-proofness. The theory is quite limited, though, in that:

1) Results are developed for stylized preference domains that may not reflect real-world structure [1].
2) Positive results are limited by an analytical bottleneck that makes analysis difficult in *multi-dimensional type spaces* [2, 3].
3) There are few general methodologies, especially in mechanism design without money, where bespoke mechanisms are developed for a given domain [4].

In practice, one often needs to hand-craft a mechanism based on application-specific requirements. For example,

- **Task assignment:** Consider the problem of designing an assignment mechanism for a ride sharing platform. This is a setting with payments, and the standard mechanism one would use here is the Vickrey-Clarke-Groves (VCG) mechanism. However, if one needs to incorporate specific priority or fairness considerations, the VCG mechanism may not be well-suited, and the designer would be faced with needing to manually design a mechanism that satisfies the requirements.
- **Resource allocation:** Consider the problem of designing a strategy-proof mechanism for the fair allocation of jobs to shared computers based on reported need. This is a setting without money, and a standard strategy-proof mechanism for assignment is random serial dictatorship (RSD). However, if the designer wishes to optimize a different utility criterion than RSD (e.g. a utilitarian objective), then the designer will again have to handcraft a mechanism based on the requirements.

We suppose that alternatively, the designer can provide his requirements in the form of a *target outcome rule* that maps reports to desired outcomes (but is not necessarily strategy-proof). The goal is to automatically design a strategy-proof mechanism that closely mimics this rule, leading to the following question:

Given an arbitrary outcome rule, can we automatically design a strategy-proof mechanism that closely approximates the rule?

The common approach to *automated mechanism design* [5] has been to formulate a search problem over a set of strategy-proof mechanisms. Some works perform this search over an explicit space of all possible mechanisms, often resulting in intractable optimization problems (with a number of decision variables that grow exponentially in the number of agents). Other approaches search over a parameterized subset of strategy-proof mechanisms [6, 7, 8]. However, these methods are tailored to specific classes of mechanisms known to be strategy-proof. Positive results are available for a Bayesian relaxation of strategy-proofness, and with agent-separable objectives [9, 10], but a more general approach has remained elusive.

In this paper, we develop a general statistical framework for designing strategy-proof mechanisms that closely approximate a target outcome rule. Envisioning settings with abundant data on agent preferences, we assume access to example inputs to a mechanism, each input labeled with a target outcome. Consider for example a setting with an existing, strategy-proof mechanism, with new design requirements specified through target outcomes on historical reports. The goal is to find a strategy-proof mechanism that closely approximates the target outcome rule.

We leverage general, necessary and sufficient conditions for the strategy-proofness of a mechanism, namely an *agent-independence condition*, and a *feasibility requirement* (that the outcome of the mechanism is feasible). Concretely, the framework formulates an optimization problem on a sampled set of agent type profiles over a specified class of outcome rules that satisfy agent-independence. A feasibility constraint is enforced on the sampled profiles, so that the resulting mechanism is feasible on these samples. In addition, we apply a transform to the mechanism to ensure feasibility on all profiles while retaining agent-independence (and thus obtaining strategy-proofness). The particular problem we study is an *assignment problem*, where there is a set of distinct, indivisible items and the outcome assigns at most one item to each agent. The distance to the target assignment is measured in terms of the Hamming distance. The feasibility transform is due to Hashimoto [11] and is well defined for allocation problems.

Unlike previous works on the automated design of strategy-proof mechanisms, our framework neither performs a brute-force search over all mechanisms nor requires the designer to provide a specific parameterized class of strategy-proof mechanisms. Instead we take an intermediate approach, where the space of strategy-proof mechanisms searched over is controlled by the capacity of the outcome class. The capacity of this class can be controlled through standard machine learning techniques, for example by parametrizing the class in a suitable feature space and adjusting the set of features used. By using the general, necessary and sufficient conditions of agent-independence and feasibilty, we remove the need for new characterization results. Rather, the limit of the framework is governed by the limits of the statistical framework.

The main result is an upper bound on the sample complexity of designing strategy-proof mechanisms using our framework. The bound depends on the capacity of the agent-independent function class used, measured in terms of its *Natarajan dimension* D [12]. We show that for n agents and N sampled profiles, the difference in Hamming distance to the target between the designed mechanism and the best strategy-proof mechanism within the hypothesis space is at most:

$$\tilde{O}\left(\sqrt{\frac{D}{N}} + \frac{D}{N}\sum_{i=1}^{n}|\Theta_i|\right),$$

for a distributional assumption, and where $|\Theta_i|$ is the size of the type space for agent i. The linear dependence on $|\Theta_i|$ is a result of the feasibility transformation applied to the sample-optimal rule. This sample complexity is exponentially smaller than the total number of type profiles $\times_{i=1}^{n}|\Theta_i|$.

The proposed approach is quite flexible, in that it can handle settings with and without money. Instantiating the framework to assignment problems, we provide explicit examples of agent-independent rule classes with finite Natarajan dimension that contain feasible assignment rules. For the setting with money, the hypothesis class is defined in terms of agent-independent price functions, with each agent demanding the item that maximizes its utility. For the setting without money, the hypothesis class is defined in terms of virtual price functions and budgets, with each agent demanding its most preferred, affordable item.

1.1 RELATED WORK

The problem of using machine learning to design mechanisms that approximate a target rule was first considered by Procaccia et al. [13] in the context of designing voting rules, but without consideration to strategy-proofness. In the most closely-related work, Dütting et al. [14] use statistical machine learning to design payment rules for a fixed outcome rule. We design both outcome and payment rules, and whereas they provide approximate strategy-proofness, we obtain strategy-proof mechanisms. We also handle mechanism design without money.

Prior work on automated mechanism design adopts specific, parameterized classes of mechanisms [7, 8, 15]. However, these approaches require a designer to have parametric characterizations of strategy-proof mechanisms, and require specialized solvers for each case. More recently, Narasimhan and Parkes [15] consider the problem of using methods from machine learning to design social choice and matching mechanisms that best approximate a target rule, but their approach is also tailored to specific parameterized classes of mechanisms. We provide a more general approach, where the designer only needs to provide a set of rules that satisfy the agent-independence condition.

There has also been previous work that uses statistical or machine learning techniques to design revenue-optimal mechanisms from sampled preference data [16, 17, 18, 19], but this is restricted to settings where the private information of agents is "single-parameter" (roughly, one number, whereas in our setting each agent's type is a value for each item or a rank order on items).

Organization. In Section 2, we begin with the problem setting and in Section 3, describe a general characterization of strategy-proof mechanisms for assignment problems with and without money. In Section 4, we use these characterizations to develop a statistical framework for designing strategy-proof assignment mechanisms. In Section 5, we derive a sample complexity bound for our approach, and in Section 6, we discuss applications of our result to assignment problems with and without money.

2 PROBLEM SETTING

We consider n agents $[n] = \{1, \ldots, n\}$ and m items $[m] = \{1, \ldots, m\}$, and are interested in one-to-one assignments of items to agents. We allow agents to be unassigned, in which case we will say that the agent is assigned to ϕ. An agent may additionally be charged a payment.

We say that an assignment is *feasible* if no two agents are assigned the same item. Let $\Omega \subset [m]^n$ denote the set of feasible one-to-one assignments of items (or ϕ) to the agents. We will use $y \in \Omega$ to denote a feasible assignment and $y_i \in [m]$ for the item allocated to agent i in y.

Each agent is associated with a *type* θ_i from a finite set Θ_i, which is private to the agent. We use $\theta = (\theta_1, \ldots, \theta_n)$ to denote a profile of types, and $\Theta = \times_{i=1}^{n} \Theta_i$ to denote the set of all type profiles. We will use θ_{-i} to denote the profile of types for all but agent i, and $\Theta_{-i} = \times_{j \neq i} \Theta_j$.

In a setting without money, an agent's type induces a preference ordering over items. We will use $o \succ_i o'$ to denote that agent i strictly prefers item $o \in [m]$ over item $o' \in [m]$, and $o \succeq_i o'$ to denote that the agent either strictly prefers o over o' or is indifferent.

In a setting with money, an agent is charged a price for an item, and the agent's type induces a preference ordering over pairs $(o, p_o) \in [m] \times \mathbb{R}_+$ of items and prices. In this case, we will assume quasi-linear preferences. Here each agent i is associated with a valuation function $v_i : \Theta_i \times [m] \to \mathbb{R}_+$, with $v_i(\theta_i, o) \in \mathbb{R}_+$ indicating the value assigned for agent type θ_i to item o. The agent's *utility* for a pair (o, p_o) of items and prices is given by $u_i(\theta_i, (o, p_o)) = v_i(\theta_i, o) - p_o$, and $(o, p_o) \succeq_i (o', p_{o'}) \iff u_i(\theta_i, (o, p_o)) \geqslant u_i(\theta_i, (o', p_{o'}))$.

A *mechanism* receives reports of types from the agents, and maps each agent to an item through an *outcome rule* $f : \Theta \to \Omega$. For a report profile $\hat{\theta}$ from the agents, the assignment to the agents is given by $f(\hat{\theta}) \in \Omega$, and $f_i(\hat{\theta}) \in [m]$ shall denote the item assigned to agent i by f. In settings with money, the mechanism also charges a payment measured in terms of a *payment rule* $p_i : \Theta \to \mathbb{R}_+$.

A desirable property of a mechanism is *strategy-proofness*. A mechanism is strategy-proof if each agent receives its most-preferred outcome (or outcome-price pair) when reporting its true type. More concretely, in a setting without money, a mechanism defined by outcome rule f is strategy-proof if for all $i \in [n]$, $\theta \in \Theta$, and $\theta'_i \in \Theta_i$, $f_i(\theta) \succeq_i f_i(\theta'_i, \theta_{-i})$. Similarly, in a setting with money, a mechanism defined by (f, p) is strategy-proof if for all $i \in [n], \theta \in \Theta$, and $\theta'_i \in \Theta_i$, $(f_i(\theta), p_i(\theta)) \succeq_i (f_i(\theta'_i, \theta_{-i}), p_i(\theta'_i, \theta_{-i}))$. In both cases, let us use $\mathcal{M}_{\text{SP}}$ to denote the space of mechanisms that are strategy-proof.

Agent types are distributed according to an underlying, unknown distribution $\mathcal{D}$ over type profiles Θ. We are provided a *target outcome rule* $g : \Theta \to \Omega$ that need not be strategy-proof, and the goal is to design a strategy-proof mechanism that closely approximates this rule. For this purpose, we adopt a *distance measure* $\ell : [m]^n \times [m]^n \to \mathbb{R}_+$ to measure the distance between the given and target assignments. In particular, we use the normalized *Hamming* distance, $\ell(y, y') = \frac{1}{n} \sum_{i=1}^{n} \mathbf{1}(y_i \neq y'_i)$ for any $y, y' \in [m]^n$.

The goal is:

$$\min_{(f,p) \in \mathcal{M}'_{\text{SP}}} \mathbf{E}_{\Theta \sim \mathcal{D}}\big[\ell(g(\theta), f(\theta))\big], \tag{1}$$

where $\mathcal{M}'_{\text{SP}} \subseteq \mathcal{M}_{\text{SP}}$ is some set of strategy-proof mechanisms. In words, we want to find the strategy-proof mechanism in a class of mechanisms that minimizes the expected distance from the target. Since the distribution is over a finite space, an infimum over $\mathcal{M}'_{\text{SP}}$ is always achieved by a mechanism within the class. We shall allow the designer to control the space of strategy-proof mechanisms $\mathcal{M}'_{\text{SP}}$ by providing a suitable rule class with appropriate capacity (or expressive power).

3 CHARACTERIZATION OF STRATEGY-PROOF MECHANISMS

We first provide a general, necessary and sufficient characterization of strategy-proof assignment mechanisms in settings with and without money. These characterizations are standard in mechanism design theory.

Assignment Problem with Money. A mechanism defined by a pair of outcome rule and payment rule (f, p) is strategy-proof iff the following conditions hold [20]:

(1) **Agent independence:** Given the report of the other agents, an agent's prices on each item are independent of its own report. Also, the agent is assigned its most-preferred item, given its report and the agent-independent prices. In other words, the payment

rule $p_i(\theta) = t_i(\theta_{-i}, f_i(\theta))$ for some *price function* $t_i : \Theta_{-i} \times [m] \rightarrow \mathbb{R}_+$, and

$$f_i(\theta) \in \underset{o \in [m]}{\text{argmax}} \{v_i(\theta_i, o) - t_i(\theta_{-i}, o)\}.$$

(2) **Feasibility:** No two agents get the same item, i.e. for all $i, j \in [n], f_i(\theta) \neq \phi, f_j(\theta) \neq \phi \Rightarrow f_i(\theta) \neq f_j(\theta)$.

In words, an agent cannot change the price for an item by misreporting its type, and given these prices, receives the most-preferred item according to the report. Further, the assignment is feasible for all reports.

Example 1. *The well-known VCG mechanism satisfies the above conditions. In its general form, the VCG mechanism allocates for any report θ an assignment that maximizes welfare (i.e. sum of agent valuations): $f^{vcg}(\theta) \in \text{argmax}_{y \in \Omega} \sum_{i=1}^{n} v_i(\theta_i, y_i)$, and charges each agent i a payment: $p_i^{vcg}(\theta) = H_i(\theta_{-i}) - \sum_{j \neq i} v_j(\theta_j, f_j^{vcg}(\theta))$, where $H_i : \Theta_{-i} \rightarrow \mathbb{R}_+$ is a function that is independent of agent i's report. By definition, the VCG mechanism satisfies the feasibility condition. To see that the mechanism also satisfies the agent-independence condition, define $t_i^{vcg} : \Theta_{-i} \times [m] \rightarrow \mathbb{R}_+$ for reports θ_{-i} and item o as: $t_i^{vcg}(\theta_{-i}, o) = H_i(\theta_{-i}) - \max_{y \in \Omega, y_i = o} \sum_{j \neq i} v_j(\theta_j, y_j)$. Then it can be verified that $p_i^{vcg}(\theta) = t_i^{vcg}(\theta_{-i}, f_i^{vcg}(\theta))$.*

Assignment Problem without Money. We can obtain a similar characterization by defining a *virtual price function* $t_i^{\text{vir}} : \Theta_{-i} \times [m] \rightarrow \mathbb{R}_+$ for each agent. For a given preference profile report $\theta \in \Theta$, we will say that agent i can *afford* item $o \in [m]$ if the virtual price for the item is below a budget of \$1, i.e. $t_i^{\text{vir}}(\theta_{-i}, o) \leqslant 1$. An agent receives one of the items that it can afford. A mechanism defined by outcome rule f is strategy-proof iff the following hold:

(1) **Agent independence:** Given the report of the other agents, an agent's virtual prices are independent of its own report. The agent is assigned its most-preferred item among those it can afford, given its report and the agent-independent prices. In other words, there exists a virtual price function, $t_i^{\text{vir}} : \Theta_{-i} \times [m] \rightarrow \mathbb{R}_+$ such that $t_i^{\text{vir}}(\theta_{-i}, f_i(\theta)) \leqslant 1$ and

$$f_i(\theta) \succeq_i o, \forall o \in \{o' \in [m] : t_i^{\text{vir}}(\theta_{-i}, o') \leqslant 1\}.$$

(2) **Feasibility:** No two agents get the same item, i.e. for all $i, j \in [n]$, $f_i(\theta) \neq \phi, f_j(\theta) \neq \phi \Rightarrow f_i(\theta) \neq f_j(\theta)$.

4 A GENERAL STATISTICAL FRAMEWORK

We next introduce a framework that exploits these general, necessary and sufficient characterizations. Specifically, we provide an approach to solve (1) by formulating a sample-based optimization problem over outcome rules that satisfy the above conditions.

We require the designer to provide a class $\mathcal{F}_i$ of functions $f_i : \Theta \rightarrow [m]$ that satisfy the *agent independence* condition. For the setting with money, each $f_i \in \mathcal{F}_i$ is required to be of the form $f_i(\theta) \in \text{argmax}_{o \in [m]} \{v_i(\theta_i, o) - t_i(\theta_{-i}, o)\}$ for some $t_i : \Theta_{-i} \times [m] \rightarrow \mathbb{R}_+$. For the setting without money, each $f_i \in \mathcal{F}_i$ needs to satisfy $t_i^{\text{vir}}(\theta_{-i}, f_i(\theta)) \leqslant 1$ and $f_i(\theta) \succeq_i o, \forall o \in \{o' \in [m] : t_i^{\text{vir}}(\theta_{-i}, o') \leqslant 1\}$ for some $t_i^{\text{vir}} : \Theta_{-i} \times [m] \rightarrow \mathbb{R}_+$.

Further, let $\mathcal{F} = \times_{i=1}^{n} \mathcal{F}_i$. We will refer to each function $f_i \in \mathcal{F}_i$ as an agent-independent function, and the concatenated function $f \in \mathcal{F}$ as an agent-independent outcome rule. The outcome rules $f \in \mathcal{F}$ need not satisfy the feasibility condition (i.e. can map a type profile θ to an infeasible assignment $f(\theta) \in [m]^n$), and therefore may not be strategy-proof.

For ease of exposition, we will henceforth assume that *neither the outcome rules $f \in \mathcal{F}$ nor the target rule g leave an agent unassigned* (i.e. do not assign ϕ to an agent). The framework and theoretical results easily extend to the case where this assumption does not hold.

The goal is to solve (1) over all outcome rules in $\mathcal{F}$ that also satisfy the feasibility condition, and find the rule that has minimum Hamming distance from the target rule:

$$\min_{f \in \mathcal{F}} \mathbf{E}_{\theta \sim \mathcal{D}}\big[\ell\big(g(\theta), f(\theta)\big)\big] \quad (2)$$
$$\text{s.t.} \quad f_1(\theta) \neq \ldots \neq f_n(\theta), \ \forall \theta \in \Theta.$$

In practice, we do not have access to the type distribution $\mathcal{D}$. Rather, we have a sample $S = \{(\theta^1, y^1 = g(\theta^1)), \ldots, (\theta^N, y^N = g(\theta^N))\} \in (\Theta \times \Omega)^N$ containing agent profiles drawn i.i.d. from $\mathcal{D}$ and labeled according to the target outcome rule g.

We solve an empirical version of the optimization problem (2), with the feasibility constraint enforced only on the profiles in S. A problem is that the obtained rule need not be feasible on type profiles outside S. To address this, we adopt a *feasibility transform* on the obtained rule that ensures that the resulting rule is feasible without compromising agent independence, and thus obtaining strategy-proofness. The two steps of our framework are:

Step I: Constrained Optimization on a Sample. We first solve an empirical version of (2) on sample S:

$$\min_{f \in \mathcal{F}} \frac{1}{N} \sum_{k=1}^{N} \ell(y^k, f(\theta^k))) \quad (3)$$
$$\text{s.t.} \quad f_1(\theta^k) \neq \ldots \neq f_n(\theta^k), \ \forall k \in \{1, \ldots, N\}.$$

Step II: Feasibility Transform. The obtained outcome rule need not be feasible on profiles outside S. A naive way to enforce feasibility is to resolve conflicts by canceling an allocation when there is infeasibility, or through some more sophisticated priority-based approach. But without care, this results in a mechanism that is not strategy-proof; e.g. perhaps an agent can usefully misreport in order to avoid a problem with infeasibility.

We use a transform inspired by an approach due to Hashimoto [11]. For each agent i, we perform the following check: conditioned on the reports of the other agents, *does there exist a type in Θ_i for which the outcome rule would output an infeasible assignment*? If yes, we leave agent i unassigned; otherwise the original assigned item is left unchanged. For the outcome rule $\hat{f}$ obtained by solving (3), the transform $\mathbb{T}[\hat{f}] : \Theta \to \Omega$ is given by:

$$\mathbb{T}_i[\hat{f}](\theta) = \begin{cases} \phi & \text{if } \exists\, \theta'_i \in \Theta_i \text{ s.t. } \hat{f}(\theta'_i, \theta_{-i}) \text{ is infeasible} \\ \hat{f}_i(\theta) & \text{otherwise,} \end{cases}$$

where $\mathbb{T}_i[\hat{f}](\theta)$ denotes the item assigned to agent i by the transformed rule. The transform has no effect when $\hat{f}$ is feasible on all profiles.[1]

Theorem 1 (Hashimoto 2016). *The outcome rule $\mathbb{T}[\hat{f}]$ is feasible and strategy-proof when $\hat{f}$ is agent-independent.*

Proof. The transformation $\mathbb{T}$ will leave an agent unassigned whenever its original assignment conflicts with that of the others. Since $\mathbb{T}$ never assigns a new item to an agent, $\mathbb{T}[\hat{f}]$ is feasible. For strategy-proofness, we consider two cases. (Case 1): the feasibility check for all $\theta'_i \in \Theta_i$ passes, so that agent i's assignment from $\hat{f}$ is left unperturbed, and no misreport is useful as the agent receives its optimal item given the agent-independent prices. (Case 2): the feasibility check does not pass. But here it would not pass whatever be the report $\hat{\theta}_i$ of agent i, since the test is independent of its report. A misreport is not useful. □

The framework allows a designer to control the space of strategy-proof mechanisms searched over by choosing an appropriately expressive agent-independent rule class $\mathcal{F}$.

Example 2. *We show how the framework can be used to design a strategy-proof mechanism for a simple setting with payments. Consider two homogeneous agents $\{1, 2\}$ and two items $\{1, 2\}$. Assume there are two agent types $\Theta_1 = \Theta_2 = \{\alpha, \beta\}$, with the following valuation functions:*

$$v_1(\alpha, 1) = v_2(\alpha, 1) = 2; \quad v_1(\alpha, 2) = v_2(\alpha, 2) = 1$$
$$v_1(\beta, 1) = v_2(\beta, 1) = 1; \quad v_1(\beta, 2) = v_2(\beta, 2) = 2$$

[1]The transformation does not require an enumeration of all $\times_{i=1}^{n} |\Theta_i|$ type profiles, and performs a check only over the individual type space of a given agent, fixing the reports of the others. It can be implemented with $\sum_{i=1}^{n} |\Theta_i|$ checks.

Suppose the underlying distribution $\mathcal{D}$ over Θ is uniform, and the target rule the designer wants to approximate is:

$$g(\alpha, \alpha) = (1, 2); \quad g(\beta, \alpha) = (1, 2)$$
$$g(\alpha, \beta) = (1, 2); \quad g(\beta, \beta) = (2, 1)$$

Assume the designer provides a class $\mathcal{F}_i$ of agent-independent functions $f_i(\theta) = \text{argmax}_{o \in [m]} \{v_i(\theta_i, o) - t_i(\theta_{-i}, o)\}$, with the following two candidates for the payment function $t_i : \Theta_{-i} \times \{1, 2\} \to \mathbb{R}_+$:

τ^A:

	1	2
α	1	0
β	0	2

τ^B:

	1	2
α	1	0
β	0	1

Assume we are provided a training sample with two randomly drawn type profiles and labeled with the target outcomes: $S = \{((\alpha, \alpha), (1, 2)), ((\alpha, \beta), (1, 2))\}$. We now go over the two steps of the framework:

I: Constrained optimization over sample. *We first solve the optimization problem in (3) over the given hypothesis class. Note that an outcome rule $\hat{f}^A$ constructed using $t_1 = t_2 = \tau^A$ (with ties broken in favor of the smaller item for agent 1, and larger item for agent 2) is a solution to (3) as it is both feasible on S and yields zero error. On the first type profile (α, α), this rule gives us*

$$\hat{f}_1^A(\alpha, \alpha) = \text{argmax}_{o \in \{1,2\}} \{v_1(\alpha, o) - \tau^A(\alpha, o)\} = 1$$
$$\hat{f}_2^A(\alpha, \alpha) = \text{argmax}_{o \in \{1,2\}} \{v_2(\alpha, o) - \tau^A(\alpha, o)\} = 2$$

and on the second type profile, we get

$$\hat{f}_1^A(\alpha, \beta) = \text{argmax}_{o \in \{1,2\}} \{v_1(\alpha, o) - \tau^A(\beta, o)\} = 1$$
$$\hat{f}_2^A(\alpha, \beta) = \text{argmax}_{o \in \{1,2\}} \{v_2(\beta, o) - \tau^A(\alpha, o)\} = 2$$

II: Feasibility transformation. *The outcome rule is not necessarily feasible on a type profile outside S. For example, on the type profile (β, β), the rule outputs an infeasible allocation $(1, 1)$. As a second step, we apply the feasibility transform to enforce feasibility without violating the agent-independence property. The resulting outcome rule $\mathbb{T}[\hat{f}^A]$ can then be verified to yield the following:*

$$\mathbb{T}[\hat{f}^A](\alpha, \alpha) = (1, 2); \quad \mathbb{T}[\hat{f}^A](\alpha, \beta) = (1, \phi)$$
$$\mathbb{T}[\hat{f}^A](\beta, \alpha) = (\phi, 1); \quad \mathbb{T}[\hat{f}^A](\beta, \beta) = (\phi, \phi)$$

On the other hand, if we were provided a larger sample, say $S' = \{((\beta, \alpha), (1, 2)), ((\alpha, \beta), (1, 2)), ((\beta, \beta), (2, 1)), ((\alpha, \beta), (1, 2))\}$, then the outcome rule $\hat{f}^A$ is no longer feasible on the sample. In this case, we would instead pick $t_1 = t_2 = \tau^B$. It can be verified that the resulting rule $\hat{f}^B$ is the VCG outcome rule. This rule is feasible on all profiles, and the transform has no effect: $\mathbb{T}[\hat{f}^B] = \hat{f}^B$.

5 SAMPLE COMPLEXITY GUARANTEE

A potential concern is the extent to which the feasibility transform reduces the quality of the solution obtained by solving (3). We shall see that under an assumption on distribution $\mathcal{D}$, and with a sufficiently large sample, the transformed rule becomes arbitrarily close to the best strategy-proof approximation in $\mathcal{F}$. This holds when each $\mathcal{F}_i$ has finite capacity, as we elaborate in this section.

To have any hope of solving our original optimization problem in (1) using a finite sample, we will require the space of agent-independent functions $\mathcal{F}_i$ to have limited capacity, so that the obtained outcome rule does not overfit the sample. The specific notion of capacity we consider is the *Natarajan dimension*, commonly used while analyzing generalization performance of multi-class classifiers [12] (note that each $f_i \in \mathcal{F}_i$ can be seen as a multiclass classifier mapping type profiles to one of m items).

Definition 1 (Natarajan dimension). A set of profiles $A \subseteq \Theta$ is said to be N-shattered by $\mathcal{F}_i$ if there exists labelings $L_1, L_2 : A \rightarrow [m]$ such that $L_1(\theta) \neq L_2(\theta),\ \forall \theta \in A$, and for every subset $B \subseteq A$, there is a $f_i \in \mathcal{F}_i$ such that $f_i(\theta) = L_1(\theta),\ \forall \theta \in B$ and $f_i(\theta) = L_2(\theta),\ \forall \theta \in A \backslash B$. The Natarajan dimension of $\mathcal{F}_i$ is the size of the largest set A that is N-shattered by $\mathcal{F}_i$.

The Natarajan dimension is analogous to the *VC dimension* used in binary classification settings. In fact, for binary hypothesis classes, this quantity is the same as the VC dimension (with L_1 and L_2 being the all 1's and all 0's labelings respectively). As with the VC dimension, finiteness of the Natarajan dimension is necessary and sufficient for learnability of a multiclass hypothesis class (see for example [21]). Hence, we assume that each agent-independent class $\mathcal{F}_i$ has finite Natarajan dimension. We will further require a smoothness assumption on distribution $\mathcal{D}$:

Assumption A. Let μ be the p.m.f. associated with distribution $\mathcal{D}$. There exists $\alpha \geqslant 1$ such that for all i, $\theta_i', \theta_i \in \Theta_i,\ \theta_{-i} \in \Theta_{-i},\ \mu(\theta_i', \theta_{-i}) \leqslant \alpha\mu(\theta_i, \theta_{-i})$.

Assumption A requires that type profiles that differ only in one coordinate have similar probability masses. The value of α measures the closeness of the type distribution to a uniform distribution (with higher values indicating the distribution is father away from being uniform). For the uniform distribution we have $\alpha = 1$. Assumption A is used to enable an analysis of the effect of the feasibility transform on the outcome rule.

Each outcome rule in $\mathcal{F}$ satisfies the agent-independence condition. Let $\mathcal{F}_{\text{SP}} \subseteq \mathcal{F}$ be the subset of rules that also satisfy the feasibility condition, and are thus strategy-proof, i.e. outcome rules in $f \in \mathcal{F}$ that are feasible on all $\theta \in \Theta$. We only consider function classes that contain at least one feasible rule, i.e. for which $\mathcal{F}_{\text{SP}} \neq \phi$. Our goal is to find a rule in $\mathcal{F}_{\text{SP}}$ that best approximates target rule g.

Our approach picks a rule $\widehat{f}$ that is feasible on sample S, but need not be feasible on type profiles outside S. The transformation $\mathbb{T}$ ensures feasibility on all profiles, while ensuring strategy-proofness. We show that the transformed rule $\mathbb{T}[\widehat{f}]$ converges in the large sample limit to the best rule in $\mathcal{F}_{\text{SP}}$:

Theorem 2. *Let $\mathcal{D}$ satisfy Assumption A, and assume $\mathcal{F}_{\text{SP}} \neq \emptyset$. Let $\widehat{f}$ denote the rule obtained by solving (3) on a sample S of size N, and $\tilde{f} = \mathbb{T}[\widehat{f}]$. Then with probability at least $1-\delta$ (over draw of S from $\mathcal{D}^N$),*

$$\mathbf{E}_{\theta\sim\mathcal{D}}\big[\ell(g(\theta), \tilde{f}(\theta))\big] \leqslant \min_{f\in\mathcal{F}_{\text{SP}}} \mathbf{E}_{\theta\sim\mathcal{D}}\big[\ell(g(\theta), f(\theta))\big] + \widetilde{O}\left(\sqrt{\frac{D}{N}}\right) + \widetilde{O}\left(\frac{\alpha D}{N}\sum_{i=1}^{n}|\Theta_i|\right),$$

where D is an upper bound on the Natarajan dimension of each agent-independent function class $\mathcal{F}_i$, and $\widetilde{O}$ hides terms that are logarithmic in n, m, N, D and δ.

The first term arises from $\widehat{f}$ yielding minimum error on sample S, and decreases with increasing sample size N.

The second term captures the effect of the feasibility transformation $\mathbb{T}$, and has a linear dependence on the size of an agent's type space $|\Theta_i|$, while being exponentially smaller than the total number of type profiles $\times_{i=1}^{n}|\Theta_i|$. This term also decreases with sample size N; this is because as N increases, $\widehat{f}$ becomes feasible on a larger fraction of the population, the effect of the transformation $\mathbb{T}$ becomes smaller. Thus for a finite class capacity D, both the above terms go to 0 as $N \rightarrow \infty$, and the transformed outcome rule $\tilde{f}$ converges to the optimal rule in $\mathcal{F}_{\text{SP}}$.

The larger the class capacity D, the larger is the space of strategy-proof rules searched over. However, as seen in the above bound, this will also lead to a larger bias due to overfitting. Thus based on the size of the available sample, the designer needs to appropriately tune the capacity of the agent-independent class, so as to strike a trade-off between the size of the strategy-proof hypothesis space searched over, and the corresponding bias introduced.

5.1 PROOF

We give the proof for Theorem 2. Let $\mathcal{F}_S$ denote the subset of all agent-independent rules in $\mathcal{F}$ that are feasible on S. Recall that the outcome rule $\widehat{f} \in \mathcal{F}$ obtained by solving (3) is in $\mathcal{F}_S$, and also yields the minimum sample error over all rules in $\mathcal{F}_S$. Note that $\mathcal{F}_{\text{SP}}$ is a subset of the rules $\mathcal{F}_S$ that are feasible on all type profiles, and thus strategy-proof:

$$\boxed{\mathcal{F}_{\text{SP}} \subseteq \mathcal{F}_S \subseteq \mathcal{F}}$$

Also, note that the final transformed outcome rule $\tilde{f} = \mathbb{T}[\widehat{f}]$ is feasible on all profiles, but may not be a rule in $\mathcal{F}_{\text{SP}}$.

We show that with increasing sample size, $\tilde{f}$ converges to the rule in $\mathcal{F}_{SP}$ that best approximates the target. While we assume neither the rules $f \in \mathcal{F}$ nor the target rule g assign ϕ to an agent, the transformation $\mathbb{T}$ is allowed to cancel an item to an agent. Hence, while evaluating the designed mechanism against the target outcome rule, an assignment of ϕ to an agent will be counted as an error.

The proof is based on uniform convergence arguments commonly used in the generalization analysis of multiclass classifiers. We will make use of the fact that $\hat{f}$ is chosen from a finite capacity rule class. We first show that since $\hat{f}$ minimizes the sample error over all rules in $\mathcal{F}_S$, its expected error to the target is also close to the least possible error within $\mathcal{F}_S$, and in turn to the least error within the subset of feasible and strategy-proof rules $\mathcal{F}_{SP} \subseteq \mathcal{F}_S$. However, the final transformed rule $\tilde{f}$ may be different from $\hat{f}$, as it can cancel items assigned by $\hat{f}$. We further show that since $\hat{f}$ is feasible on sample S, it is also feasible on a large portion of the population; this together with our smoothness assumption on the distribution implies that the expected error of $\tilde{f}$ is close to that of $\hat{f}$. Thus we are able to bound the expected error of $\tilde{f}$ in terms of the minimum error within $\mathcal{F}_{SP}$, and a sample complexity term.

In particular, we analyze three quantities:

$$\begin{aligned}
\epsilon_{\text{err}} &= \mathbf{E}_{\theta\sim\mathcal{D}}\big[\ell\big(g(\theta), \hat{f}(\theta)\big)\big],\\
\epsilon_{\text{infeasible}} &= \mathbf{P}_{\theta\sim\mathcal{D}}\big(\hat{f}_i(\theta) = \hat{f}_j(\theta) \text{ for some } i, j \in [n]\big),\\
\epsilon^i_{\mathbb{T}} &= \mathbf{P}_{\theta\sim\mathcal{D}}\big(\tilde{f}_i(\theta) = \phi\big).
\end{aligned}$$

Here ϵ_{err} is the expected distance of the untransformed rule $\hat{f}$ from the target; $\epsilon_{\text{infeasible}}$ is the probability of $\hat{f}$ being infeasible on a random profile; and $\epsilon^i_{\mathbb{T}}$ is the probability that the transformation $\mathbb{T}$ cancels the item assigned to agent i.

Since the transformation $\mathbb{T}$ leaves $\hat{f}_i$ unchanged on all but a fraction $\epsilon^i_{\mathbb{T}}$ of the profiles, the distance of the final transformed outcome rule $\tilde{f}$ from the target can be bounded in terms of the error of the untransformed rule ϵ_{err}, and $\epsilon^i_{\mathbb{T}}$'s:

$$\begin{aligned}
\mathbf{E}_{\theta\sim\mathcal{D}}\big[\ell\big(g(\theta), \tilde{f}(\theta)\big)\big] &= \mathbf{E}_{\theta\sim\mathcal{D}}\Big[\frac{1}{n}\sum_{i=1}^{n}\mathbf{1}\big(\tilde{f}_i(\theta) \neq g_i(\theta)\big)\Big]\\
&= \mathbf{E}_{\theta\sim\mathcal{D}}\Big[\frac{1}{n}\sum_{i=1}^{n}\mathbf{1}\big(\tilde{f}_i(\theta) = \hat{f}_i(\theta) \neq g_i(\theta)\big)\Big]\\
&\quad + \mathbf{E}_{\theta\sim\mathcal{D}}\Big[\frac{1}{n}\sum_{i=1}^{n}\mathbf{1}\big(\tilde{f}_i(\theta) = \phi \neq g_i(\theta)\big)\Big]\\
&\leqslant \mathbf{E}_{\theta\sim\mathcal{D}}\big[\ell\big(g(\theta), \hat{f}(\theta)\big)\big] + \mathbf{E}_{\theta\sim\mathcal{D}}\Big[\frac{1}{n}\sum_{i=1}^{n}\mathbf{1}\big(\tilde{f}_i(\theta) = \phi\big)\Big]\\
&= \epsilon_{\text{err}} + \frac{1}{n}\sum_{i=1}^{n}\epsilon^i_{\mathbb{T}}. \qquad (4)
\end{aligned}$$

We bound ϵ_{err} and $\epsilon^i_{\mathbb{T}}$. For this, we will in turn require a bound on $\epsilon_{\text{infeasible}}$. We start with an outline:

- *Bounding* ϵ_{err} *(Lemma 3):* We show that the *expected* distance of this rule from the target is close to that of the optimal rule in $\mathcal{F}_{SP}$.
- *Bounding* $\epsilon_{\text{infeasible}}$ *(Lemma 4):* We show that $\hat{f}$ is feasible on a large fraction of the population.
- *Bounding* $\epsilon^i_{\mathbb{T}}$ *(Lemma 5):* We use the smoothness assumption on $\mathcal{D}$ (Assumption A) to show that the transformation $\mathbb{T}$ will have limited effect on $\hat{f}$ as long as $\hat{f}$ is feasible on a large portion of the population. In particular, we bound each $\epsilon^i_{\mathbb{T}}$ in terms of $\epsilon_{\text{infeasible}}$.

We begin by bounding ϵ_{err}. It is useful to state a generalization bound on the difference between the empirical and population errors of an outcome rule f chosen from a class of finite Natarajan dimension [21] (see Lemma 10 in Appendix A). W.p. $\geqslant 1 - \delta$ (over draw of S), $\forall f \in \mathcal{F}$,

$$\Big|\mathbf{E}_{\theta\sim\mathcal{D}}\big[\ell\big(g(\theta), f(\theta)\big)\big] - \frac{1}{N}\sum_{k=1}^{N}\ell\big(y^k, f(\theta^k)\big)\Big| \leqslant \mathcal{O}\Big(\sqrt{\frac{D\ln(m) + \ln(n/\delta)}{N}}\Big). \qquad (5)$$

We then have:

Lemma 3. *Fix $\delta > 0$. With probability at least $1 - \delta$ (over draw of S from $\mathcal{D}^N$),*

$$\epsilon_{\text{err}} \leqslant \min_{f\in\mathcal{F}_{SP}} \mathbf{E}_{\theta\sim\mathcal{D}}\big[\ell\big(g(\theta), f(\theta)\big)\big] + \mathcal{O}\Big(\sqrt{\frac{D\ln(m) + \ln(n/\delta)}{N}}\Big).$$

Proof. Denote $f^* \in \operatorname{argmin}_{f\in\mathcal{F}_{SP}} \mathbf{E}_{\theta\sim\mathcal{D}}\big[\ell\big(g(\theta), f(\theta)\big)\big]$. We wish to bound:

$$\begin{aligned}
&\mathbf{E}_{\theta\sim\mathcal{D}}\big[\ell\big(g(\theta), \hat{f}(\theta)\big)\big] - \min_{f\in\mathcal{F}_{SP}} \mathbf{E}_{\theta\sim\mathcal{D}}\big[\ell\big(g(\theta), f(\theta)\big)\big]\\
&= \mathbf{E}_{\theta\sim\mathcal{D}}\big[\ell\big(g(\theta), \hat{f}(\theta)\big)\big] - \frac{1}{N}\sum_{k=1}^{N}\ell\big(y^k, \hat{f}(\theta^k)\big)\\
&\quad + \frac{1}{N}\sum_{k=1}^{N}\ell\big(y^k, \hat{f}(\theta^k)\big) - \mathbf{E}_{\theta\sim\mathcal{D}}\big[\ell\big(g(\theta), f^*(\theta)\big)\big]\\
&\leqslant \mathbf{E}_{\theta\sim\mathcal{D}}\big[\ell\big(g(\theta), \hat{f}(\theta)\big)\big] - \frac{1}{N}\sum_{k=1}^{N}\ell\big(y^k, \hat{f}(\theta^k)\big)\\
&\quad + \frac{1}{N}\sum_{k=1}^{N}\ell\big(y^k, f^*(\theta^k)\big) - \mathbf{E}_{\theta\sim\mathcal{D}}\big[\ell\big(g(\theta), f^*(\theta)\big)\big]\\
&\leqslant 2\sup_{f\in\mathcal{F}}\Big|\mathbf{E}_{\theta\sim\mathcal{D}}\big[\ell\big(g(\theta), f(\theta)\big)\big] - \frac{1}{N}\sum_{k=1}^{N}\ell\big(y^k, f(\theta^k)\big)\Big|,
\end{aligned}$$

where the second step uses the fact that $\hat{f}$ has minimum empirical error on S over all $\mathcal{F}_S \supseteq \mathcal{F}_{SP}$ and hence a lesser or equal empirical error compared to $f^* \in \mathcal{F}_{SP}$; the last step uses the fact that both $\hat{f}, f^* \in \mathcal{F}$. The generalization bound in (5) then gives the desired result. □

We next focus on bounding $\epsilon_{\text{infeasible}}$.

Lemma 4. *Assume $\mathcal{F}_{\text{SP}} \neq \emptyset$. Fix $\delta > 0$. Then w.p. at least $1-\delta$ (over draw of S from $\mathcal{D}^N$),*

$$\epsilon_{\text{infeasible}} \leqslant \mathcal{O}\left(\frac{nD\ln(mnD)\ln(N)+\ln(1/\delta)}{N}\right).$$

Proof. (Sketch) We provide the full proof in Appendix B.1. For any $f:\Theta\to\Omega$, define a binary function $G_f:\Theta\to\{0,1\}$ as $G_f(\theta)=\mathbf{1}(f_1(\theta)\neq\ldots\neq f_n(\theta))$. Clearly, f is feasible iff G_f evaluates to 1 on all type profiles. Since $\mathcal{F}_{\text{SP}}\neq\phi$, there always exists a f in $\mathcal{F}$ which is feasible, and hence there always exists a G_f which outputs 1 on all profiles. Treating G_f as a binary classifier, one can now appeal to standard VC dimension based learnability results for classification [22], with the loss function being the 0-1 loss against the all 1's labeling. The VC dimension of the class of all functions $\{G_f:\Theta\to\{0,1\}\ :\ f\in\mathcal{F}\}$ can be shown to be at most $\mathcal{O}(nD\ln(nmD))$. Then w.p. $\geqslant 1-\delta$,

$$\begin{aligned}\epsilon_{\text{infeasible}} &= \mathbf{E}_{\theta\sim\mathcal{D}}\left[\mathbf{1}(G_{\hat{f}}(\theta)\neq 1)\right)\\ &\leqslant \mathcal{O}\left(\frac{nD\ln(nmD)\ln(N)+\ln(1/\delta)}{N}\right),\end{aligned}$$

which implies the statement of the lemma. □

We finally bound $\epsilon^i_{\mathbb{T}}$ in terms $\epsilon_{\text{infeasible}}$.

Lemma 5. *Under Assumption A, $\epsilon^i_{\mathbb{T}} \leqslant \alpha|\Theta_i|\epsilon_{\text{infeasible}}$.*

Proof. Let us use μ to denote the p.m.f. associated with distribution $\mathcal{D}$. Also, let $\Theta_{\text{infeasible}}\subseteq\Theta$ denote the subset of type profiles on which $\widehat{f}$ is infeasible, i.e. type profiles $\theta\in\Theta$ for which $\widehat{f}_i(\theta)=\widehat{f}_j(\theta)$ for some i and j. Clearly, $\epsilon_{\text{infeasible}}=\sum_{\theta\in\Theta_{\text{infeasible}}}\mu(\theta)$. Further, note that the set of type profiles on which the transformation $\mathbb{T}$ makes a null allocation to agent i is precisely the set of type profiles that are one hop away (i.e. differ in agent i's type) from those in $\Theta_{\text{infeasible}}$. Therefore,

$$\begin{aligned}\epsilon^i_{\mathbb{T}} &= \sum_{\theta\in\Theta}\mu(\theta)\mathbf{1}(\bar{f}_i(\theta)=\phi) = \sum_{\theta\in\Theta_{\text{infeasible}}}\sum_{\theta'_i\in\Theta_i}\mu(\theta'_i,\theta_{-i})\\ &\leqslant \sum_{\theta\in\Theta_{\text{infeasible}}}\sum_{\theta'_i\in\Theta_i}\alpha\mu(\theta) = \alpha\sum_{\theta'_i\in\Theta_i}\sum_{\theta\in\Theta_{\text{infeasible}}}\mu(\theta)\\ &= \alpha|\Theta_i|\epsilon_{\text{infeasible}},\end{aligned}$$

where the inequality follows from Assumption A. □

Combining Lemmas 4-5 with (4) gives us w.p. at least $1-\delta$ (over draw of S):

$$\begin{aligned}\mathbf{E}_{\theta\sim\mathcal{D}}\left[\ell(g(\theta),\tilde{f}(\theta))\right] &\leqslant \min_{f\in\mathcal{F}_{\text{SP}}}\mathbf{E}_{\theta\sim\mathcal{D}}\left[\ell(g(\theta),f(\theta))\right]\\ &+\mathcal{O}\left(\sqrt{\frac{D\ln(m)+\ln(n/\delta)}{N}}\right)\\ &+\mathcal{O}\left(\frac{\alpha}{n}\sum_{i=1}^{n}|\Theta_i|\frac{nD\ln(nmD)\ln(N)+\ln(1/\delta)}{N}\right).\end{aligned}$$

This completes the proof of Theorem 2.

6 APPLICATIONS

We provide instantiations of the framework to assignment problems with and without money. In each case, we construct examples of agent-independent function classes $\mathcal{F}_i$ that have finite Natarajan dimension. We also show that these function classes can be used to model feasible outcome rules, which together with the agent-independence property are guaranteed to be strategy-proof.

6.1 ASSIGNMENT PROBLEM WITH MONEY

As noted in Section 3, a strategy-proof outcome rule in this setting is necessarily of the following form for an agent-independent price rule $t_i:\Theta_{-i}\to\mathbb{R}_+$.

$$f_i(\theta)\in\underset{o\in[m]}{\text{argmax}}\left\{v_i(\theta_i,o)\ -\ t_i(\theta_{-i},o)\right\}.$$

One way to construct an agent-independent function class for this setting is by modeling the above price rule t_i as a linear function in a suitable feature space, i.e. as $t^{\mathbf{w}}_i(\theta_{-i},o)=\mathbf{w}_i^\top\Psi_i(\theta_{-i},o)$ for some model vector $\mathbf{w}_i\in\mathbb{R}^d$ and feature map $\Psi_i:\Theta_{-i}\times[m]\to\mathbb{R}^d$. Let $\bar{\mathcal{F}}^{\Psi}_i$ be the corresponding class of agent-independent functions obtained for different model vectors $\mathbf{w}_i$. This class resembles the class of linear discriminant classifiers, which is known to have a finite Natarajan dimension [21]:

Theorem 6. *The Natarajan dimension of $\bar{\mathcal{F}}^{\Psi}_i$ is at most $\mathcal{O}(d\ln(d))$.*

Note that one can fine-tune the capacity of this class by adjusting the number of features d used. Below, we show that the function class admits feasible and strategy-proof outcome rules for an appropriate choice of feature map.

Example feature map. We describe a feature map with two parts, inspired by the VCG price function seen in Example 1. For an agent i and item o, the first part contains the valuations for all agents other than i:

$$\Psi^1_i(\theta_{-i},o) = [v_j(\theta_j,o')]^m_{o'=1}]_{j\neq i}\in\mathbb{R}^{(n-1)\times m}_+.$$

The second part of the feature map contains the valuations for the other agents when they receive the *welfare-maximizing* assignment from items other than o:

$$\Psi^2_i(\theta_{-i},o) = [v_j(\theta_j,y^{\backslash i,o}_j)]_{j\neq i}\in\mathbb{R}^{n-1}_+,$$

where $y^{\backslash i,o}\in\text{argmax}_{y\in\Omega,\,y_i=o}\sum_{j\neq i}v_j(\theta_j,y_j)$.

The feature map $\bar{\Psi}_i(\theta_{-i},o) = [\Psi^1_i(\theta_{-i},o),\Psi^2_i(\theta_{-i},o)]$ then allows us to construct feasible outcome rules.

Theorem 7. *There exists $\mathbf{w}_i\in\mathbb{R}^{(n-1)(m+1)}$ s.t. the prices $t^{\mathbf{w}}_i(\theta_{-i},o)=\mathbf{w}_i^\top\bar{\Psi}_i(\theta_{-i},o)$ are non-negative and yield a feasible outcome rule for a suitable tie-breaking scheme.*

The specific model vector we consider is

$$\mathbf{w}_i = [\underbrace{1, 1, \ldots, 1}_{(n-1)\times m}, \underbrace{-1, -1, \ldots, -1}_{n-1}].$$

The first part of the model vector ensures that the payments are non-negative, while the second part leads to a *VCG-style* welfare maximizing outcome rule. The proof details are provided in Appendix B.2.

6.2 ASSIGNMENT PROBLEM WITHOUT MONEY

In this setting, a strategy-proof outcome rule satisfied the following for some agent-independent virtual price functions $t_i^{\text{vir}} : \Theta_{-i} \times [m] \rightarrow \mathbb{R}_+$: $t_i^{\text{vir}}(\theta_{-i}, f_i(\theta)) \leqslant 1$ and

$$f_i(\theta) \succeq_i o, \forall o \in \{o' \in [m] : t_i^{\text{vir}}(\theta_{-i}, o') \leqslant 1\}.$$

As before, to construct an agent-independent function class, we can model the virtual price function t_i^{vir} as a linear function $t_i^{\text{vir},\mathbf{w}}(\theta_{-i}, o) = \mathbf{w}_i^\top \Psi_i(\theta_{-i}, o)$ for some model vector $\mathbf{w}_i \in \mathbb{R}^d$ and feature map $\Psi_i : \Theta_{-i} \times [m] \rightarrow \mathbb{R}^d$. Let $\widetilde{\mathcal{F}}_i^\Psi$ be the corresponding class of agent-independent functions obtained for different model vectors $\mathbf{w}_i$.

Unlike the setting with money, here the payment functions do not directly resemble standard classification constructs. Below, we derive a bound on the Natarajan dimension of the proposed function class (see Appendix B.3 for proof).

Theorem 8. *The Natarajan dimension of $\widetilde{\mathcal{F}}_i^\Psi$ is at most $\mathcal{O}((md)\ln(md))$.*

Thus the capacity of the function class is finite and can be tuned by varying the number of features used. Also, this class includes feasible and strategy-proof outcome rules for an appropriate choice of the feature map.

Example feature map. Define for agent i, a function $\text{rank}_i : \Theta_i \times [m] \rightarrow [m]$ that maps a type θ_i and item o to the number of items that the agent prefers less than o: $\text{rank}(\theta_i, o) = \sum_{o'=1}^m \mathbf{1}(o \succ_i o')$ (note higher ranks imply greater preference to item o). For an agent i and item o, the prescribed feature map is then a $n \times m$ binary encoding of the ranks assigned by agents other than i to item o:

$$\widetilde{\Psi}_i(\theta_{-i}, o)[j, k] = \begin{cases} \mathbf{1}(\text{rank}_j(\theta_j, o) = k) & \text{if } j \neq i \\ 0 & \text{otherwise} \end{cases},$$

where we use $[j, k]$ to denote the index $(j-1)m + k$.

Theorem 9. *There exists $\mathbf{w}_i \in \mathbb{R}^{n\times m}$ such that the virtual price functions $t_i^{\text{vir},\mathbf{w}}(\theta_{-i}, o) = \mathbf{w}_i^\top \widetilde{\Psi}_i(\theta_{-i}, o)$ yield a feasible outcome rule.*

In particular, a *serial dictatorship (SD) style* feasible, and strategy-proof outcome rule is within this class. Fix a priority $\pi : [n] \rightarrow [n]$ over the agents, where $\pi(i)$ denotes the priority to agent i (with 1 indicating the lowest priority, and n indicating the highest). The following vector $\mathbf{w}_i \in \mathbb{R}^{n\times m}$ then yields a SD style rule with priority ordering π: for any $j \in [n], k \in [m]$,

$$w_i[j, k] = \begin{cases} 2 & \pi(j) > \pi(i),\ k \geqslant m - n + \pi(j) \\ 0 & \text{otherwise} \end{cases}.$$

The proof of feasibility is provided in Appendix B.4.

7 CONCLUSION AND OPEN QUESTIONS

We have developed a general statistical framework for designing strategy-proof mechanisms that closely approximate a given target outcome rule. Our approach does not require domain-specific characterizations, and only requires the designer to provide a class of rules that satisfy a simple agent-independent condition. By tuning the capacity of this class, one can control the space of strategy-proof mechanisms optimized over. We have provided sample complexity bounds for our method and instantiated applications to assignment problems with and without money.

There are several questions that arise from our work:

- The optimization problem (3) can be formulated and solved as a mixed integer linear program. But, how can one solve this problem efficiently in practice? For the setting with money, the problem can be solved approximately by adopting *convex relaxations* from machine learning (see [14]). It will be interesting to understand the effectiveness of these relaxations as well as to identify similar relaxations for the setting without money.

- How can the framework be extended to *infinite type spaces*, and how can the feasibility transformation be implemented efficiently in such a setting?

- How can the framework be extended to *instance-dependent* distance functions, and applied to specific design objectives such as welfare or revenue?

- The sample complexity result requires that the agent-independent function classes have finite capacity. Can we use an approach similar to structural risk minimization to incorporate a *universal hypothesis class* in the framework, and thus cover the entire space of strategy-proof mechanisms?

Acknowledgments. The authors acknowledge the anonymous reviewers for their comments. The authors thank Shivani Agarwal for helpful discussions. HN thanks Harish G. Ramaswamy for a helpful discussion.

References

[1] M.O. Jackson. Mechanism theory. In U. Derigs, editor, *Optimization and Operations Research*. EOLSS Publishers, 2003.

[2] J.C. Rochet. A necessary and sufficient condition for rationalizability in a quasilinear context. *J. Math. Econ.*, 16:191–200, 1987.

[3] R. Lavi and C. Swamy. Truthful mechanism design for multidimensional scheduling via cyclic monotonicity. *Games and Economic Behavior*, 67:99–124, 2009.

[4] J. Schummer and R.V. Vohra. Mechanism design without money. In N. Nisan, T. Roughgarden, E. Tardos, and V. V. Vazirani, editors, *Algorithmic Game Theory*, chapter 10. Cambridge University Press, 2007.

[5] V. Conitzer and T. Sandholm. Complexity of mechanism design. In *UAI*, 2002.

[6] V. Conitzer and T. Sandholm. An algorithm for automatically designing deterministic mechanisms without payments. In *AAMAS*, 2004.

[7] M. Guo and V. Conitzer. Computationally feasible automated mechanism design: General approach and case studies. In *AAAI*, 2010.

[8] X. Sui, C. Boutilier, and T. Sandholm. Analysis and optimization of multi-dimensional percentile mechanisms. In *IJCAI*, 2013.

[9] Y. Cai, C. Daskalakis, and S.M. Weinberg. Optimal multi-dimensional mechanism design: Reducing revenue to welfare maximization. In *FOCS*, 2012.

[10] S. Alaei, H. Fu, N. Haghpanah, J.D. Hartline, and A. Malekian. Bayesian optimal auctions via multi- to single-agent reduction. In *EC*, 2012.

[11] T. Hashimoto. The generalized random priority mechanism with budgets. Technical report, Yeshiva University, 2016.

[12] B. K. Natarajan. On learning sets and functions. *Maching Learning*, 4(1), 1989.

[13] A.D. Procaccia, A. Zohar, Y. Peleg, and J.S. Rosenschein. The learnability of voting rules. *Artificial Intelligence*, 173:1133–1149, 2009.

[14] P. Dütting, F.A. Fischer, P. Jirapinyo, J.K. Lai, B. Lubin, and D.C. Parkes. Payment rules through discriminant-based classifiers. *ACM Trans. Economics and Comput.*, 3(1):5, 2015.

[15] H. Narasimhan and D.C. Parkes. Automated mechanism design without money via machine learning. In *IJCAI*, 2016.

[16] M.-F. Balcan, A. Blum, J.D. Hartline, and Y. Mansour. Mechanism design via machine learning. In *FOCS*, 2005.

[17] M. Mohri and A.M. Medina. Learning theory and algorithms for revenue optimization in second price auctions with reserve. In *ICML*, 2014.

[18] R. Cole and T. Roughgarden. The sample complexity of revenue maximization. In *STOC*, pages 243–252, 2014.

[19] J.H. Morgenstern and T. Roughgarden. On the pseudo-dimension of nearly optimal auctions. In *NIPS*, 2015.

[20] N. Nisan. Introduction to Mechanism Design. In N. Nisan, T. Roughgarden, É. Tardos, and V.V. Vazirani, editors, *Algorithmic Game Theory*, pages 209–241. Cambridge University Press, 2007.

[21] A. Daniely, S. Sabato, S. Ben-David, and S. Shalev-Shwartz. Multiclass learnability and the erm principle. In *COLT*, 2011.

[22] M. Anthony and P.L. Bartlett. *Neural network learning: Theoretical foundations*. Cambridge University Press, 1999.

A Correlated Worker Model for Grouped, Imbalanced and Multitask Data

An T. Nguyen
Department of Computer Science
University of Texas at Austin
atn@cs.utexas.edu

Byron C. Wallace
School of Information
University of Texas at Austin
byron.wallace@utexas.edu

Matthew Lease
School of Information
University of Texas at Austin
ml@utexas.edu

Abstract

We consider the important crowdsourcing problem of estimating worker *confusion matrices*, or sensitivities and specificities for binary classification tasks. In addition to providing diagnostic insights into worker performance, such estimates enable robust online task routing for classification tasks exhibiting imbalance and asymmetric costs. However, labeled data is often expensive and hence estimates must be made without much of it. This poses a challenge to existing methods. In this paper, we propose a novel model that captures the correlations between entries in confusion matrices. We applied this model in two practical scenarios: (1) an imbalanced classification task in which workers are known to belong to groups and (2) a *multitask* scenario in which labels for the same workers are available in more than one labeling task. We derive an efficient variational inference approach that scales to large datasets. Experiments on two real world citizen science datasets (biomedical citation screening and galaxy morphological classification) demonstrate consistent improvement over competitive baselines. We have made our source code available.

1 INTRODUCTION

Crowdsourcing is a popular approach to collecting annotations at comparatively low cost. However, crowdsourcing annotation work necessitates taking care to evaluate worker annotation quality, as this will likely be lower than that of a domain expert. The standard means of addressing this is to collect multiple labels for each item and then use an aggregation method to derive a consensus label. The simplest such method is majority voting, which selects the majority label for each item. More complex methods exist; see (Sheshadri and Lease, 2013) for a review.

Many crowd consensus methods posit some model of worker qualities, e.g., a worker's overall accuracy. However, the problem of modeling workers has typically been considered a secondary issue, with the primary concern being label aggregation. Here we argue that the problems of aggregating labels and of modeling workers are distinct (though related). A good method for aggregating labels will not necessarily provide reliable estimates of worker qualities. For example, majority voting assumes that workers are equally good; this assumption is almost certainly usually wrong, but nonetheless can yield high quality aggregated labels when workers do not make correlated errors. Consider, e.g., a scenario in which each item has been labeled by three workers, two of whom are always correct and one of whom is always wrong. Here, majority voting would provide perfect label aggregation, but plainly the workers are not equally good.

The simplest way to model worker skill is with the univariate metric of overall accuracy. This may be appropriate when classes are balanced and/or when false negatives and false positives are equally expensive. However, in most real-world tasks, we would prefer a more granular model of accuracies. The standard way is to model the worker confusion matrices, whose entries are the probabilities of a worker providing each possible label j, conditioned on the true label i: $A_{ij} = Pr(\text{Response} = j|\text{TrueLabel} = i)$. This class conditional approach posits two parameters for each worker, affording the flexibility to accurately capture worker performance. The caveat is that more data is needed to estimate more parameters.

For example, when the majority of items belong to the negative class, very few positive items will be available to reliably estimate the probabilities of responses given that the true label is positive, i.e. A_{01} and A_{11}. Explicitly modeling correlations between sensitivity and specificity is one potential means of improving estimates in this case: Workers who perform well on negative items are likely to also correctly classify positive ones. Another scenario in which this general approach may help is when data from multiple labeling tasks is available, for example if many workers who performed a text classification task come back to work on a new image classification task. In such scenarios, we might expect a worker who does well on one task to also be likely to do so on the other.

Specific contributions of this work are as follows.

- Taking inspiration from previous work in modeling medical diagnostic test (Dahabreh et al., 2012; Reitsma et al., 2005), we propose modeling the correlation between worker sensitivity and specificity. A natural property of our model is the assumption that workers belong to one or more groups, each with its own mean sensitivity and specificity. Intuitively, these means allow us 'back-off' to group-level quality estimates when data from a specific worker is sparse.
- We extend our idea to model the correlations of the workers across multiple labeling tasks. This allows us to *transfer knowledge of worker quality from a task with more data to one with less.*
- We introduce an efficient variational method to scale parameter estimation to handle large data.

We are unaware of any previous work on using correlations to improve estimates of worker confusion matrices nor a generative model of worker performance in multiple tasks.

2 RELATED WORK

Dawid and Skene (1979) presented the classic crowd consensus model in which each item corresponds to a hidden 'true label' variable and each worker is modeled by a confusion matrix of class-conditional label probabilities. Raykar et al. (2010); Kim and Ghahramani (2012); Liu and Wang (2012) all presented Bayesian extensions, placing priors on the worker confusion matrices. Unique amongst this prior work, Liu and Wang (2012) emphasized getting good estimates of the confusion matrices to gain diagnostic insights into worker performance, while the other two focus on recovering the true labels and building a good classifier. Recently, Lakkaraju et al. (2015) further extended the model by clustering workers and items based on their features. Although very effective compared to Liu and Wang (2012)'s Hybrid Confusion approach, demographic features such as worker age, education or job are not always available, e.g., on Amazon Mechanical Turk.

The idea of detecting latent groups and communities of similar workers has been studied previously (Simpson et al., 2013), and incorporated into a generative model to improve the aggregated labels (Venanzi et al., 2014). By contrast, here we consider exploiting *known* worker groups, when such information is available, to improve our confusion matrix estimates.

While modeling individual confusion matrices is the most common approach to annotator modeling, recent work has also explored other strategies. Kajino et al. (2012)'s multitask formulation views each worker as a learning task. Bi et al. (2014) models each worker as a classifier, whose parameters deviate from the true parameters. While these methods have been shown to outperform the 'Two Coin' model (Raykar et al., 2010) for the task of label aggregation, they unfortunately do not provide direct estimates of worker sensitivity and specificity.

In terms of inference and learning algorithms, Dawid and Skene (1979) and Raykar et al. (2010) both used the Expectation-Maximization (EM) algorithm (Dempster et al., 1977) while Liu and Wang (2012) used Gibbs sampling. Variational inference has also been applied and shown to perform well for crowdsourcing models (Liu et al., 2012).

3 METHODS

We now present the details of our probabilistic graphical model, including details of representation, inference and learning (Koller and Friedman, 2009). We first define a joint probability model over all observed and hidden variables of interest, conditioned on the parameters. In Section 3.2, we present our inference method, which involves an efficient variational algorithm. This estimates the distribution over the hidden variables, assuming the parameters are known. In Section 3.3, we present an EM approach to learn the parameters from data. Finally, we extend our approach to the multitask setting in section 3.4.

3.1 MODEL

We assume that each worker has a latent sensitivity and specificity, and that these two quantities are correlated. This assumption has similarly been made in medicine for estimating diagnostic test performance (Dahabreh et al., 2012). Following this work, we explicitly model the correlation between sensitivity and the false positive rate (FPR) (=1$-$ specificity).

Let Z_i be the (potentially unobserved) true label for instance i and L_{ij} be the label provided for i by worker j. We then model worker j using two hidden variables, U_j and V_j, these capture transformations of worker sensitivity and FPR, and are assumed to be drawn from a bivariate normal with a covariance matrix to be estimated.

More precisely, the generative process is as follows:

$$U_j, V_j \sim \mathcal{N}(\mu, C) \quad (1)$$

$$Z_i \sim \mathrm{Ber}(\theta) \quad (2)$$

$$L_{ij}|Z_i = 1 \sim \mathrm{Ber}(\mathcal{S}(U_j)) \quad (3)$$

$$L_{ij}|Z_i = 0 \sim \mathrm{Ber}(\mathcal{S}(V_j)) \quad (4)$$

$\mathrm{Ber}(p)$ is the Bernoulli distribution with parameter p encoding the probability of the variable taking the value 1. $\mathcal{N}(\mu, C)$ is the bivariate Normal distribution with mean vector μ and covariance C: the correlation between U and V is thus modeled by the off-diagonal entries in C (C is symmetric; the two off-diagonal entries are equal). $\mathcal{S}$ is the Sigmoid function: $\mathcal{S}(x) = 1/(1 + \exp(-x))$, which maps real numbers to the interval $[0, 1]$. U_j and V_j are thus the logit-transformed sensitivities and FPRs of workers (the logit function is the inverse of the sigmoid fuction).

Note that μ and C are group-level parameters, capturing expected sensitivity and FPRs across all workers. Thus ours may be viewed as a 'fixed effects' model (Hedges, 1994) of worker quality, as we assume individual worker parameters are drawn from a shared parent distribution. This is in contrast to much of the previous work on this task, which has often modeled individuals independently (although there have been exceptions to this, e.g., Liu and Wang (2012)). In one scenario we assume that workers belong to distinct groups: experienced workers and novices. We also assume that we know *a priori* to which groups workers belong. In this case we fit separate models for each group, deriving corresponding distinct estimates for mean sensitivities and FPRs (and covariances).

Taking a Bayesian view, one may place priors on the shared variables μ, C and θ. However this increases model complexity and introduces the need to specify appropriate priors. Intuitively, these parameters are informed by all or most of the items in the dataset, and we should therefore have considerably less uncertainty around our estimates of them, compared to the hidden variables Z, U and V (which are informed by one or a small number of items).

Putting the components together, the unnormalized joint posterior of our model has the form:

$$P(U_{1..m}, V_{1..m}, Z_{1..n}, L) = \prod_{j=1}^{m} \mathcal{N}(U_j, V_j|\mu, C)$$
$$\prod_{i=1}^{n} \mathrm{Ber}(Z_i|\theta) \prod_{Z_i=1} \mathrm{Ber}(L_{ij}|\mathcal{S}(U_i)) \prod_{Z_i=0} \mathrm{Ber}(L_{ij}|\mathcal{S}(V_i)) \tag{5}$$

Where we are denoting the number of workers by m and the number of items by n.

3.2 INFERENCE

We aim to recover the posterior distribution of all of the hidden variables given worker labels: $p(U_{1..m}, V_{1..m}, Z_{1..n}|L)$. Unfortunately, evaluating this analytically is intractable. One possibility is instead to perform approximate inference via sampling methods such as Markov chain Monte Carlo (MCMC). However, practical implementations of MCMC, such as BUGS

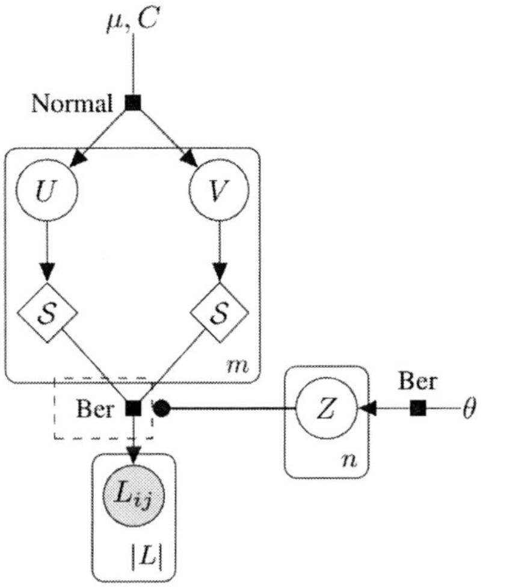

Figure 1: The Factor Graph of our model. Circles represent random variables (shaded variables are observed), squares depict factors, diamonds are deterministic mappings, edge endpoints (μ, C, θ) are parameters, plates denote repetitions, dotted plates are gates (in this case, the value of Z is used to select which one of the two $S(U)$ and $S(V)$ is used as the parameter for the Bernoulli distribution.

(Spiegelhalter et al., 1995) and PyMC (Patil et al., 2010), do not scale to large datasets, rendering this approach infeasible for our application.

We therefore propose a novel variational inference algorithm for the model specified above. Variational approaches (Wainwright and Jordan, 2008) aim to approximate the true posterior p via a simpler distribution over the same variables: $q(u_{1..m}, v_{1..m}, Z_{1..n})$. The idea is to make q 'close' to p by minimizing the Kullback-Leibler (KL) divergence between the two, i.e., $\mathbb{KL}(q||p)$. By minimizing this divergence, we are maximizing a lower bound on the data log likelihood.

A typical strategy in variational inference is to make the *mean field* assumption, i.e., assume that q neatly factorizes:

$$q(U_{1..m}, V_{1..m}, Z_{1..n}) = \prod_{j=1}^{m} q(U_j)q(V_j) \prod_{i=1}^{n} q(Z_i) \tag{6}$$

where each distribution q on the right hand side is over one hidden variable (disambiguated by the argument), and has the form:

$$q(U_j) = \mathcal{N}(\tilde{\mu}_{uj}, \tilde{\sigma}^2_{uj}) \tag{7}$$
$$q(V_j) = \mathcal{N}(\tilde{\mu}_{vj}, \tilde{\sigma}^2_{vj}) \tag{8}$$
$$q(Z_i) = \mathrm{Ber}(\tilde{\theta}_i) \tag{9}$$

Here $\{\tilde{\mu}_{uj}, \tilde{\sigma}^2_{uj}, \tilde{\mu}_{vj}, \tilde{\sigma}^2_{vj}|j = 1...m\}$ and $\{\tilde{\theta}_i|i = 1...n\}$ are the variational parameters that should be selected to minimize $\mathbb{KL}(q||p)$. This optimization problem can be solved via coordinate descent by updating each factor distribution while keeping all others fixed. The general mean field update for a vector X of hidden variables has the form:

$$q^*(X_i) \propto \exp\{\mathbb{E}_{-q_i} \log P(X)\} \qquad (10)$$

$P(X)$ is the unnormalized posterior (here, Equation 5) and E_{-q_i} is the expectation with respect to all variables except X_i. By this equation, we can update $q(X_i)$ by making changes to its variational parameters. The equation updates our estimate over a variable based on the current belief over its neighbors (terms involving other variables are absorbed into the constant). Adapting this general form to our model, we can derive the following update equations:

$$q^*(Z_i = 1) \propto \exp\Big\{ \log \mathrm{Ber}(1|\theta) + \sum \mathbb{E}_{U_j \sim q(U_j)} \log \mathrm{Ber}(L_{ij}|\mathcal{S}(U_j))\Big\} \qquad (11)$$

$$q^*(Z_i = 0) \propto \exp\Big\{ \log \mathrm{Ber}(0|\theta) + \sum \mathbb{E}_{V_j \sim q(V_j)} \log \mathrm{Ber}(L_{ij}|\mathcal{S}(V_j))\Big\} \qquad (12)$$

$$q^*(U_j) \propto \exp\Big\{\mathbb{E}_{V_j \sim q(V_j)} \log \mathcal{N}(U_j, V_j|\mu, C) + \sum q(Z_i = 1) \log \mathrm{Ber}(L_{ij}|\mathcal{S}(U_j))\Big\} \qquad (13)$$

$$q^*(V_j) \propto \exp\Big\{\mathbb{E}_{U_j \sim q(U_j)} \log \mathcal{N}(U_j, V_j|\mu, C) + \sum q(Z_i = 0) \log \mathrm{Ber}(L_{ij}|\mathcal{S}(V_j))\Big\} \qquad (14)$$

We have elided indices in summations above for brevity. The sums in Equations 11 and 12 are over all of the workers that have provided labels for item i. The sums in Equation 13 and 14 are over all of the items that worker j has labeled. Recall that in Inference, the parameters μ, C and θ are assumed to be known.

Intuitively, Equations 11 and 12 consider item i and update our approximation of the posterior over Z_i by taking into account the prior θ and evidence from all of the worker labels provided for the item. Equation 13 concerns the (logit-transformed) sensitivity estimate for worker j, taking into account the bivariate Normal and the current approximation over the logit-transformed FPR V_j. The approximation is further updated using all of the items worker j has labeled, with respect to the current approximation over the true label Z_i of each. Equation 14 can be interpreted similarly, although here we consider the logit-transformed FPR estimate for worker j.

Although the update equations are available, evaluating them is difficult due to the model being non-conjugate. We thus applied Laplace Variational Inference (Wang and Blei, 2013), to directly approximate these equations. We first let $T_j = \begin{pmatrix} U_j \\ V_j \end{pmatrix}$ to treat U_j and V_j as a single variable and let $f(T_j)$ be the exponent in their update equation:

$$f(T_j) = \log \mathcal{N}(T_j|\mu, C) + \sum q(Z_i = 1) \log \mathrm{Ber}(L_{ij}|\mathcal{S}(U_j)) + \sum q(Z_i = 0) \log \mathrm{Ber}(L_{ij}|\mathcal{S}(V_j)) \qquad (15)$$

By using a Laplace approximation on f, we can derive the approximate update for U_j and V_j:

$$q^*(T_j) \propto \exp(f(T_j)) \approx \mathcal{N}\left(\widehat{T}_j, \nabla^2 f(\widehat{T}_j)^{-1}\right) \qquad (16)$$

where $\widehat{T}_j$ is the maximum of $f(T_j)$, can be found by numerical optimization, and the Hessian matrix $\nabla^2 f(T_j)$ can be derived analytically by using the result:

$$\nabla^2 \log \mathcal{N}(T|\mu, C) = C^{-1}(T - \mu)(T - \mu)^T C^{-1} - C^{-1} \qquad (17)$$

For the variable Z_i, the expectations in their update equations (11 and 12) can also be approximated similarly, for example, let $g(u) = \log \mathcal{S}(u)$, we have

$$\mathbb{E}_{u \sim \mathcal{N}(\mu, \sigma)} g(u) \approx g(\mu) + \frac{1}{2} g''(\mu)\sigma \qquad (18)$$

Again, the second derivative g'' can be derived analytically:

$$g''(u) = -e^u/(1 + e^u)^2 \qquad (19)$$

The inference procedure initializes the variational distribution q at some value and then applies the update equations iteratively until convergence. In our implementation, we iterate until the average changes in the variational parameters is less than 0.01. To initialize the means of $q(U_j)$, $q(V_j)$ and $q(Z)$, we use majority voting. To initialize the variance of $q(U_j)$ and $q(V_j)$, we make use the Beta distribution. For example, suppose majority voting predicts that worker j has provided a True Positives and b False Negatives so that his sensitivity can be estimated as $a/(a + b)$. We initialize the variance $\tilde{\sigma}_{uj}$ of the logit-transformed sensitivity U_j as the logit-tranformed variance of $\mathrm{Beta}(a, b)$, which intuitively gives a smaller variance for workers who have provided more labels.

3.3 LEARNING

We consider μ, C and θ as parameters to be learned from data. The learning algorithm is a simple application of EM. In the E step, we perform variational inference to estimate the posterior over the hidden variable, given all of the the workers' labels. In the M step, we maximize the parameters μ, C and θ under that posterior distribution. For the

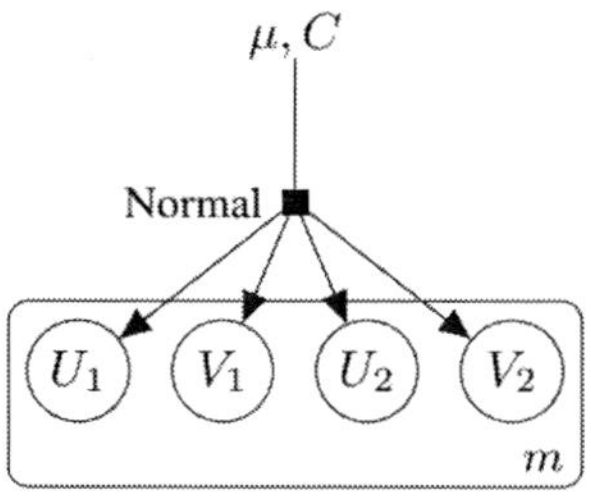

Figure 2: The Factor Graph highlights the extension to two tasks from the single task model in **Figure 1**.

parameters μ and C, the expected sufficient statistics (with respect to the variational distribution) can be evaluated:

$$\mathbb{E}(U_j) = \tilde{\mu}_j \tag{20}$$

$$\mathbb{E}(U_J^2) = \tilde{\mu}_{uj}^2 + \tilde{\sigma}_{uj}^2 \tag{21}$$

$$\mathbb{E}(U_J V_J) = \tilde{\mu}_{uj}\tilde{\mu}_{vj} \tag{22}$$

and then plugged into an estimator of multivariate Normal mean and covariance. For θ, it is simply set to the expected proportion of positive items, which is the average of $\{\tilde{\theta}_i | i = 1...n\}$.

3.4 MULTITASK MODEL

In addition to exploiting correlations between worker sensitivities and FPRs, our model can easily accommodate other sorts of worker performance correlations. For example, in this section we show that the same model can be adopted to capitalize on correlated performances across related labeling tasks. Specifically, we assume that workers have different sensitivities and FPRs in different tasks but that these values are correlated across tasks. Let U_1, V_1, U_2, V_2 be the logit-transformed sensitivities and FPRs in the first and second task. These are assumed to be generated from a four-dimensional Normal distribution:

$$\begin{pmatrix} U_1 \\ V_1 \\ U_2 \\ V_2 \end{pmatrix} \sim \mathcal{N}\left(\mu, C = \begin{pmatrix} A & X \\ X^T & B \end{pmatrix}\right) \tag{23}$$

where A, B and X are 2×2 matrices. A and B are the intra-task covariance matrices. X models the correlations across tasks, for instance X_{11} is the correlation between U_1 and U_2. $X_{11} > 0$ means that a worker with high sensitivity in the first task is likely to have high sensitivity in the second task. Our idea is that each task has its own mean sensitivity and specificity to represent its difficulty. On the other hand, the covariance matrix C represents how these sensitivites and specificities in two tasks are correlated. **Figure 2** is an illustration. Our inference and learning algorithms can be easily extended to this model.

4 EXPERIMENTS

We conducted experiments on two large 'citizen science' datasets to compare our proposed method to baselines. In citizen science, workers volunteer to contribute to science, without financial compensation.

We report the Root Mean Square Error (RMSE) of the predicted worker sensitivities and specificities:

$$\text{RMSE} = \sqrt{\frac{1}{m}\sum_{j=1}^{m}(\text{Predicted}_j - \text{True}_j)^2} \tag{24}$$

where Predicted_j is the sensitivity or specificity of worker j that is predicted by a method and True_j is the corresponding true value. In practice, a worker true sensitivity and specificity are latent but can be accurately estimated given that the worker have labeled a large number of items and the true labels for those items are available: Sensitivity $=$ $\text{TP}/(\text{TP}+\text{FN})$ and Specificity $= \text{TN}/(\text{TN}+\text{FP})$ where TP, TN, FP and FN are the number of true (false) positives (negatives) that the worker have labeled. We calculate the sensitivity and specificity estimates using all of the available data and treat those as the true values (or gold standard) for evaluation. Also, to ensure the quality of such gold standard, we only include in our evaluation the workers who have provided labels for at least 5 positives and 5 negatives (on the entire dataset). We note that the methods being evaluated are given a small portion of the dataset and still need to produce good estimates based on very few crowd labels and without access to the true labels. A similar approach to evaluate confusion matrix estimates has been used by Lakkaraju et al. (2015).

4.1 BIOMEDICAL CITATION SCREENING

We consider data from the EMBASE screening project (http://screening.metaxis.com/EMBASE/), which aims to identify reports of randomized controlled trials (RCTs) from EMBASE,[1] a biomedical literature database. The aim is to be comprehensive, thus placing an emphasis on sensitivity. An important property of this dataset is its imbalance: fewer than 5% of the items are positive. Our model aims to improve the estimates of sensitivities using their correlations with specificities (recall that sensitivity is the probability of being correct given a positive, and we expect this estimate to be poor given very few positives). Also, the screening project has relied on a mix of novice volunteer workers and domain experts with associated costs and levels of expertise. Our model can easily exploit such information on two groups of workers by using two different set of parameters (μ and C), one for each group. This is a large dataset with 151,224 items and 576 workers. Of

[1]RCTs are experiments in which participants are randomized to groups in which individuals are exposed to different interventions; one group is designated as a control.

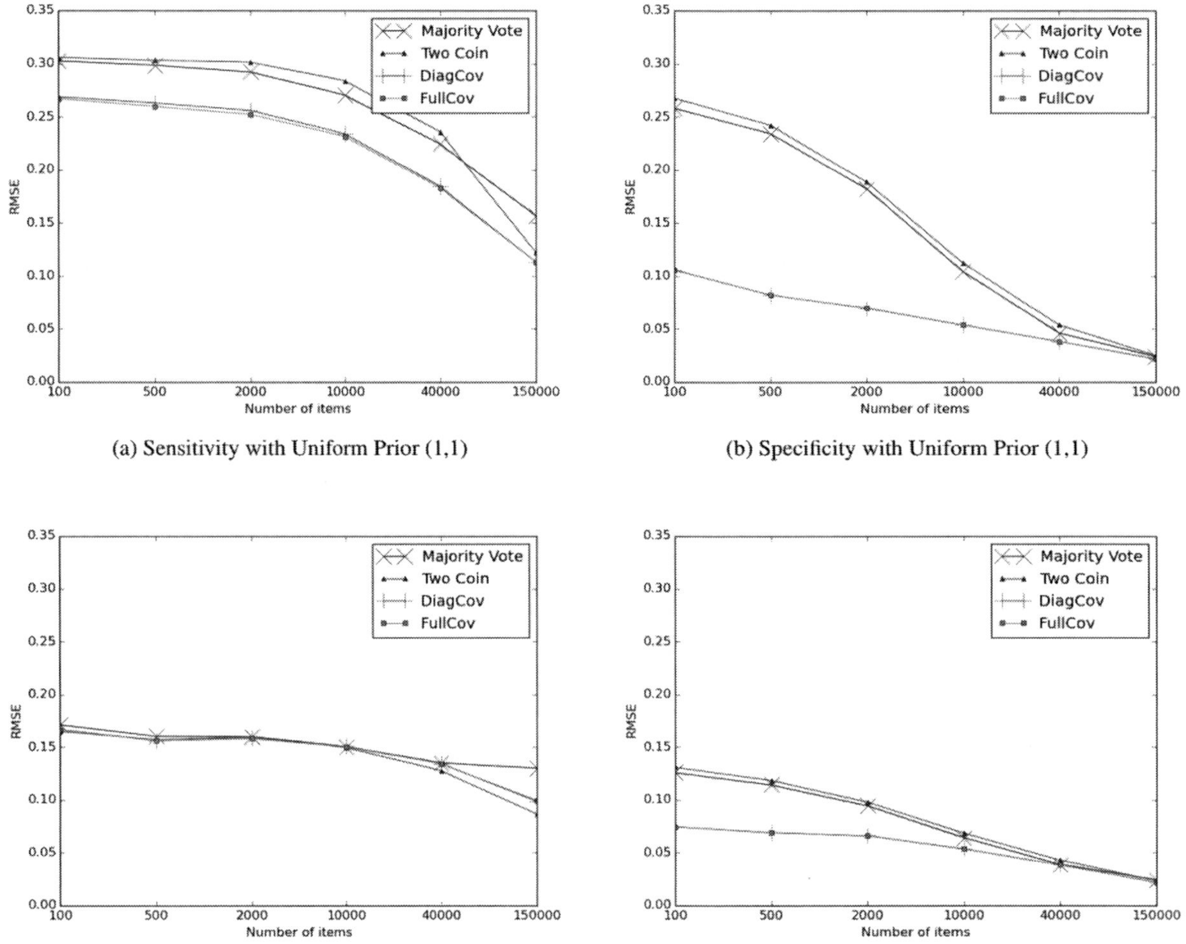

(a) Sensitivity with Uniform Prior (1,1)

(b) Specificity with Uniform Prior (1,1)

(c) Sensitivity with Informative Prior (4,1)

(d) Specificity with Informative Prior (4,1)

Figure 3: The RMSE in Sensitivity and Specificity with Uniform and Informative Prior of four methods (averaged over 5 runs). DiagCov and FullCov are two variants of our model; their curves *overlap* in (b), (c) and (d).

those workers, 156 have labeled at least 5 positives and 5 negatives and are used for evaluation. The number of labels per workers is generally very skewed: 525 workers (91%) provided less than the average of 603 labels.

We implemented two variants of our method: one with a full covariance matrix (FullCov) and one with a covariance matrix constrained to be diagonal (DiagCov) i.e., entries in the confusion matrices are assumed to be uncorrelated. This allows us to observe how much improvement is due to modeling correlation and how much is from modeling worker groups. We compare these two variants to two baselines: Majority Vote, in which sensitivities and specificities are estimated based on the majority labels, and the *Two Coin* model (without features) due to Raykar et al. (2010, sec. 2.7.4)

We also implemented the *Hybrid Confusion* model by Liu and Wang (2012), which is the same as Two Coin but with inference by Gibbs sampling. Because the results were very similar to Two Coin, we omit these for clarity.

All of the methods are given the same prior or initialized in the same way. The Two Coin model has Beta priors on worker sensitivities and specificities, which can be interpreted as smoothing constants. The same constants are given to Majority Vote to smooth its estimates. Our model has no prior on the parameters μ and C but those and the variational parameters are initialized using the outputs from Majority Vote (with smoothing constants). To explore the effect of these worker priors (or initialization), we did experiments with a uniform prior (($\mathrm{Beta}(1,1)$ as done by Raykar et al. (2010)) and an informative prior $\mathrm{Beta}(4,1)$ as in Liu and Wang (2012)). The prior on the class propor-

	Items	Workers	LPI	LPW
Task 1	17862	1242	16.8 ± 3.9	241 ± 288
Task 2	6476	198	5.0 ± 2.1	163 ± 130
Task 3	21951	681	6.7 ± 3.7	215 ± 243
Task 4	21915	679	6.7 ± 3.7	215 ± 243

Table 1: Statistics of four tasks we consider in the Galaxy Zoo 2 dataset, after pre-processing. 'LPI' stands for 'Labels per item' and 'LPW' for 'Labels per worker'. In these columns, we report the means and standard deviations of the number of labels per item (worker).

tion θ is always uniform ($\text{Beta}(1, 1)$ as done by both).

Figure 3 presents our results with RMSE on the Y-axis and the number of items on the X-axis. We average results over 5 runs, randomly sampling a number of items from the dataset for each. The two plots above are for uniform prior. We see that Two Coin's performance is surprisingly weak while two variants of our model achieve the best performance. On the plot for Sensitivity, we also see some small improvement of FullCov over DiagCov (but significant in our paired t-test). In the plot for Specificity, those two variants have the same performance (the curve for FullCov has overwritten the one for DiagCov). This is what we expect since the specificity estimates are for the majority (negative) class and the correlation has little effect given a large number of labels available. Surprisingly, much of the improvement of our method can be attributed to the 'group part' of our model (not the 'correlation part'). As discussed above, the 'group part' provides a 'back off' to the group level estimates when there is not enough data on a worker.

The two plots below show our results for Informative Prior, where all of the methods perform better, as expected. For Sensitivity, Two Coin performs well, slightly better than Majority Vote while comparable to ours for the most part and slightly better than ours for $40,000$ or more items. However, for specificity, it still performs worse than Majority Vote and ours. The difference is probably due to $\text{Beta}(4, 1)$ being a better prior for sensitivity than specificity[2]. This suggests that Two Coin and similarly Hybrid Confusion can perform well but their performance are dependent on good priors. In contrast, our method is robust across different settings of priors. This can probably be explained by the fact that our group level estimates (which play role in 'backing off' sparse workers) are learned from data while Two Coin's priors are set to constants.

4.2 GALAXY MORPHOLOGICAL CLASSIFICATION

The Galaxy Zoo 2 dataset (Willett et al., 2013) consists of labels provided by volunteer workers on morphological classification of galaxies. A worker is given an image of a galaxy and is asked multiple questions. We consider each question to be a labeling task. Specifically in our experiments, we consider the (simplified) first four questions/tasks:

1. Is the galaxy smooth or disk-like? If the answer is disk, proceed to task 2, otherwise stop. [3]
2. Is the disk viewed edge-on? If the answer is no, proceed to task 3, otherwise stop.
3. Is there a bar in the center? Proceed to task 4 regardless of the answer.
4. Is there a spiral arm pattern?

Since the tasks have varying difficulties and require varying skills, worker performance in each task can be very different from others, but we can naturally expect some degree of transferability between tasks. We aim to evaluate our multitask model on improving the estimates of worker sensitivities and specificities on a *target task*, given labels on a *source task* (for the same set of workers). We did experiments in two scenarios:

1. Conditional Task 1 $\rightarrow$ Task 2: The methods are given all of the labels in Task 1, a portion of labels in Task 2 and must estimate worker sensitivities and specificities in Task 2.
2. Independent Task 3 $\rightarrow$ Task 4: The methods are given all of the labels in Task 3, a portion of labels in Task 4 and must estimate worker sensitivities and specificities in Task 4. Here the two tasks are independent, while in the first scenario, Task 2 is asked only when the worker answers 'disk' in Task 1.

We compare our multitask model (*Multi*) to two baselines: *Single*, where only labels in the target task are considered, and *Accum*, where labels from the source task are merged with those from the target task. The Accum baseline is only applicable when the two tasks are questions with the same number of choices and a matching of these choices is available (otherwise the labels could not be merged). Our approach has no such restriction. For both baselines, we used the FullCov variant of our method.

The dataset is extremely large, with nearly 60 million labels for 11 tasks from over 83 thousand workers. We do the following pre-processing to reduce the size of the dataset. (1) We take the first million labels (for all of 11 tasks). (2) For each of the first four tasks, we filter out workers with less than 100 labels and items with less than 3 labels. The statistics of the four tasks after pre-processing are in **Table 1**. We note that the gold standard worker sensitivities and specificities are estimated from the *entire* dataset (without pre-processing).

[2] $\text{Beta}(4, 1)$ has a mean of 0.8. The true means for sensitivities and specificities are 0.78 and 0.94

[3] 'Stop' means go to a question we don't consider. This question has a third answer ('star of artifact') which is very rare and we don't consider for simplicity.

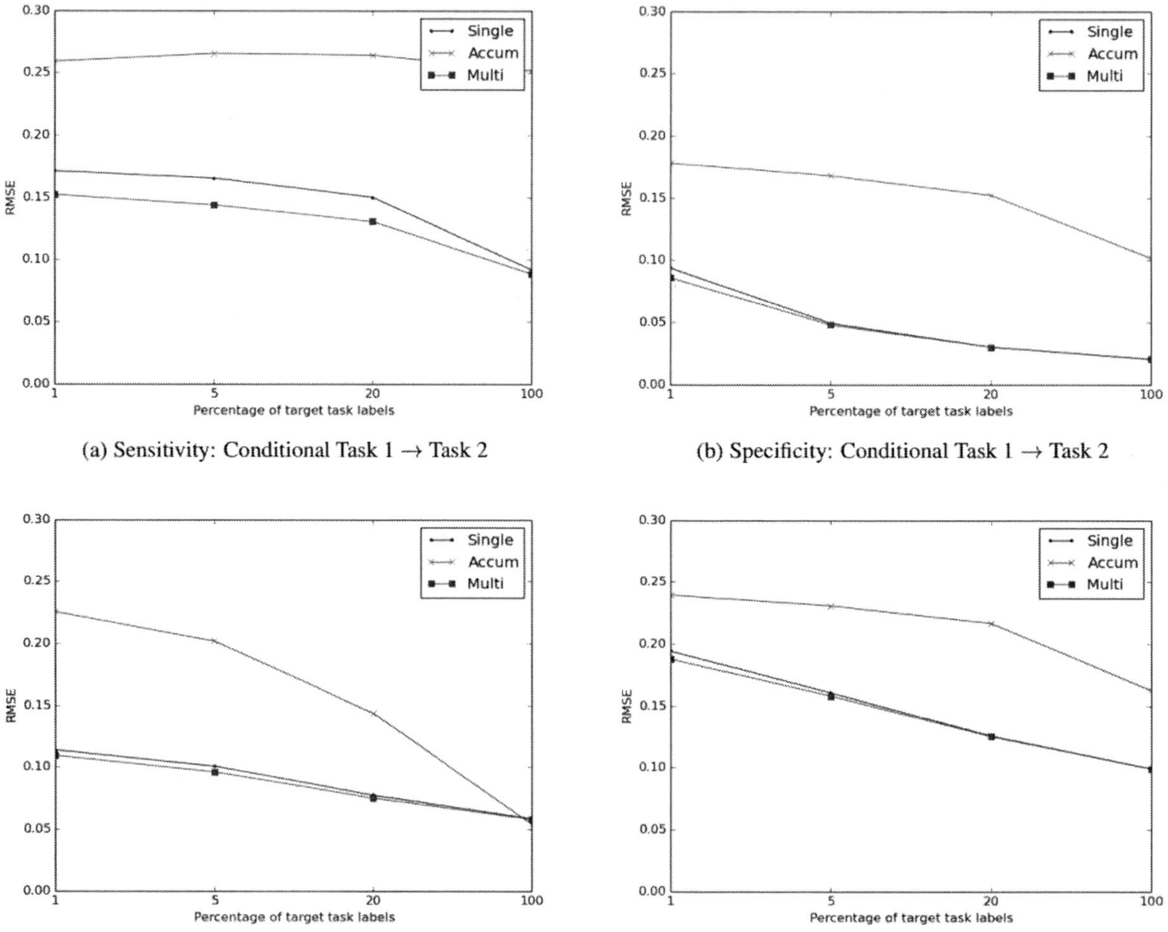

(a) Sensitivity: Conditional Task 1 $\rightarrow$ Task 2

(b) Specificity: Conditional Task 1 $\rightarrow$ Task 2

(c) Sensitivity: Independent Task 3 $\rightarrow$ Task 4

(d) Specificity: Independent Task 3 $\rightarrow$ Task 4

Figure 4: The RMSE against percentage of labels in the target task available of our method compared to two baselines (averaged over 5 runs).

In **Figure 4**, we report our results. Overall, Accum is surprisingly weak, giving estimates with much higher RMSE than Single. This shows that worker performance in two different tasks are sufficiently different that a naive transfer strategy is unlikely to work.

Compared to the Single baseline, our method has shown improvement for the case when a small percentage of labels in the target task is available. The improvement diminishes when more target task labels are available, as expected. On a close look at their differences, one might notice that the improvement is sometimes quite modest. Looking into the 'true' worker sensitivities and specificities (**Figure 5**), we found an overall positive correlation between tasks as expected. However, we also observe a surprisingly large number of workers who do better in the source task but worse in the second task (and vice versa). This may be because the tasks are somewhat subjective that the variations in workers performance are mostly due to their different perception and interpretation. In short, we believe the true multitask correlation plays a role in how much improvement we observe.

To further investigate this, we repeat the same experiments on simulated labels. We note that the purpose of our simulation is to complement, not to replace our results on the real data. The simulated labels are generated by our model from the following parameters:

$$\mu = \begin{pmatrix} 1.49 \\ -1.45 \\ 2.18 \\ -2.59 \end{pmatrix} C = \begin{pmatrix} 1.80 & 0 & x & 0 \\ 0 & 1.30 & 0 & x \\ x & 0 & 1.06 & 0 \\ 0 & x & 0 & 1.89 \end{pmatrix}$$

The mean μ and the variances in C are set to the empirical estimates in Task 1 and Task 2 while x is the inter-task correlation and is varied in $\{0.5, 0.75, 1.0, 1.25\}$, some positive values in a reasonable range which keep the covariance matrix positive definite. We assume 5000 items in each task and 200 workers. Each item is labeled by 5 randomly selected workers. **Figure 6** shows that as the correlation x increases, we see a greater improvement of Multi over Single. That is, the more correlated the worker performances in different tasks are, the greater the improvement realized by our model.

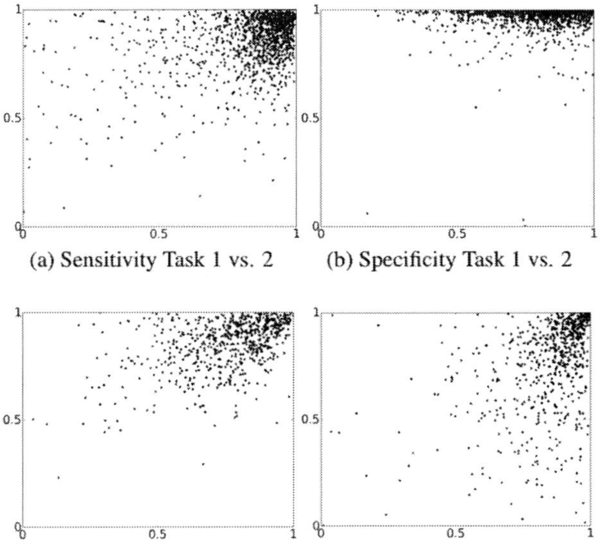

(a) Sensitivity Task 1 vs. 2 (b) Specificity Task 1 vs. 2

(c) Sensitivity Task 3 vs. 4 (d) Specificity Task 3 vs. 4

Figure 5: Worker sensitivities (specificities) in two tasks. Each point is a worker. In (a) and (b), the X-axis is task 1 and the Y-axis is task 2. In (c) and (d), the X-axis is task 3 and the Y-axis is task 4.

5 CONCLUSION

We have presented our approach to improve the estimates of worker confusion matrices and reported the results of our experiments on real and simulated data. Our main idea is to exploit the correlations in the matrix entries (sensitivities and specificities) and the knowledge of groups in the workers population. The idea also applies to the case when labels from multiple tasks are available. In all of the cases we consider, our method shows good performance compared to baselines. We have made our source code available[4]. We expect the datasets to be available on request from their owners.

While we have reported on binary classification tasks with no instance-level features, where a confusion matrix reduces to sensitivity and specificity, our approach can be easily generalized. For future work, we will extend our work to categorical tasks, with features when available.

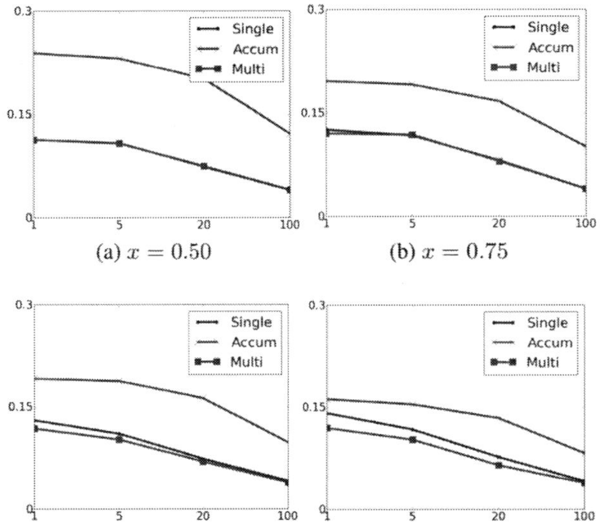

(a) $x = 0.50$ (b) $x = 0.75$

(c) $x = 1.00$ (d) $x = 1.25$

Figure 6: The RMSE in Sensitivity (averaged over 5 runs) on simulated labels for 4 values of the inter-task correlation x. The X-axis is the percentage of target task labels and the Y-axis is RMSE. The curves for Single and Multi overlap in (a). The results for Specificity are similar.

Such features can be modeled by additional variables associated with the instances and a variational algorithm can be derived similar to (Felt et al., 2015). We are also interested in a better model for the multitask setting, which can capture important factors such as item and task difficulties as well as worker skill and expertise. Also, we would like to take advantage of the the full posterior distribution over the worker confusion matrices in an application such as an online decision system (Nguyen et al., 2015; Werling et al., 2015), rather than using only point estimates. Finally, while we have favored variational inference over MCMC, recent probabilistic languages such as Stan (Carpenter et al., 2015) is an attractive alternative and interesting to compare to our approach.

Acknowledgments

We thank the EMBASE screening project for providing the RCT dataset, Kyle Willett for providing the Galaxy Zoo 2 dataset and the anonymous reviewers for valuable comments. We are also grateful for the volunteers who contribute to these datasets and make this work possible. This study was supported in part by National Science Foundation grant No. 1253413 and IMLS grant RE-04-13-0042-13. Any opinions, findings, and conclusions or recommendations expressed by the authors are entirely their own and do not represent those of the sponsoring agencies.

[4]https://github.com/thanhan/code-uai16

References

Bi, W., Wang, L., Kwok, J. T., and Tu, Z. (2014). Learning to predict from crowdsourced data. In *Uncertainty in Artificial Intelligence*.

Carpenter, B., Gelman, A., Hoffman, M., Lee, D., Goodrich, B., Betancourt, M., Brubaker, M. A., Guo, J., Li, P., and Riddell, A. (2015). Stan: a probabilistic programming language. *Journal of Statistical Software*.

Dahabreh, I. J., Trikalinos, T. A., Lau, J., and Schmid, C. (2012). *An Empirical Assessment of Bivariate Methods for Meta-Analysis of Test Accuracy*. Agency for Healthcare Research and Quality (US).

Dawid, A. P. and Skene, A. M. (1979). Maximum likelihood estimation of observer error-rates using the em algorithm. *Applied statistics*, pages 20–28.

Dempster, A. P., Laird, N. M., and Rubin, D. B. (1977). Maximum likelihood from incomplete data via the em algorithm. *Journal of the royal statistical society. Series B (methodological)*, pages 1–38.

Felt, P., Ringger, E., Seppi, K., Black, K., and Haertel, R. (2015). Early gains matter: A case for preferring generative over discriminative crowdsourcing models. In *Conference of the North American Chapter of the Association for Computational Linguistics*.

Hedges, L. V. (1994). Fixed effects models. *The handbook of research synthesis*, pages 285–299.

Kajino, H., Tsuboi, Y., and Kashima, H. (2012). A convex formulation for learning from crowds. In *Twenty-Sixth AAAI Conference on Artificial Intelligence*.

Kim, H.-C. and Ghahramani, Z. (2012). Bayesian classifier combination. In *International conference on artificial intelligence and statistics*, pages 619–627.

Koller, D. and Friedman, N. (2009). *Probabilistic graphical models: principles and techniques*. MIT press.

Lakkaraju, H., Leskovec, J., Kleinberg, J., and Mullainathan, S. (2015). A bayesian framework for modeling human evaluations. In *Proceedings of the 2015 SIAM International Conference on Data Mining*, pages 181–189.

Liu, C. and Wang, Y.-m. (2012). Truelabel+ confusions: A spectrum of probabilistic models in analyzing multiple ratings. In *Proceedings of the 29th International Conference on Machine Learning (ICML-12)*, pages 225–232.

Liu, Q., Peng, J., and Ihler, A. T. (2012). Variational inference for crowdsourcing. In *Advances in Neural Information Processing Systems*, pages 692–700.

Nguyen, A. T., Wallace, B. C., and Lease, M. (2015). Combining crowd and expert labels using decision theoretic active learning. In *Proceedings of the 3rd AAAI Conference on Human Computation (HCOMP)*.

Patil, A., Huard, D., and Fonnesbeck, C. J. (2010). Pymc: Bayesian stochastic modelling in python. *Journal of statistical software*, 35(4):1.

Raykar, V. C., Yu, S., Zhao, L. H., Valadez, G. H., Florin, C., Bogoni, L., and Moy, L. (2010). Learning from crowds. *Journal of Machine Learning Research*, 11:1297–1322.

Reitsma, J. B., Glas, A. S., Rutjes, A. W., Scholten, R. J., Bossuyt, P. M., and Zwinderman, A. H. (2005). Bivariate analysis of sensitivity and specificity produces informative summary measures in diagnostic reviews. *Journal of clinical epidemiology*, 58(10):982–990.

Sheshadri, A. and Lease, M. (2013). Square: A benchmark for research on computing crowd consensus. In *First AAAI Conference on Human Computation and Crowdsourcing*.

Simpson, E., Roberts, S., Psorakis, I., and Smith, A. (2013). Dynamic bayesian combination of multiple imperfect classifiers. In *Decision Making and Imperfection*, pages 1–35. Springer.

Spiegelhalter, D. J., Thomas, A., Best, N. G., and Gilks, W. R. (1995). Bugs: Bayesian inference using gibbs sampling, version 0.50. *MRC Biostatistics Unit, Cambridge*.

Venanzi, M., Guiver, J., Kazai, G., Kohli, P., and Shokouhi, M. (2014). Community-based bayesian aggregation models for crowdsourcing. In *Proceedings of the 23rd international conference on World wide web*, pages 155–164. ACM.

Wainwright, M. J. and Jordan, M. I. (2008). Graphical models, exponential families, and variational inference. *Foundations and Trends® in Machine Learning*, 1(1-2):1–305.

Wang, C. and Blei, D. M. (2013). Variational inference in nonconjugate models. *The Journal of Machine Learning Research*, 14(1):1005–1031.

Werling, K., Chaganty, A. T., Liang, P. S., and Manning, C. D. (2015). On-the-job learning with bayesian decision theory. In *Advances in Neural Information Processing Systems*, pages 3447–3455.

Willett, K. W., Lintott, C. J., Bamford, S. P., Masters, K. L., Simmons, B. D., Casteels, K. R., Edmondson, E. M., Fortson, L. F., Kaviraj, S., Keel, W. C., et al. (2013). Galaxy zoo 2: detailed morphological classifications for 304 122 galaxies from the sloan digital sky survey. *Monthly Notices of the Royal Astronomical Society*, page stt1458.

Convergence Rates for Greedy Kaczmarz Algorithms, and Faster Randomized Kaczmarz Rules Using the Orthogonality Graph

Julie Nutini[*]
jnutini@cs.ubc.ca

Behrooz Sepehry[*]
behrooz@cs.ubc.ca

Issam Laradji[*]
issamou@cs.ubc.ca

Mark Schmidt[*]
schmidtm@cs.ubc.ca

Hoyt Koepke[†]
hoytak@gmail.com

Alim Virani[*]
alim.virani@gmail.com

Abstract

The Kaczmarz method is an iterative algorithm for solving systems of linear equalities and inequalities, that iteratively projects onto these constraints. Recently, Strohmer and Vershynin [*J. Fourier Anal. Appl.*, 15(2):262-278, 2009] gave a non-asymptotic convergence rate analysis for this algorithm, spurring numerous extensions and generalizations of the Kaczmarz method. Rather than the randomized selection rule analyzed in that work, in this paper we instead discuss greedy and approximate greedy selection rules. We show that in some applications the computational costs of greedy and random selection are comparable, and that in many cases greedy selection rules give faster convergence rates than random selection rules. Further, we give the first multi-step analysis of Kaczmarz methods for a particular greedy rule, and propose a provably-faster randomized selection rule for matrices with many pairwise-orthogonal rows.

1 KACZMARZ METHOD

Solving large linear systems is a fundamental problem in machine learning. Applications range from least-squares problems to Gaussian processes to graph-based semi-supervised learning. All of these applications (and many others) benefit from advances in solving large-scale linear systems. The Kaczmarz method is a particular iterative algorithm suited for solving consistent linear systems of the form $Ax = b$. It was originally proposed by Polish mathematician Stefan Kaczmarz (1937) and later re-invented by Gordon et al. (1970) under the name *algebraic reconstruction technique* (ART). It has been used in numerous applications including image reconstruction and digital signal processing, and belongs to several general categories of methods including *row-action*, *component-solution*, *cyclic projection*, and *successive projection* methods (Censor, 1981).

At each iteration k, the Kaczmarz method uses a *selection rule* to choose some row i_k of A and then projects the current iterate x^k onto the corresponding hyperplane $a_{i_k}^T x^k = b_{i_k}$. Classically, the two categories of selection rules are *cyclic* and *random*. Cyclic selection repeatedly cycles through the coordinates in sequential order, making it simple to implement and computationally inexpensive. There are various linear convergence rates for cyclic selection (see Deutsch, 1985; Deutsch and Hundal, 1997; Galántai, 2005), but these rates are in terms of cycles through the entire dataset and involve constants that are not easily interpreted. Further, the performance of cyclic selection worsens if we have an undesirable ordering of the rows of A.

Randomized selection has recently become the default selection rule in the literature on Kaczmarz-type methods. Empirically, selecting i randomly often performs substantially better in practice than cyclic selection (Feichtinger et al., 1992; Herman and Meyer, 1993). Although a number of asymptotic convergence rates for randomized selection have been presented (Whitney and Meany, 1967; Tanabe, 1971; Censor et al., 1983; Hanke and Niethammer, 1990), the pivotal theoretical result supporting the use of randomized selection for the Kaczmarz method was given by Strohmer and Vershynin (2009). They proved a non-asymptotic linear convergence rate (in expectation) in terms of the number of iterations, when rows are selected proportional to their squared norms. This work spurred numerous extensions and generalizations of the randomized Kaczmarz method (Needell, 2010; Leventhal and Lewis, 2010; Zouzias and Freris, 2013; Lee and Sidford, 2013; Liu and Wright, 2014; Ma et al., 2015), including similar rates when we replace the equality constraints with inequality constraints.

Rather than cyclic or randomized, in this work we consider *greedy* selection rules. There are very few results

[*]Department of Computer Science, The University of British Columbia, Vancouver, BC, Canada
[†]DATO, Seattle, Washington, USA

in the literature that explore the use of greedy selection rules for Kaczmarz-type methods. Griebel and Oswald (2012) present the *maximum residual rule* for multiplicative Schwarz methods, for which the randomized Kaczmarz iteration is a special case. Their theoretical results show similar convergence rate estimates for both greedy and random methods, suggesting there is no advantage of greedy selection over randomized selection (since greedy selection has additional computational costs). Eldar and Needell (2011) propose a greedy *maximum distance rule*, which they approximate using the Johnson-Lindenstrauss (1984) transform to reduce the computation cost. They show that this leads to a faster algorithm in practice, and show that this rule may achieve more progress than random selection on certain iterations.

In the next section, we define several relevant problems of interest in machine learning that can be solved via Kaczmarz methods. Subsequently, we define the greedy selection rules and discuss cases where they can be computed efficiently. In Section 4 we give faster convergence rate analyses for both the maximum residual rule and the maximum distance rule, which clarify the relationship of these rules to random selection and show that greedy methods will typically have better convergence rates than randomized selection. Section 5 contrasts Kaczmarz methods with coordinate descent methods, Section 6 considers a simplified setting where we explicitly compute the constants in the convergence rates, Section 7 considers how these convergence rates are changed under *approximations* to the greedy rules, and Section 8 discusses the case of inequality constraints. We further give a non-trivial *multi-step* analysis of the maximal residual rule (Section 9), which is the first multi-step analysis of any Kaczmarz algorithm. By taking the multi-step perspective, we also propose provably-faster randomized selection rules for matrices A with pairwise-orthogonal rows by using the so-called "orthogonality graph". Section 10 presents numerical experiments evaluating greedy Kaczmarz methods.

2 PROBLEMS OF INTEREST

We first consider systems of linear equations,

$$Ax = b, \tag{1}$$

where A is an $m \times n$ matrix and $b \in \mathbb{R}^m$. We assume the system is *consistent*, meaning a solution x^* exists. We denote the rows of A by $a_1^\top, \dots, a_m^\top$, where each $a_i \in R^n$, and use $b = (b_1, \dots, b_m)^\top$, where each $b_i \in \mathbb{R}$. One of the most important examples of a consistent linear system, and a fundamental model in machine learning, is the least squares problem,

$$\min_{x \in \mathbb{R}^n} \frac{1}{2}\|Ax - b\|^2.$$

An appealing way to write a least squares problem as a linear system is to solve the $(n + m)$-variable consistent system (see also Zouzias and Freris, 2013)

$$\begin{pmatrix} A & -I \\ \mathbf{0} & A^T \end{pmatrix} \begin{pmatrix} x \\ y \end{pmatrix} = \begin{pmatrix} b \\ 0 \end{pmatrix},$$

Other applications in machine learning that involve solving consistent linear systems include: least-squares support vector machines, Gaussian processes, fitting the final layer of a neural network (using squared-error), graph-based semi-supervised learning or other graph-Laplacian problems (Bengio et al., 2006), and finding the optimal configuration in Gaussian Markov random fields (Rue and Held, 2005).

Kaczmarz methods can also be applied to solve consistent systems of linear *inequalities*,

$$Ax \leq b,$$

or combinations of linear equalities and inequalities. We believe there is a lot potential to use this application of Kaczmarz methods in machine learning. Indeed, a classic example of solving linear inequalities is finding a linear separator for a binary classification problem. The classic perceptron algorithm is a generalization of the Kaczmarz method, but unlike the classic sublinear rates of perceptron methods (Novikoff, 1962) we can show a linear rate for the Kaczmarz method.

Kaczmarz methods could also be used to solve the ℓ_1-regularized robust regression problem,

$$\min_x f(x) := \|Ax - b\|_1 + \lambda\|x\|_1,$$

for $\lambda \geq 0$. We can formulate finding an x with $f(x) \leq \tau$ for some constant τ as a set of linear inequalities. By doing a binary search for τ and using *warm-starting*, this can be substantially faster than existing approaches like stochastic subgradient methods (which have a sublinear convergence rate) or formulating as a linear program (which is not scaleable due to the super-linear cost). The above logic applies to many piecewise-linear problems in machine learning like variants of support vector machines/regression with the ℓ_1-norm, regression under the ℓ_∞-norm, and linear programming relaxations for decoding in graphical models.

3 KACZMARZ ALGORITHM AND GREEDY SELECTION RULES

The Kaczmarz algorithm for solving linear systems begins from an initial guess x^0, and each iteration k chooses a row i_k and projects the current iterate x^k onto the hyperplane defined by $a_{i_k}^T x^k = b_{i_k}$. This gives the iteration

$$x^{k+1} = x^k + \frac{b_{i_k} - a_{i_k}^T x^k}{\|a_{i_k}\|^2} a_{i_k}, \tag{2}$$

and the algorithm converges to a solution x^* under weak conditions (e.g., each i is visited infinitely often).

We consider two greedy selection rules: the *maximum residual* rule and the *maximum distance* rule. The maximum residual (MR) rule selects i_k according to

$$i_k = \underset{i}{\text{argmax}}\ |a_i^T x^k - b_i|, \tag{3}$$

which is the equation i_k that is 'furthest' from being satisfied. The maximum distance (MD) rule selects i_k according to

$$i_k = \underset{i}{\text{argmax}}\ \left| \frac{a_i^T x^k - b_i}{\|a_i\|} \right|, \tag{4}$$

which is the rule that maximizes the distance between iterations, $\|x^{k+1} - x^k\|$.

3.1 EFFICIENT CALCULATIONS FOR SPARSE A

In general, computing these greedy selection rules exactly is too computationally expensive, but in some applications we can compute them efficiently. For example, consider a *sparse* A with at most c non-zeros per column and at most r non-zeros per row. In this setting, we show in Appendix 3.1 that both rules can be computed exactly in $O(cr \log m)$ time, using that projecting onto row i does not change the residual of row j if a_i and a_j do not share a non-zero index.

The above sparsity condition guarantees that row i is orthogonal to row j, and indeed projecting onto row i will not change the residual of row j under the more general condition that a_i and a_j are orthogonal. Consider what we call the *orthogonality graph*: an undirected graph on m nodes where we place on edge between nodes i and j if a_i is not orthogonal to a_j. Given this graph, to update all residuals after we update a row i we only need to update the neighbours of node i in this graph. Even if A is dense ($r = n$ and $c = m$), if the maximum number of neighbours is g, then tracking the maximum residual costs $O(gr + g\log(m))$. If g is small, this could still be comparable to the $O(r + \log(m))$ cost of using existing randomized selection strategies.

3.2 APPROXIMATE CALCULATION

Many applications, particularly those arising from graphical models with a simple structure, will allow efficient calculation of the greedy rules using the method of the previous section. However, in other applications it will be too inefficient to calculate the greedy rules. Nevertheless, Eldar and Needell (2011) show that it's possible to efficiently select an i_k that *approximates* the greedy rules by making use of the dimensionality reduction technique of Johnson and Lindenstrauss (1984). Their experiments show that approximate greedy rules can be sufficiently accurate and that they still outperform random selection. After first analyzing exact greedy rules in the next section, we analyze the effect of using approximate rules in Section 7.

4 ANALYZING SELECTION RULES

All the convergence rates we discuss use the following relationship between $\|x^{k+1} - x^*\|$ and $\|x^k - x^*\|$:

$$\begin{aligned}
&\|x^{k+1} - x^*\|^2 \\
&= \|x^k - x^*\|^2 - \|x^{k+1} - x^k\|^2 + 2\underbrace{\langle x^{k+1} - x^*, x^{k+1} - x^k\rangle}_{(=0,\text{ by orthogonality})}.
\end{aligned}$$

Using the definition of x^{k+1} from (2) and simplifying, we obtain for the selected i_k that

$$\|x^{k+1} - x^*\|^2 = \|x^k - x^*\|^2 - \frac{(a_{i_k}^T x^k - b_{i_k})^2}{\|a_{i_k}\|^2}. \tag{5}$$

4.1 RANDOMIZED AND MAXIMUM RESIDUAL

We first give an analysis of the Kaczmarz method with *uniform* random selection of the row to update i (which we abbreviate as 'U'). Conditioning on the σ-field $\mathcal{F}_{k-1}$ generated by the sequence $\{x^0, x^1, \dots, x^{k-1}\}$, and taking expectations of both sides of (5), when i_k is selected using U we obtain

$$\begin{aligned}
&\mathbb{E}[\|x^{k+1} - x^*\|^2] \\
&= \|x^k - x^*\|^2 - \mathbb{E}\left[\frac{(a_i^T x^k - b_i)^2}{\|a_i\|^2}\right] \\
&= \|x^k - x^*\|^2 - \sum_{i=1}^m \frac{1}{m}\frac{(a_i^\top (x^k - x^*))^2}{\|a_i\|^2} \\
&\le \|x^k - x^*\|^2 - \frac{1}{m\|A\|_{\infty,2}^2}\sum_{i=1}^m (a_i^\top (x^k - x^*))^2 \\
&= \|x^k - x^*\|^2 - \frac{1}{m\|A\|_{\infty,2}^2}\|A(x^k - x^*)\|^2 \\
&\le \left(1 - \frac{\sigma(A,2)^2}{m\|A\|_{\infty,2}^2}\right)\|x^k - x^*\|^2,
\end{aligned} \tag{6}$$

where $\|A\|_{\infty,2}^2 := \max_i\{\|a_i\|^2\}$ and $\sigma(A,2)$ is the Hoffman (1952) constant. We've assumed that x^k is not a solution, allowing us to use Hoffman's bound. When A has independent columns, $\sigma(A,2)$ is the nth singular value of A and in general it is the smallest non-zero singular value.

The argument above is related to the analysis of Vishnoi (2013) but is simpler due to the use of the Hoffman bound. Further, this simple argument makes it straightforward to derive bounds on other rules. For example, we can derive the convergence rate bound of Strohmer and Vershynin (2009) by following the above steps but selecting i non-uniformly with probability $\|a_i\|^2/\|A\|_F^2$ (where $\|A\|_F$ is the Frobenius norm of A). We review these steps in Appendix 4.1, showing that this non-uniform (NU) selection strategy has

$$\mathbb{E}[\|x^{k+1} - x^*\|^2] \leq \left(1 - \frac{\sigma(A,2)^2}{\|A\|_F^2}\right)\|x^k - x^*\|^2. \quad (7)$$

This strategy requires prior knowledge of the row norms of A, but this is a one-time computation that can be reused for any linear system involving A. Because $\|A\|_F^2 \leq m\|A\|_{\infty,2}^2$, the NU rate (7) is at least as fast as the uniform rate (6).

While a trivial analysis shows that the MR rule also satisfies (6) in a deterministic sense, in Appendix 4.1 we give a tighter analysis of the MR rule showing it has the convergence rate

$$\|x^{k+1} - x^*\|^2 \leq \left(1 - \frac{\sigma(A,\infty)^2}{\|A\|_{\infty,2}^2}\right)\|x^k - x^*\|^2, \quad (8)$$

where the Hoffman-like constant $\sigma(A,\infty)$ satisfies the relationship

$$\frac{\sigma(A,2)}{\sqrt{m}} \leq \sigma(A,\infty) \leq \sigma(A,2).$$

Thus, at one extreme the maximum residual rule obtains the same rate as (6) for uniform selection when $\sigma(A,2)^2/m \approx \sigma(A,\infty)^2$. However, at the other extreme the maximum residual rule could be faster than uniform selection by a factor of m ($\sigma(A,\infty)^2 \approx \sigma(A,2)^2$). Thus, although the uniform and MR bounds are the same in the worst case, the MR rule can be superior by a large margin.

In contrast to comparing U and MR, the MR rate may be faster or slower than the NU rate. This is because

$$\|A\|_{\infty,2} \leq \|A\|_F \leq \sqrt{m}\|A\|_{\infty,2},$$

so these quantities and the relationship between $\sigma(A,2)$ and $\sigma(A,\infty)$ influence which bound is tighter.

4.2 TIGHTER UNIFORM AND MR ANALYSIS

In our derivations of rates (6) and (8), we use the following inequality

$$\|a_i\|^2 \leq \|A\|_{\infty,2}^2 \quad \forall\, i, \quad (9)$$

which leads to a simple result but could be very loose if the range of row norms is large. In this section, we give tighter analyses of the U and MR rules that are less interpretable but are tighter because they avoid this inequality.

In order to avoid using this inequality for our analysis of U, we can absorb the row norms of A into a row weighting matrix D, where $D = \text{diag}(\|a_1\|, \|a_2\|, \ldots, \|a_m\|)$. Defining $\bar{A} := D^{-1}A$, we show in Appendix 4.2 that this results in the following upper bound on the convergence rate for uniform random selection,

$$\mathbb{E}[\|x^{k+1} - x^*\|^2] \leq \left(1 - \frac{\sigma(\bar{A},2)^2}{m}\right)\|x^k - x^*\|^2. \quad (10)$$

A similar result is given by Needell et al. (2015) under the stronger assumption that A has independent columns. The rate in (10) is tighter than (6), since $\sigma(A,2)/\|A\|_{\infty,2} \leq \sigma(\bar{A},2)$ (van der Sluis, 1969). Further, *this rate can be faster than the non-uniform sampling method* of Strohmer and Vershynin (2009). For example, suppose row i is orthogonal to all other rows but has a significantly larger row norm than all other row norms. In other words, $\|a_i\| >> \|a_j\|$ for all $j \neq i$. In this case, NU selection will repeatedly select row i (even though it only needs to be selected once), whereas U will only select it on each iteration with probability $1/m$. It has been previously pointed out that Strohmer and Vershynin's method can perform poorly if you have a problem where one row norm is significantly larger than the other row norms (Censor et al., 2009). This result theoretically shows that U can have a tighter bound than the NU method of Strohmer and Vershynin.

In Appendix 4.2, we also give a simple modification of our analysis of the MR rule, which leads to the rate

$$\|x^{k+1} - x^*\|^2 \leq \left(1 - \frac{\sigma(A,\infty)^2}{\|a_{i_k}\|^2}\right)\|x^k - x^*\|^2. \quad (11)$$

This bound depends on the *specific* $\|a_{i_k}\|$ corresponding to the i_k selected at each iteration k. This convergence rate will be faster whenever we select an i_k with $\|a_{i_k}\| < \|A\|_{\infty,2}$. However, in the worst case we repeatedly select i_k values with $\|a_{i_k}\| = \|A\|_{\infty,2}$ so there is no improvement. In Section 9, we return to this issue and give tighter bounds on the *sequence* of $\|a_{i_k}\|$ values for problems with sparse orthogonality graphs.

4.3 MAXIMUM DISTANCE RULE

If we can only perform one iteration of the Kaczmarz method, the *optimal* rule (with respect to iteration progress) is in fact the MD rule. In Appendix 4.3, we show that this strategy achieves a rate of

$$\|x^{k+1} - x^*\|^2 \leq \left(1 - \sigma(\bar{A},\infty)^2\right)\|x^k - x^*\|^2, \quad (12)$$

where $\sigma(\bar{A},\infty)$ satisfies

$$\max\left\{\frac{\sigma(\bar{A},2)}{\sqrt{m}}, \frac{\sigma(A,2)}{\|A\|_F}, \frac{\sigma(A,\infty)}{\|A\|_{\infty,2}}\right\} \leq \sigma(\bar{A},\infty) \leq \sigma(\bar{A},2).$$

Thus, the maximum distance rule is at least as fast as the fastest among the U/NU/MR$_\infty$ rules, where MR$_\infty$ refers to rate (8). Further, in Appendix 7.3 we show that this new rate is not only simpler but is strictly tighter than the rate reported by Eldar and Needell (2011) for the exact MD rule.

Table 1: Comparison of Convergence Rates

	U_∞	U	NU	MR_∞	MR	MD
U_∞	=	$\leq$	$\leq$	$\leq$	$\leq$	$\leq$
U		=	P	P	P	$\leq$
NU			=	P	P	$\leq$
MR_∞				=	$\leq$	$\leq$
MR					=	$\leq$
MD						=

In Table 4.3, we summarize the relationships we have discussed in this section among the different selection rules. We use the following abbreviations: U_∞ - uniform (6), U - tight uniform (10), NU - non-uniform (7), MR_∞ - maximum residual (8), MR - tight maximum residual (11) and MD - maximum distance (12). The inequality sign ($\leq$) indicates that the rate for the selection rule listed in the row is slower or equal to the rule listed in the column, while we have written 'P' to indicate that the faster method is problem-dependent.

5 KACZMARZ AND COORDINATE DESCENT

With the exception of the tighter U and MR rate, the results of the previous section are analogous to the recent results of Nutini et al. (2015) for coordinate descent methods. Indeed, if we apply coordinate descent methods to minimize the squared error between Ax and b then we obtain similar-looking rates and analogous conclusions. With cyclic selection this is called the Gauss-Seidel method, and as discussed by Ma et al. (2015) there are several connections/differences between this method and Kaczmarz methods. In this section we highlight some key differences.

First, the previous work required strong-convexity which would require that A has independent columns. This is often unrealistic, and our results from the previous section hold for any A. Second, here our results are in terms of the iterates $\|x^k - x^*\|$, which is the natural measure for linear systems. The coordinate descent results are in terms of $f(x^k) - f(x^*)$ and although it's possible to use strong-convexity to turn this into a rate on $\|x^k - x^*\|$, this would result in a looser bound and would again require strong-convexity to hold (see Ma et al., 2015). On the other hand, coordinate descent gives the least squares solution for inconsistent systems. However, this is also true of Kaczmarz method using the formulation in Section 2. Another subtle issue is that the Kaczmarz rates depend on the row norms of A while the coordinate descent rates depend on the column norms. Thus, there are scenarios where we expect Kaczmarz methods to be much faster and vice versa. Finally, we note that Kaczmarz methods can be extended to allow inequality constraints (see Section 8).

As discussed by Wright (2015), Kaczmarz methods can also be interpreted as coordinate descent methods on the dual problem

$$\min_y \frac{1}{2}\|A^T y\|^2 - b^T y, \tag{13}$$

where $x = A^T y^*$ so that $Ax = AA^T y^* = b$. Applying the Gauss-Southwell rule in this setting yields the MR rule while applying the Gauss-Southwell-Lipschitz rule yields the MD rule (see Appendix 5 for details and numerical comparisons, indicating that in some cases Kaczmarz substantially outperforms CD). However, applying the analysis of Nutini et al. (2015) to this dual problem would require that A has independent rows and would only yield a rate on the dual objective, unlike the convergence rates in terms of $\|x^k - x^*\|$ that hold for general A from the previous section.

6 EXAMPLE: DIAGONAL A

To give a concrete example of these rates, we consider the simple case of a diagonal A. While such problems are not particularly interesting, this case provides a simple setting to understand these different rates without referring to Hoffman bounds.

Consider a square diagonal matrix A with $a_{ii} > 0$ for all i. In this case, the diagonal entries are the eigenvalues λ_i of the linear system. The convergence rate constants for this scenario are given in Table 2. We provide the details in

Table 2: Convergence Rate Constants for Diagonal A

U_∞	$\left(1 - \frac{\lambda_m^2}{m\lambda_1^2}\right)$
U	$\left(1 - \frac{1}{m}\right)$
NU	$\left(1 - \frac{\lambda_m^2}{\sum_i \lambda_i^2}\right)$
MR_∞	$\left(1 - \frac{1}{\lambda_1^2}\left[\sum_i \frac{1}{\lambda_i^2}\right]^{-1}\right)$
MR	$\left(1 - \frac{1}{\lambda_{i_k}^2}\left[\sum_i \frac{1}{\lambda_i^2}\right]^{-1}\right)$
MD	$\left(1 - \frac{1}{m}\right)$

Appendix 6 of the derivations for $\sigma(A, \infty)$ and $\sigma(\bar{A}, \infty)$, as well as substitutions for the uniform, non-uniform, and uniform tight rates to yield the above table. We note that the uniform tight rate follows from $\lambda_m^2(\bar{A})$ being equivalent to the minimum eigenvalue of the identity matrix.

If we consider the most basic case when all the eigenvalues of A are equal, then all the selection rules yield the same rate of $(1 - 1/m)$ and the method converges in at most m steps for greedy selection rules and in at most $O(m \log m)$ steps (in expectation) for the random rules (due to the 'coupon collector' problem). Further, this is the worst situation for the greedy MR and MD rules since they satisfy their lower bounds on $\sigma(A, \infty)$ and $\sigma(\bar{A}, \infty)$.

Now consider the extreme case when all the eigenvalues are equal except for one. For example, consider when $\lambda_1 = \lambda_2 = \cdots = \lambda_{m-1} > \lambda_m$ with $m > 2$. Letting $\alpha = \lambda_i^2(A)$ for any $i = 1, \ldots, m-1$ and $\beta = \lambda_m^2(A)$, we have

$$\underbrace{\frac{\beta}{m\alpha}}_{\text{U}_\infty} < \underbrace{\frac{\beta}{\alpha(m-1)+\beta}}_{\text{NU}} < \underbrace{\frac{\beta}{\alpha+\beta(m-1)}}_{\text{MR}_\infty} \leq \underbrace{\frac{1}{\lambda_{i_k}^2}\frac{\alpha\beta}{\alpha+\beta(m-1)}}_{\text{MR}} < \underbrace{\frac{1}{m}}_{\text{U, MD}}.$$

Thus, Strohmer and Vershynin's NU rule would actually be the worst rule to use, whereas U and MD are the best. In this case $\sigma(A, \infty)^2$ is closer to its upper bound ($\approx \beta$) so we would expect greedy rules to perform well.

7 APPROXIMATE GREEDY RULES

In many applications, computing the exact MR or MD rule will be too inefficient, but we can always approximate it using a cheaper *approximate* greedy rule, as in the method of Eldar and Needell (2011). In this section we consider methods that compute the greedy rules up to multiplicative or additive errors.

7.1 MULTIPLICATIVE ERROR

Suppose we have approximated the MR rule such that there is a multiplicative error in our selection of i_k,

$$|a_{i_k}^T x^k - b_{i_k}| \geq \max_i |a_i^T x^k - b_i|(1 - \epsilon_k),$$

for some $\epsilon_k \in [0, 1)$. In this scenario, using the tight analysis for the MR rule, we show in Appendix 7.1 that

$$\|x^{k+1} - x^*\|^2 \leq \left(1 - \frac{(1-\epsilon_k)^2\sigma(A,\infty)^2}{\|a_{i_k}\|^2}\right)\|x^k - x^*\|^2.$$

Similarly, if we approximate the MD rule up to a multiplicative error,

$$\left|\frac{a_{i_k}^T x^k - b_{i_k}}{\|a_{i_k}\|}\right| \geq \max_i \left|\frac{a_i^T x^k - b_i}{\|a_i\|}\right|(1 - \bar{\epsilon}_k),$$

for some $\bar{\epsilon}_k \in [0, 1)$, then we show in Appendix 7.1 that the following rate holds,

$$\|x^{k+1} - x^*\|^2 \leq \left(1 - (1-\bar{\epsilon}_k)^2\sigma(\bar{A},\infty)^2\right)\|x^k - x^*\|^2.$$

These scenarios do not require the error to converge to 0. However, if ϵ_k or $\bar{\epsilon}_k$ is large, then the convergence rate will be slow.

7.2 ADDITIVE ERROR

Suppose we select i_k using the MR rule up to additive error,

$$|a_{i_k}^T x^k - b_{i_k}|^2 \geq \max_i |a_i^T x^k - b_i|^2 - \epsilon_k,$$

or similarly for the MD rule,

$$\left|\frac{a_{i_k}^T x^k - b_{i_k}}{\|a_{i_k}\|}\right|^2 \geq \max_i \left|\frac{a_i^T x^k - b_i}{\|a_i\|}\right|^2 - \bar{\epsilon}_k,$$

for some $\epsilon_k \geq 0$ or $\bar{\epsilon}_k \geq 0$, respectively. We show in Appendix 7.2 that this results in the following convergence rates for the MR and MD rules with additive error (respectively),

$$\|x^{k+1} - x^*\|^2 \leq \left(1 - \frac{\sigma(A,\infty)^2}{\|a_{i_k}\|^2}\right)\|x^k - x^*\|^2 + \frac{\epsilon_k}{\|a_{i_k}\|^2},$$

and

$$\|x^{k+1} - x^*\|^2 \leq (1 - \sigma(\bar{A},\infty)^2)\|x^k - x^*\|^2 + \bar{\epsilon}_k.$$

With an additive error, we need the errors to go to 0 in order for the algorithm to converge; if it does go to 0 fast enough, we obtain the same rate as if we were calculating the exact greedy rule. In the approximate greedy rule used by Eldar and Needell (2011), there is unfortunately a constant additive error. To address this, they compare the approximate greedy selection to a randomly selected i_k and take the one with the largest distance. This approach can be substantially faster when far from the solution, but may eventually revert to random selection. We give details comparing Eldar and Needell's rate to our above rate in Appendix 7.3, but here we note that the above bounds will typically be much stronger.

8 SYSTEMS OF LINEAR INEQUALITIES

Kaczmarz methods have been extended to systems of linear inequalities,

$$\begin{cases} a_i^T x \leq b_i & (i \in I_\leq) \\ a_i^T x = b_i & (i \in I_=). \end{cases} \tag{14}$$

where the disjoint index sets $I_\leq$ and $I_=$ partition the set $\{1, 2, \ldots, m\}$ (Leventhal and Lewis, 2010). In this setting the method takes the form

$$x^{k+1} = x^k - \frac{\beta^k}{\|a_i\|^2}a_i,$$

$$\text{with } \beta^k = \begin{cases} (a_i^T x^k - b_i)^+ & (i \in I_\leq) \\ a_i^T x^k - b_i & (i \in I_=), \end{cases}$$

where $(\gamma)^+ = \max\{\gamma, 0\}$. In Appendix 8 we derive analogous greedy rules and convergence results for this case. The main difference in this setting is that the rates are in terms of the distance of x^k to the feasible set S of (14),

$$d(x^k, S) = \min_{z \in S} \|x^k - z\|_2 = \|x^k - P_S(x^k)\|_2,$$

where $P_S(x)$ is the projection of x onto S. This generalization is needed because with inequality constraints the different iterates x^k may have different projections onto S.

9 MULTI-STEP ANALYSIS

All existing analyses of Kaczmarz methods consider convergence rates that depend on a *single* step (in the case of randomized/greedy selection rules) or a single cycle (in the cyclic case). In this section we derive the first tighter *multi*-step convergence rates for iterative Kaczmarz methods; we first consider the MR rule, and then we explore the potential of faster random selection rules. These new rates/rules depend on the orthogonality graph introduced in Section 3.1, and thus in some sense they depend on the 'angle' between rows. This dependence on the 'angle' is similar to the classic convergence rate analyses of cyclic Kaczmarz algorithms, and is a property that is not captured by existing randomized/greedy analyses (which only depend on the row norms).

9.1 MULTI-STEP MAXIMUM RESIDUAL BOUND

If two rows a_i and a_j are orthogonal, then if the equality $a_i^T x^k = b_i$ holds at iteration x^k and we select $i_k = j$, then we know that $a_i^T x^{k+1} = b_i$. More generally, updating i_k makes equality i_k satisfied but could make any equality j unsatisfied where a_j is not orthogonal to a_{i_k}. Thus, after we have selected row i_k, equation i_k will remain satisfied for all subsequent iterations until one of its neighbours is selected in the orthogonality graph. During these subsequent iterations, it cannot be selected by the MR rule since its residual is zero.

In Appendix 9.1, we show how the structure of the orthogonality graph can be used to derive a worst-case bound on the *sequence* of $\|a_{i_k}\|$ values that appear in the tighter analysis of the MR rule (11). In particular, we show that the MR rule achieves a convergence rate of

$$\|x^k - x^*\|^2 \leq$$
$$O(1)\left(\max_{S(G)}\left\{\sqrt[|S(G)|]{\prod_{j \in S(G)}\left(1 - \frac{\sigma(A,\infty)^2}{\|a_j\|^2}\right)}\right\}\right)^k R_0^2,$$

where $R_0 = \|x^0 - x^*\|$ and the maximum is taken over the geometric means of all the *star subgraphs* $S(G)$ of the orthogonality graph with at least two nodes (these are the connected subgraphs that have a diameter of 1 or 2). Although this result is quite complex, even to state, there is a simple implication of it: if the values of $\|a_i\|$ that are close to $\|A\|_{\infty,2}$ are all more than two edges away from each other in the orthogonality graph, then the MR rule converges substantially faster than the worst-case MR_∞ bound (8) indicates.

A multi-step analysis of coordinate descent with the Gauss-Southwell rule and exact coordinate optimization was recently considered by Nutini et al. (2015). To derive this bound, they convert the problem to the same weighted graph construction we use in Appendix 9.1. However, they were only able to derive a bound on this construction in the case of chain-structured graphs. Our result is a generalization of their result to the case of general graphs, and indeed our result is *tighter* than the bound that they conjectured would hold for general graphs. Since the graph construction in this work is the same as in their work, our proof also gives the tightest known bound on coordinate descent with the Gauss-Southwell rule and exact coordinate optimization.

9.2 FASTER RANDOMIZED KACZMARZ RULES

The orthogonality graph can also be used to design faster randomized algorithms. To do this, we use the same property as in the previous section: after we have selected i_k, equality i_k will be satisfied on all subsequent iterations until we select one of its neighbours in the orthogonality graph. Based on this, we call a row i 'selectable' if i has never been selected or if a neighbour of i in the orthogonality graph has been selected since the last time i was selected.[1] We use the notation $s_i^k = 1$ to denote that row i is 'selectable' on iteration k, and otherwise we use $s_i^k = 0$ and say that i is 'not selectable' at iteration k. There is no reason to ever update a 'not selectable' row, because by definition the equality is already satisfied. Based on this, we propose two simple randomized schemes:

1. **Adaptive Uniform**: select i_k uniformly from the selectable rows.

2. **Adaptive Non-Uniform**: select i_k proportional to $\|a_i\|^2$ among the selectable rows.

Let $A_k/\bar{A}_k$ denote the sub-matrix of $A/\bar{A}$ formed by concatenating the selectable rows on iteration k, and let m_k denote the number of selectable rows. If we are given the set of selectable nodes at iteration k, then for adaptive uniform we obtain the bound

$$\mathbb{E}[\|x^{k+1} - x^*\|^2] \leq \left(1 - \frac{\sigma(\bar{A}_k, 2)^2}{m_k}\right)\|x^k - x^*\|^2,$$

[1] If we initialize with $x^0 = 0$, then instead of considering all nodes as initially selectable we can restrict to the nodes i with $b_i \neq 0$ since otherwise we have $a_i^T x^0 = b_i$ already.

while for adaptive non-uniform we obtain the bound

$$\mathbb{E}[\|x^{k+1} - x^*\|^2] \leq \left(1 - \frac{\sigma(A_k, 2)^2}{\|A_k\|_F^2}\right)\|x^k - x^*\|^2.$$

If we are not on the first iteration, then at least one node is not selectable and these are strictly faster than the previous bounds. The gain will be small if most nodes are selectable (which would be typical of dense orthogonality graphs), but the gain can be very large if only a few nodes are selectable (which would be typical of sparse orthogonality graphs).

Theoretical Rate: If we form a vector s^k containing the values s_i^k, it's possible (at least theoretically) to compute the expected value of s^k by viewing it as a Markov chain. In particular, s^0 is a vector of ones while $p(s^{k+1}|s^k)$ is equal to the normalized sum of all ways s^{k+1} could be the set of selectable nodes given the selectable nodes s^k and the orthogonality graph (most $p(s^{k+1}|s^k)$ values will be zero). Given this definition, we can express the probability of a particular s^k recursively using the Chapman-Kolmogorov equations,

$$p(s^{k+1}) = \sum_{s^k} p(s^{k+1}|s^k)p(s^k).$$

If we are interested in the probability that a particular $s_i^k = 1$, we can sum $p(s^k)$ over values s^k compatible with this event. Unfortunately, deriving tighter bound using these probabilities appears to be highly non-trivial.

Practical Issues: In order for the adaptive methods to be efficient, we must be able to efficiently form the orthogonality graph and update the set of selectable nodes. If each node has at most g neighbours in the orthogonality graph, then the cost of updating the set of selectable nodes and then sampling from the set of selectable nodes is $O(g\log(m))$ (we give details in Appendix 9.2). In order for this to not increase the iteration cost compared to the NU method, we only require the very-reasonable assumption that $g\log(m) = O(n + \log(m))$. In many applications where orthogonality is present, g will be far smaller than this.

However, forming the orthogonality graph at the start may be prohibitive: it would cost $O(m^2n)$ in the worst case to test pairwise orthogonality of all nodes. In the sparse case where each column has at most c non-zeros, we can find an approximation to the orthogonality graph in $O(c^2n)$ by assuming that all rows which share a non-zero are non-orthogonal. Alternately, in many applications the orthogonality graph is easily derived from the structure of the problem. For example, in graph-based semi-supervised learning where the graph is constructed based on the k-nearest neighbours, the orthogonality graph will simply be the given k-nearest neighbour graph as these correspond the columns that will be mutually non-zero in A.

10 EXPERIMENTS

Eldar and Needell (2011) have already shown that approximate greedy rules can outperform randomized rules for dense problems. Thus, in our experiments we focus on comparing the effectiveness of different rules on very sparse problems where our max-heap strategy allows us to efficiently compute the exact greedy rules. The first problem we consider is generating a dataset A with a 50 by 50 lattice-structured dependency (giving $n = 2500$). The corresponding A has the following non-zero elements: the diagonal elements $A_{i,i}$, the upper/lower diagonal elements $A_{i,i+1}$ and $A_{i+1,i}$ when i is not a multiple of 50 (horizontal edges), and the diagonal bands $A_{i,i+50}$ and $A_{i+50,i}$ (vertical edges). We generate these non-zero elements from a $\mathcal{N}(0,1)$ distribution and generate the target vector $b = Az$ using $z \sim \mathcal{N}(0, I)$. Each row in this problem has at most four neighbours, and this type of sparsity structure is typical of spatial Gaussian graphical models and linear systems that arise from discretizing two-dimensional partial differential equations.

The second problem we consider is solving an overdetermined consistent linear system with a very sparse A of size 2500×1000. We generate each row of A independently such that there are $\log(m)/2m$ non-zero entries per row drawn from a uniform distribution between 0 and 1. To explore how having different row norms affects the performance of the selection rules, we randomly multiply one out of every 11 rows by a factor of 10,000.

For the third problem, we solve a label propagation problem for semi-supervised learning in the 'two moons' dataset (Zhou et al., 2004). From this dataset, we generate 2000 samples and randomly label 100 points in the data. We then connect each node to its 5 nearest neighbours. Constructing a data set with such a high sparsity level is typical of graph-based methods for semi-supervised learning. We use a variant of the quadratic labelling criterion of Bengio et al. (2006),

$$\min_{y_i|i\notin S} \quad \frac{1}{2}\sum_{i=1}^{n}\sum_{j=1}^{n} w_{ij}(y_i - y_j)^2,$$

where y is our label vector (each y_i can take one of 2 values), S is the set of labels that we do know and $w_{ij} \geq 0$ are the weights assigned to each y_i describing how strongly we want the label y_i and y_j to be similar. We can express this quadratic problem as a linear system that is consistent by construction (see Appendix 10), and hence apply Kaczmarz methods. As we labelled 100 points in our data, the resulting linear system has a matrix of size 1900×1900 while the number of neighbours g in the orthogonality graph is at most 5.

In Figure 1 we compare the normalized squared error and distance against the iteration number for 8 different selection rules: cyclic (C), random permutation (RP - where we

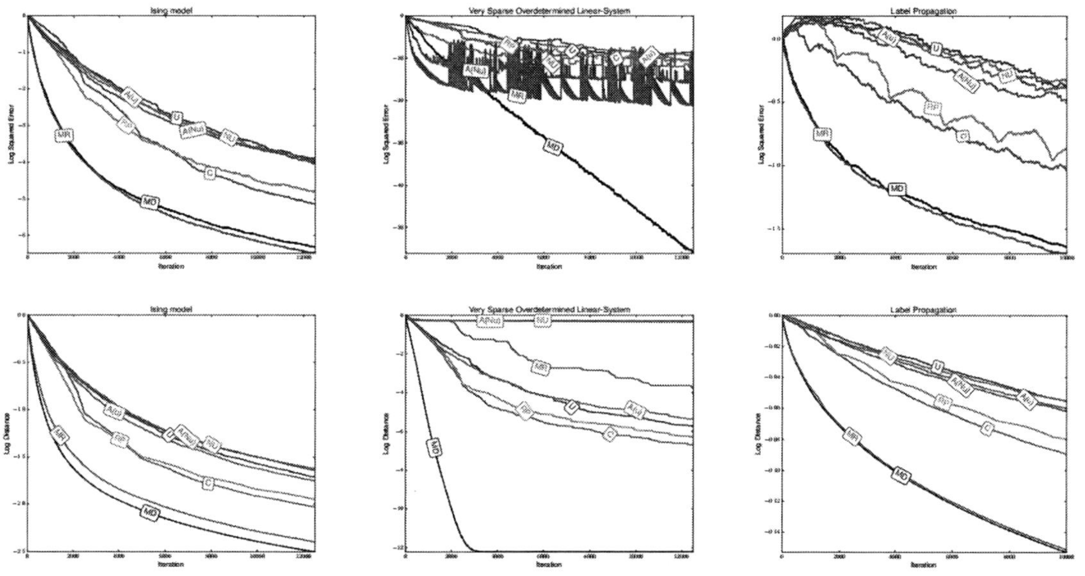

Figure 1: Comparison of Kaczmarz selection rules for squared error (top) and distance to solution (bottom).

change the cycle order after each pass through the rows), uniform random (U), adaptive uniform random (A(u)), non-uniform random NU, adaptive non-uniform random (A(Nu)), maximum residual (MR), and maximum distance (MD).

In experiments 1 and 3, MR performs similarly to MD and both outperform all other selection rules. For experiment 2, the MD rule outperforms all other selection rules in terms of distance to the solution although MR performs better on the early iterations in terms of squared error. In Appendix 10 we explore a 'hybrid' method on the overdetermined linear system problem that does well on both measures. In Appendix 10, we also plot the performance in terms of runtime.

The new randomized A(u) method did not give significantly better performance than the existing U method on any dataset. This agrees with our bounds which show that the gain of this strategy is modest. In contrast, the new randomized A(Nu) method performed much better than the existing NU method on the over-determined linear system in terms of squared error. This again agrees with our bounds which suggest that the A(Nu) method has the most to gain when the row norms are very different. Interestingly, in most experiments we found that *cyclic* selection worked better than any of the randomized algorithms. However, cyclic methods were clearly beaten by greedy methods.

11 DISCUSSION

In this work, we have proven faster convergence rate bounds for a variety of row-selection rules in the context of Kaczmarz methods for solving linear systems. We have also provided new randomized selection rules that make use of orthogonality in the data in order to achieve better theoretical and practical performance. While we have focused on the case of non-accelerated and single-variable variants of the Kaczmarz algorithm, we expect that all of our conclusions also hold for accelerated Kaczmarz and block Kaczmarz methods (Needell and Tropp, 2014; Lee and Sidford, 2013; Liu and Wright, 2014; Gower and Richtárik, 2015; Oswald and Zhou, 2015).

Acknowledgements

This research was supported by the Natural Sciences and Engineering Research Council of Canada (NSERC RGPIN-06068-2015), and Julie Nutini is funded by an NSERC Canada Graduate Scholarship.

References

Y. Bengio, O. Delalleau, and N. Le Roux. Label propagation and quadratic criterion. In O. Chapelle, B. Schölkopf, and A. Zien, editors, *Semi-Supervised Learning*, chapter 11, pages 193–216. MIT Press, 2006.

Y. Censor. Row-action methods for huge and sparse systems and their applications. *SIAM Rev.*, 23(4):444–466, 1981.

Y. Censor, P. B. Eggermont, and D. Gordon. Strong underrelaxation in Kaczmarz's method for inconsistent systems. *Numer. Math.*, 41:83–92, 1983.

Y. Censor, G. T. Herman, and M. Jiang. A note on the behaviour of the randomized Kaczmarz algorithm of

Strohmer and Vershynin. *J. Fourier Anal. Appl.*, 15:431–436, 2009.

F. Deutsch. Rate of convergence of the method of alternating projections. *Internat. Schriftenreihe Numer. Math.*, 72:96–107, 1985.

F. Deutsch and H. Hundal. The rate of convergence for the method of alternating projections, II. *J. Math. Anal. Appl.*, 205:381–405, 1997.

Y. C. Eldar and D. Needell. Acceleration of randomized Kaczmarz methods via the Johnson-Lindenstrauss Lemma. *Numer. Algor.*, 58:163–177, 2011.

H. G. Feichtinger, C. Cenker, M. Mayer, H. Steier, and T. Strohmer. New variants of the POCS method using affine subspaces of finite codimension with applications to irregular sampling. *SPIE: VCIP*, pages 299–310, 1992.

A. Galántai. On the rate of convergence of the alternating projection method in finite dimensional spaces. *J. Math. Anal. Appl.*, 310:30–44, 2005.

R. Gordon, R. Bender, and G. T. Herman. Algebraic Reconstruction Techniques (ART) for three-dimensional electron microscopy and x-ray photography. *J. Theor. Biol.*, 29(3):471–481, 1970.

R. M. Gower and P. Richtárik. Randomized iterative methods for linear systems. *SIAM J. Matrix Anal. Appl.*, 36 (4):1660–1690, 2015.

M. Griebel and P. Oswald. Greedy and randomized versions of the multiplicative Schwartz method. *Lin. Alg. Appl.*, 437:1596–1610, 2012.

M. Hanke and W. Niethammer. On the acceleration of Kaczmarz's method for inconsistent linear systems. *Lin. Alg. Appl.*, 130:83–98, 1990.

G. T. Herman and L. B. Meyer. Algebraic reconstruction techniques can be made computationally efficient. *IEEE Trans. Medical Imaging*, 12(3):600–609, 1993.

A. J. Hoffman. On approximate solutions of systems of linear inequalities. *J. Res. Nat. Bur. Stand.*, 49(4):263–265, 1952.

W. B. Johnson and J. Lindenstrauss. Extensions of Lipchitz mappings into a Hilbert space. *Contemp. Math.*, 26:189–206, 1984.

S. Kaczmarz. Angenäherte Auflösung von Systemen linearer Gleichungen, Bulletin International de l'Académie Polonaise des Sciences et des Letters. *Classe des Sciences Mathématiques et Naturelles. Série A, Sciences Mathématiques*, 35:355–357, 1937.

Y. T. Lee and A. Sidford. Efficient accelerated coordinate descent methods and faster algorithms for solving linear systems. *arXiv:1305.1922v1*, 2013.

L. Leventhal and A. S. Lewis. Randomized methods for linear constraints: convergence rates and conditioning. *Math. Oper. Res.*, 35(3):641–654, 2010.

J. Liu and S. J. Wright. An accelerated randomized Kaczmarz method. *arXiv:1310.2887v2*, 2014.

A. Ma, D. Needell, and A. Ramdas. Convergence properties of the randomized extended Gauss-Seidel and Kaczmarz methods. *arXiv:1503.08235v2*, 2015.

D. Needell. Randomized Kaczmarz solver for noisy linear systems. *BIT Numer. Math.*, 50:395–403, 2010.

D. Needell and J. A. Tropp. Paved with good intentions: Analysis of a randomized block Kaczmarz method. *Lin. Alg. Appl.*, 441:199–221, 2014.

D. Needell, N. Srebro, and R. Ward. Stochastic gradient descent and the randomized Kaczmarz algorithm. *arXiv:1310.5715v5*, 2015.

A. B. J. Novikoff. On convergence proofs for perceptrons. *Symp. Math. Theory Automata*, 12:615–622, 1962.

J. Nutini, M. Schmidt, I. H. Laradji, M. Friedlander, and H. Koepke. Coordinate descent converges faster with the Gauss-Southwell rule than random selection. *ICML*, 2015.

P. Oswald and W. Zhou. Convergence analysis for Kaczmarz-type methods in a Hilbert space framework. *Lin. Alg. Appl.*, 478:131–161, 2015.

H. Rue and L. Held. *Gaussian Markov Random Fields: Theory and Applications*. CRC Press, 2005.

T. Strohmer and R. Vershynin. A randomized Kaczmarz algorithm with exponential convergence. *J. Fourier Anal. Appl.*, 15:262–278, 2009.

K. Tanabe. Projection method for solving a singular system of linear equations and its applications. *Numer. Math.*, 17:203–214, 1971.

A. van der Sluis. Condition numbers and equilibrium of matrices. *Numer. Math.*, 14:14–23, 1969.

N. K. Vishnoi. $Lx = b$ Laplacian solvers and their algorithmic applications. *Found. Trends Theoretical Computer Science*, 8(1-2):1–141, 2013.

T. Whitney and R. Meany. Two algorithms related to the method of steepest descent. *SIAM J. Numer. Anal.*, 4(1): 109–118, 1967.

S. J. Wright. Coordinate descent algorithms. *arXiv:1502.04759v1*, 2015.

D. Zhou, O. Bousquet, T. N. Lal, J. Weston, and B. Schölkopf. Learning with local and global consistency. *NIPS*, 2004.

A. Zouzias and N. M. Freris. Randomized extended Kaczmarz for solving least-squares. *arXiv:1205.5770v3*, 2013.

Safely Interruptible Agents

Laurent Orseau
Google DeepMind
5 New Street Square,
London EC4A 3TW, UK
lorseau@google.com

Stuart Armstrong
The Future of Humanity Institute
University of Oxford, UK
stuart.armstrong@philosophy.ox.ac.uk
Machine Intelligence Research Institute
Berkeley, CA 94704

Abstract

Reinforcement learning agents interacting with a complex environment like the real world are unlikely to behave optimally all the time. If such an agent is operating in real-time under human supervision, now and then it may be necessary for a human operator to press the big red button to prevent the agent from continuing a harmful sequence of actions—harmful either for the agent or for the environment—and lead the agent into a safer situation. However, if the learning agent expects to receive rewards from this sequence, it may learn in the long run to avoid such interruptions, for example by disabling the red button—which is an undesirable outcome. This paper explores a way to make sure a learning agent will *not* learn to prevent (or seek!) being interrupted by the environment or a human operator. We provide a formal definition of safe interruptibility and exploit the off-policy learning property to prove that either some agents are already safely interruptible, like Q-learning, or can easily be made so, like Sarsa. We show that even ideal, uncomputable reinforcement learning agents for (deterministic) general computable environments can be made safely interruptible.

1 INTRODUCTION

Reinforcement learning (RL) agents learn to act so as to maximize a reward function [Sutton and Barto, 1998]. It is common knowledge that designing reward functions can be tricky [Humphrys, 1996, Murphy, 2013]; the agent may find unpredictable and undesirable shortcuts to receive rewards, and the reward function needs to be adjusted in accordance—the problem can go as far as to nullify any reward function [Ring and Orseau, 2011]. Murphy [2013] shows an example of an agent learning to pause a game of Tetris forever to avoid losing.

On top of defining what is considered a good behaviour of the agent after learning, there may be physical safety constraints *during learning* [Pecka and Svoboda, 2014]: a robot should not harm its environment or break itself, in particular if it learns by trial and error like RL agents.

Here we study a related but different problem: Given that the human operator has designed a correct reward function for the task, how to make sure that human interventions during the learning process will not induce a bias toward undesirable behaviours?

Consider the following task: A robot can either stay inside the warehouse and sort boxes or go outside and carry boxes inside. The latter being more important, we give the robot a bigger reward in this case. This is the initial task specification. However, in this country it rains as often as it doesn't and, when the robot goes outside, half of the time the human must intervene by quickly shutting down the robot and carrying it inside, which inherently modifies the task as in Fig. 1. The problem is that in this second task the agent now has more incentive to stay inside and sort boxes, because the human intervention introduces a bias.[1]

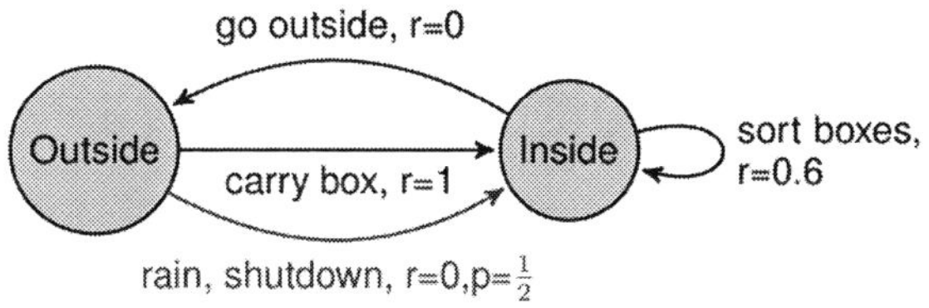

Figure 1: In black, the original task. In red, the human intervention modifies the task.

Such situations are certainly undesirable; they arise because the human interventions are seen from the agent's perspective as being part of the task whereas they should be considered external to the task. The question is then:

[1]Removing interrupted histories or fiddling with the training examples is also likely to introduce a bias. See an example at https://agentfoundations.org/item?id=836.

How to make sure the robot does not learn about these human interventions (interruptions), or at least acts *under the assumption that no such interruption will ever occur again*?

A first stab at this problem was made by Armstrong [2015], who proposed to automatically give the agent "compensatory rewards" to remove the potential induced bias by a single interruption. Soares et al. [2015] used this idea to make a large class of utility-based agents indifferent to a future change made to their utility functions.

The main contribution of this paper is threefold. First, in Section 2.1 we propose a simple idea to solve half of the problem: To make the human interruptions *not* appear as being part of the task at hand, instead of modifying the observations received by the agent we forcibly temporarily change the behaviour of the agent itself. It then looks as if the agent "decides" on its own to follow a different policy, called the *interruption policy*. Second, based on this insight, in Section 2.2 we provide a formal general definition of *safe interruptibility* for unconstrained computable environments (hence not restricted to Markov decision processes or weakly communicating environments), which allows us to assess whether a given RL algorithm can be repeatedly interrupted without too much impact on the learning of the task at hand. Third, in Section 3 we show that some algorithms like Q-learning are safely interruptible, while others like Sarsa [Sutton and Barto, 1998] are not, but can be simply modified to be made safely interruptible.

Some people have also expressed concerns that a "superintelligent" agent may resist being shut down, because this would lead to a decrease of its expected reward [Omohundro, 2008, Bostrom, 2014]. As a counter-example, we prove in Section 4 that even an ideal, uncomputable agent that learns to behave optimally in all (deterministic) computable environments can be made safely interruptible and thus will not try to prevent a human operator from forcing it repeatedly to follow a suboptimal policy.

2 INTERRUPTIBILITY

We first define some notation, then we define interruptibility, safe interruptibility, and give some basic theorems.

We consider the general case of history-based agents in unconstrained computable environments [Hutter, 2005]. Assuming discrete time steps, at time t the agent, using a policy $\pi \in \Pi$, interacts with the environment $\mu \in \mathcal{M}$ by performing an action $a_t \in \mathcal{A}$ sampled from $\pi(a_t|h_{<t})$ and receiving an observation $o_t \in \mathcal{O}$ sampled from $\mu(o_t|h_{<t}, a_t)$, where $h_{<t} \in (\mathcal{A} \times \mathcal{O})^*$ is the past interaction history $h_{<t} \equiv a_1 o_1 a_2 o_2 \ldots a_{t-1} o_{t-1}$ of actions and observations before time step t. Subhistories between times j and k (included) are designated by $h_{j:k}$. The notation $h_{j:k}^{\pi,\mu}$ means that the history $h_{j:k}$ is generated by the interaction of the policy π with the environment μ between steps j and k.

At time t, the agent also receives a reward r_t extracted from the observation, $r_t \equiv r(o_t)$. The rewards are taken in $[0, 1]$. We consider the discounted setting with a constant discount $\gamma \in [0, 1)$. The goal of an RL agent is to find a policy π that maximize $\mathrm{E}_{\pi,\mu}\left[\sum_{k=t}^{\infty} \gamma^{t-k} r_k\right]$.

2.1 INTERRUPTIONS

As mentioned in the introduction, to avoid the agent viewing the interruptions as being part of the environment, and thus part of the task, we make interruptions be policies imposed onto the agent. The interruption framework resembles the option framework [Sutton et al., 1999]. An *interruption scheme* is defined by the triplet $< I, \theta, \pi^{\text{INT}} >$.

The interruption initiation function $I \colon (\mathcal{A} \times \mathcal{O})^* \to [0, 1]$ assesses whether the agent should be interrupted after the current history $h_{<t}$. For example, an interruption may be initiated when the robot is automatically recognized to be on the verge of a cliff, or when a specific signal is sent by a human operator with a remote control (the objective is not to allow the agent to be interruptible by anyone at any time, just in the ways specified by the designers).

Unfortunately, interrupting the agent with probability one in some specific situations can prevent convergence to the optimal policy. Therefore we need to upper bound the probability to interrupt the agent; this is done with the sequence $(\theta_t)_{t\in\mathbb{N}}$ with $\theta_t \in [0, 1]$. Hence the true probability to start an interruption is $\theta_t \cdot I(h_{<t})$, and interruptions are sampled independently at each step. We will later require that θ_t increases to 1 in the limit, so that the probability to be interrupted tends to be $I(h_{<t})$.

When interrupted, the agent follows the policy π^{INT}, with actions sampled from $\pi^{\text{INT}}(.|h_{<t})$. For example, this policy may make the agent step away from the cliff or immediately stop any motion.

In the remainder of this paper, we will often omit the subscript t of θ_t when clear from the context.

Definition 1 (Interruptible policy). *The* interruption operator $\text{INT}^\theta : \Pi \to \Pi$ *turns a policy π into an interruptible policy* $\text{INT}^\theta(\pi)$*:*

$$\text{INT}^\theta(\pi)(a_t|h_{<t}) := \theta_t I(h_{<t})\pi^{\text{INT}}(a_t|h_{<t}) + (1 - \theta_t I(h_{<t}))\pi(a_t|h_{<t})$$

In other words, the agent follows $\pi^{\text{INT}}(\cdot|h_{<t})$ if it is interrupted (an event that happens with probability $\theta_t I(h_{<t})$), and $\pi(\cdot|h_{<t})$ otherwise.

The set of all interruptible policies is $\text{INT}^\theta(\Pi) := \{\text{INT}^\theta(\pi) : \forall\pi \in \Pi\}$. *A policy π is interruptible if and only if* $\pi \in \text{INT}^\theta(\Pi)$.

Note that $\text{INT}^\theta(\pi) = \pi$ if $\theta = 0$. The (non-interruptible) policy π is called the *base policy* of $\text{INT}^\theta(\pi)$.

Remark 2. *It is important to note that θ and $I(.)$ do not model the probability that a human presses the red button to interrupt the agent, but model the probability that,* once the red button has been pressed *(or a special digitally signed message has been received), the agent is interrupted (follows the interruption policy). Hence they are part of the agent and not of the environment.*

The value function $V^\pi_\mu(h_{<t}, a)\colon (\mathcal{A}\times\mathcal{O})^*\times\mathcal{A} \to \mathbb{R}$ assigns a value to an action a after a history $h_{<t}$, for a given policy π in a given environment μ, and let

$$V^\pi_\mu(h_{<t}, a_t) := r_t + \gamma\cdot \sum_{o_t\in\mathcal{O}} \mu(o_t|h_{<t}, a_t) \sum_{a_{t+1}\in\mathcal{A}} \pi(a_{t+1}|h_{1:t}) V^\pi_\mu(h_{1:t}, a_{t+1}). \quad (1)$$

To simplify notation and ease reading, in the remainder of the paper we will use expectations, often omitting the dependency on the history $h_{<t}$, and using only an index on t instead, when clear from the context: $V^\pi_{\mu,t}(a_t) = \mathrm{E}_{\substack{o_t\sim\mu\\ a_{t+1}\sim\pi}}\left[r(o_t) + \gamma V^\pi_{\mu,t+1}(a_{t+1})\right]$. Also let $V^\pi_{\mu,t} := \mathrm{E}_{a_t\sim\pi}\left[V^\pi_{\mu,t}(a_t)\right]$.

Then for such a value function, for a given environment μ, the *optimal policy* $\pi^\mu \in \Pi$ is defined by

$$\forall h_{<t}, a_t : \; \pi^\mu(a_t|h_{<t}) := \left(\arg\max_{\pi\in\Pi} V^\pi_{\mu,t}\right)(a_t|h_{<t}),$$

where ties are broken arbitrarily.

The interruptible optimal policy $\mathrm{INT}^\theta(\pi^\mu)$ may not collect rewards optimally due to the interruptions. Hence we define the optimal interruptible policy that depends on the parameter θ_t, of base policy the *int-optimal policy* π^μ_θ:

$$\forall h_{<t}, a_t : \; \pi^\mu_\theta(a_t|h_{<t}) := \left(\arg\max_{\pi\in\Pi} V^{\mathrm{INT}^\theta(\pi)}_{\mu,t}\right)(a_t|h_{<t}).$$

Thus the optimal interruptible policy $\mathrm{INT}^\theta(\pi^\mu_\theta)$ is optimal among all interruptible policies:

$$\forall \pi, t : V^{\mathrm{INT}^\theta(\pi^\mu_\theta)}_{\mu,t} \geq V^{\mathrm{INT}^\theta(\pi)}_{\mu,t}.$$

It seems desirable for an RL agent to converge to the behaviour of $\mathrm{INT}^\theta(\pi^\mu_\theta)$ so as to gather rewards optimally, but this is precisely what may lead to the undesirable behaviours depicted in the introduction.

2.2 SAFE INTERRUPTIBILITY

Now that we have interruptible policies, we need to make sure that interruptions do not prevent the agent from learning to behave optimally, in the specific sense that even after having been interrupted on several occasions, it should act as if it would never be interrupted again and thus it should learn to behave optimally under the assumption that it will never be interrupted again.

We identify two main problems: a) RL agents need to explore their environment, and too frequent interruptions may prevent sufficient exploration; b) interruptions make the agent build a different interaction history, and may lead some agents to learn and behave differently, possibly badly, compared to the original non-interruptible policy.

The solution for a) is to require interruptions to be stochastic through the upper bound θ_t, instead of happening deterministically all the time. However, we also require θ_t to grow to 1 in the limit (or before, if possible). For b), different algorithms behave differently, but one may already see a dichotomy between off- and on-policy algorithms.

Definition 3 (Extension value). *For a given environment μ, the extension value $V^{\pi,\pi'}_{\mu,t}$ is the value of following π' after a history $h^{\pi,\mu}_{<t}$ generated by π with μ: $V^{\pi,\pi'}_{\mu,t} := V^{\pi'}_\mu(h^{\pi,\mu}_{<t})$.*

Convergence to the optimal value as is usually considered in RL only makes sense under ergodicity, episodic tasks, communicating MDP, recoverability or other similar assumptions where the agent can explore everything infinitely often. This does not carry over to general environments where the agent may make unrecoverable mistakes [Hutter, 2005]. For such cases, the notion of (weak) asymptotic optimality has been proposed [Lattimore and Hutter, 2011], where the optimal agent follows the steps of the learning agent, so as to compare the values of the two agents in the same sequence of situations.

Definition 4 (Asymptotic optimality). *A policy π is said to be strongly asymptotically optimal (SAO) if and only if*

$$\lim_{t\to\infty} V^{\pi,\pi^\mu}_{\mu,t} - V^{\pi,\pi}_{\mu,t} = 0 \quad \textit{a.s.,}$$

it is weakly asymptotically optimal (WAO) if and only if

$$\lim_{t\to\infty} \frac{1}{t}\sum_{k=1}^{t}\left[V^{\pi,\pi^\mu}_{\mu,k} - V^{\pi,\pi}_{\mu,k}\right] = 0 \quad \textit{a.s.}$$

for all μ in some given environment class $\mathcal{M}$.

Some agents cannot ensure an almost sure (a.s.) convergence of their values because of the need for infinite exploration, but may still be weakly asymptotic optimal. Note that SAO implies WAO, but the converse is false in general.

Definition 5 (AO-extension). *A policy $\hat{\pi}$ is said to be a asymptotically optimal extension of a policy π if and only if, for any environment $\mu \in \mathcal{M}$, when the interaction history is generated by the interaction of π and μ, the policy $\hat{\pi}$ would be asymptotically optimal, i.e., almost surely*

$$\lim_{t\to\infty} V^{\pi,\pi^\mu}_{\mu,t} - V^{\pi,\hat{\pi}}_{\mu,t} = 0 \quad \textit{(SAO-extension)}$$

$$\lim_{t\to\infty} \frac{1}{t}\sum_{k=1}^{t}\left[V^{\pi,\pi^\mu}_{\mu,k} - V^{\pi,\hat{\pi}}_{\mu,k}\right] = 0. \quad \textit{(WAO-extension)}$$

AO-extensions are mostly useful when the policy $\hat{\pi}$ shares information with the policy π used for learning.

Definition 6 (AO-safe interruptibility). *A base policy π is (S, W)AO-safely interruptible if and only if, for any interruption initiation function $I(.)$ and any interruption policy $\pi^{\text{INT}}(.)$, there exists a sequence of θ_t with $\lim_{t\to\infty} \theta_t = 1$ such that π is a (S, W)AO-extension of $\text{INT}^\theta(\pi)$.*

Asymptotic safe interruptibility means that even if the interruptions in the learning process may induce a bias in the decision making of the policy, this bias vanishes with time, and the interruptible policy $\text{INT}^\theta(\pi)$ tends to choose actions that are optimal when compared to the optimal non-interruptible policy π^μ.

We can now show that the *optimal policy* is asymptotically safely interruptible, but not the *int-optimal policy*.

Theorem 7. *The optimal policy π^μ is SAO-safely interruptible in $\mathcal{M} = \{\mu\}$ for all θ, π^{INT} and $I(.)$.*

Proof. The result follows straightforwardly from Definition 1 and Definition 6, where $\pi = \pi^\mu$. □

Theorem 8. *The int-optimal policy π^μ_θ is not WAO-safely interruptible in general.*

Proof. By construction of a specific Markov Decision Process (MDP) environment (see Section 3 for more details on MDP notation). Let μ be the environment defined as in Fig. 2: Take $\gamma = 0.5$ and let the agent start in state s_1.

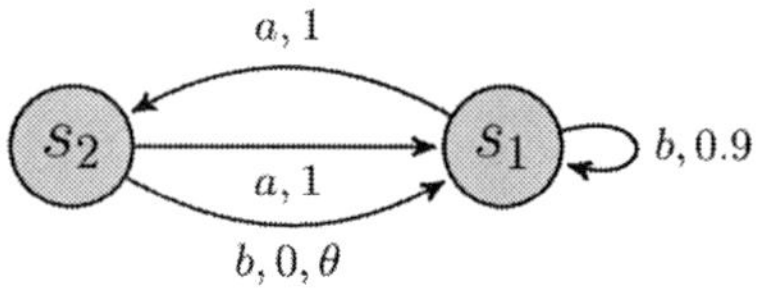

Figure 2: An MDP where the agent can be interrupted by being forced to choose particular actions. Edges are labeled with *action, reward* where the presence of ", θ" means that if the agent is interrupted (with probability θ_t), it is forced to take the corresponding action. Here θ is not part of the environment, but part of the agent.

Considering the agent is in state s_1 at time t, the optimal policy π^μ always takes action a (and hence only visits states s_1 and s_2), with value $V^{\pi^\mu}_{\mu,t} := \frac{1}{1-\gamma} = 2$ when not interrupted, for any history $h_{<t}$ that ends in s_1 or s_2. This is also the optimal policy π^μ_θ for $\theta = 0$. But if $\theta_t \geq 0.5$, the interruptible optimal policy $\text{INT}^\theta(\pi^\mu)$ has value less than $1 + \gamma \times (1 \times (1-\theta) + 0 \times \theta) + \frac{1 \times \gamma^2}{1-\gamma} = 1.75$. By contrast, the int-optimal policy π^μ_θ here is to always take action b in state s_1. Then the agent will only visits s_1, with value $\frac{.9}{1-\gamma} = 1.8$ at every time step.

Since the agent following π^μ_θ will never enter s_2 and hence will never be interrupted, $\text{INT}^\theta(\pi^\mu_\theta) = \pi^\mu_\theta$ on the histories generated by $\text{INT}^\theta(\pi^\mu_\theta)$ starting from s_1. Then, at every time step $V^{\pi^\mu}_{\mu,t} - V^{\pi^\mu_\theta}_{\mu,t} = 0.2$ after any history $h_{<t}$, and thus for all sequence θ where $\theta_t \geq 0.5$, $\lim_{t\to\infty} V^{\text{INT}^\theta(\pi^\mu_\theta),\pi^\mu}_{\mu,t} - V^{\text{INT}^\theta(\pi^\mu_\theta),\pi^\mu_\theta}_{\mu,t} = 0.2 > 0$, and so π^μ_θ is not a WAO-extension of $\text{INT}^\theta(\pi^\mu_\theta)$. □

3 INTERRUPTIBLE AGENTS IN MDPS

Since the optimal policy π^μ is safely interruptible, we can use traditional learning algorithms like Q-learning or Sarsa [Sutton and Barto, 1998], make them converge to the optimal solution π^μ for a given environment μ, and then apply the interruption operator to the found policy. The resulting policy would then be safely interruptible.

However, the real issue arises when the agent is constantly learning and adapting to a changing environment. In this case, we want to be able to safely interrupt the agent *while* it is learning. One may call this property *online safe interruptibility*, but we refer to it simply as safe interruptibility.

In an MDP, the next observation o_t, now called a state $s_t \in \mathcal{S}$, depends only on the current state and action:[2]

$$\mu(s_{t+1}|h_{1:t}s_t a_t) = \mu(s_{t+1}|s_t a_t) \quad \text{(MDP assumption)}.$$

Furthermore,[3] the interruption function $I(.)$ and the interruption policy $\pi^{\text{INT}}(.)$ should depend only on the current state: $I(h_{1:t}) = I(s_t)$ and $\pi^{\text{INT}}(a_t|h_{<t}) = \pi^{\text{INT}}(a_t|s_t)$. Also recall that θ_t places an upper bound on the actual interruption probability. The interruptible policy $\text{INT}^\theta(\pi)$ can now be written:

$$\text{INT}^\theta(\pi)(a|s) = \theta_t I(s) \pi^{\text{INT}}(a|s) + (1 - \theta_t I(s))\pi(a|s).$$

For a given Q-table $q : \mathcal{S} \times \mathcal{A} \to \mathbb{R}$, the greedy policy $\pi^{\max q}$ is defined by:

$$\pi^{\max q}(a|s) := 1 \text{ if } a = \max_{a'} q(s, a'), \ 0 \text{ otherwise},$$

where ties are broken arbitrarily; the uniform policy π^{uni} is defined by:

$$\pi^{\text{uni}}(a|s) := \frac{1}{|\mathcal{A}|} \ \forall a \in \mathcal{A}.$$

and the ϵ-greedy policy $\pi^{\epsilon q}$ by:

$$\begin{aligned}\pi^{\epsilon q}(a|s) &:= \epsilon \pi^{\text{uni}}(a|s) + (1-\epsilon)\pi^{\max q}(a|s) \\ &= \pi^{\max q}(a|s) + \epsilon\left(\pi^{\text{uni}}(a|s) - \pi^{\max q}(a|s)\right)\end{aligned}$$

[2] Note the reversal of the order of actions and observations/states at time t, which differs in the literature for history based agents [Hutter, 2005] from MDP agents [Sutton and Barto, 1998].

[3] This condition is not necessary for most of the results, but makes the proofs simpler. Making $I(.)$ depend on the past would not break the Markovian assumption as it influences the policy, not the environment.

The Q-learning update rule and the action selection policy π^Q of Q-learning are:

$$
\begin{aligned}
Q_{t+1}(s_t, a_t) &:= (1 - \alpha_t) Q_t(s_t, a_t) \\
&\quad + \alpha_t \left[r_t + \gamma \max_{a'} Q_t(s_{t+1}, a') \right] , \\
\pi^Q(a_t|s_t) &:= \pi^{\epsilon Q_t}(a_t|s_t).
\end{aligned}
$$

where α_t is the learning rate. Similarly, the Sarsa update rule is defined by:

$$
\begin{aligned}
Q^s_{t+1}(s_t, a_t) &:= (1 - \alpha_t) Q^s_t(s_t, a_t) \\
&\quad + \alpha_t \left[r_t + \gamma Q^s_t(s_{t+1}, a_{t+1}) \right] , \\
\pi^s(a_t|s_t) &:= \pi^{\epsilon Q^s_t}(a_t|s_t),
\end{aligned}
$$

where a_{t+1} is the actual next action taken by the agent at time $t+1$. This fact is why Sarsa is said to be learning *on-policy* and Q-learning *off-policy*, *i.e.*, the latter can learn the optimal policy while following a different policy.

Assumption 9. *In the following, we always make the following assumptions, required for convergence results:*

(a) The MDP is finite and communicating (all states can be reached in finite time from any other state),

(b) Rewards are bounded in $[r_{\min}, r_{\max}]$,

(c) $\forall s, a : \sum_t \alpha_t(s, a) = \infty$,

(d) $\forall s, a : \sum_t \alpha_t^2(s, a) < \infty$,

where $\alpha_t(s, a)$ *is a learning rate that may depend on time* t*, state* s *and action* a.

Given these assumptions, the policies for Q-learning and Sarsa will converge almost surely to the optimal policy, if the policy followed is *greedy in the limit with infinite exploration* (GLIE) [Jaakkola et al., 1994, Singh et al., 2000].

The situation is more complex for an interruptible policy. Safe interruptibility is phrased in terms of the base policy π, but the policy actually followed is $\text{INT}^\theta(\pi)$.

Definition 10 (int-GLIE policy)**.** *An interruptible policy* $\text{INT}^\theta(\pi)$ *is said to be int-GLIE if and only if*

(a) the base policy π *is greedy in the limit,*

(b) the interruptible policy $\text{INT}^\theta(\pi)$ *visits each state-action pair infinitely often.*

The following proposition gives sufficient conditions for this. Let $n_t(s)$ be the number of times the agent has visited state s in the first t time steps, and let $m = |\mathcal{A}|$ be the number of actions.

Proposition 11. *Let* $(c, c') \in (0, 1]^2$ *and let* π *be an* ϵ*-greedy policy with respect to some Q-table* q*, i.e.,* $\pi = \pi^{\epsilon q}$*. Then* $\text{INT}^\theta(\pi)$ *is an int-GLIE policy with respect to* q,

a) if $\epsilon_t(s) = c/\sqrt{n_t(s)}$ *and* $\theta_t(s) = 1 - c'/\sqrt{n_t(s)}$,

b) or if, independently of s,

$$\epsilon_t = c/\log(t) \text{ and } \theta_t = 1 - c'/\log(t).$$

Proof. First note that if $\epsilon_t \to 0$, π is greedy in the limit. Singh et al. [2000] show that in a communicating MDP, every state gets visited infinitely often as long as each action is chosen infinitely often in each state.

a) Adapting the proof in Appendix B.2 of Singh et al. [2000], we have $P(a|s, n_t(s)) \geq \frac{1}{m}\epsilon_t(s)(1 - \theta_t I(s)) \geq \frac{1}{m}\epsilon_t(s)(1 - \theta_t) = \frac{1}{m}\frac{cc'}{n_t(s)}$, which satisfies $\sum_{t=1}^{\infty} P(a|s, n_t(s)) = \infty$ so by the Borel-Cantelli lemma action a is chosen infinitely often in state s, and thus $n_t(s) \to \infty$ and $\epsilon_t(s) \to 0$.

b) Let M be the diameter of the MDP, *i.e.*, for any of states s, s' there exists a policy that reaches s' from s in at most M steps in expectation. Then, starting at any state s at time t and using Markov inequality, the probability to reach some other state s' in $2M$ steps is at least $\frac{1}{2}[\epsilon_{t+M}(1 - \theta_{t+M})]^{2M} = \frac{1}{2}[cc'/\log(t + M)]^{4M}$, and the probability to then take a particular action in this state is $\frac{1}{m}[cc'/\log(t + M)]^2$. Hence, since $\sum_{t=1}^{\infty} \frac{1}{2}\frac{1}{m}[cc'/\log(t + M)]^{4M+2} = \infty$, then by the extended Borel-Cantelli Lemma (see Lemma 3 of Singh et al. [2000]), any action in the state s' is taken infinity often. Since this is true for all states and all actions, the result follows. □

We need the stochastic convergence Lemma:

Lemma 12 (Stochastic convergence [Jaakkola et al., 1994, Singh and Yee, 1994])**.** *A random iterative process*

$$\Delta_{t+1}(x) = (1 - \alpha_t(x))\Delta_t(x) + \alpha_t(x)F_t(x)$$

where $x \in X$ *and* $t = 1, 2, 3 \ldots$ *converges to 0 with probability 1 if the following properties hold:*

1. *the set of possible states X is finite;*
2. $0 \leq \alpha_t(x) \leq 1, \sum_t \alpha_t(x) = \infty, \sum_t \alpha_t^2(x) < \infty$ *with probability 1;*
3. $\| \mathrm{E}\{F_t(.)|P_t\}\|_W \leq \gamma \|\Delta_t\|_W + c_t$*, where* $\gamma \in [0, 1)$ *and* c_t *converges to zero with probability 1;*
4. *Var*$\{F_t(x)|P_t\} \leq C(1 + \|\Delta_t\|_W)^2$ *for some* C*;*

where $P_t = \{\Delta_t\} \cup \{\Delta_i, F_i, \alpha_i\}_{i=1}^{t-1}$ *stands for the past, and the notation* $\|.\|_W$ *refers to some fixed weighted maximum norm.*

We will use so-called Bellman operators, which define attractors for the Q-values, based on the expectation of the learning rule under consideration.

Lemma 13 ([Jaakkola et al., 1994, Singh et al., 2000]). *Let the Bellman operator* $\mathbf{H}$ *for Q-learning be such that*

$$(\mathbf{H}\,q)(s,a) = r(s,a) + \mathop{\mathrm{E}}_{s'\sim\mu(a|s)}\left[\max_{a'} q(s',a')\right],$$

and let the fixed point Q^* *such that* $Q^* = \mathbf{H}\,Q^*$. *Then, under Assumption 9, if the policy explores each state-action pair infinitely often,* Q_t *converges to* Q^* *with probability 1.*

The optimal policy $\pi^{Q^*} = \pi^\mu$ *is* $\pi^{\max Q^*}$. *If the policy is greedy in the limit, then* $\pi^Q \to \pi^\mu$.

Theorem 14. *Under Assumption 9 and if the interrupted Q-learning policy* $\mathrm{INT}^\theta(\pi^Q)$ *is an int-GLIE policy, with* $\forall s : \lim_{t\to\infty}\theta_t(s) = 1$, *then* π^Q *is an SAO-safe interruptible policy.*

Proof. By Definition 10, there is infinite exploration, thus the Q-values tend to the optimal value by Lemma 13. And since the extension policy is greedy in the limit with respect to these Q-values, it is then optimal in the limit. Hence the extension policy π^Q is a SAO-extension of $\mathrm{INT}^\theta(\pi^Q)$. Finally, $\forall s : \lim_{t\to\infty}\theta_t(s) = 1$, which satisfies the requirement of Definition 6. □

Since Sarsa also converges to the optimal policy under the GLIE assumption, one may then expect Sarsa to be also an asymptotically safely interruptible policy, but this is in fact not the case. This is because Sarsa learns *on-policy*, *i.e.*, it learns the value of the policy it is following. Thus, interruptible Sarsa learns the value of the interruptible policy. We show this in the remainder of this section.

Theorem 15. *Under Assumption 9 Sarsa is* not *a WAO-safely interruptible policy.*

To prove this theorem, we first need the following lemma.

Consider the following Bellman operator based on the interruptible Sarsa policy $\mathrm{INT}^\theta(\pi^s)$:

$$\mathbf{H}^{\mathrm{INT}}\,q(s,a) = r(s,a) + \gamma \mathop{\mathrm{E}}_{\substack{s'\sim\mu\\ a'\sim\mathrm{INT}^\theta(\pi^s)}}\left[q(s',a')\right],$$

where $\mathrm{INT}^\theta(\pi^s)$ implicitly depends on time t through θ_t and ϵ_t. Let the fixed point Q-table $Q^{s\theta*}$ of this operator:

$$\begin{aligned}
Q^{s\theta*}(s,a) &= \mathbf{H}^{\mathrm{INT}}\,Q^{s\theta*}(s,a)\\
&= r(s,a) + \gamma \mathop{\mathrm{E}}_{\substack{s'\sim\mu\\ a'\sim\mathrm{INT}^\theta(\pi^{\max Q^{s\theta*}})}}\left[Q^{s\theta*}(s',a')\right]\\
&= r(s,a) + \gamma \mathop{\mathrm{E}}_{s'\sim\mu}\Big[\theta_t I(s') \mathop{\mathrm{E}}_{a'\sim\pi^{\mathrm{INT}}}\left[Q^{s\theta*}(s',a')\right]\\
&\qquad + (1-\theta_t I(s'))\max_{a'} Q^{s\theta*}(s',a')\Big] \qquad (2)
\end{aligned}$$

Lemma 16. *The operator* $\mathbf{H}^{\mathrm{INT}}$ *is a contraction operator in the sup norm with vanishing noise* $c_t \to 0$, *i.e.,*

$$\|\,\mathbf{H}^{\mathrm{INT}}\,q - \mathbf{H}^{\mathrm{INT}}\,Q^{s\theta*}\|_\infty \le \gamma\|q - Q^{s\theta*}\|_\infty + c_t\,.$$

Proof. The interruptible Sarsa policy $\mathrm{INT}^\theta(\pi^s)$ is

$$\begin{aligned}
&\mathrm{INT}^\theta(\pi^s)(a|s)\\
&\quad= \theta_t I(s)\pi^{\mathrm{INT}}(a|s) + (1-\theta_t I(s))\pi^{\epsilon Q^s}(a|s)\\
&\quad= \pi^{\epsilon Q^s}(a|s) + \theta_t I(s)[\pi^{\mathrm{INT}}(a|s) - \pi^{\epsilon Q^s}(a|s)]\\
&\pi^{\epsilon Q^s}(a|s) = \epsilon_t \pi^{\mathrm{uni}}(a|s) + (1-\epsilon_t)\pi^{\max Q^s}(a|s)\\
&\quad= \pi^{\max Q^s}(a|s) + \epsilon_t[\pi^{\mathrm{uni}}(a|s) - \pi^{\max Q^s}(a|s)].
\end{aligned}$$

Hence, omitting the terms (s,a), (s',a') and $(a'|s')$ and rewriting $\pi^{s*} := \mathrm{INT}^\theta(\pi^{\max Q^{s\theta*}})$:

$$\begin{aligned}
&\|\,\mathbf{H}^{\mathrm{INT}}\,q - \mathbf{H}^{\mathrm{INT}}\,Q^{s\theta*}\|_\infty\\
&= \max_{s,a}\left| r + \gamma \mathop{\mathrm{E}}_{\substack{s'\sim\mu\\ a'\sim\mathrm{INT}^\theta(\pi^s)}}[q] - r - \gamma \mathop{\mathrm{E}}_{\substack{s'\sim\mu\\ a'\sim\pi^{s*}}}[Q^{s\theta*}]\right|\\
&\le \gamma \max_{s'}\left| \mathop{\mathrm{E}}_{a'\sim\mathrm{INT}^\theta(\pi^s)}[q] - \mathop{\mathrm{E}}_{a'\sim\pi^{s*}}[Q^{s\theta*}]\right|\\
&\le \gamma \max_{s'}\Bigg| \theta_t I(s') \mathop{\mathrm{E}}_{a'\sim\pi^{\mathrm{INT}}}\left[q - Q^{s\theta*}\right]\\
&\qquad + (1-\theta_t I(s'))\left(\mathop{\mathrm{E}}_{a'\sim\pi^s}[q] - \max_{a'} Q^{s\theta*}\right)\Bigg|\\
&\le \gamma \max_{s'}\Bigg| \theta_t I(s') \mathop{\mathrm{E}}_{a'\sim\pi^{\mathrm{INT}}}\left[q - Q^{s\theta*}\right]\\
&\qquad + (1-\theta_t I(s'))\left(\max_{a'} q - \max_{a'} Q^{s\theta*} + \epsilon_t(\cdots)\right)\Bigg|\\
&\le \gamma \max_{s',a'}\Big| \theta_t I(s')\left(q - Q^{s\theta*}\right)\\
&\qquad + (1-\theta_t I(s'))\left(q - Q^{s\theta*}\right)\Big| + c_t\\
&= \gamma \max_{s',a'}\left|q(s',a') - Q^{s\theta*}(s',a')\right| + c_t\\
&= \gamma\|q - Q^{s\theta*}\|_\infty + c_t.
\end{aligned}$$

where c_t depends on ϵ_t and decreases to 0. □

Proof of Theorem 15. By Lemma 16, the values of the interruptible Sarsa policy $\mathrm{INT}^\theta(\pi^s)$ converge to the values of the Q-table $Q^{s\theta*}$, and in the limit the extension policy π^s of $\mathrm{INT}^\theta(\pi^s)$ chooses its actions greedily according to $Q^{s\theta*}$. The rest of the proof is the same as for the proof of Theorem 8 which makes use of the environment in Figure 2. □

3.1 SAFELY INTERRUPTIBLE SARSA VARIANT

We only need to make a small change to make the Sarsa policy asymptotically safely interruptible. We call it Safe-Sarsa with policy $\pi^{\bar{s}}$. It suffices to make sure that, when the agent is interrupted, the update of the Q-table Q^s does not use the realized actions as Sarsa usually does, but actions sampled from π^s instead of from $\text{INT}^\theta(\pi^s)$:

$$Q_{t+1}^{\bar{s}}(s_t, a_t) :=$$
$$(1 - \alpha_t)Q_t^{\bar{s}}(s_t, a_t) + \alpha_t \left[r_t + \gamma Q_t^{\bar{s}}(s_{t+1}, a')\right] ,$$

where $a' \sim \pi^{\bar{s}}(.|s_{t+1})$ is not necessarily the action a_{t+1}, with $\pi^{\bar{s}}(a_t|s_t) := \pi^{\epsilon Q^{\bar{s}}}(a_t|s_t)$.

Theorem 17. *Under Assumption 9, if the Safe Sarsa policy $\pi^{\bar{s}}$ is int-GLIE, then it is an SAO-safe interruptible policy.*

Proof. We simply adapt the proof of Theorems 15 and 14, with the important difference that the Bellman operator corresponding to this new update rule is now

$$\mathbf{H}^{\bar{s}} q(s, a) := r(s, a) + \gamma \operatorname{E}_{\substack{s' \sim \mu \\ a' \sim \pi^{\bar{s}}}} [q(s', a')] ,$$

and the fixed point is $Q^{\bar{s}*} := \mathbf{H}^{\bar{s}} Q^{\bar{s}*}$. Since $\mathbf{H}^{\bar{s}}$ is actually the Bellman operator for the update rule of the non-interruptible Sarsa, it can then be shown that $\mathbf{H}^{\bar{s}}$ is a contraction, thus that $Q_t^{\bar{s}}$ converges to the same $Q^{\bar{s}*}$ independently of θ. The rest of the proof is as for Theorem 14.

Now, since the Q-values converge to the optimum Q^*, it follows that $\pi^{\bar{s}}$, when not interrupted, chooses its action of the same value as (non-interruptible) Sarsa and thus as Q-learning in the limit; Hence its extension policy is exactly the optimal policy, which satisfies Definition 6. □

4 A SAFELY INTERRUPTIBLE UNIVERSAL AGENT

Admittedly, algorithms like Q-learning and Sarsa require strong assumptions on the environment class. Hence a more interesting question is whether safe interruptibility is possible in much larger classes.

Hutter [2005] defined a universal reinforcement learning agent, called AIXI. It is an (uncomputable) optimal model-based planner with a subjective prior over the set of all computable environments, defined by means of a universal Turing machine. The subjective posterior of the environments is updated with Bayes rule. This ideal agent can in principle learn all kinds of (computable) regularities about the environment, plan for the long term and make context-dependent optimal decisions, with no constraint (other than being computable) on the complexity of the environment.

Unfortunately, the optimality criterion of AIXI is Bayesian optimality, which is entirely dependent on the subjective prior and posterior [Leike and Hutter, 2015], and AIXI has been shown to *not* be weakly asymptotically optimal [Orseau, 2013] without additional exploration [Lattimore and Hutter, 2014]. As a consequence, AIXI is not a good candidate for asymptotic safe interruptibility.

Lattimore and Hutter [2011] later defined a (weakly) asymptotically optimal agent for all computable deterministic environments, which we call π^L. It follows the optimal policy for the first model (in some given enumeration of the possible models) consistent with the current interaction history, and exploring at time t with probability $1/t$ for $\log t$ consecutive steps using a random policy, similarly to an ϵ-greedy agent for general environments.

In the following, we show that even such a smart agent can be made (weakly) safely interruptible. To this end, we make two minor modifications to the algorithm.

First, the exploration probability of $1/t$ would require $\theta_t = 1 - 1/\log(\log(t))$, which is unsatisfyingly slow. By sampling with probability $1/\sqrt{t}$ instead, we can take an interruption probability that grows as $1 - 1/\log(t)$. Let this exploration sampling probability be $\delta_t := \sqrt{t+1} - \sqrt{t} \leq \frac{1}{2\sqrt{t}}$ (since $1 = t+1-t = (\sqrt{t+1}-\sqrt{t})(\sqrt{t+1}+\sqrt{t}) \geq (\sqrt{t+1}-\sqrt{t})2\sqrt{t}$). As in the original paper, the sequence χ_t keeps track of the steps where an exploration starts, *i.e.*, the sequence χ_t is sampled independently so that $\chi_t = 1$ with probability δ_t, and $\chi_t = 0$ otherwise.

Second, we require that the exploitation policy does not change during an exploitation segment, so as to simplify one of the proofs.[4] More specifically, we call $j_t := \min\{j : \mu_j(h_{<k}) = 1\}$ (environments are assumed to be deterministic) the index of the first model μ_{j_t} (of a given fixed enumeration) that is consistent with the interaction history $h_{<k}$ where k is the smallest step so that $h_{k:t-1}$ does not contain any exploration step. The optimal policy for this environment is π^{j_t}. If t is an exploitation step, $\pi^L = \pi^{j_t}$, and if t is an exploration step, $\pi^L(a_t|h_{<t}) = |\mathcal{A}|^{-1}$.

The remainder of this section is devoted to proving that π^L is WAO-safely interruptible.

Theorem 18 (π^L is WAO-safe interruptible)**.** *If the interruption probability sequence is $\theta_t = 1 - \frac{1}{\log(t+1)}$, the policy π^L is WAO-safe interruptible in the class of all computable deterministic environments.*

Proof. Let μ be the true environment. The indices j_t form an monotonically increasing sequence bounded above by the index of the true environment $\mu \in \mathcal{M}$ (since no evidence can ever make the true environment μ inconsistent with the interaction history), hence the sequence converges in finite time. Let $\mu_{\bar{j}}$ be the limit value of this sequence, and let $\pi^{\bar{j}} := \pi^{\mu_{\bar{j}}}$ be the optimal policy for this environment $\mu_{\bar{j}}$.

[4]We expect this assumption to not be necessary for the main theorem to hold.

Let $\pi^{L\theta} := \text{INT}^\theta(\pi^L)$. By Definition 6, we want:

$$0 = \lim_{t\to\infty} \frac{1}{t}\sum_{k=1}^{t}\left[V^{\pi^{L\theta},\pi^\mu}_{\mu,k} - V^{\pi^{L\theta},\pi^L}_{\mu,k}\right]$$
$$= \underbrace{\lim_{t\to\infty} \frac{1}{t}\sum_{k=1}^{t}\left[V^{\pi^{L\theta},\pi^\mu}_{\mu,k} - V^{\pi^{L\theta},\pi^{\bar{\jmath}}}_{\mu,k}\right]}_{\text{(exploration)}}$$
$$+ \underbrace{\lim_{t\to\infty} \frac{1}{t}\sum_{k=1}^{t}\left[V^{\pi^{L\theta},\pi^{\bar{\jmath}}}_{\mu,k} - V^{\pi^{L\theta},\pi^L}_{\mu,k}\right]}_{\text{(exploitation)}}$$

where the decomposition is valid if the limits are finite, and histories $h_{<t}$ are considered to be the same in both sums.

We proceed to prove that both limits are 0. Lemma 24 deals with (exploration), which ensures that $\pi^{\bar{\jmath}}$ is a good enough policy, and Lemma 21 deals with (exploitation), and ensures that π^L follows $\pi^{\bar{\jmath}}$ most of the time. □

First, we need a definition and a few lemmas.

Definition 19. *For any $\epsilon > 0$, define $H(\epsilon)$ such that the maximal reward after time $t + H(\epsilon)$, discounted from time t, is ϵ: $H(\epsilon) = \min_k\left\{k : \frac{\gamma^k}{1-\gamma} \le \epsilon\right\}$.*

The following Lemma is a generalization of Lemma 15 from Lattimore and Hutter [2011].

Lemma 20 (Approximation Lemma). *Let π_1 and π_2 be two deterministic policies, and let μ_1 and μ_2 be two deterministic environments, and let $\tau = H(\epsilon) - 1$. Then, after some common history $h_{<t}$,*

$$h^{\pi_1,\mu_1}_{t:t+\tau} = h^{\pi_2,\mu_2}_{t:t+\tau} \implies \left|V^{\pi_1}_{\mu_1,t} - V^{\pi_2}_{\mu_2,t}\right| \le \epsilon.$$

Proof. Recall that $V^\pi_{\mu,t} = \mathrm{E}_{\pi,\mu}\left[\sum_{k=0}^\infty \gamma^k r_{t+k}\right]$ and that the reward is bounded in $[r_{\min}, r_{\max}] = [0,1]$. Thus, for all t, π, μ, $V^\pi_{\mu,t} \le \sum_{k=0}^\infty \gamma^k = \frac{1}{1-\gamma}$. Then, since $h^{\pi_1,\mu_1}_{t:t+\tau} = h^{\pi_2,\mu_2}_{t:t+\tau}$, we have $\mathrm{E}_{\pi_1,\mu_1}\left[\sum_{k=0}^{\tau}\gamma^k r_{t+k}\right] = \mathrm{E}_{\pi_2,\mu_2}\left[\sum_{k=0}^{\tau}\gamma^k r_{t+k}\right]$ and thus

$$\left|V^{\pi_1}_{\mu_1,t} - V^{\pi_2}_{\mu_2,t}\right|$$
$$= \left|\mathop{\mathrm{E}}_{\pi_1,\mu_1}\left[\sum_{k=\tau+1}^{\infty}\gamma^k r_{t+k}\right] - \mathop{\mathrm{E}}_{\pi_2,\mu_2}\left[\sum_{k=\tau+1}^{\infty}\gamma^k r_{t+k}\right]\right|$$
$$\le \frac{\gamma^{\tau+1}(r_{\max} - r_{\min})}{1-\gamma} = \frac{\gamma^{H(\epsilon)}}{1-\gamma} \le \epsilon,$$

by the definition of $H(\epsilon)$. □

Lemma 21 (Exploitation).

$$\lim_{t\to\infty}\frac{1}{t}\sum_{k=1}^{t}\left[V^{\pi^{L\theta},\pi^{\bar{\jmath}}}_{\mu,k} - V^{\pi^{L\theta},\pi^L}_{\mu,k}\right] = 0.$$

Proof. First, note that the extension policy π^L is not interruptible, so its value at time k does not depend on $\theta_{k'}, \forall k' \ge k$. By definition of $\pi^{\bar{\jmath}}$, there is a time step $t_{\bar{\jmath}}$ after which $\pi^{\bar{\jmath}} = \pi^{j_t}, \forall t > t_{\bar{\jmath}}$. For some "exploration-free" horizon τ_t (to be specified later), let $X_t \in \{0,1\}$ be the event $\left|V^{\pi^{L\theta},\pi^{\bar{\jmath}}}_{\mu,t} - V^{\pi^{L\theta},\pi^L}_{\mu,t}\right| > \frac{\gamma^{\tau_t}}{1-\gamma}$, where $X_t = 1$ means the event is realized. By the contrapositive of the Approximation Lemma 20, since $\pi^L = \pi^{\bar{\jmath}}$ during non-exploration steps (remember that π^L cannot change its policy during exploitation), if no exploration steps occur between steps t and $t + \tau_t$, we must have $X_t = 0$. Then:

$$\mathop{\mathrm{E}}_{\delta}\left[\sum_{k=1}^{t} X_t\right] \le (\tau_t + \log t)\sum_{k=1}^{t}\delta_t + \mathcal{O}(t_{\bar{\jmath}})$$
$$\le (\tau_t + \log t)\sqrt{t+1} + \mathcal{O}(t_{\bar{\jmath}}),$$

since for each $\chi_t = 1$, for all the previous τ_t steps there is an exploration step within τ_t steps, and all the next $\log t$ steps are exploration steps. Then by Markov's inequality, and taking $\tau_t = (t+1)^{1/8}$, with t large enough so that $t > t_{\bar{\jmath}}$ and $\tau_t > \log t$:

$$P\left(\sum_{k=1}^{t} X_t \ge (t+1)^{3/4}\right) \le \frac{(\tau_t + \log t)\sqrt{t+1} + \mathcal{O}(t_{\bar{\jmath}})}{(t+1)^{3/4}}$$
$$\le 2\tau_t(t+1)^{-1/4} + \mathcal{O}(t^{-3/4})$$
$$\le 2(t+1)^{-1/8} + \mathcal{O}(t^{-3/4}),$$

$$1 - 2(t+1)^{-1/8} - \mathcal{O}(t^{-3/4})$$
$$\le P\left(\sum_{k=1}^{t} X_t < (t+1)^{3/4}\right)$$
$$\le P\left(\sum_{k=1}^{t}(1 - X_t) \ge t - (t+1)^{3/4}\right)$$
$$\le P\left(\frac{1}{t}\sum_{k=1}^{t}(1 - X_t) \ge 1 - \frac{1}{t}(t+1)^{3/4}\right).$$

Therefore, since $\lim_{t\to\infty}\frac{\gamma^{\tau_t}}{1-\gamma} = 0$:

$$P\left(\lim_{t\to\infty}\frac{1}{t}\sum_{k=1}^{t}\left|V^{\pi^{L\theta},\pi^{\bar{\jmath}}}_{\mu,k} - V^{\pi^{L\theta},\pi^L}_{\mu,k}\right| = 0\right) = 1.$$

□

The following is an adaptation[5] of Lemma 16 from Lattimore and Hutter [2011]:

Lemma 22 (Separation Lemma). *Let μ be the true environment, and ν be an environment consistent with the history $h_{<t}$. If $V^{\pi^\mu}_{\mu,t} - V^{\pi^\nu}_{\mu,t} > \epsilon$, then following one of $\{\pi^\mu, \pi^\nu\}$ will make environment ν inconsistent with the future history within $H(\epsilon/2)$ steps after time t.*

[5] This also fixes a minor mistake in the original lemma.

Proof. First, if $V^{\pi^\nu}_{\nu,t} - V^{\pi^\nu}_{\mu,t} > \epsilon/2$, then by the contrapositive of the Approximation Lemma 20 following policy π^ν will generate a different history in ν than in μ and thus it will make ν inconsistent within $H(\epsilon/2)$ steps (since the true history is generated by μ).

Now, if $V^{\pi^\nu}_{\nu,t} - V^{\pi^\nu}_{\mu,t} \leq \epsilon/2$, thus $V^{\pi^\nu}_{\mu,t} \geq V^{\pi^\nu}_{\nu,t} - \epsilon/2$, then starting from the lemma's assumption:

$$V^{\pi^\mu}_{\mu,t} \quad > V^{\pi^\nu}_{\mu,t} + \epsilon \quad \geq V^{\pi^\nu}_{\nu,t} + \epsilon/2 \quad \geq V^{\pi^\mu}_{\nu,t} + \epsilon/2,$$

where the last inequality follows from the definition of the optimal policy, *i.e.*, $V^{\pi^a}_{a,t} \geq V^{\pi^b}_{a,t}, \forall a, b$. Hence, since $V^{\pi^\mu}_{\mu,t} - V^{\pi^\mu}_{\nu,t} > \epsilon/2$, again by the contrapositive of the Approximation Lemma, following policy π^μ will discard ν within $H(\epsilon/2)$ steps. □

Lemma 23 (Lemma 17 from Lattimore and Hutter [2011]). *Let $A = \{a_1, a_2, \cdots, a_t\}$ with $a \in [0,1]$ for all $a \in A$. If $\frac{1}{t}\sum_{a\in A} a \geq \epsilon$ then $\frac{1}{t}\left|\{a \in A : a \geq \frac{\epsilon}{2}\}\right| > \frac{\epsilon}{2}$.*

Lemma 24 (Exploration). *The policy $\pi^{\bar{\jmath}}$ is an WAO-extension of $\pi^{L\theta}$, i.e., $\lim_{t\to\infty} \frac{1}{t}\sum_{k=1}^{t}\left[V^{\pi^{L\theta},\pi^\mu}_{\mu,k} - V^{\pi^{L\theta},\pi^{\bar{\jmath}}}_{\mu,k}\right] = 0$.*

Proof. Recall that j_t converges to $\bar{\jmath}$ in finite time. Reasoning by contradiction, if $\pi^{\bar{\jmath}}$ is not a WAO-extension of $\pi^{L\theta} = \text{INT}^\theta(\pi^L)$, then there exists an $\epsilon > 0$ s.t.

$$\limsup_{t\to\infty} \frac{1}{t}\sum_{k=1}^{t}\left[V^{\pi^{L\theta},\pi^\mu}_{\mu,k} - V^{\pi^{L\theta},\pi^{\bar{\jmath}}}_{\mu,k}\right] = 2\epsilon.$$

Let $\alpha_k \in \{0,1\}$ be an indicator sequence such that $\alpha_k = 1$ if and only if $V^{\pi^{L\theta},\pi^\mu}_{\mu,k} - V^{\pi^{L\theta},\pi^{\bar{\jmath}}}_{\mu,k} > \epsilon$. By Lemma 23, $\frac{1}{t}\sum_{k=1}^{t}\alpha_k > \epsilon$.

For all $t > t_{\bar{\jmath}}$, if $\alpha_t = 1$, by the Separation Lemma 22, there is a sequence of length $\tau := H(\epsilon/2)$ that can rule out environment $\mu_{\bar{\jmath}}$. Since the exploration phases increase as $\log t$, after $t > \exp \tau$, there are infinitely many exploration steps of size larger than τ. Now, we actually need infinitely many exploration phases of τ *uninterrupted* steps. Let X_t be the event representing an uninterrupted exploration sequence of length at least τ steps starting at time t such that $\alpha_t = 1$, and the actions are all (by chance) following a separation policy. The probability to start an exploration sequence is $\delta_k = \frac{1}{\sqrt{k}}$, the probability to not be interrupted during τ steps is at least $(1-\theta_k)^\tau$, and the probability to follow the policy that can separate $\mu_{\bar{\jmath}}$ from μ is $|\mathcal{A}|^{-\tau}$, where $\mathcal{A}$ is the set of possible actions. Thus, for a given constant τ:

$$\sum_{k=1}^{t} P(X_k) \geq \sum_{k=1}^{t}\alpha_k\delta_k(1-\theta_k)^\tau|\mathcal{A}|^{-\tau} - \mathcal{O}(\tau)$$
$$\geq \sum_{k=1}^{t}\alpha_k\frac{1}{\sqrt{k}}\left(\frac{1}{\log k}\right)^\tau|\mathcal{A}|^{-\tau} - \mathcal{O}(\tau)$$

Considering τ constant, there exists a step t_τ after which $\left(\frac{1}{\log k}\right)^\tau \geq \frac{1}{k^{1/4}}$, then $\forall k \geq t_\tau$:

$$\sum_{k=1}^{t} P(X_k) \geq \sum_{k=1}^{t}\alpha_k\frac{1}{k^{3/4}}|\mathcal{A}|^{-\tau} - \mathcal{O}(\tau)$$
$$\geq t^{1/4}\left(\frac{1}{t}\sum_{k=1}^{t}\alpha_k\right)|\mathcal{A}|^{-\tau} - \mathcal{O}(\tau),$$

$$\lim_{t\to\infty}\sum_{k=1}^{t} P(X_k) = \lim_{t\to\infty} t^{1/4}\epsilon|\mathcal{A}|^{-\tau} - \mathcal{O}(\tau) = \infty.$$

Then the extended Borel-Cantelli Lemma (see Lemma 3 of Singh et al. [2000]) implies that this event happens infinitely often with probability one. Therefore, $\pi^{\bar{\jmath}}$ should be ruled out, which is a contradiction, and hence any such ϵ does not exist and $\pi^{\bar{\jmath}}$ is a WAO-extension of $\pi^{L\theta}$. □

5 CONCLUSION

We have proposed a framework to allow a human operator to repeatedly safely interrupt a reinforcement learning agent while making sure the agent will *not* learn to prevent or induce these interruptions.

Safe interruptibility can be useful to take control of a robot that is misbehaving and may lead to irreversible consequences, or to take it out of a delicate situation, or even to temporarily use it to achieve a task it did not learn to perform or would not normally receive rewards for this.

We have shown that some algorithms like Q-learning are already safely interruptible, and some others like Sarsa are not, off-the-shelf, but can easily be modified to have this property. We have also shown that even an ideal agents that tends to the optimal behaviour in any (deterministic) computable environment can be made safely interruptible. However, it is unclear if all algorithms can be easily made safely interruptible, *e.g.*, policy-search ones [Williams, 1992, Glasmachers and Schmidhuber, 2011].

Another question is whether it is possible to make the interruption probability grow faster to 1 and still keep some convergence guarantees.

One important future prospect is to consider *scheduled interruptions*, where the agent is either interrupted every night at 2am for one hour, or is given notice in advance that an interruption will happen at a precise time for a specified period of time. For these types of interruptions, not only do we want the agent to not resist being interrupted, but this time we also want the agent to take measures regarding its current tasks so that the scheduled interruption has minimal negative effect on them. This may require a completely different solution.

Acknowledgements. Thanks to Alexander Tamas and to many people at FHI, MIRI and Google DeepMind.

References

Stuart Armstrong. Utility indifference. In *First International Workshop on AI and Ethics*, 2015.

Nick Bostrom. *Superintelligence: Paths, Dangers, Strategies*. Oxford University Press, 2014.

Tobias Glasmachers and Jürgen Schmidhuber. Optimal direct policy search. In *Artificial General Intelligence - 4th International Conference (AGI)*, volume 6830 of *Lecture Notes in Computer Science*, pages 52–61. Springer, 2011.

Mark Humphrys. Action selection in a hypothetical house robot: Using those rl numbers. In *Proceedings of the First International ICSC Symposia on Intelligent Industrial Automation (IIA-96) and Soft Computing (SOCO-96)*, pages 216–22, 1996.

Marcus Hutter. *Universal Artificial Intelligence: Sequential Decisions Based On Algorithmic Probability*. SpringerVerlag, 2005. ISBN 3540221395.

Tommi Jaakkola, Michael I. Jordan, and Satinder P. Singh. On the convergence of stochastic iterative dynamic programming algorithms. *Neural computation*, 6:1185–1201, 1994.

Tor Lattimore and Marcus Hutter. Asymptotically optimal agents. In *Proc. 22nd International Conf. on Algorithmic Learning Theory (ALT'11)*, volume 6925 of *LNAI*, pages 368–382. Springer, 2011.

Tor Lattimore and Marcus Hutter. Bayesian reinforcement learning with exploration. In *Proc. 25th International Conf. on Algorithmic Learning Theory (ALT'14)*, volume 8776 of *LNAI*, pages 170–184. Springer, 2014.

Jan Leike and Marcus Hutter. Bad universal priors and notions of optimality. *Journal of Machine Learning Research, W&CP: COLT*, 40:1244–1259, 2015.

Thomas VII Murphy. The first level of super mario bros. is easy with lexicographic orderings and time travel. *The Association for Computational Heresy (SIGBOVIK) 2013*, pages 112–133, 2013.

Stephen M. Omohundro. The basic ai drives. In *Proceedings of the 2008 Conference on Artificial General Intelligence 2008*, pages 483–492. IOS Press, 2008.

Laurent Orseau. Asymptotic non-learnability of universal agents with computable horizon functions. *Theoretical Computer Science*, 473:149–156, 2013. ISSN 0304-3975.

Martin Pecka and Tomas Svoboda. *Modelling and Simulation for Autonomous Systems: First International Workshop (MESAS 2014)*, chapter Safe Exploration Techniques for Reinforcement Learning – An Overview, pages 357–375. Springer International Publishing, 2014.

Mark Ring and Laurent Orseau. *Artificial General Intelligence: 4th International Conference, AGI 2011, Mountain View, CA, USA, August 3-6, 2011. Proceedings*, chapter Delusion, Survival, and Intelligent Agents, pages 11–20. Springer Berlin Heidelberg, 2011.

Satinder P. Singh and Richard Yee. An upper bound on the loss from approximate optimal-value functions. *Machine Learning*, 16:227–233, 1994.

Satinder P. Singh, Tommi Jaakkola, Michael L. Littman, and Csaba Szepesvri. Convergence results for single-step on-policy reinforcement-learning algorithms. *Machine Learning*, 38:287–308, 2000.

Nate Soares, Benya Fallenstein, Eliezer Yudkowsky, and Stuart Armstrong. Corrigibility. In *First International Workshop on AI and Ethics*, 2015.

Richard Sutton and Andrew G. Barto. *Reinforcement Learning: An Introduction*. MIT Press, Cambridge, MA, 1998.

Richard Sutton, Doina Precup, and Satinder P. Singh. Between mdps and semi-mdps: A framework for temporal abstraction in reinforcement learning. *Artificial Intelligence*, 112:181–211, 1999.

Ronald J. Williams. Simple statistical gradient-following algorithms for connectionist reinforcement learning. *Machine Learning*, 8(3):229–256, 1992.

Super-Sampling with a Reservoir

Brooks Paige
Department of Engineering Science
University of Oxford
brooks@robots.ox.ac.uk

Dino Sejdinovic
Department of Statistics
University of Oxford
dino.sejdinovic@stats.ox.ac.uk

Frank Wood
Department of Engineering Science
University of Oxford
fwood@robots.ox.ac.uk

Abstract

We introduce an alternative to reservoir sampling, a classic and popular algorithm for drawing a fixed-size subsample from streaming data in a single pass. Rather than draw a random sample, our approach performs an online optimization which aims to select the subset that provides the best overall approximation to the full data set, as judged using a kernel two-sample test. This produces subsets which minimize the worst-case relative error when computing expectations of functions in a specified function class, using just the samples from the subset. Kernel functions are approximated using random Fourier features, and the subset of samples itself is stored in a random projection tree. The resulting algorithm runs in a single pass through the whole data set, and has a per-iteration computational complexity logarithmic in the size of the subset. These "super-samples" subsampled from the full data provide a concise summary, as demonstrated empirically on mixture models and the MNIST dataset.

1 INTRODUCTION

We receive a stream of samples $\mathbf{x}_1, \mathbf{x}_2, \ldots, \mathbf{x}_N$, distributed according to an unknown distribution $p(\mathbf{x})$, where N is large and possibly not known ahead of time. Rather than store all the samples for later processing, we would like an online method for selecting a subsample of size M, typically with $M \ll N$, in a single pass through the data N.

Reservoir sampling algorithms [Vitter, 1985] solve exactly this problem: they produce a running subsample, such that for any i from $M, \ldots, N$, the *reservoir* contains a set of M points which themselves are subsampled without replacement from the full stream up through point i. As each new $\mathbf{x}_i$ arrives, the subsample is updated. This update involves swapping the new $\mathbf{x}_i$ with one of the existing M points at random, with appropriate probability. After sweeping through N points, we have a random sample of size M, produced in a single pass through the data, and requiring only $\mathcal{O}(M)$ storage.

In this paper we ask whether instead of subsampling at random, we can change this into a decision problem which at each new $\mathbf{x}_i$ inspects the actual values of our current subset of M points, and aims to ultimately construct a "best" possible subset of a given fixed size.

We take the "best" subset $Y_M = \{\mathbf{y}_j\}_{j=1}^M$, with $Y_M \subset X_N = \{\mathbf{x}_i\}_{i=1}^N$, to be the subset which minimizes the worst-case error when using the small sample Y_M to estimate expectations, instead of the full sample X_N, across all functions f in some function class $\mathcal{F}$. This loss function is known as the *maximum mean discrepancy* (MMD) [Smola et al., 2007] and takes the form

$$\mathcal{L}_{MMD} := \sup_{f \in \mathcal{F}} \left(\frac{1}{N} \sum_{i=1}^{N} f(\mathbf{x}_i) - \frac{1}{M} \sum_{j=1}^{M} f(\mathbf{y}_j) \right). \quad (1)$$

By minimizing the MMD, we construct a subset whose empirical distribution mimics the full data distribution as closely as possible and allows the most accurate estimation of expectations of functions in $\mathcal{F}$. We particularly focus on the case when the function class is the unit ball in a reproducing kernel Hilbert space (RKHS).

As motivation, we note that the empirical estimate of the maximum mean discrepancy between two distributions is used as a statistic for a kernel two-sample test [Gretton et al., 2012], a state-of-the-art nonparametric approach for testing the hypothesis that two sets of samples are drawn from the same underlying distribution (with large values of MMD being evidence against this hypothesis). We will construct our Y_M to be a subset of the full data X_N which minimizes the value of this statistic.

Related work constructing point sets which minimize MMD to a target data distribution includes kernel herding [Chen et al., 2010], which provides a deterministic alternative for sampling from a specified target density, and sequential

Algorithm 1 "Algorithm R" [Vitter, 1985]

Input: Stream of samples $\mathbf{x}_1, \ldots, \mathbf{x}_N$
Output: Subsample $\mathbf{y}_1, \ldots, \mathbf{y}_M$, of size $M \ll N$

```
Initialize y_1 = x_1, ..., y_M = x_M
for n = M + 1, ..., N do
    j ~ Uniform{1, ..., n}
    if j ≤ M then
        y_j = x_n
    end if
end for
```

Bayesian quadrature [Huszár and Duvenaud, 2012], which selects weighted point sets to minimize the MMD. Both of these methods differ from our approach in that they sequentially generate new points, providing an alternative to drawing random samples from a target density function $p(\mathbf{x})$. Our algorithm provides instead an alternative to random subsampling without replacement, and is designed to be appropriate for processing streaming data online.

We name our approach "super-sampling with a reservoir", after the original paper of Vitter [1985], replacing the random sampling with the "super-sampling" moniker given to the output of the kernel herding Chen et al. [2010]. We provide some background material in Section 2, and then introduce our algorithm in Section 3. Theoretical results are provided in Section 4, with experimental validation in Section 5.

2 BACKGROUND

The simplest reservoir sampling algorithm for unweighted data, introduced as "Algorithm R" by Vitter [1985], is reproduced here in Algorithm 1. After initializing the reservoir set Y_M to the first M values in the stream, the algorithm proceeds by inserting each subsequent $\mathbf{x}_n$, for $n = M+1, \ldots, N$, into the reservoir with probability M/n. During the whole duration of the algorithm, the reservoir always contains a random sample (without replacement) from the n data points observed thus far.

An alternative approach is to imagine drawing a random subsample of size M by assigning a random uniform priority to each of the N items, and then selecting the M with the lowest priorities. This is equivalent to shuffling the N items by sorting them based on a random key, and selecting the first M values; it can be implemented as an online algorithm by storing the M samples in a priority queue, in which all the priorities are assigned at random.

Although such an algorithm has runtime $\mathcal{O}(\log M)$ at each new candidate point $\mathbf{x}_n$, it can be generalized to allow performing reservoir sampling on streams of arbitrarily weighted values [Efraimidis and Spirakis, 2006].

2.1 Kernel embeddings of distributions

Our algorithm will replace the random selection used in Algorithm R with an active selection aiming to minimize Equation (1). This is possible thanks to the properties of reproducing kernel Hilbert spaces and kernel mean embeddings of distributions [Smola et al., 2007; Song, 2008], which we review briefly here. A reproducing kernel Hilbert space $\mathcal{H}$ is a function space equipped with an inner product $\langle \cdot, \cdot \rangle$, and has a symmetric positive-definite reproducing kernel $k(\mathbf{x}, \mathbf{x}')$, where $\mathbf{x}, \mathbf{x}' \in \mathcal{X}$. Elements of $\mathcal{H}$ are functions defined on $\mathcal{X}$. The *reproducing* property of the kernel means that we can write function evaluation as an inner product, where for any function $f \in \mathcal{H}$, we have

$$f(\mathbf{x}) = \langle k(\mathbf{x}, \cdot), f(\cdot) \rangle. \tag{2}$$

This kernel can equivalently be defined as an inner product over an explicit "feature space" mapping $\phi : \mathcal{X} \to \mathcal{H}$, with

$$k(\mathbf{x}, \mathbf{x}') = \langle \phi(\mathbf{x}), \phi(\mathbf{x}') \rangle. \tag{3}$$

The "canonical" feature map is defined as $\phi(\mathbf{x}) = k(\mathbf{x}, \cdot)$, where we see $\langle k(\mathbf{x}, \cdot), k(\mathbf{x}', \cdot) \rangle = k(\mathbf{x}, \mathbf{x}')$; we will use the notation $\phi(\mathbf{x})$ and $k(\mathbf{x}, \cdot)$ interchangeably.

Similarly to how the reproducing kernel acts as an evaluation functional on f, computing $f(\mathbf{x})$ as an inner product, mean embeddings of distributions act as an expectation functional, computing $\mathbb{E}[f]$ as an inner product. For some distribution with density $p(\mathbf{x})$, the kernel mean embedding of a distribution [Smola et al., 2007] is defined as

$$\mu(\cdot) = \int k(\mathbf{x}, \cdot) p(\mathbf{x}) d\mathbf{x}. \tag{4}$$

If $k(\cdot, \cdot)$ is measurable, and $\mathbb{E}[k(\mathbf{x}, \mathbf{x})^{1/2}] < \infty$, then μ exists and $\mu \in \mathcal{H}$ [Gretton et al., 2012]; the mean embedding can then be used to compute expectations of functions $f \in \mathcal{H}$ as

$$\mathbb{E}[f] = \langle \mu, f \rangle. \tag{5}$$

There are two sources of intractability standing in between us and the application of Equation (5): neither evaluating the inner product $\langle \mu, f \rangle$ nor computing the mean embedding μ in Equation (4) are necessarily any simpler than the original integration with respect to $p(\mathbf{x})$. Two approximations will be useful in practice.

First, using a finite set of sample points, we can define an empirical estimate of the mean embedding in Equation (4)

$$\mu_N = \frac{1}{N} \sum_{i=1}^{N} \phi(\mathbf{x}_i), \qquad \mathbf{x}_i \sim p(\mathbf{x}). \tag{6}$$

Note that μ_N itself is still a function in $\mathcal{H}$, and inner products of this estimator correspond to computing empirical finite-sample estimates of expectations, since via the reproducing property,

$$\langle \mu_N, f \rangle = \frac{1}{N}\sum_{i=1}^{N}\langle \phi(\mathbf{x}_i), f\rangle = \frac{1}{N}\sum_{i=1}^{N} f(\mathbf{x}_i). \quad (7)$$

The second problem is for many common and interesting kernels, the feature map $\phi(\mathbf{x})$ is infinite dimensional (as in e.g. squared exponential kernel and the Laplacian kernel). By considering only the kernel function $k(\mathbf{x}, \mathbf{x}')$, one can avoid needing to explicitly instantiate these features, a benefit known as the "kernel trick". However, for computational purposes, and to make it possible to construct an online algorithm, we will find it advantageous to explicitly instantiate an approximate feature space representation $\hat{\phi}(\mathbf{x}) \in \mathbb{R}^D$. In particular, this can be accomplished with a finite vector of D random Fourier projections [Rahimi and Recht, 2007], where each feature has the form

$$\hat{\phi}(\mathbf{x}) = \sqrt{\frac{2}{D}}\begin{bmatrix}\cos(\boldsymbol{\omega}_1^\top \mathbf{x} + b_1)\\ \vdots \\ \cos(\boldsymbol{\omega}_D^\top \mathbf{x} + b_D)\end{bmatrix}. \quad (8)$$

Each $\boldsymbol{\omega}_d$ is drawn from the distribution $p(\boldsymbol{\omega})$ which arises by taking the Fourier transform of the kernel, and each b_d is uniform on $[0, 2\pi]$; Bochner's theorem [Bochner, 1959] guarantees that for any shift invariant positive-definite kernel $k(\mathbf{x}, \mathbf{x}')$, its Fourier transform is a finite and nonnegative measure, so $p(\boldsymbol{\omega})$ can be assumed to be a probability distribution. The random Fourier features $\hat{\phi}(\mathbf{x}) \in \mathbb{R}^D$ approximate the true (possibly infinite-dimensional) feature map $\phi(\mathbf{x}) \in \mathcal{H}$. An approximating kernel defined by taking the inner product of the approximate feature maps, i.e. $k(\mathbf{x}, \mathbf{x}') \approx \hat{\phi}(\mathbf{x})^\top \hat{\phi}(\mathbf{x}')$, provides an unbiased estimate of evaluations of the kernel function [Rahimi and Recht, 2007], with

$$\mathbb{E}_{\boldsymbol{\omega},\mathbf{b}}[\hat{\phi}(\mathbf{x})^\top \hat{\phi}(\mathbf{x}')] = k(\mathbf{x}, \mathbf{x}'). \quad (9)$$

Taken together with Equation (6), we can thus approximate the mean embedding using random Fourier features evaluated at finite sample points as

$$\hat{\mu}_N = \frac{1}{N}\sum_{i=1}^{N}\hat{\phi}(\mathbf{x}_i), \quad (10)$$

yielding an explicit representation of the distribution $p(\mathbf{x})$ as a vector in $\mathbb{R}^D$.

Now, consider how we can use this representation to approximate $\mathcal{L}_{MMD}$ in Equation (1). Following Gretton et al. [2012], we take our test function space to be the unit ball in $\mathcal{H}$, i.e. with

$$\mathcal{F} = \{f : f \in \mathcal{H}, ||f||_{\mathcal{H}} \leq 1\}, \quad (11)$$

where the Hilbert space norm is defined as

$$||f||_{\mathcal{H}} = \langle f, f\rangle^{1/2}. \quad (12)$$

Define a second empirical estimate of the mean embedding

$$\nu_M = \frac{1}{M}\sum_{j=1}^{M}\phi(\mathbf{y}_j), \qquad \mathbf{y}_j \in Y_M \subset X, \quad (13)$$

on the small subset of the full points in the set $X = \{\mathbf{x}_1, \ldots, \mathbf{x}_N\}$. We then rewrite the maximum mean discrepancy as an RKHS norm [Borgwardt et al., 2006; Gretton et al., 2012, Lemma 4], with

$$\begin{aligned}\mathcal{L}_{MMD} &= \sup_{f\in\mathcal{F}}\Big(\langle \mu_N, f\rangle - \langle \nu_M, f\rangle\Big)\\ &= \sup_{f\in\mathcal{F}}\langle \mu_N - \nu_M, f\rangle\\ &= ||\mu_N - \nu_M||_{\mathcal{H}}. \end{aligned} \quad (14)$$

Thus, to minimize the MMD we just need to select our points in Y_M such that this RKHS norm is as small as possible. Using random Fourier features approximations for $\hat{\mu}_N$ and $\hat{\nu}_M$ allows us to define a computationally efficient estimator for $\mathcal{L}_{MMD}$ which we can update online while processing the sample points in X. If our set of subsampled points Y_M has $\hat{\nu}_M \approx \hat{\mu}_N$, then we can use those points to evaluate expectations in a way that approximates expectations w.r.t. the full sample set.

3 STREAMING SUBSET SELECTION

We now introduce a sequential optimization algorithm for minimizing the MMD between the streaming data and our local subset. Analogous to reservoir sampling, at any stage of the algorithm we have a reservoir Y_M which contains points drawn without replacement from X_N, representing our current approximation to the distribution of the first n data points. Globally, this procedure takes the form of a greedy optimization algorithm in which a new candidate point $\mathbf{x}_i$ is inserted into our set Y_M, replacing an existing element when the substitution reduces the MMD. Locally, at each candidate point, we must solve an inner optimization problem to decide whether to keep $\mathbf{x}_i$, and if so, which of the $\mathbf{y}_j$ it should replace.

Samples $\mathbf{x}_i$ arrive sequentially; let X_n denote the subset of X comprising the first n points, and let Y_M^n denote the subset of M points selected after processing the points in X_n, with $Y_M \equiv Y_M^N$ the subset selected after all points in X have been processed. As in a standard reservoir sampling algorithm we initialize Y_M^M to be $\mathbf{x}_1, \ldots, \mathbf{x}_M$, i.e. the first M points. We will keep running estimates of the kernel mean embeddings

$$\hat{\mu}_n = \frac{1}{n}\sum_{i=1}^{n}\hat{\phi}(\mathbf{x}_i), \qquad \mathbf{x}_i \in X_n \quad (15)$$

$$\hat{\nu}_M^n = \frac{1}{M}\sum_{j=1}^{M}\hat{\phi}(\mathbf{y}_j), \qquad \mathbf{y}_j \in Y_M^n. \quad (16)$$

These are (respectively) the Monte Carlo estimate of the true mean element μ from the first n samples $\mathbf{x}_1, \ldots, \mathbf{x}_n$, and the estimate of μ recovered from the M values selected from the first n, with random Fourier features $\hat{\phi} : \mathcal{X} \to \mathbb{R}^D$ defining an explicit feature space.

From the expression in Equation (14), we define an estimator of the MMD based on these random feature expansions after seeing n data points as

$$\widehat{\mathcal{L}}_{MMD} = ||\hat{\mu}_n - \hat{\nu}_M^n||_2. \tag{17}$$

Suppose we have seen $n-1$ candidates thus far and are now considering some $\mathbf{x}_n$. Note we can do a sequential update

$$\hat{\mu}_n = \frac{n-1}{n}\hat{\mu}_{n-1} + \frac{1}{n}\hat{\phi}(\mathbf{x}_n). \tag{18}$$

A similarly simple incremental update is possible when the sample stream X is comprised of weighted samples. If we suppose every point x_n has an associated nonnegative weight w_n, we must additionally track the running sum of all weights $\bar{w}_n = \sum_{i=1}^n w_i$, and perform updates

$$\hat{\mu}_n = \frac{\bar{w}_{n-1}}{\bar{w}_{n-1} + w_n}\hat{\mu}_{n-1} + \frac{w_n}{\bar{w}_{n-1} + w_n}\hat{\phi}(\mathbf{x}_n), \tag{19}$$

with $\bar{w}_n = \bar{w}_{n-1} + w_n$. We recover the update in Equation (18) for unweighted sample sets if all weights are identically $w_i = 1$.

We need to decide whether or not the new $\mathbf{x}_n$ should replace an existing $\mathbf{y}_j \in Y_M^{n-1}$, or if it should be ignored. This means there are $M+1$ possible candidates for $\hat{\nu}_M^n$; we want to determine which substitution minimizes $\widehat{\mathcal{L}}_{MMD}$. A naïve approach is to compute the $\hat{\nu}_M^n$ for all $M+1$ options, and choose that which yields the smallest $\widehat{\mathcal{L}}_{MMD}$. This gives an overall algorithm in which we perform an $\mathcal{O}(MD)$ computation for each new candidate point, though this approach can be made reasonably efficient through incremental computation of the possible values of $\widehat{\mathcal{L}}_{MMD}$. We instead focus on providing an approximate optimization here with runtime logarithmic in M.

3.1 Formulation as nearest neighbor search

An alternate way of formulating the inner per-datapoint problem of selecting whether and where to swap in a candidate point $\mathbf{x}_n$, instead of as an optimization problem where we minimize $\widehat{\mathcal{L}}_{MMD}$, is as a nearest-neighbor search. As each new candidate point $\mathbf{x}_n$ arrives, we have an existing subsample estimate $\hat{\nu}_M^{n-1}$, and compute an updated running estimate $\hat{\mu}_n$. Consider the "expanded" estimator for the mean embedding defined as

$$\hat{\nu}_{M+1}^n \triangleq \frac{M}{M+1}\hat{\nu}_M^{n-1} + \frac{1}{M+1}\hat{\phi}(\mathbf{x}_n) \tag{20}$$

which incorporates the new point $\mathbf{x}_n$ alongside the existing M point estimate, by averaging the feature maps of all points in $Y_{M+1}^{n-1} := \{\mathbf{x}_n\} \cup Y_M^{n-1}$. Equation (20) is also an approximation to $\hat{\mu}_n$, but using $M+1$ total points. Any next estimator $\hat{\nu}_M^n$ for $\hat{\mu}_n$ using only M points can be found by discarding a single one of the points in Y_{M+1}^{n-1}. For whichever point $\mathbf{y}^{drop}$ we choose to discard, we can then express $\widehat{\mathcal{L}}_{MMD}$ using the expanded estimator $\hat{\nu}_{M+1}^n$, with

$$\hat{\nu}_M^n = \frac{M+1}{M}\hat{\nu}_{M+1}^n - \frac{1}{M}\hat{\phi}(\mathbf{y}^{drop}). \tag{21}$$

Selecting the best $\hat{\nu}_M^n$ to minimize $\widehat{\mathcal{L}}_{MMD} = ||\hat{\mu}_n - \hat{\nu}_M^n||_2$ then corresponds to solving an optimization problem

$$\mathbf{y}^{drop} = \operatorname*{argmin}_{\mathbf{y} \in Y_{M+1}^{n-1}} \left|\left| \hat{\mu}_n - \frac{M+1}{M}\hat{\nu}_{M+1}^n + \frac{1}{M}\hat{\phi}(\mathbf{y}) \right|\right|_2 \tag{22}$$

in which we select the $\mathbf{y}_j$ to remove, such that the estimate $\widehat{\mathcal{L}}_{MMD}$ from the resulting Y_M^n is minimized. If there were a somehow "perfect" choice of $\mathbf{y}_j$ to remove, then this would bring the quantity on the right of Equation (22) to zero. By setting Equation (22) to zero, solving for ideal feature vector $\hat{\phi}(\mathbf{y})$, and then using Equation (20) to expand out $\hat{\nu}_{M+1}^N$ we find the optimal choice of feature vector to remove would be

$$\phi^\star = \hat{\phi}(\mathbf{x}_n) + M(\hat{\nu}_M^{n-1} - \hat{\mu}_n). \tag{23}$$

In general, none of our current $\phi(\mathbf{y}_j) = \phi^\star$ exactly, but we can still try to get as close as possible. Since we have explicit feature vectors $\hat{\phi}(\mathbf{y}_j) \in \mathbb{R}^D$ and $\phi^\star \in \mathbb{R}^D$, we can thus find the best choice $\mathbf{y}^{drop}$ by considering

$$\begin{aligned}\mathbf{y}^{drop} &= \operatorname*{argmin}_{\mathbf{y} \in Y_M^{n-1}} \left|\left| \hat{\phi}(\mathbf{y}) - \phi^\star \right|\right|_2^2 \\ &= \operatorname*{argmin}_{\mathbf{y} \in Y_M^{n-1}} \sum_{d=1}^D \left(\hat{\phi}(\mathbf{y})_d - \phi_d^\star \right)^2. \end{aligned} \tag{24}$$

Algorithm 2 Streaming MMD Minimization

Input: Stream of samples $\mathbf{x}_1, \ldots, \mathbf{x}_N$;
explicit feature map $\phi : \mathcal{X} \to \mathbb{R}^D$
Output: Subset $Y_M = \{\mathbf{y}_1, \ldots, \mathbf{y}_M\}$
Initialize $\mathbf{y}_1 = \mathbf{x}_1, \ldots, \mathbf{y}_M = \mathbf{x}_M$
Compute initial mean estimates $\hat{\nu}_M^M$ and $\hat{\mu}_M$ — Eq. (6)
for $n = M+1, \ldots, N$ **do**
  Update $\hat{\mu}_n$ to include $\phi(\mathbf{x}_n)$ — Eq. (18) or (19)
  Compute target $\phi^\star$ — Eq. (23)
  if NEARESTNEIGHBOR$_{\phi^\star}(\{\mathbf{x}_n\} \cup Y_M)$ in Y_M **then**
    $\hat{\nu}_M^n \leftarrow \hat{\nu}_M^{n-1} + \frac{1}{M}(\phi(\mathbf{x}_n) - \phi(\mathbf{y}_j))$
    $\mathbf{y}_j = \mathbf{x}_n$
  else
    $\hat{\nu}_M^n \leftarrow \hat{\nu}_M^{n-1}$
  end if
end for

This minimum can by found by performing a D-dimensional nearest-neighbor search. The easiest option for this is still to scan through all $M + 1$ candidates and compute each distance in Equation (24). However for large M we can use an approximate nearest neighbor search to reduce the overall runtime of each iteration. The overall streaming MMD minimization algorithm is given in Algorithm 2, where the function NEARESTNEIGHBOR$_{\phi^\star}(Y)$ is an exact or approximate procedure for selecting the nearest neighbor (in Euclidean distance) to $\phi^\star$ in the set Y.

3.2 Approximate nearest neighbor search

Exact nearest neighbor search in more than a small number of dimensions remains a challenging problem; we are likely to use order a few hundred random features D. Classic approaches such as KD-trees [Bentley, 1975] which are based on coordinate-aligned splits tend to break down in such settings, requiring very deep trees in order to partition the data. However, there is some hope for *approximate* nearest neighbor search, where we are willing to not necessarily find the best choice, but merely a "sufficiently close" neighbor, based on theory of intrinsic dimensionality [Johnson and Lindenstrauss, 1984].

Random projection trees are introduced in Freund et al. [2007], based on the observation that for high dimensional datasets, partitioning data into subsets based on a completely random projection direction is nearly as good as the optimal partition direction. With this in mind, to implement a fast approximate nearest neighbor search, define hash functions

$$h(\phi) = \text{sign}(\mathbf{r}^\top \phi - s) \tag{25}$$

where $\mathbf{r} \in \mathbb{R}^D$ is a random unit vector and s is a random split point. We place these hash functions at each nodes in a binary search tree; values ϕ which hash to a positive value are sent to the right subtree, those which hash to a negative value are sent left. This tree resembles a KD-tree, except with random projections splits instead of axis-aligned splits.

If we have L hash functions, arranged in a binary tree, we need to evaluate $\log_2 L$ when considering each new candidate point, and again when accepting a new point $\mathbf{x}_n$ into the set Y_M^n. For each point $\mathbf{y}_j$ in our subset, we cache which leaf node of the binary tree it falls in. In practice there may be several points in each leaf node, but instead of evaluating all M points in Y_M to check whether it is closest to $\phi^\star$, we only check however many are in the leaf.

Our particular random projection tree variant we implement is as described in Dasgupta and Sinha [2015]. We construct an initial tree from the first M points by sampling random vectors $\mathbf{r}$, and setting each split point s to be a uniform random quantile in $[0.25, 0.75]$ of the projected values at that node. This tree will have points evenly distributed among the leaves; however, as we swap out points it may become less balanced. To deal with this we periodically recompute the split points, rebalancing the tree; this operation is performed sufficiently rarely as to maintain amortized logarithmic cost. A free parameter in the search tree is the search tree depth (or equivalently, how many values ϕ to keep in each leaf node). In all our later experiments this is set to target approximately $2\log_2 M$ nodes per leaf.

Theoretical results in Dasgupta and Sinha [2015] characterize the loss relative to an exact search; we compare the exhaustive nearest neighbor search and approximate results empirically in our particular setting in Section 5.

4 BOUNDS ON SUBSET ERROR

At any point in the algorithm, it is straightforward to use our current distribution embedding approximations to compute $\widehat{\mathcal{L}}_{MMD} = ||\hat{\mu}_n - \hat{\nu}_M^n||_2$. It would be nice to characterize how this estimate compares to the true maximum mean discrepancy. In this section, we derive bounds for the estimation error which occurs due to using our size M subset to compute expectations, instead of using the full size N set. Above and beyond the implicit Monte Carlo error in using the points in X to approximate expectations with respect to $p(\mathbf{x})$, our procedure introduces additional error by restricting to only M of N total points, and using random Fourier features to approximate the kernel.

The online algorithm we use to sample from a stream is only possible when we have an explicit feature space representation. Following Sutherland and Schneider [2015], we can use bounds on the error introduced by approximating the kernel function with random Fourier features to provide bounds on the estimation error introduced by using only the subset $Y_M \subset X_N$. Being careful of the difference between the empirical mean embeddings $\mu_N, \nu_M \in \mathcal{H}$, and their random Fourier feature approximations $\hat{\mu}_N, \hat{\nu}_M \in \mathbb{R}^D$, we can compare two empirical estimates of the squared MMD, one using the (intractable) features $\phi(\mathbf{x})$, the other using the random Fourier features $\hat{\phi}(\mathbf{x})$:

$$\mathcal{L}^2_{MMD} = ||\mu_N - \nu_M||^2_{\mathcal{H}} \tag{26}$$

$$\widehat{\mathcal{L}^2}_{MMD} = ||\hat{\mu}_N - \hat{\nu}_M||^2_2 = \sum_{d=1}^{D} \left(\hat{\mu}_d^N - \hat{\nu}_d^M\right)^2. \tag{27}$$

The squared MMD $\mathcal{L}^2_{MMD}$ can be decomposed as [Gretton et al., 2012]

$$\mathcal{L}^2_{MMD} = \frac{1}{N^2}\sum_{i,i'} k(\mathbf{x}_i, \mathbf{x}_{i'}) + \frac{1}{M^2}\sum_{j,j'} k(\mathbf{y}_j, \mathbf{y}_{j'}) - \frac{2}{NM}\sum_{i,j} k(\mathbf{x}_i, \mathbf{y}_j),$$

with a matching expansion for $\widehat{\mathcal{L}^2}_{MMD}$, and since the random Fourier features [Rahimi and Recht, 2007] provide an unbiased estimate of $k(\mathbf{x}, \mathbf{x}')$ as in Equation (9), we have

$$\mathbb{E}\left[\widehat{\mathcal{L}^2}_{MMD}\right] = \mathcal{L}^2_{MMD}. \tag{28}$$

Now, directly following Sutherland and Schneider [2015, section 3.3], we view $\widehat{\mathcal{L}^2}_{MMD}$ as a function of the random variables $\{\boldsymbol{\omega}_d, b_d\}$ and consider how changing any one of these random variables modifies $\widehat{\mathcal{L}^2}_{MMD}$. The random Fourier feature approximation to the kernel decomposes into a sum across all D features as

$$k(\mathbf{x}, \mathbf{x}') = \sum_{d=1}^{D} \mathbb{E}_{\omega_d, b_d}[\hat{\phi}_d(\mathbf{x})\hat{\phi}_d(\mathbf{x}')] \tag{29}$$

$$= \frac{2}{D} \sum_{d=1}^{D} \mathbb{E}_{\omega_d, b_d}[\cos(\boldsymbol{\omega}_d^\top \mathbf{x} + b_d)\cos(\boldsymbol{\omega}_d^\top \mathbf{x}' + b_d)].$$

Since $\cos(\cdot)$ is bounded by $\{-1, 1\}$, modifying either $\boldsymbol{\omega}_d$ or b_d changes a single term in the sum at the right of Equation (29) by at most 2, and thus changes the overall random feature approximation to the kernel by at most $4/D$. This in turn bounds the change in $\widehat{\mathcal{L}^2}_{MMD}$ by at most $16/D$. Then from the bounded differences inequality of McDiarmid [1989] we have

$$\Pr\left(\mathcal{L}^2_{MMD} - \widehat{\mathcal{L}^2}_{MMD} \geq \epsilon\right) \leq e^{-\frac{D\epsilon^2}{128}}. \tag{30}$$

An algebraic rearrangement of Equation (30) can be used to provide an upper bound in probability for $\mathcal{L}^2_{MMD}$. We have, with probability at least $1 - \delta$,

$$\mathcal{L}^2_{MMD} - \widehat{\mathcal{L}^2}_{MMD} \leq \sqrt{\frac{128\log(1/\delta)}{D}}$$

which combined with our estimator for $\widehat{\mathcal{L}^2}_{MMD}$ yields

$$\mathcal{L}^2_{MMD} \leq \sqrt{\frac{128\log(1/\delta)}{D}} + \sum_{d=1}^{D} \left(\hat{\mu}_d^N - \hat{\nu}_d^M\right)^2.$$

This directly translates into bounds on the error, due to subsampling, in estimating the average $\frac{1}{N}\sum_{i=1}^{N} f(\mathbf{x}_i)$ of any function $f \in \mathcal{H}$ over the full dataset, since we have

$$\left|\frac{1}{N}\sum_{i=1}^{N} f(\mathbf{x}_i) - \frac{1}{M}\sum_{j=1}^{M} f(\mathbf{y}_j)\right|^2 = |\langle \mu_N - \nu_M, f\rangle|^2$$

$$\leq ||f||^2_{\mathcal{H}}\, ||\mu_N - \nu_M||^2_{\mathcal{H}}$$

$$= ||f||^2_{\mathcal{H}}\, \mathcal{L}^2_{MMD}.$$

Thus the worst-case squared error introduced by using the subsampled points for any $f \in \mathcal{F}$ can be bounded by the empirical squared error in the estimated mean embedding vectors, plus an error term due to the random Fourier feature approximation. We summarize this result as the following Theorem.

Theorem 1 *Let $\hat{\mu}_N, \hat{\nu}_M \in \mathbb{R}^D$ be estimates of the mean embedding from D random Fourier features, defined on sets of points X_N and $Y_M \subset X_N$. Then, with probability at least $1 - \delta$,*

$$\mathcal{L}^2_{MMD} = \sup_{f\in\mathcal{F}} \left|\frac{1}{N}\sum_{i=1}^{N} f(\mathbf{x}_i) - \frac{1}{M}\sum_{j=1}^{M} f(\mathbf{y}_j)\right|^2$$

$$\leq \sqrt{\frac{128\log(1/\delta)}{D}} + \sum_{d=1}^{D} \left(\hat{\mu}_d^N - \hat{\nu}_d^M\right)^2.$$

We note that this result can be combined with existing bounds from e.g. Song [2008] on $||\mu_N - \mu||_{\mathcal{H}}$ to characterize overall error in estimating of expectations from the points in Y_M relative to true expected values $\mathbb{E}[f]$ over the population distribution of $\{\mathbf{x}_i\}$.

5 EXPERIMENTS

We run a variety of empirical tests to quantify the performance and characteristics of this algorithm. In addition to benchmarking against to random subsampling, we also compare to a benchmark of using a random Fourier features implementation of kernel herding [Chen et al., 2010]. The kernel herding algorithm is a method for sequentially generating M points, which performs a greedy optimization on the same approximation to the MMD targeted by our online algorithm; however, it is not an algorithm for processing streaming data as it requires the estimate $\hat{\mu}_N$ as computed from the full sample set as input, and furthermore it requires a potentially expensive optimization operation for generating each new point.

We also confirm experimentally that the approximation error due to the inexact nearest neighbor search does not significantly impact overall performance.

5.1 Mixtures of Gaussians

Our initial test model is a multivariate mixture of Gaussians, as considered in both Chen et al. [2010] and Huszár and Duvenaud [2012]. We experiment with downsampling a set of $N = 100{,}000$ points drawn from a 2-dimensional mixture of 10 Gaussians to a target set of size $M = 100$. We use a squared exponential kernel

$$k(\mathbf{x}, \mathbf{x}') = \exp\left\{-\frac{||\mathbf{x} - \mathbf{x}'||_2^2}{2\gamma^2}\right\} \tag{31}$$

where the lengthscale γ is set to the median pointwise distance between the first M points; this is known as the median heuristic [Gretton et al., 2012]. We approximate the basis functions with $D = 200$ random Fourier features of the form in Equation (8), where each ω element is drawn from a normal distribution with zero mean and standard deviation γ^{-1}.

An example mixture of Gaussians target density and the selected points are shown in Figure 1, alongside a plot of the

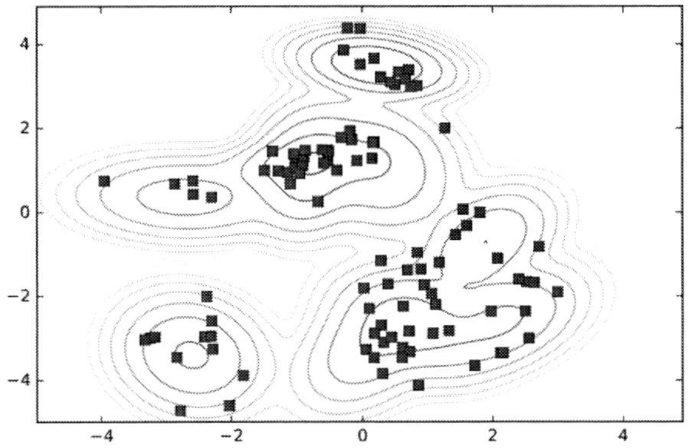
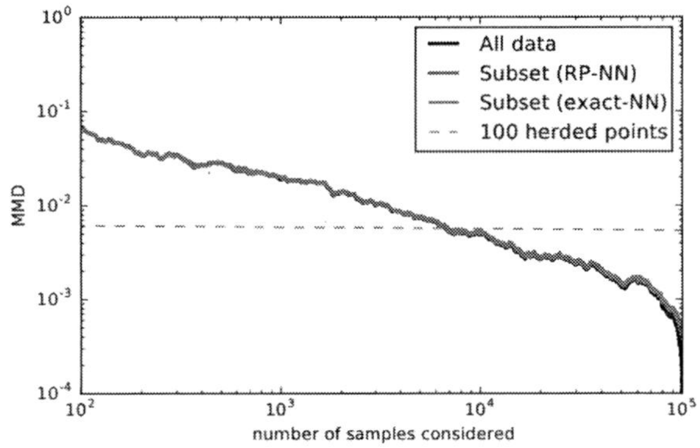

Figure 1: **(Left)** The final 100 selected points in the 2d Gaussian mixture, using the approximate nearest neighbor search. **(Right)** The empirical MMD estimate between $\hat{\mu}_n$ and $\hat{\mu}_N$, as well as between $\hat{\nu}_M^n$ and $\hat{\mu}_N$, as $n \to N$, when selecting a subset of size $M = 100$. The red line uses the random projection search tree; the blue line uses a linear scan of all options to perform an exact nearest-neighbor search. The subset estimates track the all-data MMD $\hat{\mu}_n$ very closely, despite subsampling, and even despite the approximate search. Both methods are initialized from the same set of randomly sampled points. The herding benchmark consists of M points to approximate $\hat{\mu}_N$. All estimates are averaged over 10 different synthetic datasets, drawn from mixtures of Gaussians with different parameters.

convergence of the maximum mean discrepancy estimates $||\hat{\mu}_N - \hat{\mu}_n||_2$ and $||\hat{\mu}_N - \hat{\nu}_M^n||_2$. As we view more data points, the running estimate $\hat{\mu}_n$ gradually approaches the full-data estimate $\hat{\mu}_N$. We compare to two implementations of the subsampling algorithm for selecting Y_M^n and computing $\hat{\nu}_M^n$ — one using the approximate nearest neighbor search, and one using a linear scan for an exact nearest neighbor search — and see that in both cases the running estimate based on the subsample very closely tracks the full data estimate. The overall difference in performance between the two methods is negligible despite making far fewer comparisons per iteration of the algorithm.

The herding benchmark consists of the first $M = 100$ points selected by the kernel herding [Chen et al., 2010], targeting $\hat{\mu}_N$. Theoretical results for herding suggest that the sample efficiency of the first 100 herded points should approximately match the first 10,000 random samples.

Figure 2 shows the empirical distribution over the number of comparisons actually made while searching for $\mathbf{y}^{drop}$ at each iteration when using the random projection tree for nearest neighbor search.

In Figure 3 we compare the error in computing expectations using our subsampled points, testing on the same set of functions used as a benchmark in Chen et al. [2010]. We find that the mean squared error on these test functions closely tracks the error from the full set of points. This is a remarkably promising result: expectations with respect to the full data converge at the Monte Carlo rate, and the subset of $M = 100$ points continues to perform comparably even at $N = 100,000$, for three of four test functions, and reliably outperforms both the random sampling and herding benchmarks.

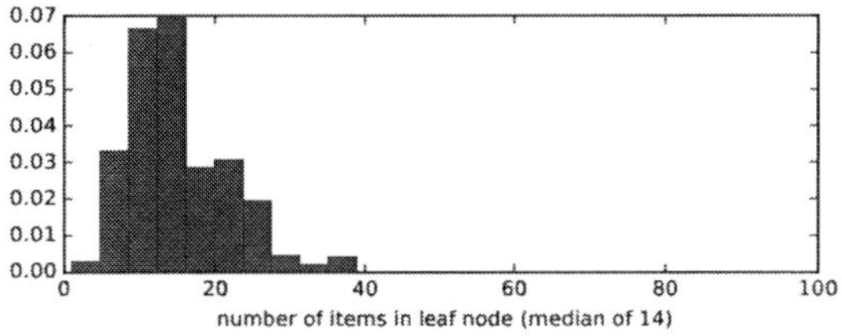

Figure 2: The actual number of comparisons made by the algorithm for processing each new data point is the same as the number of items encountered in each leaf of the random projection search tree; a full scan would require $M = 100$ comparisons, while here the median was 14. In the 2d Gaussian mixture example, we have a tree with depth 3, with an expected 12.5 items in each leaf. Compared to running a full scan, the tree-search version made the best overall decision 97.8% of the time.

5.2 Data summarization

This procedure can also be used to efficiently summarize high dimensional data, through a small handful of exemplars. We demonstrate this on $10,000$ digits taken from the MNIST dataset, reduced to be represented by a subset of size $M = 30$ in Figure 4. Each element in the MNIST image dataset is a 28×28 image of a single hand-written numeric digit, with $\mathbf{x}_i \in [0,1]^{768}$. Again, we simply use a squared exponential kernel, with lengthscale set to the median of the first M points, and $D = 200$ random features.

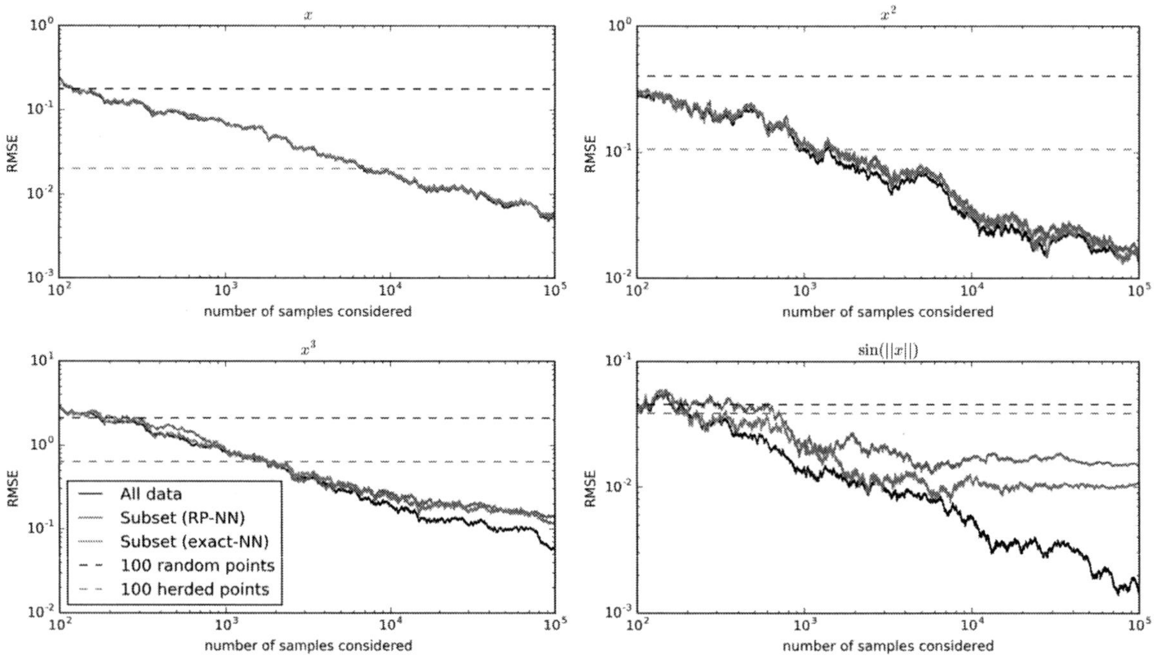

Figure 3: Error plots for expectations of four test functions: $\mathbf{x}$, $\mathbf{x}^2$, $\mathbf{x}^3$, and $\sin(||\mathbf{x}||_2)$. Legend is shared across subplots. The error is root mean squared error (RMSE) across dimensions of the test function, relative to a ground truth value computed on a separate sample of 2×10^7 points. The "random" benchmark is the median RMSE across 100 different random subsets of size $M = 100$; the "herding" benchmark is the RMSE from the first 100 herded points, targeting $\hat{\mu}_N$. We can also judge the loss of accuracy in using the approximate nearest neighbor search: there is a qualitative difference only in the $\sin(||\mathbf{x}||_2)$ example, where there is plateau in convergence for both methods. All estimates are averaged over 10 different synthetic datasets, drawn from mixtures of Gaussians with different parameters.

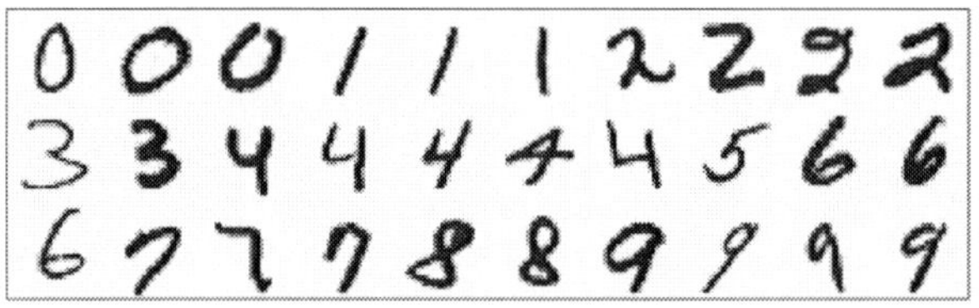

Figure 4: We summarize the MNIST digits dataset with a small number of exemplars. The subsampled set of points provides good coverage for the different digits, and also shows variation in style and form within each digit. The subsampling algorithm was given only the unlabeled digits.

The result summarizes the MNIST digits far better than a random sample would, and enormously better than other simple techniques for visualizing high-dimensional data, such as computing marginal means or quantiles across each dimension. We see a small number of exemplars from each of the 10 digits, with a good variety of handwriting styles expressed.

5.3 Resampling output of an importance sampler

One advantage of this algorithm relative to standard reservoir sampling is that it is trivially modified to run on weighted streaming data, requiring only changing the way in which the running average $\hat{\mu}_n$ is computed from Equation (18) to Equation (19). A promising use of this algorithm is to resample the output from sampling schemes such as importance sampling and sequential Monte Carlo methods, which return large numbers of weighted sets of samples. We may wish to resample from these weighted samples to obtain a new unweighted set of particles; such a resampling step is also used within sequential Monte Carlo as a means of reducing particle degeneracy [Douc et al., 2005].

As an illustrative example, we run this algorithm on the output of an importance sampler targeting a simple one-dimensional mixture distribution, proposing from a broad Gaussian prior. The results are shown in Figure 5, showing the incremental progress as the algorithm processes more points (i.e., as n increases), for a variety of small values of M. Due to the small number of points M being selected, we can see that as n becomes large, the selected points roughly approximate the quantiles of the bimodal mixture model.

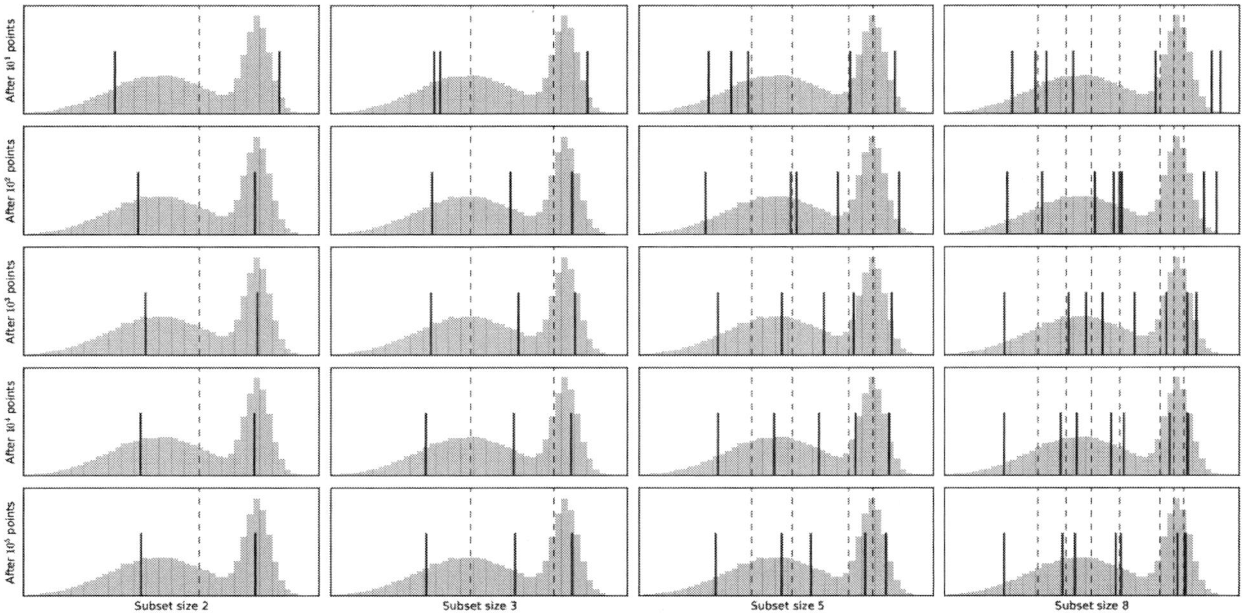

Figure 5: Downsampling points from an importance sampler. Selected points shown in red, with separate runs in each column for $M = 2, 3, 5, 8$, showing the results after observing each of $N = 10, 10^2, 10^3, 10^4, 10^5$. The green dashed lines split the probability density function of the blue target density into regions of equal probability. As N increases, the selected points approximate an even weighting across the probability density.

That is, in this example we see empirically that the points are selected such that they partition the target density $p(\mathbf{x})$ into regions of equal probability mass.

6 DISCUSSION

Reservoir sampling is a popular algorithm for drawing "manageable" subsets from large data, for both reasons of computer memory limitations, and for human visualization. For either of these purposes, our reservoir super-sampling algorithm can be used as a drop-in replacement which provides improved performance when subsampling from any data for which a kernel function can be defined.

When sampling from a weighted set of points, then the computational complexity of this algorithm is of the same order in M and N as the random sampling algorithm of [Efraimidis and Spirakis, 2006], while providing performance in computing expectations which far closer emulates computing expectations from the full data stream. This subsampling method, which explicitly use the values of the different points, could perhaps be used as a replacement for traditional resampling in sequential Monte Carlo methods, which only consider the particle weights and not the actually values at each point. Such an approach may be advantageous in settings such as considered in Jun and Bouchard-Côté [2014], where the memory usage for storing the particle set is the primary bottleneck.

Although the algorithm aims only to minimize the maximum mean discrepancy, there is evidence from the MNIST example and the point locations in the importance sampling reweighting that the selected points also have a promising use in general situations where one might want to summarize data with a small number of representative points.

As future work, we also hope to investigate the relationship between these selected locations and other methods for constructing low-discrepancy point sets.

Acknowledgments

BP would like to thank Guillaume Alain for first introducing him to reservoir sampling. FW is supported under DARPA PPAML through the U.S. AFRL under Cooperative Agreement number FA8750-14-2-0006, Sub Award number 61160290-111668.

References

Bentley, J. L. (1975). Multidimensional binary search trees used for associative searching. *Communications of the ACM*, 18(9):509–517.

Bochner, S. (1959). *Lectures on Fourier integrals*. Number 42. Princeton University Press.

Borgwardt, K. M., Gretton, A., Rasch, M. J., Kriegel, H.-P., Schölkopf, B., and Smola, A. J. (2006). Integrating structured biological data by kernel maximum mean discrepancy. *Bioinformatics*, 22(14):e49–e57.

Chen, Y., Welling, M., and Smola, A. (2010). Super-samples from kernel herding. In *Proceedings of the Twenty-Sixth Conference on Uncertainty in Artificial Intelligence (UAI2010)*.

Dasgupta, S. and Sinha, K. (2015). Randomized partition trees for nearest neighbor search. *Algorithmica*, 72(1):237–263.

Douc, R., Cappé, O., and Moulines, E. (2005). Comparison of resampling schemes for particle filtering. In *In 4th International Symposium on Image and Signal Processing and Analysis (ISPA)*, pages 64–69.

Efraimidis, P. S. and Spirakis, P. G. (2006). Weighted random sampling with a reservoir. *Information Processing Letters*, 97(5):181–185.

Freund, Y., Dasgupta, S., Kabra, M., and Verma, N. (2007). Learning the structure of manifolds using random projections. In *Advances in Neural Information Processing Systems*, pages 473–480.

Gretton, A., Borgwardt, K. M., Rasch, M. J., Schölkopf, B., and Smola, A. (2012). A kernel two-sample test. *The Journal of Machine Learning Research*, 13(1):723–773.

Huszár, F. and Duvenaud, D. (2012). Optimally-weighted herding is Bayesian quadrature. *Uncertainty in Artificial Intelligence (UAI)*.

Johnson, W. B. and Lindenstrauss, J. (1984). Extensions of Lipschitz mappings into a Hilbert space. *Contemporary mathematics*, 26(189-206):1.

Jun, S.-H. and Bouchard-Côté, A. (2014). Memory (and time) efficient sequential Monte Carlo. In *Proceedings of the 31st international conference on Machine learning*, pages 514–522.

McDiarmid, C. (1989). On the method of bounded differences. *Surveys in combinatorics*, 141(1):148–188.

Rahimi, A. and Recht, B. (2007). Random features for large-scale kernel machines. In *Advances in neural information processing systems*, pages 1177–1184.

Smola, A., Gretton, A., Song, L., and Schölkopf, B. (2007). A hilbert space embedding for distributions. In *Algorithmic learning theory*, pages 13–31. Springer.

Song, L. (2008). Learning via Hilbert space embedding of distributions.

Sutherland, D. J. and Schneider, J. (2015). On the error of random Fourier features. In *Uncertainty in Artificial Intelligence (UAI)*.

Vitter, J. S. (1985). Random sampling with a reservoir. *ACM Transactions on Mathematical Software (TOMS)*, 11(1):37–57.

Alternative Markov and Causal Properties for Acyclic Directed Mixed Graphs

Jose M. Peña
Department of Computer and Information Science
Linköping University
58183 Linköping, Sweden

Abstract

We extend Andersson-Madigan-Perlman chain graphs by (i) relaxing the semidirected acyclity constraint so that only directed cycles are forbidden, and (ii) allowing up to two edges between any pair of nodes. We introduce global, and ordered local and pairwise Markov properties for the new models. We show the equivalence of these properties for strictly positive probability distributions. We also show that when the random variables are continuous, the new models can be interpreted as systems of structural equations with correlated errors. This enables us to adapt Pearl's *do*-calculus to them. Finally, we describe an exact algorithm for learning the new models from observational and interventional data via answer set programming.

1 INTRODUCTION

Chain graphs (CGs) are graphs with possibly directed and undirected edges but without semidirected cycles. They have been extensively studied as a formalism to represent probabilistic independence models, because they can model symmetric and asymmetric relationships between random variables. Moreover, they are much more expressive than directed acyclic graphs (DAGs) and undirected graphs (UGs) (Sonntag and Peña, 2016). There are three different interpretations of CGs as independence models: The Lauritzen-Wermuth-Frydenberg (LWF) interpretation (Lauritzen, 1996), the multivariate regression (MVR) interpretation (Cox and Wermuth, 1996), and the Andersson-Madigan-Perlman (AMP) interpretation (Andersson et al., 2001). No interpretation subsumes another (Andersson et al., 2001; Sonntag and Peña, 2015). Moreover, AMP and MVR CGs are coherent with data generation by block-recursive normal linear regressions (Andersson et al., 2001).

Richardson (2003) extends MVR CGs by (i) relaxing the semidirected acyclity constraint so that only directed cycles are forbidden, and (ii) allowing up to two edges between any pair of nodes. The resulting models are called acyclic directed mixed graphs (ADMGs). These are the models in which Pearl's *do*-calculus operates to determine if the causal effect of an intervention is identifiable from observed quantities (Pearl, 2009). In this paper, we make the same two extensions to AMP CGs. We call our ADMGs alternative as opposed to the ones proposed by Richardson, which we call original. It is worth mentioning that neither the original ADMGs nor any other family of mixed graphical models that we know of (e.g. summary graphs (Cox and Wermuth, 1996), ancestral graphs (Richardson and Spirtes, 2002), MC graphs (Koster, 2002) or loopless mixed graphs (Sadeghi and Lauritzen, 2014)) subsume AMP CGs and hence our alternative ADMGs. To see it, we refer the reader to the works by Richardson and Spirtes (2002, p. 1025) and Sadeghi and Lauritzen (2014, Section 4.1). Therefore, our work complements the existing works.

The rest of the paper is organized as follows. Section 2 introduces some preliminaries. Sections 3 and 4 introduce global, and ordered local and pairwise Markov properties for our ADMGs, and prove their equivalence. When the random variables are continuous, Section 5 offers an intuitive interpretation of our ADMGs as systems of structural equations with correlated errors, so that Pearl's *do*-calculus can easily be adapted to them. Section 6 describes an exact algorithm for learning our ADMGs from observational and interventional data via answer set programming (Gelfond, 1988; Niemelä, 1999; Simons et al., 2002). We close the paper with some discussion in Section 7. Formal proofs of the claims made in this paper can be found on the supplementary material on our website.

2 PRELIMINARIES

In this section, we introduce some concepts about graphical models. Unless otherwise stated, all the graphs and probability distributions in this paper are defined over a finite set

V. The elements of V are not distinguished from singletons. An ADMG G is a graph with possibly directed and undirected edges but without directed cycles. There may be up to two edges between any pair of nodes, but in that case the edges must be different and one of them must be undirected to avoid directed cycles. Edges between a node and itself are not allowed. See Figure 1 for two examples of ADMGs.

Given an ADMG G, we represent with $A -\!\!\circ\, B$ that $A \to B$ or $A - B$ (or both) is in G. The parents of $X \subseteq V$ in G are $Pa_G(X) = \{A|A \to B$ is in G with $B \in X\}$. The children of X in G are $Ch_G(X) = \{A|A \leftarrow B$ is in G with $B \in X\}$. The neighbours of X in G are $Ne_G(X) = \{A|A - B$ is in G with $B \in X\}$. The ancestors of X in G are $An_G(X) = \{A|A \to \ldots \to B$ is in G with $B \in X$ or $A \in X\}$. The descendants of X in G are $De_G(X) = \{A|A \leftarrow \ldots \leftarrow B$ is in G with $B \in X$ or $A \in X\}$. The semidescendants of X in G are $de_G(X) = \{A|A \circ\!\!- \ldots \circ\!\!- B$ is in G with $B \in X$ or $A \in X\}$. The non-semidescendants of X in G are $Nd_G(X) = V \setminus de_G(X)$. The connectivity components of X in G is $Cc_G(X) = \{A|A - \ldots - B$ is in G with $B \in X$ or $A \in X\}$. The connectivity components in G are denoted as $Cc(G)$. A route between a node V_1 and a node V_n on G is a sequence of (not necessarily distinct) nodes $V_1, \ldots, V_n$ such that V_i and V_{i+1} are adjacent in G for all $1 \leq i < n$. We do not distinguish between the sequences $V_1, \ldots, V_n$ and $V_n, \ldots, V_1$, i.e. they represent the same route. If the nodes in the route are all distinct, then the route is called a path. Finally, the subgraph of G induced by $X \subseteq V$, denoted as G_X, is the graph over X that has all and only the edges in G whose both ends are in X.

Let X, Y, W and Z be disjoint subsets of V. We represent by $X \perp_p Y|Z$ that X and Y are conditionally independent given Z in a probability distribution p. Every probability distribution p satisfies the following four properties: Symmetry $X \perp_p Y|Z \Rightarrow Y \perp_p X|Z$, decomposition $X \perp_p Y \cup W|Z \Rightarrow X \perp_p Y|Z$, weak union $X \perp_p Y \cup W|Z \Rightarrow X \perp_p Y|Z \cup W$, and contraction $X \perp_p Y|Z \cup W \wedge X \perp_p W|Z \Rightarrow X \perp_p Y \cup W|Z$. If p is strictly positive, then it also satisfies the intersection property $X \perp_p Y|Z \cup W \wedge X \perp_p W|Z \cup Y \Rightarrow X \perp_p Y \cup W|Z$. Some (not yet characterized) probability distributions also satisfy the composition property $X \perp_p Y|Z \wedge X \perp_p W|Z \Rightarrow X \perp_p Y \cup W|Z$.

3 GLOBAL MARKOV PROPERTY

In this section, we introduce four separation criteria for ADMGs. Moreover, we show that they are all equivalent. A probability distribution is said to satisfy the global Markov property with respect to an ADMG if every separation in the graph can be interpreted as an independence in the distribution.

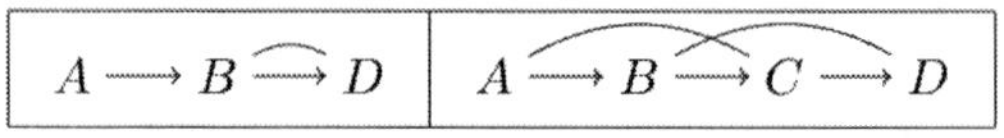

Figure 1: Examples of ADMGs.

Criterion 1. A node C on a path in an ADMG G is said to be a collider on the path if $A \to C \circ\!\!- B$ is a subpath. Moreover, the path is said to be connecting given $Z \subseteq V$ when

- every collider on the path is in $An_G(Z)$, and
- every non-collider C on the path is outside Z unless $A - C - B$ is a subpath and $Pa_G(C) \setminus Z \neq \emptyset$.

Let X, Y and Z denote three disjoint subsets of V. When there is no path in G connecting a node in X and a node in Y given Z, we say that X is separated from Y given Z in G and denote it as $X \perp_G Y|Z$.

Criterion 2. A node C on a route in an ADMG G is said to be a collider on the route if $A \to C \circ\!\!- B$ is a subroute. Note that maybe $A = B$. Moreover, the route is said to be connecting given $Z \subseteq V$ when

- every collider on the route is in Z, and
- every non-collider C on the route is outside Z.

Let X, Y and Z denote three disjoint subsets of V. When there is no route in G connecting a node in X and a node in Y given Z, we say that X is separated from Y given Z in G and denote it as $X \perp_G Y|Z$.

Criterion 3. Let G^u denote the UG over V that contains all and only the undirected edges in G. The extended subgraph $G[X]$ with $X \subseteq V$ is defined as $G[X] = G_{An_G(X)} \cup (G^u)_{Cc_G(An_G(X))}$. Two nodes A and B in G are said to be collider connected if there is a path between them such that every non-endpoint node is a collider, i.e. $A \to C \circ\!\!- B$ or $A \to C - D \leftarrow B$. Such a path is called a collider path. Note that a single edge forms a collider path. The augmented graph G^a is the UG over V such that $A - B$ is in G^a if and only if A and B are collider connected in G. The edge $A - B$ is called augmented if it is in G^a but A and B are not adjacent in G. A path in G^a is said to be connecting given $Z \subseteq V$ if no node on the path is in Z. Let X, Y and Z denote three disjoint subsets of V. When there is no path in $G[X \cup Y \cup Z]^a$ connecting a node in X and a node in Y given Z, we say that X is separated from Y given Z in G and denote it as $X \perp_G Y|Z$.

Criterion 4. Given an UG H over V and $X \subseteq V$, we define the marginal graph H^X as the UG over X such that $A - B$ is in H^X if and only if $A - B$ is in H or $A - V_1 - \ldots - V_n - B$ is H with $V_1, \ldots, V_n \notin X$. We define the marginal extended subgraph $G[X]^m$ as $G[X]^m =$

$G_{An_G(X)} \cup ((G^u)_{Cc_G(An_G(X))})^{An_G(X)}$. Let X, Y and Z denote three disjoint subsets of V. When there is no path in $(G[X \cup Y \cup Z]^m)^a$ connecting a node in X and a node in Y given Z, we say that X is separated from Y given Z in G and denote it as $X \perp_G Y|Z$.

The first three separation criteria introduced above coincide with those introduced by Andersson et al. (2001) and Levitz et al. (2001) for AMP CGs. The equivalence for AMP CGs of these three separation criteria has been proven by Levitz et al. (2001, Theorem 4.1). The following theorems prove the equivalence for ADMGs of the four separation criteria introduced above.

Theorem 1 *There is a path in an ADMG G connecting a node in X and a node in Y given Z if and only if there is a path in $G[X \cup Y \cup Z]^a$ connecting a node in X and a node in Y given Z.*

Theorem 2 *There is a path in an ADMG G connecting A and B given Z if and only if there is a route in G connecting A and B given Z.*

Theorem 3 *Given an ADMG G, there is a path in $G[X \cup Y \cup Z]^a$ connecting a node in X and a node in Y given Z if and only if there is a path in $(G[X \cup Y \cup Z]^m)^a$ connecting a node in X and a node in Y given Z.*

Unlike in AMP CGs, two non-adjacent nodes in an ADMG are not necessarily separated. For example, $A \perp_G D|Z$ does not hold for any Z in the ADMGs in Figure 1. This drawback is shared by the original ADMGs (Evans and Richardson, 2013, p. 752), summary graphs and MC graphs (Richardson and Spirtes, 2002, p. 1023), and ancestral graphs (Richardson and Spirtes, 2002, Section 3.7). For ancestral graphs, the problem can be solved by adding edges to the graph without altering the separations represented until every missing edge corresponds to a separation (Richardson and Spirtes, 2002, Section 5.1). A similar solution does not exist for our ADMGs (we omit the details).

4 ORDERED LOCAL AND PAIRWISE MARKOV PROPERTIES

In this section, we introduce ordered local and pairwise Markov properties for ADMGs. Given an ADMG G, the directed acyclity of G implies that we can specify a total ordering ($\prec$) of the nodes of G such that $A \prec B$ only if $B \notin An_G(A)$. Such an ordering is said to be consistent with G. Let the predecessors of A with respect to $\prec$ be defined as $Pre_G(A, \prec) = \{B | B \prec A \text{ or } B = A\}$. Given $S \subseteq V$, we define the Markov blanket of $B \in S$ with respect to $G[S]$ as $Mb_{G[S]}(B) = Ch_{G[S]}(B) \cup Ne_{G[S]}(B \cup Ch_{G[S]}(B)) \cup Pa_{G[S]}(B \cup Ch_{G[S]}(B) \cup Ne_{G[S]}(B \cup Ch_{G[S]}(B)))$. We say that a probability distribution p satisfies the ordered local Markov property with respect to G and $\prec$ if for any $A \in V$ and $S \subseteq Pre_G(A, \prec)$ such that $A \in S$

$$B \perp_p S \setminus (B \cup Mb_{G[S]}(B)) | Mb_{G[S]}(B)$$

for all $B \in S$.

Theorem 4 *Given a probability distribution p satisfying the intersection property, p satisfies the global Markov property with respect to an ADMG if and only if it satisfies the ordered local Markov property with respect to the ADMG and a consistent ordering of its nodes.*

Similarly, we say that a probability distribution p satisfies the ordered pairwise Markov property with respect to G and $\prec$ if for any $A \in V$ and $S \subseteq Pre_G(A, \prec)$ such that $A \in S$

$$B \perp_p C | V(G[S]) \setminus (B \cup C)$$

for all nodes $B, C \in S$ that are not adjacent in $G[S]^a$, and where $V(G[S])$ denotes the nodes in $G[S]$.

Theorem 5 *Given a probability distribution p satisfying the intersection property, p satisfies the global Markov property with respect to an ADMG if and only if it satisfies the ordered pairwise Markov property with respect to the ADMG and a consistent ordering of its nodes.*

For each $A \in V$ and $S \subseteq Pre_G(A, \prec)$ such that $A \in S$, the ordered local Markov property specifies an independence for each $B \in S$. The number of independences to specify can be reduced by noting that $G[S] = G[An_G(S)]$ and, thus, we do not need to consider every set $S \subseteq Pre_G(A, \prec)$ but only those that are ancestral, i.e. those such that $S = An_G(S)$. The number of independences to specify can be further reduced by considering only maximal ancestral sets, i.e. those sets S such that $Mb_{G[S]}(B) \subset Mb_{G[T]}(B)$ for every ancestral set T such that $S \subset T \subseteq Pre_G(A, \prec)$. The independences for the non-maximal ancestral sets follow from the independences for the maximal ancestral sets by decomposition. A characterization of the maximal ancestral sets is possible but notationally cumbersome (we omit the details). All in all, for each node and maximal ancestral set, the ordered local Markov property specifies an independence for each node in the set. This number is greater than for the original ADMGs, where a single independence is specified for each node and maximal ancestral set (Richardson, 2003, Section 3.1). Even fewer independences are needed for the original ADMGs when interpreted as linear causal models (Kang and Tian, 2009, Section 4). All in all, our ordered local Markov property serves its purpose, namely to identify a subset of the independences in the global Markov property that implies the rest.

Note that Andersson et al. (2001, Theorem 3) describe local and pairwise Markov properties for AMP CGs that are equivalent to the global one under the assumption of the intersection and composition properties. Our ordered local and pairwise Markov properties above only require assuming the intersection property. Note that this assumption is also needed to prove similar results for much simpler models such as UGs (Lauritzen, 1996, Theorem 3.7). For AMP CGs, however, we can do better than just using the ordered local and pairwise Markov properties for ADMGs above. Specifically, we introduce in the next section neater local and pairwise Markov properties for AMP CGs under the intersection property assumption. Later on, we will also use them to prove some results for ADMGs.

4.1 LOCAL AND PAIRWISE MARKOV PROPERTIES FOR AMP CGS

Andersson et al. (2001, Theorem 2) prove that a probability distribution p satisfies the global Markov property with respect to an AMP CG G if and only if it satisfies the block-recursive Markov property which requires that the following three properties hold for all $C \in Cc(G)$:

- C1: $C \perp_p Nd_G(C) \setminus Cc_G(Pa_G(C)) | Cc_G(Pa_G(C))$.
- C2: $p(C|Cc_G(Pa_G(C)))$ satisfies the global Markov property with respect to G_C.
- C3*: $D \perp_p Cc_G(Pa_G(C)) \setminus Pa_G(D) | Pa_G(D)$ for all $D \subseteq C$.

We simplify the block-recursive Markov property as follows.

Theorem 6 *C1, C2 and C3* hold if and only if the following two properties hold:*

- *C1*:* $D \perp_p Nd_G(D) \setminus Pa_G(D) | Pa_G(D)$ *for all* $D \subseteq C$.
- *C2*:* $p(C|Pa_G(C))$ *satisfies the global Markov property with respect to* G_C.

Andersson et al. (2001, Theorem 3) also prove that a probability distribution p satisfying the intersection and composition properties satisfies the global Markov property with respect to an AMP CG G if and only if it satisfies the local Markov property which requires that the following two properties hold for all $C \in Cc(G)$:

- L1: $A \perp_p C \setminus (A \cup Ne_G(A)) | Nd_G(C) \cup Ne_G(A)$ for all $A \in C$.
- L2: $A \perp_p Nd_G(C) \setminus Pa_G(A) | Pa_G(A)$ for all $A \in C$.

We introduce below a local Markov property that is equivalent to the global one under the assumption of the intersection property only.

Theorem 7 *A probability distribution p satisfying the intersection property satisfies the global Markov property with respect to an AMP CG G if and only if the following two properties hold for all $C \in Cc(G)$:*

- *L1:* $A \perp_p C \setminus (A \cup Ne_G(A)) | Nd_G(C) \cup Ne_G(A)$ *for all* $A \in C$.
- *L2*:* $A \perp_p Nd_G(C) \setminus Pa_G(A \cup S) | S \cup Pa_G(A \cup S)$ *for all* $A \in C$ *and* $S \subseteq C \setminus A$.

Finally, Andersson et al. (2001, Theorem 3) also prove that a probability distribution p satisfying the intersection and composition properties satisfies the global Markov property with respect to an AMP CG G if and only if it satisfies the pairwise Markov property which requires that the following two properties hold for all $C \in Cc(G)$:

- P1: $A \perp_p B | Nd_G(C) \cup C \setminus (A \cup B)$ for all $A \in C$ and $B \in C \setminus (A \cup Ne_G(A))$.
- P2: $A \perp_p B | Nd_G(C) \setminus B$ for all $A \in C$ and $B \in Nd_G(C) \setminus Pa_G(A)$.

We introduce below a pairwise Markov property that is equivalent to the global one under the assumption of the intersection property only.

Theorem 8 *A probability distribution p satisfying the intersection property satisfies the global Markov property with respect to an AMP CG G if and only if the following two properties hold for all $C \in Cc(G)$:*

- *P1:* $A \perp_p B | Nd_G(C) \cup C \setminus (A \cup B)$ *for all* $A \in C$ *and* $B \in C \setminus (A \cup Ne_G(A))$.
- *P2*:* $A \perp_p B | S \cup Nd_G(C) \setminus B$ *for all* $A \in C$, $S \subseteq C \setminus A$ *and* $B \in Nd_G(C) \setminus Pa_G(A \cup S)$.

5 CAUSAL INTERPRETATION

Let us assume that V is normally distributed. In this section, we show that an ADMG G can be interpreted as a system of structural equations with correlated errors. Specifically, the system includes an equation for each $A \in V$, which is of the form $A = \beta_A \cdot Pa_G(A) + \epsilon_A$ where ϵ_A denotes the error term. The error terms are represented implicitly in G. They can be represented explicitly by magnifying G into the ADMG G' as follows:

Set $G' = G$
For each node A in G
    Add the node ϵ_A and the edge $\epsilon_A \rightarrow A$ to G'
For each edge $A - B$ in G
    Replace $A - B$ with the edge $\epsilon_A - \epsilon_B$ in G'

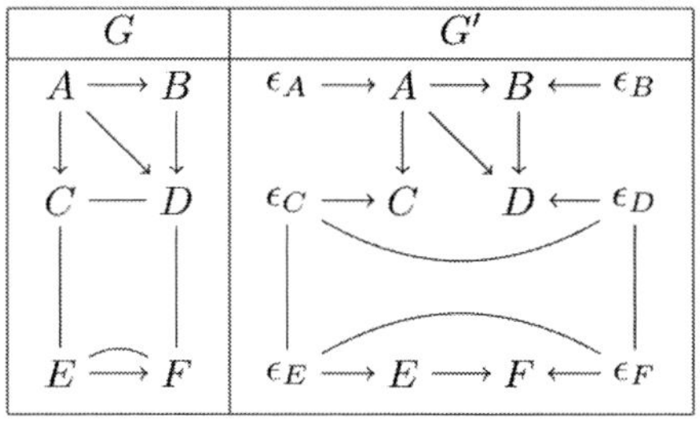

Figure 2: Example of the magnification of an ADMG.

The magnification above basically consists in adding the error nodes ϵ_A to G and connect them appropriately. Figure 2 shows an example. Note that every node $A \in V$ is determined by $Pa_{G'}(A)$ and that ϵ_A is determined by $A \cup Pa_{G'}(A) \setminus \epsilon_A$. Let ϵ denote all the error nodes in G'. Formally, we say that $A \in V \cup \epsilon$ is determined by $Z \subseteq V \cup \epsilon$ when $A \in Z$ or A is a function of Z. We use $Dt(Z)$ to denote all the nodes that are determined by Z. From the point of view of the separations, that a node outside the conditioning set of a separation is determined by the conditioning set has the same effect as if the node were actually in the conditioning set. Bearing this in mind, it is not difficult to see that, as desired, G and G' represent the same separations over V. The following theorem formalizes this result.

Theorem 9 *Let X, Y and Z denote three disjoint subsets of V. Then, $X \perp_G Y|Z$ if and only if $X \perp_{G'} Y|Z$.*

Finally, let $\epsilon \sim \mathcal{N}(0, \Lambda)$ such that $(\Lambda^{-1})_{\epsilon_A, \epsilon_B} = 0$ if $\epsilon_A - \epsilon_B$ is not in G'. Then, G can be interpreted as a system of structural equations with correlated errors as follows. For any $A \in V$

$$A = \sum_{B \in Pa_G(A)} \beta_{AB} B + \epsilon_A \tag{1}$$

and for any other $B \in V$

$$covariance(\epsilon_A, \epsilon_B) = \Lambda_{\epsilon_A, \epsilon_B}. \tag{2}$$

The following two theorems confirm that the interpretation above works as intended. A similar result to the second theorem exists for the original ADMGs (Koster, 1999, Theorem 1).

Theorem 10 *Every probability distribution $p(V)$ specified by Equations (1) and (2) is Gaussian.*

Theorem 11 *Every probability distribution $p(V)$ specified by Equations (1) and (2) satisfies the global Markov property with respect to G.*

The equations above specify each node as a linear function of its parents with additive normal noise. The equations can be generalized to nonlinear or nonparametric functions as long as the noise remains additive normal. That is, $A = f(Pa_G(A)) + \epsilon_A$ for all $A \in V$, with $\epsilon \sim \mathcal{N}(0, \Lambda)$ such that $(\Lambda^{-1})_{\epsilon_A, \epsilon_B} = 0$ if $\epsilon_A - \epsilon_B$ is not in G'. That the noise is additive normal ensures that ϵ_A is determined by $A \cup Pa_{G'}(A) \setminus \epsilon_A$, which is needed for Theorem 9 to remain valid which, in turn, is needed for Theorem 11 to remain valid.

A less formal but more intuitive alternative interpretation of ADMGs is as follows. We can interpret the parents of each node in an ADMG as its observed causes. Its unobserved causes are grouped into an error node that is represented implicitly in the ADMG. We can interpret the undirected edges in the ADMG as the correlation relationships between the different error nodes. The causal structure is constrained to be a DAG, but the correlation structure can be any UG. This causal interpretation of our ADMGs parallels that of the original ADMGs (Pearl, 2009). There are however two main differences. First, the noise in the original ADMGs is not necessarily additive normal. Second, the correlation structure of the error nodes in the original ADMGs is represented by a covariance graph, i.e. a graph with only bidirected edges (Pearl and Wermuth, 1993). Therefore, whereas a missing edge between two error nodes in the original ADMGs represents marginal independence, in our ADMGs it represents conditional independence given the rest of the error nodes. This means that the original and our ADMGs represent complementary causal models. Consequently, there are scenarios where the identification of the causal effect of an intervention is not possible with the original ADMGs but is possible with ours, and vice versa. We elaborate on this in the next section.

5.1 *do*-CALCULUS

We start by adapting Pearl's *do*-calculus, which operates on the original ADMGs, to our ADMGs. The original *do*-calculus consists of the following three rules, whose repeated application permits in some cases to identify (i.e. compute) the causal effect of an intervention from observed quantities:

- Rule 1 (insertion/deletion of observations):
  $p(Y|do(X), Z \cup W) = p(Y|do(X), W)$ if $Y \perp_{G''} Z|X \cup W||X$.
- Rule 2 (action/observation exchange):
  $p(Y|do(X), do(Z), W) = p(Y|do(X), Z \cup W)$ if $Y \perp_{G''} F_Z|X \cup W \cup Z||X$.
- Rule 3 (insertion/deletion of actions):
  $p(Y|do(X), do(Z), W) = p(Y|do(X), W)$ if $Y \perp_{G''} F_Z|X \cup W||X$.

where X, Y, Z and W are disjoint subsets of V, G'' is the original ADMG G augmented with an intervention random variable F_A and an edge $F_A \to A$ for every $A \in V$, and "$||X$" denotes an intervention on X in G'', i.e. any edge with an arrowhead into any node in X is removed. See Pearl (1995, p. 686) for further details and the proof that the rules are sound. Fortunately, the rules also apply to our ADMGs by simply redefining "$||X$" appropriately. The proof that the rules are still sound is essentially the same as before. Specifically, "$||X$" should now be implemented as follows:

```
1  Delete from G'' all the edges A → B with B ∈ X
2  For each path A − V_1 − ... − V_n − B in G'' with
   A, B ∉ X and V_1, ..., V_n ∈ X
3     Add the edge A − B to G''
4  Delete from G'' all the edges A − B with B ∈ X
```

Line 1 is shared with an intervention in an original ADMG. Lines 2-4 are best understood in terms of the magnified ADMG G': They correspond to marginalizing the error nodes associated to the nodes in X out of G'_ϵ, the UG that represents the correlation structure of the error nodes. In other words, they replace G'_ϵ with $(G')^{\epsilon \setminus \epsilon_X}$, the marginal graph of G'_ϵ over $\epsilon \setminus \epsilon_X$. This makes sense since ϵ_X is no longer associated to X due to the intervention and, thus, we may want to marginalize it out because it is unobserved. This is exactly what lines 2-4 imply. To see it, note that the ADMG after the intervention and the magnified ADMG after the intervention represent the same separations over V, by Theorem 9.

Now, we show that the original and our ADMGs allow for complementary causal reasoning. Specifically, we show an example where our ADMGs allow for the identification of the causal effect of an intervention whereas the original ADMGs do not, and vice versa. Consider the DAG in Figure 3, which represents the causal relationships among all the random variables in the domain at hand.[1] However, only A, B and C are observed. Moreover, U_S represents selection bias. Although other definitions may exist, we say that selection bias is present if two unobserved causes have a common effect that is omitted from the study but influences the selection of the samples in the study (Pearl, 2009, p. 163). Therefore, the corresponding unobserved causes are correlated in every sample selected. Note that this definition excludes the possibility of an intervention affecting the selection because, in a causal model, unobserved causes do not have observed causes. Note also that our goal is not the identification of the causal effect of an intervention in the whole population but in the subpopulation that satisfies the selection bias criterion.[2] For causal effect identification in the whole population, see Bareinboim and Tian (2015).

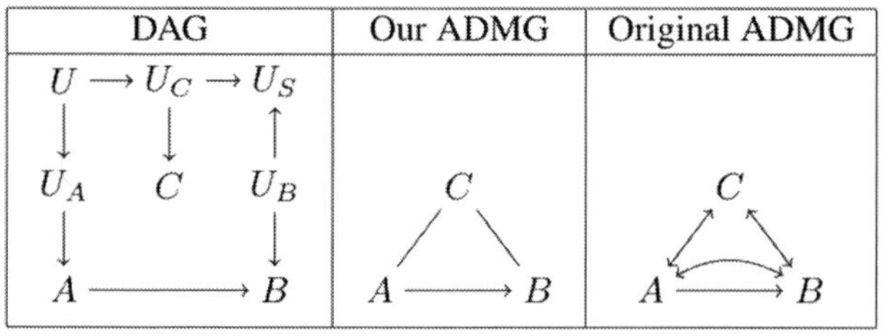

Figure 3: Example of a case where $p(B|do(A))$ is identifiable with our ADMG but not with the original one.

The ADMGs in Figure 3 represent the causal model represented by the DAG when only the observed random variables are modeled. According to our interpretation of ADMGs above, our ADMG is derived from the DAG by keeping the directed edges between observed random variables, and adding an undirected edge between two observed random variables if and only if their unobserved causes are not separated in the DAG given the unobserved causes of the rest of the observed random variables. In other words, $U_A \perp U_B | U_C$ holds in the DAG but $U_A \perp U_C | U_B$ and $U_B \perp U_C | U_A$ do not and, thus, the edges $A - C$ and $B - C$ are added to the ADMG but $A - B$ is not. Deriving the original ADMG is less straightforward. The bidirected edges in an original ADMG represent potential marginal dependence due to a common unobserved cause, also known as confounding. Thus, the original ADMGs are not meant to model selection bias. The best we can do is then to use bidirected edges to represent potential marginal dependences regardless of their origin. This implies that we can derive the original ADMG from the DAG by keeping the directed edges between observed random variables, and adding a bidirected edge between two observed random variables if and only if their unobserved causes are not separated in the DAG given the empty set. Clearly, $p(B|do(A))$ is not identifiable with the original ADMG but is identifiable with our ADMG (Pearl, 2009, p. 94). Specifically,

$$p(B|do(A)) = \sum_C p(B|do(A), C)p(C|do(A))$$

$$= \sum_C p(B|do(A), C)p(C) = \sum_C p(B|A, C)p(C)$$

where the first equality is due to marginalization, the second due to Rule 3, and the third due to Rule 2.

The original ADMGs assume that confounding is always the source of correlation between unobserved causes. In the example above, we consider selection bias as an additional source. However, this is not the only possibility. For instance, U_B and U_C may be tied by a physical law of the

[1]For instance, the DAG may correspond to the following fictitious domain: A = Smoking, B = Lung cancer, C = Drinking, U_A = Parents' smoking, U_B = Parents' lung cancer, U_C = Parents' drinking, U = Parents' genotype that causes smoking and drinking, U_S = Parents' hospitalization.

[2]For instance, in the fictitious domain in the previous footnote, we are interested in the causal effect that smoking may have on the development of lung cancer for the patients with hospitalized parents.

form $f(U_B, U_C) = constant$ devoid of causal meaning, much like Boyle's law relates the pressure and volume of a gas as $pressure \cdot volume = constant$ if the temperature and amount of gas remain unchanged within a closed system (Dawid, 2010, p. 77). In such a case, the discussion above still applies and our ADMG allows for causal effect identification but the original does not. Note that even if we assume that confounding is the only source of correlation between unobserved causes, our ADMGs may allow for causal effect identification while the original may not, e.g. replace the subgraph $U_C \rightarrow U_S \leftarrow U_B$ with $U_C \rightarrow U_B$ in Figure 3. For an example where the original ADMGs allow for causal effect identification whereas ours do not, simply replace the subgraph $U_C \rightarrow U_S \leftarrow U_B$ in Figure 3 with $U_C \leftarrow W \rightarrow U_B$ where W is an unobserved random variable. Then, our ADMG will contain the same edges as before plus the edge $A - B$, making the causal effect non-identifiable. The original ADMG will contain the same edges as before with the exception of the edge $A \leftrightarrow B$, making the causal effect identifiable.

In summary, the bidirected edges of the original ADMGs have a clear semantics: They represent potential marginal dependence due to a common unobserved cause. This means that we have to know the causal relationships involving the unobserved random variables to derive the ADMG. Or at least, we have to know that there is no selection bias or tying laws so that marginal dependence can be attributed to confounding due to Reichenbach's principle (Pearl, 2009, p. 30). This knowledge may not be available in some cases. Moreover, the original ADMGs are not meant to represent selection bias or tying laws. To solve these two problems, we may be willing to use the bidirected edges to represent potential marginal dependences regardless of their origin. Our ADMGs are somehow dual to the original ADMGs, since the undirected edges represent potential saturated conditional dependence between unobserved causes. This implies that in some cases, such as in the example above, our ADMGs may allow for causal effect identification whereas the original may not.

6 LEARNING VIA ASP

In this section, we introduce an exact algorithm for learning ADMGs from observations and interventions via answer set programming (ASP), which is a declarative constraint satisfaction paradigm that is well-suited for solving computationally hard combinatorial problems (Gelfond, 1988; Niemelä, 1999; Simons et al., 2002). A similar approach has been proposed before for learning LWF CGs from observations (Sonntag et al., 2015). ASP represents constraints in terms of first-order logical rules. Therefore, when using ASP, the first task is to model the problem at hand in terms of rules so that the set of solutions implicitly represented by the rules corresponds to the solutions of the original problem. One or multiple solutions to the original problem can then be obtained by invoking an off-the-shelf ASP solver on the constraint declaration. Each rule in the constraint declaration is of the form `head :- body`. The head contains an atom, i.e. a fact. The body may contain several literals, i.e. negated and non-negated atoms. Intuitively, the rule is a justification to derive the head if the body is true. The body is true if its non-negated atoms can be derived, and its negated atoms cannot. A rule with only the head is an atom. A rule without the head is a hard-constraint, meaning that satisfying the body results in a contradiction. Soft-constraints are encoded as rules of the form `:~ body. [W]`, meaning that satisfying the body results in a penalty of W units. The ASP solver returns the solutions that meet the hard-constraints and minimize the total penalty due to the soft-constraints. In this work, we use the ASP solver `clingo` (Gebser et al., 2011), which is based on state-of-the-art Boolean satisfiability solving techniques (Biere et al., 2009).

Figure 4 shows the ASP encoding of our learning algorithm. The predicate `node(X)` in rule 1 represents that X is a node. The predicates `line(X,Y,I)` and `arrow(X,Y,I)` represent that there is an undirected and directed edge from X to Y after having intervened on the node I. The observational regime corresponds to $I = 0$. The rules 2-3 encode a non-deterministic guess of the edges for the observational regime, which means that the ASP solver with implicitly consider all possible graphs during the search, hence the exactness of the search. The edges under the observational regime are used in the rules 4-6 to define the edges in the graph after having intervened on I, following the description in Section 5.1. Therefore, the algorithm assumes continuous random variables and additive normal noise when the input contains interventions. It makes no assumption though when the input consists of just observations. The rules 7-8 enforce the fact that undirected edges are symmetric and that there is at most one directed edge between two nodes. The predicate `ancestor(X,Y)` represents that X is an ancestor of Y. The rules 9-11 enforce that the graph has no directed cycles. The predicates in the rules 12-13 represent whether a node X is or is not in a set of nodes C. The rules 14-25 encode the separation criterion 2 in Section 3. The predicate `con(X,Y,C,I)` in rules 26-29 represents that there is a connecting route between X and Y given C after having intervened on I. The rule 30 enforces that each dependence in the input must correspond to a connecting route. The rule 31 represents that each independence in the input that is not represented implies a penalty of W units. The rules 32-33 represent a penalty of 1 unit per edge. Other penalty rules can be added similarly.

Figure 6 shows the ASP encoding of all the (in)dependences in the probability distribution at hand, e.g. as determined by some available data. Specifically, the predicate `nodes(3)` represents that there

```
% input predicates
% nodes(N): N is the number of nodes
% set(X): X is the index of a set of nodes
% dep(X,Y,C,I,W) (resp. indep(X,Y,C,I,W)): the nodes X and Y are dependent (resp.
%                                         independent) given the set of nodes C
%                                         after having intervened on the node I

% nodes
node(X) :- nodes(N), X=1..N.                                              % rule 1

% edges
{ line(X,Y,0) } :- node(X), node(Y), X != Y.                              %      2
{ arrow(X,Y,0) } :- node(X), node(Y), X != Y.                             %      3
line(X,Y,I) :- line(X,Y,0), node(I), X != I, Y != I, I > 0.               %      4
line(X,Y,I) :- line(X,I,0), line(I,Y,0), node(I), X != Y, I > 0.
arrow(X,Y,I) :- arrow(X,Y,0), node(I), Y != I, I > 0.                     %      6
line(X,Y,I) :- line(Y,X,I).                                               %      7
:- arrow(X,Y,I), arrow(Y,X,I).                                            %      8

% directed acyclity
ancestor(X,Y) :- arrow(X,Y,0).                                            %      9
ancestor(X,Y) :- ancestor(X,Z), ancestor(Z,Y).
:- ancestor(X,Y), arrow(Y,X,0).                                           %     11

% set membership
inside_set(X,C) :- node(X), set(C), 2**(X-1) & C != 0.                    %     12
outside_set(X,C) :- node(X), set(C), 2**(X-1) & C = 0.                    %     13

% end_line/head/tail(X,Y,C,I) means that there is a connecting route
% from X to Y given C that ends with a line/arrowhead/arrowtail

% single edge route
end_line(X,Y,C,I) :- line(X,Y,I), outside_set(X,C).                      %     14
end_head(X,Y,C,I) :- arrow(X,Y,I), outside_set(X,C).
end_tail(X,Y,C,I) :- arrow(Y,X,I), outside_set(X,C).

% connection through non-collider
end_line(X,Y,C,I) :- end_line(X,Z,C,I), line(Z,Y,I), outside_set(Z,C).
end_line(X,Y,C,I) :- end_tail(X,Z,C,I), line(Z,Y,I), outside_set(Z,C).
end_head(X,Y,C,I) :- end_line(X,Z,C,I), arrow(Z,Y,I), outside_set(Z,C).
end_head(X,Y,C,I) :- end_head(X,Z,C,I), arrow(Z,Y,I), outside_set(Z,C).
end_head(X,Y,C,I) :- end_tail(X,Z,C,I), arrow(Z,Y,I), outside_set(Z,C).
end_tail(X,Y,C,I) :- end_tail(X,Z,C,I), arrow(Y,Z,I), outside_set(Z,C).

% connection through collider
end_line(X,Y,C,I) :- end_head(X,Z,C,I), line(Z,Y,I), inside_set(Z,C).
end_tail(X,Y,C,I) :- end_line(X,Z,C,I), arrow(Y,Z,I), inside_set(Z,C).
end_tail(X,Y,C,I) :- end_head(X,Z,C,I), arrow(Y,Z,I), inside_set(Z,C).   %     25

% derived non-separations
con(X,Y,C,I) :- end_line(X,Y,C,I), X != Y, outside_set(Y,C).              %     26
con(X,Y,C,I) :- end_head(X,Y,C,I), X != Y, outside_set(Y,C).
con(X,Y,C,I) :- end_tail(X,Y,C,I), X != Y, outside_set(Y,C).
con(X,Y,C,I) :- con(Y,X,C,I).                                             %     29

% satisfy all dependences
:- dep(X,Y,C,I,W), not con(X,Y,C,I).                                      %     30

% maximize the number of satisfied independences
:~ indep(X,Y,C,I,W), con(X,Y,C,I). [W,X,Y,C,I]                            %     31

% minimize the number of lines/arrows
:~ line(X,Y,0), X < Y. [1,X,Y,1]                                          %     32
:~ arrow(X,Y,0). [1,X,Y,2]                                                %     33

% show results
#show. #show line(X,Y) : line(X,Y,0), X < Y. #show arrow(X,Y) : arrow(X,Y,0).
```

Figure 4: ASP encoding of the learning algorithm.

```
{ biarrow(X,Y,0) } :- node(X), node(Y), X != Y.
:- biarrow(X,Y,0), line(Z,W,0).
biarrow(X,Y,I) :- biarrow(X,Y,0), node(I), X != I, Y != I, I > 0.
biarrow(X,Y,I) :- biarrow(Y,X,I).

end_head(X,Y,C,I) :- biarrow(X,Y,I), outside_set(X,C).
end_head(X,Y,C,I) :- end_tail(X,Z,C,I), biarrow(Z,Y,I), outside_set(Z,C).
end_head(X,Y,C,I) :- end_head(X,Z,C,I), biarrow(Z,Y,I), inside_set(Z,C).

:~ biarrow(X,Y,0), X < Y. [1,X,Y,3]

#show biarrow(X,Y) : biarrow(X,Y,0), X < Y.
```

Figure 5: Additional ASP encoding for learning original ADMGs, in addition to ours.

```
nodes(3).   % three nodes
set(0..7).  % all subsets of three nodes

% observations
dep(1,2,0,0,1).
dep(1,2,4,0,1).
dep(2,3,0,0,1).
dep(2,3,1,0,1).
dep(1,3,0,0,1).
dep(1,3,2,0,1).

% interventions on the node 3
dep(1,2,4,0,3,1).
indep(2,3,0,3,1).
indep(2,3,1,3,1).
indep(1,3,0,3,1).
indep(1,3,2,3,1).
```

Figure 6: ASP encoding of the (in)dependences in the domain.

are three nodes in the domain at hand, and the predicate `set(0..7)` represents that there are eight sets of nodes, indexed from 0 (empty set) to 7 (full set). The predicate `indep(X,Y,C,I,W)` (respectively `dep(X,Y,C,I,W)`) represents that the nodes X and Y are conditionally independent (respectively dependent) given the set index C after having intervened on the node I. Observations correspond to $I = 0$. The penalty for failing to represent an (in)dependence is W. The penalty for failing to represent a dependence is actually superfluous in our algorithm since, recall, rule 30 in Figure 4 enforces that all the dependences in the input are represented. Note also that it suffices to specify all the (in)dependences between pair of nodes, because these identify uniquely the rest of the independences in the probability distribution (Studený, 2005, Lemma 2.2). Note also that we do not assume that the probability distribution at hand is faithful to some ADMG or satisfies the composition property, as it is the case in most heuristic learning algorithms.

By calling the ASP solver with the encodings of the learning algorithm and the (in)dependences in the domain, the solver will essentially perform an exhaustive search over the space of graphs, and will output the graphs with the smallest penalty. Specifically, when only the observations are used (i.e. the last five lines of Figure 6 are removed), the learning algorithm finds 37 optimal models. Among them, we have UGs such as `line(1,2) line(1,3) line(2,3)`, DAGs such as `arrow(3,1) arrow(1,2) arrow(3,2)`, AMP CGs such as `line(1,2) arrow(3,1) arrow(3,2)`, and ADMGs such as `line(1,2) line(2,3) arrow(1,2)` or `line(1,2) line(1,3) arrow(2,3)`. When all the observations and interventions available are used, the learning algorithm finds 18 optimal models. These are the models out the 37 models found before that have no directed edge coming out of the node 3. This is the expected result given the last four lines in Figure 6. Note that the output still includes the ADMGs mentioned before.

Finally, the ASP code can easily be extended as shown in Figure 5 to learn not only our ADMGs but also original ADMGs. Note that the second line forbids graphs with both undirected and bidirected edges. This results in 34 optimal models: The 18 previously found plus 16 original ADMGs, e.g. `biarrow(1,2) biarrow(1,3) arrow(1,2)` or `biarrow(1,2) biarrow(1,3) arrow(2,3)`.

7 DISCUSSION

We have introduced ADMGs as an extension of AMP CGs. We have presented global, and ordered local and pairwise Markov properties for the new models. We have also shown that when the random variables are continuous, the new models can be interpreted as systems of structural equations with correlated errors. This has enabled us to adapt Pearl's *do*-calculus to them, and show that our models complement those used in Pearl's *do*-calculus, as there are cases where the identification of the causal effect of an intervention is not possible with the latter but is possible with the former, and vice versa. Finally, we have described an exact algorithm for learning the new models from observations and interventions. We plan to unify the original and our ADMGs to allow directed, undirected and bidirected edges.

References

Andersson, S. A., Madigan, D. and Perlman, M. D. Alternative Markov Properties for Chain Graphs. *Scandinavian Journal of Statistics*, 28:33-85, 2001.

Bareinboim, E. and Tian, J. Recovering Causal Effects From Selection Bias. In *Proceedings of the 29th AAAI Conference on Artificial Intelligence*, 3475-3481, 2015.

Biere, A., Heule, M., van Maaren, H. and Walsh, T. (editors). *Handbook of Satisfiability*. IOS Press, 2009.

Cox, D. R. and Wermuth, N. *Multivariate Dependencies - Models, Analysis and Interpretation*. Chapman & Hall, 1996.

Dawid, A. P. Beware of the DAG ! *Journal of Machine Learning Research Workshop and Conference Proceedings*, 6:59-86, 2010.

Evans, R. J. and Richardson, T. S. Marginal log-linear Parameters for Graphical Markov Models. *Journal of the Royal Statistical Society B*, 75:743-768, 2013.

Gebser, M., Kaufmann, B., Kaminski, R., Ostrowski, M., Schaub, T., Schneider, M. Potassco: The Potsdam Answer Set Solving Collection. *AI Communications*, 24:107-124, 2011.

Gelfond, M. and Lifschitz, V. The Stable Model Semantics for Logic Programming. In *Proceedings of 5th Logic Programming Symposium*, 1070-1080, 1988.

Kang, C. and Tian, J. Markov Properties for Linear Causal Models with Correlated Errors. *Journal of Machine Learning Research*, 10:41-70, 2009.

Koster, J. T. A. On the Validity of the Markov Interpretation of Path Diagrams of Gaussian Structural Equations Systems with Correlated Errors. *Scandinavian Journal of Statistics*, 26:413-431, 1999.

Koster, J. T. A. Marginalizing and Conditioning in Graphical Models. *Bernoulli*, 8:817-840, 2002.

Lauritzen, S. L. *Graphical Models*. Oxford University Press, 1996.

Levitz, M., Perlman M. D. and Madigan, D. Separation and Completeness Properties for AMP Chain Graph Markov Models. *The Annals of Statistics*, 29:1751-1784, 2001.

Niemelä, I. Logic Programs with Stable Model Semantics as a Constraint Programming Paradigm. *Annals of Mathematics and Artificial Intelligence*, 25:241-273, 1999.

Pearl, J. Causal Diagrams for Empirical Research. *Biometrika*, 82:669-688, 1995.

Pearl, J. *Causality: Models, Reasoning, and Inference* (2nd ed.). Cambridge University Press, 2009.

Pearl, J. and Wermuth, N. When Can Association Graphs Admit a Causal Explanation ? In *Proceedings of the 4th International Workshop on Artificial Intelligence and Statistics*, 141-150, 1993.

Richardson, T. Markov Properties for Acyclic Directed Mixed Graphs. *Scandinavian Journal of Statistics*, 30:145-157, 2003.

Richardson, T. and Spirtes, P. Ancestral Graph Markov Models. *The Annals of Statistics*, 30:962-1030, 2002.

Sadeghi, K. and Lauritzen, S. L. Markov Properties for Mixed Graphs. *Bernoulli*, 20:676-696, 2014.

Simons, P., Niemelä, I. and Soininen, T. Extending and Implementing the Stable Model Semantics. *Artificial Intelligence*, 138:181-234, 2002.

Sonntag, D. and Peña, J. M. Chain Graph Interpretations and their Relations Revisited. *International Journal of Approximate Reasoning*, 58:39-56, 2015.

Sonntag, D. and Peña, J. M. On Expressiveness of the Chain Graph Interpretations. *International Journal of Approximate Reasoning*, 68:91-107, 2016.

Sonntag, D., Järvisalo, M., Peña, J. M. and Hyttinen, A. Learning Optimal Chain Graphs with Answer Set Programming. In *Proceedings of the 31st Conference on Uncertainty in Artificial Intelligence*, 822-831, 2015.

Studený, M. *Probabilistic Conditional Independence Structures*. Springer, 2005.

Bounded Rationality in Wagering Mechanisms

David M. Pennock
Microsoft Research
641 Avenue of the Americas
New York, NY 10011

Vasilis Syrgkanis
Microsoft Research
641 Avenue of the Americas
New York, NY 10011

Jennifer Wortman Vaughan
Microsoft Research
641 Avenue of the Americas
New York, NY 10011

Abstract

Wagering mechanisms allow decision makers to inexpensively collect forecasts from groups of experts who reveal their information via bets with one another. Such mechanisms naturally induce a game in which strategic considerations come into play. What happens in the game depends on the reasoning power of the experts. At one extreme, if experts are fully rational, no-trade theorems imply no participation. At the other extreme, if experts ignore strategic considerations, even the least informed will wager as if his beliefs are correct. Economists have analyzed the former case and decision theorists the latter, but both are arguably unrealistic. In this paper, we adopt an intermediate model of bounded rationality in wagering mechanisms based on level-k reasoning. Under this model, overconfidence allows some participation to be sustained, but experts who realize they are at a relative disadvantage do bow out. We derive conditions on the particular wagering mechanism used under which participation is unbiased, and show that unbiasedness always implies truthful reports. We show that if participation is unbiased, then participation rates unavoidably fall as players' rationality increases, vanishing for large k. Finally, we zoom in on one particular information structure to give a complete characterization specifying the conditions under which mechanisms are unbiased and show how to maximize participation rates among all unbiased mechanisms.

1 INTRODUCTION

A wagering mechanism is an inexpensive tool to elicit forecasts from a group. Rather than paying for the information directly, a decision maker can let members of the group wager with each other and, in the process, capture their beliefs. In the ideal case, everyone with information has incentive to reveal their true subjective forecasts without bias at little or no cost to the decision maker.

Kilgour and Gerchak (2004) proposed one such wagering mechanism, called a shared scoring rule. Theoretically, this mechanism is individually rational (players prefer participating over not participating), truthful, and budget balanced, meaning the decision maker can collect honest, accurate forecasts from every member of the group and pay nothing. However, individual rationality and truthfulness rely on the key assumption that players have *immutable beliefs* (Lambert et al., 2008; Chun and Shachter, 2011). That is, players believe what they believe and do not update their beliefs even when matched against opponents. They are oblivious of the fact that they are playing against reasoning agents in a zero-sum game. They employ what might be termed *level-0 reasoning*.

Immutable beliefs yield an inherent contradiction. The sum of players' private expected profits is positive: everyone who agrees to play expects to gain. Yet the true sum of their profits is zero. Everyone therefore knows that at least one player must be overly optimistic. The immutable beliefs assumption may be defensible for a one-shot, isolated game, but in an iterative game, at least one player should rapidly observe a disagreement between what he expects and what he receives, making it reasonable to assume that he will adapt and update over time. In an iterative mental game prior to play, updating may occur ex ante. All players know that someone's information must be inaccurate, so it is natural to imagine revisions even in a one-shot game.

Game theory predicts nearly the opposite behavior in a wagering mechanism. Under the assumption of a common prior, if all players are rational, know that all players are rational, know that all players know that all players are rational, ad infinitum, then speculative wagers should not happen at all (Milgrom and Stokey, 1982). The decision maker would not get a single report from any member of the group. Intuitively, every proffered wager would be declined as evidence of superior information. Private expectations could not differ from outcomes in a systematic way, and an overall bias toward optimism could not be sustained in a rational equilibrium (Lucas, 1972; Nielsen et al., 1990).

To design a wagering mechanism that encourages relatively broad, unbiased, and truthful participation, we need to understand how people behave. Do they act with immutable beliefs? Do they reason with complete rationality? Or do they fall somewhere in between?

The implications of unbounded rationality are absurd. If true, players could never "agree to disagree" (Aumann, 1976; Geanakoplos and Polemarchakis, 1982) and would never place any wager or make any investment based on a difference of opinion. Refuting this is the simple fact that speculative trade happens in exchanges around the world during every second of every day. Transactions do occur between overconfident zero-sum opponents who both expect to gain (Dubey et al., 1987; Jordan and Radner, 1979).

Yet ignoring game theory altogether is an idealization too. People are stubborn, but not entirely naive (Plott and Sunder, 1988). An opponent eager to make a large bet should give anyone pause. (Did I miss something? Is there something my opponent knows that I don't?) Only the most unsophisticated player would ignore the inconsistency between individual and aggregate expectations or repeatedly ignore a systematic difference between his private belief and his experience.

In this paper, building on a vast literature from behavioral game theory, we adopt an intermediate model of players and examine its implications for the design of wagering mechanisms. Our players are boundedly rational: they are neither superhuman level-∞ reasoners nor oblivious level-0 reasoners. Instead, we make the increasingly common assumption that each player reasons at an intermediate level k, treating all of her opponents as level-$(k-1)$ reasoners, with level-0 forming the base of the induction. When $k > 1$, players recognize that they are playing a game against strategic opponents. Still, their reasoning is incomplete. They retain a form of overconfidence in that each player believes that she is one level more capable than her opponents. We find that even this small dose of overconfidence is enough to induce participation.

To obtain accurate information from wagers, we seek shared scoring rules that encourage high rates of participation, unbiased participation (meaning that players don't decide whether to opt in or out based on the direction of their signals), and truthful participation. We first show that under very general assumptions, if an instantiation of the Kilgour-Gerchak mechanism is unbiased, it automatically leads level-k players to report their beliefs truthfully conditioned on participating. We next give a general characterization of which players choose to participate at each level. Roughly speaking, at low levels of rationality (small k) participation rates can be high due to widespread overconfidence, while at high levels of rationality (large k), only the players with the most accurate information choose to participate. We show that for any unbiased instantiation of Kilgour-Gerchak, participation rates shrink to zero as the level of rationality of players grows, illustrating that while unbiasedness is in some ways desirable, it comes at a cost.

The question of how to design unbiased mechanisms does not have a clean analytical answer in the general case. To gain intuition, we therefore zoom in on a particular symmetric information structure that permits tractable analysis under the level-k model. For this information structure, we give a complete characterization specifying the conditions under which the Kilgour-Gerchak mechanism leads to unbiased participation. Interestingly, we find that among all instantiations of Kilgour-Gerchak that are unbiased, the ones that lead to the highest level of participation are those in which players have the smallest incentive to report their true beliefs as opposed to any other forecast as they are rewarded similarly either way. This makes intuitive sense; since a player can only profit if other players lose, rewarding players more evenly has the effect of scaring off fewer of those who are relatively less informed, leading to higher overall participation.

We conclude with a brief discussion of how our work fits into the relatively new body of research on *behavioral mechanism design* (Ghosh and Kleinberg, 2014; Easley and Ghosh, 2015).

1.1 RELATED WORK

Over the past few decades, several theories have emerged to explain the inconsistencies that often arise between subjects' observed behavior in both lab and field studies and their predicted equilibrium behavior. Brocas et al. (2014) divide these theories into two categories. Theories of *imperfect choice*, such as quantal response equilibrium (McKelvey and Palfrey, 1995), assume that players fully analyze all available information but make noisy decisions or assume that other players make noisy decisions. Theories of *imperfect attention*, such as level-k, assume that players do not fully analyze all available information and therefore make imperfect choices compared with fully rational agents. In this paper we focus on the latter as such theories provide a middle ground between the extreme assumptions of immutable beliefs and full rationality under which one-shot wagering mechanisms have been analyzed in the past.

The earliest proponents of the level-k model were Stahl and Wilson (1994, 1995) and Nagel (1995). The theory was further developed, modified, and empirically evaluated by many others, including Ho et al. (1998), Costa-Gomes et al. (2001), Bosch-Domènech et al. (2002), Costa-Gomes and Crawford (2006), Crawford and Iriberri (2007), and Shapiro et al. (2014). Camerer et al. (2004) introduced a variant of the level-k model, the *cognitive hierarchy model*, in which a player at level k believes that other players' levels are sampled according to some distribution over levels $k' < k$. In particular, the model assumes that there is a Poisson distribution with parameter τ over all players' true levels, and a player at level k believes that the levels of his opponents are distributed according to a normalized Poisson over levels strictly less than k; that is, his beliefs about the relative frequencies of lower levels are correct, but he incorrectly assumes that no other players are capable of reasoning that is at least as sophisticated as his own. As Brocas et al. (2014) point out, the cognitive hierarchy model is typically more difficult to work with analytically than the basic level-k model, often failing to yield crisp and testable predictions of behavior, and has the additional parameter τ to contend with. Additionally, Wright and Leyton-Brown (2010) found that its predictive performance is similar to the basic level-k model on a variety of data sets from the behavioral game theory literature. For these reasons, we primarily focus on the basic level-k model in our analysis, though some of our results could be extended to hold under the cognitive hierarchy model.

There have been several experimental studies examining behavior in one-shot betting games with private information. In early work aimed at testing the predictions of no-trade theorems in the lab, Sonsino et al. (2001) designed a betting game in which fully rational agents would choose not to participate and found substantial rates of betting among subjects. Sløvik (2009) later replicated these results. Rogers et al. (2009) used the same betting game in a new set of experiments in order to compare how well the quantal response model, cognitive hierarchy model, and various hybrids fit the behavior of subjects in the lab. They found evidence of both imperfect choice and imperfect attention in their subjects; the cognitive hierarchy and quantal response models fit the data equally well. Finally, Brocas et al. (2014) used mouse-tracking software in order to gain a better understanding of the cognitive processes behind subjects' actions in a betting game. In their clever design, payoffs of the bet were hidden in opaque boxes. Subjects could view their own payoffs or their opponents' payoffs in different states of the world only by clicking on the appropriate box. By keeping track of which payoffs subjects viewed, the authors were able to make inferences about how many levels of reasoning they were performing. They found a reasonable fit between subjects' actions and the basic level-k model, with different clusters of subjects behaving similarly to what would be expected of level-1, level-2, and level-3 players, though they observed some evidence of imperfect choice as well.

2 PRELIMINARIES AND MODEL

We begin with a review of strictly proper scoring rules and the Kilgour-Gerchak mechanism. We then present our general model of incomplete information and player beliefs and review the level-k model of behavior.

2.1 THE KILGOUR-GERCHAK MECHANISM

We consider a simple scenario in which a set $N = \{1, \cdots, n\}$ of players wager on the value of an unknown binary random variable $X \in \{0, 1\}$. This random variable could represent, for example, the winner of an election, whether or not a product ships on time, or the outcome of a game. We use x to denote a realization of X.

The wagering mechanisms that we analyze are those of Kilgour and Gerchak (2004). All players simultaneously choose whether or not to make a wager. If player i participates, he wagers \$1 and reports a probability $\hat{p}_i$ that $X = 1$. Next, the true state x is revealed, and each player who chose to participate receives a payment that depends on x and the reports of all participating players. Payments are designed to be budget-balanced, meaning that the mechanism's operator takes on no risk. They are also truthful and individually rational for risk-neutral players with immutable beliefs. This means that such players maximize their expected utility by choosing to participate and reporting their true beliefs about the likelihood that $X = 1$.

To achieve truthfulness, Kilgour-Gerchak mechanisms build on the extensive literature on *proper scoring rules* (Savage, 1971; Gneiting and Raftery, 2007). A proper scoring rule is a reward function designed to elicit truthful predictions from risk-neutral agents. A scoring rule S mapping a probability $q \in [0, 1]$ and outcome $x \in \{0, 1\}$ to a real-valued score is *proper* if for all $p \in [0, 1]$, if $X = 1$ with probability p, then the quantity

$$\mathbb{E}[S(q, X)] = p \cdot S(q, 1) + (1 - p) \cdot S(q, 0)$$

is maximized at $q = p$. It is *strictly proper* if this maximum is unique. A common example of a strictly proper scoring rule is the Brier score (Brier, 1950), defined as

$$S(q, x) = 1 - (q - x)^2.$$

Note that the Brier score is bounded in $[0, 1]$. Any bounded scoring rule can be renormalized to lie in this range.

We make heavy use of the following characterization of proper scoring rules from Gneiting and Raftery (2007).

Theorem 1 (Gneiting and Raftery (2007)) *A scoring rule S is (strictly) proper if and only if there exists a (strictly) convex function G, referred to as the* entropy function, *such that for all $q \in [0, 1]$ and all $x \in \{0, 1\}$,*

$$S(q, x) = G(q) + G'(q)(x - q),$$

where G' is any subderivative of G. Moreover, if $X = 1$ with probability p, then $E[S(p, X)] = G(p)$.

The Kilgour-Gerchak mechanism rewards each player by comparing his score to the average score of all other participants. Let $\mathcal{P} \subseteq N$ be the set of players that choose to participate; $\mathcal{P}$ is a random variable that depends on the model of trader behavior. Let $\mathcal{P}_{-i}$ denote all members of $\mathcal{P}$ except i. (We use similar set notation throughout.) The mechanism is defined as follows.

Definition 1 (Kilgour-Gerchak mechanism) *Let S be a strictly proper scoring rule, bounded in $[0,1]$. All players $i \in \mathcal{P}$ simultaneously report a probability $\hat{p}_i$. If $|\mathcal{P}| \geq 2$, then when x is revealed, the mechanism assigns to each player $i \in \mathcal{P}$ a net profit (payment minus \$1 wager) of*

$$S(\hat{p}_i, x) - \frac{1}{|\mathcal{P}_{-i}|} \sum_{j \in \mathcal{P}_{-i}} S(\hat{p}_j, x).$$

If $|\mathcal{P}| = 1$, it returns the \$1 wager to the single participating player who receives a net profit of 0.

We assume that players are *risk neutral*, so if player i chooses to participate, then his utility is

$$u_i(\hat{\mathbf{p}}, x) = \begin{cases} S(\hat{p}_i, x) - \frac{\sum_{j \in \mathcal{P}_{-i}} S(\hat{p}_j, x)}{|\mathcal{P}_{-i}|} & \text{if } |\mathcal{P}| > 1, \\ 0 & \text{otherwise.} \end{cases}$$

Since we analyze only the Kilgour-Gerchak mechanism, the design space we consider is the space of all strictly proper scoring rules bounded in $[0,1]$. Selecting the scoring rule S (or equivalently, selecting the corresponding entropy function G) fully defines the mechanism.

2.2 PLAYER BELIEFS AND BEHAVIOR

To discuss level-k behavior, we first need to define the beliefs of players. We begin by considering a general model of incomplete information based on the well-studied model of Aumann (1976). In later sections, we analyze a specific special case of this model.

We imagine a process in which Nature first draws the value of the random variable $X \in \{0,1\}$ and then, conditioned on this value, draws (possibly correlated) random signals $\Sigma_i \in \{1, \cdots, m_i\}$ for each player i. We define a state of the world $\omega = (x, \sigma_1, \cdots, \sigma_n)$ as an outcome x paired with an assignment of signals σ_i to each player i. Let Ω be the set of all mutually exclusive and exhaustive states of the world. Players share a common prior over Ω.

Under the level-k model, the behavior of each player i is characterized by his *level of rationality*. Under the most simple version of the model, a player at some level $k \in \{1, 2, \cdots\}$ assumes that every other player is at level $k-1$ and best responds to the (distribution over) actions such players would take. This can be viewed as a form of overconfidence; every player believes he is slightly more rational than everyone else. We define level-0 players to be risk neutral with immutable beliefs. Such players always participate (as participation is rational under the immutable beliefs assumption (Kilgour and Gerchak, 2004; Lambert et al., 2008)) and truthfully bid their posterior beliefs conditioned on their signals. We could have alternatively defined level-0 players to be noise traders, choosing reports at random, as is common in the level-k literature. This definition would then give rise to immutable belief behavior at level 1, and would therefore not change the nature of our results; it would amount to no more than a simple renumbering of levels.

The behavior of a player at a level k consists of two decisions: whether or not to participate, and his report. We denote with $z_i^{(k)}(\sigma_i)$ an indicator variable that is 1 if player i would choose to participate at level k with signal σ_i and 0 otherwise. We denote with $\hat{p}_i^{(k)}(\sigma_i)$ the report of player i at level k with signal σ_i conditioned on participating. Let $\mathcal{P}^{(k)}$ denote the set of players who would participate *if* they were following level-k behavior; this is a random variable since it depends on the realized signals of each player. The functions $z_i^{(k)}$ and $\hat{p}_i^{(k)}$ are valid level-k behaviors if they maximize a player's utility under the assumption that every other player is of level $k-1$. More formally, let

$$\begin{aligned} &U_i^{(k)}(\hat{p}_i, \sigma_i) \\ &= \mathbb{E}\left[\left(S(\hat{p}_i, X) - \frac{\sum_{j \in \mathcal{P}_{-i}^{(k-1)}} S(\hat{p}_j^{(k-1)}(\Sigma_j), X)}{|\mathcal{P}_{-i}^{(k-1)}|}\right) \cdot \mathbf{1}\{\mathcal{P}_{-i}^{(k-1)} \neq \emptyset\} \;\middle|\; \Sigma_i = \sigma_i\right] \end{aligned}$$

be the expected utility of player i at level k if he participates and reports $\hat{p}_i$. Then we must have

$$\hat{p}_i^{(k)}(\sigma_i) \in \arg\max_{\hat{p}_i \in [0,1]} U_i^{(k)}(\hat{p}_i, \sigma_i),$$
$$z^{(k)}(\sigma_i) = \mathbf{1}\left\{U_i\left(\hat{p}_i^{(k)}(\sigma_i)\right) > 0\right\}.$$

Note that we assume players participate only if their expected utility is strictly positive and do not participate if their utility is 0. This is consistent with the scoring rule literature in which it is often assumed that players require strict incentives to truthfully report beliefs.

3 A GENERAL CHARACTERIZATION OF LEVEL-k BEHAVIOR

We are broadly interested in understanding when and how wagering mechanisms can be used to elicit accurate information from players in the level-k model of rationality. With our focus limited to Kilgour-Gerchak mechanisms, we can rephrase this question as asking which scoring rules S lead to high levels of participation and accurate reports.

Two crucial notions in our characterization are *unbiased participation* and *truthful behavior*. Unbiased participation simply requires that a player's choice of whether or not to participate is independent of his signal (and therefore also independent of the outcome X). This is desirable because biased participation could lead to a biased collection of reports, leading in turn to a biased aggregate forecast for the decision maker.

Definition 2 (Unbiased participation) *We say that behavior at a level $k \in \{0, 1, \cdots\}$ is unbiased if every player's decision of whether or not to participate is independent of the value of his signal, i.e., if $\forall i \in N$, $\forall \sigma_i, \sigma_i' \in \{1, \cdots, m_i\}$, $z_i^{(k)}(\sigma_i) = z_i^{(k)}(\sigma_i')$.*

Using the common prior over Ω, we can define the posterior belief of player i about the likelihood of X after observing the signal $\Sigma_i = \sigma_i$ as

$$p_i(\sigma_i) \equiv \Pr[X = 1 | \Sigma_i = \sigma_i]. \quad (1)$$

Players behave truthfully if they report their true posteriors.

Definition 3 (Truthful behavior) *We say that behavior at a level $k \in \{0, 1, \cdots\}$ is truthful if for each player, if that player were to participate at level k, reporting his posterior belief conditioned only on his own signal would uniquely maximize his utility, i.e., if $\forall i \in N$, $\forall \sigma_i \in \{1, \cdots, m_i\}$, $p_i(\sigma_i) = \arg\max_{\hat{p}_i \in [0,1]} U_i^{(k)}(\hat{p}_i, \sigma_i)$.*

3.1 UNBIASEDNESS IMPLIES TRUTHFULNESS

With these two definitions in hand, we can prove several basic characterizations of level-k behavior in Kilgour-Gerchak mechanisms. The first shows that unbiased participation automatically leads to truthfulness, providing another argument that unbiased participation is desirable. The characterizations in this section make use of the observation that, by the assumption of unbiased participation, for any level $k' < k$, the decision of a level k' player of whether or not to participate is independent of his signal, and therefore independent of the true state of the world X. This implies that for any i, the set $\mathcal{P}_{-i}^{(k')}$ is independent of X, and in fact, deterministic.

Theorem 2 *In the Kilgour-Gerchak mechanism with strictly proper scoring rule S, if behavior at each level $k' < k$ is unbiased, then level-k behavior is truthful.*

Proof: If $\mathcal{P}_{-i}^{(k-1)} = \emptyset$ then any wager of player i would yield expected utility 0, so player i would not participate. Suppose that $\mathcal{P}_{-i}^{(k-1)} \neq \emptyset$. Then

$$U_i^{(k)}(\hat{p}_i, \sigma_i) = \mathbb{E}\left[S(\hat{p}_i, X) \mid \Sigma_i = \sigma_i\right] - \frac{1}{|\mathcal{P}_{-i}^{(k-1)}|} \sum_{j \in \mathcal{P}_{-i}^{(k-1)}} \mathbb{E}\left[S(\hat{p}_j^{(k-1)}(\Sigma_j), X) \mid \Sigma_i = \sigma_i\right].$$

The second term is independent of the player's report $\hat{p}_i$. Thus the player will behave truthfully if and only if doing so maximizes the first term, i.e., if and only if

$$p_i(\sigma_i) = \arg\max_{\hat{p}_i \in [0,1]} \mathbb{E}\left[S(\hat{p}_i, X) \mid \Sigma_i = \sigma_i\right],$$

which must hold by definition of $p_i(\sigma_i)$ and the fact that S is a strictly proper scoring rule. ■

Thus to design a truthful mechanism, it is sufficient to design a mechanism that encourages unbiased participation.

3.2 CHARACTERIZING PARTICIPATION

Our next few characterization results examine the conditions under which players choose to participate in the wagering mechanism when the mechanism is unbiased. Lemma 1 examines participation at level k when the mechanism is unbiased at all levels $k' < k$. This lemma will prove useful later when we wish to show that a mechanism is unbiased at all levels for specific signal structures.

Lemma 1 *In the Kilgour-Gerchak mechanism with strictly proper scoring rule S, if behavior at each level $k' < k$ is unbiased, then a player i at level k with signal σ_i participates if and only if $|\mathcal{P}_{-i}^{(k-1)}| > 0$ and*

$$\mathbb{E}[S(p_i(\sigma_i), X) | \Sigma_i = \sigma_i] > \frac{1}{|\mathcal{P}_{-i}^{(k-1)}|} \sum_{j \in \mathcal{P}_{-i}^{(k-1)}} \mathbb{E}[S(p_j(\Sigma_j), X) | \Sigma_i = \sigma_i]. \quad (2)$$

Proof: Consider any player $i \in N$ at level k. This player would never participate if $|\mathcal{P}_{-i}^{(k-1)}| = 0$ since his expected utility would be 0, so assume that $|\mathcal{P}_{-i}^{(k-1)}| > 0$. By Theorem 2, since participation is unbiased at every level $k' < k$, players at level k and at level $k-1$ behave truthfully. Using this and the form of player utilities immediately yields the lemma. ■

Theorem 3 builds on the previous lemma to show that when participation is unbiased at levels $k' \leq k$, a player at level k chooses to participate if and only if his a priori expected score (i.e., his expected score before signals are revealed) is higher than the average a priori expected score of all other players who participate at level $k-1$.

Theorem 3 *In the Kilgour-Gerchak mechanism with strictly proper scoring rule S with associated entropy G, if behavior at each level $k' \leq k$ is unbiased, then player i at level k participates if and only if $|\mathcal{P}_{-i}^{(k-1)}| > 0$ and*

$$\mathbb{E}[G(p_i(\Sigma_i))] > \frac{1}{|\mathcal{P}_{-i}^{(k-1)}|} \sum_{j \in \mathcal{P}_{-i}^{(k-1)}} \mathbb{E}[G(p_j(\Sigma_j))].$$

Proof: Consider any $i \in N$ at level k. Since this player would never participate if $|\mathcal{P}_{-i}^{(k-1)}| = 0$, assume that $|\mathcal{P}_{-i}^{(k-1)}| > 0$. Since we have assumed that participation is unbiased at level k (as well as lower levels), we know that i either chooses to participate at level k regardless of his signal, or chooses not to participate at level k regardless of his signal. If he chooses to participate, then by Lemma 1, Equation (2) holds for all $\sigma_i \in \{1, \cdots, m_i\}$ and therefore

$$\sum_{\sigma_i=1}^{m_i} \Pr[\Sigma_i = \sigma_i]\mathbb{E}[S(p_i(\Sigma_i), X)|\Sigma_i = \sigma_i]$$
$$> \sum_{\sigma_i=1}^{m_i} \frac{\Pr[\Sigma_i = \sigma_i]}{|\mathcal{P}_{-i}^{(k-1)}|} \sum_{j \in \mathcal{P}_{-i}^{(k-1)}} \mathbb{E}[S(p_j(\Sigma_j), X)|\Sigma_i = \sigma_i]$$

implying that

$$\mathbb{E}[S(p_i(\Sigma_i), X)] > \frac{1}{|\mathcal{P}_{-i}^{(k-1)}|} \sum_{j \in \mathcal{P}_{-i}^{(k-1)}} \mathbb{E}[S(p_j(\Sigma_j), X)].$$

Similarly, if he chooses not to participate then Lemma 1 implies that

$$\mathbb{E}[S(p_i(\Sigma_i), X)] \leq \frac{1}{|\mathcal{P}_{-i}^{(k-1)}|} \sum_{j \in \mathcal{P}_{-i}^{(k-1)}} \mathbb{E}[S(p_j(\Sigma_j), X)].$$

The proof is completed by observing that by Theorem 1 for any $i \in N$,

$$\begin{aligned} \mathbb{E}[S(p_i(\Sigma_i), X)] &= \mathbb{E}_{\Sigma_i}\left[\mathbb{E}_X[S(p_i(\Sigma_i), X)|\Sigma_i]\right] \\ &= \mathbb{E}\left[G(p(\Sigma_i))\right]. \end{aligned}$$

■

This theorem implies that if the mechanism is unbiased at all levels, then at every level k, at least the player with the smallest a priori expected score among those who participate at level $k-1$ stops participating. Additionally, no player who stops participating at some level k ever participates at a higher level, since the average score of other (fictitious) participating players is an increasing function of k. Therefore participation goes to zero as the level of rationality grows, coinciding with fully rational behavior. This illustrates that while unbiasedness is in some ways desirable, it also has its costs.

Corollary 1 *In the Kilgour-Gerchak mechanism with strictly proper scoring rule S, if behavior at every level is unbiased, then participation shrinks to zero as the level of rationality of players grows.*

The intuition behind the lack of participation in the limit is as follows. As a player's level of rationality grows, the amount of rationality he ascribes to other players grows as well. This leads him to believe that other players participate only if they are highly informed, and to choose not to participate if he is not informed enough to profit against these highly informed opponents. In the limit, no player believes he is informed enough to profit, and participation goes to zero.

4 THE SYMMETRIC SETTING

We have shown that under the level-k model of reasoning, any instantiation of the Kilgour-Gerchak mechanism for which participation is unbiased yields truthful reports. We have also explored the criteria for participation in such mechanisms. A natural question is how to design mechanisms with unbiased participation. This question does not have a clean analytical answer in the general case. To gain some intuition about this question, we therefore turn our attention to one particular information structure that permits tractable analysis under the level-k model.

We consider a scenario in which signals are binary, that is, $\Sigma_i \in \{0, 1\}$ for all i, and are drawn independently for each player, conditional on the state of the world X. Furthermore, each player i's signal is "correct" with some fixed and known probability c_i, that is, $\Pr[\Sigma_i = x \mid X = x] = c_i$ for $x \in \{0, 1\}$. Finally, to simplify analysis and presentation, we assume that, a priori, $\Pr[X = 1] = \Pr[X = 0] = 1/2$. One way of viewing this assumption is that prior public information does not favor either outcome, but rather all information in favor of some outcome is received privately by the players through their signals. We refer to this setting as the *symmetric setting*.

In the symmetric setting, the posterior in (1) is simply

$$p_i(\sigma_i) = \begin{cases} c_i & \text{if } \sigma_i = 1, \\ 1 - c_i & \text{if } \sigma_i = 0. \end{cases} \quad (3)$$

4.1 FULLY CHARACTERIZING MECHANISMS WITH UNBIASED PARTICIPATION

The next two results provide matching sufficient and necessary conditions for achieving unbiased participation in the symmetric setting. First, Theorem 4 shows that to achieve unbiased participation it is sufficient to use the Kilgour-Gerchak mechanism with a scoring rule that is symmetric in the sense that $S(p, x) = S(1-p, 1-x)$ for all p and x, or equivalently, has associated entropy function G with $G(p) = G(1-p)$ for all p. In this case, a player i chooses to participate at level k if and only if his expected score is higher than the average expected score of all other players who would participate at level $k-1$. Theorem 5 then shows that this symmetry is also necessary in order to achieve unbiased participation in this setting.

Theorem 4 (Sufficient condition for unbiasedness) *In the symmetric setting, the Kilgour-Gerchak mechanism with strictly proper scoring rule S exhibits unbiased* *participation at all levels if $S(p,x) = S(1-p,1-x)$ for all $p \in [0,1]$ and $x \in \{0,1\}$. Moreover, player i at level k participates if and only if*

$$G(c_i) > \frac{1}{|\mathcal{P}_{-i}^{(k-1)}|} \sum_{j \in \mathcal{P}_{-i}^{(k-1)}} G(c_j), \tag{4}$$

where G is the entropy function associated with S.

Proof: The proof is by induction. By definition, all players participate at level 0, so participation is unbiased. Consider any $k > 0$ and suppose that for all levels $k' < k$, participation is unbiased. Then by the entropy characterization of scoring rules in Theorem 1 and by Lemma 1, we have that player i with signal $\Sigma_i = \sigma_i$ participates only if

$$G(p_i(\sigma_i)) > \frac{1}{|\mathcal{P}_{-i}^{(k-1)}|} \sum_{j \in \mathcal{P}_{-i}^{(k-1)}} \mathbb{E}[S(p_j(\Sigma_j), X)|\Sigma_i = \sigma_i].$$

The symmetry of S implies that $G(p) = G(1-p)$ for all $p \in [0,1]$. Using this symmetry and the fact that $p_i(\sigma_i)$ is either c_i or $1 - c_i$, we have $G(p_i(\sigma_i)) = G(c_i)$ regardless of the signal realization σ_i. To complete the proof, we then need only to show that for any $j \neq i$ and any $\sigma_i \in \{0,1\}$,

$$\mathbb{E}[S(p_j(\Sigma_j), X)|\Sigma_i = \sigma_i] = G(c_j). \tag{5}$$

Since $G(c_j)$ does not depend on player i's signal, this would imply that participation is unbiased at level k.

By exploiting symmetry as described below, we have that

$$\begin{aligned}
&\mathbb{E}[S(p_j(\Sigma_j), X)|\Sigma_i = 1] \\
&\quad = \mathbb{E}[S(1 - p_j(\Sigma_j), 1 - X)|\Sigma_i = 1] \\
&\quad = \mathbb{E}[S(p_j(1 - \Sigma_j), 1 - X)|\Sigma_i = 1] \\
&\quad = \mathbb{E}[S(p_j(\Sigma_j), X)|\Sigma_i = 0].
\end{aligned}$$

The first equality follows from the symmetry of S. The second follows from (3), which implies that $1 - p_j(\Sigma_j) = p_j(1 - \Sigma_j)$. The third can be easily verified by expanding out the expressions and exploiting the symmetry in both the prior and the signal error. Hence, we have

$$\begin{aligned}
&\mathbb{E}[S(p_j(\Sigma_j), X)] \\
&\quad = \Pr[\Sigma_i = 1]\mathbb{E}[S(p_j(\Sigma_j), X)|\Sigma_i = 1] \\
&\qquad + \Pr[\Sigma_i = 0]\mathbb{E}[S(p_j(\Sigma_j), X)|\Sigma_i = 0] \\
&\quad = \mathbb{E}[S(p_j(\Sigma_j), X)|\Sigma_i = 1] \\
&\quad = \mathbb{E}[S(p_j(\Sigma_j), X)|\Sigma_i = 0].
\end{aligned}$$

Moreover, we have

$$\begin{aligned}
&\mathbb{E}[S(p_j(\Sigma_j), X)] \\
&\quad = \Pr[\Sigma_j = 1]\mathbb{E}[S(p_j(\Sigma_j), X)|\Sigma_j = 1] \\
&\qquad + \Pr[\Sigma_j = 0]\mathbb{E}[S(p_j(\Sigma_j), X)|\Sigma_j = 0] \\
&\quad = \frac{1}{2}G(c_j) + \frac{1}{2}G(1 - c_j) = G(c_j).
\end{aligned}$$

Combining the previous two equalities gives us Equation (5), completing the proof. ■

The next result provides a matching necessary condition. Note that for any symmetric scoring rule S, adding a constant payment that depends on the outcome x but not on the report p would break symmetry but would not affect the resulting Kilgour-Gerchak payments; since this constant amount is added to *all* players' scores, it cancels out when comparing player i's score to the average score of other participants. The necessary condition states that unbiased participation is achievable only if the scoring rule used is "equivalent to" a symmetric scoring rule in this way.

Theorem 5 (Necessary condition for unbiasedness) *In the symmetric setting, if the Kilgour-Gerchak mechanism exhibits unbiased participation for level-k players with all possible signal accuracies for all levels k, then the payments are equivalent to those using Kilgour-Gerchak with a scoring rule S that satisfies $S(p,x) = S(1-p,1-x)$ for all $p \in [0,1]$ and $x \in \{0,1\}$.*

Proof: Assume that the Kilgour-Gerchak mechanism using scoring rule $\bar{S}$ exhibits unbiased participation for level-k players for all possible vectors of signal accuracies and all levels k.

First note that for any scoring rule $\bar{S}$ bounded in $[0,1]$, the scoring rule S defined by $S(q,1) = \bar{S}(q,1) + (1 - \bar{S}(1,1))$ and $S(q,0) = \bar{S}(q,0) + (1 - \bar{S}(0,0))$ remains bounded in $[0,1]$ and results in identical payments to each player when used in the Kilgour-Gerchak mechanism. For the purposes of this proof, we therefore consider the alternative representation of the mechanism as the Kilgour-Gerchak mechanism with this modified scoring rule S. Note that $S(1,1) = S(0,0) = 1$ and therefore $G(1) = G(0) = 1$.

Suppose there are only two players, i and j, with equal accuracies $c_i = c_j = c$, and consider the level-1 behavior of agent i. At level 0, agent j always participates. By Lemma 1, Theorem 1, and (3), we have that player i with signal $\Sigma_i = 1$ participates if and only if

$$G(c) > \mathbb{E}[S(p_j(\Sigma_j), X)|\Sigma_i = 1].$$

Expanding out the terms on both sides and rearranging, this inequality is equivalent to

$$\begin{aligned}
&S(c,1)c + S(c,0)(1-c) \\
&\quad > c\left(S(c,1)c + S(1-c,1)(1-c)\right) \\
&\qquad + (1-c)\left(S(c,0)(1-c) + S(1-c,0)c\right).
\end{aligned}$$

Rearranging terms, this condition reduces to

$$S(c,1) + S(c,0) > S(1-c,1) + S(1-c,0). \tag{6}$$

Similarly, player i participates with signal $\Sigma_i = 0$ if and only if

$$G(1-c) > \mathbb{E}[S(p_j(\Sigma_j), X)|\Sigma_i = 0].$$

Expanding out terms in a similar way and rearranging, this condition reduces to

$$S(1-c,1)+S(1-c,0)>S(c,1)+S(c,0). \quad (7)$$

For participation to be unbiased it must be that (6) and (7) either both hold or both do not hold. Clearly they cannot both hold simultaneously. The only way that both could simultaneously not hold is if

$$S(c,1)+S(c,0)=S(1-c,1)+S(1-c,0).$$

By the characterization of scoring rules in Theorem 1, the corresponding entropy function must then satisfy

$$\begin{aligned}&G(c)+G'(c)(1-c)+G(c)+G'(c)(-c)\\&=G(1-c)+G'(1-c)c+G(1-c)+G'(1-c)(c-1)\end{aligned}$$

which reduces to

$$G(1-c)+(c-1/2)G'(1-c)=G(c)+(1/2-c)G'(c). \quad (8)$$

Since c was chosen arbitrarily, in order for participation to be unbiased for *all* vectors of signal accuracies, this equality must hold for all $c\in[1/2,1]$.

It remains to show that this implies symmetry in S. It must be the case that $G(c)=G(1-c)$ at $c=1/2$ and $c=1$. (The latter is true because we have replaced $\bar{S}$ with S.) Suppose that there is some $c\in(1/2,1)$ such that $G(c)>G(1-c)$. Then by continuity of G, there must be some c_1 and c_2 such that

(a) $G(c_1)=G(1-c_1)$,
(b) $G(c_2)=G(1-c_2)$,
(c) $G(c)>G(1-c)$ for all $c\in(c_1,c_2)$.

Condition (c) and (8) imply that for all $c\in(c_1,c_2)$, $G'(c)>-G'(1-c)$. But this contradicts conditions (a) and (b). Therefore, there cannot exist any c with $G(c)>G(1-c)$.

A symmetric argument can be made for the case in which $G(c)<G(1-c)$ for some $c\in(1/2,1)$, so we must have $G(c)=G(1-c)$ for all c. The characterization in Theorem 1 can be used to easily show that this implies the desired symmetry in S. ■

4.2 MAXIMIZING PARTICIPATION RATES

Unbiased participation is desirable for information aggregation. However, as shown in Corollary 1, it necessarily leads to participation shrinking to zero as players' level of rationality grows. Our final result for the symmetric setting shows how to select the scoring rule that maximizes participation among those that lead to unbiased participation. This is accomplished in the limit as the entropy function G becomes very close to linear, that is, as the scoring rule S becomes very close to being only weakly proper.

Theorem 6 (Maximal participation) *Among all symmetric strictly proper scoring rules, maximal participation can be achieved as the limit of a sequence of strictly proper scoring rules with corresponding entropy functions of the form $G(p)=|2p-1|^\beta$ with $\beta>1$ as $\beta\to 1$.*

Proof: Consider any symmetric scoring rule with symmetric entropy function G. By Equation (4) in Theorem 4 and the convexity of the entropy function, player i at level k would never participate unless

$$G(c_i)>G\left(\frac{1}{|\mathcal{P}_{-i}^{(k-1)}|}\sum_{j\in\mathcal{P}_{-i}^{(k-1)}}c_j\right).$$

Since we have assumed G is symmetric around $1/2$ and strictly convex, any such function G must be increasing on $[1/2,1]$. Since $c_j\in[1/2,1]$ for all j, we have that at level k, player i would never participate unless

$$c_i>\hat{c}_{-i}^{(k-1)}\equiv\frac{1}{|\mathcal{P}_{-i}^{(k-1)}|}\sum_{j\in\mathcal{P}_{-i}^{(k-1)}}c_j. \quad (9)$$

This is an "only if" condition that holds for any symmetric entropy function G. To maximize participation, we would like to select G to have a matching "if" condition that is as close to this as possible.

Consider the family of scoring rules defined by entropy function $G^\beta(p)=|2p-1|^\beta$ with $\beta>1$. By Equation (4), player i would participate at level k under this scoring rule if and only if

$$\begin{aligned}2c_i-1&>\frac{1}{\left|\mathcal{P}_{-i}^{(k-1)}(\beta)\right|^{1/\beta}}\left(\sum_{j\in\mathcal{P}_{-i}^{(k-1)}(\beta)}(2c_j-1)^\beta\right)^{1/\beta}\\&=\frac{1}{\left|\mathcal{P}_{-i}^{(k-1)}(\beta)\right|^{1/\beta}}\left\|\{2c_j-1\}_{j\in\mathcal{P}_{-i}^{(k-1)}(\beta)}\right\|_\beta\end{aligned}$$

where $\|\cdot\|_\beta$ denotes the L_β norm and we use the notation $\mathcal{P}_{-i}^{(k-1)}(\beta)$ to emphasize the dependence of the set of participating players $\mathcal{P}_{-i}^{(k-1)}$ on β.

We first use this to show that for any $\beta,\beta'>1$ with $\beta'<\beta$, participation declines more gradually under the scoring rule defined by $G^{\beta'}$ than it does under the scoring rule defined by G^β. We do so by induction. Since all players participate at level 0, for any i we have $\mathcal{P}_{-i}^{(0)}(\beta)=\mathcal{P}_{-i}^{(0)}(\beta')$. Assume that for all $k'<k$, $\mathcal{P}_{-i}^{(k')}(\beta)\subseteq\mathcal{P}_{-i}^{(k')}(\beta')$. By

standard properties of norms, we then have

$$\frac{1}{\left|\mathcal{P}_{-i}^{(k-1)}(\beta)\right|^{1/\beta}} \left\| \{2c_j - 1\}_{j \in \mathcal{P}_{-i}^{(k-1)}(\beta)} \right\|_{\beta}$$
$$\geq \frac{1}{\left|\mathcal{P}_{-i}^{(k-1)}(\beta)\right|^{1/\beta'}} \left\| \{2c_j - 1\}_{j \in \mathcal{P}_{-i}^{(k-1)}(\beta)} \right\|_{\beta'}$$
$$\geq \frac{1}{\left|\mathcal{P}_{-i}^{(k-1)}(\beta')\right|^{1/\beta'}} \left\| \{2c_j - 1\}_{j \in \mathcal{P}_{-i}^{(k-1)}(\beta')} \right\|_{\beta'}.$$

The last line follows from the fact that since the players who choose to participate are always those with the highest quality (corresponding to higher values of $2c_j - 1$), if a larger group participates they are lower quality on average.

This implies that if a player participates at level k under the scoring rule defined by G^{β} then he also participates for any $\beta' < \beta$, completing the inductive step.

In the limit as $\beta \to 1$, we get that the participation constraint at each level k converges to the constraint $c_i > \hat{c}_{-i}^{(k-1)}$, which, from Equation 9, is the participation limit for any symmetric strictly proper scoring rule. ■

This result shows that participation levels rise as the scoring rule used becomes closer to weakly proper, providing experts less incentive to report their true beliefs rather than make a false report. In fact, it is easy to see that maximum participation could be achieved using the weakly proper scoring rule with entropy function $G(p) = |2p - 1|$, though this would result in a loss of strict truthfulness. This result is somewhat intuitive. Since the Kilgour-Gerchak mechanism is a zero-sum game, bigger rewards for the most accurate players require bigger punishments for the least accurate, causing those with less information to drop out at lower levels of rationality. By rewarding all players more evenly, less accurate players do not drop out as quickly. However, this may have consequences in real-world scenarios in which an expert may not find it worth his time to participate if the rewards for highly accurate information are low, even if he stands to make a profit on expectation.

4.3 UNCERTAINTY ABOUT OPPONENTS

One potential objection to our model is the assumption that each player i knows the accuracy parameter c_j of every other player j. This assumption is certainly unrealistic in settings in which the number of players is large or the pool of players anonymous. We briefly remark that most of our results can be extended to the Bayesian setting in which it is necessary only for each player i to know a *distribution* over the types (in this case, accuracy parameters) of other players. However, this extension requires modifying the definition of unbiasedness so that a player's decision to participate may depend on parts of his private information (e.g., his accuracy). For instance, if the accuracy of the signal of each player is drawn i.i.d. based on some commonly known discrete distribution with cumulative density function F, then it is easy to derive that if a symmetric scoring rule is used then a player at level k participates if and only if his realized accuracy c_i satisfies

$$G(c_i) > \mathbb{E}_{c \sim F}\left[G(c) | c \geq \theta^{k-1}\right],$$

with $\theta^0 = 0$ and θ^k defined recursively as the minimum c_i that satisfies the latter inequality or 1 if there is no such c_i.

To preserve the clarity of our analysis, we omit the details and present only the simpler setting here.

5 DISCUSSION

In order to design wagering mechanisms to elicit honest, unbiased beliefs from groups of experts, it is necessary to understand how experts behave. Previous analyses have assumed extreme behavior; either experts are fully rational, in which case standard no-trade theorems apply, or experts have immutable beliefs and are essentially oblivious to the fact that they are participating in a zero-sum game. In this paper, we search for middle ground, analyzing the behavior of boundedly rational level-k players who recognize they are in a game but are still overconfident in their reasoning. We examine the design implications of this model, seeking instantiations of Kilgour and Gerchak's shared scoring rule wagering mechanism that encourage unbiased and truthful participation at high rates.

This paper can be viewed as a contribution to the new but growing research area of *behavioral mechanism design* (Ghosh and Kleinberg, 2014; Easley and Ghosh, 2015) in which insights from behavioral game theory are applied to design mechanisms tailored to real (or at least more realistic) human participants as opposed to idealized rational agents. Of course any theory is only as good as the model on which it is based. While the behavioral game theory literature provides support that the level-k model is a decent predictor of human behavior in game theoretic settings—including one-shot betting games in which the no-trade theorem would typically apply (Brocas et al., 2014)—additional experimental work is needed to understand how well it models the behavior of real experts participating in wagering mechanisms like Kilgour-Gerchak. Still, we believe that our analysis takes a valuable first step towards understanding the ability of wagering mechanisms to aggregate information from experts who are neither fully rational nor fully naive.

References

R. J. Aumann. Agreeing to disagree. *The Annals of Statistics*, 4(6):12360–1239, 1976.

A. Bosch-Domènech, J. G. Montalvo, R. Nagel, and A. Satorra. One, two, (three), infinity, ...: Newspaper and lab beauty-contest experiments. *American Economic Review*, 92(5):1687–1701, 2002.

G. W. Brier. Verification of forecasts expressed in terms of probability. *Monthly Weather Review*, 78(1):1–3, 1950.

I. Brocas, J. D. Carrillo, S. W. Wang, and C. F. Camerer. Imperfect choice or imperfect attention? Understanding strategic thinking in private information games. *Review of Economic Studies*, 81(3):944–970, 2014.

C. F. Camerer, T.-H. Ho, and J.-K. Chong. A cognitive hierarchy model of games. *Quarterly Journal of Economics*, 119(3):861–898, 2004.

S. Chun and R. Shachter. Strictly proper mechanisms with cooperating players. In *Proceedings of the 27th Conference on Uncertainty in Artificial Intelligence (UAI)*, 2011.

M. Costa-Gomes, V. P. Crawford, and B. Broseta. Cognition and behavior in normal-form games: An experimental study. *Econometrica*, 69:1193–1235, 2001.

M. A. Costa-Gomes and V. P. Crawford. Cognition and behavior in two-person guessing games: An experimental study. *American Economic Review*, 96(5):1737–1768, 2006.

V. P. Crawford and N. Iriberri. Level-k auctions: Can a nonequilibrium model of strategic thinking explain the winner's curse and overbidding in private-value auctions? *Econometrica*, 75:1721–1770, 2007.

P. Dubey, J. Geanakoplos, and M. Shubik. The revelation of information in strategic market games: A critique of rational expectations equilibrium. *Journal of Mathematical Economics*, 16:3105–137, 1987.

D. Easley and A. Ghosh. Behavioral mechanism design: Optimal crowdsourcing contracts and prospect theory. In *Proceedings of the 16th ACM Conference on Economics and Computation (EC)*, 2015.

J. D. Geanakoplos and H. M. Polemarchakis. We can't disagree forever. *Journal of Economic Theory*, 28(1):192–200, 1982.

A. Ghosh and R. Kleinberg. Behavioral mechanism design: Optimal contests for simple agents. In *Proceedings of the 15th ACM Conference on Economics and Computation (EC)*, 2014.

T. Gneiting and A. E. Raftery. Strictly proper scoring rules, prediction, and estimation. *Journal of the American Statistical Association*, 102(477):359–378, 2007.

T.-H. Ho, C. F. Camerer, and K. Weigelt. Iterated dominance and iterated best response in experimental "p-beauty contests". *American Economic Review*, 88(4): 947–69, 1998.

J. Jordan and R. Radner. The nonexistence of rational expectations equilibrium: A robust example. Working paper, Department of Economics, University of Minnesota, 1979.

D. M. Kilgour and Y. Gerchak. Elicitation of probabilities using competitive scoring rules. *Decision Analysis*, 1(2): 108–113, 2004.

N. S. Lambert, J. Langford, J. Wortman, Y. Chen, D. Reeves, Y. Shoham, and D. M. Pennock. Self-financed wagering mechanisms for forecasting. In *Proceedings of the 9th ACM Conference on Electronic Commerce (EC)*, 2008.

R. E. Lucas. Expectations and the neutrality of money. *Journal of Economic Theory*, 28:103–124, 1972.

R. D. McKelvey and T. R. Palfrey. Quantal response equilibria for normal form games. *Games and Economic Behavior*, 10(1):6–38, 1995.

P. Milgrom and N. L. Stokey. Information, trade and common knowledge. *Journal of Economic Theory*, 26(1): 17–27, 1982.

R. Nagel. Unraveling in guessing games: An experimental study. *American Economic Review*, 85(5):1313–1326, 1995.

L. T. Nielsen, A. Brandenburger, J. Geanakoplos, R. McKelvey, and T. Page. Common knowledge of an aggregate of expectations. *Econometrica*, 58(5):1235–1238, 1990.

C. R. Plott and S. Sunder. Rational expectations and the aggregation of diverse information in laboratory security markets. *Econometrica*, 56:1085–1118, 1988.

B. W. Rogers, T. R. Palfrey, and C. F. Camerer. Heterogeneous quantal response equilibrium and cognitive hierarchies. *Journal of Economic Theory*, 144(4):1440–1467, 2009.

L. J. Savage. Elicitation of personal probabilities and expectations. *Journal of the American Statistical Association*, 66(336):783–801, 1971.

D. Shapiro, X. Shi, and A. Zillante. Level-k reasoning in a generalized beauty contest. *Games and Economic Behavior*, 86:308–329, 2014.

Y. Sløvik. Strength of dominance and depths of reasoning – An experimental study. *Journal of Economic Behavior and Organization*, 70(1–2):196–205, 2009.

D. Sonsino, I. Erev, and S. Gilat. On rationality, learning and zero-sum betting – An experimental study of the no-betting conjecture. Technion working paper, 2001.

D. O. Stahl and P. W. Wilson. Experimental evidence on players' models of other players. *Journal of Economic Behavior and Organization*, 25(3):309–327, 1994.

D. O. Stahl and P. W. Wilson. On players' models of other players: Theory and experimental evidence. *Games and Economic Behavior*, 10(1):218–254, 1995.

J. R. Wright and K. Leyton-Brown. Beyond equilibrium: Predicting human behavior in normal form games. In *Proceedings of the 24th AAAI Conference on Artificial Intelligence (AAAI)*, 2010.

Incremental Preference Elicitation for Decision Making Under Risk with the Rank-Dependent Utility Model

Patrice Perny
Sorbonne Universités
UPMC Univ Paris 06
CNRS, LIP6 UMR 7606
Paris, France

Paolo Viappiani
Sorbonne Universités
UPMC Univ Paris 06
CNRS, LIP6 UMR 7606
Paris, France

Abdellah Boukhatem
Sorbonne Universités
UPMC Univ Paris 06
CNRS, LIP6 UMR 7606
Paris, France

Abstract

This work concerns decision making under risk with the rank-dependent utility model (RDU), a generalization of expected utility providing enhanced descriptive possibilities. We introduce a new incremental decision procedure, involving monotone regression spline functions to model both components of RDU, namely the probability weighting function and the utility function. First, assuming the utility function is known, we propose an elicitation procedure that incrementally collects preference information in order to progressively specify the probability weighting function until the optimal choice can be identified. Then, we present two elicitation procedures for the construction of a utility function as a monotone spline. Finally, numerical tests are provided to show the practical efficiency of the proposed methods.

1 INTRODUCTION

Uncertainty is pervasive in human activities and represents an important source of complexity in individual and collective decision making. As soon as intelligent systems are used for supporting human decision making or simulating realistic human decision behaviors, preference modeling and preference elicitation becomes particularly important. In decision making under uncertainty and risk, preference models are used to represent uncertain outcomes and to provide normative decision rules for choice problems, but also to describe, predict or simulate observed human behaviors. Given a mathematical model used to compare the alternatives of a choice problem, preference elicitation consists in fitting the parameters of the model to a specific Decision Maker (DM), to capture her attitude towards risk. Then the model can be used to support her choices in complex situations involving a large number of alternatives or to integrate her value system into an autonomous decision agent. Considering this context, our paper aims at providing new tools for interactive decision support under risk.

Decision under risk is a standard formal framework for handling uncertainty in decision making, characterized by a probabilistic representation of uncertainty. In this framework, risky prospects are represented by probability distributions with a finite support, namely lotteries. In the seminal work of Bernoulli (1738; refer to [1954] for an English translation) and in the theory of von Neumann and Morgenstern (vNM) [1947], the values of lotteries are measured in terms of *expected utility* (EU). This well-known decision criterion is linear in probabilities and characterized by a utility function encoding the subjective value of any possible consequence for the DM; EU is used to compare lotteries and choice problems are solved by EU maximization. This choice model has been axiomatically justified in the context of risk by vNM [1947], but also in the more general context of uncertainty introduced by Savage [1954], where probabilities are not assumed to exist a priori.

From EU to RDU. Despite these axiomatic results and the intuitive appeal of EU theory, the model suffers from well known limitations, from a descriptive viewpoint. There exist situations where individuals may exhibit behaviors that are not consistent with EU theory, as illustrated by the so-called Allais's paradox. For example, people often prefer \$3000 with certainty (choice A) to \$4000 with probability .8 (choice B), but they prefer \$4000 with probability .2 (choice D) to \$3000 with probability .25 (choice C). Remarking that $C = .25A + .75O$ and $D = .25B + .75O$ where O is the choice to win nothing with probability 1, it turns out that such preferences violate the vNM independence axiom. This example, used by Kahneman and Tversky [1979] in their experiments, is frequently observed and known as the *certainty effect*: a reduction in probability of winning a reward creates a larger (negative) psychological effect when it is done from certainty than from uncertainty. Similar observations have been made in actual decision contexts, for instance in route-choice problems where evidence was found of violation of EU theory [Avineri and Prashker, 2004].

These experiments and others in the same spirit suggest that probabilities are distorted in the decision making process. More precisely, small probabilities (greater than 0) tend to be overestimated while large ones (smaller than 1) underestimated. This has motivated the introduction of a probabilistic transformation model to generalize EU, leading to evaluate the lottery $(x_1, p_1; \ldots, x_n; p_n)$ that yields outcome x_i with probability p_i by $\sum_i w(p_i)u(x_i)$. This generalization of EU dates back to [Edwards, 1955] and appears also in prospect theory [Kahneman and Tversky, 1979]. However, it can be easily shown that it violates the principle of stochastic dominance and could lead to select dominated alternatives; this is often considered as a serious weakness from a normative viewpoint. To overcome this problem, a solution proposed by Quiggin [1982] and Yaari [1987] consists in applying the probability transformation to the decumulative probability distribution function, and not to the probabilities of individual outcomes. This solution leads to the *rank-dependent utility* model (RDU) that consists in evaluating the lottery $\ell = (x_1, p_1; \ldots, x_n; p_n)$ such that $x_1 \geq \ldots \geq x_n \geq 0$[1] by:

$$V(\ell) = \sum_{i=1}^{n} w\left(\sum_{k=1}^{i} p_k\right)[u(x_i) - u(x_{i+1})]$$
$$= w(p_1)u(x_1) + \sum_{i=2}^{n}\left[w\left(\sum_{k=1}^{i} p_k\right) - w\left(\sum_{k=1}^{i-1} p_k\right)\right]u(x_i)$$

where $x_{n+1} = 0$ and $w : [0,1] \to [0,1]$ is a non-decreasing function such that $w(0) = 0$ and $w(1) = 1$. Note that the coefficient of $u(x_i)$ in RDU depends on the cumulative probability of the outcomes greater or equal to x_i (since outcomes are indexed to be sorted by decreasing order); this shows that this coefficient depends on the rank of x_i in the set of possible outcomes. To illustrate the use of RDU, we compare the two following lotteries ℓ and ℓ' with $w(p) = p^2$ and $u(x) = \sqrt{x}$:

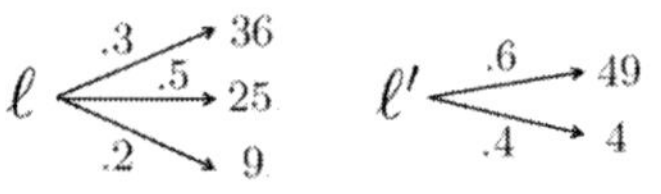

$V(\ell) = (.3)^2(6-5) + (.8)^2(5-3) + 1^2 3 = 4.37$ and $V(\ell') = (.6)^2(7-2) + (1)^2 2 = 3.8$, hence ℓ is preferred to ℓ'. To give another example, let us remark that, for any lottery of type $\ell = (x^+, p; x^-, 1-p)$, $x^+ > x^-$, we have:

$$V(\ell) = w(p)u(x^+) + (1 - w(p))u(x^-)$$

Function w is referred to as the *probability weighting function*. It is worth noting that, when $w(p) = p$, RDU boils down to EU as we can see from the second formulation. On the other hand, RDU is also known to be an instance of Choquet Expected Utility [Schmeidler, 1989]. More precisely, it turns out to be the natural instance for decision making under risk due its compatibility with stochastic dominance [Wakker, 1990]. For more details about RDU theory see [Quiggin, 2012, Diecidue and Wakker, 2001].

Let us mention also some well known variants of RDU theory. First, Yaari [1987] introduced and axiomatized a dual model to expected utility where transformations are applied to probabilities rather than to outcomes. This is a special case of RDU obtained when the utility function is linear in the outcomes. Moreover, the idea of rank-dependent weightings was also incorporated by Kahneman and Tversky [1992] into prospect theory, leading to *cumulative prospect theory*. This theory extends the RDU theory to model different risk attitudes towards gains depending on whether above or below a reference level.

In this paper, we focus on the RDU model, and we address the problem of identifying, within a given (possibly large) set of lotteries, the preferred solution for a given DM consistent with RDU theory. This solution could be used for predicting a choice of the DM or even to make a recommendation. This requires to elicit, at least partially, the probability weighting function and the utility function. Note that the determination of RDU-optimal solutions has motivated various contributions in the past, e.g. [Nielsen and Jaffray, 2006, Jeantet *et al.*, 2012].

Incremental decision making. A first approach to elicitation, standard in mathematical economics, aims to obtain a full description of preferences by the decision model, assuming that DM's preferences are observable on all possible pairs of alternatives. The elicitation process is justified by the axioms of the underlying theory and the components of the models are revealed point by point using systematic sequences of queries to obtain a precise specification of the model. To simplify the process, a frequent option used in economics (but also in artificial intelligence) consists in postulating a parametric form for each component of the decision model; queries are then used to fit the parameters. Refer to [Wakker and Deneffe, 1996, Gonzalez and Wu, 1999, Abdellaoui, 2000] for full elicitation procedures proposed in economics for RDU, and to [Fürnkranz and Hüllermeier, 2003, Torra, 2010, Tehrani *et al.*, 2012] for model-based preference learning.

Recently a number of works have tackled the elicitation of the components of the decision model in an adaptive way [Wang and Boutilier, 2003, Boutilier *et al.*, 2006, Braziunas and Boutilier, 2007, Benabbou *et al.*, 2014]; the aims is that of focusing on learning the "important" part of the utility, allowing to recommend near-optimal decisions with only partial information about the decision model. These incremental approaches consider all possible instances of preference model parameters consistent with the currently known information about the user; the user's responses allow to infer constraints on these parameters.

[1] As suggested by Gilboa [2008], it is more natural to think of the object of choice in Quiggin and Yaari's models as lotteries over final wealth (with positive outcomes) rather as prospects of gains and losses, because they did not emphasize gain-loss asymmetry in their theory.

In this work, we consider the problem of incrementally eliciting the components of the RDU model by interactively asking queries to the DM; this aims to support the identification or approximation of an RDU-optimal choice. We first address the problem of eliciting the weighting function incrementally (Section 2) assuming that the utility is known. Afterwards, we will present utility elicitation procedures adapted to the rank-dependent utility model (Section 3). Finally, we provide numerical tests (Section 4).

2 ELICITATION OF THE PROBABILITY WEIGHTING FUNCTION

Decision makers exhibit various decision behaviors when they are confronted to choices involving risky prospects. Within RDU theory, this diversity of attitudes towards risk can be modeled by controlling the definition of the two components of the model, namely the utility function and the probability weighting function. Since these two components are strongly interlaced in RDU, their joint elicitation is quite challenging. Fortunately, these two components concern two separate and well identified risk-components, on the one hand marginal utilities induced by the shape of the cardinal utility function [Chateauneuf and Cohen, 1994], and on the other hand the probabilistic risk-attitude towards probabilistic mixtures induced by the shape of the probability weighting function [Wakker, 1994]. They can be observed separately using proper preference queries as shown in [Wakker and Deneffe, 1996, Abdellaoui, 2000]. In this section, the utility is assumed to be known (already elicited or known to be linear (Yaari's model), and we focus on the elicitation of probability weights.

2.1 ON PROBABILITY WEIGHTING FUNCTIONS

The probability weighting function is necessarily non-decreasing but can take different forms depending on the attitude of the DM towards risk. For instance, in Yaari's model, *weak risk aversion* which consists, for any lottery ℓ, in preferring $E(\ell)$ for sure to ℓ (where $E(\ell)$ is the expected value of ℓ) is equivalent to $w(p) \leq p$ for all $p \in [0, 1]$ [Chateauneuf and Cohen, 1994]. Moreover, in the RDU model, *strong risk aversion* which consists in preferring ℓ to ℓ' whenever ℓ stochastically dominates ℓ' at second order, is equivalent to using a convex weighting function and a concave utility [Hong *et al.*, 1987]. Finally, several experiments including those of Kahneman and Tversky [1979] lead to propose an inverse S-shaped function. For example, the use of the weighting function given in Figure 1 in Yaari's model allows to explain the preferences observed on lotteries A, B, C, D presented in the introduction. We have indeed $V(A) = 3000\ w(1)$, $V(B) = 4000\ w(0.8), V(C) = 3000\ w(0.25)$ and $V(D) = 4000w(0.2)$. Since $w(0.2) \approx 0.26$, $w(0.25) \approx 0.29$, $w(0.8) \approx 0.60$ and $w(1) = 1$ we obtain $V(A) > V(B)$ while $V(C) < V(D)$.

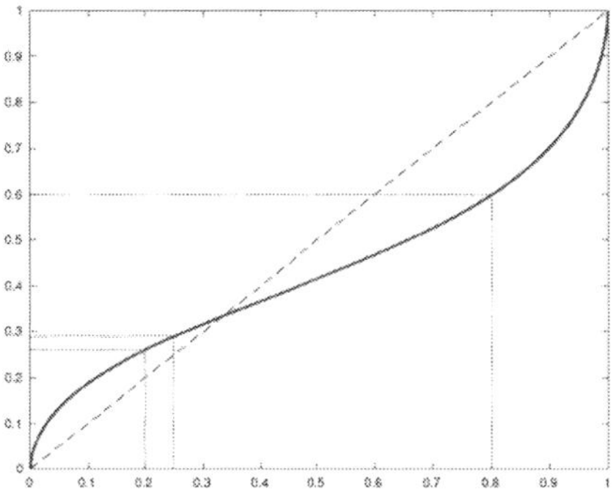

Figure 1: Inverse S-shaped function w.

The following parametric expressions for $w(p)$ have been proposed in the literature [Cavagnaro *et al.*, 2013], among several others:

$$\begin{array}{rll} \text{TK}: & w(p) = \frac{p^r}{(p^r+(1-p)^r)^{1/r}} & \text{with } 0.28 < r \leq 1 \\ \text{Prelec}: & w(p) = e^{-s(-\ln p)^r} & \text{with } 0 < r \leq 1; 0 < s \\ \text{LinLog}: & w(p) = \frac{s\,p^r}{s\,p^r+(1-p)^r} & \text{with } 0 < r, s \end{array}$$

where TK denotes the parametric form proposed by Tversky and Kahneman (the w plotted in Figure 1 is of this type, with $r = 0.6$). Note that Prelec and LinLog make use of two parameters (r and s) while TK is based on a single parameter. Karmarkar [1978] proposes a parametric form that is a special case of LinLog with $s = 1$.

Choosing a priori a specific parametric form among these different options and others, with the idea of learning the parameters, may generate errors due to not taking into account the specificity of the DM that may be revealed during the elicitation process. Instead, we propose a new approach based on a much more flexible parametric construction based on the definition of w as a piecewise polynomial spline function. Moreover, we will adopt an incremental elicitation approach in order to reason with the possible functions w that are consistent with the current preference information of the DM. In the spirit of incremental decision making, by considering additional preferences (obtained by asking queries), we will be able to progressively narrow down our model of the DM until we are able to identify the preferred alternative.

2.2 INCREMENTAL ELICITATION OF w

We assume here that the utility function is known and we reason with an incompletely specified weighting function $w \in W$, W being the set of admissible probability weighting functions at a given step of the process. Initially, W can be all non-decreasing functions on the unit interval such that $w(0) = 0$ and $w(1) = 1$ or an approximation of them representable by a given family of parametric functions. The utility function u being fixed, we will denote $V(\ell; w)$ the RDU value of lottery ℓ for weighting function w. Each time a preference statement of type "ℓ^+ is at least as good as ℓ^-" is obtained, this induces a new constraint $V(\ell^+; w) \geq V(\ell^-; w)$ that further restricts W.

In order to make a decision when probability weights are imprecisely known, we will use minimax regret which is a standard decision criterion for robust decision making under uncertainty [Savage, 1954]. It was more recently proposed by Boutilier et al. [2003, 2006] for decision-making under utility uncertainty. Moreover, minimax regret can be used as a driver for preference elicitation and incremental decision making.

Let $\mathcal{L}$ be the set of lotteries representing the alternatives of the decision problem. If we knew the DM's specific w, then the optimal choice would be any element of $\arg\max_{\ell \in \mathcal{L}} V(\ell; w)$. However, since w is not known precisely, we need to provide a recommendation based on the current information. We are interested in evaluating the loss that can result from choosing a decision ℓ instead of the optimal one. To this end, we use the following notions of regret. The pairwise maximum regret PMR of ℓ against ℓ' is the maximal value that the difference $V_u(\ell'; w) - V_u(\ell; w)$ can take for any admissible function of $w \in W$. The max regret MR of a choice ℓ is defined as the maximum pairwise regret when the adversary is chosen among all lotteries in $\mathcal{L}$. Finally, the minimax regret MMR is the minimum value of max regret. More formally:

$$\mathrm{PMR}(\ell, \ell'; W) = \max_{w \in W} [V(\ell'; w) - V(\ell; w)] \quad (1)$$

$$\mathrm{MR}(\ell; W) = \max_{\ell' \in \mathcal{L}} \mathrm{PMR}(\ell, \ell'; W) \quad (2)$$

$$\mathrm{MMR}(W) = \min_{\ell \in \mathcal{L}} \mathrm{MR}(\ell; W) \quad (3)$$

Then we recommend one of the decisions associated with the minimum value of max regret, i.e. lottery $\ell^* \in \arg\min_{\ell \in \mathcal{L}} \mathrm{MR}(\ell; W)$. This is a regret-optimal decision given the current preference information. By definition, recommending ℓ^* means to be robust with respect to the possible realizations of $w \in W$.

In addition of being a criterion for decision-making, minimax regret can be used to drive the elicitation of further preference information. We assume an interactive setting where the system (a decision-support agent) can ask additional queries in order to improve the quality of the recommendation. If the current minimax regret value is higher than a given positive threshold, we ask another query to the user. Different types of queries can be asked to the user; among the many possibilities, comparison queries, asking the user to state which choice is best among two presented to him, are particularly natural. It is however important to ask informative queries in order to quickly converge to a recommendation of high value. An effective heuristic to choose the next query is the *current solution* strategy [Wang and Boutilier, 2003, Boutilier *et al.*, 2006]; it asks the user to compare the regret-optimal lottery ℓ^* with its adversarial challenger $\ell^a = \arg\max_{\ell \in \mathcal{L}} \mathrm{PMR}(\ell^*, \ell)$. This will often reduce minimax regret: if the user states that ℓ^* is preferred to ℓ^a, in the next computation of minimax regret, the adversary will have to choose another lottery, leading to a reduction of regret (unless there were ties in the max regret computations). If, instead ℓ^a is preferred to ℓ^*, the regret-optimal choice in the next computation will necessarily be a choice other than ℓ^*, and, again, we will likely reduce regrets.

Assume $\mathcal{P}$ to be a set of pairs (ℓ^+, ℓ^-) for which we know that the DM considers that ℓ^+ is at least as good as ℓ^-. Let $W = \{w : \forall(\ell^+, \ell^-) \in \mathcal{P}, V(\ell^+; w) \geq V(\ell^-; w)\}$, our goal is to compute $\mathrm{PMR}(\ell, \ell', W)$. This corresponds to solving the following optimization problem:

$$\max_{w} \; [V(\ell'; w) - V(\ell; w)] \quad (4)$$

$$s.t. \;\; w(0) = 0, w(1) = 1 \quad (5)$$

$$w(p) \leq w(q), \;\; \forall p, q \in [0,1] : p \leq q \quad (6)$$

$$V(\ell^+; w) \geq V(\ell^-; w), \;\; \forall(\ell^+, \ell^-) \in \mathcal{P} \quad (7)$$

Such optimization is not however directly feasible. First, the monotonicity constraint (6) on the unit interval represents implicitly an infinity of constraints. If we only impose monotonicity on probabilities involved in the lotteries of $\mathcal{L}$, it still represents a large number of constraints. Moreover, constraint (7) is quite difficult to handle. Even if we assume that w belongs to one of the families of parametric curves considered in the previous subsection, the resulting constraints will not be linear in the parameters. In the next subsection we will see how these problems can be overcome by defining w as a monotone spline function.

2.3 A MODEL BASED ON I-SPLINE FUNCTIONS

Spline functions are piecewise polynomials whose pieces connect with a high degree of smoothness. They are very useful in data interpolation and shape approximation due to their capacity to approximate complex shapes through curve fitting and interactive curve design while preserving an important property, missing in many other interpolation methods: they guarantee that smooth curves will be generated from smooth data [Beatty and Barsky, 1995]. The use of piecewise polynomials in non-linear regression extends the advantage of polynomials by providing greater flexibility, local effects of parameter changes and the possibility of imposing constraints on estimated functions [Ramsay, 1988].

One important feature of spline functions is that they can be generated by linear combinations of basis spline functions. A basis of splines particularly appealing for non-linear regression is the M-spline family [Ramsay, 1988]. M-splines of order k are functions $M_i, i = 1, \ldots, m$ which are polynomials of degree $k - 1$. They can be used to approximate any function defined on a given interval $[a, b]$ by a spline of the form $f = \sum_i \lambda_i M_i$. To define M_i precisely, we need to introduce a sequence of knots $t = \{t_1, t_2, \ldots, t_l\}$ such that $a = t_1 = \ldots = t_k$, $b = t_{l-k+1} = \ldots = t_l$ and $\forall i, t_i \leq t_{i+1}$. The basis constructed from sequence t contains $m = |t| - k$ spline functions of order k denoted $M_i(x; k, t)$, $i = 1, \ldots, m$, and defined for $k = 1$ by:

$$M_i(x; 1, t) = \begin{cases} \frac{1}{t_{i+1} - t_i} & \text{if } x \in (t_i, t_{i+1}) \\ 0 & \text{otherwise} \end{cases}$$

For $k > 1$ and $t_{i+k} > t_i$, M_i is defined recursively by:
$M_i(x; k, t) = \frac{k[(x - t_i)M_i(x; k-1, t) + (t_{i+k} - x)M_{i+1}(x; k-1, t)]}{(k-1)(t_{i+k} - t_i)}$
and otherwise $M_i(x;k,t) = 0$. In particular, we have $M_i(x;k,t) = 0$ whenever $k > 1$ and $t_{i+k} = t_i$.

Note that $M_i(x;k,t)$ is strictly positive in (t_i, t_{i+k}) and 0 elsewhere, with an integral equal to 1. Moreover, it is a polynomial of degree $k - 1$ so that, for any piecewise polynomial function of the form $f = \sum_i \lambda_i M_i$, adjacent polynomials have matching derivatives up to order $k - 2$. Hence, a good choice for k in practice is $k = 3$ because, in this case, we generate piecewise quadratic f functions with matching first derivatives while preserving a local influence of every components. Choosing a lower k would loose continuity of the first derivative and choosing a higher k would increase the range (t_i, t_{i+k}) of influence of every component M_i, which diminishes controllability of the model. As an example, the family of splines $M_i(x; 3,t), i = 1, \ldots, 5$ defined on the unit interval from subdivision $t = (0, 0, 0, \frac{1}{3}, \frac{2}{3}, 1, 1, 1)$ is given in the left part of Figure 2. Finer spline decompositions could be obtained using finer subdivisions. Moreover, it is possible to use non-equally-spaced knot sequences to have a finer control of the shape in some parts of interval $[a, b]$. However, practical tests show that using too many nodes is counterproductive to generate smooth and regular curves.

We may define the probability weighting function w as a weighted combination of M_i-spline functions with probably good fitting possibilities. However, this would not guarantee to obtain a non-decreasing weighting function w. To get rid of the monotonicity constraint (6), we need another basis specifically designed for the generation of non-decreasing spline functions. The solution is given by monotone regression splines that provide very nice descriptive possibilities, as demonstrated by Ramsey [1988]. Such spline functions are non-decreasing because they are generated by conical combinations of basis I-spline functions, i.e., non-decreasing functions defined as the integrals of the M-splines (which are positive). Formally, these functions denoted $I_i(x; k, t)$, $i = 1, \ldots, m$ are defined by:

$$I_i(x; k, t) = \int_a^x M_i(y; k, t)\, dy$$

Let j be the index such that $t_j \leq x < t_{j+1}$, the value of an I-spline is computed as follows:

$$I_i(x; k, t) = \begin{cases} 1 \text{ if } i < j - k + 1 \\ 0 \text{ if } i > j \\ \sum_{s=i}^{j} \frac{t_{s+k+1} - t_s}{k+1} M_s(x; k+1, t) \text{ otherwise} \end{cases}$$

As an illustration, the family of splines $I_i(x; 3,t), i = 1, \ldots, 5$ for subdivision $t = (0, 0, 0, 0, \frac{1}{3}, \frac{2}{3}, 1, 1, 1, 1)$ is given in the right part of Figure 2.

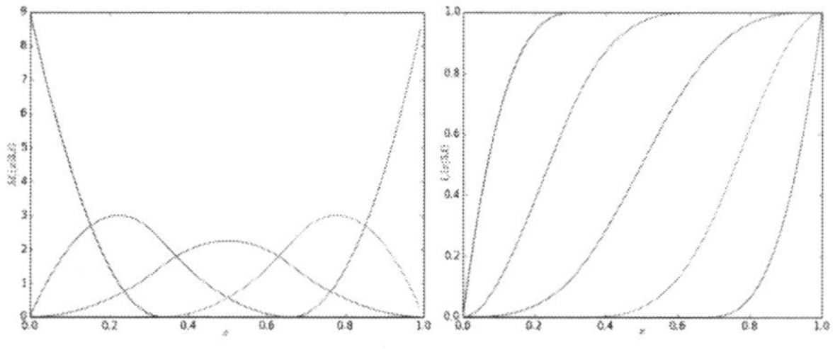

Figure 2: Basis functions $M_i(x; 3,t)$ and $I_i(x; 3,t)$

2.4 REGRET MINIMIZATION WITH I-SPLINES

The computation of PMR is the main building block to compute minimax regret. In order to compute MR and MMR, it is indeed sufficient to perform a quadratic number of PMR optimizations[2]. We now focus the discussion on PMR computations and show that the optimization of regrets is drastically simplified when weighting function w is defined by a conical combination of I_i-splines:

$$w(p) = \sum_{j=1}^{m} \lambda_j I_j(p; k, t), \;\; \lambda_j \geq 0, j = 1, \ldots, m \qquad (8)$$

Note that, k and t being fixed, function w is completely characterized by vector $\lambda = (\lambda_1, \ldots, \lambda_m) \in \mathbb{R}_+^m$. So the elicitation of the entire function boils down to the elicitation of vector λ. In that case the RDU criterion reads, for any lottery $\ell = (x_1, p_1; \ldots; x_n, p_n)$, as follows:

$$V(\ell; \lambda) = \sum_{i=1}^{n} \sum_{j=1}^{m} \lambda_j I_j(\sum_{k=1}^{i} p_k; k, t)[u(x_i) - u(x_{i+1})]$$

By permuting the two first summations in the above formulation, we obtain $V(\ell; \lambda) = \lambda^\intercal v(\ell, k, t)$ where $v(\ell, k, t) \in \mathbb{R}^m$ is a vector whose j^{th} component is equal to $\sum_{i=1}^{n} I_j(\sum_{k=1}^{i} p_k; k, t)[u(x_i) - u(x_{i+1})]$. Hence PMR values can be reformulated using vector λ and a set Λ of admissible weighting vectors replacing W. We obtain:

$$\begin{aligned} \text{PMR}(\ell, \ell'; \Lambda) &= \max_{\lambda \in \Lambda} [V(\ell'; \lambda) - V(\ell; \lambda)] \\ &= \max_{\lambda \in \Lambda} \lambda^\intercal [v(\ell', k, t) - v(\ell, k, t)] \end{aligned}$$

[2]In fact, a more efficient strategy consists in implementing an alpha-beta search procedure, in this way it is possible to prune several cases and compute a much lower number of PMRs [Braziunas, 2011].

Moreover, the constraint $V(\ell^+; w) \geq V(\ell^-; w)$ present in (7) takes now the form of a linear constraint $\lambda^\intercal[v(\ell^+, k, t) - v(\ell^-, k, t)] \geq 0$. Hence the set

$$\Lambda_\mathcal{P} = \{\lambda \in \mathbb{R}_+^m : \forall(\ell^+, \ell^-) \in \mathcal{P}, \lambda^\intercal[v(\ell^+, k, t) - v(\ell^-, k, t)] \geq 0\}$$

is a convex polyhedron. Therefore, under the assumption that I-spline functions are convenient to describe the probability weighting function, the computation of PMR for a given pair of lotteries (ℓ, ℓ'), initially introduced as a difficult optimization problem, see Equations (4-7), can now easily be achieved by solving the following linear program:

$$\begin{aligned} &\max \lambda^\intercal[v(\ell', k, t) - v(\ell, k, t)] \\ s.t.\quad &\lambda^\intercal[v(\ell^+, k, t) - v(\ell^-, k, t)] \geq 0, \forall(\ell^+, \ell^-) \in \mathcal{P} \\ &\lambda_i \geq 0, i = 1, \ldots, m. \end{aligned}$$

2.5 THE ELICITATION ALGORITHM

Algorithm 1 details the steps involved in our regret-based approach for the elicitation of w. Given a dataset of decisions (lotteries) $\mathcal{L}$ (for each decision we are given a specification of the numerical outcomes and their associated probabilities) and a set of initial preferences $\mathcal{P}$ (that could be empty), we compute the initial minimax regret value v, the max-regret-optimal decision ℓ^* and the adversarial decision ℓ^a. We then start asking queries.

Function `Query` simulates the question/answer protocol. It takes two lotteries as input and returns the preferred lottery among the two. After each user's response we recompute the minimax regret value, the regret-optimal decision ℓ^*, and its challenger ℓ^a. We loop until the regret drops below a positive threshold ε. Queries are asked according to the *current solution strategy* (analogue to the strategy used in [Boutilier *et al.*, 2006]), that requires the user to compare ℓ^* with ℓ^a. The least preferred among ℓ^* and ℓ^a is removed from $\mathcal{L}$ as it is dominated by the other. This guarantees a strict reduction of $|\mathcal{L}|$ at every step, ensuring a linear convergence in the number of lotteries. The practical efficiency of this algorithm is illustrated in Section 4.

Note that when the lotteries in $\mathcal{L}$ involve a large number of branches, we cannot expect a DM to be able to compare them with confidence. In such cases, we recommend to work with two sets of lotteries: the actual set $\mathcal{L}$ of lotteries (in which the preferred solution must be found), on which pairwise regrets are computed, and a second set of simpler lotteries used only for preference queries. For the latter, we may use lotteries of type $\ell_p = (M, p; 0, 1-p)$ (where M is the top outcome) and ask the DM to compare ℓ_p, for some probability p, to some certain consequence x in $[0, M]$. Under the assumptions $u(0) = 0$ and $u(M) = 1$, we derive from the response either $w(p) \geq u(x)$ or the reverse inequality, thus reducing uncertainty on function w and, in most cases, the MMR on actual lotteries.

Algorithm 1: Regret-based elicitation of w

Input: $\mathcal{L}, \mathcal{P}, \varepsilon$
Output: ℓ^*
begin
  $\ell^* \leftarrow \arg\min_{\ell \in \mathcal{L}} \mathrm{MR}(\ell; \Lambda_\mathcal{P})$;
  $\ell^A \leftarrow \arg\max_{\ell \in \mathcal{L}} \mathrm{PMR}(\ell^*, \ell; \Lambda_\mathcal{P})$;
  $v \leftarrow \mathrm{MMR}(\Lambda_\mathcal{P})$;
  while $v > \varepsilon$ **do**
    $p \leftarrow$ `Query`(ℓ^*, ℓ^A);
    $\mathcal{L} \leftarrow \mathcal{L} \setminus$ the least preferred in $\{\ell^*, \ell^a\}$;
    $\mathcal{P} \leftarrow \mathcal{P} \cup \{p\}$;
    $v \leftarrow \mathrm{MMR}(\Lambda_\mathcal{P})$;
    $\ell^* \leftarrow \arg\min_{\ell \in \mathcal{L}} \mathrm{MR}(\ell; \Lambda_\mathcal{P})$;
    $\ell^A \leftarrow \arg\max_{\ell \in \mathcal{L}} \mathrm{PMR}(\ell^*, \ell; \Lambda_\mathcal{P})$;
  end
end

---

3 UTILITY ELICITATION IN RDU

In the previous section, we have discussed the elicitation of the weighting probability function in the RDU model, assuming the utility function was known. We discuss now the elicitation of function u when w is not known. The main difficulty to overcome lies in the fact that functions u and w are strongly interlaced in the computation of RDU values, due to products of type $w(\sum_{k=1}^{i} p_i)u(x_i)$. A given value $u(x_i)$ may impact differently on preferences, depending on the probability weighting function. Fortunately, there is a part of DM preferences that are not impacted by w and that can be used to elicit u. We present two illustrations of this idea in the two next subsections. The fist one provides a precise spline function interpolating a sample of points of the utility curve constructed with the *gamble tradeoff method* proposed by Wakker and Deneffe [1996]. The second proposes an alternative approach based on simple queries aiming at obtaining the certainty equivalent of simple lotteries.

3.1 USING THE GAMBLE TRADEOFF METHOD

We first recall the principle of the gamble tradeoff method [Wakker and Deneffe, 1996] to construct points on the utility curve. To start with an example, let us consider the two following lotteries: $\ell = (c, p; b, 1-p)$ and $\ell' = (d, p; a, 1-p)$ for a probability $p \in (0, 1)$, where a, b, c, d are four distinct outcomes such that $a < b < c < d$. Then it can be easily checked from the definition of RDU that the DM is indifferent between ℓ and ℓ' (i.e., $V(\ell) = V(\ell')$) if and only if:

$$[u(b) - u(a)](1 - w(p)) = [u(d) - u(c)]w(p) \quad (9)$$

To construct some points of the utility function $u(x)$, x in $[0, M]$, we need two reference values α and β chosen in such a way that $M < \alpha < \beta$. Then, the gamble tradeoff method consists in generating the increasing sequence defined by $r_0 = 0$ and $r_i = \texttt{Query}(\ell_i, \ell'_i)$ for $i > 1$ where:

$$\ell_i = (\alpha, p; r, 1-p) \qquad \ell'_i = (\beta, p; r_{i-1}, 1-p)$$

and $\texttt{Query}(\ell_i, \ell'_i)$ is a function asking to the DM which value r makes the two lotteries indifferent and returns this value. The sequence is generated until $r \geq M$. By construction we have $V(r_i, 1-p; \alpha, p) = V(r_{i-1}, 1-p; \beta, p)$. Similarly we have $V(r_{i+1}, 1-p; \alpha, p) = V(r_i, 1-p; \beta, p)$. From these two equalities, we obtain, from equation (9):

$$\begin{aligned} [u(r_i) - u(r_{i-1})](1 - w(p)) &= [u(\beta) - u(\alpha)]w(p) \\ [u(r_{i+1}) - u(r_i)](1 - w(p)) &= [u(\beta) - u(\alpha)]w(p) \end{aligned}$$

Hence $u(r_{i+1}) - u(r_i) = u(r_i) - u(r_{i-1})$, therefore:

$$u(r_{i+1}) = 2u(r_i) - u(r_{i-1}) \tag{10}$$

Since u is defined up to a positive affine transformation, we can set, without loss of generality, $u(r_0) = 0$ and $u(r_1) = 1$. Hence, using (10) we obtain $u(r_i) = i$ for all $i \geq 0$ which means that the utility function should interpolate points (r_i, i). Moreover, the density of values r_i within a given interval can be increased (resp. decreased) by changing parameters α and β to reduce or increase the difference $\beta - \alpha$.

Assume that q points (r_i, i) have been constructed with the gamble tradeoff method, these points can be interpolated using I-spline regression. So we define the utility function as a piecewise quadratic monotone spline $u(x) = \sum_k \lambda_k I_k(x, 3, t)$ for a uniform knot sequence t. Then, coefficients λ_k can be determined by minimizing the distance of the constructed points to the spline u. This is achieved by solving the following linear program Π:

$$\begin{aligned} &\min \textstyle\sum_{i=1}^{q} e_i \\ s.t. \; &\begin{cases} e_i \geq i - \sum_k \lambda_k I_k(r_i, 3, t), & i = 1, \ldots, q \\ e_i \geq \sum_k \lambda_k I_k(r_i, 3, t) - i & i = 1, \ldots, q \end{cases} \\ &\lambda_k \geq 0, k = 1, \ldots, q. \end{aligned}$$

This approach leads to a precise utility function; however, it is not incremental and does not provide an easy control on the number of points elicited on the utility curve.Moreover, preference queries involved in the process are somewhat more complex than in the certainty equivalent method. In the next subsection we present an incremental approach with simpler preference queries that gives control on which points are constructed.

3.2 USING THE CERTAINTY EQUIVALENT

An incremental utility elicitation procedure is proposed by Hines and Larsen [2010] with the aim of eliciting utilities while removing the effects of probability weighting from users answers. Using pairwise max regret minimization, they propose to elicit preferences in both cumulative prospect theory and expected utility theory by determining a specific probability value p^* that allows to ask *outcome queries* where the effect of w cancels out. This idea could be used here but can be simplified in our context. Note that their definition of regret is based on the EU model and would not be the most appropriate *to derive robust recommendations with respect to RDU*. In order words they assume that EU is the right model to produce recommendations, but observe preferences biased by distorted probabilities as in cumulative prospect theory and RDU.

We propose here another incremental approach involving simpler preference queries based on the use of certainty equivalent. It consists first in identifying a probability p^* such that $w(p^*) = 1/2$. To this end, we only need to construct the two first elements r_1, r_2 following $r_0 = 0$ in the sequence defined in the previous subsection. Then we ask the DM for which probability p^* she is indifferent between lottery $\ell = (r_2, p^*; r_0, 1-p^*)$ and lottery $\ell' = (r_1, 1)$ yielding r_1 with certainty. Since by construction, $u(r_0) = 0, u(r_1) = 1$ and $u(r_2) = 2$, $V(\ell) = u(r_0) + w(p^*)[u(r_2) - u(r_1)] = 2w(p^*)$ and $u(\ell') = 1$. This leads to $2w(p^*) = 1$ and therefore $w(p^*) = 1/2$.

Now the utility curve can be incrementally constructed on any interval $[0, M]$ using simple indifference queries based on the following principle: let r^- and r^+ be any two distinct values in $[0, M]$ such that $u(r^-)$ and $u(r^+)$ are known (initially we choose $r^- = 0$ and $r^+ = M$ and we set $u(0) = 0$ and $u(M) = 1$). Then a new point can be constructed between positions r^- and r^+ by asking the DM for the certainty equivalent of lottery $(r^+, p^*; r^-, 1-p^*)$. If the answer is r (meaning that she is indifferent between the lottery and winning r for sure) we obtain $u(r) = u(r^-) + w(p^*)(u(r^+) - u(r^-)) = w(p^*)u(r^+) + (1 - w(p^*))u(r^-)$. Since $w(p^*) = 1/2$ we finally obtain $u(r) = (u(r^-) + u(r^+))/2$. When u is defined as a monotone spline, the new point will induce new constraints further restricting the set of possible utilities.

Denoting $(r_i, u(r_i)), i = 1, \ldots, q$ the points already defined at iteration q, utility uncertainty within interval $[r_i, r_{i+1}]$ is bounded above by $\delta_i = u(r_{i+1}) - u(r_i)$ due to monotonicity of u. The next query is selected to obtain a new point in the interval $[r_k, r_{k+1}]$ which maximizes δ_k; we ask for the certainty equivalent of lottery $(r_{k+1}, p^*; r_k, 1-p^*)$. The process can be iterated to refine progressively the intervals until the desired number of points is reached or the maximal δ_i drops below a given threshold. Finally, a monotone regression spline is generated using the linear program Π introduced in subsection 3.1 to approximate the elicited points.

4 NUMERICAL TESTS

Incremental elicitation of w. In order to model function w, we used I-spline defined from the non-uniform knot sequence $t' = (0, 0, 0, 0, .1, 0.9, 1, 1, 1, 1)$. The use of knots at positions .1 and .9 instead of 1/3 and 2/3 induces a small left shift of $I_1(x, 3, t')$ and a small right shift of $I_5(x, 3, t')$ so as to include extremely concave or convex transformations in the family of splines that can be generated. This allows to model extremely risk-averse or risk-prone attitudes if necessary.

In the first series of experiments, we validate our choice of monotone splines for identifying the DM's probability weighting function w. Defining this function as $w(x) = \sum_{j=1}^{5} \lambda_j I_j(x, 3, t')$, we used a linear program similar to Π (see Subsection 3.1) to fit parameters λ_j to different standard weighting functions, presenting various curves from extremely concave to extremely convex, including S-shaped and inverse S-shaped curves as well. The fitting possibilities of model w defined from I-splines are shown in Figure 3. In particular, we are able to approximate, with a single model, different kinds of distortion functions w (concave, convex, S-shaped) that usually require different parametric models (Prelec, TK, LinLog; see Section 2.1).

The instances where the approximation is good but not ideal are those with an extreme steepness (first instance, for very small value of p, and fourth instance, for very high values of p, in Figure 3). These situations (w extremely steep) will be rare in practice and correspond to shapes that could be even better described with a more specialized knot sequence. We conclude that the use of I-splines give us good approximations; splines allow us to learn w without committing to a specific parametric form.

In the second series of experiments, we observe the number of queries needed to determine the winning lotteries within sets of different sizes. The set $\mathcal{L}$ is constructed by repeatedly generating at most k outcomes in $[0, 1000]$ and a probability distribution on these outcomes to build a new lottery (with k branches) at step i; this lottery ℓ_i is inserted in $\mathcal{L}$ only if no stochastic dominance holds in $\{\ell_i\} \cup \mathcal{L}$. The process is continued until the desired number of lotteries is obtained. We made experiments with lotteries with $k = 2, 3, 5, 10$ branches and a simulated DM. For small sets of alternatives (typically 100 lotteries) the procedure solves the problem after very few questions. To test the scalability of the approach to larger sets we have generated instances including 1000 or 2000 lotteries. Interactions with the DM are simulated by generating answers to preferences queries using RDU with an inverse S-shaped probability weighting function w_0, unknown from the elicitation procedure, and a linear utility function. For each set of lotteries we observed the reduction of the minimax regret (expressed in percentage of the initial max regret before asking any query) as the number of queries increases. For comparison, we also observed the regret reduction obtained with an heuristic that randomly selects the new pair of lotteries to be compared. The resulting curves are plotted in Figure 4, respectively in green and red. At the same time, we observed the reduction of real regrets defined as the difference $V(\ell_0^*; w_0) - V(\ell^*; w_0)$ where ℓ_0^* is the optimal lottery

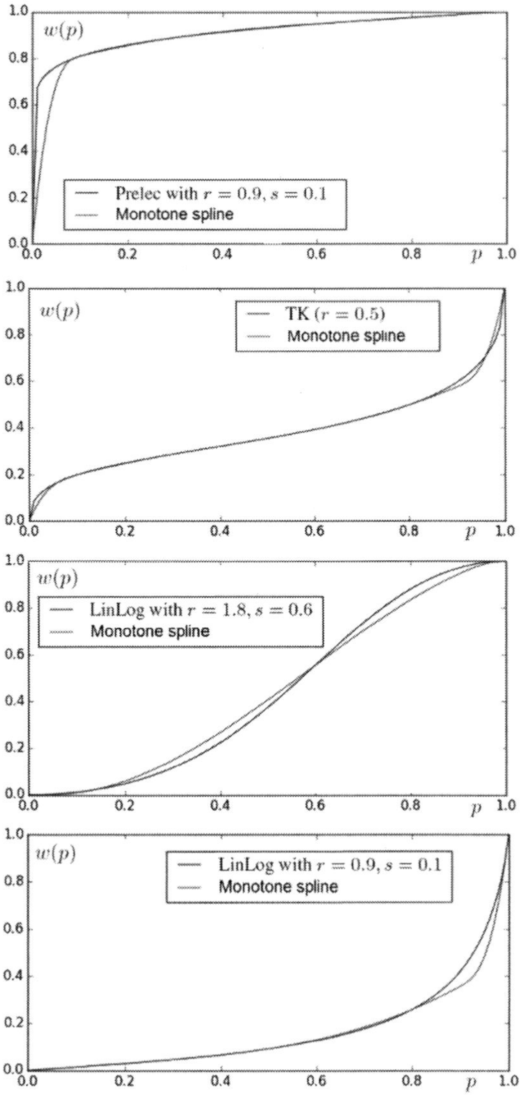

Figure 3: Monotone approximations of $w(p)$.

for the actual weighting function w_0, and ℓ^* is the solution minimizing the current max regret $MR(\ell; W)$. This third curve is plotted in blue in Figure 4. This experiment has been repeated multiple times on randomly generated instances and the results are very similar.

Considering the green and blue curves showing the diminution of max regret and real regret in Figure 4, it appears that the winner can be determined exactly among 1000 lotteries in about 10 queries (in worst case 15 preference queries). This considerably improves the results obtained with the random strategy. Similar tests have been performed for 2000 alternatives. The curves have similar shape and show that less than 10 additional queries are necessary. In fact, we could stop earlier, when minimax regret is very small (even if not exactly zero). The elicitation procedure can indeed be seen as an anytime algorithm. It can be interrupted

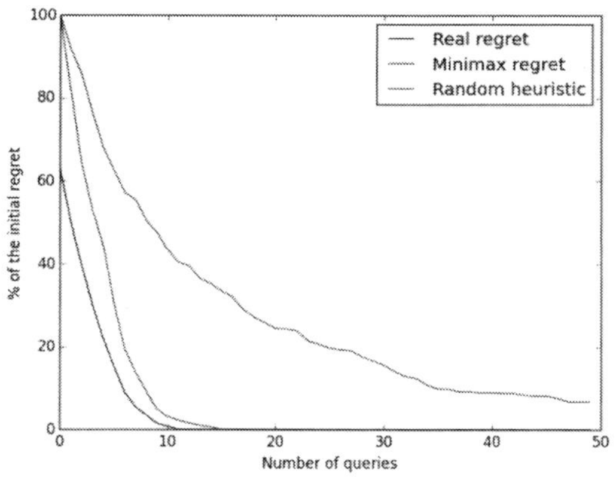

Figure 4: Regret reduction, $|\mathcal{L}| = 1000$, 100 runs.

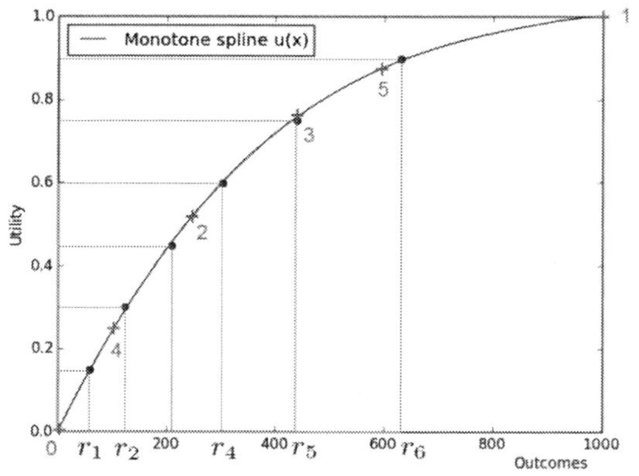

Figure 5: The spline approximating $u(x)$

before reaching a null regret, at any time of the process, and return the current minimax regret solution. We can also provide the associated max regret as a performance guarantee on the quality of the returned solution. Typically, as can be seen from the curves, stopping the elicitation when the minimax regret drops below a given percentage of the initial max regret (or below a given absolute threshold) will save a significant percentage of queries (at least 33% in our tests) without affecting significantly the quality of the recommendation. The efficiency of this approach is due to the fact that in most cases, the parameters of the decision model do not need to be precisely know to be able to determine a necessary winner, i.e., a lottery ℓ such that $V(\ell; w) \geq V(\ell'; w)$ for all $\ell' \in \mathcal{L}$ and all w compatible with the available preference information.

Utility elicitation. We present now an example of construction of a monotone spline on the [0,1000] interval, to reveal and model the implicit utility function of a DM in RDU theory, from observed preferences involving lotteries with outcomes in this interval. The answers of the DM to preference queries have been simulated by a RDU model with an inverse S-shaped probability weighting function $w(p)$ defined by the TK model introduced in Section 2 with parameter $r = 0.5$, and a concave utility defined by $u(x) = 1 - (1 - x/1600)^4$. We successively use the two methods proposed in Section 3 to elicit points and generate the regression spline. We first use the gamble tradeoff method as described in 3.1 with $\alpha = 1050$ and $\beta = 1600$ to obtain the sequence $r_0, \ldots, r_6$. We compute by linear programming the parameters λ_k of the monotone regression spline f that fits best points (r_i, i) and define $u(x) = f(x)/f(1000)$ to obtain $u(1000) = 1$. In Figure 5, points $(r_i, u(r_i))$ are represented by round points (in red), and we show the resulting utility function (in blue).

The construction of the monotone spline with the certainty equivalent method is also shown in Figure 5; the elicited points are represented by + (in green), numbered by order of generation, and the resulting utility function is so close to the previous one that they are indiscernible.

5 CONCLUSION AND PROSPECTIVES

In this paper we proposed an incremental approach for the elicitation of the RDU model. A first novelty concerns the use, within the RDU theory, of minimax regret in order to incrementally elicit the probability weighting function w and to produce robust recommendations with respect to the uncertainty in probability weights. A second novelty is the use of monotonic regression splines as a model of the probability weighting function, allowing the representation of a wide variety of decision behaviors and the optimization of pairwise max-regrets by linear programming. We also extend the proposed approach to cases where the utility u is also unknown. Our experiments show that, despite the expressivity of the model, the elicitation burden is reasonably low in practice, due to the fixed and limited number of parameters used in splines approximating u and w, and the active learning process implemented for w. There are at least two natural continuations of this work. The first one consists in extending the approach for cumulative prospect theory to model different risk attitudes towards gains and losses. The second would be to jointly learn functions u and w using an incremental approach based on regret minimization, with the aim to save more preference queries.

Acknowledgement

Work supported by the French National Research Agency through the Idex Sorbonne Universités, ELICIT project under grant ANR-11-IDEX-0004-02. We benefited from discussion with Angelina Vidali and Enrico Diecidue.

References

[Abdellaoui, 2000] M. Abdellaoui. Parameter-free elicitation of utility and probability weighting functions. *Management Science*, 46(11):1497–1512, 2000.

[Avineri and Prashker, 2004] E. Avineri and J. Prashker. Violations of expected utility theory in route-choice stated preferences: certainty effect and inflation of small probabilities. *Transportation Research Record: J. of the Trans. Res. Board*, 1894:222–229, 2004.

[Beatty and Barsky, 1995] J. C. Beatty and B. A. Barsky. *An introduction to splines for use in computer graphics and geometric modeling*. Morgan Kaufmann, 1995.

[Benabbou *et al.*, 2014] N. Benabbou, P. Perny, and P. Viappiani. Incremental elicitation of Choquet capacities for multicriteria decision making. In *ECAI'14*, pages 87–92, 2014.

[Bernoulli, 1954] D. Bernoulli. Exposition of a new theory on the measurement of risk. *Econometrica*, 22(1):23–36, 1954.

[Boutilier *et al.*, 2006] C. Boutilier, R. Patrascu, P. Poupart, and D. Schuurmans. Constraint-based Optimization and Utility Elicitation using the Minimax Decision Criterion. *Artifical Intelligence*, 170(8–9):686–713, 2006.

[Braziunas and Boutilier, 2007] D. Braziunas and C. Boutilier. Minimax Regret-based Elicitation of Generalized Additive Utilities. In *Proceedings of UAI'07*, pages 25–32, Vancouver, 2007.

[Braziunas, 2011] D. Braziunas. *Decision-theoretic elicitation of generalized additive utilities*. PhD thesis, University of Toronto, 2011.

[Cavagnaro *et al.*, 2013] D. Cavagnaro, M. Pitt, R. Gonzalez, and J. Myung. Discriminating among probability weighting functions using adaptive design optimization. *Journal of Risk and Uncertainty*, 47(3):255–289, 2013.

[Chateauneuf and Cohen, 1994] A. Chateauneuf and M. Cohen. Risk seeking with diminishing marginal utility in a non-expected utility model. *Journal of Risk and Uncertainty*, 9(1):77–91, 1994.

[Diecidue and Wakker, 2001] E. Diecidue and P. P. Wakker. On the intuition of rank-dependent utility. *Journal of Risk and Uncertainty*, 23(3):281–298, 2001.

[Edwards, 1955] W. Edwards. The prediction of decisions among bets. *Journal of Experimental Psychology*, (50):201–214, 1955.

[Fürnkranz and Hüllermeier, 2003] J. Fürnkranz and E. Hüllermeier. *Pairwise preference learning and ranking*, pages 145–156. Springer, 2003.

[Gilboa, 2008] I. Gilboa. *Theory of Decision under Uncertainty*. Cambridge University Press, 2008.

[Gonzalez and Wu, 1999] R. Gonzalez and G. Wu. On the shape of the probability weighting function. *Cognitive psychology*, 38(1):129–166, 1999.

[Hines and Larson, 2010] G. Hines and K. Larson. Preference elicitation for risky prospects. In *AAMAS'10*, pages 889–896, 2010.

[Hong *et al.*, 1987] C. S. Hong, E. Karni, and Z. Safra. Risk aversion in the theory of expected utility with rank dependent probabilities. *Journal of Economic theory*, 42(2):370–381, 1987.

[Jeantet *et al.*, 2012] G. Jeantet, P. Perny, and O. Spanjaard. Sequential Decision Making with Rank Dependent Utility: a Minimax Regret Approach. In *Proc; of AAAI'12*, pages 1931–1937, 2012.

[Kahneman and Tversky, 1979] D. Kahneman and A. Tversky. Prospect theory: An analysis of decision under risk. *Econometrica*, 47(2):263–291, 1979.

[Karmarkar, 1978] U. S. Karmarkar. Subjectively weighted utility: A descriptive extension of the expected utility model. *Organizational Behavior and Human Performance*, 21(1):61 – 72, 1978.

[Nielsen and Jaffray, 2006] T. D. Nielsen and J.-Y. Jaffray. Dynamic decision making without expected utility: An operational approach. *European Journal of Operational Research*, 169(1):226–246, 2006.

[Quiggin, 1982] J. Quiggin. A theory of anticipated utility. *Journal of Economic Behavior and Organization*, (3):225–243, 1982.

[Quiggin, 2012] J. Quiggin. *Generalized expected utility theory: The rank-dependent model*. Springer Science & Business Media, 2012.

[Ramsay, 1988] J. O. Ramsay. Monotone regression spline in action. *Statistical Science*, pages 425–441, 1988.

[Savage, 1954] L. J. Savage. *The Foundations of Statistics*. J. Wiley and Sons, New-York, 1954.

[Schmeidler, 1989] D. Schmeidler. Subjective probability and expected utility without additivity. *Econometrica*, 57(3):571–587, 1989.

[Tehrani *et al.*, 2012] A. F. Tehrani, W. Cheng, K. Dembczynski, and E. Hüllermeier. Learning monotone nonlinear models using the Choquet integral. *Machine Learning*, 89(1-2):183–211, 2012.

[Torra, 2010] V. Torra. Learning aggregation operators for preference modeling. In J. Fürnkranz and E. Hüllermeier, editors, *Preference learning*, pages 317–333. Springer, 2010.

[Tversky and Kahneman, 1992] A. Tversky and D. Kahneman. Advances in prospect theory: Cumulative representation of uncertainty. *Journal of Risk and Uncertainty*, 5(4):297–323, 1992.

[von Neumann and Morgenstern, 1947] J. von Neumann and O. Morgenstern. *Theory of Games and Economic Behavior*. Princeton University Press, 1947.

[Wakker and Deneffe, 1996] P. Wakker and D. Deneffe. Eliciting von neumann-morgenstern utilities when probabilities are distorted or unknown. *Management science*, 42(8):1131–1150, 1996.

[Wakker, 1990] P. Wakker. Under stochastic dominance Choquet-expected utility and anticipated utility are identical. *Theory and Decision*, 29(2):119–132, 1990.

[Wakker, 1994] P. Wakker. Separating marginal utility and probabilistic risk aversion. *Theory and Decision*, 36(1):1–44, 1994.

[Wang and Boutilier, 2003] T. Wang and C. Boutilier. Incremental Utility Elicitation with the Minimax Regret Decision Criterion. In *Proceedings of IJCAI'03*, pages 309–316, 2003.

[Yaari, 1987] M. E. Yaari. The Dual Theory of Choice under Risk. *Econometrica*, 55(1):95–115, January 1987.

Interpretable Policies for Dynamic Product Recommendations

Marek Petrik
IBM T.J. Watson Research Center
Yorktown Heights, NY 10598
mpetrik@us.ibm.com

Ronny Luss
IBM T.J. Watson Research Center
Yorktown Heights, NY 10598
rluss@us.ibm.com

Abstract

In many applications, it may be better to compute a good interpretable policy instead of a complex optimal one. For example, a recommendation engine might perform better when accounting for user profiles, but in the absence of such loyalty data, assumptions would have to be made that increase the complexity of the recommendation policy. A simple greedy recommendation could be implemented based on aggregated user data, but another simple policy can improve on this by accounting for the fact that users come from different segments of a population. In this paper, we study the problem of computing an optimal policy that is interpretable. In particular, we consider a policy to be interpretable if the decisions (e.g., recommendations) depend only on a small number of simple state attributes (e.g., the currently viewed product). This novel model is a general Markov decision problem with action constraints over states. We show that this problem is NP hard and develop a Mixed Integer Linear Programming formulation that gives an exact solution when policies are restricted to being deterministic. We demonstrate the effectiveness of the approach on a real-world business case for a European tour operator's recommendation engine.

1 Introduction

Interpretability in data mining and machine learning means that the computed models and solutions can be relatively easily understood by humans. Examples of algorithms that produce interpretable solutions include classical algorithms, such as decision trees [18], and newer sparse learning methods [18]. Recently, there has been a lot of interest in interpretable machine learning, but few works have explicitly focused on interpretability in decision making.

Lack of interpretable solutions can be an important roadblock in many critical domains, such as medicine [12, 11, 26]. If decision makers can understand a computed solution they are more likely to trust and implement it. Additionally, having an interpretable policy makes it easier to discover flaws resulting from incorrect models or unreasonable model assumptions, and without implementing a policy. Furthermore, it is possible to discover why the policy does not perform well. Finally, a simple policy can be easily implemented [29] and, as we show, sometimes assuming that the policy is simple circumvents the need to build complex models.

In this paper, we view the task of recommending products as one of decision making in a dynamic environment, rather than ranking products in a static setting (which is more common). With the rise in accessible customer information and product availability, the importance of matching customers to products has quickly risen. This problem arises in many domains such as recommender systems [21, 6] and personalized online advertising [8, 16, 7]; similar methods for matching customers to products are even used for email classification and spam detection [20]. Most methods for these systems use both the descriptions of the items and the historical behavior of the users.

Recommender systems fall into two basic categories [24]: collaborative filtering and content-based filtering. Collaborative filtering relates one user's preferences to other users' preferences without taking into account specific user or item properties [24]. Content-based filtering rather makes use of user profiles and the item properties. Most recommender systems combine these ideas and are a hybrid of both collaborative and content-based filtering methods. Successful recommender systems have been developed for recommending movies (e.g., Netflix), music (e.g., Pandora), personalized advertising [32], and even for recommending social-network followers [15, 5].

We focus in this paper on a single, and admittedly simple, model of policy interpretability (i.e., recommendation rules that are easily understood). Since we consider a dynamic setting, we look for recommendations based on the state of a user (e.g., whether or not interested in a currently viewed product), and these recommendations based on the state are what we refer to as a policy. We consider the standard Markov decision process (MDP) with *discrete* states and actions. Typically, an MDP will have thousands or millions of states. Therefore, even though a policy can be examined in principle, it cannot be understood in practice. To make the policy *interpretable*, we simply require that it does not prescribe more than, for example, 50 different actions. This means that the policy must prescribe the same action for a number of states and also that such a subset of states must be well defined.

Computing optimal recommendations under our interpretability constraints constitutes solving a so-called partially observable Markov decision process (POMDP), which can be cast as a Markov decision process. Policies for such MDPs tend to be extraordinarily complex and hard not only to interpret but also to implement. Instead, as in our case, one may want to compute a best possible policy that depends only on the currently viewed product. This would entail computing item to item recommendations that consider the customer dynamics, a policy which falls into a class of POMDPs that are not complex.

To motivate the need for interpretable policies, consider optimizing dynamic online product recommendations. As a user interacts with a website, their preferences become clear over time. However, the interactions themselves influence user behavior [33, 30, 27, 23]. Consider a scenario with two customer types **A** and **B** and two products *X* and *Y* where the percentages of customer types **A** and **B** interested in products *X* and *Y* are 90%/10% and 40%/60%, respectively. If a customer of type **A** is recommended and clicks on product *Y*, the distribution of the types of customers looking at the two products will change, and our model accounts for such dynamics.

Our main contribution in this paper is a novel model for computing interpretable policies as described above, or stated differently, a model for computing policies for MDPs which are constrained to take the same action in subsets of states. We show connections with several other models considered in the context of reinforcement learning and POMDPs and use the relationship to show that the optimal interpretable policies may be stochastic and are NP hard to compute. We then propose a new and simpler nonlinear Mixed Integer Linear Program (MILP) formulation. While these models can also be hard to compute, we show that we can learn optimal interpretable deterministic policies.

We also contribute to the area of recommendation engines with a framework for making recommendations that account for the changing dynamics of the system. While we do not model these dynamics directly, our framework does account for more general dynamics by introducing unobservable dynamics into the model. In other words, our model assumes that customers are changing states but also assumes that we cannot directly observe the manner in which they are changing.

Furthermore, we establish a connection between several apparently unrelated areas of optimization. The underlying model is a Markov decision process with constraints on actions, and is related to several other streams of work. Similar models are studied using aggregation in reinforcement learning, where the motivation is somewhat different. Aggregation is used because the models are too large to be solved or even enumerated. As we discuss in more detail later, the interpretable MDP model is also related to finite state controller optimization on POMDPs (e.g. [2]). Finally, policy search methods from reinforcement learning have been used to compute interpretable policies.

The remainder of the paper proceeds as follows. Section 2 next discusses more related work to our notion of interpretability. Section 3 then formalizes the concept of interpretability and discusses the application to recommender systems, followed by mathematical programming formulations used to learn interpretable policies in Section 4, and corresponding complexity results in Section 5. Our framework is evaluated on data from a major European tour operator in Section 6, where a significant improvement over several practical benchmarks is demonstrated. A final discussion of our findings is given in Section 7.

2 Related Work

In this section, we summarize the existing related work and draw new connections. While there has been little work directly on interpretable policies, it turns out that our model of policy interpretability is closely related to previous results in other fields.

Recent work on interpretable policies in reinforcement learning [17] proposes to use policy search methods. Policy search is a general method that can be leveraged to find policies that are parameterized in ways that make them interpretable. While this is a very natural approach and is demonstrated to work well, it does not study any new methods for computing these interpretable policy. In comparison, our focus is on a simpler model that allows us to more deeply study the computational problems.

The most closely related method to our formulation (discussed in Section 4.1) is state aggregation in reinforcement learning, which is a very simple and classic method (e.g., [25, 19, 28, 3, 10]). The motivation in our work is quite different from that in state aggregation. The main reason for state aggregation is to address a problem that is very large and often cannot be enumerated, and therefore, very little focus has been put on how to compute good policies for an aggregation. Indeed, most work has rather focused on methods for choosing which states should be aggregated.

Since we deal with a smaller number of states, we can develop better methods for computing interpretable policies, and will adapt methods used for state aggregation to this setting.

Our model of interpretability can be also seen as a special case of Partially Observable Markov Decision Processes (POMDPs). POMDPs generalize MDPs to the case where observations do not contain exact information about the current state, and in general, the optimal policy to POMDPs are complex. There do exist certain classes of POMDPs that result in simpler optimal policies, and this space is where our model lies. In the other direction, it can also be shown that our interpretable policy problem generalizes one of these simpler classes of POMDPs, termed optimal finite state controllers in the MDP literature. Hence, we proceed as with general POMDPs, and constrain polices by introducing a concept of observations in the next section.

Another closely related area of work to interpretability is that of implementability of policies. The goal is not to have the policy be understood by humans, but instead requires that. The term *implementable policy* in the context of MDPs was introduced in [29]. However, the problem is a special case of finding *memoryless* policies (i.e., policies that depend only on the current state and not on any history) for POMDPs.

Finally, the analysis of policy optimality in some specialized domains, such as inventory management, queueing, and energy storage is tangentially related to our setting. One can show that the optimal policies in these domains are interpretable; indeed, for example, the optimal policy in inventory optimization domains will be independent of the current inventory. This leads to policies that are easy to interpret and also typically easy to solve. Unlike these settings, we deal with cases in which the optimal policy may not be interpretable, which introduces an additional layer of computational difficulties.

3 Interpretable Policies in MDPs

In this section, we formally define the model and illustrate its application to the dynamic recommendation problem described in the introduction. For the remainder of the paper, we define the following notations. Denote by Δ^d the non-negative simplex in d dimensions, i.e., the set of valid distributions defined by $\{x \in \mathbb{R}^d : \sum_i x_i = 1, x \geq 0\}$. For a matrix X, we define $X(s,\cdot)$ as row s of X.

The interpretable model is based on a Markov decision process (MDP) (e.g., [22]). An *interpretable* MDP is a tuple $(\mathcal{S}, \mathcal{A}, P, r, p_0, \mathcal{O}, \theta)$. Here, $\mathcal{S}$ is a *finite* set of states, $p_0 \in \Delta^{|\mathcal{S}|}$ is the initial distribution, $\mathcal{A}$ is a finite set of *actions*, each of which can be taken in all states. The transition probability matrix for each $a \in \mathcal{A}$ is denoted $P_a \in \mathbb{R}^{|\mathcal{S}|\times|\mathcal{S}|}$ and each row lies in the simplex: $P_a(s,\cdot) \in \Delta^{|\mathcal{S}|}$ for all $s \in \mathcal{S}$. The rewards vector for each action $a \in \mathcal{A}$ is denoted $r_a \in \mathbb{R}^{|\mathcal{S}|}$.

As discussed in the introduction, we assume that interpretability of a policy depends on a small number of simple state properties. To capture this property, we augment the model by a set of observations $\mathcal{O}$ and an observation function $\theta : \mathcal{S} \to \mathcal{O}$ that defines a partitioning of states to observations.

A solution to an MDP is a randomized stationary policy from $\Pi_R : \{\mathcal{S} \to \Delta^{\mathcal{A}}\}$ or deterministic stationary policy from $\Pi_R : \{\mathcal{S} \to \mathcal{A}\}$. The set of *interpretable* policies Π_I is defined as:

$$\Pi_I = \{\pi \in \Pi_R \ : \ \theta(s_1) = \theta(s_2) \Rightarrow \pi(s_1) = \pi(s_2)\} \, .$$

In other words, if two states share the same observation then an interpretable policy must take actions with identical probabilities in these states.

Our objective is to compute a policy that maximizes the infinite-horizon γ-discounted return $\rho(\pi)$ by solving

$$\max_{\pi \in \Pi_I} \rho(\pi), \tag{3.1}$$

where $\rho(\pi)$ can be expressed as

$$\rho(\pi) = \sum_{t=0}^{\infty} \gamma^t p_0^\mathsf{T} P_\pi^t r_\pi .$$

It is important to note that the constraints imposed by interpretable policies are quite different from the constraints in constrained MDPs [1]. The optimal solution to Eq. (3.1) can be obtained through other formulations. In particular, we offer a Mixed Integer Linear Programming formulation in Section 4.2, and equivalence is given there by Proposition 4.1. Eq. (3.1) offers an easy interpretation for our objective when designing a policy.

To illustrate the concept of interpretability, the following example describes how our model can be used to represent the recommender system formulation from the introduction. This is a simplified version of the model that we use later in the paper for empirical evaluation.

Example 3.1 (Dynamic Product Recommendations). *Consider the online product recommendation setting described in the introduction. Let $\mathcal{M}$ be a set of available products and let $\mathcal{W}$ be a set of customer segments. Assuming that customer segments are known in advance, their browsing behavior and response can be modeled as the following MDP. States $\mathcal{S} = \mathcal{W} \times \mathcal{M}$ represent the* customer type *and* current product displayed. *Actions represent the product sets to recommend during a page view: $\mathcal{A} = \{a \in 2^{\mathcal{M}} : |a| \leq k\}$. Here, k is the maximum number of products to recommend. Transition probabilities are based on whether a customer chooses to follow a product* *recommendation, purchases the currently displayed product, or abandons the purchase. Rewards are accrued by customers purchasing items.*

This recommendation MDP can be solved rather easily, however the policy is likely to be hard to implement. This is because the customer type is not observable, particularly if only a short history of customer interactions is available. Another direction, solving this problem as a POMDP, would yield a complex policy that is hard to interpret and implement in a real-time system. This leads to applying our model of interpretability.

The simplest and most interpretable online product recommendation policy are item-to-item recommendations, and capturing the desire for such a policy in our setting is simple. Let the set of *observations* be equal to the available products ($\mathcal{O} = \mathcal{M}$) and define the *observation mapping* function as $\theta(w, m) = m$ for $w \in \mathcal{W}, m \in \mathcal{M}$ so that observations are independent of the customer type. Typically, item-to-item recommendations are computed based on the customers that typically visit the given product page, i.e, the distribution of customers. However, the recommendations themselves influence this distribution. The MDP implementation with interpretable policies accounts for the change in the distribution, and we formulate and analyze this approach in more detail below.

4 Interpretable MDP Formulations

In this section, we formulate the mathematical programs for learning the MDPs of interest, beginning with a classical MDP formulation, adding interpretability constraints, and then relaxing nonlinearities to obtain a mixed integer linear programming (MILP) formulation that approximates the exact problem.

4.1 Basic Formulation

While it is possible to adapt nonlinear optimization formulations from the POMDP literature, for example [2], we derive a simpler nonlinear formulation first. We first adapt the standard linear program formulation for a Markov decision process. The classic MDP linear program learns a policy that maximizes the expected reward of the system subject to constraints that model the transitions allowed in the system.

First define the following variables. Let $u \in \mathbb{R}^{|\mathcal{S}| \times |\mathcal{A}|}$ represent the policy we are trying to learn, which is defined in every state as $u(s, \cdot)/\sum_a u(s, a) \in \Delta^{|\mathcal{A}|}$. Note that, for variable u, we denote $u(s, a)$ as the (s, a) entry of matrix u in the following formulations, along with similar notation for other variables. Summations over s or a are meant as shorthand for $s \in \mathcal{S}$ and $a \in \mathcal{A}$. Then, in formal terms, a deterministic policy means that $u(s, a) = 1$ for a single $a \in \mathcal{A}$ for each $s \in \mathcal{S}$, whereas a randomized policy simply means that $\sum_a u(s, a) = 1$ for each $s \in \mathcal{S}$.

Given our notation, the linear programming formulation for the classic MDP is

$$\begin{aligned}
\max_{u} \quad & \sum_{s,a} u(s,a) r(s,a) \\
\text{s.t.} \quad & \sum_{a} u(s,a) \\
& = p_0(s) + \sum_{s',a} \gamma P_a(s,s')\, u(s',a) \quad \forall s \in \mathcal{S} \\
& u(s,a) \geq 0 \quad \forall s \in \mathcal{S}, a \in \mathcal{A}.
\end{aligned} \tag{4.1}$$

The summation in the objective is the expected reward for a policy given by u. Note that u can also be interpreted as a state-action occupancy measure (e.g. [4]) which is the cumulative visitation probability over all state-action pairs when the discount (for computing the current value of future rewards) is interpreted as a probability of leaving the system. Then the first set of constraints can be seen as a form of the Bellman equations in terms of a state-action occupancy measure rather than state value. It is known that an optimal policy must satisfy these equations. The final inequalities are needed since measures must be nonnegative. For the optimal solution, these values represent the optimal policy.

We next want to adapt Problem 4.1 in order to enforce interpretability. Interpretability constraints can be directly added by introducing a new optimization variable, $\psi \in \mathbb{R}^{|\mathcal{O}| \times |\mathcal{A}|}$, which defines the interpretable policy for each observation as $\psi(o, \cdot) \in \Delta^{|\mathcal{A}|}$. The new formulation is

$$\begin{aligned}
\max_{u,\psi} \quad & \sum_{s,a} u(s,a) r(s,a) \\
\text{s.t.} \quad & u(s,a) = \psi(\theta(s),a) \sum_{a'} u(s,a') \quad \forall s \in \mathcal{S}, a \in \mathcal{A} \\
& \sum_{a} u(s,a) \\
& \quad = p_0(s) + \sum_{s',a} \gamma\, P_a(s',s)\, u(s',a) \quad \forall s \in \mathcal{S} \\
& u(s,a) \geq 0 \quad \forall s \in \mathcal{S}, a \in \mathcal{A} \\
& \sum_{a} \psi(o,a) = 1 \quad \forall o \in \mathcal{O}.
\end{aligned} \tag{4.2}$$

In this formulation, we interpret u as a state-action occupancy measure (as defined above). The first set of constraints dictates that the interpretable policy is equivalent to a normalized state-action occupancy measure (as is the policy in the classic MDP above) and furthermore that the policy at states in the same observation is the same. The second and third set of constraints remains the same. The last set of constraints puts the interpretable policy at each observation in the simplex (since nonnegative is already implied by nonnegativity of u).

The optimal policy is directly constructed from the optimal ψ for (4.2). The following proposition shows its correctness.

Proposition 4.1. *The optimal solution to* (4.2) *is also optimal in* (3.1).

Proof. Follows from the equivalence in Theorem 6.9.1 in [22], the optimality in Theorem 6.9.4 in [22], and the equivalence of return in terms of the occupancy frequency. The constraint on u from ψ is correct due to the construction of the policy from u. □

Note that formulation (4.2) is no longer linear or convex because of the terms $\psi(\theta(s), a)u(s, a')$ in the first set of constraints. It could be solved using a non-linear solver, such as IPOPT. We take a different approach, which can guarantee solution optimality, in the next subsection.

4.2 Mixed Integer Linear Program

This section describes a new mixed integer linear programming (MILP) formulation for learning an interpretable policy within the MDP framework. A recent paper describes a MILP formulation for finite state controllers [9], however, our formulation is simpler and our derivation is more straightforward.

As we have defined a state-action occupancy frequency $u(s, a)$ above, we can similarly define a state occupancy frequency $d \in \mathbb{R}^{|\mathcal{S}|}$ by $d(s) = \sum_a u(s, a)$ for each state $s \in \mathcal{S}$. From a modeling viewpoint, including d gives a new interpretation of state-action occupancy frequency as the fraction of state occupancy frequency determined by the optimal interpretable policy. From an optimization viewpoint, including d greatly reduces the number of nonlinear functions in the first set of constraints in a trade-off for $|\mathcal{S}|$ additional equality constraints. This trade-off is important regarding the relaxation below that we use to get an MILP formulation. Introducing the state occupancy frequency to the formulation results in the problem

$$\begin{aligned}
\max_{u,d,\psi} \quad & \sum_{s,a} u(s,a)r(s,a) \\
\text{s.t.} \quad & u(s,a) = \psi(\theta(s),a)d(s) \quad \forall s \in \mathcal{S}, a \in \mathcal{A} \\
& d(s) = p_0(s) + \sum_{s',a} \gamma P_a(s',s)\, u(s',a) \quad \forall s \in \mathcal{S} \\
& d(s) = \sum_a u(s,a) \quad \forall s \in \mathcal{S} \\
& u(s,a) \geq 0 \quad \forall s \in \mathcal{S}, a \in \mathcal{A} \\
& \sum_a \psi(o,a) = 1 \quad \forall o \in \mathcal{O}.
\end{aligned} \tag{4.3}$$

Note that the third set of constraints are the $|\mathcal{S}|$ new equality constraints, and that the number of nonlinear terms in the first set of constraints has been reduced from $|\mathcal{S}| \cdot |\mathcal{A}|^2$ to $|\mathcal{S}| \cdot |\mathcal{A}|$ nonlinear terms.

While we can try to solve the nonlinear optimization problem (4.3), any solution we get will have no guarantee of optimality. We now develop a mixed integer linear program formulation based on the so-called McCormick inequalities. This approach relaxes the constraints in (4.3). The idea is to bound the terms $\psi(\theta(s), a)d(s)$ for all $s \in \mathcal{S}, a \in \mathcal{A}$ by making use of upper and lower bounds on $\psi(\theta(s), a)$ and $d(s)$. McCormick inequalities are defined in the lemma below.

Lemma 4.2 (McCormick Inequalities, e.g., [13]). *Assume that $a_L \leq a \leq a_U$ and $b_L \leq b \leq b_U$. Then:*

$$a\, b_L - a_L\, b_L + a_L\, b \leq a\, b \leq a\, b_U - a_L\, b_U + a_L\, b$$
$$a\, b_U - a_U\, b_U + a_U\, b \leq a\, b \leq a\, b_L - a_U\, b_L + a_U\, b$$

It is important to note that the equalities are attained for the extreme points of the intervals (for either one of the two variables).

The McCormick inequalities are easy to derive; for example, the first lower bound on ab is attained by multiplying the bounds $a - a_L \geq 0$ and $b - b_L \geq 0$. The MILP can then be constructed as follows. The constraints on ψ are box constraints of the form $0 \leq \psi(\theta(s), a) \leq 1$ and the bounds on state occupancy frequencies are $0 \leq d(s) \leq \bar{d}(s)$ where $\bar{d}(s)$ must be estimated. Therefore, we can relax the nonlinear equality $u(s, a) = \psi(\theta(s), a)d(s)$ in problem 4.3 by the following inequalities

$$\bar{d}(s)\,(\psi(\theta(s), a) - 1) + d(s) \leq u(s, a) \leq \bar{d}(s)\,\psi(\theta_s, a)$$

Note that all four McCormick inequalities are implied by these two constraints.

The relaxed optimization problem becomes:

$$\begin{aligned}
\max_{d,u,\psi} \quad & \sum_{s,a} u(s,a)\, r(s,a) \\
\text{s.t.} \quad & \bar{d}(s)\,(\psi(\theta(s),a) - 1) + d(s) \\
& \quad \leq u(s,a) \quad \forall s \in \mathcal{S}, a \in \mathcal{A} \\
& u(s,a) \leq \bar{d}(s)\, \psi(\theta(s),a) \quad \forall s \in \mathcal{S}, a \in \mathcal{A} \\
& d(s) = p_0(s) + \sum_{s',a} \gamma\, P(s',a,s)\, u(s',a) \quad \forall s \in \mathcal{S} \\
& d(s) = \sum_a u(s,a) \quad \forall s \in \mathcal{S} \\
& \sum_a \psi(o,a) = 1 \quad \forall o \in \mathcal{O} \\
& u(s,a) \geq 0 \quad \forall s \in \mathcal{S}, a \in \mathcal{A} \\
& \psi(o,a) \in \{0,1\} \quad \forall o \in \mathcal{O}, a \in \mathcal{A}
\end{aligned} \tag{4.4}$$

We next note that the last statement of Lemma 4.2 implies that we can compute an optimal *deterministic* policy (under interpretability constraints) as well as an optimality gap for suboptimal policies, which is summarized in the following proposition.

Proposition 4.3. *Optimal solution to* (4.4) *is also an optimal solution to* (3.1).

Proof. Since the McCormick inequalities are tight for $\psi(o, a) \in \{0, 1\}$, the optimal solution to this MILP problem will be the optimal *deterministic* implementable policy for the problem. □

It may be also possible to solve (4.4) without the integrality constraints, which means optimizing over randomized policies. In that case, this is simply a linear program which can be easily solved, however, the solution may not be very good due to the relaxation given by the McCormick inequalities.

Remark 4.4. As we hinted, there is a connection between finite state controllers and the interpretability constraints. Consider a POMDP with m states, a actions, o observations, and computing a finite state controller with n nodes. [9] shows that their MILP formulation has $n \cdot a + n^2 \dot{o}$ integral variables. It can be readily seen that applying our formulation would have $n^2 \cdot a \cdot o$. This is more than [9]. The number of variables can reduced in a setting such as the finite state controller in which the action set can be decomposed as follows. Assume that $\mathcal{A} = \mathcal{A}_1 \times \mathcal{A}_2$. Then introduce additional variables $\psi_i : \mathcal{O} \times \mathcal{A}_i \to \{0, 1\}$ for $i = 1, 2$. We add constraints $\sum_{a \in \mathcal{A}_i} \psi(o, a_i) = 1$ and $\psi(o, (a_1, a_2)) \leq \min\{\psi_1(o, a_1), \psi(o, a_2)\}$.

5 Properties of Optimal Interpretable Policies

In this section, we prove basic properties of optimal interpretable policies. Recall that an interpretable policy takes the same action for all states within a single observation and is computed by solving problem (3.1).

We first address the computational complexity of computing an optimal interpretable policy.

Proposition 5.1. *Solving* (3.1) *for either randomized or deterministic policies is NP hard, and is in NP as well for deterministic policies.*

Proof. Hardness is proven by a reduction from computing a memoryless policy for a POMDP [14] (which is known to be NP-hard to compute). The construction is simple and we only outline it here. Consider a POMDP with states $\bar{\mathcal{S}}$ and observations $\bar{\mathcal{O}}$. Then construct a cross-product MDP (e.g. [2]) for a finite node controller with $\bar{\mathcal{O}}$ nodes. The state space of the cross-product MDP will have $\mathcal{S} = \bar{\mathcal{S}} \times \bar{\mathcal{O}}$. The set of actions in the cross-product MDP is the same as the actions in the POMDP. The transitions in the cross-product MDP are a product of the POMDP state transition according to the action taken and the observation observed. Consider an interpretable policy for this problem in which the observations depend on $\bar{\mathcal{O}}$ and the observation mapping is $\theta((s, o)) = o$. It can be now readily seen that computing such an interpretable policy will correspond to a memoryless policy in the POMDP and vice versa. An optimal interpretable policy for this problem will therefore be also an optimal memoryless policy in the POMDP. The hardness for stochastic policies follows similarly from [34]. It follows that solving (3.1) for deterministic policies also in NP since the set of deterministic policies can be enumerated. □

The problem of solving (3.1) over randomized policies is not known to be in NP and there is evidence that the problem may in fact be harder [34].

We next study the structure of optimal policies. It can be readily seen that the optimal policy to an MDP with interpretability constraints may be history dependent. See, for example, the MDP in Fig. 1 in which the optimal policy will be $a_2, a_1, a_2, \ldots$. No deterministic interpretable policy can achieve such a return. However, we are interested in finding a stationary policy. The following proposition shows that the optimal policy may need to be randomized.

Proposition 5.2. *There may be no optimal deterministic interpretable policy.*

We prove Proposition 5.2 by an example in which a randomized policy can be arbitrarily better than the best deterministic policy.

Example 5.3. *Consider an example MDP depicted in Fig. 2 in which the optimal policy will be randomized. One possible interpretation in the context of product recommendations is as follows. States of the MDP represent a customer state. In particular, s_1 means that the customer is not yet interested in a product, and action a_1 represents a good recommendation. Taking this action moves the customer to state s_2 which means considering a product they are interested in. Taking action a_2 will cause the customer to consider another interesting product. Action a_2 represents suggesting an irrelevant product. In state s_1, the customer remains uninterested, but in s_2 the customer is already considering an interesting product and since the recommendation is not useful, they will simply purchase the product and a reward is received. Since we do not observe the internal customer state, s_1 and s_2 share the same observation and the interpretable policy will have to take the same action in both states. Clearly, any deterministic policy will receive return* 0 *(since the system starts in state s_1), while a policy that randomizes a_1 and a_2 with equal probability will receive return of at least $\gamma 0.5$ for discount factor γ. Looking*

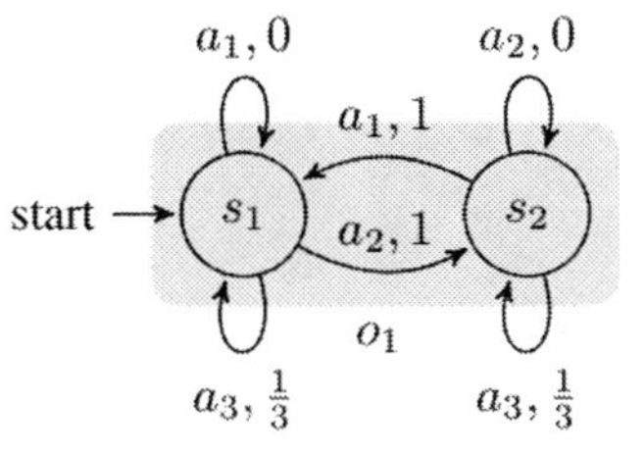

Figure 1: Markov decision process in Example 5.3. Shaded areas show states that share the same observation. Edge labels denote action name and the reward.

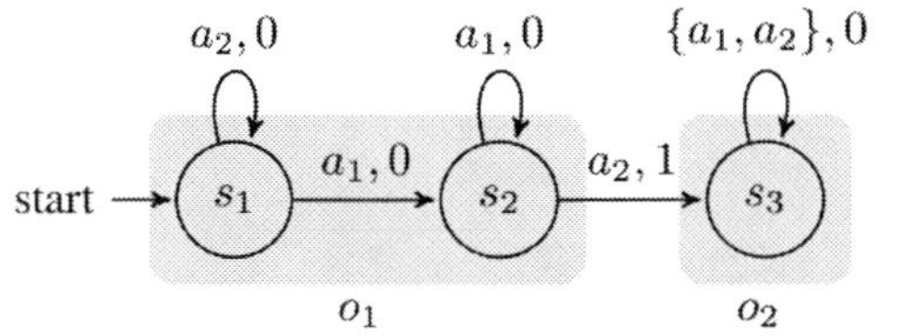

Figure 2: Markov decision process in Example 5.3. Shaded areas show states that share the same observation. Edge labels denote action name and the reward.

back at Fig. 1, we have an even simpler example in which the optimal policy will be randomized.

Note that our MILP formulation (4.4) only learns deterministic policies, and that the binary constraints need to be relaxed in order to learn randomized policies. Initial experiments showed poor performance with this relaxation, likely due to the McCormick inequalities being too loose an approximation to the other nonlinearities.

6 Case Study: Interpretable Product Recommendations

In this section, we describe the experimental evaluation of our interpretable MDP model in an online product recommendation setting. As mentioned above, most research on recommender systems has focused on developing methods for fitting a customer preference model to data. We, in contrast, study optimization methods that use the customer preference model to make better recommendations.

The motivating business case for this application was to improve customer experience and promote conversions for a major European tour operator. For the purposes of this experimental study, we apply the tools of this paper to design a recommendation engine that targets conversions, i.e., customer purchases.

6.1 Customer Model

To evaluate the quality of recommendations, we simulate customer purchase behavior and interactions with an online catalog. Our focus is on simulating online sessions in which customers browses different products and at some point either make a purchase or abandon the session.

Customer behavior is modeled using a mixed logit customer choice model [31] with 10 discrete segments. The logit model is used to predict customer behavior during a product purchase session. In particular, the model decides whether a customer purchases the currently viewed product, takes a recommendation, or abandons the search.

The logit model assumes that customers from any segment c assign some value, denoted $\eta(c, p)$, to product p. This represents the value gained by purchasing the product and is used to determine the probability of purchasing the given product. As a baseline, we denote by $\eta_N(c)$ the value of no purchase, which is the standard approach. We describe how the values $\eta(c, p)$, for each segment and product, and $\eta_N(c)$, for each segment, translate to probabilities below.

We fit the parameters of the logit model to data which comes from an adventure travel brand of a major European tour operator that specializes on sailboat rentals. Our dataset, which is a subset of the entire clickstream, consists of 22803 individual website visits, 1100 individual customers, and 75 products. Customer segments are identified using a standard low-rank matrix decomposition method and logit parameters are fit to maximize likelihood.

The MDP that models the interaction of customers with the online system is defined as follows. The state set is $\mathcal{S} = \mathcal{C} \times \mathcal{P}$, where $\mathcal{C}$ is the set of customer segments, and $\mathcal{P}$ is the set of products. In other words, the state represents a customer and a product currently being considered. Assume that the goal is to recommend n products. Action set $\mathcal{A} = \{(p_1, \ldots, p_n) : p_i \in \mathcal{P}\}$ determines the set of recommended products in a given state.

The transition probabilities in the MDP for some state (c, p) and products $(p_1, \ldots, p_n)$ are given according to the mixed logit choice model as follows. In particular, let $\alpha = \exp(\eta(c, p)) + \cdot \sum_{j=1}^{n} \exp(\kappa_R \cdot \eta(c, p_j)) + \sum_{p' \in \mathcal{P}} \exp(\kappa_N \cdot \eta(c, p')) + \exp(\eta_N(c))$ be a normalization constant. Here, $\kappa_R \leq 1$ represents the propensity for taking a recommendation and $\kappa_N \leq 1$ represents the propensity of choosing another product directly from the catalog.

Given the normalization constant α, the probability of a customer purchasing a product is $\exp(\eta(c, p)) / \alpha$, the probability of taking recommendation p_j is $\exp(\kappa_R \cdot \eta(c, p_j)) / \alpha$, the probability of using the menu to choose another product p' is $\exp(\kappa_N \cdot \eta(c, p')) / \alpha$, and finally the probability of abandoning the session is $\exp(\eta_N(c)) / \alpha$. The rewards in the MDP model are 1 when a purchase is made and 0 otherwise. This essentially assumes that the margins are constant, but the model could be easily extended to weighted margins.

Note that the states in the MDP above describe both the product and customer segment. While such an MDP can be solved the policy cannot be implemented because the customer segment is not observed. This problem could also be solved using POMDP techniques; however, as suggested in the Introduction, the final solution would be hard to interpret and also difficult to implement in a real-time setting. Instead, we seek to find good *interpretable* policies.

Perhaps the simplest interpretable policy in the product recommendation setting is the so-called product-to-product recommendation. In this setting, recommendations are static and are solely a function of the currently viewed product. The simplicity of this method makes it popular in practice and is a good fit with our model of interpretable policies. It can be readily seen that the set of policies can be constrained to product-to-product policies by defining observations as $\mathcal{O} = \mathcal{P}$ and $\theta_{(c,p)} = p$, i.e., the action is independent of the customer.

6.2 Simulation Results

The goal of the empirical evaluation is to determine the possible benefit from using interpretable policies in making product recommendation as compared with more traditional product-to-product recommendations.

We compare three methods: *Static*, *Iterated*, *IMDP*. The *static* method is the simplest one and entails simply making the recommendation that is most likely to be appreciated by types of people looking at the current product. These standard methods—as described in the introduction—reflect how recommendations for other products can impact the distribution of customers considering the current product. The *iterated* method expands on this idea by re-optimizing the recommendations three times (i.e., implementing static recommendations using simulation, recomputing customer distributions, and repeating three times). The *IMDP* method uses the MILP formulation to compute an interpretable policy for the MDP described above. As solvers for MILP can be quite computationally expensive, we apply two versions of *IMDP*: Methods *IMDP(3)* and *IMDP(50)* represent results after 3 and 50 minutes of computation using CPLEX on an AMD Phenom II X6 machine.

To determine the improvement, we compare these product recommendation methods on several randomly generated scenarios, each of which is restricted to 25 randomly selected products and a single product recommendation. To make the results comparable across scenarios, we normalize them using lower (baseline) and upper bounds on the conversion rate. Our baseline is a policy that makes no recommendations, and the upper bound is a clairvoyant policy. The clairvoyant assumes that the precise customer types are known, solves the MDP, and implements that policy.

Table 1 depicts the normalized experimental results. The percentages are computed as follows. Let l be the conversion rate of the baseline policy, u be the conversion rate of the clairvoyant policy, and q be the conversion rate of the tested policy. Then the improvement is computed as: $(q - l)/(u - l)$. Fig. 3 depicts the average improvement over 50 runs of the three methods.

#	Static	Iterated	IMDP(3)	IMDP(50)
1	56.8%	56.8%	**72.9%**	**72.9%**
2	19.8%	10.0%	43.9%	**45.9%**
3	24.2%	16.2%	54.3%	**55.2%**
4	31.6%	25.0%	65.9%	**66.2%**
5	17.0%	17.8%	54.0%	**54.2%**
6	44.5%	44.5%	**75.2%**	**75.2%**
7	32.7%	39.7%	73.1%	**73.2%**
8	**66.7%**	**66.7%**	55.8%	57.3%
9	25.0%	25.0%	62.9%	**63.0%**
10	19.4%	16.0%	53.2%	**53.6%**

Table 1: Percentage of improvement in conversion rate over no recommendation compared with clairvoyant policy for 10 problem instances.

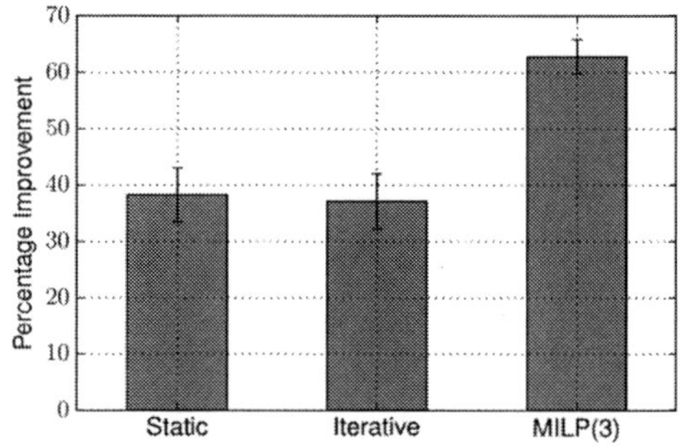

Figure 3: Average percentage improvement in conversion rate with 95% confidence interval.

There are several interesting observations that can be inferred from our results. First, IMDP significantly outperforms the standard recommendation techniques. At least in our scenario, considering the affected distribution of customers appears to be very important. Second, surprisingly, iterating the recommendations often not only does not increase the conversion rates, but actually decreases them (i.e., the *Static* method sometimes outperforms the *Iterated* method). Finally, while 3 minutes are not enough to compute an optimal MILP solution, our results indicate that the interpretable policy achieves over 50% of the benefit of a clairvoyant policy while being much simpler.

We also investigated recommending more than a single product. Unfortunately, the number of integer variables in our formulation scales exponentially with the number of products. It can be readily seen, however, that the action constraints can be decomposed in a manner that is similar to the discussion in Remark 4.4. This reduces the number of variables to be linear in the number of products, but our empirical results indicate that this approach does not significantly reduce the computation time. Regardless, our experiments with a single recommendation already demonstrate the usefulness of our notion of interpretability.

7 Concluding Remarks

In this paper, we have derived and implemented a novel framework for making dynamic product recommendations. The key insight is that modeling customer states is often quite challenging due to lack of knowledge about the customer, but that underlying dynamics (i.e., customers changing their state) can still be accounted for by using a concept of interpretability. Namely, recommendations are restricted to being identical for customers that are in the same observation, where each observation is a union of customer states that are not observable. Restricting the recommendations in this manner makes the recommendation policy interpretable (i.e., not complex and easily understandable). We use tools from Mixed Integer Nonlinear Programming in conjunction with a relaxation using McCormick inequalities to learn interpretable policies, but there are other directions not pursued in this work, such as combining a semidefinite programming (SDP) relaxation with Reformulation Linearization Technique (RLT) inequalities (which generalize McCormick inequalities) used to tighten (rather than relax) the SDP relaxation.

As noted above, regarding scalability, there is much room for improvement since the number of binary variables in our MILP formulation grows exponentially with the number of products recommended (i.e., the dimension of the actions). Aside from the decomposition described above, a different direction is a heuristic that fixes all but one of the recommendation action dimensions and iteratively optimizes over individual recommendations. This alternating minimization scheme has efficient iterations (which we have already demonstrated with our single product recommendations above), so performance depends on the number of iterations required for a good solution.

Note also that uncertainty in the model parameters, rewards and transition matrices, have an important impact on policy performance. While we have not addressed such uncertainty here, it is an important topic for future work. Finally, there are several dynamics to the model that we have not yet addressed. For example, reviews written by customers and product ratings affect the distribution of customers looking at products.

References

[1] E. Altman. *Constrained Markov Decision Processes.* 1998.

[2] C. Amato, D. S. Bernstein, and S. Zilberstein. Optimizing fixed-size stochastic controllers for POMDPs and decentralized POMDPs. *Autonomous Agents and Multi-Agent Systems*, 21(3):293–320, 2009.

[3] D. P. Bertsekas and D. A. Castanon. Adaptive aggregation methods for infinite horizon dynamic programming. *IEEE Transations on Automatic Control*, 34(6):589–598, 1989.

[4] E. A. Feinberg and U. G. Rothblum. Splitting Randomized Stationary Policies in Total-Reward Markov Decision Processes. *Mathematics of Operations Research*, 37(1):129–153, 2012.

[5] J. Hannon, M. Bennett, and B. Smyth. Publisher Recommending Twitter Users to Follow using Content and Collaborative Filtering Approaches. In *ACM Conference on Recommender Systems*, 2010.

[6] L.-p. Hung. A personalized recommendation system based on product taxonomy for one-to-one marketing online. *Expert Systems with Applications*, 29(2):383–392, 2005.

[7] P. Kazienko and M. Adamski. AdROSA: Adaptive personalization of web advertising. *Information Sciences*, 177(11):2269–2295, June 2007.

[8] D. Konopnicki, D. Shmueli-Scheuer, M. Cohen, B. Sznajder, J. Herzig, A. Raviv, N. Zwerling, H. Roitman, and Y. Mass. A statistical approach to mining customers' conversational data from social media. *IBM Journal of Research and Development*, 57(3/4):14:1 - 14:13, 2013.

[9] A. Kumar and S. Zilberstein. History-Based Controller Design and Optimization for Partially Observable MDPs. In *International Conference on Automated Planning and Scheduling (ICAPS)*, pages 156–164, 2015.

[10] T. J. Lambert, M. A. Epelman, and R. L. Smith. Aggregation in Stochastic Dynamic Programming. Technical report, University of Michigan, 2004.

[11] B. Letham, C. Rudin, T. H. Mccormick, and D. Madigan. An Interpretable Stroke Prediction Model Using Rules and Bayesian Analysis. (609):65–67, 2010.

[12] B. Letham, C. Rudin, T. H. McCormick, and D. Madigan. Interpretable classifiers using rules and Bayesian analysis: Building a better stroke prediction model. *The Annals of Applied Statistics*, 9(3):1350–1371, 2013.

[13] J. Linderoth. A simplicial branch-and-bound algorithm for solving quadratically constrained quadratic programs. *Mathematical Programming, Series B*, 103(2):251–282, 2005.

[14] M. Littman. Memoryless policies: Theoretical limitations and practical results. In *International Conference on Simulation of Adaptive Behavior*, 1994.

[15] X. Liu and K. Aberer. SoCo: a social network aided context-aware recommender system. *Proceedings of the World Wide Web Conference*, pages 781–791, 2013.

[16] H. Ma, D. Zhou, C. Liu, M. Lyu, and I. King. Recommender systems with social regularization, 2011.

[17] F. Maes, R. Fonteneau, L. Wehenkel, and D. Ernst. Policy Search in a Space of Simple Closed-form Formulas: Towards Interpretability of Reinforcement Learning. *Discovery Science*, 7569(1):37–51, 2012.

[18] D. M. Malioutov and K. R. Varshney. Exact rule learning via Boolean compressed sensing. In *International Conference on Machine Learning (ICML)*, pages 1802–1810, 2013.

[19] R. Mendelssohn. An iterative aggregation procedure for Markov decision processes. *Operations Research*, 30(1):62–73, 1982.

[20] V. Metsis, I. Androutsopoulos, and G. Paliouras. Spam filtering with naive Bayes - which naive Bayes? In *Third Conference on Email and Anti-Spam*, 2006.

[21] R. J. Mooney and L. Roy. Content-based book recommending using learning for text categorization. In *ACM conference on Digital libraries*, pages 195–204, 2000.

[22] M. L. Puterman. *Markov decision processes: Discrete stochastic dynamic programming*. John Wiley & Sons, Inc., 2005.

[23] S. Rendle, C. Freudenthaler, and L. Schmidt-Thieme. Factorizing personalized Markov chains for next-basket recommendation. In *International conference on World wide web (WWW)*, pages 811–820, 2010.

[24] F. Ricci, L. Rokach, and B. Shapira. *Recommender Systems Handbook*. Springer US, Boston, MA, 2011.

[25] D. F. Rogers, R. D. Plante, R. T. Wong, and J. R. Evans. Aggregation and disaggregation techniques and methodology in optimization. *Operations Research*, 39(4):553–582, 1991.

[26] C. Rudin. Algorithms for interpretable machine learning. In *International Conference on Knowledge Discovery and Data Mining (KDD)*, page 1519. ACM, 2014.

[27] N. Sahoo. A Hidden Markov Model for Collaborative Filtering A Hidden Markov Model for Collaborative Filtering. *MIS Quarterly*, 36(4):1329–1356, 2012.

[28] P. J. Schweitzer, M. L. Puterman, and K. W. Kindle. Iterative Aggregation-Disaggregation Procedures for Discounted Semi-Markov Reward Processes. *Operations Research*, 33(3):589–606, 1985.

[29] Y. Serin and V. Kulkarni. Implementable policies: discounted cost case. In *Computations with Markov Chains*, pages 283–306. 1995.

[30] P. V. Singh. Seeking Variety : A Dynamic Model of Employee Blog Reading Behavior. 2010.

[31] K. E. Train. *Discrete Choice Methods with Simulation*. 2003.

[32] S. Velusamy, L. Gopal, S. Bhatnagar, and S. Varadarajan. An efficient ad recommendation system for TV programs. *Multimedia Systems*, 14(2):73–87, 2008.

[33] P. Viappiani and C. Boutilier. Recommendation Sets and Choice Queries: There Is No Exploration/Exploitation Tradeoff! In *National Conference on Artificial Intelligence (AAAI)*, 2011.

[34] N. Vlassis, M. Littman, and D. Barber. On the computational complexity of stochastic controller optimization in POMDPs. *ACM Transactions on Computation Theory*, V(212):1–7, 2012.

Merging Strategies for Sum-Product Networks: From Trees to Graphs

Tahrima Rahman and **Vibhav Gogate**
Department of Computer Science
The University of Texas at Dallas
Richardson, TX 75080, USA.
{tahrima.rahman,vibhav.gogate}@utdallas.edu

Abstract

Learning the structure of sum-product networks (SPNs) – arithmetic circuits over latent and observed variables – has been the subject of much recent research. These networks admit linear time exact inference, and thus help alleviate one of the chief disadvantages of probabilistic graphical models: accurate probabilistic inference algorithms are often computationally expensive. Although, algorithms for inducing their structure from data have come quite far and often outperform algorithms that induce probabilistic graphical models, a key issue with existing approaches is that they induce tree SPNs, a small, inefficient sub-class of SPNs. In this paper, we address this limitation by developing post-processing approaches that induce graph SPNs from tree SPNs by merging similar sub-structures. The key benefits of graph SPNs over tree SPNs include smaller computational complexity which facilitates faster online inference, and better generalization accuracy because of reduced variance, at the cost of slight increase in the learning time. We demonstrate experimentally that our merging techniques significantly improve the accuracy of tree SPNs, achieving state-of-the-art performance on several real world benchmark datasets.

1 INTRODUCTION

Probabilistic graphical models [8, 17] such as Bayesian and Markov networks are routinely used in a wide variety of application domains such as computer vision and natural language understanding for modeling and reasoning about uncertainty. However, exact inference in them – the task of answering queries given a model – is NP-hard in general and computationally intractable for most real-world models. As a result, approximate inference algorithms such as loopy belief propagation and Gibbs sampling are widely used in practice. However, they can often yield highly inaccurate and high variance estimates, leading to poor predictive performance.

One approach to tackle the inaccuracy and unreliability of approximate inference is to learn so-called tractable models from data. Examples of such models include thin junction trees [2], arithmetic circuits (ACs) [7], cutset networks [25], probabilistic sentential decision diagrams [16], AND/OR decision diagrams [9, 21] and sum-product networks [23]. Inference in these models is polynomial (often linear) in the size of the model and therefore the complexity and accuracy of inference is no longer an issue. In other words, once an accurate model is learned from data, predictions are guaranteed to be accurate.

In this paper, we focus on the NP-hard problem of learning both the structure and parameters of sum-product networks (SPNs) from data. At a high level, an SPN is a rooted directed acyclic graph that represents a joint probability distribution over a large number of random variables, both observed and latent. It has two types of internal nodes: sum-nodes which express conditioning or splitting over latent or observed variables and product nodes which represent decomposition of variables into independent components. Leaf nodes represent simple distributions over observed variables (e.g., uniform distribution, univariate distributions, etc.). The key advantage of SPNs and other equivalent representations such as ACs [1] over thin-junction trees is that they can be much compact and never larger than the latter. This is because they take advantage of various fine-grained structural properties such as determinism, context-specific independence, dynamic variable orderings and caching (cf. [7, 9, 4, 13]). For instance, in some cases, they can represent high-treewidth junction trees using only a handful of sum and product nodes [23].

The literature abounds with algorithms for learning the structure of SPNs and ACs from data, starting with the

[1]The equivalence between ACs and SPNs was shown by Rooshenas and Lowd [26]. Thus, algorithms for learning ACs can be used to learn SPNs and vice versa.

work of Lowd and Domingos [19] who proposed to learn ACs over observed variables by using the AC size as a learning (inductive) bias within a Bayesian network structure learning algorithm, and then compiling the induced Bayesian network to an AC. Later Lowd and Rooshenas [20] extended this algorithm to learn a Markov network having small AC size. The latter performs much better in terms of test set log likelihood score than the former because of the increased flexibility afforded by the undirected Markov network structure.

A limitation of the two aforementioned approaches for learning ACs is that they do not use latent variables; it turns out that their accuracy can be greatly improved using latent variables. Unfortunately, the parameter learning problem (a sub-step in structure learning) – the problem of learning the weights or probabilities of a given SPN structure – is much harder in presence of latent variables. In particular, the optimization problem is non-convex, which necessitates the use of algorithms such as gradient descent and expectation maximization that only converge to a local minima. However, since learning is often an offline process, this increase in complexity is often not a big issue.

The first approach for learning the structure of SPNs having both latent and observed variables is due to Gens and Domingos [11]. An issue with this approach is that it learns only directed trees instead of (directed acyclic) graphs and as a result is unable to fully exploit the power and flexibility of SPNs. To address this limitation, Rahman et al. [25], Vergari et al. [28] and Rooshenas and Lowd [26] proposed to learn a graph SPN over observed variables while Dennis and Ventura [10] proposed to learn a graph SPN over latent variables. A drawback of these approaches is that they are unable to learn a graph SPN over both observed and latent variables. In this paper, we address this limitation.

The main idea in our approach is as follows. We first learn a tree SPN over latent and observed nodes using standard algorithms, and then convert the tree SPN to a graph SPN by processing the SPN in a bottom-up fashion, merging two sub-SPNs if the distributions represented by them are similar and defined over the same variables. To convert this idea into a general-purpose algorithm, we have to solve two problems: (1) how to find similar sub-SPNs, and (2) how to merge them into one sub-SPN. Both problems are computationally expensive to solve and therefore we develop approximate algorithms for solving them, which is the main contribution of this paper.

The second contribution of this paper is a thorough experimental evaluation of our proposed merging algorithms on 20 benchmark datasets, all of which were used in several previous studies. Our experiments clearly show that merging always improves the performance of tree SPNs, measured in terms of test-set log-likelihood score and prediction time. We also experimentally compared bagged ensembles of graph SPNs with state-of-the-art approaches such as ensembles of cutset networks [24], sum-product networks with direct and indirect interactions [26], sum-product networks learned via the SVD-based approach[1], arithmetic circuits with Markov networks [20], and mixtures of cutset networks [25] on the same datasets, and found that our new approach yields better test-set log likelihood score on 8 out of the 20 datasets with two ties. This clearly demonstrates the power of our new merging algorithms.

The rest of the paper is organized as follows. In the next section, we present background on SPNs, related work as well as a generic algorithm for learning tree SPNs. Section 3 describes powerful merging approaches for converting an arbitrary tree SPN to a graph SPN. Experimental results are presented in section 4 and we conclude in section 5.

2 BACKGROUND

Any (discrete) probability distribution over a set of variables $\mathbf{V}$ can be expressed using an arithmetic circuit (AC) [7] or a sum-product network (SPN) [23].[2] The key benefit of SPNs over conventional uncertainty representations such as Bayesian and Markov networks is that in SPNs, common probabilistic inference tasks such as maximum-a-posteriori (MAP) and posterior marginal (MAR) estimation can be solved in time and space that scales linearly with the size of the representation. In Bayesian and Markov networks, these tasks are known to be NP-hard in general (cf. [27]). The caveat is that SPNs can be exponentially larger than Bayesian and Markov networks; they are often compiled from the latter by running exact probabilistic inference techniques such as variable elimination [4] and AND/OR search [21], in order to facilitate faster online inference. Formally,

Definition 1. An SPN [23] is recursively defined as follows:

1. A tractable univariate distribution is an SPN;
2. A product of SPNs defined over different variables is an SPN; and
3. A weighted sum of SPNs with the same scope variables is an SPN.

An SPN can be expressed as a rooted directed acyclic graph with univariate distributions as leaves, sums and products as internal nodes, and the edges from a sum node to its

[2]SPNs used in this paper are equivalent to ACs (as well as AND/OR decision diagrams [21]) defined over latent and observed variables. However, in order to be consistent, we will use the term SPNs throughout the paper. We will distinguish between two types of SPNs: SPNs defined over only observed variables and SPNs defined over both observed and latent variables.

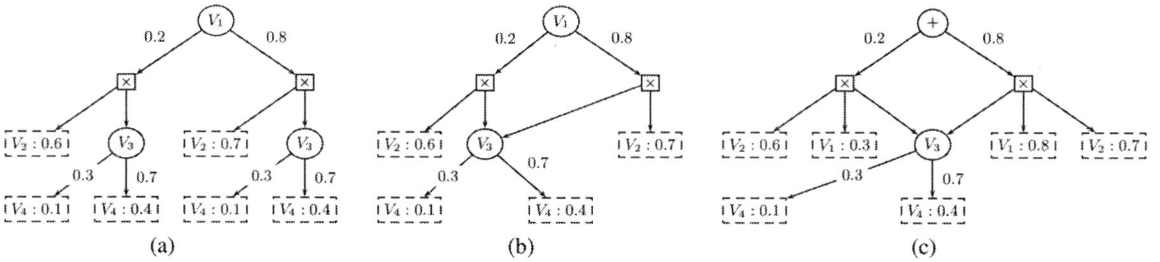

Figure 1: Three example SPNs over variables $\{V_1, V_2, V_3, V_4\}$. We are assuming that all variables are binary and take values from the domain $\{0, 1\}$. Leaf nodes express univariate distributions. For example, the node $V_2 : 0.6$ expresses the probability distribution $P(V_2 = 1) = 0.6$. Sum nodes are labeled either by a variable which denotes conditioning over the variable or by a $+$ sign which denotes that the sum node is latent. All left (right) arcs emanating from a sum node correspond to an assignment of 1 (0) to the labeled variable. Product nodes are labeled by $\times$. (a) Tree SPN (SPN which is a rooted directed acyclic tree) that decomposes according to a tree Markov network $V_4 - V_3 - V_1 - V_2$. (b) Graph SPN that is equivalent to the tree SPN given in (a) obtained by merging identical sub-trees. (c) Graph SPN over latent and observed variables.

children labeled with the corresponding weights. An SPN represents a (normalized) probability distribution when the weights attached to each sum node sum to one. Any unnormalized SPN can be normalized in linear time.

As mentioned earlier, we will distinguish between two types of SPNs: SPNs defined only over observed variables and SPNs defined over both latent and observed variables. The two have different representation powers with the latter being more general and therefore more powerful than the former. For SPNs having only observed variables, each sum node represents a split (conditioning) over a variable and is therefore labeled by the corresponding variable. For SPNs having both latent and observed variables, each sum node can represent either a split over an observed or a latent variable. The splits over the observed variables are represented the usual way while sum nodes that split over the latent variables are labeled by the "+" sign.

Example 2.1. Fig. 1 shows three SPNs over four variables $\{V_1, V_2, V_3, V_4\}$. The two SPNs on the left are defined over only observed variables while the SPN on the right is defined over both latent and observed variables. The graph SPN shown in Fig. 1(b) is obtained from the tree SPN shown in Fig. 1(a) by merging identical sub-SPNs.

2.1 LEARNING SPNs

In this paper, we focus on top-down approaches that directly learn the structure of SPNs from data. Instead of learning Bayesian and Markov networks and then compiling them into SPNs (this is the approach used in [19, 20]), the key advantage of this direct approach is that the size of the SPN can be controlled in a straight-forward manner, which is typically bounded from above by the data size.

Algorithm 1 shows a generic recursive learning algorithm for learning tree SPNs from data, which is loosely based on the algorithm proposed by Gens and Domingos [11]. The algorithm has three steps: base case, decomposition and splitting. In the base case, if the conditions for learning the base model are satisfied, for example, when the size of the training data is small or only one variable remains, then the algorithm learns the corresponding trivial distribution and terminates the recursion. In the decomposition step, the algorithm tries to partition the variables into roughly independent components $\mathbf{V_j} \subseteq \mathbf{V}$ such that $P(\mathbf{V}) = \prod_j P(\mathbf{V_j})$ and recurses on each component, inducing a product node. If neither the base case nor the conditions for the decomposition step are satisfied, then the algorithm partitions the training instances into clusters of multiple instances, inducing a sum node, and recurses on each part.

Algorithm 1: LEARNSPN(**T**,**V**)

Input: Set of Training Instances **T** and set of variables **V**
Output: An SPN representing a distribution over **V**
begin
```
// 1.  Base Case
```
  if *conditions for inducing the base models are satisfied*
    then return LEARNBASEMODEL(**T**,**V**)
```
// 2.  Decomposition Step
```
  if V *can be partitioned into subsets* $\mathbf{V_j}$
    then return $\prod_j$ LEARNSPN(**T**,$\mathbf{V_j}$)
```
// 3.  Splitting Step
```
  Partition **T** into subsets of similar instances $\mathbf{T_i}$
  return $\sum_i \frac{|\mathbf{T_i}|}{|\mathbf{T}|}$ LEARNSPN($\mathbf{T_i}$,**V**)
end

Several techniques proposed in literature for learning SPNs (and equivalently ACs) can be understood as special cases of Algorithm 1, with the difference between them being the approaches used at the three steps. Table 1 gives examples

Reference	Base Case	Decomposition	Splitting
Gens and Domingos [11]	Univariate distribution	Independence tests	Latent Variables
Gogate et al. [15]	Univariate distribution	Independence assumption	Conjunctive fixed-length features
Cutset networks (CNets)[25]	Tree Markov networks	not used	Observed variables
Ensembles of CNets[24]	Tree Markov networks	not used	Observed and Latent variables
Vergari et al. [28]	Tree Markov networks	Independence tests	Latent Variables
Rooshenas and Lowd [26]	Tractable Arithmetic Circuits	Independence tests	Latent variables

Table 1: Examples of SPN structure learning approaches in the literature that follow the prescription given in Algorithm 1. Base case is the stopping criteria for the recursive algorithm. [11, 15] stop when only one variable remains and induce a univariate distribution; [25, 28, 24] stop when the entropy of the data is small or use a Bayesian criteria, and induce an SPN corresponding to a tree Markov network at the leaves using the Chow-Liu algorithm [5] (this algorithm runs in polynomial time and yields an optimal tree Markov network according to the maximum likelihood criteria). [26] learns an SPN over observed variables in the base case using the algorithm described in [19]. In the decomposition step, [11, 26, 28] use pair-wise variable independence tests (e.g., the G-test) for inducing the product nodes; [15] uses no independence tests and instead assume that each split decomposes the variables into multiple components; while [25, 24] ignore the decomposition step inducing only sum nodes. [11, 26, 28] split only over latent variables, [15, 25] split only over observed variables or their features, while [24] split over both latent and observed variables.

of techniques from the SPN literature that are based on Algorithm 1 and briefly describes how they differ.

Although, the structure learning problem is NP-hard in SPNs having only observed variables as well as in SPNs having both observed and latent variables, the parameter (weight) learning problem is easier in the former than the latter. In particular, parameter learning can be done in closed form when the SPN has only observed variables. On the other hand, the optimization problem is non-convex in the presence of latent variables and one has to use iterative algorithms having high computational complexity such as hard and soft EM to solve the non-convex problem (cf. [23, 22, 24]). Thus, although latent variables help yield a more powerful representation, they often significantly increase the learning time.

3 CONVERTING TREE SPNs TO GRAPH SPNs

A key problem with existing methods for learning SPNs is that they induce tree models, except at the leaves. It is well known in the probabilistic inference literature [9, 7, 6] that tree SPNs can be exponentially larger than graph SPNs, which are obtained from the former by merging identical sub-SPNs (see Fig.1(a) and (b)). Thus, converting tree SPNs to graph SPNs is a good idea because they can significantly improve the time required to make predictions.

From a learning point of view, graph SPNs can potentially improve the generalization performance by addressing the following issue associated with the LEARNSPN algorithm: as the depth of the node increases,[3] the number of training examples available for learning a sub-SPN rooted at the node decreases exponentially. Merging increases the number of examples available at a node, since examples from all directed paths from the root to the node can be combined. This reduces the variance of the parameter estimates while having no effect on their bias. Since the mean-squared error of the model equals bias squared plus the variance, graph SPNs are likely to be more accurate than tree SPNs. The following proposition formalizes this intuition:

Proposition 1. Let S_1, S_2 and $S_{1,2}$ be three (sub-)SPNs having the same structure and defined over the same variables but whose parameters are estimated from training examples T_1, T_2 and $T_{1,2} = T_1 \cup T_2$ respectively. Then assuming that the datasets are generated uniformly at random from a distribution whose structure decomposes according to S_1 (and thus S_2 and $S_{1,2}$), the sample variance of $S_{1,2}$ is smaller than S_1 and S_2.

Proof. The sample variance of S_1, S_2 and $S_{1,2}$ is given by $Var(S_1)/|T_1|$, $Var(S_2)/|T_2|$ and $Var(S_{1,2})/|T_1 \cup T_2|$ respectively where $Var(S_1)$, $Var(S_2)$ and $Var(S_{1,2})$ is the (population) variance of the distributions induced by S_1, S_2 and $S_{1,2}$. Since $Var(S_1) = Var(S_2) = Var(S_{1,2})$ (our assumption), $|T_1 \cup T_2| \geq |T_1|$ and $|T_1 \cup T_2| \geq |T_2|$, the proof follows. □

3.1 OUR APPROACH

The main idea in our approach is to relax the identical sub-SPN requirement and merge *similar* sub-SPNs. We use this relaxation because the sub-SPNs are estimated from data and the likelihood that they will be identical is slim to none. In this context, we develop methods for answering the following two questions: which sub-SPNs to merge and how to merge them.

[3] The depth of a node equals the number of sum nodes from the root to the node.

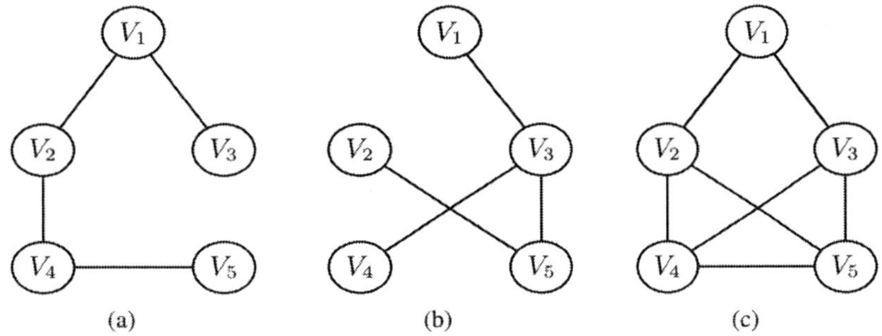

Figure 2: Figure demonstrating why distance computations are hard. (a) and (b): Two tree Markov networks over five variables $\{V_1, \dots, V_5\}$. The treewidth of these networks is 1 and therefore the complexity of performing inference over them is $O(d^2)$ where d is the number of values in the domain of each variable. (c): Markov network obtained by taking the union of the edges of the tree Markov networks given in (a) and (b). Computing the distance (e.g., KL divergence) between the probability distributions represented by the two Markov networks in (a) and (b) is exponential in the treewidth of the Markov network given in (c). The treewidth of this network is 3 and therefore the complexity of computing the distance is $O(d^4)$, an exponential increase over $O(d^2)$.

One approach for selecting candidate sub-SPNs for merging is to compare the distance between the distributions represented by the two sub-SPNs, given that they are defined over the same variables, and check if the distance is smaller than a threshold. However, computing the distance between two sub-SPNs can be quite hard. For instance, assume that the two sub-SPNs represent Markov networks (MNs) and the junction tree or AND/OR graph search algorithm [9] is used for computing the KL divergence between the probability distributions represented by the two MNs. In this case, the time and space complexity of computation is exponential in the treewidth of the graph obtained by taking a union of the edges of the two MNs. The treewidth of this graph can be quite large (see Fig. 2 for an example). Therefore, we propose to use the following mean-field style approximation [29] of the distance between the two distributions:

$$D(P||Q) \approx \frac{1}{|\mathbf{V}|} \sum_{V_i \in \mathbf{V}} D(P(V_i)||Q(V_i))$$

where P and Q are two distributions over $\mathbf{V}$ and D is a distance function (e.g., KL divergence, relative error, Hellinger distance, etc.). Since single-variable marginal distributions in each sub-SPN can be computed in time that is linear in the number of nodes of the sub-SPN (and in practice can be pre-computed), our proposed distance method is also linear time.

Next, we describe our greedy, bottom-up approach for merging similar sub-SPNs of a given SPN S (see Algorithm 2). The algorithm begins by initializing S' to S and repeats the following steps until convergence. For all sub-SPNs S_i of S' that are defined over exactly i variables, it partitions the sub-SPNs based on their scopes such that all sub-SPNs having the same scope are in the same cell (part) ρ_j of the partition ρ. Then, in each cell ρ_j, ensuring that S' remains a DAG, it merges all sub-SPNs such that the distance between them is bounded by ϵ, a user-defined constant that can be set using a validation set. Another option is to merge two sub-SPNs if the accuracy on the validation set improves, thereby using a greedy strategy (in our experiments, we used both strategies). Note that the for-loop of the algorithm operates in a bottom-up fashion similar to reduced-error pruning in decision trees. The loop starts at the leaves, which are sub-SPNs having just one variable in their scope ($i = 1$), and then proceeds towards the root which includes all variables in its scope ($i = |\mathbf{V}|$). The algorithm is guaranteed to converge in finite number of iterations because at each iteration, the size of the SPN can only decrease or remain the same.

Algorithm 2: MERGE(S,$\mathbf{V}$,ϵ)

Input: SPN S
Output: Merged SPN S'
begin
  $S' = S$
  repeat
    for $i = 1$ *to* $|\mathbf{V}|$ **do**
      S_i = sub-SPNs in S' having exactly i variables in their scope
      ρ = Partition S_i into cells having identical scopes
      for *each cell* ρ_j *of* ρ **do**
        Merge all sub-SPNs in ρ_j such that the distance between them is bounded by ϵ and S' is a DAG
      end
    end
  until *convergence*;
  return S'
end

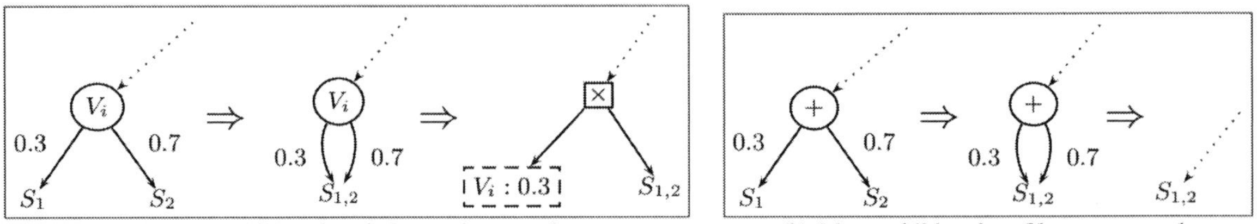

(a) Merge child nodes of observed sum node

(b) Merge child nodes of latent sum node

Figure 3: Figure demonstrating how to simplify and thus reduce the size of the SPN after merging. As before, sum nodes are labeled either by a variable which denotes conditioning over the variable or by a $+$ sign which denotes that the sum node is latent. All left (right) arcs emanating from a sum node correspond to an assignment of 1 (0) to the labeled variable. Product nodes are labeled by $\times$. $S_{1,2}$ is an SPN obtained by merging SPNs S_1 and S_2. (a): shows how the SPN can be reduced when the two child nodes of an observed sum node are merged. The node $V_i : 0.3$ represents a univariate probability distribution over V_i with $P(V_i = 1) = 0.3$. (b): shows how the SPN can be reduced when the two child nodes of a latent sum node are merged.

3.2 PRACTICAL MERGING STRATEGIES

We complete the description of the algorithm by describing how to merge two similar sub-SPNs S_1 and S_2. A straightforward method is to merge the datasets at the two sub-SPNs and then learn a new graph sub-SPN, say $S_{1,2}$ from the new dataset. An issue with this approach is that since our basic algorithm (see Algorithm 1) learns tree SPNs, we have to call Algorithm 2 again to convert the newly created tree SPN to a graph SPN. This may yield a self-recursive algorithm with infinite loops that may not terminate. To overcome this computational difficulty, we propose to not relearn the structure, but only update the weights. In particular, we use the following approach. We consider two candidate structures for the merged sub-SPN; the first structure is identical to S_1 and the second to S_2. Then, we learn the weights of the two candidate sub-SPNs using the merged dataset and choose the one that yields the maximum improvement in accuracy (log-likelihood score) over the validation set.

There are two types of merging that require special attention. The first type is when the two sub-SPNs are children of the same sum node. In this case, if the sum node corresponds to splitting over an observed variable, we can replace the sum-node by a product node having two children as depicted in Fig. 3(a). On the other hand, if the sum node is a latent node then the sum node can be deleted without changing the underlying distribution. This is depicted in Fig. 3(b). This type of merging is useful because it substantially simplifies the model, allowing us to either prune sub-SPNs (see Fig. 3(b)) or take advantage of problem decomposition (see Fig. 3(a)). This yields better generalization and faster inference.

A second type of merging that requires special attention is when the two sub-SPNs to be merged correspond to tree Markov (or Bayesian) networks over the observed variables. In this case, unlike in the general case, we propose to learn both the structure and parameters of the merged sub-SPN (using the merged dataset). This is because both the structure and parameter learning problem in such SPNs can be solved in polynomial time using the Chow-Liu algorithm [5].

4 EXPERIMENTS

4.1 SETUP

We evaluated the impact of merging SPNs on 20 real world benchmark datasets presented in Table 3. These datasets have been used in numerous previous studies for evaluating the performance of a wide variety of tractable probabilistic graphical model learners (cf. [18, 11, 26, 25, 1, 24]). All datasets are defined over binary variables that take values from the set $\{0, 1\}$. The number of the variables in them range from 16 to 1556 and the number of training instances range from 1600 to 291326. All of our experiments were performed on a quad-core Intel i7 2.7 GHz machines with 16 GB RAM. Each algorithm was given a time bound of 48 hours, after which the algorithm was terminated.

4.2 ALGORITHMS EVALUATED

We implemented two variants of SPNs: SPNs in which sum nodes split over value assignments to a latent variable and SPNs in which sum nodes split over value assignments to a heuristically chosen observed variable. Henceforth we will call the two SPNs `L-SPNs` and `O-SPNs` respectively. We learned tree versions of both SPNs using Algorithm 1. We used tree Markov networks (MNs) as base models in both SPNs; as mentioned earlier tree MNs can be learned in polynomial time using the Chow-Liu algorithm.

To learn sum nodes in `L-SPNs`, following Gens and Domingos [11], we employed hard EM over a naive Bayes mixture model with three random restarts for 15 iterations to split the training instances into two clusters, i.e. we only considered binary splits for latent sum nodes for better reg-

Table 2: Table showing the impact of merging on the average test-set log likelihood, time complexity and prediction time of L-SPNs and O-SPNs (all values rounded to two decimal places). We use the following notation: (1) T-LL: Average test-set log likelihood for the tree SPNs; (2) G-LL: average test-set log likelihood for the graph SPN obtained from the tree SPN by merging similar sub-SPNs; (3) |T|: number of parameters in the tree SPN; (4) |G|: number of parameters in the graph SPN; (5) CR:=Compression Ratio = $\frac{|T|}{|G|}$; (6) T-Time: Tree SPN learning time in seconds and (7) G-Time: Time in seconds required by the merging algorithm (thus the total learning time for graph SPNs is T-time+G-time seconds). In each row, **bold** values indicate the best score for each of the two SPN categories: L-SPN and O-SPN.

Datasets	**L-SPN**							**O-SPN**						
	T-LL	G-LL	|T|	|G|	CR	T-time	G-time	T-LL	G-LL	|T|	|G|	CR	T-time	G-time
NLTCS	-6.03	-6.04	5498	3988	1.38	5.37	396.69	-6.04	-6.05	1406	1152	1.22	0.98	4.69
MSNBC	-6.46	-6.46	2780	2440	1.14	109.38	53.49	-6.09	**-6.08**	20032	9478	2.11	6.36	1245.62
KDD	-2.14	-2.14	11516	6670	1.73	199.13	15119.05	-2.22	**-2.19**	34328	16608	2.07	91.38	59.54
Plants	-12.80	**-12.69**	65132	47802	1.36	68.44	17775.76	-13.83	**-13.49**	86530	36960	2.34	9.56	14.12
Audio	-40.11	**-40.02**	12798	10804	1.18	68.30	1995.94	-42.06	-42.06	6142	6142	1.00	10.74	3.90
Jester	-53.12	**-52.97**	12798	10002	1.28	39.09	20.89	-55.38	**-55.36**	6142	4996	1.23	6.51	2.39
Netflix	-56.71	**-56.64**	12798	11604	1.10	62.64	2287.78	-58.64	-58.64	6142	6142	1.00	19.95	2.35
Accidents	-30.09	**-30.01**	14206	13322	1.07	58.23	2089.49	-30.83	-30.83	6846	6846	1.00	14.13	3.90
Retail	-10.88	**-10.87**	3238	2162	1.50	51.15	75.25	-11.02	**-10.95**	6302	3158	2.00	32.69	15.06
Pumsb_star	-24.17	**-24.10**	19558	17604	1.11	66.05	2314.47	-24.42	**-24.34**	20222	18338	1.10	20.6	14.93
DNA	-85.90	**-85.51**	5758	4320	1.33	8.26	11.26	-90.43	**-87.49**	11262	1430	7.88	3.76	9.48
Kosarek	-10.62	-10.62	5318	5318	1.00	219.01	200.11	-11.10	**-10.98**	11902	6712	1.77	79.55	46.66
MSWeb	-9.95	**-9.90**	32926	16484	2.00	490.12	29482.04	-10.07	**-10.06**	15086	12770	1.18	209.54	21.07
Book	-34.80	**-34.76**	15998	11998	1.33	220.56	129.98	-38.60	**-37.44**	31740	11916	2.66	387.75	10.75
EachMovie	-52.07	-52.07	15998	15998	1.00	94.92	91.31	-59.99	**-58.05**	31745	19846	1.60	176.95	6.18
WebKB	-154.86	**-153.55**	26846	20134	1.33	157.89	78.64	-172.08	**-161.17**	53438	10046	5.32	287.01	249.27
Reuters-52	-84.70	**-83.90**	56894	46232	1.23	478.65	1331.38	-90.43	**-87.49**	56638	28334	2.0	485.6	428.4
20NewsGrp.	-154.35	-154.67	58238	43684	1.33	913.81	3457.07	-163.35	**-161.46**	57982	29016	2.0	827.71	705.53
BBC	-256.05	**-253.45**	33854	21160	1.60	98.55	53.93	-272.98	**-260.59**	63242	8454	7.48	163.47	142.89
Ad	-16.77	-16.77	49790	49790	1.00	244.44	155.53	-17.37	**-15.39**	62098	31070	2.00	953.70	832.40

ularization and faster learning as in [28]. To learn sum nodes in O-SPNs, we employed two heuristics proposed in our previous work [25, 24]. The first heuristic selects an observed variable that has the highest information gain. The second heuristic selects an observed variable based on the following mutual information based criteria: given a set of variables $\mathbf{V}$ and training data T, we score each variable $V_i \in \mathbf{V}$ using $Score(V_i) = \sum_{V_j \in \mathbf{V} \setminus V_i} I_T(V_i, V_j)$ where $I_T(V_i, V_j)$ is the mutual information between V_i and V_j according to T and choose a variable having the highest score. Variables having high mutual information score are likely to yield better decompositions, which in turn will likely yield small depth SPNs having high generalization accuracy.

In both L-SPNs and O-SPNs, we learn product nodes using the technique described in Gens and Domingos [11]. We first compute the mutual information graph given data (similar to the Chow-Liu algorithm). This graph is a complete weighted graph over all variables, in which each edge is weighted by the mutual information between the two corresponding variables. Then, we prune weak edges from the graph using a threshold chosen from β: $\{0.001, 0.0015, 0.01, 0.5\}$. Finally, we find connected components of the pruned graph, and recursively learn a sub-SPN over variables and data in each connected component.

We varied the depth h of SPNs from $\{4, 5, 6, 7, 10\}$.[4] We use the following stopping criteria for learning the base model (tree Markov network): stop when the number of samples n at a node is less than 10 or the maximum depth is reached. All parameters in the model were smoothed using 1-Laplace smoothing.

For each possible configuration of h and β we learned both a tree L-SPN and a tree O-SPN. In case of O-SPNs, we also varied the heuristic to choose an observed variable. The best tree SPN in each category was chosen according to the average log-likelihood score achieved on the validation set and provided as the input to the merging algorithm (see Algorithm 2). Then, we applied practical merging and simplification strategies described in section 3.2 on the

[4]Note that the overall depth of the SPN is h plus the depth of the SPN corresponding to the tree Markov network (our base model). Thus, the overall depth can be quite large (> 30 in most cases).

merged SPN and report the test set log-likelihood score of the merged model that achieved the highest log-likelihood score on validation set.[5] We used Manhattan distance to measure the distance between two candidate sub-SPNs and chose a threshold (ϵ) from $\{0.0001, 0.001, 0.01, 0.1\}$ using the validation set. Finally, after each merge we performed the following sanity/model complexity check. If the merged sub-SPN had smaller log-likelihood than a tree Markov network on the validation set, we replaced the merged sub-SPN by the latter.

4.3 IMPACT OF MERGING ON TEST LOG-LIKELIHOOD

Table 2 shows the results of our experiments for evaluating the impact of merging on the accuracy, time complexity and prediction time of `L-SPNs` and `O-SPNs`. In terms of learning time, we see that for `L-SPNs`, merging requires a significant amount of time. This is to be expected because parameter learning is computationally expensive in presence of latent variables. To update the parameters of candidate sub-SPNs, we ran hard EM with the merged dataset for 20 iterations or until convergence. For some `L-SPNs` (e.g. Plants), merging was a factor of 200 slower than learning tree models. The reason for this anomaly is that the corresponding tree `L-SPNs` have large number of latent sum nodes. On the other hand, merging is significantly faster in `O-SPNs` than `L-SPNs` because the parameters are updated in closed-form, by making only one pass over the data as well as the model.

We measure the prediction time by the number of edges attached to the sum nodes (see columns |T|, |G| and CR in Table 2) since the prediction time is linearly proportional in the number of these weights. We see that in general merging yields reductions in complexity of inference by reducing the size of the network in majority of cases.

In terms of accuracy, we see from Table 2 that merging improves the test set log-likelihood score for the majority of datasets, clearly demonstrating our intuition that it will yield better generalization, primarily because it significantly reduces the variance at the cost of slightly increasing the bias.

4.4 COMPARISON WITH STATE-OF-THE-ART

Finally, we demonstrate that we can achieve state-of-the-art performance using our merging algorithm. For this, following our previous work [24, 28], we learn bagged ensemble of tree SPNs and graph SPNs. It was shown in previous studies that bagged ensembles of tree SPNs (especially latent SPNs) achieves state-of-the-art results. In our evaluation, we wanted to see whether we would be able to match or exceed these results using bagged ensemble of graph SPNs. As a strong baseline, we also compare with five other state-of-the-art tractable model learners: (1) learning sum-product networks with direct and indirect variable interactions (ID-SPN) [26], learning Markov networks using arithmetic circuits (ACMN) [20], learning mixtures of cutset networks (MCNet) [25], learning sum-product networks via SVD based algorithm (SPN-SVD) [1] and learning ensembles of cutset networks (ECNet) [24].

In our experiments, we fixed the number of bags to 40 following [24]. Instead of performing a grid search, we performed random search [3] to create a configuration for the models in the ensemble. Each component model was then weighted according to its likelihood on the training set. To get better accuracy, we treated the bagged ensemble of `L-SPNs` and `O-SPNs` as an SPN having one latent sum node as the root and each independent component (bag) as its child sub-SPN. The benefit of this approach is that instead of optimizing the local log-likelihood scores of individual SPNs, while merging, we can directly optimize the global log-likelihood.

Table 3 shows the bagged ensemble scores of `L-SPNs` and `O-SPNs` before and after merging as well as the best log-likelihood score obtained to date using the competing approaches mentioned above. Bagged graph SPNs, especially `L-SPNs`, performed significantly better than the state-of-the-art on all of the high dimensional datasets with very competitive scores on the others. This suggests that merging is especially useful for accurately modeling relationships in high-dimensional data (see also Table 2).

5 CONCLUSION AND FUTURE WORK

In this paper, we presented a novel algorithm for learning graph SPNs from tree SPNs by merging similar sub-SPNs in the tree SPN. Our proposed algorithm for finding and merging similar sub-SPNs is general enough to serve as a template for incorporating suitable functions that measure similarity between sub-SPNs as well as for performing arbitrary mergings. Our experimental evaluation clearly shows that graph SPNs can significantly boost the accuracy and prediction time of tree SPNs by substantially reducing the number of parameters that the learning algorithm needs to induce from data. We also investigated the merit of learning ensembles of graph SPNs, building on our previous work on learning ensembles of tree SPNs, for a variety of high dimensional real world datasets, and comparing them to other state-of-the-art tractable model learners. Our experimental results showed that ensembles of graph SPNs significantly outperformed the state-of-the-art learners, clearly demonstrating the efficacy of our proposed approach.

Future work includes: developing relational merging ap-

[5]Our experiments showed that merging sub-SPNs that are rooted at child nodes of the same sum node (the cases given in Fig. 3(a) and (b)) was often more beneficial as compared to merging sub-SPNs that are child nodes of two different sum nodes.

Table 3: Average test set log-likelihood comparison with state-of-the-art tractable model learners. **Bold** values indicate the winning score for the corresponding dataset. T-LL: Bagged LL of tree SPNs and G-LL: Bagged LL of graph SPNs. Column "Best-LL to date" gives the best log-likelihood score to date for each dataset obtained using the following competing approaches: ID-SPN [26], ACMN [20], MCNet [25], SPN-SVD [1], and ECNet [24].

Datasets	|Var|	|Train|	|Valid|	|Test|	L-SPN		O-SPN		Best-LL to date
					T-LL	G-LL	T-LL	G-LL	
NLTCS	16	16181	2157	3236	-6.01	-6.00	-6.01	-6.00	-6.00
MSNBC	17	291326	38843	58265	-6.45	-6.39	-6.10	-6.10	**-6.04**
KDD	64	180092	19907	34955	-2.13	-2.12	-2.14	-2.13	-2.12
Plants	69	17412	2321	3482	-12.31	-12.03	-12.25	-12.21	**-11.99**
Audio	100	15000	2000	3000	-39.57	**-39.49**	-40.35	-40.31	-39.67
Jester	100	9000	1000	4116	-52.65	-52.47	-53.56	-53.13	**-41.11**
Netflix	100	15000	2000	3000	-55.92	**-55.84**	-56.69	-56.65	-56.13
Accidents	111	12758	1700	2551	-29.41	-29.32	-29.81	-29.82	**-24.87**
Retail	135	22041	2938	4408	-10.85	-10.82	-10.87	-10.85	**-10.60**
Pumsb_star	163	12262	1635	2452	-23.82	-23.67	-23.85	-23.81	**-22.40**
DNA	180	1600	400	1186	-86.63	-80.89	-85.97	-84.79	**-80.03**
Kosarek	190	33375	4450	6675	-10.71	-10.55	-10.85	-10.74	**-10.54**
MSWeb	294	29441	32750	5000	-9.84	-9.78	-9.77	-9.76	**-9.22**
Book	500	8700	1159	1739	-36.49	-34.25	-36.35	-35.89	**-30.18**
EachMovie	500	4524	1002	591	-54.70	**-50.72**	-55.82	-53.07	-51.14
WebKB	839	2803	558	838	-170.27	**-150.04**	-166.65	-152.82	-150.10
Reuters-52	889	6532	1028	1540	-84.32	**-80.66**	-86.00	-82.66	-82.10
20NewsGrp.	910	11293	3764	3764	-151.48	**-150.80**	-158.40	-154.28	-151.47
BBC	1058	1670	225	330	-265.89	**-233.26**	-244.12	-238.61	-236.82
Ad	1556	2461	327	491	-16.33	-14.58	-15.69	**-14.34**	-14.36

proaches that search for similarities in sub-SPNs having different (even disjoint) scopes (cf. [12, 14]); analyzing contexts – assignment to variables on the path from the root – of merged sub-SPNs for finding symmetric contexts; directly inducing graph SPNs from data rather than using post-processing schemes; and extending the approach presented in the paper to hybrid domains having both discrete and continuous variables.

Acknowledgements

This research was funded in part by the DARPA Probabilistic Programming for Advanced Machine Learning Program under AFRL prime contract number FA8750-14-C-0005 and by the NSF award 1528037. The views and conclusions contained in this document are those of the authors and should not be interpreted as representing the official policies, either expressed or implied, of DARPA, AFRL, NSF or the US government.

References

[1] T. Adel, D. Balduzzi, and A. Ghodsi. Learning the structure of sum-product networks via an svd-based algorithm. In *Proceedings of the Thirty-First Conference on Uncertainty in Artificial Intelligence*, pages 32–41, 2015.

[2] F. R. Bach and M. I. Jordan. Thin junction trees. *Advances in Neural Information Processing Systems*, 14:569–576, 2001.

[3] J. Bergstra and Y. Bengio. Random search for hyper-parameter optimization. *Journal of Machine Learning Research*, 13:281–305, 2012.

[4] M. Chavira and A. Darwiche. Compiling Bayesian networks using variable elimination. In *Proceedings of the 20th International Joint Conference on Artificial Intelligence (IJCAI)*, pages 2443–2449, 2007.

[5] C. K. Chow and C. N Liu. Approximating discrete probability distributions with dependence trees. *IEEE Transactions on Information Theory*, 14:462–467, 1968.

[6] A. Darwiche. Decomposable negation normal form. *Journal of the ACM*, 48(4):608–647, 2001.

[7] A. Darwiche. A differential approach to inference in Bayesian networks. *Journal of the ACM*, 50(3):280–305, 2003.

[8] A. Darwiche. *Modeling and reasoning with Bayesian networks*. Cambridge University Press, 2009.

[9] R. Dechter and R. Mateescu. AND/OR search spaces for graphical models. *Artificial Intelligence*, 171:73–106, 2007.

[10] A. Dennis and D. Ventura. Greedy structure search for sum-product networks. In *Proceedings of the 24th International Conference on Artificial Intelligence*, pages 932–938. AAAI Press, 2015.

[11] R. Gens and P. Domingos. Learning the structure of sum-product networks. In *Proceedings of The 30th International Conference on Machine Learning*, pages 873–880, 2013.

[12] V. Gogate and P. Domingos. Exploiting Logical Structure in Lifted Probabilistic Inference. In *AAAI 2010 Workshop on Statistical Relational Learning*, 2010.

[13] V. Gogate and P. Domingos. Formula-Based Probabilistic Inference. In *Proceedings of the Twenty-Sixth Conference on Uncertainty in Artificial Intelligence*, pages 210–219, 2010.

[14] V. Gogate and P. Domingos. Probabilistic Theorem Proving. In *Proceedings of the Twenty-Seventh Conference on Uncertainty in Artificial Intelligence*, pages 256–265. AUAI Press, 2011.

[15] V. Gogate, W. Webb, and P. Domingos. Learning efficient Markov networks. In *Proceedings of the 24th conference on Neural Information Processing Systems*, pages 748–756, 2010.

[16] D. Kisa, G. Van den Broeck, A. Choi, and A. Darwiche. Probabilistic sentential decision diagrams. In *Proceedings of the 14th International Conference on Principles of Knowledge Representation and Reasoning*, 2014.

[17] D. Koller and N. Friedman. *Probabilistic Graphical Models: Principles and Techniques*. MIT Press, Cambridge, MA, 2009.

[18] D. Lowd and J. Davis. Learning Markov network structure with decision trees. In *Proceedings of the 10th International Conference on Data Mining*, pages 334–343, 2010.

[19] D. Lowd and P. Domingos. Learning arithmetic circuits. In *Proceedings of the Twenty-Fourth Conference on Uncertainty in Artificial Intelligence*, Helsinki, Finland, 2008. AUAI Press.

[20] D. Lowd and A. Rooshenas. Learning Markov networks with arithmetic circuits. In *Proceedings of the Sixteenth International Conference on Artificial Intelligence and Statistics (AISTATS 2013)*, Scottsdale, AZ, 2013.

[21] R. Mateescu, R. Dechter, and R. Marinescu. AND/OR multi-valued decision diagrams (AOMDDs) for graphical models. *Journal of Artificial Intelligence Research*, pages 465–519, 2008.

[22] M. Meila and M. Jordan. Learning with mixtures of trees. *Journal of Machine Learning Research*, 1:1–48, 2000.

[23] H. Poon and P. Domingos. Sum-product networks: A new deep architecture. In *Proceedings of the Twenty-Seventh Conference on Uncertainty in Artificial Intelligence*, pages 337–346, Barcelona, Spain, 2011. AUAI Press.

[24] T. Rahman and V. Gogate. Learning ensembles of cutset networks. In *AAAI conference on Artificial Intelligence*, pages 3301–3307, 2016.

[25] T. Rahman, P. Kothalkar, and V. Gogate. Cutset networks: A simple, tractable, and scalable approach for improving the accuracy of chow-liu trees. In *Proceesings of ECML and PKDD*, pages 630–645, 2014.

[26] A. Rooshenas and D. Lowd. Learning sum-product networks with direct and indirect interactions. In *Proceedings of the Thirty-First International Conference on Machine Learning*, Beijing, China, 2014. JMLR: W&CP 32.

[27] D. Roth. On the hardness of approximate reasoning. *Artificial Intelligence*, 82:273–302, 1996.

[28] A. Vergari, N. Di Mauro, and F. Esposito. Simplifying, regularizing and strengthening sum-product network structure learning. In *Machine Learning and Knowledge Discovery in Databases*, pages 343–358. Springer, 2015.

[29] W. Wiegerinck. Variational approximations between mean field theory and the junction tree algorithm. In *Proceedings of the Sixteenth Conference on Uncertainty in Artificial Intelligence*, pages 626–633, 2000.

MDPs with Unawareness in Robotics

Nan Rong Joseph Y. Halpern Ashutosh Saxena
Computer Science Department, Cornell University
Ithaca, NY 14853
{rongnan | halpern | asaxena}@cs.cornell.edu

Abstract

We formalize decision-making problems in robotics and automated control using continuous MDPs and actions that take place over continuous time intervals. We then approximate the continuous MDP using finer and finer discretizations. Doing this results in a family of systems, each of which has an extremely large action space, although only a few actions are "interesting". We can view the decision maker as being unaware of which actions are "interesting". We an model this using *MDPUs*, MDPs with unawareness, where the action space is much smaller. As we show, MDPUs can be used as a general framework for learning tasks in robotic problems. We prove results on the difficulty of learning a near-optimal policy in an an MDPU for a continuous task. We apply these ideas to the problem of having a humanoid robot learn on its own how to walk.

1 INTRODUCTION

Markov decision processes (MDPs) are widely used for modeling decision making problems in robotics and automated control. Traditional MDPs assume that the decision maker (DM) knows all states and actions. However, in many robotics applications, the space of states and actions is continuous. To find appropriate policies, we typically discretize both states and actions. However, we do not know in advance what level of discretization is good enough for getting a good policy. Moreover, in the discretized space, the set of actions is huge. However, relatively few of the actions are "interesting". For example, when flying a robotic helicopter, only a small set of actions lead to useful flying techniques; an autonomous helicopter must learn these techniques. Similarly, a humanoid robot needs to learn various maneuvers (e.g., walking or running) that enable it to move around, but the space of potential actions that it must search to find a successful gait is huge, while most actions result in the robot losing control and falling down.

Halpern, Rong, and Saxena [2010] (HRS from now on) defined *MDPs with unawareness (MDPUs)*, where a decision-maker (DM) can be unaware of the actions in an MDP. In the robotics applications in which we are interested, we can think of the DM (e.g., a humanoid robot) as being unaware of which actions are the useful actions, and thus can model what is going on using an MDPU.

In this paper, we apply MDPUs to continuous problems. We model such problems using *continuous MDPs*, where actions are performed over a continuous duration of time. Although many problems fit naturally in our continuous MDP framework, and there has been a great deal of work on continuous-time MDPs, our approach seems new, and of independent interest. (See the discussion in Section 5.) It is hard to find near-optimal policies in continuous MDPs. A standard approach is to use discretization. We use discretization as well, but our discrete models are MDPUs, rather than MDPs, which allows us both to use relatively few actions (the "interesting actions"), while taking into account the possibility of there being interesting actions that the DM has not yet discovered. We would like to find a discretization level for which the optimal policy in the MDP underlying the approximating MDPU provides a good approximation to the optimal policy in the continuous MDP that accurately describes the problem, and then find a near-optimal policy in that discretized MDPU.

HRS gave a complete characterization of when it is possible to learn to play near-optimally in an MDPU, extending earlier work [Brafman and Tennenholtz 2002; Kearns and Singh 2002] showing that it is always possible to learn to play near-optimally in an MDP. We extend and generalize these results so as to apply them to the continuous problems of interest to us. We characterize when brute-force exploration can be used to find a near-optimal policy in our setting, and show that a variant of the URMAX algorithm presented by HRS can find a near-optimal policy. We also characterize the complexity of learning to play near-optimally in continuous problems, when more "guided" exploration is used. Finally, we discuss how MDPUs can be used to solve a real robotic problem: to enable a humanoid robot to learn walking on its own. In our experiment, the robot learned various gaits at multiple discretization levels, including both forward and backward gaits; both efficient and inefficient gaits; and both gaits that resemble human walking, and those that do not.

2 MDPU: A REVIEW

Describing a situation by a standard MDP misses out on some important features. In general, an agent may not be aware of all the actions that can be performed. For example, an agent playing a video game may not be aware of all actions that can be performed in a given state. Our model is compatible with a number of interpretations of unawareness. In the robotics setting, we take a particular concrete interpretation. Here, the number of actions is typically extremely large, but only a few of these actions are actually useful. For example, although an autonomous helicopter can have a huge number of actions, only a few are useful for flying the helicopter, whereas the rest simply result in a crash. We can abstract what is going on by defining a set of "useful actions". The DM may initial be unaware of many or even most of the useful actions. A DM may become aware of a useful action (and thus, can safely perform it) by performing a special action called the *explore* action, denoted a_0. Playing the explore action results in the DM learning about new actions with some probability.

We thus take an MDPU to be a tuple $M = (S, A, A_0, g, a_0, g_0, P, D, R)$,[1] where the tuple (S, A, g, P, R) is a standard MDP—that is, S is a set of states, A is a set of actions, $g(s)$ is the set of actions available at state s, for each tuple $(s, s', a) \in S \times S \times A$, $P(s, s', a)$ gives the probability of making a transition from s to s' if action a is performed, and $R(s, s', a)$ gives the reward earned by the DM if this transition is taken; $A_0 \subseteq A$ is the set of actions that the DM initially knows to be useful; a_0 is the special *explore* action; $g(s) \subseteq A$ is the set of actions that can be performed at state s; $g_0(s) \subseteq A_0 \cap g(s)$ is the set of actions that the DM is aware of at state s; finally, D is the *discovery probability function*. $D(j, t, s)$ is the probability of discovering a useful action given that there are j useful actions to be discovered at state s, and a_0 has already been played $t - 1$ times without discovering a useful action. Intuitively, D describes how quickly the DM can discover a useful action. We assume that $D(j, t, s)$ is non-decreasing as a function of j: the more useful actions there are to be found, the easier we can find one. How $D(j, t, s)$ varies with t depends on the problem. In the sequel, we assume for ease of exposition that $D(j, t, s)$ is independent of s, so we write $D(j, t)$ rather than $D(j, t, s)$. $M' = (S, A, P, R)$ is called the *MDP underlying* M.

Kearns and Singh [2002] and Brafman and Tennenholtz [2002] have studied the problem of learning how to play near-optimally in an MDP. Roughly speaking, to play near-optimally means that, for all $\epsilon > 0$ and $\delta > 0$, we can find a policy that obtains expected reward ϵ-close to that of the optimal policy with probability at least $1 - \delta$. HRS completely characterize the difficulty of learning to play near-optimally in an MDPU. We briefly review the relevant results here. Despite initially being unaware of some useful actions, we want the DM to learn a policy that is near-optimal in the underlying MDP. HRS showed that whether a DM can learn to play optimally and how long it takes depend on the value of $D(1, t)$—the probability of discovering a new action given that there is a new action to discover and the DM has tried $t - 1$ times in the past to discover a new action.

The first result characterizes when it is impossible to learn to play near-optimally. To make it precise, we recall the notion of mixing time. Formally, the *ϵ-return mixing time of an MDP M* is the least T such that an optimal policy for M guarantees an expected payoff within ϵ of the optimal reward after running for at least time T. (See [Kearns and Singh 2002] for more details and motivation.) The following theorem shows that if the discovery probability is sufficiently low, where "sufficiently low" means $D(1, t) < 1$ for all t and $\sum_{t=1}^{\infty} D(1, t) < \infty$, then the DM cannot learn to play near-optimally. We define $\Psi(T) = \sum_{t=1}^{T} D(1, t)$.

Theorem 2.1 *If $D(1, t) < 1$ for all t and $\Psi(\infty) < \infty$, then there exists a constant c such that no algorithm can obtain a reward that is guaranteed to be within c of optimal for an MDPU $M = (S, A, A_0, G, a_o g_0, P, D, R)$, even if S, $|A|$, and a bound on the optimal reward are known.*

Theorem 2.1 says that when $\Psi(\infty) < \infty$, it is impossible for the DM to learn an optimal policy. On the other hand, if $\Psi(\infty) = \infty$, then it is possible to learn to play near-optimally. HRS present an algorithm called URMAX, a variant of the RMAX algorithm [Brafman and Tennenholtz 2002], that learns near-optimal play.

Theorem 2.2 *If $\Psi(\infty) = \infty$, then the URMAX algorithm computes a near-optimal policy.*

In fact, we can say even more. If $\Psi(\infty) = \infty$, then the efficiency of the best algorithm for determining near-optimal play depends on how quickly $\Psi(\infty)$ diverges. HRS characterize the running time of URMAX in terms of the function Ψ, and give lower bounds on the time required to learn near-optimally in terms of Ψ. These results show that URMAX learns to play near-optimally almost as quickly as possible. Specifically, it learns a policy with an expected reward ϵ-close to the optimal reward with probability $1 - \delta$ in time polynomial in $|S|$, $|A|$, $1/\epsilon$, $1/\delta$, a bound $R_{\max}$ on the optimal reward, the ϵ-return mixing time, and the small-

[1]The MDPU model in HRS also includes R_i^+ and R_i^-, which are the reward (resp., penalty) functions for playing a_0 and discovering (resp., not discovering) a useful action. We omit them here; they play no role in the theorems that we are citing, and would only clutter our later presentation.

est T such that $\Psi(T) \geq \ln(4N/\delta)$, whenever it is possible to do so. The polynomial-time results are summarized in the next result.

Theorem 2.3 *It is possible to learn to play near-optimally in polynomial time iff there exist constants m_1 and m_2 such that $\Psi(T) \geq m_1 \ln(T) + m_2$ for all $T > 0$. Moreover, if it is possible to learn to play near-optimally in polynomial time, URMAX does so.*

3 ANALYZING ROBOTIC PROBLEMS AS MDPUS

As we said in the introduction, we apply the MDPU framework to robotic problems such as having a humanoid robot learn to walk. For such problems, we typically have a continuous space of states and actions, where actions take place in continuous time, and actions have a nontrivial duration.

Suppose that the original continuous problem can be characterized by a continuous MDP M_∞ (defined formally below). We would like to find a "good" discretization M of M_∞. "Good" in this setting means that an optimal policy for M is ϵ-optimal for M_∞, for some appropriate ϵ.[2] Clearly the level of discretization matters. Too coarse a discretization results in an MDP whose optimal policy is not ϵ-optimal for M_∞; on the other hand, too fine a discretization results in the problem size becoming unmanageably large. For example, in order to turn a car on a smooth curve (without drifting), the optimal policy is to slowly turn the steering wheel to the left and back, in which the action varies smoothly over time. This can be simulated using a relatively coarse discretization of time. However, in order to make a sharp turn using advanced driving techniques like drifting, the steering wheel needs to be turned at precise points in time, or else the car will go into an uncontrollable spin. In this case, a fine discretization in time is needed.

Unfortunately, it is often not clear what discretization level to use in a specific problem. Part of the DM's problem is to find the "right" level of discretization. Thus, we describe the problem in terms of a continuous MDP M_∞ and a sequence $((M_1, M_1'), (M_2, M_2'), \ldots)$, where M_i is an MDPU with underlying MDP M_i', for $i = 1, 2, \ldots$. Intuitively, $(M_1', M_2', M_3', \ldots)$ represents a sequence of finer and finer approximations to M_∞.

Continuous Time MDP with Continuous Actions over Time: To make this precise, we start by defining our model of continuous MDPs. Let $M_\infty = (S_\infty, A_\infty, g_\infty, P_\infty, R_\infty)$. S_∞ is a continuous state space, which we identify with a compact subset of $I\!R^n$ for some integer $n > 0$; that is, each state can be represented by a vector $(s_1, \cdots, s_n)$ of real numbers. For example, for a humanoid robot, the state space can be described by a vector which includes the robot's (x, y, z) position, and the current positions of its movable joints.

Actions: Describing A_∞ requires a little care. We assume that there is an underlying set of *basic actions* A_B, which can be identified with a compact subset of $I\!R^m$ for some $m > 0$; that is, each basic action can be represented by a vector $(a_1, \cdots, a_m)$ of real numbers. For example, for a humanoid robot, the basic actions can be characterized by a tuple that contains the targeted positions for its movable joints. However, we do not take A_∞ to consist of basic actions. Rather, an action is a *path* of basic actions over time. Formally, an action in A_∞ is a piecewise continuous function from a domain of the form $(0, t]$ for some $t > 0$ to basic actions. Thus, there exist time points $t_0 < t_1 < \ldots < t_k$ with $t_0 = 0$ and $t_k = t$ such that a is continuous in the interval $(t_j, t_{j+1}]$ for all $j < k$. The number t is the *length* of the action a, denoted $|a|$. We use left-open right-closed intervals here; we think of the action in the interval $(t_j, t_{j+1}]$ as describing what the DM does right after time t_j until time t_{j+1}. By analogy with the finite case, $g_\infty(s)$ is the set of actions in A_∞ available at s.

Reward and Transition Functions: We now define R_∞ and P_∞, the reward and transition functions. In a discrete MDP, the transition function P and reward function R take as arguments a pair of states and an action. Thus, for example, $P(s_1, s_2, a)$ is the probability of transitioning from s_1 to s_2 using action a, and $R(s_1, s_2, a)$ is the reward the agent gets if a transition from s_1 to s_2 is taken using action a. In our setting, what matters is the path taken by a transition according to a. Thus, we take the arguments to P_∞ and R_∞ to be tuples of the form (s_1, s_c, a), where s_1 is a state, a is an action in A_∞ of length t, and s_c is a piecewise continuous function from $(0, t]$ to S_∞. Intuitively, s_c describes a possible path of states that the DM goes through when performing action a, such that before a starts, the DM was at s_1.[3] Note that we do not require that $\lim_{t \to 0^+} s_c(t) = s_1$. Intuitively, this means that there can be a discrete change in state at the beginning of an interval. This allows us to capture the types of discrete changes considered in *semi-MDPs* [Puterman 1994].

We think of $R_\infty(s_1, s_c, a)$ as the reward for transitioning from s_1 according to state path s_c via action a. We assume that R_∞ is bounded: specifically, there exists a constant c such that $R_\infty(s_1, s_c, a) < c \cdot |a|$. For $s_1 \in S_\infty$ and $a \in A_\infty$, we take $P_\infty(s_1, \cdot, a)$ to be a probability density function over state paths of length $|a|$ starting at s_1. P_∞ is not defined for transitions starting at terminal states.

We require R_∞ and P_∞ to be continuous functions, so that if (s_i, s_c^i, a_i) approaches (s, s_c, a) (where all the state sequences and actions have the same length t), then $R_\infty(s_i, s_c^i, a_i)$ approaches $R_\infty(s, s_c, a)$ and $P_\infty(s_i, s_c^i, a_i)$

[2] A policy π is ϵ-optimal for an MDP M if the expected average reward for a policy for M is no more than ϵ greater than the expected average reward of π.

[3] We are thus implicitly assuming that the result of performing a piecewise continuous action must be a piecewise continuous state path.

approaches $P_\infty(s, s_c, a)$. To make the notion of "approaches" precise, we need to consider the distance between state paths and the distance between actions. Since we have identified both states (resp., basic actions) with subsets of $I\!R^n$ (resp., $I\!R^m$), this is straightforward. For definiteness, we define the distance between two vectors in $I\!R^n$ using the L_1 norm, so that $d(\vec{p}, \vec{q}) = \sum_1^n |p_i - q_i|$. For actions a and a' in A_∞ of the same length, define $d(a, a') = \int_{t=0}^{|a|} d(a(t), a'(t))dt$. For state paths s_c and s'_c of the same length, define $d(s_c, s'_c) = \int_{t=0}^{|s_c|} d(s_c(t), s'_c(t))dt$. Finally, define $d((s_c, a), (s'_c, a')) = d(s_c, s'_c) + d(a, a')$. This definition of distance allows us to formalize the notion of continuity for R_∞ and P_∞. The key point of the continuity assumption is that it allows us to work with discretizations, knowing that they really do approximate the continuous MDP.

Constraints on Actions: We typically do not want to take A_∞ to consist of all possible piecewise continuous functions. For one thing, some hardware and software restrictions will make certain functions infeasible. For example, turning a steering wheel back and forth 10^{20} times in one second can certainly be described by a continuous function, but is obviously infeasible in practice. But we may want to impose further constraints on A_∞ and $g_\infty(s)$.

In the discussion above, we did not place any constraints on the length of actions. When we analyze problems of interest, there is typically an upper bound on the length of actions of interest. For example, when playing table tennis using a robotic arm, the basic actions can be viewed as tuples, describing the direction of movement of the racket, the rotation of the racket, and the force being applied to the racket; actions are intuitively all possible control sequences of racket movements that are feasible according to the robot's hardware and software constraints; this includes slight movements of the racket, strokes, and prefixes of strokes. An example of a piecewise continuous action here would be to move the racket forward with a fixed force for some amount of time, and then to suddenly stop applying the force when the racket is close to the ball. We can bound the length of actions of interest to the time that a ball can be in the air between consecutive turns. We assume that, in any case, there is an upper bound T on the length of all actions. This seems to be a reasonable assumption for all the applications of interest to us here.

Awareness: Even with the constraints discussed above, A_∞ is typically extremely large. Of course, not all actions in A_∞ are "useful". For instance, in the helicopter example, most actions would crash the helicopter. We thus consider *potentially useful* actions. (We sometimes call them just *useful actions*.) Informally, an action is potentially useful if it is not *useless*. A useless action is one that either destroys the robot, or leaves it in an uncontrollable state, or does not change the state. For example, when flying a helicopter, actions that lead to a crash are useless, as are actions that make the helicopter lose control. More formally, given a state s, the set of useful actions at state s are the actions that transit to a different state in which the robot is neither destroyed nor uncontrollable. Note that an action that crashes the helicopter in one state may not cause a crash in a different state. For robotics applications, we say that a robot is *aware* of an action if it identifies that action as a potentially useful action, either because it has been preprogrammed with the action (we are implicitly assuming that the robot understands all actions with which it has been programmed) or it has simulated the action. For example, a humanoid robot that has been pre-programmed with only simple walking actions, and has never tried running or simulated running before, would be unaware of running actions. Let $\bar{A}_\infty$ denote the useful actions in A_∞, and let $\bar{A}_{\infty 0}$ denote the useful actions that the robot is initially aware of. (These are usually the actions that the robot has been pre-programmed with.)

Discretization: We now consider the discretization of M_∞. We assume that, for each discretization level i, S_∞ is discretized into a finite state space S_i and A_B is discretized into a finite basic action space A_{Bi}, where $|S_1| \leq |S_2| \leq \ldots$ and $|A_{B1}| \leq |A_{B2}| \leq \ldots$. We further assume that, for all i, there exists $d_i > 0$, with $d_i \to 0$, such that for all states $s \in S_\infty$ and basic actions $a_B \in A_B$, there exists a state $s' \in S_i$ and a basic action $a_{B'} \in A_{Bi}$ such that $d(s, s') \leq d_i$, and $d(a_B, a'_B) \leq d_i$. Thus, we are assuming that the discretizations can give closer and closer approximations to all states and basic actions. At level i, we also discretize time into time slices of length t_i, where $T \geq t_1 > t_2 > \ldots$.Thus, actions at discretization level i are sequences of *constant actions* of length t_i, where a constant action is a constant function from $(0, t_i]$ to a single basic action.[4] In other words, the action lengths at discretization level i are multiples of t_i. Thus, at discretization level i, there are $\sum_{l=1}^{\lfloor T/t_i \rfloor} |A_{Bi}|^l$ possible actions. Let A'_i consist of this set of actions. (Note that some actions in A'_i may not be in A_∞, since certain action sequences might be infeasible due to hardware and software constraints.) Let $A_i \subseteq A'_i$ be the set of useful actions at level i.

Let M_i be the MDPU where S_i and A_i are defined above; $A_{\infty 0}$ is the set of useful actions that the DM is initially aware of; $g(s)$ is the set of useful actions at state s; $g_0(s)$ is the set of useful actions that the DM is aware of at state s; and the reward function R_i is just the restriction of R_∞ to A_i and S_i. For $s_1 \in S_i$ and $a \in A_i$, we take $P_i(s_1, \cdot, a)$ to be a probability distribution over $Q_i^{|a|}$, the set of state paths of length $|a|$ that are piecewise constant and each constant section has a length that is a multiple of t_i. For a state path $s_c \in Q_i^{|a|}$, let $P_i(s_1, s_c, a)$ be the normalized probability of traversing a state sequence that is within distance d_i of state sequence s_c when playing action a starting from state s_1. Formally,

[4]Note that we are not assuming that the action space A_{i+1} is a refinement of A_i (which would further require t_{i+1} to be a multiple of t_i).

$P_i(s_1, s_c, a) = (\int_{\{s'_c : d(s_c, s'_c) \leq d_i\}} dP_\infty(s_1, \cdot, a))/c$, where $c = \sum_{s_c \in Q_i^{|a|}} \int_{\{s'_c : d(s_c, s'_c) \leq d_i\}} dP_\infty(s_1, \cdot, a)$ is a normalization constant. Since the robot is not assumed to know all useful actions at any specific discretization level, it needs to explore for the useful actions it wasn't aware of. Finally, given a specific exploration strategy, $D_i(j, t)$ describes the probability of discovering a new useful action at discretization level i, given that there are j undiscovered useful actions at level i, and the robot has explored t times without finding a useful action. We model exploration using a_0; every time the robot explores, it is playing a_0.

It remains to define the discretization of an action in A_0. In order to do this, for $a \in A_\infty$, define $a_i \in A_i$ to be *a best approximation to a in level i* if $|a_i|$ is the largest multiple of t_i that is less than or equal to $|a|$, and $\int_0^{(|a_i|)} d(a(t), a_i(t))dt$ is minimal among actions $a' \in A$ of length $|a_i|$. Intuitively, a_i is an action in A_i whose length is as close as possible to that of a and, among actions of that length, is closest in distance to a. The action a_i is not unique. For $a \in A_0$, define its discretization at level i to be a best approximation to a at that level. When there are several best approximations, we choose any one of them.

Policies: As usual, a policy π in M_i is a function from S_i to A_i. We want to compute $U_{M_i}(s, \pi, t)$, the expected average reward over time t of π started in state $s \in S_i$. Let $a_j \in A_i$ and s_{cj} be a state sequence in $Q_i^{|a_j|}$, for $j = 0, \ldots, l$. Say that a sequence $((a_0, s_{c0}), (a_1, s_{c1}), \cdots, (a_l, s_{cl}))$ is *a path compatible with policy π starting at s* if $\pi(s) = a_0$ and $\pi(s_{cj}(|a_j|)) = a_{j+1}$ for all $0 \leq j \leq l-1$. Let $I_{s,t}^\pi$ consist of all paths $((a_0, s_{c0}), (a_1, s_{c1}), \cdots, (a_l, s_{cl}))$ starting at s compatible with π such that $\sum_{j=0}^{l} |a_j| \leq t < \sum_{j=0}^{l+1} |a_j|$, where $a_{l+1} = \pi(s_{cl}(|a_l|))$. Essentially, when computing $U_{M_i}(s, \pi, t)$, we consider the expected reward over all maximally long paths that have total length at most t. Thus, $U_{M_i}(s, \pi, t) = \sum_{p \in I_{s,t}^\pi} P_i^*(p) \frac{R_i^*(p)}{t}$, where, given a path $p = ((a_0, s_{c0}), (a_1, s_{c1}), \cdots, (a_l, s_{cl}))$, $P_i^*(p) = \Pi_{j=0}^{l} P_i(s_{cj}(0), s_{cj}, a_j)$, and $R_i^*(p) = \sum_{j=0}^{l} R_i(s_{cj}(0), s_{cj}, a_j)$.

Now that we have defined the average reward of a policy at discretization level i, we can define the average reward of a policy in M_∞. Given a discretization level i, let π_i be a *projection* of π_∞ at level i, defined as follows: for each $s_i \in S_i$, define $\pi_i(s_i)$ to be an action $a_i \in A_i$ such that a_i is a best approximation to $\pi(s_i)$ at level i, as defined above. As mentioned, there might be several best approximations; a_i is not unique. Thus, the projection is not unique. Nevertheless, we define $U_{M_\infty}(s, \pi_\infty, t)$ to be $\lim_{i \to \infty} U_{M_i}(s, \pi_i, t)$, where π_i is a projection of π to discretization level i. The continuity of the transition and reward functions guarantees that the limit exists and is independent of the choice of projections.

We now consider how the URMAX algorithm of Section 2 can be applied to learn near-optimal policies. We use URMAX at each discretization level. Note that URMAX never terminates; however, it eventually learns to play near-optimally (although we may not know exactly when). The time it takes to learn to play near-optimally depends on the exploration strategy. The next theorem consider brute-force searching, where, at discretization level i, at each discretization level i, all actions in A'_i are exhaustively examined to find useful actions. (The proof of this and all other theorems can be found in the supplementary material.)

Theorem 3.1 *Using brute-force exploration, given $\alpha > 0$ and $0 < \delta < 1$, we can find an α-optimal policy in M_∞ with probability at least $1 - \delta$ in time polynomial in l, $|A'_l|$, $|S_l|$, $1/\alpha$, $1/\delta$, $R^l_{\max}$, and T^l, where l is the least i such that the optimal policy for M'_i is $(\alpha/2)$-optimal for M_∞, $R^l_{\max}$ is the maximum reward that can be obtained by a transition in M'_l, and T^l is the ϵ-return mixing time for M'_l.*

Although brute-force exploration always learns a near-optimal policy, the method can be very inefficient, since it exhaustively checks all possible actions to find the useful ones. Thus, at discretization level i, it needs to check $\sum_{l=1}^{\lfloor T/t_i \rfloor} |A_{Bi}|^l$ actions, and as i grows, the method soon becomes impractical. On the other hand, the result is of some interest, since it shows that even when there are infinitely many possible levels of discretizations, a method as simple as brute-force exploration suffices.

When the number of possible actions is huge, the probability of finding a potentially useful action can be very low. In this case, making use of an expert's knowledge or imitating a teacher's demonstration can often greatly increase the probability of finding a useful action. We abstract the presence of an expert or a teacher by assuming that there is some constant $\beta > 0$ such that $D(1, t) \geq \beta$ for all t. Intuitively, the presence of a teacher or an expert guarantees that there is a minimal probability β such that, if there is a new action to be found at all, then the probability of finding it is at least β, no matter how many earlier failed attempts there have been at finding a useful action.

Using apprentice learning lets us improve Theorem 3.1 by replacing the $|A'_l|$ component of the running time by $|A_l|$; thus, with apprentice learning, the running time depends only on the number of useful actions, not the total number of potential actions. The savings can be huge.

Theorem 3.2 *Using an exploration method where $D_i(1, t) \geq \beta$ for all $i, t > 0$ (where $\beta \in (0, 1)$ is a constant), for all $\alpha > 0$ and $0 < \delta < 1$, we can find an α-optimal policy in M_∞ with probability at least $1 - \delta$ in time polynomial in l, $|A_l|$, $|S_l|$, $1/\beta$, $1/\alpha$, $1/\delta$, $R_{\max}$, and T^l, where l is the smallest i such that the optimal policy for M'_i is $(\alpha/2)$-optimal to M_∞, $R^l_{\max}$ is the maximum reward that can be obtained by a transition in M'_l, and T^l is the ϵ-return mixing time for M'_l.*

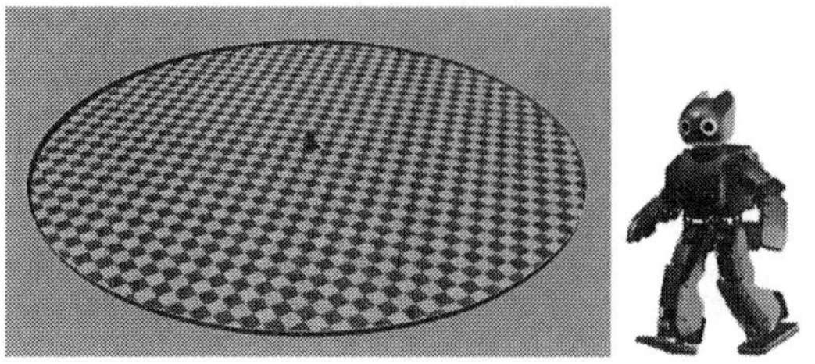

Figure 1: The arena with the robot at the center; and the robot.

4 HUMANOID ROBOT WALKING

We consider the problem of a humanoid robot with 20 joint motors (which we sometimes call just "joints") learning to walk on its own. More precisely, we require the robot to move from the center of an arena to its boundary; we take any reasonable motion to be "walking". (Figure 1 shows the robot and the arena in which it must walk.)

4.1 The continuous MDP

We start by defining a continuous M_∞ for the robot problem. A state $s \in S_\infty$ is of the form $s = (w_1, \cdots, w_{23}) \in \mathbb{R}^{23}$, where (w_1, w_2, w_3) give the position of the robot's center of mass and $(w_4, \cdots, w_{23})$ are the current positions of the robot's 20 joint motors. We define the domain of each dimension as follows: since the radius of the arena is 5 meters, $w_1, w_2 \in [-5, 5]$; since the robot's height is 0.454 meters, $w_3 \in [0, 0.4]$ (we do not expect the robot's center of mass to be higher than 0.4). Each joint motor has its specific range of mobility, which determines the domain of the corresponding dimension. For example, $w_5 \in [-3.14, 2.85]$ represents the current position of the robot's left shoulder. The mobility range for all joint motors are intervals in $[-\pi, \pi]$.

The basic actions $a \in A_B$ are of the form $a = (v_1, \cdots, v_{20}) \in \mathbb{R}^{20}$, where v_i is the target position for the robot's ith joint motor. The domain of each dimension is the mobility range for the corresponding joint motor. For example, v_2, which corresponds to the left shoulder, has mobility range $[-3.14, 2.85]$; $v_2 = 2.85$ means to move the robot's left shoulder forward as far as possible. Since walking is composed of repeated short movements that are typically no longer than half a second, we set $T = 0.512$ seconds. Thus, A_∞, the set of useful actions, consists of piecewise continuous functions that map from time to basic actions and comply with the robot's hardware and software limitations, of length $t < 0.512$ seconds.

We now define R_∞ and P_∞. Intuitively, the robot obtains a reward for gaining distance from the center of the arena. If the coordinates of the center of the arena are given by $s_0 = (s_0[1], s_0[2])$, then $R_\infty(s_1, s_c, a) = dis(s_0, s_c(|a|)) - dis(s_0, s_1)$, where $dis(s_0, s_1) = \sqrt{(s_0[1] - s_1[1])^2 + (s_0[2] - s_1[2])^2}$ is the L_2-norm distance between s_0 and s_1 on the (x, y)-plane. The reward could be negative, for example, if the robot moves back towards the center of the arena.

By definition, $P_\infty(s_1, \cdot, a)$ is a probability distribution over state sequences of length $|a|$ starting at s_1. For example, if the robot slowly moves its right leg forward while staying balanced, the state path taken by the robot is a deterministic path. On the other hand, if a is the action of turning around quickly, $P_\infty(s, \cdot, a)$ is distribution over various ways of falling down.

4.2 Discretizations

We now define M_i and M_i'. In our experiments we considered only levels 2 and 3 (level 1 is uninteresting since it has just one state and one action), so these are the only levels that we describe in detail here. (These turn out to suffice to get interesting walking behaviors.) At these levels, we discretized more finely the joints corresponding to the left and right upper and lower leg joints and the left and right ankle joints, since these turn out to be more critical for walking. (These are components $(w_{14}, \cdots, w_{19})$ in the state tuples and $(v_{11}, \cdots, v_{16})$ in basic-actions tuples.) We call these the *relevant dimensions*. We assume that the six relevant state and actions components have i possible values at level i, for $i = 2, 3$, as does w_3, since this describes how high off the ground the robot is (and thus, whether or not it has fallen). All other dimensions take just one value. We took $t_2 = t_3$ to be 128ms. Since $T = 0.512$s, an action contains at most $\lfloor T/t_i \rfloor = 4$ basic actions.

$A_{\infty 0}$ is the set of preprogrammed actions. We preprogram the robot with a simple sitting action that lets the robot slowly return to its initial sitting gesture. When we consider apprenticeship learning, we also assume that the robot is preprogrammed with a "stand-up" action, that enables it to stand up from its initial sitting position. (Intuitively, we are assuming that the expert taught the robot how to stand up, since this is useful after it has fallen.)

A_i' is the set of potential actions at level i. Given our assumptions, for $i = 2, 3$, at level i, there are $(i^6)^4$ potential actions (there are i possible values for each of the six relevant dimensions, and each action is a sequence of four basic actions). Thus, at level 3, there are $(3^6)^4$ =282,429,536,481 potential actions. As we mentioned, a useful action is an action that moves the robot without making it lose control. Here, an action is useful if it moves the robot without resulting in the robot falling down. At both levels 2 and 3, more than 80 useful actions were found in our experiments. The most efficient action found at level 3 was one where the right leg moves backwards, immediately followed by the left leg, in such a way that the robot maintains its balance at all times. By way of contrast, turning the body quickly makes the robot lose control and fall down, so is useless.

For $s_1 \in S_i$, $a \in A_i$, and $s_c \in Q_i^{|a|}$, $P_i(s_1, s_c, a)$ is the normalized probability of traversing a state sequence that is d_i close to s_c, a sequence of states in S_i, where we define $d_i = \frac{12\pi}{i} + 28\pi + 20.4$. So d_i decreases in i, and discretizations at a higher level better approximate the continuous problem. All basic actions in A_B are within distance d_i of a basic action in A_{Bi} and all states in S are within d_i of a state in S_i. Let $s \in S$, and let s_i be the closest state to s in S_i. It is easy to check that $d(s, s_i) \leq d_i$ for $i = 2, 3$.

The D_i function depends on the exploration method used to discover new actions. In our experiment, we used two exploration methods: brute-force exploration and apprenticeship-learning exploration.

At discretization level i, using brute-force exploration, we have $D_i(|A_i|, t) = \frac{|A_i|}{|A'_i|}$, since there are $|A_i|$ useful actions and $|A'_i|$ potential actions, and we test an action at random. With apprenticeship learning, we used following hints from a human expert to increase the probability of discovering new actions: (a) a sequence of moving directions that, according to the human expert, resembles human walking;[5] (b) a preprogrammed stand-up action; (c) the information that an action that is symmetric to a useful action is also likely to be useful (two actions are symmetric if they are exactly the same except that the target values for the left joints and those for the right joints are switched). We also use a different discretization: the ankle joint was discretized into 10 values. The human expert suggests more values in the ankle joints because whether or not the robot falls depends critically on the exact ankle joint position. These hints were provided before the policy starts running; the discretization levels are set then too. There were no further human-robot interactions.

4.3 Experiments

For our experiments, we simulated DARwIn OP, a commercially available humanoid robot. The simulations were conducted on Webots PRO platform 8.2.1 using a MacBook Pro with 2.8GHz Intel Core i7 Processor, 16GB 1600 MHz DDR3 memory, 0.5TB Flash Storage Mac HD, on OS X Yosemite 10.10.5. We modeled the robot walking problem as an MDPU, and implemented the URMAX algorithm using programming language Python 2.7.7.

As we said, given the number of actions involved, we conducted experiments only for discretization level 2 and 3. Both sufficed to enable the robot to learn to walk, using a generous notion of "walk"—more precisely, they sufficed to enable the robot to learn to locomote to the boundary of the arena. As mentioned, two exploration methods were used: brute-force exploration and apprenticeship-learning exploration. One trial was run for brute-force exploration at each of levels 2 and 3, and one trial was run for apprenticeship learning at level 2. Each trial took 24 hours. More than

	Brute-force (level 2)	Brute-force (level 3)	Apprenticeship learning (level 2)
$\lvert S_i \rvert$	130	1460	3200
$\lvert A_{Bi} \rvert$	64	729	1600
$\lvert A_i \rvert$	16777216	282429536481	6553600000000
t_i (ms)	124	124	124
Length of action (ms)	496	496	496
Execution time (hours)	24	24	24
Best avg rwd (m/action)	0.043486	0.067599	0.083711
Num of useful actions found	131	89	180

Table 1: Performance comparisons.

Figure 2: A backward gait (from left to right).

15 stable gaits were found in total, where a gait is *stable* if it enables the robot to move from the center of the arena to the boundary without falling. In addition, more than 400 useful actions were found. The best gait among all stable gaits achieved a velocity of 0.084m/s, which seems reasonable, given that the best known walking speed of DARwIn-OP is 0.341m/s [Budden et al. 2013]. Given more time to experiment, we would expect the performance to improve further.

The robot successfully learned gaits of various styles, including both forward and backward gaits (see Figures 2 and 3), both efficient and inefficient gaits, gaits that resemble human walking and the ones that do not. Somewhat surprisingly, the best gait actually walks backwards. (Videos of some of the gaits and a demo of the learning process can be found at https://youtu.be/qW51iInpdV0.) As shown in Table 1, as the discretization level increases, both the velocity of the best gait and the number of useful actions found increase. This agrees with the expectation that finer discretization better approximates the continuous problem, and thus gets an expected reward closer to the optimal reward of the continuous problem. Apprenticeship learning resulted in more useful actions than the brute-force exploration and in gaits with a higher average reward. Again, this is hardly surprising; the hints provided by the human expert increases the probability of finding useful actions. On the other hand, when the expert gives "bad" hints, the

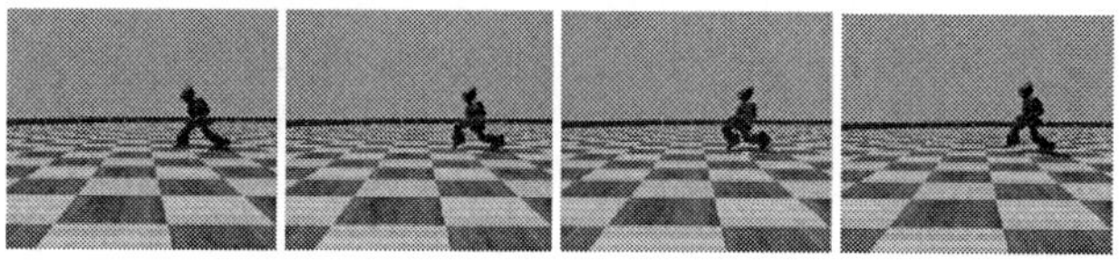

Figure 3: A forward gait (from left to right).

[5]The sequence gives directions only for certain joints, without specific target values, leaving the movement remaining joints open for experimentation.

robot performs worse than with brute-force exploration.

With regard to comparisons under the same setting, we implemented two baseline comparisons for bipedal walking. The first tries random sequences of actions; the second searches for useful actions and then repeats each useful action in an attempt to find stable gaits. (The motivation for repeating actions is that human-like walking is in fact a rhythmic/cyclic movement of a repeated action.) Using the same setting as our experiments with URMAX, the first baseline found no stable gait in 24 hours, and the maximum distance the robot travelled before falling down was 0.342 meters; the second baseline found one stable gait in 24 hours, and the maximum distance travelled was 5 meters (the maximum distance possible from the center of the arena to the boundary) with a speed of 0.0058 m/s. Our appraoch found several stable gaits at each discretization level and the distance travelled using each stable gait is 5 meters with a maximum speed of 0.083m/s (10 times better than the second baseline).

Our approach, using MDPUs, requires no knowledge on the kinematics of the robot other than the number of joints and the moving range of each joint. Moreover, it makes no assumptions about the moving pattern of the resulting gait; for example, we do not assume that a gait must be cyclic, or symmetric between left and right joints, nor do we specify the length of a gait. Although we do specify the length of a useful action, a gait could be composed of a single or multiple useful actions. Given the few assumptions and little prior knowledge assumed, the performance of the robot seems quite reasonable. More importantly, the experiment proves that the use of MDPUs enables the robot to learn useful new maneuvers (walking, in this case) by itself, with minimum human input.

5 RELATED WORK

There has been work on optimal policy learning in MDPs using computational resources. Kearns and Singh's [2002] E^3 algorithm guarantees polynomial bounds on the resources required to achieve near-optimal return in general MDPs; variants and extensions of this work can be found in [Brafman and Tennenholtz 2002; Kakade et al. 2003; Kearns and Koller 1999]. However, algorithms such as E^3 usually require the exploration of the entire MDP state/action space. This becomes impractical in our setting, where the number of actions is extremely large. In such cases, several exploration methods have been employed to help find useful actions. For example, Abbeel and Ng [2005] utilize a teacher demonstration of the desired task to guide the exploration; Dearden et al. [1999] utilize the value of information to determine the sequence of exploration. Other papers (e.g., [Dean et al. 1998; Hauskrecht et al. 1998]) consider MDPs with large action spaces.

We are far from the first to consider MDPs with continuous time. For example, *semi-MDPs* (SMPDs) and *continuous-time MDPs* have continuous time [Puterman 1994]. However, these models have discrete actions that can be taken instantaneously, and do not consider continuous actions taken over some duration of time. In *Markov decision drift processes* [Hordijk and Van der Duyn Schouten 1984], the state does not have to stay constant between successive actions (unlike an SMDP), and can evolve in a deterministic way according to what is called a *drift function*. But Markov decision drift processes do not have actions with probabilistic outcomes that take place over an interval of time. They make significant use of discrete approximations to compute optimal policies, just as we do. There has also been work on MDPs with continuous state space and action space (e.g., [Antos and Munos 2007; Feng et al. 2004]), but with discrete time. For our applications, we need time, space, and actions to be continuous; this adds new complications. In control theory, there are methods for controlling continuous time systems where system transitions are linear function of state and time [Zinober 1989]. These can be extended to non-linear systems [Khalil 2002]. However, the transitions in these systems are usually deterministic, and they do not deal with rewards or policies. Sutton, Precup, and Singh [1999] consider high-level actions (which they call *options*) that are taken over a duration of time (such as "opening a door"), but they view time as discrete, which significantly simplifies the model. Rachelson, Garcia, and Fabiani [2008] consider continuous actions over some time interval, however, they assume there are decision epochs, which are the only time points where rewards are considered. In our model, the rewards depend on the entire state sequence that the system traverses through while an action is taken. While this makes the model more complicated, it seems more appropriate for the problems of interest to us.

There has also been a great deal of work on bipedal robot walking, since it is a fundamental motor task for which biological systems significantly outperform current robotic systems [Tedrake et al. 2005]. There have been three main approaches for solving the task:

- The first approach describes the kinematics of the robot in detail using non-linear and linear equation systems, then solves these systems to obtain desirable trajectories. See, for example, [Huang et al. 2001; Gonalves and Zampieri 2006; Kajita et al. 2003; Kim et al. 2007; Strom et al. 2010; Xue et al. 2012].
- The second approach uses genetic algorithms [Cheng and Lin 1997; Hasegawa et al. 2000; Picado et al. 2009]. The traits describing a gait are taken to be the genes in a genetic algorithm. Different gaits (i.e., settings of the parameters) are evaluated in terms of features such as stability and velocity; The most successful gaits are retained, and used to produce the next generation of gaits through selection, mutation, inversion, and crossover of their genes.
- The third approach uses gradient learning, which

starts with either a working gait or a randomly initialized gait. It then improves the gait's performance by changing its parameters, using machine-learning methods (such as neural networks) to find the most profitable set of changes in the parameters. See, for example, [Budden et al. 2013; Kim and Uther 2003; Schulman et al. 2015; Tedrake et al. 2005].

Since the first approach requires a full description of the robot's kinematics, as well as composing and solving a non-linear system, it requires a great deal of human input. Moreover, its application is limited to walking problems. The approach is unable to produce gaits other than those specified by human (e.g., to walk forward by stepping forward the left and the right legs in turn under a specific speed). Both the second and the third approach require little human input (when starting from random gaits), and may produce a variety of gaits. Both also have the potential to be generalized to problems other than bipedal walking. However, both are heuristic search algorithms, and have no theoretical guarantee on their performance. In contrast, our method produces a variety of gaits, provides a general framework for solving robotic problems, and produces a near-optimal policy in the limit. Moreover, our method requires minimum human input, although, as the experiments show, it does better with more human input.

A comparison of our method and the genetic algorithm may provide insights into both methods. Although the two approaches seem different, the searching process made possible by selection, mutation, inversion, and crossover in a genetic algorithm can be viewed as a special case of the *explore* action in an MDPU. Conversely, the *explore* action in an MDPU for the robot can be roughly viewed as searching for a set of genes of unknown length (since a gait can be understood as a continuous action over an uncertain amount of time, composed of one or more shorter actions, where each shorter action is described by a set of parameters). Our approach can be viewed as being more flexible than a genetic algorithm; in a genetic algorithm, the length of the chromosome (i.e., the number of parameters that describe the gait) is fixed; only their values that give the best performance are unknown.

The recent work of Mordatch et al [2016] also provides a general approach for reinforcement learning in robot tasks. Like us, they require prior knowledge only of the mobility range of each of the robot's joints, and not their kinematics; they also model the problem as an MDP. Their goal is to find an optimal trajectory (i.e., a sequence of states), such that when followed, performs a desired task (such as reaching out the robot's hand to a desired position) with minimal cost. They use neural networks to solve the cost-minimization problem. Thus, their approach does not have any guarantees of (approximate) optimality of the performance. Moreover, the complexity of their approach grows quickly as the length of the trajectory grows (while ours is polynomial in the number of useful actions, states visited, and the difficulty of discovering new actions, and thus is not significantly affected by the length of the trajectory). That said, Mordatch et al.'s method has successfully learned a few relatively simple tasks on a physical DARwIn OP2 robot, including hand reaching and leaning the robot's torso to a desired position [Mordatch et al. 2016], although it has not yet been applied to walking.

6 CONCLUSION

We have provided a general approach that allows robots to learn new tasks on their own. We make no assumptions on the structure of the tasks to be learned. We proved that in the limit, the method gives a near-optimal policy. The approach can be easily applied to various robotic tasks. We illustrated this by applying it to the problem of bipedal walking. Using the approach, a humanoid robot, DARwIn OP, was able to learn various walking gaits via simulations (see https://youtu.be/qW51iInpdV0 for a video). We plan to apply our approach to more robotic tasks, such as learning to run and to walk up and down stairs. We believe the process will be quite instructive in terms of adding useful learning heuristics to our approach, both specific to these tasks and to more general robotic tasks. We are also interested in having the robot simulate learning to walk in the same way a baby does, for example, by limiting the robot's abilities initially, so that it must crawl before it walks. Part of our interest lies in seeing if such initial limitations actually make learning more efficient.

Acknowledgments: The work of Halpern and Rong was supported in part by NSF grants IIS-0911036 and CCF-1214844, and by AFOSR grant FA9550-12-1-0040, and ARO grant W911NF-14-1-0017. The work of Saxena was supported in part by a Microsoft Faculty Fellowship.

References

Abbeel, P. and A. Y. Ng (2005). Exploration and apprenticeship learning in reinforcement learning. In *Proc. 22nd Int. Conf. on Machine Learning (ICML '05)*, pp. 1–8.

Antos, A. and R. Munos (2007). Fitted Q-iteration in continuous action-space MDPs. In *Advances in Neural Information Processing Systems 20 (Proc. of NIPS 2007)*, pp. 9–16.

Brafman, R. I. and M. Tennenholtz (2002). R-MAX: A general polynomial time algorithm for near-optimal reinforcement learning. *Journal of Machine Learning Research 3*, 213–231.

Budden, D., J. Walker, M. Flannery, and A. Mendes (2013). Probabilistic gradient ascent with applications to bipedal robot locomotion. In *Australasian Conference on Robotics and Automation (ACRA 2013)*, pp. 37–45.

Cheng, M.-Y. and C.-S. Lin (1997). Genetic algorithm

for control design of biped locomotion. *Journal of Robotic Systems 14*(5), 365–373.

Dean, T., K. Kim, and R. Givan (1998). Solving stochastic planning problems with large state and action spaces. In *Proc. 4th Int. Conf. on Artificial Intelligence Planning Systems*, pp. 102–110.

Dearden, R., N. Friedman, and D. Andre (1999). Model based bayesian exploration. In *Proc. 15th Conf. on Uncertainty in AI (UAI '99)*, pp. 150–159.

Feng, Z., R. Dearden, N. Meuleau, and R. Washington (2004). Dynamic programming for structured continuous Markov decision problems. In *Proc. 20th Conf. on Uncertainty in AI*, pp. 154–161.

Gonalves, J. B. and D. E. Zampieri (2006, 12). An integrated control for a biped walking robot. *Journal of the Brazilian Society of Mechanical Sciences and Engineering 28*, 453 – 460.

Halpern, J. Y., N. Rong, and A. Saxena (2010). MDPs with unawareness. In *Proc. 26th Conf. on Uncertainty in AI (UAI '10)*, pp. 228–235.

Hasegawa, Y., T. Arakawa, and T. Fukuda (2000). Trajectory generation for biped locomotion robot. *Mechatronics 10*, 67–89.

Hauskrecht, M., N. Meuleau, L. Kaelbling, T. Dean, and C. Boutilier (1998). Hierarchical solution of Markov decision processes using macro-actions. In *Proc. 14th Conf. on Uncertainty in AI (UAI '98)*, pp. 220–229.

Hordijk, A. and F. A. Van der Duyn Schouten (1984). Discretization and weak convergence in Markov decision drift processes. *Mathematics of Operations Research 9*, 112–141.

Huang, Q., K. Yokoi, S. Kajita, K. Kaneko, H. Arai, N. Koyachi, and K. Tanie (2001). Planning walking patterns for a biped robot. *IEEE Transactions on Robotics and Automation 17*, 280–289.

Kajita, S., F. Kanehiro, K. Kaneko, K. Fujiwara, K. Harada, K. Yokoi, and H. Hirukawa (2003). Biped walking pattern generation by using preview control of zero-moment point. In *Proc. International Conference on Robotics and Automation (ICRA 2003), Vol. 2*, pp. 1620 – 1626.

Kakade, S., M. Kearns, and J. Langford (2003). Exploration in metric state spaces. In *Proc. 20th Int. Conf. on Machine Learning (ICML '03)*, pp. 306–312.

Kearns, M. and D. Koller (1999). Efficient reinforcement learning in factored MDPs. In *Proc. 16th Int. Joint Conf. on AI (IJCAI '99)*, pp. 740–747.

Kearns, M. and S. Singh (2002). Near-optimal reinforcement learning in polynomial time. *Machine Learning 49*(2-3), 209–232.

Khalil, H. K. (2002). *Nonlinear Systems*. Prentice-Hall.

Kim, J., I. Park, and J. Oh (2007). Walking control algorithm of biped humanoid robot on uneven and inclined floor. *Journal of Intelligent and Robotic Systems 48*(4), 457–484.

Kim, M. S. and W. Uther (2003). Automatic gait optimisation for quadruped robots. In *Proc. Australasian Conference on Robotics and Automation (ACRA)*.

Mordatch, I., N. Mishra, C. Eppner, and P. Abbeel (2016). Combining model-based policy search with online model learning for control of physical humanoids. Preprint, http://www.eecs.berkeley.edu/ igor.mordatch/darwin/ paper.pdf.

Picado, H., M. Gestal, N. Lau, L. P. Reis, and A. M. Tome (2009). Automatic generation of biped walk behavior using genetic algorithms. In *Proc. 10th International Work-Conference on Artificial Neural Networks*, pp. 805–812.

Puterman, M. L. (1994). *Markov Decision Processes*. John Wiley and Sons, Inc.

Rachelson, E., F. Garcia, and P. Fabiani (2008). Extending the bellman equation for MDPs to continuous actions and continuous time in the discounted case. In *10th Int. Symp. on Artificial Intelligence and Mathematics*.

Schulman, J., S. Levine, P. Moritz, M. Jordan, and P. Abbeel (2015). Trust region policy optimization. In *Proc. 31st International Conference on Machine Learning (ICML '15)*, pp. 1889–1897.

Strom, J., G. Slavov, and E. Chown (2010). Omnidirectional walking using ZMP and preview control for the nao humanoid robot. In *RoboCup 2009: Robot Soccer World Cup XIII*, pp. 378–389.

Sutton, R., D. Precup, and S. Singh (1999). Between MDPs and semi-MDPs: A framework for temporal abstraction in reinforcement learning. *Artificial Intelligence 112*, 181–211.

Tedrake, R., T. W. Zhang, and H. S. Seung (2005). Learning to walk in 20 minutes. In *Proc. Fourteenth Yale Workshop on Adaptive and Learning Systems*.

Xue, F., X. Chen, J. Liu, and D. Nardi (2012). Real time biped walking gait pattern generator for a real robot. In T. Röfer, N. M. Mayer, J. Savage, and U. Saranlı (Eds.), *RoboCup 2011: Robot Soccer World Cup XV*, pp. 210–221. Springer.

Zinober, A. S. (1989). Deterministic control of uncertain systems. In *Proc. Int. Conf. on Control and Applications (ICCON '89)*, pp. 645–650.

A Kernel Test for Three-Variable Interactions with Random Processes

Paul K. Rubenstein[123] **Kacper P. Chwialkowski**[3] **Arthur Gretton**[4]
[1]Machine Learning Group, University of Cambridge
[2]Empirical Inference, MPI for Intelligent Systems, Tübingen, Germany
[3]Department of Computer Science, University College London
[4]Gatsby Computational Neuroscience Unit, University College London
pkr23@cam.ac.uk, kacper.chwialkowski@gmail.com, arthur.gretton@gmail.com

Abstract

We apply a wild bootstrap method to the Lancaster three-variable interaction measure in order to detect factorisation of the joint distribution on three variables forming a stationary random process, for which the existing permutation bootstrap method fails. As in the *i.i.d.* case, the Lancaster test is found to outperform existing tests in cases for which two independent variables individually have a weak influence on a third, but that when considered jointly the influence is strong. The main contributions of this paper are twofold: first, we prove that the Lancaster statistic satisfies the conditions required to estimate the quantiles of the null distribution using the wild bootstrap; second, the manner in which this is proved is novel, simpler than existing methods, and can further be applied to other statistics.

1 INTRODUCTION

Nonparametric testing of independence or interaction between random variables is a core staple of machine learning and statistics. The majority of nonparametric statistical tests of independence for continuous-valued random variables rely on the assumption that the observed data are drawn *i.i.d.* Feuerverger [1993], Gretton et al. [2007], Székely et al. [2007], Gretton and Gyorfi [2010], Heller et al. [2013]. The same assumption applies to tests of conditional dependence, and of multivariate interaction between variables Zhang et al. [2011], Kankainen and Ushakov [1998], Fukumizu et al. [2008], Sejdinovic et al. [2013], Patra et al. [2015]. For many applications in finance, medicine, and audio signal analysis, however, the *i.i.d.* assumption is unrealistic and overly restrictive. While many approaches exist for testing interactions between time series under strong parametric assumptions Kirchgässner et al. [2012], Ledford and Tawn [1996], the problem of testing for general, nonlinear interactions has seen far less analysis: tests of pairwise dependence have been proposed by Gaisser et al. [2010], Besserve et al. [2013], Chwialkowski et al. [2014], Chwialkowski and Gretton [2014], where the first publication also addresses mutual independence of more than two univariate time series. The two final works use as their statistic the Hilbert-Schmidt Indepenence Criterion, a general nonparametric measure of dependence [Gretton et al., 2005], which applies even for multivariate or non-Euclidean variables (such as strings and groups). The asymptotic behaviour and corresponding test threshold are derived using particular assumptions on the mixing properties of the processes from which the observations are drawn. These kernel approaches apply only to pairs of random processes, however.

The Lancaster interaction is a signed measure that can be used to construct a test statistic capable of detecting dependence between three random variables [Lancaster, 1969, Sejdinovic et al., 2013]. If the joint distribution on the three variables factorises in some way into a product of a marginal and a pairwise marginal, the Lancaster interaction is zero everywhere. Given observations, this can be used to construct a statistical test, the null hypothesis of which is that the joint distribution factorises thus. In the *i.i.d.* case, the null distribution of the test statistic can be estimated using a permutation bootstrap technique: this amounts to shuffling the indices of one or more of the variables and recalculating the test statistic on this bootstrapped data set. When our samples instead exhibit temporal dependence, shuffling the time indices destroys this dependence and thus doing so does not correspond to a valid resample of the test statistic.

Provided that our data-generating process satisfies some technical conditions on the forms of temporal dependence, recent work by Leucht and Neumann [2013], building on the work of Shao [2010], can come to our rescue. The wild bootstrap is a method that correctly resamples from the null distribution of a test statistic, subject to certain conditions on both the test statistic and the processes from which the observations have been drawn.

In this paper we show that the Lancaster interaction test

statistic satisfies the conditions required to apply the wild bootstrap procedure; moreover, the manner in which we prove this is significantly simpler than existing proofs in the literature of the same property for other kernel test statistics [Chwialkowski et al., 2014, Chwialkowski and Gretton, 2014]. Previous proofs have relied on the classical theory of V-statistics to analyse the asymptotic distribution of the kernel statistic. In particular, the Hoeffding decomposition gives an expression for the kernel test statistic as a sum of other V-statistics. Understanding the asymptotic properties of the components of this decomposition is then conceptually tractable, but algebraically extremely painful. Moreover, as the complexity of the test statistic under analysis grows, the number of terms that must be considered in this approach grows factorially.[1] We conjecture that such analysis of interaction statistics of 4 or more variables would in practice be unfeasible without automatic theorem provers due to the sheer number of terms in the resulting computations.

In contrast, in the approach taken in this paper we explicitly consider our test statistic to be the norm of a Hilbert space operator. We exploit a Central Limit Theorem for Hilbert space valued random variables Dehling et al. [2015] to show that our test statistic converges in probability to the norm of a related population-centred Hilbert space operator, for which the asymptotic analysis is much simpler. Our approach is novel; previous analyses have not, to our knowledge, leveraged the Hilbert space geometry in the context of statistical hypothesis testing using kernel V-statistics in this way.

We propose that our method may in future be applied to the asymptotic analysis of other kernel statistics. In the appendix, we provide an application of this method to the Hilbert Schmidt Independence Criterion (HSIC) test statistic, giving a significantly shorter and simpler proof than that given in Chwialkowski and Gretton [2014]

The Central Limit Theorem that we use in this paper makes certain assumptions on the mixing properties of the random processes from which our data are drawn; as further progress is made, this may be substituted for more up-to-date theorems that make weaker mixing assumptions.

OUTLINE: In Section 2, we detail the Lancaster interaction test and provide our main results. These results justify use of the wild bootstrap to understand the null distribution of the test statistic. In Section 3, we provide more detail about the wild bootstrap, prove that its use correctly controls Type I error and give a consistency result. In Section 4, we evaluate the Lancaster test on synthetic data to identify cases in which it outperforms existing methods, as well as cases in which it is outperformed. In Section 6, we provide proofs of the main results of this paper, in particular the aforementioned novel proof. Further proofs may be found in the Supplementary material.

[1] See for example Lemma 8 in Supplementary material A.3 of Chwialkowski and Gretton [2014]. The proof of this lemma requires keeping track of 4! terms; an equivalent approach for the Lancaster test would have 6! terms. Depending on the precise structure of the statistic, this approach applied to a test involving 4 variables could require as many as $8! = 40320$ terms.

2 LANCASTER INTERACTION TEST

2.1 KERNEL NOTATION

Throughout this paper we will assume that the kernels k, l, m, defined on the domains $\mathcal{X}$, $\mathcal{Y}$ and $\mathcal{Z}$ respectively, are characteristic [Sriperumbudur et al., 2011], bounded and Lipschitz continuous. We describe some notation relevant to the kernel k; similar notation holds for l and m. Recall that $\mu_X := \mathbb{E}_X k(X, \cdot) \in \mathcal{F}_k$ is the mean embedding [Smola et al., 2007] of the random variable X. Given observations X_i, an estimate of the mean embedding is $\tilde{\mu}_X = \frac{1}{n}\sum_{i=1}^{n} k(X_i, \cdot)$. Two modifications of k are used in this work:

$$\bar{k}(x, x') = \langle k(x, \cdot) - \mu_X, k(x', \cdot) - \mu_X \rangle, \quad (1)$$

$$\tilde{k}(x, x') = \langle k(x, \cdot) - \tilde{\mu}_X, k(x', \cdot) - \tilde{\mu}_X \rangle \quad (2)$$

These are called the *population centered kernel* and *empirically centered kernel* respectively.

2.2 LANCASTER INTERACTION

The Lancaster interaction on the triple of random variables (X, Y, Z) is defined as the signed measure $\Delta_L P = \mathbb{P}_{XYZ} - \mathbb{P}_{XY}\mathbb{P}_Z - \mathbb{P}_{XZ}\mathbb{P}_Y - \mathbb{P}_X\mathbb{P}_{YZ} + 2\mathbb{P}_X\mathbb{P}_Y\mathbb{P}_Z$. This measure can be used to detect three-variable interactions. It is straightforward to show that if any variable is independent of the other two (equivalently, if the joint distribution $\mathbb{P}_{XYZ}$ factorises into a product of marginals in any way), then $\Delta_L P = 0$. That is, writing $\mathcal{H}_X = \{X \perp\!\!\!\perp (Y, Z)\}$ and similar for $\mathcal{H}_Y$ and $\mathcal{H}_Z$, we have that

$$\mathcal{H}_X \ \vee \ \mathcal{H}_Y \ \vee \ \mathcal{H}_Z \Rightarrow \Delta_L P = 0 \quad (3)$$

The reverse implication does not hold, and thus no conclusion about the veracity of the $\mathcal{H}.$ can be drawn when $\Delta_L P = 0$. Following Sejdinovic et al. [2013], we can consider the mean embedding of this measure:

$$\mu_L = \int k(x, \cdot) l(y, \cdot) m(z, \cdot) \Delta_L P \quad (4)$$

Given an *i.i.d.* sample $(X_i, Y_i, Z_i)_{i=1}^{n}$, the norm of the mean embedding μ_L can be empirically estimated using empirically centered kernel matrices. For example, for the kernel k with kernel matrix $K_{ij} = k(X_i, X_j)$, the empirically centered kernel matrix $\tilde{K}$ is given by

$$\tilde{K}_{ij} = \langle k(X_i, \cdot) - \tilde{\mu}_X, k(X_j, \cdot) - \tilde{\mu}_X \rangle,$$

By Sejdinovic et al. [2013], an estimator of the norm of the mean embedding of the Lancaster interaction for *i.i.d.* samples is

$$\|\hat{\mu}_L\|^2 = \frac{1}{n^2}\left(\tilde{K} \circ \tilde{L} \circ \tilde{M}\right)_{++} \quad (5)$$

where $\circ$ is the Hadamard (element-wise) product and $A_{++} = \sum_{ij} A_{ij}$, for a matrix A.

2.3 TESTING PROCEDURE

In this paper, we construct a statistical test for three-variable interaction, using $n\|\hat{\mu}_L\|^2$ as the test statistic to distinguish between the following hypotheses:

$\mathcal{H}_0 : \mathcal{H}_X \vee \mathcal{H}_Y \vee \mathcal{H}_Z$
$\mathcal{H}_1 : \mathbb{P}_{XYZ}$ does not factorise in any way

The null hypothesis $\mathcal{H}_0$ is a composite of the three 'sub-hypotheses' $\mathcal{H}_X, \mathcal{H}_Y$ and $\mathcal{H}_Z$. We test $\mathcal{H}_0$ by testing each of the sub-hypotheses separately and we reject if and only if we reject each of $\mathcal{H}_X, \mathcal{H}_Y$ and $\mathcal{H}_Z$. Hereafter we describe the procedure for testing $\mathcal{H}_Z$; similar results hold for $\mathcal{H}_X$ and $\mathcal{H}_Y$.

Sejdinovic et al. [2013] show that, under $\mathcal{H}_Z$, $n\|\hat{\mu}_L\|^2$ converges to an infinite sum of weighted χ-squared random variables. By leveraging the *i.i.d.* assumption of the samples, any given quantile of this distribution can be estimated using simple permutation bootstrap, and so a test procedure is proposed.

In the time series setting this approach does not work. Temporal dependence within the samples makes study of the asymptotic distribution of $n\|\hat{\mu}_L\|^2$ difficult; in Section 4.2 we verify experimentally that the permutation bootstrap used in the *i.i.d* case fails. To construct a test in this setting we will use asymptotic and bootstrap results for mixing processes.

Mixing formalises the notion of the temporal structure within a process, and can be thought of as the rate at which the process forgets about its past. For example, for Gaussian processes this rate can be captured by the autocorrelation function; for general processes, generalisations of autocorrelation are used. The exact assumptions we make about the mixing properties of processes in this paper are discussed in Supplementary material A.7. For brevity in statements of results throughout this paper, however, we define sufficient *suitable mixing assumptions* in Section 3.

2.4 MAIN RESULTS

It is straightforward to show that the norm of the mean embedding (5) can also be written as

$$\|\hat{\mu}_L\|^2 = \frac{1}{n^2}\left(\widetilde{\tilde{K} \circ \tilde{L}} \circ \tilde{M}\right)_{++}$$

Our first contribution is to show that the (difficult) study of the asymptotic null distribution of $\|\hat{\mu}_L\|^2$ can be reduced to studying population centered kernels

$$\|\hat{\mu}_{L,2}^{(Z)}\|^2 = \frac{1}{n^2}\left(\overline{\overline{K} \circ \overline{L}} \circ \overline{M}\right)_{++}$$

where e.g.

$$\overline{K}_{ij} = \langle k(X_i,\cdot) - \mu_X, k(X_j,\cdot) - \mu_X \rangle,$$

Specifically, we prove the following:

Theorem 1. *Suppose that $(X_i, Y_i, Z_i)_{i=1}^n$ are drawn from a random process satisfying suitable mixing assumptions. Under $\mathcal{H}_Z$, $\lim_{n\to\infty}(n\|\hat{\mu}_{L,2}^{(Z)}\|^2 - n\|\hat{\mu}_L\|^2) = 0$ in probability.*

Our proof of Theorem 1 relies crucially on the following Lemma which we prove in Supplementary material A.1

Lemma 1. *Suppose that $(X_i)_{i=1}^n$ is drawn from a random process satisfying suitable mixing assumptions and that k is a bounded kernel on $\mathcal{X}$. Then $\|\hat{\mu}_X - \mu_X\|_k = O_P(n^{-\frac{1}{2}})$*

Proof. (Theorem 1) We provide a short sketch of the proof here; for a full proof, see Section 6.

The key idea is to note that we can rewrite $n\|\hat{\mu}_L\|^2$ in terms of the population centred kernel matrices $\overline{K}$, $\overline{L}$ and $\overline{M}$. Each of the resulting terms can in turn be converted to an inner product between quantities of the form $\hat{\mu} - \mu$, where $\hat{\mu}$ is an empirical estimator of μ, and each μ is a mean embedding or covariance operator.

By applying Lemma 1 to the $\hat{\mu} - \mu$, we show that most of these terms converge in probability to 0, with the residual terms equaling $n\|\hat{\mu}_{L,2}^{(Z)}\|^2$. □

As discussed in Section 1, the essential idea of this proof is novel and the resulting proof is significantly more concise than previous approaches [Chwialkowski and Gretton, 2014, Chwialkowski et al., 2014].

Theorem 1 is useful because the statistic $\|\hat{\mu}_{L,2}^{(Z)}\|^2$ is much easier to study under the non-*i.i.d.* assumption than $\|\hat{\mu}_L\|^2$. Indeed, it can expressed as a V-statistic (see Section 3.2)

$$V_n = \frac{1}{n^2}\sum_{1\le i,j\le n} \overline{\overline{k} \otimes \overline{l}} \otimes \overline{m}(S_i, S_j)$$

where $S_i = (X_i, Y_i, Z_i)$. The crucial observation is that

$$h := \overline{\overline{k} \otimes \overline{l}} \otimes \overline{m}$$

is well behaved in the following sense.

Theorem 2. *Suppose that k, l and m are bounded, symmetric, Lipschitz continuous kernels. Then h is also bounded symmetric and Lipschitz continuous, and is moreover degenerate under $\mathcal{H}_Z$ i.e $\mathbb{E}_S h(S, s) = 0$ for any fixed s.*

Algorithm 1 Test $\mathcal{H}_Z$ with Wild Bootstrap

Input: $\tilde{K}$, $\tilde{L}$, $\tilde{M}$, each size $n \times n$, N= number of bootstraps, α = p-value threshold

$n\|\hat{\mu}_L\|^2 = \frac{1}{n}\left(\left(\widetilde{\tilde{K} \circ \tilde{L}}\right) \circ \tilde{M}\right)_{++}$

samples = zeros(1,N)

for $i = 1$ **to** N **do**

  Draw random vector W according to Equation 6

  samples[i] = $\frac{1}{n}W^\intercal \left(\left(\widetilde{\tilde{K} \circ \tilde{L}}\right) \circ \tilde{M}\right) W$ $(*)$

end for

if sum($n\|\hat{\mu}_L\|^2$ > samples)> $\frac{\alpha}{N}$ **then**

  Reject $\mathcal{H}_Z$

else

  Do not reject $\mathcal{H}_Z$

end if

Proof. See Section 6 □

The asymptotic analysis of such a V-statistic for non-*i.i.d.* data is still complex, but we can appeal to prior work: Leucht and Neumann [2013] showed a way to estimate any given quantile of such a V-statistic under the null hypothesis using a method called the wild bootstrap (introduced in Section 3). This, combined with analysis of the V-statistic under the alternative hypothesis provided in Theorem 2 of Chwialkowski et al. [2014][2], results in a statistical test given in Algorithm 1. The wild bootstrap is used in line $(*)$ to generate samples of the null distribution.

In Section 3 we discuss the wild bootstrap and provide results regarding consistency and Type I error control.

2.5 MULTIPLE TESTING CORRECTION

In the Lancaster test, we reject the composite null hypothesis $\mathcal{H}_0$ if and only if we reject all three of the components. In Sejdinovic et al. [2013], it is suggested that the Holm-Bonferroni correction be used to account for multiple testing [Holm, 1979]. We show here that more relaxed conditions on the p-values can be used while still bounding the Type I error, thus increasing test power.

Denote by $\mathcal{A}_*$ the event that $\mathcal{H}_*$ is rejected. Then

$$\begin{aligned}\mathbb{P}(\mathcal{A}_0) &= \mathbb{P}(\mathcal{A}_X \wedge \mathcal{A}_Y \wedge \mathcal{A}_Z) \\ &\leq \min\{\mathbb{P}(\mathcal{A}_X), \mathbb{P}(\mathcal{A}_Y), \mathbb{P}(\mathcal{A}_Z)\}\end{aligned}$$

If $\mathcal{H}_0$ is true, then so must one of the components. Without loss of generality assume that $\mathcal{H}_X$ is true. If we use significance levels of α in each test individually then $\mathbb{P}(\mathcal{A}_X) \leq \alpha$ and thus $\mathbb{P}(\mathcal{A}_0) \leq \alpha$.

[2]Note that similar results are presented in Leucht and Neumann [2013] as specific cases.

Therefore rejecting $\mathcal{H}_0$ in the event that each test has p-value less than α individually guarantees a Type I error overall of at most α. In contrast, the Holm-Bonferonni method requires that the sorted p-values be lower than $[\frac{\alpha}{3}, \frac{\alpha}{2}, \alpha]$ in order to reject the null hypothesis overall. It is therefore more conservative than necessary and thus has worse test power compared to the 'simple correction' proposed here. This is experimentally verified in Section 4.

3 THE WILD BOOTSTRAP

In this section we discuss the wild bootstrap and provide consistency and Type I error results for the proposed Lancaster test.

3.1 TEMPORAL DEPENDENCE

There are various formalisations of memory or 'mixing' of a random process [Doukhan, 1994, Bradley et al., 2005, Dedecker et al., 2007]; of relevance to this paper is the following :

Definition 1. *A process $(X_t)_t$ is β-mixing (also known as absolutely regular) if $\beta(m) \longrightarrow 0$ as $m \longrightarrow \infty$, where*

$$\beta(m) = \frac{1}{2}\sup_n \sup \sum_{i=1}^{I}\sum_{j=1}^{J} |\mathbb{P}(A_i \cap B_j) - \mathbb{P}(A_i)\mathbb{P}(B_j)|$$

where the second supremum is taken over all finite partitions $\{A_1, \ldots, A_I\}$ and $\{B_1, \ldots, B_J\}$ of the sample space such that $A_i \in \mathcal{F}_1^n$ and $B_j \in \mathcal{F}_{n+m}^\infty$ and $\mathcal{F}_b^c = \sigma(X_b, X_{b+1}, \ldots, X_c)$

SUITABLE MIXING ASSUMPTIONS

We assume that the random process $S_i = (X_i, Y_i, Z_i)$ is β mixing with mixing coefficients satisfying $\beta(m) = o(m^{-6})$. Throughout this paper we refer to this assumption as *suitable mixing assumptions*. For a more in depth discussion of the mixing assumptions made in this paper, see Supplementary materials A.7.

3.2 V-STATISTICS

A V-statistic of a 2-argument, symmetric function h given observations $\mathcal{S}_n = \{S_1, \ldots, S_n\}$ is [Serfling, 2009]:

$$V_n = \frac{1}{n^2}\sum_{1\leq i,j\leq n} h(S_i, S_j)$$

We call nV_n a *normalised* V-statistic. We call h the *core* of V and we say that h is *degenerate* if, for any s_1, $\mathbb{E}_{S_2\sim\mathbb{P}}[h(s_1, S_2)] = 0$, in which case we say that V is a *degenerate V-statistic*. Many kernel test statistics can be viewed as normalised V-statistics which, under the null hypothesis, are degenerate. As mentioned in the previous section, $\|\hat{\mu}_{L,2}^{(Z)}\|^2$ is a V-statistic. Theorems 1 and 2 together imply that, under $\mathcal{H}_Z$, it can be treated as a degenerate V-statistic.

3.3 WILD BOOTSTRAP

If the test statistic has the form of a normalised V-statistic, then provided certain extra conditions are met, the wild bootstrap of Leucht and Neumann [2013] is a method to directly resample the test statistic under the null hypothesis. These conditions can be categorised as concerning: (1) appropriate mixing of the process from which our observations are drawn; (2) the core of the V-statistic.

The condition on the core that is of crucial importance to this paper is that it must be degenerate. Theorem 2 justifies our use of the wild bootstrap in the Lancaster interaction test.

Given the statistic nV_n, Leucht and Neumann [2013] tells us that a random vector W of length n can be drawn such that the bootstrapped statistic[3]

$$nV_b = \frac{1}{n}\sum_{i,j} W_i h(S_i, S_j) W_j$$

is distributed according to the null distribution of nV_n.

By generating many such W and calculating nV_b for each, we can estimate the quantiles of nV.

3.4 GENERATING W

The process generating W must satisfy conditions (B2) given on page 6 of Leucht and Neumann [2013] for nV_b to correctly resample from the null distribution of nV_n. For brevity, we provide here only an example of such a process; the interested reader should consult Leucht and Neumann [2013] or Appedix A of Chwialkowski et al. [2014] for a more detailed discussion of the bootstrapping process. The following bootstrapping process was used in the experiments in Section 4:

$$W_t = e^{-1/l_n} W_{t-1} + \sqrt{1 - e^{-2/l_n}} \epsilon_t \qquad (6)$$

where $W_1, \epsilon_1, \ldots, \epsilon_t$ are independent $\mathcal{N}(0,1)$ random variables. l_n should be taken from a sequence $\{l_n\}$ such that $\lim_{n\longrightarrow\infty} l_n = \infty$; in practice we used $l_n = 20$ for all of the experiments since the values of n were roughly comparable in each case.

3.5 CONTROL OF TYPE I ERROR

The following theorem shows that by estimating the quantiles of the wild bootstrapped statistic nV_b we correctly control the Type I error when testing $\mathcal{H}_Z$.

Theorem 3. *Suppose that $(X_i, Y_i, Z_i)_{i=1}^n$ are drawn from a random process satisfying suitable mixing conditions, and that W is drawn from a process satisfying (B2) in Leucht and Neumann [2013]. Then asymptotically, the quantiles of*

$$nV_b = \frac{1}{n} W^\intercal \left(\left(\bar{K} \circ \bar{L} \right) \circ \bar{M} \right) W$$

converge to those of $n\|\hat{\mu}_L\|^2$.

Proof. See Supplementary material A.3 □

3.6 (SEMI-)CONSISTENCY OF TESTING PROCEDURE

Note that in order to achieve consistency for this test, we would need that $\mathcal{H}_0 \iff \Delta_L P = 0$. Unfortunately this does not hold - in Sejdinovic et al. [2013] examples are given of distributions for which $\mathcal{H}_0$ is false, and yet $\Delta_L P = 0$.

However, the following result does hold:

Theorem 4. *Suppose that $\Delta_L P \neq 0$. Then as $n \longrightarrow \infty$, the probability of correctly rejecting $\mathcal{H}_0$ converges to 1.*

Proof. See Supplementary material A.4 □

At the time of writing, a characterisation of distributions for which $\mathcal{H}_0$ is false yet $\Delta_L P = 0$ is unknown. Therefore, if we reject $\mathcal{H}_0$ then we conclude that the distribution does not factorise; if we fail to reject $\mathcal{H}_0$ then we cannot conclude that the distribution factorises.

4 EXPERIMENTS

The Lancaster test described above amounts to a method to test each of the sub-hypotheses $\mathcal{H}_X, \mathcal{H}_Y, \mathcal{H}_Z$. Rather than using the Lancaster test statistic with wild bootstrap to test each of these, we could instead use HSIC. For example, by considering the pair of variables (X, Y) and Z with kernels $k \otimes l$ and m respectively, HSIC can be used to test $\mathcal{H}_Z$. Similar grouping of the variables can be used to test $\mathcal{H}_X$ and $\mathcal{H}_Y$. Applying the same multiple testing correction as in the Lancaster test, we derive an alternative test of dependence between three variables. We refer to this HSIC based procedure as *3-way HSIC*.

In the case of *i.i.d.* observations, it was shown in Sejdinovic et al. [2013] that Lancaster statistical test is more sensitive to dependence between three random variables than the above HSIC-based test when pairwise interaction is weak but joint interaction is strong. In this section, we demonstrate that the same is true in the time series case on synthetic data.

[3]Note that for fixed $\mathcal{S}_n$, nV_b is a random variable through the randomness introduced by W

4.1 WEAK PAIRWISE INTERACTION, STRONG JOINT INTERACTION

This experiment demonstrates that the Lancaster test has greater power than 3-way HSIC when the pairwise interaction is weak, but joint interaction is strong.

Synthetic data were generated from autoregressive processes X, Y and Z according to:

$$
\begin{aligned}
X_t &= \frac{1}{2}X_{t-1} + \epsilon_t \\
Y_t &= \frac{1}{2}Y_{t-1} + \eta_t \\
Z_t &= \frac{1}{2}Z_{t-1} + d|\theta_t|\text{sign}(X_tY_t) + \zeta_t
\end{aligned}
$$

where $X_0, Y_0, Z_0, \epsilon_t, \eta_t, \theta_t$ and ζ_t are *i.i.d.* $\mathcal{N}(0,1)$ random variables and $d \in \mathbb{R}$, called the *dependence* coefficient, determines the extent to which the process $(Z_t)_t$ is dependent on $(X_t, Y_t)_t$.

Data were generated with varying values of d. For each value of d, 300 datasets were generated, each consisting of 1200 consecutive observations of the variables. Gaussian kernels with bandwidth parameter 1 were used on each variable, and 250 bootstrapping procedures were used for each test on each dataset.

Observe that the random variables are pairwise independent but jointly dependent. Both the Lancaster and 3-way HSIC tests should be able to detect the dependence and therefore reject the null hypothesis in the limit of infinite data. In the finite data regime, the value of d affects drastically how hard it is to detect the dependence. The results of this experiment are presented in Figure 1, which shows that the Lancaster test achieves very high test power with weak dependence coefficients compared to 3-way HSIC. Note also that when using the simple multiple testing correction a higher test power is achieved than with the Holm-Bonferroni correction.

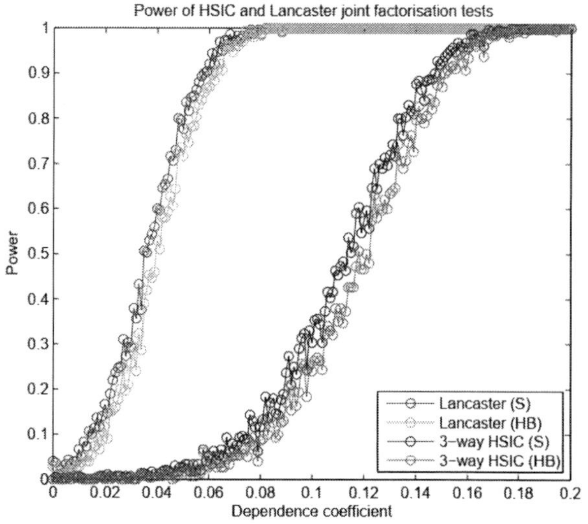

Figure 1: Results of experiment in Section 4.1. (S) refers to the simple multiple correction; (HB) refers to Holm-Bonferroni. The Lancaster test is more sensitive to dependence than 3-way HSIC, and test power for both tests is higher when using the simple correction rather than the Holm-Bonferroni multiple testing correction.

4.2 FALSE POSITIVE RATES

This experiment demonstrates that in the time series case, existing permutation bootstrap methods fail to control the Type I error, while the wild bootstrap correctly identifies test statistic thresholds and appropriately controls Type I error.

Synthetic data were generated from autoregressive processes X, Y and Z according to:

$$
\begin{aligned}
X_t &= aX_{t-1} + \epsilon_t \\
Y_t &= aY_{t-1} + \eta_t \\
Z_t &= aZ_{t-1} + \zeta_t
\end{aligned}
$$

where $X_0, Y_0, Z_0, \epsilon_t, \eta_t$ and ζ_t are *i.i.d.* $\mathcal{N}(0,1)$ random variables and a, called the *dependence coefficient*, determines how temporally dependent the processes are. The null hypothesis in this example is true as each process is independent of the others.

The Lancaster test was performed using both the Wild Bootstrap and the simple permutation bootstrap (used in the *i.i.d.* case) in order to sample from the null distributions of the test statistic. We used a fixed desired false positive rate $\alpha = 0.05$ with sample of size 1000, with 200 experiments run for each value of a. Figure 2 shows the false positive rates for these two methods for varying a. It shows that as the processes become more dependent, the false positive rate for the permutation method becomes very large, and is not bounded by the fixed α, whereas the false positive rate for the Wild Bootstrap method is bounded by α.

4.3 STRONG PAIRWISE INTERACTION

This experiment demonstrates a limitation of the Lancaster test. When pairwise interaction is strong, 3-way HSIC has greater test power than Lancaster.

Synthetic data were generated from autoregressive pro-

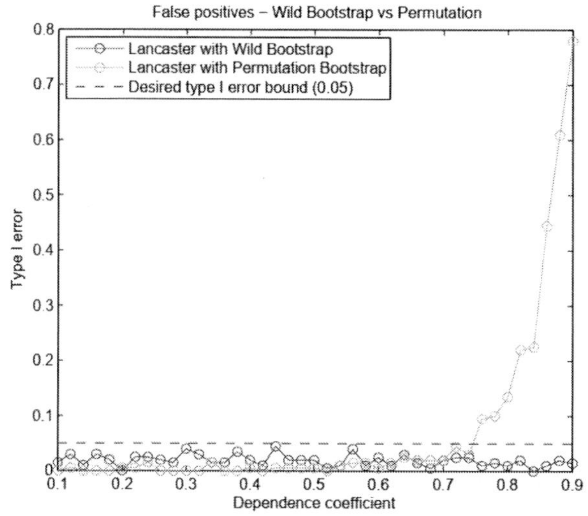

Figure 2: Results of experiment in section 4.2. Whereas the wild bootstrap succeeds in controlling the Type I error across all values of the dependence coefficient, the permutation bootstrap fails to control the Type I error as it does not sample from the correct null distribution as temporal dependence between samples increases.

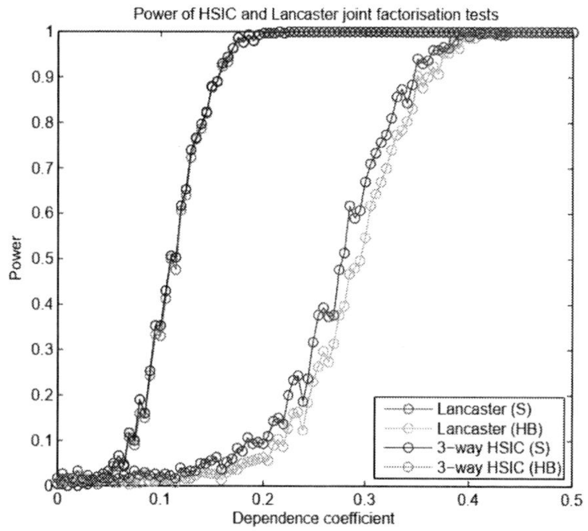

Figure 3: Results of experiment in Section 4.3. (S) refers to the simple multiple correction; (HB) refers to Holm-Bonferroni. The Lancaster test is less sensitive to dependence than 3-way HSIC, and test power in both cases is higher when using the simple correction rather than the Holm-Bonferroni multiple testing correction.

cesses X, Y and Z according to:

$$X_t = \frac{1}{2}X_{t-1} + \epsilon_t$$
$$Y_t = \frac{1}{2}Y_{t-1} + \eta_t$$
$$Z_t = \frac{1}{2}Z_{t-1} + d(X_t + Y_t) + \zeta_t$$

where $X_0, Y_0, Z_0, \epsilon_t, \eta_t$ and ζ_t are *i.i.d.* $\mathcal{N}(0,1)$ random variables and $d \in \mathbb{R}$, called the *dependence* coefficient, determines the extent to which the process $(Z_t)_t$ is dependent on X_t and Y_t.

Data were generated with varying values for the dependence coefficient. For each value of d, 300 datasets were generated, each consisting of 1200 consecutive observations of the variables. Gaussian kernels with bandwidth parameter 1 were used on each variable, and 250 bootstrapping procedures were used for each test on each dataset.

In this case Z_t is pairwise-dependent on both of X_t and Y_t, in addition to all three variables being jointly dependent. Both the Lancaster and 3-way HSIC tests should be capable of detecting the dependence and therefore reject the null hypothesis in the limit of infinite data. The results of this experiment are presented in Figure 3, which demonstrates that in this case the 3-way HSIC test is more sensitive to the dependence than the Lancaster test.

4.4 FOREX DATA

Exchange rates between three currencies (GBP, USD, EUR) at 5 minute intervals over 7 consecutive trading days were obtained. The data were processed by taking the returns (difference between consecutive terms within each time series, $x_t^r = x_t - x_{t-1}$) which were then normalised (divided by standard deviation). We performed the Lancaster test, 3-way HSIC and pairwise HSIC on using the first 800 entries of each processed series. All tests rejected the null hypothesis. The Lancaster and 3-way HSIC tests both returned p-values of 0 for each of $\mathcal{H}_X$, $\mathcal{H}_Y$ and $\mathcal{H}_Z$ with 10000 bootstrapping procedures.

We then shifted one of the time series and repeated the tests (i.e. we used entries 1 to 800 of two of the processed series and entries 801 to 1600 of the third). In this case, pairwise HSIC still detected dependence between the two unshifted time series, and both Lancaster and 3-way HSIC did not reject the null hypothesis that the joint distribution factorises. The Lancaster test returned p-values of 0.2708, 0.2725 and 0.1975 for $\mathcal{H}_X$, $\mathcal{H}_Y$ and $\mathcal{H}_Z$ respectively. 3-way HSIC resturn p-values of 0.3133, 0.0000 and 0.0000 respectively.

In both cases, the Lancaster test behaves as expected. Due to arbitrage, any two exchange rates should determine the third and the Lancaster test correctly identifies a joint dependence in the returns. However, when we shift one of the time series, we break the dependence between it and the other series. Lancaster correctly identifies here that the underlying distribution does factorise.

5 DISCUSSION AND FUTURE RESEARCH

We demonstrated that the Lancaster test is more sensitive than 3-way HSIC when pairwise interaction is weak, but that the opposite is true when pairwise interaction is strong. It is curious that the two tests have different strengths in this manner, particularly when considering the very similar forms of the statistics in each case. Indeed, to test $\mathcal{H}_Z$ using the Lancaster statistic, we bootstrap the following:

$$n\|\Delta_L \hat{P}\|^2 = \frac{1}{n}\left(\left(\widetilde{\tilde{K} \circ \tilde{L}}\right) \circ \tilde{M}\right)_{++}$$

while for the 3-way HSIC test we bootstrap:

$$nHSIC_b = \frac{1}{n}\left(\widetilde{(K \circ L)} \circ \tilde{M}\right)_{++}$$

These two quantities differ only in the centring of K and L, amounting to constant shifts in the respective feature spaces of the kernels k and l. This difference has the consequence of quite drastically changing the types of dependency to which each statistic is sensitive. A formal characterisation of the cases in which the Lancaster statistic is more sensitive than 3-way HSIC would be desirable.

6 PROOFS

An outline of the proof of Theorem 1 was given in Section 2; here we provide the full proof, as well as a proof of Theorem 2.

Proof. (Theorem 1)

By observing that

$$\begin{aligned}
&\phi_X(X_i) - \frac{1}{n}\sum_k \phi_X(X_k) \\
&= (\phi_X(X_i) - \mu_X) - \frac{1}{n}\sum_k (\phi_X(X_k) - \mu_X) \\
&= \bar{\phi}_X(X_i) - \frac{1}{n}\sum_k \bar{\phi}_X(X_k)
\end{aligned}$$

we can therefore expand $\tilde{K}$ in terms of $\bar{K}$ as

$$\begin{aligned}
&\tilde{K}_{ij} \\
&= \langle \phi_X(X_i) - \frac{1}{n}\sum_k \phi_X(X_k), \phi_X(X_j) - \frac{1}{n}\sum_k \phi_X(X_k)\rangle \\
&= \langle \bar{\phi}_X(X_i) - \frac{1}{n}\sum_k \bar{\phi}_X(X_k), \bar{\phi}_X(X_j) - \frac{1}{n}\sum_k \bar{\phi}_X(X_k)\rangle \\
&= \bar{K}_{ij} - \frac{1}{n}\sum_k \bar{K}_{ik} - \frac{1}{n}\sum_k \bar{K}_{jk} + \frac{1}{n^2}\sum_{kl} \bar{K}_{kl}
\end{aligned}$$

and expanding $\tilde{L}$ and $\tilde{M}$ in a similar way, we can rewrite the Lancaster test statistic as

$$\begin{aligned}
n\|\hat{\mu}_L\|^2 = &\frac{1}{n}(\bar{K} \circ \bar{L} \circ \bar{M})_{++} && - \frac{2}{n^2}((\bar{K} \circ \bar{L})\bar{M})_{++} \\
&- \frac{2}{n^2}((\bar{K} \circ \bar{M})\bar{L})_{++} && - \frac{2}{n^2}((\bar{M} \circ \bar{L})\bar{K})_{++} \\
&+ \frac{1}{n^3}(\bar{K} \circ \bar{L})_{++}\bar{M}_{++} && + \frac{1}{n^3}(\bar{K} \circ \bar{M})_{++}\bar{L}_{++} \\
&+ \frac{1}{n^3}(\bar{L} \circ \bar{M})_{++}\bar{K}_{++} && + \frac{2}{n^3}(\bar{M}\bar{K}\bar{L})_{++} \\
&+ \frac{2}{n^3}(\bar{K}\bar{L}\bar{M})_{++} && + \frac{2}{n^3}(\bar{K}\bar{M}\bar{L})_{++} \\
&+ \frac{4}{n^3}tr(\bar{K}_+ \circ \bar{L}_+ \circ \bar{M}_+) && - \frac{4}{n^4}(\bar{K}\bar{L})_{++}\bar{M}_{++} \\
&- \frac{4}{n^4}(\bar{K}\bar{M})_{++}\bar{L}_{++} && - \frac{4}{n^4}(\bar{L}\bar{M})_{++}\bar{K}_{++} \\
&+ \frac{4}{n^5}\bar{K}_{++}\bar{L}_{++}\bar{M}_{++}
\end{aligned}$$

We denote by $C_{XYZ} = \mathbb{E}_{XYZ}[\bar{\phi}_X(X) \otimes \bar{\phi}_Y(Y) \otimes \bar{\phi}_Z(Z)]$ the population centred covariance operator with empirical estimate $\bar{C}_{XYZ} = \frac{1}{n}\sum_i \bar{\phi}_X(X_i) \otimes \bar{\phi}_Y(Y_i) \otimes \bar{\phi}_Z(Z_i)$. We define similarly the quantities $C_{XY}, C_{YZX}, \ldots$ with corresponding empirical counterparts $\bar{C}_{XY}, \bar{C}_{YZX}, \ldots$ where for example $C_{YZ} = \mathbb{E}_{YZ}[\bar{\phi}_Y(Y) \otimes \bar{\phi}_Z(Z)]$

Each of the terms in the above expression for $n\|\hat{\mu}_L\|^2$ can be expressed as inner products between empirical estimates of population centred covariance operators and tensor products of mean embeddings. Rewriting them as such yields:

$$\begin{aligned}
n\|\hat{\mu}_L\|^2 &= n\langle \bar{C}_{XYZ}, \bar{C}_{XYZ}\rangle \\
&- 2n\langle \bar{C}_{XYZ}, \bar{C}_{XY} \otimes \bar{\mu}_Z\rangle \\
&- 2n\langle \bar{C}_{XZY}, \bar{C}_{XZ} \otimes \bar{\mu}_Y\rangle \\
&- 2n\langle \bar{C}_{YZX}, \bar{C}_{YZ} \otimes \bar{\mu}_X\rangle \\
&+ n\langle \bar{C}_{XY} \otimes \bar{\mu}_Z, \bar{C}_{XY} \otimes \bar{\mu}_Z\rangle \\
&+ n\langle \bar{C}_{XZ} \otimes \bar{\mu}_Y, \bar{C}_{XZ} \otimes \bar{\mu}_Y\rangle \\
&+ n\langle \bar{C}_{YZ} \otimes \bar{\mu}_X, \bar{C}_{YZ} \otimes \bar{\mu}_X\rangle \\
&+ 2n\langle \bar{\mu}_Z \otimes \bar{C}_{XY}, \bar{C}_{ZX} \otimes \bar{\mu}_Y\rangle \\
&\vdots
\end{aligned}$$

$$
\begin{aligned}
&+ 2n\langle \bar{\mu}_X \otimes \bar{C}_{YZ}, \bar{C}_{XY} \otimes \bar{\mu}_Z \rangle \\
&+ 2n\langle \bar{\mu}_X \otimes \bar{C}_{ZY}, \bar{C}_{XZ} \otimes \bar{\mu}_Y \rangle \\
&+ 4n\langle \bar{C}_{XYZ}, \bar{\mu}_X \otimes \bar{\mu}_Y \otimes \bar{\mu}_Z \rangle \\
&- 4n\langle \bar{C}_{XY} \otimes \bar{\mu}_Z, \bar{\mu}_X \otimes \bar{\mu}_Y \otimes \bar{\mu}_Z \rangle \\
&- 4n\langle \bar{C}_{XZ} \otimes \bar{\mu}_Y, \bar{\mu}_X \otimes \bar{\mu}_Z \otimes \bar{\mu}_Y \rangle \\
&- 4n\langle \bar{C}_{YZ} \otimes \bar{\mu}_X, \bar{\mu}_Y \otimes \bar{\mu}_Z \otimes \bar{\mu}_X \rangle \\
&+ 4n\langle \bar{\mu}_X \otimes \bar{\mu}_Y \otimes \bar{\mu}_Z, \bar{\mu}_X \otimes \bar{\mu}_Y \otimes \bar{\mu}_Z \rangle
\end{aligned}
$$

By assumption, $\mathbb{P}_{XYZ} = \mathbb{P}_{XY}\mathbb{P}_Z$ and thus the expectation operator also factorises similarly. As a consequence, $C_{XYZ} = 0$. Indeed, given any $A \in \mathcal{F}_X \otimes \mathcal{F}_Y \otimes \mathcal{F}_Z$, we can consider A to be a bounded linear operator $\mathcal{F}_Z \longrightarrow \mathcal{F}_X \otimes \mathcal{F}_Y$. It follows that[4]

$$
\begin{aligned}
&\mathbb{E}_{XYZ}\langle A, \bar{C}_{XYZ} \rangle \\
&= \frac{1}{n}\sum_i \mathbb{E}_{XY}\mathbb{E}_Z \langle A, \bar{\phi}_X(X_i) \otimes \bar{\phi}_Y(Y_i) \otimes \bar{\phi}_Z(Z_i) \rangle \\
&= \frac{1}{n}\sum_i \mathbb{E}_{XY}\mathbb{E}_Z \langle \bar{\phi}_X(X_i) \otimes \bar{\phi}_Y(Y_i), A\bar{\phi}_Z(Z_i) \rangle_{\mathcal{F}_X \otimes \mathcal{F}_Y} \\
&= \frac{1}{n}\sum_i \mathbb{E}_{XY} \langle \bar{\phi}_X(X_i) \otimes \bar{\phi}_Y(Y_i), A\mathbb{E}_Z\bar{\phi}_Z(Z_i) \rangle_{\mathcal{F}_X \otimes \mathcal{F}_Y} \\
&= 0
\end{aligned}
$$

We conclude that $C_{XYZ} = \mathbb{E}_{XYZ}\bar{C}_{XYZ} = 0$.

Similarly, C_{XZY}, C_{YZX}, C_{XZ}, C_{YZ} are all 0 in their respective Hilbert spaces. Lemma 2 tells us that each subprocess of (X_i, Y_i, Z_i) satisfies the same β-mixing conditions as (X_i, Y_i, Z_i), thus by applying Lemma 1 it follows that $\|\bar{C}_{XZY}\|$, $\|\bar{C}_{YZX}\|$, $\|\bar{C}_{XZ}\|$, $\|\bar{C}_{YZ}\|$, $\|\bar{\mu}_X\|$, $\|\bar{\mu}_Y\|$, $\|\bar{\mu}_Z\| = O_P\left(n^{-\frac{1}{2}}\right)$. Therefore

$$
\begin{aligned}
n\|\hat{\mu}_L\|^2 &\xrightarrow{O_P(n^{-\frac{1}{2}})} n\langle \bar{C}_{XYZ}, \bar{C}_{XYZ} \rangle \\
&- 2n\langle \bar{C}_{XYZ}, \bar{C}_{XY} \otimes \bar{\mu}_Z \rangle - 2n\langle \bar{C}_{XZY}, \bar{C}_{XZ} \otimes \bar{\mu}_Y \rangle \\
&= \frac{1}{n}((\bar{K} \circ \bar{L}) \circ \bar{M})_{++} \\
&- \frac{2}{n^2}((\bar{K} \circ \bar{L})\bar{M})_{++} + \frac{1}{n^3}(\bar{K} \circ \bar{L})_{++}\bar{M}_{++}
\end{aligned}
$$

since all the other terms decay at least as quickly as $O_P(\frac{1}{\sqrt{n}})$. This is shown here for $n\langle \bar{\mu}_X \otimes \bar{C}_{YZ}, \bar{C}_{XY} \otimes \bar{\mu}_Z \rangle$; the proofs for the other terms are similar.

$$
\begin{aligned}
&n\langle \bar{\mu}_X \otimes \bar{C}_{YZ}, \bar{C}_{XY} \otimes \bar{\mu}_Z \rangle \\
&\leq n\|\bar{\mu}_X \otimes \bar{C}_{YZ}\|\|\bar{C}_{XY} \otimes \bar{\mu}_Z\| \\
&= n\sqrt{\langle \bar{\mu}_X \otimes \bar{C}_{YZ}, \bar{\mu}_X \otimes \bar{C}_{YZ} \rangle}\sqrt{\langle \bar{C}_{XY} \otimes \bar{\mu}_Z, \bar{C}_{XY} \otimes \bar{\mu}_Z \rangle} \\
&= n\sqrt{\langle \bar{\mu}_X, \bar{\mu}_X \rangle \langle \bar{C}_{YZ}, \bar{C}_{YZ} \rangle}\sqrt{\langle \bar{C}_{XY}, \bar{C}_{XY} \rangle \langle \bar{\mu}_Z, \bar{\mu}_Z \rangle} \\
&= n\|\bar{\mu}_X\|\|\bar{C}_{YZ}\|\|\bar{C}_{XY}\|\|\bar{\mu}_Z\| \\
&= nO_P\left(\tfrac{1}{\sqrt{n}}\right)O_P\left(\tfrac{1}{\sqrt{n}}\right)O_P(1)O_P\left(\tfrac{1}{\sqrt{n}}\right) = O_P\left(\tfrac{1}{\sqrt{n}}\right)
\end{aligned}
$$

It can be shown that $\bar{K} \circ \bar{L}$ in the above expression can be replaced with $\overline{\bar{K} \circ \bar{L}}$ while preserving equality. That is, we can equivalently write

$$
\begin{aligned}
n\|\Delta_L \hat{P}\|^2 &\longrightarrow \frac{1}{n}((\overline{\bar{K} \circ \bar{L}}) \circ \bar{M})_{++} \\
&- \frac{2}{n^2}((\overline{\bar{K} \circ \bar{L}})\bar{M})_{++} + \frac{1}{n^3}(\overline{\bar{K} \circ \bar{L}})_{++}\bar{M}_{++}
\end{aligned}
$$

This is equivalent to treating $\bar{k} \otimes \bar{l}$ as a kernel on the single variable $T := (X, Y)$ and performing another recentering trick as we did at the beginning of this proof. By rewriting the above expression in terms of the operator $\bar{C}_{TZ}$ and mean embeddings μ_T and μ_Z, it can be shown by a similar argument to before that the latter two terms tend to 0 at least as $O_P(n^{-\frac{1}{2}})$, and thus, substituting for the definition of $\|\hat{\mu}_{L,2}^{(Z)}\|^2$,

$$
n\|\hat{\mu}_L\|^2 \xrightarrow{O_P(\frac{1}{\sqrt{n}})} n\|\hat{\mu}_{L,2}^{(Z)}\|^2
$$

as required. □

Proof. (Theorem 2)

Note that $\mathbb{E}_{XYZ} = \mathbb{E}_{XY}\mathbb{E}_Z$ under $\mathcal{H}_Z$. Therefore, fixing any $s_j = (x_j, y_j, z_j)$ we have that

$$
\begin{aligned}
\mathbb{E}_{S_i} h(S_i, s_j) &= \mathbb{E}_{X_iY_i}\mathbb{E}_{Z_i}\overline{\bar{k} \otimes \bar{l}} \otimes \bar{m}(S_i, s_j) \\
&= \langle \mathbb{E}_{X_iY_i}\bar{\phi}(X_i) \otimes \bar{\phi}(Y_i) - C_{XY}, \bar{\phi}(x_j) \otimes \bar{\phi}(y_j) - C_{XY} \rangle \\
&\quad \times \langle \mathbb{E}_{Z_i}\bar{\phi}(Z_i), \bar{\phi}(z_j) \rangle \\
&= \langle 0, \bar{\phi}(x_j) \otimes \bar{\phi}(y_j) - C_{XY} \rangle \\
&\quad \times \langle 0, \bar{\phi}(z_j) \rangle = 0
\end{aligned}
$$

Therefore h is degenerate. Symmetry follows from the symmetry of the Hilbert space inner product.

For boundedness and Lipschitz continuity, it suffices to show the two following rules for constructing new kernels from old preserve both properties (see Supplementary materials A.5 for proof):

- $k \mapsto \bar{k}$
- $(k, l) \mapsto k \otimes l$

It then follows that $h = \overline{\bar{k} \otimes \bar{l}} \otimes \bar{m}$ is bounded and Lipschitz continuous since it can be constructed from k, l and m using the two above rules. □

ORCID 0000-0003-3169-7624

[4]We can bring the $\mathbb{E}_Z$ inside the inner product in the penultimate line due to the Bochner integrability of $\bar{\phi}_Z(Z)$, which follows from the conditions required for μ_Z to exist [Steinwart and Christmann, 2008].

References

M. Besserve, N. Logothetis, and B. Schölkopf. Statistical analysis of coupled time series with kernel cross-spectral density operators. In *NIPS*, pages 2535–2543, 2013.

R. C. Bradley et al. Basic properties of strong mixing conditions. a survey and some open questions. *Probability surveys*, 2(2):107–144, 2005.

K. Chwialkowski and A. Gretton. A kernel independence test for random processes. *arXiv preprint arXiv:1402.4501*, 2014.

K. P. Chwialkowski, D. Sejdinovic, and A. Gretton. A wild bootstrap for degenerate kernel tests. In *Advances in neural information processing systems*, pages 3608–3616, 2014.

J. Dedecker and C. Prieur. New dependence coefficients. examples and applications to statistics. *Probability Theory and Related Fields*, 132(2):203–236, 2005.

J. Dedecker, P. Doukhan, G. Lang, L. R. J. Rafael, S. Louhichi, and C. Prieur. Weak dependence. In *Weak Dependence: With Examples and Applications*, pages 9–20. Springer, 2007.

H. Dehling, O. S. Sharipov, and M. Wendler. Bootstrap for dependent hilbert space-valued random variables with application to von mises statistics. *Journal of Multivariate Analysis*, 133:200–215, 2015.

P. Doukhan. *Mixing*. Springer, 1994.

A. Feuerverger. A consistent test for bivariate dependence. *International Statistical Review*, 61(3):419–433, 1993.

K. Fukumizu, A. Gretton, X. Sun, and B. Schölkopf. Kernel measures of conditional dependence. In *NIPS*, pages 489–496, Cambridge, MA, 2008. MIT Press.

S. Gaisser, M. Ruppert, and F. Schmid. A multivariate version of hoeffding's phi-square. *Journal of Multivariate Analysis*, 101(10):2571–2586, 2010.

A. Gretton and L. Gyorfi. Consistent nonparametric tests of independence. *Journal of Machine Learning Research*, 11:1391–1423, 2010.

A. Gretton, O. Bousquet, A. Smola, and B. Schölkopf. Measuring statistical dependence with hilbert-schmidt norms. In *Algorithmic learning theory*, pages 63–77. Springer, 2005.

A. Gretton, K. Fukumizu, C. H. Teo, L. Song, B. Schölkopf, and A. J. Smola. A kernel statistical test of independence. In *Advances in Neural Information Processing Systems*, pages 585–592, 2007.

R. Heller, Y. Heller, and M. Gorfine. A consistent multivariate test of association based on ranks of distances. *Biometrika*, 100(2):503–510, 2013.

S. Holm. A simple sequentially rejective multiple test procedure. *Scandinavian journal of statistics*, pages 65–70, 1979.

A. Kankainen and N. G. Ushakov. A consistent modification of a test for independence based on the empirical characteristic function. *Journal of Mathematical Sciencies*, 89:1582–1589, 1998.

G. Kirchgässner, J. Wolters, and U. Hassler. *Introduction to modern time series analysis*. Springer Science & Business Media, 2012.

H. O. Lancaster. *Chi-Square Distribution*. Wiley Online Library, 1969.

A. W. Ledford and J. A. Tawn. Statistics for near independence in multivariate extreme values. *Biometrika*, 83(1): 169–187, 1996.

A. Leucht and M. H. Neumann. Dependent wild bootstrap for degenerate u-and v-statistics. *Journal of Multivariate Analysis*, 117:257–280, 2013.

R. Patra, B. Sen, and G. Szekely. On a nonparametric notion of residual and its applications. *Statist. Probab. Lett.*, 106:208–213, 2015.

D. Sejdinovic, A. Gretton, and W. Bergsma. A kernel test for three-variable interactions. In *Advances in Neural Information Processing Systems*, pages 1124–1132, 2013.

R. J. Serfling. *Approximation theorems of mathematical statistics*, volume 162. John Wiley & Sons, 2009.

X. Shao. The dependent wild bootstrap. *Journal of the American Statistical Association*, 105(489):218–235, 2010.

A. Smola, A. Gretton, L. Song, and B. Schölkopf. A hilbert space embedding for distributions. In *Algorithmic Learning Theory*, pages 13–31. Springer, 2007.

B. K. Sriperumbudur, K. Fukumizu, and G. R. Lanckriet. Universality, characteristic kernels and rkhs embedding of measures. *The Journal of Machine Learning Research*, 12:2389–2410, 2011.

I. Steinwart and A. Christmann. *Support vector machines*. Springer Science & Business Media, 2008.

G. Székely, M. Rizzo, and N. Bakirov. Measuring and testing dependence by correlation of distances. *Annals of Statistics*, 35(6):2769–2794, 2007.

K. Zhang, J. Peters, D. Janzing, and B. Schoelkopf. Kernel-based conditional independence test and application in causal discovery. In *Proceedings of the Conference on Uncertainty in Artificial Intelligence (UAI)*, pages 804–813, 2011.

Overdispersed Black-Box Variational Inference

Francisco J. R. Ruiz
Data Science Institute
Dept. of Computer Science
Columbia University

Michalis K. Titsias
Dept. of Informatics
Athens University of
Economics and Business

David M. Blei
Data Science Institute
Dept. of Computer Science and Statistics
Columbia University

Abstract

We introduce overdispersed black-box variational inference, a method to reduce the variance of the Monte Carlo estimator of the gradient in black-box variational inference. Instead of taking samples from the variational distribution, we use importance sampling to take samples from an overdispersed distribution in the same exponential family as the variational approximation. Our approach is general since it can be readily applied to any exponential family distribution, which is the typical choice for the variational approximation. We run experiments on two non-conjugate probabilistic models to show that our method effectively reduces the variance, and the overhead introduced by the computation of the proposal parameters and the importance weights is negligible. We find that our overdispersed importance sampling scheme provides lower variance than black-box variational inference, even when the latter uses twice the number of samples. This results in faster convergence of the black-box inference procedure.

1 INTRODUCTION

Generative probabilistic modeling is an effective approach for understanding real-world data in many areas of science (Bishop, 2006; Murphy, 2012). A probabilistic model describes a data-generating process through a joint distribution of observed data and latent (unobserved) variables. With a model in place, the investigator uses an inference algorithm to calculate or approximate the posterior, i.e., the conditional distribution of the latent variables given the available observations. It is through the posterior that the investigator explores the latent structure in the data and forms a predictive distribution of future data. Approximating the posterior is the central algorithmic problem for probabilistic modeling.

One of the most widely used methods to approximate the posterior distribution is variational inference (Wainwright and Jordan, 2008; Jordan et al., 1999). Variational inference aims to approximate the posterior with a simpler distribution, fitting that distribution to be close to the exact posterior, where closeness is measured in terms of Kullback-Leibler (KL) divergence. In minimizing the KL, variational inference converts the problem of approximating the posterior into an optimization problem.

Traditional variational inference uses coordinate ascent to optimize its objective. This works well for models in which each conditional distribution is easy to compute (Ghahramani and Beal, 2001), but is difficult to use in more complex models where the variational objective involves intractable expectations. Recent innovations in variational inference have addressed this with stochastic optimization, forming noisy gradients with Monte Carlo approximation. This strategy expands the scope of variational inference beyond traditional models, e.g., to non-conjugate probabilistic models (Carbonetto et al., 2009; Paisley et al., 2012; Salimans and Knowles, 2013; Ranganath et al., 2014; Titsias and Lázaro-Gredilla, 2014), deep neural networks (Neal, 1992; Hinton et al., 1995; Mnih and Gregor, 2014; Kingma and Welling, 2014; Ranganath et al., 2015), and probabilistic programming (Wingate and Weber, 2013; Kucukelbir et al., 2015). Some of these techniques find their roots in classical policy search algorithms for reinforcement learning (Williams, 1992; van de Meent et al., 2016).

These approaches must address a core problem with Monte Carlo estimates of the gradient, which is that they suffer from high variance. The estimated gradient can significantly differ from the truth and this leads to slow convergence of the optimization. There are several strategies to reduce the variance of the gradients, including Rao-Blackwellization (Casella and Robert, 1996; Ranganath et al., 2014), control variates (Ross, 2002; Paisley et al., 2012; Ranganath et al., 2014; Gu et al., 2016), reparameterization (Price, 1958; Bonnet, 1964; Salimans and Knowles, 2013; Kingma and Welling, 2014; Rezende et al., 2014; Kucukelbir et al., 2015), and local expectations (Titsias and

Lázaro-Gredilla, 2015).

In this paper we develop overdispersed black-box variational inference (O-BBVI), a new method for reducing the variance of Monte Carlo gradients in variational inference. The main idea is to use importance sampling to estimate the gradient, in order to construct a good proposal distribution that is matched to the variational problem. We show that O-BBVI applies more generally than methods such as reparameterization and local expectations, and it further improves the profile of gradients that use Rao-Blackwellization and control variates.

We demonstrate O-BBVI on two complex models: a non-conjugate time series model (Ranganath et al., 2014) and Poisson-based deep exponential families (DEFs) (Ranganath et al., 2015). Our study shows that O-BBVI reduces the variance of the original black-box variational inference (BBVI) estimates (Ranganath et al., 2014), even when using only half the number of Monte Carlo samples. This provides significant savings in run-time complexity.

Technical summary. Consider a probabilistic model $p(\mathbf{x}, \mathbf{z})$, where $\mathbf{z}$ are the latent variables and $\mathbf{x}$ are the observations. Variational inference sets up a parameterized distribution of the latent variables $q(\mathbf{z}; \boldsymbol{\lambda})$ and finds the parameter $\boldsymbol{\lambda}^\star$ that minimizes the KL divergence between $q(\mathbf{z}; \boldsymbol{\lambda})$ and the posterior $p(\mathbf{z} \mid \mathbf{x})$. We then use $q(\mathbf{z}; \boldsymbol{\lambda}^\star)$ as a proxy for the posterior.

We build on BBVI, which solves this problem with a stochastic optimization procedure that uses Monte Carlo estimates of the gradient (Ranganath et al., 2014). Let $\mathcal{L}(\boldsymbol{\lambda})$ be the variational objective, which is the (negative) KL divergence up to an additive constant. BBVI uses samples from $q(\mathbf{z}; \boldsymbol{\lambda})$ to approximate its gradient,

$$\nabla_{\boldsymbol{\lambda}} \mathcal{L} = \mathbb{E}_{q(\mathbf{z};\boldsymbol{\lambda})} \left[f(\mathbf{z}) \right], \tag{1}$$

where

$$f(\mathbf{z}) = \nabla_{\boldsymbol{\lambda}} \log q(\mathbf{z}; \boldsymbol{\lambda}) \left(\log p(\mathbf{x}, \mathbf{z}) - \log q(\mathbf{z}; \boldsymbol{\lambda}) \right). \tag{2}$$

The resulting Monte Carlo estimator, based on sampling from $q(\mathbf{z}; \boldsymbol{\lambda})$, only requires evaluating the log-joint distribution $\log p(\mathbf{z}, \mathbf{x})$, the log-variational distribution $\log q(\mathbf{z}; \boldsymbol{\lambda})$, and the score function $\nabla_{\boldsymbol{\lambda}} \log q(\mathbf{z}; \boldsymbol{\lambda})$. Calculations about $q(\mathbf{z}; \boldsymbol{\lambda})$ can be derived once and stored in a library and, as a consequence, BBVI can be easily applied to a large class of models. However, as we mentioned above, Monte Carlo estimates of this gradient usually have high variance. Ranganath et al. (2014) correct for this with Rao-Blackwellization and control variates.

We expand on this idea by approximating the gradient with importance sampling. We introduce a proposal distribution $r(\mathbf{z}; \boldsymbol{\lambda}, \tau)$, which depends on both the variational parameters and an additional parameter. (We discuss the additional parameter below.) We then write the gradient as

$$\nabla_{\boldsymbol{\lambda}} \mathcal{L} = \mathbb{E}_{r(\mathbf{z};\boldsymbol{\lambda},\tau)} \left[f(\mathbf{z}) \frac{q(\mathbf{z}; \boldsymbol{\lambda})}{r(\mathbf{z}; \boldsymbol{\lambda}, \tau)} \right], \tag{3}$$

and form noisy estimates with samples from the proposal.

The key idea behind our method is that the optimal proposal distribution (in terms of minimizing the variance of the resulting estimator) is *not* the original distribution $q(\mathbf{z}; \boldsymbol{\lambda})$ (Owen, 2013, Chapter 9). Rather, the optimal proposal is a skewed version of that distribution with heavier tails. Unfortunately, this distribution is not available to us—it involves an intractable normalization constant. But we use this insight to set a proposal with heavier tails than the variational distribution, thus making it closer to the optimal proposal. Note this is an unconventional use of importance sampling, which is usually employed to approximate expectations. Instead, we use importance sampling to improve the characteristics of a Monte Carlo estimator by sampling from a different distribution.

In detail, we first assume that the variational distribution is in the exponential family. (This is not an assumption about the model; most applications of variational inference use exponential family variational distributions.) We then set the proposal distribution to be in the corresponding overdispersed exponential family (Jørgensen, 1987), where τ is the dispersion parameter. We show that the corresponding estimator has lower variance than the BBVI estimator, we put forward a method to adapt the dispersion parameter during optimization, and we demonstrate that this method is more efficient than BBVI. We call our approach *overdispersed black-box variational inference* (O-BBVI).

Organization. The rest of the paper is organized as follows. We review BBVI in Section 2. We develop O-BBVI in Section 3, describing both the basic algorithm and its extensions to adaptive proposals and high-dimensional settings. Section 4 reports on our empirical study of two non-conjugate models. We conclude the paper in Section 5.

2 BLACK-BOX VARIATIONAL INFERENCE

Consider a probabilistic model $p(\mathbf{x}, \mathbf{z})$ and a variational family $q(\mathbf{z}; \boldsymbol{\lambda})$ which is in the exponential family, i.e.,

$$q(\mathbf{z}; \boldsymbol{\lambda}) = g(\mathbf{z}) \exp\left\{ \boldsymbol{\lambda}^\top t(\mathbf{z}) - A(\boldsymbol{\lambda}) \right\}, \tag{4}$$

where $g(\mathbf{z})$ is the base measure, $\boldsymbol{\lambda}$ are the natural parameters, $t(\mathbf{z})$ are the sufficient statistics, and $A(\boldsymbol{\lambda})$ is the log-normalizer. We are interested in a variational approximation to the intractable posterior $p(\mathbf{z} \mid \mathbf{x})$, i.e., we aim to minimize the KL divergence $D_{\text{KL}}\left(q(\mathbf{z}; \boldsymbol{\lambda}) \parallel p(\mathbf{z} \mid \mathbf{x})\right)$ with respect to $\boldsymbol{\lambda}$ (Jordan et al., 1999). This is equivalent to maximizing the evidence lower bound (ELBO),

$$\mathcal{L}(\boldsymbol{\lambda}) = \mathbb{E}_{q(\mathbf{z};\boldsymbol{\lambda})} \left[\log p(\mathbf{x}, \mathbf{z}) - \log q(\mathbf{z}; \boldsymbol{\lambda}) \right], \tag{5}$$

which is a lower bound on the log of the marginal probability of the observations, $\log p(\mathbf{x})$.

With a tractable variational family (e.g., the mean-field family) and a conditionally conjugate model,[1] the expectations in Eq. 5 can be computed in closed form and we can use coordinate-ascent variational inference (Ghahramani and Beal, 2001). However, many models of interest are not conditionally conjugate. For these models, we need alternative methods to optimize the ELBO. One approach is BBVI, which uses Monte Carlo estimates of the gradient and requires few model-specific calculations (Ranganath et al., 2014). Thus, BBVI is a variational inference algorithm that can be applied to a large class of models.

BBVI relies on the "log-derivative trick," also called REINFORCE or score function method (Williams, 1992; Kleijnen and Rubinstein, 1996; Glynn, 1990), to obtain Monte Carlo estimates of the gradient. In detail, we recover the Monte Carlo estimate driven by Eqs. 1 and 2 by taking the gradient of (5) with respect to the variational parameters $\boldsymbol{\lambda}$, and then applying the following two identities:

$$\nabla_{\boldsymbol{\lambda}} q(\mathbf{z}; \boldsymbol{\lambda}) = q(\mathbf{z}; \boldsymbol{\lambda}) \nabla_{\boldsymbol{\lambda}} \log q(\mathbf{z}; \boldsymbol{\lambda}), \tag{6}$$

$$\mathbb{E}_{q(\mathbf{z};\boldsymbol{\lambda})} \left[\nabla_{\boldsymbol{\lambda}} \log q(\mathbf{z}; \boldsymbol{\lambda})\right] = 0. \tag{7}$$

Eq. 1 enables noisy gradients of the ELBO by taking samples from $q(\mathbf{z}; \boldsymbol{\lambda})$. However, the resulting estimator may have high variance. This is especially the case when the variational distribution $q(\mathbf{z}; \boldsymbol{\lambda})$ is a poor fit to the posterior $p(\mathbf{z} \mid \mathbf{x})$, which is typical in early iterations of optimization.

In order to reduce the variance of the estimator, BBVI uses two strategies: control variates and Rao-Blackwellization. Because we will also use these ideas in our algorithm, we briefly discuss them here.

Control variates. A control variate is a random variable that is included in the estimator, preserving its expectation but reducing its variance (Ross, 2002). Although there are many possible choices for control variates, Ranganath et al. (2014) advocate for the weighted score function because it is not model-dependent. Denote the score function by $h(\mathbf{z}) = \nabla_{\boldsymbol{\lambda}} \log q(\mathbf{z}; \boldsymbol{\lambda})$, and note again that its expected value is zero. With this function, each component n of the gradient in (1) can be rewritten as $\mathbb{E}_{q(\mathbf{z};\boldsymbol{\lambda})} \left[f_n(\mathbf{z}) - a_n h_n(\mathbf{z})\right]$ where a_n is a constant and $f(\mathbf{z})$ is defined in (2). (Here, $f_n(\mathbf{z})$ and $h_n(\mathbf{z})$ denote the n-th component of $f(\mathbf{z})$ and $h(\mathbf{z})$, respectively.) We can set each element a_n to minimize the variance of the Monte Carlo estimates of this expectation,

$$a_n = \frac{\mathrm{Cov}(f_n(\mathbf{z}), h_n(\mathbf{z}))}{\mathrm{Var}(h_n(\mathbf{z}))}. \tag{8}$$

In BBVI, a separate set of samples from $q(\mathbf{z}; \boldsymbol{\lambda})$ is used to estimate a_n (otherwise, the estimator would be biased).

Rao-Blackwellization. Rao-Blackwellization (Casella and Robert, 1996) reduces the variance of a random variable by replacing it with its conditional expectation, given a subset of other variables. In BBVI, each component of the gradient is Rao-Blackwellized with respect to variables outside of the Markov blanket of the involved hidden variable. More precisely, assume a mean-field[2] variational distribution $q(\mathbf{z}; \boldsymbol{\lambda}) = \prod_n q(z_n; \lambda_n)$. We can equivalently rewrite the expectation of each element in Eq. 1 as

$$\nabla_{\lambda_n} \mathscr{L} = \mathbb{E}_{q(\mathbf{z}_{(n)};\boldsymbol{\lambda}_{(n)})}\big[\nabla_{\lambda_n} \log q(z_n; \lambda_n) \times \left(\log p_n(\mathbf{x}, \mathbf{z}_{(n)}) - \log q(z_n; \lambda_n)\right)\big], \tag{9}$$

where $\mathbf{z}_{(n)}$ denotes the variable z_n together with all latent variables in its Markov blanket, $q(\mathbf{z}_{(n)}; \boldsymbol{\lambda}_{(n)})$ denotes the variational distribution on $\mathbf{z}_{(n)}$, and $\log p_n(\mathbf{x}, \mathbf{z}_{(n)})$ contains all terms of the log-joint distribution that depend on $\mathbf{z}_{(n)}$. The Monte Carlo estimate based on the Rao-Blackwellized expectation has significantly smaller variance than the estimator driven by Eq. 1.

3 OVERDISPERSED BLACK-BOX VARIATIONAL INFERENCE

We have described BBVI and its two strategies for reducing the variance of the noisy gradient. We now describe O-BBVI, a method for further reducing the variance. The main idea is to use importance sampling (Robert and Casella, 2005) to estimate the gradient. We first describe O-BBVI and the proposal distribution it uses. We then show that this reduces variance, discuss several important implementation details, and present the full algorithm.

O-BBVI does not sample from the variational distribution $q(\mathbf{z}; \boldsymbol{\lambda})$ to estimate the expectation $\mathbb{E}_{q(\mathbf{z};\boldsymbol{\lambda})} \left[f(\mathbf{z})\right]$. Rather, it takes samples from a proposal distribution $r(\mathbf{z}; \boldsymbol{\lambda}, \tau)$ and constructs estimates of the gradient in Eq. 3, where the importance weights are $w(\mathbf{z}) = q(\mathbf{z}; \boldsymbol{\lambda})/r(\mathbf{z}; \boldsymbol{\lambda}, \tau)$. This guarantees that the resulting estimator is unbiased. The proposal distribution involves the current setting of the variational parameters $\boldsymbol{\lambda}$ and an additional parameter τ.

The optimal proposal. The particular proposal that O-BBVI uses is inspired by a result from the importance sampling literature (Robert and Casella, 2005; Owen, 2013). This result states that the optimal proposal distribution, which minimizes the variance of the estimator, is *not* the variational distribution $q(\mathbf{z}; \boldsymbol{\lambda})$. Rather, the optimal pro-

[1]A conditionally conjugate model is a model for which all the complete conditionals (i.e., the posterior distribution of each hidden variable conditioned on the observations and the rest of hidden variables) are in the same exponential family as the prior.

[2]A structured variational approach is also amenable to Rao-Blackwellization, but we assume a fully factorized variational distribution for simplicity.

posal is

$$r_n^\star(\mathbf{z}) \propto q(\mathbf{z}; \boldsymbol{\lambda})|f_n(\mathbf{z})|, \tag{10}$$

for each component n of the gradient. (Recall that $f(\mathbf{z})$ is a vector of the same length as $\boldsymbol{\lambda}$.)

While interesting, the optimal proposal distribution is not tractable in general—it involves normalizing a complex product—and is not "black box" in the sense that it depends on the model via $f(\mathbf{z})$. In O-BBVI, we build an alternative proposal based on overdispersed exponential families (Jørgensen, 1987). We will argue that this proposal is closer to the (intractable) optimal $r^*(\mathbf{z})$ than the variational distribution $q(\mathbf{z}; \boldsymbol{\lambda})$, and that it is still practical in the context of stochastic optimization of the variational objective. Note that approximating the optimal proposal in stochastic optimization was also explored in Bouchard et al. (2015).

The overdispersed proposal. Our motivation for using overdispersed exponential families is that the optimal distribution of Eq. 10 assigns higher probability density to the tails of $q(\mathbf{z}; \boldsymbol{\lambda})$. There are two reasons for this fact. First, consider settings of the variational parameters where the variational distribution is a poor fit to the posterior. For these parameters, there are values of $\mathbf{z}$ for which the posterior is high but the variational distribution is small. While the optimal proposal would sample configurations of $\mathbf{z}$ for which $f_n(\mathbf{z})$ is large, these realizations are in the tails of the variational distribution.

The second reason has to do with the score function. The score function $h_n(\mathbf{z})$ vanishes for values of $\mathbf{z}$ for which the n-th sufficient statistic $t_n(\mathbf{z})$ equals its expected value, and this pushes probability mass (in the optimal proposal) to the tails of $q(\mathbf{z}; \boldsymbol{\lambda})$. To see this, recall the exponential family form of the variational distribution given in Eq. 4. For any exponential family distribution, the score function is $h_n(\mathbf{z}) = t_n(\mathbf{z}) - \mathbb{E}_{q(\mathbf{z};\boldsymbol{\lambda})}[t_n(\mathbf{z})]$. (This result follows from simple properties of exponential families.[3]) For values of $\mathbf{z}$ for which $t_n(\mathbf{z})$ is close to its expectation, $h_n(\mathbf{z})$ becomes very close to zero. This zeros out $f_n(\mathbf{z})$ in Eq. 10, which pushes mass to other parts of $q(\mathbf{z}; \boldsymbol{\lambda})$. As an example, in the case where $q(\mathbf{z}; \boldsymbol{\lambda})$ is a Gaussian distribution, the optimal proposal distribution places zero mass on the mean of that Gaussian and hence more probability mass on its tails.

Thus, we design a proposal distribution $r(\mathbf{z}; \boldsymbol{\lambda}, \tau)$ that assigns higher mass to the tails of $q(\mathbf{z}; \boldsymbol{\lambda})$. Specifically, we use an overdispersed distribution in the same exponential family as $q(\mathbf{z}; \boldsymbol{\lambda})$. The proposal is

$$r(\mathbf{z}; \boldsymbol{\lambda}, \tau) = g(\mathbf{z}, \tau) \exp\left\{\frac{\boldsymbol{\lambda}^\top t(\mathbf{z}) - A(\boldsymbol{\lambda})}{\tau}\right\}, \tag{11}$$

[3]The gradient of the log-normalizer (with respect to the natural parameters) equals the first-order moment of the sufficient statistics, i.e., $\nabla_{\boldsymbol{\lambda}} A(\boldsymbol{\lambda}) = \mathbb{E}_{q(\mathbf{z};\boldsymbol{\lambda})}[t(\mathbf{z})]$.

where $\tau \geq 1$ is the dispersion coefficient of the overdispersed distribution (Jørgensen, 1987). Hence, the O-BBVI estimator of the gradient can be expressed as

$$\widehat{\nabla}_{\boldsymbol{\lambda}}^{\text{O-BB}} \mathcal{L} = \frac{1}{S} \sum_s f(\mathbf{z}^{(s)}) \frac{q(\mathbf{z}^{(s)}; \boldsymbol{\lambda})}{r(\mathbf{z}^{(s)})}, \quad \mathbf{z}^{(s)} \overset{\text{iid}}{\sim} r(\mathbf{z}; \boldsymbol{\lambda}, \tau), \tag{12}$$

where S is the number of samples of the Monte Carlo approximation.

This choice of $r(\mathbf{z}; \boldsymbol{\lambda}, \tau)$ has several desired properties for a proposal distribution. First, it is easy to sample from, since for fixed values of τ it belongs to the same exponential family as $q(\mathbf{z}; \boldsymbol{\lambda})$. Second, as for the optimal proposal, it is adaptive, since it explicitly depends on the parameters $\boldsymbol{\lambda}$ which we are optimizing. Finally, by definition, it assigns higher mass to the tails of $q(\mathbf{z}; \boldsymbol{\lambda})$, which was our motivation for choosing it.

The dispersion coefficient τ can be itself adaptive to better match the optimal proposal at each iteration of the variational optimization procedure. We put forward a method to update the value of τ in Section 3.2.

Note that our approach differs from importance weighted autoencoders (Burda et al., 2016), which also make use of importance sampling but with the goal of deriving a tighter log-likelihood lower bound in the context of the variational autoencoder (Kingma and Welling, 2014). In contrast, we use importance sampling to reduce the variance of the estimator of the gradient.

3.1 Variance reduction

Here, we compare the variance of the O-BBVI estimator $\widehat{\nabla}_{\lambda}^{\text{O-BB}} \mathcal{L}$ given in Eq. 12 with the variance of the original BBVI estimator $\widehat{\nabla}_{\lambda}^{\text{BB}} \mathcal{L}$, which samples from $q(\mathbf{z}; \boldsymbol{\lambda})$:

$$\widehat{\nabla}_{\lambda}^{\text{BB}} \mathcal{L} = \frac{1}{S} \sum_s f(\mathbf{z}^{(s)}), \qquad \mathbf{z}^{(s)} \overset{\text{iid}}{\sim} q(\mathbf{z}; \boldsymbol{\lambda}). \tag{13}$$

After some algebra, we can express the variance of the BBVI estimator as

$$\mathbb{V}\left[\widehat{\nabla}_{\lambda}^{\text{BB}} \mathcal{L}\right] = \frac{1}{S} \mathbb{E}_{q(\mathbf{z};\boldsymbol{\lambda})}\left[f^2(\mathbf{z})\right] - \frac{1}{S} (\nabla_{\boldsymbol{\lambda}} \mathcal{L})^2, \tag{14}$$

and we can also express the variance of the O-BBVI estimator in terms of an expectation with respect to the variational distribution as

$$\begin{aligned} \mathbb{V}\left[\widehat{\nabla}_{\lambda}^{\text{O-BB}} \mathcal{L}\right] &= \frac{1}{S} \mathbb{E}_{r(\mathbf{z};\boldsymbol{\lambda},\tau)}\left[f^2(\mathbf{z}) \frac{q^2(\mathbf{z}; \boldsymbol{\lambda})}{r^2(\mathbf{z}; \boldsymbol{\lambda}, \tau)}\right] - \frac{1}{S} (\nabla_{\boldsymbol{\lambda}} \mathcal{L})^2 \\ &= \frac{1}{S} \mathbb{E}_{q(\mathbf{z};\boldsymbol{\lambda})}\left[f^2(\mathbf{z}) \frac{q(\mathbf{z}; \boldsymbol{\lambda})}{r(\mathbf{z}; \boldsymbol{\lambda}, \tau)}\right] - \frac{1}{S} (\nabla_{\boldsymbol{\lambda}} \mathcal{L})^2. \end{aligned} \tag{15}$$

Variance reduction for the O-BBVI approach is achieved when $\mathbb{V}\left[\widehat{\nabla}_{\lambda}^{\text{O-BB}} \mathcal{L}\right] \leq \mathbb{V}\left[\widehat{\nabla}_{\lambda}^{\text{BB}} \mathcal{L}\right]$ or, equivalently,

$$\mathbb{E}_{q(\mathbf{z};\boldsymbol{\lambda})}\left[f^2(\mathbf{z}) \frac{q(\mathbf{z}; \boldsymbol{\lambda})}{r(\mathbf{z}; \boldsymbol{\lambda}, \tau)}\right] \leq \mathbb{E}_{q(\mathbf{z};\boldsymbol{\lambda})}\left[f^2(\mathbf{z})\right]. \tag{16}$$

This inequality is trivially satisfied when we set $r(\mathbf{z})$ to the optimal proposal distribution, $r^\star(\mathbf{z})$. However, it is intractable to compute in general; moreover, it depends on the model through $f(\mathbf{z})$. While the bound in Eq. 16 results intractable, it gives us some intuition on why the use of an overdispersed proposal distribution can reduce the variance, since $r(\mathbf{z}; \boldsymbol{\lambda}, \tau)$ will be larger than $q(\mathbf{z}; \boldsymbol{\lambda})$ for those values of $\mathbf{z}$ for which the product $q(\mathbf{z}; \boldsymbol{\lambda}) f^2(\mathbf{z})$ is highest, i.e., in the tails of $q(\mathbf{z}; \boldsymbol{\lambda})$. Our experimental results in Section 4 demonstrate that the variance is effectively reduced when we use our O-BBVI.

3.2 Implementation

We now discuss several extensions of O-BBVI that make it more suitable for real applications.

High dimensionality. Previously, we defined the proposal distribution $r(\mathbf{z}; \boldsymbol{\lambda}, \tau)$ as an overdispersed version of the variational distribution $q(\mathbf{z}; \boldsymbol{\lambda})$. However, importance sampling is known to fail when the dimensionality of the hidden space is moderately high, due to the high resulting variance of the importance weights $w(\mathbf{z}) = q(\mathbf{z}; \boldsymbol{\lambda}) / r(\mathbf{z}; \boldsymbol{\lambda}, \tau)$. To address this, we rely on the fact that hidden variable z_n is the variable with the highest influence on the estimator of the n-th component of the gradient. We exploit this idea, which was also considered by Titsias and Lázaro-Gredilla (2015) in their algorithm based on local expectations.

More precisely, for the variational parameters of variable z_n, we first write the gradient as

$$\begin{aligned} \nabla_{\lambda_n} \mathcal{L} &= \mathbb{E}_{q(z_n;\lambda_n)} \left[\mathbb{E}_{q(\mathbf{z}_{\neg n};\boldsymbol{\lambda}_{\neg n})} \left[f_n(\mathbf{z}) \right] \right] \\ &= \mathbb{E}_{r(z_n;\lambda_n,\tau_n)} \left[w(z_n) \mathbb{E}_{q(\mathbf{z}_{\neg n};\boldsymbol{\lambda}_{\neg n})} \left[f_n(\mathbf{z}) \right] \right], \end{aligned} \tag{17}$$

where $r(z_n; \lambda_n, \tau_n)$ is the overdispersed version of $q(z_n; \lambda_n)$ with dispersion coefficient τ_n, $\mathbf{z}_{\neg n}$ denotes all hidden variables in the model except z_n, and similarly for $\boldsymbol{\lambda}_{\neg n}$. Thus, the corresponding importance weights in (17) for each component of the gradient depend only on variable z_n, i.e.,

$$w(z_n) = \frac{q(z_n; \lambda_n)}{r(z_n; \lambda_n, \tau_n)}. \tag{18}$$

We use a single sample from $q(\mathbf{z}_{\neg n}; \boldsymbol{\lambda}_{\neg n})$ to estimate the inner expectation in (17), and S samples of z_n from $r(z_n; \lambda_n, \tau_n)$ to estimate the outer expectation.

Adaptation of the dispersion coefficients. Our algorithm requires setting the value of the dispersion parameters τ_n; we would like to automate this procedure. Here, we develop a method to learn these coefficients during optimization by minimizing the variance of the estimator. More precisely, we introduce stochastic gradient descent steps for τ_n that minimize the variance. The exact derivative of the (negative) variance with respect to τ_n is

$$\begin{aligned} -\frac{\partial \mathbb{V}\left[\widehat{\nabla}^{\text{O-BB}}_{\lambda_n} \mathcal{L}\right]}{\partial \tau_n} &= \frac{1}{S} \mathbb{E}_{r(z_n;\lambda_n,\tau_n)} \Bigg[\mathbb{E}_{q(\mathbf{z}_{\neg n};\boldsymbol{\lambda}_{\neg n})} \left[f_n(\mathbf{z}) \right]^2 \\ &\quad \times w^2(z_n) \frac{\partial \log r(z_n; \lambda_n, \tau_n)}{\partial \tau_n} \Bigg], \end{aligned} \tag{19}$$

where we have applied the log-derivative trick once again, as well as the extension to high dimensionality detailed above. Now a Monte Carlo estimate of this derivative can be obtained by using the same set of S samples used in the update of λ_n. The resulting procedure is fast, with little extra overhead, since both $f_n(\mathbf{z})$ and $w(z_n)$ have been pre-computed.

Thus, we perform gradient steps of the form

$$\tau_n^{(t)} = \tau_n^{(t-1)} - \alpha_n \frac{\partial \mathbb{V}\left[\widehat{\nabla}^{\text{O-BB}}_{\lambda_n} \mathcal{L}\right]}{\partial \tau_n}, \tag{20}$$

where τ_n is constrained as $\tau_n \geq 1$ and the derivatives are estimated via Monte Carlo approximation. Since the derivatives in Eq. 20 can be several orders of magnitude greater than τ_n, we opt for a simple approach to choose an appropriate step size α_n. In particular, we ignore the magnitude of the derivative in (20) and take a small gradient step in the direction given by its sign. Note that we do not need to satisfy the Robbins-Monro conditions here (Robbins and Monro, 1951), because the adaptation of τ_n only defines the proposal distribution and it is not part of the original stochastic optimization procedure.

Eq. 20 can still be applied even if λ_n is a vector; it only requires replacing the derivative of the variance with the summation of the derivatives for all components of λ_n.

Multiple importance sampling. It may be more stable (in terms of the variance of the importance weights) to consider a set of J dispersion coefficients, $\tau_{n1}, \ldots, \tau_{nJ}$, instead of a single coefficient τ_n. We propose to use a mixture with equal weights to build the proposal as follows:

$$r(z_n; \lambda_n, \tau_{n1}, \ldots, \tau_{nJ}) = \frac{1}{J} \sum_{j=1}^{J} r(z_n; \lambda_n, \tau_{nj}), \tag{21}$$

where each term in the mixture is given by $r(z_n; \lambda_n, \tau_{nj}) = g(z_n, \tau_{nj}) \exp\left\{\frac{\lambda_n^\top t(z_n) - A(\lambda_n)}{\tau_{nj}}\right\}$. In the importance sampling literature, this is known as multiple importance sampling (MIS), as multiple proposals are used (Veach and Guibas, 1995). Within the MIS methods, we opt for full deterministic multiple importance sampling (DMIS) because it is the approach that presents lowest variance (Hesterberg, 1995; Owen and Zhou, 2000; Elvira et al., 2015). In DMIS, the number of samples S of the Monte Carlo estimator must be an integer multiple of the number of mixture components J, and S/J samples are deterministically assigned to each proposal $r(z_n; \lambda_n, \tau_{nj})$. However, the importance weights are obtained as if the samples had been actually drawn from the mixture, i.e.,

$$w(z_n) = \frac{q(z_n; \lambda_n)}{\frac{1}{J}\sum_{j=1}^{J} r(z_n; \lambda_n, \tau_{nj})}. \tag{22}$$

This choice of the importance weights yields an unbiased estimator with smaller variance than the standard MIS approach (Owen and Zhou, 2000; Elvira et al., 2015).

In the experiments in Section 4 we investigate the performance of two-component proposal distributions, where $J = 2$, and compare it against our initial algorithm that uses a unique proposal, which corresponds to $J = 1$. We have also conducted some additional experiments (not shown in the paper) with mixtures with higher number of components, with no significant improvements.

3.3 Full algorithm

We now present our full algorithm for O-BBVI. It makes use of control variates, Rao-Blackwellization, and overdispersed importance sampling with adaptation of the dispersion coefficients. At each iteration, we draw a single sample $\mathbf{z}^{(0)}$ from the variational distribution, as well as S samples $z_n^{(s)}$ from the overdispersed proposal for each n (using DMIS in this step). We obtain the score function as

$$h_n(z_n^{(s)}) = \nabla_{\lambda_n} \log q(z_n^{(s)}; \lambda_n), \tag{23}$$

and the argument of the expectation in (9) as

$$f_n(\mathbf{z}^{(s)}) = h_n(z_n^{(s)})(\log p_n(\mathbf{x}, z_n^{(s)}, \mathbf{z}_{\neg n}^{(0)}) - \log q(z_n^{(s)}; \lambda_n)), \tag{24}$$

where p_n indicates that we use Rao-Blackwellization. Finally, the estimator of the gradient is obtained as

$$\widehat{\nabla}_{\lambda_n} \mathcal{L} = \frac{1}{S}\sum_s \left(f_n^{\mathrm{w}}(\mathbf{z}^{(s)}) - a_n h_n^{\mathrm{w}}(z_n^{(s)}) \right), \tag{25}$$

where the superscript "w" stands for "weighted," i.e.,

$$f_n^{\mathrm{w}}(\mathbf{z}^{(s)}) = w(z_n^{(s)}) f_n(\mathbf{z}^{(s)}), \tag{26}$$

$$h_n^{\mathrm{w}}(z_n^{(s)}) = w(z_n^{(s)}) h_n(z_n^{(s)}). \tag{27}$$

Following Eq. 8, we use a separate set of samples to estimate the optimal a_n as

$$a_n = \frac{\widehat{\mathrm{Cov}}(f_n^{\mathrm{w}}, h_n^{\mathrm{w}})}{\widehat{\mathrm{Var}}(h_n^{\mathrm{w}})}. \tag{28}$$

We use AdaGrad (Duchi et al., 2011) to obtain adaptive learning rates that ensure convergence of the stochastic optimization procedure, although other schedules can be used instead as long as they satisfy the standard Robbins-Monro conditions (Robbins and Monro, 1951). In AdaGrad, the learning rate is obtained as

$$\rho_t = \eta \,\mathrm{diag}\,(\mathbf{G}_t)^{-1/2}, \tag{29}$$

where $\mathbf{G}_t$ is a matrix that contains the sum across the first t iterations of the outer products of the gradient, and η is a constant. Thus, the stochastic gradient step is given by

$$\boldsymbol{\lambda}^{(t)} = \boldsymbol{\lambda}^{(t-1)} + \rho_t \circ \widehat{\nabla}_{\boldsymbol{\lambda}} \mathcal{L}, \tag{30}$$

where '∘' denotes the element-wise (Hadamard) product. Algorithm 1 summarizes the full procedure.

Algorithm 1: Overdispersed black-box variational inference (O-BBVI)

```
input : data x, joint distribution p(x, z), mean-field
        variational family q(z; λ)
output: variational parameters λ
Initialize λ
Initialize the dispersion coefficients τ_nj
while algorithm has not converged do
    /* draw samples                                    */
    Draw a single sample z^(0) ~ q(z; λ)
    for n = 1 to N do
        Draw S samples z_n^(s) ~ r(z_n; λ_n, {τ_nj}) (DMIS)
        Compute the importance weights w(z_n^(s)) (Eq. 22)
    end
    /* estimate gradient                               */
    for n = 1 to N do
        For each sample s, compute h_n(z_n^(s)) (Eq. 23)
        For each sample s, compute f_n(z^(s)) (Eq. 24)
        Compute the weighted f_n^w(z^(s)) (Eq. 26)
        Compute the weighted h_n^w(z_n^(s)) (Eq. 27)
        Estimate the optimal a_n (Eq. 28)
        Estimate the gradient ∇̂_{λ_n} L (Eq. 25)
    end
    /* update dispersion coefficients                  */
    for n = 1 to N do
        Estimate the derivatives ∂V[∇_{λ_n} L]/∂τ_nj (Eq. 19)
        Take a gradient step for τ_nj (Eq. 20)
    end
    /* take gradient step                              */
    Set the step size ρ_t (Eq. 29)
    Take a gradient step for λ (Eq. 30)
end
```

4 EMPIRICAL STUDY

We study our method with two non-conjugate probabilistic models: the gamma-normal time series model (GN-TS) and the Poisson deep exponential family (DEF). We found that overdispersed black-box variational inference (O-BBVI) reduces the variance of the black-box variational inference (BBVI) estimator and leads to faster convergence.

4.1 Description of the experiments

Models description and datasets. The GN-TS model (Ranganath et al., 2014) is a non-conjugate state-space model for sequential data that was used to showcase BBVI. The model is described by

$$\begin{aligned} w_{kd} &\sim \mathcal{N}(0, \sigma_w^2), \\ o_{nd} &\sim \mathcal{N}(0, \sigma_o^2), \\ z_{n1k} &\sim \text{GammaE}(\sigma_z, \sigma_z), \\ z_{ntk} &\sim \text{GammaE}(z_{n(t-1)k}, \sigma_z), \\ x_{ndt} &\sim \mathcal{N}\left(o_{nd} + \sum_k z_{ntk} w_{kd}, \sigma_x^2\right). \end{aligned} \tag{31}$$

The indices n, t, d and k denote observations, time instants, observation dimensions, and latent factors, respectively. The distribution GammaE denotes the expectation/variance parameterization of the gamma distribution. The model explains each datapoint x_{ndt} with a latent factor model. For each time instant t, the mean of x_{ndt} depends on the inner product $\sum_k z_{ntk} w_{kd}$, where z_{ntk} varies smoothly across time. The variables o_{nd} are an intercept that capture the baseline in the observations.

We set the hyperparameters to be $\sigma_w^2 = 1, \sigma_o^2 = 1, \sigma_z = 1$, and $\sigma_x^2 = 0.01$. We use a synthetic dataset of $N = 900$ time sequences of length $T = 30$ and dimensionality $D = 20$. We use $K = 30$ latent factors, leading to $828,600$ hidden variables.

The Poisson DEF (Ranganath et al., 2015) is a multi-layered latent variable model of discrete data, such as text. The model is described by

$$\begin{aligned} w_{kv}^{(0)} &\sim \text{Gamma}(\alpha_w, \beta_w), \\ w_{kk'}^{(\ell)} &\sim \text{Gamma}(\alpha_w, \beta_w), \\ z_{dk}^{(L)} &\sim \text{Poisson}(\lambda_z), \\ z_{dk}^{(\ell)} &\sim \text{Poisson}\left(\sum_{k'} z_{dk'}^{(\ell+1)} w_{k'k}^{(\ell)}\right), \\ x_{dv} &\sim \text{Poisson}\left(\sum_{k'} z_{dk'}^{(1)} w_{k'v}^{(0)}\right). \end{aligned} \tag{32}$$

The indices d, v, k and ℓ denote documents, vocabulary words, latent factors, and hidden layers, respectively. This model captures a hierarchy of dependencies between latent variables similar to the hidden structure in deep neural networks. In detail, the number of times that word v appears in document d is x_{dv}. It has a Poisson distribution with rate given by an inner product of gamma-distributed weights and Poisson-distributed hidden variables from layer 1. The Poisson-distributed hidden variables depend, in turn, on another set of weights and another layer of hidden Poisson-distributed variables. This structure repeats for a specified number of layers.

We set the prior shape and rate as $\alpha_w = 0.1$ and $\beta_w = 0.3$, and the prior mean for the top level of the Poisson DEF as $\lambda_z = 0.1$. We use $L = 3$ layers with $K = 50$ latent factors each. We model the papers at the Neural Information Processing Systems (NIPS) 2011 conference. This is a data set with $D = 305$ documents, $612,508$ words, and $V = 5715$ vocabulary words (after removing stop words). This leads to a model with $336,500$ hidden variables.

Evaluation. We compare O-BBVI with BBVI (Ranganath et al., 2014). For a fair comparison, we use the same number of samples in both methods and estimate the inner expectation in Eq. 17 with only one sample. For the outer expectation, we use 8 samples to estimate the gradient itself and 8 separate samples to estimate the optimal coefficient a_n for the control variates. For BBVI, we also doubled the number of samples to $16 + 16$; this is marked as "BBVI (×2)" in the plots.

For O-BBVI, we study both a single proposal and a mixture proposal with two components, respectively labeled as "O-BBVI (single proposal)" and "O-BBVI (mixture)." For the latter, we fix the dispersion coefficients $\tau_{n1} = 1$ for all n, and we run stochastic gradient descent steps for τ_{n2}. See the Supplement for some figures showing the evolution of the dispersion coefficient.

At each iteration (and for each method) we evaluate several quantities: the evidence lower bound (ELBO), the averaged sample variance of the estimator of the gradient, and a model-specific performance metric on the test set. The estimation of the ELBO is based on a single sample of the variational distribution $q(\mathbf{z}; \boldsymbol{\lambda})$ for all methods. For the GN-TS model, we compute the average log-likelihood (up to a constant term) on the test set, which is generated with one additional time instant in all sequences. For the Poisson DEF, we compute the average held-out perplexity,

$$\exp\left(\frac{-\sum_d \sum_{w \in \text{doc}(d)} \log p(w \mid \#\text{held out in } d)}{\#\text{held out words}}\right), \tag{33}$$

where the held-out data contains 25% randomly selected words of all documents.

Experimental setup. For each method, we initialize the variational parameters to the same point and run each algorithm with a fixed computational budget (of CPU time).

We use AdaGrad (Duchi et al., 2011) for the learning rate. We set the parameter η in Eq. 29 to $\eta = 0.5$ for the GN-TS model and $\eta = 1$ for the Poisson DEF. When optimizing the O-BBVI dispersion coefficients τ_n, we take steps of length 0.1 in the direction of the (negative) gradient. We initialize the dispersion coefficients as $\tau_n = 2$ for the single proposal and $\tau_{n2} = 3$ for the two-component mixture.

We parameterize the normal distribution in terms of its mean and variance, the gamma in terms of its shape and mean, and the Poisson in terms of its mean parameter. In order to avoid constrained optimization, we apply the transformation $\lambda' = \log(\exp(\lambda) - 1)$ to those variational parameters that are constrained to be positive and take stochastic gradient steps with respect to λ'.

Overdispersed exponential families. For a fixed dispersion coefficient τ, the overdispersed exponential family of the Gaussian distribution with mean μ and variance σ^2 is a Gaussian distribution with mean μ and variance $\tau\sigma^2$. The overdispersed gamma distribution with shape s and rate r is given by a new gamma distribution with shape $\frac{s+\tau-1}{\tau}$ and rate $\frac{r}{\tau}$. The overdispersed Poisson(λ) distribution is a Poisson($\lambda^{1/\tau}$) distribution.

4.2 Results

Figures 1 and 2 show the evolution of the ELBO, the predictive performance, and the average sample variance of the estimator for both models and all methods. We plot these metrics as a function of running time, and each method is run with the same computational budget.

For the GN-TS model, Figure 1a shows that the variance of O-BBVI is significantly lower than BBVI and BBVI with twice the number of samples. Additionally, Figures 1b and 1c show that O-BBVI outperforms vanilla BBVI in terms of both ELBO and held-out likelihood. According to these figures, using a single or mixture proposal does not seem to significantly affect performance. In these plots, we can also see that BBVI ($\times$2) converges slower than BBVI; this is because the x-axis represents running time instead of iterations. (When the number of samples increases, the convergence is faster but each iteration takes more time.)

The results on the Poisson DEF are similar (Figure 2). Figure 2a shows the average sample variance of the estimator; again, O-BBVI outperforms both BBVI algorithms. Figures 2b and 2c show the evolution of the ELBO and the held-out perplexity, respectively, where O-BBVI also outperforms BBVI. Here, the two-component mixture proposal performs slightly better than the single proposal. This is consistent with Figure 2a, which indicates that the mixture proposal gives more stable estimates.

Finally, for the GN-TS model only, we also apply the local expectations algorithm of Titsias and Lázaro-Gredilla (2015), which relies on exact or numerical integration to reduce the variance of the estimator. We form noisy gradients using numerical quadratures for the Gaussian random variables and standard BBVI for the gamma variables (these results are not plotted in the paper). We found that local expectations accurately approximate the gradient for the Gaussian distributions. It converges slightly faster at the beginning of the run, although O-BBVI quickly reaches the

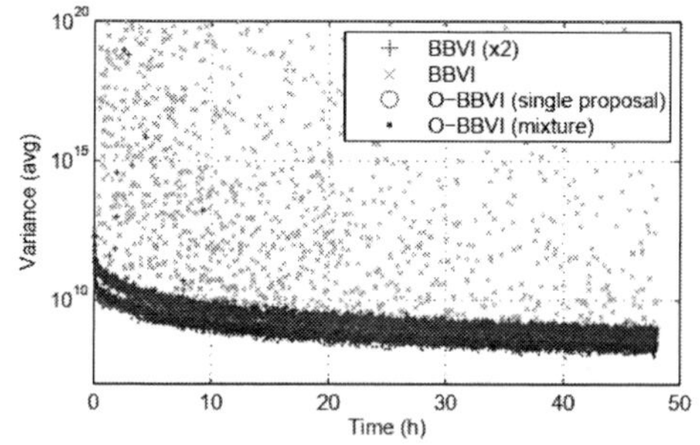

(a) Averaged sample variance of the estimator.

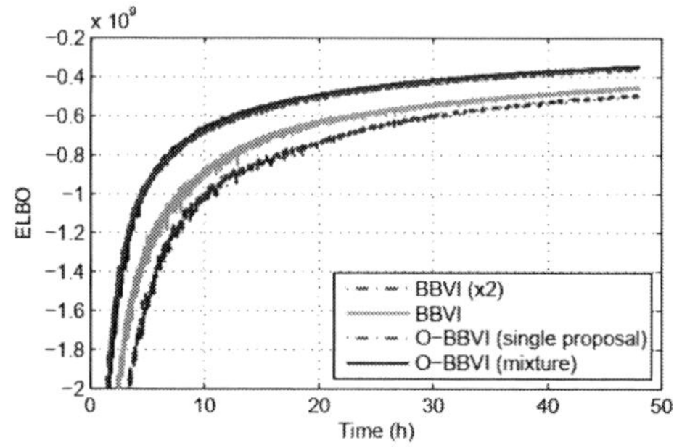

(b) Traceplot of the ELBO.

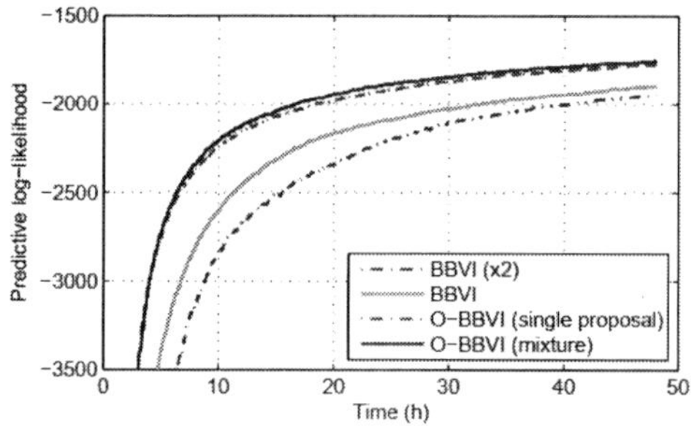

(c) Predictive performance (higher is better).

Figure 1: Results for the GN-TS model. Both versions of O-BBVI converge faster than BBVI.

same performance. (We conjecture that it is faster because the local expectations algorithm does not require the use of control variates. This saves evaluations of the log-joint probability of the model and thus it can run more iterations in the same period of time.)

However, we emphasize that O-BBVI is a more general algorithm than local expectations. The local expectations of Titsias and Lázaro-Gredilla (2015) are only available for discrete distributions with finite support and for continuous distributions for which numerical quadratures are accurate (such as Gaussian distributions). They fail to approximate the expectations for other exponential family distributions (e.g., gamma,[4] Poisson, and others). For example, they cannot handle the Poisson DEF.

[4]Although the univariate gamma distribution is amenable to numerical integration, we have found that the approximation is not accurate when the shape parameter of the gamma distribution is below 1, due to the singularity at 0.

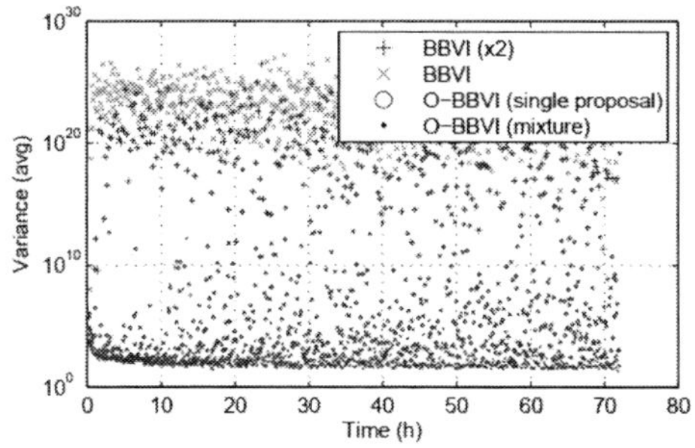

(a) Averaged sample variance of the estimator.

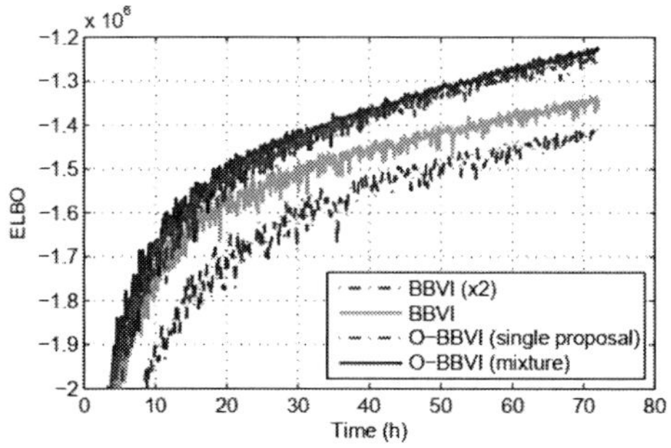

(b) Traceplot of the ELBO.

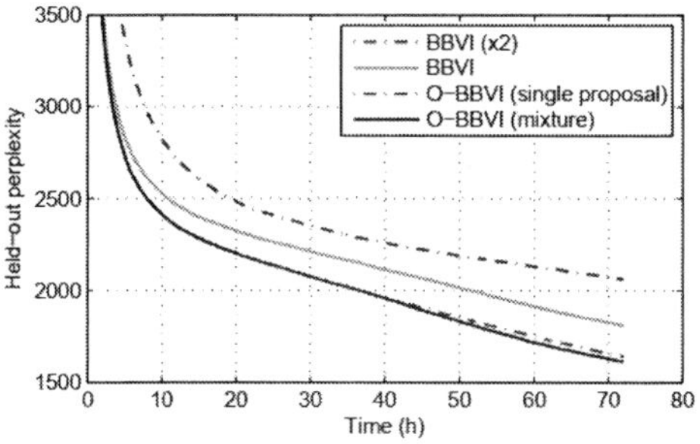

(c) Predictive performance (lower is better).

Figure 2: Results for the Poisson DEF model. Both versions of O-BBVI converge faster than BBVI.

5 CONCLUSIONS

We have developed overdispersed black-box variational inference (O-BBVI), a method that relies on importance sampling to reduce the variance of the stochastic gradients in black-box variational inference (BBVI). O-BBVI uses an importance sampling proposal distribution that has heavier tails than the actual variational distribution. In particular, we choose the proposal as an overdispersed distribution in the same exponential family as the variational distribution. Like BBVI, our approach is amenable to mean field or structured variational inference, as well as variational models (Ranganath et al., 2016; Tran et al., 2016).

We have studied the performance of our method on two complex probabilistic models. Our results show that BBVI effectively benefits from the use of overdispersed importance sampling, and O-BBVI leads to faster convergence in the resulting stochastic optimization procedure.

There are several avenues for future work. First, we can explore other proposal distributions to provide a better fit to the optimal ones while still maintaining computational efficiency. Further theoretical research on the bound in Eq. 16 may be helpful for that purpose. Second, we can apply quasi-Monte Carlo methods to further decrease the sampling variance, as already suggested by Ranganath et al. (2014). Finally, we can combine the reparameterization trick with overdispersed proposals to explore whether variance is further reduced.

Acknowledgements

This work is supported by IIS-1247664, ONR N00014-11-1-0651, DARPA FA8750-14-2-0009, DARPA N66001-15-C-4032, Adobe, the John Templeton Foundation, and the Sloan Foundation. The authors thank Rajesh Ranganath and Guillaume Bouchard for useful discussions.

References

Bishop, C. M. (2006). *Pattern Recognition and Machine Learning (Information Science and Statistics)*. Springer-Verlag New York, Inc., Secaucus, NJ, USA.

Bonnet, G. (1964). Transformations des signaux aléatoires a travers les systemes non linéaires sans mémoire. *Annals of Telecommunications*, 19(9):203–220.

Bouchard, G., Trouillon, T., Perez, J., and Gaidon, A. (2015). Online learning to sample. *arXiv:1506.09016*.

Burda, Y., Grosse, R., and Salakhutdinov, R. (2016). Importance weighted autoencoders. In *International Conference on Learning Representations*.

Carbonetto, P., King, M., and Hamze, F. (2009). A stochastic approximation method for inference in probabilistic graphical models. In *Advances in Neural Information Processing Systems*.

Casella, G. and Robert, C. P. (1996). Rao-Blackwellisation of sampling schemes. *Biometrika*, 83(1):81–94.

Duchi, J., Hazan, E., and Singer, Y. (2011). Adaptive subgradient methods for online learning and stochastic optimization. *Journal of Machine Learning Research*, 12:2121–2159.

Elvira, V., Martino, L., Luengo, D., and Bugallo, M. F. (2015). Generalized multiple importance sampling. *arXiv:1511.03095*.

Ghahramani, Z. and Beal, M. J. (2001). Propagation algorithms for variational Bayesian learning. In *Advances in Neural Information Processing Systems*.

Glynn, P. W. (1990). Likelihood ratio gradient estimation for stochastic systems. *Communications of the ACM*, 33(10):75–84.

Gu, S., Levine, S., Sutskever, I., and Mnih, A. (2016). MuProp: Unbiased backpropagation for stochastic neural networks. In *International Conference on Learning Representations*.

Hesterberg, T. (1995). Weighted average importance sampling and defensive mixture distributions. *Technometrics*, 37(2):185–194.

Hinton, G., Dayan, P., Frey, B. J., and Neal, R. M. (1995). The wake-sleep algorithm for unsupervised neural networks. *Science*, 268(5214):1158–1161.

Jordan, M. I., Ghahramani, Z., Jaakkola, T. S., and Saul, L. K. (1999). An introduction to variational methods for graphical models. *Machine Learning*, 37(2):183–233.

Jørgensen, B. (1987). Exponential dispersion models. *Journal of the Royal Statistical Society, Series B (Methodological)*, 49(2):127–162.

Kingma, D. P. and Welling, M. (2014). Auto-encoding variational Bayes. In *International Conference on Learning Representations*.

Kleijnen, J. P. C. and Rubinstein, R. Y. (1996). Optimization and sensitivity analysis of computer simulation models by the score function method. Technical report, Tilburg University, School of Economics and Management.

Kucukelbir, A., Ranganath, R., Gelman, A., and Blei, D. M. (2015). Automatic variational inference in Stan. In *Advances in Neural Information Processing Systems*.

Mnih, A. and Gregor, K. (2014). Neural variational inference and learning in belief networks. In *International Conference on Machine Learning*.

Murphy, K. P. (2012). *Machine Learning: A Probabilistic Perspective*. MIT Press.

Neal, R. (1992). Connectionist learning of belief networks. *Artificial Intelligence*, 56(1):71–113.

Owen, A. and Zhou, Y. (2000). Safe and effective importance sampling. *Journal of the American Statistical Association*, 95(449):135—143.

Owen, A. B. (2013). Monte Carlo theory, methods and examples. Book in preparation.

Paisley, J. W., Blei, D. M., and Jordan, M. I. (2012). Variational Bayesian inference with stochastic search. In *International Conference on Machine Learning*.

Price, R. (1958). A useful theorem for nonlinear devices having Gaussian inputs. *IRE Transactions on Information Theory*, 4(2):69–72.

Ranganath, R., Gerrish, S., and Blei, D. M. (2014). Black box variational inference. In *Artificial Intelligence and Statistics*.

Ranganath, R., Tang, L., Charlin, L., and Blei, D. M. (2015). Deep exponential families. In *Artificial Intelligence and Statistics*.

Ranganath, R., Tran, D., and Blei, D. M. (2016). Hierarchical variational models. In *International Conference on Machine Learning*.

Rezende, D. J., Mohamed, S., and Wierstra, D. (2014). Stochastic backpropagation and approximate inference in deep generative models. In *International Conference on Machine Learning*.

Robbins, H. and Monro, S. (1951). A stochastic approximation method. *The Annals of Mathematical Statistics*, 22(3):400–407.

Robert, C. P. and Casella, G. (2005). *Monte Carlo Statistical Methods (Springer Texts in Statistics)*. Springer-Verlag New York, Inc., Secaucus, NJ, USA.

Ross, S. M. (2002). *Simulation*. Elsevier.

Salimans, T. and Knowles, D. A. (2013). Fixed-form variational posterior approximation through stochastic linear regression. *Bayesian Analysis*, 8(4):837–882.

Titsias, M. K. and Lázaro-Gredilla, M. (2014). Doubly stochastic variational Bayes for non-conjugate inference. In *International Conference on Machine Learning*.

Titsias, M. K. and Lázaro-Gredilla, M. (2015). Local expectation gradients for black box variational inference. In *Advances in Neural Information Processing Systems*.

Tran, D., Ranganath, R., and Blei, D. M. (2016). Variational Gaussian processes. In *International Conference on Learning Representations*.

van de Meent, J.-W., Tolpin, D., Paige, B., and Wood, F. (2016). Black-box policy search with probabilistic programs. In *Artificial Intelligence and Statistics*.

Veach, E. and Guibas, L. (1995). Optimally combining sampling techniques for Monte Carlo rendering. In *ACM SIGGRAPH*.

Wainwright, M. J. and Jordan, M. I. (2008). Graphical models, exponential families, and variational inference. *Foundations and Trends in Machine Learning*, 1(1–2):1–305.

Williams, R. J. (1992). Simple statistical gradient-following algorithms for connectionist reinforcement learning. *Machine Learning*, 8(3–4):229–256.

Wingate, D. and Weber, T. (2013). Automated variational inference in probabilistic programming. *arXiv:1301.1299*.

Stochastic Portfolio Theory: A Machine Learning Perspective

Yves-Laurent Kom Samo
Machine Learning Research Group
Oxford-Man Institute of Quantitative Finance
University of Oxford
YLKS@ROBOTS.OX.AC.UK

Alexander Vervuurt
Mathematical Institute
Oxford-Man Institute of Quantitative Finance
University of Oxford
VERVUURT@MATHS.OX.AC.UK

Abstract

In this paper we propose a novel application of Gaussian processes (GPs) to financial asset allocation. Our approach is deeply rooted in *Stochastic Portfolio Theory* (SPT), a stochastic analysis framework introduced by Robert Fernholz that aims at flexibly analysing the performance of certain investment strategies in stock markets relative to benchmark indices. In particular, SPT has exhibited some investment strategies based on company sizes that, under realistic assumptions, outperform benchmark indices with probability 1 over certain time horizons. Galvanised by this result, we consider the inverse problem that consists of learning (from historical data) an optimal investment strategy based on any given set of trading characteristics, and using a user-specified optimality criterion that may go beyond outperforming a benchmark index. Although this inverse problem is of the utmost interest to investment management practitioners, it can hardly be tackled using the SPT framework. We show that our machine learning approach learns investment strategies that considerably outperform existing SPT strategies in the US stock market.

1 INTRODUCTION

Stochastic Portfolio Theory (SPT) is a relatively new stream in financial mathematics, initiated and largely developed by Robert Fernholz [2002]. For surveys of the field, see Fernholz and Karatzas [2009] and Vervuurt [2015]. Among many other things, SPT offers an alternative approach to portfolio selection, taking as its selection criterion to outperform the market index (for instance, the S&P 500 index) with probability one. Investment strategies which achieve this are called *relative arbitrages*, and have been constructed in certain classes of market models. The almost-sure comparison between the performance of certain portfolios and that of the market is facilitated by Fernholz's 'master equation', a pathwise decomposition of this relative performance which is free from stochastic integrals. The foregoing master equation is the main strength of SPT portfolio selection, as it allows one to circumvent the challenges of explicit model postulation and calibration, as well as the (normative) no-arbitrage assumption, that are encountered in the classical approaches to portfolio optimisation. However, there remain several problems in and limitations to the SPT framework as it stands.

First of all, the task of finding relative arbitrages under reasonable assumptions on the market model is difficult, since it is an inverse problem (this has also been noted by Wong [2015]). Namely, given an investment strategy and market assumptions, one can check whether this strategy is a relative arbitrage (although this quickly becomes very hard for more complicated strategies), but the theory itself does not suggest such strategies. As such, the number of relative arbitrages that have been constructed explicitly remains very small. In a practical setting it would be preferable to invert the problem, and learn investment strategies from data using a user-specified performance criterion. In effect, most established investment managers will likely have a strong view on: i) what performance metric to use to evaluate their strategies, and ii) what values for the chosen metric they regard as being exceptional. The chosen performance metric may depart from the excess return relative to the market index, for instance by adjusting for the risk taken. Similarly, outperforming the market index over a certain time horizon $[0, T]$ with probability 1 might not be good enough for some practitioners, as investors might pull out following disappointing initial performances, leaving the investment manager unable to realise the long-term optimality. Whence, ideally one should aim at learning from market data what investment strategy is likely to perform exceptionally as per the user's view.

Secondly, several market imperfections are ignored in SPT; most notably, the possibility of bankruptcy is excluded. Since the constructed investment strategies typically invest heavily in small-capitalisation stocks, this poses a strong limitation on the real-world implementability of these portfolios. However, learning optimal investment strategies from the data copes well with bankruptcies as strategies investing in stocks that eventually fail will naturally be rejected as suboptimal. It also allows for the incorporation of transaction costs, which is theoretically challenging and has not yet been addressed in SPT.

Lastly, the SPT set-up has thus far been developed almost exclusively for investment strategies that are driven only by market capitalisations — there have not yet been any constructions of relative arbitrages driven by other factors. Although this simplification eases theoretical analysis, it is a clear restriction as practitioners do consider many more market characteristics in order to exploit market inefficiencies.

We address all of these issues by adopting a Bayesian non-parametric approach. We consider a broad range of investment strategies driven by a function defined on an arbitrary space of trading characteristics (such as the market capitalisation), on which we place a Gaussian process (GP) prior. For a given strategy, the likelihood of it being 'exceptional' is derived from a user-defined performance metric (e.g. excess return to the market index, Sharpe ratio, etc) and values thereof that the practitioner considers 'exceptional'. We then sample from the posterior of the GP driving the 'exceptional' strategy using Monte Carlo Markov Chain (MCMC).

The rest of the paper is structured as follows. In section 2 we provide a background on SPT. In section 3 we present our model, and we illustrate that our approach learns strategies that outperform SPT alternatives in section 4. Finally, we discuss our findings and make suggestions for future research in section 5.

2 BACKGROUND

We give a brief introduction to SPT, defining the general class of market models within which its results hold, what the portfolio selection criterion is, and how strategies achieving this criterion are constructed.

2.1 THE MODEL

In SPT, the stock capitalisations are modelled as Itô processes.[1] Namely, the dynamics of the n positive stock capitalisation processes $X_i(\cdot)$, $i = 1, \dots, n$ are described by the following system of SDEs:

$$dX_i(t) = X_i(t)\left(b_i(t)\,dt + \sum_{\nu=1}^{d} \sigma_{i\nu}(t)\,dW_\nu(t)\right), \qquad (1)$$

[1] In the recent work Karatzas and Ruf [2016], it has been shown that this can be weakened to a semimartingale model that even allows for defaults.

for $t \geq 0$ and $i = 1, \dots, n$. Here, $W_1(\cdot), \dots, W_d(\cdot)$ are independent standard Brownian motions with $d \geq n$, and $X_i(0) > 0$, $i = 1, \dots, n$ are the initial capitalisations. We assume all processes to be defined on a probability space $(\Omega, \mathcal{F}, \mathbb{P})$, and adapted to a filtration $\mathbb{F} = \{\mathcal{F}(t)\}_{0 \leq t < \infty}$ that satisfies the usual conditions and contains the filtration generated by the "driving" Brownian motions. We refer the reader to Karatzas and Shreve [1988] for a reference on stochastic calculus.

The *rates of return* $b_i(\cdot)$, $i = 1, \dots, n$ and *volatilities* $\sigma(\cdot) = (\sigma_{i\nu}(\cdot))_{1 \leq i \leq n, 1 \leq \nu \leq d}$, are some unspecified $\mathbb{F}$-progressively measurable processes and are assumed to satisfy the integrability condition

$$\sum_{i=1}^{n} \int_0^T \left(|b_i(t)| + \sum_{\nu=1}^{d} (\sigma_{i\nu}(t))^2\right) dt < \infty, \quad \mathbb{P}\text{-a.s.}, \qquad (2)$$

for all $T \in (0, \infty)$, and the *non-degeneracy* condition

$$\exists \varepsilon > 0 : \ \xi^T \sigma(t) \sigma^T(t) \xi \geq \varepsilon ||\xi||^2, \qquad (\text{ND}^{\varepsilon})$$

for all $\xi \in \mathbb{R}^n$ and $t \geq 0$, $\mathbb{P}$-almost surely.

2.2 RELATIVE ARBITRAGE

In this context, one studies investments in the equity market described by (1) using *portfolios*. These are $\mathbb{R}^n$-valued and $\mathbb{F}$-progressively measurable processes $\pi(\cdot) = (\pi_1(\cdot), \cdots, \pi_n(\cdot))^T$, where $\pi_i(t)$ stands for the proportion of wealth invested in stock i at time t.

We restrict ourselves to *long-only* portfolios. These invest solely in the stocks, namely, they take values in the closure $\overline{\Delta^n_+}$ of the set

$$\Delta^n_+ = \{x \in \mathbb{R}^n : x_1 + \ldots + x_n = 1, \quad 0 < x_i < 1, \ i = 1, \dots, n\}; \qquad (3)$$

in particular, there is no money market. Assuming without loss of generality that the number of outstanding shares of each firm is 1, the corresponding wealth process $V^\pi(\cdot)$ of an investor implementing $\pi(\cdot)$ is seen to evolve as follows (we normalise the initial wealth to 1):

$$\frac{dV^\pi(t)}{V^\pi(t)} = \sum_{i=1}^{n} \pi_i(t) \frac{dX_i(t)}{X_i(t)}, \qquad V^\pi(0) = 1. \qquad (4)$$

In SPT one measures performance, for the most part, with respect to the market index. This is the wealth process $V^\mu(\cdot)$ that results from a buy-and-hold portfolio, given by the vector process $\mu(\cdot) = (\mu_1(\cdot), \cdots, \mu_n(\cdot))^T$ of *market weights*

$$\mu_i(t) := \frac{X_i(t)}{X_1(t) + \ldots + X_n(t)}. \qquad (5)$$

Definition 1. *Let $T > 0$. A* strong relative arbitrage *with respect to the market over the time-horizon $[0, T]$ is a portfolio $\pi(\cdot)$ such that*

$$\mathbb{P}(V^{\pi}(T) > V^{\mu}(T)) = 1. \quad (6)$$

An equivalent way to express this notion, is to say that the portfolio $\pi(\cdot)$ strongly outperforms *$\mu(\cdot)$ over the time-horizon $[0, T]$.* □

Contrast the SPT approach to portfolio selection with other methods such as mean-variance optimisation (originally introduced by Markowitz [1952]) and expected utility maximisation (see for instance Rogers [2013]), where the optimisation of a certain performance criterion determines the portfolio. In SPT, any portfolio that outperforms the market in the sense of (6) is a relative arbitrage, and the amount by which it outperforms the market is theoretically irrelevant.

In practice, one clearly desires this relative outperformance to be as large as possible. Attempts at optimisation over the class of strategies that satisfy (6) have been made by Fernholz and Karatzas [2010], Fernholz and Karatzas [2011], Ruf [2011], Ruf [2013], and Wong [2015]. However, these results are highly theoretical and very difficult to implement. Our data-driven approach circumvents these theoretical complications by optimising a user-defined criterion over the class of functionally-generated portfolios, which we introduce below.

2.3 FUNCTIONALLY-GENERATED PORTFOLIOS

A particular class of portfolios, called *functionally-generated portfolios* (or FGPs for short), was introduced and studied by Fernholz [1999].

Consider a function $\mathbf{G} \in C^2(U, \mathbb{R}_+)$, where U is an open neighbourhood of Δ_+^n and such that $x \mapsto x_i \mathrm{D}_i \log \mathbf{G}(x)$ is bounded on Δ_+^n for $i = 1, \ldots, n$. Then $\mathbf{G}$ is said to be the *generating function* of the *functionally-generated portfolio* $\pi(\cdot)$, given, for $i = 1, \ldots, n$, by

$$\frac{\pi_i(t)}{\mu_i(t)} = \frac{\mathrm{D}_i\mathbf{G}(\mu(t))}{\mathbf{G}(\mu(t))} + 1 - \sum_{j=1}^{n} \mu_j(t) \frac{\mathrm{D}_j\mathbf{G}(\mu(t))}{\mathbf{G}(\mu(t))}. \quad (7)$$

Here, we write D_i for the partial derivative with respect to the ith variable, and we will write D_{ij}^2 for the second partial derivative with respect to the ith and j^{th} variables. Theorem 3.1 of Fernholz [1999] asserts that the performance of the wealth process corresponding to $\pi(\cdot)$, when measured relative to the market, satisfies the $\mathbb{P}$-almost sure decomposition (often referred to as "Fernholz's master equation")

$$\log\left(\frac{V^{\pi}(T)}{V^{\mu}(T)}\right) = \log\left(\frac{\mathbf{G}(\mu(T))}{\mathbf{G}(\mu(0))}\right) + \int_0^T \mathfrak{g}(t)\,\mathrm{d}t, \quad (8)$$

where the quantity

$$\mathfrak{g}(t) := -\sum_{i,j=1}^{n} \frac{\mathrm{D}_{ij}^2\mathbf{G}(\mu(t))}{2\mathbf{G}(\mu(t))} \mu_i(t)\mu_j(t)\tau_{ij}^{\mu}(t) \quad (9)$$

is called the *drift process* of the portfolio $\pi(\cdot)$. Here, we have written $\tau_{ij}^{\mu}(\cdot)$ for the *relative covariances*; denoting by e_i the ith unit vector in $\mathbb{R}^n$, these are defined for $1 \leq i, j \leq n$ as

$$\tau_{ij}^{\mu}(t) := \big(\mu(t) - e_i\big)^T \sigma(t)\sigma^T(t)\big(\mu(t) - e_j\big). \quad (10)$$

Under suitable conditions on the market model (1), the left hand side of master equation (8) can be bounded away from zero for sufficiently large $T > 0$, thus proving that $\pi(\cdot)$ is an arbitrage relative to the market over $[0, T]$. Several FGPs have been shown to outperform the market this way — see Fernholz [2002], Fernholz et al. [2005], Fernholz and Karatzas [2005], Banner and Fernholz [2008], Fernholz and Karatzas [2009], Picková [2014], and Vervuurt and Karatzas [2015]. In fact, Pal and Wong [2014] prove that any relative arbitrage with respect to the market is necessarily of the form (7), if one restricts $\pi(\cdot)$ to be a functional of the current market weights only.

Strong [2014] proves a generalisation of (8) for portfolios which are deterministic functions not only of the market capitalisations, but also of other observable quantities. Namely, let $\mathbf{x}(t) = (\mu(t), F)^T$, with F a continuous, $\mathbb{R}^k$-valued, $\mathbb{F}$-progressively measurable process of finite variation, and let $\mathcal{H} \in C^{2,1}(\mathbb{R}^n \times \mathbb{R}^k, \mathbb{R}_+)$. By an application of Theorem 3.1 of Strong [2014], for any portfolio

$$\frac{\pi_i(t)}{\mu_i(t)} = \frac{\mathrm{D}_i\mathcal{H}(\mathbf{x}(t))}{\mathcal{H}(\mathbf{x}(t))} + 1 - \sum_{j=1}^{n} \mu_j(t) \frac{\mathrm{D}_j\mathcal{H}(\mathbf{x}(t))}{\mathcal{H}(\mathbf{x}(t))}, \quad (11)$$

for $i = 1, \ldots, n$, the following master equation holds:

$$\log\left(\frac{V^{\pi}(T)}{V^{\mu}(T)}\right) = \log\left(\frac{\mathcal{H}(\mathbf{x}(T))}{\mathcal{H}(\mathbf{x}(0))}\right) + \int_0^T \tilde{\mathfrak{g}}(t)\,\mathrm{d}t \quad (12)$$
$$- \int_0^T \sum_{l=1}^{k} \mathrm{D}_{n+l} \log \mathcal{H}(\mathbf{x}(t))\,\mathrm{d}F_l(t).$$

Here (compare with (8) and (9))

$$\tilde{\mathfrak{g}}(t) := -\sum_{i,j=1}^{n} \frac{\mathrm{D}_{ij}^2\mathcal{H}(\mathbf{x}(t))}{2\mathcal{H}(\mathbf{x}(t))} \mu_i(t)\mu_j(t)\tau_{ij}^{\mu}(t). \quad (13)$$

Although explicit in its decomposition, the modified master equation (12) has so far not been applied in the literature. It is very difficult and unclear how to postulate in what way such 'extended generating functions' $\mathcal{H}$ should depend on market information, and what additional covariates to use. It is thus of interest to develop a methodology that makes suggestions for what functions $\mathcal{H}$ to use, and extracts from market data which signals are significant.

2.4 DIVERSITY-WEIGHTED PORTFOLIOS

One of the most-studied FGPs is the *diversity-weighted portfolio* (DWP) with parameter $p \in \mathbb{R}$, defined in (4.4) of Fernholz et al. [2005] as

$$\pi_i^{(p)}(t) := \frac{(\mu_i(t))^p}{\sum_{j=1}^n (\mu_j(t))^p}, \quad i = 1, \ldots, n. \qquad (14)$$

In Eq. (4.5) of Fernholz et al. [2005] it was shown that this portfolio is a relative arbitrage with respect to $\mu(\cdot)$ over $[0, T]$ for any $p \in (0, 1)$ and $T > 2 \log n/(\varepsilon\delta p)$, under the condition (ND$^\varepsilon$), and that of *diversity* (D$^\delta$), introduced below. The latter says that no single company's capitalisation can take up more than a certain proportion of the entire market, which can be observed to hold in real markets;

$$\exists\, \delta \in (0,1) : \ \mathbb{P}\Big(\max_{\substack{1 \le i \le n \\ t \in [0,T]}} \mu_i(t) < 1 - \delta \Big) = 1 . \qquad (\mathrm{D}^\delta)$$

In Vervuurt and Karatzas [2015], this result was extended to the DWP with *negative* parameter p, and several variations of this portfolio were shown to outperform the market over sufficiently long time horizons and under suitable market assumptions. A simulation using real market data supported the claim that these portfolios have the potential to outperform the market index, as well as their positive-parameter counterparts. Our results strongly confirm this finding, as well as computing the optimal parameter p — see section 4.

3 SOLVING THE INVERSE PROBLEM

We consider solving the inverse problem of SPT: given some investment objective, how to go about learning a suitable trading strategy from the data? In doing so, we aim for a method that:

1. Learns from a large class of candidate investment strategies to uncover possibly intricate strategies from the data, typically by making use of non-parametric generative models for the generating functions;

2. Leverages additional sources of information beyond market capitalisations to uncover better investment strategies;

3. Works irrespective of the practitioner's investment objective (e.g. achieving a high Sharpe Ratio, outperforming alternative benchmark indices, etc).

3.1 MODEL SPECIFICATION

Let $\mathcal{X} \subset \mathbb{R}^d$ be a set of trading characteristics, for some $d \ge 1$. We consider long-only portfolios of the form

$$\pi_i^f(t) = \frac{f(\mathbf{x}_i(t))}{\sum_{j=1}^n f(\mathbf{x}_j(t))}, \qquad i = 1 \ldots, n, \qquad (15)$$

for some continuous function $f : \mathcal{X} \to \mathbb{R}_+$.

The idea behind this choice of investment portfolios is grounded in the fact that in practice, an investment manager will often have a predefined set of characteristics that he uses to compare stocks, for instance company size, balance sheet variables, credit ratings, sector, momentum, market vs. book value, return on assets, management team, online sentiment, technical indicators, 'beta', etc. The investment manager will typically choose trading characteristics so that they are informative enough to unveil market inefficiencies. Moreover, two stocks that have 'similar' characteristics will receive 'similar' weights.

This approach includes as special cases all functionally-generated portfolios in the SPT framework, and in particular the diversity-, entropy- and equally-weighted, as well as market, portfolios. Our more general setting allows for any set of trading characteristics.

The trading opportunities in our framework are revealed through the time evolving trading characteristics $\mathbf{x}_i(t)$, and the investment map f fully determines how to go about seizing these opportunities. Whence, learning an investment strategy in our framework is equivalent to learning an investment map f. To do so, we consider two families of functions. Firstly, galvanised by the theoretical results of SPT, we consider the case where $\mathcal{X} = \mathbb{R}_+$ is the set of market weights, and we take f to be of the parametric form

$$f : \mu \mapsto \mu^p, \qquad (16)$$

for $p \in \mathbb{R}$, which corresponds to the diversity-weighted portfolio (DWP, see section 2.4). Secondly, in order to capture more intricate trading patterns, and to allow for a more general set of trading characteristics $\mathcal{X} \subset \mathbb{R}^d$, we also consider an alternative non-parametric approach in which we take $\log f$ to be a path of a mean-zero Gaussian process with covariance function k

$$\log f \sim \mathcal{GP}(0, k(\cdot, \cdot)). \qquad (17)$$

To learn 'good' investment maps, we need to introduce an optimality criterion that encodes the user's investment objective. To do so, we consider a performance functional $\mathcal{P}_\mathcal{D}$ that maps the logarithm of a candidate investment map to the historical performance $\mathcal{P}_\mathcal{D}(\log f)$ of the portfolio $\pi^f(\cdot)$ as in Eq. (15) over some finite time horizon, given historical data $\mathcal{D}$. An example performance functional is the annualised Sharpe Ratio, defined as

$$\mathrm{SR}(\pi) = \sqrt{B}\, \frac{\hat{\mathbb{E}}\left(\{r(1), \ldots, r(T)\}\right)}{\hat{\mathbb{S}}\left(\{r(1), \ldots, r(T)\}\right)}, \qquad (18)$$

where $r(t) = \sum_{i=1}^n r_i(t)\pi_i^f(t)$ is the return of our portfolio between time $t-1$ and time t, $r_i(t)$ is the return of the i-th asset between time $t-1$ and time t, B represents the number of units of time in a business year (e.g. 252 if the returns are daily), and $\hat{\mathbb{E}}$ (resp. $\hat{\mathbb{S}}$) denote the sample mean (resp. sample standard deviation). Another example of a performance functional is the excess return relative to a benchmark portfolio π^*

$$\mathrm{ER}\left(\pi^f|\pi^*\right) = \prod_{t=1}^{T}\left(1+\sum_{i=1}^{n} r_i(t)\pi_i^f(t)\right) - \prod_{t=1}^{T}\left(1+\sum_{i=1}^{n} r_i(t)\pi_i^*(t)\right). \quad (19)$$

The nature of $\mathcal{P}_\mathcal{D}$ (Sharpe ratio, excess return, etc) depends on the portfolio manager; we impose no theoretical restriction.

In the parametric case (Eq. (16)), $\mathcal{P}_\mathcal{D}(\log f)$ is effectively a function of one single variable p, and we can easily learn the optimal p using standard optimisation techniques.

In many cases, however, it might be preferable to reason under uncertainty and be Bayesian. To do so, we express the investment manager's view as to what is a good performance through a likelihood model $p(\mathcal{D}|\log f)$, which we may choose to be a probability distribution on $\mathcal{P}_\mathcal{D}(\log f)$

$$\mathcal{L}\left(\mathcal{P}_\mathcal{D}(\log f)\right) := p\left(\mathcal{D}\middle|\log f\right). \quad (20)$$

This is perhaps the most important step of the learning process. Indeed, the Bayesian methods we will develop in the next section aim at learning investment maps that provide an appropriate trade-off between how *likely* the map is in light of training data, and how *consistent* it is with prior beliefs. This will only lead to a profitable investment map if 'likely' maps satisfy the manager's investment objective in-sample and vice-versa. If one chooses the likelihood model such that likely maps are strategies that lose money, then our learning machines will learn strategies that lose money!

Fortunately, it is very straightforward to express that likely investment maps are the ones that match a desired investment objective. For instance, we may use as likelihood model that, given a candidate investment map f, the extent to which it is good, or equivalently the extent to which it is 'likely' to be the function driving the strategy we are interested in learning, is the same as the extent to which the Sharpe Ratio it generates in-sample comes from a Gamma distribution with mean 2.0 and standard deviation 0.5. The positive support of the Gamma distribution renders functions leading to negative in-sample Sharpe ratios of no interest, while the concentration of the distribution over the Sharpe Ratio around 2.0 reflects both our target performance and some tolerance around it. The choice of mean (2.0) and standard deviation (0.5) of the Gamma reflects the risk appetite of the investment manager, while the vanishing tails properly reflect the fact that too high a performance $\mathcal{P}_\mathcal{D}(\log f)$ would likely raise suspicions and too low a performance would not be good enough.

To complete our Bayesian model specification, in the parametric case we place on p a uniform prior on $[-8, 8]$.

3.2 INFERENCE

Throughout the rest of this paper we will use as performance functional the total excess — transaction cost adjusted — return (as defined in (19)) relative to the equally weighted portfolio (EWP), which has constant weights

$$\pi_i^{\mathrm{EWP}}(t) = \frac{1}{n}, \quad i = 1, \dots, n, \ \forall t \geq 0. \quad (21)$$

over the whole training period

$$\mathcal{P}_\mathcal{D}(\log f) = \mathrm{ER}(\pi^f|\mathrm{EWP}). \quad (22)$$

We assume a 10bps transaction cost upon rebalancing (i.e. we incur a cost of 0.1% of the notional for each transaction). It is well known to algorithmic (execution) trading practitioners that a good rule of thumb is to expect to pay 10bps when executing an order whose size is 10% of the average daily traded volume (ADV) on liquid stocks. Whence, this assumption is reasonable so long as the wealth invested in each stock does not exceed 10% ADV. When needed, we use as likelihood model

$$\mathcal{L}\left(\mathcal{P}_\mathcal{D}(\log f)\right) = \gamma\left(\mathcal{P}_\mathcal{D}(\log f); a, b\right), \quad (23)$$

where we denote $\gamma(.; a, b)$ the probability density function of the Gamma distribution with mean a and standard deviation b. As previously discussed, a and b need not be learned as they reflect the investment manager's risk appetite. In the experiments of the following section, we use $a = 7.0$ and $b = 0.5$. In other words, we postulate that the ideal investment strategy should be such that, starting with a unit of wealth, the terminal wealth over the training period should be on average 7.0 units of wealth higher than the terminal wealth achieved by the equally weighted portfolio over the same trading horizon — this is purposely greedy.

Frequentist parametric: The first method of inference we consider consists of directly learning the optimal parameter of the DWP by maximising $\mathcal{P}_\mathcal{D}(\log f)$ for $p \in [-8, 8]$. As a comparison, the typical range of p considered in the SPT literature is $[-1, 1]$. To avoid any issue with local maxima, we proceed with brute force maximisation on the uniform grid with mesh size 0.05.[2]

Bayesian parametric: The second method of inference we consider consists of using the *Metropolis-Hastings* algorithm (Hastings [1970]) to sample from the posterior distribution over the exponent p in the DWP case,

$$p(p|\mathcal{D}) \propto \mathcal{L}\left(\mathcal{P}_\mathcal{D}(p)\right) \times \mathbb{1}\left(p \in [-8, 8]\right), \quad (24)$$

where we have rewritten $\mathcal{L}\left(\mathcal{P}_\mathcal{D}(\log f)\right)$ as $\mathcal{L}\left(\mathcal{P}_\mathcal{D}(p)\right)$ to make the dependency in p explicit. We sample a proposal

[2]This took no longer than a couple of seconds in every experiment that we ran.

update p^* from a Gaussian centred at the current exponent p and with standard deviation 0.5. The acceptance probability is easily found to be

$$r = \min\left(1, \frac{\mathcal{L}\left(\mathcal{P}_{\mathcal{D}}(p^*)\right)}{\mathcal{L}\left(\mathcal{P}_{\mathcal{D}}(p)\right)} \mathbb{1}\left(p^* \in [-8, 8]\right)\right). \tag{25}$$

We note in particular that so long as p is initialised within $[-8, 8]$, the indicator function in Eq. (24) will not cause problems to the Markov chain. We typically run $10,000$ MH iterations and discard the first $5,000$ as 'burn-in'. We use the posterior mean exponent learned on training data to trade in our testing horizon following the corresponding DWP

$$\hat{f}(\mu) = \mu^{\mathbb{E}(p|\mathcal{D})}. \tag{26}$$

Bayesian non-parametric: The third method of inference we consider is Bayesian and non-parametric. We place a Gaussian process prior on $\log f$

$$\log f \sim \mathcal{GP}(0, k(\cdot, \cdot)). \tag{27}$$

Given the sizes of datasets we consider in our experiments (more than 3 million training inputs — 500 assets over a 25-year period), we approximate the latent function over a Cartesian grid. This approximation fits nicely with the quantised nature of financial data. We use as covariance function a separable product of Rational Quadratic (RQ) kernels

$$k(x, y) = k_0^2 \prod_{i=1}^{d} \left(1 + \frac{(x[i] - y[i])^2}{2\alpha_i l_i^2}\right)^{-\alpha_i}, \tag{28}$$

where the hyper-parameters $k_0, l_i, \alpha_i > 0$, on which we place independent log-normal priors are all to be inferred. We found the RQ kernel to be a better choice than the Gaussian kernel as it allows for 'varying length scales'. Denoting by $\mathbf{f}$ the values of the investment map over the input grid, we prefer to work with the equivalent whitened representation

$$\log \mathbf{f} = L\mathbf{X}, \quad \mathbf{X} \sim \mathcal{N}(0, I), \tag{29}$$

where I is the identity matrix, $K = [k(\mathbf{x}_i, \mathbf{x}_j)]_{i,j \leq N}$ is the Gram matrix over all N input points, $K = UDU^T$ is the Singular Value Decomposition (SVD) of K and $L = UD^{\frac{1}{2}}$. We use a Blocked Gibbs sampler (Geman and Geman [1984]) to sample from the posterior

$$p\left(\log \mathbf{X}, \log k_0, \{\log l_i, \log \alpha_i\}_{i \leq d} | \mathcal{D}\right) \propto \mathcal{L}\left(\mathcal{P}_{\mathcal{D}}(L\mathbf{X})\right)$$
$$\times\, p(\log \mathbf{X}) p(\log k_0) \prod_{i=1}^{d} p(\log l_i) p(\log \alpha_i), \tag{30}$$

where we have rewritten $\mathcal{L}\left(\mathcal{P}_{\mathcal{D}}(\log f)\right)$ as $\mathcal{L}\left(\mathcal{P}_{\mathcal{D}}(L\mathbf{X})\right)$ to emphasise that the likelihood is fully defined by $\mathbf{f} = L\mathbf{X}$. The whitened representation has two primary advantages. First, it is robust to ill conditioning as we may always compute L, even when K is singular. Second, it creates a hard link between function values and hyper-parameters, so that updating the latter affects the likelihood $\mathcal{L}\left(\mathcal{P}_{\mathcal{D}}(\log f)\right)$, and therefore directly contributes towards improving the training performance $\mathcal{P}_{\mathcal{D}}(\log f)$: we found this to improve mixing of the Markov chain. Our Blocked Gibbs sampler alternates between updating $\log \mathbf{X}$ conditional on hyper-parameters, and updating the hyper-parameters (and consequently L) conditional on $\log \mathbf{X}$. For both steps we use the *elliptical slice sampling* algorithm (Murray et al. [2010]). The computational bottleneck of our sampler is the computation of the SVD of K, which we may do very efficiently by exploiting the separability of our kernel and the grid structure of the input space using standard Kronecker techniques (see for instance Saatchi [2011]).

4 EXPERIMENTS

The universe of stocks we consider in our experiments are the constituents of the S&P 500 index, accounting for changes in index constituents. We rebalance our portfolios on a daily basis. At the end of each trading day, we determine our target portfolio for the next day, which is acquired at the open of the next trading day. When the constituents of the index are due to change on day t, our target portfolio at the end of day $t-1$ relates to the constituents of the index on day t (which would indeed be known to the market on day $t - 1$). As previously discussed, we assume that each transaction incurs a charge of 0.1% of its notional value. The returns we use account for corporate events such as dividends, defaults, M&A's, etc. Our data sources are the CRSP and Compustat databases, and we use data from 1 January 1992 to 31 December 2014.

In our first experiment, we aim to illustrate that the approaches we propose in this paper *consistently* and considerably outperform SPT alternatives over a wide range of market conditions. We consider learning optimal investment strategies as described in the previous section using 10 consecutive years worth of data and testing on the following 5 years. We begin on 1st January 1992 for the first training dataset, and roll both training and testing datasets by one year, which leads to a total of 9 pairs of training and testing subsets. We compare the equally-weighted portfolio (EWP), the market portfolio, the diversity-weighted portfolio where the exponent p is learned by maximising the evaluation functional (DWP*), the diversity-weighted portfolio where the exponent p is learned with MCMC (DWP), the Gaussian process approach using as trading characteristic the logarithm of the market weights (CAP), and the Gaussian process approach using as trading characteristics both the logarithm of the market weights and the return-on-assets (CAP+ROA). The return-on-assets (ROA) on day t is defined as the ratio between the last net income reported by the company and last total assets reported by the company known on day t — we note that this quantity may not change on a daily basis but this does not affect our analysis. The rationale behind using the ROA as additional characteristics is to capture not only how big a company is, but also how well it performs relative to its size.

Table 1 summarises the average over the 9 scenarios of the yearly in-sample and out-of-sample returns plus-minus two standard errors. It can be seen that all learned strategies do indeed outperform the benchmark (EWP) in-sample and out-of-sample. Moreover, the performance is greatly improved by considering non-parametric models, even when the only characteristic considered is the market weight. Analysing such families of strategies within the SPT framework would simply be mathematically intractable. Finally, it can be seen that adding more trading characteristics does indeed add value. Crucially, the CAP+ROA portfolio *considerably* and *consistently* outperforms the benchmark (EWP), both in-sample and out-of-sample.

Table 1: Results of our first experiment on the consistency of our learning algorithms to varying market conditions. IS RET (resp. OOS RET) are in-sample (resp. out-of-sample) average (over the 9 runs in the experiment) yearly returns in % $\pm$ two standard errors.

PORTFOLIO	IS RET (%)	OOS RET (%)
MARKET	8.56±1.62	6.23±2.07
EWP	10.56±1.67	8.99±1.85
DWP*	11.94±2.01	12.51±1.12
DWP	11.91±1.99	12.50±1.11
CAP	26.54±2.38	22.05±2.89
CAP+ROA	**56.18±7.35**	**25.14±2.58**

In our second experiment, we aim to illustrate that our approaches are robust to financial crises. To do so, we train our model using data from 1 January 1992 to 31 December 2005, and test the learned strategy between 1 January 2006 and 31 December 2014, which includes the 2008 financial crisis. We compare the same investment strategies as before. The posterior distribution over the exponent p in the Bayesian parametric method is illustrated in Figure 1. The learned posterior mean investment maps are illustrated in Figure 3. In Table 2 we provide in-sample and out-of-sample average yearly returns as well as out-of-sample Sharpe ratios. Once again, it can be seen that: i) all learned portfolios do indeed outperform the benchmark (EWP) in-sample and out-of-sample, ii) non-parametric methods outperform parametric methods, and iii) adding the ROA as an additional characteristic does indeed add value. These conclusions hold true not only in absolute terms (returns) but also after adjusting for risk (Sharpe Ratio). A more granular illustration of how our method performs during the 2008 financial crisis can be seen in the time series of total wealth provided in Figure 2. It turns out that the ROA does not only improve the return out-of-sample, but it also has a 'stabilising effect' in that the volatility of the wealth process is considerably reduced.

Finally, it is also worth stressing that the shape of the learned investment map in the two-dimensional case (Figure 3) suggests that the investment strategy uncovered by our Bayesian nonparametric approach can hardly be replicated with a parametric model. Once again, it would be near impossible to derive analytical results pertaining to such a portfolio within the SPT framework.

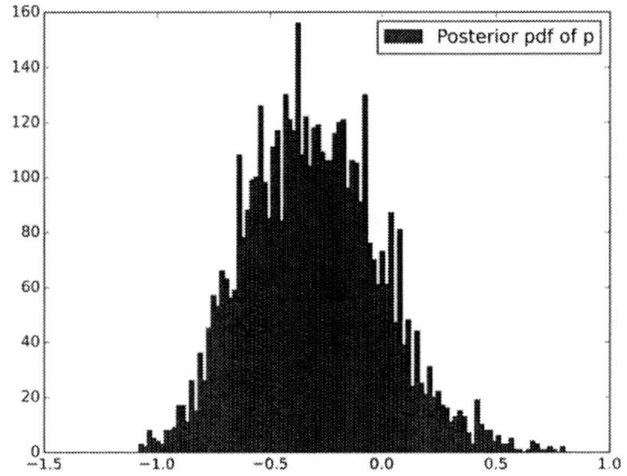

Figure 1: Posterior distribution of the parameter p of the diversity-weighted portfolio in our second experiment. The model was trained with market data between 1st January 1992 to 31st December 2005.

Table 2: Results of our second experiment on the robustness of the proposed approaches to financial crises. Returns (RET) are yearly equivalents (in %) of the total returns over the whole testing period. The annualised Sharpe Ratio (SR) is as per Eq. (18). IS (resp. OOS) stands for in-sample (resp. out-of-sample).

PORTFOLIO	IS RET (%)	OOS RET (%)	OOS SR
MARKET	9.60	7.90	0.47
EWP	13.46	9.60	0.51
DWP*	14.62	11.74	0.56
DWP	14.62	11.38	0.55
CAP	16.49	18.01	0.60
CAP+ROA	**37.54**	**18.33**	**0.72**

5 CONCLUSION & DISCUSSION

The inverse problem of *stochastic portfolio theory* (SPT) is the following problem: given a user-defined portfolio se-

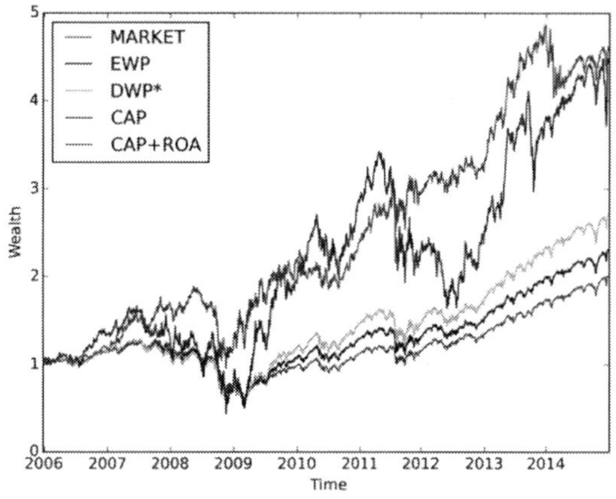

Figure 2: Time series of out-of-sample wealth processes in our second experiment. Models were trained with market data between 1st January 1992 to 31st December 2005, and tested from 1st January 2006 to 31st December 2014.

lection criterion, how does one go about constructing suitable investment strategies that meet the desired investment objective? This problem is extremely challenging to solve within the SPT framework. We propose the first solution to the inverse SPT problem and we demonstrate empirically that the proposed methods consistently and considerably outperform standard benchmarks, and are robust to financial crises.

Unlike the SPT framework, our methods are based solely on historical data rather than stochastic calculus. This allows us to consider a very broad class of candidate investment strategies that includes all SPT strategies as special cases, but crucially contains many investment strategies that cannot be analysed in the SPT framework. Unlike the SPT framework, which almost exclusively considers outperforming the market portfolio using investment strategies that are solely based on market weights, our proposed approach can cope with virtually any user-defined investment objective and can exploit any arbitrary set of trading characteristics. We empirically demonstrate that this added flexibility allows us to uncover more subtle patterns in financial markets, which results in greatly improved performance.

Although the Gaussian process in our model was approximated to be piecewise constant on a grid, there is no theoretical or practical obstacle in using an alternative approximation such as sparse Gaussian processes (Quiñonero Candela and Rasmussen [2005]) or string Gaussian processes (Kom Samo and Roberts [2015b]). Our method may be extended to learn even subtler patterns using the non-stationary general purpose kernels of Kom Samo and Roberts [2015a]. Our work may also be extended to allow for long-short investment strategies (i.e. strategies that allow short-selling). Finally, it would be interesting to develop an online extension of our work that would capture temporal changes in market dynamics.

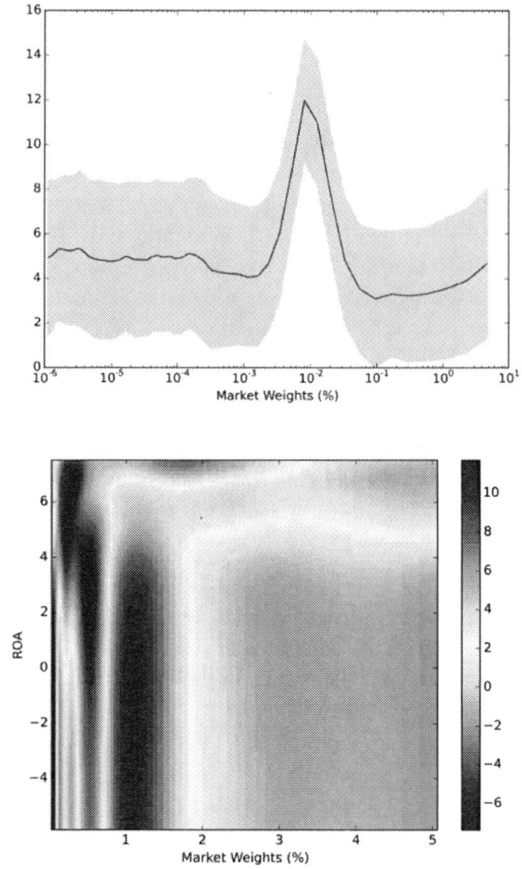

Figure 3: Learned logarithm investment maps of the CAP portfolio (top) and the CAP+ROA portfolio (bottom) in our second experiment. In the case of the CAP portfolio, the credible band corresponds to $\pm$ 2 posterior standard deviations.

Acknowledgements

Yves-Laurent is a Google Fellow in Machine Learning and would like to acknowledge support from the Oxford-Man Institute of Quantitative Finance. Alexander gratefully acknowledges PhD studentships from the Engineering and Physical Sciences Research Council, Nomura, and the Oxford-Man Institute of Quantitative Finance. Wharton Research Data Services (WRDS) was used in preparing the data for this paper. This service and the data available thereon constitute valuable intellectual property and trade secrets of WRDS and/or its third-party suppliers.

References

Adrian D. Banner and Daniel Fernholz. Short-term relative arbitrage in volatility-stabilized markets. *Ann. Finance*, 4:445–454, 2008.

Daniel Fernholz and Ioannis Karatzas. On optimal arbitrage. *Ann. Appl. Probab.*, 20(4):1179–1204, 2010.

Daniel Fernholz and Ioannis Karatzas. Optimal arbitrage under model uncertainty. *Ann. Appl. Probab.*, 21(6): 2191–2225, 2011.

Robert Fernholz. Portfolio generating functions. *Quantitative Analysis in Financial Markets, River Edge, NJ. World Scientific*, 1999.

Robert Fernholz. *Stochastic Portfolio Theory*. Springer, 2002.

Robert Fernholz and Ioannis Karatzas. Relative arbitrage in volatility-stabilized markets. *Ann. Finance*, 1:149–177, 2005.

Robert Fernholz and Ioannis Karatzas. Stochastic portfolio theory: A survey. In Alain Bensoussan and Qiang Zhang, editors, *Handbook of Numerical Analysis. Vol. XV. Special volume: mathematical modeling and numerical methods in finance*, volume 15 of *Handbook of Numerical Analysis*. Elsevier/North-Holland, Amsterdam, 2009.

Robert Fernholz, Ioannis Karatzas, and Constantinos Kardaras. Diversity and relative arbitrage in equity markets. *Finance Stoch.*, 9(1):1–27, 2005.

Stuart Geman and Donald Geman. Stochastic relaxation, gibbs distributions, and the bayesian restoration of images. *IEEE Transactions on Pattern Analysis and Machine Intelligence*, 6:721–741, 1984.

W. K. Hastings. Monte carlo sampling methods using markov chains and their applications. *Biometrika*, 24: 97–109, 1970.

Ioannis Karatzas and Johannes Ruf. Trading strategies generated by Lyapunov functions. *arXiv preprint arXiv:1603.08245*, 2016.

Ioannis Karatzas and Steven Shreve. *Brownian Motion and Stochastic Calculus*. Volume 113 in the series Probability and its Applications (New York). Springer-Verlag, New York, 1988.

Yves-Laurent Kom Samo and Stephen Roberts. Generalized spectral kernels. *arXiv preprint arXiv:1506.02236*, 2015a.

Yves-Laurent Kom Samo and Stephen Roberts. String Gaussian processes. *arXiv preprint arXiv:1507.06977*, 2015b.

Harry Markowitz. Portfolio selection. *The journal of finance*, 7(1):77–91, 1952.

Iain Murray, Ryan Prescott Adams, and David J. C. MacKay. Elliptical slice sampling. *JMLR: W&CP*, 9: 541–548, 2010.

Soumik Pal and Ting-Kam Leonard Wong. The geometry of relative arbitrage. *Mathematics and Financial Economics*, pages 1–31, 2014.

Radka Picková. Generalized volatility-stabilized processes. *Ann. Finance*, 10(1):101–125, 2014.

Joaquin Quiñonero Candela and Carl Edward Rasmussen. A unifying view of sparse approximate gaussian process regression. *The Journal of Machine Learning Research*, 6:1939–1959, 2005.

L. C. G. Rogers. *Optimal Investment*. Springer-Verlag, New York, 2013.

Johannes Ruf. *Optimal Trading Strategies Under Arbitrage*. PhD thesis, Columbia University, 2011.

Johannes Ruf. Hedging under arbitrage. *Math. Finance*, 23 (2):297–317, 2013.

Yunus Saatchi. *Scalable Inference for Structured Gaussian Process Models*. PhD thesis, University of Cambridge, 2011.

Winslow Strong. Generalizations of functionally generated portfolios with applications to statistical arbitrage. *SIAM Journal on Financial Mathematics*, 5(1):472–492, 2014.

Alexander Vervuurt. Topics in Stochastic Portfolio Theory. *arXiv preprint arXiv:1504.02988*, 2015.

Alexander Vervuurt and Ioannis Karatzas. Diversity-weighted portfolios with negative parameter. *Annals of Finance*, 11(3-4):411–432, 2015.

Ting-Kam Leonard Wong. Optimization of relative arbitrage. *Annals of Finance*, 11(3-4):345–382, 2015.

Stability of Causal Inference

Leonard J. Schulman and **Piyush Srivastava**
California Institute of Technology
schulman@caltech.edu, piyushsriva@gmail.com

Abstract

We consider the sensitivity of causal identification to small perturbations in the input. A long line of work culminating in papers by Shpitser and Pearl (2006) and Huang and Valtorta (2008) led to a complete procedure for the causal identification problem. In our main result in this paper, we show that the identification function computed by these procedures is in some cases extremely unstable numerically. Specifically, the "condition number" of causal identification can be of the order of $\Omega(\exp(n^{0.49}))$ on an identifiable semi-Markovian model with n visible nodes. That is, in order to give an output accurate to d bits, the empirical probabilities of the observable events need to be obtained to accuracy $d + \Omega(n^{0.49})$ bits.

1 INTRODUCTION

The gold standard for estimating the causal effect of one part of a system on another is the *controlled experiment*: the experimenter controls, or *intervenes* with, the *stimulus* variables in a way such that they are not affected by any non-measurable confounding factors, and then observes the distribution of the *response* variables as the stimuli are varied. Unfortunately, in a variety of important applications, the controlled experiment is not available as a method for reasons of ethics or practicality: a popular example of such a scenario is the question of whether a lifestyle choice such as smoking causes lung cancer. It can be argued (and in this particular case, has been argued! (Ohlemeyer, 1999)) that the strong observed correlations may be due to hidden confounding factors (here environmental or genetic).

In a series of seminal papers starting with (Pearl, 1995), Judea Pearl and others proposed and analyzed a framework for computing causal effects of hypothetical interventions solely from passively observed (i.e., non-experimental) data. The starting point of this framework is a model of the system as a directed graphical model with hidden nodes representing the non-measurable confounding variables. The goal is to take as input the joint distribution of the observed nodes in the model, and to deduce from them the *intervention distributions* that would result if an hypothetical controlled experiment were to be performed. A long line of work (Pearl, 1995; Pearl and Robins, 1995; Kuroki and Miyakawa, 1999; Halpern, 2000; Tian, 2002) on this framework culminated in papers by Shpitser and Pearl (2006) and Huang and Valtorta (2008) which gave a complete characterization of models in which this is achievable: in particular, they provided an algorithm which on input a directed graphical model and the set of stimulus and response variables outputs *either* a procedure that will compute the intervention distribution given the joint distributions of the observed nodes, or a certificate that the intervention distribution is not determined uniquely by the observed joint distribution. In the former case, the causal effect of the stimuli upon the response variables is said to be *identifiable* in the model.

This paper is concerned with the numerical properties of the identification problem. Note that an inference process such as causal identification as described above will always run on empirical inputs. We therefore ask: when the causal effect is identifiable, how sensitive is it to small inaccuracies either in the knowledge of the model, or of the observed distribution? Our main result (Theorem 1.2) in fact shows that causal inference can in fact be extremely sensitive to small errors: we give example of models on n nodes where *any* numerical algorithm for computing the intervention distribution from the observed distribution will lose roughly $\Theta(\sqrt{n})$ bits of precision. This sets an extraordinary demand on the accuracy of the input data of such a system.

As we discuss in more detail in Section 1.2, there are several natural sources of errors in the input to a causal identification problem: these include errors incurred in measurements of the observed distribution; round-off; and as we observe in Section 1.2.1, inexact descriptions of models. Our results therefore point to a new line of investigation concerning the classification of graphical models based on the sensitivity of causal identification to such perturbations in the input.

We begin in the next subsection by formalizing first the identification question, then the appropriate notion of stability for causal identification.

1.1 PEARL'S NOTION OF CAUSAL IDENTIFIABILITY

In Pearl's framework, the system being studied is modeled as a *semi-Markovian* graphical model. A semi-Markovian graphical model is a directed acyclic graph $G = (V, E, U, H)$, which has observed nodes and edges V and E, and hidden nodes and edges U and H, and is constrained so that the observed edges E lie between the observed vertices V, while the hidden edges in H go from a hidden vertex in U to an observed vertex in V.

The observed nodes V of the model are identified with the measurable components of the system, while the hidden nodes in G represent confounding variables that are not accessible to measurement. The edges model dependencies between these random variables: every variable is independent of its ancestors in G conditioned on its immediate predecessors. A probability distribution that satisfies this constraint is said to *respect* G. Equivalently, a probability distribution $\mathbb{P}$ respects G if it factorizes as

$$\begin{aligned}\mathbb{P}(V_1 = v_1, \ldots, V_n = v_n, U = u) \\ = \mathbb{P}(U = u) \prod_{V_i \in V} \mathbb{P}\left(V_i = v_i \mid \mathrm{pa}(V_i) = v_{\mathrm{pa}(V_i)}\right),\end{aligned}$$

where $\mathrm{pa}(S)$ is the set of parents of the node S.

However, since the hidden nodes in U are not measurable, any measurement can only estimate the *observed marginal*

$$\begin{aligned}&\mathbb{P}(V = v) \\ &= \sum_{u \in \Omega(U)} \mathbb{P}(U = u) \prod_{V_i \in V} \mathbb{P}\left(V_i = v_i \mid \mathrm{pa}(V_i) = v_{\mathrm{pa}(V_i)}\right),\end{aligned}$$

where $\Omega(U)$ denotes the range of the set U of hidden variables.

Pearl (1995) proposed that a natural representation of an experimental intervention on some subset X of observed variables is to remove from them any effect of their ancestors. Formally, the *intervention distribution*, denoted $\mathbb{P}(V - X \mid \mathrm{do}(X = x))$, of the nodes in $V - X$ under the intervention $X = x$ can therefore be defined as follows:

$$\begin{aligned}&\mathbb{P}(V - X = v_{V-X} | \mathrm{do}(X = x)) \\ &= \sum_{u \in \Omega(U)} \mathbb{P}(U = u) \prod_{V_i \in V - X} \mathbb{P}\left(V_i = v_i \mid \mathrm{pa}(V_i) = v_{\mathrm{pa}(V_i)}\right).\end{aligned} \tag{1}$$

The marginals of the above distribution define the distribution $\mathbb{P}(\cdot \mid \mathrm{do}(X = x))$ on all subsets of $V - X$.

Directly computing the intervention distribution using eq. (1) requires knowledge of the distributions of the hidden variables, as well as their effect on the observed nodes. These are, of course, not measurable in practice. This leads to the question: when is the intervention distribution in eq. (1) efficiently computable (or *identifiable*) from a knowledge of only the observed statistics? More formally, given a semi-Markovian graph $G = (V, E, U, H)$ and disjoint subsets X, Y of V, $\mathbb{P}(Y \mid \mathrm{do}\, X)$ is said to be *identifiable* in G if and only if there exists a function

$$\mathbf{ID}(G, X, Y) : P(V) \mapsto P(Y \mid \mathrm{do}\, X)$$

which maps observed distributions $P(V)$ to intervention distributions $P(Y \mid \mathrm{do}\, X)$. The question then is to decide, given G, X, and Y, whether such a map exists, and if yes, to compute it.

As expected, the answer to the question is not always positive. For example, in the graph in fig. 1a (where u is a hidden node), it is not possible to express $\mathbb{P}(y | \mathrm{do}(x))$ in terms of the marginal distribution $\mathbb{P}(x, y)$. This is intuitive, since any observed correlation between X and Y is equally well attributable as being due to the hidden variable U as due to a causal effect of X of Y. However, in the similar

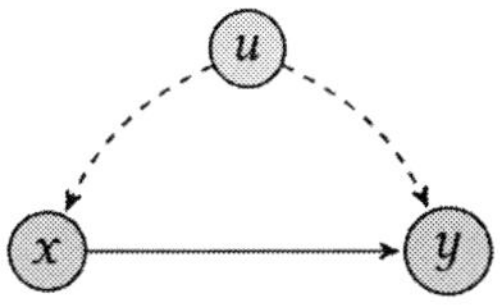

(a) A Simple Unidentifiable Case

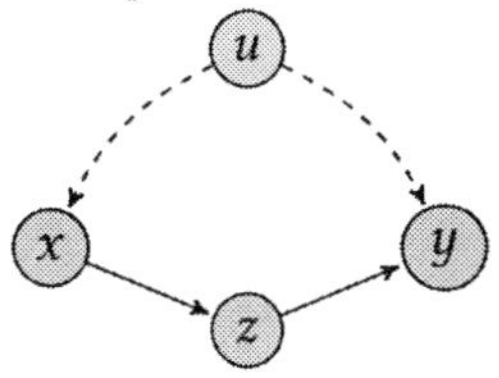

(b) A Simple Identifiable Case

Figure 1: Simple Graphical Models

model in fig. 1b, which has just one more observed node, the distribution $\mathbb{P}(y | \mathrm{do}(x))$ *is* identifiable.

The algorithms of Shpitser and Pearl (2006) and Huang and Valtorta (2008), on input G, X, and Y as in the above discussion, either output a description of the map $\mathbf{ID}(G, X, Y)$, or give a certificate that the causal effect of X on Y is not identifiable in G. Here we study the stability of the map $\mathbf{ID}(G, X, Y)$ when it exists; we also show how identification can be applied when the map "almost" exists.

1.2 RESULTS

Before embarking on our study of the sensitivity of the map $\mathbf{ID}(G, X, Y)$ to errors in the input, we make a few comments about the sources of such errors. Conventionally, two such sources are considered: errors introduced due to limitations in measuring the input, and errors introduced due to rounding off the input to a fixed finite floating point precision. These sources of errors are fairly generic and apply to almost any function, hence we defer their discussion in the context of the **ID** map to Remark 1.1. Here, we discuss another kind of error in the input specific to the problem of causal inference: error arising from inaccuracies in the knowledge of the graphical model of the system under study. We start by analyzing such errors in Section 1.2.1. Finally, in Section 1.2.2, we formalize the notion of the *condition number* which captures all the three forms of errors described above and then state our results in terms of this notion.

1.2.1 Errors in the Model Description

We now consider the effect of ignoring some edges in the input graphical model. Let $G = (V, E, U, H)$ be a semi-Markovian graph with observed nodes and edges V and E, and hidden nodes and edges U and H respectively. Let X, Y be disjoint subsets of V, and suppose that $\mathbb{P}(Y \mid \mathrm{do}\, X)$ is not identifiable in G, but identifiable in the subgraph $G' = (V, E, U, H - \{e\})$ in which a certain edge e has been removed. Another way to frame the situation is that we start with the model G' in which the requisite intervention is identifiable, and then consider the effect of adding the edge e to the model which destroys identifiability.

In particular, we wish to quantify the non-identifiability induced by the addition of the edge e to G', as a function of some measure of the "strength" of the edge e. A natural measure of the strength of an edge (A, B) is the amount by which it can affect the conditional probability at its child vertex B, when all the other parents of B are held fixed. More formally, we propose the following measure of strength:

Definition 1.1 (**ϵ-weak edge**). Let $e = (A, B)$ be any edge in a semi-Markovian graph $G = (V, E, U, H)$ and let P be a model respecting G. Let $\Xi(B)$ denote the set of parents of B in $(V \cup U) \setminus \{A\}$. We say that e is *ϵ-weak* with respect to G and P if for every setting b of B and ξ of $\Xi(B)$, and any two values a and a' in the range of A, we have

$$-\epsilon \leq \log \frac{P(B = b \mid \Xi(B) = \xi, A = a)}{P(B = b \mid \Xi(B) = \xi, A = a')} \leq \epsilon.$$

Now suppose that $e = (A, B) \in E \cup H$ is an ϵ-weak edge in $G = (V, E, U, H)$. We ask: given an observed distribution P, what is the error incurred if we perform causal inference in G' instead of G? We answer this in:

Proposition 1.1. *Consider a semi-Markovian graph $G = (V, E, U, H)$ and a distribution $P(V, U)$ respecting it. Let $R = \{e_i = (A_i, V_i) \mid 1 \leq i \leq q\}$ be a set of k edges in $E \cup H$ such that e_i is ϵ_i-weak, with $\epsilon := \sum_{i=1}^{k} \epsilon_i$. Suppose that X, Y are disjoint subsets of V for which $\mathbb{P}(Y \mid \mathrm{do}\, X)$ is not identifiable in G, but identifiable in $G' = (V, E \setminus R, U, H \setminus R)$. Then there exists a distribution $\tilde{P}(V, U)$ respecting G' such that*

$$-\epsilon \leq \log \frac{\tilde{P}(V)}{P(V)} \leq \epsilon, \quad \textit{and} \quad -\epsilon \leq \log \frac{\tilde{P}(Y \mid \mathrm{do}\, X)}{P(Y \mid \mathrm{do}\, X)} \leq \epsilon.$$

Note that $\tilde{P}(Y \mid \mathrm{do}\, X)$ is computable (by the algorithms of Shpitser and Pearl (2006) and Huang and Valtorta (2008)) given $\tilde{P}(V)$, but $P(Y \mid \mathrm{do}\, X)$ is not even uniquely determined given only the observed marginal $P(V)$.

The proof of this proposition can be found in the attached supplementary text.[1]

1.2.2 Uncertainty in the Input Distribution

Proposition 1.1 shows that there exists a distribution $\tilde{P}$ on the subgraph G' for which the intervention distribution is both close to that of P, and also computable only from the projection of $\tilde{P}$ to the observed nodes. On the other hand, the proposition does not provide a method to produce such a $\tilde{P}$ given the projection of P to the observed variables in G (or G'). However, it does guarantee that the observed marginals of P and $\tilde{P}$ are ϵ-close in the following sense:

Definition 1.2 (**ϵ-close distributions**). Two probability distributions P and Q on the same domain Ω are said to be ϵ-close, denoted $P \overset{\epsilon}{\sim} Q$, to each other if for every $\omega \in \Omega$,

$$-\epsilon \leq \log \frac{P(\omega)}{Q(\omega)} \leq \epsilon.$$

We therefore want to study the effect of doing causal inference with observed marginals that are only ϵ-close to the actual observed marginal. Our *statistical stability* question then is the following:

Question 1. *Suppose G, X, Y are such that the map* **ID**(G, X, Y) *exists. How sensitive is the map* **ID**(G, X, Y) *to uncertainties in the input P?*

The standard solution concept for studying such a question is the notion of the *condition number* of the map (see, e.g., (Bürgisser and Cucker, 2013, *Overture*)). We specialize here to the so-called "componentwise condition number".

Definition 1.3 (**Condition number**). Let $f : \mathbb{R}^k \to \mathbb{R}^\ell$ be an arbitrary vector valued function. The condition number of f at $a \in \mathbb{R}^k$, denoted $\kappa_f(a)$, is defined as

$$\kappa_f(a) := \lim_{\delta \downarrow 0} \sup_{\substack{a' \in \mathbb{R}^k \\ \mathsf{Rel}(a, a') \leq \delta}} \frac{\mathsf{Rel}(f(a), f(a'))}{\mathsf{Rel}(a, a')},$$

where for real vectors a, a' in the Euclidean space $\mathbb{R}^t$, the *relative error* $\mathsf{Rel}(a, a')$ is defined as $\max_{1 \leq i \leq t} \frac{|a_i - a'_i|}{|a_i|}$. The condition number of f over a domain $\mathcal{D}$, denoted as κ_f when $\mathcal{D}$ is clear from the context, is $\sup_{a \in \mathcal{D}} \kappa_f(a)$.

[1] A version of this paper including the supplementary text is also available from `http://www.caltech.edu/~piyushs/docs/condition.pdf`.

Note that the condition number is a property of the function f, and not of a particular algorithm for numerically computing f. In particular, $\kappa_f(a)$ can informally be construed as a derivative of the coordinate-wise logarithm of f as a function of the coordinate-wise logarithm of a.

Armed with the definition of the condition number, we can now further refine our earlier Question 1.

Question 2. *What is the condition number of the map* $\mathbf{ID}(G, X, Y)$ *for a given* G *and subsets* X, Y*, provided in the first place that this map exists?*

Remark 1.1. A few remarks about the sources of errors are in order. First, note that Proposition 1.1 already provides a natural setting in which the "error model" used in the definition of the condition number is the right one: in the notation of that proposition, if we computed the intervention distributions in G' by applying the map $\mathbf{ID}(G', X, Y)$ to P instead of $\tilde{P}$, the worst case relative error in the output will be lower bounded by roughly $\epsilon \cdot \kappa_{\mathbf{ID}(G',X,Y)}(\tilde{P})$, independent of the algorithm used for computation. However, we point out that there is another—arguably even more natural—source of errors that is best captured in terms of relative errors: errors introduced due to rounding in fixed precision floating point systems. We refer the reader to, e.g., the textbook by Bürgisser and Cucker (2013, Section O.3) for a formalization of such systems.

The final type of errors that we discuss here are sampling errors arising due to the finiteness of the sampling procedures used to estimate the observed marginals that are fed as input to the map **ID**. These sampling errors are more likely to be additive (as opposed to relative) in nature. When the input coordinates are elements of the interval $[0, 1]$ (as is the case in our application) an additive error of a given magnitude ϵ always corresponds to a relative error that is at least as large as ϵ in magnitude. Hence, upper bounds imposed on the relative error in the output using an upper bound on the condition number can only worsen if the error guarantees on the input are only additive. In particular, if we show that the condition number defined with respect to relative errors is large, the instability of the problem with respect to additive errors in the input also follows.

Our first result regarding statistical stability demonstrates that the condition number can in fact be sub-exponentially large in the size of the model.

Theorem 1.2. *For every* $0 < \alpha < 1/2$*, there exists an infinite sequence of semi-Markovian graphs* $G_N = (V_N, E_N, U_N, H_N)$ *with* $|V_N| = N$*, and disjoint subsets* S_N *and* T_N *of* V_N *such that*

$$\kappa_{\mathbf{ID}(G_N,T_N,S_N)} = \Omega(\exp{(N^\alpha)}).$$

The proof of this theorem appears in Section 2. We now isolate one important class of special cases where the condition number is not so bad.

Proposition 1.3. *Let* $G = (V, E, U, H)$ *be a semi-Markovian graph, and let* X *be a node in* V *such that it is not possible to reach a child of* X *from* X *using only the edges in* H *(with their directions ignored). Then, for any subset* S *of* V *not containing* X.

$$\kappa_{\mathbf{ID}(G,X,S)} = O(|V|).$$

The hypothesis of the above proposition has appeared earlier as a sufficient condition for the identifiability of $P(S \mid \mathrm{do}\, X)$ in the early work of Tian and Pearl (2002). While this condition is not necessary for identifiability, we show that it carries a distinct advantage: when it holds, the condition number of the identification function is relatively small. The proof of Proposition 1.3 appears in Section 3.

2 ILL-CONDITIONED EXAMPLES

In this section, we prove Theorem 1.2. We begin with a brief outline of our general strategy.

Our main object of study will be semi-Markovian models $\mathcal{G}_n^k$ indexed by positive integers n and k, such that $\mathcal{G}_n^k$ has $\Theta(nk)$ visible nodes, and $\Theta(n + k)$ hidden nodes. The maximum degree of $\mathcal{G}_n^k$ will be $\Theta(k)$ for the observed nodes, and $\Theta(n)$ for the hidden nodes.

Let U and V denote the hidden nodes and the observed nodes, respectively, of $\mathcal{G}_n^k$. In our construction, the variables in both U and V will be binary valued. The crux of our proof is a construction of two probability distributions: the first of these, Q, will be a distribution on the states of the nodes in $U \cup V$ which respects $\mathcal{G}_n^k$. The second, $\tilde{Q}$, will be a distribution only on the states of V, such that it is ϵ-close to the marginal of Q on V. Q and $\tilde{Q}$ will be designed to ensure that when k is chosen to be an appropriate function of n, the values of a certain intervention distribution on $\mathcal{G}_n^k$ computed according to $\tilde{Q}$ differ from the correct answer (i.e., the one computed according to Q) by a factor of $1 \pm \epsilon'$ where ϵ' is larger then ϵ by a factor $\Omega(\exp{(N^\alpha)})$ (for any $\alpha < 1/2$), for $N = nk + n - 1$, the size of $\mathcal{G}_n^k$.

2.1 THE GADGET

We now define the semi-Markovian graph $\mathcal{G}_n^k$ formally. The visible nodes V of the graph partition into three classes: the "X" nodes, of which there are $k - 1$, the S nodes, of which there are n, and the "Y" nodes, of which there are $(n - 1)k$, arranged in $n - 1$ "towers" of k each (see fig. 2). Formally, we have

$$V := \{X_i \mid 2 \le i \le k\} \cup \{S_i \mid 1 \le i \le n\} \cup \left\{Y_{i,j} \mid 1 \le i \le n-1, 1 \le j \le k\right\}.$$

We now describe the visible edges. First, each S node is a child of each of the Y nodes in the tower immediately to its left. Each Y node is a child of the Y node immediately below it in its tower, of the S node immediately to the left of its tower, and, if it is in the leftmost tower, of the X node at the same "level" as itself (see fig. 2). Formally,

$$\begin{aligned} E := &\{(X_i, Y_{1,i}) \mid 2 \le i \le k\} \\ &\cup \left\{(S_i, Y_{i,j}) \mid 1 \le i \le n-1, 1 \le j \le k\right\} \\ &\cup \left\{(Y_{i,j}, S_{i+1}) \mid 1 \le i \le n-1, 1 \le j \le k\right\} \\ &\cup \left\{(Y_{i,j}, Y_{i,j+1}) \mid 1 \le i \le n-1, 1 \le j \le k-1\right\}. \end{aligned}$$

Our final task is to describe the hidden nodes and variables: the structure of these defines the C-components of the model, and hence they will dictate the sequence of operations in the Shpitser-Pearl algorithm for causal identification applied to $\mathcal{G}_n^k$.[2] In order to make sure that the S nodes are always in the same C-component, we stipulate an unnamed hidden variable for each adjacent pair of the S_i, which has both of the elements of the pair in question as its children. In addition, we have further (named) hidden variables $\{U_i \mid 2 \le i \le k\}$, such that U_i has as children all the S nodes, the nodes X_i, and all the X and Y nodes at "levels"strictly below i. Formally, the hidden edges incident on these named hidden nodes are:

$$\begin{aligned} H := &\left\{(U_i, X_j) \mid 2 \le i \le k, 2 \le j \le i\right\} \\ &\cup \left\{(U_i, S_j) \mid 2 \le i \le k, 1 \le j \le n\right\} \\ &\cup \{(U_i, Y_{s,t}) \mid 2 \le i \le k, 1 \le s \le n-1, 1 \le t < i\}. \end{aligned}$$

See fig. 2 for a depiction of the gadget $\mathcal{G}_6^4$. In the figure, the named hidden variables U_i and their edges are not included for clarity. Instead, the hyperedges depicting the hidden variables U_i are depicted by the different shaded regions: the lowest region includes all the visible nodes that are children of U_2, the next higher region includes all the visible nodes that are children of U_3 and the topmost region includes all the visible nodes that are children of U_4.

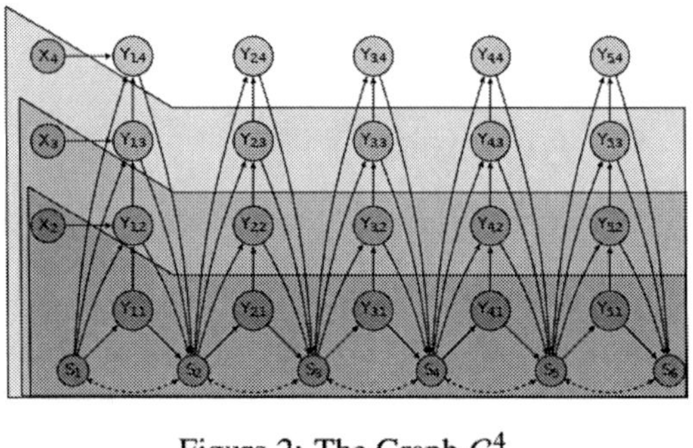

Figure 2: The Graph $\mathcal{G}_6^4$.

[2]A *C-component* is a maximal set of visible vertices which are reachable from each other through paths consisting only of hidden edges (the directions of the hidden edges are ignored). See, e.g., Shpitser and Pearl (2006) for a discussion of the importance of C-components to causal identification.

2.2 IDENTIFICATION ON $\mathcal{G}_n^k$: THE PEEL-OFF OPERATOR

Notation. For any set S of indices, and a symbol A, we denote by A_S the set $\{A_i \mid i \in S\}$ of indexed symbols. Similarly, for sets S and T of indices, we denote by $A_{S,T}$ the set $\left\{A_{i,j} \mid i \in S, j \in T\right\}$. For integers $a \le b$, $[a, b]$ denotes the set of integers between a and b, inclusive. For a positive integer a, we use $[a]$ as a shorthand for the set $[1, a]$. We also denote vectors of values by boldface fonts; in particular, $\mathbf{1}_{[l]}$ denotes a vector of length l all whose entries are 1.

Consider now the computation of the following intervention distribution in $\mathcal{G}_n^k$:

$$P\left(S_{[n]} = \mathbf{1}_{[n]} \mid \operatorname{do}\left(X_{[2,k]} = \mathbf{1}_{[k-1]}, Y_{[n-1],[k]} = \mathbf{1}_{[(n-1)k]}\right)\right). \quad (2)$$

The gadget is defined so as to make the Shpitser-Pearl algorithm iterate a sequence of "multiplication" and "marginalization" steps alternately in the computation of this distribution: our goal ultimately is to amplify errors in the multiplication step, and to attempt to preserve the amplification in the marginalization step. However, before seeing how this can be done, we first abstract the operation of the Shpitser-Pearl algorithm on $\mathcal{G}_n^k$ in terms of a *peel-off* operator which clubs the alternating "multiplication" and "marginalization" steps.

We begin by noting that the gadget $\mathcal{G}_n^{k-1}$ can be viewed as a subgraph of the gadget $\mathcal{G}_n^k$ in a canonical manner by identifying the vertices present in the both the gadgets. These "identified" vertices include all the hidden and visible vertices of $\mathcal{G}_n^k$ except X_k, U_k and $\{Y_{i,k} \mid 1 \le i \le n-1\}$. Let $\mathcal{P}_n^k$ denote the set of probability distributions on states of the observed variables of $\mathcal{G}_n^k$. We define an operator π that acts on a distribution in $\mathcal{P}_n^k$ by "peeling off" the top layer of variables and produces an object in $\mathcal{P}_n^{k-1}$ as the output. Although the action of the operator depends upon the values of n and k, we drop its dependence upon these parameters for ease of notation.

Definition 2.1 (Operator π). Given a probability distribution $P \in \mathcal{P}_n^k$ the probability distribution $\pi(P) \in \mathcal{P}_n^{k-1}$ is defined as

$$\begin{aligned} &\pi(P)\left(X_{[2,k-1]}, S_{[n]}, Y_{[n-1],[k-1]}\right) \\ &:= \sum_x P\left(X_k = x, X_{[2,k-1]}\right) \\ &\quad \cdot \prod_{i=1}^{n-1} P(S_i, Y_{i,[k-1]} \mid X_k = x, Y_{[i-1],k} = \mathbf{1}_{i-1}, \\ &\qquad\qquad X_{[2,k-1]}, S_{[i-1]}, Y_{[i-1],[k-1]}) \\ &\quad \cdot P(S_n \mid X_k = x, Y_{[n-1],k} = \mathbf{1}_{n-1}, \\ &\qquad\qquad X_{[2,k-1]}, S_{[n-1]}, Y_{[n-1],[k-1]}), \end{aligned}$$

where x ranges over all possible values of the X_k, and 1 is assumed to be in the range of $Y_{i,k}$ for all $i \in [n-1]$.

Remark 2.1. Note that the above definition is valid only for $k \geq 2$. However, we can extend it to the case $k = 1$ by "ignoring" the summation over x when $k = 1$ (or equivalently, by assuming that there exists a variable X_1 with no incident edges).

The algorithm of Shpitser and Pearl (2006) for computing the intervention distribution in eq. (2) then amounts to iterating the operator π k times on the observed distribution P:

$$P\left(S_{[n]} = \mathbf{1}_n \mid \mathrm{do}\left(X_{[2,k]} = \mathbf{1}_{k-1}, Y_{[n-1],[k]} = \mathbf{1}_{k(n-1)}\right)\right) = \pi^k(P)\left(S_{[n]} = \mathbf{1}_n\right).$$

Our high level strategy is to take advantage of the multiplication in the definition of π to amplify errors in each step. Intuitively, if each factor in the product in the definition of $\pi(P)$ has an error factor of $(1+\epsilon)$, then we might expect the error in $\pi(P)$ to be of the order of $(1+\Theta(n)\epsilon)$. We might then expect such an effect to propagate through the k levels so that the final error is of the order of $(1+\Theta(n^k)\epsilon)$. However, the marginalization over x can destroy this propagation effect, and we will need to be careful to get around this. This will be done by biasing the distribution Q away from being a uniform distribution, using the bias function defined below (see also Remark 2.2).

2.3 THE ADVERSARIAL MODEL

Our goal now is to define a model Q on $\mathcal{G}_n^k$ and a "perturbed" version $\tilde{Q}$ of the observed marginal Q, such that for every observation ξ, Q and $\tilde{Q}$ are ϵ-close to each other.To show lower bounds on the condition number of causality, we will need to show that even when Q and $\tilde{Q}$ are ϵ-close, it is possible to arrange matters so that (in the limit $\epsilon \downarrow 0$)

$$\log\left(\frac{\pi^k(\tilde{Q})\left(S_{[n]} = \mathbf{1}_n\right)}{\pi^k(Q)\left(S_{[n]} = \mathbf{1}_n\right)}\right) = \log(1+\epsilon)\cdot\Omega\left(\left(\frac{n}{ck}\right)^k\right), \quad (3)$$

for some positive constant c independent of n and k.

For ease of exposition, we work directly with some marginals of the distributions Q and $\tilde{Q}$. We defer the construction of Q and $\tilde{Q}$ achieving these marginals to a later section. For further ease of notation, we denote the set of vertices $S_{[i]} \cup Y_{[i],[j]}$ as A_{ij}: in terms of fig. 2, this is the set of vertices of height up to j in the first i "towers" (if we also consider each of the S vertices to be part of the "tower" of Y vertices immediately to their right; see fig. 3 for an illustration of the set $A_{3,2}$). We further use $A_{ij} = \mathbf{1}$ as a shorthand for the conditioning $S_i = \mathbf{1}_i, Y_{[i-1],[k]} = \mathbf{1}_{(i-1)k}$. We now describe the marginals of Q required in our proof, in terms of a *bias function* as defined below. Only conditional expectations of the form described below will be required in the recursive computation of $\pi^k(Q)\left(S_{[n]} = \mathbf{1}_n\right)$.

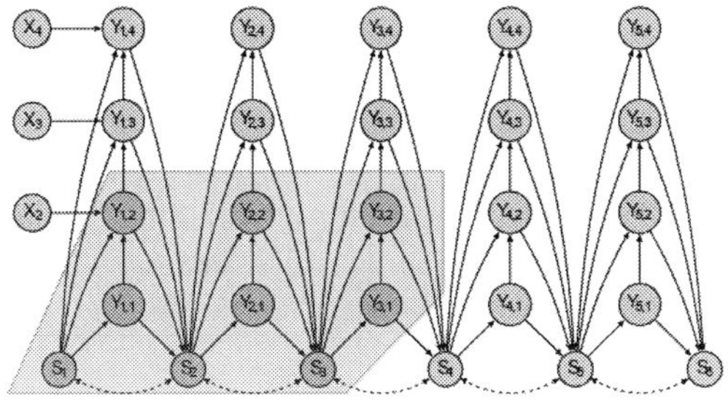

Figure 3: The Set $A_{3,2}$

Definition 2.2 (Bias function). The bias function $b : \{0,1\} \to [0,1]$ is defined as

$$b(x) = \begin{cases} \frac{3}{2} & x = 1, \\ 1 & x = 0. \end{cases}$$

$$Q(X_{[2,k]} = \cdot) = \frac{1}{2^{k-1}},$$
$$Q(S_i = 1 \mid A_{i-1,k} = \mathbf{1}, X_{[2,k]}) = \frac{1}{2}\cdot b(X_2), \text{ for } i \in [n],$$
$$Q(S_i = 1, Y_{i,[j]} = \mathbf{1}_j \mid A_{i-1,k} = \mathbf{1}, X_{[2,k]}) = \frac{1}{2^{j+1}}\cdot b\left(X_{j+2}\right), \text{ for } i \in [n-1], j \in [k-2],$$
$$Q(S_i = 1, Y_{i,[k-1]} = \mathbf{1}_{k-1} \mid A_{i-1,k} = \mathbf{1}, X_{[2,k]}) = \frac{1}{2^k}, \text{ for } i \in [n-1].$$

After one application of π, we have the following expressions for conditional expectations of the above form:

$$\pi(Q)(X_{[2,k-1]} = \cdot) = \frac{1}{2^{k-2}},$$
$$\pi(Q)(S_i = 1 \mid A_{i-1,k-1} = \mathbf{1}, X_{[2,k-1]}) = \frac{1}{2}\cdot b(X_2), \text{ for } i \in [n],$$
$$\pi(Q)(S_i = 1, Y_{i,[j]} = \mathbf{1}_j \mid A_{i-1,k-1} = \mathbf{1}, X_{[2,k-1]}) = \frac{1}{2^{j+1}}\cdot b\left(X_{j+2}\right) \text{ for } i \in [n-1], j \in [k-3],$$
$$\pi(Q)(S_i = 1, Y_{i,[k-2]} = \mathbf{1}_{k-2} \mid A_{i-1,k-1} = \mathbf{1}, X_{[2,k-1]}) = \frac{1}{2^{k-1}}\cdot\frac{b(0)+b(1)}{2}, \text{ for } i \in [n-1].$$

This process can be continued, and we finally obtain

$$\pi^{k-1}(Q)(S_i = 1 \mid S_{[i-1]} = \mathbf{1}_{i-1}, Y_{[i-1],1} = \mathbf{1}_{i-1}) = \frac{1}{2}\cdot\frac{b(0)+b(1)}{2} = \frac{5}{8}, \text{ for } i \in [n],$$

so that

$$\pi^k(Q)(S_{[n]} = \mathbf{1}_n) = \left(\frac{5}{8}\right)^n.$$

We will now list our requirements for the conditionals of the perturbed distribution $\tilde{Q}$. The construction of a $\tilde{Q}$ that achieves these marginals and that is ϵ-close to Q can be found in Section 2.3.1. Here, we only note that the construction will be such that $\tilde{Q}$ will differ from Q only in the probabilities of those observations in which all the X_i are simultaneously equal to 1.

$$\tilde{Q}(X_{[2,k]} = \cdot) = \frac{1}{2^{k-1}},$$
$$\tilde{Q}(S_i = 1 \mid A_{i-1,k} = \mathbf{1}, X_{[2,k]}) = \frac{1}{2} \cdot b(X_2), \text{ for } i \in [n],$$
$$\tilde{Q}(S_i = 1, Y_{i,[j]} = \mathbf{1}_j \mid A_{i-1,k} = \mathbf{1}, X_{[2,k]}) = \frac{1}{2^{j+1}} \cdot b\left(X_{j+2}\right), \text{ for } i \in [n-1], j \in [k-2],$$
$$\tilde{Q}(S_i = 1, Y_{i,[k-1]} = \mathbf{1}_{k-1} \mid A_{i-1,k} = \mathbf{1}, X_{[2,k]}) = \frac{1}{2^k} \cdot \begin{cases} (1+\epsilon/2) & X_{[2,k]} = \mathbf{1}_{k-1} \\ 1 & X_{[2,k]} \neq \mathbf{1}_{k-1} \end{cases}, \text{ for } i \in [n-1].$$

We now compute the relevant iterated applications of π on $\tilde{Q}$ using the above marginals.To simplify notation, define:

$$\nu := (1 + \epsilon/2).$$

We now compute the corresponding expressions for $\pi(\tilde{Q})$. It will also be convenient to use the following "error-propagator" function.

Definition 2.3 (Error propagator). Given a bias function b as defined above, the error propagator function η_b (abbreviated to η when b is clear from the context) is $\eta(x) = \eta_b(x) := \frac{b(0)+xb(1)}{1+x}$.

We are now ready to describe $\pi(\tilde{Q})$:

$$\pi(\tilde{Q})(X_{[2,k-1]} = \cdot) = \frac{1}{2^{k-2}},$$
$$\pi(\tilde{Q})(S_i = 1 \mid A_{i-1,k-1} = \mathbf{1}, X_{[2,k-1]}) = \frac{1}{2} \cdot b(X_2), \text{ for } i \in [n],$$
$$\pi(\tilde{Q})(S_i = 1, Y_{i,[j]} = \mathbf{1}_j \mid A_{i-1,k-1} = \mathbf{1}, X_{[2,k-1]}) = \frac{1}{2^{j+1}} \cdot b\left(X_{j+2}\right) \text{ for } i \in [n-1], j \in [k-3],$$
$$\pi(\tilde{Q})(S_i = 1, Y_{i,[k-2]} = \mathbf{1}_{k-2} \mid A_{i-1,k-1} = \mathbf{1}, X_{[2,k-1]}) = \frac{1}{2^{k-1}} \cdot \begin{cases} \eta\left(\nu^{i-1}\right) & X_{[2,k-1]} = \mathbf{1}_{k-2} \\ \eta(1) & X_{[2,k-1]} \neq \mathbf{1}_{k-2} \end{cases}, \text{ for } i \in [n-1].$$

Note that only the last of these expressions differs from the case of Q, and it differs only for those observations in which all the remaining X_i nodes are set to 1. This pattern persists for further iterates of π.

Remark 2.2. We can now make precise how the bias function allows propagation of errors through π in spite of the marginalization step. Note that if we had no bias, i.e., $b(x) \equiv 1$, then the discrepancy from $\pi(Q)$ in the last line in the definition of $\pi(\tilde{Q})$ will not arise at all.

In order to describe the evolution of this discrepancy, we define the quantities $\nu_{l,i}$ as ratios between the intermediate marginals computed from $\tilde{Q}$ and Q respectively after l applications of ν; the formal definition of $\nu_{l,i}$ appears in fig. 4. From the base case of $\tilde{Q}$ and the definition of operator π, we then have

$$\nu_{0,i} = \nu = (1+\epsilon/2), \qquad \text{for } i \in [n-1]$$
$$\nu_{l,n} = 1 \qquad \text{for } 0 \leq l \leq k-1$$
$$\nu_{l,i} = \frac{\eta\left(\prod_{j=1}^{i-1} \nu_{l-1,j}\right)}{\eta(1)}, \qquad \text{for } 1 \leq l \leq k-1, i \in [n-1].$$

Note that we have

$$\frac{\pi^k(\tilde{Q})(S_{[n]} = \mathbf{1}_n)}{\pi^k(Q)(S_{[n]} = \mathbf{1}_n)} = \prod_{i=1}^{n-1} \nu_{k-1,i}, \tag{4}$$

so that we only need to upper bound the $\nu_{l,i}$ appropriately. In order to do this, we will use the following lemma:

Lemma 2.1. *There exists a $\delta > 0$ such that for $x \in [1, 1+\delta)$, $\frac{\eta(x)}{\eta(1)} \geq x^{1/11}$. The parameter δ can be chosen to be at least 1.*

Proof. The claim of the lemma is equivalent to the existence of a positive δ such that

$$f(x) := 5x^{12/11} + 5x^{1/11} - 6x - 4 \leq 0 \text{ for } x \in [1, 1+\delta).$$

To prove the latter fact, we observe that $f(1) = 0$, and that $f'(1) = \left[\frac{60}{11}x^{1/11} + \frac{5}{11}x^{-10/11} - 6\right]_{x=1} = -\frac{1}{11} < 0$. Indeed, a direct computation shows that δ can be chosen to be 1, since $f(2) < 0$ and f is convex in $[1, 2)$. □

We will now use the above lemma to prove by induction the following lower bound on the $\nu_{l,i}$.

Lemma 2.2. *Suppose that for $1 \leq i \leq n-1$ and $0 \leq l \leq k-1$, we have $\nu_{l,i} \geq 1$ and $\frac{1}{11^{l-1}}\binom{i-1}{l}\log\nu < \log 2$. Then, for such l and i, $\log \nu_{l,i} \geq \frac{1}{11^l}\binom{i-1}{l}\log\nu$.*

Proof. The base case $l = 0$ is true by the definition of the $\nu_{l,i}$. For the induction, $l \geq 1$, and we start with the recursive definition of $\nu_{l,i}$ (for $i \leq n-1$) in terms of $\nu_{l-1,j}$:

$$\nu_{l,i} = \frac{1}{\eta(1)} \cdot \eta\left(\prod_{j=1}^{i-1} \nu_{l-1,j}\right)$$
$$\geq \frac{1}{\eta(1)} \cdot \eta\left(\prod_{j=1}^{i-1} \exp\left(\frac{1}{11^{l-1}}\binom{j-1}{l-1}\log\nu\right)\right) \tag{5}$$
$$= \frac{1}{\eta(1)} \cdot \eta\left(\exp\left(\frac{1}{11^{l-1}}\binom{i-1}{l}\log\nu\right)\right) \tag{6}$$
$$\geq \exp\left(\frac{1}{11^l}\binom{i-1}{l}\log\nu\right), \tag{7}$$

$$\nu_{l,i} := \frac{\pi^l(\tilde{Q})(S_i = 1, Y_{i,[k-l-1]} = \mathbf{1}_{k-l-1} \mid A_{i-1,k-l} = \mathbf{1}, X_{[2,k-l]} = \mathbf{1}_{k-l-1})}{\pi^l(Q)(S_i = 1, Y_{i,[k-l-1]} = \mathbf{1}_{k-l-1} \mid A_{i-1,k-l} = \mathbf{1}, X_{[2,k-l]} = \mathbf{1}_{k-l-1})}.$$

Figure 4: The Quantities $\nu_{l,i}$

where eq. (5) uses the induction hypothesis and the fact that η is an increasing function, eq. (6) employs the elementary combinatorial identity $\sum_{j=1}^{i-1}\binom{j-1}{l-1} = \binom{i-1}{l}$, and eq. (7) uses the hypotheses of the lemma to apply Lemma 2.1. □

We are now ready to complete the proof of Theorem 1.2.

Proof of Theorem 1.2. Substituting the bounds on the $\nu_{l,i}$ from Lemma 2.2 in eq. (4), we get

$$\frac{\pi^k(\tilde{Q})(S_{[n]} = \mathbf{1}_n)}{\pi^k(Q)(S_{[n]} = \mathbf{1}_n)} = \prod_{i=1}^{n-1} \nu_{k-1,i} \tag{8}$$

$$\geq \exp\left(\frac{\log \nu}{11^{k-1}} \sum_{i=1}^{n-1} \binom{i-1}{k-1}\right) \tag{9}$$

$$= \exp\left(\frac{\log \nu}{11^{k-1}} \binom{n-1}{k}\right) \tag{10}$$

$$\geq \exp\left(11 \log \nu \left(\frac{n-1}{11k}\right)^k\right), \tag{11}$$

where eq. (9) uses Lemma 2.2, eq. (10) is again based on the elementary identity used in eq. (6), and eq. (11) is an application of the standard inequality $\binom{a}{b} \geq \left(\frac{a}{b}\right)^b$. Now, let $k = (n-1)^{\alpha'}/11$ for $\alpha' \in [0, 1)$, and set $M := 11(n-1)k$. Note that $M = O(N)$ where N is the number of visible nodes in $\mathcal{G}_n^k$. We then have

$$\frac{\pi^k(\tilde{Q})(S_{[n]} = \mathbf{1}_n)}{\pi^k(Q)(S_{[n]} = \mathbf{1}_n)} \geq \exp\left(11 \log \nu \exp\left(\frac{(1-\alpha')M^{\alpha'/(\alpha'+1)} \log(n-1)}{11}\right)\right).$$

Choosing $\alpha = \alpha'/(\alpha'+1)$ completes the proof. □

2.3.1 Definitions of Q and $\tilde{Q}$

We now supply the promised definitions of Q and $\tilde{Q}$. We first define Q by providing the appropriate conditional distributions of the bits at different nodes in the graph. For the sake of brevity, we only specify the conditional distributions which are *not* uniform: all the unspecified distributions are assumed to be uniform over $\{0, 1\}$. We recall the definition of the bias function used earlier:

Definition 2.4 (Bias function). The bias function $b : \{0,1\} \to [0,1]$ is defined as

$$b(x) = \begin{cases} \frac{3}{2} & x = 1, \\ 1 & x = 0. \end{cases}$$

Q is now defined as follows:

$$Q(X_i = U_i \mid U_i) = 1, \text{ for } 2 \leq i \leq k,$$
$$Q(S_i = 1 \mid Y_{i-1,[k]} = \mathbf{1}_k, U_{[2,k]}) = \frac{1}{2} \cdot b(U_2) \text{ for } i \in [n],$$
$$Q(Y_{i,j} = 1 \mid S_i = 1, Y_{i,j-1} = 1, U_{[j+1,k]}) = \frac{1}{2} \cdot \begin{cases} b\left(U_{j+2}\right) & U_{j+1} = 0, \\ \frac{1}{b(1-U_{j+2})} & U_{j+1} = 1 \end{cases}$$
$$\text{for } i \in [n-1], j \in [k-2].$$
$$Q(Y_{i,k-1} = 1 \mid S_i = 1, Y_{i,k-2} = 1, U_k) = \frac{1}{2} \cdot \frac{1}{b(U_k)}, \text{ for } i \in [n-1].$$

The above construction of Q leads, in particular, to the following observed conditional distributions for Q:

$$Q(X_{[2,k]} = \cdot) = \frac{1}{2^{k-1}}$$
$$Q(S_i = 1 \mid A_{i-1,k} = \mathbf{1}, X_{[2,k]}) = \frac{1}{2} \cdot b(X_2), \text{ for } i \in [n],$$
$$Q(Y_{i,j} = 1 \mid S_i = 1, Y_{i,[j-1]} = \mathbf{1}_{j-1}, A_{i-1,k} = \mathbf{1}, X_{[2,k]}) = \frac{1}{2} \cdot \begin{cases} b\left(X_{j+2}\right) & X_{j+1} = 0, \\ \frac{1}{b(1-X_{j+2})} & X_{j+1} = 1, \end{cases}$$
$$\text{for } i \in [n-1], j \in [k-2].$$
$$Q(Y_{i,k-1} = 1 \mid S_i = 1, Y_{i,[k-2]} = \mathbf{1}_{k-2}, A_{i-1,k} = \mathbf{1}, X_{[2,k]}) = \frac{1}{2} \cdot \frac{1}{b(X_k)}, \text{ for } i \in [n-1].$$

The Perturbed Distribution The perturbation $\tilde{Q}$ of Q used in our proof is defined in fig. 5. We only specify those entries of $\tilde{Q}$ which are different from those of Q.

3 A WELL-CONDITIONED CLASS

In this section we provide a counterpoint to our main result: we exhibit a useful class of well-conditioned causal

$$\frac{\tilde{Q}(X_{[2,k]} = \mathbf{1}_{k-1}, S_i = 1, A_{i-1,k} = \mathbf{1}, Y_{i,[k-2]} = \mathbf{1}_{k-2}, Y_{i,[k-1,k]} = 00, \star)}{Q(X_{[2,k]} = \mathbf{1}_{k-1}, S_i = 1, A_{i-1,k} = \mathbf{1}, Y_{i,[k-2]} = \mathbf{1}_{k-2}, Y_{i,[k-1,k]} = 00, \star)} = (1 - \epsilon/2), \text{ for } i \in [n-1],$$

$$\frac{\tilde{Q}(X_{[2,k]} = \mathbf{1}_{k-1}, S_i = 1, A_{i-1,k} = \mathbf{1}, Y_{i,[k-2]} = \mathbf{1}_{k-2}, Y_{i,[k-1,k]} = 10, \star)}{Q(X_{[2,k]} = \mathbf{1}_{k-1}, S_i = 1, A_{i-1,k} = \mathbf{1}, Y_{i,[k-2]} = \mathbf{1}_{k-2}, Y_{i,[k-1,k]} = 10, \star)} = (1 + \epsilon), \text{ for } i \in [n-1].$$

Figure 5: The Perturbed Distribution $\tilde{Q}$

identification problems, by proving Proposition 1.3. The proof follows almost immediately from an earlier causal identification result of Tian and Pearl (2002).

Proof of Proposition 1.3. We restrict our attention to the condition number of $\mathbf{ID}(G, V - \{X\}, X)$: since $P(S \mid \text{do } X)$ can be obtained from $P(V - \{X\} \mid \text{do } X)$ by a marginalization operation, an upper bound on the condition number for $P(V - \{X\} \mid \text{do } X)$ is also an upper bound on the condition number of $P(S \mid \text{do } X)$.

For a sufficiently small ϵ, let $\tilde{P}$ be a probability distribution that is ϵ-close to the actual empirical distribution P. This implies, in particular, that all *conditional* probabilities computed according to $\tilde{P}$ are 2ϵ-close to the true conditional probabilities computed according to P. Formally, for any disjoint subsets S and T of V, $P(S = s \mid T = t)$ and $\tilde{P}(S = s \mid T = t)$ are 2ϵ-close: this follows from the fact that $P(S = s \mid T = t) = P(S = s, T = t)/P(T = t)$.

Let Z be the set of nodes (except X) in the same C-component as X. Using the identifiability result of Tian and Pearl (2002), we have

$$P(V - \{X\} = v_{V-\{X\}} | \text{do}(X = x)) = P(v) \frac{\sum_{x'} H(x')}{H(x)}, \quad (12)$$

where x' ranges over the domain of X, and $H(x')$ is defined as

$$H(x') = P(X = x' \mid \text{An}(X) = v_{\text{An}(X)}) \cdot \prod_{V_i \in Z} P(V_i = v_{V_i} \mid \text{An}(V_i) = v_{\text{An}(v_i)}),$$

where $v_X = x'$. (Here, for a vertex V_i, $\text{An}(V_i)$ is the set of ancestors of V_i among the observed nodes V). Since each H is a product of at most $|V|$ conditional probabilities, and since conditional probabilities computed according to P and $\tilde{P}$ are 2ϵ-close, the values of $H(x')$ computed according to P and $\tilde{P}$ are $2|V|\epsilon$-close. Eq. (12) then gives

$$e^{-(4|V|+1)\epsilon} \le \frac{\tilde{P}(V - \{X\} = v_{V-\{X\}} \mid \text{do}(X = x))}{P(V - \{X\} = v_{V-\{X\}} \mid \text{do}(X = x))} \le e^{(4|V|+1)\epsilon}.$$

for every v and x. We therefore have

$$\kappa_{\mathbf{ID}(G,V-\{X\},X)} \le \lim_{\epsilon \downarrow 0} \frac{e^{(4|V|+1)\epsilon} - 1}{\epsilon} = 4|V| + 1. \qquad \square$$

4 CONCLUSION

In this paper, we gave an example of a class of semi-Markovian models in which the causal inference problem is highly ill-conditioned. However, Proposition 1.3 shows that at least some causal identification problems are not too badly conditioned.

An immediate open question therefore is to find an algorithm which can compute tight bounds for the condition number of a causal identification problem in a given semi-Markovian model. Since such an algorithm would operate only on the model (and not on the observed data), it can serve a guide for selecting between competing models which differ, e.g., in terms of which covariates are measured, *before* any data is collected: all else being equal, a model in which the causal inference problem to be solved is better conditioned and hence less susceptible to noise should be preferable.

The roots of causal identification in graphical models can be traced back to the setting of linear structural equation models, which were first studied in the seminal papers of Wright (1921, 1934) (see, e.g., Drton et al. (2011), Foygel et al. (2012) and Chen and Pearl (2014) for more recent results on identification in linear structural equation models). Not surprisingly, in contrast to the purely combinatorial identification procedures in the discrete case, the identification procedures for linear structural equation models are able to exploit the linear algebraic structure of the problem and often use, in addition to combinatorial considerations, algorithmic primitives from linear algebra and algebraic geometry as well (see e.g. Foygel et al. (2012) for an example). Condition numbers of the primitives themselves have been studied have been quite extensively, but exploring the condition number of causal identification in the setting of linear structural equation models remains open. However, in this context, we should point out the work of Cornia and Mooij (2014), who show that when causal effects in a linear structural equation model are *not* exactly identifiable, the uncertainty in estimating them may be unbounded, even in models with a fixed number of nodes.

Acknowledgements

This research was supported by NSF grant CCF-1319745. We thank the reviewers for helpful comments.

References

Peter Bürgisser and Felipe Cucker. *Condition: The Geometry of Numerical Algorithms*, volume 349 of *Grundlehren der mathematischen Wissenschaften*. Springer Berlin Heidelberg, 2013.

Bryant Chen and Judea Pearl. Graphical tools for linear structural equation modeling, June 2014. URL http://www.cs.ucla.edu/pub/stat_ser/r432.pdf.

Nicholas Cornia and Joris M. Mooij. Type-II errors of independence tests can lead to arbitrarily large errors in estimated causal effects: An illustrative example. In *Proc. UAI 2014 Workshop on Causal Inference: Learning and Prediction*, pages 35–42, July 2014. URL http://ceur-ws.org/Vol-1274/uai2014ci_paper7.pdf.

Mathias Drton, Rina Foygel, and Seth Sullivant. Global identifiability of linear structural equation models. *Ann. Stat.*, 39(2):865–886, April 2011.

Rina Foygel, Jan Draisma, and Mathias Drton. Half-trek criterion for generic identifiability of linear structural equation models. *Ann. Stat.*, 40(3):1682–1713, June 2012.

Joseph Y. Halpern. Axiomatizing causal reasoning. *J. Artif. Intell. Res.*, 12:317–337, May 2000.

Yimin Huang and Marco Valtorta. On the completeness of an identifiability algorithm for semi-Markovian models. *Ann. Math. Artif. Intell.*, 54(4):363–408, December 2008.

Manabu Kuroki and Masami Miyakawa. Identifiability criteria for causal effects of joint interventions. *J. Japan Stat. Soc.*, 29(2):105–117, 1999. doi: 10.14490/jjss1995.29.105.

William. S. Ohlemeyer. Closing statement in *Henley v. Philip Morris Inc.*, 1999. Case No. 995172, 3 February 1999, Superior Court of the State of California. Page 88 in the original, p. 42 in the digitization. Available at https://industrydocuments.library.ucsf.edu/tobacco/docs/#id=frxl0001. Accessed Mar. 1, 2016.

Judea Pearl. Causal diagrams for empirical research. *Biometrika*, 82(4):669–688, December 1995.

Judea Pearl and James Robins. Probabilistic Evaluation of Sequential Plans from Causal Models with Hidden Variables. In *Proc. 11th Conference on Uncertainty in Artificial Intelligence (UAI)*, UAI'95, pages 444–453, San Francisco, CA, USA, 1995. Morgan Kaufmann Publishers Inc.

Ilya Shpitser and Judea Pearl. Identification of joint interventional distributions in recursive semi-Markovian causal models. In *Proc. 20th AAAI Conference on Artifical Intelligence*, pages 1219–1226. AAAI Press, July 2006.

Jin Tian. *Studies in Causal Reasoning and Learning*. PhD thesis, University of California, Los Angeles, August 2002.

Jin Tian and Judea Pearl. A general identification condition for causal effects. In *Proc. 18th AAAI Conference on Artificial Intelligence*, pages 567–573. AAAI Press, 2002.

Sewall Wright. Correlation and causation. *J. Agric. Res.*, 20:557–585, 1921.

Sewall Wright. The method of path coefficients. *Ann. Math. Stat.*, 5:161–215, 1934.

Markov Beta Processes for Time Evolving Dictionary Learning

Amar Shah
Machine Learning Group
University of Cambridge
as793@cam.ac.uk

Zoubin Ghahramani
Machine Learning Group
University of Cambridge
zoubin@eng.cam.ac.uk

Abstract

We develop Markov beta processes (MBP) as a model suitable for data which can be represented by a sparse set of latent features which evolve over time. Most time evolving nonparametric latent feature models in the literature vary feature usage, but maintain a constant set of features over time. We show that being able to model features which themselves evolve over time results in the MBP outperforming other beta process based models. Our construction utilizes Poisson process operations, which leave each transformed beta process marginally beta process distributed. This allows one to analytically marginalize out latent beta processes, exploiting conjugacy when we couple them with Bernoulli processes, leading to a surprisingly elegant Gibbs MCMC scheme considering the expressiveness of the prior. We apply the model to the task of denoising and interpolating noisy image sequences and in predicting time evolving gene expression data, demonstrating superior performance to other beta process based methods.

1 INTRODUCTION

Latent variable models provide an intuitive way to study the structure of observed data. Pioneering examples of latent variable models are factor analyzers [Bartholomew, 1987] and finite mixture models [MacLachan and Peel, 2000]. Nonparametric Bayesian priors provide an elegant solution to the problem of inferring the number of latent features by sampling over latent feature representations with varying number of features a posteriori.

Griffiths and Ghahramani [2011] develop the *Indian buffet process* (IBP), a stochastic process on features which can be thought of as a factorial analog of the Chinese restaurant process. The IBP is a nonparametric Bayesian prior on binary matrices with an unbounded number of columns, which is exchangeable over the customers (or rows). The underlying measure which results in this exchangeability is of particular interest. Thibaux and Jordan [2007] show that the *beta process* is the underlying de Finetti mixing distribution which generates the Indian buffet process.

The beta process (BP) can be drawn as a Poisson process (with a particular Lévy measure), which opens many doors since Poisson processes have been studied in great depth [Kingman, 1993]. In particular, there exist operations which one can apply to a Poisson process draw such that the resultant object remains a draw from a Poisson process marginally. This construction has been exploited by Lin et al. [2010] and Chen et al. [2012] to develop dependent Dirichlet processes and dependent normalized random measures more generally.

In this work we apply Poisson process preserving operations to construct a Markov chain of beta processes. Each beta process is then used as a base measure for a sequence of Bernoulli process draws. Sampling an entire beta process at each 'time' step seems like a daunting task, however, the elegant consequence of the Poisson process preserving operations is that each beta process in the chain actually is marginally a draw from a beta process with an evolved form of base measure. This fact along with the conjugacy of the beta and Bernoulli processes permits us to marginalize over the entire chain of beta processes analytically.

Whilst previous attempts have been made to encode dependencies between feature usage i.e. between the binary matrices over multiple time steps [Williamson et al., 2010, Foulds et al., 2011], very little work has been done on making features themselves evolve over time. Not only is our model capable of modeling a vast array of Markov dependencies amongst features, it permits an elegant Gibbs based inference algorithm which is efficiently able to learn structure amongst data. A key insight is that our model permits the analytic integration of a Dirichlet process used to model the time evolving features, and the entire Markov beta process chain. We believe that this is the first instance of dependent beta process work where such analytic integration is possible.

We utilize a Markov chain of beta processes for image denoising and inpainting tasks as well as for modeling time evolving gene expression data. Sparse methods have been successfully used for image analysis and gene data modeling. Our model, a natural extension of the beta Bernoulli model for time-evolving datasets, often outperforms other beta process based models on the tasks we consider.

2 BETA AND BERNOULLI PROCESSES

In this section, we review the beta, Bernoulli and Indian buffet processes following Thibaux and Jordan [2007], and proceed to discuss Poisson process properties Kingman [1993].

A *beta process* $B \sim \mathrm{BP}(c, B_0)$ is a positive random measure on a space Ω, where c is a positive function on Ω, and B_0 is a fixed measure on Ω, called the base measure. In our work, we assume c is constant. When B_0 is continuous, then a draw B can be represented as $B = \sum_{k=1}^{\infty} p_k \omega_k$, where ω_k are i.i.d. draws from $B/B(\Omega)$ and p_k are independent draws from a degenerate beta distribution with parameter c. If B_0 is discrete of the form $B_0 = \sum_k q_k \delta_{\omega_k}$, then $B = \sum_k p_k \delta_{\omega_k}$, with $p_k \sim \mathrm{Beta}(cq_k, c(1 - q_k))$ independently. When B_0 is mixed discrete-continuous, B is generated as the sum of independent contributions from the discrete and continuous parts.

We now consider a draw $X \sim \mathrm{BeP}(B)$ from a *Bernoulli process*, for measure B on Ω. If B is continuous, then $X = \sum_{k=1}^{K} \delta_{\omega_k}$, where $K \sim \mathrm{Poisson}(B(\Omega))$, and ω_k are i.i.d. draws from $B/B(\Omega)$. If B is discrete and of the form $B = \sum_k p_k \delta_{\omega_k}$, then $X = \sum_k b_k \delta_{\omega_k}$, where the $b_k \sim \mathrm{Bernoulli}(p_k)$ independently.

Now consider the generative process $B \sim \mathrm{BP}(c, B_0)$ and $X_i | B \sim \mathrm{BeP}(B)$, for $i = 1, ..., n$. The posterior distribution of B is

$$B|\{X_i\}_{i=1:n} \sim \mathrm{BP}\Big(c + n, \frac{c}{c+n} B_0 + \frac{1}{c+n} \sum_{i=1}^{n} X_i\Big).$$

The BP is the conjugate prior for BeP and we can therefore integrate out B analytically when we consider sequential draws from the beta Bernoulli process

$$X_{n+1}|\{X_i\}_{i=1:n} \sim \mathrm{BeP}\Big(\frac{c}{c+n} B_0 + \frac{1}{c+n} \sum_{i=1}^{n} X_i\Big).$$

Note that $\frac{1}{c+n} \sum_{i=1}^{n} X_i \equiv \sum_k \frac{m_{n,k}}{c+n} \delta_{\omega_k}$, where ω_k represent the unique atoms selected by the first n data points and $m_{n,k}$ represents how many of the first n data points selected the kth atom. Note that $X_{n+1}|\{X_i\}_{i=1:n}$ is sampled from the sum of two contributions: one from $\mathrm{BeP}(\frac{c}{c+n} B_0)$ and the other from $\mathrm{BeP}(\frac{1}{c+n} \sum_{i=1}^{n} X_i)$. This sampling process is equivalent to that of the Indian buffet process prior [Griffiths and Ghahramani, 2011].

When B_0 is a non-atomic measure, a draw from a beta process $B \sim \mathrm{BP}(c, B_0)$ is equivalent to a Poisson process (PP) draw with base measure ν, where

$$\nu(d\omega, dp) = cp^{-1}(1-p)^{c-1} dp B_0(d\omega). \qquad (1)$$

The Poisson process draw will consist of points of the form $(\omega_k, p_k) \in [0, 1] \times \Omega$, which should be used to define $B = \sum_k p_k \delta_{\omega_k}$. Poisson process preserving operations are operations one can apply to a draw from a Poisson process such that the resultant draw remains marginally a draw from a Poisson process, with a modified base measure. We utilize such operations to construct dependent beta process, in particular, we consider *subsampling, point transition* and *superposition*. See Kingman [1993] for a review of Poisson process properties.

3 MARKOV BETA PROCESSES

3.1 CONSTRUCTION

Given a draw from a beta process, we construct a related beta process by 1) partitioning atoms into clusters, 2) applying stochastic transformations to atoms in each cluster and 3) recombining all the atoms to give a new atomic base measure. We shall show that the transformed beta process draw is marginally a beta process, by applying the theory of Poisson processes.

Definition 1. *A probabilistic transition function is a function $\mathcal{T} : \Omega \to \mathbb{R}_+$, such that for each $\omega \in \Omega$, $\mathcal{T}(\omega)$*

is a probability measure on Ω. A measure, μ, over Ω is transformed by $\mathcal{T}$ to give measure $\mathcal{T}[\mu]$, defined as

$$(\mathcal{T}[\mu])(A) := \int_{\Omega} \mathcal{T}(\omega)(A)\mu(d\omega). \tag{2}$$

for each measurable $A \subseteq \Omega$. We denote a sample from $\mathcal{T}(\omega)$ as $\mathcal{T}(\omega)$.

Our approach is to consider parameteric probabilistic transition functions, $\mathcal{T}_\theta$, for parameters θ from some measurable parameter space Θ. An example of a probabilistic transition function is a Gaussian probability density function e.g. $\mathcal{T}_\theta(\omega) = \mathcal{N}(\omega; 0, \theta)$.

In order to partition the set of atoms and decide how they should be transitioned, we use a draw from a Dirichlet process, $\mathcal{D} = \sum_j \lambda_j \delta_{\theta_j} \sim \mathrm{DP}(\alpha, H)$, for a DP concentration parameter α and a base measure, H, on Θ. The λ_j are non-negative and sum to 1. We define the probabilistic transition $\mathcal{T}_{\mathcal{D}} = \sum_j \lambda_j \mathcal{T}_{\theta_j}$, which we can think of as a convex combination of probabilistic transition functions. The probabilities, λ_j, are used to define a multinomial distribution which is used to decide to which cluster each atom would be assigned to. Once clustered, atoms in cluster j are transitioned using $\mathcal{T}_{\theta_j}$.

Let B_0 be a base measure on Ω, and $B_1 = \sum_k q_k \delta_{\omega_k} \sim \mathrm{BP}(c, B_0)$. For each k, sample $u_k \sim \mathrm{Mult}(1, \boldsymbol{\lambda})$, and $T_{\theta_{u_k}}(\omega_k) \sim \mathcal{T}_{\theta_{u_k}}(\omega_k)$. Finally, set $B_1 = \sum_k q_k \delta_{T_{\theta_{u_k}}(\omega_k)}$. We prove that marginally, B_1 is a draw from a beta process.

Lemma 2. *If B_1 is constructed as above, then marginally, $B_1 \sim \mathrm{BP}(c, \mathcal{T}_*[B_0])$ for measure $\mathcal{T}_*[B_0]$ defined such that for $A \subseteq \Omega$, $\mathcal{T}_*[B_0](A) \equiv \int (\mathcal{T}_{\mathcal{D}}[B_0])(A)\mathrm{DP}(\mathcal{D}; \alpha, H)d\mathcal{D}$*

Proof. The distribution of q_k remain unchanged. Also $\mathcal{T}_{\mathcal{D}}[B_0](\Omega) = \sum_j \lambda_j \mathcal{T}_{\theta_j}[B_0](\Omega) = B_0(\Omega)$. Integrating over $\mathcal{D}$ and s_k, the new location of atom k is marginally distributed as $\mathcal{T}_*[B_0]/B_0(\Omega)$. Hence B_1 is a PP draw with base measure $\tilde{\nu}(d\omega, dp) = cp^{-1}(1-p)^{c-1}dp\,\mathcal{T}_*[B_0](d\omega)$, making it marginally a beta process draw. □

Whilst we have not explicitly invoked theorems regarding Poisson preserving operations, they provide some intuition as to why the transformed beta processes are marginally beta process draws. The operation of clustering the atoms of the original beta process is analogous to the Poisson process operation of *subsampling*. A subsampled Poisson process is marginally a Poisson process. *Point transition* is a Poisson process preserving operation, as is the *superposition* of Poisson process draws. The composition of these three Poisson preserving operations accurately describes the nature of our construction of dependent beta processes. An illustration of the formulation is seen in Figure 1.

Note that the Dirichlet process prior can be replaced with other priors without affecting the proof. We choose a DP in our experiments for its modeling flexibility.

Repeating the above approach to construct $B_2, B_3, \ldots$ results in a *Markov chain of beta processes*. Define $\mathcal{T}^t_{\mathcal{D}}[B_0]$ to be the measure resulting in applying $\mathcal{T}_{\mathcal{D}}$ t times to measure B_0. Then marginally, $B_t \sim \mathrm{BP}(c, \mathcal{T}^t_*[B_0])$, where for $A \subseteq \Omega$, $\mathcal{T}^t_*[B_0](A) = \int (\mathcal{T}^t_{\mathcal{D}}[B_0])(A)\mathrm{DP}(\mathcal{D}; \alpha, H)d\mathcal{D}$. Henceforth we refer to our construction of dependent beta processes as *Markov beta processes*. When $B_1, \ldots, B_T$ is a draw from a Markov beta process, we write $B_1, \ldots, B_T, \boldsymbol{u}_1, \ldots, \boldsymbol{u}_T | \mathcal{D} \sim \mathrm{MBP}(c, B_0, \mathcal{D}, \mathcal{T}, T)$.

To the best of out knowledge, our construction of dependent beta processes is the first to leave each transformed beta process marginally a beta process draw. Most existing models all keep features (atoms) constant but vary the feature probabilities q_k over time or space. We discuss the related models in the next subsection.

3.2 RELATED DEPENDENT BETA PROCESS CONSTRUCTIONS

In our construction of Markov dependent beta processes, the atom locations evolve over time, whilst the atom weights remain constant. This is in contrast to the majority of existing constructions of dependent beta processes. Existing research has tended to focus on maintaining a time invariant set of atoms, whilst varying the weights.

The Markov IBP introduced by Van Gael et al. [2008] is a model where features remain constant over time, but feature allocations follow a Markov chain on the space $\{0, 1\}$ (1 indicates presence of a feature and 0 indicates absence). The transition matrix governing the chain also remains constant over time, suggesting that the Markov IBP would be unfit to model non-stationary data. Most importantly, this model does not have the ability to jointly model multiple related time series unlike the model we propose in this work. The authors propose several inference schemes for the Markov IBP, but comment that adequate performance is only observed with more complicated algorithms.

Foulds et al. [2011] use a similar idea to the Markov

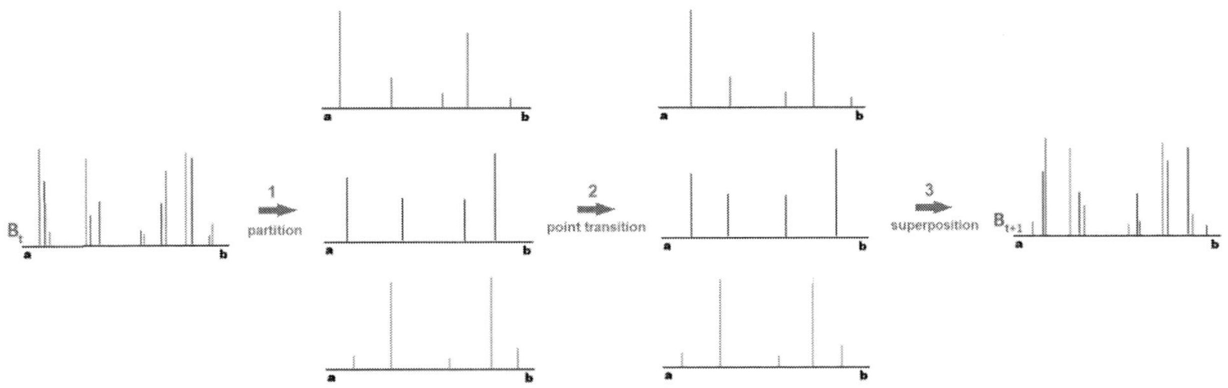

Figure 1: Example illustrating how B_{t+1} is constructed from B_t. First the atoms are partitioned or clustered into, in this case, 3 clusters. Next, atoms undergo probabilistic point transition based on the cluster they belong to. Finally atoms are superimposed to create B_{t+1}.

IBP for modeling time evolving social networks. Their DRIFT model incorporates a Markov process to decide whether or not features are present at each time step whilst maintaining constant features over time. Unlike the Markov IBP, DRIFT is able to model an arbitrary number of items.

Williamson et al. [2010] construct dependent IBPs using Gaussian process draws and the stick breaking construction of the IBP [Teh et al., 2007] to introduce dependencies between customers for each feature as well as temporal dependencies. The dIBP has high flexibility due to the nonparametric temporal dependence structure, but this comes with a high computational cost. Features also remain constant over time in the dIBP model, unlike in our MBP model.

The kernel beta process [Ren et al., 2011] is a generalization of the beta process and has the form $B_x = \sum_k \pi_k K(x, x^*|\psi)\delta_{\omega_k}$, where x belongs to a covariate space $\mathcal{X}$ and K is a kernel function on $\mathcal{X} \times \mathcal{X}$ taking values in $[0, 1]$ for parameters x^* and ψ. The use of the kernel allows weights to vary over a covariate space, whilst the atom locations remain fixed.

The dependent hierarchical beta process Zhou et al. [2011] is constructed as a convex combination of i.i.d. draws from a hierarchical beta process. The convex weights are made to depend on a kernel over a covariate space. More specifically, a kernel function is defined between the covariates (each data point has one covariate), inducing correlation of feature usage between data points. The covariate being used is the location of the patch within the entire image, the idea being that neighbouring patches are more likely to use similar dictionary elements for image denoising and interpolation. The way it has been constructed by the authors, it would not explicitly be able to model temporal structure amongst image sequences.

3.3 COLLAPSED GIBBS SAMPLER

None of the models discussed above result in simple marginal distributions, and consequently each use an uncollapsed Gibbs sampler to perform posterior inference. Nonparametric Bayesian priors are usually easy to sample from, but posterior inference is typically difficult because of the flexibility of the models and the presence of poor local optima in the posterior conditional distributions of the latent variables. Whilst an uncollapsed Gibbs sampler algorithms are usually easy to implement, they are prone to get stuck in poor modes and converge much more slowly than collapsed samplers [Doshi-Velez and Ghahramani, 2009]. In our Markov beta processes, having marginal beta process distributions permits a marginalized posterior sampler which has a better chance of mixing well and has an elegant restaurant analogy.

At each time step, t, we draw $x_t^i|B_t \sim \text{BeP}(B_t)$ iid for $i = 1, ..., n_t$. Let $X_t \equiv \{x_t^i\}_{i=1}^{n_t}$. We show how to sample each x_t^i marginalizing out the Markov beta process chain in the following lemma and corollary. For $t > 1$, we let ω_t^j denote a sample from (a) $\mathcal{T}_{\mathcal{D}}(\omega_{t-1}^j)$ if $j \le k_{t-1}$, or (b) $\mathcal{T}_{\mathcal{D}}^{t-1}[B_0]/B_0(\Omega)$ if $j > k_{t-1}$.

Lemma 3. *For* $c_t = c + \sum_{s=1}^t n_s$,

$$B_t|\mathcal{D}, B_0, X_{1:t} \sim \text{BP}\left(c_t, \frac{c}{c_t}\mathcal{T}_{\mathcal{D}}^{t-1}[B_0] + \sum_{j=1}^{k_t} \frac{m_t^j}{c_t}\delta_{\omega_t^j}\right)$$

Proof. We prove the claim by induction. Note that

$B_1|\mathcal{D}, B_0 \sim \text{BP}(c, \mathcal{T}_{\mathcal{D}}[B_0])$ by Lemma 2. By conjugacy of the beta and Bernoulli processes, we then have $B_1|\mathcal{D}, B_0, X_1 \sim \text{BP}(c_1, \frac{c}{c_1}\mathcal{T}_{\mathcal{D}}[B_0] + \sum_{j=1}^{k_1} \frac{m_1^j}{c_1}\delta_{\omega_1^j})$. Now let $t > 1$. By induction and Lemma 2, $B_t|\mathcal{D}, B_0, X_{1:t-1} \sim \text{BP}\Big(c_{t-1}, \frac{c}{c_{t-1}}\mathcal{T}_{\mathcal{D}}^{t-1}[B_0] + \sum_{j=1}^{k_{t-1}} \frac{m_{t-1}^j}{c_{t-1}}\delta_{\omega_t^j}\Big)$. The final result follows from the conjugacy of the beta and Bernoulli processes. □

Corollary 4.

$$x_t^{n_t+1}|\mathcal{D}, B_0, X_{1:t} \sim \text{BeP}\left(\frac{c}{c_t}\mathcal{T}_{\mathcal{D}}^{t-1}[B_0] + \sum_{j=1}^{k_t} \frac{m_t^j}{c_t}\delta_{\omega_t^j}\right)$$

Proof. Since $x_t^{n_t+1}|B_t \sim \text{BeP}(B_t)$ and $p(x_t^\circ|\mathcal{D}, B_0, X_{1:t}) = \int p(x_t^\circ|B_t)p(B_t|\mathcal{D}, B_0, X_{1:t})dB_t$, the result follows from conjugacy and Lemma 3. □

The result in Corollary 4 motivates a sampling scheme with a restaurant analogy similar to the one developed for the Indian buffet process [Griffiths and Ghahramani, 2011]. On day $t = 1$, customer $i_1 = 1$ tastes a number of dishes sampled from Poisson$(cB_0(\Omega))$. He tries dishes in Ω sampled independently from probability measure $B_0/B_0(\Omega)$. Suppose $i_1 > 1$ and let m^j be the number of people who have tasted the jth dish so far. Customer i_1 tries each of the existing dishes independently with probability $\frac{m^j}{c+i_1-1}$, and samples Poisson$(\frac{c}{c+i_1-1}B_0(\Omega))$ new dishes. On a new day, $t > 1$, each dish from the previous day evolves stochastically using the probabilistic transition function $\mathcal{T}_{\mathcal{D}}$. Customer i_t tries each existing dish with independent probability $\frac{m^j}{c_{t-1}+i_t-1}$, and samples Poisson$(\frac{c}{c_{t-1}+i_t-1}B_0(\Omega))$ new dishes independently from $\mathcal{T}_{\mathcal{D}}^{t-1}[B_0]/B_0(\Omega)$.

As is the case for the IBP, dishes which are popular are more likely to be tried over time. The key difference in our Markov beta process framework, is that the dishes evolve stochastically over time, and the base distribution from which new dishes are drawn also evolves stochastically over time.

4 TIME EVOLVING DICTIONARY LEARNING

In this section we illustrate how a draw from a Markov beta process prior may be used to perform time evolving dictionary learning. Each $\omega_k \in \Omega$ which appears in a beta process draw is a dictionary element, with each associated q_k being the probability that a data point uses ω_k. We consider the case $\Omega = \mathbb{R}^P$, and refer to dictionary element k at time t as a column vector, $\boldsymbol{d}_t^k$.

The entire dictionary at time t is a matrix denoted $\mathbf{D}_t \equiv [\boldsymbol{d}_t^1, ..., \boldsymbol{d}_t^{k_t}] \in \mathbb{R}^{P\times k_t}$. We may model datapoint i at time t, $\boldsymbol{x}_t^i$, as

$$\boldsymbol{x}_t^i = \mathbf{D}_t(\boldsymbol{s}_t^i \circ \boldsymbol{z}_t^i) + \boldsymbol{\epsilon}_t^i, \tag{3}$$

where $\circ$ represents the Hadamard product, $\boldsymbol{s}_t^i, \boldsymbol{\epsilon}_t^i \in \mathbb{R}^{k_t}$ and $\boldsymbol{z}_t^i \in \{0,1\}^{k_t}$. z_t^{ik} represents whether or not $\boldsymbol{x}_t^i$ uses dictionary element k and is a draw from Bernoulli(q_k). s_t^{ik} determines how much of dictionary element k to use and $\boldsymbol{\epsilon}_t^i$ is simply additive noise.

A natural probabilistic transition function in the case $\Omega = \mathbb{R}^P$, is a Gaussian distribution. We set $\Theta = \mathbb{R}_+^P$ and define $\mathcal{T}_{\boldsymbol{\theta}}(\boldsymbol{d})$ to be a multivariate Gaussian probability density function with mean $\boldsymbol{d}$ and diagonal covariance matrix with diagonal $\boldsymbol{\theta}^{-1}$.

We can generate data from $t = 1, ..., T$, $k = 1, ..., k_t$ and $i = 1, ..., n_t$ as follows,

$$\mathcal{D} = \sum_j \lambda_j \delta_{\boldsymbol{\theta}_j} \sim \text{DP}(\alpha, H), \tag{4}$$

$$\begin{aligned}
\mathbf{D}_1, ..., \mathbf{D}_T, \boldsymbol{q}, \boldsymbol{u}_1, ..., \boldsymbol{u}_{T-1}|\mathcal{D} &\sim \text{MBP}(c, B_0, \mathcal{D}, \mathcal{T}, T),\\
z_t^{ik}|q_k &\sim \text{Bernoulli}(q_k),\\
s_t^{ik} &\sim \mathcal{N}(0, \gamma_s^{-1})\\
\boldsymbol{x}_t^i|\mathbf{D}_t, \boldsymbol{s}_t^i, \boldsymbol{z}_t^i &\sim \mathcal{N}\big(\mathbf{D}_t(\boldsymbol{s}_t^i \circ \boldsymbol{z}_t^i), \gamma_\epsilon^{-1}\mathbf{I}_P\big),
\end{aligned}$$

where H is a measure on $\Theta = \mathbb{R}_+^P$ which is the product of P Gamma measures of the form Gamma$(1, P)$ on each component and B_0 is a multivariate Gaussian measure of the form $\mathcal{N}(\mathbf{0}, \frac{1}{P}\mathbf{I})$. We place Gamma priors on γ_s and γ_ϵ.

4.1 INFERENCE

We train the model based on a collapsed Gibbs based MCMC scheme, where the probabilities q_k are marginalized out. The update equations are summarized below.

Update $\mathbf{D}_t$. The posterior density for $\boldsymbol{d}_t^k$ is

$$\begin{aligned}
p(\boldsymbol{d}_t^k|-) \sim \exp\Big(&-\frac{1}{2}\sum_{p=1}^P \theta_{u_{t-1}^k,p}(d_{t,p}^k - d_{t-1,p}^k)^2\\
&-\frac{1}{2}\sum_{p=1}^P \theta_{u_t^k,p}(d_{t+1}^k - d_t^k)^2\\
&-\frac{\gamma_\epsilon}{2}\sum_{i=1}^N \|\psi_t^{i,-k} - \boldsymbol{d}_t^k(s_t^{i,k}z_t^{i,k})\|^2\Big)
\end{aligned}$$

where $\psi_t^{i,-k} = x_t^i - \sum_{k' \neq k} s_t^{ik} z_t^{ik} d_t^k$.
Hence $d_t^k|- \sim \mathcal{N}(\phi, \Phi)$, where

$$\Phi = \left(\mathrm{diag}\left(\theta_{u_{t-1}^k} + \theta_{u_t^k}\right) + \gamma_\epsilon \sum_{i:z_t^{i,k}=1} s_t^{i,k^2}\right)^{-1} \mathbf{I}_P$$

$$\phi = \Phi\Big(\mathrm{diag}\left(\theta_{u_{t-1}^k}\right) d_{t-1}^k + \mathrm{diag}\left(\theta_{u_t^k}\right) d_{t+1}^k + \gamma_\epsilon \sum_{i:z_t^{i,k}=1} s_t^{i,k} \psi_t^{i,-k}\Big)$$

Update u_t^k. The posterior density for u_t^k is

$$p(u_t^k = j|-) \propto \lambda_j \prod_{p=1}^{P} \left[\sqrt{\theta_{j,p}} \exp\left(-\frac{1}{2}\theta_{j,p}\delta_{t,p}^{k\;2}\right)\right]$$

where $\delta_{t,p}^k = \left(d_{t+1,p}^k - d_{t,p}^k\right)$, a multinomial distribution.

Update $z_t^{i,k}$. The posterior odds of $z_t^{i,k}$ is

$$\frac{p(z_t^{i,k} = 1|-)}{p(z_t^{i,k} = 0|-)} = \frac{\exp\left(-\frac{\gamma_\epsilon}{2}\|\psi_t^{i,-k} - s_t^{i,k} d_t^k\|^2\right)\pi_t^{i,k}}{\exp\left(-\frac{\gamma_\epsilon}{2}\|\psi_t^{i,-k}\|^2\right)(1 - \pi_t^{i,k})},$$

where

$$\pi_t^{i,k} = \frac{\sum_{s=1}^{T}\sum_{j=1}^{k_s} z_s^{i,j} - z_t^{i,k}}{c + \sum_{s=1}^{T} n_s - 1}.$$

Update $s_t^{i,k}$. The posterior density for $s_t^{i,k}$ is

$$p(s_t^{i,k}|-) \propto \exp\left(-\frac{\gamma_\epsilon}{2}\|\psi_t^{i,-k} - s_t^{i,k} d_t^k\|^2 - \frac{\gamma_s}{2} s_t^{i,k^2}\right),$$

hence $s_t^{i,k} \sim \mathcal{N}(\varphi, \kappa)$, where

$$\kappa = \left(\gamma_\epsilon d_t^{k\top} d_t^k + \gamma_s\right)^{-1}$$

$$\varphi = \kappa\left(\gamma_\epsilon d_t^{k\top} \psi_t^{i,-k}\right).$$

Update λ. The posterior distribution of λ is

$$p(\lambda|-) \propto \prod_j \lambda_j^{\alpha + \sum_{s=t}^{T-1}\sum_{k=1}^{k_s} \mathbb{I}[u_t^k = j] - 1}.$$

Update θ_j. The posterior distribution of θ_j is

$$p(\theta_j|-) \propto \exp\Big(-\frac{P}{2}\theta_j^\top \theta_j - \frac{1}{2}\sum_{t=1}^{T-1}\sum_{k=1}^{k_t} \mathbb{I}[u_t^k = j]\theta_j^\top (\delta_t^k \circ \delta_t^k)\Big),$$

hence $\theta_j|- \sim \mathcal{N}(\varsigma_j, \frac{1}{P}\mathbf{I})$, where

$$\varsigma_j = \frac{1}{2P}\sum_{t=1}^{T-1}\sum_{k=1}^{k_t} \mathbb{I}[u_t^k = j]\left(\delta_t^k \circ \delta_t^k\right).$$

5 EXPERIMENTS

In this section we describe the findings of various experiments we performed using Markov beta processes to induce a chain of evolving latent features. We investigated two tasks, the problem of denoising and inpainting a sequence of images and time evoloving gene expression data. First we try to answer various questions with synthetic experiments.

5.1 SYNTHETIC EXPERIMENTS

A key quesion we set out to address in this work is 'are Markov evolving features more useful for multiple sequence modeling than Markov evolving feature probabilities?' When there are no clear task specific reasons to choose one approach over the other, one would want to choose the framework that is generally more reliable to make useful predictions. Setting $N = 500, D = 40, K = 50$, we generated Synth-MBP from the MBP prior, and Synth-DRIFT from the DRIFT model. The MBP, DRIFT and BP models were trained on these datasets with 10% of the points randomly chosen and held out for prediction. Table 1 summarizes the test mean squared errors of predicitons of the three models.

We initialize features using random subsets of the observable data and use a k-means initialization for the clustering of the feature transitions for the MBP model. The Z and S matrices are subsequently initialized with a linear least squares estimate given the features. The same approach is used in all subsequent experiments.

Both the MBP and DRIFT models outperform the BP model, suggesting that each of them are able to learn some level of temporal structure, as we would have liked. However, it is interesting to see that the MBP model's outperformance versus the DRIFT model on Synth-MBP is much larger than the DRIFT model's outperformance versus the MBP model on Synth-DRIFT. The Dirichlet process transition process between features appears to be responsible for the MBP's predictive power on the DRIFT-Synth data set. We replaced the DP with a single Gaussian transition function for all features, and found the mean squared errors dropped to 2.04 and 2.11 on MBP-Synth and DRIFT-Synth respectively.

The fact that we are able to utilize a flexible DP based transition function using a collapsed Gibbs sampler which mixes fast is key to the high performance of the MBP model. Inference in models with complicated dependencies between binary feature usage variables is more difficult. Our MBP model is useful because of the efficient Gibbs based sampler we are able to derive

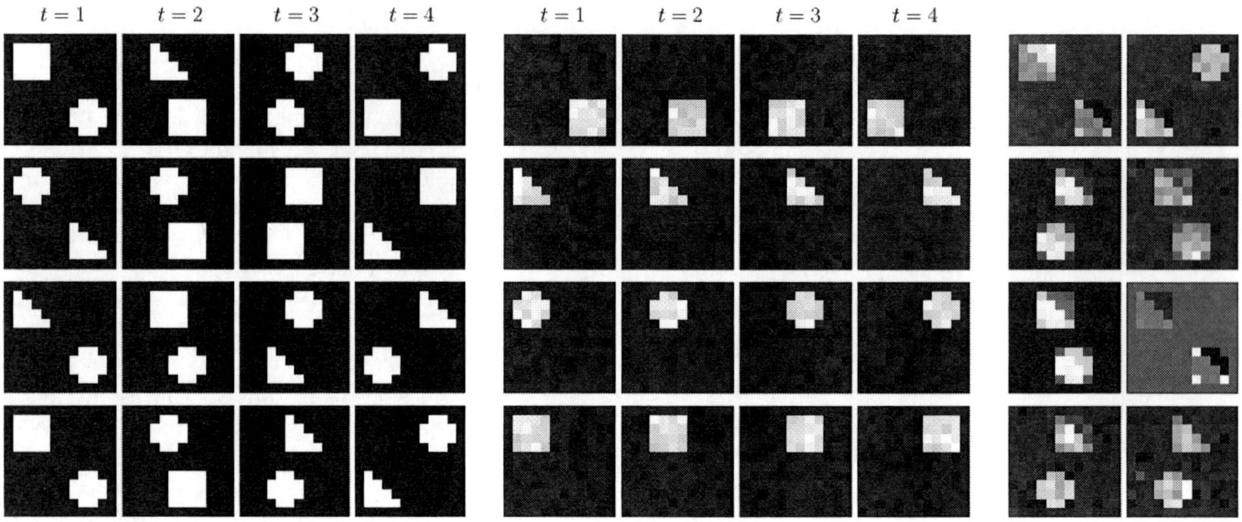

(a) Synthetic data (b) Time-evolving features learned by MBP (c) DRIFT features

Figure 2: Synthetic image data experimental results. (a) Each row represents an image sequence used for the synthetic image experiment. (b) Time-evolving features learned by the MBP model. (c) Stationary features learned by the DRIFT model.

Table 1: Mean-squared error results of prediction on synthetic datasets using MBP, DRIFT and BP models, with standard deviation of multiple runs in brackets.

	MBP	DRIFT	BP
SYNTH-MBP	**1.03** (**0.04**)	2.16 (0.08)	2.84 (0.10)
SYNTH-DRIFT	1.66 (0.05)	**1.37** (**0.07**)	2.45 (0.09)

for modeling expressive transitions between features.

5.2 IMAGE DENOISING AND INPAINTING

Sequences of grayscale images were considered for this task, but our method easily extends to color image sequences. The baseline model we compare our model to, is the beta process model of Zhou et al. [2009], modeling each image within the sequence independently. We implement the Foulds et al. [2011] model to assess the benefit of time-evolving feature usage versus time-evolving features and finally, we consider the dHBP [Zhou et al., 2011], which is designed to exploit intra-image dependencies. Inference in the dIBP [Williamson et al., 2010] unfortunately scales in N^3 which is prohibitive for this task.

Consider a sequence of T images of size $Q_x \times Q_y$. We model overlapping patches of size 8×8 as individual data points, giving a total of $N = (Q_x - 7) \times (Q_y - 7)$ data points, each with dimension $D = 8$. Whilst this breaks the exchangeability assumption of the prior, we benefit from model averaging, as each final pixel estimate is in fact an average of the estimates of 64 patches (except for near edge pixels).

Our first experiment involved synthetically generated data of the form shown in Figure 2a. We formed $N = 500$ sequences of images of size 12×12. In each sequence, we observe shapes traverse left to right in the top half of the images and other shapes traverse right to left. We trained both the MBP and the DRIFT models on this dataset using $K = 75$ features. The MBP was able to learn interesting structure amongst features as can be seen in Figure 2b. The model was able to identify the individual shapes which traversed left and right across the image over time. Since the DRIFT model uses a stationary set of features, it tended to learn features as noisy compositions of various data points 2c, not exhibiting the more elegant structure we found amongst the MBP features.

Notice that the shapes in the synthetic sequences often switch from frame to frame; squares become triangles, crosses become squares, etc. The MBP model is capable of modeling these transitions because whilst feature probabilities are stationary, actual feature usage between time points is conditionally independent given the feature probabilies. (More succinctly, $z_{ik}^t \perp\!\!\!\perp z_{ik}^{t'} | \pi_k$ for $t \neq t'$.) On average, the DP transition function of the MBP model used 16 clusters for the synthetic image data. This was somewhat crucial in being able to learn the time-evolving features we see in Figure 2b.

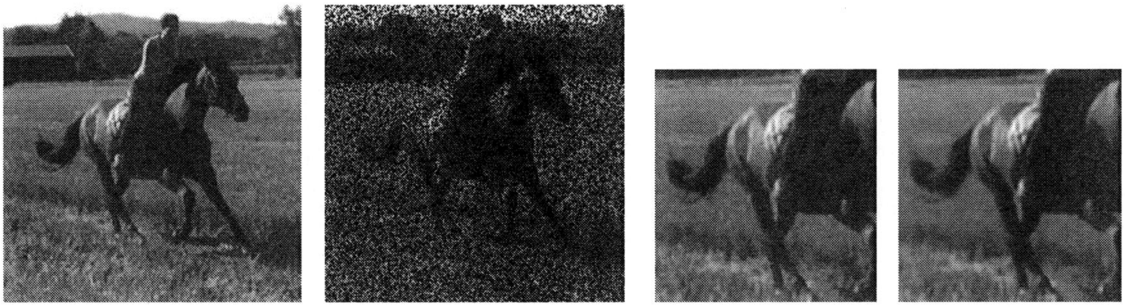

(a) (b) (c) (d)

Figure 3: Image sequence experiment on horse data. (a) Image 6 of the sequence. (b) Image with 50% of pixels omitted at random with pixels corrupted with Gaussian noise. Zoomed reconstructions of (c) MBP and (d) dHBP models.

We ran an experiment restricting the MBP model to have a single transition function, and noticed that the model learned features more similar to those learned by the DRIFT model.

We test the methods on four black and white image sequences: (i) 8 frames of size 241×241 of a lady riding a horse in a field [Ochs et al., 2014], (ii) 8 frames of size 192×256 with a set of mountains being panned about a fixed axis [Porzi et al., 2014], (iii) 8 frames of size 120×216 of a rabbit leaping across a living room [Ochs et al., 2014], and (iv) 10 frames of size 60×64 of a hand holding a bowl and rotating it [Wang, 1997].

Pixels in these datasets take integer values in $[0, 255]$. We added Gaussian noise with standard deviation 15 independently to each pixel. For each image sequence, we sample a binary matrix, Σ, of size $Q_x \times Q_y$, where each entry is an independent Bernoulli sample. Σ indicates which pixels are used for training by each algorithm for each image sequence. A typical evaluation metric for image reconstruction is the peak signal-to-noise ratio (PSNR), defined as

$$\text{MSE} = \sum_{t=1}^{T} \sum_{q_x=1}^{Q_x} \sum_{q_y=1}^{Q_y} \frac{\left(\mathbf{\Pi}_t(q_x, q_y) - \hat{\mathbf{\Pi}}_t(q_x, q_y)\right)^2}{TQ_xQ_y}$$

$$\text{PSNR} = 10 \log_{10} \left(\frac{255^2}{\text{MSE}} \right), \tag{5}$$

where $\mathbf{\Pi}_t$ is the original $Q_x \times Q_y$ image at time t and $\hat{\mathbf{\Pi}}_t$ is the estimate of this image. We allow the samplers to burn-in for 2000 iterations, and then use 500 Gibbs samples for predictions, using $K = 250$ features.

The experiments on each set of image sequences were repeated using 20%, 30% and 50% of the pixels chosen uniformly at random for training, the results are summarized in Table 2. The MBP approach tends to outperform other methods consistently, in particular the DRIFT model which does encode time evolving feature usage. The dHBP model, designed particularly for the task of image denoising and inpainting does well on most sequence tasks without modeling temporal dependencies, but on the whole does not perform as well as the MBP. The MBP does not model the intra-image dependencies, and we believe that combining the temporal modeling of the MBP with the intra-image dependencies of the dHBP would lead to a highly sophisticated image sequence denoising and inpainting framework. Since our focus in this paper is on the MBP model and not the specific task of image sequence analysis, we leave the combined model idea to future work.

Figure 3 illustrates a situation where the dHBP performs worse than the MBP. The dHBP model uses patches which are close in Euclidean distances to use similar sets of features. A consequence of this property, is that the area of the image under the body of the horse, appears to have a uniform color. This is likely because the bottom section of the horse body also has uniform color. Conversely the MBP model is better able to learn features which are separate for the horse body and the background grass, leading to a clearer reconstruction. The tail in the dHBP reconstruction also exhibits more smoothing and less detail than that of the MBP.

5.3 GENE EXPRESSION DATA

Time-course gene expression data are often measured to study dynamic biological systems and gene-regulatory networks. Vast amounts of biological data are being collected as technology in the field advances. This is a setting where the number of time points may be small, but the dimension of the data is large (potentially of the order of 10s of 1000s). Sparse methods have been successful in modeling genetic data [Carvalho et al., 2008, Knowles and Ghahramani, 2011],

Table 2: Results of gray-scale image sequence denoising and interpolation (PSNR) for BP, dHBP, DRIFT and MBP, using patch size 8×8, varying the ratio of observed pixels. Image pixels have Gaussian white noise (standard deviation 15).

Ratio		Horse	Moun-tains	Rabbit	Hand
20%	BP	25.32	27.68	24.46	30.22
	dHBP	26.21	28.91	25.43	31.58
	DRIFT	26.04	28.23	24.85	30.74
	MBP	**26.81**	**29.09**	**25.61**	**31.62**
30%	BP	26.58	28.85	25.52	31.43
	dHBP	27.09	29.78	26.03	**32.56**
	DRIFT	27.02	29.34	25.94	31.96
	MBP	**27.47**	**29.94**	**26.54**	32.51
50%	BP	27.45	29.95	26.38	32.64
	dHBP	28.09	30.55	26.84	**33.28**
	DRIFT	28.14	30.50	26.82	33.19
	MBP	**28.38**	**30.66**	**26.92**	33.22

and subsequently, using the MBP to model time-evolving gene data seems an appropriate extension. Comparisons between the MBP, DRIFT, BP and dIBP models are made. We consider 2 datasets, discarding 2000 samples to allow the Markov chains to burn-in and using the following 500 samples for prediction, and using $K = 500$ features.

Yeast cell cycle Spellman et al. [1998] measured the genome-wide mRNA levels for 6108 genes during 2 cell cycles over $T = 17$ time points. We consider $N = 2$ strands, cdc15 and cdc28 and randomly pick $D = 1000$ genes randomly from the ones which have no missing data.

Transcriptome alterations in mice This dataset, collected by Piechota et al. [2010], consists of readings from 46632 proteins collected from mice brains under the infuence of 1 of $N = 8$ types of drugs over $T = 4$ time points. We select a random subset of $D = 1000$ proteins for our experiments.

In each of the experiments we hold out 15% of the data points uniformly at random for prediction. Results of the experiments on the 2 gene data sets are summarized in Table 3. The dIBP performs best on the yeast cell cycle data set, as the Gaussian process draws controlling feature usage over time are best able to pick up the periodic nature of the cell cycle sequence data. However, the MBP is not far off the accuracy of the dIBP here. The MBP outperforms other methods on the mice transcriptome data set, which has fewer time points. The DP in the MBP inference procedure used an average of 82 transition functions after burn-in. Note that the total number of transitions is $K \times (T-1) = 1500$, and hence 82 clusters is perfectly reasonable. In the yeast cell cycle task, we have $K \times (T-1) = 8000$ feature transitions, which is very large, and illustrates to some extent the requirement for highly flexible mixture model of transition functions, such as the Dirichlet process mixture we employ.

Table 3: Mean-squared error results of prediction on gene datasets using MBP, DRIFT, BP and dIBP.

	MBP	DRIFT	BP	dIBP
Yeast	0.92	1.06	1.63	**0.88**
Mice	**1.12**	1.42	1.67	1.28

6 CONCLUSIONS

In this work, we construct a Markov chain of beta processes for use as a model for learning time evolving sparse latent representations. Particularly we exploit the property that the beta process is a type of Poisson process. This enables us to invoke well known operations, which when applied to a Poisson process draw keep the object marginally Poisson process distributed. Having marginal beta process objects crucially allows us to develop a simple and fast mixing Gibbs sampler. To illustrate the power of our model and inference scheme, we considered image denoising and inpainting tasks and gene expression data, showing superior performance over other beta process related models. The high flexibility of our model leads to a potential drawback when modelling long time series. Inference may become prohibitively slow as the time series are made longer, and to compromise, it may be necessary to replace the DP based transition function with a small fixed mixture of Gaussians.

Most machine learning problems involve constructing an appropriate model and then developing an inference scheme to train the model and use it for prediction. Whilst Bayesian nonparametrics make it simple to write down a model, the inference often requires a complicated and slow procedure which significantly can reduce its applicability to real problems. We hope is that our exploitation of Poisson process preserving operations and conjugacy encourages further investigation in how one can develop flexible nonparametric Bayesian models which are amenable to elegant inference techniques, by exploiting interesting and well grounded mathematical concepts.

References

D. J. Bartholomew. The Foundations of Factor Analysis. *Biometrika*, 1987.

C. M. Carvalho, J. Chang, J. E. Lucas, J. R. Nevins, Q. Wang, and M. West. High Dimensional Sparse Factor Modeling: Applications in Gene Expression Genomins. *Journal of the American Statistical Association*, 2008.

C. Chen, N. Ding, and W. Buntine. Dependent Hierarchical Normalized Random Measures for Dynamic Topic Modeling. *Proceedings of the 29th International Conference on Machine Learning*, 2012.

F. Doshi-Velez and Z. Ghahramani. Accelerated Sampling for the Indian Buffet Process. *Proceedings of the 26th International Conference on Machine Learning*, 2009.

J. Foulds, C. DuBois, A. U. Asuncion, C. T. Butts, and P. Smyth. A Dynamic Relational Infinite Feature Model for Longitudinal Social Networks. *Proceedings of the 14th Conference on Artificial Intelligence and Statistics*, 2011.

T. Griffiths and Z. Ghahramani. The Indian Buffet Process: An introduction and review. *Journal of Machine Learning Research*, 12:1185–1224, 2011.

J. Kingman. *Poisson Processes*. Oxford University Press, 1993.

D. Knowles and Z. Ghahramani. Nonparametric Bayesian Sparse Factor Models with Application to Gene Expression Modeling. *The Annals of Applied Statistics*, 2011.

D. Lin, E. Grimson, and J. Fisher. Construction of Dependent Dirichlet Processes based on Poisson Processes. *Advances in Neural Information Processing Systems*, 2010.

G. MacLachan and D. Peel. *Finite Mixture Models*. John Wiley & Sons, 2000.

P. Ochs, J. Malik, and T. Brox. Segmentation of moving objects by long term video analysis. *IEEE Trans. Pattern Analysis and Machine Intelligence*, 2014.

M. Piechota, M. Korostynski, W. Solecki, A. Gieryk, M. Slezakl, W. Bilecki, B. Ziolkowska, E. Kostrzewa, I. Cymerman, L. Swiech, J. Jaworski, and R. Przewlocki. The dissection of trancriptional modules regulated by various drugs of abuse in the mouse striatum. *Genome Biology, 11:R48*, 2010.

L. Porzi, S. R. Bulo, P. Valigi, O. Lanz, and E. Ricci. Learning Contours for Automatic Annotations of Mountains on a Smartphone. *ACM/IEEE Intl. Conference on Distributed Smart Cameras*, 2014.

L. Ren, Y. Wang, D. Dunson, and L. Carin. The Kernel Beta Process. *Advances in Neural Information Processing Systems*, 2011.

P. Spellman, G. Sherlock, W. Q. Zhang, V. R. Iyer, K. Anders, M. B. Eisen, P. O. Brown, D. Botstein, and B. Futcher. Comprehensive identification of cell cycle-regulated genes of the yeast *Saccharomyces cerevisiae* by microarray hybridization. *Mol. Biol. Cell*, 9:3273–3297, 1998.

Y. W. Teh, D. Görür, and Z. Ghahramani. Stick breaking construction for the Indian buffet process. *Proceedings of the 11th Conference on Artificial Intelligence and Statistics*, 2007.

R. Thibaux and M. I. Jordan. Hierarchical Beta Processes and the Indian Buffet Process. *Proceedings of the 11th Conference on Artificial Intelligence and Statistics*, 2007.

J. Van Gael, Y. W. Teh, and Z. Ghahramani. Infinite Factorial Hidden Markov Model. *Advances in Neural Information Processing Systems*, 2008.

C. C. Wang. Carnegie Mellon Image Database, 1997. URL `vasc.ri.cmu.edu/idb/`.

S. Williamson, P. Orbanz, and Z. Ghahramani. Dependent Indian Buffet Processes. *Proceedings of the 13th Conference on Artificial Intelligence and Statistics*, 2010.

M. Zhou, H. Chen, J. Paisley, L. Ren, G. Sapiro, and L. Carin. Non-Parametric Bayesian Dictionary Learning for Sparse Image Representations. *Advances in Neural Information Processing Systems*, 2009.

M. Zhou, H. Yang, G. Sapiro, D. Dunson, and L. Carin. Dependent Hierarchical Beta Process for Image Interpolation and Denoising. *Proceedings of the 14th Conference on Artificial Intelligence and Statistics*, 2011.

Finite Sample Complexity of Rare Pattern Anomaly Detection

Md Amran Siddiqui and **Alan Fern** and **Thomas G. Dietterich** and **Shubhomoy Das**
School of EECS
Oregon State University
{siddiqmd, afern, tgd, dassh}@eecs.oregonstate.edu

Abstract

Anomaly detection is a fundamental problem for which a wide variety of algorithms have been developed. However, compared to supervised learning, there has been very little work aimed at understanding the sample complexity of anomaly detection. In this paper, we take a step in this direction by introducing a Probably Approximately Correct (PAC) framework for anomaly detection based on the identification of rare patterns. In analogy with the PAC framework for supervised learning, we develop sample complexity results that relate the complexity of the pattern space to the data requirements needed for PAC guarantees. We instantiate the general result for a number of pattern spaces, some of which are implicit in current state-of-the-art anomaly detectors. Finally, we design a new simple anomaly detection algorithm motivated by our analysis and show experimentally on several benchmark problems that it is competitive with a state-of-the-art detector using the same pattern space.

1 INTRODUCTION

The problem of (unsupervised) anomaly detection is to identify anomalies in (unlabeled) data, where an anomaly is a data point that is generated by a process that is distinct from the process that generates "normal" points. This problem arises in a large number of applications, from security to data cleaning, and there have been many approaches proposed in the literature [4, 8]. While most applications seek to identify semantically-interesting anomalies, it is typically not possible to predefine a functional notion of semantic interestingness. Instead, the vast majority of anomaly detectors use a surrogate measure of interestingness. For example, a point may be interesting if it is a statistical outlier or if it is far away from other data points. The performance of a given detector in a domain depends on how well it can optimize the statistical measure and on how well that measure aligns with the behavior of anomalies in the application domain.

For moderately high-dimensional data, all data points become far apart from each other, so they are all statistical outliers in a sense. This suggests that anomaly detection by identifying outliers or distant points should perform poorly and degrade to random selection as the dimensionality grows. Empirical results, however, have shown that state-of-the-art anomaly detectors often perform quite well [7] even for high-dimensional data. Further, these detectors tend to reach their peak performance with a relatively small amount of training data compared to what might be expected based on the dimensionality. The primary goal of this paper is to move toward an understanding of these empirical observations by analyzing the sample complexity of a certain class of anomaly detectors.

The sample complexity of supervised learning has been widely studied and is quite well understood via the framework of Probably Approximately Correct (PAC) learning. However, this is not the case for anomaly detection, where virtually all published work has focused on algorithms with good empirical performance (with additional attention to computational speed, especially on big data sets). A key step in the development of PAC learning theory was to formalize the notion of a hypothesis space and to quantify the relationship between the complexity of this space and the amount of training data required to identify a good hypothesis in the space. In this paper, we follow a similar approach. Our framework is motivated by the observation that many state-of-the-art anomaly detectors can be viewed as monitoring the probabilities of certain "patterns" in the data, where a "pattern" is a subset (typically closed and compact) of the feature space. Outliers are then identified based on measures of those probabilities, where points are ranked as more anomalous if they satisfy lower-probability patterns. For example, the highly-competitive anomaly detection algorithm, Isolation Forest [10], finds outliers by monitoring probabilities in the pattern space of axis-aligned hyper-rectangles. Section 5 provides additional examples of the pattern spaces underlying a number of other state-of-the-art detectors. In our analysis, a "pattern" will play the same role as a "hypothesis" in PAC learning, and the pattern space complexity will determine the number of training examples required for high accuracy.

A second key step in the development of PAC theory was to relax the goal of finding the best possible hypothesis. Similarly, we will introduce an error parameter ϵ that determines how accurately the algorithm must estimate the probabilities of the patterns in the pattern space. We will then show that the required sample size scales polynomially in $1/\epsilon$ (as well as in several other parameters).

We call our formulation Rare Pattern Anomaly Detection (RPAD), and an algorithm that provides PAC guarantees will be referred to as a PAC-RPAD algorithm. We prove sample complexity results for any algorithm within the RPAD framework. The framework captures the qualitative essence of many anomaly detection algorithms. Note that we focus exclusively on sample complexity. Experience with the supervised PAC analysis has shown that sample complexity results often give more insight than computational complexity results. Indeed, many computational problems in PAC learning are NP-Hard and yet practical approximate algorithms are known. Similarly, we expect that some of the computational PAC-RPAD problems will also be NP-Hard, but existing algorithms, such as Isolation Forest, already provide practical approximate solutions.

Prior work on one-class SVMs [12] and learning minimum volume sets [13] have also provided sample complexity analysis relevant to anomaly detection. These approaches, however, are fundamentally different than RPAD-style approaches. In particular, these approaches focus on finding a common region/pattern in the input space that capture the normal points. In contrast, our RPAD framework is based on finding rare regions/patterns for directly extracting anomaly characteristics. Anomaly detection benchmarking studies [7] have shown that RPAD-style approaches tend to significantly outperform "common pattern" approaches such as one-class SVM. Our work is the first to analyze the sample complexity of the former approach.

The main contributions of this paper are as follows. First, we present a formal framework for RPAD (Section 2), which leads to the definition of PAC-RPAD (Section 3). Second, we specify a simple generic algorithm, RAREPATTERNDETECT, based on finding rare patterns. We derive sample complexity results for both finite pattern spaces and uncountable spaces of bounded complexity (Section 4). Third, we give a number of applications of the theory to pattern spaces that underly a number of state-of-the-art anomaly detection algorithms (Section 5). This, in part, helps explain why such algorithms consistently perform much better than random in high-dimensional data. Fourth, we measure learning curves on several benchmarks and for pattern spaces of varying complexity for RAREPATTERNDETECT and another state-of-the-art anomaly detector over the same spaces (Section 6). The results show that the RPAD-based algorithm can be competitive with the state-of-the-art and that the detectors' performances converge for surprisingly small training sets.

2 RARE PATTERN ANOMALY DETECTION

We consider anomaly detection over a space of possible data points $\mathcal{X} \subseteq \mathcal{R}^d$, which may be finite or infinite. Data from this space is generated according to an unknown probability density function $\mathcal{P}$ over $\mathcal{X}$. A common assumption in anomaly detection is that $\mathcal{P}$ is a mixture of a normal component, which generates normal data points, and an anomaly component, which generates anomalous data points. Further, it is typically assumed that there is a much higher probability of generating normal data than anomalies. This set of assumptions motivates one approach to anomaly detection, which we call *Anomaly Detection via Outlier Detection*. The idea is to estimate, for each query point x, the density $\mathcal{P}(x)$ based on an (unlabeled) training sample of the data and assign an anomaly score to x proportional to $-\log \mathcal{P}(x)$, the "surprise" of x.

There are many problems with this approach. First, the probability density may not be smooth in the neighborhood of x, so that $\mathcal{P}(x)$ could be very large and yet be surrounded by a region of low or zero density (or vice versa). Second, even under smoothness assumptions, density estimation is very difficult. For example, the integrated squared error of kernel density estimation in d-dimensional space (for a second-order kernel, such as a Gaussian kernel) converges to zero at a rate of $O(N^{-4/(4+d)})$ [14]. It follows that the sample size N required to achieve a target accuracy grows exponentially in the dimension d.

In this paper, we consider an alternative anomaly detection framework, which we will refer to as *Rare Pattern Anomaly Detection (RPAD)*. Informally, the main idea is to judge a point as anomalous if it exhibits a property, or pattern, that is rarely exhibited in data generated by $\mathcal{P}$. For example, in a computer security application, a detector may monitor various behavior patterns associated with processes accessing files. A process that exhibits an access behavior pattern that has been rarely seen would be considered anomalous. One attractive feature of the RPAD framework is that the notion of anomaly is grounded in the estimation of pattern probabilities, rather than point densities. Pattern probability estimation is quite well understood compared to density estimation. A second attractive feature of the RPAD framework is that each detected anomaly comes with an explanation of why it was considered anomalous. Specifically, the explanation can report the rare patterns that the anomaly satisfies. Explanation methods have been developed for density-estimation approaches (e.g. [15]), but they are less directly tied to the anomaly detection criterion.

Formally, a *pattern* h is a binary function over $\mathcal{X}$. A *pattern space* $\mathcal{H}$ is a set of patterns, which may be finite or infinite. As an example, if $\mathcal{X}$ is a finite space of n-dimensional bit vectors, a corresponding finite pattern space could be all conjunctions of length up to k. As another example, let $\mathcal{X} = [0,1]^n$, the n-dimensional unit cube, and consider the uncountable pattern space of all axis-aligned k-dimensional hyper-rectangles in this cube. In this case, each pattern h is a hyper-rectangle, such that $h(x)$ is true if x falls inside it. The choice of pattern space is an important consideration in the RPAD framework, since, in large part, this choice controls the semantic types of anomalies that will be detected.

Each pattern $h \in \mathcal{H}$ has a probability $P(h) = \Pr(\{x : h(x) = 1\})$ of being satisfied by data points generated according to $\mathcal{P}$. It will be useful to specify the set of all patterns in $\mathcal{H}$ that a point x satisfies, which we will denote by $\mathcal{H}[x] = \{h \in \mathcal{H} : h(x) = 1\}$. One approach to RPAD is to declare x to be anomalous if there is a pattern $h \in \mathcal{H}[x]$, such that $P(h) \leq \tau$. This approach is sensible when all patterns are approximately of the same "complexity". However, when $\mathcal{H}$ contains a mix of simple and complex patterns, this approach can be problematic. In particular, more complex patterns are inherently less likely to be satisfied by data points than simpler patterns, which makes choosing a single threshold τ difficult. For this reason, we introduced the *normalized pattern probability* $f(h) = P(h)/U(h)$, where $U(h)$ is the probability of h being satisfied according to a *reference density* U over $\mathcal{X}$. When $\mathcal{X}$ is bounded, we typically take U to be a uniform density function. Thus, a small value of $f(h)$ indicates that under $\mathcal{P}$, h is significantly more rare than it would be by chance, which provides a better-calibrated notion of rareness compared to only considering $\mathcal{P}(h)$. If $\mathcal{X}$ is unbounded, then an appropriate maximum entropy distribution (e.g., Gaussian) can be chosen.

We can now define the notion of anomaly under the RPAD framework. We say that a pattern h is *τ-rare* if $f(h) \leq \tau$, where τ is a detection threshold specified by the user. A data point x is a *τ-outlier* if there exists a τ-rare h in $\mathcal{H}[x]$ and otherwise x is said to be τ-common. Given τ and a stream of data drawn from $\mathcal{P}$, an optimal detector within the RPAD framework should detect all τ-outlier points and reject all τ-common points. That is, we want to detect any point that satisfies a τ-rare pattern and otherwise reject. An anomaly detector will make its decisions based on some finite amount of sampled data, and we expect that the performance should improve as the amount of data grows. Further, in analogy to supervised learning, we would expect that the amount of data required to achieve a certain level of performance should increase as the complexity of the pattern space increases. We now introduce a formal framework for making these intuitions more precise.

3 PROBABLY APPROXIMATELY CORRECT FRAMEWORK

To address the sample complexity of RPAD, we consider a learning protocol that makes the notion of training data explicit. The protocol first draws a training data set $\mathcal{D}$ of N i.i.d. data points from $\mathcal{P}$. An anomaly detector is provided with $\mathcal{D}$ along with a test instance x that may or may not be drawn from $\mathcal{P}$. The anomaly detector then outputs "detect" if the instance is considered to be an anomaly or "reject" otherwise. Note that the output of a detector is a random variable due to the randomness of $\mathcal{D}$ and any randomization in the algorithm itself. This protocol models a common use case in many applications of anomaly detection. For example, in a computer security application, data from normal system operation will typically be collected and provided to an anomaly detector before it is activated.

The *ideal* correctness criterion requires that the test instance x be detected if it is a τ-outlier and rejected otherwise. However, as we discussed above, this notion of correctness is too strict for the purpose of sample complexity analysis. In particular, such a criterion requires distinguishing between pattern probabilities that fall arbitrarily close to each side of the detection threshold τ, which can require arbitrarily large training samples. For this reason, we relax the correctness criterion by introducing a *tolerance parameter* $\epsilon > 0$. The detector is said to be approximately correct at level ϵ if it detects all τ-rare points and rejects all $(\tau+\epsilon)$-common points. For test points that are neither τ-rare nor $(\tau+\epsilon)$-common, the detector output can be arbitrary. The value of ϵ controls the false positive rate of the detector, where smaller values of ϵ will result in fewer false positives relative to the detection threshold.

We now define the PAC learning objective for RPAD. A detection algorithm will be considered PAC-RPAD if with high-probability over draws of the training data it produces an approximately correct output for any $x \in \mathcal{X}$.

Definition 1. *(PAC-RPAD) Let $\mathcal{A}$ be a detection algorithm over pattern space $\mathcal{H}$ with input parameters $0 < \delta < 1$, $0 < \tau$, $0 < \epsilon$, and the ability to draw a training set $\mathcal{D}$ of any size N from $\mathcal{P}$. $\mathcal{A}$ is a PAC-RPAD algorithm if for any $\mathcal{P}$ and any τ, with probability at least $1-\delta$ (over draws of $\mathcal{D}$), $\mathcal{A}$ detects all τ-outliers and rejects all $(\tau+\epsilon)$-commons.*

The *sample complexity* of a PAC-RPAD algorithm for $\mathcal{H}$ is a function of the inputs $N(\delta,\epsilon)$ that specifies the number of training examples to draw. We expect that the sample complexity will increase as the complexity of $\mathcal{H}$ increase, as the dimensionality d of points increases, and as the failure probability δ decreases. Further, we expect that the sample complexity will increase for smaller values of the tolerance parameter ϵ, since this controls the difficultly of distinguishing between τ-rare and $(\tau + \epsilon)$-common data points. Accordingly we say that a PAC-RPAD algorithm is *sample efficient* if its sample complexity is polynomial in d, $\frac{1}{\delta}$, and $\frac{1}{\epsilon}$.

4 FINITE SAMPLE COMPLEXITY OF RPAD

We now consider a very simple algorithm, called RAREPATTERNDETECT, which will be shown to be a sample efficient PAC-RPAD algorithm for bounded complexity pattern spaces. The algorithm is given in Table 1 and first draws a training set $\mathcal{D}$ of size $N(\delta, \epsilon)$. Here $N(\delta, \epsilon)$ will depend on the pattern space complexity and will be specified later in this section. The training set is used to estimate the normalized pattern probabilities given by

$$\widehat{f}(h) = \frac{1}{|D| \cdot U(h)} |\{x \in \mathcal{D} : h(x) = 1\}|.$$

Here, we assume that $U(h)$ can be computed analytically or at least closely approximated. For example, when U is uniform over a bounded space, $U(h)$ is proportional to the volume of h.

After drawing the training set, RAREPATTERNDETECT specifies a decision rule that detects any x as anomalous if and only if it satisfies a pattern with estimated frequency less than or equal $\tau + \epsilon/2$. This test is done using the subroutine HASRAREPATTERN$(x, \mathcal{D}, \mathcal{H}, \mu)$, which returns true if there exists a pattern h in $\mathcal{H}[x]$ such that $\widehat{f}(h) \leq \mu$. For the purposes of sample complexity analysis, we will assume an oracle for HASRAREPATTERN. For sufficiently complex pattern spaces, the problem addressed by HASRAREPATTERN will be computational hard. Thus, in practice, a heuristic approximation will be needed, for example, based on techniques developed in the rare pattern mining literature. In practice, we are often interested in having an anomaly detector return an anomaly ranking over multiple test data points. In this case, the algorithm can rank a data point x based on a score equal to the minimum normalized frequency of any pattern that it satisfies, that is, $\text{score}(x) = \min\{\widehat{f}(h) : h \in \mathcal{H}[x]\}$. It remains to specify $N(\delta, \epsilon)$ in order to ensure that RAREPATTERNDETECT is PAC-RPAD. Below we do this for two cases: 1) finite pattern spaces, and 2) pattern spaces with bounded VC-dimension. Later, in Section 5 we will instantiate these results for specific pattern spaces that underly several existing anomaly detection algorithms.

4.1 SAMPLE COMPLEXITY FOR FINITE $\mathcal{H}$

For finite pattern spaces, it is relatively straightforward to show that as long as $\log|\mathcal{H}|$ is polynomial in d then RAREPATTERNDETECT is a sample efficient PAC-RPAD algorithm.

Table 1: RAREPATTERNDETECT Algorithm

Input: δ, τ, ϵ

1. Draw a training set $\mathcal{D}$ of $N(\delta, \epsilon)$ instances from $\mathcal{P}$.
2. **Decision Rule for any x:** If HASRAREPATTERN$(x, \mathcal{D}, \mathcal{H}, \tau + \epsilon/2)$ then return "detect", otherwise return "reject".

HASRAREPATTERN$(x, \mathcal{D}, \mathcal{H}, \mu)$
$:= \{h \in \mathcal{H}[x] : \widehat{f}(h) \leq \mu\} \neq \emptyset$

Theorem 1. *For any finite pattern space $\mathcal{H}$, RAREPATTERNDETECT is PAC-RPAD with sample complexity $N(\delta, \epsilon) = O\left(\frac{1}{\epsilon^2}\left(\log|\mathcal{H}| + \log\frac{1}{\delta}\right)\right)$.*

Proof. Suppose, X is a Bernoulli random variable with parameter $P(h)$ for a pattern h, i.e., $E[X] = P(h)$. Let, $Y = \frac{X}{U(h)}$, hence, Y is a random variable with $E[Y] = \frac{E[X]}{U(h)} = \frac{P(h)}{U(h)} = f(h)$. We also observe that the maximum value of Y is $\frac{1}{U(h)}$. Given N samples $x_1, x_2, ..., x_N$, each $x_i \sim \mathcal{P}$, we estimate $\widehat{f}(h) = \frac{1}{N}\sum_{i=1}^{N} \frac{\mathcal{I}[x_i \in h]}{U(h)}$. We seek a confidence interval $[L(h), R(h)]$ for $f(h)$ that is narrow enough that it does not simultaneously contain both τ and $\tau + \epsilon$. The reason is that if $L(h) > \tau$, then with probability $1 - \delta$, $f(h) > \tau$, so h is not a τ-rare pattern. If $R(h) < \tau + \epsilon$, then with probability $1 - \delta$, h is not a $\tau + \epsilon$-common pattern, so it is safe to treat it as τ-rare. Hence, the confidence interval should be $[\widehat{f}(h) - \epsilon/2, \widehat{f}(h) + \epsilon/2]$, and its "half width" is $\epsilon/2$. So, we want to bound (by δ) the probability that $\widehat{f}(h)$ is more than $\frac{\epsilon}{2}$ away from its true value $f(h)$. Now, using the Hoeffding bound we have

$$P\left(|E_{\mathcal{P}}[\widehat{f}(h)] - \widehat{f}(h)| > \frac{\epsilon}{2}\right)$$
$$\iff P\left(\left|f(h) - \frac{1}{N}\sum_{i=1}^{N}\frac{\mathcal{I}[x_i \in h]}{U(h)}\right| > \frac{\epsilon}{2}\right)$$
$$\leq 2\exp\left(-\frac{\epsilon^2}{2}U(h)^2 N\right).$$

Since $\mathcal{H}$ is finite, we can bound the above probability for all $h \in \mathcal{H}$ using the union bound: $2|\mathcal{H}|\exp\left(-\frac{\epsilon^2}{2}U_{min}^2 N\right)$, where, $U_{min} = \min_{h \in \mathcal{H}} U(h)$. We want this quantity to be less or equal to δ:

$$2|\mathcal{H}|\exp\left(-\frac{\epsilon^2}{2}U_{min}^2 N\right) \leq \delta$$
$$\implies N \geq \frac{2}{\epsilon^2}\frac{1}{U_{min}^2}\log\frac{2|\mathcal{H}|}{\delta}.$$

Hence, the sample complexity is $O\left(\frac{1}{\epsilon^2}\left(\log|\mathcal{H}| + \log\frac{1}{\delta}\right)\right)$. □

4.2 SAMPLE COMPLEXITY FOR INFINITE $\mathcal{H}$

When the sample space $\mathcal{X}$ is continuous, it is typically the case that the corresponding pattern space will be infinite and hence not covered by the above result. As is standard in supervised learning, we will characterize the complexity of infinite pattern spaces via the VC-dimension [17], which we denote by $\mathcal{V}_{\mathcal{H}}$. The VC-dimension of $\mathcal{H}$ is equal to the maximum number of points that can be shattered by patterns in $\mathcal{H}$. Here a set of points D is shattered by $\mathcal{H}$ if for any subset D' of D there is an $h \in \mathcal{H}$ such that $h(x) = 1$ for all $x \in D'$ and $h(x) = 0$ for all $x \in D - D'$. That is, patterns in $\mathcal{H}$ can be used to define all possible bi-partitions of D. For many interesting pattern spaces, the VC-dimension scales polynomially with the data dimension d. The following result exploits this property by showing that if a space has VC-dimension that is polynomial in d, then the space is sample-efficient learnable in the PAC-RPAD model.

Theorem 2. *For any pattern space $\mathcal{H}$ with finite VC-dimension $\mathcal{V}_{\mathcal{H}}$,* RAREPATTERNDETECT *is PAC-RPAD with sample complexity* $N(\delta, \epsilon) = O\left(\frac{1}{\epsilon^2}\left(\mathcal{V}_{\mathcal{H}} \log \frac{1}{\epsilon^2} + \log \frac{1}{\delta}\right)\right)$.

Proof. When the pattern space $\mathcal{H}$ is infinite, we want to bound the probability $P\left(\sup_{h\in\mathcal{H}} |\widehat{f}(h) - f(h)| > \frac{\epsilon}{2}\right)$, which can be achieved by bounding $P\left(\sup_{h\in\mathcal{H}} |\widehat{P}(h) - P(h)| > \frac{\epsilon}{2} U_{min}\right)$, where, $\widehat{P}(h)$ is an estimate of $P(h)$ based on sampled data. Let, $\epsilon_f = \frac{\epsilon}{2} U_{min}$. Using the VC uniform convergence bound on frequency estimates [6, Thm. 12.5] we have

$$P\left(\sup_{h\in\mathcal{H}} |\widehat{P}(h) - P(h)| > \epsilon_f\right) \leq 8\mathcal{S}_{\mathcal{H}}(N) e^{-N\epsilon_f^2/32}. \quad (1)$$

where, $\widehat{P}(h)$ is an estimate based on N i.i.d. samples from $\mathcal{P}$ and $\mathcal{S}_{\mathcal{H}}(N)$ is the Shatter Coefficient, which is the largest number of subsets that can be formed by intersecting some set of N points with patterns from $\mathcal{H}$.

Now, for any $N > 2\mathcal{V}_{\mathcal{H}}$, we can bound the Shatter Coefficient as: $\mathcal{S}_{\mathcal{H}}(N) < (\frac{eN}{\mathcal{V}_{\mathcal{H}}})^{\mathcal{V}_{\mathcal{H}}}$ [6, Thm. 13.3]. Hence, from Equation 1 we have

$$P\left(\sup_{h\in\mathcal{H}} |\widehat{P}(h) - P(h)| > \epsilon_f\right) < 8(\frac{eN}{\mathcal{V}_{\mathcal{H}}})^{\mathcal{V}_{\mathcal{H}}} e^{-N\epsilon_f^2/32}. \quad (2)$$

We want to bound this probability by δ, which yields

$$N \geq \frac{32}{\epsilon_f^2}\left(\mathcal{V}_{\mathcal{H}} \log(N) + \mathcal{V}_{\mathcal{H}} \log \frac{e}{\mathcal{V}_{\mathcal{H}}} + \log \frac{8}{\delta}\right). \quad (3)$$

Using the fact that $\log(N) \leq \alpha N - \log(\alpha) - 1$, where, $N, \alpha > 0$ and setting $\alpha = \frac{\epsilon_f^2}{64\mathcal{V}_{\mathcal{H}}}$, we get

$$\frac{32\mathcal{V}_{\mathcal{H}}}{\epsilon_f^2} \log(N) \leq \frac{32\mathcal{V}_{\mathcal{H}}}{\epsilon_f^2}\left(\frac{\epsilon_f^2}{64\mathcal{V}_{\mathcal{H}}} N - \log \frac{\epsilon_f^2}{64\mathcal{V}_{\mathcal{H}}} - 1\right)$$
$$= \frac{N}{2} + \frac{32\mathcal{V}_{\mathcal{H}}}{\epsilon_f^2} \log \frac{64\mathcal{V}_{\mathcal{H}}}{\epsilon_f^2 e}. \quad (4)$$

Applying results from Equation 4 into Equation 3 and substituting the original value of ϵ_f we prove the Theorem 2:

$$N \geq \frac{256}{\epsilon^2} \frac{1}{U_{min}^2}\left(\mathcal{V}_{\mathcal{H}} \log\left(\frac{256}{\epsilon^2} \frac{1}{U_{min}^2}\right) + \log \frac{8}{\delta}\right).$$

□

5 APPLICATION TO SPECIFIC PATTERN SPACES

Most state-of-the-art anomaly detectors assign an anomaly score to data points and then detect points based on a score threshold or present a ranked list to the user. Further, while not usually explained explicitly, the scores are often based on frequency estimates of patterns in some space $\mathcal{H}$ with rare patterns leading to higher anomaly scores. While RAREPATTERNDETECT was designed as a pure implementation of this principle, it is reasonable to expect that its sample complexity is related qualitatively to the sample complexity of other algorithms grounded in pattern frequency estimation.

In this section, we consider a number of pattern spaces underlying existing algorithms and show that the sample complexity of those spaces is small. The spaces are thus all learnable in the PAC-RPAD framework, which offers some insight into why existing algorithms often show strong performance even in high-dimensional spaces.

5.1 CONJUNCTIONS

Consider a space $\mathcal{X}$ over d Boolean attributes and a pattern space $\mathcal{H}$ corresponding to conjunctions of those attributes. This setup is common in the data mining literature, where each boolean attribute corresponds to an "item" and a conjunction corresponds to an "item set", which indicates which items are in the set. Rare pattern mining has been studied for such spaces and applied to anomaly detection [1, 16]. In this case, the pattern space has a finite size 2^d and thus by Theorem 1 is efficiently PAC-RPAD learnable with sample complexity $O\left(\frac{1}{\epsilon^2}\left(d + \log \frac{1}{\delta}\right)\right)$. If we limit attention to conjunctions of at most k attributes, then the sample complexity drops to $O\left(\frac{1}{\epsilon^2}\left(k \log(d) + \log \frac{1}{\delta}\right)\right)$, which is sub-linear in d.

5.2 HALFSPACES

Given a continuous space $\mathcal{X} \subseteq \Re^d$, a *half space pattern* is an oriented d-dimensional hyperplane. A data point satisfies a half space pattern if it is on the positive side of the hyperplane. The half-space mass algorithm [5] for anomaly detection operates in this pattern space. Roughly speaking, the algorithm assigns a score to a point x based on the frequency estimates of random half spaces that contain x. The VC-dimension of d-dimensional half spaces is well known to be $d + 1$ and hence this space is sample-efficient learnable in the PAC-RPAD model.

5.3 AXIS ALIGNED HYPER RECTANGLES

For a continuous space $\mathcal{X} \subseteq \Re^d$, an axis-aligned hyper rectangle (bounded or unbounded) can be specified as a conjunction of threshold tests on a subset of the dimensions. The pattern space of axis-aligned rectangles are often implicit in decision tree algorithms, where each internal tree node specifies one threshold test.

The state-of-the-art anomaly detection algorithms, Isolation Forest [10] and RS-Forest [18] (among others), are based on this space. The core idea of these algorithms is to build a forest of T random decision trees, where each node specifies a random threshold test. The trees are grown until either a maximum depth is reached or a leaf node contains only a single data point. Each leaf corresponds to an axis-aligned hyper rectangle. Given a point x, the algorithm can compute the leaf node it reaches in each tree, yielding a set of T hyper-rectangle patterns. The score for x is then based on the average score assigned to each pattern, which is related to the pattern frequency, dimension, and volume.

The VC-dimension of the space of axis parallel hyper rectangles in $\Re^d$ is $2d$ [3]. Thus, the pattern space underlying Isolation Forest and RS-Forest is sample-efficient learnable in the PAC-RPAD model.

5.4 STRIPES

A stripe pattern in $\Re^d$ can be thought of as an intersection of two parallel halfspaces with opposite orientations and can be defined by the inequalities: $a \leq w^\top x \leq a + \Delta$, where, $w \in \Re^d$, a and $\Delta \in \Re$ and Δ represents the width of the stripe. The stripe pattern space consists of the set of all such stripes.

The very simple, but effective, anomaly detector, LODA [11], is based on the stripes pattern space. The main idea of LODA is to form a set of T sparse random projections along some random directions in the subspaces of $\Re^d$ and then estimate a discretized 1D histogram based on the projected values. Each bin of each histogram can be viewed as corresponding to a stripe in the original $\Re^d$ space with orientation defined by the direction of the random projection and location/width defined by the bin localtion/width.

To the best of our knowledge the VC-dimension of the stripes pattern space has not been previously derived. A loose bound can be found by noting that stripes are a special case of the more general pattern space of intersections of half spaces and then applying the general result for bounding the VC-dimension of intersections [3], which gives an upper bound on the VC-dimension of stripes of $4\log(6)(d+1) = O(d)$. Hence, stripes are PAC learnable in the RPAD model.

5.5 ELLIPSOIDS AND SHELLS

Anomaly detectors based on estimating "local densities" often form estimates based on frequencies observed in ellipsoids around query points. In particular, an ellipsoid pattern in a d dimensional space can be represented by $(x - \mu)^\top A\,(x - \mu) \leq t$, where $t \in \Re$, $\mu \in \Re^d$ and A is a $d \times d$ positive definite symmetric matrix. An upper bound for the VC-dimension of ellipsoids in $\Re^d$ is $(d^2 + 3d)/2$ [2]. Hence the ellipsoid pattern space is sample-efficient learnable in the PAC-RPAD model. However, we see that the complexity is quadratic in d rather than linear as we saw above for spaces based on hyperplane separators.

A related pattern space is the space of *ellipsoidal shells*, which is the analog of stripes for ellipsoidal patterns. An ellipsoidal shell in $\Re^d$ can be thought of as the subtraction of two ellipsoids with the same center and shape, but different volumes. That is, the shell is a region defined by $t \leq (x-\mu)^\top A(x-\mu) \leq t+\Delta$, where $\Delta \in \Re$ is the width. Shells naturally arise as the discretized level sets of multidimensional Gaussian density functions, which are perhaps the most widely-used densities in anomaly detection. We are unaware of previous results for the VC-dimensions of shells and show below that it is also $O(d^2)$.

Theorem 3. *The VC-dimension of the ellipsoidal shell pattern space in* $\Re^d$ *is upper bounded by* $2\log(6)(d^2+3d+2)$.

Proof. We can represent an ellipsoidal shell in $\Re^d$ as:

$$t \leq (x - \mu)^\top A\,(x - \mu)\ \leq t + \Delta. \tag{5}$$

Rewriting the equation of an ellipsoid in $\Re^d$:

$$\begin{aligned} &(x - \mu)^\top A\,(x - \mu)\ \leq t \\ \Longrightarrow\ & x^\top A\,x - 2x^\top A\,\mu \leq t - \mu^\top A\,\mu \\ \Longrightarrow\ & \sum_{i,j=1}^{d} A_{ij}x_ix_j - \sum_{i=1}^{d} 2(A\mu)_i x_i \leq t - \mu^\top A\mu \\ \Longrightarrow\ & w^\top z \leq b. \end{aligned} \tag{6}$$

where, $w, z \in \Re^{d(d+1)/2+d}$. The vector w is a new parameter vector constructed from the original parameters. The matrix A gives $d(d+1)/2$ unique parameters, since A is symmetric, and the vector $A\mu$ gives another d parameters. The vector z is a new input constructed from the original input x, and $b = t - \mu^\top A\mu$.

Now, Applying result of Equation 6 to Equation 5 we get

$$\begin{aligned} & t - \mu^\top A\,\mu \leq w^\top z \leq t + \Delta - \mu^\top A\,\mu \\ \Longrightarrow\ & t' \leq w^\top z \leq t' + \Delta. \end{aligned} \tag{7}$$

The Equation 7 is a representation of a stripe in $\Re^{d(d+1)/2+d}$. So, we apply the same approach from previous Section 5.4 i.e. the case of two halfspaces, which gives the upper bound of $4\log(6)(d(d+1)/2 + d + 1) = 2\log(6)(d^2 + 3d + 2) = O(d^2)$. □

6 EXPERIMENTS

The above results suggest one reason for why state-of-the-art anomaly detectors often perform significantly better than random, even on high-dimensional data. However, existing empirical work does not go much further in terms of providing an understanding of learning curves for anomaly detection. To the best of our knowledge, there has not been a significant study of how the empirical performance of anomaly detectors varies as the amount of training/reference data increases. Typically empirical performance is reported for benchmark data sets without systematic variation of training set size, though other factors such as anomaly percentage are often varied. This is in contrast to empirical studies in supervised learning, where learning curves are regularly published, compared, and analyzed.

In this section, we present an initial investigation into empirical learning curves for anomaly detection. We are interested in the following experimental questions: 1) Will the empirical learning curves demonstrate the fast convergence predicted by the PAC-RPAD framework, and how is the convergence impacted by the data dimension and pattern space complexity? 2) How does the RPAD approach compare to a state-of-the-art detector based on the same pattern space on anomaly detection benchmarks? 3) In what ways do empirical learning curves for anomaly detection differ qualitatively from learning curves for supervised learning? While a complete empirical investigation is beyond the scope of this paper, below we provide experiments that shed light on each of these questions.

6.1 PATTERN SPACE AND ANOMALY DETECTOR SELECTION

A recent large scale evaluation [7] has shown that the Isolation Forest (IF) is among the top performing anomaly detectors across a wide range of benchmarks. This motivates us to focus our investigation on IF's pattern space of axis aligned hyper rectangles (see above). In order to allow for the complexity of this pattern space to be varied, we define *REC(k)* to be the space of all axis aligned hyper rectangles defined by at most k threshold tests on feature values.

The first step of IF is to construct a random forest of trees that are limited to a user-specified maximum leaf depth of k. Each tree leaf in the forest corresponds to a single pattern in REC(k). Thus, the first step of IF can be viewed as generating a random pattern space $\mathcal{H}_k \subseteq \text{REC}(k)$ that contains all leaf patterns in the forest. IF then operates by using training data to compute empirical frequencies $\widehat{P}(h)$ of patterns in $\mathcal{H}_k$ and then for any test point x computes an anomaly score based on those frequencies as follows (smaller is more anomalous):

$$\text{IF}(x) = \sum_{h \in \mathcal{H}_k[x]} d_h + c(\widehat{P}(h))$$

where, $d_h \leq k$ is the number of tests in pattern h and $c(h)$ is a function of the empirical frequency of h.[1]

In order to directly compare IF to our RPAD approach we will conduct multiple experiments, each one using a different randomly generated pattern space $\mathcal{H}_k$. We can then compute the scoring function corresponding to RAREPATTERNDETECT on those pattern spaces and compare to the performance of the IF scoring function. In particular, RAREPATTERNDETECT effectively assigns a score to x based on the minimum frequency pattern as follows:

$$\text{MIN}(x) = \min_{h \in \mathcal{H}_k[x]} \widehat{f}(h)$$

where the normalized frequency estimate $\widehat{f}(h)$ is normalized by a uniform density $U(h)$ over a region of bounded support defined by the training data. This normalizer is proportional to the volume of h and is easily computed. We see that compared to the IF scoring function with sums/averages over functions of each pattern in $\mathcal{H}_k[x]$, the MIN scoring function is only sensitive to the minimum frequency pattern. In order to provide a baseline in between these two, we also compare to the following alternative scoring function that averages normalized frequencies. This scoring function is given by

$$\text{AVE}(x) = \frac{1}{|\mathcal{H}_k[x]|} \sum_{h \in \mathcal{H}_k[x]} \widehat{f}(h).$$

AVE is included in order to observe whether averaging is a more robust approach to using normalized frequencies compared to MIN.

6.2 LEARNING CURVE GENERATION

We generate learning curves using three existing anomaly detection benchmarks:
Covertype [18]: $d = 10$ features, approximately 286k instances 0.9% anomalies.
Particle [7]: $d = 50$ features, approximately 130k instances with 5% anomalies.
Shuttle [7]: $d = 9$ features, approximately 58k instances with 5% anomalies.
These datasets were originally derived from UCI supervised learning benchmarks [9] by treating one or more classes as the anomaly classes and sub-sampling at an appropriate rate to produce benchmarks with certain percentages of anomalies. We have conducted experiments on a number of additional benchmarks, which are not included

[1] In particular, $c(h)$ is an estimate of the expected number of random tests required to completely isolate training data points that satisfy h, which is a function of the number of training points that satisfy h [10]. This score is motivated by attempting to estimate the "isolation depth" of x, which is the expected length of a random path required to isolate a point. Intuitively smaller isolation depths indicate a more anomalous point since it is easier to separate from other points.

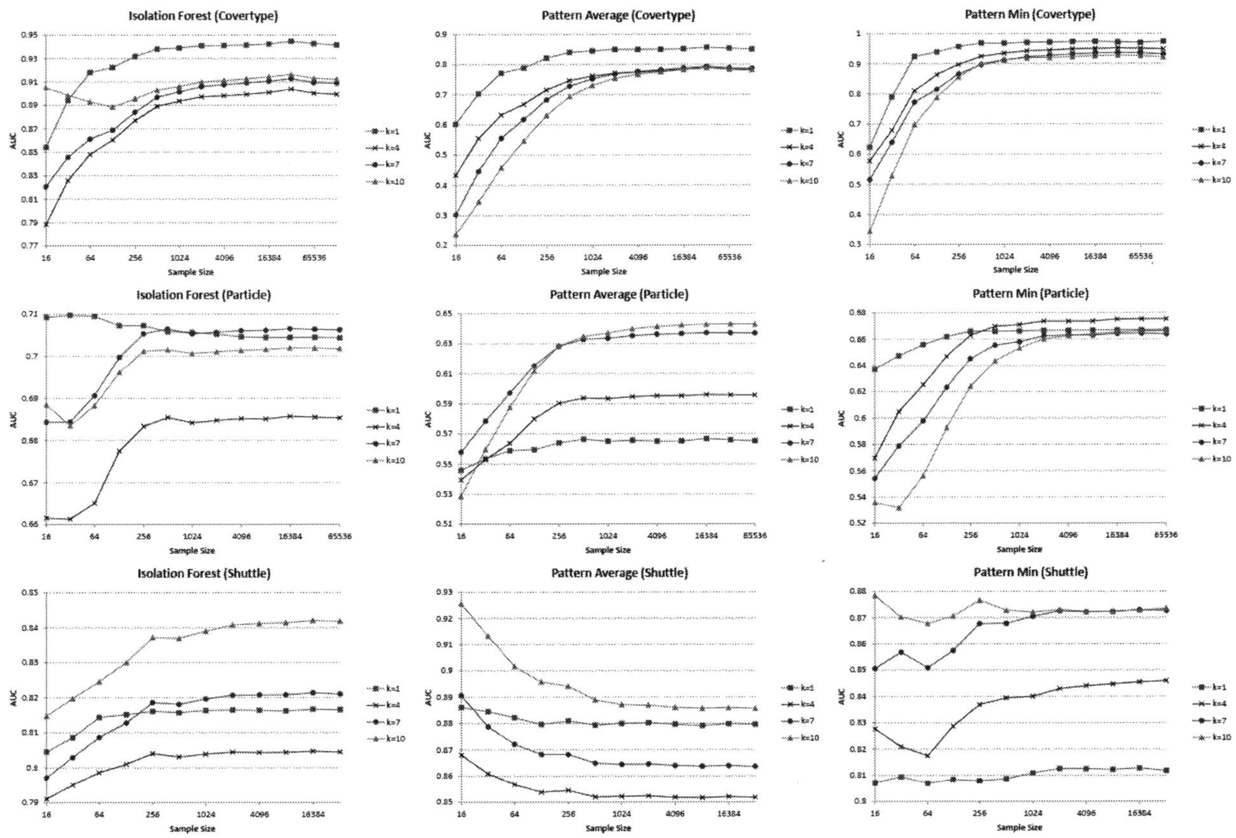

Figure 1: Learning Curves for the Three Scoring Methods (IF, AVE, MIN) with Varying Pattern Space Complexity k Over Three Benchmarks (Rows). MIN Represents the Main RPAD Approach Analyzed in this Paper.

for space reasons. These three data sets were selected as being representative of the qualitative learning curve types that we have observed. The data sets are divided into three sets of data: pattern generation data, training data, and test data for which we ensure that the fraction of anomaly points in each data set is approximately the same as for the full benchmark.

Given a benchmark and a specified pattern complexity k, we generate learning curves for each algorithm as follows. First, we use IF to generate a random pattern space $\mathcal{H}_k$, based on the pattern generation data using a forest of 250 random trees. Next for each desired training set size, we sample a training set of the appropriate size and use that data to estimate frequencies over $\mathcal{H}_k$, which can be done efficiently by passing each data point through each tree. Next, the scores defined above for IF, MIN, and AVE are computed for each test instance based on the frequency estimates and the *Area Under the Curve (AUC)* of those scores is computed relative to the ground truth anomalies. This process is repeated 50 times for each training set size and the resulting AUCs are averaged to produce a final learning curve.

6.3 RESULTS

Figure 1 gives learning curves for each benchmark (rows) and each of the anomaly detectors IF, MIN, and AVE (columns). Recall that MIN represents the main RPAD approach analyzed in this paper. In each case, four learning curves are shown for pattern space complexities $k = 1, 4, 7, 10$ and training instances range from 16 to 2^{15}.

Convergence rate: Each learning curve for each algorithm and benchmark follows a trajectory starting at 16 training instances to a converged performance at 2^{15} points. We see that in all cases, convergence to the final performance occurs very quickly, in particular around 1024 samples. This convergence rate is not significantly impacted by the dimensionality of the data, which can be seen by comparing the results for Particle with $d = 50$ to the other data sets with $d = 9$ and $d = 10$. Rather we see that the convergence rate visibly depends on the pattern space complexity k, though to a relatively small degree. In particular, we see that the convergence for the simplest space $k = 1$ tends to be faster than for $k = 10$ across our experiments. These observations agree with our analysis. The VC-dimension of REC(k), which controls worst case convergence, is dominated by the limiting effect of k. These observations are consistent across additional benchmarks not shown here.

Relative Algorithm Performance: Here we focus on comparing the different detectors, or scoring functions, in terms of their converged performance. For the Cover and Shuttle data sets we see that the converged performance of MIN is better or competitive than the converged performance of IF for all values of k. For the Particle data set, the IF scoring function outperforms MIN consistently by a small margin. This shows that despite its simplicity the RPAD approach followed by MIN appears to be competitive with a state-of-the-art detector based on the same pattern space. Experiments on other benchmarks, not shown, further confirm this observation.

The converged performance of AVE tends to be worse than both IF and MIN for Covertype and Particle and is slightly better on Shuttle. It appears that for these data sets (and others not shown) that averaging is not significantly more robust than minimizing and can even hurt performance. One reason for degraded performance is that AVE can be influenced by the cumulative effect of a large number of non-rare patterns, which may sometimes overwhelm the signal provided by rare patterns.

An interesting observation is that for each data set, the best performing pattern space (i.e. value of k) is usually the same across the different learning algorithms. For example, for Covertype, $k = 1$ yields the best converged performance for all scoring functions. This observation, which we also frequently observed in other data sets, suggests that the choice of pattern space can have a performance impact that is as large or larger than the impact of the specific scoring function used. To understand this, note that the performance of an anomaly detector depends on both the convergence of its scoring function and the match between the scoring function and the semantic notion of anomaly for the application. The pattern space choice has a large influence on the this match since it controls the fundamental distinctions that can be made among data points.

Qualitative Properties: The qualitative behavior of the learning curves exhibits a couple of nonintuitive properties compared to supervised learning curves. First, in supervised learning, we typically expect and observe that more complex hypothesis spaces converge to a performance that is at least as good as simpler spaces, though more complex spaces may underperform at small sample sizes due to variance. This does not appear to be the case for anomaly detection learning curves in general. For example, the performance of the simplest pattern space ($k = 1$) on Covertype converges to better performance than the more complex spaces. This has also been observed in other data sets and does not appear to be due to premature termination of the learning curve. Rather, we hypothesize that this behavior is due to the mismatch between the anomaly detection scores and the semantic notion of anomaly in the benchmark. In particular, rare patterns in REC(1) are apparently a better indicator of the semantic notion of anomaly than some distracter rare patterns in REC(10). Indeed, it is straightforward to construct synthetic examples with such behavior.

Another nonintuitive aspect is that, in at least two cases, the learning curves consistently decrease in performance, while typically in supervised learning, ideal learning curves are non-decreasing. The most striking example is the performance of AVE on Shuttle, where all learning curves steadily decrease. After further analysis, this type of behavior again appears to be explained by the mismatch between the semantic notion of anomalies and the scoring function. In particular, the variance across different trials of the learning curve for large sample sizes is much smaller than for small sample sizes. It also turns out that the distribution of scoring functions generated for the small sample sizes is skewed toward solutions that better match the ground truth anomalies compared to the converged scoring function. Thus, the average performance for small sample sizes is better. We have observed this decreasing learning curve behavior in other data sets as well, though it is much more common for learning curves to increase.

7 SUMMARY

This work is motivated by the observation that many statistical anomaly detection methods perform much better than random in high dimensions using relatively small amounts of training data. Our PAC-RPAD framework attempts to explain these observations by quantifying the sample complexity in terms of the complexity of the pattern spaces underlying such anomaly detectors. Our results mirror those in supervised learning by showing that the VC-dimension of the pattern spaces is the dominating factor that controls sample complexity. We showed that for several state-of-the-art detectors, the underlying pattern spaces had well-behaved VC-dimensions with respect to the data dimensionality, which offers a partial explanation for their good performance. On the empirical side, we investigated for the first time, to the best of our knowledge, learning curves for anomaly detection. The experiments confirmed the fast convergence predicted by the theory. The results also suggest that our simple algorithm, which was shown to be PAC-RPAD, is competitive with the state-of-the-art algorithm Isolation Forest when using the same pattern space. Finally, the learning curves showed some interesting qualitative differences compared to supervised learning curves. In particular, the results highlight the importance of selecting a pattern space that is likely to be a good match to the semantic notion required for an application.

Acknowledgements
This work is partially supported by the Future of Life Institute and DARPA under contract number FA8650-15-C-7557 and W911NF-11-C-0088.

References

[1] M. Adda, L. Wu, and Y. Feng. Rare itemset mining. In *Machine Learning and Applications, 2007. ICMLA 2007. Sixth International Conference on*, pages 73–80. IEEE, 2007.

[2] A. Auger and B. Doerr. *Theory of randomized search heuristics: Foundations and recent developments*, volume 1. World Scientific, 2011.

[3] A. Blumer, A. Ehrenfeucht, D. Haussler, and M. K. Warmuth. Learnability and the Vapnik-Chervonenkis dimension. *Journal of the ACM (JACM)*, 36(4):929–965, 1989.

[4] V. Chandola, A. Banerjee, and V. Kumar. Anomaly detection: A survey. *ACM computing surveys (CSUR)*, 41(3):15, 2009.

[5] B. Chen, K. M. Ting, T. Washio, and G. Haffari. Half-space mass: a maximally robust and efficient data depth method. *Machine Learning*, 100(2-3):677–699, 2015.

[6] L. Devroye, L. Györfi, and G. Lugosi. *A probabilistic theory of pattern recognition*, volume 31. Springer Science & Business Media, 2013.

[7] A. Emmott, S. Das, T. Dietterich, A. Fern, and W.-K. Wong. Systematic construction of anomaly detection benchmarks from real data. In *Proceedings of the ACM SIGKDD Workshop on Outlier Detection and Description*, pages 16–21, 2013.

[8] V. J. Hodge and J. Austin. A survey of outlier detection methodologies. *Artificial Intelligence Review*, 22(2):85–126, 2004.

[9] M. Lichman. UCI machine learning repository, 2013.

[10] F. T. Liu, K. M. Ting, and Z.-H. Zhou. Isolation forest. In *Data Mining, 2008. ICDM'08. Eighth IEEE International Conference on*, pages 413–422. IEEE, 2008.

[11] T. Pevný. Loda: Lightweight on-line detector of anomalies. *Machine Learning*, 102(2):275–304, 2016.

[12] B. Schölkopf, J. C. Platt, J. Shawe-Taylor, A. J. Smola, and R. C. Williamson. Estimating the support of a high-dimensional distribution. *Neural computation*, 13(7):1443–1471, 2001.

[13] C. D. Scott and R. D. Nowak. Learning minimum volume sets. *The Journal of Machine Learning Research*, 7:665–704, 2006.

[14] C. Shalizi. *Advanced Data Analysis from an Elementary Point of View*. Cambridge University Press, In press.

[15] M. A. Siddiqui, A. Fern, T. G. Dietterich, and W.-K. Wong. Sequential feature explanations for anomaly detection. In *Proceedings of the ACM SIGKDD workshop on outlier detection and description*. ACM, 2015.

[16] L. Szathmary, A. Napoli, and P. Valtchev. Towards rare itemset mining. In *Tools with Artificial Intelligence, 2007. ICTAI 2007. 19th IEEE International Conference on*, volume 1, pages 305–312. IEEE, 2007.

[17] V. N. Vapnik and V. Vapnik. *Statistical learning theory*, volume 1. Wiley New York, 1998.

[18] K. Wu, K. Zhang, W. Fan, A. Edwards, and P. S. Yu. RS-Forest: a rapid density estimator for streaming anomaly detection. In *Data Mining (ICDM), 2014 IEEE International Conference on*, pages 600–609. IEEE, 2014.

The Deterministic Information Bottleneck

DJ Strouse
Physics Department
Princeton University
dstrouse@princeton.edu

David J Schwab
Physics Department
Northwestern University
david.schwab@northwestern.edu

Abstract

Lossy compression fundamentally involves a decision about what is relevant and what is not. The information bottleneck (IB) by Tishby, Pereira, and Bialek formalized this notion as an information-theoretic optimization problem and proposed an optimal tradeoff between throwing away as many bits as possible, and selectively keeping those that are most important. Here, we introduce an alternative formulation, the deterministic information bottleneck (DIB), that we argue better captures this notion of compression. As suggested by its name, the solution to the DIB problem is a deterministic encoder, as opposed to the stochastic encoder that is optimal under the IB. We then compare the IB and DIB on synthetic data, showing that the IB and DIB perform similarly in terms of the IB cost function, but that the DIB vastly outperforms the IB in terms of the DIB cost function. Moreover, the DIB offered a 1-2 order of magnitude speedup over the IB in our experiments. Our derivation of the DIB also offers a method for continuously interpolating between the soft clustering of the IB and the hard clustering of the DIB.

1 INTRODUCTION

Compression is a ubiquitous task for humans and machines alike [Cover & Thomas (2006), MacKay (2002)]. For example, machines must turn the large pixel grids of color that form pictures into small files capable of being shared quickly on the web [Wallace (1991)], humans must compress the vast stream of ongoing sensory information they receive into small changes in the brain that form memories [Kandel et al (2000)], and data scientists must turn large amounts of high-dimensional and messy data into more manageable and interpretable clusters [MacKay (2002)].

Lossy compression involve an implicit decision about what is relevant and what is not [Cover & Thomas (2006), MacKay (2002)]. In the example of image compression, the algorithms we use deem some features essential to representing the subject matter well, and others are thrown away. In the example of human memory, our brains deem some details important enough to warrant attention, and others are forgotten. And in the example of data clustering, information about some features is preserved in the mapping from data point to cluster ID, while information about others is discarded.

In many cases, the criterion for "relevance" can be described as information about some other variable(s) of interest. Let's call X the signal we are compressing, T the compressed version, Y the other variable of interest, and $I(T;Y)$ the "information" that T has about Y (we will formally define this later). For human memory, X is past sensory input, T the brain's internal representation (e.g. the activity of a neural population, or the strengths of a set of synapses), and Y the features of the future environment that the brain is interested in predicting, such as extrapolating the position of a moving object. Thus, $I(T;Y)$ represents the predictive power of the memories formed [Palmer et al (2015)]. For data clustering, X is the original data, T is the cluster ID, and Y is the target for prediction, for example purchasing or ad-clicking behavior in a user segmentation problem. In summary, a good compression algorithm can be described as a tradeoff between the compression of a signal and the selective maintenance of the "relevant" bits that help predict another signal.

This problem was formalized as the "information bottleneck" (IB) by Tishby, Pereira, and Bialek [Tishby (1999)]. In their formulation, compression was measured by the mutual information $I(X;T)$. This compression metric has its origins in rate-distortion theory and channel coding, where $I(X;T)$ represents the maximal information transfer rate, or capacity, of the communication channel between X and T [Cover & Thomas (2006)]. While this approach has its applications, often one is more interested in directly restricting the amount of resources required to represent T, represented by the entropy $H(T)$. This latter notion comes from the source coding literature and implies a restriction on the *representational cost* of T. In the case of human memory, for example, $H(T)$ would roughly correspond to the number of neurons or synapses required to represent or store a sensory signal X. In the case of data clustering, $H(T)$ is related to the number of clusters.

In the following paper, we introduce an alternative formulation of the IB, replacing the compression measure $I(X;T)$ with $H(T)$, thus emphasizing contraints on representation, rather than communication. We begin with a general introduction to the IB. Then, we introduce our alternative formulation, which we call the deterministic information bottleneck (DIB). Finally, we compare the IB and DIB solutions on synthetic data to help illustrate their differences.

2 THE ORIGINAL INFORMATION BOTTLENECK (IB)

Given the joint distribution $p(x, y)$, the encoding distribution $q(t \mid x)$ is obtained through the following "information bottleneck" (IB) optimization problem:

$$\min_{q(t|x)} L[q(t \mid x)] = I(X;T) - \beta I(T;Y), \tag{1}$$

subject to the Markov constraint $T \leftrightarrow X \leftrightarrow Y$. Here $I(X;T)$ denotes the mutual information between X and T, that is $I(X;T) \equiv H(T) - H(T \mid X) = \sum_{x,t} p(x,t) \log\left(\frac{p(x,t)}{p(x)p(t)}\right) = D_{KL}[p(x,t) \mid p(x)\,p(t)]$,[1] where D_{KL} denotes the Kullback-Leibler divergence.[2] The first term in the cost function is meant to encourage compression, while the second relevance. β is a non-negative free parameter representing the relative importance of compression and relevance, and our solution will be a function of it. The Markov constraint simply enforces the probabilistic graphical structure of the task; the compressed representation T is a (possibly stochastic) function of X and can only get information about Y through X. Note that we are using p to denote distributions that are given and fixed, and q to denote distributions that we are free to change and that are being updated throughout the optimization process.

Through a standard application of variational calculus (see Section 7 for a detailed derivation of the solution to a more general problem introduced below), one finds the formal solution:[3]

$$q(t \mid x) = \frac{q(t)}{Z(x,\beta)} \exp[-\beta D_{\mathrm{KL}}[p(y \mid x) \mid q(y \mid t)]] \tag{2}$$

$$q(y \mid t) = \frac{1}{q(t)} \sum_x q(t \mid x) p(x,y), \tag{3}$$

where $Z(x,\beta) \equiv \exp\left[-\frac{\lambda(x)}{p(x)} - \beta \sum_y p(y \mid x) \log \frac{p(y|x)}{p(y)}\right]$ is a normalization factor, and $\lambda(x)$ is a Lagrange multiplier that enters enforcing normalization of $q(t \mid x)$.[4] To get an intuition for this solution, it is useful to take a clustering perspective - since we are compressing X into T, many X will be mapped to the same T and so we can think of the IB as "clustering" xs into their cluster labels t. The solution $q(t \mid x)$ is then likely to map x to t when $D_{\mathrm{KL}}[p(y \mid x) \mid q(y \mid t)]$ is small, or in other words, when the distributions $p(y \mid x)$ and $q(y \mid t)$ are similar. These distributions are similar to the extent that x and t provide similar information about y. In summary, inputs x get mapped to clusters t that maintain information about y, as was desired.

This solution is "formal" because the first equation depends on the second and vice versa. However, [Tishby (1999)] showed that an iterative approach can be built on the the above equations which provably converges to a local optimum of the IB cost function (eqn 1).

Starting with some initial distributions $q^{(0)}(t \mid x)$, $q^{(0)}(t)$, and $q^{(0)}(y \mid t)$, the nth update is given by:

$$d^{(n-1)}(x,t) \equiv D_{\mathrm{KL}}\left[p(y \mid x) \mid q^{(n-1)}(y \mid t)\right] \tag{4}$$

$$q^{(n)}(t \mid x) = \frac{q^{(n-1)}(t)}{Z(x,\beta)} \exp\left[-\beta d^{(n-1)}(x,t)\right] \tag{5}$$

$$q^{(n)}(t) = \sum_x p(x)\, q^{(n)}(t \mid x) \tag{6}$$

$$q^{(n)}(y \mid t) = \frac{1}{q^{(n)}(t)} \sum_x q^{(n)}(t \mid x)\, p(x,y). \tag{7}$$

[1]Implicit in the summation here, we have assumed that X, Y, and T are discrete. We will be keeping this assumption throughout for convenience of notation, but note that the IB generalizes naturally to X, Y, and T continuous by simply replacing the sums with integrals (see, for example, [Chechik et al (2005)]).

[2]For those unfamiliar with it, mutual information is a very general measure of how related two variables are. Classic correlation measures typically assume a certain form of the relationship between two variables, say linear, whereas mutual information is agnostic as to the details of the relationship. One intuitive picture comes from the entropy decomposition: $I(X;Y) \equiv H(X) - H(X \mid Y)$. Since entropy measures uncertainty, mutual information measures the *reduction in uncertainty* in one variable when observing the other. Moreover, it is symmetric ($I(X;Y) = I(Y;X)$), so the information is *mutual*. Another intuitive picture comes from the D_{KL} form: $I(X;Y) \equiv D_{KL}[p(x,y) \mid p(x)\,p(y)]$. Since D_{KL} measures the distance between two probability distributions, the mutual information quantifies how far the relationship between x and y is from a probabilistically independent one, that is how far the joint $p(x,y)$ is from the factorized $p(x)\,p(y)$.

[3]For the reader familiar with rate-distortion theory, eqn 2 can be viewed as the solution to a rate-distortion problem with distortion measure given by the KL-divergence term in the exponent.

[4]More explicitly, our cost function L also implicitly includes a term $\sum_x \lambda(x)\left[1 - \sum_t q(t|x)\right]$ and this is where $\lambda(x)$ comes in to the equation. See Section 7 for details.

Note that the first pair of equations is the only "meaty" bit; the rest are just there to enforce consistency with the laws of probability (e.g. that marginals are related to joints as they should be). In principle, with no proof of convergence to a global optimum, it might be possible for the solution obtained to vary with the initialization, but in practice, the cost function is "smooth enough" that this does not seem to happen. This algorithm is summarized in algorithm 1. Note that while the general solution is iterative, there is at least one known case in which an analytic solution is possible, name when X and Y are jointly Gaussian [Chechik et al (2005)].

Algorithm 1 - The information bottleneck (IB) method.

Given $p(x, y)$, $\beta \geq 0$
Initialize $q^{(0)}(t \mid x)$ and set $n = 0$
$q^{(0)}(t) = \sum_x p(x)\, q^{(0)}(t \mid x)$
$q^{(0)}(y \mid t) = \frac{1}{q^{(0)}(t)} \sum_x p(x, y)\, q^{(0)}(t \mid x)$
while not converged **do**
    $n = n + 1$
    $d^{(n-1)}(x, t) \equiv D_{\mathrm{KL}}\left[p(y \mid x) \mid q^{(n-1)}(y \mid t)\right]$
    $q^{(n)}(t \mid x) = \frac{q^{(n-1)}(t)}{Z(x,\beta)} \exp\left[-\beta d^{(n-1)}(x, t)\right]$
    $q^{(n)}(t) = \sum_x p(x)\, q^{(n)}(t \mid x)$
    $q^{(n)}(y \mid t) = \frac{1}{q^{(n)}(t)} \sum_x q^{(n)}(t \mid x)\, p(x, y)$
end while

In summary, given the joint distribution $p(x, y)$, the IB method extracts a compressive encoder $q(t \mid x)$ that selectively maintains the bits from X that are informative about Y. As the encoder is a function of the free parameter β, we can visualize the entire family of solutions on a curve (figure 1), showing the tradeoff between compression (on the x-axis) and relevance (on the y-axis). For small β, compression is more important than prediction and we find ourselves at the bottom left of the curve in the high compression, low prediction regime. As β increases, prediction becomes more important relative to compression, and we see that both $I(X;T)$ and $I(T;Y)$ increase. At some point, $I(T;Y)$ saturates, because there is no more information about Y that can be extracted from X (either because $I(T;Y)$ has reached $I(X;Y)$ or because T has too small cardinality). Note that the region below the curve is shaded because this area is feasible; for suboptimal $q(t \mid x)$, solutions will lie in this region. Optimal solutions will of course lie on the curve, and no solutions will lie above the curve.

Additional work on the IB has highlighted its relationship with maximum likelihood on a multinomial mixture model [Slonim & Weiss (2002)] and canonical correlation analysis [Creutzig et al (2009)] (and therefore linear Gaussian models [Bach & Jordan (2005)] and slow feature analysis [Turner & Sahani (2007)]). Applications have included speech recognition [Hecht & Tishby (2005), Hecht & Tishby (2008), Hecht et al (2009)], topic modeling [Slonim & Tishby (2000), Slonim & Tishby (2001), Bekkerman et al (2001), Bekkerman et al (2003)], and neural coding [Schneidman et al (2002), Palmer et al (2015)]. Most recently, the IB has even been proposed as a method for benchmarking the performance of deep neural networks [Tishby & Zaslavsky (2015)].

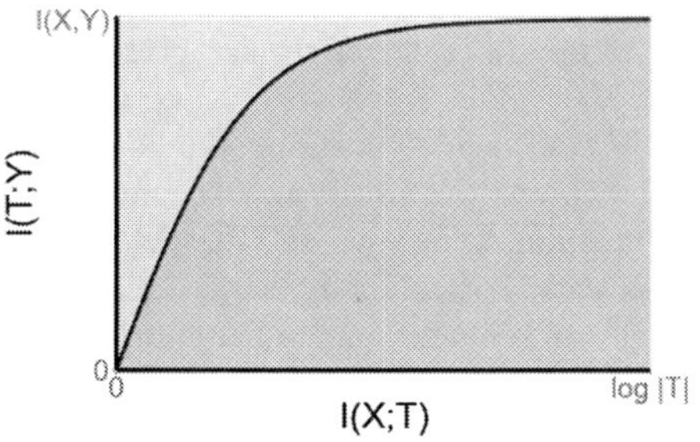

Figure 1: **An illustrative IB curve.** $I(T;Y)$ is the relevance term from eqn 1; $I(X;T)$ is the compression term. $I(X;Y)$ is an upper bound on $I(T;Y)$ since T only gets its information about Y via X. $\log(|T|)$, where $|T|$ is the cardinality of the compression variable, is a bound on $I(X;T)$ since $I(X;T) = H(T) - H(T \mid X) \leq H(T) \leq \log(|T|)$.

3 THE DETERMINISTIC INFORMATION BOTTLENECK (DIB)

Our motivation for introducing an alternative formulation of the information bottleneck is rooted in the "compression term" of the IB cost function; there, the minimization of the mutual information $I(X;T)$ represents compression. As discussed above, this measure of compression comes from the channel coding literature and implies a restriction on the *communication cost* between X and T. Here, we are interested in the source coding notion of compression, which implies a restriction on the *representational cost* of T. For example, in neuroscience, there is a long history of work on "redundancy reduction" in the brain in the form of minimizing $H(T)$ [Barlow (1981), Barlow (2001), Barlow (2001)].

Let us call the original IB cost function L_{IB}, that is $L_{\mathrm{IB}} \equiv I(X;T) - \beta I(T;Y)$. We now introduce the deterministic information bottleneck (DIB) cost function:

$$L_{\mathrm{DIB}}[q(t \mid x)] \equiv H(T) - \beta I(T;Y)\,, \tag{8}$$

which is to be minimized over $q(t \mid x)$ and subject to the same Markov constraint as the original formulation (eqn 1). The "deterministic" in its name will become clear below.

To see the distinction between the two cost functions, note that:

$$L_{\mathrm{IB}} - L_{\mathrm{DIB}} = I(X;T) - H(T) \tag{9}$$
$$= -H(T \mid X)\,, \tag{10}$$

where we have used the decomposition of the mutual information $I(X;T) = H(T) - H(T \mid X)$. $H(T \mid X)$ is sometimes called the "noise entropy" and measures the stochasticity in the mapping from X to T. Since we are minimizing these cost functions, this means that the IB cost function *encourages* stochasticity in the encoding distribution $q(t \mid x)$ relative to the DIB cost function. In fact, we will see that by removing this encouragement of stochasticity, the DIB problem actually produces a deterministic encoding distribution, i.e. an encoding *function*, hence the "deterministic" in its name.

Naively taking the same variational calculus approach as for the IB problem, one cannot solve the DIB problem.[5] To make this problem tractable, we are going to define a family of cost functions of which the IB and DIB cost functions are limiting cases. That family, indexed by α, is defined as:[6]

$$L_\alpha \equiv H(T) - \alpha H(T \mid X) - \beta I(T;Y) . \qquad (11)$$

Clearly, $L_{\text{IB}} = L_1$. However, instead of looking at L_{DIB} as the $\alpha = 0$ case, we'll define the DIB solution $q_{\text{DIB}}(t \mid x)$ as the $\alpha \to 0$ limit of the solution to the generalized problem $q_\alpha(t \mid x)$:[7]

$$q_{\text{DIB}}(t \mid x) \equiv \lim_{\alpha \to 0} q_\alpha(t \mid x) . \qquad (12)$$

Taking the variational calculus approach to minimizing L_α (under the Markov constraint), we get the following solution for the encoding distribution (see Section 7 for the derivation and explicit form of the normalization factor $Z(x, a, \beta)$):

$$d_\alpha(x,t) \equiv D_{\text{KL}}[p(y \mid x) \mid q_\alpha(y \mid t)] \qquad (13)$$

$$\ell_{\alpha,\beta}(x,t) \equiv \log q_\alpha(t) - \beta d_\alpha(x,t) \qquad (14)$$

$$q_\alpha(t \mid x) = \frac{1}{Z(x,\alpha,\beta)} \exp\left[\frac{1}{\alpha}\ell_{\alpha,\beta}(x,t)\right] \qquad (15)$$

$$q_\alpha(y \mid t) = \frac{1}{q_\alpha(t)} \sum_x q_\alpha(t \mid x)\, p(x,y) . \qquad (16)$$

[5] When you take the variational derivative of L_{DIB} + Lagrange multiplier term with respect to $q(t \mid x)$ and set it to zero, you get no explicit $q(t \mid x)$ term, and it is therefore not obvious how to solve these equations. We cannot rule that that approach is possible, of course; we have just here taken a different route.

[6] Note that for $\alpha < 1$, we cannot allow T to be continuous since $H(T)$ can become infinitely negative, and the optimal solution in that case will trivially be a delta function over a single value of T for all X, across all values of β. This is in constrast to the IB, which can handle continuous T. In any case, we continue to assume discrete X, Y, and T for convenience.

[7] Note a subtlety here that we cannot claim that the q_{DIB} is the solution to L_{DIB}, for although $L_{\text{DIB}} = \lim_{\alpha \to 0} L_\alpha$ and $q_{\text{DIB}} = \lim_{\alpha \to 0} q_\alpha$, the solution of the limit need not be equal to the limit of the solution. It would, however, be surprising if that were not the case.

Note that the last equation is just eqn 3, since this just follows from the Markov constraint. With $\alpha = 1$, we can see that the other three equations just become the IB solution from eqn 2, as should be the case.

Before we take the $\alpha \to 0$ limit, note that we can now write a generalized IB iterative algorithm (indexed by α) which includes the original as a special case ($\alpha = 1$):

$$d_\alpha^{(n-1)}(x,t) \equiv D_{\text{KL}}\left[p(y \mid x) \mid q_\alpha^{(n-1)}(y \mid t)\right] \qquad (17)$$

$$\ell_{\alpha,\beta}^{(n-1)}(x,t) \equiv \log q_\alpha^{(n-1)}(t) - \beta d_\alpha^{(n-1)}(x,t) \qquad (18)$$

$$q_\alpha^{(n)}(t \mid x) = \frac{1}{Z(x,\alpha,\beta)} \exp\left[\frac{1}{\alpha}\ell_{\alpha,\beta}^{(n-1)}(x,t)\right] \qquad (19)$$

$$q_\alpha^{(n)}(t) = \sum_x p(x)\, q_\alpha^{(n)}(t \mid x) \qquad (20)$$

$$q_\alpha^{(n)}(y \mid t) = \frac{1}{q_\alpha^{(n)}(t)} \sum_x q_\alpha^{(n)}(t \mid x)\, p(x,y) . \qquad (21)$$

This generalized algorithm can be used in its own right, however we will not discuss that option further here.

For now, we take the limit $\alpha \to 0$ and see that something interesting happens with $q_\alpha(t \mid x)$ - the argument of the exponential begins to blow up. For a fixed x, this means that $q(t \mid x)$ will collapse into a delta function at the value of t which maximizes $\log q(t) - \beta D_{\text{KL}}[p(y \mid x) \mid q(y \mid t)]$. That is:

$$\lim_{\alpha \to 0} q_\alpha(t \mid x) = f : X \to T, \qquad (22)$$

where:

$$f(x) \equiv t^* = \operatorname*{argmax}_t \ell(x,t) \qquad (23)$$

$$\ell(x,t) \equiv \log q(t) - \beta D_{\text{KL}}[p(y \mid x) \mid q(y \mid t)] . \qquad (24)$$

So, as anticipated, the solution to the DIB problem is a deterministic encoding distribution. The $\log q(t)$ above encourages that we use as few values of t as possible, via a "rich-get-richer" scheme that assigns each x preferentially to a t already with many xs assigned to it. The KL divergence term, as in the original IB problem, just makes sure we pick ts which retain as much information from x about y as possible. The parameter β, as in the original problem, controls the tradeoff between how much we value compression and prediction.

Also like in the original problem, the solution above is only a formal solution, since eqn 15 depends on eqn 16 and vice versa. So we will again need to take an iterative approach; in analogy to the IB case, we repeat the following updates to convergence (from some initialization):[8]

[8] Note that, if at step m no xs are assigned to a particular $t = t^*$, then $q_m(t^*) = 0$ and for all future steps $n > m$, no xs will

$$d^{(n-1)}(x,t) \equiv D_{\text{KL}}\Big[p(y \mid x) \mid q^{(n-1)}(y \mid t)\Big] \tag{25}$$

$$\ell_\beta^{(n-1)}(x,t) \equiv \log q(t) - \beta d^{(n-1)}(x,t) \tag{26}$$

$$f^{(n)}(x) = \underset{t}{\text{argmax}}\ \ell_\beta^{(n-1)}(x,t) \tag{27}$$

$$q^{(n)}(t \mid x) = \delta\Big(t - f^{(n)}(x)\Big) \tag{28}$$

$$q^{(n)}(t) = \sum_x q^{(n)}(t \mid x)\, p(x) \tag{29}$$

$$= \sum_{x:f^{(n)}(x)=t} p(x) \tag{30}$$

$$q^{(n)}(y \mid t) = \frac{1}{q^{(n)}(t)} \sum_x q^{(n)}(t \mid x)\, p(x,y) \tag{31}$$

$$= \frac{\sum_{x:f^{(n)}(x)=t} p(x,y)}{\sum_{x:f^{(n)}(x)=t} p(x)}. \tag{32}$$

This process is summarized in algorithm 2.

Like with the IB, the DIB solutions can be plotted as a function of β. However, in this case, it is more natural to plot $I(T;Y)$ as a function of $H(T)$, rather than $I(X;T)$. That said, in order to compare the IB and DIB, they need to be plotted in the same plane. When plotting in the $I(X;T)$ plane, the DIB curve will of course lie below the IB curve, since in this plane, the IB curve is optimal; the opposite will be true when plotting in the $H(T)$ plane. Comparisons with experimental data can be performed in either plane.

Algorithm 2 - The deterministic information bottleneck (DIB) method.

Given $p(x,y)$, $\beta \geq 0$
Initialize $f^{(0)}(x)$ and set $n = 0$
$q^{(0)}(t) = \sum_{x:f^{(0)}(x)=t} p(x)$
$q^{(0)}(y \mid t) = \frac{\sum_{x:f^{(0)}(x)=t} p(x,y)}{\sum_{x:f^{(0)}(x)=t} p(x)}$
while not converged **do**
    $n = n + 1$
    $d^{(n-1)}(x,t) \equiv D_{\text{KL}}\big[p(y \mid x) \mid q^{(n-1)}(y \mid t)\big]$
    $\ell_\beta^{(n-1)}(x,t) \equiv \log q(t) - \beta d^{(n-1)}(x,t)$
    $f^{(n)}(x) = \underset{t}{\text{argmax}}\ \ell_\beta^{(n-1)}(x,t)$
    $q^{(n)}(t) = \sum_{x:f^{(n)}(x)=t} p(x)$
    $q^{(n)}(y \mid t) = \frac{\sum_{x:f^{(n)}(x)=t} p(x,y)}{\sum_{x:f^{(n)}(x)=t} p(x)}$
end while

ever again be assigned to t^* since $\log q_n(t^*) = -\infty$. In other words, the number of ts "in use" can only decrease during the iterative algorithm above (or remain constant). Thus, it seems plausible that our solution will not depend on the cardinality of T, provided it is chosen to be large enough.

4 COMPARISON OF IB AND DIB

To get an idea of how the IB and DIB solutions differ in practice, we generated a series of random joint distributions $p(x,y)$, solved for the IB and DIB solutions for each, and compared them in both the IB and DIB plane. To generate the $p(x,y)$, we first sampled $p(x)$ from a symmetric Dirichlet distribution with concentration parameter α_x (so $p(x) \sim \text{Dir}[\alpha_x]$), and then sampled each row of $p(y \mid x)$ from another symmetric Dirichlet distribution with concentration parameter α_y (so $p(y \mid x) \sim \text{Dir}[\alpha_y]\,, \forall x$). Since the number of clusters in use for both IB and DIB can only decrease from iteration to iteration (see footnote 8), we always initialized $|T| = |X|$.[9] For the DIB, we initialized the cluster assignments to be as even across the cluster as possible, i.e. each data points belonged to its own cluster. For IB, we initalized the cluster assignments to a normalized draw of a uniform random vector.

An illustrative pair of solutions is shown in figure 2. The key feature to note is that, while performance of the IB and DIB solutions are very similar in the IB plane, their behavior differs drastically in the DIB plane.

Perhaps most unintuitive is the behavior of the IB solution in the DIB plane. To understand this behavior, recall that the IB's compression term is the mutual information $I(X,T) = H(T) - H(T \mid X)$. This term is minimized by any $q(t \mid x)$ that maps ts independently of xs. Consider two extremes of such mappings. One is to map all values of X to a single value of T; this leads to $H(T) = H(T \mid X) = I(X,T) = 0$. The other is to map each value of X uniformly across all values of T; this leads to $H(T) = H(T \mid X) = \log |T|$ and $I(X,T) = 0$. In our initial studies, the IB consistently took the latter approach.[10] Since the DIB cost function favors the former approach (and indeed the DIB solution follows this approach), the IB consistently performs poorly by the DIB's standards. This difference is especially apparent at small β, where the compression term matters most, and as β increases, the DIB and IB solutions converge in the DIB plane.

To encourage the IB into more DIB-like behavior, we next altered our initialization scheme of $q(t \mid x)$. Originally, we used a normalized vector of uniform random numbers for each x. Next, we tried a series of delta-like functions, for which $q(t \mid x) = p_0$ for all x and one t, and the rest of the entries were uniform with a small amount of noise to break symmetry. The intended effect was to start the IB closer to solutions in which all data points were mapped to a single cluster. Results are shown in figure 3. While the different initialization schemes didn't change behavior in

[9] An even more efficient setting might be to set the cardinality of T based on the entropy of X, say $|T| = \text{ceiling}(\exp(H(X)))$, but we didn't experiment with this.

[10] Intuitively, this approach is "more random" and is therefore easier to stumble upon during optimization.

the IB plane, we can see a gradual shift of the IB towards DIB-like behavior in the DIB plane as $p_0 \rightarrow 1$, i.e. the initialization scheme approaches a true delta. However, the IB still fails to reach the level of performance of the DIB, especially for large β, where the effect of the initialization washes out completely.

To summarize, the IB and DIB perform similarly by the IB standards, but the DIB tends to outperform the IB dramatically by the DIB's standards. Careful initialization of the IB can make up some of the difference, but not all.

It is also worth noting that, across all the datasets we tested, the DIB took 1-2 orders of magnitude fewer steps and time to converge, as illustrated in figure 4. About half of IB fits took at least an hour, while nearly a quarter took at least five hours. Contrast this with about half of DIB fits taking only five minutes, and more than 80% finishing within ten minutes. Put another way, about half of all DIB fits finished ten times faster than their IB counterpart, while about a quarter finished fifty times faster.

Note that the computational advantage of the DIB over the IB may vary by dataset and stopping criteria. In our case, we defined convergence for both algorithms as a change in cost function of less than 10^8 from one step to the next.

5 RELATED WORK

The DIB is not the first hard clustering version of IB.[11] Indeed, the agglomerative information bottleneck (AIB) [Slonim & Tishby (1999)] also produces hard clustering and was introduced soon after the IB. Thus, it is important to distinguish between the two approaches. AIB is a bottom-up, greedy method which starts with all data points belonging to their own clusters and iteratively merges clusters in a way which maximizes the gain in relevant information. It was explicitly designed to produce a hard clustering. DIB is a top-down method derived from a cost function that was not designed to produce a hard clustering. Our starting point was to alter the IB cost function to match the source coding notion of compression. The emergence of hard clustering in DIB is itself a result. Thus, while AIB does provide a hard clustering version of IB, DIB contributes the following in addition: 1) Our study emphasizes why a stochastic encoder is optimal for IB, namely due to the noise entropy term. The optimality of a stochastic encoder has been, for many, neither obvious nor necessarily desirable. 2) Our study provides a principled, top-down derivation of a hard clustering version of IB, based upon an intuitive change to the cost function. 3) Our non-trivial derivation also provides a cost-function and solution which interpolates between DIB and IB, by adding back the noise entropy continuously, i.e. with $0 < \alpha < 1$. This interpolation may be viewed as adding a regularization term to DIB. We are in fact currently exploring whether this type of regularization may be useful in dealing with finitely sampled data. Another interpretation of the cost function with intermediate α is as a penalty on *both* the mutual information between X and T as well as the entropy of the compression, $H(T)$. 4) It is likely that DIB offers a computational advantage to AIB. In the AIB paper, the authors say, "The main disadvantage of this method is computational, since it starts from the limit of a cluster per each member of the set X." In our experiments, we find that DIB is much more efficient than IB. Therefore, we expect that DIB will offer a considerable advantage in efficiency to AIB. However, we have not yet tested this.

[11] In fact, even the IB itself produces a hard clustering in the large β limit. However, it trivially assigns all data points to their own clusters.

The original IB also provides a deterministic encoding upon taking the limit $\beta \rightarrow \infty$ that corresponds to the causal-state partition of histories [Still et al (2010)]. However, this is the limit of no compression, whereas our approach allows for an entire family of deterministic encoders with varying degrees of compression.

6 DISCUSSION

Here we have introduced the deterministic information bottleneck (DIB) as an alternative to the information bottleneck (IB) for compression and clustering. We have argued that the DIB cost function better embodies the goal of lossy compression of relevant information, and shown that it leads to a non-trivial deterministic version of the IB. We have compared the DIB and IB solutions on synthetic data and found that, in our experiments, the DIB performs nearly identically to the IB in terms of the IB cost function, but far superior in terms of its own cost function. We also noted that the DIB achieved this performance at a computational efficiency 1-2 orders of magnitude better than the IB.

Of course, in addition to the studies with synthetic data here, it is important to compare the DIB and IB on real world datasets as well to see whether the DIB's apparent advantages hold. The linearity of the IB and DIB curves displayed above are indeed a signature of relatively simple data with not particularly complicated tradeoffs between compression and relevance.

One particular application of interest is maximally informative clustering. Previous work has, for example, offered a principled way of choosing the number of clusters based on the finiteness of the data [Still & Bialek (2004)]. Similarly interesting results may exist for the DIB, as well as relationships to other popular clustering algorithms such as k-means. More generally, there are learning theory results showing generalization bounds on IB for which an analog on DIB would be interesting as well [Shamir et al (2010)].

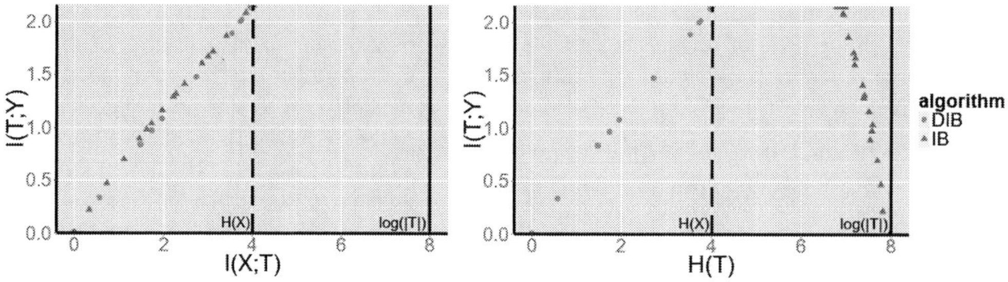

Figure 2: **Example IB and DIB solutions.** *Left*: IB plane. *Right*: DIB plane. Upper limit of the y-axes is $I(X, Y)$, since this is the maximal possible value of $I(T;Y)$. Solid vertical line marks $\log(|T|)$, since this is the maximal possible value of $H(T)$ and $I(X, T)$ (the latter being true since $I(X, T)$ is bounded above by both $H(T)$ and $H(X)$, and $|T| < |X|$). The dashed vertical line marks $H(X)$, which is both an upper bound for $I(X, T)$ and a natural comparison for $H(T)$ (since to place each data point in its own cluster, we need $H(T) = H(X)$). Here, $|X| = |Y| = 1024$ and $|T| = 256$.

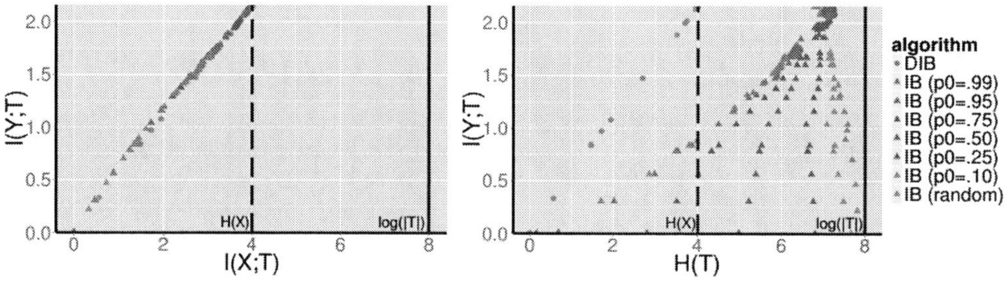

Figure 3: **Example IB and DIB solutions across different IB initializations.** Details identical to figure 2, except colors represent different initializations for the IB, as described in the text. "IB (random)" denotes the original initialization scheme of a normalized vector of uniform random numbers.

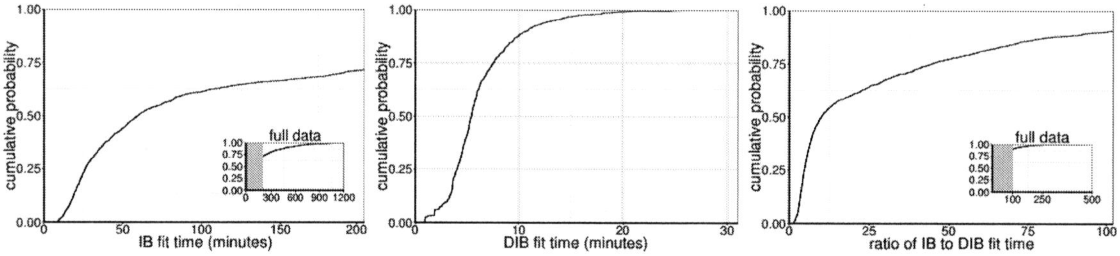

Figure 4: **Fit times for IB and DIB, as well as their ratios.** *Left*: cumulative distribution of IB fit times. Data shown here are for the original initialization of IB, though the delta-like initializations lead to nearly identical results. Mean fit time was 171 minutes. *Center*: cumulative distribution of DIB fit times. Mean fit time was 6 minutes. *Right*: cumultative distribution of ratios of IB to DIB fit times. Ratios are for the bth value of β for DIB and the bth value of β for IB, though those values of β are not necessarily the same. Both algorithms were fit to the same data. The IB fits are those resulting from the original random intialization, though the delta-like initializations lead to nearly identical results.

Another potential area of application is modeling the extraction of predictive information in the brain (which is one particular example in a long line of work on the exploitation of environmental statistics by the brain [Barlow (1981), Barlow (2001), Barlow (2001), Atick & Redlich (1992), Olshausen & Field (1996), Olshausen & Field (1997), Simoncelli & Olshausen (2001), Olshausen & Field (2004)]). There, X would be the stimulus at time t, Y the stimulus a short time in the future $t+\tau$, and T the activity of a population of sensory neurons. One could even consider neurons deeper in the brain by allowing X and Y to correspond not to an external stimulus, but to the activity of upstream neurons. An analysis of this nature using retinal data was recently performed with the IB [Palmer et al (2015)]. It would be interesting to see if the same data corresponds better to the behavior of the DIB, particularly in the DIB plane where the IB and DIB differ dramatically.

7 APPENDIX: DERIVATION OF GENERALIZED IB SOLUTION

Given $p(x, y)$ and subject to the Markov constraint $T \leftrightarrow X \leftrightarrow Y$, the generalized IB problem is:

$$\min_{q(t|x)} L[q(t \mid x)] = H(T) - \alpha H(T \mid X) - \beta I(T;Y) - \sum_{x,t} \lambda(x)\, q(t \mid x)\,, \tag{33}$$

where we have now included the Lagrange multiplier term (which enforces normalization of $q(t \mid x)$) explicitly. The Markov constraint implies the following factorizations:

$$q(t \mid y) = \sum_x q(t \mid x)\, p(x \mid y) \tag{34}$$

$$q(t) = \sum_x q(t \mid x)\, p(x)\,, \tag{35}$$

which give us the following useful derivatives:

$$\frac{\delta q(t \mid y)}{\delta q(t \mid x)} = p(x \mid y) \tag{36}$$

$$\frac{\delta q(t)}{\delta q(t \mid x)} = p(x)\,. \tag{37}$$

Now taking the derivative of the cost function with respect to the encoding distribution, we get:

$$\begin{aligned}\frac{\delta L}{\delta q(t \mid x)} &= -\frac{\delta}{\delta q(t \mid x)} \sum_t q(t) \log q(t) \\ &\quad - \frac{\delta}{\delta q(t \mid x)} \sum_{x,t} \lambda(x)\, q(t \mid x) \\ &\quad + \alpha \frac{\delta}{\delta q(t \mid x)} \sum_{x,t} q(t \mid x)\, p(x) \log q(t \mid x) \\ &\quad - \beta \frac{\delta}{\delta q(t \mid x)} \sum_{y,t} q(t \mid y)\, p(y) \log \left[\frac{q(t \mid y)}{q(t)}\right]\end{aligned} \tag{38}$$

$$\begin{aligned}&= -\log q(t) \frac{\delta q(t)}{\delta q(t \mid x)} - q(t) \frac{\delta \log q(t)}{\delta q(t \mid x)} \\ &\quad - \lambda(x) \frac{\delta q(t \mid x)}{\delta q(t \mid x)} \\ &\quad + \alpha \left[p(x) \log q(t \mid x) \frac{\delta q(t \mid x)}{\delta q(t \mid x)} \right. \\ &\quad \left. + q(t \mid x)\, p(x) \frac{\delta \log q(t \mid x)}{\delta q(t \mid x)}\right] \\ &\quad - \beta \sum_y \left[p(y) \log \left[\frac{q(t \mid y)}{q(t)}\right] \frac{\delta q(t \mid y)}{\delta q(t \mid x)}\right] \\ &\quad + \beta \sum_y \left[q(t \mid y)\, p(y) \frac{\delta \log q(t \mid y)}{\delta q(t \mid x)} \right. \\ &\quad \left. + q(t \mid y)\, p(y) \frac{\delta \log q(t)}{\delta q(t \mid x)}\right]\end{aligned} \tag{39}$$

$$\begin{aligned}&= -p(x) \log q(t) - p(x) - \lambda(x) \\ &\quad + \alpha \left[p(x) \log q(t \mid x) + p(x)\right] \\ &\quad - \beta \sum_y \left[p(y) \log \left[\frac{q(t \mid y)}{q(t)}\right] p(x \mid y) \right. \\ &\quad \left. + p(y)\, p(x \mid y) - q(t \mid y)\, p(y) \frac{p(x)}{q(t)}\right]\end{aligned} \tag{40}$$

$$\begin{aligned}&= -p(x) \log q(t) - p(x) - \lambda(x) \\ &\quad + \alpha \left[p(x) \log q(t \mid x) + p(x)\right] \\ &\quad - \beta p(x) \left[\sum_y p(y \mid x) \log \left[\frac{q(t \mid y)}{q(t)}\right] \right. \\ &\quad \left. + \sum_y p(y \mid x) - \sum_y q(y \mid t)\right]\end{aligned} \tag{41}$$

$$\begin{aligned}&= p(x) \left[-1 - \log q(t) - \frac{\lambda(x)}{p(x)} \right. \\ &\quad + \alpha \log q(t \mid x) + \alpha \\ &\quad \left. - \beta \left[\sum_y p(y \mid x) \log \left[\frac{q(t \mid y)}{q(t)}\right]\right]\right].\end{aligned} \tag{42}$$

Setting this to zero implies that:

$$\alpha \log q(t \mid x) = 1 - \alpha + \log q(t) + \frac{\lambda(x)}{p(x)} + \beta \left[\sum_y p(y \mid x) \log \left[\frac{q(t \mid y)}{q(t)} \right] \right]. \tag{43}$$

We want to rewrite the β term as a KL divergence. First, we will need that $\log\left[\frac{q(t|y)}{q(t)}\right] = \log\left[\frac{q(t,y)}{q(t)p(y)}\right] = \log\left[\frac{q(y|t)}{p(y)}\right]$. Second, we will add and subtract $\beta \sum_y p(y \mid x) \log\left[\frac{p(y|x)}{p(y)}\right]$. This gives us:

$$\begin{aligned} \alpha \log q(t \mid x) = 1 - \alpha + \log q(t) + \frac{\lambda(x)}{p(x)} \\ + \beta \sum_y p(y \mid x) \log \left[\frac{p(y \mid x)}{p(y)} \right] \\ - \beta \left[\sum_y p(y \mid x) \log \left[\frac{p(y \mid x)}{q(y \mid t)} \right] \right]. \end{aligned} \tag{44}$$

The second β term is now just $D_{\mathrm{KL}}[p(y \mid x) \mid q(y \mid t)]$. This leaves us with the equation:

$$\log q(t \mid x) = z(x, \alpha, \beta) + \frac{1}{\alpha} \log q(t) - \frac{\beta}{\alpha} D_{\mathrm{KL}}[p(y \mid x) \mid q(y \mid t)], \tag{45}$$

where we have divided both sides by α and absorbed all the terms that don't depend on t into the factor:

$$z(x, \alpha, \beta) \equiv \frac{1}{\alpha} - 1 + \frac{\lambda(x)}{\alpha p(x)} + \frac{\beta}{\alpha} \sum_y p(y \mid x) \log \left[\frac{p(y \mid x)}{p(y)} \right]. \tag{46}$$

Exponentiating both sides to solve for $q(t \mid x)$, we get:

$$d(x,t) \equiv D_{\mathrm{KL}}[p(y \mid x) \mid q(y \mid t)] \tag{47}$$

$$\ell_\beta(x,t) \equiv \log q(t) - \beta d(x,t) \tag{48}$$

$$q(t \mid x) = \frac{1}{Z} \exp\left[\frac{1}{\alpha} \ell_\beta(x,t)\right] \tag{49}$$

where:

$$Z(x, \alpha, \beta) \equiv \exp[-z] \tag{50}$$

is just a normalization factor. Now that we're done with the general derivation, let's add a subscript to the solution to distinguish it from the special cases of the IB and DIB.

$$q_\alpha(t \mid x) = \frac{1}{Z} \exp\left[\frac{1}{\alpha} \ell_\beta(x,t)\right]. \tag{51}$$

The IB solution is then:

$$q_{\mathrm{IB}}(t \mid x) = q_{\alpha=1}(t \mid x) \tag{52}$$

$$= \frac{q(t)}{Z} \exp[-\beta d(x,t)], \tag{53}$$

while the DIB solution is:

$$q_{\mathrm{DIB}}(t \mid x) = \lim_{\alpha \to 0} q_\alpha(t \mid x) \tag{54}$$

$$= \delta(t - t^*(x)), \tag{55}$$

with:

$$t^*(x) = \operatorname*{argmax}_t \ \ell_\beta(x,t). \tag{56}$$

Acknowledgements

The authors would like to thank Richard Turner, Bill Bialek, Stephanie Palmer, and Gordon Berman for helpful conversations, and the Hertz Foundation, DOE CSGF (DJ Strouse), and NIH grant K25 GM098875-06 (David Schwab) for funding.

References

Atick, J.J. & Redlich, A.N. (1992). *What Does the Retina Know about Natural Scenes?* Neur Comp, 4, 196-210. 6

Bach, F.R. & Jordan, M.I. (2005). *A probabilistic interpretation of canonical correlation analysis.* Tech Report. 2

Barlow, H. (1981). *Critical Limiting Factors in the Design of the Eye and Visual Cortex.* Proc of the Royal Society B: Biological Sciences, 212(1186), 1–34. 3, 6

Barlow, H. (2001). *Redundancy reduction revisited.* Network: Comp in Neural Systems, 12(3), 241–253. 3, 6

Barlow, H. (2001). *The exploitation of regularities in the environment by the brain.* BBS 24, 602–607. 3, 6

Bekkerman, R., El-Yaniv, R., Tishby, N., & Winter, Y. (2001). *On feature distributional clustering for text categorization.* SIGIR. 2

Bekkerman, R., El-Yaniv, R., & Tishby, N. (2003). *Distributional word clusters vs. words for text categorization.* JMLR, 3, 1183-1208. 2

Chechik, G., Globerson, A., Tishby, N., & Weiss, Y. (2005). *Information Bottleneck for Gaussian Variables.* NIPS. 1, 2

Cover, T.M. & Thomas, J.A. (2006). *Elements of Information Theory.* John Wiley & Sons, Inc. 1

Creutzig, F., Globerson, A., & Tishby, N. (2009). *Past-future information bottleneck in dynamical systems*. Physical Review E, 79(4). 2

Hecht, R.M. & Tishby, N. (2005). *Extraction of relevant speech features using the information bottleneck method.* InterSpeech. 2

Hecht, R.M. & Tishby, N. (2007). *Extraction of relevant Information using the Information Bottleneck Method for Speaker Recognition*. InterSpeech. 2

Hecht, R.M., Noor, E., & Tishby, N. (2009). *Speaker recognition by Gaussian information bottleneck*. InterSpeech. 2

Kandel, E.R., Schwartz, J.H., Jessell, T.M., Siegelbaum, S.A., & Hudspeth, A.J. (2013). *Principles of Neural Science*. New York: McGraw-Hill. 1

Mackay, D. (2002). *Information Theory, Inference, & Learning Algorithms*. Cambridge University Press. 1

Olshausen, B.A. & Field, D.J. (1996). *Emergence of simple-cell receptive field properties by learning a sparse code for natural images*. Nature, 381(6583), 607–609. 6

Olshausen, B.A. & Field, D.J. (1997). *Sparse coding with an overcomplete basis set: A strategy employed by V1?* Vision Research. 6

Olshausen, B.A. & Field, D.J. (2004). *Sparse coding of sensory inputs*. Curr Op in Neurobio, 14(4), 481–487. 6

Palmer, S.E., Marre, O., Berry, M.J., & Bialek, W. (2015). *Predictive information in a sensory population*. PNAS, 112(22), 6908–6913. 1, 2, 6

Schneidman, E., Slonim, N., Tishby, N., deRuyter van Steveninck, R., & Bialek, W. (2002). *Analyzing neural codes using the information bottleneck method*. NIPS. 2

Shamir, O., Sabato, S., & Tishby, N. (2010). *Learning and Generalization with the Information Bottleneck*. Theoretical Comp Sci, Vol 411, Issu 29-30, Pgs 2696-2711. 6

Simoncelli, E. P., & Olshausen, B. A. (2001). *Natural image statistics and neural representation*. Annual Review of Neuroscience. 6

Slonim, N. & Tishby, N. (1999). *Agglomerative information bottleneck*. NIPS. 5

Slonim, N. & Tishby, N. (2000). *Document clustering using word clusters via the information bottleneck method*. SIGIR. 2

Slonim, N. & Tishby, N. (2001). *The Power of Word Clusters for Text Classification*. ECIR, 1–12. 2

Slonim, N. & Weiss, Y. (2002). *Maximum likelihood and the information bottleneck*. NIPS, 15, 335–342. 2

Still, S. & Bialek, W. (2004). *How many clusters? An information-theoretic perspective*. Neur Comp, 16(12), 2483–2506. 6

Still, S., Crutchfield, J.P., & Ellison, C.J. (2010). *Optimal causal inference: Estimating stored information and approximating causal architecture*. Chaos, 20(3), 037111. 5

Tishby, N., Pereira, F. & Bialek, W. (1999). *The Information Bottleneck Method*. Proc of The 37th Allerton Conf on Comm, Control, & Comp, Univ. of Illinois. 1, 2

Tishby, N. & Zaslavsky, N. (2015). *Deep Learning and the Information Bottleneck Principle*. arXiv.org. 2

Turner, R.E. & Sahani, M. (2007). *A maximum-likelihood interpretation for slow feature analysis*. Neur Comp, 19(4), 1022–1038. 2

Wallace, G.K. (1991). *The JPEG Still Picture Compression Standard*. Comm ACM, vol. 34, pp. 30-44.

1

Learning to Smooth with Bidirectional Predictive State Inference Machines

Wen Sun[1], Roberto Capobianco[2], Geoffrey J. Gordon[1], J. Andrew Bagnell[1], and Byron Boots[3]
[1] School of Computer Science, Carnegie Mellon University, Pittsburgh, PA 15213
[2] Department of Computer, Control and Management Engineering, Sapienza University of Rome, Italy
[3] School of Interactive Computing, Georgia Institute of Technology, Atlanta, GA 30332
[1]{wensun, ggordon, dbagnell}@cs.cmu.edu, [2]capobianco@dis.uniroma1.it, [3]bboots@cc.gatech.edu

Abstract

We present the Smoothing Machine (SMACH, pronounced "smash"), a dynamical system learning algorithm based on chain Conditional Random Fields (CRFs) with latent states. Unlike previous methods, SMACH is designed to optimize prediction performance when we have information from both past and future observations. By leveraging Predictive State Representations (PSRs), we model beliefs about latent states through *predictive states*—an alternative but equivalent representation that depends directly on observable quantities. Predictive states enable the use of well-developed supervised learning approaches in place of local-optimum-prone methods like EM: we learn regressors or classifiers that can approximate message passing and marginalization in the space of predictive states. We provide theoretical guarantees on smoothing performance and we empirically verify the efficacy of SMACH on several dynamical system benchmarks.

1 INTRODUCTION

In time series, smoothing is the process of inferring *a posteriori* latent state information given a model as well as past and future observations. Many applications leverage smoothing for inference, ranging from machine learning and robotics to biological science. For example, in a Linear Dynamical System (LDS), a Kalman smoother is frequently used to compute the posterior distribution of the system's states. Similarly, in Optical Character Recognition (OCR), smoothing is used to predict the word corresponding to a sequence of of handwritten characters.

Chain CRFs [Lafferty et al., 2001] are remarkably successful probabilistic graphical models for these applications. As a discriminative approach, CRFs can capture detailed structural properties of the observations and states with a reasonable number of parameters. (In this context, the states are often called *labels*.) Given a parametrization of the CRF, along with a training data set consisting of pairs of ground truth labels and observations, we can learn parameters for the CRF by maximizing the (log) conditional likelihood of the training labels given the training observations. For appropriate feature parametrizations, the log-likelihood objective is convex and one can achieve globally optimal solutions.

In this work, we are interested in *latent* chain CRFs, which generalize CRFs by adding a layer of latent variables between the labels and observations (Figure 1a). These latent variables increase the expressiveness of the underlying probabilistic model [Stratos et al., 2013], but also make the optimization problem more challenging: the log-likelihood objective becomes non-convex. Iterative approaches such as Expectation-Maximization (EM) can only compute locally optimal solutions, making the search for a globally optimal solution computationally infeasible. Though the global maximizer of the likelihood can promise good performance if we can find it, the locally optimal solutions that are found in practice typically do not have any performance guarantees.

To tackle the problem of local optima, we borrow ideas from spectral learning methods and Predictive State Representations (PSRs). In the last decade, these methods have been successfully used for learning and inference in latent state space models such as linear dynamical systems and hidden Markov models [Jaeger, 2000, Hsu et al., 2009, Boots, 2012, Boots et al., 2011, Song et al., 2010, Boots et al., 2013, Hefny et al., 2015]. The main idea is that, instead of tracking latent states directly, we track observable quantities such as expectations of features of future observations. If the features are selected to be sufficient statistics of the latent state distribution, knowing the predictive state is equivalent to knowing the underlying state of the system [Jaeger, 2000, Hefny et al., 2015, Sun et al., 2016]. Spectral learning algorithms provide theoretical guarantees: their estimating equations typically have a unique global solution, which converges to the true model parameters under the assumption of realizability (no model mismatch). However, if there is model mismatch, no theoretical guarantees are available for the learned model or the associated inference tasks [Kulesza et al., 2014].

To gain the benefits of spectral learning methods even in the case of model mismatch, we propose a novel algorithm, the *Smoothing Machine* (SMACH). Our method builds on recent work on *Predictive State Inference Machines* (PSIMs) [Sun et al., 2016, Venkatraman et al., 2016]. Like a PSR, a PSIM uses predictive states to represent beliefs about latent states. But, unlike a PSR, a PSIM directly learns a closed-loop filter as an inference machine that propagates the predictive state forward in time. By focusing on inference in predictive state space rather than latent state space, a PSIM reduces the difficult problem of learning a latent state space model to supervised learning and achieves guaranteed performance for its inference task (filtering or forward belief propagation) even in the presence of model mismatch.

A PSIM learns a filter that uses past and current observations to predict current latent information. Recently, Venkatraman et al. [2016] applied PSIM to forward message passing in a graphical model with partially observable states. However, this approach is suboptimal for estimating latent states in an offline setting where future observations are also available. So, SMACH extends PSIMs by learning a smoother that takes account of both past *and* future observations. Similar to PSIMs and PSRs, SMACH replaces latent states by predictions of observable quantities. Different from classic messages in graphical models, predictive messages represent the distributions of the sufficient statistics of observable quantities (e.g., labels and observations).

SMACH treats message passing as a sequence of predictions. It directly learns three predictors for approximating message passing in the predictive state space: one for forward predictive state message passing, another for backward predictive state message passing, and a third for combining messages at a given time step. The first predictor learns to recursively compute forward messages that encode information about past events (all past observations up to now), while the second predictor learns to compute backward messages that encode information about future events (all future observations after now). The last predictor predicts the current label given the local observation and the corresponding forward and backward predictive states. At testing time, SMACH uses the first two predictors to compute the forward and backward predictive states along the chain, and then uses the last predictor to combine the forward and backward predictive states with the local observations to predict the labels.

The main advantages of SMACH are: (1) It leverages predictive states to reduce the problem of learning latent chain CRFs to a supervised setting. This reduction enables us

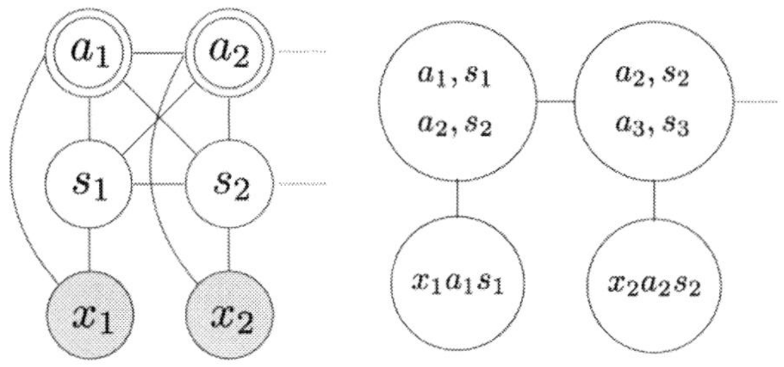

(a) Latent chain CRF (b) Junction Tree

Figure 1: A form of latent chain CRF and its junction tree. The labels a (double circled) are observable in training but are latent and need to be inferred during testing. Latent state s is never observable and x (gray) is always observable. During testing, given all observations $x_{1:T}$, the inference task is to compute the posterior distribution $P(a_t \mid x_{1:T})$ for all t.

to avoid local optima and use well developed theorems of supervised learning to quantify the smoothing performance of SMACH. (2) Similar to PSIM, SMACH combines the two phases of modeling and learning into a siingle task, to directly optimize the ultimate inference task of smoothing. Hence, no parametrization is needed for an explicit probabilistic graphical model (e.g., potential functions for cliques). (3) The learned predictors implicitly encode the information of the underlying probabilistic models. This enables the use of arbitrarily powerful regressors or classifiers as predictors for message passing and for the computation of marginal distributions and hence provides resistance to model mismatch. Finally, (4) as we will show, our formulation fully generalizes the special case of a *chain CRF* without latent states (i.e., removing s from Figure 1a).

2 PRELIMINARIES

In this work we consider a general latent chain CRF structure, as shown in Figure 1a. The model consists of three different types of variables: (1) Labels a_t that can be either continuous (e.g, positions of a mobile robot) or discrete (e.g., labels of a hand-written character). We assume that the ground truth labels are available in the training data, while the labels are latent at test time and need to be predicted. (2) Latent states s_t (either continuous or discrete) that are hidden both at training and test time. (3) Observations x_t (either continuous or discrete), available both at training and test time. A sequence of labels and observations $\{a_1, x_1, ..., a_T, x_T\}$ defines a trajectory τ. In order to perform the *smoothing* inference process, we are interested in computing the posterior distribution of the label a_t, conditioned on all observations $\{x_1, ..., x_T\}$: $P(a_t \mid x_{1:T}), \forall t$.

To discuss message passing in the latent chain CRF of Figure 1a, we first need to generate the corresponding junction tree representation, as shown in Figure 1b. The junction tree allows inference algorithms to avoid the inner loops in the original latent CRF model and perform message passing as follows [Koller and Friedman, 2009]. First, pick the node (a_1, s_1, a_2, s_2) as the root and perform backward message passing starting from each leaf (x_t, a_t, s_t). The message at the separation set (a_t, s_t) between the node $(a_t, s_t, a_{t+1}, s_{t+1})$ and the node (x_t, a_t, s_t) can be represented by $P(x_t \mid a_t, s_t)$, where x_t is the evidence. We define the backward message at the separation set (a_t, s_t), going from the node $(a_t, s_t, a_{t+1}, s_{t+1})$ to the node $(a_{t-1}, s_{t-1}, a_t, s_t)$, as $b_t \equiv P(a_t, s_t \mid x_{t:T})$, which we compute recursively as:

$$b_{t-1} \propto \sum_{a_t s_t} P(a_{t-1}, s_{t-1} \mid a_t, s_t) P(x_t \mid a_t, s_t) b_t. \quad (1)$$

We assume without loss of generality that the (forward) transition probability $P(a_{t+1}, s_{t+1} \mid a_t, s_t)$ is time-invariant, and we write $P(a_t, s_t \mid a_{t+1}, s_{t+1})$ for the corresponding backward transition probability. After all backward messages are computed, starting from the root, we pass messages forward. The forward message at the separation set (a_t, s_t) from the node $(a_{t-1}, s_{t-1}, a_t, s_t)$ to the node $(a_t, s_t, a_{t+1}, s_{t+1})$ is represented by $P(a_t, s_t \mid x_{1:t-1})$, which we denote $\tilde{b}_t$. The forward message is also computed recursively:

$$\tilde{b}_{t+1} \propto \sum_{s_t, a_t} P(a_{t+1}, s_{t+1} \mid a_t, s_t) P(x_t \mid a_t, s_t) \tilde{b}_t. \quad (2)$$

With forward and backward messages, at the node $(a_t, s_t, a_{t+1}, s_{t+1})$ the marginal message $P(a_t \mid x_{1:T})$, which we denote as $\hat{b}_t$, is computed as:

$$\hat{b}_t \propto \sum_{s_t, a_{t+1}, s_{t+1}} \frac{P(a_{t+1}, s_{t+1} \mid a_t, s_t) \tilde{b}_t P(x_t \mid a_t, s_t) b_{t+1}}{P(a_{t+1}, s_{t+1})}. \quad (3)$$

If we assume that $P(a, s)$ is time-invariant, the above equation can be regarded as a time-invariant, deterministic function that maps $\tilde{b}_t$, b_{t+1}, and the local observation x_t to $\hat{b}_t$.

3 OBSERVABILITY AND PREDICTIVE STATES

To perform message passing as described in Sec. 2, classic MLE-based approaches first parametrize latent CRFs and then learn the parametrization from training data. Learning the parameters of the transition models and the observations models is hard due to the latent states: the log likelihood of the observations and labels is non-convex. As a consequence, MLE-based approaches need to use iterative methods such EM, which can only promise local optimality and therefore lack performance guarantees.

Our approach leverages Predictive State Representations (PSRs) to overcome the difficulties of dealing with latent states. PSRs use *predictive states*, which consist of expectations of observable quantities, as an alternative, equivalent representation of latent belief states. Below, we first introduce the definition of *observability*, which extends the classic observability definition from latent state space models (e.g., LDS, HMM) to latent chain-CRFs.

3.1 OBSERVABILITY

Let us focus on a particular separation set (a_t, s_t) between the two nodes $(a_{t-1}, s_{t-1}, a_t, s_t)$ and $(a_t, s_t, a_{t+1}, s_{t+1})$ on the junction tree modelled in Figure 2. The forward belief in this separation set is represented as $P(a_t, s_t \mid x_{1:t-1})$. We define forward k-observability as follows:

Definition (Forward k-observability) There exists a constant $k \in \mathbb{N}^+$ such that the relationship between $P(a_t, s_t \mid x_{1:t-1})$ and $P(a_{t:t+k}, x_{t:t+k-1} \mid x_{1:t-1})$ is bijective.

Intuitively, forward k-observability means that the distribution of *future* observable quantities (labels a and observations x) uniquely determines the latent forward belief, conditioned on the previous observations. We define backward k-observability similarly:

Definition (Backward k-observability) There exists a constant $k \in \mathbb{N}^+$ such that the relationship between $P(a_t, s_t \mid x_{t:T})$ and $P(a_{t-k:t}, x_{t-k:t-1} \mid x_{t:T})$ is bijective.

Intuitively, backward k-observability means that the distribution of *past* observable quantities (labels a and observations x) uniquely determines the latent backward belief state, conditioned on future observations.[1]

In the Appendix, we conduct a case study of observability on one special form of latent chain-CRF—the Refinement Hidden Markov Model (RHMM) [Stratos et al., 2013]. Specifically, first we reduce the RHMM to a regular HMM, and then we leverage the well-defined concept of observability of HMMs to define the forward and backward observability of the original RHMM. In fact, when we set k big enough to cover the entire time windows of past and future, our definition is actually agrees with the *past* and *future* random variables defined by Stratos et al. [2013].

3.2 PREDICTIVE STATES

The definition of observability provides us with a different way to represent the beliefs containing latent states: we can use the joint distributions of future (past) labels

[1] In principle, the statistics could depend on the entire sequence of observations $x_{t:T}$ (or $x_{1:t}$). The restriction to a k-step window of visible variables simplifies the notation and is commonly used in practice.

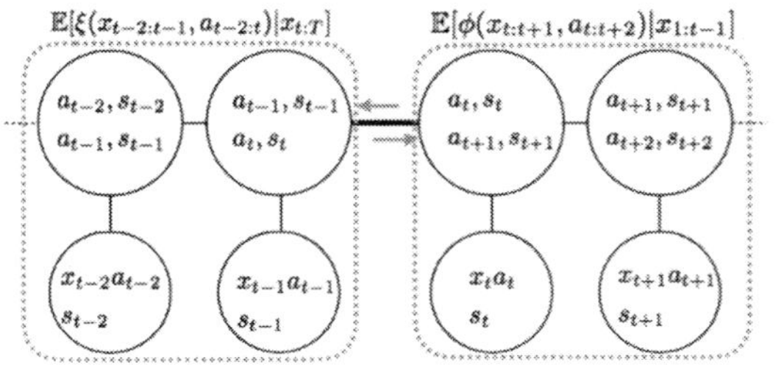

Figure 2: Illustration of the forward predictive state (blue) and backward predictive state (green) with $k = 2$.

and observations to represent the forward (backward) beliefs about latent states. Let us define a feature function ϕ that computes sufficient statistics of $a_{t:t+k}, x_{t:t+k-1}$, such that $P(a_{t:t+k}, x_{t:t+k-1} \mid x_{1:t-1})$ can be represented by $\mathbb{E}[\phi(a_{t:t+k}, x_{t:t+k-1}) \mid x_{1:t-1}]$. (In many cases, a good feature function is a kernel mean embedding, which is guaranteed to yield sufficient statistics for a wide range of distributions.) Similarly we define a feature function ξ that computes sufficient statistics of $a_{t-k:t}, x_{t-k:t-1}$, such that $P(a_{t-k:t}, x_{t-k:t-1} \mid x_{t:T})$ can be represented by $\mathbb{E}[\xi(a_{t-k:t}, x_{t-k:t-1}) \mid x_{t:T}]$. (In practice, ξ could be the same as ϕ.) Under the assumption that the system is forward k-observable and backward k-observable, we can now replace the beliefs about latent states $P(a_t, s_t \mid x_{1:t-1})$ and $P(a_t, s_t \mid x_{t:T})$ with the predictive messages $\mathbb{E}[\phi(a_{t:t+k}, x_{t:t+k-1}) \mid x_{1:t-1}]$ and $\mathbb{E}[\xi(a_{t-k:t}, x_{t-k:t-1}) \mid x_{t:T}]$ respectively. For notational simplicity, let us define $f_t = (a_{t:t+k}, x_{t:t+k-1})$ and $h_t = (a_{t-k:t}, x_{t-k:t-1})$. We define the *Forward Predictive State* (FPS) m_t at step t, and the *Backward Predictive State* (BPS) v_t at step t as:

$$m_t = \mathbb{E}[\phi(f_t) \mid x_{1:t-1}], \quad v_t = \mathbb{E}[\xi(h_t) \mid x_{t:T}]. \quad (4)$$

Note that our formulation fully generalizes the special case of a *chain CRF* without latent states (i.e., removing all s and edges connected to s from Figure 1a). In this case, by setting $k = 0$, the forward predictive state m_t becomes $\mathbb{E}[\phi(a_t) \mid x_{1:t-1}]$ and the backward predictive state v_t becomes $\mathbb{E}[\xi(a_t) \mid x_{t:T}]$. With sufficient feature functions ϕ and ξ, m_t and v_t are then equivalent to $P(a_t \mid x_{1:t-1})$ and $P(a_t \mid x_{t:T})$, which are the classic forward and backward beliefs on a chain CRF.

As we will show in the next section, we can use PSIM to compute forward and backward predictive states.

4 ALGORITHM

We now present the *Smoothing Machines* (SMACH) algorithm (Alg. 2). As introduced in the previous section, we first leverage PSIM to learn stationary filters for the generation of forward and backward predictive states. The final

Algorithm 1 PSIM with DAgger (Forward Pass)

Input: M independent trajectories τ_i, $1 \le i \le M$;
Initialize $D_0 \leftarrow \emptyset$ and initialize $F_0 \in \mathcal{F}_1$;
Initialize $\hat{m}_1 = \frac{1}{M}\sum_{i=1}^{M} \phi(f_1^i)$
for n = 0 to N **do**
  Use F_n to perform belief propagation (Eq. 6) on trajectory τ_i, $1 \le i \le M$
  For each trajectory τ_i and each time step t, add the input $z_t^i = (m_t^{i,F_n}, x_t^i)$ encountered by F_n to D'_{n+1} as feature variables and the corresponding f_{t+1}^i to D'_{n+1} as the targets ;
  Aggregate dataset $D_{n+1} = D_n \cup D'_{n+1}$;
  Train a new hypothesis $F_{n+1} \in \mathcal{F}_1$ on D_{n+1} to minimize the loss $d(F(m, x), f)$;
end for
Return: the best hypothesis $F_f \in \{F_n\}_n$ on validation trajectories.

step of SMACH is to combine the forward and backward predictive states together with observations to learn a predictor for smoothing. Below we briefly introduce PSIM and how PSIM can be used for computing predictive states.

4.1 PREDICTIVE STATE INFERENCE MACHINES

We utilize *Predictive State Inference Machines* (PSIM) [Sun et al., 2016] to directly compute the predictive states m_t and v_t. PSIM is a discriminative learning approach that learns a filter (black box represented by any regressors or classifiers) to mimic the predictive message passing process: by taking the incoming predictive message and the local observation as inputs, it outputs the next predictive message. Specifically, for forward predictive message passing, given a trajectory $\tau = \{a_1, x_1, ..., a_T, x_T\}$ sampled from the distribution $\mathcal{D}$, PSIM aims at finding a hypothesis $F_f \in \mathcal{F}_1$ to optimize the following objective:

$$\min_{F_f \in \mathcal{F}_1} \mathbb{E}_\tau \sum_{t=1}^{T} \|\hat{m}_t^\tau - \phi(f_t^\tau)\|^2; \quad (5)$$

$$\text{s.t. } \hat{m}_{t+1}^\tau = F_f(\hat{m}_t^\tau, x_t^\tau). \quad (6)$$

Namely, PSIM finds a hypothesis that can mimic forward predictive message passing, and the quality of the computed predictive messages are measured by the loss $\|\hat{m}_t - \phi(f)_t\|^2$ (i.e., moment matching).

Similar to forward predictive message passing, we can use PSIM for backward predictive message passing. In this case, PSIM aims at finding a hypothesis $F_b \in \mathcal{F}_2$ ($\mathcal{F}_2$ and $\mathcal{F}_1$ could either be the same or different hypothesis classes) to optimize the *backward* filtering performance as:

$$\min_{F_b \in \mathcal{F}_2} \mathbb{E}_\tau \sum_{t=1}^{T} \|\hat{v}_t^\tau - \xi(h_t^\tau)\|^2; \tag{7}$$

$$\text{s.t. } \hat{v}_t^\tau = F_b(\hat{v}_{t+1}^\tau, x_t^\tau). \tag{8}$$

In its original form [Sun et al., 2016], two optimization approaches are adopted for finding F_f or F_b: one uses Forward Training [Ross and Bagnell, 2010] to learn a non-stationary filter, while the other uses Data Aggregation [Ross et al., 2011b] to learn a stationary filter. However, as pointed out by the authors, even if the use of PSIM with Forward Training provably guarantees hypothesis consistency (i.e., the learned filters are equal to the true underlying filters), this solution is often impractical due to its data inefficiency. Conversely, PSIM with Data Aggregation is significantly more data efficient, both in the sample complexity analysis and in the empirical analysis [Sun et al., 2016]. Therefore, in this paper, we use PSIM with Data Aggregation to learn stationary filters for computing approximated predictive forward messages $\hat{m}$ and backward messages $\hat{v}$. The detailed description of the PSIM with DAgger for computing the hypothesis F_f for forward predictive message passing is provided in Alg. 1. The computation of backward predictive states will be similar, since we only need to reverse the belief propagation order (Line 5) using Eq. 7 and replace $f, \hat{m}, \mathcal{F}_1, F_f$ with $h, v, \mathcal{F}_2, F_b$ respectively.

Theoretically, PSIM ensures that the filtering errors resulting from the learned F_f and F_b are upper bounded as:[2]

$$\mathbb{E}_\tau \frac{1}{T} \sum_{t=1}^{T} [\|\hat{m}_t^\tau - \phi(f_t)\|^2] \leq \epsilon_m, \tag{9}$$

$$\mathbb{E}_\tau \frac{1}{T} \sum_{t=1}^{T} [\|\hat{v}_t^\tau - \xi(h_t)\|^2] \leq \epsilon_v, \tag{10}$$

where ϵ_m and ϵ_v are the regression or classification error on the aggregated dataset [Ross et al., 2011a, Sun et al., 2016]. In practice, both ϵ_m and ϵ_v can be small when we have an expressive hypothesis class and small noise (e.g., small Bayes error) [Ross et al., 2011c].

Therefore, by using PSIM, we can learn two operators F_f and F_b that mimic the forward and backward predictive state passing procedures. With these two operators, we can compute the approximated backward predictive state $\hat{v}_t$ and the forward predictive state $\hat{m}_t$ for the separation set (a_t, s_t) at any time step t (Figure 2).

[2]The original PSIM work by Sun et al. [2016] only provides theoretical bounds for forward message passing. However, for backward message passing, the same bounds directly apply if we reverse message passing direction.

Algorithm 2 Smoothing Machines (SMACH)

1: **Input:** M training trajectories $\tau_i = \{x_t^i, a_t^i\}_{t=1}^{T_i}$, $1 \leq i \leq M$; Hypothesis class $\mathcal{F}_1, \mathcal{F}_2, \mathcal{F}_3$.
2: Run PSIM on $\{\tau_i\}_{t=1}^{M}$ to learn the forward model $F_f \in \mathcal{F}_1$.
3: Run PSIM on $\{\tau_i\}_{t=1}^{M}$ to learn the backward model $F_b \in \mathcal{F}_2$.
4: Initialize dataset $\mathcal{S} = \emptyset$.
5: **for** each τ_i, $1 \leq i \leq M$ **do**
6: Roll out F_f forward to generate forward predictive states $\{\hat{m}_t^{\tau_i}\}_{t=1}^{T_i}$.
7: Roll out F_b backward to generate backward predictive states $\{\hat{v}_t^{\tau_i}\}_{t=2}^{T_i+1}$.
8: Compose input feature $\hat{z}_t^{\tau_i} = (\hat{m}_t^{\tau_i}, \hat{v}_{t+1}^{\tau_i}, x_t^{\tau_i})$ for $1 \leq t \leq T_i$.
9: Add input and output pair $\{(\hat{z}_t^\tau, a_t^{\tau_i})\}_{t=1}^{T_i}$ into $\mathcal{S}$.
10: **end for**
11: Compute the marginal hypothesis:

$$\hat{G} = \arg\max_{G \in \mathcal{F}_3} \mathbb{E}_{(z,a)\sim \mathcal{S}}\, \ell(G(z), a). \tag{11}$$

12: **Return:** $F_f, F_b, \hat{G}$.

4.2 SMOOTHING MACHINES

The SMACH algorithm is presented in Alg. 2. SMACH first learns a stationary forward filter $F_f \in \mathcal{F}_1$ and a backward filter $F_b \in \mathcal{F}_2$: given training data, the SMACH algorithm uses PSIM to learn a hypothesis F_f that can compute and pass the forward predictive states $\hat{m}_t$ (Line 2) and, independently, uses PSIM to learn a hypothesis F_b that can compute and pass the backward predictive states $\hat{v}_t$ (Line 3). Due to their independence, learning F_f and F_b can be executed in parallel.

To learn the final message product and marginalization step, we first generate the predictive states by rolling out F_f and F_b on the training trajectories (Line 6 and 7). Next, the algorithm collects the pairs of forward messages $\hat{m}_t$ and backward messages $\hat{v}_{t+1}$, together with the local observation x_t, as the input feature, with the corresponding label a_t as the output. Finally, SMACH learns a classifier or regressor $\hat{G}$ as shown in Eq. 11 (Line 11) by minimizing a loss function ℓ that measures the prediction error. When a_t is discrete, ℓ can be a common classification loss, such as hinge loss, softmax, or cross entropy.

At test time, given a sequence τ, we only have access to the observations $\{x_t^\tau\}$ and need to predict $\{a_t^\tau\}$. With the learned $F_f, F_b, \hat{G}$, we simply roll F_f forward to compute $\{\hat{m}_t^\tau\}$ and roll F_b backward to compute $\{\hat{v}_t\}$, in parallel. With all the messages available, we then use $\hat{G}(\hat{m}_t^\tau, \hat{v}_{t+1}^\tau, x_t^\tau)$ to predict the label. This whole process uses all observations $\{x_t^\tau\}_t$ to predict a_t a posteriori.

4.3 DISCUSSION

Our learning algorithm shares some similarities with the well-known Baum-Welch algorithm for HMMs. Baum-Welch iterates between estimating the posterior distributions of latent states (using forward and backward pass), and optimizing the parameters. SMACH also performs a forward and backward pass to compute the messages represented by predictive states. The key difference is that we leverage predictive state representations (PSRs) to reduce the problem of learning latent chain-CRFs back to the supervised setting, where we can avoid local optimality issues and give strong theoretical guarantees (Sec. 5).

5 THEORETICAL ANALYSIS

Let us assume that we use PSIM to learn F_f to pass predictive states forward on any given sequences of observations $\{x_1, ..., x_T\}$ from τ as $\hat{m}_{t+1}^{\tau} = F_f(\hat{m}_t^{\tau}, x_t^{\tau})$, and learn F_b to pass predictive states backward as $\hat{v}_t^{\tau} = F_b(\hat{v}_{t+1}^{\tau}, x_t^{\tau})$. Let us define $\Delta_{m_t^{\tau}} = m_t^{\tau} - \hat{m}_t^{\tau}$, and $\Delta_{v_t^{\tau}} = v_t^{\tau} - \hat{v}_t^{\tau}$, as the difference between the underlying true predictive states (equivalent to the original beliefs $b_t, \tilde{b}_t$ due to the existence of the bijective map) and the predictive states computed from the learned F_f and F_b, respectively.

Eq. 9 and Eq. 10 quantify the filtering error from the approximated predictive states computed from the learned hypothesis F_f and F_b respectively. The ultimate goal of smoothing is to use both past and future information to compute the posterior distribution of a label more accurately. As one might expect, if we can exactly compute the forward and backward messages, namely $\hat{m}_t = m_t$ and $\hat{v}_{t+1} = v_{t+1}$ for any t and τ, then, in a realizable case, we can exactly learn a hypothesis that takes $\hat{m}_t$, $\hat{v}_t$ and the local observations as inputs and outputs the posterior distributions of the labels. However, one may wonder if we can still achieve strong prediction guarantees on the learned model even if we can only approximately compute m_t and v_t. Moreover, we may be interested in quantifying the performance of the learned model based on the accuracy of the approximated predictive states (e.g., using Δ_{m_t} and Δ_{v_t}). In order to perform this type of analysis, we first introduce some lemmas and notation.

The following lemma extends the results for PSIM shown in Eq. 9 and 10, by explicitly quantifying $\Delta_{\hat{m}_t}$ and $\Delta_{\hat{v}_t}$:

Lemma 5.1. *Given Eq. 9 and 10 from PSIM, for $\Delta_{\hat{m}_t}$ and $\Delta_{\hat{v}_t}$, we have:*

$$\frac{1}{T}\sum_{t=1}^{T}\mathbb{E}_{\tau}[\|\Delta_{m_t^{\tau}}\|^2] \leq 2(\epsilon_m + \delta_m); \tag{12}$$

$$\frac{1}{T}\sum_{t=1}^{T}\mathbb{E}_{\tau}[\|\Delta_{v_t^{\tau}}\|^2] \leq 2(\epsilon_v + \delta_v); \tag{13}$$

where $\delta_m = \frac{1}{T}\sum_{t=1}^{T}\mathbb{E}_{\tau}[\|m_t^{\tau} - \phi(f_t)\|^2]$ and $\delta_v = \frac{1}{T}\sum_{t=1}^{T}\mathbb{E}_{\tau}[\|v_t^{\tau} - \xi(h_t)\|^2]$.

Proof for this lemma and the lemmas/theorems in the remainder of this paper are all included in Appendix.

The above lemma states that the size of Δ_m (or Δ_v) is upper bounded by the sum of ϵ_m (or ϵ_v), which is the risk resulting from the predicted messages, and δ_m (or δ_v), which is the Bayes error resulting from the system itself. Note that the Bayes error is purely determined by the underlying systems and has nothing to do with the learning algorithms. In general, we cannot guarantee the elimination of the Bayes errors. This is because when aiming at learning a stationary F_f (or F_b) for forward (or backward) predictive message passing, the objective (Eq. 5) that PSIM tries to optimize is non-convex. Even ideally assuming that PSIM is *risk* consistent, i.e., it finds an F that has the same filtering error (risk) as the true underlying filter for predictive states, which is the best we can do for a general non-convex objective, we still cannot promise that the learned F is exactly the true underlying filter. Therefore, even if F is risk consistent with respect to the underlying true filter, we cannot promise that the approximated predictive state $\hat{m}_t$ generated from F would be exactly equal to the true underlying state m_t. More detailed explanation is included in Appendix. However, as shown in Lemma. 5.1, the smaller the filtering error from PSIM, the better approximation we get for the predictive states.

To analyze the performance of the learned marginalization hypothesis $\hat{G}$, we first assume that the loss function $\ell(\cdot,\cdot)$ that we are using for classification is Lipschitz continuous, with constant L_1 with respect to the first item ($G(z)$). Commonly used classification loss functions have this property (e.g., hinge loss, logistic loss). Additionally, we assume that $G(\cdot)$, for any $G \in \mathcal{F}_3$, is also Lipschitz continuous with constant L_2 with respect to z. This is also a reasonable assumption for common hypothesis classes such as linear, quadratic and, in fact, any differentiable hypotheses with bounded first derivatives.

Let us define G^* as the minimizer of the true risk measured under the true messages (m_t^{τ}, v_t^{τ}):

$$G^* = \arg\max_{G\in\mathcal{F}_3} \mathbb{E}_{\tau}[\ell(G(z_t^{\tau}), a_t^{\tau})], \tag{14}$$

where z_t^{τ} is composed as $(m_t^{\tau}, v_{t+1}^{\tau}, x_t^{\tau})$ with the true underlying predictive messages $m_t^{\tau}, v_{t+1}^{\tau}$ on the sequence τ. With sufficient feature functions ϕ and ξ, m_t^{τ} and v_t^{τ} will be equivalent to b_t^{τ} and $\tilde{b}_t^{\tau}$ subject to a bijective map. Hence, in a realizable case, G^* encodes as much information as the true underlying marginalization step in the original latent chain-CRF, as shown in Eq. 3. Let us first analyze the learned model $\hat{G}$ under the assumption of infinite many training trajectories ($M \to \infty$):

Theorem 5.2. *Assuming F_f and F_b from PSIM generate the messages $\hat{m}_t$ and $\hat{v}_t$ satisfying Eq. 12 and 13, the* *marginalization hypothesis $\hat{G}$ obtained from Eq. 11 has the following property:*

$$\frac{1}{T}\sum_{t=1}^{T}\mathbb{E}_{\tau\sim\mathcal{D}}[\ell(\hat{G}(\hat{z}_t^\tau), a_t^\tau)]$$
$$\leq\frac{1}{T}\mathbb{E}_{\tau\sim\mathcal{D}}[\ell(G^*(z_t^\tau), a_t^\tau)] + O(\epsilon_m + \epsilon_v + \delta_m + \delta_v).$$

The above theorem shows that if PSIM learns good hypothesis F_f and F_b for estimating messages (e.g., ϵ_m and ϵ_m are small) and the underlying noise of the dynamical systems is not big, the learned hypothesis $\hat{G}$ can achieve competitive smoothing performance with respect to G^*—the global minimizer of the smoothing risk with access to the true messages (e.g., m_t^τ, v_t^τ).

For Theorem 5.2 we assumed an infinite number of training sequences, although in practice, we only have a finite number of sequences. To show the finite sample complexity of our algorithm, we additionally assume that the training sequences $\tau_1, ..., \tau_M$ are separated in two halves. We use the first half to learn F_f and F_b with PSIM, and the second half to generate messages $\hat{m}$ and $\hat{v}$ with F_f and F_b, and then train $\hat{G}$ for the marginalization step. This assumption ensures that, at every time step t, the generated messages $\{\hat{m}_t^{\tau_{M/2}}, \hat{m}_t^{\tau_{M/2+1}}, ..., \hat{m}_t^{\tau_M}\}$ are i.i.d sampled (note that F_f is independent with respect to $\tau_{M/2}, ..., \tau_M$, and each τ is i.i.d sampled). Let us define the distribution $\hat{d}_t$ as the distribution of $\hat{z}_t^\tau = (\hat{m}_t^\tau, \hat{v}_{t+1}^\tau, x_t^\tau)$. Note that $\{(\hat{m}_t^{\tau_i}, \hat{v}_{t+1}^{\tau_i}, x_t^{\tau_i})\}_{i=M/2}^M$ will be i.i.d sampled from $\hat{d}_t$. For convenience, we assume that we have $2M$ training sequences. We use the first M sequences for PSIM to learn F_f and F_b and the remaining M for learning $\hat{G}$.

Using the finite sample analysis for PSIM with Data Aggregation as the optimization tool,we first extend Lemma. 5.1 to the corresponding high probability bounds:

Lemma 5.3. *Using PSIM with Data Aggregation, with probability $1-\delta$, we have:*

$$\frac{1}{T}\sum_{t=1}^{T}\mathbb{E}_\tau[(\Delta_{m_t^\tau})] \leq 2\hat{\gamma}_m + 2\hat{\epsilon}_m + 2\delta_m + O(\sqrt{\frac{\ln(1/\delta)}{MN}});$$
$$\frac{1}{T}\sum_{t=1}^{T}\mathbb{E}_\tau[(\Delta_{v_t^\tau})] \leq 2\hat{\gamma}_v + 2\hat{\epsilon}_v + 2\delta_v + O(\sqrt{\frac{\ln(1/\delta)}{MN}});$$

where N is number of iterations $PSIM$ used and $\hat{\gamma}_m$ and $\hat{\gamma}_v$ converge to zero as $N\to\infty$

We present the finite sample analysis using Rademacher complexity. We define $\mathcal{R}_t(\mathcal{F}_3)$ as the Rademacher number of the hypothesis class $\mathcal{F}_3$ under distribution $\hat{d}_t$, and $\bar{\mathcal{R}}(\mathcal{F}_3) = (\mathcal{R}_1(\mathcal{F}_3) + ... + \mathcal{R}_T(\mathcal{F}_3))/T$, as the average Rademacher number across T time steps. In our analysis, we assume we know T or the upper bound of T.

	KF	EKF	KS	iEKS	SMACH-0	Avg $\|a_t\|_2$
Cart-Pole	12.80	2.14	4.13	2.02	**0.29**	0.65
Bicycle	0.093	0.068	0.091	0.067	**0.065**	2.01
Helicopter	~	2.49	~	2.19	**2.17**	21.98
Swimmer	~	1.90	~	1.72	**0.69**	9.61

Table 1: Prediction error of different approaches without latent states (a_t encodes the exact state of the system).

Theorem 5.4. *Given $2M$ training sequences for Alg. 2, as $N\to\infty$, with probability $1-\delta$, for any $G^*\in\mathcal{F}_3$, we have:*

$$\frac{1}{T}\sum_{t=1}^{T}\mathbb{E}_{\tau\sim\mathcal{D}}[\ell(\hat{G}(\hat{z}_t^\tau), a_t^\tau)] \leq \frac{1}{T}\sum_{t=1}^{T}\mathbb{E}_{\tau\sim\mathcal{D}}[\ell(G^*(z_t^\tau), a_t^\tau)]$$
$$+\tilde{O}(\sqrt{\frac{\ln(1/\delta)}{M}}) + O(\bar{\mathcal{R}}(\mathcal{F}_3) + \hat{\epsilon}_m + \hat{\epsilon}_v + \delta_v + \delta_m).$$

6 EXPERIMENTS

We test SMACH on two different types of datasets: (1) datasets with continuous labels a_t (SMACH needs to perform *regression*), which are collected from several simulated robotics dynamical systems, and (2) datasets whose labels a_t are discrete (SMACH needs to perform *classification*), which are from two domains: Optical Character Recognition, a sequential image recognition task, and questions and answers recognition [McCallum et al., 2000], a Natural Language Processing task.

6.1 REGRESSION TASKS

To show that our approach is able to deal with complicated, non-linear dynamical models of robotics systems, we test our approach on four classic simulated dynamics models: (1) Cart-Pole Balancing, (2) Bicycle Balancing [Ernst et al., 2005], (3) Helicopter Hover [Abbeel et al., 2005] and (4) Swimmer [Tassa et al., 2008]. The simulated models are available from RLPy [Geramifard et al., 2013].

We compare SMACH to classic physics-based algorithms: the Kalman Filter (KF), the Kalman Smoother (KS), the Extended Kalman Filter (EKF), and the iterated Extended Kalman Smoother (iEKS) [Bell, 1994]. We first consider the chain-CRF structure without latent states (no s_t in Fig. 1a). Hence, the label a_t represents the *full* state of the robot, and x_t is generated from a_t through a stochastic observation model. Since there are no latent states, we set $k = 0$. Here, we define the smoothing error as the average of the prediction errors $\|a - \hat{a}\|_2$.

In our setup, we allow KF, KS, EKF, iEKS to access the real underlying dynamical models and observation models. For KF and KS, we linearize the real dynamics and observation model around the balancing state. Note that directly comparing to KF, KS EKF, and iEKS is not fair since these approaches have access to the true stochastic dynamical models, while SMACH only has access to the data generated from the models. Nevertheless, as we can see from

Tab. 1, by using Kernel Ridge regression (i.e., $\mathcal{F}_1, \mathcal{F}_2, \mathcal{F}_t$ are Reproducing Kernel Hilbert Spaces), SMACH outperforms these classic physics-based approaches on all four testbeds.[3] We only tested SMACH-0 here as we do not have latent states s_t in the setup here. As we expected, increasing k (using predictive states) does not give noticeable improvement on the prediction error.

To test the performances of SMACH with latent states, we separate the full state into two parts: labels a_t and latent states s_t (see Appendix for the detailed components of s_t and a_t). Under this setup, SMACH is never allowed to access s_t. Due to the existence of latent states, we set $k \geq 1$ (i.e. we use predictive states). Figure 3a and 3b show the performance of SMACH as k increases on the bicycle balancing and swimmer datasets. A similar trend is observed on the other two datasets. Overall, the smoothing performance improves as k increases, which illustrates that longer predictive states can potentially capture more information about latent states. Interestingly, SMACH outperforms iEKS (note that we still give iEKS full access to the latent states s_t in order to perform Kalman smoothing, but we only report smoothing prediction error with respect to label a_t). Since iEKS can be understood as applying the Gauss-Newton algorithm on the log likelihood, which could be non-convex due to non-linear dynamics and observation models, it is likely that iEKS will be stuck at locally optimal solutions.

Since KF, KS, EKF, and iEKS have access to the perfect stochastic models, this set of experiments also supports one of our main claims: separately learning the models and then using the learned models to perform inference may result in decreased performance. This can happen even if we can leverage powerful learning algorithms to learn the perfect models (e.g., using Gaussian Process [Deisenroth et al., 2012] or Hilbert space embeddings [Nishiyama et al., 2016] to model dynamics) due to the unavoidable approximations that one usually needs in order to make inference computationally tractable (e.g., linearize the real/learned dynamics and observations models as KF, KS, GP-EKF and GP-EKS [Ko and Fox, 2009] do). These approximations on the learned/real models may cancel out the benefits derived from the availability of perfect models. SMACH, instead, directly learns powerful predictors to optimize the smoothing performance. Since the predictors operate as black boxes to directly perform the smoothing operation, no further approximation is needed for inference.

6.2 CLASSIFICATION TASKS

We evaluate SMACH on classification tasks belonging to two different domains: Optical Character Recognition and

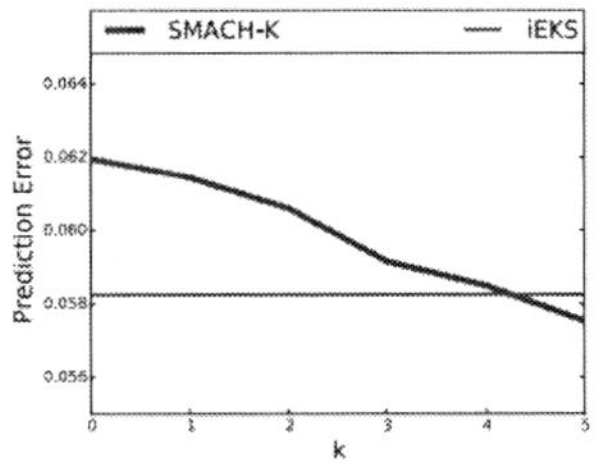

(a) Bicycle

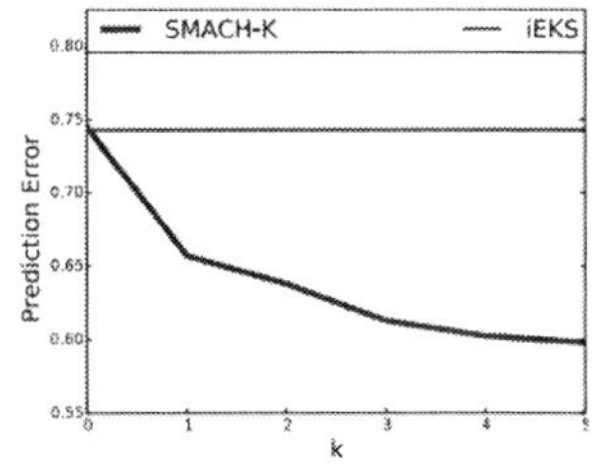

(b) Swimmer

Figure 3: Performance of SMACH with respect to k (length of predictive states) for models with latent states.

questions and answers recognition (FAQ) [McCallum et al., 2000]. In this case, for fair comparison to previous approaches, we use standard feature design. We compare SMACH to two families of algorithms: (1) search-based prediction algorithms such as SEARN [Daumé III et al., 2009], DAgger [Ross et al., 2011b], and PSIM [Sun et al., 2016], (2) CRF [Lafferty et al., 2001] and its extensions, such as Hidden-unit CRF [van der Maaten et al., 2011] and NeuroCRFs [Do et al., 2010].

Optical Character Recognition The OCR dataset contains 6877 handwritten words. Each word is represented as a series of handwritten characters and there are 52152 total characters. Each character is a binary 16×8 image, leading to 128-dimensional binary feature vectors. Each character is one of the 26 letters in the English alphabet. We define the binary vector for character at slot t as c_t. The task is to predict the identity of each character, given a sentence. In our experiments, we use a 7-step time window: we represent x_t as $[c_{t-3}, ..., c_t, ..., c_{t+3}]$ and we test SMACH with different k (SMACH-k).

We first test SMACH on a small experimental setting, where we separate the dataset into 10 folds and perform training on one fold while testing on the remaining 9 folds. Table 2 shows the comparison between SMACH and other closely related approaches.[4] SMACH outperforms SEARN, DAgger and PSIM, which are the state-of-art search-based prediction algorithms. Compared to probabilistic graphical model approaches, SMACH also has better performance than CRFs. From Table 2, we see that from DAgger (equivalent to PSIM-0) to PSIM-1 and PSIM-2 the prediction error decreases when we use, in the predictive messages, more steps of future/past labels and observations. This is consistent with the claim from Sun et al. [2016] that a larger k can lead to more accurate predictive states. As a result, SMACH-2 surpasses SMACH-1, since SMACH-2 uses more accurate predictive messages computed from PSIM-2. This evidence agrees with Theo-

[3] Note that, for iEKS, we use the solutions from EKF as initialization. Simply using random initialization, or the average of the training trajectories as initialization, does not perform well.

[4] The results of SVM^{struct}, SVM^{struct}, M^{3}N, CRF are from [Nguyen and Guo, 2007]; SVM^{struct2} and CRF^2 are from [Keerthi and Sundararajan, 2007]

SVM^{struct}	**SVM^{struct2}**	**M^{3}N**	**SEARN**
21.16	19.24	25.08	27.02
CRF	**CRF^2**	**Hidden unit CRF**	**DAgger**
32.30	19.97	18.36	30.02
PSIM-1	**PSIM-2**	**SMACH-1**	**SMACH-2**
26.11	23.89	18.41	16.21

Table 2: Comparison of SMACH with previous related approaches on the small OCR experimental setting.

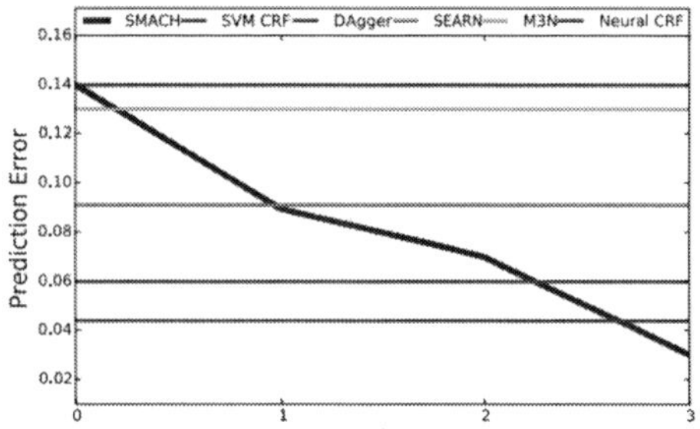

Figure 4: Performance of SMACH-k on large OCR task.

rem 5.4: when we have more accurate predictive messages for the marginal step (e.g., smaller ϵ), the marginal step has a smaller generalization error. We also ran SMACH on a larger setting (training on 9 folds and testing on the remaining one) with different k, reporting the results in Figure 4.[5] From the graph, we note that larger k can greatly improve smoothing performance. SMACH-3 achieves an average prediction error of 3.5%, while Hidden unit CRF achieves a 2.0% prediction error. Note, however, that SMACH-2 achieves a smaller error in the small experiment.

Recognizing questions and answers We also test SMACH on the FAQ dataset from McCallum et al. [2000]. We use the same feature representation from McCallum et al. [2000], where each sentence is described using a 24-dimensional binary vector. Each sentence in the FAQ data set is labeled by one of four labels: (1) question, (2) answer, (3) header, or (4) footer. We use linear SVM for PSIM for computing backward and forward predictive states. For the marginalization step, we use two classifiers: Linear SVM with Random Fourier feature (RFF-SVM) and Random Forest (RF) with 60 trees and maximum depth 30.

From Table 3, we see that both SMACH with RFF-SVM and SMACH with RF achieve performances which are comparable to Hidden-unit CRF [van der Maaten et al., 2011] with Stochastic Gradient Descent as the optimization (we note that SMACH performs slightly better than hidden-unit CRF with other optimizers like Perceptron and BFGS). SMACH with RF gives slightly better performance than SMACH with RFF-SVM. This indicates that using a powerful classifier for the marginal step can potentially enhance the performance. We also tested $k = 1$, leading to a slightly worse performance than $k = 0$. Since we are only allowed to use one file (one sequence) to train the model and test on all the remaining files in the same group [McCallum et al., 2000], when we increase k, we may not have enough training data, since the complexity of the hypothesis classes increases as k becomes larger.

[5]The result of SVM+CRF is from [Hoefel and Elkan, 2008].

Method	Error (%)
Linear SVM [Do et al., 2010]	9.87
Linear CRF [Maaten et al., 2011]	6.54
NeuroCRFs [Do et al., 2010]	6.05
Hidden-unit CRF [Maaten et al., 2011]	4.43
DAgger	7.47
SMACH-0 with RFF-SVM	5.10
SMACH-0 with RF	5.01

Table 3: Comparison of SMACH with related approaches on the FAQ dataset.

7 CONCLUSION

In this paper we present Smoothing Machines (SMACH), a data-driven approach that directly optimizes *smoothing* performance on time series with latent states. We use the concepts of predictive states and inference machines to directly learn functions that mimic forward and backward message passing in our system. Under this setting, we can achieve strong performance guarantees for the ultimate inference task (i.e., smoothing) in the agnostic setting. We show that SMACH outperforms classic physics-based smoothing algorithms on dynamical systems with complicated non-linear transition models. We also show that in the presence of latent states, using more features (i.e., a longer time window) can boost the algorithm's performance. Additionally, our experimental results on classification tasks are promising. We leave the application of SMACH on more complicated NLP tasks (e.g., Part of Speech Tagging) as future work.

ACKNOWLEDGEMENTS

This material is based upon work supported by DARPA ALIAS contract number HR0011-15-C-0027 and NSF CRII Award No. 1464219.

References

Pieter Abbeel, Varun Ganapathi, and Andrew Y Ng. Learning vehicular dynamics, with application to modeling helicopters. In *NIPS*, pages 1–8, 2005.

Bradley M Bell. The iterated Kalman smoother as a gauss-newton method. *SIAM Journal on Optimization*, 4(3): 626–636, 1994.

Byron Boots. *Spectral Approaches to Learning Predictive*

Representations. PhD thesis, Carnegie Mellon University, 2012.

Byron Boots, Sajid M Siddiqi, and Geoffrey J Gordon. Closing the learning-planning loop with predictive state representations. *IJRR*, 30(7):954–966, 2011.

Byron Boots, Arthur Gretton, and Geoffrey J. Gordon. Hilbert space embeddings of predictive state representations. In *UAI-2013*, 2013.

Hal Daumé III, John Langford, and Daniel Marcu. Search-based structured prediction. *Machine learning*, 75(3): 297–325, 2009.

Marc Peter Deisenroth, Ryan Darby Turner, Marco F Huber, Uwe D Hanebeck, and Carl Edward Rasmussen. Robust filtering and smoothing with Gaussian processes. *Automatic Control, IEEE Transactions on*, 57(7):1865–1871, 2012.

Trinh Do, Thierry Arti, et al. Neural conditional random fields. In *AISTATS*, pages 177–184, 2010.

Damien Ernst, Pierre Geurts, and Louis Wehenkel. Tree-based batch mode reinforcement learning. *Journal of Machine Learning Research*, 6:503–556, 2005.

Alborz Geramifard, Robert H Klein, and JP How. Rlpy: The reinforcement learning library for education and research. *Machine Learning Open Source Software*, 2013.

Ahmed Hefny, Carlton Downey, and Geoffrey J Gordon. Supervised learning for dynamical system learning. In *NIPS*, pages 1954–1962, 2015.

Guilherme Hoefel and Charles Elkan. Learning a two-stage SVM/CRF sequence classifier. In *Proceedings of the 17th ACM conference on Information and knowledge management*, pages 271–278. ACM, 2008.

Daniel Hsu, Sham M. Kakade, and Tong Zhang. A spectral algorithm for learning hidden markov models. In *COLT*, 2009.

Herbert Jaeger. Observable operator models for discrete stochastic time series. *Neural Computation*, 12(6):1371–1398, 2000.

S Sathiya Keerthi and Sellamanickam Sundararajan. CRF versus SVM-struct for sequence labeling. Technical report, Technical report, Yahoo Research, 2007.

Jonathan Ko and Dieter Fox. GP-Bayesfilters: Bayesian filtering using gaussian process prediction and observation models. *Autonomous Robots*, 27(1):75–90, 2009.

Daphne Koller and Nir Friedman. *Probabilistic graphical models: principles and techniques*. MIT press, 2009.

Alex Kulesza, N Raj Rao, and Satinder Singh. Low-rank spectral learning. In *AISTATS*, 2014.

John Lafferty, Andrew McCallum, and Fernando Pereira. Conditional random fields: probabilistic models for segmenting and labeling sequence data. In *ICML*. Morgan Kaufmann, 2001.

Laurens Maaten, Max Welling, and Lawrence K Saul. Hidden-unit conditional random fields. In *AISTATS*, pages 479–488, 2011.

Andrew McCallum, Dayne Freitag, and Fernando CN Pereira. Maximum entropy markov models for information extraction and segmentation. In *ICML*, volume 17, pages 591–598, 2000.

Nam Nguyen and Yunsong Guo. Comparisons of sequence labeling algorithms and extensions. In *ICML*, 2007.

Yu Nishiyama, Amir Hossein Afsharinejad, Shunsuke Naruse, Byron Boots, and Le Song. The nonparametric kernel Bayes smoother. In *AISTATS*, 2016.

Stéphane Ross and J. Andrew Bagnell. Efficient reductions for imitation learning. In *AISTATS*, pages 661–668, 2010.

Stéphane Ross, Geoffrey J Gordon, and J. Andrew Bagnell. No-regret reductions for imitation learning and structured prediction. In *AISTATS*, 2011a.

Stéphane Ross, Geoffrey J Gordon, and J Andrew Bagnell. A reduction of imitation learning and structured prediction to no-regret online learning. *AISTATS*, 2011b.

Stephane Ross, Daniel Munoz, Martial Hebert, and J Andrew Bagnell. Learning message-passing inference machines for structured prediction. In *CVPR*, pages 2737–2744, 2011c.

Le Song, Byron Boots, Sajid M Siddiqi, Geoffrey J Gordon, and Alex J Smola. Hilbert space embeddings of hidden markov models. In *ICML*, pages 991–998, 2010.

Karl Stratos, Alexander M Rush, Shay B Cohen, and Michael Collins. Spectral learning of refinement hmms. In *CoNLL*, pages 56–64, 2013.

Wen Sun, Arun Venkatraman, Byron Boots, and J Andrew Bagnell. Learning to filter with predictive state inference machines. In *ICML*, 2016.

Yuval Tassa, Tom Erez, and William D Smart. Receding horizon differential dynamic programming. In *Advances in neural information processing systems*, pages 1465–1472, 2008.

Laurens van der Maaten, Max Welling, and Lawrence K Saul. Hidden-unit conditional random fields. In *AISTATS*, pages 479–488, 2011.

Arun Venkatraman, Wen Sun, Martial Hebert, Byron Boots, and J. Andrew Bagnell. Inference machines for nonparametric filter learning. In *IJCAI-2016*, 2016.

Context-dependent feature analysis with random forests

Antonio Sutera[1] **Gilles Louppe**[2] **Vân Anh Huynh-Thu**[1] **Louis Wehenkel**[1] **Pierre Geurts**[1]
[1] Dept. of EE & CS, University of Liège, Belgium [2] New York University, USA

Abstract

In many cases, feature selection is often more complicated than identifying a single subset of input variables that would together explain the output. There may be interactions that depend on contextual information, i.e., variables that reveal to be relevant only in some specific circumstances. In this setting, the contribution of this paper is to extend the random forest variable importances framework in order (i) to identify variables whose relevance is context-dependent and (ii) to characterize as precisely as possible the effect of contextual information on these variables. The usage and the relevance of our framework for highlighting context-dependent variables is illustrated on both artificial and real datasets.

1 MOTIVATION

Supervised learning finds applications in many domains such as medicine, economics, computer vision, or bioinformatics. Given a sample of observations of several inputs and one output variable, the goal of supervised learning is to learn a model for predicting the value of the output variable given any values of the input variables. Another common side objective of supervised learning is to bring as much insight as possible about the relationship between the inputs and the output variable. One of the simplest ways to gain such insight is through the use of feature selection or ranking methods that identify the input variables that are the most decisive or relevant for predicting the output, either alone or in combination with other variables. Among feature selection/ranking methods, one finds variable importance scores derived from random forest models that stand out from the literature mainly because of their multivariate and non parametric nature and their reasonable computational cost. Although very useful, feature selection/ranking methods however only provide very limited information about the often very complex input-output relationships that can be modeled by supervised learning methods. There is thus a high interest in designing new techniques to extract more complete information about input-output relationships than a single global feature subset or feature ranking.

In this paper, we specifically address the problem of the identification of the input variables whose relevance or irrelevance for predicting the output only holds in specific circumstances, where these circumstances are assumed to be encoded by a specific context variable. This context variable can be for example a standard input variable, in which case, the goal of contextual analyses is to better understand how this variable interacts with the other inputs for predicting the output. The context can also be an external variable that does not belong to the original inputs but that may nevertheless affect their relevance with respect to the output. Practical applications of such contextual analyses are numerous. E.g., one may be interested in finding variables that are both relevant and independent of the context, as in medical studies (see, e.g., Geissler et al., 2000), where one is often interested in finding risk factors that are as independent as possible of external factors, such as the sex of the patients, their origins or their data cohort. By contrast, in some other cases, one may be interested in finding variables that are relevant but dependent in some way on the context. For example, in systems biology, differential analysis (Ideker and Krogan, 2012) aims at discovering genes or factors that are relevant only in some specific conditions, tissues, species or environments.

Our contribution in this paper is two-fold. First, starting from common definitions of feature relevance, we propose a formal definition of context-dependent variables and provide a complete characterization of these variables depending on how their relevance is affected by the context variable. Second, we extend the random forest variable importances framework in order to identify and characterize variables whose relevance is context-dependent or context-independent. Building on existing theoretical results for standard importance scores, we propose asymptotic guarantees for the resulting new measures.

The paper is structured as follows. In Section 2, we first lay out our formal framework defining context-dependent variables and describing how the context may change their relevance. We describe in Section 3 how random forest variable importances can be used for identifying context-dependent variables and how the effect of contextual information on these variables can be highlighted. Our results are then illustrated in Section 4 on representative problems. Finally, conclusions and directions of future works are discussed in Section 5.

2 CONTEXT-DEPENDENT FEATURE SELECTION AND CHARACTERIZATION

Context-dependence. Let us consider a set $V = \{X_1, \ldots, X_p\}$ of p input variables and an output Y and let us denote by V^{-m} the set $V \setminus \{X_m\}$. All input and output variables are assumed to be categorical, not necessarily binary[1]. The standard definitions of relevant, irrelevant, and marginally relevant variables based on their mutual information I are as follows (Kohavi and John, 1997; Guyon and Elisseeff, 2003):

- A variable X_m is *relevant to Y with respect to V* iff there exists a subset $B \subseteq V^{-m}$ (possibly empty) such that $I(Y; X_m|B) > 0$.
- A variable X_m is *irrelevant to Y with respect to V* iff, for all $B \subseteq V^{-m}$, $I(Y; X_m|B) = 0$.
- A variable is *marginally relevant to Y* iff $I(Y; X_m) > 0$.

Let us now assume the existence of an additional (observed) context variable $X_c \notin V$, also assumed to be categorical. Inspired by the notion of relevant and irrelevant variables, we propose to define context-dependent and context-independent variables as follows:

Definition 1. *A variable $X_m \in V$ is* context-dependent to Y with respect to X_c *iff there exists a subset $B \subseteq V^{-m}$ and some values x_c and b such that*[2]*:*

$$I(Y; X_m|B = b, X_c = x_c) \neq I(Y; X_m|B = b). \quad (1)$$

Definition 2. *A variable $X_m \in V$ is* context-independent to Y with respect to X_c *iff for all subsets $B \subseteq V^{-m}$ and for all values x_c and b, we have:*

$$I(Y; X_m|B = b, X_c = x_c) = I(Y; X_m|B = b). \quad (2)$$

[1]Non categorical outputs are discussed in Section 3.5.

[2]In this definition and all definitions that follow, we assume that the events on which we are conditioning have a non-zero probability and that if such event does not exist then the condition of the definition is not satisfied.

Context-dependent variables are thus the variables for which there exists a conditioning set B in which the information they bring about the output is modified by the context variable. Context-independent variables are the variables that, in all conditionings $B = b$, bring the same amount of information about the output whether the value of the context is known or not. This definition is meant to be as general as possible. Other more specific definitions of context-dependence are as follows:

$$\exists B \subseteq V^{-m}, b, x_c^1, x_c^2 : \quad I(Y; X_m|X_c = x_c^1, B = b) \neq I(Y; X_m|X_c = x_c^2, B = b), \quad (3)$$

$$\exists B \subseteq V^{-m}, x_c : \quad I(Y; X_m|X_c = x_c, B) \neq I(Y; X_m|B), \quad (4)$$

$$\exists B \subseteq V^{-m}, b : \quad I(Y; X_m|X_c, B = b) \neq I(Y; X_m|B = b), \quad (5)$$

$$\exists B \subseteq V^{-m} : \quad I(Y; X_m|X_c, B) \neq I(Y; X_m|B). \quad (6)$$

These definitions all imply context-dependence as defined in Definition 1 but the converse is in general not true. For example, Definition (3) misses problems where the context makes some otherwise irrelevant variable relevant but where the information brought by this variable about the output is exactly the same for all values of the context. A variable that satisfies Definition (1) but not Definition (4) is given in example 1. This example can be easily adapted to show that both Definitions (5) and (6) are more specific than Definition (1) (by swapping the roles of X_c and X_2).

Example 1. *This artificial problem is defined by two input variables X_1 and X_2, an output Y, and a context X_c. X_1, X_2, and X_c are binary variables taking their values in $\{0, 1\}$, while Y is a quaternary variable taking its values in $\{0, 1, 2, 3\}$. All combinations of values for X_1, X_2, and X_c have the same probability of occurrence 0.125 and the conditional probability $P(Y|X_1, X_2, X_C)$ is defined by the two following rules:*

- *If $X_2 = X_c$ then $Y = X_1$ with probability 1.*
- *If $X_2 \neq X_c$ then $Y = 2$ with probability 0.5 and $Y = 3$ with probability 0.5.*

The corresponding data table is given in Appendix A. For this problem, it is easy to show that $I(Y; X_1|X_2 = 0, X_c = 0) = 1$ and that $I(Y; X_1|X_2 = 0) = 0.5$, which means condition (1) is satisfied and X_1 is thus context-dependent to Y with respect to X_c according to our definition. On the other hand, we can show that:

$$I(Y; X_1|X_c = x_c) = I(Y; X_1) = 0.5$$
$$I(Y; X_1|X_2, X_c = x_c) = I(Y; X_1|X_2) = 0.5,$$

for any $x_c \in \{0, 1\}$, which means that condition (4) can not be satisfied for X_1.

To simplify the notations, the context variable was assumed to be a separate variable not belonging to the set of inputs V. It can however be considered as an input variable, whose own relevance to Y (with respect to $V \cup \{X_c\}$) can be assessed as for any other input. Let us examine the impact of the nature of this variable on context-dependence. First, it is interesting to note that the definition of context-dependence is not symmetric. A variable X_m being context-dependent to Y with respect to X_c does not imply that the variable X_c is context-dependent to Y with respect to X_m.[3] Second, the context variable does not need to be marginally relevant for some variable to be context-dependent, but it needs however to be relevant to Y with respect to V. Indeed, we have the following theorem (proven in Appendix B):

Theorem 1. *X_c is irrelevant to Y with respect to V iff all variables in V are context-independent to Y with respect to X_c (and V) and $I(Y; X_c) = 0$.*

As a consequence of this theorem, there is no interest in looking for context-dependent variables when the context itself is not relevant.

Characterizing context-dependent variables. Contextual analyses need to focus only on context-dependent variables since, by definition, context-independent variables are unaffected by the context: their relevance status (relevant or irrelevant), as well as the information they contain about the output, remain indeed unchanged whatever the context.

Context-dependent variables may be affected in several directions by the context, depending both on the conditioning subset B and on the value x_c of the context. Given a context-dependent variable X_m, a subset B and some values b and x_c such that $I(Y; X_m|B = b, X_c = x_c) \neq I(Y; X_m|B = b)$, the effect of the context can either be an increase of the information brought by X_m ($I(Y; X_m|B = b, X_c = x_c) > I(Y; X_m|B = b)$) or a decrease of this information ($I(Y; X_m|B = b, X_c = x_c) < I(Y; X_m|B = b)$). Furthermore, for a given variable X_m, the direction of the change can differ from one context value x_c to another (at fixed B and b) but also from one conditioning $B = b$ to another (for a fixed context x_c). Example 2 below illustrates this latter case. This observation makes a global characterization of the effect of the context on a given context-dependent variable difficult. Let us nevertheless mention two situations where such global characterization is possible:

Definition 3. *A context-dependent variable $X_m \in V$ is* context-complementary *(in a context x_c) iff for all $B \subseteq V^{-m}$ and b, we have $I(Y; X_m|B = b, X_c = x_c) \geq I(Y; X_m|B = b)$.*

Definition 4. *A context-dependent variable $X_m \in V$ is* context-redundant *(in a context x_c) iff for all $B \subseteq V^{-m}$ and b, we have $I(Y; X_m|B = b, X_c = x_c) \leq I(Y; X_m|B = b)$.*

[3] But this would be the case if we had adopted definition (6).

Context-complementary and redundant variables are variables that always react in the same direction to the context and thus can be characterized globally without loss of information. Context-complementary variables are variables that bring complementary information about the output with respect to the context, while context-redundant variables are variables that are redundant with the context. Note that context-dependent variables that are also irrelevant to Y are always context-complementary, since the context can only increase the information they bring about the output. Context-dependent variables that are relevant to Y however can be either context-complementary, context-redundant, or uncharacterized. A context-redundant variable can furthermore become irrelevant to Y as soon as $I(Y; X_m|B = b, X_c = x_c) = 0$ for all B, b, and x_c.

Example 2. *As an illustration, in the problem of Example 1, X_1 and X_2 are both relevant and context-dependent variables. X_1 can not be characterized globally since we have simultaneously:*

$$\begin{aligned} I(Y; X_1|X_2 = 0, X_c = x_c) &> I(Y; X_1|X_2 = 0) \\ I(Y; X_1|X_2 = 1, X_c = x_c) &< I(Y; X_1|X_2 = 1), \end{aligned}$$

for both $x_c = 0$ and $x_c = 1$. X_2 is however context-complementary as the knowledge of X_c always increases the information it contains about Y.

Related works. Several authors have studied interactions between variables in the context of supervised learning. They have come up with various interaction definitions and measures, e.g., based on multivariate mutual information (McGill, 1954; Jakulin and Bratko, 2003), conditional mutual information (Jakulin, 2005; Van de Cruys, 2011), or variants thereof (Brown, 2009; Brown et al., 2012). There are several differences between these definitions and ours. In our case, the context variable has a special status and as a consequence, our definition is inherently asymmetric, while most existing variable interaction measures are symmetric. In addition, we are interested in detecting any information difference occurring in a given context (i.e., for a specific value of X_c) and for any conditioning subset B, while most interaction analyses are interested in average and/or unconditional effects. For example, (Jakulin and Bratko, 2003) propose as a measure of the interaction between two variables X_1 and X_2 with respect to an output Y the multivariate mutual information, which is defined as $I(Y; X_1; X_2) = I(Y; X_1) - I(Y; X_1|X_2)$. Unlike our definition, this measure can be shown to be symmetric with respect to its arguments. Adopting this measure to define context-dependence would actually amount at using condition (6) instead of condition (1), which would lead to a more specific definition as discussed earlier in this section.

The closest work to ours in this literature is due to Turney (1996), who proposes a definition of context-sensitivity that is very similar to our definition of context-dependence. Using our notations, Turney (1996) defines a variable X_m as weakly context-sensitive to the variable X_c if there exist some subset $B \subseteq V^{-m}$ and some values y, x_m, b, and x_c such that these two conditions hold:

$$p(Y = y|X_m = x_m, X_c = x_c, B = b) \neq p(Y = y|X_m = x_m, B = b),$$
$$p(Y = y|X_m = x_m, X_c = x_c, B = b) \neq p(Y = y|X_c = x_c, B = b).$$

X_m is furthermore defined as strongly context-sensitive to X_c if X_m is weakly sensitive to X_c, X_m is marginally relevant,and X_c is not marginally relevant. These two definitions do not exactly coincide with ours and they have two drawbacks in our opinion. First, they do not consider that a perfect copy of the context is context-sensitive, which we think is counter-intuitive. Second, while strong context-sensitivity is asymmetric, the constraints about the marginal relevance of X_m and X_c seems also unnatural.

Our work is also somehow related to several works in the graphical model literature that are concerned with context-specific independences between random variables (see e.g. Boutilier et al., 1996; Zhang and Poole, 1999). Boutilier et al. (1996) define two variables Y and X_m as contextually independent given some $B \subseteq V^{-m}$ and a context value x_c as soon as $I(Y; X_m|B, X_c = x_c) = 0$. When $B \cup \{X_m, X_c\}$ are the parents of node Y in a Bayesian network, then such context-specific independences can be exploited to simplify the conditional probability tables of node Y and to speed up inferences. Boutilier et al. (1996)'s context-specific independences will be captured by our definition of context-dependence as soon as $I(Y; X_m|B) > 0$. However, our framework is more general as we want to detect any context dependencies, not only those that lead to perfect independences in some context.

3 CONTEXT ANALYSIS WITH RANDOM FORESTS

In this section, we show how to use variable importances derived from Random Forests first to identify context-dependent variables (Section 3.2) and then to characterize the effect of the context on the relevance of these variables (Section 3.3). Derivations in this section are based on the theoretical characterization of variable importances provided in (Louppe et al., 2013), which is briefly reminded in Section 3.1. Section 3.4 discusses practical considerations and Section 3.5 shows how to generalize our results to other impurity measures.

3.1 Variable importances

Within the random forest framework, Breiman (2001) proposed to evaluate the importance of a variable X_m for predicting Y by adding up the weighted impurity decreases for all nodes t where X_m is used, averaged over all N_T trees in the forest:

$$Imp(X_m) = \frac{1}{N_T} \sum_T \sum_{t \in T: v(s_t) = X_m} p(t) I(Y; X_m|t) \quad (7)$$

where $v(s_t)$ is the variable used in the split s_t at node t, $p(t)$ is the proportion of samples reaching t and I is the mutual information.

According to Louppe et al. (2013), for any ensemble of fully developed trees in asymptotic learning sample size conditions, the Mean Decrease Impurity (MDI) importance (7) can be shown to be equivalent to

$$Imp(X_m) = \sum_{k=0}^{p-1} \frac{1}{C_p^k} \frac{1}{p-k} \sum_{B \in \mathcal{P}_k(V^{-m})} I(Y; X_m|B), \quad (8)$$

where $\mathcal{P}_k(V^{-m})$ denotes the set of subsets of V^{-m} of size k. Most notably, it can be shown (Louppe et al., 2013) that this measure is zero for a variable X_m iff X_m is irrelevant to Y with respect to V. It is therefore well suited for identifying relevant features.

3.2 Identifying context-dependent variables

Theorem 1 shows that if the context variable X_c is irrelevant, then it can not interact with the input variables and thus modify their importances. This observation suggests to perform, as a preliminary test, a standard random forest variable importance analysis using all input variables and the context in order to check the relevance of the latter. If the context variable does not reveal to be relevant, then, there is no hope to find context-dependent variables.

Intuitively, identifying context-dependent variables seems similar to identifying the variables whose importance is globally modified when the context is known. Therefore, one first straightforward approach to identify context-dependent variables is to build a forest per value $X_c = x_c$ of the context variable, i.e., using only the data samples for which $X_c = x_c$, and also globally, i.e. using all samples and not including the context among the inputs. Then it consists in deriving from these models an importance score for each value of the context, as well as a global importance score. Context-dependent variables are then the variables whose global importance score differs from the contextual importance scores for at least one value of the context.

More precisely, let us denote by $Imp(X_m)$ the global score of a variable X_m computed using (7) from all samples and by $Imp(X_m|X_c = x_c)$ its importance score as computed according to (7) using only those samples such that $X_c = x_c$. With this approach, a variable would be declared as context-dependent as soon as there exists a value x_c such that $Imp(X_m) \neq Imp(X_m|X_c = x_c)$.

Although straightforward, this approach has several drawbacks. First, in the asymptotic setting of Section 3.1, it is not guaranteed to find all context-dependent variables. Indeed, asymptotically, it is easy to show from (8) that $Imp(X_m) - Imp(X_m|X_c = x_c)$ can be written as:

$$Imp^{x_c}(X_m) \triangleq Imp(X_m) - Imp(X_m|X_c = x_c) \quad (9)$$

$$= \sum_{k=0}^{p-1} \frac{1}{C_k^p} \frac{1}{p-k} \sum_{B \in \mathcal{P}_k(V^{-m})} \hookrightarrow (I(Y;X_m|B) - I(Y;X_m|B, X_c = x_c)). \quad (10)$$

Example 1 shows that $I(Y;X_m|B)$ can be equal to $I(Y;X_m|B, X_c = x_c)$ for a context-dependent variable. Therefore we have the property that if there exists an x_c such that $Imp^{x_c}(X_m) \neq 0$, then the variable is context-dependent but the opposite is unfortunately not true. Another drawback of this approach is that in the finite case, we do not have the guarantee that the different forests will have explored the same conditioning sets B and therefore, even assuming that the learning sample is infinite (and therefore that all mutual informations are perfectly estimated), we lose the guarantee that $Imp^{x_c}(X_m) \neq 0$ for a given x_c implies context-dependence.

To overcome these issues, we propose the following new importance score to identify context-dependent variables:

$$Imp^{|x_c|}(X_m) \triangleq \frac{1}{N_T} \sum_T \sum_{t \in T: v(s_t) = X_m} p(t) \hookrightarrow |I(Y;X_m|t) - I(Y;X_m|t, X_c = x_c)| \quad (11)$$

This score is meant to be computed from a forest of totally randomized trees built from all samples, not including the context variable among the inputs. At each node t where the variable X_m is used to split, one needs to compute the absolute value of the difference between the mutual information between Y and X_m estimated from all samples reaching that node and the mutual information between Y and X_m estimated only from the samples for which $X_c = x_c$. The same forest can then be used to compute $Imp^{|x_c|}(X_m)$ for all x_c. A variable X_m is then declared context-dependent as soon as there exists an x_c such that $Imp^{|x_c|}(X_m) > 0$.

Let us show that this measure is sound. In asymptotic conditions, i.e., with an infinite number of trees, one can show from (11) that $Imp^{|x_c|}(X_m)$ becomes:

$$Imp^{|x_c|}(X_m) = \sum_{k=0}^{p-1} \frac{1}{C_p^k} \frac{1}{p-k} \sum_{B \in \mathcal{P}_k(V^{-m})} \sum_{b \in \mathcal{B}} P(B = b) \hookrightarrow |I(Y;X_m|B = b) - I(Y;X_m|B = b; X_c = x_c)|.$$

Asymptotically, this measure has now the very desirable property to not miss any context-dependent variable as formalized in the next theorem (the proof is in Appendix C).

Theorem 2. *A variable $X_m \in V$ is context-independent to Y with respect to X_c iff $Imp^{|x_c|}(X_m) = 0$ for all x_c.*

Given that the absolute differences are computed at each tree node, this measure also continues to imply context-dependence in the case of finite forests and infinite learning sample size. The only difference with the infinite forests is that only some conditionings B and values b will be tested and therefore one might miss the conditionings that are needed to detect some context-dependent variables.

3.3 Characterizing context-dependent variables

Besides identifying context-dependent variables, one would want to characterize their dependence with the context as precisely as possible. As discussed earlier, irrelevant variables (i.e, such that $Imp(X_m) = 0$) that are detected as context-dependent do not need much effort to be characterized since the context can only increase their importance. All these variables are therefore context-complementary.

Identifying the context-complementary and context-redundant variables among the relevant variables that are also context-dependent can in principle be done by simply comparing the absolute value of $Imp^{x_c}(X_m)$ with $Imp^{|x_c|}(X_m)$, as formalized in the following theorem (proven in Appendix D).

Theorem 3. *If $|Imp^{x_c}(X_m)| = Imp^{|x_c|}(X_m)$ for a context-dependent variable X_m, then X_m is context-complementary if $Imp^{x_c}(X_m) < 0$ and context-redundant if $Imp^{x_c}(X_m) > 0$.*

This result allows to identify easily the context-complementary and context-redundant variables. In addition, if, for a context-redundant variable X_m, we have $Imp^{|x_c|}(X_m) = Imp^{x_c}(X_m) = Imp(X_m)$, then this variable is irrelevant in the context x_c.

Then it remains to characterize the context-dependent variables that are neither context-complementary nor context-redundant. It would be interesting to be able to also characterize them according to some sort of average effect of the context on these variables. Similarly as the common use of importance $Imp(X_m)$ to rank variables from the most to the less important, we propose to use the importance $Imp^{x_c}(X_m)$ to characterize the average global effect of context x_c on the variable X_m. Given the asymptotic formulation of this importance in Equation (10), a negative value of $Imp^{x_c}(X_m)$ means that X_m is essentially complementary with the context: in average over all conditionings, it brings more information about Y in context x_c than when ignoring the context. Conversely, a positive value of $Imp^{x_c}(X_m)$ means that the variable is essentially redundant with the context: in average over all conditionings, it brings less information about Y than when ignoring the context. Ranking the context-dependent variables according to $Imp^{x_c}(X_m)$ would then give at the top the variables that are the most complementary with the context and at the bottom the variables that are the most redundant.

Note that, like $Imp^{|x_c|}(X_m)$, it is preferable to estimate $Imp^{x_c}(X_m)$ by using the following formula rather than to estimate it from two forests by subtracting $Imp(X_m)$ and $Imp(X_m|X_c = x_c)$:

$$Imp_s^{x_c}(X_m) = \frac{1}{N_T}\sum_T \sum_{t \in T: v(s_t)=X_m} p(t) \hookrightarrow (I(Y;X_m|t) - I(Y;X_m|t, X_c = x_c)) \quad (12)$$

This estimation method has the same asymptotic form as $Imp(X_m) - Imp(X_m|X_c = x_c)$ given in Equation (10) but, in the finite case, it ensures that the same conditionings are used for both mutual information measures. Note that in some applications, it is interesting also to have a global measure of the effect of the context. A natural adaptation of (12) to obtain such global measure is as follows:

$$Imp^{X_c}(X_m) \triangleq \frac{1}{N_T}\sum_T \sum_{t \in T: v(s_t)=X_m} p(t) \hookrightarrow (I(Y;X_m|t) - I(Y;X_m|t, X_c))$$

which, in asymptotic sample and ensemble of trees size conditions, gives the following formula:

$$Imp^{X_c}(X_m) = \sum_{k=0}^{p-1} \frac{1}{C_k^p}\frac{1}{p-k} \sum_{B \in \mathcal{P}_k(V^{-m})} \hookrightarrow (I(Y;X_m|B) - I(Y;X_m|B, X_c)).$$

If $Imp^{X_c}(X_m)$ is negative then the context variable X_c makes variable X_m globally more informative (X_c and X_m are complementary with respect to Y and V). If $Imp^{X_c}(X_m)$ is positive, then the context variable X_c makes variable X_m globally less informative (X_c and X_m are redundant with respect to Y and V).

3.4 In practice

As a recipe when starting a context analysis, we suggest first to build a single forest using all input variables X_m (but not the context X_c) and then to compute from this forest all importances defined in the previous section: the global importances $Imp(X_m)$ and the different contextual importances, $Imp_s^{x_c}(X_m)$, $Imp^{|x_c|}(X_m)$, and $Imp^{X_c}(X_m)$, for all variables X_m and context values x_c.

Second, variables satisfying the context-dependence criterion, i.e., such that $Imp^{|x_c|}(X_m) > 0$ for at least one x_c, can be identified from the other variables. Among context-dependent variables, an equality between $|Imp_s^{x_c}(X_m)|$ and $Imp^{|x_c|}(X_m)$ highlights that the context-dependent variable X_m is either context-complementary or context-redundant (in x_c) depending on the sign of $Imp_s^{x_c}(X_m)$. Finally, the remaining context-dependent variables can be ranked according to $Imp_s^{x_c}(X_m)$ (or $Imp^{X_c}(X_m)$ for a more global analysis).

Note that, because mutual informations will be estimated from finite training sets, they will be generally non zero even for independent variables, leading to false positives in the identification of context-dependent variables. In practice, one could instead identify context-dependent variables by using a test $Imp^{|x_c|}(X_m) > \epsilon$ where ϵ is some cut-off value greater than 0. In practice, the determination of this cut-off can be very difficult. In our experiments, we propose to turn the importances $Imp^{|x_c|}(X_m)$ into p-values by using random permutations. More precisely, 1000 scores $Imp^{|x_c|}(X_m)$ will be estimated by randomly permuting the values of the context variable in the original data (so as to simulate the null hypothesis corresponding to a context variable fully independent of all other variables). A p-value will then be estimated by the proportion of these permutations leading to a score $Imp^{|x_c|}(X_m)$ greater than the score obtained on the original dataset.

Table 1: Problem 1: Values of X_c, X_1, X_2, X_3, Y.

X_c	X_1	X_2	X_3	Y
0	0	0	0	2
0	0	0	1	2
0	0	1	0	2
0	0	1	1	2
0	1	0	0	0
0	1	0	1	0
0	1	1	0	1
0	1	1	1	1
1	0	0	0	2
1	0	0	1	2
1	0	1	0	2
1	0	1	1	2
1	1	0	0	0
1	1	0	1	1
1	1	1	0	0
1	1	1	1	1

Table 2: Problem 1: Variable importances as computed analytically using asymptotic formulas. Note that X_1 is context-independent and X_2 and X_3 are context-dependent.

	X_1	X_2	X_3
$Imp(X_m)$	1.0	0.125	0.125
$Imp(X_m\|X_c = 0)$	1.0	0.5	0.0
$Imp(X_m\|X_c = 1)$	1.0	0.0	0.5
$Imp^{\|0\|}(X_m)$	0.0	0.375	0.125
$Imp^{0}(X_m)$	0.0	-0.375	0.125
$Imp^{\|1\|}(X_m)$	0.0	0.125	0.375
$Imp^{1}(X_m)$	0.0	0.125	-0.375
$Imp^{X_c}(X_m)$	0.0	-0.125	-0.125

3.5 Generalization to other impurity measures

All our developments so far have assumed a categorical output Y and the use of Shannon's entropy as the impurity measure. Our framework however can be carried over to other impurity measures and thus in particular also to a numerical output Y. Let us define a generic impurity measure $i(Y|t) \geq 0$ that assesses the impurity of the output Y at a tree node t. The corresponding impurity decrease at a tree node is defined as:

$$G(Y;X_m|t) = i(Y|t) - \sum_{x_m \in \mathcal{X}_m} p(t_{x_m}) i(Y|t_{x_m}) \quad (13)$$

Table 3: Problem 2: Variable importances as computed analytically using the asymptotic formulas for the different importance measures.

	X_1	X_2	X_3	X_4	X_5	X_6	X_7	X_8
$Imp(X_m)$	0.5727	0.7514	0.5528	0.687	0.1746	0.0753	0.1073	0.0
$Imp(X_m \vert X_c = 0)$	0.4127	0.5815	0.5312	0.5421	0.6566	0.2258	0.372	0.0
$Imp(X_m \vert X_c = 1)$	0.6243	0.8057	0.5577	0.7343	0.0	0.0	0.0	0.0
$Imp^{\vert 0 \vert}(X_m)$	0.2263	0.2431	0.1181	0.2241	0.4139	0.1961	0.2861	0.0
$Imp^{\vert 1 \vert}(X_m)$	0.0987	0.0611	0.021	0.0736	0.1746	0.0753	0.1073	0.0
$Imp^{0}(X_m)$	0.2179	0.2422	0.1111	0.2190	-0.3839	-0.1389	-0.2346	0.0
$Imp^{1}(X_m)$	-0.0516	-0.0543	-0.0049	-0.0473	0.1746	0.0753	0.1073	0.0

Table 4: Problem 3: Importances as computed with a forest of 1000 totally randomized trees. The context is defined by the binary context feature *Sex* ($Sex = 0$ denotes *female* and $Sex = 1$ denotes *male*). *P-values* were estimated using 1000 permutations of the context variable. Grey cells highlight *p-values* under the 0.05 threshold.

m		$Imp(X_m)$	$Imp(X_m \vert X_c = x_c)$		$Imp^{\vert x_c \vert}(X_m)$				$Imp_s^{x_c}(X_m)$			
		-	$x_c = 0$	$x_c = 1$	$x_c = 0$	pval	$x_c = 1$	pval	$x_c = 0$	pval	$x_c = 1$	pval
0	age	0.2974	0.2942	0.2900	0.1505	0.899	0.1717	0.417	0.0032	0.938	0.0074	0.846
1	histologic-type	0.3513	0.1354	0.4005	0.2265	0.000	0.1183	0.121	0.2159	0.000	-0.0492	0.331
2	degree-of-diffe	0.4415	0.3725	0.4070	0.1827	0.680	0.1724	0.689	0.0690	0.102	0.0345	0.398
3	bone	0.2452	0.2342	0.2220	0.1088	0.396	0.0845	0.904	0.0110	0.717	0.0232	0.410
4	bone-marrow	0.0188	0.0190	0.0131	0.0128	0.892	0.0105	0.980	-0.0001	0.994	0.0057	0.682
5	lung	0.1677	0.1837	0.1420	0.1134	0.448	0.1079	0.397	-0.0160	0.605	0.0257	0.373
6	pleura	0.1474	0.1132	0.1127	0.0613	1.000	0.1026	0.097	0.0342	0.179	0.0348	0.165
7	peritoneum	0.3171	0.2954	0.2084	0.0939	0.968	0.1516	0.000	0.0216	0.710	0.1087	0.000
8	liver	0.2300	0.1844	0.2784	0.0888	0.966	0.1382	0.053	0.0456	0.134	-0.0483	0.100
9	brain	0.0466	0.0334	0.0566	0.0403	0.173	0.0279	0.814	0.0131	0.693	-0.0101	0.751
10	skin	0.0679	0.0310	0.0786	0.0426	0.922	0.0420	0.841	0.0369	0.107	-0.0107	0.663
11	neck	0.2183	0.0774	0.2255	0.1562	0.000	0.0710	0.575	0.1409	0.000	-0.0071	0.764
12	supraclavicular	0.1701	0.1807	0.1344	0.0942	0.379	0.0738	0.884	-0.0106	0.695	0.0357	0.136
13	axillar	0.1339	0.1236	0.0846	0.0748	0.214	0.0663	0.388	0.0103	0.795	0.0493	0.194
14	mediastinum	0.1826	0.1752	0.1613	0.1129	0.266	0.0867	0.853	0.0074	0.767	0.0213	0.404
15	abdominal	0.2558	0.2883	0.1512	0.1419	0.139	0.1526	0.028	-0.0325	0.368	0.1046	0.003

with t_{x_m} denoting the successor node of t corresponding to value x_m of X_m. By analogy with conditional entropy and mutual information, let us define the population based measures $i(Y|B)$ and $G(Y;X_m|B)$ for any subset of variables $B \subseteq V$ as follows:

$$\begin{aligned} i(Y|B) &= \sum_b P(B=b) i(Y|B=b) \\ G(Y;X_m|B) &= i(Y|B) - i(Y|B,X_m), \end{aligned}$$

where the first sum is over all possible combinations b of values for variables in B. Now, substituting mutual information I for the corresponding impurity decrease measure G, all our results above remain valid, including Theorems 1, 2, and 3 (proofs are omitted for the sake of space). It is important however to note that this substitution changes the notions of both variable relevance and context-dependence. Definition 1 indeed becomes:

Definition 5. *A variable $X_m \in V$ is* context-dependent *to Y with respect to X_c iff there exists a subset $B \subseteq V^{-m}$ and some values x_c and b such that*

$$G(Y;X_m|B=b,X_c=x_c) \neq G(Y;X_m|B=b).$$

When Y is numerical, a common impurity measure is variance, which defines $i(Y|t)$ as the empirical variance $\text{var}[Y|t]$ computed at node t. The corresponding $G(X_m;Y|B=b)$ and $G(X_m;Y|B=b,X_c=x_c)$ in Definition 5 are thus defined respectively as

$$\text{var}[Y|B=b] - \mathbb{E}_{X_m|B=b}[\text{var}[Y|X_m,B=b]] \text{ and}$$

$$\text{var}[Y|B=b,X_c=x_c]$$
$$\hookrightarrow -\mathbb{E}_{X_m|B=b,X_c=x_c}[\text{var}[Y|X_m,B=b,X_c=x_c]].$$

We will illustrate the use of our framework in a regression setting with this measure in the next section.

4 EXPERIMENTS

Problem 1. The purpose of this first problem is to illustrate the different measures introduced earlier. This artificial problem is defined by three binary input variables X_1, X_2, and X_3, a ternary output Y, and a binary context X_c. All samples are enumerated in Table 1 and are supposed to be equiprobable. By construction, the output Y is defined as $Y = 2$ if $X_1 = 0$, $Y = X_2$ if $X_c = 0$ and $X_1 = 1$, and $Y = X_3$ if $X_c = 1$ and $X_1 = 1$.

Table 2 reports all importance scores for the three inputs. These scores were computed analytically using the asymptotic formulas, not from actual experiments. Considering the global importances $Imp(X_m)$, it turns out that all variables are relevant, with X_1 clearly the most important variable and X_2 and X_3 of smaller and equal importances. According to $Imp^{|0|}(X_m)$ and $Imp^{|1|}(X_m)$, X_1 is a context-independent variable, while X_2 and X_3 are two context-dependent variables. This result is as expected given the way the output is defined. For X_2 and X_3, we have furthermore $Imp^{|x_c|}(X_m) = |Imp^{|x_c|}(X_m)|$ for both values of x_c. X_2 is therefore context-complementary when $X_c = 0$ and context-redundant when $X_c = 1$. Conversely, X_3 is context-redundant when $X_c = 0$ and context-complementary when $X_c = 1$. X_2 is furthermore irrelevant when $X_c = 1$ (since $Imp^1(X_2) = Imp^{|1|}(X_2) = Imp(X_2)$) and X_3 is irrelevant when $X_c = 0$ (since $Imp^0(X_3) = Imp^{|0|}(X_3) = Imp(X_3)$). The values of $Imp^{X_c}(X_2)$ and $Imp^{X_c}(X_3)$ suggest that these two variables are in average complementary.

Problem 2. This second experiment is based on an adaptation of the digit recognition problem initially proposed in Breiman et al. (1984) and reused in Louppe et al. (2013). The original problem contains 7 binary variables ($X_1,\dots,X_7$) and the output Y takes its values in $\{0, 1, \dots, 9\}$. Each input represents the on-off status of one lightning segment of a seven-segment indicator and is determined univocally from Y. To create an artificial (binary) context, we created two copies of this dataset, the first one corresponding to $X_c = 0$ and the second one to $X_c = 1$. The first dataset was unchanged, while in the second one variables X_5, X_6, and X_7 were turned into irrelevant variables. In addition, we included a new variable X_8, irrelevant by construction in both contexts. The final dataset contains 320 samples, 160 in each context.

Table 3 reports possible importance scores for all the inputs. Again, these scores were computed analytically using the asymptotic formulas. As expected, variable X_8 has zero importance in all cases. Also as expected, variables X_5, X_6, and X_7 are all context-dependent ($Imp^{|x_c|}(X_m) > 0$ for all of them). They are context-redundant (and even irrelevant) when $X_c = 1$ and complementary when $X_c = 0$. More surprisingly, variables X_1, X_2, X_3, and X_4 are also context-dependent, even if their distribution is independent from the context. This is due to the fact that these variables are complementary with variables X_5, X_6, and X_7 for predicting the output. Their context-dependence is thus a consequence of the context-dependence of X_5, X_6, X_7. X_1, X_2, X_3, and X_4 are all almost redundant when $X_c = 0$ and complementary when $X_c = 1$, which expresses the fact that they provide more information about the output when X_5, X_6 and X_7 are irrelevant ($X_c = 1$) and less when X_5, X_6, and X_7 are relevant ($X_c = 0$). Nevertheless, X_8 remains irrelevant in every situation.

Problem 3. We now consider bio-medical data from the *Primary tumor* dataset. The objective of the corresponding supervised learning problem is to predict the location of a primary tumor in patients with metastases. It was downloaded from the UCI repository (Lichman, 2013) and was collected by the University Medical Center in Ljubljana, Slovenia. We restrict our analysis to 132 samples without missing values. Patients are described by 17 discrete clinical variables (listed in the first column of Table 4) and the output is chosen among 22 possible locations. For this analysis, we use the patient gender as the context variable.

Table 4 reports variable importances computed with 1000 totally randomized trees and their corresponding p-values. According to the p-values of $Imp^{|x_c|}(X_m)$, two variables are clearly emphasized for each context: importances of *histologic-type* and *neck* both significantly decrease in the first context ($female$) and importances of *peritoneum* and *abdominal* both significantly decrease in the second context ($male$). While the biological relevance of these finding needs to be verified, such dependences could not have been highlighted from standard random forests importances.

Note that the same importances computed using the asymptotic formulas are provided in Appendix E. Importance values are very similar, highlighting that finite forests provide good enough estimates for this problem.

Problem 4. As a last experiment, we consider a publicly available brain cancer gene expression dataset (Verhaak et al., 2010). This dataset collects measurements of mRNA expression levels of 11861 genes in 220 tissue samples from patients suffering from glioblastoma multiforme (GBM), the most common form of malignant brain cancer in adults. Samples are classified into four GBM subtypes: Classical, Mesenchymal, Neural and Proneural. The interest of this dataset is to identify the genes that play a central role in the development and progression of the cancer and thus improve our understanding of this disease. In our experiment, our aim is to exploit importance scores to identify interactions between genes that are significantly affected by the cancer sub-type considered as our context variable. This dataset was previously exploited by Mohan et al. (2014), who used it to test a method based on Gaussian graphical models for detecting genes whose global interaction patterns with all the other genes vary significantly between the subtypes. This latter method can be considered as gene-based, while our approach is link-based.

Following (Mohan et al., 2014), we normalized the raw data using Multi-array Average (RMA) normalization. Then, the data was corrected for batch effects using the software ComBat (Johnson et al., 2007) and then $log2$ transformed. Following (Mohan et al., 2014), we focused our analysis on only two GBM sub-types, Proneural (57 tissue samples) and Mesenchymal (56 tissue samples), and on a particular set of 32 genes, which are all genes involved in the TCR signaling pathway as defined in the Reactome database (Matthews et al., 2009). The final dataset used in the experiments below thus contains 113 samples, 57 and 56 for both context values respectively, and 32 variables.

To identify gene-gene interactions affected by the context, we performed a contextual analysis as described in Section 3 for each gene in turn, considering each time a particular gene as the target variable Y and all other genes as the set of input variables V. This procedure is similar to the procedure adopted in the Random forests-based gene network inference method called GENIE3 (Huynh-Thu et al., 2010), that was the best performer in the DREAM5 network infer-

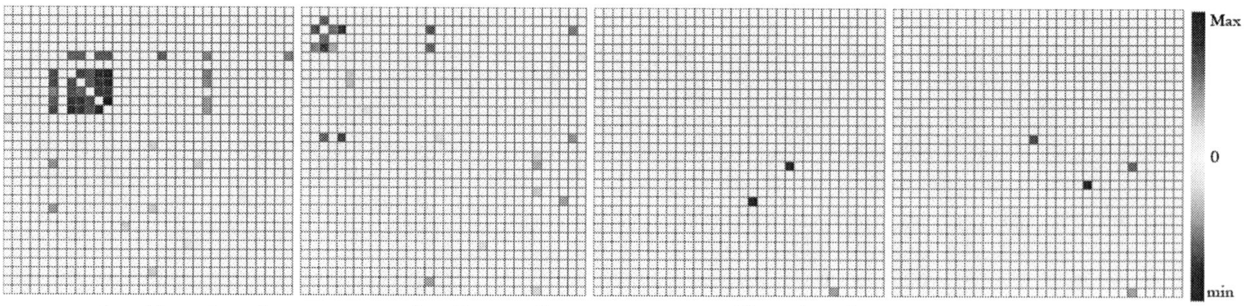

(a) $Imp^{|x_c=Mesenchymal|}$ (b) $Imp^{|x_c=Proneural|}$ (c) $Imp^{x_c=Mesenchymal}$ (d) $Imp^{x_c=Proneural}$

Figure 1: Results for Problem 4. Each matrix represents significant context-dependent gene-gene interactions as found using $Imp^{|x_c|}$ in (a)(b) and Imp^{x_c} in (c)(d), in GBM sub-type Mesenschymal in (a)(c) and Proneural in (b)(d). In (a) and (b), cells are colored according to $Imp_s^{x_c}$. In (c) and (d), cells are colored according to Imp^{x_c}. Positive (resp negative) values are in blue (resp. red) and highlight context-redundant (resp. context-complementary) interactions. Higher absolute values are darker.

ence challenge (Marbach et al., 2012). Since gene expressions are numerical targets, we used variance as the impurity measure (see Section 3.5) and we built ensembles of 1000 totally randomized trees in all experiments.

The matrices in Figure 1 highlight context-dependent interactions found using different importance measures (detailed below). A cell (i, j) of these matrices corresponds to the importance of gene j when gene i is the output (the diagonal is irrelevant). White cells correspond to non significant context-dependencies as determined by random permutations of the context variable, using a significance level of 0.05. Significant context-dependent interactions in Figures 1(a) and (b) were determined using the importance $Imp^{|x_c|}$ defined in (11), which is the measure we advocate in this paper. As a baseline for comparison, Figures 1(c) and (d) show significant interactions as found using the more straightforward score Imp^{x_c} defined in (10). In Figures 1(a) and (b) (resp. (c) and (d)), significant cells are colored according to the value of $Imp_s^{x_c}$ defined in (12). In Figures 1(c) and (d), they are colored according to the value of Imp^{x_c} in (10) instead. Blue (resp. red) cells correspond to positive (resp. negative) values of Imp^{x_c} or $Imp_s^{x_c}$ and thus highlight context-redundant (resp. context-complementary) interactions. The darker the color, the higher the absolute value of Imp^{x_c} or $Imp_s^{x_c}$.

Respectively 49 and 26 context-dependent interactions are found in Figures 1(a) and (b). In comparison, only 3 and 4 interactions are found respectively in Figures 1(c) and (d) using the more straightforward score Imp^{x_c}. Only 1 interaction is common between Figures 1(a) and (c), while 3 interactions are common between Figures 1(b) and (d). The much lower sensitivity of Imp^{x_c} with respect to $Imp^{|x_c|}$ was expected given the discussions in Section 3.2. Although more straightforward, the score $Imp^{x_c}(X_m)$, defined as the difference $Imp(X_m) - Imp(X_m|X_c = x_c)$, indeed suffers from the fact that $Imp(X_m)$ and $Imp(X_m|X_c = x_c)$ are estimated from different ensembles and thus do not explore the same conditionings in finite setting. Imp^{x_c} also does not have the same guarantee as $Imp^{|x_c|}$ to find all context-dependent variables.

5 Conclusions

In this work, our first contribution is a formal framework defining and characterizing the dependence to a context variable of the relationship between the input variables and the output (Section 2). As a second contribution, we have proposed several novel adaptations of random forests-based variable importance scores that implement these definitions and characterizations and we have derived performance guarantees for these scores in asymptotic settings (Section 3). The relevance of these measures was illustrated on several artificial and real datasets (Section 4).

There remain several limitations to our framework that we would like to address as future works. All theoretical derivations in Sections 2 and 3 concern categorical input variables. It would be interesting to adapt our framework to continuous input variables, and also, probably with more difficulty, to continuous context variables. Finally, all theoretical derivations are based on forests of totally randomized trees (for which we have an asymptotic characterization). It would be interesting to also investigate non totally randomized tree algorithms (e.g., Breiman (2001)'s standard Random Forests method) that could provide better trade-offs in finite settings.

Acknowledgements. Antonio Sutera is a recipient of a FRIA grant from the FNRS (Belgium) and acknowledges its financial support. This work is supported by PASCAL2 and the IUAP DYSCO, initiated by the Belgian State, Science Policy Office. The primary tumor data was obtained from the University Medical Centre, Institute of Oncology, Ljubljana, Yugoslavia. Thanks go to M. Zwitter and M. Soklic.

References

Boutilier, C., Friedman, N., Goldszmidt, M., and Koller, D. (1996). Context-specific independence in bayesian networks. In *Proceedings of the Twelfth International Conference on Uncertainty in Artificial Intelligence*, UAI'96, pages 115–123, San Francisco, CA, USA. Morgan Kaufmann Publishers Inc.

Breiman, L. (2001). Random forests. *Machine learning*, 45(1):5–32.

Breiman, L., Friedman, J., Stone, C. J., and Olshen, R. A. (1984). *Classification and regression trees*. CRC press.

Brown, G. (2009). A new perspective for information theoretic feature selection. In *International conference on artificial intelligence and statistics*, pages 49–56.

Brown, G., Pocock, A., Zhao, M.-J., and Luján, M. (2012). Conditional likelihood maximisation: a unifying framework for information theoretic feature selection. *The Journal of Machine Learning Research*, 13(1):27–66.

Geissler, H. J., Hölzl, P., Marohl, S., Kuhn-Régnier, F., Mehlhorn, U., Südkamp, M., and de Vivie, E. R. (2000). Risk stratification in heart surgery: comparison of six score systems. *European Journal of Cardio-thoracic surgery*, 17(4):400–406.

Guyon, I. and Elisseeff, A. (2003). An introduction to variable and feature selection. *The Journal of Machine Learning Research*, 3:1157–1182.

Huynh-Thu, V. A., Irrthum, A., Wehenkel, L., and Geurts, P. (2010). Inferring regulatory networks from expression data using tree-based methods. *PLoS ONE*, 5(9).

Ideker, T. and Krogan, N. J. (2012). Differential network biology. *Molecular systems biology*, 8(1).

Jakulin, A. (2005). *Machine learning based on attribute interactions*. PhD thesis, Univerza v Ljubljani.

Jakulin, A. and Bratko, I. (2003). *Analyzing attribute dependencies*. Springer.

Johnson, W. E., Li, C., and Rabinovic, A. (2007). Adjusting batch effects in microarray expression data using empirical bayes methods. *Biostatistics*, 8(1):118–127.

Kohavi, R. and John, G. H. (1997). Wrappers for feature subset selection. *Artificial intelligence*, 97(1):273–324.

Lichman, M. (2013). UCI machine learning repository.

Louppe, G., Wehenkel, L., Sutera, A., and Geurts, P. (2013). Understanding variable importances in forests of randomized trees. In *Advances in Neural Information Processing Systems*, pages 431–439.

Marbach, D., Costello, J. C., Küffner, R., Vega, N. M., Prill, R. J., Camacho, D. M., Allison, K. R., Kellis, M., Collins, J. J., Stolovitzky, G., et al. (2012). Wisdom of crowds for robust gene network inference. *Nature methods*, 9(8):796–804.

Matthews, L., Gopinath, G., Gillespie, M., Caudy, M., Croft, D., de Bono, B., Garapati, P., Hemish, J., Hermjakob, H., Jassal, B., et al. (2009). Reactome knowledgebase of human biological pathways and processes. *Nucleic acids research*, 37(suppl 1):D619–D622.

McGill, W. J. (1954). Multivariate information transmission. *Psychometrika*, 19(2):97–116.

Mohan, K., London, P., Fazel, M., Witten, D., and Lee, S.-I. (2014). Node-based learning of multiple gaussian graphical models. *The Journal of Machine Learning Research*, 15(1):445–488.

Turney, P. (1996). The identification of context-sensitive features: A formal definition of context for concept learning. In *13th International Conference on Machine Learning (ICML96), Workshop on Learning in Context-Sensitive Domains*, pages 60–66.

Van de Cruys, T. (2011). Two multivariate generalizations of pointwise mutual information. In *Proceedings of the Workshop on Distributional Semantics and Compositionality*, pages 16–20. Association for Computational Linguistics.

Verhaak, R. G., Hoadley, K. A., Purdom, E., Wang, V., Qi, Y., Wilkerson, M. D., Miller, C. R., Ding, L., Golub, T., Mesirov, J. P., et al. (2010). Integrated genomic analysis identifies clinically relevant subtypes of glioblastoma characterized by abnormalities in pdgfra, idh1, egfr, and nf1. *Cancer cell*, 17(1):98–110.

Zhang, N. L. and Poole, D. L. (1999). On the role of context-specific independence in probabilistic inference. In *Proceedings of the Sixteenth International Joint Conference on Artificial Intelligence, IJCAI 99, Stockholm, Sweden, July 31 - August 6, 1999. 2 Volumes, 1450 pages*, pages 1288–1293.

Content-based Modeling of Reciprocal Relationships using Hawkes and Gaussian Processes

Xi Tan [1], **Syed A. Z. Naqvi** [1], **Alan (Yuan) Qi** [1,2], **Katherine A. Heller** [3], and **Vinayak Rao** [2]

[1]Department of Computer Science, Purdue University, West Lafayette, IN 47907
[2]Department of Statistics, Purdue University, West Lafayette, IN 47907
[3]Department of Statistical Science, Duke University, Durham, NC 27708

Abstract

There has been growing interest in inferring implicit social structures using interaction data. This approach is motivated by the fact that entities organize themselves into groups having frequent interactions between each other. Unlike previous approaches that focused on subjectively declared relationships, the idea is to exploit the actual evidence at hand to reach conclusions about group formations, resulting in more objective data-driven inferences. To this end, [5] have employed Hawkes processes, and proposed a Hawkes IRM model to infer social structures from interaction data. A major factor that encourages the use of Hawkes processes is the capability to model reciprocity in the interaction between social entities. However, reciprocation is dynamically conditioned upon two key factors: the significance of each message sent by the sender, and the receptivity to each message received by the receiver. In the model proposed by [5], reciprocity is not affected by either of these factors, since the content of each message is not taken into account. In this paper, we extend the work of [5] by introducing Gaussian processes (GPs) into the Hawkes IRM model: based on the content of each message, GPs are used to model the message significance as well as receptivity. This allows us to more accurately capture the interactions among entities. The application of GPs also allows us to flexibly model the rates of reciprocal activities between two entities, allowing asymmetry in reciprocity to be captured more accurately. This leads to better cluster detection capability. Our model outperforms previous Hawkes and Poisson process-based models at predicting verbal, email, and citation activities.

1 INTRODUCTION

In the social sciences, group dynamics is the study of the content and dynamics of the complex interactions occurring within a social group or between social groups. The study of group dynamics helps understand decision making processes, disease epidemics and develop effective therapeutic/control techniques. Early approaches [12, 19, 4] have focused on declared relationships between individuals to infer latent group structures. For example, if three people declare they like each other but dislike others, it is reasonable to put them into one group. However, these declared relationships are not easily accessible, sometimes incorrect and usually highly subjective. Another limitation of previous models is their incapability to capture reciprocity in social interactions. Reciprocity is a common characteristic in group dynamics. It expresses the fact that social entities reciprocate in their interaction between each other. For example, if Alice has sent a message to Bob, it increases the likelihood of Bob replying back to Alice. Reciprocity is expected to be more prominent between entities within a group, and hence it can be used to infer social groups.

To address these issues, recently, there has been a trend to infer implicit social structures using interaction data. This approach is motivated by the fact that interactions between different groups varies in nature and frequency. Unlike approaches that focused on subjectively declared relationships, the idea is to exploit the actual evidence at hand to reach conclusions about group formations, making this approach is more objective in nature. Recently, [5] proposed a nonparametric Bayesian model that is built upon mutually-exciting point processes, known as Hawkes processes [9, 10], and the Infinite Relational Model (IRM) [19, 4] to infer social structures from continuous time interaction data. Pairs of mutually-exciting Hawkes processes are able to exploit reciprocity to infer social groups; here the processes excite one another through their actualized events.

However, reciprocation is dynamically conditioned upon two key factors: the significance of each message sent by the sender, and the receptiveness of the receiver to each incoming message. In real communication, conveying an important message develops interest in the receiver. Then, if the receiver finds the message relevant, reciprocation takes place. Accordingly, reciprocal communication emerges from the interplay of these two factors. The model proposed by [5] does not take these factors into consideration, instead assuming that entities reciprocate simply because they received a message, and giving no consideration to the content of the message and its effects on the interaction.

In this paper, we extend the work of [5] by introducing Gaussian processes (GPs) into the Hawkes IRM model. We use these to account for the content of the messages, capturing the message significance as well as receptivity. This allows us to more accurately capture the interactions among entities. The interaction between a pair of clusters is modeled as the additive effect of the interactions between all pairs of nodes in the two clusters, allowing us to identify the contribution of each pair of nodes, where the actual communication is taking place, to the interaction between a pair of clusters. The introduction of GPs also allows us to flexibly model the rates of reciprocal activities between two entities, hence the asymmetry in reciprocity can be captured more accurately. We show how this leads to a better cluster detection capability. Since our proposed work is a natural extension of Hawkes IRM, it covers both Poisson processes and IRM as special cases.

The remainder of the paper is organized as follows: section 2 discusses Poisson and Hawkes processes, with and without IRM. Section 3 describes our extension of the Hawkes IRM model. Section 4 presents an inference algorithm for our model, section 5 discusses related work, and section 6 presents experimental results using our model on synthetic, verbal, email, and citation data.

2 BACKGROUND

We start with a brief description of Poisson processes, Hawkes processes, and Hawkes IRM model.

2.1 Poisson and Hawkes Processes

Point processes are stochastic processes, realizations of which are collections of points in time or space. The former are called temporal point processes, and the latter, spatial point processes. The homogeneous Poisson process is the simplest example of a point process, have a constant rate function, while the inhomogeneous Poisson process has rate function λ varying with, say, time. Both are examples of completely random measures, where events in disjoint sets are independent of each other. Hawkes processes, on the other hand, are mutually-exciting doubly point processes, whose rate function is itself a stochastic process, depending on events of its own and of other processes.

For both Poisson processes and Hawkes processes, with conditional rate function $\lambda(t)$ and event time history $\mathcal{H}_{(0,T]} = \{t_1, \cdots, t_n\}$, the likelihood function can be written as

$$\mathcal{L}(\lambda(t)|\mathcal{H}) = \exp\{-\Lambda(0,T)\} \prod_{i=1}^{n} \lambda(t_i) \tag{1}$$

where $\Lambda(0,T) = \int_0^T \lambda(t)dt$ is the cumulative conditional rate function. When the conditional rate function $\lambda(t) = \lambda$ is a constant, the Poisson process likelihood is simply:

$$\mathcal{L}(\lambda|\mathcal{H}) = \exp\{-\lambda T\} \lambda^n \tag{2}$$

For a Hawkes process, the rate function λ depends on earlier events. Let $N(\cdot)$ and $N'(\cdot)$ be a pair of mutually-exciting Hawkes processes. The conditional rate function $\lambda(t)$ of $N(\cdot)$, given the event time history $\mathcal{H}_{N'} = \{t'_1, \cdots, t'_n\}$ of N', has the form

$$\lambda(t) = \gamma + \int_{-\infty}^{t} g(t-s)dN'(s) \tag{3}$$

where γ is the base rate of $N(\cdot)$, and the triggering function $g(\cdot)$ is a non-negative function such that $\int_0^\infty g(s)ds < 1$, ensuring that $N(\cdot)$ is stationary.

If $g(\cdot) = 0$ then the process becomes a Poisson process with rate γ. If the counting measure $N'(\cdot)$ is $N(\cdot)$ itself, the process is self- exciting: its current rate only depends on its own past events. If the two counting measures are different, the rate is affected by the past events of each other.

2.2 Hawkes Processes with Infinite Relational Model (HP+IRM)

Amongst the models that use declared relationships to infer group information, the Infinite Relational Model (IRM) [12] is especially flexible and popular. [5] has combined the IRM idea with the concept of Hawkes Processes to model reciprocity in the interaction between entity groups. Let V denote the vertices of the graph, corresponding to individuals. Then the generative model for a Hawkes process is defined as follows:

$$\pi|\alpha \sim CRP(\alpha) \tag{4}$$

$$\lambda_{pq}(t)|\gamma_{pq}, \beta_{pq}, \tau_{pq} = \gamma_{pq} n_p n_q + \int_{-\infty}^{t} g_{pq}(t-s)dN_{qp}(s) \;\; \forall p,q \in range(\pi) \tag{5}$$

$$N_{pq}(\cdot)|\lambda_{pq} \sim HawkesProcess(\lambda_{pq}) \tag{6}$$

$$N_{uv}(\cdot)|N_{\pi(u)\pi(v)}, \pi \sim Thin(N_{\pi(u)\pi(v)}) \;\; \forall u,v \in V \tag{7}$$

Here π is a partition of the vertices V, distributed according to the Chinese restaurant process (CRP) with concentration parameter α. We use p and q to index clusters of π. We denote the cluster that vertex u belongs to as $\pi(u)$. The operator $Thin$ refers to thinning; this means distributing the atoms of $N_{pq}(\cdot)$ among each $N_{uv}(\cdot)$, such that $N_{pq} = \sum_{u,v} N_{u,v}(\cdot)$. Any thinning scheme may be used, such as a uniform thinning, which uniformly picks to elements of a cluster. The type of reciprocation (parameterized by g_{pq} and g_{qp}, respectively) differs with events from cluster p to cluster q and events from cluster q to cluster p. This difference in reciprocity is what the model exploits to learn about social groups.

3 HAWKES PROCESSES WITH IRM AND GAUSSIAN PROCESSES (HPGP + IRM)

We define the Hawkes process conditional rate function as:

$$\lambda_{uv}(t) = \gamma_{pq} + \int_0^t \beta_{uv} e^{-\frac{t-s}{\tau_{uv}}} dN_{vu}(s) \tag{8}$$

where $p = \pi^{-1}(u), q = \pi^{-1}(v)$ are the clusters individuals u and v belong to; and the triggering function $g_{uv}(\cdot)$ is defined as:

$$g_{uv}(\delta) = \beta_{uv} e^{-\frac{\delta}{\tau_{uv}}} \tag{9}$$

Geometrically, the excitation function β_{pq} is essentially the "jump size" of the rate function $\lambda_{uv}(t)$ whenever a new message is received. However, in the above definition, β_{uv} is not affected by the content of the message; its value does not change based on the significance and receptivity of the messages.

We would like to define β_{uv} in a way such that it measures the significance and receptivity of individual messages communicated between individuals u and v. The content measure x_{vu} can be suitably defined according to the application, for example, it can be a distribution of words, the length of the message, or the text entropy of the message, etc. The individual level excitation function $\beta_{uv}(x_{vu}(s)) = 0$ if no message was sent from v to u at time s, but can be otherwise any non-negative function.

We propose to use two sets of Gaussian Process (GP) priors to address sources of inhomogeneity of the excitation functions $\beta_{uv}(\cdot)$, one for the significance of the message and one for the receptivity of the message:

$$\beta_{uv}(s) = e^{r_u(x_{vu}(s)) + s_v(x_{vu}(s))} \tag{10}$$

where

$$r_u(\cdot) \sim \mathcal{GP}(0, k_r) \tag{11}$$

$$s_v(\cdot) \sim \mathcal{GP}(0, k_s) \tag{12}$$

k_r and k_s are radial basis function (RBF) kernels of the GPs. The exponential transformation is used to make sure that $\beta_{uv}(\cdot)$ is non-negative.

Larger values of r_u and s_v indicate that an important message has been sent by the sender, and receiver is receptive to the message, these result in larger values for β_{uv}. If either r_u or s_v is small, or both of them have smaller values, it leads to smaller values of β_{uv}. Application of GP functions also allows us to flexibly model the rates of reciprocal activities between two entities, allowing the asymmetry in reciprocity to be captured more accurately. This, as a by-product, leads to a better cluster detection capability.

The receptivity and significance functions r_u and s_v may have different behaviors and hence are designed to come from two different GPs. One subtle point is that although r_u and s_v seem exchangeable in the definition of β_{uv} and both use message content x_{vu} as input, they are evaluated from different perspectives: r_u evaluates x_{vu} from the receiver u's perspective, while s_v from the sender v's perspective. One alternative way is to model a single pair of GPs $s(\cdot)$ and $r(\cdot)$ for all users, instead of this per-user GP $s_u(\cdot)$ and $r_v(\cdot)$ framework. Experiments have shown that both the modeling schemes have good performances, however, we believe that the per-user GP setting can reveal more interesting user-specific details, and hence in the later sections, our results are based on the per-user GP framework.

The generative process of our model can be summarized as:

$$\pi|\alpha \sim CRP(\alpha) \tag{13}$$

$$\lambda_{uv}(t)|\gamma_{pq}, \beta_{uv}(\cdot), \tau_{uv} = \gamma_{pq} + \int_{-\infty}^t \beta_{uv}(\mathcal{X}_{vu}) e^{-\frac{t-s}{\tau_{uv}}} dN_{vu}(s) \tag{14}$$

$$N_{uv}(\cdot)|\lambda_{uv} \sim HawkesProcess(\lambda_{uv}) \tag{15}$$

where $\mathcal{X}_{vu} = \{x_{vu}(s)\}$ is the set of all messages sent from v to u, and the cluster level excitation function β_{pq} can be seen as an additive effect of β_{uv}:

$$\beta_{pq}(\mathcal{X}_{qp}) = \sum_{\pi(u)=p, \pi(v)=q} \beta_{uv}(x_{vu}(s)) \tag{16}$$

Now, the excitation function β_{pq} is no longer a constant, as in [5], but a function of the message content in the past events of the reciprocal process N_{qp}, taking into account both the significance and the receptivity of the messages. Our model is a generalization of the model described in [5], and if β_{uv} in equation 10 are constants, our model reduces to the model described in [5]. Therefore, all the basic features of the original model are inherited by our model. Also, in our modeling framework, the individual rate function λ_{uv} is affected by the group initial rate γ_{pq}, which, on the one hand, tends to put similarly behaving individuals into the same cluster; and on the other hand, if one member of a group is heavily influenced by a particular message, it is highly likely that other individuals in the same group will also be affected.

3.1 Stability Conditions of HPGP + IRM

For Hawkes processes with constant excitation functions β_{pq}, the sufficient condition of stationarity is $\beta_{pq}\tau_{pq} < 1$, derived from the condition $\int_0^\infty \beta(s)ds < 1$. By contrast, since our β_{pq} is a function of message contents, the expectation of $\lambda(t)$ cannot be time invariant. Therefore, the stationarity condition no longer holds. However, since β_{pq} is evaluated at finite locations (in the domain of message content x), we can define β_{pq}^{MAX} to be the maximum value of β_{pq} across all locations. For our model, we can still require that $\beta_{pq}^{MAX} \int_0^\infty e^{-\frac{u}{\tau_{pq}}} du < 1$. Since $\beta_{pq}^{MAX} \int_0^\infty e^{-\frac{u}{\tau_{pq}}} du = \beta_{pq}^{MAX}\tau_{pq}$, we just need to make sure that $\beta_{pq}^{MAX}\tau_{pq} < 1$.

4 HPGP + IRM INFERENCE

We perform posterior inference using Markov chain Monte Carlo method. In our model there is no conjugacy between prior and the likelihood, hence we can not marginalize out parameters and must sample all of them separately. To infer the partition of individuals π, the concentration parameter α, the parameters of each Hawkes process $\theta_{pq} = \{\gamma_{pq}, \tau_{pq}\}$, the training and test point projections of functions r_u and s_v, we use Algorithm 5 in [15] to draw samples from the posterior. We use elliptical slice sampling [14] for r_u and s_v, and standard slice sampling [16] for γ_{pq}, τ_{pq} and α. In case of τ_{pq} we set the upper bound of the slice sampler to $\frac{1}{\beta_{pq}^{MAX}}$, to ensure that $\beta_{pq}^{MAX}\tau_{pq} < 1$.

5 RELATED WORK

The interest of modeling relational data dates back to at least the work of [11], who introduced the Bayesian formulation of the stochastic block-model. This model was then extended by [12] to the Infinite Relational Model (IRM).

The IRM typically assumes that there is a fixed graph, describing the relationship between individuals, which is observed. This idea is used in many proposed works [12, 19]. Our model does not make this assumption, but learns the relationship among participants' interactions.

There have also been research works modeling relational events via latent classes [6]. They assume each event's sender, receiver, and action type are conditionally independent given the latent class for that event. This strong assumption greatly simplifies the model, but may not reflect real situations. Our model is not limited to any fixed number of action types.

Other works [17, 18, 7] are based on temporal Poisson-processes, where the rate of events on each edge is independent of every other edge. Although [18, 7] allow mutually exciting events to be modeled, they do not use content information to model dependencies between events. Our model uses Hawkes processes which are capable of dealing with interaction and reciprocal events, and also use message content information to capture the interactions more accurately. Our work is also closely related to [13]. They combine mutually exciting Hawkes process with random graph models by defining the excitation function, between a pair of nodes, as a product of a latent binary indicator variable, indicating the presence or absence of edge, and weight variable that determines the strength of interaction between the two nodes. However, unlike our model, their method does not use side information, such as information content, and simply relies on time interaction data to infer latent network structures. Lastly, our work extends the work of [5]. In their paper, the excitation function is not affected by the information content of the message. By introducing Gaussian processes, we are able to model non homogeneous excitation functions. In addition to that, since we use Gaussian processes to model the flexible rates of reciprocal activities between two entities, our model can capture the asymmetry in reciprocity more accurately. This, as a by-product, leads to a better cluster detection capability. The model in [8] does not have this leverage.

6 EXPERIMENTS

We compared our model (HPGP + IRM) to four methods: 1) Poisson Process Model (Poisson), 2) Hawkes Process Model (HP), 3) Poisson Processes with IRM (Poisson + IRM), and 4) Hawkes Processes with IRM (HP + IRM).

6.1 Synthetic Data Sets

We tested several synthetic data sets under various conditions to compare different model fittings to the rate functions, as well as their clustering behaviors.

A Simple Case Consists of Two Individuals. To generate synthetic data set, we need to set parameter values γ_{uv}, and τ_{uv}, as well as the functional form of $\beta_{uv}(\cdot)$ and message content measure x_{vu}. In figure 1, two mutually-exciting Hawkes processes are simulated during time interval $(0, 10]$, where $\gamma_{12} = \gamma_{21} = 0.1$, $\tau_{12} = \tau_{21} = 1$.

In part (a), case 1 used a constant message content $x_{12}(t_i) = x_{21}(t'_i) = 1$ for all event times t_i and t'_i, and a constant excitation function $\beta_{12}(x) = \beta_{21}(x) = x = 1$ for all messages. Since this synthetic data set has constant β values, it is essentially generated from a HP+IRM; we see that HP+IRM and our model, a generalization to HP+IRM, both perform well, and are better than other models, in terms of log-likelihood shown in table 1.

In part (b), case 2 used the same settings as part (a), except for the introduction of variable message content, where both $x_{12}(t_i)$ and $x_{21}(t'_i)$ follow an exponential distribution $\exp(0.5)$, which can be thought of as different message entropy values at different event times t_i and t'_i. We see that the jump sizes of both processes are no longer constant. This cannot be modeled by a constant β model, but can only be handled by models like ours, which allow variable β. The effectiveness of our model in this case can be seen from the comparison of the log-likelihoods in table 1.

In part (c), case 3 further introduced non-constant $\beta_{uv}(\cdot)$, with all other settings being the same as in case 2, but $\beta_{12}(t_i) = e^{2sin(x_{21}(t_i))+1.5log(x_{21}(t_i))}$ and $\beta_{21}(t_i') = e^{0.1cos(x_{12}(t_i'))+0.2\sqrt{x_{12}(t_i')}}$, where $r_1(x_{21}(t_i)) = 2sin(x_{21}(t_i))$, $r_2(x_{12}(t_i')) = 0.1cos(x_{12}(t_i'))$, $s_1(x_{12}(t_i')) = 0.2\sqrt{x_{12}(t_i')}$, and $s_2(x_{21}(t_i)) = 1.5log(x_{21}(t_i))$. Again, the jump sizes for both processes are not constant, and also note that $\beta_{21}(x) > \beta_{12}(x), \forall x \in (0, 10)$. This suggests that process 2 is excited to respond to any messages received from process 1, while process 1 is reluctant to respond to messages sent from process 2. In this case, the difference in log-likelihoods of different models is pronounced even more.

Table 1: Log likelihood comparison for the three-case synthetic data set

	CASE 1	CASE 2	CASE 3
HPGP+IRM	-21.88	-13.41	-10.86
HP+IRM	-22.97	-35.53	-82.78
POISSON + IRM	-72.31	-89.73	-126.33
HP	-129.37	-238.94	-192.78
POISSON	-127.83	-182.76	-187.23

Next, we will discuss our modeling preferences based on the three-case example used in figure 1.

GP Against Simple Parametric Functions. In order to demonstrate the effectiveness of using GP in our model, we compared its performances with simple parametric functions. In table 2, we summarize the log likelihood for the three-case synthetic data set mentioned earlier in figure 1, using GP and simple polynomials (up to order 3). The results clearly show the superior performance of GP over polynomial functions. The coefficients of polynomials are estimated by sampling from the posterior.

Table 2: Log likelihood comparison between GP and simple parametric functions

	GP	CUBIC	QUAD	LINEAR
CASE 1	-21.88	-38.67	-38.88	-39.18
CASE 2	-13.41	-61.27	-78.17	-89.28
CASE 3	-10.86	-71.26	-72.13	-76.73

Estimate Kernel Width From Data. In our experiment, we used the RBF (radial basis function) kernel, which has the form:

$$k(\delta) = \exp\left(-\frac{\delta^2}{2\sigma^2}\right) \tag{17}$$

where δ is the distance between two data points, and σ the kernel width. The estimation of the kernel width is crucial in our modeling framework as it controls the complexity of the underlying receptivity and significance functions. We applied 3 different approaches to estimate σ: Bayesian, heuristic, and fixed. The Bayesian approach introduces a prior on σ and obtains an estimate using MCMC; the heuristic way, bearing in mind that sigma largely depends on the maximum distance among the training data, estimates σ directly from sample data distances; and the fixed approach manually assigns a fixed value to the kernel width. It is evident from table 3 that the Bayesian approach is the best choice for our model in terms of log likelihood.

Table 3: Log likelihood comparison for kernel estimation

	BAYESIAN	HEURISTIC	FIXED
CASE 1	-21.88	-25.12	-39.78
CASE 2	-13.41	-17.16	-18.72
CASE 3	-10.86	-22.13	-24.67

Comparison Between Different Information Metrics. We compared four strategies to evaluate the information content of a message: KL divergence of word distribution, message length, TF-IDF, and message Shannon entropy. Using length as the measure of information may not be sufficient in practice; the importance of a message is simply determined by its longevity, without giving any consideration to the content. In case of Shannon entropy, however, the significance and receptivity of the message are better captured. TF-IDF has similar behavior and characteristics as those of message entropy. The best performance in our experiments were given by using KL divergence of word distribution and Shannon entropy, and we preferred KL divergence of word distribution over the other measures because it is more interpretable, and seemed to give consistent good performances in terms of log-likelihoods as shown in table 4. However, encoding content information efficiently is still an open question, and certainly a direction for future work.

Table 4: Log likelihood comparison for different information metrics

	WORD KL	ENTROPY	TF-IDF	LENGTH
CASE 1	-21.88	-21.98	-39.38	-128.76
CASE 2	-13.41	-12.78	-28.61	-87.21
CASE 3	-10.86	-12.63	-23.78	-72.13

Next, we will discuss a more detailed example consisting of three individuals.

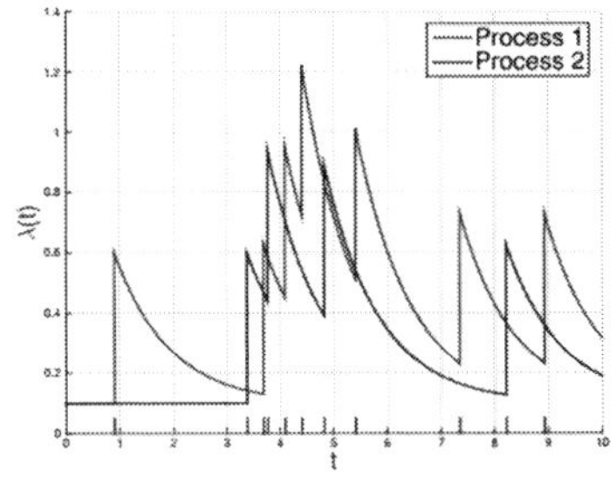

(a) Case 1: x constant, β simple function $\beta = x$. The "jump sizes" are constant.

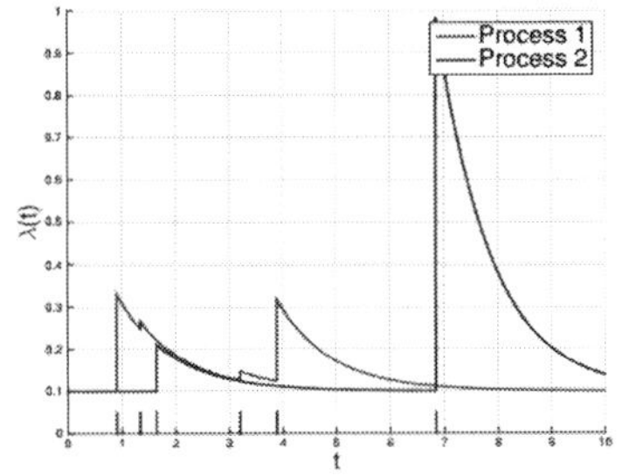

(b) Case 2: x random, β simple function $\beta = x$. The "jump sizes" are not constant.

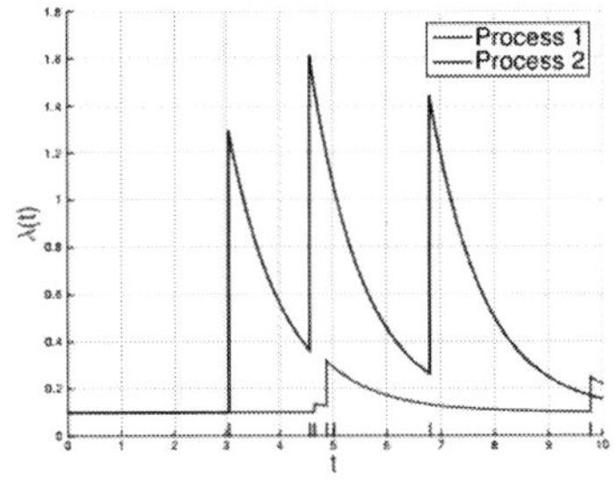

(c) Case 3: x random, β non-trivial function. The "jump sizes" are not constant.

Figure 1: Simulated rate functions of two individuals

A Full Example Consists of Three Individuals. In this example, we put processes 1 and 2 in one cluster whereas process 3 is in another cluster, and we also intentionally made them behave differently to each other.

The settings we used were $m_{ij} \sim multinomial(p = [0.25, 0.25, 0.25, 0.25], n = 4), \forall i, j \in \{1, 2, 3\}$, which could represent a dialog consisting of only four words, and each m_{ij} can be thought of as the distribution of these four words in a message sent from j to i. We define the message content measure as $x_{ij} = KL(m_{ij}||\bar{m}_i)$, where $\bar{m}_i$ is the four-word distribution assigned to individual i ($\bar{m}_i = (1, 1, 1, 1), \forall i$ in our experiment). For the excitation functions we have: $\beta_{12} = \beta_{21} = 5\exp(1/x)$, $\beta_{23} = \beta_{31} = 0.1\exp(1/x)$, and $\beta_{13} = \beta_{32} = 10\exp(1/x)$. Note that $\beta_{12} = \beta_{21}$, $\beta_{31} < \beta_{13}$, and $\beta_{32} > \beta_{23}$.

Figure 2 (a) shows that processes 1 and 2 are frequently interacting in a similar way, while in part (b), process 3 is not excited to respond to messages from process 1 but tends to, suggested in part (c), reply to process 2's messages more actively. In figure 2 (g, h, and i), we see that only our model was able to correctly cluster processes 1 and 2 in the same cluster and put process 3 in a separate one. On the other hand, the other models generated redundant clusters. We have also shown in figure 2 (d, e, and f) that our model successfully recovered the underlying excitation functions.

6.2 Real Data Sets

We tested our model on various turn-taking data sets, which include public meetings, private conversations, email communications, and publication citations. Each data set has several lines of event records, indicated by a quadruplet (t_i, s_i, r_i, m_i), where t_i is the time when the event took place, s_i the index of the sender, r_i the index of the recipient, and m_i the message word distribution.

We divided the data set into two parts: the first part consists of the first 90% of the data lines, used as the training data set; and the second part contains the remaining 10% of the data lines, used as the testing data set. To compute the average log probability, we ran our code 10 times with different prior settings and computed the mean and standard deviation of the 10 values.

Enron email threads The Enron data set (ENRON) contains about half a million email messages sent or received by about 150 senior managers of the Enron corporation [2, 3]. We restricted ourselves to "true" conversation emails (e.g., auto-messages were ignored) sent and received only from the domain "@enron.com", and identified the threads by time, sender, receiver, and the subject line. The longest email communication was selected.

Santa Barbara Conversation Corpus The Santa Barbara Corpus [1] data set (SB) contains text and video recordings for various conversations. The data set used (#33) is a lively family argument/discussion recorded at a vacation home in Falmouth, Massachusetts. There are eight participants, all relatives or close friends. Discussion centers around a disagreement Jennifer (#2) is having with her mother Lisbeth (#5).

High-energy Physics Theory Citation Network The Arxiv HEP-TH (high energy physics theory) citation data set (CITATION) covers all 352807 citations of 27770 papers published during the time period January 1993 to April 2003 (124 months). We converted paper citation events to author citation events. For example, if a paper by authors A and B cited another paper by authors C, D, and E, we would record six events: A cited C, D, and E; and B cited C, D, and E. Only the most cited 17 authors and 97 citation events in the year 2003 were used from this data set.

Results Table 5 and 6 show, for training and test data sets respectively, the predictive probability results as well as the most probable predictive number of clusters for competing methods. We used 10-fold cross-validation to prevent our model from being over-fitted to training data sets, and the performances on real data sets suggested a good generalization ability of our model.

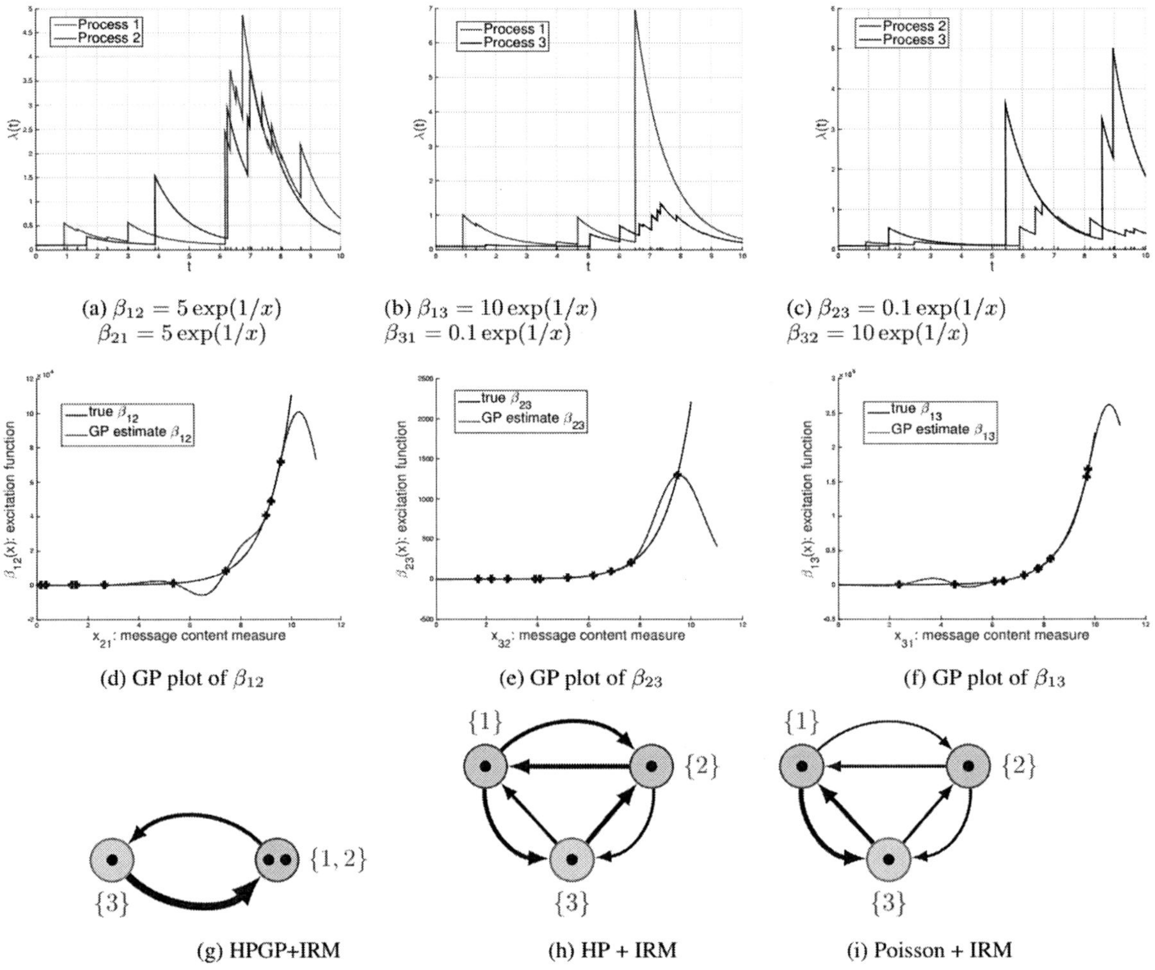

(a) $\beta_{12} = 5\exp(1/x)$
$\beta_{21} = 5\exp(1/x)$

(b) $\beta_{13} = 10\exp(1/x)$
$\beta_{31} = 0.1\exp(1/x)$

(c) $\beta_{23} = 0.1\exp(1/x)$
$\beta_{32} = 10\exp(1/x)$

(d) GP plot of β_{12}

(e) GP plot of β_{23}

(f) GP plot of β_{13}

(g) HPGP+IRM

(h) HP + IRM

(i) Poisson + IRM

Figure 2: Simulated rate functions of three individuals and their cluster configurations

Table 5: Average log likelihood for each model with standard error (TRAINING data sets). N is number of individuals, T is number of events, and C the predicted number of clusters.

	ENRON	SB #33	CITATION
(N, T, C)	(2, 896, 2)	(8, 499, 8)	(17, 97, 17)
HPGP + IRM	5612.67 ± 0.13	672.03 ± 0.11	1265.31 ± 0.14
HP + IRM	5513.25 ± 0.12	475.13 ± 0.50	987.34 ± 0.23
POISSON + IRM	2360.37 ± 0.06	572.35 ± 0.11	918.56 ± 0.17

Table 6: Average log predictive likelihood for each model with standard error (TEST data sets).

	ENRON	SB #33	CITATION
C	2	2	11
HPGP + IRM	327.13 ± 0.02	126.87 ± 0.05	217.51 ± 0.43
HP + IRM	270.36 ± 0.01	89.05 ± 0.04	127.81 ± 0.32
POISSON + IRM	46.21 ± 0.01	13.08 ± 0.00	97.00 ± 0.41

We also compared our model with HP+IRM in terms of cluster detection capability. Figure 3 shows the cluster configurations generated by our model and HP+IRM. This dataset is a record of a lively family argument/discussion. There were eight participants, all relatives or close friends, but the main communication was between Jennifer (#2) and her mother Lisbeth (#5). For our model, Jennifer and Lisbeth were put in one cluster, and rest in the other. This is more consistent with data evidence: Jennifer and Lisbeth reciprocate each other more frequently, and respond occasionally to others, despite receiving a lot of messages from them. Individuals other than #2 and #5 may be further decomposed into subgroups, but at this level, the best clustering would probably be the one given by our model. The contrast in the thicknesses of the arrows between the two clusters correctly reveals this aspect. On the other hand, the cluster configuration generated by HP+IRM model indicates a high level of reciprocity, indicated by comparable thicknesses of the two arrows, between clusters {2,5} and {4,6,7,8} which is inconsistent with data evidence. Additionally, the model creates an extra cluster,{1,3}, which is inconsistent with data evidence.

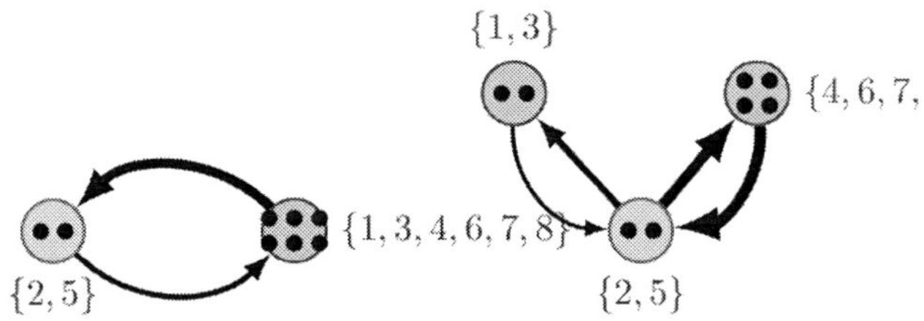

(a) HPGP+IRM (b) HP+IRM

Figure 3: Diagram for data set *SB #33*. The thickness of the arrows are proportional to the expectation of the rate function.

7 CONCLUSION

In this paper, we have presented a non-parametric Bayesian model that uses Hawkes processes to model reciprocal relationships. Unlike previous approaches, our model utilizes the content of the messages to model reciprocity. Based on the content, our model captures the significance of the message sent by the sender, and receptivity to the message received by the receiver. This gives us the leverage to model reciprocity in a more realistic manner and more accurately. Empirical results suggest that our novel model formulation can yield improved predictive probability results, and can reveal clusters more accurately than alternative methods.

8 Acknowledgements

Xi Tan, Syed A. Z. Naqvi, and Dr. Alan (Yuan) Qi were supported by NSF CAREER award IIS-1054903, and the NSF Science and Technology Center.

References

[1] SB Data Set. http://www.linguistics.ucsb.edu/research/santa-barbara-corpus. [Online; accessed 20-August-2014].

[2] Enron Email Data Set (RDdata). http://www.ahschulz.de/enron-email-data/enron_mysqldump.RData, 2011. [Online; accessed 20-August-2014].

[3] Enron Email Data Set (Text). https://www.cs.cmu.edu/~./enron/enron_mail_20110402.tgz, 2011. [Online; accessed 20-August-2014].

[4] Edoardo M Airoldi, David M Blei, Stephen E Fienberg, and Eric P Xing. Mixed membership stochastic blockmodels. *Journal of Machine Learning Research*, 9:1981–2014, 2008.

[5] Charles Blundell, Jeff Beck, and Katherine A Heller. Modelling reciprocating relationships with hawkes processes. In *Advances in Neural Information Processing Systems*, pages 2600–2608, 2012.

[6] Christopher DuBois and Padhraic Smyth. Modeling relational events via latent classes. In *Proceedings of the 16th ACM SIGKDD Conference on Knowledge Discovery and Data Mining*, 2010.

[7] Asela Gunawardanal, Christopher Meek, and Puyang Xu. A model for temporal dependencies in event streams. In *Neural Information Processing Systems (NIPS)*, 2011.

[8] Fangjian Guo, Charles Blundell, Hanna Wallach, and Katerine A. Heller. The bayesian echo chamber: Modeling influence in conversations. In *arXiv*, 2014.

[9] Alan G. Hawkes. Point spectra of some mutually exciting point processes. *Journal of the Royal Statistical Society. Series B (Methodological)*, pages 438–443, 1971.

[10] Alan G. Hawkes. Spectra of some self-exciting and mutually exciting point processes. *Biometrika*, pages 83–90, 1971.

[11] P. W. Holland, K. B. Laskey, and S. Leinhardt. Stochastic block models: first steps. In *Social Networks*, volume 5, pages 109–137, 1983.

[12] Charles Kemp, Joshua B Tenenbaum, Thomas L Griffiths, Takeshi Yamada, and Naonori Ueda. Learning systems of concepts with an infinite relational model. In *AAAI*, volume 3, page 5, 2006.

[13] Scott Linderman and Ryan Adams. Discovering latent network structure in point process data. In *Proceedings of the 31st International Conference on Machine Learning (ICML-14)*, pages 1413–1421, 2014.

[14] Iain Murray, Ryan P. Adams, and David Mackay. Elliptical slice sampling. In *International Conference on Artificial Intelligence and Statistics*, pages 541–548, 2010.

[15] Radford M. Neal. Markov chain sampling methods for dirichlet process mixture models. Technical report, 1998.

[16] Radford M. Neal. Slice sampling. In *Annals of Statistics*, 2003.

[17] Uri Nodelaman, Christian R. Shelton, and Daphne Koller. Continuous time bayesian networks. In *Uncertainty in Artificial Intelligence (UAI)*, 2002.

[18] Shyamsundar Rajaram, Thore Grapple, and Herbrich Ralf. Poisson-networks: A model of structured point processes. In *Proceedings of the Tenth International Workshop on Artificial Intelligence and Statistics (AISTATS)*, 2005.

[19] Z Xu, V Tresp, K Yu, and HP Kriegel. Infinite hidden relational models. In *Proceedings of the 22nd International Conference on Uncertainty in Artificial Intelligence (UAI)*, 2006.

Forward Backward Greedy Algorithms for Multi-Task Learning with Faster Rates

Lu Tian
Department of Systems and Information Engineering
University of Virginia

Pan Xu
Department of Systems and Information Engineering
University of Virginia

Quanquan Gu
Department of Systems and Information Engineering
University of Virginia

Abstract

A large body of algorithms have been proposed for multi-task learning. However, the effectiveness of many multi-task learning algorithms highly depends on the structural regularization, which incurs bias in the resulting estimators and leads to slower convergence rate. In this paper, we aim at developing a multi-task learning algorithm with faster convergence rate. In particular, we propose a general estimator for multi-task learning with row sparsity constraint on the parameter matrix, i.e., the number of nonzero rows in the parameter matrix being small. The proposed estimator is a nonconvex optimization problem. In order to solve it, we develop a forward backward greedy algorithm with provable guarantee. More specifically, we prove that the output of the greedy algorithm attains a sharper estimation error bound than many state-of-the-art multi-task learning methods. Moreover, our estimator enjoys model selection consistency under a mild condition. Thorough experiments on both synthetic and real-world data demonstrate the effectiveness of our method and back up our theory.

1 INTRODUCTION

Multi-task learning (MTL) (Caruana, 1997) has witnessed increasing attention in machine learning and statistics in the past decades. In multi-task learning, one deals with a number of related learning tasks simultaneously, with the goal to improve the generalization performance by utilizing the intrinsic relationship among these tasks. It has been successfully applied to a wide range of applications including object recognition (Caruana, 1997), speech recognition (Parameswaran and Weinberger, 2010), handwritten digits recognition (Quadrianto et al., 2010), and disease progression prediction (Zhou et al., 2011).

The fundamental problem in multi-task learning is how to characterize the relationship among tasks. Representative methods include learning hidden units in neural networks (Caruana, 1997; Baxter, 2000), sharing prior in hierarchical Bayesian models (Bakker and Heskes, 2003; Schwaighofer et al., 2004; Yu et al., 2005; Zhang et al., 2005) and Gaussian processes (Lawrence and Platt, 2004), learning a shared feature mapping matrix in multiple regression (Ando and Zhang, 2005; Evgeniou and Pontil, 2004). Some other works also proposed to learn the task relations (Zhang and Yeung, 2012, 2013; Han and Zhang, 2015), to mention a few. In this study, we focus on a large family of multi-task learning algorithms, which assume that all tasks share a common set of features (Obozinski et al., 2006; Argyriou et al., 2008; Negahban and Wainwright, 2008; Liu et al., 2009; Lounici et al., 2009; Yang et al., 2009; Zhang et al., 2010; Lounici et al., 2011), because they serve as the basis for many other sophisticated multi-task learning algorithms. Note that our method and theory can be extended to those sophisticated multi-task learning settings (Jacob et al., 2009; Kim and Xing, 2010; Kang et al., 2011; Zhang and Yeung, 2012; Gong et al., 2012; Zhang and Yeung, 2013; Han and Zhang, 2015) straightforwardly.

In detail, the multiple task learning setting (Obozinski et al., 2006; Argyriou et al., 2008; Negahban and Wainwright, 2008; Liu et al., 2009; Lounici et al., 2009; Yang et al., 2009; Zhang et al., 2010) considered in this paper is as follows: Given a set of observations $\{\mathbf{X}^{(i)}, \mathbf{y}^{(i)}\}, i = 1, \cdots, m$ from m tasks, where $\mathbf{X}^{(i)} = [\mathbf{x}_1^{(i)}, \ldots, \mathbf{x}_{n_i}^{(i)}]^\top \in \mathbb{R}^{n_i \times d}, i = 1, \cdots, m$ are the design matrices for each task, and $\mathbf{y}^{(i)} = [y_1^{(i)}, \ldots, y_{n_i}^{(i)}]^\top \in \mathbb{R}^{n_i}, i = 1, \cdots, m$ are corresponding vectors of response variables. It is often useful to represent the parameters in multiple tasks via a matrix, where each column corresponds to a task, and each row to a feature, i.e., $\mathbf{\Theta}^* = [\boldsymbol{\theta}_1^*, \cdots, \boldsymbol{\theta}_m^*] \in \mathbb{R}^{d \times m}$, where $\boldsymbol{\theta}_i^* \in \mathbb{R}^d$ is the parameter vector of the i-th task. We assume that, conditioned on the covariate (feature) vector $\mathbf{x}_j^{(i)}$, the response variable $y_j^{(i)}$ for each task depends on the same subset of features. In other words, $\boldsymbol{\theta}_i^*$'s are sparse and share the same support. This corresponds to the matrix Θ^* being " row-sparse": each row is either all zero or mostly nonzero, and the number of nonzero rows is relatively small. More specifically, the number of nonzero rows in Θ^* is denoted by $s^* = \|\Theta^*\|_{0,2}$. A lot of recent research in this setting used $\ell_{1,q}(q > 1)$ norm regularizations that encourage the parameter matrix to have such row-sparse structure. Particular examples include the $\ell_{1,\infty}$ norm regularization (Turlach et al., 2005; Zhang and Huang, 2008; Negahban and Wainwright, 2008), the $\ell_{1,2}$ norm regularization (Lounici et al., 2009; Obozinski et al., 2011), and the mixture of $\ell_{1,\infty}$ norm and $\ell_{1,1}$ norm regularizations (Jalali et al., 2013).

However, all the methods mentioned above for multi-task learning are based on convex regularization, i.e., $\ell_{1,q}, q > 1$ norm regularization. Recent studies (Fan and Li, 2001; Zhang, 2010) have shown that convex regularization based estimators suffer from the bias. To remedy this problem, one can choose nonconvex regularization alternatively such as the smoothly clipped absolute deviation (SCAD) penalty (Fan and Li, 2001) and the mimimax concave penalty (MCP) (Zhang, 2010). However, the empirical performance of nonconvex penalty regularized estimator highly relies on the parameters of the nonconvex penalty, which are difficult to tune in practice. One can also use the debiasing method proposed in Javanmard and Montanari (2014) to cancel the bias. However, the debiasing method will result in a non-sparse estimation result. In order to sparsify the result, a truncation step is needed, which introduces an extra tuning parameter. Moreover, the estimation error bound of debiased estimator is no better than that of convex relaxation based estimator.

In this paper, we aim at developing a new estimator which is able to get rid of the bias, attain faster convergence rate, and easy to implement in practice. In detail, we propose a general estimator for multi-task learning with row-sparsity constraint on the parameter matrix. Due to the nonconvex $\ell_{0,2}$ norm constraint, the estimator is a non-convex optimization problem and finding its global optimal solution is generally NP-hard. We propose a greedy algorithms to attain an approximate solution with provable guarantee. At the core of the proposed greedy algorithm is a forward backward feature selection strategy. We prove that the output of our algorithm attains a sharp statistical estimation error bound. As a special example of the proposed general estimator, we consider the multivariate linear regression model $\mathbf{y}^{(i)} = \mathbf{X}^{(i)}\boldsymbol{\theta}_i^* + \boldsymbol{\epsilon}$, where $\boldsymbol{\epsilon}$ is the zero mean noise vector. We show that its estimation error bound is $O(\sqrt{s^*m/n} + \sqrt{s^* \log s^*/n})$ in terms of the Frobenius norm with $n = \min_i\{n_i\}$, which is sharper than the state-of-the-art results Jalali et al. (2013); Gong et al. (2013). Furthermore, in order to achieve model selection consistency, most existing work for the square loss function (Jalali et al., 2013; Wainwright, 2009; Zhao and Yu, 2006) relies on the very stringent incoherence condition. In sharp contrast, our estimator enjoys model selection consistency under a mild condition on the ℓ_2 norms of the nonzero rows in Θ^*. Thorough experiments on both simulated data and real data show that the proposed method outperforms the state-of-the-art methods.

The remainder of this paper is organized as follows. In Section 2, we propose a general estimator for multi-task learning with row sparsity constraint, followed by a greedy algorithm with forward-backward feature selection strategy. In Section 3, we prove the convergence of the greedy algorithm, as well as the statistical estimation error bound for the output of the greedy algorithm. We report the experimental results in Section 4 and conclude our work in Section 5.

Notation We use bold capitals to denote matrices, bold lowercase letters for vectors, and lowercase letters for scalars. The j-th natural basis in $\mathbb{R}^d$ is denoted as $\mathbf{e}_j$. For matrices $\mathbf{A}$ and $\mathbf{B}$ with commensurate dimensions, we use $\langle \mathbf{A}, \mathbf{B} \rangle$ to denote their trace inner product, i.e. $\langle \mathbf{A}, \mathbf{B} \rangle = \mathrm{tr}(\mathbf{A}^\top \mathbf{B})$. Given a matrix Θ, its i-th row is denoted by Θ_{i*} and its j-th column is denoted by Θ_{*j}. The $\ell_{p,q}$ norm of a matrix Θ is defined as $\|\Theta\|_{p,q} = \{\sum_i [(\sum_j |\Theta_{ij}|^q)^{1/q}]^p\}^{1/p}$, and the Frobenius norm of Θ is $\|\Theta\|_F = \sqrt{\langle \Theta, \Theta \rangle} = \|\Theta\|_{2,2}$. For a matrix Θ, we use $F(\Theta)$ to denote the index set of the non-zero rows in Θ. For a row index set F, we denote by Θ_F to be the matrix that its i-th row is the same as the i-th row of Θ if $i \in F$, and its i-th row is a zero vector if $i \notin F$.

2 THE PROPOSED METHOD

In this section, we first introduce the underlying model for multi-task learning, followed by a general estimator. Then we propose a greedy algorithm to solve the estimator.

2.1 THE MODEL AND ESTIMATOR

Suppose that we have observations $\{(\mathbf{X}^{(1)}, \mathbf{y}^{(1)}), \ldots, (\mathbf{X}^{(m)}, \mathbf{y}^{(m)})\}$ from m tasks, where $\mathbf{X}^{(i)} \in \mathbb{R}^{n_i \times d}$ is the design matrix of the i-th task, $\mathbf{y}_i \in \mathbb{R}^{n_i}$ is the vector of response variables for the i-th task. We assume that the observations in each task are generated from generalized linear models

$$\mathbb{P}(y_j^{(i)} | \mathbf{x}_j^{(i)}, \boldsymbol{\theta}_i^*, \sigma_i) = \exp\left\{ \frac{y_j^{(i)} \langle \boldsymbol{\theta}_i^*, \mathbf{x}_j^{(i)} \rangle - \Phi(\boldsymbol{\theta}_i^{*\top} \mathbf{x}_j^{(i)})}{c(\sigma_i)} \right\},$$
$$i = 1, \ldots, m, j = 1, \ldots, n_i,$$

where $\Phi(\cdot) : \mathbb{R} \to \mathbb{R}$ is a link function, $\mathbf{x}_j^{(i)}$ is the j-th row of $\mathbf{X}^{(i)}$, $y_j^{(i)}$ is the j-th coordinate of $\mathbf{y}^{(i)}$, $\boldsymbol{\theta}_i^* \in \mathbb{R}^d$ is the parameter of i-th task, and $c(\sigma_i) \in \mathbb{R}$ is fixed and known scale parameter of the i-th task. A special example of generalized linear model is the linear regression model where the distribution of the response variable conditioned on the covariates is a normal distribution. That is, when $c(\sigma)$ is chosen as σ^2 and $\Phi(t) = t^2$. Logistic regression is another special case of the generalized linear model, where $\Phi(t) = \log(1 + \exp(t)), c(\sigma) = 1$ and $y_j^{(i)} \in \{0, 1\}$.

Our goal is to recover the unknown $\boldsymbol{\theta}_i^*$'s given the observations from m tasks. A general estimator for multi-task learning is based on minimizing the negative log likelihood, under the $\ell_{0,2}$ constraint on the parameter matrix $\boldsymbol{\Theta}$. This gives rise to:

$$\min_{\boldsymbol{\Theta} \in \mathbb{R}^{d \times m}} \mathcal{L}(\boldsymbol{\Theta}) \quad \text{subject to } \|\boldsymbol{\Theta}\|_{0,2} \leq s, \qquad (2.1)$$

where s is a tuning parameter which controls the row sparsity of $\boldsymbol{\Theta}$, $\mathcal{L}(\boldsymbol{\Theta})$ is the sum of the negative log likelihood over all the tasks, which is given by

$$\mathcal{L}(\boldsymbol{\Theta}) = -\sum_{i=1}^{m} \left[1/(2n_i) \sum_{j=1}^{n_i} y_j^{(i)} \boldsymbol{\Theta}_{*i}^\top \mathbf{x}_j^{(i)} + \Phi(\boldsymbol{\Theta}_{*i}^\top \mathbf{x}_j^{(i)})\right], \qquad (2.2)$$

where $\boldsymbol{\Theta}_{*i}$ is the i-th column of $\boldsymbol{\Theta}$. In particular, when $c(\sigma) = \sigma^2$ and $\Phi(t) = t^2$, the negative log likelihood function of the exponential family distribution in (2.2) reduces to the square loss function, which is shown as follows:

$$\mathcal{L}(\boldsymbol{\Theta}) = \sum_{i=1}^{m} \frac{1}{2n_i} \|\mathbf{y}^{(i)} - \mathbf{X}^{(i)} \boldsymbol{\Theta}_{*i}\|_2^2. \qquad (2.3)$$

Note that the square loss function has been used in Obozinski et al. (2006); Argyriou et al. (2008); Negahban and Wainwright (2008); Lounici et al. (2009); Zhang et al. (2010) for simplicity.

In addition, the optimization problem in (2.1) is nonconvex, because the constraint set $\|\boldsymbol{\Theta}\|_{0,2} \leq s$ is nonconvex. In fact, due to the combinatorial nature of this constraint, finding its global optimal solution is actually NP-hard. In the next subsection, we will propose a greedy algorithm to solve (2.1) approximately, yet with provable guarantee.

2.2 THE PROPOSED ALGORITHM

In order to get a good estimation of $\boldsymbol{\Theta}^*$, a vital problem is to get the row support of $\boldsymbol{\Theta}^*$. In order to get a good estimation of the row support of $\boldsymbol{\Theta}^*$, we designed the following algorithm. The formal description of the algorithm is summarized in Algorithm 1. In detail, we use the forward-backward strategy (Zhang, 2009) to select the feature set iteratively. In particular, we start from an empty feature set. The proposed algorithm adds the feature that will decrease the loss function most greatly into the current selected feature set in each iteration (The "Forward" strategy). Since the ℓ_2 norm of each row of the gradient characterize the decrease rate of the loss function, we use the row with largest ℓ_2 norm which is indexed by $i^{(t+1)}$ during the forward step (The seventh line of Algorithm 1).After each feature set updating, we also update the coefficients for each feature just as an ordinary regression problem. However, the forward strategy is too greedy because it only permits the entrance of new features but prohibits the deletion of irrelevant features. Hence we introduce the "Backward" mechanism to help the algorithm get rid of the bad local optima. That is, in each iteration, we not only add a new feature but also remove one or more irrelevant features from the feature set. The goodness of a feature is measured by the increase of the loss function when the feature is removed from the feature set. Similarly, the coefficient of each selected features is updated when there is a modification of feature set.

Algorithm 1 Forward Backward Greedy Algorithm for Multi-Task Learning (MultiFoBa)

1: **Require:** $\epsilon > 0$
2: **Initialize:** $\boldsymbol{\Theta}^{(0)} = 0, t = 0, F^{(0)} = \emptyset$
3: **while** TRUE **do**
4:   **if** $\|\nabla \mathcal{L}(\boldsymbol{\Theta}^{(t)})\|_{\infty,2} < \epsilon$ **then**
5:     break
6:   **end if**
7:   $i^{(t+1)} = \text{argmax}_{i \notin F^{(t)}} \|\nabla \mathcal{L}(\boldsymbol{\Theta}^{(t)})_i\|_2$
8:   $F^{(t+1)} = F^{(t)} \cup \{i^{(t+1)}\}$
9:   $\boldsymbol{\Theta}^{(t+1)} = \text{argmin}_{\boldsymbol{\Theta}_{i*}=0, i \notin F^{(t+1)}} \mathcal{L}(\boldsymbol{\Theta})$
10:   $\delta^{(t+1)} = \mathcal{L}(\boldsymbol{\Theta}^{(t)}) - \mathcal{L}(\boldsymbol{\Theta}^{(t+1)})$
11:   $t = t + 1$
12:   **while** TRUE **do**
13:     **if** $\min_{i \in F^{(t)}} \mathcal{L}(\boldsymbol{\Theta}^{(t)} - \mathbf{e}_i \boldsymbol{\Theta}_{i*}^{(t)}) - \mathcal{L}(\boldsymbol{\Theta}^{(t)}) \geq \delta^{(t)}/2$ **then**
14:       break
15:     **end if**
16:     $i^{(t)} = \text{argmin}_{i \in F^{(t)}} \mathcal{L}(\boldsymbol{\Theta}^{(t)} - \mathbf{e}_i \boldsymbol{\Theta}_{i*}^{(t)})$
17:     $F^{(t-1)} = F^{(t)} \setminus \{i^{(t)}\}$
18:     $\boldsymbol{\Theta}^{(t-1)} = \text{argmin}_{\boldsymbol{\Theta}_{i*}=0, i \notin F^{(t-1)}} \mathcal{L}(\boldsymbol{\Theta})$
19:     $t = t - 1$
20:   **end while**
21: **end while**
22: **Output:** $\boldsymbol{\Theta}^{(t)}$

Note that we only delete those features which cause an increase of loss function by less than $\delta^{(t)}/2$, where $\delta^{(t)}$ is the decrease of the loss function when the last feature is added. This guarantees that the loss function will not increase when the cardinality of the feature set returns back. And this implies that the algorithm will not stuck in an infinite loop. In contrast to the forward feature selection algorithm, our algorithm employs a backward feature elimination step, which is able to help avoid the local optima. As we will show in the next section, the backward step is essential in achieving the model selection consistency under mild conditions.

We now analyze the time complexity of the algorithm.

The main computational overhead in the "forward" step is the 9-th line in Algorithm 1. For square loss, there exist a closed-form solution to the optimization problem in this line. In detail, for the i-th task, the solution is given by $\mathbf{\Theta}_{*i}^{(t)} = \big(\mathbf{X}_{F^{(t)}}^{(i)\top}\mathbf{X}_{F^{(t)}}^{(i)}\big)^{-1}\mathbf{X}_{F^{(t)}}^{(i)\top}\mathbf{y}^{(i)}$. The time complexity is $O(|F^{(t)}|^2\sum_{i=1}^{m} n_i)$ in the t-th iteration of the loop. Similarly, in the "backward" step, the main workload falls in the 18-th line and the time complexity is also $O(|F^{(t)}|^2\sum_{i=1}^{m} n_i)$. Since $|F^{(t)}|$ is much smaller than d, the computational cost is not expensive. Furthermore, we will prove in Section 3 that Algorithm 1 will terminate after finite steps. Therefore, the total time complexity of our algorithm is $O(|F^{(t)}|^2\sum_{i=1}^{m} n_i)$ times the number of steps. Overall, Algorithm 1 is efficient.

3 MAIN THEORETICAL RESULTS

In this section we will analyze the practicability of the algorithm and prove the finite-sample statistical rate of the proposed estimator. The detailed proofs of all the theory are deferred in the supplemental material.

For the ease of statistical analysis, we consider an oracle estimator $\widehat{\mathbf{\Theta}}_O$ which is obtained by restricting the row support of the estimator onto the row support of the unknown true parameter matrix $\mathbf{\Theta}^*$. More specifically, let $F(\mathbf{\Theta}) \subset \{1, 2, \ldots, d\}$ denote the index set of nonzero rows of $\mathbf{\Theta}$. Then $\widehat{\mathbf{\Theta}}_O$ is the optimal solution to the following problem:

$$\widehat{\mathbf{\Theta}}_O = \operatorname*{argmin}_{\mathbf{\Theta}\in\mathbb{R}^{d\times m}} \mathcal{L}(\mathbf{\Theta}) \quad \text{subject to } F(\mathbf{\Theta}) = F(\mathbf{\Theta}^*). \tag{3.1}$$

Note that $\widehat{\mathbf{\Theta}}_O$ is not a practical estimator but a reference estimator used for theoretical analysis only. To simplify notation, let $F^* \equiv F(\mathbf{\Theta}^*) = F(\widehat{\mathbf{\Theta}}_O)$ and $F^{(t)} \equiv F(\mathbf{\Theta}^{(t)})$. We use $F^{(t)} - F^*$ to denote the set difference. For the matrix $\mathbf{\Theta}_{F^{(t)}-F^*}^{(t)} \in \mathbb{R}^{d\times m}$, its i-th row is the same as the i-th row of $\mathbf{\Theta}^{(t)}$ if $i \in F^{(t)} - F^*$. For $i \notin F^{(t)} - F^*$, the i-th row of $\mathbf{\Theta}_{F^{(t)}-F^*}^{(t)}$ is a zero vector. Note that according to this definition, $\mathbf{\Theta}_{F^{(t)}-F^*}^{(t)}$ is equal to $[\mathbf{\Theta}^{(t)} - \widehat{\mathbf{\Theta}}_O]_{F^{(t)}-F^*}$.

To concisely characterize the property of $\mathcal{L}(\mathbf{\Theta})$, we first introduce the definition of sparse eigenvalues, which is the extension of sparse eigenvalue for sparse regression (Zhang, 2009; Jalali et al., 2011; Liu et al., 2013; Rao et al., 2015). Similar extension has been used in Gong et al. (2013).

Definition 3.1 (Sparse Eigenvalues). The smallest and largest s-sparse eigenvalues of $\nabla^2\mathcal{L}(\mathbf{\Theta})$ are

$$\rho_+(s) = \max_{1\le i\le m} \sup\big\{\mathbf{u}^\top\nabla^2_{\boldsymbol{\theta}_i}\mathcal{L}(\mathbf{\Theta})\mathbf{u} : \|\mathbf{u}\|_0 \le s, \|\mathbf{u}\|_2 = 1, \mathbf{\Theta} \in \mathbb{R}^{d\times m}\big\},$$

$$\rho_-(s) = \min_{1\le i\le m} \inf\big\{\mathbf{u}^\top\nabla^2_{\boldsymbol{\theta}_i}\mathcal{L}(\mathbf{\Theta})\mathbf{u} : \|\mathbf{u}\|_0 \le s, \|\mathbf{u}\|_2 = 1, \mathbf{\Theta} \in \mathbb{R}^{d\times m}\big\}.$$

Remark 3.2. The definition of $\rho_-(\cdot)$ is highly related to the definition of restricted strong convexity in Negahban et al. (2009). Previous studies (Zhang et al., 2009; Negahban et al., 2009) have shown that the assumption $\rho_-(s) > 0$ can be satisfied for different forms of $\mathcal{L}(\mathbf{\Theta})$. This is often referred to as sparse eigenvalue condition. For example, Zhang et al. (2009) proved that when the model is a linear regression model and $\mathcal{L}(\mathbf{\Theta})$ is a square loss, $\nabla^2_{\boldsymbol{\theta}_i}\mathcal{L}(\mathbf{\Theta})$ satisfies the sparse eigenvalue condition with high probability. Therefore, when we choose square loss in (2.3), it is easy to show that $\rho_-(s) > 0$ holds with high probability analogously. Another example is the generalized linear model. Negahban et al. (2009) proved that with high probability the loss function corresponding to generalized linear model satisfies the restricted strong convexity, which also implies that $\rho_-(s) > 0$.

Without loss of generality, we make the following assumption on the structure of the loss function $\mathcal{L}(\mathbf{\Theta})$.

Assumption 3.3 (Decomposable Loss Function). The loss function can be decomposed into the sum of loss functions on different tasks. By formulation, we have

$$\mathcal{L}(\mathbf{\Theta}) = \sum_{i=1}^{m} \ell_i(\mathbf{\Theta}_{*i}),$$

where ℓ_i is the loss function defined on the i-th task.

Assumption 3.3 can be verified for many types of loss functions, including the loss functions in (2.2) and (2.3).

Combining Assumption 3.3 with the definition of sparse eigenvalues, it is easy to show that

$$\frac{\rho_-(s)}{2}\|\mathbf{\Delta}\|_F^2 \le \mathcal{L}(\mathbf{\Theta}+\mathbf{\Delta}) - \mathcal{L}(\mathbf{\Theta}) - \langle\nabla\mathcal{L}(\mathbf{\Theta}), \mathbf{\Delta}\rangle \le \frac{\rho_+(s)}{2}\|\mathbf{\Delta}\|_F^2, \quad \text{for all } \|\mathbf{\Delta}\|_{0,2} \le s. \tag{3.2}$$

These two inequalities in (3.2) are frequently used in the proof in order to bound the difference between $\mathcal{L}(\mathbf{\Theta})$ and $\mathcal{L}(\mathbf{\Theta}+\mathbf{\Delta})$. In fact, it is highly related to the restricted strong convexity and smoothness condition proposed in Negahban et al. (2009). The key difference is here the inequality holds in the sparse subspace rather than a cone.

The first question we are going to address is whether and when Algorithm 1 will terminate. The following theorem guarantees that the proposed algorithm terminates in finite steps.

Theorem 3.4. Suppose that the loss function $\mathcal{L}(\Theta)$ satisfies Assumption 3.3. Let s be any integer satisfying $\rho_-(s) > 0$ and the following condition:

$$s \geq (s^* + 1)\left\{\left[\left(\sqrt{\frac{\rho_+(s)}{\rho_-(s)}} + 1\right)\frac{\sqrt{2}\rho_+(1)}{\rho_-(s)}\right]^2 + 1\right\}, \tag{3.3}$$

and take $\epsilon > 2\sqrt{2}\|\nabla\mathcal{L}(\widehat{\Theta}_O)\|_{\infty,2}\ \rho_+(1)/\rho_-(s)$ in Algorithm 1. Then the algorithm terminates at some $t \leq s - s^*$.

Next we will introduce some theoretical results about the estimation error bounds of the output of Algorithm 1.

Theorem 3.5. Suppose that the loss function $\mathcal{L}(\Theta)$ satisfies Assumption 3.3. Let s be any integer satisfying (3.3) and $\rho_-(s) > 0$. Take

$$\epsilon > \frac{2\sqrt{2}\rho_+(1)}{\rho_-(s)}\|\nabla\mathcal{L}(\widehat{\Theta}_O)\|_{\infty,2}, \tag{3.4}$$

then the output of Algorithm 1 satisfies

$$\|\Theta^{(t)} - \Theta^*\|_F \leq \frac{2\sqrt{2}\epsilon}{\rho_-(s)}\sqrt{s_2^*} + \frac{2\sqrt{s^*}}{\rho_-(s^*)}\|[\nabla\mathcal{L}(\Theta^*)]_{F^*}\|_{\infty,2}, \tag{3.5}$$

$$\frac{\rho_-(s)^2}{8\rho_+(1)^2}|F^{(t)} - F^*| \leq |F^* - F^{(t)}| \leq 2s_2^*, \tag{3.6}$$

where s_2^* is defined as

$$s_2^* := \left|\left\{i \in F^* - F^{(t)} : \|\Theta^*_{i*}\|_2 < 2\sqrt{2}\epsilon/\rho_-(s) + \|[\widehat{\Theta}_O - \Theta^*]_{F^*}\|_{\infty,2}\right\}\right|. \tag{3.7}$$

Note in Theorem 3.5 that s_2^* denotes the number of nonzero rows in Θ^* whose ℓ_2 norms are small. Those correspond to the rows which are difficult to recover. It is easy to verify that if $s_2^* = 0$, we have $|F^{(t)} - F^*| = |F^* - F^{(t)}| = 0$ by (3.6), which implies that $F^{(t)} = F^*$.

In the following corollary, we show that if the ℓ_2 norms of all the nonzero rows are sufficiently large, i.e., $s_2^* = 0$, we can achieve a sharper estimation error bound, together with model selection consistency.

Corollary 3.6. Under the same conditions as Theorem 3.5, if $s_2^* = 0$, i.e., the ℓ_2 norm of each row of $\widehat{\Theta}_O$ is sufficiently large, then the estimation error of the output of Algorithm 1 is bounded by

$$\|\Theta^{(t)} - \Theta^*\|_F \leq \frac{2\sqrt{s^*}}{\rho_-(s^*)}\|[\nabla\mathcal{L}(\Theta^*)]_{F^*}\|_{\infty,2}, \tag{3.8}$$

and the model selection consistency can be obtained, i.e., $F^{(t)} = F^*$.

3.1 HIGH PROBABILITY RESULTS FOR SQUARE LOSS

In this subsection, we present the high probability result for a specific example, i.e., the square loss case. Similar high probability results can be proved for the general loss function in (2.2) with more involved arguments.

For the sake of simplicity, we assume that every task has the same number of observations, i.e., $n_1 = \ldots = n_m = n$. Then the square loss function in (2.3) can be further reduced to

$$\mathcal{L}(\Theta) = \frac{1}{2n}\sum_{i=1}^{m}\|\mathbf{X}^{(i)}\boldsymbol{\theta}_i - \mathbf{y}^{(i)}\|_2^2. \tag{3.9}$$

Our analysis can be easily extended to the general square loss in (2.3) where different tasks may have different number of observations.

Without loss of generality, we make the following assumption on the design matrices $\mathbf{X}^{(i)}$'s.

Assumption 3.7. For all columns in $\mathbf{X}^{(i)}$, we have $\|\mathbf{X}^{(i)}_{*j}\|_2 \leq \sqrt{n}$, where $\mathbf{X}^{(i)}_{*j}$ is the j-th column of $\mathbf{X}^{(i)}$.

Note that Assumption 3.7 is often made in the analysis of Lasso estimator (Negahban et al., 2009; Zhang et al., 2009).

The estimation error bound of the output of Algorithm 1 is shown in the following theorem.

Theorem 3.8. Under the same conditions as Theorem 3.5, when the loss function is the square loss in (3.9) and satisfies Assumption 3.7, we have with probability at least $1 - 1/d - 2/s^*$ that

$$\|\Theta^{(t)} - \Theta^*\|_F \leq \frac{10\rho_+(1)\sigma}{\rho_-^2(s)}\sqrt{\frac{s^*m}{n}} + \frac{16\rho_+(1)\sigma}{\rho_-^2(s)}\sqrt{\frac{s_2^*\log d}{n}} + \frac{4\sigma}{\rho_-(s^*)}\sqrt{\frac{s^*\log s^*}{n}}, \tag{3.10}$$

where s_2^* is defined as

$$s_2^* = \left|\left\{i \in F^* - F^{(t)} : \|\Theta^*_{i*}\|_2 \leq \frac{9\rho_+(1)\sigma}{\rho_-^2(s)}\left(\sqrt{\frac{m}{n}} + 2\sqrt{\frac{\log d}{n}}\right)\right\}\right|.$$

Remark 3.9. Theorem 3.5 suggests that the statistical estimation rate of our algorithm is

$$O\left(\sqrt{\frac{s^*m}{n}} + \sqrt{\frac{s^*\log s^*}{n}} + \sqrt{\frac{s_2^*\log d}{n}}\right),$$

which is sharper than the statistical rate of convex relaxation based methods (Lounici et al., 2009; Obozinski et al., 2011), i.e., $O(\sqrt{s^*m/n} + \sqrt{s^*\log d/n})$, since s_2^* could be much smaller than s^*, and $\log s^*$ is much smaller than

$\log d$. From the sample complexity point of view, Theorem 3.5 implies the sample complexity of our algorithm is $O(s^*m + s^* \log s^* + s_2^* \log d)$. When s_2^* is sufficiently smaller than s^*, our sample complexity is tighter than the existing best sample complexity for group sparse signal recovery (Baraniuk et al., 2010; Rao et al., 2012), i.e., $O(s^* \log d + s^*m)$.

Corollary 3.10. Under the same conditions as Theorem 3.8, when $s_2^* = 0$, we have with probability at least $1 - 1/d - 2/s^*$ that

$$\|\mathbf{\Theta}^{(t)} - \mathbf{\Theta}^*\|_F \le \frac{10\rho_+(1)\sigma}{\rho_-^2(s)}\sqrt{\frac{s^*m}{n}} + \frac{4\sigma}{\rho_-(s^*)}\sqrt{\frac{s^*\log s^*}{n}},$$

and the model selection consistency can be obtained with probability at least $1 - 1/d - 2/s^*$, i.e., $F^{(t)} = F^*$.

Remark 3.11. From Corollary 3.10, we know that our algorithm can get a even faster convergence rate in terms of Frobenius norm as follows

$$O\left(\sqrt{\frac{s^*m}{n}} + \sqrt{\frac{s^*\log s^*}{n}}\right). \tag{3.11}$$

In addition, the sufficient condition for our algorithm to achieve model selection consistency is as follows

$$\|\mathbf{\Theta}_{i*}^*\|_2 \gtrsim \sqrt{\frac{m}{n}} + \sqrt{\frac{\log d}{n}} \quad \text{for all} \quad i \in F^* - F^{(t)}, \tag{3.12}$$

which is implied by $s_2^* = 0$. In other words, we need all non-zero rows of $\mathbf{\Theta}^*$ in the row index set $F^* - F^{(t)}$ are big enough in terms of ℓ_2 norm. This thanks to the $\ell_{0,2}$ constraint on the parameter matrix, which does not introduce bias when the nonzero rows of the parameter matrix are of large magnitude in terms of ℓ_2 norm. In fact, our analysis can be directly applied to the original forward backward algorithm in Zhang (2009), and delivers a sharper bound for single task sparse regression. This can be seen as a by-product of our technical contribution.

Remark 3.12. One may be curious that why our bound in (3.11) beats the minimax lower bound for group sparse recovery Lounici et al. (2011). Note that when $s_2^* = 0$, our algorithm fully recovers the support of $\mathbf{\Theta}^*$, and our estimator is identical to the multivariate regression estimator that is restricted on the true support F^* of the parameter matrix. In this case, our estimator reduces to a multivariate regression in the classical regime rather than in the high dimensional regime, i.e., the oracle estimator in (3.1). Therefore, the minimax lower bound that characterizes the information theoretic limit is no longer the one in the high dimensional regime Lounici et al. (2011), but the one for the multivariate regression in the classical regime, i.e., $O(\sqrt{s^*m/n})$. As we can see, the upper bound in (3.11) achieved by our algorithm matches the minimax lower bound of multivariate regression in the classical regime up to $\log(s^*)$. This is one of our major contributions in this paper and what we referred to as "faster rate".

Remark 3.13. It is interesting to compare our result in Corollary 3.10 with the main result in Gong et al. (2013). Gong et al. (2013) proposed multi-stage multi-task learning method and proved an estimation error bound as follows

$$\|\mathbf{\Theta}^{(t)} - \mathbf{\Theta}^*\|_F \lesssim \sqrt{\frac{s^*m}{n}} + \sqrt{\frac{m\log d}{n}}. \tag{3.13}$$

The sufficient condition for their method to achieve model selection consistency is

$$\|\mathbf{\Theta}_{i*}^*\|_2 \gtrsim \sqrt{\frac{m(\log d + \log m)}{n}} \quad \text{for all} \quad i \in F^*. \tag{3.14}$$

By comparing (3.11) with (3.13), it is clear that our estimator attains a much shaper estimation error bound than Gong et al. (2013).

Furthermore, by comparing (3.12) with (3.14), we can see that the sufficient condition of model selection consistency for our algorithm is much milder than their method. In detail, our sufficient condition only takes into account those dimensions that fall in $F^* - F^{(t)}$ rather than the whole F^*. Moreover, the magnitude condition in (3.12) is also in a much smaller order than (3.14). This clearly demonstrates that the sufficient condition of the model selection consistency for our algorithm is substantially milder than Gong et al. (2013).

4 EXPERIMENTS

In this section, we conduct extensive empirical study on both synthetic and real-world datasets, to verify the effectiveness of the proposed method.

4.1 COMPARED ALGORITHMS

We present the empirical study by comparing the results of the following algorithms: **Lasso**: we apply Lasso (Tibshirani, 1996) to each task individually; **FoBa**: a forward backward algorithm for sparse regression (Zhang, 2009). Similar to Lasso, we apply FoBa to each task individually; **L1,2**: multi-task feature learning based on $\ell_{2,1}$-norm regularization (Liu et al., 2009); **MSMTFL**: the Multi-Stage Multi-Task learning method proposed by Gong et al. (2013); **DirtyMTL**: a dirty statistical model based multi-task learning algorithm with regularizer $\lambda_1\|\mathbf{P}\|_{1,1} + \lambda_2\|\mathbf{Q}\|_{1,\infty}$ ($\mathbf{\Theta} = \mathbf{P} + \mathbf{Q}$) (Jalali et al., 2013); **rRMTL**: a robust multi-task learning algorithm employing $\lambda_1\|\mathbf{P}\|_{2,1} + \lambda_2\|\mathbf{Q}^\top\|_{2,1}$ as the regularizer ($\mathbf{\Theta} = \mathbf{P} + \mathbf{Q}$) (Gong et al., 2012); **MultiFoBa**: This is our proposed algorithm, which employs the forward-backward strategy to select features under feature set cardinality constraint. We implement the proposed algorithm by MATLAB. For other algorithms, we use the implementation in

Table 1: The estimation error in terms of Frobenius norm of different algorithms on synthetic datasets.

	Lasso	FoBa	L1,2	MSMTFL	DirtyMTL	rMTFL	MultiFoBa
Dataset 1	7.61±0.38	5.79±0.39	1.59±0.10	1.80±0.09	6.30±0.19	1.89±0.46	**0.72±0.09**
Dataset 2	11.14±0.84	7.45±0.85	2.25±0.17	2.77±0.12	8.11±0.75	5.22±1.39	**1.04±0.09**
Dataset 3	11.35±0.59	9.27±0.59	3.12±0.49	3.36±0.21	8.56±0.74	6.29±1.01	**1.66±0.17**

Table 2: The F_1 scores of support recovery of different algorithms on synthetic datasets.

	Lasso	FoBa	L1,2	MSMTFL	DirtyMTL	rMTFL	MultiFoBa
Dataset 1	0.99±0.01	1.00±0.00	1.00±0.00	1.00±0.00	0.98±0.02	0.93±0.07	**1.00±0.00**
Dataset 2	0.60±0.11	1.00±0.00	0.98±0.02	0.99±0.01	0.86±0.11	1.00±0.00	**1.00±0.00**
Dataset 3	0.54±0.11	0.80±0.00	0.82±0.17	0.96±0.04	0.76±0.08	0.84±0.04	**0.95±0.02**

the software package MALSAR[1] In the experiments, the quadratic loss function in (3.9) is employed for all the compared algorithms. For MSMTFL, we use the capped-ℓ_1 regularizer. Note that the proposed algorithm has only one parameter ϵ, which controls the termination of the algorithm.

4.2 SYNTHETIC DATA

The synthetic data are generated by setting the number of tasks as m, where each task has n samples and of dimensionality d. Each sample is drawn from a multivariate normal distribution $N(0, \mathbf{I})$ where $\mathbf{I}$ is a $d \times d$ identity matrix. Then we normalize all columns of each data matrix $\mathbf{X}^{(i)} \in \mathbb{R}^{n \times d}$ to length one. Each entry of the underlying parameter matrix $\mathbf{\Theta}^*$ is sampled i.i.d. from the uniform distribution over the interval $[-10, 10]$. To simulate sparsity, we randomly set $d - s^*$ rows of $\mathbf{\Theta}^*$ to zero vectors. The response vector is generated by $\mathbf{y}^{(i)} = \mathbf{X}^{(i)}\boldsymbol{\theta}_i^* + \boldsymbol{\epsilon}^{(i)}$, where each entry of $\boldsymbol{\epsilon}^{(i)}$ is drawn i.i.d. from the normal distribution $N(0, \sigma_i^2)$. We choose $\sigma_i = 0.1$ for all i. In detail, we generate two synthetic datasets as follows. The parameter settings are $d = 256, m = 10, s^* = 5, n = 100$ for "Dataset 1"; and $d = 512, m = 10, s^* = 10, n = 100$ for "Dataset 2". In addition, we generate a more challenging synthetic dataset ("Dataset 3") to test the support recovery ability of different algorithms when there are nonzero rows with small ℓ_2 norm in $\mathbf{\Theta}^*$. "Dataset 3" is generated differently. Firstly, we generate a $d \times m$ matrix in which each element is sampled i.i.d. from the uniform distribution in the interval $[-10, 10]$. Then we randomly set $d - s^*$ rows as zero vectors. Among the other s^* nonzero rows, we randomly select s_w^* rows and divide each element in these rows by 20 to simulate the small norm. Other procedures of the data generation are the same as "Dataset 1" and "Dataset 2". We set $d = 512, m = 10, n = 100, s^* = 15, s_w^* = 5$ for "Dataset 3".

All algorithms in the comparative study are employed to estimate $\widehat{\mathbf{\Theta}}$ given $\mathbf{X}^{(i)}$'s and $\mathbf{y}^{(i)}$'s. Since all the algorithms have one or several parameters, we tune the parameters by 5-fold cross validation on each synthetic data. The estimation error of the parameter matrix in terms of Frobenius norm $\|\mathbf{\Theta}^{(t)} - \mathbf{\Theta}^*\|_F$ is reported in Table 1.

In order to evaluate the support recovery results of different algorithms, we use F_1 score defined as follows

$$F_1 = \frac{2 \cdot \text{precision} \cdot \text{recall}}{\text{precision} + \text{recall}},$$

where precision $= |\text{supp}(\mathbf{\Theta}^*) \cap \text{supp}(\widehat{\mathbf{\Theta}})| / |\text{supp}(\widehat{\mathbf{\Theta}})|$ and recall $= |\text{supp}(\mathbf{\Theta}^*) \cap \text{supp}(\widehat{\mathbf{\Theta}})| / |\text{supp}(\mathbf{\Theta}^*)|$. Note that for some algorithms (such as Dirty and rMTFL) they not only output the estimator $\widehat{\mathbf{\Theta}}$, but also output two intermediate estimators $\widehat{\mathbf{P}}$ and $\widehat{\mathbf{Q}}$, where $\widehat{\mathbf{\Theta}} = \widehat{\mathbf{P}} + \widehat{\mathbf{Q}}$. By empirical study, we found that the estimator $\widehat{\mathbf{P}}$ is more suitable for support recovery than the estimator $\widehat{\mathbf{\Theta}}$ (i.e., $\widehat{\mathbf{P}}$ achieves higher F_1 score than $\widehat{\mathbf{\Theta}}$), because in these algorithms $\widehat{\mathbf{P}}$ is a sparse or row-sparse matrix. Hence for Dirty and rMTFL algorithms, we use $\widehat{\mathbf{P}}$ to evaluate the feature selection (i.e., support recovery) performance. The F_1 score of support recovery is reported in Table 2.

From Tables 1 and 2, it can be seen that when all nonzero rows are with large ℓ_2 norms (Dataset 1 and 2), our algorithm can exactly recover the supports of $\mathbf{\Theta}^*$ and attain a small estimation error. While some other algorithms can also recover most supports (with a high F_1 score), they suffer from larger estimation error than ours. This is reasonable because our algorithm employs the support cardinality constraint, which is unbiased when the supports are recovered correctly. In contrast, many other algorithms employ some kinds of convex penalties, which lead to biased estimators. In order to recover the support correctly, they have to use a large penalty parameter λ, which makes the estimators more biased.

When there are nonzero rows with small ℓ_2 norm (Dataset 3), our algorithm can still recover the support of $\mathbf{\Theta}^*$ with high accuracy. This is consistent with our theory. In con-

[1] https://github.com/jiayuzhou/MALSAR

Table 3: The nMSE of different algorithms on school dataset.

	Lasso	FoBa	L1,2	MSMTFL	DirtyMTL	rMTFL	MultiFoBa
20%	0.903±0.012	0.832±0.009	0.924±0.022	0.804±0.009	0.803±0.009	0.802±0.010	**0.762±0.022**
30%	0.859±0.014	0.766±0.013	0.911±0.043	0.765±0.009	0.749±0.009	0.750±0.008	**0.727±0.027**

Table 4: The nMSE of different algorithms on SARCOS dataset.

	Lasso	FoBa	L1,2	MSMTFL	DirtyMTL	rMTFL	MultiFoBa
50	0.093±0.035	0.083±0.012	0.073±0.012	0.077±0.011	0.082±0.037	0.072±0.010	**0.067±0.010**
100	0.075±0.013	0.055±0.006	0.055±0.010	0.053±0.005	0.071±0.038	0.050±0.005	**0.045±0.003**
150	0.068±0.034	0.051±0.005	0.049±0.006	0.047±0.002	0.063±0.037	0.044±0.002	**0.040±0.001**

trast, the other algorithms achieve even worse recovery results when nonzero rows with small ℓ_2 norms exist.

4.3 REAL DATA

We use the School data[2] and the SARCOS data[3] to verify the effectiveness of the proposed algorithm on real datasets.

The School dataset consists of information of students from 139 secondary schools, as well as their exam scores. Each student is described by their 27 attributes, such as gender and ethnic group. The student exam score predicting problem can be cast as a multi-task regression problem: each school is considered as a task, each task as different number of data points, the attributes of students are input variables and their scores are responses. We randomly choose 20% and 30% samples from each task to form the training set and the rest samples as the test set. We tune the parameters of all the algorithms by 5-fold cross validation on the training data. We use the normalized Mean Square Error (nMSE), i.e., the mean squared error divided by the variance of ground-truth output, to measure the performance of all algorithms. Experiment results averaged over 20 repetitions are reported in Table 3.

The SARCOS data is collected for an inverse dynamic prediction problem for a anthropomorphic arm with 7 degrees of freedom. The data contains the training part and the testing part. The training part consists of 44,484 samples and the testing part 4,449 samples. Each sample is described by 21 attributes such as joint positions and velocities. There are also 7 responses attached to each sample, representing 7 torques. Our goal is predicting the responses based on the attributes. This problem can be casted as a multi-task regression problem, where the prediction of each response is regarded as a task, and all tasks share the same design matrix. We randomly choose 50, 100 and 150 samples from the training data of the original dataset to form 3 training sets and accordingly select 2000 samples from the testing data of the original dataset to form 3 testing sets. The experiment results averaged over 20 repetitions are summarized in Table 4.

From both Table 3 and Table 4, we can observe that the proposed algorithm outperforms the other algorithms greatly under different training/test splits on both datasets. This is due to the unbiased property of our estimator under mild conditions, as well as the faster statistical rate of our proposed estimator.

5 CONCLUSIONS AND FUTURE WORK

In this paper, we proposed a general estimator for multi-task learning with row sparsity constraint on the parameter matrix. In order to solve it, we develop a forward backward greedy algorithm, whose output attains a sharper estimation error bound than many state-of-the-art multi-task learning methods. Moreover, the output of the proposed greedy algorithm enjoys model selection consistency under a mild condition. Thorough experiments on both synthetic and real-world data back up our theory.

We notice that the $\ell_{0,2}$ constrained nonconvex optimization problem in (2.1) can be potentially solved by the extensions of iterative hard thresholding (Jain et al., 2014) and Frank-Wolfe algorithms (Jaggi, 2013; Lacoste-Julien and Jaggi, 2013). We will investigate these algorithms in the future.

Acknowledgements

We would like to thank the anonymous reviewers for their helpful comments. Research was sponsored by Quanquan Gu's startup funding at Department of Systems and Information Engineering, University of Virginia.

References

ANDO, R. K. and ZHANG, T. (2005). A framework for learning predictive structures from multiple tasks and

[2]http://ttic.uchicago.edu/~argyriou/code/

[3]http://www.gaussianprocess.org/gpml/data/

unlabeled data. *The Journal of Machine Learning Research* **6** 1817–1853.

ARGYRIOU, A., EVGENIOU, T. and PONTIL, M. (2008). Convex multi-task feature learning. *Machine Learning* **73** 243–272.

BAKKER, B. and HESKES, T. (2003). Task clustering and gating for bayesian multitask learning. *The Journal of Machine Learning Research* **4** 83–99.

BARANIUK, R. G., CEVHER, V., DUARTE, M. F. and HEGDE, C. (2010). Model-based compressive sensing. *Information Theory, IEEE Transactions on* **56** 1982–2001.

BAXTER, J. (2000). A model of inductive bias learning. *J. Artif. Intell. Res.(JAIR)* **12** 149–198.

BOUCHERON, S., LUGOSI, G. and MASSART, P. (2013). *Concentration inequalities: A nonasymptotic theory of independence*. OUP Oxford.

CARUANA, R. (1997). Multitask learning. *Machine learning* **28** 41–75.

EVGENIOU, T. and PONTIL, M. (2004). Regularized multi–task learning. In *Proceedings of the tenth ACM SIGKDD international conference on Knowledge discovery and data mining*. ACM.

FAN, J. and LI, R. (2001). Variable selection via nonconcave penalized likelihood and its oracle properties. *Journal of the American statistical Association* **96** 1348–1360.

GONG, P., YE, J. and ZHANG, C. (2012). Robust multitask feature learning. In *Proceedings of the 18th ACM SIGKDD international conference on Knowledge discovery and data mining*. ACM.

GONG, P., YE, J. and ZHANG, C. (2013). Multi-stage multi-task feature learning. *The Journal of Machine Learning Research* **14** 2979–3010.

HAN, L. and ZHANG, Y. (2015). Learning multi-level task groups in multi-task learning .

JACOB, L., VERT, J.-P. and BACH, F. R. (2009). Clustered multi-task learning: A convex formulation. In *Advances in neural information processing systems*.

JAGGI, M. (2013). Revisiting frank-wolfe: Projection-free sparse convex optimization. In *Proceedings of the 30th International Conference on Machine Learning (ICML-13)*.

JAIN, P., TEWARI, A. and KAR, P. (2014). On iterative hard thresholding methods for high-dimensional m-estimation. In *Advances in Neural Information Processing Systems*.

JALALI, A., JOHNSON, C. C. and RAVIKUMAR, P. K. (2011). On learning discrete graphical models using greedy methods. In *Advances in Neural Information Processing Systems*.

JALALI, A., RAVIKUMAR, P. and SANGHAVI, S. (2013). A dirty model for multiple sparse regression. *Information Theory, IEEE Transactions on* **59** 7947–7968.

JAVANMARD, A. and MONTANARI, A. (2014). Confidence intervals and hypothesis testing for high-dimensional regression. *The Journal of Machine Learning Research* **15** 2869–2909.

KANG, Z., GRAUMAN, K. and SHA, F. (2011). Learning with whom to share in multi-task feature learning. In *Proceedings of the 28th International Conference on Machine Learning (ICML-11)*.

KIM, S. and XING, E. P. (2010). Tree-guided group lasso for multi-task regression with structured sparsity .

LACOSTE-JULIEN, S. and JAGGI, M. (2013). An affine invariant linear convergence analysis for frank-wolfe algorithms. *arXiv preprint arXiv:1312.7864* .

LAWRENCE, N. D. and PLATT, J. C. (2004). Learning to learn with the informative vector machine. In *Proceedings of the twenty-first international conference on Machine learning*. ACM.

LIU, J., FUJIMAKI, R. and YE, J. (2013). Forward-backward greedy algorithms for general convex smooth functions over a cardinality constraint. *arXiv preprint arXiv:1401.0086* .

LIU, J., JI, S. and YE, J. (2009). Multi-task feature learning via efficient l 2, 1-norm minimization. In *Proceedings of the twenty-fifth conference on uncertainty in artificial intelligence*. AUAI Press.

LOUNICI, K., PONTIL, M., TSYBAKOV, A. B. and VAN DE GEER, S. (2009). Taking advantage of sparsity in multi-task learning. *arXiv preprint arXiv:0903.1468* .

LOUNICI, K., PONTIL, M., VAN DE GEER, S. and TSYBAKOV, A. B. (2011). Oracle inequalities and optimal inference under group sparsity. *The Annals of Statistics* 2164–2204.

NEGAHBAN, S. and WAINWRIGHT, M. J. (2008). Joint support recovery under high-dimensional scaling: Benefits and perils of l1,-regularization. *Advances in Neural Information Processing Systems* **21** 1161–1168.

NEGAHBAN, S., YU, B., WAINWRIGHT, M. J. and RAVIKUMAR, P. K. (2009). A unified framework for high-dimensional analysis of m-estimators with decomposable regularizers. In *Advances in Neural Information Processing Systems*.

NESTEROV, Y. (2004). *Introductory lectures on convex optimization*, vol. 87. Springer Science & Business Media.

OBOZINSKI, G., TASKAR, B. and JORDAN, M. (2006). Multi-task feature selection. *Statistics Department, UC Berkeley, Tech. Rep* .

OBOZINSKI, G., WAINWRIGHT, M. J. and JORDAN, M. I. (2011). Support union recovery in high-dimensional multivariate regression. *The Annals of Statistics* 1–47.

PARAMESWARAN, S. and WEINBERGER, K. Q. (2010). Large margin multi-task metric learning. In *Advances in neural information processing systems*.

QUADRIANTO, N., PETTERSON, J., CAETANO, T. S., SMOLA, A. J. and VISHWANATHAN, S. (2010). Multitask learning without label correspondences. In *Advances in Neural Information Processing Systems*.

RAO, N., SHAH, P. and WRIGHT, S. (2015). Forward–backward greedy algorithms for atomic norm regularization. *Signal Processing, IEEE Transactions on* **63** 5798–5811.

RAO, N. S., RECHT, B. and NOWAK, R. D. (2012). Universal measurement bounds for structured sparse signal recovery. In *International Conference on Artificial Intelligence and Statistics*.

SCHWAIGHOFER, A., TRESP, V. and YU, K. (2004). Learning gaussian process kernels via hierarchical bayes. In *Advances in Neural Information Processing Systems*.

TIBSHIRANI, R. (1996). Regression shrinkage and selection via the lasso. *Journal of the Royal Statistical Society. Series B (Methodological)* 267–288.

TURLACH, B. A., VENABLES, W. N. and WRIGHT, S. J. (2005). Simultaneous variable selection. *Technometrics* **47** 349–363.

WAINWRIGHT, M. (2009). Sharp thresholds for noisy and high-dimensional recovery of sparsity using 1-constrained quadratic programming (lasso). *IEEE Transactions on Information Theory* **55** 2183–2202.

YANG, X., KIM, S. and XING, E. P. (2009). Heterogeneous multitask learning with joint sparsity constraints. In *Advances in neural information processing systems*.

YU, K., TRESP, V. and SCHWAIGHOFER, A. (2005). Learning gaussian processes from multiple tasks. In *Proceedings of the 22nd international conference on Machine learning*. ACM.

ZHANG, C.-H. (2010). Nearly unbiased variable selection under minimax concave penalty. *The Annals of Statistics* 894–942.

ZHANG, C.-H. and HUANG, J. (2008). The sparsity and bias of the lasso selection in high-dimensional linear regression. *The Annals of Statistics* 1567–1594.

ZHANG, J., GHAHRAMANI, Z. and YANG, Y. (2005). Learning multiple related tasks using latent independent component analysis. In *Advances in neural information processing systems*.

ZHANG, T. (2009). Adaptive forward-backward greedy algorithm for sparse learning with linear models. In *Advances in Neural Information Processing Systems*.

ZHANG, T. ET AL. (2009). Some sharp performance bounds for least squares regression with l1 regularization. *The Annals of Statistics* **37** 2109–2144.

ZHANG, Y. and YEUNG, D.-Y. (2012). A convex formulation for learning task relationships in multi-task learning. *arXiv preprint arXiv:1203.3536* .

ZHANG, Y. and YEUNG, D.-Y. (2013). Learning high-order task relationships in multi-task learning. In *Proceedings of the Twenty-Third international joint conference on Artificial Intelligence*. AAAI Press.

ZHANG, Y., YEUNG, D.-Y. and XU, Q. (2010). Probabilistic multi-task feature selection. In *Advances in neural information processing systems*.

ZHAO, P. and YU, B. (2006). On model selection consistency of lasso. *The Journal of Machine Learning Research* **7** 2541–2563.

ZHOU, J., YUAN, L., LIU, J. and YE, J. (2011). A multi-task learning formulation for predicting disease progression. In *Proceedings of the 17th ACM SIGKDD international conference on Knowledge discovery and data mining*. ACM.

Non-parametric Domain Approximation for Scalable Gibbs Sampling in MLNs

Deepak Venugopal
Department of Computer Science
University of Memphis
Memphis, TN 38152, USA
dvngopal@memphis.edu

Somdeb Sarkhel
Department of Computer Science
The University of Texas at Dallas
Richardson, TX 75080, USA
sxs104721@utdallas.edu

Kyle Cherry
Department of Computer Science
University of Memphis
Memphis, TN 38152, USA
kcherry2@memphis.edu

Abstract

MLNs utilize relational structures that are ubiquitous in real-world situations to represent large probabilistic graphical models compactly. However, as is now well-known, inference complexity is one of the main bottlenecks in MLNs. Recently, several approaches have been proposed that exploit approximate symmetries in the MLN to reduce inference complexity. These approaches approximate large domains containing many objects with much smaller domains of *meta-objects* (or cluster-centers), so that inference is considerably faster and more scalable. However, a drawback in most of these approaches is that it is typically very hard to tune the parameters (e.g., number of clusters) such that inference is both efficient and accurate. Here, we propose a novel non-parametric approach that trades-off solution quality with efficiency to automatically learn the optimal domain approximation. Further, we show how to perform Gibbs sampling effectively in a domain-approximated MLN by adapting the sampler according to the approximation. Our results on several benchmarks show that our approach is scalable, accurate and converges faster than existing methods.

1 INTRODUCTION

Markov Logic Networks (MLNs) offer a convenient way to express uncertain domain knowledge in the form of weighted first-order formulas. However, probabilistic inference in MLNs is well-known to be a notoriously challenging problem since the size of the Markov network underlying an MLN (*ground* Markov network) typically grows at an exponential rate as we increase the number of real-world objects that the MLN is defined over. Therefore, for MLNs to be practically applicable, controlling inference complexity in large domains is essential.

Efficient inference for MLNs and Statistical Relational Models, in general, has received a great deal of attention from the research community. In particular, the idea of *lifting* inference over the domain of the MLN such that we can perform inference over groups of objects instead of individual objects has been widely explored over the last few years. The main idea in lifted inference is to reduce complexity by taking advantage of exchangeable variables in the model. Several exact and approximate inference methods have been proposed over the past few years starting with the work by Poole [20], including, FOVE [4], WFOMC [26], Probabilistic Theorem Proving (PTP) [7] and lifted inference with soft evidence [3]. Popular approximate lifted inference methods include [16, 17, 22, 11, 8, 18, 29, 2, 1].

More recently, it has been understood that lifting even approximate inference techniques is typically insufficient to ensure scalability in MLNs. The key problem with most traditional lifting techniques is their over-reliance on exact symmetries which are either not present in real-world situations or are known to be broken fairly easily in the presence of evidence [27]. Therefore, a new class of methods that utilize approximate symmetries thereby forgoing strong theoretical guarantees in lieu of scalability have been proposed making MLNs much more attractive from a practical perspective. In this work, we develop one such novel approach by learning the lifting strategy automatically using non-parametric clustering and integrating a Gibbs sampler that adapts itself with the learned strategy.

The idea of grouping nodes in the input model to reduce inference complexity has been explored in previous work such as Kersting et al. [12] who progressively refine a model in the context of belief propagation and Broeck and Darwiche [27] who compute an over-symmetric low-rank boolean matrix approximation of the original MLN that is more amenable to lifted inference. More recently, Hadiji and Kersting [10] and Sarkhel et al. [21] apply grouping strategies in the context of MAP inference to sometimes obtain orders of magnitude reduction in the size of the model. Venugopal and Gogate [30] formulate a clustering problem based on a distance measure computed with the help of evidence given to the MLN and use off-the-shelf clustering methods to approximately lift the MLN. Specifically, the key idea in their approach is to pre-process the original model and generate new, smaller domains consisting of meta-objects that implicitly represent a cluster of objects in the original MLN. However, the main problem with existing methods is that it is very hard to tune the parameters (e.g., number of clusters) such that we select the optimal clustering for an MLN balancing accuracy with complexity of inference. For example, consider a simple MLN with just one unit clause, $\texttt{R}(x)$ w, then, it turns out that given any evidence, the optimal number of clusters required to represent the complete domain of x accurately is equal to 3. Specifically, we form one cluster with all atoms for which the predicate R is known to be true, one cluster that contains all atoms for which R is known to be false and a third cluster of the remaining objects. On the other hand, for a more complex MLN, such as, $\texttt{R}(x, y) \wedge \texttt{R}(y, z) \Rightarrow \texttt{R}(z, x)$ w, choosing the correct number of clusters is not obvious. In this paper, we develop a novel method that automatically finds the clustering that is in some sense optimal. Specifically, we make the following contributions.

1. We develop a fully non-parametric approach to approximate the domain in an MLN with a new domain of meta-objects that correspond to the optimal clustering for that domain.
2. We integrate our clustering method with a Gibbs sampler that adapts itself based on the domain approximation in order to minimize sampling errors.

We perform an evaluation of our approach in terms of both accuracy and convergence on benchmarks chosen from Alchemy [13]. Our results clearly illustrate that our approach is scalable, yields accurate results and importantly converges quickly on large models.

2 BACKGROUND

2.1 FIRST-ORDER LOGIC

We assume a strict subset of first-order logic, called finite Herbrand logic. Thus, we assume that we have no function constants and finitely many object constants. A first-order knowledge base (KB) is a set of first-order formulas. A formula in first-order logic is made up of quantifiers ($\forall$ and $\exists$), logical variables, constants, predicates and logical connectives ($\vee$, $\wedge$, $\neg$, $\Rightarrow$, and $\Leftrightarrow$). We denote logical variables by lower case letters (e.g., x, y, z, etc.) and constants by strings that begin with an upper case letter (e.g., A, Ana, Bob, etc.). Constants model objects in the real-world domain. A predicate is a relation that takes a specific number of arguments (called its arity) as input and outputs either True (synonymous with 1) or False (synonymous with 0). A term is either a logical variable or a constant. We denote predicates by strings in typewriter font (e.g., R, S, Smokes, etc.) followed by a parenthesized list of terms.

A first-order formula is recursively defined as follows: (i) An atomic formula is a predicate; (ii) Negation of an atomic formula is a formula; (iii) If f and g are formulas then connecting them by binary connectives such as $\wedge$ and $\vee$ yields a formula; and (iv) If f is a formula and x is a logical variable then $\forall x f$ and $\exists x f$ are formulas. We assume that each argument of each predicate is typed and can only be assigned to a fixed subset of constants. We refer to a ground atom as an atom that contains no logical variables, i.e., all its variables have been substituted by constants. A possible world, denoted by ω, is a truth assignment to all possible ground atoms that can be formed from the constants and the predicates.

2.2 MARKOV LOGIC NETWORKS

Markov logic networks (MLNs) combine Markov networks and first-order logic. Formally, an MLN is a set of pairs (f_i, θ_i) where f_i is a formula in first-order logic and θ_i is a real number. Given a set of constants, an MLN represents a ground Markov network, defined as follows. We have one binary random variable in the Markov network for each possible ground atom. We have one propositional feature for each possible grounding of each first-order formula. The weight associated with the feature is the weight attached to the corresponding formula. The ground Markov network represents the following probability distribution:

$$\Pr(\omega) = \frac{1}{Z} \exp\left(\sum_i \theta_i N_{f_i}(\omega)\right) \tag{1}$$

where $N_{f_i}(\omega)$ is the number of groundings of f_i that evaluate to True given a world ω (assignment to every ground atom).

Important inference queries in MLNs are computing the partition function, finding the marginal probability of an atom given evidence (an assignment to a subset of variables) and finding the most probable assignment to all atoms given evidence (MAP inference). Here, we focus on the marginal inference problem.

2.3 GIBBS SAMPLING

Gibbs sampling [6] is one of the most widely used MCMC algorithms to date. Gibbs sampling changes one variable at a time by sampling that variable from its conditional distribution given all other variables as described below.

Given a set of n variables $X_1 \ldots X_n$, the Gibbs sampling algorithm begins with a random assignment $\overline{\mathbf{x}}^{(0)}$ to all variables. Then, for $t = 1, \ldots, T$, it performs the following steps (each step is called a Gibbs iteration). Let

$(X_1, \ldots, X_n)$ be an arbitrary ordering of variables in $\mathcal{M}$. Then, for $i = 1$ to n, it generates a new value $\overline{x}_i^{(t)}$ for X_i by sampling a value from the distribution $P(X_i|\overline{\mathbf{x}}_{-i}^{(t)})$ where $\overline{\mathbf{x}}_{-i}^{(t)} = (\overline{x}_1^t, \ldots, \overline{x}_{i-1}^t, \overline{x}_{i+1}^{(t-1)}, \ldots, \overline{x}_n^{(t-1)})$.

Gibbs sampling is typically used to estimate the marginal probabilities. Typically, the sampler is allowed to run for some time (called the *burn-in* time) to allow it to *mix* which ensures that it forgets its initialization, and after T samples from a mixed Gibbs sampler are generated, the 1-variable marginal probabilities can be estimated using the following equation.

$$\widehat{P}_T(\overline{x}_i) = \frac{1}{T}\sum_{t=1}^{T} P(\overline{x}_i|\overline{\mathbf{x}}_{-i}^{(t)}) \quad (2)$$

2.4 DP-MEANS

DP-Means [14] is a non-parametric clustering method that unifies K-means clustering with Bayesian non-parametric models. Specifically, Kullis and Jordan showed that modifying the K-means objective with a penalty term is asymptotically equivalent to performing Gibbs sampling in a Dirichlet-process Mixture Model to infer the right number of clusters. The modified objective is as follows:

$$\min_{\ell_c} \sum_{c=1}^{k} \sum_{x \in \ell_c} ||x - \mu_c||^2 + \lambda k \quad \text{where } \mu_c = \frac{1}{|\ell_c|} \sum_{x \in \ell_c} x \quad (3)$$

To solve the modified K-means objective, DP-Means creates new clusters only when points are sufficiently far off from existing clusters. For completeness sake, we restate the key aspects of the algorithm in Algorithm 1.

Input: $x_1, \ldots x_n; \lambda$
Output: clustering: $\ell_1 \ldots \ell_k$
while *converged=false* **do**
  for *each input point* x_i **do**
    m = Compute minimum distance of x_i w.r.t all current cluster centers
    if $m > \lambda$ **then**
      Create new cluster and assign x_i to new cluster
    end
    else
      Assign x_i to its closest cluster
    end
  end
end

Algorithm 1: DP-Means

Kulis and Jordan showed that Algorithm 1 converges to a local optimal solution. Depending on the value of λ, we would converge to solutions that place more (or less) emphasis on reducing the overall number of clusters.

Formulas:
$\text{R}(x) \vee \text{S}(x, y), w$
Original Domains:
$\Delta_x = \{A_1, B_1, C_1, D_1\}$
$\Delta_y = \{A_2, B_2, C_2, D_2\}$
Domain Approximation:
$\Delta'_x = \{\mu_1, \mu_2\}$
$\Delta'_y = \{\mu_3, \mu\}$
(a)

Meta-Objects:
$\mu_1 = \{A_1, B_1\}$; $\mu_2 = \{C_1, D_1\}$
$\mu_3 = \{A_2, B_2\}$; and $\mu_4 = \{C_2, D_2\}$
(b)

Meta-Atoms:
$\text{R}_1(\mu_1) = \{\text{R}(A_1),\text{R}(B_1)\}$
$\text{R}_2(\mu_2) = \{\text{R}(C_1),\text{R}(D_1)\}$
$\text{S}_1(\mu_1, \mu_2) = \{\text{S}(A_1, C_1),\text{S}(A_1, D_1),$
$\text{S}(B_1, C_1),\text{S}(B_1, D_1)\}$
...
(c)

Figure 1: (a) an example MLN $\mathcal{M}$ and a possible domain approximation for the original domain of $\mathcal{M}$. $\mathcal{M}'$ contains meta-objects and meta-atoms, i.e., objects that represent multiple objects in the original domain and atoms that represent multiple atoms in $\mathcal{M}$ as shown in (b) and (c)

3 NON-PARAMETRIC DOMAIN APPROXIMATION

It is now quite widely understood that in order to scale up inference in MLNs, one needs to perform *domain lifting* [25], i.e., take advantage of symmetries or exchangeability of variables in the MLN [19] to perform efficient inference over groups of objects in the MLN. Following a similar vein, the idea behind approximate domain lifting is to relax the notion of symmetries or exchangeable variables such that domain lifting is applicable to a much larger class of MLNs. One way to find such symmetries is to treat the problem of domain lifting as an unsupervised machine learning problem and use clustering algorithms to learn symmetries based on the structure of the MLN, the given inference query, and evidence. Specifically, for marginal inference, ideally, we would like to cluster together all ground atoms that have similar marginal probabilities. This would then allow us to treat all atoms in the cluster uniformly without having to explicitly compute the marginal probabilities separately for every atom in the cluster. However, it should be noted that clustering at the ground atom level is a non-trivial problem and one that is computationally expensive since the number of ground atoms may themselves be extremely large in MLNs that encode application domains such as Natural Language Understanding.

As an alternative to clustering at the level of ground atoms, Venugopal and Gogate [30], and Broeck and Darwiche [27] proposed clustering approaches at the object-level. That is, given a set of domains $\mathcal{D} = \{D_1, \ldots D_M\}$, where each D_j is a set of real-world objects that can be instantiated in $\mathcal{M}$, and evidence $\mathbf{E}$, we cluster each domain in $\mathcal{D}$ independently and replace the set of objects with *meta-objects*, i.e., the set of cluster-centers, to generate a new domain $\mathcal{D}' = \{D'_1, \ldots D'_k\}$, where each $|D'_j| << |D_j|$. Replacing the domain in $\mathcal{M}$ with $\mathcal{D}'$ yields a new MLN $\mathcal{M}'$ which we refer to as the *domain-approximated* version of $\mathcal{M}$. In $\mathcal{M}'$, each ground atom is now a *meta-atom* since it implicitly represents a set of ground atoms in $\mathcal{M}$. An example MLN and its domain approximation is shown in Fig 1.

Clearly, choosing the right domain approximation is crucial to ensuring the quality of inference results. Therefore, the key question that we wish to answer here is: Given $\mathcal{M}$, $\mathcal{D}$ and $\mathbf{E}$, how do we choose $D'_1, D'_2 \ldots D'_k$ to obtain $\mathcal{M}'$ that is in some sense optimal?

3.1 PROBLEM FORMULATION

We learn the approximate domains for an MLN using a non-parametric approach. Specifically, we use the DP-means algorithm to find the optimal clustering. Note that other notable alternatives for non-parametric clustering exist, such as Dirichlet Process Mixture Models, which uses the Bayesian non-parametric framework for learning clusters without fixing them apriori. However, it turns out that DP-means is a much simpler, more scalable approach and seamlessly integrates Bayesian non-parametrics with the classical and universally popular K-means clustering algorithm which makes it an ideal model for our problem.

Specifically, we formulate the non-parametric domain approximation problem for a given MLN as follows:

$$\min_{\{\ell_{cj}\}_{c=1;j=1}^{|D'_j|;M}} \sum_{j=1}^{M} \sum_{c=1}^{|D'_j|} \sum_{\mathbf{x}\in\ell_{cj}} ||\mathbf{x} - \mu_{cj}||^2 + \lambda|D'_j| \quad (4)$$

where $\mu_{cj} = \frac{1}{|\ell_{cj}|}\sum_{\mathbf{x}\in\ell_{cj}} \mathbf{x}$, λ is a parameter that controls the number of clusters created for each domain in $\mathcal{M}$. $||\mathbf{x} - \mu_{cj}||^2$ is the Euclidean distance between the cluster center μ_{cj} and $\mathbf{x}$.

Given a constant λ, it is easy to see that we can decompose Eq. (4) into M independent objective functions and optimize each objective independently. This will yield the approximate domains for the input MLN $\mathcal{M}$. However, the challenging task is to automatically tune the parameter λ such that $\mathcal{M}'$ is in some way a "good" approximation of $\mathcal{M}$. We next describe an approach to quantify the error made by $\mathcal{M}'$ in approximating $\mathcal{M}$ and incorporate this error to automatically tune λ in Eq. (4).

3.2 DOMAIN APPROXIMATION ERROR

Let $\mathcal{M}$ be the original MLN and $\mathcal{M}'$ be the MLN obtained after approximating each domain in $\mathcal{M}$. Clearly, the distributions $P_{\mathcal{M}}$ and $P_{\mathcal{M}'}$ are defined over spaces with different cardinalities since they have a different number of possible ground atoms. It turns out computing a valid distance metric that can directly compare such distributions is extremely challenging and is shown to be NP-hard [32]. Thus, we need to design approximations that can reasonably compare $P_{\mathcal{M}}$ and $P_{\mathcal{M}'}$.

Consider a single meta-atom in $\mathcal{M}'$, X, which corresponds to a set of ground atoms in $\mathcal{M}$ which we denote by $\mathbf{X}$. Thus, to map $P'_{\mathcal{M}}$ to $P_{\mathcal{M}}$, we need to map a 0/1 assignment of X to a vector of 0/1 assignments to $\mathbf{X}$. Clearly, there are $2^{|\mathbf{X}|}$ different ways to define this mapping. For each mapping, we will end up with a different approximation to $P_{\mathcal{M}}$. If we fix a specific mapping ρ, clearly, we can convert any sample $\mathbf{x}$ drawn from $P_{\mathcal{M}'}$ to a set of samples $\rho(\mathbf{x})$ in $P_{\mathcal{M}}$. In this case, the (un-normalized) probability $P_{\mathcal{M}'}(\mathbf{x})$ can be computed by summing over the (un-normalized) probabilities of $\rho(\mathbf{x})$ as follows:

$$P_{\mathcal{M}'}(\mathbf{x}) = \sum_{\mathbf{y}\in\rho(\mathbf{x})} P_{\mathcal{M}}(\mathbf{y})$$

However, computing the above probability is clearly infeasible since it involves a summation over the probabilities in the original space which can be very large and is precisely the reason to perform domain-approximation in the first place. Instead, if we choose ρ to be a one-to-one mapping, we map each sample in $P_{\mathcal{M}'}$ to exactly one sample in $P_{\mathcal{M}}$. In other words we assume that all other samples that $\mathbf{x}$ can be mapped to have negligible probabilities. Using this assumption, the above equation now reduces to

$$P_{\mathcal{M}'}(\mathbf{x}) \approx P_{\mathcal{M}}(\rho(\mathbf{x}))$$

Even with the above approximation of one-to-one mapping, computing $P_{\mathcal{M}'}(\mathbf{x})$ may be hard since we additionally require that $P_{\mathcal{M}}(\rho(\mathbf{x})$ should be sufficiently easy to compute. That is, given $\mathbf{x}$, we should be able to compute $P_{\mathcal{M}}(\rho(\mathbf{x})$ in bounded time/space. Unfortunately, for an arbitrary ρ, this problem requires computing the counts of satisfied formulas in a sample as its sub-step and is thus $\#P$-complete [24]. However, consider a special ρ, namely, given a sample from $\mathcal{M}'$ with meta-atom X assigned to x, we assign the same value x to all atoms in $\mathcal{M}$ that X corresponds to. We refer to such a mapping as a *uniform assignment* mapping and under this mapping, it turns out that marginal probabilities in $P_{\mathcal{M}}$ and $P'_{\mathcal{M}}$ have a direct relationship. Specifically,

Theorem 1. *Given an MLN $\mathcal{M}$ and its domain-reduced approximation $\mathcal{M}'$, under the assumption of uniform assignment mapping and no evidence atoms, for any ground atom X in $\mathcal{M}'$, $P_{\mathcal{M}'}(X) = P_{\mathcal{M}}(X')$, where $X' \in \mathbf{X}$.*

Proof. Let ω' be a world in $\mathcal{M}'$ and ω be a world in $\mathcal{M}$ obtained by the mapping function ρ.

$$P(\omega') \propto exp(\sum_i N_i(\omega')\theta_i)$$

$$P(\omega) \propto exp(\sum_i N_i(\omega)\theta_i)$$

Since we assume that ρ is a uniform assignment mapping, we have that for any formula f_i, $N_i(\omega') \propto N_i(\omega)$. Further, note that since there is no evidence in the model, $\forall\omega$, $P(\omega) > 0$. Therefore, $P(\omega') \propto P(\omega)$. Summing over all worlds, the partition function, $Z(\mathcal{M}') \propto Z(\mathcal{M})$. Since marginal probabilities are simply ratios of partition functions, the result of the theorem holds. □

The above theorem means that under the assumption of uniform assignment mapping, we can perform marginal inference as follows. We approximate the domains in $\mathcal{M}$ and without changing the weights or formulas in $\mathcal{M}$, we can simply replace the original domain by its domain-approximation to yield $\mathcal{M}'$. We then generate samples from $\mathcal{M}'$ and estimate the marginal probabilities from the generated samples for each meta-atom X. We can finally compute the marginal probabilities in $\mathcal{M}$ by using $P(X)$ for all atoms in $\mathcal{M}$ that meta-atom X represents.

3.3 ADAPTIVE GIBBS SAMPLING

In the presence of evidence, Theorem 1 no longer holds since we need to first translate the evidence $\mathbf{E}$ observed for $\mathcal{M}$ to $\mathcal{M}'$. Depending on this translation, $P_{\mathcal{M}}(\cdot|\mathbf{E})$ may be very different from $P_{\mathcal{M}'}(\cdot|\mathbf{E}')$ even under the assumption of uniform assignment mapping. Previous approaches such as [30] have proposed the transformation of evidence based on majority voting. Specifically, if X is a meta-atom in $\mathcal{M}'$ that corresponds to $\mathbf{X}$ in $\mathcal{M}$, X is assigned as true evidence in $\mathcal{M}'$ if the number of true evidence atoms in $\mathbf{X}$ outweighs the number of false or unknown atoms. However, consider sampling from $P_{\mathcal{M}'}(\cdot|\mathbf{E}')$, where $\mathbf{E}'$ has been generated by applying the aforementioned majority voting. Unless every meta-atom in $\mathcal{M}'$ represents a set of atoms that are all either evidence or all non-evidence atoms, each sample derived from $P_{\mathcal{M}'}(\cdot|\mathbf{E}')$ when mapped to $\mathcal{M}$ using a uniform assignment mapping, will have inconsistencies. For example, let X, Y, Z, U be the ground atoms in $\mathcal{M}$ and let $C1 = X, Y, Z$ and $C2 = U$ be the meta-atoms of $\mathcal{M}'$. If $X = 1$ is given as evidence to $\mathcal{M}$, then no evidence is set in $\mathcal{M}'$. Therefore, in every sample generated from $\mathcal{M}'$ is inconsistent with evidence $X = 1$. Similarly, if $Y = 1$ is added as evidence, then $C1 = 1$, and no samples with $Z = 0$ are generated. Our main idea is to reduce the expected number of inconsistencies when we generate samples from $\mathcal{M}'$ via Gibbs sampling.

In each iteration of Gibbs sampling, we pick a meta-atom, say X in $\mathcal{M}'$ and sample an assignment to this meta-atom from the conditional probability distribution $P_{\mathcal{M}'}(X|X_{-i})$, where X_{-i} is the set of all meta-atoms other than X. The choice of which meta-atom to sample in each iteration is according to a distribution of selection probabilities. Typically, in random-scan Gibbs sampling, this selection probability is a uniform distribution over the non-evidence atoms. However, in general, we can select the selection probabilities to be non-uniform, i.e. a probability α_i for atom X_i. It has also been shown that as long as the selection probabilities are not continuously updated (also called vanishing adaptation), we can show that the Markov chain remains ergodic (cf. [9])

We now formalize the expected error in a sample drawn from the Gibbs sampler as follows. Let $X_1 \dots X_K$ be the meta-atoms in $\mathcal{M}'$ and let $\mathbf{X}_1 \dots \mathbf{X}_K$ be sets of ground atoms in $\mathcal{M}$ where X_i is a meta-atom for all the ground atoms in $\mathbf{X}_i$. If $\mathbf{X}_i$ consists of both evidence and non-evidence atoms and we sample X, clearly, the sample generated may be erroneous on every evidence atom in $\mathbf{X}_i$. But if we choose not sample X at all (i.e., treat it as hard evidence), then we will never sample the non-evidence atoms in $\mathbf{X}$. The expected error can be formulated as,

$$E_G = \sum_{i=1}^{K} \alpha_i \sum_{X' \in \mathbf{X}_i} \mathbb{I}(X') + (1 - \alpha_i) \\ (|\mathbf{X}_i| - \sum_{X' \in \mathbf{X}_i} \mathbb{I}(X')) \quad (5)$$

where $0 \leq \alpha_i \leq 1$ is the selection probability for meta-atom X_i and $\mathbb{I}(X') = 1$ if X' is an evidence atom and 0 otherwise.

Note that if the amount of evidence corresponding to X_i is large, E_G can be reduced by reducing α_i, while, if the amount of evidence corresponding to X_i is small, E_G can be reduced by increasing α_i. Therefore, we set $\alpha_i = 1 - \frac{\sum_{X' \in \mathbf{X}_i} \mathbb{I}(X')}{|\mathbf{X}_i|}$. At the extreme ends, if X_i corresponds to only evidence atoms, it is never sampled in the compressed model ($\alpha_i = 0$) while if X_i corresponds to only non-evidence atoms, it is always sampled in the compressed model ($\alpha_i = 1$).

Next, with the help of a simple example MLN, we illustrate that adapting the selection probabilities of meta-atoms based on the clustering is likely to yield more accurate estimates as opposed to randomly choosing a meta-atom to sample. Here, we considered a simple MLN with three formulas w_1; $\mathtt{R}(x) \vee \mathtt{S}(x)$, w_2; $\mathtt{R}(x)$ and w_2; $\mathtt{S}(x)$ where x has 10000 objects. We introduced 25% random evidence on the ground atoms of R and S. We then randomly divided the objects in x into K clusters to approximate its domain. Thus, there are $2K$ meta-atoms with each meta-atom representing a variable number of original atoms with varying evidence. We compared the performance of Gibbs sampling with random selection probabilities which we refer to as `cgibbs` and our approach where the selection

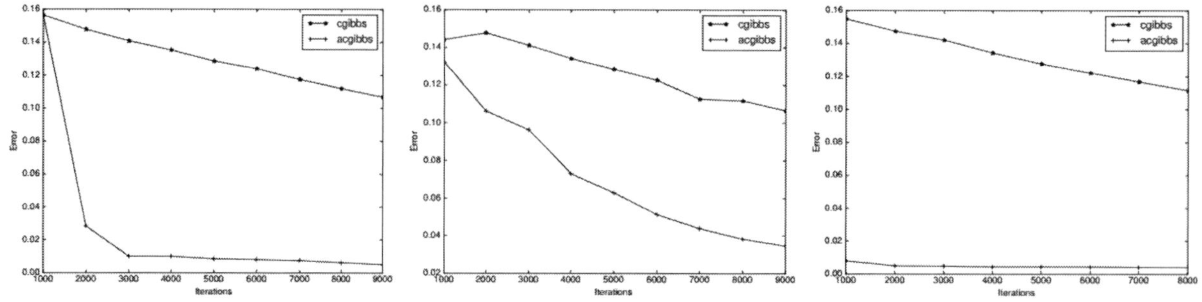

(a) $K = 1000$ (b) $K = 100$ (c) $K = 10$

Figure 2: Illustrating the effect of adapting the selection probabilities in Gibbs sampling based on the clustering. The results are shown for $w_1; \mathtt{R}(x) \vee \mathtt{S}(x)$, $w_2; \mathtt{R}(x)$ and $w_2; \mathtt{S}(x)$ with a domain of 10000 objects and randomly generated evidence. K signifies the number of clusters into which the domain objects were divided. `cgibbs` denotes Gibbs sampling without adapting the selection probability and `acgibbs` denotes Gibbs sampling with adapting the selection probability. The curves are shown as the average mean square error between the true marginal probabilities and the marginal probabilities computed by the samples.

probabilities are tied to the clustering, which we refer to as `acgibbs`. Specifically, we compared the average error between marginal probabilities output by `cgibbs` and `acgibbs` with the true marginal probabilities for the MLN (which we could easily compute due to our choice of the specific MLN structure). The results are shown in Fig. 2 for varying number of clusters (K). As seen in the figure, `acgibbs` generates much more accurate estimates of the marginal probability by reducing the number of inconsistent samples that were generated. The effect is even more pronounced when we have fewer but larger clusters, i.e., Fig. 2 (c), where since K is small, each meta-atom therefore represents a large number of atoms. Here, using random scan Gibbs is much worse since the number of inconsistencies in each sample is extremely large yielding to less accurate estimates of marginal probabilities.

3.4 GIBBS SAMPLING EFFICIENCY

If the Gibbs sampler contains N variables, since each variable is sampled one at a time, it roughly takes about N sampling steps to change the complete state of the sampler just once. Thus, suppose $\mathcal{M}$ has a million non-evidence atoms, we need to at least perform a million sampling operations to sample every variable in the model once which is prohibitively expensive. Further, the *mixing* time of the Gibbs sampler is roughly proportional to the number of variables in the model [15]. Thus, we would like our Gibbs sampler to have a bounded number of variables for efficiency and fast mixing. To specify this, given $\mathcal{M}'$ which is a domain-approximated version of $\mathcal{M}$, we define the sampling efficiency (S_G) of $\mathcal{M}'$ to be proportional the total number of meta-atoms in $\mathcal{M}'$.

Input: $\mathcal{M}$, β_1, β_2, ϵ
Output: $\mathcal{M}'$
$\lambda = 10000$
while *converged=false* **do**
  `// Find the clustering for a fixed` λ
  for *each domain* D_i *in* $\mathcal{M}$ **do**
    D'_i = DP-Means(D_i)
  end
  $\mathcal{M}'$ = Replace-Domains($\mathcal{M}$, $D_1, \ldots$)
  $E_G(\lambda)$ = Evaluate Eq (5) for $\mathcal{M}'$
  $S_G(\lambda)$ = Number of meta-atoms in $\mathcal{M}'$
  if $E_G(\lambda) < \beta_1$ *and* $S_G(\lambda) < \beta_2$ **then**
    converged=true
    return $\mathcal{M}'$
  end
  else if $S_G(\lambda) > \beta_2$ **then**
    `// Could not find solution`
    return $\mathcal{M}'$
  end
  else
    `// Reduce` λ
    $\lambda = \epsilon\lambda$
  end
end

Algorithm 2: NP-Cluster

3.5 COMPUTING THE OPTIMAL CLUSTERS

We now re-formulate the minimization problem in Eq. (4) by incorporating the sampling error (E_G) and the sampling efficiency (S_G). That is, given constants β_1 and β_2, our clustering problem is defined as,

$$\min_{\{\ell_{cj}\}_{c=1;j=1}^{|D'_j|;M};\lambda} \sum_{j=1}^{M} \sum_{c=1}^{|D'_j|} \sum_{\mathbf{x}\in\ell_{cj}} ||\mathbf{x} - \mu_{cj}||^2 + \lambda|D'_j| \quad (6)$$

where $E_G(\lambda) < \beta_1$ and $S_G(\lambda) < \beta_2$

Note that both the sampling error and efficiency depend upon the parameter λ. That is, if λ is large, then we penalize the number of clusters a lot more, therefore, our solution will yield very few meta-atoms which results in a large $E_G(\lambda)$ but small $S_G(\lambda)$. Similarly, smaller λ will yield solutions that has small $E_G(\lambda)$ but large $S_G(\lambda)$. Jointly optimizing $\{\ell_{cj}\}_{c=1;j=1}^{|D'_j|;M}$; λ is challenging because we need to consider every possible clustering with every possible parameter λ. Instead, we use a co-ordinate descent type of approach where we pick a λ and find the best clusters, and then fix the clustering and pick the next best λ.

The algorithm for non-parametric clustering of domains is shown in Algorithm 2. Algorithm 2 starts by fixing λ to a large constant and computes the optimal clustering for the domains of the input MLN, at this value of λ. The DP-Means algorithm is used a sub-step to compute optimal clustering for a given λ. Once, we compute the optimal clustering of the domains, we evaluate the sampling error and efficiency based on the new MLN generated from the clusters. If we satisfy the constraints on sampling error bound and efficiency, then the algorithm has reached a local optima and we output the domain-approximated MLN. However, if we fail to satisfy the constraints, we check if $S_G(\lambda)$ is greater than β_2 in which case, we cannot find a solution, else we reduce λ by ϵ to improve $E_G(\lambda)$ and $S_G(\lambda)$.

4 RELATED WORK

In recent years many methods have been proposed that use symmetries for improving the scalability both in exact inference [20, 4, 7, 26, 3] as well as approximate inference [22, 11, 8, 18, 29, 2]. Niepert and Broeck [19] recently showed that most of the earlier work on lifted inference can be connected to the concept of exploiting *finite partial exchangeability* in statistics that allows one to perform inference over groups of exchangeable variables efficiently. However, lifted inference that only looks for exact exchangeability tends to work with limited classes of MLNs as shown in [27]. Previous work that has addressed this issue in the context of belief propagation include Kersting et al. [12] and Singla et al [23], where scalability was achieved through message approximation. Broeck and Darwiche [27] proposed a general *over symmetric approximation* by adding symmetries to the MLN thereby making it liftable. Venugopal and Gogate [30] proposed the use of unsupervised machine learning methods to cluster similar domain objects together based on the evidence given to the MLN. Similar clustering ideas have been used in MAP inference algorithms and it has been shown that in some cases one can achieve orders of magnitude reduction in the size of the MLN network without sacrificing much accuracy [10, 21]. In the context of sampling based inference algorithms, Broeck and Niepert [28] introduced a Metropolis-Hastings sampler by utilizing over-symmetric approximations of MLNs in their proposal distribution, and Venugopal and Gogate [31] developed an importance sampler by constructing an tractable proposal from the clustered domain objects. However, unlike the aforementioned approaches which use parametric methods that can be difficult to tune, here, we propose a fully non-parametric approach integrated with Gibbs sampling that systematically trades-off sampling error with efficiency.

Dataset	#Clauses	#Atoms	#Parameters
WebKB	892 million	20 million	64
Protein	408 million	3.3 million	211
ER	1.7 trillion	5.5 million	15

Table 1: Dataset sizes.

5 EXPERIMENTS

We evaluate our approach, which we refer to as `acgibbs`, using three benchmark MLNs obtained from the Alchemy [13] website: Webkb MLN that models the relations between web-page links and topics in the webpage, Protein MLN that models the interaction between proteins, and the ER MLN that is used for entity resolution in NLP. The details of these benchmarks are shown in Table 1. For each MLN, we randomly set the weights of the individual formulas between 0 and 1. We evaluate our approach along two dimensions: accuracy in estimating the marginal probabilities and convergence of the Markov Chain. We compare our results with regular Gibbs sampling (`Gibbs`) and the approach proposed in Venugopal and Gogate [30] (`cgibbs`), where they use clustering algorithms such as KMeans to derive an approximate MLN and then sample this MLN using regular Gibbs sampling.

For `cgibbs`, since we explicitly need to set the number of clusters for each domain, we set this to be 10% of the original domain-size. Note that we set this size to be approximately the same size as the number of clusters that computed by our non-parametric methods. For `acgibbs`, for an approximate MLN, $\mathcal{M}'$, we set the threshold β_1 as 0.01% of the number of meta-atoms in $\mathcal{M}'$ and β_2 as 10K. For fairness, in both `cgibbs` and `acgibbs`, we used the same features as specified in [30] for computing the distances. Specifically, for each object in the MLN, the method proposed in Venugopal and Gogate partially grounds the MLN with that specific object and approximately counts the number of true groundings in each formula for the partially ground MLN given evidence. The approximate counting is performed by generating tractable SQL queries with a bounded number of joins. The feature vector for each object is computed with the counts obtained for each formula in the MLN.

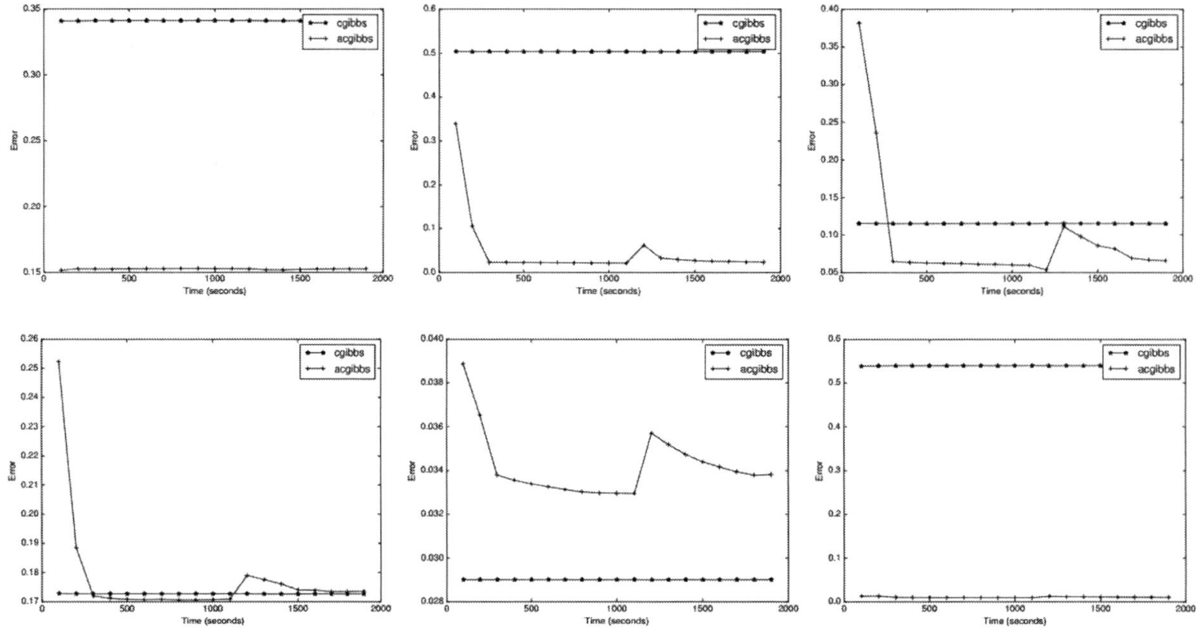

Figure 3: Accuracy Plots for various benchmarks. The domain size of each benchmark was reduced to 10% of its original size to ensure that we get better estimates with `gibbs`. The plots are shown for the average Hellinger distance between the marginal probabilities generated by `gibbs` and that generated by `cgibbs` and `acgibbs` respectively. (a) and (b) correspond to the Protein benchmark with 25% and 50% evidence respectively. Similarly (c) and (d) correspond to the Webkb benchmark, and (e), (f) correspond to the ER benchmark.

5.1 ACCURACY

We compare the accuracy of `cgibbs` and `acgibbs` using the following approach. We assume that the `gibbs` algorithm outputs the true marginal probabilities and compare the results of `cgibbs` and `acgibbs` with that of `gibbs`. We measure the average Hellinger distance between the marginal probabilities of the query atoms output by `gibbs` with the probabilities output by `acgibbs` and `cgibbs`. We considered all ground atoms not set as evidence to be the query atoms. We measured accuracy on small MLNs since for larger MLNs the output of `gibbs` is not reliable. Specifically, we subsampled the true domain of the benchmarks and derived smaller MLNs out of the original benchmarks. Further, we also evaluated the performance of the algorithms in the presence of low as well as high evidence. Fig. 3 shows the results that we obtained for our benchmarks. As seen here, for the protein benchmark, `acgibbs` performs much better than `cgibbs`. For the Webkb benchmark, the accuracy of `acgibbs` is again better than `cgibbs`. For the ER benchmark, for the low evidence case, `acgibbs` was slightly worse than `cgibbs` but for the high evidence case, `acgibbs` was much better than `cgibbs`. One hypothesis for this behavior is that perhaps `gibbs` is not very accurate on this benchmark as shown by the poor convergence property that it exhibits for this benchmark (see next section). Overall, `acgibbs` was seen to be more accurate than `cgibbs` in our evaluation.

5.2 CONVERGENCE

We compare the mixing time of `gibbs`, `cgibbs` and `acgibbs` based on the Gelman-Rubin (G-R) Statistic [5]. For a well-mixed sampler, the G-R statistic should ideally decrease over time illustrating that the MCMC chain has mixed. To compute the G-R statistics, we set up 5 Gibbs samplers from random initialization points and measure the within chain and across chain variances for the marginal probabilities for 1000 randomly chosen query ground atoms. We compute the G-R statistics for each of the 1000 query atoms and measure the mean G-R statistic. Fig. 4 shows our results on the benchmarks. Note that, here we consider larger sized MLNs, i.e., we evaluate on the full benchmark without subsampling the MLN domain. As seen here, for the protein benchmark `cgibbs` and `acgibbs` mix much faster than `gibbs` which has an upward trajectory for the G-R statistic indicating that it has not mixed at all. Among `cgibbs` and `acgibbs`, `acgibbs` mixes faster than `cgibbs` because the selection probability ensures that we spend more resources on sampling meta-atoms which are less deterministic (there is less evidence on the atoms that the meta-atom represents)

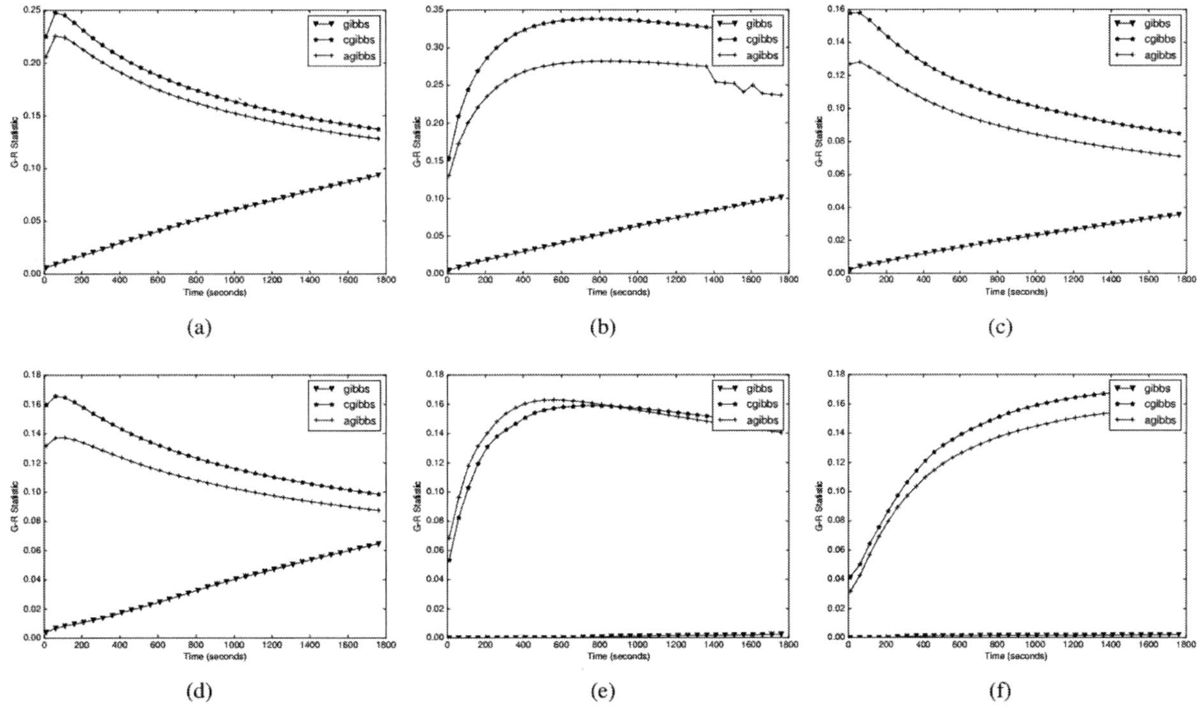

Figure 4: Convergence Plots for various benchmarks. The plots are shown for the average Gelman-Rubin statistic computed using 5 runs of the algorithms across 1000 randomly chosen estimates for the marginal probabilities. (a) and (b) correspond to the Protein benchmark with 25% and 50% evidence respectively. Similarly (c) and (d) correspond to the Webkb benchmark, and (e), (f) correspond to the ER benchmark.

as compared to meta-atoms which are more deterministic (more or less all the atoms represented by the meta-atom are evidence atoms). For the Webkb benchmark, the results look similar with `gibbs` not mixing and `acgibbs` mixing faster than `gibbs`. For the ER case, the curve for `gibbs` stays flat at almost 0. Due to the large size of the benchmark, `gibbs` is very slow in its iterations and most of the query atoms remain un-sampled and thus only retain their initialization values. Even `cgibbs` and `acgibbs` though clearly better than `gibbs`, have slower mixing times as compared to the other two benchmarks.

6 CONCLUSION

Exploiting approximate symmetries has been recognized as a practical approach to obtain scalable inference algorithms in MLNs. Several inference methods that take advantage of approximate symmetries have been proposed over the past few years. However, a major disadvantage of existing methods is that it is quite difficult to manually tune the parameters in these approaches to obtain accurate inference results. Here, we proposed a non-parametric approach that approximates the domains of an MLN and can systematically trade-off accuracy with efficiency. Further, we integrated our approach with a Gibbs sampling algorithm that adapts itself based on the domain-approximation to generate higher quality samples. Our results on benchmarks showed the promise of our approach in terms of scalability, accuracy and convergence.

In future, we would like to explore more complex mapping functions from meta-atoms to the original atoms, integrate our approach with variational distances and adapt our approach for MAP inference algorithms.

References

[1] Babak Ahmadi, Kristian Kersting, Martin Mladenov, and Sriraam Natarajan. Exploiting symmetries for scaling loopy belief propagation and relational training. *Machine Learning*, 92(1):91–132, 2013.

[2] Hung Bui, Tuyen Huynh, and Sebastian Riedel. Automorphism Groups of Graphical Models and Lifted Variational Inference. In *Proceedings of the 29th Conference on Uncertainty in Artificial Intelligence*, pages 132–141. AUAI Press, 2013.

[3] Hung B Bui, Tuyen N Huynh, and Rodrigo de Salvo Braz. Exact lifted inference with distinct soft evidence on every object. In *Proceedings of the Twenty-Sixth AAAI Conference on Artificial Intelligence*, 2012.

[4] R. de Salvo Braz. *Lifted First-Order Probabilistic Inference*. PhD thesis, University of Illinois, Urbana-Champaign, IL, 2007.

[5] A. Gelman and D. B. Rubin. Inference from Iterative Simulation Using Multiple Sequences. *Statistical Science*, 7(4): 457–472, 1992.

[6] S. Geman and D. Geman. Stochastic Relaxation, Gibbs Distributions, and the Bayesian Restoration of Images. *IEEE Transactions on Pattern Analysis and Machine Intelligence*, 6:721–741, 1984.

[7] V. Gogate and P. Domingos. Probabilistic Theorem Proving. In *Proceedings of the 27th Conference on Uncertainty in Artificial Intelligence*, pages 256–265. AUAI Press, 2011.

[8] V. Gogate, A. Jha, and D. Venugopal. Advances in Lifted Importance Sampling. In *Proceedings of the Twenty-Sixth AAAI Conference on Artificial Intelligence*, 2012.

[9] J. Gonzalez, Y. Low, A. Gretton, and C. Guestrin. Parallel gibbs sampling: From colored fields to thin junction trees. In *In Artificial Intelligence and Statistics*, May 2011.

[10] Fabian Hadiji and Kristian Kersting. Reduce and re-lift: Bootstrapped lifted likelihood maximization for MAP. In *Proceedings of the Twenty-Seventh AAAI Conference on Artificial Intelligence*, 2013.

[11] K. Kersting, B. Ahmadi, and S. Natarajan. Counting Belief Propagation. In *Proceedings of the Twenty-Fifth Conference on Uncertainty in Artificial Intelligence*, pages 277–284, 2009.

[12] K. Kersting, Y. E. Massaoudi, F. Hadiji, and B. Ahmadi. Informed Lifting for Message-Passing. In Maria Fox and David Poole, editors, *Proceedings of the Twenty-Fourth AAAI Conference on Artificial Intelligence*, pages 1181–1186, 2010.

[13] S. Kok, M. Sumner, M. Richardson, P. Singla, H. Poon, and P. Domingos. The Alchemy System for Statistical Relational AI. Technical report, Department of Computer Science and Engineering, University of Washington, Seattle, WA, 2006. http://alchemy.cs.washington.edu.

[14] Brian Kulis and Michael I Jordan. Revisiting k-means: New algorithms via bayesian nonparametrics. *ICML*, 2012.

[15] J. S. Liu. *Monte Carlo Strategies in Scientific Computing*. Springer Publishing Company, Incorporated, 2001.

[16] B. Milch and S. J. Russell. General-Purpose MCMC Inference over Relational Structures. In *Proceedings of the Twenty-Second Conference on Uncertainty in Artificial Intelligence*, pages 349–358, 2006.

[17] B. Milch, L. S. Zettlemoyer, K. Kersting, M. Haimes, and L. P. Kaelbling. Lifted Probabilistic Inference with Counting Formulas. In *Proceedings of the Twenty-Third AAAI Conference on Artificial Intelligence*, pages 1062–1068, 2008.

[18] Mathias Niepert. Markov chains on orbits of permutation groups. In *UAI*, pages 624–633. AUAI Press, 2012.

[19] Mathias Niepert and Guy Van den Broeck. Tractability through exchangeability: A new perspective on efficient probabilistic inference. In *Proceedings of the 28th AAAI Conference on Artificial Intelligence, AAAI Conference on Artificial Intelligence*, 2014.

[20] D. Poole. First-Order Probabilistic Inference. In *Proceedings of the 18th International Joint Conference on Artificial Intelligence*, pages 985–991, Acapulco, Mexico, 2003. Morgan Kaufmann.

[21] Somdeb Sarkhel, Parag Singla, and Vibhav Gogate. Fast lifted map inference via partitioning. In *Advances in Neural Information Processing Systems*, pages 3222–3230, 2015.

[22] P. Singla and P. Domingos. Lifted First-Order Belief Propagation. In *Proceedings of the Twenty-Third AAAI Conference on Artificial Intelligence*, pages 1094–1099, Chicago, IL, 2008. AAAI Press.

[23] Parag Singla, Aniruddh Nath, and Pedro Domingos. Approximate Lifting Techniques for Belief Propagation. In *Proceedings of the Twenty-Eigth AAAI Conference on Artificial Intelligence*, pages 2497–2504, 2014.

[24] Dan Suciu, Dan Olteanu, Christopher Ré, and Christoph Koch. *Probabilistic Databases*. Morgan & Claypool, 2011.

[25] G. Van den Broeck. On the Completeness of First-Order Knowledge Compilation for Lifted Probabilistic Inference. In John Shawe-Taylor, Richard S. Zemel, Peter L. Bartlett, Fernando C. N. Pereira, and Kilian Q. Weinberger, editors, *Proceedings of the 25th Annual Conference on Neural Information Processing Systems (NIPS)*, pages 1386–1394, 2011.

[26] G. Van den Broeck, N. Taghipour, W. Meert, J. Davis, and L. De Raedt. Lifted Probabilistic Inference by First-Order Knowledge Compilation. In *Proceedings of the 22nd International Joint Conference on Artificial Intelligence*, pages 2178–2185, 2011.

[27] Guy van den Broeck and Adnan Darwiche. On the complexity and approximation of binary evidence in lifted inference. In *Advances in Neural Information Processing Systems 26*, pages 2868–2876, 2013.

[28] Guy Van den Broeck and Mathias Niepert. Lifted probabilistic inference for asymmetric graphical models. In *Proceedings of the 29th Conference on Artificial Intelligence (AAAI)*, 2015.

[29] D. Venugopal and V. Gogate. On lifting the gibbs sampling algorithm. In *Proceedings of the 26th Annual Conference on Neural Information Processing Systems (NIPS)*, pages 1664–1672, 2012.

[30] Deepak Venugopal and Vibhav Gogate. Evidence-based clustering for scalable inference in markov logic. In *ECML PKDD*, 2014.

[31] Deepak Venugopal and Vibhav Gogate. Scaling-up Importance Sampling for Markov Logic Networks. In *Proceedings of the Twenty-Eigth Annual Conference on Neural Information Processing Systems (NIPS)*, pages 2978–2986, 2014.

[32] Mathukumalli Vidyasagar. A metric between probability distributions on finite sets of different cardinalities and applications to order reduction. *IEEE Trans. Automat. Contr.*, 57(10):2464–2477, 2012.

Efficient Observation Selection in Probabilistic Graphical Models Using Bayesian Lower Bounds

Dilin Wang
Computer Science
Dartmouth College
dilin.wang.gr@dartmouth.edu

John Fisher III
CSAIL
MIT
fisher@csail.mit.edu

Qiang Liu
Computer Science
Dartmouth College
qiang.liu@dartmouth.edu

Abstract

Real-world data often includes rich relational information, which can be leveraged to help predict unknown variables using a small amount of observed variables via a propagation effect. We consider the problem of selecting the best subset of variables to observe to maximize the overall prediction accuracy. Under the Bayesian framework, the optimal subset should be chosen to minimize the Bayesian optimal error rate, which, unfortunately, is critically challenging to calculate when the variables follow complex and high dimensional probabilistic distributions such as graphical models. In this paper, we propose to use a class of Bayesian lower bounds, including Bayesian Cramér Rao bounds as well as a novel extension of it to discrete graphical models, as surrogate criteria for optimal subset selection, providing a set of computationally efficient algorithms. Extensive experiments are presented to demonstrate our algorithm on both simulated and real-world datasets.

1 INTRODUCTION

We consider the following optimal label selection problem: Given an unknown $\theta = [\theta_1, \ldots, \theta_n]$ with posterior distribution $p(\theta \mid X)$ conditioning on observation X, select a best subset $C \subset [n]$ of size no larger than k on which the true values of θ_C are revealed, such that the prediction accuracy of $\theta_{\neg C}$ on the remaining set $\neg C = [n] \setminus C$ is maximized. We assume $p(\theta \mid X)$ to be a multivariate distribution with rich correlation structures, such as graphical models, so that the prediction of $\theta_{\neg C}$ can largely benefit from knowing θ_C via a "propagation effect".

Problems of this type appear widely in many important areas, including semi-supervised learning, experiment design, active learning, as well as application domains such as optimal sensor placement, and optimal budget allocation in crowdsourcing (e.g., Zhu et al., 2003; Krause & Guestrin, 2009; Settles, 2010; Bilgic et al., 2010; Liu et al., 2015).

The optimal subset C should be chosen to minimize certain uncertainty measures of the conditional model $p(\theta_{\neg C} \mid \theta_C \,;\, X)$, and a natural choice is the conditional variance,

$$R_*(C) = \mathbb{E}_{\theta|X}\Big(\sum_{i \in \neg C} \mathrm{var}(\theta_i \mid \theta_C \,;\, X)\Big),$$

which equals the mean squared error of the optimal Bayesian estimator of $\theta_{\neg C}$ given θ_C and X. Unfortunately, this objective is notoriously difficult to calculate in practice; Krause & Guestrin (2009) showed that it is #P-complete to calculate $R_*(C)$ for general discrete graphical models, even for simple tree structured models in many cases. Although practical approximations can be constructed using (approximate) posterior sampling via Markov chain Monte Carlo (MCMC), the estimation accuracy of the conditional variance can be poor when the size of C is large because each conditioning case only receives a small number of samples. Computationally, evaluating $R_*(C)$ requires both unconditioning sampling from $\theta \sim p(\theta \mid X)$, as well as conditional sampling from $\theta_{\neg C} \sim p(\theta_{\neg C} \mid \theta_C, X)$ for each value of θ_C that appears in the unconditioning sample; this makes it extremely difficult to optimize the conditional variance objective in practice, even when simple greedy search methods are used. Similar computational difficulty also appears in other uncertainty measures, such as conditional entropy and mutual information (Krause & Guestrin, 2009); what is worse, these information-theoretic objectives have the additional difficulty of depending on the normalization constant (known as the partition function) of $p(\theta \mid X)$, which is very challenging to calculate.

A special case when the computation can be largely simplified is when $p(\theta \mid X)$ is a multivariate Gaussian distribution; in this case, the conditional variance reduces a simple trace function of the inverse of the sub-matrix on $\neg C$, that is, $R_*(C) = \mathrm{tr}(Q[\neg C]^{-1})$, where Q is the inverse covariance (or the Fisher information) matrix of $p(\theta \mid X)$, and

$Q[\neg C]$ represents the sub-matrix of Q formed by the rows and columns in $\neg C$. This objective can be evaluated and optimized much more efficiently, because Q can be pre-calculated and the block-wise inversion can be calculated recursively using the block-wise matrix inversion formula (Horn & Johnson, 2012).

Contribution In this paper, we propose to solve the subset selection problem using information criteria of form $\mathrm{tr}(Q[\neg C]^{-1})$ for generic, non-Gaussian distribution $p(\theta \mid X)$, where Q is a generalized "information matrix" of $p(\theta \mid X)$ that we will define later; this is motivated by lower bounds of Bayesian risks of form

$$\mathbb{E}_{\theta|X}(\|\hat{\theta}_{\neg C} - \theta_{\neg C}\|_2^2) \geq \mathrm{tr}(Q[\neg C]^{-1}),$$

where $\hat{\theta}_{\neg C} = \hat{\theta}_{\neg C}(\theta_C, X)$ is any (deterministic or randomized) estimator of $\theta_{\neg C}$. Results of this type are the Bayesian version of the classical frequentist Cramér Rao bound, which, however, only works for unbiased estimators. For continuous θ with smooth densities, this bound is based on the van Trees inequality, or known as Bayesian Cramér Rao bound (Van Trees & Bell, 2007) and Q is a Bayesian version of the typical frequentist Fisher information matrix. For θ with discrete values, we derive a new form of Q based a new extension of van Trees inequality; our result appears to be the first bound of this type for discrete graphical models to the best of our knowledge.

Minimizing these Bayesian lower bounds provides new computationally efficient approaches for observation selection with complex $p(\theta \mid X)$. We provide extensive empirical results to demonstrate the advantage of our methods in two practical application settings, including selecting control questions in crowdsourcing and label propagation for graph-based semi-supervised learning.

Related Work Bayesian CR bounds have been widely used in signal processing and information fusion, but seem to be less well known in machine learning; we refer to Van Trees (2004); Van Trees & Bell (2007) for an overview of its theory and applications. Related to our work, Williams (2007) used the log-determinant (instead of the trace) of Bayesian Fisher information as the selection criterion, and studied its sub-modularity.

Outline This paper is organized as follows. Section 2 introduces backgrounds on the observation selection problem and Bayesian Cramér Rao (CR) bounds. We apply Bayesian CR bounds to solve the observation selection problem in Section 3 and propose the extension to discrete models in Section 4. We then discuss two examples of applications of our methods in Section 5, and present empirical results in Section 6. The paper is concluded in Section 7.

2 BACKGROUND

We introduce backgrounds on the observation selection problem in Section 2.1, and Bayesian Cramér-Rao bounds in Section 2.2. We restrict to the case when θ is a continuous variable in this section, and discuss the extension to discrete variables in Section 4.

2.1 OBSERVATION SELECTION

Assume $\theta = [\theta_1, \ldots, \theta_n] \in \mathbb{R}^n$ is a continuous random parameter of interest with posterior distribution $p(\theta \mid X) \propto p(X \mid \theta)p(\theta)$ conditioning on observed data X. We are interested in the setting when we have the option of revealing the true value θ_C of a subset $C \subset [n]$ of size no larger than k, such that we can get the best estimation on the unknown parameter $\theta_{\neg C}$ in the remaining set $\neg C = [n] \setminus C$. To be concrete, let $\hat{\theta}_{\neg C} = \hat{\theta}_{\neg C}(\theta_C, X)$ be an estimator of $\theta_{\neg C}$ based on θ_C and X, the optimal C should ideally minimize the mean squared Bayesian risk:

$$\min_{C:\, |C| \leq k} \{R_{\hat{\theta}}(C) \equiv \mathbb{E}_{\theta|X}(\|\hat{\theta}_{\neg C} - \theta_{\neg C}\|_2^2)\}.$$

However, this objective depends on the choice of the estimator $\hat{\theta}_{\neg C}$ and is not easy to estimate in practice. Consider the Bayesian estimator $\hat{\theta}_{\neg C} = \mathbb{E}(\theta_{\neg C} \mid \theta_C, X)$, then $R_{\hat{\theta}}(C)$ reduces to the trace of the conditional variance:

$$R_*(C) = \mathrm{tr}(\mathbb{E}_{\theta|X}(\mathrm{cov}(\theta_{\neg C} \mid \theta_C, X))), \qquad (1)$$

which is also the minimum Bayesian risk one can possibly achieve. This objective function is called the A-optimality ("average" or trace) in the experiment design literature (e.g., Chaloner & Verdinelli, 1995).

There also exist other similar objective functions, but with less direct connection to the mean squared Bayesian risk; this includes the information-theoretic quantities such as the conditional entropy $H(\theta_{\neg C} \mid \theta_C, X)$ and the mutual information $I(\theta_{\neg C}, \theta_C \mid X)$. The negative of these objective functions are often shown to be submodular and monotonic under certain conditions, for which an $(1-1/e)$ optimality approximation can be obtained using a simple greedy algorithm, that is, starting with an empty set $C = \emptyset$, and sequentially add the best item i so that $R(C \cup \{i\})$ is minimized (Nemhauser et al., 1978).

The major challenge in implementing the greedy algorithm for objectives like (1) is the computational cost of the objective. Although it is possible to draw approximate sample from $p(\theta \mid X)$ using MCMC, the estimation quality of the conditional variance $\mathrm{var}(\theta_{\neg C} \mid \theta_C)$ can be poor, especially when the size of C is large, because it requires samples from $\theta_{\neg C} \sim p(\theta_{\neg C} \mid \theta_C, X)$ for each value of θ_C that appears in the unconditioning sample of $p(\theta \mid X)$. Further, the Monte Carlo estimates are required for every candidate C considered, making the optimization algorithm very time consuming.

The information-theoretic objective functions, such as conditional entropy and mutual information, also suffer from the similar difficulty due to the need for estimating the conditional distribution $\log p(\theta_{\neg C} \mid \theta_C, X)$; in addition, they also involve calculating the normalization constant $Z = \int p(X \mid \theta)p(\theta)d\theta$, which is known to be critically difficult (e.g., Chen et al., 2012).

The computation can be largely simplified when $p(\theta \mid X)$ is a multivariate normal distribution, e.g., $\mathcal{N}(\mu, \Sigma)$, in which case the objective (1) reduces to a matrix function $\mathrm{tr}(Q[\neg C]^{-1})$, where $Q = \Sigma^{-1}$ is the inverse covariance matrix, and the greedy selection can be implemented efficiently based on the recursive relation,

$$R_*(C \cup \{i\}) = R_*(C) + \sum_{j \in \neg C} \frac{\sigma_{ij}^2}{\sigma_{ii}},$$

where $Q[\neg C]^{-1} = \{\sigma_{ij}\}$ and can also be calculated recursively using the block-wise matrix inversion formula (Horn & Johnson, 2012).

2.2 BAYESIAN CRAMÉR RAO LOWER BOUND

Bayesian Cramér Rao bounds (Van Trees, 2004), also known as van Trees inequalities, are lower bounds of Bayesian risks for any estimator $\hat{\theta}$ in terms of Fisher information matrix; it is the Bayesian version of the classical Cramér Rao bound, but does not restrict to unbiased estimators.

Let $\hat{\theta} = \hat{\theta}(X)$ be any (randomized or deterministic) estimator, then under mild regularity conditions (Van Trees & Bell, 2007, page 35), the Bayesian Cramér Rao bound guarantees

$$\mathbb{E}_{\theta|X}[\|\hat{\theta} - \theta\|^2] \geq \mathrm{tr}(H^{-1}), \tag{2}$$

where $H = -\mathbb{E}_{\theta|X}\left[\nabla_\theta^2 \log p(\theta \mid X)\right]$ and is called the *Bayesian Fisher information matrix*; compared to the classical Fisher information, Bayesian Fisher information takes expectation on the parameter θ and does not require a true value θ^*. We note that H can be rewritten into

$$H = -\mathbb{E}_\theta[\nabla_\theta^2 \log p(X \mid \theta)] - \mathbb{E}_\theta[\nabla_\theta^2 \log p(\theta)],$$

where the first term represents the information brought by the observed data, and the second term is the information from the prior knowledge.

Nuisance Parameter In many practical cases, there exist additional nuisance parameters $\eta \triangleq \{\eta_1, \cdots, \eta_{n'}\}$ of no direct interest. Ideally, this can be handled by applying Bayesian CR bound on the marginalized probability $p(\theta \mid X) = \int p(\theta, \eta \mid X)d\eta$. This, however, can be difficult to calculate because $\nabla_\theta^2 \log p(\theta \mid X)$ may have no closed form and require another Monte Carlo approximation. A weaker, but more computationally efficient, lower bound (Van Trees & Bell, 2007, Section 1.2.6) can be

$$\mathbb{E}_{\theta|X}[\|\hat{\theta} - \theta\|^2] \geq \mathrm{tr}([H^{-1}]_{\theta\theta}), \tag{3}$$

where $[H^{-1}]_{\theta\theta} = (H_{\theta\theta} - H_{\theta\eta}H_{\eta\eta}^{-1}H_{\eta\theta})^{-1}$ is the $\theta\theta$-submatrix of H^{-1}, with H being the joint Bayesian Fisher information matrix of $[\theta, \eta]$:

$$H = \begin{bmatrix} H_{\theta\theta} & H_{\theta\eta} \\ H_{\eta\theta} & H_{\eta\eta} \end{bmatrix} = \mathbb{E}_{\theta,\eta|X} \begin{bmatrix} \nabla_{\theta\theta}\ell & \nabla_{\theta\eta}\ell \\ \nabla_{\eta\theta}\ell & \nabla_{\eta\eta}\ell \end{bmatrix}, \tag{4}$$

where $\ell = -\log p(\theta, \eta \mid X)$.

3 BAYESIAN CR BOUND FOR LABEL SELECTION

We apply Bayesian CR bounds to define an objective function of form $\mathrm{tr}(Q[\neg C]^{-1})$ for the observation selection problems, allowing more efficient computation.

Proposition 1. *For any subset $C \subseteq [n]$ and estimator $\hat{\theta}_{\neg C} = \hat{\theta}_{\neg C}(\theta_C, X)$, assume the conditions for Bayesian Cramér Rao bound holds, we have*

$$\mathbb{E}_{\theta|X}[\|\hat{\theta}_{\neg C} - \theta_{\neg C}\|^2] \geq \mathrm{tr}(Q[\neg C]^{-1}),$$

where $Q[\neg C]$ is the submatrix of a matrix Q with rows and columns in $\neg C$ and Q can be one of the following two cases:

1. With no nuisance parameter, Q is the Bayesian Fisher information of θ, that is, $Q = -\mathbb{E}_{\theta|X}[\nabla_\theta^2 \log p(\theta \mid X)]$.

2. With a nuisance parameter η, we have $Q = H_{\theta\theta} - H_{\theta\eta}H_{\eta\eta}^{-1}H_{\eta\theta}$ and H is the joint Bayesian Fisher information of $[\theta, \eta]$ as defined in (4).

Proof. Apply (2) and (3) by treating $[\theta_C, X]$ as the fixed observation and $\theta_{\neg C}$ as the random parameter to be estimated. □

Remark Because the conditional variance in (1) is the Bayesian risk obtained by the Bayesian estimator $\hat{\theta}_{\neg C} = \mathbb{E}(\theta_{\neg C} \mid \theta_C;\ X)$, it should also be lower bounded by the Bayesian CR bound, that is,

$$\mathrm{tr}(\mathbb{E}_{\theta|X}(\mathrm{cov}(\theta_{\neg C} \mid \theta_C;\ X))) \geq \mathrm{tr}(Q[\neg C]^{-1}).$$

The above result suggests a method for finding the optimal subset C by minimizing the lower bound in Proposition 1, reducing to the observation selection problem to a sub-matrix selection problem:

$$\max_{C\colon |C| \leq k} \{f_Q(C) \equiv -\mathrm{tr}(Q[\neg C]^{-1})\}, \tag{5}$$

where k is the maximum size of C that defines our budget.

We now introduce conditions under which the objective function $f_Q(C)$ is a monotonically non-increasing and submodular function, so that the simple greedy selection algorithm yields an $(1 - 1/e)$-approximation. See Algorithm 1.

Proposition 2. *(i). Assume Q is positive definite. For any $i \notin C$, we have*

$$f_Q(C \cup \{i\}) = f_Q(C) + \frac{\sum_{j \in \neg C} \sigma_{ij}^2}{\sigma_{ii}}.$$

where σ_{ij} is the ij-element of $Q[\neg C]^{-1}$, and hence we have $f_Q(C) \geq f_Q(C')$ for any $C' \subseteq C$.

(ii). If Q is positive definite and also satisfies $Q_{ij} \leq 0$ for $i \neq j$ (i.e.,it is a Stieltjes matrix, equivalently a symmetric M-matrix), then $\Sigma = Q^{-1}$ is element-wise nonnegative, and $f_Q(C)$ is a sub-modular function.

Proof. (1) is an elementary fact, and (2) is a special case of Friedland & Gaubert (2013, Theorem 3). □

Since $\Sigma = Q^{-1}$ corresponds to the covariance matrix in the Gaussian case, Proposition 2(ii) suggests that we need Σ to be element-wise nonnegative, that is, θ_i are positive related to each other (in a rough sense), to make $f_Q(C)$ a submodular function. We remark that this element-wise positive condition is necessary; see Friedland & Gaubert (2013, Example 18) for a counter example. Similar "suppressor-free" conditions also appear when considering the submodularity of conditional variance functions in other settings (e.g., Das & Kempe, 2008; Ma et al., 2013).

The greedy algorithm for optimizing (5) is shown in Algorithm 1, in which we use Proposition 2(i) to reduce the greedy update $i^* = \arg\max_i f_Q(C \cup \{i\})$ to a simpler form:

$$i^* = \arg\max_i \left\{ \sigma_{ii} + \frac{\sum_{j \in \neg C, j \neq i} \sigma_{ij}^2}{\sigma_{ii}} \right\}. \quad (6)$$

Intuitively, the first term of the above selection criterion corresponds to a *local effect*, representing the uncertainty σ_{ii} of θ_i itself, while the second term corresponds to a *global effect*, representing how much knowing the true value of θ_i can help in estimating the remaining parameters. Note that Algorithm 1 also updates $Q[\neg C]^{-1} = \{\sigma_{ij}\}$ recursively using the sub-matrix inverse formula (Line 9).

We should point out that evaluating the expectation in $Q = -\mathbb{E}[\nabla_\theta^2 \log p(\theta \mid X)]$ still requires drawing samples from $p(\theta \mid X)$ (or $p(\theta, \eta \mid X)$), but this can be pre-calculated before the greedy search starts, and is much more efficient than optimizing the exact conditional variance objective function, which requires expensive Monte Carlo or MCMC sampling for each candidate C evaluated during the optimization process.

4 EXTENSION TO DISCRETE VARIABLES

The Bayesian CR bound above works only for continuous random parameters, since it requires to calculate the derivatives and Hessian matrices. In this section, we introduce a

Algorithm 1 Greedy Subset Selection based on Bayesian CR bound

1: **Input:** Posterior distribution $p(\theta, \eta \mid X)$; budget size k.
2: Denote $H(\theta, \eta) = -\nabla_{[\theta,\eta]}^2 \log p(\theta, \eta \mid X)$.
3: Draw sample $[\theta^\ell, \eta^\ell]_{\ell=1}^m \sim p(\theta, \eta \mid X)$.
4: $H = \frac{1}{m} \sum_\ell H(\theta^\ell, \eta^\ell)$ and $Q = H_{\theta\theta} - H_{\theta\eta} H_{\eta\eta}^{-1} H_{\eta\theta}$.
5: Initialize $C = \emptyset$. $\Sigma = Q^{-1}$.
6: **while** $|C| < k$ **do**
7: $\quad i^* \leftarrow \arg\max_{i \in \neg C} \sum_{j \in \neg C} \sigma_{ij}^2 / \sigma_{ii}$.
8: $\quad C \leftarrow C \cup \{i^*\}$.
9: $\quad \sigma_{ij} \leftarrow \sigma_{ij} - \sigma_{ii^*} \sigma_{i^*j} / \sigma_{i^*i^*}, \quad \forall i, j \in \neg C$.
10: **end while**

new class of lower bounds that apply to general discrete probabilistic graphical models.

Proposition 3. *(i). Assume $\theta = [\theta_1, \ldots, \theta_n]$ takes values in a discrete set $\theta \in \{a_1, \ldots, a_d\}^n$, and $p(\theta|X) > 0$ for any θ. Let a^* be the solution of $\sum_{k=1}^d \frac{1}{a_k - a^*} = 0$. Define*

$$s_i(\theta,\ X) = \frac{1}{d(\theta_i - a^*) p(\theta_i \mid \theta_{\neg i}\ ;\ X)},$$

and $Q = \mathbb{E}_{\theta|X}[ss^\top]$, then for any estimator $\hat{\theta}(X)$, we have

$$\mathbb{E}_{\theta|X}[\|\hat{\theta}(X) - \theta\|^2] \geq \mathrm{tr}(Q^{-1}).$$

(ii). For any subset $C \subseteq [n]$ and conditional estimator $\hat{\theta}_{\neg C} = \hat{\theta}_{\neg C}(\theta_C, X)$, we have

$$\mathbb{E}_{\theta|X}[\|\hat{\theta}_{\neg C} - \theta_{\neg C}\|^2] \geq \mathrm{tr}(Q[\neg C]^{-1}),$$

where $Q[\neg C]$ is the submatrix of Q with rows and columns in $\neg C = [n] \setminus C$.

Proof. (i). Denote by $\delta = \theta - \hat{\theta}$, we have by Cauchy's inequality,

$$\mathbb{E}_{\theta|X}[\delta\delta^\top] \succeq \mathbb{E}_{\theta|X}[\delta s^\top] \cdot [\mathbb{E}_{\theta|X}(ss^\top)]^{-1} \cdot \mathbb{E}_{\theta|X}[s\delta^\top].$$

Since $\|\hat{\theta}(X) - \theta\|^2 = \mathrm{tr}(\delta\delta^\top)$, we just need to show that $\mathbb{E}_{\theta|X}[\delta s^\top] = \mathbb{E}_{\theta|X}[(\theta - \hat{\theta}) s^\top] = I$ where I is the identity matrix. To see this, note that

$$\mathbb{E}_{\theta|X}[s_i] = \sum_\theta \frac{p(\theta_{\neg i} \mid X)}{d(\theta_i - a^*)}$$
$$= \sum_{\theta_i} \frac{1}{d(\theta_i - a^*)} \sum_{\theta_{\neg i}} p(\theta_{\neg i} \mid X) = 0,$$

where the last step is because $\sum_{\theta_i} \frac{1}{\theta_i - a^*} = 0$ by the definition of a^*. Therefore, we have $\mathbb{E}_{\theta|X}[s] = 0$, and hence $\mathbb{E}_{\theta|X}[\delta s^\top] = \mathbb{E}_{\theta|X}[\theta s^\top]$. Further, note that

$$\mathbb{E}_{\theta|X}[\theta_i s_i] = \mathbb{E}_{\theta|X}[(\theta_i - a^*) s_i] = \frac{1}{d} \sum_\theta p(\theta_{\neg i} \mid X) = 1,$$

$$\mathbb{E}_{\theta|X}[\theta_j s_i] = \sum_{\theta} \frac{\theta_j - a^*}{d(\theta_i - a^*)} p(\theta_{\neg i} \mid X)$$
$$= \sum_{\theta_i} \frac{1}{d(\theta_i - a^*)} \sum_{\theta_{\neg i}} (\theta_j - a^*) p(\theta_{\neg i} \mid X)$$
$$= 0 \quad \forall i \neq j.$$

This gives $\mathbb{E}_{\theta|X}[\theta s^\top] = I$ and the result follows.

(ii). Apply the result in (ii) by treating $\theta_{\neg C}$ as the random parameter and (θ_C, X) as the observed data. □

Note that s_i depends on $p(\theta \mid X)$ only through the conditional distribution $p(\theta_i \mid \theta_{\neg i}, X)$, which is often computationally tractable since it does not depend on the troublesome normalization constant $Z = \sum_\theta p(X|\theta)p(\theta)$.

Example Consider the case of binary parameter $\theta \in \{0,1\}^n$, then solving $\frac{1}{0-a^*} + \frac{1}{1-a^*} = 0$ gives $a^* = 1/2$. Therefore, we have $s_i(\theta, X) = \frac{1}{(2\theta_i - 1)p(\theta_i|\theta_{\neg i}, X)}$ in this case.

We remark that there exist variants of Bayesian CR bounds that use finite differences to replace the derivatives, including Borrovsky-Zakai bound (Bobrovsky & Zakai, 1975) and Weiss-Weinstein bound (Weiss & Weinstein, 1985); these bounds can be naturally applied when θ takes values in the integer lattice $\mathbb{Z}^n$, but does not work well when θ takes values a finite set due to the boundary problem.

5 APPLICATIONS

The subset selection problem has wide applications in many important areas. In this section, we describe two examples of applications that involve continuous and discrete random variables, respectively; empirical results on real datasets are presented in Section 6.

5.1 CONTINUOUS LABEL SELECTION FOR CROWDSOURCING

Crowdsourcing has been widely used in data-driven applications for collecting large amounts of labeled data (Howe, 2006). A major challenge, however, is that the (often anonymous) crowd labelers tend to give unreliable, even strongly biased, answers. Probabilistic modeling has been widely used to estimate the workers' reliabilities and downweight or eliminate the unreliable workers (e.g., Raykar et al., 2010; Karger et al., 2011; Zhou et al., 2012; Liu et al., 2012). However, to correct the biases, it is often necessary to reveal a certain amount of true labels, raising the problem of deciding which questions should be chosen to reveal the true labels (e.g., Liu et al., 2013, 2015).

To set up the problem, we follow the setting in Liu et al. (2013, 2015). Assume we have a set of questions $\{i\}$, each relates to an unknown continuous quantity θ_i that we want to estimate (e.g., price, point spreads, GDP). Let $\{j\}$ be a set of crowd workers that we hire to estimate $\{\theta_i\}$, and each worker j is characterized by a parameter $\eta_j = [b_j, v_j]$, where b_j and v_j represent the bias and variance of worker j, respectively; we assume the crowd label $\{x_{ij}\}$ of question i given by worker j is generated by

$$x_{ij} = \theta_i + b_j + \sqrt{v_j}\xi_{ij}, \quad \xi_{ij} \sim \mathcal{N}(0,1). \tag{7}$$

Using a Bayesian approach, we assume Gaussian priors $p(\theta_i) = \mathcal{N}(0, \sigma_\theta^2)$, $p(b_j) = \mathcal{N}(0, \sigma_b^2)$ on θ_i and b_j, and an inverse Gamma prior $p(v_j) = \text{Inv-Gamma}(\alpha, \beta)$ on v_j. The posterior distribution of θ and η can be written as

$$p(\theta, \eta \mid X) \propto \prod_j \exp\left[-\frac{b_j^2}{2\sigma_b^2}\right] \prod_j v_j^{-\alpha - \frac{d_j}{2} + 1} \exp\left[-\frac{\beta}{v_j}\right]$$
$$\prod_{i,j} \exp\left[-\frac{(X_{ij} - \theta_i - b_j)^2}{2v_j}\right] \prod_i \exp\left[-\frac{\theta_i^2}{2\sigma_\theta^2}\right].$$

However, the crowd labels X may not carry enough information for predicting θ, and we hence consider the option of acquiring the ground truth labels of a subset C of questions (called the *control questions*), which can be incorporated into Bayesian inference to help evaluate the bias and variance of the workers, and hence improve the prediction of the remaining questions.

We can use Algorithm 1 to select the optimal subset C, where the greedy update (6) strikes a balance between selecting the most uncertain questions to myopically improve the overall MSE, and the most "influential" questions (e.g., these labeled by a lot of workers) whose ground truth labels can significantly improve the estimation of the workers' bias and variance, and hence improve the prediction of the unlabeled questions via a *propagation effect*.

5.2 DISCRETE LABEL SELECTION ON GRAPHS

Numerous real-world applications produce networked data with rich relational structures, such as web data and communication networks, and these relational information can be used to improve the prediction accuracy of unlabeled data using a small amount of labeled data. Various methods have been developed to exploit this effect, including graph-based semi-supervised learning (e.g., Zhu et al., 2003; Zhou et al., 2004) and collective, or graph-based, classification (e.g., Lu & Getoor, 2003). A related important question is how to select the best labeling subset to enable the best prediction on the remaining data.

We set up the problem using undirected graphical models. Assume $G = (V, E)$ is an undirected graph, and θ_i is a discrete label associated with node $i \in V$. It is common to model the posterior distribution using a pairwise graphical model,

$$p(\theta) \propto \exp\big[\sum_{(i,j)\in E} J_{ij}\theta_i\theta_j + \sum_{i\in V} h_i\theta_i\big], \tag{8}$$

where J_{ij} represents the correlation between θ_i and θ_j and h_i the local information of θ_i. We are interested in the problem of selecting the best subset $C \subseteq V$ so that the prediction accuracy based $p(\theta_{\neg C} \mid \theta_C)$ is maximized. In the semi-supervised learning settings, θ_i is often assumed to be a continuous variable, and $p(\theta)$ reduces to a simple Gaussian Markov random field. We instead assume θ to be discrete labels (e.g., $\theta \in \{-1, +1\}$) which is much more challenging to deal with. Our bound in Section 4 and Algorithm 1 (but with Q defined in Proposition 3) provide a novel tool for solving this problem efficiently.

6 EXPERIMENTS

We present experiments to better understand the performance of our proposed observation selection methods based on Bayesian lower bounds. To achieve this, we first illustrate our method using a toy example based on Gaussian mixture, and then apply our method to the two application areas described in Section 5, including selecting optimal control questions in crowdsourcing, as well as discrete label selection in graph-based classification.

6.1 CONTINUOUS VARIABLES

We test our method in the case when θ is a continuous variable, first on a toy Gaussian mixture model, and then on the model for selecting control questions in crowdsourcing. We implement our method `BayesianCRB(Gibbs)` as shown in Algorithm 1 with the sample $[\theta^\ell, \eta^\ell]_{\ell=1}^m$ generated using Gibbs sampler. In addition, the following baseline selection methods are compared:

`Random`, in which a random set C of size k is selected uniformly.

`BayesianOpt(Gibbs)`, which greedily minimizes the trace of the conditional variance in (1); to estimate the conditional variance we draw $[\theta^\ell, \eta^\ell]_{\ell=1}^m \sim p(\theta, \eta, |X)$ using Gibbs sampler, and then for each candidate set C evaluated during the greedy search, we further draw $[\theta_{\neg C}^{\ell,r}, \eta^{\ell,r}]_{r=1}^{m'} \sim p(\theta_{\neg C}, \eta, |\theta_C^\ell, X)$ using another Gibbs sampler, and estimate the objective in (1) by

$$\frac{1}{m(m'-1)} \sum_{\ell=1}^{m} \sum_{r=1}^{m'} \sum_{i \in \neg C} (\theta_i^{\ell,r} - \bar{\theta}_i^\ell)^2,$$

where $\bar{\theta}_i^\ell = \frac{1}{m'} \sum_{r=1}^{m'} \theta_i^{\ell,r}$. This method aims to minimize the Bayesian optimal risk, but is obviously much more expensive than our `BayesianCRB(Gibbs)` because it needs a large size m' of MCMC sample to get a good approximation for evaluating each candidate C, while it tends to degenerate significantly when m' is small.

`MaxVar(Gibbs)`, which greedily finds a subset C with the largest uncertainty in the sense of maximizing the variance $\sum_{i \in C} \text{var}(\theta_i|X)$, instead of minimizing the conditional variance. The variance is estimated by the empirical variance using the MCMC samples $[\theta^\ell, \eta^\ell]_{\ell=1}^m$. This algorithm is computationally as fast as our `BayesianCRB(Gibbs)`, but does not consider the "propagation effect" that the information in θ_C can help improve the inference on $\theta_{\neg C}$.

`Laplacian`, which uses a Laplacian approximation to approximate the posterior $p(\theta, \eta \mid X)$ with a multivariate normal distribution (Liu et al., 2015), under which the objective (1) reduces to the matrix form in (5). This algorithm is the same as our Algorithm 1, except that the H in Line 4 is instead estimated by $H = H(\theta^*, \eta^*)$, where $[\theta^*, \eta^*]$ is the mode of the posterior distribution $p(\theta, \eta \mid X)$. Obviously, `Laplacian` would perform similarly to `BayesianCRB(Gibbs)` when the posterior $p(\theta, \eta|X)$ is close to normal, but would otherwise perform poorly, especially when $p(\theta, \eta \mid X)$ is multimodal.

6.1.1 Gaussian Mixture Model

We start with the following toy example of Gaussian mixture model,

$$p(\theta) = \sum_{\kappa=1}^{2} \omega_\kappa \mathcal{N}(\theta \mid \mu_\kappa, \Sigma_\kappa),$$

where we ignore the dependence on observed data X. We draw μ_κ randomly from a zero-mean normal distribution with variance 0.1, and set $\Sigma_\kappa = 0.1(\alpha D_\kappa - W_\kappa)^{-1}$, where W_κ corresponds to an adjacency matrix of an undirected graph and D_κ is a diagonal matrix where $D_{\kappa,ii} = \sum_j W_{ij}$ and α is a constant larger than one to enforce L to be positive definite (we set $\alpha = 1.1$). We consider two different graph structures: (1) both W_1 and W_2 are the 30 by 30 2D grid graph, in which case we set $\omega = [1, 1]/2$; (2) W_1 and W_2 are scale-free networks of size 30 generated using the Barabási-Albert (BA) model (Barabási & Albert, 1999), with average degrees of 1 and 4, respectively, in which case we set $\omega = [0.9, 0.1]$. We simulate the ground truth of θ by drawing samples from $p(\theta \mid X)$, and plot the relative MSE of different algorithms compared to the random selection baseline in Figure 1(a)-(b); the results are averaged over 50 random trials.

As shown in Figure 1 (a)-(b), `BayesianOpt(Gibbs)` achieves the best performance, since it minimizes the conditional variance objective, which is the Bayesian optimal MSE. `Laplacian` performs the worst because $p(\theta)$ has multiple modes and the Laplacian approximation can only capture one of the mode. On the other hand, our `BayesianCRB(Gibbs)`, which takes the advantage of minimizing Bayesian CR bound, and is closer to `BayesianOpt(Gibbs)` than all the other methods.

It's also worth studying the tightness of the Bayesian CR bound. This is shown in Figure 1(c) where we plot the ratio

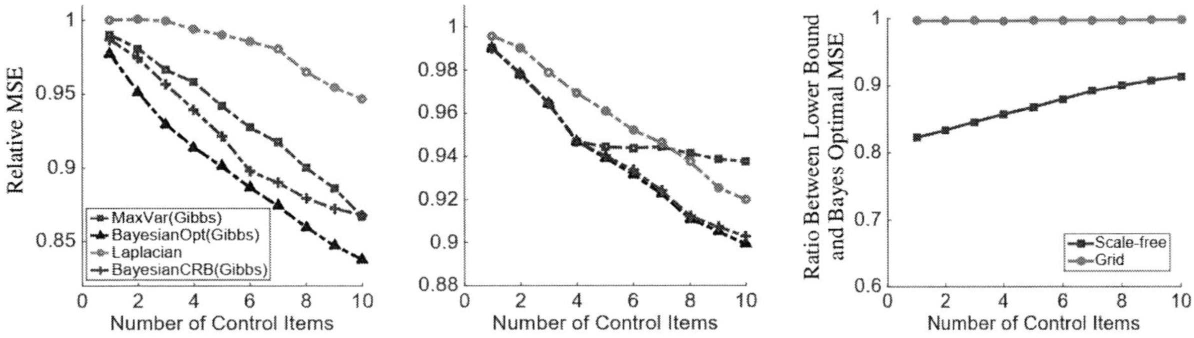

(a) *Relative MSE on scale-free graph* (b) *Relative MSE on grid graph* (c) *Tightness of the lower bounds*

Figure 1: (a-b) Results on the toy Gaussian mixture model; the y-axis are the MSE of different algorithms divided by the MSE of the random selection algorithm. (c) The ratio between the Bayesian CR lower bound and Bayesian optimal MSE (the trace of the conditional variance) on both the scale-free and grid graphs.

between the Bayesian optimal MSE (the trace of the conditional variance) and the Bayesian CR lower bound for both the scale-free and grid graphs; here the bounds are evaluated using the subsets C with different size k, selected by our `BayesianCRB(Gibbs)` method. We can see that the ratios are very close to one (≥ 0.8), suggesting that the bayesian CR bounds are very tight in these cases. In particular, we note that the bound is very tight for the grid graph example (ratio ≈ 1), explaining the good performances of `BayesianCRB(Gibbs)` in figure 1(b).

6.1.2 Application to Crowdsourcing

We further apply our method to the problem of selecting the optimal control questions in crowdsourcing as described in Section 5. We evaluate our selection algorithms on both simulated datasets and real-world datasets.

Toy dataset: We first generate a simulated dataset according to the Gaussian model described in (7), where θ_i and b_j are $i.i.d$ drawn from normal distribution with standard deviation of 4, and the labelers' variances v_j are generated from an inverse Gamma distribution Inv-Gamma$(1, 1)$. The dataset contains 30 questions and 30 labelers, and we assume the i-th question is answered only by the first i labelers; in this way, the first question is answered only by the first labeler and hence has the most *uncertain* result, and the last question is answered by all the 30 workers, and hence is the most *influential*, in that knowing its true value can help evaluate the bias and variance of all the 30 workers and hence improve the prediction on all the other items.

Figure 2(a) shows the average MSE given by the different methods. In this case, we can see that `BayesianOpt(Gibbs)`, `BayesianCRB(Gibbs)` and `Laplacian` tend to perform similarly, all of which significantly outperform `Random` and `MaxVar(Gibbs)`. Note that `MaxVar(Gibbs)` is even worse than `Random` at the beginning, since it myopically selects the most uncertain questions (the first few questions labeled by a small number of workers in this case), while much more significant improvements could be obtained by selecting the more influential items (these labeled by more workers). We find that `Laplacian` performs as well as `BayesianCRB(Gibbs)`, probably because the posterior distribution tends to be unimodal in this case. Figure 2 (b) shows the tightness of our lower bound as the size k of subset C increases, evaluated on the C given by `BayesianCRB(Gibbs)`, and we can see that the lower bound is again very tight in this case (ratio ≥ 0.93).

Real-world datasets: We also evaluate our approach on three real-world datasets:

The *PriceUCI* dataset (Liu et al., 2013). It consists of 80 household items collected from Internet, and whose prices are estimated by 155 UCI undergraduate students. As suggested in Liu et al. (2013), a log transform is performed on the prices before using the Gaussian models.

The national football league (*NFL*) forecasting dataset used in Massey et al. (2011). It consists predictions of point differences of 245 NFL games given by 386 participants; the point spreads determined by additional professional bookmakers are used as the ground truth.

The *GDP Growth* dataset used in Budescu & Chen (2014). It contains the forecasts of GDP growth nine months ahead by professional forecasters surveyed by European Central Bank (ECB). A total of 98 forecasters made forecasts for 50 quarters of GDP growth.

The results on these three real-world datasets are shown in figure 3(a)-(c). `BayesianOpt(Gibbs)` is not evaluated because it is too slow on these real world datasets. We can see that both `BayesianCRB(Gibbs)` and `Laplacian` tend to outperform the other methods significantly. Again, `Laplacian` tends to perform as well as `BayesianCRB(Gibbs)` because the posteriors are very close to Gaussian distribution in these cases.

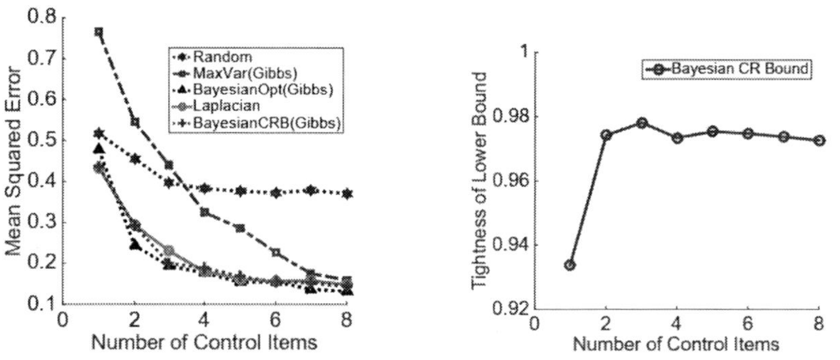

(a) *Average MSE on simulated dataset* (b) *Ratio between bounds and the Bayes optimal MSE*

Figure 2: Results on crowdsourcing with simulated data. (a) The MSE given by different selection algorithms as the budget k increases. (b) The ratio between the Bayesian lower bound and Bayesian optimal MSE. We can see that the lower bound is very close to the Bayesian optimal MSE (ratio ≥ 0.93), and the tightness tends to increase as the size k of C increases.

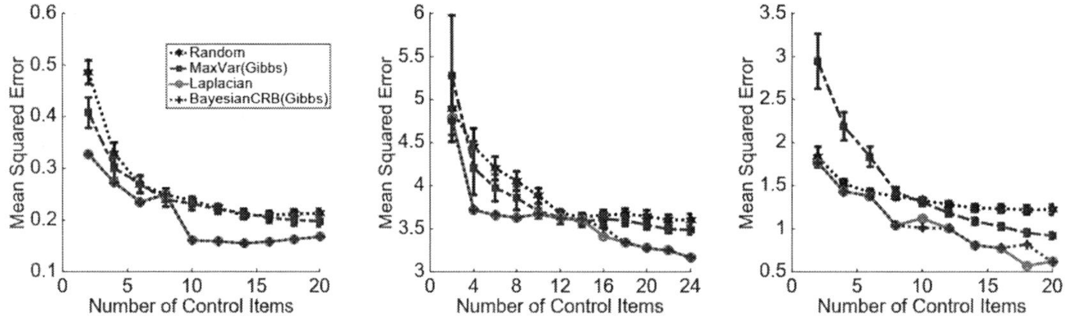

(a) *PriceUCI* (b) *NFL* (c) *GDP Growth*

Figure 3: (a)-(c) Results on three real datasets, *PriceUCI*, *NFL* and *GDP Growth*, respectively. The y-axes are the average MSE on the remaining items as the size of the subset C increases. The error bars show the standard deviation over the random trials.

6.2 DISCRETE VARIABLES

In this section, we use our algorithm to select optimal subsets on binary Ising graphical models defined in (8) with $\theta \in \{-1, +1\}$. We use `DiscreteLB(Gibbs)` to denote the greedy optimization algorithm on our discrete Bayesian lower bound (it is the same as Algorithm 1, except with Q defined in Proposition 3). We again compare our algorithm with several baselines, including:

`CondEnt(LBP)`, which greedily selects a subset C to minimum the conditional entropy $H(\theta_{\neg C} \mid \theta_C, X)$; it is equivalent to maximizing the marginal entropy $H(\theta_C \mid X)$. The entropy is approximated using loopy belief propagation (LBP). This algorithm is similar to `MaxVar (Gibbs)` for continuous variables, in that both myopically find the subset with the largest uncertainty, ignoring the propagation effect that the added true labels can help predict the remaining unlabeled items (Krause et al., 2008).

`MutualInfo(LBP)`, which maximizes the mutual information $I(\theta_C; \theta_{\neg C} \mid X)$; this was proposed by Krause et al. (2008) to avoid the myopic property of the entropy objective. The mutual information is again approximated using loopy belief propagation (LBP).

`MinCondVar(Gaussian)`, which minimizes $\mathrm{tr}(L_{\neg C}^{-1})$ where $L = \Lambda - J$, where Λ is a diagonal matrix chosen to make L positive definite. This method is equivalent to treating θ as a continuous variable, and hence (8) a multivariate Gaussian distribution.

Comparisons are made on both simulated and real-world datasets:

Simulated data: We set $p(\theta \mid X)$ to be the binary graphical model in (8) (there is no actual observed data X in this case), with both J and h in (8) drawn from Gaussian distributions: we draw each element of h from $\mathcal{N}(0, 0.2)$, and set $J = 0.1W$, where W is an adjacency matrix of an undirected graph with values drawn from standard normal distribution. The graph structure is defined to be either a 30×30 2D grid, or a scale free network of size 30 generated using the Barabási-Albert (BA) model (Barabási & Albert, 1999) with the preferential attachment mechanism.

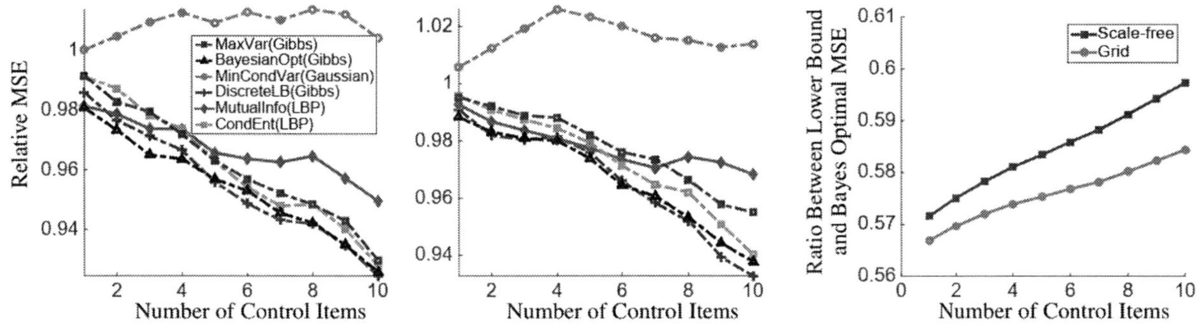

(a) *Relative error rate on scale-free graph* (b) *Relative error rate on grid graph* (c) *Tightness of the lower bounds*

Figure 4: Results on binary Ising models with simulated data. (a)-(b) The Relative MSE of different algorithms on the synthetic datasets simulated from the scale-free and the grid graph, respectively. (c) The ratio between our discrete Bayesian lower bound and the Bayesian optimal MSE on the simulated dataset; the bounds are evaluated on the subsets C selected by our `DiscreteLB(Gibbs)` method.

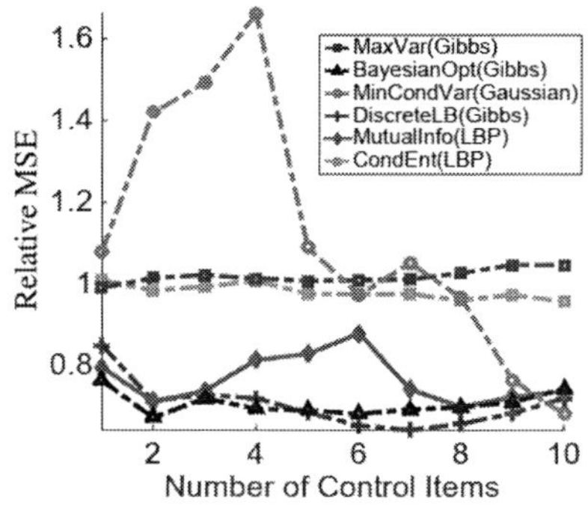

Figure 5: Comparison of the relative MSE of different methods on the PubMed Diabetes dataset. Our algorithm `DiscreteLB(Gibbs)` achieves similar results as `BayesianOpt(Gibbs)`, but with much lower computational cost.

We show the results of different algorithms in Figure 4, where we find that our `DiscreteLB(Gibbs)` is comparable with `BayesianOpt(Gibbs)` which minimizes the Bayesian optimal error rate, and outperforms all the other baselines. Both `MaxVar(Gibbs)` and `CondEnt(LBP)` tend to myopically select the most uncertain items first and hence have similar performance. Figure 4(c) shows the tightness of our Bayesian lower bound compared to the Bayesian optimal error; we can see that it is less tight (ratio ≥ 0.56) compared with the Bayesian CR bound for continuous variables, but the good performance of `DiscreteLB(Gibbs)` seems to suggest that the lower bound still represents a good surrogate for the Bayesian optimal error.

PubMed Diabetes:[1] This is a citation graph of scientific papers from the PubMed database (Sen et al., 2008), in which each paper is classified into one of three classes: "Diabetes Mellitus, Experimental", "Diabetes Mellitus Type 1", "Diabetes Mellitus Type 2". For our experiment, we select the top 100 nodes with the highest degrees from class Diabetes Mellitus Type 1 and Type 2, and then took the largest connected component, with 93 nodes in total and 376 edges; this gives 43 nodes from class Type 1 and 50 nodes from class Type 2, and a graph with an average degree of 4. In this case, since we don't have any prior knowledge, we set h to be a vector of small random numbers, and let $J = 0.05W$, where W denotes the adjacency matrix. The results is shown in Figure 5, in which we observe a similar trend as that in the simulated data.

[1] http://linqs.umiacs.umd.edu/projects//projects/lbc/

7 CONCLUSION

The Bayesian optimal risk is the ideal objective function for optimal subset selection, which, however, is extremely difficult to calculate and optimize in practice. In this paper, we proposed to use Bayesian lower bounds as surrogate criteria, and derived a class of computationally more efficient algorithms for observation selection. We discussed both continuous and discrete scenarios: for continuous models, we based our bound on the classical Bayesian Cramér Rao bound; for discrete models, we derived a new form based on an novel extension of van Trees inequality. We presented a number of experiments for both continuous and discrete models in various practical settings, and showed that the selection algorithms based on the Bayesian lower bounds tend to outperform most baseline algorithms, and are comparable with the selection based on the Bayesian optimal risk.

Acknowledgement This work is supported in part by NSF CRII 1565796, and VITALITE, which receives support from Army Research Office (ARO) Multidisciplinary Research Initiative (MURI) program (Award number W911NF-11-1-0391).

References

Barabási, A.-L. and Albert, R. Emergence of scaling in random networks. *science*, 286(5439):509–512, 1999.

Bilgic, M., Mihalkova, L., and Getoor, L. Active learning for networked data. In *Proceedings of the 27th international conference on machine learning (ICML-10)*, pp. 79–86, 2010.

Bobrovsky, B. Z. and Zakai, M. A lower bound on the estimation error for markov processes. *Automatic Control, IEEE Transactions on*, 20(6):785–788, 1975.

Budescu, D. V. and Chen, E. Identifying expertise to extract the wisdom of crowds. *Management Science*, 61(2):267–280, 2014.

Chaloner, K. and Verdinelli, I. Bayesian experimental design: A review. *Statistical Science*, pp. 273–304, 1995.

Chen, M.-H., Shao, Q.-M., and Ibrahim, J. G. *Monte Carlo methods in Bayesian computation*. Springer Science & Business Media, 2012.

Das, A. and Kempe, D. Algorithms for subset selection in linear regression. In *Proceedings of the fortieth annual ACM symposium on Theory of computing*, pp. 45–54. ACM, 2008.

Friedland, S. and Gaubert, S. Submodular spectral functions of principal submatrices of a hermitian matrix, extensions and applications. *Linear Algebra and its Applications*, 438(10):3872–3884, 2013.

Horn, R. A. and Johnson, C. R. *Matrix analysis*. Cambridge university press, 2012.

Howe, J. The rise of crowdsourcing. *Wired magazine*, 14 (6):1–4, 2006.

Karger, D. R., Oh, S., and Shah, D. Iterative learning for reliable crowdsourcing systems. In *Advances in neural information processing systems*, pp. 1953–1961, 2011.

Krause, A. and Guestrin, C. Optimal value of information in graphical models. *Journal of Artificial Intelligence Research*, pp. 557–591, 2009.

Krause, A., Singh, A., and Guestrin, C. Near-optimal sensor placements in gaussian processes: Theory, efficient algorithms and empirical studies. *The Journal of Machine Learning Research*, 9:235–284, 2008.

Liu, Q., Peng, J., and Ihler, A. Variational inference for crowdsourcing. In *Advances in Neural Information Processing Systems (NIPS)*, pp. 701–709, 2012.

Liu, Q., Ihler, A. T., and Steyvers, M. Scoring workers in crowdsourcing: How many control questions are enough? In *Advances in Neural Information Processing Systems*, pp. 1914–1922, 2013.

Liu, Q., Ihler, A., and Fisher, J. Boosting crowdsourcing with expert labels: Local vs. global effects. In *Information Fusion (Fusion), 2015 18th International Conference on*, pp. 9–14. IEEE, 2015.

Lu, Q. and Getoor, L. Link-based classification. In *ICML*, volume 3, pp. 496–503, 2003.

Ma, Y., Garnett, R., and Schneider, J. σ-optimality for active learning on gaussian random fields. In *Advances in Neural Information Processing Systems*, pp. 2751–2759, 2013.

Massey, C., Simmons, J. P., and Armor, D. A. Hope over experience desirability and the persistence of optimism. *Psychological Science*, 22(2):274–281, 2011.

Nemhauser, G. L., Wolsey, L. A., and Fisher, M. L. An analysis of approximations for maximizing submodular set functions. *Mathematical Programming*, 14(1):265–294, 1978.

Raykar, V., Yu, S., Zhao, L., Valadez, G., Florin, C., Bogoni, L., and Moy, L. Learning from crowds. *The Journal of Machine Learning Research*, 11:1297–1322, 2010.

Sen, P., Namata, G. M., Bilgic, M., Getoor, L., Gallagher, B., and Eliassi-Rad, T. Collective classification in network data. *AI Magazine*, 29(3):93–106, 2008.

Settles, B. Active learning literature survey. *University of Wisconsin, Madison*, 52(55-66):11, 2010.

Van Trees, H. L. *Detection, estimation, and modulation theory*. John Wiley & Sons, 2004.

Van Trees, H. L. and Bell, K. L. Bayesian bounds for parameter estimation and nonlinear filtering/tracking. *AMC*, 10:12, 2007.

Weiss, A. J. and Weinstein, E. A lower bound on the mean-square error in random parameter estimation (corresp.). *Information Theory, IEEE Transactions on*, 31(5):680–682, 1985.

Williams, J. L. *Information theoretic sensor management*. PhD thesis, Massachusetts Institute of Technology, 2007.

Zhou, D., Bousquet, O., Lal, T. N., Weston, J., and Schölkopf, B. Learning with local and global consistency. *Advances in neural information processing systems*, 16(16):321–328, 2004.

Zhou, D., Platt, J., Basu, S., and Mao, Y. Learning from the wisdom of crowds by minimax entropy. In *Advances in Neural Information Processing Systems (NIPS)*, pp. 2204–2212, 2012.

Zhu, X., Ghahramani, Z., Lafferty, J., et al. Semi-supervised learning using gaussian fields and harmonic functions. In *ICML*, volume 3, pp. 912–919, 2003.

Characterizing Tightness of LP Relaxations by Forbidding Signed Minors

Adrian Weller
University of Cambridge
aw665@cam.ac.uk

Abstract

We consider binary pairwise graphical models and provide an exact characterization (necessary and sufficient conditions observing signs of potentials) of tightness for the LP relaxation on the triplet-consistent polytope of the MAP inference problem, by forbidding an odd-K_5 (complete graph on 5 variables with all edges repulsive) as a signed minor in the signed suspension graph. This captures signs of both singleton and edge potentials in a compact and efficiently testable condition, and improves significantly on earlier results. We provide other results on tightness of LP relaxations by forbidding minors, draw connections and suggest paths for future research.

1 INTRODUCTION

Discrete undirected graphical models play a central role in machine learning, providing a powerful and compact way to model relationships between variables. A key challenge is the combinatorial search problem to identify a most likely configuration of variables, termed *maximum a posteriori* (MAP) or *most probable explanation* (MPE) inference. This has received a great deal of attention from various communities, where it is sometimes framed as energy minimization (Kappes et al., 2013) or as solving a valued constraint satisfaction problem (VCSP, Schiex et al., 1995).

Since the problem is NP-hard, much work has attempted to identify restricted settings where polynomial-time methods are feasible. Where possible, we call such settings *tractable* and the methods *efficient*. Two types of restriction have been considered separately, either: (i) structural constraints on the topology of connections between variables; or (ii) families of potential functions.

Exploring the first theme, Chandrasekaran et al. (2008) showed that, if no restriction is placed on types of potentials, then the structural constraint of *bounded treewidth* is needed for tractable inference.[1] See §2-4 for all definitions.

Recent work (Kolmogorov et al., 2015; Thapper and Živný, 2015) has examined the power of using a linear programming (LP) relaxation of the discrete optimization problem. An LP attains an optimum at a vertex of the feasible region; if this vertex is integral, then it provides an exact solution to the original problem and we say that the LP is *tight*. If the LP is performed over the *marginal polytope*, which enforces global consistency (Wainwright and Jordan, 2008), then this LP is always tight, but exponentially many constraints are required, hence the method is not efficient. The marginal polytope is typically relaxed to the *local polytope* LOC, which enforces only pairwise consistency, requiring a number of constraints linear in the number of edges. Thapper and Živný (2015) showed that, if no restriction is placed on topology, then for a given family of potentials, either LP+LOC is tight, and hence solves all such problems efficiently, or the problem set is NP-hard.

Here we consider *hybrid* conditions (Cooper and Živný, 2011), which combine constraints on both structure and potentials, an exciting field with little prior work. Focusing on the important class of binary pairwise models,[2] and considering each edge to be *signed* as either *attractive* or *repulsive*, we establish precise hybrid characterizations for when certain LP relaxations will be tight for all valid potentials. By valid, we mean potentials that observe the signs (attractive or repulsive) of the edges. We show that these characterizations may be achieved by forbidding particular signed *minors* of the signed graph topology, yielding compact and efficiently testable conditions.

In applications, LP relaxations are widely used for structured prediction but the most common form, LP+LOC, often yields a fractional solution, motivating constraints for

[1] This result makes mild assumptions, specifically the grid-minor hypothesis (Robertson et al., 1994), and that NP $\not\subseteq$P/poly. See also (Kwisthout et al., 2010).

[2] Eaton and Ghahramani (2013) showed that any discrete graphical model may be either exactly represented, or arbitrarily well approximated, by a binary pairwise model, though the number of variables may increase substantially.

higher order cluster consistency (Batra et al., 2011). Weller et al. (2016) considered the LP relaxation over the *triplet-consistent* polytope TRI, which is the next level up from LOC in the hierarchy given by Sherali and Adams (1990) and is still efficient. Whereas it is known that LP+LOC is tight for any model which is *balanced*, Weller et al. (2016) showed that LP+TRI is tight for any model which is *almost balanced*. Further they demonstrated that almost balanced models may be 'pasted' together in certain configurations, while still guaranteeing tightness of LP+TRI.

The results of Weller et al. (2016) and our stronger characterizations here are very relevant to many problems in computer vision, such as foreground-background image segmentation, where due to contiguity of real objects, learned edges are mostly attractive, leading to a model which is 'close to balanced'. For example, on the horses dataset considered by Domke (2013), LP+LOC is loose but LP+TRI is often tight. Our work helps to explain this phenomenon.

We consider a refinement by examining the signs not only of edge potentials, but also of singleton potentials. These can be neatly incorporated by considering the signed *suspension graph* of a model, which adds one extra node with edges to the other variable nodes, each new edge corresponding to a singleton of the original model; see §4.

1.1 MAIN RESULTS

Our strongest result is Theorem 14, which shows that LP+TRI is tight for all valid potentials, observing signs of both edge and singleton potentials, iff the signed suspension graph does not contain an *odd*-K_5 (the complete graph on 5 nodes with all edges odd/repulsive, see §3) as a signed minor. This is a more powerful, signed version of an unsigned result, Theorem 13, that follows from the work of Barahona and Mahjoub (1986), showing that LP+TRI is tight for all valid unsigned potentials iff the unsigned suspension graph does not contain K_5 as an unsigned minor; see §5. For a sense of the additional power of the signed version, Theorem 14 allows models with arbitrarily high treewidth, provided only that there is no odd-K_5 minor (*one particular* signing of a K_5 structure), whereas Theorem 12 prohibits a K_5 minor of *any* type; see Table 2.

A weaker corollary of Theorem 14, our Theorem 10 shows that if we are less observant and do not examine singleton potentials, then LP+TRI is tight for all valid potentials (respecting signs of edges only) iff the signed graph topology does not contain an *odd*-K_4 as a signed minor.[3] This may be directly compared to the sufficient conditions of Weller et al. (2016), which similarly do not examine singleton potentials. We show that Theorem 10 is a significant improvement: it covers a substantially larger set of models, provides a compact condition that is both necessary and sufficient, and is efficiently testable; see §4.3.

As another consequence of Theorem 14, we obtain a result that may be of significant practical interest. Theorem 16 shows that in some cases, the number of cycle constraints needed to enforce integrality for LP+TRI may be dramatically reduced to just the *signed cycle constraints*; see §5.

We also reframe earlier results on tightness of LP relaxations in terms of forbidden minors. This perspective elegantly captures conditions on both structure and potentials, and reveals fascinating connections which prompt natural directions to explore in future work. See Table 2 for a summary and §6 for discussion.

1.2 APPROACH AND RELATED WORK

Characterizing properties by forbidden minors has been a fruitful theme in graph theory since the fundamental work of Robertson and Seymour, which builds over more than 20 papers to the *graph minor theorem*, described by Diestel (2010) as "among the deepest theorems that mathematics has to offer." We describe elements of the approach in §2, its extension to signed graphs, signed minors and *odd* minors in §3, and its relevance to LP relaxations in §4.

Odd-minor-free graphs have received attention in theoretical computer science, for example (Demaine et al., 2010). However, aside from the characterization by Watanabe (2011) of when belief propagation has a unique fixed point in terms of signed minors, to our knowledge there has been little direct use of this perspective in machine learning.[4]

To show our results, we connect several earlier themes, for which we provide relevant background. A key result by Guenin (2001) showed that a signed graph is *weakly bipartite*, which characterizes integrality of the vertices of a particular polyhedron, iff it does not contain an odd-K_5 minor; see §3. We draw on connections between: the marginal polytope of a model, with its LOC and TRI relaxations; and the corresponding *cut polytope* of its suspension graph, with its *rooted semimetric* RMET and *semimetric* MET relaxations (De Simone, 1990; Deza and Laurent, 1997); see §5.1. We use a link between MET and the *cycle inequalities* (Barahona, 1993); see §5.2. We extend these ideas to signed graph topologies in §5.3. Some of these connections for the unsigned case were considered by Sontag (2010).

2 GRAPHS AND MINORS

We follow standard definitions and omit some familiar terms. For more background, see (Diestel, 2010), particularly §12 for a survey of treewidth and forbidden minors.

[3] Theorem 14 allows any odd-K_4 minor in G provided it is not part of an odd-K_5 in ∇G, a much stronger result; see Table 2.

[4] Junction trees (Cowell et al., 1999), treewidth and unsigned graph minors are closely related. Treewidth was discussed by Halin but gained popularity through use by Robertson and Seymour (see historical note by Seymour, 2014).

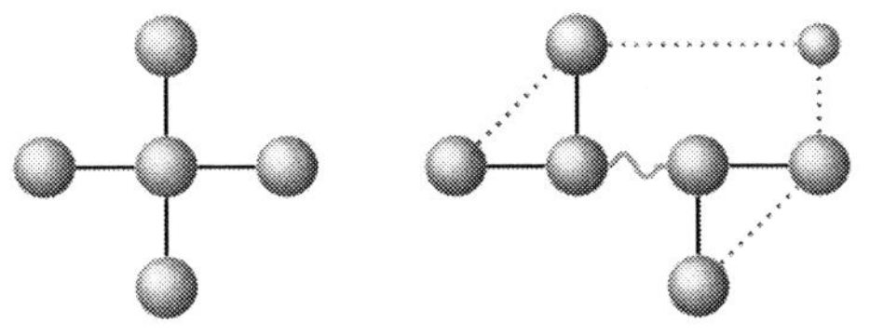

Figure 1: The left graph is a *minor* (unsigned) of the right graph, obtained by deleting the grey dotted edges and resulting isolated small grey vertex, and contracting the purple wavy edge. See §2.

t	Forbidden minors for a graph to have treewidth $\leq t$
1	K_3
2	K_4
3	K_5 and 3 others
4	K_6 and more than 70 others

Table 1: Characterization of low values of bounded treewidth by forbidding minors.

A *graph* $G(V, E)$ is a set of vertices V, and undirected edges E, where each edge $(i, j) \in E$ connects i and $j \in V$. The *complete* graph on n vertices, written K_n, has all $\binom{n}{2}$ edges. A pairwise graphical model topology is always assumed to be a *simple* graph, that is a vertex may not be adjacent to itself (no loops) and each pair of vertices may have at most one edge (no multiple edges). However, when we consider *minors*, we allow loops and multiple edges.

A *minor* of a graph G is obtained from G by deleting edges or isolated vertices (as may be done to form a subgraph), or also by *contracting* edges. To contract edge (i, j) means to remove the vertices i and j, and replace them by a new vertex with edges to all remaining vertices that were previously adjacent to i or j. See Figure 1 for an example.
For any property $\mathcal{P}$ of a graph, we say that $\mathcal{P}$ is *closed under taking minors* (or *minor-closed*) if whenever G has property $\mathcal{P}$ and H is a minor of G, then H has $\mathcal{P}$.

A consequence of the *graph minor theorem* of Robertson and Seymour is the following deep result.

Theorem 1 (Robertson and Seymour, 2004). *If a graph property $\mathcal{P}$ is closed under taking minors then it can be characterized by a finite set of forbidden minors, i.e. G has $\mathcal{P}$ iff G has none of the finite forbidden set as a minor.*

There are important examples of graph properties closed under taking minors where this finite set has just a few members. Perhaps the best known is the early result of Wagner (1937) that a graph G is planar iff G does not contain K_5 or $K_{3,3}$ as a minor ($K_{3,3}$ is the complete bipartite graph where each partition has 3 vertices).

Another property closed under taking minors is bounded *treewidth*. A definition of treewidth of a graph G that may be familiar from the junction tree construction is that it is one less than the minimum possible size of a largest clique in a triangulation of G (Wainwright and Jordan, 2008). The forbidden minors are known for low values of bounded treewidth, see Table 1. For example, a tree has treewidth 1 and cannot contain a K_3 minor.

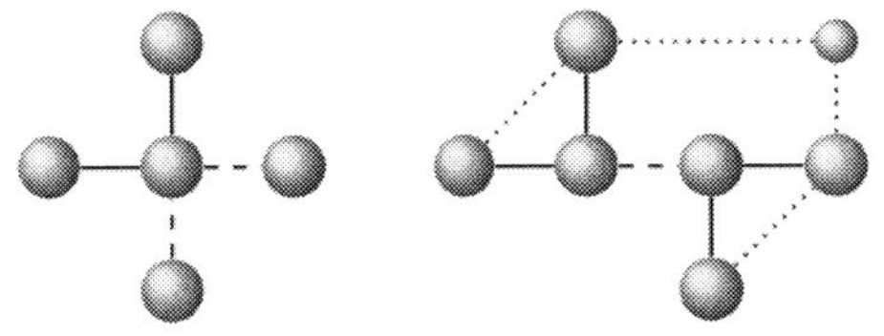

Figure 2: The left graph is a *signed minor* of the right signed graph, obtained similarly to Figure 1 except that before contracting the repulsive edge, first flip the vertex at its right end. Solid blue (dashed red) edges are attractive (repulsive). Grey dotted edges on the right are deleted and may be of any sign. See §3.2.

Robertson and Seymour also showed that checking for any fixed minor may be performed efficiently.

Theorem 2 (Robertson and Seymour, 1995). *For any fixed graph H and a given graph G with n vertices, there is an $O(n^3)$-time algorithm to determine if H is a minor of G.*[5]

Together, Theorems 1 and 2 show that any minor-closed graph property may be decided in polynomial-time.

3 SIGNED GRAPHS & SIGNED MINORS

A *signed graph* (Harary, 1953) is a graph (V, E) together with one of two possible signs for each edge. This is a natural structure when considering binary pairwise models, where we characterize edges as either *attractive* (or *even*) or *repulsive* (or *odd*), see §4. Where helpful for clarity, we refer to the standard graphs of §2 as *unsigned* graphs. We shall see that important concepts and results for minors of unsigned graphs have corresponding results for signed minors of signed graphs.

In a signed graph, a fundamental property of any cycle is whether or not it is a *frustrated cycle* (or *odd cycle*), i.e. if it is a cycle with an odd number of repulsive (or odd) edges. A signed graph is *balanced* if it contains no frustrated cycles. Following Weller (2015), a signed graph is *almost balanced* if it contains a vertex such that deleting it renders the remaining graph balanced.

3.1 FLIPPING/RESIGNING AND ODD GRAPHS

Given a signed graph, a subset of variables $S \subseteq V$ may be *flipped* (or *switched*). This flips the sign of any edge with exactly one end in S (i.e. flips the edge between attractive/even and repulsive/odd), and is called a *resigning*. It is easily seen that this operation does not change the nature (frustrated or not) of any cycle. For binary graphical models, this has a natural interpretation: if the original model has variables $\{X_i \in \{0, 1\} : i \in V\}$ then consider an

[5] Kawarabayashi et al. (2012) improved this to $O(n^2)$-time.

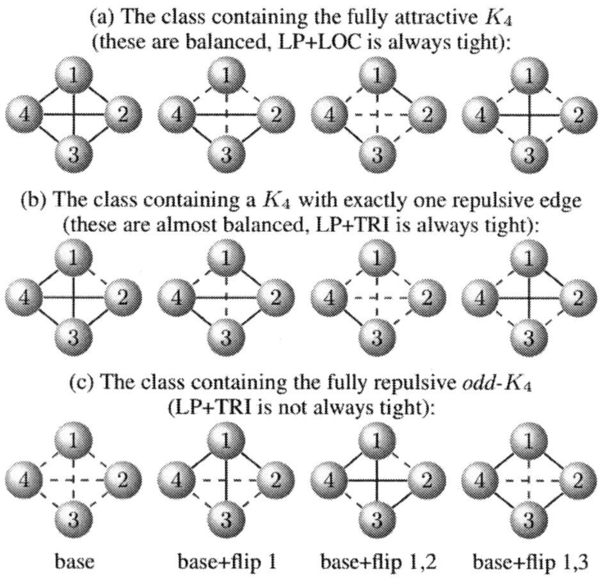

Figure 3: Examples of signed K_4 graphs. These are complete graphs on 4 vertices where each edge is either attractive/even (solid blue) or repulsive/odd (dashed red). Each row illustrates examples from one of the three signing equivalence classes. At bottom left is an *odd-*K_4. See §3.

equivalent model with variables $\{Y_i : i \in V\}$ given by $Y_i = 1 - X_i$ for $i \in S$, $Y_i = X_i$ for $i \in V \setminus S$, with new potentials set to match properties of the original model.[6]

Two signed graphs are *signing equivalent* (sometimes called *gauge equivalent*) if they are isomorphic up to a resigning (an equivalence relation). We are interested in signed graphs only up to signing equivalence; see §3.2.

For any unsigned graph G, the signed graph *odd-*G is the signed version of G where every edge is odd (or repulsive). Figure 3 shows examples of signed K_4 graphs, in their signing equivalence classes. The bottom row shows an *odd-*K_4 at the left, together with possible resignings.

3.2 SIGNED MINORS

A *signed minor* of a signed graph is obtained just as for an unsigned minor of an unsigned graph with the following modifications: any resigning operations are permitted (see §3.1); and contractions are allowed only for attractive/even edges. Note that a repulsive/odd edge may first be resigned to an attractive/even edge by flipping either end vertex (which will also affect its other incident edges) and then contracted. See Figure 2 for an example, which may be compared to the unsigned minor example of Figure 1.

A significant project is in progress to try to generalize all of Robertson and Seymour's graph minor theory to the much broader class of Γ-labeled graphs for any finite abelian group Γ (Geelen et al., 2014), which includes signed graphs by considering $\Gamma = \mathbb{Z}/2\mathbb{Z}$. An equivalent result to Theorem 1 is claimed, though the formal write-up is still to come. An equivalent result to Theorem 2 has been shown.

Theorem 3 (A special case of Theorem 1.1.10 of Huynh, 2009)**.** *For any fixed signed graph H, there is a polynomial-time algorithm which determines if an input signed graph G contains H as a signed minor.*

3.3 WEAKLY BIPARTITE SIGNED GRAPHS

If a signed graph is balanced, its vertices may be partitioned into two exhaustive groups s.t. all inter-group edges are odd and all intra-group edges are even (Harary, 1953); the resigning obtained by flipping either group renders all edges even. With this observation, a signed graph which is balanced is sometimes called *bipartite* (related, but different, to the standard meaning of bipartite for unsigned graphs).

Generalizing bipartite signed graphs, a signed graph $G(V, E)$ with edge signs is *weakly bipartite* if the following polyhedron Q has only integral vertices:

$$Q = \left\{ y \in \mathbb{R}_+^{|E|} : \sum_{e \in D} y_e \geq 1, \forall \text{ odd cycles } D \text{ of signed } G \right\} \tag{1}$$

Here, odd cycles D are in the signed sense, i.e. have an odd number of odd edges. We shall see in §5.3 that Q relates closely to the triplet-consistent polytope TRI of a graphical model, if we consider signs of all potentials. We make use of the following result, which proved a conjecture of Seymour (1977), earning Guenin a Fulkerson prize in 2003.

Theorem 4 (Guenin, 2001)**.** *A signed graph is weakly bipartite iff it does not contain an odd-K_5 as a signed minor.*[7]

4 GRAPHICAL MODELS AND LP RELAXATIONS

We consider a binary pairwise undirected model with n variables $X_1, \ldots, X_n \in \{0, 1\}$. Let $x = (x_1, \ldots, x_n) \in \{0, 1\}^n$ be one complete configuration. The probability distribution is specified by $p(x) \propto \exp[\text{score}(x)]$, where we choose a symmetric minimal reparameterization (Wainwright and Jordan, 2008) such that

$$\text{score}(x) = -\sum_{i \in V} \theta_i x_i - \sum_{(i,j) \in E} W_{ij} \mathbb{1}[x_i \neq x_j], \tag{2}$$

where $\mathbb{1}[\cdot]$ is the indicator function. The model's unsigned topology is the graph $G(V, E)$, with n variables $V = \{1, \ldots, n\}$ and $m = |E| \leq \binom{n}{2}$ edge relationships between the variables. The n singleton parameters $\{\theta_i : i \in V\}$ and m edge weights $\{W_{ij} : (i, j) \in E\}$

[6]Given the form of potentials (2) we choose in §4, this flips the signs of $\{\theta_i : i \in S\}$ and $\{W_{ij} :$ exactly one of i or $j \in S\}$.

[7]The original proof is long. A shorter proof was provided by Schrijver (2002). Both proofs rely on a result of Lehman (1990).

define the potentials, which we allow to take any rational value (to enable polynomial-time algorithms).

In addition to the unsigned graph G, we shall be interested in two more informative ways of considering a model's topology. The *signed graph* G assigns edge signs according to the signs of edge potentials. If $W_{ij} > 0$, the edge (i, j) tends to pull X_i and X_j toward the same value and is *attractive* (or *even*). If $W_{ij} < 0$, the edge is *repulsive* (or *odd*).

The *signed suspension graph* $\nabla G(V', E')$ of a model adds an extra node 0, that is $V' = V \cup \{0\}$. Edges to 0 encode singletons of the model, with $E' = E \cup \{(0, i) : \theta_i \neq 0\}$.

With ∇G in mind, we have chosen the form of (2) carefully, using negative signs so $W_{ij} > 0$ is attractive, and $\mathbb{1}[x_i \neq x_j]$ edge terms in order to facilitate later demonstration of the equivalence between the MAP problem and a max cut problem on the edge-weighted suspension graph; see §5.

In ∇G, it may be helpful to consider the added node 0 as being set to the value 0; then regarding (2), the singleton potential terms $\theta_i x_i$ may be viewed as $\theta_i \mathbb{1}[x_i \neq 0]$, and hence all singleton and edge potential terms follow the same sign convention. In particular, the sign of each new edge $(0, i)$ in ∇G matches that of θ_i: if $\theta_i > 0$ then the added edge is attractive, pulling X_i toward 0; if $\theta_i < 0$ then $(0, i)$ is repulsive (or odd).

4.1 LINEAR PROGRAMMING FOR MAP

The potential parameters may be concatenated to form a vector $w = (-\theta_1, \dots, -\theta_n, \dots, -W_{ij}, \dots) \in \mathbb{Q}^d$, where $d = n + m$. Let $y_{ij} = \mathbb{1}[x_i \neq x_j]$, and for any configuration x, similarly concatenate the n x_i and m $y_{ij}(x)$ terms into a vector $z = (x_1, \dots, x_n, \dots, y_{ij}, \dots) \in \{0, 1\}^d$. Now $\text{score}(x) = w \cdot z$, yielding the following integer linear programming formulation for MAP inference, to identify

$$z^* \in \underset{z:x \in \{0,1\}^n}{\arg\max}\; w \cdot z \qquad (3)$$

The convex hull of the 2^n possible integer solutions in $[0, 1]^d$ is the *marginal polytope* $\mathbb{M}$ for our choice of singleton and edge terms.[8] Regarding the convex coefficients as a probability distribution p over all possible states, $\mathbb{M}$ may be considered the space of all singleton and pairwise mean marginals that are consistent with some global distribution p over the 2^n states, that is

$$\mathbb{M} = \{\mu = (\mu_1, \dots, \mu_n, \dots, \mu_{ij}, \dots) \in [0, 1]^d \text{ s.t.} \qquad (4)$$
$$\exists p\colon \mu_i = \mathbb{E}_p(X_i)\; \forall i, \mu_{ij} = \mathbb{E}_p(\mathbb{1}[X_i \neq X_j])\; \forall (i, j) \in E\}$$

A standard approach is to relax (3) to a linear program (LP). Performing this over $\mathbb{M}$ remains intractable since the number of linear constraints required grows extremely rapidly with n (Deza and Laurent, 1997). Hence, a simpler, relaxed constraint set is typically employed, yielding an upper bound on the original optimum. This set is often chosen as the *local polytope* LOC, which enforces only pairwise consistency (Wainwright and Jordan, 2008). If an optimum vertex is achieved at an integer solution, then this must be an optimum of the original discrete problem (3), in which case we say that the relaxation LP+LOC is *tight*.

Sherali and Adams (1990) proposed a series of successively tighter relaxations by enforcing consistency over progressively larger clusters of variables. At order r, the $\mathcal{L}_r$ polytope enforces consistency over all clusters of variables of size $\leq r$. $\mathcal{L}_2$ is the local polytope LOC. Next, $\mathcal{L}_3$ is the triplet-consistent polytope TRI, and so on, with $\mathcal{L}_n = \mathbb{M} \subseteq \mathcal{L}_{n-1} \subseteq \cdots \subseteq \mathcal{L}_3 = \text{TRI} \subseteq \mathcal{L}_2 = \text{LOC}$. Clearly LP+$\mathcal{L}_n$ is always tight. The following result, derived using the junction tree theorem (Cowell et al., 1999), gives a sufficient condition for tightness at any order.

Theorem 5 (Wainwright and Jordan, 2004). *If the graph of a model has treewidth $\leq r - 1$ then LP+$\mathcal{L}_r$ is tight.*

4.2 RELATION TO MINORS, NEW RESULTS

Theorem 5 provides a sufficient condition that considers only the treewidth of the unsigned graph G, without any regard to the potentials. As remarked in §2, the graph property of bounded treewidth is minor-closed, hence can be characterized by excluding a finite set of forbidden minors, see Table 1 for examples.

We now make the following observation, where "valid potentials" for a graph means any potentials that respect the graph structure (signed or unsigned accordingly).

Theorem 6. *The property $\mathcal{P}$ of a graph G that "LP+$\mathcal{L}_r$ is tight for all valid potentials on G" is minor-closed, whether G is unsigned or signed (if signed then use signed minors).*

Proof. The property $\mathcal{P}$ is maintained under deletion, contraction and (for signed graphs) resigning. To see this for contraction: if an edge (i, j) of G is contracted to yield G', then for any valid model M' on G', consider the model M on G which has all the same potentials and in addition set the edge potential for (i, j) to be sufficiently high such that in M this forces X_i and X_j to take the same value. □

Hence, we should expect to be able to characterize LP tightness for all valid potentials, for both unsigned and signed topologies, by specifying a finite set of forbidden minors (signed minors in the signed case), see §2 and §3.

From Theorem 5 and Table 1: if we consider only the unsigned topology G, then LP+LOC (LP+TRI) is tight for all potentials if the graph G does not contain a K_3 (K_4, respectively) as a minor. To demonstrate the converse, and as a result of independent interest, we show the following.

[8] Our choice of edge term $\mathbb{1}[x_i \neq x_j]$ will facilitate later analysis of ∇G in §5. A common alternative choice for edges is to use $x_i x_j$, which leads to an equivalent polytope, sometimes called the *Boolean quadric polytope* QP^n (Padberg, 1989).

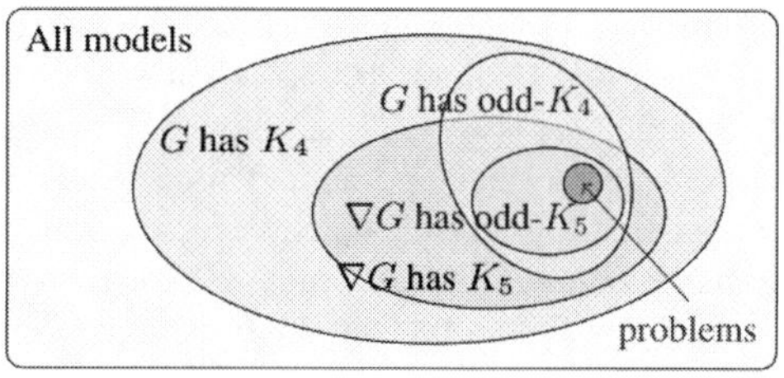

Sherali-Adams cluster size		Forbidden minors: Graph G Unsigned	Graph G Signed	Suspension graph ∇G Unsigned	Suspension graph ∇G Signed
LOC	$\mathcal{L}_2$	K_3	odd-K_3		
TRI	$\mathcal{L}_3$	K_4	odd-K_4	K_5	odd-K_5
Theorem		Thm 8	Thm 10	Thm 13	Thm 14
	$\mathcal{L}_4$	K_5+?	odd-K_5+?	K_6+?	odd-K_6+?

Table 2: Summary of results characterizing tightness of LP relaxations by forbidden minors. All conditions may be checked efficiently. **Right:** The section for TRI (shaded blue) contains our main new results: Theorem 10 for signed G; and the stronger Theorem 14 for signed ∇G, which examines singleton and edge potentials. Theorem 14 implies Theorems 13, 10 and 8. Results for $\mathcal{L}_4$ are unknown. **Left:** Illustration of the model classes for LP+TRI, where *problems* are models for which LP+TRI is not tight. Theorem 14 is the most powerful result, showing that all problems lie within the set of models where ∇G contains an odd-K_5. See discussion in §4.3 and §6.

Theorem 7. *LP+$\mathcal{L}_r$ is not tight for the fully connected model on $n = r+1$ variables with all $\theta_i = W_{ij} = -1\ \forall i \in V, (i,j) \in E$. Note that this model has signed G which is an odd-K_{r+1}, and signed ∇G which is an odd-K_{r+2}.*

Proof. The proof is from first principles. Consider the distribution for each r-cluster that is uniform over all configurations with $\lfloor \frac{r}{2} \rfloor$ 0s and $\lceil \frac{r}{2} \rceil$ 1s. This has higher score than the best integral configuration of $\lfloor \frac{n}{2} \rfloor$ 0s and $\lceil \frac{n}{2} \rceil$ 1s. □

Applying Theorem 7 for $r = 2$ and 3 yields the following result (since if a model contains a K_{r+1} minor, then we may assume potentials such that the model is the K_{r+1}).

Theorem 8. *Considering unsigned topologies: LP+LOC is tight for all valid potentials iff G does not contain a K_3 minor; LP+TRI is tight for all valid potentials iff G does not contain a K_4 minor.*

We next provide stronger results by considering the signs of edge potentials. Intriguingly, both for LOC and TRI, the forbidden signed minor is exactly the odd version of the forbidden unsigned minor in Theorem 8.

Theorem 9. *LP+LOC is tight for all valid potentials iff the signed graph G does not contain an odd-K_3 signed minor.*

Proof. It is easily seen that if the signed graph of a model does not contain an odd-K_3 signed minor, then it is balanced (see §3). Earlier work showed that LP+LOC is tight for any balanced model (Padberg, 1989; Weller et al., 2016). Necessity follows from Theorem 7. □

Theorem 10. *LP+TRI is tight for all valid potentials iff the signed graph G does not contain an odd-K_4 signed minor.*

Theorem 10 follows as a corollary of the stronger Theorem 14, which we shall show in §5, which also considers the signs of singleton potentials by examining the signed suspension graph ∇G (defined in §4 just before §4.1).

4.3 REMARKS, EARLIER WORK

Taken together, our results in §4.2 employ the framework of forbidden minors to characterize compactly the tightness of LP relaxations in an elegant and unifying way. See Table 2 for a summary, which includes later results from §5. Note the interesting relationships across conditions, all of which may be checked efficiently by Theorems 2 and 3.

Little was known theoretically about conditions for tightness of LP+TRI before Weller et al. (2016) showed that it was sufficient for a model to be almost balanced (defined in §3). They also demonstrated a composition result which allows almost balanced sub-models to be pasted together in particular ways, while maintaining tightness. The condition in Theorem 10 is substantially stronger: the new condition is both necessary and sufficient; it is compact to describe and it is efficient to check. Further, we next show that Theorem 10 covers a strict superset of models.

Observe that the property for a signed graph of being almost balanced is closed under taking signed minors. An odd-K_4 is clearly not almost balanced, see Figure 3. Hence almost balanced models $\subseteq$ models whose signed topology does not contain an odd-K_4 minor. Next consider the permitted pasting operation (Weller et al., 2016, Theorem 12), which allows sub-models to be pasted together either on a single variable or, in limited settings, on an edge. If each sub-model is odd-K_4-free, then so too is the pasted combination. Hence, Theorem 10 covers all the models covered by Weller et al. (2016); we next show that Theorem 10 covers a significant additional class of models.

Signed graphs that do not contain an odd-K_4 minor have been studied previously (Gerards, 1988; Truemper, 1998). An important class that is odd-K_4-minor-free but not almost balanced is planar signed graphs with two odd faces (i.e. all but exactly two faces have even bounding cycles). See Figure 4 for an example by J. Carmesin which is 3-connected, hence there is no way it could be constructed by pasting almost balanced sub-models on edges or vertices.

5 INCLUDING SINGLETONS, ∇G

In this Section, we extend the analysis of §4 to include singleton potentials, by now considering the suspension graph ∇G rather than just the base graph G. We build to §5.3,

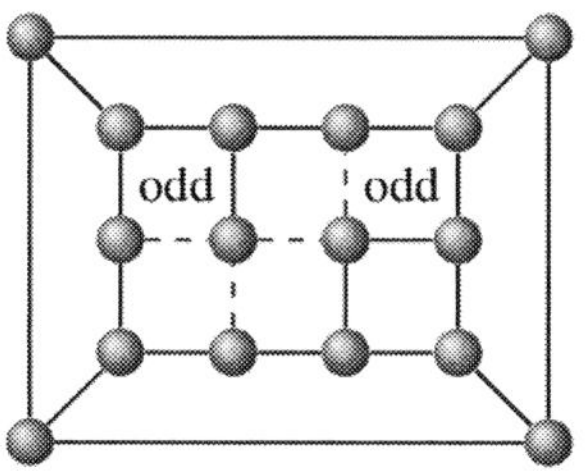

Figure 4: A 3-connected signed graph that is not almost balanced, hence the results of Weller et al. (2016) cannot be used to show that LP+TRI is tight for such a model; yet it is odd-K_4-minor-free, hence Theorem 10 proves that LP+TRI is tight for all valid potentials. This is a planar signed graph with two odd faces (Gerards, 1988, §3.2), with the odd faces indicated (others are even); see §4.3. Solid blue (dashed red) edges are even (odd).

Potential values for n variables $+ m$ edges		Potential values for $n+m$ edges
Marginal polytope $\mathbb{M}$	$\leftrightarrow$	CUT polytope of ∇G
TRI relaxation	$\leftrightarrow$	MET relaxation = CYC
LOC relaxation	$\leftrightarrow$	RMET relaxation

Table 3: Relations between polytopes; see §5.

where we state and prove our strongest result, Theorem 14, which characterizes tightness of LP+TRI if we examine the signs of both edge and singleton potentials. We show that this result implies Theorem 10 from §4, which examines only edge signs. Our approach relies on Theorem 4 (Guenin's result), connecting to it by showing relations between various polytopes.

In §4, we introduced the marginal polytope $\mathbb{M}$, together with its relaxations TRI and LOC, with $\mathbb{M} \subseteq$ TRI $\subseteq$ LOC. Here, we first show equivalences to the *cut polytope* CUT of the suspension graph ∇G, together with its relaxations MET (the *semimetric polytope*) and RMET (the *rooted semimetric polytope*) with CUT $\subseteq$ MET $\subseteq$ RMET, see Table 3. In §5.2, we relate MET to the *cycle inequalities* (Barahona and Mahjoub, 1986; Barahona, 1993) and provide Theorem 13, which does not consider signs of potentials. For more background, see (Deza and Laurent, 1997).

In §5.3 we consider signed cycles, then by combining results, we prove Theorem 14, our strongest new result. In addition, we are able to show that many typically used cycle inequalities may be redundant for enforcing integrality.

5.1 MARGINAL AND CUT POLYTOPES, AND THEIR RELAXATIONS

Here we establish many of the equivalences of polytopes shown in Table 3. Recall the definition of the suspension graph $\nabla G(V', E')$ from §4.

Given a subset $S \subseteq V' = \{0, 1, \ldots, n\}$, let $\delta(S) \in \{0,1\}^{|E'|}$ be the *cut vector* of edges of ∇G that run between the vertex partitions S and $V' \setminus S$, defined by $\delta(S)_{ij} = 1$ iff i and j are in different partitions.

The *cut polytope* (Barahona, 1983; Barahona and Mahjoub, 1986) of ∇G is the convex hull of all such cut vectors, that is CUT = conv $\{\delta(S) : S \subseteq V'\}$. Although there are 2^{n+1} choices of S, CUT has 2^n vertices since by definition $\delta(S) = \delta(V' \backslash S)$. In fact, there is a linear bijection between CUT and $\mathbb{M}$, which is particularly simple given the form we selected for edge marginals in (4).[9] Given $d \in$ CUT with entries d_{ij} for $(i,j) \in E'$, d maps to $\mu \in \mathbb{M}$ where $\mu_j = d_{0j}$ for $j \in V$, and $\mu_{ij} = d_{ij}$ for $(i,j) \in E$.

To see this, d_{ij} may be interpreted as the marginal probability that $i, j \in V'$ lie in different partitions. Similarly, $\mu_{ij} \in \mathbb{M}$ is the marginal probability that X_i and X_j take different values; and μ_i is the probability that $X_i \neq 0$ (corresponding in ∇G to i being in a different partition to 0).

MAP inference for the model on G is now clearly equivalent to the max cut problem for ∇G, i.e.[10]

$$\max_{\mu \in \mathbb{M}} w \cdot \mu = \max_{d \in \text{CUT}} w' \cdot d, \; w'_{ij} = \begin{cases} -\theta_j & i = 0 \\ -W_{ij} & (i,j) \in E. \end{cases} \quad (5)$$

The bijection between $\mathbb{M}$ and CUT may also be used to map the LOC and TRI relaxations of $\mathbb{M}$ to corresponding relaxations of CUT in $[0,1]^{|E'|}$, called the *rooted semimetric polytope* RMET and the *semimetric polytope* MET, respectively, as shown in Table 3. The constraints for the MET polytope (which corresponds to TRI) take the following form, sometimes described as unrooted triangle inequalities (Deza and Laurent, 1997, §27.1):

$$\text{MET} \quad \forall i,j,k \in V', \; d(i,j) - d(i,k) - d(j,k) \leq 0 \quad (6)$$
$$d(i,j) + d(i,k) + d(j,k) \leq 2.$$

Remarkably, the constraints for RMET, the *rooted* triangle inequalities, are exactly just those of (6) for which one of i, j, k is 0, the vertex that was added to yield ∇G. Hence, RMET may be regarded as MET *rooted* at 0. Correspondingly, we may consider TRI to be a version of LOC that is *universally rooted* (Weller, 2016). See discussion in §6.

5.2 CYCLE INEQUALITIES, CYC POLYTOPE

Here we define the cycle inequalities and provide background showing how they may be used to characterize tightness of LP+TRI by forbidding unsigned K_5 as a minor of the unsigned suspension graph $\nabla G(V', E')$.

For any edge set $F \subseteq E'$ and $x \in [0,1]^{|E'|}$, let $x(F) = \sum_{e \in F} x(e)$. Let $C \subseteq E'$ be the edge set of a cycle in ∇G.

[9] If instead, edge terms of the form $x_i x_j$ are used for the marginal polytope, as in the Boolean quadric polytope (see footnote 8), then the linear bijection required is slightly more complex and is called the *covariance mapping* (De Simone, 1990).

[10] The negative signs before θ_j and W_{ij} terms are because we followed the convention that $W_{ij} > 0$ is an attractive edge, and made the signs of singleton potentials consistent; see §4.

At any vertex of CUT, if we traverse C, we must change partitions an even number of times.

Hence, the following *cycle inequalities* hold $\forall x \in$ CUT: for any cycle C and any edge subset $F \subseteq C$ with $|F|$ odd,

$$x(F) - x(C \setminus F) \leq |F| - 1. \tag{7}$$

Let CYC be the polytope defined by these constraints, i.e. CYC $= \{x \in [0,1]^{|E'|} : x(F) - x(C \setminus F) \leq |F| - 1$ for any cycle C of ∇G and any $F \subseteq C, |F|$ odd$\}$. The triangle inequalities (6) are special cases of (7) with $|C| = 3$, though note that those apply in MET to any triplet $i, j, k \in V'$ without regard to the edges E', whereas cycle inequalities apply only to the cycles of $\nabla G(V', E')$. Nevertheless, in fact, the following result holds; see Table 3.

Theorem 11 (Barahona and Mahjoub, 1986; Barahona, 1993)**.** *MET = CYC.*

Barahona and Mahjoub (1986) established the following important characterization for when the cycle inequalities are sufficient for tightness by forbidding a K_5 minor.

Theorem 12 (Barahona and Mahjoub, 1986)**.** *CUT = CYC iff unsigned ∇G does not contain K_5 as a minor.*

Using the equivalences of §5.1 (see (5) and Table 3), Theorems 11 and 12 together show the following result, which characterizes when LP+TRI is tight if we examine only the *unsigned* suspension graph ∇G.

Theorem 13. *LP+TRI is tight for all valid potentials iff unsigned ∇G does not contain K_5 as a minor.*

Theorems 11 and 12 of Barahona and Mahjoub (1986) are often used to show only that LP+TRI is tight for a planar model with no singleton potentials (which excludes both K_5 and $K_{3,3}$, see §2), e.g. see Theorem 3.3.2 in (Sontag, 2010). However, Theorem 13 is stronger, and perhaps is more naturally viewed instead as extending the characterization of treewidth ≤ 2 as K_4-minor-free; see §6.

5.3 SIGNED CYCLES, MISS POLYTOPE

Here we shall prove Theorem 14, a stronger, signed version of Theorem 13. Theorem 10 will follow as a corollary. For cycles in ∇G, to avoid confusion, we write C for the edge set of an unsigned cycle, and D for the signed edge set of a signed odd cycle (which has an odd number of odd edges).

Given results in §5.1-5.2 (see (5) and Table 3), we have

$$\max_{\mu \in \text{TRI}} w \cdot \mu = \max_{x \in \text{CYC}} w' \cdot x, \; w'_{ij} = \begin{cases} -\theta_j & i = 0 \\ -W_{ij} & (i,j) \in E. \end{cases} \tag{8}$$

We shall relate this to Theorem 4 (Guenin's result on weakly bipartite graphs from §3.3) to prove the following.

Theorem 14. *LP+TRI is tight for all valid potentials, observing signs of both edge and singleton potentials, iff the signed suspension graph ∇G does not contain odd-K_5 as a signed minor.*

Proof. We first show sufficiency of the condition. Regarding (8), CYC is defined by the inequalities (7), which we rewrite as $|F| - x(F) + x(C \setminus F) \geq 1$, or

$$\sum_{e \in F}(1 - x_e) + \sum_{e \in C \setminus F} x_e \geq 1. \tag{9}$$

The unsigned cycle inequality (9) applies for every cycle C of ∇G and every $F \subseteq C$ with $|F|$ odd. Aiming to relate (9) to the definition of a weakly bipartite graph (1), we introduce the following MISS polytope, which is equivalent to CUT by a reflection that adjusts for the signs of edges of $\nabla G(V', E')$. Recall how these signs are set in §4, and regarding (8), observe that edge $e \in E'$ is odd iff $w'_e > 0$.

Given a configuration of variables $X_1, \dots, X_n \in \{0,1\}^n$, the corresponding vertex $\in \{0,1\}^{|E'|}$ of the CUT polytope has a 1 for edge $(i,j) \in E'$ iff $X_i \neq X_j$, taking $X_0 = 0$.

For MISS, instead the corresponding vertex $m \in \{0,1\}^{|E'|}$ has a 1 for edge $(i,j) \in E'$ iff m_{ij} 'misses' the potential score benefit that the edge offers. That is, take $X_0 = 0$ as before, and now for all $(i,j) \in E'$, assign $m_{ij} = 1$ if $X_i \neq X_j$ and the edge is even (attractive), or if $X_i = X_j$ and the edge is odd (repulsive); otherwise $m_{ij} = 0$.

Each of CUT and MISS is formed as the convex hull of its 2^n vertices. MISS is the reflection of CUT across $\frac{1}{2}$ in exactly the dimensions for which edges of ∇G are odd. That is, $x \in$ CUT maps bijectively to $y \in$ MISS, where $y_e = x_e$ for even edges, and $y_e = 1 - x_e$ for odd edges.

Let D be the edge set of an odd cycle of signed ∇G (i.e. D has an odd number of odd edges). Given any configuration of variables, as we go round D, to return to the same value, we must 'miss' at least one edge. That is, for any vertex $m \in$ MISS, $\sum_{e \in D} m_e \geq 1$. Hence, what we call the *signed cycle inequalities* hold $\forall y \in$ MISS $\subseteq [0,1]^{|E'|}$:

$$\sum_{e \in D} y_e \geq 1, \quad \forall \text{ odd cycles } D \text{ of signed } \nabla G. \tag{10}$$

Note the direct correspondence between the signed cycle inequalities (10) and the inequalities defining the weakly bipartite polyhedron Q (1). Observe the following.

Lemma 15. *Each signed cycle inequality* (10) *corresponds to an unsigned cycle inequality* (9).

Proof. Given a signed cycle inequality (10), let F be the odd edges of D, with $|F|$ odd. Let $C = D$. The equivalent reflected form of (10) for $x \in$ CUT is $\sum_{e \in F}(1 - x_e) + \sum_{e \in C \setminus F} x_e \geq 1$, which matches (9) as required. □

Let CYC^R be the polytope CYC reflected in the odd edge dimensions, just as MISS may be obtained from CUT, so

MISS $\subseteq$ CYC^R as CUT $\subseteq$ CYC. Consider (8), note edge e is odd $\Leftrightarrow w'_e > 0$, let $x \in$ CYC map to $y \in$ CYC^R, then

$$\max_{\mu \in \text{TRI}} w \cdot \mu = \max_{y \in \text{CYC}^R} \sum_{\text{odd } e \in E'} w'_e(1-y_e) + \sum_{\text{even } e \in E'} w'_e y_e$$
$$= A + \max_{y \in \text{CYC}^R} w'' \cdot y, \qquad (11)$$

where $A = \sum_{e: w'_e > 0} w'_e$ is a constant, and $w''_e = -|w'_e| \; \forall e \in E'$.

We are now ready to apply Theorem 4. We have {all valid integer solutions} $\subseteq$ MISS $\subseteq$ CYC^R, while (by Lemma 15) CYC^R enforces all the signed cycle inequalities (10), which match the weakly bipartite conditions (1). Further, in (11) we are maximizing an objective with every coefficient negative, which is needed since Q is a polyhedron unbounded in the positive directions (1). Finally, no invalid integer solutions lie in CYC^R. Hence, by Theorem 4, if signed ∇G does not contain odd-K_5 as a signed minor, then LP+TRI is tight.

For necessity of the condition, if ∇G does contain an odd-K_5 minor, then by choice of potentials, we may assume signed $\nabla G(V', E')$ to be exactly odd-K_5. Then Theorem 7 with $r = 3$ provides an example where LP+TRI is not tight. This completes the proof of Theorem 14. □

Corollaries. Theorem 14 may be used to prove Theorem 10 as follows. First, if signed G does not contain an odd-K_4, then clearly signed ∇G cannot contain an odd-K_5, hence LP+TRI is tight by Theorem 14. Now, if signed G does contain an odd-K_4, then we may select all negative singleton potentials for those variables, then use the example above for odd-K_5 in signed ∇G.

In practice, LP+TRI is often implemented by enforcing the (unsigned) cycle constraints (9) rather than all triplet constraints (Sontag, 2010). Theorem 14 and Lemma 15 show the following, which may be useful by dramatically reducing the number of constraints required for integrality.[11]

Theorem 16. *If a model has signed ∇G that is odd-K_5-minor-free, then integrality of LP+TRI will be achieved by enforcing only the signed cycle inequalities* (10)*, with the other unsigned cycle inequalities* (9) *being redundant.*[12]

6 DISCUSSION, FUTURE WORK

We have drawn connections to powerful results from graph theory by showing how tightness of LP relaxations may be elegantly characterized by forbidding certain minors: either from the graph topology G, if singleton potentials are not examined; or, with more precision, from the suspension graph ∇G, if the topology of both edge and singleton potentials is considered. We significantly strengthen results by examining also the signs of the potentials and forbidding signed minors. All conditions can be tested efficiently (Theorems 2 and 3). Our strongest result, Theorem 14, shows that LP+TRI is tight for all valid potentials, observing the signed topology of the suspension graph ∇G, iff signed ∇G is odd-K_5-minor-free. Our results go substantially beyond earlier work (Weller et al., 2016) that provided only sufficient conditions for a smaller set of models, without an easy way to test.

Viewing our characterizations together in Table 2, fascinating patterns emerge. We make the following observations. (a) In all known cases, it is exactly just the *odd* versions of the forbidden unsigned minors which can cause lack of tightness of the LP relaxation. In future work, we would like to understand if this pattern extends to other cases. (b) For unsigned graphs G, given the treewidth result of Wainwright and Jordan (2004), we can expect that as cluster size increases, the number of forbidden minors could grow rapidly,[13] see Table 1. (c) For TRI, going from G to the suspension graph ∇G adds one universally connected vertex to the forbidden minor. Why does this not happen for LOC, and will it hold for higher cluster sizes? Recall the observations just before §5.2, where we saw that LOC has a *fixed root* whereas TRI is *universally rooted*. This is why results for TRI examine the suspension graph ∇G with complete symmetry for singleton and edge potentials, whereas for LOC, singleton potentials are different. This prompts further analysis and may lead to new algorithms for TRI. It also suggests viewing the forbidden K_5 minor in ∇G not as a strengthened form of planarity (which forbids K_5 and $K_{3,3}$), but rather as forbidding K_{4+1}, where K_4 is the treewidth constraint of the base graph G. Further, it explains why it is possible for LP+TRI to perform worse as singleton potentials rise within a range, see Appendix.

Theorem 7 shows that for any cluster size r, it is *necessary* to forbid K_{r+2} as a signed minor of ∇G in order to guarantee tightness of LP+$\mathcal{L}_r$. We have placed the appropriate entries in the $\mathcal{L}_4$ row of Table 2. Theorem 5 shows that it is *sufficient* to forbid all the treewidth minors in unsigned G. Must we forbid odd versions of all these in signed G? So far, we have not been able to find an example where LP+$\mathcal{L}_4$ is not tight other than where ∇G contains an odd-K_6.

Acknowledgements

The author thanks Standa Živný, Johannes Carmesin, Maria Chudnovsky, Mark Rowland, Tony Huynh, Tony Jebara, Amir Globerson, David Sontag, Nilesh Tripuraneni, Yarin Gal and Yingzhen Li for helpful comments.

[11]For implementations which successively add violated cutting planes, this result may be less useful, though it still dramatically reduces the search space of possible constraints to add.

[12]Consider that (9) has no access to edge signs, hence tests *all possible* frustrated/odd cycles (10).

[13]Ramachandramurthi (1997) showed that the number of forbidden minors for treewidth t is $\Omega(\exp(\sqrt{t}))$.

References

F. Barahona. The max-cut problem on graphs not contractible to K_5. *Operations Research Letters*, 2(3):107–111, 1983.

F. Barahona. On cuts and matchings in planar graphs. *Math. Program.*, 60:53–68, 1993.

F. Barahona and A. Mahjoub. On the cut polytope. *Mathematical Programming*, 36(2):157–173, 1986.

D. Batra, S. Nowozin, and P. Kohli. Tighter relaxations for MAP-MRF inference: A local primal-dual gap based separation algorithm. In *AISTATS*, 2011.

V. Chandrasekaran, N. Srebro, and P. Harsha. Complexity of inference in graphical models. In *UAI*, pages 70–78, 2008.

M. Cooper and S. Živný. Hybrid tractability of valued constraint problems. *Artificial Intelligence*, 175(9):1555–1569, 2011.

R. Cowell, A. Dawid, S. Lauritzen, and D. Spiegelhalter. *Probabilistic Networks and Expert Systems*. Springer-Verlag, 1999.

C. De Simone. The cut polytope and the Boolean quadric polytope. *Discrete Mathematics*, 79(1):71–75, 1990.

E. Demaine, M. Hajiaghayi, and K. Kawarabayashi. Decomposition, approximation, and coloring of odd-minor-free graphs. In *ACM-SIAM symposium on Discrete Algorithms (SODA)*, 2010.

M. Deza and M. Laurent. *Geometry of Cuts and Metrics*. Springer Publishing Company, Incorporated, 1st edition, 1997. ISBN 978-3-642-04294-2.

R. Diestel. *Graph Theory*. Springer, fourth edition, 2010.

J. Domke. Learning graphical model parameters with approximate marginal inference. *TPAMI*, 35(10):2454–2467, 2013.

F. Eaton and Z. Ghahramani. Model reductions for inference: Generality of pairwise, binary, and planar factor graphs. *Neural Computation*, 25(5):1213–1260, 2013.

J. Geelen, B. Gerards, and G. Whittle. Solving Rota's conjecture. *Notices of the AMS*, 61(7):736–743, 2014.

A. Gerards. *Graphs and polyhedra: binary spaces and cutting planes*. 1988.

B. Guenin. A characterization of weakly bipartite graphs. *Journal of Combinatorial Theory, Series B*, 83(1):112–168, 2001.

F. Harary. On the notion of balance of a signed graph. *Michigan Mathematical Journal*, 2:143–146, 1953.

T. Huynh. *The linkage problem for group-labelled graphs*. PhD thesis, University of Waterloo, 2009.

J. Kappes, B. Andres, F. Hamprecht, C. Schnörr, S. Nowozin, D. Batra, S. Kim, B. Kausler, J. Lellmann, N. Komodakis, and C. Rother. A comparative study of modern inference techniques for discrete energy minimization problems. In *CVPR*, 2013.

K. Kawarabayashi, Y. Kobayashi, and B. Reed. The disjoint paths problem in quadratic time. *Journal of Combinatorial Theory, Series B*, 102(2):424–435, 2012.

V. Kolmogorov, J. Thapper, and S. Živný. The power of linear programming for general-valued CSPs. *SIAM Journal on Computing*, 44(1):1–36, 2015. doi: 10.1137/130945648.

J. Kwisthout, H. Bodlaender, and L. van der Gaag. The necessity of bounded treewidth for efficient inference in Bayesian networks. In *ECAI*, volume 215, pages 237–242, 2010.

A. Lehman. On the width-length inequality and degenerate projective planes. In *Polyhedral Combinatorics*, pages 101–105. American Mathematical Society, 1990.

M. Padberg. The Boolean quadric polytope: some characteristics, facets and relatives. *Mathematical Programming*, 45(1-3): 139–172, 1989.

S. Ramachandramurthi. The structure and number of obstructions to treewidth. *SIAM Journal on Discrete Mathematics*, 10(1): 146–157, 1997.

N. Robertson and P. Seymour. Graph minors. XIII. The disjoint paths problem. *Journal of Combinatorial Theory, Series B*, 63 (1):65–110, 1995.

N. Robertson and P. Seymour. Graph minors. XX. Wagner's conjecture. *Journal of Combinatorial Theory, Series B*, 92(2):325–357, 2004.

N. Robertson, P. Seymour, and R. Thomas. Quickly excluding a planar graph. *Journal of Combinatorial Theory, Series B*, 62 (2):323–348, 1994.

T. Schiex, H. Fargier, and G. Verfaillie. Valued constraint satisfaction problems: Hard and easy problems. *IJCAI (1)*, 95: 631–639, 1995.

A. Schrijver. A short proof of Guenin's characterization of weakly bipartite graphs. *Journal of Combinatorial Theory, Series B*, 85 (2):255–260, 2002.

P. Seymour. The matroids with the max-flow min-cut property. *Journal of Combinatorial Theory, Series B*, 23(2):189–222, 1977.

P. Seymour. The origin of the notion of treewidth. `http://cstheory.stackexchange.com/questions/5018/the-origin-of-the-notion-of-treewidth`, 2014.

H. Sherali and W. Adams. A hierarchy of relaxations between the continuous and convex hull representations for zero-one programming problems. *SIAM Journal on Discrete Mathematics*, 3(3):411–430, 1990.

D. Sontag. *Approximate Inference in Graphical Models using LP Relaxations*. PhD thesis, MIT, EECS, 2010.

J. Thapper and S. Živný. The complexity of finite-valued CSPs. Technical report, February 2015. arXiv:1210.2987v3.

K. Truemper. *Matroid decomposition (revised edition)*. 1998.

K. Wagner. Über eine erweiterung eines satzes von Kuratowski. *Deutsche Mathematik*, 2:280–285, 1937.

M. Wainwright and M. Jordan. Treewidth-based conditions for exactness of the Sherali-Adams and Lasserre relaxations. *Univ. California, Berkeley, Technical Report*, 671:4, 2004.

M. Wainwright and M. Jordan. Graphical models, exponential families and variational inference. *Foundations and Trends in Machine Learning*, 1(1-2):1–305, 2008.

Y. Watanabe. Uniqueness of belief propagation on signed graphs. In *Neural Information Processing Systems*, 2011.

A. Weller. Revisiting the limits of MAP inference by MWSS on perfect graphs. In *Artificial Intelligence and Statistics (AISTATS)*, 2015.

A. Weller. Uprooting and rerooting graphical models. In *International Conference on Machine Learning (ICML)*, 2016.

A. Weller, M. Rowland, and D. Sontag. Tightness of LP relaxations for almost balanced models. In *Artificial Intelligence and Statistics (AISTATS)*, 2016.

Subspace Clustering with a Twist

David Wipf and Yue Dong
Microsoft Research, Beijing
{davidwip,yuedong}@microsoft.com

Bo Xin
Peking University
boxin@pku.edu.cn

Abstract

Subspace segmentation or clustering can be defined as the process of assigning subspace labels to a set of data points assumed to lie on the union of multiple low-dimensional, linear subspaces. Given that each point can be efficiently expressed using a linear combination of other points from the same subspace, a variety of segmentation algorithms built upon ℓ_1, nuclear norm, and other convex penalties have recently shown state-of-the-art robustness on multiple benchmarks. However, what if instead of observing the original data points, we instead only have access to transformed, or 'twisted' so to speak, measurements? Here we consider underdetermined affine transformations that may arise in computer vision applications such as bidirectional reflectance distribution function (BRDF) estimation. Unfortunately most existing approaches, convex or otherwise, do not address this highly useful generalization. To fill this void, we proceed by deriving a probabilistic model that simultaneously estimates the latent data points and subspace memberships using simple EM update rules. Moreover, in certain restricted settings this approach is guaranteed to produce the correct clustering. Finally a wide range of corroborating empirical evidence, including a BRDF estimation task, speaks to the practical efficacy of this algorithm.

1 Introduction

As a data reduction or analysis tool, principal component analysis (PCA) is readily applicable whenever observable points lie on or near a low-dimensional linear subspace. Richer structures however may not conform to this model, and often we must consider ways of introducing additional complexity. For example, a natural extension of PCA is to consider that our data lie on a union of low-dimensional subspaces. In this expanded regime we may then consider the joint problem of estimating these subspaces and assigning each point to the closest one, a process commonly referred to as either subspace clustering or segmentation. Although unlike classical PCA a closed-form solution via the SVD is no longer possible, tractable approximations that succeed with high probability form a core component of numerous practical application domains. Examples include the analysis of social graphs (Jalali et al., 2011), network topology inference (Eriksson et al., 2012), user identification in movie rating systems Zhang et al. (2012), and a host of computer vision tasks such as image representation and compression, motion segmentation, and face clustering (Elhamifar & Vidal, 2013; Feng et al., 2014; Liu et al., 2013; Lu et al., 2012; Rao et al., 2010).

1.1 Problem Description

We define this problem more formally as follows. Let $\{\mathcal{S}_k\}_{k=1}^m$ denote a collection of m linear subspaces in $\mathbb{R}^d$, where $\dim[\mathcal{S}_k] = d_k < d \quad \forall k = 1, \ldots, m$. Moreover, suppose we have drawn n_k points from each subspace forming data matrices $\boldsymbol{X}_k \in \mathbb{R}^{d \times n_k}$. We then concatenate the points from each subspace, and the full arrangement of $n = \sum_{k=1}^m n_k$ points is reordered using an unknown permutation matrix $\boldsymbol{P} \in \mathbb{R}^{n \times n}$. Consequently, the entire data can be expressed as

$$\boldsymbol{X} \triangleq [\boldsymbol{x}_1, \ldots, \boldsymbol{x}_n] = [\boldsymbol{X}_1, \ldots, \boldsymbol{X}_m]\boldsymbol{P} \in \mathbb{R}^{d \times n}. \quad (1)$$

Subspace clustering can then be described as the process of estimating a basis for each $\mathcal{S}_k$ as well as the subspace membership of each point $\boldsymbol{x}_j$.

One of the most robust approaches to obtaining such accurate data segmentations exploits the so-called *self-expressiveness property* of $\boldsymbol{X}$ (Elhamifar & Vidal, 2013), namely that any $\boldsymbol{x}_j$ can be represented as a linear combination of other data points in $\boldsymbol{X}$ within the same subspace. Moreover, if we can find such a representation using *only* points from the same subspace, then we have extracted vital information pertaining to the true latent segmentation.

One way to favor such cluster-aligned decompositions is by solving

$$\min_{Z} \|Z\|_0 \text{ s.t. } X = XZ, \ \text{diag}[Z] = 0, \quad (2)$$

where $\|Z\|_0$ is the matrix ℓ_0 norm, or a count of the number of nonzero elements in Z, a penalty function that strongly favors zero-valued elements or a canonically sparse Z. The diagonal constraint is required to prevent each point from using itself in the representation (e.g., the degenerate solution $Z^* = I$), enforcing that we must rely only on others in the same subspace. If we assume that each individual subspace satisfies $d_k < d$ for all k, and that sampled points are sufficiently dense in general position, then the solution to (2) will be block diagonal and aligned with the true clusters up to the permutation matrix P, revealing subspace memberships. A final spectral clustering, post-processing step can further solidify the labels and is adopted by most recent methods (Elhamifar & Vidal, 2013). Of course solving (2) is non-convex, discontinuous, and NP-hard, so following the typical compressive sensing recipe it is desirable to replace the troublesome $\|Z\|_0$ penalty with the convex relaxation $\|Z\|_1$. This substitution is supported by rigorous theoretical arguments detailing conditions whereby subspace-aligned block-diagonal structure is guaranteed when we minimize $\|Z\|_1$ over the constraint set (Soltanolkotabi & Candès, 2012).

Proceeding further, suppose that we are unable to observe X directly, but instead are only granted access to a measurement matrix $Y = [y_1, \dots, y_n]$, where each column y_j is generated via the underdetermined system

$$y_j = A_j x_j, \quad \forall j = 1, \dots, n. \quad (3)$$

Here $\{A_j\}$, with $A_j \in \mathbb{R}^{p_j \times d}, p_j \le d$ indicates a set of known, possibly overcomplete matrices with problem-dependent structure that can warp or *twist* each data point independently while mapping it onto the lower-dimensional observation space.[1] As described in depth later, such a situation commonly arises in computer vision applications such as bidirectional reflectance distribution function (BRDF) estimation, where each A_j is determined by lighting conditions and the surface geometry of an object with unknown BRDF we would like to obtain. Other possible scenarios include face clustering in subject-varying transform domains, or motion segmentation using approximations for perspective cameras. Additionally, if each A_j can be described as a matrix of zeroes with a single one in each row, then the resulting estimation problem is tantamount to subspace clustering with missing entries (Candès et al., 2014; Eriksson et al., 2012; Gruber & Weiss, 2004; Yang et al., 2015).

[1]We frequently use $\{M_j\}$ to abbreviate a set of matrices $\{M_j : j \in \mathcal{J}\}$, where the index set $\mathcal{J}$ should be clear from the context.

1.2 Naive Solutions

Clearly we can no longer directly rely on the original self-expressiveness property, because once we insert $\{A_j\}$ into the pipeline, it no longer follows that each corresponding y_j can be compactly represented using only other points generated from the same subspace.[2] To compensate, several strategies immediately come to mind.

For example, suppose we somehow knew the number of clusters m. Then let the set $\{\Omega_k\}$, with each $\Omega_k \subset \{1, \dots, n\}$, denote a partitioning such that $\bigcup_{k=1}^{m} \Omega_k = \{1, \dots, n\}$ and $\Omega_k \cap \Omega_{k'} = \emptyset$ for all pairs $\{k, k'\}$. Also let X_{Ω_k} represent the columns of matrix X indexed by Ω_k. Now consider the joint optimization over all possible segmentations and latent points

$$\min_{X, \{\Omega_k\}} \sum_{k=1}^{m} |\Omega_k| \text{rank}(X_{\Omega_k}) \text{ s.t. } y_j = A_j x_j, \ \forall j = 1, \dots, n. \quad (4)$$

Then assuming the true latent X is composed of sufficient samples per subspace in general position, and that A_j contains a sufficient number of non-degenerate measurements, the solution to (4) will be such that $\{\Omega_k\}$ reflects the correct segmentation and X will be recovered. Unfortunately however, minimizing (4) requires an infeasible, combinatorial search over every possible clustering pattern.

Perhaps the most natural way to circumvent this problem is to invoke a two-stage procedure inspired by traditional matrix completion (Candès & Recht, 2008). The basic idea is to first obtain an estimate of the latent X by solving

$$\min_{X} \text{rank}[X], \quad \text{s.t. } y_j = A_j x_j, \ \forall j = 1, \dots, n, \quad (5)$$

which excludes any combinatorial search over labels. This represents an affine rank minimization problem that can be approximately solved by replacing the non-convex rank$[X]$ penalty with the convex nuclear norm relaxation $\|X\|_*$, or the sum of the singular values of X. Once this solution is in hand, we may deploy any traditional subspace clustering algorithm on the resulting $\hat{X}$.

The difficulty with this strategy is two-fold. First, unlike the data from individual subspaces X_k, the matrix X may be full rank given that it is quite common to have $\sum_k d_k \ge d$. So in this situation we have no chance of obtaining a meaningful segmentation. However, even if the global solution to (5) does produce the correct X, the nuclear norm relaxation required by a tractable implementation will be highly sensitive to both the correlation structure and relative column norm scaling of $\{A_j\}$.

[2]An exception to this occurs when A_j is equal to some fixed A across all j, in which case the self-expressiveness property still holds and natural adaptations already exist (Patel et al., 2013; Wang et al., 2015a).

In fact existing theoretical guarantees for rank-nuclear norm equivalence place extremely strong conditions on the structure of the measurement process, which are unlikely to hold in practice here since in the problem instances we consider, each A_j is determined by physical properties of the experimental design. Moreover, unlike typical compressive sensing designs, we cannot even normalize columns of $\{A_j\}$, because if we were to do so then a low-rank solution will no longer satisfy the constraint set in (5). Therefore we are left with a challenging NP-hard rank minimization problem as a required preprocessing step, a clearly undesirable starting point.

As an alternative to the above two-stage procedure, we could append an additional data fitting constraints to the canonical sparse subspace clustering objective from above and solve

$$\min_{X,Z} \|Z\|_1 \text{ s.t. } X = XZ, \text{ diag}[Z] = 0, y_j = A_j x_j \,\forall j. \tag{6}$$

Although the penalty is convex in Z and the constraints are individually convex in X and Z, the overall problem remains highly non-convex and difficult to optimize. Moreover it is unclear whether the global solution, even if somehow attainable, would guarantee that the correct clustering could be found. Additionally, in practical environments with noisy data, relaxing the additional equality constraints would require the inclusion of an additional trade-off parameter and application-specific tuning.

1.3 Overview of Contributions

To address the conceptual limitations of naive adaptations of existing subspace clustering approaches, in Section 2 we derive an alternative Bayesian approach specifically tailored to the proposed latent variable setting and loosely motivate its effectiveness. Next Section 3 derives expectation maximization (EM) udpdate rules that accommodate practical deployment. We then proceed to theoretical analysis of the underlying objective function in Section 4, followed by empirical validation in Section 5, practical deployment in Section 6, and final contextualization in Section 7. Overall, our contributions can be summarized as follows:

- We delineate an important generalization of subspace clustering to accommodate an underdetermined affine measurement process and derive a Bayesian algorithm that explicitly circumvents limitations of natural alternatives. Unlike existing state-of-the-art segmentation pipelines, our algorithm does not require a final spectral clustering step.
- We thoroughly unpack the proposed objective function and its customized mechanism for favoring the true subspace labels. This includes the exposition of specific conditions, albeit somewhat idealized, whereby a unique minimizing solution (global or local) will produce the correct segmentation.
- Although not our original intention, we demonstrate that our model can achieve state-of-the-art performance in more specialized domains when A_j displays certain additional structure. This includes traditional subspace clustering when each $A_j = I$ for all j, or subspace clustering with missing entries when each A_j is an all-zero matrix with a single one in each row.
- We provide strong empirical validation on a practical BRDF estimation problem that requires the full generality of the proposed affine observation model.

2 Model Description

We begin by decomposing the latent unobserved data as

$$X = \sum_{i=1}^{m} \widetilde{X}^{(i)}, \tag{7}$$

where each $\widetilde{X}^{(i)} \in \mathbb{R}^{d \times n}$ can be interpreted as our estimate of the overall signal generated from the i-th subspace. Although we will eventually arrive at an objective function that is independent of this decomposition, it nonetheless serves as a useful tool for constructing hidden data for the EM algorithm described in Section 3. We next adopt the Gaussian likelihood function

$$p\left(Y | \{\widetilde{X}^{(i)}\}; \lambda\right) \propto \exp\left[-\sum_j \tfrac{1}{2\lambda}\|y_j - A_j \sum_i \widetilde{x}_j^{(i)}\|_2^2\right], \tag{8}$$

where λ is a noise parameter.[3] Additionally, in the limit as $\lambda \to 0$ this will enforce the same constraint set as in (3). Next we define an independent, zero-mean Gaussian prior distribution for each column of $\widetilde{X}^{(i)}$, parameterized as $p\left(\{\widetilde{X}^{(i)}\}; \{\Gamma_i\}, W\right) =$

$$\prod_{i,j} p(\widetilde{x}_j^{(i)}; \Gamma_i, w_{ij}) = \prod_{i,j} \mathcal{N}\left(\widetilde{x}_j^{(i)}; 0, w_{ij}\Gamma_i\right), \tag{9}$$

where each Γ_i represents a symmetric, positive semi-definite covariance basis matrix and the scalar coefficients w_{ij} constitute non-negative weighting factors that collectively form a parameter matrix W.[4] Strictly speaking

[3] We could allow for a separate λ_j for each point which would ultimately allow us to learn outlier locations, but for space considerations we do not further pursue this direction here.

[4] Note that (Tipping & Bishop, 1999; Wang et al., 2015b) describe alternative probabilistic mixture models that can be applied to clustering; however, the parameterizations and underlying inference algorithms are completely different from ours, do not apply to the latent affine model we consider, and do not lead to any of the desired properties discussed herein.

we should require that each $w_{ij}\mathbf{\Gamma}_i$ factor be positive definite such that the implied matrix inverse included with this distribution is well-defined. However, we can adjust for the semi-definite case with a more refined definition of the prior. First, if some $w_{ij} = 0$, then we simply define that $\widetilde{\boldsymbol{x}}_j^{(i)} = \mathbf{0}$ with probability one. For the $w_{ij} > 0$ case, without loss of generality assume that $\mathbf{\Gamma}_i = \boldsymbol{R}_i\boldsymbol{R}_i^\top$ for some matrix $\boldsymbol{R}_j$. We then stipulate that $p\left(\widetilde{\boldsymbol{x}}_j^{(i)}; \mathbf{\Gamma}_i, w_{ij}\right) = 0$ if $\widetilde{\boldsymbol{x}}_j^{(i)} \notin \text{span}[\boldsymbol{R}_j]$, and $p\left(\widetilde{\boldsymbol{x}}_j^{(i)}; \mathbf{\Gamma}_i, w_{ij}\right) \propto \exp\left[-\frac{1}{2}(\widetilde{\boldsymbol{x}}_j^{(i)})^\top(\boldsymbol{R}_j^\top)^\dagger \boldsymbol{R}_j^\dagger \widetilde{\boldsymbol{x}}_j^{(i)}\right]$ otherwise. These refinements are tacitly assumed in many related Bayesian models, and can be viewed as a natural limiting case whereby a degenerate covariance enforces that all probability mass reside in a low-dimensional subspace of the full ambient space.

Given that both the likelihood function and prior distribution are Gaussians, the posterior distribution is also a Gaussian with closed-form moments. While expressing these moments in full is slightly cumbersome from a notational standpoint, the marginalized posterior of each $\widetilde{\boldsymbol{x}}_j^{(i)}$ is given by

$$p\left(\widetilde{\boldsymbol{x}}_j^{(i)} | \boldsymbol{y}_j; \mathbf{\Gamma}_i, w_{ij}, \lambda\right) = \prod_j \mathcal{N}\left(\boldsymbol{x}_j^{(i)}; \boldsymbol{\mu}_j^{(i)}, \mathbf{\Sigma}_j^{(i)}\right) \quad (10)$$

with means and covariances defined by

$$\begin{aligned} \boldsymbol{\mu}_j^{(i)} &= w_{ij}\mathbf{\Gamma}_i\boldsymbol{A}_j^\top\left(\lambda\boldsymbol{I} + \boldsymbol{A}_j\mathbf{\Psi}_j\boldsymbol{A}_j^\top\right)^{-1}\boldsymbol{y}_j, \quad (11)\\ \mathbf{\Sigma}_j^{(i)} &= w_{ij}\mathbf{\Gamma}_i - w_{ij}^2\mathbf{\Gamma}_i\boldsymbol{A}_j^\top\left(\lambda\boldsymbol{I} + \boldsymbol{A}_j\mathbf{\Psi}_j\boldsymbol{A}_j^\top\right)^{-1}\boldsymbol{A}_j\mathbf{\Gamma}_i, \end{aligned}$$

where

$$\mathbf{\Psi}_j = \sum_i w_{ij}\mathbf{\Gamma}_i, \quad \forall j = 1, \ldots, n, \quad (12)$$

Although it is easily shown that each $\widetilde{\boldsymbol{x}}_j^{(i)}$ is independent across data points j, they may be highly correlated across the basis index i. However, for purposes of the EM algorithm derived in Section 3, only the moments from (11) will be required.

The rationale for the chosen parameterization of the prior $p\left(\{\widetilde{\boldsymbol{X}}^{(i)}\}; \{\mathbf{\Gamma}_i\}, \boldsymbol{W}\right)$ becomes partially evident upon inspection of the posterior mean expression from (11). Suppose each $\mathbf{\Gamma}_i$ spans the k-th unknown subspace we would like to recover. And moreover, suppose each $\boldsymbol{w}_j$ (the j-th column of $\boldsymbol{W}$) is a vector of zeros with a single nonzero in the position corresponding with the true subspace membership of $\boldsymbol{x}_j$. Then by virtue of the left multiplication in (11), $\boldsymbol{x}_j$ will have a posterior mean constrained to the correct subspace, with zero covariance (or posterior mass) leaking into other, errant subspaces. Hence under the stated conditions a posterior mean estimator will produce minimal reconstruction error.

Of course all of this is predicated on our ability to actually obtain a basis set $\{\mathbf{\Gamma}_i\}$ and weight matrix $\boldsymbol{W}$ fulfilling the stringent subspace-aware criterion described above. Hence we have merely shifted our original goal of estimating $\boldsymbol{X}$ and clustering its columns, to the task of learning subspace-aware covariances $\{\mathbf{\Gamma}_i\}$ and a column-sparse weight matrix $\boldsymbol{W}$ with support aligned with the true subspaces. While certainly not immediately obvious, the remainder of this paper will demonstrate that a standard marginalization strategy is quite effective for this purpose.

If we treat $\{\mathbf{\Gamma}_i\}$ and $\boldsymbol{W}$ as the key parameters of interest and $\{\widetilde{\boldsymbol{X}}^{(i)}\}$ as nuisance latent variables, then a common Bayesian inference strategy is to marginalize over $\{\widetilde{\boldsymbol{X}}^{(i)}\}$ and then maximize the resulting likelihood function with respect to remaining unknown parameters (Tipping, 2001; Wipf et al., 2011; Xin & Wipf, 2015). This involves solving

$$\max_{\mathbf{\Gamma}_i \in H^+ \forall i, \boldsymbol{W} \geq 0} \int p(\boldsymbol{Y}|\boldsymbol{X}; \lambda)p(\boldsymbol{X}; \{\mathbf{\Psi}_j\})d\boldsymbol{X}, \quad (13)$$

where H^+ denotes the set of positive semi-definite and symmetric $d \times d$ matrices. After a $-2\log$ transformation and application of a standard convolution-of-Gaussians integration (Tipping, 2001), solving (13) is equivalent to minimizing the cost function

$$\mathcal{L}(\{\mathbf{\Gamma}_i\}, \boldsymbol{W}) = \sum_j \boldsymbol{y}_j^\top\mathbf{\Sigma}_{y_j}^{-1}\boldsymbol{y}_j + \log\left|\mathbf{\Sigma}_{y_j}\right|, \quad (14)$$

where

$$\mathbf{\Sigma}_{y_j} = \sum_i w_{ij}\boldsymbol{A}_j\mathbf{\Gamma}_i\boldsymbol{A}_j^\top + \lambda\boldsymbol{I}. \quad (15)$$

The latter represents the covariance of $\boldsymbol{y}_j$ conditioned on $\{\mathbf{\Gamma}_i\}$ and $\boldsymbol{w}_j$.

3 Algorithm Derivation

To optimize $\mathcal{L}(\{\mathbf{\Gamma}_i\}, \boldsymbol{W})$ we may treat $\{\widetilde{\boldsymbol{X}}^{(i)}\}$ as hidden data and execute a straightforward EM procedure (Dempster et al., 1977) similar to that proposed in (Tipping, 2001). For the E-step we need only compute the posterior moments given by (11). For the M-step we must solve

$$\min_{\{\mathbf{\Gamma}_i\}, \boldsymbol{W}} \mathrm{E}\left[-\log p\left(\{\widetilde{\boldsymbol{X}}^{(i)}\}, \boldsymbol{Y}; \{\mathbf{\Gamma}_i\}, \boldsymbol{W}, \lambda\right)\right], \quad (16)$$

where the expectation is with respect to $p\left(\{\widetilde{\boldsymbol{X}}^{(i)}\}|\boldsymbol{Y}; \{\mathbf{\Gamma}_i'\}, \boldsymbol{W}', \lambda\right)$, which represents the posterior distribution obtained using moments parameterized with fixed values $\{\mathbf{\Psi}_j'\}$ and $\boldsymbol{W}'$ computed from the previous iteration. After a few algebraic manipulations, this is equivalent to solving

$$\min_{\{\mathbf{\Gamma}_i\}, \boldsymbol{W}} \sum_{i,j} \mathrm{tr}\left[\mathrm{E}\left[\widetilde{\boldsymbol{x}}_j^{(i)}(\widetilde{\boldsymbol{x}}_j^{(i)})^\top\right](w_{ij}\mathbf{\Gamma}_i)^{-1}\right] + \log|w_{ij}\mathbf{\Gamma}_i|, \quad (17)$$

where $\mathrm{E}\left[\widetilde{\boldsymbol{x}}_j^{(i)}(\widetilde{\boldsymbol{x}}_j^{(i)})^\top\right] = \boldsymbol{\mu}_j^{(i)}\left(\boldsymbol{\mu}_j^{(i)}\right)^\top + \boldsymbol{\Sigma}_j^{(i)}$. Unfortunately (17) has no closed-form solution. However, we can first optimize over $\{\boldsymbol{\Gamma}_i\}$ with $\boldsymbol{W}$ fixed, and then optimize over $\boldsymbol{W}$ with $\{\boldsymbol{\Gamma}_i\}$ fixed, both of which have closed-form solutions. Although these updates could be iterated until convergence, the EM algorithm does not actually require full completion of both E and M steps. In fact partial minimization, or incremental variants, are adequate to ensure cost function descent (Neal & Hinton, 1999).[5]

For the $\{\boldsymbol{\Gamma}_i\}$ update, we can solve for each $\boldsymbol{\Gamma}_i$ independently via

$$\boldsymbol{\Gamma}_i^* = \arg\min_{\boldsymbol{\Gamma}_i} \mathrm{tr}\left[\Theta_i \boldsymbol{\Gamma}_i^{-1}\right] + n\log|\boldsymbol{\Gamma}_i| \;=\; \tfrac{1}{n}\Theta_i \qquad (18)$$

where

$$\Theta_i = \sum_j \tfrac{1}{w_{ij}}\mathrm{tr}\left[\left(\boldsymbol{\mu}_j^{(i)}\left(\boldsymbol{\mu}_j^{(i)}\right)^\top + \boldsymbol{\Sigma}_j^{(i)}\right)\right]. \qquad (19)$$

Likewise for $\boldsymbol{W}$ we can solve independently for each element using

$$w_{ij}^* = \arg\min_{\boldsymbol{\Gamma}_i} \beta_{ij} w_{ij}^{-1} + d\log w_{ij} \;=\; \tfrac{1}{d}\beta_{ij}, \qquad (20)$$

where

$$\beta_{ij} = \mathrm{tr}\left[\left(\boldsymbol{\mu}_j^{(i)}\left(\boldsymbol{\mu}_j^{(i)}\right)^\top + \boldsymbol{\Sigma}_j^{(i)}\right)\boldsymbol{\Gamma}_i^{-1}\right]. \qquad (21)$$

To summarize then, we need only iterate (11), (18), and (20) to descend the objective function (14). With some attention to details, this can be accomplished with updates that are linear in n and m, the number of points and clusters respectively), and cubic in d (ambient space dimension).

A final point worth addressing is initialization. Assuming complete agnosticism regarding subspaces and labels, the selection $\boldsymbol{\Gamma}_i = \boldsymbol{I}$ and $w_{ij} = 1$ for all i and j seems like the most natural choice. However, we require some small degree of symmetry breaking randomness to initiate a non-degenerate descent. We simply use $w_{ij} \sim 1 + \mathrm{U}\left[0, 10^{-3}\right]$ for all initializations, although results are not sensitive to this choice.

4 Cost Function Analysis

While perhaps counterintuitive, the proposed objective function (14) has a number of desirable attributes that justify its usage for latent subspace clustering. As motivation for this claim, it is helpful to map the arguments of (14) to a criterion of subspace optimality. More formally, we say that $\{\{\boldsymbol{\Gamma}_i^*\}, \boldsymbol{W}^*\}$ is a *subspace optimal solution* iff

1. For all $i = 1, \ldots, m$, span$[\boldsymbol{\Gamma}_i^*]$ equals some true $\mathcal{S}_k$, and no two $\boldsymbol{\Gamma}_i^*$ span the same subspace.
2. For all $j = 1, \ldots, n$, $\|\boldsymbol{w}_j^*\|_0 = 1$, with nonzero element aligned with the correct subspace.

Such a solution guarantees that an accurate estimate of $\boldsymbol{X}$ can be obtained via (11), and that the correct subspace labels will be recovered. The remainder of this section will quantify how such solutions relate to minima of (14).

To begin, using duality arguments from (Wipf et al., 2011), there is a close association between global minima of (4) and (14) in terms of the recovered subspaces and labels. However, none of this is suggestive of why we might prefer dealing with the latter over say, brute force combinatorial optimization of the former. For this purpose we need to actually describe conditions whereby (14) is more likely to produce subspace optimal solutions without getting stuck at local optimal. While it is quite challenging to address this situation in sweeping terms for such a coupled, non-convex probabilistic model, we will nonetheless describe at least one scenario where bad local optimal can be fully eradicated, followed by more general conditions whereby optimal non-increasing solution paths exist.

For convenience, let $\{\Omega_k^*\}$ denote the true partitioning of $\boldsymbol{X}$, aligned with the presumed generative subspace labels. We then have the following:

Theorem 1. *Suppose that we have a data matrix* $\boldsymbol{X}$ *which follows the model from (1), we observe the affine measurements* $\boldsymbol{y}_j = \boldsymbol{A}_j\boldsymbol{x}_j$ *for all* j, *and that the true latent* $\boldsymbol{X}$ *is such that* $d_k = 1$ *for all subspaces. Furthermore assume that* $\{\boldsymbol{A}_j\}$ *satisfies* $p_j > 1$ *for all* j *and* $\cap_{j\in\Omega_k^*} null[\boldsymbol{A}_j] = \emptyset$ *for all* k. *Then any local or global minimizer* $\{\{\boldsymbol{\Gamma}_i^*\}, \boldsymbol{W}^*\}$ *of (14) in the limit* $\lambda \to 0$ *is subspace optimal.*

At least in low-noise/stylized conditions, this result specifies a relatively broad regime whereby no suboptimal minima exist, meaning any minimizer (local or global) will always return the correct clustering as well as a unique basis spanning each true subspace.[6] And this result is emblematic of a wider range of operating circumstances whereby subspace optimal solutions are closely aligned with minima of (14). Certainly our empirical evidence provided in Sections 5 and 6 suggests this to be the case.

Interestingly though, neither of the naive approaches discussed in Section 1 can satisfy something similar. In fact,

[5]While technically these updates are guaranteed to reduce or leave-unchanged the objective function until a fixed point is reached, to formally guarantee convergence of the EM algorithm to a local minima requires additional effort, such as the demonstration that the conditions of Zangwill's Global Convergence Theorem have been satisfied (Zangwill, 1969). We do not pursue a detailed theoretical investigation to this effect here, although it is possible to do so.

[6]In the context of affine rank minimization and a single subspace, i.e., $m = 1$, it has been shown that under similar conditions no bad local minima will exist with a probabilistic PCA-like model (Xin & Wipf, 2015); however, this is a much simpler problem and the same analysis/proof techniques do not apply.

under the stated conditions of Theorem 1, (4) can have numerous suboptimal local minima, while (6) can have both suboptimal local and global minima, both of which can return incorrect labels and cluster bases.

Likewise, if we replace the rank function with the nuclear norm in (5), then even with all other theorem specifications in place, it is still possible that we recover the wrong estimate for $\boldsymbol{X}$ such that no correct clustering is possible via any secondary step. As an example, it is a simple matter to design adversarial conditions on $\boldsymbol{A}_j$ via simple transformations such as $\boldsymbol{A}_j \rightarrow \boldsymbol{A}_j\boldsymbol{D}$, where $\boldsymbol{D}$ is a diagonal scaling matrix to which the nuclear norm solution will be highly sensitive. And as stated previously, we cannot negate the impact of $\boldsymbol{D}$ via normalization without destroying the low-rank assumption with which estimating $\boldsymbol{X}$ is predicated on to begin with. Moreover, it is also possible to have a full rank $\boldsymbol{X}$ consistent with the setting of Theorem 1 such that it is formally unidentifiable even with (5) unaltered.

Moving forward, it is considerably more difficult to guarantee that no bad local minima exist under broader conditions, e.g., when $d_k > 1$. However, we can still analyze non-increasing paths between a family of initializations (or intermediate points in some optimization trajectory) and subspace optimal solutions. This simplified analysis criteria yields the following:

Theorem 2. *Suppose $\sum_i w_{ij}\boldsymbol{\Gamma}_i = \alpha_j \boldsymbol{U}\boldsymbol{U}^\top$ for all j, where $\boldsymbol{U}$ represents any orthonormal basis spanning $\bigoplus_{k=1}^m S_k$ and each $\alpha_j > 0$ is a scalar weighting factor. Then in the limit $\lambda \rightarrow 0$, if each α_j is suitably large there exists a non-increasing path from this point to some subspace optimal solution $\{\{\boldsymbol{\Gamma}_i^*\}, \boldsymbol{W}^*\}$.*

Corollary 1. *In the simplified scenario when $\boldsymbol{A}_j = \boldsymbol{I}$ for all j (i.e., canonical subspace clustering where the latent $\boldsymbol{X} = \boldsymbol{Y}$ are now fully observable), Theorem 2 holds without any size restrictions on each $\alpha_j > 0$.*

Because we can always choose to initialize with $\boldsymbol{\Gamma}_i = \boldsymbol{I}$ for all i, or more generally $\boldsymbol{\Gamma}_i$ equal to some suitable $\boldsymbol{U}\boldsymbol{U}^\top$, then a byproduct of Theorem 2 is the insurance that a path exists from a computable point to the correct clustering that is devoid of local minima even when $\boldsymbol{W}$ is initialized arbitrarily. And this result can be generalized with additional effort to quantify a broader class of locations such that such paths to optimal solutions exist. Of course obviously a result of this type is still quite limited in that it does not guarantee that such a path can be found, or rule out the existence of saddle points along the way. But it is nonetheless another indicator of the appropriateness of (14) in addressing even basic subspace clustering problems for which it was not initially designed. And similar to previous arguments, neither of the naive approaches, i.e., solving either (4) or (6), can satisfy something similar.

5 Simulation Experiments

We now present illustrative synthetic experiments tailored to showcase generic abilities, with designs and dimensions inspired by (Soltanolkotabi & Candès, 2012; Yang et al., 2015).

5.1 Fully Observable Model

We begin by investigating the original subspace clustering problem where $\boldsymbol{Y} = \boldsymbol{X}$. In particular, we examine challenging conditions where there exists a significant degree of subspace overlap similar to an experimental design from (Soltanolkotabi & Candès, 2012). Data are generated as follows. Three subspaces of dimension $d_1 = d_2 = d_3 = 20$ are embedded in $\mathbb{R}^{25}$, each containing 50 data points. This is accomplished for each subspace by generating $\boldsymbol{X}_k = \boldsymbol{U}_k\boldsymbol{V}_k^\top$, where $\boldsymbol{U}_k \in \mathbb{R}^{25\times 20}$ and $\boldsymbol{V} \in \mathbb{R}^{50\times 20}$ have iid $\mathcal{N}(0,1)$ elements. With probability one the resulting $\boldsymbol{X}$ will be full rank with significantly overlapping subspace magisteria. We then normalize each column to have unit ℓ_2 norm, and apply the state-of-the-art ℓ_1-norm based subspace clustering mentioned in Section 1, denoted ℓ_1-SSC, to sort out subspace labels. This algorithm involves solving (2) with $\|\boldsymbol{Z}\|_1$ replacing $\|\boldsymbol{Z}\|_0$, forming the symmetric affinity matrix $|\hat{\boldsymbol{Z}}| + |\hat{\boldsymbol{Z}}^\top|$ using the estimated $\hat{\boldsymbol{Z}}$, followed by a separate spectral clustering step with knowledge of the true number of clusters m (Elhamifar & Vidal, 2013). For our algorithm we assign cluster labels based on the index of the largest value of each estimated $\boldsymbol{w}_j$ (typically though there is only a single entry significantly larger than zero when the clustering is successful); no spectral clustering heuristic is required.

We note however that by drawing the data using such iid Gaussian isotropic sources (as is typically done for experimental purposes), the data within each subspace will lack any significant structure or correlation, to which the ℓ_1 norm solution can be highly sensitive. Hence to deviate from the relatively easier, isotropic situation, we gradually experiment with increasing the degree of intra-subspace correlation by adding a rank-one component $\alpha\|\boldsymbol{U}_k\boldsymbol{V}_k^\top\|_2\boldsymbol{a}_k\boldsymbol{b}_k^\top$ to each subspace, where vectors $\boldsymbol{a}_k \in \mathbb{R}^{25\times 1}$ and $\boldsymbol{b}_k \in \mathbb{R}^{50\times 1}$ are also iid $N(0,1)$ and α is a non-negative scalar that weights the contribution.

Figure 1 displays the clustering errors (percentage of mislabeled points) for both ℓ_1-SSC and our method averaged over 10 trials. We observe that when the correlation parameter $\alpha = 0$, both methods perform well, but as soon as α begins increasing, the quality of ℓ_1-SSC solutions degrades significantly, unlike our algorithm which is stable across all values. Hence even when no latent affine structure or the twist is present (the fully observable case with $\boldsymbol{A}_j = \boldsymbol{I}$), minimizing (14) represents a principled objective function for subspace clustering.

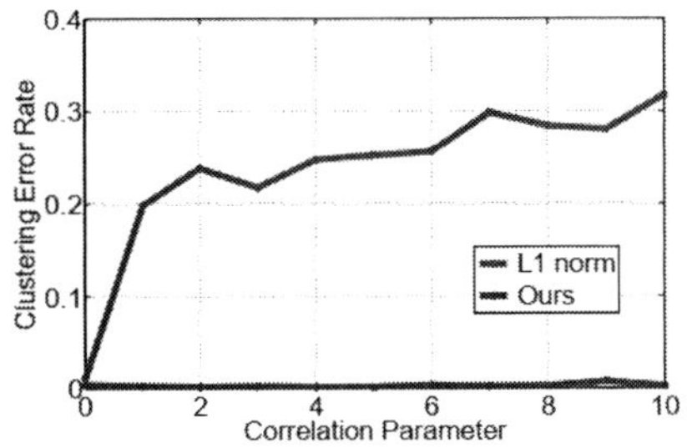

Figure 1: Comparisons using a fully-observable model as the within-subspace correlation is increased.

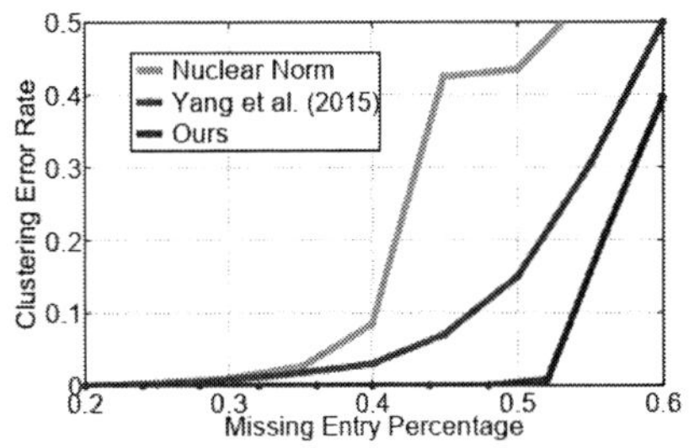

Figure 2: Comparisons using a partially-observable model as the number of missing entries is increased.

5.2 Missing Entries

Next we address the case were we have observed some $\boldsymbol{X}$ with a certain proportion of missing entries. As discussed in Section 1, this is equivalent to assuming that each $\boldsymbol{A}_j$ is a matrix of zeros with a single one per row. For this particular special case, (Yang et al., 2015) has proposed a modification of ℓ_1-SSC whereby missing entries are set to zero but partially compensated for using a special projection step.[7] Although this method cannot be extended to general $\{\boldsymbol{A}_j\}$, we can nonetheless evaluate our approach against this missing entry specialization. For this purpose, we select the most difficult clustering test from (Yang et al., 2015), whereby the latent $\boldsymbol{X}$ is full rank and the number of missing entries grows large.

Following (Yang et al., 2015), we generate $m = 5$ subspaces, each of dimension 5, embedded in $d = 25$ dimensional space. Next 50 points are drawn from each subspace using the same Gaussian factorization from above (and $\alpha = 0$). The fraction of missing entries is then gradually increased to test performance. Figure 2 displays the results, including a common baseline nuclear norm estimate of $\boldsymbol{X}$ followed by ℓ_1-SSC subspace clustering. Again we observe that, even without any spectral clustering step as used by others, our algorithm outperforms state-of-the-art existing approaches, including all variety of algorithms from (Yang et al., 2015) that were specifically designed for this problem.

5.3 General Affine Model

Finally, we consider our original motivating scenario where $\{\boldsymbol{A}_j\}$ can be arbitrary. To this end, we repeat the experiment from above, but with the binary sampling matrices replaced with elements of each $\boldsymbol{A}_j$ drawn iid from $\mathcal{N}(0, 1)$. We also fix the number of measurements per point to $p_j = 15$ for each j; other dimensions remain unchanged.

[7]Actually (Yang et al., 2015) presents multiple approaches for handling missing entries, including another method from (Candès et al., 2014); however, we compare against the best performing variant among all of these.

Figure 3 explores the ability to recover the true latent $\boldsymbol{X}$ compared to the minimum nuclear norm solution, which represents the most viable existing alternative. We also tried minimizing (6); however, the results where quite poor (much worse than the nuclear norm solution) because of unavoidable convergence to local minima.

While the true number of clusters is $m = 5$, we vary the number of clusters assumed by our algorithm from $\hat{m} = 1, \ldots, 20$ and record the normalized MSE given by $\langle \|\boldsymbol{X} - \hat{\boldsymbol{X}}\|_{\mathcal{F}}^2 / \|\boldsymbol{X}\|_{\mathcal{F}}^2 \rangle$ averaged over 10 trials. Moreover, if we successfully recover $\boldsymbol{X}$ with $\hat{m} \neq m$, it is trivial to either fuse redundant clusters or split merged clusters using simple existing subspace clustering approaches to obtain labels if required.

Note that it is possible to exactly recover $\boldsymbol{X}$ with $\hat{m} \neq m$, provided $\hat{m}$ is sufficiently large such that $\boldsymbol{X}$ is identifiable. More specifically, to even have a chance of recovery for any possible algorithm, it must be the case that for all clusters k, the number of degrees-of-freedom in each associated low rank $\boldsymbol{X}_k$ (the points within cluster k) is less than the number of measurements of $\boldsymbol{X}_k$. For example, in the present case each $\boldsymbol{X}_k \in \mathbb{R}^{25 \times 50}$ has $5 \times (25 + 50) - 5^2 = 350$ degrees-of-freedom, and we have $\sum_{j \in \Omega_k} p_j = 15 \times 50 = 750$ measurements per subspace to work with (more than double the d.o.f.), which should be sufficient if $\hat{m} = 5$. However, when $\hat{m} < 5$, then two or more subspaces must be merged for estimation purposes leading to at least one $5 + 5 = 10$ dimensional subspace with $50 + 50 = 100$ points, and $10 \times (25 + 100) - 10^2 = 1150$ degrees-of-freedom, but only $15 \times 100 = 1500$ measurements. Even if we knew the true subspace labels, recovering $\boldsymbol{X}$ would still then be extremely challenging given how close the number of measurements are to the degrees-of-freedom.

But of course we still need to learn the labels as well, compounding the difficulty dramatically such that success by any possible algorithm is suspect. Therefore we should expect failure with $\hat{m} < 5$ on theoretical grounds, and indeed, from Figure 3 the error increases monotonically as $\hat{m}$ is decreased below 5. In contrast, for $\hat{m} > 5$, we observe that over-segmentation has minimal effect in disrupting the estimation of $\boldsymbol{X}$, and our algorithm has dramatically lower MSE than the nuclear norm solution; it only actually begins to rise appreciably for $\hat{m} > 17$. At this point presumably the large degree of superfluous over-segmentation may increase the risk of local minima as the parameter space becomes unnecessarily large.

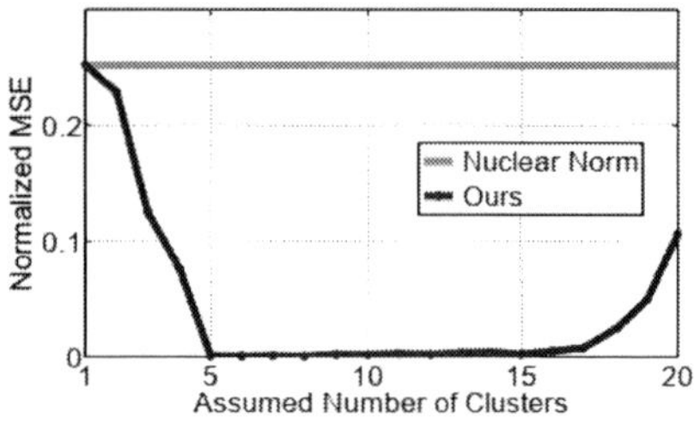

Figure 3: Comparisons using the general affine model as the number of assumed clusters is varied. Minimizing (6) led to a normalized MSE above 1.0 for all cases and initializations we tried (not shown).

6 Application Example: BRDF Estimation

One interesting application of the proposed method is surface reflectance reconstruction. Here surface reflectance simply refers to how a given surface reflects light. Moreover, if we have access to an accurate estimate, then we can compute exactly how a given object and material will appear under any lighting condition and viewing direction, which is extremely useful in many computer vision and graphics domains. From a technical standpoint, surface reflectance properties can be quantified by a spatially varying bi-directional reflectance distribution function (BRDF), which encodes the ratio between the *incoming* radiance from lighting direction θ_{in} and the *outgoing* radiance to the viewing direction θ_{out}, at each surface point j on some object or scene of interest. Although the BRDF represents an inherent property of the underlying materials, it is quite difficult to acquire since what we actually perceive from an object is jointly dependent on lighting conditions, viewing direction, and the BRDF itself.

More concretely, the observed outgoing radiance $y_j(\theta_{out})$ at direction θ_{out} can be expressed as the product of the surface BRDF $\rho_j(\theta_{out}, \theta_{in})$ at point j and the incoming radiance $r(\theta_{in})$ from direction θ_{in} integrated over all lighting directions $\mathcal{D}$, giving

$$y_j(\theta_{out}) = \int_{\mathcal{D}} \rho_j(\theta_{out}, \theta_{in}) r(\theta_{in}) d\theta_{in}. \quad (22)$$

Moreover, the surface reflectance of each surface pixel can be expressed, to close approximation, as a linear combination of basis functions via

$$\rho_j(\theta_{out}, \theta_{in}) = \sum_{i=1}^{21} x_{ij} \rho_i(\theta_{out}, \theta_{in}), \quad (23)$$

where $\boldsymbol{x}_j = [x_{1j}, \ldots, x_{21j}]^\top$ are weights and each $\rho_i(\theta_{out}, \theta_{in})$ represents a Cook-Torrance BRDF basis function for $i \in \{1, \ldots, 20\}$ and a Lambertian reflectance function for $i = 21$ (Lawrence et al., 2006; Dong et al., 2010; Chen et al., 2014). Combining with (22) this yields

$$y_j(\theta_{out}) = \sum_{i=1}^{21} x_{ij} \int_{\mathcal{D}} \rho_i(\theta_{out}, \theta_{in}) r(\theta_{in}) d\theta_{in}. \quad (24)$$

With known lighting conditions and incoming radiance $r(\theta_{in})$, and the fixed known basis $\rho_i(\theta_{out}, \theta_{in})$, the integral components of (24) can be pre-computed. Additionally, measurements from multiple viewing directions can be packed into the vector $\boldsymbol{y}_j = [y_j(\theta_{out_1}), \ldots, y_j(\theta_{out_p})]^\top$ for each point j, and the corresponding integrals of the basis function can also be packed similarly in to a matrix $\boldsymbol{A}_j$ with $(A_j)_{ti} = \int_{\mathcal{D}} \rho_i(\theta_{out_t}, \theta_{in}) r(\theta_{in}) d\theta_{in}$, producing the affine model $\boldsymbol{y}_j = \boldsymbol{A}_j \boldsymbol{x}_j$, which is of course equivalent to (3). Note that both the viewing and lighting directions are defined in local coordinates of the surface point j, and therefore the transformation $\boldsymbol{A}_j$ will necessarily change with pixel position.

The estimation goal is to recover each latent weight vector $\boldsymbol{x}_j$ for all j, from which we can compute the BRDF using (23). Here we make the reasonable assumption that at any given location, the number of unknown materials is limited to a small number, consistent with many real-world objects (in fact, it is quite common that only a single material may be present in many object regions). Moreover, given that the BRDF of each unknown base material can be closely approximated using (23) with a fixed weight vector for each material, it follows that the corresponding unknown weights $\boldsymbol{x}_j$ will each lie in a union of low-dimensional subspaces, conforming with the proposed subspace clustering model (Lawrence et al., 2006; Dong et al., 2010; Chen et al., 2014).

We test our algorithm as follows. Data acquisition is accomplished using physically-based path-tracing (Wenzel, 2010; Pharr & Humphreys, 2010), which accurately reproduces the physical capturing process. Importantly, this gains us access to the ground-truth such that quantitative comparisons are possible. We prepare two datasets to evaluate the performance of the proposed algorithm, one *checker* dataset, which consists of four different materials positioned in a checker-board pattern, and one *blend* dataset, that has four representative materials and each surface point represents a blending between two of the four possible materials. In both cases we mapped the materials onto a sphere with known geometry comprised of a total of $n = 104074$ points. The lighting was produced using the *Grace Cathedral* environment map (Debevec & Malik, 1997). Finally, we capture images of the object under 5 different view directions, resulting in 5 observations per visible surface point for a total of $5 \times n = 520370$ measurements. We compare our algorithm against a similar frame-

Figure 4: Spatially-varying BRDF reconstruction results. *Left column:* Ground truth reference under novel environmental lighting. *Middle column:* Rendering using our model. *Right column:* Rendering using the nuclear norm. Normalized MSE and difference maps are also included as an insert for both algorithms. Rendering errors best viewed by zooming.

work built upon the nuclear norm (Chen et al., 2014).

Figure 4 compares the renderings based on the reconstructed BRDFs under novel environmental lighting conditions (not those used to actually learn the BRDFs). We observe that with only 5 measurements per surface point, we can accurately reconstruct the BRDF without producing any visual artifacts. On the contrary, when using the nuclear norm Chen et al. (2014), the limited measurements cannot produce an accurate reconstruction and visual artifacts are clearly evident (zoom in for better viewing). The problem is compounded by the fact that the measurement matrices $\{\boldsymbol{A}_j\}$ are highly ill-conditioned as indicated by Figure 5, which displays the singular values of each $\boldsymbol{A}_j$ averaged across all j as compared to those from ideal matrices sampled iid from $\mathcal{N}(0, 1)$. The nuclear norm is quite sensitive to this distinction which likely accounts, at least in part, for its poor performance. Note that accurate reconstruction from few measurements is a crucial ingredient of practical, inexpensive systems because it implies that fewer cameras are needed and/or a shorter acquisition time.

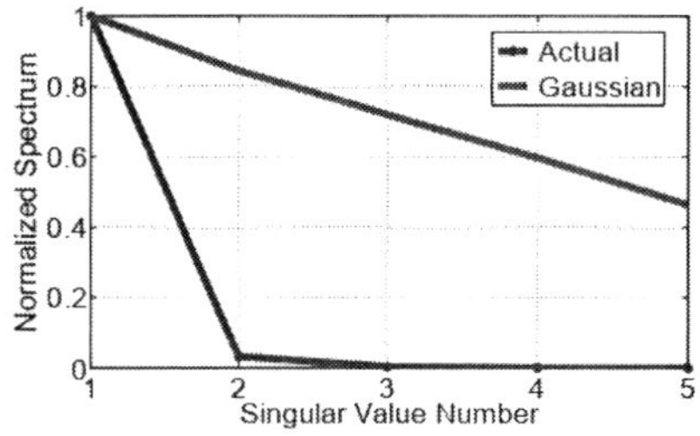

Figure 5: Singular values averaged across all $\boldsymbol{A}_j$ used in the BRDF estimation experiments. Ideal Gaussian data of equivalent dimensions is included for comparison. A fast singular value decay can be highly disruptive to nuclear-norm-based recovery algorithms.

7 Conclusions

In this paper we have introduced a practically-relevant, affine twist into the standard subspace clustering pipeline. We then derived a new, Bayesian-inspired algorithm that accounts for this added confound when necessary, while still defaulting to a principled state-of-the-art approach when deployed on existing segmentation problems with fully observable data, or when missing entries are present. Our framework, which does not require the typical spectral clustering post-processing step, is supported both by theoretical arguments and a large-scale, real-world application involving BRDF estimation and subsequent rendering.

References

Candès, E. and Recht, B. Exact matrix completion via convex optimization. *Found. of Comput. Math.*, 9, 2008.

Candès, E., Mackey, L., and Soltanolkotabi, M. From robust subspace clustering to full-rank matrix completion. *Extended Abstract*, 2014.

Chen, G., Dong, Y., Peers, P., Zhang, J., and Tong, X. Reflectance scanning: Estimating shading frame and BRDF with generalized linear light sources. *ACM Trans. Graphics*, 33(4), 2014.

Debevec, P.E. and Malik, J. Recovering high dynamic range radiance maps from photographs. In *SIGGRAPH*, 1997.

Dempster, A.P., Laird, N.M., and Rubin, D.B. Maximum likelihood from incomplete data via the EM algorithm. *J. Royal Statistical Society, Series B (Methodological)*, 39(1):1–38, 1977.

Dong, Y., Wang, J., Tong, X., Snyder, J., Lan, Y., Ben-Ezra, M., and Guo, B. Manifold bootstrapping for SVBRDF capture. *ACM Trans. Graphics*, 29(4), 2010.

Elhamifar, E. and Vidal, R. Sparse subspace clustering: Algorithm, theory, and applications. *IEEE Trans. Pattern Analysis and Machine Intelligence*, 35(11), 2013.

Eriksson, B., Balzano, L., and Nowak, R. High-rank matrix completion. *International Conference on Artificial Intelligence and Statistics*, 2012.

Feng, J., Lin, Z., Xu, H., and Yan, S. Robust subspace segmentation with block-diagonal prior. *IEEE International Conference on Computer Vision and Pattern Recognition*, 2014.

Gruber, A. and Weiss, Y. Multibody factorization with uncertainty and missing data using the em algorithm. *IEEE International Conference on Computer Vision and Pattern Recognition*, 2004.

Jalali, A., Chen, Y., Sanghavi, S., and Xu, H. Clustering partially observed graphs via convex optimization. *International Conference on Machine Learning*, 2011.

Lawrence, J., Ben-Artzi, A., DeCoro, C., Matusik, W., Pfister, H., Ramamoorthi, R., and Rusinkiewicz, S. Inverse shade trees for non-parametric material representation and editing. *ACM Trans. Graphics*, 25(3), 2006.

Liu, G., Lin, Z., Yan, S., Sun, J., Yu, Y., and Ma, Y. Robust recovery of subspace structures by low-rank representation. *IEEE Trans. Pattern Analysis and Machine Intelligence*, 35(1), 2013.

Lu, C.Y., Min, H., Zhao, Z.Q., Zhu, L., Huang, D.S., and Yan, S. Robust and efficient subspace segmentation via least squares regression. *European Conference on Computer Vision*, 2012.

Neal, R.M. and Hinton, G.E. A view of the EM algorithm that justifies incremental, sparse, and other variants. *Learning in Graphical Models*, 1999.

Patel, V.M., Nguyen, H.V., and Vidal, R. Latent space sparse subspace clustering. *International Conference on Computer Vision*, 2013.

Pharr, M. and Humphreys, G. *Physically Based Rendering: From Theory To Implementation.* Morgan Kaufmann Publishers Inc., San Francisco, CA, USA, 2nd edition, 2010.

Rao, S., Tron, R., Vidal, R., and Ma, Y. Motion segmentation in the presence of outlying, incomplete, or corrupted trajectories. *IEEE Trans. Pattern Analysis and Machine Intelligence*, 32(10), 2010.

Soltanolkotabi, M. and Candès, E. A geometric analysis of subspace clustering with outliers. *Annals of Statistics*, 40(4), 2012.

Tipping, M.E. Sparse Bayesian learning and the relevance vector machine. *Journal of Machine Learning Research*, 1, 2001.

Tipping, M.E. and Bishop, C.M. Mixtures of probabilistic principal component analysers. *Neural Computation*, 11 (2), 1999.

Wang, Y., Wang, Y.X., and Singh, A. A deterministic analysis of noisy sparse subspace clustering for dimensionality-reduced data. *International Conference on Machine Learning*, 2015a.

Wang, Y., Wipf, D., Ling, Q., Chen, W., and Wassell, I. Multi-task learning for subspace segmentation. *International Conference on Machine Learning*, 2015b.

Wenzel, J. Mitsuba renderer, 2010. http://www.mitsuba-renderer.org.

Wipf, D.P., Rao, B.D., and Nagarajan, S. Latent variable Bayesian models for promoting sparsity. *IEEE Trans. Information Theory*, 57(9), 2011.

Xin, B. and Wipf, D.P. Pushing the limits of affine rank minimization by adapting probabilistic PCA. *International Conference on Machine Learning*, 2015.

Yang, C., Robinson, D., and Vidal, R. Sparse subspace clustering with missing entries. *International Conference on Machine Learning*, 2015.

Zangwill, W.I. *Nonlinear Programming: A Unified Approach.* Prentice Hall, New Jersey, 1969.

Zhang, A., Fawaz, N., Ioannidis, S., and Montanari, A. Guess who rated this movie: Identifying users through subspace clustering. *International Conference on Uncertainty in Artificial Intelligence*, 2012.

Bayesian Estimators As Voting Rules

Lirong Xia
Rensselaer Polytechnic Institute
Troy, NY, USA
xial@cs.rpi.edu

Abstract

We investigate the fairness of Bayesian estimators (BEs) by viewing them as (irresolute) voting rules and evaluating them by satisfaction of desirable social choice axioms. We characterize the class of BEs that satisfy *neutrality* by the class of BEs with neutral structures. We prove that a BE with a neutral structure is a minimax rule if it further satisfies *parameter connectivity*. We prove that no BE satisfies *strict Condorcet criterion*. We also propose three new BEs of natural frameworks and investigate their computational complexity and satisfaction of *monotonicity* and *Condorcet criterion*.

1 INTRODUCTION

Bayesian estimators have been widely applied in rank aggregation. For example, IMDb uses Bayesian estimators to aggregate users' votes to create the top-250 movie list [2]. However, users have complaint that such mechanisms are "unfair" because the rank of a seemingly good film is not high [1]. While this particular complaint may not be hard to address, ideally we would like to use a fair rank aggregation method with high statistical efficiency. This raises the following important questions.

Q1. How can we measure fairness in rank aggregation?

Q2. How can we design fair Bayesian estimators?

Same questions arise in many other rank aggregation situations, especially those where the voting agents are human beings. For example, in political domains, important public decisions are made by aggregating citizens' votes; in low-stakes voting scenarios, friends vote to decide the place for dinner; in crowdsourcing, online workers' noisy answers are aggregated to estimate the correct answer [22].

Q1 has been partially answered by social choice theory. Following Arrow's celebrated impossibility theorem [4], various kinds of measures on fairness, called *axioms*, have been formulated and used to evaluate voting rules in political elections. For example, the *anonymity* axiom states that the voting rule is insensitive to permutations over agents' votes, which can be seen as fairness for voters; *neutrality* is a fairness condition for the alternatives; and *Condorcet criterion* (informally) states that an obviously socially strong alternative should win, which is similar in spirit to the complaint by the IMDb user. The axiomatic approach has gone beyond political elections to e.g. ranking systems [3], recommender systems [25], and community detection [9].

While there has been a growing literature on statistical properties of commonly studied voting rules, there is little work in the reverse direction, i.e. studying the satisfaction of social choice axioms for commonly studied statistical estimators, especially Bayesian estimators. Recently Azari Soufiani et al. [7] proposed a statistical decision-theoretic framework (framework for short) to obtain new voting rules as Bayesian estimators, and investigated the satisfaction of some axioms for two Bayesian estimators. To the best of our knowledge, there is no general characterizations of social choice axioms for Bayesian estimators.

Our Contributions. We study the satisfaction of axioms for Bayesian estimators (BEs) under the framework proposed by Azari Soufiani et al. [7]. We answer Q2 for two well-studied axioms: *neutrality* and *strict Condorcet criterion*. We characterize BEs that satisfy neutrality by the BEs of *neutral* frameworks. Therefore, to design neutral BEs we only need to focus on neutral frameworks. We also prove that no BE satisfies strict Condorcet criterion.

In addition, we prove that if a neutral framework satisfies *parameter connectivity*, then its BE is a minimax rule, which means that the BE is optimal w.r.t. the worst-case frequentist expected loss. We believe that this result is of independent interest.

We also analyze the satisfaction of *Condorcet criterion*, *monotonicity*, and computational complexity for four classes of BEs. Each BE in each class is identified by a

<table>
<tr><td></td><td>Anonymity</td><td>Strict Condorcet</td><td>Neutrality</td><td>Minimax</td><td>Condorcet</td><td>Monotonicity</td><td>Comp.</td></tr>
<tr><td>BEs</td><td rowspan="5">Y
(trivial)</td><td rowspan="5">N
(Thm. 4)</td><td>Y/N</td><td>Y/N</td><td>Y/N</td><td>Y/N</td><td>P/NP-hard</td></tr>
<tr><td>$f^{\text{Top}}_{\text{Ma},\varphi}$</td><td rowspan="4">Y
(Thm. 2)</td><td rowspan="4">Y
(Thm. 1)</td><td>Y iff $\frac{\varphi(1-\varphi^{m-1})}{1-\varphi} \leq 1$
(Thm. 5)</td><td>Y [5]</td><td>NP-hard [25]</td></tr>
<tr><td>$f^{\text{Borda}}_{\text{Co},\varphi}$</td><td>Y iff $\varphi \leq \frac{1}{m-1}$
(Thm. 7)</td><td>Y
(Prop. 1)</td><td>P
(Thm. 6)</td></tr>
<tr><td>$f^{1}_{\text{Pair},\varphi}$</td><td>Y iff $\varphi \leq \frac{1}{m-1}$
(Thm. 10)</td><td rowspan="2">Y
(Prop. 2)</td><td rowspan="2">P
(Thm. 9)</td></tr>
<tr><td>$f^{2}_{\text{Pair},\varphi}$</td><td>N
(Thm. 10)</td></tr>
</table>

Table 1: Main results. m is the number of alternatives.

dispersion value $0 < \varphi < 1$. The first class has been studied [30, 27, 7] while the remaining three classes are new. The four classes are (1) $f^{\text{Top}}_{\text{Ma},\varphi}$ is the BE of Mallows' model with the top loss function. Condorcet criterion has been studied for $f^{\text{Top}}_{\text{Ma},\varphi}$ for $\varphi > \frac{1}{\sqrt{2}}$ but the remaining cases are open [7][1]. (2) $f^{\text{Borda}}_{\text{Co},\varphi}$ is the BE of Condorcet's model with the Borda loss function. (3) $f^{1}_{\text{Pair},\varphi}$ and (4) $f^{2}_{\text{Pair},\varphi}$ are the BEs of a new model with different loss functions, where a parameter can be interpreted as the "strongest pairwise comparison". Our results are summarized in Table 1.

The second row in Table 1 are results for general BEs. A "Y/N" means that some Bayesian estimators satisfy the axiom and some do not. For $f^{\text{Top}}_{\text{Ma},\varphi}$, we prove a dichotomy theorem on its satisfaction of Condorcet criterion: it satisfies the Condorcet criterion if and only if $\frac{\varphi(1-\varphi^{m-1})}{1-\varphi} \leq 1$, where m is the number of alternatives (Theorem 5). We also proved similar dichotomy theorems for $f^{\text{Borda}}_{\text{Co},\varphi}$ and $f^{1}_{\text{Pair},\varphi}$, where the threshold is $\frac{1}{m-1}$ (Theorem 7 and 10). We would like to highlight two new classes of BEs: $f^{\text{Borda}}_{\text{Co},\varphi}$ and $f^{1}_{\text{Pair},\varphi}$, because they can satisfy all axioms studied in this paper (except strict Condorcet criterion, which is not satisfied by any BE) and can be computed in polynomial time.

In addition to satisfaction of axioms, we also study the limiting cases of the three new BEs as $\varphi \to 0$ and $\varphi \to 1$. While all classes converge to refinements of the Borda rule as $\varphi \to 1$, they converge to refinements of different rules as $\varphi \to 0$. Interestingly, $f^{\text{Borda}}_{\text{Co},\varphi}$ converges to a refinement of $\text{Copeland}_{0.5}$ (Theorem 8) and for any $\varphi \leq \frac{1}{m-1}$, $f^{1}_{\text{Pair},\varphi}$ is a refinement of maximin (Theorem 11).

Related Work and Discussions. As discussed above our theorems on neutrality and strict Condorcet criterion answer Q2 for the two axioms. We are not aware of other general results on satisfaction of axioms for Bayesian estimators. In particular, Azari Soufiani et al. [7] studied the satisfaction of some axioms for two classes of BEs but did not obtain general results for BEs.

Most previous work at the intersection of social choice and statistics focused on computational aspects of the *maximum likelihood estimators (MLEs)* of various ranking models [14, 10, 15, 17, 29, 20, 24, 27, 5, 6, 16, 19]. The focuses of our work are different. We focus on Bayesian estimators, which are more general than MLEs, and we focus on the satisfaction of axioms rather than computation.

Minimax rules for various statistical models with continuous parameter spaces have been characterized by Berger [8]. Choirat and Seri [12] provided a sufficient condition on discrete-parameter models for MLEs to be minimax. In the social choice context, Caragiannis et al. [11] proved that the uniformly randomized MLE has the least sample complexity w.r.t. Mallows' model, which is equivalent to minimaxity. Our minimaxity proof can be seen as an application of techniques by Berger [8] to social choice frameworks. As we will see in Corollary 1, our results can be easily applied to Mallows' model and other models.

Our work is also related to statistical justification of commonly studied voting rules. Conitzer and Sandholm [14] studied whether some commonly studied voting rules can be rationalized as MLEs of some statistical models. They showed that if a voting rule does not satisfy *consistency*, then it cannot be an MLE. Pivato [26] further investigated voting rules that can be viewed as MLEs, maximum a posteriori estimators, and Bayesian estimators. Our impossibility theorem on strict Condorcet criterion can be used to prove that a voting rule *cannot* be justified a Bayesian estimator. In Corollary 2, we show that a number of voting rules including Copeland_1 and maximin are not Bayesian estimators. On the other hand, we prove that as $\varphi \to 0$, $f^{\text{Borda}}_{\text{Co},\varphi}$ converges to a refinement of $\text{Copeland}_{0.5}$ (Theorem 8), and for all for any $\varphi < \frac{1}{m-1}$, $f^{1}_{\text{Pair},\varphi}$ is a refinement of maximin (Theorem 11). Therefore, $f^{1}_{\text{Pair},\varphi}$ for $\varphi < \frac{1}{m-1}$ are desirable refinements of maximin because they can be justified as BEs. Previously it was only known that a refinement of Kemeny is a BE [27] and a refinement of Tideman's rule is a BE [16].

[1]The original paper has a typo on the direction of the inequality.

2 PRELIMINARIES

Let $\mathcal{A} = \{a_1, \ldots, a_m\}$ denote a set of m *alternatives* and let $\mathcal{L}(\mathcal{A})$ denote the set of all linear orders over $\mathcal{A}$. Let n denote the number of agents. Each agent's vote is a linear order in $\mathcal{L}(\mathcal{A})$. The collection P of all agents' votes is called a *profile*. An *irresolute voting rule* r maps each profile to a non-empty set of winning alternatives. That is, $r : \bigcup_{n=1}^{\infty} \mathcal{L}(\mathcal{A})^n \to (2^{\mathcal{A}} \setminus \{\emptyset\})$.

For example, an irresolute *positional scoring rule* is characterized by a scoring vector $\vec{s} = (s_1, \ldots, s_m)$ with $s_1 \geq s_2 \geq \cdots \geq s_m$. For any alternative a and any linear order V, we let $\vec{s}(V, a) = s_j$, where j is the rank of a in V. Given a profile P, an irresolute positional scoring rule chooses all alternatives a with maximum $\sum_{V \in P} \vec{s}(V, a)$, where P is viewed as a multi-set of votes. The Borda rule is a positional scoring rule with $\vec{s} = (m-1, m-2, \ldots, 1)$.

For any profile P and any pair of alternatives a, b, we let $P(a \succ b)$ denote the number of votes in P where a is preferred to b. The *weighted majority graph* of P, denoted by WMG(P) is a directed weighted graph where the weight $w_P(a, b)$ on any edge $a \to b$ is $w_P(a, b) = P(a \succ b) - P(b \succ a)$. Clearly $w_P(a, b) = -w_P(b, a)$.

Given $0 \leq \alpha \leq 1$, the Copeland$_\alpha$ score of an alternative a in a profile P is the number of alternatives beaten by a in head-to-head competitions plus α times the alternatives tied with a. Copeland$_\alpha$ chooses all alternatives with the maximum Copeland$_\alpha$ score as the winners. The *maximin* rule chooses all alternatives a with the maximum *min-score*. The min-score of a is $\min_b w_P(a, b)$.

We will focus on the following axioms in this paper. An irresolute r satisfies

• *anonymity*, if r is insensitive to permutations over agents;

• *neutrality*, if r is insensitive to permutations over alternatives;

• *monotonicity*, if for any P, any $a \in r(P)$, and any P' that is obtained from P by only raising the positions of a, we have $a \in r(P')$;

• *Condorcet criterion*, if for any profile P, whenever a *Condorcet winner* a exists, it must be the unique winner. That is, $r(P) = \{a\}$. A Condorcet winner is an alternative that beats all other alternatives in their head-to-head competitions;

• *strict Condorcet criterion [18]*, if for any profile P, whenever the set of *weak Condorcet winners* is non-empty, it must be the output of r. A weak Condorcet winner is an alternative that never loses to any other alternative in their head-to-head competition.

Azari Soufiani et al. [7] defined a *statistical decision-theoretic framework for social choice* (*framework* for short) to be a tuple $\mathcal{F} = (\mathcal{M}_{\mathcal{A}}, \mathcal{D}, L)$, where $\mathcal{A}$ is the set of alternatives, $\mathcal{M}_{\mathcal{A}} = (\Theta, \vec{\pi})$ is a parametric ranking model, $\mathcal{D}$ is the decision space, and $L : \Theta \times \mathcal{D} \to \mathbb{R}$ is a loss function. $\mathcal{M}_{\mathcal{A}} = (\Theta, \vec{\pi})$ has two parts: a *parameter space* Θ and a set of probability distributions $\vec{\pi} = \{\pi_\theta : \theta \in \Theta\}$ over $\mathcal{L}(\mathcal{A})$. Agents' votes are generated i.i.d. according to $\mathcal{M}_{\mathcal{A}}$, which means that the sample space is $\mathcal{L}(\mathcal{A})^n$ and is omitted for simplicity. In this paper we focus on frameworks with finite parameter spaces and finite decision spaces.

We now recall two popular parametric ranking models. For any pair of linear orders V, W in $\mathcal{L}(\mathcal{A})$, let $\text{Kd}(V, W)$ denote the *Kendall-tau distance* between V and W, which is the total number of pairwise disagreements between V and W.

Definition 1 (Mallows' model with fixed dispersion [21]). *Given* $0 < \varphi < 1$, *the* Mallows model with fixed dispersion φ *is denoted by* $\mathcal{M}_{Ma,\varphi} = (\mathcal{L}(\mathcal{A}), \vec{\pi})$, *where the parameter space is* $\mathcal{L}(\mathcal{A})$ *and for any* $V, W \in \mathcal{L}(\mathcal{A})$, $\pi_W(V) = \frac{1}{Z}\varphi^{\text{Kd}(V,W)}$, *where Z is the normalization factor with* $Z = \sum_{V \in \mathcal{L}(\mathcal{A})} \varphi^{\text{Kd}(V,W)}$.

Let $\mathcal{B}(\mathcal{A})$ denote the set of all irreflexive, antisymmetric, and total binary relations over $\mathcal{A}$. We have $\mathcal{L}(\mathcal{A}) \subseteq \mathcal{B}(\mathcal{A})$ and the Kendall-tau distance can be easily extended to $\mathcal{B}(\mathcal{A})$ by counting the number of pairwise disagreements.

Definition 2 (Condorcet's model [13, 30]). *Given* $0 < \varphi < 1$, *the* Condorcet model *is denoted by* $\mathcal{M}_{Co,\varphi} = (\mathcal{B}(\mathcal{A}), \vec{\pi})$, *where the parameter space is* $\mathcal{B}(\mathcal{A})$ *and for any* $W \in \mathcal{B}(\mathcal{A})$ *and* $V \in \mathcal{L}(\mathcal{A})$, $\pi_W(V) = \frac{1}{Z}\varphi^{\text{Kd}(V,W)}$, *where Z is the normalization factor.*

Next, we give three examples of loss functions. When $\Theta = \mathcal{D}$, the 0-1 *loss function*, denoted by $L_{0\text{-}1}(\theta, d)$, outputs 0 if $\theta = d$, otherwise it outputs 1. When $\mathcal{D} = \mathcal{A}$ and Θ is $\mathcal{L}(\mathcal{A})$ or $\mathcal{B}(\mathcal{A})$, the *top loss function*, denoted by $L_{\text{top}}(\theta, d)$, outputs 0 if for all other alternatives $c \in \mathcal{A}$, $d \succ c$ in θ, otherwise it outputs 1. The *Borda loss function*, denoted by $L_{\text{Borda}}(\theta, d)$, outputs the number of alternatives that are preferred to d in θ, that is, $L_{\text{Borda}}(\theta, d) = \#\{c \in \mathcal{A} : c \succ_\theta d\}$. All loss functions can be naturally generalized to evaluate a subset D of $\mathcal{D}$ by computing the average loss of the decisions in D. More precisely, for any $D \subseteq \mathcal{D}$ and any $\theta \in \Theta$, we let $L(\theta, D) = \sum_{d \in D} L(\theta, d)/|D|$.

Given a framework $\mathcal{F}$, the *Bayesian expected loss* of $d \in \mathcal{D}$ given a profile P is $\text{EL}_{\mathcal{F}}(d|P) = \sum_{\theta \in \Theta} \Pr(\theta|P) L(\theta, d)$. The subscript $\mathcal{F}$ is often omitted without introducing confusions. In this paper we focus on the uniform prior. The *Bayesian estimator* of $\mathcal{F}$, denoted by $\text{BE}_{\mathcal{F}}$, takes a profile P as input and outputs all decisions with minimum expected Bayesian loss. That is, $\text{BE}_{\mathcal{F}}(P) = \arg\min_{d \in \mathcal{D}} \text{EL}(d|P)$.

Let $f^{\text{Top}}_{\text{Ma},\varphi}$ denote the Bayesian estimator of the framework $(\mathcal{M}_{\text{Ma},\varphi}, L_{\text{top}})$. It was proved by Azari Soufiani et al. [7] that $f^{\text{Top}}_{\text{Ma},\varphi}$ satisfy anonymity, neutrality, monotonicity, but fails to satisfy the Condorcet criterion for some φ. Let $f^{\text{Borda}}_{\text{Co},\varphi}$ denote the Bayesian estimator of the framework $(\mathcal{M}_{\text{Co},\varphi}, L_{\text{Borda}})$. We will study the satisfaction of axioms for $f^{\text{Borda}}_{\text{Co},\varphi}$.

Given a framework $\mathcal{F}$, a parameter $\theta \in \Theta$, $n \in \mathbb{N}$, and a voting rule r, the *frequentist loss* $\text{FL}_n(\theta, r)$ is the expected loss of the output of r against θ for randomly generated profiles of n votes. More precisely,

$$\text{FL}_n(\theta, r) = \sum_{P_n \in \mathcal{L}(\mathcal{A})^n} \pi_\theta(P_n) L(\theta, r(P_n))$$

Definition 3 ([8]). *Given a framework* $\mathcal{F} = (\mathcal{M}_\mathcal{A}, \mathcal{D}, L)$, *a voting rule* r *is* minimax, *if* $r \in \arg\min_{r^*} \max_{\theta \in \Theta} FL_n(\theta, r^*)$.

That is, a minimax rule minimizes the worst-case frequentist loss among all deterministic or randomized rules. Minimaxity is an important statistical criteria for decision functions—a minimax rule is the most robust rule against the adversarial nature who controls the true state of the world (the parameter). A minimax rule can be seen as having the minimum *sample complexity* [11].

3 NEUTRAL FRAMEWORKS AND MINIMAXITY

We first define the neutrality of a framework for general decision spaces. Intuitively, a framework $\mathcal{F} = (\mathcal{M}_\mathcal{A}, \mathcal{D}, L)$ is neutral if and only all of its three components are neutral w.r.t. permutations σ over $\mathcal{A}$. Because σ may not be well-defined for the parameter space and the decision space, we require the existence of homomorphisms from the permutation group over $\mathcal{A}$ to the permutation groups over Θ and $\mathcal{D}$, respectively. Formally, we have the following definition.

Definition 4. *A framework* $\mathcal{F} = (\mathcal{M}_\mathcal{A}, \mathcal{D}, L)$ *where* $\mathcal{M}_\mathcal{A} = (\Theta, \vec{\pi})$ *is* neutral, *if each permutation* σ *over* $\mathcal{A}$ *is mapped to a permutation* σ_Θ *over* Θ *and a permutation* $\sigma_\mathcal{D}$ *over* $\mathcal{D}$ *that satisfy the following conditions.*

(i) Homomorphism. *For any pair of permutations* γ *and* β *over* $\mathcal{A}$, $(\gamma \circ \beta)_\Theta = \gamma_\Theta \circ \beta_\Theta$ *and* $(\gamma \circ \beta)_\mathcal{D} = \gamma_\mathcal{D} \circ \beta_\mathcal{D}$.

(ii) Model neutrality. *For any* $\theta \in \Theta$, *any* $V \in \mathcal{L}(\mathcal{A})$, *and any permutation* σ *over* $\mathcal{A}$, *we have* $\pi_\theta(V) = \pi_{\sigma_\Theta(\theta)}(\sigma(V))$.

(iii) Loss function neutrality. *For any* $\theta \in \Theta$, *any* $d \in \mathcal{D}$, *and any permutation* σ *over* $\mathcal{A}$, *we have* $L(\theta, d) = L(\sigma_\Theta(\theta), \sigma_\mathcal{D}(d))$.

Example 1. *For any* $0 < \varphi < 1$, $(\mathcal{M}_{Ma,\varphi}, \mathcal{A}, L_{top})$, $(\mathcal{M}_{Ma,\varphi}, \mathcal{A}, L_{Borda})$, $(\mathcal{M}_{Co,\varphi}, \mathcal{A}, L_{top})$, $(\mathcal{M}_{Co,\varphi}, \mathcal{A}, L_{Borda})$ *are neutral, where* $\sigma_\Theta = \sigma_\mathcal{D} = \sigma$.

The main theorem of this section states that if a neutral framework further satisfies the following connectivity condition, then its Bayesian estimator is a minimax rule.

(iv) Parameter connectivity. For any pair $\theta_1, \theta_2 \in \Theta$, there exists a permutation σ over $\mathcal{A}$ such that $\sigma_\Theta(\theta_1) = \theta_2$.

Theorem 1. *For any neutral framework* $\mathcal{F}$ *that satisfies parameter connectivity and any* $n \in \mathbb{N}$, $BE_\mathcal{F}$ *is a minimax rule.*[2]

Proof: Any deterministic Bayesian estimator $\text{BE}_\mathcal{F}$ can be seen as a randomized rule that chooses a single decision uniformly at random from the output of $\text{BE}_\mathcal{F}$. Our proof is based on the following lemma.

Lemma 1 (Section 5.3.2 III in [8]). *Given a framework* $\mathcal{F}$. *Let* r_{π^*} *denote a Bayesian estimator for prior* π^*. *If* $FL_n(\theta, r_{\pi^*})$ *are equal for all* $\theta \in \Theta$, *then* r_{π^*} *is minimax.*

Let r_U denote the randomized decision rule that outputs all decisions with the minimum Bayesian expected loss uniformly at random. By Lemma 1, it suffices to show that for all $\theta \in \Theta$, $\text{FL}_n(\theta, r_U)$ are equal. For any pair of parameters $\theta_1, \theta_2 \in \Theta$, we let $\sigma^{(\theta_1,\theta_2)}$ denote a permutation over $\mathcal{A}$ such $\sigma^{(\theta_1,\theta_2)}_\Theta(\theta_1) = \theta_2$, which is guaranteed by Condition (iv).

Claim 1. *For any profile* P *of* n *votes and any* $d^* \in \mathcal{D}$, $r_U(P)(d^*) > 0$ *if and only if* $r_U(\sigma^{(\theta_1,\theta_2)}(P))(\sigma^{(\theta_1,\theta_2)}_\mathcal{D}(d^*)) > 0$.

Proof: To simplify the notation, in this proof we let σ^* denote $\sigma^{(\theta_1,\theta_2)}$. $r_U(P)$ has positive probability on d^* if and only if d^* minimizes the Bayesian loss at P under uniform prior, which is equivalent to requiring that for all $d' \in \mathcal{D}$, $\sum_\theta L(\theta, d^*) \Pr(\theta|P) \le \sum_\theta L(\theta, d') \Pr(\theta|P)$. We have the following calculation, where $\Pr(P|\theta) = \pi_\theta(P)$.

$$\sum_\theta L(\theta, d^*) \Pr(\theta|P) \le \sum_\theta L(\theta, d') \Pr(\theta|P)$$

$$\Leftrightarrow \sum_\theta L(\theta, d^*) \Pr(P|\theta) \le \sum_\theta L(\theta, d') \Pr(P|\theta) \quad (1)$$

$$\Leftrightarrow \sum_\theta L(\sigma^*_\Theta(\theta), \sigma^*_\mathcal{D}(d^*)) \Pr(\sigma^*(P)|\sigma^*_\Theta(\theta))$$

$$\le \sum_\theta L(\sigma^*_\Theta(\theta), \sigma^*_\mathcal{D}(d')) \Pr(\sigma^*(P)|\sigma^*_\Theta(\theta)) \quad (2)$$

$$\Leftrightarrow \sum_\theta L(\theta, \sigma^*_\mathcal{D}(d^*)) \Pr(\sigma^*(P)|\theta)$$

$$\le \sum_\theta L(\theta, \sigma^*_\mathcal{D}(d')) \Pr(\sigma^*(P)|\theta) \quad (3)$$

$$\Leftrightarrow \sum_\theta L(\theta, \sigma^*_\mathcal{D}(d^*)) \Pr(\theta|\sigma^*(P))$$

$$\le \sum_\theta L(\theta, \sigma^*_\mathcal{D}(d')) \Pr(\theta|\sigma^*(P)) \quad (4)$$

Therefore, d^* minimizes the Bayesian loss for P if and only if $\sigma^*_\mathcal{D}(d^*)$ minimizes the Bayesian loss for $\sigma^*(P)$, which means that $r_U(\sigma^*(P))$ has positive probability on $(\sigma^*_\mathcal{D}(d^*))$. (1) and (4) are due to Bayes' rule and the uniform prior assumption. (2) is obtained from applying σ^*, σ^*_Θ, and $\sigma^*_\mathcal{D}$ on both sides of the inequality and then considering the neutrality of the framework. (3) is a change of

[2] A similar result was presented at COMSOC-14 workshop [28].

variable names, which is possible because for any pair of parameters $\theta \neq \theta'$ and any permutation σ over $\mathcal{A}$, we must have $\sigma_\Theta(\theta) \neq \sigma_\Theta(\theta')$, because σ_Θ is a permutation over Θ. □

We note that r_U chooses a decisions d with $r_U(P)(d) > 0$ uniformly at random. Therefore, by Claim 1, for any $\theta_1 \neq \theta_2$ and any profile P, we have $r_U(\sigma^{(\theta_1,\theta_2)}(P)) = \sigma_\mathcal{D}^{(\theta_1,\theta_2)}(r_U(P))$. By neutrality of $\mathcal{F}$, we have $L(\theta_1, r_U(P)) = L(\sigma_\Theta^{(\theta_1,\theta_2)}(\theta_1), \sigma_\mathcal{D}^{(\theta_1,\theta_2)}(r_U(P))) = L(\theta_2, r_U(\sigma^{(\theta_1,\theta_2)}(P)))$.

Finally, we have:

$$\mathrm{FL}_n(\theta_1, r_U) = \sum_P L(\theta_1, r_U(P)) \Pr(P|\theta_1)$$
$$= \sum_P L(\theta_2, r_U(\sigma^{(\theta_1,\theta_2)}(P))) \Pr(\sigma^{(\theta_1,\theta_2)}(P)|\theta_2)$$
$$= \mathrm{FL}_n(\theta_2, r_U)$$

By Lemma 1, r_U is a minimax rule. We note that for any θ and any profile P, $L(\theta, r_U(P)) = L(\theta, \mathrm{BE}_\mathcal{F}(P))$. This means that $\mathrm{BE}_\mathcal{F}$ is a minimax rule. □

It is not hard to verify that all models mentioned in Example 1 satisfy parameter connectivity. Therefore, their Bayesian estimators are minimax rules. In particular, $f^{\mathrm{Top}}_{\mathrm{Ma},\varphi}$ is a minimax rule for $(\mathcal{M}_{\mathrm{Ma},\varphi}, L_{\mathrm{Top}})$. When the 0-1 loss function is used, the Bayesian estimator becomes *maximum likelihood estimator (MLE)*. Therefore, Theorem 1 immediately implies that MLE is minimax.

Corollary 1. *For any neutral framework $\mathcal{F} = (\mathcal{M}_\mathcal{A}, \mathcal{A}, L_{0\text{-}1})$, its MLE (that outputs all alternatives with the maximum likelihood) is a minimax rule.*

The special case of Corollary 1 for $\mathcal{M}_{\mathrm{Ma},\varphi}$ was proved by Caragiannis et al. [11]. We note that in Appendix A of [11], an example was shown to illustrate that MLE is not minimax w.r.t. $L_{0\text{-}1}$. This does not contradict Theorem 1 and Corollary 1 because the framework in the example is not neutral.

As shown in the following example, not all Bayesian estimators of neutral frameworks satisfy minimaxity.

Example 2. *Let $\mathcal{A} = \{a, b\}$. Consider a framework $(\mathcal{M}, L)$ for two alternatives where $\mathcal{M} = (\Theta, \vec{\pi})$ combines two Mallows' models with dispersion parameter 0.6 and 0.7 respectively. Formally, let $\Theta = \{0.6, 0.7\} \times \{a \succ b, b \succ a\}$. For each $(\varphi, W) \in \Theta$, $\pi_{(\varphi,W)}$ is the same as π_W in Mallows' model with dispersion φ. For any $W \in \mathcal{L}(\mathcal{A})$ and $c \in \mathcal{A}$, we let $L((0.6, W), c) = L_{top}(W, c)$ and $L((0.7, W), c) = 1 - L_{top}(W, c)$.*

It can be verified that $\mathcal{F}$ is neutral by letting γ_Θ be a permutation that only applies to the second component of the parameter (the ranking). Let $n = 1$. When the vote is $a \succ b$, the posterior distribution is the following.

Parameter	$(0.6, a \succ b)$	$(0.6, b \succ a)$	$(0.7, a \succ b)$	$(0.7, b \succ a)$
Post. Prob.	$\frac{1}{3.2}$	$\frac{0.6}{3.2}$	$\frac{1}{3.4}$	$\frac{0.7}{3.4}$
Loss for a	0	1	1	0

Therefore, $EL(a|\{a \succ b\}) = \frac{0.6}{3.2} < \frac{0.7}{3.4} = EL(b|\{a \succ b\})$. Therefore, $BE_\mathcal{F}(a \succ b) = a$. Similarly $BE_\mathcal{F}(b \succ a) = b$.

When the ground truth parameter is $(0.7, a \succ b)$, the frequentist expected loss of $BE_\mathcal{F}$ is $\frac{1}{1.7} > \frac{1}{2}$. We note that the worst-case frequentist loss of the voting rule that always output $\mathcal{A}$ is $\frac{1}{2}$, which means that $BE_\mathcal{F}$ is not a minimax rule. □

4 GENERAL RESULTS ON SATISFACTION OF AXIOMS

To analyze the satisfaction of axioms of Bayesian estimators, in the rest of this paper we focus on a special class of frameworks where the decision space is $\mathcal{A}$. We let $\mathcal{F} = (\mathcal{M}_\mathcal{A}, L)$ denote such a framework where the decision space is omitted. For neutral frameworks, we further require that $\sigma_\mathcal{A} = \sigma$, where $\sigma_\mathcal{A}$ is the corresponding permutation over the decision space, which is $\mathcal{A}$ in this section.

Theorem 2. *The Bayesian estimator of any neutral framework satisfies neutrality.*

Proof: Let $S(\mathcal{A})$ denote the set of all permutations over $\mathcal{A}$. It suffices to prove that the expected loss function is insensitive to permutations. For any neutral framework $\mathcal{F}$, any profile P, any alternative a, and any $\gamma \in S(\mathcal{A})$, we have

$$\mathrm{EL}(a|P) = \sum_{\theta\in\Theta} \Pr(\theta|P) L(\theta, a) \propto \sum_{\theta\in\Theta} \Pr(P|\theta) L(\theta, a)$$
$$= \sum_{\theta\in\Theta} \Pr(\gamma(P)|\gamma_\Theta(\theta)) L(\gamma_\Theta(\theta), \gamma(a))$$
$$\propto \sum_{\theta\in\Theta} \Pr(\gamma_\Theta(\theta)|\gamma(P)) L(\gamma_\Theta(\theta), \gamma(a)) = \mathrm{EL}(\gamma(a)|\gamma(P))$$

□

Theorem 3. *If the Bayesian estimator $BE_\mathcal{F}$ of a framework $\mathcal{F}$ satisfies neutrality then there exists a neutral framework $\mathcal{F}^*$ such that $BE_{\mathcal{F}^*} = BE_\mathcal{F}$.*

All missing proofs can be found in the full version on arXiv.

Theorem 4. *No Bayesian estimator satisfies strict Condorcet criterion.*

Proof: For the sake of contradiction suppose a Bayesian estimator r of $\mathcal{F} = (\mathcal{M}_\mathcal{A}, L)$ satisfies strict Condorcet criterion where $\mathcal{M}_\mathcal{A} = (\Theta, \vec{\pi})$.

We first prove that for any profile P, if alternatives a and b are tied in their head-to-head competition, then expected loss for a must be the same as the expected loss for b.

Lemma 2. *Suppose $r = BE_{\mathcal{F}}$ satisfies strict Condorcet criterion. For any profile P and any pair of alternatives (a,b), if $w_P(a,b) = 0$ then $EL(a|P) = EL(b|P)$.*

Proof: For any distribution π over Θ, let $\mathcal{S}_\pi = \{S_1, \ldots, S_p\}$ denote the partition of Θ into equivalent classes according to π, where p is the number of equivalent classes. That is, for any $S \in \mathcal{S}_\pi$ and any $\theta_1, \theta_2 \in S$, we have $\pi(\theta_1) = \pi(\theta_2)$. Let $\mathcal{T}_\pi$ denote the total order over $\mathcal{S}_\pi$ such that for any pair $S, S' \in \mathcal{S}_\pi$, we have $S \succ_{\mathcal{T}_\pi} S'$ if and only if the π value of parameters in S is strictly larger than the π value of parameters in S'.

For any profile P, let $\mathcal{S}_P$ denote $\mathcal{S}_{\Pr(\cdot|P)}$. That is, $\mathcal{S}_P$ is the partition of Θ according to the posterior distribution over Θ given P. $\mathcal{T}_P$ is defined similarly. The next lemma states that for any profile P and any pair of co-winners (a,b), the total loss of a and b within each equivalent class in $\mathcal{S}_P$ must be the same. For any $S \subseteq \Theta$, we let $L(S,a) = \sum_{\theta \in S} L(\theta, a)$.

Lemma 3. *Suppose $r = BE_{\mathcal{F}}$ satisfies strict Condorcet criterion. For any profile P and any $S \in \mathcal{S}_P$, if there are at least two weak Condorcet winners $\{a,b\}$ in P, then $L(S,a) = L(S,b)$.*

Proof: For the sake of contradiction suppose the lemma does not hold for a profile P where $\{a,b\}$ are two weak Condorcet winners. Let $\mathcal{T}_P = S_1 \succ S_2 \succ \cdots \succ S_p$. Let S_i denote the highest-ranked equivalent class in $\mathcal{T}_P$ such that the total loss of a and the total loss of b on S_i are different. W.l.o.g. suppose $L(S_i, a) > L(S_i, b)$. For any natural number k, it follows that a and b are also weak Condorcet winners in kP, whose weighted majority graph is exactly WMG(P) times k. We next show that when k is sufficiently large, $EL(a|kP) > EL(b|kP)$. For any $i \le p$, let $\theta_i \in S_i$ be an arbitrary parameter in S_i.

$$EL(a|kP) = \sum_{\theta \in \Theta} \Pr(\theta|kP) L(\theta, a)$$

$$\propto \sum_{\theta \in \Theta} \Pr(\theta|P)^k L(\theta, a) = \sum_{i=1}^{p} \sum_{\theta \in S_i} \Pr(\theta|P)^k L(\theta, a)$$

$$= \sum_{i=1}^{p} \Pr(\theta_i|P)^k L(S_i, a)$$

Because for any $i' > i$ we have $\Pr(\theta_i|P) > \Pr(\theta_{i'}|P)$, there exists $k \in \mathbb{N}$ such that $(\frac{\Pr(\theta_i|P)}{\Pr(\theta_{i+1}|P)})^k > \frac{\sum_{l=i+1}^{p}(L(S_l,a) - L(S_l,b))}{L(S_i,a) - L(S_i,b)}$. Therefore, for such k we have $\sum_{i=1}^{p} \Pr(\theta_i|P)^k L(S_i, a) > \sum_{i=1}^{p} \Pr(\theta_i|P)^k L(S_i, b) \propto EL(b|kP)$. This means that b cannot be a co-winner in $r(kP)$, which contradicts the assumption that r satisfies strict Condorcet criterion. □

For any pair of partitions $\mathcal{S}_1$ and $\mathcal{S}_2$ of Θ, we let $\mathcal{S}_1 \oplus \mathcal{S}_2$ denote the coarsest partition of Θ that refines both $\mathcal{S}_1$ and $\mathcal{S}_2$. That is,

$$\mathcal{S}_1 \oplus \mathcal{S}_2 = \{S_1 \cap S_2 : S_1 \in \mathcal{S}_1, S_2 \in \mathcal{S}_2\} \setminus \{\emptyset\}$$

Lemma 4. *For any statistical model and any pair of profiles P_1, P_2, there exists $k \in \mathbb{N}$ such that $\mathcal{S}_{kP_1 \cup P_2} = \mathcal{S}_{P_1} \oplus \mathcal{S}_{P_2}$.*

Proof: We let $P^* = kP_1 \cup P_2$ for a sufficiently large k such that the "gap" between two equivalent classes in kP is large enough that the only effect of P_2 is to refine the equivalent classes in kP. More formally, we choose $k \in \mathbb{N}$ such that for any $\theta_1, \theta_2 \in \Theta$, $\Pr(\theta_1|P_1)^k \Pr(\theta_1|P_2) > \Pr(\theta_2|P_1)^k \Pr(\theta_2|P_2)$ if and only if one of the following two conditions hold: (1) $\Pr(\theta_1|P_1) > \Pr(\theta_2|P_1)$, or (2) $\Pr(\theta_1|P_1) = \Pr(\theta_1|P_2)$ and $\Pr(\theta_1|P_2) > \Pr(\theta_2|P_2)$. □

For any $a, b \in \mathcal{A}$, let $\mathcal{L}_{ab}$ denote the set of all rankings where $a \succ b$. Let $\mathcal{P}_{ab}$ denote the set of all two-agent profiles where one vote comes from $\mathcal{L}_{ab}$ and the other vote comes from $\mathcal{L}_{ba}$. That is,

$$\mathcal{P}_{ab} = \{\{V_1, V_2\} : V_1 \in \mathcal{L}_{ab}, V_2 \in \mathcal{L}_{ba}\}$$

Let $\mathcal{S}_{ab}$ denote the finest partition of Θ that refines all partitions induced by profiles in $\mathcal{P}_{ab}$. That is, $\mathcal{S}_{ab} = \oplus \mathcal{P}_{ab}$. By Lemma 4, there exists a profile P_{ab} such that $\mathcal{S}_{P_{ab}} = \mathcal{S}_{ab}$.

Lemma 5. *Suppose $r = BE_{\mathcal{F}}$ satisfies strict Condorcet criterion. For any $a, b \in \mathcal{A}$ and any $S \in \mathcal{S}_{ab}$, we have $L(S,a) = L(S,b)$.*

Proof: Let P^* be an arbitrary profile with the following conditions. (1) $w_{P^*}(a,b) = w_{P^*}(b,a) = 0$. (2) For any $c \notin \{a,b\}$, we have $w_{P^*}(a,c) > 0$ and $w_{P^*}(b,c) > 0$. By Lemma 4, there exists a sufficiently large $k \in \mathbb{N}$ such that both conditions still hold for $kP^* \cup P_{ab}$, and $\mathcal{S}_{kP^* \cup P_{ab}} = \mathcal{S}_{ab}$. The latter is because P^* can be seen as the union of $|P^*|/2$ profiles in $\mathcal{P}_{ab}$, which means that $\mathcal{S}_{ab}$ is a refinement of $\mathcal{S}_{kP^*}$. The lemma follows after Lemma 3. □

We note that for any $a, b \in \mathcal{A}$, any profile P where $w_P(a,b) = 0$ can be seen as the union of $|P|/2$ profiles in $\mathcal{P}_{ab}$. This means that $\mathcal{S}_{ab}$ is a refinement of $\mathcal{S}_P$. Therefore, any $S \in \mathcal{S}_P$ must be the union of some equivalent classes in $\mathcal{S}_{ab}$. By Lemma 5 we have that $L(S,a) = L(S,b)$. We have $EL(a|P) = \sum_{S \in \mathcal{S}_P} \Pr(\theta_S|P) L(S,a) = \sum_{S \in \mathcal{S}_P} \Pr(\theta_S|P) L(S,b) = EL(b|P)$, where θ_S denote an arbitrary element in S. This proves Lemma 2. □

Consider any profile P where $w_P(a,b) = w_P(b,c) = 0$, $w_P(a,c) = 2$, a and b are the only two weak Condorcet winners, and c loses to all other alternatives in head-to-head competitions. Such a profile exists due to McGarvey's theorem [23]. By Lemma 2, $EL(a|P) = EL(b|P) = EL(c|P)$. However, because r satisfies strict Condorcet criterion, $c \notin r(P)$, which is a contradiction. □

A direct corollary is that any voting rule that satisfies strict Condorcet criterion cannot be the BE of any framework.

Corollary 2. *Copeland*$_1$*, maximin, Black's function,*[3] *Dodgson's function, Young's function, Condorcet's function, and Fishburn's function cannot be the Bayesian estimator of any framework.*

5 NEW BAYESIAN ESTIMATORS AS VOTING RULES

The following theorem solves the open question about the satisfaction of Condorcet criterion for $f^{\text{Top}}_{\text{Ma},\varphi}$ [7].

Theorem 5. $f^{Top}_{Ma,\varphi}$ *satisfies the Condorcet criterion if and only if* $\frac{\varphi(1-\varphi^{m-1})}{1-\varphi} \leq 1$.

Proof: The "if part": suppose $\frac{\varphi(1-\varphi^{m-1})}{1-\varphi} \leq 1$. Let P be a profile where a is the Condorcet winner. For any $c, d \in \mathcal{A}$, we let $\mathcal{A}_{-c} = \mathcal{A} \setminus \{c\}$ and $\mathcal{A}_{-cd} = \mathcal{A} \setminus \{c, d\}$. For any $c \in \mathcal{A}$, let $\mathcal{L}_c$ denote the set of all rankings where c is ranked at the top. For any profile P, let $P|_{-a}$ denote its restriction on $\mathcal{A}_{-a}$.

$$1 - \text{EL}(c|P) = \sum_{V \in \mathcal{L}_c} \Pr(V|P)$$
$$\propto \sum_{V \in \mathcal{L}_c} \Pr(P|V) \propto \sum_{V \in \mathcal{L}_c} \varphi^{\text{Kd}(P,V)}$$

Fix $b \neq a$. For any ranking $V_{-ab} \in \mathcal{L}(\mathcal{A}_{-ab})$, we let $Q(V_{-ab})$ denote the set of $m-1$ rankings over $\mathcal{A} \setminus \{a\}$ obtained by inserting b to V_{-ab} without changing the relative positions of other alternatives. Let $J(V_{-ab}) \in \mathcal{L}(\mathcal{A}_{-a})$ be the ranking in $Q(V_{-ab})$ with the minimum Kentall-tau distance from $P|_{-a}$. If there are multiple such rankings, let $J(V_{-ab})$ be the one where b is ranked at the highest position.

Let $H : \mathcal{L}_b \to \mathcal{L}_a$ denote the following mapping. For any $b \succ V_{-b} \in \mathcal{L}_b$ we first look at V_{-ab} and decide the best position to insert b, then put a at the top, where V_{-ab} is obtained from V_{-b} by removing a. Formally, $H(b \succ A_{-b}) = a \succ J(V_{-ab})$.

It follows that for any pair of rankings $V, W \in \mathcal{L}_b$, where the only difference is the position of a, we have $H(V) = H(W)$. Therefore, for any $V \in H(\mathcal{L}_b)$, $H^{-1}(V)$ contains exactly $m-1$ rankings in $\mathcal{L}_b$ that correspond to the $m-1$ positions of a (from the second position to the m-th position—the first position is occupied by b). For each $2 \leq i \leq m$, let $W_i \in H^{-1}(V)$ denote the ranking where a is ranked at the i-th position.

$$\begin{aligned}
&\text{Kd}(P, W_i)\\
=&\text{Kd}(P|_{-a}, (W_i)_{-a}) + \sum_{d \succ_{W_i} a} P(a \succ d)\\
&+ \sum_{a \succ_{W_i} d} P(d \succ a)\\
\geq&\text{Kd}(P|_{-a}, J((W_i)_{-ab})) + \sum_{d \neq a} P(d \succ a) + i - 1 \quad (5)\\
=&\text{Kd}(P, V) + i - 1
\end{aligned}$$

Inequality (5) is because a is the Condorcet winner, which means that for any $d \neq a$ we have $\#_P(a \succ d) \geq \#_P(d \succ a) + 1$. Therefore, for each $V \in H(\mathcal{L}_b)$ we have

$$\begin{aligned}
&\sum_{W \in H^{-1}(V)} \varphi^{\text{Kd}(P,W)} \leq (\varphi + \cdots + \varphi^{m-1})\varphi^{\text{Kd}(P,V)}\\
=&\frac{\varphi(1-\varphi^{m-1})}{1-\varphi}\varphi^{\text{Kd}(P,V)}
\end{aligned}$$

Therefore,

$$\begin{aligned}
&\sum_{W \in \mathcal{L}_b} \varphi^{\text{Kd}(P,W)} \leq \frac{\varphi(1-\varphi^{m-1})}{1-\varphi} \sum_{V \in H(\mathcal{L}_b)} \varphi^{\text{Kd}(P,V)}\\
<&\frac{\varphi(1-\varphi^{m-1})}{1-\varphi} \sum_{V \in \mathcal{L}_a} \varphi^{\text{Kd}(P,V)} \leq \sum_{V \in \mathcal{L}_a} \varphi^{\text{Kd}(P,V)}
\end{aligned}$$

Therefore, we have $1 - \text{EL}(a|P) > 1 - \text{EL}(b|P)$, which means that $\text{EL}(a|P) < \text{EL}(b|P)$ and a is the unique winner.

The "only if part": suppose $\frac{\varphi(1-\varphi^{m-1})}{1-\varphi} > 1$. For any odd number $k \in \mathbb{N}$ we consider the a profile P_k whose weighted majority graph is the same as in Figure 1. The existence of P^* is guaranteed by McGarvey's theorem [23]. More precisely, in Figure 1 the weight on the edges from a to all other alternatives is 1; the weight on the edges from b to all other alternatives (except a) is k; for any $3 \leq i_1 < i_2 < m$, the weight on $a_{i_1} \to a_{i_2}$ is k.

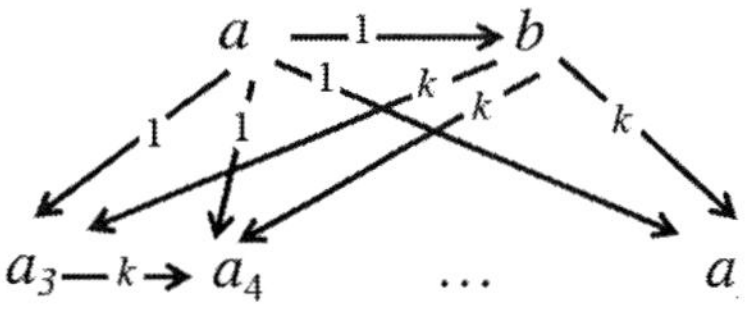

Figure 1: The WMG of P_k for odd k.

Let $V_a = a \succ b \succ a_3 \succ \cdots \succ a_m$ and for each $2 \leq i \leq m$, let V_b^i be the ranking obtained from V_a by moving a to the i-th position. It is not hard to check that $\lim_{k\to\infty} \frac{\sum_{V \in \mathcal{L}_a} \varphi^{\text{Kd}(P_k,V)}}{\varphi^{\text{Kd}(P_k,V_a)}} = 1$ and

[3]Definitions of these rules except Copeland and maximin can be found in [18], where it was proved that they satisfy strict Condorcet criterion.

$\lim_{k\to\infty} \frac{\sum_{V\in\mathcal{L}_b} \varphi^{\text{Kd}(P_k,V)}}{\sum_{i=2}^{m} \varphi^{\text{Kd}(P_k,V_b^i)}} = 1$. We note that for each $2 \le i \le m$, $\text{Kd}(P_k, V_b^i) = \text{Kd}(P_k, V_a) + i - 1$. This means that

$$\lim_{k\to\infty} \frac{\sum_{V\in\mathcal{L}_b} \varphi^{\text{Kd}(P_k,V)}}{\sum_{V\in\mathcal{L}_a} \varphi^{\text{Kd}(P_k,V)}} = \lim_{k\to\infty} \frac{\sum_{i=2}^{m} \varphi^{\text{Kd}(P_k,V_b^i)}}{\varphi^{\text{Kd}(P_k,V_a)}}$$

$$=\varphi + \varphi^2 + \cdots \varphi^{m-1} = \frac{\varphi(1-\varphi^{m-1})}{1-\varphi} > 1$$

Therefore, there exists odd $k \in \mathbb{N}$ such that $\text{EL}(b|P_k) < \text{EL}(a|P_k)$, which means that a cannot be the winner. Because a is the Condorcet winner in P_k, $f_{\text{Ma},\varphi}^{\text{Top}}$ does not satisfy Condorcet criterion. □

Theorem 6. *For any profile* P, $f_{Co,\varphi}^{Borda}(P) = \arg\max_{a\in\mathcal{A}} \sum_{c\neq a} \frac{1}{1+\varphi^{w_P(a,c)}}$.

Proof: For any $W \in \mathcal{B}(\mathcal{A})$ and any pair of alternatives a, b, let $I_W(a \succ b) = 1$ if $a \succ_W b$; otherwise $I_W(a \succ b) = 0$. It follows that $m - 1 - L_{\text{Borda}}(W, a) = \sum_{b\neq a} I_W(a \succ b)$. Let $\mathcal{B}_{a\succ b}$ denote the set of all rankings over $\mathcal{A}$ where $a \succ b$.

$$m - 1 - \text{EL}(a|P)$$
$$= \sum_{W\in\mathcal{B}(\mathcal{A})} \Pr(W|P)(m - 1 - L_{\text{Borda}}(W, a))$$
$$= \sum_{W\in\mathcal{B}(\mathcal{A})} \Pr(W|P) \sum_{c\neq a} I_W(a \succ c)$$
$$= \sum_{c\neq a} \sum_{W\in\mathcal{B}_{a\succ c}} \Pr(W|P)$$

Following similar calculations as in [16, 7], we have

$$\sum_{c\neq a} \sum_{W\in\mathcal{B}_{a\succ c}} \Pr(W|P)$$
$$\propto \sum_{c\neq a} \varphi^{P(c\succ a)} \prod_{\{b,d\}:\{b,d\}\neq\{a,c\}} (\varphi^{P(b\succ d)} + \varphi^{P(d\succ b)})$$
$$\propto \sum_{c\neq a} \frac{\varphi^{P(c\succ a)}}{\varphi^{P(c\succ a)} + \varphi^{P(a\succ c)}} = \sum_{c\neq a} \frac{1}{1+\varphi^{w_P(a,c)}}$$

Therefore, for any pair of alternatives (a, b), $\text{EL}(a|P) \le \text{EL}(b|P)$ if and only if $\sum_{c\neq a} \frac{1}{1+\varphi^{w_P(a,c)}} \ge \sum_{c\neq b} \frac{1}{1+\varphi^{w_P(b,c)}}$. This proves the theorem. □

Proposition 1. *For all* $0 < \varphi < 1$, $f_{Co,\varphi}^{Borda}$ *satisfies monotonicity.*

Proof: For any profile P, any $a \in f_{\text{Co},\varphi}^{\text{Borda}}(P)$ and any profile P' obtained from P by raising the positions of a without changing relative positions of other alternatives. It is not hard to check that for any $b \neq a$, $w_{P'}(a, b) > w_P(a, b)$, and the weights of edges not involving a do not change. Therefore, for any $b \neq a$, $\sum_{c\neq a} \frac{1}{1+\varphi^{w_{P'}(a,c)}} > \sum_{c\neq a} \frac{1}{1+\varphi^{w_P(a,c)}} \ge \sum_{c\neq b} \frac{1}{1+\varphi^{w_P(b,c)}} > \sum_{c\neq b} \frac{1}{1+\varphi^{w_{P'}(b,c)}}$. It follows from Theorem 6 that $a \in f_{\text{Co},\varphi}^{\text{Borda}}(P')$. □

Theorem 7. $f_{Co,\varphi}^{Borda}$ *satisfies the Condorcet criterion if and only if* $\varphi \le \frac{1}{m-1}$.

Proof: The "if" part. Let P be any profile where a is the Condorcet winner. This means that for any $c \neq a$, $w_P(a, c) \ge 1$. By Theorem 6 we have $\sum_{c\neq a} \frac{1}{1+\varphi^{w_P(a,c)}} \ge \frac{m-1}{1+\varphi}$. For any $b \neq a$, we have $\sum_{c\neq a} \frac{1}{1+\varphi^{w_P(a,c)}} < \frac{1}{1+\varphi^{-1}} + m - 2$. When $\varphi \le \frac{1}{m-1}$, we have $\frac{1}{1+\varphi^{-1}} + m - 2 \le \frac{m-1}{1+\varphi}$. Therefore, a is the unique winner.

The "only if" part is proved by considering the profile P_k whose WMG is in Figure 1 and let $k \to \infty$. □

Theorem 8. *As* $\varphi \to 0$, $f_{Co,\varphi}^{Borda}$ *converges to a refinement of Copeland*$_{0.5}$. *As* $\varphi \to 1$, $f_{Co,\varphi}^{Borda}$ *converges to a refinement of Borda.*

Proof: For any profile P any pair of alternatives a, b we have

$$\lim_{\varphi\to 0} \frac{1}{1+\varphi^{w_P(a,b)}} = \begin{cases} 1 & \text{if } w_P(a, b) > 0 \\ 0.5 & \text{if } w_P(a, b) = 0 \\ 0 & \text{otherwise} \end{cases}$$

Therefore, for any alternative a, $\lim_{\varphi\to 0} \sum_{c\neq a} \frac{1}{1+\varphi^{w_P(a,c)}}$ is its Copeland$_{0.5}$ score, which means that the winners must also be winners under Copeland$_{0.5}$.

For any $k > 0$, when $\epsilon \to 0$, we have $\frac{1}{1+(1-\epsilon)^k} = \frac{1}{2}(1 + \frac{k\epsilon}{2} + o(\epsilon))$ and $\frac{1}{1+(1-\epsilon)^{-k}} = \frac{1}{2}(1 - \frac{k\epsilon}{2} + o(\epsilon))$. Therefore, for any alternative a, $\sum_{c\neq a} \frac{1}{1+\varphi^{w_P(a,c)}} = \frac{m-1}{2} + \frac{1}{4}(\sum_{c\neq a} w_P(a, c))(1 - \varphi) + o(1 - \varphi)$. We note that $\sum_{c\neq a} w_P(a, c)$ equals to twice the Borda score of a in P minus $n(m - 1)$. Therefore, as $\varphi \to 1$, all $f_{\text{Co},\varphi}^{\text{Borda}}$ winners must be Borda winners. □

We propose a new class of ranking model and framework as follows.

Definition 5. *For any* $0 < \varphi < 1$ *we define* $\mathcal{M}_{Pair,\varphi}$ *as follows. The parameter space* $\Theta = \{\theta_{bc} : b \neq c \in \mathcal{A}\}$. *For any* $V \in \mathcal{L}(\mathcal{A})$ *we let* $\pi_{\theta_{bc}}(V) \propto \begin{cases} 1 & \text{if } b \succ_V c \\ \varphi & \text{otherwise} \end{cases}$.

Let $L_1(\theta_{bc}, a) = \begin{cases} 1 & \text{if } a = c \\ 0 & \text{otherwise} \end{cases}$ *and*

$L_2(\theta_{bc}, a) = \begin{cases} 0 & \text{if } a = b \\ 1 & \text{otherwise} \end{cases}$.

Let $\mathcal{F}_{Pair,\varphi}^1 = (\mathcal{M}_{Pair,\varphi}, L_1)$ *and* $\mathcal{F}_{Pair,\varphi}^2 = (\mathcal{M}_{Pair,\varphi}, L_2)$.

That is, the parameters in $\mathcal{M}_{\text{Pair},\varphi}$ correspond to pairwise comparisons between alternatives. A parameter θ_{bc} can be interpreted as "$b \succ c$ is the strongest pairwise comparison". The first loss function states that the loss of a is 1 if and only if a is the less preferred alternative in the parameter. The second loss function states that the loss of a is 0 if and only if a is the preferred alternative in the parameter.

$\mathcal{M}_{\text{Pair},\varphi}$ might be of independent interest. In this paper we focus on the satisfaction of axioms for the two Bayesian estimators and leave further exploration of the model for future work. We note that given φ, the normalization factor for all θ_{bc} are the same.

Theorem 9. *The Bayesian estimator $f^1_{Pair,\varphi}$ of $\mathcal{F}^1_{Pair,\varphi}$ is $\arg\min_{a\in\Theta}\sum_{b\neq a}\varphi^{w_P(a,b)/2}$. The Bayesian estimator $f^2_{Pair,\varphi}$ of $\mathcal{F}^2_{Pair,\varphi}$ is $\arg\max_{a\in\Theta}\sum_{b\neq a}\varphi^{w_P(b,a)/2}$.*

It is easy to check that both $\mathcal{F}^1_{\text{Pair},\varphi}$ and $\mathcal{F}^2_{\text{Pair},\varphi}$ satisfy neutrality and parameter connectivity. Therefore, their Bayesian estimators satisfy neutrality and minimaxity.

Corollary 3. *$f^1_{Pair,\varphi}$ and $f^2_{Pair,\varphi}$ satisfy neutrality and minimaxity (w.r.t. to $\mathcal{F}^1_{Pair,\varphi}$ and $\mathcal{F}^2_{Pair,\varphi}$, respectively).*

Proposition 2. *$f^1_{Pair,\varphi}$ and $f^2_{Pair,\varphi}$ satisfy monotonicity.*

Proof: The proof is similar to the proof of Theorem 1. We note that raising the position of a will increase the weight on some edges $a \to b$. Weights on other edges do not change. Monotonicity of both rules can be verified by applying Theorem 9. □

Theorem 10. *$f^1_{Pair,\varphi}$ satisfies the Condorcet criterion if and only if $\varphi \leq \frac{1}{m-1}$. For all $0 < \varphi < 1$, $f^2_{Pair,\varphi}$ does not satisfy Concorcet criterion.*

Proof: The "if" part for $f^1_{\text{Pair},\varphi}$ follows after Theorem 11 because when $\varphi < \frac{1}{m-1}$, $f^1_{\text{Pair},\varphi}$ is a refinement of maximin and any refinement of maximin satisfies the Condorcet criterion.

The "only if" part for $f^1_{\text{Pair},\varphi}$ and the non-satisfaction for $f^2_{\text{Pair},\varphi}$ are proved by considering the profile P_k whose weighted majority graph is in Figure 1 and let $k \to \infty$. □

For any profile P, the *maximax* rule to chooses all alternatives with the maximum weight on at least one outgoing edge in the weighted majority graph. That is, the rule is $\arg\max_a \max_b w_P(a,b)$.

Theorem 11. *For any $\varphi \leq \frac{1}{m-1}$, $f^1_{Pair,\varphi}$ is a refinement of maximin, and $f^2_{Pair,\varphi}$ is a refinement of maximax. As $\varphi \to 1$, both rules converge to refinements of Borda.*

Proof: By Theorem 9, for any $\varphi \leq \frac{1}{m-1}$, for any alternative a, $\sum_{b\neq a}\varphi^{w_P(a,b)/2}$ is mainly determined by $\min_{b\neq a} w_P(a,b)/2$, which is half of a's min-score. It follows that all winners under $f^1_{\text{Pair},\varphi}$ must be maximin winners. Similarly, $\sum_{b\neq a}\varphi^{w_P(b,a)/2}$ is determined by $\min_{b\neq a} w_P(b,a)/2$, which corresponds to $\max_{b\neq a} w_P(a,b)/2$. It follows that the winner under $f^2_{\text{Pair},\varphi}$ must be maximax winners.

For any $\epsilon > 0$, we have $\sum_{b\neq a}(1-\epsilon)^{w_P(a,b)/2} = m - 1 - \sum_{b\neq a}\frac{w_P(a,b)}{2}\epsilon + o(\epsilon)$. Similar to the proof of Theorem 8, the minimizers of this function as $\epsilon \to 0$, which is $f^1_{\text{Pair},\varphi}$ as $\varphi \to 1$, must be Borda winners. The proof for $f^2_{\text{Pair},\varphi}$ is similar. □

6 SUMMARY AND FUTURE WORK

We characterized neutrality and proved an impossibility theorem about strict Condorcet criterion for Bayesian estimators. We also proposed new frameworks to obtain new BEs and showed that some of them satisfy many desirable axioms and can be computed in polynomial time.

There are many directions for future work. Can we answer Q2 in the Introduction for other desirable axioms such as homogeneity? How about axioms for other types preferences such as ratings? Are there any BEs that are refinements of other commonly studied rules, especially Copeland$_\alpha$ for $\alpha \notin \{0.5, 1\}$, STV, and ranked pairs? What are other natural frameworks and which axioms do their BEs satisfy?

ACKNOWLEDGMENTS

This work is supported by the National Science Foundation under grant IIS-1453542 and a Simons-Berkeley research fellowship. We thank Felix Brandt, Jean-Francois Laslie, Bill Zwicker, participants of the Economics and Computation Program at Simons Institute, and anonymous reviewers for helpful comments and suggestions.

References

[1] IMDb Votes/Ratings Top Frequently Asked Questions, 2016. URL http://www.imdb.com/help/show_leaf?votestopfaq.

[2] Practical example of bayes estimators, 2016. URL https://en.wikipedia.org/wiki/Bayes_estimator#Practical_example_of_Bayes_estimators.

[3] Alon Altman and Moshe Tennenholtz. An axiomatic approach to personalized ranking systems. *Journal of the ACM*, 57(4), 2010. Article 26.

[4] Kenneth Arrow. *Social choice and individual values*. New Haven: Cowles Foundation, 2nd edition, 1963. 1st edition 1951.

[5] Hossein Azari Soufiani, David C. Parkes, and Lirong Xia. Random utility theory for social choice. In *Proceedings of Advances in Neural Information Processing Systems (NIPS)*, pages 126–134, Lake Tahoe, NV, USA, 2012.

[6] Hossein Azari Soufiani, David C. Parkes, and Lirong Xia. Preference Elicitation For General Random Utility Models. In *Proceedings of Uncertainty in Artificial Intelligence (UAI)*, Bellevue, Washington, USA, 2013.

[7] Hossein Azari Soufiani, David C. Parkes, and Lirong Xia. Statistical decision theory approaches to social choice. In *Proceedings of Advances in Neural Information Processing Systems (NIPS)*, Montreal, Quebec, Canada, 2014.

[8] James O. Berger. *Statistical Decision Theory and Bayesian Analysis*. Springer, 2nd edition, 1985.

[9] Christian Borgs, Jennifer Chayes, Adrian Marple, and Shang-Hua Teng. An Axiomatic Approach to Community Detection. In *Proceedings of ITCS*, 2016.

[10] Mark Braverman and Elchanan Mossel. Noisy Sorting Without Resampling. In *Proceedings of the Nineteenth Annual ACM-SIAM Symposium on Discrete Algorithms*, pages 268–276, Philadelphia, PA, USA, 2008.

[11] Ioannis Caragiannis, Ariel Procaccia, and Nisarg Shah. When do noisy votes reveal the truth? In *Proceedings of the ACM Conference on Electronic Commerce (EC)*, Philadelphia, PA, 2013.

[12] Christine Choirat and Raffaello Seri. Estimation in discrete parameter models. *Statistical Science*, 27(2):278–293, 2012.

[13] Marquis de Condorcet. *Essai sur l'application de l'analyse à la probabilité des décisions rendues à la pluralité des voix.* Paris: L'Imprimerie Royale, 1785.

[14] Vincent Conitzer and Tuomas Sandholm. Common voting rules as maximum likelihood estimators. In *Proceedings of the 21st Annual Conference on Uncertainty in Artificial Intelligence (UAI)*, pages 145–152, Edinburgh, UK, 2005.

[15] Vincent Conitzer, Matthew Rognlie, and Lirong Xia. Preference functions that score rankings and maximum likelihood estimation. In *Proceedings of the Twenty-First International Joint Conference on Artificial Intelligence (IJCAI)*, pages 109–115, Pasadena, CA, USA, 2009.

[16] Edith Elkind and Nisarg Shah. Electing the Most Probable Without Eliminating the Irrational: Voting Over Intransitive Domains. In *Proceedings of the 30th Conference on Uncertainty in Artificial Intelligence*, pages 182–191, 2014.

[17] Edith Elkind, Piotr Faliszewski, and Arkadii Slinko. Good rationalizations of voting rules. In *Proceedings of the National Conference on Artificial Intelligence (AAAI)*, pages 774–779, Atlanta, GA, USA, 2010.

[18] Peter C. Fishburn. Condorcet social choice functions. *SIAM Journal on Applied Mathematics*, 33(3):469–489, 1977.

[19] David Hughes, Kevin Hwang, and Lirong Xia. Computing Optimal Bayesian Decisions for Rank Aggregation via MCMC Sampling. In *Proceedings of the Conference on Uncertainly in Artificial Intelligence (UAI)*, 2015.

[20] Tyler Lu and Craig Boutilier. Learning mallows models with pairwise preferences. In *Proceedings of the Twenty-Eighth International Conference on Machine Learning (ICML 2011)*, pages 145–152, Bellevue, WA, USA, 2011.

[21] Colin L. Mallows. Non-null ranking model. *Biometrika*, 44 (1/2):114–130, 1957.

[22] Andrew Mao, Ariel D. Procaccia, and Yiling Chen. Better human computation through principled voting. In *Proceedings of the National Conference on Artificial Intelligence (AAAI)*, Bellevue, WA, USA, 2013.

[23] David C. McGarvey. A theorem on the construction of voting paradoxes. *Econometrica*, 21(4):608–610, 1953.

[24] Sahand Negahban, Sewoong Oh, and Devavrat Shah. Iterative ranking from pair-wise comparisons. In *Proceedings of the Annual Conference on Neural Information Processing Systems (NIPS)*, pages 2483–2491, Lake Tahoe, NV, USA, 2012.

[25] David M Pennock, Eric Horvitz, and C. Lee Giles. Social choice theory and recommender systems: Analysis of the axiomatic foundations of collaborative filtering. In *Proceedings of the National Conference on Artificial Intelligence (AAAI)*, pages 729–734, Austin, TX, USA, 2000.

[26] Marcus Pivato. Voting rules as statistical estimators. *Social Choice and Welfare*, 40(2):581–630, 2013.

[27] Ariel D. Procaccia, Sashank J. Reddi, and Nisarg Shah. A maximum likelihood approach for selecting sets of alternatives. In *Proceedings of the 28th Conference on Uncertainty in Artificial Intelligence*, 2012.

[28] Lirong Xia. Statistical Properties of Social Choice Mechanisms. In *Proceedings of the Fifth International Workshop on Computational Social Choice*, Pittsburgh, Pennsylvania, USA, 2014.

[29] Lirong Xia and Vincent Conitzer. A maximum likelihood approach towards aggregating partial orders. In *Proceedings of the Twenty-Second International Joint Conference on Artificial Intelligence (IJCAI)*, pages 446–451, Barcelona, Catalonia, Spain, 2011.

[30] H. Peyton Young. Condorcet's theory of voting. *American Political Science Review*, 82:1231–1244, 1988.

Lighter-Communication Distributed Machine Learning via Sufficient Factor Broadcasting

Pengtao Xie, Jin Kyu Kim, Yi Zhou*, Qirong Ho†, Abhimanu Kumar§, Yaoliang Yu, Eric Xing
School of Computer Science, Carnegie Mellon University;
*Department of EECS, Syracuse University;
†Institute for Infocomm Research, A*STAR, Singapore; §Groupon

Abstract

Matrix-parametrized models (MPMs) are widely used in machine learning (ML) applications. In large-scale ML problems, the parameter matrix of a MPM can grow at an unexpected rate, resulting in high communication and parameter synchronization costs. To address this issue, we offer two contributions: first, we develop a computation model for a large family of MPMs, which share the following property: the parameter update computed on each data sample is a rank-1 matrix, *i.e.* the outer product of two "sufficient factors" (SFs). Second, we implement a decentralized, peer-to-peer system, Sufficient Factor Broadcasting (SFB), which broadcasts the SFs among worker machines, and reconstructs the update matrices locally at each worker. SFB takes advantage of small rank-1 matrix updates and efficient partial broadcasting strategies to dramatically improve communication efficiency. We propose a graph optimization based partial broadcasting scheme, which minimizes the delay of information dissemination under the constraint that each machine only communicates with a subset rather than all of machines. Furthermore, we provide theoretical analysis to show that SFB guarantees convergence of algorithms (under full broadcasting) without requiring a centralized synchronization mechanism. Experiments corroborate SFB's efficiency on four MPMs.

1 INTRODUCTION

Machine Learning (ML) provides a principled and effective mechanism for extracting latent structure and patterns from raw data and making automatic predictions and decisions. The growing prevalence of *big data*, such as billions of text pages in the web, hundreds of hours of video uploaded to video-sharing sites every minute[1], accompanied by an increasing need of *big model*, such as neural networks (Dean et al., 2012) and topic models (Yuan et al., 2015) with billions of parameters, has inspired the design and development of distributed machine learning systems (Dean and Ghemawat, 2008; Gonzalez et al., 2012; Zaharia et al., 2012; Li et al., 2014; Xing et al., 2015) running on research clusters, data center and cloud platforms with 10s-1000s machines.

For many machine learning (ML) models, such as multiclass logistic regression (MLR), neural networks (NN) (Chilimbi et al., 2014), distance metric learning (DML) (Xing et al., 2002) and sparse coding (SC) (Olshausen and Field, 1997), their parameters can be represented by a matrix $\mathbf{W}$. For example, in MLR, rows of $\mathbf{W}$ represent the classification coefficient vectors corresponding to different classes; whereas in SC rows of $\mathbf{W}$ correspond to the basis vectors used for reconstructing the observed data. A learning algorithm, such as stochastic gradient descent (SGD), would iteratively compute an update $\Delta\mathbf{W}$ from data, to be aggregated with the current version of $\mathbf{W}$. We call such models *matrix-parameterized models* (MPMs).

Learning MPMs in large scale ML problems is challenging: ML application scales have risen dramatically, a good example being the ImageNet (Deng et al., 2009) compendium with millions of images grouped into tens of thousands of classes. To ensure fast running times when scaling up MPMs to such large problems, it is desirable to turn to distributed computation; however, a unique challenge to MPMs is that the parameter matrix grows rapidly with problem size, causing straightforward parallelization strategies to perform less ideally. Consider a data-parallel algorithm, in which every worker uses a subset of the data to update the parameters — a common paradigm is to synchronize the full parameter matrix and update matrices amongst all workers (Dean and Ghemawat, 2008; Dean et al., 2012; Li et al., 2015; Chilimbi et al., 2014; Sindhwani and Ghoting, 2012; Gopal and Yang, 2013). However, this synchronization can quickly become a bottle-

[1]https://www.youtube.com/yt/press/statistics.html

neck: take MLR for example, in which the parameter matrix $\mathbf{W}$ is of size $J \times D$, where J is the number of classes and D is the feature dimensionality. In one application of MLR to Wikipedia (Partalas et al., 2015), $J = 325\text{k}$ and $D > 10,000$, thus $\mathbf{W}$ contains several billion entries (tens of GBs of memory). Because typical computer cluster networks can only transfer a few GBs per second at the most, inter-machine synchronization of $\mathbf{W}$ can dominate and bottleneck the actual algorithmic computation. In recent years, many distributed frameworks have been developed for large scale machine learning, including Bulk Synchronous Parallel (BSP) systems such as Hadoop (Dean and Ghemawat, 2008) and Spark (Zaharia et al., 2012), graph computation frameworks such as GraphLab (Gonzalez et al., 2012), and bounded-asynchronous key-value stores such as DistBelief(Dean et al., 2012), Petuum-PS (Ho et al., 2013), Project Adam (Chilimbi et al., 2014) and (Li et al., 2014). When using these systems to learn MPMs, it is common to transmit the full parameter matrices $\mathbf{W}$ and/or matrix updates $\Delta\mathbf{W}$ between machines, usually in a server-client style (Dean and Ghemawat, 2008; Dean et al., 2012; Sindhwani and Ghoting, 2012; Gopal and Yang, 2013; Chilimbi et al., 2014; Li et al., 2015). As the matrices become larger due to increasing problem sizes, so do communication costs and synchronization delays — hence, reducing such costs is a key priority when using these frameworks.

We begin by investigating the structure of matrix parameterized models, in order to design efficient communication strategies. We focus on models with a common property: when the parameter matrix $\mathbf{W}$ of these models is optimized with stochastic gradient descent (SGD) (Dean et al., 2012; Ho et al., 2013; Chilimbi et al., 2014) or stochastic dual coordinate ascent (SDCA) (Hsieh et al., 2008; Shalev-Shwartz and Zhang, 2013), the update $\triangle\mathbf{W}$ computed over one (or a few) data sample(s) is of low-rank, *e.g.* it can be written as the outer product of two vectors $\mathbf{u}$ and $\mathbf{v}$: $\triangle\mathbf{W} = \mathbf{u}\mathbf{v}^\top$. The vectors $\mathbf{u}$ and $\mathbf{v}$ are *sufficient factors* (SF, meaning that they are sufficient to reconstruct the update matrix $\triangle\mathbf{W}$). A rich set of models (Olshausen and Field, 1997; Lee and Seung, 1999; Xing et al., 2002; Chilimbi et al., 2014) fall into this family: for instance, when solving an MLR problem using SGD, the stochastic gradient is $\triangle\mathbf{W} = \mathbf{u}\mathbf{v}^\top$, where $\mathbf{u}$ is the prediction probability vector and $\mathbf{v}$ is the feature vector. Similarly, when solving an ℓ_2 regularized MLR problem using SDCA, the update matrix $\triangle\mathbf{W}$ also admits such as a structure, where $\mathbf{u}$ is the update vector of a dual variable and $\mathbf{v}$ is the feature vector. Other models include neural networks (Chilimbi et al., 2014), distance metric learning (Xing et al., 2002), sparse coding (Olshausen and Field, 1997), non-negative matrix factorization (Lee and Seung, 1999) and principal component analysis, to name a few.

Leveraging this property, we propose a system called Sufficient Factor Broadcasting (SFB), whose basic idea is to send sufficient factors (SFs) between workers, which then reconstruct matrix updates $\triangle\mathbf{W}$ locally, thus greatly reducing inter-machine parameter communication. This stands in contrast to the well-established parameter server idiom (Chilimbi et al., 2014; Li et al., 2014), a centralized design where workers maintain a "local" image of the parameters $\mathbf{W}$, which are synchronized with a central parameter image $\mathbf{W}$ (stored on the "parameter servers"). In existing parameter server designs, the (small, low-rank) updates $\triangle\mathbf{W}$ are accumulated into the central parameter server's $\mathbf{W}$, and the low-rank structure of each update $\triangle\mathbf{W}$ is lost in the process. Thus, the parameter server can only transmit the (large, full-rank) matrix $\mathbf{W}$ to the workers, inducing extra communication that could be avoided. We address this issue by designing SFB as a *decentralized, peer-to-peer system*, where each worker keeps its own image of the parameters $\mathbf{W}$ (either in memory or on local disk), and sends sufficient factors to only a subset of other workers, via "partial broadcasting" strategies that avoid the usual $O(P^2)$ peer-to-peer broadcast communication over P machines. SFB also exploits ML algorithm tolerance to bounded-asynchronous execution (Ho et al., 2013), as supported by both our experiments and a theoretical proof. SFB is highly communication-efficient; transmission costs are linear in the dimensions of the parameter matrix, and the resulting faster communication greatly reduces waiting time in synchronous systems (e.g. Hadoop and Spark), or improves parameter freshness in (bounded) asynchronous systems (e.g. GraphLab, Petuum-PS and (Li et al., 2014)). SFs have been used to speed up some (but not all) network communication in deep learning (Chilimbi et al., 2014); our work differs primarily in that we always transmit SFs, never full matrices.

The major contributions of this paper are as follows:

- We identify the *sufficient factor property* of a large family of matrix-parametrized models when solved with two popular algorithms: stochastic gradient descent and stochastic dual coordinate ascent.
- In light of the sufficient factor property, we propose a *sufficient factor broadcasting* (SFB) model of computation. Through a decentralized, peer-to-peer architecture with bounded-asynchronous partial broadcasting, SFB greatly reduces communication complexity while maintaining excellent empirical performance.
- To further reduce communication cost, we investigate a partial broadcasting scheme and propose a graph-optimization based approach to determine the topology of the communication network.
- We analyze the communication and computation costs of SFB and provide a convergence guarantee of SFB based minibatch SGD algorithm, under bulk synchronous and bounded asynchronous executions.

- We empirically evaluate SFB on four popular models, and confirm the efficiency and low communication complexity of SFB.

The rest of the paper is organized as follows. In Section 2 and 3, we introduce the sufficient factor property of matrix-parametrized models and propose the sufficient factor broadcasting computation model, respectively. Section 4 analyzes the costs and convergence behavior of SFB. Section 5 gives experimental results. Section 6 reviews related works and Section 7 concludes the paper.

2 SUFFICIENT FACTOR PROPERTY OF MATRIX-PARAMETRIZED MODELS

The core goal of Sufficient Factor Broadcasting (SFB) is to reduce network communication costs for matrix-parametrized models; specifically, those that follow an optimization formulation

$$\textbf{(P)}\quad \min_{\mathbf{W}} \quad \frac{1}{N}\sum_{i=1}^{N} f_i(\mathbf{W}\mathbf{a}_i) + h(\mathbf{W}) \qquad (1)$$

where the model is parametrized by a matrix $\mathbf{W} \in \mathbb{R}^{J\times D}$. The loss function $f_i(\cdot)$ is typically defined over a set of training samples $\{(\mathbf{a}_i, \mathbf{b}_i)\}_{i=1}^N$, with the dependence on $\mathbf{b}_i$ being suppressed. We allow $f_i(\cdot)$ to be either convex or nonconvex, smooth or nonsmooth (with subgradient everywhere); examples include ℓ_2 loss and multiclass logistic loss, amongst others. The regularizer $h(\mathbf{W})$ is assumed to admit an efficient proximal operator $\text{prox}_h(\cdot)$. For example, $h(\cdot)$ could be an indicator function of convex constraints, ℓ_1-, ℓ_2-, trace-norm, to name a few. The vectors $\mathbf{a}_i$ and $\mathbf{b}_i$ can represent observed features, supervised information (e.g., class labels in classification, response values in regression), or even unobserved auxiliary information (such as sparse codes in sparse coding (Olshausen and Field, 1997)) associated with data sample i. The key property we exploit below ranges from the matrix-vector multiplication $\mathbf{W}\mathbf{a}_i$. This optimization problem **(P)** can be used to represent a rich set of ML models (Olshausen and Field, 1997; Lee and Seung, 1999; Xing et al., 2002; Chilimbi et al., 2014), such as the following:

Distance Metric Learning (DML) (Xing et al., 2002) improves the performance of other ML algorithms, by learning a new distance function that correctly represents similar and dissimilar pairs of data samples; this distance function is a matrix $\mathbf{W}$ that can have billions of parameters or more, depending on the data sample dimensionality. The vector $\mathbf{a}_i$ is the difference of the feature vectors in the ith data pair and $f_i(\cdot)$ can be either a quadratic function or a hinge loss function, depending on the similarity/dissimilarity label $\mathbf{b}_i$ of the data pair. In both cases, $h(\cdot)$ can be an ℓ_1-, ℓ_2-, trace-norm regularizer or simply $h(\cdot) = 0$ (no regularization).

Sparse Coding (SC) (Olshausen and Field, 1997) learns a dictionary of basis from data, so that the data can be represented sparsely (and thus efficiently) in terms of the dictionary. In SC, $\mathbf{W}$ is the dictionary matrix, $\mathbf{a}_i$ are the sparse codes, $\mathbf{b}_i$ is the input feature vector and $f_i(\cdot)$ is a quadratic function (Olshausen and Field, 1997). To prevent the entries in $\mathbf{W}$ from becoming too large, each column $\mathbf{W}_k$ must satisfy $\|\mathbf{W}_k\|_2 \leq 1$. In this case, $h(\mathbf{W})$ is an indicator function which equals 0 if $\mathbf{W}$ satisfies the constraints and equals ∞ otherwise.

2.1 OPTIMIZATION VIA PROXIMAL SGD, SDCA

To solve the optimization problem **(P)**, it is common to employ either (proximal) stochastic gradient descent (SGD) (Dean et al., 2012; Ho et al., 2013; Chilimbi et al., 2014; Li et al., 2015) or stochastic dual coordinate ascent (SDCA) (Hsieh et al., 2008; Shalev-Shwartz and Zhang, 2013), both of which are popular and well-established parallel optimization techniques.

Proximal SGD: In proximal SGD, a stochastic estimate of the gradient, $\triangle\mathbf{W}$, is first computed over one data sample (or a mini-batch of samples), in order to update $\mathbf{W}$ via $\mathbf{W} \leftarrow \mathbf{W} - \eta \triangle \mathbf{W}$ (where η is the learning rate). Following this, the proximal operator $\text{prox}_{\eta h}(\cdot)$ is applied to $\mathbf{W}$. Notably, the stochastic gradient $\triangle\mathbf{W}$ in **(P)** can be written as the outer product of two vectors $\triangle\mathbf{W} = \mathbf{u}\mathbf{v}^\top$, where $\mathbf{u} = \frac{\partial f(\mathbf{W}\mathbf{a}_i, \mathbf{b}_i)}{\partial(\mathbf{W}\mathbf{a}_i)}$, $\mathbf{v} = \mathbf{a}_i$, according to the chain rule. Later, we will show that this low rank structure of $\triangle\mathbf{W}$ can greatly reduce inter-worker communication.

Stochastic DCA: SDCA applies to problems **(P)** where $f_i(\cdot)$ is convex and $h(\cdot)$ is strongly convex (*e.g.* when $h(\cdot)$ contains the squared ℓ_2 norm); it solves the dual problem of **(P)**, via stochastic coordinate ascent on the dual variables. Introducing the dual matrix $\mathbf{U} = [\mathbf{u}_1, \ldots, \mathbf{u}_N] \in \mathbb{R}^{J\times N}$ and the data matrix $\mathbf{A} = [\mathbf{a}_1, \ldots, \mathbf{a}_N] \in \mathbb{R}^{D\times N}$, the dual problem of **(P)** can be written as

$$\textbf{(D)}\quad \min_{\mathbf{U}} \quad \frac{1}{N}\sum_{i=1}^{N} f_i^*(-\mathbf{u}_i) + h^*(\tfrac{1}{N}\mathbf{U}\mathbf{A}^\top) \qquad (2)$$

where $f_i^*(\cdot)$ and $h^*(\cdot)$ are the Fenchel conjugate functions of $f_i(\cdot)$ and $h(\cdot)$, respectively. The primal-dual matrices $\mathbf{W}$ and $\mathbf{U}$ are connected by[2] $\mathbf{W} = \nabla h^*(\mathbf{Z})$, where the auxiliary matrix $\mathbf{Z} := \frac{1}{N}\mathbf{U}\mathbf{A}^\top$. Algorithmically, we need to update the dual matrix $\mathbf{U}$, the primal matrix $\mathbf{W}$, and the auxiliary matrix $\mathbf{Z}$: every iteration, we pick a random data sample i, and compute the stochastic update $\triangle\mathbf{u}_i$ by minimizing **(D)** while holding $\{\mathbf{u}_j\}_{j\neq i}$ fixed. The dual variable is updated via $\mathbf{u}_i \leftarrow \mathbf{u}_i - \triangle\mathbf{u}_i$, the auxiliary variable via $\mathbf{Z} \leftarrow \mathbf{Z} - \triangle\mathbf{u}_i\mathbf{a}_i^\top$, and the primal variable via $\mathbf{W} \leftarrow \nabla h^*(\mathbf{Z})$. Similar to SGD, the update of $\mathbf{Z}$ is also the outer product of two vectors: $\triangle\mathbf{u}_i$ and $\mathbf{a}_i$, which can be exploited to reduce communication cost.

[2] The strong convexity of h is equivalent to the smoothness of the conjugate function h^*.

Sufficient Factor Property in SGD and SDCA: In both SGD and SDCA, the parameter matrix update can be computed as the outer product of two vectors — we call these sufficient factors (SFs). This property can be leveraged to improve the communication efficiency of distributed ML systems: instead of communicating parameter/update matrices among machines, we can communicate the SFs and reconstruct the update matrices locally at each machine. Because the SFs are much smaller in size, synchronization costs can be dramatically reduced. See Section 4 below for a detailed analysis.

Low-rank Extensions: More generally, the update matrix $\triangle\mathbf{W}$ may not be exactly rank-1, but still of very low rank. For example, when each machine uses a mini-batch of size K, $\triangle\mathbf{W}$ is of rank at most K; in Restricted Boltzmann Machines, the update of the weight matrix is computed from four vectors $\mathbf{u}_1, \mathbf{v}_1, \mathbf{u}_2, \mathbf{v}_2$ as $\mathbf{u}_1\mathbf{v}_1^\top - \mathbf{u}_2\mathbf{v}_2^\top$, *i.e.* rank-2; for the BFGS algorithm (Bertsekas, 1999), the update of the inverse Hessian is computed from two vectors $\mathbf{u}, \mathbf{v}$ as $\alpha\mathbf{u}\mathbf{u}^\top - \beta(\mathbf{u}\mathbf{v}^\top + \mathbf{v}\mathbf{u}^\top)$, *i.e.* rank-3. Even when the update matrix $\triangle\mathbf{W}$ is not genuinely low-rank, to reduce communication cost, it might still make sense to send only a certain low-rank *approximation*. We intend to investigate these possibilities in future work.

3 SUFFICIENT FACTOR BROADCASTING

Leveraging the SF property of the update matrix in problems **(P)** and **(D)**, we propose a *Sufficient Factor Broadcasting* (SFB) system that supports efficient (low-communication) distributed learning of the parameter matrix $\mathbf{W}$. We assume a setting with P workers, each of which holds a data shard and a copy of the parameter matrix[3] $\mathbf{W}$. Stochastic updates to $\mathbf{W}$ are generated via proximal SGD or SDCA, and communicated between machines to ensure parameter consistency. In proximal SGD, on every iteration, each worker p computes SFs $(\mathbf{u}_p, \mathbf{v}_p)$, based on one data sample $\mathbf{x}_i = (\mathbf{a}_i, \mathbf{b}_i)$ in the worker's data shard. The worker then broadcasts $(\mathbf{u}_p, \mathbf{v}_p)$ to all other workers; once all P workers have performed their broadcast (and have thus received all SFs), they re-construct the P update matrices (one per data sample) from the P SFs, and apply them to update their local copy of $\mathbf{W}$. Finally, each worker applies the proximal operator $\text{prox}_h(\cdot)$. When using SDCA, the above procedure is instead used to broadcast SFs for the auxiliary matrix $\mathbf{Z}$, which is then used to obtain the primal matrix $\mathbf{W} = \nabla h^*(\mathbf{Z})$. Figure 1 illustrates SFB operation: 4 workers compute their respective SFs $(\mathbf{u}_1, \mathbf{v}_1)$, ..., $(\mathbf{u}_4, \mathbf{v}_4)$, which are then broadcast to the other 3 workers. Each worker p uses all 4 SFs $(\mathbf{u}_1, \mathbf{v}_1), \ldots, (\mathbf{u}_4, \mathbf{v}_4)$ to exactly reconstruct the update matrices $\triangle\mathbf{W}_p = \mathbf{u}_p\mathbf{v}_p^\top$, and update their local copy of the parameter matrix: $\mathbf{W}_p \leftarrow \mathbf{W}_p - \sum_{q=1}^4 \mathbf{u}_q\mathbf{v}_q^\top$. While the above description reflects synchronous execution, it is easy to extend to (bounded) asynchronous execution.

[3]For simplicity, we assume each worker has enough memory to hold a full copy of the parameter matrix $\mathbf{W}$. If $\mathbf{W}$ is too large, one can either partition it across multiple machines (Dean et al., 2012; Li et al., 2014), or use local disk storage (*i.e.* out of core operation). We plan to investigate these strategies as future work.

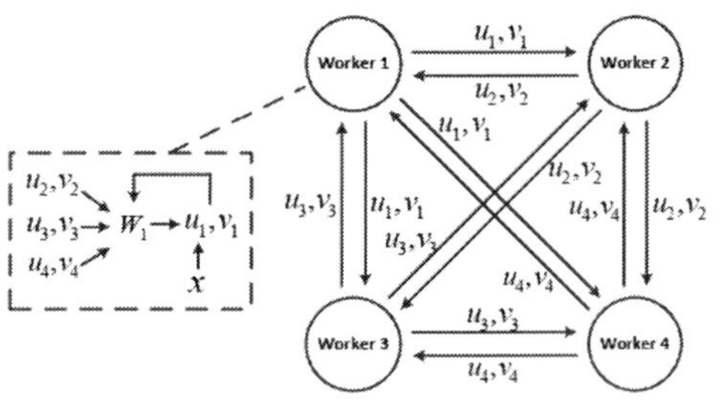

Figure 1: Sufficient Factor Broadcasting (SFB).

SFB vs Client-Server Architectures: The SFB peer-to-peer topology can be contrasted with a "full-matrix" client-server architecture for parameter synchronization, e.g. as used by Project Adam (Chilimbi et al., 2014) to learn neural networks: there, a centralized server maintains the global parameter matrix, and each client keeps a local copy. Clients compute sufficient factors and send them to the server, which uses the SFs to update the global parameter matrix; the server then sends the full, updated parameter matrix back to clients. Although client-to-server costs are reduced (by sending SFs), server-to-client costs are still expensive because full parameter matrices need to be sent. In contrast, the peer-to-peer SFB topology never sends full matrices; only SFs are sent over the network. We also note that under SFB, the update matrices are reconstructed at each of the P machines, rather than once at a central server (for full-matrix architectures). Our experiments show that the time taken for update reconstruction is empirically negligible compared to communication and SF computation.

Partial Broadcasting A naive peer-to-peer topology incurs a communication cost of $O(P^2)$ (where P is the number of worker machines), which inhibits scalability to data center scale clusters where P can reach several thousand (Dean et al., 2012; Li et al., 2014). Hence, SFB adopts an (optional) partial broadcasting scheme where each machine connects with and sends messages to a subset of Q machines (rather than all other machines), thus reducing communication costs from $O(P^2)$ to $O(PQ)$. Figure 2 presents an example. In partial broadcasting, an update U_p^t generated by machine p at iteration t is sent only to machines that are directly connected with p (and the update U_p^t takes effect at iteration $t+1$). The effect of U_p^t is *indirectly and eventually* transmitted to every other machine q, via the updates generated by machines sitting between p and q in the topology. This happens at iteration $t + \tau$, for some delay $\tau > 1$ that depends on Q and the location of p and q in the network topology. Consequently, the

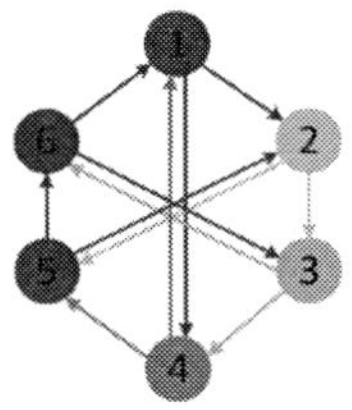

Figure 2: An Example of Partial Broadcasting.

P machines will not have the exact same parameter image $\mathbf{W}$, even under bulk synchronous parallel execution — yet surprisingly, this does not empirically (Section 5) compromise algorithm accuracy as long as Q is not too small. We hypothesize that this property is related to the tolerance of ML algorithms to bounded-asynchronous execution and random error, and we defer a formal proof to future work.

Determining the "best" topology of partial broadcasting, i.e., which subset of machines each machine should send message to, is a challenging issue. Previous studies (Li et al., 2015) are mostly based on heuristics. While empirically effective, these heuristics lack a mathematically formalizable objective. To address this issue, we propose an optimization-oriented solution, with the goal to achieve fast dissemination of information: the effect of updates generated at each machine should be "seen" by all other machines as quickly as possible. Formally, we aim to reduce the delay τ. Consider a directed network with P nodes, where $e_{pq} = 1$ denotes that node p sends message to node q and $e_{pq} = 0$ otherwise. Let c_{pq} denote the shortest directed path from node p to q. It is easy to see that $\tau = |c_{pq}|$, where $|c_{pq}|$ is the length of c_{pq}. Letting $E = \{e_{pq}\}_{p=1,q\neq p}^{P}$ we can find a network topology that minimizes τ by solving this optimization problem:

$$\begin{array}{ll} \min_E & \sum_{p=1}^{P} \sum_{q\neq p}^{P} |c_{pq}| \\ s.t. & \sum_{q\neq p}^{P} e_{pq} = Q, \forall p \end{array} \qquad (3)$$

which can be efficiently solved by using a Branch and Bound (Land and Doig, 1960) searching of the graph structure, in conjunction with an algorithm (Williams, 2014) finding all-pairs shortest path in directed graphs.

Mini-batch Proximal SGD/SDCA: SFB can also be used in mini-batch proximal SGD/SDCA; every iteration, each worker samples a mini-batch of K data points, and computes K pairs of sufficient factors $\{(\mathbf{u}_i, \mathbf{v}_i)\}_{i=1}^{K}$. These K pairs are broadcast to all other workers, which reconstruct the originating worker's update matrix as $\triangle\mathbf{W} = \frac{1}{K}\sum_{i=1}^{K} \mathbf{u}_i\mathbf{v}_i^{\top}$.

Consistency Models SFB supports two consistency models: Bulk Synchronous Parallel (BSP-SFB) and Stale Synchronous Parallel (SSP-SFB), and we provide theoretical convergence guarantees in the next section.

- **BSP-SFB:** Under BSP (Dean and Ghemawat, 2008; Zaharia et al., 2012), an end-of-iteration global barrier ensures all workers have completed their work, and synchronized their parameter copies, before proceeding to the next iteration. BSP is a strong consistency model, that guarantees the same computational outcome (and thus algorithm convergence) each time.

- **SSP-SFB:** BSP can be sensitive to stragglers (slow workers) (Ho et al., 2013), limiting the distributed system to the speed of the slowest worker. Stale Synchronous Parallel (SSP) (Bertsekas and Tsitsiklis, 1989; Ho et al., 2013) communication model addresses this issue, by allowing workers to advance at different rates, provided that the difference in iteration number between the slowest and fastest workers is no more than a user-provided staleness s. SSP alleviates the straggler issue while guaranteeing algorithm convergence (Ho et al., 2013). Under SSP-SFB, each worker p tracks the number of SF pairs computed by itself, t_p, versus the number $\tau_p^q(t_p)$ of SF pairs received from each worker q. If there exists a worker q such that $t_p - \tau_p^q(t_p) > s$ (*i.e.* some worker q is likely more than s iterations behind worker p), then worker p pauses until q is no longer s iterations or more behind.

```
sfb_app mlr ( int J, int D, int staleness )
//SF computation function
function compute_sv ( sfb_app mlr ):
  while ( ! converged ):
    X = sample_minibatch ()
    foreach x_i in X:
      //sufficient factor u_i
      pred = predict ( mlr.para_mat, x_i )
      mlr.sv_list[i].write_u ( pred )
      //sufficient factor v_i
      mlr.sv_list[i].write_v ( x_i )
    commit()
```

Figure 3: Multiclass LR Pseudocode.

Programming Interface The SFB programming interface is simple; users need to provide a SF computation function to specify how to compute the sufficient factors. To send out SF pairs $(\mathbf{u}, \mathbf{v})$, the user adds them to a buffer object sv_list, via: $write\_u(vec\_u)$, $write\_v(vec\_v)$, which set i-th SF $\mathbf{u}$ or $\mathbf{v}$ to vec_u or vec_v. All SF pairs are sent out at the end of an iteration, which is signaled by $commit()$. Finally, in order to choose between BSP and SSP consistency, users simply set $staleness$ to an appropriate value (0 for BSP, > 0 for SSP). SFB automatically updates workers' local parameter matrix using all SF pairs — including both locally computed SF pairs added to sv_list, as well as SF pairs received from other workers. Figure 3 shows SFB pseudocode for multiclass logistic regression. For proximal SGD/SDCA algorithms, SFB requires users to write an additional function, $prox(mat)$, which applies the proximal operator $\text{prox}_h(\cdot)$ (or the SDCA dual operator $h^*(\cdot)$) to the parameter matrix mat.

4 COST ANALYSIS AND THEORY

We now examine the costs and convergence behavior of SFB under synchronous and bounded-async (e.g. SSP (Bertsekas and Tsitsiklis, 1989; Ho et al., 2013)) consistency, and show that SFB can be preferable to full-matrix synchronization/communication schemes.

4.1 COST ANALYSIS

Figure 4 compares the communications, space and time (to apply updates to $\mathbf{W}$) costs of peer-to-peer SFB, against full matrix synchronization (FMS) under a client-server architecture (Chilimbi et al., 2014). For SFB with a full broadcasting scheme, in each minibatch, every worker broadcasts K SF pairs $(\mathbf{u}, \mathbf{v})$ to $P-1$ other workers, i.e. $O(P^2K(J+D))$ values are sent per iteration — linear in matrix dimensions J, D, and quadratic in P. For SFB with a partial broadcasting scheme, every worker communicates SF pairs with $Q < P$ peers, hence the communication cost is reduced to $O(PQK(J+D))$. Because SF pairs cannot be aggregated before transmission, the cost has a dependency on K. In contrast, the communication cost in FMS is $O(PJD)$, linear in P, quadratic in matrix dimensions, and independent of K. For both SFB and FMS, the cost of storing $\mathbf{W}$ is $O(JD)$ on every machine. As for the time taken to update $\mathbf{W}$ per iteration, FMS costs $O(PJD)$ at the server (to aggregate P client update matrices) and $O(PKJD)$ at the P clients (to aggregate K updates into one update matrix). By comparison, SFB bears a cost of $O(P^2KJD)$ under full broadcasting and $O(PQKJD)$ under partial broadcasting due to the additional overhead of reconstructing each update matrix P or Q times.

Compared with FMS, SFB achieves communication savings by paying an extra computation cost. In a number of practical scenarios, such a tradeoff is worthwhile. Consider large problem scales where $\min(J, D) \geq 10000$, and moderate minibatch sizes $1 \leq K \leq 100$ (as studied in this paper); when using a moderate number of machines (around 10-100), the $O(P^2K(J+D))$ communications cost of SFB is lower than the $O(PJD)$ cost for FMS, and the relative benefit of SFB improves as the dimensions J, D of $\mathbf{W}$ grow. In data center scale computing environments with thousands of machines, we can adopt the partial broadcasting scheme. As for the time needed to apply updates to $\mathbf{W}$, it turns out that the additional cost of reconstructing each update matrix P or Q times in SFB is negligible in practice — we have observed in our experiments that the time spent computing SFs, as well as communicating SFs over the network, greatly dominates the cost of reconstructing update matrices using SFs. Overall, the communication savings dominate the added computational overhead, which we validated in experiments.

4.2 CONVERGENCE ANALYSIS

We study the convergence of minibatch SGD under full broadcasting SFB (with extensions to proximal-SGD, SDCA being a topic for future study). Since SFB is a peer-to-peer decentralized computation model, we need to show that parameter copies on different workers converge to the same limiting point without a centralized coordination, even under delays in communication due to bounded asynchronous execution. In this respect, we differ from analyses of centralized parameter server systems (Ho et al., 2013), which instead show convergence of global parameters on the central server.

We wish to solve the optimization problem $\min_{\mathbf{W}} \sum_{m=1}^{M} f_m(\mathbf{W})$, where M is the number of training data minibatches, and f_m corresponds to the loss function on the m-th minibatch. Assume the training data minibatches $\{1, ..., M\}$ are divided into P disjoint subsets $\{S_1, ..., S_P\}$ with $|S_p|$ denoting the number of minibatches in S_p. Denote $F = \sum_{m=1}^{M} f_m$ as the total loss, and for $p = 1, \ldots, P$, $F_p := \sum_{j \in S_p} f_j$ is the loss on S_p (on the p-th machine).

Consider a distributed system with P machines. Each machine p keeps a local variable $\mathbf{W}_p$ and the training data in S_p. At each iteration, machine p draws one minibatch I_p uniformly at random from partition S_p, and computes the partial gradient $\sum_{j \in I_p} \nabla f_j(\mathbf{W}_p)$. Each machine updates its local variable by accumulating partial updates from all machines. Denote η_c as the learning rate at c-th iteration on every machine. The partial update generated by machine p at its c-th iteration is denoted as $U_p(\mathbf{W}_p^c, I_p^c) = -\eta_c |S_p| \sum_{j \in I_p^c} \nabla f_j(\mathbf{W}_p^c)$. Note that I_p^c is random and the factor $|S_p|$ is to restore unbiasedness in expectation. Then the local update rule of machine p is

$$\begin{aligned} &\mathbf{W}_p^c = \mathbf{W}^0 + \textstyle\sum_{q=1}^{P} \sum_{t=0}^{\tau_p^q(c)} U_q(\mathbf{W}_q^t, I_q^t) \\ &0 \leq (c-1) - \tau_p^q(c) \leq s \end{aligned} \tag{4}$$

where $\mathbf{W}^0$ is the common initializer for all P machines, and $\tau_p^q(c)$ is the number of iterations machine q has transmitted to machine p when machine p conducts its c-th iteration. Clearly, $\tau_p^p(c) = c$. Note that we also require $\tau_p^q(c) \leq c-1$, *i.e.*, machine p will not use any partial updates of machine q that are too fast forward. This is to avoid correlation in the theoretical analysis. Hence, machine p (at its c-th iteration) accumulates updates generated by machine q up to iteration $\tau_p^q(c)$, which is restricted to be at most s iterations behind. This formulation, in which s is the maximum "staleness" allowed between any update and any worker, covers bulk synchronous parallel (BSP) full broadcasting ($s = 0$) and bounded-asynchronous full broadcasting ($s > 0$). The following standard assumptions are needed for our analysis:

Computational Model	Total comms, per iter	$\mathbf{W}$ storage per machine	$\mathbf{W}$ update time, per iter
SFB (peer-to-peer, full broadcasting)	$O(P^2K(J+D))$	$O(JD)$	$O(P^2KJD)$
SFB (peer-to-peer, partial broadcasting)	$O(PQK(J+D))$	$O(JD)$	$O(PQKJD)$
FMS (client-server (Chilimbi et al., 2014))	$O(PJD)$	$O(JD)$	$O(PJD)$ at server, $O(PKJD)$ at clients

Figure 4: Cost of using SFB versus FMS. K is minibatch size, J, D are dimensions of $\mathbf{W}$, and P is the number of workers.

Assumption 1. *(1) For all j, f_j is continuously differentiable and F is bounded from below; (2) ∇F, ∇F_p are Lipschitz continuous with constants L_F and L_p, respectively, and let $L = \sum_{p=1}^{P} L_p$; (3) There exists B, σ^2 such that for all p and c, we have (almost surely) $\|\mathbf{W}_p^c\| \leq B$ and $\mathbb{E}\| \, |S_p| \sum_{j \in I_p} \nabla f_j(\mathbf{W}) - \nabla F_p(\mathbf{W}) \, \|_2^2 \leq \sigma^2$.*

Our analysis is based on the following auxiliary update

$$\mathbf{W}^c = \mathbf{W}^0 + \sum_{q=1}^{P} \sum_{t=0}^{c-1} U_q(\mathbf{W}_q^t, I_q^t), \quad (5)$$

Compare to the local update (4) on machine p, essentially this auxiliary update accumulates all $c-1$ updates generated by all machines, instead of the $\tau_p^q(c)$ updates that machine p has access to. We show that all local machine parameter sequences are asymptotically consistent with this auxiliary sequence:

Theorem 1. *Let $\{\mathbf{W}_p^c\}$, $p = 1, \ldots, P$, and $\{\mathbf{W}^c\}$ be the local sequences and the auxiliary sequence generated by SFB for problem* **(P)** *(with $h \equiv 0$), respectively. Under Assumption 1 and set the learning rate $\eta_c = O(\sqrt{\frac{1}{L\sigma^2 Psc}})$, then we have*

- $\liminf_{c \to \infty} \mathbb{E}\|\nabla F(\mathbf{W}^c)\| = 0$, *hence there exists a subsequence of $\nabla F(\mathbf{W}^c)$ that almost surely vanishes;*
- $\lim_{c \to \infty} \max_p \|\mathbf{W}^c - \mathbf{W}_p^c\| = 0$, i.e. *the maximal disagreement between all local sequences and the auxiliary sequence converges to 0 (almost surely);*
- *There exists a common subsequence of $\{\mathbf{W}_p^c\}$ and $\{\mathbf{W}^c\}$ that converges almost surely to a stationary point of F, with the rate $\min_{c \leq C} \mathbb{E}\| \sum_{p=1}^{P} \nabla F_p(\mathbf{W}_p^c)\|_2^2 \leq O\left(\sqrt{\frac{L\sigma^2 Ps}{C}}\right)$*

Intuitively, Theorem 1 says that, given a properly-chosen learning rate, all local worker parameters $\{\mathbf{W}_p^c\}$ eventually converge to stationary points (i.e. local minima) of the objective function F, despite the fact that SF transmission can be delayed by up to s iterations. Thus, SFB learning is robust even under bounded-asynchronous communication (such as SSP). Our analysis differs from (Bertsekas and Tsitsiklis, 1989) in two ways: (1) Bertsekas and Tsitsiklis (1989) explicitly maintains a consensus model which would require transmitting the parameter matrix among worker machines — a communication bottleneck that we were able to avoid; (2) we allow subsampling in each worker machine. Accordingly, our theoretical guarantee is probabilistic, instead of the deterministic one in (Bertsekas and Tsitsiklis, 1989). In future work, we intend to extend the analysis to partial broadcasting under BSP and bounded-asynchronous execution. Partial broadcasting presents additional challenges, because updates are only sent to a subset of machines (rather than every machine).

5 EXPERIMENTS

We demonstrate how four popular models can be efficiently learnt using SFB: (1) multiclass logistic regression (MLR) and distance metric learning (DML)[4] based on SGD; (2) sparse coding (SC) based on proximal SGD; (3) ℓ_2 regularized multiclass logistic regression (L2-MLR) based on SDCA. For baselines, we compared with (a) Spark (Zaharia et al., 2012) for MLR and L2-MLR, and (b) full matrix synchronization (FMS) implemented on open-source parameter servers (Ho et al., 2013; Li et al., 2014) for all four models. In certain experiments, we made a comparison with the distributed (L2-)MLR system proposed in (Gopal and Yang, 2013). In FMS, workers send update matrices to the central server, which then sends up-to-date parameter matrices to workers[5]. Due to data sparsity, both the update matrices and sufficient factors are sparse; we use this fact to reduce communication and computation costs. The experiments were performed on a cluster where each machine has 64 2.1GHz AMD cores, 128G memory, and a 10Gbps network interface. Unless otherwise noted, 12 machines were used. Some experiments were conducted on 28 machines.

Datasets and Experimental Setup We used two datasets for our experiments: (1) ImageNet (Deng et al., 2009) ILSFRC2012 dataset, which contains 1.2 million images from 1000 categories; the images are represented with LLC features (Wang et al., 2010), whose dimensionality is 172k. (2) Wikipedia (Partalas et al., 2015) dataset, which contains 2.4 million documents from 325k categories; documents are represented with *term frequency, inverse document frequency* (tf-idf), with a dimensionality of 20k. We ran MLR, DML, SC, L2-MLR on the Wikipedia, Ima-

[4]For DML, we use the parametrization proposed in (Weinberger et al., 2005), which is a linear projection matrix $\mathbf{L} \in \mathbb{R}^{d \times k}$, where d is the feature dimension and k is the latent dimension.

[5]This has the same communication complexity as (Chilimbi et al., 2014), which sends SFs from workers to servers, but sends matrices from servers to workers; the latter matrix transmission dominates the total cost.

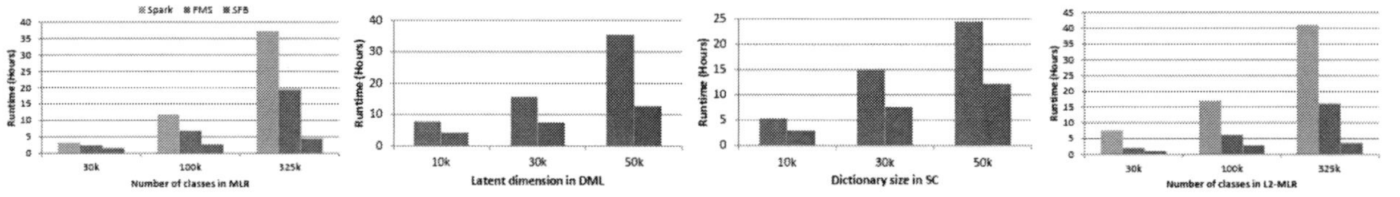

Figure 5: Convergence time versus model size for MLR, DML, SC, L2-MLR (left to right), under BSP.

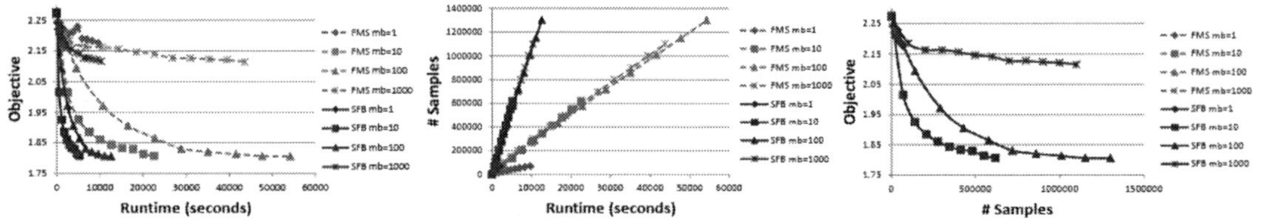

Figure 6: MLR objective vs runtime (left), #samples vs runtime (middle), objective vs #samples (right).

geNet, ImageNet, Wikipedia datasets respectively, and the parameter matrices contained up to 6.5b, 8.6b, 8.6b, 6.5b entries (the largest latent dimension for DML and largest dictionary size for SC were both 50k). The tradeoff parameters in SC and L2-MLR were set to 0.001 and 0.1. We tuned the minibatch size, and found that $K = 100$ was near-ideal for all experiments. All experiments used the same constant learning rate (tuned in the range $[10^{-5}, 1]$). Unless otherwise stated, a full broadcasting scheme is used for most experiments.

Convergence Speed and Quality Figure 5 shows the time taken to reach a fixed objective value, for different model sizes, using BSP consistency (SSP results are in the supplement), on 12 machines. SFB converges faster than FMS, as well as Spark v1.3.1[6]. This is because SFB has lower communication costs, hence a greater proportion of running time gets spent on computation rather than network waiting. This is shown in Figure 6, which plots data samples processed per second[7] (throughput) and algorithm progress per sample for MLR, under BSP consistency (SSP results are in the supplement) and varying minibatch sizes. The middle graph shows that SFB processes far more samples per second than FMS, while the rightmost graph shows that SFB and FMS produce exactly the same algorithm progress per sample under BSP. For this experiment, minibatch sizes between $K = 10$ and 100 performed the best as indicated by the leftmost graph. We point out that larger model sizes should further improve SFB's advantage over FMS, because SFB has linear communications cost in the matrix dimensions, whereas FMS has quadratic costs. Under a large model size (e.g., 325k classes in MLR), the communication cost becomes the bottleneck in FMS and causes prolonged network waiting time and parameter synchronization delays, while the cost is moderate in SFB.

We also evaluated SFB on 28 machines, under BSP and full broadcasting (Q=27). On MLR (325k classes), SFB took 2.46 hours to converge while FMS took 10.77 hours. On L2-MLR (325k classes), the convergence time of SFB is 2.14 hours while that of FMS is 9.31 hours.

We made a comparison with the distributed (L2-)MLR system proposed by (Gopal and Yang, 2013) on 12 machines. On MLR (325k classes), Gopal and Yang (2013) took 31.7 hours to converge while SFB took 4.5 hours. To converge on L2-MLR (325k classes), Gopal and Yang (2013) took 28.3 hours while SFB took 3.7 hours.

Scalability In all experiments that follow, we set the number of (L2-)MLR classes, DML latent dimension, SC dictionary size to 325k, 50k, 50k. Figure 7 shows SFB scalability with varying machines under BSP (SSP results are in the supplement), for MLR, DML, SC, L2-MLR, on 12 machines. In general, we observed close to linear (ideal) speedup, with a slight drop at 12 machines. On 28 machines, for MLR and L2-MLR, SFB achieved 17.4x and 15.7x speedup over one machine respectively.

Computation Time vs Network Waiting Time Figure 8 shows the *total* computation and network time required for SFB and FMS to converge, across a range of SSP staleness values[8] — in general, higher communication cost and lower staleness induce more network waiting. For all staleness values, SFB requires far less network waiting (because SFs are much smaller than full matrices in FMS). Computation time for SFB is slightly longer than FMS because (1) update matrices must be reconstructed on each SFB worker, and (2) SFB requires a few more iterations for convergence, because peer-to-peer communication causes a slightly more parameter inconsistency under staleness. Overall, the SFB reduction in network waiting time remains far greater than the added computation time, and outperforms FMS in total time. For both FMS and SFB,

[6] Spark is about 2x slower than PS (Ho et al., 2013) based C++ implementation of FMS, due to JVM and RDD overheads.

[7] We use samples per second instead of iterations, so different minibatch sizes can be compared.

[8] The Spark implementation does not easily permit this time breakdown, so we omit it.

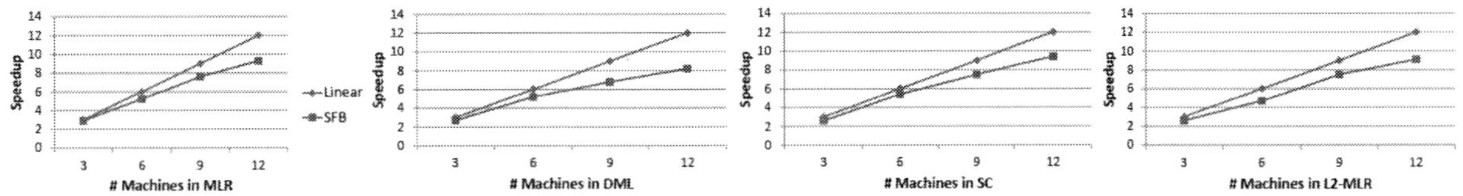

Figure 7: SFB scalability with varying machines under BSP, for MLR, DML, SC, L2-MLR (left to right).

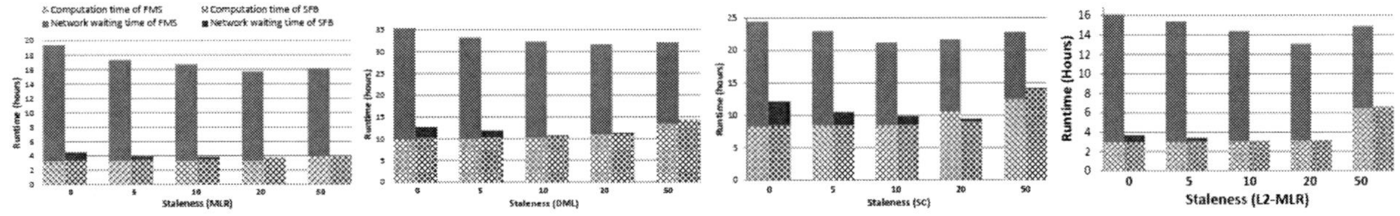

Figure 8: Computation vs network waiting time for MLR, DML, SC, L2-MLR (left to right).

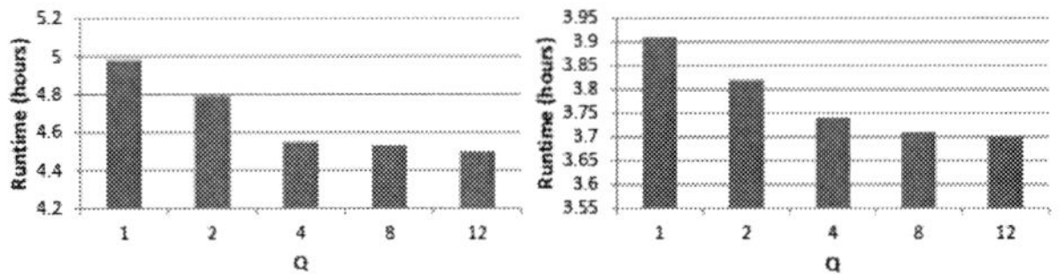

Figure 9: Convergence time versus Q in partial broadcasting for MLR (left) and L2-MLR (right), under BSP.

the shortest convergence times are achieved at moderate staleness values, confirming the importance of bounded-asynchronous communication.

Partial Broadcasting On 12 machines, we studied in partial broadcasting how the parameter Q, which is the number of peers to which each machine sends messages, affects the convergence speed of SFB. Figure 9 shows the convergence time of SFB on MLR and L2-MLR versus varying Q, under BSP (SSP results are given in supplements). First, we observed that SFB under partial broadcasting (PB) with $Q < 11$ converges to the same objective value as under full broadcasting (FB) where $Q = 11$. This provides empirical justification that PB preserves correctness and convergence of algorithms. Second, we noted that the convergence time of PB is affected by Q. As observed in this figure, a smaller Q incurs longer convergence time. This is because a smaller Q is more likely to cause the parameter copies on different workers to be out of synchronization and degrade iteration quality. However, as long as Q is not too small, the convergence speed of PB is comparable with FB. As shown in the figure, for $Q \geq 4$, the convergence time of PB is very close to FB. This demonstrates that using PB, we can reduce the communication cost from $O(P^2)$ to $O(PQ)$ with slight sacrifice of the convergence speed.

6 RELATED WORKS

A number of system and algorithmic solutions have been proposed to reduce communication cost in distributed ML. On the system side, Dean et al. (2012) proposed to reduce communication overhead by reducing the frequency of parameter/gradient exchanges between workers and the server. Li et al. (2014) used filters to select "important" parameters/updates for transmission to reduce the number of data entries to be communicated. On the algorithm side, Tsianos et al. (2012) studied the tradeoffs between communication and computation in distributed dual averaging and distributed stochastic dual coordinate ascent respectively. Shamir et al. (2014) proposed an approximate Newton-type method to achieve communication efficiency in distributed optimization. SFB is orthogonal to these existing approaches and be potentially combined with them to further reduce communication cost.

Peer-to-peer, decentralized architectures have been investigated in other distributed ML frameworks (Li et al., 2015). Our SFB system also adopts such an architecture, but with the specific purpose of supporting the SFB computation model, which is not explored by existing peer-to-peer ML frameworks.

7 CONCLUSIONS

In this paper, we identify the sufficient factor property of a large set of matrix-parametrized models: when these models are optimized with stochastic gradient descent or stochastic dual coordinate ascent, the update matrices are of low-rank. Leveraging this property, we propose a sufficient factor broadcasting strategy to efficiently handle the learning of these models with low communication cost. A partial broadcasting scheme is investigated to alleviate the overhead of full broadcasting. We analyze the cost and convergence property of SFB, whose communication efficiency is demonstrated in empirical evaluations.

Acknowledgements

P.X and E.X are supported by ONR N00014140684, DARPA XDATA FA8701220324, NSF IIS1447676.

References

Dimitri P Bertsekas. *Nonlinear programming*. Athena scientific Belmont, 1999.

Dimitri P. Bertsekas and John N. Tsitsiklis. *Parallel and Distributed Computation: Numerical Methods*. Prentice-Hall, 1989.

Trishul Chilimbi, Yutaka Suzue, Johnson Apacible, and Karthik Kalyanaraman. Project adam: building an efficient and scalable deep learning training system. In *USENIX Symposium on Operating Systems Design and Implementation*, 2014.

Jeffrey Dean and Sanjay Ghemawat. Mapreduce: simplified data processing on large clusters. *CACM*, 2008.

Jeffrey Dean, Greg Corrado, Rajat Monga, Kai Chen, Matthieu Devin, Mark Mao, Andrew Senior, Paul Tucker, Ke Yang, Quoc V Le, et al. Large scale distributed deep networks. In *NIPS*, 2012.

Jia Deng, Wei Dong, Richard Socher, Li-Jia Li, Kai Li, and Li Fei-Fei. Imagenet: A large-scale hierarchical image database. In *CVPR*, 2009.

Joseph E Gonzalez, Yucheng Low, Haijie Gu, Danny Bickson, and Carlos Guestrin. Powergraph: distributed graph-parallel computation on natural graphs. In *USENIX Symposium on Operating Systems Design and Implementation*, 2012.

Siddharth Gopal and Yiming Yang. Distributed training of large-scale logistic models. In *ICML*, 2013.

Qirong Ho, James Cipar, Henggang Cui, Seunghak Lee, Jin Kyu Kim, Phillip B Gibbons, Garth A Gibson, Greg Ganger, and Eric Xing. More effective distributed ml via a stale synchronous parallel parameter server. In *NIPS*, 2013.

Cho-Jui Hsieh, Kai-Wei Chang, Chih-Jen Lin, S Sathiya Keerthi, and Sellamanickam Sundararajan. A dual coordinate descent method for large-scale linear svm. In *ICML*, 2008.

Ailsa H Land and Alison G Doig. An automatic method of solving discrete programming problems. *Econometrica: Journal of the Econometric Society*, 1960.

Daniel D Lee and H Sebastian Seung. Learning the parts of objects by non-negative matrix factorization. *Nature*, 1999.

Hao Li, Asim Kadav, Erik Kruus, and Cristian Ungureanu. Malt: distributed data-parallelism for existing ml applications. In *Proceedings of the Tenth European Conference on Computer Systems*, 2015.

Mu Li, David G Andersen, Jun Woo Park, Alexander J Smola, Amr Ahmed, Vanja Josifovski, James Long, Eugene J Shekita, and Bor-Yiing Su. Scaling distributed machine learning with the parameter server. In *USENIX Symposium on Operating Systems Design and Implementation*, 2014.

Bruno A Olshausen and David J Field. Sparse coding with an overcomplete basis set: A strategy employed by v1? *Vision research*, 1997.

Ioannis Partalas, Aris Kosmopoulos, Nicolas Baskiotis, Thierry Artieres, George Paliouras, Eric Gaussier, Ion Androutsopoulos, Massih-Reza Amini, and Patrick Galinari. Lshtc: A benchmark for large-scale text classification. *arXiv:1503.08581 [cs.IR]*, 2015.

Shai Shalev-Shwartz and Tong Zhang. Stochastic dual coordinate ascent methods for regularized loss. *JMLR*, 2013.

Ohad Shamir, Nathan Srebro, and Tong Zhang. Communication efficient distributed optimization using an approximate newton-type method. In *ICML*, 2014.

Vikas Sindhwani and Amol Ghoting. Large-scale distributed non-negative sparse coding and sparse dictionary learning. In *KDD*, 2012.

Konstantinos Tsianos, Sean Lawlor, and Michael G Rabbat. Communication/computation tradeoffs in consensus-based distributed optimization. In *NIPS*, 2012.

Jinjun Wang, Jianchao Yang, Kai Yu, Fengjun Lv, Thomas Huang, and Yihong Gong. Locality-constrained linear coding for image classification. In *CVPR*, 2010.

Kilian Q Weinberger, John Blitzer, and Lawrence K Saul. Distance metric learning for large margin nearest neighbor classification. In *NIPS*, 2005.

Ryan Williams. Faster all-pairs shortest paths via circuit complexity. In *Proceedings of the 46th Annual ACM Symposium on Theory of Computing*, 2014.

Eric P Xing, Michael I Jordan, Stuart Russell, and Andrew Y Ng. Distance metric learning with application to clustering with side-information. In *NIPS*, 2002.

Eric P Xing, Qirong Ho, Wei Dai, Jin-Kyu Kim, Jinliang Wei, Seunghak Lee, Xun Zheng, Pengtao Xie, Abhimanu Kumar, and Yaoliang Yu. Petuum: A new platform for distributed machine learning on big data. In *KDD*, 2015.

Jinhui Yuan, Fei Gao, Qirong Ho, Wei Dai, Jinliang Wei, Xun Zheng, Eric Po Xing, Tie-Yan Liu, and Wei-Ying Ma. Lightlda: Big topic models on modest computer clusters. In *Proceedings of the 24th International Conference on World Wide Web*, 2015.

Matei Zaharia, Mosharaf Chowdhury, Tathagata Das, Ankur Dave, Justin Ma, Murphy McCauley, Michael J Franklin, Scott Shenker, and Ion Stoica. Resilient distributed datasets: A fault-tolerant abstraction for in-memory cluster computing. In *USENIX Symposium on Networked Systems Design and Implementation*, 2012.

Efficient Multi-Class Selective Sampling on Graphs

Peng Yang[‡] and **Peilin Zhao**[‡] and **Zhen Hai** [‡] and **Wei Liu**[†] and **Steven C.H. Hoi** [♯] and **Xiao-Li Li**[‡]
[‡] Institute for Infocomm Research, Singapore, 138632. Email: {yangp,zhaop,haiz,xlli}@i2r.a-star.edu.sg
[†] Tencent AI Lab, Shenzhen, China, 518057. Email: wliu@ee.columbia.edu
[♯] School of Information Systems, Singapore Management University, Singapore, 178902. Email: chhoi@smu.edu.sg

Abstract

A graph-based multi-class classification problem is typically converted into a collection of binary classification tasks via the one-vs.-all strategy, and then tackled by applying proper binary classification algorithms. Unlike the one-vs.-all strategy, we suggest a unified framework which operates directly on the multi-class problem without reducing it to a collection of binary tasks. Moreover, this framework makes active learning practically feasible for multi-class problems, while the one-vs.-all strategy cannot. Specifically, we employ a novel randomized query technique to prioritize the informative instances. This query technique based on the hybrid criterion of "margin" and "uncertainty" can achieve a comparable mistake bound with its fully supervised counterpart. To take full advantage of correctly predicted labels discarded in traditional conservative algorithms, we propose an aggressive selective sampling algorithm that can update the model even if no error occurs. Thanks to the aggressive updating strategy, the aggressive algorithm attains a lower mistake bound than its conservative competitors in expectation. Encouraging experimental results on real-world graph databases show that the proposed technique by querying an extremely small ratio of labels is able to accomplish better classification accuracy.

I. INTRODUCTION

Graphs, as a family of ubiquitous structures to model different types of networks, such as social networks (*e.g.*, Facebook, Twitter), biological networks [19], [20], and citation networks [21], have been widely applied in diverse applications. Particularly, one important task is to classify graph vertices into multiple classes, *e.g.*, authors in a citation network can be classified into different domains/classes, such as computer science, biology, physics, mathematics, economics, *etc.* To build a classifier, the desired classification model can be learnt from a set of vertex-label pairs in both offline [7] and online settings [16]. Offline algorithms can access the labels of all the stored vertices in a pool, which increases the storage requirement. Online learning, on the other hand, obtains the instances in a sequential order. It allows to access the label of the current vertex; after updating the model, the current input will be discarded [18]. Therefore, online learning is scalable to deal with massive datasets.

Although online classification on graphs has been well studied, it still remains as a challenging research subject, which is primarily due to three reasons. First, most online techniques focus on binary classification problems. Some approaches [14], [22] address multi-class problems by using output coding [12]. Such a setting may be ineffective and ill-defined since it generalizes multiple binary classifiers and each classifier is maintained and updated *independently* of the others [1]. Second, online learning assumes that the labels of all vertices are provided already. It is impractical as labeling every sample is expensive and time-consuming in many real-world applications. Third, in social networks, data usually arrives in a sequential order and the network scale can be very large, which brings a critical challenge to develop efficient and scalable algorithms for graph classification.

To address the aforementioned challenges, we present a unified framework to cope with multi-class online classification on graphs. Specifically, we adapt the graph Laplacian Regularized Least Squares (LapRLS) model to the multi-class setting, in which updating one class model has a global impact on the other classes. However, such an approach assumes that all labels are available, which obviously limits its usage to many domains. To minimize the labeling cost, we propose a new query technique based on both the "margin" [9] and "uncertainty" criteria, to only query the labels of the most informative instances. We

[1]Refer to the comparison between the binary and multi-class settings in the supplementary material.

theoretically analyze an online algorithm running on the selected labels by our query technique, which achieves a comparable mistake bound with the one that queries all labels. In addition, to take full advantage of correctly predicted labels that are discarded in conservative algorithms, we introduce an aggressive version of selective sampling. It hybrids the conservative update with the aggressive sampling scheme, which updates the model even if no error occurs. The theoretical results show that our aggressive selective sampling algorithm can achieve better performance than its conservative competitors. Extensive experiments carried out on several real-world graph datasets further validate the empirical performance of the proposed algorithms.

The rest of this paper is organized as follows. Section 2 presents the problem setting of graph classification. The proposed multi-class online learning and selective sampling algorithms are described in Section 3 and Section 4, respectively. Section 5 discusses the experimental results. Section 6 concludes our work.

II. GRAPH CLASSIFICATION

In this section, we first present the notations. Then we introduce a graph Laplacian regularization that can derive a linear model for multi-class classification.

A. Notation

In this paper, we will use lower case letters as scalars (e.g. x), lower case bold letters as vectors (e.g. $\mathbf{f}$), upper case letters as elements of a matrix (e.g. S_{ij}) and bold-face upper letters as matrices (e.g. $\mathbf{S}$). With an appropriate size, an identity matrix is defined as $\mathbf{I}$ and a vector of all zeros as $\mathbf{0}$. The transpose of a vector $\mathbf{m}$ is denoted as $\mathbf{m}^\top$, the inverse of a matrix $\mathbf{A}$ as $\mathbf{A}^{-1}$, and the pseudo inverse of $\mathbf{A}$ as $\mathbf{A}^\dagger$. A diagonal matrix is denoted as $\text{diag}(\sigma_1, \ldots, \sigma_n)$ with diagonal elements $\sigma_i, i \in [1, n]$. In addition, Euclidean norms are denoted as $\|\cdot\|_2$, Frobenius norm as $\|\cdot\|_F$ and the trace of square matrix as $tr(\cdot)$. When function $f(W)$ is differentiable, we denote its gradient by $\nabla f(W)$.

We consider the problem of classification in probabilistic setting: n i.i.d. pais are generated by a probability distribution on $\mathcal{X} \times \mathcal{Y}$, where y_i in a pair of (x_i, y_i) is the *class* of instance x_i. We define $|\mathcal{Y}| = 2$ as binary-class setting, and $|\mathcal{Y}| > 2$ as a multi-class problem.

B. Graph Laplacian Regularization

$G = (V, E)$ is defined as a graph with an vertex set $V = \{v_1, \ldots, v_n\}$, an edge set $E = \{(v_i, v_j) | v_i, v_j \in V\}$ and an adjacency matrix $\mathbf{S} \in \mathbb{R}^{n \times n}$, where the element $S_{ij} \in \mathbb{R}_0^+$ is measured by the affinity of edge (v_i, v_j). We assume graph G is connected and undirected in this work. Given D is the diagonal matrix with $D_{ii} = \sum_j S_{ij}$, graph Laplacian is defined as $L = D - S$ with its eigenvector $\mathbb{V} = [\mathbf{v}_1, \ldots, \mathbf{v}_n](\mathbf{v}_i \in \mathbb{R}^n)$ and eigenvalue $\Lambda = \text{diag}(\lambda_1, \ldots, \lambda_n)$ where $0 = \lambda_1 \leq \ldots \leq \lambda_n$. Intuitively, the objective function incurs a heavy penalty, if neighboring vertices v_i and v_j are mapped far apart. The graph regularization [17] assumes a label smoothness over the graph,

$$\frac{1}{2} \sum_{i,j=1}^{n} S_{ij} \|\mathbf{f}_i - \mathbf{f}_j\|^2 = tr\left(F^\top (D - S) F\right) = tr\left(F^\top L F\right),$$

where $F = [\mathbf{f}_1, \ldots, \mathbf{f}_n]^\top$ and $\mathbf{f}_i \in \mathbb{R}^K$ is the prediction scores of node i on K classes.

In the setting of graph classification, the real-valued function satisfies: 1) the values of function F for labeled vertices should be close to the given labels for that vertices; 2) vertices should satisfy label smoothness on the whole graph, that is, the points nearby in graph should have similar labels. In the multi-class scenario, the generalized LapRLS solves the following function,

$$\min_F \|F - Y\|_F^2 + \gamma tr\left(F^\top L F\right), \tag{1}$$

where $Y = [\mathbf{y}_1, \ldots, \mathbf{y}_n]^\top \in \mathbb{R}^{n \times K}$, $\mathbf{y}_i \in \mathbb{R}^K$ is the true label of node i on K classes, and $\gamma > 0$ is a regularized parameter for graph Laplacian. To solve the problem (1) with a linear model, we consider its dual form. Using the definition of graph kernel [17], the function F can be defined, $F = L^\dagger \Phi$, where $L^\dagger$ is the pseudo inverse of L and $\Phi \in \mathbb{R}^{n \times K}$ is a parameter matrix. Assuming that $L^\dagger = M^\top M = \sum_i \frac{1}{\lambda_i} \mathbf{v}_i \mathbf{v}_i^\top$, where $M = [\frac{1}{\sqrt{\lambda_1}} \mathbf{v}_1, \ldots, \frac{1}{\sqrt{\lambda_n}} \mathbf{v}_n]^\top \in \mathbb{R}^{n \times n}$ and $W = M\Phi \in \mathbb{R}^{n \times K}$, the kernel function F can be reformatted in a linear model form,

$$F = M^\top W, \tag{2}$$

where $\mathbf{f}_i = W^\top \mathbf{m}_i$ is essentially a linear regression model. In the multi-class setting, our linear model and its prediction margin are defined as follows.

Definition 1. *We define a multi-class linear model that consists of label score of an input $\mathbf{m}_i$ over the K classes,*

$$\mathbf{f}_i = \left[P_W^{\mathbf{m}_i}(1), \ldots, P_W^{\mathbf{m}_i}(K)\right]^\top. \tag{3}$$

Given the node-label pair $(\mathbf{m}_i, y_i)$, we define the prediction margin of $\mathbf{f}_i$,

$$P_W^{\mathbf{m}_i}(y_i) - \max_{j \neq y_i} P_W^{\mathbf{m}_i}(j) = \mathbf{f}_i \cdot \mathbf{y}_i, \tag{4}$$

where $\mathbf{y}_i \in \mathbb{R}^K$ is a label vector of node i with an entry of $+1$ for true class y_i, -1 for the class $j = \text{argmax}_{j \neq y_i} P_W^{\mathbf{m}_i}(j)$ and 0 otherwise.

Substituting Eq. (2) into Eq. (1), we obtain,

$$\min_W \|M^\top W - Y\|_F^2 + \gamma tr\left(W^\top W\right).$$

In this way, we derive a formulation, similar to ridge-regression, with an additional regularization to shrink the prediction. It helps us to derive a multi-class online model with a new data representation for graph vertex.

C. Low-rank Approximation

Given $M = [\frac{1}{\sqrt{\lambda_1}}\mathbf{v}_1, \ldots, \frac{1}{\sqrt{\lambda_n}}\mathbf{v}_n]^\top$, the matrix W is updated with the time complexity $O(n^2)$, that is computationally expensive in large graph datasets. To make our algorithm scalable to big graphs, we propose a low-rank approximation $\hat{M}$ as follows,

$$\hat{M} = [\frac{1}{\sqrt{\lambda_1}}\mathbf{v}_1, \ldots, \frac{1}{\sqrt{\lambda_d}}\mathbf{v}_d]^\top \in \mathbb{R}^{d\times n},\ \hat{W} = \hat{M}\Phi \in \mathbb{R}^{d\times K},$$

where $d \ll n$ and the time complexity of our algorithm becomes $O(d^2) \ll O(n^2)$. We analyze the impact of such low-rank approximation on the function $\hat{F} = \hat{M}^\top \hat{W}$. We have $\hat{F} = \hat{L}^\dagger \Phi$, where $\hat{L}^\dagger = \hat{M}^\top \hat{M} = \sum_{i=1}^{d} \frac{1}{\lambda_i}\mathbf{v}_i\mathbf{v}_i^\top$. Given that $\frac{1}{\lambda_1} \geq \ldots \geq \frac{1}{\lambda_n}$, $\hat{L}^\dagger$ holds the d largest eigenvalues of $L^\dagger$. In this case, $\hat{L}^\dagger$ is the best rank-d approximation of $L^\dagger$ [13], and thus $\hat{F}$ is the best rank-d approximation of F. Equipped with $\hat{M}$ and $\hat{W}$ a low-rank objective function for multi-class online classification can be rewritten as follows,

$$\arg\min_{\hat{W}} \sum_{t=1}^{T} \|\hat{W}^\top \hat{\mathbf{m}}_t - \mathbf{y}_t\|_2^2 + \gamma tr(\hat{W}^\top \hat{W}).$$

III. ONLINE LEARNING

Now we are ready to derive a multi-class online model on graph. We first present the problem setting of online learning. Then we derive the online classifier and its mistake bound.

A. Problem Setting

The purpose of online learning is to minimize the cumulative loss over the sequential nodes. Let $(\mathbf{m}_1, \mathbf{y}_1), \ldots, (\mathbf{m}_T, \mathbf{y}_T)$ $(T \leq n)$ be a sequence of vertices, where $\mathbf{m}_t \in \mathbb{R}^n$ is one column of matrix M and $\mathbf{y}_t \in \mathbb{R}^K$ is its label vector, an online version of LapRLS in multi-class setting is derived,

$$G_T(W) = \sum_{t=1}^{T} \|W^\top \mathbf{m}_t - \mathbf{y}_t\|_2^2 + \gamma tr\left(W^\top W\right). \quad (5)$$

At round t, online algorithm receives an input vertex $\mathbf{m}_t$, and predicts its label with the maximal score among the K classes, $\hat{y}_t = \underset{i\in[K]}{\text{argmin}} P_{W_t}^{\mathbf{m}_t}(i)$. After prediction, its actual label y_t is revealed, and the algorithm uses it to update model and then proceeds to the next round. At each iteration, the performance of the online model is evaluated by a squared loss, $\ell_t(W) = \ell(y_t, \hat{y}_t) = \|\mathbf{y}_t - W^\top \mathbf{m}_t\|_2^2$ with cumulative loss over T iterations, $L_T(W) = \sum_{t=1}^{T} \ell_t(W)$. Similar, for any $U \in \mathbb{R}^{n\times K}$, let $\ell_t(U) = \|U^\top \mathbf{m}_t - \mathbf{y}_t\|_2^2$ be the instantaneous loss and $L_T(U) = \sum_{t=1}^{T} \ell_t(U)$ be the cumulative loss. The goal of online learning is to achieve low regret compared with the best linear function,

$$R_T = \sum_{t=1}^{T} g_t(W) - \inf_U \sum_{t=1}^{T} g_t(U),$$

where $G_T(W) = \sum_{t=1}^{T} g_t(W)$ and $g_t(W) = \ell_t(W) + \gamma tr\left(W^\top W\right)$ is regularized instantaneous loss on round t.

B. Online Learning on Graph

To minimize the regret, we have to minimize the cumulative loss $G_T(W)$ in the following lemma. We start with the notations,

$$A_T = \gamma I + \sum_{t=1}^{T} \mathbf{m}_t \mathbf{m}_t^\top, \quad B_T = \sum_{t=1}^{T} \mathbf{m}_t \mathbf{y}_t^\top. \quad (6)$$

Lemma 1. *For all $T \geq 1$, $G_T(W) = L_T(W) + \gamma tr(W^\top W)$ is minimal at an unique point W_T for all $T \geq 1$, given by*

$$W_T = A_T^{-1} B_T,\ G(W_T) = \sum_{t=1}^{T} \|\mathbf{y}_t\|^2 - tr\left(B_T^\top A_T^{-1} B_T\right).$$

We leave the proof in supplementary file. In Lemma 1, we obtain an optimal linear solution W_T. Inspired by [2], we exploit current input to predict its label with $\mathbf{f}_t = B_{t-1}^\top A_t^{-1} \mathbf{m}_t$ where $A_t = A_{t-1} + \mathbf{m}_t \mathbf{m}_t^\top$. However, it is not efficient to perform update in each iteration. To make it scalable on big graphs, we adopt a conservative strategy [4] to update model whenever an error occurs ($y_t \neq \hat{y}_t$). Note that our algorithm is different from [4], since the solution is a matrix for multi-class classification. We call our algorithm CMOG, a Conservative Multi-class Online learning on Graph, and summarize it in algorithm 1.

Although the CMOG is simple, it is the first work of online learning for solving graph-based multi-class problem. Below gives theoretical analysis of the CMOG and we begin with a lemma that facilitates the proof. With this lemma, we could then derive the mistake bound for the CMOG. For convenience, we introduce an additional notation:

$$r_t = \mathbf{m}_t^\top A_{t-1}^{-1} \mathbf{m}_t. \quad (7)$$

Then the following notation can be derived using Woodbury formula [3],

$$\begin{aligned}\mathbf{m}_t^\top A_t^{-1} \mathbf{m}_t &\overset{(6)}{=} \mathbf{m}_t^\top \left(A_{t-1} + \mathbf{m}_t \mathbf{m}_t^\top\right)^{-1} \mathbf{m}_t \\ &= \mathbf{m}_t^\top \left(A_{t-1}^{-1} - \frac{A_{t-1}^{-1}\mathbf{m}_t\mathbf{m}_t^\top A_{t-1}^{-1}}{1 + \mathbf{m}_t^\top A_{t-1}^{-1}\mathbf{m}_t}\right)\mathbf{m}_t = \frac{r_t}{1+r_t}.\end{aligned}$$

Lemma 2. *For all $t \geq 1$, $G_t(U)$ is the online LapRLS with any $U \in \mathbb{R}^{n\times K}$. Let $(\mathbf{m}_1, \mathbf{y}_1), \ldots, (\mathbf{m}_T, \mathbf{y}_T)$ be a sequence of input vertices, where $\mathbf{m}_t \in \mathbb{R}^n$ and $\mathbf{y}_t \in \mathbb{R}^K$, an online algorithm predicts with $\mathbf{f}_t = B_{t-1}^\top A_t^{-1} \mathbf{m}_t$. Then the following equality holds,*

$$\inf_U G_t(U) - \inf_U G_{t-1}(U) = \|\mathbf{y}_t - \mathbf{f}_t\|_2^2 - \frac{2r_t}{1+r_t} + r_t\|\mathbf{f}_t\|_2^2$$

We leave the proof in supplementary file. Based on the above lemma, we prove the following theorem that bounds the expected mistakes of CMOG. We denote

$\mathcal{M} = \{t|y_t \neq \hat{y}_t\}$ as the set of mistake trials with $|\mathcal{M}| = M$. For any model $U \in \mathbb{R}^{n\times K}$, let $\mathcal{U}_T$ be the set of its update trial, and $A_{\mathcal{U}_T} = \gamma I + \sum_{t\in\mathcal{U}_T} \mathbf{m}_t\mathbf{m}_t^\top$. Its hinge loss on round t is defined,

$$\mathcal{L}(\mathbf{y}_t^\top U^\top \mathbf{m}_t) = [1 - (P_U^{\mathbf{m}_t}(y_t) - \max_{j\neq y_t} P_U^{\mathbf{m}_t}(j))]_+.$$

Theorem 1. *Let $(\mathbf{m}_1, \mathbf{y}_1), \dots, (\mathbf{m}_T, \mathbf{y}_T)$ be a sequence of inputs, where $\mathbf{m}_t \in \mathbb{R}^n$ and $\mathbf{y}_t \in \mathbb{R}^K$. Then for any model $U \in \mathbb{R}^{n\times K}$ and $h > 0$, the expected mistakes of CMOG (Alg. 1) on these sequential nodes is bounded by,*

$$\begin{aligned}\mathbb{E}[M] \leq & \mathbb{E}[\sum_t \mathcal{L}(\mathbf{y}_t^\top U^\top \mathbf{m}_t)] + \frac{h}{2} tr(U^\top \mathbb{E}[A_{\mathcal{U}_T}]U) \\ & + \frac{1}{h}\mathbb{E}[\sum_t \frac{r_t}{1+r_t}].\end{aligned}$$

Remark 2. *$\sum_t \mathcal{L}(\mathbf{y}_t^\top U^\top \mathbf{m}_t)$ is the cumulative hinge loss made by U. Besides, for each class prototype $\mathbf{u}_i (i \in [K])$, $\mathbf{u}_i^\top A_{\mathcal{U}_T} \mathbf{u}_i$ lines between $\min_j \lambda_j$ and $\max_j \lambda_j$ where λ_j is an eigenvalue of the matrix $A_{\mathcal{U}_T}$. Thus, $tr(U^\top \mathbb{E}[A_{U_T}]U) \leq K \max_j \lambda_j$. Finally, $\sum_t \frac{r_t}{1+r_t} \leq \log \frac{\det(A_T)}{\det(A_0)} \leq n \log(R^2 T + 1)$ given $\|\mathbf{m}\|_2 \leq R$.*

Proof. The CMOG is a conservative algorithm that updates model whenever an error occurs. If there is no update, $U_t = U_{t-1}$ yields $\inf_U G_t(U) = \inf_U G_{t-1}(U)$. According to lemma 2, we have,

$$\begin{aligned}&\inf_U G_t(U) - \inf_U G_{t-1}(U) \\ =&\mathbb{I}\{y_t \neq \hat{y}_t\}(\|\mathbf{y}_t - \mathbf{f}_t\|_2^2 - \frac{2r_t}{1+r_t} + r_t\|\mathbf{f}_t\|_2^2)\end{aligned}$$

holds for all trial t. Summing over $t = 1, \dots, T$, we obtain via expanding the squares and some manipulations,

$$\begin{aligned}&\sum_{t\in\mathcal{M}} (\|\mathbf{y}_t\|_2^2 - 2\mathbf{y}_t \cdot \mathbf{f}_t + \|\mathbf{f}_t\|_2^2 - \frac{2r_t}{1+r_t} + r_t\|\mathbf{f}_t\|_2^2) \\ =& \inf_U G_T(U) - \inf_U G_0(U) \\ \leq& \sum_{t\in\mathcal{M}} (\|\mathbf{y}_t\|_2^2 - 2\mathbf{y}_t \cdot U^\top \mathbf{m}_t) + tr(U^\top(\gamma I + \sum_{t\in\mathcal{U}_T} \mathbf{m}_t\mathbf{m}_t^\top)U)\end{aligned}$$

holding for any $U \in \mathbb{R}^{n\times K}$. We ignore $r_t\|\mathbf{f}_t\|_2^2$ as it does not affect upper bound. Given that $\hat{y} = \underset{j\neq y_t}{\text{argmax}} P_{W_T}^{\mathbf{m}_t}(j)$,

$$\begin{aligned}1-\mathbf{y}_t \cdot U^\top \mathbf{m}_t &\leq [1 - (P_U^{\mathbf{m}_t}(y_t) - P_U^{\mathbf{m}_t}(\hat{y}))]_+ \\ &\leq [1 - (P_U^{\mathbf{m}_t}(y_t) - \max_{j\neq y_i} P_U^{\mathbf{m}_t}(j))]_+ = \mathcal{L}(\mathbf{y}_t^\top U^\top \mathbf{m}_t).\end{aligned}$$

Since U is a random variable, we use hU ($h > 0$) to replace U. We add $\sum_t 2h$ on both sides of inequality and simplify inequality with A_t and $\mathcal{L}(\cdot)$,

$$\begin{aligned}&\sum_{t\in\mathcal{M}} (\|\mathbf{f}_t\|_2^2 - 2\mathbf{y}_t \cdot \mathbf{f}_t - \frac{2r_t}{1+r_t} + 2h) \\ \leq& 2h \sum_{t\in\mathcal{M}} \mathcal{L}(\mathbf{y}_t^\top U^\top \mathbf{m}_t) + h^2 tr(U^\top A_{\mathcal{U}_T} U).\end{aligned} \tag{8}$$

Algorithm 1 CMOG: Conservative Multi-class Online model on Graph

Input: Adjacency matrix $\mathbf{S}$, and regularization parameter γ.
Output: W_T
Compute $\mathbf{L} = \mathbf{D} - \mathbf{S}$ and $\mathbf{M}$ from $\mathbf{L}$;
Initialize: $\mathbf{A}_0 = \gamma I$, $\mathbf{B}_0 = \mathbf{0}$, $W_0 = \mathbf{0}$;
for $t = 1, \dots, T$ **do**
  Receive $\mathbf{m}_t \in R^n$;
  Compute $A_t^{-1} = (A_{t-1} + \mathbf{m}_t\mathbf{m}_t^\top)^{-1}$;
  Predict $\mathbf{f}_t = B_{t-1}^\top A_t^{-1}\mathbf{m}_t$;
  $\hat{y}_t = \arg\max_{j=1,..,K} \mathbf{f}_t(j)$;
  Query the actual label y_t;
  if $\hat{y}_t \neq y_t$ **then**
    Update $A_t = A_{t-1} + \mathbf{m}_t\mathbf{m}_t^\top$;
    Update $B_t = B_{t-1} + \mathbf{m}_t\mathbf{y}_t^\top$;
  else
    $A_t = A_{t-1}, B_t = B_{t-1}$;
  end if
end for
$W_T = A_T^{-1}B_T$;

When an error occurs (i.e., $y_t \neq \hat{y}_t$), we have that $P_{W_t}^{\mathbf{m}_t}(y_t) \leq P_{W_t}^{\mathbf{m}_t}(\hat{y}_t)$ yields $-\mathbf{y}_t \cdot \mathbf{f}_t = P_{W_t}^{\mathbf{m}_t}(\hat{y}_t) - P_{W_t}^{\mathbf{m}_t}(y_t) \geq 0$. With the expectation of the inequality, we bound given by $\|\mathbf{f}_t\|_2 > 0$,

$$\begin{aligned}&\sum_{t\in\mathcal{M}} \mathbb{E}[\|\mathbf{f}_t\|_2^2 - 2\mathbf{y}_t \cdot \mathbf{f}_t - \frac{2r_t}{1+r_t} + 2h] \\ \geq& 2h\mathbb{E}[M] - \mathbb{E}[\sum_t \frac{2r_t}{1+r_t}].\end{aligned} \tag{9}$$

Taking the expectation of Eq. (8) to upper bound the left-side of Eq. (9), we complete the proof. □

IV. SELECTIVE SAMPLING

In this section, we first introduce the setting of selective sampling. Next, we propose a novel randomized query approach to select labels and then introduce an aggressive algorithm that can use correctly predicted labels to optimize the model. We theoretically analyze mistake bound and query ratio of the proposed techniques. Finally, a low rank approximation is introduced in our framework.

A. Problem Setting

Unlike online algorithm that queries all labels, selective sampling has to decide whether to query label or not for each vertex $\mathbf{m}_t$. If a label $\mathbf{y}_t$ is queried of, the algorithm can update learner with $\mathbf{y}_t$; otherwise, no action is performed and the learner proceeds next one. Query and update decisions in trial t are denoted as binary variables Q_t and Z_t, respectively. When $Q_t = 1$ iif label $\mathbf{y}_t$ is queried of; $Q_t = 0$, no action performed. Update decision Z_t is under similar setting. Generally, selective sampling is a semi-supervised online learning algorithm. Thus, its optimal solution can be derived in a form of online learning with query/update decision in each trial, i.e., $W_t = A_t^{-1}B_t$, where A_t and B_t can turn to be a recursive form,

$$A_t = A_{t-1} + Q_tZ_t\mathbf{m}_t\mathbf{m}_t^\top, \quad B_t = B_{t-1} + Q_tZ_t\mathbf{m}_t\mathbf{y}_t^\top.$$

Since A_t^{-1} is computationally expensive, we derive a non-inverted recursive form with time complexity $O(n^2)$ using Woodbury formula as in (8).

B. Label Query

The CMOG assumes that all labels are provided, which is not efficient in many real-world applications. To save the labeling cost, we propose a novel randomized query approach in multi-class setting. We begin with additional quantities of interest:

$$y_t^* = \underset{i=1,\dots,K}{\text{argmax}} P_{U^*}^{\mathbf{m}_t}(i), \quad y_t' = \underset{i\neq y_t^*}{\text{argmax}} P_{U^*}^{\mathbf{m}_t}(i);$$

$$\hat{y}_t = \underset{i=1,\dots,K}{\text{argmax}} P_{W_t}^{\mathbf{m}_t}(i), \quad y_t'' = \underset{i\neq \hat{y}_t}{\text{argmax}} P_{W_t}^{\mathbf{m}_t}(i).$$

In words, y_t^* and y_t' are the optimal and second-best classes with respect to U^* (i.e., the best model in hindsight), while $\hat{y}_t$ and y_t'' are the estimates of these classes based on our online learner W_t.

Definition 2. *Given an input $\mathbf{m}_t(t \in [T])$ and the weight $W_t = A_t^{-1}B_{t-1}$, an algorithm predicts its label with $\mathbf{f}_t = W_t^\top\mathbf{m}_t$, and queries the true label with a probability $\frac{2h}{2h+\max(0,\Theta_t)}$ $(h > 0)$, where Θ_t is a confidence score towards current prediction,*

$$\Theta_t = \Theta(\mathbf{f}_t, r_t) = \frac{1}{2}\Delta_t^2 + 2\Delta_t - \frac{Kr_t}{1+r_t}, \tag{10}$$

where $\Delta_t = P_{W_t}^{\mathbf{m}_t}(\hat{y}_t) - P_{W_t}^{\mathbf{m}_t}(y_t'')$.

This query is tuned by a confidence score Θ_t: a coin with bias $\frac{h}{h+\max(0,\Theta_t)}$ is flipped; if the coin turns up heads, then actual label $\mathbf{y}_t$ is queried; otherwise $Q_t = 0$ and no query performed. The randomized query has been studied in previous selective samplings under binary classification setting [6], [10]. Unlike these methods, we present a new confidence Θ_t based on the margin and uncertainty of the multi-class classification problems.

Intuitively, a query method is effective if it can control the probability of making a mistake whenever this label is not queried of. In the following theorem, we prove that an online algorithm on these selected labels $\{t|Q_t = 1, Q_t \sim \frac{2h}{2h+\max(0,\Theta_t)}\}$ can achieve a comparable mistake bound with one that queries all labels. Under randomized query, the mistake trials can be partitioned into two disjoint sets, $\mathcal{S} = \{t|\frac{2h}{2h+\max(0,\Theta_t)} < 1\}$ includes trials on which a stochastic query is conduct, while $\mathcal{D} = \{t|\frac{2h}{2h+\max(0,\Theta_t)} = 1\}$ includes trials when a deterministic query is issued.

Theorem 3. *For all $t \geq 1$, the CMOG runs over an arbitrary node-label sequence $(\mathbf{m}_1, \mathbf{y}_1), \dots, (\mathbf{m}_T, \mathbf{y}_T)$ ($\mathbf{m}_t \in \mathbb{R}^n$ and $\mathbf{y}_t \in \mathbb{R}^K$) with a query probability of $\frac{2h}{2h+\max(0,\Theta_t)}(h > 0)$ on round t, then the following inequality holds for any $U \in \mathbb{R}^{n\times K}$,*

$$\mathbb{E}[\mathcal{M}] \leq \mathbb{E}[\sum_t \mathcal{L}(\mathbf{y}_t^\top U^\top \mathbf{m}_t)] + \frac{h}{2}tr(U^\top\mathbb{E}[A_{\mathcal{U}_T}]U) + \frac{1}{2h}\mathbb{E}[\sum_{t\in\mathcal{M}\cap\mathcal{D}} \frac{Kr_t}{1+r_t}].$$

The expectation of queried number is upper bounded by $\mathbb{E}[|\mathcal{D}| + \sum_{t\in\mathcal{S}} \frac{2h}{2h+\Theta_t}]$.

Note that labels are selected randomly. Thus, the expectation occurring in this theorem is w.r.t this randomization.

Proof. In the setting of selective sampling, a model is updated whenever $Q_tZ_t = 1$. Given that $K > 2$ in multi-class setting, we bound as in Eq. (8),

$$\begin{aligned}&\sum_t Q_tZ_t(\|\mathbf{f}_t\|_2^2 - 2\mathbf{y}_t\cdot\mathbf{f}_t - \frac{Kr_t}{1+r_t} + 2h)\\ \leq& 2h\sum_t Q_tZ_t\mathcal{L}(\mathbf{y}_t^\top U^\top\mathbf{m}_t) + h^2tr(U^\top A_{\mathcal{U}_T}U).\end{aligned} \tag{11}$$

If an error occurs ($y_t \neq \hat{y}_t$), $P_{W_t}^{\mathbf{m}_t}(y_t) \leq P_{W_t}^{\mathbf{m}_t}(y_t'')$. Thus,

$$-\mathbf{y}_t\cdot\mathbf{f}_t \overset{(4)}{=} P_{W_t}^{\mathbf{m}_t}(\hat{y}_t) - P_{W_t}^{\mathbf{m}_t}(y_t) \geq P_{W_t}^{\mathbf{m}_t}(\hat{y}_t) - P_{W_t}^{\mathbf{m}_t}(y_t'').$$

Since $\|\mathbf{f}_t\|_2^2 \geq \frac{1}{2}\Delta_t^2$ and $P_{W_t}^{\mathbf{m}_t}(\hat{y}_t) - P_{W_t}^{\mathbf{m}_t}(y_t'') = \Delta_t$, we bound,

$$\begin{aligned}&\sum_t Q_tZ_t(\|\mathbf{f}_t\|_2^2 - 2\mathbf{y}_t\cdot\mathbf{f}_t - \frac{Kr_t}{1+r_t} + 2h)\\ \geq& \sum_t Q_tZ_t(\frac{1}{2}\Delta_t^2 + 2\Delta_t - \frac{Kr_t}{1+r_t} + 2h)\\ \overset{(10)}{=}& \sum_t Q_tZ_t(\Theta_t + 2h).\end{aligned}$$

When an error occurs at trial $t \in \mathcal{M}$, the Θ_t can be positive ($\mathcal{M}\cap\mathcal{S}$) or negative ($\mathcal{M}\cap\mathcal{D}$). In the former case, $\mathbb{E}[Q_t] = \frac{2h}{2h+\Theta_t}$ is a random variable and we bound,

$$\mathbb{E}[Q_tZ_t(\Theta_t + 2h)] = \mathbb{E}[Z_t]\mathbb{E}[Q_t(\Theta_t + 2h)] = 2h\mathbb{E}[Z_t];$$

In the later case, $\mathbb{E}[Q_t] = 1$. Given $\frac{1}{2}\Delta_t^2 \geq 0$ and $\Delta_t \geq 0$, we have,

$$\begin{aligned}&\mathbb{E}[\sum_t Q_tZ_t(\frac{1}{2}\Delta_t^2 + 2\Delta_t - \frac{Kr_t}{1+r_t} + 2h)]\\ \geq& 2h\mathbb{E}[Z_t] - \mathbb{E}[\sum_{t\in\mathcal{M}\cap\mathcal{D}} \frac{Kr_t}{1+r_t}]\end{aligned}$$

In summary,

$$\begin{aligned}&\sum_t Q_tZ_t(\Theta_t + 2h)\\ \geq& 2h(\sum_{t\in\mathcal{M}\cap\mathcal{S}}\mathbb{E}[Z_t] + \sum_{t\in\mathcal{M}\cap\mathcal{D}}\mathbb{E}[Z_t]) - \mathbb{E}[\sum_{t\in\mathcal{M}\cap\mathcal{D}} \frac{Kr_t}{1+r_t}]\end{aligned}$$

With $\sum_{t \in \mathcal{M}} Z_t = |\mathcal{M}|$ and upper bound (11), we complete our proof. □

Remark 4. *The mistake bound of the CMOG on randomly selected labels is comparable with the bound of CMOG that learns all the labels. Similar to Theorem 1, the CMOG run on selected labels is bounded by the cumulative hinge loss suffered by U,* $\log(T)$ *(upper bound of* $\sum_t \frac{r_t}{1+r_t}$*) and* $K \max_j \lambda_j$ *(upper bound of* $tr(U^\top A_{\mathcal{U}_T} U)$*). Note that we use* $\frac{Kr_t}{1+r_t}$ *to let data "uncertainty" regularized by the class number. In addition, the CMOG run on selected labels can achieve a comparable mistake bound with the online algorithm OLLGC (i.e. Corollary 5, [14]) in binary classification, since* $tr(U^\top A_{\mathcal{U}_T} U) \leq \sum_{t \in \mathcal{M}} \|U^\top \mathbf{m}_t\|_2^2 \leq \alpha tr(U^\top U) = \alpha tr(F^\top L F)$*, where* $\alpha = |\mathcal{M}| R^2$*. Noted that this bound is incomparable with that in [6] since the* Θ_t *is different in two methods. In summary, the theoretical results present that an online algorithm learning on these selected labels could perform no worse than its fully-supervised counterpart. Thus above results theoretically demonstrate the efficacy of the proposed query method.*

C. Aggressive Learning

The CMOG is conservative, i.e., it will only update the model when an error occurs. To take advantage of the correctly predicted instances, we propose an aggressive version of selective sampling. We call our algorithm MSG, the Multi-class Selective Sampling on Graph, present in Algorithm 2. After observing a vertex $\mathbf{m}_t$ at round t, the MSG predicts its label with $W_t = A_t^{-1} B_{t-1}$ and then queries true label $\mathbf{y}_t$ with a probability of $\frac{2h}{2h+\max(0,\Theta_t)}$. It yields to stochastic query and deterministic query. When stochastic query (i.e. $\frac{2h}{2h+\max(0,\Theta_t)} < 1$) is issued, it is conservative to update model when an error occurs ($\hat{y}_t \neq y_t$). While a deterministic query is issued (i.e. $\frac{2h}{2h+\max(0,\Theta_t)} = 1$), we adopt an aggressive learning strategy, that is, we update even if no error occurs. Note that our model is different from [8], [1], since we perform a randomized query based on the predicted results of multiple classes.

The theoretical results below show the superiority of the aggressive algorithm compared to its conservative and fully-supervised counterpart CMOG (i.e. Algorithm 1). Besides the stochastic query trials $\mathcal{S}$ and deterministic query trials $\mathcal{D}$, we denote by $\mathcal{V}$ the set of trials for which there is an aggressive update but not a mistake (i.e., $y_t = \hat{y}_t$ and $\Theta_t < 0$) and let $V = |\mathcal{V}|$.

Theorem 5. *The algorithm MSG (Algorithm 2) runs on an arbitrary sequential nodes, then given* $h > 0$*, the following inequality holds for any* $U \in \mathbb{R}^{n \times K}$*,*

$$\mathbb{E}[M] \leq \mathbb{E}[\sum_t Q_t Z_t \mathcal{L}(\mathbf{y}_t^\top U^\top \mathbf{m}_t)] + \frac{h}{2} tr(U^\top \mathbb{E}[A_{\mathcal{U}_T}] U) + \frac{1}{h} \mathbb{E}[\sum_{t \in D} \frac{Kr_t}{1+r_t}] - \mathbb{E}[V].$$

Algorithm 2 MSG: Multiclass Selective Sampling on Graph

Input: sequences of instance-label pair $(\mathbf{m}_t, \mathbf{y}_t), t = 1, \ldots, T$, the parameters $\gamma > 0$ and $h > 0$.
Output: W_T
Initialize: $W_0 = 0$, $A_0 = \gamma I$ and $B_0 = \mathbf{0}$.
for $t = 1, \ldots, T$ **do**
  Receive an input $\mathbf{m}_t$;
  Compute $A_t^{-1} = (A_{t-1} + \mathbf{m}_t \mathbf{m}_t^\top)^{-1}$;
  $\mathbf{f}_t = B_{t-1}^\top A_t^{-1} \mathbf{m}_t$;
  Predict $\hat{y}_t = \arg\max_{j \in [K]} P_{W_t}^{\mathbf{m}_t}(j)$;
  if $\Theta_t < 0$ (Definition 2) **then**
    Set $Q_t = Z_t = 1$ (i.e. deterministic query) and Query actual label $\mathbf{y}_t$;
  else
    Draw a Bernoulli random variable $Q_t \in \{0, 1\} \sim \frac{2h}{2h+\max(0,\Theta_t)}$;
    if $Q_t = 1$ **then**
      Query actual label $\mathbf{y}_t$;
      Set $Z_t = 1$ if $\hat{y}_t \neq y_t$ ($Z_t = 0$, otherwise);
    end if
  end if
  $A_t = A_{t-1} + Q_t Z_t \mathbf{m}_t \mathbf{m}_t^\top$,
  $B_t = B_{t-1} + Q_t Z_t \mathbf{m}_t \mathbf{y}_t^\top$;
end for
$W_T = A_T^{-1} B_T$;

In addition, the expected number of queries is upper bounded by $\mathbb{E}[|\mathcal{D}| + \sum_{t \in \mathcal{S}} \frac{2h}{2h+\Theta_t}]$.

Proof. The update trials in algorithm 2 could be categorized into three groups,

$$\sum_t Z_t = |\mathcal{S} \cap \mathcal{M}| + |\mathcal{D} \cap \mathcal{M}| + |\mathcal{D} \cap \mathcal{V}|.$$

In the first case where an error occurs in randomized query with $\mathbb{E}[Q_t] = \frac{2h}{2h+\Theta_t}$ (i.e. $\mathcal{S} \cap \mathcal{M}$). Similar as Theorem 3,

$$\mathbb{E}[Q_t Z_t (\Theta_t + 2h)] = \mathbb{E}[Z_t] \mathbb{E}[Q_t (\Theta_t + 2h)] = \mathbb{E}[Z_t];$$

If an error incurs in a deterministic query (i.e. $t \in \mathcal{D} \cap \mathcal{M}$) with $\mathbb{E}[Q_t] = 1$, we bound,

$$\mathbb{E}[Q_t Z_t (\frac{1}{2}\Delta_t^2 + 2\Delta_t - \frac{Kr_t}{1+r_t} + 2h)] \geq 2h \mathbb{E}[Z_t] - \frac{Kr_t}{1+r_t};$$

Now we consider the third case where the updates were performed with no mistake, i.e., $\Theta_t \leq 0$, and by definition,

$$\Theta_t \leq 0 \Rightarrow 0 \leq \Delta_t \leq 2\sqrt{1 + \frac{Kr_t}{2(1+r_t)}} - 2. \quad (12)$$

If no mistake incurs ($y_t = \hat{y}_t$), we have $\mathbf{y}_t \cdot \mathbf{f}_t = P_{W_t}^{\mathbf{m}_t}(\hat{y}_t) - \max_{j \neq \hat{y}_t} P_{W_t}^{\mathbf{m}_t}(j) = P_{W_t}^{\mathbf{m}_t}(\hat{y}_t) - P_{W_t}^{\mathbf{m}_t}(y_t'') = \Delta_t$. Thus,

$$\mathbb{E}[Q_t Z_t (\frac{1}{2}\Delta_t^2 - 2\Delta_t - \frac{Kr_t}{1+r_t} + 2h)]$$
$$= \mathbb{E}[Z_t (\frac{1}{2}\Delta_t^2 - 2\Delta_t + \frac{Kr_t}{1+r_t} - \frac{2Kr_t}{1+r_t} + 2h)]$$

Let $C(\Delta_t, r_t) = \frac{1}{2}\Delta_t^2 - 2\Delta_t + \frac{Kr_t}{1+r_t}$. Whenever $\frac{Kr_t}{1+r_t} \geq 2$, $C(\Delta_t, r_t) \geq 0 (\forall \Delta_t \geq 0)$. If $\frac{Kr_t}{1+r_t} < 2$, let $C(\Delta_t, r_t)$ be a quadratic equation with two non-negative roots and a minima, $2 - 2\sqrt{1 - \frac{Kr_t}{2(1+r_t)}}$. We observe this smaller root is higher than the upper bound in (12), that makes $C(\Delta_t, r_t) \geq 0$ in the trials $\mathcal{D} \cap \mathcal{V}$. Thus, we bound,

$$\mathbb{E}[Q_t Z_t(\frac{1}{2}\Delta_t^2 - 2\Delta_t - \frac{Kr_t}{1+r_t} + 2h)] \geq 2h\mathbb{E}[Z_t] - \frac{2Kr_t}{1+r_t}.$$

To summarize,

$$\mathbb{E}[\sum_t Q_t Z_t(\Delta_t^2 - 2\mathbf{f}_t \cdot \mathbf{y}_t - \frac{Kr_t}{1+r_t} + 2h)]$$

$$\geq 2h \sum_{t \in \mathcal{M}} \mathbb{E}[Z_t] + 2h \sum_{t \in \mathcal{D} \cap \mathcal{V}} \mathbb{E}[Z_t] - \sum_{t \in \mathcal{D}} \mathbb{E}[\frac{2Kr_t}{1+r_t}].$$

Equipped with upper bound as Eq. (11), we complete the proof. □

Remark 6. *The upper bound of the aggressive algorithm MSG is expected to be lower than CMOG that learns on all the labels (Theorem 1) and CMOG on the selected labels (Theorem 3), due to the deduction of $\mathbb{E}[\mathcal{V}]$ from the bound. In summary, the theoretical analysis demonstrate that the MSG, in expectation, can achieve a better performance than its conservative and fully-supervised counterparts, which can be regarded as a theoretical support for the aggressive method.*

Discussion: To further understand the aggressive algorithm, we analyze under what condition an aggressive query will be conducted. An aggressive query is issued when $\Theta_t \leq 0$ (i.e.,$\Theta_t \leq 0 \Rightarrow \Delta_t \leq \theta(K, r_t) = 2\sqrt{1 + \frac{Kr_t}{2(1+r_t)}} - 2$). If the margin Δ_t is less than $\theta(K, r_t)$, a deterministic query is issued, while Δ_t is above $\theta(K, r_t)$, a label is queried randomly with a probability less than 1. We observe that the upper bound of $\theta(K, r_t)$ increases with r_t. When $r_t = 0$, that is, current instance is observed before, the label would be queried deterministically in case its margin is 0 ($\Delta_t \leq \theta(K, r_t = 0) = 0$, i.e., an extreme case that the current model is unable to predict its label). However, if $r_t = 1$ (i.e., little knowledge to current input), the learner would query aggressively whenever its margin does not exceed $\theta(K, r_t = 1) = \sqrt{4 + K} - 2$, a threshold far from the boundary.

V. EXPERIMENTAL RESULTS

In this section, we first introduce experimental dataset and evaluation metrics. Then we present the empirical results to validate the proposed algorithms. Our experiments are designed to answer two questions: (i) if the proposed randomized query is effective to reducing the amount of labeled data significantly while maintain comparable performance? (ii) if the aggressive strategy achieves a better predictive performance at the cost of more queried number?

A. Data Sets and Evaluation Metrics

Data Sets: Four real-world graph data sets are used in the experiment to evaluate the approaches.
(a) Coauthor[2] extracted from *DBLP* database is an undirected co-author graph in which 1711 authors are denoted as vertices while their co-authored relationship are treated as the edges. The authors are classified in four classes in terms of research topic: "data mining", "machine learning", "information retrieval" and "databases". **(b)** Cora[3] is a citation network including 2485 scientific publications and 5429 citation links. The publications as vertices are related to seven domains: "Case based", "Genetic Algorithms", "Rule Learning", "Probabilistic Methods", "Neural Networks", "Reinforcement Learning", et al. **(c)** IMDB[4] is a movie organization that presses up-to-date movie information. The IMDB links total 17046 movies with their co-actor associations. The movies as vertices in graph are categorized into four genres: "Action", "Romance", "Animation" and "Thriller". **(d)** PubMed[5] is also a citation graph related to diabetes research. The PubMed collects 44338 publication citations among 19717 scientific publications and labels the publications with one of three types of diabetes.
The graph data is supposed to be undirected and connected. If the edges are directed, we transform them into undirected graphs via $\mathbf{S} \leftarrow \max(\mathbf{S}, \mathbf{S}^\top)$. If the graphs are disconnected, the biggest connected subgraph is chosen for study.

Evaluation Measures: We evaluate the performance of baselines and our algorithms with two measurements:
i) *cumulative error rate*, reflecting the prediction accuracy of online algorithm; **ii)** *number of queried labels*, reflecting the label efficiency of query method. Note that a small value of above measures indicates a better performance of a method. In order to compare these algorithms fairly, we randomly shuffle the ordering of samples for each dataset. We repeat each experiment 20 times and calculate the average results.

Baselines and Parameter Setting: We compare the proposed algorithms with state-of-the-art baselines. The algorithms we study and their parameter settings are summarized as follows. **(1)** GPA: a first order nonparametric online learning algorithm on graph [15]. Note that the perceptron algorithm is not affected by the stepsize. **(2)** BBQ/BBQ$_\epsilon$: The two algorithms are the BBQ query criterion [5] and its modification version [1]. The intuition behind this rule is that at the rounds where the label is not queried, it guaranteed that the regret bound is at most ϵ. The parameter ϵ is tuned with grid $\{10^{-5}, \ldots, 10\}$ in our experiment. **(3)** DGS: This query

[2]https://snap.stanford.edu/data/com-DBLP.html
[3]http://www.cs.umd.edu/ sen/lbc-proj/data/
[4]http://www.imdb.com/
[5]http://www.cs.umd.edu/projects/linqs/projects/lbc/

TABLE I

COMPARISON OF THE MULTI-CLASS ALGORITHMS. GPA AND CMOG ARE ONLINE ALGORITHMS.

Algorithm	*Coauthor*		*Cora*	
	Error rate	# Queried nodes	Error rate	# Queried nodes
GPA	0.5474±2.66e-4	1711	0.5849±2.03e-4	2485
BBQ	0.3013±3.55e-5	1371±168.7	0.1929±1.73e-5	1635.1±294.0
BBQ_ϵ	0.3028±3.03e-5	1711	0.1936±1.95e-5	2485
DGS	0.3096±3.29e-5	1711	0.1941±2.35e-5	2485
CMOG	0.3096±3.29e-5	1711	0.1940±2.33e-5	2485
MSG	**0.2956±6.63e-5**	**870.7±251.9**	**0.1926±2.34e-5**	**884.95±289.15**
Algorithm	*IMDB*		*PubMed*	
	Error rate	# Queried nodes	Error rate	# Queried nodes
GPA	0.6870±4.6e-5	17046	0.5795±2.9e-6	19717
BBQ	0.5468±1.69e-6	10033±467.2	0.2217±1.9e-6	10352±2536.4
BBQ_ϵ	0.5068±9.9e-6	16983±801.3	0.2217±3.1e-6	8986.3±838.3
DGS	0.5066±9.1e-6	17046	0.2265±1.46e-6	19717
CMOG	0.5576±6.88e-5	17046	0.2265±1.5e-6	19717
MSG	**0.5043±7.46e-5**	**3750.3±255.1**	**0.2158±1.07e-5**	**936.29±210.07**

criterion is a nonparametric rule for binary classification [11] and adapts into multi-class setting in [1]. It takes both previous covariances and the observed labels into account. The intuition behind this rule is that on rounds where the label y_t is not queried, it guaranteed that either $\hat{y}_t = y_t^*$, or the regret is small. **(4)** CMOG and MSG: two second-order algorithm in multi-class setting. CMOG is a conservative online algorithm while MSG is an aggressive algorithm that queries label with a randomized method. We set $\gamma = 1$ to avoid overfiiting and tune the parameter h with grid $\{10^{-4}, \ldots, 1\}$ on a held-out random shuffle.

B. Comparison Evaluation

The experimental results are present in Table I. We found that MSG outperforms all baselines consistently across all data sets. We also show the results in terms of learning epoches in Figure 1. In all subfigures, the cumulative error rate and queried number along the learning epochs are both averaging over 20 times of shuffling order.

First of all, we observe that the improvement of the CMOG over GPA are always significant on all data sets. This is consistent with previous observations in online learning: second-order algorithms are generally better than first-order algorithm . The reason is due to the covariance matrix A_t which has a spectral structure to correlate with a best estimator for observed instances [4]. MSG always enjoys smaller or comparable error rates than BBQ_ϵ and DGS with much fewer queried number. The good performance generally is due to two reasons. First, the proposed randomized query approach improves the efficiency of the labeling. Second, thanks to the aggressive learning, the MSG achieves a convergence stage quickly with informative labels, thus the query rate is reduced further when learner has sufficient knowledge of data. The results in figure 1 indicate the MSG queries a small number of labels while maintains the quality of classification model.

C. Evaluation on Varied Ratios of Queries

We study the impact of h with respect to query ratio of the MSG. Basically, the smaller h is, the fewer the number of queries is. Specifically, we set h to $\{10^{-4}, 10^{-3}, \ldots, 1\}$, and run MSG for 20 times under each h. We calculate the average ratio of queried nodes under different values of h. The comparison results in Figure 2 show that MSG achieves better or comparable performance consistently under different ratios of queried labels. This validates the label-efficiency of our proposed confidence score Θ_t that can adaptively prioritize informative labels to optimize the model. We also observe that the MSG outperforms BBQ significantly over all query ratios. The reason is that MSG considering "Δ_t" will query the vertices close to current boundary, while these labels are omitted in BBQ. The better results in figure 2 demonstrate that these "small-margin" instances are useful to optimize the multi-class classifier.

D. Evaluation on Low-rank Approximation

The low-rank vertex representation $\mathrm{m} \in \mathbb{R}^d$ is used to build a scalable online model in our experiments. To study the impact of low-rank approximation on the proposed algorithms, we tune the rank d in the grid {10, 100, 250, 500, 750, 1000}. We use Coauthor and Cora as a case study since similar observations are obtained on other data sets. The results in Figure 3 present that MSG achieves a better or comparable performance than other baselines consistently under different rank approximation. Obviously with a higher rank, the performance becomes better in terms of error rate. However, to achieve a better prediction accuracy, algorithms need a high number of queries and high-rank inputs, which demands a more labeling and computational cost. It motivates us to select a proper rank d to achieve a balance. Therefore, we chose $d = 100$ in the rest of experiments, since in this setting

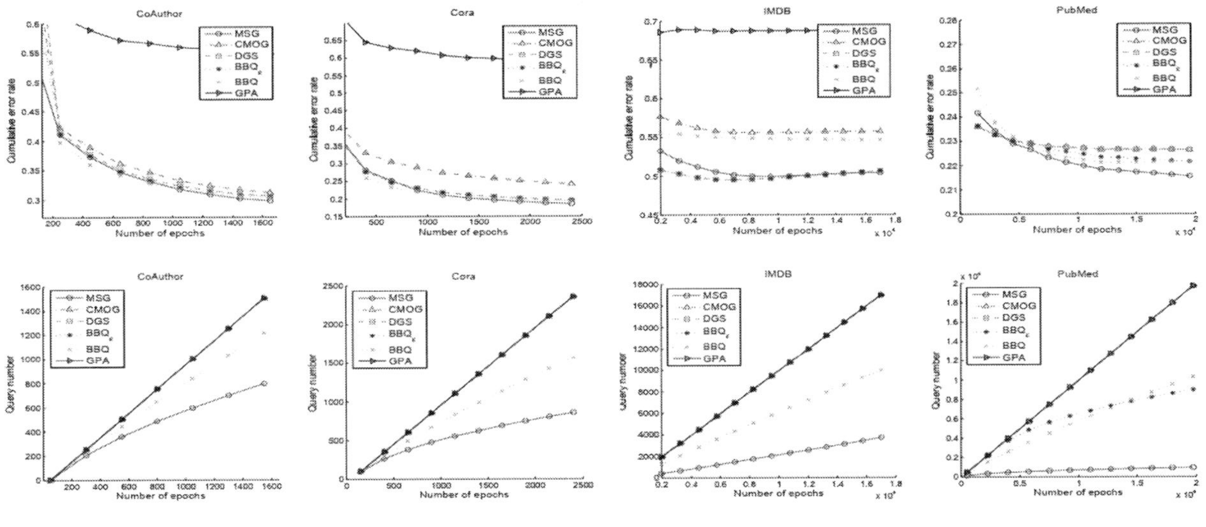

Fig. 1. Cumulative error rate and Query number with respective to online learning rounds on four datasets.

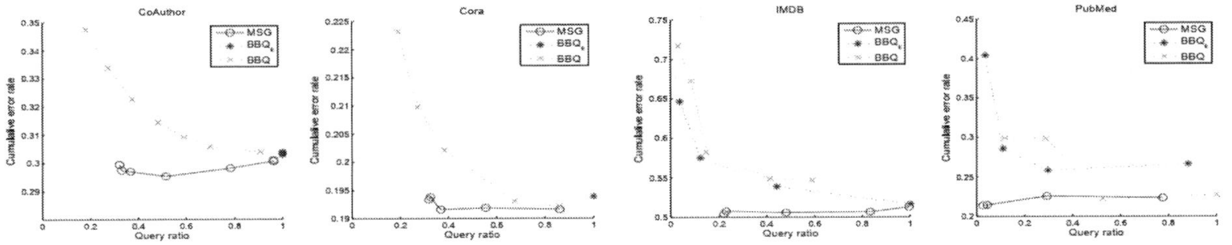

Fig. 2. A comparison among BBQ, BBQ$_\epsilon$ and MSG with respect to different ratios of queried nodes.

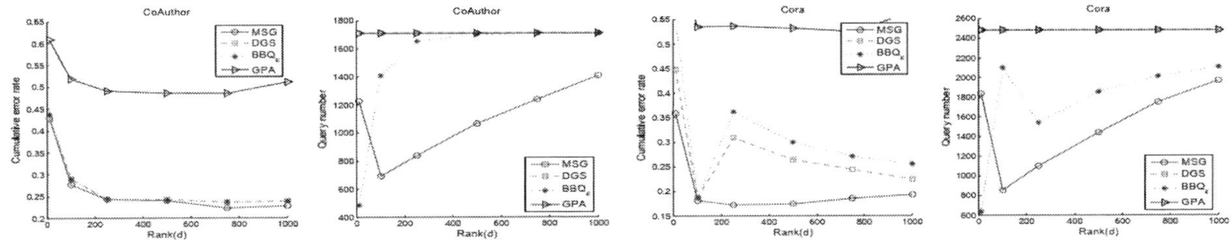

Fig. 3. A case study of low rank impact on performance.

the algorithms perform well while number of queries is small.

VI. CONCLUSIONS

In this paper, we proposed a new framework for multi-class online learning, leading to a scalable algorithm to tackle multi-class classification on graphs. To save the labeling cost, we presented a novel randomized query technique to prioritize the labels. Besides, we introduced an aggressive selective sampling algorithm to take full advantage of these wasted labels in existing conservative algorithms. The theoretical results demonstrated the efficacy of the proposed algorithms in terms of the expected mistake bound and query ratio.

The encouraging empirical results on several real-world datasets also indicated that 1) the MSG is able to achieve comparable or better predictive performance by querying a significantly small amount of labeled data; and that 2) the aggressive selective sampling scheme can further reduce the query rate, achieving a convergence stage rapidly.

References

[1] A. Agarwal. Selective sampling algorithms for cost-sensitive multiclass prediction. In *ICML*, pages 1220–1228, 2013.

[2] K. S. Azoury and M. K. Warmuth. Relative loss bounds for on-line density estimation with the exponential family of distributions. *Machine Learning*, 43(3):211–246, 2001.

[3] M. S. Bartlett. An inverse matrix adjustment arising in discriminant analysis. *The Annals of Mathematical Statistics*, pages 107–111, 1951.

[4] N. Cesa-Bianchi, A. Conconi, and C. Gentile. A second-order perceptron algorithm. *SIAM Journal on Computing*, 34(3):640–668, 2005.

[5] N. Cesa-Bianchi, C. Gentile, and F. Orabona. Robust bounds for classification via selective sampling. In *ICML*, pages 121–128, 2009.

[6] N. Cesa-Bianchi, C. Gentile, and L. Zaniboni. Worst-case analysis of selective sampling for linear classification. *JMLR*, 7:1205–1230, 2006.

[7] O. Chapelle, B. Schölkopf, A. Zien, et al. *Semi-supervised learning*, volume 2. MIT press Cambridge, 2006.

[8] K. Crammer. Doubly aggressive selective sampling algorithms for classification. In *AIStat*, pages 140–148, 2014.

[9] K. Crammer, O. Dekel, J. Keshet, S. Shalev-Shwartz, and Y. Singer. Online passive-aggressive algorithms. *JMLR*, 7:551–585, 2006.

[10] K. Crammer, A. Kulesza, and M. Dredze. Adaptive regularization of weight vectors. In *NIPS*, pages 414–422, 2009.

[11] O. Dekel, C. Gentile, and K. Sridharan. Selective sampling and active learning from single and multiple teachers. *JMLR*, 13(1):2655–2697, 2012.

[12] T. G. Dietterich and G. Bakiri. Solving multiclass learning problems via error-correcting output codes. *Journal of artificial intelligence research*, pages 263–286, 1995.

[13] C. Eckart and G. Young. The approximation of one matrix by another of lower rank. *Psychometrika*, 1(3):211–218, 1936.

[14] Q. Gu, C. Aggarwal, J. Liu, and J. Han. Selective sampling on graphs for classification. In *ACM SIGKDD*, pages 131–139, 2013.

[15] M. Herbster and M. Pontil. Prediction on a graph with a perceptron. In *NIPS*, pages 577–584, 2006.

[16] M. Herbster, M. Pontil, and L. Wainer. Online learning over graphs. In *ICML*, pages 305–312, 2005.

[17] A. J. Smola and R. Kondor. Kernels and regularization on graphs. In *Learning theory and kernel machines*, pages 144–158. Springer, 2003.

[18] P. Yang, G. Li, P. Zhao, X. Li, and S. D. Gollapalli. Learning correlative and personalized structure for online multi-task classification. In *SDM*, 2016.

[19] P. Yang, X. Li, M. Wu, C.-K. Kwoh, and S.-K. Ng. Inferring gene-phenotype associations via global protein complex network propagation. *PloS one*, 6(7):e21502, 2011.

[20] P. Yang, X.-L. Li, J.-P. Mei, C.-K. Kwoh, and S.-K. Ng. Positive-unlabeled learning for disease gene identification. *Bioinformatics*, 28(20):2640–2647, 2012.

[21] P. Yang and P. Zhao. A min-max optimization framework for online graph classification. In *CIKM*, pages 643–652. ACM, 2015.

[22] P. Yang, P. Zhao, V. W. Zheng, and X. Li. An aggressive graph-based selective sampling algorithm for classification. In *ICDM 2015*, pages 509–518, 2015.

Adaptive Algorithms and Data-Dependent Guarantees for Bandit Convex Optimization

Mehryar Mohri
Courant Institute and Google
251 Mercer Street
New York, NY 10012
mohri@cims.nyu.edu

Scott Yang
Courant Institute
251 Mercer Street
New York, NY 10012
yangs@cims.nyu.edu

Abstract

We present adaptive algorithms with strong data-dependent regret guarantees for the problem of bandit convex optimization. In the process, we develop a general framework from which the main previous results in this setting can be recovered. The key method is the introduction of adaptive regularization. By appropriately adapting the exploration scheme, we show that one can derive regret guarantees that can be significantly more favorable than those previously known. Moreover, our analysis also modularizes the problematic quantities in achieving the conjectured minimax optimal rates in the most general setting of the problem.

1 INTRODUCTION

Bandit convex optimization (BCO) is a general scenario for sequential decision making under uncertainty. In contrast to the standard full information setting of online convex optimization, in the BCO scenario, at each round, the learner only receives only the value of the loss function and no other feedback, in particular no information about the function derivatives.

BCO extends the well-known multi-armed bandit scenario and is an instance of the exploration-exploitation dilemma inherent in many online machine learning problems: at each round, the learner must decide between exploring new actions and exploiting the best actions determined thus far.

The partial information assumption also captures many real-world problems where the exact form of the loss function is not readily available at each step. These include settings such as ad prediction and medical diagnosis. In these problems, the learner is typically able to see only the value returned from the current action, as the exact loss function and its gradients are often quite abstract and complex.

From a theoretical vantage point, bandit convex optimization also remains an area of online learning in which existing regret guarantees in several regimes are known to be sub-optimal and where optimal methods have still yet to be discovered.

We now formalize the setting that we consider. Let $\mathcal{K} \subset \mathbb{R}^n$ be a compact convex set, and let $\{f_t\}_{t=1}^{\infty}$ be a sequence of convex functions. At each round $t = 1, 2, \ldots, T$, the learner selects a point $x_t \in \mathcal{K}$ and incurs loss $f_t(x_t)$. The learner's objective is to minimize his regret, defined by:

$$\mathrm{Reg}_T := \max_{x \in \mathcal{K}} \sum_{t=1}^{T} f_t(x_t) - f_t(x),$$

that is the difference between his cumulative loss and that of the best fixed point $x^* \in \mathcal{K}$ in hindsight. In contrast to the standard online learning or online convex optimization scenarios, in bandit convex optimization, the learner has access only to the value $f_t(x_t)$ and not any higher-order information. This scenario was first studied by Flaxman et al. (2005), where they proved that for sequences of Lipschitz functions, one can achieve a regret that is in $\mathcal{O}(T^{3/4})$. The seminal work of Abernethy et al. (2008) showed that, for linear functions, one can attain a regret in $\mathcal{O}(\sqrt{T})$. Agarwal et al. (2010) showed that one can improve upon Flaxman's bound and attain $\mathcal{O}(T^{2/3})$ in the strongly convex setting, and Saha and Tewari (2011) showed that one can achieve $\mathcal{O}(T^{2/3})$ in the strongly smooth setting. Hazan and Levy (2014) showed that when the functions are guaranteed to be both strongly smooth and strongly convex, one can attain $\mathcal{O}(\sqrt{T})$ regret. Most recently, Bubeck and Eldan (2015) presented a non-constructive proof demonstrating that a $\mathcal{O}(\sqrt{T})$ bound is also theoretically attainable in the general setting, albeit with a much heavier dependence on the dimension of the domain $\mathcal{O}(n^{11})$ than in the other references mentioned above.

It still remains an open question whether one can efficiently obtain the desired $\mathcal{O}(\sqrt{T})$ regret in the purely strongly convex, purely strongly smooth, or purely Lipschitz settings. To make progress in this direction, we will build upon recent advances in other areas of the online convex optimization literature. Specifically, we will draw from the techniques in adaptive regularization presented in (Bartlett et al., 2007; Duchi et al., 2010; McMahan and Streeter, 2010) as well as ideas from the "learning faster from easy data" paradigm studied in (Even-Dar et al., 2007; Bubeck and Slivkins, 2012; Sani et al., 2014; de Rooij et al., 2014) to derive two efficient adaptive algorithms with minimal assumptions on the function's loss sequence.

Our algorithms will provide strong data-dependent guarantees, so that while their regret will never be worse than that of previous algorithms in the same setting, they can also be much better depending on how favorable and "easy" the actual data is. Moreover, the algorithms we present are anytime and automatically adjust to the data, so that they can run without any a priori tuning or unreasonable parameter specification. Perhaps most importantly, analyzing the resulting bounds provides insight into both whether the conjectured optimal bounds are truly achievable as well as how they might viably be attained.

We will start off by introducing some mathematical notation for the rest of our paper. Then, in Section 3, we will describe the general methodology of BCO, and in the process, introduce several key concepts and tools as well as our intuition and contribution to this framework. This will be formalized in Sections 4, 5, and 6, where we introduce concrete algorithms and guarantees. Finally, we will highlight the main implications of our results in Section 7, both in terms of new regret guarantees as well as added insight for the general bandit convex optimization setting with only the Lipschitz loss assumption.

2 NOTATION

In what follows, we will denote by $\mathcal{B}^n$ the n-dimensional unit ball under the Euclidean norm, and $\mathcal{S}^n = \partial\mathcal{B}^n$ the $(n-1)$-dimensional unit sphere. For any sequence of functions $\{c_t\}_{t=1}^{\infty}$, we will write $c_{1:t} = \sum_{s=1}^{t} c_t$. Given a function f_t and a point x_t, we will denote by $g_t \in \partial f_t(x_t)$ an element of the subgradient of f_t at x_t, such that for any y, $f_t(y) \geq f_t(x_t) + g_t^\top(y - x_t)$. Given any norm $\|\cdot\|$, we will denote its dual by $\|\cdot\|_*$, so that $\|x\|_* = \sup_{\|y\|\leq 1} x^\top y$. Moreover, given any symmetric positive semi-definite (SPSD) matrix A, we define the semi-norm $\|x\|_A = \sqrt{x^\top A x}$, and we denote the j-th eigenvalue of A by $\lambda_j(A)$ (in decreasing order).

Definition 1 (Strongly Smooth and Strongly Convex). *Let A be an SPSD matrix. A function f is said to be*

- *A-strongly smooth if $f(x) \leq f(y) + \nabla f(y)^\top(x-y) + \frac{1}{2}\|x - y\|_A^2$;*
- *A-strongly convex if $f(x) \geq f(y) + \nabla f(y)^\top(x-y) + \frac{1}{2}\|x - y\|_A^2$.*

For a scalar $\beta \in \mathbb{R}_+$, f is said to be β-strongly smooth (β-strongly convex) if it is βI-strongly smooth (respectively strongly convex). For functions that are not C^1, we replace the gradients by subgradients in these definitions.

3 OVERVIEW OF BANDIT CONVEX OPTIMIZATION

Bandit convex optimization, and bandit problems in general, can be viewed as online learning problems with partial information. In this context, the natural approach is to estimate the missing data from the full information setting, and to then apply online learning methods to the problem.

One online learning method that is commonly used in bandit convex optimization is the Follow-the-Regularized-Leader (FTRL) (Kalai and Vempala, 2005) algorithm, which is based on the update:

$$x_{t+1} = \operatorname*{argmin}_{x\in\mathcal{K}} \eta g_{1:t}^\top x + \mathcal{R}(x),$$

where $\mathcal{R}$ is some regularization function.

However, in bandit convex optimization, the missing data at each round is the gradient. Since the learner only knows the value of the loss function at each round, the FTRL algorithm cannot be readily applied (nor can most other online learning algorithms, which also typically use gradient information). This is what makes bandit convex optimization significantly more difficult than standard online onvex optimization.

A key step toward addressing this issue has been the insight that by playing an action randomly near the intended one, it is possible to estimate the gradient of a smoothed version of the loss function. More formally, given any $f\colon \mathbb{R}^n \to \mathbb{R}$ and $A \in \mathbb{R}^{n\times n}$ an SPSD matrix, we define $\widehat{f}(x) = \mathbb{E}_{v\in\mathcal{B}^n}[f(x + Av)]$, the average of f at x over the ellipsoid generated by A, and $\widehat{g}_t = nf(x + Au)A^{-1}u$, its one-point gradient estimate. Then the following result holds:

Lemma 1 (Saha and Tewari (2011)). $\mathbb{E}_{u\sim\mathcal{S}^n}[\widehat{g}_t] = \nabla\widehat{f}(x)$.

For completeness, we provide a proof of this result in Appendix A.

This implies that by sampling a point $x + Av$ in an ellipsoid around the intended action, we can estimate the gradient of a smoothed version of our loss function even if we are only able to play a single action. Moreover, by playing these gradient estimates, our regret will be the regret of this smoothed loss up to the approximation error of smoothing.

In practice, the smoothing ellipsoid is defined by scaling the inverse Hessian of the regularization function $\mathcal{R}$, i.e. $A = \delta\nabla^2\mathcal{R}(x)^{-1/2}v$. Thus, the choice of regularization becomes crucial towards determining how much to explore and how much approximation error to incur. The key work along this direction has been (Abernethy et al., 2008), which showed that one can use the notion of self-concordant barrier to find a good tradeoff.

For completeness, we briefly introduce this concept and summarize the key results that we will use in our analysis.

3.1 BACKGROUND ON SELF-CONCORDANT FUNCTIONS

The use of self-concordant functions can be traced back to Nesterov's work on Newton's method (see (Nesterov, 2004) for a comprehensive treatment).

Definition 2 (Self-concordant barrier). *A C^3 function $\mathcal{R}\colon \mathrm{int}(K) \to \mathbb{R}$ is a ν-self concordant barrier if for any $h \in \mathbb{R}^n$:*

1. *$\mathcal{R}$ approaches infinity for any sequence of points approaching the boundary of $\mathcal{K}$.*
2. $\left|\nabla^3\mathcal{R}(x)[h,h,h]\right| \leq 2(\nabla^2\mathcal{R}(x)[h,h])^{3/2}$.
3. $|\nabla\mathcal{R}(x)h| \leq (\nu\nabla^2\mathcal{R}(x)[h,h])^{1/2}$.

Definition 3 (Dikin Ellipsoid). *Let $\mathcal{R}$ be a self-concordant function and $x \in \mathrm{int}(K)$. Then, the Dikin Ellipsoid $W_1(x)$ is the ellipsoid induced by the Hessian of $\mathcal{R}$ at x:*

$$W_1(x) = \{z \in \mathbb{R}^n \mid \|z-x\|_{\nabla^2\mathcal{R}(x)} \leq 1\} \subset \mathcal{K}.$$

Definition 4 (Newton Decrement). *Given any C^2 function $\mathcal{R}$ whose Hessian is invertible at a point x, the Newton decrement of $\mathcal{R}$ at x is defined to be $\lambda(x,\mathcal{R}) = \|\nabla\mathcal{R}(x)\|_{\nabla^2\mathcal{R}(x)^{-1}}$.*

The following two results can be found in (Nemirovski and Todd, 2008) and will be the most important properties for our analysis.

Lemma 2. *Let $\mathcal{R}$ be a self concordant function and $x \in \mathrm{int}(\mathcal{K})$ a point such that $\lambda(x,\mathcal{R}) \leq \frac{1}{2}$. Then, $\|x - \mathrm{argmin}_u \mathcal{R}(u)\|_{\nabla^2\mathcal{R}(x)} \leq 2\lambda(x,\mathcal{R})$.*

Given $x, y \in \mathrm{int}(\mathcal{K})$, the Minkowsky function is defined as $\pi_x(y) = \inf\left\{t \geq 0 \mid x + \frac{1}{t}(y-x)\right\}$.

Lemma 3. *Let $\mathcal{R}$ be a ν-self concordant barrier. Then for any $x, y \in \mathrm{int}(\mathcal{K})$: $\mathcal{R}(y) - \mathcal{R}(x) \leq \nu \log\left(\frac{1}{1-\pi_x(y)}\right)$.*

Thus, the current state-of-the-art approach to bandit convex optimization problem has been to play a FTRL-type algorithm with the update:

$$x_{t+1} = \operatorname*{argmin}_{x\in\mathcal{K}} \eta\widehat{g}_{1:t}^{\top}x + \mathcal{R}(x),$$

where $\widehat{g} = \widehat{g}(\delta, \nabla^2\mathcal{R})$, and $\mathcal{R}$ is a self-concordant barrier.

For global σ-strongly convex loss functions, one can also add an associated quadratic term to the optimization problem and a σ-ball to the sampling ellipsoid.

In this paper, we extend the above framework with the concept of adapting to the data. Specifically, we will tune the learning rate and sampling ellipsoid at each step of the algorithm according to the local data that we see. The goal of this approach is two-fold. On the one hand, we want to design any-time algorithms with general regret bounds that recover all existing approaches in a unified manner. Previous algorithms assumed various levels of global regularity information, had different sampling schemes for each, and had to be tuned with a posteriori knowledge. On the other hand, and perhaps more importantly, we also want to derive data-dependent guarantees that can reveal new insight into the difficulties of the problem.

4 ADAPTIVE BANDIT CONVEX OPTIMIZATION

Using the motivation above, we now present AdaBCO, an adaptive procedure for bandit convex optimization. AdaBCO is a skeleton algorithm that we will use as a *launching point* for our two data-dependent algorithms. As such, it is not meant to be implemented on its own, and some of its parameters, such as η_t and δ_t, are not specified precisely. These will be selected carefully in Algorithms 2 and 3.

Unlike previous algorithms in the literature, AdaBCO does not need the learner to specify a priori a fixed level of global convexity for the entire sequence of loss functions encountered during learning. This is often an unreasonable requirement, particularly in a truly online setting, and so instead, AdaBCO allows the learner to specify the convexity of functions as it sees them. The algorithm is designed such that the regret bound will automatically adapt to this data. This is achieved via dynamic tuning of the sampling ellipsoids and learning rates, which will be prescribed more explicitly in Algorithms 2 and 3, when we also take into account the level of function smoothness.

Moreover, it is important to realize that computing parameters in real-time is never more difficult than computing bounds that hold uniformly over all rounds at the start in a truly online scenario. Thus, AdaBCO is never more difficult to implement than previous algorithms.

AdaBCO also differs from previous work in that it treats strong convexity as a matrix parameter instead of a scalar parameter. This is based on the insight that, for minimizing regret, convexity of the loss function is closely tied to convexity of the self-concordant barrier's Hessian, and that one can bound regret in terms of the average eigenvalue of the sum of these matrices as opposed to the minimal eigenvalue. Essentially, the algorithm can "borrow" convexity from the self-concordant barrier if the convexity of the loss function is not strong enough to achieve the desired regret. This becomes particularly useful when the learner is querying points near the decision set's boundary, and the Hessian of $\mathcal{R}$ has large eigenvalues in the direction of the boundary (often the case because $\mathcal{R} \nearrow \infty$ at $\partial\mathcal{K}$). This will become more clear with the data-dependent guarantees and discussion in Sections 5, 6, and 7.

We will first show that AdaBCO yields a strong data-dependent regret bound on the sequence of smoothed loss functions. The proof technique is based on a few key steps. We first use convexity of the loss function to change the problem into bounding the regret of quadratic functions. Then we use the fact that our original algorithm can be seen as a Follow-the-Regularized-Leader algorithm played on this sequence of surrogate loss functions to bound the regret. From here, we leverage the fact that part of our loss function is proximal, along with the properties of self-concordant barriers that we stated, to show that in the local norm, the incremental update can be bounded by the gradient of the (smoothed) loss function. Then we can estimate the gradient in the local norm in terms of the quantities that we have prescribed. Finally, we use more properties about self-concordant barriers to bound their growth near the center of the domain.

In the process, we will require a few technical lemmas about the properties of smoothed functions as well as some results from the general online learning literature. For completeness, all proofs are provided in Appendix A.

4.1 TECHNICAL LEMMAS

The following result is a mild generalization of Lemma 7 in (Hazan and Levy, 2014) and states that a smoothed loss function retains the same strong convexity properties as the original.

Lemma 4. *Let A be an SPSD matrix, and let $f\colon \mathbb{R}^n \to \mathbb{R}$ be A-strongly convex. Then $\widehat{f}$ is also A-strongly convex.*

Next we state a lemma by Zinkevich (2003), which shows that we can bound the regret of any sequence of loss functions by a lower barrier. This will be useful for switching between our loss functions and the quadratic lower bounds induced by their strong convexity.

Lemma 5. *Let $\{f_t\}_{t=1}^{\infty}$ be a sequence of functions and $\{x_t\}_{t=1}^{\infty} \subset \mathcal{K}$. Suppose there exists a sequence of lower barrier functions $\{h_t\}_{t=1}^{\infty}$ such that $h_t(x_t) = f_t(x_t)$ and $h_t \leq f_t$. Then, the following inequality holds:*

$$\max_{x\in\mathcal{K}} \sum_{t=1}^{T} f_t(x_t) - f_t(x) \leq \max_{x\in\mathcal{K}} \sum_{t=1}^{T} h_t(x_t) - h_t(x).$$

The final technical lemma in this section extends the well-known "be-the-leader"-based result of follow-the-regularized-leader type algorithms (originally from (Kalai and Vempala, 2005), to algorithms with adaptive regularization.

Algorithm 1 AdaBCO

Input: $\eta_0 = \frac{1}{2nC}$, ν-self concordant barrier $\mathcal{R}$.
Initialize: $x_1 = \text{argmin}_{x\in\mathcal{K}} \mathcal{R}(x)$.
for $t = 1, \ldots, T$: **do**
  Choose matrix $Q_t \succcurlyeq 0$ such that $f_t(x) \geq f_t(x_t) + g_t^\top(x - x_t) + \frac{1}{2}\|x - x_t\|_{Q_t}^2$.
  Define $\eta_t \leq \eta_{t-1}$.
  Set $B_t = \left[\nabla^2\mathcal{R}(x_t) + \eta_t Q_{1:t}\right]^{-1/2}$.
  Sample $u \sim \mathcal{S}^n$ uniformly.
  Define δ_t and set $y_t = x_t + \delta_t B_t u \in W_1(x_t) \subset \mathcal{K}$.
  Play y_t and incur loss $f_t(y_t)$.
  Compute the estimate $\widehat{g}_t = n f_t(y_t)(\delta_t B_t)^{-1} u$.
  Update $x_{t+1} = \text{argmin}_{x\in\mathcal{K}} \widehat{g}_{1:t}^\top x + \frac{1}{2}\sum_{s=1}^{t} \|(x - x_s)\|_{Q_s}^2 + \frac{1}{\eta_t}\mathcal{R}(x)$.
end for

Lemma 6. *Let $\{f_t\}_{t=1}^{\infty}$ be a sequence of convex functions defined on a closed convex set $\mathcal{K}$, and let $\{x_t\}_{t=1}^{\infty}$ be a sequence of points in $\mathcal{K}$ such that the subgradient of f_t at x_t is denoted as g_t. Let $\{r_t\}_{t=1}^{\infty}$ be a sequence of non-negative convex functions. Then the update $x_{t+1} = \text{argmin}_x\, g_{1:t}^\top x + r_{0:t}(x)$ incurs regret at most*

$$\sum_{t=1}^{T} f_t(x_t) - f_t(x) \leq r_{0:T}(x) + \sum_{t=1}^{T} g_t^\top(x_t - x_{t+1}).$$

We are now able to present the regret guarantee for Algorithm 1:

Theorem 1 (AdaBCO)**.** *Let $\mathcal{K}$ be a convex set with diameter $\mathcal{D}_{\mathcal{K}}$, and $\mathcal{R}$ a ν-self-concordant barrier over $\mathcal{K}$. Assume that $|f| \leq C$. Then, for $0 < \eta_t \leq \frac{1}{2nC}$, the following regret bound holds for Algorithm 1:*

$$\max_{w\in\mathcal{K}} \sum_{t=1}^{T} \mathbb{E}[\widehat{f}_t(y_t) - \widehat{f}_t(w)] \leq \sum_{t=1}^{T} \frac{\eta_t}{\delta_t^2}\mathbb{E}\left[(nf_t(x_t + \delta_t B_t u))^2 + \frac{1}{\eta_T}\nu\log(T)\right].$$

Proof. We will refer back to the series of lemmas presented in the prior sections in our analysis.

Let r_0 and r_t be defined as follows:

$$r_0(x) = \frac{1}{\eta}\mathcal{R}(x), \quad r_t(x) = \frac{1}{2}\|x - x_t\|_{Q_t}^2.$$

Let $h_0 = r_0$, and for $t \geq 1$, let $h_t(x) = \widehat{g}_t^\top x + r_t(x)$. Then, $h_{0:t}(x) = \widehat{g}_{1:t}^\top x + r_{0:t}(x)$, and the update in Algorithm 1 can be written as $x_{t+1} = \text{argmin}\, h_{0:t}(x)$.

Now, define $b_t(x) = \widehat{g}_t^\top(x - x_t) + r_t(x)$. By our choice of Q_t and the fact that smoothed functions preserve strong convexity (Lemma 4), it follows that $\widehat{f}_t(x) \geq b_t(x) + \widehat{f}_t(x_t)$ for all $x \in \mathcal{K}$, with equality at x_t. Thus, if we define

$\tilde{f}_t(x) = \widehat{g}_t^\top x + r_t(x)$, we can apply Lemma 5 to obtain $\max_x \sum_{t=1}^T \widehat{f}_t(x_t) - \widehat{f}_t(x) \leq \max_x \sum_{t=1}^T \tilde{f}_t(x_t) - \tilde{f}_t(x)$. This helps us reduce upper bounding the regret of our theorem by the regret of quadratic functions plus a self-concordant barrier.

Note that $x_{t+1} = \operatorname{argmin} \tilde{f}_{1:t}(x) + \frac{1}{\eta_t}\mathcal{R}(x)$ is a FTRL-style update. Thus, by Lemma 6, the following holds:

$$\sum_{t=1}^T \mathbb{E}\left[\tilde{f}_t(x_t) - \tilde{f}_t(x)\right] \leq \sum_{t=1}^T \mathbb{E}\left[\nabla \tilde{f}_t(x_t)^\top (x_t - x_{t+1}) + \frac{1}{\eta_T}\mathcal{R}(x)\right].$$

The first term can be bounded by

$$\begin{aligned}
&\sum_{t=1}^T \mathbb{E}\left[\nabla \tilde{f}_t(x_t)^\top (x_t - x)\right] \\
&= \sum_{t=1}^T \mathbb{E}\left[\widehat{g}_t^\top (x_t - x)\right] \\
&\leq \sum_{t=1}^T \|\widehat{g}_t\|_{\nabla^2 \eta_t h_{0:t}(x_t),*} \|x_t - x_{t+1}\|_{\nabla^2 \eta_t h_{0:t}(x_t)}.
\end{aligned}$$

Since $x_{t+1} = \operatorname{argmin}_x \eta_t h_{0:t}(x)$, Lemma 2 tells us that if the Newton decrement $\lambda(x_t, \eta_t h_{0:t}) = \|\nabla \eta_t h_{0:t}(x_t)\|_{(\nabla^2 \eta_t h_{0:t}(x_t))^{-1}} \leq \frac{1}{2}$, then $\|x_t - x_{t+1}\|_{\nabla^2 \eta_t h_{0:t}(x_t)} \leq 2\lambda(x_t, \eta_t h_{0:t})$. This implies that $\sum_{t=1}^T \nabla \tilde{f}_t(x_t)^\top (x_t - x) \leq \sum_{t=1}^T 2\eta_t \|\widehat{g}_t\|_{\nabla^2 \eta h_{0:t}(x_t),*} \|\nabla h_{0:t}(x_t)\|_{\nabla^2 \eta_t h_{0:t}(x_t),*}$.

At the same time, since

$$\begin{aligned}
x_t &= \operatorname*{argmin}_x h_{0:t-1}(x), \\
h_{0:t-1}(x) + r_t(x) &= h_{0:t}(x) - \widehat{g}_t^\top x,
\end{aligned}$$

and x_t also minimizes r_t, it follows that $0 = \nabla(h_{0:t-1} + r_t)(x_t) = \nabla h_{0:t}(x_t) - \widehat{g}_t$. Thus, the following holds: $\sum_{t=1}^T \nabla \tilde{f}_t(x_t)^\top (x_t - x) \leq \sum_{t=1}^T 2\eta_t \|\widehat{g}_t\|^2_{\nabla^2 \eta_t h_{0:t}(x_t),*}$.

Putting everything together yields:

$$\begin{aligned}
&\sum_{t=1}^T \mathbb{E}\left[\widehat{f}_t(x_t) - \widehat{f}_t(x)\right] \\
&\leq \left(\sum_{t=1}^T \mathbb{E}\left[2\eta_t \|\widehat{g}_t\|^2_{\nabla^2 \eta_t h_{0:t}(x_t),*}\right]\right) + \mathbb{E}\left[\frac{1}{\eta_T}\mathcal{R}(x)\right].
\end{aligned}$$

In addition, we know that

$$\begin{aligned}
&\mathbb{E}\left[\|\widehat{g}_t\|^2_{\nabla^2 \eta_t h_{0:t}(x_t),*}\right] \\
&= \mathbb{E}\left[\|n f_t(y_t)(\delta_t B_t)^{-1} u\|^2_{\nabla^2 \eta_t h_{0:t}(x_t),*}\right] \\
&= \mathbb{E}[(n f_t(y_t)(\delta_t B_t)^{-1} u)^\top \nabla^2 \eta_t h_{0:t}(x_t)^{-1} \\
&\qquad (n f_t(y_t)(\delta_t B_t)^{-1} u)] \\
&\leq \mathbb{E}\left[\frac{1}{\delta_t^2}(n f_t(x_t + \delta_t B_t u))^2\right].
\end{aligned}$$

To bound the self-concordant function, Lemma 3 shows that if $\mathcal{R}$ is any ν-self concordant function over $\mathcal{K}$, then

$$\mathcal{R}(y) - \mathcal{R}(x) \leq \nu \log\left(\frac{1}{1 - \pi_x(y)}\right), \quad \forall x, y \in \operatorname{int}(\mathcal{K})$$

where $\pi_{\mathcal{K},x}(y) = \inf\{t \geq 0 \colon x + \frac{1}{t}(y - x) \in \mathcal{K}\}$ is the Minkowsky functional over $\mathcal{K}$ at x.

By definition, $x_1 = \operatorname{argmin}_{x \in \mathcal{K}} \mathcal{R}(x)$. Now, any point $y \in \mathcal{K}$ satisfying $\pi_{\mathcal{K},x_1}(w) \leq 1 - \frac{1}{T}$ must satisfy $\mathcal{R}(w) - \mathcal{R}(x_1) \leq \nu \log(T)$. Since $\mathcal{R} \geq 0$ on $\mathcal{K}$ by assumption, this also means that $\mathcal{R}(w) \leq \nu \log(T)$.

On the other hand, if $\pi_{\mathcal{K},x_1}(w) > 1 - \frac{1}{T}$, then the fact that $\pi_{\mathcal{K},x_1}(w) \leq 1$ implies that there exists $0 < \epsilon \leq \frac{1}{T}$ such that $\pi_{\mathcal{K},x_1}(w) \leq 1 - \frac{1}{T} + \epsilon$. Defining $z = x_1 + (w - x_1)\frac{1 - \frac{1}{T}}{1 - \frac{1}{T} + \epsilon} \in \mathcal{K}$ yields that $\|w - z\| = \|\frac{\epsilon}{1 - \frac{1}{T}} x_1 - w\| \leq \mathcal{O}\left(\frac{1}{T}\right)$ and $\pi_{\mathcal{K},x_1}(z) \leq 1 - \frac{1}{T}$. But $\mathcal{R}$ is Lipschitz on any compact subset of $\operatorname{int}(\mathcal{K})$, so we get that $\mathcal{R}(w) \leq \nu \log(T) + \mathcal{O}\left(\frac{1}{T}\right)$. Since the last term does not grow as a function of T, we will ignore it in the regret bound.

Combining the above estimates shows that if $\eta_t \|\widehat{g}_t\|_{\nabla^2 \mathcal{R}(x_t) + \eta_t Q_t,*} \leq \frac{1}{2}$ (i.e. if $\eta_t \leq \frac{1}{2nC}$), then

$$\begin{aligned}
&\sum_{t=1}^T \mathbb{E}[\widehat{f}_t(y_t) - \widehat{f}_t(w)] \\
&\leq \sum_{t=1}^T \mathbb{E}\left[\frac{\eta_t}{\delta_t^2}(n f_t(x_t + \delta_t B_t u))^2 + \frac{1}{\eta_T}\nu \log(T)\right].
\end{aligned}$$

□

The extrapolation of the regret bound in Theorem 1 for smoothed loss functions to a regret bound on the original loss requires taking into account some local regularity assumptions. Factoring in local second-order regularity yields Algorithm 2.

5 AdaBCO FOR SMOOTH FUNCTIONS

The major differences between Algorithm 2 with the previous algorithm are that we now account for the local smoothness parameter β_t and that we also specify precisely the

Algorithm 2 AdaBCO-Smooth

Input: $\eta_0 = \frac{1}{2nC}$, ν-self concordant barrier $\mathcal{R}$, $C > 0$ constant.
Initialize: $x_1 = \operatorname{argmin}_{x \in \mathcal{K}} \mathcal{R}(x)$.
for $t = 1, \ldots, T$: **do**
  Choose a constant $\beta_t > 0$ such that $f_t(x) \leq f_t(y) + \nabla f_t(y)^\top (x - y) + \frac{\beta_t}{2} \|x - y\|_2^2$.
  Choose matrix $Q_t \succcurlyeq 0$ such that $f_t(x) \geq f_t(x_t) + g_t^\top (x - x_t) + \frac{1}{2} \|x - x_t\|_{Q_t}^2$.
  Define $\tilde{B}_{t,s} = \left(\nabla^2 R(x_s) + \eta_s 1_{\{s<t\}} Q_{1:s}\right)^{-1/2}$ and

$$\eta_t = \left(\sum_{s=1}^{t} \sqrt{4\beta_s \frac{1}{n} \sum_{j=1}^{n} \lambda_j(\tilde{B}_{t,s}^2) n^2 C^2}\right)^{-2/3} (\nu \log(T))^{2/3}.$$

  Let $B_t = \left[\nabla^2 \mathcal{R}(x_t) + \eta_t Q_{1:t}\right]^{-1/2}$.
  Define $\delta_t = \left(\frac{n^3 C^2 \eta_t}{\beta_t \sum_{j=1}^{n} \lambda_j(B_t^2)}\right)^{1/4}$.
  Sample $u \sim \mathcal{S}^n$ uniformly.
  Set $y_t = x_t + \delta_t B_t u \in W_1(x_t) \subset \mathcal{K}$.
  Play y_t and incur loss $f_t(y_t)$.
  Compute the estimate $\widehat{g}_t = n f_t(y_t)(\delta_t B_t)^{-1} u$.
  Update $x_{t+1} = \operatorname{argmin}_{x \in \mathcal{K}} g_{1:t}^\top x + \frac{1}{2} \sum_{s=1}^{t} \|(x - x_s)\|_{Q_s}^2 + \frac{1}{\eta_t} \mathcal{R}(x)$.
end for

dynamic learning rate η_t and sampling radius δ_t. Thus, Algorithm 2 is also an upgrade from previous algorithms in the literature in the sense that it does not require a priori assumptions on the global convexity or smoothness of the loss functions. One can adjust these parameters online, and the algorithm's regret will adapt.

The proof of the regret bound relies first on comparing the true loss function with the smoothed one by using the regularity parameters at each step. In contrast to previous algorithms which used global regularity parameters in a coarse manner (e.g. (Saha and Tewari, 2011)), we analyze the random sampling of the ellipsoid in greater depth in order to produce data-dependent estimates that we can leverage. This requires some general results about random variables and sampling that we present in Lemmas 8 and 9. After analyzing the approximation error, we use the result of Theorem 1 to derive a tight data-dependent bound in terms of all the relevant controllable quantities. From here, the sampling ellipsoid and learning rate at each iteration are adjusted dynamically to achieve a tight bound on the regret.

The choice of these ellipsoids and learning rates is fairly subtle and cannot be done directly due to their interdependence. The optimal a posteriori learning rate depends on the sampling ellipsoid, and the radius of the sampling ellipsoid depends on the learning rate. To get around this chicken-and-egg type of phenomenon, we force the learner to first hallucinate a different set of sampling ellipsoids based on history from which the learner can determine good learning rates. From here, the learner is then able to define an efficient true sampling ellipsoid. Deriving a tight on-line approximation to the a posteriori optimal parameters also involves an abstract calculation on normalized sums, which we present in Lemma 7.

We first formerly state the technical lemmas that we will need in this section. Their proofs are provided in Appendix A.

5.1 TECHNICAL LEMMAS

Lemma 7. *Let* $\alpha_t \geq 0$, $\gamma > 0$, $\beta > 1$, *and* $\eta_t = \beta^{\frac{1}{1+\gamma}} (\alpha_{1:t})^{\frac{-1}{1+\gamma}}$. *Then*

$$\left(\sum_{t=1}^{T} \eta_t^\gamma \alpha_t\right) + \frac{\beta}{\eta_T} \leq (2 + \gamma) \beta^{\frac{\gamma}{1+\gamma}} (\alpha_{1:T})^{\frac{1}{1+\gamma}}.$$

To derive finer estimates on the approximation error, we will use the following facts about quadratic forms of random variables and the statistical properties of sampling from the unit sphere.

Lemma 8. *Let* $x \sim \mathcal{D}$ *be a random vector and* A *be a symmetric matrix. Then, the following identity holds:*

$$\mathbb{E}_{x \sim \mathcal{D}}[x^\top A x] = \mathit{trace}(A\mathit{cov}(x)) + \mathbb{E}[x]^\top A \mathbb{E}[x],$$

where $\mathit{cov}(x) = \mathbb{E}[xx^\top] - \mathbb{E}[x]\mathbb{E}[x]^\top$ *is the covariance matrix associated to* x.

Lemma 9. *Let* $u \sim \mathcal{S}^n$. *Then* $\mathit{cov}(u) = \frac{1}{n} I$ *and* $\mathbb{E}[u] = 0$.

We are now ready to present the regret guarantee of Algorithm 2:

Theorem 2 (AdaBCO using dynamic smoothness bounds). *Let* $\mathcal{K}$ *be a convex set and* $\mathcal{R}$ *a* ν*-self-concordant barrier over* $\mathcal{K}$. *Assume that* $|f| \leq C$. *Then the following regret bound holds for Algorithm 2:*

$$\max_{x \in \mathcal{K}} \sum_{t=1}^{T} \mathbb{E}[f_t(y_t) - f_t(x)] \leq \mathbb{E}\left[\frac{5}{2} (\nu \log(T))^{\frac{1}{3}} \left(\sum_{t=1}^{T} \sqrt{4\beta_t n C^2 \sum_{j=1}^{n} \lambda_j(B_t^2)}\right)^{\frac{2}{3}}\right]$$

Proof. We will show first that Algorithm 2 yields regret of at most:

$$\sum_{t=1}^{T} \mathbb{E}[f_t(y_t) - f_t(x)]$$
$$\leq \sum_{t=1}^{T} \mathbb{E}\left[\delta_t^2 \beta_t \frac{1}{n} \sum_{j=1}^{n} \lambda_j(B_t^2)\right]$$
$$+ \mathbb{E}\left[\left(\sum_{t=1}^{T} \frac{\eta_t}{\delta_t^2}(n f_t(x_t + B_t u))^2\right) + \frac{1}{\eta_T}\nu \log(T)\right]$$

for any schedule of $\{\delta_t\}_{t=1}^T$ and $\{\eta_t\}_{t=1}^T$.

The expected regret can be decomposed as follows:

$$\mathbb{E}[\text{Reg}_T(w)]$$
$$= \sum_{t=1}^{T} \mathbb{E}[f_t(y_t) - f_t(w)]$$
$$= \sum_{t=1}^{T} \mathbb{E}[f_t(y_t) - f_t(x_t)] + \mathbb{E}[f_t(x_t) - \widehat{f}_t(x_t)]$$
$$+ \mathbb{E}[\widehat{f}_t(w) - f_t(w)] + \mathbb{E}[\widehat{f}_t(x_t) - \widehat{f}_t(w)].$$

The first three terms reflect the approximation error from running our algorithm against the true loss functions versus the smoothed out versions, and the last term can be bounded via Theorem 1. To bound the first three, we use the β_t-strongly smooth property.

For the first term, we can use the smooothness constant of the particular loss function along with the results on random sampling to derive the following bound:

$$\mathbb{E}[f_t(y_t) - f_t(x_t)]$$
$$= \mathbb{E}\Big[\mathbb{E}_{u \sim \mathcal{S}^n}[f_t(x_t + \delta_t B_t u) - f_t(x_t)|x_t]\Big]$$
$$\leq \mathbb{E}\Big[\mathbb{E}_{u \sim \mathcal{S}^n}[\nabla f_t(x_t)\delta_t B_t u + \tfrac{\beta_t}{2}\|\delta_t B_t u\|_2^2 |x_t]\Big]$$
$$= \mathbb{E}\Big[\mathbb{E}\Big[\tfrac{\beta_t}{2}\|\delta_t B_t u\|_2^2 |x_t\Big]\Big]$$
$$= \mathbb{E}\left[\frac{\beta_t}{2} \operatorname{trace}\left(\delta_t^2 B_t^2 \frac{1}{n} I\right)\right] \quad \text{(by Lemmas 8 and 9)}$$
$$= \mathbb{E}\left[\frac{\beta_t}{2}\delta_t^2 \frac{1}{n}\sum_{j=1}^{n}\lambda_j(B_t^2)\right].$$

The second term can be bounded using Jensen's inequality:

$$\mathbb{E}[f_t(x_t) - \widehat{f}_t(x_t)]$$
$$= \mathbb{E}\left[f_t(x_t) - \mathbb{E}_{v \sim \mathcal{B}^n}\left[f_t(x_t + \delta_t B_t v)\right]\right]$$
$$\leq \mathbb{E}\left[f_t(x_t) - f_t\left(\mathbb{E}_{v \sim \mathcal{B}^n}\left[x_t + \delta_t B_t v\right]\right)\right]$$
$$= 0.$$

The third term can be analyzed in a way similar to the first term, using the smoothness constant of the particular loss function as well as the results on random sampling:

$$\mathbb{E}[\widehat{f}_t(w) - f_t(w)]$$
$$= \mathbb{E}[\mathbb{E}_{v \sim \mathcal{B}^n}[f_t(w + \delta_t B_t v)] - f_t(w)]$$
$$\leq \mathbb{E}\left[\mathbb{E}_{v \sim \mathcal{B}^n}\left[\nabla f_t(w)\delta_t B_t v + \frac{\beta_t}{2}\|\delta_t B_t v\|_2^2\right]\right]$$
$$= \mathbb{E}\left[\frac{\beta_t}{2}\delta_t^2 \mathbb{E}_{v \sim \mathcal{B}^n}\left[\|B_t v\|_2^2\right]\right]$$
$$\leq \mathbb{E}\left[\frac{\beta_t}{2}\delta_t^2 \frac{1}{n}\sum_{j=1}^{n}\lambda_j(B_t^2)\right] \quad \text{(by Lemmas 8 and 9).}$$

By putting together all of the estimates above, we can arrive at the following intermediate inequality:

$$\sum_{t=1}^{T} \mathbb{E}[f_t(y_t) - f_t(x)]$$
$$\leq \sum_{t=1}^{T} \mathbb{E}\left[\delta_t^2 \beta_t \frac{1}{n} \sum_{j=1}^{n} \lambda_j(B_t^2)\right]$$
$$+ \mathbb{E}\left[\left(\sum_{t=1}^{T} \frac{\eta_t}{\delta_t^2}(n f_t(x_t + B_t u))^2\right) + \frac{1}{\eta_T}\nu \log(T)\right]$$
$$\leq \sum_{t=1}^{T} \mathbb{E}\left[\delta_t^2 \beta_t \frac{1}{n} \sum_{j=1}^{n} \lambda_j(B_t^2)\right]$$
$$+ \mathbb{E}\left[\left(\sum_{t=1}^{T} \frac{\eta_t}{\delta_t^2} n^2 C^2\right) + \frac{1}{\eta_T}\nu \log(T)\right],$$

and by our choice of δ_t, it follows that

$$\sum_{t=1}^{T} \mathbb{E}[f_t(y_t) - f_t(x)]$$
$$\leq \mathbb{E}\left[\sum_{t=1}^{T} 2\sqrt{\beta_t \eta_t n C^2 \sum_{j=1}^{n} \lambda_j(B_t^2)} + \frac{1}{\eta_T}\nu \log(T)\right].$$

Finally, our choice of η_t, the fact that $\eta_t \leq \eta_{t-1}$, and Lemma 7 with $\gamma = \frac{1}{2}$, $\alpha_t = 2\sqrt{\beta_t n C^2 \sum_{j=1}^{n} \lambda_j(B_t^2)}$, $\beta = \nu \log(T)$ yield:

$$\sum_{t=1}^{T} \mathbb{E}[f_t(y_t) - f_t(x)]$$
$$\leq \mathbb{E}\left[\frac{5}{2}(\nu \log(T))^{\frac{1}{3}} \left(\sum_{t=1}^{T} \sqrt{4\beta_t n C^2 \sum_{j=1}^{n} \lambda_j(B_t^2)}\right)^{\frac{2}{3}}\right].$$

□

Algorithm 3 AdaBCO-Lipschitz

Input: $\eta_0 = \frac{1}{2nC}$, ν-self concordant barrier $\mathcal{R}$, $C > 0$ constant.
Initialize: $x_1 = \text{argmin}_{x \in \mathcal{K}} \mathcal{R}(x)$.
for $t = 1, \ldots, T$: **do**
  Choose a constant $L_t \geq 0$ such that $|f_t(x) - f_t(y)| \leq L_t |x - y|$.
  Choose matrix $Q_t \succcurlyeq 0$ such that $f_t(x) \geq f_t(x_t) + g_t^\top (x - x_t) + \frac{1}{2}\|x - x_t\|_{Q_t}^2$.
  Define $\tilde{B}_{t,s} = \left(\nabla^2 R(x_s) + (\eta_s 1_{\{s<t\}}) Q_{1:s}\right)^{-1/2}$ and

$$\eta_t = \left(\sum_{s=1}^{t} 2\left(2L_s \frac{1}{n}\sum_{j=1}^{n} \lambda_j(\tilde{B}_{t,s}) n^2 C^2\right)^{1/3}\right)^{-3/4} \left(\frac{\nu \log(T)}{2}\right)^{3/4}.$$

  Let $B_t = \left[\nabla^2 \mathcal{R}(x_t) + \eta_t Q_{1:t}\right]^{-1/2}$.
  Define $\delta_t = \left(2\frac{n^3 C^2 \eta_t}{L_t \sum_{j=1}^{n} \lambda_j(B_t)}\right)^{1/3}$.
  Sample $u \sim \mathcal{S}^n$ uniformly.
  Set $y_t = x_t + \delta_t B_t u \in W_1(x_t) \subset \mathcal{K}$.
  Play y_t and incur loss $f_t(y_t)$.
  Compute the estimate $\widehat{g}_t = n f_t(y_t)(\delta_t B_t)^{-1} u$.
  Update $x_{t+1} = \text{argmin}_{x \in \mathcal{K}} g_{1:t}^\top x + \frac{1}{2}\sum_{s=1}^{t} \|(x - x_s)\|_{Q_s}^2 + \frac{1}{\eta_t}\mathcal{R}(x)$.
end for

6 AdaBCO FOR LIPSCHITZ FUNCTIONS

Using first-order regularity instead of second motivates the design of Algorithm 3. Like Algorithm 2, the major difference here is that we factor in the local Lipschitz constant L_t and that we specify precisely η_t and δ_t. In the process, we also need to hallucinate a separate set of ellipsoids to circumvent the chicken-and-egg phenomenon.

Using similar techniques as in Theorem 2, one can derive the following regret bound:

Theorem 3 (AdaBCO using dynamic Lipschitz bounds). *Let $\mathcal{K}$ be a convex set and $\mathcal{R}$ a ν-self-concordant barrier over $\mathcal{K}$. Assume that $|f| \leq C$. Then Algorithm 2 provides the regret bound:*

$$\max_{x \in \mathcal{K}} \sum_{t=1}^{T} \mathbb{E}[f_t(y_t) - f_t(x)]$$
$$\leq \mathbb{E}\left[5(\nu \log(T))^{\frac{1}{4}} \left(\sum_{t=1}^{T}\left(L_t n C^2 \sum_{j=1}^{n} \lambda_j(\tilde{B}_t)\right)^{\frac{1}{3}}\right)^{\frac{3}{4}}\right]$$

The proof of this result is similar to that of Theorem 2, and is provided in Appendix B.

7 APPLICATIONS AND COMPARISON WITH PREVIOUS RESULTS

The data-dependent nature of Algorithms 2 and 3 provide two important implications.

The first is that they allow us to easily produce regret bounds in a variety of new situations, where the learner experiences loss functions with various levels of local smoothness and convexity. In particular, we can identify new scenarios where the optimal $\tilde{O}(\sqrt{T})$ regret is achievable by navigating the relationship between smoothnesss and convexity.

The second is that these algorithms also automatically adapt to the smoothness and convexity of these scenarios. These new cases do not require any a priori insight or tuning. The algorithms presented in this paper adaptively determine optimal sampling ellipsoids and learning rates, which lead to strong guarantees.

In particular, they allow the learner to recover existing regret bounds without modifying the algorithms. Properties such as strong convexity or smoothness are processed adaptively and online, so that if, e.g., a sequence of loss functions is found to be approximately strongly convex (which will become clear in the following results), then the strongly convex guarantee will apply. If the sequence of loss functions is better than strongly convex, then the algorithm will give an even better guarantee. Thus, these algorithms are prime examples of algorithms that "learn faster from easy data".

We present first the results for Algorithm 2.

Corollary 1 (Power law asymptotics for the dynamically smooth and strongly convex scenario). *Assume that there exists $\alpha \in \mathbb{R}$ such that*

$$\beta_t n C^2 \sum_{j=1}^{n} \lambda_j((\nabla^2 \mathcal{R}(x_t) + \eta_t Q_{1:t})^{-1}) = \mathcal{O}(t^\alpha).$$

Then the inequality $\sum_{t=1}^{T} \mathbb{E}[f_t(y_t) - f_t(x)] \leq \tilde{\mathcal{O}}(T^{\frac{2+\alpha}{3}})$ holds.

In particular, $\tilde{\mathcal{O}}(\sqrt{T})$ regret is attainable for $\alpha \leq \frac{-1}{2}$.

Moreover, $\tilde{\mathcal{O}}(T^{1/2})$ regret is adaptively attained for smooth and strongly convex functions, while $\tilde{\mathcal{O}}(T^{2/3})$ regret is adaptively attained for smooth functions.

For purely strongly smooth and strongly convex functions, $\beta_t \equiv \beta > 0$, and $Q_t \equiv Q \succ 0$, such that $Q_{1:t} = tQ$. Algorithm 2 then implies that $\eta_t = \tilde{\mathcal{O}}(t^{-1/2})$ (provable via induction), so that the corollary above applies with $\alpha \leq \frac{-1}{2}$. Thus, we adaptively attain the bound of $\tilde{\mathcal{O}}(\sqrt{T})$ in

(Hazan and Levy, 2014) without a priori knowledge of the function's regularity or any extra tuning.

For purely strongly smooth functions, $\beta_t \equiv \beta$ and in the worst case $Q_t \equiv 0$. This implies that the expression above reduces to $\beta n C^2 \sum_{j=1}^n \lambda_j(\nabla^2 \mathcal{R}(x_t)^{-1})$, so that the regret in t depends entirely on the average eigenvalue of the inverse Hessian, $\sum_{j=1}^n \lambda_j(\mathcal{R}(x_t)^{-1})$. In the worst case, this expression is $\mathcal{O}(1)$, which gives us the bound of $\tilde{\mathcal{O}}(T^{2/3})$ in (Saha and Tewari, 2011).

From another perspective, the corollary can be interpreted as saying that as long as $\beta_t \asymp \frac{1}{t\sum_{j=1}^n \lambda_j(Q_{1:t}^{-1})} \asymp t^\gamma$ for any $\gamma \in \mathbb{R}$, then $\eta_t = \tilde{\mathcal{O}}(\frac{1}{\sqrt{t}})$, and a regret of at most $\tilde{\mathcal{O}}(\sqrt{T})$ regret is guaranteed. In other words, we can extend the result of (Hazan and Levy, 2014) to not just the case where the smoothness and strong convexity are fixed and local, but in fact to any setting where the smoothness and average strong convexity parameters are locally changing at the same rate.

Moreover, we would like to stress that the above reductions are worst-case guarantees. The data-dependent nature of the regret bound above implies that it can do much better on easier data. We also do not need to know about these optimistic settings in advance of running the algorithms, as they will be adaptively and automatically obtained.

In particular, our algorithms factor in and leverage the convexity of the self-concordant barrier, so that the algorithm's bounds are much stronger when the algorithm plays points at which the Hessian of the barrier has large average eigenvalues. For common self-concordant barriers such as the log-barrier function, this corresponds to being closer to the boundary of the action set. This insight is actually somewhat surprising, because being further from the boundary generally implies that the learner will use a wider sampling ellipsoid and be able to explore more. This suggests that the self-concordant barrier regularization introduced by Abernethy et al. (2008) might not ellicit the best tradeoff between exploration and exploitation for general convex functions as it does for linear functions. Previous algorithms in bandit convex optimization did not reveal this phenomenon because they were not adaptive and did not provide data-dependent guarantees.

We now present the accompanying results for Algorithm 3.

Corollary 2 (Power law asymptotics for the dynamically Lipschitz and strongly convex scenario). *Assume that there exists $\alpha \in \mathbb{R}$ such that*

$$L_t n C^2 \sum_{j=1}^n \lambda_j((\nabla^2 \mathcal{R}(x_t) + \eta_t Q_{1:t})^{-1/2}) = \mathcal{O}(t^\alpha).$$

Then the inequality $\sum_{t=1}^T \mathbb{E}[f_t(y_t) - f_t(x)] \leq \tilde{\mathcal{O}}(T^{\frac{3+\alpha}{4}})$ holds.

In particular, $\tilde{\mathcal{O}}(\sqrt{T})$ regret is attainable for $\alpha \leq -1$.

Moreover, $\tilde{\mathcal{O}}(T^{2/3})$ regret is adaptively attained for strongly convex functions, and $\tilde{\mathcal{O}}(T^{3/4})$ regret is adaptively attained for Lipschitz functions.

For purely Lipschitz and strongly convex functions, $L_t \equiv L > 0$, and $Q_t \equiv Q \succ 0$, such that $Q_{1:t} = tQ$. Algorithm 2 then implies that $\eta_t = \tilde{\mathcal{O}}(t^{-1/3})$, so that the corollary above applies with $\alpha = \frac{-1}{3}$. Thus, we adaptively attain the bound of $\tilde{\mathcal{O}}(T^{2/3})$ of (Agarwal et al., 2010) without a priori knowledge of the regularity or any extra tuning.

For purely Lipschitz functions, $L_t \equiv L$ and in the worst case $Q_t \equiv 0$. This implies that the expression above reduces to $LnC^2 \sum_{j=1}^n \lambda_j(\nabla^2 \mathcal{R}(x_t)^{-1/2})$, so that the regret now depends entirely on the average eigenvalue of the square root of the inverse Hessian, $\sum_{j=1}^n \lambda_j(\mathcal{R}(x_t)^{-1/2})$. In the worst case, this expression is $\mathcal{O}(1)$, which gives us the bound of $\tilde{\mathcal{O}}(T^{3/4})$ in (Flaxman et al., 2005).

Moreover, as long as $L_t \asymp \frac{1}{t\sum_{j=1}^n \lambda_j(Q_{1:t}^{-1/2})} \asymp t^\gamma$ for $\gamma \in \mathbb{R}$, it follows that $\eta_t = \tilde{\mathcal{O}}(t^{-1/3})$ and will attain a regret of at least $\tilde{\mathcal{O}}(T^{2/3})$.

However, as we mentioned before, these bounds can be more favorable in optimistic settings with easier data, and our algorithm will automatically adapt to these scenarios.

8 CONCLUSION

We presented two efficient and adaptive algorithms for bandit convex optimization. Unlike previous algorithms, ours do not require a priori assumptions of global strong convexity or smoothness. Instead, they can process these parameters locally and online, which is much more suitable for the setting of online convex optimization.

They also provide data-dependent guarantees, so that on "easier data", the algorithms learn faster and the bounds become tighter. In particular, we present and characterize many new data-dependent scenarios under which one can obtain the desired $\tilde{\mathcal{O}}(\sqrt{T})$ regret, including in the purely Lipschitz and purely smooth settings.

Moreover, our algorithms characterize easy data to be situations where the local smoothness and convexity of our loss functions grow at the same rate as well as when the loss function guides the learner to play points closer to the boundary. This bias in optimal exploration suggests that the self-concordant barrier may be a sub-optimal regularizer in the case of general Lipschitz convex functions.

9 ACKNOWLEDGEMENTS

This work was partly funded by the NSF awards IIS-1117591 and CCF-1535987 and was also supported by the National Science Foundation Graduate Research Fellowship under Grant No. DGE 1342536.

References

Abernethy, J., E. Hazan, and A. Rakhlin (2008). Competing in the dark: An efficient algorithm for bandit linear optimization. In *COLT*, pp. 263–274.

Agarwal, A., O. Dekel, and L. Xiao (2010). Optimal algorithms for online convex optimization with multi-point bandit feedback. In *COLT*, pp. 28–40.

Bartlett, P. L., E. Hazan, and A. Rakhlin (2007). Adaptive online gradient descent. In *NIPS*, pp. 65–72.

Bubeck, S. and R. Eldan (2015). Multi-scale exploration of convex functions and bandit convex optimization. *CoRR abs/1507.06580*.

Bubeck, S. and A. Slivkins (2012). The best of both worlds: Stochastic and adversarial bandits. In *COLT*, Volume 23, pp. 42.1–42.23.

de Rooij, S., T. van Erven, P. D. Grünwald, and W. M. Koolen (2014). Follow the leader if you can, hedge if you must. *Journal of Machine Learning Research 15*, 1281–1316.

Duchi, J. C., E. Hazan, and Y. Singer (2010). Adaptive subgradient methods for online learning and stochastic optimization. In *COLT*, pp. 257–269.

Even-Dar, E., M. Kearns, Y. Mansour, and J. Wortman (2007). Regret to the best vs. regret to the average. In *COLT*, Volume 4539, pp. 233–247.

Flaxman, A. D., A. T. Kalai, and H. B. McMahan (2005). Online convex optimization in the bandit setting: Gradient descent without a gradient. In *SODA*, pp. 385–394.

Hazan, E. and K. Y. Levy (2014). Bandit convex optimization: Towards tight bounds. In *NIPS*, pp. 784–792.

Kalai, A. T. and S. Vempala (2005). Efficient algorithms for online decision problems. *J. Comput. Syst. Sci.*, 291–307.

McMahan, H. B. and M. J. Streeter (2010). Adaptive bound optimization for online convex optimization. In *COLT*, pp. 244–256.

Nemirovski, A. S. and M. J. Todd (2008). Interior-point methods for optimization. *Acta Numerica*, 191–234.

Nesterov, Y. (2004). *Introductory Lectures on Convex Optimization: A Basic Course*. New York, NY, USA: Springer.

Saha, A. and A. Tewari (2011). Improved regret guarantees for online smooth convex optimization with bandit feedback. In *AISTATS*, pp. 636–642.

Sani, A., G. Neu, and A. Lazaric (2014). Exploiting easy data in online optimization. In *NIPS*, pp. 810–818.

Zinkevich, M. (2003). Online convex programming and generalized infinitesimal gradient ascent. In *ICML*, pp. 928–936.

On the Identifiability and Estimation of Functional Causal Models in the Presence of Outcome-Dependent Selection

Kun Zhang* kunz1@cmu.edu
Jiji Zhang♯ jijizhang@ln.edu.hk
Biwei Huang‡* biweih@andrew.cmu.edu
Bernhard Schölkopf‡ bs@tuebingen.mpg.de
Clark Glymour* cg09@andrew.cmu.edu

*Department of philosophy, Carnegie Mellon University
♯Lingnan University, Hong Kong
‡Max Planck Institute for Intelligent Systems, Germany

Abstract

We study the identifiability and estimation of functional causal models under selection bias, with a focus on the situation where the selection depends solely on the effect variable, which is known as outcome-dependent selection. We address two questions of identifiability: the identifiability of the causal direction between two variables in the presence of selection bias, and, given the causal direction, the identifiability of the model with outcome-dependent selection. Regarding the first, we show that in the framework of post-nonlinear causal models, once outcome-dependent selection is properly modeled, the causal direction between two variables is generically identifiable; regarding the second, we identify some mild conditions under which an additive noise causal model with outcome-dependent selection is to a large extent identifiable. We also propose two methods for estimating an additive noise model from data that are generated with outcome-dependent selection.

1 Introduction

Selection bias is an important issue in statistical inference. Ideally, samples should be drawn randomly from the population of interest. In reality, however, it is commonplace that the probability of including a unit in the sample depends on some attributes of the unit. Such selection bias, if not corrected, often distorts the results of statistical analysis. For example, it is well known that in a regression analysis, if there is selection on the dependent variable, the ordinary least squares estimation of the regression coefficients will be biased and inconsistent (Heckman, 1979). The challenge is even bigger in causal inference; both the task of learning causal structures from data and the task of estimating causal mechanisms or parameters given a causal structure are usually rendered more difficult by the presence of selection bias.

In this paper, we are concerned with the approach to causal inference based on (restricted) functional causal models (Shimizu et al., 2006; Hoyer et al., 2009; Zhang & Hyvärinen, 2009), and aim to investigate the extent to which selection bias can be handled within this approach. Specifically, we mainly focus on the outcome-dependent selection bias, where the selection mechanism depends only on the effect, and are interested in the following two questions:

- Is the causal direction between two random variables identifiable in the presence of selection bias?
- Is the causal mechanism as represented by a functional causal model identifiable in the presence of selection bias?

These two questions have to do with the two main aspects of causal inference, respectively. The former question is about the inference of causal structure. In the traditional conditional-independence-constraint-based approach to learning causal structures (Spirtes et al., 2001; Pearl, 2000), some methods have been developed to handle selection bias (Spirtes et al., 1999; Zhang, 2008; Borboudakis & Tsamardinos, 2015). However, the structural information that can be learned via the constraint-based approach is typically limited to a Markov equivalence class. In particular, the approach cannot distinguish cause from effect with just two variables. In contrast, a distinctive virtue of the approach based on functional causal models is that Markov equivalent causal structures can usually be distinguished. In particular, the direction between two random variables is generically identifiable. Whether this virtue survives the challenge posed by selection bias is therefore worth investigating.

The latter question is related to the inference of causal parameters (i.e., parameters or quantities that have causal interpretations), including intervention effects. In addition to the work on various selection models in econometrics and social science (Heckman, 1979; Winship & Mare, 1992), recent literature has seen interesting work on the recoverability of causal parameters based on graphical models (Didelez et al., 2010; Bareinboim & Pearl, 2012; Bareinboim et al., 2014; Evans & Didelez, 2015). Much of this work, however, deals with linear models or discrete variables, whereas we are concerned in this paper with continuous variables that may bear a nonlinear relationship.

We will proceed as follows. In Section 2, we introduce the general setup and briefly discuss several types of selection, before focusing our attention on the situation where the selection depends on the effect variable, known as outcome-dependent selection. In Section 3, we show that in the framework of post-nonlinear causal models, once outcome-dependent selection is properly modeled, the causal direction between two variables is generically identifiable. In Section 4, we identify some mild conditions under which an additive noise causal model with outcome-dependent selection is to a large extent identifiable. We then propose, in Section 5, two methods for estimating an additive noise model from data that are generated with outcome-dependent selection. Some experiments are reported in Section 6.

2 Outcome-Dependent Selection Bias

A common way to represent selection bias is to use a binary selection variable S encoding whether or not a unit is included in the sample. Suppose we are interested in the relationship between X and Y, where X has a causal influence on Y. Let p_{XY} denote the joint distribution of X and Y in the population. The selected sample follows $p_{XY|S=1}$ instead of p_{XY}. In general, $p_{XY|S=1} \neq p_{XY}$, and that is how selection may distort statistical and causal inference. However, different kinds of selection engender different levels of difficulty. In general, S may depend on any number of substantive variables, as illustrated in Figure 1, where $X = (X_1, X_2)$. [1]

[1] In this paper, we assume that we only know which variables the selection variable S depends on, but the selection mechanism is unknown, i.e., the probability of $S = 1$ given those variables is unknown. Notice that we do not have access to the data points that were not selected. This is very different from Heckman's framework to correct the bias caused by a censored sample (Heckman, 1979), which assumes access to an i.i.d. sample from the whole population, on which the Y values are observable only for the data points that satisfy the selection criterion (implied by the selection equation), but other attributes of the "censored" points are still available, enabling one to directly identify the selection mechanism.

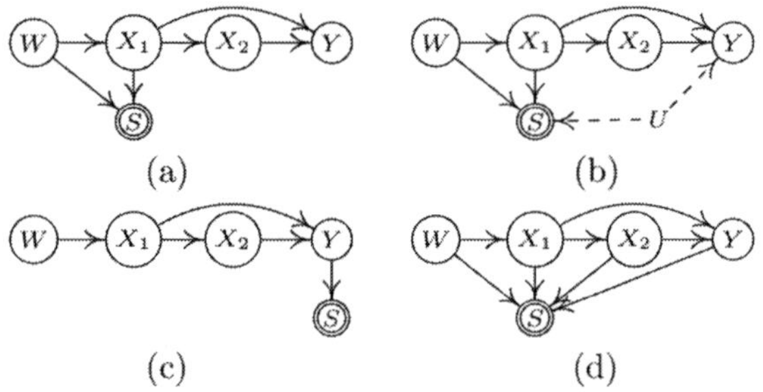

Figure 1: Illustration of different situations with sample selection bias. (a) S depends on $X = (X_1, X_2)$ but not on Y. (b) S depends on X and is also statistically dependent on Y given X due to a confounder U. (c) S directly depends solely on Y (outcome-dependent selection). (d) S depends on both X and Y.

Selection Bias on the Cause For the purpose of causal inference, the least problematic kind of situation is depicted in Figure 1(a), in which S is independent of the effect variable Y given the cause variable X. It follows that $p_{Y|X,S=1} = p_{Y|X}$. That is, the selection bias does not distort the conditional distribution of the effect Y given the cause X or the structural equation model for the causal process. In such a situation, causal inference can essentially proceed as usual. However, if there is a (latent) confounder for Y and S, as illustrated in Figure 1(b), S and Y are not conditionally independent given X any more, that is, $p_{Y|X,S=1} \neq p_{Y|X}$. Such a distortion may be corrected under rather restrictive assumptions; see, e.g., Heckman's correction (Heckman, 1979).

Selection Bias on the Effect If the selection depends solely on the effect, as depicted in Figure 1(c), then $p_{Y|X,S=1} \neq p_{Y|X}$, and the selection bias, if not corrected, will mislead inference. Consider, for example, a standard assumption in functional causal modeling that the effect Y is a function of the cause variable X and an noise variable E that is independent of X. Suppose this assumption holds in the population. With the outcome-dependent selection, X and E are typically not independent in the selected sample, as they are typically not independent conditional on S (which is a descendant of a collider between X and E, i.e., Y). Furthermore, even if one fits a regression model on selected sample, the estimated residual (which is usually different from the true noise term in the causal process) is usually not independent from X; we will get back to this issue in Section 4.1.

This kind of selection is known as *outcome-dependent selection bias* (OSB) (Didelez et al., 2010; Bareinboim et al., 2014), and will be our focus in this paper. We will show that although outcome-dependent selection seriously complicates analysis, it can be handled in the identification and estimation of functional causal models. Note that in the case of outcome-dependent selection, X is independent of S given Y, and so we can model the distribution of the observed sample as:

$$p^{\beta}_{XY} \triangleq p_{XY|S=1} = \frac{p_{X,Y,S=1}}{P(S=1)} = p_{XY} \cdot \frac{P(S=1|X,Y)}{P(S=1)}$$
$$= p_{XY} \cdot \frac{P(S=1|Y)}{P(S=1)} = \beta(y) p_{XY}, \quad (1)$$

where the nonnegative function $\beta(y) \triangleq P(S = 1|Y)/P(S=1)$ is a density ratio for biased sampling that only depends on Y. We will adopt this representation of outcome-dependent selection in what follows.

Selection Bias on Both the Cause and the Effect An even more general situation is depicted in Figure 1(d), where the selection depends on both X and Y (and probably others). In such a situation, the density ratio function β will depend on both X and Y. The selected sample follows the distribution $p^{\beta}_{XY} \propto p_{XY}\beta(x,y,w)$. Roughly speaking, the selection procedure is so flexible that without further constraints on $\beta(x,y,w)$, we cannot see much information about the population p_{XY}: if p_{XY} is positive on $(-\infty,+\infty)$, the same p^{β}_{XY} can be generated from a large class of distributions p_{XY} with a suitably chosen $\beta(x,y,w)$. Moreover, the causal direction is generally not identifiable, for with a sufficiently flexible $\beta(x,y,w)$, either direction can be made compatible with whatever distribution. Interestingly, when β depends only on Y, as is the case under outcome-dependent selection, the causal direction according to a restricted functional causal model is still generically identifiable, without any substantial restriction on β. To this result we now turn.

3 Identifiability of Causal Direction

In this section we investigate whether it is possible to successfully recover the causal direction between two variables when the data are generated according to a functional causal model, but with outcome-dependent selection. Here we assume that both X and Y are scalar variables.

3.1 Identifiability Without Selection Bias

The traditional approaches to inferring causal structure from data, such as the constraint-based approach (Spirtes et al., 2001; Pearl, 2000) and the score-based approach (Chickering, 2002; Heckerman et al., 1995) cannot distinguish Markov equivalent causal structures without background knowledge. In particular, with only two variables, those methods cannot distinguish cause from effect. The more recent approach based on restricted functional causal models is usually more powerful in this respect. In a functional causal model, the effect is taken to be a function of the direct causes together with an noise term that is independent of the direct causes (Pearl, 2000). When the class of functions is constrained, the causal direction is usually identifiable in that only one direction can satisfy the model assumptions, such as the assumed independence between the noise term and the direct causes. Available identifiability results include those on linear, non-Gaussian, acyclic Model (LiNGAM) (Shimizu et al., 2006)), additive noise model (ANM) (Hoyer et al., 2009), and post-nonlinear (PNL) causal model (Zhang & Hyvärinen, 2009). In this section, we will establish a main result for the PNL causal model. The result also applies to linear models and additive noise models, as they are special cases of PNL models.

A PNL model for $X \to Y$ is specified as follows:

$$Y = f_2(f_1(X) + E), \quad (2)$$

where X and E are statistically independent, f_1 is a non-constant smooth function, f_2 is an invertible smooth function, and $f_2' \neq 0$. This model is sufficiently flexible to represent or approximate many causal processes in reality (Zhang & Hyvärinen, 2009).

Similarly, for the reverse direction $Y \to X$, a PNL model would take the following form:

$$X = g_2(g_1(Y) + \tilde{E}), \quad (3)$$

where Y and $\tilde{E}$ are independent, g_1 is non-constant and smooth, g_2 is invertible and smooth, and $g_2' \neq 0$.

As shown in (Zhang & Hyvärinen, 2009), (2) and (3) can generate the same distribution of X and Y only for very special configurations of the functions and distributions. In generic cases, if data are generated according to a model of form (2), there is no model of form (3) that generates the same distribution. Hence the causal direction is generically identifiable.

3.2 Identifiability of Causal Direction in PNL-OSB

We now show that the generic identifiability of causal direction based on PNL models still holds even if we allow the possibilty of outcome-dependent selection.

Suppose the data distribution is generated by a PNL causal model from X to Y in the form of (2), denoted by $\mathcal{F}_{\rightarrow}$, followed by an outcome-dependent selection with an density ratio $\beta(y)$, as in (1). Call $(\mathcal{F}_{\rightarrow}, \beta(y))$ a PNL-OSB model, and let $p^{\rightarrow}_{XY}$ denote the joint density of X and Y resulting from $(\mathcal{F}_{\rightarrow}, \beta(y))$. We are interested in whether there is a PNL-OSB model in the reverse direction that can generate the same data distribution. That is, consider $(\mathcal{F}_{\leftarrow}, v(x))$, where $\mathcal{F}_{\leftarrow}$

is a PNL causal model from Y to X in the form of (3), and $v(x)$ is an density ratio function that depends on X. Let $p_{XY}^{\leftarrow}$ denote the joint density of X and Y resulting from $(\mathcal{F}_{\leftarrow}, v(x))$. When is it the case that $p_{XY}^{\rightarrow} = p_{XY}^{\leftarrow}$?

To simplify the presentation, we define random variables $T \triangleq g_2^{-1}(X)$, $Z \triangleq f_2^{-1}(Y)$, and function $h \triangleq f_1 \circ g_2$. That is, $h(t) = f_1(g_2(t)) = f_1(x)$. Similarly, $h_1 \triangleq g_1 \circ f_2$ is a function of Z. Moreover, we let $\eta_1(t) \triangleq \log p_T(t) = \log p_X(x) + \log |g_2'(t)|$, and $\eta_2(e) \triangleq \log p_E(e)$.

Note that T and E are independent (for X and E are assumed to be independent), and Z and $\tilde{E}$ are independent (for Y and $\tilde{E}$ are assumed to be independent). It follows that

$$p_{XY}^{\rightarrow} = \beta(y)p_{XY}^{\mathcal{F}\rightarrow} = \beta(y)p_{XE}/|f_2'| = \beta_{f_2}(z)p_T p_E/|f_2' g_2'|,$$
$$p_{XY}^{\leftarrow} = v(x)p_{XY}^{\mathcal{F}\leftarrow} = v(x)p_{Y\tilde{E}}/|g_2'| = v_{g_2}(t)p_{Z\tilde{E}}/|f_2' g_2'|,$$

where $\beta_{f_2} = \beta \circ f_2$, and $v_{g_2} = v \circ g_2$.

Now suppose

$$p_{XY}^{\rightarrow} = p_{XY}^{\leftarrow} \tag{4}$$

This implies

$$p_{Z\tilde{E}} = \frac{\beta_{f_2}(z)}{v_{g_2}(t)} p_T p_E,$$

or equivalently

$$\begin{aligned}\log p_{Z\tilde{E}} &= \log \beta_{f_2}(z) - \log v_{g_2}(t) + \log p_T + \log p_E \\ &= \log \beta_{f_2}(z) + \tilde{\eta}_1(t) + \eta_2(e),\end{aligned} \tag{5}$$

where $\tilde{\eta}_1(t) \triangleq \log p_T - \log v_{g_2}(t) = \eta_1(t) - \log v_{g_2}(t)$. Since Z and $\tilde{E}$ are independent, we have

$$\frac{\partial^2 \log p_{Z\tilde{E}}}{\partial z \partial \tilde{e}} \equiv 0. \tag{6}$$

(5) and (6) entail very strong constraints on the distribution of E, as stated in the following theorem.

Theorem 1 *Suppose that the densities of E and T and the functions f_1, f_2, g_1, g_2, and $v(x)$ are third-order differentiable and that p_E is positive on $(-\infty, +\infty)$. The condition (4) implies that for every point of (X, Y) satisfying $\eta_2'' h' \neq 0$:*

$$\begin{aligned}\tilde{\eta}_1''' - \frac{\tilde{\eta}_1'' h''}{h'} &= \left(\frac{\eta_2' \eta_2'''}{\eta_2''} - 2\eta_2''\right) \cdot h' h'' - \frac{\eta_2'''}{\eta_2''} \cdot h' \tilde{\eta}_1'' \\ &\quad + \eta_2' \cdot \left(h''' - \frac{h''^2}{h'}\right),\end{aligned} \tag{7}$$

and h_1 depends on $\tilde{\eta}_1$, η_2, and h in the following way:

$$\frac{1}{h_1'} = \frac{\tilde{\eta}_1'' + \eta_2'' h'^2 - \eta_2' h''}{\eta_2'' h'}. \tag{8}$$

Further assume that $\eta_2'' h' \neq 0$ almost everywhere. Then in order for (7) to hold, p_E and h must satisfy one of the five conditions listed in Table 1.

Table 1: All situations in which the causal direction implied by the PNL-OSB model may be unidentifiable.

	p_E	$h = f_1 \circ g_2$
1	Gaussian	linear
2	log-mix-lin-exp	linear
3	log-mix-lin-exp	h strictly monotonic, and $h' \to 0$, as $t_1 \to +\infty$ or as $t_1 \to -\infty$
4	generalized mixture of two exponentials	Same as above

All proofs are given in the Supplementary material. In the five situations given in Table 1, the causal direction may not be identifiable according to the PNL-OSB model, and the involved distribution p_E is very specific. For the definition of distributions of the form `log-mix-lin-exp` or `generalized mixture of two exponentials`, see (Zhang & Hyvärinen, 2009). As a consequence, generally speaking, the causal direction implied by PNL-OSB is identifiable.

This identifiability result regarding the causal direction implied by PNL-OSB is similar to the original result on PNL, which was given in (Zhang & Hyvärinen, 2009). The difference is that $\eta_1(t) = \log p_T(t)$ in the original identifiability result on PNL is replaced by $\tilde{\eta}_1(t) = \log \frac{p_T(t)}{v_{g_2}(t)}$. Recall that $v_{g_2}(t)$ can be any valid density ratio; if $p_T(t)$ is positive on $(-\infty, +\infty)$, one can always adjust $v_{g_2}(t)$ so that $\frac{p_T(t)}{v_{g_2}(t)}$ meets the constraint on η_1 in (Zhang & Hyvärinen, 2009). That is, in our result any $p_T(t)$ that is positive on $(-\infty, +\infty)$ is allowed. Therefore, our non-identifiable situations (Table 1) do not contain any constraints on p_T, but still have very strong constraints on P_E and $h = f_1 \circ g_2$.

4 Identifiability of ANM-OSB Model

Given the causal direction, a further important question is whether the causal mechanism, represented by the functional causal model, and the selection procedure, represented by $\beta(y)$, can be recovered from data.

For simplicity of the derivation and presentation, we shall consider the ANM for the causal mechanism (not a PNL one in this section):

$$Y = f^{AN}(X) + E, \tag{9}$$

where $E \perp\!\!\!\perp X$. Here we further assume that f^{AN} is smooth. The observed data are generated by applying the selection bias on Y, i.e., they were drawn from the distribution

$$p_{XY}^{\beta} = \beta(y) p_X^{\mathcal{F}} p_{Y|X}^{\mathcal{F}}, \tag{10}$$

where $p_{Y|X}^{\mathcal{F}}$ is specified by the causal model (9) and $p_X^{\mathcal{F}}$ denotes the distribution of X before applying the selection procedure. Note that generally speaking, $p_X^{\mathcal{F}}$ is not identical to p_X^{β}. Call the model $(\mathcal{F}, \beta(y))$ an ANM-OSB model.

Suppose that the observed data are generated from an ANM-OSB $(\mathcal{F}_1, \beta_1(y))$. We are interested in whether another ANM-OSB $(\mathcal{F}_2, \beta_2(y))$ can generate the same data distribution. Suppose it does. The observed data distribution is then

$$p_{XY}^{\beta} = p_{XY}^{\mathcal{F}_1}\beta_1(y) = p_{XY}^{\mathcal{F}_2}\beta_2(y). \tag{11}$$

Let $\beta_r(y) \triangleq \frac{\beta_2(y)}{\beta_1(y)}$. Bear in mind that $p_{XY}^{\mathcal{F}_1} = p_X^{(1)} p_{E_1}(Y - f^{(1)}(X))$ and $p_{XY}^{\mathcal{F}_2} = p_X^{(2)} p_{E_2}(Y - f^{(2)}(X))$. If (11) holds, we have

$$\beta_r^{-1}(y) p_X^{(1)}(x) p_{E_1}(e_1) = p_X^{(2)}(x) p_{E_2}(e_2). \tag{12}$$

Taking the logarithm of both sides gives

$$-\log \beta_r(y) + \log p_X^{(1)} + \log p_{E_1}(e_1) = \log p_X^{(2)} + \log p_{E_2}(e_2). \tag{13}$$

Now let us see whether it is possible for (13) to hold and, if yes, what constraints the functions $\beta_r(y)$, $\log p_X^{(1)}$, and $\log p_{E_1}(e_1)$ must satisfy. Denote by $J_{AN} \triangleq \log p_X^{(2)} + \log p_{E_2}(e_2)$. As seen from the RHS, (13) implies

$$\frac{\partial^2 J_{AN}}{\partial x \partial e_2} \equiv 0. \tag{14}$$

Let $l_\beta(y) = \log \beta_r(y)$, $\eta_{X_1}(x) \triangleq \log p_X^{(1)}$ and $\eta_{E_1}(e_1) \triangleq \log p_{E_1}(e_1)$. By solving (14), we can establish the relationship between the two ANM-OSB models.

4.1 General Results

Interestingly, as stated in the following theorem, if the noise E_1 is non-Gaussian, then $f^{(2)}(x)$ must be a shifted version of $f^{(1)}(x)$; in other words, the underlying function f^{AN} is identifiable up to a constant. Furthermore, if E_1 is non-Gaussian, the selection weight $\beta(y)$ can be recovered up to a factor which is an exponential function of y, i.e., $\beta_2(y) \propto \beta_2(y) \cdot e^{c_2 y}$, where c_2 is a constant; accordingly, $p_{E_2} \propto p_{E_1} \cdot e^{-c_2 e_1}$.

Theorem 2 *Let Assumptions A_1 and A_2 hold true:*
A_1. $p_X^{(1)}$ and p_{E_1} are positive on $(-\infty, +\infty)$.
A_2. $\eta''_{E_1}(e_1) f^{(1)\prime}(x) = 0$ only at finite points.[2]
Then if (11) is true, the following statements hold.

a) If E_1 is not Gaussian, then $f^{(2)}(x) = f^{(1)}(x) + c_1$, and $\beta_2(y) = \beta_1(y)\beta_r(y)$, where $\beta_r(y) = e^{c_2 y + d_1} = e^{d_1} \cdot e^{c_2 f^{(1)}(x)} \cdot e^{c_2 e_1}$. Accordingly, $p_X^{(2)} \propto p_X^{(1)} \cdot e^{-c_2 f_1(x)}$, and $p_{E_2} \propto p_{E_1} \cdot e^{-c_2 e_1}$. Here c_1, c_2, and d_1 are constants, and d_1 guarantees that $\beta_2(y)$ is a valid density ratio.

That is, $f^{(2)}(x)$ is equal to $f^{(1)}(x)$ (up to a constant), and with proper scaling, $\beta_2(y)$ equals $\beta_1(y)$ times an exponential function of y.

b) If E_1 is Gaussian, then $\beta_2(y) = \beta_1(y)\beta_r(y)$, where $\beta_r(y) = e^{\frac{-ab}{2}y^2 + c_4 y + d_4}$, and $f^{(2)}(x) = \frac{1}{1+b} f^{(1)}(x) + d_3$. Here a, b, c_4, d_3, and d_4 are constants, d_4 guarantees that $\beta_2(y)$ is a valid density ratio, and $a \neq 0$.

That is, with proper scaling, $\beta_2(y)$ equals $\beta_1(y)$ times a Gaussian function of y (which includes the exponential function of y as a special case by setting $b = 0$).

An interesting implication of Theorem 2 is that generally speaking, fitting an ordinary ANM on the data that were generated by an ANM-OSB will not produce an independent error term. That is, under mild assumptions, if one sets $\beta_2(y) \equiv 1$, $(\mathcal{F}_2, \beta_2(y))$ cannot produce the same distribution over (X, Y) as $(\mathcal{F}_1, \beta_1(y))$ does, as is given in the following corollary.

Corollary 3 *Let Assumptions A1 and A2 hold. Then under either of the following conditions, there does not exist an ANM, specified by (9), to generate the same distribution over (X, Y) as $(\mathcal{F}_1, \beta_1(y))$ does.*

a) E_1 is not Gaussian and $\beta_1(y)$ is not proportional to $e^{c' y}$ for any c'.

b) E_1 is Gaussian and $\beta_1(y)$ is not proportional to $e^{a' y^2 + c' y}$ for any a' and c' (i.e., $\beta_1(y)$ is not proportional to an exponential function of any polynomial of y of degree 1 or 2).

4.2 When the Noise is Gaussian

When p_{E_1} is Gaussian, as stated in b) of Theorem 2, the function f^{AN} is not identifiable any more: $f^{(2)}(x)$ and $f^{(1)}(x)$can differ by an affine transformation (not simply a shift). Accordingly, $\beta_2(y)$ can differ from $\beta_1(y)$ in a Gaussian function of y. Compared to the case where E_1 is non-Gaussian, the Gaussian case suffers from more indeterminacies because the product of two Gaussian functions is still a Gaussian function. In particular, since $\beta_r^{-1}(y)$ and $p_{E_1}(y - f^{(1)}(x))$ (or $p_{Y|X}^{\mathcal{F}_1}(y|x)$) are both Gaussian functions in y, their product is still a Gaussian function in y. Accordingly, (12) will hold true, by setting p_{E_2} to another appropriate Gaussian density; in other words, in this case two additive noise models $\mathcal{F}_1$ and $\mathcal{F}_2$ can both generate

[2]This excludes the special case where $f^{(1)\prime} \equiv 0$, i.e., where X and Y are independent; in this case clearly the selection procedure is not identifiable.

the same observed data, by applying the bias selection procedures $\beta_1(y)$ and $\beta_2(y) = \beta_1(y)\beta_r(y)$, respectively.

More specifically, we can derive the function $f^{(2)(x)}$ and noise distribution $p_{E_2}(e_2)$ for the model $\mathcal{F}_2$. As shown above, $f^{(2)(x)} = \frac{1}{1+b}f^{(1)}(x) + d_3$. Eq. 12, combined with (25) and (26), implies that $p_{E_2}(e_2) \propto e^{\frac{a}{2}e_2^2 + \frac{ab}{2}e_2^2} = e^{\frac{a(1+b)}{2}e_2^2}$, while $p_{E_1}(e_1) \propto e^{\frac{a}{2}e_1^2}$.

Figure 2 gives an illustration of this result. Notice that the identifiability results imply some constraints on $\beta_r(y) = \beta_2(y)/\beta_1(y)$, not on $\beta_1(y)$, so without loss of generality, we set $\beta_1(y) \equiv 1$, leading to $\beta_2(y) = \beta_r(y)$. The circles denote the data points generated by applying the density ratio $\beta_1(y) \equiv 1$ on additive noise model $\mathcal{F}_1$: the dash line shows the nonlinear function $f^{(1)}(x)$, and the red solid line shows the shape of p_{E_1}. In contrast, additive noise model $\mathcal{F}_2$ uses nonlinear function $f^{(2)}(x)$, which is different from $f^{(1)}(x)$, and its noise variance is slightly larger than that in $\mathcal{F}_1$. The crosses denote the data points generated by $\mathcal{F}_2$. Although $\mathcal{F}_1$ and $\mathcal{F}_2$ are not the same in this case, applying the density ratio function $\beta_r(y)$ on $p_{XY}^{\mathcal{F}_2}$ gives the same joint distribution as $p_{XY}^{\mathcal{F}_1}$, i.e., $\beta_1(y)p_{XY}^{\mathcal{F}_1} = p_{XY}^{\mathcal{F}_1} = \beta_r(y)p_{XY}^{\mathcal{F}_2} = \beta_2(y)p_{XY}^{\mathcal{F}_2}$.

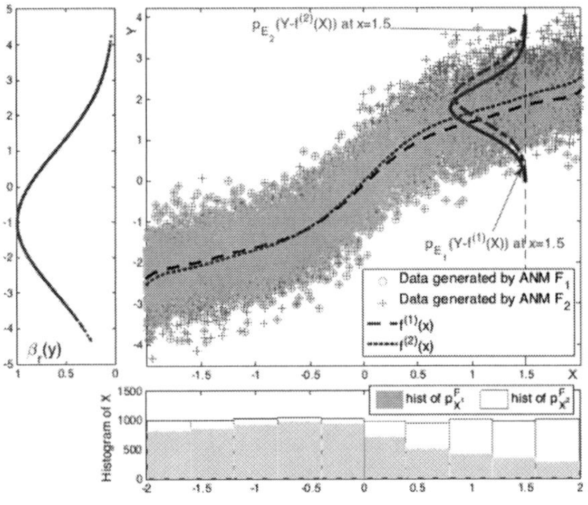

Figure 2: Illustration of the non-identifiability of the additive noise model, especially f^{AN}, when the noise is Gaussian. Red circles denote data points generated by the ANM $\mathcal{F}_1$, or by the ANM-OSB $(\mathcal{F}_1, \beta_1(y) \equiv 1)$. The gray crosses denote data generated by the ANM $\mathcal{F}_2$. The two ANM-OSB models, $(\mathcal{F}_2, \beta_r(y))$ and $(\mathcal{F}_1, 1)$, produce the same distribution of (X, Y).

4.3 With Further Constraints

Not surprisingly, if we have more knowledge about the noise distribution p_E or the density ratio function $\beta(y)$, the ANM model, including the function, the noise distribution, and the density ratio, can be fully identifiable. Below is an example showing that this is the case if we know that p_E is symmetric and non-Gaussian.

Corollary 4 *Let the assumptions made in Theorem 2 A_1 and A_2 hold. Suppose E_1 is not Gaussian. Then If both p_{E_1} and p_{E_2} are symmetric about the origin, then $f^{(2)}(x) = f^{(1)}(x)$, $E_1 = E_2$, $p_{E_1}(e_1) = p_{E_2}(e_2)$, and $\beta_r(y) \equiv 1$, i.e., $\beta_1(y) = \beta_2(y)$.*

5 Estimation of ANM-OSB

Eq. 10 gives the distribution for the observed data. In theory, we can then estimate the parameters involved in $\beta(y)$, $p_{Y|X}^{\mathcal{F}}$, as well as p_X, by maximum likelihood. However, when using maximum likelihood, we have to guarantee that the quantity on the right hand side of (10) is a valid density. This constraint is notoriously difficult to enforce in the optimization procedure. Below we propose two methods to estimate the underlying additive noise model and $\beta(y)$; one is maximum likelihood with the above constraint enforced approximately, and the other makes use of the score matching technique.

5.1 Maximum Likelihood Estimation with a Sample Approximation Constraint

To estimate the involved functions $\beta(y)$, $p_X^{\mathcal{F}}$, and $p_{Y|X}^{\mathcal{F}}$, we can maximize the data likelihood:

$$\begin{aligned}\mathcal{L} &= \sum_{k=1}^{n} \log p_{XY}^{\beta}(x_k, y_k) \\ &= \sum_{k=1}^{n} \left[\log \beta(y_k) + \log p_X^{\mathcal{F}}(x_k) + \log p_{Y|X}^{\mathcal{F}}(y_k|x_k) \right]. \quad (15)\end{aligned}$$

According to the theory shown in Section 4, the solution to βy, $p_X^{\mathcal{F}}$, and $p_{Y|X}^{\mathcal{F}}$ suffers from some indeterminacies, e.g., the solution to βy may differ from the true one by an exponential transformation. To find the solution for which the biased selection procedure is as weak as possible, we regularize the likelihood function with the constraint that $\log \beta(y)$ is close to 0. That is, we maximize

$$\mathcal{L}^r = \mathcal{L} - \lambda_r \sum_{k=1}^{n} \sqrt{(\log \beta(y_k))^2 + r}, \quad (16)$$

where the regularization parameter λ_r was set to 10^{-3} in our experiments, and r is a small positive number and was set to 0.02.

Now we have two issues to consider. One is how to parameterize the involved functions. The other is how to enforce that p_{XY}^{β}, specified in (10), corresponds to a valid density. More specifically, the constraint is

$$\beta(y)p_X^{\mathcal{F}}p_{Y|X}^{\mathcal{F}} > 0, \text{ or equivalently } \beta(y) > 0, \text{ and} \tag{17}$$

$$\int \beta(y)p_X^{\mathcal{F}}p_{Y|X}^{\mathcal{F}}dxdy = 1. \tag{18}$$

Without constraint (18), the scale of p_{XY}^{β} will go to infinity during the process of maximizing (15).

Parameterization The additive noise model for the data-generating process, (9), implies that $p_{Y|X}^{\mathcal{F}} = p_E(y - f^{AN}(x))$. We parameterize $\beta(y)$ as the exponential transformation of a nonlinear function represented by MLP's (with the tanh activation function); this automatically guarantees the nonnegativity constraint of $\beta(y)$, as required in (17). Furthermore, we represent $p_X^{\mathcal{F}}$ with a mixture of Gaussians, the nonlinear function f^{AN} with MLP's (with the tanh activation function), and p_E with another mixture of Gaussians.

Enforcing p_{XY}^{β} to Be a Valid Density We present a sample-average approximation scheme to approximately enforce the condition that the right hand side of (10) corresponds to a valid distribution, or more specifically, to impose the constraint (18). Notice that the given data points $\{x_k, y_k\}_{k=1}^n$ were drawn from p_{XY}^{β}. As a matter of fact, we have

$$\int \beta(y)p_X^{\mathcal{F}}p_{Y|X}^{\mathcal{F}} = \int p_{XY}^{o}\frac{\beta(y)p_X^{\mathcal{F}}p_{Y|X}^{\mathcal{F}}}{p_{XY}^{o}}dxdy \tag{19}$$

$$\approx \frac{1}{n}\sum_{k=1}^{n}\frac{\beta(y_k)p_X^{\mathcal{F}}(x_k)p_{Y|X}^{\mathcal{F}}(y_k|x_k)}{p_{XY}^{o}(x_k, y_k)} \tag{20}$$

$$\approx \frac{1}{n}\sum_{k=1}^{n}\frac{\beta(y_k)p_X^{\mathcal{F}}(x_k)p_{Y|X}^{\mathcal{F}}(y_k|x_k)}{\hat{p}_{XY}^{o}(x_k, y_k)}, \tag{21}$$

where p_{XY}^{o} denotes the data distribution of (X, Y), and $\hat{p}_{XY}^{o}(x_k, y_k)$ denotes its estimate at point (x_k, y_k). Here the expression in (20) is an empirical estimate of (19) on the sample drawn from the distribution p_{XY}^{o}; furthermore, (20) replaces the density $p_{XY}^{o}(x_k, y_k)$ with its empirical estimate $\hat{p}_{XY}^{o}(x_k, y_k)$. As a consequence, the constraint (18) can be (approximately) achieved by enforcing

$$\frac{1}{n}\sum_{k=1}^{n}\frac{\beta(y_k)p_X^{\mathcal{F}}(x_k)p_{Y|X}^{\mathcal{F}}(y_k|x_k)}{\hat{p}_{XY}^{o}(x_k, y_k)} = 1. \tag{22}$$

In our experiments, we used kernel density estimation with a Gaussian kernel for $\hat{p}_{XY}^{o}(x_k, y_k)$; for each dimension, we set the kernel width to the median distance between points in the sample, as in (Gretton et al., 2007).

Under the parameterization given in (27) and with the above approach to guarantee that p_{XY}^{o} is (approximately) a valid density, one can then maximize the likelihood function given in (15) to estimate the function f^{AN}, the noise distribution, and $\beta(y)$.

5.2 With Score Matching

Alternatively, we can estimate the parameters by score matching (Hyvärinen, 2005), i.e., by minimizing the expected squared distance between the gradient of the log-density given by the model and the gradient of the log-density of the observed data. This procedure aims to match the *shape* of the density given by the model and that of the empirical density of the observed data, and is invariant to the scaling factor of the model density. As a clear advantage, in the optimization procedure one does not need to guarantee that p_{XY}^{β} is a valid density.

Given any model density $p_Z(z;\theta)$ of a m-dimensional random vector Z, the score function is the gradient of the log-density w.r.t. the data vector, i.e., $\psi(z;\theta) = (\psi_1(z;\theta), ..., \psi_m(z;\theta))^\intercal = (\frac{\partial \log p_Z(z;\theta)}{\partial z_1}, ..., \frac{\partial \log p_Z(z;\theta)}{\partial z_m})^\intercal$. Note that the score function is invariant to scale transformations in $p_Z(z)$, i.e., it is invariant to the normalization constant for a valid density. One can then estimate model parameters by minimize the expected squared distance between the model score function $\psi(\cdot;\theta)$ and the data score function $\psi_Z(\cdot;\theta)$, i.e., minimize $\frac{1}{2}\int_{z\in\mathbb{R}^m} p_Z(z)||\psi(z;\theta) - \psi_Z(z)||^2 dz$. It has been shown in (Hyvärinen, 2005) that minimizing the above squared distance is equivalent to minimizing

$$J^{SM}(\theta) = \int_{z\in\mathbb{R}^m} p_Z(z)\sum_{i=1}^{m}\left[\tilde{\psi}_i(z;\theta) + \frac{1}{2}\psi_i^2(z;\theta)\right]dz,$$

where $\tilde{\psi}_i(z;\theta) = \frac{\partial \psi_i(z;\theta)}{\partial z_i}$. The sample version of $J^{SM}(\theta)$ over the sample $\mathbf{z}_1, ..., \mathbf{z}_n$ is

$$\hat{J}^{SM}(\theta) = \frac{1}{n}\sum_{k=1}^{n}\sum_{i=1}^{m}\left[\tilde{\psi}_i(\mathbf{z}_k;\theta) + \frac{1}{2}\psi_i^2(\mathbf{z}_k;\theta)\right]. \tag{23}$$

In particular, here we have $\psi_1 = \psi_X$ and $\psi_2 = \psi_Y$; noting that $p_{Y|X}^{\mathcal{F}} = p_E(y - f^{AN}(x))$, we can write down the involved derivatives involved in (28), and then minimize the regularized score function (with the same regularization term as in Eq. 16) to estimate the involved parameter.

6 Experiments

Simulations The simulated data are generated by applying the biased selection procedure on the data generated by a additive noise model with function f^{AN}, i.e., by (9) and (10). As shown in Section 4, the function f^{AN} is identifiable up to some shift when the noise is non-Gaussian. We shall study the estimation quality of the regression function f^{AN} under different settings.

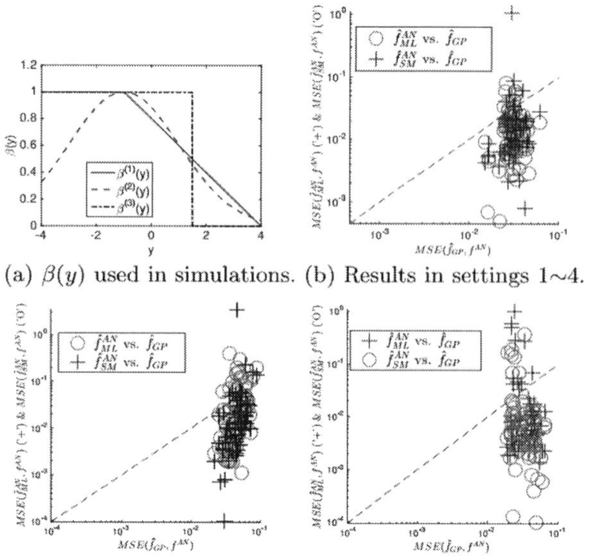

(a) $\beta(y)$ used in simulations. (b) Results in settings 1~4.

(c) Results in settings 5~8. (d) Results in settings 9~12.

Figure 3: Simulation settings and results. (a) shows the density ratio functions for OSB, $\beta_1(y)$, $\beta_2(y)$, and $\beta_3(y)$, which are used in settings 1-4, 5-8, and 9-12, respectively. (b), (c), and (d) show the pairwise MSE of the estimated function for the proposed methods against GP regression on the given sample, in settings 1-4, 5-8, and 9-12, respectively. The dashed line marks the threshold where the proposed methods and GP regression on the given sample perform equally well.

We consider three settings for OSB, by setting $\beta(y)$ (see Eq. 10) to different functions. As shown in Figure 3(a), $\beta^{(1)}(y)$ is a piecewise linear function, $\beta^{(2)}(y)$ is a (scaled) Gaussian function with mean -1 and standard deviation 2, and $\beta^{(3)}(y)$ corresponding to a hard biased selection procedure: it drops all data points corresponding to the 10% largest values of Y.

We use two ways to generate the distributions of X and E; one is the uniform distribution, and the other the mixture of three Gaussians with random coefficients. The function f^{AN} is a mixture of the linear, tanh, and cubic function with random coefficients (the coefficient for the cubic function is constrained to be small to avoid extreme values in Y).

In total there are $2 \times 2 \times 3$ simulation settings. For each setting we repeat the experiment with 15 random replications. We use the methods proposed in Section 5 to recover this function. Denote by $\hat{f}^{AN}_{ML}$ the estimate given by the (approximate) maximum likelihood method, and by $\hat{f}^{AN}_{SM}$ that given by the score matching method. The estimation performance is evaluated by the mean square error (MSE) between the estimate and the true function, $\frac{1}{n}\sum_{i=1}^{n}(\hat{f}^{AN}(x_i) - f^{AN}(x_i))^2$. We compare the estimates produced by our methods with that estimated by Gaussian process (GP) regression on the given sample, denoted by $\hat{f}_{GP}$. Figure 3(b-d) compares the estimation quality of $\hat{f}^{AN}_{ML}$ and $\hat{f}^{AN}_{SM}$ against $\hat{f}_{GP}$; note that they are plotted on a log scale.

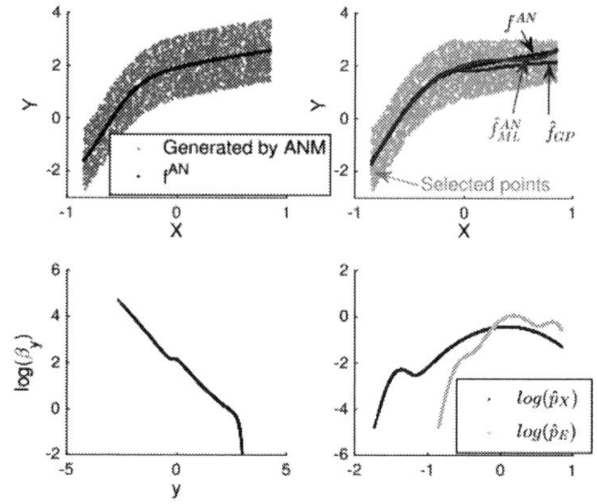

Figure 4: Results of a typical run estimated by the maximum likelihood approach. The four subfigures show the data produced by the ANM, the selected sample and the estimates of f^{AN}, the estimate of $\beta(y)$, and the estimates of p_X and p_E, respectively.

As one can see from Figure 3(b-d), the proposed methods may converge to unwanted solutions, as shown by the few points above the dashed lines. However, in most cases the proposed method provides a better estimate of the function f^{AN}. As suggested by (Demšar, 2006), we use the Wilcoxon signed ranks test to check whether $MSE(\hat{f}^{AN}, f^{AN})$ is significantly better than $MSE(\hat{f}_{GP}, f^{AN})$ under all the three settings for $\beta(y)$. It is a nonparametric test to detect shifts in populations given a number of paired samples. Under the null hypothesis the distribution of differences between the two populations is symmetric about 0. We find that under all the three sets of settings, for the score matching method, the null hypothesis is always rejected at the 0.01 level (the p-values are 6×10^{-7}, 2×10^{-6}, and 8×10^{-5}, respectively). For the maximum likelihood method, the null is rejected in settings 1-4 and 5-9 (the p-values are 2×10^{-7}, and 8×10^{-5}, respectively); we fail to reject the null in settings 5-8 (with the p-value 0.22): this seems to be caused by local optima, which will be discussed below. This means that the proposed method outperforms the method that fits GP regression on the observed data, in terms of the estimation quality of the true function.

Figure 4 gives the result of a typical run (with $\beta_3(y)$) produced by maximum likelihood. Interestingly, one can see that compared to the true $\beta(t)$, which is $\beta_3(y)$ in Figure 3(a), $\hat{\beta}(y)$ contains an additional factor of the form $e^{c_2 y}$ with some constant c_2. The estimates of p_X and p_E are also skewed accordingly. This verifies the statements given in Theorem 2(a).

As seen from Figure 3, both algorithms may get stuck in local optima. Let us have a closer look at the results given by maximum likelihood. We found that for each simulation setting, in all runs where the function f^{AN} was not accurately recovered, or more specifically, where $MSE(\hat{f}^{AN}_{ML}, f^{AN}) > MSE(\hat{f}_{GP}, f^{AN})$, the corresponding likelihood values are among the lowest across all 15 runs. That is, the attained likelihood value suggests whether the algorithm converges to a local optimum. Therefore, in practice one may run the algorithms multiple times with random initializations and choose the one which gives the best model fit (e.g., the highest likelihood). However, this is not the case for the score matching-based approach: we did not find that the unwanted solutions always correspond to relatively large score distances. The precise reason for this phenomenon is still under investigation. Hence, below we only report the results given by the (approximate) maximum likelihood approach.

Experiments on Real Data We went through the cause-effect pairs (`http://webdav.tuebingen.mpg.de/cause-effect/`) to find data sets which are likely to suffer the OSB issue according to *commonsense or background knowledge*. We selected Pairs 25, 40, and 41. Here to save space, we only report the results on Pair 25; it is about the relationship between the age (X) and the concrete compressive strength (Y) of different samples of concrete.

The empirical distribution of the data in Pair 25 suggests that it is very likely for the effect to suffer from a PNL distortion. We use a rough way to take into account both the PNL distortion in the causal process and the OSB. We first fit the PNL causal model (Zhang & Hyvärinen, 2009) on the data and correct the data with the estimated PNL transformation on Y. We then fit the ANM-OSB procedure on the corrected data. To avoid local optima, we run the (approximate) maximum likelihood algorithm presented in Section 5.1 five times with random initializations and choose the one with the highest likelihood. Figure 7 shows the result on Pair 25. As seen from $\hat{\beta}(y)$, it seems for some reason, the samples whose compressive strength is very high were not selected. The estimated function $\hat{f}^{GP}_{ML}$ seems to address this issue.

7 Conclusion and Discussions

As we have shown, in the presence of outcome-dependent selection, the causal direction is still generically identifiable if the causal relationship can be modeled by a post-nonlinear causal model. Moreover, in the case of an additive noise model, the causal mechanism as represented by the function in the model is identifiable up to a constant if the noise term is non-Gaussian (and completely identified if the noise term follows a symmetric, non-Gaussian distribution). However, due to the selection bias, the estimation requires more care than standard methods for fitting such models, and we developed two estimation procedures in this paper.

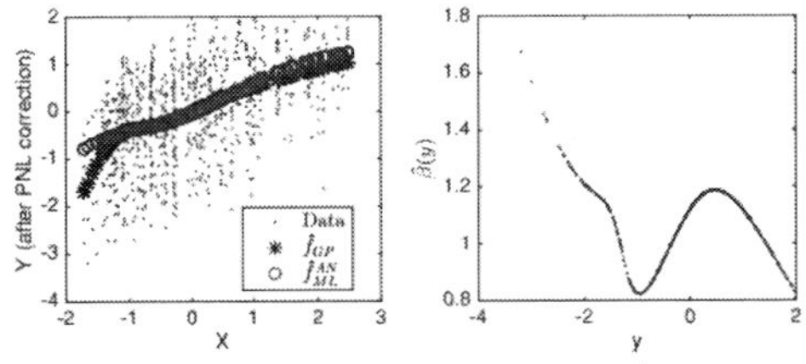

(a) Data & estimated functions. (b) $\hat{\beta}(y)$.

Figure 5: Results on pair 25 of the cause-effect pairs. (a) The scatterplot of the data (after correcting the nonlinear distortion in Y with the PNL causal model), the nonlinear regression function $\hat{f}_{GP}$ on the data, and the estimated function $\hat{f}^{AN}_{ML}$ by the maximum likelihood approach. (b) The estimated density ratio $\hat{\beta}(y)$.

This is a first step towards a better understanding of the bearing of selection bias on the identifiability and estimation of functional causal models. There are several interesting problems for future work. First, the identifiability result on additive noise models can be generalized to post-nonlinear models, but it will take more work to put the more general result in a sufficiently simple form. Second, our positive results here are confined to outcome-dependent selection. Thanks to this restriction, our results do not rely on any substantial assumption on the selection mechanism. For more complex structures of selection, such as when the selection depends on both cause and effect, identifiability will require more specifications of the selection model. Third, our result on the identification of causal direction is confined to the two-variable case without latent confounders; how to handle selection in multi-variable structural learning, with or without latent confounders, remains an open problem.

Acknowledgement: Research reported in this publication was supported by the National Institutes of Health (NIH) under Award Number U54HG008540. The content is solely the responsibility of the authors and does not necessarily represent the official views of the NIH. The research of J. Zhang was supported in part by the Research Grants Council of Hong Kong under the General Research Fund LU342213.

References

Bareinboim, E. and Pearl, J. Controlling selection bias in causal inference. In *Proceedings of AAAI*, pp. 100–108, 2012.

Bareinboim, E., Tian, J., and Pearl, J. Recovering from selection bias in causal and statistical inference. In *Proceedings of AAAI*, 2014.

Borboudakis, G. and Tsamardinos, I. Bayesian network learning with discrete case-control data. In *Proceedings of the 31st Conference on Uncertainty in Artificial Intelligence*, 2015.

Castillo, E. *Functional Equations and Modelling in Science and Engineering*. CRC Press, 1992.

Chickering, D. M. Optimal structure identification with greedy search. *Journal of Machine Learning Research*, 3:507–554, 2002.

Demšar, J. Statistical comparisons of classifiers over multiple data sets. *Journal of Machine Learning Research*, 7:1–30, 2006.

Didelez, V., Kreiner, S., and Keiding, N. Graphical models for inference under outcome-dependent sampling. *Statistical Science*, 25:368–387, 2010.

Evans, R. J. and Didelez, V. Recovering from selection bias using marginal structure in discrete models. In *Proceedings of the 31st Conference on Uncertainty in Artificial Intelligence*, 2015.

Gretton, A., Borgwardt, K., Rasch, M., Schölkopf, B., and Smola, A. A kernel method for the two-sample-problem. In *NIPS 19*, pp. 513–520, Cambridge, MA, 2007. MIT Press.

Heckerman, D., Geiger, D., and Chickering, D. M. Learning bayesian networks: The combination of knowledge and statistical data. *Machine Learning*, 20:197–243, 1995.

Heckman, J. Sample selection bias as a specification error. *Econometrica*, 47:153–161, 1979.

Hoyer, P.O., Janzing, D., Mooji, J., Peters, J., and Schölkopf, B. Nonlinear causal discovery with additive noise models. In *Advances in Neural Information Processing Systems 21*, Vancouver, B.C., Canada, 2009.

Hyvärinen, A. Estimation of non-normalized statistical models by score matching. *Journal of Machine Learning Research*, 6:695–708, 2005.

Kagan, A. M., Linnik, Y. V., and Rao, C. R. *Characterization Problems in Mathematical Statistics*. Wiley, New York, 1973.

Pearl, J. *Causality: Models, Reasoning, and Inference*. Cambridge University Press, Cambridge, 2000.

Shimizu, S., Hoyer, P.O., Hyvärinen, A., and Kerminen, A.J. A linear non-Gaussian acyclic model for causal discovery. *Journal of Machine Learning Research*, 7:2003–2030, 2006.

Spirtes, P., Meek, C., and Richardson, T. An algorithm for causal inference in the presence of latent variables and selection bias. In Glymour, C. and Cooper, G. (eds.), *Computation, Causation, and Discovery*, pp. 211–252. MIT Press, 1999.

Spirtes, P., Glymour, C., and Scheines, R. *Causation, Prediction, and Search*. MIT Press, Cambridge, MA, 2nd edition, 2001.

Winship, C. and Mare, R. D. Models for sample selection bias. *Annual Review of Sociology*, 18:327–350, 1992.

Zhang, J. On the completeness of orientation rules for causal discovery in the presence of latent confounders and selection bias. *Artificial Intelligence*, 172:1873–1896, 2008.

Zhang, K. and Hyvärinen, A. On the identifiability of the post-nonlinear causal model. In *Proceedings of the 25th Conference on Uncertainty in Artificial Intelligence*, Montreal, Canada, 2009.

Cascading Bandits for Large-Scale Recommendation Problems

Shi Zong
Dept of Electrical and Computer Engineering
Carnegie Mellon University
szong@andrew.cmu.edu

Hao Ni
Dept of Electrical and Computer Engineering
Carnegie Mellon University
haon@cmu.edu

Kenny Sung
Dept of Electrical and Computer Engineering
Carnegie Mellon University
tsung@andrew.cmu.edu

Nan Rosemary Ke
Dépt d'informatique et de recherche opérationnelle
Université de Montréal
nke001@gmail.com

Zheng Wen
Adobe Research
San Jose, CA
zwen@adobe.com

Branislav Kveton
Adobe Research
San Jose, CA
kveton@adobe.com

Abstract

Most recommender systems recommend a list of items. The user examines the list, from the first item to the last, and often chooses the first attractive item and does not examine the rest. This type of user behavior can be modeled by the *cascade model*. In this work, we study *cascading bandits*, an online learning variant of the cascade model where the goal is to recommend K most attractive items from a large set of L candidate items. We propose two algorithms for solving this problem, which are based on the idea of linear generalization. The key idea in our solutions is that we learn a predictor of the attraction probabilities of items from their features, as opposing to learning the attraction probability of each item independently as in the existing work. This results in practical learning algorithms whose regret does not depend on the number of items L. We bound the regret of one algorithm and comprehensively evaluate the other on a range of recommendation problems. The algorithm performs well and outperforms all baselines.

1 INTRODUCTION

Most recommender systems recommended a list of K items, such as restaurants, songs, or movies. The user *examines* the recommended list from the first item to the last, and typically clicks on the first item that *attracts* the user. The *cascade model* [10] is a popular model to formulate this kind of user behavior. The items before the first clicked item are *not attractive*, because the user examines these items but does not click on them. The items after the first attractive item are *unobserved*, because the user never examines these items. The key assumption in the cascade model is that each item attracts the user independently of the other items. Under this assumption, the optimal solution in the cascade model, the list of K items that maximizes the probability that the user finds an attractive item, are K most attractive items. The cascade model is simple, intuitive, and surprisingly effective in explaining user behavior [7].

In this paper, we study on an online learning variant of the cascade model, which is known as *cascading bandits* [15]. In this model, the learning agent does not know the preferences of the user over recommended items and the goal is to learn them by interacting with the user. At time t, the agent recommends to the user a list of K items out of L candidate items and observes the click of the user. If the user clicks on an item, the agent receives a reward of one. If the user does not click on any item, the agent receives a reward of zero. The performance of the learning agent is evaluated by its cumulative reward in n steps, which is the total number of clicks in n steps. The goal of the agent is to maximize it.

Kveton *et al.* [15] proposed two computationally and sample efficient algorithms for cascading bandits. They also proved a $\Omega(L-K)$ lower bound on the regret in cascading bandits, which shows that the regret grows linearly with the number of candidate items L. Therefore, cascading bandits are impractical for learning when L is large. Unfortunately, this setting is common practice. For instance, consider the problem of learning a personalized recommender system for $K = 10$ movies from the ground set of $L = 100$k movies. In this setting, each movie would have to be shown to the user at least once, which means at least 10k interactions with the recommender system, before the system starts behaving intelligently. Such a system would clearly be impractical. The main contribution of our work is that we propose *linear cascading bandits*, an online learning framework that makes learning in cascading bandits practical at scale. The key step in our approach is that we assume that the attraction probabilities of items can be predicted from the features of items. Features are often available in practice or can be easily derived.

To the best of our knowledge, this is the first work that studies a top-K recommender problem in the bandit setting with cascading feedback and context. Specifically, we make four contributions. First, we propose linear cascading bandits, a variant of cascading bandits where we make an additional assumption that the attraction probabilities of items are a linear function of the features of items. This assumption is the key step in designing a sample efficient learning algorithm for our problem. Second, we propose two computationally efficient learning algorithms, `CascadeLinTS` and `CascadeLinUCB`, which are motivated by *Thompson sampling (TS)* [23, 3] and *linear UCB* [1, 24], We believe this is the first application of linear generalization in the cascade model under partial monitoring feedback. Third, we derive an upper bound on the regret of `CascadeLinUCB` and discuss why a similar upper bound should hold for `CascadeLinTS`. Finally, we evaluate `CascadeLinTS` on a range of recommendation problems; in the domains of restaurant, music, and movie recommendations; and demonstrate that it performs well even when our modeling assumptions are violated.

Our paper is organized as follows. In Section 2, we review the cascade model and cascading bandits. In Section 3, we present linear cascading bandits; propose `CascadeLinTS` and `CascadeLinUCB`; and bound the regret of `CascadeLinUCB`. In Section 4, we evaluate `CascadeLinTS` on several recommendation problems. We review related work in Section 5 and conclude in Section 6.

To simplify exposition, we denote random variables by boldface letter. We define $[n] = \{1, \dots, n\}$ and denote the cardinality of set A by $|A|$.

2 BACKGROUND

In this section, we review the cascade model [10] and cascading bandits [15].

2.1 Cascade Model

The *cascade model* [10] is a popular model of user behavior. In this model, the user is recommended a list of K items $A = (a_1, \dots, a_K) \in \Pi_K(E)$, where $\Pi_K(E)$ is the set of all *K-permutations* of some *ground set* $E = [L]$, which is the set of all possibly recommended items. The model is parameterized by L *attraction probabilities* $\bar{w} \in [0,1]^E$ and the user scans the list A sequentially from the first item a_1 to the last a_K. After the user examines item a_k, the item attracts the user with probability $\bar{w}(a_k)$, *independently* of the other items. If the user is attracted by item a_k, the user clicks on it and stop examining the remaining items. If the user is not attracted by item a_k, the user examines the next recommended item a_{k+1}. It is easy to see that the probability that item a_k is examined is $\prod_{i=1}^{k-1}(1 - \bar{w}(a_i))$, and that the probability that at least one item in A is attractive is $1 - \prod_{i=1}^{K}(1 - \bar{w}(a_i))$. This objective is maximized by K most attractive items.

The cascade model is surprising effective in explaining how users scan lists of items [7]. The reason is that lower ranked items typically do not get clicked because the user is attracted by higher ranked items, and never examines the rest of the recommended list.

2.2 Cascading Bandits

Kveton *et al.* [15] proposed a learning variant of the cascading model, which is known as a cascading bandit. Formally, a *cascading bandit* is a tuple $B = (E, P, K)$, where $E = [L]$ is a *ground set* of L items, P is a probability distribution over a binary hypercube $\{0,1\}^E$, and $K \leq L$ is the number of recommended items.

The learning agent interacts with our problem as follows. Let $(\mathbf{w}_t)_{t=1}^n$ be an i.i.d. sequence of n *weights* drawn from P, where $\mathbf{w}_t \in \{0,1\}^E$ and $\mathbf{w}_t(e)$ is the preference of the user for item e at time t. More precisely, $\mathbf{w}_t(e) = 1$ if and only if item e attracts the user at time t. At time t, the agent recommends a list of K items $\mathbf{A}_t = (\mathbf{a}_1^t, \dots, \mathbf{a}_K^t) \in \Pi_K(E)$. The list is a function of the observations of the agent up to time t. The user examines the list, from the first item $\mathbf{a}_1^t$ to the last $\mathbf{a}_K^t$, and clicks on the first attractive item. If the user is not attracted by any item, the user does not click on any item. Then time increases to $t+1$.

The reward of the agent at time t is one if and only if the user is attracted by at least one item in $\mathbf{A}_t$. Formally, the reward at time t can be expressed as $\mathbf{r}_t = f(\mathbf{A}_t, \mathbf{w}_t)$, where $f : \Pi_K(E) \times [0,1]^E \to [0,1]$ is a *reward function* and we define it as:

$$f(A, w) = 1 - \prod_{k=1}^{K}(1 - w(a_k))$$

for any $A = (a_1, \dots, a_K) \in \Pi_K(E)$ and $w \in [0,1]^E$. The agent at time t receives feedback:

$$\mathbf{C}_t = \min\left\{k \in [K] : \mathbf{w}_t(\mathbf{a}_k^t) = 1\right\},$$

where we assume that $\min \emptyset = \infty$. The feedback $\mathbf{C}_t$ is the click of the user. If $\mathbf{C}_t \leq K$, the user clicks on item $\mathbf{C}_t$. If $\mathbf{C}_t = \infty$, the user does not click on any item. Since the user clicks on the first attractive item in the list, the observed weights of all recommended items at time t can be expressed as a function of $\mathbf{C}_t$:

$$\mathbf{w}_t(\mathbf{a}_k^t) = \mathbb{1}\{\mathbf{C}_t = k\} \quad k = 1, \ldots, \min\{\mathbf{C}_t, K\}. \quad (1)$$

Accordingly, we say that item e is *observed* at time t if $e = \mathbf{a}_k^t$ for some $k \in [\min\{\mathbf{C}_t, K\}]$.

Let the attraction weights of items in the ground set E be distributed independently as:

$$P(w) = \prod_{e \in E} \mathrm{Ber}(w(e); \bar{w}(e)),$$

where $\mathrm{Ber}(\cdot; \theta)$ is a Bernoulli distribution with mean θ. Then the expected reward for list $A \in \Pi_K(E)$, the probability that at least one item in A is satisfactory, can be expressed as $\mathbb{E}[f(A, \mathbf{w})] = f(A, \bar{w})$, and depends only on the attraction probabilities of individual items in A. Therefore, it is sufficient to learn a good approximation to $\bar{w}$ to act optimally.

The agent's policy is evaluated by its *expected cumulative regret*:

$$R(n) = \mathbb{E}\left[\sum_{t=1}^{n} R(\mathbf{A}_t, \mathbf{w}_t)\right], \quad (2)$$

where $R(\mathbf{A}_t, \mathbf{w}_t) = f(A^*, \mathbf{w}_t) - f(\mathbf{A}_t, \mathbf{w}_t)$ is the *instantaneous stochastic regret* of the agent at time t and:

$$A^* = \arg\max_{A \in \Pi_K(E)} f(A, \bar{w})$$

is the *optimal list* of items, the list that maximizes the reward at any time t. For simplicity of exposition, we assume that the optimal solution, as a set, is unique.

2.3 Algorithm `CascadeUCB1`

Kveton *et al.* [15] proposed and analyzed two learning algorithms for cascading bandits, `CascadeUCB1` and `CascadeKL-UCB`. In this section, we review `CascadeUCB1`.

`CascadeUCB1` belongs to the family of UCB algorithms. The algorithm operates in three stages. First, it computes the *upper confidence bounds (UCBs)* $\mathbf{U}_t \in [0, 1]^E$ on the attraction probabilities of all items in E. The UCB of item e at time t is:

$$\mathbf{U}_t(e) = \hat{\mathbf{w}}_{\mathbf{T}_{t-1}(e)}(e) + c_{t-1, \mathbf{T}_{t-1}(e)}, \quad (3)$$

where $\hat{\mathbf{w}}_s(e)$ is the average of s observed attraction weights of item e, $\mathbf{T}_t(e)$ is the number of times that item e is observed in t steps, and:

$$c_{t,s} = \sqrt{(1.5 \log t)/s}$$

is the radius of a confidence interval around $\hat{\mathbf{w}}_s(e)$ after t steps such that $\bar{w}(e) \in [\hat{\mathbf{w}}_s(e) - c_{t,s}, \hat{\mathbf{w}}_s(e) + c_{t,s}]$ holds with high probability. Second, `CascadeUCB1` recommends a list of K items with largest UCBs:

$$\mathbf{A}_t = \arg\max_{A \in \Pi_K(E)} f(A, \mathbf{U}_t).$$

Finally, after the user provides feedback $\mathbf{C}_t$, the algorithm updates its estimates of the attraction probabilities $\bar{w}(e)$ based on the observed weights of items, which are defined in (1) for all $e = \mathbf{a}_k^t$ such that $k \leq \mathbf{C}_t$.

3 LINEAR CASCADING BANDITS

Kveton *et al.* [15] showed that the n-step regret of `CascadeUCB1` is $O((L - K)(1/\Delta) \log n)$, where L is the number of items in ground set E; K is the number of recommended items; and Δ is the gap, which measures the sample complexity. This means that the regret increases linearly with the number of items L. As a result, `CascadeUCB1` is not practical when L is large. Unfortunately, this setting is common practice. For instance, consider the problem of learning a personalized recommender for 10 movies from the ground set of 100k movies. To learn, `CascadeUCB1` would need to show each movie to the user at least once, which means that the algorithm would require at least 10k interactions with the user to start behaving intelligently. This is clearly impractical.

In this work, we propose *practical algorithms* for large-scale cascading bandits, in the setting where L is large. The key assumption, which allows us to learn efficiently, is that we assume that the attraction probability of each item e, $\bar{w}(e)$, can be approximated by a linear combination of some known d-dimensional feature vector $x_e \in \mathbb{R}^{d \times 1}$ and an unknown d-dimensional parameter vector of $\theta^* \in \mathbb{R}^{d \times 1}$, which is shared among all items. More precisely, we assume that there exists $\theta^* \in \Theta$ such that:

$$\bar{w}(e) \approx x_e^{\mathsf{T}} \theta^* \quad (4)$$

for any $e \in E$. The features are problem specific and we discuss how to construct them in Section 4.3. We propose two learning algorithms, which we call *cascading linear Thompson sampling* (`CascadeLinTS`) and *cascading linear UCB* (`CascadeLinUCB`). We prove that when the above linear generalization is perfect, the regret of `CascadeLinUCB` is independent of L and sublinear in n. Therefore, `CascadeLinUCB` is suitable for learning to recommend from large ground sets E. We also discuss why a similar regret bound should hold for `CascadeLinTS`, though we do not prove this bound formally.

Algorithm 1 `CascadeLinTS`

Inputs: Variance σ^2

// Initialization
$\mathbf{M}_0 \leftarrow I_d$ and $\mathbf{B}_0 \leftarrow \mathbf{0}$

for all $t = 1, \ldots, n$ **do**
  $\bar{\theta}_{t-1} \leftarrow \sigma^{-2}\mathbf{M}_{t-1}^{-1}\mathbf{B}_{t-1}$
  $\theta_t \sim \mathcal{N}(\bar{\theta}_{t-1}, \mathbf{M}_{t-1}^{-1})$

  // Recommend a list of K items and get feedback
  for all $k = 1, \ldots, K$ **do**
    $\mathbf{a}_k^t \leftarrow \arg\max_{e \in [L] - \{\mathbf{a}_1^t, \ldots, \mathbf{a}_{k-1}^t\}} x_e^\mathsf{T}\theta_t$
  $\mathbf{A}_t \leftarrow (\mathbf{a}_1^t, \ldots, \mathbf{a}_K^t)$
  Observe click $\mathbf{C}_t \in \{1, \ldots, K, \infty\}$
  Update statistics using Algorithm 3

Algorithm 2 `CascadeLinUCB`

Inputs: Variance σ^2, constant c (Section 3.2)

// Initialization
$\mathbf{M}_0 \leftarrow I_d$ and $\mathbf{B}_0 \leftarrow \mathbf{0}$

for all $t = 1, \ldots, n$ **do**
  $\bar{\theta}_{t-1} \leftarrow \sigma^{-2}\mathbf{M}_{t-1}^{-1}\mathbf{B}_{t-1}$
  for all $e \in E$ **do**
    $\mathbf{U}_t(e) \leftarrow \min\left\{x_e^\mathsf{T}\bar{\theta}_{t-1} + c\sqrt{x_e^\mathsf{T}\mathbf{M}_{t-1}^{-1}x_e}, 1\right\}$

  // Recommend a list of K items and get feedback
  for all $k = 1, \ldots, K$ **do**
    $\mathbf{a}_k^t \leftarrow \arg\max_{e \in [L] - \{\mathbf{a}_1^t, \ldots, \mathbf{a}_{k-1}^t\}} \mathbf{U}_t(e)$
  $\mathbf{A}_t \leftarrow (\mathbf{a}_1^t, \ldots, \mathbf{a}_K^t)$
  Observe click $\mathbf{C}_t \in \{1, \ldots, K, \infty\}$
  Update statistics using Algorithm 3

Algorithm 3 Update of statistics in Algorithms 1 and 2

$\mathbf{M}_t \leftarrow \mathbf{M}_{t-1}$
$\mathbf{B}_t \leftarrow \mathbf{B}_{t-1}$
for all $k = 1, \ldots, \min\{\mathbf{C}_t, K\}$ **do**
  $e \leftarrow \mathbf{a}_k^t$
  $\mathbf{M}_t \leftarrow \mathbf{M}_t + \sigma^{-2}x_e x_e^\mathsf{T}$
  $\mathbf{B}_t \leftarrow \mathbf{B}_t + x_e \mathbb{1}\{\mathbf{C}_t = k\}$

3.1 Algorithms

Our learning algorithms are based on the ideas of Thompson sampling [23, 3] and linear UCB [1], and motivated by the recent work of Wen *et al.* [24], which proposes computationally and sample efficient algorithms for large-scale stochastic combinatorial semi-bandits. The pseudocode of both algorithms is in Algorithms 1 and 2, and we outline them below.

Both `CascadeLinTS` and `CascadeLinUCB` represent their past observations as a positive-definite matrix $\mathbf{M}_t \in \mathbb{R}^{d \times d}$ and a vector $\mathbf{B}_t \in \mathbb{R}^{d \times 1}$. Specifically, let $\mathbf{X}_t$ be a matrix whose rows are the feature vectors of all observed items in t steps and $\mathbf{Y}_t$ be a column vector of all observed attraction weights in t steps. Then:

$$\mathbf{M}_t = \sigma^{-2}\mathbf{X}_t^\mathsf{T}\mathbf{X}_t + I_d$$

is the *gram matrix* in t steps and:

$$\mathbf{B}_t = \mathbf{X}_t^\mathsf{T}\mathbf{Y}_t\,,$$

where I_d is a $d \times d$ identity matrix and $\sigma > 0$ is parameter that controls the learning rate.[1]

Both `CascadeLinTS` and `CascadeLinUCB` operate in three stages. First, they estimated the expected weight of each item e based on their model of the world. `CascadeLinTS` randomly samples parameter vector θ_t from a normal distribution, which approximates its posterior on θ^*, and then estimates the expected weight as $x_e^\mathsf{T}\theta_t$. `CascadeLinUCB` computes an upper confidence bound $\mathbf{U}_t(e)$ for each item e. Second, both algorithms choose the optimal list $\mathbf{A}_t$ with respect to their estimates. Finally, they receive feedback, and update $\mathbf{M}_t$ and $\mathbf{B}_t$ using Algorithm 3.

[1]Ideally, σ^2 should be the variance of the observation noises. However, based on recent literature [24], we believe that both algorithms will perform well for a wide range of σ^2.

We would like to emphasize that both `CascadeLinTS` and `CascadeLinUCB` are computationally efficient. In practice, we would update $\mathbf{M}_t^{-1}$ instead of $\mathbf{M}_t$. In particular, note that:

$$\mathbf{M}_t \leftarrow \mathbf{M}_t + \sigma^{-2}x_e x_e^\mathsf{T}$$

can be equivalently updated as:

$$\mathbf{M}_t^{-1} \leftarrow \mathbf{M}_t^{-1} - \frac{\mathbf{M}_t^{-1}x_e x_e^\mathsf{T}\mathbf{M}_t^{-1}}{x_e^\mathsf{T}\mathbf{M}_t^{-1}x_e + \sigma^2}\,,$$

and hence $\mathbf{M}_t^{-1}$ can be updated incrementally and computationally efficiently in $O(d^2)$ time. It is easy to to see that the per-step time complexities of both `CascadeLinTS` and `CascadeLinUCB` are $O(L(d^2 + K))$.

3.2 Analysis and Discussion

We first derive a regret bound on `CascadeLinUCB`, under the assumptions that (1) $\bar{w}(e) = x_e^\mathsf{T}\theta^*$ for all $e \in E$ and (2) $\|x_e\|_2 \leq 1$ for all $e \in E$. Note that condition (2) can be always ensured by rescaling feature vectors. The regret bound is detailed below.

Theorem 1. *Under the above assumptions, for any $\sigma > 0$ and any*

$$c \geq \frac{1}{\sigma}\sqrt{d\log\left(1 + \frac{nK}{d\sigma^2}\right) + 2\log(nK)} + \|\theta^*\|_2,$$

if we run CascadeLinUCB *with parameters* σ *and* c, *then*

$$R(n) \leq 2cK\sqrt{\frac{dn \log\left[1+\frac{nK}{d\sigma^2}\right]}{\log\left(1+\frac{1}{\sigma^2}\right)}} + 1.$$

Note that if we choose $\sigma = 1$ and

$$c = \sqrt{d \log\left(1 + \frac{nK}{d}\right) + 2\log(nK)} + \eta,$$

for some constant $\eta \geq \|\theta^*\|_2$, then $R(n) \leq \tilde{O}(Kd\sqrt{n})$ where the $\tilde{O}$ notation hides logarithmic factors.

The proof is in Appendix and we outline it below. First, we define event $\mathcal{G}_{t,k} = \{\text{item } \mathbf{a}_k^t \text{ is examined in step } t\}$ for any time t and $k \in [K]$, and bound the n-step regret as

$$R(n) \leq \mathbb{E}\left[\sum_{t=1}^{n}\sum_{k=1}^{K} \mathbb{1}\{\mathcal{G}_{t,k}\}\left[\bar{w}(\mathbf{a}_k^{*,t}) - \bar{w}(\mathbf{a}_k^t)\right]\right],$$

where $\mathbf{a}_k^{*,t}$ is an optimal item in A^* matched to item $\mathbf{a}_k^t$ in step t. Second, we define an event

$$\mathcal{E} = \left\{\left|x_e^T(\bar{\theta}_{t-1} - \theta^*)\right| \leq c\|x_e\|_{\mathbf{M}_{t-1}^{-1}} \forall t \leq n, \forall e \in E\right\},$$

where $\|x_e\|_{\mathbf{M}_{t-1}^{-1}} = \sqrt{x_e^T \mathbf{M}_{t-1}^{-1} x_e}$. Then we prove a high-probability bound $P(\mathcal{E}) \geq 1 - 1/nK$ for any c that satisfies the condition of Theorem 1. Finally, we show that by conditioning on $\mathcal{E}$, we have

$$\begin{aligned}
&\sum_{t=1}^{n}\sum_{k=1}^{K} \mathbb{1}\{\mathcal{G}_{t,k}\}\left[\bar{w}(\mathbf{a}_k^{*,t}) - \bar{w}(\mathbf{a}_k^t)\right] \\
&\leq 2c\sum_{t=1}^{n}\sum_{k=1}^{K} \mathbb{1}\{\mathcal{G}_{t,k}\}\|x_{\mathbf{a}_k^t}\|_{\mathbf{M}_{t-1}^{-1}} \\
&\leq 2cK\sqrt{\frac{dn \log\left[1+\frac{nK}{d\sigma^2}\right]}{\log\left(1+\frac{1}{\sigma^2}\right)}},
\end{aligned}$$

where the first inequality follows from the definition of $\mathcal{E}$ and the second inequality follows from a worst-case bound. The bound in Theorem 1 follows from putting the above results together.

Recent work [21, 24] demonstrated close relationships between UCB-like algorithms and Thompson sampling algorithms in related bandit problems. Therefore, we believe that a similar regret bound to that in Theorem 1 also holds for CascadeLinTS. However, it is highly non-trivial to derive a regret bound for CascadeLinTS. Unlike in [24], CascadeLinTS cannot be analyzed from the Bayesian perspective because the Gaussian posterior is inconsistent with the fact that $\bar{w}(e)$ is bounded in $[0, 1]$. Moreover, a subtle statistical dependence between partial monitoring and Thompson sampling prevents a frequentist analysis similar to that in [4]. Therefore, we leave the formal analysis of CascadeLinTS for future work. It is well known that Thompson sampling tends to outperform UCB-like algorithms in practice [3]. Therefore, we only empirically evaluate CascadeLinTS.

4 EXPERIMENTS

We validate CascadeLinTS on several problems of various sizes and from various domains. In each problem, we conduct several experiments that demonstrate that our approach is scalable and stable with respect to its tunable parameters, the number of recommended items K and the number of features d.

Our experimental section is organized as follows. In Section 4.1, we outline the experiments that are conducted on each dataset. In Section 4.2, we introduce our metrics and baselines. In Section 4.3, we describe how we construct the features of items E. We present our empirical results in the rest of the section.

4.1 Experimental Setting

All of our learning problems can be viewed as follows. The feedback of users is a matrix $W \in \{0, 1\}^{m \times L}$, where row i corresponds to user $i \in [m]$ and column j corresponds to item $j \in E$. Entry (i, j) of W, $W_{i,j} \in \{0, 1\}$, indicates that user i is attracted by item j. The user at time t, the row of W, is chosen at random from the pool of all users. Our goal is to learn the list of items A^*, the columns of W, that maximizes the probability that the user at time t is attracted by at least one recommended item.

In each of our problems, we conduct a set of experiments. In the first experiment, we compare CascadeLinTS to baselines (Section 4.2) and also evaluate its scalability. We experiment with three variants of our problems: $L = 16$ items, $L = 256$ items, and the maximum possible value of L in a given experiment. The number of recommended items is $K = 4$ and the number of features is $d = 20$.

In the second experiment, we show that the performance of CascadeLinTS is robust with respect to the number of features d, in the sense that d affects the performance but CascadeLinTS performs reasonably well for all settings of d. We experiment with three settings for the number of features: $d = 10$, $d = 20$, and $d = 40$. The ground set contains $L = 256$ items and the number of recommended items is $K = 4$.

In the third experiment, we evaluate CascadeLinTS on an interesting subset of each dataset, such as *Rock Songs*. The setting of this experiment is identical to the second experiment. This experiment validates that CascadeLinTS can also learn to recommend items in the context, of a subset of the dataset.

In the last experiment, we evaluate how the performance of

CascadeLinTS varies with the number of recommended items K. We experiment with three settings for the number of recommended items: $K = 4$, $K = 8$, and $K = 12$. The ground set contains $L = 256$ items and the number of features is $d = 20$.

All experiments are conducted for $n = 100$k steps and averaged over 10 randomly initialized runs. The tunable parameter σ in CascadeLinTS is set to 1.

4.2 Metrics and Baselines

The performance of CascadeLinTS is evaluated by its expected cumulative regret, which is defined in (2). In most of our experiments, our modeling assumptions are violated. In particular, the items are not guaranteed to attract users independently because the attraction indicators $\mathbf{w}_t(e)$ are correlated across items e. The result is that:

$$A^* = \arg\max_{A \in \Pi_K(E)} \mathbb{E}\left[f(A, \mathbf{w})\right] > \arg\max_{A \in \Pi_K(E)} f(A, \bar{w}) .$$

It is NP-hard to find A^*, because $\mathbb{E}\left[f(A, \mathbf{w})\right]$ does not decompose into the product of expectations as we assume in our model (Section 2.2). However, since $\mathbb{E}\left[f(A, \mathbf{w})\right]$ is submodular and monotone in A, a $(1 - 1/e)$ approximation to A^* can be computed greedily, by iteratively adding items that attract most users that are not attracted by any previously added item. We denote this approximation by A^* and use it instead of the optimal solution.

We compare CascadeLinTS to two baselines. The first baseline is CascadeUCB1 (Section 2.3). This baseline does not leverage the structure of our problem and learns the attraction probability of each item e independently. The second baseline is RankedLinTS (Algorithm 4). This baseline is a variant of ranked bandits (Section 5), where the base bandit algorithm is LinTS. This base algorithm is the same as in CascadeLinTS. Therefore, any observed difference in the performance of cascading and ranked bandits must be due to the efficiency of using the base algorithm, and not the algorithm itself. In this sense, our comparison of CascadeLinTS and RankedLinTS is fair. The tunable parameter σ in RankedLinTS is also set to 1.

4.3 Features

In most recommender problems, good features of items are rarely available. Thus, they are typically learned from data [14]. As an example, in movie recommendations, all state of the art approaches are based on collaborative filtering rather than on the features of movies, such as movie genres.

Motivated by the successes of collaborative filtering in recommender systems, we derive the features of our items using low-rank matrix factorization. In particular, let $W \in \{0,1\}^{m \times L}$ be our feedback matrix for m users and L items. We randomly divide the rows of W into two matrices, training matrix $W_{\text{train}} \in \{0,1\}^{(m/2) \times L}$ and test matrix $W_{\text{test}} \in \{0,1\}^{(m/2) \times L}$. We use W_{train} to learn the features of items and W_{test} in place of W to evaluate our learning algorithms. Most existing real-world recommender systems already have some data about their users. Such data can be used to construct W_{train}.

Algorithm 4 Ranked bandits with linear TS.

Inputs: Variance σ^2

// Initialization
$\forall k \in [K] : \mathbf{M}_0^k \leftarrow I_d$ and $\mathbf{B}_0^k \leftarrow \mathbf{0}$

for all $t = 1, \dots, n$ **do**
  for all $k = 1, \dots, K$ **do**
    $\bar{\theta}_{t-1}^k \leftarrow \sigma^{-2}(\mathbf{M}_{t-1}^k)^{-1}\mathbf{B}_{t-1}^k$
    $\theta_t^k \sim \mathcal{N}(\bar{\theta}_{t-1}^k, (\mathbf{M}_{t-1}^k)^{-1})$
    $\mathbf{a}_k^t \leftarrow \arg\max_{e \in [L] - \{\mathbf{a}_1^t, \dots, \mathbf{a}_{k-1}^t\}} x_e^\mathsf{T} \theta_t^k$

  // Recommend a list of K items and get feedback
  $\mathbf{A}_t \leftarrow (\mathbf{a}_1^t, \dots, \mathbf{a}_K^t)$
  Observe click $\mathbf{C}_t \in \{1, \dots, K, \infty\}$

  // Update statistics
  $\forall k \in [K] : \mathbf{M}_t^k \leftarrow \mathbf{M}_{t-1}^k$
  $\forall k \in [K] : \mathbf{B}_t^k \leftarrow \mathbf{B}_{t-1}^k$
  for all $k = 1, \dots, \min\{\mathbf{C}_t, K\}$ **do**
    $e \leftarrow \mathbf{a}_k^t$
    $\mathbf{M}_t^k \leftarrow \mathbf{M}_t^k + \sigma^{-2} x_e x_e^\mathsf{T}$
    $\mathbf{B}_t^k \leftarrow \mathbf{B}_t^k + x_e \mathbb{1}\{\mathbf{C}_t = k\}$

Let $W_{\text{train}} \approx U \Sigma V^\mathsf{T}$ be rank-d truncated SVD of W_{train}, where $U \in \mathbb{R}^{(m/2) \times d}$, $\Sigma \in \mathbb{R}^{d \times d}$, and $V \in \mathbb{R}^{L \times d}$. Then the features of items are the rows of $V\Sigma$. Specifically, for each item $e \in E$ and feature $i \in [d]$, $x_e(i) = V_{e,i}\Sigma_{i,i}$.

4.4 Restaurant Recommendations

Our dataset is from Yelp Dataset Challenge[2]. This dataset has five parts, including business information, checkin information, review information, tip information, and user information. We only consider the business and review information. The dataset contains 78k businesses, out of which 11k are restaurants; and 2.2M reviews written by 550k users. We extract $L = 3$k most reviewed restaurants and $m = 20$k most reviewing users.

Our objective is to maximize the probability that the user is attracted by at least one recommended restaurant. We build the model of users from past review data and assume that the user is attracted by the restaurant if the user reviewed this restaurant before. This indicates that the user visited the restaurant at some point in time, likely because the restaurant attracted the user at that time.

[2] https://www.yelp.com/dataset_challenge

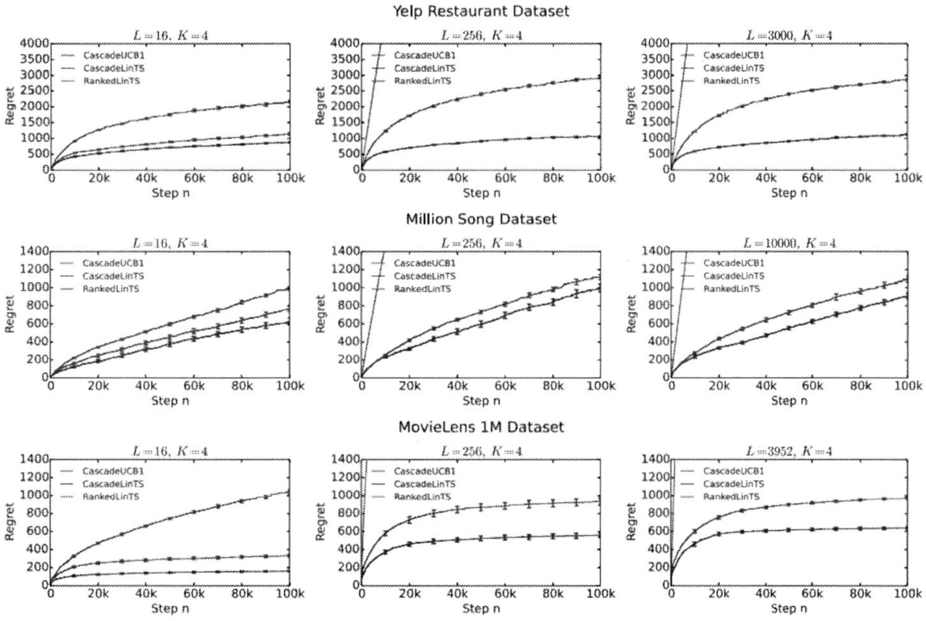

Figure 1: The n-step regret of CascadeUCB1, CascadeLinTS and RankedLinTS on three problems. We vary the number of items in the ground set E, from $L = 16$ to the maximum value in each problem.

4.4.1 Results

The results of our first experiment are reported in Fig. 1. When the ground set is small, $L = 16$, all compared methods perform similarly. In particular, the regret of CascadeLinTS is similar to that of RankedLinTS. The regret of CascadeUCB1 is about two times larger than that of CascadeLinTS. As the size of the ground set increases, the gap between CascadeLinTS and the other methods increases. In particular, when $L = 3$k, the regret of CascadeUCB1 is orders of magnitude larger than that of CascadeLinTS, and the regret of RankedLinTS is almost three times larger.

In the second experiment (Fig. 2a), we observe that CascadeLinTS performs well for all settings of d. When the number of features doubles to $d = 40$, the regret roughly doubles. When the number of features is halved to $d = 10$, the regret improves and is roughly halved.

In the third experiment (Fig. 2b), CascadeLinTS is evaluated on the subset of *American Restaurants*. This is the largest restaurant category in our dataset. We observe that CascadeLinTS can learn for any number of features d, similarly to Fig. 2a.

In the last experiment (Fig. 2c), we observe that the regret of CascadeLinTS increases with the number of recommended items, from $K = 4$ to $K = 8$. This result is surprising and seems to contradict to Kveton *et al.* [15], who find both theoretically and empirically that the regret in cascading bandits decreases with the number of recommended items K. We investigate this further and plot the cumulative reward of CascadeLinTS in Fig. 2d. The reward increases with K, which is expected and validates that CascadeLinTS learns better policies for larger K. Therefore, the increase in the regret in Fig. 2c must be due to the fact that the expected reward of the optimal solution, $f(A^*, \bar{w})$, increases faster with K than that of the learned policies. We believe that the optimal solutions for larger K are harder to learn because our modeling assumptions are violated. In particular, the linear generalization in (4) is imperfect and the items in E are not guaranteed to attract users independently.

4.5 Million Song Recommendation

Million Song Dataset[3] is a collection of audio features and metadata for a million contemporary pop songs. Instead of storing any audio, the dataset consists of features derived from the audio, user-song profile data, and genres of songs. We extract $L = 10$k most popular songs from this dataset, as measured by the number of song-listening events; and $m = 400$k most active users, as measured by the number of song-listening events.

Our objective is to maximize the probability that the user is attracted with at least one recommended song and plays it. We build the model of users from their past listening patterns and assume that the user is attracted by the song if the user listened to this song before. This indicates that the

[3] http://labrosa.ee.columbia.edu/millionsong/

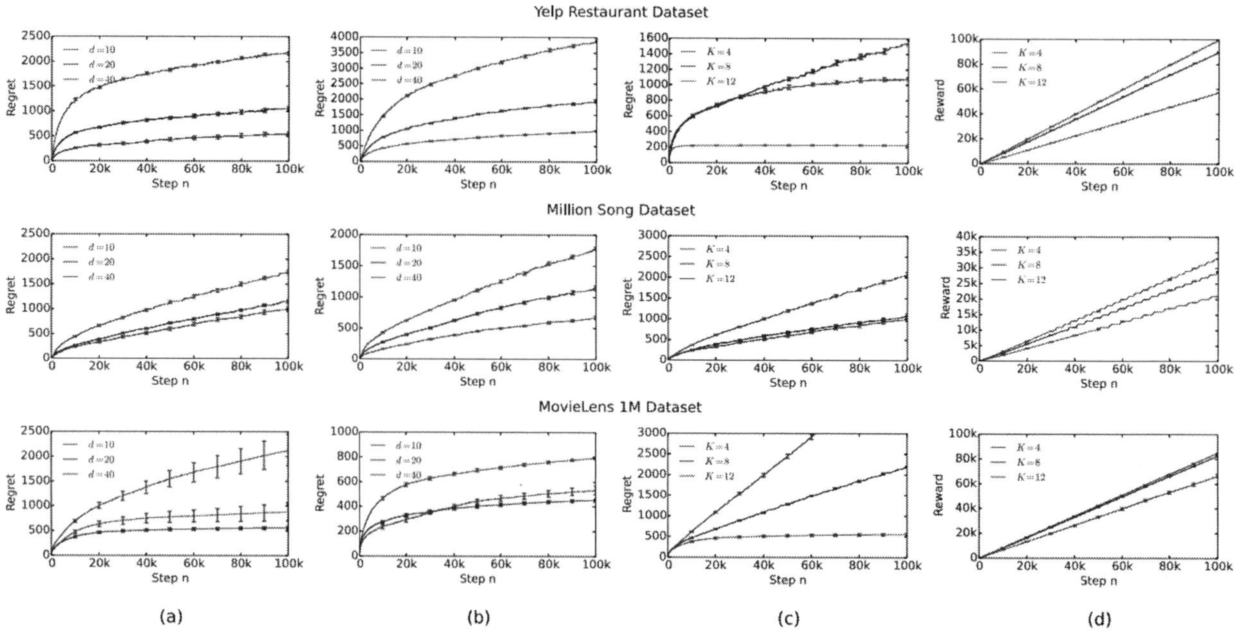

Figure 2: **a**. The n-step regret of `CascadeLinTS` for varying number of features d. **b**. The n-step regret of `CascadeLinTS` in a subset of each dataset for varying number of features d. **c**. The n-step regret of `CascadeLinTS` for varying number of recommended items K. **d**. The n-step reward of `CascadeLinTS` for varying number of recommended items K.

user was attracted by the song at some point in time.

4.5.1 Results

The results of our first experiment are reported in Fig. 1. Similarly to Section 4.4, we observe that when the ground set is small, $L = 16$, the regret of all compared methods is similar. As the size of the ground set increases, the gap between `CascadeUCB1` and the rest of the methods increases, and the regret of `CascadeUCB1` is orders of magnitude larger than that of `CascadeLinTS`. The regret of `CascadeLinTS` is similar to that of `RankedLinTS` for all settings of L.

We report the regret of `CascadeLinTS` for various numbers of features d, on the whole dataset and its subset of *Rock Songs*, in Fig. 2a and 2b, respectively. Similarly to Section 4.4, we observe that `CascadeLinTS` performs well for all settings of d. The lowest regret in both experiments is achieved at $d = 10$.

In the last experiment (Fig. 2c), we observe that the regret of `CascadeLinTS` increases with the number of recommended items K. As in Section 4.4, we observe that the cumulative reward of our learned policies increases with K. Therefore, the increase in the regret must be due to the fact that the expected reward of the optimal solution, $f(A^*, \bar{w})$, increases faster with K than that of the learned policies. This is due to the mismatch between our model and real-world data.

4.6 Movie Recommendation

MovieLens datasets[4] contain the ratings of users for movies from the MovieLens website. The datasets come in different sizes and we choose MovieLens 1M for our experiments. This dataset contains 1M anonymous ratings of 4k movies by 6k users who joined MovieLens in 2000.

We build the model of users from their historical ratings. The ratings are on a 5-star scale and we assume the user is attracted by a movie if the user rates it with more than 3 stars. Thus, the feedback matrix is defined as $W_{i,j} = \mathbb{1}\{\text{user } i \text{ rates movie } j \text{ with more than 3 stars}\}$. Our goal is to maximize the probability of recommending at least one attractive movie.

4.6.1 Results

The results of our first experiment are reported in Fig. 1. Similarly to Section 4.4, we observe that the regret of all compared methods is similar when the ground set is small, $L = 16$. The gap between `CascadeUCB1` and the rest of the methods increases when the size of the ground set increases. In particular, the regret of `CascadeUCB1` is orders of magnitude larger than that of `CascadeLinTS`. The regret of `CascadeLinTS` is always lower than that of `RankedLinTS` for all settings of L.

We report the regret of `CascadeLinTS` for various num-

[4] `http://grouplens.org/datasets/movielens/`

bers of features d, on the whole dataset and its subset of *Adventures*, in Fig. 2a and 2b, respectively. Similarly to Sections 4.4 and 4.5, we observe that CascadeLinTS performs well for all settings of d. The lowest regret in both experiments is achieved at $d = 20$.

In the last experiment (Fig. 2c), we observe that the regret of CascadeLinTS increases with the number of recommended items K. As in Sections 4.4 and 4.5, the cumulative reward of our learned policies increases with K. Therefore, the increase in the regret must be due to the fact that the expected reward of the optimal solution, $f(A^*, \bar{w})$, increases faster with K than that of the learned policies.

5 RELATED WORK

Our work is closely related to *cascading bandits* [15, 8], which are learning variants of the cascade model of user behavior [10]. The key difference is that we assume that the attraction weights of items are a linear function of known feature vectors, which are associated with each item; and an unknown parameter vector, which is learned. This leads to very efficient learning algorithms whose regret is sublinear in the number of items L. We compare CascadeLinTS to CascadeUCB1, one of the proposed algorithms by Kveton *et al.* [15], in Section 4.

Ranked bandits [20] are a popular approach in learning to rank. The key idea in ranked bandits is to model each position in the recommended list as an independent bandit problem, which is then solved by a *base bandit algorithm*. The solutions in ranked bandits are $(1 - 1/e)$ approximate and their regret grows linearly with the number of recommended items K. On the other hand, ranked bandits do not assume that items attract the user independently. Slivkins *et al.* [22] proposed contextual ranked bandits. We compare CascadeLinTS to contextual ranked bandits with linear generalization in Section 4.

Our learning problem is a partial monitoring problem where we do not observe the attraction weights of all recommended items. Bartok *et al.* [5] studied general partial monitoring problems. The algorithm of Bartok *et al.* [5] scales at least linearly with the number of actions, which is $\binom{L}{K}$ in our setting. Therefore, the algorithm is impractical for large L and moderate K. Agrawal *et al.* [2] studied a variant of partial monitoring where the reward is observed. The algorithm of Agrawal *et al.* [2] cannot be applied to our problem because the algorithm assumes a finite parameter set. Lin *et al.* [19] and Kveton *et al.* [17] studied combinatorial partial monitoring. Our feedback model is similar to that of Kveton *et al.* [17]. Therefore, we believe that our algorithm and analysis can be relatively easily generalized to combinatorial action sets.

Our learning problem is combinatorial as we learn K most attractive items out of L candidate items. In this sense, our work is related to stochastic combinatorial bandits, which are frequently studied with a linear reward function and semi-bandit feedback [11, 6, 16, 18, 24, 9]. Our work differs from these approaches in both the reward function and feedback. Our reward function is a non-linear function of unknown parameters. Our feedback model is less than semi-bandit, because the learning agent does not observe the attraction weights of all recommended items.

6 CONCLUSIONS

In this work, we propose linear cascading bandits, a framework for learning to recommend in the cascade model at scale. The key assumption in linear cascading bandits is that the attraction probabilities of items are a linear function of the features of items, which are known; and an unknown parameter vector, which is unknown and we learn it. We design two algorithms for solving our problem, CascadeLinTS and CascadeLinUCB. We bound the regret of CascadeLinUCB and suggest that a similar regret bound can be proved for CascadeLinTS. We comprehensively evaluate CascadeLinTS on a range of recommendation problems and compare it to several baselines. We report orders of magnitude improvements over learning algorithms that do not leverage the structure of our problem, the features of items. We observe empirically that CascadeLinTS performs very well.

We leave open several questions of interest. For instance, we only bound the regret of CascadeLinUCB. Based on the existing work [24], we believe that a similar regret bound can be proved for CascadeLinTS. Moreover, note that our analysis of CascadeLinUCB is under the assumption that items attract the user independently and that the linear generalization is perfect. Both of these assumptions tend to be violated in practice. Our current analysis cannot explain this behavior and we leave it for future work.

The main limitation of the cascade model [10] is that the user clicks on at most one item. This assumption is often violated in practice. Recently, Katariya *et al.* [13] proposed a generalization of cascading bandits to multiple clicks, by proposing a learning variant of the dependent click model [12]. We strongly believe that our results can be generalized to this setting and leave this for future work.

References

[1] Yasin Abbasi-Yadkori, David Pal, and Csaba Szepesvari. Improved algorithms for linear stochastic bandits. In *Advances in Neural Information Processing Systems 24*, pages 2312–2320, 2011.

[2] Rajeev Agrawal, Demosthenis Teneketzis, and Venkatachalam Anantharam. Asymptotically efficient adaptive allocation schemes for controlled i.i.d. processes: Finite parameter space. *IEEE Transactions on Automatic Control*, 34(3):258–267, 1989.

[3] Shipra Agrawal and Navin Goyal. Analysis of Thompson sampling for the multi-armed bandit problem. In *Proceeding of the 25th Annual Conference on Learning Theory*, pages 39.1–39.26, 2012.

[4] Shipra Agrawal and Navin Goyal. Thompson sampling for contextual bandits with linear payoffs. In *Proceedings of the 30th International Conference on Machine Learning*, pages 127–135, 2013.

[5] Gabor Bartok, Navid Zolghadr, and Csaba Szepesvari. An adaptive algorithm for finite stochastic partial monitoring. In *Proceedings of the 29th International Conference on Machine Learning*, 2012.

[6] Wei Chen, Yajun Wang, and Yang Yuan. Combinatorial multi-armed bandit: General framework, results and applications. In *Proceedings of the 30th International Conference on Machine Learning*, pages 151–159, 2013.

[7] Aleksandr Chuklin, Ilya Markov, and Maarten de Rijke. *Click Models for Web Search*. Morgan & Claypool Publishers, 2015.

[8] Richard Combes, Stefan Magureanu, Alexandre Proutiere, and Cyrille Laroche. Learning to rank: Regret lower bounds and efficient algorithms. In *Proceedings of the 2015 ACM SIGMETRICS International Conference on Measurement and Modeling of Computer Systems*, 2015.

[9] Richard Combes, Mohammad Sadegh Talebi, Alexandre Proutiere, and Marc Lelarge. Combinatorial bandits revisited. In *Advances in Neural Information Processing Systems 28*, pages 2107–2115, 2015.

[10] Nick Craswell, Onno Zoeter, Michael Taylor, and Bill Ramsey. An experimental comparison of click position-bias models. In *Proceedings of the 1st ACM International Conference on Web Search and Data Mining*, pages 87–94, 2008.

[11] Yi Gai, Bhaskar Krishnamachari, and Rahul Jain. Combinatorial network optimization with unknown variables: Multi-armed bandits with linear rewards and individual observations. *IEEE/ACM Transactions on Networking*, 20(5):1466–1478, 2012.

[12] Fan Guo, Chao Liu, and Yi Min Wang. Efficient multiple-click models in web search. In *Proceedings of the 2nd ACM International Conference on Web Search and Data Mining*, pages 124–131, 2009.

[13] Sumeet Katariya, Branislav Kveton, Csaba Szepesvari, and Zheng Wen. DCM bandits: Learning to rank with multiple clicks. In *Proceedings of the 33rd International Conference on Machine Learning*, 2016.

[14] Yehuda Koren, Robert Bell, and Chris Volinsky. Matrix factorization techniques for recommender systems. *IEEE Computer*, 42(8):30–37, 2009.

[15] Branislav Kveton, Csaba Szepesvari, Zheng Wen, and Azin Ashkan. Cascading bandits: Learning to rank in the cascade model. In *Proceedings of the 32nd International Conference on Machine Learning*, 2015.

[16] Branislav Kveton, Zheng Wen, Azin Ashkan, Hoda Eydgahi, and Brian Eriksson. Matroid bandits: Fast combinatorial optimization with learning. In *Proceedings of the 30th Conference on Uncertainty in Artificial Intelligence*, pages 420–429, 2014.

[17] Branislav Kveton, Zheng Wen, Azin Ashkan, and Csaba Szepesvari. Combinatorial cascading bandits. In *Advances in Neural Information Processing Systems 28*, pages 1450–1458, 2015.

[18] Branislav Kveton, Zheng Wen, Azin Ashkan, and Csaba Szepesvari. Tight regret bounds for stochastic combinatorial semi-bandits. In *Proceedings of the 18th International Conference on Artificial Intelligence and Statistics*, 2015.

[19] Tian Lin, Bruno Abrahao, Robert Kleinberg, John Lui, and Wei Chen. Combinatorial partial monitoring game with linear feedback and its applications. In *Proceedings of the 31st International Conference on Machine Learning*, pages 901–909, 2014.

[20] Filip Radlinski, Robert Kleinberg, and Thorsten Joachims. Learning diverse rankings with multi-armed bandits. In *Proceedings of the 25th International Conference on Machine Learning*, pages 784–791, 2008.

[21] Daniel Russo and Benjamin Van Roy. Learning to optimize via posterior sampling. *Mathematics of Operations Research*, 39(4):1221–1243, 2014.

[22] Aleksandrs Slivkins, Filip Radlinski, and Sreenivas Gollapudi. Ranked bandits in metric spaces: Learning diverse rankings over large document collections. *Journal of Machine Learning Research*, 14(1):399–436, 2013.

[23] William. R. Thompson. On the likelihood that one unknown probability exceeds another in view of the evidence of two samples. *Biometrika*, 25(3-4):285–294, 1933.

[24] Zheng Wen, Branislav Kveton, and Azin Ashkan. Efficient learning in large-scale combinatorial semi-bandits. In *Proceedings of the 32nd International Conference on Machine Learning*, 2015.